Peterson's®
Two-Year
Colleges
2016

About Peterson's®

Peterson's® is excited to be celebrating 50 years of trusted educational publishing. It's a milestone we're quite proud of, as we continue to provide the most accurate, dependable, high-quality education content in the field, providing you with everything you need to succeed. No matter where you are on your academic or professional path, you can rely on Peterson's® publications and its online information at **www.petersons.com** for the most up-to-date education exploration data, expert test-prep tools, and the highest quality career success resources—everything you need to achieve your educational goals.

For more information, contact Peterson's, 3 Columbia Circle, Suite 205, Albany, NY 12203-5158; 800-338-3282 Ext. 54229; or visit us online at **www.petersons.com**.

Sustainability—Its Importance to Peterson's

What does sustainability mean to Peterson's? As a leading publisher, we are aware that our business has a direct impact on vital resources—most importantly the raw material used to make our books. Peterson's is proud that its products are printed at SFI Chain-of-Custody certified facilities and that all of its books are printed on SFI certified paper with 10 percent post-consumer waste using vegetable-based ink.

Supporting the Sustainable Forestry Initiative® (SFI®) means that we only use vendors—from paper suppliers to printers—who have undergone rigorous certification audits by independent parties to demonstrate that they meet the standards.

Peterson's continuously strives to find new ways to incorporate responsible sourcing throughout all aspects of its business.

Contents

A Note from the Peterson's® Editors

For more than 40 years, Peterson's has given students and parents the most comprehensive, up-to-date information on undergraduate institutions in the United States. Peterson's researches the data published in *Peterson's Two-Year Colleges* each year. The information is furnished by the colleges and is accurate at the time of publishing.

This guide also features advice and tips on the college search and selection process, such as how to decide if a two-year college is right for you, how to approach transferring between colleges, and what's in store for adults returning to college. If you seem to be getting more, not less, anxious about choosing and getting into the right college, *Peterson's Two-Year Colleges* provides just the right help, giving you the information you need to make important college decisions and ace the admission process.

Opportunities abound for students, and this guide can help you find what you want in a number of ways:

"What You Need to Know About Two-Year Colleges" outlines the basic features and advantages of two-year colleges. "Surviving Standardized Tests" gives an overview of the common examinations students take prior to attending college. "Who's Paying for This? Financial Aid Basics" provides guidelines for financing your college education. "Frequently Asked Questions About Transferring" takes a look at the two-year college scene from the perspective of a student who is looking toward the day when he or she may pursue additional education at a four-year institution. "Returning to School: Advice for Adult Students" is an analysis of the pros and cons (mostly pros) of returning to college after already having begun a professional career. "Coming to America: Tips for International Students Considering Study in the U.S." is an article written particularly for students overseas who are considering a U.S. college education. "Community Colleges and the Green Economy" offers information on some exciting "green" programs at community colleges throughout the United States, as well as two insightful essays by Mary F. T. Spilde, President, Lane Community College and Tom Sutton, Director of Wind Energy and Technical Services, Kalamazoo Valley Community College. Finally, "How to Use This Guide" gives details on the data in this guide: what terms mean and why they're here.

- If you already have specifics in mind, such as a particular institution or major, turn to the easy-to-use **Two-Year Colleges At-a-Glance Chart** or **Indexes.** You can look up a particular feature—location and programs offered—or use the alphabetical index and immediately find the colleges that meet your criteria.

- For information about particular colleges, turn to the **Profiles of Two-Year Colleges** section. Here, our comprehensive college profiles are arranged alphabetically by state. They provide a complete picture of need-to-know information about every accredited two-year college—from admission to graduation, including expenses, financial aid, majors, and campus safety. All the information you need to apply is placed together at the conclusion of each college **Profile.** Display ads, which appear near some of the institutions' profiles, have been provided and paid for by those colleges or universities that wished to supplement their profile data with additional information about their institution.

- In addition, two-page narrative descriptions, which appear in the **Featured Two-Year Colleges** section, are paid for and written by college officials and offer great detail about each college. They are edited to provide a consistent format across entries for your ease of comparison.

Peterson's publishes a full line of books—education exploration, test prep, financial aid, and career preparation. Peterson's publications can be found at high school guidance offices, college libraries and career centers, and your local bookstore and library. Peterson's books are also available as eBooks and online at www.petersonsbooks.com.

We welcome any comments or suggestions you may have about this publication. Your feedback will help us make educational dreams possible for you—and others like you.

Colleges will be pleased to know that Peterson's helped you in your selection. Admissions staff members are more than happy to answer questions, address specific problems and help in any way they can. The editors at Peterson's wish you great success in your college search.

NOTICE: Certain portions of or information contained in this book have been submitted and paid for by the educational institution identified, and such institutions take full responsibility for the accuracy, timeliness, completeness and functionality of such content. Such portions or information include (i) each display ad in the "Profiles" section from pages 51 through 362 that comprises a half or full page of information covering a single educational institution, and (ii) each two-page description in the "Featured Two-Year Colleges" section from pages 364 through 373.

The College Admissions Process: An Overview

What You Need to Know About Two-Year Colleges

David R. Pierce

Two-year colleges—better known as community colleges—are often called "the people's colleges." With their open-door policies (admission is open to individuals with a high school diploma or its equivalent), community colleges provide access to higher education for millions of Americans who might otherwise be excluded from higher education. Community college students are diverse and of all ages, races, and economic backgrounds. While many community college students enroll full-time, an equally large number attend on a part-time basis so they can fulfill employment and family commitments as they advance their education.

Community colleges can also be referred to as either technical or junior colleges, and they may either be under public or independent control. What unites two-year colleges is that they are regionally accredited, postsecondary institutions, whose highest credential awarded is the associate degree. With few exceptions, community colleges offer a comprehensive curriculum, which includes transfer, technical, and continuing education programs.

IMPORTANT FACTORS IN A COMMUNITY COLLEGE EDUCATION

The student who attends a community college can count on receiving high-quality instruction in a supportive learning community. This setting frees the student to pursue his or her own goals, nurture special talents, explore new fields of learning, and develop the capacity for lifelong learning.

From the student's perspective, four characteristics capture the essence of community colleges:

1. They are community-based institutions that work in close partnership with high schools, community groups, and employers in extending high-quality programs at convenient times and places.

2. Community colleges are cost effective. Annual tuition and fees at public community colleges average approximately half those at public four-year colleges and less than 15 percent of private four-year institutions. In addition, since most community colleges are generally close to their students' homes, these students can also save a significant amount of money on the room, board, and transportation expenses traditionally associated with a college education.

3. Community colleges provide a caring environment, with faculty members who are expert instructors, known for excellent teaching and meeting students at the point of their individual needs, regardless of age, sex, race, current job status, or previous academic preparation. Community colleges join a strong curriculum with a broad range of counseling and career services that are intended to assist students in making the most of their educational opportunities.

4. Many offer comprehensive programs, including transfer curricula in such liberal arts programs as chemistry, psychology, and business management, that lead directly to a baccalaureate degree and career programs that prepare students for employment or assist those already employed in upgrading their skills. For those students who need to strengthen their academic skills, community colleges also offer a wide range of developmental programs in mathematics, languages, and learning skills, designed to prepare the student for success in college studies.

GETTING TO KNOW YOUR TWO-YEAR COLLEGE

The first step in determining the quality of a community college is to check the status of its accreditation. Once you have established that a community college is appropriately accredited, find out as much as you can about the programs and services it has to offer. Much of that information can be found in materials the college provides. However, the best way to learn about a college is to visit in person.

During a campus visit, be prepared to ask a lot of questions. Talk to students, faculty members, administrators, and counselors about the college and its programs, particularly those in which you have a special interest. Ask about available certificates and associate degrees. Don't be shy. Do what you can to dig below the surface. Ask college officials about the transfer rate to four-year colleges. If a college emphasizes student services, find out what particular assistance is offered, such as educational or career guidance. Colleges are eager to provide you with the information you need to make informed decisions.

COMMUNITY COLLEGES CAN SAVE YOU MONEY

If you are able to live at home while you attend college, you will certainly save money on room and board, but it does cost something to commute. Many two-year colleges offer you instruction in your own home through online learning programs or through home study courses that can save both time and money. Look into all the options, and be sure to add up all the costs of attending various colleges before deciding which is best for you.

FINANCIAL AID

Many students who attend community colleges are eligible for a range of federal financial aid programs, state aid, and on-campus jobs. Your high school counselor or the financial aid officer at a community college will also be able to help you. It is in your interest to apply for financial aid months in advance of the date you intend to start your college program, so find out early what assistance is available to you. While many community colleges are able to help students who make a last-minute decision to attend college, either through short-term loans or emergency grants, if you are considering entering college and think you might need financial aid, it is best to find out as much as you can as early as you can.

WORKING AND GOING TO SCHOOL

Many two-year college students maintain full-time or part-time employment while they earn their degrees. Over the years, a steadily growing number of students have chosen to attend community colleges while they fulfill family and employment responsibilities. To enable these students to balance the demands of home, work, and school, most community colleges offer classes at night and on weekends.

For the full-time student, the usual length of time it takes to obtain an associate degree is two years. However, your length of study will depend on the course load you take: the fewer credits you earn each term, the longer it will take you to earn a degree. To assist you in moving more quickly toward earning your degree, many community colleges now award credit through examination or for equivalent knowledge gained through relevant life experiences. Be certain to find out the credit options that are available to you at the college in which you are interested. You may discover that it will take less time to earn a degree than you first thought.

PREPARATION FOR TRANSFER

Studies have repeatedly shown that students who first attend a community college and then transfer to a four-year college or university do at least as well academically as the students who entered the four-year institutions as freshmen. Most community colleges have agreements with nearby four-year institutions to make transfer of credits easier. If you are thinking of transferring, be sure to meet with a counselor or faculty adviser before choosing your courses. You will want to map out a course of study with transfer in mind. Make sure you also find out the credit-transfer requirements of the four-year institution you might want to attend.

ATTENDING A TWO-YEAR COLLEGE IN ANOTHER REGION

Although many community colleges serve a specific county or district, they are committed (to the extent of their ability) to the goal of equal educational opportunity without regard to economic status, race, creed, color, sex, or national origin. Independent two-year colleges recruit from a much broader geographical area—throughout the United States and, increasingly, around the world.

Although some community colleges do provide on-campus housing for their students, most do not. However, even if on-campus housing is not available, most colleges do have housing referral services.

NEW CAREER OPPORTUNITIES

Community colleges realize that many entering students are not sure about the field in which they want to focus their studies or the career they would like to pursue. Often, students discover fields and careers they never knew existed. Community colleges have the resources to help students identify areas of career interest and to set challenging occupational goals.

Once a career goal is set, you can be confident that a community college will provide job-relevant, technical education. About half of the students who take courses for credit at community colleges do so to prepare for employment or to acquire or upgrade skills for their current job. Especially helpful in charting a career path is the assistance of a counselor or a faculty adviser, who can discuss job opportunities in your chosen field and help you map out your course of study.

In addition, since community colleges have close ties to their communities, they are in constant contact with leaders in business, industry, organized labor, and public life. Community colleges work with these individuals and their organizations to prepare students for direct entry into the world of work. For example, some community colleges have established partnerships with local businesses and industries to provide specialized training programs. Some also provide the academic portion of apprenticeship training, while others offer extensive job-shadowing and cooperative education opportunities. Be sure to examine all of the career-preparation opportunities offered by the community colleges in which you are interested.

David R. Pierce is the former President of the American Association of Community Colleges.

Surviving Standardized Tests

WHAT ARE STANDARDIZED TESTS?

Colleges and universities in the United States use tests to help evaluate applicants' readiness for admission or to place them in appropriate courses. The tests that are most frequently used by colleges are the ACT® of American College Testing, Inc., and the College Board's SAT®. In addition, the Educational Testing Service (ETS) offers the TOEFL® test, which evaluates the English-language proficiency of nonnative speakers. The tests are offered at designated testing centers located at high schools and colleges throughout the United States and U.S. territories and at testing centers in various countries throughout the world.

Upon request, special accommodations for students with documented visual, hearing, physical, or learning disabilities are available. Examples of special accommodations include tests in Braille or large print and such aids as a reader, recorder, magnifying glass, or sign language interpreter. Additional testing time may be allowed in some instances. Contact the appropriate testing program or your guidance counselor for details on how to request special accommodations.

THE ACT®

The ACT® is a standardized college entrance examination that measures knowledge and skills in English, mathematics, reading, and science reasoning and the application of these skills to future academic tasks. The ACT® consists of four multiple-choice tests.

Test 1: English
- 75 questions, 45 minutes
- Usage and mechanics
- Rhetorical skills

Test 2: Mathematics
- 60 questions, 60 minutes
- Pre-algebra
- Elementary algebra
- Intermediate algebra
- Coordinate geometry
- Plane geometry
- Trigonometry

Test 3: Reading
- 40 questions, 35 minutes
- Prose fiction
- Humanities
- Social studies
- Natural sciences

Test 4: Science
- 40 questions, 35 minutes
- Data representation
- Research summary
- Conflicting viewpoints

Each section is scored from 1 to 36 and is scaled for slight variations in difficulty. Students are not penalized for incorrect responses. The composite score is the average of the four scaled scores. The ACT® Plus Writing includes the four multiple-choice tests and a writing test, which measures writing skills emphasized in high school English classes and in entry-level college composition courses.

- To prepare for the ACT®, ask your guidance counselor for a free guidebook, "Preparing for the ACT®," or download it at www.act.org/aap/pdf/Preparing-for-the-ACT.pdf. Besides providing general test-preparation information and additional test-taking strategies, this guidebook provides full-length practice tests, including a Writing test, information about the optional Writing Test, strategies to prepare for the tests, and what to expect on test day.

DON'T FORGET TO . . .

- ☐ Take the SAT® or ACT® before application deadlines.
- ☐ Note that test registration deadlines precede test dates by about six weeks.
- ☐ Register to take the TOEFL® test if English is not your native language and you are planning on studying at a North American college.
- ☐ Contact the College Board or American College Testing, Inc., in advance if you need special accommodations when taking tests.

THE SAT®

The SAT® measures developed critical reading and mathematical reasoning abilities as they relate to successful performance in college. It is intended to supplement the secondary school record and other information about the student in assessing readiness for college. There is one unscored, experimental section on the exam, which is used for equating and/or pretesting purposes and can cover either the mathematics or critical reading area.

Critical Reading
- 67 questions, 70 minutes
- Sentence completion
- Passage-based reading

Mathematics
- 54 questions, 70 minutes
- Multiple-choice
- Student-produced response (grid-ins)

Writing
- 49 questions plus essay, 60 minutes
- Identifying sentence errors

- Improving paragraphs
- Improving sentences
- Essay

Students receive one point for each correct response and lose a fraction of a point for each incorrect response (except for student-produced responses). These points are totaled to produce the raw scores, which are then scaled to equalize the scores for slight variations in difficulty for various editions of the test. The critical reading, writing, and mathematics scaled scores range from 200–800 per section. The total scaled score range is from 600–2400.

Changes to the SAT

The SAT® is changing in the spring of 2016! According to the College Board, the redesigned SAT® will have these sections: Evidence-Based Reading and Writing, Math, and the Essay. It will be based on 1600 points—the top scores for the Math section and the Evidence-Based Reading and Writing section will be 800, and the Essay score will be reported separately.

According to the College Board's website, the "Eight Key Changes" are the following:

- **Relevant Words in Context:** Students will need to interpret the meaning of words based on the context of the passage in which they appear. The focus will be on "relevant" words—not obscure ones.

- **Command of Evidence:** In addition to demonstrating writing skills, students will need to show that they're able to interpret, synthesize, and use evidence found in a wide range of sources.

- **Essay Analyzing a Source:** Students will read a passage and explain how the author builds an argument, supporting support their claims with actual data from the passage.

- **Math Focused on Three Key Areas:** Problem Solving and Data Analysis (using ratios, percentages, and proportional reasoning to solve problems in science, social science, and career contexts), the Heart of Algebra (mastery of linear equations and systems), and Passport to Advanced Math (more complex equations and the manipulation they require).

- **Problems Grounded in Real-World Contexts:** All of the questions will be grounded in the real world, directly related to work performed in college.

- **Analysis in Science and in Social Studies:** Students will need to apply reading, writing, language, and math skills to answer questions in contexts of science, history, and social studies.

- **Founding Documents and Great Global Conversation:** Students will find an excerpt from one of the Founding Documents—such as the Declaration of Independence, the Constitution, and the Bill of Rights—or a text from the "Great Global Conversation" about freedom, justice, and human dignity.

- **No Penalty for Wrong Answers:** Students will earn points for the questions they answer correctly.

If you'll be taking the test after March 2016, you should check out the College Board's website at https://www.collegeboard.org/delivering-opportunity/sat/redesign for the most up-to-date information.

Top 10 Ways Not to Take the Test

10. Cramming the night before the test.
9. Not becoming familiar with the directions before you take the test.
8. Not becoming familiar with the format of the test before you take it.
7. Not knowing how the test is graded.
6. Spending too much time on any one question.
5. Second-guessing yourself.
4. Not checking spelling, grammar, and sentence structure in essays.
3. Writing a one-paragraph essay.
2. Forgetting to take a deep breath to keep from—
1. Losing It!

SAT SUBJECT TESTS™

Subject Tests are required by some institutions for admission and/or placement in freshman-level courses. Each Subject Test measures one's knowledge of a specific subject and the ability to apply that knowledge. Students should check with each institution for its specific requirements. In general, students are required to take three Subject Tests (one English, one mathematics, and one of their choice).

Subject Tests are given in the following areas: biology, chemistry, Chinese, French, German, Italian, Japanese, Korean, Latin, literature, mathematics, modern Hebrew, physics, Spanish, U.S. history, and world history. These tests are 1 hour long and are primarily multiple-choice tests. Three Subject Tests may be taken on one test date.

Scored like the current SAT®, students gain a point for each correct answer and lose a fraction of a point for each incorrect answer. The raw scores are then converted to scaled scores that range from 200 to 800.

THE TOEFL® INTERNET-BASED TEST (IBT)

The Test of English as a Foreign Language Internet-Based Test (TOEFL® iBT) is designed to help assess a student's grasp of English if it is not the student's first language. Performance on the TOEFL® test may help interpret scores on the critical reading sections of the SAT®. The test consists of four integrated sections: speaking, listening, reading, and writing. The TOEFL® iBT emphasizes integrated skills. The paper-based versions of the TOEFL® will continue to be administered in certain countries where the Internet-based version has not yet been introduced. For further information, visit www.toefl.org.

WHAT OTHER TESTS SHOULD I KNOW ABOUT?

The AP Program

This program allows high school students to try college-level work and build valuable skills and study habits in the process. Subject matter is explored in more depth in AP courses than in other high school classes. A qualifying score on an AP test— which varies from school to school—can earn you college credit or advanced placement. Getting qualifying grades on enough exams can even earn you a full year's credit and sophomore standing at more than 1,500 higher-education institutions. There are more than thirty AP courses across multiple subject areas, including art history, biology, and computer science. Speak to your guidance counselor for information about your school's offerings.

College-Level Examination Program (CLEP)

The CLEP enables students to earn college credit for what they already know, whether it was learned in school, through independent study, or through other experiences outside of the classroom. More than 2,900 colleges and universities now award credit for qualifying scores on one or more of the 33 CLEP exams. The exams, which are 90 minutes in length and are primarily multiple choice, are administered at participating colleges and universities. For more information, check out the website at www.collegeboard.com/clep.

WHAT CAN I DO TO PREPARE FOR THESE TESTS?

Know what to expect. Get familiar with how the tests are structured, how much time is allowed, and the directions for each type of question. Get plenty of rest the night before the test and eat breakfast that morning.

There are a variety of products, from books to software to videos, available to help you prepare for most standardized tests. Find the learning style that suits you best. As for which products to buy, there are two major categories— those created by the test-makers and those created by private companies. The best approach is to talk to someone who has been through the process and find out which product or products he or she recommends.

Some students report significant increases in scores after participating in coaching programs. Longer-term programs (40 hours) seem to raise scores more than short-term programs (20 hours), but beyond 40 hours, score gains are minor. Math scores appear to benefit more from coaching than critical reading scores.

Resources

There is a variety of ways to prepare for standardized tests— find a method that fits your schedule and your budget. But you should definitely prepare. Far too many students walk into these tests cold, either because they find standardized tests frightening or annoying or they just haven't found the time to study. The key is that these exams are standardized. That means these tests are largely the same from administration to administration; they always test the same concepts. They have to, or else you couldn't compare the scores of people who took the tests on different dates. The numbers or words may change, but the underlying content doesn't.

So how do you prepare? At the very least, you should review relevant material, such as math formulas and commonly used vocabulary words, and know the directions for each question type or test section. You should take at least one practice test and review your mistakes so you don't make them again on the test day. Beyond that, you know best how much preparation you need. You'll also find lots of material in libraries or bookstores to help you: books and software from the test- makers and from other publishers (including Peterson's) or live courses that range from national test-preparation companies to teachers at your high school who offer classes.

Who's Paying for This?
Financial Aid Basics

A college education can be expensive—costing more than $150,000 for four years at some of the higher priced private colleges and universities. Even at the lower-cost state colleges and universities, the cost of a four-year education can approach $60,000. Determining how you and your family will come up with the necessary funds to pay for your education requires planning, perseverance, and learning as much as you can about the options that are available to you. But before you get discouraged, College Board statistics show that 53 percent of full-time students attend four-year public and private colleges with tuition and fees less than $9,000, while 20 percent attend colleges that have tuition and fees more than $36,000. College costs tend to be less in the western states and higher in New England.

Paying for college should not be looked at as a four-year financial commitment. For many families, paying the total cost of a student's college education out of current income and savings is usually not realistic. For families that have planned ahead and have financial savings established for higher education, the burden is a lot easier. But for most, meeting the cost of college requires the pooling of current income and assets and investing in longer-term loan options. These family resources, together with financial assistance from state, federal, and institutional sources, enable millions of students each year to attend the institution of their choice.

FINANCIAL AID PROGRAMS

There are three types of financial aid:

1. Gift-aid—Scholarships and grants are funds that do not have to be repaid.

2. Loans—Loans must be repaid, usually after graduation; the amount you have to pay back is the total you've borrowed plus any accrued interest. This is considered a source of self-help aid.

3. Student employment—Student employment is a job arranged for you by the financial aid office. This is another source of self-help aid.

The federal government has four major grant programs—the Federal Pell Grant, the Federal Supplemental Educational Opportunity Grant, Academic Competitiveness Grants (ACG), and National SMART (Science and Mathematics Access to Retain Talent) grants. ACG and SMART grants are limited to students who qualify for a Pell Grant and are awarded to a select group of students. Overall, these grants are targeted to low-to-moderate income families with significant financial need. The federal government also sponsors a student employment program called the Federal Work-Study Program, which offers jobs both on and off campus, and several loan programs, including those for students and for parents of undergraduate students.

There are two types of student loan programs: subsidized and unsubsidized. The subsidized Federal Direct Loan and the Federal Perkins Loan are need-based, government-subsidized loans. Students who borrow through these programs do not have to pay interest on the loan until after they graduate or leave school. The unsubsidized Federal Direct Loan and the Federal Direct PLUS Loan Program are not based on need, and borrowers are responsible for the interest while the student is in school. These loans are administered by different methods. Once you choose your college, the financial aid office will guide you through this process.

After you've submitted your financial aid application and you've been accepted for admission, each college will send you a letter describing your financial aid award. Most award letters show estimated college costs, how much you and your family are expected to contribute, and the amount and types of aid you have been awarded. Most students are awarded aid from a combination of sources and programs. Hence, your award is often called a financial aid "package."

SOURCES OF FINANCIAL AID

Millions of students and families apply for financial aid each year. Financial aid from all sources exceeds $143 billion per year. The largest single source of aid is the federal government, which will award more than $100 billion this year.

The next largest source of financial aid is found in the college and university community. Most of this aid is awarded to students who have a demonstrated need based on the Federal Methodology. Some institutions use a different formula, the Institutional Methodology (IM), to award their own funds in conjunction with other forms of aid. Institutional aid may be either need-based or non-need based. Aid that is not based on need is usually awarded for a student's academic performance (merit awards), specific talents or abilities, or to attract the type of students a college seeks to enroll.

Another source of financial aid is from state government. All states offer grant and/or scholarship aid, most of which is need-based. However, more and more states are offering substantial merit-based aid programs. Most state programs award aid only to students attending college in their home state.

Other sources of financial aid include:

- Private agencies
- Foundations
- Corporations
- Clubs
- Fraternal and service organizations

- Civic associations
- Unions
- Religious groups that award grants, scholarships, and low-interest loans
- Employers that provide tuition reimbursement benefits for employees and their children

More information about these different sources of aid is available from high school guidance offices, public libraries, college financial aid offices, directly from the sponsoring organizations, and online at www.petersons.com/college-search/scholarship-search.aspx.

HOW NEED-BASED FINANCIAL AID IS AWARDED

When you apply for aid, your family's financial situation is analyzed using a government-approved formula called the Federal Methodology. This formula looks at five items:

1. Demographic information of the family
2. Income of the parents
3. Assets of the parents
4. Income of the student
5. Assets of the student

This analysis determines the amount you and your family are expected to contribute toward your college expenses, called your Expected Family Contribution, or EFC. If the EFC is equal to or more than the cost of attendance at a particular college, then you do not demonstrate financial need. However, even if you don't have financial need, you may still qualify for aid, as there are grants, scholarships, and loan programs that are not need-based.

If the cost of your education is greater than your EFC, then you do demonstrate financial need and qualify for assistance. The amount of your financial need that can be met varies from school to school. Some are able to meet your full need, while others can only cover a certain percentage of need. Here's the formula:

Cost of Attendance
− Expected Family Contribution
= Financial Need

The EFC remains constant, but your need will vary according to the costs of attendance at a particular college. In general, the higher the tuition and fees at a particular college, the higher the cost of attendance will be. Expenses for books and supplies, room and board, transportation, and other miscellaneous items are included in the overall cost of attendance. It is important to remember that you do not have to be low-income to qualify for financial aid. Many middle and upper-middle income families qualify for need-based financial aid.

APPLYING FOR FINANCIAL AID

Every student must complete the Free Application for Federal Student Aid (FAFSA) to be considered for financial aid. The FAFSA is available from your high school guidance office,

many public libraries, colleges in your area, or directly from the U.S. Department of Education.

Students are encouraged to apply for federal student aid on the Web. The electronic version of the FAFSA can be accessed at http://www.fafsa.ed.gov. Both the student and at least one parent must apply for a federal PIN at http:// www.pin.ed.gov. The PIN serves as your electronic signature when applying for aid on the Web.

To award their own funds, some colleges require an additional application, the CSS/Financial Aid PROFILE® form. The PROFILE asks supplemental questions that some colleges and awarding agencies feel provide a more accurate assessment of the family's ability to pay for college. It is up to the college to decide whether it will use only the FAFSA or both the FAFSA and the PROFILE. PROFILE applications are available from the high school guidance office and on the Web. Both the paper application and the website list those colleges and programs that require the PROFILE application.

If Every College You're Applying to for Fall 2016 Requires the FAFSA

. . . then it's pretty simple: Complete the FAFSA after January 1, 2016, being certain to send it in before any college-imposed deadlines. (You are not permitted to send in the 2016–17 FAFSA before January 1, 2016.) Most college FAFSA application deadlines are in February or early March. It is easier if you have all your financial records for the previous year available, but if that is not possible, you are strongly encouraged to use estimated figures.

After you send in your FAFSA, either with the paper application or electronically, you'll receive a Student Aid Report (SAR) that includes all of the information you reported and shows your EFC. If you provided an e-mail address, the SAR is sent to you electronically; otherwise, you will receive a SAR or SAR Acknowledgment in the mail, which lists your FAFSA information but may require you to make any corrections on the FAFSA website. Be sure to review the SAR, checking to see if the information you reported is accurately represented. If you used estimated numbers to complete the FAFSA, you may have to resubmit the SAR with any corrections to the data. The college(s) you have designated on the FAFSA will receive the information you reported and will use that data to make their decision. In many instances, the colleges to which you've applied will ask you to send copies of your and your parents' federal income tax returns for 2015, plus any other documents needed to verify the information you reported.

If a College Requires the PROFILE

Step 1: Register for the CSS/Financial Aid PROFILE in the fall of your senior year in high school. You can apply for the PROFILE online at http://profileonline.collegeboard.com/prf/index.jsp. Registration information with a list of the colleges that require the PROFILE is available in most high school guidance offices. There is a fee for using the Financial Aid PROFILE application ($25 for the first college, which includes the $9 application fee, and $16 for each additional college). You must pay for the service by credit card when you register. If you do not have a credit card, you will be billed. A limited number of fee waivers are automatically granted to first-time applicants based on the financial information provided on the PROFILE.

Step 2: Fill out your customized CSS/Financial Aid PROFILE. Once you register, your application will be immediately available online and will have questions that all students must complete, questions which must be completed by the student's parents (unless the student is independent and the colleges or programs selected do not require parental information), and *may* have supplemental questions needed by one or more of your schools or programs. If required, those will be found in Section Q of the application.

In addition to the PROFILE application you complete online, you may also be required to complete a Business/ Farm Supplement via traditional paper format. Completion of this form is not a part of the online process. If this form is required, instructions on how to download and print the supplemental form are provided. If your biological or adoptive parents are separated or divorced and your colleges and programs require it, your noncustodial parent may be asked to complete the Noncustodial PROFILE.

Once you complete and submit your PROFILE application, it will be processed and sent directly to your requested colleges and programs.

IF YOU DON'T QUALIFY FOR NEED-BASED AID

If you are not eligible for need-based aid, you can still find ways to lessen your burden.

Here are some suggestions:

- Search for merit scholarships. You can start at the initial stages of your application process. College merit awards are increasingly important as more and more colleges award these to students they especially want to attract. As a result, applying to a college at which your qualifications put you at the top of the entering class may give you a larger merit award. Another source of aid to look for is private scholarships that are given for special skills and talents. Additional information can be found at www.finaid.org.

- Seek employment during the summer and the academic year. The student employment office at your college can help you locate a school-year job. Many colleges and local businesses have vacancies remaining after they have hired students who are receiving Federal Work-Study Program financial aid.

- Borrow through the unsubsidized Federal Direct Loan program. This is generally available to all students. The terms and conditions are similar to the subsidized loans. The biggest difference is that the borrower is responsible for the interest while still in college, although the government permits students to delay paying the interest right away and add the accrued interest to the total amount owed. You must file the FAFSA to be considered.

- After you've secured what you can through scholarships, working, and borrowing, you and your parents will be expected to meet your share of the college bill (the Expected Family Contribution). Many colleges offer monthly payment plans that spread the cost over the academic year. If the monthly payments are too high, parents can borrow through the Federal Direct PLUS Loan Program, through one of the many private education loan programs available, or through home equity loans and lines of credit. Families seeking assistance in financing college expenses should inquire at the financial aid office about what programs are available at the college. Some families seek the advice of professional financial advisers and tax consultants.

Frequently Asked Questions About Transferring

Muriel M. Shishkoff

Among the students attending two-year colleges are a large number who began their higher education knowing they would eventually transfer to a four-year school to obtain their bachelor's degree. There are many reasons why students go this route. Upon graduating from high school, some simply do not have definite career goals. Although they don't want to put their education on hold, they prefer not to pay exorbitant amounts in tuition while trying to "find themselves." As the cost of a university education escalates—even in public institutions—the option of spending the freshman and sophomore years at a two-year college looks attractive to many students. Others attend a two-year college because they are unable to meet the initial entrance standards—a specified grade point average (GPA), standardized test scores, or knowledge of specific academic subjects—required by the four-year school of their choice. Many such students praise the community college system for giving them the chance to be, academically speaking, "born again." In addition, students from other countries often find that they can adapt more easily to language and cultural changes at a two-year school before transferring to a larger, more diverse four-year college.

If your plan is to attend a two-year college with the ultimate goal of transferring to a four-year school, you will be pleased to know that the increased importance of the community college route to a bachelor's degree is recognized by all segments of higher education. As a result, many two-year schools have revised their course outlines and established new courses in order to comply with the programs and curricular offerings of the universities. Institutional improvements to make transferring easier have also proliferated at both the two-and four-year levels. The generous transfer policies of the Pennsylvania, New York, and Florida state university systems, among others, reflect this attitude; these systems accept all credits from students who have graduated from accredited community colleges.

If you are interested in moving from a two-year college to a four-year school, the sooner you make up your mind that you are going to make the switch, the better position you will be to transfer successfully (that is, without having wasted valuable time and credits). The ideal point at which to make such a decision is **before** you register for classes at your two-year school; a counselor can help you plan your course work with an eye toward fulfilling the requirements needed for your major course of study.

Naturally, it is not always possible to plan your transferring strategy that far in advance, but keep in mind that the key to a successful transfer is **preparation,** and preparation takes time—time to think through your objectives and time to plan the right classes to take.

As students face the prospect of transferring from a two-year to a four-year school, many thoughts and concerns about this complicated and often frustrating process race through their minds. Here are answers to the questions that are most frequently asked by transferring students.

Q Does every college and university accept transfer students?

A Most four-year institutions accept transfer students, but some do so more enthusiastically than others. Graduating from a community college is an advantage at, for example, Arizona State University and the University of Massachusetts Boston; both accept more community college transfer students than traditional freshmen. At the University at Albany, SUNY, graduates of two-year transfer programs within the State University of New York System are given priority for upper-division (i.e., junior-and senior-level) vacancies.

Schools offering undergraduate work at the upper division only are especially receptive to transfer applications. On the other hand, some schools accept only a few transfer students; others refuse entrance to sophomores or those in their final year. Princeton University requires an "excellent academic record and particularly compelling reasons to transfer." Check the catalogs of several colleges for their transfer requirements before you make your final choice.

Q Do students who go directly from high school to a four-year college do better academically than transfer students from community colleges?

A On the contrary: some institutions report that transfers from two-year schools who persevere until graduation do *better* than those who started as freshmen in a four-year college.

Q Why is it so important that my two-year college be accredited?

A Four-year colleges and universities accept transfer credits only from schools formally recognized by a regional, national, or professional educational agency. This accreditation signifies that an institution or program of study meets or exceeds a minimum level of educational quality necessary for meeting stated educational objectives.

Q After enrolling at a four-year school, may I still make up necessary courses at a community college?

A Some institutions restrict credit after transfer to their own facilities. Others allow students to take a limited number of transfer courses after matriculation, depending on the subject matter. A few provide opportunities for cross-registration or dual enrollment, which means taking classes on more than one campus.

Q What do I need to do to transfer?

A First, send for your high school and college transcripts. Having chosen the school you wish to transfer to, check its admission requirements against your transcripts. If you find that you are admissible, file an application as early as possible before the deadline. Part of the process will be asking your former schools to send official transcripts to the admission office, i.e., not the copies you used in determining your admissibility.

Plan your transfer program with the head of your new department as soon as you have decided to transfer. Determine the recommended general education pattern and necessary preparation for your major. At your present school, take the courses you will need to meet transfer requirements for the new school.

Q What qualifies me for admission as a transfer student?

A Admission requirements for most four-year institutions vary. Depending on the reputation or popularity of the school and program you wish to enter, requirements may be quite selective and competitive. Usually, you will need to show satisfactory test scores, an academic record up to a certain standard, and completion of specific subject matter.

Transfer students can be eligible to enter a four-year school in a number of ways: by having been eligible for admission directly upon graduation from high school, by making up shortcomings in grades (or in subject matter not covered in high school) at a community college, or by satisfactory completion of necessary courses or credit hours at another postsecondary institution. Ordinarily, students coming from a community college or from another four-year institution must meet or exceed the receiving institution's standards for freshmen and show appropriate college-level course work taken since high school. Students who did not graduate from high school can present proof of proficiency through results on the the GED® Test, the HiSET® Exam, or another state-approved high school equivalency test.

Q Are exceptions ever made for students who don't meet all the requirements for transfer?

A Extenuating circumstances, such as disability, low family income, refugee or veteran status, or athletic talent, may permit the special enrollment of students who would not otherwise be eligible but who demonstrate the potential for academic success. Consult the appropriate office—the Educational Opportunity Program, the disabled students' office, the athletic department, or the academic dean—to see whether an exception can be made in your case.

Q How far in advance do I need to apply for transfer?

A Some schools have a rolling admission policy, which means that they process transfer applications as they are received, all year long. With other schools, you must apply during the priority filing period, which can be up to a year before you wish to enter. Check the date with the admission office at your prospective campus.

Q Is it possible to transfer courses from several different institutions?

A Institutions ordinarily accept the courses that they consider transferable, regardless of the number of accredited schools involved. However, there is the danger of exceeding the maximum number of credit hours that can be transferred from all other schools or earned through credit by examination, extension courses, or correspondence courses. The limit placed on transfer credits varies from school to school, so read the catalog carefully to avoid taking courses you won't be able to use. To avoid duplicating courses, keep attendance at different campuses to a minimum.

Q What is involved in transferring from a semester system to a quarter or trimester system?

A In the semester system, the academic calendar is divided into two equal parts. The quarter system is more aptly named trimester, since the academic calendar is divided into three equal terms (not counting a summer session). To convert semester units into quarter units or credit hours, simply multiply the semester units by one and a half. Conversely, multiply quarter units by two thirds to come up with semester units. If you are used to a semester system of fifteen- to sixteen-week courses, the ten-week courses of the quarter system may seem to fly by.

Q Why might a course be approved for transfer credit by one four-year school but not by another?

A The beauty of postsecondary education in the United States lies in its variety. Entrance policies and graduation requirements are designed to reflect and serve each institution's mission. Because institutional policies vary so widely, schools may interpret the subject matter of a course from quite different points of view. Given that the granting of transfer credit indicates that a course is viewed as being, in effect, parallel to one offered by the receiving institution, it is easy to see how this might be the case at one university and not another.

Q Must I take a foreign language to transfer?

A Foreign language proficiency is often required for admission to a four-year institution; such proficiency also often figures in certain majors or in the general education pattern. Often, two or three years of a single language in high school will do the trick. Find out if scores received on Advanced Placement (AP®) examinations, placement examinations given by the foreign language department, or SAT Subject Tests™ will be accepted in lieu of college course work.

Q Will the school to which I'm transferring accept pass/ no pass, pass/fail, or credit/no credit grades in lieu of letter grades?

A Usually, a limit is placed on the number of these courses you can transfer, and there may be other restrictions as well. If you want to use other-than-letter grades for the fulfillment of general education requirements or lower-division (freshman and sophomore) preparation for the major, check with the receiving institution.

Q Which is more important for transfer—my grade point average or my course completion pattern?

A Some schools believe that your past grades indicate academic potential and overshadow prior preparation for a specific degree program. Others require completion of certain introductory courses before transfer to prepare you for upper-division work in your major. In any case, appropriate course selection will cut down the time to graduation and increase your chances of making a successful transfer.

Q What happens to my credits if I change majors?

A If you change majors after admission, your transferable course credit should remain fairly intact. However, because you may need extra or different preparation for your new major, some of the courses you've taken may now be useful only as electives. The need for additional lower-level preparation may mean you're staying longer at your new school than you originally planned. On the other hand, you may already have taken courses that count toward your new major as part of the university's general education pattern.

Excerpted from *Transferring Made Easy: A Guide to Changing Colleges Successfully,* by Muriel M. Shishkoff, © 1991 by Muriel M. Shishkoff (published by Peterson's).

Returning to School: Advice for Adult Students

Sandra Cook, Ph.D.
Associate Vice President for Enrollment Management, San Diego State University

Many adults think for a long time about returning to school without taking any action. One purpose of this article is to help the "thinkers" finally make some decisions by examining what is keeping them from action. Another purpose is to describe not only some of the difficulties and obstacles that adult students may face when returning to school but also tactics for coping with them.

If you have been thinking about going back to college, and believing that you are the only person your age contemplating college, you should know that approximately 7 million adult students are currently enrolled in higher education institutions. This number represents 50 percent of total higher education enrollments. The majority of adult students are enrolled at two-year colleges.

There are many reasons why adult students choose to attend a two-year college. Studies have shown that the three most important criteria that adult students consider when choosing a college are location, cost, and availability of the major or program desired. Most two-year colleges are public institutions that serve a geographic district, making them readily accessible to the community. Costs at most two-year colleges are far less than at other types of higher education institutions. For many students who plan to pursue a bachelor's degree, completing their first two years of college at a community college is an affordable means to that end. If you are interested in an academic program that will transfer to a four-year institution, most two-year colleges offer the "general education" courses that compose most freshman and sophomore years. If you are interested in a vocational or technical program, two-year colleges excel in providing this type of training.

SETTING THE STAGE

There are three different "stages" in the process of adults returning to school. The first stage is uncertainty. Do I really want to go back to school? What will my friends or family think? Can I compete with those 18-year-old whiz kids? Am I too old? The second stage is choice. Once the decision to return has been made, you must choose where you will attend. There are many criteria to use in making this decision. The third stage is support. You have just added another role to your already-too-busy life. There are, however, strategies that

will help you accomplish your goals—perhaps not without struggle, but with grace and humor nonetheless. Let's look at each of these stages.

UNCERTAINTY

Why are you thinking about returning to school? Is it to

- fulfill a dream that had to be delayed?
- become more educationally well-rounded?
- fill an intellectual void in your life?

These reasons focus on personal growth.

If you are returning to school to

- meet people and make friends
- attain and enjoy higher social status and prestige among friends, relatives, and associates
- understand/study a cultural heritage
- have a medium in which to exchange ideas

You are interested in social and cultural opportunities.

If you are like most adult students, you want to

- qualify for a new occupation
- enter or reenter the job market
- increase earnings potential
- qualify for a more challenging position in the same field of work

You are seeking career growth.

Understanding the reasons why you want to go back to school is an important step in setting your educational goals and will help you to establish some criteria for selecting a college. However, don't delay your decision because you have not been able to clearly define your motives. Many times, these aren't clear until you have already begun the process, and they may change as you move through your college experience.

Assuming you agree that additional education will benefit you, what is it that keeps you from returning to school? You may have a litany of excuses running through your mind:

- I don't have time.
- I can't afford it.
- I'm too old to learn.
- My friends will think I'm crazy.

- I'll be older than the teachers and other students.
- My family can't survive without me to take care of them every minute.
- I'll be X years old when I finish.
- I'm afraid.
- I don't know what to expect.

And that is just what these are—excuses. You can make school, like anything else in your life, a priority or not. If you really want to return, you can. The more you understand your motivation for returning to school and the more you understand what excuses are keeping you from taking action, the easier your task will be.

If you think you don't have time: The best way to decide how attending class and studying can fit into your schedule is to keep track of what you do with your time each day for several weeks. Completing a standard time-management grid (each day is plotted out by the half hour) is helpful for visualizing how your time is spent. For each 3-credit-hour class you take, you will need to find 3 hours for class plus 6 to 9 hours for reading-studying-library time. This study time should be spaced evenly throughout the week, not loaded up on one day. It is not possible to learn or retain the material that way. When you examine your grid, see where there are activities that could be replaced with school and study time. You may decide to give up your bowling league or some time in front of the TV. Try not to give up sleeping, and don't cut out every moment of free time. Here are some suggestions that have come from adults who have returned to school:

- Enroll in a time-management workshop. It helps you rethink how you use your time.
- Don't think you have to take more than one course at a time. You may eventually want to work up to taking more, but consider starting with one. (It is more than you are taking now!)
- If you have a family, start assigning to them those household chores that you usually do—and don't redo what they do.
- Use your lunch hour or commuting time for reading.

If you think you cannot afford it: As mentioned earlier, two-year colleges are extremely affordable. If you cannot afford the tuition, look into the various financial aid options. Most federal and state funds are available to full- and part-time students. Loans are also available. While many people prefer not to accumulate a debt for school, these same people will think nothing of taking out a loan to buy a car. After five or six years, which is the better investment? Adult students who work should look into whether their company has a tuition-reimbursement policy. There are also private scholarships, available through foundations, service organizations, and clubs, that are focused on adult learners. Your public library, the Web, and a college financial aid adviser are three excellent sources for reference materials regarding financial aid.

If you think you are too old to learn: This is pure myth. A number of studies have shown that adult learners perform as well as, or better than, traditional-age students.

If you are afraid your friends will think you're crazy: Who cares? Maybe they will, maybe they won't. Usually, they will admire your courage and be just a little jealous of your ambition (although they'll never tell you that). Follow your dreams, not theirs.

If you are concerned because the teachers or students will be younger than you: Don't be. The age differences that may be apparent in other settings evaporate in the classroom. If anything, an adult in the classroom strikes fear into the hearts of some 18-year-olds because adults have been known to be prepared, ask questions, be truly motivated, and be there to learn!

If you think your family will have a difficult time surviving while you are in school: If you have done everything for them up to now, they might struggle. Consider this an opportunity to help them become independent and self-sufficient. Your family can only make you feel guilty if you let them. You are not abandoning them; you are becoming an educational role model. When you are happy and working toward your goals, everyone benefits. Admittedly, it sometimes takes time for them to realize this. For single parents, there are schools that offer support groups, child care, and cooperative babysitting.

If you're appalled at the thought of being X years old when you graduate in Y years: How old will you be in Y years if you don't go back to school?

If you are afraid or don't know what to expect: Know that these are natural feelings when one encounters any new situation. Adult students find that their fears usually dissipate once they begin classes. Fear of trying is usually the biggest roadblock to the reentry process.

No doubt you have dreamed up a few more reasons for not making the decision to return to school. Keep in mind that what you are doing is making up excuses, and you are using these excuses to release you from the obligation to make a decision about your life. The thought of returning to college can be scary. Anytime anyone ventures into unknown territory, there is a risk, but taking risks is a necessary component of personal and professional growth. It is your life, and you alone are responsible for making the decisions that determine its course. Education is an investment in your future.

CHOICE

Once you have decided to go back to school, your next task is to decide where to go. If your educational goals are well defined (e.g., you want to pursue a degree in order to change careers), then your task is a bit easier. But even if your educational goals are still evolving, do not defer your return. Many students who enter higher education with a specific major in mind change that major at least once.

Most students who attend a public two-year college choose the community college in the district in which they live. This is generally the closest and least expensive option if the school offers the programs you want. If you are planning to begin your education at a two-year college and then transfer to a four-year school, there are distinct advantages to choosing your four-year school early. Many community and four-year colleges have "articulation" agreements that designate what credits from the two-year school will transfer to the four-year college and how. Some four-year institutions accept an associate degree as equivalent to the freshman and sophomore years, regardless of the courses you have taken. Some four-year schools accept two-year college work only on a course-by-course basis. If you can identify which school you will transfer to, you can know in advance exactly how your two-year credits will apply, preventing an unexpected loss of credit or time.

Each institution of higher education is distinctive. Your goal in choosing a college is to come up with the best student-institution fit—matching your needs with the offerings and characteristics of the school. The first step in choosing a college is to determine what criteria are most important to you in attaining your educational goals. Location, cost, and program availability are the three main factors that influence an adult student's college choice. In considering location, don't forget that some colleges have conveniently located branch campuses. In considering cost, remember to explore your financial aid options before ruling out an institution because of its tuition. Program availability should include not only the major in which you are interested, but also whether or not classes in that major are available when you can take them.

Some additional considerations beyond location, cost, and programs are:

- Does the school have a commitment to adult students and offer appropriate services, such as child care, tutoring, and advising?
- Are classes offered at times when you can take them?
- Are there academic options for adults, such as credit for life or work experience, credit by examination (including CLEP), credit for military service, or accelerated programs?
- Is the faculty sensitive to the needs of adult learners?

Once you determine which criteria are vital in your choice of an institution, you can begin to narrow your choices. There are myriad ways for you to locate the information you desire. Many newspapers publish a "School Guide" several times a year in which colleges and universities advertise to an adult student market. In addition, schools themselves publish catalogs, class schedules, and promotional materials that contain much of the information you need, and they are yours for the asking. Many colleges sponsor information sessions and open houses that allow you to visit the campus and ask questions. An appointment with an adviser is a good way to assess the fit

between you and the institution. Be sure to bring your questions with you to your interview.

SUPPORT

Once you have made the decision to return to school and have chosen the institution that best meets your needs, take some additional steps to ensure your success during your crucial first semester. Take advantage of institutional support and build some social support systems of your own. Here are some ways of doing just that:

- Plan to participate in any orientation programs. These serve the threefold purpose of providing you with a great deal of important information, familiarizing you with the campus and its facilities, and giving you the opportunity to meet and begin networking with other students.
- Take steps to deal with any academic weaknesses. Take mathematics and writing placement tests if you have reason to believe you may need some extra help in these areas. It is not uncommon for adult students to need a math refresher course or a program to help alleviate math anxiety. Ignoring a weakness won't make it go away.
- Look into adult reentry programs. Many institutions offer adults workshops focusing on ways to improve study skills, textbook reading, test-taking, and time-management skills.
- Build new support networks by joining an adult student organization, making a point of meeting other adult students through workshops, or actively seeking out a "study buddy" in each class—that invaluable friend who shares and understands your experience.
- Incorporate your new status as "student" into your family life. Doing your homework with your children at a designated "homework time" is a valuable family activity and reinforces the importance of education.
- Make sure you take a reasonable course load in your first semester. It is far better to have some extra time on your hands and to succeed magnificently than to spend the entire semester on the brink of a breakdown. Also, whenever possible, try to focus your first courses not only on requirements, but also on areas of personal interest.
- Faculty members, advisers, and student affairs personnel are there to help you during difficult times—let them assist you as often as necessary.

After completing your first semester, you will probably look back in wonder at why you thought going back to school was so imposing. Certainly, it's not without its occasional exasperations. But, as with life, keeping things in perspective and maintaining your sense of humor make the difference between just coping and succeeding brilliantly.

Coming to America: Tips for International Students Considering Study in the U.S.

Introduction: Why Study in the United States?

Are you thinking about going to a college or university in the United States? If you're looking at this book, you probably are! All around the world, students like you, pursuing higher education, are considering that possibility. They envision themselves on modern, high-tech campuses in well-known cities, surrounded by American students, taking classes and having fun. A degree from a U.S. school would certainly lead to success and fortune, either back in your home country or perhaps even in the United States, wouldn't it?

It can be done—but becoming a student at a college or university in the U.S. requires academic talent, planning, time, effort, and money. While there may be only a small number of institutions of higher learning in your country, there are more than 2,800 four-year colleges and universities in the United States. Choosing one, being accepted, and then traveling and becoming a student in America is a big undertaking.

If this is your dream, here is some helpful information and expert tips from professionals who work with international students at colleges and universities throughout the United States.

Timing and Planning

The journey to a college or university in the U.S. often starts years in advance. Most international students choose to study in the U.S. because of the high quality of academics. Your family may also have a lot of input on this decision, too.

"We always tell students they should be looking in the sophomore year, visiting in the junior year, and applying in the senior year," says Father Francis E. Chambers, OSA, D.Min., Associate Director of International Admission at Villanova University. He stresses that prospective students need to be taking challenging courses in the years leading up to college. "We want to see academic rigor. Most admission decisions are based on the first six semesters—senior year is too late."

Heidi Gregori-Gahan, Assistant Provost for International Programs at the University of Southern Indiana agrees that it's important to start early. "Plan ahead and do your homework. There is so much to choose from—so many schools, programs, degrees, and experiences. It can be overwhelming."

While students in some countries may pay an agent to help them get into a school in the United States, Gregori-Gahan often directs potential international students to EducationUSA (http://educationusa.state.gov), a U.S. State Department network of over 400 international student advising centers in more than 170 countries. "They are there to provide unbiased information about studying in the United States and help you understand the process and what you need to do."

Two to three years of advance planning is also recommended by Daphne Durham, who has been an international student adviser at Harvard, Suffolk University, Valdosta State University, and the University of Georgia. She points out that the academic schedule in other countries is often different than that of the United States, so you need to synchronize your calendar accordingly.

You will have to take several tests in order to gain admission to a U.S. school, so it's important to know when those tests are given in your country, then register and take them so your scores will be available when you apply. Even if you have taken English in school, you will probably have to take The Test of English as a Foreign Language (TOEFL®), but some schools also accept the International English Language Testing Sytem (IELTS). You will probably also have to take the SAT® or ACT® tests, which are achievement or aptitude tests, and are usually required of all students applying for admission, not just international students.

"Make sure you understand how the international admissions process works at the school or schools you want to attend," says Durham. "What test scores are needed and when? Does the school have a fixed calendar or rolling admissions?" Those are just some of the many factors that can impact your application and could make a difference in when you are able to start school.

"Every university is unique in what's required and what they need to do. Even navigating each school's different website can be challenging," explains Gregori-Gahan.

Searching for Schools

This book contains information on thousands of four-year colleges and universities, and it will be a valuable resource for you in your search and application process. But with so many options, how do you decide which school you should attend?

"Where I find a big difference with international students is if their parents don't recognize the school, they don't apply to the school," says Fr. Chambers. "They could be overlooking a lot of great schools. They have to look outside the box."

The school Gregori-Gahan represents is in Evansville, Indiana, and it probably isn't familiar to students abroad. "Not many people have heard of anything beyond New York and California and maybe Florida. I like to tell students that this is 'real America.' But happy international students on our campus have recruited others to come here."

She points out that Internet technology has made a huge difference in the search process for international students. Websites full of information, live chat, webinars, virtual tours, and admission interviews via Skype have made it easier for potential students to connect with U.S. institutions, get more information, and be better able to visualize the campus.

One thing than will help narrow your search for a school is knowing specifically what you want to study. You need to know what the course of study is called in the United States, what it means, and what is required in order to study that subject. You also need to consider your future plans. What are your goals and objectives? What do you plan to do after earning your degree?

"If you're going to overcome the hurdles and get to a U.S. school, you have to have a directed path chosen," says Durham.

The other thing that could help your search process is finding a school that is a good fit.

Fit Is Important

You want your clothing and shoes to fit you properly and be comfortable, so a place where you will spend four or more years of your life studying should also be comfortable and appropriate for you. So how can you determine if a particular school is a good fit?

"We really recommend international students visit first. Yes, there are websites and virtual tours, but there's still nothing that beats an in-person visit," says Fr. Chambers. He estimates that 50 to 60 percent of Villanova's international students visited the campus before enrolling.

"It can be hard to get a sense of a place—you're so far away and you're probably not going to set foot on campus until you arrive," says Gregori-Gahan. "There is a high potential for culture shock."

You need to ask yourself what is important to you in a campus environment, then do some homework to ensure that the schools you are considering meet those needs. Here are some things to consider when it comes to fit:

- **Location:** Is it important for you to be in a well-known city or is a part of the United States that is unfamiliar a possibility? "Look at geographic areas, but also cost of living," recommends Durham. "Be sure to factor in transportation costs also, especially if you plan to return to your home country regularly."
- **Student population:** Some small schools have just 1,000 students while larger ones may have 30,000 students or more.
- **Familiar faces:** Is it important for you to be at a school with others from your home nation or region?

- **Climate:** Some students want a climate similar to where they live now, but others are open and curious about seasons and weather conditions they may not have ever experienced. "We do have four seasons here," says Gregori-Gahan. "Sometimes students who come here from tropical regions are concerned about the winters. The first snow is so exciting, but after that, students may not be aware of how cold it really is."
- **Amenities:** Do you want to find your own housing or choose a school where the majority of students live on campus? Is there public transportation available or is it necessary to walk or have a bicycle or car? Does the school or community have access to things that are important to you culturally and meet the traditions you want to follow?
- **Campus size:** Some campuses are tightly compacted into a few city blocks but others cover hundreds of acres of land. "International students are amazed by how green and spacious our campus is, with blooming flowers, trees, and lots of grass," says Gregori-Gahan.
- **Academic offerings:** Does this school offer the program you want to study? Can you complete it in four years or perhaps sooner? What sort of internship and career services are available?
- **Finances:** Can you afford to attend this school? Is there any sort of financial assistance available for international students?
- **Support services:** Durham suggests students look carefully at each school's offerings for international students. "Does the school have online guidance for getting your visa? Is ESL tutoring available? Does the school offer host family or community friend programs?" She also suggests you look for campus support groups for students from your country or region.

Looking at the listings and reading the in-depth descriptions in this book can help you search for a school that is a good fit for you.

Government Requirements

The one thing that every international student must have in order to study in the United States is a student visa. Having accurate advice and following all the necessary steps regarding the visa process is essential to being able to enter this country and start school.

As you schedule your tests and application deadlines, you must also consider how long it will take to get your visa. This varies depending on where you live; in some countries, extensive background checks are required. The subject you plan to study can also impact your visa status; it does help to have a major rather than be undeclared. The U.S. State Department website, http://travel.state.gov/content/visas/english/study-exchange.html, can give you an idea of how long it will take.

In addition to the visa, you will also need a Form I-20, which is a U.S. government immigration form. You must have that form when you get to the United States.

"It's very different from being a tourist. You need to be prepared to meet with an immigration officer and be interviewed about your college," explains Durham. "Where you are going, why you are going, where the school is located, what you are studying and so on."

You also need to keep in mind that there are reporting requirements once you are a student in the U.S. Every semester, your adviser has to report to the government to confirm that you are enrolled in and attending school in order for you to stay in the United States.

Finances

Part of the visa process includes having the funds to pay for the cost of your schooling and support yourself. Finances are a huge hurdle in the process of becoming a college student in the United States.

"It's crucial. So many foreign systems offer 'free' higher education to students. How is your family going to handle the ongoing expense of attending college for four years or longer in the United States?" Durham reiterates that planning ahead is key because there are so many details. Student loans require a U.S.-based cosigner. Each school has its own financial aid deadlines. You have to factor in your own government's requirements, such currency exchange and fund transfers.

The notion that abundant funds are available to assist international students is not true. Sometimes state schools may offer diversity waivers or there may be special scholarship opportunities for international students. But attending school in the U.S. is still a costly venture.

"We do offer financial aid to international students, but they still have to be able to handle a large portion of the costs. Full-need scholarships are not likely," explained Fr. Chambers. "Sometimes students think that once they get here, it will all work out and the funds will be there. But the scenario for the first year has to be repeated each year they are on campus.

Once You Arrive…

You've taken your tests, researched schools, found a good fit, applied, got accepted, arranged the financing, gotten your visa and I-20, and made it to the campus in the United States. Now what?

You can expect the school where you have enrolled to be welcoming and helpful, but within reason. If you arrive on a weekend, or at a time outside of the time when international students are scheduled to arrive, the assistance you need may not be available to you.

Every school offers different levels of assistance to international students. For instance, Villanova offers a full-service office that can assist students with everything from visas, to employment, to finding a place for students to stay over breaks.

Fr. Chambers attends the international student orientation session to greet the students he's worked with through the recruitment and application process. "But I rarely see an international student after that. I think that bodes well for them being integrated into the entire university."

"Those of us who work with international students are really working to help them adjust," says Gregori-Gahan. "International students get here well before school starts so they can get over jet lag. We have orientation sessions and pair them with peer advisers who help them navigate the first few days, and we assure them that we are there for them."

Students should be open to their new setting, but they should be prepared that things may not be at all how they had envisioned during their planning and searching process. "While you may think you'll meet lots of Americans, don't underestimate the importance of community with your traditional home culture and people," says Durham.

Don't Make These Mistakes

The journey to college attendance in the United States is a long one, with many steps. The experts warn about mistakes to avoid along the way.

"Not reading through everything thoroughly and not understanding what the program of study really is and what will it cost. You have to be really clear on the important details," says Gregori-Gahan.

"Every school does things differently," cautions Fr. Chambers. "International students must be aware of that as they are applying."

Durham stresses that going to school in the United States is too big a decision to leave to someone else. "Students need to know about their school—they have to be in charge of their application."

"It involves a lot of work to be successful and happy and not surprised by too many things," Gregori-Gahan says.

Hopefully now, you are more informed and better prepared to pursue your dream of studying at a college or university in the United States.

Community Colleges and the Green Economy

Community colleges are a focal point for state and national efforts to create a green economy and workforce. As the United States transforms its economy into a "green" one, community colleges are leading the way—filling the need for both educated technicians whose skills can cross industry lines as well as those technicians who are able to learn new skills as technologies evolve.

Community colleges have been at the heart of the Obama administration's economic recovery strategy, with $12 billion allocated over this decade. President Obama has extolled community colleges as "the unsung heroes of America's education system," essential to our country's success in the "global competition to lead in the growth of industries of the twenty-first century." With the support of state governments, and, more importantly, local and international business partners, America's community colleges are rising to meet the demands of the new green economy. Community colleges are training individuals to work in fields such as renewable energy, energy efficiency, wind energy, green building, and sustainability. The programs are as diverse as the campuses housing them.

Here is a quick look at just some of the exciting "green" programs available at community colleges throughout the United States.

At Mesalands Community College in Tucumcari, New Mexico, the North American Wind Research and Training Center provides state-of-the-art facilities for research and training qualified technicians in wind energy technology to help meet the need for an estimated 170,000 new positions in the industry by 2030. The Center includes a facility for applied research in collaboration with Sandia National Laboratories—the first-ever such partnership between a national laboratory and a community college. It also provides associate degree training for wind energy technicians, meeting the fast-growing demand for "windsmiths" in the western part of the country—jobs that pay $45,000–$60,000 per year. For more information, visit http://www.mesalands.edu.

Cape Cod Community College (CCCC) in Massachusetts has become one of the nation's leading colleges in promoting and integrating sustainability and green practices throughout all campus operations and technical training programs. Ten years ago, Cape Wind Associates, Cape Cod's first wind farm, provided $50,000 to jumpstart CCCC's wind technician program—considered a state model for community-based clean energy workforce development and education. In addition, hundreds of CCCC students have earned associate degrees in environmental technology and environmental studies, as well as certificate programs in coastal zone management, environmental site assessment, solar thermal technology, and more. Visit http://www.capecod.edu/web/natsci/env/programs for more information.

At Oakland Community College in Michigan, more than 350 students are enrolled in the college's Renewable Energies and Sustainable Living program and its related courses. Students gain field experience refurbishing public buildings with renewable materials, performing energy audits for the government, and working with small businesses and hospitals to reduce waste and pollution. To learn more, visit http://www.oaklandcc.edu/est/.

In 2007, Columbia Gorge Community College in Oregon became the first community college in the Pacific Northwest to offer training programs for the windpower generation industry. The college offers a one-year certificate and a two-year Associate of Applied Science (A.A.S.) degree in renewable energy technology. The Renewable Energy Technology program was designed in collaboration with industry partners from the wind energy industry and the power generation industry. Students are prepared for employment in a broad range of industries, including hydro-generation, wind-generation, automated manufacturing, and engineering technology, and the College plans to add solar array technology to this list as well. For more information, visit http://www.cgcc.cc.or.us/Academics/WindTechnologyPage.cfm.

Central Carolina Community College (CCCC) in Pittsboro, North Carolina, has been leading the way in "green" programs for more than a decade. It offered a sustainable agriculture class at its Chatham campus in 1996 and soon became the first community college in the nation to offer an Associate in Applied Science degree in sustainable agriculture and the first in North Carolina to offer an associate degree in biofuels. In addition, it was the first North Carolina community college to offer a North American Board of Certified Energy Practitioners (NABCEP)–approved solar PV panel installation course as part of its green building/renewable energy program. In 2010, CCCC added an associate degree in sustainable technology and launched its new Natural Chef culinary arts program. The College also offers an ecotourism certificate as well as certificates in other green programs. For more information about Central Carolina Community College's green programs, visit http://www.cccc.edu/green.

At Metropolitan Community College in Omaha, Nebraska, the Continuing Education Department in partnership with Pro-Train is offering green/renewable energy/sustainability online training courses. The courses are designed to provide students with the workforce skills necessary for many in-demand green-collar occupations. Green/Renewable Energy courses include Building Energy Efficient Level, Fundamentals of Solar Hot Water Heating, Green Building Sales (or Technical) Professional, and more. Sustainability Green Supply Chain Training courses include such courses as Alternative Energy Operations, Carbon Strategies, Green Building for Contractors, and Sustainability 101. For more information, visit www.theknowledgebase.org/metropolitan/.

At Cascadia Community College in Bothell, Washington, thanks to a grant from Puget Sound Energy (PSE), students in the Energy Informatics class designed a kiosk screen that shows the energy usage and solar generation at the local 21 Acres Center for Local Food and Sustainable Living. The PSE grant supports the classroom materials for renewable energy education and the Web-based monitoring software that allows students and interested community members to track how much energy is being generated as the weather changes. For more information, visit http://www.cascadia.edu/Default.aspx.

At Grand Rapids Community College, the federally funded Pathways to Prosperity program has successfully prepared low-income residents for jobs in fields such as renewable energy. More than 200 people have completed the program, which began in 2010 thanks to a $4-million grant from the Department of Labor, and found jobs in industries ranging from energy-efficient building construction to alternative energy and sustainable manufacturing. For additional information, check out http://cms.grcc.edu/workforce-training/pathways-prosperity.

Established in 2008, the Green Institute at Heartland Community College in Normal, Illinois, supports a wide range of campus initiatives, educational programs, and community activities that are related to sustainability, energy conservation, renewable energy, recycling, retro-commissioning, and other environmental technologies. For more information, visit http://www.heartland.edu/greenInstitute/.

Most of California's 112 community colleges offer some type of green-tech classes. These include photovoltaic panel installation and repair, green construction practices, and biotechnology courses leading to careers in agriculture, medicine, and environmental forensics. For additional information, check out http://www.californiacommunitycolleges.cccco.edu/ProgramstoWatch/MoreProgramstoWatch/GreenTechnology.aspx.

Linn-Benton Community College (LBCC) in Albany, Oregon, is now offering training for the Oregon Green Technology Certificate. Oregon Green Tech is a federally funded program that is designed to prepare entry-level workers with foundational skills for a variety of industries associated with or in support of green jobs. Students learn skills in green occupations that include green energy production; manufacturing, construction, installation, monitoring, and repair of equipment for solar, wind, wave, and bio-energy; building retro-fitting; process

recycling; hazardous materials removal work; and more. LBCC is one of ten Oregon community colleges to provide training for the Green Technology Certificate, offered through the Oregon Consortium and Oregon Workforce Alliance. Visit http://www.linnbenton.edu for additional information.

The Santa Fe Community College Sustainable Technology Center in New Mexico offers several green jobs training programs along with various noncredit courses. It also provides credit programs from certificates in green building systems, environmental technology training, and solar energy training as well as an Associate in Applied Science (A.A.S.) degree in environmental technology. For more information, go online to http://www.sfcc.edu/sustainable_technologies_center.

In Colorado, Red Rocks Community College (RRCC) offers degree and certificate programs in renewable energy (solar photovoltaic, solar thermal, and wind energy technology), energy and industrial maintenance, energy operations and process technology, environmental technology, water quality management, and energy audit. RRCC has made a commitment to the national challenge of creating and sustaining a green workforce and instructs students about the issues of energy, environmental stewardship, and renewable resources across the college curriculum. For more information, visit http://www.rrcc.edu/green/.

At GateWay Community College in Phoenix, Arizona, graduates of the Environmental Science program now work for the U.S. Geological Survey (USGS), the Arizona Department of Environmental Quality (ADEQ), the Occupational Safety and Health Administration (OSHA), and municipalities across the state and region, as well as private consultants and environmental organizations. For additional information, check out http://www.gatewaycc.edu/environment.

During the past 3.5 years, 17 Illinois community colleges and their partners have created 35 certificate and degree programs to prepare students for careers in green industry sectors. Over 185 courses were created and piloted, online and on-site, in communities across Illinois. The courses were created using open-source materials, with the intent to be shared with other colleges and universities through the Department of Labor's Trade Adjustment Assistance Community College and Career Training (TAACCCT) Grant Program repository.

Next you'll find two essays about other green community college programs. The first essay was written by the president of Lane Community College in Eugene, Oregon, about the role Lane and other community colleges are playing in creating a workforce for the green economy. Then, read a first-hand account of the new Wind Turbine Training Program at Kalamazoo Valley Community College in Kalamazoo, Michigan—a program that has more applicants than spaces and one whose students are being hired BEFORE they even graduate. It's clear that there are exciting "green" programs at community colleges throughout the United States.

The Role of Community Colleges in Creating a Workforce for the Green Economy

by Mary F.T. Spilde, President
Lane Community College

Community colleges are expected to play a leadership role in educating and training the workforce for the green economy. Due to close connections with local and regional labor markets, colleges assure a steady supply of skilled workers by developing and adapting programs to respond to the needs of business and industry. Further, instead of waiting for employers to create job openings, many colleges are actively engaged in local economic development to help educate potential employers to grow their green business opportunities and to participate in the creation of the green economy.

As the green movement emerges there has been confusion about what constitutes a green job. It is now clear that many of the green jobs span several economic sectors such as renewable energy, construction, manufacturing, transportation and agriculture. It is predicted that there will be many middle skill jobs requiring more than a high school diploma but less than a bachelor's degree. This is precisely the unique role that community colleges play. Community colleges develop training programs, including pre-apprenticeship, that ladder the curriculum to take lower skilled workers through a relevant and sequenced course of study that provides a clear pathway to career track jobs. As noted in *Going Green: The Vital Role of Community Colleges in Building a Sustainable Future and Green Workforce* by the National Council for Workforce Education and the Academy for Educational Development, community colleges are strategically positioned to work with employers to redefine skills and competencies needed by the green workforce and to create the framework for new and expanded green career pathways.

While there will be new occupations such as solar and wind technologists, the majority of the jobs will be in the energy management sector—retrofitting the built environment. For example, President Obama called for retrofitting more than 75 percent of federal buildings and more than 2 million homes to make them more energy-efficient. The second major area for growth will be the "greening" of existing jobs as they evolve to incorporate green practices. Both will require new knowledge, skills and abilities. For community colleges, this means developing new programs that meet newly created industry standards and adapting existing programs and courses to integrate green skills. The key is to create a new talent pool of environmentally conscious, highly skilled workers.

These two areas show remarkable promise for education and training leading to high wage/high demand jobs:

- Efficiency and energy management: There is a need for auditors and energy efficiency experts to retrofit existing buildings. Consider how much built environment we have in this country, and it's not difficult to see that this is where the vast amount of jobs are now and will be in the future.
- Greening of existing jobs: There are few currently available jobs that environmental sustainability will not impact.

Whether it is jobs in construction, such as plumbers, electricians, heating and cooling technicians, painters, and building supervisors, or chefs, farmers, custodians, architects, automotive technicians and interior designers, all will need to understand how to lessen their impact on the environment.

Lane Community College offers a variety of degree and certificate programs to prepare students to enter the energy efficiency fields. Lane has offered an Energy Management program since the late 1980s—before it was hip to be green! Students in this program learn to apply basic principles of physics and analysis techniques to the description and measurement of energy in today's building systems, with the goal of evaluating and recommending alternative energy solutions that will result in greater energy efficiency and energy cost savings. Students gain a working understanding of energy systems in today's built environment and the tools to analyze and quantify energy efficiency efforts. The program began with an emphasis in residential energy efficiency/solar energy systems and has evolved to include commercial energy efficiency and renewable energy system installation technology.

The Renewable Energy Technician program is offered as a second-year option within the Energy Management program. Course work prepares students for employment designing and installing solar electric and domestic hot water systems. Renewable Energy students, along with Energy Management students, take a first-year curriculum in commercial energy efficiency giving them a solid background that includes residential energy efficiency, HVAC systems, lighting, and physics and math. In the second year, Renewable Energy students diverge from the Energy Management curriculum and take course work that starts with two courses in electricity fundamentals and one course in energy economics. In the following terms, students learn to design, install, and develop a thorough understanding of photovoltaics and domestic hot water systems.

Recent additions to Lane's offerings are Sustainability Coordinator and Water Conservation Technician degrees. Both programs were added to meet workforce demand.

Lane graduates find employment in a wide variety of disciplines and may work as facility managers, energy auditors, energy program coordinators, or control system specialists, for such diverse employers as engineering firms, public and private utilities, energy equipment companies, and departments of energy and as sustainability leaders within public and private sector organizations.

Lane Community College also provides continuing education for working professionals. The Sustainable Building Advisor (SBA) Certificate Program is a nine-month, specialized training program for working professionals. Graduate are able to advise employers or clients on strategies and tools for implementing sustainable building practices. Benefits from participating in the SBA program often include saving long-term building operating costs; improving the environmental, social, and economic viability of the region; and reducing environmental impacts and owner liability—not to mention the chance to improve one's job skills in a rapidly growing field.

The Building Operators Certificate is a professional development program created by The Northwest Energy Efficiency Council. It is offered through the Northwest Energy Education Institute at Lane. The certificate is designed for operations and maintenance staff working in public or private commercial buildings. It certifies individuals in energy and resource-efficient operation of building systems at two levels: Level I–Building System Maintenance and Level II–Equipment Troubleshooting and Maintenance.

Lane Community College constantly scans the environment to assess workforce needs and develop programs that provide highly skilled employees. Lane, like most colleges, publishes information in its catalog on workforce demand and wages so that students can make informed decisions about program choice.

Green jobs will be a large part of a healthy economy. Opportunities will abound for those who take advantage of programs with a proven record of connecting with employers and successfully educating students to meet high skills standards.

Establishing a World-Class Wind Turbine Technician Academy

by Thomas Sutton, Director of Wind Energy and Technical Services
Kalamazoo Valley Community College

When Kalamazoo Valley Community College (KVCC) decided it wanted to become involved in the training of utility-grade technicians for wind-energy jobs, early on the choice was made to avoid another "me too" training course.

Our program here in Southwest Michigan, 30 miles from Lake Michigan, had to meet industry needs and industry standards.

It was also obvious from the start that the utility-grade or large wind industry had not yet adopted any uniform training standards in the United States.

Of course, these would come, but why should the college wait when European standards were solidly established and working well in Germany, France, Denmark and Great Britain?

As a result, in 2009, KVCC launched its Wind Turbine Technician Academy, the first of its kind in the United States. The noncredit academy runs 8 hours a day, five days a week, for twenty-four weeks of intense training in electricity, mechanics, wind dynamics, safety, and climbing. The college developed this program rather quickly—in eight months—to fast-track individuals into this emerging field.

KVCC based its program on the training standards forged by the Bildungszentrum fur Erneuerebare Energien (BZEE)—the Renewable Energy Education Center. Located in Husum, Germany, the BZEE was created and supported by major wind-turbine manufacturers, component makers, and enterprises that provide operation and maintenance services.

As wind-energy production increased throughout Europe, the need for high-quality, industry-driven, international standards emerged. The BZEE has become the leading trainer for wind-turbine technicians across Europe and now in Asia.

With the exception of one college in Canada, the standards were not yet available in North America. When Kalamazoo Valley realized it could be the first college or university in the United States to offer this training program—that was enough motivation to move forward.

For the College to become certified by the BZEE, it needed to hire and send an electrical instructor and a mechanical instructor to Germany for six weeks of "train the trainer." The instructors not only had to excel in their respective fields, they also needed to be able to climb the skyscraper towers supporting megawatt-class turbines—a unique combination of skills to possess. Truly, individuals who fit this job description don't walk through the door everyday—but we found them! Amazingly, we found a top mechanical instructor who was a part-time fireman and comfortable with tall ladder rescues and a skilled electrical instructor who used to teach rappelling off the Rockies to the Marine Corps.

In addition to employing new instructors, the College needed a working utility-grade nacelle that could fit in its training lab that would be located in the KVCC Michigan Technical Education Center. So one of the instructors traveled to Denmark and purchased a 300-kilowatt turbine.

Once their own training was behind them and the turbine was on its way from the North Sea, the instructors quickly turned to crafting the curriculum necessary for our graduates to earn both an academy certificate from KVCC and a certification from the BZEE.

Promoting the innovative program to qualified potential students across the country was the next step. News releases were published throughout Michigan, and they were also picked up on the Internet. Rather quickly, KVCC found itself with more than 500 requests for applications for a program built for 16 students.

Acceptance into the academy includes a medical release, a climbing test, reading and math tests, relevant work experience, and, finally, an interview. Students in the academy's pioneer class, which graduated in spring 2010, ranged in age from their late teens to early 50s. They hailed from throughout Michigan, Indiana, Ohio, and Illinois as well as from Puerto Rico and Great Britain.

The students brought with them degrees in marketing, law, business, science, and architecture, as well as entrepreneurial experiences in several businesses, knowledge of other languages, military service, extensive travel, and electrical, computer, artistic, and technical/mechanical skills.

Kalamazoo Valley's academy has provided some high-value work experiences for the students in the form of two collaborations with industry that has allowed them to maintain and/or repair actual utility-grade turbines, including those at the 2.5 megawatt size. This hands-on experience will add to the attractiveness of the graduates in the market place. Potential employers were recently invited to an open house where they could see the lab and meet members of this pioneer class.

The College's Turbine Technician Academy has also attracted a federal grant for $550,000 to expand its program through additional equipment purchases. The plan is to erect our own climbing tower. Climbing is a vital part of any valid program, and yet wind farms cannot afford to shut turbines down just for climb-training. The funds were put to use engineering, fabricating, and erecting a wind training tower that incorporated all of the necessary components to teach competency-based work at heights safety training.

When the students are asked what best distinguishes the Kalamazoo Valley program, their answers point to the experienced instructors and the working lab, which is constantly changing to offer the best training experiences. Students also consistently report that the hands-on field experience operating and maintaining the five large turbines during the course has set them apart at companies where they work.

Industry continues to tell us that community colleges need to offer fast-track training programs of this caliber if the nation is to reach the U.S. Department of Energy's goal of 20 percent renewable energy by 2030. This would require more than 1,500 new technicians each year.

The Wind Turbine Technician Academy continues the process improvements as directed by industry input. The academy not only holds the BZEE certification, it is also one of the few American Wind Energy Association (AWEA) Seal of Approval schools in the nation.

With that in mind, KVCC plans to host several BZEE orientation programs for other community colleges in order to encourage them to consider adopting the European training standards and start their own programs.

Meanwhile, applications are continuing to stream in from across the country for the next Wind Turbine Technician Academy program at Kalamazoo Valley Community College. For more information about the program, visit http://www.kvccgrovescenter.com/career/wtta.

How to Use This Guide

Peterson's *Two-Year Colleges 2016* contains a wealth of information for anyone interested in colleges offering associate degrees. This section details the criteria that institutions must meet to be included in this guide and provides information about research procedures used by Peterson's.

QUICK-REFERENCE CHART

The **Two-Year Colleges At-a-Glance Chart** is a geographically arranged table that lists colleges by name and city within the state, or country in which they are located. Areas listed include the United States, Canada, and other countries; the institutions are included because they are accredited by recognized U.S. accrediting bodies (see **Criteria for Inclusion** section).

The At-a-Glance chart contains basic information that enables you to compare institutions quickly according to broad characteristics such as degrees awarded, enrollment, application requirements, financial aid availability, and numbers of sports and majors offered. A dagger (†) after the institution's name indicates that an institution has an entry in the **Featured Two-Year Colleges** section.

Column 1: Degrees Awarded

C= *college transfer associate degree:* the degree awarded after a "university-parallel" program, equivalent to the first two years of a bachelor's degree.

T= *terminal associate degree:* the degree resulting from a one- to three-year program providing training for a specific occupation.

B= *bachelor's degree (baccalaureate):* the degree resulting from a liberal arts, science, professional, or preprofessional program normally lasting four years, although in some cases an accelerated program can be completed in three years.

M= *master's degree:* the first graduate (postbaccalaureate) degree in the liberal arts and sciences and certain professional fields, usually requiring one to two years of full-time study.

D= *doctoral degree* (research/scholarship, professional practice, or other)

Column 2: Institutional Control

Private institutions are designated as one of the following:

Ind = *independent* (nonprofit)

I-R = *independent-religious:* nonprofit; sponsored by or affiliated with a particular religious group or having a nondenominational or interdenominational religious orientation.

Prop = *proprietary* (profit-making)

Public institutions are designated by the source of funding, as follows:

Fed = *federal*

St = *state*

Comm = *commonwealth* (Puerto Rico)

Terr = *territory* (U.S. territories)

Cou = *county*

Dist = *district:* an administrative unit of public education, often having boundaries different from units of local government.

City = *city*

St-L = *state and local:* local may refer to county, district, or city.

St-R = *state-related:* funded primarily by the state but administratively autonomous.

Column 3: Student Body

M= *men only* (100% of student body)

PM = *coed, primarily men*

W= *women only* (100% of student body)

PW = *coed, primarily women*

M/W = *coeducational*

Column 4: Undergraduate Enrollment

The figure shown represents the number of full-time and part-time students enrolled in undergraduate degree programs as of fall 2014.

Columns 5–7: Enrollment Percentages

Figures are shown for the percentages of the fall 2014 undergraduate enrollment made up of students attending part-time (column 5) and students 25 years of age or older (column 6). Also listed is the percentage of students in the last graduating class who completed a college-transfer associate program and went directly on to four-year colleges (column 7).

For columns 8 through 15, the following letter codes are used: Y = yes; N = no; R = recommended; S = for some.

Columns 8–10: Admission Policies

The information in these columns shows whether the college has an open admission policy (column 8) whereby virtually all applicants are accepted without regard to standardized test scores, grade average, or class rank; whether a high school equivalency certificate is accepted in place of a high school diploma for admission consideration (column 9); and whether a high school transcript (column 10) is required as part of the application process. In column 10, the combination of the codes R and S indicates that a high school transcript is recommended for all applicants (R) or required for some (S).

Columns 11–12: Financial Aid

These columns show which colleges offer the following types of financial aid: need-based aid (column 11) and part-time jobs (column 12), including those offered through the federal government's Federal Work-Study program.

Columns 13–15: Services and Facilities

These columns show which colleges offer the following: career counseling (column 13) on either an individual or group basis, job placement services (column 14) for individual students, and college-owned or -operated housing facilities (column 16) for noncommuting students.

Column 16: Sports

This figure indicates the number of sports that a college offers at the intramural and/or intercollegiate levels.

Column 17: Majors

This figure indicates the number of major fields of study in which a college offers degree programs.

PROFILES OF TWO-YEAR COLLEGES AND SPECIAL MESSAGES

The **Profiles of Two-Year Colleges** contain basic data in capsule form for quick review and comparison. The following outline of the **Profile** format shows the section headings and the items that each section covers. Any item that does not apply to a particular college or for which no information was supplied is omitted from that college's **Profile.** Display ads, which appear near some of the institution's profiles, have been provided and paid for by those colleges that chose to supplement their profile with additional information.

Bulleted Highlights

The bulleted highlights section features important information, for quick reference and comparison. The number of possible bulleted highlights that an ideal **Profile** would have if all questions were answered in a timely manner follow. However, not every institution provides all of the information necessary to fill out every bulleted line. In such instances, the line will not appear.

First Bullet

Institutional control: Private institutions are designated as independent (nonprofit), proprietary (profit-making), or independent, with a specific religious denomination or affiliation. Nondenominational or interdenominational religious orientation is possible and would be indicated.

Public institutions are designated by the source of funding. Designations include federal, state, province, commonwealth (Puerto Rico), territory (U.S. territories), county, district (an administrative unit of public education, often having boundaries different from units of local government), city, state and local (local may refer to county, district, or city), or state-related (funded primarily by the state but administratively autonomous).

Religious affiliation is also noted here.

Institutional type: Each institution is classified as one of the following:

> *Primarily two-year college:* Awards baccalaureate degrees, but the vast majority of students are enrolled in two-year programs.

> *Four-year college:* Awards baccalaureate degrees; may also award associate degrees; does not award graduate (postbaccalaureate) degrees.

> *Upper-level institution:* Awards baccalaureate degrees, but entering students must have at least two years of previous college-level credit; may also offer graduate degrees.

> *Comprehensive institution:* Awards baccalaureate degrees; may also award associate degrees; offers graduate degree programs, primarily at the master's, specialist's, or professional level, although one or two doctoral programs may be offered.

> *University:* Offers four years of undergraduate work plus graduate degrees through the doctorate in more than two academic or professional fields.

Founding date: If the year an institution was chartered differs from the year when instruction actually began, the earlier date is given.

System or administrative affiliation: Any coordinate institutions or system affiliations are indicated. An institution that has separate colleges or campuses for men and women but shares facilities and courses is termed a coordinate institution. A formal administrative grouping of institutions, either private or public, of which the college is a part, or the name of a single institution with which the college is administratively affiliated, is a system.

Second Bullet

Setting: Schools are designated as urban (located within a major city), suburban (a residential area within commuting distance of a major city), small-town (a small but compactly settled area not within commuting distance of a major city), or rural (a remote and sparsely populated area). The phrase *easy access to...* indicates that the campus is within an hour's drive of the nearest major metropolitan area that has a population greater than 500,000.

Third Bullet

Endowment: The total dollar value of funds and/or property donated to the institution or the multicampus educational system of which the institution is a part.

Fourth Bullet

Student body: An institution is coed (coeducational—admits men and women), primarily (80 percent or more) women, primarily men, women only, or men only.

Undergraduate students: Represents the number of full-time and part-time students enrolled in undergraduate degree programs as of fall 2014. The percentage of full-time undergraduates and the percentages of men and women are given.

Category Overviews

Undergraduates

For fall 2014, the number of full- and part-time undergraduate students is listed. This list provides the number of states and U.S. territories, including the District of Columbia and Puerto Rico (or for Canadian institutions, provinces and territories), and other countries from which undergraduates come. Percentages of undergraduates who are part-time or full-time students; transfers in; live on campus; out-of-state; Black or African American, non-Hispanic/Latino; Hispanic/Latino; Asian, non-Hispanic/Latino; Native Hawaiian or other Pacific Islander, non-Hispanic/Latino; American Indian or Alaska Native, non-Hispanic/Latino are given.

Retention: The percentage of freshmen (or, for upper-level institutions, entering students) who returned the following year for the fall term.

Freshmen

Admission: Figures are given for the number of students who applied for fall 2014 admission, the number of those who were admitted, and the number who enrolled. Freshman statistics include the average high school GPA; the percentage of freshmen who took the SAT and received critical reading, writing, and math scores above 500, above 600, and above 700; as well as the percentage of freshmen taking the ACT who received a composite score of 18 or higher.

Faculty

Total: The total number of faculty members; the percentage of full-time faculty members as of fall 2014; and the percentage of full-time faculty members who hold doctoral/first professional/ terminal degrees.

Student-faculty ratio: The school's estimate of the ratio of matriculated undergraduate students to faculty members teaching undergraduate courses.

Majors

This section lists the major fields of study offered by the college.

Academics

Calendar: Most colleges indicate one of the following: 4-1-4, 4-4-1, or a similar arrangement (two terms of equal length plus an abbreviated winter or spring term, with the numbers referring to months); semesters; trimesters; quarters; 3-3 (three courses for each of three terms); modular (the academic year is divided into small blocks of time; courses of varying lengths

are assembled according to individual programs); or standard year (for most Canadian institutions).

Degrees: This names the full range of levels of certificates, diplomas, and degrees, including prebaccalaureate, graduate, and professional, that are offered by this institution:

Associate degree: Normally requires at least two but fewer than four years of full-time college work or its equivalent.

Bachelor's degree (baccalaureate): Requires at least four years but not more than five years of full-time college-level work or its equivalent. This includes all bachelor's degrees in which the normal four years of work are completed in three years and bachelor's degrees conferred in a five-year cooperative (work-study plan) program. A cooperative plan provides for alternate class attendance and employment in business, industry, or government. This allows students to combine actual work experience with their college studies.

Master's degree: Requires the successful completion of a program of study of at least the full-time equivalent of one but not more than two years of work beyond the bachelor's degree.

Doctoral degree (doctorate; research/scholarship, professional, or other): The highest degree in graduate study. The doctoral degree classification includes Doctor of Education, Doctor of Juridical Science, Doctor of Public Health, Doctor of Philosophy, Doctor of Podiatry, Doctor of Veterinary Medicine, and many more.

Post-master's certificate: Requires completion of an organized program of study of 24 credit hours beyond the master's degree but does not meet the requirements of academic degrees at the doctoral level.

Special study options: Details are next given here on study options available at each college:

Accelerated degree program: Students may earn a bachelor's degree in three academic years.

Academic remediation for entering students: Instructional courses designed for students deficient in the general competencies necessary for a regular postsecondary curriculum and educational setting.

Adult/continuing education programs: Courses offered for nontraditional students who are currently working or are returning to formal education.

Advanced placement: Credit toward a degree awarded for acceptable scores on College Board Advanced Placement (AP) tests.

Cooperative (co-op) education programs: Formal arrangements with off-campus employers allowing students to combine work and study in order to gain degree-related experience, usually extending the time required to complete a degree.

Distance learning: For-credit courses that can be accessed off-campus via cable television, the Internet, satellite, DVD, correspondence course, or other media.

Double major: A program of study in which a student concurrently completes the requirements of two majors.

English as a second language (ESL): A course of study designed specifically for students whose native language is not English.

External degree programs: A program of study in which students earn credits toward a degree through a combination of independent study, college courses, proficiency examinations, and personal experience. External degree programs require minimal or no classroom attendance.

Freshmen honors college: A separate academic program for talented freshmen.

Honors programs: Any special program for very able students offering the opportunity for educational enrichment, independent study, acceleration, or some combination of these.

Independent study: Academic work, usually undertaken outside the regular classroom structure, chosen or designed by the student with departmental approval and instructor supervision.

Internships: Any short-term, supervised work experience usually related to a student's major field, for which the student earns academic credit. The work can be full-or part-time, on or off-campus, paid or unpaid.

Off-campus study: A formal arrangement with one or more domestic institutions under which students may take courses at the other institution(s) for credit.

Part-time degree program: Students may earn a degree through part-time enrollment in regular session (daytime) classes or evening, weekend, or summer classes.

Self-designed major: Program of study based on individual interests, designed by the student with the assistance of an adviser.

Services for LD students: Special help for learning-disabled students with resolvable difficulties, such as dyslexia.

Study abroad: An arrangement by which a student completes part of the academic program studying in another country. A college may operate a campus abroad or it may have a cooperative agreement with other U.S. institutions or institutions in other countries.

Summer session for credit: Summer courses through which students may make up degree work or accelerate their program.

Tutorials: Undergraduates can arrange for special in-depth academic assignments (not for remediation) working with faculty members one-on-one or in small groups.

ROTC: Army, Naval, or Air Force Reserve Officers' Training Corps programs offered either on campus, at a branch campus [designated by a (b)], or at a cooperating host institution [designated by (c)].

Unusual degree programs: Nontraditional programs such as a 3-2 degree program, in which three years of liberal arts study is followed by two years of study in a professional field at another institution (or in a professional division of the same institution), resulting in two bachelor's degrees or a bachelor's and a master's degree.

Student Life

Housing options: The institution's policy about whether students are permitted to live off-campus or are required to live on campus for a specified period; whether freshmen-only, coed, single-sex, cooperative, and disabled student housing options are available; whether campus housing is leased by the school and/or provided by a third party; whether freshman applicants are given priority for college housing. The phrase *college housing not available* indicates that no college-owned or -operated housing facilities are provided for undergraduates and that noncommuting students must arrange for their own accommodations.

Activities and organizations: Lists information on drama-theater groups, choral groups, marching bands, student-run campus newspapers, student-run radio stations, and social organizations (sororities, fraternities, eating clubs, etc.) and how many are represented on campus.

Campus security: Campus safety measures including 24-hour emergency response devices (telephones and alarms) and patrols by trained security personnel, student patrols, late-night transport-escort service, and controlled dormitory access (key, security card, etc.).

Student services: Information provided indicates services offered to students by the college, such as legal services, health clinics, personal-psychological counseling, and women's centers.

Athletics

Membership in one or more of the following athletic associations is indicated by initials.

NCAA: National Collegiate Athletic Association

NAIA: National Association of Intercollegiate Athletics

NCCAA: National Christian College Athletic Association

NJCAA: National Junior College Athletic Association

USCAA: United States Collegiate Athletic Association

CIS: Canadian Interuniversity Sports

The overall NCAA division in which all or most intercollegiate teams compete is designated by a roman numeral I, II, or

III. All teams that do not compete in this division are listed as exceptions.

Sports offered by the college are divided into two groups: intercollegiate (**M** or **W** following the name of each sport indicates that it is offered for men or women) and intramural. An **s** in parentheses following an **M** or **W** for an intercollegiate sport indicates that athletic scholarships (or grants-in-aid) are offered for men or women in that sport, and a c indicates a club team as opposed to a varsity team.

Standardized Tests

The most commonly required standardized tests are the ACT®, SAT®, and SAT Subject Tests™. These and other standardized tests may be used for selective admission, as a basis for counseling or course placement, or for both purposes. This section notes if a test is used for admission or placement and whether it is required, required for some, or recommended.

In addition to the ACT and SAT, the following standardized entrance and placement examinations are referred to by their initials:

ABLE: Adult Basic Learning Examination

ACT ASSET: ACT Assessment of Skills for Successful Entry and Transfer

ACT PEP: ACT Proficiency Examination Program

CAT: California Achievement Tests

CELT: Comprehensive English Language Test

CPAt: Career Programs Assessment

CPT: Computerized Placement Test

DAT: Differential Aptitude Test

LSAT: Law School Admission Test

MAPS: Multiple Assessment Program Service

MCAT: Medical College Admission Test

MMPI: Minnesota Multiphasic Personality Inventory

OAT: Optometry Admission Test

PAA: Prueba de Aptitud Académica (Spanish-language version of the SAT)

PCAT: Pharmacy College Admission Test

PSAT/NMSQT: Preliminary SAT National Merit Scholarship Qualifying Test

SCAT: Scholastic College Aptitude Test

SRA: Scientific Research Association (administers verbal, arithmetical, and achievement tests)

TABE: Test of Adult Basic Education

TASP: Texas Academic Skills Program

TOEFL: Test of English as a Foreign Language (for international students whose native language is not English)

WPCT: Washington Pre-College Test

Costs

Costs are given for the 2015–16 academic year or for the 2014–15 academic year if 2015–16 figures were not yet available. Annual expenses may be expressed as a comprehensive fee (including full-time tuition, mandatory fees, and college room and board) or as separate figures for full-time tuition, fees, room and board, or room only. For public institutions where tuition differs according to residence, separate figures are given for area or state residents and for nonresidents. Part-time tuition is expressed in terms of a per-unit rate (per credit, per semester hour, etc.) as specified by the institution.

The tuition structure at some institutions is complex in that freshmen and sophomores may be charged a different rate from that for juniors and seniors, a professional or vocational division may have a different fee structure from the liberal arts division of the same institution, or part-time tuition may be prorated on a sliding scale according to the number of credit hours taken. Tuition and fees may vary according to academic program, campus/location, class time (day, evening, weekend), course/credit load, course level, degree level, reciprocity agreements, and student level. Room and board charges are reported as an average for one academic year and may vary according to the board plan selected, campus/location, type of housing facility, or student level. If no college-owned or -operated housing facilities are offered, the phrase *college housing not available* will appear in the Housing section of the Student Life paragraph.

Tuition payment plans that may be offered to undergraduates include tuition prepayment, installment payments, and deferred payment. A tuition prepayment plan gives a student the option of locking in the current tuition rate for the entire term of enrollment by paying the full amount in advance rather than year by year. Colleges that offer such a prepayment plan may also help the student to arrange financing.

The availability of full or partial undergraduate tuition waivers to minority students, children of alumni, employees or their children, adult students, and senior citizens may be listed.

Financial Aid

The number of Federal Work Study and/or part-time jobs and average earnings are listed. Financial aid deadlines are given as well.

Applying

Application and admission options include the following:

Early admission: Highly qualified students may matriculate before graduating from high school.

Early action plan: An admission plan that allows students to apply and be notified of an admission decision well in advance of the regular notification dates. If accepted, the candidate is not committed to enroll; students may reply to the offer under the college's regular reply policy.

Early decision plan: A plan that permits students to apply and be notified of an admission decision (and financial aid offer, if applicable) well in advance of the regular notification date. Applicants agree to accept an offer of admission and to withdraw their applications from other colleges. Candidates who are not accepted under early decision are automatically considered with the regular applicant pool, without prejudice.

Deferred entrance: The practice of permitting accepted students to postpone enrollment, usually for a period of one academic term or year.

Application fee: The fee required with an application is noted. This is typically nonrefundable, although under certain specified conditions it may be waived or returned.

Requirements: Other application requirements are grouped into three categories: required for all, required for some, and recommended. They may include an essay, standardized test scores, a high school transcript, a minimum high school grade point average (expressed as a number on a scale of 0 to 4.0, where 4.0 equals A, 3.0 equals B, etc.), letters of recommendation, an interview on campus or with local alumni, and, for certain types of schools or programs, special requirements such as a musical audition or an art portfolio.

Application deadlines and notification dates: Admission application deadlines and dates for notification of acceptance or rejection are given either as specific dates or as **rolling** and **continuous.** Rolling means that applications are processed as they are received, and qualified students are accepted as long as there are openings. Continuous means that applicants are notified of acceptance or rejection as applications are processed up until the date indicated or the actual beginning of classes. The application deadline and the notification date for transfers are given if they differ from the dates for freshmen. Early decision and early action application deadlines and notification dates are also indicated when relevant.

Admissions Contact

The name, title, and phone number of the person to contact for application information are given at the end of the Profile. The admission office address is listed in most cases. Toll-free phone numbers may also be included. The admission office fax number and e-mail address, if available, are listed, provided the school wanted them printed for use by prospective students. Finally, the URL of the institution's Web site is provided.

Additional Information

Each college that has a **Featured Two-Year College Description** in the guide will have a cross-reference appended to the Profile, referring you directly to that **Featured Two-Year College Description.**

FEATURED TWO-YEAR COLLEGES

These narrative descriptions provide an inside look at certain colleges, shifting the focus to a variety of other factors that should also be considered. The descriptions provide a wealth of statistics that are crucial components in the college decision-making equation—components such as tuition, financial aid, and major fields of study. Prepared exclusively by college officials, the descriptions are designed to help give students a better sense of the individuality of each institution, in terms that include campus environment, student activities, and lifestyle. Such quality-of-life intangibles can be the deciding factors in the college selection process. The absence of any college or university does not constitute an editorial decision on the part of Peterson's. In essence, these descriptions are an open forum for colleges, on a voluntary basis, to communicate their particular message to prospective college students. The colleges included have paid a fee to Peterson's to provide this information. The **Featured Two-Year Colleges** are edited to provide a consistent format across entries for your ease of comparison.

INDEXES

Institutional Changes Since *Peterson's® Two-Year Colleges 2015*

Here you will find an alphabetical listing of institutions that have recently closed, merged with other institutions, or changed their name or status.

Associate Degree Programs at Two-and Four-Year Colleges

These indexes present hundreds of undergraduate fields of study that are currently offered most widely according to the colleges' responses on *Peterson's Annual Survey of Undergraduate Institutions.* The majors appear in alphabetical order, each followed by an alphabetical list of the schools that offer an associate-level program in that field. Liberal Arts and Studies indicates a general program with no specified major. The terms used for the majors are those of the U.S. Department of Education Classification of Instructional Programs (CIPs). Many institutions, however, use different terms. Readers should refer to the **Featured Two-Year Colleges** two-page descriptions in this book for the school's exact terminology. In addition, although the term "major" is used in this guide, some colleges may use other terms, such as "concentration," "program of study," or "field."

DATA COLLECTION PROCEDURES

The data contained in the **Profiles** of Two-Year Colleges and **Indexes** were researched in winter and spring 2015 through *Peterson's Annual Survey of Undergraduate Institutions.* Questionnaires were sent to the more than 1,950 colleges that meet the outlined inclusion criteria. All data included in this edition have been submitted by officials (usually admission and financial aid officers, registrars, or institutional research personnel) at the colleges themselves. All usable information received in time for publication has been included. The omission of any particular item from the **Profiles** of Two-Year Colleges and **Indexes** listing signifies either that the item is not applicable to that institution or that data were not available. Because of the comprehensive editorial review that takes place in our offices and because all material comes directly from college officials, Peterson's has every reason to believe that the information presented in this guide is accurate at the time of printing. However, students should check with a specific college or university at the time of application to verify such figures as tuition and fees, which may have changed since the publication of this volume.

CRITERIA FOR INCLUSION IN THIS BOOK

Peterson's Two-Year Colleges 2016 covers accredited institutions in the United States, U.S. territories, and other countries that award the associate degree as their most popular undergraduate offering (a few also offer bachelor's, master's, or doctoral degrees). The term two-year college is the commonly used designation for institutions that grant the associate degree, since two years is the normal duration of the traditional associate degree program. However, some programs may be completed in one year, others require three years, and, of course, part-time programs may take a considerably longer period. Therefore, "two-year college" should be understood as a conventional term that accurately describes most of the institutions included in this guide but which should not be taken literally in all cases. Also included are some non-degree-granting institutions, usually branch campuses of a multicampus system, which offer the equivalent of the first two years of a bachelor's degree, transferable to a bachelor's degree–granting institution.

To be included in this guide, an institution must have full accreditation or be a candidate for accreditation (preaccreditation) status by an institutional or specialized accrediting body recognized by the U.S. Department of Education or the Council for Higher Education Accreditation (CHEA). Institutional accrediting bodies, which review each institution as a whole, include the six regional associations of schools and colleges (Middle States, New England, North Central, Northwest, Southern, and Western), each of which is responsible for a specified portion of the United States and its territories. Other institutional accrediting bodies are national in scope and accredit specific kinds of institutions (e.g., Bible colleges, independent colleges, and rabbinical and Talmudic schools). Program registration by the New York State Board of Regents is considered to be the equivalent of institutional accreditation, since the board requires that all programs offered by an institution meet its standards before recognition is granted. This guide also includes institutions outside the United States that are accredited by these U.S. accrediting bodies. There are recognized specialized or professional accrediting bodies in more than forty different fields, each of which is authorized to accredit institutions or specific programs in its particular field. For specialized institutions that offer programs in one field only, we designate this to be the equivalent of institutional accreditation. A full explanation of the accrediting process and complete information on recognized, institutional (regional and national), and specialized accrediting bodies can be found online at www.chea.org or at www.ed.gov/admins/finaid/accred/index.html.

Quick-Reference Chart

Two-Year Colleges At-a-Glance

This chart includes the names and locations of accredited two-year colleges in the United States, Canada, and other countries and shows institutions' responses to the *Peterson's Annual Survey of Undergraduate Institutions*. If an institution submitted incomplete data, one or more columns opposite the institution's name is blank. A dagger after the school name indicates that the institution has one or more entries in the *Featured Two-Year Colleges* section. If a school does not appear, it did not report any of the information.

Y—Yes; N—No; R—Recommended; S—For Some

Column key (left to right after Student Body): Undergraduate Enrollment · Percent Attending Part-Time · Percent 25 Years of Age or Older · Percent of Grads Going on to Four-Year Colleges · Open Admissions · High School Equivalency Certificate Accepted · High School Transcript Required · Need-Based Aid Available · Part-Time Jobs Available · Career Counseling Available · Job Placement Services Available · College Housing Available · Number of Sports Available · Number of Majors Offered

Degrees Awarded: College Transfer Associate (C), Terminal Associate (T), Bachelor's (B), Master's (M), Doctoral (D)

Institution	Location	Degrees	Control	Student Body	Undergrad Enroll.	% PT	% 25+	% to 4-Yr	Open Adm.	HS Equiv	HS Transcript	Need-Based Aid	PT Jobs	Career Couns.	Job Place.	College Housing	# Sports	# Majors
UNITED STATES																		
Alabama																		
Alabama Southern Community College	Monroeville	C,T	St	M/W	1,349													
Bevill State Community College	Jasper	C,T	St	M/W	3,490	48	31	22	Y	Y	Y	Y	Y	Y	Y	Y		13
Bishop State Community College	Mobile	C,T	St	M/W	3,900	44												
Community College of the Air Force	Maxwell Gunter AFB	T	Fed	M/W	297,469				Y	Y	Y			Y		N	N	12	49
Gadsden State Community College	Gadsden	C,T	St	M/W	5,289	48	34	14	Y	Y	Y	Y	Y	Y	Y	Y	N		23
George C. Wallace Community College	Dothan	C,T	St	M/W	4,854	54	37		Y	Y	Y	Y	Y	Y	Y	Y	N	N	4	2	28
H. Councill Trenholm State Technical College	Montgomery	T	St	M/W	1,338		80		Y	Y	Y	Y	Y	Y	Y		N		18
ITT Technical Institute	Bessemer	T,B	Prop	M/W														
ITT Technical Institute	Madison	T,B	Prop	M/W														
ITT Technical Institute	Mobile	T,B	Prop	M/W														
James H. Faulkner State Community College	Bay Minette	C,T	St	M/W	3,323	36	39		Y	Y	Y	Y	Y	Y	Y	Y		6	18
Jefferson State Community College	Birmingham	C,T	St	M/W	8,516	65	34		Y	Y	S	Y	Y	Y	Y		N		19
J. F. Drake State Community and Technical College	Huntsville	C,T	St	M/W	1,258	40	57		Y	Y	Y	Y	Y	Y	Y		N		21
Lawson State Community College	Birmingham	C,T	St	M/W	3,031	41												
Lurleen B. Wallace Community College	Andalusia	C,T	St	M/W	1,599	37	22		Y	Y		Y	Y				N	3	10
Marion Military Institute	Marion	C	St	M/W	418	2												
Northwest-Shoals Community College	Muscle Shoals	C	St	M/W	3,858	52	27	15	Y	Y	Y	Y	Y				N	3	16
Reid State Technical College	Evergreen	T	St	M/W	549	50	34		Y		Y	Y	Y	Y	Y	Y	N		4
Shelton State Community College	Tuscaloosa	C,T	St	M/W	5,068	51												
Snead State Community College	Boaz	C,T	St	M/W	2,161	29												
Alaska																		
Ilisagvik College	Barrow	C	St	M/W	257	81												
University of Alaska Southeast, Sitka Campus	Sitka	C,T,B,M	St	M/W	1,552		65		Y	Y	Y			Y		N		12
American Samoa																		
American Samoa Community College	Pago Pago	C,T,B	Terr	M/W	1,276	44	12	0	Y	Y		Y	Y	Y	Y	N	8	25
Arizona																		
Arizona Western College	Yuma	C,T	St-L	M/W	7,702	67	30		Y				Y	Y	Y	Y	Y	7	64
Brown Mackie College–Phoenix	Phoenix	T,B	Prop	M/W														
Brown Mackie College–Tucson	Tucson	T,B	Prop	M/W														
Carrington College–Mesa	Mesa	T	Prop	M/W	691	10												
Carrington College–Phoenix	Phoenix	T	Prop	M/W	676													
Carrington College–Phoenix Westside	Phoenix	T	Prop	M/W	513	30												
Carrington College–Tucson	Tucson	T	Prop	M/W	440	1												
Chandler-Gilbert Community College	Chandler	C,T	St-L	M/W	14,500	71				Y				Y	Y		N	6	37
Cochise College	Douglas	C,T	St-L	M/W	4,540	61	44	41	Y			R	Y	Y			Y	3	51
Coconino Community College	Flagstaff	C,T	St	M/W	3,698	73												
CollegeAmerica–Flagstaff	Flagstaff	C,T,B	Priv	M/W	205		0	47	Y	Y		Y	Y	Y	Y	Y	Y		5
Eastern Arizona College	Thatcher	C,T	St-L	M/W	6,379	72	53	3	Y			R	Y	Y	Y		Y	10	52
Glendale Community College	Glendale	C,T	St-L	M/W	21,361	66												
ITT Technical Institute	Phoenix	T,B	Prop	M/W														
ITT Technical Institute	Phoenix	T,B	Prop	M/W														
ITT Technical Institute	Tucson	T,B	Prop	M/W														
Mesa Community College	Mesa	C,T	St-L	M/W	22,000					Y			Y	Y	Y		N	11	36
Mohave Community College	Kingman	C,T	St	M/W	4,744	77	47		Y	Y				Y			N		34
Penn Foster College	Scottsdale	T,B	Prop	M/W	28,900	100			Y	Y	Y						N		23
Phoenix College	Phoenix	C,T	Cou	M/W	12,676					Y							N	6	56
Pima Community College	Tucson	C,T	St-L	M/W	26,613													
Scottsdale Community College	Scottsdale	C,T	St-L	M/W	9,863	70	30		Y					Y	Y		N	12	22
Sessions College for Professional Design	Tempe	T	Prop	M/W														
Tohono O'odham Community College	Sells	C,T	Pub	M/W	269	91	74	25	Y	Y	Y			Y			N	1	6
Arkansas																		
Arkansas Northeastern College	Blytheville	C,T	St	M/W	1,425	62	45		Y	Y	R	Y	Y	Y	Y	N	4	11
Arkansas State University–Newport	Newport	C,T	St	M/W	2,057	53												
College of the Ouachitas	Malvern	C,T	St	M/W	1,501	61												
Cossatot Community College of the University of Arkansas	De Queen	C,T	St	M/W	1,575													
ITT Technical Institute	Little Rock	T,B	Prop	M/W														
Mid-South Community College	West Memphis	C,T	St	M/W	1,793	61												
NorthWest Arkansas Community College	Bentonville	C,T	St-L	M/W	8,020	65												
University of Arkansas Community College at Batesville	Batesville	C,T	St	M/W	1,315	43	40		Y	Y		Y	Y	Y	Y	Y	N		10
University of Arkansas Community College at Hope	Hope	C,T	St	M/W	1,360	51	37		Y			Y	Y	Y	Y	N		13
University of Arkansas Community College at Morrilton	Morrilton	C,T	St	M/W	1,995	43	36		Y			Y	Y	Y	Y	N	5	17
California																		
Academy of Couture Art	Beverly Hills	C,T,B	Prop	M/W														
American Academy of Dramatic Arts	Hollywood	C	Ind	M/W	282		11		N	Y	Y	Y	Y	Y	Y	N		1
Antelope Valley College	Lancaster	C,T	St-L	M/W	14,598	77	38		Y			Y	Y	Y	Y	Y	N	12	45
Barstow Community College	Barstow	C,T	St-L	M/W	4,791													
Berkeley City College	Berkeley	C,T	St-L	M/W	7,645													

This chart includes the names and locations of accredited two-year colleges in the United States, Canada, and other countries and shows institutions' responses to the *Peterson's Annual Survey of Undergraduate Institutions*. If an institution submitted incomplete data, one or more columns opposite the institution's name is blank. A dagger after the school name indicates that the institution has one or more entries in the *Featured Two-Year Colleges* section. If a school does not appear, it did not report any of the information.

Y—Yes; N—No; R—Recommended; S—For Some

Column headings (left to right): Degrees Awarded — College Transfer Associate (C), Terminal Associate (T), Bachelor's (B), Master's (M), Doctoral (D); Institutional Control — County, District, City, State and Local, State-Related, Federal, State, Commonwealth, Proprietary, Territory, Independent, Independent-Religious; Student Body — Men, Primarily Men, Women, Primarily Women, Coed; Undergraduate Enrollment; Percent Attending Part-Time; Percent 25 Years of Age or Older; Percent of Grads Going on to Four-Year Colleges; High School Equivalency Certificate Accepted; Open Admissions; High School Transcript Required; Need-Based Aid Available; Part-Time Jobs Available; Career Counseling Available; Job Placement Services Available; College Housing Available; Number of Sports Offered; Number of Majors Offered

Institution	Location	Degrees Awarded	Inst. Control	Student Body	Undergrad Enrollment	% Part-Time	% 25+	% Grads to 4-Yr	HS Equiv Accepted	Open Admissions	HS Transcript Req	Need-Based Aid	Part-Time Jobs	Career Counseling	Job Placement	College Housing	# Sports	# Majors
Butte College	Oroville	C,T	St-L	M/W	12,290	57												
Ca&nnada College	Redwood City	C,T	St-L	M/W	6,250	72	31		Y	Y	R	Y	Y	Y	Y	N	5	44
Carrington College–Citrus Heights	Citrus Heights	T	Prop	M/W	451	7												
Carrington College–Pleasant Hill	Pleasant Hill	T	Prop	M/W	589	13												
Carrington College–Pomona	Pomona	T	Prop	M/W	301	20												
Carrington College–Sacramento	Sacramento	T	Prop	M/W	1,267	10												
Carrington College–San Jose	San Jose	T	Prop	M/W	693	4												
Carrington College–San Leandro	San Leandro	T	Prop	M/W	521	3												
Carrington College–Stockton	Stockton	T	Prop	M/W	465	8												
Citrus College	Glendora	C	St-L	M/W	12,920	62			Y	Y	Y	Y	Y	Y	Y		10	59
Coastline Community College	Fountain Valley	C	St-L	M/W	9,487		72		Y		R	Y	Y	Y	Y	N		1
College of Marin	Kentfield	C,T	St-L	M/W	6,000				Y		R	Y	Y	Y	Y	N	8	55
College of the Canyons	Santa Clarita	C,T	St-L	M/W	18,064	64	35		Y		R	Y	Y	Y	Y	N	11	55
College of the Desert	Palm Desert	C,T	St-L	M/W	9,259	61	33		Y	Y		Y	Y	Y		N	11	61
Columbia College	Sonora	C,T	St-L	M/W	2,667	69												
Copper Mountain College	Joshua Tree	C,T	St	M/W	2,500													
Cosumnes River College	Sacramento	C,T	Dist	M/W	14,545													
De Anza College	Cupertino	C,T	St-L	M/W	23,833	57												
Deep Springs College	Deep Springs	C	Ind	CM	28		0	75		Y			Y		Y		13	1
Feather River College	Quincy	C,T	St-L	M/W	1,785	64												
FIDM/Fashion Institute of Design & Merchandising, Los Angeles Campus†	Los Angeles	C,T,B	Prop	M/W	3,142	12	14		N	Y	Y		Y	Y	Y	Y	Y		20
FIDM/Fashion Institute of Design & Merchandising, Orange County Campus	Irvine	C,T	Prop	PW	156	4	5		N	Y	Y			Y	Y	Y	Y		12
FIDM/Fashion Institute of Design & Merchandising, San Francisco Campus	San Francisco	C,T,B	Prop	M/W	527	12	17		N	Y	Y			Y	Y	Y	N		11
FIDM/The Fashion Institute of Design & Merchandising, San Diego Campus	San Diego	C,T	Prop	PW	142	6	12		N	Y	Y			Y	Y	Y	Y		7
Fullerton College	Fullerton	C,T	St-L	M/W	24,423	65												
Gavilan College	Gilroy	C,T	St-L	M/W	5,267	66												
Golden West College	Huntington Beach	C,T	St-L	M/W	12,394	65	29		Y	Y	R	Y	Y	Y	Y	N	9	31
Imperial Valley College	Imperial	C,T	St-L	M/W	7,413													
ITT Technical Institute	Culver City	T,B	Prop	M/W														
ITT Technical Institute	Lathrop	T,B	Prop	M/W														
ITT Technical Institute	National City	T,B	Prop	M/W														
ITT Technical Institute	Oakland	T,B	Prop	M/W														
ITT Technical Institute	Orange	T,B	Prop	M/W														
ITT Technical Institute	Oxnard	C,T,B	Prop	M/W														
ITT Technical Institute	Rancho Cordova	T,B	Prop	M/W														
ITT Technical Institute	San Bernardino	T,B	Prop	M/W														
ITT Technical Institute	San Dimas	T,B	Prop	M/W														
ITT Technical Institute	Sylmar	T,B	Prop	M/W														
ITT Technical Institute	Torrance	T,B	Prop	M/W														
Lake Tahoe Community College	South Lake Tahoe	C,T	St-L	M/W	5,700													
Los Angeles Mission College	Sylmar	C,T	St-L	M/W	8,990	78												
Los Angeles Trade-Technical College	Los Angeles	C,T	St-L	M/W	13,194	68	47				R	Y	Y	Y		N	4	34
MiraCosta College†	Oceanside	C,T	St	M/W	14,687	66	32		Y			Y	Y			N	2	39
Modesto Junior College	Modesto	C,T	St-L	M/W	19,307	64												
Mt. San Antonio College	Walnut	C,T	St-L	M/W	28,481	63			Y		S	Y	Y	Y	Y	N	15	77
Mt. San Jacinto College	San Jacinto	C,T	St-L	M/W	14,170	64												
Ohlone College	Fremont	C,T	St-L	M/W	11,318	72	45		Y		S	Y	Y	Y	Y	N	8	77
Orange Coast College	Costa Mesa	C,T	St-L	M/W	20,521	59	28		Y			Y	Y	Y	Y	N	14	98
Oxnard College	Oxnard	C	St	M/W	6,867	72												
Palomar College	San Marcos	C	St-L	M/W	22,535	64	37		Y			Y	Y			N	14	95
Pasadena City College	Pasadena	C,T	St-L	M/W	26,611	61	28		Y				Y	Y	Y	N	13	74
Rio Hondo College	Whittier	C,T	St-L	M/W	26,490		40		Y				Y	Y	Y	N	10	4
San Diego City College	San Diego	C	St-L	M/W	16,930													
San Diego Miramar College	San Diego	C	St-L	M/W	10,650		48		Y			Y	Y	Y	Y	N	4	35
San Joaquin Delta College	Stockton	C,T	Dist	M/W	16,587	57	27		Y			Y	Y	Y	Y	N	18	57
San Joaquin Valley College	Bakersfield	T	Prop	M/W	959		37		N	Y	S		Y	Y				9
San Joaquin Valley College	Chula Vista	T	Prop	M/W	26		81											1
San Joaquin Valley College	Fresno	T	Prop	M/W	1,051		37		Y				Y	Y		N		8
San Joaquin Valley College	Hanford	T	Prop	M/W	333		40											4
San Joaquin Valley College	Hesperia	T	Prop	M/W	877		34											7
San Joaquin Valley College	Lancaster	T	Prop	M/W	292		40											10
San Joaquin Valley College	Ontario	T	Prop	M/W	998		33		N	Y			Y	Y		N		1
San Joaquin Valley College	Rancho Cordova	T	Prop	M/W	192		70		N	Y			Y	Y	Y	N		6
San Joaquin Valley College	Salida	T	Prop	M/W	489		38		N	Y			Y	Y				6
San Joaquin Valley College	Temecula	T	Prop	M/W	631		45											16
San Joaquin Valley College	Visalia	T	Prop	M/W	1,364		48		N	Y	S		Y	Y		N		16
San Joaquin Valley College–Fresno Aviation Campus	Fresno	T	Prop	PM	123		61		N	Y	S		Y	Y	Y			1
San Joaquin Valley College–Online	Visalia	T	Prop	M/W	1,002		71		N				Y					5
Santa Monica College	Santa Monica	C,T	St-L	M/W	30,000	64												
Santa Rosa Junior College	Santa Rosa	C,T	St-L	M/W	22,008													
Sierra College	Rocklin	C,T	St	M/W	19,416	72	32		Y			Y	Y		Y	Y	13	61
Victor Valley College	Victorville	C,T	St	M/W	7,030	60	31		Y			Y	Y	Y	Y	N	12	41

Colorado

Institution	Location	Degrees Awarded	Inst. Control	Student Body	Undergrad Enrollment	% Part-Time	% 25+	% Grads to 4-Yr	HS Equiv Accepted	Open Admissions	HS Transcript Req	Need-Based Aid	Part-Time Jobs	Career Counseling	Job Placement	College Housing	# Sports	# Majors
Arapahoe Community College	Littleton	C,T	St	M/W	9,745	79	45		Y			Y	Y	Y	Y	N	15	24
Colorado Northwestern Community College	Rangely	C,T	St	M/W					Y	Y	Y	Y	Y	Y	Y	Y	11	14

This chart includes the names and locations of accredited two-year colleges in the United States, Canada, and other countries and shows institutions' responses to the *Peterson's Annual Survey of Undergraduate Institutions.* If an institution submitted incomplete data, one or more columns opposite the institution's name is blank. A dagger after the school name indicates that the institution has one or more entries in the *Featured Two-Year Colleges* section. If a school does not appear, it did not report any of the information.

Y—Yes; N—No; R—Recommended; S—For Some

Column headers (left to right): Institution | Location | Degrees Awarded — College Transfer Associate (C); Terminal Associate (T); Bachelor's (B); Master's (M); Doctoral (D) | Institutional Control — Independent, Independent-Religious, Proprietary; County District, City, State and Local, State-Related; Federal, State Commonwealth, Territory | Student Body — Men, Primarily Men, Women, Primarily Women, Coed | Undergraduate Enrollment | Percent Attending Part-Time | Percent 25 Years of Age or Older | Percent of Grads Going on to Four-Year Colleges | Open Admissions | High School Equivalency Certificate Accepted | High School Transcript Required | Need-Based Aid Required | Part-Time Jobs Available | Career Counseling Available | Job Placement Services Available | College Housing Available | Number of Sports Offered | Number of Majors Offered

Institution	Location	Deg	Ctrl	SB	Enroll	%PT	%25+	%Grad	OpenAdm	HSEquiv	HSTrans	NeedAid	PTJobs	Career	JobPlace	Housing	Sports	Majors
Community College of Aurora	Aurora	C,T	St	M/W	7,617	80			Y			S	Y	Y	Y	Y		13
Community College of Denver	Denver	C,T	St	M/W	10,296	76			Y				Y	Y	Y	Y	N		27
Front Range Community College	Westminster	C,T	St	M/W	19,619	69	43		Y				Y	Y	Y	Y	N	23	27
IBMC College	Fort Collins	T	Priv	M/W	1,020		67			Y	Y	Y	Y	Y	Y			15
IntelliTec College	Grand Junction	C	Prop	M/W						Y	Y	Y		Y				4
ITT Technical Institute	Aurora	T,B	Prop	M/W														
ITT Technical Institute	Westminster	T,B	Prop	M/W														
Lamar Community College	Lamar	C,T	St	M/W	902	49	18		Y	Y		Y	Y	Y		Y	7	29
Lincoln College of Technology	Denver	T	Prop	PM	952													
Morgan Community College	Fort Morgan	C,T	St	M/W	1,837	78			Y		R	Y	Y	Y	Y	N		10
Northeastern Junior College	Sterling	C,T	St	M/W	1,776	45	21		Y		R	R	Y	Y	Y	Y	15	58
Otero Junior College	La Junta	C,T	St	M/W	1,449	32	11		Y		R	R	Y	Y	Y	Y	6	24
Pueblo Community College	Pueblo	C,T	St	M/W	5,921	62	56	4	Y			Y	Y	Y	Y	N		36
Trinidad State Junior College	Trinidad	C,T	St	M/W	1,783	51	43		Y	Y		Y	Y	Y	Y	Y	7	38
Connecticut																		
Gateway Community College	New Haven	C,T	St	M/W	8,201	68	42		Y	Y	Y	Y	Y	Y	Y	N	4	35
Goodwin College	East Hartford	C,T,B	Ind	M/W	3,440	82			Y	Y	Y	Y	Y	Y	Y	N	4	28
Housatonic Community College	Bridgeport	C,T	St	M/W	5,286				Y	Y	Y	Y	Y	Y	Y			24
Manchester Community College	Manchester	C,T	St	M/W	7,300	66	32		Y	Y	Y	Y	Y			N	4	31
Northwestern Connecticut Community College	Winsted	C,T	St	M/W	1,549	70												
Norwalk Community College	Norwalk	C,T	St	M/W	6,363	65			Y	Y	Y	Y	Y					34
St. Vincent's College	Bridgeport	C,T,B	I-R	M/W	751		66		N	Y	Y	Y	Y	Y		N		5
Three Rivers Community College	Norwich	C,T	St	M/W	4,530	67	42		Y	Y	R	Y	Y	Y		N	2	35
Tunxis Community College	Farmington	C,T	St	M/W	4,225	62	38	25	Y	Y	Y	Y	Y	Y		N		19
Delaware																		
Delaware Technical & Community College, Jack F. Owens Campus	Georgetown	C,T	St	M/W	4,429	55												
Delaware Technical & Community College, Stanton/Wilmington Campus	Newark	C,T	St	M/W	7,035	63												
Delaware Technical & Community College, Terry Campus	Dover	C,T	St	M/W	2,955	57			Y	Y	S	Y	Y			N	3	44
Florida																		
Broward College	Fort Lauderdale	C,T,B	St	M/W	43,715	70												
Brown Mackie College–Miami	Miramar	T,B	Prop	M/W														
Chipola College	Marianna	C,T,B	St	M/W	2,090	58	37		Y	Y	Y	Y	Y	Y	Y	N	4	19
College of Central Florida	Ocala	C,T,B	St-L	M/W	8,210	63	43		Y	Y	Y	Y	Y	Y	Y	N	5	75
Daytona State College	Daytona Beach	C,T,B	St	M/W	14,951	63	44		Y	Y	Y	Y	Y	Y	Y	N	9	52
Eastern Florida State College	Cocoa	C,T,B	St	M/W	16,711	65												
Florida Gateway College	Lake City	C,T,B	St	M/W	2,912	71	33		Y	Y	S	Y	Y	Y	Y	N		18
Florida SouthWestern State College	Fort Myers	C,T,B	St-L	M/W	15,705	66	32		Y	Y	Y	Y	Y	Y	Y		3	29
Florida State College at Jacksonville	Jacksonville	C,T,B	St	M/W	25,514	69	45		Y	Y	S	Y	Y	Y	Y		11	61
Gulf Coast State College	Panama City	C,T,B	St	M/W	6,271	65	43		Y	Y	Y	Y	Y	Y	Y	N	4	43
Hillsborough Community College	Tampa	C,T	St	M/W	27,298	58	37		Y	Y	Y	Y	Y	Y	Y		5	37
ITT Technical Institute	Fort Lauderdale	T,B	Prop	M/W														
ITT Technical Institute	Fort Myers	T,B	Prop	M/W														
ITT Technical Institute	Hialeah	T,B	Prop	M/W														
ITT Technical Institute	Jacksonville	T,B	Prop	M/W														
ITT Technical Institute	Lake Mary	T,B	Prop	M/W														
ITT Technical Institute	Orlando	T,B	Prop	M/W														
ITT Technical Institute	Pensacola		Prop	M/W														
ITT Technical Institute	St. Petersburg	T,B	Prop	M/W														
ITT Technical Institute	Tallahassee	T,B	Prop	M/W														
ITT Technical Institute	Tampa	T,B	Prop	M/W														
Miami Dade College	Miami	C,T,B	St-L	M/W	66,046	60	34		Y	Y	Y	Y	Y	Y	Y	N	4	191
Northwest Florida State College	Niceville	C,T,B	St-L	M/W	6,938	60												
Pasco-Hernando State College	New Port Richey	C,T,B	St	M/W	10,206	61	62		Y	Y	Y	Y	Y	Y		N	6	18
Pensacola State College	Pensacola	C,B	St	M/W	10,317	62	38		Y	Y	Y	Y	Y	Y	Y	N	16	103
Seminole State College of Florida	Sanford	C,T,B	St-L	M/W	18,422	66	39	87	Y	Y	Y	Y	Y	Y	Y	N	3	50
Southeastern College–Greenacres	Greenacres	T	Prop	M/W	433							Y						15
Southern Technical College	Orlando	C	Prop	M/W	1,445				Y	Y				Y	Y	N		4
South Florida State College	Avon Park	C,T,B	St	M/W	2,699	64	35		Y	Y	Y	Y	Y	Y	Y	N	6	162
Tallahassee Community College	Tallahassee	C,T	St-L	M/W	13,049	53	25		Y	Y	Y	Y	Y	Y	Y	N	6	38
Ultimate Medical Academy Clearwater	Clearwater	T	Prop	M/W								Y			Y	Y	N		1
Ultimate Medical Academy Online	Clearwater	T	Prop	M/W											Y	Y	N		7
Ultimate Medical Academy Tampa	Tampa	T	Prop	M/W								Y			Y	Y	N		2
Georgia																		
Albany Technical College	Albany	T	St	M/W	3,894	46												
Athens Technical College	Athens	T	St	M/W	4,563	72												
Atlanta Technical College	Atlanta	T	St	M/W	4,859	64												
Augusta Technical College	Augusta	T	St	M/W	4,379	60												
Bainbridge State College	Bainbridge	C,T	St	M/W	2,470		42		Y		S	Y	Y	Y	Y	N	2	33
Brown Mackie College–Atlanta	Atlanta	T	Prop	M/W														
Central Georgia Technical College	Warner Robins	T	St	M/W	7,796	59												
Chattahoochee Technical College	Marietta	T	St	M/W	10,470	67												
Coastal Pines Technical College	Waycross	T	St	M/W	1,180	68												
Columbus Technical College	Columbus	T	St	M/W	3,739	62												
Darton State College	Albany	C,T,B	St	M/W	5,620	54	43	39	Y	Y	S	Y	Y	Y	Y	Y	14	67

This chart includes the names and locations of accredited two-year colleges in the United States, Canada, and other countries and shows institutions' responses to the *Peterson's Annual Survey of Undergraduate Institutions*. If an institution submitted incomplete data, one or more columns opposite the institution's name is blank. A dagger after the school name indicates that the institution has one or more entries in the *Featured Two-Year Colleges* section. If a school does not appear, it did not report any of the information.

Y—Yes; N—No; R—Recommended; S—For Some

Institution	Location	Degrees Awarded	Institutional Control	Student Body	Undergraduate Enrollment	Percent Attending Part-Time	Percent 25 Years of Age or Older	Percent of Grads Going on to Four-Year Colleges	Open Admissions	High School Equivalency Certificate Accepted	High School Transcript Required	Need-Based Aid Available	Part-Time Jobs Available	Career Counseling Available	Job Placement Services Available	College Housing Available	Number of Sports Offered	Number of Majors Offered
Georgia Highlands College	Rome	C,T,B	St	M/W	5,359	51	25		N	Y	Y	Y	Y	Y			N	12	36
Georgia Military College	Milledgeville	C	St-L	M/W	7,069	46													
Georgia Northwestern Technical College	Rome	T	St	M/W	6,051	65													
Georgia Piedmont Technical College	Clarkston	T	St	M/W	4,431	67													
Gordon State College	Barnesville	C,T,B	St	M/W	4,189														
Gupton-Jones College of Funeral Service	Decatur	T	Ind	M/W	149		48		Y	Y	Y	Y		Y	Y	N	N		1
Gwinnett Technical College	Lawrenceville	T	St	M/W	7,180	68		19	Y	Y	Y	Y		Y	Y		N		27
ITT Technical Institute	Atlanta	T,B	Prop	M/W															
ITT Technical Institute	Duluth	T,B	Prop	M/W															
ITT Technical Institute	Kennesaw	T,B	Prop	M/W															
Lanier Technical College	Oakwood	T	St	M/W	3,579	71													
Moultrie Technical College	Moultrie	T	St	M/W	2,058	62													
North Georgia Technical College	Clarkesville	T	St	M/W	2,441	58													
Oconee Fall Line Technical College	Sandersville	T	St	M/W	1,869	70													
Ogeechee Technical College	Statesboro	T	St	M/W	2,216	61													
Savannah Technical College	Savannah	T	St	M/W	4,784	63													
Southeastern Technical College	Vidalia	T	St	M/W	1,533	71													
Southern Crescent Technical College	Griffin	T	St	M/W	5,177	59													
South Georgia State College	Douglas	C,B	St	M/W	2,579	27													
South Georgia Technical College	Americus	T	St	M/W	1,828	47													
Southwest Georgia Technical College	Thomasville	T	St	M/W	1,546	71													
West Georgia Technical College	Waco	T	St	M/W	6,915	68													
Wiregrass Georgia Technical College	Valdosta	T	St	M/W	3,966	65													
Guam																		
Guam Community College	Mangilao	T	Terr	M/W	2,458	60	29		Y	Y	Y	Y	Y				N		22
Hawaii																		
Hawaii Tokai International College	Kapolei	C,T	Ind	M/W	89		0	90	N	Y	Y	Y					Y		1
Honolulu Community College	Honolulu	C,T	St	M/W	4,368	63													
University of Hawaii Maui College	Kahului	C,T,B	St	M/W	4,071	64													
Idaho																		
Brown Mackie College–Boise	Boise	T,B	Prop	M/W															
Carrington College–Boise	Boise	T	Prop	M/W	552	10													
College of Southern Idaho	Twin Falls	T	St-L	M/W	8,473	72	43		Y	Y	Y		Y	Y	Y		Y	13	72
College of Western Idaho	Nampa	C,T	St	M/W	9,204														
Eastern Idaho Technical College	Idaho Falls	T	St	M/W	756	57	58		Y	Y	Y	Y	Y	Y	Y	Y	N		12
ITT Technical Institute	Boise	T,B	Prop	M/W															
Illinois																		
Black Hawk College	Moline	C,T	St-L	M/W	6,574	61													
City Colleges of Chicago, Olive-Harvey College	Chicago	C,T	St-L	M/W	4,572	57			Y	Y	S	Y	Y	Y	Y		N	3	18
Danville Area Community College	Danville	C,T	St-L	M/W	3,207	67	43		Y	Y	Y	Y	Y	Y	Y		N	5	31
Elgin Community College	Elgin	C,T	St-L	M/W	11,285	67	42		Y		S		Y	Y	Y		N	8	35
Fox College	Bedford Park	T	Priv	M/W	387												N		6
Harper College	Palatine	C,T	St-L	M/W	14,957		36		Y		Y		Y	Y	Y		N	12	66
Highland Community College	Freeport	C,T	St-L	M/W	1,730	44	34		Y	Y	R,S	Y	Y	Y			N	6	22
Illinois Eastern Community Colleges, Frontier Community College	Fairfield	C,T	St-L	M/W	2,218	90	58		Y	Y	Y	Y	Y	Y	Y		N	2	15
Illinois Eastern Community Colleges, Lincoln Trail College	Robinson	C,T	St-L	M/W	1,032	61	37		Y	Y	Y	Y	Y	Y	Y		N	3	14
Illinois Eastern Community Colleges, Olney Central College	Olney	C,T	St-L	M/W	1,398	55	34		Y	Y	Y	Y	Y	Y	Y		N	3	15
Illinois Eastern Community Colleges, Wabash Valley College	Mount Carmel	C,T	St-L	M/W	4,239	87	47		Y	Y	Y	Y	Y	Y	Y		N	3	20
ITT Technical Institute	Arlington Heights	T,B	Prop	M/W															
ITT Technical Institute	Oak Brook	T,B	Prop	M/W															
ITT Technical Institute	Orland Park	T,B	Prop	M/W															
Kankakee Community College	Kankakee	C,T	St-L	M/W	3,378	59	45	24	Y	Y	Y	Y	Y	Y	Y		N	5	42
Kaskaskia College	Centralia	C,T	St-L	M/W	4,905	65	15		Y	Y	Y	Y	Y	Y	Y		N	9	43
Kishwaukee College	Malta	C,T	St-L	M/W	4,475	55	27		Y		R,S	Y	Y	Y			N	4	29
Lake Land College	Mattoon	C,T	St-L	M/W	6,351	56			Y		R	Y	Y	Y	Y		N	9	37
Lincoln Land Community College	Springfield	C,T	Dist	M/W	7,020	57													
McHenry County College	Crystal Lake	C,T	St-L	M/W	7,023	62	34		Y		R	Y	Y	Y			N	6	27
Moraine Valley Community College	Palos Hills	C,T	St-L	M/W	15,286	57	25	85	Y		R	Y	Y	Y			N	9	39
Northwestern College	Chicago	C,T	Prop	M/W	1,082	56	61		N	Y	Y	Y	Y				N		10
Oakton Community College	Des Plaines	C,T	Dist	M/W	9,880		39		Y	Y	R		Y				N	10	30
Rend Lake College	Ina	C,T	St	M/W	2,714	46													
Richland Community College	Decatur	C,T	Dist	M/W	3,152	68	49		Y		Y	Y	Y	Y			N		28
Rock Valley College	Rockford	C,T	Dist	M/W	8,150	55	35		Y		Y	Y	Y	Y			N	9	32
Sauk Valley Community College	Dixon	C,T	Dist	M/W	2,220	55													
Shawnee Community College	Ullin	C,T	St-L	M/W	1,781	47	33		Y	Y	Y	Y	Y	Y			N	4	30
South Suburban College	South Holland	C,T	St-L	M/W	4,514		42		Y	Y	Y	Y	Y	Y			N	5	23
Southwestern Illinois College	Belleville	C,T	Dist	M/W	10,545	56	39		Y	Y	Y	Y	Y	Y			N	5	60
Spoon River College	Canton	C,T	St	M/W	1,784	60													
Vet Tech Institute at Fox College	Tinley Park	T	Priv	M/W	151							Y					N		1
Waubonsee Community College	Sugar Grove	C,T	Dist	M/W	10,721	68													
Indiana																		
Ancilla College	Donaldson	C,T	I-R	M/W	400	23	11		Y	Y	Y	Y	Y	Y	Y	Y	Y	7	18
Brown Mackie College–Fort Wayne	Fort Wayne	T,B	Prop	M/W															

This chart includes the names and locations of accredited two-year colleges in the United States, Canada, and other countries and shows institutions' responses to the *Peterson's Annual Survey of Undergraduate Institutions*. If an institution submitted incomplete data, one or more columns opposite the institution's name is blank. A dagger after the school name indicates that the institution has one or more entries in the *Featured Two-Year Colleges* section. If a school does not appear, it did not report any of the information.

Y—Yes; N—No; R—Recommended; S—For Some

Name	City	Degrees Awarded	Institutional Control	Student Body	Undergrad Enrollment	% Attending Part-Time	% 25 Yrs or Older	% Grads to 4-Yr Colleges	HS Equiv Cert Accepted	Open Admissions	HS Transcript Required	Need-Based Aid Available	Part-Time Jobs Available	Career Counseling Available	Job Placement Services Available	College Housing Available	# Sports Offered	# Majors Offered
Brown Mackie College–Indianapolis	Indianapolis	T,B	Prop	M/W														
Brown Mackie College–Merrillville	Merrillville	T,B	Prop	M/W														
Brown Mackie College–Michigan City	Michigan City	T,B	Prop	M/W														
Brown Mackie College–South Bend	South Bend	T,B	Prop	PW														
International Business College	Indianapolis	T	Priv	M/W	399						Y		Y			Y		11
ITT Technical Institute	Fort Wayne	T,B	Prop	M/W														
ITT Technical Institute	Merrillville	T,B	Prop	M/W														
ITT Technical Institute	Newburgh	T,B	Prop	M/W														
Ivy Tech Community College–Bloomington	Bloomington	C,T	St	M/W	6,477	61												
Ivy Tech Community College–Central Indiana	Indianapolis	C,T	St	M/W	21,978	68												
Ivy Tech Community College–Columbus	Columbus	C,T	St	M/W	4,578	72												
Ivy Tech Community College–East Central	Muncie	C,T	St	M/W	7,466	56												
Ivy Tech Community College–Kokomo	Kokomo	C,T	St	M/W	3,948	60												
Ivy Tech Community College–Lafayette	Lafayette	C,T	St	M/W	6,398	56												
Ivy Tech Community College–North Central	South Bend	C,T	St	M/W	7,182	71												
Ivy Tech Community College–Northeast	Fort Wayne	C,T	St	M/W	9,102	65												
Ivy Tech Community College–Northwest	Gary	C,T	St	M/W	9,942	65												
Ivy Tech Community College–Richmond	Richmond	C,T	St	M/W	3,095	66												
Ivy Tech Community College–Southeast	Madison	C,T	St	M/W	2,881	66												
Ivy Tech Community College–Southern Indiana	Sellersburg	C,T	St	M/W	4,892	74												
Ivy Tech Community College–Southwest	Evansville	C,T	St	M/W	5,475	67												
Ivy Tech Community College–Wabash Valley	Terre Haute	C,T	St	M/W	5,364	64												
Vet Tech Institute at International Business College	Fort Wayne	T	Priv	M/W	127											Y		1
Vet Tech Institute at International Business College	Indianapolis	T	Priv	M/W	124					Y						Y	Y	1
Vincennes University	Vincennes	C,T,B	St	M/W	19,205	68			Y	Y	Y	Y					Y	8	125
Iowa																		
Brown Mackie College–Quad Cities	Bettendorf	T	Prop	M/W														
Des Moines Area Community College	Ankeny	C,T	St-L	M/W	22,324	60	41		Y		S	Y	Y	Y	Y	Y	8	50
Hawkeye Community College	Waterloo	C,T	St-L	M/W	5,291	50	28		Y	Y	Y	Y	Y	Y	Y	N	9	39
Iowa Central Community College	Fort Dodge	C,T	St-L	M/W	5,654	47		26	Y	Y	Y	Y	Y	Y	Y	Y	12	35
Iowa Lakes Community College	Estherville	C,T	St-L	M/W	2,340		25		Y	Y		Y	Y	Y	Y	Y	19	183
ITT Technical Institute	Clive	T,B	Prop	M/W														
Northeast Iowa Community College	Calmar	C,T	St-L	M/W	4,934	67	20		Y		R	Y	Y	Y	Y	N	7	29
North Iowa Area Community College	Mason City	C	St-L	M/W	2,955	52			Y	Y	S	Y	Y	Y	Y	N	10	40
St. Luke's College	Sioux City	C,T,B	Ind	M/W	251	38		25	N	Y	Y	Y	Y	Y	Y	N		4
Southeastern Community College	West Burlington	C	St-L	M/W	2,987	52	27		Y			Y	Y	Y	Y	Y	6	29
Western Iowa Tech Community College	Sioux City	C,T	St	M/W	6,331	61	41		Y		Y	R	Y	Y	Y	Y	8	56
Kansas																		
Allen Community College	Iola	C,T	St-L	M/W	2,741		20		Y		Y	Y	Y	Y	Y	Y	12	66
Brown Mackie College–Kansas City	Lenexa	T,B	Prop	M/W														
Brown Mackie College–Salina	Salina	T,B	Prop	M/W														
Cloud County Community College	Concordia	C,T	St-L	M/W	2,406	64	34		Y	Y	Y	Y	Y	Y	Y		8	19
Donnelly College	Kansas City	C,T,B	I-R	M/W	463	33	34	11	Y	Y	R	Y	Y	Y	Y	Y		4
Garden City Community College	Garden City	C,T	Cou	M/W	1,997	46												
Hutchinson Community College	Hutchinson	C,T	St-L	M/W	5,723	60	28	70	Y	Y	Y		Y	Y			Y	12	55
Independence Community College	Independence	C,T	St	M/W	1,031	44												
Manhattan Area Technical College	Manhattan	C,T	St-L	M/W	825	40												
Wichita Area Technical College	Wichita	C,T	Dist	M/W	2,936	63												
Wright Career College	Overland Park	C,T,B	Prop	M/W	71													
Wright Career College	Wichita	T,B	Prop	M/W	362	65												
Kentucky																		
Brown Mackie College–Hopkinsville	Hopkinsville	T	Prop	M/W														
Brown Mackie College–Louisville	Louisville	T,B	Prop	M/W														
Brown Mackie College–Northern Kentucky	Fort Mitchell	C,B	Prop	M/W														
Elizabethtown Community and Technical College	Elizabethtown	C,T	St	M/W	7,353	62	46			Y	S			Y	Y	N		24
Gateway Community and Technical College	Florence	C	St	M/W	4,639	72			Y	Y	Y			Y		N	N		15
Hopkinsville Community College	Hopkinsville	C,T	St	M/W	3,609	55			Y	Y	R	Y	Y	Y	Y	N	5	20
ITT Technical Institute	Louisville	T,B	Prop	M/W														
Maysville Community and Technical College	Maysville	C,T	St	M/W	3,478	58	46		Y	Y	Y	Y	Y	Y	Y	N		12
Owensboro Community and Technical College	Owensboro	C,T	St	M/W	4,162	61	39	15	Y	Y	Y	Y	Y	Y	Y	N		23
Somerset Community College	Somerset	C,T	St	M/W	1,210	28	49		Y	Y	Y	Y	Y		N	N		18
Spencerian College	Louisville	T,B	Prop	PW	500	39			Y	Y	Y		Y	Y	Y	N	Y	8
Spencerian College–Lexington	Lexington	T	Prop	M/W	99		60		Y	Y	Y	Y	Y	Y	Y	Y		10
Sullivan College of Technology and Design	Louisville	C,T,B	Prop	M/W	365	38	50		N	Y	Y		Y	Y	Y	Y		45
West Kentucky Community and Technical College	Paducah	C,T	St	M/W	4,668	49												
Louisiana																		
Bossier Parish Community College	Bossier City	C,T	St	M/W	15,910	33	39		Y	Y		Y		Y	Y	N	10	35
Career Technical College	Monroe	T	Prop	M/W	576	22	56		N	Y	Y			Y	Y	N		12
Delgado Community College	New Orleans	C,T	St	M/W	18,698	58	59		Y		R,S	Y	Y	Y	Y	N	8	37
ITI Technical College	Baton Rouge	T	Prop	M/W	585		50	1			Y			Y		N		8
ITT Technical Institute	Baton Rouge	T,B	Prop	M/W														
ITT Technical Institute	St. Rose	T,B	Prop	M/W														
Louisiana Delta Community College	Monroe	C,T	St	M/W	4,933	54	40			Y								15
Nunez Community College	Chalmette	C,T	St	M/W	2,597	46	52		Y		S	Y	Y	Y	Y	N	2	8
Southern University at Shreveport	Shreveport	C,T	St	M/W	2,988	30	32			Y		Y	Y	Y	Y	Y	3	36
South Louisiana Community College	Lafayette	C,T	St	M/W	6,032	46	20		Y	Y	Y		Y	Y	Y	N		29
Sowela Technical Community College	Lake Charles	C,T	St	M/W	3,411	47	30		Y	Y	Y			Y	Y	N		12

This chart includes the names and locations of accredited two-year colleges in the United States, Canada, and other countries and shows institutions' responses to the *Peterson's Annual Survey of Undergraduate Institutions*. If an institution submitted incomplete data, one or more columns opposite the institution's name is blank. A dagger after the school name indicates that the institution has one or more entries in the *Featured Two-Year Colleges* section. If a school does not appear, it did not report any of the information.

Degrees Awarded: College Transfer Associate (C), Terminal Associate (T), Bachelor's (B), Master's (M), Doctoral (D)

Y—Yes; N—No; R—Recommended; S—For Some

Column headings (left to right): Institution | City | Degrees Awarded | Institutional Control | Student Body | Undergraduate Enrollment | Percent Attending Part-Time | Percent 25 Years of Age or Older | Percent of Grads Going on to Four-Year Colleges | Open Admissions | High School Equivalency Certificate Accepted | High School Transcript Required | Need-Based Aid Available | Part-Time Jobs Available | Career Counseling Available | Job Placement Services Available | College Housing Available | Number of Sports Offered | Number of Majors Offered

Maine

Institution	City	Deg	Ctrl	Body	Enroll	%PT	%25+	%Grad	OA	Equiv	Trans	Need	PTJob	Career	JobPl	Hous	Sports	Majors
Beal College	Bangor	T	Prop	M/W	464	22			N	Y	Y	Y	Y	Y	Y	Y	6	25
Central Maine Community College	Auburn	C,T	St	M/W	3,162	56	38		Y	Y	Y	Y	Y	Y	Y	N	7	31
Kennebec Valley Community College	Fairfield	C,T	St	M/W	2,401	75	44		Y	Y	Y	Y	Y	Y	Y	N		
The Landing School	Arundel	C,T	Ind	M/W	81			80		Y	Y	Y			Y		Y		1
Maine College of Health Professions	Lewiston	T	Ind	M/W	210	72	74		N	Y	Y	Y				Y		3
Southern Maine Community College	South Portland	C,T	St	M/W	7,131	58												
York County Community College	Wells	C,T	St	M/W	1,699	69	42		Y	Y	Y	Y	Y	Y	Y	N	10	17

Maryland

Institution	City	Deg	Ctrl	Body	Enroll	%PT	%25+	%Grad	OA	Equiv	Trans	Need	PTJob	Career	JobPl	Hous	Sports	Majors
Anne Arundel Community College	Arnold	C,T	St-L	M/W	15,274	71	37		Y		Y	Y	Y	Y	Y	N	8	47
Carroll Community College	Westminster	C,T	St-L	M/W	3,661	63	30		Y		Y	Y	Y	Y	Y	N		33
Cecil College	North East	C	Cou	M/W	2,551	60	33		Y	Y	Y	Y	Y	Y	Y	N	8	42
Chesapeake College	Wye Mills	C,T	St-L	M/W	2,069	63	35		Y	Y	Y	Y	Y	Y	Y	N	5	24
College of Southern Maryland	La Plata	C,T	St-L	M/W	8,411	63	33		Y		R	Y	Y	Y	Y	N	7	37
The Community College of Baltimore County	Baltimore	C,T	Cou	M/W	23,136	68				Y	Y		Y			N	8	56
Frederick Community College	Frederick	C,T	St-L	M/W	6,031	66	35		Y		R	Y	Y	Y	Y	N	7	32
Garrett College	McHenry	C,T	St-L	M/W	712	19	13		Y	Y	Y	Y	Y	Y	Y	Y	9	13
Hagerstown Community College	Hagerstown	C,T	St-L	M/W	4,615	75	31		Y		S	Y	Y	Y	Y		12	29
Harford Community College	Bel Air	C,T	St-L	M/W	6,713	62	29	50	Y			Y	Y	Y			13	58
Howard Community College	Columbia	C,T	St-L	M/W	9,920	62	37		Y		S	Y	Y	Y	Y	N	6	48
ITT Technical Institute	Owings Mills	T,B	Prop	M/W														
Montgomery College	Rockville	C,T	St-L	M/W	25,517	65	31	61	Y		R	Y	Y	Y	Y		9	44
Wor-Wic Community College	Salisbury	C,T	St-L	M/W	3,107	71	41		Y		R		Y	Y		N		23

Massachusetts

Institution	City	Deg	Ctrl	Body	Enroll	%PT	%25+	%Grad	OA	Equiv	Trans	Need	PTJob	Career	JobPl	Hous	Sports	Majors
Bay State College †	Boston	C,T,B	Ind	M/W	1,098													
Benjamin Franklin Institute of Technology	Boston	C,T,B	Ind	M/W	493	13			Y	Y	Y		Y	Y	Y	Y	3	16
Berkshire Community College	Pittsfield	C,T	St	M/W	2,400	66												
Bristol Community College	Fall River	C,T	St	M/W	9,335	53												
Bunker Hill Community College	Boston	C,T	St	M/W	14,253	68			Y	Y		Y	Y	Y	Y	N	4	56
Dean College	Franklin	C,T,B	Ind	M/W	1,292	17	1		N	Y	Y	Y	Y	Y	Y	Y	8	19
Greenfield Community College	Greenfield	C,T	St	M/W	2,127	64	42		Y	Y	S	Y	Y	Y		N		34
Holyoke Community College	Holyoke	C,T	St	M/W	6,604	54	34		Y		Y	Y	Y	Y		N	8	21
ITT Technical Institute	Norwood	T,B	Prop	M/W														
ITT Technical Institute	Wilmington	T,B	Prop	M/W														
Massachusetts Bay Community College	Wellesley Hills	C,T	St	M/W	5,369	65	49		Y	Y		Y	Y	Y	Y	N	9	30
Middlesex Community College	Bedford	C,T	St	M/W	9,205	62	35		Y	Y	S	Y	Y	Y	Y	N	3	33
Mount Wachusett Community College	Gardner	C,T	St	M/W	4,336	59	46		Y	Y	Y	Y	Y	Y	Y	N	8	29
Northern Essex Community College	Haverhill	C,T	St	M/W	6,963	67	36		Y	Y	Y	Y	Y	Y	Y	N	11	58
North Shore Community College	Danvers	C,T	St	M/W	7,412	65	41	45	Y	Y	S	Y	Y	Y	Y	N	2	40
Quinsigamond Community College	Worcester	C,T	St	M/W	8,453	61	35		Y	Y	Y	Y		Y	Y	N	6	42
Springfield Technical Community College	Springfield	C,T	St	M/W	6,622	53	41		Y	Y	Y	Y	Y	Y	Y	N	8	56

Michigan

Institution	City	Deg	Ctrl	Body	Enroll	%PT	%25+	%Grad	OA	Equiv	Trans	Need	PTJob	Career	JobPl	Hous	Sports	Majors
Delta College	University Center	C,T	Dist	M/W	9,842	63	34		Y		R	Y	Y	Y	Y	N	6	64
Glen Oaks Community College	Centreville	C,T	St-L	M/W	1,221	57												
Gogebic Community College	Ironwood	C,T	St-L	M/W	1,199	46												
Grand Rapids Community College	Grand Rapids	C,T	Dist	M/W	15,668	68	36		Y	Y	Y	Y	Y	Y	Y	N	6	44
ITT Technical Institute	Canton	T,B	Prop	M/W														
ITT Technical Institute	Dearborn	T,B	Prop	M/W														
ITT Technical Institute	Swartz Creek	C,B	Prop	M/W														
ITT Technical Institute	Troy	T,B	Prop	M/W														
ITT Technical Institute	Wyoming	T,B	Prop	M/W														
Jackson College	Jackson	C,T	Cou	M/W	5,665	58												
Kalamazoo Valley Community College	Kalamazoo	C,T	St-L	M/W	11,113		37		Y	Y	Y	Y	Y	Y	Y	N	6	34
Kellogg Community College	Battle Creek	C,T	St-L	M/W	5,647	72	38		Y		S	Y	Y	Y	Y	N	5	35
Kirtland Community College	Roscommon	C,T	Dist	M/W	1,773	70	47		Y	Y		Y	Y	Y	Y	N	3	32
Lansing Community College	Lansing	C,T	St-L	M/W	17,562	62												
Macomb Community College	Warren	C,T	Dist	M/W	22,914	67	36		Y			Y	Y	Y	Y	N	11	72
Monroe County Community College	Monroe	C,T	Cou	M/W				45	Y	Y	Y		Y	Y	Y	N	2	42
Montcalm Community College	Sidney	C,T	St-L	M/W	1,832	71	55		Y		R	Y	Y			N	1	23
Mott Community College	Flint	C,T	Dist	M/W	8,937	73	45		Y		Y	Y	Y	Y	Y	N	7	45
Northwestern Michigan College	Traverse City	C,T,B	St-L	M/W	4,609	56	37		Y	Y	S	Y	Y	Y	Y	Y	7	45
Oakland Community College	Bloomfield Hills	C,T	St-L	M/W	26,405	69												
Saginaw Chippewa Tribal College	Mount Pleasant	C,T	Ind	M/W	150	61					Y							3
St. Clair County Community College	Port Huron	C,T	St-L	M/W	4,127	61			Y		Y	Y	Y	Y	Y	N	5	27
Schoolcraft College	Livonia	C,T	Dist	M/W	11,542	67	35		Y	Y	R,S	Y	Y	Y	Y	N	5	36
Southwestern Michigan College	Dowagiac	C,T	St-L	M/W	2,567	52	25		Y	Y	Y	Y	Y			Y	7	26
Wayne County Community College District	Detroit	C,T	St-L	M/W	16,310	80	48		Y		Y	Y	Y	Y	Y	N	5	39

Minnesota

Institution	City	Deg	Ctrl	Body	Enroll	%PT	%25+	%Grad	OA	Equiv	Trans	Need	PTJob	Career	JobPl	Hous	Sports	Majors
Alexandria Technical and Community College	Alexandria	C,T	St	M/W	2,525		21		Y	Y	Y	Y	Y	Y	Y	N	4	27
Anoka-Ramsey Community College	Coon Rapids	C,T	St	M/W	7,807		24		Y	Y	S	Y	Y	Y	Y	N	10	25
Anoka-Ramsey Community College, Cambridge Campus	Cambridge	C,T	St	M/W	2,313		26		Y	Y	S	Y	Y	Y	Y	N	7	25
Anoka Technical College	Anoka	C,T	St	M/W	2,237		44		Y	Y	Y	Y	Y	Y	Y	N		23
Century College	White Bear Lake	C,T	St	M/W	9,386	61	43		Y	Y	Y	Y	Y	Y	Y	N	11	42
Duluth Business University	Duluth	T,B	Prop	PW	182	43	53				Y		Y	Y	Y	N		8
Dunwoody College of Technology	Minneapolis	T,B	Ind	PM	1,070	18	32		N	Y	Y	Y	Y	Y	Y	N		25
Hennepin Technical College	Brooklyn Park	C,T	St	M/W	5,985	66	51		Y		R	Y	Y	Y	Y	N		35

This chart includes the names and locations of accredited two-year colleges in the United States, Canada, and other countries and shows institutions' responses to the *Peterson's Annual Survey of Undergraduate Institutions*. If an institution submitted incomplete data, one or more columns opposite the institution's name is blank. A dagger after the school name indicates that the institution has one or more entries in the *Featured Two-Year Colleges* section. If a school does not appear, it did not report any of the information.

Column key

Degrees Awarded: College Transfer Associate (C), Terminal Associate (T), Bachelor's (B), Master's (M), Doctoral (D)

Institutional Control: County District City, State and Local, State-Related / Federal, State Commonwealth, Territory / Independent, Independent-Religious, Proprietary

Student Body: Men, Primarily Men, Women, Primarily Women, Coed

Y—Yes; N—No; R—Recommended; S—For Some

Institution	City	Deg.	Control	Student Body	Undergrad Enroll.	% Part-Time	% to 4-Yr	% 25+	HS Equiv. Cert.	HS Transcript Req.	Open Adm.	Need-Based Aid	Part-Time Jobs	Career Couns.	Job Place.	Housing	# Sports	# Majors
The Institute of Production and Recording	Minneapolis	T	Prop	M/W	242	37												
ITT Technical Institute	Brooklyn Center	T,B	Prop	M/W														
ITT Technical Institute	Eden Prairie	T,B	Prop	M/W														
Lake Superior College	Duluth	C,T	St	M/W	5,050	58												
Mesabi Range College	Virginia	C,T	St	M/W	1,451	39	37		Y	Y	Y	Y	Y	Y	Y	Y	13	16
Minneapolis Business College	Roseville	T	Priv	M/W	235					Y								
Minneapolis Community and Technical College	Minneapolis	C,T	St	M/W	9,465	66			Y	Y	Y	Y	Y	Y	Y	N	6	42
Minnesota School of Business–Brooklyn Center	Brooklyn Center	C,T,B	Prop	M/W	169	41												
Minnesota School of Business–Plymouth	Plymouth	C,T,B	Prop	M/W	190	44												
Minnesota State College–Southeast Technical	Winona	C,T	St	M/W	2,136	54	48		Y	Y	Y	Y	Y	Y				27
Minnesota West Community and Technical College	Pipestone	C,T	St	M/W	3,182				Y	Y	Y	Y	Y				7	42
Normandale Community College	Bloomington	C,T	St	M/W					Y	Y	S	Y	Y	Y	Y	N	10	23
North Hennepin Community College	Brooklyn Park	C,T	St	M/W	7,178	72			Y	Y	R	Y	Y	Y	Y	N	10	29
Northland Community College	Thief River Falls	C,T	St	M/W	3,629				Y	Y	R	Y	Y	Y		N	13	52
Northwest Technical College	Bemidji	T	St	M/W	1,088	64	51		Y	Y	Y	Y	Y					16
Rainy River Community College	International Falls	C,T	St	M/W	267	13	54		Y	Y	R	Y	Y	Y	Y	Y	16	5
Ridgewater College	Willmar	C,T	St	M/W	3,753				Y	Y	Y	Y	Y	Y	Y	N	9	51
Riverland Community College	Austin	C,T	St	M/W	3,014		39		Y	Y	Y	Y	Y	Y	Y	Y	5	30
Mississippi																		
Copiah-Lincoln Community College	Wesson	C,T	St-L	M/W	3,157	21	6		Y	Y	Y	Y	Y	Y	Y	Y	8	42
Hinds Community College	Raymond	C,T	St-L	M/W	11,832	35	32				Y	Y	Y	Y	Y	Y	14	103
Mississippi Delta Community College	Moorhead	C,T	Dist	M/W	2,950	22												
Mississippi Gulf Coast Community College	Perkinston	C,T	Dist	M/W	10,074	31												
Northwest Mississippi Community College	Senatobia	C,T	St-L	M/W	6,300													
Missouri																		
Brown Mackie College–St. Louis	Fenton	T,B	Prop	M/W														
Cottey College	Nevada	C,B	Ind	CW	284													
Crowder College	Neosho	C,T	St-L	M/W	5,710	54	30		Y	Y	Y	Y	Y	Y	Y		4	46
Culinary Institute of St. Louis at Hickey College	St. Louis	T	Priv	M/W	91					Y								1
East Central College	Union	C,T	Dist	M/W	3,900	53												
ITT Technical Institute	Arnold	T,B	Prop	M/W														
ITT Technical Institute	Earth City	T,B	Prop	M/W														
ITT Technical Institute	Kansas City	T,B	Prop	M/W														
Jefferson College	Hillsboro	C,T	Dist	M/W	4,883	48			Y	Y	Y	Y	Y	Y	Y		6	28
Metro Business College	Jefferson City	T	Prop	M/W	142	20												
Metropolitan Community College–Kansas City	Kansas City	C,T	St-L	M/W	19,234	60												
Mineral Area College	Park Hills	C,T	Dist	M/W	4,508	36												
Missouri State University–West Plains	West Plains	C,T	St	M/W	2,123	38												
Ozarks Technical Community College	Springfield	C,T	Dist	M/W	14,396				Y	Y	Y	Y	Y	Y	Y	N		34
Pinnacle Career Institute–North Kansas City	Kansas City	T	Prop	M/W	147				Y	Y	Y	Y			Y			
St. Charles Community College	Cottleville	C,T	St	M/W	7,153	52	26		Y	Y	R,S	Y	Y	Y	Y		3	41
St. Louis Community College	St. Louis	C,T	Pub	M/W	21,218	59	41		Y	Y	S	Y	Y	Y	Y	N	5	51
State Fair Community College	Sedalia	C,T	Dist	M/W	4,983	50	32		Y	Y			Y	Y	Y	Y	1	29
Vet Tech Institute at Hickey College	St. Louis	T	Priv	M/W	126													1
Montana																		
Flathead Valley Community College	Kalispell	C,T	St-L	M/W	2,216	51												
Great Falls College Montana State University	Great Falls	C,T	St	M/W	1,756	53	47	43	Y	Y	Y	Y	Y					20
Helena College University of Montana	Helena	C,T	St	M/W	1,430	53												
Nebraska																		
ITT Technical Institute	Omaha	T,B	Prop	M/W														
Mid-Plains Community College	North Platte	C,T	Dist	M/W	2,143	60	34		Y	Y	Y	Y	Y	Y	Y	N	5	18
Nebraska Indian Community College	Macy	C,T	Fed	M/W	120	55	47	50	Y			Y	Y	Y	Y	N		13
Northeast Community College	Norfolk	C,T	St-L	M/W	5,145	57												
Wright Career College	Omaha	T,B	Prop	M/W	306	69												
Nevada																		
Carrington College–Las Vegas	Las Vegas	T	Prop	M/W	255	12												
Carrington College–Reno	Reno	T	Prop	M/W	333	24												
Great Basin College	Elko	C,T,B	St	M/W	3,128	69	40		Y	Y		Y	Y	Y	Y	Y	3	30
ITT Technical Institute	Henderson	T,B	Prop	M/W														
ITT Technical Institute	North Las Vegas	T,B	Prop	M/W														
Truckee Meadows Community College	Reno	C,T	St	M/W	11,106	75	40	35	Y	Y	S	Y	Y	Y	Y	N		51
Western Nevada College	Carson City	C,T,B	St	M/W	4,032	65	48		Y	Y	S	Y	Y	Y		N	2	27
New Hampshire																		
Lakes Region Community College	Laconia	C,T	St	M/W	1,179	58	39		Y	Y	Y	Y				N		23
River Valley Community College	Claremont	C,T	St	M/W	982	64			Y	Y	Y	Y				N		
St. Joseph School of Nursing	Nashua	C,T	Ind	M/W	144	56	76		N	Y		Y	Y			N		
White Mountains Community College	Berlin	C,T	St	M/W	845	69	46		Y	Y	Y	Y				N		19
New Jersey																		
Burlington County College	Pemberton	C,T	Cou	M/W	9,438	49	34		Y	Y	R	Y	Y	Y	Y	N	6	57
Camden County College†	Blackwood	C,T	St-L	M/W	15,670	46	39		Y	Y	R	S	Y	Y	Y	N	5	40
County College of Morris	Randolph	C,T	Cou	M/W	8,096			24	Y	Y	Y	Y	Y	Y	Y	N	12	30
Cumberland County College	Vineland	C,T	St-L	M/W	3,844		34		Y	Y	Y	Y	Y	Y	Y	N	7	20
Hudson County Community College	Jersey City	C,T	St-L	M/W	9,203	35	32		Y	Y	Y					N		17
ITT Technical Institute	Marlton	T	Prop	M/W														

This chart includes the names and locations of accredited two-year colleges in the United States, Canada, and other countries and shows institutions' responses to the *Peterson's Annual Survey of Undergraduate Institutions*. If an institution submitted incomplete data, one or more columns opposite the institution's name is blank. A dagger after the school name indicates that the institution has one or more entries in the *Featured Two-Year Colleges* section. If a school does not appear, it did not report any of the information.

Y—Yes; N—No; R—Recommended; S—For Some

Name	City	Degrees Awarded	Institutional Control	Student Body	Undergraduate Enrollment	Percent Attending Part-Time	Percent 25 Years of Age or Older	Percent of Grads Going on to Four-Year Colleges	Open Admissions	High School Equivalency Certificate Accepted	High School Transcript Required	Need-Based Aid Available	Part-Time Jobs Available	Career Counseling Available	Job Placement Services Available	College Housing Available	Number of Sports Offered	Number of Majors Offered
Mercer County Community College	Trenton	C,T	St-L	M/W	8,501	64												
Middlesex County College	Edison	C,T	Cou	M/W	12,064				Y	Y	Y	Y	Y			N	7	40
Ocean County College	Toms River	C,T	Cou	M/W	9,296	47	26		Y		S	Y	Y	Y		N	13	21
Raritan Valley Community College	Branchburg	C,T	St-L	M/W	8,214	58	22				S	Y	Y	Y	Y	Y	N		57
Salem Community College	Carneys Point	C,T	Cou	M/W	1,107	46	29		Y	Y	Y		Y	Y	Y		N		33
Sussex County Community College	Newton	C,T	St-L	M/W	3,732	45												
New Mexico																		
Brown Mackie College–Albuquerque	Albuquerque	T,B	Prop	M/W														
Carrington College–Albuquerque	Albuquerque	T	Prop	M/W	647	16												
ITT Technical Institute	Albuquerque	T,B	Prop	M/W														
New Mexico Junior College	Hobbs	C,T	St-L	M/W	3,222		52		Y			Y	Y	Y		Y	10	52
New Mexico State University–Alamogordo	Alamogordo	C,T	St	M/W	3,371	70												
San Juan College	Farmington	C,T	St	M/W	7,786	71	58		Y	Y		Y	Y	Y	Y	N	13	53
Southwestern Indian Polytechnic Institute	Albuquerque	C,T	Fed	M/W	481	12	40	1	Y	Y	Y	Y	Y	Y	Y	Y	3	12
University of New Mexico–Los Alamos Branch	Los Alamos	C,T	St	M/W	744	74			N	Y	Y	Y	Y	Y	Y			
New York																		
American Academy of Dramatic Arts–New York	New York	T	Ind	M/W	253	20		0	N	Y	Y	Y	Y	Y		Y		1
The Belanger School of Nursing	Schenectady	C,T	Ind	PW	124	70	78				Y	Y	Y			N	1	6
Berkeley College–Westchester Campus	White Plains	C,T,B	Prop	M/W	450	8	21		N	Y	Y	Y	Y	Y	Y	Y	3	6
Borough of Manhattan Community College of the City University of New York	New York	C,T	St-L	M/W	26,623	36	25		Y	Y	Y	Y	Y	Y		N	4	27
Bronx Community College of the City University of New York	Bronx	C,T	St-L	M/W	11,368	42												
Cayuga County Community College	Auburn	C,T	St-L	M/W	3,269	39	40		Y	Y	Y	Y	Y	Y		Y	8	35
Clinton Community College	Plattsburgh	C,T	St-L	M/W	1,347	28	18	35	Y	Y	Y	Y	Y	Y	Y	Y	4	17
The College of Westchester	White Plains	C,T,B	Prop	M/W	1,125	21	35		N	Y	Y	Y	Y	Y	Y	N		8
Columbia-Greene Community College	Hudson	C,T	St-L	M/W	2,043	58	28			Y	Y	Y	Y	Y		N	5	17
Corning Community College	Corning	C,T	St-L	M/W	4,520	53	30		Y	Y	Y	Y	Y	Y		Y	8	64
Dutchess Community College	Poughkeepsie	C,T	St-L	M/W	9,905	53	17		Y	Y	Y	Y	Y	Y		Y	6	31
Elmira Business Institute	Elmira	C,T	Priv	PW	98	24												
Erie Community College	Buffalo	C,T	St-L	M/W	2,880	24	43		Y	Y	Y	Y	Y	Y		N	10	16
Erie Community College, North Campus	Williamsville	C,T	St-L	M/W	5,855	34	34		Y	Y	Y	Y	Y	Y		N	10	32
Erie Community College, South Campus	Orchard Park	C,T	St-L	M/W	3,935	41	21		Y	Y	Y	Y	Y	Y		N	10	21
Fashion Institute of Technology†	New York	C,T,B,M	St-L	PW	9,567	22	20		N	Y	Y	Y	Y	Y	Y	Y	8	23
Finger Lakes Community College	Canandaigua	C,T	St-L	M/W	6,800	51	33		Y	Y	Y	Y	Y	Y	Y	Y	9	57
Fiorello H. LaGuardia Community College of the City University of New York	Long Island City	C,T	St-L	M/W	20,153	45	35	46	Y	Y	Y	Y	Y	Y		N	7	43
Genesee Community College	Batavia	C,T	St-L	M/W	6,883	54	35		Y	Y	Y	Y	Y	Y		Y	13	91
Herkimer County Community College	Herkimer	C,T	St-L	M/W	3,223	35												
Institute of Design and Construction	Brooklyn	C,T	Ind	M/W	103	58												
Island Drafting and Technical Institute	Amityville	C,T	Prop	PM	110		45	0	Y	Y	R		Y	Y		N		8
ITT Technical Institute	Albany	T	Prop	M/W														
ITT Technical Institute	Getzville	T	Prop	M/W														
ITT Technical Institute	Liverpool	T	Prop	M/W														
Jamestown Business College	Jamestown	T,B	Prop	M/W	318	1	34		N	Y	Y		Y	Y		N	8	4
Jamestown Community College	Jamestown	C,T	St-L	M/W	3,368	26	28	54	Y	Y	Y	Y	Y	Y	Y	Y	10	28
Jefferson Community College	Watertown	C,T	St-L	M/W	3,931	43			N	Y	Y	Y	Y	Y	Y	Y	6	36
Kingsborough Community College of the City University of New York	Brooklyn	C,T	St-L	M/W	17,495	42	23		Y	Y	Y	Y	Y	Y		N	7	40
Long Island Business Institute	Flushing	C	Prop	PW	391	27	65	0	Y	Y	Y			Y	Y	N		7
Mohawk Valley Community College	Utica	C,T	St-L	M/W	7,149	44	33		Y		S	Y	Y	Y	Y	Y	13	50
Monroe Community College	Rochester	C,T	St-L	M/W	15,335	39	41		Y	Y	Y	Y	Y	Y	Y	Y	18	67
Nassau Community College	Garden City	C,T	St-L	M/W	22,310	40	23		Y	Y	Y	Y	Y	Y		N	18	53
New York Career Institute	New York	T	Prop	PW	702													
Niagara County Community College	Sanborn	C,T	St-L	M/W	6,486	38	26		Y	Y	Y	Y	Y	Y		Y	11	42
Onondaga Community College	Syracuse	C,T	St-L	M/W	12,841	49												
Plaza College	Forest Hills	C,T,B	Prop	M/W	726				N	Y		Y		Y	Y	N		7
Queensborough Community College of the City University of New York	Bayside	C,T	St-L	M/W	16,182	41	21		Y	Y	Y	Y	Y	Y		N	11	21
Rockland Community College	Suffern	C,T	St-L	M/W	7,434	44	35		Y		Y	Y	Y	Y		N	11	41
St. Elizabeth College of Nursing	Utica	T	Ind	M/W	159	55												
State University of New York College of Technology at Alfred	Alfred	C,T,B	St	M/W	3,661	9	14		N	Y	Y	Y	Y	Y	Y	Y	17	57
Sullivan County Community College	Loch Sheldrake	C,T	St-L	M/W	1,647	43	25	42	Y	Y	Y	Y	Y	Y	Y	Y	14	37
TCI–The College of Technology	New York	C,T	Prop	M/W	3,020													
Tompkins Cortland Community College	Dryden	C,T	St-L	M/W	5,560	58	29	0	Y	Y	Y	Y	Y	Y		Y	22	36
Trocaire College	Buffalo	T,B	Ind	PW	1,467	54	48	0	N	Y	Y	Y	Y	Y		N		14
Ulster County Community College	Stone Ridge	C,T	St-L	M/W	3,540	50	23	59	Y	Y	Y	Y	Y	Y		N	7	26
Westchester Community College	Valhalla	C,T	St-L	M/W	13,916	46	27		Y	Y	Y	Y	Y	Y		N	11	50
Wood Tobe–Coburn School	New York	T	Priv	M/W	476				N	Y		Y				N		9
North Carolina																		
Alamance Community College	Graham	C,T	St	M/W	4,614	43	44		Y	Y	Y	Y	Y	Y		N	4	28
Cape Fear Community College	Wilmington	C,T	St	M/W	9,300	55	42		Y	Y	S	Y	Y	Y		N	6	35
Carolinas College of Health Sciences	Charlotte	T	Pub	M/W	438	87												
Carteret Community College	Morehead City	C,T	St	M/W	1,872	57	53		Y	Y	S	Y	Y	Y		N		17
Catawba Valley Community College	Hickory	C,T	St-L	M/W	4,561	61	35		Y	Y	Y	Y	Y	Y		N	4	34
Central Carolina Community College	Sanford	C,T	St-L	M/W	4,900	56												
Cleveland Community College	Shelby	C,T	St	M/W	2,990	66			Y	Y	Y	Y	Y	Y	Y	N		27

This chart includes the names and locations of accredited two-year colleges in the United States, Canada, and other countries and shows institutions' responses to the *Peterson's Annual Survey of Undergraduate Institutions*. If an institution submitted incomplete data, one or more columns opposite the institution's name is blank. A dagger after the school name indicates that the institution has one or more entries in the *Featured Two-Year Colleges* section. If a school does not appear, it did not report any of the information.

Y—Yes; N—No; R—Recommended; S—For Some

Degrees Awarded: College Transfer Associate (C), Terminal Associate (T), Bachelor's (B), Master's (M), Doctoral (D)

Institution	Location	Degrees Awarded	Institutional Control	Student Body	Undergraduate Enrollment	Percent Attending Part-Time	Percent 25 Years of Age or Older	Percent of Grads Going on to Four-Year Colleges	Open Admissions	High School Equivalency Certificate Accepted	High School Transcript Required	Need-Based Aid Available	Part-Time Jobs Available	Career Counseling Available	Job Placement Services Available	College Housing Available	Number of Sports Offered	Number of Majors Offered
Fayetteville Technical Community College	Fayetteville	C,T	St	M/W	12,103	60	61	11	Y	Y	S	Y	Y	Y	Y	N	5	51
Forsyth Technical Community College	Winston-Salem	C,T	St	M/W	9,148	59	45		Y	Y	S	Y	Y	Y	Y	N	N	49
Guilford Technical Community College	Jamestown	C,T	St-L	M/W	12,430	53	46		Y	Y	S	Y	Y	Y	Y	N	4	54
Halifax Community College	Weldon	C,T	St-L	M/W	1,293	47	40		Y	Y	Y	Y	Y	Y		N		15
Harrison College	Morrisville	C,T	Prop	M/W	200	21												
Haywood Community College	Clyde	C,T	St-L	M/W	2,127		50		Y	Y	Y		Y	Y	Y	N	6	34
ITT Technical Institute	Cary	T,B	Prop	M/W														
ITT Technical Institute	Charlotte	T,B	Prop	M/W														
ITT Technical Institute	High Point	T,B	Prop	M/W														
James Sprunt Community College	Kenansville	C,T	St	M/W	1,213	54	38	1	Y	Y	Y	Y	Y	Y		N	2	17
Johnston Community College	Smithfield	C,T	St	M/W	4,021	55	40		Y	Y	Y	Y	Y	Y	Y	N	1	13
King's College	Charlotte	T	Priv	M/W	381											Y		9
Lenoir Community College	Kinston	C,T	St	M/W	3,251	60	39		Y	Y	Y	Y	Y	Y	Y	N	3	25
Living Arts College	Raleigh	B	Prop	M/W	578													
Mitchell Community College	Statesville	C,T	St	M/W	3,514	56												
Montgomery Community College	Troy	C,T	St	M/W	863	60	40		Y	Y	Y	Y	Y	Y		N		13
Piedmont Community College	Roxboro	C,T	St	M/W	1,475				Y	Y	S	Y	Y	Y	Y	N	1	25
Pitt Community College	Greenville	C,T	St-L	M/W	8,902	48												
Randolph Community College	Asheboro	C,T	St	M/W	2,771	63	31	52	Y	Y						N		27
Richmond Community College	Hamlet	C,T	St	M/W	2,664	58	42		Y	Y	Y	Y	Y			N		23
Southeastern Community College	Whiteville	C,T	St	M/W	1,402	45												
South Piedmont Community College	Polkton	C,T	St	M/W	2,658	72	33		Y	Y	Y	Y	Y	Y	Y	N		29
Southwestern Community College	Sylva	C,T	St	M/W	2,689													
Wayne Community College	Goldsboro	C,T	St-L	M/W	3,837	53												
North Dakota																		
Bismarck State College	Bismarck	C,T,B	St	M/W	4,062	42												
Dakota College at Bottineau	Bottineau	C,T	St	M/W	852		33		Y	Y	Y	Y	Y	Y	Y	Y	9	72
Lake Region State College	Devils Lake	C,T	St	M/W	1,988	73			Y	Y	S	Y	Y	Y	Y	Y	9	15
North Dakota State College of Science	Wahpeton	C,T	St	M/W	3,168	46												
Williston State College	Williston	C,T	St	M/W	883	52	23		Y	Y	Y	Y	Y	Y	Y	Y	5	18
Ohio																		
The Art Institute of Cincinnati	Cincinnati	T,B	Ind	M/W	34	12	22	0	N	Y	Y		Y	Y		N		1
Bowling Green State University-Firelands College	Huron	C,T,B	St	M/W	2,287	48	39		Y	Y	Y	Y	Y	Y	N	N	5	25
Bradford School	Columbus	T	Priv	PW	449								Y			Y		5
Brown Mackie College–Akron	Akron	T,B	Prop	M/W														
Brown Mackie College–Cincinnati	Cincinnati	T,B	Prop	M/W														
Brown Mackie College–Findlay	Findlay	T,B	Prop	M/W														
Brown Mackie College–North Canton	Canton	T,B	Prop	M/W														
Central Ohio Technical College	Newark	T	St	M/W	3,648	73												
Cincinnati State Technical and Community College	Cincinnati	C,T	St	M/W	10,707	67	49		Y	Y	Y		Y	Y	Y	N	4	63
Clark State Community College	Springfield	C,T	St	M/W	5,653	70												
Columbus Culinary Institute at Bradford School	Columbus	T	Priv	M/W	148											Y		1
Columbus State Community College	Columbus	C,T	St	M/W	25,249	65												
Davis College	Toledo	T	Prop	M/W	193	74	73		N	Y	Y	Y	Y	Y	Y	N		12
Eastern Gateway Community College	Steubenville	C,T	St-L	M/W	3,182	53	40		Y	Y	S	Y	Y	Y	Y	N	2	21
Edison Community College	Piqua	C,T	St	M/W	3,042	74	54		Y	Y	Y		Y	Y	Y	N	3	41
Good Samaritan College of Nursing and Health Science	Cincinnati	T,B	Prop	M/W	353	64	45			Y	Y	Y	Y			N		1
Hocking College	Nelsonville	C,T	St	M/W	4,094		28		Y	Y	Y	Y				Y	10	39
International College of Broadcasting	Dayton	C,T	Priv	M/W	88		35		Y	Y	Y		Y	Y	Y	N		1
ITT Technical Institute	Akron	T,B	Prop	M/W														
ITT Technical Institute	Columbus	T,B	Prop	M/W														
ITT Technical Institute	Dayton	T,B	Prop	M/W														
ITT Technical Institute	Hilliard	T,B	Prop	M/W														
ITT Technical Institute	Maumee	T,B	Prop	M/W														
ITT Technical Institute	Norwood	C,B	Prop	M/W														
ITT Technical Institute	Strongsville	T,B	Prop	M/W														
ITT Technical Institute	Warrensville Heights	T,B	Prop	M/W														
ITT Technical Institute	Youngstown	T,B	Prop	M/W														
Kent State University at Ashtabula	Ashtabula	C,B	St	M/W	2,278	49	50		Y	Y	Y	Y	Y	Y	Y	N	1	22
Kent State University at East Liverpool	East Liverpool	C,B,M	St	M/W	1,481	45	11		Y	Y	Y	Y	Y	Y	Y	N		13
Kent State University at Salem	Salem	C,B	St	M/W	1,844	33	41		Y	Y	Y	Y	Y	Y	Y	N	5	21
Kent State University at Trumbull	Warren	C,B	St	M/W	2,796	35	43		Y	Y	Y	Y	Y	Y	Y	N		22
Kent State University at Tuscarawas	New Philadelphia	C,B	St	M/W	2,266	41	38		Y	Y	Y	Y	Y	Y	Y	N	2	21
Lakeland Community College	Kirtland	C,T	St-L	M/W	8,250	65				Y	Y	Y	Y	Y	Y	N	6	39
Lorain County Community College	Elyria	C,T	St-L	M/W	11,574	72	41		Y	Y	S	Y	Y	Y	Y	N	6	72
Northwest State Community College	Archbold	C,T	St	M/W	3,614	80	53		Y	Y	Y	Y	Y			N	5	51
Ohio Business College	Hilliard	T	Prop	M/W						Y	Y							
Ohio Business College	Sandusky	C	Prop	M/W	265	36	71							Y	Y		N		8
The Ohio State University Agricultural Technical Institute	Wooster	C,T	St	M/W	757	7	8		Y	Y	Y		Y	Y	N	Y	10	34
Owens Community College	Toledo	C,T	St	M/W	12,572	66	32		Y	Y	Y		Y	Y		N	11	45
School of Advertising Art	Kettering	T	Prop	M/W	142	3	1	2	N	Y	Y			Y		N		1
Southern State Community College	Hillsboro	C,T	St	M/W	2,431	52												
Stark State College	North Canton	C,T	St-R	M/W	14,097	71	46			Y	Y	Y		Y	Y	N		49
Terra State Community College	Fremont	C,T	St	M/W	2,603	68			Y	Y	Y		Y	Y	Y	N	6	67
The University of Akron Wayne College	Orrville	C,T,B	St	M/W	2,353	53												
University of Cincinnati Clermont College	Batavia	C,T,B	St	M/W	3,246	42	32		Y	Y	Y		Y	Y	Y	N	6	37
Vet Tech Institute at Bradford School	Columbus	T	Priv	M/W	156											Y		1
Wright State University–Lake Campus	Celina	C,T,B,M	St	M/W	1,115	32	22		N	Y	Y		Y	Y	Y	Y	2	27

This chart includes the names and locations of accredited two-year colleges in the United States, Canada, and other countries and shows institutions' responses to the *Peterson's Annual Survey of Undergraduate Institutions*. If an institution submitted incomplete data, one or more columns opposite the institution's name is blank. A dagger after the school name indicates that the institution has one or more entries in the *Featured Two-Year Colleges* section. If a school does not appear, it did not report any of the information.

Y—Yes; N—No; R—Recommended; S—For Some

Institution	Location	Degrees Awarded	Institutional Control	Student Body	Undergraduate Enrollment	Percent Attending Part-Time	Percent 25 Years of Age or Older	Percent of Grads Going on to Four-Year Colleges	High School Equivalency Certificate Accepted	Open Admissions	High School Transcript Required	Need-Based Aid Available	Part-Time Jobs Available	Job Placement Services Available	Career Counseling Available	College Housing Available	Number of Sports Offered	Number of Majors Offered
Oklahoma																		
Brown Mackie College–Oklahoma City	Oklahoma City	T,B	Prop	M/W														
Brown Mackie College–Tulsa	Tulsa	T,B	Prop	M/W														
Carl Albert State College	Poteau	C,T	St	M/W	2,460	44	35		Y		Y	Y	Y	Y	Y	Y	6	29
Clary Sage College	Tulsa	T	Prop	PW	312		50		Y	Y	Y			Y	Y	N	N		3
Community Care College	Tulsa	T	Prop	PW	587		52		Y	Y	Y	Y		Y	Y	N	N		13
ITT Technical Institute	Tulsa	T,B	Prop	M/W														
Oklahoma City Community College	Oklahoma City	C,T	St	M/W	13,391	65	39		Y		S	Y	Y	Y	Y	Y	N	8	72
Oklahoma State University Institute of Technology	Okmulgee	C,T,B	St	M/W	2,624	27	31		Y	Y	Y	Y	Y			Y	N	7	25
Oklahoma State University, Oklahoma City	Oklahoma City	C,T,B	St	M/W	6,712	68	49		Y	Y	Y	Y	Y	Y	Y	Y	N		46
Oklahoma Technical College	Tulsa	T	Prop	M/W	182		50		Y	Y				Y	Y	N	N		4
Seminole State College	Seminole	C,T	St	M/W	1,895	44	36		Y			Y		Y	Y	Y	N	7	27
Tulsa Community College	Tulsa	C,T	St	M/W	17,253	65	44		Y			Y	Y	Y	Y	Y	N	5	55
Western Oklahoma State College	Altus	C,T	St	M/W	1,690	60												
Wright Career College	Oklahoma City	C,T,B	Prop	M/W	254	29												
Wright Career College	Tulsa	C,T,B	Prop	M/W	309	64												
Oregon																		
Central Oregon Community College	Bend	C,T	Dist	M/W	6,312	57	47		Y	Y			Y	Y	Y	Y	Y	12	56
Clatsop Community College	Astoria	C,T	Cou	M/W	1,071	58												
Columbia Gorge Community College	The Dalles	C,T	St	M/W	1,245	56												
ITT Technical Institute	Portland	T,B	Prop															
Lane Community College	Eugene	C,T	St-L	M/W	11,002	55												
Linn-Benton Community College	Albany	C,T	St-L	M/W	5,617	54												
Oregon Coast Community College	Newport	C,T	Pub	M/W	489	57			Y				Y			Y	N		5
Rogue Community College	Grants Pass	C,T	St-L	M/W	5,099	62	49		Y	Y		Y	Y	Y	Y		5	25
Treasure Valley Community College	Ontario	C,T	St-L	M/W	2,443	50												
Umpqua Community College	Roseburg	C,T	St-L	M/W	2,046	53	42		Y		R	Y	Y	Y	Y	Y	N	2	53
Pennsylvania																		
Antonelli Institute	Erdenheim	T	Prop	M/W	189				Y	Y		Y	Y			Y			2
Bradford School	Pittsburgh	T	Priv	M/W	439					Y			Y			Y			11
Bucks County Community College	Newtown	C,T	Cou	M/W	8,979	66	30	55	Y	Y	Y	Y	Y	Y	Y	N	10	59
Butler County Community College	Butler	C,T	Cou	M/W	3,570		29		Y	Y	Y	Y	Y	Y	Y	N	6	62
Cambria-Rowe Business College	Indiana	C,T	Prop	M/W	93	1		0		Y	Y			Y	Y	N		6
Cambria-Rowe Business College	Johnstown	C,T	Prop	PW	142	1												
Career Training Academy	Pittsburgh	T	Prop	M/W	70		49	0		Y			Y	Y		Y		3
Commonwealth Technical Institute	Johnstown	T	St	M/W	222		11		Y		Y	R,S	Y	Y	Y	Y		6
Community College of Allegheny County	Pittsburgh	C,T	Cou	M/W	17,148	65	45			Y		R	Y	Y		N	15	115
Community College of Philadelphia	Philadelphia	C,T	St-L	M/W	39,500		53	58	Y	Y		S	Y	Y	Y	N	8	38
Harrisburg Area Community College	Harrisburg	C,T	St-L	M/W	20,230	70	41		Y			S	Y	Y	Y	N	5	86
ITT Technical Institute	Dunmore	T	Prop	M/W														
ITT Technical Institute	Harrisburg	T	Prop	M/W														
ITT Technical Institute	Levittown	T	Prop	M/W														
ITT Technical Institute	Philadelphia		Prop	M/W														
ITT Technical Institute	Pittsburgh		Prop	M/W														
ITT Technical Institute	Plymouth Meeting	T	Prop	M/W														
ITT Technical Institute	Tarentum	T	Prop	M/W														
JNA Institute of Culinary Arts	Philadelphia	T	Prop	M/W	59		30											1
Lehigh Carbon Community College	Schnecksville	C,T	St-L	M/W	6,779	63	33	44	Y		S	Y	Y	Y	Y	N	7	61
Luzerne County Community College	Nanticoke	C,T	Cou	M/W	6,049	54	36		Y	Y	R	Y	Y	Y	Y	N	10	74
Manor College	Jenkintown	C,T	I-R	M/W	780	40	31	30	N	Y	Y	Y	Y	Y	Y		2	18
Montgomery County Community College	Blue Bell	C,T	Cou	M/W	12,805	66	34	66	Y	Y	Y	Y	Y	Y	Y	N	13	55
New Castle School of Trades	New Castle	T	Ind	PM	601		0			Y			Y			N		7
Northampton Community College	Bethlehem	C,T	St-L	M/W	10,531	57	34	65	Y		R,S	Y	Y	Y	Y	N	10	62
Penn State DuBois	DuBois	C,T,B	St-R	M/W	615	24	19		N	Y	Y	Y	Y			N	7	127
Penn State Fayette, The Eberly Campus	Lemont Furnace	C,T,B	St-R	M/W	717	19	20		N	Y	Y	Y	Y			N	11	124
Penn State Mont Alto	Mont Alto	C,T,B	St-R	M/W	940	28	20		N	Y	Y	Y	Y			Y	10	120
Penn State Shenango	Sharon	C,T,B	St-R	M/W	539	43	49		N	Y	Y	Y	Y			N	7	124
Pennsylvania Highlands Community College	Johnstown	C,T	St-L	M/W	2,470	63			Y	Y	Y	Y	Y	Y	Y	N	6	28
Pennsylvania Institute of Technology	Media	C,T	Ind	M/W	661	33	46		Y	Y	Y	Y	Y	Y	Y	N	1	11
Pittsburgh Technical Institute	Oakdale	T	Prop	M/W	1,841													
Reading Area Community College	Reading	C,T	Cou	M/W	4,198	78	37		Y	R,S	Y	Y	Y	Y		N		36
South Hills School of Business & Technology	State College	T	Prop	M/W	630	9	27		N	Y	Y		Y	Y	Y	N		11
Triangle Tech, Pittsburgh	Pittsburgh	C,T	Prop	PM	103													
Vet Tech Institute	Pittsburgh	T	Priv	M/W	385					Y		Y			Y			1
Westmoreland County Community College	Youngwood	C,T	Cou	M/W	5,638	52	36		Y			Y	Y	Y	Y	N	8	78
The Williamson Free School of Mechanical Trades	Media	T	Ind	CM	270													
Puerto Rico																		
Humacao Community College	Humacao	T,B	Ind	M/W	639	26	35											10
Rhode Island																		
Community College of Rhode Island	Warwick	C,T	St	M/W	17,553	70	38		Y	Y		Y	Y	Y	Y	N	8	48
South Carolina																		
Brown Mackie College–Greenville	Greenville	T,B	Prop	M/W														
Denmark Technical College	Denmark	C,T	St	M/W	1,678	15	53		Y	Y	Y	Y	Y	Y	Y	Y	2	8
Forrest College	Anderson	C,T	Prop	M/W	120	28	62			Y	Y	Y	Y	Y	Y			10
Greenville Technical College	Greenville	C,T	St	M/W	12,592	61	40		Y	Y	Y	Y	Y	Y	Y	N	7	34
Horry-Georgetown Technical College	Conway	C,T	St-L	M/W	7,660	62	45		Y		S	Y	Y	Y	Y	N		9

This chart includes the names and locations of accredited two-year colleges in the United States, Canada, and other countries and shows institutions' responses to the *Peterson's Annual Survey of Undergraduate Institutions*. If an institution submitted incomplete data, one or more columns opposite the institution's name is blank. A dagger after the school name indicates that the institution has one or more entries in the *Featured Two-Year Colleges* section. If a school does not appear, it did not report any of the information.

Y—Yes; N—No; R—Recommended; S—For Some

Institution	City	Degrees	Control	Body	Enroll.	% PT	% 25+	% →4-Yr	Open Adm.	HS Equiv.	HS Trans.	Need Aid	PT Jobs	Career	Job Place.	Housing	Sports	Majors
ITT Technical Institute	Columbia	T,B	Prop	M/W														
ITT Technical Institute	Greenville	T,B	Prop	M/W														
ITT Technical Institute	Myrtle Beach	T,B	Prop	M/W														
ITT Technical Institute	North Charleston	T,B	Prop	M/W														
Midlands Technical College	Columbia	C,T	St-L	M/W	11,424	54	38	37	Y		R	Y	Y	Y	Y	N	7	49
Northeastern Technical College	Cheraw	C,T	St-L	M/W	976	54												
Spartanburg Community College	Spartanburg	C,T	St	M/W	5,495	53	20		Y	Y	Y	Y	Y	Y	Y			19
Spartanburg Methodist College	Spartanburg	C,T	I-R	M/W	793	2	1	81	N	Y	Y	Y	Y	Y	Y	Y	12	5
Technical College of the Lowcountry	Beaufort	C,T	St	M/W	2,529	71	0			Y		Y	Y	Y		N		19
Trident Technical College	Charleston	C,T	St-L	M/W	16,139	55	49		Y	Y	S	Y	Y	Y	Y	N		39
University of South Carolina Salkehatchie	Allendale	C,T	St	M/W	1,076		25			Y	Y	Y	Y			N	4	1
University of South Carolina Union	Union	C,B	St	M/W	500	50	33		N	Y	Y	Y				N	1	2
South Dakota																		
Kilian Community College	Sioux Falls	C,T	Ind	M/W	253	87												
Lake Area Technical Institute	Watertown	T	St	M/W	1,728	19			Y	Y	Y	Y	Y	Y	Y	N	4	27
Mitchell Technical Institute	Mitchell	T	St	M/W	1,245	28	24		Y	Y	Y	Y	Y	Y	Y	Y	6	28
Sisseton-Wahpeton College	Sisseton	C,T	Fed	M/W	165	39	42		Y	Y	Y	Y	Y	Y	Y			12
Southeast Technical Institute	Sioux Falls	T	St	M/W	2,467	32			Y	Y	Y	Y	Y	Y	Y	N		21
Western Dakota Technical Institute	Rapid City	T	St	M/W	876	22	44		Y	Y	Y	Y	Y	Y	Y	N		21
Tennessee																		
Chattanooga College—Medical, Dental and Technical Careers	Chattanooga	C	Prop	M/W	330													
Cleveland State Community College	Cleveland	C,T	St	M/W	3,522	49	28	60	Y	Y	Y	Y	Y	Y	Y	N	8	13
Dyersburg State Community College	Dyersburg	C,T	St	M/W	2,847	60	33			Y	Y	Y	Y	Y	Y		8	20
Fountainhead College of Technology	Knoxville	C,T,B	Prop	M/W	180		90		Y	Y	Y	Y		Y	Y	N		8
ITT Technical Institute	Chattanooga	T,B	Prop	M/W														
ITT Technical Institute	Cordova	T,B	Prop	M/W														
ITT Technical Institute	Johnson City	T,B	Prop	M/W														
ITT Technical Institute	Knoxville	T,B	Prop	M/W														
ITT Technical Institute	Nashville	T,B	Prop	M/W														
Jackson State Community College	Jackson	C,T	St	M/W	4,926				Y	Y	S	Y	Y	Y	Y	N	3	13
John A. Gupton College	Nashville	C,T	Ind	M/W	129	48	55		N	Y	Y		Y	Y	Y			1
Lincoln College of Technology	Nashville	T	Prop	PM	1,375													
Motlow State Community College	Tullahoma	C,T	St	M/W	3,901	50	59		Y	Y	Y	Y	Y	Y	Y	N	8	8
Roane State Community College	Harriman	C,T	St	M/W	5,832	60	34		Y	Y	Y	Y	Y	Y	Y	N	8	42
Volunteer State Community College	Gallatin	C,T	St	M/W	7,664	56	28		Y	Y	Y	Y	Y	Y	Y	N	3	21
Walters State Community College	Morristown	C,T	St	M/W	6,005	48	25		Y	Y	Y	Y	Y	Y	Y	N	5	20
Texas																		
Alvin Community College	Alvin	C,T	St-L	M/W	4,837	72	0		Y	Y	S	Y	Y	Y	Y	N	2	47
Amarillo College	Amarillo	C,T	St-L	M/W			36		Y		Y	Y	Y	Y	Y	N	5	83
Austin Community College District	Austin	C,T	St-L	M/W	40,949		43		Y		Y	Y	Y	Y	Y	N	3	90
Brookhaven College	Farmers Branch	C,T	Cou	M/W	12,403	83	46		Y		Y		Y	Y	Y	N	5	27
Cedar Valley College	Lancaster	C,T	St	M/W	6,953	78	45	32		Y	Y	Y	Y	Y	Y	N	4	21
Central Texas College	Killeen	C,T	St-L	M/W	21,647	83			Y	Y	Y	Y	Y	Y	Y	Y	10	49
Clarendon College	Clarendon	C,T	St-L	M/W	1,214	53												
Coastal Bend College	Beeville	C,T	Cou	M/W	3,776	64	26		Y	Y	Y	Y	Y	Y	Y	Y	13	20
College of the Mainland	Texas City	C,T	St-L	M/W	4,188	73												
Collin County Community College District	McKinney	C,T	St-L	M/W	27,991	65	30		Y	Y	Y	Y	Y	Y	Y	N	2	49
Culinary Institute LeNotre	Houston	T	Prop	M/W	403													
Dallas Institute of Funeral Service	Dallas	C,T	Ind	M/W	141		52		Y	Y	Y	Y				N		1
El Centro College	Dallas	C,T	Cou	M/W	10,101	77	46				S	Y	Y	Y	Y	N		37
Frank Phillips College	Borger	C,T	St-L	M/W	1,148	56												
Galveston College	Galveston	C,T	St-L	M/W	2,131	73												
Grayson College	Denison	C,T	St-L	M/W	5,014	58												
Houston Community College	Houston	C,T	St-L	M/W	58,276	70	45		Y	Y	S	Y	Y	Y	Y			60
ITT Technical Institute	Arlington	T,B	Prop	M/W														
ITT Technical Institute	Austin	T,B	Prop	M/W														
ITT Technical Institute	DeSoto	T,B	Prop	M/W														
ITT Technical Institute	Houston	T,B	Prop	M/W														
ITT Technical Institute	Houston	T,B	Prop	M/W														
ITT Technical Institute	Richardson	T,B	Prop	M/W														
ITT Technical Institute	San Antonio	T,B	Prop	M/W														
ITT Technical Institute	San Antonio	T,B	Prop	M/W														
ITT Technical Institute	Waco	T,B	Prop	M/W														
ITT Technical Institute	Webster	T,B	Prop	M/W														
KD College Conservatory of Film and Dramatic Arts	Dallas	C,T	Prop	M/W	236		44		Y	Y	Y	Y		Y		N		3
Kilgore College	Kilgore	C,T	St-L	M/W	5,768	55	30		Y	Y	Y	Y	Y	Y	Y	Y	7	62
Lamar State College–Orange	Orange	C,T	St	M/W	2,426	59												
Lone Star College–CyFair	Cypress	C,T	St-L	M/W	20,384	70	29		Y	Y				Y		N		30
Lone Star College–Kingwood	Kingwood	C,T	St-L	M/W	12,837	68	34		Y	Y			Y	Y		N	1	17
Lone Star College–Montgomery	Conroe	C,T	St-L	M/W	13,254	67	33		Y	Y			Y	Y	Y	N		14
Lone Star College–North Harris	Houston	C,T	St-L	M/W	17,721	70	42		Y	Y		Y	Y	Y	Y		15	22
Lone Star College–Tomball	Tomball	C,T	St-L	M/W	9,361	69	36		Y	Y		Y	Y	Y	Y			15
Lone Star College–University Park	Houston	C,T	St-L	M/W	9,261	70	28		Y			R		Y		N		4
Mountain View College	Dallas	C,T	St-L	M/W	9,068	77												
Navarro College	Corsicana	C,T	St-L	M/W	9,999	61	28		Y	Y	Y	Y	Y	Y	Y	Y	7	55
North Central Texas College	Gainesville	C,T	St-L	M/W	10,109	65	25	2	Y	Y	Y	Y	Y	Y	Y		15	42
Northeast Texas Community College	Mount Pleasant	C,T	St-L	M/W	3,282	66												

This chart includes the names and locations of accredited two-year colleges in the United States, Canada, and other countries and shows institutions' responses to the *Peterson's Annual Survey of Undergraduate Institutions*. If an institution submitted incomplete data, one or more columns opposite the institution's name is blank. A dagger after the school name indicates that the institution has one or more entries in the *Featured Two-Year Colleges* section. If a school does not appear, it did not report any of the information.

Y—Yes; N—No; R—Recommended; S—For Some

Institution	Location	Degrees Awarded	Institutional Control	Student Body	Undergraduate Enrollment	Percent Attending Part-Time	Percent 25 Years of Age or Older	Percent of Grads Going on to Four-Year Colleges	Open Admissions	High School Equivalency Certificate Accepted	High School Transcript Required	Need-Based Aid Required	Part-Time Jobs Available	Career Counseling Available	Job Placement Services Available	College Housing Available	Number of Sports Available	Number of Majors Offered
Panola College	Carthage	C,T	St-L	M/W	2,564	49	32					R,S	Y	Y	Y	Y	7	16
Paris Junior College	Paris	C,T	St-L	M/W	5,086	56	26		Y	Y	R	Y	Y	Y	Y	Y	10	62
St. Philip's College	San Antonio	C,T	Dist	M/W	10,238	83	41		Y	Y	Y	Y			N		5	68
San Jacinto College District	Pasadena	C,T	St-L	M/W	27,911	75	29	23	Y	Y	Y			Y		N	11	78
South Plains College	Levelland	C,T	St-L	M/W	9,444	54												
Tarrant County College District	Fort Worth	C,T	Cou	M/W	50,439	65												
Temple College	Temple	C,T	Dist	M/W	5,506	67												
Texarkana College	Texarkana	C,T	St-L	M/W	4,111													
Texas State Technical College Harlingen	Harlingen	C,T	St	M/W	5,225	59	27		Y	Y	Y	Y	Y	Y	Y	Y	11	29
Texas State Technical College Waco	Waco	C,T	St	M/W	7,269	26												
Trinity Valley Community College	Athens	C,T	St-L	M/W	5,172	48	35		Y	Y	Y	Y	Y	Y	Y	Y	7	55
Tyler Junior College	Tyler	C,T	St-L	M/W	11,168	44	26		Y	Y	Y	Y	Y	Y	Y	Y	11	86
Vet Tech Institute of Houston	Houston	T	Priv	M/W	196											N		1
Victoria College	Victoria	C,T	Cou	M/W	4,169	72	37		Y	Y	Y	Y	Y	Y	Y	N	6	14
Western Texas College	Snyder	C,T	St-L	M/W	2,473	72												
Utah																		
ITT Technical Institute	Murray	T,B	Prop	M/W														
LDS Business College	Salt Lake City	C,T	I-R	M/W	2,191	27												
Nightingale College	Ogden	B	Prop	M/W						Y	Y	Y						
Salt Lake Community College	Salt Lake City	C,T	St	M/W	29,537	73	38		Y				Y	Y	Y	N	6	69
Snow College	Ephraim	C,T	St	M/W	4,605	39												
Vermont																		
Community College of Vermont	Montpelier	C,T	St	M/W	6,619													
Landmark College	Putney	T,B	Ind	M/W	514	4	6	92	N	Y	Y	Y	Y	Y	Y	Y	13	73
New England Culinary Institute	Montpelier	C,B	Prop	M/W	422		32		N	Y	Y	Y	Y	Y	Y			3
Virginia																		
Central Virginia Community College	Lynchburg	C,T	St	M/W	4,519		21		Y	Y			Y	Y	Y		1	19
Dabney S. Lancaster Community College	Clifton Forge	C,T	St	M/W	1,284	76	29				R		Y	Y	Y	N	2	17
Eastern Shore Community College	Melfa	C,T	St	M/W	857													
ITT Technical Institute	Chantilly	T,B	Prop	M/W														
ITT Technical Institute	Norfolk	T,B	Prop	M/W														
ITT Technical Institute	Richmond	T,B	Prop	M/W														
ITT Technical Institute	Salem	T,B	Prop	M/W														
ITT Technical Institute	Springfield	T,B	Prop	M/W														
John Tyler Community College	Chester	C,T	St	M/W	9,875	73	35		Y	Y	R	Y	Y	Y	Y	N	3	22
J. Sargeant Reynolds Community College	Richmond	C,T	St	M/W	11,949	72	46	3	Y	Y	Y	Y	Y	Y	Y	N		55
Mountain Empire Community College	Big Stone Gap	C,T	St	M/W	2,924													
Northern Virginia Community College	Annandale	C,T	St	M/W	51,803	62	42		Y	Y	S	Y	Y	Y	Y	N	4	35
Patrick Henry Community College	Martinsville	C,T	St	M/W	3,163													
Piedmont Virginia Community College	Charlottesville	C,T	St	M/W	5,554	78	33		Y		S	Y	Y	Y		N	8	
Rappahannock Community College	Glenns	C,T	St-L	M/W	3,555				Y			Y	Y	Y	Y	N	1	11
Southwest Virginia Community College	Richlands	C,T	St	M/W	2,546	53	26		Y	Y	Y	Y	Y			N		12
Virginia Western Community College	Roanoke	C,T	St	M/W	8,652	83	38	72	Y	Y	R,S	Y	Y	Y		N	3	25
Wytheville Community College	Wytheville	C,T	St	M/W	3,468		33		Y			Y		Y	Y	N	2	21
Washington																		
Bellingham Technical College	Bellingham	C,T	St	M/W	2,864		61		Y		S	Y	Y	Y		N		25
Big Bend Community College	Moses Lake	C,T	St	M/W	1,991	28	33		Y		S	Y	Y	Y	Y	Y	4	18
Carrington College–Spokane	Spokane	T	Prop	M/W	538													
Cascadia Community College	Bothell	C,T	St	M/W	2,670	60												
Clark College	Vancouver	C,T	St	M/W	10,911	52	36						Y	Y		N	8	37
Grays Harbor College	Aberdeen	C,T	St	M/W	1,966	33												
ITT Technical Institute	Everett	T,B	Prop	M/W														
ITT Technical Institute	Seattle	T,B	Prop	M/W														
ITT Technical Institute	Spokane Valley	T,B	Prop	M/W														
Lower Columbia College	Longview	C,T	St	M/W	3,152	48			Y		R	Y	Y	Y		N	5	20
Northwest School of Wooden Boatbuilding	Port Hadlock	T	Ind	M/W									Y	Y	Y	N		1
Olympic College	Bremerton	C,T,B	St	M/W	8,058		49		Y		S	Y	Y	Y	Y	Y	8	22
Renton Technical College	Renton	C,T,B	St	M/W	9,301				Y		S	Y	Y	Y		N		19
Shoreline Community College	Shoreline	C	St	M/W	8,591													
Walla Walla Community College	Walla Walla	C,T	St	M/W	5,109	42												
Wenatchee Valley College	Wenatchee	C,T	St-L	M/W	3,510	27			Y		S	Y	Y	Y		Y	10	39
Whatcom Community College	Bellingham	C,T	St	M/W	6,233		34		Y				Y	Y	Y	N	6	14
West Virginia																		
Blue Ridge Community and Technical College	Martinsburg	C,T	St	M/W	5,553	80	49		Y	Y	Y			Y	Y	N		25
ITT Technical Institute	Huntington	T	Prop	M/W														
Mountain State College	Parkersburg	T	Prop	M/W	176	1	55		N	Y		Y	Y	Y		N		7
Potomac State College of West Virginia University	Keyser	C,T,B	St	M/W	1,540	20	14		Y	Y	Y	Y	Y	Y	Y	Y	10	54
West Virginia Junior College–Bridgeport	Bridgeport	C,T	Prop	M/W	389		30		Y		R	Y	Y	Y		N		5
Wisconsin																		
Blackhawk Technical College	Janesville	C,T	Dist	M/W	2,522	60												
Chippewa Valley Technical College	Eau Claire	C,T	Dist	M/W	5,617	56												
Fox Valley Technical College	Appleton	T	St-L	M/W	10,488	75	47		Y	Y		Y	Y	Y	Y	N	3	57
Gateway Technical College	Kenosha	T	St-L	M/W	7,410	81			Y			Y	Y	Y	Y	N		48
ITT Technical Institute	Green Bay	T,B	Prop	M/W														
ITT Technical Institute	Greenfield	T,B	Prop	M/W														

This chart includes the names and locations of accredited two-year colleges in the United States, Canada, and other countries and shows institutions' responses to the *Peterson's Annual Survey of Undergraduate Institutions*. If an institution submitted incomplete data, one or more columns opposite the institution's name is blank. A dagger after the school name indicates that the institution has one or more entries in the *Featured Two-Year Colleges* section. If a school does not appear, it did not report any of the information.

Degrees Awarded: College Transfer Associate (C); Terminal Associate (T); Bachelor's (B); Master's (M); Doctoral (D)

Y—Yes; N—No; R—Recommended; S—For Some

Institution	Location	Degrees Awarded	Institutional Control	Student Body	Undergraduate Enrollment	Percent Attending Part-Time	Percent 25 Years of Age or Older	Percent of Grads Going on to Four-Year Colleges	Open Admissions	High School Equivalency Certificate Accepted	High School Transcript Required	Need-Based Aid Required	Part-Time Jobs Available	Job Placement Services Available	Career Counseling Services Available	College Housing Available	Number of Sports Offered	Number of Majors Offered
ITT Technical Institute	Madison	T,B	Prop	M/W														
Moraine Park Technical College	Fond du Lac	C,T	Dist	M/W	6,613		55						Y	Y	Y	N		37
Northcentral Technical College	Wausau	C,T	Dist	M/W	4,401	62	50		N	Y	Y	Y	Y	Y	Y	N	6	29
University of Wisconsin–Fond du Lac	Fond du Lac	C	St	M/W	626		18		N	Y	Y	Y	Y	Y	Y	N	6	1
University of Wisconsin–Fox Valley	Menasha	C,T	St	M/W	1,797	42	25	70		Y	Y	Y	Y	Y	Y	N	7	1
University of Wisconsin–Sheboygan	Sheboygan	C	St	M/W	769	60				Y	Y	Y	Y	Y	Y	N	7	1
University of Wisconsin–Waukesha	Waukesha	C,B	St	M/W	2,239	52	28		N	Y	Y	Y	Y	Y	Y	N	11	1
Waukesha County Technical College	Pewaukee	T	St-L	M/W	8,692	80	53		Y				Y	Y	Y	N		40
Wisconsin Indianhead Technical College	Shell Lake	T	Dist	M/W	3,045	60	52		Y							N		24
Wyoming																		
Casper College	Casper	C,T	St-L	M/W	3,993	57	33	40	Y	Y	Y	Y	Y	Y	Y	Y	10	101
Central Wyoming College	Riverton	C,T	St-L	M/W	2,036	64	39	48	Y		R		Y	Y	Y	Y	17	54
Eastern Wyoming College	Torrington	C,T	St-L	M/W	1,750	62					R	Y	Y	Y	Y	Y	4	42
Laramie County Community College	Cheyenne	C,T	Dist	M/W	4,271	57	39		Y	Y	S		Y	Y	Y		11	62
Northwest College	Powell	C,T	St-L	M/W	1,652	38	25		Y	Y	Y		Y	Y	Y	Y	10	60
Sheridan College	Sheridan	C,T	St-L	M/W	4,374	68	32		Y		R,S		Y	Y	Y	Y	13	47
Western Wyoming Community College	Rock Springs	C,T	St-L	M/W	3,621	66	6	7	Y		R	Y		Y	Y	Y	5	84

OTHER COUNTRIES

Mexico

Institution	Location	Degrees Awarded	Institutional Control	Student Body	Undergraduate Enrollment	Percent Attending Part-Time	Percent 25 Years of Age or Older	Percent of Grads Going on to Four-Year Colleges	Open Admissions	High School Equivalency Certificate Accepted	High School Transcript Required	Need-Based Aid Required	Part-Time Jobs Available	Job Placement Services Available	Career Counseling Services Available	College Housing Available	Number of Sports Offered	Number of Majors Offered
Westhill University	Sante Fe	T,B,M	Ind	M/W	1,206					Y	N	Y				N	5	3

Profiles
of Two-Year
Colleges

ALABAMA

Alabama Southern Community College
Monroeville, Alabama

- **State-supported** 2-year, founded 1965, part of Alabama Community College System
- **Rural** 80-acre campus
- **Coed**

Undergraduates 28% Black or African American, non-Hispanic/Latino; 0.4% Hispanic/Latino; 0.3% Asian, non-Hispanic/Latino; 0.8% American Indian or Alaska Native, non-Hispanic/Latino; 0.1% Two or more races, non-Hispanic/Latino; 0.5% Race/ethnicity unknown; 0.1% international. *Retention:* 57% of full-time freshmen returned.
Faculty *Student/faculty ratio:* 17:1.
Academics *Calendar:* semesters. *Degree:* certificates and associate. *Special study options:* academic remediation for entering students, adult/continuing education programs, advanced placement credit, part-time degree program, summer session for credit.
Student Life *Campus security:* 24-hour patrols.
Athletics Member NJCAA.
Standardized Tests *Recommended:* ACT (for admission).
Costs (2014–15) *Tuition:* state resident $3616 full-time; nonresident $7232 full-time. Full-time tuition and fees vary according to course load. Part-time tuition and fees vary according to course load. *Required fees:* $928 full-time.
Applying *Options:* electronic application, early admission. *Required:* high school transcript.
Freshman Application Contact Alabama Southern Community College, PO Box 2000, Monroeville, AL 36461. *Phone:* 251-575-3156 Ext. 8252. *Website:* http://www.ascc.edu/.

Bevill State Community College
Jasper, Alabama

- **State-supported** 2-year, founded 1969, part of Alabama Community College System
- **Rural** 245-acre campus with easy access to Birmingham
- **Endowment** $148,059
- **Coed,** 3,490 undergraduate students, 52% full-time, 64% women, 36% men

Undergraduates 1,808 full-time, 1,682 part-time. 14% Black or African American, non-Hispanic/Latino; 1% Hispanic/Latino; 0.4% Asian, non-Hispanic/Latino; 0.2% American Indian or Alaska Native, non-Hispanic/Latino; 0.7% Two or more races, non-Hispanic/Latino; 2% Race/ethnicity unknown. *Retention:* 61% of full-time freshmen returned.
Freshmen *Admission:* 905 enrolled.
Faculty *Total:* 316, 36% full-time, 16% with terminal degrees. *Student/faculty ratio:* 17:1.
Majors Administrative assistant and secretarial science; child-care and support services management; computer and information sciences; drafting and design technology; electrician; emergency medical technology (EMT paramedic); general studies; heating, ventilation, air conditioning and refrigeration engineering technology; industrial electronics technology; legal assistant/paralegal; liberal arts and sciences/liberal studies; registered nursing/registered nurse; tool and die technology.
Academics *Calendar:* semesters. *Degree:* certificates and associate. *Special study options:* academic remediation for entering students, adult/continuing education programs, advanced placement credit, cooperative education, distance learning, honors programs, off-campus study, part-time degree program, services for LD students, summer session for credit.
Library 166,771 titles, an OPAC, a Web page.
Student Life *Housing Options:* coed. Campus housing is university owned. *Activities and Organizations:* drama/theater group, choral group, Student Government Association, Campus Ministries, Circle K, Outdoors men Club, Students Against Destructive Decisions. *Campus security:* 24-hour emergency response devices.
Costs (2014–15) *Tuition:* state resident $2712 full-time, $113 per credit hour part-time; nonresident $5424 full-time, $226 per credit hour part-time. Full-time tuition and fees vary according to course load and program. Part-time tuition and fees vary according to course load and program. *Required fees:* $711 full-time, $29 per credit hour part-time. *Room and board:* $1850. Room and board charges vary according to board plan and location. *Payment plan:* installment. *Waivers:* employees or children of employees.

Financial Aid Of all full-time matriculated undergraduates who enrolled in 2013, 88 Federal Work-Study jobs (averaging $1807).
Applying *Options:* electronic application, early admission, deferred entrance. *Required:* high school transcript. *Application deadlines:* rolling (freshmen), rolling (transfers).
Freshman Application Contact Bevill State Community College, 1411 Indiana Avenue, Jasper, AL 35501. *Phone:* 205-387-0511 Ext. 5813. *Website:* http://www.bscc.edu/.

Bishop State Community College
Mobile, Alabama

- **State-supported** 2-year, founded 1965, part of Alabama Community College System
- **Urban** 9-acre campus
- **Coed**

Undergraduates 2,175 full-time, 1,725 part-time. Students come from 8 states and territories; 32 other countries; 3% are from out of state; 62% Black or African American, non-Hispanic/Latino; 1% Hispanic/Latino; 2% Asian, non-Hispanic/Latino; 0.2% Native Hawaiian or other Pacific Islander, non-Hispanic/Latino; 0.7% American Indian or Alaska Native, non-Hispanic/Latino; 0.9% Two or more races, non-Hispanic/Latino; 0.4% Race/ethnicity unknown; 2% international; 10% transferred in. *Retention:* 41% of full-time freshmen returned.
Faculty *Student/faculty ratio:* 23:1.
Academics *Calendar:* semesters. *Degree:* certificates and associate. *Special study options:* academic remediation for entering students, accelerated degree program, adult/continuing education programs, advanced placement credit, cooperative education, distance learning, independent study, internships, part-time degree program, services for LD students, summer session for credit.
Student Life *Campus security:* 24-hour emergency response devices and patrols, 24-hour electronic alert system.
Athletics Member NJCAA.
Costs (2014–15) *Tuition:* state resident $2712 full-time, $111 per credit hour part-time; nonresident $5424 full-time, $222 per credit hour part-time. Full-time tuition and fees vary according to course load. Part-time tuition and fees vary according to course load. *Required fees:* $696 full-time, $29 per credit hour part-time.
Financial Aid Of all full-time matriculated undergraduates who enrolled in 2013, 299 Federal Work-Study jobs (averaging $2400).
Applying *Options:* electronic application, early admission, deferred entrance. *Required:* high school transcript.
Freshman Application Contact Bishop State Community College, 351 North Broad Street, Mobile, AL 36603-5898. *Phone:* 251-405-7000. *Toll-free phone:* 800-523-7235. *Website:* http://www.bishop.edu/.

Calhoun Community College
Decatur, Alabama

Freshman Application Contact Admissions Office, Calhoun Community College, PO Box 2216, Decatur, AL 35609-2216. *Phone:* 256-306-2593. *Toll-free phone:* 800-626-3628. *Fax:* 256-306-2941. *E-mail:* admissions@calhoun.edu. *Website:* http://www.calhoun.edu/.

Central Alabama Community College
Alexander City, Alabama

Freshman Application Contact Ms. Donna Whaley, Central Alabama Community College, 1675 Cherokee Road, Alexander City, AL 35011-0699. *Phone:* 256-234-6346 Ext. 6232. *Toll-free phone:* 800-634-2657. *Website:* http://www.cacc.edu/.

Chattahoochee Valley Community College
Phenix City, Alabama

Freshman Application Contact Chattahoochee Valley Community College, 2602 College Drive, Phenix City, AL 36869-7928. *Phone:* 334-291-4929. *Website:* http://www.cv.edu/.

Community College of the Air Force
Maxwell Gunter Air Force Base, Alabama

- **Federally supported** 2-year, founded 1972, part of Air University
- **Suburban** campus
- **Coed,** 297,469 undergraduate students, 100% full-time, 18% women, 82% men

Undergraduates 297,469 full-time.
Freshmen *Admission:* 14,261 applied, 14,261 admitted, 14,261 enrolled.
Faculty *Total:* 6,070, 100% full-time.
Majors Aeronautics/aviation/aerospace science and technology; airframe mechanics and aircraft maintenance technology; air traffic control; apparel and textile marketing management; atmospheric sciences and meteorology; automobile/automotive mechanics technology; avionics maintenance technology; biomedical technology; cardiovascular technology; clinical/medical laboratory technology; commercial and advertising art; communications technology; construction engineering technology; criminal justice/law enforcement administration; dental assisting; dental laboratory technology; dietetics; educational/instructional technology; educational leadership and administration; electrical, electronic and communications engineering technology; environmental health; environmental studies; finance; fire science/firefighting; health/health-care administration; hematology technology; hotel/motel administration; human resources management; industrial technology; legal assistant/paralegal; logistics, materials, and supply chain management; management information systems; medical radiologic technology; mental health counseling; metallurgical technology; music performance; nuclear medical technology; occupational safety and health technology; office management; ophthalmic laboratory technology; parks, recreation and leisure; pharmacy technician; physical therapy technology; physiology; public relations/image management; purchasing, procurement/acquisitions and contracts management; security and loss prevention; social work; surgical technology.
Academics *Calendar:* continuous. *Degrees:* certificates and associate (courses conducted at 125 branch locations worldwide for members of the U.S. Air Force). *Special study options:* academic remediation for entering students, adult/continuing education programs, advanced placement credit, distance learning, independent study, internships, off-campus study.
Library Air Force Library Service with an OPAC, a Web page.
Student Life *Housing:* college housing not available. *Campus security:* 24-hour emergency response devices and patrols. *Student services:* health clinic, personal/psychological counseling, legal services.
Athletics *Intramural sports:* badminton W, basketball M/W, bowling M/W, cross-country running M/W, football M, golf M/W, racquetball M/W, softball M/W, table tennis M/W, tennis M/W, volleyball M/W, weight lifting M/W.
Standardized Tests *Required:* Armed Services Vocational Aptitude Battery (for admission).
Costs (2014–15) *Comprehensive fee:* Air Force Tuition Assistance (TA) provides 100% tuition and fees for courses taken by active duty personnel.
Applying *Options:* electronic application. *Required:* high school transcript, interview, military physical, good character, criminal background check. *Application deadlines:* rolling (freshmen), rolling (transfers). *Notification:* continuous (freshmen), continuous (transfers).
Freshman Application Contact S.M. Sgt. Gwendolyn Ford, Chief of Admissions Flight, Community College of the Air Force, Community College of the Air Force, 100 South Turner Blvd., Maxwell Air Force Base, Maxwell - Gunter AFB, AL 36114-3011. *Phone:* 334-649-5081. *Fax:* 334-649-5015. *E-mail:* gwendolyn.ford@us.af.mil.
Website: http://www.au.af.mil/au/ccaf/.

Enterprise State Community College
Enterprise, Alabama

Director of Admissions Mr. Gary Deas, Associate Dean of Students/Registrar, Enterprise State Community College, PO Box 1300, Enterprise, AL 36331-1300. *Phone:* 334-347-2623 Ext. 2233. *E-mail:* gdeas@eocc.edu.
Website: http://www.escc.edu/.

Fortis College
Mobile, Alabama

Admissions Office Contact Fortis College, 7033 Airport Boulevard, Mobile, AL 36608. *Toll-free phone:* 888-369-8131.
Website: http://www.fortis.edu/.

Fortis College
Montgomery, Alabama

Admissions Office Contact Fortis College, 3470 Eastdale Circle, Montgomery, AL 36117. *Toll-free phone:* 855-4-FORTIS.
Website: http://www.fortis.edu/.

Fortis College
Montgomery, Alabama

Admissions Office Contact Fortis College, 3736 Atlanta Highway, Montgomery, AL 36109.
Website: http://www.fortis.edu/.

Fortis Institute
Birmingham, Alabama

Admissions Office Contact Fortis Institute, 100 London Parkway, Suite 150, Birmingham, AL 35211.
Website: http://www.fortis.edu/.

Gadsden State Community College
Gadsden, Alabama

- **State-supported** 2-year, founded 1965, part of Alabama Community College System
- **Small-town** 275-acre campus with easy access to Birmingham
- **Coed,** 5,289 undergraduate students, 52% full-time, 59% women, 41% men

Undergraduates 2,751 full-time, 2,538 part-time. Students come from 23 states and territories; 45 other countries; 8% are from out of state; 20% Black or African American, non-Hispanic/Latino; 3% Hispanic/Latino; 0.5% Asian, non-Hispanic/Latino; 0.2% Native Hawaiian or other Pacific Islander, non-Hispanic/Latino; 1% American Indian or Alaska Native, non-Hispanic/Latino; 2% Two or more races, non-Hispanic/Latino; 2% Race/ethnicity unknown; 2% international; 5% transferred in; 2% live on campus.
Freshmen *Admission:* 1,315 enrolled.
Faculty *Total:* 319, 49% full-time. *Student/faculty ratio:* 17:1.
Majors Accounting technology and bookkeeping; administrative assistant and secretarial science; child-care and support services management; civil engineering technology; clinical/medical laboratory technology; communication and journalism related; computer and information sciences; court reporting; criminal justice/police science; drafting and design technology; electrical, electronic and communications engineering technology; emergency medical technology (EMT paramedic); general studies; heating, ventilation, air conditioning and refrigeration engineering technology; industrial mechanics and maintenance technology; legal assistant/paralegal; liberal arts and sciences/liberal studies; manufacturing engineering technology; radiologic technology/science; registered nursing/registered nurse; sales, distribution, and marketing operations; substance abuse/addiction counseling; tool and die technology.
Academics *Calendar:* semesters. *Degree:* certificates and associate. *Special study options:* academic remediation for entering students, adult/continuing education programs, advanced placement credit, cooperative education, distance learning, English as a second language, external degree program, honors programs, internships, part-time degree program, services for LD students, study abroad, summer session for credit. *ROTC:* Army (b).
Library Meadows Library with 115,901 titles, 7,080 audiovisual materials, an OPAC, a Web page.
Student Life *Housing Options:* coed. Campus housing is university owned. *Activities and Organizations:* drama/theater group, choral group, National Society of Leadership and Success, Student Government Association, Circle K, International Club, Cardinal Spirit Club. *Campus security:* 24-hour patrols. *Student services:* personal/psychological counseling.
Athletics Member NJCAA. *Intercollegiate sports:* basketball M(s)/W(s), softball W(s), tennis M(s), volleyball W(s).
Costs (2015–16) *Tuition:* state resident $2760 full-time, $115 per credit hour part-time; nonresident $5520 full-time, $230 per credit hour part-time. Full-time tuition and fees vary according to reciprocity agreements. Part-time tuition and fees vary according to reciprocity agreements. *Required fees:* $456 full-time, $19 part-time. *Room and board:* $3600. *Waivers:* minority students, adult students, senior citizens, and employees or children of employees.
Applying *Options:* electronic application, early admission, deferred entrance. *Required:* high school transcript. *Application deadlines:* rolling (freshmen), rolling (transfers).
Freshman Application Contact Mrs. Jennie Dobson, Admissions and Records, Gadsden State Community College, PO Box 227, 1001 George

Wallace Drive, Gadsden, AL 35902-0227. *Phone:* 256-549-8210. *Toll-free phone:* 800-226-5563. *Fax:* 256-549-8205. *E-mail:* info@gadsdenstate.edu. *Website:* http://www.gadsdenstate.edu/.

George Corley Wallace State Community College
Selma, Alabama

Director of Admissions Ms. Sunette Newman, Registrar, George Corley Wallace State Community College, PO Box 2530, Selma, AL 36702. *Phone:* 334-876-9305.
Website: http://www.wccs.edu/.

George C. Wallace Community College
Dothan, Alabama

- **State-supported** 2-year, founded 1949, part of The Alabama Community College System
- **Rural** 258-acre campus
- **Coed,** 4,854 undergraduate students, 46% full-time, 64% women, 36% men

Undergraduates 2,251 full-time, 2,603 part-time. Students come from 30 states and territories; 5% are from out of state; 31% Black or African American, non-Hispanic/Latino; 2% Hispanic/Latino; 0.7% Asian, non-Hispanic/Latino; 0.1% Native Hawaiian or other Pacific Islander, non-Hispanic/Latino; 0.5% American Indian or Alaska Native, non-Hispanic/Latino; 1% Two or more races, non-Hispanic/Latino; 0.1% Race/ethnicity unknown; 48% transferred in. *Retention:* 56% of full-time freshmen returned.
Freshmen *Admission:* 1,109 enrolled.
Faculty *Total:* 241, 52% full-time.
Majors Accounting; administrative assistant and secretarial science; autobody/collision and repair technology; automobile/automotive mechanics technology; business administration and management; cabinetmaking and millwork; carpentry; clinical/medical laboratory technology; computer and information sciences; computer science; criminal justice/police science; drafting and design technology; electrical, electronic and communications engineering technology; electrician; emergency medical technology (EMT paramedic); heating, air conditioning, ventilation and refrigeration maintenance technology; heating, ventilation, air conditioning and refrigeration engineering technology; industrial mechanics and maintenance technology; licensed practical/vocational nurse training; machine tool technology; medical/clinical assistant; medical radiologic technology; physical therapy technology; radiologic technology/science; registered nursing/registered nurse; respiratory care therapy; tool and die technology; welding technology.
Academics *Calendar:* semesters. *Degree:* certificates, diplomas, and associate. *Special study options:* academic remediation for entering students, adult/continuing education programs, advanced placement credit, cooperative education, distance learning, English as a second language, independent study, off-campus study, part-time degree program.
Library Learning Resources Centers with 45,000 titles, 1,300 audiovisual materials, an OPAC.
Student Life *Housing:* college housing not available. *Activities and Organizations:* drama/theater group, student-run newspaper. *Campus security:* 24-hour patrols. *Student services:* personal/psychological counseling.
Athletics Member NJCAA. *Intercollegiate sports:* baseball M(s), softball W(s).
Standardized Tests *Recommended:* SAT or ACT (for admission).
Costs (2014–15) *Tuition:* state resident $3390 full-time, $113 per credit hour part-time; nonresident $6780 full-time, $226 per credit hour part-time. Full-time tuition and fees vary according to reciprocity agreements. Part-time tuition and fees vary according to reciprocity agreements. *Required fees:* $570 full-time, $19 per credit hour part-time. *Waivers:* senior citizens and employees or children of employees.
Financial Aid Of all full-time matriculated undergraduates who enrolled in 2013, 82 Federal Work-Study jobs (averaging $1975).
Applying *Options:* early admission. *Required:* high school transcript. *Application deadlines:* rolling (freshmen), rolling (transfers).
Freshman Application Contact Mr. Keith Saulsberry, Director, Enrollment Services/Registrar, George C. Wallace Community College, 1141 Wallace Drive, Dothan, AL 36303. *Phone:* 334-983-3521 Ext. 2470. *Toll-free phone:* 800-543-2426. *Fax:* 334-983-3600. *E-mail:* ksaulsberry@wallace.edu.
Website: http://www.wallace.edu/.

H. Councill Trenholm State Technical College
Montgomery, Alabama

- **State-supported** 2-year, founded 1962, part of Alabama Department of Postsecondary Education
- **Urban** 83-acre campus with easy access to Montgomery
- **Coed,** 1,338 undergraduate students

Undergraduates Students come from 2 states and territories; 1% are from out of state; 59% Black or African American, non-Hispanic/Latino; 1% Hispanic/Latino; 1% Asian, non-Hispanic/Latino; 0.3% Two or more races, non-Hispanic/Latino; 0.2% Race/ethnicity unknown; 0.1% international. *Retention:* 55% of full-time freshmen returned.
Freshmen *Admission:* 1,886 applied, 493 admitted.
Faculty *Total:* 99, 59% full-time, 18% with terminal degrees. *Student/faculty ratio:* 13:1.
Majors Accounting technology and bookkeeping; administrative assistant and secretarial science; automotive engineering technology; child-care and support services management; computer and information sciences; culinary arts; dental assisting; diagnostic medical sonography and ultrasound technology; drafting and design technology; electrician; emergency medical technology (EMT paramedic); graphic communications related; heating, ventilation, air conditioning and refrigeration engineering technology; industrial mechanics and maintenance technology; machine tool technology; manufacturing engineering technology; medical/clinical assistant; radiologic technology/science.
Academics *Calendar:* semesters. *Degree:* certificates, diplomas, and associate. *Special study options:* academic remediation for entering students, adult/continuing education programs, advanced placement credit, cooperative education, distance learning, external degree program, independent study, internships, part-time degree program, services for LD students, summer session for credit.
Library Trenholm State Learning Resources plus 2 others with 66,678 titles, 1,173 audiovisual materials, an OPAC, a Web page.
Student Life *Housing:* college housing not available. *Activities and Organizations:* Student Government Association, College Ambassadors, Photography Club, Skills USA - VICA, Student Leadership Academy. *Student services:* personal/psychological counseling.
Standardized Tests *Required for some:* ACT (for admission).
Costs (2015–16) *Tuition:* state resident $3390 full-time, $113 per credit hour part-time; nonresident $6780 full-time, $226 per credit hour part-time. *Required fees:* $780 full-time, $26 per credit hour part-time. *Payment plan:* installment. *Waivers:* senior citizens and employees or children of employees.
Applying *Options:* electronic application, early admission. *Required:* high school transcript. *Application deadlines:* rolling (freshmen), rolling (out-of-state freshmen), rolling (transfers).
Freshman Application Contact Mrs. Tennie McBryde, Registrar, H. Councill Trenholm State Technical College, Montgomery, AL 36108. *Phone:* 334-420-4306. *Toll-free phone:* 866-753-4544. *Fax:* 334-420-4201. *E-mail:* tmcbryde@trenholmstate.edu.
Website: http://www.trenholmstate.edu/.

ITT Technical Institute
Bessemer, Alabama

- **Proprietary** primarily 2-year, founded 1994, part of ITT Educational Services, Inc.
- **Suburban** campus
- **Coed**

Academics *Calendar:* quarters. *Degrees:* associate and bachelor's.
Student Life *Campus security:* 24-hour emergency response devices.
Freshman Application Contact Director of Recruitment, ITT Technical Institute, 6270 Park South Drive, Bessemer, AL 35022. *Phone:* 205-497-5700. *Toll-free phone:* 800-488-7033.
Website: http://www.itt-tech.edu/.

ITT Technical Institute
Madison, Alabama

- **Proprietary** primarily 2-year, part of ITT Educational Services, Inc.
- **Coed**

Academics *Degrees:* associate and bachelor's.
Freshman Application Contact Director of Recruitment, ITT Technical Institute, 9238 Madison Boulevard, Suite 500, Madison, AL 35758. *Phone:* 256-542-2900. *Toll-free phone:* 877-628-5960.
Website: http://www.itt-tech.edu/.

ITT Technical Institute

Mobile, Alabama

- **Proprietary** primarily 2-year, part of ITT Educational Services, Inc.
- **Coed**

Academics *Degrees:* associate and bachelor's.
Freshman Application Contact Director of Recruitment, ITT Technical Institute, Office Mall South, 3100 Cottage Hill Road, Building 3, Mobile, AL 36606. *Phone:* 251-472-4760. *Toll-free phone:* 877-327-1013.
Website: http://www.itt-tech.edu/.

James H. Faulkner State Community College

Bay Minette, Alabama

- **State-supported** 2-year, founded 1965, part of Alabama College System
- **Small-town** 105-acre campus
- **Coed,** 3,323 undergraduate students, 64% full-time, 63% women, 37% men

Undergraduates 2,139 full-time, 1,184 part-time. 3% are from out of state; 9% live on campus.
Freshmen *Admission:* 988 enrolled.
Faculty *Total:* 227, 38% full-time, 2% with terminal degrees. *Student/faculty ratio:* 15:1.
Majors Administrative assistant and secretarial science; agricultural economics; business administration and management; commercial and advertising art; computer and information sciences; criminal justice/law enforcement administration; dental assisting; environmental engineering technology; general studies; hospitality administration; landscaping and groundskeeping; legal assistant/paralegal; liberal arts and sciences/liberal studies; licensed practical/vocational nurse training; mass communication/media; parks, recreation and leisure facilities management; registered nursing/registered nurse; surgical technology.
Academics *Calendar:* semesters. *Degree:* certificates and associate. *Special study options:* academic remediation for entering students, adult/continuing education programs, advanced placement credit, cooperative education, honors programs, internships, part-time degree program, services for LD students.
Library Austin R. Meadows Library with 53,100 titles, an OPAC.
Student Life *Housing Options:* men-only, women-only. Campus housing is university owned. *Activities and Organizations:* drama/theater group, student-run newspaper, choral group, Student Government Association, Pow-Wow Leadership Society, Phi Theta Kappa, Association of Computational Machinery, Phi Beta Lambda, national fraternities. *Campus security:* 24-hour emergency response devices and patrols, controlled dormitory access. *Student services:* personal/psychological counseling.
Athletics Member NJCAA. *Intercollegiate sports:* baseball M(s), basketball M(s)/W(s), golf M(s), softball W(s), tennis M(s)/W(s), volleyball W(s). *Intramural sports:* basketball M, tennis M/W, volleyball M/W.
Costs (2014–15) *Tuition:* state resident $4260 full-time, $113 per credit hour part-time; nonresident $7650 full-time, $226 per credit hour part-time. Full-time tuition and fees vary according to course level, course load, program, and student level. Part-time tuition and fees vary according to course level, course load, program, and student level. *Required fees:* $1000 full-time, $29 per credit hour part-time, $29 per credit hour part-time. *Room and board:* $5800. Room and board charges vary according to board plan and housing facility. *Waivers:* employees or children of employees.
Applying *Options:* early admission, deferred entrance. *Required:* high school transcript. *Application deadlines:* rolling (freshmen), rolling (transfers). *Notification:* continuous until 8/18 (freshmen), continuous until 8/18 (transfers).
Freshman Application Contact Ms. Carmelita Mikkelsen, Director of Admissions and High School Relations, James H. Faulkner State Community College, 1900 Highway 31 South, Bay Minette, AL 36507. *Phone:* 251-580-2213. *Toll-free phone:* 800-231-3752. *Fax:* 251-580-2285. *E-mail:* cmikkelsen@faulknerstate.edu.
Website: http://www.faulknerstate.edu/.

Jefferson Davis Community College

Brewton, Alabama

Director of Admissions Ms. Robin Sessions, Registrar, Jefferson Davis Community College, PO Box 958, Brewton, AL 36427-0958. *Phone:* 251-867-4832.
Website: http://www.jdcc.edu/.

Jefferson State Community College

Birmingham, Alabama

- **State-supported** 2-year, founded 1965, part of Alabama Community College System
- **Suburban** 351-acre campus
- **Endowment** $1.2 million
- **Coed,** 8,516 undergraduate students, 35% full-time, 61% women, 39% men

Undergraduates 2,965 full-time, 5,551 part-time. Students come from 59 other countries; 2% are from out of state; 22% Black or African American, non-Hispanic/Latino; 5% Hispanic/Latino; 2% Asian, non-Hispanic/Latino; 0.1% Native Hawaiian or other Pacific Islander, non-Hispanic/Latino; 0.2% American Indian or Alaska Native, non-Hispanic/Latino; 3% Two or more races, non-Hispanic/Latino; 0.5% international. *Retention:* 53% of full-time freshmen returned.
Freshmen *Admission:* 1,648 enrolled. *Average high school GPA:* 2.84.
Faculty *Total:* 442, 33% full-time. *Student/faculty ratio:* 20:1.
Majors Accounting technology and bookkeeping; administrative assistant and secretarial science; child-care and support services management; clinical/medical laboratory technology; computer and information sciences; construction engineering technology; criminal justice/police science; emergency medical technology (EMT paramedic); engineering technology; fire services administration; funeral service and mortuary science; general studies; hospitality administration; liberal arts and sciences/liberal studies; office management; physical therapy technology; radiologic technology/science; registered nursing/registered nurse; veterinary/animal health technology.
Academics *Calendar:* semesters. *Degree:* certificates and associate. *Special study options:* academic remediation for entering students, adult/continuing education programs, advanced placement credit, distance learning, English as a second language, honors programs, independent study, internships, part-time degree program, services for LD students, summer session for credit. *ROTC:* Army (c), Air Force (c).
Library Jefferson State Libraries plus 4 others with 334,343 titles, 1,498 audiovisual materials, an OPAC, a Web page.
Student Life *Housing:* college housing not available. *Activities and Organizations:* choral group, Student Government Association, Phi Theta Kappa, Sigma Kappa Delta, Jefferson State Ambassadors, Students in Free Enterprise (SIFE). *Campus security:* 24-hour patrols.
Costs (2014–15) *Tuition:* state resident $4320 full-time, $144 per semester hour part-time; nonresident $7710 full-time, $257 per semester hour part-time. Full-time tuition and fees vary according to course load. Part-time tuition and fees vary according to course load. *Waivers:* senior citizens and employees or children of employees.
Applying *Options:* electronic application, early admission, early action, deferred entrance. *Required for some:* high school transcript. *Application deadline:* rolling (freshmen). *Notification:* continuous (freshmen), continuous (transfers).
Freshman Application Contact Mrs. Lillian Owens, Director of Admissions and Retention, Jefferson State Community College, 2601 Carson Road, Birmingham, AL 35215-3098. *Phone:* 205-853-1200 Ext. 7990. *Toll-free phone:* 800-239-5900. *Fax:* 205-856-6070. *E-mail:* lowens@jeffstateonline.com.
Website: http://www.jeffstateonline.com/.

J. F. Drake State Community and Technical College

Huntsville, Alabama

- **State-supported** 2-year, founded 1961, part of Alabama Community College System
- **Urban** 6-acre campus
- **Coed,** 1,258 undergraduate students, 60% full-time, 55% women, 45% men

Undergraduates 754 full-time, 504 part-time. Students come from 1 other state; 2 other countries; 4% are from out of state; 23% transferred in.
Freshmen *Admission:* 1,205 admitted, 347 enrolled.
Faculty *Total:* 72, 35% full-time, 7% with terminal degrees. *Student/faculty ratio:* 17:1.
Majors Accounting; accounting technology and bookkeeping; administrative assistant and secretarial science; automobile/automotive mechanics technology; automotive engineering technology; commercial and advertising art; computer and information sciences; cosmetology; culinary arts; drafting and design technology; electrical, electronic and communications engineering technology; electrician; heating, ventilation, air conditioning and refrigeration engineering technology; industrial electronics technology; industrial mechanics and maintenance technology; information science/studies; licensed

practical/vocational nurse training; machine tool technology; medical/clinical assistant; multi/interdisciplinary studies related; tool and die technology.
Academics *Calendar:* semesters. *Degree:* certificates and associate. *Special study options:* academic remediation for entering students, cooperative education, internships, part-time degree program, services for LD students.
Library S.C. O'Neal Library and Technology Center with 24,676 titles, 2,247 audiovisual materials, an OPAC, a Web page.
Student Life *Housing:* college housing not available. *Activities and Organizations:* Phi Beta Lambda, SKILLS - USA. *Campus security:* 24-hour patrols.
Costs (2015–16) *Tuition:* state resident $2712 full-time, $113 per credit hour part-time; nonresident $5424 full-time, $226 per credit hour part-time. Full-time tuition and fees vary according to course load. Part-time tuition and fees vary according to course load. *Required fees:* $672 full-time, $28 per credit hour part-time. *Waivers:* senior citizens and employees or children of employees.
Applying *Options:* electronic application, deferred entrance. *Required:* high school transcript. *Application deadlines:* rolling (freshmen), rolling (transfers). *Notification:* continuous (freshmen), continuous (transfers).
Freshman Application Contact Mrs. Kristin Treadway, Pre-Admissions Coordinator, J. F. Drake State Community and Technical College, Huntsville, AL 35811. *Phone:* 256-551-3111 Ext. 704. *Toll-free phone:* 888-413-7253. *E-mail:* sudeall@drakestate.edu.
Website: http://www.drakestate.edu/.

Lawson State Community College
Birmingham, Alabama

- **State-supported** 2-year, founded 1949, part of Alabama Community College System
- **Urban** 30-acre campus
- **Coed**

Undergraduates 1,791 full-time, 1,240 part-time. Students come from 14 states and territories; 1 other country; 1% are from out of state; 75% Black or African American, non-Hispanic/Latino; 1% Hispanic/Latino; 0.4% Asian, non-Hispanic/Latino; 0.2% Native Hawaiian or other Pacific Islander, non-Hispanic/Latino; 0.1% American Indian or Alaska Native, non-Hispanic/Latino; 0.8% Two or more races, non-Hispanic/Latino; 8% Race/ethnicity unknown; 0.1% international; 7% transferred in; 1% live on campus. *Retention:* 52% of full-time freshmen returned.
Faculty *Student/faculty ratio:* 17:1.
Academics *Calendar:* semesters. *Degree:* certificates and associate. *Special study options:* academic remediation for entering students, adult/continuing education programs, advanced placement credit, cooperative education, distance learning, honors programs, internships, part-time degree program, services for LD students, summer session for credit.
Student Life *Campus security:* 24-hour emergency response devices and patrols, controlled dormitory access.
Athletics Member NJCAA.
Costs (2014–15) *Tuition:* state resident $3420 full-time, $114 per credit hour part-time; nonresident $6840 full-time, $228 per credit hour part-time. *Required fees:* $850 full-time, $28 per credit hour part-time. *Room and board:* $4760; room only: $3000.
Financial Aid Of all full-time matriculated undergraduates who enrolled in 2013, 91 Federal Work-Study jobs (averaging $3000).
Applying *Options:* electronic application. *Required:* high school transcript.
Freshman Application Contact Mr. Jeff Shelley, Director of Admissions and Records, Lawson State Community College, 3060 Wilson Road, SW, Birmingham, AL 35221-1798. *Phone:* 205-929-6361. *Fax:* 205-923-7106. *E-mail:* jshelley@lawsonstate.edu.
Website: http://www.lawsonstate.edu/.

Lurleen B. Wallace Community College
Andalusia, Alabama

- **State-supported** 2-year, founded 1969, part of Alabama Community College System
- **Small-town** 200-acre campus
- **Coed,** 1,599 undergraduate students, 63% full-time, 60% women, 40% men

Undergraduates 1,010 full-time, 589 part-time. Students come from 8 states and territories; 8 other countries; 3% are from out of state; 27% Black or African American, non-Hispanic/Latino; 1% Hispanic/Latino; 0.6% Asian, non-Hispanic/Latino; 0.4% American Indian or Alaska Native, non-

Hispanic/Latino; 1% Two or more races, non-Hispanic/Latino; 0.2% international; 19% transferred in.
Freshmen *Admission:* 490 enrolled.
Faculty *Total:* 97, 58% full-time, 6% with terminal degrees. *Student/faculty ratio:* 17:1.
Majors Administrative assistant and secretarial science; child-care and support services management; computer and information sciences; diagnostic medical sonography and ultrasound technology; emergency medical technology (EMT paramedic); forest technology; general studies; industrial electronics technology; liberal arts and sciences/liberal studies; registered nursing/registered nurse.
Academics *Calendar:* semesters. *Degree:* certificates and associate. *Special study options:* academic remediation for entering students, cooperative education, distance learning, honors programs, independent study, part-time degree program, summer session for credit.
Library Lurleen B. Wallace Library plus 2 others with 36,003 titles, 2,427 audiovisual materials, an OPAC, a Web page.
Student Life *Housing:* college housing not available. *Activities and Organizations:* drama/theater group, choral group, Student Government Association, Student Ambassadors, Interclub Council, Campus Civitan, Christian Student Ministries. *Student services:* personal/psychological counseling.
Athletics Member NJCAA. *Intercollegiate sports:* baseball M(s), basketball M(s)/W(s), softball W(s).
Costs (2014–15) *Tuition:* state resident $3390 full-time, $113 per credit hour part-time; nonresident $6780 full-time, $226 per credit hour part-time. Full-time tuition and fees vary according to course load. Part-time tuition and fees vary according to course load. *Required fees:* $840 full-time, $28 per credit hour part-time. *Payment plan:* installment. *Waivers:* senior citizens and employees or children of employees.
Applying *Required:* high school transcript. *Application deadlines:* rolling (freshmen), rolling (out-of-state freshmen), rolling (transfers).
Freshman Application Contact Lurleen B. Wallace Community College, PO Box 1418, Andalusia, AL 36420-1418. *Phone:* 334-881-2273.
Website: http://www.lbwcc.edu/.

Marion Military Institute
Marion, Alabama

- **State-supported** 2-year, founded 1842, part of Alabama Community College System
- **Rural** 130-acre campus with easy access to Birmingham
- **Coed**

Undergraduates 411 full-time, 7 part-time. Students come from 40 states and territories; 66% are from out of state; 23% Black or African American, non-Hispanic/Latino; 10% Hispanic/Latino; 4% Asian, non-Hispanic/Latino; 0.5% Native Hawaiian or other Pacific Islander, non-Hispanic/Latino; 1% American Indian or Alaska Native, non-Hispanic/Latino; 3% Two or more races, non-Hispanic/Latino; 1% Race/ethnicity unknown; 6% transferred in; 100% live on campus. *Retention:* 38% of full-time freshmen returned.
Faculty *Student/faculty ratio:* 16:1.
Academics *Calendar:* semesters. *Degree:* associate. *Special study options:* academic remediation for entering students, English as a second language, services for LD students. *ROTC:* Army (b), Air Force (c).
Student Life *Campus security:* night patrols by trained security personnel.
Athletics Member NJCAA.
Standardized Tests *Required:* SAT or ACT (for admission).
Costs (2014–15) *Tuition:* state resident $6000 full-time; nonresident $12,000 full-time. *Required fees:* $2778 full-time. *Room and board:* $3950.
Financial Aid Of all full-time matriculated undergraduates who enrolled in 2013, 29 Federal Work-Study jobs (averaging $210).
Applying *Options:* electronic application, deferred entrance. *Application fee:* $30. *Required:* high school transcript, minimum 2.0 GPA.
Freshman Application Contact Mrs. Brittany Crawford, Director of Admissions, Marion Military Institute, 1101 Washington Street, Marion, AL 36756. *Phone:* 800-664-1842. *Toll-free phone:* 800-664-1842. *Fax:* 334-683-2383. *E-mail:* bcrawford@marionmilitary.edu.
Website: http://www.marionmilitary.edu/.

Northeast Alabama Community College
Rainsville, Alabama

Freshman Application Contact Northeast Alabama Community College, PO Box 159, Rainsville, AL 35986-0159. *Phone:* 256-228-6001 Ext. 2325.
Website: http://www.nacc.edu/.

Northwest-Shoals Community College
Muscle Shoals, Alabama

- **State-supported** 2-year, founded 1963, part of Alabama Department of Postsecondary Education
- **Small-town** 210-acre campus
- **Endowment** $727,778
- **Coed,** 3,858 undergraduate students, 48% full-time, 55% women, 45% men

Undergraduates 1,859 full-time, 1,999 part-time. Students come from 3 states and territories; 1 other country; 2% are from out of state; 11% Black or African American, non-Hispanic/Latino; 4% Hispanic/Latino; 0.3% Asian, non-Hispanic/Latino; 0.1% Native Hawaiian or other Pacific Islander, non-Hispanic/Latino; 0.8% American Indian or Alaska Native, non-Hispanic/Latino; 0.1% Two or more races, non-Hispanic/Latino; 3% Race/ethnicity unknown; 0.3% international; 6% transferred in.
Freshmen *Admission:* 812 applied, 812 admitted, 812 enrolled.
Faculty *Total:* 150, 52% full-time, 5% with terminal degrees. *Student/faculty ratio:* 24:1.
Majors Administrative assistant and secretarial science; child-care and support services management; child development; computer and information sciences; criminal justice/police science; drafting and design technology; emergency medical technology (EMT paramedic); environmental engineering technology; general studies; industrial electronics technology; industrial mechanics and maintenance technology; liberal arts and sciences/liberal studies; medical/clinical assistant; multi/interdisciplinary studies related; registered nursing/registered nurse; salon/beauty salon management.
Academics *Calendar:* semesters. *Degree:* certificates and associate. *Special study options:* academic remediation for entering students, accelerated degree program, adult/continuing education programs, advanced placement credit, cooperative education, distance learning, honors programs, independent study, internships, part-time degree program, services for LD students, summer session for credit.
Library Larry W. McCoy Learning Resource Center and James Glasgow Library with 60,799 titles, 3,368 audiovisual materials, an OPAC.
Student Life *Housing:* college housing not available. *Activities and Organizations:* choral group, Student Government Association, Science Club, Phi Theta Kappa, Baptist Campus Ministry, Northwest-Shoals Singers. *Campus security:* 24-hour emergency response devices.
Athletics *Intramural sports:* basketball M/W, football M/W, tennis M/W.
Standardized Tests *Required:* ACT Compass Placement Test for English and Math (for admission).
Costs (2015–16) *Tuition:* state resident $3450 full-time, $115 per credit hour part-time; nonresident $6900 full-time, $230 per credit hour part-time. *Required fees:* $810 full-time, $27 per credit hour part-time. *Waivers:* senior citizens and employees or children of employees.
Financial Aid Of all full-time matriculated undergraduates who enrolled in 2014, 43 Federal Work-Study jobs (averaging $2445). *Financial aid deadline:* 6/1.
Applying *Options:* electronic application. *Required:* high school transcript. *Application deadlines:* rolling (freshmen), rolling (transfers). *Notification:* continuous (transfers).
Freshman Application Contact Mr. Tom Carter, Assistant Dean of Recruitment, Admissions and Financial Aid, Northwest-Shoals Community College, PO Box 2545, Muscle Shoals, AL 35662. *Phone:* 256-331-5263. *Fax:* 256-331-5366. *E-mail:* tom.carter@nwscc.edu.
Website: http://www.nwscc.edu/.

Reid State Technical College
Evergreen, Alabama

- **State-supported** 2-year, founded 1966, part of Alabama Community College System
- **Rural** 26-acre campus
- **Coed,** 549 undergraduate students, 50% full-time, 61% women, 39% men

Undergraduates 276 full-time, 273 part-time. Students come from 2 states and territories; 1% are from out of state; 44% Black or African American, non-Hispanic/Latino; 0.5% Hispanic/Latino; 0.2% Asian, non-Hispanic/Latino; 0.7% American Indian or Alaska Native, non-Hispanic/Latino; 0.7% Two or more races, non-Hispanic/Latino; 0.4% Race/ethnicity unknown.
Freshmen *Admission:* 93 applied, 93 admitted, 93 enrolled.
Faculty *Total:* 31, 77% full-time, 13% with terminal degrees. *Student/faculty ratio:* 12:1.
Majors Administrative assistant and secretarial science; child-care and support services management; computer and information sciences; electrical, electronic and communications engineering technology.
Academics *Calendar:* semesters. *Degree:* certificates and associate. *Special study options:* academic remediation for entering students, adult/continuing

education programs, double majors, independent study, internships, part-time degree program, services for LD students, summer session for credit.
Library Edith A. Gray Library with 4,157 titles, 298 audiovisual materials, a Web page.
Student Life *Housing:* college housing not available. *Activities and Organizations:* Student Government Association, Phi Beta Lambda, National Vocational-Technical Society, Ambassadors, Who's Who. *Campus security:* 24-hour emergency response devices, day and evening security guard. *Student services:* personal/psychological counseling.
Costs (2015–16) *Tuition:* state resident $3480 full-time, $116 per credit part-time; nonresident $6960 full-time, $232 per credit part-time. Full-time tuition and fees vary according to course load and program. Part-time tuition and fees vary according to course load and program. *Required fees:* $900 full-time, $30 per credit part-time. *Payment plan:* deferred payment. *Waivers:* senior citizens and employees or children of employees.
Financial Aid Of all full-time matriculated undergraduates who enrolled in 2013, 35 Federal Work-Study jobs (averaging $1500).
Applying *Options:* early admission. *Required:* high school transcript. *Application deadlines:* rolling (freshmen), rolling (transfers).
Freshman Application Contact Dr. Alesia Stuart, Public Relations/Marketing/Associate Dean of Workforce Development, Reid State Technical College, Evergreen, AL 36401-0588. *Phone:* 251-578-1313 Ext. 108. *E-mail:* akstuart@rstc.edu.
Website: http://www.rstc.edu/.

Remington College–Mobile Campus
Mobile, Alabama

Freshman Application Contact Remington College–Mobile Campus, 828 Downtowner Loop West, Mobile, AL 36609-5404. *Phone:* 251-343-8200. *Toll-free phone:* 800-560-6192.
Website: http://www.remingtoncollege.edu/.

Shelton State Community College
Tuscaloosa, Alabama

- **State-supported** 2-year, founded 1979, part of Alabama Community College System
- **Small-town** 202-acre campus with easy access to Birmingham
- **Coed**

Undergraduates 2,468 full-time, 2,600 part-time. 5% are from out of state; 34% Black or African American, non-Hispanic/Latino; 0.5% Hispanic/Latino; 1% Asian, non-Hispanic/Latino; 0.3% American Indian or Alaska Native, non-Hispanic/Latino; 1% Two or more races, non-Hispanic/Latino; 7% Race/ethnicity unknown; 0.4% international; 9% transferred in. *Retention:* 58% of full-time freshmen returned.
Faculty *Student/faculty ratio:* 25:1.
Academics *Calendar:* semesters. *Degree:* certificates, diplomas, and associate. *Special study options:* academic remediation for entering students, accelerated degree program, adult/continuing education programs, advanced placement credit, cooperative education, distance learning, double majors, part-time degree program, services for LD students, summer session for credit. *ROTC:* Army (c), Air Force (c).
Student Life *Campus security:* 24-hour emergency response devices and patrols.
Athletics Member NJCAA.
Costs (2014–15) *Tuition:* state resident $3330 full-time, $113 per credit part-time; nonresident $6660 full-time, $226 per credit part-time. Full-time tuition and fees vary according to course load and reciprocity agreements. Part-time tuition and fees vary according to course load and reciprocity agreements. *Required fees:* $570 full-time, $19 per credit part-time.
Applying *Options:* electronic application. *Required:* high school transcript.
Freshman Application Contact Ms. Sharon Chastine, Secretary to the Associate Dean of Student Services Enrollment, Shelton State Community College, 9500 Old Greensboro Road, Tuscaloosa, AL 35405. *Phone:* 205-391-2309. *Fax:* 205-391-3910. *E-mail:* schastine@sheltonstate.edu.
Website: http://www.sheltonstate.edu/.

Snead State Community College
Boaz, Alabama

- **State-supported** 2-year, founded 1898, part of Alabama College System
- **Small-town** 42-acre campus with easy access to Birmingham
- **Coed**

Undergraduates 1,538 full-time, 623 part-time.
Faculty *Student/faculty ratio:* 23:1.
Academics *Calendar:* semesters. *Degree:* certificates and associate. *Special study options:* academic remediation for entering students, accelerated degree program, adult/continuing education programs, advanced placement credit,

distance learning, independent study, internships, part-time degree program, services for LD students, student-designed majors, summer session for credit.
Student Life *Campus security:* 24-hour patrols.
Athletics Member NJCAA.
Costs (2014–15) *Tuition:* state resident $3390 full-time, $113 per credit hour part-time; nonresident $6780 full-time, $226 per credit hour part-time. *Required fees:* $930 full-time. *Room and board:* $3187; room only: $2150.
Financial Aid Of all full-time matriculated undergraduates who enrolled in 2013, 45 Federal Work-Study jobs.
Applying *Options:* electronic application, early admission, deferred entrance. *Required:* high school transcript. *Required for some:* interview.
Freshman Application Contact Dr. Jason Watts, Chief Academic Officer, Snead State Community College, PO Box 734, Boaz, AL 35957-0734. *Phone:* 256-840-4118. *Fax:* 256-593-7180. *E-mail:* jwatts@snead.edu.
Website: http://www.snead.edu/.

Southern Union State Community College
Wadley, Alabama

Freshman Application Contact Admissions Office, Southern Union State Community College, PO Box 1000, Roberts Street, Wadley, AL 36276. *Phone:* 256-395-5157. *E-mail:* info@suscc.edu.
Website: http://www.suscc.edu/.

Virginia College in Huntsville
Huntsville, Alabama

Freshman Application Contact Director of Admission, Virginia College in Huntsville, 2021 Drake Avenue SW, Huntsville, AL 35801. *Phone:* 256-533-7387. *Fax:* 256-533-7785.
Website: http://www.vc.edu/.

Virginia College in Mobile
Mobile, Alabama

Admissions Office Contact Virginia College in Mobile, 3725 Airport Boulevard, Suite 165, Mobile, AL 36608.
Website: http://www.vc.edu/.

Virginia College in Montgomery
Montgomery, Alabama

Admissions Office Contact Virginia College in Montgomery, 6200 Atlanta Highway, Montgomery, AL 36117-2800.
Website: http://www.vc.edu/.

Wallace State Community College
Hanceville, Alabama

Director of Admissions Jennifer Hill, Director of Admissions, Wallace State Community College, PO Box 2000, 801 Main Street, Hanceville, AL 35077-2000. *Phone:* 256-352-8278. *Toll-free phone:* 866-350-9722.
Website: http://www.wallacestate.edu/.

ALASKA

Alaska Career College
Anchorage, Alaska

Admissions Office Contact Alaska Career College, 1415 East Tudor Road, Anchorage, AK 99507.
Website: http://www.alaskacareercollege.edu/.

Alaska Christian College
Soldotna, Alaska

Admissions Office Contact Alaska Christian College, 35109 Royal Place, Soldotna, AK 99669.
Website: http://www.akcc.org/.

Charter College
Anchorage, Alaska

Director of Admissions Ms. Lily Sirianni, Vice President, Charter College, 2221 East Northern Lights Boulevard, Suite 120, Anchorage, AK 99508. *Phone:* 907-277-1000. *Toll-free phone:* 888-200-9942.
Website: http://www.chartercollege.edu/.

Ilisagvik College
Barrow, Alaska

- **State-supported** 2-year, founded 1995
- **Rural** 7-acre campus
- **Endowment** $3.5 million
- **Coed**

Undergraduates 50 full-time, 207 part-time. Students come from 3 states and territories; 3 other countries; 2% Black or African American, non-Hispanic/Latino; 2% Hispanic/Latino; 7% Asian, non-Hispanic/Latino; 4% Native Hawaiian or other Pacific Islander, non-Hispanic/Latino; 58% American Indian or Alaska Native, non-Hispanic/Latino; 1% Race/ethnicity unknown; 0.8% international; 3% transferred in; 10% live on campus.
Faculty *Student/faculty ratio:* 6:1.
Academics *Calendar:* semesters. *Degree:* certificates, diplomas, and associate. *Special study options:* academic remediation for entering students, cooperative education, distance learning, double majors, English as a second language, independent study, internships, off-campus study, part-time degree program, services for LD students, summer session for credit.
Student Life *Campus security:* 24-hour emergency response devices and patrols, controlled dormitory access.
Standardized Tests *Recommended:* ACT ASSET or ACT Compass Test.
Costs (2014–15) *Tuition:* state resident $3000 full-time, $125 per credit part-time; nonresident $3000 full-time, $125 per credit part-time. Full-time tuition and fees vary according to course load and program. Part-time tuition and fees vary according to course load and program. *Required fees:* $460 full-time, $60 per term part-time, $60 per term part-time. *Room and board:* $6600; room only: $4000. Room and board charges vary according to housing facility. *Payment plans:* installment, deferred payment.
Applying *Options:* deferred entrance. *Required:* high school transcript, minimum 2.0 GPA. *Required for some:* copy of Alaska Native Shareholder/Native American Tribal Affiliation card if native.
Freshman Application Contact Janelle Everett, Recruiter, Ilisagvik College, PO Box 749, Barrow, AK 99723. *Phone:* 907-852-1799. *Toll-free phone:* 800-478-7337. *Fax:* 907-852-2729. *E-mail:* janelle.everett@ilisagvik.edu.
Website: http://www.ilisagvik.edu/.

University of Alaska Anchorage, Kenai Peninsula College
Soldotna, Alaska

Freshman Application Contact Ms. Shelly Love Blatchford, Admission and Registration Coordinator, University of Alaska Anchorage, Kenai Peninsula College, 156 College Road, Soldotna, AK 99669-9798. *Phone:* 907-262-0311. *Toll-free phone:* 877-262-0330.
Website: http://www.kpc.alaska.edu/.

University of Alaska Anchorage, Kodiak College
Kodiak, Alaska

Freshman Application Contact University of Alaska Anchorage, Kodiak College, 117 Benny Benson Drive, Kodiak, AK 99615-6643. *Phone:* 907-486-1235. *Toll-free phone:* 800-486-7660.
Website: http://www.koc.alaska.edu/.

University of Alaska Anchorage, Matanuska-Susitna College
Palmer, Alaska

Freshman Application Contact Ms. Sandra Gravley, Student Services Director, University of Alaska Anchorage, Matanuska-Susitna College, PO Box 2889, Palmer, AK 99645-2889. *Phone:* 907-745-9712. *Fax:* 907-745-9747. *E-mail:* info@matsu.alaska.edu.
Website: http://www.matsu.alaska.edu/.

University of Alaska, Prince William Sound Community College
Valdez, Alaska

Freshman Application Contact Shelia Mann, University of Alaska, Prince William Sound Community College, PO Box 97, Valdez, AK 99686-0097. *Phone:* 907-834-1600. *Toll-free phone:* 800-478-8800. *Fax:* 907-834-1691. *E-mail:* studentservices@pwscc.edu.
Website: http://www.pwscc.edu/.

University of Alaska Southeast, Ketchikan Campus
Ketchikan, Alaska

Freshman Application Contact Admissions Office, University of Alaska Southeast, Ketchikan Campus, 2600 7th Avenue, Ketchikan, AK 99901-5798. *Phone:* 907-225-6177. *Toll-free phone:* 888-550-6177. *Fax:* 907-225-3895. *E-mail:* ketch.info@uas.alaska.edu.
Website: http://www.ketch.alaska.edu/.

University of Alaska Southeast, Sitka Campus
Sitka, Alaska

- **State-supported** primarily 2-year, founded 1962, part of University of Alaska System
- **Small-town** campus
- **Coed,** 1,552 undergraduate students

Undergraduates Students come from 10 states and territories; 2 other countries.
Faculty *Total:* 59, 32% full-time. *Student/faculty ratio:* 13:1.
Majors Business administration and management; criminal justice/law enforcement administration; elementary education; fishing and fisheries sciences and management; general studies; health information/medical records administration; health information/medical records technology; health services/allied health/health sciences; liberal arts and sciences/liberal studies; nursing assistant/aide and patient care assistant/aide; social sciences; special education.
Academics *Calendar:* semesters. *Degrees:* certificates, diplomas, associate, bachelor's, and master's. *Special study options:* academic remediation for entering students, adult/continuing education programs, advanced placement credit, cooperative education, distance learning, double majors, English as a second language, independent study, internships, off-campus study, part-time degree program, services for LD students, study abroad, summer session for credit.
Library Egan Library with 80,050 titles, an OPAC, a Web page.
Student Life *Housing:* college housing not available. *Options:* coed. Campus housing is provided by a third party. *Activities and Organizations:* Student Government Association, Phi Theta Kappa Honor Society. *Campus security:* 24-hour emergency response devices. *Student services:* personal/psychological counseling.
Costs (2015–16) *One-time required fee:* $50. *Tuition:* state resident $4224 full-time, $176 per credit part-time; nonresident $4224 full-time, $176 per credit part-time. Full-time tuition and fees vary according to degree level, location, and program. Part-time tuition and fees vary according to degree level, location, and program. UAS Sitka campus programs have no nonresident tuition rates. *Required fees:* $856 full-time, $36 per credit part-time. *Room and board:* room only: $4800. Room and board charges vary according to housing facility. *Payment plan:* installment. *Waivers:* senior citizens and employees or children of employees.
Applying *Options:* electronic application, early admission, deferred entrance. *Application fee:* $35. *Required:* high school transcript, minimum 2.0 GPA. *Required for some:* essay or personal statement. *Application deadlines:* rolling (freshmen), rolling (out-of-state freshmen), rolling (transfers). *Notification:* continuous (freshmen), continuous (out-of-state freshmen), continuous (transfers).
Freshman Application Contact Ms. Teal Gordon, Admissions Representative, University of Alaska Southeast, Sitka Campus, UAS Sitka, 1332 Seward Ave., Sitka, AK 99835. *Phone:* 907-747-7726. *Toll-free phone:* 800-478-6653. *Fax:* 907-747-7731. *E-mail:* ktgordon@uas.alaska.edu.
Website: http://www.uas.alaska.edu/.

AMERICAN SAMOA

American Samoa Community College
Pago Pago, American Samoa

- **Territory-supported** primarily 2-year, founded 1969
- **Rural** 20-acre campus
- **Endowment** $3.1 million
- **Coed,** 1,276 undergraduate students, 56% full-time, 63% women, 37% men

Undergraduates 716 full-time, 560 part-time. Students come from 5 other countries; 0.5% Asian, non-Hispanic/Latino; 92% Native Hawaiian or other Pacific Islander, non-Hispanic/Latino; 0.2% Race/ethnicity unknown; 7% international; 0.2% transferred in. *Retention:* 100% of full-time freshmen returned.
Freshmen *Admission:* 472 applied, 454 admitted, 452 enrolled. *Test scores:* SAT critical reading scores over 500: 17%; SAT math scores over 500: 16%; SAT writing scores over 500: 13%; SAT critical reading scores over 600: 5%; SAT math scores over 600: 2%; SAT writing scores over 600: 2%.
Faculty *Total:* 61. *Student/faculty ratio:* 25:1.
Majors Accounting; agricultural business and management; agriculture; architectural drafting and CAD/CADD; art; autobody/collision and repair technology; automobile/automotive mechanics technology; business administration and management; civil engineering; construction trades; criminal justice/safety; education; electrical, electronic and communications engineering technology; family and consumer economics related; forensic science and technology; health services/allied health/health sciences; human services; liberal arts and sciences/liberal studies; marine science/merchant marine officer; music; natural resources/conservation; office occupations and clerical services; political science and government; pre-law studies; welding technology.
Academics *Calendar:* semesters. *Degrees:* certificates, associate, and bachelor's. *Special study options:* academic remediation for entering students, adult/continuing education programs, cooperative education, double majors, English as a second language, honors programs, independent study, internships, off-campus study, part-time degree program, services for LD students, student-designed majors, summer session for credit. *ROTC:* Army (b).
Library ASCC Learning Resource Center/ Library plus 1 other with 40,000 titles, an OPAC.
Student Life *Housing:* college housing not available. *Activities and Organizations:* student-run newspaper, Student Government Association, Phi Theta Kappa, ASCC Research Foundation Student Club, Fa'aSamoa (Samoan Culture) Club, Journalism Club. *Campus security:* 24-hour patrols. *Student services:* personal/psychological counseling.
Athletics *Intramural sports:* basketball M/W, football M/W, golf M/W, rugby M, soccer M, tennis M/W, track and field M/W, volleyball M/W.
Standardized Tests *Recommended:* SAT (for admission), ACT (for admission), SAT or ACT (for admission), SAT and SAT Subject Tests or ACT (for admission), SAT Subject Tests (for admission).
Costs (2014–15) *Tuition:* territory resident $3300 full-time, $110 per credit part-time; nonresident $3600 full-time, $120 per credit part-time. Full-time tuition and fees vary according to course load. Part-time tuition and fees vary according to course load. *Required fees:* $250 full-time, $125 per term part-time. *Payment plan:* installment. *Waivers:* employees or children of employees.
Financial Aid Of all full-time matriculated undergraduates who enrolled in 2013, 689 applied for aid, 689 were judged to have need. 102 Federal Work-Study jobs (averaging $528). *Average percent of need met:* 94%. *Average financial aid package:* $7310. *Average need-based gift aid:* $7549. *Financial aid deadline:* 9/10.
Applying *Options:* electronic application, early admission, deferred entrance. *Application deadline:* rolling (freshmen). *Notification:* continuous (freshmen).
Freshman Application Contact Elizabeth Leuma, Admissions Officer, American Samoa Community College, PO Box 2609, Pago Pago 96799, American Samoa. *Phone:* 684-699-9155 Ext. 411. *Fax:* 684-699-1083.
Website: http://www.amsamoa.edu/.

ARIZONA

Arizona Automotive Institute
Glendale, Arizona

Director of Admissions Director of Admissions, Arizona Automotive Institute, 6829 North 46th Avenue, Glendale, AZ 85301-3597. *Phone:* 623-

934-7273 Ext. 211. *Toll-free phone:* 800-321-5861 (in-state); 800-321-5961 (out-of-state). *Fax:* 623-937-5000. *E-mail:* info@azautoinst.com. *Website:* http://www.aai.edu/.

Arizona College
Glendale, Arizona

Freshman Application Contact Admissions Department, Arizona College, 4425 West Olive Avenue, Suite 300, Glendale, AZ 85302-3843. *Phone:* 602-222-9300. *E-mail:* lhicks@arizonacollege.edu.
Website: http://www.arizonacollege.edu/.

Arizona Western College
Yuma, Arizona

- **State and locally supported** 2-year, founded 1962, part of Arizona State Community College System
- **Rural** 640-acre campus
- **Coed,** 7,702 undergraduate students, 33% full-time, 57% women, 43% men

Undergraduates 2,562 full-time, 5,140 part-time. Students come from 29 states and territories; 36 other countries; 4% are from out of state; 3% Black or African American, non-Hispanic/Latino; 68% Hispanic/Latino; 1% Asian, non-Hispanic/Latino; 0.3% Native Hawaiian or other Pacific Islander, non-Hispanic/Latino; 1% American Indian or Alaska Native, non-Hispanic/Latino; 1% Two or more races, non-Hispanic/Latino; 3% Race/ethnicity unknown; 3% international; 7% live on campus.
Freshmen *Admission:* 1,862 enrolled.
Faculty *Total:* 398, 32% full-time. *Student/faculty ratio:* 21:1.
Majors Accounting; agricultural business and management; agriculture; American Indian/Native American studies; architectural technology; biology/biological sciences; business administration and management; business/commerce; CAD/CADD drafting/design technology; carpentry; chemistry; civil engineering technology; computer and information sciences; computer graphics; construction management; construction trades related; criminal justice/law enforcement administration; crop production; culinary arts; data entry/microcomputer applications; dramatic/theater arts; early childhood education; electrical, electronic and communications engineering technology; elementary education; emergency medical technology (EMT paramedic); engineering; English; environmental science; family and consumer sciences/human sciences; fine/studio arts; fire science/firefighting; general studies; geology/earth science; health and physical education/fitness; health services/allied health/health sciences; heating, air conditioning, ventilation and refrigeration maintenance technology; history; hospitality administration; industrial technology; legal administrative assistant/secretary; logistics, materials, and supply chain management; manufacturing engineering technology; marketing/marketing management; massage therapy; mass communication/media; mathematics; music; office management; parks, recreation and leisure facilities management; philosophy; physics; plumbing technology; political science and government; prenursing studies; psychology; radio and television broadcasting technology; radiologic technology/science; secondary education; social sciences; solar energy technology; Spanish; water quality and wastewater treatment management and recycling technology; welding technology; work and family studies.
Academics *Calendar:* semesters. *Degree:* certificates and associate. *Special study options:* academic remediation for entering students, adult/continuing education programs, advanced placement credit, cooperative education, distance learning, English as a second language, honors programs, independent study, part-time degree program, services for LD students, summer session for credit.
Library Arizona Western College and NAU-Yuma Library with 112,111 titles, 6,121 audiovisual materials, an OPAC, a Web page.
Student Life *Housing Options:* coed, men-only, women-only. Campus housing is university owned. *Activities and Organizations:* drama/theater group, student-run newspaper, radio and television station, choral group, Student Government Association, Spirit Squad, Dance Team, Students in Free Enterprise (SIFE), International Students Team, national fraternities, national sororities. *Campus security:* 24-hour emergency response devices and patrols, student patrols, late-night transport/escort service. *Student services:* health clinic, personal/psychological counseling.
Athletics Member NJCAA. *Intercollegiate sports:* baseball M(s), basketball M(s)/W(s), football M(s), soccer M(s)/W(s), softball W(s), volleyball W(s). *Intramural sports:* cheerleading M(c)/W(c).
Standardized Tests *Required for some:* SAT or ACT (for admission).
Costs (2015–16) *Tuition:* state resident $2340 full-time, $78 per credit part-time; nonresident $9330 full-time, $311 per credit part-time. Full-time tuition and fees vary according to course load, program, and reciprocity agreements. Part-time tuition and fees vary according to course load, program, and reciprocity agreements. *Room and board:* $6740; room only: $2240. Room and board charges vary according to board plan and housing facility. *Payment plan:* installment. *Waivers:* senior citizens and employees or children of employees.
Financial Aid Of all full-time matriculated undergraduates who enrolled in 2013, 350 Federal Work-Study jobs (averaging $1500). 100 state and other part-time jobs (averaging $1800).
Applying *Options:* electronic application, early admission, deferred entrance. *Application deadlines:* rolling (freshmen), rolling (out-of-state freshmen), rolling (transfers).
Freshman Application Contact Nicole D Harral, Interim Director of Admissions/Registrar, Arizona Western College, PO Box 929, Yuma, AZ 85366. *Phone:* 928-344-7600. *Toll-free phone:* 888-293-0392. *Fax:* 928-344-7712. *E-mail:* nicole.harral@azwestern.edu.
Website: http://www.azwestern.edu/.

Brown Mackie College–Phoenix
Phoenix, Arizona

- **Proprietary** primarily 2-year, part of Education Management Corporation
- **Coed**

Academics *Degrees:* diplomas, associate, and bachelor's.
Freshman Application Contact Brown Mackie College–Phoenix, 13430 North Black Canyon Highway, Suite 190, Phoenix, AZ 85029. *Phone:* 602-337-3044. *Toll-free phone:* 866-824-4793.
Website: http://www.brownmackie.edu/phoenix/.

Brown Mackie College–Tucson
Tucson, Arizona

- **Proprietary** primarily 2-year, founded 1972, part of Education Management Corporation
- **Suburban** campus
- **Coed**

Academics *Degrees:* diplomas, associate, and bachelor's.
Freshman Application Contact Brown Mackie College–Tucson, 4585 East Speedway, Suite 204, Tucson, AZ 85712. *Phone:* 520-319-3300.
Website: http://www.brownmackie.edu/tucson/.

Carrington College–Mesa
Mesa, Arizona

- **Proprietary** 2-year, founded 1977, part of Carrington Colleges Group, Inc.
- **Suburban** campus
- **Coed**

Undergraduates 624 full-time, 67 part-time. 1% are from out of state; 5% Black or African American, non-Hispanic/Latino; 33% Hispanic/Latino; 3% Asian, non-Hispanic/Latino; 0.7% Native Hawaiian or other Pacific Islander, non-Hispanic/Latino; 12% American Indian or Alaska Native, non-Hispanic/Latino; 0.7% Two or more races, non-Hispanic/Latino; 1% Race/ethnicity unknown; 9% transferred in.
Faculty *Student/faculty ratio:* 26:1.
Academics *Calendar:* semesters. *Degree:* certificates and associate.
Applying *Required:* essay or personal statement, high school transcript, interview.
Freshman Application Contact Carrington College–Mesa, 1001 West Southern Avenue, Suite 130, Mesa, AZ 85210.
Website: http://carrington.edu/.

Carrington College–Phoenix
Phoenix, Arizona

- **Proprietary** 2-year, founded 1976, part of Carrington Colleges Group, Inc.
- **Urban** campus
- **Coed**

Undergraduates 676 full-time. 1% are from out of state; 8% Black or African American, non-Hispanic/Latino; 54% Hispanic/Latino; 0.4% Asian, non-Hispanic/Latino; 0.6% Native Hawaiian or other Pacific Islander, non-Hispanic/Latino; 8% American Indian or Alaska Native, non-Hispanic/Latino; 1% Two or more races, non-Hispanic/Latino; 1% Race/ethnicity unknown; 8% transferred in.
Faculty *Student/faculty ratio:* 35:1.
Academics *Calendar:* continuous. *Degree:* certificates and associate.

Applying *Required:* essay or personal statement, high school transcript, interview.
Freshman Application Contact Carrington College–Phoenix, 8503 North 27th Avenue, Phoenix, AZ 85051.
Website: http://carrington.edu/.

Carrington College–Phoenix Westside
Phoenix, Arizona

- **Proprietary** 2-year, part of Carrington Colleges Group, Inc.
- **Urban** campus
- **Coed**

Undergraduates 358 full-time, 155 part-time. 2% are from out of state; 9% Black or African American, non-Hispanic/Latino; 27% Hispanic/Latino; 4% Asian, non-Hispanic/Latino; 1% Native Hawaiian or other Pacific Islander, non-Hispanic/Latino; 4% American Indian or Alaska Native, non-Hispanic/Latino; 1% Two or more races, non-Hispanic/Latino; 3% Race/ethnicity unknown; 2% transferred in.
Faculty *Student/faculty ratio:* 16:1.
Academics *Calendar:* semesters. *Degree:* certificates and associate.
Applying *Required:* essay or personal statement, high school transcript, interview.
Freshman Application Contact Carrington College–Phoenix Westside, 2701 West Bethany Home Road, Phoenix, AZ 85017.
Website: http://carrington.edu/.

Carrington College–Tucson
Tucson, Arizona

- **Proprietary** 2-year, founded 1984, part of Carrington Colleges Group, Inc.
- **Suburban** campus
- **Coed**

Undergraduates 437 full-time, 3 part-time. 0.5% are from out of state; 4% Black or African American, non-Hispanic/Latino; 61% Hispanic/Latino; 0.2% Asian, non-Hispanic/Latino; 0.5% Native Hawaiian or other Pacific Islander, non-Hispanic/Latino; 5% American Indian or Alaska Native, non-Hispanic/Latino; 1% Two or more races, non-Hispanic/Latino; 2% Race/ethnicity unknown; 8% transferred in.
Faculty *Student/faculty ratio:* 38:1.
Academics *Calendar:* semesters modular courses are offered. *Degree:* certificates and associate.
Applying *Required:* essay or personal statement, high school transcript, interview.
Freshman Application Contact Carrington College–Tucson, 201 N. Bonita Avenue, Tucson, AZ 85745.
Website: http://carrington.edu/.

Central Arizona College
Coolidge, Arizona

Freshman Application Contact Dr. James Moore, Dean of Records and Admissions, Central Arizona College, 8470 North Overfield Road, Coolidge, AZ 85128. *Phone:* 520-494-5261. *Toll-free phone:* 800-237-9814. *Fax:* 520-426-5083. *E-mail:* james.moore@centralaz.edu.
Website: http://www.centralaz.edu/.

Chandler-Gilbert Community College
Chandler, Arizona

- **State and locally supported** 2-year, founded 1985, part of Maricopa County Community College District System
- **Suburban** 188-acre campus with easy access to Phoenix
- **Coed,** 14,500 undergraduate students, 29% full-time, 53% women, 47% men

Undergraduates 4,238 full-time, 10,262 part-time. 4% Black or African American, non-Hispanic/Latino; 22% Hispanic/Latino; 6% Asian, non-Hispanic/Latino; 0.4% Native Hawaiian or other Pacific Islander, non-Hispanic/Latino; 2% American Indian or Alaska Native, non-Hispanic/Latino; 3% Two or more races, non-Hispanic/Latino; 13% Race/ethnicity unknown; 0.5% international; 2% transferred in.
Freshmen *Admission:* 1,691 enrolled.
Faculty *Total:* 617, 21% full-time. *Student/faculty ratio:* 25:1.
Majors Accounting; accounting technology and bookkeeping; airline pilot and flight crew; business administration and management; business administration, management and operations related; business/commerce; business, management, and marketing related; computer and information sciences; computer and information sciences and support services related; computer programming; computer programming (vendor/product certification); computer systems analysis; computer systems networking and telecommunications; criminal justice/safety; data entry/microcomputer applications; data modeling/warehousing and database administration; dietetic technology; dietitian assistant; dramatic/theater arts; electromechanical technology; elementary education; fine/studio arts; general studies; information technology; kinesiology and exercise science; liberal arts and sciences and humanities related; liberal arts and sciences/liberal studies; lineworker; massage therapy; mechanic and repair technologies related; music management; organizational behavior; physical sciences; psychology; registered nursing/registered nurse; social work; visual and performing arts.
Academics *Calendar:* semesters. *Degree:* certificates, diplomas, and associate. *Special study options:* academic remediation for entering students, advanced placement credit, English as a second language, freshman honors college, honors programs, independent study, part-time degree program, services for LD students, study abroad, summer session for credit.
Library Chandler-Gilbert Community College Library with an OPAC, a Web page.
Student Life *Housing:* college housing not available. *Activities and Organizations:* student-run newspaper, radio station, choral group. *Campus security:* 24-hour emergency response devices and patrols, late-night transport/escort service. *Student services:* personal/psychological counseling.
Athletics Member NJCAA. *Intercollegiate sports:* baseball M, basketball M/W, golf M/W, soccer M/W, softball W, volleyball W.
Costs (2014–15) *Tuition:* state resident $2016 full-time, $84 per credit hour part-time; nonresident $7800 full-time, $325 per credit hour part-time. Full-time tuition and fees vary according to reciprocity agreements. Part-time tuition and fees vary according to reciprocity agreements. *Required fees:* $30 full-time, $15 per term part-time. *Payment plans:* installment, deferred payment. *Waivers:* employees or children of employees.
Applying *Options:* electronic application.
Freshman Application Contact Ryan Cain, Coordinator of Enrollment Services, Chandler-Gilbert Community College, 2626 East Pecos Road, Chandler, AZ 85225-2479. *Phone:* 480-732-7044. *E-mail:* ryan.cain@cgc.edu.
Website: http://www.cgc.maricopa.edu/.

Cochise College
Douglas, Arizona

- **State and locally supported** 2-year, founded 1962, part of Cochise County Community College District
- **Rural** 607-acre campus with easy access to Tucson
- **Coed,** 4,540 undergraduate students, 39% full-time, 54% women, 46% men

Undergraduates 1,779 full-time, 2,761 part-time. Students come from 18 states and territories; 1 other country; 6% are from out of state; 6% Black or African American, non-Hispanic/Latino; 44% Hispanic/Latino; 2% Asian, non-Hispanic/Latino; 0.6% Native Hawaiian or other Pacific Islander, non-Hispanic/Latino; 0.7% American Indian or Alaska Native, non-Hispanic/Latino; 2% Two or more races, non-Hispanic/Latino; 2% Race/ethnicity unknown; 0.4% international; 18% transferred in; 2% live on campus. *Retention:* 56% of full-time freshmen returned.
Freshmen *Admission:* 1,942 applied, 1,942 admitted, 880 enrolled. *Average high school GPA:* 2.67.
Faculty *Total:* 325, 26% full-time. *Student/faculty ratio:* 16:1.
Majors Administrative assistant and secretarial science; adult and continuing education; agricultural business and management; air and space operations technology; airline pilot and flight crew; air transportation related; art; art teacher education; automobile/automotive mechanics technology; avionics maintenance technology; biology/biological sciences; building construction technology; business administration and management; chemistry; computer and information systems security; computer programming; computer science; computer systems networking and telecommunications; criminal justice/police science; culinary arts; digital communication and media/multimedia; dramatic/theater arts; early childhood education; economics; electrical, electronic and communications engineering technology; elementary education; emergency medical technology (EMT paramedic); engineering; English; equestrian studies; fire science/firefighting; general studies; health and physical education/fitness; history teacher education; humanities; information science/studies; intelligence; journalism; logistics, materials, and supply chain management; mathematics; mechatronics, robotics, and automation engineering; music; philosophy; physics; psychology; registered nursing/registered nurse; respiratory care therapy; social sciences; social work; speech communication and rhetoric; welding technology.
Academics *Calendar:* semesters. *Degrees:* certificates and associate (profile includes campuses in Douglas and Sierra Vista AZ). *Special study options:* academic remediation for entering students, adult/continuing education programs, advanced placement credit, cooperative education, distance learning, English as a second language, honors programs, independent study,

internships, part-time degree program, services for LD students, summer session for credit.

Library Charles Di Peso plus 1 other with 110,129 titles, 6,650 audiovisual materials, an OPAC, a Web page.

Student Life *Housing Options:* coed, special housing for students with disabilities. Campus housing is university owned. *Activities and Organizations:* drama/theater group, student-run newspaper, choral group, The Art Club, Phi Theta Kappa, Psi Beta, Tabletop Gaming Club, Literary Guild. *Campus security:* 24-hour emergency response devices and patrols. *Student services:* personal/psychological counseling.

Athletics Member NJCAA. *Intercollegiate sports:* baseball M(s), basketball M(s)/W(s), soccer W(s).

Costs (2015–16) *Tuition:* state resident $2310 full-time, $77 per credit hour part-time; nonresident $7500 full-time, $250 per credit hour part-time. Full-time tuition and fees vary according to course load, program, and reciprocity agreements. Part-time tuition and fees vary according to course load, program, and reciprocity agreements. *Room and board:* $6440. Room and board charges vary according to housing facility. *Payment plan:* installment. *Waivers:* senior citizens and employees or children of employees.

Financial Aid Of all full-time matriculated undergraduates who enrolled in 2013, 1,157 applied for aid, 966 were judged to have need. In 2013, 31 non-need-based awards were made. *Average financial aid package:* $5383. *Average need-based loan:* $3447. *Average need-based gift aid:* $3431. *Average non-need-based aid:* $1282. *Financial aid deadline:* 6/15.

Applying *Options:* electronic application, deferred entrance. *Recommended:* high school transcript. *Application deadlines:* rolling (freshmen), rolling (out-of-state freshmen), rolling (transfers). *Notification:* continuous (freshmen), continuous (out-of-state freshmen), continuous (transfers).

Freshman Application Contact Ms. Debbie Quick, Director of Admissions and Records, Cochise College, 4190 West Highway 80, Douglas, AZ 85607-6190. *Phone:* 520-515-3640. *Toll-free phone:* 800-593-9567. *Fax:* 520-515-5452. *E-mail:* quickd@cochise.edu.
Website: http://www.cochise.edu/.

Coconino Community College
Flagstaff, Arizona

- **State-supported** 2-year, founded 1991
- **Small-town** 5-acre campus
- **Endowment** $322,526
- **Coed**

Undergraduates 1,009 full-time, 2,689 part-time. Students come from 10 states and territories; 1% are from out of state; 1% Black or African American, non-Hispanic/Latino; 14% Hispanic/Latino; 1% Asian, non-Hispanic/Latino; 0.4% Native Hawaiian or other Pacific Islander, non-Hispanic/Latino; 21% American Indian or Alaska Native, non-Hispanic/Latino; 4% Two or more races, non-Hispanic/Latino; 2% Race/ethnicity unknown.

Faculty *Student/faculty ratio:* 18:1.

Academics *Calendar:* semesters. *Degree:* certificates and associate. *Special study options:* academic remediation for entering students, adult/continuing education programs, distance learning, honors programs, independent study, internships, part-time degree program, study abroad, summer session for credit. *ROTC:* Army (b), Air Force (b).

Student Life *Campus security:* 24-hour emergency response devices, student patrols, late-night transport/escort service, security patrols while campuses are open; electronic access throughout the campuses with security cards.

Costs (2014–15) *Tuition:* state resident $2256 full-time, $89 per credit hour part-time; nonresident $7596 full-time, $312 per credit hour part-time. Full-time tuition and fees vary according to program. Part-time tuition and fees vary according to program. *Required fees:* $150 full-time.

Financial Aid Of all full-time matriculated undergraduates who enrolled in 2013, 25 Federal Work-Study jobs (averaging $4000).

Applying *Options:* electronic application.

Freshman Application Contact Veronica Hipolito, Director of Student Services, Coconino Community College, 2800 South Lone Tree Road, Flagstaff, AZ 86001. *Phone:* 928-226-4334 Ext. 4334. *Toll-free phone:* 800-350-7122. *Fax:* 928-226-4114. *E-mail:* veronica.hipolito@coconino.edu.
Website: http://www.coconino.edu/.

CollegeAmerica–Flagstaff
Flagstaff, Arizona

- **Private** primarily 2-year
- **Small-town** campus
- **Coed**, 205 undergraduate students, 100% full-time, 75% women, 25% men

Undergraduates 205 full-time. 1% Black or African American, non-Hispanic/Latino; 11% Hispanic/Latino; 60% American Indian or Alaska Native, non-Hispanic/Latino; 0.5% Two or more races, non-Hispanic/Latino.

Freshmen *Admission:* 121 enrolled.

Faculty *Total:* 14, 64% full-time. *Student/faculty ratio:* 15:1.

Majors Business administration and management; computer science; computer systems networking and telecommunications; health/health-care administration; medical/health management and clinical assistant.

Academics *Calendar:* quarters modules. *Degrees:* associate and bachelor's. *Special study options:* academic remediation for entering students, internships.

Library Main Library plus 1 other.

Student Life *Housing:* college housing not available.

Costs (2014–15) *Tuition:* $42,411 per degree program part-time. Full-time tuition and fees vary according to course load, degree level, program, and reciprocity agreements. No tuition increase for student's term of enrollment. Tuition cost varies by program. Prospective students should contact the school for current tuition costs. *Payment plan:* installment. *Waivers:* minority students, adult students, and employees or children of employees.

Applying *Required:* essay or personal statement, high school transcript, interview, references.

Freshman Application Contact CollegeAmerica–Flagstaff, 399 South Malpais, Flagstaff, AZ 86001. *Phone:* 928-213-6060 Ext. 1402. *Toll-free phone:* 800-622-2894.
Website: http://www.collegeamerica.edu/.

Diné College
Tsaile, Arizona

Freshman Application Contact Mrs. Louise Litzin, Registrar, Diné College, PO Box 67, Tsaile, AZ 86556. *Phone:* 928-724-6633. *Toll-free phone:* 877-988-DINE. *Fax:* 928-724-3349. *E-mail:* louise@dinecollege.edu.
Website: http://www.dinecollege.edu/.

Eastern Arizona College
Thatcher, Arizona

- **State and locally supported** 2-year, founded 1888, part of Arizona State Community College System
- **Small-town** campus
- **Endowment** $3.6 million
- **Coed**, 6,379 undergraduate students, 28% full-time, 54% women, 46% men

Undergraduates 1,783 full-time, 4,596 part-time. Students come from 19 other countries; 4% are from out of state; 3% Black or African American, non-Hispanic/Latino; 20% Hispanic/Latino; 1% Asian, non-Hispanic/Latino; 0.4% Native Hawaiian or other Pacific Islander, non-Hispanic/Latino; 7% American Indian or Alaska Native, non-Hispanic/Latino; 0.9% Two or more races, non-Hispanic/Latino; 3% Race/ethnicity unknown; 0.8% international; 37% transferred in; 5% live on campus.

Freshmen *Admission:* 623 applied, 623 admitted, 1,224 enrolled.

Faculty *Total:* 361, 26% full-time, 8% with terminal degrees. *Student/faculty ratio:* 18:1.

Majors Anthropology; art; art teacher education; automobile/automotive mechanics technology; biology/biological sciences; business administration and management; business, management, and marketing related; business operations support and secretarial services related; business teacher education; chemistry; civil engineering technology; commercial and advertising art; cosmetology; criminal justice/law enforcement administration; criminal justice/police science; diesel mechanics technology; drafting and design technology; dramatic/theater arts; early childhood education; elementary education; emergency medical technology (EMT paramedic); English; entrepreneurship; environmental biology; fire science/firefighting; foreign languages and literatures; forestry; geology/earth science; health and physical education/fitness; health/medical preparatory programs related; history; industrial electronics technology; industrial mechanics and maintenance technology; information science/studies; liberal arts and sciences/liberal studies; machine shop technology; mathematics; mining technology; multi/interdisciplinary studies related; music; pharmacy technician; physics; political science and government; premedical studies; pre-pharmacy studies; psychology; registered nursing/registered nurse; secondary education; sociology; technology/industrial arts teacher education; welding technology; wildlife biology.

Academics *Calendar:* semesters. *Degree:* certificates and associate. *Special study options:* academic remediation for entering students, adult/continuing education programs, advanced placement credit, cooperative education, distance learning, double majors, independent study, internships, part-time degree program, services for LD students, study abroad, summer session for credit.

Library Alumni Library with an OPAC, a Web page.

Student Life *Housing Options:* men-only, women-only. Campus housing is university owned. *Activities and Organizations:* drama/theater group, choral group, marching band, Latter-Day Saints Student Association, Criminal Justice

Student Association, Multicultural Council, Phi Theta Kappa, Mark Allen Dorm Club. *Campus security:* 24-hour emergency response devices, late-night transport/escort service, controlled dormitory access, 20-hour patrols by trained security personnel. *Student services:* personal/psychological counseling.

Athletics Member NJCAA. *Intercollegiate sports:* baseball M(s), basketball M(s)/W(s), football M(s), golf M/W, softball W(s), volleyball W(s). *Intramural sports:* basketball M/W, racquetball M/W, swimming and diving M/W, table tennis M/W, tennis M/W, volleyball M/W.

Costs (2014–15) *One-time required fee:* $150. *Tuition:* state resident $2000 full-time, $95 per credit part-time; nonresident $9200 full-time, $215 per credit part-time. Full-time tuition and fees vary according to program. Part-time tuition and fees vary according to program. *Room and board:* $6610. Room and board charges vary according to board plan. *Waivers:* senior citizens and employees or children of employees.

Financial Aid Of all full-time matriculated undergraduates who enrolled in 2013, 2,329 applied for aid, 2,104 were judged to have need, 44 had their need fully met. In 2013, 89 non-need-based awards were made. *Average percent of need met:* 18%. *Average financial aid package:* $4984. *Average need-based gift aid:* $4809. *Average non-need-based aid:* $3962.

Applying *Options:* electronic application, early admission, deferred entrance. *Recommended:* high school transcript. *Application deadlines:* rolling (freshmen), rolling (transfers). *Notification:* continuous (freshmen). **Freshman Application Contact** Suzette Udall, Records Assistant, Eastern Arizona College, 615 North Stadium Avenue, Thatcher, AZ 85552-0769. *Phone:* 928-428-8904. *Toll-free phone:* 800-678-3808. *Fax:* 928-428-3729. *E-mail:* admissions@eac.edu.
Website: http://www.eac.edu/.

Estrella Mountain Community College
Avondale, Arizona

Freshman Application Contact Estrella Mountain Community College, 3000 North Dysart Road, Avondale, AZ 85392. *Phone:* 623-935-8812.
Website: http://www.emc.maricopa.edu/.

Fortis College
Phoenix, Arizona

Admissions Office Contact Fortis College, 555 North 18 Street, Suite 110, Phoenix, AZ 85006.
Website: http://www.fortis.edu/.

GateWay Community College
Phoenix, Arizona

Freshman Application Contact Director of Admissions and Records, GateWay Community College, 108 North 40th Street, Phoenix, AZ 85034. *Phone:* 602-286-8200. *Fax:* 602-286-8200. *E-mail:* enroll@gatewaycc.edu.
Website: http://www.gatewaycc.edu/.

Glendale Community College
Glendale, Arizona

- **State and locally supported** 2-year, founded 1965, part of Maricopa County Community College District System
- **Suburban** 222-acre campus with easy access to Phoenix
- **Coed**

Undergraduates 7,335 full-time, 14,026 part-time. *Retention:* 58% of full-time freshmen returned.

Academics *Calendar:* semesters. *Degree:* certificates and associate. *Special study options:* academic remediation for entering students, adult/continuing education programs, advanced placement credit, cooperative education, distance learning, double majors, English as a second language, freshman honors college, honors programs, internships, off-campus study, part-time degree program, services for LD students, study abroad, summer session for credit. *ROTC:* Army (c), Air Force (c).

Student Life *Campus security:* 24-hour patrols, student patrols, late-night transport/escort service.

Athletics Member NJCAA.

Costs (2014–15) *Tuition:* state resident $1944 full-time; nonresident $7608 full-time. Full-time tuition and fees vary according to course load, program, and reciprocity agreements. Part-time tuition and fees vary according to course load, program, and reciprocity agreements. *Required fees:* $30 full-time.

Financial Aid Of all full-time matriculated undergraduates who enrolled in 2012, 150 Federal Work-Study jobs (averaging $2300).

Applying *Options:* electronic application. *Required for some:* high school transcript.
Freshman Application Contact Ms. Mary Blackwell, Dean of Enrollment Services, Glendale Community College, 6000 West Olive Avenue, Glendale, AZ 85302. *Phone:* 623-435-3305. *Fax:* 623-845-3303. *E-mail:* admissions.recruitment@gccaz.edu.
Website: http://www.gc.maricopa.edu/.

Golf Academy of America
Chandler, Arizona

Admissions Office Contact Golf Academy of America, 2031 N. Arizona Avenue, Suite 2, Chandler, AZ 85225.
Website: http://www.golfacademy.edu/.

ITT Technical Institute
Phoenix, Arizona

- **Proprietary** primarily 2-year, founded 1972, part of ITT Educational Services, Inc.
- **Urban** campus
- **Coed**

Academics *Calendar:* quarters. *Degrees:* associate and bachelor's.
Financial Aid Of all full-time matriculated undergraduates who enrolled in 2013, 10 Federal Work-Study jobs (averaging $4000).
Freshman Application Contact Director of Recruitment, ITT Technical Institute, 10220 North 25th Avenue, Suite 100, Phoenix, AZ 85021. *Phone:* 602-749-7900. *Toll-free phone:* 877-221-1132.
Website: http://www.itt-tech.edu/.

ITT Technical Institute
Phoenix, Arizona

- **Proprietary** primarily 2-year, part of ITT Educational Services, Inc.
- **Coed**

Academics *Calendar:* quarters. *Degrees:* associate and bachelor's.
Freshman Application Contact Director of Recruitment, ITT Technical Institute, 1840 N. 95th Avenue, Suite 132, Phoenix, AZ 85037. *Phone:* 623-474-7900. *Toll-free phone:* 800-210-1178.
Website: http://www.itt-tech.edu/.

ITT Technical Institute
Tucson, Arizona

- **Proprietary** primarily 2-year, founded 1984, part of ITT Educational Services, Inc.
- **Urban** campus
- **Coed**

Academics *Calendar:* quarters. *Degrees:* associate and bachelor's.
Freshman Application Contact Director of Recruitment, ITT Technical Institute, 1455 West River Road, Tucson, AZ 85704. *Phone:* 520-408-7488. *Toll-free phone:* 800-870-9730.
Website: http://www.itt-tech.edu/.

Le Cordon Bleu College of Culinary Arts in Scottsdale
Scottsdale, Arizona

Director of Admissions Le Cordon Bleu College of Culinary Arts in Scottsdale, 8100 East Camelback Road, Suite 1001, Scottsdale, AZ 85251-3940. *Toll-free phone:* 888-557-4222.
Website: http://www.chefs.edu/Scottsdale/.

Mesa Community College
Mesa, Arizona

- **State and locally supported** 2-year, founded 1965, part of Maricopa County Community College District System
- **Urban** 160-acre campus with easy access to Phoenix
- **Coed**, 22,000 undergraduate students

Majors Accounting; administrative assistant and secretarial science; agricultural business and management; agricultural mechanization; agronomy and crop science; art; automobile/automotive mechanics technology; biology/biological sciences; business administration and management; child development; criminal justice/law enforcement administration; data processing and data processing technology; drafting and design technology; electrical, electronic and communications engineering technology; engineering technology; family and consumer sciences/human sciences; fashion merchandising; finance; fire science/firefighting; heavy equipment maintenance technology; horticultural science; industrial technology; insurance; interior design; liberal arts and sciences/liberal studies; library and information science; marketing/marketing management; mathematics; medical administrative assistant and medical secretary; music; ornamental horticulture; pre-engineering; quality control technology; real estate; registered nursing/registered nurse; teacher assistant/aide.

Academics *Calendar:* semesters. *Degree:* certificates and associate. *Special study options:* academic remediation for entering students, adult/continuing education programs, advanced placement credit, cooperative education, distance learning, English as a second language, freshman honors college, honors programs, independent study, off-campus study, part-time degree program, services for LD students, student-designed majors, study abroad, summer session for credit. *ROTC:* Army (c), Air Force (c).

Library Information Commons with an OPAC, a Web page.

Student Life *Housing:* college housing not available. *Activities and Organizations:* drama/theater group, student-run newspaper, choral group, MECHA, International Student Association, American Indian Association, Asian/Pacific Islander Club. *Campus security:* 24-hour emergency response devices and patrols, student patrols. *Student services:* personal/psychological counseling, legal services.

Athletics Member NJCAA. *Intercollegiate sports:* baseball M, basketball M/W, cross-country running M, football M, golf M/W, soccer M/W, softball W, tennis M/W, track and field M/W, volleyball W, wrestling M. *Intramural sports:* basketball M/W, cross-country running M, football M/W, tennis M/W, track and field M/W, volleyball M/W, wrestling M/W.

Costs (2015–16) *Tuition:* state resident $2016 full-time; nonresident $7800 full-time. Full-time tuition and fees vary according to course load and reciprocity agreements. Part-time tuition and fees vary according to course load and reciprocity agreements. *Required fees:* $30 full-time. *Payment plan:* installment. *Waivers:* employees or children of employees.

Applying *Options:* electronic application, early admission, deferred entrance. *Application deadlines:* 8/18 (freshmen), 8/18 (transfers). *Notification:* continuous (freshmen).

Freshman Application Contact Dr. Barbara Boros, Dean, Enrollment Services, Mesa Community College, 1833 West Southern Avenue, Mesa, AZ 85202-4866. *Phone:* 480-461-7342. *Toll-free phone:* 866-532-4983. *Fax:* 480-844-3117. *E-mail:* admissionsandrecords@mesacc.edu. *Website:* http://www.mesacc.edu/.

Mohave Community College
Kingman, Arizona

- **State-supported** 2-year, founded 1971
- **Small-town** 160-acre campus
- **Coed,** 4,744 undergraduate students, 23% full-time, 64% women, 36% men

Undergraduates 1,082 full-time, 3,662 part-time. Students come from 19 states and territories; 5% are from out of state; 1% Black or African American, non-Hispanic/Latino; 20% Hispanic/Latino; 2% Asian, non-Hispanic/Latino; 0.5% Native Hawaiian or other Pacific Islander, non-Hispanic/Latino; 2% American Indian or Alaska Native, non-Hispanic/Latino; 2% Two or more races, non-Hispanic/Latino; 2% Race/ethnicity unknown.

Freshmen *Admission:* 804 enrolled.

Faculty *Total:* 344, 23% full-time. *Student/faculty ratio:* 14:1.

Majors Accounting; art; automobile/automotive mechanics technology; building/construction finishing, management, and inspection related; business administration and management; computer and information sciences related; computer programming (specific applications); computer science; criminal justice/police science; culinary arts; dental assisting; dental hygiene; drafting and design technology; education; emergency medical technology (EMT paramedic); English; fire science/firefighting; heating, air conditioning, ventilation and refrigeration maintenance technology; history; information technology; legal assistant/paralegal; liberal arts and sciences/liberal studies; mathematics; medical/clinical assistant; personal and culinary services related; pharmacy technician; physical therapy technology; psychology; registered nursing/registered nurse; sociology; substance abuse/addiction counseling; surgical technology; truck and bus driver/commercial vehicle operation/instruction; welding technology.

Academics *Calendar:* semesters. *Degree:* certificates and associate. *Special study options:* academic remediation for entering students, adult/continuing education programs, cooperative education, distance learning, English as a second language, independent study, part-time degree program, summer session for credit.

Library Mohave Community College Library with 45,849 titles, an OPAC, a Web page.

Student Life *Housing:* college housing not available. *Activities and Organizations:* Art Club, Phi Theta Kappa, Computer Club (MC4), Science Club, student government. *Campus security:* late-night transport/escort service.

Costs (2014–15) *Tuition:* state resident $2400 full-time, $80 per credit hour part-time; nonresident $8400 full-time, $280 per credit hour part-time. Full-time tuition and fees vary according to program. Part-time tuition and fees vary according to program. *Required fees:* $210 full-time, $7 per credit hour part-time. *Payment plans:* installment, deferred payment. *Waivers:* employees or children of employees.

Applying *Options:* electronic application, early admission, deferred entrance. *Application deadlines:* rolling (freshmen), rolling (transfers). *Notification:* continuous (freshmen), continuous (transfers).

Freshman Application Contact Ms. Ana Masterson, Dean of Student Services, Mohave Community College, 1971 Jagerson Ave, Kingman, AZ 86409. *Phone:* 928-757-0803. *Toll-free phone:* 888-664-2832. *Fax:* 928-757-0808. *E-mail:* amasterson@mohave.edu. *Website:* http://www.mohave.edu/.

Northland Pioneer College
Holbrook, Arizona

Freshman Application Contact Ms. Suzette Willis, Coordinator of Admissions, Northland Pioneer College, PO Box 610, Holbrook, AZ 86025. *Phone:* 928-536-6271. *Toll-free phone:* 800-266-7845. *Fax:* 928-536-6212. *Website:* http://www.npc.edu/.

Paradise Valley Community College
Phoenix, Arizona

Freshman Application Contact Paradise Valley Community College, 18401 North 32nd Street, Phoenix, AZ 85032-1200. *Phone:* 602-787-7020. *Website:* http://www.pvc.maricopa.edu/.

The Paralegal Institute, Inc.
Scottsdale, Arizona

Freshman Application Contact Patricia Yancy, Director of Admissions, The Paralegal Institute, Inc., 2933 West Indian School Road, Drawer 11408, Phoenix, AZ 85061-1408. *Phone:* 602-212-0501. *Toll-free phone:* 800-354-1254. *Fax:* 602-212-0502. *E-mail:* paralegalinst@mindspring.com. *Website:* http://www.theparalegalinstitute.edu/.

Penn Foster College
Scottsdale, Arizona

- **Proprietary** primarily 2-year
- **Coed,** 28,900 undergraduate students, 60% women, 40% men

Undergraduates 28,900 part-time. Students come from 50 states and territories; 5 other countries.

Faculty *Total:* 164, 26% full-time, 7% with terminal degrees.

Majors Accounting; building construction technology; business administration and management; computer and information sciences; computer installation and repair technology; criminal justice/law enforcement administration; early childhood education; engineering technology; fashion merchandising; finance; graphic design; health/health-care administration; health information/medical records technology; hospitality administration; human resources management; industrial electronics technology; legal assistant/paralegal; marketing/marketing management; marketing research; medical/clinical assistant; retail management; roofing; veterinary/animal health technology.

Academics *Degrees:* certificates, associate, and bachelor's. *Special study options:* academic remediation for entering students, accelerated degree program, cooperative education, distance learning, external degree program, independent study, internships, off-campus study, part-time degree program, services for LD students.

Library Penn Foster College Online Library.

Student Life *Housing:* college housing not available. *Activities and Organizations:* Online Community hosts academic interest groups, clubs, etc. that are open to students around the world.

Costs (2015–16) *Tuition:* $79 per credit part-time. Part-time tuition and fees vary according to course load and program. *Payment plan:* installment.

Applying *Options:* electronic application. *Application fee:* $75. *Required:* high school transcript. *Application deadlines:* rolling (freshmen), rolling (out-of-state freshmen).

Freshman Application Contact Admissions, Penn Foster College, 14300 North Northsight Boulevard, Suite 120, Scottsdale, AZ 85260. *Phone:* 480-315-4950. *Toll-free phone:* 800-471-3232. *Website:* http://www.pennfostercollege.edu/.

Phoenix College
Phoenix, Arizona

- **County-supported** 2-year, founded 1920, part of Maricopa County Community College District System
- **Urban** 58-acre campus
- **Coed,** 12,676 undergraduate students, 27% full-time, 61% women, 39% men

Undergraduates 3,421 full-time, 9,255 part-time. 11% Black or African American, non-Hispanic/Latino; 41% Hispanic/Latino; 3% Asian, non-Hispanic/Latino; 0.2% Native Hawaiian or other Pacific Islander, non-Hispanic/Latino; 3% American Indian or Alaska Native, non-Hispanic/Latino; 0.1% Two or more races, non-Hispanic/Latino; 0.1% Race/ethnicity unknown; 0.5% international. *Retention:* 60% of full-time freshmen returned.
Faculty *Total:* 766, 21% full-time. *Student/faculty ratio:* 17:1.
Majors Accounting; administrative assistant and secretarial science; architectural drafting and CAD/CADD; art; banking and financial support services; building/home/construction inspection; business administration and management; business/commerce; child-care and support services management; civil engineering technology; clinical/medical laboratory technology; commercial and advertising art; commercial photography; computer and information sciences; computer graphics; computer systems analysis; construction management; criminal justice/safety; culinary arts; dental assisting; dental hygiene; dramatic/theater arts; elementary education; emergency medical technology (EMT paramedic); family and community services; family and consumer sciences/human sciences; fashion/apparel design; fashion merchandising; fine/studio arts; fire science/firefighting; food service systems administration; forensic science and technology; general studies; graphic design; health information/medical records technology; histologic technology/histotechnologist; human services; interior design; legal assistant/paralegal; liberal arts and sciences/liberal studies; marketing/marketing management; massage therapy; medical/clinical assistant; medical office assistant; music management; natural sciences; organizational behavior; parks, recreation and leisure; physical sciences; recording arts technology; registered nursing/registered nurse; sign language interpretation and translation; surveying technology; teacher assistant/aide; visual and performing arts; web page, digital/multimedia and information resources design.
Academics *Calendar:* semesters. *Degree:* certificates, diplomas, and associate. *Special study options:* academic remediation for entering students, adult/continuing education programs, advanced placement credit, cooperative education, distance learning, English as a second language, freshman honors college, honors programs, independent study, internships, off-campus study, part-time degree program, services for LD students, study abroad, summer session for credit. *ROTC:* Army (c), Navy (c), Air Force (c).
Library Fannin Library with 225,767 titles, 8,436 audiovisual materials, an OPAC, a Web page.
Student Life *Housing:* college housing not available. *Activities and Organizations:* drama/theater group, choral group, Student Leadership Council (SLC), MEChA Movimiento Estudiantil Chicanos de Aztlan, ALE Asociacion Latina Estudiantil, Rainbow Spectrum - Gay, Straight, Whatever alliance, International Club. *Campus security:* 24-hour emergency response devices and patrols, student patrols, late-night transport/escort service. *Student services:* personal/psychological counseling.
Athletics Member NCAA, NJCAA. All NCAA Division II. *Intercollegiate sports:* baseball M(s), basketball M(s)/W(s), football M(s), soccer M(s)/W(s), softball W(s), volleyball W(s).
Costs (2014–15) *Tuition:* area resident $2016 full-time, $84 per credit hour part-time; state resident $8616 full-time, $359 per credit hour part-time; nonresident $8616 full-time, $359 per credit hour part-time. Full-time tuition and fees vary according to reciprocity agreements. Part-time tuition and fees vary according to course load and reciprocity agreements. *Required fees:* $30 full-time, $15 per term part-time. *Payment plan:* installment. *Waivers:* employees or children of employees.
Financial Aid Of all full-time matriculated undergraduates who enrolled in 2013, 220 Federal Work-Study jobs (averaging $4800).
Applying *Options:* electronic application, early admission, deferred entrance. *Application deadlines:* rolling (freshmen), rolling (out-of-state freshmen), rolling (transfers). *Notification:* continuous (freshmen), continuous (out-of-state freshmen), continuous (transfers).
Freshman Application Contact Ms. Brenda Stark, Director of Admissions, Registration, and Records, Phoenix College, 1202 West Thomas Road, Phoenix, AZ 85013. *Phone:* 602-285-7503. *Fax:* 602-285-7813. *E-mail:* kathy.french@pcmail.maricopa.edu.
Website: http://www.pc.maricopa.edu/.

Pima Community College
Tucson, Arizona

- **State and locally supported** 2-year, founded 1966
- **Urban** 486-acre campus with easy access to Tucson
- **Coed**

Undergraduates 5% Black or African American, non-Hispanic/Latino; 41% Hispanic/Latino; 3% Asian, non-Hispanic/Latino; 0.3% Native Hawaiian or other Pacific Islander, non-Hispanic/Latino; 2% American Indian or Alaska Native, non-Hispanic/Latino; 3% Two or more races, non-Hispanic/Latino.
Academics *Calendar:* semesters. *Degrees:* certificates, diplomas, associate, and postbachelor's certificates. *Special study options:* academic remediation for entering students, adult/continuing education programs, advanced placement credit, cooperative education, distance learning, English as a second language, honors programs, independent study, internships, off-campus study, part-time degree program, services for LD students, student-designed majors, summer session for credit. *ROTC:* Army (c), Navy (c), Air Force (c).
Athletics Member NJCAA.
Applying *Options:* electronic application.
Freshman Application Contact Terra Benson, Director of Admissions and Registrar, Pima Community College, 4905B East Broadway Boulevard, Tucson, AZ 85709-1120. *Phone:* 520-206-4640. *Fax:* 520-206-4790. *E-mail:* tbenson@pima.edu.
Website: http://www.pima.edu/.

Pima Medical Institute
Mesa, Arizona

Freshman Application Contact Pima Medical Institute, 2160 S. Power Road, Mesa, AZ 85209. *Phone:* 480-898-9898.
Website: http://www.pmi.edu/.

Pima Medical Institute
Mesa, Arizona

Freshman Application Contact Admissions Office, Pima Medical Institute, 957 South Dobson Road, Mesa, AZ 85202. *Phone:* 480-644-0267 Ext. 225. *Toll-free phone:* 800-477-PIMA (in-state); 888-477-PIMA (out-of-state).
Website: http://www.pmi.edu/.

Pima Medical Institute
Tucson, Arizona

Freshman Application Contact Admissions Office, Pima Medical Institute, 3350 East Grant Road, Tucson, AZ 85716. *Phone:* 520-326-1600 Ext. 5112. *Toll-free phone:* 800-477-PIMA (in-state); 888-477-PIMA (out-of-state).
Website: http://www.pmi.edu/.

The Refrigeration School
Phoenix, Arizona

Freshman Application Contact Ms. Heather Haskell, The Refrigeration School, 4210 East Washington Street. *Phone:* 602-275-7133. *Toll-free phone:* 888-943-4822. *Fax:* 602-267-4811. *E-mail:* heather@rsiaz.edu.
Website: http://www.refrigerationschool.com/.

Rio Salado College
Tempe, Arizona

Freshman Application Contact Laurel Redman, Director, Instruction Support Services and Student Development, Rio Salado College, 2323 West 14th Street, Tempe 85281. *Phone:* 480-517-8563. *Toll-free phone:* 800-729-1197. *Fax:* 480-517-8199. *E-mail:* admission@riomail.maricopa.edu.
Website: http://www.rio.maricopa.edu/.

Scottsdale Community College
Scottsdale, Arizona

- **State and locally supported** 2-year, founded 1969, part of Maricopa County Community College District System
- **Urban** 160-acre campus with easy access to Phoenix
- **Coed,** 9,863 undergraduate students, 30% full-time, 53% women, 47% men

Undergraduates 2,985 full-time, 6,878 part-time. Students come from 36 states and territories; 36 other countries; 4% are from out of state; 5% Black or African American, non-Hispanic/Latino; 15% Hispanic/Latino; 3% Asian, non-Hispanic/Latino; 0.3% Native Hawaiian or other Pacific Islander, non-

Hispanic/Latino; 5% American Indian or Alaska Native, non-Hispanic/Latino; 2% Two or more races, non-Hispanic/Latino; 8% Race/ethnicity unknown; 1% international; 10% transferred in.

Faculty *Total:* 570, 30% full-time, 15% with terminal degrees. *Student/faculty ratio:* 17:1.

Majors Accounting; administrative assistant and secretarial science; business administration and management; criminal justice/law enforcement administration; culinary arts; dramatic/theater arts; electrical, electronic and communications engineering technology; environmental design/architecture; equestrian studies; fashion merchandising; finance; hospitality administration; hotel/motel administration; information science/studies; interior design; mathematics; medical administrative assistant and medical secretary; photography; public administration; real estate; registered nursing/registered nurse; special products marketing.

Academics *Calendar:* semesters. *Degree:* certificates, diplomas, and associate. *Special study options:* academic remediation for entering students, adult/continuing education programs, advanced placement credit, cooperative education, English as a second language, honors programs, internships, off-campus study, part-time degree program, services for LD students, study abroad, summer session for credit.

Library Scottsdale Community College Library with an OPAC, a Web page.

Student Life *Housing:* college housing not available. *Activities and Organizations:* drama/theater group, student-run newspaper, radio station, choral group, Student Leadership Forum, International Community Club, Phi Theta Kappa, Music Industry Club, SCC ASID-Interior Design group. *Campus security:* 24-hour emergency response devices and patrols, student patrols, late-night transport/escort service, 24-hour automatic surveillance cameras. *Student services:* personal/psychological counseling.

Athletics Member NCAA, NJCAA. All NCAA Division II. *Intercollegiate sports:* baseball M, basketball M/W, cross-country running M/W, football M, golf M/W, soccer M/W, softball W, volleyball W. *Intramural sports:* archery M/W, badminton M/W, basketball M/W, racquetball M/W, track and field M/W, volleyball M/W.

Costs (2015–16) *Tuition:* state resident $2520 full-time, $84 per credit part-time; nonresident $9750 full-time, $325 per credit part-time. Full-time tuition and fees vary according to program and reciprocity agreements. Part-time tuition and fees vary according to program and reciprocity agreements. *Required fees:* $30 full-time, $15 per term part-time. *Payment plan:* deferred payment. *Waivers:* employees or children of employees.

Financial Aid Of all full-time matriculated undergraduates who enrolled in 2013, 75 Federal Work-Study jobs (averaging $2000). *Financial aid deadline:* 7/15.

Applying *Options:* electronic application, early admission. *Application deadline:* rolling (freshmen). *Notification:* continuous (freshmen).

Freshman Application Contact Ms. Fran Vitale, Director of Admissions and Records, Scottsdale Community College, 9000 East Chaparral Road, Scottsdale, AZ 85256. *Phone:* 480-423-6133. *Fax:* 480-423-6200. *E-mail:* fran.Vitale@scottsdalecc.edu.
Website: http://www.scottsdalecc.edu/.

Sessions College for Professional Design
Tempe, Arizona

- **Proprietary** 2-year
- **Coed**

Academics *Degree:* certificates and associate. *Special study options:* adult/continuing education programs, part-time degree program.

Costs (2014–15) *Tuition:* $11,700 full-time, $350 per credit part-time. Full-time tuition and fees vary according to course load. Part-time tuition and fees vary according to course load. No tuition increase for student's term of enrollment. *Required fees:* $200 full-time.

Applying *Options:* early admission. *Application fee:* $50. *Required:* essay or personal statement, high school transcript, portfolio.

Freshman Application Contact Mhelanie Hernandez, Director of Admissions, Sessions College for Professional Design, 350 South Mill Avenue, Suite B-104, Tempe, AZ 85281. *Phone:* 480-212-1704. *Toll-free phone:* 800-258-4115. *E-mail:* admissions@sessions.edu.
Website: http://www.sessions.edu/.

South Mountain Community College
Phoenix, Arizona

Director of Admissions Dean of Enrollment Services, South Mountain Community College, 7050 South Twenty-fourth Street, Phoenix, AZ 85040. *Phone:* 602-243-8120.
Website: http://www.southmountaincc.edu/.

Southwest Institute of Healing Arts
Tempe, Arizona

Director of Admissions Katie Yearous, Student Advisor, Southwest Institute of Healing Arts, 1100 East Apache Boulevard, Tempe, AZ 85281. *Phone:* 480-994-9244. *Toll-free phone:* 888-504-9106. *E-mail:* joannl@swiha.net.
Website: http://www.swiha.org/.

Tohono O'odham Community College
Sells, Arizona

- **Public** 2-year, founded 1998
- **Rural** 42-acre campus
- **Endowment** $138,720
- **Coed,** 269 undergraduate students, 9% full-time, 60% women, 40% men

Undergraduates 25 full-time, 244 part-time. Students come from 7 states and territories; 2% are from out of state; 1% Black or African American, non-Hispanic/Latino; 0.7% Hispanic/Latino; 0.4% Native Hawaiian or other Pacific Islander, non-Hispanic/Latino; 94% American Indian or Alaska Native, non-Hispanic/Latino; 0.7% Two or more races, non-Hispanic/Latino; 10% live on campus. *Retention:* 43% of full-time freshmen returned.

Freshmen *Admission:* 15 enrolled.

Faculty *Total:* 33, 52% full-time. *Student/faculty ratio:* 8:1.

Majors Business administration and management; child development; computer systems analysis; early childhood education; human services; liberal arts and sciences/liberal studies.

Academics *Calendar:* semesters. *Degree:* certificates, diplomas, and associate. *Special study options:* academic remediation for entering students, adult/continuing education programs, cooperative education, distance learning, double majors, part-time degree program, services for LD students, summer session for credit.

Library Tohono O'odham Community College Library plus 2 others with 7,886 titles, 1,398 audiovisual materials, an OPAC, a Web page.

Student Life *Housing:* college housing not available. *Options:* men-only, women-only. Campus housing is university owned. *Activities and Organizations:* Student Senate, AISIS, Archery Club, Chess Club. *Student services:* personal/psychological counseling.

Athletics *Intercollegiate sports:* basketball M(s)/W(s).

Costs (2014–15) *Tuition:* state resident $1656 full-time, $69 per credit hour part-time; nonresident $3696 full-time, $154 per credit hour part-time. *Required fees:* $20 full-time, $10 per course part-time. *Payment plan:* installment. *Waivers:* employees or children of employees.

Applying *Application fee:* $25. *Required:* high school transcript. *Recommended:* interview. *Application deadlines:* rolling (freshmen), rolling (transfers). *Notification:* continuous (freshmen), continuous (transfers).

Freshman Application Contact Jennifer Hill, Admissions, Tohono O'odham Community College, TOCC, P.O. Box 3129, Sells, AZ 85634. *Phone:* 520-383-8401. *E-mail:* jhill@tocc.edu.
Website: http://www.tocc.edu/.

Universal Technical Institute
Avondale, Arizona

Freshman Application Contact Director of Admission, Universal Technical Institute, 10695 West Pierce Street, Avondale, AZ 85323. *Phone:* 623-245-4600. *Toll-free phone:* 800-510-5072. *Fax:* 623-245-4601.
Website: http://www.uti.edu/.

Yavapai College
Prescott, Arizona

Freshman Application Contact Mrs. Sheila Jarrell, Admissions, Registration, and Records Manager, Yavapai College, 1100 East Sheldon Street, Prescott, AZ 86301-3297. *Phone:* 928-776-2107. *Toll-free phone:* 800-922-6787. *Fax:* 928-776-2151. *E-mail:* registration@yc.edu.
Website: http://www.yc.edu/.

ARKANSAS

Arkansas Northeastern College
Blytheville, Arkansas

- **State-supported** 2-year, founded 1975
- **Small-town** 80-acre campus with easy access to Memphis
- **Endowment** $187,500
- **Coed,** 1,425 undergraduate students, 38% full-time, 66% women, 34% men

Undergraduates 538 full-time, 887 part-time. Students come from 4 states and territories; 17% are from out of state; 30% Black or African American, non-Hispanic/Latino; 4% Hispanic/Latino; 0.6% Asian, non-Hispanic/Latino; 0.1% Native Hawaiian or other Pacific Islander, non-Hispanic/Latino; 0.4% American Indian or Alaska Native, non-Hispanic/Latino; 1% Two or more races, non-Hispanic/Latino; 6% transferred in. *Retention:* 50% of full-time freshmen returned.

Freshmen *Admission:* 501 applied, 501 admitted, 274 enrolled. *Average high school GPA:* 2.85.

Majors Business/commerce; criminal justice/police science; general studies; industrial mechanics and maintenance technology; industrial production technologies related; industrial technology; marketing/marketing management; metallurgical technology; middle school education; multi/interdisciplinary studies related; registered nursing/registered nurse.

Academics *Calendar:* semesters. *Degree:* certificates and associate. *Special study options:* academic remediation for entering students, adult/continuing education programs, advanced placement credit, distance learning, double majors, part-time degree program, summer session for credit.

Library Adams/Vines Library with 15,493 titles, 682 audiovisual materials, an OPAC.

Student Life *Housing:* college housing not available. *Activities and Organizations:* drama/theater group, choral group, Gamma Beta Phi, Association of Childhood Education International, Nursing Club, Cultural Diversity, Adult Student Association. *Campus security:* 24-hour patrols.

Athletics *Intramural sports:* badminton M/W, basketball M, football M, volleyball M/W.

Costs (2014–15) *Tuition:* area resident $1736 full-time, $62 per credit hour part-time; state resident $2016 full-time, $72 per credit hour part-time; nonresident $3416 full-time, $122 per credit hour part-time. Full-time tuition and fees vary according to course load. Part-time tuition and fees vary according to course load. *Required fees:* $218 full-time, $6 per credit hour part-time, $25 per term part-time. *Payment plans:* installment, deferred payment. *Waivers:* senior citizens and employees or children of employees.

Financial Aid Of all full-time matriculated undergraduates who enrolled in 2013, 42 Federal Work-Study jobs (averaging $2500).

Applying *Options:* deferred entrance. *Recommended:* high school transcript. *Application deadlines:* rolling (freshmen), rolling (transfers). *Notification:* continuous (freshmen), continuous (transfers).

Freshman Application Contact Arkansas Northeastern College, PO Box 1109, Blytheville, AR 72316. *Phone:* 870-762-1020. *Fax:* 870-763-1654. *Website:* http://www.anc.edu/.

Arkansas State University–Beebe
Beebe, Arkansas

Freshman Application Contact Mr. Ronald Hudson, Coordinator of Student Recruitment, Arkansas State University–Beebe, PO Box 1000, Beebe, AR 72012. *Phone:* 501-882-8860. *Toll-free phone:* 800-632-9985. *E-mail:* rdhudson@asub.edu.
Website: http://www.asub.edu/.

Arkansas State University–Mountain Home
Mountain Home, Arkansas

Freshman Application Contact Ms. Delba Parrish, Admissions Coordinator, Arkansas State University–Mountain Home, 1600 South College Street, Mountain Home, AR 72653. *Phone:* 870-508-6180. *Fax:* 870-508-6287. *E-mail:* dparrish@asumh.edu.
Website: http://www.asumh.edu/.

Arkansas State University–Newport
Newport, Arkansas

- **State-supported** 2-year, founded 1989, part of Arkansas State University System
- **Rural** 189-acre campus
- **Endowment** $2.0 million
- **Coed**

Undergraduates 963 full-time, 1,094 part-time. Students come from 4 states and territories; 2 other countries; 8% are from out of state; 13% Black or African American, non-Hispanic/Latino; 3% Hispanic/Latino; 0.3% Asian, non-Hispanic/Latino; 0.1% Native Hawaiian or other Pacific Islander, non-Hispanic/Latino; 0.4% American Indian or Alaska Native, non-Hispanic/Latino; 3% Two or more races, non-Hispanic/Latino; 5% Race/ethnicity unknown; 0.7% international; 21% transferred in.

Faculty *Student/faculty ratio:* 14:1.

Academics *Calendar:* semesters. *Degree:* certificates, diplomas, and associate. *Special study options:* academic remediation for entering students, adult/continuing education programs, advanced placement credit, cooperative education, distance learning, external degree program, independent study, internships, off-campus study, part-time degree program, services for LD students, summer session for credit.

Standardized Tests *Required:* SAT or ACT or ACT Compass (for admission).

Costs (2014–15) *Tuition:* state resident $2160 full-time, $90 per credit hour part-time; nonresident $3528 full-time, $147 per credit hour part-time. *Required fees:* $288 full-time.

Financial Aid Of all full-time matriculated undergraduates who enrolled in 2013, 19 Federal Work-Study jobs (averaging $4500).

Applying *Options:* electronic application. *Required:* high school transcript.

Freshman Application Contact Arkansas State University–Newport, 7648 Victory Boulevard, Newport, AR 72112. *Phone:* 870-512-7800. *Toll-free phone:* 800-976-1676.
Website: http://www.asun.edu/.

Black River Technical College
Pocahontas, Arkansas

Director of Admissions Director of Admissions, Black River Technical College, 1410 Highway 304 East, Pocahontas, AR 72455. *Phone:* 870-892-4565.
Website: http://www.blackrivertech.edu/.

Bryan University
Rogers, Arkansas

Admissions Office Contact Bryan University, 3704 W. Walnut Street, Rogers, AR 72756.
Website: http://www.bryanu.edu/.

College of the Ouachitas
Malvern, Arkansas

- **State-supported** 2-year, founded 1972
- **Small-town** 11-acre campus with easy access to Little Rock
- **Coed**

Undergraduates 584 full-time, 917 part-time. 12% Black or African American, non-Hispanic/Latino; 4% Hispanic/Latino; 0.7% Asian, non-Hispanic/Latino; 0.1% Native Hawaiian or other Pacific Islander, non-Hispanic/Latino; 0.5% American Indian or Alaska Native, non-Hispanic/Latino; 3% Two or more races, non-Hispanic/Latino; 0.2% international.

Academics *Calendar:* semesters. *Degree:* certificates and associate. *Special study options:* academic remediation for entering students, accelerated degree program, advanced placement credit, cooperative education, distance learning, double majors, freshman honors college, honors programs, independent study, internships, part-time degree program, services for LD students, summer session for credit.

Student Life *Campus security:* 24-hour patrols.

Standardized Tests *Recommended:* SAT or ACT (for admission), ACT Compass or ASSET.

Costs (2014–15) *Tuition:* state resident $2550 full-time, $85 per credit part-time; nonresident $5100 full-time, $170 per credit part-time. Full-time tuition and fees vary according to program. Part-time tuition and fees vary according to program. No tuition increase for student's term of enrollment. *Required fees:* $950 full-time, $24 per credit part-time, $21 per term part-time.

Financial Aid Of all full-time matriculated undergraduates who enrolled in 2013, 18 Federal Work-Study jobs (averaging $2400).

Applying *Options:* electronic application, early admission, deferred entrance. *Required:* high school transcript.

Freshman Application Contact Mrs. Shanea Nelson, Student Success Coordinator, College of the Ouachitas, One College Circle, Malvern, AR 72104. *Phone:* 501-337-5000 Ext. 1177. *Toll-free phone:* 800-337-0266. *Fax:* 501-337-9382. *E-mail:* snelson@coto.edu. *Website:* http://www.coto.edu/.

Cossatot Community College of the University of Arkansas
De Queen, Arkansas

- **State-supported** 2-year, founded 1991, part of University of Arkansas System
- **Rural** 30-acre campus
- **Endowment** $76,785
- **Coed**

Undergraduates Students come from 8 states and territories; 1 other country; 2% are from out of state; 11% Black or African American, non-Hispanic/Latino; 18% Hispanic/Latino; 0.9% Asian, non-Hispanic/Latino; 0.3% Native Hawaiian or other Pacific Islander, non-Hispanic/Latino; 3% American Indian or Alaska Native, non-Hispanic/Latino.

Faculty *Student/faculty ratio:* 15:1.

Academics *Calendar:* semesters. *Degree:* certificates and associate. *Special study options:* academic remediation for entering students, accelerated degree program, advanced placement credit, cooperative education, distance learning, double majors, honors programs, independent study, internships, off-campus study, part-time degree program, services for LD students, summer session for credit.

Student Life *Campus security:* Daytime campus police force. Evening patrol by city police force.

Costs (2014–15) *Tuition:* area resident $1710 full-time, $61 per credit hour part-time; state resident $2010 full-time, $72 per credit hour part-time; nonresident $4560 full-time, $157 per credit hour part-time. *Required fees:* $502 full-time, $251 per term part-time.

Financial Aid Of all full-time matriculated undergraduates who enrolled in 2013, 14 Federal Work-Study jobs (averaging $2700).

Applying *Options:* electronic application. *Recommended:* high school transcript.

Freshman Application Contact Mrs. Tommi Cobb, Admissions Coordinator, Cossatot Community College of the University of Arkansas, 183 College Drive, DeQueen, AR 71832. *Phone:* 870-584-4471 Ext. 1158. *Toll-free phone:* 800-844-4471. *Fax:* 870-642-5088. *E-mail:* tcobb@cccua.edu. *Website:* http://www.cccua.edu/.

Crowley's Ridge College
Paragould, Arkansas

Freshman Application Contact Amanda Drake, Director of Admissions, Crowley's Ridge College, 100 College Drive, Paragould, AR 72450-9731. *Phone:* 870-236-6901. *Toll-free phone:* 800-264-1096. *Fax:* 870-236-7748. *E-mail:* njoneshi@crc.pioneer.paragould.ar.us. *Website:* http://www.crc.edu/.

East Arkansas Community College
Forrest City, Arkansas

Freshman Application Contact Ms. Sharon Collier, Director of Enrollment Management/Institutional Research, East Arkansas Community College, 1700 Newcastle Road, Forrest City, AR 72335-2204. *Phone:* 870-633-4480. *Toll-free phone:* 877-797-3222. *Fax:* 870-633-3840. *E-mail:* dadams@eacc.edu. *Website:* http://www.eacc.edu/.

ITT Technical Institute
Little Rock, Arkansas

- **Proprietary** primarily 2-year, founded 1993, part of ITT Educational Services, Inc.
- **Urban** campus
- **Coed**

Academics *Calendar:* quarters. *Degrees:* associate and bachelor's.

Freshman Application Contact Director of Recruitment, ITT Technical Institute, 12200 Westhaven Drive, Little Rock, AR 72211. *Phone:* 501-565-5550. *Toll-free phone:* 800-359-4429. *Website:* http://www.itt-tech.edu/.

Mid-South Community College
West Memphis, Arkansas

- **State-supported** 2-year, founded 1993
- **Suburban** 80-acre campus with easy access to Memphis
- **Endowment** $967,261
- **Coed**

Undergraduates 703 full-time, 1,090 part-time. Students come from 3 states and territories; 3 other countries; 5% are from out of state; 53% Black or African American, non-Hispanic/Latino; 0.4% Hispanic/Latino; 0.6% Asian, non-Hispanic/Latino; 0.1% Native Hawaiian or other Pacific Islander, non-Hispanic/Latino; 0.3% American Indian or Alaska Native, non-Hispanic/Latino; 4% Two or more races, non-Hispanic/Latino; 0.5% international; 7% transferred in. *Retention:* 34% of full-time freshmen returned.

Faculty *Student/faculty ratio:* 14:1.

Academics *Calendar:* semesters. *Degree:* certificates and associate. *Special study options:* academic remediation for entering students, adult/continuing education programs, advanced placement credit, distance learning, independent study, internships, part-time degree program, services for LD students, summer session for credit.

Student Life *Campus security:* 24-hour emergency response devices, security during class hours.

Standardized Tests *Required:* SAT, ACT or ACT Compass (for admission).

Costs (2014–15) *Tuition:* area resident $1080 full-time; state resident $1320 full-time; nonresident $3600 full-time. *Required fees:* $144 full-time.

Financial Aid Of all full-time matriculated undergraduates who enrolled in 2013, 39 Federal Work-Study jobs (averaging $1676).

Applying *Options:* early admission.

Freshman Application Contact Jeremy Reece, Director of Admissions, Mid-South Community College, 2000 West Broadway, West Memphis, AR 72301. *Phone:* 870-733-6786. *Toll-free phone:* 866-733-6722. *Fax:* 870-733-6719. *E-mail:* jreece@midsouthcc.edu. *Website:* http://www.midsouthcc.edu/.

National Park Community College
Hot Springs, Arkansas

Director of Admissions Dr. Allen B. Moody, Director of Institutional Services/Registrar, National Park Community College, 101 College Drive, Hot Springs, AR 71913. *Phone:* 501-760-4222. *E-mail:* bmoody@npcc.edu. *Website:* http://www.npcc.edu/.

North Arkansas College
Harrison, Arkansas

Freshman Application Contact Mrs. Charla Jennings, Director of Admissions, North Arkansas College, 1515 Pioneer Drive, Harrison, AR 72601. *Phone:* 870-391-3221. *Toll-free phone:* 800-679-6622. *Fax:* 870-391-3339. *E-mail:* charlam@northark.edu. *Website:* http://www.northark.edu/.

NorthWest Arkansas Community College
Bentonville, Arkansas

- **State and locally supported** 2-year, founded 1989
- **Urban** 77-acre campus
- **Coed**

Undergraduates 2,843 full-time, 5,177 part-time. Students come from 21 states and territories; 2% are from out of state; 7% transferred in. *Retention:* 50% of full-time freshmen returned.

Faculty *Student/faculty ratio:* 19:1.

Academics *Calendar:* semesters. *Degree:* certificates and associate. *Special study options:* academic remediation for entering students, accelerated degree program, adult/continuing education programs, advanced placement credit, cooperative education, distance learning, double majors, English as a second language, honors programs, independent study, internships, part-time degree program, services for LD students, student-designed majors, summer session for credit. *ROTC:* Army (c), Air Force (c).

Student Life *Campus security:* 24-hour emergency response devices and patrols.

Costs (2014–15) *Tuition:* area resident $2250 full-time, $75 per credit hour part-time; state resident $3675 full-time, $123 per credit hour part-time; nonresident $5250 full-time, $175 per credit hour part-time. *Required fees:* $837 full-time, $24 per credit hour part-time, $55 per term part-time.

Applying *Options:* electronic application. *Application fee:* $10. *Required:* high school transcript.
Freshman Application Contact NorthWest Arkansas Community College, One College Drive, Bentonville, AR 72712. *Phone:* 479-636-9222. *Toll-free phone:* 800-995-6922. *Fax:* 479-619-4116. *E-mail:* admissions@nwacc.edu. *Website:* http://www.nwacc.edu/.

Ozarka College
Melbourne, Arkansas

Freshman Application Contact Ms. Dylan Mowery, Director of Admissions, Ozarka College, PO Box 10, Melbourne, AR 72556. *Phone:* 870-368-7371 Ext. 2013. *Toll-free phone:* 800-821-4335. *E-mail:* dmmowery@ozarka.edu. *Website:* http://www.ozarka.edu/.

Phillips Community College of the University of Arkansas
Helena, Arkansas

Director of Admissions Mr. Lynn Boone, Registrar, Phillips Community College of the University of Arkansas, PO Box 785, Helena, AR 72342-0785. *Phone:* 870-338-6474.
Website: http://www.pccua.edu/.

Pulaski Technical College
North Little Rock, Arkansas

Freshman Application Contact Mr. Clark Atkins, Director of Admissions, Pulaski Technical College, 3000 West Scenic Drive, North Little Rock, AR 72118. *Phone:* 501-812-2734. *Fax:* 501-812-2316. *E-mail:* catkins@pulaskitech.edu.
Website: http://www.pulaskitech.edu/.

Remington College–Little Rock Campus
Little Rock, Arkansas

Director of Admissions Brian Maggio, Director of Recruitment, Remington College–Little Rock Campus, 19 Remington Drive, Little Rock, AR 72204. *Phone:* 501-312-0007. *Fax:* 501-225-3819. *E-mail:* brian.maggio@remingtoncollege.edu.
Website: http://www.remingtoncollege.edu/.

Rich Mountain Community College
Mena, Arkansas

Director of Admissions Dr. Steve Rook, Dean of Students, Rich Mountain Community College, 1100 College Drive, Mena, AR 71953. *Phone:* 479-394-7622 Ext. 1400.
Website: http://www.rmcc.edu/.

Shorter College
North Little Rock, Arkansas

Director of Admissions Mr. Keith Hunter, Director of Admissions, Shorter College, 604 Locust Street, North Little Rock, AR 72114-4885. *Phone:* 501-374-6305.
Website: http://www.shortercollege.edu/.

South Arkansas Community College
El Dorado, Arkansas

Freshman Application Contact Dr. Stephanie Tully-Dartez, Director of Enrollment Services, South Arkansas Community College, PO Box 7010, El Dorado, AR 71731-7010. *Phone:* 870-864-7142. *Toll-free phone:* 800-955-2289. *Fax:* 870-864-7109. *E-mail:* dinman@southark.edu.
Website: http://www.southark.edu/.

Southeast Arkansas College
Pine Bluff, Arkansas

Freshman Application Contact Ms. Barbara Dunn, Director of Admissions, Southeast Arkansas College, 1900 Hazel Street, Pine Bluff, AR 71603. *Phone:* 870-543-5957. *Toll-free phone:* 888-SEARK TC (in-state); 888-SEARC TC (out-of-state). *Fax:* 870-543-5957. *E-mail:* bdunn@seark.edu. *Website:* http://www.seark.edu/.

Southern Arkansas University Tech
Camden, Arkansas

Freshman Application Contact Mrs. Beverly Ellis, Admissions Analyst, Southern Arkansas University Tech, PO Box 3499, Camden, AR 71711-1599. *Phone:* 870-574-4558. *Fax:* 870-574-4478. *E-mail:* bellis@sautech.edu. *Website:* http://www.sautech.edu/.

University of Arkansas Community College at Batesville
Batesville, Arkansas

- **State-supported** 2-year, part of University of Arkansas System
- **Small-town** campus
- **Coed,** 1,315 undergraduate students, 57% full-time, 67% women, 33% men

Undergraduates 750 full-time, 565 part-time. Students come from 2 states and territories; 3% Black or African American, non-Hispanic/Latino; 5% Hispanic/Latino; 0.9% Asian, non-Hispanic/Latino; 0.2% Native Hawaiian or other Pacific Islander, non-Hispanic/Latino; 0.9% American Indian or Alaska Native, non-Hispanic/Latino; 4% Two or more races, non-Hispanic/Latino; 0.4% Race/ethnicity unknown; 0.2% international; 4% transferred in. *Retention:* 60% of full-time freshmen returned.
Freshmen *Admission:* 262 enrolled.
Faculty *Student/faculty ratio:* 19:1.
Majors Aircraft powerplant technology; business/commerce; criminal justice/safety; early childhood education; electrical/electronics equipment installation and repair; emergency medical technology (EMT paramedic); liberal arts and sciences/liberal studies; medical office management; multi/interdisciplinary studies related; registered nursing/registered nurse.
Academics *Calendar:* semesters. *Degree:* certificates and associate. *Special study options:* academic remediation for entering students, adult/continuing education programs, advanced placement credit, cooperative education, distance learning, double majors, English as a second language, external degree program, independent study, internships, off-campus study, part-time degree program, services for LD students, student-designed majors, summer session for credit.
Library University of Arkansas Community College at Batesville Library with an OPAC, a Web page.
Student Life *Housing:* college housing not available. *Activities and Organizations:* choral group, Student Government Association, Phi Kappa Theta, Circle K International, Non-Traditional Students Organization, Renaissance Club. *Campus security:* trained security officers during operations hours, security cameras, emergency alerts systems.
Standardized Tests *Recommended:* ACT (for admission), ACT, ASSET, Compass, and SAT tests are all accepted for admissions purposes. Minimum reading scores must be met for admission to the colleges.
Financial Aid Of all full-time matriculated undergraduates who enrolled in 2013, 49 Federal Work-Study jobs (averaging $1311).
Applying *Options:* electronic application. *Required:* high school transcript, Composite score of 15 or higher on ACT; or a Reading score of 63 or higher on the Compass test. *Application deadlines:* rolling (freshmen), rolling (transfers). *Notification:* continuous (freshmen), continuous (transfers).
Freshman Application Contact Ms. Amy Foree, Enrollment Specialist, University of Arkansas Community College at Batesville, PO Box 3350, Batesville, AR 72503. *Phone:* 870-612-2113. *Toll-free phone:* 800-508-7878. *Fax:* 870-612-2129. *E-mail:* amy.foree@uaccb.edu.
Website: http://www.uaccb.edu/.

University of Arkansas Community College at Hope
Hope, Arkansas

- **State-supported** 2-year, founded 1966, part of University of Arkansas System
- **Rural** 60-acre campus
- **Coed,** 1,360 undergraduate students, 49% full-time, 67% women, 33% men

Undergraduates 666 full-time, 694 part-time. Students come from 5 states and territories; 7% are from out of state; 37% Black or African American, non-Hispanic/Latino; 7% Hispanic/Latino; 0.4% Asian, non-Hispanic/Latino; 0.1% Native Hawaiian or other Pacific Islander, non-Hispanic/Latino; 0.8% American Indian or Alaska Native, non-Hispanic/Latino; 0.2% Two or more races, non-Hispanic/Latino; 6% transferred in. *Retention:* 42% of full-time freshmen returned.
Freshmen *Admission:* 540 applied, 540 admitted, 278 enrolled. *Average high school GPA:* 2.86. *Test scores:* ACT scores over 18: 136%; ACT scores over 24: 27%; ACT scores over 30: 1%.

Faculty *Total:* 91, 44% full-time, 11% with terminal degrees. *Student/faculty ratio:* 15:1.

Majors Business/commerce; child-care and support services management; computer and information sciences; education (multiple levels); electrical, electronic and communications engineering technology; emergency medical technology (EMT paramedic); funeral service and mortuary science; general studies; human services; liberal arts and sciences/liberal studies; medical office management; multi/interdisciplinary studies related; registered nursing/registered nurse.

Academics *Calendar:* semesters. *Degree:* certificates, diplomas, and associate. *Special study options:* academic remediation for entering students, accelerated degree program, advanced placement credit, distance learning, double majors, independent study, internships, off-campus study, part-time degree program, services for LD students, summer session for credit.

Library University of Arkansas Community College at Hope Library with a Web page.

Student Life *Housing:* college housing not available. *Activities and Organizations:* Phi Theta Kappa, Arkansas Licensed Practical Nursing Association, Campus Crusaders for Christ, Technical and Industrial Club, Fine Arts Club. *Campus security:* 24-hour emergency response devices, on-campus security during class hours.

Standardized Tests *Recommended:* SAT or ACT (for admission), ACT Compass.

Costs (2015–16) *Tuition:* area resident $1860 full-time, $61 per credit part-time; state resident $2040 full-time, $66 per credit part-time; nonresident $4080 full-time, $131 per credit part-time. *Required fees:* $520 full-time, $15 per term part-time, $8 per term part-time. *Payment plan:* installment. *Waivers:* senior citizens and employees or children of employees.

Financial Aid Of all full-time matriculated undergraduates who enrolled in 2013, 1,071 were judged to have need. *Average indebtedness upon graduation:* $2625.

Applying *Options:* early admission. *Required:* high school transcript. *Application deadlines:* rolling (freshmen), rolling (out-of-state freshmen), rolling (transfers). *Notification:* continuous (freshmen), continuous (out-of-state freshmen), continuous (transfers).

Freshman Application Contact University of Arkansas Community College at Hope, PO Box 140, Hope, AR 71802. *Phone:* 870-772-8174.
Website: http://www.uacch.edu/.

University of Arkansas Community College at Morrilton
Morrilton, Arkansas

- **State-supported** 2-year, founded 1961, part of University of Arkansas System
- **Rural** 79-acre campus
- **Coed,** 1,995 undergraduate students, 57% full-time, 60% women, 40% men

Undergraduates 1,146 full-time, 849 part-time. Students come from 6 states and territories; 1 other country; 0.8% are from out of state; 9% Black or African American, non-Hispanic/Latino; 6% Hispanic/Latino; 0.7% Asian, non-Hispanic/Latino; 0.1% Native Hawaiian or other Pacific Islander, non-Hispanic/Latino; 0.2% American Indian or Alaska Native, non-Hispanic/Latino; 4% Two or more races, non-Hispanic/Latino; 0.3% Race/ethnicity unknown; 10% transferred in.

Freshmen *Admission:* 1,215 applied, 751 admitted, 511 enrolled. *Average high school GPA:* 2.86. *Test scores:* ACT scores over 18: 72%; ACT scores over 24: 16%; ACT scores over 30: 1%.

Faculty *Total:* 87, 60% full-time, 9% with terminal degrees. *Student/faculty ratio:* 22:1.

Majors Autobody/collision and repair technology; automobile/automotive mechanics technology; business/commerce; child development; commercial and advertising art; computer and information sciences; computer technology/computer systems technology; criminal justice/law enforcement administration; drafting and design technology; education (multiple levels); forensic science and technology; general studies; heating, air conditioning, ventilation and refrigeration maintenance technology; liberal arts and sciences/liberal studies; petroleum technology; registered nursing/registered nurse; surveying technology.

Academics *Calendar:* semesters. *Degree:* certificates and associate. *Special study options:* academic remediation for entering students, advanced placement credit, cooperative education, distance learning, double majors, internships, part-time degree program, services for LD students, summer session for credit.

Library E. Allen Gordon Library with 27,079 titles, 1,862 audiovisual materials, an OPAC, a Web page.

Student Life *Housing:* college housing not available. *Activities and Organizations:* drama/theater group, Student Engagement and Leadership Organization, Phi Theta Kappa, Petroleum Students Organization, Practical Nurses Organization, Computer Information Systems Club. *Campus security:* 24-hour emergency response devices, late-night transport/escort service, campus alert system through phone call, text message and/or e-mail. *Student services:* personal/psychological counseling.

Athletics *Intramural sports:* basketball M/W, football M/W, table tennis M/W, ultimate Frisbee M/W, volleyball M/W.

Standardized Tests *Recommended:* SAT or ACT (for admission), ACT Compass.

Costs (2014–15) *Tuition:* area resident $2535 full-time, $85 per credit hour part-time; state resident $2745 full-time, $92 per credit hour part-time; nonresident $3840 full-time, $128 per credit hour part-time. Full-time tuition and fees vary according to course load and program. Part-time tuition and fees vary according to course load and program. *Required fees:* $1170 full-time, $39 per credit hour part-time. *Payment plan:* installment. *Waivers:* senior citizens and employees or children of employees.

Financial Aid Of all full-time matriculated undergraduates who enrolled in 2014, 997 applied for aid, 877 were judged to have need, 60 had their need fully met. 20 Federal Work-Study jobs (averaging $1897). In 2014, 38 non-need-based awards were made. *Average percent of need met:* 48%. *Average financial aid package:* $5768. *Average need-based loan:* $2537. *Average need-based gift aid:* $4083. *Average non-need-based aid:* $1611. *Financial aid deadline:* 7/1.

Applying *Options:* electronic application, early admission, deferred entrance. *Required:* high school transcript. *Required for some:* immunization records and prior college transcript(s). *Application deadlines:* rolling (freshmen), rolling (transfers). *Notification:* continuous (freshmen), continuous (transfers).

Freshman Application Contact Ms. Terry McCoy, Coordinator of Recruitment, University of Arkansas Community College at Morrilton, 1537 University Boulevard, Morrilton, AR 72110. *Phone:* 501-977-2053. *Toll-free phone:* 800-264-1094. *Fax:* 501-977-2123. *E-mail:* mullins@uaccm.edu. *Website:* http://www.uaccm.edu/.

CALIFORNIA

Academy of Couture Art
Beverly Hills, California

- **Proprietary** primarily 2-year
- **Urban** campus with easy access to Los Angeles
- **Coed**

Academics *Degrees:* associate and bachelor's. *Special study options:* double majors, English as a second language.

Student Life *Campus security:* 24-hour emergency response devices and patrols.

Freshman Application Contact Academy of Couture Art, 8484 Wilshire Boulevard, Suite 730, Beverly Hills, CA 90211. *Phone:* 310-360-8888. *Website:* http://www.academyofcoutureart.edu/.

Advanced College
South Gate, California

Admissions Office Contact Advanced College, 13180 Paramount Boulevard, South Gate, CA 90280.
Website: http://www.advancedcollege.edu/.

Advanced Computing Institute
Los Angeles, California

Admissions Office Contact Advanced Computing Institute, 3470 Wilshire Boulevard 11th Floor, Los Angeles, CA 90010-3911.
Website: http://www.advancedcomputinginstitute.edu/.

Advanced Training Associates
El Cajon, California

Admissions Office Contact Advanced Training Associates, 1810 Gillespie Way, Suite 104, El Cajon, CA 92020. *Toll-free phone:* 800-720-2125.
Website: http://www.advancedtraining.edu/.

Allan Hancock College
Santa Maria, California

Freshman Application Contact Ms. Adela Esquivel Swinson, Director of Admissions and Records, Allan Hancock College, 800 South College Drive,

Santa Maria, CA 93454-6399. *Phone:* 805-922-6966 Ext. 3272. *Toll-free phone:* 866-342-5242. *Fax:* 805-922-3477.
Website: http://www.hancockcollege.edu/.

American Academy of Dramatic Arts
Hollywood, California

- **Independent** 2-year, founded 1974
- **Urban** 4-acre campus with easy access to Los Angeles
- **Endowment** $1.7 million
- **Coed,** 282 undergraduate students, 100% full-time, 59% women, 41% men

Undergraduates 282 full-time. Students come from 36 states and territories; 26 other countries; 54% are from out of state; 7% Black or African American, non-Hispanic/Latino; 10% Hispanic/Latino; 1% Asian, non-Hispanic/Latino; 0.4% Native Hawaiian or other Pacific Islander, non-Hispanic/Latino; 0.8% American Indian or Alaska Native, non-Hispanic/Latino; 14% Two or more races, non-Hispanic/Latino; 25% international; 0.7% transferred in.
Freshmen *Admission:* 1,612 applied, 325 admitted, 146 enrolled.
Faculty *Total:* 50, 18% full-time, 2% with terminal degrees. *Student/faculty ratio:* 12:1.
Majors Dramatic/theater arts.
Academics *Calendar:* semesters. *Degree:* certificates, diplomas, and associate. *Special study options:* internships, services for LD students.
Library Bryn Morgan Library with 12,500 titles, 1,500 audiovisual materials.
Student Life *Housing:* college housing not available. *Activities and Organizations:* choral group. *Campus security:* 24-hour emergency response devices, 8-hour patrols by trained security personnel. *Student services:* personal/psychological counseling.
Costs (2015–16) *Tuition:* $29,900 full-time. *Required fees:* $750 full-time. *Payment plan:* installment.
Financial Aid Of all full-time matriculated undergraduates who enrolled in 2013, 15 Federal Work-Study jobs (averaging $2000).
Applying *Options:* electronic application, deferred entrance. *Application fee:* $50. *Required:* essay or personal statement, high school transcript, 2 letters of recommendation, interview, audition. *Recommended:* minimum 2.0 GPA. *Application deadlines:* rolling (freshmen), rolling (transfers). *Notification:* continuous (freshmen), continuous (transfers).
Freshman Application Contact Steven Hong, Director of Admissions, American Academy of Dramatic Arts, 1336 North La Brea Avenue, Hollywood, CA 90028. *Phone:* 323-464-2777 Ext. 103. *Toll-free phone:* 800-222-2867. *E-mail:* shong@aada.edu.
Website: http://www.aada.edu/.

American Career College
Anaheim, California

Director of Admissions Susan Pailet, Senior Executive Director of Admission, American Career College, 1200 North Magnolia Avenue, Anaheim, CA 92801. *Phone:* 714-952-9066. *Toll-free phone:* 877-832-0790. *E-mail:* info@americancareer.com.
Website: http://americancareercollege.edu/.

American Career College
Los Angeles, California

Director of Admissions Tamra Adams, Director of Admissions, American Career College, 4021 Rosewood Avenue, Los Angeles, CA 90004-2932. *Phone:* 323-668-7555. *Toll-free phone:* 877-832-0790. *E-mail:* info@americancareer.com.
Website: http://americancareercollege.edu/.

American Career College
Ontario, California

Director of Admissions Juan Tellez, Director of Admissions, American Career College, 3130 East Sedona Court, Ontario, CA 91764. *Phone:* 951-739-0788. *Toll-free phone:* 877-832-0790. *E-mail:* info@americancareer.com.
Website: http://americancareercollege.edu/.

American River College
Sacramento, California

Freshman Application Contact American River College, 4700 College Oak Drive, Sacramento, CA 95841-4286. *Phone:* 916-484-8171.
Website: http://www.arc.losrios.edu/.

Antelope Valley College
Lancaster, California

- **State and locally supported** 2-year, founded 1929, part of California Community College System
- **Suburban** 135-acre campus with easy access to Los Angeles
- **Endowment** $3.6 million
- **Coed,** 14,598 undergraduate students, 23% full-time, 59% women, 41% men

Undergraduates 3,294 full-time, 11,304 part-time. 20% Black or African American, non-Hispanic/Latino; 44% Hispanic/Latino; 1% Asian, non-Hispanic/Latino; 2% Native Hawaiian or other Pacific Islander, non-Hispanic/Latino; 0.4% American Indian or Alaska Native, non-Hispanic/Latino; 5% Two or more races, non-Hispanic/Latino; 1% Race/ethnicity unknown; 3% international.
Freshmen *Admission:* 5,517 applied, 5,517 admitted, 7,161 enrolled.
Faculty *Total:* 593, 29% full-time, 7% with terminal degrees.
Majors Administrative assistant and secretarial science; aircraft powerplant technology; airframe mechanics and aircraft maintenance technology; apparel and textiles; autobody/collision and repair technology; automobile/automotive mechanics technology; avionics maintenance technology; biology/biological sciences; business administration and management; business/commerce; childcare and support services management; child development; cinematography and film/video production; computer and information sciences; computer graphics; computer programming; construction engineering technology; corrections; criminal justice/law enforcement administration; criminal justice/police science; data processing and data processing technology; drafting and design technology; electrical, electronic and communications engineering technology; engineering; engineering technology; family and consumer sciences/home economics teacher education; fiber, textile and weaving arts; fire prevention and safety technology; foods, nutrition, and wellness; health and physical education/fitness; heating, air conditioning, ventilation and refrigeration maintenance technology; interior design; liberal arts and sciences/liberal studies; marketing/marketing management; mathematics; medical administrative assistant and medical secretary; music; ornamental horticulture; photography; physical sciences; real estate; registered nursing/registered nurse; teacher assistant/aide; welding technology; work and family studies.
Academics *Calendar:* semesters. *Degree:* certificates and associate. *Special study options:* academic remediation for entering students, adult/continuing education programs, advanced placement credit, cooperative education, distance learning, English as a second language, honors programs, independent study, part-time degree program, services for LD students, student-designed majors, study abroad, summer session for credit. *ROTC:* Army (c), Navy (c), Air Force (c).
Library Antelope Valley College Library with 52,502 titles, an OPAC, a Web page.
Student Life *Housing:* college housing not available. *Activities and Organizations:* drama/theater group, student-run newspaper, choral group. *Campus security:* 24-hour emergency response devices and patrols, late-night transport/escort service. *Student services:* personal/psychological counseling.
Athletics *Intercollegiate sports:* baseball M, basketball M/W, cross-country running M/W, football M, golf M/W, soccer W, softball W, tennis W, track and field M/W, volleyball W. *Intramural sports:* basketball M/W, golf M/W, swimming and diving M/W, tennis M/W, volleyball M/W, weight lifting M/W.
Costs (2015–16) *Tuition:* state resident $1104 full-time, $46 per credit part-time; nonresident $5664 full-time, $236 per credit part-time. *Required fees:* $40 full-time, $46 per credit part-time, $20 per term part-time. *Payment plan:* installment.
Applying *Options:* electronic application, early admission. *Required:* high school transcript. *Recommended:* assessment. *Application deadlines:* rolling (freshmen), rolling (transfers). *Notification:* continuous (freshmen), continuous (transfers).
Freshman Application Contact Welcome Center, Antelope Valley College, 3041 West Avenue K, SSV Building, Lancaster, CA 93536. *Phone:* 661-722-6300 Ext. 6331.
Website: http://www.avc.edu/.

APT College
Carlsbad, California

Director of Admissions Monica Hoffman, Director of Admissions/Registrar, APT College, 5751 Palmer Way, Suite D, PO Box 131717, Carlsbad, CA 92013. *Phone:* 800-431-8488. *Toll-free phone:* 800-431-8488. *Fax:* 888-431-8588. *E-mail:* aptc@aptc.com.
Website: http://www.aptc.edu/.

Ashdown College of Health Sciences
Redlands, California

Admissions Office Contact Ashdown College of Health Sciences, 101 E. Redlands Boulevard, Suite 285, Redlands, CA 92373.
Website: http://ashdowncollege.edu/.

Aviation & Electronic Schools of America
Colfax, California

Freshman Application Contact Admissions Office, Aviation & Electronic Schools of America, 111 South Railroad Street, PO Box 1810, Colfax, CA 95713-1810. *Phone:* 530-346-6792. *Toll-free phone:* 800-345-2742. *Fax:* 530-346-8466. *E-mail:* aesa@aesa.com.
Website: http://www.aesa.com/.

Bakersfield College
Bakersfield, California

Freshman Application Contact Bakersfield College, 1801 Panorama Drive, Bakersfield, CA 93305-1299. *Phone:* 661-395-4301.
Website: http://www.bakersfieldcollege.edu/.

Barstow Community College
Barstow, California

- **State and locally supported** 2-year, founded 1959, part of California Community College System
- **Small-town** 50-acre campus
- **Coed**

Faculty *Student/faculty ratio:* 35:1.
Academics *Calendar:* semesters. *Degree:* certificates and associate. *Special study options:* academic remediation for entering students, adult/continuing education programs, cooperative education, English as a second language, external degree program, part-time degree program, services for LD students, student-designed majors, summer session for credit.
Student Life *Campus security:* evening security personnel.
Costs (2014–15) *Tuition:* state resident $1104 full-time, $46 per unit part-time; nonresident $5400 full-time, $239 per unit part-time. Full-time tuition and fees vary according to course load. Part-time tuition and fees vary according to course load. *Payment plans:* installment, deferred payment.
Applying *Options:* early admission, deferred entrance. *Recommended:* high school transcript.
Freshman Application Contact Barstow Community College, 2700 Barstow Road, Barstow, CA 92311-6699. *Phone:* 760-252-2411 Ext. 7236.
Website: http://www.barstow.edu/.

Berkeley City College
Berkeley, California

- **State and locally supported** 2-year, founded 1974, part of California Community College System
- **Urban** campus with easy access to San Francisco, Oakland
- **Coed**

Undergraduates 1% are from out of state; 18% Black or African American, non-Hispanic/Latino; 12% Hispanic/Latino; 16% Asian, non-Hispanic/Latino; 0.5% Native Hawaiian or other Pacific Islander, non-Hispanic/Latino; 0.5% American Indian or Alaska Native, non-Hispanic/Latino; 3% Two or more races, non-Hispanic/Latino; 31% Race/ethnicity unknown.
Faculty *Student/faculty ratio:* 35:1.
Academics *Calendar:* semesters. *Degree:* certificates and associate. *Special study options:* academic remediation for entering students, adult/continuing education programs, advanced placement credit, cooperative education, distance learning, double majors, English as a second language, independent study, internships, off-campus study, part-time degree program, services for LD students, student-designed majors, study abroad, summer session for credit.
Student Life *Campus security:* 24-hour patrols.
Standardized Tests *Required:* Matriculating students must take a math and English assessment test (for admission).
Costs (2014–15) *Tuition:* state resident $1380 full-time, $46 per credit part-time; nonresident $7770 full-time, $259 per credit part-time. Full-time tuition and fees vary according to class time, course load, and program. Part-time tuition and fees vary according to class time, course load, and program. *Required fees:* $296 full-time, $46 per credit part-time, $296 per year part-time.

Financial Aid Of all full-time matriculated undergraduates who enrolled in 2013, 48 Federal Work-Study jobs (averaging $3000).
Applying *Required:* assessment test in Math and English for matriculating students. *Recommended:* high school transcript.
Freshman Application Contact Dr. May Kuang-chi Chen, Vice President of Student Services, Berkeley City College, 2050 Center Street, Berkeley, CA 94704. *Phone:* 510-981-2820. *Fax:* 510-841-7333. *E-mail:* mrivas@peralta.edu.
Website: http://www.berkeleycitycollege.edu/.

Blake Austin College
Vacaville, California

Admissions Office Contact Blake Austin College, 611-K Orange Drive, Vacaville, CA 95687.
Website: http://www.blakeaustincollege.edu/.

Bryan College
Gold River, California

Freshman Application Contact Bryan College, 2317 Gold Meadow Way, Gold River, CA 95670. *Phone:* 916-649-2400. *Toll-free phone:* 866-649-2400.
Website: http://www.bryancollege.edu/.

Bryan University
Los Angeles, California

Admissions Office Contact Bryan University, 3580 Wilshire Boulevard, Los Angeles, CA 90010.
Website: http://losangeles.bryanuniversity.edu/.

Butte College
Oroville, California

- **State and locally supported** 2-year, founded 1966, part of California Community College System
- **Rural** 928-acre campus with easy access to Sacramento
- **Coed**

Undergraduates 5,330 full-time, 6,960 part-time. 3% Black or African American, non-Hispanic/Latino; 15% Hispanic/Latino; 6% Asian, non-Hispanic/Latino; 0.4% Native Hawaiian or other Pacific Islander, non-Hispanic/Latino; 2% American Indian or Alaska Native, non-Hispanic/Latino; 0.1% Two or more races, non-Hispanic/Latino; 1% international.
Faculty *Student/faculty ratio:* 25:1.
Academics *Calendar:* semesters. *Degree:* certificates and associate. *Special study options:* academic remediation for entering students, accelerated degree program, adult/continuing education programs, advanced placement credit, cooperative education, distance learning, double majors, English as a second language, honors programs, independent study, internships, part-time degree program, services for LD students, study abroad, summer session for credit.
Student Life *Campus security:* 24-hour emergency response devices and patrols, student patrols.
Applying *Options:* electronic application, early admission, deferred entrance. *Required for some:* high school transcript.
Freshman Application Contact Mr. Brad Zuniga, Director of Recruitment, Outreach and New Student Orientation, Butte College, 3536 Butte Campus Drive, Oroville, CA 95965-8399. *Phone:* 530-895-2948.
Website: http://www.butte.edu/.

Cabrillo College
Aptos, California

Freshman Application Contact Tama Bolton, Director of Admissions and Records, Cabrillo College, 6500 Soquel Drive, Aptos, CA 95003-3194. *Phone:* 831-477-3548. *Fax:* 831-479-5782. *E-mail:* tabolton@cabrillo.edu.
Website: http://www.cabrillo.edu/.

Cambridge Junior College
Yuba City, California

Freshman Application Contact Admissions Office, Cambridge Junior College, 990-A Klamath Lane, Yuba City, CA 95993. *Phone:* 530-674-9199. *Fax:* 530-671-7319.
Website: http://cambridge.edu/.

Cañada College
Redwood City, California

- **State and locally supported** 2-year, founded 1968, part of San Mateo County Community College District System
- **Suburban** 131-acre campus with easy access to San Francisco, San Jose
- **Coed,** 6,250 undergraduate students, 28% full-time, 64% women, 36% men

Undergraduates 1,739 full-time, 4,511 part-time. 1% are from out of state; 4% Black or African American, non-Hispanic/Latino; 37% Hispanic/Latino; 8% Asian, non-Hispanic/Latino; 6% Native Hawaiian or other Pacific Islander, non-Hispanic/Latino; 0.2% American Indian or Alaska Native, non-Hispanic/Latino; 16% Two or more races, non-Hispanic/Latino; 3% Race/ethnicity unknown; 2% international; 8% transferred in. *Retention:* 79% of full-time freshmen returned.

Freshmen *Admission:* 394 applied, 394 enrolled.

Faculty *Total:* 263, 29% full-time. *Student/faculty ratio:* 25:1.

Majors Accounting technology and bookkeeping; administrative assistant and secretarial science; animation, interactive technology, video graphics and special effects; anthropology; apparel and textile manufacturing; archeology; area studies related; art; biological and physical sciences; biology/biological sciences; business administration and management; chemistry; child-care provision; computer science; computer systems networking and telecommunications; dramatic/theater arts; economics; engineering; English; fashion/apparel design; geography; health and physical education/fitness; history; humanities; human services; interior design; international relations and affairs; legal assistant/paralegal; liberal arts and sciences/liberal studies; linguistics; medical/clinical assistant; music; network and system administration; philosophy; physics; political science and government; psychology; radiologic technology/science; retailing; small business administration; sociology; Spanish; speech communication and rhetoric; sport and fitness administration/management.

Academics *Calendar:* semesters. *Degree:* certificates and associate. *Special study options:* academic remediation for entering students, accelerated degree program, adult/continuing education programs, advanced placement credit, cooperative education, distance learning, double majors, English as a second language, honors programs, independent study, internships, part-time degree program, services for LD students, study abroad, summer session for credit. *ROTC:* Army (c), Navy (c), Air Force (c).

Library Library with an OPAC.

Student Life *Housing:* college housing not available. *Activities and Organizations:* drama/theater group, choral group. *Campus security:* 12-hour patrols by trained security personnel. *Student services:* health clinic, personal/psychological counseling.

Athletics *Intercollegiate sports:* baseball M, basketball M, golf W, soccer M/W, tennis W.

Costs (2015–16) *Tuition:* state resident $1380 full-time, $46 per unit part-time; nonresident $7950 full-time, $265 per unit part-time. *Required fees:* $60 full-time, $46 part-time, $28 per term part-time. *Payment plan:* installment.

Financial Aid Of all full-time matriculated undergraduates who enrolled in 2012, 35 Federal Work-Study jobs (averaging $2600).

Applying *Options:* electronic application. *Recommended:* high school transcript. *Application deadlines:* rolling (freshmen), rolling (transfers).

Freshman Application Contact Cañada College, 4200 Farm Hill Boulevard, Redwood City, CA 94061-1099. *Phone:* 650-306-3125.

Website: http://www.canadacollege.edu/.

Carrington College–Citrus Heights
Citrus Heights, California

- **Proprietary** 2-year, part of Carrington Colleges Group, Inc.
- **Coed**

Undergraduates 420 full-time, 31 part-time. 9% Black or African American, non-Hispanic/Latino; 15% Hispanic/Latino; 2% Asian, non-Hispanic/Latino; 1% Native Hawaiian or other Pacific Islander, non-Hispanic/Latino; 0.7% American Indian or Alaska Native, non-Hispanic/Latino; 4% Two or more races, non-Hispanic/Latino; 12% Race/ethnicity unknown; 17% transferred in.

Faculty *Student/faculty ratio:* 37:1.

Academics *Degree:* certificates and associate.

Applying *Required:* essay or personal statement, high school transcript, interview.

Freshman Application Contact Carrington College–Citrus Heights, 7301 Greenback Lane, Suite A, Citrus Heights, CA 95621.

Website: http://carrington.edu/.

Carrington College–Pleasant Hill
Pleasant Hill, California

- **Proprietary** 2-year, founded 1997, part of Carrington Colleges Group, Inc.
- **Coed**

Undergraduates 512 full-time, 77 part-time. 14% Black or African American, non-Hispanic/Latino; 28% Hispanic/Latino; 13% Asian, non-Hispanic/Latino; 3% Native Hawaiian or other Pacific Islander, non-Hispanic/Latino; 0.7% American Indian or Alaska Native, non-Hispanic/Latino; 3% Two or more races, non-Hispanic/Latino; 1% Race/ethnicity unknown; 0.3% international; 17% transferred in.

Faculty *Student/faculty ratio:* 20:1.

Academics *Calendar:* semesters. *Degree:* certificates and associate.

Costs (2014–15) *Tuition:* $17,671 per degree program part-time. Full-time tuition and fees vary according to program. Part-time tuition and fees vary according to program. Total costs vary by program. Tuition provided is for largest program (Medical Assisting).

Applying *Required:* essay or personal statement, high school transcript, interview.

Freshman Application Contact Carrington College–Pleasant Hill, 380 Civic Drive, Suite 300, Pleasant Hill, CA 94523.

Website: http://carrington.edu/.

Carrington College–Pomona
Pomona, California

- **Proprietary** 2-year
- **Coed**

Undergraduates 240 full-time, 61 part-time. 4% Black or African American, non-Hispanic/Latino; 59% Hispanic/Latino; 5% Asian, non-Hispanic/Latino; 1% Native Hawaiian or other Pacific Islander, non-Hispanic/Latino; 0.7% American Indian or Alaska Native, non-Hispanic/Latino; 1% Two or more races, non-Hispanic/Latino; 3% Race/ethnicity unknown; 2% international; 14% transferred in.

Faculty *Student/faculty ratio:* 22:1.

Academics *Degree:* certificates and associate.

Costs (2014–15) *Tuition:* $32,351 per degree program part-time. Total costs vary by program. Tuition provided is for largest program (Veterinary Technology).

Freshman Application Contact Carrington College–Pomona, 901 Corporate Center Drive, Suite 300, Pomona, CA 91768. *Toll-free phone:* 877-206-2106.

Website: http://carrington.edu/.

Carrington College–Sacramento
Sacramento, California

- **Proprietary** 2-year, founded 1967, part of Carrington Colleges Group, Inc.
- **Coed**

Undergraduates 1,145 full-time, 122 part-time. 10% are from out of state; 13% Black or African American, non-Hispanic/Latino; 20% Hispanic/Latino; 12% Asian, non-Hispanic/Latino; 2% Native Hawaiian or other Pacific Islander, non-Hispanic/Latino; 1% American Indian or Alaska Native, non-Hispanic/Latino; 7% Two or more races, non-Hispanic/Latino; 6% Race/ethnicity unknown; 0.1% international; 13% transferred in.

Faculty *Student/faculty ratio:* 23:1.

Academics *Calendar:* semesters. *Degree:* certificates and associate.

Standardized Tests *Required:* Entrance test administered by Carrington College California (for admission).

Costs (2014–15) *Tuition:* $19,429 per degree program part-time. Full-time tuition and fees vary according to program. Part-time tuition and fees vary according to program. Total costs vary by program. Tuition provided is for largest program (Dental Assisting).

Applying *Required:* essay or personal statement, high school transcript, interview.

Freshman Application Contact Carrington College–Sacramento, 8909 Folsom Boulevard, Sacramento, CA 95826.

Website: http://carrington.edu/.

Carrington College–San Jose
San Jose, California

- **Proprietary** 2-year, founded 1999, part of Carrington Colleges Group, Inc.
- **Coed**

Undergraduates 662 full-time, 31 part-time. 1% are from out of state; 2% Black or African American, non-Hispanic/Latino; 45% Hispanic/Latino; 16%

Asian, non-Hispanic/Latino; 4% Native Hawaiian or other Pacific Islander, non-Hispanic/Latino; 1% American Indian or Alaska Native, non-Hispanic/Latino; 3% Two or more races, non-Hispanic/Latino; 0.3% Race/ethnicity unknown; 0.6% international; 17% transferred in.
Faculty *Student/faculty ratio:* 20:1.
Academics *Calendar:* semesters. *Degree:* certificates and associate.
Standardized Tests *Required:* Entrance test administered by Carrington College California (for admission).
Costs (2014–15) *Tuition:* $32,351 per degree program part-time. Full-time tuition and fees vary according to program. Part-time tuition and fees vary according to program. Total costs vary by program. Tuition provided is for largest program (Veterinary Technology).
Applying *Required:* essay or personal statement, high school transcript, interview.
Freshman Application Contact Carrington College–San Jose, 6201 San Ignacio Avenue, San Jose, CA 95119.
Website: http://carrington.edu/.

Carrington College–San Leandro
San Leandro, California

- **Proprietary** 2-year, founded 1986, part of Carrington Colleges Group, Inc.
- **Coed**

Undergraduates 505 full-time, 16 part-time. 20% Black or African American, non-Hispanic/Latino; 40% Hispanic/Latino; 9% Asian, non-Hispanic/Latino; 5% Native Hawaiian or other Pacific Islander, non-Hispanic/Latino; 0.2% American Indian or Alaska Native, non-Hispanic/Latino; 5% Two or more races, non-Hispanic/Latino; 1% Race/ethnicity unknown; 0.2% international; 17% transferred in.
Faculty *Student/faculty ratio:* 35:1.
Academics *Calendar:* semesters. *Degree:* certificates and associate.
Standardized Tests *Required:* Entrance test administered by Carrington Colleges California (for admission).
Costs (2014–15) *Tuition:* $17,671 per degree program part-time. Full-time tuition and fees vary according to program. Part-time tuition and fees vary according to program. Total costs vary by program. Tuition provided is for largest program (Medical Assisting).
Applying *Required:* essay or personal statement, high school transcript, interview.
Freshman Application Contact Carrington College–San Leandro, 15555 East 14th Street, Suite 500, San Leandro, CA 94578.
Website: http://carrington.edu/.

Carrington College–Stockton
Stockton, California

- **Proprietary** 2-year
- **Coed**

Undergraduates 430 full-time, 35 part-time. 12% Black or African American, non-Hispanic/Latino; 42% Hispanic/Latino; 7% Asian, non-Hispanic/Latino; 2% Native Hawaiian or other Pacific Islander, non-Hispanic/Latino; 2% American Indian or Alaska Native, non-Hispanic/Latino; 3% Two or more races, non-Hispanic/Latino; 1% Race/ethnicity unknown; 12% transferred in.
Faculty *Student/faculty ratio:* 49:1.
Academics *Degree:* certificates and associate.
Costs (2014–15) *Tuition:* $32,351 per degree program part-time. Full-time tuition and fees vary according to program. Part-time tuition and fees vary according to program. Total costs vary by program. Tuition provided is for largest program (Veterinary Technology).
Freshman Application Contact Carrington College–Stockton, 1313 West Robinhood Drive, Suite B, Stockton, CA 95207.
Website: http://carrington.edu/.

Casa Loma College–Van Nuys
Los Angeles, California

Admissions Office Contact Casa Loma College–Van Nuys, 6725 Kester Avenue, Los Angeles, CA 91405.
Website: http://www.casalomacollege.edu/.

Cerritos College
Norwalk, California

Director of Admissions Ms. Stephanie Murguia, Director of Admissions and Records, Cerritos College, 11110 Alondra Boulevard, Norwalk, CA 90650-6298. *Phone:* 562-860-2451. *E-mail:* smurguia@cerritos.edu.
Website: http://www.cerritos.edu/.

Cerro Coso Community College
Ridgecrest, California

Freshman Application Contact Mrs. Heather Ootash, Counseling/Matriculation Coordinator, Cerro Coso Community College, 3000 College Heights Boulevard, Ridgecrest, CA 93555. *Phone:* 760-384-6291. *Fax:* 760-375-4776. *E-mail:* hostash@cerrocoso.edu.
Website: http://www.cerrocoso.edu/.

Chabot College
Hayward, California

Director of Admissions Paulette Lino, Director of Admissions and Records, Chabot College, 25555 Hesperian Boulevard, Hayward, CA 94545-5001. *Phone:* 510-723-6700.
Website: http://www.chabotcollege.edu/.

Chaffey College
Rancho Cucamonga, California

Freshman Application Contact Erlinda Martinez, Coordinator of Admissions, Chaffey College, 5885 Haven Avenue, Rancho Cucamonga, CA 91737-3002. *Phone:* 909-652-6610. *E-mail:* erlinda.martinez@chaffey.edu.
Website: http://www.chaffey.edu/.

Charter College
Canyon Country, California

Admissions Office Contact Charter College, 27125 Sierra Highway, Suite 329, Canyon Country, CA 91351.
Website: http://www.chartercollege.edu/.

Citrus College
Glendora, California

- **State and locally supported** 2-year, founded 1915, part of California Community College System
- **Small-town** 104-acre campus with easy access to Los Angeles
- **Coed,** 12,920 undergraduate students, 38% full-time, 53% women, 47% men

Undergraduates 4,931 full-time, 7,989 part-time. 5% Black or African American, non-Hispanic/Latino; 59% Hispanic/Latino; 8% Asian, non-Hispanic/Latino; 0.2% Native Hawaiian or other Pacific Islander, non-Hispanic/Latino; 0.2% American Indian or Alaska Native, non-Hispanic/Latino; 3% Two or more races, non-Hispanic/Latino; 1% Race/ethnicity unknown; 3% international.
Freshmen *Admission:* 9,207 applied, 9,207 admitted, 2,312 enrolled.
Faculty *Total:* 508, 30% full-time. *Student/faculty ratio:* 33:1.
Majors Administrative assistant and secretarial science; art; automobile/automotive mechanics technology; behavioral sciences; biological and physical sciences; biology/biological sciences; business administration and management; business/commerce; child development; computer and information sciences related; computer graphics; computer science; construction trades related; cosmetology; criminal justice/law enforcement administration; criminal justice/police science; dance; dance related; data processing and data processing technology; dental assisting; diesel mechanics technology; drafting and design technology; dramatic/theater arts; electrical, electronic and communications engineering technology; engineering; engineering technology; English; English language and literature related; French; German; health and physical education/fitness; history; hydrology and water resources science; Japanese; journalism; liberal arts and sciences/liberal studies; library and archives assisting; library and information science; licensed practical/vocational nurse training; mathematics; mechanical engineering/mechanical technology; modern languages; music; natural sciences; photography; physical education teaching and coaching; physical sciences; psychology; public administration; real estate; recording arts technology; registered nursing/registered nurse; security and loss prevention; social sciences; sociology; Spanish; speech communication and rhetoric; visual and performing arts; water quality and wastewater treatment management and recycling technology.
Academics *Calendar:* semesters. *Degree:* certificates, diplomas, and associate. *Special study options:* academic remediation for entering students, advanced placement credit, cooperative education, distance learning, double majors, English as a second language, honors programs, part-time degree program, services for LD students, study abroad, summer session for credit.
Library Hayden Library with 42,000 titles, 7,000 audiovisual materials, an OPAC, a Web page.

Student Life *Activities and Organizations:* drama/theater group, student-run newspaper, choral group, Student Government, Alpha Gamma Sigma (A.G.S.), Veterans Network, International Friendship Club, Citrus Business Association (C.B.A.). *Campus security:* 24-hour patrols, student patrols, late-night transport/escort service. *Student services:* health clinic, personal/psychological counseling, legal services.

Athletics *Intercollegiate sports:* baseball M, basketball M/W, cross-country running M/W, football M, golf M/W, soccer M/W, softball W, swimming and diving W, volleyball W, water polo M/W.

Costs (2014–15) *Tuition:* state resident $1380 full-time, $46 per unit part-time; nonresident $6210 full-time, $207 per unit part-time. Full-time tuition and fees vary according to course load. Part-time tuition and fees vary according to course load. *Required fees:* $70 full-time.

Financial Aid Of all full-time matriculated undergraduates who enrolled in 2013, 141 Federal Work-Study jobs (averaging $5500).

Applying *Options:* electronic application, early decision. *Required:* high school transcript. *Application deadline:* rolling (freshmen).

Freshman Application Contact Admissions and Records, Citrus College, Glendora, CA 91741-1899. *Phone:* 626-914-8511. *Fax:* 626-914-8613. *E-mail:* admissions@citruscollege.edu.

Website: http://www.citruscollege.edu/.

City College of San Francisco
San Francisco, California

Freshman Application Contact Ms. Mary Lou Leyba-Frank, Dean of Admissions and Records, City College of San Francisco, 50 Phelan Avenue, San Francisco, CA 94112-1821. *Phone:* 415-239-3291. *Fax:* 415-239-3936. *E-mail:* mleyba@ccsf.edu.

Website: http://www.ccsf.edu/.

Coastline Community College
Fountain Valley, California

- **State and locally supported** 2-year, founded 1976, part of Coast Community College District System
- **Urban** campus with easy access to Orange County
- **Coed,** 9,487 undergraduate students

Undergraduates 9% Black or African American, non-Hispanic/Latino; 24% Hispanic/Latino; 26% Asian, non-Hispanic/Latino; 2% Native Hawaiian or other Pacific Islander, non-Hispanic/Latino; 0.7% American Indian or Alaska Native, non-Hispanic/Latino; 3% Two or more races, non-Hispanic/Latino; 6% Race/ethnicity unknown.

Faculty *Total:* 282, 15% full-time. *Student/faculty ratio:* 32:1.

Majors Liberal arts and sciences/liberal studies.

Academics *Calendar:* semesters. *Degree:* certificates and associate. *Special study options:* academic remediation for entering students, accelerated degree program, adult/continuing education programs, advanced placement credit, cooperative education, distance learning, double majors, English as a second language, external degree program, honors programs, independent study, internships, off-campus study, part-time degree program, services for LD students, study abroad, summer session for credit.

Library Coastline Virtual Library plus 1 other with an OPAC, a Web page.

Student Life *Housing:* college housing not available. *Campus security:* 24-hour emergency response devices. *Student services:* health clinic, personal/psychological counseling.

Costs (2015–16) *Tuition:* state resident $1104 full-time, $46 per unit part-time; nonresident $5544 full-time, $231 per unit part-time. No tuition increase for student's term of enrollment. *Required fees:* $32 full-time, $46 per unit part-time, $46 per unit part-time.

Financial Aid Of all full-time matriculated undergraduates who enrolled in 2014, 8,176 applied for aid, 7,655 were judged to have need, 3 had their need fully met. 37 Federal Work-Study jobs (averaging $4000). *Average percent of need met:* 13%. *Average financial aid package:* $4227. *Average need-based loan:* $2930. *Average need-based gift aid:* $4156. *Financial aid deadline:* 8/15.

Applying *Options:* electronic application, early admission. *Recommended:* high school transcript. *Application deadlines:* rolling (freshmen), rolling (transfers).

Freshman Application Contact Jennifer McDonald, Director of Admissions and Records, Coastline Community College, 11460 Warner Avenue, Fountain Valley, CA 92708-2597. *Phone:* 714-241-6163.

Website: http://www.coastline.edu/.

College of Alameda
Alameda, California

Freshman Application Contact College of Alameda, 555 Ralph Appezzato Memorial Parkway, Alameda, CA 94501-2109. *Phone:* 510-748-2204.

Website: http://alameda.peralta.edu/.

College of Marin
Kentfield, California

- **State and locally supported** 2-year, founded 1926, part of California Community College System
- **Suburban** 410-acre campus with easy access to San Francisco
- **Coed,** 6,000 undergraduate students

Undergraduates 7% Black or African American, non-Hispanic/Latino; 25% Hispanic/Latino; 8% Asian, non-Hispanic/Latino; 0.3% Native Hawaiian or other Pacific Islander, non-Hispanic/Latino; 0.2% American Indian or Alaska Native, non-Hispanic/Latino; 5% Two or more races, non-Hispanic/Latino; 2% Race/ethnicity unknown; 1% international.

Faculty *Total:* 323.

Majors Accounting technology and bookkeeping; animation, interactive technology, video graphics and special effects; architectural technology; art; autobody/collision and repair technology; automobile/automotive mechanics technology; biological and physical sciences; biology/biological sciences; business administration and management; business/commerce; chemistry; child-care provision; cinematography and film/video production; computer science; computer systems networking and telecommunications; court reporting; criminal justice/police science; dance; data modeling/warehousing and database administration; dental assisting; design and visual communications; dramatic/theater arts; engineering; engineering technology; English; ethnic, cultural minority, gender, and group studies related; film/cinema/video studies; foreign languages and literatures; French; geography; geology/earth science; health and physical education/fitness; history; humanities; interior design; international relations and affairs; landscaping and groundskeeping; liberal arts and sciences/liberal studies; machine tool technology; mass communication/media; mathematics; medical administrative assistant and medical secretary; medical/clinical assistant; music; office management; physical sciences; physics; plant nursery management; political science and government; psychology; real estate; registered nursing/registered nurse; social sciences; Spanish; speech communication and rhetoric.

Academics *Calendar:* semesters. *Degree:* certificates and associate. *Special study options:* academic remediation for entering students, advanced placement credit, cooperative education, distance learning, double majors, English as a second language, part-time degree program, services for LD students, summer session for credit.

Library Main Library plus 1 other.

Student Life *Housing:* college housing not available. *Activities and Organizations:* drama/theater group, student-run newspaper. *Campus security:* 24-hour emergency response devices and patrols. *Student services:* health clinic, personal/psychological counseling.

Athletics *Intercollegiate sports:* baseball M, basketball M/W, soccer M/W, softball W, swimming and diving M/W, track and field M/W, volleyball W, water polo M/W.

Costs (2015–16) *Tuition:* state resident $1380 full-time, $46 per credit hour part-time; nonresident $7650 full-time, $255 per credit hour part-time. Full-time tuition and fees vary according to course load. Part-time tuition and fees vary according to course load. *Required fees:* $46 per credit hour part-time. *Payment plan:* installment.

Applying *Options:* electronic application, early admission. *Application deadlines:* rolling (freshmen), rolling (transfers).

Freshman Application Contact College of Marin, 835 College Avenue, Kentfield, CA 94904. *Phone:* 415-485-9414.

Website: http://www.marin.edu/.

College of San Mateo
San Mateo, California

Director of Admissions Mr. Henry Villareal, Dean of Admissions and Records, College of San Mateo, 1700 West Hillsdale Boulevard, San Mateo, CA 94402-3784. *Phone:* 650-574-6590. *E-mail:* csmadmission@smccd.edu.

Website: http://www.collegeofsanmateo.edu/.

College of the Canyons
Santa Clarita, California

- **State and locally supported** 2-year, founded 1969, part of California Community College System
- **Suburban** 224-acre campus with easy access to Los Angeles
- **Coed,** 18,064 undergraduate students, 36% full-time, 48% women, 52% men

Undergraduates 6,465 full-time, 11,599 part-time. Students come from 42 other countries; 1% are from out of state; 5% Black or African American, non-Hispanic/Latino; 45% Hispanic/Latino; 8% Asian, non-Hispanic/Latino; 0.2% Native Hawaiian or other Pacific Islander, non-Hispanic/Latino; 0.2% American Indian or Alaska Native, non-Hispanic/Latino; 0.8% Two or more races, non-Hispanic/Latino; 0.8% Race/ethnicity unknown; 0.7% international.
Freshmen *Admission:* 3,779 applied, 3,779 admitted, 2,681 enrolled.
Faculty *Total:* 713, 25% full-time. *Student/faculty ratio:* 17:1.
Majors Accounting technology and bookkeeping; administrative assistant and secretarial science; animation, interactive technology, video graphics and special effects; architectural drafting and CAD/CADD; art; athletic training; automobile/automotive mechanics technology; biological and physical sciences; building/construction site management; business administration and management; child-care provision; cinematography and film/video production; clinical/medical laboratory technology; computer science; computer systems networking and telecommunications; criminal justice/police science; dramatic/theater arts; English; fire prevention and safety technology; French; geography; geology/earth science; graphic design; health and physical education/fitness; history; hospitality administration; hotel/motel administration; humanities; interior design; journalism; legal assistant/paralegal; liberal arts and sciences/liberal studies; mathematics; music; parks, recreation and leisure; philosophy; photography; physics; political science and government; pre-engineering; psychology; radio and television; real estate; registered nursing/registered nurse; restaurant, culinary, and catering management; sales, distribution, and marketing operations; sign language interpretation and translation; small business administration; social sciences; sociology; Spanish; speech communication and rhetoric; surveying technology; water quality and wastewater treatment management and recycling technology; welding technology.
Academics *Calendar:* semesters. *Degree:* certificates and associate. *Special study options:* academic remediation for entering students, accelerated degree program, adult/continuing education programs, advanced placement credit, cooperative education, distance learning, double majors, English as a second language, honors programs, internships, part-time degree program, services for LD students, summer session for credit.
Library College of the Canyons Library with 57,390 titles, 5,168 audiovisual materials, an OPAC, a Web page.
Student Life *Housing:* college housing not available. *Activities and Organizations:* drama/theater group, choral group, Gamma Beta Phi, Alpha Delta Nu Nursing Honor Society, Psychology Club, COC Sports Medicine Club, Society of Hispanic Professional Engineers. *Campus security:* 24-hour emergency response devices, late-night transport/escort service. *Student services:* health clinic, personal/psychological counseling, women's center.
Athletics *Intercollegiate sports:* baseball M, basketball M/W, cross-country running M/W, football M, golf M/W, ice hockey M(c), soccer M/W, softball W, swimming and diving M/W, track and field M/W, volleyball W.
Costs (2015–16) *Tuition:* state resident $1154 full-time, $46 per unit part-time; nonresident $5474 full-time, $226 per unit part-time. Full-time tuition and fees vary according to course load. Part-time tuition and fees vary according to course load. *Required fees:* $50 full-time.
Financial Aid Of all full-time matriculated undergraduates who enrolled in 2012, 15,496 applied for aid, 9,185 were judged to have need.
Applying *Options:* electronic application. *Recommended:* high school transcript. *Application deadlines:* rolling (freshmen), rolling (transfers). *Notification:* continuous (freshmen), continuous (transfers).
Freshman Application Contact Ms. Jasmine Ruys, Director, Admissions and Records and Online Services, College of the Canyons, 26455 Rockwell Canyon Road, Santa Clarita, CA 91355. *Phone:* 661-362-3280. *Fax:* 661-254-7996. *E-mail:* jasmine.ruys@canyons.edu.
Website: http://www.canyons.edu/.

College of the Desert
Palm Desert, California

- **State and locally supported** 2-year, founded 1959, part of California Community College System
- **Small-town** 160-acre campus
- **Coed,** 9,259 undergraduate students, 39% full-time, 54% women, 46% men

Undergraduates 3,629 full-time, 5,630 part-time. 8% are from out of state; 4% Black or African American, non-Hispanic/Latino; 65% Hispanic/Latino;

3% Asian, non-Hispanic/Latino; 0.2% Native Hawaiian or other Pacific Islander, non-Hispanic/Latino; 0.3% American Indian or Alaska Native, non-Hispanic/Latino; 2% Two or more races, non-Hispanic/Latino; 1% Race/ethnicity unknown; 2% international; 4% transferred in. *Retention:* 75% of full-time freshmen returned.
Freshmen *Admission:* 1,976 applied, 1,976 admitted, 1,520 enrolled.
Faculty *Total:* 423, 24% full-time. *Student/faculty ratio:* 29:1.
Majors Agribusiness; agriculture; anthropology; applied horticulture/horticulture operations; architectural technology; art; automobile/automotive mechanics technology; biological and physical sciences; biology/biological sciences; building/construction site management; business administration and management; business/commerce; chemistry; child-care and support services management; computer graphics; computer science; creative writing; criminal justice/police science; crop production; culinary arts; dietetic technology; drafting and design technology; dramatic/theater arts; economics; English; environmental science; environmental studies; fire science/firefighting; French; geography; geology/earth science; health and physical education/fitness; heating, air conditioning, ventilation and refrigeration maintenance technology; history; hospitality administration; humanities; information technology; Italian; journalism; liberal arts and sciences/liberal studies; licensed practical/vocational nurse training; mass communication/media; mathematics; multi/interdisciplinary studies related; music; natural resources/conservation; office management; parks, recreation and leisure facilities management; philosophy; physics; political science and government; psychology; registered nursing/registered nurse; resort management; social sciences; sociology; Spanish; speech communication and rhetoric; substance abuse/addiction counseling; turf and turfgrass management; vehicle maintenance and repair technologies.
Academics *Calendar:* semesters. *Degree:* certificates, diplomas, and associate. *Special study options:* academic remediation for entering students, adult/continuing education programs, distance learning, double majors, English as a second language, freshman honors college, honors programs, independent study, part-time degree program, services for LD students, study abroad, summer session for credit.
Library College of the Desert Library with an OPAC, a Web page.
Student Life *Housing:* college housing not available. *Activities and Organizations:* drama/theater group, student-run newspaper, radio station, choral group, Student Nursing Association, Phi Theta Kappa, Gay Straight Alliance, International Club, Support and Education for Local Media and Arts (SELMA) SELMA Grows COD. *Campus security:* 24-hour emergency response devices and patrols, late-night transport/escort service. *Student services:* health clinic, personal/psychological counseling.
Athletics Member NJCAA. *Intercollegiate sports:* baseball M, basketball M/W, cross-country running M/W, fencing M/W, football M, golf M/W, soccer M/W, softball W, tennis M/W, track and field M/W, volleyball W.
Costs (2014–15) *Tuition:* state resident $1289 full-time, $46 per unit part-time; nonresident $6609 full-time, $236 per unit part-time. Full-time tuition and fees vary according to course load and program. Part-time tuition and fees vary according to course load and program. *Required fees:* $38 full-time, $0 per unit part-time, $20 per term part-time. *Payment plan:* installment. *Waivers:* employees or children of employees.
Applying *Options:* electronic application. *Application deadlines:* rolling (freshmen), rolling (transfers). *Notification:* continuous (freshmen), continuous (transfers).
Freshman Application Contact College of the Desert, 43-500 Monterey Avenue, Palm Desert, CA 92260-9305. *Phone:* 760-346-8041 Ext. 7441. *Website:* http://www.collegeofthedesert.edu/.

College of the Redwoods
Eureka, California

Freshman Application Contact Director of Enrollment Management, College of the Redwoods, 7351 Tompkins Hill Road, Eureka, CA 95501-9300. *Phone:* 707-476-4100. *Toll-free phone:* 800-641-0400. *Fax:* 707-476-4400. *Website:* http://www.redwoods.edu/.

College of the Sequoias
Visalia, California

Freshman Application Contact Ms. Lisa Hott, Director for Admissions, College of the Sequoias, 915 South Mooney Boulevard, Visalia, CA 93277-2234. *Phone:* 559-737-4844. *Fax:* 559-737-4820. *Website:* http://www.cos.edu/.

College of the Siskiyous
Weed, California

Freshman Application Contact Recruitment and Admissions, College of the Siskiyous, 800 College Avenue, Weed, CA 96094-2899. *Phone:* 530-938-5555. *Toll-free phone:* 888-397-4339. *E-mail:* admissions-weed@siskyous.edu.
Website: http://www.siskiyous.edu/.

Columbia College
Sonora, California

- **State and locally supported** 2-year, founded 1968, part of Yosemite Community College District System
- **Rural** 200-acre campus
- **Endowment** $296,432
- **Coed**

Undergraduates 826 full-time, 1,841 part-time. 1% Black or African American, non-Hispanic/Latino; 14% Hispanic/Latino; 2% Asian, non-Hispanic/Latino; 0.4% Native Hawaiian or other Pacific Islander, non-Hispanic/Latino; 2% American Indian or Alaska Native, non-Hispanic/Latino; 4% Two or more races, non-Hispanic/Latino; 3% Race/ethnicity unknown; 8% transferred in.
Faculty *Student/faculty ratio:* 19:1.
Academics *Calendar:* semesters. *Degree:* certificates and associate. *Special study options:* academic remediation for entering students, adult/continuing education programs, advanced placement credit, cooperative education, distance learning, double majors, English as a second language, independent study, internships, off-campus study, part-time degree program, services for LD students, summer session for credit.
Student Life *Campus security:* 24-hour emergency response devices and patrols, late-night transport/escort service.
Costs (2014–15) *Tuition:* state resident $1150 full-time, $46 per credit part-time; nonresident $6046 full-time, $268 per credit part-time. *Required fees:* $52 full-time, $35 per term part-time.
Financial Aid Of all full-time matriculated undergraduates who enrolled in 2010, 2,616 applied for aid, 2,232 were judged to have need. 29 Federal Work-Study jobs (averaging $1672). In 2010, 30. *Average non-need-based aid:* $100.
Applying *Options:* electronic application, early admission. *Required for some:* high school transcript, All new students are required to complete the matriculation process that may include assessment testing, orientation and advisement.
Freshman Application Contact Admissions Office, Columbia College, 11600 Columbia College Drive, Sonora, CA 95370. *Phone:* 209-588-5231. *Fax:* 209-588-5337. *E-mail:* ccadmissions@yosemite.edu.
Website: http://www.gocolumbia.edu/.

Community Christian College
Redlands, California

Freshman Application Contact Enrique D. Melendez, Assistant Director of Admissions, Community Christian College, 251 Tennessee Street, Redlands, CA 92373. *Phone:* 909-222-9556. *Fax:* 909-335-9101. *E-mail:* emelendez@cccollege.edu.
Website: http://www.cccollege.edu/.

Concorde Career College
Garden Grove, California

Freshman Application Contact Chris Becker, Director, Concorde Career College, 12951 Euclid Street, Suite 101, Garden Grove, CA 92840. *Phone:* 714-703-1900. *Fax:* 714-530-4737. *E-mail:* cbecker@concorde.edu.
Website: http://www.concorde.edu/.

Concorde Career College
North Hollywood, California

Freshman Application Contact Madeline Volker, Director, Concorde Career College, 12412 Victory Boulevard, North Hollywood, CA 91606. *Phone:* 818-766-8151. *Fax:* 818-766-1587. *E-mail:* mvolker@concorde.edu.
Website: http://www.concorde.edu/.

Concorde Career College
San Bernardino, California

Admissions Office Contact Concorde Career College, 201 East Airport Drive, San Bernardino, CA 92408.
Website: http://www.concorde.edu/.

Concorde Career College
San Diego, California

Admissions Office Contact Concorde Career College, 4393 Imperial Avenue, Suite 100, San Diego, CA 92113.
Website: http://www.concorde.edu/.

Contra Costa College
San Pablo, California

Freshman Application Contact Admissions and Records Office, Contra Costa College, San Pablo, CA 94806. *Phone:* 510-235-7800 Ext. 7500. *Fax:* 510-412-0769. *E-mail:* A&R@contracosta.edu.
Website: http://www.contracosta.edu/.

Copper Mountain College
Joshua Tree, California

- **State-supported** 2-year, founded 1966
- **Rural** 26-acre campus
- **Endowment** $102,297
- **Coed**
- 90% of applicants were admitted

Undergraduates 1,712 full-time, 788 part-time. 7% Black or African American, non-Hispanic/Latino; 13% Hispanic/Latino; 4% Asian, non-Hispanic/Latino; 2% American Indian or Alaska Native, non-Hispanic/Latino; 7% Race/ethnicity unknown.
Academics *Calendar:* semesters. *Degree:* certificates and associate. *Special study options:* academic remediation for entering students, advanced placement credit, distance learning, English as a second language, honors programs, independent study, internships, off-campus study, services for LD students, summer session for credit.
Student Life *Campus security:* 24-hour emergency response devices.
Costs (2014–15) *Tuition:* state resident $1384 full-time; nonresident $8430 full-time.
Applying *Options:* electronic application.
Freshman Application Contact Greg Brown, Executive Vice President for Academic and Student Affairs, Copper Mountain College, 6162 Rotary Way, Joshua Tree, CA 92252. *Phone:* 760-366-3791. *Toll-free phone:* 866-366-3791. *Fax:* 760-366-5257. *E-mail:* gbrown@cmccd.edu.
Website: http://www.cmccd.edu/.

Cosumnes River College
Sacramento, California

- **District-supported** 2-year, founded 1970, part of Los Rios Community College District System
- **Suburban** 180-acre campus with easy access to Sacramento
- **Coed**

Undergraduates 14,545 full-time.
Faculty *Student/faculty ratio:* 34:1.
Academics *Calendar:* semesters. *Degree:* certificates and associate. *Special study options:* academic remediation for entering students, accelerated degree program, adult/continuing education programs, advanced placement credit, cooperative education, distance learning, double majors, English as a second language, freshman honors college, honors programs, independent study, internships, off-campus study, part-time degree program, services for LD students, study abroad, summer session for credit.
Student Life *Campus security:* 24-hour emergency response devices and patrols, student patrols, late-night transport/escort service.
Financial Aid Of all full-time matriculated undergraduates who enrolled in 2013, 139 Federal Work-Study jobs (averaging $2000).
Applying *Options:* electronic application, early admission.
Freshman Application Contact Admissions and Records, Cosumnes River College, 8401 Center Parkway, Sacramento, CA 95823-5799. *Phone:* 916-691-7411.
Website: http://www.crc.losrios.edu/.

Crafton Hills College
Yucaipa, California

Director of Admissions Larry Aycock, Admissions and Records Coordinator, Crafton Hills College, 11711 Sand Canyon Road, Yucaipa, CA 92399-1799. *Phone:* 909-389-3663. *E-mail:* laycock@craftonhills.edu. *Website:* http://www.craftonhills.edu/.

Cuesta College
San Luis Obispo, California

Freshman Application Contact Cuesta College, PO Box 8106, San Luis Obispo, CA 93403-8106. *Phone:* 805-546-3130 Ext. 2262. *Website:* http://www.cuesta.edu/.

Cuyamaca College
El Cajon, California

Freshman Application Contact Ms. Susan Topham, Dean of Admissions and Records, Cuyamaca College, 900 Rancho San Diego Parkway, El Cajon, CA 92019-4304. *Phone:* 619-660-4302. *Fax:* 619-660-4575. *E-mail:* susan.topham@gcccd.edu. *Website:* http://www.cuyamaca.net/.

Cypress College
Cypress, California

Freshman Application Contact Admissions Office, Cypress College, 9200 Valley View, Cypress, CA 90630-5897. *Phone:* 714-484-7346. *Fax:* 714-484-7446. *E-mail:* admissions@cypresscollege.edu. *Website:* http://www.cypresscollege.edu/.

De Anza College
Cupertino, California

- **State and locally supported** 2-year, founded 1967, part of California Community College System
- **Suburban** 112-acre campus with easy access to San Francisco, San Jose
- **Coed**

Undergraduates 10,365 full-time, 13,468 part-time. 4% Black or African American, non-Hispanic/Latino; 23% Hispanic/Latino; 35% Asian, non-Hispanic/Latino; 0.5% Native Hawaiian or other Pacific Islander, non-Hispanic/Latino; 0.5% American Indian or Alaska Native, non-Hispanic/Latino; 5% Two or more races, non-Hispanic/Latino; 6% Race/ethnicity unknown.
Faculty *Student/faculty ratio:* 36:1.
Academics *Calendar:* quarters. *Degree:* certificates, diplomas, and associate. *Special study options:* academic remediation for entering students, adult/continuing education programs, advanced placement credit, cooperative education, distance learning, English as a second language, external degree program, honors programs, independent study, internships, part-time degree program, services for LD students, student-designed majors, study abroad, summer session for credit. *ROTC:* Army (c), Air Force (c).
Student Life *Campus security:* 24-hour emergency response devices, student patrols, late-night transport/escort service.
Athletics Member NCAA. All Division II.
Costs (2014–15) *Tuition:* state resident $1494 full-time; nonresident $6048 full-time, $149 per credit hour part-time. Full-time tuition and fees vary according to course load. Part-time tuition and fees vary according to course load. *Required fees:* $167 full-time, $31 per credit part-time, $49 per term part-time.
Freshman Application Contact De Anza College, 21250 Stevens Creek Boulevard, Cupertino, CA 95014-5793. *Phone:* 408-864-8292. *Website:* http://www.deanza.fhda.edu/.

Deep Springs College
Deep Springs, California

- **Independent** 2-year, founded 1917
- **Rural** 3000-acre campus
- **Endowment** $18.0 million
- **Men only,** 28 undergraduate students, 100% full-time

Undergraduates 28 full-time. Students come from 14 states and territories; 3 other countries; 83% are from out of state; 4% Hispanic/Latino; 14% Asian, non-Hispanic/Latino; 4% Two or more races, non-Hispanic/Latino; 14% international; 50% transferred in; 100% live on campus. *Retention:* 93% of full-time freshmen returned.
Freshmen *Admission:* 14 enrolled. *Test scores:* SAT critical reading scores over 500: 100%; SAT math scores over 500: 100%; SAT writing scores over 500: 100%; SAT critical reading scores over 600: 100%; SAT math scores over 600: 100%; SAT writing scores over 600: 100%; SAT critical reading scores over 700: 83%; SAT math scores over 700: 58%; SAT writing scores over 700: 75%; ACT scores over 30: 100%.
Faculty *Total:* 16, 19% full-time, 81% with terminal degrees. *Student/faculty ratio:* 4:1.
Majors Liberal arts and sciences/liberal studies.
Academics *Calendar:* six 7-week terms. *Degree:* associate. *Special study options:* distance learning, independent study, internships, services for LD students, summer session for credit.
Library Deep Springs College with 30,000 titles.
Student Life *Housing:* on-campus residence required through sophomore year. *Options:* men-only, cooperative. Campus housing is university owned. Freshman campus housing is guaranteed. *Activities and Organizations:* drama/theater group, choral group, Student Self-Government, Labor Program, Applications Committee, Review Committee, Curriculum Committee. *Campus security:* 24-hour emergency response devices, late-night transport/escort service. *Student services:* personal/psychological counseling, legal services.
Athletics *Intramural sports:* archery M, basketball M, cross-country running M, equestrian sports M, football M, riflery M, rock climbing M, soccer M, swimming and diving M, table tennis M, ultimate Frisbee M, water polo M, weight lifting M.
Standardized Tests *Required for some:* SAT or ACT (for admission).
Costs (2014–15) *Comprehensive fee:* includes mandatory fees ($250). Every student accepted to Deep Springs receives a scholarship covering tuition, room, and board.
Applying *Required:* essay or personal statement, high school transcript, 2 letters of recommendation, interview.
Freshman Application Contact Jack Davis, Chair, Applications Committee, Deep Springs College, HC 72, Box 45001, Dyer, NV 89010-9803. *Phone:* 760-872-2000. *Fax:* 760-874-0314. *E-mail:* apcom@deepsprings.edu. *Website:* http://www.deepsprings.edu/.

Diablo Valley College
Pleasant Hill, California

Freshman Application Contact Ileana Dorn, Director of Admissions and Records, Diablo Valley College, Pleasant Hill, CA 94523-1529. *Phone:* 925-685-1230 Ext. 2330. *Fax:* 925-609-8085. *E-mail:* idorn@dvc.edu. *Website:* http://www.dvc.edu/.

East Los Angeles College
Monterey Park, California

Freshman Application Contact Mr. Jeremy Allred, Associate Dean of Admissions, East Los Angeles College, 1301 Avenida Cesar Chavez, Monterey Park, CA 91754. *Phone:* 323-265-8801. *Fax:* 323-265-8688. *E-mail:* allredjp@elac.edu. *Website:* http://www.elac.edu/.

East San Gabriel Valley Regional Occupational Program & Technical Center
West Covina, California

Admissions Office Contact East San Gabriel Valley Regional Occupational Program & Technical Center, 1501 West Del Norte Avenue, West Covina, CA 91790. *Website:* http://www.esgvrop.org/.

El Camino College
Torrance, California

Director of Admissions Mr. William Mulrooney, Director of Admissions, El Camino College, 16007 Crenshaw Boulevard, Torrance, CA 90506-0001. *Phone:* 310-660-3418. *Toll-free phone:* 866-ELCAMINO. *Fax:* 310-660-6779. *E-mail:* wmulrooney@elcamino.edu. *Website:* http://www.elcamino.edu/.

Empire College
Santa Rosa, California

Freshman Application Contact Ms. Dahnja Barker, Admissions Officer, Empire College, 3035 Cleveland Avenue, Santa Rosa, CA 95403. *Phone:* 707-546-4000. *Toll-free phone:* 877-395-8535.
Website: http://www.empcol.edu/.

Evergreen Valley College
San Jose, California

Freshman Application Contact Evergreen Valley College, 3095 Yerba Buena Road, San Jose, CA 95135-1598. *Phone:* 408-270-6423.
Website: http://www.evc.edu/.

Feather River College
Quincy, California

- **State and locally supported** 2-year, founded 1968, part of California Community College System
- **Rural** 150-acre campus
- **Coed**

Undergraduates 639 full-time, 1,146 part-time. 15% are from out of state; 13% Black or African American, non-Hispanic/Latino; 20% Hispanic/Latino; 5% Asian, non-Hispanic/Latino; 1% Native Hawaiian or other Pacific Islander, non-Hispanic/Latino; 3% American Indian or Alaska Native, non-Hispanic/Latino; 0.7% Two or more races, non-Hispanic/Latino; 5% Race/ethnicity unknown; 2% international; 16% transferred in. *Retention:* 52% of full-time freshmen returned.
Faculty *Student/faculty ratio:* 23:1.
Academics *Calendar:* semesters. *Degree:* certificates, diplomas, and associate. *Special study options:* academic remediation for entering students, adult/continuing education programs, advanced placement credit, cooperative education, distance learning, double majors, honors programs, independent study, part-time degree program, services for LD students, summer session for credit.
Student Life *Campus security:* student patrols.
Costs (2014–15) *Tuition:* state resident $1380 full-time, $46 per credit part-time; nonresident $7230 full-time, $241 per credit part-time. *Room and board:* room only: $4250.

Financial Aid Of all full-time matriculated undergraduates who enrolled in 2013, 22 Federal Work-Study jobs (averaging $750). 103 state and other part-time jobs (averaging $1504).
Applying *Options:* electronic application.
Freshman Application Contact Leslie Mikesell, Director of Admissions and Records, Feather River College, 570 Golden Eagle Avenue, Quincy, CA 95971-9124. *Phone:* 530-283-0202. *Toll-free phone:* 800-442-9799. *E-mail:* lmikesell@frc.edu.
Website: http://www.frc.edu/.

FIDM/Fashion Institute of Design & Merchandising, Los Angeles Campus
Los Angeles, California

- **Proprietary** primarily 2-year, founded 1969, part of The Fashion Institute of Design and Merchandising/FIDM
- **Urban** campus
- **Coed**, 3,142 undergraduate students, 88% full-time, 90% women, 10% men

Undergraduates 2,773 full-time, 369 part-time. Students come from 65 other countries; 32% are from out of state; 6% Black or African American, non-Hispanic/Latino; 23% Hispanic/Latino; 12% Asian, non-Hispanic/Latino; 0.7% Native Hawaiian or other Pacific Islander, non-Hispanic/Latino; 0.4% American Indian or Alaska Native, non-Hispanic/Latino; 3% Two or more races, non-Hispanic/Latino; 7% Race/ethnicity unknown; 14% international; 16% transferred in; 10% live on campus. *Retention:* 96% of full-time freshmen returned.
Freshmen *Admission:* 1,348 applied, 698 admitted, 446 enrolled.
Faculty *Total:* 275, 27% full-time. *Student/faculty ratio:* 21:1.
Majors Apparel and accessories marketing; apparel and textile manufacturing; apparel and textile marketing management; apparel and textiles; business administration and management; business, management, and marketing related; cinematography and film/video production; commercial and advertising art; consumer merchandising/retailing management; costume design; design and visual communications; fashion/apparel design; fashion merchandising; graphic design; industrial and product design; interdisciplinary studies; interior design; logistics, materials, and supply chain management; marketing/marketing management; metal and jewelry arts.
Academics *Calendar:* quarters. *Degrees:* associate and bachelor's (also includes Orange County Campus). *Special study options:* academic remediation for entering students, adult/continuing education programs,

FIDM. Creative careers begin here.

L.A.

S.D.

O.C.

S.F.

IT'S MORE THAN A COLLEGE, IT'S FIDM.

- Bachelor's, Associates & Advanced Study Degree programs
- Accredited by WASC & NASAD
- 26 professionally-based majors
- Curriculum with built in work experience
- Faculty of industry professionals
- Unparalleled industry partnerships
- Powerful global network of more than 60,000 alumni
- 4 California campuses: Los Angeles, San Francisco, Orange County & San Diego

Visit fidm.edu or call 800.624.1200
Text FIDM4year to 57682
Msg & Data Rates Apply. Reply STOP to cancel, HELP for help.

advanced placement credit, cooperative education, distance learning, English as a second language, independent study, internships, part-time degree program, services for LD students, study abroad, summer session for credit.
Library FIDM Los Angeles Campus Library plus 1 other with 30,242 titles, 8,019 audiovisual materials, an OPAC, a Web page.
Student Life *Housing Options:* coed, men-only, women-only. Campus housing is leased by the school. *Activities and Organizations:* Cross-Cultural Student Alliance, Fashion Industry Club, Phi Theta Kappa Honor Society, Student Council, MODE. *Campus security:* 24-hour emergency response devices and patrols, late-night transport/escort service. *Student services:* personal/psychological counseling.
Standardized Tests *Recommended:* SAT or ACT (for admission).
Costs (2014–15) *Tuition:* $28,965 full-time. Full-time tuition and fees vary according to course load and program. Part-time tuition and fees vary according to course load and program. *Required fees:* $965 full-time. *Payment plan:* installment. *Waivers:* employees or children of employees.
Financial Aid Of all full-time matriculated undergraduates who enrolled in 2013, 88 Federal Work-Study jobs (averaging $2935).
Applying *Options:* electronic application, deferred entrance. *Application fee:* $225. *Required:* essay or personal statement, high school transcript, minimum 2.0 GPA, 3 letters of recommendation, interview, major-determined project. *Application deadlines:* rolling (freshmen), rolling (out-of-state freshmen), rolling (transfers).
Freshmen Application Contact Ms. Susan Aronson, Director of Admissions, FIDM/Fashion Institute of Design & Merchandising, Los Angeles Campus, Los Angeles, CA 90015. *Phone:* 213-624-1201. *Toll-free phone:* 800-624-1200. *Fax:* 213-624-4799. *E-mail:* saronson@fidm.com. *Website:* http://www.fidm.edu/.

See display on previous page and page 370 for the College Close-Up.

FIDM/Fashion Institute of Design & Merchandising, Orange County Campus
Irvine, California

- **Proprietary** 2-year, founded 1981, part of The Fashion Institute of Design and Merchandising/FIDM
- **Coed, primarily women,** 156 undergraduate students, 96% full-time, 94% women, 6% men

Undergraduates 150 full-time, 6 part-time. Students come from 4 other countries; 16% are from out of state; 2% Black or African American, non-Hispanic/Latino; 26% Hispanic/Latino; 12% Asian, non-Hispanic/Latino; 2% Native Hawaiian or other Pacific Islander, non-Hispanic/Latino; 1% American Indian or Alaska Native, non-Hispanic/Latino; 6% Two or more races, non-Hispanic/Latino; 3% Race/ethnicity unknown; 3% international; 23% transferred in. *Retention:* 81% of full-time freshmen returned.
Freshmen *Admission:* 265 applied, 175 admitted, 106 enrolled.
Faculty *Total:* 21, 19% full-time. *Student/faculty ratio:* 15:1.
Majors Apparel and textile marketing management; apparel and textiles; commercial and advertising art; consumer merchandising/retailing management; design and visual communications; fashion/apparel design; fashion merchandising; fiber, textile and weaving arts; graphic design; industrial technology; interior design; marketing/marketing management.
Academics *Calendar:* quarters. *Degree:* associate. *Special study options:* academic remediation for entering students, adult/continuing education programs, advanced placement credit, cooperative education, distance learning, English as a second language, independent study, internships, part-time degree program, services for LD students, study abroad, summer session for credit.
Library FIDM Orange County Campus Library plus 1 other with 4,069 titles, 3,515 audiovisual materials, an OPAC, a Web page.
Student Life *Activities and Organizations:* MODE, Student Council, Phi Theta Kappa- National Honor Society, Fashion Industry Club, Cross-Cultural Student Alliance. *Campus security:* 24-hour emergency response devices, late-night transport/escort service. *Student services:* personal/psychological counseling.
Costs (2014–15) *Tuition:* $28,965 full-time. Full-time tuition and fees vary according to course load and program. Part-time tuition and fees vary according to course load and program. *Required fees:* $965 full-time. *Payment plan:* installment. *Waivers:* employees or children of employees.
Applying *Options:* deferred entrance. *Application fee:* $225. *Required:* essay or personal statement, high school transcript, minimum 2.0 GPA, 3 letters of recommendation, interview, entrance requirement project. *Application deadlines:* rolling (freshmen), rolling (out-of-state freshmen), rolling (transfers). *Notification:* continuous (freshmen), continuous (out-of-state freshmen), continuous (transfers).
Freshman Application Contact Admissions, FIDM/Fashion Institute of Design & Merchandising, Orange County Campus, 17590 Gillette Avenue,

Irvine, CA 92614-5610. *Phone:* 949-851-6200. *Toll-free phone:* 888-974-3436. *Fax:* 949-851-6808.
Website: http://www.fidm.edu/.

FIDM/Fashion Institute of Design & Merchandising, San Francisco Campus
San Francisco, California

- **Proprietary** primarily 2-year, founded 1973, part of The Fashion Institute of Design and Merchandising/FIDM
- **Urban** campus
- **Coed,** 527 undergraduate students, 88% full-time, 92% women, 8% men

Undergraduates 463 full-time, 64 part-time. Students come from 14 other countries; 7% are from out of state; 3% Black or African American, non-Hispanic/Latino; 24% Hispanic/Latino; 19% Asian, non-Hispanic/Latino; 2% Native Hawaiian or other Pacific Islander, non-Hispanic/Latino; 0.8% American Indian or Alaska Native, non-Hispanic/Latino; 4% Two or more races, non-Hispanic/Latino; 6% Race/ethnicity unknown; 6% international; 19% transferred in. *Retention:* 89% of full-time freshmen returned.
Freshmen *Admission:* 258 applied, 139 admitted, 99 enrolled. *Test scores:* ACT scores over 18: 100%; ACT scores over 24: 40%; ACT scores over 30: 10%.
Faculty *Total:* 62, 19% full-time. *Student/faculty ratio:* 17:1.
Majors Apparel and accessories marketing; apparel and textiles; business, management, and marketing related; commercial and advertising art; consumer merchandising/retailing management; design and visual communications; fashion/apparel design; fashion merchandising; graphic design; interdisciplinary studies; interior design.
Academics *Calendar:* quarters. *Degrees:* associate and bachelor's. *Special study options:* academic remediation for entering students, adult/continuing education programs, advanced placement credit, cooperative education, distance learning, English as a second language, honors programs, independent study, internships, off-campus study, part-time degree program, services for LD students, study abroad, summer session for credit.
Library FIDM San Francisco Library plus 1 other with 8,676 titles, 4,069 audiovisual materials, an OPAC, a Web page.
Student Life *Housing:* college housing not available. *Activities and Organizations:* MODE, Student Council, Phi Theta Kappa- National Honor Society, Fashion Industry Club, Cross-Cultural Student Alliance. *Campus security:* 24-hour emergency response devices and patrols. *Student services:* personal/psychological counseling.
Standardized Tests *Recommended:* SAT or ACT (for admission).
Costs (2014–15) *Tuition:* $28,965 full-time. Full-time tuition and fees vary according to course load and program. Part-time tuition and fees vary according to course load and program. *Required fees:* $965 full-time. *Payment plan:* installment. *Waivers:* employees or children of employees.
Applying *Options:* electronic application, deferred entrance. *Application fee:* $225. *Required:* essay or personal statement, high school transcript, 3 letters of recommendation, interview, major-determined project. *Application deadlines:* rolling (freshmen), rolling (out-of-state freshmen), rolling (transfers).
Freshman Application Contact Ms. Susan Aronson, Director of Admissions, FIDM/Fashion Institute of Design & Merchandising, San Francisco Campus, San Francisco, CA 94108. *Phone:* 213-624-1201. *Toll-free phone:* 800-422-3436. *Fax:* 415-296-7299. *E-mail:* info@fidm.com. *Website:* http://www.fidm.edu/.

FIDM/The Fashion Institute of Design & Merchandising, San Diego Campus
San Diego, California

- **Proprietary** 2-year, founded 1985, part of The Fashion Institute of Design and Merchandising/FIDM
- **Urban** campus
- **Coed, primarily women,** 142 undergraduate students, 94% full-time, 94% women, 6% men

Undergraduates 133 full-time, 9 part-time. Students come from 5 other countries; 17% are from out of state; 4% Black or African American, non-Hispanic/Latino; 37% Hispanic/Latino; 8% Asian, non-Hispanic/Latino; 3% Native Hawaiian or other Pacific Islander, non-Hispanic/Latino; 1% American Indian or Alaska Native, non-Hispanic/Latino; 1% Two or more races, non-Hispanic/Latino; 5% Race/ethnicity unknown; 4% international; 25% transferred in. *Retention:* 86% of full-time freshmen returned.
Freshmen *Admission:* 150 applied, 88 admitted, 67 enrolled. *Test scores:* ACT scores over 18: 100%; ACT scores over 24: 40%; ACT scores over 30: 10%.
Faculty *Total:* 24, 8% full-time. *Student/faculty ratio:* 15:1.

Majors Apparel and accessories marketing; commercial and advertising art; consumer merchandising/retailing management; design and visual communications; fashion/apparel design; fashion merchandising; interior design.

Academics *Calendar:* quarters. *Degree:* associate. *Special study options:* academic remediation for entering students, adult/continuing education programs, advanced placement credit, cooperative education, distance learning, English as a second language, independent study, internships, part-time degree program, services for LD students, study abroad, summer session for credit.

Library FIDM San Diego Campus Library plus 1 other with 7,027 titles, 4,194 audiovisual materials, an OPAC.

Student Life *Activities and Organizations:* MODE, Student Council, Phi Theta Kappa- National Honor Society, Fashion Industry Club, Cross-Cultural Student Alliance. *Campus security:* 24-hour emergency response devices and patrols. *Student services:* personal/psychological counseling.

Standardized Tests *Recommended:* SAT or ACT (for admission).

Costs (2014–15) *Tuition:* $28,965 full-time. Full-time tuition and fees vary according to course load and program. Part-time tuition and fees vary according to course load and program. *Required fees:* $965 full-time. *Payment plan:* installment. *Waivers:* employees or children of employees.

Applying *Options:* electronic application, deferred entrance. *Application fee:* $225. *Required:* essay or personal statement, high school transcript, minimum 2.0 GPA, 3 letters of recommendation, interview, major-determined project. *Application deadlines:* rolling (freshmen), rolling (out-of-state freshmen), rolling (transfers).

Freshman Application Contact Ms. Susan Aronson, Director of Admissions, FIDM/The Fashion Institute of Design & Merchandising, San Diego Campus, San Diego, CA 92101. *Phone:* 213-624-1200 Ext. 5400. *Toll-free phone:* 800-243-3436. *Fax:* 619-232-4322. *E-mail:* info@fidm.com. *Website:* http://www.fidm.edu/.

Folsom Lake College
Folsom, California

Freshman Application Contact Admissions Office, Folsom Lake College, 10 College Parkway, Folsom, CA 95630. *Phone:* 916-608-6500. *Website:* http://www.flc.losrios.edu/.

Foothill College
Los Altos Hills, California

Freshman Application Contact Ms. Shawna Aced, Registrar, Foothill College, Admissions and Records, 12345 El Monte Road, Los Altos Hills, CA 94022. *Phone:* 650-949-7771. *E-mail:* acedshawna@hda.edu. *Website:* http://www.foothill.edu/.

Four-D College
Colton, California

Admissions Office Contact Four-D College, 1020 East Washington Street, Colton, CA 92324. *Website:* http://www.4dcollege.edu/.

Fremont College
Cerritos, California

Freshman Application Contact Natasha Dawson, Director of Admissions, Fremont College, 18000 Studebaker Road, Suite 900A, Cerritos, CA 90703. *Phone:* 562-809-5100. *Toll-free phone:* 800-373-6668. *Fax:* 562-809-5100. *E-mail:* info@fremont.edu. *Website:* http://www.fremont.edu/.

Fremont College
Los Angeles, California

Admissions Office Contact Fremont College, 3440 Wilshire Boulevard, 10th Floor, Los Angeles, CA 90010. *Toll-free phone:* 800-373-6668. *Website:* http://www.fremont.edu/.

Fresno City College
Fresno, California

Freshman Application Contact Office Assistant, Fresno City College, 1101 East University Avenue, Fresno, CA 93741-0002. *Phone:* 559-442-4600 Ext. 8604. *Fax:* 559-237-4232. *E-mail:* fcc.admissions@fresnocitycollege.edu. *Website:* http://www.fresnocitycollege.edu/.

Fullerton College
Fullerton, California

- **State and locally supported** 2-year, founded 1913, part of California Community College System
- **Suburban** 79-acre campus with easy access to Los Angeles
- **Coed**

Undergraduates 8,538 full-time, 15,885 part-time. 4% Black or African American, non-Hispanic/Latino; 55% Hispanic/Latino; 13% Asian, non-Hispanic/Latino; 0.4% Native Hawaiian or other Pacific Islander, non-Hispanic/Latino; 0.8% American Indian or Alaska Native, non-Hispanic/Latino; 1% Race/ethnicity unknown; 4% transferred in. *Retention:* 78% of full-time freshmen returned.

Faculty *Student/faculty ratio:* 29:1.

Academics *Calendar:* semesters. *Degree:* certificates and associate. *Special study options:* academic remediation for entering students, adult/continuing education programs, advanced placement credit, cooperative education, English as a second language, honors programs, part-time degree program, services for LD students, study abroad, summer session for credit. *ROTC:* Army (c), Navy (c), Air Force (c).

Financial Aid *Financial aid deadline:* 6/30.

Applying *Options:* electronic application, early admission.

Freshman Application Contact Fullerton College, 321 East Chapman Avenue, Fullerton, CA 92832-2095. *Phone:* 714-992-7076. *Website:* http://www.fullcoll.edu/.

Gavilan College
Gilroy, California

- **State and locally supported** 2-year, founded 1919, part of California Community College System
- **Rural** 150-acre campus with easy access to San Jose
- **Coed**

Undergraduates 1,767 full-time, 3,500 part-time. Students come from 5 states and territories; 0.1% are from out of state; 3% Black or African American, non-Hispanic/Latino; 51% Hispanic/Latino; 6% Asian, non-Hispanic/Latino; 0.4% Native Hawaiian or other Pacific Islander, non-Hispanic/Latino; 0.6% American Indian or Alaska Native, non-Hispanic/Latino; 1% Two or more races, non-Hispanic/Latino; 5% Race/ethnicity unknown; 100% transferred in. *Retention:* 69% of full-time freshmen returned.

Faculty *Student/faculty ratio:* 30:1.

Academics *Calendar:* semesters. *Degree:* certificates, diplomas, and associate. *Special study options:* academic remediation for entering students, adult/continuing education programs, advanced placement credit, cooperative education, distance learning, English as a second language, honors programs, independent study, internships, part-time degree program, services for LD students, study abroad, summer session for credit.

Student Life *Campus security:* 24-hour emergency response devices.

Financial Aid Of all full-time matriculated undergraduates who enrolled in 2013, 50 Federal Work-Study jobs (averaging $2000). *Financial aid deadline:* 6/30.

Freshman Application Contact Gavilan College, 5055 Santa Teresa Boulevard, Gilroy, CA 95020-9599. *Phone:* 408-848-4754. *Website:* http://www.gavilan.edu/.

Glendale Career College
Glendale, California

Admissions Office Contact Glendale Career College, 240 North Brand Boulevard, Lower Level, Glendale, CA 91203. *Website:* http://www.glendalecareer.com/.

Glendale Community College
Glendale, California

Freshman Application Contact Ms. Sharon Combs, Dean, Admissions, and Records, Glendale Community College, 1500 North Verdugo Road, Glendale, CA 91208. *Phone:* 818-240-1000 Ext. 5910. *E-mail:* scombs@glendale.edu. *Website:* http://www.glendale.edu/.

Golden West College
Huntington Beach, California

- **State and locally supported** 2-year, founded 1966, part of Coast Community College District System
- **Suburban** 122-acre campus with easy access to Los Angeles
- **Endowment** $7.6 million
- **Coed,** 12,394 undergraduate students, 35% full-time, 53% women, 47% men

Undergraduates 4,394 full-time, 8,000 part-time. 1% are from out of state; 2% Black or African American, non-Hispanic/Latino; 32% Hispanic/Latino; 28% Asian, non-Hispanic/Latino; 0.5% Native Hawaiian or other Pacific Islander, non-Hispanic/Latino; 0.3% American Indian or Alaska Native, non-Hispanic/Latino; 4% Two or more races, non-Hispanic/Latino; 1% Race/ethnicity unknown; 2% international. *Retention:* 71% of full-time freshmen returned.

Freshmen *Admission:* 11,210 applied, 11,210 admitted, 2,298 enrolled.

Faculty *Total:* 534, 24% full-time. *Student/faculty ratio:* 33:1.

Majors Accounting; administrative assistant and secretarial science; architectural engineering technology; art; automobile/automotive mechanics technology; biological and physical sciences; biology/biological sciences; business administration and management; commercial and advertising art; consumer merchandising/retailing management; cosmetology; criminal justice/law enforcement administration; criminal justice/police science; drafting and design technology; electrical, electronic and communications engineering technology; engineering technology; graphic and printing equipment operation/production; humanities; journalism; legal administrative assistant/secretary; liberal arts and sciences/liberal studies; marketing/marketing management; mathematics; music; natural sciences; ornamental horticulture; physical sciences; radio and television; real estate; registered nursing/registered nurse; sign language interpretation and translation.

Academics *Calendar:* semesters (summer session). *Degree:* certificates and associate. *Special study options:* academic remediation for entering students, adult/continuing education programs, advanced placement credit, cooperative education, distance learning, English as a second language, external degree program, honors programs, independent study, internships, part-time degree program, services for LD students, student-designed majors, study abroad, summer session for credit. *ROTC:* Air Force (c).

Library Golden West College Library plus 1 other with 95,000 titles, an OPAC, a Web page.

Student Life *Housing:* college housing not available. *Activities and Organizations:* drama/theater group, student-run newspaper, choral group. *Campus security:* 24-hour emergency response devices and patrols, late-night transport/escort service. *Student services:* health clinic, personal/psychological counseling, legal services.

Athletics Member NJCAA. *Intercollegiate sports:* baseball M, cross-country running M/W, football M, soccer M/W, softball W, swimming and diving M/W, track and field M/W, volleyball M/W, water polo M/W.

Costs (2014–15) *Tuition:* state resident $1104 full-time, $46 per unit part-time; nonresident $5544 full-time, $219 per unit part-time. Full-time tuition and fees vary according to course load and program. Part-time tuition and fees vary according to course load and program. *Required fees:* $72 full-time, $36 per year part-time. *Waivers:* minority students, children of alumni, adult students, senior citizens, and employees or children of employees.

Applying *Options:* early admission. *Required for some:* essay or personal statement. *Recommended:* high school transcript. *Application deadlines:* rolling (freshmen), rolling (transfers). *Notification:* continuous (freshmen), continuous (transfers).

Freshman Application Contact Golden West College, PO Box 2748, 15744 Golden West Street, Huntington Beach, CA 92647-2748. *Phone:* 714-892-7711 Ext. 58965.

Website: http://www.goldenwestcollege.edu/.

Golf Academy of America
Carlsbad, California

Director of Admissions Ms. Deborah Wells, Admissions Coordinator, Golf Academy of America, 1950 Camino Vida Roble, Suite 125, Carlsbad, CA 92008. *Phone:* 760-414-1501. *Toll-free phone:* 800-342-7342. *E-mail:* sdga@sdgagolf.com.

Website: http://www.golfacademy.edu/.

Grossmont College
El Cajon, California

Freshman Application Contact Admissions Office, Grossmont College, 8800 Grossmont College Drive, El Cajon, CA 92020-1799. *Phone:* 619-644-7186.

Website: http://www.grossmont.edu/.

Gurnick Academy of Medical Arts
San Mateo, California

Admissions Office Contact Gurnick Academy of Medical Arts, 2121 South El Camino Real, Building C 2000, San Mateo, CA 94403.

Website: http://www.gurnick.edu/.

Hartnell College
Salinas, California

Director of Admissions Director of Admissions, Hartnell College, 411 Central Avenue, Salinas, CA 93901. *Phone:* 831-755-6711. *Fax:* 831-759-6014.

Website: http://www.hartnell.edu/.

ICDC College
Huntington Park, California

Admissions Office Contact ICDC College, 6812 Pacific Boulevard, Huntington Park, CA 33409.

Website: http://icdccollege.edu/.

Imperial Valley College
Imperial, California

- **State and locally supported** 2-year, founded 1922, part of California Community College System
- **Rural** 160-acre campus
- **Endowment** $832,061
- **Coed**

Undergraduates Students come from 12 states and territories; 3% are from out of state.

Academics *Calendar:* semesters. *Degree:* certificates and associate. *Special study options:* academic remediation for entering students, accelerated degree program, adult/continuing education programs, advanced placement credit, double majors, English as a second language, part-time degree program, services for LD students, student-designed majors, summer session for credit.

Student Life *Campus security:* student patrols.

Costs (2014–15) *Tuition:* state resident $1326 full-time, $46 per unit part-time; nonresident $7486 full-time, $220 per unit part-time. *Required fees:* $39 full-time, $19 per term part-time. *Payment plans:* installment, deferred payment.

Applying *Application fee:* $23. *Required for some:* high school transcript. *Recommended:* high school transcript.

Freshman Application Contact Imperial Valley College, 380 East Aten Road, PO Box 158, Imperial, CA 92251-0158. *Phone:* 760-352-8320 Ext. 200.

Website: http://www.imperial.edu/.

Institute of Technology
Clovis, California

Admissions Office Contact Institute of Technology, 564 W. Herndon Avenue, Clovis, CA 93612.

Website: http://www.it-colleges.edu/.

Irvine Valley College
Irvine, California

Director of Admissions Mr. John Edwards, Director of Admissions, Records, and Enrollment Services, Irvine Valley College, 5500 Irvine Center Drive, Irvine, CA 92618. *Phone:* 949-451-5416.

Website: http://www.ivc.edu/.

ITT Technical Institute
Culver City, California

- **Proprietary** primarily 2-year, part of ITT Educational Services, Inc.
- **Coed**

Academics *Calendar:* quarters. *Degrees:* associate and bachelor's.
Freshman Application Contact Director of Recruitment, ITT Technical Institute, 6101 W. Centinela Avenue, Suite 180, Culver City, CA 90230. *Phone:* 310-417-5800. *Toll-free phone:* 800-215-6151.
Website: http://www.itt-tech.edu/.

ITT Technical Institute
Lathrop, California

- **Proprietary** primarily 2-year, founded 1997, part of ITT Educational Services, Inc.
- **Coed**

Academics *Calendar:* quarters. *Degrees:* associate and bachelor's.
Freshman Application Contact Director of Recruitment, ITT Technical Institute, 16916 South Harlan Road, Lathrop, CA 95330. *Phone:* 209-858-0077. *Toll-free phone:* 800-346-1786.
Website: http://www.itt-tech.edu/.

ITT Technical Institute
National City, California

- **Proprietary** primarily 2-year, founded 1981, part of ITT Educational Services, Inc.
- **Suburban** campus
- **Coed**

Academics *Calendar:* quarters. *Degrees:* associate and bachelor's.
Freshman Application Contact Director of Recruitment, ITT Technical Institute, 401 Mile of Cars Way, National City, CA 91950. *Phone:* 619-327-1800. *Toll-free phone:* 800-883-0380.
Website: http://www.itt-tech.edu/.

ITT Technical Institute
Oakland, California

- **Proprietary** primarily 2-year, part of ITT Educational Services, Inc.
- **Coed**

Academics *Calendar:* quarters. *Degrees:* associate and bachelor's.
Freshman Application Contact Director of Recruitment, ITT Technical Institute, 7901 Oakport Street, Suite 3000, Oakland, CA 94621. *Phone:* 510-553-2800. *Toll-free phone:* 877-442-5833.
Website: http://www.itt-tech.edu/.

ITT Technical Institute
Orange, California

- **Proprietary** primarily 2-year, founded 1982, part of ITT Educational Services, Inc.
- **Suburban** campus
- **Coed**

Academics *Calendar:* quarters. *Degrees:* associate and bachelor's.
Financial Aid Of all full-time matriculated undergraduates who enrolled in 2013, 20 Federal Work-Study jobs (averaging $5000).
Freshman Application Contact Director of Recruitment, ITT Technical Institute, 4000 West Metropolitan Drive, Suite 100, Orange, CA 92868. *Phone:* 714-941-2400.
Website: http://www.itt-tech.edu/.

ITT Technical Institute
Oxnard, California

- **Proprietary** primarily 2-year, founded 1993, part of ITT Educational Services, Inc.
- **Urban** campus
- **Coed**

Academics *Calendar:* quarters. *Degrees:* associate and bachelor's.
Freshman Application Contact Director of Recruitment, ITT Technical Institute, 2051 Solar Drive, Suite 150, Oxnard, CA 93036. *Phone:* 805-988-0143. *Toll-free phone:* 800-530-1582.
Website: http://www.itt-tech.edu/.

ITT Technical Institute
Rancho Cordova, California

- **Proprietary** primarily 2-year, founded 1954, part of ITT Educational Services, Inc.
- **Urban** campus
- **Coed**

Academics *Calendar:* quarters. *Degrees:* associate and bachelor's.
Freshman Application Contact Director of Recruitment, ITT Technical Institute, 10863 Gold Center Drive, Rancho Cordova, CA 95670-6034. *Phone:* 916-851-3900. *Toll-free phone:* 800-488-8466.
Website: http://www.itt-tech.edu/.

ITT Technical Institute
San Bernardino, California

- **Proprietary** primarily 2-year, founded 1987, part of ITT Educational Services, Inc.
- **Urban** campus
- **Coed**

Academics *Calendar:* quarters. *Degrees:* associate and bachelor's.
Freshman Application Contact Director of Recruitment, ITT Technical Institute, 670 East Carnegie Drive, San Bernardino, CA 92408. *Phone:* 909-806-4600. *Toll-free phone:* 800-888-3801.
Website: http://www.itt-tech.edu/.

ITT Technical Institute
San Dimas, California

- **Proprietary** primarily 2-year, founded 1982, part of ITT Educational Services, Inc.
- **Suburban** campus
- **Coed**

Academics *Calendar:* quarters. *Degrees:* associate and bachelor's.
Financial Aid Of all full-time matriculated undergraduates who enrolled in 2013, 20 Federal Work-Study jobs (averaging $4500).
Freshman Application Contact Director of Recruitment, ITT Technical Institute, 650 West Cienega Avenue, San Dimas, CA 91773. *Phone:* 909-971-2300. *Toll-free phone:* 800-414-6522.
Website: http://www.itt-tech.edu/.

ITT Technical Institute
Sylmar, California

- **Proprietary** primarily 2-year, founded 1982, part of ITT Educational Services, Inc.
- **Urban** campus
- **Coed**

Academics *Calendar:* quarters. *Degrees:* associate and bachelor's.
Freshman Application Contact Director of Recruitment, ITT Technical Institute, 12669 Encinitas Avenue, Sylmar, CA 91342-3664. *Phone:* 818-364-5151. *Toll-free phone:* 800-363-2086 (in-state); 800-636-2086 (out-of-state).
Website: http://www.itt-tech.edu/.

ITT Technical Institute
Torrance, California

- **Proprietary** primarily 2-year, founded 1987, part of ITT Educational Services, Inc.
- **Urban** campus
- **Coed**

Academics *Calendar:* quarters. *Degrees:* associate and bachelor's.
Financial Aid Of all full-time matriculated undergraduates who enrolled in 2013, 6 Federal Work-Study jobs (averaging $4000).
Freshman Application Contact Director of Recruitment, ITT Technical Institute, 2555 West 190th Street, Suite 125, Torrance, CA 90504. *Phone:* 310-965-5900.
Website: http://www.itt-tech.edu/.

Kaplan College, Bakersfield Campus
Bakersfield, California

Freshman Application Contact Kaplan College, Bakersfield Campus, 1914 Wible Road, Bakersfield, CA 93304. *Phone:* 661-836-6300. *Toll-free phone:* 800-935-1857.
Website: http://www.kaplancollege.com/.

Kaplan College, Chula Vista Campus
Chula Vista, California

Freshman Application Contact Kaplan College, Chula Vista Campus, 555 Broadway, Chula Vista, CA 91910. *Phone:* 877-473-3052. *Toll-free phone:* 800-935-1857.
Website: http://www.kaplancollege.com/.

Kaplan College, Fresno Campus
Clovis, California

Freshman Application Contact Kaplan College, Fresno Campus, 44 Shaw Avenue, Clovis, CA 93612. *Phone:* 559-325-5100. *Toll-free phone:* 800-935-1857.
Website: http://www.kaplancollege.com/.

Kaplan College, Modesto Campus
Salida, California

Freshman Application Contact Kaplan College, Modesto Campus, 5172 Kiernan Court, Salida, CA 95368. *Phone:* 209-543-7000. *Toll-free phone:* 800-935-1857.
Website: http://www.kaplancollege.com/.

Kaplan College, North Hollywood Campus
North Hollywood, California

Freshman Application Contact Ms. Renee Codner, Director of Admissions, Kaplan College, North Hollywood Campus, 6180 Laurel Canyon Boulevard, Suite 101, North Hollywood, CA 91606. *Phone:* 818-763-2563 Ext. 240. *Toll-free phone:* 800-935-1857. *E-mail:* rcodner@mariccollege.edu.
Website: http://www.kaplancollege.com/.

Kaplan College, Palm Springs Campus
Palm Springs, California

Freshman Application Contact Kaplan College, Palm Springs Campus, 2475 East Tahquitz Canyon Way, Palm Springs, CA 92262. *Phone:* 760-778-3540. *Toll-free phone:* 800-935-1857.
Website: http://www.kaplancollege.com/.

Kaplan College, Riverside Campus
Riverside, California

Freshman Application Contact Kaplan College, Riverside Campus, 4040 Vine Street, Riverside, CA 92507. *Phone:* 951-276-1704. *Toll-free phone:* 800-935-1857.
Website: http://www.kaplancollege.com/.

Kaplan College, Sacramento Campus
Sacramento, California

Freshman Application Contact Kaplan College, Sacramento Campus, 4330 Watt Avenue, Suite 400, Sacramento, CA 95821. *Phone:* 916-649-8168. *Toll-free phone:* 800-935-1857.
Website: http://www.kaplancollege.com/.

Kaplan College, San Diego Campus
San Diego, California

Freshman Application Contact Kaplan College, San Diego Campus, 9055 Balboa Avenue, San Diego, CA 92123. *Phone:* 858-279-4500. *Toll-free phone:* 800-935-1857.
Website: http://www.kaplancollege.com/.

Kaplan College, Vista Campus
Vista, California

Freshman Application Contact Kaplan College, Vista Campus, 2022 University Drive, Vista, CA 92083. *Phone:* 760-630-1555. *Toll-free phone:* 800-935-1857.
Website: http://www.kaplancollege.com/.

Lake Tahoe Community College
South Lake Tahoe, California

- **State and locally supported** 2-year, founded 1975, part of California Community College System
- **Small-town** 164-acre campus
- **Coed**

Academics *Calendar:* quarters. *Degree:* certificates and associate. *Special study options:* academic remediation for entering students, advanced placement credit, cooperative education, distance learning, double majors, English as a second language, independent study, internships, part-time degree program, services for LD students, study abroad, summer session for credit.
Student Life *Campus security:* 24-hour emergency response devices, late-night transport/escort service.
Costs (2014–15) *Tuition:* state resident $1395 full-time, $31 per unit part-time; nonresident $7650 full-time, $170 per unit part-time. Full-time tuition and fees vary according to course load. Part-time tuition and fees vary according to course load.
Financial Aid Of all full-time matriculated undergraduates who enrolled in 2013, 15 Federal Work-Study jobs (averaging $1500).
Applying *Options:* electronic application, early admission. *Recommended:* high school transcript.
Freshman Application Contact Office of Admissions and Records, Lake Tahoe Community College, One College Drive, South Lake Tahoe, CA 96150. *Phone:* 530-541-4660 Ext. 211. *Fax:* 530-541-7852. *E-mail:* admissions@ltcc.edu.
Website: http://www.ltcc.edu/.

Laney College
Oakland, California

Freshman Application Contact Mrs. Barbara Simmons, District Admissions Officer, Laney College, 900 Fallon Street, Oakland, CA 94607-4893. *Phone:* 510-466-7369.
Website: http://www.laney.edu/.

Las Positas College
Livermore, California

Director of Admissions Mrs. Sylvia R. Rodriguez, Director of Admissions and Records, Las Positas College, 3000 Campus Hill Drive, Livermore, CA 94551. *Phone:* 925-373-4942.
Website: http://www.laspositascollege.edu/.

Lassen Community College District
Susanville, California

Freshman Application Contact Mr. Chris J. Alberico, Registrar, Lassen Community College District, Highway 139, PO Box 3000, Susanville, CA 96130. *Phone:* 530-257-6181.
Website: http://www.lassencollege.edu/.

Le Cordon Bleu College of Culinary Arts in Los Angeles
Pasadena, California

Director of Admissions Nora Sandoval, Registrar, Le Cordon Bleu College of Culinary Arts in Los Angeles, 530 East Colorado Boulevard, Pasadena, CA 91101. *Phone:* 626-229-1300. *Fax:* 626-204-3905. *E-mail:* nsandoval@la.chefs.edu.
Website: http://www.chefs.edu/Los-Angeles/.

Le Cordon Bleu College of Culinary Arts in San Francisco
San Francisco, California

Director of Admissions Ms. Nancy Seyfert, Vice President of Admissions, Le Cordon Bleu College of Culinary Arts in San Francisco, 350 Rhode Island Street, San Francisco, CA 94103. *Phone:* 800-229-2433 Ext. 275. *Toll-free phone:* 800-229-2433 (in-state); 800-BAYCHEF (out-of-state).
Website: http://www.chefs.edu/San-Francisco/.

Long Beach City College
Long Beach, California

Director of Admissions Mr. Ross Miyashiro, Dean of Admissions and Records, Long Beach City College, 4901 East Carson Street, Long Beach, CA 90808-1780. *Phone:* 562-938-4130.
Website: http://www.lbcc.edu/.

Los Angeles City College
Los Angeles, California

Freshman Application Contact Elaine Geismar, Director of Student Assistance Center, Los Angeles City College, 855 North Vermont Avenue, Los Angeles, CA 90029-3590. *Phone:* 323-953-4340.
Website: http://www.lacitycollege.edu/.

Los Angeles County College of Nursing and Allied Health
Los Angeles, California

Freshman Application Contact Admissions Office, Los Angeles County College of Nursing and Allied Health, 1237 North Mission Road, Los Angeles, CA 90033. *Phone:* 323-226-4911.
Website: http://www.ladhs.org/wps/portal/CollegeOfNursing.

Los Angeles Harbor College
Wilmington, California

Freshman Application Contact Los Angeles Harbor College, 1111 Figueroa Place, Wilmington, CA 90744-2397. *Phone:* 310-233-4091.
Website: http://www.lahc.edu/.

Los Angeles Mission College
Sylmar, California

- **State and locally supported** 2-year, founded 1974, part of Los Angeles Community College District System
- **Urban** 22-acre campus with easy access to Los Angeles
- **Coed**

Undergraduates 1,941 full-time, 7,049 part-time. 3% Black or African American, non-Hispanic/Latino; 75% Hispanic/Latino; 4% Asian, non-Hispanic/Latino; 0.1% Native Hawaiian or other Pacific Islander, non-Hispanic/Latino; 0.2% American Indian or Alaska Native, non-Hispanic/Latino; 1% Two or more races, non-Hispanic/Latino; 3% Race/ethnicity unknown; 1% international; 8% transferred in. *Retention:* 70% of full-time freshmen returned.
Academics *Calendar:* semesters. *Degree:* certificates and associate. *Special study options:* academic remediation for entering students, adult/continuing education programs, advanced placement credit, cooperative education, distance learning, double majors, English as a second language, external degree program, independent study, internships, off-campus study, part-time degree program, services for LD students, study abroad, summer session for credit.
Student Life *Campus security:* 24-hour emergency response devices and patrols, late-night transport/escort service.
Financial Aid Of all full-time matriculated undergraduates who enrolled in 2013, 40 Federal Work-Study jobs (averaging $4000).
Applying *Options:* early admission.
Freshman Application Contact Los Angeles Mission College, 13356 Eldridge Avenue, Sylmar, CA 91342-3245.
Website: http://www.lamission.edu/.

Los Angeles Pierce College
Woodland Hills, California

Director of Admissions Ms. Shelley L. Gerstl, Dean of Admissions and Records, Los Angeles Pierce College, 6201 Winnetka Avenue, Woodland Hills, CA 91371-0001. *Phone:* 818-719-6448.
Website: http://www.piercecollege.edu/.

Los Angeles Southwest College
Los Angeles, California

Director of Admissions Dan W. Walden, Dean of Academic Affairs, Los Angeles Southwest College, 1600 West Imperial Highway, Los Angeles, CA 90047-4810. *Phone:* 323-242-5511.
Website: http://www.lasc.edu/.

Los Angeles Trade-Technical College
Los Angeles, California

- **State and locally supported** 2-year, founded 1925, part of Los Angeles Community College District System
- **Urban** 25-acre campus
- **Coed,** 13,194 undergraduate students, 32% full-time, 51% women, 49% men

Undergraduates 4,160 full-time, 9,034 part-time.
Freshmen *Admission:* 342 enrolled.
Faculty *Total:* 443, 45% full-time.
Majors Accounting; architectural engineering technology; automobile/automotive mechanics technology; business administration and management; carpentry; chemical engineering; commercial and advertising art; computer engineering technology; computer programming; construction engineering technology; cosmetology; culinary arts; data processing and data processing technology; drafting and design technology; electrical, electronic and communications engineering technology; engineering; fashion/apparel design; fashion merchandising; graphic and printing equipment operation/production; heating, air conditioning, ventilation and refrigeration maintenance technology; heavy equipment maintenance technology; hydrology and water resources science; industrial technology; information science/studies; journalism; labor and industrial relations; liberal arts and sciences/liberal studies; mechanical engineering/mechanical technology; photography; pipefitting and sprinkler fitting; real estate; registered nursing/registered nurse; transportation and materials moving related; welding technology.
Academics *Calendar:* semesters. *Degree:* certificates, diplomas, and associate. *Special study options:* academic remediation for entering students, adult/continuing education programs, advanced placement credit, cooperative education, English as a second language, part-time degree program, services for LD students, summer session for credit.
Library Los Angeles Trade-Technical College Library with 80,200 titles, an OPAC, a Web page.
Student Life *Housing:* college housing not available. *Campus security:* 24-hour patrols, student patrols, late-night transport/escort service. *Student services:* health clinic, personal/psychological counseling, women's center.
Athletics *Intercollegiate sports:* basketball M/W, cross-country running M/W, tennis M, track and field M/W.
Applying *Recommended:* high school transcript. *Application deadline:* 9/7 (freshmen).
Freshman Application Contact Los Angeles Trade-Technical College, 400 West Washington Boulevard, Los Angeles, CA 90015-4108. *Phone:* 213-763-7127.
Website: http://www.lattc.edu/.

Los Angeles Valley College
Van Nuys, California

Director of Admissions Mr. Florentino Manzano, Associate Dean, Los Angeles Valley College, 5800 Fulton Avenue, Van Nuys, CA 91401-4096. *Phone:* 818-947-2353. *E-mail:* manzanf@lavc.edu.
Website: http://www.lavc.cc.ca.us/.

Los Medanos College
Pittsburg, California

Freshman Application Contact Ms. Gail Newman, Director of Admissions and Records, Los Medanos College, 2700 East Leland Road, Pittsburg, CA 94565-5197. *Phone:* 925-439-2181 Ext. 7500.
Website: http://www.losmedanos.net/.

Mendocino College
Ukiah, California

Freshman Application Contact Mendocino College, 1000 Hensley Creek Road, Ukiah, CA 95482-0300. *Phone:* 707-468-3103.
Website: http://www.mendocino.edu/.

Merced College
Merced, California

Freshman Application Contact Ms. Cherie Davis, Associate Registrar, Merced College, 3600 M Street, Merced, CA 95348-2898. *Phone:* 209-384-6188. *Fax:* 209-384-6339.
Website: http://www.mccd.edu/.

Merritt College
Oakland, California

Freshman Application Contact Ms. Barbara Simmons, District Admissions Officer, Merritt College, 12500 Campus Drive, Oakland, CA 94619-3196. *Phone:* 510-466-7369. *E-mail:* hperdue@peralta.cc.ca.us. *Website:* http://www.merritt.edu/.

MiraCosta College
Oceanside, California

- **State-supported** 2-year, founded 1934, part of California Community College System
- **Suburban** 131-acre campus with easy access to San Diego
- **Endowment** $5.0 million
- **Coed,** 14,687 undergraduate students, 34% full-time, 56% women, 44% men

Undergraduates 5,024 full-time, 9,663 part-time. 2% are from out of state; 3% Black or African American, non-Hispanic/Latino; 33% Hispanic/Latino; 6% Asian, non-Hispanic/Latino; 0.5% Native Hawaiian or other Pacific Islander, non-Hispanic/Latino; 0.3% American Indian or Alaska Native, non-Hispanic/Latino; 7% Two or more races, non-Hispanic/Latino; 2% Race/ethnicity unknown; 1% international.

Freshmen *Admission:* 2,768 enrolled.

Faculty *Total:* 634, 23% full-time. *Student/faculty ratio:* 23:1.

Majors Accounting technology and bookkeeping; administrative assistant and secretarial science; adult development and aging; architectural technology; art; biological and physical sciences; biomedical technology; business administration and management; child-care and support services management; child-care provision; computer programming; computer science; computer systems networking and telecommunications; criminal justice/police science; dance; data entry/microcomputer applications; drafting and design technology; history; hospitality administration; liberal arts and sciences/liberal studies; licensed practical/vocational nurse training; mathematics; medical/clinical assistant; music; office management; photographic and film/video technology; plant nursery management; psychology; psychology related; real estate; recording arts technology; registered nursing/registered nurse; restaurant, culinary, and catering management; sales, distribution, and marketing operations; small business administration; sociology; surgical technology; theater design and technology; web/multimedia management and webmaster.

Academics *Calendar:* semesters. *Degree:* certificates, diplomas, and associate. *Special study options:* academic remediation for entering students, accelerated degree program, adult/continuing education programs, advanced placement credit, cooperative education, distance learning, double majors, English as a second language, honors programs, independent study, internships, part-time degree program, services for LD students, student-designed majors, study abroad, summer session for credit.

Library MiraCosta College Library with an OPAC, a Web page.

Student Life *Housing:* college housing not available. *Activities and Organizations:* drama/theater group, student-run newspaper, choral group, Inter Varsity Christian Fellowship, Accounting and Business Club, Backstage Players (Drama), Gay Straight Alliance, Puente Diversity Network. *Campus security:* 24-hour emergency response devices, student patrols, late-night transport/escort service, trained security personnel during class hours. *Student services:* health clinic, personal/psychological counseling.

Athletics *Intercollegiate sports:* basketball M/W, soccer M/W.

Costs (2014–15) *Tuition:* state resident $1288 full-time, $46 per unit part-time; nonresident $5188 full-time, $185 per unit part-time. Full-time tuition and fees vary according to course load. Part-time tuition and fees vary according to course load. *Required fees:* $48 full-time, $48 per year part-time.

Applying *Options:* electronic application, early admission, deferred entrance. *Application deadlines:* rolling (freshmen), rolling (transfers).

Freshman Application Contact Jane Sparks, Interim Director of Admissions and Records, MiraCosta College, One Barnard Drive, Oceanside, CA 92057. *Phone:* 760-795-6620. *Toll-free phone:* 888-201-8480. *E-mail:* admissions@miracosta.edu. *Website:* http://www.miracosta.edu/.

See display on this page and page 372 for the College Close-Up.

Mission College
Santa Clara, California

Director of Admissions Daniel Sanidad, Dean of Student Services, Mission College, 3000 Mission College Boulevard, Santa Clara, CA 95054-1897. *Phone:* 408-855-5139. *Website:* http://www.missioncollege.org/.

Modesto Junior College

Modesto, California

- **State and locally supported** 2-year, founded 1921, part of Yosemite Community College District System
- **Urban** 229-acre campus
- **Coed**

Undergraduates 6,874 full-time, 12,433 part-time. 4% transferred in. *Retention:* 73% of full-time freshmen returned.

Faculty *Student/faculty ratio:* 29:1.

Academics *Calendar:* semesters. *Degree:* certificates and associate. *Special study options:* academic remediation for entering students, adult/continuing education programs, advanced placement credit, cooperative education, distance learning, English as a second language, honors programs, independent study, part-time degree program, services for LD students, study abroad, summer session for credit.

Student Life *Campus security:* 24-hour emergency response devices and patrols, late-night transport/escort service.

Financial Aid Of all full-time matriculated undergraduates who enrolled in 2011, 4,538 applied for aid, 4,537 were judged to have need, 4,537 had their need fully met. 278 Federal Work-Study jobs (averaging $4749). *Average percent of need met:* 100. *Average financial aid package:* $5088. *Average need-based gift aid:* $4942.

Applying *Options:* electronic application. *Recommended:* high school transcript.

Freshman Application Contact Ms. Martha Robles, Dean of Student Services and Support, Modesto Junior College, 435 College Avenue, Modesto, CA 95350. *Phone:* 209-575-6470. *Fax:* 209-575-6859. *E-mail:* mjcadmissions@mail.yosemite.cc.ca.us.

Website: http://www.mjc.edu/.

Monterey Peninsula College

Monterey, California

Director of Admissions Ms. Vera Coleman, Registrar, Monterey Peninsula College, 980 Fremont Street, Monterey, CA 93940-4799. *Phone:* 831-646-4007. *E-mail:* vcoleman@mpc.edu.

Website: http://www.mpc.edu/.

Moorpark College

Moorpark, California

Freshman Application Contact Ms. Katherine Colborn, Registrar, Moorpark College, 7075 Campus Road, Moorpark, CA 93021-2899. *Phone:* 805-378-1415.

Website: http://www.moorparkcollege.edu/.

Moreno Valley College

Moreno Valley, California

Freshman Application Contact Jamie Clifton, Director, Enrollment Services, Moreno Valley College, 16130 Lasselle Street, Moreno Valley, CA 92551. *Phone:* 951-571-6293. *E-mail:* admissions@mvc.edu.

Website: http://www.mvc.edu/.

Mt. San Antonio College

Walnut, California

- **State and locally supported** 2-year, founded 1946, part of California Community College System
- **Suburban** 421-acre campus with easy access to Los Angeles
- **Coed,** 28,481 undergraduate students, 37% full-time, 51% women, 49% men

Undergraduates 10,499 full-time, 17,982 part-time. Students come from 21 states and territories; 139 other countries; 1% are from out of state; 5% Black or African American, non-Hispanic/Latino; 59% Hispanic/Latino; 18% Asian, non-Hispanic/Latino; 0.4% Native Hawaiian or other Pacific Islander, non-Hispanic/Latino; 0.2% American Indian or Alaska Native, non-Hispanic/Latino; 3% Two or more races, non-Hispanic/Latino; 2% Race/ethnicity unknown; 2% international. *Retention:* 79% of full-time freshmen returned.

Freshmen *Admission:* 4,835 enrolled.

Faculty *Total:* 1,260, 30% full-time. *Student/faculty ratio:* 26:1.

Majors Accounting; administrative assistant and secretarial science; advertising; agricultural business and management; agriculture; airframe mechanics and aircraft maintenance technology; airline pilot and flight crew; air traffic control; animal sciences; apparel and textiles; architectural engineering technology; avionics maintenance technology; biological and physical sciences; building/construction finishing, management, and inspection related; business administration and management; business teacher education; child development; civil engineering technology; commercial and advertising art; computer and information sciences; computer engineering technology; computer graphics; computer science; corrections; criminal justice/police science; dairy science; data processing and data processing technology; drafting and design technology; drafting/design engineering technologies related; electrical, electronic and communications engineering technology; emergency medical technology (EMT paramedic); engineering technology; English language and literature related; family and consumer sciences/human sciences; fashion merchandising; finance; fire science/firefighting; forest technology; health and physical education/fitness; heating, air conditioning, ventilation and refrigeration maintenance technology; horticultural science; hotel/motel administration; humanities; industrial and product design; industrial radiologic technology; interior design; journalism; kindergarten/preschool education; landscape architecture; legal administrative assistant/secretary; legal assistant/paralegal; machine tool technology; marketing/marketing management; materials science; mathematics; medical administrative assistant and medical secretary; mental health counseling; music; occupational safety and health technology; ornamental horticulture; parks, recreation and leisure; parks, recreation and leisure facilities management; photography; physical sciences related; pre-engineering; quality control technology; radio and television; real estate; registered nursing/registered nurse; respiratory care therapy; sign language interpretation and translation; social sciences; surveying technology; transportation and materials moving related; visual and performing arts; welding technology; wildlife, fish and wildlands science and management.

Academics *Calendar:* semesters. *Degree:* certificates, diplomas, and associate. *Special study options:* academic remediation for entering students, adult/continuing education programs, advanced placement credit, cooperative education, distance learning, double majors, English as a second language, honors programs, independent study, part-time degree program, services for LD students, study abroad, summer session for credit. *ROTC:* Army (b), Air Force (b).

Library Learning Resources Center with 97,996 titles, 9,933 audiovisual materials, an OPAC, a Web page.

Student Life *Housing:* college housing not available. *Activities and Organizations:* drama/theater group, student-run radio station, choral group, Alpha Gamma Sigma, Muslim Student Association, student government, Asian Student Association, Kasama-Filipino Student Organization. *Campus security:* 24-hour emergency response devices and patrols, late-night transport/escort service. *Student services:* health clinic, personal/psychological counseling, women's center.

Athletics *Intercollegiate sports:* badminton W, baseball M, basketball M/W, cheerleading M/W, cross-country running M/W, football M, golf M/W, soccer M/W, softball W, swimming and diving M/W, tennis M/W, track and field M/W, volleyball M/W, water polo M/W, wrestling M.

Costs (2014–15) *Tuition:* state resident $1288 full-time, $46 per unit part-time; nonresident $7424 full-time, $216 per unit part-time. Full-time tuition and fees vary according to course load and program. Part-time tuition and fees vary according to course load and program. *Required fees:* $60 full-time, $58 per term part-time.

Applying *Options:* electronic application, early admission, deferred entrance. *Required for some:* high school transcript. *Notification:* continuous (freshmen), continuous (transfers).

Freshman Application Contact Dr. George Bradshaw, Dean of Enrollment Management, Mt. San Antonio College, Walnut, CA 91789. *Phone:* 909-274-5570 Ext. 4505.

Website: http://www.mtsac.edu/.

Mt. San Jacinto College

San Jacinto, California

- **State and locally supported** 2-year, founded 1963, part of California Community College System
- **Suburban** 180-acre campus with easy access to San Diego
- **Endowment** $1.6 million
- **Coed**

Undergraduates 5,105 full-time, 9,065 part-time. Students come from 4 states and territories; 8% Black or African American, non-Hispanic/Latino; 43% Hispanic/Latino; 6% Asian, non-Hispanic/Latino; 0.5% Native Hawaiian or other Pacific Islander, non-Hispanic/Latino; 0.5% American Indian or Alaska Native, non-Hispanic/Latino; 5% Two or more races, non-Hispanic/Latino; 2% Race/ethnicity unknown; 7% transferred in. *Retention:* 70% of full-time freshmen returned.

Faculty *Student/faculty ratio:* 27:1.

Academics *Calendar:* semesters. *Degree:* certificates, diplomas, and associate. *Special study options:* academic remediation for entering students, adult/continuing education programs, advanced placement credit, distance learning, double majors, English as a second language, honors programs, off-campus study, part-time degree program, services for LD students, study abroad, summer session for credit.

Student Life *Campus security:* part-time trained security personnel.

Costs (2014–15) *One-time required fee:* $6. *Tuition:* state resident $1380 full-time, $46 per credit part-time; nonresident $6930 full-time, $231 per credit part-time. *Required fees:* $280 full-time, $140 per term part-time.

Financial Aid Of all full-time matriculated undergraduates who enrolled in 2013, 109 Federal Work-Study jobs (averaging $1114). 125 state and other part-time jobs (averaging $1000).

Applying *Options:* early admission. *Recommended:* high school transcript.

Freshman Application Contact Mt. San Jacinto College, 1499 North State Street, San Jacinto, CA 92583-2399. *Phone:* 951-639-5212.

Website: http://www.msjc.edu/.

MTI College
Sacramento, California

Freshman Application Contact Director of Admissions, MTI College, 5221 Madison Avenue, Sacramento, CA 95841. *Phone:* 916-339-1500. *Fax:* 916-339-0305.

Website: http://www.mticollege.edu/.

Napa Valley College
Napa, California

Director of Admissions Mr. Oscar De Haro, Vice President of Student Services, Napa Valley College, 2277 Napa-Vallejo Highway, Napa, CA 94558-6236. *Phone:* 707-253-3000. *Toll-free phone:* 800-826-1077. *E-mail:* odeharo@napavalley.edu.

Website: http://www.napavalley.edu/.

National Career College
Panorama City, California

Admissions Office Contact National Career College, 14355 Roscoe Boulevard, Panorama City, CA 91402.

Website: http://www.nccusa.edu/.

Norco College
Norco, California

Freshman Application Contact Mark DeAsis, Director, Enrollment Services, Norco College, 2001 Third Street, Norco, CA 92860. *E-mail:* admissionsnorco@norcocollege.edu.

Website: http://www.norcocollege.edu/.

Ohlone College
Fremont, California

- **State and locally supported** 2-year, founded 1967, part of California Community College System
- **Suburban** 530-acre campus with easy access to San Jose
- **Coed,** 11,318 undergraduate students, 28% full-time, 47% women, 53% men

Undergraduates 3,211 full-time, 8,138 part-time. Students come from 11 states and territories; 40 other countries; 0.2% are from out of state; 4% Black or African American, non-Hispanic/Latino; 18% Hispanic/Latino; 30% Asian, non-Hispanic/Latino; 0.7% Native Hawaiian or other Pacific Islander, non-Hispanic/Latino; 0.2% American Indian or Alaska Native, non-Hispanic/Latino; 5% Two or more races, non-Hispanic/Latino; 19% Race/ethnicity unknown; 3% international; 13% transferred in. *Retention:* 55% of full-time freshmen returned.

Freshmen *Admission:* 861 enrolled.

Faculty *Total:* 451, 25% full-time. *Student/faculty ratio:* 27:1.

Majors Accounting; administrative assistant and secretarial science; American Sign Language (ASL); anthropology; art; biology/biological sciences; biotechnology; broadcast journalism; business administration and management; child development; commercial and advertising art; communication; computer and information sciences; computer and information systems security; computer engineering; computer programming; computer science; computer systems networking and telecommunications; computer typography and composition equipment operation; consumer services and advocacy; costume design; criminal justice/law enforcement administration; criminal justice/police science; deaf studies; drafting and design technology; early childhood education; economics; electrical, electronic and communications engineering technology; engineering; English; environmental science; environmental studies; family and consumer sciences/human sciences; fashion merchandising; fine arts related; food

science; foods, nutrition, and wellness; geography; geology/earth science; health professions related; history; human development and family studies; interior design; journalism; kindergarten/preschool education; kinesiology and exercise science; liberal arts and sciences/liberal studies; marketing/marketing management; mass communication/media; mathematics; medical administrative assistant and medical secretary; medical/clinical assistant; music; music history, literature, and theory; music performance; music technology; music theory and composition; natural sciences; network and system administration; philosophy; physical sciences; physical therapy; physical therapy technology; physics; pre-engineering; psychology; radio and television; radio and television broadcasting technology; real estate; registered nursing/registered nurse; respiratory care therapy; sign language interpretation and translation; social sciences; sociology; Spanish; theater design and technology; theater/theater arts management.

Academics *Calendar:* semesters. *Degrees:* certificates and associate (profile includes campuses in Fremont and Newark CA). *Special study options:* academic remediation for entering students, adult/continuing education programs, advanced placement credit, cooperative education, distance learning, double majors, English as a second language, external degree program, honors programs, internships, off-campus study, part-time degree program, services for LD students, student-designed majors, study abroad, summer session for credit. *ROTC:* Army (c), Air Force (c).

Library Ohlone College Library plus 1 other with 67,849 titles, 100 audiovisual materials, an OPAC, a Web page.

Student Life *Housing:* college housing not available. *Activities and Organizations:* drama/theater group, student-run newspaper, radio and television station, choral group, Associated Students of Ohlone (ASOC), American Sign Language Club (ASL Club), Asian Pacific American Student Association, M.E.Ch.A. Club (Spanish: Movimiento Estudiantil Chican@ de Aztlan), Science and Math Seminar Series (Science, Math, and Engineering). *Campus security:* 24-hour emergency response devices and patrols, late-night transport/escort service. *Student services:* health clinic, personal/psychological counseling.

Athletics *Intercollegiate sports:* baseball M, basketball M/W, soccer M/W, softball W, swimming and diving M/W, tennis M/W, volleyball M/W, water polo M.

Costs (2015–16) *Tuition:* state resident $1162 full-time; nonresident $6394 full-time.

Financial Aid Of all full-time matriculated undergraduates who enrolled in 2013, 35 Federal Work-Study jobs (averaging $1800).

Applying *Options:* early admission. *Required for some:* high school transcript. *Application deadlines:* rolling (freshmen), rolling (out-of-state freshmen), rolling (transfers). *Notification:* continuous (freshmen), continuous (out-of-state freshmen), continuous (transfers).

Freshman Application Contact Ohlone College, 43600 Mission Boulevard, Fremont, CA 94539-5884. *Phone:* 510-659-6107.

Website: http://www.ohlone.edu/.

Orange Coast College
Costa Mesa, California

- **State and locally supported** 2-year, founded 1947, part of Coast Community College District
- **Suburban** 164-acre campus with easy access to Los Angeles
- **Endowment** $10.8 million
- **Coed,** 20,521 undergraduate students, 41% full-time, 48% women, 52% men

Undergraduates 8,386 full-time, 12,135 part-time. Students come from 69 other countries; 2% are from out of state; 2% Black or African American, non-Hispanic/Latino; 32% Hispanic/Latino; 21% Asian, non-Hispanic/Latino; 0.3% Native Hawaiian or other Pacific Islander, non-Hispanic/Latino; 0.2% American Indian or Alaska Native, non-Hispanic/Latino; 4% Two or more races, non-Hispanic/Latino; 3% Race/ethnicity unknown; 4% international; 7% transferred in.

Freshmen *Admission:* 3,677 enrolled.

Faculty *Total:* 650, 37% full-time. *Student/faculty ratio:* 35:1.

Majors Accounting; administrative assistant and secretarial science; aeronautics/aviation/aerospace science and technology; airline pilot and flight crew; anthropology; architectural engineering technology; art; athletic training; avionics maintenance technology; behavioral sciences; biology/biological sciences; building/home/construction inspection; business administration and management; cardiovascular technology; chemistry; child-care and support services management; child-care provision; cinematography and film/video production; clinical laboratory science/medical technology; commercial and advertising art; communications technology; computer engineering technology; computer graphics; computer programming; computer programming (specific applications); computer typography and composition equipment operation; construction engineering technology; culinary arts; dance; data entry/microcomputer applications related; data processing and data processing technology; dental hygiene; dietetics; drafting and design technology; dramatic/theater arts; economics; electrical and power transmission installation; electrical, electronic and communications engineering technology; electrical/electronics equipment installation and repair; emergency medical technology (EMT paramedic); engineering; English; family and consumer economics related; family and consumer sciences/human sciences; fashion merchandising; film/cinema/video studies; food science; foods, nutrition, and wellness; food technology and processing; French; geography; geology/earth science; German; health professions related; heating, air conditioning, ventilation and refrigeration maintenance technology; history; horticultural science; hotel/motel administration; housing and human environments; human development and family studies; humanities; industrial and product design; industrial radiologic technology; information science/studies; interior design; journalism; kindergarten/preschool education; kinesiology and exercise science; liberal arts and sciences/liberal studies; machine shop technology; machine tool technology; marine maintenance and ship repair technology; marketing/marketing management; mass communication/media; mathematics; medical administrative assistant and medical secretary; medical/clinical assistant; music; music management; natural sciences; nuclear medical technology; ornamental horticulture; philosophy; photography; physical education teaching and coaching; physics; political science and government; religious studies; respiratory care therapy; restaurant, culinary, and catering management; retailing; selling skills and sales; social sciences; sociology; Spanish; special products marketing; welding technology; word processing.

Academics *Calendar:* semesters plus summer session. *Degree:* certificates and associate. *Special study options:* academic remediation for entering students, adult/continuing education programs, advanced placement credit, cooperative education, distance learning, double majors, English as a second language, external degree program, freshman honors college, honors programs, internships, off-campus study, part-time degree program, services for LD students, student-designed majors, study abroad, summer session for credit. *ROTC:* Army (c), Air Force (c).

Library Library plus 1 other with 112,783 titles, 3,240 audiovisual materials, an OPAC, a Web page.

Student Life *Housing:* college housing not available. *Activities and Organizations:* drama/theater group, student-run newspaper, choral group, Architecture Club, Circle K, Doctors of Tomorrow, Speech, Theater, and Debate, Vietnamese Student Association. *Campus security:* 24-hour emergency response devices and patrols, student patrols, late-night transport/escort service. *Student services:* health clinic, personal/psychological counseling, legal services.

Athletics *Intercollegiate sports:* baseball M, basketball M/W, bowling M(c)/W(c), crew M/W, cross-country running M/W, football M, golf M/W, soccer M/W, softball W, swimming and diving M/W, tennis M/W, track and field M/W, volleyball W, water polo M/W.

Costs (2015–16) *Tuition:* state resident $1288 full-time, $46 per unit part-time; nonresident $6208 full-time, $219 per unit part-time. Full-time tuition and fees vary according to program. Part-time tuition and fees vary according to program. *Required fees:* $902 full-time, $140 per term part-time. *Payment plan:* installment.

Financial Aid Of all full-time matriculated undergraduates who enrolled in 2013, 108 Federal Work-Study jobs (averaging $3000). *Financial aid deadline:* 5/28.

Applying *Options:* electronic application. *Application deadlines:* rolling (freshmen), rolling (transfers). *Notification:* continuous (freshmen), continuous (transfers).

Freshman Application Contact Efren Galvan, Director of Admissions, Records and Enrollment Technology, Orange Coast College, 2701 Fairview Road, Costa Mesa, CA 92926. *Phone:* 714-432-5774. *E-mail:* egalvan@occ.cccd.edu.
Website: http://www.orangecoastcollege.edu/.

Oxnard College
Oxnard, California

- **State-supported** 2-year, founded 1975, part of Ventura County Community College District System
- **Urban** 119-acre campus
- **Endowment** $1.7 million
- **Coed**

Undergraduates 1,927 full-time, 4,940 part-time. 3% Black or African American, non-Hispanic/Latino; 71% Hispanic/Latino; 5% Asian, non-Hispanic/Latino; 0.3% American Indian or Alaska Native, non-Hispanic/Latino; 2% Two or more races, non-Hispanic/Latino; 0.6% Race/ethnicity unknown; 0.1% international; 3% transferred in.

Faculty *Student/faculty ratio:* 30:1.

Academics *Calendar:* semesters. *Degree:* certificates, diplomas, and associate. *Special study options:* academic remediation for entering students, accelerated degree program, advanced placement credit, distance learning, double majors, English as a second language, honors programs, independent study, part-time degree program, services for LD students, summer session for credit.

Student Life *Campus security:* 24-hour patrols.

Costs (2014–15) *Tuition:* state resident $0 full-time; nonresident $6440 full-time, $230 per unit part-time. *Required fees:* $1350 full-time, $46 per unit part-time, $62 per year part-time.

Financial Aid Of all full-time matriculated undergraduates who enrolled in 2013, 80 Federal Work-Study jobs (averaging $3000).

Applying *Options:* electronic application, early admission. *Recommended:* high school transcript.

Freshman Application Contact Mr. Joel Diaz, Registrar, Oxnard College, 4000 South Rose Avenue, Oxnard, CA 93033-6699. *Phone:* 805-986-5843. *Fax:* 805-986-5943. *E-mail:* jdiaz@vcccd.edu.
Website: http://www.oxnardcollege.edu/.

Palomar College
San Marcos, California

- **State and locally supported** 2-year, founded 1946, part of California Community College System
- **Suburban** 156-acre campus with easy access to San Diego
- **Coed,** 22,535 undergraduate students, 36% full-time, 44% women, 56% men

Undergraduates 8,107 full-time, 14,428 part-time.

Freshmen *Admission:* 4,166 enrolled.

Faculty *Total:* 1,305, 21% full-time. *Student/faculty ratio:* 21:1.

Majors Accounting technology and bookkeeping; administrative assistant and secretarial science; advertising; airline pilot and flight crew; animation, interactive technology, video graphics and special effects; apparel and textile marketing management; archeology; architectural drafting and CAD/CADD; architectural technology; art; astronomy; autobody/collision and repair technology; automobile/automotive mechanics technology; aviation/airway management; biological and physical sciences; biology/biological sciences; broadcast journalism; building/home/construction inspection; business administration and management; business/commerce; cabinetmaking and millwork; carpentry; ceramic arts and ceramics; chemistry; child-care and support services management; child-care provision; commercial and advertising art; computer graphics; computer programming; computer systems networking and telecommunications; construction trades related; dance; dental assisting; design and visual communications; desktop publishing and digital imaging design; diesel mechanics technology; drafting and design technology; dramatic/theater arts; drawing; drywall installation; economics; education; electrical/electronics drafting and CAD/CADD; electrician; emergency medical technology (EMT paramedic); English; family and community services; family and consumer sciences/human sciences; fashion/apparel design; film/cinema/video studies; fire prevention and safety technology; foreign languages and literatures; forensic science and technology; French; geography; geography related; geology/earth science; graphic and printing equipment operation/production; graphic design; homeland security; humanities; information technology; insurance; interior design; international business/trade/commerce; journalism; kinesiology and exercise science; legal studies; liberal arts and sciences/liberal studies; library and archives assisting; masonry; mathematics; medical administrative assistant and medical secretary; metal and jewelry arts; music; parks, recreation and leisure; photographic and film/video technology; pre-engineering; psychology; public administration; radio and television; real estate; registered nursing/registered nurse; sculpture; sheet metal technology; sign language interpretation and translation; social sciences; sociology; special education–early childhood; speech communication and rhetoric; substance abuse/addiction counseling; water quality and wastewater treatment management and recycling technology; web page, digital/multimedia and information resources design; welding technology; women's studies.

Academics *Calendar:* semesters. *Degree:* certificates and associate. *Special study options:* academic remediation for entering students, advanced placement credit, cooperative education, distance learning, English as a second language, internships, part-time degree program, services for LD students, study abroad, summer session for credit.

Library Palomar College Library with 108,000 titles, an OPAC, a Web page.

Student Life *Housing:* college housing not available. *Activities and Organizations:* drama/theater group, student-run newspaper, radio and television station, choral group, SNAP (Student Nursing Association of Palomar College), Alpha Omega Rho Chapter of Phi Theta Kappa (International Honor Society), Active Minds, Student Veterans Organization, MEChA (Chicano Organization). *Campus security:* 24-hour patrols, student patrols, late-night transport/escort service. *Student services:* health clinic, personal/psychological counseling.

Athletics *Intercollegiate sports:* baseball M, basketball M/W, football M, golf M, soccer M/W, softball W, swimming and diving M/W, tennis M/W, track and field M/W, volleyball M/W, water polo M/W, wrestling M. *Intramural sports:*

basketball M/W, bowling M, golf M, skiing (downhill) M/W, soccer M, softball W, tennis M, volleyball M, water polo M, wrestling M.

Costs (2015–16) *Tuition:* state resident $1104 full-time, $46 per unit part-time; nonresident $6024 full-time, $251 per unit part-time. *Required fees:* $50 full-time, $1 per credit hour part-time, $19 per term part-time.

Applying *Options:* electronic application. *Application deadlines:* rolling (freshmen), rolling (transfers). *Notification:* continuous (freshmen), continuous (transfers).

Freshman Application Contact Dr. Kendyl Magnuson, Director of Enrollment Services, Palomar College, 1140 W Mission Rd, San Marcos, CA 92069. *Phone:* 760-744-1150 Ext. 2171. *Fax:* 760-744-2932. *E-mail:* kmagnuson@palomar.edu. *Website:* http://www.palomar.edu/.

Palo Verde College
Blythe, California

Freshman Application Contact Diana Rodriguez, Vice President of Student Services, Palo Verde College, 1 College Drive, Blythe, CA 92225. *Phone:* 760-921-5428. *Fax:* 760-921-3608. *E-mail:* diana.rodriguez@paloverde.edu. *Website:* http://www.paloverde.edu/.

Pasadena City College
Pasadena, California

- **State and locally supported** 2-year, founded 1924, part of California Community College System
- **Urban** 55-acre campus with easy access to Los Angeles
- **Coed,** 26,611 undergraduate students, 39% full-time, 52% women, 48% men

Undergraduates 10,401 full-time, 16,210 part-time. Students come from 26 states and territories; 150 other countries; 1% are from out of state; 5% Black or African American, non-Hispanic/Latino; 49% Hispanic/Latino; 23% Asian, non-Hispanic/Latino; 0.1% Native Hawaiian or other Pacific Islander, non-Hispanic/Latino; 0.1% American Indian or Alaska Native, non-Hispanic/Latino; 9% Two or more races, non-Hispanic/Latino; 1% Race/ethnicity unknown; 4% international; 8% transferred in. *Retention:* 84% of full-time freshmen returned.

Freshmen *Admission:* 5 applied, 5,144 enrolled.

Faculty *Total:* 1,296, 29% full-time. *Student/faculty ratio:* 20:1.

Majors Accounting; accounting technology and bookkeeping; administrative assistant and secretarial science; animation, interactive technology, video graphics and special effects; anthropology; architecture; art; audiology and speech-language pathology; automobile/automotive mechanics technology; biochemistry; biological and physical sciences; biology/biological sciences; broadcast journalism; building/home/construction inspection; business administration and management; business automation/technology/data entry; chemistry; child development; cinematography and film/video production; classics and classical languages; computer/information technology services administration related; computer science; computer technology/computer systems technology; construction trades; cosmetology; cosmetology, barber/styling, and nail instruction; criminal justice/law enforcement administration; dance; data entry/microcomputer applications related; dental assisting; dental hygiene; dental laboratory technology; desktop publishing and digital imaging design; digital communication and media/multimedia; drafting and design technology; dramatic/theater arts; electrical and electronic engineering technologies related; electrical and electronics engineering; engineering technology; fashion/apparel design; fashion merchandising; fire prevention and safety technology; food service and dining room management; graphic and printing equipment operation/production; graphic design; history; hospitality administration; humanities; industrial electronics technology; international business/trade/commerce; international/global studies; legal assistant/paralegal; liberal arts and sciences/liberal studies; library science related; licensed practical/vocational nurse training; machine shop technology; marketing/marketing management; mathematics; mechanical engineering; medical/clinical assistant; medical insurance/medical billing; medical office assistant; photography; photojournalism; psychology; radio and television; radio and television broadcasting technology; radiologic technology/science; registered nursing/registered nurse; sociology; Spanish; speech communication and rhetoric; theater design and technology; welding technology.

Academics *Calendar:* semesters. *Degree:* certificates and associate. *Special study options:* academic remediation for entering students, adult/continuing education programs, advanced placement credit, distance learning, double majors, English as a second language, honors programs, independent study,

internships, part-time degree program, services for LD students, study abroad, summer session for credit.

Library Pasadena City College Library plus 1 other with 180,789 titles, 12,079 audiovisual materials, an OPAC, a Web page.

Student Life *Housing:* college housing not available. *Activities and Organizations:* drama/theater group, student-run newspaper, choral group, marching band. *Campus security:* 24-hour emergency response devices and patrols, late-night transport/escort service, cadet patrols. *Student services:* health clinic, personal/psychological counseling.

Athletics *Intercollegiate sports:* badminton M/W, baseball M, basketball M/W, cheerleading W(c), cross-country running M/W, football M, soccer M/W, softball W, swimming and diving M/W, tennis M/W, track and field M/W, volleyball W, water polo W. *Intramural sports:* water polo M(c).

Costs (2015–16) *Tuition:* state resident $1628 full-time, $46 per unit part-time; nonresident $3312 full-time, $193 per unit part-time. *Required fees:* $3256 full-time.

Applying *Options:* electronic application. *Application deadlines:* rolling (freshmen), rolling (transfers). *Notification:* continuous (freshmen), continuous (transfers).

Freshman Application Contact Pasadena City College, 1570 East Colorado Boulevard, Pasadena, CA 91106-2041. *Phone:* 626-585-7284. *Fax:* 626-585-7915. *Website:* http://www.pasadena.edu/.

Pima Medical Institute
Chula Vista, California

Freshman Application Contact Admissions Office, Pima Medical Institute, 780 Bay Boulevard, Suite 101, Chula Vista, CA 91910. *Phone:* 619-425-3200. *Toll-free phone:* 800-477-PIMA (in-state); 888-477-PIMA (out-of-state). *Website:* http://www.pmi.edu/.

Platt College
Alhambra, California

Director of Admissions Mr. Detroit Whiteside, Director of Admissions, Platt College, 1000 South Fremont A9W, Alhambra, CA 91803. *Phone:* 323-258-8050. *Toll-free phone:* 888-866-6697 (in-state); 888-80-PLATT (out-of-state). *Website:* http://www.plattcollege.edu/.

Platt College
Ontario, California

Director of Admissions Ms. Jennifer Abandonato, Director of Admissions, Platt College, 3700 Inland Empire Boulevard, Suite 400, Ontario, CA 91764. *Phone:* 909-941-9410. *Toll-free phone:* 888-80-PLATT. *Website:* http://www.plattcollege.edu/.

Porterville College
Porterville, California

Director of Admissions Ms. Judy Pope, Director of Admissions and Records/Registrar, Porterville College, 100 East College Avenue, Porterville, CA 93257-6058. *Phone:* 559-791-2222. *Website:* http://www.pc.cc.ca.us/.

Professional Golfers Career College
Temecula, California

Freshman Application Contact Mr. Gary Gilleon, Professional Golfers Career College, 26109 Ynez Road, Temecula, CA 92591. *Phone:* 951-719-2994 Ext. 1021. *Toll-free phone:* 800-877-4380. *Fax:* 951-719-1643. *E-mail:* garygilleon@golfcollege.edu. *Website:* http://www.golfcollege.edu/.

Reedley College
Reedley, California

Freshman Application Contact Admissions and Records Office, Reedley College, 995 North Reed Avenue, Reedley, CA 93654. *Phone:* 559-638-0323. *Fax:* 559-637-2523. *Website:* http://www.reedleycollege.edu/.

Rio Hondo College
Whittier, California

- **State and locally supported** 2-year, founded 1960, part of California Community College System
- **Suburban** 128-acre campus with easy access to Los Angeles
- **Coed,** 26,490 undergraduate students

Undergraduates Students come from 5 states and territories; 40 other countries; 2% Black or African American, non-Hispanic/Latino; 72% Hispanic/Latino; 9% Asian, non-Hispanic/Latino; 0.1% Native Hawaiian or other Pacific Islander, non-Hispanic/Latino; 0.2% American Indian or Alaska Native, non-Hispanic/Latino; 0.9% Two or more races, non-Hispanic/Latino; 7% Race/ethnicity unknown; 0.1% international.
Faculty *Total:* 546, 32% full-time. *Student/faculty ratio:* 30:1.
Majors Business teacher education; criminal justice/law enforcement administration; liberal arts and sciences/liberal studies; registered nursing/registered nurse.
Academics *Calendar:* semesters. *Degree:* certificates and associate. *Special study options:* academic remediation for entering students, adult/continuing education programs, advanced placement credit, English as a second language, honors programs, part-time degree program, services for LD students, study abroad, summer session for credit. *ROTC:* Army (c), Navy (c), Air Force (c).
Library Learning Resource Center plus 1 other with 94,143 titles, a Web page.
Student Life *Housing:* college housing not available. *Activities and Organizations:* drama/theater group, student-run newspaper, radio station, choral group. *Campus security:* 24-hour patrols, late-night transport/escort service. *Student services:* health clinic, personal/psychological counseling, women's center, legal services.
Athletics *Intercollegiate sports:* baseball M, basketball M/W, cross-country running M/W, soccer M/W, softball W, swimming and diving M/W, tennis M/W, volleyball W, water polo M/W, wrestling M.
Costs (2015–16) *Tuition:* state resident $46 per credit part-time; nonresident $239 per credit part-time. Full-time tuition and fees vary according to course load. Part-time tuition and fees vary according to course load.
Financial Aid Of all full-time matriculated undergraduates who enrolled in 2013, 150 Federal Work-Study jobs (averaging $3200). 35 state and other part-time jobs (averaging $3200). *Financial aid deadline:* 5/1.
Applying *Options:* early admission. *Application deadlines:* 7/10 (freshmen), 7/10 (transfers). *Notification:* continuous (freshmen), continuous (transfers).
Freshman Application Contact Rio Hondo College, 3600 Workman Mill Road, Whittier, CA 90601-1699. *Phone:* 562-692-0921 Ext. 3415.
Website: http://www.riohondo.edu/.

Riverside City College
Riverside, California

Freshman Application Contact Joy Chambers, Dean of Enrollment Services, Riverside City College, Riverside, CA 92506. *Phone:* 951-222-8600. *Fax:* 951-222-8037. *E-mail:* admissionsriverside@rcc.edu.
Website: http://www.rcc.edu/.

Sacramento City College
Sacramento, California

Director of Admissions Mr. Sam T. Sandusky, Dean, Student Services, Sacramento City College, 3835 Freeport Boulevard, Sacramento, CA 95822-1386. *Phone:* 916-558-2438.
Website: http://www.scc.losrios.edu/.

Saddleback College
Mission Viejo, California

Freshman Application Contact Admissions Office, Saddleback College, 28000 Marguerite Parkway, Mission Viejo, CA 92692. *Phone:* 949-582-4555. *Fax:* 949-347-8315. *E-mail:* earaiza@saddleback.edu.
Website: http://www.saddleback.edu/.

Sage College
Moreno Valley, California

Admissions Office Contact Sage College, 12125 Day Street, Building L, Moreno Valley, CA 92557-6720. *Toll-free phone:* 888-755-SAGE.
Website: http://www.sagecollege.edu/.

The Salvation Army College for Officer Training at Crestmont
Rancho Palos Verdes, California

Freshman Application Contact Capt. Brian Jones, Director of Curriculum, The Salvation Army College for Officer Training at Crestmont, 30840 Hawthorne Boulevard, Rancho Palos Verdes, CA 90275. *Phone:* 310-544-6442. *Fax:* 310-265-6520.
Website: http://www.crestmont.edu/.

San Bernardino Valley College
San Bernardino, California

Director of Admissions Ms. Helena Johnson, Director of Admissions and Records, San Bernardino Valley College, 701 South Mount Vernon Avenue, San Bernardino, CA 92410-2748. *Phone:* 909-384-4401.
Website: http://www.valleycollege.edu/.

San Diego City College
San Diego, California

- **State and locally supported** 2-year, founded 1914, part of San Diego Community College District System
- **Urban** 60-acre campus with easy access to San Diego, Tijuana
- **Endowment** $166,270
- **Coed**

Undergraduates 13% Black or African American, non-Hispanic/Latino; 47% Hispanic/Latino; 9% Asian, non-Hispanic/Latino; 0.5% Native Hawaiian or other Pacific Islander, non-Hispanic/Latino; 0.3% American Indian or Alaska Native, non-Hispanic/Latino; 7% Race/ethnicity unknown.
Faculty *Student/faculty ratio:* 35:1.
Academics *Calendar:* semesters. *Degree:* certificates and associate. *Special study options:* academic remediation for entering students, adult/continuing education programs, cooperative education, distance learning, English as a second language, external degree program, honors programs, independent study, off-campus study, part-time degree program, services for LD students, student-designed majors, summer session for credit. *ROTC:* Air Force (c).
Student Life *Campus security:* 24-hour emergency response devices and patrols, late-night transport/escort service.
Costs (2014–15) *Tuition:* state resident $1380 full-time, $46 per unit part-time; nonresident $7080 full-time, $236 per unit part-time. Full-time tuition and fees vary according to course load. Part-time tuition and fees vary according to course load. *Required fees:* $60 full-time.
Financial Aid Of all full-time matriculated undergraduates who enrolled in 2010, 90 Federal Work-Study jobs (averaging $3844). 19 state and other part-time jobs (averaging $2530).
Applying *Options:* electronic application. *Required for some:* high school transcript.
Freshman Application Contact Ms. Lou Humphries, Registrar/Supervisor of Admissions, Records, Evaluations and Veterans, San Diego City College, 1313 Park Boulevard, San Diego, CA 92101-4787. *Phone:* 619-388-3474. *Fax:* 619-388-3505. *E-mail:* lhumphri@sdccd.edu.
Website: http://www.sdcity.edu/.

San Diego Mesa College
San Diego, California

Freshman Application Contact Ms. Cheri Sawyer, Admissions Supervisor, San Diego Mesa College, 7250 Mesa College Drive, San Diego, CA 92111. *Phone:* 619-388-2686. *Fax:* 619-388-2960. *E-mail:* csawyer@sdccd.edu.
Website: http://www.sdmesa.edu/.

San Diego Miramar College
San Diego, California

- **State and locally supported** 2-year, founded 1969, part of San Diego Community College District
- **Suburban** 120-acre campus
- **Coed,** 10,650 undergraduate students

Majors Accounting; administrative assistant and secretarial science; airframe mechanics and aircraft maintenance technology; anthropology; applied mathematics; art; automobile/automotive mechanics technology; avionics maintenance technology; biology/biological sciences; business administration and management; chemistry; corrections; criminal justice/law enforcement administration; criminal justice/police science; developmental and child psychology; emergency medical technology (EMT paramedic); English; fine/studio arts; fire science/firefighting; geography; humanities; information science/studies; legal assistant/paralegal; liberal arts and sciences/liberal studies; mathematics; occupational safety and health technology; philosophy; physical education teaching and coaching; physical sciences; physics; psychology; social sciences; sociology; Spanish; transportation and materials moving related.

Academics *Calendar:* semesters. *Degree:* certificates and associate. *Special study options:* academic remediation for entering students, accelerated degree program, adult/continuing education programs, advanced placement credit, cooperative education, distance learning, double majors, English as a second language, honors programs, independent study, part-time degree program, services for LD students, student-designed majors, study abroad, summer session for credit.

Library Miramar College Library with 19,301 titles, 901 audiovisual materials, an OPAC.

Student Life *Housing:* college housing not available. *Activities and Organizations:* student-run newspaper. *Campus security:* 24-hour emergency response devices and patrols. *Student services:* health clinic, personal/psychological counseling.

Athletics *Intercollegiate sports:* basketball M, water polo M/W. *Intramural sports:* tennis M/W, volleyball M.

Applying *Options:* electronic application.

Freshman Application Contact Ms. Dana Stack, Admissions Supervisor, San Diego Miramar College, 10440 Black Mountain Road, San Diego, CA 92126-2999. *Phone:* 619-536-7854. *E-mail:* dstack@sdccd.edu. *Website:* http://www.sdmiramar.edu/.

San Joaquin Delta College
Stockton, California

- **District-supported** 2-year, founded 1935, part of California Community College System
- **Urban** 165-acre campus with easy access to Sacramento
- **Coed,** 16,587 undergraduate students, 43% full-time, 59% women, 41% men

Undergraduates 7,187 full-time, 9,400 part-time. Students come from 20 states and territories; 0.2% are from out of state; 10% Black or African American, non-Hispanic/Latino; 43% Hispanic/Latino; 17% Asian, non-Hispanic/Latino; 0.5% Native Hawaiian or other Pacific Islander, non-Hispanic/Latino; 0.4% American Indian or Alaska Native, non-Hispanic/Latino; 5% Two or more races, non-Hispanic/Latino; 0.6% Race/ethnicity unknown; 0.2% international; 5% transferred in. *Retention:* 77% of full-time freshmen returned.

Freshmen *Admission:* 8,815 applied, 8,815 admitted, 3,531 enrolled.

Faculty *Total:* 492, 40% full-time. *Student/faculty ratio:* 27:1.

Majors Accounting; agricultural business and management; agricultural mechanization; agriculture; animal sciences; anthropology; art; automobile/automotive mechanics technology; biology/biological sciences; broadcast journalism; business administration and management; chemistry; civil engineering technology; commercial and advertising art; comparative literature; computer science; construction engineering technology; corrections; criminal justice/police science; crop production; culinary arts; dance; dramatic/theater arts; economics; electrical, electronic and communications engineering technology; engineering; engineering related; engineering technology; English; family and consumer sciences/human sciences; fashion merchandising; fire science/firefighting; geology/earth science; heating, air conditioning, ventilation and refrigeration maintenance technology; history; humanities; journalism; liberal arts and sciences/liberal studies; licensed practical/vocational nurse training; machine tool technology; mathematics; mechanical engineering/mechanical technology; music; natural resources management and policy; natural sciences; ornamental horticulture; philosophy; photography; physical education teaching and coaching; physical sciences; political science and government; psychology; registered nursing/registered nurse; religious studies; rhetoric and composition; social sciences; sociology.

Academics *Calendar:* semesters. *Degree:* certificates and associate. *Special study options:* academic remediation for entering students, adult/continuing education programs, advanced placement credit, cooperative education, distance learning, English as a second language, honors programs, independent study, part-time degree program, services for LD students, summer session for credit.

Library Goleman Library plus 1 other with 124,755 titles, 6,184 audiovisual materials, an OPAC, a Web page.

Student Life *Housing:* college housing not available. *Activities and Organizations:* drama/theater group, student-run newspaper, radio station, choral group. *Campus security:* 24-hour emergency response devices and patrols, late-night transport/escort service. *Student services:* personal/psychological counseling, legal services.

Athletics Member NJCAA. *Intercollegiate sports:* baseball M, basketball M/W, cross-country running M/W, fencing M/W, football M, golf M/W, soccer M/W, softball W, swimming and diving M/W, tennis M/W, track and field M/W, volleyball W, water polo M/W, wrestling M. *Intramural sports:*

badminton M/W, basketball M/W, bowling M/W, soccer M/W, swimming and diving M/W, tennis M/W, ultimate Frisbee M/W, volleyball M/W, weight lifting M/W.

Costs (2014–15) *Tuition:* state resident $1104 full-time; nonresident $6432 full-time.

Financial Aid Of all full-time matriculated undergraduates who enrolled in 2013, 4,169 applied for aid, 3,781 were judged to have need, 10 had their need fully met. 203 Federal Work-Study jobs (averaging $2798). *Average percent of need met:* 34%. *Average financial aid package:* $5639. *Average need-based loan:* $2588. *Average need-based gift aid:* $5339. *Average indebtedness upon graduation:* $8977.

Applying *Options:* electronic application, early admission. *Application deadlines:* rolling (freshmen), rolling (transfers). *Notification:* continuous (freshmen), continuous (transfers).

Freshman Application Contact Ms. Karen Sea, Registrar, San Joaquin Delta College, 5151 Pacific Avenue, Stockton, CA 95207. *Phone:* 209-954-5635. *Fax:* 209-954-5769. *E-mail:* admissions@deltacollege.edu. *Website:* http://www.deltacollege.edu/.

San Joaquin Valley College
Bakersfield, California

- **Proprietary** 2-year, founded 1977, part of San Joaquin Valley College
- **Suburban** campus with easy access to Bakersfield
- **Coed,** 959 undergraduate students, 100% full-time, 70% women, 30% men

Undergraduates 959 full-time. 5% Black or African American, non-Hispanic/Latino; 58% Hispanic/Latino; 2% Asian, non-Hispanic/Latino; 0.4% Native Hawaiian or other Pacific Islander, non-Hispanic/Latino; 2% American Indian or Alaska Native, non-Hispanic/Latino; 4% Two or more races, non-Hispanic/Latino; 1% Race/ethnicity unknown; 3% international. *Retention:* 76% of full-time freshmen returned.

Faculty *Total:* 66, 39% full-time. *Student/faculty ratio:* 24:1.

Majors Business administration and management; corrections; heating, ventilation, air conditioning and refrigeration engineering technology; homeland security, law enforcement, firefighting and protective services related; medical/clinical assistant; medical insurance/medical billing; pharmacy technician; respiratory care therapy; surgical technology.

Academics *Degree:* certificates and associate.

Student Life *Activities and Organizations:* CAMA Club, RACT Club, Business Club, Student Council, National Technical Honor Society.

Applying *Required for some:* essay or personal statement, high school transcript, interview. *Application deadlines:* rolling (freshmen), rolling (transfers). *Notification:* continuous (freshmen), continuous (transfers).

Freshman Application Contact Enrollment Services Director, San Joaquin Valley College, 201 New Stine Road, Bakersfield, CA 93309. *Phone:* 661-834-0126. *Toll-free phone:* 866-544-7898. *Fax:* 661-834-8124. *E-mail:* admissions@sjvc.edu. *Website:* http://www.sjvc.edu/campuses/central-california/bakersfield.

San Joaquin Valley College
Chula Vista, California

- **Proprietary** 2-year, founded 2012
- **Urban** campus with easy access to San Diego
- **Coed,** 26 undergraduate students, 100% full-time, 92% women, 8% men

Undergraduates 26 full-time. 19% Hispanic/Latino; 27% Asian, non-Hispanic/Latino; 4% Native Hawaiian or other Pacific Islander, non-Hispanic/Latino; 4% Two or more races, non-Hispanic/Latino; 4% international.

Faculty *Student/faculty ratio:* 4:1.

Majors Dental hygiene.

Academics *Degree:* associate.

Freshman Application Contact San Joaquin Valley College, 303 H Street, Chula Vista, CA 91910. *Website:* http://www.sjvc.edu/campuses/southern-california/san-diego.

San Joaquin Valley College
Fresno, California

- **Proprietary** 2-year, part of San Joaquin Valley College
- **Urban** campus with easy access to Fresno
- **Coed,** 1,051 undergraduate students, 100% full-time, 74% women, 26% men

Undergraduates 1,051 full-time. 4% Black or African American, non-Hispanic/Latino; 58% Hispanic/Latino; 5% Asian, non-Hispanic/Latino; 0.4% Native Hawaiian or other Pacific Islander, non-Hispanic/Latino; 1% American Indian or Alaska Native, non-Hispanic/Latino; 5% Two or more races, non-

Hispanic/Latino; 2% Race/ethnicity unknown; 2% international. *Retention:* 82% of full-time freshmen returned.
Faculty *Total:* 47, 40% full-time, 4% with terminal degrees. *Student/faculty ratio:* 38:1.
Majors Corrections; heating, ventilation, air conditioning and refrigeration engineering technology; medical/clinical assistant; medical office assistant; office occupations and clerical services; pharmacy technician; surgical technology; veterinary/animal health technology.
Academics *Degree:* certificates and associate.
Student Life *Housing:* college housing not available. *Activities and Organizations:* Associated Student Body, American Medical Technologists, State and County Dental Assistants Association, Arts and Entertainment.
Applying *Required for some:* essay or personal statement, 1 letter of recommendation, interview. *Application deadlines:* rolling (freshmen), rolling (transfers). *Notification:* continuous (freshmen), continuous (transfers).
Freshman Application Contact Enrollment Services Director, San Joaquin Valley College, 295 East Sierra Avenue, Fresno, CA 93710. *Phone:* 559-448-8282. *Fax:* 559-448-8250. *E-mail:* admissions@sjvc.edu.
Website: http://www.sjvc.edu/campuses/central-california/fresno/.

San Joaquin Valley College
Hanford, California

- **Proprietary** 2-year
- **Small-town** campus with easy access to Fresno
- **Coed,** 333 undergraduate students, 100% full-time, 81% women, 19% men

Undergraduates 333 full-time. 3% Black or African American, non-Hispanic/Latino; 79% Hispanic/Latino; 2% Asian, non-Hispanic/Latino; 0.6% Native Hawaiian or other Pacific Islander, non-Hispanic/Latino; 2% American Indian or Alaska Native, non-Hispanic/Latino; 6% Two or more races, non-Hispanic/Latino; 0.6% Race/ethnicity unknown; 5% international.
Faculty *Total:* 12, 25% full-time. *Student/faculty ratio:* 55:1.
Majors Criminal justice/law enforcement administration; medical/clinical assistant; medical insurance/medical billing; office occupations and clerical services.
Academics *Degree:* certificates and associate.
Freshman Application Contact San Joaquin Valley College, 215 West 7th Street, Hanford, CA 93230.
Website: http://www.sjvc.edu/campuses/central-california/hanford/.

San Joaquin Valley College
Hesperia, California

- **Proprietary** 2-year, part of San Joaquin Valley College
- **Suburban** campus with easy access to San Bernadino
- **Coed,** 877 undergraduate students, 100% full-time, 66% women, 34% men

Undergraduates 877 full-time. 11% Black or African American, non-Hispanic/Latino; 51% Hispanic/Latino; 2% Asian, non-Hispanic/Latino; 1% Native Hawaiian or other Pacific Islander, non-Hispanic/Latino; 1% American Indian or Alaska Native, non-Hispanic/Latino; 5% Two or more races, non-Hispanic/Latino; 3% Race/ethnicity unknown; 1% international. *Retention:* 89% of full-time freshmen returned.
Faculty *Total:* 32, 47% full-time, 3% with terminal degrees. *Student/faculty ratio:* 49:1.
Majors Criminal justice/law enforcement administration; heating, air conditioning, ventilation and refrigeration maintenance technology; industrial technology; medical/clinical assistant; medical insurance/medical billing; office occupations and clerical services; pharmacy technician.
Academics *Degree:* certificates and associate.
Freshman Application Contact San Joaquin Valley College, 9331 Mariposa Road, Hesperia, CA 92344.
Website: http://www.sjvc.edu/campuses/southern-california/victor-valley/.

San Joaquin Valley College
Lancaster, California

- **Proprietary** 2-year, founded 2012, part of San Joaquin Valley College
- **Suburban** campus
- **Coed,** 292 undergraduate students, 100% full-time, 79% women, 21% men

Undergraduates 292 full-time. 23% Black or African American, non-Hispanic/Latino; 48% Hispanic/Latino; 1% Asian, non-Hispanic/Latino; 2% Native Hawaiian or other Pacific Islander, non-Hispanic/Latino; 1% American Indian or Alaska Native, non-Hispanic/Latino; 7% Two or more races, non-Hispanic/Latino; 0.7% Race/ethnicity unknown; 2% international. *Retention:* 78% of full-time freshmen returned.

Faculty *Total:* 24, 29% full-time, 4% with terminal degrees. *Student/faculty ratio:* 29:1.
Majors Corrections; heating, air conditioning, ventilation and refrigeration maintenance technology; industrial mechanics and maintenance technology; medical/clinical assistant; medical office assistant; office occupations and clerical services; pharmacy technician.
Academics *Degree:* certificates and associate.
Freshman Application Contact San Joaquin Valley College, 42135 10th Street West, Lancaster, CA 93534.
Website: http://www.sjvc.edu/campuses/southern-california/antelope-valley/.

San Joaquin Valley College
Ontario, California

- **Proprietary** 2-year, part of San Joaquin Valley College
- **Urban** campus with easy access to Los Angeles
- **Coed,** 998 undergraduate students, 100% full-time, 60% women, 40% men

Undergraduates 998 full-time. 6% Black or African American, non-Hispanic/Latino; 61% Hispanic/Latino; 5% Asian, non-Hispanic/Latino; 2% Native Hawaiian or other Pacific Islander, non-Hispanic/Latino; 0.4% American Indian or Alaska Native, non-Hispanic/Latino; 6% Two or more races, non-Hispanic/Latino; 2% Race/ethnicity unknown; 2% international. *Retention:* 78% of full-time freshmen returned.
Faculty *Student/faculty ratio:* 22:1.
Majors Construction management; corrections; dental hygiene; heating, air conditioning, ventilation and refrigeration maintenance technology; industrial mechanics and maintenance technology; medical/clinical assistant; medical office assistant; office occupations and clerical services; pharmacy technician; respiratory care therapy.
Academics *Degree:* certificates and associate.
Student Life *Housing:* college housing not available. *Activities and Organizations:* Students in Free Enterprise (SIFE), Associated Student Body, Fitness Club, Ambassador Club, Diversity Club.
Applying *Required for some:* essay or personal statement, interview. *Application deadlines:* rolling (freshmen), rolling (transfers). *Notification:* continuous (freshmen), continuous (transfers).
Freshman Application Contact Enrollment Services Director, San Joaquin Valley College, 4580 Ontario Mills Parkway, Ontario, CA 91764. *Phone:* 909-948-7582. *Fax:* 909-948-3860. *E-mail:* admissions@sjvc.edu.
Website: http://www.sjvc.edu/campuses/southern-california/ontario/.

San Joaquin Valley College
Rancho Cordova, California

- **Proprietary** 2-year, part of San Joaquin Valley College
- **Suburban** campus with easy access to Sacramento
- **Coed,** 192 undergraduate students, 100% full-time, 54% women, 46% men

Undergraduates 192 full-time. 2% Black or African American, non-Hispanic/Latino; 8% Hispanic/Latino; 17% Asian, non-Hispanic/Latino; 6% Native Hawaiian or other Pacific Islander, non-Hispanic/Latino; 5% Two or more races, non-Hispanic/Latino; 4% Race/ethnicity unknown; 5% international.
Faculty *Student/faculty ratio:* 27:1.
Majors Respiratory therapy technician.
Academics *Degree:* certificates and associate.
Student Life *Housing:* college housing not available. *Activities and Organizations:* Associated Student Body, Diversity Committee.
Applying *Required for some:* essay or personal statement, interview. *Application deadlines:* rolling (freshmen), rolling (transfers). *Notification:* continuous (freshmen), continuous (transfers).
Freshman Application Contact Enrollment Services Director, San Joaquin Valley College, 11050 Olson Drive, Suite 210, Rancho Cordova, CA 95670. *Phone:* 916-638-7582. *Fax:* 916-638-7553. *E-mail:* admissions@sjvc.edu.
Website: http://www.sjvc.edu/campuses/northern-california/rancho-cordova/.

San Joaquin Valley College
Salida, California

- **Proprietary** 2-year, part of San Joaquin Valley College
- **Suburban** campus
- **Coed,** 489 undergraduate students, 100% full-time, 71% women, 29% men

Undergraduates 489 full-time. Students come from 1 other state; 4% Black or African American, non-Hispanic/Latino; 49% Hispanic/Latino; 6% Asian, non-Hispanic/Latino; 2% Native Hawaiian or other Pacific Islander, non-Hispanic/Latino; 0.4% American Indian or Alaska Native, non-

Hispanic/Latino; 3% Two or more races, non-Hispanic/Latino; 2% Race/ethnicity unknown; 3% international. *Retention:* 63% of full-time freshmen returned.
Faculty *Student/faculty ratio:* 34:1.
Majors Industrial technology; massage therapy; medical/clinical assistant; medical office assistant; office occupations and clerical services; pharmacy technician.
Academics *Degree:* certificates and associate.
Student Life *Activities and Organizations:* Associated Student Body, Book Club.
Applying *Required for some:* essay or personal statement, interview. *Application deadlines:* rolling (freshmen), rolling (transfers). *Notification:* continuous (freshmen), continuous (transfers).
Freshman Application Contact Enrollment Services Director, San Joaquin Valley College, 5380 Pirrone Road, Salida, CA 95368. *Phone:* 209-543-8800. *Fax:* 209-543-8320. *E-mail:* admissions@sjvc.edu.
Website: http://www.sjvc.edu/campuses/northern-california/modesto/.

San Joaquin Valley College
Temecula, California

- **Proprietary** 2-year, part of San Joaquin Valley College
- **Urban** campus with easy access to Los Angeles
- **Coed,** 631 undergraduate students, 100% full-time, 72% women, 28% men

Undergraduates 631 full-time. 8% Black or African American, non-Hispanic/Latino; 39% Hispanic/Latino; 7% Asian, non-Hispanic/Latino; 3% Native Hawaiian or other Pacific Islander, non-Hispanic/Latino; 1% American Indian or Alaska Native, non-Hispanic/Latino; 6% Two or more races, non-Hispanic/Latino; 2% Race/ethnicity unknown; 5% international. *Retention:* 77% of full-time freshmen returned.
Faculty *Student/faculty ratio:* 27:1.
Majors Heating, air conditioning, ventilation and refrigeration maintenance technology; medical/clinical assistant; medical office assistant; office occupations and clerical services; pharmacy technician; respiratory care therapy.
Academics *Degree:* certificates and associate.
Freshman Application Contact Robyn Whiles, Enrollment Services Director, San Joaquin Valley College, 27270 Madison Avenue, Suite 103, Temecula, CA 92590. *Phone:* 559-651-2500. *E-mail:* admissions@sjvc.edu.
Website: http://www.sjvc.edu/campuses/southern-california/temecula/.

San Joaquin Valley College
Visalia, California

- **Proprietary** 2-year, founded 1977, part of San Joaquin Valley College
- **Suburban** campus with easy access to Fresno
- **Coed,** 1,364 undergraduate students, 100% full-time, 69% women, 31% men

Undergraduates 1,364 full-time. 3% Black or African American, non-Hispanic/Latino; 54% Hispanic/Latino; 5% Asian, non-Hispanic/Latino; 0.7% Native Hawaiian or other Pacific Islander, non-Hispanic/Latino; 0.7% American Indian or Alaska Native, non-Hispanic/Latino; 4% Two or more races, non-Hispanic/Latino; 2% Race/ethnicity unknown; 3% international. *Retention:* 60% of full-time freshmen returned.
Faculty *Total:* 115, 40% full-time. *Student/faculty ratio:* 20:1.
Majors Business/commerce; computer and information sciences and support services related; corrections; dental hygiene; health and medical administrative services related; heating, ventilation, air conditioning and refrigeration engineering technology; human resources management; industrial technology; licensed practical/vocational nurse training; medical administrative assistant and medical secretary; medical/clinical assistant; medical office assistant; pharmacy technician; physician assistant; registered nursing/registered nurse; respiratory care therapy.
Academics *Calendar:* continuous. *Degree:* certificates and associate. *Special study options:* academic remediation for entering students.
Library SJVC Visalia Campus Library.
Student Life *Housing:* college housing not available. *Activities and Organizations:* Associated Student Body, Students in Free Enterprise (SIFE), American Medical Technologists, National and Technical Honor Society. *Campus security:* late-night transport/escort service, full-time security personnel.
Applying *Required for some:* essay or personal statement, high school transcript, interview. *Application deadlines:* rolling (freshmen), rolling (transfers). *Notification:* continuous (freshmen), continuous (transfers).
Freshman Application Contact Susie Topjian, Enrollment Services Director, San Joaquin Valley College, 8400 West Mineral King Boulevard, Visalia, CA

93291. *Phone:* 559-651-2500. *Fax:* 559-734-9048. *E-mail:* admissions@sjvc.edu.
Website: http://www.sjvc.edu/campuses/central-california/visalia/.

San Joaquin Valley College–Fresno Aviation Campus
Fresno, California

- **Proprietary** 2-year, part of San Joaquin Valley College
- **Urban** campus with easy access to Fresno
- **Coed, primarily men,** 123 undergraduate students, 100% full-time, 3% women, 97% men

Undergraduates 123 full-time. 2% Black or African American, non-Hispanic/Latino; 32% Hispanic/Latino; 14% Asian, non-Hispanic/Latino; 0.8% Native Hawaiian or other Pacific Islander, non-Hispanic/Latino; 2% American Indian or Alaska Native, non-Hispanic/Latino; 3% Two or more races, non-Hispanic/Latino; 2% Race/ethnicity unknown; 2% international. *Retention:* 75% of full-time freshmen returned.
Faculty *Student/faculty ratio:* 24:1.
Majors Airframe mechanics and aircraft maintenance technology.
Academics *Calendar:* semesters. *Degree:* associate.
Student Life *Housing:* college housing not available. *Activities and Organizations:* RC Club (radio controlled airplane).
Costs (2015–16) *Tuition:* $30,210 full-time.
Applying *Required for some:* essay or personal statement, high school transcript, interview. *Application deadlines:* rolling (freshmen), rolling (transfers). *Notification:* continuous (freshmen), continuous (transfers).
Freshman Application Contact Enrollment Services Coordinator, San Joaquin Valley College–Fresno Aviation Campus, 4985 East Anderson Avenue, Fresno, CA 93727. *Phone:* 559-453-0123. *Fax:* 599-453-0133. *E-mail:* admissions@sjvc.edu.
Website: http://www.sjvc.edu/campuses/central-california/fresno-aviation/.

San Joaquin Valley College–Online
Visalia, California

- **Proprietary** 2-year, part of San Joaquin Valley College
- **Suburban** campus
- **Coed,** 1,002 undergraduate students, 100% full-time, 88% women, 12% men

Undergraduates 1,002 full-time. 31% Black or African American, non-Hispanic/Latino; 16% Hispanic/Latino; 1% Asian, non-Hispanic/Latino; 0.3% Native Hawaiian or other Pacific Islander, non-Hispanic/Latino; 0.7% American Indian or Alaska Native, non-Hispanic/Latino; 6% Two or more races, non-Hispanic/Latino; 8% Race/ethnicity unknown; 0.9% international.
Faculty *Total:* 20, 35% full-time, 20% with terminal degrees.
Majors Business administration and management; construction management; human resources management and services related; medical/clinical assistant; medical office management.
Academics *Calendar:* continuous. *Degree:* certificates and associate.
Applying *Options:* electronic application. *Required for some:* essay or personal statement, interview. *Application deadlines:* rolling (freshmen), rolling (transfers). *Notification:* continuous (freshmen), continuous (transfers).
Freshman Application Contact Enrollment Services Director, San Joaquin Valley College–Online, 8344 West Mineral King Avenue, Visalia, CA 93291. *E-mail:* admissions@sjvc.edu.
Website: http://www.sjvc.edu/online-programs/.

San Jose City College
San Jose, California

Freshman Application Contact Mr. Carlo Santos, Director of Admissions/Registrar, San Jose City College, 2100 Moorpark Avenue, San Jose, CA 95128-2799. *Phone:* 408-288-3707. *Fax:* 408-298-1935.
Website: http://www.sjcc.edu/.

Santa Ana College
Santa Ana, California

Freshman Application Contact Mrs. Christie Steward, Admissions Clerk, Santa Ana College, 1530 West 17th Street, Santa Ana, CA 92706-3398. *Phone:* 714-564-6053.
Website: http://www.sac.edu/.

Santa Barbara Business College
Bakersfield, California

Admissions Office Contact Santa Barbara Business College, 5300 California Avenue, Bakersfield, CA 93309.
Website: http://www.sbbcollege.edu/.

Santa Barbara Business College
Santa Maria, California

Admissions Office Contact Santa Barbara Business College, 303 East Plaza Drive, Santa Maria, CA 93454.
Website: http://www.sbbcollege.edu/.

Santa Barbara City College
Santa Barbara, California

Freshman Application Contact Ms. Allison Curtis, Director of Admissions and Records, Santa Barbara City College, Santa Barbara, CA 93109. *Phone:* 805-965-0581 Ext. 2352. *Fax:* 805-962-0497. *E-mail:* admissions@sbcc.edu. *Website:* http://www.sbcc.edu/.

Santa Monica College
Santa Monica, California

- **State and locally supported** 2-year, founded 1929, part of California Community College System
- **Urban** 40-acre campus with easy access to Los Angeles
- **Coed**

Undergraduates 10,722 full-time, 19,278 part-time. 6% are from out of state; 9% Black or African American, non-Hispanic/Latino; 37% Hispanic/Latino; 11% Asian, non-Hispanic/Latino; 0.3% Native Hawaiian or other Pacific Islander, non-Hispanic/Latino; 0.2% American Indian or Alaska Native, non-Hispanic/Latino; 4% Two or more races, non-Hispanic/Latino; 1% Race/ethnicity unknown; 11% international. *Retention:* 65% of full-time freshmen returned.
Academics *Calendar:* semester plus optional winter and summer terms. *Degree:* certificates and associate. *Special study options:* academic remediation for entering students, adult/continuing education programs, advanced placement credit, cooperative education, distance learning, English as a second language, honors programs, independent study, internships, part-time degree program, services for LD students, study abroad, summer session for credit. *ROTC:* Army (c).
Student Life *Campus security:* 24-hour emergency response devices and patrols, student patrols, late-night transport/escort service.
Athletics Member NJCAA.
Costs (2014–15) *Tuition:* state resident $1104 full-time, $46 per unit part-time; nonresident $7800 full-time, $325 per unit part-time. *Required fees:* $101 full-time.
Financial Aid Of all full-time matriculated undergraduates who enrolled in 2013, 450 Federal Work-Study jobs (averaging $3000).
Applying *Options:* early admission. *Required:* high school transcript.
Freshman Application Contact Santa Monica College, 1900 Pico Boulevard, Santa Monica, CA 90405-1628. *Phone:* 310-434-4774.
Website: http://www.smc.edu/.

Santa Rosa Junior College
Santa Rosa, California

- **State and locally supported** 2-year, founded 1918, part of California Community College System
- **Urban** 100-acre campus with easy access to San Francisco
- **Endowment** $41.3 million
- **Coed**

Undergraduates 6,830 full-time, 15,178 part-time. Students come from 36 other countries; 3% are from out of state; 3% Black or African American, non-Hispanic/Latino; 31% Hispanic/Latino; 4% Asian, non-Hispanic/Latino; 1% Native Hawaiian or other Pacific Islander, non-Hispanic/Latino; 0.8% American Indian or Alaska Native, non-Hispanic/Latino; 4% Two or more races, non-Hispanic/Latino; 6% Race/ethnicity unknown.
Faculty *Student/faculty ratio:* 22:1.
Academics *Calendar:* semesters. *Degree:* certificates and associate. *Special study options:* academic remediation for entering students, adult/continuing education programs, advanced placement credit, cooperative education, distance learning, English as a second language, independent study, internships, off-campus study, part-time degree program, services for LD students, study abroad, summer session for credit.

Student Life *Campus security:* 24-hour emergency response devices and patrols, student patrols.
Athletics Member NJCAA.
Costs (2014–15) *One-time required fee:* $40. *Tuition:* state resident $0 full-time; nonresident $5832 full-time, $243 per unit part-time. Full-time tuition and fees vary according to course load. Part-time tuition and fees vary according to course load. *Required fees:* $1104 full-time, $46 per unit part-time, $20 per term part-time. *Payment plans:* installment, deferred payment.
Financial Aid Of all full-time matriculated undergraduates who enrolled in 2009, 135 Federal Work-Study jobs (averaging $2210). 43 state and other part-time jobs (averaging $7396).
Applying *Options:* electronic application, early admission.
Freshman Application Contact Ms. Freyja Pereira, Director, Admissions, Records and Enrollment Services, Santa Rosa Junior College, 1501 Mendocino Avenue, Santa Rosa, CA 95401. *Phone:* 707-527-4512. *Fax:* 707-527-4798. *E-mail:* admininfo@santarosa.edu.
Website: http://www.santarosa.edu/.

Santiago Canyon College
Orange, California

Freshman Application Contact Tuyen Nguyen, Admissions and Records, Santiago Canyon College, 8045 East Chapman Avenue, Orange, CA 92869. *Phone:* 714-628-4902.
Website: http://www.sccollege.edu/.

Shasta College
Redding, California

Director of Admissions Dr. Kevin O'Rorke, Dean of Enrollment Services, Shasta College, PO Box 496006, 11555 Old Oregon Trail, Redding, CA 96049-6006. *Phone:* 530-242-7669.
Website: http://www.shastacollege.edu/.

Sierra College
Rocklin, California

- **State-supported** 2-year, founded 1936, part of California Community College System
- **Suburban** 327-acre campus with easy access to Sacramento
- **Coed,** 19,416 undergraduate students, 28% full-time, 57% women, 43% men

Undergraduates 5,355 full-time, 14,061 part-time. 1% are from out of state; 4% transferred in; 1% live on campus.
Freshmen *Admission:* 24,000 applied, 24,000 admitted, 2,112 enrolled.
Faculty *Total:* 870, 18% full-time. *Student/faculty ratio:* 25:1.
Majors Accounting; administrative assistant and secretarial science; agriculture; American Sign Language (ASL); animal/livestock husbandry and production; apparel and textile manufacturing; apparel and textile marketing management; applied horticulture/horticulture operations; architectural drafting and CAD/CADD; art; automobile/automotive mechanics technology; biological and physical sciences; biology/biological sciences; business administration and management; business/commerce; cabinetmaking and millwork; chemistry; child development; commercial photography; computer and information sciences and support services related; computer installation and repair technology; computer programming; computer systems networking and telecommunications; construction trades; corrections; criminal justice/police science; data entry/microcomputer applications; digital communication and media/multimedia; electrical/electronics equipment installation and repair; engineering; English; equestrian studies; fire science/firefighting; forestry; general studies; geology/earth science; graphic design; hazardous materials management and waste technology; health and physical education/fitness; industrial electronics technology; information technology; liberal arts and sciences/liberal studies; licensed practical/vocational nurse training; manufacturing engineering technology; mathematics; mechanical drafting and CAD/CADD; music; network and system administration; parks, recreation and leisure; philosophy; physics; psychology; real estate; registered nursing/registered nurse; rhetoric and composition; sales, distribution, and marketing operations; small business administration; social sciences; visual and performing arts; web page, digital/multimedia and information resources design; women's studies.
Academics *Calendar:* semesters. *Degree:* certificates and associate. *Special study options:* academic remediation for entering students, accelerated degree program, advanced placement credit, distance learning, double majors, English as a second language, honors programs, independent study, internships, off-campus study, part-time degree program, services for LD students, study abroad, summer session for credit.
Library Leary Resource Center plus 1 other with 69,879 titles, an OPAC, a Web page.

Student Life *Housing Options:* coed. Campus housing is university owned. *Activities and Organizations:* drama/theater group, student-run newspaper, choral group, Drama Club, student government, Art Club, band, Aggie Club. *Campus security:* 24-hour emergency response devices and patrols, late-night transport/escort service. *Student services:* health clinic, personal/psychological counseling.

Athletics *Intercollegiate sports:* baseball M, basketball M/W, football M, golf M/W, soccer W, softball W, swimming and diving M/W, tennis M/W, volleyball W, water polo M/W, wrestling M. *Intramural sports:* archery M/W, badminton M/W, basketball M/W, tennis M/W, volleyball M/W.

Costs (2014–15) *Tuition:* state resident $1380 full-time, $46 per credit hour part-time; nonresident $5790 full-time, $193 per credit hour part-time. Full-time tuition and fees vary according to course load. Part-time tuition and fees vary according to course load. *Required fees:* $38 full-time, $19 per term part-time. *Room and board:* $3600. *Payment plan:* installment.

Financial Aid Of all full-time matriculated undergraduates who enrolled in 2013, 112 Federal Work-Study jobs (averaging $4400). 14 state and other part-time jobs (averaging $4644). *Average financial aid package:* $5779. *Average need-based loan:* $3726. *Average need-based gift aid:* $5309.

Applying *Options:* electronic application, early admission. *Application deadline:* rolling (freshmen). *Notification:* continuous (freshmen), continuous (transfers).

Freshman Application Contact Sierra College, 5000 Rocklin Road, Rocklin, CA 95677-3397. *Phone:* 916-660-7341.
Website: http://www.sierracollege.edu/.

Skyline College
San Bruno, California

Freshman Application Contact Terry Stats, Admissions Office, Skyline College, 3300 College Drive, San Bruno, CA 94066-1698. *Phone:* 650-738-4251. *E-mail:* stats@smccd.net.
Website: http://skylinecollege.edu/.

Solano Community College
Fairfield, California

Freshman Application Contact Solano Community College, 4000 Suisun Valley Road, Fairfield, CA 94534. *Phone:* 707-864-7000 Ext. 4313.
Website: http://www.solano.edu/.

South Coast College
Orange, California

Director of Admissions South Coast College, 2011 West Chapman Avenue, Orange, CA 92868. *Toll-free phone:* 877-568-6130.
Website: http://www.southcoastcollege.com/.

Southwestern College
Chula Vista, California

Freshman Application Contact Director of Admissions and Records, Southwestern College, 900 Otay Lakes Road, Chula Vista, CA 91910-7299. *Phone:* 619-421-6700 Ext. 5215. *Fax:* 619-482-6489.
Website: http://www.swc.edu/.

Stanbridge College
Irvine, California

Admissions Office Contact Stanbridge College, 2041 Business Center Drive, Irvine, CA 92612.
Website: http://www.stanbridge.edu/.

SUM Bible College & Theological Seminary
Oakland, California

Freshman Application Contact Admissions, SUM Bible College & Theological Seminary, 735 105th Avenue, Oakland, CA 94603. *Phone:* 510-567-6174. *Toll-free phone:* 888-567-6174. *Fax:* 510-568-1024.
Website: http://www.sum.edu/.

Taft College
Taft, California

Freshman Application Contact Nichole Cook, Admissions/Counseling Technician, Taft College, 29 Emmons Park Drive, Taft, CA 93268-2317. *Phone:* 661-763-7790. *Fax:* 661-763-7758. *E-mail:* ncook@taftcollege.edu.
Website: http://www.taftcollege.edu/.

Unitek College
Fremont, California

Admissions Office Contact Unitek College, 4670 Auto Mall Parkway, Fremont, CA 94538.
Website: http://www.unitekcollege.edu/.

Valley College of Medical Careers
West Hills, California

Admissions Office Contact Valley College of Medical Careers, 8399 Topanga Canyon Boulevard, Suite 200, West Hills, CA 91304.
Website: http://www.vcmc.edu/.

Ventura College
Ventura, California

Freshman Application Contact Ms. Susan Bricker, Registrar, Ventura College, 4667 Telegraph Road, Ventura, CA 93003-3899. *Phone:* 805-654-6456. *Fax:* 805-654-6357. *E-mail:* sbricker@vcccd.net.
Website: http://www.venturacollege.edu/.

Victor Valley College
Victorville, California

- **State-supported** 2-year, founded 1961, part of California Community College System
- **Small-town** 253-acre campus with easy access to Los Angeles
- **Coed,** 7,030 undergraduate students, 40% full-time, 57% women, 43% men

Undergraduates 2,812 full-time, 4,218 part-time. 3% are from out of state; 7% transferred in. *Retention:* 69% of full-time freshmen returned.

Freshmen *Admission:* 1,259 enrolled.

Faculty *Student/faculty ratio:* 26:1.

Majors Administrative assistant and secretarial science; agricultural teacher education; art; automobile/automotive mechanics technology; biological and physical sciences; biology/biological sciences; building/construction finishing, management, and inspection related; business administration and management; business/commerce; child-care and support services management; child development; computer and information sciences; computer programming (specific applications); computer science; construction engineering technology; criminal justice/police science; dramatic/theater arts; electrical, electronic and communications engineering technology; fire prevention and safety technology; fire science/firefighting; food technology and processing; horticultural science; humanities; information science/studies; kindergarten/preschool education; liberal arts and sciences/liberal studies; management information systems; mathematics; music; natural sciences; ornamental horticulture; physical sciences; real estate; registered nursing/registered nurse; respiratory care therapy; science technologies related; social sciences; teacher assistant/aide; trade and industrial teacher education; vehicle maintenance and repair technologies related; welding technology.

Academics *Calendar:* semesters. *Degree:* certificates, diplomas, and associate. *Special study options:* academic remediation for entering students, accelerated degree program, advanced placement credit, cooperative education, distance learning, double majors, English as a second language, honors programs, independent study, internships, off-campus study, part-time degree program, services for LD students, study abroad, summer session for credit.

Library Learning Resource Center with an OPAC, a Web page.

Student Life *Housing:* college housing not available. *Activities and Organizations:* drama/theater group, student-run newspaper, choral group, Black Student Union, Drama Club, rugby, Phi Theta Kappa. *Campus security:* 24-hour emergency response devices and patrols, late-night transport/escort service, part-time trained security personnel. *Student services:* health clinic, personal/psychological counseling.

Athletics Member NCAA, NJCAA. *Intercollegiate sports:* baseball M, basketball M/W, cross-country running M/W, football M, golf M, soccer M/W, softball W, tennis M/W, track and field M/W, volleyball W, wrestling M. *Intramural sports:* rock climbing M/W.

Costs (2014–15) *Tuition:* state resident $1104 full-time, $46 per credit part-time; nonresident $5736 full-time, $193 per credit part-time. *Required fees:* $10 full-time. *Payment plan:* installment.
Financial Aid *Average need-based loan:* $6168. *Average need-based gift aid:* $3707.
Applying *Application deadline:* rolling (freshmen). *Notification:* continuous (freshmen).
Freshman Application Contact Ms. Greta Moon, Director of Admissions and Records (Interim), Victor Valley College, 18422 Bear Valley Road, Victorville, CA 92395. *Phone:* 760-245-4271. *Fax:* 760-843-7707. *E-mail:* moong@vvc.edu.
Website: http://www.vvc.edu/.

West Coast Ultrasound Institute
Beverly Hills, California
Admissions Office Contact West Coast Ultrasound Institute, 291 S. La Cienega Boulevard, Suite 500, Beverly Hills, CA 90211.
Website: http://wcui.edu/.

West Hills Community College
Coalinga, California
Freshman Application Contact Sandra Dagnino, West Hills Community College, 300 Cherry Lane, Coalinga, CA 93210-1399. *Phone:* 559-934-3203. *Toll-free phone:* 800-266-1114. *Fax:* 559-934-2830. *E-mail:* sandradagnino@westhillscollege.com.
Website: http://www.westhillscollege.com/.

West Hills Community College–Lemoore
Lemoore, California
Admissions Office Contact West Hills Community College–Lemoore, 555 College Avenue, Lemoore, CA 93245.
Website: http://www.westhillscollege.com/.

West Los Angeles College
Culver City, California
Director of Admissions Mr. Len Isaksen, Director of Admissions, West Los Angeles College, 9000 Overland Avenue, Culver City, CA 90230-3519. *Phone:* 310-287-4255.
Website: http://www.lacolleges.net/.

West Valley College
Saratoga, California
Freshman Application Contact Ms. Barbara Ogilive, Supervisor, Admissions and Records, West Valley College, 14000 Fruitvale Avenue, Saratoga, CA 95070-5698. *Phone:* 408-741-4630. *E-mail:* barbara_ogilvie@westvalley.edu.
Website: http://www.westvalley.edu/.

Woodland Community College
Woodland, California
Admissions Office Contact Woodland Community College, 2300 East Gibson Road, Woodland, CA 95776.
Website: http://www.yccd.edu/woodland/.

Yuba College
Marysville, California
Director of Admissions Dr. David Farrell, Dean of Student Development, Yuba College, 2088 North Beale Road, Marysville, CA 95901-7699. *Phone:* 530-741-6705.
Website: http://www.yccd.edu/.

COLORADO

Aims Community College
Greeley, Colorado
Freshman Application Contact Ms. Susie Gallardo, Admissions Technician, Aims Community College, Box 69, 5401 West 20th Street, Greeley, CO 80632-0069. *Phone:* 970-330-8008 Ext. 6624. *E-mail:* wgreen@chiron.aims.edu.
Website: http://www.aims.edu/.

Arapahoe Community College
Littleton, Colorado
- **State-supported** 2-year, founded 1965, part of Colorado Community College and Occupational Education System
- **Suburban** 52-acre campus with easy access to Denver
- **Endowment** $730,363
- **Coed,** 9,745 undergraduate students, 21% full-time, 57% women, 43% men

Undergraduates 2,064 full-time, 7,681 part-time. Students come from 13 other countries; 6% are from out of state; 3% Black or African American, non-Hispanic/Latino; 14% Hispanic/Latino; 3% Asian, non-Hispanic/Latino; 0.3% Native Hawaiian or other Pacific Islander, non-Hispanic/Latino; 0.7% American Indian or Alaska Native, non-Hispanic/Latino; 4% Two or more races, non-Hispanic/Latino; 5% Race/ethnicity unknown; 0.9% international; 12% transferred in. *Retention:* 47% of full-time freshmen returned.
Freshmen *Admission:* 2,166 applied, 2,166 admitted, 1,004 enrolled. *Average high school GPA:* 2.96.
Faculty *Total:* 494, 21% full-time. *Student/faculty ratio:* 20:1.
Majors Accounting technology and bookkeeping; architectural engineering technology; automobile/automotive mechanics technology; banking and financial support services; business administration and management; civil engineering technology; clinical/medical laboratory technology; computer and information sciences; computer and information sciences and support services related; criminal justice/law enforcement administration; electrical, electronic and communications engineering technology; emergency medical technology (EMT paramedic); engineering technology; funeral service and mortuary science; graphic design; health and physical education/fitness; health information/medical records technology; interior design; legal assistant/paralegal; liberal arts and sciences/liberal studies; medical office management; physical therapy technology; registered nursing/registered nurse; system, networking, and LAN/WAN management.
Academics *Calendar:* semesters. *Degree:* certificates, diplomas, and associate. *Special study options:* academic remediation for entering students, accelerated degree program, adult/continuing education programs, advanced placement credit, cooperative education, distance learning, double majors, English as a second language, external degree program, honors programs, independent study, internships, off-campus study, part-time degree program, services for LD students, student-designed majors, study abroad, summer session for credit. *ROTC:* Army (c), Navy (c), Air Force (c).
Library Weber Center for Learning Resources plus 1 other with 48,693 titles, 2,000 audiovisual materials, an OPAC, a Web page.
Student Life *Housing:* college housing not available. *Activities and Organizations:* drama/theater group, choral group, F.A.S.T Club (First Aid Survival Training), Phi Theta Kappa, History Club, Jewelry Club, ASID (American Society of Interior Designers). *Campus security:* 24-hour emergency response devices and patrols, late-night transport/escort service. *Student services:* personal/psychological counseling.
Athletics *Intramural sports:* baseball M(c)/W, basketball M, football M, ice hockey M, rock climbing M/W, skiing (cross-country) M/W, skiing (downhill) M/W, soccer M/W, softball M/W, swimming and diving M/W, table tennis M/W, tennis M/W, ultimate Frisbee M/W, volleyball M/W, weight lifting M.
Standardized Tests *Recommended:* ACT (for admission), SAT or ACT (for admission).
Costs (2014–15) *Tuition:* state resident $3748 full-time, $153 per credit hour part-time; nonresident $15,370 full-time, $541 per credit hour part-time. Full-time tuition and fees vary according to program. Part-time tuition and fees vary according to program. *Required fees:* $197 full-time, $28 per semester hour part-time. *Payment plan:* installment. *Waivers:* employees or children of employees.
Financial Aid Of all full-time matriculated undergraduates who enrolled in 2013, 100 Federal Work-Study jobs (averaging $4200). 200 state and other part-time jobs (averaging $4200).
Applying *Options:* electronic application, early admission, deferred entrance. *Application deadlines:* rolling (freshmen), rolling (out-of-state freshmen),

rolling (transfers). *Notification:* continuous (freshmen), continuous (out-of-state freshmen), continuous (transfers).

Freshman Application Contact Arapahoe Community College, 5900 South Santa Fe Drive, PO Box 9002, Littleton, CO 80160-9002. *Phone:* 303-797-5623.

Website: http://www.arapahoe.edu/.

Bel–Rea Institute of Animal Technology
Denver, Colorado

Director of Admissions Ms. Paulette Kaufman, Director, Bel-Rea Institute of Animal Technology, 1681 South Dayton Street, Denver, CO 80247. *Phone:* 303-751-8700. *Toll-free phone:* 800-950-8001. *E-mail:* admissions@bel-rea.com.

Website: http://www.bel-rea.com/.

CollegeAmerica–Colorado Springs
Colorado Springs, Colorado

Freshman Application Contact CollegeAmerica–Colorado Springs, 2020 N. Academy Boulevard, Colorado Springs, CO 80909. *Phone:* 719-637-0600. *Toll-free phone:* 800-622-2894.

Website: http://www.collegeamerica.edu/.

CollegeAmerica–Denver
Denver, Colorado

Freshman Application Contact Admissions Office, CollegeAmerica–Denver, 1385 South Colorado Boulevard, Denver, CO 80222. *Phone:* 303-300-8740. *Toll-free phone:* 800-622-2894.

Website: http://www.collegeamerica.edu/.

CollegeAmerica–Fort Collins
Fort Collins, Colorado

Director of Admissions Ms. Anna DiTorrice-Mull, Director of Admissions, CollegeAmerica–Fort Collins, 4601 South Mason Street, Fort Collins, CO 80525-3740. *Phone:* 970-223-6060 Ext. 8002. *Toll-free phone:* 800-622-2894.

Website: http://www.collegeamerica.edu/.

Colorado Academy of Veterinary Technology
Colorado Springs, Colorado

Admissions Office Contact Colorado Academy of Veterinary Technology, 2766 Janitell Road, Colorado Springs, CO 80906.

Website: http://www.coloradovettech.com/.

Colorado Northwestern Community College
Rangely, Colorado

- **State-supported** 2-year, founded 1962, part of Colorado Community College and Occupational Education System
- **Rural** 150-acre campus
- **Coed**

Freshmen *Admission:* 497 applied, 497 admitted.

Majors Accounting; aircraft powerplant technology; airline pilot and flight crew; banking and financial support services; cosmetology; dental hygiene; early childhood education; emergency medical technology (EMT paramedic); equestrian studies; general studies; liberal arts and sciences/liberal studies; natural resources/conservation; registered nursing/registered nurse; small business administration.

Academics *Calendar:* semesters. *Degree:* certificates and associate. *Special study options:* academic remediation for entering students, adult/continuing education programs, advanced placement credit, distance learning, double majors, independent study, internships, part-time degree program, services for LD students, student-designed majors, summer session for credit.

Library Colorado Northwestern Community College Library - Rangely plus 1 other with 22,000 titles, 9,612 audiovisual materials, an OPAC.

Student Life *Housing:* on-campus residence required for freshman year. *Options:* coed. Campus housing is university owned. Freshman applicants given priority for college housing. *Activities and Organizations:* student-run newspaper, choral group. *Campus security:* student patrols, late night transport/escort service. *Student services:* personal/psychological counseling.

Athletics Member NJCAA. *Intercollegiate sports:* baseball M(s), basketball M(s)/W(s), softball W(s), volleyball W(s). *Intramural sports:* basketball M/W, football M/W, golf M/W, racquetball M/W, skiing (cross-country) M/W, skiing (downhill) M/W, softball M/W, table tennis M/W, tennis M/W, volleyball M/W.

Standardized Tests *Recommended:* ACT (for admission).

Costs (2014–15) *Tuition:* state resident $5907 full-time, $200 per credit hour part-time; nonresident $6704 full-time, $223 per credit hour part-time. Full-time tuition and fees vary according to program. Part-time tuition and fees vary according to program. *Required fees:* $288 full-time, $8 per credit hour part-time, $13 per term part-time. *Room and board:* $6478; room only: $2356. Room and board charges vary according to board plan and housing facility. *Payment plan:* installment.

Applying *Options:* electronic application, early admission, deferred entrance. *Required:* high school transcript. *Required for some:* essay or personal statement, 3 letters of recommendation, interview. *Application deadlines:* rolling (freshmen), rolling (out-of-state freshmen), rolling (transfers). *Notification:* continuous (freshmen), continuous (out-of-state freshmen), continuous (transfers).

Freshman Application Contact Colorado Northwestern Community College, 500 Kennedy Drive, Rangely, CO 81648-3598. *Phone:* 970-675-3285. *Toll-free phone:* 800-562-1105.

Website: http://www.cncc.edu/.

Colorado School of Healing Arts
Lakewood, Colorado

Freshman Application Contact Colorado School of Healing Arts, 7655 West Mississippi Avenue, Suite 100, Lakewood, CO 80220. *Phone:* 303-986-2320. *Toll-free phone:* 800-233-7114. *Fax:* 303-980-6594.

Website: http://www.csha.net/.

Colorado School of Trades
Lakewood, Colorado

Freshman Application Contact Colorado School of Trades, 1575 Hoyt Street, Lakewood, CO 80215-2996. *Phone:* 303-233-4697 Ext. 44. *Toll-free phone:* 800-234-4594.

Website: http://www.schooloftrades.com/.

Community College of Aurora
Aurora, Colorado

- **State-supported** 2-year, founded 1983, part of Colorado Community College System
- **Suburban** campus with easy access to Denver
- **Coed,** 7,617 undergraduate students, 20% full-time, 59% women, 41% men

Undergraduates 1,528 full-time, 6,089 part-time. 21% Black or African American, non-Hispanic/Latino; 21% Hispanic/Latino; 5% Asian, non-Hispanic/Latino; 0.4% Native Hawaiian or other Pacific Islander, non-Hispanic/Latino; 0.6% American Indian or Alaska Native, non-Hispanic/Latino; 6% Two or more races, non-Hispanic/Latino; 5% Race/ethnicity unknown; 2% international.

Freshmen *Admission:* 872 enrolled.

Faculty *Student/faculty ratio:* 20:1.

Majors Accounting technology and bookkeeping; child development; cinematography and film/video production; criminal justice/law enforcement administration; emergency medical technology (EMT paramedic); fire science/firefighting; general studies; heavy equipment maintenance technology; liberal arts and sciences and humanities related; liberal arts and sciences/liberal studies; management information systems; office management; science technologies related.

Academics *Calendar:* semesters. *Degree:* certificates and associate. *Special study options:* academic remediation for entering students, adult/continuing education programs, distance learning, English as a second language, external degree program, independent study, internships, off-campus study, part-time degree program, services for LD students, summer session for credit.

Library 6,727 titles, an OPAC, a Web page.

Student Life *Activities and Organizations:* drama/theater group. *Campus security:* late-night transport/escort service. *Student services:* women's center.

Applying *Options:* early admission. *Required for some:* high school transcript. *Application deadlines:* rolling (freshmen), rolling (out-of-state freshmen), rolling (transfers). *Notification:* continuous (freshmen), continuous (out-of-state freshmen), continuous (transfers).

Freshman Application Contact Community College of Aurora, 16000 East Centre Tech Parkway, Aurora, CO 80011-9036. *Phone:* 303-360-4701.

Website: http://www.ccaurora.edu/.

Community College of Denver
Denver, Colorado

- **State-supported** 2-year, founded 1970, part of Colorado Community College System
- **Urban** 124-acre campus
- **Coed,** 10,296 undergraduate students, 24% full-time, 56% women, 44% men

Undergraduates 2,514 full-time, 7,782 part-time. 2% are from out of state; 13% Black or African American, non-Hispanic/Latino; 26% Hispanic/Latino; 5% Asian, non-Hispanic/Latino; 0.2% Native Hawaiian or other Pacific Islander, non-Hispanic/Latino; 1% American Indian or Alaska Native, non-Hispanic/Latino; 4% Two or more races, non-Hispanic/Latino; 13% Race/ethnicity unknown; 4% international. *Retention:* 53% of full-time freshmen returned.

Freshmen *Admission:* 1,550 enrolled.

Faculty *Total:* 435, 28% full-time. *Student/faculty ratio:* 25:1.

Majors Accounting; accounting technology and bookkeeping; administrative assistant and secretarial science; business administration and management; child development; computer and information sciences; dental hygiene; drafting and design technology; electroneurodiagnostic/electroencephalographic technology; general studies; graphic design; human services; legal assistant/paralegal; liberal arts and sciences/liberal studies; licensed practical/vocational nurse training; machine shop technology; management information systems; mental health counseling; office management; quality control and safety technologies related; radiologic technology/science; registered nursing/registered nurse; science technologies related; teacher assistant/aide; teaching assistants/aides related; veterinary/animal health technology; welding technology.

Academics *Calendar:* semesters. *Degree:* certificates and associate. *Special study options:* academic remediation for entering students, accelerated degree program, adult/continuing education programs, advanced placement credit, cooperative education, distance learning, double majors, English as a second language, external degree program, freshman honors college, honors programs, independent study, internships, off-campus study, part-time degree program, services for LD students, study abroad, summer session for credit. *ROTC:* Army (c).

Library Auraria Library with an OPAC, a Web page.

Student Life *Housing:* college housing not available. *Activities and Organizations:* student-run newspaper, choral group, Phi Theta Kappa, Black Student Alliance, La Mision, SAFI, Chinese Culture Club. *Campus security:* 24-hour emergency response devices and patrols, late-night transport/escort service. *Student services:* health clinic, personal/psychological counseling.

Athletics *Intramural sports:* archery M/W, badminton M/W, basketball M/W, bowling M/W, cross-country running M/W, equestrian sports M/W, fencing M/W, field hockey M/W, football M/W, golf M/W, gymnastics M/W, racquetball M/W, riflery M/W, rugby M/W, skiing (cross-country) M/W, skiing (downhill) M/W, soccer M/W, swimming and diving M/W, table tennis M/W, tennis M/W, track and field M/W, volleyball M/W, weight lifting M/W.

Costs (2015–16) *Tuition:* state resident $2998 full-time, $125 per credit hour part-time; nonresident $12,296 full-time, $512 per credit hour part-time. Full-time tuition and fees vary according to course load, location, program, and reciprocity agreements. Part-time tuition and fees vary according to course load, location, program, and reciprocity agreements. *Payment plan:* installment.

Applying *Options:* electronic application, early admission, deferred entrance. **Freshman Application Contact** Mr. Michael Rusk, Dean of Students, Community College of Denver, PO Box 173363, Campus Box 201, Denver, CO 80127-3363. *Phone:* 303-556-6325. *Fax:* 303-556-2431. *E-mail:* enrollment_services@ccd.edu. *Website:* http://www.ccd.edu/.

Concorde Career College
Aurora, Colorado

Admissions Office Contact Concorde Career College, 111 North Havana Street, Aurora, CO 80010. *Website:* http://www.concorde.edu/.

Ecotech Institute
Aurora, Colorado

Admissions Office Contact Ecotech Institute, 1400 South Abilene Street, Aurora, CO 80012. *Website:* http://www.ecotechinstitute.com/.

Everest College
Aurora, Colorado

Freshman Application Contact Everest College, 14280 East Jewell Avenue, Suite 100, Aurora, CO 80014. *Phone:* 303-745-6244. *Toll-free phone:* 888-741-4270. *Website:* http://www.everest.edu/.

Everest College
Colorado Springs, Colorado

Director of Admissions Director of Admissions, Everest College, 1815 Jet Wing Drive, Colorado Springs, CO 80916. *Phone:* 719-630-6580. *Toll-free phone:* 888-741-4270. *Fax:* 719-638-6818. *Website:* http://www.everest.edu/.

Everest College
Thornton, Colorado

Freshman Application Contact Admissions Office, Everest College, 9065 Grant Street, Thornton, CO 80229-4339. *Phone:* 303-457-2757. *Toll-free phone:* 888-741-4270. *Fax:* 303-457-4030. *Website:* http://www.everest.edu/.

Front Range Community College
Westminster, Colorado

- **State-supported** 2-year, founded 1968, part of Community Colleges of Colorado System
- **Suburban** 90-acre campus with easy access to Denver
- **Endowment** $457,964
- **Coed,** 19,619 undergraduate students, 31% full-time, 56% women, 44% men

Undergraduates 6,120 full-time, 13,499 part-time. Students come from 46 states and territories; 27 other countries; 2% are from out of state; 2% Black or African American, non-Hispanic/Latino; 14% Hispanic/Latino; 3% Asian, non-Hispanic/Latino; 0.2% Native Hawaiian or other Pacific Islander, non-Hispanic/Latino; 0.9% American Indian or Alaska Native, non-Hispanic/Latino; 3% Two or more races, non-Hispanic/Latino; 6% Race/ethnicity unknown; 1% international; 14% transferred in. *Retention:* 57% of full-time freshmen returned.

Freshmen *Admission:* 5,793 applied, 5,793 admitted, 2,511 enrolled.

Faculty *Total:* 1,170, 22% full-time. *Student/faculty ratio:* 20:1.

Majors Accounting technology and bookkeeping; animation, interactive technology, video graphics and special effects; applied horticulture/horticulture operations; architectural engineering technology; automobile/automotive mechanics technology; business administration and management; CAD/CADD drafting/design technology; computer and information sciences; computer systems networking and telecommunications; early childhood education; energy management and systems technology; general studies; health information/medical records technology; heating, ventilation, air conditioning and refrigeration engineering technology; holistic health; hospitality administration; interior design; legal assistant/paralegal; liberal arts and sciences and humanities related; liberal arts and sciences/liberal studies; medical office assistant; registered nursing/registered nurse; science technologies related; sign language interpretation and translation; veterinary/animal health technology; welding technology; wildlife, fish and wildlands science and management.

Academics *Calendar:* semesters. *Degree:* certificates and associate. *Special study options:* academic remediation for entering students, advanced placement credit, cooperative education, distance learning, double majors, English as a second language, freshman honors college, honors programs, independent study, internships, off-campus study, part-time degree program, services for LD students, student-designed majors, study abroad, summer session for credit. *ROTC:* Army (c), Air Force (c).

Library College Hill Library plus 2 others with an OPAC, a Web page.

Student Life *Housing:* college housing not available. *Activities and Organizations:* drama/theater group, student-run newspaper, Student Government Association, Student Colorado Registry of Interpreters for the Deaf, Students in Free Enterprise (SIFE), Gay Straight Alliance, Recycling Club. *Campus security:* 24-hour patrols, late-night transport/escort service. *Student services:* personal/psychological counseling.

Costs (2014–15) *Tuition:* state resident $2998 full-time, $125 per credit hour part-time; nonresident $12,296 full-time, $512 per credit hour part-time. Full-time tuition and fees vary according to program. Part-time tuition and fees vary according to program. *Required fees:* $367 full-time, $367 per year part-time. *Payment plan:* installment. *Waivers:* employees or children of employees.

Applying *Options:* electronic application, early admission, deferred entrance. **Freshman Application Contact** Ms. Yolanda Espinoza, Registrar, Front Range Community College, Westminster, CO 80031. *Phone:* 303-404-5000. *Fax:* 303-439-2614. *E-mail:* yolanda.espinoza@frontrange.edu. *Website:* http://www.frontrange.edu/.

Heritage College
Denver, Colorado

Freshman Application Contact Admissions Office, Heritage College, 4704 Harlan Street, Suite 100, Denver, CO 80212. *Website:* http://www.heritage-education.com/.

IBMC College
Fort Collins, Colorado

- **Private** 2-year, founded 1987
- **Suburban** campus with easy access to Denver
- **Coed,** 1,020 undergraduate students, 100% full-time, 85% women, 15% men
- 92% of applicants were admitted

Undergraduates 1,020 full-time. 2% are from out of state; 1% Black or African American, non-Hispanic/Latino; 20% Hispanic/Latino; 0.5% Asian, non-Hispanic/Latino; 0.2% Native Hawaiian or other Pacific Islander, non-Hispanic/Latino; 0.6% American Indian or Alaska Native, non-Hispanic/Latino; 1% Two or more races, non-Hispanic/Latino. *Retention:* 72% of full-time freshmen returned.
Freshmen *Admission:* 1,064 applied, 977 admitted, 355 enrolled.
Faculty *Total:* 115, 40% full-time, 3% with terminal degrees. *Student/faculty ratio:* 10:1.
Majors Accounting technology and bookkeeping; aesthetician/esthetician and skin care; business administration and management; computer support specialist; cosmetology; barber/styling, and nail instruction; dental assisting; hair styling and hair design; legal administrative assistant/secretary; legal assistant/paralegal; massage therapy; medical administrative assistant and medical secretary; medical/clinical assistant; nail technician and manicurist; office occupations and clerical services; pharmacy technician.
Academics *Calendar:* continuous. *Degree:* certificates, diplomas, and associate. *Special study options:* accelerated degree program, adult/continuing education programs, cooperative education, honors programs, internships, summer session for credit.
Library IBMC College plus 8 others with 175,000 titles, 125 audiovisual materials.
Student Life *Housing:* college housing not available. *Activities and Organizations:* Alpha Beta Kappa, Circle of Hope, Relay for Life, Peer Mentoring, Peer Tutor.
Standardized Tests *Required:* Wonderlic Assessment (for admission).
Costs (2015–16) *One-time required fee:* $100. *Tuition:* $12,240 full-time. Full-time tuition and fees vary according to course load and program. Part-time tuition and fees vary according to course load and program. No tuition increase for student's term of enrollment. *Payment plans:* tuition prepayment, installment. *Waivers:* children of alumni and employees or children of employees.
Financial Aid Of all full-time matriculated undergraduates who enrolled in 2014, 935 applied for aid, 885 were judged to have need, 666 had their need fully met. 31 Federal Work-Study jobs (averaging $3122). *Average percent of need met:* 72%. *Average financial aid package:* $7500. *Average need-based loan:* $4270. *Average need-based gift aid:* $3205. *Average indebtedness upon graduation:* $12,249.
Applying *Options:* electronic application. *Application fee:* $75. *Required:* high school transcript, interview. *Application deadline:* rolling (freshmen).
Freshman Application Contact Mr. Jimmy Henig, Regional Director of Admissions, IBMC College, 3842 South Mason Street, Fort Collins, CO 80525. *Phone:* 970-223-2669. *Toll-free phone:* 800-495-2669. *E-mail:* jjohnson@ibmc.edu. *Website:* http://www.ibmc.edu/.

IntelliTec College
Colorado Springs, Colorado

Director of Admissions Director of Admissions, IntelliTec College, 2315 East Pikes Peak Avenue, Colorado Springs, CO 80909-6030. *Phone:* 719-632-7626. *Toll-free phone:* 800-748-2282. *Website:* http://www.intelliteccollege.edu/.

IntelliTec College
Grand Junction, Colorado

- **Proprietary** 2-year
- **Small-town** campus
- **Coed**

Faculty *Student/faculty ratio:* 22:1.
Majors Accounting and business/management; automotive engineering technology; clinical/medical laboratory assistant; environmental engineering technology.
Academics *Calendar:* continuous. *Degree:* certificates, diplomas, and associate.
Student Life *Housing:* college housing not available.
Applying *Required:* high school transcript, interview.
Freshman Application Contact Admissions, IntelliTec College, 772 Horizon Drive, Grand Junction, CO 81506. *Phone:* 970-245-8101. *Toll-free phone:* 800-748-2282. *Fax:* 970-243-8074. *Website:* http://www.intelliteccollege.edu/.

IntelliTec Medical Institute
Colorado Springs, Colorado

Director of Admissions Michelle Squibb, Admissions Representative, IntelliTec Medical Institute, 2345 North Academy Boulevard, Colorado Springs, CO 80909. *Phone:* 719-596-7400. *Toll-free phone:* 800-748-2282. *Website:* http://www.intelliteccollege.edu/.

ITT Technical Institute
Aurora, Colorado

- **Proprietary** primarily 2-year
- **Coed**

Academics *Degrees:* associate and bachelor's.
Freshman Application Contact Director of Recruitment, ITT Technical Institute, 12500 East Iliff Avenue, Suite 100, Aurora, CO 80014. *Phone:* 303-695-6317. *Toll-free phone:* 877-832-8460. *Website:* http://www.itt-tech.edu/.

ITT Technical Institute
Westminster, Colorado

- **Proprietary** primarily 2-year, founded 1984, part of ITT Educational Services, Inc.
- **Suburban** campus
- **Coed**

Academics *Calendar:* quarters. *Degrees:* associate and bachelor's.
Freshman Application Contact Director of Recruitment, ITT Technical Institute, 8620 Wolff Court, Suite 100, Westminster, CO 80031. *Phone:* 303-288-4488. *Toll-free phone:* 800-395-4488. *Website:* http://www.itt-tech.edu/.

Lamar Community College
Lamar, Colorado

- **State-supported** 2-year, founded 1937, part of Colorado Community College and Occupational Education System
- **Small-town** 125-acre campus
- **Endowment** $58,000
- **Coed,** 902 undergraduate students, 51% full-time, 57% women, 43% men

Undergraduates 463 full-time, 439 part-time. Students come from 27 states and territories; 4 other countries; 11% are from out of state; 4% Black or African American, non-Hispanic/Latino; 25% Hispanic/Latino; 0.2% Asian, non-Hispanic/Latino; 0.2% Native Hawaiian or other Pacific Islander, non-Hispanic/Latino; 1% American Indian or Alaska Native, non-Hispanic/Latino; 3% Two or more races, non-Hispanic/Latino; 5% Race/ethnicity unknown; 4% international; 8% transferred in; 20% live on campus. *Retention:* 58% of full-time freshmen returned.
Freshmen *Admission:* 466 applied, 466 admitted, 162 enrolled.
Faculty *Total:* 52, 35% full-time. *Student/faculty ratio:* 19:1.
Majors Accounting; agricultural business and management; agriculture; agronomy and crop science; animal sciences; animal training; biological and physical sciences; biology/biological sciences; business administration and management; computer programming; computer science; computer typography and composition equipment operation; construction trades; cosmetology; criminal justice/safety; data processing and data processing technology; emergency medical technology (EMT paramedic); entrepreneurship; equestrian studies; farm and ranch management; history;

information science/studies; liberal arts and sciences/liberal studies; licensed practical/vocational nurse training; management information systems; marketing/marketing management; medical office computer specialist; pre-engineering; registered nursing/registered nurse.

Academics *Calendar:* semesters. *Degree:* certificates, diplomas, and associate. *Special study options:* academic remediation for entering students, adult/continuing education programs, advanced placement credit, cooperative education, distance learning, double majors, English as a second language, independent study, internships, part-time degree program, services for LD students, student-designed majors, summer session for credit.

Library Learning Resources Center with 27,729 titles, an OPAC.

Student Life *Housing:* on-campus residence required for freshman year. *Options:* coed. Campus housing is university owned. *Campus security:* 24-hour emergency response devices and patrols, student patrols, late-night transport/escort service, controlled dormitory access. *Student services:* health clinic, personal/psychological counseling.

Athletics Member NJCAA. *Intercollegiate sports:* baseball M(s), basketball M(s)/W(s), equestrian sports M(s)/W(s), golf M(s), soccer M(c), softball W(s), volleyball W(s).

Costs (2014–15) *Tuition:* state resident $2868 full-time, $120 per credit hour part-time; nonresident $5363 full-time, $223 per credit hour part-time. *Required fees:* $355 full-time. *Room and board:* $5760. *Payment plan:* installment. *Waivers:* employees or children of employees.

Financial Aid Of all full-time matriculated undergraduates who enrolled in 2012, 16 Federal Work-Study jobs (averaging $2000). 81 state and other part-time jobs (averaging $2000).

Applying *Options:* electronic application, early admission. *Application deadlines:* 9/16 (freshmen), 9/16 (transfers).

Freshman Application Contact Director of Admissions, Lamar Community College, 2401 South Main Street, Lamar, CO 81052-3999. *Phone:* 719-336-1592. *Toll-free phone:* 800-968-6920. *E-mail:* admissions@lamarcc.edu. *Website:* http://www.lamarcc.edu/.

Lincoln College of Technology
Denver, Colorado

- **Proprietary** 2-year, founded 1963
- **Urban** campus
- **Coed, primarily men**

Academics *Calendar:* eight 6-week terms. *Degree:* certificates, diplomas, and associate. *Special study options:* cooperative education, services for LD students, summer session for credit.

Student Life *Campus security:* 24-hour emergency response devices and patrols.

Applying *Application fee:* $25.

Freshman Application Contact Lincoln College of Technology, 11194 East 45th Avenue, Denver, CO 80239. *Phone:* 800-347-3232 Ext. 43032. *Website:* http://www.lincolnedu.com/campus/denver-co/.

Morgan Community College
Fort Morgan, Colorado

- **State-supported** 2-year, founded 1967, part of Colorado Community College and Occupational Education System
- **Small-town** 20-acre campus with easy access to Denver
- **Coed,** 1,837 undergraduate students, 22% full-time, 64% women, 36% men

Undergraduates 412 full-time, 1,425 part-time. Students come from 3 states and territories; 1% are from out of state. *Retention:* 69% of full-time freshmen returned.

Freshmen *Admission:* 158 enrolled.

Faculty *Total:* 147, 22% full-time. *Student/faculty ratio:* 14:1.

Majors Accounting; administrative assistant and secretarial science; automobile/automotive mechanics technology; biological and physical sciences; business administration and management; business/managerial economics; business teacher education; liberal arts and sciences/liberal studies; occupational therapy; physical therapy.

Academics *Calendar:* semesters. *Degree:* certificates and associate. *Special study options:* academic remediation for entering students, adult/continuing education programs, advanced placement credit, distance learning, double majors, internships, part-time degree program, services for LD students, summer session for credit.

Library Learning Resource Center with 13,800 titles, 1,096 audiovisual materials, an OPAC, a Web page.

Student Life *Housing:* college housing not available. *Activities and Organizations:* student-run newspaper.

Costs (2014–15) *Tuition:* state resident $2997 full-time, $125 per credit hour part-time; nonresident $12,297 full-time, $512 per credit hour part-time. Full-time tuition and fees vary according to course load, program, and reciprocity

agreements. Part-time tuition and fees vary according to course load, program, and reciprocity agreements. *Required fees:* $396 full-time. *Payment plan:* installment. *Waivers:* employees or children of employees.

Applying *Options:* electronic application, early admission, deferred entrance. *Recommended:* high school transcript. *Application deadlines:* rolling (freshmen), rolling (transfers).

Freshman Application Contact Ms. Kim Maxwell, Morgan Community College, 920 Barlow Road, Fort Morgan, CO 80701-4399. *Phone:* 970-542-3111. *Toll-free phone:* 800-622-0216. *Fax:* 970-867-6608. *E-mail:* kim.maxwell@morgancc.edu. *Website:* http://www.morgancc.edu/.

Northeastern Junior College
Sterling, Colorado

- **State-supported** 2-year, founded 1941, part of Colorado Community College and Occupational Education System
- **Small-town** 65-acre campus
- **Endowment** $5.6 million
- **Coed,** 1,776 undergraduate students, 55% full-time, 56% women, 44% men

Undergraduates 981 full-time, 795 part-time. Students come from 31 states and territories; 5 other countries; 8% are from out of state; 7% Black or African American, non-Hispanic/Latino; 12% Hispanic/Latino; 0.5% Asian, non-Hispanic/Latino; 0.1% Native Hawaiian or other Pacific Islander, non-Hispanic/Latino; 0.8% American Indian or Alaska Native, non-Hispanic/Latino; 3% Two or more races, non-Hispanic/Latino; 7% Race/ethnicity unknown; 0.4% international; 4% transferred in; 31% live on campus. *Retention:* 59% of full-time freshmen returned.

Freshmen *Admission:* 1,608 applied, 1,608 admitted, 414 enrolled. *Average high school GPA:* 2.81.

Faculty *Total:* 77, 64% full-time, 5% with terminal degrees. *Student/faculty ratio:* 21:1.

Majors Accounting; agricultural business and management; agricultural economics; agricultural mechanization; agricultural teacher education; agriculture; agronomy and crop science; anatomy; animal sciences; applied mathematics; art; art teacher education; automobile/automotive mechanics technology; biological and physical sciences; biology/biological sciences; business administration and management; business teacher education; child development; clinical laboratory science/medical technology; computer engineering technology; computer science; corrections; cosmetology; criminal justice/police science; dramatic/theater arts; drawing; economics; education; elementary education; emergency medical technology (EMT paramedic); English; equestrian studies; family and consumer sciences/human sciences; farm and ranch management; fine/studio arts; health professions related; history; humanities; journalism; kindergarten/preschool education; legal administrative assistant/secretary; liberal arts and sciences/liberal studies; licensed practical/vocational nurse training; marketing/marketing management; mathematics; medical administrative assistant and medical secretary; music; music teacher education; natural sciences; physical education teaching and coaching; physical sciences; pre-engineering; psychology; registered nursing/registered nurse; social sciences; social work; trade and industrial teacher education; zoology/animal biology.

Academics *Calendar:* semesters. *Degree:* certificates and associate. *Special study options:* academic remediation for entering students, accelerated degree program, adult/continuing education programs, advanced placement credit, cooperative education, distance learning, double majors, English as a second language, honors programs, independent study, internships, part-time degree program, services for LD students, summer session for credit.

Library Monahan Library with 103,442 titles, an OPAC, a Web page.

Student Life *Housing:* on-campus residence required for freshman year. *Options:* coed, women-only. Campus housing is university owned. Freshman applicants given priority for college housing. *Activities and Organizations:* drama/theater group, choral group, Associated Student Government, Post Secondary Agriculture (PAS), Crossroads, NJC Ambassadors, Business Club. *Campus security:* 24-hour emergency response devices, late-night transport/escort service, controlled dormitory access. *Student services:* health clinic, personal/psychological counseling.

Athletics Member NCAA, NJCAA. All NCAA Division I. *Intercollegiate sports:* baseball M(s), basketball M(s)/W(s), equestrian sports M(s)/W(s), golf M(s)/W(s), soccer M(s), softball W(s), volleyball W(s). *Intramural sports:* badminton M/W, baseball M/W, basketball M/W, bowling M/W, cheerleading M/W, football M, golf M/W, racquetball M/W, soccer M/W, softball M/W, tennis M/W, ultimate Frisbee M/W, volleyball M/W, weight lifting M/W.

Costs (2014–15) *Tuition:* state resident $3747 full-time, $125 per credit hour part-time; nonresident $5621 full-time, $187 per credit hour part-time. Full-time tuition and fees vary according to course load. Part-time tuition and fees vary according to course load. *Required fees:* $599 full-time, $23 per credit hour part-time, $13 per term part-time. *Room and board:* $6376; room only: $3000. Room and board charges vary according to board plan and housing

facility. *Payment plan:* installment. *Waivers:* senior citizens and employees or children of employees.
Applying *Options:* electronic application, early admission, deferred entrance. *Recommended:* high school transcript. *Application deadlines:* rolling (freshmen), rolling (out-of-state freshmen), rolling (transfers). *Notification:* continuous until 8/1 (freshmen), continuous (out-of-state freshmen), continuous until 8/1 (transfers).
Freshman Application Contact Mr. Terry Ruch, Director of Admissions, Northeastern Junior College, 100 College Avenue, Sterling, CO 80751-2399. *Phone:* 970-521-7000. *Toll-free phone:* 800-626-4637. *E-mail:* terry.ruch@njc.edu.
Website: http://www.njc.edu/.

Otero Junior College
La Junta, Colorado

- **State-supported** 2-year, founded 1941, part of Colorado Community College System
- **Rural** 40-acre campus
- **Endowment** $1.5 million
- **Coed,** 1,449 undergraduate students

Undergraduates Students come from 20 states and territories; 10 other countries; 9% are from out of state; 3% Black or African American, non-Hispanic/Latino; 29% Hispanic/Latino; 0.8% Asian, non-Hispanic/Latino; 0.5% Native Hawaiian or other Pacific Islander, non-Hispanic/Latino; 1% American Indian or Alaska Native, non-Hispanic/Latino; 6% Race/ethnicity unknown; 3% international. *Retention:* 53% of full-time freshmen returned.
Faculty *Student/faculty ratio:* 19:1.
Majors Administrative assistant and secretarial science; agricultural business and management; automobile/automotive mechanics technology; biological and physical sciences; biology/biological sciences; business administration and management; child development; comparative literature; data processing and data processing technology; dramatic/theater arts; elementary education; history; humanities; kindergarten/preschool education; legal administrative assistant/secretary; liberal arts and sciences/liberal studies; mathematics; medical administrative assistant and medical secretary; modern languages; political science and government; pre-engineering; psychology; registered nursing/registered nurse; social sciences.
Academics *Calendar:* semesters. *Degree:* certificates and associate. *Special study options:* academic remediation for entering students, adult/continuing education programs, advanced placement credit, distance learning, external degree program, honors programs, internships, part-time degree program, summer session for credit.
Library Wheeler Library with 36,701 titles, an OPAC.
Student Life *Housing:* on-campus residence required for freshman year. *Options:* men-only, women-only. Campus housing is university owned. *Activities and Organizations:* drama/theater group, student-run newspaper, choral group. *Campus security:* 24-hour patrols, late-night transport/escort service.
Athletics Member NJCAA. *Intercollegiate sports:* baseball M(s), basketball M(s)/W(s), golf M(s)/W(s), soccer M(s)/W(s), softball W(s), volleyball W(s). *Intramural sports:* basketball M/W, volleyball M/W.
Costs (2014–15) *Tuition:* state resident $2998 full-time; nonresident $5363 full-time. Full-time tuition and fees vary according to course load. Part-time tuition and fees vary according to course load. *Required fees:* $274 full-time. *Room and board:* $6122. Room and board charges vary according to board plan and housing facility. *Payment plans:* installment, deferred payment. *Waivers:* senior citizens.
Financial Aid Of all full-time matriculated undergraduates who enrolled in 2013, 30 Federal Work-Study jobs (averaging $2000). 100 state and other part-time jobs (averaging $2000).
Applying *Options:* electronic application, early admission. *Recommended:* high school transcript. *Application deadlines:* 8/30 (freshmen), 8/30 (transfers). *Notification:* continuous (freshmen), continuous (transfers).
Freshman Application Contact Mrs. Rana Brown, Registrar, Otero Junior College, 1802 Colorado Ave., La Junta, CO 81050. *Phone:* 719-384-6831. *Fax:* 719-384-6933. *E-mail:* Rana.Brown@ojc.edu.
Website: http://www.ojc.edu/.

Pikes Peak Community College
Colorado Springs, Colorado

Freshman Application Contact Pikes Peak Community College, 5675 South Academy Boulevard, Colorado Springs, CO 80906-5498. *Phone:* 719-540-7041. *Toll-free phone:* 866-411-7722.
Website: http://www.ppcc.edu/.

Pima Medical Institute
Aurora, Colorado

Admissions Office Contact Pima Medical Institute, 13750 E. Mississippi Avenue, Aurora, CO 80012. *Toll-free phone:* 800-477-PIMA.
Website: http://www.pmi.edu/.

Pima Medical Institute
Colorado Springs, Colorado

Freshman Application Contact Pima Medical Institute, 3770 Citadel Drive North, Colorado Springs, CO 80909. *Phone:* 719-482-7462.
Website: http://www.pmi.edu/.

Pima Medical Institute
Denver, Colorado

Freshman Application Contact Admissions Office, Pima Medical Institute, 7475 Dakin Street, Denver, CO 80221. *Phone:* 303-426-1800. *Toll-free phone:* 800-477-PIMA (in-state); 888-477-PIMA (out-of-state).
Website: http://www.pmi.edu/.

Pueblo Community College
Pueblo, Colorado

- **State-supported** 2-year, founded 1933, part of Colorado Community College System
- **Urban** 35-acre campus
- **Endowment** $1.1 million
- **Coed,** 5,921 undergraduate students, 38% full-time, 59% women, 41% men

Undergraduates 2,255 full-time, 3,666 part-time. Students come from 23 states and territories; 4 other countries; 1% are from out of state; 3% Black or African American, non-Hispanic/Latino; 29% Hispanic/Latino; 1% Asian, non-Hispanic/Latino; 4% American Indian or Alaska Native, non-Hispanic/Latino; 0.2% Two or more races, non-Hispanic/Latino; 7% Race/ethnicity unknown; 8% transferred in. *Retention:* 59% of full-time freshmen returned.
Freshmen *Admission:* 2,075 applied, 2,075 admitted, 1,468 enrolled.
Faculty *Total:* 427, 26% full-time. *Student/faculty ratio:* 16:1.
Majors Accounting technology and bookkeeping; animation, interactive technology, video graphics and special effects; autobody/collision and repair technology; automobile/automotive mechanics technology; business administration and management; business automation/technology/data entry; communications technology; computer and information sciences; cooking and related culinary arts; cosmetology; criminal justice/law enforcement administration; dental assisting; dental hygiene; early childhood education; electrical, electronic and communications engineering technology; electromechanical and instrumentation and maintenance technologies related; emergency medical technology (EMT paramedic); engineering technology; fire science/firefighting; general studies; liberal arts and sciences and humanities related; liberal arts and sciences/liberal studies; library and archives assisting; machine shop technology; manufacturing engineering technology; medical office management; occupational therapist assistant; physical therapy technology; psychiatric/mental health services technology; radiologic technology/science; registered nursing/registered nurse; respiratory care therapy; science technologies related; surgical technology; web page, digital/multimedia and information resources design; welding technology.
Academics *Calendar:* semesters. *Degree:* certificates and associate. *Special study options:* academic remediation for entering students, accelerated degree program, advanced placement credit, cooperative education, distance learning, double majors, English as a second language, honors programs, independent study, internships, part-time degree program, services for LD students, summer session for credit.
Library PCC Library with 39,332 titles, 15,870 audiovisual materials, an OPAC, a Web page.
Student Life *Housing:* college housing not available. *Activities and Organizations:* drama/theater group, choral group, Phi Theta Kappa, Welding Club, Culinary Arts Club, Performing Arts Club, Art Club. *Campus security:* 24-hour emergency response devices and patrols, late-night transport/escort service. *Student services:* health clinic, personal/psychological counseling.
Costs (2015–16) *Tuition:* state resident $4722 full-time, $157 per credit hour part-time; nonresident $15,371 full-time, $512 per credit hour part-time. Full-time tuition and fees vary according to location and program. Part-time tuition and fees vary according to location and program. *Required fees:* $1199 full-time, $20 per credit hour part-time, $56 per term part-time. *Payment plans:* installment, deferred payment.

Financial Aid Of all full-time matriculated undergraduates who enrolled in 2013, 84 Federal Work-Study jobs (averaging $3500). 254 state and other part-time jobs (averaging $3500). *Average financial aid package:* $5647.
Applying *Options:* electronic application, early admission, deferred entrance. *Application deadlines:* rolling (freshmen), rolling (out-of-state freshmen), rolling (transfers). *Notification:* continuous until 9/1 (freshmen), continuous until 9/1 (out-of-state freshmen), continuous until 9/1 (transfers).
Freshman Application Contact Mrs. Barbara Benedict, Director of Admissions and Records, Pueblo Community College, 900 West Orman Avenue, Pueblo, CO 81004. *Phone:* 719-549-3039. *Toll-free phone:* 888-642-6017. *Fax:* 719-549-3012. *E-mail:* barbara.benedict@pueblocc.edu. *Website:* http://www.pueblocc.edu/.

Red Rocks Community College
Lakewood, Colorado

Freshman Application Contact Admissions Office, Red Rocks Community College, 13300 West 6th Avenue, Lakewood, CO 80228-1255. *Phone:* 303-914-6360. *Fax:* 303-914-6919. *E-mail:* admissions@rrcc.edu. *Website:* http://www.rrcc.edu/.

Redstone College–Denver
Broomfield, Colorado

Freshman Application Contact Redstone College–Denver, 10851 West 120th Avenue, Broomfield, CO 80021. *Phone:* 303-466-7383. *Toll-free phone:* 877-801-1025.
Website: http://www.redstone.edu/.

Trinidad State Junior College
Trinidad, Colorado

- **State-supported** 2-year, founded 1925, part of Colorado Community College and Occupational Education System
- **Small-town** 17-acre campus
- **Coed,** 1,783 undergraduate students, 49% full-time, 58% women, 42% men

Undergraduates 882 full-time, 901 part-time. Students come from 33 states and territories; 8 other countries; 13% are from out of state; 2% Black or African American, non-Hispanic/Latino; 41% Hispanic/Latino; 0.7% Asian, non-Hispanic/Latino; 0.1% Native Hawaiian or other Pacific Islander, non-Hispanic/Latino; 1% American Indian or Alaska Native, non-Hispanic/Latino; 2% Two or more races, non-Hispanic/Latino; 8% Race/ethnicity unknown; 1% international; 8% transferred in; 12% live on campus. *Retention:* 60% of full-time freshmen returned.
Freshmen *Admission:* 281 enrolled.
Faculty *Total:* 161, 31% full-time. *Student/faculty ratio:* 13:1.
Majors Agricultural business and management; aquaculture; automobile/automotive mechanics technology; biological and physical sciences; biology/biological sciences; business administration and management; business automation/technology/data entry; chemistry; construction/heavy equipment/earthmoving equipment operation; construction trades; counseling psychology; criminal justice/law enforcement administration; diesel mechanics technology; dramatic/theater arts; early childhood education; education; emergency medical technology (EMT paramedic); English; environmental engineering technology; fire science/firefighting; general studies; gunsmithing; heavy equipment maintenance technology; liberal arts and sciences/liberal studies; lineworker; manufacturing engineering technology; massage therapy; medical office assistant; natural resources management and policy; nursing assistant/aide and patient care assistant/aide; occupational safety and health technology; physical education teaching and coaching; pre-engineering; psychology; registered nursing/registered nurse; science technologies related; welding technology; wildland/forest firefighting and investigation.
Academics *Calendar:* semesters. *Degree:* certificates, diplomas, and associate. *Special study options:* academic remediation for entering students, accelerated degree program, adult/continuing education programs, advanced placement credit, cooperative education, distance learning, double majors, English as a second language, independent study, internships, part-time degree program, services for LD students, student-designed majors, summer session for credit.
Library Freudenthal Memorial Library with 49,396 titles, 1,574 audiovisual materials, an OPAC.
Student Life *Housing Options:* men-only, women-only. Campus housing is university owned. *Activities and Organizations:* drama/theater group. *Campus security:* 24-hour emergency response devices, trained security personnel patrol after campus hours.

Athletics Member NJCAA. *Intercollegiate sports:* baseball M(s), basketball M(s), golf M(s), soccer M(s)/W(s), softball W(s), volleyball W(s). *Intramural sports:* riflery M/W.
Costs (2014–15) *One-time required fee:* $25. *Tuition:* state resident $3747 full-time, $125 per credit hour part-time; nonresident $6704 full-time, $223 per credit hour part-time. Full-time tuition and fees vary according to course load, program, and reciprocity agreements. Part-time tuition and fees vary according to course load, program, and reciprocity agreements. *Required fees:* $424 full-time, $10 per credit hour part-time. *Room and board:* $6110. Room and board charges vary according to board plan. *Payment plan:* installment. *Waivers:* senior citizens and employees or children of employees.
Applying *Options:* deferred entrance. *Required:* high school transcript. *Application deadlines:* rolling (freshmen), rolling (out-of-state freshmen), rolling (transfers). *Notification:* continuous (freshmen), continuous (out-of-state freshmen), continuous (transfers).
Freshman Application Contact Bernadine DeGarbo, Student Services Administrative Assistant, Trinidad State Junior College, 600 Prospect Street, Trinidad, CO 81082. *Phone:* 719-846-5621. *Toll-free phone:* 800-621-8752. *Fax:* 719-846-5620. *E-mail:* Bernadine.degarbo@trinidadstate.edu. *Website:* http://www.trinidadstate.edu/.

CONNECTICUT

Asnuntuck Community College
Enfield, Connecticut

Freshman Application Contact Timothy St. James, Director of Admissions, Asnuntuck Community College, 170 Elm Street, Enfield, CT 06082-3800. *Phone:* 860-253-3087. *Fax:* 860-253-3014. *E-mail:* tstjames@acc.commnet.edu.
Website: http://www.acc.commnet.edu/.

Capital Community College
Hartford, Connecticut

Freshman Application Contact Ms. Jackie Phillips, Director of the Welcome and Advising Center, Capital Community College, 950 Main Street, Hartford, CT 06103. *Phone:* 860-906-5078. *Toll-free phone:* 800-894-6126. *E-mail:* jphillips@ccc.commnet.edu.
Website: http://www.ccc.commnet.edu/.

Gateway Community College
New Haven, Connecticut

- **State-supported** 2-year, founded 1992, part of Connecticut Community – Technical College System
- **Urban** 5-acre campus with easy access to New York City
- **Coed,** 8,201 undergraduate students, 32% full-time, 59% women, 41% men

Undergraduates 2,590 full-time, 5,611 part-time. 26% Black or African American, non-Hispanic/Latino; 22% Hispanic/Latino; 4% Asian, non-Hispanic/Latino; 0.2% American Indian or Alaska Native, non-Hispanic/Latino; 2% Two or more races, non-Hispanic/Latino; 4% Race/ethnicity unknown; 0.5% international; 9% transferred in.
Freshmen *Admission:* 3,522 applied, 3,428 admitted, 1,376 enrolled.
Faculty *Total:* 581, 18% full-time, 3% with terminal degrees. *Student/faculty ratio:* 17:1.
Majors Accounting; automobile/automotive mechanics technology; avionics maintenance technology; biomedical technology; business administration and management; computer and information sciences related; computer engineering related; computer engineering technology; computer graphics; computer typography and composition equipment operation; consumer merchandising/retailing management; data entry/microcomputer applications; data processing and data processing technology; dietetics; electrical, electronic and communications engineering technology; engineering-related technologies; engineering technology; fashion merchandising; fire science/firefighting; gerontology; hotel/motel administration; human services; industrial radiologic technology; industrial technology; kindergarten/preschool education; legal administrative assistant/secretary; liberal arts and sciences/liberal studies; mechanical engineering/mechanical technology; medical administrative assistant and medical secretary; mental health counseling; nuclear medical technology; registered nursing/registered nurse; special products marketing; substance abuse/addiction counseling; word processing.
Academics *Calendar:* semesters. *Degree:* certificates and associate. *Special study options:* academic remediation for entering students, adult/continuing

education programs, advanced placement credit, distance learning, English as a second language, external degree program, independent study, internships, off-campus study, part-time degree program, services for LD students, summer session for credit.

Library Gateway Community College Library plus 2 others with 46,090 titles, 3,121 audiovisual materials, an OPAC, a Web page.

Student Life *Housing:* college housing not available. *Activities and Organizations:* drama/theater group, student-run newspaper. *Campus security:* late-night transport/escort service. *Student services:* personal/psychological counseling, women's center.

Athletics Member NJCAA. *Intercollegiate sports:* baseball M, basketball M/W, soccer M, softball W.

Financial Aid Of all full-time matriculated undergraduates who enrolled in 2014, 69 Federal Work-Study jobs (averaging $1070). 64 state and other part-time jobs (averaging $3084).

Applying *Options:* early admission, deferred entrance. *Application fee:* $20. *Required:* high school transcript. *Required for some:* essay or personal statement, interview. *Application deadlines:* 9/1 (freshmen), 9/1 (transfers). *Notification:* continuous until 9/1 (freshmen), continuous until 9/1 (transfers).

Freshman Application Contact Mr. Joseph Carberry, Director of Enrollment Management, Gateway Community College, 20 Church Street, New Haven, CT 06510. *Phone:* 203-285-2011. *Toll-free phone:* 800-390-7723. *Fax:* 203-285-2018. *E-mail:* Jcarberry@gatewayct.edu.
Website: http://www.gwcc.commnet.edu/.

Goodwin College
East Hartford, Connecticut

- **Independent** primarily 2-year, founded 1999
- **Suburban** 660-acre campus with easy access to Hartford
- **Coed,** 3,440 undergraduate students, 18% full-time, 82% women, 18% men

Undergraduates 612 full-time, 2,828 part-time. 3% are from out of state; 22% Black or African American, non-Hispanic/Latino; 17% Hispanic/Latino; 2% Asian, non-Hispanic/Latino; 0.1% Native Hawaiian or other Pacific Islander, non-Hispanic/Latino; 0.3% American Indian or Alaska Native, non-Hispanic/Latino; 2% Two or more races, non-Hispanic/Latino; 0.2% Race/ethnicity unknown; 0.1% international; 14% transferred in. *Retention:* 62% of full-time freshmen returned.

Freshmen *Admission:* 480 applied, 318 enrolled.

Faculty *Total:* 312, 29% full-time, 21% with terminal degrees. *Student/faculty ratio:* 10:1.

Majors Business administration and management; business/commerce; child-care and support services management; child development; criminal justice/law enforcement administration; criminal justice/safety; dental hygiene; environmental studies; family systems; health services/allied health/health sciences; histologic technician; homeland security; homeland security, law enforcement, firefighting and protective services related; human services; liberal arts and sciences/liberal studies; logistics, materials, and supply chain management; medical/clinical assistant; medical insurance coding; medical insurance/medical billing; nonprofit management; occupational therapist assistant; office management; operations management; opticianry; organizational behavior; quality control technology; registered nursing/registered nurse; respiratory care therapy.

Academics *Calendar:* semesters. *Degrees:* certificates, associate, and bachelor's. *Special study options:* academic remediation for entering students, adult/continuing education programs, advanced placement credit, distance learning, double majors, English as a second language, internships, off-campus study, part-time degree program, services for LD students, summer session for credit.

Library Hoffman Family Library with an OPAC.

Student Life *Housing:* college housing not available. *Activities and Organizations:* choral group. *Campus security:* 24-hour emergency response devices, late-night transport/escort service, evening security patrolman. *Student services:* personal/psychological counseling.

Athletics *Intramural sports:* basketball M, football M/W, soccer M/W, softball M/W.

Costs (2014–15) *Tuition:* $18,900 full-time, $590 per credit hour part-time. Full-time tuition and fees vary according to course load and program. Part-time tuition and fees vary according to course load and program. *Required fees:* $500 full-time. *Payment plan:* installment. *Waivers:* employees or children of employees.

Applying *Options:* electronic application, early admission, deferred entrance. *Application fee:* $50. *Required:* essay or personal statement, high school transcript, minimum 2.0 GPA, medical exam. *Recommended:* 2 letters of recommendation, interview.

Freshman Application Contact Mr. Nicholas Lentino, Assistant Vice President for Admissions, Goodwin College, One Riverside Drive, East Hartford, CT 06118. *Phone:* 860-727-6765. *Toll-free phone:* 800-889-3282. *Fax:* 860-291-9550. *E-mail:* nlentino@goodwin.edu.
Website: http://www.goodwin.edu/.

Housatonic Community College
Bridgeport, Connecticut

- **State-supported** 2-year, founded 1965, part of Connecticut State Colleges & Universities (ConnSCU)
- **Urban** 4-acre campus with easy access to New York City
- **Coed,** 5,286 undergraduate students

Undergraduates 31% Black or African American, non-Hispanic/Latino; 28% Hispanic/Latino; 4% Asian, non-Hispanic/Latino; 0.2% Native Hawaiian or other Pacific Islander, non-Hispanic/Latino; 0.2% American Indian or Alaska Native, non-Hispanic/Latino; 2% Two or more races, non-Hispanic/Latino.

Faculty *Total:* 399, 18% full-time. *Student/faculty ratio:* 13:1.

Majors Accounting; administrative assistant and secretarial science; art; avionics maintenance technology; business administration and management; child development; clinical/medical laboratory technology; commercial and advertising art; computer typography and composition equipment operation; criminal justice/law enforcement administration; data processing and data processing technology; environmental studies; humanities; human services; journalism; liberal arts and sciences/liberal studies; mathematics; mental health counseling; physical therapy; pre-engineering; public administration; registered nursing/registered nurse; social sciences; substance abuse/addiction counseling.

Academics *Calendar:* semesters. *Degree:* certificates and associate. *Special study options:* academic remediation for entering students, adult/continuing education programs, advanced placement credit, cooperative education, distance learning, double majors, English as a second language, honors programs, independent study, internships, part-time degree program, services for LD students, summer session for credit. *ROTC:* Army (c). *Unusual degree programs:* nursing with Bridgeport Hospital.

Library Housatonic Community College Library with 30,000 titles, an OPAC, a Web page.

Student Life *Activities and Organizations:* drama/theater group, student-run newspaper, Student Senate, Association of Latin American Students, Community Action Network, Drama Club. *Campus security:* 24-hour emergency response devices, late-night transport/escort service. *Student services:* health clinic, personal/psychological counseling, women's center.

Costs (2014–15) *Tuition:* state resident $3866 full-time, $143 per credit hour part-time; nonresident $11,558 full-time, $429 per credit hour part-time. *Required fees:* $424 full-time, $5 per credit hour part-time, $124 per term part-time. *Payment plan:* installment. *Waivers:* senior citizens and employees or children of employees.

Financial Aid Of all full-time matriculated undergraduates who enrolled in 2013, 70 Federal Work-Study jobs (averaging $2850).

Applying *Options:* electronic application, deferred entrance. *Application fee:* $20. *Required:* high school transcript. *Required for some:* interview. *Application deadlines:* rolling (freshmen), rolling (transfers). *Notification:* continuous (freshmen), continuous (transfers).

Freshman Application Contact Mr. Earl Graham, Director of Admissions, Housatonic Community College, 900 Lafayette Boulevard, Bridgeport, CT 06604-4704. *Phone:* 203-332-5102.
Website: http://www.hctc.commnet.edu/.

Manchester Community College
Manchester, Connecticut

- **State-supported** 2-year, founded 1963, part of Connecticut State Colleges & Universities (ConnSCU)
- **Small-town** campus
- **Coed,** 7,300 undergraduate students, 34% full-time, 53% women, 47% men

Undergraduates 2,517 full-time, 4,783 part-time. 18% Black or African American, non-Hispanic/Latino; 16% Hispanic/Latino; 5% Asian, non-Hispanic/Latino; 0.1% Native Hawaiian or other Pacific Islander, non-Hispanic/Latino; 0.2% American Indian or Alaska Native, non-Hispanic/Latino; 2% Two or more races, non-Hispanic/Latino; 5% Race/ethnicity unknown; 0.1% international; 16% transferred in. *Retention:* 62% of full-time freshmen returned.

Freshmen *Admission:* 2,907 applied, 2,589 admitted, 1,452 enrolled.

Faculty *Total:* 501, 23% full-time. *Student/faculty ratio:* 21:1.

Majors Accounting; administrative assistant and secretarial science; business administration and management; clinical/medical laboratory technology; commercial and advertising art; criminal justice/law enforcement administration; dramatic/theater arts; engineering science; fine/studio arts; general studies; hotel/motel administration; human services; industrial engineering; industrial technology; information science/studies; journalism;

kindergarten/preschool education; legal administrative assistant/secretary; legal assistant/paralegal; liberal arts and sciences/liberal studies; management information systems; marketing/marketing management; medical administrative assistant and medical secretary; music; occupational therapist assistant; physical therapy technology; respiratory care therapy; social work; speech communication and rhetoric; surgical technology; teacher assistant/aide.

Academics *Calendar:* semesters. *Degree:* certificates and associate. *Special study options:* adult/continuing education programs, part-time degree program.

Student Life *Housing:* college housing not available.

Athletics Member NJCAA. *Intercollegiate sports:* baseball M, basketball M/W, soccer M/W, softball W.

Costs (2014–15) *Tuition:* state resident $3432 full-time; nonresident $10,316 full-time. *Required fees:* $434 full-time. *Payment plan:* installment. *Waivers:* senior citizens and employees or children of employees.

Financial Aid *Financial aid deadline:* 8/13.

Applying *Options:* electronic application. *Application fee:* $20. *Required:* high school transcript.

Freshman Application Contact Director of Admissions, Manchester Community College, PO Box 1046, Manchester, CT 06045-1046. *Phone:* 860-512-3210. *Fax:* 860-512-3221.

Website: http://www.manchestercc.edu/.

Middlesex Community College
Middletown, Connecticut

Freshman Application Contact Mensimah Shabazz, Director of Admissions, Middlesex Community College, Middletown, CT 06457-4889. *Phone:* 860-343-5742. *Fax:* 860-344-3055. *E-mail:* mshabazz@mxcc.commnet.edu.

Website: http://www.mxcc.commnet.edu/.

Naugatuck Valley Community College
Waterbury, Connecticut

Freshman Application Contact Ms. Lucretia Sveda, Director of Enrollment Services, Naugatuck Valley Community College, Waterbury, CT 06708. *Phone:* 203-575-8016. *Fax:* 203-596-8766. *E-mail:* lsveda@nvcc.commnet.edu.

Website: http://www.nvcc.commnet.edu/.

Northwestern Connecticut Community College
Winsted, Connecticut

- **State-supported** 2-year, founded 1965, part of Connecticut State Colleges & Universities (ConnSCU)
- **Small-town** 5-acre campus with easy access to Hartford
- **Coed**

Undergraduates 457 full-time, 1,092 part-time. Students come from 3 states and territories; 0.5% are from out of state; 2% Black or African American, non-Hispanic/Latino; 8% Hispanic/Latino; 1% Asian, non-Hispanic/Latino; 0.1% Native Hawaiian or other Pacific Islander, non-Hispanic/Latino; 1% Two or more races, non-Hispanic/Latino; 3% Race/ethnicity unknown; 0.1% international; 9% transferred in. *Retention:* 55% of full-time freshmen returned.

Academics *Calendar:* semesters. *Degree:* certificates and associate. *Special study options:* academic remediation for entering students, distance learning, English as a second language, independent study, internships, part-time degree program, services for LD students, summer session for credit.

Student Life *Campus security:* evening security patrols.

Costs (2014–15) *Tuition:* state resident $3432 full-time; nonresident $10,296 full-time. *Required fees:* $434 full-time.

Applying *Options:* deferred entrance. *Application fee:* $20.

Freshman Application Contact Admissions Office, Northwestern Connecticut Community College, Park Place East, Winsted, CT 06098-1798. *Phone:* 860-738-6330. *Fax:* 860-738-6437. *E-mail:* admissions@nwcc.commnet.edu.

Website: http://www.nwcc.commnet.edu/.

Norwalk Community College
Norwalk, Connecticut

- **State-supported** 2-year, founded 1961, part of Connecticut State Colleges & Universities (ConnSCU)
- **Suburban** 30-acre campus with easy access to New York City
- **Coed,** 6,363 undergraduate students, 35% full-time, 57% women, 43% men

Undergraduates 2,258 full-time, 4,105 part-time. 1% are from out of state; 19% Black or African American, non-Hispanic/Latino; 33% Hispanic/Latino; 4% Asian, non-Hispanic/Latino; 0.2% Native Hawaiian or other Pacific Islander, non-Hispanic/Latino; 0.2% American Indian or Alaska Native, non-Hispanic/Latino; 1% Two or more races, non-Hispanic/Latino; 6% Race/ethnicity unknown; 2% international; 6% transferred in. *Retention:* 67% of full-time freshmen returned.

Freshmen *Admission:* 948 enrolled.

Faculty *Total:* 408, 26% full-time. *Student/faculty ratio:* 19:1.

Majors Accounting; administrative assistant and secretarial science; architectural engineering technology; art; business administration and management; commercial and advertising art; computer and information systems security; computer systems networking and telecommunications; construction engineering technology; criminal justice/law enforcement administration; early childhood education; engineering science; finance; fine/studio arts; fire science/firefighting; general studies; graphic design; hotel/motel administration; human services; information science/studies; information technology; interior design; kinesiology and exercise science; legal assistant/paralegal; liberal arts and sciences/liberal studies; marketing/marketing management; medical office management; parks, recreation and leisure; psychology; registered nursing/registered nurse; respiratory care therapy; restaurant/food services management; speech communication and rhetoric; web page, digital/multimedia and information resources design.

Academics *Calendar:* semesters. *Degree:* certificates and associate. *Special study options:* academic remediation for entering students, advanced placement credit, cooperative education, distance learning, English as a second language, independent study, internships, part-time degree program, services for LD students, summer session for credit.

Library Everett I. L. Baker Library with an OPAC, a Web page.

Student Life *Housing:* college housing not available. *Activities and Organizations:* drama/theater group, student-run newspaper, choral group, Student World Assembly, Accounting Club, Literature Club, Art Club, Phi Theta Kappa. *Campus security:* late-night transport/escort service, all buildings are secured each evening; there are foot patrols and vehicle patrols by security from 7 am to 11pm. *Student services:* personal/psychological counseling, women's center.

Costs (2014–15) *Tuition:* state resident $3432 full-time; nonresident $10,296 full-time. *Required fees:* $434 full-time. *Payment plan:* installment. *Waivers:* senior citizens and employees or children of employees.

Financial Aid Of all full-time matriculated undergraduates who enrolled in 2012, 53 Federal Work-Study jobs (averaging $2800). 20 state and other part-time jobs (averaging $2800).

Applying *Options:* electronic application, deferred entrance. *Required:* high school transcript, 4 math courses, 3 science courses, 2 labs; immunization form.

Freshman Application Contact Mr. Curtis Antrum, Admissions Counselor, Norwalk Community College, 188 Richards Avenue, Norwalk, CT 06854-1655. *Phone:* 203-857-7060. *Fax:* 203-857-3335. *E-mail:* admissions@ncc.commnet.edu.

Website: http://www.ncc.commnet.edu/.

Quinebaug Valley Community College
Danielson, Connecticut

Freshman Application Contact Dr. Toni Moumouris, Director of Admissions, Quinebaug Valley Community College, 742 Upper Maple Street, Danielson, CT 06239. *Phone:* 860-774-1130 Ext. 318. *Fax:* 860-774-7768. *E-mail:* qu_isd@commnet.edu.

Website: http://www.qvcc.commnet.edu/.

St. Vincent's College
Bridgeport, Connecticut

- **Independent** primarily 2-year, founded 1991, affiliated with Roman Catholic Church
- **Urban** campus with easy access to New York City
- **Coed,** 751 undergraduate students, 10% full-time, 87% women, 13% men

Undergraduates 78 full-time, 673 part-time. Students come from 3 states and territories; 1 other country; 11% Black or African American, non-

Hispanic/Latino; 12% Hispanic/Latino; 3% Asian, non-Hispanic/Latino; 0.1% American Indian or Alaska Native, non-Hispanic/Latino; 11% Race/ethnicity unknown; 18% transferred in.

Freshmen *Admission:* 78 applied, 30 admitted, 14 enrolled.

Faculty *Student/faculty ratio:* 13:1.

Majors Cardiovascular technology; general studies; medical/clinical assistant; medical radiologic technology; registered nursing/registered nurse.

Academics *Calendar:* semesters. *Degrees:* certificates, associate, and bachelor's. *Special study options:* academic remediation for entering students, advanced placement credit, distance learning, part-time degree program, summer session for credit.

Library Daniel T. Banks Health Science Library.

Student Life *Housing:* college housing not available. *Campus security:* 24-hour patrols, late-night transport/escort service. *Student services:* personal/psychological counseling.

Standardized Tests *Recommended:* SAT or ACT (for admission).

Costs (2015–16) *Tuition:* $14,280 full-time. *Payment plan:* installment. *Waivers:* employees or children of employees.

Financial Aid Of all full-time matriculated undergraduates who enrolled in 2012, 89 applied for aid, 78 were judged to have need, 5 had their need fully met. *Average percent of need met:* 38%. *Average financial aid package:* $10,050. *Average need-based loan:* $3189. *Average need-based gift aid:* $5401.

Applying *Options:* electronic application, deferred entrance. *Required:* high school transcript. *Recommended:* minimum 3.0 GPA. *Application deadlines:* rolling (freshmen), rolling (transfers).

Freshman Application Contact Mr. Joseph Marrone, Director of Admissions and Recruitment Marketing, St. Vincent's College, 2800 Main Street, Bridgeport, CT 06606-4292. *Phone:* 203-576-5515. *Toll-free phone:* 800-873-1013. *Fax:* 203-576-5893. *E-mail:* jmarrone@stvincentscollege.edu. *Website:* http://www.stvincentscollege.edu/.

Three Rivers Community College
Norwich, Connecticut

- **State-supported** 2-year, founded 1963, part of Connecticut State Colleges & Universities (ConnSCU)
- **Suburban** 40-acre campus with easy access to Hartford
- **Coed,** 4,530 undergraduate students, 33% full-time, 59% women, 41% men

Undergraduates 1,487 full-time, 3,043 part-time. Students come from 5 states and territories; 1% are from out of state; 8% Black or African American, non-Hispanic/Latino; 15% Hispanic/Latino; 4% Asian, non-Hispanic/Latino; 0.3% Native Hawaiian or other Pacific Islander, non-Hispanic/Latino; 0.6% American Indian or Alaska Native, non-Hispanic/Latino; 4% Two or more races, non-Hispanic/Latino; 4% Race/ethnicity unknown; 0.2% international; 8% transferred in. *Retention:* 58% of full-time freshmen returned.

Freshmen *Admission:* 878 enrolled.

Faculty *Total:* 283, 29% full-time. *Student/faculty ratio:* 17:1.

Majors Accounting; accounting technology and bookkeeping; airframe mechanics and aircraft maintenance technology; architectural drafting and CAD/CADD; architectural engineering technology; banking and financial support services; business/commerce; child-care and support services management; civil engineering technology; computer engineering technology; construction management; criminal justice/police science; e-commerce; education; electrical, electronic and communications engineering technology; engineering science; engineering technology; entrepreneurship; environmental engineering technology; fine/studio arts; fire services administration; general studies; graphic design; hospitality administration; kinesiology and exercise science; laser and optical technology; liberal arts and sciences/liberal studies; management information systems; manufacturing engineering technology; marketing/marketing management; mechanical engineering/mechanical technology; nuclear/nuclear power technology; psychiatric/mental health services technology; registered nursing/registered nurse; sport and fitness administration/management.

Academics *Calendar:* semesters. *Degrees:* certificates and associate (engineering technology programs are offered on the Thames Valley Campus; liberal arts, transfer and career programs are offered on the Mohegan Campus). *Special study options:* adult/continuing education programs, part-time degree program.

Library Three Rivers Community College Learning Resource Center plus 1 other with an OPAC.

Student Life *Housing:* college housing not available. *Activities and Organizations:* student-run newspaper. *Campus security:* 24-hour emergency response devices, late-night transport/escort service, 14-hour patrols by trained security personnel.

Athletics *Intramural sports:* baseball M(c)/W(c), golf M(c)/W(c).

Costs (2014–15) *Tuition:* state resident $3432 full-time, $143 per credit hour part-time; nonresident $10,296 full-time, $429 per credit hour part-time. Full-time tuition and fees vary according to course load and reciprocity agreements.

Part-time tuition and fees vary according to course load and reciprocity agreements. *Required fees:* $434 full-time, $77 per credit hour part-time. *Payment plan:* installment. *Waivers:* senior citizens and employees or children of employees.

Financial Aid Of all full-time matriculated undergraduates who enrolled in 2010, 1,135 applied for aid, 967 were judged to have need, 266 had their need fully met. *Average percent of need met:* 48%. *Average financial aid package:* $2631. *Average need-based loan:* $3308. *Average need-based gift aid:* $2409.

Applying *Options:* electronic application, early admission, deferred entrance. *Recommended:* high school transcript. *Application deadlines:* rolling (freshmen), rolling (transfers). *Notification:* continuous (freshmen), continuous (transfers).

Freshman Application Contact Admissions Office, Three Rivers Community College, CT. *Phone:* 860-215-9296. *E-mail:* admissions@ trcc.commnet.edu. *Website:* http://www.trcc.commnet.edu/.

Tunxis Community College
Farmington, Connecticut

- **State-supported** 2-year, founded 1969, part of Connecticut State Colleges & Universities (ConnSCU), Board of Regents for Higher Education
- **Suburban** 12-acre campus with easy access to Hartford
- **Coed,** 4,225 undergraduate students, 38% full-time, 56% women, 44% men

Undergraduates 1,586 full-time, 2,639 part-time. Students come from 6 states and territories; 2% are from out of state; 8% Black or African American, non-Hispanic/Latino; 17% Hispanic/Latino; 4% Asian, non-Hispanic/Latino; 0.2% Native Hawaiian or other Pacific Islander, non-Hispanic/Latino; 0.2% American Indian or Alaska Native, non-Hispanic/Latino; 5% Race/ethnicity unknown. *Retention:* 61% of full-time freshmen returned.

Freshmen *Admission:* 776 enrolled.

Faculty *Total:* 239, 28% full-time, 12% with terminal degrees. *Student/faculty ratio:* 17:1.

Majors Accounting; administrative assistant and secretarial science; art; business administration and management; commercial and advertising art; corrections; criminal justice/law enforcement administration; data processing and data processing technology; dental hygiene; design and applied arts related; engineering; engineering technology; forensic science and technology; human services; information science/studies; kindergarten/preschool education; liberal arts and sciences/liberal studies; marketing/marketing management; medical administrative assistant and medical secretary.

Academics *Calendar:* semesters. *Degree:* certificates and associate. *Special study options:* academic remediation for entering students, adult/continuing education programs, cooperative education, distance learning, double majors, English as a second language, honors programs, independent study, internships, part-time degree program, services for LD students, summer session for credit.

Library Tunxis Community College Library with 33,866 titles, an OPAC.

Student Life *Housing:* college housing not available. *Activities and Organizations:* drama/theater group, student-run newspaper, Phi Theta Kappa, Student American Dental Hygiene Association (SADHA), Human Services Club, student newspaper, Criminal Justice Club. *Campus security:* 24-hour emergency response devices.

Costs (2015–16) *Tuition:* state resident $143 per semester hour part-time; nonresident $429 per semester hour part-time. *Required fees:* $124 per term part-time. *Payment plan:* installment. *Waivers:* senior citizens and employees or children of employees.

Applying *Options:* deferred entrance. *Application fee:* $20. *Required:* high school transcript. *Application deadlines:* rolling (freshmen), rolling (transfers).

Freshman Application Contact Ms. Tamika Davis, Director of Admissions, Tunxis Community College, 271 Scott Swamp Road, Farmington, CT 06032. *Phone:* 860-773-1494. *Fax:* 860-606-9501. *E-mail:* pmccluskey@tunxis.edu. *Website:* http://www.tunxis.edu/.

DELAWARE

Delaware College of Art and Design
Wilmington, Delaware

Freshman Application Contact Ms. Allison Gullo, Delaware College of Art and Design, 600 North Market Street, Wilmington, DE 19801. *Phone:* 302-622-8867 Ext. 111. *Fax:* 302-622-8870. *E-mail:* agullo@dcad.edu. *Website:* http://www.dcad.edu/.

Delaware Technical & Community College, Jack F. Owens Campus
Georgetown, Delaware

- **State-supported** 2-year, founded 1967, part of Delaware Technical and Community College System
- **Small-town** campus
- **Coed**

Undergraduates 1,981 full-time, 2,448 part-time. 19% Black or African American, non-Hispanic/Latino; 7% Hispanic/Latino; 2% Asian, non-Hispanic/Latino; 0.1% Native Hawaiian or other Pacific Islander, non-Hispanic/Latino; 0.6% American Indian or Alaska Native, non-Hispanic/Latino; 2% Two or more races, non-Hispanic/Latino; 0.8% Race/ethnicity unknown; 3% international. *Retention:* 55% of full-time freshmen returned.

Academics *Calendar:* semesters. *Degree:* certificates, diplomas, and associate. *Special study options:* part-time degree program.

Student Life *Campus security:* 24-hour emergency response devices, late-night transport/escort service.

Athletics Member NJCAA.

Financial Aid Of all full-time matriculated undergraduates who enrolled in 2013, 250 Federal Work-Study jobs (averaging $2000).

Applying *Options:* electronic application, early admission, deferred entrance. *Application fee:* $10. *Required for some:* high school transcript.

Freshman Application Contact Ms. Claire McDonald, Admissions Counselor, Delaware Technical & Community College, Jack F. Owens Campus, PO Box 610, Georgetown, DE 19947. *Phone:* 302-856-5400. *Fax:* 302-856-9461.

Website: http://www.dtcc.edu/.

Delaware Technical & Community College, Stanton/Wilmington Campus
Newark, Delaware

- **State-supported** 2-year, founded 1968, part of Delaware Technical and Community College System
- **Urban** campus
- **Coed**

Undergraduates 2,616 full-time, 4,419 part-time. 28% Black or African American, non-Hispanic/Latino; 10% Hispanic/Latino; 4% Asian, non-Hispanic/Latino; 0.2% Native Hawaiian or other Pacific Islander, non-Hispanic/Latino; 0.4% American Indian or Alaska Native, non-Hispanic/Latino; 2% Two or more races, non-Hispanic/Latino; 2% Race/ethnicity unknown; 2% international. *Retention:* 52% of full-time freshmen returned.

Academics *Calendar:* semesters. *Degree:* certificates, diplomas, and associate. *Special study options:* part-time degree program.

Student Life *Campus security:* 24-hour emergency response devices, late-night transport/escort service.

Athletics Member NJCAA.

Applying *Options:* electronic application, early admission, deferred entrance. *Application fee:* $10. *Required for some:* high school transcript.

Freshman Application Contact Ms. Rebecca Bailey, Admissions Coordinator, Wilmington, Delaware Technical & Community College, Stanton/Wilmington Campus, 333 Shipley Street, Wilmington, DE 19713. *Phone:* 302-571-5343. *Fax:* 302-577-2548.

Website: http://www.dtcc.edu/.

Delaware Technical & Community College, Terry Campus
Dover, Delaware

- **State-supported** 2-year, founded 1972, part of Delaware Technical and Community College System
- **Small-town** campus
- **Coed,** 2,955 undergraduate students, 43% full-time, 64% women, 36% men

Undergraduates 1,285 full-time, 1,670 part-time. 29% Black or African American, non-Hispanic/Latino; 6% Hispanic/Latino; 2% Asian, non-Hispanic/Latino; 0.1% Native Hawaiian or other Pacific Islander, non-Hispanic/Latino; 0.4% American Indian or Alaska Native, non-Hispanic/Latino; 3% Two or more races, non-Hispanic/Latino; 2% Race/ethnicity unknown; 0.8% international. *Retention:* 52% of full-time freshmen returned.

Freshmen *Admission:* 1,351 applied, 1,351 admitted, 591 enrolled.

Majors Accounting; agricultural business and management; architectural engineering technology; bilingual and multilingual education; biomedical technology; business administration and management; business automation/technology/data entry; business/commerce; civil engineering technology; commercial and advertising art; computer and information sciences; computer engineering technology; computer systems networking and telecommunications; computer technology/computer systems technology; construction management; criminal justice/law enforcement administration; criminal justice/police science; culinary arts; digital communication and media/multimedia; drafting and design technology; early childhood education; e-commerce; education (multiple levels); electrical, electronic and communications engineering technology; electromechanical technology; elementary education; emergency medical technology (EMT paramedic); energy management and systems technology; entrepreneurship; hotel/motel administration; human resources management; human services; interior design; kindergarten/preschool education; legal administrative assistant/secretary; management information systems; marketing/marketing management; mathematics teacher education; medical/clinical assistant; middle school education; office management; photography; registered nursing/registered nurse; substance abuse/addiction counseling.

Academics *Calendar:* semesters. *Degree:* certificates, diplomas, and associate. *Special study options:* part-time degree program.

Student Life *Housing:* college housing not available. *Campus security:* 24-hour emergency response devices, late-night transport/escort service.

Athletics Member NJCAA. *Intercollegiate sports:* lacrosse M(s), soccer M(s)/W(s), softball W(s).

Financial Aid Of all full-time matriculated undergraduates who enrolled in 2013, 50 Federal Work-Study jobs (averaging $1500).

Applying *Options:* electronic application, early admission, deferred entrance. *Application fee:* $10. *Required for some:* high school transcript.

Freshman Application Contact Mrs. Maria Harris, Admissions Officer, Delaware Technical & Community College, Terry Campus, 100 Campus Drive, Dover, DE 19904. *Phone:* 302-857-1020. *Fax:* 302-857-1296. *E-mail:* terry-info@dtcc.edu.

Website: http://www.dtcc.edu/.

DISTRICT OF COLUMBIA

Radians College
Washington, District of Columbia

Admissions Office Contact Radians College, 1025 Vermont Avenue, NW, Suite 200, Washington, DC 20005.

Website: http://www.radianscollege.edu/.

FLORIDA

ATA Career Education
Spring Hill, Florida

Admissions Office Contact ATA Career Education, 7351 Spring Hill Drive, Suite 11, Spring Hill, FL 34606.

Website: http://www.atafl.edu/.

Aviator College of Aeronautical Science & Technology
Fort Pierce, Florida

Admissions Office Contact Aviator College of Aeronautical Science & Technology, 3800 St. Lucie Boulevard, Fort Pierce, FL 34946.

Website: http://www.aviator.edu/FlightCollege.

Broward College
Fort Lauderdale, Florida

- **State-supported** primarily 2-year, founded 1960, part of Florida College System
- **Urban** campus with easy access to Miami
- **Coed**

Undergraduates 13,327 full-time, 30,388 part-time. Students come from 143 other countries; 35% Black or African American, non-Hispanic/Latino; 34% Hispanic/Latino; 3% Asian, non-Hispanic/Latino; 0.2% Native Hawaiian or other Pacific Islander, non-Hispanic/Latino; 0.2% American Indian or Alaska

Native, non-Hispanic/Latino; 2% Two or more races, non-Hispanic/Latino; 4% Race/ethnicity unknown; 3% international; 3% transferred in.
Faculty *Student/faculty ratio:* 30:1.
Academics *Calendar:* trimesters. *Degrees:* certificates, diplomas, associate, and bachelor's. *Special study options:* academic remediation for entering students, accelerated degree program, adult/continuing education programs, advanced placement credit, cooperative education, distance learning, English as a second language, honors programs, part-time degree program, services for LD students, student-designed majors, study abroad, summer session for credit. *ROTC:* Army (b).
Student Life *Campus security:* 24-hour emergency response devices and patrols, late-night transport/escort service.
Athletics Member NJCAA.
Financial Aid *Financial aid deadline:* 7/1.
Applying *Options:* electronic application, early admission, deferred entrance. *Application fee:* $35. *Required for some:* high school transcript.
Freshman Application Contact Mr. Willie J. Alexander, Associate Vice President for Student Affairs/College Registrar, Broward College, 225 East Las Olas Boulevard, Fort Lauderdale, FL 33301. *Phone:* 954-201-7471. *Fax:* 954-201-7466. *E-mail:* walexand@broward.edu.
Website: http://www.broward.edu/.

Brown Mackie College–Miami
Miramar, Florida

- **Proprietary** primarily 2-year, part of Education Management Corporation
- **Coed**

Academics *Degrees:* diplomas, associate, and bachelor's.
Freshman Application Contact Brown Mackie College–Miami, 3700 Lakeside Drive, Miramar, FL 33027. *Phone:* 305-341-6600. *Toll-free phone:* 866-505-0335.
Website: http://www.brownmackie.edu/miami/.

Cambridge Institute of Allied Health and Technology
Delray Beach, Florida

Admissions Office Contact Cambridge Institute of Allied Health and Technology, 5150 Linton Boulevard, Suite 340, Delray Beach, FL 33484.
Website: http://www.cambridgehealth.edu/.

Chipola College
Marianna, Florida

- **State-supported** primarily 2-year, founded 1947
- **Rural** 105-acre campus
- **Coed,** 2,090 undergraduate students, 42% full-time, 63% women, 37% men

Undergraduates 881 full-time, 1,209 part-time. Students come from 7 states and territories; 6 other countries; 8% are from out of state; 15% Black or African American, non-Hispanic/Latino; 4% Hispanic/Latino; 0.6% Asian, non-Hispanic/Latino; 0.1% Native Hawaiian or other Pacific Islander, non-Hispanic/Latino; 0.7% American Indian or Alaska Native, non-Hispanic/Latino; 3% Two or more races, non-Hispanic/Latino; 7% transferred in.
Freshmen *Admission:* 684 applied, 578 admitted, 188 enrolled. *Average high school GPA:* 2.5. *Test scores:* SAT critical reading scores over 500: 16%; SAT math scores over 500: 36%; ACT scores over 18: 81%; SAT critical reading scores over 600: 4%; SAT math scores over 600: 12%; ACT scores over 24: 25%; ACT scores over 30: 3%.
Faculty *Total:* 127, 31% full-time, 13% with terminal degrees. *Student/faculty ratio:* 24:1.
Majors Accounting; agriculture; agronomy and crop science; art; biological and physical sciences; business administration and management; clinical laboratory science/medical technology; computer and information sciences related; computer science; education; finance; liberal arts and sciences/liberal studies; mass communication/media; mathematics teacher education; pre-engineering; registered nursing/registered nurse; science teacher education; secondary education; social work.
Academics *Calendar:* semesters. *Degrees:* certificates, associate, and bachelor's. *Special study options:* academic remediation for entering students, adult/continuing education programs, advanced placement credit, distance learning, honors programs, independent study, part-time degree program, services for LD students, summer session for credit.
Library Chipola Library with 37,740 titles.

Student Life *Housing:* college housing not available. *Activities and Organizations:* drama/theater group, student-run newspaper, choral group, Drama/Theater Group. *Campus security:* night security personnel.
Athletics Member NJCAA. *Intercollegiate sports:* baseball M(s), basketball M(s)/W(s), softball W(s).
Costs (2014–15) *Tuition:* state resident $3060 full-time, $102 per semester hour part-time; nonresident $8891 full-time, $296 per semester hour part-time. Full-time tuition and fees vary according to degree level. Part-time tuition and fees vary according to degree level. *Required fees:* $40 full-time.
Applying *Options:* early admission. *Required:* high school transcript. *Application deadlines:* rolling (freshmen), rolling (transfers). *Notification:* continuous (freshmen), continuous (transfers).
Freshman Application Contact Mrs. Kathy L. Rehberg, Registrar, Chipola College, 3094 Indian Circle, Marianna, FL 32446-3065. *Phone:* 850-718-2233. *Fax:* 850-718-2287. *E-mail:* rehbergk@chipola.edu.
Website: http://www.chipola.edu/.

City College
Altamonte Springs, Florida

Director of Admissions Ms. Kimberly Bowden, Director of Admissions, City College, 177 Montgomery Road, Altamonte Springs, FL 32714. *Phone:* 352-335-4000. *Fax:* 352-335-4303. *E-mail:* kbowden@citycollege.edu.
Website: http://www.citycollege.edu/.

City College
Fort Lauderdale, Florida

Freshman Application Contact City College, 2000 West Commercial Boulevard, Suite 200, Fort Lauderdale, FL 33309. *Phone:* 954-492-5353. *Toll-free phone:* 866-314-5681.
Website: http://www.citycollege.edu/.

City College
Gainesville, Florida

Freshman Application Contact Admissions Office, City College, 7001 Northwest 4th Boulevard, Gainesville, FL 32607. *Phone:* 352-335-4000.
Website: http://www.citycollege.edu/.

City College
Miami, Florida

Freshman Application Contact Admissions Office, City College, 9300 South Dadeland Boulevard, Suite PH, Miami, FL 33156. *Phone:* 305-666-9242. *Fax:* 305-666-9243.
Website: http://www.citycollege.edu/.

College of Business and Technology
Miami, Florida

Freshman Application Contact Ms. Ivis Delgado, Admissions Representative, College of Business and Technology, 8230 West Flagler Street, Miami, FL 33144. *Phone:* 305-273-4499 Ext. 2204. *Toll-free phone:* 866-626-8842. *Fax:* 305-485-4411. *E-mail:* admissions@cbt.edu.
Website: http://www.cbt.edu/.

College of Business and Technology–Cutler Bay Campus
Cutler Bay, Florida

Admissions Office Contact College of Business and Technology–Cutler Bay Campus, 19151 South Dixie Highway, Cutler Bay, FL 33157.
Website: http://www.cbt.edu/.

College of Business and Technology–Flagler Campus
Miami, Florida

Admissions Office Contact College of Business and Technology–Flagler Campus, 8230 W. Flagler Street, Miami, FL 33144.
Website: http://www.cbt.edu/.

College of Business and Technology–Hialeah Campus
Hialeah, Florida

Admissions Office Contact College of Business and Technology–Hialeah Campus, 935 West 49 Street, # 203, Hialeah, FL 33012.
Website: http://www.cbt.edu/.

College of Central Florida
Ocala, Florida

- **State and locally supported** primarily 2-year, founded 1957, part of Florida Community College System
- **Small-town** 139-acre campus
- **Endowment** $64.5 million
- **Coed,** 8,210 undergraduate students, 37% full-time, 63% women, 37% men

Undergraduates 3,066 full-time, 5,144 part-time. Students come from 61 other countries; 1% are from out of state; 14% Black or African American, non-Hispanic/Latino; 14% Hispanic/Latino; 2% Asian, non-Hispanic/Latino; 0.3% Native Hawaiian or other Pacific Islander, non-Hispanic/Latino; 0.4% American Indian or Alaska Native, non-Hispanic/Latino; 8% Race/ethnicity unknown; 1% international; 1% transferred in.
Freshmen *Admission:* 3,452 applied, 2,132 admitted, 1,597 enrolled.
Faculty *Total:* 393, 34% full-time, 12% with terminal degrees. *Student/faculty ratio:* 21:1.
Majors Accounting technology and bookkeeping; advertising; agribusiness; agriculture; animal sciences; architecture; art; biology/biological sciences; business administration and management; business administration, management and operations related; business/commerce; chemistry; clinical laboratory science/medical technology; computer and information sciences; construction engineering technology; criminal justice/law enforcement administration; criminology; dental assisting; drafting and design technology; dramatic/theater arts; early childhood education; economics; elementary education; emergency medical technology (EMT paramedic); engineering; engineering technology; English; environmental studies; equestrian studies; family and consumer sciences/human sciences; fire science/firefighting; foreign languages and literatures; forestry; health information/medical records technology; health/medical preparatory programs related; health services/allied health/health sciences; history; humanities; human services; information technology; interior architecture; journalism; landscaping and groundskeeping; legal assistant/paralegal; liberal arts and sciences and humanities related; liberal arts and sciences/liberal studies; library and information science; marketing/marketing management; mathematics; medical radiologic technology; music; music teacher education; occupational therapy; office management; parks, recreation and leisure; philosophy; physical education teaching and coaching; physical therapy; physical therapy technology; physics; pre-law studies; premedical studies; pre-pharmacy studies; pre-veterinary studies; psychology; registered nursing/registered nurse; religious studies; restaurant, culinary, and catering management; secondary education; social sciences; social work; sociology; special education; statistics; veterinary/animal health technology.
Academics *Calendar:* semesters. *Degrees:* certificates, diplomas, associate, and bachelor's. *Special study options:* academic remediation for entering students, adult/continuing education programs, advanced placement credit, cooperative education, distance learning, English as a second language, freshman honors college, honors programs, independent study, internships, part-time degree program, services for LD students, summer session for credit.
Library Clifford B. Stearns Learning Resources Center with 135,621 titles, 21,511 audiovisual materials, an OPAC, a Web page.
Student Life *Housing:* college housing not available. *Activities and Organizations:* drama/theater group, student-run newspaper, choral group, Inspirational Choir, Model United nations, Performing Arts, Phi Theta Kappa (PTK), Student Nurses Association. *Campus security:* 24-hour emergency response devices and patrols, student patrols, late-night transport/escort service. *Student services:* personal/psychological counseling.
Athletics Member NJCAA. *Intercollegiate sports:* baseball M(s), basketball M(s)/W(s), softball W(s), volleyball W(s). *Intramural sports:* bowling M/W.
Standardized Tests *Recommended:* SAT (for admission), ACT (for admission), SAT or ACT (for admission), SAT and SAT Subject Tests or ACT (for admission), SAT Subject Tests (for admission).
Costs (2014–15) *Tuition:* state resident $2388 full-time, $80 per credit part-time; nonresident $9552 full-time, $318 per credit part-time. Full-time tuition and fees vary according to course level, degree level, program, and student level. Part-time tuition and fees vary according to course level, degree level, program, and student level. *Required fees:* $825 full-time, $28 per credit hour part-time. *Payment plan:* deferred payment. *Waivers:* employees or children of employees.

Applying *Options:* electronic application, early admission. *Application fee:* $30. *Required:* high school transcript. *Application deadlines:* rolling (freshmen), rolling (transfers). *Notification:* continuous (freshmen), continuous (transfers).
Freshman Application Contact Ms. Devona Sewell, Registrar, Admission and Records, College of Central Florida, 3001 SW College Road, Ocala, FL 34474. *Phone:* 352-237-2111 Ext. 1398. *Fax:* 352-873-5882. *E-mail:* sewelld@cf.edu.
Website: http://www.cf.edu/.

Concorde Career Institute
Jacksonville, Florida

Admissions Office Contact Concorde Career Institute, 7259 Salisbury Road, Jacksonville, FL 32256.
Website: http://www.concorde.edu/.

Concorde Career Institute
Miramar, Florida

Admissions Office Contact Concorde Career Institute, 10933 Marks Way, Miramar, FL 33025.
Website: http://www.concorde.edu/.

Concorde Career Institute
Orlando, Florida

Admissions Office Contact Concorde Career Institute, 3444 McCrory Place, Orlando, FL 32803.
Website: http://www.concorde.edu/.

Concorde Career Institute
Tampa, Florida

Admissions Office Contact Concorde Career Institute, 4202 West Spruce Street, Tampa, FL 33607-4127.
Website: http://www.concorde.edu/.

Daytona College
Ormond Beach, Florida

Admissions Office Contact Daytona College, 469 South Nova Road, Ormond Beach, FL 32174-8445.
Website: http://www.daytonacollege.edu/.

Daytona State College
Daytona Beach, Florida

- **State-supported** primarily 2-year, founded 1958, part of Florida Community College System
- **Suburban** 100-acre campus with easy access to Orlando
- **Endowment** $6.3 million
- **Coed,** 14,951 undergraduate students, 37% full-time, 60% women, 40% men

Undergraduates 5,583 full-time, 9,368 part-time. Students come from 130 other countries; 4% are from out of state; 13% Black or African American, non-Hispanic/Latino; 13% Hispanic/Latino; 2% Asian, non-Hispanic/Latino; 0.2% Native Hawaiian or other Pacific Islander, non-Hispanic/Latino; 0.5% American Indian or Alaska Native, non-Hispanic/Latino; 2% Two or more races, non-Hispanic/Latino; 1% Race/ethnicity unknown; 0.4% international; 5% transferred in.
Freshmen *Admission:* 1,805 admitted, 1,572 enrolled. *Test scores:* SAT critical reading scores over 500: 40%; SAT math scores over 500: 32%; SAT writing scores over 500: 25%; ACT scores over 18: 66%; SAT critical reading scores over 600: 8%; SAT math scores over 600: 7%; SAT writing scores over 600: 4%; ACT scores over 24: 14%; SAT critical reading scores over 700: 1%; SAT math scores over 700: 1%; ACT scores over 30: 1%.
Faculty *Total:* 879, 35% full-time, 17% with terminal degrees. *Student/faculty ratio:* 21:1.
Majors Accounting; administrative assistant and secretarial science; architectural engineering technology; automobile/automotive mechanics technology; biology teacher education; business administration and management; child development; communications technology; computer and information sciences related; computer engineering; computer engineering related; computer graphics; computer/information technology services administration related; computer programming; computer programming (specific applications); computer science; computer systems networking and

telecommunications; computer technology/computer systems technology; criminal justice/law enforcement administration; criminal justice/police science; culinary arts; dental hygiene; drafting and design technology; electrical, electronic and communications engineering technology; elementary education; emergency medical technology (EMT paramedic); engineering; fire science/firefighting; health information/medical records administration; hospitality administration; hotel/motel administration; human services; industrial radiologic technology; industrial technology; information technology; interior design; kindergarten/preschool education; legal assistant/paralegal; machine shop technology; mathematics teacher education; medical administrative assistant and medical secretary; occupational therapist assistant; photographic and film/video technology; physical therapy; plastics and polymer engineering technology; radio and television; registered nursing/registered nurse; respiratory care therapy; robotics technology; secondary education, special education–early childhood; tourism and travel services management.

Academics *Calendar:* semesters. *Degrees:* certificates, diplomas, associate, bachelor's, and postbachelor's certificates. *Special study options:* academic remediation for entering students, adult/continuing education programs, advanced placement credit, cooperative education, distance learning, double majors, English as a second language, external degree program, freshman honors college, honors programs, independent study, internships, off-campus study, part-time degree program, services for LD students, study abroad, summer session for credit. *ROTC:* Army (c), Air Force (c).

Library Mary Karl Memorial Learning Resources Center plus 1 other with 85,904 titles, 14,052 audiovisual materials, an OPAC, a Web page.

Student Life *Housing:* college housing not available. *Activities and Organizations:* drama/theater group, student-run newspaper, choral group, Rotaract, Student Government Association, Student Occupational Therapy Club, Massage Therapy Club, Student Paralegal Club, national fraternities, national sororities. *Campus security:* 24-hour emergency response devices and patrols, late-night transport/escort service. *Student services:* personal/psychological counseling, women's center.

Athletics Member NJCAA. *Intercollegiate sports:* baseball M(s), basketball M(s)/W(s), golf W(s), softball W(s), volleyball W(s). *Intramural sports:* basketball M/W, football M/W, soccer M/W, table tennis M/W, tennis M/W.

Costs (2014–15) *Tuition:* state resident $1940 full-time, $81 per credit hour part-time; nonresident $7621 full-time, $318 per credit hour part-time. Full-time tuition and fees vary according to course load and degree level. Part-time tuition and fees vary according to course load and degree level. *Required fees:* $740 full-time, $24 per credit hour part-time. *Payment plan:* installment.

Financial Aid Of all full-time matriculated undergraduates who enrolled in 2013, 4,148 applied for aid, 3,780 were judged to have need, 1,991 had their need fully met. 193 Federal Work-Study jobs (averaging $1299). In 2013, 334 non-need-based awards were made. *Average need-based loan:* $1839. *Average need-based gift aid:* $1479. *Average non-need-based aid:* $798.

Applying *Options:* electronic application, early admission, deferred entrance. *Required:* high school transcript. *Application deadlines:* rolling (freshmen), rolling (transfers). *Notification:* continuous (freshmen), continuous (transfers).

Freshman Application Contact Dr. Karen Sanders, Director of Admissions and Recruitment, Daytona State College, 1200 International Speedway Boulevard, Daytona Beach, FL 32114. *Phone:* 386-506-3050. *E-mail:* SanderK@daytonastate.edu.
Website: http://www.daytonastate.edu/.

Eastern Florida State College
Cocoa, Florida

- **State-supported** primarily 2-year, founded 1960, part of Florida Community College System
- **Suburban** 100-acre campus with easy access to Orlando
- **Coed**

Undergraduates 5,929 full-time, 10,782 part-time. Students come from 67 other countries; 11% Black or African American, non-Hispanic/Latino; 10% Hispanic/Latino; 2% Asian, non-Hispanic/Latino; 0.3% Native Hawaiian or other Pacific Islander, non-Hispanic/Latino; 0.6% American Indian or Alaska Native, non-Hispanic/Latino; 3% Two or more races, non-Hispanic/Latino; 1% Race/ethnicity unknown; 0.7% international.

Faculty *Student/faculty ratio:* 23:1.

Academics *Calendar:* semesters. *Degrees:* certificates, associate, and bachelor's. *Special study options:* academic remediation for entering students, accelerated degree program, adult/continuing education programs, advanced placement credit, cooperative education, distance learning, double majors, English as a second language, external degree program, honors programs, independent study, internships, part-time degree program, services for LD students, study abroad, summer session for credit. *ROTC:* Army (b), Air Force (b).

Student Life *Campus security:* 24-hour emergency response devices and patrols

Athletics Member NJCAA.

Costs (2014–15) *Tuition:* state resident $2496 full-time, $104 per credit part-time; nonresident $9738 full-time, $406 per credit part-time. Full-time tuition and fees vary according to degree level and program. Part-time tuition and fees vary according to degree level and program. *Required fees:* $20 full-time, $10 per term part-time.

Financial Aid Of all full-time matriculated undergraduates who enrolled in 2013, 200 Federal Work-Study jobs (averaging $2244). 200 state and other part-time jobs (averaging $2000).

Applying *Options:* electronic application, early admission. *Application fee:* $30. *Required:* high school transcript.

Freshman Application Contact Ms. Stephanie Burnette, Registrar, Eastern Florida State College, 1519 Clearlake Road, Cocoa, FL 32922-6597. *Phone:* 321-433-7271. *Fax:* 321-433-7172. *E-mail:* cocoaadmissions@brevardcc.edu.
Website: http://www.easternflorida.edu/.

Everest University
Orange Park, Florida

Freshman Application Contact Admissions Office, Everest University, 805 Wells Road, Orange Park, FL 32073. *Phone:* 904-264-9122.
Website: http://www.everest.edu/.

Florida Career College
Miami, Florida

Director of Admissions Mr. David Knobel, President, Florida Career College, 1321 Southwest 107 Avenue, Suite 201B, Miami, FL 33174. *Phone:* 305-553-6065. *Toll-free phone:* 888-852-7272.
Website: http://www.careercollege.edu/.

Florida College of Natural Health
Maitland, Florida

Freshman Application Contact Admissions Office, Florida College of Natural Health, 2600 Lake Lucien Drive, Suite 140, Maitland, FL 32751. *Phone:* 407-261-0319. *Toll-free phone:* 800-393-7337.
Website: http://www.fcnh.com/.

Florida College of Natural Health
Miami, Florida

Director of Admissions Admissions Coordinator, Florida College of Natural Health, 7925 Northwest 12th Street, Suite 201, Miami, FL 33126. *Phone:* 305-597-9599. *Toll-free phone:* 800-599-9599. *Fax:* 305-597-9110.
Website: http://www.fcnh.com/.

Florida College of Natural Health
Pompano Beach, Florida

Freshman Application Contact Admissions Office, Florida College of Natural Health, 2001 West Sample Road, Suite 100, Pompano Beach, FL 33064. *Phone:* 954-975-6400. *Toll-free phone:* 800-541-9299.
Website: http://www.fcnh.com/.

Florida Gateway College
Lake City, Florida

- **State-supported** primarily 2-year, founded 1962, part of Florida Community College System
- **Small-town** 132-acre campus with easy access to Jacksonville
- **Coed,** 2,912 undergraduate students, 29% full-time, 65% women, 35% men

Undergraduates 831 full-time, 2,081 part-time. Students come from 2 states and territories; 11% Black or African American, non-Hispanic/Latino; 5% Hispanic/Latino; 1% Asian, non-Hispanic/Latino; 0.4% American Indian or Alaska Native, non-Hispanic/Latino; 0.7% Two or more races, non-Hispanic/Latino; 0.9% Race/ethnicity unknown; 0.1% international; 3% transferred in.

Freshmen *Admission:* 348 enrolled.

Faculty *Total:* 188, 35% full-time, 7% with terminal degrees. *Student/faculty ratio:* 14:1.

Majors Computer and information sciences; computer programming; corrections; criminal justice/law enforcement administration; early childhood education; emergency medical technology (EMT paramedic); engineering technology; graphic design; health information/medical records administration; health services administration; information technology; liberal arts and sciences/liberal studies; logistics, materials, and supply chain management; natural resources/conservation; office management; physical therapy technology; registered nursing/registered nurse; veterinary/animal health technology.

Academics *Calendar:* semesters. *Degrees:* certificates, diplomas, associate, bachelor's, and postbachelor's certificates. *Special study options:* academic remediation for entering students, accelerated degree program, adult/continuing education programs, advanced placement credit, cooperative education, distance learning, English as a second language, honors programs, independent study, off-campus study, part-time degree program, services for LD students, summer session for credit.

Library Wilson S. Rivers Library and Media Center with 101,800 titles, an OPAC, a Web page.

Student Life *Housing:* college housing not available. *Activities and Organizations:* drama/theater group, choral group, Anime Club, Art Club, FGC Board Game Club, Gay Straight Alliance, Rotaract. *Campus security:* 24-hour emergency response devices and patrols. *Student services:* personal/psychological counseling.

Costs (2014–15) *Tuition:* state resident $2368 full-time, $103 per credit hour part-time; nonresident $11,747 full-time, $392 per credit hour part-time. Full-time tuition and fees vary according to course level, course load, degree level, program, reciprocity agreements, and student level. Part-time tuition and fees vary according to course level, course load, degree level, program, reciprocity agreements, and student level. *Required fees:* $731 full-time. *Payment plans:* installment, deferred payment. *Waivers:* employees or children of employees.

Applying *Options:* electronic application. *Required for some:* high school transcript. *Application deadlines:* 8/6 (freshmen), 8/6 (transfers). *Notification:* continuous (freshmen), continuous (transfers).

Freshman Application Contact Admissions, Florida Gateway College, 149 SE College Place, Lake City, FL 32025-8703. *Phone:* 386-755-4236. *E-mail:* admissions@fgc.edu.
Website: http://www.fgc.edu/.

Florida Keys Community College
Key West, Florida

Director of Admissions Ms. Cheryl A. Malsheimer, Director of Admissions and Records, Florida Keys Community College, 5901 College Road, Key West, FL 33040-4397. *Phone:* 305-296-9081 Ext. 201.
Website: http://www.fkcc.edu/.

The Florida School of Traditional Midwifery
Gainseville, Florida

Freshman Application Contact Admissions Office, The Florida School of Traditional Midwifery, 810 East University Avenue, 2nd Floor, Gainseville, FL 32601. *Phone:* 352-338-0766. *Fax:* 352-338-2013. *E-mail:* info@midwiferyschool.org.
Website: http://www.midwiferyschool.org/.

Florida SouthWestern State College
Fort Myers, Florida

- **State and locally supported** primarily 2-year, founded 1962, part of Florida College System
- **Urban** 413-acre campus
- **Endowment** $46.1 million
- **Coed,** 15,705 undergraduate students, 34% full-time, 61% women, 39% men

Undergraduates 5,387 full-time, 10,318 part-time. Students come from 39 states and territories; 95 other countries; 2% are from out of state; 11% Black or African American, non-Hispanic/Latino; 26% Hispanic/Latino; 2% Asian, non-Hispanic/Latino; 0.2% Native Hawaiian or other Pacific Islander, non-Hispanic/Latino; 0.3% American Indian or Alaska Native, non-Hispanic/Latino; 2% Two or more races, non-Hispanic/Latino; 5% Race/ethnicity unknown; 2% international; 3% transferred in; 3% live on campus. *Retention:* 61% of full-time freshmen returned.

Freshmen *Admission:* 4,972 applied, 3,994 admitted, 2,993 enrolled. *Average high school GPA:* 2.93. *Test scores:* SAT critical reading scores over 500: 33%; SAT math scores over 500: 25%; SAT critical reading scores over 600: 5%; SAT math scores over 600: 5%.

Faculty *Total:* 646, 27% full-time, 36% with terminal degrees. *Student/faculty ratio:* 27:1.

Majors Accounting technology and bookkeeping; architectural technology; biology/biotechnology laboratory technician; biology teacher education; business administration and management; business administration, management and operations related; cardiovascular technology; child-care

provision; civil engineering technology; computer programming; computer systems networking and telecommunications; criminal justice/law enforcement administration; dental hygiene; early childhood education; elementary education; emergency medical technology (EMT paramedic); English/language arts teacher education; fire prevention and safety technology; forensic science and technology; health information/medical records technology; homeland security, law enforcement, firefighting and protective services related; legal assistant/paralegal; liberal arts and sciences/liberal studies; management information systems; mathematics teacher education; medical radiologic technology; registered nursing/registered nurse; respiratory care therapy; science teacher education.

Academics *Calendar:* semesters. *Degrees:* certificates, associate, and bachelor's. *Special study options:* academic remediation for entering students, accelerated degree program, advanced placement credit, cooperative education, distance learning, double majors, English as a second language, honors programs, independent study, internships, off-campus study, part-time degree program, services for LD students, study abroad, summer session for credit.

Library Richard H. Rush Library with 65,655 titles, 35,773 audiovisual materials, an OPAC, a Web page.

Student Life *Housing Options:* Campus housing is university owned. *Activities and Organizations:* drama/theater group, choral group. *Campus security:* 24-hour emergency response devices and patrols, controlled dormitory access.

Athletics Member NJCAA. *Intramural sports:* basketball M/W, soccer M/W, volleyball M/W.

Costs (2014–15) *Tuition:* state resident $2436 full-time, $81 per credit hour part-time; nonresident $9750 full-time, $325 per credit hour part-time. Full-time tuition and fees vary according to degree level. Part-time tuition and fees vary according to degree level. *Required fees:* $904 full-time, $30 per credit hour part-time. *Room and board:* $8860; room only: $6000. *Payment plan:* installment. *Waivers:* employees or children of employees.

Applying *Options:* electronic application, early admission, deferred entrance. *Application fee:* $30. *Required:* high school transcript. *Application deadlines:* 8/14 (freshmen), 8/14 (transfers). *Notification:* continuous (freshmen), continuous (transfers).

Freshman Application Contact Mr. Mark Bukowski, Director of Admissions, Florida SouthWestern State College, 8099 College Parkway, Fort Myers, FL 33919. *Phone:* 239-489-9362 Ext. 1362. *E-mail:* Lauren.Willison@edison.edu.
Website: http://www.fsw.edu/.

Florida State College at Jacksonville
Jacksonville, Florida

- **State-supported** primarily 2-year, founded 1963, part of Florida College System
- **Urban** 844-acre campus
- **Endowment** $44.6 million
- **Coed,** 25,514 undergraduate students, 31% full-time, 60% women, 40% men

Undergraduates 7,819 full-time, 17,695 part-time. 25% Black or African American, non-Hispanic/Latino; 7% Hispanic/Latino; 4% Asian, non-Hispanic/Latino; 0.5% Native Hawaiian or other Pacific Islander, non-Hispanic/Latino; 0.3% American Indian or Alaska Native, non-Hispanic/Latino; 2% Two or more races, non-Hispanic/Latino; 12% Race/ethnicity unknown; 0.8% international; 6% transferred in.

Freshmen *Admission:* 3,195 enrolled.

Faculty *Total:* 1,180, 34% full-time, 29% with terminal degrees. *Student/faculty ratio:* 21:1.

Majors Airframe mechanics and aircraft maintenance technology; airline pilot and flight crew; animation, interactive technology, video graphics and special effects; architectural technology; autobody/collision and repair technology; automobile/automotive mechanics technology; automotive engineering technology; aviation/airway management; biology/biotechnology laboratory technician; biomedical sciences; biomedical technology; business administration and management; business administration, management and operations related; cardiovascular technology; child-care and support services management; child-care provision; clinical/medical laboratory technology; computer graphics; computer/information technology services administration related; computer systems networking and telecommunications; criminal justice/law enforcement administration; criminal justice/police science; crisis/emergency/disaster management; culinary arts; dental hygiene; drafting and design technology; early childhood education; emergency medical technology (EMT paramedic); engineering technology; environmental science; finance; fire prevention and safety technology; fire science/firefighting; fire services administration; funeral service and mortuary science; health information/medical records technology; histologic technician; homeland security, law enforcement, firefighting and protective services related; hotel/motel administration; information technology; interior design; legal assistant/paralegal; liberal arts and sciences/liberal studies; logistics, materials, and supply chain management; marketing/marketing management; mass communication/media; medical radiologic technology; network and system administration; occupational therapist assistant; office management; operations management; ophthalmic technology; physical therapy technology; real estate; registered nursing/registered nurse; respiratory care therapy; restaurant, culinary, and catering management; special education–individuals with hearing impairments; theater design and technology; transportation/mobility management; web page, digital/multimedia and information resources design.

Academics *Calendar:* semesters. *Degrees:* certificates, diplomas, associate, and bachelor's. *Special study options:* academic remediation for entering students, accelerated degree program, adult/continuing education programs, advanced placement credit, cooperative education, distance learning, double majors, English as a second language, honors programs, independent study, internships, off-campus study, part-time degree program, services for LD students, study abroad, summer session for credit. *ROTC:* Navy (c).

Library Florida State College at Jacksonville Library and Learning Commons plus 7 others with 174,406 titles, 10,878 audiovisual materials, an OPAC, a Web page.

Student Life *Activities and Organizations:* drama/theater group, student-run newspaper, radio and television station, choral group, Phi Theta Kappa, Forensic Team, Brain Bowl Team, International Student Association, DramaWorks. *Campus security:* 24-hour emergency response devices and patrols, late-night transport/escort service. *Student services:* personal/psychological counseling, women's center.

Athletics Member NJCAA. *Intercollegiate sports:* baseball M(s), basketball M(s)/W(s), softball W(s), tennis W(s), volleyball W(s). *Intramural sports:* badminton M/W, basketball M/W, bowling M/W, football M/W, golf M/W, soccer M/W, softball M/W, table tennis M/W, tennis M/W, volleyball M/W.

Costs (2014–15) *Tuition:* state resident $2470 full-time, $103 per credit hour part-time; nonresident $9583 full-time, $399 per credit hour part-time. Full-time tuition and fees vary according to degree level and program. Part-time tuition and fees vary according to degree level and program. *Required fees:* $320 full-time. *Payment plan:* installment. *Waivers:* employees or children of employees.

Applying *Options:* electronic application, early admission, deferred entrance. *Application fee:* $25. *Required for some:* high school transcript. *Application deadlines:* rolling (freshmen), rolling (out-of-state freshmen), rolling (transfers).

Freshman Application Contact Dr. Peter Biegel, Registrar, Florida State College at Jacksonville, 501 West State Street, Jacksonville, FL 32202. *Phone:* 904-632-5112. *Toll-free phone:* 888-873-1145. *E-mail:* pbiegel@fscj.edu. *Website:* http://www.fscj.edu/.

Florida Technical College
DeLand, Florida

Freshman Application Contact Mr. Bill Atkinson, Director, Florida Technical College, 1199 South Woodland Boulevard, 3rd Floor, DeLand, FL 32720. *Phone:* 386-734-3303. *Fax:* 386-734-5150. *Website:* http://www.ftccollege.edu/.

Florida Technical College
Orlando, Florida

Director of Admissions Ms. Jeanette E. Muschlitz, Director of Admissions, Florida Technical College, 12900 Challenger Parkway, Orlando, FL 32826. *Phone:* 407-678-5600. *Website:* http://www.ftccollege.edu/.

Fortis College
Largo, Florida

Admissions Office Contact Fortis College, 6565 Ulmerton Road, Largo, FL 33771. *Website:* http://www.fortis.edu/.

Fortis College
Orange Park, Florida

Admissions Office Contact Fortis College, 700 Blanding Boulevard, Suite 16, Orange Park, FL 32065. *Website:* http://www.fortis.edu/.

Fortis College
Winter Park, Florida

Freshman Application Contact Admissions Office, Fortis College, 1573 West Fairbanks Avenue, Suite 100, Winter Park, FL 32789. *Phone:* 407-843-3984. *Toll-free phone:* 855-4-FORTIS. *Fax:* 407-843-9828. *Website:* http://www.fortis.edu/.

Fortis Institute
Fort Lauderdale, Florida

Admissions Office Contact Fortis Institute, 4850 W. Oakland Park Boulevard, Suite 200, Fort Lauderdale, FL 33313. *Website:* http://www.fortis.edu/.

Fortis Institute
Miami, Florida

Admissions Office Contact Fortis Institute, 9035 Sunset Drive, Suite 200, Miami, FL 33173. *Website:* http://www.fortis.edu/.

Fortis Institute
Palm Springs, Florida

Director of Admissions Campus Director, Fortis Institute, 1630 South Congress Avenue, Palm Springs, FL 33461. *Phone:* 561-304-3466. *Toll-free phone:* 877-606-3382. *Fax:* 561-304-3471. *Website:* http://www.fortis.edu/.

Fortis Institute
Pensacola, Florida

Admissions Office Contact Fortis Institute, 4081 East Olive Road, Suite B, Pensacola, FL 32514. *Website:* http://www.fortis.edu/.

Fortis Institute
Port St. Lucie, Florida

Admissions Office Contact Fortis Institute, 9022 South US Highway 1, Port St. Lucie, FL 34952. *Website:* http://www.fortis.edu/.

Golf Academy of America
Apopka, Florida

Admissions Office Contact Golf Academy of America, 510 South Hunt Club Boulevard, Apopka, FL 32703. *Website:* http://www.golfacademy.edu/.

Gulf Coast State College
Panama City, Florida

- **State-supported** primarily 2-year, founded 1957, part of Florida College System
- **Urban** 80-acre campus
- **Endowment** $30.1 million
- **Coed,** 6,271 undergraduate students, 35% full-time, 61% women, 39% men

Undergraduates 2,224 full-time, 4,047 part-time. Students come from 15 states and territories; 2% are from out of state; 11% Black or African American, non-Hispanic/Latino; 5% Hispanic/Latino; 3% Asian, non-Hispanic/Latino; 0.6% American Indian or Alaska Native, non-Hispanic/Latino; 3% Two or more races, non-Hispanic/Latino; 3% Race/ethnicity unknown; 0.1% international; 3% transferred in.

Freshmen *Admission:* 853 enrolled.

Faculty *Total:* 303, 34% full-time. *Student/faculty ratio:* 18:1.

Majors Accounting technology and bookkeeping; animation, interactive technology, video graphics and special effects; automation engineer technology; business administration and management; business administration, management and operations related; CAD/CADD drafting/design technology; child-care provision; civil engineering technology; communications technology; computer/information technology services administration related; computer programming; computer programming (vendor/product certification); computer systems networking and telecommunications; construction engineering technology; criminal justice/law enforcement administration; dental hygiene; diagnostic medical sonography and ultrasound technology; digital arts; digital communication and media/multimedia; early childhood education; electrical, electronic and communications engineering technology; emergency medical technology (EMT paramedic); engineering technology; fire prevention and safety technology; forensic science and technology; health services/allied health/health sciences; hospitality administration; liberal arts and sciences/liberal studies; management information systems; manufacturing engineering technology; medical administrative assistant and medical secretary; medical radiologic technology; music technology; network and system administration; nuclear medical technology; office management; physical therapy technology; registered nursing/registered nurse; respiratory care therapy; restaurant, culinary, and catering management; surgical technology; transportation/mobility management; web page, digital/multimedia and information resources design.

Academics *Calendar:* semesters. *Degrees:* certificates, associate, and bachelor's. *Special study options:* academic remediation for entering students, accelerated degree program, adult/continuing education programs, advanced placement credit, cooperative education, distance learning, double majors, English as a second language, external degree program, honors programs, independent study, off-campus study, part-time degree program, services for LD students, summer session for credit.

Library Gulf Coast State College Library with 144,513 titles, an OPAC, a Web page.

Student Life *Housing:* college housing not available. *Activities and Organizations:* drama/theater group, student-run newspaper, television station, choral group. *Campus security:* 24-hour patrols, late-night transport/escort service, patrols by trained security personnel during campus hours. *Student services:* personal/psychological counseling.

Athletics Member NJCAA. *Intercollegiate sports:* baseball M(s), basketball M(s)/W(s), softball W(s), volleyball W(s).

Costs (2015–16) *Tuition:* state resident $2370 full-time, $99 per credit hour part-time; nonresident $8635 full-time, $360 per credit hour part-time. Full-time tuition and fees vary according to degree level. Part-time tuition and fees vary according to degree level. *Required fees:* $620 full-time, $26 per credit hour part-time.

Financial Aid Of all full-time matriculated undergraduates who enrolled in 2013, 145 Federal Work-Study jobs (averaging $3200). 60 state and other part-time jobs (averaging $2600).

Applying *Options:* electronic application, early admission, deferred entrance. *Application fee:* $20. *Required:* high school transcript. *Application deadlines:* rolling (freshmen), rolling (transfers). *Notification:* continuous (freshmen).

Freshman Application Contact Mrs. Donna Newell, Application Process Specialist, Gulf Coast State College, 5230 West U.S. Highway 98, Panama City, FL 32401. *Phone:* 850-769-1551 Ext. 2936. *Fax:* 850-913-3308. *E-mail:* dnewell@gulfcoast.edu.
Website: http://www.gulfcoast.edu/.

Heritage Institute
Fort Myers, Florida

Admissions Office Contact Heritage Institute, 6630 Orion Drive, Fort Myers, FL 33912.
Website: http://heritage-education.com/.

Heritage Institute
Jacksonville, Florida

Admissions Office Contact Heritage Institute, 4130 Salisbury Road, Suite 1100, Jacksonville, FL 32216.
Website: http://www.heritage-education.com/.

Hillsborough Community College
Tampa, Florida

- **State-supported** 2-year, founded 1968, part of Florida College System
- **Urban** campus with easy access to Tampa, Clearwater, St. Petersburg
- **Coed,** 27,298 undergraduate students, 42% full-time, 57% women, 43% men

Undergraduates 11,391 full-time, 15,907 part-time. Students come from 36 states and territories; 133 other countries; 0.8% are from out of state; 17% Black or African American, non-Hispanic/Latino; 26% Hispanic/Latino; 3% Asian, non-Hispanic/Latino; 0.2% Native Hawaiian or other Pacific Islander, non-Hispanic/Latino; 0.5% American Indian or Alaska Native, non-Hispanic/Latino; 24% Two or more races, non-Hispanic/Latino; 12% Race/ethnicity unknown; 3% international; 26% transferred in.

Freshmen *Admission:* 5,066 enrolled.

Faculty *Total:* 1,669, 18% full-time, 13% with terminal degrees. *Student/faculty ratio:* 22:1.

Majors Accounting technology and bookkeeping; aquaculture; architectural engineering technology; biology/biotechnology laboratory technician; business administration and management; child-care and support services management; cinematography and film/video production; computer/information technology services administration related; computer programming (specific applications); computer systems analysis; computer technology/computer systems technology; criminal justice/law enforcement administration; dental hygiene; diagnostic medical sonography and ultrasound technology; dietitian assistant; electrical, electronic and communications engineering technology; emergency medical technology (EMT paramedic); engineering technology; environmental control technologies related; executive assistant/executive secretary; fire prevention and safety technology; hospitality administration; legal assistant/paralegal; liberal arts and sciences/liberal studies; management information systems and services related; medical radiologic technology; nuclear medical technology; operations management; opticianry; optometric technician; psychiatric/mental health services technology; registered nursing/registered nurse; respiratory care therapy; restaurant, culinary, and catering management; restaurant/food services management; special education–individuals with hearing impairments; veterinary/animal health technology.

Academics *Calendar:* semesters. *Degree:* certificates and associate. *Special study options:* academic remediation for entering students, advanced placement credit, cooperative education, distance learning, English as a second language, honors programs, independent study, internships, off-campus study, part-time degree program, services for LD students, study abroad, summer session for credit. *ROTC:* Army (c), Air Force (c).

Library Dale Mabry plus 5 others with an OPAC, a Web page.

Student Life *Housing Options:* Campus housing is provided by a third party. *Activities and Organizations:* drama/theater group, student-run newspaper, radio station, choral group. *Campus security:* 24-hour emergency response devices and patrols, late-night transport/escort service, emergency call boxes. *Student services:* personal/psychological counseling.

Athletics Member NJCAA. *Intercollegiate sports:* baseball M(s), basketball M(s)/W(s), softball W(s), tennis W(s), volleyball W(s).

Standardized Tests *Required:* Degree-seeking students may need to provide scores from PERT, CPT, FCLEPT, ACT or SAT prior to registering for classes. Test scores may be no more than 2 years old. Exemptions may be made for active military service and graduates from Florida Public High-Schools (for admission).

Costs (2014–15) *Tuition:* state resident $2505 full-time, $104 per credit hour part-time; nonresident $9111 full-time, $380 per credit hour part-time. *Payment plan:* installment. *Waivers:* employees or children of employees.

Applying *Options:* electronic application, early admission. *Required:* high school transcript. *Application deadlines:* rolling (freshmen), rolling (out-of-state freshmen), rolling (transfers).

Freshman Application Contact Ms. Jennifer Williams, College Registrar, Hillsborough Community College, PO Box 31127, Tampa, FL 33631-3127. *Phone:* 813-259-6565. *E-mail:* jwilliams301@hccfl.edu.
Website: http://www.hccfl.edu/.

Institute of Technical Arts
Casselberry, Florida

Admissions Office Contact Institute of Technical Arts, 493 Semoran Boulevard, Casselberry, FL 70475.
Website: http://www.myfiaa.com/.

ITT Technical Institute
Bradenton, Florida

Freshman Application Contact Director of Recruitment, ITT Technical Institute, 8039 Cooper Creek Boulevard, Bradenton, FL 34201. *Phone:* 941-309-9200. *Toll-free phone:* 800-342-8684.
Website: http://www.itt-tech.edu/.

ITT Technical Institute
Fort Lauderdale, Florida

- **Proprietary** primarily 2-year, founded 1991, part of ITT Educational Services, Inc.
- **Suburban** campus
- **Coed**

Academics *Calendar:* quarters. *Degrees:* associate and bachelor's.

Freshman Application Contact Director of Recruitment, ITT Technical Institute, 3401 South University Drive, Fort Lauderdale, FL 33328-2021. *Phone:* 954-476-9300. *Toll-free phone:* 800-488-7797.
Website: http://www.itt-tech.edu/.

ITT Technical Institute
Fort Myers, Florida
- **Proprietary** primarily 2-year
- **Coed**

Academics *Degrees:* associate and bachelor's.
Freshman Application Contact Director of Recruitment, ITT Technical Institute, 13500 Powers Court, Suite 100, Fort Myers, FL 33912. *Phone:* 239-603-8700. *Toll-free phone:* 877-485-5313.
Website: http://www.itt-tech.edu/.

ITT Technical Institute
Hialeah, Florida
- **Proprietary** primarily 2-year, founded 1996, part of ITT Educational Services, Inc.
- **Coed**

Academics *Calendar:* quarters. *Degrees:* associate and bachelor's.
Freshman Application Contact Director of Recruitment, ITT Technical Institute, 5901 NW 183rd Street, Suite 100, Hialeah, FL 33015. *Phone:* 305-477-3080.
Website: http://www.itt-tech.edu/.

ITT Technical Institute
Jacksonville, Florida
- **Proprietary** primarily 2-year, founded 1991, part of ITT Educational Services, Inc.
- **Urban** campus
- **Coed**

Academics *Calendar:* quarters. *Degrees:* associate and bachelor's.
Financial Aid Of all full-time matriculated undergraduates who enrolled in 2013, 5 Federal Work-Study jobs.
Freshman Application Contact Director of Recruitment, ITT Technical Institute, 7011 A.C. Skinner Parkway, Suite 140, Jacksonville, FL 32256. *Phone:* 904-573-9100. *Toll-free phone:* 800-318-1264.
Website: http://www.itt-tech.edu/.

ITT Technical Institute
Lake Mary, Florida
- **Proprietary** primarily 2-year, founded 1989, part of ITT Educational Services, Inc.
- **Suburban** campus
- **Coed**

Academics *Calendar:* quarters. *Degrees:* associate and bachelor's.
Freshman Application Contact Director of Recruitment, ITT Technical Institute, 1400 South International Parkway, Lake Mary, FL 32746. *Phone:* 407-936-0600. *Toll-free phone:* 866-489-8441.
Website: http://www.itt-tech.edu/.

ITT Technical Institute
Orlando, Florida
- **Proprietary** primarily 2-year, part of ITT Educational Services, Inc.
- **Coed**

Academics *Calendar:* quarters. *Degrees:* associate and bachelor's.
Freshman Application Contact Director of Recruitment, ITT Technical Institute, 8301 Southpark Circle, Suite 100, Orlando, FL 32819. *Phone:* 407-371-6000. *Toll-free phone:* 877-201-4367.
Website: http://www.itt-tech.edu/.

ITT Technical Institute
Pensacola, Florida
- **Proprietary** 2-year
- **Coed**

Freshman Application Contact Director of Recruiting, ITT Technical Institute, 6913 North 9th Avenue, Pensacola, FL 32504. *Phone:* 850-483-5700. *Toll-free phone:* 877-290-8248.
Website: http://www.itt-tech.edu/.

ITT Technical Institute
St. Petersburg, Florida
- **Proprietary** primarily 2-year, part of ITT Educational Services, Inc.
- **Coed**

Academics *Degrees:* associate and bachelor's.
Freshman Application Contact Director of Recruitment, ITT Technical Institute, 877 Executive Center Drive W., Suite 100, St. Petersburg, FL 33702. *Phone:* 727-209-4700. *Toll-free phone:* 866-488-5084.
Website: http://www.itt-tech.edu/.

ITT Technical Institute
Tallahassee, Florida
- **Proprietary** primarily 2-year
- **Coed**

Academics *Degrees:* associate and bachelor's.
Freshman Application Contact Director of Recruitment, ITT Technical Institute, 2639 North Monroe Street, Building A, Suite 100, Tallahassee, FL 32303. *Phone:* 850-422-6300. *Toll-free phone:* 877-230-3559.
Website: http://www.itt-tech.edu/.

ITT Technical Institute
Tampa, Florida
- **Proprietary** primarily 2-year, founded 1981, part of ITT Educational Services, Inc.
- **Suburban** campus
- **Coed**

Academics *Calendar:* quarters. *Degrees:* associate and bachelor's.
Freshman Application Contact Director of Recruitment, ITT Technical Institute, 4809 Memorial Highway, Tampa, FL 33634-7151. *Phone:* 813-885-2244. *Toll-free phone:* 800-825-2831.
Website: http://www.itt-tech.edu/.

Key College
Dania Beach, Florida
Director of Admissions Mr. Ronald H. Dooley, President and Director of Admissions, Key College, 225 East Dania Beach Boulevard, Dania Beach, FL 33004. *Phone:* 954-581-2223 Ext. 23. *Toll-free phone:* 877-421-6149.
Website: http://www.keycollege.edu/.

Lake-Sumter State College
Leesburg, Florida
Freshman Application Contact Ms. Bonnie Yanick, Enrollment Specialist, Lake-Sumter State College, 9501 U.S. Highway 441, Leesburg, FL 34788-8751. *Phone:* 352-365-3561. *Fax:* 352-365-3553. *E-mail:* admissinquiry@lscc.edu.
Website: http://www.lssc.edu/.

Le Cordon Bleu College of Culinary Arts in Miami
Miramar, Florida
Freshman Application Contact Admissions Office, Le Cordon Bleu College of Culinary Arts in Miami, 3221 Enterprise Way, Miramar, FL 33025. *Phone:* 954-628-4000. *Toll-free phone:* 888-569-3222.
Website: http://www.chefs.edu/Miami/.

Le Cordon Bleu College of Culinary Arts in Orlando
Orlando, Florida
Admissions Office Contact Le Cordon Bleu College of Culinary Arts in Orlando, 8511 Commodity Circle, Suite 100, Orlando, FL 32819. *Toll-free phone:* 888-793-3222.
Website: http://www.chefs.edu/Orlando/.

Lincoln College of Technology
West Palm Beach, Florida

Director of Admissions Mr. Kevin Cassidy, Director of Admissions, Lincoln College of Technology, 2410 Metrocentre Boulevard, West Palm Beach, FL 33407. *Phone:* 561-842-8324 Ext. 117. *Fax:* 561-842-9503. *Website:* http://www.lincolnedu.com/.

Lincoln Technical Institute
Fern Park, Florida

Admissions Office Contact Lincoln Technical Institute, 7275 Estapona Circle, Fern Park, FL 32730. *Website:* http://www.lincolnedu.com/.

Management Resources College
Miami, Florida

Admissions Office Contact Management Resources College, 10 NW LeJeune Road, Miami, FL 33126. *Website:* http://www.mrc.edu/.

Meridian College
Sarasota, Florida

Admissions Office Contact Meridian College, 7020 Professional Parkway East, Sarasota, FL 34240. *Website:* http://www.meridian.edu/.

Miami Dade College
Miami, Florida

- **State and locally supported** primarily 2-year, founded 1960, part of Florida College System
- **Urban** campus
- **Endowment** $163.0 million
- **Coed,** 66,046 undergraduate students, 40% full-time, 58% women, 42% men

Undergraduates 26,157 full-time, 39,889 part-time. Students come from 43 states and territories; 180 other countries; 0.4% are from out of state; 16% Black or African American, non-Hispanic/Latino; 68% Hispanic/Latino; 1% Asian, non-Hispanic/Latino; 0.1% Native Hawaiian or other Pacific Islander, non-Hispanic/Latino; 0.1% American Indian or Alaska Native, non-Hispanic/Latino; 0.3% Two or more races, non-Hispanic/Latino; 3% Race/ethnicity unknown; 5% international; 2% transferred in.

Freshmen *Admission:* 22,978 applied, 22,978 admitted, 12,860 enrolled.

Faculty *Total:* 2,566, 29% full-time, 22% with terminal degrees. *Student/faculty ratio:* 29:1.

Majors Accounting technology and bookkeeping; administrative assistant and secretarial science; aeronautics/aviation/aerospace science and technology; agriculture; airline pilot and flight crew; air traffic control; American studies; anthropology; architectural drafting and CAD/CADD; architectural engineering technology; architectural technology; art; Asian studies; audiology and speech-language pathology; automation engineer technology; aviation/airway management; banking and financial support services; behavioral sciences; biology/biological sciences; biology teacher education; biomedical technology; biotechnology; business administration and management; business administration, management and operations related; business automation/technology/data entry; CAD/CADD drafting/design technology; chemistry; chemistry teacher education; child-care provision; child development; cinematography and film/video production; civil engineering technology; clinical/medical laboratory technology; commercial and advertising art; community health services counseling; comparative literature; computer engineering technology; computer graphics; computer installation and repair technology; computer programming; computer programming (specific applications); computer programming (vendor/product certification); computer science; computer software technology; computer support specialist; computer systems networking and telecommunications; computer technology/computer systems technology; construction engineering technology; cooking and related culinary arts; corrections; corrections and criminal justice related; court reporting; criminal justice/law enforcement administration; criminal justice/police science; culinary arts; customer service support/call center/teleservice operation; dance; dental hygiene; diagnostic medical sonography and ultrasound technology; dietetics; dietetic technology; drafting and design technology; dramatic/theater arts; early childhood education; economics; education; education related; education (specific levels and methods) related; electrical and electronic engineering technologies related; electrical, electronic and communications engineering technology;

electrician; elementary education; emergency medical technology (EMT paramedic); engineering; engineering related; engineering technology; English; entrepreneurship; environmental engineering technology; environmental science; finance; fire prevention and safety technology; fire science/firefighting; food science; forensic science and technology; forestry; French; funeral service and mortuary science; general studies; geology/earth science; German; health information/medical records administration; health information/medical records technology; health/medical preparatory programs related; health professions related; health services/allied health/health sciences; heating, air conditioning, ventilation and refrigeration maintenance technology; heating, ventilation, air conditioning and refrigeration engineering technology; histologic technician; histologic technology/histotechnologist; history; homeland security, law enforcement, firefighting and protective services related; horticultural science; hospitality administration; hotel/motel administration; humanities; human services; industrial technology; information science/studies; information technology; interior design; international relations and affairs; Italian; journalism; kindergarten/preschool education; landscaping and groundskeeping; Latin American studies; legal administrative assistant/secretary; legal assistant/paralegal; liberal arts and sciences/liberal studies; logistics, materials, and supply chain management; management information systems; manufacturing engineering technology; marketing/marketing management; massage therapy; mass communication/media; mathematics; mathematics teacher education; medical/clinical assistant; medical radiologic technology; middle school education; music; music performance; music teacher education; music technology; natural sciences; network and system administration; nonprofit management; nuclear medical technology; office management; operations management; ophthalmic technology; opticianry; ornamental horticulture; parks, recreation and leisure; pharmacy technician; philosophy; phlebotomy technology; photographic and film/video technology; photography; physical education teaching and coaching; physical sciences; physical therapy technology; physician assistant; physics; physics teacher education; pipefitting and sprinkler fitting; plant nursery management; plumbing technology; political science and government; Portuguese; pre-engineering; psychology; public administration; radio and television; radio and television broadcasting technology; radiologic technology/science; real estate; recording arts technology; registered nursing/registered nurse; respiratory care therapy; respiratory therapy technician; restaurant, culinary, and catering management; restaurant/food services management; science teacher education; security and loss prevention; sheet metal technology; sign language interpretation and translation; social sciences; social work; sociology; Spanish; special education; special education–individuals with hearing impairments; substance abuse/addiction counseling; teacher assistant/aide; telecommunications technology; theater design and technology; tourism and travel services management; veterinary/animal health technology; web page, digital/multimedia and information resources design.

Academics *Calendar:* 16-16-6-6. *Degrees:* certificates, associate, bachelor's, and postbachelor's certificates. *Special study options:* academic remediation for entering students, accelerated degree program, adult/continuing education programs, advanced placement credit, cooperative education, distance learning, English as a second language, freshman honors college, honors programs, independent study, internships, off-campus study, part-time degree program, services for LD students, study abroad, summer session for credit. *ROTC:* Army (b), Air Force (b).

Library Miami Dade College Learning Resources plus 9 others with 397,647 titles, 46,010 audiovisual materials, an OPAC, a Web page.

Student Life *Housing:* college housing not available. *Activities and Organizations:* drama/theater group, student-run newspaper, radio and television station, choral group, Student Government Association, Phi Theta Kappa, Phi Beta Lambda (Business), Future Educators of America Professional, Kappa Delta Pi Honor Society (Education), national fraternities. *Campus security:* 24-hour emergency response devices and patrols, late-night transport/escort service, Emergency Mass Notification System (EMNS), campus sirens and public address systems, In Case of Crisis smart phone application. *Student services:* health clinic, personal/psychological counseling.

Athletics Member NCAA, NJCAA. All NCAA Division I. *Intercollegiate sports:* baseball M(s), basketball M(s)/W(s), softball W(s), volleyball W(s).

Costs (2015–16) *One-time required fee:* $30. *Tuition:* state resident $1987 full-time, $83 per credit hour part-time; nonresident $7947 full-time, $331 per credit hour part-time. Full-time tuition and fees vary according to course load, degree level, and program. Part-time tuition and fees vary according to course load, degree level, and program. *Required fees:* $803 full-time, $33 per credit hour part-time. *Waivers:* employees or children of employees.

Financial Aid Of all full-time matriculated undergraduates who enrolled in 2013, 800 Federal Work-Study jobs (averaging $5000). 125 state and other part-time jobs (averaging $5000).

Applying *Options:* electronic application, early admission. *Application fee:* $30. *Required:* high school transcript. *Required for some:* Some programs such as Honors College and Medical programs have additional admissions

requirements. *Application deadlines:* rolling (freshmen), rolling (out-of-state freshmen), rolling (transfers). *Notification:* continuous (freshmen), continuous (out-of-state freshmen), continuous (transfers).
Freshman Application Contact Ms. Ferne Creary, Interim College Registrar, Miami Dade College, 11011 SW 104th Street, Miami, FL 33176. *Phone:* 305-237-2206. *Fax:* 305-237-2532. *E-mail:* fcreary@mdc.edu.
Website: http://www.mdc.edu/.

North Florida Community College
Madison, Florida

Freshman Application Contact Mr. Bobby Scott, North Florida Community College, 325 Northwest Turner Davis Drive, Madison, FL 32340. *Phone:* 850-973-9450. *Toll-free phone:* 866-937-6322. *Fax:* 850-973-1697.
Website: http://www.nfcc.edu/.

Northwest Florida State College
Niceville, Florida

- **State and locally supported** primarily 2-year, founded 1963, part of Florida College System
- **Small-town** 264-acre campus
- **Endowment** $28.6 million
- **Coed**

Undergraduates 2,758 full-time, 4,180 part-time. Students come from 12 states and territories; 4% are from out of state; 9% Black or African American, non-Hispanic/Latino; 7% Hispanic/Latino; 3% Asian, non-Hispanic/Latino; 0.4% Native Hawaiian or other Pacific Islander, non-Hispanic/Latino; 0.5% American Indian or Alaska Native, non-Hispanic/Latino; 3% Two or more races, non-Hispanic/Latino; 3% Race/ethnicity unknown; 0.5% international; 7% transferred in.
Faculty *Student/faculty ratio:* 26:1.
Academics *Calendar:* semesters plus summer sessions. *Degrees:* certificates, associate, and bachelor's. *Special study options:* academic remediation for entering students, accelerated degree program, adult/continuing education programs, advanced placement credit, distance learning, English as a second language, independent study, internships, part-time degree program, services for LD students, study abroad, summer session for credit. *ROTC:* Army (b).
Student Life *Campus security:* 24-hour patrols.
Athletics Member NJCAA.
Standardized Tests *Required for some:* ACT, SAT I, ACT ASSET, MAPS, or PERT are used for placement not admission.
Costs (2014–15) *Tuition:* state resident $2313 full-time, $77 per credit part-time; nonresident $9252 full-time, $308 per credit part-time. Full-time tuition and fees vary according to course level, degree level, program, and reciprocity agreements. Part-time tuition and fees vary according to course level, degree level, program, and reciprocity agreements. *Required fees:* $811 full-time, $27 per credit part-time. *Payment plans:* tuition prepayment, deferred payment.
Applying *Options:* electronic application. *Required:* high school transcript.
Freshman Application Contact Ms. Karen Cooper, Director of Admissions, Northwest Florida State College, 100 College Boulevard, Niceville, FL 32578. *Phone:* 850-729-4901. *Fax:* 850-729-5206. *E-mail:* cooperk@nwfsc.edu.
Website: http://www.nwfsc.edu/.

Pasco-Hernando State College
New Port Richey, Florida

- **State-supported** primarily 2-year, founded 1972, part of Florida College System
- **Suburban** 142-acre campus with easy access to Tampa
- **Coed,** 10,206 undergraduate students, 39% full-time, 61% women, 39% men

Undergraduates 4,004 full-time, 6,202 part-time. Students come from 50 states and territories; 7 other countries; 2% are from out of state; 4% Black or African American, non-Hispanic/Latino; 14% Hispanic/Latino; 2% Asian, non-Hispanic/Latino; 0.2% Native Hawaiian or other Pacific Islander, non-Hispanic/Latino; 0.4% American Indian or Alaska Native, non-Hispanic/Latino; 3% Two or more races, non-Hispanic/Latino; 2% Race/ethnicity unknown; 0.2% international. *Retention:* 53% of full-time freshmen returned.
Freshmen *Admission:* 1,811 enrolled.
Faculty *Total:* 377, 33% full-time, 18% with terminal degrees. *Student/faculty ratio:* 26:1.
Majors Business administration and management; computer programming related; computer programming (specific applications); computer systems networking and telecommunications; computer technology/computer systems technology; criminal justice/law enforcement administration; dental hygiene; drafting and design technology; e-commerce; emergency medical technology

(EMT paramedic); human services; information technology; legal assistant/paralegal; liberal arts and sciences/liberal studies; marketing/marketing management; radiologic technology/science; registered nursing/registered nurse; web page, digital/multimedia and information resources design.
Academics *Calendar:* semesters. *Degrees:* certificates, diplomas, associate, and bachelor's. *Special study options:* academic remediation for entering students, accelerated degree program, adult/continuing education programs, advanced placement credit, cooperative education, distance learning, double majors, honors programs, independent study, internships, off-campus study, part-time degree program, services for LD students, summer session for credit. *ROTC:* Army (c).
Library Alric Pottberg Library plus 1 other with 91,950 titles, an OPAC, a Web page.
Student Life *Housing:* college housing not available. *Activities and Organizations:* drama/theater group, choral group, Student Government Association, Phi Theta Kappa, Phi Beta Lambda, Human Services, Legal Eagles. *Campus security:* Security Personnel while college classes are being held. *Student services:* personal/psychological counseling.
Athletics Member NJCAA. *Intercollegiate sports:* baseball M(s), basketball M(s), cross-country running W(s), softball W(s), volleyball W(s). *Intramural sports:* cheerleading M/W.
Standardized Tests *Recommended:* SAT and SAT Subject Tests or ACT (for admission), PERT.
Costs (2014–15) *Tuition:* state resident $3155 full-time, $105 per credit hour part-time; nonresident $12,032 full-time, $401 per credit hour part-time. Full-time tuition and fees vary according to degree level and program. Part-time tuition and fees vary according to degree level and program. *Payment plan:* installment.
Financial Aid Of all full-time matriculated undergraduates who enrolled in 2013, 83 Federal Work-Study jobs (averaging $3201).
Applying *Options:* electronic application. *Application fee:* $25. *Required:* high school transcript. *Application deadlines:* rolling (freshmen), rolling (out-of-state freshmen), rolling (transfers). *Notification:* continuous (freshmen), continuous (out-of-state freshmen), continuous (transfers).
Freshman Application Contact Ms. Estela Carrion, Director of Admissions and Student Records, Pasco-Hernando State College, 10230 Ridge Road, New Port Richey, FL 34654-5199. *Phone:* 727-816-3261. *Toll-free phone:* 877-TRY-PHSC. *Fax:* 727-816-3389. *E-mail:* carrioe@phsc.edu.
Website: http://www.phsc.edu/.

Pensacola State College
Pensacola, Florida

- **State-supported** primarily 2-year, founded 1948, part of Florida College System
- **Urban** 130-acre campus
- **Coed,** 10,317 undergraduate students, 38% full-time, 60% women, 40% men

Undergraduates 3,888 full-time, 6,429 part-time. Students come from 16 states and territories; 1% are from out of state; 15% Black or African American, non-Hispanic/Latino; 6% Hispanic/Latino; 3% Asian, non-Hispanic/Latino; 0.4% Native Hawaiian or other Pacific Islander, non-Hispanic/Latino; 0.8% American Indian or Alaska Native, non-Hispanic/Latino; 6% Two or more races, non-Hispanic/Latino; 1% Race/ethnicity unknown; 0.3% international; 2% transferred in.
Freshmen *Admission:* 1,554 enrolled.
Faculty *Total:* 599, 30% full-time, 6% with terminal degrees. *Student/faculty ratio:* 23:1.
Majors Accounting; accounting technology and bookkeeping; administrative assistant and secretarial science; agricultural business and management; agriculture; art; art teacher education; biochemistry; biology/biological sciences; botany/plant biology; building/property maintenance; business administration and management; business administration, management and operations related; business/commerce; chemical technology; chemistry; child-care and support services management; child-care provision; civil engineering technology; commercial and advertising art; communications technology; computer and information sciences; computer and information sciences related; computer and information systems security; computer engineering; computer programming; computer programming (specific applications); computer programming (vendor/product certification); computer science; computer systems analysis; construction engineering technology; consumer services and advocacy; cooking and related culinary arts; criminal justice/law enforcement administration; cyber/computer forensics and counterterrorism; dental hygiene; diagnostic medical sonography and ultrasound technology; dietetics; drafting and design technology; dramatic/theater arts; early childhood education; education; electrical, electronic and communications engineering technology; elementary education; emergency medical technology (EMT paramedic); engineering; engineering technology; English; executive assistant/executive secretary; fire prevention

and safety technology; fire science/firefighting; food service systems administration; foods, nutrition, and wellness; forensic science and technology; geology/earth science; graphic design; hazardous materials management and waste technology; health/health-care administration; health information/medical records administration; health information/medical records technology; history; homeland security related; hospitality administration; hotel/motel administration; hotel, motel, and restaurant management; information science/studies; journalism; landscaping and groundskeeping; legal administrative assistant/secretary; legal assistant/paralegal; liberal arts and sciences/liberal studies; management information systems; management information systems and services related; management science; mathematics; medical radiologic technology; music; music teacher education; natural resources management and policy; nursing assistant/aide and patient care assistant/aide; nursing science; ornamental horticulture; pharmacy technician; philosophy; photography; physical therapy technology; physics; pre-dentistry studies; pre-law studies; premedical studies; prenursing studies; pre-pharmacy studies; pre-veterinary studies; psychology; registered nursing/registered nurse; religious studies; restaurant, culinary, and catering management; small business administration; sociology; special education; telecommunications technology; veterinary/animal health technology; zoology/animal biology.

Academics *Calendar:* semesters. *Degrees:* certificates, diplomas, associate, and bachelor's. *Special study options:* academic remediation for entering students, adult/continuing education programs, advanced placement credit, cooperative education, distance learning, double majors, English as a second language, external degree program, honors programs, independent study, part-time degree program, services for LD students, summer session for credit. *ROTC:* Army (b).

Library Edward M. Chadbourne Library plus 3 others with 145,834 titles, 8,724 audiovisual materials, an OPAC, a Web page.

Student Life *Housing:* college housing not available. *Activities and Organizations:* drama/theater group, student-run newspaper, choral group. *Campus security:* 24-hour emergency response devices and patrols, late-night transport/escort service. *Student services:* health clinic, personal/psychological counseling.

Athletics Member NJCAA. *Intercollegiate sports:* baseball M(s), basketball M(s)/W(s), softball W(s), volleyball W. *Intramural sports:* archery M/W, badminton M/W, basketball M/W, bowling M/W, cross-country running M/W, gymnastics M/W, racquetball M/W, sailing M/W, swimming and diving M/W, tennis M/W, track and field M/W, volleyball M/W, weight lifting M/W, wrestling M.

Costs (2014–15) *One-time required fee:* $30. *Tuition:* state resident $2510 full-time, $105 per credit hour part-time; nonresident $10,075 full-time, $420 per credit hour part-time. Full-time tuition and fees vary according to degree level. Part-time tuition and fees vary according to degree level. *Payment plan:* deferred payment. *Waivers:* senior citizens and employees or children of employees.

Financial Aid Of all full-time matriculated undergraduates who enrolled in 2013, 120 Federal Work-Study jobs (averaging $3000).

Applying *Options:* electronic application, early admission. *Application fee:* $30. *Required:* high school transcript. *Application deadlines:* 8/30 (freshmen), 8/30 (transfers). *Notification:* continuous until 8/30 (freshmen), continuous until 8/30 (transfers).

Freshman Application Contact Susan Desbrow, Registrar, Pensacola State College, 1000 College Blvd, Pensacola, FL 32504. *Phone:* 850-484-1605. *Fax:* 850-484-1020. *E-mail:* kdutremble@pensacolastate.edu. *Website:* http://www.pensacolastate.edu/.

Praxis Institute
Miami, Florida

Admissions Office Contact Praxis Institute, 1850 SW 8th Street, 4th Floor, Miami, FL 33135.
Website: http://the-praxisinstitute.com/.

Professional Hands Institute
Miami, Florida

Admissions Office Contact Professional Hands Institute, 10 NW 42 Avenue, Suite 200, Miami, FL 33126.
Website: http://prohands.edu/.

Remington College–Orlando Campus
Heathrow, Florida

Admissions Office Contact Remington College–Orlando Campus, 500 International Parkway, Heathrow, FL 32746. *Toll-free phone:* 800-560-6192. *Website:* http://www.remingtoncollege.edu/.

Remington College–Tampa Campus
Tampa, Florida

Freshman Application Contact Remington College–Tampa Campus, 6302 E. Dr. Martin Luther King, Jr. Boulevard, Suite 400, Tampa, FL 33619. *Phone:* 813-932-0701. *Toll-free phone:* 800-560-6192. *Website:* http://www.remingtoncollege.edu/.

SABER College
Miami, Florida

Admissions Office Contact SABER College, 3990 W. Flagler Street, Suite 103, Miami, FL 33134.
Website: http://www.sabercollege.com/.

St. Johns River State College
Palatka, Florida

Director of Admissions Dean of Admissions and Records, St. Johns River State College, 5001 Saint Johns Avenue, Palatka, FL 32177-3897. *Phone:* 386-312-4032. *Fax:* 386-312-4289.
Website: http://www.sjrstate.edu/.

Seminole State College of Florida
Sanford, Florida

- **State and locally supported** primarily 2-year, founded 1966
- **Small-town** 200-acre campus with easy access to Orlando
- **Endowment** $14.6 million
- **Coed,** 18,422 undergraduate students, 34% full-time, 56% women, 44% men

Undergraduates 6,345 full-time, 12,077 part-time. Students come from 24 states and territories; 75 other countries; 0.2% are from out of state; 17% Black or African American, non-Hispanic/Latino; 23% Hispanic/Latino; 3% Asian, non-Hispanic/Latino; 0.3% Native Hawaiian or other Pacific Islander, non-Hispanic/Latino; 0.2% American Indian or Alaska Native, non-Hispanic/Latino; 3% Two or more races, non-Hispanic/Latino; 1% Race/ethnicity unknown; 2% international; 6% transferred in.

Freshmen *Admission:* 2,689 applied, 2,689 admitted, 2,689 enrolled.

Faculty *Total:* 780, 30% full-time, 21% with terminal degrees. *Student/faculty ratio:* 25:1.

Majors Accounting; administrative assistant and secretarial science; architectural engineering technology; automobile/automotive mechanics technology; banking and financial support services; building/construction finishing, management, and inspection related; business administration and management; child development; civil engineering technology; computer and information sciences and support services related; computer and information sciences related; computer and information systems security; computer engineering related; computer engineering technology; computer graphics; computer hardware engineering; computer/information technology services administration related; computer programming; computer programming related; computer programming (specific applications); computer programming (vendor/product certification); computer software and media applications related; computer software engineering; computer systems networking and telecommunications; construction engineering technology; criminal justice/law enforcement administration; data entry/microcomputer applications; data entry/microcomputer applications related; data modeling/warehousing and database administration; data processing and data processing technology; drafting and design technology; electrical, electronic and communications engineering technology; emergency medical technology (EMT paramedic); finance; fire science/firefighting; industrial technology; information science/studies; information technology; interior design; legal assistant/paralegal; liberal arts and sciences/liberal studies; marketing/marketing management; network and system administration; physical therapy; registered nursing/registered nurse; respiratory care therapy; telecommunications technology; web/multimedia management and webmaster; web page, digital/multimedia and information resources design; word processing.

Academics *Calendar:* semesters. *Degrees:* certificates, diplomas, associate, bachelor's, and postbachelor's certificates. *Special study options:* academic remediation for entering students, accelerated degree program, adult/continuing education programs, advanced placement credit, cooperative education, distance learning, double majors, English as a second language, external degree program, honors programs, independent study, internships, part-time degree program, services for LD students, study abroad, summer session for credit. *ROTC:* Army (b).

Library Seminole State College Library - SLM plus 8 others with 110,348 titles, 7,045 audiovisual materials, an OPAC, a Web page.

Student Life *Housing:* college housing not available. *Activities and Organizations:* drama/theater group, student-run newspaper, choral group, Phi Beta Lambda, Phi Theta Kappa, Student Government Association, Sigma Phi Gamma, Hispanic Student Association. *Campus security:* 24-hour emergency response devices and patrols, late-night transport/escort service. *Student services:* personal/psychological counseling.

Athletics Member NJCAA. *Intercollegiate sports:* baseball M(s), golf W(s), softball W(s).

Standardized Tests *Recommended:* SAT (for admission), ACT (for admission), SAT or ACT (for admission), SAT and SAT Subject Tests or ACT (for admission), SAT Subject Tests (for admission), CPT, PERT.

Costs (2014–15) *Tuition:* state resident $3131 full-time, $104 per credit hour part-time; nonresident $11,456 full-time, $382 per credit hour part-time. Full-time tuition and fees vary according to course level, course load, degree level, and program. Part-time tuition and fees vary according to course level, course load, degree level, and program. *Payment plan:* deferred payment. *Waivers:* senior citizens and employees or children of employees.

Applying *Options:* electronic application, early admission, deferred entrance. *Required:* high school transcript, minimum 2.0 GPA. *Application deadlines:* rolling (freshmen), rolling (transfers). *Notification:* continuous (freshmen), continuous (transfers).

Freshman Application Contact Ms. Pamela Mennechey, Associate Vice President - Student Recruitment and Enrollment, Seminole State College of Florida, Sanford, FL 32773-6199. *Phone:* 407-708-2050. *Fax:* 407-708-2395. *E-mail:* admissions@scc-fl.edu.
Website: http://www.seminolestate.edu/.

Southeastern College–Greenacres
Greenacres, Florida

- **Proprietary** 2-year
- **Coed,** 433 undergraduate students
- 98% of applicants were admitted

Freshmen *Admission:* 536 applied, 526 admitted.

Majors Aesthetician/esthetician and skin care; business, management, and marketing related; computer and information sciences and support services related; computer systems networking and telecommunications; emergency medical technology (EMT paramedic); health professions related; licensed practical/vocational nurse training; massage therapy; medical/clinical assistant; medical insurance coding; medical insurance/medical billing; parks, recreation and leisure facilities management; pharmacy technician; salon/beauty salon management; surgical technology.

Academics *Degree:* certificates and associate.

Costs (2014–15) *Tuition:* $16,056 full-time, $669 per term part-time. Full-time tuition and fees vary according to course load and program. Part-time tuition and fees vary according to course load and program. *Required fees:* $1540 full-time.

Applying *Application fee:* $55. *Required:* high school transcript.

Freshman Application Contact Admissions Office, Southeastern College–Greenacres, 6812 Forest Hill Boulevard, Suite D-1, Greenacres, FL 33413.
Website: http://www.sec.edu/.

Southeastern College–Jacksonville
Jacksonville, Florida

Admissions Office Contact Southeastern College–Jacksonville, 6700 Southpoint Parkway, Suite 400, Jacksonville, FL 3216.
Website: http://www.sec.edu/.

Southeastern College–Miami Lakes
Miami Lakes, Florida

Freshman Application Contact Admissions Office, Southeastern College–Miami Lakes, 17395 NW 59th Avenue, Miami Lakes, FL 33015.
Website: http://www.sec.edu/.

Southeastern College–St. Petersburg
St. Petersburg, Florida

Admissions Office Contact Southeastern College–St. Petersburg, 11208 Blue Heron Boulevard, Suite A, St. Petersburg, FL 33716.
Website: http://www.sec.edu/.

Southern Technical College
Orlando, Florida

- **Proprietary** 2-year
- **Urban** 1-acre campus with easy access to Greater Orlando
- **Coed,** 1,445 undergraduate students, 100% full-time, 57% women, 43% men

Undergraduates 1,445 full-time. 40% Black or African American, non-Hispanic/Latino; 27% Hispanic/Latino; 0.6% Asian, non-Hispanic/Latino; 0.4% Native Hawaiian or other Pacific Islander, non-Hispanic/Latino; 0.6% American Indian or Alaska Native, non-Hispanic/Latino; 0.9% Two or more races, non-Hispanic/Latino; 2% Race/ethnicity unknown; 0.1% international.

Freshmen *Admission:* 468 admitted, 411 enrolled.

Faculty *Total:* 57, 100% full-time. *Student/faculty ratio:* 25:1.

Majors Electrical and electronics engineering; electrical/electronics maintenance and repair technology related; medical/clinical assistant; medical insurance/medical billing.

Academics *Calendar:* quarters. *Degree:* diplomas and associate. *Special study options:* academic remediation for entering students, advanced placement credit, distance learning, independent study, summer session for credit.

Library STC Library with 4,572 titles, 210 audiovisual materials.

Student Life *Housing:* college housing not available. *Activities and Organizations:* Alpha Beta Kappa Honors Socieity. *Campus security:* evening security guard.

Costs (2014–15) *Tuition:* $16,455 full-time. *Payment plan:* installment.

Applying *Required:* self attestation at time of application that student has met admissions criteria of high school diploma or GED completion. *Application deadlines:* rolling (freshmen), rolling (transfers). *Notification:* continuous (freshmen), continuous (transfers).

Freshman Application Contact Mr. Robinson Elie, Director of Admissions, Southern Technical College, 1485 Florida Mall Avenue, Orlando, FL 32809. *Phone:* 407-438-6000. *Toll-free phone:* 877-347-5492. *E-mail:* relie@southerntech.edu.
Website: http://www.southerntech.edu/.

Southern Technical College
Tampa, Florida

Director of Admissions Admissions, Southern Technical College, 3910 Riga Boulevard, Tampa, FL 33619. *Phone:* 813-630-4401. *Toll-free phone:* 877-347-5492.
Website: http://www.southerntech.edu/locations/tampa/.

South Florida State College
Avon Park, Florida

- **State-supported** primarily 2-year, founded 1965, part of Florida State College System
- **Rural** 228-acre campus with easy access to Tampa-St. Petersburg, Orlando
- **Endowment** $5.0 million
- **Coed,** 2,699 undergraduate students, 36% full-time, 62% women, 38% men

Undergraduates 970 full-time, 1,729 part-time. 3% are from out of state; 10% Black or African American, non-Hispanic/Latino; 29% Hispanic/Latino; 2% Asian, non-Hispanic/Latino; 0.4% Native Hawaiian or other Pacific Islander, non-Hispanic/Latino; 0.1% American Indian or Alaska Native, non-Hispanic/Latino; 1% Two or more races, non-Hispanic/Latino; 2% Race/ethnicity unknown; 1% international; 0.9% transferred in.

Freshmen *Admission:* 736 applied, 736 admitted, 568 enrolled. *Average high school GPA:* 3.03.

Faculty *Total:* 145, 45% full-time, 18% with terminal degrees. *Student/faculty ratio:* 16:1.

Majors Accounting; accounting technology and bookkeeping; actuarial science; advertising; aerospace, aeronautical and astronautical/space engineering; agribusiness; agricultural economics; agricultural engineering; agricultural teacher education; agriculture; American studies; animal sciences; anthropology; applied mathematics; architecture; art; art history, criticism and conservation; art teacher education; astronomy; atmospheric sciences and meteorology; audiology and speech-language pathology; banking and financial support services; biochemistry; biological and physical sciences; biology/biological sciences; biomedical technology; botany/plant biology; business administration and management; business administration, management and operations related; business/commerce; business/managerial economics; business teacher education; chemical engineering; chemistry; chemistry related; city/urban, community and regional planning; civil engineering; civil engineering technology; clinical laboratory science/medical technology; computer and information sciences; computer engineering;

computer engineering technology; computer programming; construction engineering technology; criminal justice/law enforcement administration; criminal justice/safety; dental hygiene; dietetics; dramatic/theater arts; early childhood education; economics; electrical and electronics engineering; electrical, electronic and communications engineering technology; elementary education; emergency medical technology (EMT paramedic); engineering; engineering science; engineering technology; English; English/language arts teacher education; entomology; environmental/environmental health engineering; environmental science; family and consumer sciences/home economics teacher education; finance; fine/studio arts; fire prevention and safety technology; food science; foreign languages and literatures; foreign language teacher education; forensic science and technology; forestry; French; general studies; geography; geology/earth science; gerontology; graphic design; health/health-care administration; health information/medical records administration; health services/allied health/health sciences; health teacher education; history; horticultural science; hospitality administration; humanities; human resources management; industrial engineering; information science/studies; insurance; international business/trade/commerce; international relations and affairs; jazz/jazz studies; journalism; kinesiology and exercise science; landscaping and groundskeeping; legal assistant/paralegal; liberal arts and sciences and humanities related; liberal arts and sciences/liberal studies; linguistics; management information systems; management science; marine biology and biological oceanography; marketing/marketing management; materials engineering; mathematics; mathematics teacher education; mechanical engineering; medical microbiology and bacteriology; medical radiologic technology; middle school education; multi/interdisciplinary studies related; music; music history, literature, and theory; music performance; music teacher education; music theory and composition; music therapy; nuclear engineering; occupational therapy; ocean engineering; office management; parks, recreation and leisure facilities management; pharmacy; philosophy; philosophy and religious studies related; physics; physics related; plant sciences; political science and government; psychology; public administration; public relations/image management; radio and television; real estate; registered nursing/registered nurse; religious studies; respiratory care therapy; rhetoric and composition; science teacher education; secondary education; social psychology; social sciences; social science teacher education; social work; sociology; soil science and agronomy; Spanish; special education; special education–individuals with emotional disturbances; special education–individuals with intellectual disabilities; special education–individuals with specific learning disabilities; special education–individuals with vision impairments; speech communication and rhetoric; statistics; surveying technology; systems engineering; trade and industrial teacher education; transportation/mobility management; vocational rehabilitation counseling; water, wetlands, and marine resources management; zoology/animal biology.

Academics *Calendar:* semesters. *Degrees:* certificates, diplomas, associate, and bachelor's. *Special study options:* academic remediation for entering students, adult/continuing education programs, advanced placement credit, cooperative education, distance learning, English as a second language, internships, part-time degree program, services for LD students, summer session for credit.

Library Learning Resource Center with 154,239 titles, 883 audiovisual materials, an OPAC, a Web page.

Student Life *Housing Options:* Campus housing is provided by a third party. *Activities and Organizations:* drama/theater group, student-run newspaper, choral group, Phi Theta Kappa, Phi Beta Lambda, Performing Arts Club, Anime & Gaming Club, Basketball Club. *Campus security:* 24-hour emergency response devices and patrols, late-night transport/escort service. *Student services:* personal/psychological counseling.

Athletics Member NJCAA. *Intercollegiate sports:* baseball M(s), cheerleading M/W, softball W(s), volleyball W(s). *Intramural sports:* basketball M(c)/W(c), soccer M(c)/W(c).

Costs (2014–15) *One-time required fee:* $15. *Tuition:* state resident $2505 full-time, $105 per credit hour part-time; nonresident $9463 full-time, $394 per credit hour part-time. Full-time tuition and fees vary according to degree level. Part-time tuition and fees vary according to degree level. *Room and board:* $5821; room only: $1500. *Payment plan:* installment. *Waivers:* employees or children of employees.

Applying *Options:* electronic application, early admission, deferred entrance. *Application fee:* $15. *Required:* high school transcript. *Application deadline:* rolling (freshmen). *Notification:* continuous (freshmen).

Freshman Application Contact Ms. Lynn Hintz, Admissions Director, South Florida State College, 600 West College Drive, Avon Park, FL 33825. *Phone:* 863-453-6661.

Website: http://www.southflorida.edu/.

Stenotype Institute of Jacksonville
Jacksonville, Florida

Admissions Office Contact Stenotype Institute of Jacksonville, 3563 Phillips Highway, Building E, Suite 501, Jacksonville, FL 32207. *Toll-free phone:* 800-273-5090.

Website: http://www.stenotype.edu/.

Tallahassee Community College
Tallahassee, Florida

- **State and locally supported** 2-year, founded 1966, part of Florida College System
- **Suburban** 214-acre campus
- **Endowment** $10.6 million
- **Coed,** 13,049 undergraduate students, 47% full-time, 54% women, 46% men

Undergraduates 6,141 full-time, 6,908 part-time. Students come from 27 states and territories; 79 other countries; 2% are from out of state; 33% Black or African American, non-Hispanic/Latino; 11% Hispanic/Latino; 1% Asian, non-Hispanic/Latino; 0.1% Native Hawaiian or other Pacific Islander, non-Hispanic/Latino; 0.2% American Indian or Alaska Native, non-Hispanic/Latino; 3% Two or more races, non-Hispanic/Latino; 2% Race/ethnicity unknown; 1% international; 8% transferred in. *Retention:* 59% of full-time freshmen returned.

Freshmen *Admission:* 4,834 applied, 4,834 admitted, 2,230 enrolled.

Faculty *Total:* 613, 32% full-time, 22% with terminal degrees. *Student/faculty ratio:* 26:1.

Majors Accounting technology and bookkeeping; CAD/CADD drafting/design technology; commercial and advertising art; computer graphics; computer programming; computer programming (specific applications); computer systems networking and telecommunications; construction engineering technology; corrections; criminal justice/law enforcement administration; criminal justice/police science; dental assisting; dental hygiene; diagnostic medical sonography and ultrasound technology; drafting and design technology; early childhood education; emergency medical technology (EMT paramedic); entrepreneurship; environmental science; fire science/firefighting; health information/medical records technology; homeland security related; information technology; legal assistant/paralegal; liberal arts and sciences/liberal studies; manufacturing engineering technology; masonry; medical radiologic technology; nursing assistant/aide and patient care assistant/aide; office management; pharmacy technician; physical fitness technician; registered nursing/registered nurse; respiratory care therapy; security and loss prevention; surgical technology; web page, digital/multimedia and information resources design; welding technology.

Academics *Calendar:* semesters. *Degree:* certificates and associate. *Special study options:* academic remediation for entering students, accelerated degree program, adult/continuing education programs, advanced placement credit, distance learning, English as a second language, external degree program, honors programs, independent study, off-campus study, part-time degree program, services for LD students, study abroad, summer session for credit. *ROTC:* Army (c), Navy (c), Air Force (c).

Library Tallahassee Community College Library with 97,919 titles, 7,965 audiovisual materials, an OPAC.

Student Life *Housing:* college housing not available. *Activities and Organizations:* drama/theater group, student-run newspaper, choral group, Student Government Association, International Student Organization, Phi Theta Kappa, Model United Nations, Honors Council. *Campus security:* 24-hour emergency response devices and patrols, late-night transport/escort service. *Student services:* personal/psychological counseling.

Athletics Member NJCAA. *Intercollegiate sports:* baseball M(s), basketball M(s)/W(s), softball W(s). *Intramural sports:* basketball M/W, football M/W, soccer M/W, softball M/W, volleyball M/W.

Costs (2014–15) *Tuition:* state resident $2622 full-time, $101 per credit hour part-time; nonresident $10,069 full-time, $387 per credit hour part-time. Full-time tuition and fees vary according to course load. Part-time tuition and fees vary according to course load. *Payment plan:* installment. *Waivers:* employees or children of employees.

Financial Aid Of all full-time matriculated undergraduates who enrolled in 2013, 4,479 applied for aid, 3,185 were judged to have need. 125 Federal Work-Study jobs (averaging $2600). *Average financial aid package:* $4254. *Average need-based gift aid:* $4127.

Applying *Options:* electronic application, early admission, deferred entrance. *Required:* high school transcript. *Application deadlines:* 8/1 (freshmen), 8/1 (transfers).

Freshman Application Contact Student Success Center, Tallahassee Community College, 444 Appleyard Drive, Tallahassee, FL 32304-2895. *Phone:* 850-201-8555. *E-mail:* admissions@tcc.fl.edu.

Website: http://www.tcc.fl.edu/.

Ultimate Medical Academy Clearwater
Clearwater, Florida

- **Proprietary** 2-year
- **Urban** campus with easy access to Tampa, Florida
- **Coed**

Majors Health services/allied health/health sciences.
Academics *Calendar:* continuous. *Degree:* diplomas and associate. *Special study options:* distance learning, services for LD students.
Student Life *Housing:* college housing not available.
Applying *Required:* high school transcript.
Freshman Application Contact Ultimate Medical Academy Clearwater, 1255 Cleveland Street, Clearwater, FL 33756. *Toll-free phone:* 888-205-8685. *Website:* http://www.ultimatemedical.edu/.

Ultimate Medical Academy Online
Clearwater, Florida

- **Proprietary** 2-year
- **Urban** campus
- **Coed**

Majors Health/health-care administration; health information/medical records technology; health services/allied health/health sciences; human services; medical administrative assistant and medical secretary; medical insurance/medical billing; pharmacy technician.
Academics *Degree:* diplomas and associate. *Special study options:* distance learning, services for LD students.
Student Life *Housing:* college housing not available.
Freshman Application Contact Online Admissions Department, Ultimate Medical Academy Online, 1255 Cleveland Street, Clearwater, FL 33756. *Phone:* 888-209-8848. *Toll-free phone:* 888-205-2510. *E-mail:* onlineadmissions@ultimatemedical.edu. *Website:* http://www.ultimatemedical.edu/.

Ultimate Medical Academy Tampa
Tampa, Florida

- **Proprietary** 2-year
- **Urban** campus
- **Coed**

Majors Health services/allied health/health sciences; nursing science.
Academics *Calendar:* continuous. *Degree:* diplomas and associate. *Special study options:* distance learning, services for LD students.
Student Life *Housing:* college housing not available.
Freshman Application Contact Ultimate Medical Academy Tampa, 9309 N. Florida Avenue, Suite 100, Tampa, FL 33612. *Toll-free phone:* 888-205-2510. *Website:* http://www.ultimatemedical.edu/.

Virginia College in Jacksonville
Jacksonville, Florida

Admissions Office Contact Virginia College in Jacksonville, 5940 Beach Boulevard, Jacksonville, FL 32207. *Website:* http://www.vc.edu/.

Virginia College in Pensacola
Pensacola, Florida

Admissions Office Contact Virginia College in Pensacola, 19 West Garden Street, Pensacola, FL 32502. *Website:* http://www.vc.edu/.

WyoTech Daytona
Ormond Beach, Florida

Admissions Office Contact WyoTech Daytona, 470 Destination Daytona Lane, Ormond Beach, FL 32174. *Toll-free phone:* 800-881-2AMI. *Website:* http://www.wyotech.edu/.

GEORGIA

Albany Technical College
Albany, Georgia

- **State-supported** 2-year, founded 1961, part of Technical College System of Georgia
- **Coed**

Undergraduates 2,091 full-time, 1,803 part-time. 0.4% are from out of state; 125% Black or African American, non-Hispanic/Latino; 2% Hispanic/Latino; 0.4% Asian, non-Hispanic/Latino; 0.4% Native Hawaiian or other Pacific Islander, non-Hispanic/Latino; 1% Two or more races, non-Hispanic/Latino. *Retention:* 55% of full-time freshmen returned.
Academics *Calendar:* quarters. *Degree:* certificates, diplomas, and associate. *Special study options:* distance learning.
Applying *Options:* early admission. *Application fee:* $23. *Required:* high school transcript.
Freshman Application Contact Albany Technical College, 1704 South Slappey Boulevard, Albany, GA 31701. *Phone:* 229-430-3520. *Toll-free phone:* 877-261-3113. *Website:* http://www.albanytech.edu/.

Andrew College
Cuthbert, Georgia

Freshman Application Contact Ms. Bridget Kurkowski, Director of Admission, Andrew College, 413 College Street, Cuthbert, GA 39840. *Phone:* 229-732-5986. *Toll-free phone:* 800-664-9250. *Fax:* 229-732-2176. *E-mail:* admissions@andrewcollege.edu. *Website:* http://www.andrewcollege.edu/.

Athens Technical College
Athens, Georgia

- **State-supported** 2-year, founded 1958, part of Technical College System of Georgia
- **Suburban** campus
- **Coed**

Undergraduates 1,281 full-time, 3,282 part-time. 0.3% are from out of state; 22% Black or African American, non-Hispanic/Latino; 5% Hispanic/Latino; 1% Asian, non-Hispanic/Latino; 0.2% Native Hawaiian or other Pacific Islander, non-Hispanic/Latino; 0.1% American Indian or Alaska Native, non-Hispanic/Latino; 1% Two or more races, non-Hispanic/Latino; 8% Race/ethnicity unknown; 0.6% international. *Retention:* 59% of full-time freshmen returned.
Academics *Calendar:* quarters. *Degree:* certificates, diplomas, and associate. *Special study options:* distance learning.
Financial Aid Of all full-time matriculated undergraduates who enrolled in 2013, 34 Federal Work-Study jobs (averaging $3090).
Applying *Options:* early admission. *Application fee:* $20. *Required:* high school transcript.
Freshman Application Contact Athens Technical College, 800 US Highway 29 North, Athens, GA 30601-1500. *Phone:* 706-355-5008. *Website:* http://www.athenstech.edu/.

Atlanta Metropolitan State College
Atlanta, Georgia

Freshman Application Contact Ms. Audrey Reid, Director, Office of Admissions, Atlanta Metropolitan State College, 1630 Metropolitan Parkway, SW, Atlanta, GA 30310-4498. *Phone:* 404-756-4004. *Fax:* 404-756-4407. *E-mail:* admissions@atlm.edu. *Website:* http://www.atlm.edu/.

Atlanta Technical College
Atlanta, Georgia

- **State-supported** 2-year, founded 1945, part of Technical College System of Georgia
- **Coed**

Undergraduates 1,763 full-time, 3,096 part-time. 0.6% are from out of state; 90% Black or African American, non-Hispanic/Latino; 2% Hispanic/Latino; 4% Asian, non-Hispanic/Latino; 0.1% Native Hawaiian or other Pacific Islander, non-Hispanic/Latino; 0.4% American Indian or Alaska Native, non-Hispanic/Latino; 1% Two or more races, non-Hispanic/Latino; 0.1% Race/ethnicity unknown *Retention:* 54% of full-time freshmen returned.

Academics *Calendar:* quarters. *Degree:* certificates, diplomas, and associate. *Special study options:* distance learning, study abroad.
Applying *Options:* early admission. *Application fee:* $20. *Required:* high school transcript.
Freshman Application Contact Atlanta Technical College, 1560 Metropolitan Parkway, SW, Atlanta, GA 30310. *Phone:* 404-225-4455. *Website:* http://www.atlantatech.edu/.

Augusta Technical College
Augusta, Georgia

- **State-supported** 2-year, founded 1961, part of Technical College System of Georgia
- **Urban** campus
- **Coed**

Undergraduates 1,762 full-time, 2,617 part-time. 5% are from out of state; 45% Black or African American, non-Hispanic/Latino; 3% Hispanic/Latino; 0.6% Asian, non-Hispanic/Latino; 0.1% Native Hawaiian or other Pacific Islander, non-Hispanic/Latino; 0.4% American Indian or Alaska Native, non-Hispanic/Latino; 3% Two or more races, non-Hispanic/Latino; 4% Race/ethnicity unknown; 0.1% international. *Retention:* 56% of full-time freshmen returned.
Academics *Calendar:* quarters. *Degree:* certificates, diplomas, and associate. *Special study options:* distance learning.
Applying *Options:* early admission. *Application fee:* $20. *Required:* high school transcript.
Freshman Application Contact Augusta Technical College, 3200 Augusta Tech Drive, Augusta, GA 30906. *Phone:* 706-771-4150. *Website:* http://www.augustatech.edu/.

Bainbridge State College
Bainbridge, Georgia

- **State-supported** 2-year, founded 1972, part of University System of Georgia
- **Small-town** 160-acre campus
- **Coed**, 2,470 undergraduate students, 38% full-time, 71% women, 29% men

Undergraduates 929 full-time, 1,541 part-time. Students come from 3 states and territories; 3% are from out of state; 51% Black or African American, non-Hispanic/Latino; 3% Hispanic/Latino; 0.2% Asian, non-Hispanic/Latino; 0.1% Native Hawaiian or other Pacific Islander, non-Hispanic/Latino; 0.2% American Indian or Alaska Native, non-Hispanic/Latino; 1% Two or more races, non-Hispanic/Latino; 1% Race/ethnicity unknown.
Freshmen *Admission:* 951 applied, 566 admitted.
Faculty *Total:* 123, 52% full-time, 25% with terminal degrees.
Majors Accounting; administrative assistant and secretarial science; agriculture; art; biology/biological sciences; business administration and management; business teacher education; chemistry; criminal justice/law enforcement administration; data processing and data processing technology; drafting and design technology; dramatic/theater arts; education; electrical, electronic and communications engineering technology; elementary education; English; family and consumer sciences/human sciences; forestry; health teacher education; history; information science/studies; journalism; kindergarten/preschool education; liberal arts and sciences/liberal studies; licensed practical/vocational nurse training; marketing/marketing management; mathematics; political science and government; psychology; registered nursing/registered nurse; rhetoric and composition; sociology; welding technology.
Academics *Calendar:* semesters. *Degree:* certificates and associate. *Special study options:* academic remediation for entering students, advanced placement credit, distance learning, double majors, honors programs, independent study, part-time degree program, services for LD students, study abroad, summer session for credit.
Library Bainbridge State College Library with 47,037 titles, 4,207 audiovisual materials, an OPAC.
Student Life *Housing:* college housing not available. *Activities and Organizations:* choral group, Canoe Club, BANS, LPN Club, Honors, Student Government Association. *Campus security:* 24-hour patrols. *Student services:* personal/psychological counseling.
Athletics *Intramural sports:* table tennis M/W, volleyball M/W.
Standardized Tests *Required for some:* SAT or ACT (for admission), ACT Compass.
Costs (2014–15) *Tuition:* state resident $2128 full-time, $89 per credit hour part-time; nonresident $8054 full-time, $336 per credit hour part-time. Full-time tuition and fees vary according to course load and program. Part-time tuition and fees vary according to course load and program. *Required fees:* $1046 full-time, $523 per term part-time. *Waivers:* senior citizens and employees or children of employees.

Applying *Options:* electronic application, early admission. *Required for some:* high school transcript, minimum 1.8 GPA, 3 letters of recommendation, interview, immunizations/waivers, medical records and criminal background. *Application deadlines:* rolling (freshmen), rolling (transfers). *Notification:* continuous (freshmen), continuous (transfers).
Freshman Application Contact Ms. Melanie Cleveland, Director of Admission, Bainbridge State College, 2500 East Shotwell Street, Bainbridge, GA 39819. *Phone:* 229-243-6922. *Toll-free phone:* 866-825-1715 (in-state); 888-825-1715 (out-of-state). *Fax:* 229-248-2525. *E-mail:* melanie.cleveland@bainbridge.edu.
Website: http://www.bainbridge.edu/.

Brown College of Court Reporting
Atlanta, Georgia

Admissions Office Contact Brown College of Court Reporting, 1900 Emery Street NW, Suite 200, Atlanta, GA 30318.
Website: http://www.bccr.edu/.

Brown Mackie College–Atlanta
Atlanta, Georgia

- **Proprietary** 2-year, part of Education Management Corporation
- **Urban** campus
- **Coed**

Academics *Degree:* certificates and associate.
Freshman Application Contact Brown Mackie College–Atlanta, 4370 Peachtree Road, NE, Atlanta, GA 30319. *Phone:* 404-799-4500. *Website:* http://www.brownmackie.edu/atlanta/.

Central Georgia Technical College
Warner Robins, Georgia

- **State-supported** 2-year, founded 1966, part of Technical College System of Georgia
- **Suburban** campus
- **Coed**

Undergraduates 3,191 full-time, 4,605 part-time. 2% are from out of state; 53% Black or African American, non-Hispanic/Latino; 2% Hispanic/Latino; 0.8% Asian, non-Hispanic/Latino; 0.3% American Indian or Alaska Native, non-Hispanic/Latino; 1% Two or more races, non-Hispanic/Latino; 1% Race/ethnicity unknown; 0.1% international.
Academics *Calendar:* quarters. *Degree:* certificates, diplomas, and associate. *Special study options:* distance learning.
Financial Aid Of all full-time matriculated undergraduates who enrolled in 2013, 175 Federal Work-Study jobs (averaging $2000). *Financial aid deadline:* 9/1.
Applying *Options:* early admission. *Application fee:* $15. *Required:* high school transcript.
Freshman Application Contact Central Georgia Technical College, 80 Cohen Walker Drive, Warner Robins, GA 31088. *Phone:* 770-531-6332. *Toll-free phone:* 866-430-0135.
Website: http://www.centralgatech.edu/.

Chattahoochee Technical College
Marietta, Georgia

- **State-supported** 2-year, founded 1961, part of Technical College System of Georgia
- **Suburban** campus
- **Coed**

Undergraduates 3,434 full-time, 7,036 part-time. 0.2% are from out of state; 29% Black or African American, non-Hispanic/Latino; 10% Hispanic/Latino; 1% Asian, non-Hispanic/Latino; 0.2% Native Hawaiian or other Pacific Islander, non-Hispanic/Latino; 0.8% American Indian or Alaska Native, non-Hispanic/Latino; 2% Two or more races, non-Hispanic/Latino; 0.6% Race/ethnicity unknown; 0.7% international. *Retention:* 50% of full-time freshmen returned.
Academics *Calendar:* quarters. *Degree:* certificates, diplomas, and associate. *Special study options:* distance learning.
Financial Aid Of all full-time matriculated undergraduates who enrolled in 2013, 40 Federal Work-Study jobs (averaging $2500).
Applying *Options:* early admission. *Application fee:* $15. *Required:* high school transcript.
Freshman Application Contact Chattahoochee Technical College, 980 South Cobb Drive, SE, Marietta, GA 30060. *Phone:* 770-757-3408. *Website:* http://www.chattahoocheetech.edu/.

Coastal Pines Technical College
Waycross, Georgia

- **State-supported** 2-year, part of Technical College System of Georgia
- **Small-town** campus
- **Coed**

Undergraduates 382 full-time, 798 part-time. 21% Black or African American, non-Hispanic/Latino; 2% Hispanic/Latino; 0.6% Asian, non-Hispanic/Latino; 0.1% Native Hawaiian or other Pacific Islander, non-Hispanic/Latino; 0.8% American Indian or Alaska Native, non-Hispanic/Latino; 1% Two or more races, non-Hispanic/Latino; 0.2% Race/ethnicity unknown; 0.5% international. *Retention:* 51% of full-time freshmen returned.

Academics *Calendar:* quarters. *Degree:* certificates, diplomas, and associate. *Special study options:* distance learning.

Applying *Options:* early admission. *Application fee:* $20. *Required:* high school transcript.

Freshman Application Contact Coastal Pines Technical College, 1701 Carswell Avenue, Waycross, GA 31503. *Phone:* 912-338-5251. *Toll-free phone:* 877-ED-AT-OTC.
Website: http://www.coastalpines.edu/.

Columbus Technical College
Columbus, Georgia

- **State-supported** 2-year, founded 1961, part of Technical College System of Georgia
- **Urban** campus
- **Coed**

Undergraduates 1,426 full-time, 2,313 part-time. 15% are from out of state; 53% Black or African American, non-Hispanic/Latino; 4% Hispanic/Latino; 0.6% Asian, non-Hispanic/Latino; 0.4% Native Hawaiian or other Pacific Islander, non-Hispanic/Latino; 0.9% American Indian or Alaska Native, non-Hispanic/Latino; 2% Two or more races, non-Hispanic/Latino; 1% Race/ethnicity unknown; 0.1% international. *Retention:* 46% of full-time freshmen returned.

Academics *Calendar:* quarters. *Degree:* certificates, diplomas, and associate. *Special study options:* distance learning.

Financial Aid Of all full-time matriculated undergraduates who enrolled in 2013, 6 Federal Work-Study jobs (averaging $2000).

Applying *Options:* early admission. *Application fee:* $25. *Required:* high school transcript.

Freshman Application Contact Columbus Technical College, 928 Manchester Expressway, Columbus, GA 31904-6572. *Phone:* 706-649-1901.
Website: http://www.columbustech.edu/.

Darton State College
Albany, Georgia

- **State-supported** primarily 2-year, founded 1965, part of University System of Georgia
- **Urban** 185-acre campus
- **Endowment** $1.9 million
- **Coed,** 5,620 undergraduate students, 46% full-time, 71% women, 29% men

Undergraduates 2,577 full-time, 3,043 part-time. Students come from 29 states and territories; 6 other countries; 3% are from out of state; 45% Black or African American, non-Hispanic/Latino; 3% Hispanic/Latino; 1% Asian, non-Hispanic/Latino; 0.1% Native Hawaiian or other Pacific Islander, non-Hispanic/Latino; 0.3% American Indian or Alaska Native, non-Hispanic/Latino; 0.8% Two or more races, non-Hispanic/Latino; 0.5% Race/ethnicity unknown; 0.1% international; 12% transferred in. *Retention:* 40% of full-time freshmen returned.

Freshmen *Admission:* 1,825 applied, 878 admitted, 886 enrolled. *Average high school GPA:* 2.08. *Test scores:* SAT critical reading scores over 500: 29%; SAT math scores over 500: 23%; SAT writing scores over 500: 18%; ACT scores over 18: 41%; SAT critical reading scores over 600: 5%; SAT math scores over 600: 3%; SAT writing scores over 600: 3%; ACT scores over 24: 9%; SAT critical reading scores over 700: 1%.

Faculty *Total:* 265, 50% full-time. *Student/faculty ratio:* 25:1.

Majors Accounting; agriculture; anthropology; art; art teacher education; behavioral aspects of health; biological and biomedical sciences related; biology/biological sciences; business administration and management; business teacher education; cardiovascular technology; chemistry; clinical laboratory science/medical technology; computer and information sciences; computer and information sciences and support services related; computer science; criminal justice/law enforcement administration; dance; dental hygiene; diagnostic medical sonography and ultrasound technology; drama and dance teacher education; dramatic/theater arts; economics; emergency medical technology (EMT paramedic); engineering technology; English; English/language arts teacher education; environmental studies; foreign languages and literatures; forensic science and technology; forestry; general studies; geography; health and physical education/fitness; health information/medical records administration; health information/medical records technology; health/medical preparatory programs related; histologic technician; history; history teacher education; journalism; mathematics; mathematics teacher education; middle school education; music; music teacher education; nuclear medical technology; occupational therapist assistant; philosophy; physical therapy technology; physics; political science and government; pre-dentistry studies; pre-engineering; pre-law studies; premedical studies; pre-pharmacy studies; pre-veterinary studies; psychology; registered nursing/registered nurse; respiratory care therapy; science teacher education; social work; sociology; special education; speech teacher education; trade and industrial teacher education.

Academics *Calendar:* semesters. *Degrees:* certificates, associate, bachelor's, and postbachelor's certificates. *Special study options:* academic remediation for entering students, accelerated degree program, adult/continuing education programs, advanced placement credit, cooperative education, distance learning, double majors, English as a second language, honors programs, independent study, off-campus study, part-time degree program, services for LD students, summer session for credit. *ROTC:* Army (c).

Library Weatherbee Learning Resources Center with 115,731 titles, 5,182 audiovisual materials, an OPAC, a Web page.

Student Life *Housing Options:* coed. Campus housing is provided by a third party. *Activities and Organizations:* drama/theater group, choral group, Cultural Exchange Club, Democratic, Independent, & Republican Team (D.I.R.T.), Human Services Club, Outdoor Adventure Club (OAC), Music Club. *Campus security:* 24-hour emergency response devices and patrols, student patrols, late-night transport/escort service, controlled dormitory access. *Student services:* health clinic, personal/psychological counseling.

Athletics Member NJCAA. *Intercollegiate sports:* baseball M(s), basketball W(s), cross-country running M(s)/W(s), golf M(s), soccer M(s)/W(s), softball W(s), swimming and diving M(s)/W(s), wrestling M. *Intramural sports:* badminton M/W, basketball M/W, bowling M/W, football M, racquetball M/W, table tennis M, volleyball M/W.

Standardized Tests *Required:* non-traditional students must take the ACT Compass test (for admission). *Required for some:* SAT or ACT (for admission), SAT Subject Tests (for admission). *Recommended:* SAT or ACT (for admission), SAT Subject Tests (for admission).

Costs (2014–15) *Tuition:* state resident $2660 full-time, $89 per credit hour part-time; nonresident $9822 full-time, $335 per credit hour part-time. *Required fees:* $992 full-time, $587 per term part-time. *Room and board:* $9340. Room and board charges vary according to board plan and housing facility. *Waivers:* senior citizens and employees or children of employees.

Applying *Options:* electronic application, deferred entrance. *Application fee:* $20. *Required:* minimum 2.0 GPA, proof of immunization. *Required for some:* high school transcript. *Application deadlines:* 8/1 (freshmen), 8/1 (transfers). *Notification:* continuous until 8/8 (freshmen), continuous until 8/8 (transfers).

Freshman Application Contact Darton State College, 2400 Gillionville Road, Albany, GA 31707-3098. *Phone:* 229-430-6740. *Toll-free phone:* 866-775-1214.
Website: http://www.darton.edu/.

East Georgia State College
Swainsboro, Georgia

Freshman Application Contact East Georgia State College, 131 College Circle, Swainsboro, GA 30401-2699. *Phone:* 478-289-2017.
Website: http://www.ega.edu/.

Emory University, Oxford College
Oxford, Georgia

Freshman Application Contact Emory University, Oxford College, 100 Hamill Street, PO Box 1328, Oxford, GA 30054. *Phone:* 770-784-8328. *Toll-free phone:* 800-723-8328.
Website: http://oxford.emory.edu/.

Everest Institute
Norcross, Georgia

Admissions Office Contact Everest Institute, 1750 Beaver Ruin Road, Norcross, GA 30093.
Website: http://www.everest.edu/.

Fortis College
Smyrna, Georgia

Admissions Office Contact Fortis College, 2108 Cobb Parkway SE, Smyrna, GA 30080.
Website: http://www.fortis.edu/.

Georgia Highlands College
Rome, Georgia

- **State-supported** primarily 2-year, founded 1970, part of University System of Georgia
- **Suburban** 226-acre campus with easy access to Atlanta
- **Endowment** $33,299
- **Coed,** 5,359 undergraduate students, 49% full-time, 62% women, 38% men

Undergraduates 2,604 full-time, 2,755 part-time. Students come from 16 states and territories; 18 other countries; 1% are from out of state; 17% Black or African American, non-Hispanic/Latino; 9% Hispanic/Latino; 1% Asian, non-Hispanic/Latino; 0.1% Native Hawaiian or other Pacific Islander, non-Hispanic/Latino; 0.2% American Indian or Alaska Native, non-Hispanic/Latino; 3% Two or more races, non-Hispanic/Latino; 0.8% Race/ethnicity unknown; 7% transferred in. *Retention:* 64% of full-time freshmen returned.

Freshmen *Admission:* 1,107 enrolled. *Average high school GPA:* 2.9. *Test scores:* SAT critical reading scores over 500: 34%; SAT math scores over 500: 28%; SAT writing scores over 500: 20%; ACT scores over 18: 71%; SAT critical reading scores over 600: 5%; SAT math scores over 600: 3%; SAT writing scores over 600: 1%; ACT scores over 24: 9%.

Faculty *Total:* 263, 47% full-time, 18% with terminal degrees. *Student/faculty ratio:* 21:1.

Majors Agriculture; art; biological and physical sciences; business administration and management; chemistry; clinical laboratory science/medical technology; communication and journalism related; computer and information sciences; criminal justice/police science; criminal justice/safety; dental hygiene; economics; education related; English; foreign languages and literatures; general studies; geology/earth science; health information/medical records administration; history; human services; journalism; liberal arts and sciences/liberal studies; mathematics and statistics related; music; music management; philosophy; physician assistant; physics; political science and government; pre-pharmacy studies; pre-physical therapy; psychology; registered nursing/registered nurse; respiratory therapy technician; secondary education; sociology.

Academics *Calendar:* semesters. *Degrees:* associate and bachelor's. *Special study options:* academic remediation for entering students, advanced placement credit, cooperative education, distance learning, double majors, honors programs, independent study, part-time degree program, services for LD students, study abroad, summer session for credit.

Library Georgia Highlands College Library - Floyd Campus plus 3 others with 63,746 titles, 18,244 audiovisual materials, an OPAC, a Web page.

Student Life *Housing:* college housing not available. *Activities and Organizations:* student-run newspaper, Highlands Association of Nursing Students, Green Highlands, Black Awareness Society, Political Science Association, Phi Theta Kappa. *Campus security:* 24-hour emergency response devices and patrols, emergency phone/email alert system. *Student services:* personal/psychological counseling.

Athletics Member NJCAA. *Intercollegiate sports:* baseball M(s)/W(s), basketball M(s)/W(s), softball M(s)/W(s). *Intramural sports:* basketball M/W, cheerleading M/W, football M/W, golf M/W, skiing (downhill) M/W, table tennis M/W, tennis M/W, ultimate Frisbee M/W, volleyball M/W, weight lifting M/W.

Standardized Tests *Required:* COMPASS (for admission). *Recommended:* SAT or ACT (for admission), SAT and SAT Subject Tests or ACT (for admission).

Costs (2014–15) *Tuition:* state resident $2128 full-time, $89 per hour part-time; nonresident $8054 full-time, $336 per hour part-time. Full-time tuition and fees vary according to course load. Part-time tuition and fees vary according to course load. *Required fees:* $934 full-time, $467 per term part-time. *Waivers:* senior citizens and employees or children of employees.

Financial Aid Of all full-time matriculated undergraduates who enrolled in 2013, 50 Federal Work-Study jobs (averaging $3500).

Applying *Options:* electronic application, deferred entrance. *Application fee:* $30. *Required:* high school transcript, minimum 2.0 GPA. *Required for some:* Additional requirements for Nursing. *Application deadlines:* rolling (freshmen), rolling (out-of-state freshmen), rolling (transfers). *Notification:* continuous (freshmen), continuous (out-of-state freshmen), continuous (transfers).

Freshman Application Contact Sandie Davis, Director of Admissions, Georgia Highlands College, 3175 Cedartown Highway, Rome, GA 30161.

Phone: 706-295-6339. *Toll-free phone:* 800-332-2406. *Fax:* 706-295-6341.
E-mail: sdavis@highlands.edu.
Website: http://www.highlands.edu/.

Georgia Military College
Milledgeville, Georgia

- **State and locally supported** 2-year, founded 1879, part of Georgia Independent College Association (GICA)
- **Small-town** campus
- **Endowment** $12.8 million
- **Coed**

Undergraduates 3,788 full-time, 3,281 part-time. Students come from 18 states and territories; 11 other countries; 1% are from out of state; 40% Black or African American, non-Hispanic/Latino; 0.4% Hispanic/Latino; 2% Asian, non-Hispanic/Latino; 1% American Indian or Alaska Native, non-Hispanic/Latino; 16% Race/ethnicity unknown; 0.2% international; 12% transferred in; 4% live on campus. *Retention:* 46% of full-time freshmen returned.

Faculty *Student/faculty ratio:* 15:1.

Academics *Calendar:* quarters. *Degree:* associate. *Special study options:* academic remediation for entering students, advanced placement credit, cooperative education, distance learning, double majors, off-campus study, part-time degree program, services for LD students, student-designed majors, study abroad, summer session for credit. *ROTC:* Army (b).

Student Life *Campus security:* 24-hour emergency response devices and patrols, controlled dormitory access.

Athletics Member NJCAA.

Costs (2014–15) *Tuition:* state resident $2928 full-time, $122 per credit hour part-time; nonresident $2928 full-time, $122 per credit hour part-time. Full-time tuition and fees vary according to course load and location. Part-time tuition and fees vary according to course load and location. *Required fees:* $668 full-time, $26 per credit hour part-time, $25 per term part-time. *Room and board:* $7050. Room and board charges vary according to location.

Financial Aid Of all full-time matriculated undergraduates who enrolled in 2012, 6,554 applied for aid, 6,132 were judged to have need, 282 had their need fully met. 121 Federal Work-Study jobs (averaging $1614). In 2012, 61. *Average percent of need met:* 47. *Average financial aid package:* $9567. *Average need-based loan:* $3189. *Average need-based gift aid:* $4626. *Average non-need-based aid:* $2226.

Applying *Options:* electronic application, early admission, deferred entrance. *Application fee:* $35. *Required for some:* essay or personal statement, high school transcript, interview.

Freshman Application Contact Georgia Military College, 201 East Greene Street, Old Capitol Building, Milledgeville, GA 31061-3398. *Phone:* 478-387-4948. *Toll-free phone:* 800-342-0413.
Website: http://www.gmc.cc.ga.us/.

Georgia Northwestern Technical College
Rome, Georgia

- **State-supported** 2-year, founded 1962, part of Technical College System of Georgia
- **Coed**

Undergraduates 2,135 full-time, 3,916 part-time. 0.5% are from out of state; 10% Black or African American, non-Hispanic/Latino; 8% Hispanic/Latino; 0.6% Asian, non-Hispanic/Latino; 0.0% Native Hawaiian or other Pacific Islander, non-Hispanic/Latino; 0.3% American Indian or Alaska Native, non-Hispanic/Latino; 2% Two or more races, non-Hispanic/Latino; 0.1% international. *Retention:* 51% of full-time freshmen returned.

Academics *Calendar:* quarters. *Degree:* certificates, diplomas, and associate. *Special study options:* distance learning.

Applying *Options:* early admission. *Application fee:* $15. *Required:* high school transcript.

Freshman Application Contact Georgia Northwestern Technical College, One Maurice Culberson Drive, Rome, GA 30161. *Phone:* 706-295-6933. *Toll-free phone:* 866-983-GNTC.
Website: http://www.gntc.edu/.

Georgia Perimeter College
Decatur, Georgia

Freshman Application Contact Georgia Perimeter College, 3251 Panthersville Road, Decatur, GA 30034-3897. *Phone:* 678-891-3250. *Toll-free phone:* 888-696-2780.
Website: http://www.gpc.edu/.

Georgia Piedmont Technical College
Clarkston, Georgia

- **State-supported** 2-year, founded 1961, part of Technical College System of Georgia
- **Suburban** campus
- **Coed**

Undergraduates 1,470 full-time, 2,961 part-time. 79% Black or African American, non-Hispanic/Latino; 2% Hispanic/Latino; 2% Asian, non-Hispanic/Latino; 0.2% Native Hawaiian or other Pacific Islander, non-Hispanic/Latino; 0.3% American Indian or Alaska Native, non-Hispanic/Latino; 2% Two or more races, non-Hispanic/Latino; 0.5% Race/ethnicity unknown; 2% international. *Retention:* 55% of full-time freshmen returned.

Academics *Calendar:* quarters. *Degree:* certificates, diplomas, and associate. *Special study options:* distance learning.

Financial Aid Of all full-time matriculated undergraduates who enrolled in 2010, 7,200 applied for aid, 7,100 were judged to have need. 145 Federal Work-Study jobs (averaging $4000). *Average financial aid package:* $4500. *Average need-based gift aid:* $4500.

Applying *Options:* early admission. *Application fee:* $25. *Required:* high school transcript.

Freshman Application Contact Georgia Piedmont Technical College, 495 North Indian Creek Drive, Clarkston, GA 30021-2397. *Phone:* 404-297-9522 Ext. 1229.
Website: http://www.gptc.edu/.

Gordon State College
Barnesville, Georgia

- **State-supported** primarily 2-year, founded 1852, part of University System of Georgia
- **Small-town** 125-acre campus with easy access to Atlanta
- **Endowment** $7.8 million
- **Coed**

Undergraduates Students come from 9 states and territories; 1 other country; 0.1% are from out of state.

Faculty *Student/faculty ratio:* 23:1.

Academics *Calendar:* semesters. *Degrees:* certificates, associate, and bachelor's. *Special study options:* academic remediation for entering students, accelerated degree program, adult/continuing education programs, advanced placement credit, cooperative education, honors programs, internships, off-campus study, part-time degree program, study abroad, summer session for credit.

Student Life *Campus security:* 24-hour emergency response devices and patrols, student patrols, late-night transport/escort service, controlled dormitory access, RA's and RDs (housing) and Parking Patrol (Public Safety).

Athletics Member NJCAA.

Standardized Tests *Required for some:* SAT and SAT Subject Tests or ACT (for admission).

Costs (2014–15) *Tuition:* state resident $3073 full-time; nonresident $9207 full-time. *Required fees:* $1074 full-time. *Room and board:* $9772; room only: $4410.

Financial Aid Of all full-time matriculated undergraduates who enrolled in 2013, 75 Federal Work-Study jobs (averaging $1850).

Applying *Options:* electronic application, early admission, deferred entrance. *Application fee:* $30. *Required:* high school transcript.

Freshman Application Contact Gordon State College, 419 College Drive, Barnesville, GA 30204-1762. *Phone:* 678-359-5021. *Toll-free phone:* 800-282-6504.
Website: http://www.gordonstate.edu/.

Gupton-Jones College of Funeral Service
Decatur, Georgia

- **Independent** 2-year, founded 1920, part of Pierce Mortuary Colleges, Inc.
- **Suburban** 3-acre campus with easy access to Atlanta
- **Coed,** 149 undergraduate students

Majors Mortuary science and embalming.

Academics *Calendar:* quarters. *Degree:* associate. *Special study options:* distance learning, summer session for credit.

Library Russell Millison Library with 3,500 titles, an OPAC.

Student Life *Housing:* college housing not available. *Activities and Organizations:* national fraternities.

Applying *Options:* electronic application. *Application fee:* $50. *Required:* high school transcript, health certificate. *Recommended:* minimum 3.0 GPA. *Application deadline:* rolling (freshmen).

Freshman Application Contact Ms. Felicia Smith, Registrar, Gupton-Jones College of Funeral Service, 5141 Snapfinger Woods Drive, Decatur, GA 30035-4022. *Phone:* 770-593-2257. *Toll-free phone:* 800-848-5352.
Website: http://www.gupton-jones.edu/.

Gwinnett College
Lilburn, Georgia

Admissions Office Contact Gwinnett College, 4230 Highway 29, Suite 11, Lilburn, GA 30047.
Website: http://www.gwinnettcollege.edu/.

Gwinnett Technical College
Lawrenceville, Georgia

- **State-supported** 2-year, founded 1984, part of Technical College System of Georgia
- **Suburban** 88-acre campus
- **Coed,** 7,180 undergraduate students, 32% full-time, 61% women, 39% men

Undergraduates 2,282 full-time, 4,898 part-time. 0.6% are from out of state; 34% Black or African American, non-Hispanic/Latino; 12% Hispanic/Latino; 7% Asian, non-Hispanic/Latino; 0.1% Native Hawaiian or other Pacific Islander, non-Hispanic/Latino; 0.2% American Indian or Alaska Native, non-Hispanic/Latino; 2% Two or more races, non-Hispanic/Latino; 6% Race/ethnicity unknown; 0.4% international. *Retention:* 55% of full-time freshmen returned.

Freshmen *Admission:* 1,021 enrolled.

Faculty *Total:* 404, 25% full-time. *Student/faculty ratio:* 25:1.

Majors Accounting; administrative assistant and secretarial science; automobile/automotive mechanics technology; building/construction finishing, management, and inspection related; business administration and management; computer programming; computer science; computer systems networking and telecommunications; drafting and design technology; electrical, electronic and communications engineering technology; emergency medical technology (EMT paramedic); horticultural science; hotel/motel administration; information science/studies; interior design; machine tool technology; management information systems; marketing/marketing management; medical/clinical assistant; medical radiologic technology; ornamental horticulture; photography; physical therapy; physical therapy technology; respiratory care therapy; tourism and travel services management; veterinary/animal health technology.

Academics *Calendar:* semesters. *Degree:* certificates, diplomas, and associate. *Special study options:* distance learning, English as a second language, part-time degree program, services for LD students, summer session for credit.

Library Gwinnett Technical College Library plus 1 other with 15,195 titles, 1,846 audiovisual materials, an OPAC, a Web page.

Student Life *Housing:* college housing not available. *Campus security:* 24-hour emergency response devices and patrols. *Student services:* personal/psychological counseling.

Costs (2014–15) *Tuition:* state resident $2040 full-time; nonresident $4080 full-time. Full-time tuition and fees vary according to course load and program. Part-time tuition and fees vary according to course load and program. *Required fees:* $660 full-time. *Payment plans:* tuition prepayment, installment.

Financial Aid Of all full-time matriculated undergraduates who enrolled in 2013, 20 Federal Work-Study jobs (averaging $2100).

Applying *Options:* electronic application, early admission. *Application fee:* $20. *Required:* high school transcript.

Freshman Application Contact Gwinnett Technical College, 5150 Sugarloaf Parkway, Lawrenceville, GA 30043-5702. *Phone:* 678-762-7580 Ext. 434.
Website: http://www.gwinnetttech.edu/.

Interactive College of Technology
Chamblee, Georgia

Freshman Application Contact Director of Admissions, Interactive College of Technology, 5303 New Peachtree Road, Chamblee, GA 30341. *Phone:* 770-216-2960. *Toll-free phone:* 800-447-2011. *Fax:* 770-216-2988.
Website: http://ict.edu/.

Interactive College of Technology
Gainesville, Georgia

Admissions Office Contact Interactive College of Technology, 2323-C Browns Bridge Road, Gainesville, GA 30504.
Website: http://ict.edu/.

ITT Technical Institute
Atlanta, Georgia

- **Proprietary** primarily 2-year, part of ITT Educational Services, Inc.
- **Coed**

Academics *Degrees:* associate and bachelor's.
Freshman Application Contact Director of Recruitment, ITT Technical Institute, 485 Oak Place, Suite 800, Atlanta, GA 30349. *Phone:* 404-765-4600. *Toll-free phone:* 877-488-6102 (in-state); 877-788-6102 (out-of-state). *Website:* http://www.itt-tech.edu/.

ITT Technical Institute
Duluth, Georgia

- **Proprietary** primarily 2-year, founded 2003, part of ITT Educational Services, Inc.
- **Coed**

Academics *Calendar:* quarters. *Degrees:* associate and bachelor's.
Freshman Application Contact Director of Recruitment, ITT Technical Institute, 10700 Abbotts Bridge Road, Duluth, GA 30097. *Phone:* 678-957-8510. *Toll-free phone:* 866-489-8818.
Website: http://www.itt-tech.edu/.

ITT Technical Institute
Kennesaw, Georgia

- **Proprietary** primarily 2-year, founded 2004, part of ITT Educational Services, Inc.
- **Coed**

Academics *Calendar:* quarters. *Degrees:* associate and bachelor's.
Freshman Application Contact Director of Recruitment, ITT Technical Institute, 2065 ITT Tech Way NW, Kennesaw, GA 30144. *Phone:* 770-426-2300. *Toll-free phone:* 877-231-6415 (in-state); 800-231-6415 (out-of-state). *Website:* http://www.itt-tech.edu/.

Lanier Technical College
Oakwood, Georgia

- **State-supported** 2-year, founded 1964, part of Technical College System of Georgia
- **Coed**

Undergraduates 1,042 full-time, 2,537 part-time. 0.1% are from out of state; 10% Black or African American, non-Hispanic/Latino; 11% Hispanic/Latino; 2% Asian, non-Hispanic/Latino; 0.2% Native Hawaiian or other Pacific Islander, non-Hispanic/Latino; 0.4% American Indian or Alaska Native, non-Hispanic/Latino; 0.7% Two or more races, non-Hispanic/Latino; 0.2% Race/ethnicity unknown; 0.2% international. *Retention:* 62% of full-time freshmen returned.
Academics *Calendar:* quarters. *Degree:* certificates, diplomas, and associate. *Special study options:* distance learning.
Applying *Options:* early admission. *Application fee:* $15. *Required:* high school transcript.
Freshman Application Contact Lanier Technical College, 2990 Landrum Education Drive, PO Box 58, Oakwood, GA 30566. *Phone:* 770-531-6332.
Website: http://www.laniertech.edu/.

Le Cordon Bleu College of Culinary Arts in Atlanta
Tucker, Georgia

Freshman Application Contact Admissions Office, Le Cordon Bleu College of Culinary Arts in Atlanta, 1927 Lakeside Parkway, Tucker, GA 30084. *Toll-free phone:* 888-549-8222.
Website: http://www.chefs.edu/Atlanta/.

Lincoln College of Technology
Marietta, Georgia

Admissions Office Contact Lincoln College of Technology, 2359 Windy Hill Road, SE, Suite 280, Marietta, GA 30067-8645.
Website: http://www.lincolnedu.com/campus/marietta-ga.

Miller-Motte Technical College
Augusta, Georgia

Admissions Office Contact Miller-Motte Technical College, 621 NW Frontage Road, Augusta, GA 30907. *Toll-free phone:* 866-297-0267.
Website: http://www.miller-motte.edu/.

Miller-Motte Technical College
Columbus, Georgia

Admissions Office Contact Miller-Motte Technical College, 1800 Box Road, Columbus, GA 31907.
Website: http://www.miller-motte.edu/.

Miller-Motte Technical College
Macon, Georgia

Admissions Office Contact Miller-Motte Technical College, 175 Tom Hill Sr. Boulevard, Macon, GA 31210. *Toll-free phone:* 866-297-0267.
Website: http://www.miller-motte.edu/.

Moultrie Technical College
Moultrie, Georgia

- **State-supported** 2-year, founded 1964, part of Technical College System of Georgia
- **Coed**

Undergraduates 789 full-time, 1,269 part-time. 35% Black or African American, non-Hispanic/Latino; 6% Hispanic/Latino; 0.1% Asian, non-Hispanic/Latino; 0.1% American Indian or Alaska Native, non-Hispanic/Latino; 0.1% Two or more races, non-Hispanic/Latino; 1% Race/ethnicity unknown; 0.1% international. *Retention:* 55% of full-time freshmen returned.
Academics *Calendar:* quarters. *Degree:* certificates, diplomas, and associate. *Special study options:* distance learning.
Applying *Options:* early admission. *Application fee:* $20. *Required:* high school transcript.
Freshman Application Contact Moultrie Technical College, 800 Veterans Parkway North, Moultrie, GA 31788. *Phone:* 229-528-4581.
Website: http://www.moultrietech.edu/.

North Georgia Technical College
Clarkesville, Georgia

- **State-supported** 2-year, founded 1943, part of Technical College System of Georgia
- **Coed**

Undergraduates 1,027 full-time, 1,414 part-time. 2% are from out of state; 7% Black or African American, non-Hispanic/Latino; 3% Hispanic/Latino; 0.7% Asian, non-Hispanic/Latino; 0.2% American Indian or Alaska Native, non-Hispanic/Latino; 1% Two or more races, non-Hispanic/Latino; 0.5% Race/ethnicity unknown; 0.2% international. *Retention:* 50% of full-time freshmen returned.
Academics *Calendar:* quarters. *Degree:* certificates, diplomas, and associate. *Special study options:* distance learning.
Applying *Options:* early admission. *Application fee:* $15. *Required:* high school transcript.
Freshman Application Contact North Georgia Technical College, 1500 Georgia Highway 197, North, PO Box 65, Clarkesville, GA 30523. *Phone:* 706-754-7724.
Website: http://www.northgatech.edu/.

Oconee Fall Line Technical College
Sandersville, Georgia

- **State-supported** 2-year, part of Technical College System of Georgia
- **Coed**

Undergraduates 554 full-time, 1,315 part-time. 45% Black or African American, non-Hispanic/Latino; 1% Hispanic/Latino; 0.6% Asian, non-Hispanic/Latino; 0.1% Native Hawaiian or other Pacific Islander, non-

Hispanic/Latino; 0.2% American Indian or Alaska Native, non-Hispanic/Latino; 0.8% Two or more races, non-Hispanic/Latino; 0.3% Race/ethnicity unknown; 0.1% international. *Retention:* 44% of full-time freshmen returned.
Academics *Calendar:* quarters. *Degree:* certificates, diplomas, and associate. *Special study options:* distance learning.
Applying *Options:* early admission. *Application fee:* $20. *Required:* high school transcript.
Freshman Application Contact Oconee Fall Line Technical College, 1189 Deepstep Road, Sandersville, GA 31082. *Phone:* 478-553-2050. *Toll-free phone:* 877-399-8324.
Website: http://www.oftc.edu/.

Ogeechee Technical College
Statesboro, Georgia

- **State-supported** 2-year, founded 1989, part of Technical College System of Georgia
- **Small-town** campus
- **Coed**

Undergraduates 854 full-time, 1,362 part-time. 0.9% are from out of state; 40% Black or African American, non-Hispanic/Latino; 2% Hispanic/Latino; 0.8% Asian, non-Hispanic/Latino; 0.2% American Indian or Alaska Native, non-Hispanic/Latino; 1% Two or more races, non-Hispanic/Latino. *Retention:* 60% of full-time freshmen returned.
Academics *Calendar:* quarters. *Degree:* certificates, diplomas, and associate. *Special study options:* distance learning.
Applying *Options:* early admission. *Application fee:* $25. *Required:* high school transcript.
Freshman Application Contact Ogeechee Technical College, One Joe Kennedy Boulevard, Statesboro, GA 30458. *Phone:* 912-871-1600. *Toll-free phone:* 800-646-1316.
Website: http://www.ogeecheetech.edu/.

SAE Institute Atlanta
Atlanta, Georgia

Admissions Office Contact SAE Institute Atlanta, 215 Peachtree Street, Suite 300, Atlanta, GA 30303.
Website: http://atlanta.sae.edu/.

Savannah Technical College
Savannah, Georgia

- **State-supported** 2-year, founded 1929, part of Technical College System of Georgia
- **Urban** campus
- **Coed**

Undergraduates 1,749 full-time, 3,035 part-time. 1% are from out of state; 46% Black or African American, non-Hispanic/Latino; 6% Hispanic/Latino; 2% Asian, non-Hispanic/Latino; 0.2% Native Hawaiian or other Pacific Islander, non-Hispanic/Latino; 0.3% American Indian or Alaska Native, non-Hispanic/Latino; 2% Two or more races, non-Hispanic/Latino; 0.4% Race/ethnicity unknown; 0.6% international. *Retention:* 54% of full-time freshmen returned.
Academics *Calendar:* quarters. *Degree:* certificates, diplomas, and associate. *Special study options:* distance learning.
Applying *Options:* early admission. *Application fee:* $20. *Required:* high school transcript.
Freshman Application Contact Savannah Technical College, 5717 White Bluff Road, Savannah, GA 31405. *Phone:* 912-443-5711. *Toll-free phone:* 800-769-6362.
Website: http://www.savannahtech.edu/.

Southeastern Technical College
Vidalia, Georgia

- **State-supported** 2-year, founded 1989, part of Technical College System of Georgia
- **Coed**

Undergraduates 442 full-time, 1,091 part-time. 0.3% are from out of state; 32% Black or African American, non-Hispanic/Latino; 4% Hispanic/Latino; 0.7% Asian, non-Hispanic/Latino; 0.1% American Indian or Alaska Native, non-Hispanic/Latino; 0.4% Two or more races, non-Hispanic/Latino; 0.1% Race/ethnicity unknown. *Retention:* 60% of full-time freshmen returned.
Academics *Calendar:* quarters. *Degree:* certificates, diplomas, and associate. *Special study options:* distance learning.

Applying *Options:* early admission. *Application fee:* $20. *Required:* high school transcript.
Freshman Application Contact Southeastern Technical College, 3001 East First Street, Vidalia, GA 30474. *Phone:* 912-538-3121.
Website: http://www.southeasterntech.edu/.

Southern Crescent Technical College
Griffin, Georgia

- **State-supported** 2-year, founded 1965, part of Technical College System of Georgia
- **Small-town** campus
- **Coed**

Undergraduates 2,142 full-time, 3,035 part-time. 0.1% are from out of state; 43% Black or African American, non-Hispanic/Latino; 3% Hispanic/Latino; 1% Asian, non-Hispanic/Latino; 0.1% Native Hawaiian or other Pacific Islander, non-Hispanic/Latino; 0.3% American Indian or Alaska Native, non-Hispanic/Latino; 1% Two or more races, non-Hispanic/Latino; 0.5% Race/ethnicity unknown; 0.3% international. *Retention:* 48% of full-time freshmen returned.
Academics *Calendar:* quarters. *Degree:* certificates, diplomas, and associate. *Special study options:* distance learning.
Applying *Options:* early admission. *Application fee:* $15. *Required:* high school transcript.
Freshman Application Contact Southern Crescent Technical College, 501 Varsity Road, Griffin, GA 30223. *Phone:* 770-646-6160.
Website: http://www.sctech.edu/.

South Georgia State College
Douglas, Georgia

- **State-supported** primarily 2-year, founded 1906, part of University System of Georgia
- **Small-town** 340-acre campus
- **Endowment** $286,240
- **Coed**

Undergraduates 1,877 full-time, 702 part-time. Students come from 17 states and territories; 2 other countries; 5% are from out of state; 32% Black or African American, non-Hispanic/Latino; 4% Hispanic/Latino; 0.8% Asian, non-Hispanic/Latino; 0.1% Native Hawaiian or other Pacific Islander, non-Hispanic/Latino; 0.4% American Indian or Alaska Native, non-Hispanic/Latino; 0.7% Two or more races, non-Hispanic/Latino; 0.2% international; 5% transferred in; 13% live on campus.
Faculty *Student/faculty ratio:* 27:1.
Academics *Calendar:* semesters. *Degrees:* associate and bachelor's. *Special study options:* academic remediation for entering students, adult/continuing education programs, advanced placement credit, distance learning, double majors, part-time degree program, services for LD students, study abroad, summer session for credit.
Student Life *Campus security:* 24-hour emergency response devices and patrols, controlled dormitory access.
Athletics Member NJCAA.
Applying *Options:* electronic application, early admission, deferred entrance. *Application fee:* $20. *Required:* high school transcript.
Freshman Application Contact South Georgia State College, 100 West College Park Drive, Douglas, GA 31533-5098. *Phone:* 912-260-4409. *Toll-free phone:* 800-342-6364.
Website: http://www.sgc.edu/.

South Georgia Technical College
Americus, Georgia

- **State-supported** 2-year, founded 1948, part of Technical College System of Georgia
- **Coed**

Undergraduates 976 full-time, 852 part-time. 4% are from out of state; 57% Black or African American, non-Hispanic/Latino; 2% Hispanic/Latino; 0.5% Asian, non-Hispanic/Latino; 0.1% American Indian or Alaska Native, non-Hispanic/Latino; 0.1% Two or more races, non-Hispanic/Latino; 0.3% Race/ethnicity unknown; 0.1% international. *Retention:* 60% of full-time freshmen returned.
Academics *Calendar:* quarters. *Degree:* certificates, diplomas, and associate. *Special study options:* distance learning.
Applying *Options:* early admission. *Application fee:* $20. *Required:* high school transcript.
Freshman Application Contact South Georgia Technical College, 900 South Georgia Tech Parkway, Americus, GA 31709. *Phone:* 229-931-2299.
Website: http://www.southgatech.edu/.

Southwest Georgia Technical College
Thomasville, Georgia

- **State-supported** 2-year, founded 1963, part of Technical College System of Georgia
- **Coed**

Undergraduates 443 full-time, 1,103 part-time. 4% are from out of state; 31% Black or African American, non-Hispanic/Latino; 1% Hispanic/Latino; 0.9% Asian, non-Hispanic/Latino; 0.8% American Indian or Alaska Native, non-Hispanic/Latino; 1% Two or more races, non-Hispanic/Latino; 0.2% Race/ethnicity unknown; 0.1% international. *Retention:* 58% of full-time freshmen returned.
Academics *Calendar:* quarters. *Degree:* certificates, diplomas, and associate. *Special study options:* distance learning.
Applying *Options:* electronic application, early admission. *Application fee:* $20. *Required:* high school transcript.
Freshman Application Contact Southwest Georgia Technical College, 15689 US 19 North, Thomasville, GA 31792. *Phone:* 229-225-5089.
Website: http://www.southwestgatech.edu/.

Virginia College in Augusta
Augusta, Georgia

Admissions Office Contact Virginia College in Augusta, 2807 Wylds Road Extension, Suite B, Augusta, GA 30909.
Website: http://www.vc.edu/.

Virginia College in Columbus
Columbus, Georgia

Admissions Office Contact Virginia College in Columbus, 5601 Veterans Parkway, Columbus, GA 31904.
Website: http://www.vc.edu/.

Virginia College in Macon
Macon, Georgia

Admissions Office Contact Virginia College in Macon, 1901 Paul Walsh Drive, Macon, GA 31206.
Website: http://www.vc.edu/.

Virginia College in Savannah
Savannah, Georgia

Admissions Office Contact Virginia College in Savannah, 14045 Abercorn Street, Suite 1503, Savannah, GA 31419.
Website: http://www.vc.edu/.

West Georgia Technical College
Waco, Georgia

- **State-supported** 2-year, founded 1966, part of Technical College System of Georgia
- **Coed**

Undergraduates 2,223 full-time, 4,692 part-time. 3% are from out of state; 32% Black or African American, non-Hispanic/Latino; 3% Hispanic/Latino; 0.9% Asian, non-Hispanic/Latino; 0.1% Native Hawaiian or other Pacific Islander, non-Hispanic/Latino; 0.4% American Indian or Alaska Native, non-Hispanic/Latino; 0.6% Two or more races, non-Hispanic/Latino; 2% Race/ethnicity unknown; 0.2% international. *Retention:* 55% of full-time freshmen returned.
Academics *Calendar:* quarters. *Degree:* certificates, diplomas, and associate. *Special study options:* distance learning.
Financial Aid Of all full-time matriculated undergraduates who enrolled in 2013, 68 Federal Work-Study jobs (averaging $800).
Applying *Options:* early admission. *Application fee:* $25. *Required:* high school transcript.
Freshman Application Contact West Georgia Technical College, 176 Murphy Campus Boulevard, Waco, GA 30182. *Phone:* 770-537-5719.
Website: http://www.westgatech.edu/.

Wiregrass Georgia Technical College
Valdosta, Georgia

- **State-supported** 2-year, founded 1963, part of Technical College System of Georgia
- **Suburban** campus
- **Coed**

Undergraduates 1,386 full-time, 2,580 part-time. 1% are from out of state; 33% Black or African American, non-Hispanic/Latino; 3% Hispanic/Latino; 0.5% Asian, non-Hispanic/Latino; 0.1% Native Hawaiian or other Pacific Islander, non-Hispanic/Latino; 0.2% American Indian or Alaska Native, non-Hispanic/Latino; 0.9% Two or more races, non-Hispanic/Latino; 0.2% Race/ethnicity unknown; 0.1% international. *Retention:* 51% of full-time freshmen returned.
Academics *Calendar:* quarters. *Degree:* certificates, diplomas, and associate. *Special study options:* distance learning.
Applying *Options:* early admission. *Application fee:* $15. *Required:* high school transcript.
Freshman Application Contact Wiregrass Georgia Technical College, 4089 Val Tech Road, Valdosta, GA 31602. *Phone:* 229-468-2278.
Website: http://www.wiregrass.edu/.

GUAM

Guam Community College
Mangilao, Guam

- **Territory-supported** 2-year, founded 1977
- **Small-town** 33-acre campus
- **Endowment** $8.8 million
- **Coed**, 2,458 undergraduate students, 40% full-time, 56% women, 44% men

Undergraduates 989 full-time, 1,469 part-time. 2% Black or African American, non-Hispanic/Latino; 0.4% Hispanic/Latino; 39% Asian, non-Hispanic/Latino; 55% Native Hawaiian or other Pacific Islander, non-Hispanic/Latino; 0.1% American Indian or Alaska Native, non-Hispanic/Latino; 0.6% Race/ethnicity unknown; 0.7% international; 1% transferred in.
Freshmen *Admission:* 202 applied, 202 admitted, 202 enrolled.
Faculty *Total:* 194, 59% full-time. *Student/faculty ratio:* 15:1.
Majors Accounting; architectural drafting and CAD/CADD; automobile/automotive mechanics technology; business automation/technology/data entry; computer science; computer systems networking and telecommunications; criminal justice/law enforcement administration; crisis/emergency/disaster management; culinary arts related; design and visual communications; early childhood education; education; hotel/motel administration; human services; liberal arts and sciences/liberal studies; marketing/marketing management; medical/clinical assistant; office management; restaurant, culinary, and catering management; sales, distribution, and marketing operations; surveying technology; tourism and travel services management.
Academics *Calendar:* semesters. *Degree:* certificates, diplomas, and associate. *Special study options:* academic remediation for entering students, adult/continuing education programs, advanced placement credit, cooperative education, double majors, English as a second language, honors programs, independent study, internships, off-campus study, part-time degree program, services for LD students, summer session for credit. *ROTC:* Army (c).
Library Learning Resource Center with 20,778 titles, 2,213 audiovisual materials, an OPAC.
Student Life *Housing:* college housing not available. *Campus security:* 12-hour patrols by trained security personnel. *Student services:* health clinic, personal/psychological counseling.
Costs (2015–16) *One-time required fee:* $37. *Tuition:* territory resident $3120 full-time, $130 per credit hour part-time; nonresident $3720 full-time, $155 per credit hour part-time. *Required fees:* $294 full-time, $147 per term part-time. *Waivers:* employees or children of employees.
Financial Aid Of all full-time matriculated undergraduates who enrolled in 2013, 83 Federal Work-Study jobs (averaging $940).
Applying *Options:* early admission. *Required:* high school transcript. *Application deadline:* rolling (freshmen). *Notification:* continuous (freshmen).
Freshman Application Contact Mr. Patrick L. Clymer, Registrar, Guam Community College, PO Box 23069 GMF, Barrigada, GU 96921. *Phone:* 671-735-5561. *Fax:* 671-735-5531. *E-mail:* patrick.clymer@guamcc.edu. *Website:* http://www.guamcc.edu/.

HAWAII

Hawaii Community College
Hilo, Hawaii

Director of Admissions Mrs. Tammy M. Tanaka, Admissions Specialist, Hawaii Community College, 200 West Kawili Street, Hilo, HI 96720-4091. *Phone:* 808-974-7661.
Website: http://www.hawcc.hawaii.edu/.

Hawaii Tokai International College
Kapolei, Hawaii

- **Independent** 2-year, founded 1992, part of Tokai University Educational System (Japan)
- **Suburban** 6-acre campus with easy access to Honolulu
- **Endowment** $1.3 million
- **Coed,** 89 undergraduate students, 100% full-time, 52% women, 48% men

Undergraduates 89 full-time. Students come from 25 states and territories; 64 other countries; 24% are from out of state; 11% American Indian or Alaska Native, non-Hispanic/Latino; 10% Race/ethnicity unknown; 74% international; 60% live on campus. *Retention:* 72% of full-time freshmen returned.
Freshmen *Admission:* 20 applied, 16 admitted, 25 enrolled. *Average high school GPA:* 3.54.
Faculty *Total:* 39, 36% full-time, 15% with terminal degrees. *Student/faculty ratio:* 2:1.
Majors Liberal arts and sciences/liberal studies.
Academics *Calendar:* quarters. *Degree:* certificates, diplomas, and associate. *Special study options:* academic remediation for entering students, advanced placement credit, English as a second language, part-time degree program, study abroad, summer session for credit.
Library The Learning Center with 7,000 titles, 500 audiovisual materials, an OPAC.
Student Life *Housing Options:* men-only, women-only, special housing for students with disabilities. Campus housing is university owned. Freshman applicants given priority for college housing. *Activities and Organizations:* Running Club, Kendo Club, Music Club, Baseball Club, Phi Theta Kappa International Honor Society, Student Government. *Campus security:* 24-hour patrols. *Student services:* personal/psychological counseling.
Standardized Tests *Required for some:* TOEFL score of 450 PBT for international students.
Applying *Options:* electronic application, deferred entrance. *Application fee:* $50. *Required:* essay or personal statement, high school transcript, minimum 2.5 GPA. *Required for some:* interview. *Recommended:* 1 letter of recommendation. *Application deadlines:* rolling (freshmen), rolling (out-of-state freshmen), rolling (transfers). *Notification:* continuous (freshmen), continuous (out-of-state freshmen), continuous (transfers).
Freshman Application Contact Hawaii Tokai International College, 91-971 Farrington Highway, Kapolei, HI 96707. *Phone:* 808-983-4116.
Website: http://www.hawaiitokai.edu/.

Honolulu Community College
Honolulu, Hawaii

- **State-supported** 2-year, founded 1920, part of University of Hawaii System
- **Urban** 20-acre campus
- **Coed**

Undergraduates 1,632 full-time, 2,736 part-time. Students come from 26 states and territories; 12 other countries; 2% are from out of state; 2% Black or African American, non-Hispanic/Latino; 9% Hispanic/Latino; 42% Asian, non-Hispanic/Latino; 9% Native Hawaiian or other Pacific Islander, non-Hispanic/Latino; 0.2% American Indian or Alaska Native, non-Hispanic/Latino; 28% Two or more races, non-Hispanic/Latino; 0.7% Race/ethnicity unknown; 1% international; 10% transferred in. *Retention:* 61% of full-time freshmen returned.
Faculty *Student/faculty ratio:* 16:1.
Academics *Calendar:* semesters. *Degree:* certificates and associate. *Special study options:* academic remediation for entering students, accelerated degree program, advanced placement credit, cooperative education, distance learning, English as a second language, internships, part-time degree program, services for LD students, student-designed majors, summer session for credit. *ROTC:* Army (c), Air Force (c).
Student Life *Campus security:* 24-hour emergency response devices.

Standardized Tests *Required for some:* TOEFL required for international applicants.
Costs (2014–15) *Tuition:* state resident $2766 full-time, $114 per credit part-time; nonresident $7584 full-time, $316 per credit part-time. *Required fees:* $30 full-time, $1 per credit part-time, $10 per term part-time.
Financial Aid Of all full-time matriculated undergraduates who enrolled in 2013, 30 Federal Work-Study jobs (averaging $1600).
Applying *Options:* early admission.
Freshman Application Contact Admissions Office, Honolulu Community College, 874 Dillingham Boulevard, Honolulu, HI 96817. *Phone:* 808-845-9129. *E-mail:* honcc@hawaii.edu.
Website: http://www.honolulu.hawaii.edu/.

Kapiolani Community College
Honolulu, Hawaii

Freshman Application Contact Kapiolani Community College, 4303 Diamond Head Road, Honolulu, HI 96816-4421. *Phone:* 808-734-9555.
Website: http://www.kapiolani.hawaii.edu/.

Kauai Community College
Lihue, Hawaii

Freshman Application Contact Mr. Leighton Oride, Admissions Officer and Registrar, Kauai Community College, 3-1901 Kaumualii Highway, Lihue, HI 96766. *Phone:* 808-245-8225. *Fax:* 808-245-8297. *E-mail:* arkauai@hawaii.edu.
Website: http://kauai.hawaii.edu/.

Leeward Community College
Pearl City, Hawaii

Freshman Application Contact Ms. Anna Donald, Office Assistant, Leeward Community College, 96-045 Ala Ike, Pearl City, HI 96782-3393. *Phone:* 808-455-0642.
Website: http://www.lcc.hawaii.edu/.

Remington College–Honolulu Campus
Honolulu, Hawaii

Director of Admissions Louis LaMair, Director of Recruitment, Remington College–Honolulu Campus, 1111 Bishop Street, Suite 400, Honolulu, HI 96813. *Phone:* 808-942-1000. *Fax:* 808-533-3064. *E-mail:* louis.lamair@remingtoncollege.edu.
Website: http://www.remingtoncollege.edu/.

University of Hawaii Maui College
Kahului, Hawaii

- **State-supported** primarily 2-year, founded 1967, part of University of Hawaii System
- **Rural** 77-acre campus
- **Coed**

Undergraduates 1,446 full-time, 2,625 part-time. 1% live on campus.
Academics *Calendar:* semesters. *Degrees:* certificates, associate, and bachelor's. *Special study options:* academic remediation for entering students, adult/continuing education programs, cooperative education, English as a second language, external degree program, part-time degree program, services for LD students, summer session for credit.
Student Life *Campus security:* 24-hour emergency response devices and patrols.
Costs (2014–15) *Tuition:* state resident $2736 full-time, $114 per credit part-time; nonresident $7584 full-time, $316 per credit part-time. Full-time tuition and fees vary according to course level, course load, and location. Part-time tuition and fees vary according to course level, course load, and location. *Required fees:* $126 full-time. *Room and board:* $14,766.
Financial Aid Of all full-time matriculated undergraduates who enrolled in 2013, 40 Federal Work-Study jobs (averaging $4000).
Applying *Options:* electronic application, early admission. *Application fee:* $25. *Required for some:* high school transcript.
Freshman Application Contact Mr. Stephen Kameda, Director of Admissions and Records, University of Hawaii Maui College, 310 Kaahumanu Avenue, Kahului, HI 96732. *Phone:* 808-984-3267. *Toll-free phone:* 800-479-6692. *Fax:* 808-984-3872. *E-mail:* skameda@hawaii.edu.
Website: http://maui.hawaii.edu/.

Windward Community College
Kaneohe, Hawaii

Director of Admissions Geri Imai, Registrar, Windward Community College, 45-720 Keaahala Road, Kaneohe, HI 96744-3528. *Phone:* 808-235-7430. *E-mail:* gerii@hawaii.edu.
Website: http://www.windward.hawaii.edu/.

IDAHO

Brown Mackie College–Boise
Boise, Idaho

- **Proprietary** primarily 2-year, part of Education Management Corporation
- **Coed**

Academics *Degrees:* diplomas, associate, and bachelor's.
Freshman Application Contact Brown Mackie College–Boise, 9050 West Overland Road, Suite 100, Boise, ID 83709. *Phone:* 208-321-8800.
Website: http://www.brownmackie.edu/boise/.

Carrington College–Boise
Boise, Idaho

- **Proprietary** 2-year, founded 1980, part of Carrington Colleges Group, Inc.
- **Coed**

Undergraduates 496 full-time, 56 part-time. 9% are from out of state; 2% Black or African American, non-Hispanic/Latino; 11% Hispanic/Latino; 2% Asian, non-Hispanic/Latino; 0.9% Native Hawaiian or other Pacific Islander, non-Hispanic/Latino; 1% American Indian or Alaska Native, non-Hispanic/Latino; 3% Two or more races, non-Hispanic/Latino; 0.4% Race/ethnicity unknown; 21% transferred in.
Faculty *Student/faculty ratio:* 18:1.
Academics *Calendar:* semesters. *Degree:* certificates and associate.
Costs (2014–15) *Tuition:* $54,125 per degree program part-time. Full-time tuition and fees vary according to program. Part-time tuition and fees vary according to program. Total costs vary by program. Tuition provided is for largest program (Dental Hygiene).
Applying *Required:* essay or personal statement, high school transcript, interview, Entrance test administered by Carrington College.
Freshman Application Contact Carrington College–Boise, 1122 North Liberty Street, Boise, ID 83704.
Website: http://carrington.edu/.

College of Southern Idaho
Twin Falls, Idaho

- **State and locally supported** 2-year, founded 1964
- **Small-town** 287-acre campus
- **Coed,** 8,473 undergraduate students, 28% full-time, 64% women, 36% men

Undergraduates 2,402 full-time, 6,071 part-time. 4% are from out of state; 0.8% Black or African American, non-Hispanic/Latino; 22% Hispanic/Latino; 0.9% Asian, non-Hispanic/Latino; 0.5% Native Hawaiian or other Pacific Islander, non-Hispanic/Latino; 0.9% American Indian or Alaska Native, non-Hispanic/Latino; 1% Two or more races, non-Hispanic/Latino; 3% Race/ethnicity unknown; 0.8% international; 4% live on campus.
Freshmen *Admission:* 1,059 enrolled.
Faculty *Total:* 332, 47% full-time. *Student/faculty ratio:* 21:1.
Majors Accounting; administrative assistant and secretarial science; agricultural business and management; agricultural business and management related; agriculture; American Sign Language (ASL); animal sciences; anthropology; applied horticulture/horticulture operations; aquaculture; art; autobody/collision and repair technology; automobile/automotive mechanics technology; bilingual and multilingual education; biology/biological sciences; building/construction finishing, management, and inspection related; business administration and management; cabinetmaking and millwork; chemistry; child-care and support services management; clinical laboratory science/medical technology; commercial and advertising art; computer science; computer systems networking and telecommunications; criminal justice/law enforcement administration; culinary arts; dental assisting; diesel mechanics technology; drafting and design technology; dramatic/theater arts; education; elementary education; emergency medical technology (EMT paramedic); engineering; English; entrepreneurship; equestrian studies; foreign languages and literatures; forestry; geography; geology/earth science;

history; hotel/motel administration; human services; hydrology and water resources science; liberal arts and sciences/liberal studies; library and information science; licensed practical/vocational nurse training; manufacturing engineering technology; mathematics; medical radiologic technology; music; photography; physical education teaching and coaching; physics; political science and government; pre-law studies; pre-pharmacy studies; psychiatric/mental health services technology; psychology; public health education and promotion; real estate; registered nursing/registered nurse; social sciences; sociology; speech communication and rhetoric; surgical technology; teacher assistant/aide; veterinary/animal health technology; water quality and wastewater treatment management and recycling technology; web page, digital/multimedia and information resources design; welding technology.
Academics *Calendar:* semesters. *Degree:* certificates and associate. *Special study options:* academic remediation for entering students, adult/continuing education programs, advanced placement credit, cooperative education, distance learning, English as a second language, honors programs, independent study, internships, part-time degree program, services for LD students, summer session for credit.
Library College of Southern Idaho Library with an OPAC, a Web page.
Student Life *Housing Options:* men-only, women-only. Campus housing is university owned. *Activities and Organizations:* drama/theater group, student-run newspaper, radio station, choral group, BPA, Delta Epsilon Chi, Chi Alpha (Christian Group), Vet Tech Club, Equine Club. *Campus security:* 24-hour emergency response devices and patrols, controlled dormitory access. *Student services:* health clinic, personal/psychological counseling, women's center, legal services.
Athletics Member NJCAA. *Intercollegiate sports:* baseball M(s), basketball M(s)/W(s), cheerleading M(s)/W(s), equestrian sports M(s)(c)/W(s)(c), softball W(s), volleyball M/W(s). *Intramural sports:* badminton M/W, basketball M/W, football M/W, racquetball M/W, rock climbing M/W, soccer M/W, softball M/W, tennis M/W, ultimate Frisbee M/W, volleyball M/W.
Costs (2015–16) *Tuition:* area resident $2880 full-time, $120 per credit hour part-time; state resident $3880 full-time, $170 per credit hour part-time; nonresident $6720 full-time, $280 per credit hour part-time. Full-time tuition and fees vary according to course load. Part-time tuition and fees vary according to course load. *Room and board:* $5540; room only: $2500. Room and board charges vary according to board plan. *Payment plan:* installment. *Waivers:* senior citizens and employees or children of employees.
Financial Aid Of all full-time matriculated undergraduates who enrolled in 2013, 250 Federal Work-Study jobs (averaging $2000). 100 state and other part-time jobs (averaging $2000).
Applying *Application fee:* $10. *Required:* high school transcript. *Required for some:* interview.
Freshman Application Contact Director of Admissions, Registration, and Records, College of Southern Idaho, PO Box 1238, Twin Falls, ID 83303-1238. *Phone:* 208-732-6232. *Toll-free phone:* 800-680-0274. *Fax:* 208-736-3014.
Website: http://www.csi.edu/.

College of Western Idaho
Nampa, Idaho

- **State-supported** 2-year, founded 2007
- **Rural** campus with easy access to Boise
- **Coed**

Undergraduates 2% Black or African American, non-Hispanic/Latino; 14% Hispanic/Latino; 1% Asian, non-Hispanic/Latino; 0.7% Native Hawaiian or other Pacific Islander, non-Hispanic/Latino; 1% American Indian or Alaska Native, non-Hispanic/Latino; 2% Two or more races, non-Hispanic/Latino; 13% Race/ethnicity unknown.
Faculty *Student/faculty ratio:* 22:1.
Academics *Calendar:* semesters. *Degree:* certificates and associate. *Special study options:* academic remediation for entering students, advanced placement credit, cooperative education, English as a second language, honors programs, internships, part-time degree program, services for LD students, summer session for credit.
Standardized Tests *Recommended:* SAT or ACT (for admission), ACT Compass.
Costs (2014–15) *Tuition:* area resident $1632 full-time, $136 per credit part-time; state resident $2132 full-time, $186 per credit part-time; nonresident $3600 full-time, $300 per credit part-time. Full-time tuition and fees vary according to course load. Part-time tuition and fees vary according to course load.
Applying *Options:* electronic application. *Application fee:* $25. *Required:* high school transcript.
Freshman Application Contact College of Western Idaho, 6056 Birch Lane, Nampa, ID 83687.
Website: http://cwidaho.cc/.

Eastern Idaho Technical College
Idaho Falls, Idaho

- **State-supported** 2-year, founded 1970
- **Small-town** 40-acre campus
- **Endowment** $881,885
- **Coed,** 756 undergraduate students, 43% full-time, 60% women, 40% men

Undergraduates 325 full-time, 431 part-time. Students come from 3 states and territories; 0.3% Black or African American, non-Hispanic/Latino; 18% Hispanic/Latino; 1% Asian, non-Hispanic/Latino; 1% Native Hawaiian or other Pacific Islander, non-Hispanic/Latino; 1% American Indian or Alaska Native, non-Hispanic/Latino; 0.4% Two or more races, non-Hispanic/Latino; 2% Race/ethnicity unknown; 0.6% international; 9% transferred in.
Freshmen *Admission:* 82 enrolled.
Faculty *Student/faculty ratio:* 8:1.
Majors Accounting; administrative assistant and secretarial science; automobile/automotive mechanics technology; computer systems networking and telecommunications; diesel mechanics technology; fire science/firefighting; legal assistant/paralegal; marketing/marketing management; medical/clinical assistant; registered nursing/registered nurse; surgical technology; welding technology.
Academics *Calendar:* semesters. *Degree:* certificates and associate. *Special study options:* academic remediation for entering students, adult/continuing education programs, advanced placement credit, English as a second language, part-time degree program, services for LD students, summer session for credit.
Library Richard and Lila Jordan Library plus 1 other with 21,000 titles, 158 audiovisual materials, an OPAC.
Student Life *Housing:* college housing not available. *Campus security:* 24-hour emergency response devices and patrols, controlled dormitory access. *Student services:* personal/psychological counseling.
Standardized Tests *Required for some:* ACT Compass, SAT, ACT, ASSET, or CPT.
Costs (2015–16) *Tuition:* state resident $2256 full-time, $100 per credit part-time; nonresident $8262 full-time, $199 per credit part-time. Full-time tuition and fees vary according to course load and program. Part-time tuition and fees vary according to course load and program. *Required fees:* $832 full-time, $15 per term part-time.
Financial Aid Of all full-time matriculated undergraduates who enrolled in 2013, 37 Federal Work-Study jobs (averaging $1176). 11 state and other part-time jobs (averaging $1619).
Applying *Options:* electronic application, deferred entrance. *Application fee:* $10. *Required:* high school transcript, interview. *Required for some:* essay or personal statement. *Application deadline:* rolling (freshmen).
Freshman Application Contact Hailey Mack, Career Placement and Recruiting Coordinator, Eastern Idaho Technical College, 1600 South 25th East, Idaho Falls, ID 83404. *Phone:* 208-524-5337 Ext. 35337. *Toll-free phone:* 800-662-0261. *Fax:* 208-524-0429. *E-mail:* hailey.mack@my.eitc.edu.
Website: http://www.eitc.edu/.

ITT Technical Institute
Boise, Idaho

- **Proprietary** primarily 2-year, founded 1906, part of ITT Educational Services, Inc.
- **Urban** campus
- **Coed**

Academics *Calendar:* quarters. *Degrees:* associate and bachelor's.
Financial Aid Of all full-time matriculated undergraduates who enrolled in 2013, 9 Federal Work-Study jobs (averaging $5500).
Freshman Application Contact Director of Recruitment, ITT Technical Institute, 12302 West Explorer Drive, Boise, ID 83713. *Phone:* 208-322-8844. *Toll-free phone:* 800-666-4888.
Website: http://www.itt-tech.edu/.

North Idaho College
Coeur d'Alene, Idaho

Freshman Application Contact North Idaho College, 1000 West Garden Avenue, Coeur d Alene, ID 83814-2199. *Phone:* 208-769-3303. *Toll-free phone:* 877-404-4536 Ext. 3311. *E-mail:* admit@nic.edu.
Website: http://www.nic.edu/.

ILLINOIS

Ambria College of Nursing
Hoffman Estates, Illinois

Admissions Office Contact Ambria College of Nursing, 5210 Trillium Boulevard, Hoffman Estates, IL 60192.
Website: http://www.ambria.edu/.

Black Hawk College
Moline, Illinois

- **State and locally supported** 2-year, founded 1946, part of Black Hawk College District System
- **Urban** 161-acre campus
- **Coed**

Undergraduates 2,581 full-time, 3,993 part-time. Students come from 21 states and territories; 18 other countries; 8% are from out of state; 12% Black or African American, non-Hispanic/Latino; 10% Hispanic/Latino; 4% Asian, non-Hispanic/Latino; 0.2% Native Hawaiian or other Pacific Islander, non-Hispanic/Latino; 0.3% American Indian or Alaska Native, non-Hispanic/Latino; 2% Race/ethnicity unknown; 0.3% international; 4% transferred in. *Retention:* 59% of full-time freshmen returned.
Faculty *Student/faculty ratio:* 20:1.
Academics *Calendar:* semesters. *Degree:* certificates and associate. *Special study options:* academic remediation for entering students, accelerated degree program, advanced placement credit, cooperative education, distance learning, English as a second language, independent study, internships, off-campus study, part-time degree program, services for LD students, study abroad, summer session for credit.
Student Life *Campus security:* 24-hour patrols.
Athletics Member NJCAA.
Costs (2014–15) *Tuition:* area resident $3600 full-time, $120 per credit hour part-time; state resident $6900 full-time, $230 per credit hour part-time; nonresident $7050 full-time, $235 per credit hour part-time.
Financial Aid Of all full-time matriculated undergraduates who enrolled in 2013, 157 Federal Work-Study jobs (averaging $1437). 176 state and other part-time jobs (averaging $1023).
Applying *Recommended:* high school transcript.
Freshman Application Contact Ms. Gabriella Hurtado, Recruitment Coordinator/Admissions Advisor, Black Hawk College, 6600-34th Avenue, Moline, IL 61265. *Phone:* 309-796-5341. *Toll-free phone:* 800-334-1311. *E-mail:* ghurtado@bhc.edu.
Website: http://www.bhc.edu/.

Carl Sandburg College
Galesburg, Illinois

Director of Admissions Ms. Carol Kreider, Dean of Student Support Services, Carl Sandburg College, 2400 Tom L. Wilson Boulevard, Galesburg, IL 61401-9576. *Phone:* 309-341-5234.
Website: http://www.sandburg.edu/.

City Colleges of Chicago, Harold Washington College
Chicago, Illinois

Freshman Application Contact Admissions Office, City Colleges of Chicago, Harold Washington College, 30 East Lake Street, Chicago, IL 60601-2449. *Phone:* 312-553-6010.
Website: http://hwashington.ccc.edu/.

City Colleges of Chicago, Harry S. Truman College
Chicago, Illinois

Freshman Application Contact City Colleges of Chicago, Harry S. Truman College, 1145 West Wilson Avenue, Chicago, IL 60640-5616. *Phone:* 773-907-4000 Ext. 1112.
Website: http://www.trumancollege.edu/.

City Colleges of Chicago, Kennedy-King College
Chicago, Illinois

Freshman Application Contact Admissions Office, City Colleges of Chicago, Kennedy-King College, 6301 South Halstead Street, Chicago, IL 60621. *Phone:* 773-602-5062. *Fax:* 773-602-5055. *Website:* http://kennedyking.ccc.edu/.

City Colleges of Chicago, Malcolm X College
Chicago, Illinois

Freshman Application Contact Ms. Kimberly Hollingsworth, Dean of Student Services, City Colleges of Chicago, Malcolm X College, 1900 West Van Buren Street, Chicago, IL 60612-3145. *Phone:* 312-850-7120. *Fax:* 312-850-7119. *E-mail:* khollingsworth@ccc.edu. *Website:* http://malcolmx.ccc.edu/.

City Colleges of Chicago, Olive-Harvey College
Chicago, Illinois

- **State and locally supported** 2-year, founded 1970, part of City Colleges of Chicago
- **Urban** 67-acre campus
- **Coed,** 4,572 undergraduate students, 43% full-time, 58% women, 42% men

Undergraduates 1,959 full-time, 2,613 part-time. 71% Black or African American, non-Hispanic/Latino; 9% Hispanic/Latino; 7% Asian, non-Hispanic/Latino; 0.4% American Indian or Alaska Native, non-Hispanic/Latino; 0.9% Two or more races, non-Hispanic/Latino; 4% Race/ethnicity unknown. *Retention:* 38% of full-time freshmen returned.
Freshmen *Admission:* 297 enrolled.
Faculty *Total:* 174, 33% full-time.
Majors Accounting; biological and physical sciences; business administration and management; child-care provision; crisis/emergency/disaster management; diesel mechanics technology; engineering science; fine/studio arts; general studies; homeland security; human development and family studies; information technology; liberal arts and sciences/liberal studies; logistics, materials, and supply chain management; manufacturing engineering technology; registered nursing/registered nurse; respiratory care therapy; web page, digital/multimedia and information resources design.
Academics *Calendar:* semesters. *Degree:* certificates and associate. *Special study options:* academic remediation for entering students, accelerated degree program, adult/continuing education programs, advanced placement credit, cooperative education, distance learning, English as a second language, independent study, internships, part-time degree program, services for LD students, summer session for credit.
Library Olga-Haley Library-Learning Resource Center with 70,000 titles, 1,150 audiovisual materials, an OPAC, a Web page.
Student Life *Housing:* college housing not available. *Activities and Organizations:* drama/theater group. *Campus security:* 24-hour emergency response devices and patrols. *Student services:* personal/psychological counseling, women's center.
Athletics Member NJCAA. *Intercollegiate sports:* baseball M, basketball M/W, volleyball W.
Costs (2015–16) *Tuition:* area resident $2670 full-time, $89 per credit hour part-time; state resident $6005 full-time, $200 per credit hour part-time; nonresident $7386 full-time, $246 per credit hour part-time. Full-time tuition and fees vary according to course load. Part-time tuition and fees vary according to course load. *Required fees:* $400 full-time, $80 per term part-time. *Payment plan:* installment. *Waivers:* employees or children of employees.
Financial Aid Of all full-time matriculated undergraduates who enrolled in 2013, 150 Federal Work-Study jobs (averaging $3900).
Applying *Options:* electronic application, early admission, deferred entrance. *Required for some:* high school transcript. *Application deadlines:* rolling (freshmen), rolling (out-of-state freshmen), rolling (transfers). *Notification:* continuous (freshmen), continuous (out-of-state freshmen), continuous (transfers).
Freshman Application Contact City Colleges of Chicago, Olive-Harvey College, 10001 South Woodlawn Avenue, Chicago, IL 60628-1645. *Phone:* 773-291-6372.
Website: http://oliveharvey.ccc.edu/.

City Colleges of Chicago, Richard J. Daley College
Chicago, Illinois

Freshman Application Contact City Colleges of Chicago, Richard J. Daley College, 7500 South Pulaski Road, Chicago, IL 60652-1242. *Phone:* 773-838-7606.
Website: http://daley.ccc.edu/.

City Colleges of Chicago, Wilbur Wright College
Chicago, Illinois

Freshman Application Contact Ms. Amy Aiello, Assistant Dean of Student Services, City Colleges of Chicago, Wilbur Wright College, Chicago, IL 60634. *Phone:* 773-481-8207. *Fax:* 773-481-8185. *E-mail:* aaiello@ccc.edu. *Website:* http://wright.ccc.edu/.

College of DuPage
Glen Ellyn, Illinois

Freshman Application Contact College of DuPage, IL. *E-mail:* admissions@cod.edu.
Website: http://www.cod.edu/.

College of Lake County
Grayslake, Illinois

Freshman Application Contact Director, Student Recruitment, College of Lake County, Grayslake, IL 60030-1198. *Phone:* 847-543-2383. *Fax:* 847-543-3061.
Website: http://www.clcillinois.edu/.

Coyne College
Chicago, Illinois

Admissions Office Contact Coyne College, 330 N. Green Street, Chicago, IL 60607.
Website: http://www.coynecollege.edu/.

Danville Area Community College
Danville, Illinois

- **State and locally supported** 2-year, founded 1946, part of Illinois Community College Board
- **Small-town** 50-acre campus
- **Coed,** 3,207 undergraduate students, 33% full-time, 54% women, 46% men

Undergraduates 1,069 full-time, 2,138 part-time. Students come from 4 states and territories; 1 other country; 13% Black or African American, non-Hispanic/Latino; 5% Hispanic/Latino; 1% Asian, non-Hispanic/Latino; 0.2% Native Hawaiian or other Pacific Islander, non-Hispanic/Latino; 0.4% American Indian or Alaska Native, non-Hispanic/Latino; 0.7% Two or more races, non-Hispanic/Latino; 8% Race/ethnicity unknown; 23% transferred in. *Retention:* 56% of full-time freshmen returned.
Freshmen *Admission:* 562 enrolled.
Faculty *Total:* 167, 40% full-time, 9% with terminal degrees. *Student/faculty ratio:* 20:1.
Majors Accounting technology and bookkeeping; agricultural business and management; autobody/collision and repair technology; automobile/automotive mechanics technology; business automation/technology/data entry; CAD/CADD drafting/design technology; child-care provision; computer programming (specific applications); computer systems networking and telecommunications; corrections; criminal justice/police science; electrician; energy management and systems technology; engineering; executive assistant/executive secretary; fire science/firefighting; floriculture/floristry management; general studies; health information/medical records technology; industrial electronics technology; industrial mechanics and maintenance technology; juvenile corrections; landscaping and groundskeeping; liberal arts and sciences/liberal studies; manufacturing engineering technology; medical administrative assistant and medical secretary; radiologic technology/science; registered nursing/registered nurse; selling skills and sales; teacher assistant/aide; turf and turfgrass management.
Academics *Calendar:* semesters. *Degree:* certificates and associate. *Special study options:* academic remediation for entering students, adult/continuing

education programs, advanced placement credit, cooperative education, distance learning, double majors, English as a second language, independent study, internships, part-time degree program, services for LD students, summer session for credit.

Library Library with 69,144 titles, 5,203 audiovisual materials, an OPAC.

Student Life *Housing:* college housing not available. *Activities and Organizations:* drama/theater group, choral group. *Campus security:* 24-hour emergency response devices and patrols. *Student services:* personal/psychological counseling.

Athletics Member NJCAA. *Intercollegiate sports:* baseball M(s), basketball M(s)/W(s), cheerleading W, cross-country running M(s)/W(s), softball W(s).

Costs (2015–16) *Tuition:* area resident $3300 full-time, $110 per credit hour part-time; state resident $5700 full-time, $190 per credit hour part-time; nonresident $5700 full-time, $190 per credit hour part-time. Full-time tuition and fees vary according to program. Part-time tuition and fees vary according to program. *Required fees:* $450 full-time, $15 per credit hour part-time. *Payment plan:* installment. *Waivers:* senior citizens and employees or children of employees.

Financial Aid Of all full-time matriculated undergraduates who enrolled in 2011, 60 Federal Work-Study jobs (averaging $3000). 100 state and other part-time jobs (averaging $3000).

Applying *Options:* early admission, deferred entrance. *Required:* high school transcript. *Application deadlines:* rolling (freshmen), rolling (transfers).

Freshman Application Contact Ms. Dawn Nasser, Coordinator of Recruitment, Danville Area Community College, 2000 East Main Street, Danville, IL 61832-5199. *Phone:* 217-443-8755. *Fax:* 217-443-8337. *E-mail:* dnasser@dacc.edu.
Website: http://www.dacc.edu/.

Elgin Community College
Elgin, Illinois

- **State and locally supported** 2-year, founded 1949, part of Illinois Community College Board
- **Suburban** 145-acre campus with easy access to Chicago
- **Coed,** 11,285 undergraduate students, 33% full-time, 55% women, 45% men

Undergraduates 3,780 full-time, 7,505 part-time. Students come from 4 states and territories; 15 other countries; 0.2% are from out of state; 5% Black or African American, non-Hispanic/Latino; 37% Hispanic/Latino; 6% Asian, non-Hispanic/Latino; 0.1% Native Hawaiian or other Pacific Islander, non-Hispanic/Latino; 0.2% American Indian or Alaska Native, non-Hispanic/Latino; 2% Two or more races, non-Hispanic/Latino; 3% Race/ethnicity unknown; 0.4% international; 4% transferred in. *Retention:* 77% of full-time freshmen returned.

Freshmen *Admission:* 1,357 enrolled.

Majors Accounting; administrative assistant and secretarial science; animation, interactive technology, video graphics and special effects; automobile/automotive mechanics technology; baking and pastry arts; biological and physical sciences; biology/biotechnology laboratory technician; business administration and management; CAD/CADD drafting/design technology; clinical/medical laboratory technology; computer and information systems security; criminal justice/police science; culinary arts; data entry/microcomputer applications; design and visual communications; engineering; entrepreneurship; executive assistant/executive secretary; fine/studio arts; fire science/firefighting; graphic design; health and physical education/fitness; heating, air conditioning, ventilation and refrigeration maintenance technology; industrial mechanics and maintenance technology; legal assistant/paralegal; liberal arts and sciences/liberal studies; machine tool technology; marketing/marketing management; music; physical therapy technology; radiologic technology/science; registered nursing/registered nurse; restaurant, culinary, and catering management; retailing; social work.

Academics *Calendar:* semesters. *Degree:* certificates, diplomas, and associate. *Special study options:* academic remediation for entering students, accelerated degree program, advanced placement credit, cooperative education, distance learning, double majors, English as a second language, honors programs, independent study, internships, off-campus study, part-time degree program, services for LD students, study abroad, summer session for credit.

Library Renner Academic Library & Learning Resources with an OPAC, a Web page.

Student Life *Housing:* college housing not available. *Activities and Organizations:* drama/theater group, student-run newspaper, choral group, Phi Theta Kappa Honor Society, Organization of Latin American Students, Asian Filipino Club, Amnesty International, student government. *Campus security:* grounds are patrolled Sunday-Saturday 7am-11pm during the academic year. *Student services:* personal/psychological counseling, legal services.

Athletics Member NJCAA. *Intercollegiate sports:* baseball M(s), basketball M(s)/W(s), cross-country running M(s)/W(s), golf M(s), soccer M(s)/W(s), softball W(s), tennis M(s)/W(s), volleyball W(s).

Costs (2014–15) *Tuition:* area resident $2736 full-time, $114 per credit hour part-time; state resident $9146 full-time, $381 per credit hour part-time; nonresident $11,947 full-time, $497 per credit hour part-time. *Required fees:* $10 full-time, $5 per term part-time. *Payment plan:* installment. *Waivers:* senior citizens.

Applying *Options:* electronic application. *Required for some:* high school transcript, some academic programs have additional departmental admission requirements that students must meet. *Application deadlines:* rolling (freshmen), rolling (transfers). *Notification:* continuous (freshmen), continuous (transfers).

Freshman Application Contact Admissions, Recruitment, and Student Life, Elgin Community College, 1700 Spartan Drive, Elgin, IL 60123. *Phone:* 847-214-7414. *E-mail:* admissions@elgin.edu.
Website: http://www.elgin.edu/.

Fox College
Bedford Park, Illinois

- **Private** 2-year, founded 1932
- **Suburban** campus
- **Coed,** 387 undergraduate students
- **65%** of applicants were admitted

Freshmen *Admission:* 742 applied, 484 admitted.

Majors Accounting technology and bookkeeping; administrative assistant and secretarial science; graphic design; medical/clinical assistant; physical therapy technology; veterinary/animal health technology.

Academics *Calendar:* semesters. *Degree:* diplomas and associate. *Special study options:* accelerated degree program.

Student Life *Housing:* college housing not available.

Freshman Application Contact Admissions Office, Fox College, 6640 South Cicero, Bedford Park, IL 60638. *Phone:* 708-444-4500.
Website: http://www.foxcollege.edu/.

Gem City College
Quincy, Illinois

Director of Admissions Admissions Director, Gem City College, PO Box 179, Quincy, IL 62301. *Phone:* 217-222-0391.
Website: http://www.gemcitycollege.com/.

Harper College
Palatine, Illinois

- **State and locally supported** 2-year, founded 1965, part of Illinois Community College Board
- **Suburban** 200-acre campus with easy access to Chicago
- **Coed,** 14,957 undergraduate students

Undergraduates Students come from 9 states and territories; 1% are from out of state; 5% Black or African American, non-Hispanic/Latino; 22% Hispanic/Latino; 11% Asian, non-Hispanic/Latino; 2% Native Hawaiian or other Pacific Islander, non-Hispanic/Latino; 0.2% American Indian or Alaska Native, non-Hispanic/Latino; 5% Race/ethnicity unknown.

Freshmen *Admission:* 1,769 applied, 1,635 admitted. *Average high school GPA:* 2.82. *Test scores:* ACT scores over 18: 76%; ACT scores over 24: 29%; ACT scores over 30: 4%.

Faculty *Total:* 785, 27% full-time. *Student/faculty ratio:* 8:1.

Majors Accounting; administrative assistant and secretarial science; architectural drafting and CAD/CADD; architectural engineering technology; art; banking and financial support services; biology/biological sciences; business administration and management; cardiovascular technology; chemistry; child-care provision; computer and information sciences; computer programming; computer programming (specific applications); computer science; criminal justice/law enforcement administration; cyber/computer forensics and counterterrorism; dental hygiene; diagnostic medical sonography and ultrasound technology; dietetics; dietetic technology; early childhood education; electrical, electronic and communications engineering technology; elementary education; emergency medical technology (EMT paramedic); engineering; English; environmental studies; fashion and fabric consulting; fashion/apparel design; fashion merchandising; finance; fine/studio arts; fire science/firefighting; food service systems administration; health teacher education; heating, air conditioning, ventilation and refrigeration maintenance technology; history; homeland security; hospitality administration; humanities; human services; interior design; international business/trade/commerce; legal administrative assistant/secretary; legal assistant/paralegal; liberal arts and sciences/liberal studies; marketing/marketing management; mathematics; medical administrative assistant and medical secretary; medical/clinical assistant; music; nanotechnology; philosophy; physical education teaching and coaching; physical sciences; psychology; public relations, advertising, and applied communication related; radiologic technology/science; registered nursing/registered nurse; sales, distribution, and marketing operations; small business administration; sociology and anthropology; speech communication and rhetoric; theater/theater arts management; web page, digital/multimedia and information resources design.

Academics *Calendar:* semesters. *Degree:* certificates and associate. *Special study options:* academic remediation for entering students, accelerated degree program, adult/continuing education programs, advanced placement credit, cooperative education, distance learning, English as a second language, honors programs, independent study, internships, part-time degree program, services for LD students, study abroad, summer session for credit.

Library Harper College Library with 128,068 titles, 17,540 audiovisual materials, an OPAC, a Web page.

Student Life *Housing:* college housing not available. *Activities and Organizations:* drama/theater group, student-run newspaper, radio station, choral group, Student Radio Station, Program Board, Student Senate, Nursing Club, Phi Theta Kappa. *Campus security:* 24-hour emergency response devices and patrols, late-night transport/escort service. *Student services:* health clinic, personal/psychological counseling, women's center, legal services.

Athletics Member NJCAA. *Intercollegiate sports:* baseball M, basketball M/W, cross-country running M/W, soccer M/W, softball W, track and field M/W, volleyball W, wrestling M. *Intramural sports:* baseball M, basketball M, football M, racquetball M/W, softball M/W, table tennis M/W, tennis M/W, volleyball M/W.

Costs (2015–16) *Tuition:* area resident $3412 full-time, $114 per credit hour part-time; state resident $11,123 full-time, $371 per credit hour part-time; nonresident $13,388 full-time, $446 per credit hour part-time. Full-time tuition and fees vary according to course load and program. Part-time tuition and fees vary according to course load and program. No tuition increase for student's term of enrollment. *Required fees:* $16 per credit hour part-time. *Payment plans:* installment, deferred payment. *Waivers:* senior citizens and employees or children of employees.

Financial Aid Of all full-time matriculated undergraduates who enrolled in 2013, 85 Federal Work-Study jobs (averaging $1210).

Applying *Options:* electronic application, early admission, deferred entrance. *Application fee:* $25. *Required:* high school transcript. *Application deadlines:* rolling (freshmen), rolling (transfers). *Notification:* continuous (freshmen), continuous (transfers).

Freshman Application Contact Admissions Office, Harper College, 1200 West Algonquin Road, Palatine, IL 60067. *Phone:* 847-925-6700. *Fax:* 847-925-6044. *E-mail:* admissions@harpercollege.edu. *Website:* http://goforward.harpercollege.edu/.

Heartland Community College
Normal, Illinois

Freshman Application Contact Ms. Candace Brownlee, Director of Student Recruitment, Heartland Community College, 1500 West Raab Road, Normal, IL 61761. *Phone:* 309-268-8041. *Fax:* 309-268-7992. *E-mail:* candace.brownlee@heartland.edu. *Website:* http://www.heartland.edu/.

Highland Community College
Freeport, Illinois

- **State and locally supported** 2-year, founded 1962, part of Illinois Community College Board
- **Rural** 240-acre campus
- **Coed,** 1,730 undergraduate students, 56% full-time, 60% women, 40% men

Undergraduates 965 full-time, 765 part-time. 2% are from out of state; 9% Black or African American, non-Hispanic/Latino; 3% Hispanic/Latino; 0.8% Asian, non-Hispanic/Latino; 0.1% Native Hawaiian or other Pacific Islander, non-Hispanic/Latino; 2% American Indian or Alaska Native, non-Hispanic/Latino; 3% Two or more races, non-Hispanic/Latino; 3% Race/ethnicity unknown; 3% transferred in.

Freshmen *Admission:* 633 applied, 633 admitted, 395 enrolled.

Faculty *Total:* 132, 35% full-time, 6% with terminal degrees. *Student/faculty ratio:* 16:1.

Majors Accounting; agricultural business and management; autobody/collision and repair technology; automobile/automotive mechanics technology; biological and physical sciences; child-care provision; early childhood education; emergency medical technology (EMT paramedic); engineering; general studies; graphic design; health information/medical records technology; heavy equipment maintenance technology; horse husbandry/equine science and management; industrial technology; information technology; liberal arts and sciences/liberal studies; mathematics teacher education; medical/clinical assistant; registered nursing/registered nurse; special education; teacher assistant/aide.

Academics *Calendar:* semesters. *Degree:* certificates and associate. *Special study options:* academic remediation for entering students, adult/continuing education programs, advanced placement credit, cooperative education, distance learning, English as a second language, external degree program, honors programs, independent study, internships, part-time degree program, services for LD students, student-designed majors, summer session for credit.

Library Clarence Mitchell Libarary with 1.0 million titles, 6,181 audiovisual materials, an OPAC, a Web page.

Student Life *Housing:* college housing not available. *Activities and Organizations:* drama/theater group, student-run newspaper, radio station, choral group, Phi Theta Kappa, Royal Scots, Prairie Wind, intramurals, Collegiate Choir. *Campus security:* 24-hour emergency response devices and patrols. *Student services:* personal/psychological counseling.

Athletics Member NJCAA. *Intercollegiate sports:* baseball M(s), basketball M(s)/W(s), bowling M(s)/W(s), golf M(s)/W(s), softball W(s), volleyball W(s). *Intramural sports:* basketball M/W, volleyball M/W.

Costs (2014–15) *Tuition:* $118 per credit hour part-time; state resident $188 per credit hour part-time; nonresident $198 per credit hour part-time. *Required fees:* $16 per credit hour part-time.

Financial Aid Of all full-time matriculated undergraduates who enrolled in 2013, 847 applied for aid, 732 were judged to have need, 1 had their need fully met. In 2013, 38 non-need-based awards were made. *Average percent of need met:* 38%. *Average financial aid package:* $6169. *Average need-based loan:* $3300. *Average need-based gift aid:* $5579. *Average non-need-based aid:* $4178.

Applying *Options:* electronic application, early admission, deferred entrance. *Required for some:* high school transcript, 1 letter of recommendation. *Recommended:* high school transcript. *Application deadlines:* rolling (freshmen), rolling (transfers).

Freshman Application Contact Mr. Jeremy Bradt, Director, Enrollment and Records, Highland Community College, 2998 West Pearl City Road, Freeport, IL 61032. *Phone:* 815-235-6121 Ext. 3500. *Fax:* 815-235-6130. *E-mail:* jeremy.bradt@highland.edu. *Website:* http://www.highland.edu/.

Illinois Central College
East Peoria, Illinois

Freshman Application Contact Angela Dreessen, Director of Enrollment Services and Student Life, Illinois Central College, One College Drive, East Peoria, IL 61635-0001. *Phone:* 309-694-5353. *Website:* http://www.icc.edu/.

Illinois Eastern Community Colleges, Frontier Community College
Fairfield, Illinois

- **State and locally supported** 2-year, founded 1976, part of Illinois Eastern Community Colleges System
- **Rural** 8-acre campus
- **Coed,** 2,218 undergraduate students, 10% full-time, 61% women, 39% men

Undergraduates 222 full-time, 1,996 part-time. 2% are from out of state; 0.6% Black or African American, non-Hispanic/Latino; 0.7% Hispanic/Latino; 0.4% Asian, non-Hispanic/Latino; 0.2% Race/ethnicity unknown.

Freshmen *Admission:* 79 enrolled.

Faculty *Total:* 189, 3% full-time. *Student/faculty ratio:* 19:1.

Majors Automobile/automotive mechanics technology; biological and physical sciences; business automation/technology/data entry; construction trades; corrections; emergency care attendant (EMT ambulance); engineering; executive assistant/executive secretary; fire science/firefighting; general studies; health information/medical records technology; liberal arts and sciences/liberal studies; quality control technology; registered nursing/registered nurse; sport and fitness administration/management.

Academics *Calendar:* semesters. *Degree:* certificates and associate. *Special study options:* academic remediation for entering students, adult/continuing education programs, advanced placement credit, cooperative education, distance learning, double majors, English as a second language, external degree program, independent study, part-time degree program, services for LD students, student-designed majors, summer session for credit.

Library Learning Resource Center plus 1 other with 15,318 titles, 919 audiovisual materials.

Student Life *Housing:* college housing not available.

Athletics Member NJCAA. *Intercollegiate sports:* cross-country running M/W, golf M/W.

Costs (2015–16) *Tuition:* area resident $2464 full-time, $77 per semester hour part-time; state resident $8589 full-time, $268 per semester hour part-time; nonresident $10,580 full-time, $331 per semester hour part-time. *Required fees:* $490 full-time, $15 per semester hour part-time, $5 per term part-time.

Payment plan: installment. *Waivers:* senior citizens and employees or children of employees.
Applying *Options:* early admission, deferred entrance. *Required:* high school transcript. *Application deadlines:* rolling (freshmen), rolling (transfers). *Notification:* continuous (freshmen), continuous (transfers).
Freshman Application Contact Ms. Mary Johnston, Coordinator of Registration and Records, Illinois Eastern Community Colleges, Frontier Community College, Frontier Drive, Fairfield, IL 62837. *Phone:* 618-842-3711 Ext. 4111. *Fax:* 618-842-6340. *E-mail:* johnstonm@iecc.edu. *Website:* http://www.iecc.edu/fcc/.

Illinois Eastern Community Colleges, Lincoln Trail College
Robinson, Illinois

- **State and locally supported** 2-year, founded 1969, part of Illinois Eastern Community Colleges System
- **Rural** 120-acre campus
- **Coed**, 1,032 undergraduate students, 39% full-time, 57% women, 43% men

Undergraduates 403 full-time, 629 part-time. 3% are from out of state; 2% Black or African American, non-Hispanic/Latino; 1% Hispanic/Latino; 1% Asian, non-Hispanic/Latino; 0.1% Native Hawaiian or other Pacific Islander, non-Hispanic/Latino; 0.3% American Indian or Alaska Native, non-Hispanic/Latino; 0.1% Race/ethnicity unknown.
Freshmen *Admission:* 183 enrolled.
Faculty *Total:* 83, 20% full-time. *Student/faculty ratio:* 16:1.
Majors Biological and physical sciences; business automation/technology/data entry; computer systems networking and telecommunications; construction trades; corrections; general studies; health information/medical records administration; liberal arts and sciences/liberal studies; mechanical engineering/mechanical technology; medical/clinical assistant; quality control technology; sport and fitness administration/management; teacher assistant/aide; telecommunications technology.
Academics *Calendar:* semesters. *Degree:* certificates and associate. *Special study options:* academic remediation for entering students, adult/continuing education programs, advanced placement credit, cooperative education, distance learning, double majors, English as a second language, external degree program, independent study, internships, part-time degree program, services for LD students, student-designed majors, summer session for credit.
Library Eagleton Learning Resource Center plus 1 other with 15,393 titles, 622 audiovisual materials.
Student Life *Housing:* college housing not available. *Activities and Organizations:* drama/theater group, choral group, national fraternities.
Athletics Member NJCAA. *Intercollegiate sports:* baseball M(s), basketball M(s)/W(s), softball W(s). *Intramural sports:* baseball M, basketball M, softball W.
Costs (2015–16) *Tuition:* area resident $2464 full-time, $77 per semester hour part-time; state resident $8589 full-time, $268 per semester hour part-time; nonresident $10,580 full-time, $331 per semester hour part-time. *Required fees:* $490 full-time, $15 per semester hour part-time, $5 per term part-time. *Payment plan:* installment. *Waivers:* senior citizens and employees or children of employees.
Applying *Options:* early admission, deferred entrance. *Required:* high school transcript. *Application deadlines:* rolling (freshmen), rolling (transfers). *Notification:* continuous (freshmen), continuous (transfers).
Freshman Application Contact Ms. Megan Scott, Director of Admissions, Illinois Eastern Community Colleges, Lincoln Trail College, 11220 State Highway 1, Robinson, IL 62454. *Phone:* 618-544-8657 Ext. 1137. *Fax:* 618-544-7423. *E-mail:* scottm@iecc.edu.
Website: http://www.iecc.edu/ltc/.

Illinois Eastern Community Colleges, Olney Central College
Olney, Illinois

- **State and locally supported** 2-year, founded 1962, part of Illinois Eastern Community Colleges System
- **Rural** 128-acre campus
- **Coed**, 1,398 undergraduate students, 45% full-time, 62% women, 38% men

Undergraduates 632 full-time, 766 part-time. 2% are from out of state; 1% Black or African American, non-Hispanic/Latino; 1% Hispanic/Latino; 1% Asian, non-Hispanic/Latino; 0.2% American Indian or Alaska Native, non-Hispanic/Latino; 0.1% Race/ethnicity unknown.
Freshmen *Admission:* 220 enrolled.
Faculty *Total:* 108, 41% full-time. *Student/faculty ratio:* 14:1.

Majors Accounting; autobody/collision and repair technology; automobile/automotive mechanics technology; biological and physical sciences; business administration and management; business automation/technology/data entry; engineering; general studies; human resources management; industrial mechanics and maintenance technology; information technology; liberal arts and sciences/liberal studies; medical administrative assistant and medical-secretary; medical radiologic technology; registered nursing/registered nurse.
Academics *Calendar:* semesters. *Degree:* certificates and associate. *Special study options:* academic remediation for entering students, adult/continuing education programs, advanced placement credit, cooperative education, distance learning, double majors, English as a second language, external degree program, independent study, internships, part-time degree program, services for LD students, student-designed majors, summer session for credit.
Library Anderson Learning Resources Center plus 1 other with 21,990 titles, 907 audiovisual materials.
Student Life *Housing:* college housing not available. *Activities and Organizations:* drama/theater group, student-run newspaper, choral group.
Athletics Member NJCAA. *Intercollegiate sports:* baseball M(s), basketball M(s)/W(s), softball W(s). *Intramural sports:* baseball M, basketball M/W, softball W.
Costs (2015–16) *Tuition:* area resident $2464 full-time, $77 per semester hour part-time; state resident $8589 full-time, $268 per semester hour part-time; nonresident $10,580 full-time, $331 per semester hour part-time. *Required fees:* $490 full-time, $15 per semester hour part-time, $5 per term part-time. *Payment plan:* installment. *Waivers:* senior citizens and employees or children of employees.
Applying *Options:* early admission, deferred entrance. *Required:* high school transcript. *Application deadlines:* rolling (freshmen), rolling (transfers). *Notification:* continuous (freshmen), continuous (transfers).
Freshman Application Contact Ms. Chris Webber, Assistant Dean for Student Services, Illinois Eastern Community Colleges, Olney Central College, 305 North West Street, Olney, IL 62450. *Phone:* 618-395-7777 Ext. 2005. *Fax:* 618-392-5212. *E-mail:* webberc@iecc.edu.
Website: http://www.iecc.edu/occ/.

Illinois Eastern Community Colleges, Wabash Valley College
Mount Carmel, Illinois

- **State and locally supported** 2-year, founded 1960, part of Illinois Eastern Community Colleges System
- **Rural** 40-acre campus
- **Coed**, 4,239 undergraduate students, 13% full-time, 32% women, 68% men

Undergraduates 560 full-time, 3,679 part-time. 6% are from out of state; 2% Black or African American, non-Hispanic/Latino; 1% Hispanic/Latino; 1% Asian, non-Hispanic/Latino; 0.2% Native Hawaiian or other Pacific Islander, non-Hispanic/Latino; 0.3% American Indian or Alaska Native, non-Hispanic/Latino; 0.1% Race/ethnicity unknown; 0.1% international.
Freshmen *Admission:* 231 enrolled.
Faculty *Total:* 130, 28% full-time. *Student/faculty ratio:* 35:1.
Majors Agricultural business and management; agricultural production; biological and physical sciences; business administration and management; business automation/technology/data entry; child development; diesel mechanics technology; energy management and systems technology; engineering; executive assistant/executive secretary; general studies; industrial technology; legal assistant/paralegal; liberal arts and sciences/liberal studies; machine tool technology; manufacturing engineering technology; mining technology; radio and television; social work; sport and fitness administration/management.
Academics *Calendar:* semesters. *Degree:* certificates and associate. *Special study options:* academic remediation for entering students, adult/continuing education programs, advanced placement credit, cooperative education, distance learning, double majors, English as a second language, external degree program, independent study, internships, part-time degree program, services for LD students, student-designed majors, summer session for credit.
Library Bauer Media Center plus 1 other with 33,749 titles, 1,545 audiovisual materials.
Student Life *Housing:* college housing not available. *Activities and Organizations:* drama/theater group, student-run newspaper, radio and television station, choral group.
Athletics Member NJCAA. *Intercollegiate sports:* baseball M(s), basketball M(s)/W(s), softball W(s). *Intramural sports:* baseball M, basketball M/W, softball W.
Costs (2015–16) *Tuition:* area resident $2464 full-time, $77 per semester hour part-time; state resident $8589 full-time, $268 per semester hour part-time; nonresident $10,580 full-time, $331 per semester hour part-time. *Required fees:* $490 full-time, $15 per semester hour part-time, $5 per term part-time.

Payment plan: installment. *Waivers:* senior citizens and employees or children of employees.

Applying *Options:* early admission, deferred entrance. *Required:* high school transcript. *Application deadlines:* rolling (freshmen), rolling (transfers). *Notification:* continuous (freshmen), continuous (transfers).

Freshman Application Contact Mrs. Diana Spear, Assistant Dean for Student Services, Illinois Eastern Community Colleges, Wabash Valley College, 2200 College Drive, Mt. Carmel, IL 62863. *Phone:* 618-262-8641 Ext. 3101. *Fax:* 618-262-8641. *E-mail:* speard@iecc.edu.
Website: http://www.iecc.edu/wvc/.

Illinois Valley Community College
Oglesby, Illinois

Freshman Application Contact Mr. Mark Grzybowski, Director of Admissions and Records, Illinois Valley Community College, Oglesby, IL 61348. *Phone:* 815-224-0437. *Fax:* 815-224-3033. *E-mail:* mark_grzybowski@ivcc.edu.
Website: http://www.ivcc.edu/.

ITT Technical Institute
Arlington Heights, Illinois

- **Proprietary** primarily 2-year, founded 1986, part of ITT Educational Services, Inc.
- **Suburban** campus
- **Coed**

Academics *Calendar:* quarters. *Degrees:* associate and bachelor's.

Freshman Application Contact Director of Recruitment, ITT Technical Institute, 3800 N. Wilke Road, Arlington Heights, IL 60004. *Phone:* 847-454-1800.
Website: http://www.itt-tech.edu/.

ITT Technical Institute
Oak Brook, Illinois

- **Proprietary** primarily 2-year, founded 1998, part of ITT Educational Services, Inc.
- **Coed**

Academics *Calendar:* quarters. *Degrees:* associate and bachelor's.

Freshman Application Contact Director of Recruitment, ITT Technical Institute, 800 Jorie Boulevard, Suite 100, Oak Brook, IL 60523. *Phone:* 630-472-7000. *Toll-free phone:* 877-488-0001.
Website: http://www.itt-tech.edu/.

ITT Technical Institute
Orland Park, Illinois

- **Proprietary** primarily 2-year, founded 1993, part of ITT Educational Services, Inc.
- **Suburban** campus
- **Coed**

Academics *Calendar:* quarters. *Degrees:* associate and bachelor's.

Financial Aid Of all full-time matriculated undergraduates who enrolled in 2013, 6 Federal Work-Study jobs (averaging $4000).

Freshman Application Contact Director of Recruitment, ITT Technical Institute, 11551 184th Place, Orland Park, IL 60467. *Phone:* 708-326-3200.
Website: http://www.itt-tech.edu/.

John A. Logan College
Carterville, Illinois

Director of Admissions Mr. Terry Crain, Dean of Student Services, John A. Logan College, 700 Logan College Road, Carterville, IL 62918-9900. *Phone:* 618-985-3741 Ext. 8382. *Fax:* 618-985-4433. *E-mail:* terrycrain@jalc.edu.
Website: http://www.jalc.edu/.

John Wood Community College
Quincy, Illinois

Freshman Application Contact Mr. Lee Wibbell, Director of Admissions, John Wood Community College, Quincy, IL 62305-8736. *Phone:* 217-641-4339. *Fax:* 217-224-4208. *E-mail:* admissions@jwcc.edu.
Website: http://www.jwcc.edu/.

Joliet Junior College
Joliet, Illinois

Freshman Application Contact Ms. Jennifer Kloberdanz, Director of Admissions and Recruitment, Joliet Junior College, 1215 Houbolt Road, Joliet, IL 60431. *Phone:* 815-729-9020 Ext. 2414. *E-mail:* admission@jjc.edu. *Website:* http://www.jjc.edu/.

Kankakee Community College
Kankakee, Illinois

- **State and locally supported** 2-year, founded 1966, part of Illinois Community College Board
- **Small-town** 178-acre campus with easy access to Chicago
- **Endowment** $5.3 million
- **Coed**, 3,378 undergraduate students, 41% full-time, 61% women, 39% men

Undergraduates 1,386 full-time, 1,992 part-time. Students come from 8 states and territories; 10 other countries; 1% are from out of state; 15% Black or African American, non-Hispanic/Latino; 10% Hispanic/Latino; 1% Asian, non-Hispanic/Latino; 0.1% Native Hawaiian or other Pacific Islander, non-Hispanic/Latino; 0.3% American Indian or Alaska Native, non-Hispanic/Latino; 1% Two or more races, non-Hispanic/Latino; 2% Race/ethnicity unknown; 0.1% international; 28% transferred in. *Retention:* 69% of full-time freshmen returned.

Freshmen *Admission:* 1,386 applied, 381 enrolled. *Average high school GPA:* 2.75.

Faculty *Total:* 282, 26% full-time, 5% with terminal degrees. *Student/faculty ratio:* 15:1.

Majors Administrative assistant and secretarial science; agriculture; applied horticulture/horticulture operations; art; automobile/automotive mechanics technology; biology/biological sciences; business administration and management; chemistry; clinical/medical laboratory technology; construction management; criminal justice/law enforcement administration; criminal justice/police science; desktop publishing and digital imaging design; drafting and design technology; early childhood education; education; elementary education; emergency medical technology (EMT paramedic); engineering; English; general studies; heating, air conditioning, ventilation and refrigeration maintenance technology; history; industrial electronics technology; legal assistant/paralegal; mathematics; mathematics teacher education; medical/clinical assistant; medical office assistant; physical therapy technology; physics; political science and government; psychology; radiologic technology/science; registered nursing/registered nurse; respiratory care therapy; secondary education; sociology; special education; teacher assistant/aide; visual and performing arts; welding technology.

Academics *Calendar:* semesters. *Degrees:* certificates, diplomas, and associate (also offers continuing education program with significant enrollment not reflected in profile). *Special study options:* academic remediation for entering students, advanced placement credit, distance learning, English as a second language, honors programs, independent study, internships, off-campus study, part-time degree program, services for LD students, student-designed majors, study abroad, summer session for credit. *ROTC:* Army (c).

Library Kankakee Community College Learning Resource Center with 35,308 titles, 2,299 audiovisual materials, an OPAC, a Web page.

Student Life *Housing:* college housing not available. *Activities and Organizations:* drama/theater group, Phi Theta Kappa, Hort, Student Nursing, Gay Straight Alliance, Student Advisory Council. *Campus security:* 24-hour patrols, late-night transport/escort service.

Athletics Member NJCAA. *Intercollegiate sports:* baseball M(s), basketball M(s)/W(s), soccer M(s), softball W(s), volleyball W(s).

Costs (2014–15) *Tuition:* area resident $3750 full-time, $112 per credit hour part-time; state resident $7707 full-time, $244 per credit hour part-time; nonresident $16,050 full-time, $522 per credit hour part-time. *Required fees:* $390 full-time. *Payment plan:* installment. *Waivers:* senior citizens and employees or children of employees.

Financial Aid Of all full-time matriculated undergraduates who enrolled in 2013, 70 Federal Work-Study jobs (averaging $1100). *Financial aid deadline:* 10/1.

Applying *Options:* electronic application, early admission. *Required:* high school transcript. *Application deadlines:* rolling (freshmen), rolling (out-of-state freshmen), rolling (transfers). *Notification:* continuous (freshmen), continuous (out-of-state freshmen), continuous (transfers).

Freshman Application Contact Mrs. Lindsey Zerbian, Coordinator of Admissions and Recruitment Services, Kankakee Community College, 100 College Drive, Kankakee, IL 60901. *Phone:* 815-802-8513. *Fax:* 815-802-8521. *E-mail:* lzerbian@kcc.edu.
Website: http://www.kcc.edu/.

Kaskaskia College
Centralia, Illinois

- **State and locally supported** 2-year, founded 1966, part of Illinois Community College Board
- **Rural** 195-acre campus with easy access to St. Louis
- **Endowment** $5.9 million
- **Coed,** 4,905 undergraduate students, 35% full-time, 59% women, 41% men

Undergraduates 1,716 full-time, 3,189 part-time. Students come from 3 states and territories; 5 other countries; 1% are from out of state; 7% Black or African American, non-Hispanic/Latino; 2% Hispanic/Latino; 0.5% Asian, non-Hispanic/Latino; 0.6% American Indian or Alaska Native, non-Hispanic/Latino; 6% Two or more races, non-Hispanic/Latino; 0.2% Race/ethnicity unknown; 0.1% international; 3% transferred in.
Freshmen *Admission:* 284 applied, 284 admitted, 288 enrolled.
Faculty *Total:* 237, 32% full-time, 8% with terminal degrees. *Student/faculty ratio:* 21:1.
Majors Accounting; agriculture; animal sciences; applied horticulture/horticulture operations; architectural drafting and CAD/CADD; autobody/collision and repair technology; automobile/automotive mechanics technology; biological and physical sciences; business automation/technology/data entry; business/commerce; carpentry; child-care provision; clinical/medical laboratory technology; construction management; cosmetology; criminal justice/law enforcement administration; culinary arts; dental assisting; electrical, electronic and communications engineering technology; electrician; emergency medical technology (EMT paramedic); engineering; executive assistant/executive secretary; general studies; health information/medical records technology; heating, air conditioning, ventilation and refrigeration maintenance technology; industrial mechanics and maintenance technology; information science/studies; juvenile corrections; liberal arts and sciences/liberal studies; mathematics teacher education; music; network and system administration; occupational therapist assistant; physical therapy technology; radiologic technology/science; registered nursing/registered nurse; respiratory care therapy; robotics technology; teacher assistant/aide; veterinary/animal health technology; web/multimedia management and webmaster; welding technology.
Academics *Calendar:* semesters. *Degree:* certificates and associate. *Special study options:* academic remediation for entering students, accelerated degree program, adult/continuing education programs, cooperative education, distance learning, double majors, English as a second language, honors programs, independent study, internships, off-campus study, part-time degree program, services for LD students, study abroad, summer session for credit. *ROTC:* Army (c).
Library Kaskaskia College Library with 17,313 titles, 432 audiovisual materials, an OPAC, a Web page.
Student Life *Housing:* college housing not available. *Activities and Organizations:* drama/theater group, student-run newspaper, choral group, Student Nurse Organization, Phi Theta Kappa Organization, Agriculture Club, Student Practical Nurses, B.A.S.I.C. Club. *Campus security:* 24-hour emergency response devices and patrols, late-night transport/escort service. *Student services:* personal/psychological counseling.
Athletics Member NJCAA. *Intercollegiate sports:* baseball M(s), basketball M(s)/W(s), cheerleading M(s)/W(s), cross-country running M(s)/W(s), golf M(s)/W(s), soccer W(s), softball W(s), tennis M(s), volleyball W(s).
Standardized Tests *Recommended:* ACT (for admission).
Costs (2014–15) *Tuition:* area resident $3360 full-time, $105 per credit hour part-time; state resident $6336 full-time, $198 per credit hour part-time; nonresident $12,640 full-time, $395 per credit hour part-time. Full-time tuition and fees vary according to program. Part-time tuition and fees vary according to program. *Required fees:* $448 full-time, $14 per credit hour part-time. *Payment plan:* installment. *Waivers:* senior citizens and employees or children of employees.
Financial Aid Of all full-time matriculated undergraduates who enrolled in 2013, 1,143 applied for aid, 1,039 were judged to have need, 65 had their need fully met. 17 Federal Work-Study jobs (averaging $4377). 28 state and other part-time jobs (averaging $4903). In 2013, 93 non-need-based awards were made. *Average percent of need met:* 67%. *Average financial aid package:* $6098. *Average need-based gift aid:* $4517. *Average non-need-based aid:* $2530.
Applying *Options:* electronic application, early admission, deferred entrance. *Required:* high school transcript. *Required for some:* interview. *Application deadlines:* rolling (freshmen), rolling (transfers). *Notification:* continuous (freshmen), continuous (transfers).
Freshman Application Contact Jan Ripperda, Manager of Records and Registration, Kaskaskia College, 27210 College Road, Centralia, IL 62801. *Phone:* 618-545-3041. *Toll-free phone:* 800-642-0859. *Fax:* 618-532-1990. *E-mail:* jripperda@kaskaskia.edu.
Website: http://www.kaskaskia.edu/.

Kishwaukee College
Malta, Illinois

- **State and locally supported** 2-year, founded 1967, part of Illinois Community College Board
- **Rural** 120-acre campus with easy access to Chicago
- **Coed,** 4,475 undergraduate students, 45% full-time, 54% women, 46% men

Undergraduates 2,030 full-time, 2,445 part-time. 17% Black or African American, non-Hispanic/Latino; 11% Hispanic/Latino; 2% Asian, non-Hispanic/Latino; 0.1% Native Hawaiian or other Pacific Islander, non-Hispanic/Latino; 0.6% American Indian or Alaska Native, non-Hispanic/Latino; 5% Two or more races, non-Hispanic/Latino; 1% Race/ethnicity unknown; 7% transferred in.
Freshmen *Admission:* 745 enrolled.
Faculty *Total:* 243, 33% full-time, 4% with terminal degrees.
Majors Administrative assistant and secretarial science; agricultural mechanization; airline pilot and flight crew; applied horticulture/horticulture operations; art; autobody/collision and repair technology; automobile/automotive mechanics technology; biological and physical sciences; business administration and management; CAD/CADD drafting/design technology; child-care and support services management; child-care provision; criminal justice/police science; criminal justice/safety; diesel mechanics technology; education (multiple levels); electrical, electronic and communications engineering technology; emergency medical technology (EMT paramedic); engineering; fine/studio arts; forensic science and technology; information technology; landscaping and groundskeeping; liberal arts and sciences/liberal studies; network and system administration; ornamental horticulture; radiologic technology/science; registered nursing/registered nurse; teacher assistant/aide.
Academics *Calendar:* semesters. *Degree:* certificates, diplomas, and associate. *Special study options:* academic remediation for entering students, adult/continuing education programs, advanced placement credit, cooperative education, distance learning, double majors, English as a second language, external degree program, freshman honors college, honors programs, independent study, internships, off-campus study, part-time degree program, services for LD students, study abroad, summer session for credit.
Library Kishwaukee College Library with 58,231 titles, 1,500 audiovisual materials, an OPAC, a Web page.
Student Life *Housing:* college housing not available. *Activities and Organizations:* drama/theater group, student-run newspaper, choral group. *Campus security:* 24-hour emergency response devices and patrols. *Student services:* health clinic, personal/psychological counseling.
Athletics Member NJCAA. *Intercollegiate sports:* baseball M(s), basketball M(s)/W(s), softball W(s), volleyball W(s).
Costs (2014–15) *Tuition:* area resident $3390 full-time, $113 per credit hour part-time; state resident $8820 full-time, $294 per credit hour part-time; nonresident $14,190 full-time, $473 per credit hour part-time. Full-time tuition and fees vary according to program and reciprocity agreements. Part-time tuition and fees vary according to program and reciprocity agreements. *Required fees:* $370 full-time, $12 per credit hour part-time. *Payment plans:* installment, deferred payment. *Waivers:* senior citizens and employees or children of employees.
Financial Aid *Average indebtedness upon graduation:* $4375.
Applying *Options:* electronic application, early admission, deferred entrance. *Required for some:* high school transcript. *Recommended:* high school transcript, Transcripts from all other colleges or universities previously attended. *Application deadlines:* rolling (freshmen), rolling (out-of-state freshmen), rolling (transfers). *Notification:* continuous (freshmen), continuous (out-of-state freshmen), continuous (transfers).
Freshman Application Contact Mr. Bryce Law, Coordinator-Student Outreach and Orientation, Kishwaukee College, 21193 Malta Road, Malta, IL 60150. *Phone:* 815-825-2086 Ext. 2351. *E-mail:* bryce.law@kishwaukeecollege.edu.
Website: http://www.kishwaukeecollege.edu/.

Lake Land College
Mattoon, Illinois

- **State and locally supported** 2-year, founded 1966, part of Illinois Community College Board
- **Rural** 308-acre campus
- **Endowment** $2.7 million
- **Coed,** 6,351 undergraduate students, 44% full-time, 52% women, 48% men

Undergraduates 2,809 full-time, 3,542 part-time. 1% are from out of state; 0.6% transferred in. *Retention:* 89% of full-time freshmen returned.
Freshmen *Admission:* 1,101 enrolled.

Faculty *Total:* 191, 61% full-time, 5% with terminal degrees. *Student/faculty ratio:* 21:1.

Majors Accounting technology and bookkeeping; administrative assistant and secretarial science; agricultural business and management; agricultural mechanization; agricultural production; architectural engineering technology; automobile/automotive mechanics technology; biological and physical sciences; business administration and management; child-care and support services management; civil engineering technology; computer programming (specific applications); computer systems networking and telecommunications; corrections; criminal justice/police science; dental hygiene; desktop publishing and digital imaging design; drafting and design technology; electrical, electronic and communications engineering technology; electromechanical technology; executive assistant/executive secretary; general studies; graphic and printing equipment operation/production; human services; industrial technology; information technology; legal administrative assistant/secretary; liberal arts and sciences/liberal studies; marketing/marketing management; medical administrative assistant and medical secretary; office management; physical therapy technology; printing press operation; radio and television; registered nursing/registered nurse; social work; telecommunications technology.

Academics *Calendar:* semesters. *Degree:* certificates and associate. *Special study options:* academic remediation for entering students, accelerated degree program, adult/continuing education programs, cooperative education, distance learning, English as a second language, external degree program, honors programs, internships, part-time degree program, services for LD students, summer session for credit.

Library Virgil H. Judge Learning Resource Center plus 1 other with 28,000 titles, 1,939 audiovisual materials, an OPAC.

Student Life *Housing:* college housing not available. *Activities and Organizations:* student-run newspaper, radio station, choral group, Agriculture Production and Management Club, Cosmetology Club, Agriculture Transfer Club, Phi Theta Kappa, Civil Engineering Technology Club. *Campus security:* 24-hour patrols. *Student services:* personal/psychological counseling.

Athletics Member NJCAA. *Intercollegiate sports:* baseball M(s), basketball M(s)/W(s), cheerleading W, softball W(s), tennis M(s)/W, volleyball W(s). *Intramural sports:* basketball M/W, bowling M/W, golf M/W, soccer M/W, softball M/W, volleyball M/W.

Standardized Tests *Recommended:* ACT (for admission).

Costs (2015–16) *Tuition:* area resident $2775 full-time; state resident $6599 full-time; nonresident $12,400 full-time. *Required fees:* $684 full-time.

Financial Aid Of all full-time matriculated undergraduates who enrolled in 2013, 120 Federal Work-Study jobs (averaging $1400).

Applying *Options:* electronic application, early admission. *Recommended:* high school transcript. *Application deadlines:* rolling (freshmen), rolling (transfers). *Notification:* continuous (freshmen), continuous (transfers).

Freshman Application Contact Mr. Jon VanDyke, Dean of Admission Services, Lake Land College, Mattoon, IL 61938-9366. *Phone:* 217-234-5378. *E-mail:* admissions@lakeland.cc.il.us.

Website: http://www.lakelandcollege.edu/.

Le Cordon Bleu College of Culinary Arts in Chicago
Chicago, Illinois

Freshman Application Contact Mr. Matthew Verratti, Vice President of Admissions and Marketing, Le Cordon Bleu College of Culinary Arts in Chicago, 361 West Chestnut, Chicago, IL 60610. *Phone:* 312-873-2064. *Toll-free phone:* 888-295-7222. *Fax:* 312-798-2903. *E-mail:* mverratti@chicnet.org.

Website: http://www.chefs.edu/chicago/.

Lewis and Clark Community College
Godfrey, Illinois

Freshman Application Contact Lewis and Clark Community College, 5800 Godfrey Road, Godfrey, IL 62035-2466. *Phone:* 618-468-5100. *Toll-free phone:* 800-YES-LCCC.

Website: http://www.lc.edu/.

Lincoln College
Lincoln, Illinois

Director of Admissions Gretchen Bree, Director of Admissions, Lincoln College, 300 Keokuk Street, Lincoln, IL 62656-1699. *Phone:* 217-732-3155 Ext. 256. *Toll-free phone:* 800-569-0558. *E-mail:* gbree@lincolncollege.edu.

Website: http://www.lincolncollege.edu/.

Lincoln College of Technology
Melrose Park, Illinois

Admissions Office Contact Lincoln College of Technology, 8317 W. North Avenue, Melrose Park, IL 60160.

Website: http://www.lincolnedu.com/.

Lincoln Land Community College
Springfield, Illinois

- **District-supported** 2-year, founded 1967, part of Illinois Community College Board
- **Suburban** 441-acre campus
- **Endowment** $3.5 million
- **Coed**

Undergraduates 2,985 full-time, 4,035 part-time. Students come from 4 states and territories; 11% Black or African American, non-Hispanic/Latino; 2% Hispanic/Latino; 1% Asian, non-Hispanic/Latino; 0.1% Native Hawaiian or other Pacific Islander, non-Hispanic/Latino; 0.3% American Indian or Alaska Native, non-Hispanic/Latino; 0.6% Two or more races, non-Hispanic/Latino; 3% Race/ethnicity unknown; 3% transferred in. *Retention:* 56% of full-time freshmen returned.

Faculty *Student/faculty ratio:* 21:1.

Academics *Calendar:* semesters. *Degree:* certificates and associate. *Special study options:* academic remediation for entering students, accelerated degree program, adult/continuing education programs, advanced placement credit, distance learning, English as a second language, external degree program, honors programs, independent study, internships, off-campus study, part-time degree program, services for LD students, study abroad, summer session for credit.

Student Life *Campus security:* 24-hour emergency response devices and patrols, late-night transport/escort service.

Athletics Member NJCAA.

Costs (2014–15) *Tuition:* area resident $2484 full-time, $104 per credit hour part-time; state resident $4968 full-time, $207 per credit hour part-time; nonresident $7452 full-time, $311 per credit hour part-time. Full-time tuition and fees vary according to program. Part-time tuition and fees vary according to program. *Required fees:* $264 full-time, $11 per credit hour part-time. *Payment plans:* installment, deferred payment.

Applying *Options:* electronic application, early admission, deferred entrance. *Recommended:* high school transcript.

Freshman Application Contact Mr. Ron Gregoire, Executive Director of Admissions and Records, Lincoln Land Community College, 5250 Shepherd Road, PO Box 19256, Springfield, IL 62794-9256. *Phone:* 217-786-2243. *Toll-free phone:* 800-727-4161. *Fax:* 217-786-2492. *E-mail:* ron.gregoire@llcc.edu.

Website: http://www.llcc.edu/.

MacCormac College
Chicago, Illinois

Director of Admissions Mr. David Grassi, Director of Admissions, MacCormac College, 506 South Wabash Avenue, Chicago, IL 60605-1667. *Phone:* 312-922-1884 Ext. 102.

Website: http://www.maccormac.edu/.

McHenry County College
Crystal Lake, Illinois

- **State and locally supported** 2-year, founded 1967, part of Illinois Community College Board
- **Suburban** 166-acre campus with easy access to Chicago
- **Coed,** 7,023 undergraduate students, 38% full-time, 55% women, 45% men

Undergraduates 2,642 full-time, 4,381 part-time. 0.5% are from out of state; 2% Black or African American, non-Hispanic/Latino; 14% Hispanic/Latino; 2% Asian, non-Hispanic/Latino; 0.1% Native Hawaiian or other Pacific Islander, non-Hispanic/Latino; 0.2% American Indian or Alaska Native, non-Hispanic/Latino; 2% Two or more races, non-Hispanic/Latino; 6% Race/ethnicity unknown; 0.2% international.

Freshmen *Admission:* 1,666 applied, 1,666 admitted, 1,212 enrolled. *Average high school GPA:* 2.25.

Faculty *Total:* 367, 27% full-time, 72% with terminal degrees. *Student/faculty ratio:* 20:1.

Majors Accounting; administrative assistant and secretarial science; animation, interactive technology, video graphics and special effects; applied horticulture/horticulture operations; biological and physical sciences; business administration and management; child-care provision; commercial photography; computer systems networking and telecommunications; construction management; criminal justice/police science; emergency medical technology (EMT paramedic); engineering; fine/studio arts; fire science/firefighting; general studies; health and physical education/fitness; information technology; liberal arts and sciences/liberal studies; music; occupational therapist assistant; operations management; registered nursing/registered nurse; restaurant, culinary, and catering management; robotics technology; selling skills and sales; special education.

Academics *Calendar:* semesters. *Degree:* certificates and associate. *Special study options:* academic remediation for entering students, accelerated degree program, adult/continuing education programs, advanced placement credit, cooperative education, distance learning, English as a second language, independent study, internships, part-time degree program, services for LD students, study abroad, summer session for credit.

Library McHenry County College Library with 52,045 titles, 4,730 audiovisual materials, an OPAC, a Web page.

Student Life *Housing:* college housing not available. *Activities and Organizations:* drama/theater group, student-run newspaper, radio station, choral group, Phi Theta Kappa, Student Senate, Equality Club, Writer's Block, Latinos Unidos. *Campus security:* 24-hour emergency response devices and patrols, late-night transport/escort service. *Student services:* personal/psychological counseling.

Athletics Member NJCAA. *Intercollegiate sports:* baseball M(s), basketball M(s)/W(s), soccer M(s), softball W(s), tennis M(s)/W(s), volleyball W(s).

Costs (2015–16) *Tuition:* area resident $2880 full-time, $96 per credit hour part-time; state resident $10,382 full-time, $346 per credit hour part-time; nonresident $13,213 full-time, $440 per credit hour part-time. Full-time tuition and fees vary according to course load. Part-time tuition and fees vary according to course load. *Required fees:* $284 full-time, $9 per credit hour part-time, $7 per term part-time. *Payment plan:* installment. *Waivers:* senior citizens and employees or children of employees.

Financial Aid Of all full-time matriculated undergraduates who enrolled in 2013, 200 Federal Work-Study jobs (averaging $3700). 130 state and other part-time jobs (averaging $2000).

Applying *Options:* electronic application, early admission, deferred entrance. *Application fee:* $15. *Recommended:* high school transcript. *Application deadlines:* rolling (freshmen), rolling (out-of-state freshmen), rolling (transfers). *Notification:* continuous (freshmen), continuous (out-of-state freshmen), continuous (transfers).

Freshman Application Contact Kellie Carper-Sowiak, Manager of New Student Transitions, McHenry County College, 8900 US Highway 14, Crystal Lake, IL 60012-2761. *Phone:* 815-455-8670. *E-mail:* admissions@mchenry.edu.
Website: http://www.mchenry.edu/.

Moraine Valley Community College
Palos Hills, Illinois

- **State and locally supported** 2-year, founded 1967, part of Illinois Community College Board
- **Suburban** 294-acre campus with easy access to Chicago
- **Endowment** $13.3 million
- **Coed,** 15,286 undergraduate students, 43% full-time, 53% women, 47% men

Undergraduates 6,624 full-time, 8,662 part-time. Students come from 11 states and territories; 40 other countries; 0.2% are from out of state; 9% Black or African American, non-Hispanic/Latino; 22% Hispanic/Latino; 2% Asian, non-Hispanic/Latino; 0.1% Native Hawaiian or other Pacific Islander, non-Hispanic/Latino; 0.3% American Indian or Alaska Native, non-Hispanic/Latino; 2% Two or more races, non-Hispanic/Latino; 9% Race/ethnicity unknown; 2% international; 3% transferred in. *Retention:* 70% of full-time freshmen returned.

Freshmen *Admission:* 2,200 enrolled. *Test scores:* ACT scores over 18: 69%; ACT scores over 24: 15%; ACT scores over 30: 1%.

Faculty *Total:* 735, 26% full-time, 10% with terminal degrees. *Student/faculty ratio:* 27:1.

Majors Administrative assistant and secretarial science; automobile/automotive mechanics technology; baking and pastry arts; biological and physical sciences; business administration and management; business/commerce; child-care provision; computer graphics; criminal justice/police science; design and visual communications; emergency medical technology (EMT paramedic); fire prevention and safety technology; fire science/firefighting; health information/medical records technology; health professions related; heating, air conditioning, ventilation and refrigeration maintenance technology; hospitality administration; human resources management; industrial electronics technology; liberal arts and sciences/liberal studies; management information systems; mathematics teacher education; mechanical engineering/mechanical technology; movement and mind-body therapies and education related; music; parks, recreation and leisure facilities management; polysomnography; radiologic technology/science; registered

nursing/registered nurse; respiratory care therapy; science teacher education; small business administration; special education; substance abuse/addiction counseling; system, networking, and LAN/WAN management; teacher assistant/aide; tourism and travel services management; visual and performing arts; web/multimedia management and webmaster.

Academics *Calendar:* semesters. *Degree:* certificates and associate. *Special study options:* academic remediation for entering students, accelerated degree program, adult/continuing education programs, advanced placement credit, cooperative education, distance learning, double majors, English as a second language, honors programs, independent study, internships, off-campus study, part-time degree program, services for LD students, study abroad, summer session for credit.

Library Library with 66,017 titles, 8,066 audiovisual materials, an OPAC, a Web page.

Student Life *Housing:* college housing not available. *Activities and Organizations:* drama/theater group, student-run newspaper, choral group, Student Newspaper, Speech Team, Alliance of Latin American Students, Phi Theta Kappa, Arab Student Union. *Campus security:* 24-hour emergency response devices and patrols, late-night transport/escort service, safety and security programs. *Student services:* personal/psychological counseling, women's center.

Athletics Member NJCAA. *Intercollegiate sports:* baseball M(s), basketball M(s)/W(s), cross-country running M(s)/W(s), golf M(s), soccer M(s)/W(s), softball W(s), tennis M(s)/W(s), volleyball W(s). *Intramural sports:* basketball M/W, football M, soccer M/W, volleyball M/W.

Costs (2015–16) *Tuition:* area resident $3480 full-time, $116 per credit hour part-time; state resident $8400 full-time, $280 per credit hour part-time; nonresident $9810 full-time, $327 per credit hour part-time. *Required fees:* $516 full-time, $17 per credit hour part-time, $3 per term part-time. *Payment plan:* installment. *Waivers:* senior citizens and employees or children of employees.

Financial Aid Of all full-time matriculated undergraduates who enrolled in 2013, 66 Federal Work-Study jobs (averaging $2812). 355 state and other part-time jobs (averaging $2000).

Applying *Options:* electronic application, early admission, deferred entrance. *Recommended:* high school transcript. *Application deadlines:* rolling (freshmen), rolling (transfers). *Notification:* continuous (freshmen), continuous (transfers).

Freshman Application Contact Mr. Andrew Sarata, Director, Admissions and Recruitment, Moraine Valley Community College, 9000 West College Parkway, Palos Hills, IL 60465-0937. *Phone:* 708-974-5357. *Fax:* 708-974-0681. *E-mail:* sarataa@morainevalley.edu.
Website: http://www.morainevalley.edu/.

Morrison Institute of Technology
Morrison, Illinois

Freshman Application Contact Mrs. Tammy Pruis, Admission Secretary, Morrison Institute of Technology, 701 Portland Avenue, Morrison, IL 61270. *Phone:* 815-772-7218. *Fax:* 815-772-7584. *E-mail:* admissions@morrison.tec.il.us.
Website: http://www.morrisontech.edu/.

Morton College
Cicero, Illinois

Freshman Application Contact Morton College, 3801 South Central Avenue, Cicero, IL 60804-4398. *Phone:* 708-656-8000 Ext. 401.
Website: http://www.morton.edu/.

Northwestern College
Chicago, Illinois

- **Proprietary** 2-year, founded 1902
- **Urban** 3-acre campus with easy access to Chicago, IL
- **Coed,** 1,082 undergraduate students, 44% full-time, 83% women, 17% men

Undergraduates 472 full-time, 610 part-time. 2% are from out of state; 40% Black or African American, non-Hispanic/Latino; 21% Hispanic/Latino; 1% Asian, non-Hispanic/Latino; 0.2% Native Hawaiian or other Pacific Islander, non-Hispanic/Latino; 2% American Indian or Alaska Native, non-Hispanic/Latino; 8% Two or more races, non-Hispanic/Latino; 6% Race/ethnicity unknown.

Freshmen *Admission:* 555 applied, 530 admitted, 256 enrolled.

Faculty *Total:* 92, 38% full-time.

Majors Accounting technology and bookkeeping; business administration and management; criminal justice/law enforcement administration; diagnostic medical sonography and ultrasound technology; health information/medical records technology; legal assistant/paralegal; massage therapy;

medical/clinical assistant; radiologic technology/science; registered nursing/registered nurse.

Academics *Calendar:* quarters. *Degrees:* certificates and associate (profile includes branch campuses in Bridgeview and Naperville, IL). *Special study options:* academic remediation for entering students, cooperative education, honors programs, independent study, internships, part-time degree program, summer session for credit.

Library Edward G. Schumacher Memorial Library with 12,000 titles, 100 audiovisual materials, an OPAC, a Web page.

Student Life *Housing:* college housing not available. *Student services:* personal/psychological counseling.

Standardized Tests *Recommended:* SAT or ACT (for admission).

Costs (2015–16) *Tuition:* $20,925 full-time, $465 per quarter hour part-time. *Required fees:* $370 full-time. *Payment plan:* installment.

Applying *Options:* electronic application. *Application fee:* $25. *Required:* high school transcript. *Application deadline:* rolling (freshmen).

Freshman Application Contact Northwestern College, 4829 North Lipps Avenue, Chicago, IL 60630. *Phone:* 708-233-5000. *Toll-free phone:* 888-205-2283.

Website: http://www.northwesterncollege.edu/.

Oakton Community College
Des Plaines, Illinois

- **District-supported** 2-year, founded 1969, part of Illinois Community College Board
- **Suburban** 193-acre campus with easy access to Chicago
- **Coed,** 9,880 undergraduate students

Majors Accounting technology and bookkeeping; administrative assistant and secretarial science; architectural drafting and CAD/CADD; automobile/automotive mechanics technology; banking and financial support services; biological and physical sciences; building/construction finishing, management, and inspection related; child-care provision; clinical/medical laboratory technology; computer programming; criminal justice/police science; electrical, electronic and communications engineering technology; engineering; fire science/firefighting; graphic design; health information/medical records administration; heating, ventilation, air conditioning and refrigeration engineering technology; information technology; liberal arts and sciences/liberal studies; manufacturing engineering technology; marketing/marketing management; mechanical engineering/mechanical technology; music; operations management; physical therapy technology; real estate; registered nursing/registered nurse; sales, distribution, and marketing operations; social work; substance abuse/addiction counseling.

Academics *Calendar:* semesters. *Degree:* certificates and associate. *Special study options:* academic remediation for entering students, adult/continuing education programs, advanced placement credit, distance learning, English as a second language, honors programs, independent study, internships, off-campus study, part-time degree program, services for LD students, study abroad, summer session for credit.

Library Oakton Community College Library plus 1 other with 92,000 titles, 10,500 audiovisual materials, an OPAC, a Web page.

Student Life *Housing:* college housing not available. *Activities and Organizations:* drama/theater group, student-run newspaper, choral group. *Campus security:* 24-hour emergency response devices and patrols, student patrols, late-night transport/escort service. *Student services:* health clinic, personal/psychological counseling.

Athletics Member NJCAA. *Intercollegiate sports:* baseball M, basketball M/W, cross-country running M/W, soccer M/W, softball W, tennis M/W, track and field M/W, volleyball W. *Intramural sports:* basketball M/W, cheerleading W, soccer M, table tennis M/W, volleyball M/W.

Costs (2015–16) *Tuition:* area resident $2598 full-time, $103 per semester hour part-time; state resident $6912 full-time, $288 per semester hour part-time; nonresident $8784 full-time, $366 per semester hour part-time. Full-time tuition and fees vary according to course load. Part-time tuition and fees vary according to course load. *Payment plans:* installment, deferred payment. *Waivers:* employees or children of employees.

Applying *Options:* electronic application. *Application fee:* $25. *Required for some:* interview. *Recommended:* high school transcript. *Application deadlines:* rolling (freshmen), rolling (transfers). *Notification:* continuous (freshmen), continuous (transfers).

Freshman Application Contact Mr. Ashlee Mishler, Admissions Specialist, Oakton Community College, 1600 East Golf Road, Des Plaines, IL 60016-1268. *Phone:* 847-635-1703. *Fax:* 847-635-1890. *E-mail:* amishler@oakton.edu.

Website: http://www.oakton.edu/.

Parkland College
Champaign, Illinois

Freshman Application Contact Admissions Representative, Parkland College, Champaign, IL 61821-1899. *Phone:* 217-351-2482. *Toll-free phone:* 800-346-8089. *Fax:* 217-351-2640.

Website: http://www.parkland.edu/.

Prairie State College
Chicago Heights, Illinois

Freshman Application Contact Jaime Miller, Director of Admissions, Prairie State College, 202 South Halsted Street, Chicago Heights, IL 60411. *Phone:* 708-709-3513. *E-mail:* jmmiller@prairiestate.edu.

Website: http://www.prairiestate.edu/.

Rend Lake College
Ina, Illinois

- **State-supported** 2-year, founded 1967, part of Illinois Community College Board
- **Rural** 350-acre campus
- **Coed**

Undergraduates 1,479 full-time, 1,235 part-time. 2% Black or African American, non-Hispanic/Latino; 0.5% Hispanic/Latino; 0.1% Asian, non-Hispanic/Latino; 0.3% Native Hawaiian or other Pacific Islander, non-Hispanic/Latino; 0.5% American Indian or Alaska Native, non-Hispanic/Latino; 0.1% Race/ethnicity unknown.

Faculty *Student/faculty ratio:* 25:1.

Academics *Calendar:* semesters. *Degree:* certificates and associate. *Special study options:* academic remediation for entering students, adult/continuing education programs, advanced placement credit, cooperative education, distance learning, double majors, English as a second language, honors programs, independent study, internships, off-campus study, part-time degree program, services for LD students, summer session for credit.

Student Life *Campus security:* 24-hour emergency response devices and patrols, late-night transport/escort service.

Athletics Member NJCAA.

Costs (2014–15) *Tuition:* area resident $2850 full-time, $95 per hour part-time; state resident $4455 full-time, $149 per hour part-time; nonresident $4500 full-time, $150 per hour part-time. Full-time tuition and fees vary according to course load, program, and reciprocity agreements. Part-time tuition and fees vary according to course load, program, and reciprocity agreements. *Required fees:* $90 full-time, $3 per hour part-time.

Financial Aid Of all full-time matriculated undergraduates who enrolled in 2013, 133 Federal Work-Study jobs (averaging $1000). 174 state and other part-time jobs (averaging $940).

Applying *Options:* electronic application, deferred entrance. *Required:* high school transcript.

Freshman Application Contact Mr. Jason Swann, Dean of Admissions and Enrollment Management, Rend Lake College, 468 North Ken Gray Parkway, Ina, IL 62846-9801. *Phone:* 618-437-5321 Ext. 1265. *Toll-free phone:* 800-369-5321. *Fax:* 618-437-5677. *E-mail:* swannj@rlc.edu.

Website: http://www.rlc.edu/.

Richland Community College
Decatur, Illinois

- **District-supported** 2-year, founded 1971, part of Illinois Community College Board
- **Small-town** 117-acre campus
- **Coed,** 3,152 undergraduate students, 32% full-time, 63% women, 37% men

Undergraduates 1,003 full-time, 2,149 part-time. *Retention:* 59% of full-time freshmen returned.

Freshmen *Admission:* 491 enrolled.

Faculty *Total:* 242, 40% full-time, 7% with terminal degrees. *Student/faculty ratio:* 14:1.

Majors Accounting; administrative assistant and secretarial science; agricultural business and management; automobile/automotive mechanics technology; biological and physical sciences; business administration and management; child development; computer and information sciences related; computer graphics; computer programming (specific applications); construction engineering technology; criminal justice/police science; data entry/microcomputer applications; data entry/microcomputer applications related; drafting and design technology; electrical, electronic and communications engineering technology; fire science/firefighting; food technology and processing; industrial technology; information science/studies;

insurance; legal administrative assistant/secretary; liberal arts and sciences/liberal studies; medical administrative assistant and medical secretary; pre-engineering; registered nursing/registered nurse; surgical technology; word processing.

Academics *Calendar:* semesters. *Degree:* certificates and associate. *Special study options:* academic remediation for entering students, adult/continuing education programs, advanced placement credit, distance learning, English as a second language, freshman honors college, honors programs, part-time degree program, services for LD students, student-designed majors, summer session for credit.

Library Kitty Lindsay Library with 39,452 titles, an OPAC, a Web page.

Student Life *Housing:* college housing not available. *Activities and Organizations:* student-run newspaper, Student Senate, Forensics Club, Drama Club, Black Student Association, Student Activities Board. *Campus security:* 24-hour emergency response devices and patrols. *Student services:* personal/psychological counseling.

Standardized Tests *Recommended:* ACT (for admission).

Financial Aid Of all full-time matriculated undergraduates who enrolled in 2013, 43 Federal Work-Study jobs (averaging $1339). 129 state and other part-time jobs (averaging $578).

Applying *Options:* early admission. *Required:* high school transcript. *Application deadlines:* rolling (freshmen), rolling (transfers).

Freshman Application Contact Ms. Catherine Sebok, Director of Admissions and Records, Richland Community College, Decatur, IL 62521. *Phone:* 217-875-7200 Ext. 558. *Fax:* 217-875-7783. *E-mail:* csebok@ richland.edu.

Website: http://www.richland.edu/.

Rockford Career College
Rockford, Illinois

Director of Admissions Ms. Barbara Holliman, Director of Admissions, Rockford Career College, 1130 South Alpine Road, Suite 100, Rockford, IL 61108. *Phone:* 815-965-8616 Ext. 16.

Website: http://www.rockfordcareercollege.edu/.

Rock Valley College
Rockford, Illinois

- **District-supported** 2-year, founded 1964, part of Illinois Community College Board
- **Suburban** 217-acre campus with easy access to Chicago
- **Coed,** 8,150 undergraduate students, 45% full-time, 56% women, 44% men

Undergraduates 3,652 full-time, 4,498 part-time. 10% Black or African American, non-Hispanic/Latino; 14% Hispanic/Latino; 2% Asian, non-Hispanic/Latino; 0.1% Native Hawaiian or other Pacific Islander, non-Hispanic/Latino; 0.5% American Indian or Alaska Native, non-Hispanic/Latino; 2% Two or more races, non-Hispanic/Latino; 1% Race/ethnicity unknown; 0.3% international; 3% transferred in. *Retention:* 66% of full-time freshmen returned.

Freshmen *Admission:* 1,144 enrolled.

Faculty *Total:* 462, 34% full-time.

Majors Accounting; administrative assistant and secretarial science; automobile/automotive mechanics technology; avionics maintenance technology; business administration and management; child development; computer engineering technology; computer science; computer systems networking and telecommunications; construction engineering technology; criminal justice/law enforcement administration; dental hygiene; drafting/design engineering technologies related; electrical, electronic and communications engineering technology; electrician; energy management and systems technology; fire science/firefighting; graphic and printing equipment operation/production; human services; industrial and product design; industrial technology; liberal arts and sciences/liberal studies; marketing/marketing management; pre-engineering; quality control technology; registered nursing/registered nurse; respiratory care therapy; sheet metal technology; sport and fitness administration/management; surgical technology; tool and die technology; welding technology.

Academics *Calendar:* semesters. *Degree:* certificates and associate. *Special study options:* academic remediation for entering students, adult/continuing education programs, advanced placement credit, cooperative education, distance learning, English as a second language, honors programs, independent study, internships, part-time degree program, services for LD students, student-designed majors, study abroad, summer session for credit.

Library Educational Resource Center with an OPAC, a Web page.

Student Life *Housing:* college housing not available. *Activities and Organizations:* drama/theater group, student-run newspaper, choral group, Black Student Alliance, Phi Theta Kappa, Adults on Campus, Inter-Varsity Club, Christian Fellowship. *Campus security:* 24-hour emergency response

devices and patrols, late-night transport/escort service. *Student services:* personal/psychological counseling.

Athletics Member NJCAA. *Intercollegiate sports:* baseball M, basketball M/W, golf M, soccer M/W, softball W, squash W, tennis M/W, volleyball W. *Intramural sports:* skiing (downhill) M/W.

Costs (2015–16) *Tuition:* area resident $2730 full-time, $91 per credit hour part-time; state resident $7620 full-time, $254 per credit hour part-time; nonresident $14,460 full-time, $482 per credit hour part-time. Full-time tuition and fees vary according to course load. Part-time tuition and fees vary according to course load. *Required fees:* $314 full-time. *Payment plans:* installment, deferred payment. *Waivers:* employees or children of employees.

Financial Aid Of all full-time matriculated undergraduates who enrolled in 2013, 120 Federal Work-Study jobs (averaging $1800).

Applying *Required:* high school transcript.

Freshman Application Contact Mr. Patrick Peyer, Director, Student Retention and Success, Rock Valley College, 3301 North Mulford Rd, Rockford, IL 61008. *Phone:* 815-921-4103. *Toll-free phone:* 800-973-7821. *E-mail:* p.peyer@rockvalleycollege.edu.

Website: http://www.rockvalleycollege.edu/.

Sauk Valley Community College
Dixon, Illinois

- **District-supported** 2-year, founded 1965, part of Illinois Community College Board
- **Rural** 165-acre campus
- **Endowment** $2.0 million
- **Coed**

Undergraduates 998 full-time, 1,222 part-time. 4% Black or African American, non-Hispanic/Latino; 8% Hispanic/Latino; 0.7% Asian, non-Hispanic/Latino; 0.2% Native Hawaiian or other Pacific Islander, non-Hispanic/Latino; 0.3% American Indian or Alaska Native, non-Hispanic/Latino; 0.1% Two or more races, non-Hispanic/Latino; 2% Race/ethnicity unknown. *Retention:* 59% of full-time freshmen returned.

Faculty *Student/faculty ratio:* 21:1.

Academics *Calendar:* semesters. *Degree:* certificates and associate. *Special study options:* academic remediation for entering students, accelerated degree program, adult/continuing education programs, cooperative education, distance learning, English as a second language, honors programs, independent study, internships, off-campus study, part-time degree program, services for LD students, summer session for credit.

Student Life *Campus security:* 24-hour emergency response devices and patrols, late-night transport/escort service.

Athletics Member NJCAA.

Standardized Tests *Recommended:* ACT (for admission).

Costs (2014–15) *Tuition:* area resident $2996 full-time, $107 per credit part-time; state resident $8848 full-time, $316 per credit part-time; nonresident $9604 full-time, $343 per credit part-time. Full-time tuition and fees vary according to course load and program. Part-time tuition and fees vary according to course load and program. *Required fees:* $150 full-time, $5 per credit part-time.

Financial Aid Of all full-time matriculated undergraduates who enrolled in 2014, 755 applied for aid, 499 were judged to have need. *Average percent of need met:* 36. *Average financial aid package:* $5223. *Average need-based loan:* $2955. *Average need-based gift aid:* $4556.

Applying *Options:* electronic application, early admission, deferred entrance. *Recommended:* high school transcript.

Freshman Application Contact Sauk Valley Community College, 173 Illinois Route 2, Dixon, IL 61021. *Phone:* 815-288-5511 Ext. 378.

Website: http://www.svcc.edu/.

Shawnee Community College
Ullin, Illinois

- **State and locally supported** 2-year, founded 1967, part of Illinois Community College Board
- **Rural** 163-acre campus
- **Coed,** 1,781 undergraduate students, 53% full-time, 59% women, 41% men

Undergraduates 936 full-time, 845 part-time. Students come from 3 states and territories; 2% are from out of state; 17% Black or African American, non-Hispanic/Latino; 2% Hispanic/Latino; 0.3% Asian, non-Hispanic/Latino; 0.5% American Indian or Alaska Native, non-Hispanic/Latino; 0.3% Race/ethnicity unknown; 7% transferred in.

Freshmen *Admission:* 633 applied, 633 admitted, 167 enrolled.

Faculty *Total:* 169, 24% full-time, 4% with terminal degrees. *Student/faculty ratio:* 13:1.

Majors Accounting; administrative assistant and secretarial science; agricultural business and management; agriculture; agronomy and crop science; animal sciences; automobile/automotive mechanics technology; biological and physical sciences; business administration and management; business automation/technology/data entry; child development; clinical/medical laboratory technology; computer graphics; computer systems networking and telecommunications; cosmetology; criminal justice/police science; electrical, electronic and communications engineering technology; health information/medical records technology; human services; information science/studies; legal administrative assistant/secretary; liberal arts and sciences/liberal studies; medical administrative assistant and medical secretary; occupational therapist assistant; registered nursing/registered nurse; sheet metal technology; social work; veterinary/animal health technology; welding technology; wildlife, fish and wildlands science and management.

Academics *Calendar:* semesters. *Degree:* certificates, diplomas, and associate. *Special study options:* academic remediation for entering students, accelerated degree program, adult/continuing education programs, advanced placement credit, cooperative education, distance learning, double majors, English as a second language, external degree program, independent study, internships, off-campus study, part-time degree program, services for LD students, summer session for credit.

Library Shawnee Community College Library with 46,313 titles, 1,842 audiovisual materials, an OPAC, a Web page.

Student Life *Housing:* college housing not available. *Activities and Organizations:* drama/theater group, choral group, Phi Theta Kappa, Phi Beta Lambda, Music Club, Student Senate, Future Teachers Organization. *Campus security:* 24-hour patrols. *Student services:* personal/psychological counseling.

Athletics Member NJCAA. *Intercollegiate sports:* baseball M(s), basketball M(s)/W(s), softball W(s). *Intramural sports:* weight lifting M/W.

Standardized Tests *Required for some:* ACT (for admission). *Recommended:* ACT (for admission).

Costs (2015–16) *Tuition:* area resident $2376 full-time, $99 per hour part-time; state resident $3936 full-time, $164 per hour part-time; nonresident $3984 full-time, $166 per hour part-time. *Payment plans:* installment, deferred payment. *Waivers:* senior citizens and employees or children of employees.

Financial Aid Of all full-time matriculated undergraduates who enrolled in 2013, 60 Federal Work-Study jobs (averaging $2000). 50 state and other part-time jobs (averaging $2000).

Applying *Options:* electronic application, early admission, deferred entrance. *Required:* high school transcript. *Application deadlines:* rolling (freshmen), rolling (out-of-state freshmen), rolling (transfers). *Notification:* continuous (freshmen), continuous (out-of-state freshmen), continuous (transfers).

Freshman Application Contact Mrs. Erin King, Recruiter/Advisor, Shawnee Community College, 8364 Shawnee College Road, Ullin, IL 62992. *Phone:* 618-634-3200. *Toll-free phone:* 800-481-2242. *Fax:* 618-634-3300. *E-mail:* erink@shawneecc.edu. *Website:* http://www.shawneecc.edu/.

Solex College
Wheeling, Illinois

Freshman Application Contact Solex College, 350 East Dundee Road, Wheeling, IL 60090. *Website:* http://www.solex.edu/.

Southeastern Illinois College
Harrisburg, Illinois

Freshman Application Contact Dr. David Nudo, Director of Counseling, Southeastern Illinois College, 3575 College Road, Harrisburg, IL 62946-4925. *Phone:* 618-252-5400 Ext. 2430. *Toll-free phone:* 866-338-2742. *Website:* http://www.sic.edu/.

South Suburban College
South Holland, Illinois

- **State and locally supported** 2-year, founded 1927, part of Illinois Community College Board
- **Suburban** campus with easy access to Chicago
- **Coed,** 4,514 undergraduate students, 38% full-time, 68% women, 32% men

Undergraduates 1,725 full-time, 2,789 part-time. 6% are from out of state; 64% Black or African American, non-Hispanic/Latino; 14% Hispanic/Latino; 0.4% Asian, non-Hispanic/Latino; 1% American Indian or Alaska Native, non-Hispanic/Latino; 2% Two or more races, non-Hispanic/Latino; 0.8% Race/ethnicity unknown; 0.3% international. *Retention:* 15% of full-time freshmen returned.

Freshmen *Average high school GPA:* 2.33.

Faculty *Total:* 513, 22% full-time. *Student/faculty ratio:* 20:1.

Majors Accounting; accounting technology and bookkeeping; architectural drafting and CAD/CADD; biological and physical sciences; building/home/construction inspection; CAD/CADD drafting/design technology; child-care provision; construction engineering technology; court reporting; criminal justice/safety; electrical, electronic and communications engineering technology; executive assistant/executive secretary; fine/studio arts; information technology; kinesiology and exercise science; legal assistant/paralegal; liberal arts and sciences/liberal studies; nursing administration; occupational therapist assistant; office management; radiologic technology/science; small business administration; social work.

Academics *Calendar:* semesters. *Degree:* certificates and associate. *Special study options:* academic remediation for entering students, adult/continuing education programs, advanced placement credit, cooperative education, distance learning, English as a second language, honors programs, internships, off-campus study, part-time degree program, services for LD students, study abroad, summer session for credit.

Library South Suburban College Library with 24,630 titles, 7,326 audiovisual materials, an OPAC, a Web page.

Student Life *Housing:* college housing not available. *Activities and Organizations:* drama/theater group, choral group. *Campus security:* 24-hour emergency response devices and patrols.

Athletics Member NJCAA. *Intercollegiate sports:* baseball M, basketball M/W, soccer M/W, softball W, volleyball W.

Costs (2015–16) *Tuition:* area resident $3600 full-time; state resident $9540 full-time; nonresident $11,190 full-time. Full-time tuition and fees vary according to course load and reciprocity agreements. Part-time tuition and fees vary according to course load and reciprocity agreements. *Required fees:* $533 full-time. *Payment plan:* installment. *Waivers:* senior citizens and employees or children of employees.

Applying *Options:* early admission, deferred entrance. *Required:* high school transcript. *Required for some:* essay or personal statement. *Recommended:* essay or personal statement, minimum 2.0 GPA. *Application deadlines:* rolling (freshmen), rolling (transfers). *Notification:* continuous (freshmen), continuous (transfers).

Freshman Application Contact Ms. Tiffane Jones, Admissions, South Suburban College, 15800 South State Street, South Holland, IL 60473. *Phone:* 708-596-2000 Ext. 2158. *E-mail:* admissionsquestions@ssc.edu. *Website:* http://www.ssc.edu/.

Southwestern Illinois College
Belleville, Illinois

- **District-supported** 2-year, founded 1946, part of Illinois Community College Board
- **Suburban** 341-acre campus with easy access to St. Louis
- **Endowment** $7.1 million
- **Coed,** 10,545 undergraduate students, 44% full-time, 56% women, 44% men

Undergraduates 4,591 full-time, 5,954 part-time. Students come from 13 states and territories; 1% are from out of state; 24% Black or African American, non-Hispanic/Latino; 4% Hispanic/Latino; 2% Asian, non-Hispanic/Latino; 0.4% Native Hawaiian or other Pacific Islander, non-Hispanic/Latino; 0.5% American Indian or Alaska Native, non-Hispanic/Latino; 4% Race/ethnicity unknown; 5% transferred in.

Freshmen *Admission:* 1,373 applied, 1,373 admitted, 1,373 enrolled.

Faculty *Total:* 974, 16% full-time, 6% with terminal degrees. *Student/faculty ratio:* 15:1.

Majors Accounting; administrative assistant and secretarial science; airframe mechanics and aircraft maintenance technology; airline pilot and flight crew; applied horticulture/horticulture operations; autobody/collision and repair technology; aviation/airway management; biological and physical sciences; carpentry; child-care provision; clinical/medical laboratory technology; computer and information sciences; computer/information technology services administration related; computer programming; concrete finishing; construction trades; criminal justice/law enforcement administration; data modeling/warehousing and database administration; desktop publishing and digital imaging design; electrical and power transmission installation; electrical, electronic and communications engineering technology; electrician; emergency medical technology (EMT paramedic); fine/studio arts; fire science/firefighting; general studies; health information/medical records technology; heating, air conditioning, ventilation and refrigeration maintenance technology; industrial mechanics and maintenance technology; information technology; ironworking; legal administrative assistant/secretary; legal assistant/paralegal; liberal arts and sciences/liberal studies; machine tool technology; manufacturing engineering technology; masonry; massage therapy; mathematics teacher education; mechanical drafting and CAD/CADD; medical/clinical assistant; medical office assistant; music; music teacher education; network and system administration; painting and wall covering; physical therapy technology; pipefitting and sprinkler fitting; radiologic technology/science; registered nursing/registered nurse; respiratory care therapy; restaurant, culinary, and catering management; selling skills and sales; sheet metal technology; sign language interpretation and translation; small business administration; social work; teacher assistant/aide; web/multimedia management and webmaster; welding technology.

Academics *Calendar:* semesters. *Degree:* certificates, diplomas, and associate. *Special study options:* academic remediation for entering students, accelerated degree program, adult/continuing education programs, advanced placement credit, cooperative education, distance learning, double majors, English as a second language, internships, off-campus study, part-time degree program, services for LD students, study abroad, summer session for credit. *ROTC:* Army (c), Air Force (c).

Library Southwestern Illinois College Library with 85,265 titles, 6,902 audiovisual materials, an OPAC, a Web page.

Student Life *Housing:* college housing not available. *Activities and Organizations:* drama/theater group, student-run newspaper, choral group, College Activities Board, Phi Theta Kappa, Student Nurses Association, Horticulture Club, Data Processing Management Association. *Campus security:* 24-hour emergency response devices and patrols, late-night transport/escort service. *Student services:* personal/psychological counseling.

Athletics Member NJCAA. *Intercollegiate sports:* baseball M(s), basketball M(s)/W(s), soccer M(s)/W(s), softball W(s), volleyball W(s).

Standardized Tests *Required for some:* ACT (for admission), ACT ASSET or ACT Compass.

Costs (2014–15) *Tuition:* area resident $3180 full-time, $106 per semester hour part-time; state resident $10,320 full-time, $344 per semester hour part-time; nonresident $13,650 full-time, $455 per semester hour part-time. Full-time tuition and fees vary according to program and reciprocity agreements. Part-time tuition and fees vary according to program and reciprocity agreements. *Required fees:* $150 full-time, $5 per semester hour part-time. *Payment plan:* installment. *Waivers:* senior citizens and employees or children of employees.

Financial Aid Of all full-time matriculated undergraduates who enrolled in 2013, 170 Federal Work-Study jobs (averaging $1537). 179 state and other part-time jobs (averaging $1004).

Applying *Options:* electronic application, early admission, deferred entrance. *Required:* high school transcript. *Application deadlines:* rolling (freshmen), rolling (out-of-state freshmen), rolling (transfers).

Freshman Application Contact Ms. Michelle Birk, Dean of Enrollment Services, Southwestern Illinois College, 2500 Carlyle Ave, Belleville, IL 62221. *Phone:* 618-235-2700 Ext. 5400. *Toll-free phone:* 866-942-SWIC. *Fax:* 618-222-9768. *E-mail:* michelle.birk@swic.edu. *Website:* http://www.swic.edu/.

Spoon River College
Canton, Illinois

- **State-supported** 2-year, founded 1959, part of Illinois Community College Board
- **Rural** 160-acre campus
- **Endowment** $1.5 million
- **Coed**

Undergraduates 713 full-time, 1,071 part-time. 6% Black or African American, non-Hispanic/Latino; 2% Hispanic/Latino; 0.9% Asian, non-Hispanic/Latino; 0.4% American Indian or Alaska Native, non-Hispanic/Latino; 0.2% Two or more races, non-Hispanic/Latino; 0.1% Race/ethnicity unknown; 0.1% international; 12% transferred in. *Retention:* 58% of full-time freshmen returned.

Faculty *Student/faculty ratio:* 17:1.

Academics *Calendar:* semesters. *Degree:* certificates and associate. *Special study options:* academic remediation for entering students, accelerated degree program, adult/continuing education programs, advanced placement credit, distance learning, English as a second language, freshman honors college, honors programs, internships, part-time degree program, services for LD students, summer session for credit. *ROTC:* Army (b).

Student Life *Campus security:* 24-hour emergency response devices, Night Patrol by trained security personnel.

Athletics Member NJCAA.

Costs (2014–15) *Tuition:* area resident $4050 full-time, $135 per semester hour part-time; state resident $8640 full-time, $288 per semester hour part-time; nonresident $9720 full-time, $324 per semester hour part-time. Full-time tuition and fees vary according to course load and program. Part-time tuition and fees vary according to course load and program. *Required fees:* $600 full-time, $20 per semester hour part-time.

Financial Aid Of all full-time matriculated undergraduates who enrolled in 2013, 44 Federal Work-Study jobs (averaging $1735).

Applying *Options:* electronic application, early admission, deferred entrance. *Required:* high school transcript.

Freshman Application Contact Ms. Missy Wilkinson, Dean of Student Services, Spoon River College, 23235 North County 22, Canton, IL 61520-

9801. *Phone:* 309-649-6305. *Toll-free phone:* 800-334-7337. *Fax:* 309-649-6235. *E-mail:* info@spoonrivercollege.edu. *Website:* http://www.src.edu/.

Taylor Business Institute
Chicago, Illinois

Director of Admissions Mr. Rashed Jahangir, Taylor Business Institute, 318 West Adams, Chicago, IL 60606. *Website:* http://www.tbiil.edu/.

Tribeca Flashpoint Media Arts Academy
Chicago, Illinois

Admissions Office Contact Tribeca Flashpoint Media Arts Academy, 28 North Clark Street, Chicago, IL 60602. *Website:* http://www.tfa.edu/.

Triton College
River Grove, Illinois

Freshman Application Contact Ms. Mary-Rita Moore, Dean of Admissions, Triton College, 2000 Fifth Avenue, River Grove, IL 60171. *Phone:* 708-456-0300 Ext. 3679. *Fax:* 708-583-3162. *E-mail:* mpatrice@triton.edu. *Website:* http://www.triton.edu/.

Vatterott College
Fairview Heights, Illinois

Admissions Office Contact Vatterott College, 110 Commerce Lane, Fairview Heights, IL 62208. *Toll-free phone:* 888-202-2636. *Website:* http://www.vatterott.edu/.

Vatterott College
Quincy, Illinois

Admissions Office Contact Vatterott College, 3609 North Marx Drive, Quincy, IL 62305. *Website:* http://www.vatterott.edu/.

Vet Tech Institute at Fox College
Tinley Park, Illinois

- **Private** 2-year, founded 2006
- **Suburban** campus
- **Coed,** 151 undergraduate students
- **61% of applicants were admitted**

Freshmen *Admission:* 389 applied, 236 admitted.

Majors Veterinary/animal health technology.

Academics *Calendar:* semesters. *Degree:* associate. *Special study options:* accelerated degree program, internships.

Student Life *Housing:* college housing not available.

Freshman Application Contact Admissions Office, Vet Tech Institute at Fox College, 18020 South Oak Park Avenue, Tinley Park, IL 60477. *Phone:* 888-884-3694. *Toll-free phone:* 888-884-3694. *Website:* http://chicago.vettechinstitute.edu/.

Waubonsee Community College
Sugar Grove, Illinois

- **District-supported** 2-year, founded 1966, part of Illinois Community College Board
- **Small-town** 243-acre campus with easy access to Chicago
- **Coed**

Undergraduates 3,469 full-time, 7,252 part-time. 7% Black or African American, non-Hispanic/Latino; 33% Hispanic/Latino; 3% Asian, non-Hispanic/Latino; 0.1% Native Hawaiian or other Pacific Islander, non-Hispanic/Latino; 0.1% American Indian or Alaska Native, non-Hispanic/Latino; 2% Two or more races, non-Hispanic/Latino; 3% Race/ethnicity unknown.

Academics *Calendar:* semesters. *Degree:* certificates and associate. *Special study options:* academic remediation for entering students, accelerated degree program, advanced placement credit, distance learning, English as a second language, honors programs, independent study, internships, off-campus study, part-time degree program, services for LD students, study abroad, summer session for credit. *ROTC:* Army (c).

Student Life *Campus security:* 24-hour emergency response devices and patrols, late-night transport/escort service.

Athletics Member NJCAA.

Costs (2014–15) *Tuition:* area resident $3120 full-time, $104 per credit hour part-time; state resident $8217 full-time, $274 per credit hour part-time; nonresident $8903 full-time, $297 per credit hour part-time. Full-time tuition and fees vary according to reciprocity agreements. Part-time tuition and fees vary according to reciprocity agreements. *Required fees:* $240 full-time, $8 per credit hour part-time.

Financial Aid Of all full-time matriculated undergraduates who enrolled in 2013, 23 Federal Work-Study jobs (averaging $2000).

Applying *Options:* electronic application.

Freshman Application Contact Joy Sanders, Admissions Manager, Waubonsee Community College, Route 47 at Waubonsee Drive, Sugar Grove, IL 60554. *Phone:* 630-466-7900 Ext. 5756. *Fax:* 630-466-6663. *E-mail:* admissions@waubonsee.edu.
Website: http://www.waubonsee.edu/.

Worsham College of Mortuary Science
Wheeling, Illinois

Director of Admissions President, Worsham College of Mortuary Science, 495 Northgate Parkway, Wheeling, IL 60090-2646. *Phone:* 847-808-8444.
Website: http://www.worshamcollege.com/.

INDIANA

Ancilla College
Donaldson, Indiana

- **Independent Roman Catholic** 2-year, founded 1937
- **Rural** 63-acre campus with easy access to Chicago
- **Endowment** $5.5 million
- **Coed,** 400 undergraduate students, 77% full-time, 55% women, 46% men

Undergraduates 307 full-time, 93 part-time. Students come from 10 states and territories; 3 other countries; 3% are from out of state; 11% Black or African American, non-Hispanic/Latino; 10% Hispanic/Latino; 0.3% American Indian or Alaska Native, non-Hispanic/Latino; 3% Two or more races, non-Hispanic/Latino; 0.5% international; 10% transferred in. *Retention:* 43% of full-time freshmen returned.

Freshmen *Admission:* 607 applied, 437 admitted, 159 enrolled. *Average high school GPA:* 2.45. *Test scores:* SAT critical reading scores over 500: 17%; SAT math scores over 500: 19%; SAT math scores over 600: 3%.

Faculty *Total:* 37, 41% full-time, 11% with terminal degrees. *Student/faculty ratio:* 14:1.

Majors Behavioral sciences; biological and physical sciences; business administration and management; computer and information sciences; criminal justice/safety; data processing and data processing technology; early childhood education; elementary education; environmental studies; general studies; health services/allied health/health sciences; history; kinesiology and exercise science; logistics, materials, and supply chain management; mass communication/media; registered nursing/registered nurse; secondary education; speech communication and rhetoric.

Academics *Calendar:* semesters. *Degree:* certificates and associate. *Special study options:* academic remediation for entering students, adult/continuing education programs, advanced placement credit, cooperative education, distance learning, double majors, independent study, internships, part-time degree program, services for LD students, student-designed majors, summer session for credit.

Library Gerald J. Ball Library with 22,226 titles, 822 audiovisual materials, an OPAC, a Web page.

Student Life *Housing Options:* coed. Campus housing is university owned. Freshman applicants given priority for college housing. *Activities and Organizations:* Student Government Association, Student Nursing Organization, Ancilla Student Ambassadors, Phi Theta Kappa. *Campus security:* 24-hour emergency response devices and patrols, late-night transport/escort service, controlled dormitory access. *Student services:* personal/psychological counseling.

Athletics Member NJCAA. *Intercollegiate sports:* baseball M(s), basketball M(s)/W(s), cheerleading M(s)/W(s), golf M(s)/W(s), soccer M(s)/W(s), softball W(s), volleyball W(s).

Standardized Tests *Recommended:* SAT or ACT (for admission).

Costs (2015–16) *Comprehensive fee:* $22,780 includes full-time tuition ($14,050), mandatory fees ($230), and room and board ($8500). Full-time tuition and fees vary according to course load and program. Part-time tuition: $470 per credit. Part-time tuition and fees vary according to course load and program. *Required fees:* $55 per term part-time. *Payment plan:* installment. *Waivers:* employees or children of employees.

Financial Aid Of all full-time matriculated undergraduates who enrolled in 2014, 326 applied for aid, 315 were judged to have need. 16 Federal Work-Study jobs (averaging $2301). *Average need-based loan:* $1321. *Average need-based gift aid:* $1573. *Financial aid deadline:* 2/28.

Applying *Options:* electronic application. *Required:* high school transcript. *Application deadlines:* rolling (freshmen), rolling (out-of-state freshmen), rolling (transfers).

Freshman Application Contact Mrs. Sarah Lawrence, Assistant Director of Admissions, Ancilla College, 9601 Union Road, Donaldson, IN 46513. *Phone:* 574-936-8898 Ext. 396. *Toll-free phone:* 866-ANCILLA. *Fax:* 574-935-1773. *E-mail:* admissions@ancilla.edu.
Website: http://www.ancilla.edu/.

Brown Mackie College–Fort Wayne
Fort Wayne, Indiana

- **Proprietary** primarily 2-year, part of Education Management Corporation
- **Coed**

Academics *Calendar:* quarters. *Degrees:* certificates, associate, and bachelor's.

Freshman Application Contact Brown Mackie College–Fort Wayne, 3000 East Coliseum Boulevard, Fort Wayne, IN 46805. *Phone:* 260-484-4400. *Toll-free phone:* 866-433-2289.
Website: http://www.brownmackie.edu/fortwayne/.

Brown Mackie College–Indianapolis
Indianapolis, Indiana

- **Proprietary** primarily 2-year, part of Education Management Corporation
- **Coed**

Academics *Degrees:* certificates, diplomas, associate, and bachelor's.

Freshman Application Contact Brown Mackie College–Indianapolis, 1200 North Meridian Street, Suite 100, Indianapolis, IN 46204. *Phone:* 317-554-8300. *Toll-free phone:* 866-255-0279.
Website: http://www.brownmackie.edu/indianapolis/.

Brown Mackie College–Merrillville
Merrillville, Indiana

- **Proprietary** primarily 2-year, founded 1890, part of Education Management Corporation
- **Small-town** campus
- **Coed**

Academics *Calendar:* quarters. *Degrees:* certificates, associate, and bachelor's.

Freshman Application Contact Brown Mackie College–Merrillville, 1000 East 80th Place, Suite 205S, Merrillville, IN 46410. *Phone:* 219-769-3321. *Toll-free phone:* 800-258-3321.
Website: http://www.brownmackie.edu/merrillville/.

Brown Mackie College–Michigan City
Michigan City, Indiana

- **Proprietary** primarily 2-year, part of Education Management Corporation
- **Rural** campus
- **Coed**

Academics *Calendar:* quarters. *Degrees:* certificates, associate, and bachelor's.

Freshman Application Contact Brown Mackie College–Michigan City, 1001 East US Highway 20, Michigan City, IN 46360. *Phone:* 219-877-3100. *Toll-free phone:* 800-519-2416.
Website: http://www.brownmackie.edu/michigancity/.

Brown Mackie College–South Bend
South Bend, Indiana

- **Proprietary** primarily 2-year, founded 1882, part of Education Management Corporation
- **Urban** campus
- **Coed, primarily women**

Academics *Calendar:* quarters. *Degrees:* certificates, diplomas, associate, and bachelor's.
Freshman Application Contact Brown Mackie College–South Bend, 3454 Douglas Road, South Bend, IN 46635. *Phone:* 574-237-0774. *Toll-free phone:* 800-743-2447.
Website: http://www.brownmackie.edu/southbend/.

College of Court Reporting
Hobart, Indiana

Freshman Application Contact Ms. Nicky Rodriquez, Director of Admissions, College of Court Reporting, 111 West Tenth Street, Suite 111, Hobart, IN 46342. *Phone:* 219-942-1459 Ext. 222. *Toll-free phone:* 866-294-3974. *Fax:* 219-942-1631. *E-mail:* nrodriquez@ccr.edu.
Website: http://www.ccr.edu/.

Fortis College
Indianapolis, Indiana

Admissions Office Contact Fortis College, 9001 N. Wesleyan Road, Suite 101, Indianapolis, IN 46268.
Website: http://www.fortis.edu/.

International Business College
Indianapolis, Indiana

- **Private** 2-year, founded 1889
- **Suburban** campus
- **Coed,** 399 undergraduate students
- **66%** of applicants were admitted

Freshmen *Admission:* 931 applied, 612 admitted.
Majors Accounting technology and bookkeeping; administrative assistant and secretarial science; computer programming; computer systems networking and telecommunications; dental assisting; graphic design; hotel/motel administration; legal administrative assistant/secretary; legal assistant/paralegal; medical/clinical assistant; veterinary/animal health technology.
Academics *Calendar:* semesters. *Degree:* diplomas and associate.
Freshman Application Contact Admissions Office, International Business College, 7205 Shadeland Station, Indianapolis, IN 46256. *Phone:* 317-813-2300. *Toll-free phone:* 800-589-6500.
Website: http://www.ibcindianapolis.edu/.

ITT Technical Institute
Fort Wayne, Indiana

- **Proprietary** primarily 2-year, founded 1967, part of ITT Educational Services, Inc.
- **Coed**

Academics *Calendar:* quarters. *Degrees:* associate and bachelor's.
Freshman Application Contact Director of Recruitment, ITT Technical Institute, 2810 Dupont Commerce Court, Fort Wayne, IN 46825. *Phone:* 260-497-6200. *Toll-free phone:* 800-866-4488.
Website: http://www.itt-tech.edu/.

ITT Technical Institute
Merrillville, Indiana

- **Proprietary** primarily 2-year
- **Coed**

Academics *Degrees:* associate and bachelor's.
Freshman Application Contact Director of Recruitment, ITT Technical Institute, 8488 Georgia Street, Merrillville, IN 46410. *Phone:* 219-738-6100. *Toll-free phone:* 877-418-8134.
Website: http://www.itt-tech.edu/.

ITT Technical Institute
Newburgh, Indiana

- **Proprietary** primarily 2-year, founded 1966, part of ITT Educational Services, Inc.
- **Coed**

Academics *Calendar:* quarters. *Degrees:* associate and bachelor's.
Freshman Application Contact Director of Recruitment, ITT Technical Institute, 10999 Stahl Road, Newburgh, IN 47630-7430. *Phone:* 812-858-1600. *Toll-free phone:* 800-832-4488.
Website: http://www.itt-tech.edu/.

Ivy Tech Community College–Bloomington
Bloomington, Indiana

- **State-supported** 2-year, founded 2001, part of Ivy Tech Community College System
- **Coed**

Undergraduates 2,503 full-time, 3,974 part-time. 1% are from out of state; 3% Black or African American, non-Hispanic/Latino; 2% Hispanic/Latino; 3% Asian, non-Hispanic/Latino; 0.3% American Indian or Alaska Native, non-Hispanic/Latino; 2% Two or more races, non-Hispanic/Latino; 21% Race/ethnicity unknown; 5% transferred in. *Retention:* 51% of full-time freshmen returned.
Faculty *Student/faculty ratio:* 20:1.
Academics *Calendar:* semesters. *Degree:* certificates and associate. *Special study options:* academic remediation for entering students, adult/continuing education programs, advanced placement credit, distance learning, external degree program, internships, part-time degree program, services for LD students, summer session for credit.
Student Life *Campus security:* late-night transport/escort service.
Costs (2014–15) *Tuition:* state resident $3935 full-time, $132 per credit hour part-time; nonresident $7812 full-time, $260 per credit hour part-time. *Required fees:* $120 full-time, $60 per term part-time. *Payment plans:* installment, deferred payment.
Financial Aid Of all full-time matriculated undergraduates who enrolled in 2013, 51 Federal Work-Study jobs (averaging $3259).
Applying *Options:* electronic application, deferred entrance. *Required:* high school transcript. *Required for some:* interview.
Freshman Application Contact Mr. Neil Frederick, Assistant Director of Admissions, Ivy Tech Community College–Bloomington, 200 Daniels Way, Bloomington, IN 47404. *Phone:* 812-330-6026. *Toll-free phone:* 888-IVY-LINE. *Fax:* 812-332-8147. *E-mail:* nfrederi@ivytech.edu.
Website: http://www.ivytech.edu/.

Ivy Tech Community College–Central Indiana
Indianapolis, Indiana

- **State-supported** 2-year, founded 1963, part of Ivy Tech Community College System
- **Urban** 10-acre campus
- **Coed**

Undergraduates 7,034 full-time, 14,944 part-time. 5% are from out of state; 27% Black or African American, non-Hispanic/Latino; 5% Hispanic/Latino; 2% Asian, non-Hispanic/Latino; 0.3% American Indian or Alaska Native, non-Hispanic/Latino; 3% Two or more races, non-Hispanic/Latino; 4% Race/ethnicity unknown; 5% transferred in. *Retention:* 48% of full-time freshmen returned.
Faculty *Student/faculty ratio:* 27:1.
Academics *Calendar:* semesters. *Degree:* certificates and associate. *Special study options:* academic remediation for entering students, adult/continuing education programs, advanced placement credit, cooperative education, distance learning, English as a second language, internships, off-campus study, part-time degree program, services for LD students, summer session for credit.
Student Life *Campus security:* 24-hour emergency response devices and patrols, late-night transport/escort service.
Costs (2014–15) *Tuition:* state resident $3935 full-time, $132 per credit hour part-time; nonresident $7812 full-time, $260 per credit hour part-time. *Required fees:* $120 full-time, $60 per term part-time. *Payment plans:* installment, deferred payment.
Financial Aid Of all full-time matriculated undergraduates who enrolled in 2013, 92 Federal Work-Study jobs (averaging $3766).
Applying *Options:* electronic application, early admission, deferred entrance. *Required:* high school transcript. *Required for some:* interview.
Freshman Application Contact Ms. Tracy Funk, Director of Admissions, Ivy Tech Community College–Central Indiana, 50 West Fall Creek Parkway North

Drive, Indianapolis, IN 46208-4777. *Phone:* 317-921-4371. *Toll-free phone:* 888-IVYLINE. *Fax:* 317-917-5919. *E-mail:* tfunk@ivytech.edu. *Website:* http://www.ivytech.edu/.

Ivy Tech Community College–Columbus
Columbus, Indiana

- **State-supported** 2-year, founded 1963, part of Ivy Tech Community College System
- **Small-town** campus with easy access to Indianapolis
- **Coed**

Undergraduates 1,283 full-time, 3,295 part-time. 1% are from out of state; 2% Black or African American, non-Hispanic/Latino; 2% Hispanic/Latino; 0.8% Asian, non-Hispanic/Latino; 0.4% American Indian or Alaska Native, non-Hispanic/Latino; 1% Two or more races, non-Hispanic/Latino; 21% Race/ethnicity unknown; 4% transferred in. *Retention:* 52% of full-time freshmen returned.

Faculty *Student/faculty ratio:* 18:1.

Academics *Calendar:* semesters. *Degree:* certificates and associate. *Special study options:* academic remediation for entering students, adult/continuing education programs, advanced placement credit, distance learning, internships, part-time degree program, services for LD students, summer session for credit.

Student Life *Campus security:* late-night transport/escort service, trained evening security personnel, escort service.

Costs (2014–15) *Tuition:* state resident $3935 full-time, $132 per credit hour part-time; nonresident $7812 full-time, $260 per credit hour part-time. *Required fees:* $120 full-time, $60 per term part-time. *Payment plans:* installment, deferred payment.

Financial Aid Of all full-time matriculated undergraduates who enrolled in 2013, 26 Federal Work-Study jobs (averaging $1694).

Applying *Options:* electronic application, early admission, deferred entrance. *Required:* high school transcript. *Required for some:* interview.

Freshman Application Contact Alisa Deck, Director of Admissions, Ivy Tech Community College–Columbus, 4475 Central Avenue, Columbus, IN 47203-1868. *Phone:* 812-374-5129. *Toll-free phone:* 888-IVY-LINE. *Fax:* 812-372-0331. *E-mail:* adeck@ivytech.edu. *Website:* http://www.ivytech.edu/.

Ivy Tech Community College–East Central
Muncie, Indiana

- **State-supported** 2-year, founded 1968, part of Ivy Tech Community College System
- **Suburban** 15-acre campus with easy access to Indianapolis
- **Coed**

Undergraduates 3,294 full-time, 4,172 part-time. 8% Black or African American, non-Hispanic/Latino; 2% Hispanic/Latino; 0.6% Asian, non-Hispanic/Latino; 0.5% American Indian or Alaska Native, non-Hispanic/Latino; 3% Two or more races, non-Hispanic/Latino; 7% Race/ethnicity unknown; 5% transferred in. *Retention:* 46% of full-time freshmen returned.

Faculty *Student/faculty ratio:* 18:1.

Academics *Calendar:* semesters. *Degree:* certificates and associate. *Special study options:* academic remediation for entering students, adult/continuing education programs, advanced placement credit, distance learning, internships, part-time degree program, services for LD students.

Costs (2014–15) *Tuition:* state resident $3935 full-time, $132 per credit hour part-time; nonresident $7812 full-time, $260 per credit hour part-time. *Required fees:* $120 full-time, $60 per term part-time. *Payment plans:* installment, deferred payment.

Financial Aid Of all full-time matriculated undergraduates who enrolled in 2013, 65 Federal Work-Study jobs (averaging $2666).

Applying *Options:* electronic application, early admission, deferred entrance. *Required:* high school transcript. *Required for some:* interview.

Freshman Application Contact Ms. Mary Lewellen, Ivy Tech Community College–East Central, 4301 South Cowan Road, Muncie, IN 47302-9448. *Phone:* 765-289-2291 Ext. 1391. *Toll-free phone:* 888-IVY-LINE. *Fax:* 765-289-2292. *E-mail:* mlewelle@ivytech.edu. *Website:* http://www.ivytech.edu/.

Ivy Tech Community College–Kokomo
Kokomo, Indiana

- **State-supported** 2-year, founded 1968, part of Ivy Tech Community College System
- **Small-town** 20-acre campus with easy access to Indianapolis
- **Coed**

Undergraduates 1,587 full-time, 2,361 part-time. 6% Black or African American, non-Hispanic/Latino; 3% Hispanic/Latino; 0.6% Asian, non-Hispanic/Latino; 0.7% American Indian or Alaska Native, non-Hispanic/Latino; 2% Two or more races, non-Hispanic/Latino; 3% Race/ethnicity unknown; 4% transferred in. *Retention:* 49% of full-time freshmen returned.

Faculty *Student/faculty ratio:* 15:1.

Academics *Calendar:* semesters. *Degree:* certificates and associate. *Special study options:* academic remediation for entering students, adult/continuing education programs, advanced placement credit, distance learning, internships, part-time degree program, services for LD students, summer session for credit.

Student Life *Campus security:* 24-hour emergency response devices, late-night transport/escort service.

Costs (2014–15) *Tuition:* state resident $3935 full-time, $132 per credit hour part-time; nonresident $7812 full-time, $260 per credit hour part-time. *Required fees:* $120 full-time. *Payment plans:* installment, deferred payment.

Financial Aid Of all full-time matriculated undergraduates who enrolled in 2013, 45 Federal Work-Study jobs (averaging $1829).

Applying *Options:* electronic application, early admission. *Required:* high school transcript. *Required for some:* interview.

Freshman Application Contact Mr. Mike Federspill, Director of Admissions, Ivy Tech Community College–Kokomo, 1815 East Morgan Street, Kokomo, IN 46903-1373. *Phone:* 765-459-0561 Ext. 233. *Toll-free phone:* 888-IVY-LINE. *Fax:* 765-454-5111. *E-mail:* mfedersp@ivytech.edu. *Website:* http://www.ivytech.edu/.

Ivy Tech Community College–Lafayette
Lafayette, Indiana

- **State-supported** 2-year, founded 1968, part of Ivy Tech Community College System
- **Suburban** campus with easy access to Indianapolis
- **Coed**

Undergraduates 2,792 full-time, 3,606 part-time. 4% are from out of state; 4% Black or African American, non-Hispanic/Latino; 6% Hispanic/Latino; 2% Asian, non-Hispanic/Latino; 0.5% American Indian or Alaska Native, non-Hispanic/Latino; 2% Two or more races, non-Hispanic/Latino; 9% Race/ethnicity unknown; 5% transferred in. *Retention:* 55% of full-time freshmen returned.

Faculty *Student/faculty ratio:* 19:1.

Academics *Calendar:* semesters. *Degree:* certificates and associate. *Special study options:* academic remediation for entering students, advanced placement credit, distance learning, internships, part-time degree program, services for LD students, summer session for credit.

Costs (2014–15) *Tuition:* state resident $3935 full-time, $132 per credit hour part-time; nonresident $7812 full-time, $260 per credit hour part-time. *Required fees:* $120 full-time. *Payment plans:* installment, deferred payment.

Financial Aid Of all full-time matriculated undergraduates who enrolled in 2013, 65 Federal Work-Study jobs (averaging $2222). 1 state and other part-time job (averaging $2436).

Applying *Options:* electronic application. *Required:* high school transcript. *Required for some:* interview.

Freshman Application Contact Mr. Ivan Hernanadez, Director of Admissions, Ivy Tech Community College–Lafayette, 3101 South Creasy Lane, PO Box 6299, Lafayette, IN 47903. *Phone:* 765-269-5116. *Toll-free phone:* 888-IVY-LINE. *Fax:* 765-772-9293. *E-mail:* ihernand@ivytech.edu. *Website:* http://www.ivytech.edu/.

Ivy Tech Community College–North Central
South Bend, Indiana

- **State-supported** 2-year, founded 1968, part of Ivy Tech Community College System
- **Suburban** 4-acre campus
- **Coed**

Undergraduates 2,059 full-time, 5,123 part-time. 4% are from out of state; 17% Black or African American, non-Hispanic/Latino; 9% Hispanic/Latino; 1% Asian, non-Hispanic/Latino; 0.4% American Indian or Alaska Native, non-Hispanic/Latino; 3% Two or more races, non-Hispanic/Latino; 4%

Race/ethnicity unknown; 0.1% international; 5% transferred in. *Retention:* 47% of full-time freshmen returned.

Faculty *Student/faculty ratio:* 18:1.

Academics *Calendar:* semesters. *Degree:* certificates and associate. *Special study options:* academic remediation for entering students, adult/continuing education programs, advanced placement credit, distance learning, English as a second language, internships, off-campus study, part-time degree program, services for LD students, summer session for credit.

Student Life *Campus security:* 24-hour emergency response devices and patrols, late-night transport/escort service, security during open hours.

Costs (2014–15) *Tuition:* state resident $3935 full-time, $131 per credit part-time; nonresident $7812 full-time, $260 per credit part-time. *Required fees:* $120 full-time. *Payment plans:* installment, deferred payment.

Financial Aid Of all full-time matriculated undergraduates who enrolled in 2013, 100 Federal Work-Study jobs (averaging $1538).

Applying *Options:* electronic application, early admission, deferred entrance. *Required:* high school transcript. *Required for some:* interview.

Freshman Application Contact Ms. Janice Austin, Director of Admissions, Ivy Tech Community College–North Central, 220 Dean Johnson Boulevard, South Bend, IN 46601-3415. *Phone:* 574-289-7001 Ext. 5326. *Toll-free phone:* 888-IVY-LINE. *Fax:* 574-236-7177. *E-mail:* jaustin@ivytech.edu. *Website:* http://www.ivytech.edu/.

Ivy Tech Community College–Northeast
Fort Wayne, Indiana

- **State-supported** 2-year, founded 1969, part of Ivy Tech Community College System
- **Urban** 22-acre campus
- **Coed**

Undergraduates 3,177 full-time, 5,925 part-time. 6% are from out of state; 15% Black or African American, non-Hispanic/Latino; 5% Hispanic/Latino; 2% Asian, non-Hispanic/Latino; 0.5% American Indian or Alaska Native, non-Hispanic/Latino; 3% Two or more races, non-Hispanic/Latino; 3% Race/ethnicity unknown; 6% transferred in. *Retention:* 45% of full-time freshmen returned.

Faculty *Student/faculty ratio:* 19:1.

Academics *Calendar:* semesters. *Degree:* certificates and associate. *Special study options:* adult/continuing education programs, advanced placement credit, distance learning, English as a second language, internships, part-time degree program, services for LD students, summer session for credit.

Student Life *Campus security:* 24-hour emergency response devices and patrols, late-night transport/escort service.

Costs (2014–15) *Tuition:* state resident $3935 full-time, $132 per credit hour part-time; nonresident $7812 full-time, $260 per credit hour part-time. *Required fees:* $120 full-time. *Payment plans:* installment, deferred payment.

Financial Aid Of all full-time matriculated undergraduates who enrolled in 2013, 40 Federal Work-Study jobs (averaging $4041).

Applying *Options:* early admission. *Required:* high school transcript. *Required for some:* interview.

Freshman Application Contact Robyn Boss, Director of Admissions, Ivy Tech Community College–Northeast, 3800 North Anthony Boulevard, Ft. Wayne, IN 46805-1489. *Phone:* 260-480-4211. *Toll-free phone:* 888-IVY-LINE. *Fax:* 260-480-2053. *E-mail:* rboss1@ivytech.edu. *Website:* http://www.ivytech.edu/.

Ivy Tech Community College–Northwest
Gary, Indiana

- **State-supported** 2-year, founded 1963, part of Ivy Tech Community College System
- **Urban** 13-acre campus with easy access to Chicago
- **Coed**

Undergraduates 3,431 full-time, 6,511 part-time. 3% are from out of state; 24% Black or African American, non-Hispanic/Latino; 10% Hispanic/Latino; 0.6% Asian, non-Hispanic/Latino; 0.4% American Indian or Alaska Native, non-Hispanic/Latino; 3% Two or more races, non-Hispanic/Latino; 8% Race/ethnicity unknown; 6% transferred in. *Retention:* 44% of full-time freshmen returned.

Faculty *Student/faculty ratio:* 21:1.

Academics *Calendar:* semesters. *Degree:* certificates and associate. *Special study options:* academic remediation for entering students, adult/continuing education programs, advanced placement credit, distance learning, internships, part-time degree program, services for LD students, summer session for credit.

Student Life *Campus security:* 24-hour emergency response devices, late-night transport/escort service.

Costs (2014–15) *Tuition:* state resident $3935 full-time, $131 per credit part-time; nonresident $7812 full-time, $260 per credit part-time. *Required fees:* $120 full-time.

Financial Aid Of all full-time matriculated undergraduates who enrolled in 2013, 74 Federal Work-Study jobs (averaging $2131).

Applying *Options:* electronic application, deferred entrance. *Required:* high school transcript. *Required for some:* interview.

Freshman Application Contact Ms. Twilla Lewis, Associate Dean of Student Affairs, Ivy Tech Community College–Northwest, 1440 East 35th Avenue, Gary, IN 46409-499. *Phone:* 219-981-1111 Ext. 2273. *Toll-free phone:* 888-IVY-LINE. *Fax:* 219-981-4415. *E-mail:* tlewis@ivytech.edu. *Website:* http://www.ivytech.edu/.

Ivy Tech Community College–Richmond
Richmond, Indiana

- **State-supported** 2-year, founded 1963, part of Ivy Tech Community College System
- **Small-town** 23-acre campus with easy access to Indianapolis
- **Coed**

Undergraduates 1,042 full-time, 2,053 part-time. 8% are from out of state; 10% Black or African American, non-Hispanic/Latino; 1% Hispanic/Latino; 0.6% American Indian or Alaska Native, non-Hispanic/Latino; 2% Two or more races, non-Hispanic/Latino; 2% Race/ethnicity unknown; 3% transferred in. *Retention:* 46% of full-time freshmen returned.

Faculty *Student/faculty ratio:* 19:1.

Academics *Calendar:* semesters. *Degree:* certificates and associate. *Special study options:* academic remediation for entering students, adult/continuing education programs, advanced placement credit, distance learning, independent study, internships, off-campus study, part-time degree program, services for LD students, summer session for credit.

Student Life *Campus security:* 24-hour emergency response devices, late-night transport/escort service.

Costs (2014–15) *Tuition:* state resident $3935 full-time, $132 per credit hour part-time; nonresident $7812 full-time, $260 per credit hour part-time. *Required fees:* $120 full-time. *Payment plans:* installment, deferred payment.

Financial Aid Of all full-time matriculated undergraduates who enrolled in 2013, 14 Federal Work-Study jobs (averaging $3106). 1 state and other part-time job (averaging $3380).

Applying *Options:* electronic application, early admission. *Required:* high school transcript. *Required for some:* interview.

Freshman Application Contact Christine Seger, Director of Admissions, Ivy Tech Community College–Richmond, 2325 Chester Boulevard, Richmond, IN 47374-1298. *Phone:* 765-966-2656 Ext. 1212. *Toll-free phone:* 888-IVY-LINE. *Fax:* 765-962-8741. *E-mail:* crethlake@ivytech.edu. *Website:* http://www.ivytech.edu/richmond/.

Ivy Tech Community College–Southeast
Madison, Indiana

- **State-supported** 2-year, founded 1963, part of Ivy Tech Community College System
- **Small-town** 5-acre campus with easy access to Louisville
- **Coed**

Undergraduates 977 full-time, 1,904 part-time. 6% are from out of state; 0.8% Black or African American, non-Hispanic/Latino; 0.9% Hispanic/Latino; 0.3% Asian, non-Hispanic/Latino; 0.2% American Indian or Alaska Native, non-Hispanic/Latino; 1% Two or more races, non-Hispanic/Latino; 15% Race/ethnicity unknown; 4% transferred in. *Retention:* 55% of full-time freshmen returned.

Faculty *Student/faculty ratio:* 15:1.

Academics *Calendar:* semesters. *Degree:* certificates and associate. *Special study options:* academic remediation for entering students, advanced placement credit, distance learning, internships, part-time degree program, services for LD students, summer session for credit.

Student Life *Campus security:* 24-hour emergency response devices.

Costs (2014–15) *Tuition:* state resident $3935 full-time, $132 per credit hour part-time; nonresident $7812 full-time, $260 per credit hour part-time. *Required fees:* $120 full-time, $60 per term part-time. *Payment plans:* installment, deferred payment.

Financial Aid Of all full-time matriculated undergraduates who enrolled in 2013, 26 Federal Work-Study jobs (averaging $1696).

Applying *Options:* electronic application. *Required:* high school transcript. *Required for some:* interview.

Freshman Application Contact Ms. Cindy Hutcherson, Assistant Director of Admission/Career Counselor, Ivy Tech Community College–Southeast, 590 Ivy Tech Drive, Madison, IN 47250-1881. *Phone:* 812-265-2580 Ext. 4142. *Toll-free phone:* 888-IVY-LINE. *Fax:* 812-265-4028. *E-mail:* chutcher@ivytech.edu. *Website:* http://www.ivytech.edu/.

Ivy Tech Community College–Southern Indiana
Sellersburg, Indiana

- **State-supported** 2-year, founded 1968, part of Ivy Tech Community College System
- **Small-town** 63-acre campus with easy access to Louisville
- **Coed**

Undergraduates 1,285 full-time, 3,607 part-time. 8% are from out of state; 7% Black or African American, non-Hispanic/Latino; 2% Hispanic/Latino; 0.7% Asian, non-Hispanic/Latino; 0.5% American Indian or Alaska Native, non-Hispanic/Latino; 2% Two or more races, non-Hispanic/Latino; 11% Race/ethnicity unknown; 6% transferred in. *Retention:* 48% of full-time freshmen returned.
Faculty *Student/faculty ratio:* 19:1.
Academics *Calendar:* semesters. *Degree:* certificates and associate. *Special study options:* academic remediation for entering students, adult/continuing education programs, advanced placement credit, cooperative education, distance learning, internships, part-time degree program, services for LD students, summer session for credit.
Student Life *Campus security:* late-night transport/escort service.
Costs (2014–15) *Tuition:* state resident $3935 full-time, $132 per credit hour part-time; nonresident $7812 full-time, $260 per credit hour part-time. *Required fees:* $120 full-time, $60 per term part-time.
Financial Aid Of all full-time matriculated undergraduates who enrolled in 2013, 20 Federal Work-Study jobs (averaging $5007). 1 state and other part-time job (averaging $6080).
Applying *Options:* electronic application, early admission, deferred entrance. *Required:* high school transcript. *Required for some:* interview.
Freshman Application Contact Ben Harris, Director of Admissions, Ivy Tech Community College–Southern Indiana, 8204 Highway 311, Sellersburg, IN 47172-1897. *Phone:* 812-246-3301 Ext. 4137. *Toll-free phone:* 888-IVY-LINE. *Fax:* 812-246-9905. *E-mail:* bharris88@ivytech.edu. *Website:* http://www.ivytech.edu/.

Ivy Tech Community College–Southwest
Evansville, Indiana

- **State-supported** 2-year, founded 1963, part of Ivy Tech Community College System
- **Suburban** 15-acre campus
- **Coed**

Undergraduates 1,827 full-time, 3,648 part-time. 6% are from out of state; 10% Black or African American, non-Hispanic/Latino; 1% Hispanic/Latino; 0.4% Asian, non-Hispanic/Latino; 0.3% American Indian or Alaska Native, non-Hispanic/Latino; 2% Two or more races, non-Hispanic/Latino; 7% Race/ethnicity unknown; 5% transferred in. *Retention:* 48% of full-time freshmen returned.
Faculty *Student/faculty ratio:* 18:1.
Academics *Calendar:* semesters. *Degree:* certificates and associate. *Special study options:* academic remediation for entering students, advanced placement credit, cooperative education, distance learning, independent study, internships, part-time degree program, services for LD students, summer session for credit.
Student Life *Campus security:* late-night transport/escort service.
Costs (2014–15) *Tuition:* state resident $3934 full-time, $132 per credit hour part-time; nonresident $7812 full-time, $260 per credit hour part-time. *Required fees:* $120 full-time, $60 per term part-time. *Payment plans:* installment, deferred payment.
Financial Aid Of all full-time matriculated undergraduates who enrolled in 2013, 65 Federal Work-Study jobs (averaging $2264).
Applying *Options:* electronic application, early admission, deferred entrance. *Required:* high school transcript. *Required for some:* interview.
Freshman Application Contact Ms. Denise Johnson-Kincade, Director of Admissions, Ivy Tech Community College–Southwest, 3501 First Avenue, Evansville, IN 47710-3398. *Phone:* 812-429-1430. *Toll-free phone:* 888-IVY-LINE. *Fax:* 812-429-9878. *E-mail:* ajohnson@ivytech.edu. *Website:* http://www.ivytech.edu/.

Ivy Tech Community College–Wabash Valley
Terre Haute, Indiana

- **State-supported** 2-year, founded 1966, part of Ivy Tech Community College System
- **Suburban** 55-acre campus with easy access to Indianapolis
- **Coed**

Undergraduates 1,921 full-time, 3,443 part-time. 5% are from out of state; 4% Black or African American, non-Hispanic/Latino; 0.9% Hispanic/Latino; 0.7% Asian, non-Hispanic/Latino; 0.4% American Indian or Alaska Native, non-Hispanic/Latino; 2% Two or more races, non-Hispanic/Latino; 4% Race/ethnicity unknown; 3% transferred in. *Retention:* 48% of full-time freshmen returned.
Faculty *Student/faculty ratio:* 19:1.
Academics *Calendar:* semesters. *Degree:* certificates and associate. *Special study options:* academic remediation for entering students, adult/continuing education programs, advanced placement credit, distance learning, internships, part-time degree program, services for LD students, summer session for credit.
Student Life *Campus security:* 24-hour emergency response devices.
Costs (2014–15) *Tuition:* state resident $3935 full-time, $132 per credit hour part-time; nonresident $7812 full-time, $260 per credit hour part-time. *Required fees:* $120 full-time.
Financial Aid Of all full-time matriculated undergraduates who enrolled in 2013, 51 Federal Work-Study jobs (averaging $2110). 1 state and other part-time job (averaging $2963).
Applying *Options:* electronic application, early admission, deferred entrance. *Required:* high school transcript. *Required for some:* interview.
Freshman Application Contact Mr. Michael Fisher, Director of Admissions, Ivy Tech Community College–Wabash Valley, 7999 U.S. Highway 41 South, Terre Haute, IN 47802-4898. *Phone:* 812-298-2300. *Toll-free phone:* 888-IVY-LINE. *Fax:* 812-298-2291. *E-mail:* mfisher@ivytech.edu. *Website:* http://www.ivytech.edu/.

Kaplan College, Hammond Campus
Hammond, Indiana

Freshman Application Contact Kaplan College, Hammond Campus, 7833 Indianapolis Boulevard, Hammond, IN 46324. *Phone:* 219-844-0100. *Toll-free phone:* 800-935-1857.
Website: http://www.kaplancollege.com/.

Kaplan College, Southeast Indianapolis Campus
Indianapolis, Indiana

Freshman Application Contact Director of Admissions, Kaplan College, Southeast Indianapolis Campus, 4200 South East Street, Indianapolis, IN 46227. *Phone:* 317-782-0315.
Website: http://www.kaplancollege.com/.

Lincoln College of Technology
Indianapolis, Indiana

Director of Admissions Ms. Cindy Ryan, Director of Admissions, Lincoln College of Technology, 7225 Winton Drive, Building 128, Indianapolis, IN 46268. *Phone:* 317-632-5553.
Website: http://www.lincolnedu.com/.

MedTech College
Ft. Wayne, Indiana

Admissions Office Contact MedTech College, 7230 Engle Road, Ft. Wayne, IN 46804.
Website: http://www.medtechcollege.edu/.

MedTech College
Greenwood, Indiana

Admissions Office Contact MedTech College, 1500 American Way, Greenwood, IN 46143.
Website: http://www.medtechcollege.edu/.

MedTech College
Indianapolis, Indiana

Admissions Office Contact MedTech College, 6612 East 75th Street, Suite 300, Indianapolis, IN 46250-2865.
Website: http://www.medtechcollege.com/.

Mid-America College of Funeral Service
Jeffersonville, Indiana

Freshman Application Contact Mr. Richard Nelson, Dean of Students, Mid-America College of Funeral Service, 3111 Hamburg Pike, Jeffersonville, IN 47130-9630. *Phone:* 812-288-8878. *Toll-free phone:* 800-221-6158. *Fax:* 812-288-5942. *E-mail:* macfs@mindspring.com.
Website: http://www.mid-america.edu/.

Vet Tech Institute at International Business College
Fort Wayne, Indiana

- **Private** 2-year, founded 2005
- **Suburban** campus
- **Coed**, 127 undergraduate students
- 54% of applicants were admitted

Freshmen *Admission:* 306 applied, 165 admitted.
Majors Veterinary/animal health technology.
Academics *Calendar:* semesters. *Degree:* associate. *Special study options:* accelerated degree program, internships.
Freshman Application Contact Admissions Office, Vet Tech Institute at International Business College, 5699 Coventry Lane, Fort Wayne, IN 46804. *Phone:* 800-589-6363. *Toll-free phone:* 800-589-6363.
Website: http://ftwayne.vettechinstitute.edu/.

Vet Tech Institute at International Business College
Indianapolis, Indiana

- **Private** 2-year, founded 2007
- **Suburban** campus
- **Coed**, 124 undergraduate students
- 46% of applicants were admitted

Freshmen *Admission:* 489 applied, 227 admitted.
Majors Veterinary/animal health technology.
Academics *Calendar:* semesters. *Degree:* associate. *Special study options:* accelerated degree program, internships.
Freshman Application Contact Admissions Office, Vet Tech Institute at International Business College, 7205 Shadeland Station, Indianapolis, IN 46256. *Phone:* 800-589-6500. *Toll-free phone:* 877-835-7297.
Website: http://indianapolis.vettechinstitute.edu/.

Vincennes University
Vincennes, Indiana

- **State-supported** primarily 2-year, founded 1801
- **Small-town** 160-acre campus
- **Coed**, 19,205 undergraduate students, 32% full-time, 45% women, 55% men

Undergraduates 6,175 full-time, 13,030 part-time. 13% Black or African American, non-Hispanic/Latino; 3% Hispanic/Latino; 0.6% Asian, non-Hispanic/Latino; 0.2% Native Hawaiian or other Pacific Islander, non-Hispanic/Latino; 0.3% American Indian or Alaska Native, non-Hispanic/Latino; 2% Two or more races, non-Hispanic/Latino; 9% Race/ethnicity unknown; 0.4% international.
Freshmen *Admission:* 5,965 applied, 4,860 admitted, 3,089 enrolled.
Majors Accounting technology and bookkeeping; administrative assistant and secretarial science; agricultural business and management; agricultural engineering; agriculture; aircraft powerplant technology; airline pilot and flight crew; American Sign Language (ASL); anthropology; applied horticulture/horticulture operations; architectural drafting and CAD/CADD; art; art teacher education; art therapy; autobody/collision and repair technology; automobile/automotive mechanics technology; behavioral sciences; biochemistry; biological and biomedical sciences related; biological and physical sciences; biology/biological sciences; biotechnology; building/home/construction inspection; business administration and

management; business/commerce; chemistry; chemistry related; chemistry teacher education; child-care and support services management; child-care provision; civil engineering; commercial and advertising art; communications technology; computer and information sciences; computer/information technology services administration related; computer programming; computer science; computer systems networking and telecommunications; construction trades; corrections; corrections and criminal justice related; cosmetology; criminal justice/police science; culinary arts; design and applied arts related; diesel mechanics technology; dietetics; dramatic/theater arts; early childhood education; economics; education; electrical, electronic and communications engineering technology; elementary education; emergency medical technology (EMT paramedic); engineering technology; English; English/language arts teacher education; family and consumer sciences/home economics teacher education; family and consumer sciences/human sciences; fashion merchandising; finance; fire science/firefighting; food science; foreign languages and literatures; foreign languages related; funeral service and mortuary science; geology/earth science; graphic and printing equipment operation/production; health and physical education/fitness; health information/medical records technology; history; hospitality administration; hotel/motel administration; industrial technology; journalism; legal assistant/paralegal; liberal arts and sciences/liberal studies; manufacturing engineering technology; marketing/marketing management; massage therapy; mathematics; mathematics teacher education; mechanical drafting and CAD/CADD; mechanical engineering/mechanical technology; medical radiologic technology; music; music teacher education; natural resources/conservation; nuclear medical technology; ophthalmic and optometric support services and allied professions related; parks, recreation and leisure; pharmacy technician; philosophy; photojournalism; physical education teaching and coaching; physical sciences; physical therapy technology; political science and government; pre-dentistry studies; premedical studies; pre-pharmacy studies; pre-veterinary studies; psychology; public relations/image management; radio and television broadcasting technology; recording arts technology; registered nursing/registered nurse; restaurant, culinary, and catering management; robotics technology; science teacher education; secondary education; securities services administration; security and loss prevention; sheet metal technology; social work; sociology; special education; sport and fitness administration/management; surgical technology; surveying technology; teacher assistant/aide; theater design and technology; tool and die technology; web/multimedia management and webmaster; woodworking.
Academics *Calendar:* semesters. *Degrees:* certificates, associate, and bachelor's. *Special study options:* academic remediation for entering students, accelerated degree program, adult/continuing education programs, advanced placement credit, distance learning, double majors, English as a second language, external degree program, freshman honors college, honors programs, independent study, internships, off-campus study, part-time degree program, services for LD students, student-designed majors, summer session for credit. *ROTC:* Army (b), Air Force (c).
Library Shake Learning Resource Center.
Student Life *Housing:* on-campus residence required for freshman year. *Options:* coed, men-only, women-only, special housing for students with disabilities. Campus housing is university owned. Freshman campus housing is guaranteed. *Activities and Organizations:* drama/theater group, student-run newspaper, radio and television station, choral group, national fraternities, national sororities. *Campus security:* 24-hour emergency response devices and patrols, student patrols, late-night transport/escort service, controlled dormitory access, surveillance cameras. *Student services:* health clinic, personal/psychological counseling.
Athletics Member NJCAA. *Intercollegiate sports:* baseball M, basketball M/W, bowling M, cross-country running M/W, golf M, tennis M, track and field M/W, volleyball W.
Costs (2014–15) *Tuition:* state resident $5174 full-time, $2209 per year part-time; nonresident $12,234 full-time, $5033 per year part-time. Full-time tuition and fees vary according to course level, course load, location, program, reciprocity agreements, and student level. Part-time tuition and fees vary according to course level, course load, location, program, reciprocity agreements, and student level. *Room and board:* $8732. Room and board charges vary according to board plan, gender, and housing facility. *Payment plan:* installment. *Waivers:* senior citizens and employees or children of employees.
Applying *Options:* electronic application, early admission, deferred entrance. *Application fee:* $20. *Required:* high school transcript. *Required for some:* interview. *Application deadlines:* rolling (freshmen), rolling (transfers). *Notification:* continuous until 8/1 (freshmen), continuous (transfers).
Freshman Application Contact Vincennes University, 1002 North First Street, Vincennes, IN 47591-5202. *Phone:* 812-888-4313. *Toll-free phone:* 800-742-9198.
Website: http://www.vinu.edu/.

IOWA

Brown Mackie College–Quad Cities

Bettendorf, Iowa

- **Proprietary** 2-year, part of Education Management Corporation
- **Coed**

Academics *Degree:* diplomas and associate.
Freshman Application Contact Brown Mackie College–Quad Cities, 2119 East Kimberly Road, Bettendorf, IA 52722. *Phone:* 563-344-1500. *Toll-free phone:* 888-420-1652.
Website: http://www.brownmackie.edu/quad-cities/.

Clinton Community College

Clinton, Iowa

Freshman Application Contact Mr. Gary Mohr, Executive Director of Enrollment Management and Marketing, Clinton Community College, 1000 Lincoln Boulevard, Clinton, IA 52732-6299. *Phone:* 563-336-3322. *Toll-free phone:* 800-462-3255. *Fax:* 563-336-3350. *E-mail:* gmohr@eicc.edu.
Website: http://www.eicc.edu/ccc/.

Des Moines Area Community College

Ankeny, Iowa

- **State and locally supported** 2-year, founded 1966, part of Iowa Area Community Colleges System
- **Small-town** 362-acre campus
- **Endowment** $11.1 million
- **Coed,** 22,324 undergraduate students, 40% full-time, 55% women, 45% men

Undergraduates 8,947 full-time, 13,377 part-time. Students come from 47 states and territories; 69 other countries; 6% Black or African American, non-Hispanic/Latino; 6% Hispanic/Latino; 4% Asian, non-Hispanic/Latino; 0.1% Native Hawaiian or other Pacific Islander, non-Hispanic/Latino; 0.4% American Indian or Alaska Native, non-Hispanic/Latino; 2% Two or more races, non-Hispanic/Latino; 4% Race/ethnicity unknown; 0.8% international. *Retention:* 58% of full-time freshmen returned.
Freshmen *Admission:* 5,183 enrolled.
Faculty *Total:* 326, 99% full-time. *Student/faculty ratio:* 33:1.
Majors Accounting; accounting and business/management; accounting technology and bookkeeping; agricultural/farm supplies retailing and wholesaling; apparel and accessories marketing; applied horticulture/horticultural business services related; architectural drafting and CAD/CADD; autobody/collision and repair technology; automobile/automotive mechanics technology; biomedical technology; business administration and management; child-care provision; civil engineering technology; clinical/medical laboratory technology; commercial and advertising art; communications systems installation and repair technology; computer and information sciences and support services related; computer engineering technology; computer programming (specific applications); criminal justice/law enforcement administration; culinary arts; dental hygiene; desktop publishing and digital imaging design; diesel mechanics technology; electrical, electronic and communications engineering technology; fire prevention and safety technology; funeral service and mortuary science; health/health-care administration; heating, air conditioning, ventilation and refrigeration maintenance technology; hospitality administration; industrial electronics technology; industrial mechanics and maintenance technology; information technology; language interpretation and translation; legal assistant/paralegal; liberal arts and sciences/liberal studies; licensed practical/vocational nurse training; machine tool technology; marketing/marketing management; mechanical drafting and CAD/CADD; medical administrative assistant and medical secretary; medical/clinical assistant; office management; registered nursing/registered nurse; respiratory care therapy; sales, distribution, and marketing operations; sport and fitness administration/management; surveying engineering; tool and die technology; veterinary/animal health technology.
Academics *Calendar:* semesters. *Degrees:* certificates, diplomas, and associate (profile also includes information from the Boone, Carroll, Des Moines, and Newton campuses). *Special study options:* academic remediation for entering students, adult/continuing education programs, advanced placement credit, cooperative education, distance learning, English as a second language, honors programs, off-campus study, part-time degree program, services for LD students, student-designed majors, summer session for credit.
Library DMACC District Library plus 4 others with 62,986 titles, 7,224 audiovisual materials, an OPAC, a Web page.
Student Life *Housing Options:* coed. Campus housing is university owned. *Activities and Organizations:* drama/theater group, student-run newspaper, choral group, Agri-Business Club, Horticulture Club, Hospitality Arts Club, Iowa Delta Epsilon Chi, Dental Hygienist Club. *Campus security:* 24-hour emergency response devices and patrols, late-night transport/escort service. *Student services:* health clinic, personal/psychological counseling.
Athletics Member NJCAA. *Intercollegiate sports:* baseball M(s), basketball M(s)/W(s), cross-country running W(s), golf M(s)/W(s), volleyball W(s). *Intramural sports:* badminton M/W, basketball M/W, football M/W, golf M/W, soccer M/W, volleyball M/W.
Standardized Tests *Required for some:* SAT or ACT (for admission), ACT Compass.
Costs (2014–15) *Tuition:* state resident $4170 full-time, $139 per credit hour part-time; nonresident $8340 full-time, $278 per credit hour part-time. Full-time tuition and fees vary according to course load and reciprocity agreements. Part-time tuition and fees vary according to course load and reciprocity agreements. *Room and board:* room only: $4400. Room and board charges vary according to location. *Payment plan:* installment. *Waivers:* senior citizens and employees or children of employees.
Financial Aid Of all full-time matriculated undergraduates who enrolled in 2013, 377 Federal Work-Study jobs (averaging $1055).
Applying *Options:* electronic application, early admission, deferred entrance. *Required for some:* high school transcript, interview. *Application deadlines:* rolling (freshmen), rolling (transfers).
Freshman Application Contact Mr. Michael Lentsch, Director of Enrollment Management, Des Moines Area Community College, 2006 South Ankeny Boulevard, Ankeny, IA 50021-8995. *Phone:* 515-964-6216. *Toll-free phone:* 800-362-2127. *Fax:* 515-964-6391. *E-mail:* mjleutsch@dmacc.edu.
Website: http://www.dmacc.edu/.

Ellsworth Community College

Iowa Falls, Iowa

Director of Admissions Mrs. Nancy Walters, Registrar, Ellsworth Community College, 1100 College Avenue, Iowa Falls, IA 50126-1199. *Phone:* 641-648-4611. *Toll-free phone:* 800-ECC-9235.
Website: http://www.iavalley.cc.ia.us/ecc/.

Hawkeye Community College

Waterloo, Iowa

- **State and locally supported** 2-year, founded 1966
- **Rural** 320-acre campus
- **Endowment** $2.1 million
- **Coed,** 5,291 undergraduate students, 50% full-time, 57% women, 43% men

Undergraduates 2,659 full-time, 2,632 part-time. 1% are from out of state; 10% Black or African American, non-Hispanic/Latino; 3% Hispanic/Latino; 0.8% Asian, non-Hispanic/Latino; 0.1% Native Hawaiian or other Pacific Islander, non-Hispanic/Latino; 0.3% American Indian or Alaska Native, non-Hispanic/Latino; 2% Two or more races, non-Hispanic/Latino; 0.5% international; 34% transferred in.
Freshmen *Admission:* 3,938 applied, 3,290 admitted, 1,041 enrolled. *Test scores:* ACT scores over 18: 52%; ACT scores over 24: 14%; ACT scores over 30: 3%.
Faculty *Total:* 434, 28% full-time, 7% with terminal degrees. *Student/faculty ratio:* 16:1.
Majors Accounting; agricultural/farm supplies retailing and wholesaling; agricultural power machinery operation; animal/livestock husbandry and production; applied horticulture/horticulture operations; autobody/collision and repair technology; automobile/automotive mechanics technology; carpentry; child-care provision; civil engineering technology; clinical/medical laboratory technology; commercial photography; computer/information technology services administration related; computer systems networking and telecommunications; criminal justice/police science; dental hygiene; diesel mechanics technology; digital communication and media/multimedia; electrical, electronic and communications engineering technology; emergency medical technology (EMT paramedic); energy management and systems technology; executive assistant/executive secretary; fire science/firefighting; graphic communications; human resources management; interior design; liberal arts and sciences/liberal studies; machine tool technology; manufacturing engineering technology; medical administrative assistant and medical secretary; medical insurance coding; multi/interdisciplinary studies related; natural resources management and policy; occupational therapist assistant; physical therapy technology; registered nursing/registered nurse; respiratory care therapy; sales, distribution, and marketing operations; web page, digital/multimedia and information resources design.
Academics *Calendar:* semesters. *Degree:* certificates, diplomas, and associate. *Special study options:* academic remediation for entering students, accelerated degree program, adult/continuing education programs, advanced placement credit, cooperative education, distance learning, English as a second

language, external degree program, part-time degree program, services for LD students, study abroad, summer session for credit. *ROTC:* Army (c).
Library Hawkeye Community College Library with 33,297 titles, 1,884 audiovisual materials, an OPAC, a Web page.
Student Life *Housing:* college housing not available. *Activities and Organizations:* choral group, Student Senate, Phi Theta Kappa, Student Ambassadors, Chorus, Natural Resources. *Campus security:* 24-hour patrols. *Student services:* health clinic, personal/psychological counseling, women's center.
Athletics *Intramural sports:* badminton M/W, basketball M/W, bowling M/W, football M/W, golf M/W, soccer M/W, softball M/W, table tennis M/W, volleyball M/W.
Standardized Tests *Required:* ACT Compass or the equivalent from ACT or accredited college course(s) (for admission). *Required for some:* ACT (for admission).
Costs (2014–15) *Tuition:* state resident $4060 full-time, $145 per credit hour part-time; nonresident $4760 full-time, $170 per credit hour part-time. *Required fees:* $168 full-time, $6 per credit hour part-time. *Payment plan:* installment.
Applying *Options:* electronic application, deferred entrance. *Required:* high school transcript. *Application deadlines:* rolling (freshmen), rolling (out-of-state freshmen), rolling (transfers). *Notification:* continuous (freshmen), continuous (out-of-state freshmen), continuous (transfers).
Freshman Application Contact Ms. Holly Grimm-See, Associate Director, Admissions and Recruitment, Hawkeye Community College, PO Box 8015, Waterloo, IA 50704-8015. *Phone:* 319-296-4277. *Toll-free phone:* 800-670-4769. *Fax:* 319-296-2505. *E-mail:* holly.grimm-see@hawkeyecollege.edu. *Website:* http://www.hawkeyecollege.edu/.

Indian Hills Community College
Ottumwa, Iowa

Freshman Application Contact Mrs. Jane Sapp, Admissions Officer, Indian Hills Community College, 525 Grandview Avenue, Building #1, Ottumwa, IA 52501-1398. *Phone:* 641-683-5155. *Toll-free phone:* 800-726-2585. *Website:* http://www.ihcc.cc.ia.us/.

Iowa Central Community College
Fort Dodge, Iowa

- **State and locally supported** 2-year, founded 1966
- **Small-town** 110-acre campus
- **Coed,** 5,654 undergraduate students, 53% full-time, 50% women, 50% men

Undergraduates 2,979 full-time, 2,675 part-time. Students come from 31 states and territories; 21 other countries; 4% are from out of state; 9% Black or African American, non-Hispanic/Latino; 7% Hispanic/Latino; 1% Asian, non-Hispanic/Latino; 0.2% Native Hawaiian or other Pacific Islander, non-Hispanic/Latino; 0.6% American Indian or Alaska Native, non-Hispanic/Latino; 1% Two or more races, non-Hispanic/Latino; 5% Race/ethnicity unknown; 2% international; 3% transferred in; 22% live on campus.
Freshmen *Admission:* 1,239 applied, 1,367 enrolled.
Faculty *Total:* 416, 21% full-time. *Student/faculty ratio:* 20:1.
Majors Accounting; administrative assistant and secretarial science; airline pilot and flight crew; automobile/automotive mechanics technology; aviation/airway management; biological and physical sciences; broadcast journalism; business administration and management; business teacher education; carpentry; clinical/medical laboratory technology; community organization and advocacy; computer engineering technology; criminal justice/police science; data processing and data processing technology; drafting and design technology; education; electrical, electronic and communications engineering technology; hospitality and recreation marketing; industrial radiologic technology; journalism; liberal arts and sciences/liberal studies; licensed practical/vocational nurse training; machine tool technology; mass communication/media; medical/clinical assistant; occupational therapy; physical therapy; radio and television; registered nursing/registered nurse; science teacher education; social work; sociology; telecommunications technology; welding technology.
Academics *Calendar:* semesters. *Degree:* certificates, diplomas, and associate. *Special study options:* academic remediation for entering students, adult/continuing education programs, advanced placement credit, cooperative education, distance learning, English as a second language, independent study, internships, part-time degree program, services for LD students, study abroad, summer session for credit.
Library Iowa Central Community College Library with 68,618 titles, an OPAC, a Web page.
Student Life *Housing Options:* men-only, women-only. *Activities and Organizations:* drama/theater group, student-run newspaper, radio station,

choral group, marching band, Student Senate, BPA, Phi Beta Lambda. *Campus security:* 24-hour emergency response devices and patrols, student patrols, late-night transport/escort service, controlled dormitory access. *Student services:* health clinic, personal/psychological counseling.
Athletics Member NJCAA. *Intercollegiate sports:* baseball M(s), basketball M(s)/W(s), cross-country running M/W, football M(s), golf M(s)/W(s), soccer M(s)/W(s), softball W(s), volleyball W(s), wrestling M(s). *Intramural sports:* basketball M/W, football M, golf M/W, softball W, table tennis M/W, tennis M/W, volleyball M/W, weight lifting M, wrestling M.
Costs (2014–15) *Tuition:* state resident $4290 full-time, $157 per credit part-time; nonresident $6435 full-time, $229 per credit part-time. Full-time tuition and fees vary according to course load and program. Part-time tuition and fees vary according to course load and program. *Required fees:* $420 full-time, $420 per term part-time. *Room and board:* $6150; room only: $3898. *Payment plan:* installment.
Applying *Options:* electronic application, early admission, deferred entrance. *Required:* high school transcript. *Application deadlines:* rolling (freshmen), rolling (transfers).
Freshman Application Contact Mrs. Sue Flattery, Enrollment Management Secretary, Iowa Central Community College, 330 Avenue M, Fort Dodge, IA 50501-5798. *Phone:* 515-574-1010 Ext. 2402. *Toll-free phone:* 800-362-2793. *Fax:* 515-576-7207. *E-mail:* flattery@iowacentral.com. *Website:* http://www.iccc.cc.ia.us/.

Iowa Lakes Community College
Estherville, Iowa

- **State and locally supported** 2-year, founded 1967, part of Iowa Community College System
- **Small-town** 20-acre campus
- **Endowment** $6.5 million
- **Coed,** 2,340 undergraduate students, 47% full-time, 53% women, 47% men

Undergraduates 1,090 full-time, 1,250 part-time. Students come from 37 states and territories; 10 other countries; 6% Black or African American, non-Hispanic/Latino; 7% Hispanic/Latino; 0.6% Asian, non-Hispanic/Latino; 0.3% Native Hawaiian or other Pacific Islander, non-Hispanic/Latino; 1% American Indian or Alaska Native, non-Hispanic/Latino; 0.1% Two or more races, non-Hispanic/Latino; 3% Race/ethnicity unknown; 2% international; 37% live on campus. *Retention:* 54% of full-time freshmen returned.
Freshmen *Admission:* 1,425 applied, 1,318 admitted, 383 enrolled.
Faculty *Total:* 177, 51% full-time. *Student/faculty ratio:* 18:1.
Majors Accounting; accounting technology and bookkeeping; administrative assistant and secretarial science; agribusiness; agricultural business and management; agricultural business and management related; agricultural business technology; agricultural economics; agricultural/farm supplies retailing and wholesaling; agricultural mechanics and equipment technology; agricultural mechanization; agricultural power machinery operation; agricultural production; agricultural production related; agricultural teacher education; agriculture; agronomy and crop science; airline pilot and flight crew; animal/livestock husbandry and production; animal sciences; art teacher education; astronomy; athletic training; autobody/collision and repair technology; automobile/automotive mechanics technology; aviation/airway management; behavioral sciences; biological and physical sciences; biology/biological sciences; botany/plant biology; business administration and management; business automation/technology/data entry; business machine repair; business teacher education; carpentry; chemistry; child-care provision; child development; commercial and advertising art; communication and journalism related; comparative literature; computer and information sciences related; computer graphics; computer/information technology services administration related; computer programming; computer science; computer software technology; computer systems networking and telecommunications; construction engineering technology; construction management; construction trades; consumer merchandising/retailing management; corrections; criminal justice/law enforcement administration; criminal justice/police science; crop production; culinary arts related; data entry/microcomputer applications; data processing and data processing technology; design and applied arts related; desktop publishing and digital imaging design; developmental and child psychology; early childhood education; ecology; economics; education; electrical, electronic and communications engineering technology; electrical/electronics equipment installation and repair; elementary education; emergency care attendant (EMT ambulance); energy management and systems technology; engineering technology; environmental design/architecture; environmental education; environmental engineering technology; environmental studies; family and consumer sciences/human sciences; farm and ranch management; fashion merchandising; finance; fine/studio arts; fishing and fisheries sciences and management; flight instruction; food preparation; foods and nutrition related; food service and dining room management; foreign languages and literatures; forestry; general studies; geology/earth science; graphic and printing equipment operation/production;

graphic communications; graphic design; health and physical education/fitness; health/health-care administration; heating, air conditioning, ventilation and refrigeration maintenance technology; heating, ventilation, air conditioning and refrigeration engineering technology; history; hospitality administration; hotel/motel administration; humanities; human resources management and services related; hydrology and water resources science; information technology; institutional food workers; jazz/jazz studies; journalism; keyboard instruments; kindergarten/preschool education; landscaping and groundskeeping; legal administrative assistant/secretary; legal assistant/paralegal; legal studies; liberal arts and sciences and humanities related; liberal arts and sciences/liberal studies; marine maintenance and ship repair technology; marketing/marketing management; massage therapy; mass communication/media; mathematics; medical administrative assistant and medical secretary; medical/clinical assistant; medical office assistant; medical office computer specialist; medical reception; medical transcription; merchandising, sales, and marketing operations related (general); motorcycle maintenance and repair technology; music; music teacher education; natural resources/conservation; natural sciences; office management; office occupations and clerical services; parks, recreation and leisure; percussion instruments; pharmacy; philosophy; photography; physical education teaching and coaching; physical sciences; political science and government; pre-dentistry studies; pre-engineering; pre-law studies; premedical studies; prenursing studies; pre-pharmacy studies; pre-veterinary studies; psychology; radio and television; radio and television broadcasting technology; real estate; receptionist; registered nursing/registered nurse; rehabilitation and therapeutic professions related; restaurant, culinary, and catering management; restaurant/food services management; retailing; rhetoric and composition; sales, distribution, and marketing operations; science teacher education; selling skills and sales; small business administration; small engine mechanics and repair technology; social sciences; social work; sociology; soil science and agronomy; Spanish; sport and fitness administration/management; surgical technology; system, networking, and LAN/WAN management; technology/industrial arts teacher education; trade and industrial teacher education; turf and turfgrass management; voice and opera; water, wetlands, and marine resources management; welding technology; wildlife biology; wildlife, fish and wildlands science and management; woodwind instruments; word processing.

Academics *Calendar:* semesters. *Degree:* certificates, diplomas, and associate. *Special study options:* academic remediation for entering students, accelerated degree program, adult/continuing education programs, advanced placement credit, cooperative education, distance learning, English as a second language, honors programs, independent study, internships, part-time degree program, services for LD students, summer session for credit.
Library Iowa Lakes Community College Library plus 2 others with 25,305 titles, 1,175 audiovisual materials, an OPAC.
Student Life *Housing Options:* coed, special housing for students with disabilities. Campus housing is university owned. Freshman campus housing is guaranteed. *Activities and Organizations:* drama/theater group, choral group, music, Criminal Justice, nursing clubs, Environmental Studies, Business. *Campus security:* 24-hour emergency response devices, student patrols.
Athletics Member NJCAA. *Intercollegiate sports:* baseball M(s), basketball M(s)/W(s), cheerleading W(s), cross-country running M(s)/W(s), golf M(s)/W(s), soccer M(s)/W(s), softball W(s), swimming and diving M(s)/W(s), volleyball W(s), wrestling M(s). *Intramural sports:* basketball M/W, football M/W, golf M/W, racquetball M/W, riflery M/W, skiing (cross-country) M/W, skiing (downhill) M/W, soccer M/W, softball M/W, swimming and diving M/W, table tennis M/W, tennis M/W, ultimate Frisbee M/W, volleyball M/W, weight lifting M/W, wrestling M.
Costs (2014–15) *Tuition:* state resident $5516 full-time, $155 per credit hour part-time; nonresident $5868 full-time, $166 per credit hour part-time. Full-time tuition and fees vary according to program and reciprocity agreements. Part-time tuition and fees vary according to program and reciprocity agreements. *Required fees:* $17 per credit hour part-time. *Room and board:* $6000. Room and board charges vary according to board plan and location. *Payment plan:* installment. *Waivers:* children of alumni and employees or children of employees.
Applying *Options:* electronic application. *Required for some:* interview. *Application deadlines:* rolling (freshmen), rolling (out-of-state freshmen), rolling (transfers).
Freshman Application Contact Iowa Lakes Community College, IA. *Phone:* 712-362-7923 Ext. 7923. *Toll-free phone:* 800-521-5054. *E-mail:* info@iowalakes.edu.
Website: http://www.iowalakes.edu/.

Iowa Western Community College
Council Bluffs, Iowa

Freshman Application Contact Ms. Tori Christie, Director of Admissions, Iowa Western Community College, 2700 College Road, Box 4-C, Council Bluffs, IA 51502. *Phone:* 712-325-3288. *Toll-free phone:* 800-432-5852. *E-mail:* admissions@iwcc.edu.
Website: http://www.iwcc.edu/.

ITT Technical Institute
Cedar Rapids, Iowa

Freshman Application Contact Director of Recruitment, ITT Technical Institute, 3735 Queen Court SW, Cedar Rapids, IA 52404. *Phone:* 319-297-3400. *Toll-free phone:* 877-320-4625.
Website: http://www.itt-tech.edu/.

ITT Technical Institute
Clive, Iowa

- **Proprietary** primarily 2-year, part of ITT Educational Services, Inc.
- **Coed**

Academics *Degrees:* associate and bachelor's.
Freshman Application Contact Director of Recruitment, ITT Technical Institute, 1860 Northwest 118th Street, Suite 110, Clive, IA 50325. *Phone:* 515-327-5500. *Toll-free phone:* 877-526-7312.
Website: http://www.itt-tech.edu/.

Kaplan University, Cedar Falls
Cedar Falls, Iowa

Freshman Application Contact Kaplan University, Cedar Falls, 7009 Nordic Drive, Cedar Falls, IA 50613. *Phone:* 319-277-0220. *Toll-free phone:* 866-527-5268 (in-state); 800-527-5268 (out-of-state).
Website: http://www.kaplanuniversity.edu/.

Kaplan University, Cedar Rapids
Cedar Rapids, Iowa

Freshman Application Contact Kaplan University, Cedar Rapids, 3165 Edgewood Parkway, SW, Cedar Rapids, IA 52404. *Phone:* 319-363-0481. *Toll-free phone:* 866-527-5268 (in-state); 800-527-5268 (out-of-state).
Website: http://www.kaplanuniversity.edu/.

Kaplan University, Des Moines
Urbandale, Iowa

Freshman Application Contact Kaplan University, Des Moines, 4655 121st Street, Urbandale, IA 50323. *Phone:* 515-727-2100. *Toll-free phone:* 866-527-5268 (in-state); 800-527-5268 (out-of-state).
Website: http://www.kaplanuniversity.edu/.

Kirkwood Community College
Cedar Rapids, Iowa

Freshman Application Contact Kirkwood Community College, PO Box 2068, Cedar Rapids, IA 52406-2068. *Phone:* 319-398-5517. *Toll-free phone:* 800-332-2055.
Website: http://www.kirkwood.edu/.

Marshalltown Community College
Marshalltown, Iowa

Freshman Application Contact Ms. Deana Inman, Director of Admissions, Marshalltown Community College, 3700 South Center Street, Marshalltown, IA 50158-4760. *Phone:* 641-752-7106. *Toll-free phone:* 866-622-4748. *Fax:* 641-752-8149.
Website: http://www.marshalltowncommunitycollege.com/.

Muscatine Community College
Muscatine, Iowa

Freshman Application Contact Gary Mohr, Executive Director of Enrollment Management and Marketing, Muscatine Community College, 152 Colorado Street, Muscatine, IA 52761-5396. *Phone:* 563-336-3322. *Toll-free phone:* 800-351-4669. *Fax:* 563-336-3350. *E-mail:* gmohr@eicc.edu.
Website: http://www.eicc.edu/general/muscatine/.

Northeast Iowa Community College
Calmar, Iowa

- **State and locally supported** 2-year, founded 1966, part of Iowa Area Community Colleges System
- **Rural** 210-acre campus
- **Coed,** 4,934 undergraduate students, 33% full-time, 57% women, 43% men

Undergraduates 1,647 full-time, 3,287 part-time. 12% are from out of state; 7% Black or African American, non-Hispanic/Latino; 2% Hispanic/Latino; 0.5% Asian, non-Hispanic/Latino; 0.5% American Indian or Alaska Native, non-Hispanic/Latino; 0.5% Two or more races, non-Hispanic/Latino; 6% Race/ethnicity unknown. *Retention:* 58% of full-time freshmen returned.
Freshmen *Admission:* 936 applied, 837 admitted, 625 enrolled.
Faculty *Total:* 342, 33% full-time, 8% with terminal degrees. *Student/faculty ratio:* 16:1.
Majors Accounting; administrative assistant and secretarial science; agribusiness; agricultural and food products processing; agricultural power machinery operation; agricultural production; automobile/automotive mechanics technology; business administration and management; business automation/technology/data entry; clinical/medical laboratory technology; computer programming (specific applications); construction trades; cosmetology; crop production; dairy husbandry and production; desktop publishing and digital imaging design; electrical, electronic and communications engineering technology; electrician; emergency medical technology (EMT paramedic); energy management and systems technology; fire science/firefighting; health information/medical records technology; liberal arts and sciences/liberal studies; plumbing technology; radiologic technology/science; registered nursing/registered nurse; respiratory care therapy; sales, distribution, and marketing operations; social work.
Academics *Calendar:* semesters. *Degree:* certificates, diplomas, and associate. *Special study options:* academic remediation for entering students, adult/continuing education programs, advanced placement credit, cooperative education, distance learning, double majors, external degree program, honors programs, internships, off-campus study, part-time degree program, services for LD students, summer session for credit.
Library Wilder Resource Center & Burton Payne Library plus 2 others with an OPAC, a Web page.
Student Life *Housing:* college housing not available. *Activities and Organizations:* student-run newspaper, choral group, national fraternities, national sororities. *Campus security:* security personnel on weeknights. *Student services:* personal/psychological counseling.
Athletics *Intramural sports:* basketball M/W, bowling M/W, football M, golf M/W, skiing (downhill) M/W, softball M/W, volleyball M/W.
Costs (2014–15) *Tuition:* state resident $4200 full-time, $150 per credit hour part-time; nonresident $4200 full-time, $150 per credit hour part-time. Full-time tuition and fees vary according to course load. Part-time tuition and fees vary according to course load. *Required fees:* $364 full-time, $13 per credit hour part-time. *Payment plan:* installment. *Waivers:* employees or children of employees.
Applying *Options:* electronic application. *Recommended:* high school transcript.
Freshman Application Contact Ms. Brynn McConnell, Admissions Representative, Northeast Iowa Community College, Calmar, IA 52132. *Phone:* 563-562-3263 Ext. 307. *Toll-free phone:* 800-728-CALMAR. *Fax:* 563-562-4369. *E-mail:* mcconnellb@nicc.edu. *Website:* http://www.nicc.edu/.

North Iowa Area Community College
Mason City, Iowa

- **State and locally supported** 2-year, founded 1918, part of Iowa Community College System
- **Rural** 500-acre campus
- **Coed,** 2,955 undergraduate students, 48% full-time, 54% women, 46% men

Undergraduates 1,420 full-time, 1,535 part-time. 3% Black or African American, non-Hispanic/Latino; 5% Hispanic/Latino; 1% Asian, non-Hispanic/Latino; 0.3% American Indian or Alaska Native, non-Hispanic/Latino; 1% Two or more races, non-Hispanic/Latino; 0.3% Race/ethnicity unknown; 1% international.
Freshmen *Admission:* 654 enrolled. *Test scores:* SAT critical reading scores over 500: 8%; SAT math scores over 500: 15%; SAT writing scores over 500: 15%; ACT scores over 18: 76%; ACT scores over 24: 23%; ACT scores over 30: 2%.
Faculty *Total:* 213, 38% full-time, 7% with terminal degrees. *Student/faculty ratio:* 13:1.
Majors Accounting; accounting technology and bookkeeping; administrative assistant and secretarial science; agricultural economics; agricultural/farm

supplies retailing and wholesaling; agricultural production; automobile/automotive mechanics technology; business administration and management; carpentry; clinical/medical laboratory technology; computer systems networking and telecommunications; criminal justice/police science; desktop publishing and digital imaging design; early childhood education; electrical, electronic and communications engineering technology; emergency medical technology (EMT paramedic); entrepreneurship; fire prevention and safety technology; health and medical administrative services related; heating, air conditioning, ventilation and refrigeration maintenance technology; hospitality administration; insurance; legal administrative assistant/secretary; liberal arts and sciences/liberal studies; licensed practical/vocational nurse training; manufacturing engineering technology; mechanical drafting and CAD/CADD; medical administrative assistant and medical secretary; medical/clinical assistant; multi/interdisciplinary studies related; network and system administration; nursing assistant/aide and patient care assistant/aide; physical education teaching and coaching; physical therapy technology; registered nursing/registered nurse; sales, distribution, and marketing operations; sport and fitness administration/management; tool and die technology; web page, digital/multimedia and information resources design; welding technology.
Academics *Calendar:* semesters. *Degree:* certificates, diplomas, and associate. *Special study options:* academic remediation for entering students, advanced placement credit, cooperative education, distance learning, English as a second language, honors programs, internships, part-time degree program, services for LD students, student-designed majors, study abroad, summer session for credit.
Library an OPAC, a Web page.
Student Life *Housing Options:* coed. Campus housing is university owned. *Activities and Organizations:* drama/theater group, student-run newspaper, choral group, Ski & Snowboard Club, intramurals, Student Senate, Education Club, Sport Shooting Club. *Campus security:* student patrols, late-night transport/escort service, controlled dormitory access. *Student services:* health clinic, personal/psychological counseling.
Athletics Member NJCAA. *Intercollegiate sports:* baseball M(s), basketball M(s)/W(s), cross-country running M(s)/W(s), golf M(s)/W(s), soccer M(s), softball W(s), track and field M(s)/W(s), volleyball W(s), wrestling M(s). *Intramural sports:* cheerleading W.
Costs (2014–15) *Tuition:* state resident $3922 full-time, $131 per semester hour part-time; nonresident $5884 full-time, $196 per semester hour part-time. Full-time tuition and fees vary according to course load. Part-time tuition and fees vary according to course load. *Required fees:* $780 full-time, $26 per semester hour part-time. *Room and board:* $6518. Room and board charges vary according to housing facility. *Payment plan:* installment. *Waivers:* senior citizens and employees or children of employees.
Financial Aid Of all full-time matriculated undergraduates who enrolled in 2013, 125 Federal Work-Study jobs (averaging $2000). 4 state and other part-time jobs (averaging $2000).
Applying *Options:* electronic application. *Required for some:* high school transcript. *Application deadlines:* rolling (freshmen), rolling (transfers). *Notification:* continuous (freshmen), continuous (transfers).
Freshman Application Contact Ms. Rachel McGuire, Director of Enrollment Services, North Iowa Area Community College, 500 College Drive, Mason City, IA 50401. *Phone:* 641-422-4104. *Toll-free phone:* 888-GO NIACC Ext. 4245. *Fax:* 641-422-4385. *E-mail:* request@niacc.edu. *Website:* http://www.niacc.edu/.

Northwest Iowa Community College
Sheldon, Iowa

Director of Admissions Ms. Lisa Story, Director of Enrollment Management, Northwest Iowa Community College, 603 West Park Street, Sheldon, IA 51201-1046. *Phone:* 712-324-5061 Ext. 115. *Toll-free phone:* 800-352-4907. *E-mail:* lstory@nwicc.edu. *Website:* http://www.nwicc.edu/.

St. Luke's College
Sioux City, Iowa

- **Independent** primarily 2-year, founded 1967, part of UnityPoint Health - St. Luke's (formerly St. Luke's Regional Medical Center and Iowa Health System)
- **Rural** 3-acre campus with easy access to Omaha
- **Endowment** $1.1 million
- **Coed,** 251 undergraduate students, 62% full-time, 88% women, 12% men

Undergraduates 156 full-time, 95 part-time. Students come from 19 states and territories; 3 other countries; 41% are from out of state; 4% Black or African American, non-Hispanic/Latino; 6% Hispanic/Latino; 4% Asian, non-Hispanic/Latino; 0.4% Native Hawaiian or other Pacific Islander, non-

Hispanic/Latino; 0.4% American Indian or Alaska Native, non-Hispanic/Latino; 2% Two or more races, non-Hispanic/Latino.

Freshmen *Admission:* 24 applied, 6 admitted, 5 enrolled. *Average high school GPA:* 3.51.

Faculty *Total:* 40, 63% full-time, 10% with terminal degrees. *Student/faculty ratio:* 8:1.

Majors Health services/allied health/health sciences; radiologic technology/science; registered nursing/registered nurse; respiratory care therapy.

Academics *Calendar:* semesters. *Degrees:* certificates, associate, and bachelor's. *Special study options:* advanced placement credit, cooperative education, distance learning, summer session for credit.

Library St. Luke's College with 2,854 titles, 271 audiovisual materials, an OPAC, a Web page.

Student Life *Housing:* college housing not available. *Campus security:* 24-hour emergency response devices and patrols, late-night transport/escort service. *Student services:* health clinic, personal/psychological counseling.

Standardized Tests *Required:* SAT or ACT (for admission).

Costs (2015–16) *Tuition:* $18,000 full-time, $500 per credit hour part-time. Full-time tuition and fees vary according to course load, degree level, and program. Part-time tuition and fees vary according to course load, degree level, and program. *Required fees:* $1440 full-time. *Payment plans:* installment, deferred payment.

Financial Aid Of all full-time matriculated undergraduates who enrolled in 2013, 108 applied for aid, 108 were judged to have need, 5 had their need fully met. 9 Federal Work-Study jobs (averaging $837). 4 state and other part-time jobs (averaging $522). In 2013, 3 non-need-based awards were made. *Average percent of need met:* 60%. *Average financial aid package:* $14,950. *Average need-based loan:* $5100. *Average need-based gift aid:* $5227. *Average non-need-based aid:* $1800. *Average indebtedness upon graduation:* $52,799.

Applying *Options:* electronic application. *Application fee:* $50. *Required:* essay or personal statement, high school transcript, minimum 2.5 GPA, interview. *Application deadline:* 8/1 (freshmen). *Notification:* continuous (transfers).

Freshman Application Contact Ms. Sherry McCarthy, Admissions Coordinator, St. Luke's College, 2800 Pierce St, Sioux City, IA 51104. *Phone:* 712-279-3149. *Toll-free phone:* 800-352-4660 Ext. 3149. *Fax:* 712-233-8017. *E-mail:* sherry.mccarthy@stlukescollege.edu.
Website: http://stlukescollege.edu/.

Scott Community College
Bettendorf, Iowa

Freshman Application Contact Mr. Gary Mohr, Executive Director of Enrollment Management and Marketing, Scott Community College, 500 Belmont Road, Bettendorf, IA 52722-6804. *Phone:* 563-336-3322. *Toll-free phone:* 800-895-0811. *Fax:* 563-336-3350. *E-mail:* gmohr@eicc.edu.
Website: http://www.eicc.edu/scc/.

Southeastern Community College
West Burlington, Iowa

- **State and locally supported** 2-year, founded 1968, part of Iowa Department of Education Division of Community Colleges
- **Small-town** 160-acre campus
- **Coed,** 2,987 undergraduate students, 48% full-time, 58% women, 42% men

Undergraduates 1,427 full-time, 1,560 part-time. 14% are from out of state; 5% Black or African American, non-Hispanic/Latino; 5% Hispanic/Latino; 0.7% Asian, non-Hispanic/Latino; 0.1% Native Hawaiian or other Pacific Islander, non-Hispanic/Latino; 1% American Indian or Alaska Native, non-Hispanic/Latino; 3% Two or more races, non-Hispanic/Latino; 2% Race/ethnicity unknown; 0.9% international; 2% transferred in; 17% live on campus.

Freshmen *Admission:* 1,469 applied, 1,122 admitted, 441 enrolled. *Average high school GPA:* 2.9. *Test scores:* ACT scores over 18: 69%; ACT scores over 24: 12%.

Faculty *Total:* 134, 52% full-time, 6% with terminal degrees.

Majors Accounting; administrative assistant and secretarial science; agricultural business and management; agronomy and crop science; artificial intelligence; automobile/automotive mechanics technology; biomedical technology; business administration and management; child development; computer programming; construction engineering technology; cosmetology; criminal justice/law enforcement administration; drafting and design technology; electrical, electronic and communications engineering technology; emergency medical technology (EMT paramedic); engineering related; industrial radiologic technology; information science/studies; liberal arts and sciences/liberal studies; licensed practical/vocational nurse training; machine

tool technology; mechanical engineering/mechanical technology; medical/clinical assistant; registered nursing/registered nurse; respiratory care therapy; substance abuse/addiction counseling; trade and industrial teacher education; welding technology.

Academics *Calendar:* semesters. *Degree:* certificates, diplomas, and associate. *Special study options:* adult/continuing education programs, part-time degree program.

Library Yohe Memorial Library.

Student Life *Housing Options:* coed, men-only, special housing for students with disabilities. Campus housing is university owned. *Campus security:* controlled dormitory access, night patrols by trained security personnel.

Athletics Member NJCAA. *Intercollegiate sports:* baseball M(s), basketball M(s), softball W(s), volleyball W(s). *Intramural sports:* basketball M, bowling M/W, softball M/W, volleyball M/W, weight lifting M/W.

Costs (2015–16) *Tuition:* state resident $4740 full-time, $158 per credit hour part-time; nonresident $4890 full-time, $163 per credit hour part-time. Full-time tuition and fees vary according to course load, program, and reciprocity agreements. Part-time tuition and fees vary according to course load, program, and reciprocity agreements. *Required fees:* $50 full-time. *Room and board:* $6216. Room and board charges vary according to board plan and housing facility. *Payment plan:* installment. *Waivers:* employees or children of employees.

Financial Aid Of all full-time matriculated undergraduates who enrolled in 2013, 1,220 applied for aid, 1,091 were judged to have need. In 2013, 50 non-need-based awards were made. *Average financial aid package:* $5834. *Average need-based loan:* $2879. *Average need-based gift aid:* $4445. *Average non-need-based aid:* $1795.

Applying *Options:* early admission, deferred entrance.

Freshman Application Contact Ms. Stacy White, Admissions, Southeastern Community College, 1500 West Agency Road, West Burlington, IA 52655-0180. *Phone:* 319-752-2731 Ext. 8137. *Toll-free phone:* 866-722-4692. *E-mail:* admoff@scciowa.edu.
Website: http://www.scciowa.edu/.

Southwestern Community College
Creston, Iowa

Freshman Application Contact Ms. Lisa Carstens, Admissions Coordinator, Southwestern Community College, 1501 West Townline Street, Creston, IA 50801. *Phone:* 641-782-7081 Ext. 453. *Toll-free phone:* 800-247-4023. *Fax:* 641-782-3312. *E-mail:* carstens@swcciowa.edu.
Website: http://www.swcciowa.edu/.

Vatterott College
Des Moines, Iowa

Freshman Application Contact Mr. Dana Smith, Co-Director, Vatterott College, 7000 Fleur Drive, Suite 290, Des Moines, IA 50321. *Phone:* 515-309-9000. *Toll-free phone:* 888-553-6627. *Fax:* 515-309-0366.
Website: http://www.vatterott.edu/.

Western Iowa Tech Community College
Sioux City, Iowa

- **State-supported** 2-year, founded 1966, part of Iowa Department of Education Division of Community Colleges
- **Suburban** 143-acre campus
- **Endowment** $1.0 million
- **Coed,** 6,331 undergraduate students, 39% full-time, 58% women, 42% men

Undergraduates 2,459 full-time, 3,872 part-time. Students come from 25 states and territories; 8 other countries; 14% are from out of state; 3% Black or African American, non-Hispanic/Latino; 14% Hispanic/Latino; 2% Asian, non-Hispanic/Latino; 0.4% Native Hawaiian or other Pacific Islander, non-Hispanic/Latino; 3% American Indian or Alaska Native, non-Hispanic/Latino; 3% Two or more races, non-Hispanic/Latino; 7% Race/ethnicity unknown; 0.5% international; 19% transferred in; 5% live on campus. *Retention:* 41% of full-time freshmen returned.

Freshmen *Admission:* 570 enrolled. *Test scores:* ACT scores over 18: 74%; ACT scores over 24: 12%; ACT scores over 30: 1%.

Faculty *Total:* 417, 19% full-time, 9% with terminal degrees. *Student/faculty ratio:* 20:1.

Majors Accounting; accounting technology and bookkeeping; administrative assistant and secretarial science; agricultural/farm supplies retailing and wholesaling; animation, interactive technology, video graphics and special effects; architectural engineering technology; autobody/collision and repair technology; automobile/automotive mechanics technology; biomedical technology; business administration and management; business automation/technology/data entry; carpentry; child-care provision;

cinematography and film/video production; commercial photography; computer/information technology services administration related; computer programming (specific applications); criminal justice/police science; crisis/emergency/disaster management; dental assisting; desktop publishing and digital imaging design; electrician; emergency medical technology (EMT paramedic); energy management and systems technology; finance; fire science/firefighting; game and interactive media design; heating, air conditioning, ventilation and refrigeration maintenance technology; human resources management; industrial mechanics and maintenance technology; interior design; legal assistant/paralegal; liberal arts and sciences/liberal studies; licensed practical/vocational nurse training; mechanical drafting and CAD/CADD; medical administrative assistant and medical secretary; medical/clinical assistant; medical office management; motorcycle maintenance and repair technology; multi/interdisciplinary studies related; musical instrument fabrication and repair; nursing assistant/aide and patient care assistant/aide; pharmacy technician; physical fitness technician; physical therapy technology; recording arts technology; registered nursing/registered nurse; retailing; sales, distribution, and marketing operations; securities services administration; surgical technology; teacher assistant/aide; telecommunications technology; veterinary/animal health technology; web page, digital/multimedia and information resources design; welding technology.

Academics *Calendar:* semesters. *Degree:* certificates, diplomas, and associate. *Special study options:* academic remediation for entering students, accelerated degree program, advanced placement credit, cooperative education, distance learning, double majors, English as a second language, honors programs, independent study, internships, off-campus study, part-time degree program, services for LD students, student-designed majors, study abroad, summer session for credit.

Library Western Iowa Tech Community College Library Services plus 1 other with 29,485 titles, 12,450 audiovisual materials, an OPAC, a Web page.

Student Life *Housing Options:* coed. Campus housing is university owned. *Activities and Organizations:* drama/theater group, choral group, Shakespeare Overseas Traveling Club, Habitat for Humanity, Anime Club, Leadership Academy, Police Science Club. *Campus security:* 24-hour emergency response devices and patrols, controlled dormitory access. *Student services:* personal/psychological counseling.

Athletics *Intramural sports:* basketball M/W, bowling M/W, football M/W, rugby M/W, soccer M/W, softball M/W, volleyball M/W, wrestling M/W.

Standardized Tests *Recommended:* ACT (for admission), SAT or ACT (for admission).

Costs (2014–15) *Tuition:* state resident $3216 full-time, $134 per credit hour part-time; nonresident $3240 full-time, $135 per credit hour part-time. Full-time tuition and fees vary according to class time and program. Part-time tuition and fees vary according to class time and program. *Required fees:* $408 full-time, $17 per credit hour part-time. *Room and board:* Room and board charges vary according to housing facility. *Payment plan:* installment. *Waivers:* employees or children of employees.

Financial Aid Of all full-time matriculated undergraduates who enrolled in 2013, 148 Federal Work-Study jobs (averaging $1000). 2 state and other part-time jobs (averaging $2500).

Applying *Options:* electronic application, early admission, deferred entrance. *Recommended:* high school transcript. *Application deadlines:* rolling (freshmen), rolling (out-of-state freshmen), rolling (transfers). *Notification:* continuous (freshmen), continuous (out-of-state freshmen), continuous (transfers).

Freshman Application Contact Lora VanderZwaag, Registrar, Western Iowa Tech Community College, 4647 Stone Ave, Sioux City, IA 51106. *Phone:* 712-274-6400. *Toll-free phone:* 800-352-4649 Ext. 6403. *Fax:* 712-274-6441. *E-mail:* Lora.VanderZwaag@witcc.edu. *Website:* http://www.witcc.edu/.

KANSAS

Allen Community College
Iola, Kansas

- **State and locally supported** 2-year, founded 1923, part of Kansas State Board of Regents
- **Small-town** 88-acre campus
- **Coed,** 2,741 undergraduate students, 48% full-time, 66% women, 34% men

Undergraduates 1,311 full-time, 1,430 part-time. 6% Black or African American, non-Hispanic/Latino; 7% Hispanic/Latino; 2% Asian, non-Hispanic/Latino; 1% American Indian or Alaska Native, non-Hispanic/Latino; 0.4% Race/ethnicity unknown; 0.1% international.

Faculty *Student/faculty ratio:* 22:1.

Majors Accounting; administrative assistant and secretarial science; agricultural production; architecture; art; athletic training; banking and financial support services; biology/biological sciences; business administration and management; business/commerce; business teacher education; chemistry; child development; computer science; computer systems networking and telecommunications; criminal justice/law enforcement administration; data processing and data processing technology; drafting and design technology; dramatic/theater arts; economics; electrical and electronics engineering; electrical, electronic and communications engineering technology; elementary education; emergency medical technology (EMT paramedic); engineering; engineering technology; equestrian studies; family and consumer sciences/human sciences; farm and ranch management; forestry; funeral service and mortuary science; general studies; geography; health aide; health and physical education/fitness; history; home health aide/home attendant; hospital and health-care facilities administration; humanities; industrial technology; information science/studies; journalism; language interpretation and translation; library and information science; mathematics; music; nuclear/nuclear power technology; nursing assistant/aide and patient care assistant/aide; parks, recreation and leisure facilities management; philosophy; physical therapy; physics; political science and government; pre-dentistry studies; pre-law studies; premedical studies; pre-pharmacy studies; pre-veterinary studies; psychology; religious studies; rhetoric and composition; secondary education; social work; sociology; technology/industrial arts teacher education; writing.

Academics *Calendar:* semesters. *Degree:* certificates and associate. *Special study options:* academic remediation for entering students, adult/continuing education programs, cooperative education, distance learning, English as a second language, independent study, internships, part-time degree program, services for LD students, student-designed majors, summer session for credit.

Library Learning Resource Center plus 1 other with 49,416 titles, an OPAC.

Student Life *Housing Options:* coed, men-only, women-only. Campus housing is university owned. *Activities and Organizations:* drama/theater group, student-run newspaper, choral group, intramurals, Student Senate, Biology Club, Theatre, Phi Theta Kappa. *Student services:* personal/psychological counseling.

Athletics Member NJCAA. *Intercollegiate sports:* baseball M(s), basketball M(s)/W(s), cheerleading M(s)/W(s), cross-country running M(s)/W(s), golf M(s), soccer M(s)/W(s), softball W(s), track and field M(s)/W(s), volleyball W(s). *Intramural sports:* basketball M/W, football M/W, soccer M/W, softball M/W, table tennis M/W, tennis M/W, volleyball M/W.

Costs (2015–16) *Tuition:* state resident $1920 full-time, $60 per credit part-time; nonresident $1920 full-time, $60 per credit part-time. *Required fees:* $736 full-time, $23 per credit part-time. *Room and board:* $4740.

Financial Aid Of all full-time matriculated undergraduates who enrolled in 2008, 510 applied for aid, 411 were judged to have need, 384 had their need fully met. 40 Federal Work-Study jobs (averaging $2600). 112 state and other part-time jobs (averaging $2600). In 2008, 22 non-need-based awards were made. *Average percent of need met:* 80%. *Average financial aid package:* $4738. *Average need-based loan:* $2482. *Average need-based gift aid:* $3257. *Average non-need-based aid:* $1241.

Applying *Options:* electronic application, early admission, deferred entrance. *Required:* high school transcript. *Application deadlines:* 8/24 (freshmen), 8/24 (transfers). *Notification:* continuous (freshmen), continuous (transfers).

Freshman Application Contact Rebecca Bilderback, Director of Admissions, Allen Community College, 1801 North Cottonwood, Iola, KS 66749. *Phone:* 620-365-5116 Ext. 267. *Fax:* 620-365-7406. *E-mail:* bilderback@allencc.edu. *Website:* http://www.allencc.edu/.

Barton County Community College
Great Bend, Kansas

Freshman Application Contact Ms. Tana Cooper, Director of Admissions and Promotions, Barton County Community College, 245 Northeast 30th Road, Great Bend, KS 67530. *Phone:* 620-792-9241. *Toll-free phone:* 800-722-6842. *Fax:* 620-786-1160. *E-mail:* admissions@bartonccc.edu. *Website:* http://www.bartonccc.edu/.

Brown Mackie College–Kansas City
Lenexa, Kansas

- **Proprietary** primarily 2-year, founded 1892, part of Education Management Corporation
- **Suburban** campus
- **Coed**

Academics *Calendar:* quarters. *Degrees:* certificates, diplomas, associate, and bachelor's.

Freshman Application Contact Brown Mackie College–Kansas City, 9705 Lenexa Drive, Lenexa, KS 66215. *Phone:* 913-768-1900. *Toll-free phone:* 800-635-9101.
Website: http://www.brownmackie.edu/kansascity/.

Brown Mackie College–Salina
Salina, Kansas

- **Proprietary** primarily 2-year, founded 1892, part of Education Management Corporation
- **Small-town** campus
- **Coed**

Academics *Calendar:* modular. *Degrees:* certificates, diplomas, associate, and bachelor's.

Freshman Application Contact Brown Mackie College–Salina, 2106 South 9th Street, Salina, KS 67401-2810. *Phone:* 785-825-5422. *Toll-free phone:* 800-365-0433.
Website: http://www.brownmackie.edu/salina/.

Bryan University
Topeka, Kansas

Admissions Office Contact Bryan University, 1527 SW Fairlawn Road, Topeka, KS 66604.
Website: http://www.bryanu.edu/.

Butler Community College
El Dorado, Kansas

Freshman Application Contact Mr. Glenn Lygrisse, Interim Director of Enrollment Management, Butler Community College, 901 South Haverhill Road, El Dorado, KS 67042. *Phone:* 316-321-2222. *Fax:* 316-322-3109. *E-mail:* admissions@butlercc.edu.
Website: http://www.butlercc.edu/.

Cloud County Community College
Concordia, Kansas

- **State and locally supported** 2-year, founded 1965, part of Kansas Community College System
- **Rural** 35-acre campus
- **Coed,** 2,406 undergraduate students, 36% full-time, 62% women, 38% men

Undergraduates 857 full-time, 1,549 part-time. Students come from 16 states and territories; 13 other countries; 8% are from out of state; 12% Black or African American, non-Hispanic/Latino; 11% Hispanic/Latino; 0.8% Asian, non-Hispanic/Latino; 0.9% Native Hawaiian or other Pacific Islander, non-Hispanic/Latino; 0.4% American Indian or Alaska Native, non-Hispanic/Latino; 3% Two or more races, non-Hispanic/Latino; 0.9% Race/ethnicity unknown; 2% international; 7% transferred in. *Retention:* 53% of full-time freshmen returned.

Freshmen *Admission:* 490 enrolled.

Faculty *Total:* 306, 19% full-time. *Student/faculty ratio:* 20:1.

Majors Administrative assistant and secretarial science; agricultural business and management; agricultural/farm supplies retailing and wholesaling; business administration and management; business, management, and marketing related; child-care and support services management; child development; criminal justice/police science; graphic design; journalism; legal assistant/paralegal; liberal arts and sciences/liberal studies; mechanic and repair technologies related; office occupations and clerical services; radio and television broadcasting technology; registered nursing/registered nurse; system, networking, and LAN/WAN management; teacher assistant/aide; web page, digital/multimedia and information resources design.

Academics *Calendar:* semesters. *Degree:* certificates, diplomas, and associate. *Special study options:* academic remediation for entering students, adult/continuing education programs, advanced placement credit, cooperative education, distance learning, internships, part-time degree program, services for LD students, summer session for credit.

Library 18,010 titles.

Student Life *Activities and Organizations:* drama/theater group, student-run newspaper, radio station, choral group. *Campus security:* 24-hour emergency response devices. *Student services:* health clinic.

Athletics Member NJCAA. *Intercollegiate sports:* baseball M(s), basketball M(s)/W(s), cross-country running M(s)/W(s), soccer M(s), softball W(s), tennis M(s)/W(s), track and field M(s)/W(s), volleyball W(s). *Intramural sports:* baseball M, basketball M/W, softball W, volleyball M/W.

Costs (2014–15) *Tuition:* area resident $2160 full-time, $72 per credit hour part-time; state resident $2370 full-time, $79 per credit hour part-time; nonresident $2370 full-time, $79 per credit hour part-time. Full-time tuition and fees vary according to course level, course load, location, reciprocity agreements, and student level. Part-time tuition and fees vary according to course level, course load, location, reciprocity agreements, and student level. *Required fees:* $750 full-time. *Room and board:* $5352. Room and board charges vary according to board plan and housing facility. *Payment plan:* installment. *Waivers:* senior citizens and employees or children of employees.

Financial Aid Of all full-time matriculated undergraduates who enrolled in 2013, 122 Federal Work-Study jobs (averaging $800).

Applying *Options:* early admission, deferred entrance. *Required:* high school transcript. *Application deadlines:* 9/11 (freshmen), 9/11 (transfers). *Notification:* continuous (freshmen), continuous (transfers).

Freshman Application Contact Cloud County Community College, 2221 Campus Drive, PO Box 1002, Concordia, KS 66901-1002. *Phone:* 785-243-1435 Ext. 213. *Toll-free phone:* 800-729-5101.
Website: http://www.cloud.edu/.

Coffeyville Community College
Coffeyville, Kansas

Freshman Application Contact Stacia Meek, Admissions Counselor/Marketing Event Coordinator, Coffeyville Community College, 400 West 11th Street, Coffeyville, KS 67337-5063. *Phone:* 620-252-7100. *Toll-free phone:* 877-51-RAVEN. *E-mail:* staciam@coffeyville.edu.
Website: http://www.coffeyville.edu/.

Colby Community College
Colby, Kansas

Freshman Application Contact Ms. Nikol Nolan, Admissions Director, Colby Community College, Colby, KS 67701-4099. *Phone:* 785-462-3984 Ext. 5496. *Toll-free phone:* 888-634-9350. *Fax:* 785-460-4691. *E-mail:* admissions@colbycc.edu.
Website: http://www.colbycc.edu/.

Cowley County Community College and Area Vocational–Technical School
Arkansas City, Kansas

Freshman Application Contact Ms. Lory West, Director of Admissions, Cowley County Community College and Area Vocational–Technical School, PO Box 1147, Arkansas City, KS 67005. *Phone:* 620-441-5594. *Toll-free phone:* 800-593-CCCC. *Fax:* 620-441-5350. *E-mail:* admissions@cowley.edu.
Website: http://www.cowley.edu/.

Dodge City Community College
Dodge City, Kansas

Freshman Application Contact Dodge City Community College, 2501 North 14th Avenue, Dodge City, KS 67801-2399. *Phone:* 620-225-1321.
Website: http://www.dc3.edu/.

Donnelly College
Kansas City, Kansas

- **Independent Roman Catholic** primarily 2-year, founded 1949
- **Urban** 4-acre campus
- **Endowment** $4.9 million
- **Coed,** 463 undergraduate students, 67% full-time, 71% women, 29% men

Undergraduates 310 full-time, 153 part-time. Students come from 2 states and territories; 35 other countries; 25% are from out of state; 29% Black or African American, non-Hispanic/Latino; 40% Hispanic/Latino; 10% Asian, non-Hispanic/Latino; 0.4% American Indian or Alaska Native, non-Hispanic/Latino; 5% Two or more races, non-Hispanic/Latino; 6% international; 6% transferred in; 9% live on campus. *Retention:* 45% of full-time freshmen returned.

Freshmen *Admission:* 185 enrolled.
Faculty *Total:* 56, 36% full-time. *Student/faculty ratio:* 11:1.
Majors Computer and information systems security; elementary education; liberal arts and sciences/liberal studies; nonprofit management.
Academics *Calendar:* semesters. *Degrees:* certificates, associate, and bachelor's. *Special study options:* academic remediation for entering students, advanced placement credit, distance learning, English as a second language, external degree program, honors programs, independent study, part-time degree program, services for LD students, summer session for credit.
Library Trant Memorial Library plus 1 other with 16,579 titles, 229 audiovisual materials, an OPAC, a Web page.
Student Life *Housing Options:* men-only, women-only. Campus housing is university owned and is provided by a third party. *Activities and Organizations:* Organization of Student Leadership, Student Ambassadors, Healthy Student Task Force, Men's Soccer Club, Women's Soccer Club. *Campus security:* 24-hour emergency response devices. *Student services:* personal/psychological counseling.
Standardized Tests *Recommended:* ACT (for admission).
Costs (2015–16) *Comprehensive fee:* $12,244 includes full-time tuition ($5920), mandatory fees ($100), and room and board ($6224). Full-time tuition and fees vary according to course level, course load, degree level, and program. Part-time tuition and fees vary according to course level. *Room and board:* Room and board charges vary according to housing facility. *Payment plan:* installment. *Waivers:* employees or children of employees.
Applying *Options:* electronic application, early admission, deferred entrance. *Recommended:* high school transcript. *Application deadlines:* rolling (freshmen), rolling (transfers).
Freshman Application Contact Ms. Sydney Beeler, Vice President of Enrollment and Student Affairs, Donnelly College, 608 North 18th Street, Kansas City, KS 66102. *Phone:* 913-621-8713. *Fax:* 913-621-8719. *E-mail:* admissions@donnelly.edu.
Website: http://www.donnelly.edu/.

Flint Hills Technical College
Emporia, Kansas

Freshman Application Contact Admissions Office, Flint Hills Technical College, 3301 West 18th Avenue, Emporia, KS 66801. *Phone:* 620-341-1325. *Toll-free phone:* 800-711-6947.
Website: http://www.fhtc.edu/.

Fort Scott Community College
Fort Scott, Kansas

Director of Admissions Mrs. Mert Barrows, Director of Admissions, Fort Scott Community College, 2108 South Horton, Fort Scott, KS 66701. *Phone:* 620-223-2700 Ext. 353. *Toll-free phone:* 800-874-3722.
Website: http://www.fortscott.edu/.

Garden City Community College
Garden City, Kansas

- **County-supported** 2-year, founded 1919, part of Kansas Board of Regents
- **Rural** 63-acre campus
- **Endowment** $5.9 million
- **Coed**

Undergraduates 1,069 full-time, 928 part-time. Students come from 5 other countries; 17% are from out of state; 7% Black or African American, non-Hispanic/Latino; 38% Hispanic/Latino; 3% Asian, non-Hispanic/Latino; 0.1% Native Hawaiian or other Pacific Islander, non-Hispanic/Latino; 0.7% American Indian or Alaska Native, non-Hispanic/Latino; 2% Race/ethnicity unknown; 0.3% international; 3% transferred in.
Academics *Calendar:* semesters. *Degree:* certificates and associate. *Special study options:* academic remediation for entering students, adult/continuing education programs, advanced placement credit, distance learning, English as a second language, external degree program, part-time degree program, services for LD students, student-designed majors, summer session for credit.
Student Life *Campus security:* 24-hour emergency response devices and patrols, student patrols, late-night transport/escort service, controlled dormitory access.
Athletics Member NJCAA.
Standardized Tests *Required:* ACT Compass (for admission). *Recommended:* ACT (for admission).
Costs (2014–15) *Tuition:* state resident $1760 full-time, $55 per credit hour part-time; nonresident $2368 full-time, $74 per credit hour part-time. Full-time tuition and fees vary according to course load. Part-time tuition and fees vary according to course load. *Required fees:* $960 full-time, $30 per credit hour

part-time. *Room and board:* $4950. Room and board charges vary according to board plan and housing facility.
Financial Aid Of all full-time matriculated undergraduates who enrolled in 2013, 90 Federal Work-Study jobs (averaging $1000). 100 state and other part-time jobs (averaging $900).
Applying *Required:* high school transcript.
Freshman Application Contact Office of Admissions, Garden City Community College, 801 Campus Drive, Garden City, KS 67846. *Phone:* 620-276-9531. *Toll-free phone:* 800-658-1696. *Fax:* 620-276-9650. *E-mail:* admissions@gcccks.edu.
Website: http://www.gcccks.edu/.

Heritage College
Wichita, Kansas

Admissions Office Contact Heritage College, 2800 South Rock Road, Wichita, KS 67210.
Website: http://www.heritage-education.com/.

Hesston College
Hesston, Kansas

Freshman Application Contact Joel Kauffman, Vice President of Admissions, Hesston College, Hesston, KS 67062. *Phone:* 620-327-8222. *Toll-free phone:* 800-995-2757. *Fax:* 620-327-8300. *E-mail:* admissions@hesston.edu.
Website: http://www.hesston.edu/.

Highland Community College
Highland, Kansas

Director of Admissions Ms. Cheryl Rasmussen, Vice President of Student Services, Highland Community College, 606 West Main Street, Highland, KS 66035. *Phone:* 785-442-6020. *Fax:* 785-442-6106.
Website: http://www.highlandcc.edu/.

Hutchinson Community College
Hutchinson, Kansas

- **State and locally supported** 2-year, founded 1928, part of Kansas Board of Regents
- **Small-town** 47-acre campus with easy access to Wichita
- **Coed,** 5,723 undergraduate students, 40% full-time, 54% women, 46% men

Undergraduates 2,272 full-time, 3,451 part-time. Students come from 46 states and territories; 6 other countries; 8% are from out of state; 6% Black or African American, non-Hispanic/Latino; 9% Hispanic/Latino; 0.8% Asian, non-Hispanic/Latino; 0.1% Native Hawaiian or other Pacific Islander, non-Hispanic/Latino; 0.7% American Indian or Alaska Native, non-Hispanic/Latino; 3% Two or more races, non-Hispanic/Latino; 8% Race/ethnicity unknown; 0.5% international; 5% transferred in; 8% live on campus.
Freshmen *Admission:* 2,496 applied, 2,496 admitted, 859 enrolled. *Average high school GPA:* 3.1. *Test scores:* ACT scores over 18: 72%; ACT scores over 24: 23%; ACT scores over 30: 3%.
Faculty *Total:* 470, 26% full-time, 4% with terminal degrees. *Student/faculty ratio:* 14:1.
Majors Administrative assistant and secretarial science; agricultural mechanics and equipment technology; agriculture; architectural drafting and CAD/CADD; autobody/collision and repair technology; automobile/automotive mechanics technology; biology/biological sciences; biology/biotechnology laboratory technician; business and personal/financial services marketing; business/commerce; carpentry; child-care and support services management; clinical/medical laboratory technology; communications technology; computer and information sciences; computer systems analysis; computer systems networking and telecommunications; criminal justice/police science; design and visual communications; drafting and design technology; drama and dance teacher education; education; electrical, electronic and communications engineering technology; electrical/electronics equipment installation and repair; emergency medical technology (EMT paramedic); engineering; English; family and consumer sciences/human sciences; farm and ranch management; fire science/firefighting; foreign languages and literatures; health information/medical records technology; legal assistant/paralegal; liberal arts and sciences/liberal studies; machine tool technology; manufacturing engineering technology; mathematics; mechanical drafting and CAD/CADD; medical radiologic technology; natural resources management and policy; pharmacy technician; physical sciences; physical therapy technology;

psychology; radio and television broadcasting technology; registered nursing/registered nurse; respiratory therapy technician; retailing; social sciences; speech communication and rhetoric; sport and fitness administration/management; surgical technology; visual and performing arts; web page, digital/multimedia and information resources design; welding technology.

Academics *Calendar:* semesters. *Degree:* certificates and associate. *Special study options:* academic remediation for entering students, adult/continuing education programs, advanced placement credit, cooperative education, distance learning, double majors, English as a second language, honors programs, independent study, internships, part-time degree program, services for LD students, student-designed majors, summer session for credit.

Library John F. Kennedy Library plus 1 other with 41,118 titles, 2,354 audiovisual materials, an OPAC, a Web page.

Student Life *Housing Options:* men-only, women-only. Campus housing is university owned. *Activities and Organizations:* drama/theater group, student-run newspaper, choral group, Circle K, Student Fire Fighter Association, RESET (non-denominational religious group), DragonLAN, Block & Bridle Club. *Campus security:* 24-hour emergency response devices and patrols, student patrols, late-night transport/escort service, controlled dormitory access. *Student services:* health clinic, personal/psychological counseling.

Athletics Member NJCAA. *Intercollegiate sports:* baseball M(s), basketball M(s)/W(s), cheerleading M(s)/W(s), cross-country running M(s)/W(s), football M(s), golf M(s), soccer W(s), softball W(s), track and field M(s)/W(s), volleyball W(s). *Intramural sports:* basketball M/W, football M/W, soccer M/W, table tennis M/W, tennis M/W, track and field M/W, volleyball M/W.

Costs (2014–15) *Tuition:* area resident $2112 full-time, $66 per credit hour part-time; state resident $2432 full-time, $76 per credit hour part-time; nonresident $3424 full-time, $107 per credit hour part-time. *Required fees:* $608 full-time, $19 per credit hour part-time. *Room and board:* $5361. Room and board charges vary according to board plan and housing facility. *Payment plan:* installment. *Waivers:* employees or children of employees.

Applying *Options:* electronic application, early admission, deferred entrance. *Required:* high school transcript. *Required for some:* interview, Copy of GED certificate required from GED completers. *Application deadlines:* rolling (freshmen), rolling (out-of-state freshmen), rolling (transfers). *Notification:* continuous (freshmen), continuous (out-of-state freshmen), continuous (transfers).

Freshman Application Contact Mr. Corbin Strobel, Director of Admissions, Hutchinson Community College, 1300 North Plum, Hutchinson, KS 67501. *Phone:* 620-665-3536. *Toll-free phone:* 888-GO-HUTCH. *Fax:* 620-665-3301. *E-mail:* strobelc@hutchcc.edu. *Website:* http://www.hutchcc.edu/.

Independence Community College
Independence, Kansas

- **State-supported** 2-year, founded 1925, part of Kansas Board of Regents
- **Rural** 68-acre campus
- **Coed**

Undergraduates 575 full-time, 456 part-time. Students come from 23 states and territories; 25 other countries; 30% are from out of state; 10% Black or African American, non-Hispanic/Latino; 4% Hispanic/Latino; 0.3% Asian, non-Hispanic/Latino; 0.6% Native Hawaiian or other Pacific Islander, non-Hispanic/Latino; 2% American Indian or Alaska Native, non-Hispanic/Latino; 3% Two or more races, non-Hispanic/Latino; 1% Race/ethnicity unknown; 2% international; 7% transferred in. *Retention:* 40% of full-time freshmen returned.

Faculty *Student/faculty ratio:* 11:1.

Academics *Calendar:* semesters. *Degree:* certificates and associate. *Special study options:* academic remediation for entering students, advanced placement credit, cooperative education, distance learning, part-time degree program, services for LD students, summer session for credit.

Student Life *Campus security:* controlled dormitory access, night patrol.

Athletics Member NJCAA.

Costs (2014–15) *Tuition:* area resident $1188 full-time; state resident $1270 full-time; nonresident $2590 full-time. *Required fees:* $1254 full-time. *Room and board:* $4700.

Financial Aid Of all full-time matriculated undergraduates who enrolled in 2013, 85 Federal Work-Study jobs (averaging $900).

Applying *Required:* high school transcript. *Required for some:* essay or personal statement, minimum 2.5 GPA, 2 letters of recommendation, interview.

Freshman Application Contact Ms. Brittany Thornton, Admissions Coordinator, Independence Community College, PO Box 708, 1057 W. College Avenue, Independence, KS 673001. *Phone:* 620-332-5495. *Toll-free phone:* 800-842-6063. *Fax:* 620-331-0946. *E-mail:* bthornton@indycc.edu. *Website:* http://www.indycc.edu/.

Johnson County Community College
Overland Park, Kansas

Director of Admissions Dr. Charles J. Carlsen, President, Johnson County Community College, 12345 College Boulevard, Overland Park, KS 66210-1299. *Phone:* 913-469-8500 Ext. 3806. *Website:* http://www.johnco.cc.ks.us/.

Kansas City Kansas Community College
Kansas City, Kansas

Freshman Application Contact Dr. Denise McDowell, Dean of Enrollment Management/Registrar, Kansas City Kansas Community College, Admissions Office, 7250 State Avenue, Kansas City, KS 66112. *Phone:* 913-288-7694. *Fax:* 913-288-7648. *E-mail:* dmcdowell@kckcc.edu. *Website:* http://www.kckcc.edu/.

Labette Community College
Parsons, Kansas

Freshman Application Contact Ms. Tammy Fuentez, Director of Admission, Labette Community College, 200 South 14th Street, Parsons, KS 67357-4299. *Phone:* 620-421-6700. *Toll-free phone:* 888-522-3883. *Fax:* 620-421-0180. *Website:* http://www.labette.edu/.

Manhattan Area Technical College
Manhattan, Kansas

- **State and locally supported** 2-year, founded 1965
- **Rural** 18-acre campus
- **Coed**

Undergraduates 491 full-time, 334 part-time. Students come from 11 states and territories; 1% are from out of state; 8% Black or African American, non-Hispanic/Latino; 6% Hispanic/Latino; 2% Asian, non-Hispanic/Latino; 0.8% Native Hawaiian or other Pacific Islander, non-Hispanic/Latino; 0.6% American Indian or Alaska Native, non-Hispanic/Latino; 2% Two or more races, non-Hispanic/Latino; 1% Race/ethnicity unknown; 14% transferred in. *Retention:* 80% of full-time freshmen returned.

Faculty *Student/faculty ratio:* 14:1.

Academics *Calendar:* semesters. *Degree:* certificates and associate. *Special study options:* academic remediation for entering students, adult/continuing education programs, advanced placement credit, cooperative education, distance learning, double majors, honors programs, internships, part-time degree program, services for LD students, student-designed majors, summer session for credit.

Student Life *Campus security:* late-night transport/escort service, evening security guards.

Standardized Tests *Required:* If students do not have SAT or ACT scores, then students do ACT Compass Testing to guide placement into Math and English courses (for admission).

Costs (2014–15) *Tuition:* state resident $3895 full-time, $97 per credit hour part-time; nonresident $3895 full-time, $97 per credit hour part-time. Full-time tuition and fees vary according to program. Part-time tuition and fees vary according to program. *Required fees:* $1000 full-time, $28 per credit hour part-time.

Applying *Options:* electronic application. *Application fee:* $40. *Required:* high school transcript. *Required for some:* essay or personal statement, 3 letters of recommendation, interview, Admission to pre-allied health programs have specific criteria for admission. Electric Power and Distribution requires a Class A CDL.

Freshman Application Contact Ms. Nicole Bollig, Director of Admissions, Manhattan Area Technical College, 3136 Dickens Ave., Manhattan, KS 66503. *Phone:* 785-587-2800. *Toll-free phone:* 800-352-7575. *Fax:* 913-587-2804. *E-mail:* NicoleBollig@ManhattanTech.edu. *Website:* http://www.manhattantech.edu/.

National American University
Overland Park, Kansas

Freshman Application Contact Admissions Office, National American University, 10310 Mastin Street, Overland Park, KS 66212. *Website:* http://www.national.edu/.

Neosho County Community College
Chanute, Kansas

Freshman Application Contact Ms. Lisa Last, Dean of Student Development, Neosho County Community College, 800 West 14th Street,

Chanute, KS 66720. *Phone:* 620-431-2820 Ext. 213. *Toll-free phone:* 800-729-6222. *Fax:* 620-431-0082. *E-mail:* llast@neosho.edu. *Website:* http://www.neosho.edu/.

North Central Kansas Technical College
Beloit, Kansas

Freshman Application Contact Ms. Judy Heidrick, Director of Admissions, North Central Kansas Technical College, PO Box 507, 3033 US Highway 24, Beloit, KS 67420. *Toll-free phone:* 800-658-4655. *E-mail:* jheidrick@ncktc.tec.ks.us.
Website: http://www.ncktc.edu/.

Northwest Kansas Technical College
Goodland, Kansas

Admissions Office Contact Northwest Kansas Technical College, PO Box 668, 1209 Harrison Street, Goodland, KS 67735. *Toll-free phone:* 800-316-4127.
Website: http://www.nwktc.edu/.

Pinnacle Career Institute
Lawrence, Kansas

Admissions Office Contact Pinnacle Career Institute, 1601 West 23rd Street, Suite 200, Lawrence, KS 66046-2743. *Toll-free phone:* 877-241-3097.
Website: http://www.pcitraining.edu/.

Pratt Community College
Pratt, Kansas

Freshman Application Contact Ms. Theresa Ziehr, Office Assistant, Student Services, Pratt Community College, 348 Northeast State Road 61, Pratt, KS 67124. *Phone:* 620-450-2217. *Toll-free phone:* 800-794-3091. *Fax:* 620-672-5288. *E-mail:* theresaz@prattcc.edu.
Website: http://www.prattcc.edu/.

Salina Area Technical College
Salina, Kansas

Admissions Office Contact Salina Area Technical College, 2562 Centennial Road, Salina, KS 67401.
Website: http://www.salinatech.edu/.

Seward County Community College and Area Technical School
Liberal, Kansas

Director of Admissions Dr. Gerald Harris, Dean of Student Services, Seward County Community College and Area Technical School, PO Box 1137, Liberal, KS 67905-1137. *Phone:* 620-624-1951 Ext. 617. *Toll-free phone:* 800-373-9951.
Website: http://www.sccc.edu/.

Vatterott College
Wichita, Kansas

Admissions Office Contact Vatterott College, 8853 37th Street North, Wichita, KS 67226.
Website: http://www.vatterott.edu/.

Wichita Area Technical College
Wichita, Kansas

- **District-supported** 2-year, founded 1963
- **Urban** campus
- **Endowment** $1.1 million
- **Coed**

Undergraduates 1,087 full-time, 1,849 part-time. Students come from 11 states and territories; 1% are from out of state; 16% Black or African American, non-Hispanic/Latino; 10% Hispanic/Latino; 4% Asian, non-Hispanic/Latino; 0.3% Native Hawaiian or other Pacific Islander, non-Hispanic/Latino; 2% American Indian or Alaska Native, non-Hispanic/Latino; 4% Two or more races, non-Hispanic/Latino; 8% Race/ethnicity unknown; 0.1% international; 3% transferred in. *Retention:* 58% of full-time freshmen returned.

Faculty *Student/faculty ratio:* 19:1.
Academics *Calendar:* semesters. *Degree:* certificates, diplomas, and associate. *Special study options:* academic remediation for entering students, distance learning, internships, part-time degree program, services for LD students, summer session for credit.
Student Life *Campus security:* 24-hour emergency response devices and patrols, late-night transport/escort service.
Standardized Tests *Required for some:* WorkKeys, ACT Compass and TEAS.
Costs (2014–15) *Tuition:* state resident $1890 full-time, $63 per credit hour part-time; nonresident $2280 full-time, $76 per credit hour part-time. Full-time tuition and fees vary according to course load, location, and program. Part-time tuition and fees vary according to course load, location, and program. *Required fees:* $885 full-time, $30 per credit hour part-time.
Applying *Required for some.* high school transcript.
Freshman Application Contact Mr. Andy McFayden, Director, Admissions, Wichita Area Technical College, 4004 N. Webb Road, Suite 100, Wichita, KS 67226 . *Phone:* 316-677-9400. *Fax:* 316-677-9555. *E-mail:* info@watc.edu.
Website: http://www.watc.edu/.

Wichita Technical Institute
Wichita, Kansas

Admissions Office Contact Wichita Technical Institute, 2051 S. Meridian Avenue, Wichita, KS 67213.
Website: http://www.wti.edu/.

Wright Career College
Overland Park, Kansas

- **Proprietary** primarily 2-year
- **Suburban** 5-acre campus with easy access to Kansas City
- **Coed**

Undergraduates 71 full-time. Students come from 3 states and territories; 61% are from out of state; 51% Black or African American, non-Hispanic/Latino; 3% Hispanic/Latino; 1% Two or more races, non-Hispanic/Latino; 1% transferred in.
Academics *Degrees:* associate and bachelor's. *Special study options:* adult/continuing education programs, distance learning, internships, off-campus study.
Freshman Application Contact Wright Career College, 10700 Metcalf Avenue, Overland Park, KS 66210. *Phone:* 913-385-7700. *E-mail:* info@wrightcc.edu.
Website: http://www.wrightcc.edu/.

Wright Career College
Wichita, Kansas

- **Proprietary** primarily 2-year, founded 2011
- **Suburban** campus with easy access to Wichita
- **Coed**

Undergraduates 127 full-time, 235 part-time. Students come from 1 other state; 48% Black or African American, non-Hispanic/Latino; 6% Hispanic/Latino; 0.8% Asian, non-Hispanic/Latino; 4% Two or more races, non-Hispanic/Latino; 0.6% Race/ethnicity unknown; 0.8% transferred in. *Retention:* 1% of full-time freshmen returned.
Academics *Degrees:* diplomas, associate, and bachelor's. *Special study options:* adult/continuing education programs, distance learning, internships, off-campus study.
Freshman Application Contact Wright Career College, 7700 East Kellogg, Wichita, KS 67207. *Phone:* 316-927-7700. *Toll-free phone:* 800-555-4003. *E-mail:* info@wrightcc.edu.
Website: http://www.wrightcc.edu/.

KENTUCKY

Ashland Community and Technical College
Ashland, Kentucky

Freshman Application Contact Ashland Community and Technical College, 1400 College Drive, Ashland, KY 41101-3683. *Phone:* 606-326-2008. *Toll-free phone:* 800-928-4256.
Website: http://www.ashland.kctcs.edu/.

ATA College
Louisville, Kentucky

Freshman Application Contact Admissions Office, ATA College, 10180 Linn Station Road, Suite A200, Louisville, KY 40223. *Phone:* 502-371-8330. *Fax:* 502-371-8598.
Website: http://www.ata.edu/.

Beckfield College
Florence, Kentucky

Freshman Application Contact Mrs. Leah Boerger, Director of Admissions, Beckfield College, 16 Spiral Drive, Florence, KY 41042. *Phone:* 859-371-9393. *E-mail:* lboerger@beckfield.edu.
Website: http://www.beckfield.edu/.

Big Sandy Community and Technical College
Prestonsburg, Kentucky

Director of Admissions Jimmy Wright, Director of Admissions, Big Sandy Community and Technical College, One Bert T. Combs Drive, Prestonsburg, KY 41653-1815. *Phone:* 606-886-3863. *Toll-free phone:* 888-641-4132. *E-mail:* jimmy.wright@kctcs.edu.
Website: http://www.bigsandy.kctcs.edu/.

Bluegrass Community and Technical College
Lexington, Kentucky

Freshman Application Contact Mrs. Shelbie Hugle, Director of Admission Services, Bluegrass Community and Technical College, 470 Cooper Drive, Lexington, KY 40506. *Phone:* 859-246-6216. *Toll-free phone:* 800-744-4872 (in-state); 866-744-4872 (out-of-state). *E-mail:* shelbie.hugle@kctcs.edu.
Website: http://www.bluegrass.kctcs.edu/.

Brown Mackie College–Hopkinsville
Hopkinsville, Kentucky

- **Proprietary** 2-year, part of Education Management Corporation
- **Small-town** campus
- **Coed**

Academics *Calendar:* quarters. *Degree:* diplomas and associate.
Freshman Application Contact Brown Mackie College–Hopkinsville, 4001 Fort Cambell Boulevard, Hopkinsville, KY 42240. *Phone:* 270-886-1302. *Toll-free phone:* 800-359-4753.
Website: http://www.brownmackie.edu/Hopkinsville/.

Brown Mackie College–Louisville
Louisville, Kentucky

- **Proprietary** primarily 2-year, founded 1972, part of Education Management Corporation
- **Suburban** campus
- **Coed**

Academics *Calendar:* quarters. *Degrees:* certificates, diplomas, associate, and bachelor's.
Freshman Application Contact Brown Mackie College–Louisville, 3605 Fern Valley Road, Louisville, KY 40219. *Phone:* 502-968-7191. *Toll-free phone:* 800-999-7387.
Website: http://www.brownmackie.edu/louisville/.

Brown Mackie College–Northern Kentucky
Fort Mitchell, Kentucky

- **Proprietary** primarily 2-year, founded 1927, part of Education Management Corporation
- **Suburban** campus
- **Coed**

Academics *Calendar:* quarters. *Degrees:* diplomas, associate, and bachelor's.
Freshman Application Contact Brown Mackie College–Northern Kentucky, 309 Buttermilk Pike, Fort Mitchell, KY 41017-2191. *Phone:* 859-341-5627. *Toll-free phone:* 800-888-1445.
Website: http://www.brownmackie.edu/northernkentucky/.

Daymar College
Bowling Green, Kentucky

Freshman Application Contact Mrs. Traci Henderson, Admissions Director, Daymar College, 2421 Fitzgerald Industrial Drive, Bowling Green, KY 42101. *Phone:* 270-843-6750. *Toll-free phone:* 877-258-7796. *E-mail:* thenderson@daymarcollege.edu.
Website: http://www.daymarcollege.edu/.

Daymar College
Madisonville, Kentucky

Admissions Office Contact Daymar College, 1105 National Mine Drive, Madisonville, KY 42431. *Toll-free phone:* 877-258-7796.
Website: http://www.daymarcollege.edu/.

Daymar College
Owensboro, Kentucky

Freshman Application Contact Ms. Vickie McDougal, Director of Admissions, Daymar College, 3361 Buckland Square, Owensboro, KY 42301. *Phone:* 270-926-4040. *Toll-free phone:* 877-258-7796. *Fax:* 270-685-4090. *E-mail:* info@daymarcollege.edu.
Website: http://www.daymarcollege.edu/.

Elizabethtown Community and Technical College
Elizabethtown, Kentucky

- **State-supported** 2-year, founded 1966, part of Kentucky Community and Technical College System
- **Small-town** 80-acre campus
- **Endowment** $655,000
- **Coed,** 7,353 undergraduate students, 38% full-time, 53% women, 47% men

Undergraduates 2,822 full-time, 4,531 part-time. Students come from 17 states and territories; 0.5% are from out of state; 7% Black or African American, non-Hispanic/Latino; 3% Hispanic/Latino; 0.9% Asian, non-Hispanic/Latino; 0.2% Native Hawaiian or other Pacific Islander, non-Hispanic/Latino; 0.4% American Indian or Alaska Native, non-Hispanic/Latino; 3% Two or more races, non-Hispanic/Latino; 3% Race/ethnicity unknown; 3% transferred in.
Freshmen *Admission:* 1,218 enrolled.
Faculty *Total:* 302, 47% full-time. *Student/faculty ratio:* 22:1.
Majors Automobile/automotive mechanics technology; business administration and management; child-care provision; computer and information sciences; criminal justice/law enforcement administration; data processing and data processing technology; dental hygiene; diesel mechanics technology; electrician; engineering technology; executive assistant/executive secretary; fire science/firefighting; industrial electronics technology; industrial mechanics and maintenance technology; interdisciplinary studies; liberal arts and sciences/liberal studies; medical administrative assistant and medical secretary; medical radiologic technology; quality control and safety technologies related; registered nursing/registered nurse; respiratory care therapy; social work; teacher assistant/aide; welding technology.
Academics *Calendar:* semesters. *Degree:* certificates, diplomas, and associate. *Special study options:* academic remediation for entering students, advanced placement credit, cooperative education, distance learning, internships, off-campus study, part-time degree program, services for LD students, summer session for credit.
Library ECTC Media Center.
Student Life *Housing:* college housing not available. *Activities and Organizations:* student-run newspaper. *Campus security:* late-night transport/escort service.
Standardized Tests *Recommended:* ACT (for admission).
Applying *Options:* electronic application. *Required for some:* high school transcript. *Application deadlines:* rolling (freshmen), rolling (transfers). *Notification:* continuous (freshmen), continuous (transfers).
Freshman Application Contact Elizabethtown Community and Technical College, 620 College Street Road, Elizabethtown, KY 42701. *Phone:* 270-706-8800. *Toll-free phone:* 877-246-2322.
Website: http://www.elizabethtown.kctcs.edu/.

Galen College of Nursing
Louisville, Kentucky

Admissions Office Contact Galen College of Nursing, 1031 Zorn Avenue, Suite 400, Louisville, KY 40207.
Website: http://www.galencollege.edu/.

Gateway Community and Technical College
Florence, Kentucky

- **State-supported** 2-year, founded 1961, part of Kentucky Community and Technical College System
- **Suburban** campus with easy access to Cincinnati
- **Coed,** 4,639 undergraduate students, 28% full-time, 50% women, 50% men

Undergraduates 1,305 full-time, 3,334 part-time. 9% Black or African American, non-Hispanic/Latino; 3% Hispanic/Latino; 0.7% Asian, non-Hispanic/Latino; 0.1% Native Hawaiian or other Pacific Islander, non-Hispanic/Latino; 0.2% American Indian or Alaska Native, non-Hispanic/Latino; 2% Two or more races, non-Hispanic/Latino; 3% Race/ethnicity unknown.
Freshmen *Admission:* 1,635 applied, 879 admitted, 451 enrolled.
Faculty *Student/faculty ratio:* 22:1.
Majors Business administration and management; CAD/CADD drafting/design technology; computer and information sciences; criminal justice/law enforcement administration; early childhood education; educational/instructional technology; engineering technology; fire science/firefighting; general studies; health professions related; industrial technology; manufacturing engineering technology; office occupations and clerical services; registered nursing/registered nurse; teacher assistant/aide.
Academics *Calendar:* semesters. *Degree:* certificates, diplomas, and associate. *Special study options:* academic remediation for entering students, cooperative education, distance learning, internships, part-time degree program, services for LD students, summer session for credit.
Library Main Library plus 3 others.
Student Life *Housing:* college housing not available. *Activities and Organizations:* National Technical Honor Society, Student Government Association, Speech Team, American Criminal Justice Association, Phi Theta Kappa. *Student services:* personal/psychological counseling.
Standardized Tests *Required:* ACT or ACT Compass (for admission).
Costs (2014–15) *Tuition:* state resident $3528 full-time, $147 per credit hour part-time; nonresident $12,360 full-time, $515 per credit hour part-time. Full-time tuition and fees vary according to course load. Part-time tuition and fees vary according to course load. *Required fees:* $40 per term part-time. *Payment plan:* installment. *Waivers:* senior citizens and employees or children of employees.
Applying *Options:* electronic application, early admission, deferred entrance. *Required:* high school transcript. *Application deadlines:* rolling (freshmen), rolling (out-of-state freshmen), rolling (transfers). *Notification:* continuous (freshmen), continuous (out-of-state freshmen), continuous (transfers).
Freshman Application Contact Gateway Community and Technical College, 500 Technology Way, Florence, KY 41042. *Phone:* 859-441-4500. *E-mail:* andre.washington@kctcs.edu.
Website: http://www.gateway.kctcs.edu/.

Hazard Community and Technical College
Hazard, Kentucky

Freshman Application Contact Director of Admissions, Hazard Community and Technical College, 1 Community College Drive, Hazard, KY 41701-2403. *Phone:* 606-487-3102. *Toll-free phone:* 800-246-7521.
Website: http://www.hazard.kctcs.edu/.

Henderson Community College
Henderson, Kentucky

Freshman Application Contact Ms. Teresa Hamiton, Admissions Counselor, Henderson Community College, 2660 South Green Street, Henderson, KY 42420-4623. *Phone:* 270-827-1867 Ext. 354. *Toll-free phone:* 800-696-9958.
Website: http://www.henderson.kctcs.edu/.

Hopkinsville Community College
Hopkinsville, Kentucky

- **State-supported** 2-year, founded 1965, part of Kentucky Community and Technical College System
- **Small-town** 69-acre campus with easy access to Nashville, TN
- **Coed,** 3,609 undergraduate students, 45% full-time, 66% women, 34% men

Undergraduates 1,627 full-time, 1,982 part-time. 24% Black or African American, non-Hispanic/Latino; 7% Hispanic/Latino; 1% Asian, non-Hispanic/Latino; 0.5% Native Hawaiian or other Pacific Islander, non-Hispanic/Latino; 0.5% American Indian or Alaska Native, non-Hispanic/Latino; 3% Two or more races, non-Hispanic/Latino; 1% Race/ethnicity unknown; 0.1% international; 7% transferred in. *Retention:* 52% of full-time freshmen returned.
Freshmen *Admission:* 1,627 applied, 1,627 admitted, 650 enrolled.
Faculty *Total:* 145, 47% full-time. *Student/faculty ratio:* 23:1.
Majors Administrative assistant and secretarial science; agricultural production; animal/livestock husbandry and production; business administration and management; child-care and support services management; child-care provision; computer and information sciences; criminal justice/law enforcement administration; criminal justice/police science; early childhood education; electrical, electronic and communications engineering technology; engineering technology; executive assistant/executive secretary; human services; industrial technology; liberal arts and sciences/liberal studies; multi/interdisciplinary studies related; registered nursing/registered nurse; social work; teacher assistant/aide.
Academics *Calendar:* semesters. *Degree:* certificates, diplomas, and associate. *Special study options:* academic remediation for entering students, advanced placement credit, cooperative education, distance learning, honors programs, independent study, part-time degree program, services for LD students, summer session for credit.
Library Learning Resource Center with an OPAC, a Web page.
Student Life *Housing:* college housing not available. *Activities and Organizations:* student-run newspaper, Ag Tech, Amateur Radio, Ballroom Dance, Baptist Campus Ministries, Black Men United. *Campus security:* 24-hour emergency response devices, late-night transport/escort service, security provided by trained security personnel during hours of normal operation.
Athletics *Intramural sports:* basketball M, football M, golf M, table tennis M/W, volleyball M/W.
Costs (2014–15) *Tuition:* state resident $4410 full-time, $147 per credit hour part-time; nonresident $15,450 full-time, $515 per credit hour part-time. Full-time tuition and fees vary according to reciprocity agreements. Part-time tuition and fees vary according to reciprocity agreements. *Required fees:* $120 full-time, $4 per credit hour part-time. *Payment plan:* installment. *Waivers:* senior citizens and employees or children of employees.
Financial Aid Of all full-time matriculated undergraduates who enrolled in 2013, 30 Federal Work-Study jobs (averaging $1500). *Financial aid deadline:* 6/30.
Applying *Options:* electronic application, deferred entrance. *Recommended:* high school transcript. *Application deadlines:* rolling (freshmen), rolling (out-of-state freshmen), rolling (transfers). *Notification:* continuous (freshmen), continuous (out-of-state freshmen), continuous (transfers).
Freshman Application Contact Ms. Janet Level, Student Records, Hopkinsville Community College, Room 135, English Education Center, 202 Bastogne Avenue, Fort Campbell, KY. *Phone:* 270-707-3918. *Toll-free phone:* 866-534-2224. *Fax:* 270-707-3973. *E-mail:* janet.level@kctcs.edu.
Website: http://hopkinsville.kctcs.edu/.

Interactive College of Technology
Newport, Kentucky

Admissions Office Contact Interactive College of Technology, 76 Carothers Road, Newport, KY 41701.
Website: http://ict.edu/.

ITT Technical Institute
Louisville, Kentucky

- **Proprietary** primarily 2-year, founded 1993, part of ITT Educational Services, Inc.
- **Suburban** campus
- **Coed**

Academics *Calendar:* quarters. *Degrees:* associate and bachelor's.
Freshman Application Contact Director of Recruitment, ITT Technical Institute, 9500 Ormsby Station Road, Suite 100, Louisville, KY 40223. *Phone:* 502-327-7424. *Toll-free phone:* 888-790-7427.
Website: http://www.itt-tech.edu/.

Jefferson Community and Technical College
Louisville, Kentucky

Freshman Application Contact Ms. Melanie Vaughan-Cooke, Admissions Coordinator, Jefferson Community and Technical College, Louisville, KY 40202. *Phone:* 502-213-4000. *Fax:* 502-213-2540.
Website: http://www.jefferson.kctcs.edu/.

Madisonville Community College
Madisonville, Kentucky

Director of Admissions Mr. Jay Parent, Registrar, Madisonville Community College, 2000 College Drive, Madisonville, KY 42431-9185. *Phone:* 270-821-2250.
Website: http://www.madisonville.kctcs.edu/.

Maysville Community and Technical College
Maysville, Kentucky

- **State-supported** 2-year, founded 1967, part of Kentucky Community and Technical College System
- **Rural** 12-acre campus
- **Coed,** 3,478 undergraduate students, 42% full-time, 62% women, 38% men

Undergraduates 1,466 full-time, 2,012 part-time. 3% Black or African American, non-Hispanic/Latino; 1% Hispanic/Latino; 0.2% Asian, non-Hispanic/Latino; 0.1% Native Hawaiian or other Pacific Islander, non-Hispanic/Latino; 0.2% American Indian or Alaska Native, non-Hispanic/Latino; 1% Two or more races, non-Hispanic/Latino; 1% Race/ethnicity unknown; 0.1% international.
Majors Business administration and management; computer and information sciences; electromechanical technology; engineering technology; executive assistant/executive secretary; family systems; interdisciplinary studies; liberal arts and sciences/liberal studies; machine shop technology; registered nursing/registered nurse; respiratory care therapy; welding technology.
Academics *Calendar:* semesters. *Degree:* certificates, diplomas, and associate. *Special study options:* academic remediation for entering students, adult/continuing education programs, advanced placement credit, cooperative education, distance learning, English as a second language, external degree program, honors programs, independent study, internships, off-campus study, part-time degree program, services for LD students, summer session for credit.
Library Finch Library with 36,600 titles, an OPAC, a Web page.
Student Life *Housing:* college housing not available. *Activities and Organizations:* student-run television station. *Campus security:* student patrols, evening parking lot security. *Student services:* personal/psychological counseling.
Costs (2014–15) *Tuition:* state resident $3528 full-time, $147 per credit hour part-time; nonresident $12,360 full-time, $515 per credit hour part-time. *Required fees:* $8 per credit hour part-time.
Financial Aid Of all full-time matriculated undergraduates who enrolled in 2013, 30 Federal Work-Study jobs (averaging $1960).
Applying *Options:* electronic application, early admission. *Required:* high school transcript. *Application deadlines:* rolling (freshmen), rolling (transfers). *Notification:* continuous (freshmen), continuous (transfers).
Freshman Application Contact Maysville Community and Technical College, 1755 US 68, Maysville, KY 41056. *Phone:* 606-759-7141.
Website: http://www.maysville.kctcs.edu/.

Maysville Community and Technical College
Morehead, Kentucky

Director of Admissions Patee Massie, Registrar, Maysville Community and Technical College, 609 Viking Drive, Morehead, KY 40351. *Phone:* 606-759-7141 Ext. 66184.
Website: http://www.maysville.kctcs.edu/.

MedTech College
Lexington, Kentucky

Admissions Office Contact MedTech College, 1648 McGrathiana Parkway, Suite 200, Lexington, KY 40511.
Website: http://www.medtechcollege.edu/.

National College
Danville, Kentucky

Director of Admissions James McGuire, Campus Director, National College, 115 East Lexington Avenue, Danville, KY 40422. *Phone:* 859-236-6991. *Toll-free phone:* 888-9-JOBREADY.
Website: http://www.national-college.edu/.

National College
Florence, Kentucky

Director of Admissions Mr. Terry Kovacs, Campus Director, National College, 8095 Connector Drive, Florence, KY 41042. *Phone:* 859-525-6510. *Toll-free phone:* 888-9-JOBREADY.
Website: http://www.national-college.edu/.

National College
Lexington, Kentucky

Director of Admissions Kim Thomasson, Campus Director, National College, 2376 Sir Barton Way, Lexington, KY 40509. *Phone:* 859-253-0621. *Toll-free phone:* 888-9-JOBREADY.
Website: http://www.national-college.edu/.

National College
Louisville, Kentucky

Director of Admissions Vincent C. Tinebra, Campus Director, National College, 4205 Dixie Highway, Louisville, KY 40216. *Phone:* 502-447-7634. *Toll-free phone:* 888-9-JOBREADY.
Website: http://www.national-college.edu/.

National College
Pikeville, Kentucky

Director of Admissions Tammy Riley, Campus Director, National College, 50 National College Boulevard, Pikeville, KY 41501. *Phone:* 606-478-7200. *Toll-free phone:* 888-9-JOBREADY.
Website: http://www.national-college.edu/.

National College
Richmond, Kentucky

Director of Admissions Ms. Keeley Gadd, Campus Director, National College, 125 South Killarney Lane, Richmond, KY 40475. *Phone:* 859-623-8956. *Toll-free phone:* 888-9-JOBREADY.
Website: http://www.national-college.edu/.

Owensboro Community and Technical College
Owensboro, Kentucky

- **State-supported** 2-year, founded 1986, part of Kentucky Community and Technical College System
- **Suburban** 102-acre campus
- **Coed,** 4,162 undergraduate students, 39% full-time, 59% women, 41% men

Undergraduates 1,637 full-time, 2,525 part-time. Students come from 15 states and territories; 4% are from out of state; 4% Black or African American, non-Hispanic/Latino; 2% Hispanic/Latino; 0.8% Asian, non-Hispanic/Latino; 0.1% Native Hawaiian or other Pacific Islander, non-Hispanic/Latino; 0.2% American Indian or Alaska Native, non-Hispanic/Latino; 2% Two or more races, non-Hispanic/Latino; 2% Race/ethnicity unknown; 0.1% international. *Retention:* 49% of full-time freshmen returned.
Freshmen *Admission:* 666 enrolled.
Faculty *Total:* 182, 49% full-time, 13% with terminal degrees. *Student/faculty ratio:* 20:1.
Majors Agricultural production; applied horticulture/horticulture operations; business administration and management; child-care provision; computer and information sciences; construction trades; dramatic/theater arts; emergency medical technology (EMT paramedic); engineering technology; executive assistant/executive secretary; fine/studio arts; fire science/firefighting; health and medical administrative services related; human services; liberal arts and sciences/liberal studies; mechanics and repair; medical administrative assistant and medical secretary; medical radiologic technology; precision production trades; registered nursing/registered nurse; surgical technology; teacher assistant/aide; veterinary/animal health technology.

Academics *Calendar:* semesters. *Degree:* certificates, diplomas, and associate. *Special study options:* academic remediation for entering students, adult/continuing education programs, advanced placement credit, cooperative education, distance learning, double majors, English as a second language, external degree program, honors programs, independent study, off-campus study, part-time degree program, services for LD students, student-designed majors, study abroad, summer session for credit.
Library Main Campus Library with 26,584 titles, 1,847 audiovisual materials, an OPAC, a Web page.
Student Life *Housing:* college housing not available. *Activities and Organizations:* drama/theater group, choral group, Student Government Association. *Campus security:* 24-hour emergency response devices, late-night transport/escort service.
Standardized Tests *Recommended:* SAT or ACT (for admission).
Costs (2014–15) *Tuition:* state resident $4410 full-time, $147 per credit hour part-time; nonresident $15,450 full-time, $515 per credit hour part-time. Full-time tuition and fees vary according to course load and reciprocity agreements. Part-time tuition and fees vary according to course load and reciprocity agreements. *Required fees:* $120 full-time, $4 per credit hour part-time. *Payment plan:* installment. *Waivers:* senior citizens and employees or children of employees.
Financial Aid Of all full-time matriculated undergraduates who enrolled in 2014, 36 Federal Work-Study jobs. *Financial aid deadline:* 4/1.
Applying *Options:* electronic application. *Required:* high school transcript. *Application deadlines:* rolling (freshmen), rolling (transfers). *Notification:* continuous (freshmen), continuous (transfers).
Freshman Application Contact Ms. Barbara Tipmore, Director of Counseling Services, Owensboro Community and Technical College, 4800 New Hartford Road, Owensboro, KY 42303. *Phone:* 270-686-4530. *Toll-free phone:* 866-755-6282. *E-mail:* barb.tipmore@kctcs.edu.
Website: http://www.owensboro.kctcs.edu/.

Somerset Community College
Somerset, Kentucky

- **State-supported** 2-year, founded 1965, part of Kentucky Community and Technical College System
- **Small-town** 70-acre campus
- **Coed,** 7,504 undergraduate students, 12% full-time, 9% women, 7% men

Undergraduates 866 full-time, 344 part-time. *Retention:* 60% of full-time freshmen returned.
Freshmen *Admission:* 1,282 applied, 1,282 admitted, 1,210 enrolled.
Faculty *Total:* 340, 54% full-time. *Student/faculty ratio:* 18:1.
Majors Aircraft powerplant technology; business administration and management; child-care provision; clinical/medical laboratory assistant; computer and information sciences; criminal justice/law enforcement administration; engineering technology; executive assistant/executive secretary; industrial mechanics and maintenance technology; liberal arts and sciences/liberal studies; medical administrative assistant and medical secretary; medical radiologic technology; multi/interdisciplinary studies related; physical therapy technology; registered nursing/registered nurse; respiratory care therapy; surgical technology; teacher assistant/aide.
Academics *Calendar:* semesters. *Degree:* certificates, diplomas, and associate. *Special study options:* academic remediation for entering students, adult/continuing education programs, advanced placement credit, distance learning, part-time degree program, summer session for credit.
Library Somerset Community College Library.
Student Life *Housing:* college housing not available. *Activities and Organizations:* drama/theater group, student-run newspaper.
Costs (2014–15) *Tuition:* state resident $3456 full-time, $147 per credit hour part-time; nonresident $12,096 full-time, $515 per credit hour part-time. Full-time tuition and fees vary according to course load. Part-time tuition and fees vary according to course load. *Payment plan:* installment. *Waivers:* senior citizens and employees or children of employees.
Applying *Options:* electronic application, early admission. *Required:* high school transcript. *Application deadlines:* 8/14 (freshmen), 8/14 (transfers). *Notification:* continuous (freshmen), continuous (transfers).
Freshman Application Contact Director of Admission, Somerset Community College, 808 Monticello Street, Somerset, KY 42501-2973. *Phone:* 606-451-6630. *Toll-free phone:* 877-629-9722. *E-mail:* somerset-admissions@kctcs.edu.
Website: http://www.somerset.kctcs.edu/.

Southcentral Kentucky Community and Technical College
Bowling Green, Kentucky

Director of Admissions Mark Garrett, Chief Student Affairs Officer, Southcentral Kentucky Community and Technical College, 1845 Loop Drive,

Bowling Green, KY 42101. *Phone:* 270-901-1114. *Toll-free phone:* 800-790-0990.
Website: http://www.bowlinggreen.kctcs.edu/.

Southeast Kentucky Community and Technical College
Cumberland, Kentucky

Freshman Application Contact Southeast Kentucky Community and Technical College, 700 College Road, Cumberland, KY 40823-1099. *Phone:* 606-589-2145 Ext. 13018. *Toll-free phone:* 888-274-SECC.
Website: http://www.southeast.kctcs.edu/.

Spencerian College
Louisville, Kentucky

- **Proprietary** primarily 2-year, founded 1892
- **Urban** 10-acre campus
- **Coed,** 500 undergraduate students, 61% full-time, 87% women, 13% men

Undergraduates 303 full-time, 197 part-time. Students come from 3 states and territories; 19% Black or African American, non-Hispanic/Latino; 3% Hispanic/Latino; 0.8% Asian, non-Hispanic/Latino; 0.4% Native Hawaiian or other Pacific Islander, non-Hispanic/Latino; 11% Two or more races, non-Hispanic/Latino; 6% Race/ethnicity unknown; 1% live on campus.
Freshmen *Admission:* 81 enrolled.
Majors Clinical laboratory science/medical technology; clinical/medical laboratory technology; massage therapy; medical insurance coding; radiologic technology/science; registered nursing/registered nurse; respiratory care therapy; surgical technology.
Academics *Calendar:* quarters. *Degrees:* certificates, diplomas, associate, and bachelor's. *Special study options:* distance learning, off-campus study, summer session for credit.
Library Spencerian College Learning Resource Center with 1,770 titles, 324 audiovisual materials, an OPAC, a Web page.
Student Life *Housing Options:* coed. Campus housing is university owned.
Costs (2014–15) *Comprehensive fee:* $28,545 includes full-time tuition ($17,940), mandatory fees ($1680), and room and board ($8925). Full-time tuition and fees vary according to class time and program. Part-time tuition: $299 per credit hour. Part-time tuition and fees vary according to class time and program. *Required fees:* $60 per course part-time. *Room and board:* college room only: $5940. Room and board charges vary according to housing facility. *Waivers:* employees or children of employees.
Applying *Application fee:* $50. *Required:* high school transcript. *Required for some:* essay or personal statement, interview, Some medical programs have specific selective admission criteria. *Notification:* continuous (freshmen), continuous (out-of-state freshmen), continuous (transfers).
Freshman Application Contact Spencerian College, 4627 Dixie Highway, Louisville, KY 40216. *Phone:* 502-447-1000 Ext. 7808. *Toll-free phone:* 800-264-1799.
Website: http://www.spencerian.edu/.

Spencerian College–Lexington
Lexington, Kentucky

- **Proprietary** 2-year, founded 1997, part of Sullivan University System
- **Urban** campus with easy access to Louisville
- **Coed,** 99 undergraduate students, 76% full-time, 58% women, 42% men

Undergraduates 75 full-time, 24 part-time. Students come from 2 states and territories; 1% are from out of state.
Freshmen *Average high school GPA:* 2.5.
Faculty *Total:* 29, 69% full-time. *Student/faculty ratio:* 3:1.
Majors Biomedical technology; clinical/medical laboratory technology; computer and information systems security; computer engineering technology; computer graphics; electrical and electronic engineering technologies related; electrical, electronic and communications engineering technology; massage therapy; medical office management; radiologic technology/science.
Academics *Calendar:* quarters. *Degree:* certificates, diplomas, and associate. *Special study options:* academic remediation for entering students, cooperative education, independent study, part-time degree program, services for LD students, summer session for credit.
Library Spencerian College Library with 450 titles, 25 audiovisual materials.
Student Life *Housing Options:* men-only, women-only. Campus housing is leased by the school. *Activities and Organizations:* student-run newspaper. *Campus security:* 24-hour emergency response devices.
Standardized Tests *Required for some:* ACT ASSET.
Costs (2015–16) *One-time required fee:* $50. *Tuition:* $299 per credit hour part-time. Full-time tuition and fees vary according to class time, course load,

program, and student level. Part-time tuition and fees vary according to class time, course load, program, and student level. *Required fees:* $1700 per year part-time. *Payment plans:* tuition prepayment, installment, deferred payment. *Waivers:* employees or children of employees.
Applying *Application fee:* $50. *Required:* high school transcript, interview. *Application deadline:* rolling (freshmen).
Freshman Application Contact Spencerian College–Lexington, 1575 Winchester Road, Lexington, KY 40505. *Phone:* 859-223-9608 Ext. 5430. *Toll-free phone:* 800-456-3253.
Website: http://www.spencerian.edu/.

Sullivan College of Technology and Design
Louisville, Kentucky

- **Proprietary** primarily 2-year, founded 1961, part of The Sullivan University System, Inc.
- **Suburban** 10-acre campus with easy access to Louisville
- **Coed,** 365 undergraduate students, 62% full-time, 30% women, 70% men

Undergraduates 228 full-time, 137 part-time. Students come from 3 states and territories; 13% are from out of state; 12% Black or African American, non-Hispanic/Latino; 0.3% Hispanic/Latino; 2% Asian, non-Hispanic/Latino; 0.5% Native Hawaiian or other Pacific Islander, non-Hispanic/Latino; 0.3% American Indian or Alaska Native, non-Hispanic/Latino; 13% Two or more races, non-Hispanic/Latino; 4% Race/ethnicity unknown; 5% transferred in.
Freshmen *Admission:* 52 enrolled.
Faculty *Total:* 75, 33% full-time. *Student/faculty ratio:* 9:1.
Majors Animation, interactive technology, video graphics and special effects; architectural drafting and CAD/CADD; architectural engineering technology; architecture related; artificial intelligence; CAD/CADD drafting/design technology; civil drafting and CAD/CADD; computer and information sciences; computer and information sciences and support services related; computer and information systems security; computer engineering technology; computer graphics; computer hardware engineering; computer hardware technology; computer installation and repair technology; computer programming (vendor/product certification); computer systems networking and telecommunications; computer technology/computer systems technology; desktop publishing and digital imaging design; digital communication and media/multimedia; drafting and design technology; drafting/design engineering technologies related; electrical and electronic engineering technologies related; electrical, electronic and communications engineering technology; electrical/electronics equipment installation and repair; electrical/electronics maintenance and repair technology related; electromechanical and instrumentation and maintenance technologies related; engineering technologies and engineering related; engineering technology; graphic and printing equipment operation/production; graphic communications; graphic communications related; graphic design; heating, ventilation, air conditioning and refrigeration engineering technology; housing and human environments; industrial electronics technology; industrial mechanics and maintenance technology; information technology; interior design; manufacturing engineering technology; mechanical drafting and CAD/CADD; mechanical engineering/mechanical technology; network and system administration; robotics technology; web page, digital/multimedia and information resources design.
Academics *Calendar:* quarters. *Degrees:* associate and bachelor's. *Special study options:* academic remediation for entering students, accelerated degree program, adult/continuing education programs, advanced placement credit, double majors, independent study, internships, part-time degree program, services for LD students, summer session for credit.
Library Sullivan College of Technology and Design Library plus 1 other with 30,000 titles, 370 audiovisual materials, an OPAC, a Web page.
Student Life *Housing Options:* coed. Campus housing is university owned. Freshman campus housing is guaranteed. *Activities and Organizations:* ASID, IIDA, ADDA, MAKE Club, Skills USA. *Campus security:* late-night transport/escort service, controlled dormitory access, patrols by trained security personnel while classes are in session.
Standardized Tests *Required:* ACT Compass or ACT or SAT Language and Math scores in place of Compass results (for admission). *Recommended:* SAT or ACT (for admission).
Costs (2015–16) *Comprehensive fee:* $32,005 includes full-time tuition ($20,460), mandatory fees ($1735), and room and board ($9810). Full-time tuition and fees vary according to course load, degree level, and program. Part-time tuition and fees vary according to course load, degree level, and program. No tuition increase for student's term of enrollment. *Room and board:* Room and board charges vary according to board plan. *Payment plan:* installment. *Waivers:* employees or children of employees.
Applying *Options:* electronic application, deferred entrance. *Application fee:* $50. *Required:* high school transcript, interview, Compass Exam or ACT/SAT

Scores. *Application deadlines:* rolling (freshmen), rolling (out-of-state freshmen), rolling (transfers). *Notification:* continuous (freshmen), continuous (out-of-state freshmen), continuous (transfers).
Freshman Application Contact Ms. Heather Wilson, Director of Admissions, Sullivan College of Technology and Design, 3901 Atkinson Square Drive, Louisville, KY 40218. *Phone:* 502-456-6509 Ext. 8220. *Toll-free phone:* 800-884-6528. *Fax:* 502-456-2341. *E-mail:* hwilson@sctd.edu.
Website: http://www.sctd.edu/.

West Kentucky Community and Technical College
Paducah, Kentucky

- **State-supported** 2-year, founded 1932, part of Kentucky Community and Technical College System
- **Small-town** 117-acre campus
- **Coed**

Undergraduates 2,364 full-time, 2,304 part-time. Students come from 22 states and territories; 6% are from out of state; 9% Black or African American, non-Hispanic/Latino; 2% Hispanic/Latino; 0.6% Asian, non-Hispanic/Latino; 0.3% American Indian or Alaska Native, non-Hispanic/Latino; 1% Two or more races, non-Hispanic/Latino; 1% Race/ethnicity unknown; 0.1% international. *Retention:* 61% of full-time freshmen returned.
Academics *Calendar:* semesters. *Degree:* certificates, diplomas, and associate. *Special study options:* academic remediation for entering students, adult/continuing education programs, cooperative education, distance learning, English as a second language, honors programs, independent study, internships, part-time degree program, study abroad.
Student Life *Campus security:* late-night transport/escort service, 14-hour patrols by trained security personnel.
Standardized Tests *Required:* SAT or ACT (for admission). *Recommended:* ACT (for admission).
Costs (2014–15) *Tuition:* state resident $4410 full-time, $147 per credit hour part-time; nonresident $15,450 full-time, $515 per credit hour part-time. Full-time tuition and fees vary according to reciprocity agreements. Part-time tuition and fees vary according to reciprocity agreements. *Required fees:* $120 full-time, $4 per credit hour part-time.
Financial Aid Of all full-time matriculated undergraduates who enrolled in 2013, 50 Federal Work-Study jobs (averaging $1650).
Applying *Options:* early admission. *Required for some:* high school transcript.
Freshman Application Contact Ms. Debbie Smith, Admissions Counselor, West Kentucky Community and Technical College, 4810 Alben Barkley Drive, Paducah, KY 42001. *Phone:* 270-554-3266. *E-mail:* Debbie.Smith@kctcs.edu.
Website: http://www.westkentucky.kctcs.edu/.

LOUISIANA

Baton Rouge Community College
Baton Rouge, Louisiana

Director of Admissions Nancy Clay, Interim Executive Director for Enrollment Services, Baton Rouge Community College, 201 Community College Drive, Baton Rouge, LA 70806. *Phone:* 225-216-8700. *Toll-free phone:* 800-601-4558.
Website: http://www.mybrcc.edu/.

Baton Rouge School of Computers
Baton Rouge, Louisiana

Freshman Application Contact Admissions Office, Baton Rouge School of Computers, 10425 Plaza Americana, Baton Rouge, LA 70816. *Phone:* 225-923-2524. *Toll-free phone:* 888-920-BRSC. *Fax:* 225-923-2979. *E-mail:* admissions@brsc.net.
Website: http://www.brsc.edu/.

Blue Cliff College–Shreveport
Shreveport, Louisiana

Freshman Application Contact Blue Cliff College–Shreveport, 8731 Park Plaza Drive, Shreveport, LA 71105. *Toll-free phone:* 800-516-6597.
Website: http://www.bluecliffcollege.edu/.

Bossier Parish Community College
Bossier City, Louisiana

- **State-supported** 2-year, founded 1967, part of Louisiana Community and Technical College System
- **Urban** 64-acre campus with easy access to Shreveport
- **Coed,** 15,910 undergraduate students, 67% full-time, 63% women, 37% men

Undergraduates 10,612 full-time, 5,298 part-time. 3% are from out of state; 44% Black or African American, non-Hispanic/Latino; 7% Hispanic/Latino; 0.5% Asian, non-Hispanic/Latino; 0.2% Native Hawaiian or other Pacific Islander, non-Hispanic/Latino; 0.9% American Indian or Alaska Native, non-Hispanic/Latino; 2% Two or more races, non-Hispanic/Latino; 4% Race/ethnicity unknown; 0.2% international.

Freshmen *Admission:* 2,172 enrolled. *Average high school GPA:* 2.77.

Faculty *Total:* 335, 41% full-time, 45% with terminal degrees. *Student/faculty ratio:* 31:1.

Majors Administrative assistant and secretarial science; audiovisual communications technologies related; business/commerce; child-care provision; computer/information technology services administration related; construction engineering; construction engineering technology; criminal justice/safety; culinary arts; drafting and design technology; dramatic/theater arts; education; educational/instructional technology; emergency medical technology (EMT paramedic); engineering; foods, nutrition, and wellness; general studies; hospital and health-care facilities administration; industrial mechanics and maintenance technology; industrial technology; information science/studies; liberal arts and sciences and humanities related; liberal arts and sciences/liberal studies; medical/clinical assistant; music; natural sciences; occupational therapist assistant; petroleum technology; pharmacy technician; physical therapy; physical therapy technology; recording arts technology; registered nursing/registered nurse; respiratory care therapy; visual and performing arts related.

Academics *Calendar:* semesters. *Degree:* certificates, diplomas, and associate. *Special study options:* academic remediation for entering students, adult/continuing education programs, advanced placement credit, distance learning, double majors, part-time degree program, services for LD students, summer session for credit.

Library Bossier Parish Community College Library with 29,600 titles, an OPAC.

Student Life *Housing:* college housing not available. *Activities and Organizations:* drama/theater group, student-run newspaper, choral group. *Campus security:* student patrols. *Student services:* personal/psychological counseling.

Athletics Member NJCAA. *Intercollegiate sports:* baseball M(s), basketball M(s), soccer W, softball W(s). *Intramural sports:* badminton M/W, bowling M/W, football M, racquetball M, softball M, table tennis M/W, volleyball M/W.

Costs (2014–15) *Tuition:* state resident $2980 full-time, $124 per credit hour part-time; nonresident $6883 full-time, $287 per credit hour part-time. Full-time tuition and fees vary according to course load, location, and program. Part-time tuition and fees vary according to course load, location, and program. *Required fees:* $636 full-time, $24 per credit hour part-time, $30 per term part-time. *Payment plan:* deferred payment. *Waivers:* employees or children of employees.

Financial Aid Of all full-time matriculated undergraduates who enrolled in 2013, 4,712 applied for aid, 4,313 were judged to have need, 113 had their need fully met. In 2013, 2 non-need-based awards were made. *Average percent of need met:* 36%. *Average financial aid package:* $12,921. *Average need-based loan:* $3291. *Average need-based gift aid:* $2683. *Average non-need-based aid:* $500.

Applying *Options:* early admission. *Application fee:* $15.

Freshman Application Contact Mr. Richard Cockerham HM, Registrar, Bossier Parish Community College, 6220 East Texas Street, Bossier City, LA 71111. *Phone:* 318-678-6093. *Fax:* 318-678-6390.

Website: http://www.bpcc.edu/.

Camelot College
Baton Rouge, Louisiana

Freshman Application Contact Camelot College, 2618 Wooddale Boulevard, Suite A, Baton Rouge, LA 70805. *Phone:* 225-928-3005. *Toll-free phone:* 800-470-3320.

Website: http://www.camelotcollege.com/.

Cameron College
New Orleans, Louisiana

Admissions Office Contact Cameron College, 2740 Canal Street, New Orleans, LA 70119.

Website: http://www.cameroncollege.com/.

Career Technical College
Monroe, Louisiana

- **Proprietary** 2-year, founded 1985, part of Delta Career Education Corporation
- **Small-town** campus with easy access to Shreveport
- **Coed,** 576 undergraduate students, 78% full-time, 84% women, 16% men

Undergraduates 450 full-time, 126 part-time. Students come from 2 states and territories; 1% are from out of state; 71% Black or African American, non-Hispanic/Latino; 0.7% Hispanic/Latino; 0.2% Asian, non-Hispanic/Latino; 0.3% American Indian or Alaska Native, non-Hispanic/Latino; 2% Two or more races, non-Hispanic/Latino; 0.2% Race/ethnicity unknown. *Retention:* 80% of full-time freshmen returned.

Freshmen *Admission:* 576 enrolled.

Faculty *Total:* 35, 54% full-time. *Student/faculty ratio:* 20:1.

Majors Administrative assistant and secretarial science; business administration and management; computer and information sciences and support services related; corrections and criminal justice related; legal administrative assistant/secretary; management science; massage therapy; medical/clinical assistant; medical office management; radiologic technology/science; respiratory therapy technician; surgical technology.

Academics *Calendar:* quarters. *Degree:* diplomas and associate. *Special study options:* academic remediation for entering students, adult/continuing education programs, advanced placement credit, cooperative education, double majors, independent study, internships.

Library Library & Information Resources Network.

Student Life *Housing:* college housing not available. *Activities and Organizations:* Medical Assisting Club, Surgical Technology Club, Criminal Justice Club, Rad Tech Club, Management/Information Processing Club. *Campus security:* 24-hour emergency response devices, late-night transport/escort service, evening security guard.

Standardized Tests *Required:* SLE-Wonderlic Scholastic Level Exam; Math Proficiency Exam; English Proficiency Exam (for admission).

Costs (2014–15) *One-time required fee:* $120. *Tuition:* $11,376 full-time. Full-time tuition and fees vary according to course load and program. Part-time tuition and fees vary according to course load and program. No tuition increase for student's term of enrollment. *Required fees:* $1368 full-time. *Payment plans:* tuition prepayment, installment. *Waivers:* employees or children of employees.

Applying *Options:* deferred entrance. *Application fee:* $40. *Required:* high school transcript, interview. *Application deadlines:* rolling (freshmen), rolling (out-of-state freshmen), rolling (transfers). *Notification:* continuous (freshmen), continuous (out-of-state freshmen), continuous (transfers).

Freshman Application Contact Mrs. Susan Boudreaux, Admissions Office, Career Technical College, 2319 Louisville Avenue, Monroe, LA 71201. *Phone:* 318-323-2889. *Toll-free phone:* 800-923-1947. *Fax:* 318-324-9883. *E-mail:* susan.boudreaux@careertc.edu.

Website: http://www.careertc.edu/.

Career Technical College
Shreveport, Louisiana

Admissions Office Contact Career Technical College, 1227 Shreveport-Barksdale Highway, Shreveport, LA 71105.

Website: http://www.careertc.edu/.

Central Louisiana Technical Community College
Alexandria, Louisiana

Director of Admissions Ms. Janice Bolden, Vice Chancellor of Student Services, Enrollment Management and College Registrar, Central Louisiana Technical Community College, 4311 South MacArthur Drive, Alexandria, LA 71302. *Phone:* 800-351-7611.

Website: http://www.cltcc.edu/.

Delgado Community College
New Orleans, Louisiana

- **State-supported** 2-year, founded 1921, part of Louisiana Community and Technical College System
- **Urban** 57-acre campus
- **Endowment** $2.0 million
- **Coed,** 18,698 undergraduate students, 42% full-time, 66% women, 34% men

Undergraduates 7,906 full-time, 10,792 part-time. Students come from 20 states and territories; 45% Black or African American, non-Hispanic/Latino; 8% Hispanic/Latino; 3% Asian, non-Hispanic/Latino; 0.1% Native Hawaiian or other Pacific Islander, non-Hispanic/Latino; 0.4% American Indian or Alaska Native, non-Hispanic/Latino; 2% Two or more races, non-Hispanic/Latino; 7% Race/ethnicity unknown; 0.8% international. *Retention:* 57% of full-time freshmen returned.
Freshmen *Admission:* 3,009 enrolled.
Faculty *Total:* 600, 63% full-time. *Student/faculty ratio:* 42:1.
Majors Accounting; architectural engineering technology; automobile/automotive mechanics technology; biological and physical sciences; biomedical technology; building/construction finishing, management, and inspection related; building/property maintenance; business administration and management; civil engineering technology; clinical/medical laboratory technology; commercial and advertising art; communication and journalism related; computer engineering technology; computer installation and repair technology; criminal justice/police science; data processing and data processing technology; dental hygiene; dental laboratory technology; dietetics; drafting and design technology; electrical, electronic and communications engineering technology; electrical/electronics equipment installation and repair; emergency medical technology (EMT paramedic); fire prevention and safety technology; funeral service and mortuary science; general studies; health information/medical records technology; hospitality administration; interior architecture; kindergarten/preschool education; medical radiologic technology; occupational safety and health technology; occupational therapist assistant; physical therapy technology; registered nursing/registered nurse; respiratory care therapy; sign language interpretation and translation.
Academics *Calendar:* semesters. *Degree:* certificates and associate. *Special study options:* academic remediation for entering students, advanced placement credit, cooperative education, distance learning, double majors, English as a second language, honors programs, off-campus study, part-time degree program, services for LD students, summer session for credit. *ROTC:* Army (c), Air Force (c).
Library Moss Memorial Library with 110,000 titles, an OPAC, a Web page.
Student Life *Housing:* college housing not available. *Activities and Organizations:* drama/theater group, student-run newspaper, radio station, student government, Circle K, International Club, Phi Theta Kappa, Lambda Phi Nu. *Campus security:* 24-hour patrols, late-night transport/escort service. *Student services:* health clinic, personal/psychological counseling, women's center, legal services.
Athletics Member NJCAA. *Intercollegiate sports:* baseball M(s), basketball M(s)/W(s), track and field W. *Intramural sports:* football M, golf M, soccer M, tennis M/W, volleyball M/W.
Costs (2014–15) *Tuition:* state resident $2922 full-time, $122 per credit hour part-time; nonresident $6981 full-time, $122 per credit hour part-time. Full-time tuition and fees vary according to class time, course load, degree level, location, and program. Part-time tuition and fees vary according to class time, course load, degree level, location, and program. *Required fees:* $704 full-time, $26 per credit hour part-time, $35 per term part-time. *Payment plans:* installment, deferred payment. *Waivers:* senior citizens and employees or children of employees.
Financial Aid Of all full-time matriculated undergraduates who enrolled in 2013, 308 Federal Work-Study jobs (averaging $1375).
Applying *Options:* electronic application. *Application fee:* $25. *Required for some:* high school transcript. *Recommended:* high school transcript, proof of immunization. *Application deadlines:* rolling (freshmen), rolling (transfers).
Freshman Application Contact Ms. Gwen Boute, Director of Admissions, Delgado Community College, 615 City Park Avenue, New Orleans, LA 70119. *Phone:* 504-671-5010. *Fax:* 504-483-1895. *E-mail:* enroll@dcc.edu. *Website:* http://www.dcc.edu/.

Delta College of Arts and Technology
Baton Rouge, Louisiana

Freshman Application Contact Ms. Beulah Laverghe-Brown, Admissions Director, Delta College of Arts and Technology, 7380 Exchange Place, Baton Rouge, LA 70806-3851. *Phone:* 225-928-7770. *Fax:* 225-927-9096. *E-mail:* bbrown@deltacollege.com. *Website:* http://www.deltacollege.com/.

Delta School of Business & Technology
Lake Charles, Louisiana

Freshman Application Contact Jeffery Tibodeaux, Director of Admissions, Delta School of Business & Technology, 517 Broad Street, Lake Charles, LA 70601. *Phone:* 337-439-5765. *Website:* http://www.deltatech.edu/.

Fletcher Technical Community College
Schriever, Louisiana

Director of Admissions Admissions Office, Fletcher Technical Community College, 1407 Highway 311, Schriever, LA 70395. *Phone:* 985-857-3659. *Website:* http://www.fletcher.edu/.

Fortis College
Baton Rouge, Louisiana

Director of Admissions Ms. Sheri Kirley, Associate Director of Admissions, Fortis College, 9255 Interline Avenue, Baton Rouge, LA 70809. *Phone:* 225-248-1015. *Website:* http://www.fortis.edu/.

ITI Technical College
Baton Rouge, Louisiana

- **Proprietary** 2-year, founded 1973
- **Suburban** 10-acre campus
- **Coed,** 585 undergraduate students, 100% full-time, 15% women, 85% men

Undergraduates 585 full-time. Students come from 3 states and territories; 1% are from out of state; 38% Black or African American, non-Hispanic/Latino; 2% Hispanic/Latino; 0.7% Asian, non-Hispanic/Latino; 0.9% American Indian or Alaska Native, non-Hispanic/Latino; 0.7% Two or more races, non-Hispanic/Latino. *Retention:* 81% of full-time freshmen returned.
Freshmen *Admission:* 142 enrolled.
Faculty *Total:* 51, 47% full-time, 49% with terminal degrees. *Student/faculty ratio:* 15:1.
Majors Computer technology/computer systems technology; drafting and design technology; electrical, electronic and communications engineering technology; information science/studies; information technology; instrumentation technology; manufacturing engineering technology; office occupations and clerical services.
Academics *Calendar:* quarters. *Degree:* certificates and associate. *Special study options:* internships.
Library ITI Technical College Library with 1,260 titles.
Student Life *Housing:* college housing not available. *Campus security:* electronic alarm devices are activated during non-business hours and security cameras monitor campus 24 hours.
Costs (2014–15) *Tuition:* $10,425 full-time. Full-time tuition and fees vary according to program. *Required fees:* $150 full-time. *Payment plan:* installment.
Applying *Required:* high school transcript, interview.
Freshman Application Contact Mr. Shawn Norris, Admissions Director, ITI Technical College, 13944 Airline Highway, Baton Rouge, LA 70817. *Phone:* 225-752-4230 Ext. 261. *Toll-free phone:* 888-211-7165. *Fax:* 225-756-0903. *E-mail:* snorris@iticollege.edu. *Website:* http://www.iticollege.edu/.

ITT Technical Institute
Baton Rouge, Louisiana

- **Proprietary** primarily 2-year
- **Coed**

Academics *Degrees:* associate and bachelor's.
Freshman Application Contact Director of Recruitment, ITT Technical Institute, 14111 Airline Highway, Suite 101, Baton Rouge, LA 70817. *Phone:* 225-754-5800. *Toll-free phone:* 800-295-8485. *Website:* http://www.itt-tech.edu/.

ITT Technical Institute
St. Rose, Louisiana

- **Proprietary** primarily 2-year, founded 1998, part of ITT Educational Services, Inc.
- **Coed**

Academics *Calendar:* quarters. *Degrees:* associate and bachelor's.
Freshman Application Contact Director of Recruitment, ITT Technical Institute, 140 James Drive East, St. Rose, LA 70087. *Phone:* 504-463-0338. *Toll-free phone:* 866-463-0338.
Website: http://www.itt-tech.edu/.

Louisiana Culinary Institute
Baton Rouge, Louisiana

Admissions Office Contact Louisiana Culinary Institute, 10550 Airline Highway, Baton Rouge, LA 70816. *Toll-free phone:* 877-533-3198.
Website: http://www.louisianaculinary.com/.

Louisiana Delta Community College
Monroe, Louisiana

- **State-supported** 2-year, part of Louisiana Community and Technical College System
- **Rural** 70-acre campus with easy access to Monroe, LA
- **Coed,** 4,933 undergraduate students, 46% full-time, 61% women, 39% men

Undergraduates 2,259 full-time, 2,674 part-time. Students come from 23 states and territories; 2% are from out of state; 36% Black or African American, non-Hispanic/Latino; 4% Hispanic/Latino; 0.4% Asian, non-Hispanic/Latino; 0.1% Native Hawaiian or other Pacific Islander, non-Hispanic/Latino; 0.2% American Indian or Alaska Native, non-Hispanic/Latino; 1% Two or more races, non-Hispanic/Latino; 8% Race/ethnicity unknown; 0.1% international; 5% transferred in.
Freshmen *Admission:* 576 enrolled. *Average high school GPA:* 2.41.
Faculty *Total:* 197, 46% full-time. *Student/faculty ratio:* 19:1.
Majors Administrative assistant and secretarial science; business/commerce; child-care provision; drafting and design technology; education; forensic science and technology; general studies; heating, air conditioning, ventilation and refrigeration maintenance technology; industrial electronics technology; industrial production technologies related; instrumentation technology; liberal arts and sciences and humanities related; liberal arts and sciences/liberal studies; network and system administration; registered nursing/registered nurse.
Academics *Calendar:* semesters. *Degree:* certificates, diplomas, and associate. *Special study options:* academic remediation for entering students, accelerated degree program, advanced placement credit, distance learning, double majors, internships, part-time degree program, services for LD students, summer session for credit.
Student Life *Activities and Organizations:* drama/theater group. *Student services:* personal/psychological counseling.
Standardized Tests *Required:* SAT or ACT (for admission), ACT Compass (for admission).
Costs (2014–15) *Tuition:* state resident $2922 full-time, $122 per credit hour part-time; nonresident $5988 full-time, $124 per credit hour part-time. *Required fees:* $713 full-time.
Applying *Required:* high school transcript.
Freshman Application Contact Kathy Gardner, Interim Dean of Enrollment Services, Louisiana Delta Community College, 7500 Millhaven Dr, Monroe, LA 71203. *Phone:* 318-345-9261. *Toll-free phone:* 866-500-LDCC.
Website: http://www.ladelta.edu/.

Louisiana State University at Eunice
Eunice, Louisiana

Freshman Application Contact Ms. Gracie Guillory, Director of Financial Aid, Louisiana State University at Eunice, PO Box 1129, Eunice, LA 70535-1129. *Phone:* 337-550-1282. *Toll-free phone:* 888-367-5783.
Website: http://www.lsue.edu/.

Northshore Technical Community College
Bogalusa, Louisiana

Director of Admissions Admissions Office, Northshore Technical Community College, 1710 Sullivan Drive, Bogalusa, LA 70427. *Phone:* 985-732-6640.
Website: http://www.northshorecollege.edu/.

Northwest Louisiana Technical College
Minden, Louisiana

Director of Admissions Ms. Helen Deville, Admissions Office, Northwest Louisiana Technical College, 9500 Industrial Drive, Minden, LA 71055. *Phone:* 318-371-3035. *Toll-free phone:* 800-529-1387. *Fax:* 318-371-3155.
Website: http://www.nwltc.edu/.

Nunez Community College
Chalmette, Louisiana

- **State-supported** 2-year, founded 1992, part of Louisiana Community and Technical College System
- **Suburban** 20-acre campus with easy access to New Orleans
- **Endowment** $1.4 million
- **Coed,** 2,597 undergraduate students, 36% full-time, 64% women, 36% men

Undergraduates 926 full-time, 1,671 part-time. Students come from 3 states and territories; 38% Black or African American, non-Hispanic/Latino; 5% Hispanic/Latino; 3% Asian, non-Hispanic/Latino; 0.2% Native Hawaiian or other Pacific Islander, non-Hispanic/Latino; 0.7% American Indian or Alaska Native, non-Hispanic/Latino; 2% Two or more races, non-Hispanic/Latino; 10% Race/ethnicity unknown; 0.2% international. *Retention:* 70% of full-time freshmen returned.
Freshmen *Admission:* 241 enrolled. *Average high school GPA:* 2.28.
Faculty *Total:* 102, 36% full-time. *Student/faculty ratio:* 25:1.
Majors Business/commerce; child-care provision; education; general studies; industrial technology; kindergarten/preschool education; legal assistant/paralegal; liberal arts and sciences and humanities related.
Academics *Calendar:* semesters. *Degree:* certificates, diplomas, and associate. *Special study options:* academic remediation for entering students, adult/continuing education programs, advanced placement credit, cooperative education, distance learning, double majors, independent study, internships, off-campus study, part-time degree program, services for LD students, student-designed majors, summer session for credit.
Library Nunez Community College Library with 72,500 titles, 3,128 audiovisual materials, an OPAC, a Web page.
Student Life *Housing:* college housing not available. *Campus security:* 24-hour emergency response devices, late-night transport/escort service, security cameras. *Student services:* health clinic, personal/psychological counseling.
Athletics *Intramural sports:* basketball M, football M/W.
Standardized Tests *Recommended:* ACT (for admission).
Costs (2015–16) *Tuition:* state resident $3520 full-time; nonresident $6466 full-time. Full-time tuition and fees vary according to course load and location. Part-time tuition and fees vary according to course load and location. *Required fees:* $610 full-time. *Payment plan:* installment. *Waivers:* senior citizens and employees or children of employees.
Financial Aid Of all full-time matriculated undergraduates who enrolled in 2013, 70 Federal Work-Study jobs (averaging $1452).
Applying *Options:* electronic application, early admission, deferred entrance. *Application fee:* $10. *Required for some:* high school transcript. *Application deadlines:* rolling (freshmen), rolling (transfers).
Freshman Application Contact Mrs. Becky Maillet, Nunez Community College, 3710 Paris Road, Chalmette, LA 70043. *Phone:* 504-278-6477. *E-mail:* bmaillet@nunez.edu.
Website: http://www.nunez.edu/.

Remington College–Baton Rouge Campus
Baton Rouge, Louisiana

Director of Admissions Monica Butler-Johnson, Director of Recruitment, Remington College–Baton Rouge Campus, 10551 Coursey Boulevard, Baton Rouge, LA 70816. *Phone:* 225-236-3200. *Fax:* 225-922-3250. *E-mail:* monica.johnson@remingtoncollege.edu.
Website: http://www.remingtoncollege.edu/.

Remington College–Lafayette Campus
Lafayette, Louisiana

Freshman Application Contact Remington College–Lafayette Campus, 303 Rue Louis XIV, Lafayette, LA 70508. *Phone:* 337-981-4010. *Toll-free phone:* 800-560-6192.
Website: http://www.remingtoncollege.edu/.

Remington College–Shreveport
Shreveport, Louisiana

Freshman Application Contact Marc Wright, Remington College–Shreveport, 2106 Bert Kouns Industrial Loop, Shreveport, LA 71118. *Phone:* 318-671-4000.
Website: http://www.remingtoncollege.edu/.

River Parishes Community College
Gonzales, Louisiana

Director of Admissions Ms. Allison Dauzat, Dean of Students and Enrollment Management, River Parishes Community College, 925 West Edenborne Parkway, Gonzales, LA 70737. *Phone:* 225-675-8270. *Fax:* 225-675-5478. *E-mail:* adauzat@rpcc.cc.la.us.
Website: http://www.rpcc.edu/.

South Central Louisiana Technical College
Morgan City, Louisiana

Director of Admissions Ms. Melanie Henry, Admissions Office, South Central Louisiana Technical College, 900 Youngs Road, Morgan City, LA 70380. *Phone:* 504-380-2436. *Fax:* 504-380-2440.
Website: http://www.scl.edu/.

Southern University at Shreveport
Shreveport, Louisiana

- **State-supported** 2-year, founded 1964, part of Southern University System
- **Urban** 103-acre campus
- **Endowment** $619,644
- **Coed,** 2,988 undergraduate students, 70% full-time, 69% women, 31% men

Undergraduates 2,082 full-time, 906 part-time. Students come from 5 states and territories; 1 other country; 28% are from out of state; 89% Black or African American, non-Hispanic/Latino; 0.3% Hispanic/Latino; 0.6% Asian, non-Hispanic/Latino; 0.1% Native Hawaiian or other Pacific Islander, non-Hispanic/Latino; 0.3% Two or more races, non-Hispanic/Latino; 2% international; 9% transferred in; 7% live on campus. *Retention:* 45% of full-time freshmen returned.
Freshmen *Admission:* 359 enrolled. *Average high school GPA:* 2. *Test scores:* ACT scores over 18: 8%.
Faculty *Total:* 145, 52% full-time, 8% with terminal degrees. *Student/faculty ratio:* 30:1.
Majors Accounting; accounting technology and bookkeeping; avionics maintenance technology; banking and financial support services; biology/biological sciences; business/commerce; cardiovascular technology; chemistry; clinical/medical laboratory technology; computer science; criminal justice/law enforcement administration; dental hygiene; electrical, electronic and communications engineering technology; general studies; health information/medical records administration; health information/medical records technology; hospitality administration; hotel/motel administration; human services; kindergarten/preschool education; legal assistant/paralegal; liberal arts and sciences and humanities related; mathematics; mechanical engineering/mechanical technology; medical radiologic technology; mental health counseling; physical therapy technology; public administration; radiologic technology/science; registered nursing/registered nurse; respiratory care therapy; robotics technology; sociology; surgical technology; teacher assistant/aide; tourism and travel services management.
Academics *Calendar:* semesters. *Degree:* certificates and associate. *Special study options:* academic remediation for entering students, accelerated degree program, adult/continuing education programs, advanced placement credit, cooperative education, distance learning, honors programs, internships, off-campus study, part-time degree program, student-designed majors, summer session for credit. *ROTC:* Army (c).

Library Library/Learning Resources Center plus 1 other with 24,016 audiovisual materials, an OPAC.
Student Life *Housing Options:* coed. Campus housing is provided by a third party. *Activities and Organizations:* drama/theater group, student-run newspaper, choral group, Afro-American Society, SUSLA Gospel Choir, Student Center Board, Allied Health, Engineering Club. *Campus security:* 24-hour patrols, controlled dormitory access. *Student services:* personal/psychological counseling.
Athletics Member NJCAA. *Intercollegiate sports:* basketball M(s)/W(s). *Intramural sports:* basketball M/W, cheerleading M/W, soccer M.
Standardized Tests *Required for some:* SAT or ACT (for admission). *Recommended:* ACT (for admission).
Costs (2014–15) *Tuition:* state resident $4497 full-time; nonresident $6116 full-time. Full-time tuition and fees vary according to course load, location, and program. Part-time tuition and fees vary according to course load, location, and program. *Room and board:* $10,270; room only: $7920. Room and board charges vary according to board plan. *Payment plans:* installment, deferred payment.
Applying *Required:* high school transcript.
Freshman Application Contact Ms. Danielle Anderson, Admissions Advisor, Southern University at Shreveport, 3050 Martin Luther King Jr. Drive, Shreveport, LA 71107. *Phone:* 318-670-9211. *Toll-free phone:* 800-458-1472. *Fax:* 318-670-6483. *E-mail:* danderson@susla.edu.
Website: http://www.susla.edu/.

South Louisiana Community College
Lafayette, Louisiana

- **State-supported** 2-year, part of Louisiana Community and Technical College System
- **Small-town** campus
- **Endowment** $846,166
- **Coed,** 6,332 undergraduate students, 54% full-time, 57% women, 43% men

Undergraduates 3,436 full-time, 2,896 part-time. Students come from 12 states and territories; 17 other countries; 1% are from out of state; 35% Black or African American, non-Hispanic/Latino; 3% Hispanic/Latino; 2% Asian, non-Hispanic/Latino; 0.1% Native Hawaiian or other Pacific Islander, non-Hispanic/Latino; 0.5% American Indian or Alaska Native, non-Hispanic/Latino; 2% Two or more races, non-Hispanic/Latino; 5% Race/ethnicity unknown; 0.8% international; 7% transferred in. *Retention:* 55% of full-time freshmen returned.
Freshmen *Admission:* 1,405 enrolled.
Faculty *Total:* 257, 52% full-time. *Student/faculty ratio:* 25:1.
Majors Administrative assistant and secretarial science; aircraft powerplant technology; automobile/automotive mechanics technology; business/commerce; carpentry; clinical/medical laboratory technology; computer systems networking and telecommunications; criminal justice/safety; culinary arts; desktop publishing and digital imaging design; diesel mechanics technology; drafting and design technology; education; electrician; emergency medical technology (EMT paramedic); energy management and systems technology; general studies; heating, air conditioning, ventilation and refrigeration maintenance technology; industrial electronics technology; industrial mechanics and maintenance technology; industrial radiologic technology; industrial technology; licensed practical/vocational nurse training; machine tool technology; registered nursing/registered nurse; surgical technology; surveying technology; web page, digital/multimedia and information resources design; welding technology.
Academics *Calendar:* semesters. *Degree:* certificates, diplomas, and associate. *Special study options:* academic remediation for entering students, advanced placement credit, distance learning, double majors, English as a second language, independent study, internships, part-time degree program, services for LD students, summer session for credit.
Student Life *Housing:* college housing not available.
Costs (2014–15) *Tuition:* state resident $3586 full-time, $124 per credit hour part-time; nonresident $6766 full-time, $296 per credit hour part-time. Full-time tuition and fees vary according to course load and program. Part-time tuition and fees vary according to course load and program. *Required fees:* $606 full-time, $24 per credit hour part-time, $15 per term part-time. *Payment plan:* installment. *Waivers:* employees or children of employees.
Applying *Options:* electronic application. *Required:* high school transcript.
Freshman Application Contact Director of Admissions, South Louisiana Community College, 1101 Bertrand Drive, Lafayette, LA 70506. *Phone:* 337-521-8953. *E-mail:* admissions@solacc.edu.
Website: http://www.solacc.edu/.

Sowela Technical Community College
Lake Charles, Louisiana

- **State-supported** 2-year, founded 1938, part of Louisiana Community and Technical College System
- **Urban** 77-acre campus
- **Endowment** $274,815
- **Coed,** 3,411 undergraduate students, 53% full-time, 42% women, 58% men
- 100% of applicants were admitted

Undergraduates 1,815 full-time, 1,596 part-time. Students come from 43 states and territories; 8 other countries; 2% are from out of state; 25% Black or African American, non-Hispanic/Latino; 2% Hispanic/Latino; 0.6% Asian, non-Hispanic/Latino; 0.1% Native Hawaiian or other Pacific Islander, non-Hispanic/Latino; 0.9% American Indian or Alaska Native, non-Hispanic/Latino; 2% Two or more races, non-Hispanic/Latino; 6% Race/ethnicity unknown; 0.2% international. *Retention:* 46% of full-time freshmen returned.
Freshmen *Admission:* 691 applied, 691 admitted. *Average high school GPA:* 2.7.
Faculty *Total:* 148, 52% full-time, 7% with terminal degrees. *Student/faculty ratio:* 23:1.
Majors Accounting technology and bookkeeping; administrative assistant and secretarial science; aircraft powerplant technology; commercial and advertising art; computer programming; computer systems networking and telecommunications; criminal justice/safety; culinary arts; drafting and design technology; general studies; instrumentation technology; liberal arts and sciences and humanities related.
Academics *Calendar:* semesters. *Degree:* certificates, diplomas, and associate. *Special study options:* academic remediation for entering students, accelerated degree program, adult/continuing education programs, distance learning, double majors, internships, off-campus study, part-time degree program, services for LD students, summer session for credit.
Library Library & Learning Resource Center (LLRC) plus 2 others with 7,031 titles, 631 audiovisual materials, an OPAC, a Web page.
Student Life *Housing:* college housing not available. *Options:* Campus housing is provided by a third party. *Activities and Organizations:* student-run newspaper, choral group, SkillsUSA, Student Government Association (SGA), Gamerz, Criminal Justice Club, Astronomy Club. *Campus security:* Security guard on duty. *Student services:* personal/psychological counseling.
Standardized Tests *Required:* For Placement Purposes Only: Compass, Asset, ACT, SAT (for admission).
Costs (2015–16) *Tuition:* state resident $2980 full-time, $124 per credit hour part-time; nonresident $5908 full-time, $246 per credit hour part-time. Full-time tuition and fees vary according to course load, program, and reciprocity agreements. Part-time tuition and fees vary according to course load, program, and reciprocity agreements. *Required fees:* $740 full-time, $28 per credit hour part-time, $5 per term part-time. *Payment plan:* deferred payment.
Applying *Options:* electronic application, early admission. *Required:* high school transcript, Compass Test, Asset or ACT for placement purposes, Proof of Immunization, Proof of Selective Service Status, College Transcript if applicable Note: High School transcript required for all AAS and Practical Nursing Programs. *Application deadlines:* 8/29 (freshmen), 8/29 (out-of-state freshmen), 8/29 (transfers). *Notification:* continuous (freshmen), continuous (out-of-state freshmen), continuous (transfers).
Freshman Application Contact Office of Admissions, Sowela Technical Community College, 3820 Senator J. Bennett Johnston Ave., Lake Charles, LA 70616. *Phone:* 337-421-6540. *Toll-free phone:* 800-256-0431. *Fax:* 337-491-2663.
Website: http://www.sowela.edu/.

Virginia College in Baton Rouge
Baton Rouge, Louisiana

Admissions Office Contact Virginia College in Baton Rouge, 9501 Cortana Place, Baton Rouge, LA 70815.
Website: http://www.vc.edu/.

Virginia College in Shreveport/Bossier City
Bossier City, Louisiana

Admissions Office Contact Virginia College in Shreveport/Bossier City, 2950 East Texas Street, Suite C, Bossier City, LA 71111.
Website: http://www.vc.edu/.

MAINE

Beal College
Bangor, Maine

- **Proprietary** 2-year, founded 1891
- **Small-town** 4-acre campus
- **Coed**

Undergraduates 363 full-time, 101 part-time. Students come from 1 other state; 0.9% Black or African American, non-Hispanic/Latino; 1% Hispanic/Latino; 0.6% Asian, non-Hispanic/Latino; 0.2% Native Hawaiian or other Pacific Islander, non-Hispanic/Latino; 2% American Indian or Alaska Native, non-Hispanic/Latino; 4% Race/ethnicity unknown; 10% transferred in. *Retention:* 60% of full-time freshmen returned.
Faculty *Student/faculty ratio:* 30:1.
Academics *Calendar:* modular. *Degree:* certificates, diplomas, and associate. *Special study options:* accelerated degree program, adult/continuing education programs, advanced placement credit, internships, part-time degree program, summer session for credit.
Costs (2014–15) *Tuition:* $6240 full-time, $208 per credit part-time. Full-time tuition and fees vary according to course load and program. Part-time tuition and fees vary according to course load and program.
Applying *Options:* deferred entrance. *Application fee:* $30. *Required:* essay or personal statement, high school transcript, 1 letter of recommendation, interview, Entrance exam; immunizations.
Freshman Application Contact Sue Borden, Admissions Assistant, Beal College, 99 Farm Road, Bangor, ME 04401. *Phone:* 207-947-4591. *Toll-free phone:* 800-660-7351. *Fax:* 207-947-0208. *E-mail:* admissions@bealcollege.edu.
Website: http://www.bealcollege.edu/.

Central Maine Community College
Auburn, Maine

- **State-supported** 2-year, founded 1964, part of Maine Community College System
- **Small-town** 135-acre campus
- **Endowment** $530,000
- **Coed,** 3,162 undergraduate students, 44% full-time, 55% women, 45% men

Undergraduates 1,384 full-time, 1,778 part-time. Students come from 16 states and territories; 3 other countries; 8% are from out of state; 5% Black or African American, non-Hispanic/Latino; 3% Hispanic/Latino; 1% Asian, non-Hispanic/Latino; 0.1% Native Hawaiian or other Pacific Islander, non-Hispanic/Latino; 0.9% American Indian or Alaska Native, non-Hispanic/Latino; 2% Two or more races, non-Hispanic/Latino; 6% Race/ethnicity unknown; 0.8% international; 15% transferred in; 8% live on campus.
Freshmen *Admission:* 2,448 applied, 733 admitted, 547 enrolled. *Test scores:* SAT critical reading scores over 500: 8%; SAT math scores over 500: 8%; SAT writing scores over 500: 5%; SAT critical reading scores over 600: 1%; SAT math scores over 600: 1%; SAT writing scores over 600: 1%.
Faculty *Total:* 231, 24% full-time, 1% with terminal degrees. *Student/faculty ratio:* 17:1.
Majors Accounting; accounting technology and bookkeeping; administrative assistant and secretarial science; architectural engineering technology; automobile/automotive mechanics technology; building construction technology; business administration and management; child development; civil engineering technology; computer installation and repair technology; construction trades related; criminal justice/law enforcement administration; criminal justice/safety; early childhood education; electromechanical technology; graphic and printing equipment operation/production; graphic communications; human services; liberal arts and sciences/liberal studies; licensed practical/vocational nurse training; machine tool technology; medical/clinical assistant; multi/interdisciplinary studies related; network and system administration; registered nursing/registered nurse.
Academics *Calendar:* semesters. *Degree:* certificates, diplomas, and associate. *Special study options:* academic remediation for entering students, accelerated degree program, adult/continuing education programs, advanced placement credit, cooperative education, distance learning, English as a second language, independent study, internships, part-time degree program, services for LD students, summer session for credit.
Library Central Maine Community College Library with 15,914 titles, 2 audiovisual materials, an OPAC, a Web page.
Student Life *Housing Options:* coed, men-only, women-only. Campus housing is university owned. Freshman applicants given priority for college housing. *Activities and Organizations:* drama/theater group. *Campus*

security: 24-hour emergency response devices, student patrols, controlled dormitory access, night patrols by police.

Athletics Member USCAA. *Intercollegiate sports:* baseball M, basketball M/W, golf M/W, soccer M/W, softball W. *Intramural sports:* volleyball M/W.

Standardized Tests *Recommended:* SAT (for admission), SAT and SAT Subject Tests or ACT (for admission), SAT Subject Tests (for admission).

Costs (2015–16) *Tuition:* state resident $2700 full-time, $1350 per year part-time; nonresident $5400 full-time, $2700 per year part-time. Full-time tuition and fees vary according to course load and program. Part-time tuition and fees vary according to course load and program. *Required fees:* $1050 full-time, $35 per credit hour part-time. *Room and board:* $8916; room only: $4150. Room and board charges vary according to housing facility. *Payment plan:* installment. *Waivers:* employees or children of employees.

Financial Aid Of all full-time matriculated undergraduates who enrolled in 2013, 89 Federal Work-Study jobs (averaging $1200). *Financial aid deadline:* 8/1.

Applying *Options:* electronic application, deferred entrance. *Application fee:* $20. *Required:* high school transcript. *Recommended:* essay or personal statement. *Application deadlines:* rolling (freshmen), rolling (transfers). *Notification:* continuous (freshmen), continuous (transfers).

Freshman Application Contact Ms. Joan Nichols, Admissions Assistant, Central Maine Community College, 1250 Turner Street, Auburn, ME 04210. *Phone:* 207-755-5273. *Toll-free phone:* 800-891-2002. *Fax:* 207-755-5493. *E-mail:* enroll@cmcc.edu. *Website:* http://www.cmcc.edu/.

Eastern Maine Community College
Bangor, Maine

Freshman Application Contact Mr. W. Gregory Swett, Director of Admissions, Eastern Maine Community College, 354 Hogan Road, Bangor, ME 04401. *Phone:* 207-974-4680. *Toll-free phone:* 800-286-9357. *Fax:* 207-974-4683. *E-mail:* admissions@emcc.edu. *Website:* http://www.emcc.edu/.

Kaplan University, Lewiston
Lewiston, Maine

Freshman Application Contact Kaplan University, Lewiston, 475 Lisbon Street, Lewiston, ME 04240. *Phone:* 207-333-3300. *Toll-free phone:* 866-527-5268 (in-state); 800-527-5268 (out-of-state). *Website:* http://www.kaplanuniversity.edu/.

Kaplan University, South Portland
South Portland, Maine

Freshman Application Contact Kaplan University, South Portland, 265 Western Avenue, South Portland, ME 04106. *Phone:* 207-774-6126. *Toll-free phone:* 866-527-5268 (in-state); 800-527-5268 (out-of-state). *Website:* http://www.kaplanuniversity.edu/.

Kennebec Valley Community College
Fairfield, Maine

- **State-supported** 2-year, founded 1970, part of Maine Community College System
- **Coed,** 2,401 undergraduate students, 25% full-time, 65% women, 35% men

Undergraduates 589 full-time, 1,812 part-time. Students come from 9 states and territories; 1% are from out of state; 0.9% Black or African American, non-Hispanic/Latino; 1% Hispanic/Latino; 0.7% Asian, non-Hispanic/Latino; 0.7% American Indian or Alaska Native, non-Hispanic/Latino; 1% Two or more races, non-Hispanic/Latino; 7% Race/ethnicity unknown; 0.1% international; 7% transferred in.

Freshmen *Admission:* 291 enrolled.

Faculty *Total:* 45, 100% full-time.

Majors Accounting technology and bookkeeping; agroecology and sustainable agriculture; biology/biotechnology laboratory technician; building construction technology; child development; cooking and related culinary arts; diagnostic medical sonography and ultrasound technology; drafting/design engineering technologies related; electrical, electronic and communications engineering technology; electrical/electronics maintenance and repair technology related; electrician; emergency medical technology (EMT paramedic); health information/medical records technology; heating, ventilation, air conditioning and refrigeration engineering technology; industrial mechanics and maintenance technology; liberal arts and sciences/liberal studies; lineworker; machine tool technology; management information systems; marketing/marketing management; medical

administrative assistant and medical secretary; medical/clinical assistant; mental and social health services and allied professions related; multi/interdisciplinary studies related; occupational therapist assistant; physical therapy technology; radiologic technology/science; registered nursing/registered nurse; respiratory care therapy; welding technology; wood science and wood products/pulp and paper technology.

Academics *Calendar:* semesters. *Degree:* certificates, diplomas, and associate. *Special study options:* academic remediation for entering students, accelerated degree program, adult/continuing education programs, advanced placement credit, distance learning, external degree program, independent study, internships, part-time degree program, services for LD students, summer session for credit.

Library Lunder Library plus 1 other with 19,316 titles, 2,955 audiovisual materials, an OPAC, a Web page.

Student Life *Housing:* college housing not available. *Activities and Organizations:* choral group, Phi Theta Kappa, National Society for Leadership & Success, Student Senate, Respiratory Therapy Club, KV Federal Nurses Association. *Campus security:* evening security patrol. *Student services:* personal/psychological counseling.

Athletics *Intercollegiate sports:* ice hockey M/W. *Intramural sports:* basketball M/W, bowling M/W, golf M/W, soccer M/W, softball M/W, volleyball M/W.

Standardized Tests *Required for some:* HESI nursing exam, HOBET for Allied Health programs, ACCUPLACER. *Recommended:* SAT or ACT (for admission).

Costs (2014–15) *One-time required fee:* $30. *Tuition:* state resident $2700 full-time, $90 per credit hour part-time; nonresident $5400 full-time, $180 per credit hour part-time. *Required fees:* $610 full-time, $3 per credit hour part-time. *Payment plan:* installment. *Waivers:* senior citizens and employees or children of employees.

Financial Aid Of all full-time matriculated undergraduates who enrolled in 2014, 1,971 applied for aid, 1,768 were judged to have need, 16 had their need fully met. In 2014, 11 non-need-based awards were made. *Average percent of need met:* 51%. *Average financial aid package:* $6827. *Average need-based loan:* $3025. *Average need-based gift aid:* $5176. *Average non-need-based aid:* $2090.

Applying *Options:* electronic application, deferred entrance. *Application fee:* $20. *Required:* essay or personal statement, high school transcript. *Required for some:* interview. *Application deadlines:* rolling (freshmen), rolling (transfers). *Notification:* continuous (freshmen), continuous (transfers).

Freshman Application Contact Mr. CJ (Crichton) McKenna, Assistant Director of Admissions, Kennebec Valley Community College, 92 Western Avenue, Fairfield, ME 04937-1367. *Phone:* 207-453-5155. *Toll-free phone:* 800-528-5882. *Fax:* 207-453-5011. *E-mail:* admissions@kvcc.me.edu. *Website:* http://www.kvcc.me.edu/.

The Landing School
Arundel, Maine

- **Independent** 2-year, founded 1978
- **Rural** 4-acre campus with easy access to Portland, Maine and Boston, Massachusetts
- **Coed,** 81 undergraduate students, 100% full-time, 2% women, 98% men
- 68% of applicants were admitted

Undergraduates 81 full-time. Students come from 41 states and territories; 8 other countries; 75% are from out of state; 1% Black or African American, non-Hispanic/Latino; 2% Hispanic/Latino; 1% Two or more races, non-Hispanic/Latino; 2% international. *Retention:* 84% of full-time freshmen returned.

Freshmen *Admission:* 120 applied, 81 admitted, 62 enrolled.

Faculty *Total:* 10. *Student/faculty ratio:* 9:1.

Majors Marine maintenance and ship repair technology.

Academics *Calendar:* continuous. *Degree:* diplomas and associate. *Special study options:* academic remediation for entering students, adult/continuing education programs, cooperative education, internships, services for LD students.

Library S/V Patience Learning Resource Center with an OPAC, a Web page.

Student Life *Housing:* college housing not available. *Options:* Campus housing is provided by a third party. *Activities and Organizations:* Jam Band, Hockey Club, Surf Club. *Campus security:* 24-hour emergency response devices. *Student services:* personal/psychological counseling.

Costs (2015–16) *Tuition:* $20,107 full-time. Full-time tuition and fees vary according to program. *Required fees:* $1000 full-time. *Room only:* Room and board charges vary according to housing facility. *Payment plans:* tuition prepayment, installment, deferred payment.

Applying *Options:* electronic application, early admission, deferred entrance. *Required:* essay or personal statement, high school transcript, 3 letters of recommendation, interview. *Application deadlines:* rolling (freshmen), rolling (out-of-state freshmen), rolling (transfers), rolling (early action). *Early decision deadline:* rolling (for plan 1), rolling (for plan 2). *Notification:*

continuous (freshmen), continuous (out-of-state freshmen), continuous (transfers), rolling (early decision plan 1), rolling (early decision plan 2), rolling (early action).

Freshman Application Contact Kristin Potter, Admissions Representative, The Landing School, 286 River Rd, Arundel, ME 04046. *Phone:* 207-985-7976. *E-mail:* info@landingschool.edu.
Website: http://www.landingschool.edu/.

Maine College of Health Professions
Lewiston, Maine

- **Independent** 2-year, founded 1891
- **Urban** campus
- **Coed,** 210 undergraduate students, 28% full-time, 85% women, 15% men

Undergraduates 59 full-time, 151 part-time. Students come from 2 states and territories; 2% are from out of state; 1% Black or African American, non-Hispanic/Latino; 1% Hispanic/Latino; 0.5% Asian, non-Hispanic/Latino; 0.5% Native Hawaiian or other Pacific Islander, non-Hispanic/Latino; 0.5% American Indian or Alaska Native, non-Hispanic/Latino; 2% live on campus.
Freshmen *Admission:* 7 enrolled. *Average high school GPA:* 3.75.
Faculty *Student/faculty ratio:* 10:1.
Majors Nuclear medical technology; radiologic technology/science; registered nursing/registered nurse.
Academics *Calendar:* semesters. *Degree:* associate. *Special study options:* advanced placement credit, off-campus study, services for LD students, summer session for credit.
Library Gerrish True Health Sciences Library plus 1 other with 1,975 titles, an OPAC, a Web page.
Student Life *Housing Options:* coed. Campus housing is university owned. *Activities and Organizations:* Student Communication Council, student government, Student Nurses Association. *Campus security:* 24-hour emergency response devices and patrols, late-night transport/escort service, controlled dormitory access. *Student services:* health clinic, personal/psychological counseling.
Standardized Tests *Required:* SAT or ACT (for admission), ACCUPLACER entrance exam for some programs; HESI Entrance Exam for nursing applicants (for admission).
Costs (2014–15) *Tuition:* $8092 full-time. *Required fees:* $1798 full-time. *Room only:* $2350. *Waivers:* employees or children of employees.
Financial Aid Of all full-time matriculated undergraduates who enrolled in 2010, 5 applied for aid, 4 were judged to have need. *Average financial aid package:* $17,200. *Average need-based loan:* $4000. *Average need-based gift aid:* $7700.
Applying *Application fee:* $50. *Required:* essay or personal statement, high school transcript, Entrance exam, SAT or ACT, high school or college level algebra, second math, biology, chemistry, high school transcript or GED. *Application deadline:* 1/15 (freshmen). *Notification:* 3/15 (freshmen).
Freshman Application Contact Ms. Erica Watson, Admissions Director, Maine College of Health Professions, 70 Middle Street, Lewiston, ME 04240. *Phone:* 207-795-2843. *Fax:* 207-795-2849.
Website: http://www.mchp.edu/.

Northern Maine Community College
Presque Isle, Maine

Freshman Application Contact Ms. Nancy Gagnon, Admissions Secretary, Northern Maine Community College, 33 Edgemont Drive, Presque Isle, ME 04769-2016. *Phone:* 207-768-2785. *Toll-free phone:* 800-535-6682. *Fax:* 207-768-2848. *E-mail:* ngagnon@nmcc.edu.
Website: http://www.nmcc.edu/.

Southern Maine Community College
South Portland, Maine

- **State-supported** 2-year, founded 1946, part of Maine Community College System
- **Urban** 80-acre campus
- **Coed**

Undergraduates 3,019 full-time, 4,112 part-time. 4% Black or African American, non-Hispanic/Latino; 2% Hispanic/Latino; 2% Asian, non-Hispanic/Latino; 0.1% Native Hawaiian or other Pacific Islander, non-Hispanic/Latino; 0.7% American Indian or Alaska Native, non-Hispanic/Latino; 2% Two or more races, non-Hispanic/Latino; 6% Race/ethnicity unknown; 0.5% international; 8% transferred in; 5% live on campus. *Retention:* 53% of full-time freshmen returned.
Faculty *Student/faculty ratio:* 20:1.
Academics *Calendar:* semesters. *Degree:* certificates and associate. *Special study options:* academic remediation for entering students, advanced

placement credit, distance learning, double majors, English as a second language, honors programs, independent study, internships, off-campus study, part-time degree program, services for LD students, study abroad, summer session for credit.
Student Life *Campus security:* 24-hour emergency response devices and patrols, student patrols, late-night transport/escort service, controlled dormitory access.
Athletics Member USCAA.
Standardized Tests *Recommended:* SAT or ACT (for admission), ACCUPLACER.
Financial Aid Of all full-time matriculated undergraduates who enrolled in 2013, 130 Federal Work-Study jobs (averaging $1500).
Applying *Options:* electronic application. *Application fee:* $20. *Required:* high school transcript or proof of high school graduation.
Freshman Application Contact Amy Lee, Director of Enrollment Services, Southern Maine Community College, 2 Fort Road, South, Portland, ME 04106. *Phone:* 207-741-5800. *Toll-free phone:* 877-282-2182. *Fax:* 207-741-5760. *E-mail:* alee@smccme.edu.
Website: http://www.smccme.edu/.

Washington County Community College
Calais, Maine

Director of Admissions Mr. Kent Lyons, Admissions Counselor, Washington County Community College, One College Drive, Calais, ME 04619. *Phone:* 207-454-1000. *Toll-free phone:* 800-210-6932.
Website: http://www.wccc.me.edu/.

York County Community College
Wells, Maine

- **State-supported** 2-year, founded 1994, part of Maine Community College System
- **Small-town** 84-acre campus with easy access to Boston
- **Endowment** $559,629
- **Coed,** 1,699 undergraduate students, 31% full-time, 64% women, 36% men

Undergraduates 529 full-time, 1,170 part-time. Students come from 7 states and territories; 2% are from out of state; 0.4% Black or African American, non-Hispanic/Latino; 2% Hispanic/Latino; 1% Asian, non-Hispanic/Latino; 0.1% Native Hawaiian or other Pacific Islander, non-Hispanic/Latino; 0.5% American Indian or Alaska Native, non-Hispanic/Latino; 2% Two or more races, non-Hispanic/Latino; 12% Race/ethnicity unknown; 0.4% international; 22% transferred in. *Retention:* 56% of full-time freshmen returned.
Freshmen *Admission:* 651 applied, 325 admitted, 521 enrolled.
Faculty *Total:* 143, 17% full-time, 12% with terminal degrees. *Student/faculty ratio:* 14:1.
Majors Accounting; animation, interactive technology, video graphics and special effects; architectural drafting and CAD/CADD; business administration and management; computer science; construction trades related; criminal justice/safety; culinary arts; early childhood education; education; health information/medical records technology; health services/allied health/health sciences; human services; machine tool technology; medical/clinical assistant; multi/interdisciplinary studies related; veterinary/animal health technology.
Academics *Calendar:* semesters. *Degree:* certificates and associate. *Special study options:* academic remediation for entering students, adult/continuing education programs, advanced placement credit, cooperative education, distance learning, internships, off-campus study, part-time degree program, services for LD students, summer session for credit.
Library Library and Learning Resource Center plus 1 other with 14,385 titles, 1,628 audiovisual materials, an OPAC, a Web page.
Student Life *Housing:* college housing not available. *Activities and Organizations:* Student Senate, Phi Theta Kappa. *Campus security:* 24-hour emergency response devices, late-night transport/escort service.
Athletics *Intramural sports:* basketball M/W, bowling M/W, cross-country running M/W, football M/W, ice hockey M/W, skiing (downhill) M/W, soccer M/W, softball M/W, ultimate Frisbee M/W, volleyball M/W.
Costs (2014–15) *Tuition:* state resident $2700 full-time, $90 per credit part-time; nonresident $5400 full-time, $180 per credit part-time. *Required fees:* $630 full-time. *Payment plan:* installment. *Waivers:* employees or children of employees.
Financial Aid Of all full-time matriculated undergraduates who enrolled in 2013, 585 applied for aid, 480 were judged to have need, 8 had their need fully met. In 2013, 7 non-need-based awards were made. *Average percent of need met:* 18%. *Average financial aid package:* $6019. *Average need-based loan:* $3049. *Average need-based gift aid:* $4895. *Average non-need-based aid:* $1909. *Average indebtedness upon graduation:* $11,034.

Applying *Options:* electronic application. *Required:* high school transcript, interview. *Application deadlines:* rolling (freshmen), rolling (transfers).
Freshman Application Contact Fred Quistgard, Director of Admissions, York County Community College, 112 College Drive, Wells, ME 04090. *Phone:* 207-216-4406 Ext. 311. *Toll-free phone:* 800-580-3820. *Fax:* 207-641-0837.
Website: http://www.yccc.edu/.

MARSHALL ISLANDS

College of the Marshall Islands
Majuro, Marshall Islands, Marshall Islands

Freshman Application Contact Ms. Rosita Capelle, Director of Admissions and Records, College of the Marshall Islands, PO Box 1258, Majuro, MH 96960, Marshall Islands. *Phone:* 692-625-6823. *Fax:* 692-625-7203. *E-mail:* cmiadmissions@cmi.edu.
Website: http://www.cmi.edu/.

MARYLAND

Allegany College of Maryland
Cumberland, Maryland

Freshman Application Contact Ms. Cathy Nolan, Director of Admissions and Registration, Allegany College of Maryland, Cumberland, MD 21502. *Phone:* 301-784-5000 Ext. 5202. *Fax:* 301-784-5220. *E-mail:* cnolan@allegany.edu.
Website: http://www.allegany.edu/.

Anne Arundel Community College
Arnold, Maryland

- **State and locally supported** 2-year, founded 1961
- **Suburban** 230-acre campus with easy access to Baltimore and Washington, DC
- **Coed,** 15,274 undergraduate students, 29% full-time, 60% women, 40% men

Undergraduates 4,442 full-time, 10,832 part-time. Students come from 33 states and territories; 91 other countries; 18% Black or African American, non-Hispanic/Latino; 6% Hispanic/Latino; 4% Asian, non-Hispanic/Latino; 0.3% Native Hawaiian or other Pacific Islander, non-Hispanic/Latino; 0.6% American Indian or Alaska Native, non-Hispanic/Latino; 3% Two or more races, non-Hispanic/Latino; 7% Race/ethnicity unknown; 1% international; 30% transferred in.
Freshmen *Admission:* 2,430 enrolled. *Test scores:* SAT critical reading scores over 500: 58%; SAT math scores over 500: 69%; SAT writing scores over 500: 47%; ACT scores over 18: 80%; SAT critical reading scores over 600: 10%; SAT math scores over 600: 21%; SAT writing scores over 600: 8%; ACT scores over 24: 32%; SAT critical reading scores over 700: 1%; SAT math scores over 700: 2%; SAT writing scores over 700: 1%; ACT scores over 30: 2%.
Faculty *Total:* 979, 27% full-time, 12% with terminal degrees. *Student/faculty ratio:* 16:1.
Majors Accounting technology and bookkeeping; architectural drafting and CAD/CADD; business administration and management; business administration, management and operations related; business/commerce; chemistry teacher education; child-care and support services management; clinical/medical laboratory technology; communications technologies and support services related; computer and information sciences; computer and information systems security; computer systems networking and telecommunications; criminal justice/law enforcement administration; criminal justice/police science; early childhood education; electrical and electronics engineering; electrical, electronic and communications engineering technology; engineering; English/language arts teacher education; entrepreneurship; fire prevention and safety technology; gerontology; graphic design; health and physical education/fitness; health information/medical records technology; hotel/motel administration; legal assistant/paralegal; liberal arts and sciences and humanities related; liberal arts and sciences/liberal studies; management information systems; management information systems and services related; mathematics; mathematics teacher education; mechatronics, robotics, and automation engineering; medical administrative assistant and medical secretary; medical radiologic technology;

multi/interdisciplinary studies related; occupational safety and health technology; physical therapy technology; physics teacher education; pre-law studies; psychiatric/mental health services technology; public health; registered nursing/registered nurse; Spanish language teacher education; substance abuse/addiction counseling; surgical technology.
Academics *Calendar:* semesters. *Degree:* certificates and associate. *Special study options:* academic remediation for entering students, accelerated degree program, adult/continuing education programs, advanced placement credit, cooperative education, distance learning, English as a second language, freshman honors college, honors programs, independent study, internships, part-time degree program, services for LD students, summer session for credit. *ROTC:* Army (c), Air Force (c).
Library Andrew G. Truxal Library plus 1 other with 175,000 titles, 3,130 audiovisual materials, an OPAC, a Web page.
Student Life *Housing:* college housing not available. *Activities and Organizations:* drama/theater group, student-run newspaper, choral group, Drama Club, Student Association, Black Student Union, International Student Association, Chemistry Club. *Campus security:* 24-hour emergency response devices and patrols, student patrols, late-night transport/escort service. *Student services:* health clinic, personal/psychological counseling.
Athletics Member NJCAA. *Intercollegiate sports:* baseball M(s), basketball M/W, cross-country running W, golf M, lacrosse M(s)/W(s), soccer M/W, softball W, volleyball W.
Costs (2014–15) *Tuition:* area resident $3060 full-time, $102 per credit hour part-time; state resident $5880 full-time, $196 per credit hour part-time; nonresident $10,410 full-time, $347 per credit hour part-time. Full-time tuition and fees vary according to program. Part-time tuition and fees vary according to program. *Required fees:* $770 full-time, $26 per credit hour part-time. *Payment plans:* installment, deferred payment. *Waivers:* adult students, senior citizens, and employees or children of employees.
Financial Aid Of all full-time matriculated undergraduates who enrolled in 2013, 104 Federal Work-Study jobs (averaging $1900). 55 state and other part-time jobs (averaging $1740).
Applying *Options:* electronic application, early admission, deferred entrance. *Required:* high school transcript. *Application deadlines:* rolling (freshmen), rolling (out-of-state freshmen), rolling (transfers). *Notification:* continuous (freshmen), continuous (out-of-state freshmen), continuous (transfers).
Freshman Application Contact Mr. Thomas McGinn, Director of Enrollment Development and Admissions, Anne Arundel Community College, 101 College Parkway, Arnold, MD 21012-1895. *Phone:* 410-777-2240. *Fax:* 410-777-2246. *E-mail:* 4info@aacc.edu.
Website: http://www.aacc.edu/.

Baltimore City Community College
Baltimore, Maryland

Freshman Application Contact Baltimore City Community College, 2901 Liberty Heights Avenue, Baltimore, MD 21215-7893. *Phone:* 410-462-8311. *Toll-free phone:* 888-203-1261.
Website: http://www.bccc.edu/.

Carroll Community College
Westminster, Maryland

- **State and locally supported** 2-year, founded 1993, part of Maryland Higher Education Commission
- **Suburban** 80-acre campus with easy access to Baltimore
- **Endowment** $4.8 million
- **Coed,** 3,661 undergraduate students, 37% full-time, 61% women, 39% men

Undergraduates 1,352 full-time, 2,309 part-time. Students come from 3 states and territories; 20 other countries; 2% are from out of state; 4% Black or African American, non-Hispanic/Latino; 3% Hispanic/Latino; 1% Asian, non-Hispanic/Latino; 0.1% Native Hawaiian or other Pacific Islander, non-Hispanic/Latino; 0.3% American Indian or Alaska Native, non-Hispanic/Latino; 2% Two or more races, non-Hispanic/Latino; 1% Race/ethnicity unknown; 0.2% international; 7% transferred in.
Freshmen *Admission:* 684 applied, 684 admitted, 684 enrolled.
Faculty *Total:* 265, 29% full-time, 6% with terminal degrees. *Student/faculty ratio:* 15:1.
Majors Accounting technology and bookkeeping; administrative assistant and secretarial science; architectural drafting and CAD/CADD; art; business administration and management; chemistry teacher education; child-care and support services management; computer engineering; computer graphics; criminal justice/police science; early childhood education; education; electrical and electronics engineering; elementary education; emergency medical technology (EMT paramedic); English/language arts teacher education; forensic science and technology; general studies; health information/medical records technology; health professions related; kinesiology and exercise

science; legal studies; liberal arts and sciences/liberal studies; licensed practical/vocational nurse training; management information systems; mathematics teacher education; multi/interdisciplinary studies related; music; physical therapy technology; psychology; registered nursing/registered nurse; Spanish language teacher education; theater design and technology.

Academics *Calendar:* semesters plus winter session. *Degree:* certificates and associate. *Special study options:* academic remediation for entering students, advanced placement credit, distance learning, English as a second language, honors programs, independent study, internships, part-time degree program, services for LD students, summer session for credit.

Library Carroll Community College Library with 151,001 titles, 3,426 audiovisual materials, an OPAC, a Web page.

Student Life *Housing:* college housing not available. *Activities and Organizations:* drama/theater group, choral group, Student Government Organization, S.T.E.M. Club, Campus Activities Board, Service Learning Club, Early Childhood Education Club. *Campus security:* 24-hour emergency response devices, late night security escort to parked car.

Costs (2014–15) *Tuition:* area resident $4308 full-time, $144 per credit hour part-time; state resident $6252 full-time, $208 per credit hour part-time; nonresident $8736 full-time, $291 per credit hour part-time. *Payment plan:* deferred payment. *Waivers:* senior citizens and employees or children of employees.

Financial Aid Of all full-time matriculated undergraduates who enrolled in 2013, 32 Federal Work-Study jobs (averaging $2011).

Applying *Options:* electronic application. *Required:* high school transcript. *Application deadlines:* rolling (freshmen), rolling (out-of-state freshmen), rolling (transfers). *Notification:* continuous (freshmen), continuous (out-of-state freshmen), continuous (transfers).

Freshman Application Contact Ms. Candace Edwards, Director of Admissions, Carroll Community College, 1601 Washington Road, Westminster, MD 21157. *Phone:* 410-386-8405. *Toll-free phone:* 888-221-9748. *Fax:* 410-386-8446. *E-mail:* cedwards@carrollcc.edu. *Website:* http://www.carrollcc.edu/.

Cecil College
North East, Maryland

- **County-supported** 2-year, founded 1968
- **Small-town** 159-acre campus with easy access to Baltimore
- **Coed,** 2,551 undergraduate students, 40% full-time, 62% women, 38% men

Undergraduates 1,011 full-time, 1,540 part-time. Students come from 12 states and territories; 10 other countries; 9% are from out of state; 9% Black or African American, non-Hispanic/Latino; 5% Hispanic/Latino; 1% Asian, non-Hispanic/Latino; 0.1% Native Hawaiian or other Pacific Islander, non-Hispanic/Latino; 0.5% American Indian or Alaska Native, non-Hispanic/Latino; 3% Two or more races, non-Hispanic/Latino; 0.1% Race/ethnicity unknown; 0.5% international; 4% transferred in. *Retention:* 55% of full-time freshmen returned.

Freshmen *Admission:* 499 applied, 499 admitted, 536 enrolled.

Faculty *Total:* 273, 19% full-time, 6% with terminal degrees. *Student/faculty ratio:* 12:1.

Majors Administrative assistant and secretarial science; aeronautics/aviation/aerospace science and technology; air traffic control; animation, interactive technology, video graphics and special effects; applied horticulture/horticulture operations; biology/biological sciences; biotechnology; business administration and management; business/commerce; business/corporate communications; chemistry; child-care and support services management; commercial photography; criminal justice/police science; design and visual communications; drawing; education; electrical, electronic and communications engineering technology; elementary education; emergency medical technology (EMT paramedic); English/language arts teacher education; financial planning and services; fine/studio arts; fire science/firefighting; general studies; health services/allied health/health sciences; horse husbandry/equine science and management; human resources management; liberal arts and sciences/liberal studies; logistics, materials, and supply chain management; management information systems; marketing/marketing management; mathematics; office management; photography; physics; purchasing, procurement/acquisitions and contracts management; registered nursing/registered nurse; secondary education; transportation and materials moving related; transportation/mobility management; web page, digital/multimedia and information resources design.

Academics *Calendar:* semesters. *Degree:* certificates and associate. *Special study options:* academic remediation for entering students, accelerated degree program, adult/continuing education programs, advanced placement credit, cooperative education, distance learning, double majors, English as a second language, independent study, internships, off-campus study, part-time degree program, services for LD students, summer session for credit.

Library Cecil County Veterans Memorial Library with 65,908 titles, 808 audiovisual materials, an OPAC, a Web page.

Student Life *Housing:* college housing not available. *Activities and Organizations:* drama/theater group, student government, Non-traditional Student Organization, Student Nurses Association, national fraternities. *Campus security:* 24-hour emergency response devices, late-night transport/escort service. *Student services:* personal/psychological counseling, women's center.

Athletics Member NJCAA. *Intercollegiate sports:* baseball M(s), basketball M(s)/W(s), cheerleading W, lacrosse M(c), soccer M(s)/W(s), softball W(s), tennis W(s), volleyball W(s).

Costs (2014–15) *Tuition:* area resident $3000 full-time, $100 per credit hour part-time; state resident $5700 full-time, $190 per credit hour part-time; nonresident $7050 full-time, $235 per credit hour part-time. *Required fees:* $362 full-time. *Payment plan:* deferred payment. *Waivers:* senior citizens and employees or children of employees.

Applying *Options:* electronic application, early admission, deferred entrance. *Required:* high school transcript. *Application deadlines:* rolling (freshmen), rolling (out-of-state freshmen), rolling (transfers). *Notification:* continuous (freshmen), continuous (out-of-state freshmen), continuous (transfers).

Freshman Application Contact Dr. Diane Lane, Cecil College, One Seahawk Drive, North East, MD 21901-1999. *Phone:* 410-287-1002. *Fax:* 410-287-1001. *E-mail:* dlane@cecil.edu. *Website:* http://www.cecil.edu/.

Chesapeake College
Wye Mills, Maryland

- **State and locally supported** 2-year, founded 1965
- **Rural** 170-acre campus with easy access to Baltimore and Washington, DC
- **Endowment** $3.7 million
- **Coed,** 2,069 undergraduate students, 37% full-time, 66% women, 34% men

Undergraduates 773 full-time, 1,296 part-time. 17% Black or African American, non-Hispanic/Latino; 4% Hispanic/Latino; 1% Asian, non-Hispanic/Latino; 0.1% Native Hawaiian or other Pacific Islander, non-Hispanic/Latino; 0.8% American Indian or Alaska Native, non-Hispanic/Latino; 2% Two or more races, non-Hispanic/Latino; 2% Race/ethnicity unknown; 1% international; 16% transferred in. *Retention:* 43% of full-time freshmen returned.

Freshmen *Admission:* 541 enrolled.

Faculty *Total:* 127, 43% full-time, 19% with terminal degrees. *Student/faculty ratio:* 17:1.

Majors Accounting technology and bookkeeping; business administration and management; business/commerce; child-care and support services management; computer and information sciences and support services related; computer and information systems security; computer science; corrections and criminal justice related; early childhood education; education; elementary education; emergency medical technology (EMT paramedic); engineering-related technologies; general studies; hospitality administration; legal assistant/paralegal; liberal arts and sciences and humanities related; liberal arts and sciences/liberal studies; mathematics teacher education; medical radiologic technology; mental and social health services and allied professions related; physical therapy; physics teacher education; registered nursing/registered nurse.

Academics *Calendar:* semesters. *Degree:* certificates and associate. *Special study options:* academic remediation for entering students, adult/continuing education programs, advanced placement credit, cooperative education, distance learning, English as a second language, honors programs, independent study, internships, part-time degree program, services for LD students, summer session for credit.

Library Learning Resource Center with 72,000 titles, 1,080 audiovisual materials, an OPAC, a Web page.

Student Life *Housing:* college housing not available. *Activities and Organizations:* drama/theater group. *Campus security:* 24-hour patrols. *Student services:* personal/psychological counseling, women's center.

Athletics Member NJCAA. *Intercollegiate sports:* baseball M, basketball M/W, soccer M, softball W, volleyball W.

Costs (2014–15) *Tuition:* area resident $3300 full-time, $110 per credit hour part-time; state resident $5340 full-time, $178 per credit hour part-time; nonresident $7650 full-time, $255 per credit hour part-time. *Required fees:* $1040 full-time, $32 per credit hour part-time, $25 per term part-time. *Payment plan:* installment. *Waivers:* senior citizens and employees or children of employees.

Financial Aid Of all full-time matriculated undergraduates who enrolled in 2013, 32 Federal Work-Study jobs (averaging $1482).

Applying *Options:* electronic application, early admission, deferred entrance. *Required:* high school transcript. *Application deadlines:* rolling (freshmen), rolling (out-of-state freshmen), rolling (transfers). *Notification:* continuous (freshmen), continuous (out-of-state freshmen), continuous (transfers).

Freshman Application Contact Ms. Marci Leach, Director of Student Recruitment and Outreach, Chesapeake College, PO Box 8, Wye Mills, MD 21679-0008. *Phone:* 410-822-5400. *Fax:* 410-827-5875. *E-mail:* mleach@chesapeake.edu.

Website: http://www.chesapeake.edu/.

College of Southern Maryland

La Plata, Maryland

- **State and locally supported** 2-year, founded 1958
- **Rural** 175-acre campus with easy access to Washington, DC
- **Coed,** 8,411 undergraduate students, 37% full-time, 61% women, 39% men

Undergraduates 3,087 full-time, 5,324 part-time. 26% Black or African American, non-Hispanic/Latino; 6% Hispanic/Latino; 3% Asian, non-Hispanic/Latino; 0.3% Native Hawaiian or other Pacific Islander, non-Hispanic/Latino; 0.5% American Indian or Alaska Native, non-Hispanic/Latino; 5% Two or more races, non-Hispanic/Latino; 2% Race/ethnicity unknown; 0.4% international; 7% transferred in.

Freshmen *Admission:* 1,966 enrolled.

Faculty *Total:* 513, 24% full-time, 13% with terminal degrees. *Student/faculty ratio:* 19:1.

Majors Accounting technology and bookkeeping; building/construction finishing, management, and inspection related; business administration and management; business/commerce; child-care and support services management; clinical/medical laboratory technology; communication and media related; computer and information sciences; computer and information systems security; computer engineering; computer programming; criminal justice/law enforcement administration; digital communication and media/multimedia; early childhood education; education; electrical and electronics engineering; electrician; elementary education; emergency medical technology (EMT paramedic); engineering; engineering technologies and engineering related; fire science/firefighting; health and physical education related; health information/medical records technology; homeland security; hospitality administration; information technology; legal studies; liberal arts and sciences and humanities related; liberal arts and sciences/liberal studies; lineworker; massage therapy; mental and social health services and allied professions related; multi/interdisciplinary studies related; nuclear engineering technology; physical therapy technology; registered nursing/registered nurse.

Academics *Calendar:* semesters. *Degree:* certificates and associate. *Special study options:* academic remediation for entering students, accelerated degree program, adult/continuing education programs, advanced placement credit, cooperative education, distance learning, honors programs, independent study, part-time degree program, services for LD students, study abroad, summer session for credit.

Library College of Southern Maryland Library with an OPAC, a Web page.

Student Life *Housing:* college housing not available. *Activities and Organizations:* drama/theater group, student-run newspaper, television station, choral group, Spanish Club, Nursing Student Association, Science Club, Black Student Union, BACCHUS. *Campus security:* 24-hour emergency response devices and patrols. *Student services:* personal/psychological counseling.

Athletics Member NJCAA. *Intercollegiate sports:* baseball M, basketball M/W, golf M/W, lacrosse M/W, soccer M/W, softball W, volleyball W.

Costs (2014–15) *Tuition:* area resident $4244 full-time, $115 per credit hour part-time; state resident $7306 full-time, $198 per credit hour part-time; nonresident $9446 full-time, $256 per credit hour part-time. Full-time tuition and fees vary according to course load. Part-time tuition and fees vary according to course load. *Required fees:* $794 full-time. *Payment plan:* deferred payment. *Waivers:* senior citizens and employees or children of employees.

Financial Aid Of all full-time matriculated undergraduates who enrolled in 2013, 2,067 applied for aid, 1,496 were judged to have need, 10 had their need fully met. In 2013, 12 non-need-based awards were made. *Average percent of need met:* 35%. *Average financial aid package:* $5727. *Average need-based loan:* $3115. *Average need-based gift aid:* $5347. *Average non-need-based aid:* $1090.

Applying *Options:* electronic application, early admission, deferred entrance. *Recommended:* high school transcript. *Application deadlines:* rolling (freshmen), rolling (transfers). *Notification:* continuous (freshmen), continuous (transfers).

Freshman Application Contact Admissions Department, College of Southern Maryland, PO Box 910, La Plata, MD 20646-0910. *Phone:* 301-934-2251. *Toll-free phone:* 800-933-9177. *Fax:* 301-934-7698. *E-mail:* askme@csmd.edu.

Website: http://www.csmd.edu/.

The Community College of Baltimore County

Baltimore, Maryland

- **County-supported** 2-year, founded 1957
- **Suburban** 350-acre campus with easy access to Baltimore City
- **Coed,** 23,136 undergraduate students, 32% full-time, 61% women, 39% men

Undergraduates 7,301 full-time, 15,835 part-time. 39% Black or African American, non-Hispanic/Latino; 4% Hispanic/Latino; 5% Asian, non-Hispanic/Latino; 0.2% Native Hawaiian or other Pacific Islander, non-Hispanic/Latino; 0.4% American Indian or Alaska Native, non-Hispanic/Latino; 3% Two or more races, non-Hispanic/Latino; 0.5% Race/ethnicity unknown; 4% international.

Freshmen *Admission:* 4,346 enrolled.

Faculty *Total:* 1,365, 32% full-time, 9% with terminal degrees.

Majors Accounting technology and bookkeeping; administrative assistant and secretarial science; aeronautics/aviation/aerospace science and technology; applied horticulture/horticulture operations; architectural drafting and CAD/CADD; automobile/automotive mechanics technology; biological and physical sciences; building/construction finishing, management, and inspection related; building/construction site management; business administration and management; business/commerce; chemistry teacher education; child-care and support services management; clinical/medical laboratory technology; commercial and advertising art; computer and information sciences; computer and information systems security; computer engineering; computer systems networking and telecommunications; criminal justice/police science; dental hygiene; early childhood education; education; electrical and electronics engineering; elementary education; emergency medical technology (EMT paramedic); engineering; engineering technologies and engineering related; funeral service and mortuary science; geography; heating, ventilation, air conditioning and refrigeration engineering technology; hotel/motel administration; hydraulics and fluid power technology; legal assistant/paralegal; liberal arts and sciences and humanities related; liberal arts and sciences/liberal studies; management information systems; massage therapy; mathematics teacher education; medical administrative assistant and medical secretary; medical informatics; medical radiologic technology; occupational safety and health technology; occupational therapy; parks, recreation and leisure; parks, recreation, and fitness studies related; physics teacher education; psychiatric/mental health services technology; registered nursing/registered nurse; respiratory care therapy; sign language interpretation and translation; Spanish language teacher education; substance abuse/addiction counseling; surveying technology; veterinary/animal health technology; visual and performing arts.

Academics *Calendar:* semesters. *Degree:* certificates and associate. *Special study options:* academic remediation for entering students, advanced placement credit, cooperative education, distance learning, English as a second language, honors programs, independent study, internships, off-campus study, services for LD students, study abroad, summer session for credit.

Student Life *Housing:* college housing not available. *Campus security:* 24-hour emergency response devices and patrols, late-night transport/escort service.

Athletics Member NJCAA. *Intercollegiate sports:* baseball M(s), basketball M(s)/W(s), cross-country running W(s), lacrosse M(s)/W(s), soccer M(s)/W(s), softball W(s), track and field W(s), volleyball W(s).

Standardized Tests *Recommended:* SAT or ACT (for admission).

Costs (2014–15) *Tuition:* area resident $3390 full-time, $113 per credit part-time; state resident $6480 full-time, $216 per credit part-time; nonresident $9720 full-time, $324 per credit hour part-time. Full-time tuition and fees vary according to course load. Part-time tuition and fees vary according to course load. *Required fees:* $862 full-time. *Payment plan:* installment. *Waivers:* employees or children of employees.

Applying *Options:* electronic application. *Required:* high school transcript. *Application deadlines:* rolling (freshmen), rolling (out-of-state freshmen), rolling (transfers).

Freshman Application Contact Ms. Diane Drake, Director of Admissions, The Community College of Baltimore County, 7201 Rossville Boulevard, Baltimore, MD 21237-3899. *Phone:* 443-840-4392. *E-mail:* ddrake@ccbcmd.edu.

Website: http://www.ccbcmd.edu/.

Fortis College

Landover, Maryland

Admissions Office Contact Fortis College, 4351 Garden City Drive, Landover, MD 20785.

Website: http://www.fortis.edu/.

Frederick Community College
Frederick, Maryland

- **State and locally supported** 2-year, founded 1957
- **Small-town** 100-acre campus with easy access to Baltimore and Washington, DC
- **Endowment** $10.1 million
- **Coed,** 6,031 undergraduate students, 34% full-time, 57% women, 43% men

Undergraduates 2,061 full-time, 3,970 part-time. 2% are from out of state; 14% Black or African American, non-Hispanic/Latino; 10% Hispanic/Latino; 5% Asian, non-Hispanic/Latino; 0.4% American Indian or Alaska Native, non-Hispanic/Latino; 3% Two or more races, non-Hispanic/Latino; 0.6% Race/ethnicity unknown; 0.6% international. *Retention:* 45% of full-time freshmen returned.

Freshmen *Admission:* 1,238 enrolled.

Faculty *Total:* 562, 18% full-time, 14% with terminal degrees. *Student/faculty ratio:* 11:1.

Majors Accounting; art; biology/biological sciences; building/construction finishing, management, and inspection related; business administration and management; chemistry; child development; computer science; criminal justice/law enforcement administration; drafting and design technology; early childhood education; education; elementary education; emergency medical technology (EMT paramedic); engineering; fire science/firefighting; general studies; human services; information technology; legal assistant/paralegal; liberal arts and sciences/liberal studies; mathematics; mathematics teacher education; medical administrative assistant and medical secretary; medical/clinical assistant; nuclear medical technology; political science and government; psychology; registered nursing/registered nurse; respiratory care therapy; Spanish language teacher education; surgical technology.

Academics *Calendar:* semesters. *Degree:* certificates and associate. *Special study options:* academic remediation for entering students, adult/continuing education programs, advanced placement credit, cooperative education, distance learning, English as a second language, external degree program, freshman honors college, honors programs, independent study, internships, off-campus study, part-time degree program, services for LD students, study abroad, summer session for credit.

Library FCC Library with 12,500 titles, 104 audiovisual materials, an OPAC, a Web page.

Student Life *Housing:* college housing not available. *Activities and Organizations:* drama/theater group, student-run newspaper. *Campus security:* 24-hour emergency response devices and patrols, late-night transport/escort service. *Student services:* personal/psychological counseling, women's center.

Athletics Member NJCAA. *Intercollegiate sports:* baseball M/W, basketball M/W, golf M/W, lacrosse M/W, soccer M/W, softball W, volleyball W.

Costs (2014–15) *Tuition:* area resident $4166 full-time, $116 per credit hour part-time; state resident $8246 full-time, $252 per credit hour part-time; nonresident $10,944 full-time, $342 per credit hour part-time. *Required fees:* $20 per credit hour part-time, $57 per semester part-time. *Payment plans:* installment, deferred payment. *Waivers:* senior citizens.

Financial Aid Of all full-time matriculated undergraduates who enrolled in 2013, 25 Federal Work-Study jobs (averaging $1368). 14 state and other part-time jobs (averaging $2715).

Applying *Options:* electronic application. *Recommended:* high school transcript. *Application deadlines:* rolling (freshmen), rolling (transfers). *Notification:* continuous (freshmen), continuous (transfers).

Freshman Application Contact Ms. Lisa A. Freel, Director of Admissions, Frederick Community College, 7932 Opossumtown Pike, Frederick, MD 21702. *Phone:* 301-846-2468. *Fax:* 301-624-2799. *E-mail:* admissions@frederick.edu.

Website: http://www.frederick.edu/.

Garrett College
McHenry, Maryland

- **State and locally supported** 2-year, founded 1966
- **Rural** 62-acre campus
- **Coed,** 712 undergraduate students, 81% full-time, 50% women, 50% men

Undergraduates 576 full-time, 136 part-time. Students come from 15 states and territories; 18 other countries; 24% are from out of state; 27% Black or African American, non-Hispanic/Latino; 3% Hispanic/Latino; 0.2% Asian, non-Hispanic/Latino; 0.2% American Indian or Alaska Native, non-Hispanic/Latino; 3% Two or more races, non-Hispanic/Latino; 2% international; 5% transferred in; 22% live on campus.

Freshmen *Admission:* 1,047 applied, 1,000 admitted, 219 enrolled. *Test scores:* SAT critical reading scores over 500: 38%; SAT math scores over 500: 38%; SAT writing scores over 500: 30%; ACT scores over 18: 63%; SAT critical reading scores over 600: 10%; SAT math scores over 600: 10%; SAT

writing scores over 600: 5%; ACT scores over 24: 16%; ACT scores over 30: 3%.

Faculty *Total:* 85, 28% full-time. *Student/faculty ratio:* 14:1.

Majors Business administration and management; business automation/technology/data entry; business/commerce; corrections; early childhood education; education; electrical and electronics engineering; elementary education; liberal arts and sciences and humanities related; liberal arts and sciences/liberal studies; management information systems; sport and fitness administration/management; wildlife, fish and wildlands science and management.

Academics *Calendar:* semesters. *Degree:* certificates and associate. *Special study options:* academic remediation for entering students, adult/continuing education programs, advanced placement credit, cooperative education, distance learning, double majors, external degree program, honors programs, independent study, internships, part-time degree program, services for LD students, summer session for credit.

Library Learning Resource Center with 53,293 titles, 2,975 audiovisual materials, an OPAC, a Web page.

Student Life *Housing Options:* coed, special housing for students with disabilities. Campus housing is university owned and leased by the school. *Activities and Organizations:* SGA, International Students Club, CRU. *Campus security:* 24-hour emergency response devices and patrols, controlled dormitory access. *Student services:* health clinic, personal/psychological counseling.

Athletics Member NJCAA. *Intercollegiate sports:* baseball M(s), basketball M(s)/W(s), cross-country running M/W, golf M/W, softball W, volleyball W. *Intramural sports:* basketball M/W, football M/W, rock climbing M/W, ultimate Frisbee M/W.

Standardized Tests *Recommended:* SAT or ACT (for admission).

Costs (2015–16) *Tuition:* area resident $2632 full-time, $94 per credit hour part-time; state resident $6048 full-time, $216 per credit hour part-time; nonresident $7140 full-time, $255 per credit hour part-time. Full-time tuition and fees vary according to program and reciprocity agreements. Part-time tuition and fees vary according to program and reciprocity agreements. *Required fees:* $778 full-time, $26 per credit hour part-time, $25 per term part-time. *Room and board:* $7412; room only: $5400. Room and board charges vary according to board plan and housing facility. *Payment plans:* installment, deferred payment. *Waivers:* senior citizens.

Financial Aid Of all full-time matriculated undergraduates who enrolled in 2013, 461 applied for aid, 403 were judged to have need, 43 had their need fully met. In 2013, 53 non-need-based awards were made. *Average percent of need met:* 57%. *Average financial aid package:* $7788. *Average need-based loan:* $3096. *Average need-based gift aid:* $5122. *Average non-need-based aid:* $3220.

Applying *Options:* electronic application, early admission, deferred entrance. *Required:* high school transcript. *Application deadlines:* rolling (freshmen), rolling (out-of-state freshmen), rolling (transfers). *Notification:* continuous (freshmen), continuous (out-of-state freshmen), continuous (transfers).

Freshman Application Contact Mrs. Rachelle Davis, Director of Admissions, Garrett College, 687 Mosser Road, McHenry, MD 21541. *Phone:* 301-387-3044. *Toll-free phone:* 866-55-GARRETT. *E-mail:* admissions@garrettcollege.edu.

Website: http://www.garrettcollege.edu/.

Hagerstown Community College
Hagerstown, Maryland

- **State and locally supported** 2-year, founded 1946
- **Suburban** 319-acre campus with easy access to Baltimore and Washington, DC
- **Coed,** 4,615 undergraduate students, 25% full-time, 64% women, 36% men

Undergraduates 1,174 full-time, 3,441 part-time. Students come from 14 states and territories; 19% are from out of state; 10% Black or African American, non-Hispanic/Latino; 5% Hispanic/Latino; 2% Asian, non-Hispanic/Latino; 0.2% Native Hawaiian or other Pacific Islander, non-Hispanic/Latino; 0.3% American Indian or Alaska Native, non-Hispanic/Latino; 4% Two or more races, non-Hispanic/Latino; 2% Race/ethnicity unknown; 0.5% international; 8% transferred in.

Freshmen *Admission:* 841 enrolled.

Faculty *Total:* 246, 33% full-time, 8% with terminal degrees. *Student/faculty ratio:* 17:1.

Majors Accounting technology and bookkeeping; animation, interactive technology, video graphics and special effects; biology/biotechnology laboratory technician; business administration and management; business/commerce; child-care and support services management; commercial and advertising art; computer and information sciences; computer and information systems security; criminal justice/police science; dental hygiene; early childhood education; education; elementary education; emergency medical technology (EMT paramedic); engineering; engineering technologies and engineering related; English/language arts teacher education; industrial technology; instrumentation technology; liberal arts and sciences and humanities related; liberal arts and sciences/liberal studies; management information systems; mechanical engineering/mechanical technology; medical radiologic technology; psychiatric/mental health services technology; registered nursing/registered nurse; transportation/mobility management; web page, digital/multimedia and information resources design.

Academics *Calendar:* semesters. *Degree:* certificates and associate. *Special study options:* academic remediation for entering students, accelerated degree program, adult/continuing education programs, advanced placement credit, cooperative education, distance learning, English as a second language, honors programs, independent study, internships, off-campus study, part-time degree program, services for LD students, summer session for credit.

Library William Brish Library with 48,117 titles, an OPAC, a Web page.

Student Life *Activities and Organizations:* drama/theater group, student-run newspaper, choral group, Phi Theta Kappa, Robinwood Players Theater Club, Association of Nursing Students, Radiography Club, Art and Design Club. *Campus security:* 24-hour patrols, student patrols. *Student services:* personal/psychological counseling.

Athletics Member NJCAA. *Intercollegiate sports:* baseball M(s), basketball M(s)/W(s), cross-country running M(s)/W(s), golf M/W, soccer M(s)/W, softball W(s), track and field M(s)/W(s), volleyball W(s). *Intramural sports:* cheerleading M/W, golf M/W, lacrosse M/W, table tennis M/W, tennis M/W.

Costs (2014–15) *Tuition:* area resident $2640 full-time, $110 per credit hour part-time; state resident $4128 full-time, $172 per credit hour part-time; nonresident $5424 full-time, $226 per credit hour part-time. Full-time tuition and fees vary according to course load, program, and reciprocity agreements. Part-time tuition and fees vary according to course load, program, and reciprocity agreements. *Required fees:* $468 full-time, $11 per credit hour part-time, $27 per term part-time. *Payment plan:* installment. *Waivers:* senior citizens and children of employees.

Financial Aid Of all full-time matriculated undergraduates who enrolled in 2013, 898 applied for aid, 752 were judged to have need, 48 had their need fully met. 45 Federal Work-Study jobs (averaging $1835). 317 state and other part-time jobs (averaging $2081). In 2013, 18 non-need-based awards were made. *Average percent of need met:* 50%. *Average financial aid package:* $6129. *Average need-based loan:* $3038. *Average need-based gift aid:* $4597. *Average non-need-based aid:* $825.

Applying *Options:* electronic application, early admission, deferred entrance. *Required for some:* high school transcript, selective admissions for RN, LPN, EMT, and radiography programs. *Application deadlines:* rolling (freshmen), rolling (out-of-state freshmen), rolling (transfers). *Notification:* continuous (freshmen), continuous (out-of-state freshmen), continuous (transfers).

Freshman Application Contact Mr. Kevin L Crawford, Assistant Director, Recruiting, Admissions, Records and Registration, Hagerstown Community College, 11400 Robinwood Drive, Hagerstown, MD 21742-6514. *Phone:* 240-500-2412. *Fax:* 301-791-9165. *E-mail:* klcrawford@hagerstowncc.edu. *Website:* http://www.hagerstowncc.edu/.

Harford Community College
Bel Air, Maryland

- **State and locally supported** 2-year, founded 1957
- **Small-town** 331-acre campus with easy access to Baltimore
- **Coed,** 6,713 undergraduate students, 38% full-time, 59% women, 41% men

Undergraduates 2,524 full-time, 4,189 part-time. 15% Black or African American, non-Hispanic/Latino; 5% Hispanic/Latino; 2% Asian, non-Hispanic/Latino; 0.2% Native Hawaiian or other Pacific Islander, non-Hispanic/Latino; 0.4% American Indian or Alaska Native, non-Hispanic/Latino; 3% Two or more races, non-Hispanic/Latino; 0.7% Race/ethnicity unknown; 1% international.

Freshmen *Admission:* 1,390 enrolled. *Test scores:* SAT critical reading scores over 500: 75%; SAT math scores over 500: 79%; SAT critical reading scores over 600: 26%; SAT math scores over 600: 30%; SAT critical reading scores over 700: 2%; SAT math scores over 700: 2%.

Faculty *Total:* 357, 28% full-time, 13% with terminal degrees. *Student/faculty ratio:* 21:1.

Majors Accounting; administrative assistant and secretarial science; advertising; agribusiness; agriculture; anthropology; biology/biological sciences; business administration and management; chemistry; chemistry teacher education; civil drafting and CAD/CADD; computer and information sciences; computer science; criminal justice/police science; digital arts; early childhood education; education; education (specific levels and methods) related; education (specific subject areas) related; electroneurodiagnostic/electroencephalographic technology; elementary education; engineering; engineering technology; English; English/language arts teacher education; entrepreneurship; environmental engineering technology; environmental science; fine/studio arts; general studies; graphic design; history; human resources management; information science/studies;

interior design; international relations and affairs; legal assistant/paralegal; marketing/marketing management; mass communication/media; mathematics; mathematics teacher education; medical office assistant; music; philosophy; photography; physics; physics teacher education; political science and government; psychology; registered nursing, nursing administration, nursing research and clinical nursing related; social work; sociology; Spanish language teacher education; special education; special education–early childhood; special education–elementary school; teacher assistant/aide; theater design and technology.

Academics *Calendar:* semesters. *Degree:* certificates, diplomas, and associate. *Special study options:* academic remediation for entering students, adult/continuing education programs, advanced placement credit, cooperative education, distance learning, double majors, English as a second language, honors programs, independent study, internships, part-time degree program, services for LD students, student-designed majors, study abroad, summer session for credit.

Library Harford Community College Library with 52,069 titles, 4,224 audiovisual materials, an OPAC, a Web page.

Student Life *Activities and Organizations:* drama/theater group, student-run newspaper, radio station, choral group, Student Government Association, Phi Theta Kappa, Student Nurses Association, Actor's Guild, Paralegal Club. *Campus security:* 24-hour patrols, late-night transport/escort service. *Student services:* personal/psychological counseling.

Athletics Member NJCAA. *Intercollegiate sports:* baseball M(s), basketball M(s)/W(s), cross-country running M(s)/W(s), golf M(s), lacrosse M(s)/W(s), soccer M(s)/W(s), softball W(s), tennis M(s)/W(s), volleyball W(s). *Intramural sports:* badminton M/W, basketball M/W, cheerleading M(c)/W(c), football M/W, soccer M/W, softball M/W, swimming and diving M/W, tennis M/W, volleyball M/W.

Costs (2015–16) *Tuition:* area resident $3120 full-time, $104 per credit hour part-time; state resident $5730 full-time, $191 per credit hour part-time; nonresident $8340 full-time, $78 per credit hour part-time. *Required fees:* $624 full-time, $21 per credit hour part-time. *Payment plan:* installment. *Waivers:* senior citizens and employees or children of employees.

Financial Aid Of all full-time matriculated undergraduates who enrolled in 2013, 1,428 applied for aid, 1,023 were judged to have need. 68 Federal Work-Study jobs (averaging $1901).

Applying *Options:* electronic application. *Application deadlines:* rolling (freshmen), rolling (transfers). *Notification:* continuous (transfers).

Freshman Application Contact Jennifer Starkey, Enrollment Services Associate - Admissions, Harford Community College, 401 Thomas Run Road, Bel Air, MD 21015-1698. *Phone:* 443-412-2311. *Fax:* 443-412-2169. *E-mail:* jestarkey@harford.edu. *Website:* http://www.harford.edu/.

Howard Community College
Columbia, Maryland

- **State and locally supported** 2-year, founded 1966
- **Suburban** 122-acre campus with easy access to Baltimore and Washington, DC
- **Coed,** 9,920 undergraduate students, 38% full-time, 56% women, 44% men

Undergraduates 3,729 full-time, 6,191 part-time. Students come from 5 states and territories; 111 other countries; 0.4% are from out of state; 29% Black or African American, non-Hispanic/Latino; 9% Hispanic/Latino; 11% Asian, non-Hispanic/Latino; 0.3% Native Hawaiian or other Pacific Islander, non-Hispanic/Latino; 0.3% American Indian or Alaska Native, non-Hispanic/Latino; 4% Two or more races, non-Hispanic/Latino; 3% Race/ethnicity unknown; 4% international.

Freshmen *Admission:* 1,671 enrolled.

Faculty *Total:* 962, 20% full-time, 17% with terminal degrees. *Student/faculty ratio:* 15:1.

Majors Accounting; art; biological and physical sciences; biomedical technology; biotechnology; business administration and management; cardiovascular technology; child development; clinical laboratory science/medical technology; computer and information sciences related; computer graphics; computer/information technology services administration related; computer science; computer systems networking and telecommunications; criminal justice/law enforcement administration; design and applied arts related; diagnostic medical sonography and ultrasound technology; dramatic/theater arts; electrical, electronic and communications engineering technology; elementary education; emergency medical technology (EMT paramedic); engineering; environmental studies; financial planning and services; general studies; health teacher education; information science/studies; information technology; kindergarten/preschool education; legal administrative assistant/secretary; liberal arts and sciences/liberal studies; licensed practical/vocational nurse training; medical administrative assistant and medical secretary; music; nuclear medical technology; office management; photography; physical sciences; physical therapy technology; premedical studies; pre-pharmacy studies; registered nursing/registered nurse; secondary education; social sciences; sport and fitness administration/management; substance abuse/addiction counseling; telecommunications technology; theater design and technology.

Academics *Calendar:* semesters. *Degree:* certificates and associate. *Special study options:* academic remediation for entering students, adult/continuing education programs, advanced placement credit, cooperative education, distance learning, double majors, English as a second language, external degree program, freshman honors college, honors programs, off-campus study, part-time degree program, services for LD students, study abroad, summer session for credit.

Library Howard Community College Library with 45,707 titles, 2,636 audiovisual materials, an OPAC, a Web page.

Student Life *Housing:* college housing not available. *Activities and Organizations:* drama/theater group, student-run newspaper, radio station, choral group, Phi Theta Kappa, Nursing Club, Black Leadership Organization, student newspaper, Student Government Association. *Campus security:* 24-hour emergency response devices and patrols, late-night transport/escort service. *Student services:* personal/psychological counseling.

Athletics Member NJCAA. *Intercollegiate sports:* basketball M/W, cross-country running M/W, lacrosse M/W, soccer M/W, track and field M/W, volleyball W. *Intramural sports:* basketball M/W.

Standardized Tests *Required for some:* SAT or ACT (for admission).

Costs (2014–15) *Tuition:* area resident $3810 full-time, $127 per credit hour part-time; state resident $6300 full-time, $210 per credit hour part-time; nonresident $7650 full-time, $255 per credit hour part-time. *Required fees:* $638 full-time, $21 per credit hour part-time. *Payment plan:* installment. *Waivers:* senior citizens and employees or children of employees.

Financial Aid Of all full-time matriculated undergraduates who enrolled in 2013, 571 applied for aid, 477 were judged to have need. In 2013, 31 non-need-based awards were made. *Average percent of need met:* 22%. *Average financial aid package:* $3871. *Average need-based loan:* $2525. *Average need-based gift aid:* $4032. *Average non-need-based aid:* $1288.

Applying *Options:* electronic application, early admission, deferred entrance. *Application fee:* $25. *Required for some:* essay or personal statement, high school transcript, 2 letters of recommendation. *Application deadlines:* rolling (freshmen), rolling (out-of-state freshmen), rolling (transfers). *Notification:* continuous (freshmen), continuous (out-of-state freshmen), continuous (transfers).

Freshman Application Contact Ms. Christine Palmer, Assistant Director of Admissions, Howard Community College, 10901 Little Patuxent Parkway, Columbia, MD 21044-3197. *Phone:* 443-518-4599. *Fax:* 443-518-4711. *E-mail:* admissions@howardcc.edu.
Website: http://www.howardcc.edu/.

ITT Technical Institute
Owings Mills, Maryland

- **Proprietary** primarily 2-year, founded 2005
- **Coed**

Academics *Calendar:* quarters. *Degrees:* associate and bachelor's.

Freshman Application Contact Director of Recruitment, ITT Technical Institute, 11301 Red Run Boulevard, Owings Mills, MD 21117. *Phone:* 443-394-7115. *Toll-free phone:* 877-411-6782.
Website: http://www.itt-tech.edu/.

Kaplan University, Hagerstown Campus
Hagerstown, Maryland

Freshman Application Contact Kaplan University, Hagerstown Campus, 18618 Crestwood Drive, Hagerstown, MD 21742-2797. *Phone:* 301-739-2680 Ext. 217. *Toll-free phone:* 866-527-5268 (in-state); 800-527-5268 (out-of-state).
Website: http://www.kaplanuniversity.edu/.

Lincoln College of Technology
Columbia, Maryland

Admissions Office Contact Lincoln College of Technology, 9325 Snowden River Parkway, Columbia, MD 21046.
Website: http://www.lincolnedu.com/.

Montgomery College
Rockville, Maryland

- **State and locally supported** 2-year, founded 1946
- **Suburban** 333-acre campus with easy access to Washington, DC
- **Endowment** $22.4 million
- **Coed,** 25,517 undergraduate students, 35% full-time, 53% women, 47% men

Undergraduates 8,931 full-time, 16,586 part-time. Students come from 26 states and territories; 163 other countries; 3% are from out of state; 26% Black or African American, non-Hispanic/Latino; 22% Hispanic/Latino; 11% Asian, non-Hispanic/Latino; 0.3% Native Hawaiian or other Pacific Islander, non-Hispanic/Latino; 0.3% American Indian or Alaska Native, non-Hispanic/Latino; 3% Two or more races, non-Hispanic/Latino; 0.1% Race/ethnicity unknown; 10% international; 5% transferred in.

Freshmen *Admission:* 11,107 applied, 11,107 admitted, 3,969 enrolled.

Faculty *Total:* 1,492, 33% full-time, 32% with terminal degrees. *Student/faculty ratio:* 18:1.

Majors Accounting technology and bookkeeping; American Sign Language (ASL); animation, interactive technology, video graphics and special effects; applied horticulture/horticulture operations; architectural drafting and CAD/CADD; art; automobile/automotive mechanics technology; biology/biotechnology laboratory technician; building/construction finishing, management, and inspection related; business/commerce; chemistry teacher education; child-care provision; commercial and advertising art; commercial photography; communications technologies and support services related; computer and information sciences; computer and information systems security; computer technology/computer systems technology; criminal justice/police science; crisis/emergency/disaster management; data entry/microcomputer applications; diagnostic medical sonography and ultrasound technology; early childhood education; elementary education; engineering; English/language arts teacher education; fire prevention and safety technology; geography; health information/medical records technology; hotel/motel administration; interior design; legal assistant/paralegal; liberal arts and sciences and humanities related; liberal arts and sciences/liberal studies; mathematics teacher education; medical radiologic technology; physical therapy technology; physics teacher education; psychiatric/mental health services technology; registered nursing/registered nurse; Spanish language teacher education; speech communication and rhetoric; surgical technology; web page, digital/multimedia and information resources design.

Academics *Calendar:* semesters. *Degree:* certificates and associate. *Special study options:* academic remediation for entering students, adult/continuing education programs, advanced placement credit, cooperative education, distance learning, double majors, English as a second language, external degree program, honors programs, independent study, internships, off-campus study, part-time degree program, services for LD students, study abroad, summer session for credit. *ROTC:* Air Force (c).

Library Montgomery College Library plus 4 others with 440,410 titles, 37,164 audiovisual materials, an OPAC, a Web page.

Student Life *Activities and Organizations:* drama/theater group, student-run newspaper, choral group, Math Club, International Club, Anime Society Club, Animation & Video Game Club, Soccer, Basketball, Rugby, Cricket, Tennis, Lacrosse and Swim Clubs. *Campus security:* 24-hour emergency response devices and patrols, late-night transport/escort service. *Student services:* personal/psychological counseling, women's center.

Athletics Member NJCAA. *Intercollegiate sports:* baseball M, basketball M/W, soccer M/W, softball W, tennis M/W, track and field M/W, volleyball W. *Intramural sports:* baseball M, basketball M/W, cheerleading W, cross-country running M, soccer M/W, softball W, tennis M/W, track and field M/W, volleyball W.

Costs (2014–15) *Tuition:* area resident $2760 full-time, $115 per credit hour part-time; state resident $5640 full-time, $235 per credit hour part-time; nonresident $7752 full-time, $323 per credit hour part-time. Full-time tuition and fees vary according to course load. Part-time tuition and fees vary according to course load. *Required fees:* $912 full-time, $38 per credit hour part-time. *Payment plan:* installment. *Waivers:* senior citizens and employees or children of employees.

Financial Aid Of all full-time matriculated undergraduates who enrolled in 2013, 28,000 applied for aid.

Applying *Options:* electronic application, early admission, deferred entrance. *Application fee:* $25. *Recommended:* high school transcript, interview. *Application deadlines:* rolling (freshmen), rolling (out-of-state freshmen), rolling (transfers). *Notification:* continuous (freshmen), continuous (out-of-state freshmen), continuous (transfers).

Freshman Application Contact Montgomery College, 51 Mannakee Street, Rockville, MD 20850. *Phone:* 240-567-5036.
Website: http://www.montgomerycollege.edu/.

Prince George's Community College
Largo, Maryland

Freshman Application Contact Ms. Vera Bagley, Director of Admissions and Records, Prince George's Community College, 301 Largo Road, Largo, MD 20774-2199. *Phone:* 301-322-0801. *Fax:* 301-322-0119. *E-mail:* enrollmentservices@pgcc.edu. *Website:* http://www.pgcc.edu/.

TESST College of Technology
Baltimore, Maryland

Freshman Application Contact TESST College of Technology, 1520 South Caton Avenue, Baltimore, MD 21227. *Phone:* 410-644-6400. *Toll-free phone:* 800-935-1857. *Website:* http://www.baltimore.tesst.com/.

TESST College of Technology
Beltsville, Maryland

Freshman Application Contact TESST College of Technology, 4600 Powder Mill Road, Beltsville, MD 20705. *Phone:* 301-937-8448. *Toll-free phone:* 800-935-1857. *Website:* http://www.beltsville.tesst.com/.

TESST College of Technology
Towson, Maryland

Freshman Application Contact TESST College of Technology, 803 Glen Eagles Court, Towson, MD 21286. *Phone:* 410-296-5350. *Toll-free phone:* 800-935-1857. *Website:* http://www.towson.tesst.com/.

Wor-Wic Community College
Salisbury, Maryland

- **State and locally supported** 2-year, founded 1976
- **Small-town** 202-acre campus
- **Endowment** $14.3 million
- **Coed,** 3,107 undergraduate students, 29% full-time, 64% women, 36% men

Undergraduates 909 full-time, 2,198 part-time. Students come from 11 states and territories; 2% are from out of state; 23% Black or African American, non-Hispanic/Latino; 4% Hispanic/Latino; 2% Asian, non-Hispanic/Latino; 0.1% Native Hawaiian or other Pacific Islander, non-Hispanic/Latino; 0.4% American Indian or Alaska Native, non-Hispanic/Latino; 4% Two or more races, non-Hispanic/Latino; 2% Race/ethnicity unknown; 0.4% international; 7% transferred in.
Freshmen *Admission:* 1,311 applied, 1,311 admitted, 671 enrolled.
Faculty *Total:* 176, 40% full-time, 17% with terminal degrees. *Student/faculty ratio:* 15:1.
Majors Accounting technology and bookkeeping; administrative assistant and secretarial science; biological and physical sciences; business administration and management; business/commerce; child-care and support services management; computer and information sciences; computer systems analysis; criminal justice/police science; early childhood education; education; electrical, electronic and communications engineering technology; elementary education; emergency medical technology (EMT paramedic); engineering technologies and engineering related; environmental engineering technology; hospitality administration; liberal arts and sciences and humanities related; liberal arts and sciences/liberal studies; medical radiologic technology; occupational therapist assistant; registered nursing/registered nurse; substance abuse/addiction counseling.
Academics *Calendar:* semesters. *Degree:* certificates and associate. *Special study options:* academic remediation for entering students, accelerated degree program, adult/continuing education programs, advanced placement credit, distance learning, double majors, English as a second language, honors programs, independent study, internships, part-time degree program, services for LD students, summer session for credit.
Library Patricia M. Hazel Media Center plus 4 others with a Web page.
Student Life *Housing:* college housing not available. *Activities and Organizations:* drama/theater group, Anime Club, Criminal Justice Club, Role Playing Game Association, Veterans and Military Association, Alpha Nu Omicron (PTK). *Campus security:* 24-hour emergency response devices, late-night transport/escort service, patrols by trained security personnel 9 am to midnight. *Student services:* personal/psychological counseling.
Standardized Tests *Required for some:* ACT (for admission).

Costs (2015–16) *Tuition:* area resident $3090 full-time, $103 per credit part-time; state resident $6930 full-time, $231 per credit part-time; nonresident $8520 full-time, $284 per credit part-time. *Required fees:* $510 full-time, $17 per credit part-time. *Payment plan:* installment. *Waivers:* senior citizens and employees or children of employees.
Applying *Options:* electronic application, early admission. *Recommended:* high school transcript. *Application deadlines:* rolling (freshmen), rolling (transfers).
Freshman Application Contact Mr. Richard Webster, Director of Admissions, Wor-Wic Community College, 32000 Campus Drive, Salisbury, MD 21804. *Phone:* 410-334-2895. *Fax:* 410-334-2954. *E-mail:* admissions@worwic.edu. *Website:* http://www.worwic.edu/.

MASSACHUSETTS

Bay State College
Boston, Massachusetts

- **Independent** primarily 2-year, founded 1946
- **Urban** campus
- **Coed**

Undergraduates 13% are from out of state; 26% live on campus. *Retention:* 76% of full-time freshmen returned.
Faculty *Student/faculty ratio:* 20:1.
Academics *Calendar:* semesters. *Degrees:* certificates, diplomas, associate, and bachelor's. *Special study options:* academic remediation for entering students, accelerated degree program, adult/continuing education programs, advanced placement credit, cooperative education, distance learning, English as a second language, independent study, internships, part-time degree program, study abroad, summer session for credit.
Student Life *Campus security:* late-night transport/escort service, controlled dormitory access, 14-hour patrols by trained security personnel.
Standardized Tests *Recommended:* SAT or ACT (for admission).
Costs (2014–15) *Comprehensive fee:* $36,580 includes full-time tuition ($24,780) and room and board ($11,800). Full-time tuition and fees vary according to class time, location, and program. Part-time tuition: $826 per credit. Part-time tuition and fees vary according to class time, location, and program.
Financial Aid Of all full-time matriculated undergraduates who enrolled in 2013, 20 Federal Work-Study jobs (averaging $2600).
Applying *Options:* electronic application, early admission. *Required:* high school transcript, minimum 2.3 GPA. *Recommended:* interview.
Freshman Application Contact Kimberly Odusami, Director of Admissions, Bay State College, 122 Commonwealth Avenue, Boston, MA 02116. *Phone:* 617-217-9186. *Toll-free phone:* 800-81-LEARN. *E-mail:* admissions@baystate.edu. *Website:* http://www.baystate.edu/.

See display on next page and page 364 for the College Close-Up.

Benjamin Franklin Institute of Technology
Boston, Massachusetts

- **Independent** primarily 2-year, founded 1908
- **Urban** 3-acre campus
- **Coed,** 493 undergraduate students, 87% full-time, 10% women, 90% men

Undergraduates 428 full-time, 65 part-time. 29% Black or African American, non-Hispanic/Latino; 21% Hispanic/Latino; 9% Asian, non-Hispanic/Latino; 0.2% Native Hawaiian or other Pacific Islander, non-Hispanic/Latino; 0.4% American Indian or Alaska Native, non-Hispanic/Latino; 3% Two or more races, non-Hispanic/Latino; 6% Race/ethnicity unknown; 0.8% international.
Freshmen *Admission:* 635 applied, 407 admitted, 210 enrolled. *Test scores:* SAT critical reading scores over 500: 13%; SAT math scores over 500: 24%; SAT writing scores over 500: 11%; SAT critical reading scores over 600: 5%; SAT math scores over 600: 5%; SAT writing scores over 600: 5%; SAT critical reading scores over 700: 3%; SAT writing scores over 700: 2%.
Majors Architectural drafting and CAD/CADD; architectural engineering technology; automobile/automotive mechanics technology; automotive engineering technology; bioengineering and biomedical engineering; biomedical technology; computer engineering technology; computer science; computer technology/computer systems technology; drafting and design technology; electrical and electronic engineering technologies related; electrical and power transmission installation; electrical, electronic and

communications engineering technology; engineering technology; mechanical engineering/mechanical technology; opticianry.

Academics *Calendar:* semesters. *Degrees:* certificates, associate, and bachelor's. *Special study options:* academic remediation for entering students, adult/continuing education programs, advanced placement credit, cooperative education, English as a second language, internships, off-campus study, part-time degree program, services for LD students, summer session for credit.

Library Lufkin Memorial Library with an OPAC.

Student Life *Housing Options:* coed. Campus housing is provided by a third party. Freshman campus housing is guaranteed. *Activities and Organizations:* Phi Theta Kappa, Student Government and Leadership, yearbook and video club, Green Technology Club, Women's Forum. *Campus security:* 24-hour emergency response devices. *Student services:* personal/psychological counseling.

Athletics Member NJCAA. *Intercollegiate sports:* soccer M. *Intramural sports:* basketball M/W, table tennis M/W.

Standardized Tests *Recommended:* SAT or ACT (for admission).

Costs (2014–15) *Comprehensive fee:* $32,050 includes full-time tuition ($16,950), mandatory fees ($1200), and room and board ($13,900). Full-time tuition and fees vary according to course load, degree level, and program. Part-time tuition: $707 per credit hour. Part-time tuition and fees vary according to course load, degree level, and program. *Room and board:* Room and board charges vary according to housing facility. *Payment plan:* installment. *Waivers:* employees or children of employees.

Applying *Options:* electronic application, deferred entrance. *Application fee:* $25. *Required:* high school transcript. *Recommended:* essay or personal statement, minimum 2.0 GPA, interview.

Freshman Application Contact Ms. Brittainy Johnson, Associate Director of Admissions, Benjamin Franklin Institute of Technology, Boston, MA 02116. *Phone:* 617-423-4630 Ext. 122. *Toll-free phone:* 877-400-BFIT. *Fax:* 617-482-3706. *E-mail:* bjohnson@bfit.edu. *Website:* http://www.bfit.edu/.

Berkshire Community College
Pittsfield, Massachusetts

- **State-supported** 2-year, founded 1960, part of Massachusetts Public Higher Education System
- **Rural** 180-acre campus with easy access to Hartford, CT and Albany, NY
- **Endowment** $8.7 million
- **Coed**

Undergraduates 821 full-time, 1,579 part-time. Students come from 5 states and territories; 4 other countries; 2% are from out of state; 7% Black or African American, non-Hispanic/Latino; 6% Hispanic/Latino; 2% Asian, non-Hispanic/Latino; 0.1% Native Hawaiian or other Pacific Islander, non-Hispanic/Latino; 0.3% American Indian or Alaska Native, non-Hispanic/Latino; 2% Two or more races, non-Hispanic/Latino; 3% Race/ethnicity unknown; 0.3% international; 42% transferred in. *Retention:* 48% of full-time freshmen returned.

Faculty *Student/faculty ratio:* 15:1.

Academics *Calendar:* semesters. *Degree:* certificates and associate. *Special study options:* academic remediation for entering students, accelerated degree program, adult/continuing education programs, advanced placement credit, cooperative education, distance learning, double majors, English as a second language, honors programs, independent study, internships, off-campus study, part-time degree program, services for LD students, summer session for credit.

Student Life *Campus security:* 24-hour emergency response devices and patrols, late-night transport/escort service.

Costs (2014–15) *Tuition:* state resident $624 full-time, $26 per credit hour part-time; nonresident $6240 full-time, $260 per credit hour part-time. Full-time tuition and fees vary according to class time, course load, and reciprocity agreements. Part-time tuition and fees vary according to class time, course load, and reciprocity agreements. *Required fees:* $4034 full-time, $166 per credit hour part-time, $25 per term part-time.

Financial Aid Of all full-time matriculated undergraduates who enrolled in 2013, 1,655 applied for aid, 1,483 were judged to have need. 164 Federal Work-Study jobs (averaging $508). 122 state and other part-time jobs (averaging $675). In 2013, 5. *Average financial aid package:* $5957. *Average need-based loan:* $1768. *Average need-based gift aid:* $4073. *Average non-need-based aid:* $580.

Applying *Options:* deferred entrance. *Application fee:* $10. *Required:* high school transcript. *Recommended:* interview.

Freshman Application Contact Ms. Tina Schettini, Enrollment Services, Berkshire Community College, 1350 West Street, Pittsfield, MA 01201-5786.

Phone: 413-236-1635. *Toll-free phone:* 800-816-1233. *Fax:* 413-496-9511. *E-mail:* tschetti@berkshirecc.edu. *Website:* http://www.berkshirecc.edu/.

Bristol Community College
Fall River, Massachusetts

- **State-supported** 2-year, founded 1965, part of Massachusetts Community College System
- **Urban** 105-acre campus with easy access to Boston
- **Endowment** $4.4 million
- **Coed**

Undergraduates 4,429 full-time, 4,906 part-time. Students come from 13 other countries; 6% are from out of state; 7% Black or African American, non-Hispanic/Latino; 8% Hispanic/Latino; 2% Asian, non-Hispanic/Latino; 0.1% Native Hawaiian or other Pacific Islander, non-Hispanic/Latino; 0.4% American Indian or Alaska Native, non-Hispanic/Latino; 4% Two or more races, non-Hispanic/Latino; 3% Race/ethnicity unknown; 0.1% international. **Faculty** *Student/faculty ratio:* 19:1.

Academics *Calendar:* semesters. *Degree:* certificates and associate. *Special study options:* academic remediation for entering students, accelerated degree program, adult/continuing education programs, advanced placement credit, cooperative education, distance learning, English as a second language, honors programs, independent study, internships, off-campus study, part-time degree program, services for LD students, student-designed majors, summer session for credit.

Student Life *Campus security:* 24-hour emergency response devices and patrols, late-night transport/escort service.

Athletics Member NJCAA.

Costs (2014–15) *Tuition:* state resident $720 full-time, $24 per credit part-time; nonresident $6900 full-time, $230 per credit part-time. Full-time tuition and fees vary according to course load. Part-time tuition and fees vary according to course load. *Required fees:* $4484 full-time.

Financial Aid Of all full-time matriculated undergraduates who enrolled in 2013, 205 Federal Work-Study jobs (averaging $1627). 65 state and other part-time jobs (averaging $1478).

Applying *Options:* electronic application, deferred entrance. *Application fee:* $10. *Required:* high school transcript.

Freshman Application Contact Ms. Shilo Henriques, Dean of Admissions, Bristol Community College, 777 Elsbree Street, Fall River, MA 02720. *Phone:* 508-678-2811 Ext. 2947. *Fax:* 508-730-3265. *E-mail:* Shilo.Henriques@bristolcc.edu. *Website:* http://www.bristolcc.edu/.

Bunker Hill Community College
Boston, Massachusetts

- **State-supported** 2-year, founded 1973
- **Urban** 21-acre campus
- **Endowment** $5.0 million
- **Coed,** 14,253 undergraduate students, 32% full-time, 57% women, 43% men

Undergraduates 4,550 full-time, 9,703 part-time. 27% Black or African American, non-Hispanic/Latino; 23% Hispanic/Latino; 10% Asian, non-Hispanic/Latino; 0.2% Native Hawaiian or other Pacific Islander, non-Hispanic/Latino; 0.3% American Indian or Alaska Native, non-Hispanic/Latino; 3% Two or more races, non-Hispanic/Latino; 6% Race/ethnicity unknown; 5% international; 7% transferred in.

Freshmen *Admission:* 2,395 applied, 2,395 admitted, 2,395 enrolled. **Faculty** *Total:* 735, 21% full-time. *Student/faculty ratio:* 20:1.

Majors Accounting; art; bioengineering and biomedical engineering; biology/biological sciences; biotechnology; business administration and management; business administration, management and operations related; business operations support and secretarial services related; cardiovascular technology; chemistry; clinical/medical laboratory technology; computer and information sciences and support services related; computer and information systems security; computer/information technology services administration related; computer programming; computer programming (specific applications); computer science; computer systems networking and telecommunications; criminal justice/law enforcement administration; criminal justice/police science; culinary arts; data entry/microcomputer applications; design and visual communications; diagnostic medical sonography and ultrasound technology; dramatic/theater arts; early childhood education; education; electrical/electronics maintenance and repair technology related; engineering; English; entrepreneurship; finance; fire prevention and safety technology; foreign languages and literatures; general studies; health information/medical records administration; history; hospitality administration; hospitality administration related; human services; international business/trade/commerce; legal assistant/paralegal; mass

communication/media; mathematics; medical administrative assistant and medical secretary; medical radiologic technology; music; operations management; physics; psychology; registered nursing/registered nurse; respiratory therapy technician; sociology; speech communication and rhetoric; tourism and travel services management; web page, digital/multimedia and information resources design.

Academics *Calendar:* semesters. *Degree:* certificates and associate. *Special study options:* academic remediation for entering students, accelerated degree program, advanced placement credit, cooperative education, distance learning, English as a second language, external degree program, honors programs, independent study, internships, part-time degree program, services for LD students, study abroad, summer session for credit.

Library Bunker Hill Community College Library with 46,996 titles, 20,074 audiovisual materials, an OPAC, a Web page.

Student Life *Housing:* college housing not available. *Activities and Organizations:* drama/theater group, student-run radio station, choral group, Alpha Kappa Mu Honor Society, Asian-Pacific Students Association, Music Club, Latinos Unidos Club, Haitian Students Club. *Campus security:* 24-hour emergency response devices and patrols, late-night transport/escort service. *Student services:* health clinic, personal/psychological counseling.

Athletics Member NJCAA. *Intercollegiate sports:* baseball M, basketball M/W, soccer M/W, volleyball W. *Intramural sports:* basketball M/W, volleyball M/W.

Costs (2015–16) *Tuition:* state resident $576 full-time, $24 per credit hour part-time; nonresident $5520 full-time, $230 per credit hour part-time. Full-time tuition and fees vary according to course load, program, and reciprocity agreements. Part-time tuition and fees vary according to course load, program, and reciprocity agreements. *Required fees:* $3000 full-time, $125 per credit hour part-time. *Payment plan:* installment. *Waivers:* minority students, senior citizens, and employees or children of employees.

Financial Aid Of all full-time matriculated undergraduates who enrolled in 2010, 135 Federal Work-Study jobs (averaging $2376).

Applying *Application fee:* $10. *Application deadlines:* rolling (freshmen), rolling (transfers). *Notification:* continuous (freshmen), continuous (transfers).

Freshman Application Contact Vanessa Whaley Rowley, Director of Enrollment Management and Admissions, Bunker Hill Community College, 250 New Rutherford Avenue, Boston, MA 02129. *Phone:* 617-228-3398. *Fax:* 617-228-3481. *E-mail:* admissions@bhcc.mass.edu. *Website:* http://www.bhcc.mass.edu/.

Cape Cod Community College
West Barnstable, Massachusetts

Freshman Application Contact Director of Admissions, Cape Cod Community College, 2240 Iyannough Road, West Barnstable, MA 02668-1599. *Phone:* 508-362-2131 Ext. 4311. *Toll-free phone:* 877-846-3672. *Fax:* 508-375-4089. *E-mail:* admiss@capecod.edu. *Website:* http://www.capecod.edu/.

Dean College
Franklin, Massachusetts

- **Independent** primarily 2-year, founded 1865
- **Small-town** 100-acre campus with easy access to Boston, Providence
- **Endowment** $38.9 million
- **Coed,** 1,292 undergraduate students, 83% full-time, 52% women, 48% men

Undergraduates 1,069 full-time, 223 part-time. Students come from 31 states and territories; 16 other countries; 47% are from out of state; 14% Black or African American, non-Hispanic/Latino; 5% Hispanic/Latino; 3% Asian, non-Hispanic/Latino; 0.1% Native Hawaiian or other Pacific Islander, non-Hispanic/Latino; 0.3% American Indian or Alaska Native, non-Hispanic/Latino; 3% Two or more races, non-Hispanic/Latino; 20% Race/ethnicity unknown; 10% international; 6% transferred in; 89% live on campus. *Retention:* 70% of full-time freshmen returned.

Freshmen *Admission:* 2,646 applied, 1,806 admitted, 454 enrolled. *Average high school GPA:* 2.5. *Test scores:* SAT critical reading scores over 500: 22%; SAT math scores over 500: 17%; SAT writing scores over 500: 20%; ACT scores over 18: 44%; SAT critical reading scores over 600: 4%; SAT math scores over 600: 3%; SAT writing scores over 600: 2%; ACT scores over 24: 5%; SAT critical reading scores over 700: 1%; SAT writing scores over 700: 1%.

Faculty *Total:* 151, 21% full-time, 25% with terminal degrees. *Student/faculty ratio:* 16:1.

Majors Arts, entertainment, and media management; athletic training; biology/biological sciences; business administration and management; criminal justice/safety; dance; dramatic/theater arts; early childhood education; English; environmental studies; general studies; health and wellness; history; liberal arts and sciences/liberal studies; mass communication/media;

mathematics; psychology; sociology; sport and fitness administration/management.

Academics *Calendar:* semesters. *Degrees:* certificates, diplomas, associate, and bachelor's. *Special study options:* adult/continuing education programs, advanced placement credit, cooperative education, distance learning, double majors, English as a second language, honors programs, independent study, internships, off-campus study, part-time degree program, services for LD students, student-designed majors, study abroad, summer session for credit.

Library E. Ross Anderson Library with 38,150 titles, 825 audiovisual materials, an OPAC, a Web page.

Student Life *Housing Options:* coed, men-only, women-only, special housing for students with disabilities. Campus housing is university owned. Freshman campus housing is guaranteed. *Activities and Organizations:* student-run radio station, National Society of Leadership and Success, Student Activities Committee, Residence Hall Association, International Student Association, Phi Theta Kappa. *Campus security:* 24-hour emergency response devices and patrols, late-night transport/escort service, controlled dormitory access. *Student services:* health clinic, personal/psychological counseling.

Athletics Member NJCAA. *Intercollegiate sports:* baseball M(s), basketball M(s)/W(s), football M(s), golf M, lacrosse M(s)/W(s), soccer M(s)/W(s), softball W(s), volleyball W(s). *Intramural sports:* basketball M, football M, golf M, lacrosse M, soccer M, volleyball M/W.

Standardized Tests *Recommended:* SAT or ACT (for admission).

Costs (2015–16) *Comprehensive fee:* $50,920 includes full-time tuition ($35,420), mandatory fees ($300), and room and board ($15,200). Full-time tuition and fees vary according to class time, course load, and program. Part-time tuition: $313 per credit. Part-time tuition and fees vary according to class time, course load, and program. *Required fees:* $25 per term part-time. *Room and board:* college room only: $9600. Room and board charges vary according to housing facility. *Payment plan:* installment. *Waivers:* employees or children of employees.

Applying *Options:* electronic application, early admission, early action, deferred entrance. *Required:* high school transcript. *Required for some:* audition is required for performing arts majors. *Recommended:* essay or personal statement, minimum 2.0 GPA, 1 letter of recommendation, interview. *Application deadlines:* rolling (freshmen), 12/1 (early action). *Notification:* continuous (freshmen), 1/15 (early action).

Freshman Application Contact Iris P. Godes, Assistant Vice President of Enrollment Services and Dean of Admissions, Dean College, 99 Main Street, Franklin, MA 02038. *Phone:* 508-541-1547. *Toll-free phone:* 877-TRY-DEAN. *Fax:* 508-541-8726. *E-mail:* igodes@dean.edu. *Website:* http://www.dean.edu/.

FINE Mortuary College, LLC
Norwood, Massachusetts

Freshman Application Contact Dean Marsha Wise, Admissions Office, FINE Mortuary College, LLC, 150 Kerry Place, Norwood, MA 02062. *Phone:* 781-762-1211. *Fax:* 781-762-7177. *E-mail:* mwise@fine-ne.com. *Website:* http://www.fine-ne.com/.

Greenfield Community College
Greenfield, Massachusetts

- **State-supported** 2-year, founded 1962, part of Commonwealth of Massachusetts Department of Higher Education
- **Small-town** 120-acre campus
- **Coed,** 2,127 undergraduate students, 36% full-time, 60% women, 40% men

Undergraduates 758 full-time, 1,369 part-time. 8% are from out of state; 3% Black or African American, non-Hispanic/Latino; 7% Hispanic/Latino; 4% Asian, non-Hispanic/Latino; 0.6% American Indian or Alaska Native, non-Hispanic/Latino; 3% Two or more races, non-Hispanic/Latino; 4% Race/ethnicity unknown; 11% transferred in. *Retention:* 60% of full-time freshmen returned.

Freshmen *Admission:* 370 enrolled.

Faculty *Student/faculty ratio:* 13:1.

Majors Accounting technology and bookkeeping; acting; administrative assistant and secretarial science; American studies; art; business administration and management; business/commerce; community health services counseling; computer and information sciences; computer and information sciences and support services related; criminal justice/police science; crop production; dance; early childhood education; economics; education; engineering science; English; environmental science; film/video and photographic arts related; fine/studio arts; fire prevention and safety technology; food science; health professions related; hospitality administration; international relations and affairs; liberal arts and sciences/liberal studies; music performance; natural resources/conservation related; registered nursing/registered nurse; sales,

distribution, and marketing operations; social sciences; social sciences related; women's studies.

Academics *Calendar:* semesters. *Degree:* certificates and associate. *Special study options:* academic remediation for entering students, adult/continuing education programs, advanced placement credit, cooperative education, distance learning, double majors, English as a second language, independent study, internships, part-time degree program, services for LD students, summer session for credit.

Library Greenfield Community College Library with 69,974 titles, 1,158 audiovisual materials, an OPAC, a Web page.

Student Life *Housing:* college housing not available. *Activities and Organizations:* drama/theater group, choral group, Student Senate, Art Club, Business Club, Active Minds Club, International Students Club. *Campus security:* 24-hour emergency response devices and patrols, late-night transport/escort service. *Student services:* personal/psychological counseling, women's center, legal services.

Standardized Tests *Required for some:* Psychological Corporation Practical Nursing Entrance Examination.

Costs (2015–16) *Tuition:* state resident $624 full-time; nonresident $6744 full-time. Full-time tuition and fees vary according to class time, course load, and program. Part-time tuition and fees vary according to class time, course load, and program. *Required fees:* $4334 full-time. *Payment plan:* installment. *Waivers:* senior citizens and employees or children of employees.

Applying *Options:* electronic application. *Required for some:* high school transcript, interview. *Application deadlines:* rolling (freshmen), rolling (transfers).

Freshman Application Contact Ms. Colleen Kucinski, Assistant Director of Admission, Greenfield Community College, 1 College Drive, Greenfield, MA 01301-9739. *Phone:* 413-775-1000. *Fax:* 413-773-5129. *E-mail:* admission@gcc.mass.edu. *Website:* http://www.gcc.mass.edu/.

Holyoke Community College
Holyoke, Massachusetts

- **State-supported** 2-year, founded 1946, part of Massachusetts Public Higher Education System
- **Small-town** 135-acre campus
- **Endowment** $12.9 million
- **Coed,** 6,604 undergraduate students, 46% full-time, 62% women, 38% men

Undergraduates 3,017 full-time, 3,587 part-time. Students come from 16 states and territories; 1% are from out of state; 6% Black or African American, non-Hispanic/Latino; 23% Hispanic/Latino; 2% Asian, non-Hispanic/Latino; 0.5% American Indian or Alaska Native, non-Hispanic/Latino; 3% Two or more races, non-Hispanic/Latino; 4% Race/ethnicity unknown; 0.4% international; 7% transferred in.

Freshmen *Admission:* 1,495 enrolled.

Faculty *Total:* 491, 26% full-time, 25% with terminal degrees. *Student/faculty ratio:* 17:1.

Majors Accounting technology and bookkeeping; administrative assistant and secretarial science; art; business administration and management; child-care and support services management; computer programming (specific applications); criminal justice/safety; engineering; environmental control technologies related; health and physical education/fitness; hospitality administration related; liberal arts and sciences and humanities related; liberal arts and sciences/liberal studies; medical radiologic technology; music; opticianry; registered nursing/registered nurse; retailing; social work; sport and fitness administration/management; veterinary/animal health technology.

Academics *Calendar:* semesters. *Degree:* certificates and associate. *Special study options:* academic remediation for entering students, adult/continuing education programs, advanced placement credit, cooperative education, distance learning, double majors, English as a second language, external degree program, honors programs, independent study, internships, off-campus study, part-time degree program, services for LD students, student-designed majors, study abroad, summer session for credit. *ROTC:* Army (c), Air Force (c).

Library Holyoke Community College Library plus 1 other with 61,425 titles, 5,524 audiovisual materials, an OPAC, a Web page.

Student Life *Housing:* college housing not available. *Activities and Organizations:* drama/theater group, student-run newspaper, radio station, Drama Club, Japanese Anime Club, Student Senate, LISA Club, STRIVE. *Campus security:* 24-hour emergency response devices and patrols, late-night transport/escort service. *Student services:* health clinic, personal/psychological counseling, women's center.

Athletics Member NJCAA. *Intercollegiate sports:* baseball M, basketball M/W, cross-country running M/W, golf M/W, soccer M/W, softball W, track and field M/W, volleyball W.

Costs (2014–15) *One-time required fee:* $65. *Tuition:* state resident $576 full-time, $152 per credit hour part-time; nonresident $5520 full-time, $358 per

credit hour part-time. Full-time tuition and fees vary according to course load. Part-time tuition and fees vary according to course load. *Required fees:* $3262 full-time, $95 per term part-time. *Payment plan:* installment. *Waivers:* senior citizens and employees or children of employees.
Applying *Options:* electronic application, early admission, deferred entrance. *Required:* high school transcript. *Recommended:* interview. *Application deadlines:* rolling (freshmen), rolling (transfers). *Notification:* continuous (freshmen), continuous (transfers).
Freshman Application Contact Ms. Marcia Rosbury-Henne, Director of Admissions and Transfer Affairs, Holyoke Community College, Admission Office, Holyoke, MA 01040. *Phone:* 413-552-2321. *Fax:* 413-552-2045. *E-mail:* admissions@hcc.edu.
Website: http://www.hcc.edu/.

ITT Technical Institute
Norwood, Massachusetts

- **Proprietary** primarily 2-year, founded 1990, part of ITT Educational Services, Inc.
- **Suburban** campus
- **Coed**

Academics *Calendar:* quarters. *Degrees:* associate and bachelor's.
Freshman Application Contact Director of Recruitment, ITT Technical Institute, 333 Providence Highway, Norwood, MA 02062. *Phone:* 781-278-7200. *Toll-free phone:* 800-879-8324.
Website: http://www.itt-tech.edu/.

ITT Technical Institute
Wilmington, Massachusetts

- **Proprietary** primarily 2-year, founded 2000, part of ITT Educational Services, Inc.
- **Coed**

Academics *Calendar:* quarters. *Degrees:* associate and bachelor's.
Freshman Application Contact Director of Recruitment, ITT Technical Institute, 200 Ballardvale Street, Suite 200, Wilmington, MA 01887. *Phone:* 978-658-2636. *Toll-free phone:* 800-430-5097.
Website: http://www.itt-tech.edu/.

Labouré College
Boston, Massachusetts

Director of Admissions Ms. Gina M. Morrissette, Director of Admissions, Labouré College, 2120 Dorchester Avenue, Boston, MA 02124-5698. *Phone:* 617-296-8300.
Website: http://www.laboure.edu/.

Le Cordon Bleu College of Culinary Arts in Boston
Cambridge, Massachusetts

Admissions Office Contact Le Cordon Bleu College of Culinary Arts in Boston, 215 First Street, Cambridge, MA 02142.
Website: http://www.chefs.edu/boston/.

Marian Court College
Swampscott, Massachusetts

Director of Admissions Bryan Boppert, Director of Admissions, Marian Court College, 35 Little's Point Road, Swampscott, MA 01907-2840. *Phone:* 781-309-5230. *Fax:* 781-309-5286.
Website: http://www.mariancourt.edu/.

Massachusetts Bay Community College
Wellesley Hills, Massachusetts

- **State-supported** 2-year, founded 1961
- **Suburban** 84-acre campus with easy access to Boston
- **Coed,** 5,369 undergraduate students, 35% full-time, 55% women, 45% men

Undergraduates 1,874 full-time, 3,495 part-time. Students come from 13 states and territories; 102 other countries; 2% are from out of state; 16% Black or African American, non-Hispanic/Latino; 15% Hispanic/Latino; 5% Asian, non-Hispanic/Latino; 0.7% American Indian or Alaska Native, non-Hispanic/Latino; 14% Race/ethnicity unknown; 2% international; 5% transferred in. *Retention:* 63% of full-time freshmen returned.

Freshmen *Admission:* 1,887 applied, 1,885 admitted, 1,206 enrolled.
Faculty *Total:* 346, 25% full-time. *Student/faculty ratio:* 18:1.
Majors Accounting; automotive engineering technology; biological and physical sciences; biology/biotechnology laboratory technician; business administration and management; business/commerce; chemical technology; child-care and support services management; computer and information sciences; computer engineering technology; computer science; criminal justice/law enforcement administration; drafting and design technology; engineering technology; environmental engineering technology; forensic science and technology; general studies; hospitality administration; human services; information science/studies; international relations and affairs; legal assistant/paralegal; liberal arts and sciences/liberal studies; mechanical engineering/mechanical engineering technology; medical radiologic technology; physical therapy technology; registered nursing/registered nurse; respiratory care therapy; social sciences; speech communication and rhetoric.
Academics *Calendar:* semesters. *Degree:* certificates and associate. *Special study options:* academic remediation for entering students, adult/continuing education programs, advanced placement credit, cooperative education, distance learning, honors programs, internships, part-time degree program, services for LD students, summer session for credit.
Library Perkins Library with 51,429 titles, 4,780 audiovisual materials, an OPAC, a Web page.
Student Life *Housing:* college housing not available. *Activities and Organizations:* drama/theater group, student-run newspaper, Student Government Association, Latino Student Organization, New World Society Club, Mass Bay Players, Student Occupational Therapy Association. *Campus security:* 24-hour emergency response devices and patrols. *Student services:* health clinic, personal/psychological counseling.
Athletics Member NJCAA. *Intercollegiate sports:* baseball M, basketball M/W, cross-country running M/W, golf M/W, soccer M/W, softball W, tennis M/W, volleyball W. *Intramural sports:* ice hockey M, soccer M/W.
Costs (2015–16) *Tuition:* state resident $576 full-time, $24 per credit part-time; nonresident $5520 full-time, $230 per credit part-time. Full-time tuition and fees vary according to class time, program, and reciprocity agreements. Part-time tuition and fees vary according to class time, program, and reciprocity agreements. *Required fees:* $3680 full-time, $130 per credit part-time, $20 per term part-time. *Payment plan:* installment. *Waivers:* senior citizens and employees or children of employees.
Financial Aid Of all full-time matriculated undergraduates who enrolled in 2013, 59 Federal Work-Study jobs (averaging $1840).
Applying *Options:* electronic application, deferred entrance. *Application fee:* $20. *Application deadlines:* rolling (freshmen), rolling (transfers). *Notification:* continuous (freshmen), continuous (transfers).
Freshman Application Contact Ms. Lisa Slavin, Director of Admissions, Massachusetts Bay Community College, 50 Oakland Street, Wellesley Hills, MA 02481. *Phone:* 781-239-2500. *Fax:* 781-239-1047. *E-mail:* lslavin@massbay.edu.
Website: http://www.massbay.edu/.

Massasoit Community College
Brockton, Massachusetts

Freshman Application Contact Michelle Hughes, Director of Admissions, Massasoit Community College, 1 Massasoit Boulevard, Brockton, MA 02302-3996. *Phone:* 508-588-9100. *Toll-free phone:* 800-CAREERS.
Website: http://www.massasoit.mass.edu/.

Middlesex Community College
Bedford, Massachusetts

- **State-supported** 2-year, founded 1970, part of Massachusetts Public Higher Education System
- **Suburban** 200-acre campus with easy access to Boston
- **Coed,** 9,205 undergraduate students, 38% full-time, 58% women, 42% men

Undergraduates 3,537 full-time, 5,668 part-time. 7% Black or African American, non-Hispanic/Latino; 18% Hispanic/Latino; 11% Asian, non-Hispanic/Latino; 0.1% Native Hawaiian or other Pacific Islander, non-Hispanic/Latino; 0.2% American Indian or Alaska Native, non-Hispanic/Latino; 2% Two or more races, non-Hispanic/Latino; 0.7% Race/ethnicity unknown; 1% international.
Freshmen *Admission:* 1,845 enrolled.
Majors Aircraft powerplant technology; art; biology/biological sciences; biology/biotechnology laboratory technician; business administration and management; commercial and advertising art; computer and information sciences; computer and information sciences and support services related; computer engineering technology; computer programming; criminal justice/law enforcement administration; dental assisting; dental hygiene; dental laboratory technology; diagnostic medical sonography and ultrasound

technology; electrical, electronic and communications engineering technology; electrical/electronics drafting and CAD/CADD; elementary education; engineering technologies and engineering related; fashion merchandising; fire science/firefighting; general studies; hotel/motel administration; kindergarten/preschool education; legal assistant/paralegal; liberal arts and sciences/liberal studies; medical/clinical assistant; medical radiologic technology; office occupations and clerical services; physical sciences; psychiatric/mental health services technology; registered nursing/registered nurse; web page, digital/multimedia and information resources design.

Academics *Calendar:* semesters. *Degree:* certificates and associate. *Special study options:* academic remediation for entering students, accelerated degree program, adult/continuing education programs, advanced placement credit, cooperative education, distance learning, English as a second language, honors programs, independent study, internships, off-campus study, part-time degree program, services for LD students, study abroad, summer session for credit. *ROTC:* Air Force (c).

Library Main Library plus 1 other with 52,960 titles, an OPAC, a Web page.

Student Life *Housing:* college housing not available. *Activities and Organizations:* drama/theater group, student-run newspaper. *Campus security:* 24-hour emergency response devices and patrols. *Student services:* health clinic, personal/psychological counseling, legal services.

Athletics *Intramural sports:* basketball M/W, table tennis M/W, volleyball M/W.

Standardized Tests *Required for some:* CPT.

Costs (2014–15) *Tuition:* state resident $4344 full-time; nonresident $9288 full-time. Full-time tuition and fees vary according to course load and reciprocity agreements. Part-time tuition and fees vary according to course load and reciprocity agreements. *Required fees:* $50 full-time. *Payment plan:* installment. *Waivers:* senior citizens and employees or children of employees.

Financial Aid Of all full-time matriculated undergraduates who enrolled in 2013, 68 Federal Work-Study jobs (averaging $2200).

Applying *Options:* electronic application, early admission. *Required for some:* essay or personal statement, high school transcript, 3 letters of recommendation, interview. *Application deadlines:* rolling (freshmen), rolling (transfers). *Notification:* continuous (freshmen), continuous (transfers).

Freshman Application Contact Middlesex Community College, 591 Springs Road, Bedford, MA 01730-1655. *Phone:* 978-656-3211. *Toll-free phone:* 800-818-3434.

Website: http://www.middlesex.mass.edu/.

Mount Wachusett Community College
Gardner, Massachusetts

- **State-supported** 2-year, founded 1963, part of Massachusetts Public Higher Education System
- **Small-town** 270-acre campus with easy access to Boston
- **Endowment** $4.0 million
- **Coed,** 4,336 undergraduate students, 41% full-time, 64% women, 36% men

Undergraduates 1,764 full-time, 2,572 part-time. 4% are from out of state; 7% Black or African American, non-Hispanic/Latino; 15% Hispanic/Latino; 2% Asian, non-Hispanic/Latino; 0.1% Native Hawaiian or other Pacific Islander, non-Hispanic/Latino; 0.5% American Indian or Alaska Native, non-Hispanic/Latino; 2% Two or more races, non-Hispanic/Latino; 2% Race/ethnicity unknown; 0.4% international; 7% transferred in.

Freshmen *Admission:* 1,829 applied, 1,818 admitted, 800 enrolled. *Average high school GPA:* 2.72.

Faculty *Total:* 408, 19% full-time, 15% with terminal degrees. *Student/faculty ratio:* 14:1.

Majors Allied health and medical assisting services related; alternative and complementary medical support services related; art; automobile/automotive mechanics technology; biotechnology; business administration and management; business/commerce; child-care and support services management; child development; clinical/medical laboratory technology; computer and information sciences; computer graphics; corrections; criminal justice/law enforcement administration; dental hygiene; energy management and systems technology; environmental studies; fire prevention and safety technology; general studies; health information/medical records administration; human services; legal assistant/paralegal; liberal arts and sciences/liberal studies; medical/clinical assistant; physical therapy technology; plastics and polymer engineering technology; radio and television broadcasting technology; registered nursing/registered nurse; web page, digital/multimedia and information resources design.

Academics *Calendar:* semesters. *Degree:* certificates, diplomas, and associate. *Special study options:* academic remediation for entering students, accelerated degree program, adult/continuing education programs, advanced placement credit, cooperative education, distance learning, double majors, English as a second language, honors programs, independent study, internships, part-time degree program, services for LD students, study abroad, summer session for credit. *ROTC:* Army (c).

Library LaChance Library with 47,500 titles, 450 audiovisual materials, an OPAC, a Web page.

Student Life *Housing:* college housing not available. *Activities and Organizations:* drama/theater group, student-run newspaper, choral group, Green Society Group, Dental Hygienist Club, ESL Club, Student Government Association, Student Nurses Association. *Campus security:* 24-hour emergency response devices and patrols. *Student services:* health clinic, personal/psychological counseling.

Athletics *Intramural sports:* badminton M/W, basketball M/W, football M/W, soccer M/W, softball M/W, table tennis M/W, volleyball M/W, water polo M/W.

Costs (2014–15) *Tuition:* state resident $750 full-time, $25 per credit hour part-time; nonresident $6900 full-time, $230 per credit hour part-time. Full-time tuition and fees vary according to program and reciprocity agreements. Part-time tuition and fees vary according to program and reciprocity agreements. *Required fees:* $5160 full-time, $172 per credit hour part-time, $170 per term part-time. *Payment plan:* installment. *Waivers:* senior citizens and employees or children of employees.

Financial Aid Of all full-time matriculated undergraduates who enrolled in 2013, 47 Federal Work-Study jobs (averaging $2228).

Applying *Options:* electronic application, early admission. *Required:* high school transcript. *Required for some:* 2 letters of recommendation. *Recommended:* interview. *Application deadlines:* rolling (freshmen), rolling (transfers). *Notification:* continuous (freshmen), continuous (transfers).

Freshman Application Contact Ms. Ann McDonald JD, Executive Vice President, Mount Wachusett Community College, 444 Green Street, Gardner, MA 01440-1378. *Phone:* 978-632-6600 Ext. 103. *Fax:* 978-630-9558. *E-mail:* admissions@mwcc.mass.edu.

Website: http://www.mwcc.mass.edu/.

Northern Essex Community College
Haverhill, Massachusetts

- **State-supported** 2-year, founded 1960
- **Suburban** 106-acre campus with easy access to Boston
- **Endowment** $2.9 million
- **Coed,** 6,963 undergraduate students, 33% full-time, 62% women, 38% men

Undergraduates 2,298 full-time, 4,665 part-time. Students come from 13 states and territories; 15% are from out of state; 4% Black or African American, non-Hispanic/Latino; 39% Hispanic/Latino; 2% Asian, non-Hispanic/Latino; 0.5% Native Hawaiian or other Pacific Islander, non-Hispanic/Latino; 0.2% American Indian or Alaska Native, non-Hispanic/Latino; 1% Two or more races, non-Hispanic/Latino; 1% Race/ethnicity unknown; 0.5% international. *Retention:* 62% of full-time freshmen returned.

Freshmen *Admission:* 3,000 applied, 2,800 admitted, 1,365 enrolled.

Faculty *Total:* 657, 16% full-time. *Student/faculty ratio:* 21:1.

Majors Accounting; administrative assistant and secretarial science; biological and physical sciences; business administration and management; business teacher education; civil engineering technology; commercial and advertising art; computer and information sciences; computer engineering technology; computer graphics; computer programming; computer programming related; computer programming (specific applications); computer science; computer systems networking and telecommunications; computer typography and composition equipment operation; criminal justice/law enforcement administration; dance; data processing and data processing technology; dental assisting; dramatic/theater arts; education; electrical, electronic and communications engineering technology; elementary education; engineering science; finance; general studies; health information/medical records administration; history; hotel/motel administration; human services; industrial radiologic technology; international relations and affairs; journalism; kindergarten/preschool education; legal assistant/paralegal; liberal arts and sciences/liberal studies; machine tool technology; marketing/marketing management; materials science; medical administrative assistant and medical secretary; medical transcription; mental health counseling; music; parks, recreation and leisure; physical education teaching and coaching; political science and government; radiologic technology/science; real estate; registered nursing/registered nurse; respiratory care therapy; respiratory therapy technician; sign language interpretation and translation; telecommunications technology; tourism and travel services management; web/multimedia management and webmaster; web page, digital/multimedia and information resources design; women's studies.

Academics *Calendar:* semesters. *Degree:* certificates and associate. *Special study options:* academic remediation for entering students, adult/continuing education programs, advanced placement credit, cooperative education, distance learning, double majors, English as a second language, freshman honors college, honors programs, independent study, internships, off-campus study, part-time degree program, services for LD students, study abroad, summer session for credit. *ROTC:* Air Force (c).

Library Bentley Library with 61,120 titles, an OPAC.
Student Life *Housing:* college housing not available. *Activities and Organizations:* drama/theater group, student-run newspaper. *Campus security:* 24-hour emergency response devices and patrols. *Student services:* health clinic, personal/psychological counseling, women's center.
Athletics Member NJCAA. *Intercollegiate sports:* baseball M, basketball M/W, cross-country running M/W, softball W, volleyball M/W. *Intramural sports:* basketball M/W, cross-country running M/W, football M/W, golf M/W, racquetball M/W, skiing (cross-country) M/W, skiing (downhill) M/W, weight lifting M/W.
Standardized Tests *Required:* Psychological Corporation Aptitude Test for Practical Nursing (for admission).
Costs (2014–15) *Tuition:* state resident $600 full-time, $25 per credit hour part-time; nonresident $6384 full-time, $266 per credit hour part-time. Full-time tuition and fees vary according to program and reciprocity agreements. Part-time tuition and fees vary according to program and reciprocity agreements. *Required fees:* $3720 full-time, $155 per credit hour part-time. *Payment plan:* installment. *Waivers:* employees or children of employees.
Financial Aid Of all full-time matriculated undergraduates who enrolled in 2013, 74 Federal Work-Study jobs (averaging $1759).
Applying *Options:* early admission. *Application fee:* $25. *Required:* high school transcript. *Application deadlines:* rolling (freshmen), rolling (transfers). *Notification:* continuous (freshmen), continuous (transfers).
Freshman Application Contact Ms. Laurie Dimitrov, Director of Admissions, Northern Essex Community College, Haverhill, MA 01830. *Phone:* 978-556-3616. *Fax:* 978-556-3155.
Website: http://www.necc.mass.edu/.

North Shore Community College
Danvers, Massachusetts

- **State-supported** 2-year, founded 1965
- **Suburban** campus with easy access to Boston
- **Endowment** $5.5 million
- **Coed,** 7,412 undergraduate students, 35% full-time, 60% women, 40% men

Undergraduates 2,575 full-time, 4,837 part-time. Students come from 9 states and territories; 8 other countries; 2% are from out of state; 10% Black or African American, non-Hispanic/Latino; 22% Hispanic/Latino; 4% Asian, non-Hispanic/Latino; 0.1% Native Hawaiian or other Pacific Islander, non-Hispanic/Latino; 0.2% American Indian or Alaska Native, non-Hispanic/Latino; 2% Two or more races, non-Hispanic/Latino; 3% Race/ethnicity unknown; 0.2% international; 7% transferred in.
Freshmen *Admission:* 4,139 applied, 3,601 admitted, 1,301 enrolled.
Faculty *Total:* 486, 28% full-time, 18% with terminal degrees. *Student/faculty ratio:* 17:1.
Majors Accounting; administrative assistant and secretarial science; airline pilot and flight crew; biology/biotechnology laboratory technician; business administration and management; child development; computer and information sciences related; computer engineering technology; computer graphics; computer programming; computer programming (specific applications); computer science; criminal justice/law enforcement administration; culinary arts; data entry/microcomputer applications; engineering science; fire science/firefighting; foods, nutrition, and wellness; gerontology; health professions related; hospitality administration; information science/studies; interdisciplinary studies; kindergarten/preschool education; legal administrative assistant/secretary; legal assistant/paralegal; liberal arts and sciences/liberal studies; marketing/marketing management; medical administrative assistant and medical secretary; medical radiologic technology; mental health counseling; occupational therapy; physical therapy technology; pre-engineering; registered nursing/registered nurse; respiratory care therapy; substance abuse/addiction counseling; tourism and travel services management; veterinary/animal health technology; web page, digital/multimedia and information resources design.
Academics *Calendar:* semesters. *Degree:* certificates and associate. *Special study options:* academic remediation for entering students, accelerated degree program, adult/continuing education programs, advanced placement credit, cooperative education, distance learning, English as a second language, honors programs, independent study, internships, part-time degree program, services for LD students, summer session for credit.
Library Learning Resource Center plus 2 others with 68,035 titles, 4,213 audiovisual materials, an OPAC, a Web page.
Student Life *Housing:* college housing not available. *Activities and Organizations:* drama/theater group, student-run newspaper, Program Council, student government, performing arts, student newspaper, Phi Theta Kappa, national fraternities. *Campus security:* 24-hour emergency response devices and patrols, late-night transport/escort service. *Student services:* health clinic, personal/psychological counseling, women's center.
Athletics *Intramural sports:* basketball M/W, soccer M/W.

Costs (2014–15) *Tuition:* state resident $600 full-time, $25 per credit hour part-time; nonresident $6168 full-time, $257 per credit hour part-time. *Required fees:* $3696 full-time, $156 per credit hour part-time. *Payment plan:* installment. *Waivers:* senior citizens and employees or children of employees.
Financial Aid Of all full-time matriculated undergraduates who enrolled in 2009, 1,658 applied for aid, 1,438 were judged to have need, 23 had their need fully met. 123 Federal Work-Study jobs (averaging $1359). In 2009, 11 non-need-based awards were made. *Average percent of need met:* 18%. *Average financial aid package:* $6856. *Average need-based loan:* $1639. *Average need-based gift aid:* $2522. *Average non-need-based aid:* $614.
Applying *Options:* electronic application, early admission, deferred entrance. *Required for some:* essay or personal statement, high school transcript, interview. *Application deadlines:* rolling (freshmen), rolling (transfers). *Notification:* continuous (freshmen), continuous (transfers).
Freshman Application Contact Mrs. Lisa Barrett, Academic Counselor, North Shore Community College, Danvers, MA 01923. *Phone:* 978-762-4000 Ext. 6225. *Fax:* 978-762-4015. *E-mail:* lbarrett@northshore.edu.
Website: http://www.northshore.edu/.

Quincy College
Quincy, Massachusetts

Freshman Application Contact Paula Smith, Dean, Enrollment Services, Quincy College, 34 Coddington Street, Quincy, MA 02169-4522. *Phone:* 617-984-1700. *Toll-free phone:* 800-698-1700. *Fax:* 617-984-1779. *E-mail:* psmith@quincycollege.edu.
Website: http://www.quincycollege.edu/.

Quinsigamond Community College
Worcester, Massachusetts

- **State-supported** 2-year, founded 1963, part of Massachusetts System of Higher Education
- **Urban** 57-acre campus with easy access to Boston
- **Endowment** $421,076
- **Coed,** 8,453 undergraduate students, 39% full-time, 57% women, 43% men

Undergraduates 3,337 full-time, 5,116 part-time. Students come from 17 states and territories; 21 other countries; 1% are from out of state; 12% Black or African American, non-Hispanic/Latino; 17% Hispanic/Latino; 4% Asian, non-Hispanic/Latino; 0.1% Native Hawaiian or other Pacific Islander, non-Hispanic/Latino; 0.4% American Indian or Alaska Native, non-Hispanic/Latino; 2% Two or more races, non-Hispanic/Latino; 6% Race/ethnicity unknown; 0.3% international.
Freshmen *Admission:* 3,517 applied, 2,069 admitted, 1,787 enrolled.
Faculty *Total:* 582, 24% full-time, 14% with terminal degrees. *Student/faculty ratio:* 18:1.
Majors Alternative and complementary medicine related; American Sign Language (ASL); automobile/automotive mechanics technology; bioengineering and biomedical engineering; biotechnology; business administration and management; business/commerce; computer and information systems security; computer engineering technology; computer graphics; computer programming (specific applications); computer science; computer systems analysis; criminal justice/police science; data modeling/warehousing and database administration; dental hygiene; dental services and allied professions related; electrical, electronic and communications engineering technology; electromechanical technology; elementary education; emergency medical technology (EMT paramedic); energy management and systems technology; engineering technologies and engineering related; executive assistant/executive secretary; fire services administration; general studies; health services/allied health/health sciences; hospitality administration; human services; kindergarten/preschool education; liberal arts and sciences/liberal studies; manufacturing engineering technology; medical administrative assistant and medical secretary; occupational therapy; pre-pharmacy studies; radiologic technology/science; registered nursing/registered nurse; respiratory care therapy; restaurant/food services management; telecommunications technology; trade and industrial teacher education; web page, digital/multimedia and information resources design.
Academics *Calendar:* semesters. *Degree:* certificates and associate. *Special study options:* academic remediation for entering students, accelerated degree program, advanced placement credit, cooperative education, distance learning, double majors, English as a second language, honors programs, independent study, internships, off-campus study, part-time degree program, services for LD students, summer session for credit. *ROTC:* Army (c).
Library Alden Library with 95,000 titles, 1,500 audiovisual materials, an OPAC, a Web page.
Student Life *Housing:* college housing not available. *Activities and Organizations:* drama/theater group, student-run newspaper, Phi Theta Kappa,

academic-related clubs, Student Senate, Chess Club, Business Club. *Campus security:* 24-hour emergency response devices and patrols, late-night transport/escort service. *Student services:* personal/psychological counseling.
Athletics Member NJCAA. *Intercollegiate sports:* baseball M, basketball M/W, softball W. *Intramural sports:* basketball M/W, soccer M/W, ultimate Frisbee M/W, volleyball M/W.
Costs (2014–15) *Tuition:* state resident $576 full-time, $24 per credit part-time; nonresident $5520 full-time, $230 per credit part-time. Full-time tuition and fees vary according to course load and program. Part-time tuition and fees vary according to course load and program. *Required fees:* $5094 full-time, $157 per credit part-time, $250 per term part-time. *Payment plan:* installment. *Waivers:* senior citizens and employees or children of employees.
Applying *Options:* electronic application. *Application fee:* $20. *Required:* high school transcript. *Required for some:* interview. *Application deadlines:* rolling (freshmen), rolling (out-of-state freshmen), rolling (transfers). *Notification:* continuous (freshmen), continuous (out-of-state freshmen), continuous (transfers).
Freshman Application Contact Quinsigamond Community College, 670 West Boylston Street, Worcester, MA 01606-2092. *Phone:* 508-854-4576. *Website:* http://www.qcc.edu/.

Roxbury Community College
Roxbury Crossing, Massachusetts

Director of Admissions Nancy Santos, Director, Admissions, Roxbury Community College, 1234 Columbus Avenue, Roxbury Crossing, MA 02120-3400. *Phone:* 617-541-5310.
Website: http://www.rcc.mass.edu/.

Salter College
Chicopee, Massachusetts

Admissions Office Contact Salter College, 645 Shawinigan Drive, Chicopee, MA 01020.
Website: http://www.saltercollege.com/.

Salter College
West Boylston, Massachusetts

Admissions Office Contact Salter College, 184 West Boylston Street, West Boylston, MA 01583.
Website: http://www.saltercollege-us.com/.

Springfield Technical Community College
Springfield, Massachusetts

- **State-supported** 2-year, founded 1967
- **Urban** 34-acre campus
- **Coed**, 6,622 undergraduate students, 47% full-time, 58% women, 42% men

Undergraduates 3,085 full-time, 3,537 part-time. Students come from 16 states and territories; 4% are from out of state; 16% Black or African American, non-Hispanic/Latino; 27% Hispanic/Latino; 3% Asian, non-Hispanic/Latino; 0.1% Native Hawaiian or other Pacific Islander, non-Hispanic/Latino; 0.5% American Indian or Alaska Native, non-Hispanic/Latino; 2% Two or more races, non-Hispanic/Latino; 0.6% Race/ethnicity unknown; 0.8% international; 7% transferred in.
Freshmen *Admission:* 2,948 applied, 2,564 admitted, 1,421 enrolled.
Faculty *Total:* 492, 30% full-time. *Student/faculty ratio:* 16:1.
Majors Accounting; administrative assistant and secretarial science; animation, interactive technology, video graphics and special effects; architectural engineering; automotive engineering technology; biology/biological sciences; biotechnology; building/construction finishing, management, and inspection related; business administration and management; business/commerce; chemistry; civil engineering technology; clinical/medical laboratory technology; commercial and advertising art; commercial photography; computer and information systems security; computer engineering technology; computer programming (specific applications); computer science; criminal justice/police science; dental hygiene; diagnostic medical sonography and ultrasound technology; early childhood education; electrical, electronic and communications engineering technology; electromechanical technology; elementary education; engineering; finance; fine/studio arts; fire prevention and safety technology; general studies; heating, ventilation, air conditioning and refrigeration engineering technology; landscaping and groundskeeping; laser and optical technology; liberal arts and sciences/liberal studies; marketing/marketing management; massage therapy; mathematics; mechanical engineering/mechanical technology; medical

administrative assistant and medical secretary; medical/clinical assistant; medical insurance coding; occupational therapist assistant; physical therapy technology; physics; premedical studies; radio and television broadcasting technology; radiologic technology/science; recording arts technology; registered nursing/registered nurse; respiratory care therapy; secondary education; small business administration; sport and fitness administration/management; surgical technology; telecommunications technology.
Academics *Calendar:* semesters. *Degree:* certificates and associate. *Special study options:* academic remediation for entering students, adult/continuing education programs, advanced placement credit, cooperative education, distance learning, English as a second language, honors programs, independent study, internships, off-campus study, part-time degree program, services for LD students, summer session for credit.
Library Springfield Technical Community College Library with 34,120 titles, 8,101 audiovisual materials, an OPAC, a Web page.
Student Life *Housing:* college housing not available. *Activities and Organizations:* drama/theater group, student-run newspaper, Phi Theta Kappa, Campus Civitian Club, Tech Times (student newspaper), Dental Hygiene Club, Landscape Design Club. *Campus security:* 24-hour emergency response devices and patrols, late-night transport/escort service. *Student services:* health clinic, personal/psychological counseling.
Athletics Member NJCAA. *Intercollegiate sports:* basketball M/W, golf M, soccer M/W, wrestling M. *Intramural sports:* basketball M/W, cross-country running M/W, golf M/W, skiing (cross-country) M/W, volleyball M/W, weight lifting M/W.
Standardized Tests *Required for some:* SAT (for admission).
Costs (2014–15) *Tuition:* state resident $750 full-time, $25 per credit part-time; nonresident $7260 full-time, $242 per credit part-time. Full-time tuition and fees vary according to course load and reciprocity agreements. Part-time tuition and fees vary according to course load and reciprocity agreements. No tuition increase for student's term of enrollment. *Required fees:* $4356 full-time, $138 per credit part-time, $108 per term part-time. *Payment plan:* installment. *Waivers:* senior citizens and employees or children of employees.
Applying *Options:* electronic application. *Required:* high school transcript. *Required for some:* interview. *Application deadlines:* rolling (freshmen), rolling (transfers).
Freshman Application Contact Mr. Ray Blair, Dean of Student Affairs, Springfield Technical Community College, Springfield, MA 01105. *Phone:* 413-781-7822 Ext. 4868. *E-mail:* rblair@stcc.edu.
Website: http://www.stcc.edu/.

Urban College of Boston
Boston, Massachusetts

Director of Admissions Dr. Henry J. Johnson, Director of Enrollment Services/Registrar, Urban College of Boston, 178 Tremont Street, Boston, MA 02111. *Phone:* 617-348-6353.
Website: http://www.urbancollege.edu/.

MICHIGAN

Alpena Community College
Alpena, Michigan

Freshman Application Contact Mr. Mike Kollien, Director of Admissions, Alpena Community College, 665 Johnson, Alpena, MI 49707. *Phone:* 989-358-7339. *Toll-free phone:* 888-468-6222. *Fax:* 989-358-7540. *E-mail:* kollienm@alpenacc.edu.
Website: http://www.alpenacc.edu/.

Bay de Noc Community College
Escanaba, Michigan

Freshman Application Contact Bay de Noc Community College, 2001 North Lincoln Road, Escanaba, MI 49829-2511. *Phone:* 906-786-5802 Ext. 1276. *Toll-free phone:* 800-221-2001.
Website: http://www.baycollege.edu/.

Bay Mills Community College
Brimley, Michigan

Freshman Application Contact Ms. Elaine Lehre, Admissions Officer, Bay Mills Community College, 12214 West Lakeshore Drive, Brimley, MI 49715. *Phone:* 906-248-3354. *Toll-free phone:* 800-844-BMCC. *Fax:* 906-248-3351.
Website: http://www.bmcc.edu/.

Delta College
University Center, Michigan

- **District-supported** 2-year, founded 1961
- **Rural** 640-acre campus
- **Endowment** $17.8 million
- **Coed,** 9,842 undergraduate students, 37% full-time, 55% women, 45% men

Undergraduates 3,688 full-time, 6,154 part-time. Students come from 1 other state; 1 other country; 10% Black or African American, non-Hispanic/Latino; 7% Hispanic/Latino; 0.6% Asian, non-Hispanic/Latino; 0.6% American Indian or Alaska Native, non-Hispanic/Latino; 0.3% Two or more races, non-Hispanic/Latino; 2% Race/ethnicity unknown; 0.2% international; 4% transferred in.

Freshmen *Admission:* 1,435 applied, 1,435 admitted, 1,435 enrolled.

Faculty *Total:* 531, 40% full-time. *Student/faculty ratio:* 22:1.

Majors Accounting technology and bookkeeping; administrative assistant and secretarial science; architectural engineering technology; automobile/automotive mechanics technology; building/construction finishing, management, and inspection related; building/property maintenance; business administration and management; carpentry; chemical technology; child-care provision; computer and information sciences related; computer and information systems security; computer installation and repair technology; computer programming; computer software and media applications related; computer systems networking and telecommunications; construction engineering technology; corrections; criminal justice/police science; dental assisting; dental hygiene; diagnostic medical sonography and ultrasound technology; electrical and power transmission installation; electrician; energy management and systems technology; environmental engineering technology; fine/studio arts; fire prevention and safety technology; fire science/firefighting; fire services administration; general studies; heating, air conditioning, ventilation and refrigeration maintenance technology; industrial mechanics and maintenance technology; journalism; legal assistant/paralegal; liberal arts and sciences/liberal studies; machine shop technology; manufacturing engineering technology; marketing/marketing management; mechanical engineering/mechanical technology; medical administrative assistant and medical secretary; medical radiologic technology; merchandising; peace studies and conflict resolution; physical therapy technology; pipefitting and sprinkler fitting; plumbing technology; precision metal working related; precision production related; radio and television; registered nursing/registered nurse; respiratory care therapy; retailing; salon/beauty salon management; security and loss prevention; sheet metal technology; small business administration; sport and fitness administration/management; surgical technology; technology/industrial arts teacher education; tool and die technology; water quality and wastewater treatment management and recycling technology; web/multimedia management and webmaster; welding technology.

Academics *Calendar:* semesters. *Degree:* certificates and associate. *Special study options:* academic remediation for entering students, adult/continuing education programs, advanced placement credit, cooperative education, distance learning, double majors, freshman honors college, honors programs, independent study, internships, off-campus study, part-time degree program, services for LD students, study abroad, summer session for credit.

Library Library Learning Information Center with 73,591 titles, 4,500 audiovisual materials, an OPAC, a Web page.

Student Life *Housing:* college housing not available. *Activities and Organizations:* drama/theater group, student-run newspaper, choral group, Phi Theta Kappa, DCSNA (Student Nursing Association), PTA (Physical Therapy Assistant) Club, Inter-Varsity Christian Fellowship, Chez les Napoleons (French Club). *Campus security:* 24-hour emergency response devices, student patrols, late-night transport/escort service. *Student services:* personal/psychological counseling.

Athletics Member NJCAA. *Intercollegiate sports:* baseball M(s), basketball M(s)/W(s), golf M, soccer W(s), softball W(s). *Intramural sports:* basketball M/W, football M/W.

Costs (2014–15) *Tuition:* area resident $2268 full-time, $95 per credit hour part-time; state resident $3696 full-time, $154 per credit hour part-time; nonresident $7176 full-time, $299 per credit hour part-time. Full-time tuition and fees vary according to course load. Part-time tuition and fees vary according to course load. *Required fees:* $80 full-time, $40 per term part-time. *Payment plan:* installment. *Waivers:* senior citizens and employees or children of employees.

Financial Aid Of all full-time matriculated undergraduates who enrolled in 2013, 115 Federal Work-Study jobs (averaging $2307). 67 state and other part-time jobs (averaging $2214).

Applying *Options:* electronic application, early admission, deferred entrance. *Required for some:* essay or personal statement. *Recommended:* high school transcript. *Application deadlines:* rolling (freshmen), rolling (transfers).

Freshman Application Contact Mr. Zachary Ward, Director of Admissions and Recruitment, Delta College, 1961 Delta Road, University Center, MI 48710. *Phone:* 989-686-9590. *Fax:* 989-667-2202. *E-mail:* admit@delta.edu.

Website: http://www.delta.edu/.

Glen Oaks Community College
Centreville, Michigan

- **State and locally supported** 2-year, founded 1965
- **Rural** 300-acre campus
- **Coed**

Undergraduates 531 full-time, 690 part-time. 6% Black or African American, non-Hispanic/Latino; 6% Hispanic/Latino; 1% Asian, non-Hispanic/Latino; 0.4% American Indian or Alaska Native, non-Hispanic/Latino; 3% Race/ethnicity unknown; 0.1% international; 4% transferred in.

Faculty *Student/faculty ratio:* 16:1.

Academics *Calendar:* semesters. *Degree:* certificates and associate. *Special study options:* academic remediation for entering students, advanced placement credit, distance learning, internships, part-time degree program, services for LD students, summer session for credit.

Student Life *Campus security:* 24-hour emergency response devices.

Athletics Member NJCAA.

Financial Aid Of all full-time matriculated undergraduates who enrolled in 2013, 70 Federal Work-Study jobs (averaging $1100). 38 state and other part-time jobs (averaging $1200).

Applying *Options:* electronic application. *Required:* high school transcript.

Freshman Application Contact Ms. Beverly M. Andrews, Director of Admissions/Registrar, Glen Oaks Community College, 62249 Shimmel Road, Centreville, MI 49032-9719. *Phone:* 269-294-4249. *Toll-free phone:* 888-994-7818. *Fax:* 269-467-4114. *E-mail:* thowden@glenoaks.edu.

Website: http://www.glenoaks.edu/.

Gogebic Community College
Ironwood, Michigan

- **State and locally supported** 2-year, founded 1932, part of Michigan Department of Education
- **Small-town** 195-acre campus
- **Coed**

Undergraduates 647 full-time, 552 part-time. Students come from 5 states and territories; 1 other country; 1% Black or African American, non-Hispanic/Latino; 0.8% Hispanic/Latino; 0.8% Asian, non-Hispanic/Latino; 6% American Indian or Alaska Native, non-Hispanic/Latino; 5% Race/ethnicity unknown; 0.1% international.

Academics *Calendar:* semesters. *Degree:* certificates and associate. *Special study options:* academic remediation for entering students, adult/continuing education programs, advanced placement credit, cooperative education, distance learning, honors programs, internships, part-time degree program, services for LD students, study abroad, summer session for credit.

Student Life *Campus security:* controlled dormitory access.

Athletics Member NJCAA.

Costs (2014–15) *Tuition:* area resident $3162 full-time, $102 per credit hour part-time; state resident $4464 full-time, $144 per credit hour part-time; nonresident $5363 full-time, $173 per credit hour part-time. Full-time tuition and fees vary according to course load and reciprocity agreements. Part-time tuition and fees vary according to course load and reciprocity agreements. *Required fees:* $962 full-time, $10 per credit hour part-time. *Room and board:* $6704; room only: $4004.

Financial Aid Of all full-time matriculated undergraduates who enrolled in 2013, 75 Federal Work-Study jobs (averaging $1800). 50 state and other part-time jobs (averaging $1800).

Applying *Options:* electronic application, early admission, deferred entrance. *Application fee:* $10. *Required:* high school transcript.

Freshman Application Contact Ms. Kim Zeckovich, Director of Admissions, Marketing, and Public Relations, Gogebic Community College, E4946 Jackson Road, Ironwood, MI 49938. *Phone:* 906-932-4231 Ext. 347. *Toll-free phone:* 800-682-5910. *Fax:* 906-932-2339. *E-mail:* jeanneg@gogebic.edu.

Website: http://www.gogebic.edu/.

Grand Rapids Community College
Grand Rapids, Michigan

- **District-supported** 2-year, founded 1914, part of Michigan Department of Education
- **Urban** 35-acre campus
- **Endowment** $30.8 million
- **Coed,** 15,668 undergraduate students, 32% full-time, 51% women, 49% men

Undergraduates 5,021 full-time, 10,647 part-time. Students come from 10 states and territories; 23 other countries; 1% are from out of state; 10% Black or African American, non-Hispanic/Latino; 10% Hispanic/Latino; 4% Asian, non-Hispanic/Latino; 0.1% Native Hawaiian or other Pacific Islander, non-Hispanic/Latino; 0.8% American Indian or Alaska Native, non-Hispanic/Latino; 2% Two or more races, non-Hispanic/Latino; 5% Race/ethnicity unknown; 0.1% international; 8% transferred in. *Retention:* 57% of full-time freshmen returned.
Freshmen *Admission:* 9,363 applied, 3,126 enrolled. *Average high school GPA:* 2.8. *Test scores:* ACT scores over 18: 71%; ACT scores over 24: 18%; ACT scores over 30: 1%.
Faculty *Total:* 914, 27% full-time. *Student/faculty ratio:* 21:1.
Majors Architectural technology; architecture; art; automobile/automotive mechanics technology; business administration and management; chemistry; child-care and support services management; computer and information sciences; computer and information systems security; computer programming; computer programming (specific applications); computer support specialist; computer systems networking and telecommunications; corrections; criminal justice/law enforcement administration; criminal justice/police science; culinary arts; dental hygiene; electrical, electronic and communications engineering technology; elementary education; engineering; English; fashion merchandising; foreign languages and literatures; forestry; geology/earth science; heating, air conditioning, ventilation and refrigeration maintenance technology; industrial technology; journalism; landscaping and groundskeeping; liberal arts and sciences/liberal studies; library and information science; licensed practical/vocational nurse training; medical administrative assistant and medical secretary; music; music teacher education; physical education teaching and coaching; plastics and polymer engineering technology; quality control technology; recording arts technology; registered nursing/registered nurse; restaurant, culinary, and catering management; secondary education; welding technology.
Academics *Calendar:* semesters. *Degree:* certificates and associate. *Special study options:* academic remediation for entering students, adult/continuing education programs, advanced placement credit, cooperative education, distance learning, English as a second language, honors programs, independent study, internships, off-campus study, part-time degree program, services for LD students, study abroad, summer session for credit.
Library Arthur Andrews Memorial Library with 68,397 titles, 7,987 audiovisual materials, an OPAC, a Web page.
Student Life *Housing:* college housing not available. *Activities and Organizations:* drama/theater group, student-run newspaper, choral group, Student Congress, Phi Theta Kappa, Hispanic Student Organization, Student Gamers Association, Foreign Affairs Club. *Campus security:* 24-hour emergency response devices, late-night transport/escort service. *Student services:* personal/psychological counseling.
Athletics Member NJCAA. *Intercollegiate sports:* baseball M(s), basketball M(s)/W(s), cross-country running M/W, golf M(s), softball W(s), volleyball W(s).
Standardized Tests *Recommended:* SAT or ACT (for admission).
Costs (2014–15) *Tuition:* area resident $3180 full-time, $106 per contact hour part-time; state resident $6840 full-time, $228 per contact hour part-time; nonresident $10,140 full-time, $338 per contact hour part-time. Full-time tuition and fees vary according to course load and program. Part-time tuition and fees vary according to course load and program. *Required fees:* $459 full-time, $15 per contact hour part-time, $90 per term part-time. *Payment plan:* installment. *Waivers:* employees or children of employees.
Financial Aid Of all full-time matriculated undergraduates who enrolled in 2008, 6,142 applied for aid, 4,896 were judged to have need, 1,012 had their need fully met. In 2008, 96 non-need-based awards were made. *Average financial aid package:* $4850. *Average need-based loan:* $2764. *Average need-based gift aid:* $3984. *Average non-need-based aid:* $1051.
Applying *Options:* electronic application, early admission, deferred entrance. *Required:* high school transcript. *Application deadline:* 8/30 (freshmen). *Notification:* continuous (freshmen), continuous (transfers).
Freshman Application Contact Ms. Diane Patrick, Director of Admissions, Grand Rapids Community College, Grand Rapids, MI 49503-3201. *Phone:* 616-234-4100. *Fax:* 616-234-4005. *E-mail:* dpatrick@grcc.edu.
Website: http://www.grcc.edu/.

Henry Ford Community College
Dearborn, Michigan

Freshman Application Contact Admissions Office, Henry Ford Community College, 5101 Evergreen Road, Dearborn, MI 48128-1495. *Phone:* 313-845-6403. *Toll-free phone:* 800-585-HFCC. *Fax:* 313-845-6464. *E-mail:* enroll@hfcc.edu.
Website: http://www.hfcc.edu/.

ITT Technical Institute
Canton, Michigan

- **Proprietary** primarily 2-year, founded 2002, part of ITT Educational Services, Inc.
- **Coed**

Academics *Calendar:* quarters. *Degrees:* associate and bachelor's.
Freshman Application Contact Director of Recruitment, ITT Technical Institute, 1905 South Haggerty Road, Canton, MI 48188-2025. *Phone:* 784-397-7800. *Toll-free phone:* 800-247-4477.
Website: http://www.itt-tech.edu/.

ITT Technical Institute
Dearborn, Michigan

- **Proprietary** primarily 2-year, part of ITT Educational Services, Inc.
- **Coed**

Academics *Calendar:* quarters. *Degrees:* associate and bachelor's.
Freshman Application Contact Director of Recruitment, ITT Technical Institute, 19855 W. Outer Drive, Suite L10W, Dearborn, MI 48124. *Phone:* 313-278-5208. *Toll-free phone:* 800-605-0801.
Website: http://www.itt-tech.edu/.

ITT Technical Institute
Swartz Creek, Michigan

- **Proprietary** primarily 2-year, founded 2005, part of ITT Educational Services, Inc.
- **Coed**

Academics *Calendar:* quarters. *Degrees:* associate and bachelor's.
Freshman Application Contact Director of Recruitment, ITT Technical Institute, 6359 Miller Road, Swartz Creek, MI 48473. *Phone:* 810-628-2500. *Toll-free phone:* 800-514-6564.
Website: http://www.itt-tech.edu/.

ITT Technical Institute
Troy, Michigan

- **Proprietary** primarily 2-year, founded 1987, part of ITT Educational Services, Inc.
- **Coed**

Academics *Calendar:* quarters. *Degrees:* associate and bachelor's.
Freshman Application Contact Director of Recruitment, ITT Technical Institute, 1522 East Big Beaver Road, Troy, MI 48083-1905. *Phone:* 248-524-1800. *Toll-free phone:* 800-832-6817.
Website: http://www.itt-tech.edu/.

ITT Technical Institute
Wyoming, Michigan

- **Proprietary** primarily 2-year, part of ITT Educational Services, Inc.
- **Coed**

Academics *Calendar:* quarters. *Degrees:* associate and bachelor's.
Freshman Application Contact Director of Recruitment, ITT Technical Institute, 1980 Metro Court SW, Wyoming, MI 49519. *Phone:* 616-406-1200. *Toll-free phone:* 800-632-4676.
Website: http://www.itt-tech.edu/.

Jackson College
Jackson, Michigan

- **County-supported** 2-year, founded 1928
- **Suburban** 580-acre campus with easy access to Detroit
- **Coed**

Undergraduates 2,389 full-time, 3,276 part-time. 2% are from out of state; 17% Black or African American, non-Hispanic/Latino; 9% Hispanic/Latino; 4% Two or more races, non-Hispanic/Latino; 8% Race/ethnicity unknown. *Retention:* 57% of full-time freshmen returned.

Faculty *Student/faculty ratio:* 18:1.

Academics *Calendar:* semesters. *Degree:* certificates and associate. *Special study options:* academic remediation for entering students, accelerated degree program, adult/continuing education programs, advanced placement credit, cooperative education, distance learning, double majors, English as a second language, freshman honors college, honors programs, independent study, internships, part-time degree program, services for LD students, summer session for credit.

Student Life *Campus security:* 24-hour emergency response devices and patrols, student patrols, late-night transport/escort service, controlled dormitory access.

Athletics Member NJCAA.

Applying *Options:* electronic application. *Required:* Minimum ACT of 16 is required for housing admission. *Required for some:* minimum #### GPA.

Freshman Application Contact Mr. Daniel Vainner, Registrar, Jackson College, 2111 Emmons Road, Jackson, MI 49201. *Phone:* 517-796-8425. *Toll-free phone:* 888-522-7344. *Fax:* 517-796-8446. *E-mail:* admissions@jccmi.edu.

Website: http://www.jccmi.edu/.

Kalamazoo Valley Community College

Kalamazoo, Michigan

- **State and locally supported** 2-year, founded 1966
- **Suburban** 187-acre campus
- **Coed**, 11,113 undergraduate students

Undergraduates 1% are from out of state.

Majors Accounting technology and bookkeeping; animation, interactive technology, video graphics and special effects; automobile/automotive mechanics technology; business administration and management; CAD/CADD drafting/design technology; chemical technology; computer programming; computer systems analysis; criminal justice/police science; dental hygiene; e-commerce; electrical, electronic and communications engineering technology; elementary education; emergency medical technology (EMT paramedic); engineering; engineering technology; executive assistant/executive secretary; fire science/firefighting; general studies; graphic design; heating, ventilation, air conditioning and refrigeration engineering technology; illustration; international/global studies; liberal arts and sciences/liberal studies; machine tool technology; marketing/marketing management; mechanical engineering/mechanical technology; mechanics and repair; registered nursing/registered nurse; respiratory care therapy; surgical technology; web/multimedia management and webmaster; web page, digital/multimedia and information resources design; welding technology.

Academics *Calendar:* semesters. *Degree:* certificates and associate. *Special study options:* academic remediation for entering students, advanced placement credit, cooperative education, distance learning, English as a second language, honors programs, independent study, internships, off-campus study, part-time degree program, services for LD students, student-designed majors, summer session for credit. *ROTC:* Army (c).

Library Kalamazoo Valley Community College Library with 88,791 titles, an OPAC, a Web page.

Student Life *Housing:* college housing not available. *Activities and Organizations:* choral group. *Campus security:* 24-hour emergency response devices and patrols. *Student services:* personal/psychological counseling.

Athletics Member NJCAA. *Intercollegiate sports:* baseball M(s), basketball M(s)/W(s), golf M, softball W(s), tennis W(s), volleyball W(s). *Intramural sports:* basketball M/W.

Standardized Tests *Required:* ACT (for admission).

Financial Aid Of all full-time matriculated undergraduates who enrolled in 2013, 47 Federal Work-Study jobs (averaging $2631).

Applying *Required:* high school transcript. *Application deadlines:* rolling (freshmen), rolling (transfers). *Notification:* continuous (freshmen), continuous (transfers).

Freshman Application Contact Kalamazoo Valley Community College, PO Box 4070, Kalamazoo, MI 49003-4070. *Phone:* 269-488-4207.

Website: http://www.kvcc.edu/.

Kellogg Community College

Battle Creek, Michigan

- **State and locally supported** 2-year, founded 1956, part of Michigan Department of Education
- **Urban** 120-acre campus
- **Coed**, 5,647 undergraduate students, 28% full-time, 66% women, 34% men

Undergraduates 1,589 full-time, 4,058 part-time. 12% Black or African American, non-Hispanic/Latino; 4% Hispanic/Latino; 2% Asian, non-Hispanic/Latino; 0.6% American Indian or Alaska Native, non-Hispanic/Latino; 4% Two or more races, non-Hispanic/Latino; 5% Race/ethnicity unknown; 0.2% international.

Freshmen *Admission:* 495 applied, 495 admitted, 495 enrolled.

Faculty *Total:* 393, 22% full-time, 5% with terminal degrees. *Student/faculty ratio:* 16:1.

Majors Accounting; administrative assistant and secretarial science; business administration and management; chemical technology; computer engineering technology; computer graphics; computer programming; computer programming (specific applications); computer software and media applications related; corrections; criminal justice/police science; criminal justice/safety; data entry/microcomputer applications related; dental hygiene; drafting and design technology; elementary education; emergency medical technology (EMT paramedic); engineering; executive assistant/executive secretary; general studies; heating, air conditioning, ventilation and refrigeration maintenance technology; human services; industrial technology; legal administrative assistant/secretary; legal assistant/paralegal; liberal arts and sciences/liberal studies; licensed practical/vocational nurse training; machine tool technology; medical administrative assistant and medical secretary; medical radiologic technology; physical therapy technology; pipefitting and sprinkler fitting; registered nursing/registered nurse; welding technology; word processing.

Academics *Calendar:* semesters. *Degree:* certificates and associate. *Special study options:* academic remediation for entering students, accelerated degree program, adult/continuing education programs, advanced placement credit, cooperative education, distance learning, double majors, English as a second language, freshman honors college, honors programs, independent study, internships, off-campus study, part-time degree program, services for LD students, summer session for credit.

Library Emory W. Morris Learning Resource Center with 42,131 titles, an OPAC, a Web page.

Student Life *Housing:* college housing not available. *Activities and Organizations:* drama/theater group, student-run newspaper, choral group, Tech Club, Phi Theta Kappa, Student Nurses Association, Crude Arts Club, Art League. *Campus security:* 24-hour emergency response devices and patrols, late-night transport/escort service.

Athletics Member NJCAA. *Intercollegiate sports:* baseball M(s), basketball M(s)/W(s), soccer W, softball W(s), volleyball W(s).

Standardized Tests *Required for some:* ACT (for admission), SAT or ACT (for admission).

Costs (2015–16) *Tuition:* area resident $110 full-time; state resident $170 full-time; nonresident $171 full-time. Full-time tuition and fees vary according to program. Part-time tuition and fees vary according to program. *Payment plan:* installment. *Waivers:* senior citizens and employees or children of employees.

Financial Aid Of all full-time matriculated undergraduates who enrolled in 2013, 41 Federal Work-Study jobs (averaging $2251). 43 state and other part-time jobs (averaging $2058).

Applying *Options:* electronic application, early admission. *Required for some:* high school transcript, minimum 2.0 GPA. *Application deadlines:* rolling (freshmen), rolling (transfers). *Notification:* continuous (freshmen), continuous (transfers).

Freshman Application Contact Ms. Meredith Stravers, Director of Admissions, Kellogg Community College, 450 North Avenue, Battle Creek, MI 49017. *Phone:* 269-965-3931 Ext. 2644. *Fax:* 269-965-4133. *E-mail:* straversm@kellogg.edu.

Website: http://www.kellogg.edu/.

Keweenaw Bay Ojibwa Community College

Baraga, Michigan

Freshman Application Contact Megan Shanahan, Admissions Officer, Keweenaw Bay Ojibwa Community College, 111 Beartown Road, Baraga, MI 49908. *Phone:* 909-353-4600. *E-mail:* megan@kbocc.org.

Website: http://www.kbocc.org/.

Kirtland Community College

Roscommon, Michigan

- **District-supported** 2-year, founded 1966
- **Rural** 180-acre campus
- **Coed**, 1,773 undergraduate students, 30% full-time, 61% women, 39% men

Undergraduates 540 full-time, 1,233 part-time. Students come from 4 states and territories; 2 other countries; 1% Black or African American, non-Hispanic/Latino; 2% Hispanic/Latino; 0.6% Asian, non-Hispanic/Latino; 0.1% Native Hawaiian or other Pacific Islander, non-Hispanic/Latino; 1% American Indian or Alaska Native, non-Hispanic/Latino; 1% Two or more races, non-Hispanic/Latino; 5% Race/ethnicity unknown; 0.1% international.

Freshmen *Admission:* 539 applied, 539 admitted, 227 enrolled. *Test scores:* ACT scores over 18: 51%; ACT scores over 24: 8%; ACT scores over 30: 1%.
Faculty *Total:* 126, 26% full-time. *Student/faculty ratio:* 18:1.
Majors Administrative assistant and secretarial science; animation, interactive technology, video graphics and special effects; art; automobile/automotive mechanics technology; business administration and management; cardiovascular technology; commercial photography; computer systems analysis; corrections administration; cosmetology; criminal justice/law enforcement administration; criminal justice/police science; electrical, electronic and communications engineering technology; electromechanical technology; emergency medical technology (EMT paramedic); general studies; graphic design; health information/medical records technology; heating, air conditioning, ventilation and refrigeration maintenance technology; information science/studies; legal administrative assistant/secretary; liberal arts and sciences/liberal studies; licensed practical/vocational nurse training; management information systems; medical administrative assistant and medical secretary; medical/clinical assistant; pharmacy technician; registered nursing/registered nurse; robotics technology; surgical technology; web/multimedia management and webmaster; welding technology.
Academics *Calendar:* semesters. *Degree:* certificates and associate. *Special study options:* academic remediation for entering students, adult/continuing education programs, advanced placement credit, cooperative education, distance learning, honors programs, independent study, internships, part-time degree program, services for LD students, summer session for credit.
Library Kirtland Community College Library with 33,000 titles, an OPAC.
Student Life *Housing:* college housing not available. *Campus security:* 24-hour emergency response devices, student patrols, late-night transport/escort service, campus warning siren, uniformed armed police officers, RAVE alert system (text, email, voice).
Athletics Member NJCAA. *Intercollegiate sports:* bowling M(s)/W(s), cross-country running M(s)/W(s), golf M(s)/W(s).
Standardized Tests *Recommended:* ACT (for admission).
Costs (2014–15) *Tuition:* area resident $2970 full-time, $99 per contact hour part-time; state resident $4110 full-time, $137 per contact hour part-time; nonresident $6750 full-time, $225 per contact hour part-time. *Required fees:* $535 full-time, $16 per contact hour part-time, $35 per term part-time. *Payment plan:* installment. *Waivers:* senior citizens and employees or children of employees.
Financial Aid Of all full-time matriculated undergraduates who enrolled in 2013, 50 Federal Work-Study jobs (averaging $1253). 28 state and other part-time jobs (averaging $1647).
Applying *Options:* electronic application. *Application deadlines:* rolling (freshmen), rolling (transfers). *Notification:* continuous until 8/22 (freshmen), continuous until 8/22 (transfers).
Freshman Application Contact Ms. Michelle Vyskocil, Dean of Student Services, Kirtland Community College, 10775 North Saint Helen Road, Roscommon, MI 48653. *Phone:* 989-275-5000 Ext. 248. *Fax:* 989-275-6789. *E-mail:* registrar@kirtland.edu.
Website: http://www.kirtland.edu/.

Lake Michigan College
Benton Harbor, Michigan

Freshman Application Contact Mr. Louis Thomas, Lead Admissions Specialist, Lake Michigan College, 2755 East Napier Avenue, Benton Harbor, MI 49022-1899. *Phone:* 269-927-6584. *Toll-free phone:* 800-252-1LMC. *Fax:* 269-927-6718. *E-mail:* thomas@lakemichigancollege.edu.
Website: http://www.lakemichigancollege.edu/.

Lansing Community College
Lansing, Michigan

- **State and locally supported** 2-year, founded 1957, part of Michigan Department of Education
- **Urban** 28-acre campus
- **Endowment** $7.3 million
- **Coed**

Undergraduates 6,587 full-time, 10,975 part-time. Students come from 17 states and territories; 37 other countries; 1% are from out of state; 12% Black or African American, non-Hispanic/Latino; 2% Hispanic/Latino; 3% Asian, non-Hispanic/Latino; 0.3% Native Hawaiian or other Pacific Islander, non-Hispanic/Latino; 0.7% American Indian or Alaska Native, non-Hispanic/Latino; 3% Two or more races, non-Hispanic/Latino; 10% Race/ethnicity unknown; 0.6% international.
Faculty *Student/faculty ratio:* 13:1.
Academics *Calendar:* semesters. *Degree:* certificates and associate. *Special study options:* academic remediation for entering students, adult/continuing education programs, advanced placement credit, cooperative education, distance learning, double majors, English as a second language, external

degree program, honors programs, independent study, internships, part-time degree program, services for LD students, study abroad, summer session for credit. *ROTC:* Army (c), Air Force (c).
Student Life *Campus security:* 24-hour emergency response devices and patrols, student patrols, late-night transport/escort service.
Athletics Member NJCAA.
Financial Aid Of all full-time matriculated undergraduates who enrolled in 2013, 125 Federal Work-Study jobs (averaging $2636). 122 state and other part-time jobs (averaging $2563).
Applying *Options:* electronic application, early admission, deferred entrance. *Required for some:* essay or personal statement, high school transcript, 2 letters of recommendation, interview, Special requirements for health, aviation, music, police academy, and fire academy program admissions.
Freshman Application Contact Ms. Tammy Grossbauer, Director of Admissions/Registrar, Lansing Community College, 1121 Enrollment Services, PO BOX 40010, Lansing, MI 48901. *Phone:* 517-483-1200. *Toll-free phone:* 800-644-4LCC. *Fax:* 517-483-1170. *E-mail:* grossbt@lcc.edu.
Website: http://www.lcc.edu/.

Macomb Community College
Warren, Michigan

- **District-supported** 2-year, founded 1954, part of Michigan Public Community College System
- **Suburban** 384-acre campus with easy access to Detroit
- **Endowment** $19.2 million
- **Coed,** 22,914 undergraduate students, 33% full-time, 53% women, 47% men

Undergraduates 7,514 full-time, 15,400 part-time. Students come from 4 states and territories; 12% Black or African American, non-Hispanic/Latino; 2% Hispanic/Latino; 4% Asian, non-Hispanic/Latino; 0.1% Native Hawaiian or other Pacific Islander, non-Hispanic/Latino; 0.5% American Indian or Alaska Native, non-Hispanic/Latino; 2% Two or more races, non-Hispanic/Latino; 9% Race/ethnicity unknown; 1% international. *Retention:* 56% of full-time freshmen returned.
Freshmen *Admission:* 1,338 enrolled.
Faculty *Total:* 1,002, 20% full-time, 11% with terminal degrees. *Student/faculty ratio:* 27:1.
Majors Accounting; administrative assistant and secretarial science; agriculture; architectural drafting and CAD/CADD; automobile/automotive mechanics technology; automotive engineering technology; biology/biological sciences; business administration and management; business automation/technology/data entry; business/commerce; cabinetmaking and millwork; chemistry; child-care and support services management; civil engineering technology; commercial and advertising art; computer programming; computer programming (specific applications); construction engineering technology; criminal justice/law enforcement administration; criminal justice/police science; culinary arts; drafting and design technology; drafting/design engineering technologies related; electrical, electronic and communications engineering technology; electrical/electronics equipment installation and repair; electromechanical technology; emergency medical technology (EMT paramedic); energy management and systems technology; engineering related; finance; fire prevention and safety technology; forensic science and technology; general studies; graphic and printing equipment operation/production; heating, air conditioning, ventilation and refrigeration maintenance technology; heating, ventilation, air conditioning and refrigeration engineering technology; industrial mechanics and maintenance technology; industrial technology; international/global studies; legal assistant/paralegal; legal studies; liberal arts and sciences/liberal studies; machine tool technology; manufacturing engineering technology; marketing/marketing management; mathematics; mechanical drafting and CAD/CADD; mechanical engineering/mechanical technology; mechanic and repair technologies related; medical/clinical assistant; mental health counseling; metallurgical technology; music performance; occupational therapist assistant; operations management; physical therapy technology; plastics and polymer engineering technology; plumbing technology; pre-engineering; quality control and safety technologies related; quality control technology; registered nursing/registered nurse; respiratory care therapy; robotics technology; sheet metal technology; social psychology; speech communication and rhetoric; surgical technology; surveying technology; tool and die technology; veterinary/animal health technology; welding technology.
Academics *Calendar:* semesters. *Degree:* certificates and associate. *Special study options:* academic remediation for entering students, adult/continuing education programs, advanced placement credit, cooperative education, English as a second language, honors programs, internships, off-campus study, part-time degree program, services for LD students, student-designed majors, summer session for credit.
Library Library of South Campus, Library of Center Campus with 159,226 titles, an OPAC.

Student Life *Housing:* college housing not available. *Activities and Organizations:* drama/theater group, Phi Beta Kappa, Adventure Unlimited, Alpha Rho Rho, SADD. *Campus security:* 24-hour emergency response devices and patrols, late-night transport/escort service, security phones in parking lots, surveillance cameras. *Student services:* health clinic, personal/psychological counseling.
Athletics Member NJCAA. *Intercollegiate sports:* baseball M(s), basketball M(s), cross-country running M(s)/W(s), soccer M(s), softball W(s), track and field M(s)/W(s), volleyball W(s). *Intramural sports:* baseball M, basketball M, bowling M/W, cross-country running M/W, football M/W, skiing (cross-country) M/W, skiing (downhill) M/W, volleyball M/W.
Costs (2014–15) *Tuition:* area resident $2837 full-time, $92 per credit hour part-time; state resident $4340 full-time, $140 per credit hour part-time; nonresident $5611 full-time, $181 per credit hour part-time. Full-time tuition and fees vary according to course load. Part-time tuition and fees vary according to course load. *Required fees:* $255 full-time, $5 per credit hour part-time, $50 per term part-time. *Waivers:* employees or children of employees.
Applying *Options:* early admission, deferred entrance. *Application deadlines:* rolling (freshmen), rolling (transfers).
Freshman Application Contact Mr. Brian Bouwman, Coordinator of Admissions and Transfer Credit, Macomb Community College, G312, 14500 East 12 Mile Road, Warren, MI 48088-3896. *Phone:* 586-445-7246. *Toll-free phone:* 866-MACOMB1. *Fax:* 586-445-7140. *E-mail:* stevensr@macomb.edu.
Website: http://www.macomb.edu/.

Mid Michigan Community College
Harrison, Michigan

Freshman Application Contact Jennifer Casebeer, Admissions Specialist, Mid Michigan Community College, 1375 South Clare Avenue, Harrison, MI 48625-9447. *Phone:* 989-386-6661. *E-mail:* apply@midmich.edu.
Website: http://www.midmich.edu/.

Monroe County Community College
Monroe, Michigan

- **County-supported** 2-year, founded 1964, part of Michigan Department of Education
- **Small-town** 150-acre campus with easy access to Detroit, Toledo
- **Coed**

Undergraduates Students come from 3 other countries; 4% are from out of state.
Freshmen *Admission:* 1,700 applied, 1,698 admitted. *Average high school GPA:* 2.5.
Faculty *Total:* 195, 27% full-time.
Majors Accounting; administrative assistant and secretarial science; architectural engineering technology; art; biology/biological sciences; business administration and management; child development; clinical laboratory science/medical technology; computer and information sciences related; computer engineering technology; computer graphics; computer programming (specific applications); criminal justice/police science; criminal justice/safety; culinary arts; data processing and data processing technology; drafting and design technology; electrical, electronic and communications engineering technology; elementary education; English; finance; funeral service and mortuary science; industrial technology; information technology; journalism; legal administrative assistant/secretary; liberal arts and sciences/liberal studies; marketing/marketing management; mass communication/media; mathematics; medical administrative assistant and medical secretary; physical therapy; pre-engineering; psychology; registered nursing/registered nurse; respiratory care therapy; rhetoric and composition; social work; web/multimedia management and webmaster; web page, digital/multimedia and information resources design; welding technology; word processing.
Academics *Calendar:* semesters. *Degree:* certificates and associate. *Special study options:* academic remediation for entering students, advanced placement credit, distance learning, independent study, part-time degree program, services for LD students, summer session for credit.
Library Campbell Learning Resource Center with 47,352 titles, an OPAC.
Student Life *Housing:* college housing not available. *Activities and Organizations:* drama/theater group, student-run newspaper, choral group, student government, Society of Auto Engineers, Oasis, Nursing Students Organization, Respiratory Therapy. *Campus security:* police patrols during open hours.
Athletics *Intramural sports:* soccer M/W, volleyball M/W.

Standardized Tests *Required:* ACT, ACT Compass (for admission). *Required for some:* ACT (for admission). *Recommended:* ACT (for admission).
Costs (2015–16) *Tuition:* area resident $2638 full-time, $107 per contact hour part-time; state resident $4270 full-time, $175 per contact hour part-time; nonresident $4702 full-time, $193 per contact hour part-time. Full-time tuition and fees vary according to reciprocity agreements. Part-time tuition and fees vary according to reciprocity agreements. *Required fees:* $204 full-time, $35 per term part-time. *Payment plan:* installment. *Waivers:* senior citizens and employees or children of employees.
Applying *Options:* early admission, deferred entrance. *Required:* high school transcript, Baseline cut scores on ACT or COMPASS. *Application deadline:* rolling (transfers). *Notification:* continuous (freshmen), continuous (transfers).
Freshman Application Contact Mr. Mark V. Hall, Director of Admissions and Guidance Services, Monroe County Community College, 1555 South Raisinville Road, Monroe, MI 48161. *Phone:* 734-384-4261. *Toll-free phone:* 877-YES-MCCC. *Fax:* 734-242-9711. *E-mail:* mhall@monroeccc.edu. *Website:* http://www.monroeccc.edu/.

Montcalm Community College
Sidney, Michigan

- **State and locally supported** 2-year, founded 1965, part of Michigan Department of Education
- **Rural** 240-acre campus with easy access to Grand Rapids
- **Coed,** 1,832 undergraduate students, 29% full-time, 65% women, 35% men

Undergraduates 538 full-time, 1,294 part-time. 0.4% Black or African American, non-Hispanic/Latino; 1% Hispanic/Latino; 0.2% Asian, non-Hispanic/Latino; 0.6% American Indian or Alaska Native, non-Hispanic/Latino; 2% Two or more races, non-Hispanic/Latino; 7% Race/ethnicity unknown; 0.1% international; 15% transferred in.
Freshmen *Admission:* 263 enrolled.
Faculty *Total:* 118, 25% full-time, 4% with terminal degrees. *Student/faculty ratio:* 16:1.
Majors Accounting; administrative assistant and secretarial science; automobile/automotive mechanics technology; business administration and management; child-care and support services management; child-care provision; computer installation and repair technology; corrections; cosmetology; criminal justice/law enforcement administration; data processing and data processing technology; drafting and design technology; electrical, electronic and communications engineering technology; emergency medical technology (EMT paramedic); entrepreneurship; general studies; industrial engineering; industrial technology; liberal arts and sciences/liberal studies; medical administrative assistant and medical secretary; registered nursing/registered nurse; teacher assistant/aide; welding technology.
Academics *Calendar:* semesters. *Degree:* certificates and associate. *Special study options:* academic remediation for entering students, adult/continuing education programs, advanced placement credit, cooperative education, distance learning, double majors, independent study, internships, off-campus study, part-time degree program, services for LD students, study abroad, summer session for credit.
Library Montcalm Community College Library with an OPAC, a Web page.
Student Life *Housing:* college housing not available. *Activities and Organizations:* drama/theater group, choral group, Nursing Club, Native American Club, Phi Theta Kappa, Business Club, Judo Club. *Student services:* personal/psychological counseling.
Athletics *Intramural sports:* volleyball M/W.
Costs (2014–15) *Tuition:* area resident $2880 full-time, $96 per credit hour part-time; state resident $5400 full-time, $180 per credit hour part-time; nonresident $8010 full-time, $267 per credit hour part-time. Full-time tuition and fees vary according to course load. Part-time tuition and fees vary according to course load. *Required fees:* $420 full-time, $14 per credit hour part-time. *Payment plan:* installment. *Waivers:* senior citizens and employees or children of employees.
Financial Aid Of all full-time matriculated undergraduates who enrolled in 2013, 444 were judged to have need.
Applying *Options:* electronic application, early admission, deferred entrance. *Recommended:* high school transcript.
Freshman Application Contact Ms. Debra Alexander, Associate Dean of Student Services, Montcalm Community College, 2800 College Drive, SW, Sidney, MI 48885. *Phone:* 989-328-1276. *Toll-free phone:* 877-328-2111. *E-mail:* admissions@montcalm.edu.
Website: http://www.montcalm.edu/.

Mott Community College
Flint, Michigan

- **District-supported** 2-year, founded 1923, part of Michigan Workforce Programs/Postsecondary Services/Community College Services
- **Urban** 32-acre campus with easy access to Detroit
- **Endowment** $41.5 million
- **Coed,** 8,937 undergraduate students, 27% full-time, 59% women, 41% men

Undergraduates 2,417 full-time, 6,520 part-time. Students come from 27 states and territories; 19% Black or African American, non-Hispanic/Latino; 4% Hispanic/Latino; 0.4% Asian, non-Hispanic/Latino; 0.1% Native Hawaiian or other Pacific Islander, non-Hispanic/Latino; 0.7% American Indian or Alaska Native, non-Hispanic/Latino; 3% Two or more races, non-Hispanic/Latino; 5% Race/ethnicity unknown; 4% international; 3% transferred in.
Freshmen *Admission:* 1,511 enrolled.
Faculty *Total:* 453, 32% full-time, 11% with terminal degrees. *Student/faculty ratio:* 19:1.
Majors Accounting technology and bookkeeping; architectural engineering technology; automobile/automotive mechanics technology; baking and pastry arts; biology/biological sciences; business administration and management; business/commerce; child-care provision; cinematography and film/video production; communications technology; community health services counseling; computer programming; computer programming (specific applications); computer systems networking and telecommunications; criminal justice/police science; culinary arts; dental assisting; dental hygiene; drafting and design technology; early childhood education; electrical, electronic and communications engineering technology; emergency medical technology (EMT paramedic); engineering technologies and engineering related; entrepreneurship; fire prevention and safety technology; food service systems administration; general studies; graphic design; heating, ventilation, air conditioning and refrigeration engineering technology; histologic technician; liberal arts and sciences/liberal studies; marketing/marketing management; mechanical engineering/mechanical technology; medical radiologic technology; music technology; occupational therapist assistant; photography; physical therapy technology; precision production related; registered nursing/registered nurse; respiratory care therapy; salon/beauty salon management; sign language interpretation and translation; visual and performing arts; web page, digital/multimedia and information resources design.
Academics *Calendar:* semesters. *Degree:* certificates and associate. *Special study options:* academic remediation for entering students, accelerated degree program, adult/continuing education programs, advanced placement credit, cooperative education, distance learning, double majors, English as a second language, honors programs, independent study, internships, part-time degree program, services for LD students, summer session for credit.
Library Charles Stewart Mott Library with 64,045 titles, an OPAC, a Web page.
Student Life *Housing:* college housing not available. *Activities and Organizations:* student-run newspaper, choral group, Otaku Club, L.E.R.N, Respiratory Care Student Society, Student Nurses Association, Transitions Cosmetology. *Campus security:* 24-hour emergency response devices and patrols, student patrols, late-night transport/escort service. *Student services:* health clinic, personal/psychological counseling.
Athletics Member NJCAA. *Intercollegiate sports:* baseball M(s), basketball M(s)/W(s), cross-country running M(s)/W(s), golf M(s), softball W(s), volleyball W(s). *Intramural sports:* cheerleading W(c).
Costs (2015–16) *Tuition:* area resident $3031 full-time, $126 per contact hour part-time; state resident $4402 full-time, $183 per contact hour part-time; nonresident $6274 full-time, $261 per contact hour part-time. Full-time tuition and fees vary according to course load. Part-time tuition and fees vary according to course load. *Required fees:* $637 full-time, $16 per contact hour part-time, $126 per term part-time. *Payment plan:* installment. *Waivers:* senior citizens and employees or children of employees.
Financial Aid Of all full-time matriculated undergraduates who enrolled in 2011, 16,668 applied for aid, 15,858 were judged to have need, 810 had their need fully met. 7,449 Federal Work-Study jobs (averaging $6303). In 2011, 95 non-need-based awards were made. *Average percent of need met:* 79%. *Average financial aid package:* $21,292. *Average need-based loan:* $3019. *Average need-based gift aid:* $3471. *Average non-need-based aid:* $2356.
Applying *Options:* electronic application, early admission, deferred entrance. *Required:* high school transcript. *Application deadline:* 8/31 (freshmen). *Notification:* continuous (transfers).
Freshman Application Contact Ms. Regina Broomfield, Supervisor of Admissions Operations - Admissions and Recruitment, Mott Community College, 1401 East Court Street, Flint, MI 48503. *Phone:* 810-762-0358. *Toll-free phone:* 800-852-8614. *Fax:* 810-232-9442. *E-mail:* regina.broomfield@mcc.edu.
Website: http://www.mcc.edu/.

Muskegon Community College
Muskegon, Michigan

Freshman Application Contact Ms. Darlene Peklar, Enrollment Generalist, Muskegon Community College, 221 South Quarterline Road, Muskegon, MI 49442-1493. *Phone:* 231-777-0366. *Toll-free phone:* 866-711-4622. *E-mail:* Dalene.Peklar@muskegoncc.edu.
Website: http://www.muskegoncc.edu/.

North Central Michigan College
Petoskey, Michigan

Director of Admissions Ms. Julieanne Tobin, Director of Enrollment Management, North Central Michigan College, 1515 Howard Street, Petoskey, MI 49770-8717. *Phone:* 231-439-6511. *Toll-free phone:* 888-298-6605. *E-mail:* jtobin@ncmich.edu.
Website: http://www.ncmich.edu/.

Northwestern Michigan College
Traverse City, Michigan

- **State and locally supported** primarily 2-year, founded 1951
- **Small-town** 180-acre campus
- **Coed,** 4,609 undergraduate students, 44% full-time, 59% women, 41% men

Undergraduates 2,011 full-time, 2,598 part-time. Students come from 19 states and territories; 21 other countries; 2% are from out of state; 11% transferred in. *Retention:* 61% of full-time freshmen returned.
Freshmen *Admission:* 1,909 applied, 1,054 admitted, 1,036 enrolled.
Faculty *Total:* 280, 33% full-time. *Student/faculty ratio:* 18:1.
Majors Accounting technology and bookkeeping; agricultural production related; airline pilot and flight crew; art; automobile/automotive mechanics technology; biology/biological sciences; business administration and management; business and personal/financial services marketing; business automation/technology/data entry; business, management, and marketing related; child-care and support services management; commercial and advertising art; corrections and criminal justice related; crop production; culinary arts; dental assisting; drafting and design technology; dramatic/theater arts; education; electrical, electronic and communications engineering technology; electromechanical and instrumentation and maintenance technologies related; engineering; English; executive assistant/executive secretary; forest/forest resources management; health professions related; industrial technology; landscaping and groundskeeping; legal administrative assistant/secretary; liberal arts and sciences/liberal studies; machine shop technology; management information systems; marine science/merchant marine officer; marine transportation related; maritime studies; marketing/marketing management; mathematics; medical/clinical assistant; music; ocean engineering; physical sciences; registered nursing/registered nurse; social sciences; speech communication and rhetoric; turf and turfgrass management.
Academics *Calendar:* semesters. *Degrees:* certificates, associate, and bachelor's. *Special study options:* academic remediation for entering students, adult/continuing education programs, advanced placement credit, cooperative education, distance learning, honors programs, independent study, internships, part-time degree program, services for LD students, summer session for credit.
Library Mark and Helen Osterlin Library plus 1 other with 53,050 titles, 2,316 audiovisual materials, an OPAC, a Web page.
Student Life *Housing Options:* coed. Campus housing is university owned and leased by the school. *Activities and Organizations:* drama/theater group, student-run newspaper, radio station, choral group, Residence Hall Council, Honors fraternity, student newspaper, student magazine, NMC I-dance. *Campus security:* 24-hour emergency response devices and patrols, student patrols, late-night transport/escort service, controlled dormitory access, well-lit campus. *Student services:* health clinic, personal/psychological counseling.
Athletics *Intramural sports:* basketball M/W, football M/W, golf M/W, sailing M(c)/W(c), skiing (downhill) M(c)/W(c), softball M/W, volleyball M/W.
Costs (2014–15) *Tuition:* area resident $2727 full-time, $91 per contact hour part-time; state resident $5400 full-time, $180 per contact hour part-time; nonresident $7040 full-time, $235 per contact hour part-time. Full-time tuition and fees vary according to course load and program. Part-time tuition and fees vary according to course load, program, and reciprocity agreements. *Required fees:* $859 full-time, $26 per contact hour part-time, $26 per term part-time. *Room and board:* $8725; room only: $5325. Room and board charges vary according to board plan, housing facility, and student level. *Payment plan:* installment. *Waivers:* employees or children of employees.
Financial Aid Of all full-time matriculated undergraduates who enrolled in 2013, 58 Federal Work-Study jobs (averaging $2068). 39 state and other part-time jobs (averaging $1718).

Applying *Options:* electronic application, early admission, deferred entrance. *Application fee:* $20. *Required for some:* high school transcript. *Recommended:* minimum 2.0 GPA. *Application deadlines:* rolling (freshmen), rolling (transfers). *Notification:* continuous until 8/22 (freshmen), continuous until 8/22 (transfers).
Freshman Application Contact Catheryn Claerhout, Director of Admissions, Northwestern Michigan College, 1701 E. Front St., Traverse City, MI 49686. *Phone:* 231-995-1034. *Toll-free phone:* 800-748-0566. *E-mail:* c.claerhout@nmc.edu.
Website: http://www.nmc.edu/.

Oakland Community College
Bloomfield Hills, Michigan

- **State and locally supported** 2-year, founded 1964
- **Suburban** 540-acre campus with easy access to Detroit
- **Endowment** $1.2 million
- **Coed**

Undergraduates 8,058 full-time, 18,347 part-time. Students come from 11 states and territories; 47 other countries; 0.1% are from out of state; 30% Black or African American, non-Hispanic/Latino; 3% Hispanic/Latino; 2% Asian, non-Hispanic/Latino; 0.1% Native Hawaiian or other Pacific Islander, non-Hispanic/Latino; 0.5% American Indian or Alaska Native, non-Hispanic/Latino; 2% Two or more races, non-Hispanic/Latino; 3% Race/ethnicity unknown; 4% international; 5% transferred in. *Retention:* 48% of full-time freshmen returned.
Faculty *Student/faculty ratio:* 22:1.
Academics *Calendar:* semesters. *Degree:* certificates and associate. *Special study options:* academic remediation for entering students, adult/continuing education programs, advanced placement credit, cooperative education, distance learning, English as a second language, independent study, internships, off-campus study, part-time degree program, services for LD students, study abroad, summer session for credit.
Student Life *Campus security:* 24-hour emergency response devices, late-night transport/escort service.
Athletics Member NJCAA.
Financial Aid Of all full-time matriculated undergraduates who enrolled in 2013, 3,517 applied for aid, 3,077 were judged to have need, 4 had their need fully met. 9 Federal Work-Study jobs (averaging $5061). In 2013, 53. *Average percent of need met:* 42. *Average financial aid package:* $4484. *Average need-based loan:* $1471. *Average need-based gift aid:* $4834. *Average non-need-based aid:* $1779.
Applying *Options:* electronic application, deferred entrance.
Freshman Application Contact Stephan M. Linden, Registrar, Oakland Community College, 2480 Opdyke Road, Bloomfield Hills, MI 48304-2266. *Phone:* 248-341-2192. *Fax:* 248-341-2099. *E-mail:* smlinden@oaklandcc.edu.
Website: http://www.oaklandcc.edu/.

Saginaw Chippewa Tribal College
Mount Pleasant, Michigan

- **Independent** 2-year, founded 1998
- **Small-town** campus
- **Coed,** 150 undergraduate students, 39% full-time, 61% women, 39% men

Undergraduates 58 full-time, 92 part-time. 2% Black or African American, non-Hispanic/Latino; 3% Hispanic/Latino; 84% American Indian or Alaska Native, non-Hispanic/Latino.
Freshmen *Admission:* 42 enrolled.
Faculty *Total:* 18, 39% full-time, 17% with terminal degrees. *Student/faculty ratio:* 9:1.
Majors American Indian/Native American studies; business/commerce; liberal arts and sciences/liberal studies.
Academics *Calendar:* semesters. *Degree:* associate.
Costs (2015–16) *Tuition:* $60 per contact hour part-time. Full-time tuition and fees vary according to class time, course level, course load, degree level, location, program, and student level. Part-time tuition and fees vary according to class time, course level, course load, degree level, location, program, and student level. *Required fees:* $25 per credit hour part-time. *Payment plans:* installment, deferred payment.
Applying *Options:* electronic application. *Required:* high school transcript.
Freshman Application Contact Ms. Amanda Flaugher, Admissions Officer/Registrar/Financial Aid, Saginaw Chippewa Tribal College, 2274 Enterprise Drive, Mount Pleasant, MI 48858. *Phone:* 989-775-4123. *Fax:* 989-775-4528. *E-mail:* flaugher.amanda@sagchip.org.
Website: http://www.sagchip.edu/.

St. Clair County Community College
Port Huron, Michigan

- **State and locally supported** 2-year, founded 1923, part of Michigan Department of Education
- **Small-town** 25-acre campus with easy access to Detroit
- **Coed,** 4,127 undergraduate students, 39% full-time, 59% women, 41% men

Undergraduates 1,591 full-time, 2,536 part-time. 3% Black or African American, non-Hispanic/Latino; 3% Hispanic/Latino; 0.4% Asian, non-Hispanic/Latino; 0.1% Native Hawaiian or other Pacific Islander, non-Hispanic/Latino; 1% American Indian or Alaska Native, non-Hispanic/Latino; 1% Two or more races, non-Hispanic/Latino; 4% Race/ethnicity unknown; 0.2% international. *Retention:* 55% of full-time freshmen returned.
Freshmen *Admission:* 751 enrolled.
Faculty *Total:* 254, 29% full-time. *Student/faculty ratio:* 18:1.
Majors Accounting technology and bookkeeping; automation engineer technology; business/commerce; child-care and support services management; commercial and advertising art; computer programming; computer systems networking and telecommunications; corrections; criminal justice/law enforcement administration; data processing and data processing technology; drafting and design technology; electrical, electronic and communications engineering technology; energy management and systems technology; engineering; executive assistant/executive secretary; fire science/firefighting; health information/medical records technology; liberal arts and sciences/liberal studies; manufacturing engineering technology; marketing/marketing management; massage therapy; medical administrative assistant and medical secretary; medical/clinical assistant; medical radiologic technology; office management; web/multimedia management and webmaster; welding engineering technology.
Academics *Calendar:* semesters. *Degree:* certificates and associate. *Special study options:* academic remediation for entering students, adult/continuing education programs, advanced placement credit, cooperative education, distance learning, honors programs, independent study, part-time degree program, services for LD students, summer session for credit.
Library Library plus 1 other with an OPAC, a Web page.
Student Life *Housing:* college housing not available. *Activities and Organizations:* drama/theater group, student-run newspaper, radio station, Phi Theta Kappa, Zombie Defense Council, Marketing and Management Club, Gay-Straight Alliance, Criminal Justice Club. *Campus security:* 24-hour emergency response devices, late-night transport/escort service, patrols by security until 10 pm. *Student services:* personal/psychological counseling.
Athletics Member NJCAA. *Intercollegiate sports:* baseball M(s), basketball M(s)/W(s), golf M, softball W(s), volleyball W(s).
Costs (2015–16) *Tuition:* $102 per contact hour part-time; state resident $198 per contact hour part-time; nonresident $290 per contact hour part-time. Full-time tuition and fees vary according to course load and location. Part-time tuition and fees vary according to course load and location. *Required fees:* $13 per contact hour part-time. *Payment plan:* deferred payment. *Waivers:* senior citizens and employees or children of employees.
Applying *Options:* electronic application, early admission. *Required:* high school transcript. *Application deadlines:* rolling (freshmen), rolling (transfers).
Freshman Application Contact St. Clair County Community College, 323 Erie Street, PO Box 5015, Port Huron, MI 48061-5015. *Phone:* 810-989-5501. *Toll-free phone:* 800-553-2427.
Website: http://www.sc4.edu/.

Schoolcraft College
Livonia, Michigan

- **District-supported** 2-year, founded 1961, part of Michigan Department of Education
- **Suburban** campus with easy access to Detroit
- **Coed,** 11,542 undergraduate students, 33% full-time, 54% women, 46% men

Undergraduates 3,793 full-time, 7,749 part-time. 15% Black or African American, non-Hispanic/Latino; 4% Hispanic/Latino; 4% Asian, non-Hispanic/Latino; 0.1% Native Hawaiian or other Pacific Islander, non-Hispanic/Latino; 0.7% American Indian or Alaska Native, non-Hispanic/Latino; 2% Two or more races, non-Hispanic/Latino; 7% Race/ethnicity unknown; 1% international; 25% transferred in. *Retention:* 66% of full-time freshmen returned.
Freshmen *Admission:* 2,217 enrolled.
Faculty *Total:* 501, 20% full-time. *Student/faculty ratio:* 28:1.
Majors Accounting technology and bookkeeping; biomedical technology; business administration and management; business automation/technology/data entry; business/commerce; child development; computer graphics; computer programming; computer programming (specific

applications); criminal justice/police science; culinary arts; drafting and design technology; education; electrical, electronic and communications engineering technology; emergency medical technology (EMT paramedic); engineering; environmental engineering technology; executive assistant/executive secretary; fine arts related; fire science/firefighting; general studies; health information/medical records technology; health services/allied health/health sciences; homeland security, law enforcement, firefighting and protective services related; manufacturing engineering technology; marketing/marketing management; massage therapy; metallurgical technology; pre-pharmacy studies; radio and television broadcasting technology; recording arts technology; registered nursing/registered nurse; salon/beauty salon management; small business administration; web page, digital/multimedia and information resources design; welding technology.

Academics *Calendar:* semesters. *Degree:* certificates and associate. *Special study options:* academic remediation for entering students, adult/continuing education programs, advanced placement credit, distance learning, English as a second language, honors programs, independent study, internships, part-time degree program, services for LD students, study abroad, summer session for credit.

Library Bradner Library with an OPAC, a Web page.

Student Life *Housing:* college housing not available. *Activities and Organizations:* drama/theater group, student-run newspaper, choral group, Phi Theta Kappa, The Schoolcraft Connection Newspaper, Student Activities Board, Project Playhem Gaming Club, Otaku Anime Japanese Animation Club. *Campus security:* 24-hour emergency response devices and patrols, late-night transport/escort service. *Student services:* personal/psychological counseling, women's center.

Athletics Member NJCAA. *Intercollegiate sports:* basketball M(s)/W(s), cross-country running M/W, golf M, soccer M(s)/W(s), volleyball W(s).

Costs (2014–15) *Tuition:* area resident $2790 full-time, $93 per semester hour part-time; state resident $4050 full-time, $135 per semester hour part-time; nonresident $5970 full-time, $199 per semester hour part-time. *Required fees:* $684 full-time, $20 per credit hour part-time, $42 per term part-time. *Payment plans:* installment, deferred payment. *Waivers:* senior citizens and employees or children of employees.

Financial Aid Of all full-time matriculated undergraduates who enrolled in 2013, 42 Federal Work-Study jobs (averaging $1722).

Applying *Options:* electronic application, early admission, deferred entrance. *Required for some:* high school transcript. *Recommended:* high school transcript. *Application deadlines:* rolling (freshmen), rolling (transfers).

Freshman Application Contact Ms. Nicole Wilson-Fennell, Registrar, Schoolcraft College, 18600 Haggerty Road, Livonia, MI 48152-2696. *Phone:* 734-462-4683. *Fax:* 734-462-4553. *E-mail:* gotoSC@schoolcraft.edu. *Website:* http://www.schoolcraft.edu/.

Southwestern Michigan College
Dowagiac, Michigan

- **State and locally supported** 2-year, founded 1964
- **Rural** 240-acre campus
- **Coed,** 2,567 undergraduate students, 48% full-time, 58% women, 42% men

Undergraduates 1,236 full-time, 1,331 part-time. Students come from 10 states and territories; 6 other countries; 14% are from out of state; 12% Black or African American, non-Hispanic/Latino; 6% Hispanic/Latino; 0.9% Asian, non-Hispanic/Latino; 1% American Indian or Alaska Native, non-Hispanic/Latino; 6% Two or more races, non-Hispanic/Latino; 3% Race/ethnicity unknown; 0.3% international; 28% transferred in; 18% live on campus. *Retention:* 53% of full-time freshmen returned.

Freshmen *Admission:* 2,358 applied, 2,335 admitted, 658 enrolled.

Faculty *Total:* 164, 30% full-time, 26% with terminal degrees. *Student/faculty ratio:* 19:1.

Majors Accounting technology and bookkeeping; automation engineer technology; automobile/automotive mechanics technology; business administration and management; carpentry; computer programming; computer support specialist; computer systems networking and telecommunications; criminal justice/safety; early childhood education; emergency medical technology (EMT paramedic); engineering technology; executive assistant/executive secretary; fire science/firefighting; general studies; graphic design; health information/medical records technology; industrial mechanics and maintenance technology; industrial production technologies related; liberal arts and sciences/liberal studies; machine tool technology; medical/clinical assistant; prenursing studies; professional, technical, business, and scientific writing; registered nursing/registered nurse; social work.

Academics *Calendar:* semesters. *Degree:* certificates and associate. *Special study options:* academic remediation for entering students, accelerated degree program, adult/continuing education programs, advanced placement credit, cooperative education, double majors, English as a second language, independent study, internships, part-time degree program, services for LD students, summer session for credit.

Library Fred L. Mathews Library with 36,303 titles, 3,853 audiovisual materials, an OPAC, a Web page.

Student Life *Housing Options:* coed. Campus housing is university owned. *Activities and Organizations:* drama/theater group, choral group, Advocates for All, Business Club, STEM Club, Alpha Kappa Omega, Rock Climbing Club. *Campus security:* 24-hour emergency response devices and patrols, controlled dormitory access, day and evening police patrols.

Athletics *Intramural sports:* basketball M/W, football M/W, rock climbing M/W, soccer M/W, softball M/W, tennis M/W, volleyball M/W.

Costs (2014–15) *Tuition:* area resident $2893 full-time, $111 per contact hour part-time; state resident $3751 full-time, $144 per contact hour part-time; nonresident $4082 full-time, $157 per contact hour part-time. *Required fees:* $1138 full-time, $44 per contact hour part-time. *Room and board:* $7989; room only: $5800. *Payment plan:* installment. *Waivers:* employees or children of employees.

Financial Aid Of all full-time matriculated undergraduates who enrolled in 2013, 125 Federal Work-Study jobs (averaging $1000). 75 state and other part-time jobs (averaging $1000).

Applying *Options:* electronic application, deferred entrance. *Required:* high school transcript. *Required for some:* interview. *Application deadlines:* rolling (freshmen), rolling (transfers). *Notification:* continuous (freshmen), continuous (transfers).

Freshman Application Contact Ms. Angela Palsak, Executive Director of Student Services, Southwestern Michigan College, Dowagiac, MI 49047. *Phone:* 269-782-1000 Ext. 1310. *Toll-free phone:* 800-456-8675. *Fax:* 269-782-1331. *E-mail:* apalsak@swmich.edu. *Website:* http://www.swmich.edu/.

Washtenaw Community College
Ann Arbor, Michigan

Freshman Application Contact Washtenaw Community College, 4800 East Huron River Drive, PO Box D-1, Ann Arbor, MI 48106. *Phone:* 734-973-3315. *Website:* http://www.wccnet.edu/.

Wayne County Community College District
Detroit, Michigan

- **State and locally supported** 2-year, founded 1967
- **Urban** campus
- **Coed,** 16,310 undergraduate students, 20% full-time, 66% women, 34% men

Undergraduates 3,186 full-time, 13,124 part-time. 72% Black or African American, non-Hispanic/Latino; 2% Hispanic/Latino; 1% Asian, non-Hispanic/Latino; 0.1% Native Hawaiian or other Pacific Islander, non-Hispanic/Latino; 0.5% American Indian or Alaska Native, non-Hispanic/Latino; 4% Two or more races, non-Hispanic/Latino; 10% Race/ethnicity unknown; 0.1% international; 15% transferred in.

Freshmen *Admission:* 3,390 enrolled.

Faculty *Total:* 936, 8% full-time. *Student/faculty ratio:* 24:1.

Majors Accounting technology and bookkeeping; aircraft powerplant technology; airframe mechanics and aircraft maintenance technology; art; autobody/collision and repair technology; automobile/automotive mechanics technology; biomedical technology; building/property maintenance; business administration and management; CAD/CADD drafting/design technology; child-care and support services management; computer numerically controlled (CNC) machinist technology; computer programming; corrections; criminal justice/police science; dental hygiene; digital communication and media/multimedia; e-commerce; electrical and electronic engineering technologies related; electrical, electronic and communications engineering technology; elementary education; emergency medical technology (EMT paramedic); fire prevention and safety technology; food service systems administration; general studies; heating, air conditioning, ventilation and refrigeration maintenance technology; legal assistant/paralegal; manufacturing engineering technology; mortuary science and embalming; office management; pharmacy technician; physician assistant; pre-engineering; registered nursing/registered nurse; social sciences; social work; surgical technology; veterinary/animal health technology; welding technology.

Academics *Calendar:* semesters. *Degree:* certificates and associate. *Special study options:* academic remediation for entering students, adult/continuing education programs, advanced placement credit, cooperative education, distance learning, English as a second language, honors programs, internships, part-time degree program, services for LD students, study abroad, summer session for credit.

Library Learning Resource Center plus 5 others with an OPAC, a Web page.

Student Life *Housing:* college housing not available. *Campus security:* 24-hour emergency response devices.

Athletics Member NJCAA. *Intercollegiate sports:* basketball M/W, bowling M/W, cross-country running M/W, golf M, volleyball W.
Costs (2014–15) *Tuition:* area resident $2520 full-time; state resident $2784 full-time; nonresident $3504 full-time. *Required fees:* $268 full-time. *Waivers:* senior citizens and employees or children of employees.
Financial Aid Of all full-time matriculated undergraduates who enrolled in 2013, 239 Federal Work-Study jobs (averaging $2360). 147 state and other part-time jobs (averaging $1200).
Applying *Options:* electronic application, early admission, deferred entrance. *Application deadlines:* rolling (freshmen), rolling (transfers).
Freshman Application Contact Mr. Adrian Phillips, District Associate Vice Chancellor of Student Services, Wayne County Community College District, 801 West Fort Street, Detroit, MI 48226-9975. *Phone:* 313-496-2820. *Fax:* 313-962-1643. *E-mail:* aphilli1@wcccd.edu.
Website: http://www.wcccd.edu/.

West Shore Community College
Scottville, Michigan

Freshman Application Contact Wendy Fought, Director of Admissions, West Shore Community College, PO Box 277, 3000 North Stiles Road, Scottville, MI 49454-0277. *Phone:* 231-843-5503. *Fax:* 231-845-3944. *E-mail:* admissions@westshore.edu.
Website: http://www.westshore.edu/.

MICRONESIA

College of Micronesia–FSM
Kolonia Pohnpei, Federated States of Micronesia, Micronesia

Freshman Application Contact Rita Hinga, Student Services Specialist, College of Micronesia–FSM, PO Box 159, Kolonia Pohnpei, FM 96941-0159, Micronesia. *Phone:* 691-320-3795 Ext. 15. *E-mail:* rhinga@comfsm.fm.
Website: http://www.comfsm.fm/.

MINNESOTA

Alexandria Technical and Community College
Alexandria, Minnesota

- **State-supported** 2-year, founded 1961, part of Minnesota State Colleges and Universities System
- **Small-town** 98-acre campus
- **Coed,** 2,525 undergraduate students, 55% full-time, 50% women, 50% men

Undergraduates 1,399 full-time, 1,126 part-time. Students come from 14 states and territories; 1 other country; 3% are from out of state; 2% Black or African American, non-Hispanic/Latino; 2% Hispanic/Latino; 0.7% Asian, non-Hispanic/Latino; 0.1% Native Hawaiian or other Pacific Islander, non-Hispanic/Latino; 1% American Indian or Alaska Native, non-Hispanic/Latino; 4% Race/ethnicity unknown.
Faculty *Total:* 102, 65% full-time, 4% with terminal degrees. *Student/faculty ratio:* 21:1.
Majors Accounting; automation engineer technology; business administration and management; child development; clinical/medical laboratory technology; commercial and advertising art; computer systems networking and telecommunications; criminal justice/police science; diesel mechanics technology; fashion merchandising; human services; industrial mechanics and maintenance technology; information science/studies; interior design; legal administrative assistant/secretary; legal assistant/paralegal; liberal arts and sciences/liberal studies; marketing/marketing management; mechanical drafting and CAD/CADD; medical administrative assistant and medical secretary; multi/interdisciplinary studies related; office management; physical fitness technician; pre-engineering; registered nursing/registered nurse; sales, distribution, and marketing operations; speech-language pathology assistant.
Academics *Calendar:* semesters. *Degree:* certificates, diplomas, and associate. *Special study options:* academic remediation for entering students, advanced placement credit, distance learning, double majors, independent study, internships, part-time degree program, services for LD students, student-designed majors, summer session for credit.

Library Learning Resource Center with 8,602 titles, 979 audiovisual materials, an OPAC, a Web page.
Student Life *Housing:* college housing not available. *Options:* Campus housing is provided by a third party. *Activities and Organizations:* Skills USA, Business Professionals of America, Delta Epsilon Chi, Student Senate, Phi Theta Kappa. *Campus security:* student patrols, late-night transport/escort service, security cameras inside and outside. *Student services:* personal/psychological counseling.
Athletics *Intramural sports:* basketball M/W, football M/W, softball M/W, volleyball M/W.
Costs (2014–15) *Tuition:* state resident $4817 full-time, $161 per credit part-time; nonresident $4817 full-time, $161 per credit part-time. *Required fees:* $581 full-time, $19 per credit part-time. *Room and board:* $5200. *Payment plan:* deferred payment. *Waivers:* senior citizens and employees or children of employees.
Financial Aid Of all full-time matriculated undergraduates who enrolled in 2013, 94 Federal Work-Study jobs (averaging $1871).
Applying *Options:* electronic application, early admission, deferred entrance. *Application fee:* $20. *Required:* high school transcript. *Required for some:* interview. *Recommended:* interview. *Application deadlines:* rolling (freshmen), rolling (out-of-state freshmen), rolling (transfers). *Notification:* continuous (freshmen), continuous (out-of-state freshmen), continuous (transfers).
Freshman Application Contact Janet Dropik, Admissions Office Assistant, Alexandria Technical and Community College, 1601 Jefferson Street, Alexandria, MN 56308. *Phone:* 320-762-4520. *Toll-free phone:* 888-234-1222. *Fax:* 320-762-4603. *E-mail:* admissionsrep@alextech.edu.
Website: http://www.alextech.edu/.

Anoka-Ramsey Community College
Coon Rapids, Minnesota

- **State-supported** 2-year, founded 1965, part of Minnesota State Colleges and Universities System
- **Suburban** 100-acre campus with easy access to Minneapolis-St. Paul
- **Coed,** 7,807 undergraduate students

Undergraduates 5% are from out of state; 8% Black or African American, non-Hispanic/Latino; 5% Hispanic/Latino; 4% Asian, non-Hispanic/Latino; 0.1% Native Hawaiian or other Pacific Islander, non-Hispanic/Latino; 0.5% American Indian or Alaska Native, non-Hispanic/Latino; 4% Two or more races, non-Hispanic/Latino; 2% Race/ethnicity unknown; 0.4% international. *Retention:* 53% of full-time freshmen returned.
Freshmen *Admission:* 3,301 applied, 1,394 admitted.
Faculty *Total:* 226, 50% full-time. *Student/faculty ratio:* 29:1.
Majors Accounting; accounting technology and bookkeeping; bioengineering and biomedical engineering; biology/biological sciences; biomedical technology; business administration and management; business/commerce; community health and preventive medicine; computer science; computer systems networking and telecommunications; creative writing; dramatic/theater arts; environmental science; fine/studio arts; health services/allied health/health sciences; holistic health; human resources management; interdisciplinary studies; liberal arts and sciences/liberal studies; multi/interdisciplinary studies related; music; physical therapy technology; pre-engineering; registered nursing/registered nurse; sales, distribution, and marketing operations.
Academics *Calendar:* semesters. *Degree:* certificates and associate. *Special study options:* academic remediation for entering students, accelerated degree program, advanced placement credit, cooperative education, distance learning, double majors, honors programs, independent study, internships, off-campus study, part-time degree program, services for LD students, study abroad, summer session for credit. *ROTC:* Air Force (c).
Library Coon Rapids Campus Library with 44,537 titles, 1,978 audiovisual materials, an OPAC, a Web page.
Student Life *Housing:* college housing not available. *Activities and Organizations:* drama/theater group, student-run newspaper, choral group, Theatre, Math Team, Concert Choir, Anime Association, Concert Band. *Campus security:* 24-hour emergency response devices, late-night transport/escort service. *Student services:* personal/psychological counseling.
Athletics Member NJCAA. *Intercollegiate sports:* baseball M, basketball M/W, soccer M/W, softball W, volleyball W. *Intramural sports:* basketball M/W, bowling M/W, football M/W, golf M/W, ice hockey M/W, soccer M/W, softball M/W, tennis M/W, volleyball M/W.
Costs (2015–16) *Tuition:* state resident $4349 full-time, $145 per credit part-time; nonresident $4349 full-time, $145 per credit part-time. Full-time tuition and fees vary according to course load and program. Part-time tuition and fees vary according to course load and program. *Required fees:* $657 full-time, $22 per credit part-time. *Payment plans:* installment, deferred payment. *Waivers:* senior citizens and employees or children of employees.
Financial Aid Of all full-time matriculated undergraduates who enrolled in 2012, 2,375 applied for aid, 2,281 were judged to have need, 1,655 had their

need fully met. In 2012, 15 non-need-based awards were made. *Average percent of need met:* 94%. *Average financial aid package:* $4852. *Average need-based loan:* $1925. *Average need-based gift aid:* $2262. *Average non-need-based aid:* $795.

Applying *Options:* electronic application, early admission, deferred entrance. *Required for some:* high school transcript. *Application deadlines:* rolling (freshmen), rolling (out-of-state freshmen), rolling (transfers). *Notification:* continuous (freshmen), continuous (out-of-state freshmen), continuous (transfers).

Freshman Application Contact Admissions Department, Anoka-Ramsey Community College, 11200 Mississippi Boulevard NW, Coon Rapids, MN 55433-3470. *Phone:* 763-433-1300. *Fax:* 763-433-1521. *E-mail:* admissions@anokaramsey.edu.
Website: http://www.anokaramsey.edu/.

Anoka-Ramsey Community College, Cambridge Campus
Cambridge, Minnesota

- **State-supported** 2-year, founded 1965, part of Minnesota State Colleges and Universities System
- **Small-town** campus
- **Coed,** 2,313 undergraduate students

Undergraduates 3% are from out of state; 2% Black or African American, non-Hispanic/Latino; 3% Hispanic/Latino; 2% Asian, non-Hispanic/Latino; 0.2% Native Hawaiian or other Pacific Islander, non-Hispanic/Latino; 0.3% American Indian or Alaska Native, non-Hispanic/Latino; 3% Two or more races, non-Hispanic/Latino; 0.6% Race/ethnicity unknown. *Retention:* 47% of full-time freshmen returned.

Freshmen *Admission:* 896 applied, 361 admitted.

Faculty *Total:* 53, 57% full-time. *Student/faculty ratio:* 35:1.

Majors Accounting; accounting technology and bookkeeping; bioengineering and biomedical engineering; biology/biological sciences; biomedical technology; business administration and management; business/commerce; community health and preventive medicine; computer science; computer systems networking and telecommunications; creative writing; dramatic/theater arts; environmental science; fine/studio arts; health services/allied health/health sciences; holistic health; human resources management; interdisciplinary studies; liberal arts and sciences/liberal studies; multi/interdisciplinary studies related; music; pharmacy technician; pre-engineering; registered nursing/registered nurse; sales, distribution, and marketing operations.

Academics *Calendar:* semesters. *Degree:* certificates and associate. *Special study options:* academic remediation for entering students, accelerated degree program, advanced placement credit, cooperative education, distance learning, double majors, honors programs, independent study, internships, off-campus study, part-time degree program, services for LD students, study abroad, summer session for credit. *ROTC:* Air Force (c).

Library Cambridge Campus Library with 17,406 titles, 1,240 audiovisual materials, an OPAC, a Web page.

Student Life *Housing:* college housing not available. *Activities and Organizations:* drama/theater group, student-run newspaper, choral group. *Campus security:* 24-hour emergency response devices, late-night transport/escort service. *Student services:* personal/psychological counseling.

Athletics Member NJCAA. *Intercollegiate sports:* baseball M, basketball M/W, soccer M/W, softball W, volleyball W. *Intramural sports:* bowling M/W, golf M/W, volleyball M/W.

Costs (2015–16) *Tuition:* state resident $4349 full-time; nonresident $4349 full-time. Full-time tuition and fees vary according to course load and program. Part-time tuition and fees vary according to course load and program. *Required fees:* $651 full-time. *Payment plans:* installment, deferred payment. *Waivers:* senior citizens and employees or children of employees.

Applying *Options:* electronic application, early admission, deferred entrance. *Required for some:* high school transcript. *Application deadlines:* rolling (freshmen), rolling (out-of-state freshmen), rolling (transfers). *Notification:* continuous (freshmen), continuous (out-of-state freshmen), continuous (transfers).

Freshman Application Contact Admissions Department, Anoka-Ramsey Community College, Cambridge Campus, 300 Spirit River Drive South, Cambridge, MN 55008-5704. *Phone:* 763-433-1300. *Fax:* 763-433-1841. *E-mail:* admissions@anokaramsey.edu.
Website: http://www.anokaramsey.edu/.

Anoka Technical College
Anoka, Minnesota

- **State-supported** 2-year, founded 1967, part of Minnesota State Colleges and Universities System
- **Small-town** campus with easy access to Minneapolis-St. Paul
- **Coed,** 2,237 undergraduate students

Majors Accounting; administrative assistant and secretarial science; architectural drafting and CAD/CADD; automobile/automotive mechanics technology; aviation/airway management; biomedical technology; computer numerically controlled (CNC) machinist technology; computer technology/computer systems technology; court reporting; developmental services worker; electrical, electronic and communications engineering technology; golf course operation and grounds management; health information/medical records technology; landscaping and groundskeeping; legal administrative assistant/secretary; licensed practical/vocational nurse training; mechanical drafting and CAD/CADD; medical administrative assistant and medical secretary; medical/clinical assistant; occupational therapist assistant; office management; surgical technology; welding technology.

Academics *Calendar:* semesters. *Degree:* certificates, diplomas, and associate. *Special study options:* academic remediation for entering students, advanced placement credit, cooperative education, distance learning, double majors, English as a second language, internships, part-time degree program, services for LD students.

Student Life *Housing:* college housing not available. *Campus security:* late-night transport/escort service. *Student services:* personal/psychological counseling.

Costs (2015–16) *Tuition:* state resident $5010 full-time, $167 per credit part-time; nonresident $5010 full-time, $167 per credit part-time. Full-time tuition and fees vary according to program and reciprocity agreements. Part-time tuition and fees vary according to program and reciprocity agreements. *Required fees:* $557 full-time, $19 per credit part-time. *Payment plan:* installment. *Waivers:* senior citizens and employees or children of employees.

Applying *Options:* electronic application, deferred entrance. *Required:* high school transcript. *Required for some:* interview.

Freshman Application Contact Anoka Technical College, 1355 West Highway 10, Anoka, MN 55303.
Website: http://www.anokatech.edu/.

Central Lakes College
Brainerd, Minnesota

Freshman Application Contact Ms. Rose Tretter, Central Lakes College, 501 West College Drive, Brainerd, MN 56401-3904. *Phone:* 218-855-8036. *Toll-free phone:* 800-933-0346. *Fax:* 218-855-8220. *E-mail:* cdaniels@clcmn.edu. *Website:* http://www.clcmn.edu/.

Century College
White Bear Lake, Minnesota

- **State-supported** 2-year, founded 1970, part of Minnesota State Colleges and Universities System
- **Suburban** 170-acre campus with easy access to Minneapolis-St. Paul
- **Coed,** 9,386 undergraduate students, 39% full-time, 55% women, 45% men

Undergraduates 3,629 full-time, 5,757 part-time. Students come from 41 states and territories; 54 other countries; 6% are from out of state; 10% Black or African American, non-Hispanic/Latino; 7% Hispanic/Latino; 17% Asian, non-Hispanic/Latino; 0.1% Native Hawaiian or other Pacific Islander, non-Hispanic/Latino; 0.4% American Indian or Alaska Native, non-Hispanic/Latino; 5% Two or more races, non-Hispanic/Latino; 0.5% Race/ethnicity unknown; 2% international; 45% transferred in.

Freshmen *Admission:* 2,943 applied, 2,943 admitted, 1,206 enrolled.

Faculty *Total:* 368, 52% full-time. *Student/faculty ratio:* 22:1.

Majors Accounting; administrative assistant and secretarial science; building/property maintenance; business administration and management; CAD/CADD drafting/design technology; computer and information systems security; computer science; computer systems networking and telecommunications; computer technology/computer systems technology; cosmetology; criminal justice/police science; criminal justice/safety; cyber/computer forensics and counterterrorism; dental assisting; dental hygiene; digital communication and media/multimedia; e-commerce; education; emergency medical technology (EMT paramedic); energy management and systems technology; fine/studio arts; greenhouse management; health services/allied health/health sciences; heating, air conditioning, ventilation and refrigeration maintenance technology; homeland security; law enforcement, firefighting and protective services related; horticultural science; human services; information science/studies; interior design; landscaping and groundskeeping; language interpretation and translation; liberal arts and sciences/liberal studies; marketing/marketing management; medical administrative assistant and medical secretary; multi/interdisciplinary studies related; music; orthotics/prosthetics; pre-engineering; radiologic technology/science; registered nursing/registered nurse; substance abuse/addiction counseling; teacher assistant/aide.

Academics *Calendar:* semesters. *Degree:* certificates, diplomas, and associate. *Special study options:* academic remediation for entering students, advanced placement credit, distance learning, double majors, English as a second language, honors programs, internships, part-time degree program, services for LD students, student-designed majors, summer session for credit. *ROTC:* Air Force (c).

Library Century College Library with 226,028 titles, 21,339 audiovisual materials, an OPAC, a Web page.

Student Life *Housing:* college housing not available. *Activities and Organizations:* drama/theater group, student-run newspaper, choral group, Asian Student Association, Student Senate, Phi Theta Kappa, Planning Activities Committee, Anime Club. *Campus security:* late-night transport/escort service, day patrols. *Student services:* health clinic, personal/psychological counseling.

Athletics Member NJCAA. *Intercollegiate sports:* baseball M, soccer M/W, softball W. *Intramural sports:* badminton M/W, basketball M/W, bowling M/W, football M/W, golf M/W, ice hockey M/W, soccer M/W, softball M/W, table tennis M/W, volleyball M/W.

Costs (2014–15) *Tuition:* state resident $4818 full-time, $161 per semester hour part-time; nonresident $4818 full-time, $161 per semester hour part-time. Full-time tuition and fees vary according to class time, program, and reciprocity agreements. Part-time tuition and fees vary according to class time, program, and reciprocity agreements. *Required fees:* $555 full-time, $19 per semester hour part-time. *Payment plan:* installment. *Waivers:* senior citizens and employees or children of employees.

Financial Aid Of all full-time matriculated undergraduates who enrolled in 2013, 81 Federal Work-Study jobs (averaging $2763). 85 state and other part-time jobs (averaging $2646).

Applying *Options:* electronic application, deferred entrance. *Application fee:* $20. *Required:* high school transcript. *Application deadlines:* rolling (freshmen), rolling (transfers).

Freshman Application Contact Ms. Christine Paulos, Admissions Director, Century College, 3300 Century Avenue North, White Bear Lake, MN 55110. *Phone:* 651-779-2619. *Toll-free phone:* 800-228-1978. *Fax:* 651-773-1796. *E-mail:* admissions@century.edu. *Website:* http://www.century.edu/.

Dakota County Technical College

Rosemount, Minnesota

Freshman Application Contact Mr. Patrick Lair, Admissions Director, Dakota County Technical College, 1300 East 145th Street, Rosemount, MN 55068. *Phone:* 651-423-8399. *Toll-free phone:* 877-YES-DCTC. *Fax:* 651-423-8775. *E-mail:* admissions@dctc.mnscu.edu. *Website:* http://www.dctc.edu/.

Duluth Business University

Duluth, Minnesota

- **Proprietary** primarily 2-year, founded 1891
- **Urban** 2-acre campus
- **Coed, primarily women,** 182 undergraduate students, 57% full-time, 87% women, 13% men

Undergraduates 103 full-time, 79 part-time. Students come from 6 states and territories; 24% are from out of state; 2% Black or African American, non-Hispanic/Latino; 0.5% Asian, non-Hispanic/Latino; 0.5% Native Hawaiian or other Pacific Islander, non-Hispanic/Latino; 2% American Indian or Alaska Native, non-Hispanic/Latino.

Freshmen *Admission:* 278 applied, 19 enrolled.

Majors Accounting technology and bookkeeping; business administration and management; commercial and advertising art; health information/medical records technology; massage therapy; medical/clinical assistant; phlebotomy technology; veterinary/animal health technology.

Academics *Calendar:* quarters. *Degrees:* diplomas, associate, and bachelor's.

Student Life *Housing:* college housing not available.

Applying *Application fee:* $35.

Freshman Application Contact Mr. Mark Traux, Director of Admissions, Duluth Business University, 4724 Mike Colalillo Drive, Duluth, MN 55807. *Phone:* 218-722-4000. *Toll-free phone:* 800-777-8406. *Fax:* 218-628-2127. *E-mail:* markt@dbumn.edu. *Website:* http://www.dbumn.edu/.

Dunwoody College of Technology

Minneapolis, Minnesota

- **Independent** primarily 2-year, founded 1914
- **Urban** 12-acre campus with easy access to Minneapolis-St. Paul
- **Endowment** $21.6 million
- **Coed, primarily men,** 1,070 undergraduate students, 82% full-time, 14% women, 86% men

Undergraduates 873 full-time, 197 part-time. 1% are from out of state; 7% Black or African American, non-Hispanic/Latino; 2% Hispanic/Latino; 4% Asian, non-Hispanic/Latino; 0.2% Native Hawaiian or other Pacific Islander, non-Hispanic/Latino; 0.6% American Indian or Alaska Native, non-Hispanic/Latino; 5% Two or more races, non-Hispanic/Latino; 3% Race/ethnicity unknown. *Retention:* 100% of full-time freshmen returned.

Freshmen *Admission:* 741 applied, 501 admitted, 180 enrolled. *Average high school GPA:* 2.48.

Faculty *Total:* 145, 54% full-time, 9% with terminal degrees. *Student/faculty ratio:* 9:1.

Majors Architectural drafting and CAD/CADD; architectural technology; autobody/collision and repair technology; automobile/automotive mechanics technology; building/construction site management; business administration and management; CAD/CADD drafting/design technology; computer science; computer systems networking and telecommunications; construction management; desktop publishing and digital imaging design; electrical, electronic and communications engineering technology; electrical/electronics drafting and CAD/CADD; electrician; graphic design; heating, air conditioning, ventilation and refrigeration maintenance technology; heating, ventilation, air conditioning and refrigeration engineering technology; industrial technology; interior design; medical radiologic technology; printing press operation; robotics technology; tool and die technology; web page, digital/multimedia and information resources design; welding technology.

Academics *Calendar:* semesters. *Degrees:* certificates, associate, and bachelor's. *Special study options:* academic remediation for entering students, cooperative education, distance learning, independent study, internships, study abroad, summer session for credit.

Library Learning Resource Center with 8,000 titles, 250 audiovisual materials, an OPAC, a Web page.

Student Life *Housing:* college housing not available. *Activities and Organizations:* Phi Theta Kappa, Historic Green. *Campus security:* 24-hour emergency response devices, late-night transport/escort service. *Student services:* personal/psychological counseling, women's center.

Standardized Tests *Recommended:* SAT or ACT (for admission).

Costs (2014–15) *Tuition:* $17,645 full-time. Full-time tuition and fees vary according to course level, course load, and program. Part-time tuition and fees vary according to course level, course load, and program. *Required fees:* $1446 full-time. *Payment plans:* installment, deferred payment.

Financial Aid Of all full-time matriculated undergraduates who enrolled in 2013, 635 applied for aid, 584 were judged to have need, 14 had their need fully met. 22 Federal Work-Study jobs (averaging $3410). 44 state and other part-time jobs (averaging $2369). In 2013, 7 non-need-based awards were made. *Average percent of need met:* 32%. *Average financial aid package:* $8339. *Average need-based loan:* $3770. *Average need-based gift aid:* $5698. *Average non-need-based aid:* $1333. *Average indebtedness upon graduation:* $9798.

Applying *Options:* electronic application. *Application fee:* $50. *Required:* essay or personal statement, high school transcript, minimum 2.5 GPA. *Required for some:* minimum 3.0 GPA, . *Recommended:* interview. *Application deadlines:* rolling (freshmen), rolling (out-of-state freshmen), rolling (transfers). *Notification:* continuous (freshmen), continuous (out-of-state freshmen), continuous (transfers).

Freshman Application Contact Cynthia Olson, Director of Admissions and Student Services, Dunwoody College of Technology, 818 Dunwoody Boulevard, Minneapolis, MN 55403. *Phone:* 612-374-5800. *Toll-free phone:* 800-292-4625. *Website:* http://www.dunwoody.edu/.

Fond du Lac Tribal and Community College

Cloquet, Minnesota

Freshman Application Contact Kathie Jubie, Admissions Representative, Fond du Lac Tribal and Community College, 2101 14th Street, Cloquet, MN 55720. *Phone:* 218-879-0808. *Toll-free phone:* 800-657-3712. *E-mail:* admissions@fdltcc.edu. *Website:* http://www.fdltcc.edu/.

Hennepin Technical College
Brooklyn Park, Minnesota

- **State-supported** 2-year, founded 1972, part of Minnesota State Colleges and Universities System
- **Suburban** 100-acre campus with easy access to Minneapolis-St. Paul
- **Coed,** 5,985 undergraduate students, 34% full-time, 42% women, 58% men

Undergraduates 2,063 full-time, 3,922 part-time. 7% transferred in.
Freshmen *Admission:* 654 enrolled.
Faculty *Total:* 172. *Student/faculty ratio:* 25:1.
Majors Accounting; administrative assistant and secretarial science; architectural drafting and CAD/CADD; autobody/collision and repair technology; automation engineer technology; automobile/automotive mechanics technology; business administration and management; CAD/CADD drafting/design technology; carpentry; child development; computer numerically controlled (CNC) machinist technology; computer programming; computer systems networking and telecommunications; dental assisting; desktop publishing and digital imaging design; drafting/design engineering technologies related; electrical, electronic and communications engineering technology; fire science/firefighting; graphic design; greenhouse management; heating, air conditioning, ventilation and refrigeration maintenance technology; hydraulics and fluid power technology; landscaping and groundskeeping; licensed practical/vocational nurse training; machine tool technology; management information systems; manufacturing engineering technology; medical administrative assistant and medical secretary; medium/heavy vehicle and truck technology; photography; plastics and polymer engineering technology; recording arts technology; tool and die technology; urban forestry; web page, digital/multimedia and information resources design.
Academics *Calendar:* semesters. *Degree:* certificates, diplomas, and associate. *Special study options:* academic remediation for entering students, adult/continuing education programs, advanced placement credit, cooperative education, distance learning, double majors, English as a second language, honors programs, independent study, internships, part-time degree program, services for LD students, student-designed majors, summer session for credit.
Library Main Library plus 1 other.
Student Life *Housing:* college housing not available. *Activities and Organizations:* Student Senate, Pangea, Images, Skills USA. *Campus security:* late-night transport/escort service, security service. *Student services:* personal/psychological counseling.
Costs (2015–16) *Tuition:* state resident $5142 full-time, $157 per credit part-time; nonresident $5142 full-time, $157 per credit part-time. Full-time tuition and fees vary according to program. Part-time tuition and fees vary according to program. *Required fees:* $441 full-time, $15 per credit part-time. *Payment plan:* installment. *Waivers:* senior citizens and employees or children of employees.
Financial Aid Of all full-time matriculated undergraduates who enrolled in 2013, 72 Federal Work-Study jobs (averaging $3000).
Applying *Options:* electronic application. *Recommended:* high school transcript. *Application deadlines:* rolling (freshmen), rolling (transfers). *Notification:* continuous (freshmen), continuous (transfers).
Freshman Application Contact Ms. Monir Johnson, Director of Admissions, Hennepin Technical College, 9000 Brooklyn Boulevard, Brooklyn Park, MN 55445. *Phone:* 763-488-2415. *Toll-free phone:* 800-345-4655 (in-state); 800-645-4655 (out-of-state). *Fax:* 763-550-2113. *E-mail:* monir.johnson@hennepintech.edu.
Website: http://www.hennepintech.edu/.

Herzing University
Minneapolis, Minnesota

Freshman Application Contact Ms. Shelly Larson, Director of Admissions, Herzing University, 5700 West Broadway, Minneapolis, MN 55428. *Phone:* 763-231-3155. *Toll-free phone:* 800-596-0724. *Fax:* 763-535-9205. *E-mail:* info@mpls.herzing.edu.
Website: http://www.herzing.edu/minneapolis.

Hibbing Community College
Hibbing, Minnesota

Freshman Application Contact Admissions, Hibbing Community College, 1515 East 25th Street, Hibbing, MN 55746. *Phone:* 218-262-7200. *Toll-free phone:* 800-224-4HCC. *Fax:* 218-262-6717. *E-mail:* admissions@hibbing.edu.
Website: http://www.hcc.mnscu.edu/.

The Institute of Production and Recording
Minneapolis, Minnesota

- **Proprietary** 2-year, part of Globe Education Network (GEN) which is composed of Globe University, Minnesota School of Business, Broadview University, The Institute of Production and Recording and Minnesota School of Cosmetology
- **Urban** 4-acre campus with easy access to Minneapolis-St. Paul
- **Coed**

Undergraduates 153 full-time, 89 part-time. Students come from 20 states and territories; 24% are from out of state; 10% Black or African American, non-Hispanic/Latino; 5% Hispanic/Latino; 2% Asian, non-Hispanic/Latino; 0.4% Native Hawaiian or other Pacific Islander, non Hispanic/Latino; 0.4% American Indian or Alaska Native, non-Hispanic/Latino; 5% Two or more races, non-Hispanic/Latino; 3% Race/ethnicity unknown; 0.4% international; 15% transferred in.
Academics *Degree:* associate. *Special study options:* academic remediation for entering students, accelerated degree program, adult/continuing education programs, advanced placement credit, independent study, internships, off-campus study, part-time degree program, services for LD students, summer session for credit.
Student Life *Campus security:* 24-hour emergency response devices.
Standardized Tests *Required:* ACCUPLACER is required of most applicants unless documentation of a minimum ACT composite score of 21 or documentation of a minimum composite score of 1485 on the SAT is presented (for admission).
Applying *Options:* electronic application. *Application fee:* $50. *Required:* high school transcript, interview, Certification of high school graduation or GED.
Freshman Application Contact The Institute of Production and Recording, 300 North 1st Avenue, Suite 500, Minneapolis, MN 55401.
Website: http://www.ipr.edu/.

Inver Hills Community College
Inver Grove Heights, Minnesota

Freshman Application Contact Mr. Casey Carmody, Admissions Representative, Inver Hills Community College, 2500 East 80th Street, Inver Grove Heights, MN 55076-3224. *Phone:* 651-450-3589. *Fax:* 651-450-3677. *E-mail:* admissions@inverhills.edu.
Website: http://www.inverhills.edu/.

Itasca Community College
Grand Rapids, Minnesota

Freshman Application Contact Ms. Candace Perry, Director of Enrollment Services, Itasca Community College, Grand Rapids, MN 55744. *Phone:* 218-322-2340. *Toll-free phone:* 800-996-6422. *Fax:* 218-327-4350. *E-mail:* iccinfo@itascacc.edu.
Website: http://www.itascacc.edu/.

ITT Technical Institute
Brooklyn Center, Minnesota

- **Proprietary** primarily 2-year, part of ITT Educational Services, Inc.
- **Coed**

Academics *Calendar:* quarters. *Degrees:* associate and bachelor's.
Freshman Application Contact Director of Recruitment, ITT Technical Institute, 6120 Earle Brown Drive, Suite 100, Brooklyn Center, MN 55430. *Phone:* 763-549-5900. *Toll-free phone:* 800-216-8883.
Website: http://www.itt-tech.edu/.

ITT Technical Institute
Eden Prairie, Minnesota

- **Proprietary** primarily 2-year, founded 2003, part of ITT Educational Services, Inc.
- **Coed**

Academics *Calendar:* quarters. *Degrees:* associate and bachelor's.
Freshman Application Contact Director of Recruitment, ITT Technical Institute, 7905 Golden Triangle Drive, Eden Prairie, MN 55344. *Phone:* 952-914-5300. *Toll-free phone:* 888-488-9646.
Website: http://www.itt-tech.edu/.

Lake Superior College
Duluth, Minnesota

- **State-supported** 2-year, founded 1995, part of Minnesota State Colleges and Universities System
- **Urban** 105-acre campus
- **Coed**

Undergraduates 2,108 full-time, 2,942 part-time. Students come from 28 states and territories; 6 other countries; 15% are from out of state; 4% Black or African American, non-Hispanic/Latino; 3% Hispanic/Latino; 1% Asian, non-Hispanic/Latino; 0.1% Native Hawaiian or other Pacific Islander, non-Hispanic/Latino; 2% American Indian or Alaska Native, non-Hispanic/Latino; 4% Two or more races, non-Hispanic/Latino; 1% Race/ethnicity unknown; 0.1% international; 39% transferred in.

Faculty *Student/faculty ratio:* 21:1.

Academics *Calendar:* semesters. *Degree:* certificates, diplomas, and associate. *Special study options:* academic remediation for entering students, advanced placement credit, distance learning, double majors, independent study, internships, part-time degree program, services for LD students, study abroad, summer session for credit.

Student Life *Campus security:* late-night transport/escort service.

Costs (2014–15) *Tuition:* state resident $4418 full-time; nonresident $8835 full-time. Full-time tuition and fees vary according to course load, program, and reciprocity agreements. Part-time tuition and fees vary according to course load, program, and reciprocity agreements. *Required fees:* $689 full-time. *Payment plans:* installment, deferred payment.

Financial Aid Of all full-time matriculated undergraduates who enrolled in 2013, 53 Federal Work-Study jobs (averaging $2720). 145 state and other part-time jobs (averaging $2720).

Applying *Options:* electronic application. *Application fee:* $20. *Required:* transcripts from high school, GED, or HSED and official transcripts from all previous post-secondary institutions attended. *Required for some:* high school transcript.

Freshman Application Contact Ms. Melissa Leno, Director of Admissions, Lake Superior College, 2101 Trinity Road, Duluth, MN 55811. *Phone:* 218-733-5903. *Toll-free phone:* 800-432-2884. *E-mail:* enroll@lsc.edu. *Website:* http://www.lsc.edu/.

Le Cordon Bleu College of Culinary Arts in Minneapolis/St. Paul
Mendota Heights, Minnesota

Freshman Application Contact Admissions Office, Le Cordon Bleu College of Culinary Arts in Minneapolis/St. Paul, 1315 Mendota Heights Road, Mendota Heights, MN 55120. *Phone:* 651-675-4700. *Toll-free phone:* 888-348-5222.
Website: http://www.chefs.edu/Minneapolis-St-Paul/.

Leech Lake Tribal College
Cass Lake, Minnesota

Freshman Application Contact Ms. Shelly Braford, Recruiter, Leech Lake Tribal College, PO Box 180, 6945 Littlewolf Road NW, Cass Lake, MN 56633. *Phone:* 218-335-4200 Ext. 4270. *Fax:* 218-335-4217. *E-mail:* shelly.braford@lltc.edu.
Website: http://www.lltc.edu/.

Mesabi Range College
Virginia, Minnesota

- **State-supported** 2-year, founded 1918, part of Minnesota State Colleges and Universities System
- **Small-town** 30-acre campus
- **Coed,** 1,451 undergraduate students, 61% full-time, 45% women, 55% men

Undergraduates 878 full-time, 573 part-time. Students come from 6 states and territories; 2 other countries; 4% are from out of state; 7% Black or African American, non-Hispanic/Latino; 0.5% Hispanic/Latino; 1% Asian, non-Hispanic/Latino; 4% American Indian or Alaska Native, non-Hispanic/Latino; 10% Race/ethnicity unknown; 10% live on campus.

Faculty *Total:* 203. *Student/faculty ratio:* 24:1.

Majors Administrative assistant and secretarial science; business/commerce; computer graphics; computer/information technology services administration related; computer programming related; computer programming (specific applications); computer software and media applications related; computer systems networking and telecommunications; electrical/electronics equipment installation and repair; human services; information technology; instrumentation technology; liberal arts and sciences/liberal studies; pre-

engineering; substance abuse/addiction counseling; web page, digital/multimedia and information resources design.

Academics *Calendar:* semesters. *Degree:* certificates, diplomas, and associate. *Special study options:* academic remediation for entering students, adult/continuing education programs, advanced placement credit, cooperative education, distance learning, independent study, internships, off-campus study, part-time degree program, services for LD students, student-designed majors, study abroad, summer session for credit.

Library Mesabi Library with 23,000 titles.

Student Life *Housing Options:* coed. Campus housing is provided by a third party. *Activities and Organizations:* drama/theater group, student-run newspaper, choral group, Student Senate, Human Services Club, Career Program Clubs, Student Life Club, Diversity Club. *Campus security:* late-night transport/escort service. *Student services:* personal/psychological counseling.

Athletics Member NJCAA. *Intercollegiate sports:* baseball M, basketball M/W, football M, golf M/W, softball W, volleyball W. *Intramural sports:* badminton M/W, basketball M/W, bowling M/W, field hockey M/W, football M/W, golf M/W, ice hockey M/W, skiing (cross-country) M/W, skiing (downhill) M/W, tennis M/W, volleyball M/W.

Costs (2014–15) *Tuition:* state resident $5280 full-time, $158 per credit part-time; nonresident $5670 full-time, $197 per credit part-time. Full-time tuition and fees vary according to reciprocity agreements. Part-time tuition and fees vary according to reciprocity agreements. *Required fees:* $564 full-time, $19 per credit part-time, $19 per credit part-time. *Room and board:* room only: $3936.

Financial Aid Of all full-time matriculated undergraduates who enrolled in 2011, 168 Federal Work-Study jobs (averaging $1227). 82 state and other part-time jobs (averaging $1380).

Applying *Options:* electronic application, early admission, deferred entrance. *Required:* high school transcript. *Application deadlines:* rolling (freshmen), rolling (transfers). *Notification:* continuous (freshmen), continuous (transfers).

Freshman Application Contact Ms. Brenda Kochevar, Enrollment Services Director, Mesabi Range College, Virginia, MN 55792. *Phone:* 218-749-0314. *Toll-free phone:* 800-657-3860. *Fax:* 218-749-0318. *E-mail:* b.kochevar@mesabirange.edu.
Website: http://www.mesabirange.edu/.

Minneapolis Business College
Roseville, Minnesota

- **Private** 2-year, founded 1874
- **Suburban** campus with easy access to Minneapolis-St. Paul
- **Coed,** 235 undergraduate students
- **88%** of applicants were admitted

Freshmen *Admission:* 462 applied, 405 admitted.

Majors Accounting technology and bookkeeping; administrative assistant and secretarial science; computer programming; computer systems networking and telecommunications; graphic design; hotel/motel administration; legal administrative assistant/secretary; legal assistant/paralegal; medical/clinical assistant.

Academics *Calendar:* semesters. *Degree:* diplomas and associate.

Freshman Application Contact Admissions Office, Minneapolis Business College, 1711 West County Road B, Roseville, MN 55113. *Phone:* 651-636-7406. *Toll-free phone:* 800-279-5200.
Website: http://www.minneapolisbusinesscollege.edu/.

Minneapolis Community and Technical College
Minneapolis, Minnesota

- **State-supported** 2-year, founded 1965, part of Minnesota State Colleges and Universities System
- **Urban** 22-acre campus
- **Coed,** 9,465 undergraduate students, 34% full-time, 55% women, 45% men

Undergraduates 3,210 full-time, 6,255 part-time. 31% Black or African American, non-Hispanic/Latino; 10% Hispanic/Latino; 6% Asian, non-Hispanic/Latino; 0.1% Native Hawaiian or other Pacific Islander, non-Hispanic/Latino; 2% American Indian or Alaska Native, non-Hispanic/Latino; 8% Two or more races, non-Hispanic/Latino; 2% Race/ethnicity unknown; 1% international.

Freshmen *Admission:* 1,260 enrolled.

Faculty *Total:* 397, 45% full-time, 20% with terminal degrees.

Majors Accounting; accounting technology and bookkeeping; administrative assistant and secretarial science; allied health diagnostic, intervention, and treatment professions related; animation, interactive technology, video graphics and special effects; biology/biological sciences; business administration and management; business automation/technology/data entry; chemistry; child-care and support services management; child development; cinematography and film/video production; commercial photography; community organization and advocacy; computer and information systems security; computer programming; computer systems networking and telecommunications; criminal justice/police science; criminal justice/safety; dental assisting; design and visual communications; digital communication and media/multimedia; dramatic/theater arts; education; education (multiple levels); fine/studio arts; heating, air conditioning, ventilation and refrigeration maintenance technology; human services; liberal arts and sciences/liberal studies; library and archives assisting; mathematics; network and system administration; philosophy; photographic and film/video technology; playwriting and screenwriting; polysomnography; public administration; recording arts technology; registered nursing/registered nurse; restaurant/food services management; substance abuse/addiction counseling; web page, digital/multimedia and information resources design.

Academics *Calendar:* semesters. *Degree:* certificates, diplomas, and associate. *Special study options:* academic remediation for entering students, accelerated degree program, adult/continuing education programs, advanced placement credit, distance learning, English as a second language, honors programs, independent study, internships, off-campus study, part-time degree program, services for LD students, study abroad, summer session for credit.

Library Minneapolis Community and Technical College Library plus 1 other with an OPAC, a Web page.

Student Life *Housing:* college housing not available. *Activities and Organizations:* drama/theater group, student-run newspaper, choral group, Student Senate, College Choirs, Student African American Brotherhood /B2B, Science Club, Phi Theta Kappa. *Campus security:* 24-hour emergency response devices and patrols, late-night transport/escort service. *Student services:* health clinic, personal/psychological counseling, legal services.

Athletics *Intramural sports:* badminton M/W, basketball M/W, soccer M/W, tennis M/W, volleyball M/W, weight lifting M/W.

Costs (2015–16) *Tuition:* state resident $4658 full-time; nonresident $4658 full-time. Full-time tuition and fees vary according to course load and program. Part-time tuition and fees vary according to course load and program. *Required fees:* $692 full-time. *Payment plan:* installment. *Waivers:* employees or children of employees.

Applying *Options:* electronic application, early admission, deferred entrance. *Application fee:* $20. *Required:* high school transcript. *Application deadlines:* rolling (freshmen), rolling (out-of-state freshmen), rolling (transfers). *Notification:* continuous (freshmen), continuous (out-of-state freshmen), continuous (transfers).

Freshman Application Contact Minneapolis Community and Technical College, 1501 Hennepin Avenue, Minneapolis, MN 55403. *Phone:* 612-659-6200. *Toll-free phone:* 800-247-0911. *E-mail:* admissions.office@minneapolis.edu.
Website: http://www.minneapolis.edu/.

Minneapolis Media Institute
Edina, Minnesota

Admissions Office Contact Minneapolis Media Institute, 4100 West 76th Street, Edina, MN 55435. *Toll-free phone:* 800-236-4997.
Website: http://www.mediainstitute.edu/.

Minnesota School of Business–Brooklyn Center
Brooklyn Center, Minnesota

- **Proprietary** primarily 2-year, founded 1989, part of Globe Education Network (GEN) which is composed of Globe University, Minnesota School of Business, Broadview University, The Institute of Production and Recording and Minnesota School of Cosmetology
- **Suburban** 4-acre campus with easy access to Minneapolis-St. Paul
- **Coed**

Undergraduates 100 full-time, 69 part-time. Students come from 3 states and territories; 2% are from out of state; 28% Black or African American, non-Hispanic/Latino; 4% Hispanic/Latino; 15% Asian, non-Hispanic/Latino; 2% American Indian or Alaska Native, non-Hispanic/Latino; 3% Two or more races, non-Hispanic/Latino; 18% Race/ethnicity unknown; 18% transferred in.

Academics *Calendar:* quarters. *Degrees:* certificates, diplomas, associate, and bachelor's. *Special study options:* academic remediation for entering students, accelerated degree program, adult/continuing education programs, advanced placement credit, independent study, internships, off-campus study, part-time degree program, services for LD students, summer session for credit.

Student Life *Campus security:* 24-hour emergency response devices.

Standardized Tests *Required:* ACCUPLACER is required of most applicants unless documentation of a minimum ACT composite score of 21 or

documentation of a minimum composite score of 1485 on the SAT is presented (for admission).

Applying *Options:* electronic application. *Application fee:* $50. *Required:* interview, Certification of high school graduation or GED.

Freshman Application Contact Minnesota School of Business–Brooklyn Center, 5910 Shingle Creek Parkway, Brooklyn Center, MN 55430.
Website: http://www.msbcollege.edu/.

Minnesota School of Business–Plymouth
Plymouth, Minnesota

- **Proprietary** primarily 2-year, founded 2002, part of Globe Education Network (GEN) which is composed of Globe University, Minnesota School of Business, Broadview University, The Institute of Production and Recording and Minnesota School of Cosmetology
- **Suburban** 7-acre campus with easy access to Minneapolis-St. Paul
- **Coed**

Undergraduates 107 full-time, 83 part-time. Students come from 2 states and territories; 0.5% are from out of state; 5% Black or African American, non-Hispanic/Latino; 3% Hispanic/Latino; 2% Asian, non-Hispanic/Latino; 0.5% Native Hawaiian or other Pacific Islander, non-Hispanic/Latino; 1% American Indian or Alaska Native, non-Hispanic/Latino; 4% Two or more races, non-Hispanic/Latino; 8% Race/ethnicity unknown; 15% transferred in.

Academics *Calendar:* quarters. *Degrees:* certificates, diplomas, associate, and bachelor's. *Special study options:* academic remediation for entering students, accelerated degree program, adult/continuing education programs, advanced placement credit, independent study, internships, off-campus study, part-time degree program, services for LD students, summer session for credit.

Student Life *Campus security:* 24-hour emergency response devices.

Standardized Tests *Required:* ACCUPLACER is required of most applicants unless documentation of a minimum ACT composite score of 21 or documentation of a minimum composite score of 1485 on the SAT is presented (for admission).

Applying *Options:* electronic application. *Application fee:* $50. *Required:* interview, Certification of high school graduation or GED.

Freshman Application Contact Minnesota School of Business–Plymouth, 1455 Country Road 101 North, Plymouth, MN 55447.
Website: http://www.msbcollege.edu/.

Minnesota State College–Southeast Technical
Winona, Minnesota

- **State-supported** 2-year, founded 1992, part of Minnesota State Colleges and Universities System
- **Small-town** 132-acre campus with easy access to Minneapolis-St. Paul
- **Coed,** 2,136 undergraduate students, 46% full-time, 60% women, 40% men

Undergraduates 981 full-time, 1,155 part-time. 29% are from out of state; 5% Black or African American, non-Hispanic/Latino; 3% Hispanic/Latino; 2% Asian, non-Hispanic/Latino; 0.5% American Indian or Alaska Native, non-Hispanic/Latino; 3% Two or more races, non-Hispanic/Latino; 0.7% Race/ethnicity unknown; 0.2% international; 13% transferred in. *Retention:* 35% of full-time freshmen returned.

Freshmen *Admission:* 597 admitted, 232 enrolled. *Average high school GPA:* 2.69.

Faculty *Total:* 119, 60% full-time, 4% with terminal degrees. *Student/faculty ratio:* 16:1.

Majors Accounting; accounting technology and bookkeeping; administrative assistant and secretarial science; autobody/collision and repair technology; biomedical technology; business administration and management; CAD/CADD drafting/design technology; carpentry; computer programming; computer systems networking and telecommunications; computer technology/computer systems technology; cosmetology; criminal justice/safety; early childhood education; electrical, electronic and communications engineering technology; heating, air conditioning, ventilation and refrigeration maintenance technology; industrial mechanics and maintenance technology; legal administrative assistant/secretary; massage therapy; medical administrative assistant and medical secretary; multi/interdisciplinary studies related; radiologic technology/science; registered nursing/registered nurse; retailing; sales, distribution, and marketing operations; selling skills and sales; web page, digital/multimedia and information resources design.

Academics *Calendar:* semesters. *Degree:* certificates, diplomas, and associate. *Special study options:* distance learning, double majors, internships.

Library Learning Resource Center.

Student Life *Activities and Organizations:* student-run newspaper. *Campus security:* 24-hour emergency response devices, late-night transport/escort service.

Costs (2014–15) *Tuition:* state resident $5019 full-time, $167 per credit part-time; nonresident $5019 full-time, $167 per credit part-time. Full-time tuition and fees vary according to program. Part-time tuition and fees vary according to program. *Required fees:* $598 full-time, $21 per credit part-time. *Payment plan:* installment. *Waivers:* senior citizens and employees or children of employees.

Financial Aid Of all full-time matriculated undergraduates who enrolled in 2013, 1,008 applied for aid, 934 were judged to have need, 19 had their need fully met. 48 Federal Work-Study jobs (averaging $2810). 16 state and other part-time jobs (averaging $3050). In 2013, 27 non-need-based awards were made. *Average percent of need met:* 37%. *Average financial aid package:* $6994. *Average need-based loan:* $3406. *Average need-based gift aid:* $4686. *Average non-need-based aid:* $1642. *Average indebtedness upon graduation:* $18,416.

Applying *Options:* electronic application. *Application fee:* $20. *Required:* high school transcript. *Recommended:* interview. *Application deadlines:* rolling (freshmen), rolling (out-of-state freshmen), rolling (transfers). *Notification:* continuous (freshmen), continuous (out-of-state freshmen), continuous (transfers).

Freshman Application Contact Admissions, SE Technical, Minnesota State College–Southeast Technical, 1250 Homer Road, PO Box 409, Winona, MN 55987. *Phone:* 877-853-8324. *Toll-free phone:* 800-372-8164. *Fax:* 507-453-2715. *E-mail:* enrollmentservices@southeastmn.edu.
Website: http://www.southeastmn.edu/.

Minnesota State Community and Technical College

Fergus Falls, Minnesota

Freshman Application Contact Ms. Carrie Brimhall, Dean of Enrollment Management, Minnesota State Community and Technical College, Fergus Falls, MN 56537-1009. *Phone:* 218-736-1528. *Toll-free phone:* 877-450-3322. *E-mail:* carrie.brimhall@minnesota.edu.
Website: http://www.minnesota.edu/.

Minnesota State Community and Technical College–Detroit Lakes

Detroit Lakes, Minnesota

Director of Admissions Mr. Dale Westley, Enrollment Manager, Minnesota State Community and Technical College–Detroit Lakes, 900 Highway 34, E, Detroit Lakes, MN 56501. *Phone:* 218-846-3777. *Toll-free phone:* 800-492-4836.
Website: http://www.minnesota.edu/.

Minnesota State Community and Technical College–Moorhead

Moorhead, Minnesota

Director of Admissions Laurie McKeever, Enrollment Manager, Minnesota State Community and Technical College–Moorhead, 1900 28th Avenue, South, Moorhead, MN 56560. *Phone:* 218-299-6583. *Toll-free phone:* 800-426-5603. *Fax:* 218-299-6810.
Website: http://www.minnesota.edu/.

Minnesota State Community and Technical College–Wadena

Wadena, Minnesota

Director of Admissions Mr. Paul Drange, Enrollment Manager, Minnesota State Community and Technical College–Wadena, 405 Colfax Avenue, SW, PO Box 566, Wadena, MN 56482. *Phone:* 218-631-7818. *Toll-free phone:* 800-247-2007.
Website: http://www.minnesota.edu/.

Minnesota West Community and Technical College

Pipestone, Minnesota

- **State-supported** 2-year, founded 1967, part of Minnesota State Colleges and Universities System
- **Rural** campus
- **Coed,** 3,182 undergraduate students, 36% full-time, 57% women, 43% men

Undergraduates 1,153 full-time, 2,029 part-time. 11% are from out of state; 5% Black or African American, non-Hispanic/Latino; 6% Hispanic/Latino; 3% Asian, non-Hispanic/Latino; 0.1% Native Hawaiian or other Pacific Islander, non-Hispanic/Latino; 0.9% American Indian or Alaska Native, non-Hispanic/Latino; 2% Two or more races, non-Hispanic/Latino; 5% Race/ethnicity unknown. *Retention:* 60% of full-time freshmen returned.

Freshmen *Average high school GPA:* 2.62.

Faculty *Total:* 146, 66% full-time. *Student/faculty ratio:* 21:1.

Majors Accounting; administrative assistant and secretarial science; agribusiness; agricultural and food products processing; agricultural/farm supplies retailing and wholesaling; agricultural production; agriculture; agronomy and crop science; automobile/automotive mechanics technology; biology/biotechnology laboratory technician; business administration and management; business/commerce; child-care and support services management; clinical/medical laboratory technology; computer and information systems security; computer engineering technology; computer science; computer systems networking and telecommunications; computer technology/computer systems technology; criminal justice/police science; dental assisting; diesel mechanics technology; electrical and power transmission installation; electrical and power transmission installation related; electrician; energy management and systems technology; hospital and health-care facilities administration; human services; hydraulics and fluid power technology; information technology; liberal arts and sciences and humanities related; liberal arts and sciences/liberal studies; lineworker; manufacturing engineering technology; medical administrative assistant and medical secretary; medical/clinical assistant; medical insurance coding; plumbing technology; radiologic technology/science; registered nursing/registered nurse; robotics technology; surgical technology.

Academics *Calendar:* semesters. *Degrees:* certificates, diplomas, and associate (profile contains information from Canby, Granite Falls, Jackson, and Worthington campuses). *Special study options:* academic remediation for entering students, advanced placement credit, cooperative education, distance learning, double majors, external degree program, honors programs, independent study, internships, part-time degree program, services for LD students, summer session for credit.

Library Library and Academic Resource Center plus 4 others with 44,078 titles, 4,253 audiovisual materials, an OPAC, a Web page.

Student Life *Activities and Organizations:* choral group.

Athletics Member NJCAA. *Intercollegiate sports:* baseball M, basketball M/W, cheerleading W, football M, softball W, volleyball W, wrestling M.

Standardized Tests *Required:* ACCUPLACER (for admission).

Costs (2015–16) *Tuition:* state resident $177 per credit part-time; nonresident $177 per credit part-time. Full-time tuition and fees vary according to reciprocity agreements. Part-time tuition and fees vary according to reciprocity agreements. *Required fees:* $17 per credit part-time. *Payment plan:* installment. *Waivers:* senior citizens and employees or children of employees.

Financial Aid Of all full-time matriculated undergraduates who enrolled in 2013, 2,049 applied for aid. 239 Federal Work-Study jobs (averaging $1166). 116 state and other part-time jobs (averaging $1620).

Applying *Options:* electronic application. *Application fee:* $20. *Required:* high school transcript. *Application deadlines:* rolling (freshmen), rolling (transfers).

Freshman Application Contact Ms. Crystal Strouth, College Registrar, Minnesota West Community and Technical College, 1450 Collegeway, Worthington, MN 56187. *Phone:* 507-372-3451. *Toll-free phone:* 800-658-2330. *Fax:* 507-372-5803. *E-mail:* crystal.strouth@mnwest.edu.
Website: http://www.mnwest.edu/.

National American University

Bloomington, Minnesota

Freshman Application Contact Ms. Jennifer Michaelson, Admissions Assistant, National American University, 321 Kansas City Street, Rapid City, SD 57201. *Phone:* 605-394-4827. *Toll-free phone:* 866-628-6387. *E-mail:* jmichaelson@national.edu.
Website: http://www.national.edu/.

National American University
Brooklyn Center, Minnesota

Freshman Application Contact Admissions Office, National American University, 6200 Shingle Creek Parkway, Suite 130, Brooklyn Center, MN 55430.
Website: http://www.national.edu/.

Normandale Community College
Bloomington, Minnesota

- **State-supported** 2-year, founded 1968, part of Minnesota State Colleges and Universities System
- **Suburban** 90-acre campus with easy access to Minneapolis-St. Paul
- **Coed**

Freshmen *Admission:* 2,311 applied, 2,022 admitted.
Faculty *Total:* 358, 54% full-time.
Majors Computer science; computer technology/computer systems technology; creative writing; criminal justice/police science; criminal justice/safety; dental hygiene; dietetic technology; dramatic/theater arts; elementary education; fine/studio arts; food science; hospitality administration; liberal arts and sciences/liberal studies; management information systems; manufacturing engineering technology; marketing/marketing management; medical office computer specialist; multi/interdisciplinary studies related; music; pre-engineering; registered nursing/registered nurse; special education; theater design and technology.
Academics *Calendar:* semesters. *Degree:* certificates and associate. *Special study options:* academic remediation for entering students, adult/continuing education programs, advanced placement credit, cooperative education, distance learning, English as a second language, external degree program, independent study, internships, off-campus study, part-time degree program, services for LD students, student-designed majors, study abroad, summer session for credit.
Library Library plus 1 other with 93,000 titles, 40,000 audiovisual materials, an OPAC, a Web page.
Student Life *Housing:* college housing not available. *Activities and Organizations:* drama/theater group, student-run newspaper, choral group, Program Board (NPB), Student Senate, Phi Theta Kappa, Inter-Varsity Christian Fellowship, Latino Student Club. *Campus security:* 24-hour emergency response devices, student patrols, late-night transport/escort service. *Student services:* personal/psychological counseling.
Athletics *Intramural sports:* archery M/W, badminton M/W, basketball M/W, ice hockey M/W, soccer M/W, softball M/W, table tennis M/W, tennis M/W, volleyball M/W, weight lifting M/W.
Costs (2014–15) *Tuition:* state resident $5709 full-time, $161 per credit part-time; nonresident $5709 full-time, $161 per credit part-time. Full-time tuition and fees vary according to program and reciprocity agreements. Part-time tuition and fees vary according to program and reciprocity agreements. *Required fees:* $864 full-time, $29 per credit part-time, $29 per credit part-time. *Payment plan:* installment. *Waivers:* senior citizens and employees or children of employees.
Applying *Options:* electronic application, deferred entrance. *Application fee:* $20. *Required for some:* high school transcript, GED is also accepted for admission. *Application deadlines:* 8/10 (freshmen), 8/10 (transfers). *Notification:* 8/10 (freshmen), 8/10 (transfers).
Freshman Application Contact Admissions Office, Normandale Community College, 9700 France Avenue South, Bloomington, MN 55431. *Phone:* 952-358-8201. *Toll-free phone:* 800-481-5412. *Fax:* 952-358-8230. *E-mail:* information@normandale.edu.
Website: http://www.normandale.edu/.

North Hennepin Community College
Brooklyn Park, Minnesota

- **State-supported** 2-year, founded 1966, part of Minnesota State Colleges and Universities System
- **Suburban** 80-acre campus with easy access to Minneapolis/St. Paul
- **Coed,** 7,178 undergraduate students, 28% full-time, 58% women, 42% men

Undergraduates 2,020 full-time, 5,158 part-time. Students come from 27 states and territories; 40 other countries; 24% Black or African American, non-Hispanic/Latino; 3% Hispanic/Latino; 14% Asian, non-Hispanic/Latino; 0.2% Native Hawaiian or other Pacific Islander, non-Hispanic/Latino; 1% American Indian or Alaska Native, non-Hispanic/Latino; 3% Race/ethnicity unknown; 1% international. *Retention:* 51% of full-time freshmen returned.
Freshmen *Admission:* 5,320 applied, 4,477 admitted, 1,167 enrolled.
Faculty *Total:* 307, 46% full-time. *Student/faculty ratio:* 19:1.
Majors Accounting; accounting technology and bookkeeping; biology/biological sciences; business administration and management;

chemistry; clinical/medical laboratory technology; computer science; construction management; creative writing; criminal justice/police science; criminal justice/safety; dramatic/theater arts; education; entrepreneurship; finance; fine/studio arts; graphic design; health and physical education/fitness; histologic technology/histotechnologist; legal assistant/paralegal; liberal arts and sciences/liberal studies; management information systems; marketing/marketing management; mathematics; multi/interdisciplinary studies related; music; physical education teaching and coaching; pre-engineering; registered nursing/registered nurse.
Academics *Calendar:* semesters. *Degree:* certificates and associate. *Special study options:* academic remediation for entering students, accelerated degree program, adult/continuing education programs, advanced placement credit, distance learning, double majors, English as a second language, external degree program, honors programs, independent study, internships, off-campus study, part-time degree program, services for LD students, student-designed majors, study abroad, summer session for credit. *ROTC:* Army (c), Navy (c), Air Force (c).
Library Learning Resource Center with 52,849 titles, 3,244 audiovisual materials, an OPAC, a Web page.
Student Life *Housing:* college housing not available. *Activities and Organizations:* drama/theater group, choral group, Muslim Student Association, Phy Theta Kappa, Student Anime/Game Club, Multicultural Club. *Campus security:* 24-hour emergency response devices, student patrols, late-night transport/escort service. *Student services:* personal/psychological counseling.
Athletics *Intramural sports:* basketball M/W, bowling M/W, football M/W, ice hockey M(c)/W(c), lacrosse M/W, soccer M/W, softball M/W, table tennis M/W, volleyball M/W, weight lifting M/W.
Costs (2014–15) *Tuition:* state resident $3962 full-time, $165 per credit part-time; nonresident $3962 full-time, $165 per credit part-time. Full-time tuition and fees vary according to course load and program. Part-time tuition and fees vary according to course load and program. *Required fees:* $396 full-time, $17 per credit part-time. *Payment plan:* installment. *Waivers:* senior citizens and employees or children of employees.
Applying *Options:* electronic application, early admission, deferred entrance. *Application fee:* $20. *Recommended:* high school transcript. *Application deadlines:* rolling (freshmen), rolling (transfers). *Notification:* continuous (freshmen), continuous (transfers).
Freshman Application Contact Mr. Sean Olson, Interim Director of Admissions and Outreach, North Hennepin Community College, 7411 85th Avenue North, Brooklyn Park, MN 55445. *Phone:* 763-424-0724. *Toll-free phone:* 800-818-0395. *Fax:* 763-493-0563. *E-mail:* SOlson2@nhcc.edu.
Website: http://www.nhcc.cdu/.

Northland Community College
Thief River Falls, Minnesota

- **State-supported** 2-year, founded 1965, part of Minnesota State Colleges and Universities System
- **Small-town** 239-acre campus
- **Coed,** 3,629 undergraduate students, 41% full-time, 57% women, 43% men

Undergraduates 1,472 full-time, 2,157 part-time. 5% Black or African American, non-Hispanic/Latino; 3% Hispanic/Latino; 2% Asian, non-Hispanic/Latino; 0.1% Native Hawaiian or other Pacific Islander, non-Hispanic/Latino; 4% American Indian or Alaska Native, non-Hispanic/Latino; 1% Race/ethnicity unknown; 0.7% international.
Freshmen *Admission:* 1,200 applied, 1,200 admitted.
Faculty *Total:* 171, 55% full-time. *Student/faculty ratio:* 21:1.
Majors Accounting; administrative assistant and secretarial science; aeronautics/aviation/aerospace science and technology; architectural engineering technology; autobody/collision and repair technology; automobile/automotive mechanics technology; aviation/airway management; business administration and management; cardiovascular technology; carpentry; child-care provision; child development; computer and information sciences and support services related; computer and information sciences related; computer graphics; computer science; computer software and media applications related; consumer merchandising/retailing management; criminal justice/law enforcement administration; criminal justice/police science; criminology; data entry/microcomputer applications; data entry/microcomputer applications related; data modeling/warehousing and database administration; drafting and design technology; electrical, electronic and communications engineering technology; emergency medical technology (EMT paramedic); entrepreneurship; farm and ranch management; fire prevention and safety technology; heating, air conditioning, ventilation and refrigeration maintenance technology; industrial electronics technology; information technology; liberal arts and sciences/liberal studies; licensed practical/vocational nurse training; marketing/marketing management; mass communication/media; medical administrative assistant and medical secretary; network and system administration; occupational therapist assistant; pharmacy

technician; physical therapy technology; plumbing technology; radiologic technology/science; registered nursing/registered nurse; respiratory care therapy; signal/geospatial intelligence; surgical technology; web/multimedia management and webmaster; web page, digital/multimedia and information resources design; welding technology; word processing.

Academics *Calendar:* semesters. *Degree:* certificates, diplomas, and associate. *Special study options:* academic remediation for entering students, adult/continuing education programs, advanced placement credit, cooperative education, distance learning, double majors, internships, off-campus study, part-time degree program, services for LD students, summer session for credit.

Library Northland Comm & Tech College Library plus 1 other with 42,588 titles, 3,411 audiovisual materials, an OPAC, a Web page.

Student Life *Housing:* college housing not available. *Activities and Organizations:* student-run radio station, choral group, Student Senate, PAMA, AD Nursing, PN Nursing, Fire Tech. *Campus security:* student patrols, late-night transport/escort service. *Student services:* personal/psychological counseling, women's center.

Athletics Member NJCAA. *Intercollegiate sports:* baseball M, basketball M/W, football M, softball W, volleyball W, wrestling M. *Intramural sports:* basketball M/W, bowling M/W, golf M/W, ice hockey M/W, racquetball M/W, rock climbing M/W, soccer M/W, softball M/W, volleyball M/W, weight lifting M/W.

Costs (2014–15) *Tuition:* state resident $4950 full-time, $165 per credit hour part-time; nonresident $4950 full-time, $165 per credit hour part-time. Full-time tuition and fees vary according to course load and program. Part-time tuition and fees vary according to course load and program. *Required fees:* $567 full-time, $19 per credit hour part-time. *Payment plan:* installment. *Waivers:* senior citizens and employees or children of employees.

Financial Aid Of all full-time matriculated undergraduates who enrolled in 2011, 98 Federal Work-Study jobs (averaging $2701). 68 state and other part-time jobs (averaging $2839).

Applying *Options:* electronic application, early admission, deferred entrance. *Application fee:* $20. *Required:* high school transcript. *Application deadlines:* 8/24 (freshmen), 8/24 (out-of-state freshmen), 8/24 (transfers). *Notification:* continuous (freshmen), continuous (out-of-state freshmen), continuous (transfers).

Freshman Application Contact Mrs. Nicki Carlson, Director of Enrollment Management, Northland Community College, 1101 Highway One East, Thief River Falls, MN 56701. *Phone:* 218-683-8546. *Toll-free phone:* 800-959-6282. *Fax:* 218-683-8980. *E-mail:* nicki.carlson@northlandcollege.edu. *Website:* http://www.northlandcollege.edu/.

Northwest Technical College
Bemidji, Minnesota

- **State-supported** 2-year, founded 1993, part of Minnesota State Colleges and Universities System
- **Small-town** campus
- **Coed,** 1,088 undergraduate students, 36% full-time, 72% women, 28% men

Undergraduates 397 full-time, 691 part-time. 7% are from out of state; 2% Black or African American, non-Hispanic/Latino; 2% Hispanic/Latino; 1% Asian, non-Hispanic/Latino; 0.1% Native Hawaiian or other Pacific Islander, non-Hispanic/Latino; 9% American Indian or Alaska Native, non-Hispanic/Latino; 7% Two or more races, non-Hispanic/Latino; 1% Race/ethnicity unknown; 0.1% international; 14% transferred in; 4% live on campus. *Retention:* 52% of full-time freshmen returned.

Freshmen *Admission:* 115 enrolled.

Faculty *Total:* 54, 57% full-time, 2% with terminal degrees. *Student/faculty ratio:* 16:1.

Majors Accounting; administrative assistant and secretarial science; automobile/automotive mechanics technology; business administration and management; child-care and support services management; computer systems networking and telecommunications; dental assisting; energy management and systems technology; engine machinist; industrial safety technology; industrial technology; licensed practical/vocational nurse training; manufacturing engineering technology; medical administrative assistant and medical secretary; registered nursing/registered nurse; sales, distribution, and marketing operations.

Academics *Calendar:* semesters. *Degree:* certificates, diplomas, and associate. *Special study options:* part-time degree program.

Library Northwest Technical College Learning Enrichment Center.

Student Life *Housing Options:* coed, special housing for students with disabilities. Campus housing is provided by a third party.

Costs (2014–15) *Tuition:* state resident $5190 full-time, $173 per credit part-time; nonresident $5190 full-time, $173 per credit part-time. Full-time tuition

and fees vary according to program. Part-time tuition and fees vary according to program. *Required fees:* $292 full-time, $11 per credit part-time. *Room and board:* $7470; room only: $5370. Room and board charges vary according to board plan and housing facility. *Payment plan:* installment. *Waivers:* senior citizens and employees or children of employees.

Financial Aid Of all full-time matriculated undergraduates who enrolled in 2013, 20 Federal Work-Study jobs, 21 state and other part-time jobs.

Applying *Options:* electronic application. *Application fee:* $20. *Required:* high school transcript.

Freshman Application Contact Ms. Kari Kantack-Miller, Diversity and Enrollment Representative, Northwest Technical College, 905 Grant Avenue, Southeast, Bemidji, MN 56601. *Phone:* 218-333-6645. *Toll-free phone:* 800-942-8324. *Fax:* 218-333-6694. *E-mail:* kari.kantack@ntcmn.edu. *Website:* http://www.ntcmn.edu/.

Pine Technical and Community College
Pine City, Minnesota

Freshman Application Contact Pine Technical and Community College, 900 4th Street SE, Pine City, MN 55063. *Phone:* 320-629-5100. *Toll-free phone:* 800-521-7463.
Website: http://www.pine.edu/.

Rainy River Community College
International Falls, Minnesota

- **State-supported** 2-year, founded 1967, part of Minnesota State Colleges and Universities System
- **Small-town** 80-acre campus
- **Coed,** 267 undergraduate students, 87% full-time, 56% women, 44% men

Undergraduates 231 full-time, 36 part-time. 15% Black or African American, non-Hispanic/Latino; 1% Hispanic/Latino; 1% Asian, non-Hispanic/Latino; 6% American Indian or Alaska Native, non-Hispanic/Latino; 8% international.

Faculty *Total:* 25, 40% full-time. *Student/faculty ratio:* 15:1.

Majors Administrative assistant and secretarial science; biological and physical sciences; business administration and management; liberal arts and sciences/liberal studies; pre-engineering.

Academics *Calendar:* semesters. *Degree:* certificates, diplomas, and associate. *Special study options:* academic remediation for entering students, adult/continuing education programs, advanced placement credit, cooperative education, honors programs, independent study, internships, part-time degree program, services for LD students, summer session for credit.

Library Rainy River Community College Library with 20,000 titles, an OPAC.

Student Life *Housing Options:* special housing for students with disabilities. Campus housing is university owned. *Activities and Organizations:* drama/theater group, Anishinaabe Student Coalition, Student Senate, Black Student Association. *Campus security:* 24-hour emergency response devices, late-night transport/escort service, controlled dormitory access. *Student services:* personal/psychological counseling.

Athletics Member NJCAA. *Intercollegiate sports:* basketball M/W, ice hockey W, softball W, volleyball W. *Intramural sports:* archery M/W, badminton M/W, baseball M, bowling M/W, cheerleading M/W, cross-country running M/W, ice hockey M, skiing (cross-country) M/W, skiing (downhill) M/W, swimming and diving M/W, table tennis M/W, tennis M/W, volleyball M/W, weight lifting M/W.

Costs (2014–15) *Tuition:* state resident $4729 full-time, $158 per credit part-time; nonresident $5911 full-time, $197 per credit part-time. Full-time tuition and fees vary according to course load, program, and reciprocity agreements. Part-time tuition and fees vary according to course load, program, and reciprocity agreements. *Required fees:* $594 full-time, $20 per credit part-time, $20 per credit part-time. *Room and board:* $3750; room only: $2950. Room and board charges vary according to housing facility. *Payment plan:* installment. *Waivers:* employees or children of employees.

Applying *Options:* electronic application, early admission, deferred entrance. *Application fee:* $20. *Recommended:* high school transcript. *Application deadlines:* rolling (freshmen), rolling (out-of-state freshmen), rolling (transfers). *Notification:* continuous (freshmen), continuous (out-of-state freshmen), continuous (transfers).

Freshman Application Contact Ms. Berta Hagen, Registrar, Rainy River Community College, 1501 Highway 71, International Falls, MN 56649. *Phone:* 218-285-2207. *Toll-free phone:* 800-456-3996. *Fax:* 218-285-2314. *E-mail:* berta.hagen@rainyriver.edu. *Website:* http://www.rainyriver.edu/.

Ridgewater College
Willmar, Minnesota

- **State-supported** 2-year, founded 1961, part of Minnesota State Colleges and Universities System
- **Small-town** 83-acre campus
- **Coed,** 3,753 undergraduate students, 55% full-time, 52% women, 48% men

Undergraduates 2,063 full-time, 1,690 part-time.
Faculty *Total:* 213, 47% full-time.
Majors Accounting; administrative assistant and secretarial science; agribusiness; agricultural production; agriculture; agronomy and crop science; animal/livestock husbandry and production; autobody/collision and repair technology; automobile/automotive mechanics technology; biology/biological sciences; business administration and management; carpentry; chemistry; commercial photography; computer programming; computer science; computer systems networking and telecommunications; computer technology/computer systems technology; cosmetology; criminal justice/police science; crop production; dairy husbandry and production; desktop publishing and digital imaging design; digital communication and media/multimedia; early childhood education; electrical, electronic and communications engineering technology; electrician; electromechanical technology; health information/medical records technology; instrumentation technology; legal administrative assistant/secretary; liberal arts and sciences and humanities related; liberal arts and sciences/liberal studies; machine tool technology; marketing/marketing management; mechanical drafting and CAD/CADD; medical administrative assistant and medical secretary; medical/clinical assistant; network and system administration; radiologic technology/science; recording arts technology; registered nursing/registered nurse; sales, distribution, and marketing operations; selling skills and sales; teacher assistant/aide; telecommunications technology; therapeutic recreation; tool and die technology; veterinary/animal health technology; web page, digital/multimedia and information resources design; welding technology.
Academics *Calendar:* semesters. *Degree:* certificates, diplomas, and associate. *Special study options:* academic remediation for entering students, advanced placement credit, cooperative education, distance learning, internships, off-campus study, part-time degree program, services for LD students, student-designed majors, study abroad, summer session for credit.
Library an OPAC, a Web page.
Student Life *Housing:* college housing not available. *Campus security:* 24-hour emergency response devices. *Student services:* personal/psychological counseling.
Athletics Member NJCAA. *Intercollegiate sports:* baseball M, basketball M/W, football M, soccer M, softball W, volleyball W, wrestling M. *Intramural sports:* basketball M/W, football M, golf M/W, softball M/W, weight lifting M/W.
Financial Aid Of all full-time matriculated undergraduates who enrolled in 2013, 350 Federal Work-Study jobs (averaging $3000). 133 state and other part-time jobs (averaging $2400).
Applying *Options:* electronic application. *Application fee:* $20. *Required:* high school transcript. *Required for some:* interview.
Freshman Application Contact Ms. Linda Duering, Admissions Assistant, Ridgewater College, PO Box 1097, Willmar, MN 56201-1097. *Phone:* 320-222-5976. *Toll-free phone:* 800-722-1151. *E-mail:* linda.duering@ridgewater.edu.
Website: http://www.ridgewater.edu/.

Riverland Community College
Austin, Minnesota

- **State-supported** 2-year, founded 1940, part of Minnesota State Colleges and Universities System
- **Small-town** 187-acre campus
- **Coed,** 3,014 undergraduate students, 41% full-time, 59% women, 41% men

Undergraduates 1,249 full-time, 1,765 part-time. Students come from 16 states and territories; 23 other countries; 3% are from out of state; 5% Black or African American, non-Hispanic/Latino; 11% Hispanic/Latino; 1% Asian, non-Hispanic/Latino; 0.2% Native Hawaiian or other Pacific Islander, non-Hispanic/Latino; 0.3% American Indian or Alaska Native, non-Hispanic/Latino; 2% Two or more races, non-Hispanic/Latino; 0.5% Race/ethnicity unknown; 1% international; 2% live on campus. *Retention:* 52% of full-time freshmen returned.
Freshmen *Average high school GPA:* 2.81.
Majors Administrative assistant and secretarial science; autobody/collision and repair technology; business administration and management; computer and information sciences and support services related; computer and information systems security; computer installation and repair technology; computer programming (specific applications); computer programming (vendor/product certification); computer software and media applications related; computer systems networking and telecommunications; corrections; criminal justice/police science; data entry/microcomputer applications; data entry/microcomputer applications related; diesel mechanics technology; electrical/electronics equipment installation and repair; health unit coordinator/ward clerk; human services; industrial mechanics and maintenance technology; legal administrative assistant/secretary; liberal arts and sciences/liberal studies; machine shop technology; medical administrative assistant and medical secretary; medical radiologic technology; nursing assistant/aide and patient care assistant/aide; pharmacy technician; registered nursing/registered nurse; web/multimedia management and webmaster; web page, digital/multimedia and information resources design; word processing.
Academics *Calendar:* semesters. *Degree:* certificates, diplomas, and associate. *Special study options:* academic remediation for entering students, adult/continuing education programs, advanced placement credit, distance learning, double majors, English as a second language, independent study, internships, off-campus study, part-time degree program, services for LD students, study abroad, summer session for credit.
Library Riverland Community College Library plus 2 others with 33,500 titles, an OPAC.
Student Life *Housing Options:* coed. Campus housing is provided by a third party. *Activities and Organizations:* drama/theater group, student-run newspaper, choral group, College Choir, student newspaper, Student Activities Board, Phi Theta Kappa, Theater Club. *Campus security:* late-night transport/escort service. *Student services:* personal/psychological counseling, women's center.
Athletics Member NJCAA. *Intercollegiate sports:* baseball M, basketball M/W, golf M/W, softball W, volleyball W. *Intramural sports:* basketball M.
Financial Aid Of all full-time matriculated undergraduates who enrolled in 2013, 401 applied for aid. 126 Federal Work-Study jobs (averaging $2000). 95 state and other part-time jobs (averaging $2000). *Average indebtedness upon graduation:* $7167.
Applying *Options:* electronic application, early admission. *Application fee:* $20. *Required:* high school transcript. *Application deadlines:* rolling (freshmen), rolling (transfers).
Freshman Application Contact Riverland Community College, 1900 8th Avenue, NW, Austin, MN 55912. *Phone:* 507-433-0600. *Toll-free phone:* 800-247-5039.
Website: http://www.riverland.edu/.

Rochester Community and Technical College
Rochester, Minnesota

Director of Admissions Mr. Troy Tynsky, Director of Admissions, Rochester Community and Technical College, 851 30th Avenue, SE, Rochester, MN 55904-4999. *Phone:* 507-280-3509.
Website: http://www.rctc.edu/.

St. Cloud Technical & Community College
St. Cloud, Minnesota

Freshman Application Contact Ms. Jodi Elness, Admissions Office, St. Cloud Technical & Community College, 1540 Northway Drive, St. Cloud, MN 56303. *Phone:* 320-308-5089. *Toll-free phone:* 800-222-1009. *Fax:* 320-308-5981. *E-mail:* jelness@sctcc.edu.
Website: http://www.sctcc.edu/.

Saint Paul College–A Community & Technical College
St. Paul, Minnesota

Freshman Application Contact Ms. Sarah Carrico, Saint Paul College–A Community & Technical College, 235 Marshall Avenue, Saint Paul, MN 55102. *Phone:* 651-846-1424. *Toll-free phone:* 800-227-6029. *Fax:* 651-846-1703. *E-mail:* admissions@saintpaul.edu.
Website: http://www.saintpaul.edu/.

South Central College
North Mankato, Minnesota

Freshman Application Contact Ms. Beverly Herda, Director of Admissions, South Central College, 1920 Lee Boulevard, North Mankato, MN 56003. *Phone:* 507-389-7334. *Fax:* 507-388-9951.
Website: http://southcentral.edu/.

Vermilion Community College

Ely, Minnesota

Freshman Application Contact Mr. Todd Heiman, Director of Enrollment Services, Vermilion Community College, 1900 East Camp Street, Ely, MN 55731-1996. *Phone:* 218-365-7224. *Toll-free phone:* 800-657-3608. *Website:* http://www.vcc.edu/.

White Earth Tribal and Community College

Mahnomen, Minnesota

Admissions Office Contact White Earth Tribal and Community College, 102 3rd Street NE, Mahnomen, MN 56557. *Website:* http://www.wetcc.edu/.

MISSISSIPPI

Antonelli College

Hattiesburg, Mississippi

Freshman Application Contact Mrs. Karen Gautreau, Director, Antonelli College, 1500 North 31st Avenue, Hattiesburg, MS 39401. *Phone:* 601-583-4100. *Fax:* 601-583-0839. *E-mail:* admissionsh@antonellicollege.edu. *Website:* http://www.antonellicollege.edu/.

Antonelli College

Jackson, Mississippi

Freshman Application Contact Antonelli College, 2323 Lakeland Drive, Jackson, MS 39232. *Phone:* 601-362-9991. *Website:* http://www.antonellicollege.edu/.

Blue Cliff College–Gulfport

Gulfport, Mississippi

Admissions Office Contact Blue Cliff College–Gulfport, 12251 Bernard Parkway, Gulfport, MS 39503. *Website:* http://www.bluecliffcollege.edu/.

Coahoma Community College

Clarksdale, Mississippi

Freshman Application Contact Mrs. Wanda Holmes, Director of Admissions and Records, Coahoma Community College, Clarksdale, MS 38614-9799. *Phone:* 662-621-4205. *Toll-free phone:* 866-470-1CCC. *Website:* http://www.ccc.cc.ms.us/.

Copiah-Lincoln Community College

Wesson, Mississippi

- **State and locally supported** 2-year, founded 1928, part of Mississippi Community College Board
- **Rural** 525-acre campus with easy access to Jackson
- **Endowment** $2.5 million
- **Coed,** 3,157 undergraduate students, 79% full-time, 63% women, 37% men

Undergraduates 2,509 full-time, 648 part-time. Students come from 6 states and territories; 1% are from out of state; 42% Black or African American, non-Hispanic/Latino; 1% Hispanic/Latino; 0.3% Asian, non-Hispanic/Latino; 0.3% American Indian or Alaska Native, non-Hispanic/Latino; 0.2% Two or more races, non-Hispanic/Latino; 1% Race/ethnicity unknown; 6% transferred in; 30% live on campus.

Freshmen *Admission:* 692 enrolled.

Faculty *Total:* 138.

Majors Accounting; agribusiness; agricultural business and management; agricultural business and management related; agricultural economics; agricultural/farm supplies retailing and wholesaling; agriculture; architecture; art teacher education; biological and physical sciences; biology/biological sciences; business administration and management; chemistry; child development; civil engineering technology; clinical/medical laboratory technology; computer programming; cosmetology; criminal justice/police science; data processing and data processing technology; drafting and design technology; economics; education; electrical, electronic and communications

engineering technology; elementary education; engineering; English; family and consumer sciences/home economics teacher education; farm and ranch management; food technology and processing; forestry; health teacher education; history; industrial radiologic technology; journalism; liberal arts and sciences/liberal studies; library and information science; music teacher education; physical education teaching and coaching; registered nursing/registered nurse; special products marketing; trade and industrial teacher education.

Academics *Calendar:* semesters. *Degree:* certificates and associate. *Special study options:* academic remediation for entering students, adult/continuing education programs, advanced placement credit, honors programs, part-time degree program, student-designed majors, summer session for credit.

Library Oswalt Memorial Library with 34,357 titles.

Student Life *Housing Options:* Campus housing is university owned. *Activities and Organizations:* drama/theater group, student-run newspaper, radio station, choral group, marching band. *Campus security:* 24-hour patrols. *Student services:* health clinic, personal/psychological counseling.

Athletics Member NJCAA. *Intercollegiate sports:* baseball M(s), basketball M(s)/W(s), football M(s), golf M/W, softball W, tennis M/W, track and field M. *Intramural sports:* basketball M/W, football M, golf M/W, tennis M/W, volleyball M/W.

Costs (2014–15) *Tuition:* state resident $2300 full-time, $115 per semester hour part-time; nonresident $4300 full-time, $200 per semester hour part-time. *Required fees:* $250 full-time, $13 per semester part-time. *Room and board:* $3250; room only: $1550. Room and board charges vary according to board plan and housing facility. *Waivers:* senior citizens and employees or children of employees.

Financial Aid Of all full-time matriculated undergraduates who enrolled in 2013, 125 Federal Work-Study jobs (averaging $1000).

Applying *Options:* early admission. *Required:* high school transcript. *Application deadlines:* rolling (freshmen), rolling (transfers).

Freshman Application Contact Ms. Gay Langham, Student Records Manager, Copiah-Lincoln Community College, PO Box 649, Wesson, MS 39191-0457. *Phone:* 601-643-8307. *E-mail:* gay.langham@colin.edu. *Website:* http://www.colin.edu/.

East Central Community College

Decatur, Mississippi

Director of Admissions Ms. Donna Luke, Director of Admissions, Records, and Research, East Central Community College, PO Box 129, Decatur, MS 39327-0129. *Phone:* 601-635-2111 Ext. 206. *Toll-free phone:* 877-462-3222. *Website:* http://www.eccc.edu/.

East Mississippi Community College

Scooba, Mississippi

Director of Admissions Ms. Melinda Sciple, Admissions Officer, East Mississippi Community College, PO Box 158, Scooba, MS 39358-0158. *Phone:* 662-476-5041. *Website:* http://www.eastms.edu/.

Hinds Community College

Raymond, Mississippi

- **State and locally supported** 2-year, founded 1917, part of Mississippi Community College Board
- **Small-town** 671-acre campus
- **Coed,** 11,832 undergraduate students, 65% full-time, 62% women, 38% men

Undergraduates 7,737 full-time, 4,095 part-time. Students come from 27 states and territories; 19 other countries; 3% are from out of state; 56% Black or African American, non-Hispanic/Latino; 2% Hispanic/Latino; 0.6% Asian, non-Hispanic/Latino; 0.3% American Indian or Alaska Native, non-Hispanic/Latino; 2% Two or more races, non-Hispanic/Latino; 3% Race/ethnicity unknown; 0.4% international; 88% transferred in. *Retention:* 54% of full-time freshmen returned.

Freshmen *Admission:* 2,879 enrolled.

Faculty *Total:* 734, 54% full-time. *Student/faculty ratio:* 20:1.

Majors Accounting; accounting technology and bookkeeping; administrative assistant and secretarial science; aeronautics/aviation/aerospace science and technology; agribusiness; agricultural mechanization related; agriculture; airframe mechanics and aircraft maintenance technology; applied horticulture/horticultural business services related; architectural engineering technology; architecture; art; aviation/airway management; banking and financial support services; biology/biological sciences; business/commerce; business teacher education; chemistry; child-care provision; clinical laboratory science/medical technology; clinical/medical laboratory technology; computer and information sciences; computer and information systems security;

computer installation and repair technology; computer programming; computer systems networking and telecommunications; construction engineering technology; cooking and related culinary arts; corrections and criminal justice related; court reporting; criminal justice/safety; dance; dental assisting; dental hygiene; diagnostic medical sonography and ultrasound technology; diesel mechanics technology; digital communication and media/multimedia; drafting and design technology; dramatic/theater arts; electrical, electronic and communications engineering technology; electrical/electronics equipment installation and repair; electrician; elementary education; emergency medical technology (EMT paramedic); engineering; English; family and consumer sciences/human sciences; fashion merchandising; forestry; game and interactive media design; general studies; geographic information science and cartography; geology/earth science; graphic design; health and medical administrative services related; health information/medical records administration; health information/medical records technology; health professions related; heating, air conditioning, ventilation and refrigeration maintenance technology; history; hospitality administration; housing and human environments related; institutional food workers; journalism; landscape architecture; landscaping and groundskeeping; legal assistant/paralegal; marketing/marketing management; mathematics; medical/clinical assistant; music; occupational therapy; photographic and film/video technology; physical education teaching and coaching; physical sciences; physical therapy; physical therapy technology; plumbing technology; political science and government; pre-dentistry studies; pre-law studies; premedical studies; prenursing studies; pre-pharmacy studies; pre-veterinary studies; psychology; radio and television; radio and television broadcasting technology; radiologic technology/science; real estate; registered nursing/registered nurse; respiratory care therapy; secondary education; sign language interpretation and translation; social sciences; sociology; speech communication and rhetoric; surgical technology; technology/industrial arts teacher education; telecommunications technology; tourism and travel services management; veterinary/animal health technology; welding technology.

Academics *Calendar:* semesters. *Degrees:* certificates and associate (reported data includes Raymond, Jackson Academic and Technical Center, Jackson Nursing-Allied Health Center, Rankin, Utica, and Vicksburg campus locations). *Special study options:* academic remediation for entering students, accelerated degree program, adult/continuing education programs, advanced placement credit, cooperative education, distance learning, double majors, freshman honors college, honors programs, independent study, internships, part-time degree program, services for LD students, study abroad, summer session for credit. *ROTC:* Army (b).

Library McLendon Library plus 5 others with 352,064 titles, an OPAC.

Student Life *Housing Options:* coed, men-only, women-only, special housing for students with disabilities. Campus housing is university owned. *Activities and Organizations:* drama/theater group, student-run newspaper, choral group, marching band. *Campus security:* 24-hour emergency response devices and patrols, late-night transport/escort service, controlled dormitory access. *Student services:* personal/psychological counseling, legal services.

Athletics Member NJCAA. *Intercollegiate sports:* baseball M(s), basketball M(s)/W(s), cheerleading M(s)/W(s), football M(s), golf M(s), soccer M(s)/W(s), softball W(s), tennis M(s)/W(s), track and field M(s)/W(s). *Intramural sports:* basketball M/W, bowling M/W, cross-country running M/W, football M/W, golf M/W, softball M/W, swimming and diving M/W, tennis M/W, ultimate Frisbee M/W, volleyball M/W.

Standardized Tests *Required:* Students who do not have ACT or SAT scores take the Compass test for placement purposes (for admission). *Required for some:* SAT and SAT Subject Tests or ACT (for admission).

Costs (2014–15) *Tuition:* state resident $2400 full-time, $100 per semester hour part-time; nonresident $5000 full-time, $200 per semester hour part-time. Part-time tuition and fees vary according to course load. *Required fees:* $100 full-time, $50 per term part-time. *Room and board:* $3900. Room and board charges vary according to housing facility. *Payment plan:* installment. *Waivers:* senior citizens and employees or children of employees.

Financial Aid Of all full-time matriculated undergraduates who enrolled in 2013, 300 Federal Work-Study jobs (averaging $1250). 200 state and other part-time jobs (averaging $1000).

Applying *Required:* high school transcript.

Freshman Application Contact Hinds Community College, PO Box 1100, Raymond, MS 39154-1100. *Phone:* 601-857-3280. *Toll-free phone:* 800-HINDSCC.

Website: http://www.hindscc.edu/.

Holmes Community College
Goodman, Mississippi

Director of Admissions Dr. Lynn Wright, Dean of Admissions and Records, Holmes Community College, PO Box 369, Goodman, MS 39079-0369. *Phone:* 601-472-2312 Ext. 1023. *Toll-free phone:* 800-HOLMES-4. *Website:* http://www.holmescc.edu/.

Itawamba Community College
Fulton, Mississippi

Freshman Application Contact Mr. Larry Boggs, Director of Student Recruitment and Scholarships, Itawamba Community College, 602 West Hill Street, Fulton, MS 38843. *Phone:* 601-862-8252. *E-mail:* laboggs@iccms.edu.

Website: http://www.iccms.edu/.

Jones County Junior College
Ellisville, Mississippi

Director of Admissions Mrs. Dianne Speed, Director of Admissions and Records, Jones County Junior College, 900 South Court Street, Ellisville, MS 39437-3901. *Phone:* 601-477-4025.

Website: http://www.jcjc.edu/.

Meridian Community College
Meridian, Mississippi

Freshman Application Contact Ms. Angela Payne, Director of Admissions, Meridian Community College, 910 Highway 19 North, Meridian, MS 39307. *Phone:* 601-484-8357. *Toll-free phone:* 800-MCC-THE-1. *E-mail:* apayne@meridiancc.edu.

Website: http://www.meridiancc.edu/.

Miller-Motte Technical College
Gulfport, Mississippi

Admissions Office Contact Miller-Motte Technical College, 12121 Highway 49 North, Gulfport, MS 39503. *Toll-free phone:* 866-297-0267. *Website:* http://www.miller-motte.edu/.

Mississippi Delta Community College
Moorhead, Mississippi

- **District-supported** 2-year, founded 1926, part of Mississippi State Board for Community and Junior Colleges
- **Small-town** 425-acre campus
- **Coed**

Undergraduates 2,305 full-time, 645 part-time. Students come from 6 states and territories; 64% Black or African American, non-Hispanic/Latino; 0.9% Hispanic/Latino; 0.8% Asian, non-Hispanic/Latino; 0.8% Race/ethnicity unknown; 25% live on campus. *Retention:* 58% of full-time freshmen returned.

Faculty *Student/faculty ratio:* 18:1.

Academics *Calendar:* semesters. *Degree:* certificates, diplomas, and associate. *Special study options:* academic remediation for entering students, adult/continuing education programs, advanced placement credit, part-time degree program, summer session for credit.

Student Life *Campus security:* 24-hour emergency response devices and patrols, late-night transport/escort service, controlled dormitory access.

Athletics Member NJCAA.

Standardized Tests *Required for some:* ACT (for admission).

Costs (2014–15) *Tuition:* state resident $2490 full-time, $125 per credit hour part-time; nonresident $4098 full-time, $125 per credit hour part-time. Full-time tuition and fees vary according to course load and location. Part-time tuition and fees vary according to course load and location. *Required fees:* $30 full-time. *Room and board:* $2740; room only: $940. Room and board charges vary according to board plan.

Financial Aid Of all full-time matriculated undergraduates who enrolled in 2013, 100 Federal Work-Study jobs (averaging $1400). 100 state and other part-time jobs (averaging $1400).

Applying *Options:* deferred entrance. *Required:* high school transcript.

Freshman Application Contact Mississippi Delta Community College, PO Box 668, Highway 3 and Cherry Street, Moorhead, MS 38761-0668. *Phone:* 662-246-6302.

Website: http://www.msdelta.edu/.

Mississippi Gulf Coast Community College
Perkinston, Mississippi

- **District-supported** 2-year, founded 1911
- **Small-town** 600-acre campus with easy access to New Orleans
- **Coed**

Undergraduates 6,935 full-time, 3,139 part-time. Students come from 15 states and territories; 4% are from out of state; 24% Black or African American, non-Hispanic/Latino; 3% Hispanic/Latino; 3% Asian, non-Hispanic/Latino; 0.1% Native Hawaiian or other Pacific Islander, non-Hispanic/Latino; 0.5% American Indian or Alaska Native, non-Hispanic/Latino; 2% Two or more races, non-Hispanic/Latino; 3% Race/ethnicity unknown; 7% live on campus. *Retention:* 62% of full-time freshmen returned.
Faculty *Student/faculty ratio:* 24:1.
Academics *Calendar:* semesters. *Degree:* certificates, diplomas, and associate. *Special study options:* academic remediation for entering students, adult/continuing education programs, advanced placement credit, cooperative education, distance learning, English as a second language, honors programs, independent study, internships, part-time degree program, study abroad, summer session for credit.
Student Life *Campus security:* 24-hour emergency response devices and patrols.
Athletics Member NJCAA.
Costs (2014–15) *Tuition:* state resident $1150 full-time, $115 per semester hour part-time; nonresident $2073 full-time. *Required fees:* $86 full-time. *Room and board:* $1785.
Applying *Required:* high school transcript.
Freshman Application Contact Mrs. Nichol Green, Director of Admissions, Mississippi Gulf Coast Community College, PO Box 548, Perkinston, MS 39573. *Phone:* 601-928-6264. *Fax:* 601-928-6345.
Website: http://www.mgccc.edu/.

Northeast Mississippi Community College
Booneville, Mississippi

Freshman Application Contact Office of Enrollment Services, Northeast Mississippi Community College, 101 Cunningham Boulevard, Booneville, MS 38829. *Phone:* 662-720-7239. *Toll-free phone:* 800-555-2154. *E-mail:* admitme@nemcc.edu.
Website: http://www.nemcc.edu/.

Northwest Mississippi Community College
Senatobia, Mississippi

- **State and locally supported** 2-year, founded 1927, part of Mississippi State Board for Community and Junior Colleges
- **Rural** 75-acre campus with easy access to Memphis
- **Coed**

Faculty *Student/faculty ratio:* 20:1.
Academics *Calendar:* semesters. *Degree:* associate. *Special study options:* academic remediation for entering students, adult/continuing education programs, honors programs, part-time degree program, services for LD students, summer session for credit. *ROTC:* Air Force (b).
Student Life *Campus security:* 24-hour emergency response devices, late-night transport/escort service, controlled dormitory access.
Athletics Member NJCAA.
Applying *Options:* early admission, deferred entrance. *Required:* high school transcript.
Freshman Application Contact Northwest Mississippi Community College, 4975 Highway 51 North, Senatobia, MS 38668-1701. *Phone:* 662-562-3222.
Website: http://www.northwestms.edu/.

Pearl River Community College
Poplarville, Mississippi

Freshman Application Contact Mr. J. Dow Ford, Director of Admissions, Pearl River Community College, 101 Highway 11 North, Poplarville, MS 39470. *Phone:* 601-403-1000. *E-mail:* dford@prcc.edu.
Website: http://www.prcc.edu/.

Southwest Mississippi Community College
Summit, Mississippi

Freshman Application Contact Mr. Matthew Calhoun, Vice President of Admissions and Records, Southwest Mississippi Community College, 1156 College Drive, Summit, MS 39666. *Phone:* 601-276-2001. *Fax:* 601-276-3888. *E-mail:* mattc@smcc.edu.
Website: http://www.smcc.cc.ms.us/.

Virginia College in Biloxi
Biloxi, Mississippi

Admissions Office Contact Virginia College in Biloxi, 920 Cedar Lake Road, Biloxi, MS 39532.
Website: http://www.vc.edu/.

Virginia College in Jackson
Jackson, Mississippi

Director of Admissions Director of Admissions, Virginia College in Jackson, 5841 Ridgewood Road, Jackson, MS 39211. *Phone:* 601-977-0960.
Website: http://www.vc.edu/.

MISSOURI

Brown Mackie College–St. Louis
Fenton, Missouri

- **Proprietary** primarily 2-year, part of Education Management Corporation
- **Coed**

Academics *Degrees:* diplomas, associate, and bachelor's.
Freshman Application Contact Brown Mackie College–St. Louis, #2 Soccer Park Road, Fenton, MO 63026. *Phone:* 636-651-3290.
Website: http://www.brownmackie.edu/st-louis/.

Bryan University
Columbia, Missouri

Admissions Office Contact Bryan University, 3215 LeMone Industrial Boulevard, Columbia, MO 65201. *Toll-free phone:* 855-566-0650.
Website: http://www.bryanu.edu/.

Concorde Career College
Kansas City, Missouri

Freshman Application Contact Deborah Crow, Director, Concorde Career College, 3239 Broadway, Kansas City, MO 64111-2407. *Phone:* 816-531-5223. *Fax:* 816-756-3231. *E-mail:* dcrow@concorde.edu.
Website: http://www.concorde.edu/.

Cottey College
Nevada, Missouri

- **Independent** primarily 2-year, founded 1884
- **Small-town** 51-acre campus
- **Endowment** $95,497
- **Women only**

Undergraduates 284 full-time. Students come from 40 states and territories; 21 other countries; 80% are from out of state; 4% Black or African American, non-Hispanic/Latino; 11% Hispanic/Latino; 0.4% Asian, non-Hispanic/Latino; 0.4% Native Hawaiian or other Pacific Islander, non-Hispanic/Latino; 1% American Indian or Alaska Native, non-Hispanic/Latino; 3% Two or more races, non-Hispanic/Latino; 10% international; 0.7% transferred in; 98% live on campus. *Retention:* 79% of full-time freshmen returned.
Faculty *Student/faculty ratio:* 8:1.
Academics *Calendar:* semesters. *Degrees:* associate and bachelor's. *Special study options:* advanced placement credit, distance learning, independent study, internships, part-time degree program, services for LD students, study abroad.
Student Life *Campus security:* 24-hour emergency response devices and patrols, late-night transport/escort service, controlled dormitory access.
Athletics Member NJCAA.

Standardized Tests *Required:* SAT or ACT (for admission).

Costs (2014–15) *Comprehensive fee:* $26,950 includes full-time tuition ($18,400), mandatory fees ($900), and room and board ($7650). Part-time tuition: $125 per hour. Part-time tuition and fees vary according to course load. *Required fees:* $76 per credit hour part-time. *Room and board:* college room only: $4000. Room and board charges vary according to housing facility.

Financial Aid Of all full-time matriculated undergraduates who enrolled in 2013, 236 applied for aid, 211 were judged to have need, 53 had their need fully met. In 2013, 59. *Average percent of need met:* 83. *Average financial aid package:* $19,014. *Average need-based loan:* $3376. *Average need-based gift aid:* $15,208. *Average non-need-based aid:* $10,607. *Average indebtedness upon graduation:* $13,066.

Applying *Required:* essay or personal statement, high school transcript, 1 letter of recommendation. *Recommended:* minimum 2.6 GPA, interview.

Freshman Application Contact Ms. Judi Steege, Director of Admission, Cottey College, 1000 West Austin Boulevard, Nevada, MO 64772. *Phone:* 417-667-8181. *Toll-free phone:* 888-526-8839. *Fax:* 417-667-8103. *E-mail:* enrollmgt@cottey.edu.

Website: http://www.cottey.edu/.

Court Reporting Institute of St. Louis
Clayton, Missouri

Freshman Application Contact Admissions Office, Court Reporting Institute of St. Louis, 7730 Carondelet Avenue, Suite 400, Clayton, MO 63105. *Phone:* 713-996-8300. *Toll-free phone:* 888-208-6780.

Website: http://www.cri.edu/st-louis-court-reporting-school.asp.

Crowder College
Neosho, Missouri

- **State and locally supported** 2-year, founded 1963, part of Missouri Coordinating Board for Higher Education
- **Rural** 608-acre campus
- **Coed,** 5,710 undergraduate students, 46% full-time, 64% women, 36% men

Undergraduates 2,638 full-time, 3,072 part-time. Students come from 12 states and territories; 64% are from out of state; 1% Black or African American, non-Hispanic/Latino; 8% Hispanic/Latino; 1% Asian, non-Hispanic/Latino; 0.4% Native Hawaiian or other Pacific Islander, non-Hispanic/Latino; 2% American Indian or Alaska Native, non-Hispanic/Latino; 2% Two or more races, non-Hispanic/Latino; 1% Race/ethnicity unknown; 1% international; 5% transferred in; 10% live on campus. *Retention:* 64% of full-time freshmen returned.

Freshmen *Admission:* 1,320 enrolled.

Faculty *Total:* 494, 19% full-time, 8% with terminal degrees. *Student/faculty ratio:* 12:1.

Majors Administrative assistant and secretarial science; agribusiness; agricultural mechanization; agriculture; art; autobody/collision and repair technology; automobile/automotive mechanics technology; biology/biological sciences; business administration and management; business automation/technology/data entry; computer systems analysis; computer systems networking and telecommunications; construction engineering technology; construction trades; drafting and design technology; dramatic/theater arts; education; electrical, electronic and communications engineering technology; elementary education; emergency medical technology (EMT paramedic); energy management and systems technology; environmental engineering technology; executive assistant/executive secretary; farm and ranch management; fire science/firefighting; general studies; health information/medical records technology; industrial technology; legal administrative assistant/secretary; liberal arts and sciences/liberal studies; manufacturing engineering technology; mass communication/media; mathematics; mathematics and computer science; medical administrative assistant and medical secretary; music; occupational therapist assistant; physical education teaching and coaching; physical sciences; pre-engineering; psychology; public relations/image management; registered nursing/registered nurse; solar energy technology; veterinary/animal health technology; welding technology.

Academics *Calendar:* semesters. *Degree:* certificates and associate. *Special study options:* academic remediation for entering students, adult/continuing education programs, advanced placement credit, cooperative education, English as a second language, freshman honors college, honors programs, independent study, part-time degree program, student-designed majors, study abroad, summer session for credit.

Library Bill & Margot Lee Library with 183,354 titles, 6,558 audiovisual materials, a Web page.

Student Life *Housing Options:* men-only, women-only. Campus housing is university owned. *Activities and Organizations:* drama/theater group, student-run newspaper, choral group, Phi Theta Kappa, Students in Free Enterprise (SIFE), Baptist Student Union, Student Senate, Student Ambassadors. *Campus security:* 24-hour patrols.

Athletics Member NJCAA. *Intercollegiate sports:* baseball M(s), basketball W(s), soccer M(s).

Financial Aid Of all full-time matriculated undergraduates who enrolled in 2013, 150 Federal Work-Study jobs (averaging $1000).

Applying *Application fee:* $25. *Required:* high school transcript. *Application deadlines:* rolling (freshmen), rolling (transfers). *Notification:* continuous (freshmen).

Freshman Application Contact Mr. Jim Riggs, Admissions Coordinator, Crowder College, Neosho, MO 64850. *Phone:* 417-451-3223 Ext. 5466. *Toll-free phone:* 866-238-7788. *Fax:* 417-455-5731. *E-mail:* jimriggs@crowder.edu.

Website: http://www.crowder.edu/.

Culinary Institute of St. Louis at Hickey College
St. Louis, Missouri

- **Private** 2-year, founded 2009
- **Suburban** campus
- **Coed,** 91 undergraduate students
- **83%** of applicants were admitted

Freshmen *Admission:* 167 applied, 139 admitted.

Majors Cooking and related culinary arts.

Academics *Calendar:* semesters. *Degree:* associate.

Freshman Application Contact Admissions Office, Culinary Institute of St. Louis at Hickey College, 2700 North Lindbergh Boulevard, St. Louis, MO 63114. *Phone:* 314-434-2212.

Website: http://www.ci-stl.com/.

East Central College
Union, Missouri

- **District-supported** 2-year, founded 1959
- **Rural** 207-acre campus with easy access to St. Louis
- **Endowment** $2.8 million
- **Coed**

Undergraduates 1,852 full-time, 2,048 part-time. Students come from 3 states and territories; 0.1% are from out of state; 0.6% Black or African American, non-Hispanic/Latino; 1% Hispanic/Latino; 0.4% Asian, non-Hispanic/Latino; 0.2% Native Hawaiian or other Pacific Islander, non-Hispanic/Latino; 0.3% American Indian or Alaska Native, non-Hispanic/Latino; 0.1% Two or more races, non-Hispanic/Latino; 1% Race/ethnicity unknown; 6% transferred in.

Faculty *Student/faculty ratio:* 20:1.

Academics *Calendar:* semesters. *Degree:* certificates and associate. *Special study options:* academic remediation for entering students, adult/continuing education programs, advanced placement credit, distance learning, English as a second language, honors programs, independent study, internships, off-campus study, part-time degree program, services for LD students, study abroad, summer session for credit.

Student Life *Campus security:* 24-hour emergency response devices, late-night transport/escort service.

Athletics Member NJCAA.

Costs (2014–15) *Tuition:* area resident $1800 full-time, $75 per credit hour part-time; state resident $2544 full-time, $106 per credit hour part-time; nonresident $3840 full-time, $160 per credit hour part-time. Full-time tuition and fees vary according to program. Part-time tuition and fees vary according to program. *Required fees:* $456 full-time, $19 per credit hour part-time. *Payment plans:* installment, deferred payment.

Applying *Options:* early admission, deferred entrance. *Required:* high school transcript.

Freshman Application Contact Mr. Nathaniel Mitchell, Director, Admissions, East Central College, 1964 Prairie Dell Road, Union, MO 63084. *Phone:* 636-584-6552. *E-mail:* nemitche@eastcentral.edu.

Website: http://www.eastcentral.edu/.

Everest College
Springfield, Missouri

Freshman Application Contact Admissions Office, Everest College, 1010 West Sunshine, Springfield, MO 65807-2488. *Phone:* 417-864-7220. *Toll-free phone:* 888-741-4270. *Fax:* 417-864-5697.

Website: http://www.everest.edu/.

Heritage College
Kansas City, Missouri

Freshman Application Contact Admissions Office, Heritage College, 1200 East 104th Street, Suite 300, Kansas City, MO 64131. *Phone:* 816-942-5474. *Toll-free phone:* 888-334-7339. *E-mail:* info@heritage-education.com. *Website:* http://www.heritage-education.com/.

IHM Academy of EMS
St. Louis, Missouri

Freshman Application Contact Admissions Director, IHM Academy of EMS, 2500 Abbott Place, St. Louis, MO 63143. *Phone:* 314-768-1234. *Fax:* 314-768-1595. *E-mail:* info@ihmhealthstudies.edu. *Website:* http://www.ihmacademyofems.net/.

ITT Technical Institute
Arnold, Missouri

- **Proprietary** primarily 2-year, founded 1997, part of ITT Educational Services, Inc.
- **Coed**

Academics *Calendar:* quarters. *Degrees:* associate and bachelor's.
Freshman Application Contact Director of Recruitment, ITT Technical Institute, 1930 Meyer Drury Drive, Arnold, MO 63010. *Phone:* 636-464-6600. *Toll-free phone:* 888-488-1082. *Website:* http://www.itt-tech.edu/.

ITT Technical Institute
Earth City, Missouri

- **Proprietary** primarily 2-year, founded 1936, part of ITT Educational Services, Inc.
- **Suburban** campus
- **Coed**

Academics *Calendar:* quarters. *Degrees:* associate and bachelor's.
Freshman Application Contact Director of Recruitment, ITT Technical Institute, 3640 Corporate Trail Drive, Earth City, MO 63045. *Phone:* 314-298-7800. *Toll-free phone:* 800-235-5488. *Website:* http://www.itt-tech.edu/.

ITT Technical Institute
Kansas City, Missouri

- **Proprietary** primarily 2-year, founded 2004, part of ITT Educational Services, Inc.
- **Coed**

Academics *Calendar:* quarters. *Degrees:* associate and bachelor's.
Freshman Application Contact Director of Recruitment, ITT Technical Institute, 9150 East 41st Terrace, Kansas City, MO 64133. *Phone:* 816-276-1400. *Toll-free phone:* 877-488-1442. *Website:* http://www.itt-tech.edu/.

Jefferson College
Hillsboro, Missouri

- **District-supported** 2-year, founded 1963
- **Rural** 455-acre campus with easy access to St. Louis
- **Endowment** $684,672
- **Coed,** 4,883 undergraduate students, 52% full-time, 59% women, 41% men

Undergraduates 2,549 full-time, 2,334 part-time. 2% Black or African American, non-Hispanic/Latino; 0.3% Hispanic/Latino; 0.8% Asian, non-Hispanic/Latino; 0.1% Native Hawaiian or other Pacific Islander, non-Hispanic/Latino; 0.8% American Indian or Alaska Native, non-Hispanic/Latino; 5% Race/ethnicity unknown; 0.3% international.
Freshmen *Admission:* 1,136 enrolled.
Faculty *Total:* 341, 28% full-time, 10% with terminal degrees. *Student/faculty ratio:* 19:1.
Majors Administrative assistant and secretarial science; automobile/automotive mechanics technology; business administration and management; business/commerce; child-care and support services management; computer systems networking and telecommunications; criminal justice/law enforcement administration; criminal justice/police science; culinary arts; education (specific levels and methods) related; electrical, electronic and communications engineering technology; emergency medical technology (EMT paramedic); engineering; fire prevention and safety technology; heating, air conditioning, ventilation and refrigeration maintenance technology; information technology; legal administrative assistant/secretary; liberal arts and sciences/liberal studies; licensed practical/vocational nurse training; machine tool technology; manufacturing engineering technology; medical administrative assistant and medical secretary; occupational therapist assistant; physical therapy technology; precision production related; registered nursing/registered nurse; veterinary/animal health technology; welding technology.
Academics *Calendar:* semesters. *Degree:* certificates, diplomas, and associate. *Special study options:* academic remediation for entering students, adult/continuing education programs, advanced placement credit, distance learning, English as a second language, freshman honors college, honors programs, internships, off-campus study, part-time degree program, services for LD students, summer session for credit.
Library Jefferson College Library plus 1 other with 73,443 titles, 2,805 audiovisual materials, an OPAC, a Web page.
Student Life *Housing Options:* coed. Campus housing is university owned. *Activities and Organizations:* drama/theater group, student-run newspaper, television station, choral group, Student Senate, Nursing associations, Baptist Student Unit, Phi Theta Kappa, National Technical Honors Society, national sororities. *Campus security:* 24-hour patrols, campus police department. *Student services:* health clinic, personal/psychological counseling.
Athletics Member NJCAA. *Intercollegiate sports:* baseball M(s), basketball W(s), cheerleading M(s)/W(s), soccer M(s), softball W(s), volleyball W(s).
Costs (2015–16) *One-time required fee:* $25. *Tuition:* area resident $2910 full-time, $97 per credit hour part-time; state resident $4380 full-time, $479 per credit hour part-time; nonresident $5820 full-time, $194 per credit hour part-time. Full-time tuition and fees vary according to course load and program. Part-time tuition and fees vary according to course load and program. *Required fees:* $90 full-time, $3 per credit hour part-time, $10 per term part-time. *Room and board:* $5644. Room and board charges vary according to housing facility. *Payment plan:* installment. *Waivers:* senior citizens and employees or children of employees.
Financial Aid Of all full-time matriculated undergraduates who enrolled in 2013, 2,416 applied for aid, 1,872 were judged to have need, 72 had their need fully met. 78 Federal Work-Study jobs (averaging $1415). 133 state and other part-time jobs (averaging $1345). In 2013, 145 non-need-based awards were made. *Average percent of need met:* 58%. *Average financial aid package:* $5038. *Average need-based loan:* $3020. *Average need-based gift aid:* $2625. *Average non-need-based aid:* $1996.
Applying *Options:* electronic application, early admission. *Application fee:* $25. *Required:* high school transcript. *Application deadlines:* rolling (freshmen), rolling (transfers).
Freshman Application Contact Dr. Kimberly Harvey, Director of Student Records and Admissions Services, Jefferson College, 1000 Viking Drive, Hillsboro, MO 63050-2441. *Phone:* 636-481-3205 Ext. 3205. *Fax:* 636-789-5103. *E-mail:* admissions@jeffco.edu. *Website:* http://www.jeffco.edu/.

L'Ecole Culinaire–Kansas City
Kansas City, Missouri

Admissions Office Contact L'Ecole Culinaire–Kansas City, 310 Ward Parkway, Kansas City, MO 64112-2110. *Website:* http://www.lecole.edu/kansas-city/.

L'Ecole Culinaire–St. Louis
St. Louis, Missouri

Admissions Office Contact L'Ecole Culinaire–St. Louis, 9811 South Forty Drive, St. Louis, MO 63124. *Website:* http://www.lecole.edu/st-louis/.

Metro Business College
Arnold, Missouri

Admissions Office Contact Metro Business College, 2132 Tenbrook Road, Arnold, MO 63010. *Website:* http://www.metrobusinesscollege.edu/.

Metro Business College
Cape Girardeau, Missouri

Director of Admissions Ms. Kyla Evans, Admissions Director, Metro Business College, 1732 North Kingshighway Street, Cape Girardeau, MO 63701. *Phone:* 573-334-9181. *Toll-free phone:* 888-206-4545. *Fax:* 573-334-0617. *Website:* http://www.metrobusinesscollege.edu/.

Metro Business College
Jefferson City, Missouri

- **Proprietary** 2-year, founded 1979
- **Suburban** campus
- **Coed**

Undergraduates 113 full-time, 29 part-time. Students come from 1 other state; 18% Black or African American, non-Hispanic/Latino; 2% Asian, non-Hispanic/Latino; 0.7% American Indian or Alaska Native, non-Hispanic/Latino; 4% Race/ethnicity unknown; 4% transferred in.
Faculty *Student/faculty ratio:* 11:1.
Academics *Calendar:* quarters. *Degree:* certificates, diplomas, and associate. *Special study options:* academic remediation for entering students, adult/continuing education programs, advanced placement credit, independent study, internships, part-time degree program, services for LD students, summer session for credit.
Standardized Tests *Required:* Wonderlic aptitude test (for admission).
Costs (2014–15) *Tuition:* $10,200 full-time, $1278 per term part-time. Full-time tuition and fees vary according to program. Part-time tuition and fees vary according to program. No tuition increase for student's term of enrollment. *Required fees:* $125 full-time. *Payment plans:* tuition prepayment, installment, deferred payment.
Applying *Required:* essay or personal statement, high school transcript, interview.
Freshman Application Contact Ms. Cheri Chockley, Campus Director, Metro Business College, 210 El Mercado Plaza, Jefferson City, MO 65109. *Phone:* 573-635-6600. *Toll-free phone:* 888-206-4545. *Fax:* 573-635-6999. *E-mail:* cheri@metrobusinesscollege.edu.
Website: http://www.metrobusinesscollege.edu/.

Metro Business College
Rolla, Missouri

Freshman Application Contact Admissions Office, Metro Business College, 1202 East Highway 72, Rolla, MO 65401. *Phone:* 573-364-8464. *Toll-free phone:* 888-206-4545. *Fax:* 573-364-8077. *E-mail:* inforolla@metrobusinesscollege.edu.
Website: http://www.metrobusinesscollege.edu/.

Metropolitan Community College–Kansas City
Kansas City, Missouri

- **State and locally supported** 2-year, founded 1969, part of Metropolitan Community Colleges System
- **Suburban** 420-acre campus with easy access to Kansas City
- **Endowment** $4.5 million
- **Coed**

Undergraduates 7,734 full-time, 11,500 part-time. Students come from 19 states and territories; 74 other countries; 1% are from out of state; 17% Black or African American, non-Hispanic/Latino; 9% Hispanic/Latino; 3% Asian, non-Hispanic/Latino; 0.3% Native Hawaiian or other Pacific Islander, non-Hispanic/Latino; 0.3% American Indian or Alaska Native, non-Hispanic/Latino; 6% Two or more races, non-Hispanic/Latino; 0.7% Race/ethnicity unknown; 4% transferred in. *Retention:* 52% of full-time freshmen returned.
Faculty *Student/faculty ratio:* 26:1.
Academics *Calendar:* semesters. *Degree:* certificates and associate. *Special study options:* academic remediation for entering students, accelerated degree program, adult/continuing education programs, advanced placement credit, cooperative education, distance learning, English as a second language, honors programs, independent study, internships, off-campus study, part-time degree program, services for LD students, summer session for credit.
Student Life *Campus security:* 24-hour emergency response devices and patrols, late-night transport/escort service.
Athletics Member NJCAA.
Standardized Tests *Recommended:* ACT (for admission), Placement Testing for first-time freshman.
Costs (2014–15) *Tuition:* area resident $2700 full-time, $90 per credit hour part-time; state resident $5100 full-time, $170 per credit hour part-time; nonresident $6720 full-time, $224 per credit hour part-time. Full-time tuition and fees vary according to program and reciprocity agreements. Part-time tuition and fees vary according to program and reciprocity agreements. *Required fees:* $170 full-time, $5 per credit hour part-time, $10 per term part-time.
Applying *Options:* electronic application, early admission, deferred entrance.
Freshman Application Contact Dr. Tuesday Stanley, Vice Chancellor of Student Development and Enrollment Services, Metropolitan Community College–Kansas City, 3200 Broadway, Kansas City, MO 64111-2429. *Phone:* 816-604-1253. *E-mail:* tuesday.stanley@mcckc.edu.
Website: http://www.mcckc.edu/.

Midwest Institute
Fenton, Missouri

Freshman Application Contact Admissions Office, Midwest Institute, 964 S. Highway Drive, Fenton, MO 63026. *Toll-free phone:* 800-695-5550.
Website: http://www.midwestinstitute.com/.

Midwest Institute
St. Louis, Missouri

Freshman Application Contact Admissions Office, Midwest Institute, 4260 Shoreline Drive, St. Louis, MO 63045. *Phone:* 314-344-4440. *Toll-free phone:* 800-695-5550. *Fax:* 314-344-0495.
Website: http://www.midwestinstitute.com/.

Mineral Area College
Park Hills, Missouri

- **District-supported** 2-year, founded 1922, part of Missouri Coordinating Board for Higher Education
- **Rural** 240-acre campus with easy access to St. Louis
- **Coed**

Undergraduates 2,869 full-time, 1,639 part-time. Students come from 14 states and territories; 2 other countries; 1% are from out of state; 2% Black or African American, non-Hispanic/Latino; 1% Hispanic/Latino; 0.4% Asian, non-Hispanic/Latino; 0.1% Native Hawaiian or other Pacific Islander, non-Hispanic/Latino; 0.6% American Indian or Alaska Native, non-Hispanic/Latino; 5% Race/ethnicity unknown; 0.1% international; 4% transferred in. *Retention:* 68% of full-time freshmen returned.
Faculty *Student/faculty ratio:* 14:1.
Academics *Calendar:* semesters. *Degree:* certificates and associate. *Special study options:* academic remediation for entering students, advanced placement credit, distance learning, honors programs, internships, off-campus study, part-time degree program, services for LD students, summer session for credit.
Student Life *Campus security:* 24-hour patrols.
Athletics Member NJCAA.
Costs (2014–15) *Tuition:* area resident $2820 full-time, $94 per semester hour part-time; state resident $3780 full-time, $126 per semester hour part-time; nonresident $4950 full-time, $165 per semester hour part-time. *Room and board:* room only: $3612. Room and board charges vary according to board plan and housing facility.
Financial Aid Of all full-time matriculated undergraduates who enrolled in 2013, 65 Federal Work-Study jobs (averaging $3708).
Applying *Options:* electronic application, early admission. *Application fee:* $15. *Required:* high school transcript.
Freshman Application Contact Pam Reeder, Registrar, Mineral Area College, PO Box 1000, Park Hills, MO 63601-1000. *Phone:* 573-518-2204. *Fax:* 573-518-2166. *E-mail:* preeder@mineralarea.edu.
Website: http://www.mineralarea.edu/.

Missouri College
Brentwood, Missouri

Director of Admissions Mr. Doug Brinker, Admissions Director, Missouri College, 1405 South Hanley Road, Brentwood, MO 63117. *Phone:* 314-821-7700. *Toll-free phone:* 800-216-6732. *Fax:* 314-821-0891.
Website: http://www.missouricollege.edu/.

Missouri State University–West Plains
West Plains, Missouri

- **State-supported** 2-year, founded 1963, part of Missouri State University
- **Small-town** 20-acre campus
- **Endowment** $6.4 million
- **Coed**

Undergraduates 1,310 full-time, 813 part-time. Students come from 27 states and territories; 3 other countries; 4% are from out of state; 2% Black or African American, non-Hispanic/Latino; 2% Hispanic/Latino; 1% Asian, non-Hispanic/Latino; 1% American Indian or Alaska Native, non-Hispanic/Latino; 4% Race/ethnicity unknown; 0.6% international; 5% transferred in; 4% live on campus. *Retention:* 47% of full-time freshmen returned.
Faculty *Student/faculty ratio:* 25:1.

Academics *Calendar:* semesters. *Degree:* certificates and associate. *Special study options:* academic remediation for entering students, adult/continuing education programs, advanced placement credit, cooperative education, distance learning, honors programs, internships, off-campus study, part-time degree program, services for LD students, study abroad, summer session for credit.

Student Life *Campus security:* access only with key.

Athletics Member NJCAA.

Costs (2014–15) *Tuition:* state resident $3720 full-time; nonresident $6958 full-time. Full-time tuition and fees vary according to course load, location, and program. Part-time tuition and fees vary according to course load and location. *Required fees:* $294 full-time. *Room and board:* $5480. Room and board charges vary according to board plan.

Financial Aid Of all full-time matriculated undergraduates who enrolled in 2013, 63 Federal Work-Study jobs (averaging $2000).

Applying *Options:* electronic application. *Application fee:* $15. *Required for some:* high school transcript.

Freshman Application Contact Ms. Melissa Jett, Coordinator of Admissions, Missouri State University–West Plains, 128 Garfield, West Plains, MO 65775. *Phone:* 417-255-7955. *Toll-free phone:* 888-466-7897. *Fax:* 417-255-7959. *E-mail:* melissajett@missouristate.edu. *Website:* http://wp.missouristate.edu/.

Moberly Area Community College
Moberly, Missouri

Freshman Application Contact Dr. James Grant, Dean of Student Services, Moberly Area Community College, Moberly, MO 65270-1304. *Phone:* 660-263-4110 Ext. 235. *Toll-free phone:* 800-622-2070. *Fax:* 660-263-2406. *E-mail:* info@macc.edu. *Website:* http://www.macc.edu/.

North Central Missouri College
Trenton, Missouri

Freshman Application Contact Megan Goodin, Admissions Assistant, North Central Missouri College, Trenton, MO 64683. *Phone:* 660-359-3948 Ext. 1410. *E-mail:* megoodin@mail.ncmissouri.edu. *Website:* http://www.ncmissouri.edu/.

Ozarks Technical Community College
Springfield, Missouri

- **District-supported** 2-year, founded 1990, part of Missouri Coordinating Board for Higher Education
- **Urban** campus
- **Endowment** $1.7 million
- **Coed,** 14,396 undergraduate students, 45% full-time, 48% women, 52% men

Undergraduates 6,513 full-time, 7,883 part-time. 2% are from out of state; 2% Black or African American, non-Hispanic/Latino; 2% Hispanic/Latino; 1% Asian, non-Hispanic/Latino; 0.7% American Indian or Alaska Native, non-Hispanic/Latino; 32% Race/ethnicity unknown.

Faculty *Total:* 888, 21% full-time. *Student/faculty ratio:* 22:1.

Majors Accounting; administrative assistant and secretarial science; autobody/collision and repair technology; automobile/automotive mechanics technology; business administration and management; business machine repair; computer systems networking and telecommunications; construction engineering technology; culinary arts; diesel mechanics technology; electrical, electronic and communications engineering technology; emergency medical technology (EMT paramedic); fire science/firefighting; graphic and printing equipment operation/production; health information/medical records technology; heating, air conditioning, ventilation and refrigeration maintenance technology; heavy equipment maintenance technology; hotel/motel administration; industrial technology; information science/studies; instrumentation technology; kindergarten/preschool education; liberal arts and sciences/liberal studies; machine tool technology; management information systems; mechanical drafting and CAD/CADD; occupational therapist assistant; occupational therapy; physical sciences; physical therapy technology; radio and television broadcasting technology; respiratory care therapy; turf and turfgrass management; welding technology.

Academics *Calendar:* semesters. *Degree:* certificates, diplomas, and associate. *Special study options:* academic remediation for entering students, adult/continuing education programs, cooperative education, distance learning, double majors, English as a second language, honors programs, internships, off-campus study, part-time degree program, services for LD students, summer session for credit.

Library Library plus 1 other with 6,000 titles, an OPAC, a Web page.

Student Life *Housing:* college housing not available. *Activities and Organizations:* student-run newspaper, choral group, Phi Theta Kappa. *Campus security:* 24-hour emergency response devices. *Student services:* personal/psychological counseling.

Costs (2015–16) *Tuition:* area resident $2280 full-time, $95 per credit hour part-time; state resident $3420 full-time, $143 per credit hour part-time; nonresident $4560 full-time, $190 per credit hour part-time. Tuition dollars reported are listed for Tier 1 - General Education Courses. Additional Tuition Rates are as follows: Tier 2 - Technical Education Courses - $98 per credit hour, Tier 3 - Allied Health Courses - $101 per credit hour. *Required fees:* $500 full-time, $21 per credit hour part-time, $45 per term part-time. *Payment plans:* installment, deferred payment. *Waivers:* employees or children of employees.

Financial Aid Of all full-time matriculated undergraduates who enrolled in 2013, 201 Federal Work-Study jobs.

Applying *Options:* electronic application. *Required:* high school transcript. *Application deadlines:* rolling (freshmen), rolling (out-of-state freshmen), rolling (transfers). *Notification:* continuous (freshmen), continuous (out-of-state freshmen), continuous (transfers).

Freshman Application Contact Ozarks Technical Community College, 1001 E. Chestnut Expressway, Springfield, MO 65802. *Website:* http://www.otc.edu/.

Pinnacle Career Institute
Kansas City, Missouri

Director of Admissions Ms. Ruth Matous, Director of Admissions, Pinnacle Career Institute, 1001 East 101st Terrace, Suite 325, Kansas City, MO 64131. *Phone:* 816-331-5700 Ext. 212. *Toll-free phone:* 877-241-3097. *Website:* http://www.pcitraining.edu/.

Pinnacle Career Institute–North Kansas City
Kansas City, Missouri

- **Proprietary** 2-year, part of Pinnacle Career Institute
- **Suburban** campus with easy access to Kansas City
- **Coed,** 147 undergraduate students

Academics *Calendar:* monthly modules. *Degree:* certificates, diplomas, and associate.

Applying *Options:* electronic application. *Required:* high school transcript, interview.

Freshman Application Contact Pinnacle Career Institute–North Kansas City, 11500 NW. Ambassador, Suite 221, Kansas City, MO 64153. *Phone:* 816-331-5700. *Website:* http://www.pcitraining.edu.

Ranken Technical College
St. Louis, Missouri

Director of Admissions Ms. Elizabeth Keserauskis, Director of Admissions, Ranken Technical College, 4431 Finney Avenue, St. Louis, MO 63113. *Phone:* 314-371-0233 Ext. 4811. *Toll-free phone:* 866-4-RANKEN. *Website:* http://www.ranken.edu/.

St. Charles Community College
Cottleville, Missouri

- **State-supported** 2-year, founded 1986, part of Missouri Coordinating Board for Higher Education
- **Suburban** 228-acre campus with easy access to St. Louis
- **Endowment** $77,505
- **Coed,** 7,153 undergraduate students, 48% full-time, 57% women, 43% men

Undergraduates 3,466 full-time, 3,687 part-time. Students come from 11 states and territories; 32 other countries; 6% Black or African American, non-Hispanic/Latino; 4% Hispanic/Latino; 2% Asian, non-Hispanic/Latino; 0.1% Native Hawaiian or other Pacific Islander, non-Hispanic/Latino; 0.3% American Indian or Alaska Native, non-Hispanic/Latino; 3% Two or more races, non-Hispanic/Latino; 4% Race/ethnicity unknown; 0.8% international; 7% transferred in.

Freshmen *Admission:* 6,806 applied, 6,806 admitted, 1,675 enrolled.

Faculty *Total:* 386, 27% full-time, 10% with terminal degrees. *Student/faculty ratio:* 24:1.

Majors Accounting technology and bookkeeping; biology/biological sciences; chemistry; child-care provision; civil engineering; commercial and advertising art; criminal justice/police science; drafting and design technology;

dramatic/theater arts; economics; education; education (specific subject areas) related; emergency medical technology (EMT paramedic); engineering; English; fire science/firefighting; foreign languages and literatures; French; general studies; health information/medical records technology; history; human services; industrial technology; liberal arts and sciences/liberal studies; licensed practical/vocational nurse training; marketing/marketing management; massage therapy; mathematics; mechanical engineering; medical administrative assistant and medical secretary; music history, literature, and theory; occupational therapist assistant; philosophy; political science and government; precision production related; psychology; registered nursing/registered nurse; social work; sociology; Spanish; teacher assistant/aide.

Academics *Calendar:* semesters. *Degree:* certificates and associate. *Special study options:* academic remediation for entering students, adult/continuing education programs, advanced placement credit, cooperative education, distance learning, double majors, English as a second language, honors programs, independent study, internships, part-time degree program, services for LD students, study abroad, summer session for credit.

Library Paul and Helen Schnare Library with 67,427 titles, 8,009 audiovisual materials, an OPAC, a Web page.

Student Life *Activities and Organizations:* drama/theater group, student-run newspaper, choral group, Phi Theta Kappa, Student Nurse Organization, GAMES Club, Phi Bet Lambda, Student Veterans Organization. *Campus security:* 24-hour emergency response devices and patrols, late-night transport/escort service, campus police officers on duty during normal operating hours. *Student services:* personal/psychological counseling.

Athletics Member NJCAA. *Intercollegiate sports:* baseball M(s), soccer M(s)/W(s), softball W(s).

Costs (2015–16) *Tuition:* area resident $2352 full-time, $98 per credit part-time; state resident $3528 full-time, $147 per credit part-time; nonresident $5160 full-time, $215 per credit part-time. Full-time tuition and fees vary according to course load and program. Part-time tuition and fees vary according to course load and program. *Required fees:* $120 full-time, $5 per credit part-time. *Payment plan:* installment. *Waivers:* senior citizens and employees or children of employees.

Financial Aid Of all full-time matriculated undergraduates who enrolled in 2013, 33 Federal Work-Study jobs.

Applying *Options:* electronic application, early admission, deferred entrance. *Application fee:* $10. *Required for some:* high school transcript, minimum 2.5 GPA. *Recommended:* high school transcript. *Application deadlines:* rolling (freshmen), rolling (out-of-state freshmen), rolling (transfers). *Notification:* continuous (freshmen), continuous (out-of-state freshmen), continuous (transfers).

Freshman Application Contact Ms. Kathy Brockgreitens-Gober, Dean of Enrollment Services, St. Charles Community College, 4601 Mid Rivers Mall Drive, Cottleville, MO 63376-0975. *Phone:* 636-922-8229. *Fax:* 636-922-8236. *E-mail:* regist@stchas.edu. *Website:* http://www.stchas.edu/.

St. Louis College of Health Careers
Fenton, Missouri

Admissions Office Contact St. Louis College of Health Careers, 1297 North Highway Drive, Fenton, MO 63026. *Website:* http://www.slchc.com/.

St. Louis College of Health Careers
St. Louis, Missouri

Freshman Application Contact Admissions Office, St. Louis College of Health Careers, 909 South Taylor Avenue, St. Louis, MO 63110-1511. *Phone:* 314-652-0300. *Toll-free phone:* 888-789-4820. *Fax:* 314-652-4825. *Website:* http://www.slchc.com/.

St. Louis Community College
St. Louis, Missouri

- **Public** 2-year, part of St. Louis Community College System
- **Suburban** campus with easy access to St. Louis
- **Coed,** 21,218 undergraduate students, 41% full-time, 59% women, 41% men

Undergraduates 8,682 full-time, 12,536 part-time. Students come from 27 states and territories; 106 other countries; 2% are from out of state; 35% Black or African American, non-Hispanic/Latino; 3% Hispanic/Latino; 3% Asian, non-Hispanic/Latino; 0.1% Native Hawaiian or other Pacific Islander, non-Hispanic/Latino; 0.3% American Indian or Alaska Native, non-Hispanic/Latino; 3% Two or more races, non-Hispanic/Latino; 0.8% Race/ethnicity unknown; 1% international; 8% transferred in. *Retention:* 56% of full-time freshmen returned.

Freshmen *Admission:* 3,563 enrolled.
Faculty *Total:* 1,494, 29% full-time. *Student/faculty ratio:* 19:1.
Academics *Calendar:* semesters. *Degree:* certificates and associate. *Special study options:* academic remediation for entering students, accelerated degree program, adult/continuing education programs, advanced placement credit, distance learning, English as a second language, honors programs, independent study, internships, part-time degree program, services for LD students, study abroad, summer session for credit.
Library an OPAC, a Web page.
Student Life *Housing:* college housing not available. *Activities and Organizations:* drama/theater group, student-run newspaper. *Campus security:* 24-hour emergency response devices, late-night transport/escort service. *Student services:* personal/psychological counseling.
Athletics Member NJCAA. *Intercollegiate sports:* baseball M(s), basketball M(s)/W(s), soccer M(s)/W(s), softball W(s), volleyball W(s).
Costs (2015–16) *Tuition:* area resident $2760 full-time, $92 per credit part-time; state resident $4140 full-time, $138 per credit part-time; nonresident $5790 full-time, $193 per credit part-time. Full-time tuition and fees vary according to course load. Part-time tuition and fees vary according to course load. *Required fees:* $270 full-time, $9 per credit part-time. *Payment plan:* installment. *Waivers:* senior citizens and employees or children of employees.
Applying *Options:* electronic application. *Required for some:* high school transcript, interview. *Application deadlines:* rolling (freshmen), rolling (out-of-state freshmen), rolling (transfers). *Notification:* continuous (freshmen), continuous (out-of-state freshmen), continuous (transfers).
Freshman Application Contact St. Louis Community College, 300 South Broadway, St. Louis, MO 63102. *Website:* http://www.stlcc.edu/.

Southeast Missouri Hospital College of Nursing and Health Sciences
Cape Girardeau, Missouri

Freshman Application Contact Southeast Missouri Hospital College of Nursing and Health Sciences, 2001 William Street, Cape Girardeau, MO 63701. *Phone:* 573-334-6825 Ext. 12. *Website:* http://www.sehcollege.edu/.

State Fair Community College
Sedalia, Missouri

- **District-supported** 2-year, founded 1966, part of Missouri Coordinating Board for Higher Education
- **Small-town** 128-acre campus
- **Endowment** $12.5 million
- **Coed,** 4,983 undergraduate students, 50% full-time, 65% women, 35% men

Undergraduates 2,506 full-time, 2,477 part-time. Students come from 15 states and territories; 2 other countries; 4% Black or African American, non-Hispanic/Latino; 2% Hispanic/Latino; 0.7% Asian, non-Hispanic/Latino; 0.2% Native Hawaiian or other Pacific Islander, non-Hispanic/Latino; 0.7% American Indian or Alaska Native, non-Hispanic/Latino; 6% Two or more races, non-Hispanic/Latino; 0.3% Race/ethnicity unknown; 7% transferred in. *Retention:* 59% of full-time freshmen returned.
Freshmen *Admission:* 1,091 admitted, 1,128 enrolled.
Faculty *Total:* 387, 20% full-time. *Student/faculty ratio:* 32:1.
Majors Accounting; accounting and computer science; agribusiness; applied horticulture/horticulture operations; automobile/automotive mechanics technology; building/construction site management; business administration and management; CAD/CADD drafting/design technology; child-care and support services management; computer programming (specific applications); computer systems networking and telecommunications; criminal justice/police science; dental hygiene; education (specific subject areas) related; health information/medical records technology; liberal arts and sciences/liberal studies; machine tool technology; manufacturing engineering technology; marine maintenance and ship repair technology; mechanic and repair technologies related; medical administrative assistant and medical secretary; occupational therapist assistant; physical therapy technology; radiologic technology/science; registered nursing/registered nurse; special products marketing; teacher assistant/aide; technical teacher education; web page, digital/multimedia and information resources design.
Academics *Calendar:* semesters. *Degree:* certificates and associate. *Special study options:* academic remediation for entering students, adult/continuing education programs, advanced placement credit, distance learning, English as a second language, internships, off-campus study, part-time degree program, services for LD students, summer session for credit.
Library Donald C. Proctor Library with 41,258 titles, 1,633 audiovisual materials, an OPAC, a Web page.

Student Life *Housing Options:* coed. Campus housing is university owned. *Activities and Organizations:* drama/theater group, choral group. *Campus security:* 24-hour emergency response devices, controlled dormitory access, Campus Safety Officer on campus M-Th from 11 am - 10 pm, security during evening class hours. *Student services:* personal/psychological counseling.
Athletics Member NJCAA. *Intercollegiate sports:* basketball M(s)/W(s).
Costs (2015–16) *Tuition:* area resident $3000 full-time; state resident $4200 full-time; nonresident $6000 full-time. *Room and board:* $6250. Room and board charges vary according to location.
Financial Aid Of all full-time matriculated undergraduates who enrolled in 2013, 87 Federal Work-Study jobs (averaging $1148).
Applying *Options:* electronic application. *Application deadlines:* rolling (freshmen), rolling (transfers).
Freshman Application Contact State Fair Community College, 3201 West 16th Street, Sedalia, MO 65301-2199. *Phone:* 660-596-7379. *Toll-free phone:* 877-311-7322.
Website: http://www.sfccmo.edu/.

State Technical College of Missouri
Linn, Missouri

Freshman Application Contact State Technical College of Missouri, One Technology Drive, Linn, MO 65051-9606. *Phone:* 573-897-5196. *Toll-free phone:* 800-743-TECH.
Website: http://www.statetechmo.edu/.

Texas County Technical College
Houston, Missouri

Admissions Office Contact Texas County Technical College, 6915 S. Hwy 63, Houston, MO 65483.
Website: http://www.texascountytech.edu/.

Three Rivers Community College
Poplar Bluff, Missouri

Freshman Application Contact Ms. Marcia Fields, Director of Admissions and Recruiting, Three Rivers Community College, Poplar Bluff, MO 63901. *Phone:* 573-840-9675. *Toll-free phone:* 877-TRY-TRCC. *E-mail:* trytrcc@trcc.edu.
Website: http://www.trcc.edu/.

Vatterott College
Berkeley, Missouri

Director of Admissions Ann Farajallah, Director of Admissions, Vatterott College, 8580 Evans Avenue, Berkeley, MO 63134. *Phone:* 314-264-1020. *Toll-free phone:* 888-553-6627.
Website: http://www.vatterott.edu/.

Vatterott College
Joplin, Missouri

Admissions Office Contact Vatterott College, 809 Illinois Avenue, Joplin, MO 64801. *Toll-free phone:* 800-934-6975.
Website: http://www.vatterott.edu/.

Vatterott College
Kansas City, Missouri

Admissions Office Contact Vatterott College, 4131 N. Corrington Avenue, Kansas City, MO 64117. *Toll-free phone:* 888-553-6627.
Website: http://www.vatterott.edu/.

Vatterott College
St. Charles, Missouri

Director of Admissions Gertrude Bogan-Jones, Director of Admissions, Vatterott College, 3550 West Clay Street, St. Charles, MO 63301. *Phone:* 636-978-7488. *Toll-free phone:* 888-553-6627. *Fax:* 636-978-5121. *E-mail:* ofallon@vatterott-college.edu.
Website: http://www.vatterott.edu/.

Vatterott College
St. Joseph, Missouri

Director of Admissions Director of Admissions, Vatterott College, 3709 Belt Highway, St. Joseph, MO 64506. *Phone:* 816-364-5399. *Toll-free phone:* 888-553-6627. *Fax:* 816-364-1593.
Website: http://www.vatterott.edu/.

Vatterott College
Springfield, Missouri

Freshman Application Contact Mr. Scott Lester, Director of Admissions, Vatterott College, 3850 South Campbell Avenue, Springfield, MO 65807. *Phone:* 417-831-8116. *Toll-free phone:* 888-553-6627. *Fax:* 417-831-5099. *E-mail:* springfield@vatterott-college.edu.
Website: http://www.vatterott.edu/.

Vatterott College
Sunset Hills, Missouri

Director of Admissions Director of Admission, Vatterott College, 12900 Maurer Industrial Drive, Sunset Hills, MO 63127. *Phone:* 314-843-4200. *Toll-free phone:* 888-553-6627. *Fax:* 314-843-1709.
Website: http://www.vatterott.edu/.

Vet Tech Institute at Hickey College
St. Louis, Missouri

- **Private** 2-year, founded 2007
- **Suburban** campus
- **Coed,** 126 undergraduate students
- **61%** of applicants were admitted

Freshmen *Admission:* 451 applied, 275 admitted.
Majors Veterinary/animal health technology.
Academics *Calendar:* semesters. *Degree:* associate. *Special study options:* accelerated degree program, internships.
Freshman Application Contact Admissions Office, Vet Tech Institute at Hickey College, 2780 North Lindbergh Boulevard, St. Louis, MO 63114. *Phone:* 888-884-1459. *Toll-free phone:* 888-884-1459.
Website: http://stlouis.vettechinstitute.edu/.

Wentworth Military Academy and College
Lexington, Missouri

Freshman Application Contact Capt. Mike Bellis, College Admissions Director, Wentworth Military Academy and College, 1880 Washington Avenue, Lexington, MO 64067. *Phone:* 660-259-2221 Ext. 1351. *Fax:* 660-259-2677. *E-mail:* admissions@wma.edu.
Website: http://www.wma.edu/.

MONTANA

Aaniiih Nakoda College
Harlem, Montana

Director of Admissions Ms. Dixie Brockie, Registrar and Admissions Officer, Aaniiih Nakoda College, PO Box 159, Harlem, MT 59526-0159. *Phone:* 406-353-2607 Ext. 233. *Fax:* 406-353-2898. *E-mail:* dbrockie@mail.fbcc.edu.
Website: http://www.ancollege.edu/.

Blackfeet Community College
Browning, Montana

Freshman Application Contact Ms. Deana M. McNabb, Registrar and Admissions Officer, Blackfeet Community College, PO Box 819, Browning, MT 59417-0819. *Phone:* 406-338-5421. *Toll-free phone:* 800-549-7457. *Fax:* 406-338-3272.
Website: http://www.bfcc.edu/.

Chief Dull Knife College
Lame Deer, Montana

Freshman Application Contact Director of Admissions, Chief Dull Knife College, PO Box 98, 1 College Drive, Lame Deer, MT 59043-0098. *Phone:* 406-477-6215.
Website: http://www.cdkc.edu/.

Dawson Community College
Glendive, Montana

Freshman Application Contact Dawson Community College, 300 College Drive, PO Box 421, Glendive, MT 59330-0421. *Phone:* 406-377-3396 Ext. 410. *Toll-free phone:* 800-821-8320.
Website: http://www.dawson.edu/.

Flathead Valley Community College
Kalispell, Montana

- **State and locally supported** 2-year, founded 1967, part of Montana University System
- **Small-town** 209-acre campus
- **Endowment** $6.5 million
- **Coed**

Undergraduates 1,082 full-time, 1,134 part-time. Students come from 18 states and territories; 3% are from out of state; 0.3% Black or African American, non-Hispanic/Latino; 2% Hispanic/Latino; 0.9% Asian, non-Hispanic/Latino; 0.3% Native Hawaiian or other Pacific Islander, non-Hispanic/Latino; 3% American Indian or Alaska Native, non-Hispanic/Latino; 13% Race/ethnicity unknown; 0.1% international; 8% transferred in; 1% live on campus. *Retention:* 52% of full-time freshmen returned.
Faculty *Student/faculty ratio:* 16:1.
Academics *Calendar:* semesters. *Degree:* certificates and associate. *Special study options:* academic remediation for entering students, adult/continuing education programs, advanced placement credit, cooperative education, distance learning, double majors, English as a second language, honors programs, independent study, internships, part-time degree program, services for LD students, study abroad, summer session for credit.
Standardized Tests *Required:* ACT Compass Placement Test (for admission). *Recommended:* ACT (for admission).
Costs (2014–15) *Tuition:* area resident $2761 full-time, $99 per credit hour part-time; state resident $4133 full-time, $148 per credit hour part-time; nonresident $9901 full-time, $354 per credit hour part-time. Full-time tuition and fees vary according to course load. Part-time tuition and fees vary according to course load. *Required fees:* $1076 full-time, $42 per credit hour part-time. *Payment plans:* installment, deferred payment.
Applying *Options:* electronic application, early admission, deferred entrance. *Required:* high school transcript.
Freshman Application Contact Ms. Marlene C. Stoltz, Admissions/Graduation Coordinator, Flathead Valley Community College, 777 Grandview Drive, Kalispell, MT 59901-2622. *Phone:* 406-756-3846. *Toll-free phone:* 800-313-3822. *E-mail:* mstoltz@fvcc.cc.mt.us.
Website: http://www.fvcc.edu/.

Fort Peck Community College
Poplar, Montana

Director of Admissions Mr. Robert McAnally, Vice President for Student Services, Fort Peck Community College, PO Box 398, Poplar, MT 59255-0398. *Phone:* 406-768-6329.
Website: http://www.fpcc.edu/.

Great Falls College Montana State University
Great Falls, Montana

- **State-supported** 2-year, founded 1969, part of Montana University System
- **Small-town** 40-acre campus
- **Coed,** 1,756 undergraduate students, 47% full-time, 70% women, 30% men

Undergraduates 821 full-time, 935 part-time. Students come from 27 states and territories; 1 other country; 1% are from out of state; 1% Black or African American, non-Hispanic/Latino; 4% Hispanic/Latino; 0.8% Asian, non-Hispanic/Latino; 0.3% Native Hawaiian or other Pacific Islander, non-Hispanic/Latino; 5% American Indian or Alaska Native, non-Hispanic/Latino;

4% Two or more races, non-Hispanic/Latino; 3% Race/ethnicity unknown; 9% transferred in.
Freshmen *Admission:* 397 applied, 381 admitted, 261 enrolled.
Faculty *Total:* 115, 39% full-time, 17% with terminal degrees. *Student/faculty ratio:* 18:1.
Majors Accounting technology and bookkeeping; business administration and management; computer systems networking and telecommunications; dental hygiene; emergency medical technology (EMT paramedic); entrepreneurship; graphic design; health information/medical records technology; information technology; liberal arts and sciences and humanities related; licensed practical/vocational nurse training; medical/clinical assistant; medical insurance/medical billing; medical transcription; physical therapy technology; radiologic technology/science; respiratory care therapy; surgical technology; web page, digital/multimedia and information resources design; welding technology.
Academics *Calendar:* semesters. *Degree:* certificates and associate. *Special study options:* academic remediation for entering students, advanced placement credit, distance learning, double majors, independent study, internships, off-campus study, part-time degree program, services for LD students, summer session for credit.
Library Weaver Library plus 1 other with 50,470 titles, 1,294 audiovisual materials, an OPAC, a Web page.
Student Life *Activities and Organizations:* choral group, The Associated Students of Great Falls College Montana State University, Phi Theta Kappa Honorary, Physical Therapy Assistant Club, Dental Hygiene Assistant Club, Nursing Club. *Campus security:* 24-hour emergency response devices.
Costs (2014–15) *Tuition:* state resident $2496 full-time, $104 per credit part-time; nonresident $8748 full-time, $364 per credit part-time. Full-time tuition and fees vary according to course load, location, and program. Part-time tuition and fees vary according to course load, location, and program. *Required fees:* $598 full-time, $71 per credit part-time. *Payment plan:* deferred payment. *Waivers:* minority students, senior citizens, and employees or children of employees.
Financial Aid Of all full-time matriculated undergraduates who enrolled in 2013, 783 applied for aid, 708 were judged to have need, 17 had their need fully met. In 2013, 3 non-need-based awards were made. *Average percent of need met:* 71%. *Average financial aid package:* $9632. *Average need-based loan:* $3079. *Average need-based gift aid:* $5339. *Average non-need-based aid:* $400. *Average indebtedness upon graduation:* $22,219.
Applying *Options:* electronic application, early admission. *Application fee:* $30. *Required:* high school transcript, proof of immunization. *Application deadlines:* rolling (freshmen), rolling (out-of-state freshmen), rolling (transfers). *Notification:* continuous (freshmen), continuous (out-of-state freshmen), continuous (transfers).
Freshman Application Contact Ms. Brittany Budeski, Admissions, Great Falls College Montana State University, 2100 16th Avenue South, Great Falls, MT 59405. *Phone:* 406-771-4309. *Toll-free phone:* 800-446-2698. *Fax:* 406-771-2267. *E-mail:* brittany.budeski@gfcmsu.edu.
Website: http://www.gfcmsu.edu/.

Helena College University of Montana
Helena, Montana

- **State-supported** 2-year, founded 1939, part of Montana University System
- **Small-town** campus
- **Endowment** $75,877
- **Coed**

Undergraduates 670 full-time, 760 part-time. Students come from 12 states and territories; 0.6% Black or African American, non-Hispanic/Latino; 2% Hispanic/Latino; 1% Asian, non-Hispanic/Latino; 4% American Indian or Alaska Native, non-Hispanic/Latino; 1% Two or more races, non-Hispanic/Latino; 6% Race/ethnicity unknown; 7% transferred in. *Retention:* 53% of full-time freshmen returned.
Faculty *Student/faculty ratio:* 12:1.
Academics *Calendar:* semesters. *Degree:* certificates and associate. *Special study options:* academic remediation for entering students, adult/continuing education programs, advanced placement credit, distance learning, double majors, internships, part-time degree program, services for LD students, study abroad, summer session for credit.
Student Life *Campus security:* late-night transport/escort service.
Costs (2014–15) *One-time required fee:* $28. *Tuition:* state resident $3061 full-time; nonresident $8357 full-time. Full-time tuition and fees vary according to course load. Part-time tuition and fees vary according to course load.
Financial Aid Of all full-time matriculated undergraduates who enrolled in 2008, 445 applied for aid, 334 were judged to have need. 42 Federal Work-Study jobs (averaging $1549). 22 state and other part-time jobs (averaging $1476). In 2008, 37. *Average financial aid package:* $6368. *Average need-*

based loan: $3428. *Average need-based gift aid:* $3111. *Average non-need-based aid:* $1769. *Average indebtedness upon graduation:* $14,068.
Applying *Options:* electronic application, early admission, deferred entrance. *Application fee:* $30. *Required for some:* high school transcript.
Freshman Application Contact Mr. Ryan Loomis, Admissions Representative/Recruiter, Helena College University of Montana, 1115 North Roberts Street, Helena, MT 59601. *Phone:* 406-447-6904. *Toll-free phone:* 800-241-4882.
Website: http://www.umhelena.edu/.

Little Big Horn College
Crow Agency, Montana

Freshman Application Contact Ms. Ann Bullis, Dean of Student Services, Little Big Horn College, Box 370, 1 Forest Lane, Crow Agency, MT 59022-0370. *Phone:* 406-638-2228 Ext. 50.
Website: http://www.lbhc.edu/.

Miles Community College
Miles City, Montana

Freshman Application Contact Mr. Haley Anderson, Admissions Representative, Miles Community College, 2715 Dickinson Street, Miles City, MT 59301. *Phone:* 406-874-6178. *Toll-free phone:* 800-541-9281. *E-mail:* andersonh@milescc.edu.
Website: http://www.milescc.edu/.

Salish Kootenai College
Pablo, Montana

Freshman Application Contact Ms. Jackie Moran, Admissions Officer, Salish Kootenai College, PO Box 70, Pablo, MT 59855-0117. *Phone:* 406-275-4866. *Fax:* 406-275-4810. *E-mail:* jackie_moran@skc.edu.
Website: http://www.skc.edu/.

Stone Child College
Box Elder, Montana

Director of Admissions Mr. Ted Whitford, Director of Admissions/Registrar, Stone Child College, RR1, Box 1082, Box Elder, MT 59521. *Phone:* 406-395-4313 Ext. 110. *E-mail:* uanet337@quest.ocsc.montana.edu.
Website: http://www.stonechild.edu/.

NEBRASKA

Central Community College–Columbus Campus
Columbus, Nebraska

Freshman Application Contact Ms. Erica Leffler, Admissions/Recruiting Coordinator, Central Community College–Columbus Campus, PO Box 1027, Columbus, NE 68602-1027. *Phone:* 402-562-1296. *Toll-free phone:* 877-CCC-0780. *Fax:* 402-562-1201. *E-mail:* eleffler@cccneb.edu.
Website: http://www.cccneb.edu/.

Central Community College–Grand Island Campus
Grand Island, Nebraska

Freshman Application Contact Michelle Lubken, Admissions Director, Central Community College–Grand Island Campus, PO Box 4903, Grand Island, NE 68802-4903. *Phone:* 308-398-7406 Ext. 406. *Toll-free phone:* 877-CCC-0780. *Fax:* 308-398-7398. *E-mail:* mlubken@cccneb.edu.
Website: http://www.cccneb.edu/.

Central Community College–Hastings Campus
Hastings, Nebraska

Freshman Application Contact Mr. Robert Glenn, Admissions and Recruiting Director, Central Community College–Hastings Campus, PO Box

1024, East Highway 6, Hastings, NE 68902-1024. *Phone:* 402-461-2428. *Toll-free phone:* 877-CCC-0780. *E-mail:* rglenn@cccneb.edu.
Website: http://www.cccneb.edu/.

ITT Technical Institute
Omaha, Nebraska

- **Proprietary** primarily 2-year, founded 1991, part of ITT Educational Services, Inc.
- **Urban** campus
- **Coed**

Academics *Calendar:* quarters. *Degrees:* associate and bachelor's.
Freshman Application Contact Director of Recruitment, ITT Technical Institute, 1120 North 103rd Plaza, Suite 200, Omaha, NE 68114. *Phone:* 402-331-2900. *Toll-free phone:* 800-677-9260.
Website: http://www.itt-tech.edu/.

Kaplan University, Lincoln
Lincoln, Nebraska

Freshman Application Contact Kaplan University, Lincoln, 1821 K Street, Lincoln, NE 68501-2826. *Phone:* 402-474-5315. *Toll-free phone:* 866-527-5268 (in-state); 800-527-5268 (out-of-state).
Website: http://www.kaplanuniversity.edu/.

Kaplan University, Omaha
Omaha, Nebraska

Freshman Application Contact Kaplan University, Omaha, 5425 North 103rd Street, Omaha, NE 68134. *Phone:* 402-572-8500. *Toll-free phone:* 866-527-5268 (in-state); 800-527-5268 (out-of-state).
Website: http://www.kaplanuniversity.edu/.

Little Priest Tribal College
Winnebago, Nebraska

Freshman Application Contact Little Priest Tribal College, PO Box 270, Winnebago, NE 68071. *Phone:* 402-878-2380 Ext. 112.
Website: http://www.littlepriest.edu/.

Metropolitan Community College
Omaha, Nebraska

Freshman Application Contact Ms. Maria Vazquez, Associate Vice President for Student Affairs, Metropolitan Community College, PO Box 3777, Omaha, NE 69103-0777. *Phone:* 402-457-2430. *Toll-free phone:* 800-228-9553. *Fax:* 402-457-2238. *E-mail:* mvazquez@mccneb.edu.
Website: http://www.mccneb.edu/.

Mid-Plains Community College
North Platte, Nebraska

- **District-supported** 2-year, founded 1973
- **Small-town** campus
- **Endowment** $5.5 million
- **Coed,** 2,143 undergraduate students, 40% full-time, 62% women, 38% men

Undergraduates 851 full-time, 1,292 part-time. Students come from 36 states and territories; 6 other countries; 13% are from out of state; 4% Black or African American, non-Hispanic/Latino; 8% Hispanic/Latino; 0.7% Asian, non-Hispanic/Latino; 0.2% Native Hawaiian or other Pacific Islander, non-Hispanic/Latino; 0.7% American Indian or Alaska Native, non-Hispanic/Latino; 1% Two or more races, non-Hispanic/Latino; 2% Race/ethnicity unknown; 2% international; 3% transferred in; 8% live on campus.
Freshmen *Admission:* 462 applied, 462 admitted, 462 enrolled.
Faculty *Total:* 326, 20% full-time, 2% with terminal degrees. *Student/faculty ratio:* 9:1.
Majors Administrative assistant and secretarial science; autobody/collision and repair technology; automobile/automotive mechanics technology; building/construction finishing, management, and inspection related; business administration and management; clinical/medical laboratory technology; commercial and advertising art; computer and information sciences; construction engineering technology; dental assisting; diesel mechanics technology; fire science/firefighting; heating, air conditioning, ventilation and refrigeration maintenance technology; liberal arts and sciences/liberal studies;

licensed practical/vocational nurse training; registered nursing/registered nurse; transportation and materials moving related; welding technology.

Academics *Calendar:* semesters. *Degree:* certificates, diplomas, and associate. *Special study options:* academic remediation for entering students, accelerated degree program, adult/continuing education programs, advanced placement credit, cooperative education, distance learning, double majors, English as a second language, external degree program, independent study, internships, part-time degree program, services for LD students, summer session for credit.

Library von Riesen Library-McCook Campus plus 1 other with 25,728 titles, 1,746 audiovisual materials, an OPAC, a Web page.

Student Life *Housing Options:* coed, special housing for students with disabilities. Campus housing is university owned. *Activities and Organizations:* drama/theater group, student-run newspaper, choral group, Student Senate, Phi Theta Kappa, Phi Beta Lambda, Intercollegiate Athletics, MPCC Student Nurses Association, national fraternities, national sororities. *Campus security:* controlled dormitory access, patrols by trained security personnel.

Athletics Member NJCAA. *Intercollegiate sports:* baseball M(s), basketball M(s)/W(s), golf M(s), softball W(s), volleyball W(s). *Intramural sports:* baseball M, basketball M/W, softball M/W, volleyball W.

Standardized Tests *Required for some:* ACT Compass. *Recommended:* ACT (for admission).

Costs (2014–15) *Tuition:* state resident $2370 full-time, $79 per credit hour part-time; nonresident $3090 full-time, $103 per credit hour part-time. *Required fees:* $450 full-time, $15 per credit hour part-time. *Room and board:* $6000. Room and board charges vary according to board plan, housing facility, and location. *Payment plan:* installment. *Waivers:* senior citizens and employees or children of employees.

Financial Aid Of all full-time matriculated undergraduates who enrolled in 2013, 342 applied for aid, 284 were judged to have need, 77 had their need fully met. 41 Federal Work-Study jobs (averaging $749). In 2013, 57 non-need-based awards were made. *Average percent of need met:* 79%. *Average financial aid package:* $7037. *Average need-based loan:* $2668. *Average need-based gift aid:* $5691. *Average non-need-based aid:* $1790. *Average indebtedness upon graduation:* $12,013.

Applying *Options:* electronic application, deferred entrance. *Required:* high school transcript. *Required for some:* 2 letters of recommendation, interview. *Application deadlines:* rolling (freshmen), rolling (out-of-state freshmen), rolling (transfers). *Notification:* continuous (freshmen), continuous (out-of-state freshmen), continuous (transfers).

Freshman Application Contact Mr. Michael Driskell, Area Recruiter, Mid-Plains Community College, 1101 Halligan Dr, North Platte, NE 69101. *Phone:* 308-535-3709. *Toll-free phone:* 800-658-4308 (in-state); 800-658-4348 (out-of-state). *Fax:* 308-534-5767. *E-mail:* driskellm@mpcc.edu. *Website:* http://www.mpcc.edu/.

Myotherapy Institute
Lincoln, Nebraska

Freshman Application Contact Admissions Office, Myotherapy Institute, 6020 South 58th Street, Lincoln, NE 68516. *Phone:* 402-421-7410. *Website:* http://www.myotherapy.edu/.

Nebraska College of Technical Agriculture
Curtis, Nebraska

Freshman Application Contact Kevin Martin, Assistant Admissions Coordinator, Nebraska College of Technical Agriculture, 404 East 7th Street, Curtis, NE 69025. *Phone:* 308-367-4124. *Toll-free phone:* 800-3CURTIS. *Website:* http://www.ncta.unl.edu/.

Nebraska Indian Community College
Macy, Nebraska

- **Federally supported** 2-year, founded 1979
- **Rural** 22-acre campus with easy access to Omaha
- **Endowment** $384,373
- **Coed,** 120 undergraduate students, 45% full-time, 71% women, 29% men

Undergraduates 54 full-time, 66 part-time. Students come from 3 states and territories; 22% are from out of state; 14% transferred in.

Freshmen *Admission:* 21 enrolled.

Faculty *Total:* 16, 63% full-time. *Student/faculty ratio:* 6:1.

Majors American Indian/Native American studies; building/construction finishing, management, and inspection related; business administration and

management; carpentry; child-care and support services management; corrections and criminal justice related; data entry/microcomputer applications; early childhood education; human services; information technology; liberal arts and sciences/liberal studies; natural resources/conservation; social work.

Academics *Calendar:* semesters. *Degree:* certificates and associate. *Special study options:* academic remediation for entering students, adult/continuing education programs, double majors, independent study, internships, part-time degree program, study abroad, summer session for credit.

Library Macy Library plus 1 other with 7,130 titles, 100 audiovisual materials, an OPAC.

Student Life *Housing:* college housing not available. *Activities and Organizations:* Student Senate.

Standardized Tests *Required:* Compass testing for Math and English placement (for admission).

Costs (2015–16) *One-time required fee:* $50. *Tuition:* state resident $4080 full-time, $170 per credit hour part-time; nonresident $4080 full-time, $170 per credit hour part-time. *Payment plan:* installment. *Waivers:* children of alumni, senior citizens, and employees or children of employees.

Applying *Required:* high school transcript, certificate of tribal enrollment if applicable.

Freshman Application Contact Troy Munhofen, Registrar, Nebraska Indian Community College, PO Box 428, Macy, NE 68039. *Phone:* 402-241-5922. *Toll-free phone:* 844-440-NICC. *Fax:* 402-837-4183. *E-mail:* tmunhofen@thenicc.edu. *Website:* http://www.thenicc.edu/.

Northeast Community College
Norfolk, Nebraska

- **State and locally supported** 2-year, founded 1973, part of Nebraska Coordinating Commission for Postsecondary Education
- **Small-town** 202-acre campus
- **Coed**

Undergraduates 2,200 full-time, 2,945 part-time. 1% Black or African American, non-Hispanic/Latino; 7% Hispanic/Latino; 0.4% Asian, non-Hispanic/Latino; 0.1% Native Hawaiian or other Pacific Islander, non-Hispanic/Latino; 0.7% American Indian or Alaska Native, non-Hispanic/Latino; 0.8% Two or more races, non-Hispanic/Latino; 5% Race/ethnicity unknown; 1% international; 5% transferred in; 7% live on campus. *Retention:* 68% of full-time freshmen returned.

Faculty *Student/faculty ratio:* 18:1.

Academics *Calendar:* semesters. *Degree:* certificates, diplomas, and associate. *Special study options:* academic remediation for entering students, adult/continuing education programs, advanced placement credit, cooperative education, distance learning, double majors, English as a second language, internships, off-campus study, part-time degree program, services for LD students, study abroad, summer session for credit.

Student Life *Campus security:* 24-hour patrols, controlled dormitory access.

Athletics Member NJCAA.

Costs (2014–15) *Tuition:* state resident $2475 full-time, $83 per credit part-time; nonresident $3480 full-time, $116 per credit part-time. *Required fees:* $555 full-time, $19 per credit part-time. *Room and board:* $6389; room only: $3817.

Financial Aid Of all full-time matriculated undergraduates who enrolled in 2013, 1,766 applied for aid, 1,498 were judged to have need, 205 had their need fully met. 56 Federal Work-Study jobs (averaging $1132). In 2013, 30. *Average percent of need met:* 68. *Average financial aid package:* $6426. *Average need-based loan:* $3117. *Average need-based gift aid:* $4839. *Average non-need-based aid:* $807. *Average indebtedness upon graduation:* $10,877.

Applying *Options:* electronic application, early admission. *Required for some:* essay or personal statement, high school transcript, minimum 2.0 GPA, 3 letters of recommendation, interview. *Recommended:* high school transcript.

Freshman Application Contact Tiffany Hopper, Admissions Specialist, Northeast Community College, 801 East Benjamin Avenue, PO Box 469, Norfolk, NE 68702-0469. *Phone:* 402-844-7260. *Toll-free phone:* 800-348-9033 Ext. 7260. *E-mail:* admission@northeast.edu. *Website:* http://www.northeast.edu/.

Omaha School of Massage and Healthcare of Herzing University
Omaha, Nebraska

Admissions Office Contact Omaha School of Massage and Healthcare of Herzing University, 9748 Park Drive, Omaha, NE 68127. *Website:* http://www.osmhc.com/.

Southeast Community College, Beatrice Campus

Beatrice, Nebraska

Freshman Application Contact Admissions Office, Southeast Community College, Beatrice Campus, 4771 West Scott Road, Beatrice, NE 68310. *Phone:* 402-228-3468. *Toll-free phone:* 800-233-5027. *Fax:* 402-228-2218. *Website:* http://www.southeast.edu/.

Southeast Community College, Lincoln Campus

Lincoln, Nebraska

Freshman Application Contact Admissions Office, Southeast Community College, Lincoln Campus, 8800 O Street, Lincoln, NE 68520-1299. *Phone:* 402-471-3333. *Toll-free phone:* 800-642-4075. *Fax:* 402-437-2404. *Website:* http://www.southeast.edu/.

Southeast Community College, Milford Campus

Milford, Nebraska

Freshman Application Contact Admissions Office, Southeast Community College, Milford Campus, 600 State Street, Milford, NE 68405. *Phone:* 402-761-2131. *Toll-free phone:* 800-933-7223. *Fax:* 402-761-2324. *Website:* http://www.southeast.edu/.

Universal College of Healing Arts

Omaha, Nebraska

Admissions Office Contact Universal College of Healing Arts, 8702 North 30th Street, Omaha, NE 68112-1810. *Website:* http://www.ucha.edu/.

Western Nebraska Community College

Sidney, Nebraska

Director of Admissions Mr. Troy Archuleta, Admissions and Recruitment Director, Western Nebraska Community College, 371 College Drive, Sidney, NE 69162. *Phone:* 308-635-6015. *Toll-free phone:* 800-222-9682. *E-mail:* rhovey@wncc.net. *Website:* http://www.wncc.net/.

Wright Career College

Omaha, Nebraska

- **Proprietary** primarily 2-year, founded 2011
- **Suburban** campus with easy access to Omaha
- **Coed**

Undergraduates 96 full-time, 210 part-time. Students come from 3 states and territories; 3% are from out of state; 72% Black or African American, non-Hispanic/Latino; 3% Hispanic/Latino; 0.3% Asian, non-Hispanic/Latino; 1% American Indian or Alaska Native, non-Hispanic/Latino; 2% Two or more races, non-Hispanic/Latino; 0.7% Race/ethnicity unknown; 2% transferred in. *Retention:* 1% of full-time freshmen returned.

Academics *Degrees:* diplomas, associate, and bachelor's. *Special study options:* adult/continuing education programs, distance learning, internships, off-campus study.

Freshman Application Contact Wright Career College, 3000 S. 84th Street, Omaha, NE 68124. *Phone:* 402-514-2500. *Toll-free phone:* 800-555-4003. *E-mail:* info@wrightcc.edu. *Website:* http://www.wrightcc.edu/.

NEVADA

Career College of Northern Nevada

Sparks, Nevada

Freshman Application Contact Ms. Laura Goldhammer, Director of Admissions, Career College of Northern Nevada, 1421 Pullman Drive, Sparks, NV 89434. *Phone:* 775-856-2266 Ext. 11. *Fax:* 775-856-0935. *E-mail:* lgoldhammer@ccnn4u.com. *Website:* http://www.ccnn.edu/.

Carrington College–Las Vegas

Las Vegas, Nevada

- **Proprietary** 2-year, part of Carrington Colleges Group, Inc.
- **Coed**

Undergraduates 224 full-time, 31 part-time. 3% are from out of state; 19% Black or African American, non-Hispanic/Latino; 13% Hispanic/Latino; 16% Asian, non-Hispanic/Latino; 6% Native Hawaiian or other Pacific Islander, non-Hispanic/Latino; 0.4% American Indian or Alaska Native, non-Hispanic/Latino; 4% Two or more races, non-Hispanic/Latino; 2% Race/ethnicity unknown; 24% transferred in.

Faculty *Student/faculty ratio:* 20:1.

Academics *Degree:* certificates and associate.

Applying *Required:* essay or personal statement, high school transcript, interview, Entrance test administered by Carrington College.

Freshman Application Contact Carrington College–Las Vegas, 5740 South Eastern Avenue, Las Vegas, NV 89119. *Website:* http://carrington.edu/.

Carrington College–Reno

Reno, Nevada

- **Proprietary** 2-year, part of Carrington Colleges Group, Inc.
- **Coed**

Undergraduates 254 full-time, 79 part-time. 8% are from out of state; 0.6% Black or African American, non-Hispanic/Latino; 16% Hispanic/Latino; 3% Asian, non-Hispanic/Latino; 2% Native Hawaiian or other Pacific Islander, non-Hispanic/Latino; 0.6% American Indian or Alaska Native, non-Hispanic/Latino; 2% Two or more races, non-Hispanic/Latino; 1% Race/ethnicity unknown; 14% transferred in.

Faculty *Student/faculty ratio:* 15:1.

Academics *Degree:* certificates and associate.

Applying *Required:* essay or personal statement, high school transcript, interview, Entrance test administered by Carrington College.

Freshman Application Contact Carrington College–Reno, 5580 Kietzke Lane, Reno, NV 89511. *Phone:* 775-335-2900. *Website:* http://carrington.edu/.

College of Southern Nevada

Las Vegas, Nevada

Freshman Application Contact Admissions and Records, College of Southern Nevada, 6375 West Charleston Boulevard, Las Vegas, NV 89146. *Phone:* 702-651-4060. *Website:* http://www.csn.edu/.

Everest College

Henderson, Nevada

Admissions Office Contact Everest College, 170 North Stephanie Street, 1st Floor, Henderson, NV 89074. *Toll-free phone:* 888-741-4270. *Website:* http://www.everest.edu/.

Great Basin College

Elko, Nevada

- **State-supported** primarily 2-year, founded 1967, part of Nevada System of Higher Education
- **Small-town** 45-acre campus
- **Endowment** $246,000
- **Coed,** 3,128 undergraduate students, 31% full-time, 65% women, 35% men

Undergraduates 976 full-time, 2,152 part-time. 6% are from out of state; 2% Black or African American, non-Hispanic/Latino; 16% Hispanic/Latino; 2% Asian, non-Hispanic/Latino; 0.8% Native Hawaiian or other Pacific Islander, non-Hispanic/Latino; 3% American Indian or Alaska Native, non-Hispanic/Latino; 2% Two or more races, non-Hispanic/Latino; 5% Race/ethnicity unknown; 0.1% international; 5% transferred in; 4% live on campus. *Retention:* 62% of full-time freshmen returned.

Freshmen *Admission:* 436 enrolled.

Faculty *Total:* 183, 34% full-time. *Student/faculty ratio:* 24:1.

Majors Anthropology; art; business administration and management; business/commerce; chemistry; criminal justice/safety; data processing and data processing technology; diesel mechanics technology; electrical, electronic and communications engineering technology; elementary education; English; geology/earth science; history; industrial technology; interdisciplinary studies; kindergarten/preschool education; management science; mathematics; natural resources management and policy related; office management; operations management; physics; psychology; registered nursing/registered nurse; secondary education; social sciences; social work; sociology; surveying technology; welding technology.

Academics *Calendar:* semesters. *Degrees:* certificates, associate, bachelor's, and postbachelor's certificates. *Special study options:* academic remediation for entering students, accelerated degree program, adult/continuing education programs, cooperative education, distance learning, double majors, English as a second language, external degree program, independent study, off-campus study, part-time degree program, services for LD students, summer session for credit.

Library Learning Resource Center with 315,088 titles, 2,138 audiovisual materials, an OPAC.

Student Life *Housing Options:* coed, special housing for students with disabilities. Campus housing is university owned. *Activities and Organizations:* Student Nurses Organization, Housing Central, Skills USA, Agriculture Student Organization, Colleges Against Cancer. *Campus security:* late-night transport/escort service, evening patrols by trained security personnel. *Student services:* personal/psychological counseling.

Athletics *Intramural sports:* rock climbing M/W, volleyball M/W, weight lifting M/W.

Costs (2015–16) *Tuition:* state resident $2640 full-time, $88 per credit part-time; nonresident $9285 full-time. Full-time tuition and fees vary according to course level, degree level, and reciprocity agreements. Part-time tuition and fees vary according to course level, degree level, and reciprocity agreements. *Required fees:* $165 full-time, $6 per credit part-time. *Payment plan:* deferred payment. *Waivers:* employees or children of employees.

Financial Aid Of all full-time matriculated undergraduates who enrolled in 2013, 35 Federal Work-Study jobs (averaging $1000). 50 state and other part-time jobs (averaging $1800).

Applying *Options:* electronic application, early admission, deferred entrance. *Application fee:* $10. *Application deadlines:* rolling (freshmen), rolling (out-of-state freshmen), rolling (transfers). *Notification:* continuous (freshmen), continuous (out-of-state freshmen), continuous (transfers).

Freshman Application Contact Ms. Jan King, Director of Admissions and Registrar, Great Basin College, 1500 College Parkway, Elko, NV 89801. *Phone:* 775-753-2102.
Website: http://www.gbcnv.edu/.

ITT Technical Institute
Henderson, Nevada

- **Proprietary** primarily 2-year, founded 1997, part of ITT Educational Services, Inc.
- **Coed**

Academics *Degrees:* associate and bachelor's.

Financial Aid Of all full-time matriculated undergraduates who enrolled in 2013, 6 Federal Work-Study jobs (averaging $5000).

Freshman Application Contact Director of Recruitment, ITT Technical Institute, 2300 Corporate Circle, Suite 150, Henderson, NV 89074. *Phone:* 702-558-5404. *Toll-free phone:* 800-488-8459.
Website: http://www.itt-tech.edu/.

ITT Technical Institute
North Las Vegas, Nevada

- **Proprietary** primarily 2-year, part of ITT Educational Services, Inc.
- **Coed**

Academics *Calendar:* quarters. *Degrees:* associate and bachelor's.

Freshman Application Contact Director of Recruitment, ITT Technical Institute, 3825 W. Cheyenne Avenue, Suite 600, North Las Vegas, NV 89032. *Phone:* 702-240-0967. *Toll-free phone:* 877-832-8442.
Website: http://www.itt-tech.edu/.

Kaplan College, Las Vegas Campus
Las Vegas, Nevada

Freshman Application Contact Admissions Office, Kaplan College, Las Vegas Campus, 3535 West Sahara Avenue, Las Vegas, NV 89102. *Phone:* 702-368-2338. *Toll-free phone:* 800-935-1857.
Website: http://www.kaplancollege.com/.

Le Cordon Bleu College of Culinary Arts in Las Vegas
Las Vegas, Nevada

Freshman Application Contact Admissions Office, Le Cordon Bleu College of Culinary Arts in Las Vegas, 1451 Center Crossing Road, Las Vegas, NV 89144. *Toll-free phone:* 888-551-8222.
Website: http://www.chefs.edu/Las-Vegas/.

Northwest Career College
Las Vegas, Nevada

Admissions Office Contact Northwest Career College, 7398 Smoke Ranch Road, Suite 100, Las Vegas, NV 89128.
Website: http://www.northwestcareercollege.edu/.

Pima Medical Institute
Las Vegas, Nevada

Freshman Application Contact Admissions Office, Pima Medical Institute, 3333 East Flamingo Road, Las Vegas, NV 89121. *Phone:* 702-458-9650 Ext. 202. *Toll-free phone:* 800-477-PIMA.
Website: http://www.pmi.edu/.

Truckee Meadows Community College
Reno, Nevada

- **State-supported** 2-year, founded 1971, part of Nevada System of Higher Education
- **Suburban** 63-acre campus
- **Endowment** $11.0 million
- **Coed,** 11,106 undergraduate students, 25% full-time, 55% women, 45% men

Undergraduates 2,823 full-time, 8,283 part-time. Students come from 21 states and territories; 13 other countries; 7% are from out of state; 2% Black or African American, non-Hispanic/Latino; 25% Hispanic/Latino; 6% Asian, non-Hispanic/Latino; 0.1% Native Hawaiian or other Pacific Islander, non-Hispanic/Latino; 1% American Indian or Alaska Native, non-Hispanic/Latino; 3% Two or more races, non-Hispanic/Latino; 2% Race/ethnicity unknown; 0.4% international; 5% transferred in. *Retention:* 63% of full-time freshmen returned.

Freshmen *Admission:* 1,895 applied, 1,895 admitted, 1,398 enrolled.

Faculty *Total:* 523, 29% full-time. *Student/faculty ratio:* 22:1.

Majors Administrative assistant and secretarial science; anthropology; architecture; automobile/automotive mechanics technology; biology/biological sciences; building construction technology; business administration and management; chemistry; civil engineering; computer programming; construction management; criminal justice/law enforcement administration; culinary arts; dance; dental hygiene; diesel mechanics technology; dietetics; dietetic technology; drafting and design technology; dramatic/theater arts; early childhood education; elementary education; engineering; English; entrepreneurship; environmental science; fine/studio arts; fire science/firefighting; general studies; geological and earth sciences/geosciences related; heating, ventilation, air conditioning and refrigeration engineering technology; history; landscape architecture; legal assistant/paralegal; logistics, materials, and supply chain management; manufacturing engineering technology; mathematics; mental health counseling; music; network and system administration; philosophy; physics; psychology; radiologic technology/science; registered nursing/registered nurse; special education; special education–elementary school; substance abuse/addiction counseling; veterinary/animal health technology; web/multimedia management and webmaster; welding technology.

Academics *Calendar:* semesters. *Degree:* certificates and associate. *Special study options:* academic remediation for entering students, accelerated degree program, adult/continuing education programs, advanced placement credit, cooperative education, distance learning, double majors, English as a second language, independent study, internships, part-time degree program, services for LD students, summer session for credit. *ROTC:* Army (c).

Library Elizabeth Sturm Library with an OPAC, a Web page.

Student Life *Housing:* college housing not available. *Activities and Organizations:* drama/theater group, student-run newspaper, Entrepreneurship Club, International Club, Phi Theta Kappa, Student Government Association, Student Media and Broadcasting Club. *Campus security:* 24-hour emergency response devices and patrols, late-night transport/escort service. *Student services:* personal/psychological counseling.

Costs (2015–16) *Tuition:* state resident $2925 full-time, $88 per credit hour part-time; nonresident $9570 full-time, $185 per credit hour part-time. Full-time tuition and fees vary according to course load and program. Part-time tuition and fees vary according to course load and program. *Required fees:* $165 full-time, $6 per credit hour part-time. *Payment plan:* installment. *Waivers:* employees or children of employees.

Financial Aid Of all full-time matriculated undergraduates who enrolled in 2013, 126 Federal Work-Study jobs (averaging $5000). 368 state and other part-time jobs (averaging $5000).

Applying *Options:* electronic application, early admission. *Application fee:* $10.

Freshman Application Contact Truckee Meadows Community College, 7000 Dandini Boulevard, Reno, NV 89512-3901. *Phone:* 775-673-7240. *Website:* http://www.tmcc.edu/.

Western Nevada College
Carson City, Nevada

- **State-supported** primarily 2-year, founded 1971, part of Nevada System of Higher Education
- **Small-town** 200-acre campus
- **Endowment** $257,000
- **Coed,** 4,032 undergraduate students, 35% full-time, 59% women, 41% men

Undergraduates 1,429 full-time, 2,603 part-time. 3% are from out of state; 1% Black or African American, non-Hispanic/Latino; 18% Hispanic/Latino; 2% Asian, non-Hispanic/Latino; 0.7% Native Hawaiian or other Pacific Islander, non-Hispanic/Latino; 3% American Indian or Alaska Native, non-Hispanic/Latino; 3% Two or more races, non-Hispanic/Latino; 4% Race/ethnicity unknown. *Retention:* 62% of full-time freshmen returned.

Freshmen *Admission:* 855 enrolled.

Faculty *Total:* 270, 16% full-time, 13% with terminal degrees. *Student/faculty ratio:* 29:1.

Majors Accounting; automobile/automotive mechanics technology; biology/biological sciences; business/commerce; child-care and support services management; clinical/medical laboratory technology; computer and information sciences; computer programming; construction management; corrections; criminal justice/law enforcement administration; criminal justice/police science; drafting and design technology; electrical and power transmission installation; electrical, electronic and communications engineering technology; engineering; environmental studies; fire prevention and safety technology; general studies; industrial technology; liberal arts and sciences/liberal studies; machine tool technology; management information systems; mathematics; physical sciences; registered nursing/registered nurse; welding technology.

Academics *Calendar:* semesters. *Degrees:* certificates, associate, and bachelor's. *Special study options:* academic remediation for entering students, adult/continuing education programs, advanced placement credit, cooperative education, distance learning, double majors, English as a second language, honors programs, independent study, internships, part-time degree program, services for LD students, summer session for credit.

Library Western Nevada College Library and Media Services with an OPAC, a Web page.

Student Life *Housing:* college housing not available. *Activities and Organizations:* drama/theater group, choral group, Wildcat Productions, Lone Mountain Writers, Art Club, ASL Club, Latino Student Club. *Campus security:* late-night transport/escort service. *Student services:* personal/psychological counseling.

Athletics Member NJCAA. *Intercollegiate sports:* baseball M, softball W.

Standardized Tests *Recommended:* SAT or ACT (for admission).

Costs (2015–16) *Tuition:* state resident $2640 full-time, $88 per credit part-time; nonresident $9285 full-time. Full-time tuition and fees vary according to course level, degree level, and reciprocity agreements. Part-time tuition and fees vary according to course level, degree level, and reciprocity agreements. *Required fees:* $165 full-time, $6 per credit part-time. *Payment plan:* deferred payment. *Waivers:* employees or children of employees.

Applying *Options:* early admission. *Application fee:* $15. *Required for some:* high school transcript. *Application deadlines:* rolling (freshmen), rolling (transfers).

Freshman Application Contact Admissions and Records, Western Nevada College, 2201 West College Parkway, Carson City, NV 89703. *Phone:* 775-445-2377. *Fax:* 775-445-3147. *E-mail:* wncc_aro@wncc.edu. *Website:* http://www.wnc.edu/.

NEW HAMPSHIRE

Great Bay Community College
Portsmouth, New Hampshire

Freshman Application Contact Matt Thornton, Admissions Coordinator, Great Bay Community College, 320 Corporate Drive, Portsmouth, NH 03801. *Phone:* 603-427-7605. *Toll-free phone:* 800-522-1194. *E-mail:* askgreatbay@ccsnh.edu. *Website:* http://www.greatbay.edu/.

Lakes Region Community College
Laconia, New Hampshire

- **State-supported** 2-year, part of Community College System of New Hampshire
- **Small-town** campus
- **Coed,** 1,179 undergraduate students, 42% full-time, 54% women, 46% men

Undergraduates 490 full-time, 689 part-time. Students come from 2 other countries; 3% are from out of state; 0.5% Black or African American, non-Hispanic/Latino; 1% Hispanic/Latino; 0.5% Asian, non-Hispanic/Latino; 0.1% Native Hawaiian or other Pacific Islander, non-Hispanic/Latino; 0.5% American Indian or Alaska Native, non-Hispanic/Latino; 0.9% Two or more races, non-Hispanic/Latino; 22% Race/ethnicity unknown.

Freshmen *Admission:* 311 enrolled.

Faculty *Student/faculty ratio:* 9:1.

Majors Accounting; animation, interactive technology, video graphics and special effects; automobile/automotive mechanics technology; business automation/technology/data entry; business/commerce; computer and information sciences; culinary arts; early childhood education; education; electrical/electronics equipment installation and repair; energy management and systems technology; fine/studio arts; fire prevention and safety technology; fire science/firefighting; general studies; gerontology; graphic and printing equipment operation/production; hospitality administration; human services; liberal arts and sciences/liberal studies; marine maintenance and ship repair technology; registered nursing/registered nurse; restaurant/food services management.

Academics *Calendar:* semesters accelerated terms also offered. *Degree:* associate. *Special study options:* academic remediation for entering students, adult/continuing education programs, cooperative education, distance learning, double majors, independent study, internships, part-time degree program, services for LD students, summer session for credit.

Library Hugh Bennett Library plus 1 other.

Student Life *Housing:* college housing not available. *Campus security:* 24-hour emergency response devices.

Costs (2014–15) *Tuition:* state resident $6800 full-time; nonresident $10,200 full-time. *Payment plan:* installment. *Waivers:* employees or children of employees.

Applying *Options:* electronic application, deferred entrance. *Application fee:* $20. *Required:* high school transcript. *Notification:* continuous (freshmen), continuous (out-of-state freshmen), continuous (transfers).

Freshman Application Contact Kathy Plummer, Admissions, Lakes Region Community College, Admissions Office, 379 Belmont Road, Laconia, NH 03246. *Phone:* 603-524-3207 Ext. 6410. *Toll-free phone:* 800-357-2992. *E-mail:* lrccinfo@ccsnh.edu. *Website:* http://www.lrcc.edu/.

Manchester Community College
Manchester, New Hampshire

Freshman Application Contact Ms. Jacquie Poirier, Coordinator of Admissions, Manchester Community College, 1066 Front Street, Manchester, NH 03102-8518. *Phone:* 603-668-6706 Ext. 283. *Toll-free phone:* 800-924-3445. *E-mail:* jpoirier@nhctc.edu. *Website:* http://www.mccnh.edu/.

Mount Washington College
Manchester, New Hampshire

Freshman Application Contact Mount Washington College, 3 Sundial Avenue, Manchester, NH 03103. *Phone:* 603-668-6660. *Toll-free phone:* 888-971-2190. *Website:* http://www.mountwashington.edu/.

Nashua Community College
Nashua, New Hampshire

Freshman Application Contact Ms. Patricia Goodman, Vice President of Student Services, Nashua Community College, Nashua, NH 03063. *Phone:* 603-882-6923 Ext. 1529. *Fax:* 603-882-8690. *E-mail:* pgoodman@ccsnh.edu.
Website: http://www.nashuacc.edu/.

NHTI, Concord's Community College
Concord, New Hampshire

Freshman Application Contact Mr. Francis P. Meyer, Director of Admissions, NHTI, Concord's Community College, 31 College Drive, Concord, NH 03301-7412. *Phone:* 603 271-6484 Ext. 2459. *Toll-free phone:* 800-247-0179. *E-mail:* fmeyer@ccsnh.edu.
Website: http://www.nhti.edu/.

River Valley Community College
Claremont, New Hampshire

- **State-supported** 2-year, part of Community College System of NH
- **Rural** campus
- **Coed**
- 76% of applicants were admitted

Undergraduates 351 full-time, 631 part-time. 6% are from out of state; 1% Black or African American, non-Hispanic/Latino; 2% Hispanic/Latino; 2% Asian, non-Hispanic/Latino; 4% American Indian or Alaska Native, non-Hispanic/Latino; 0.5% Two or more races, non-Hispanic/Latino; 9% Race/ethnicity unknown.
Academics *Degree:* certificates, diplomas, and associate. *Special study options:* academic remediation for entering students, distance learning, double majors, independent study, part-time degree program, services for LD students, summer session for credit.
Student Life *Campus security:* 24-hour emergency response devices, security personnel on campus during open hours of operation - 6:30 am to 10 pm.
Financial Aid Of all full-time matriculated undergraduates who enrolled in 2012, 22 Federal Work-Study jobs (averaging $1000).
Applying *Options:* electronic application. *Application fee:* $20. *Required:* high school transcript. *Required for some:* 2 letters of recommendation, interview, program specific requirements.
Freshman Application Contact River Valley Community College, 1 College Place, Claremont, NH 03743. *Phone:* 603-542-7744 Ext. 5322. *Toll-free phone:* 800-837-0658.
Website: http://www.rivervalley.edu/.

St. Joseph School of Nursing
Nashua, New Hampshire

- **Independent** 2-year, founded 1964, affiliated with Roman Catholic Church
- **Urban** campus with easy access to Boston, Portland
- **Coed,** 144 undergraduate students, 44% full-time, 90% women, 10% men

Undergraduates 63 full-time, 81 part-time. Students come from 3 states and territories; 9 other countries; 27% are from out of state; 17% Black or African American, non-Hispanic/Latino; 4% Hispanic/Latino; 2% Asian, non-Hispanic/Latino; 0.4% American Indian or Alaska Native, non-Hispanic/Latino; 3% Two or more races, non-Hispanic/Latino; 24% transferred in.
Freshmen *Admission:* 5 applied, 2 admitted, 2 enrolled. *Average high school GPA:* 3.25.
Faculty *Total:* 20, 55% full-time, 100% with terminal degrees.
Academics *Calendar:* semesters. *Degree:* associate. *Special study options:* academic remediation for entering students, advanced placement credit, services for LD students, summer session for credit.
Student Life *Housing:* college housing not available. *Campus security:* 24-hour emergency response devices and patrols, late-night transport/escort service.
Applying *Options:* electronic application. *Application fee:* $50. *Required:* essay or personal statement, high school transcript, minimum 2.5 GPA, 3 letters of recommendation, interview. *Application deadline:* 7/10 (freshmen).
Freshman Application Contact Mrs. L. Nadeau, Admissions, St. Joseph School of Nursing, 5 Woodward Avenue, Nashua, NH 03060. *Toll-free phone:* 800-370-3169.
Website: http://www.sjhacademiccenter.org/.

White Mountains Community College
Berlin, New Hampshire

- **State-supported** 2-year, founded 1966, part of Community College System of New Hampshire
- **Rural** 325-acre campus
- **Coed,** 845 undergraduate students, 31% full-time, 64% women, 36% men

Undergraduates 263 full-time, 582 part-time. Students come from 4 states and territories; 4% are from out of state; 0.2% Black or African American, non-Hispanic/Latino; 1% Hispanic/Latino; 0.4% Asian, non-Hispanic/Latino; 0.4% American Indian or Alaska Native, non-Hispanic/Latino; 0.6% Two or more races, non-Hispanic/Latino; 17% Race/ethnicity unknown; 6% transferred in.
Freshmen *Admission:* 315 applied, 288 admitted, 206 enrolled.
Faculty *Total:* 157, 17% full-time. *Student/faculty ratio:* 7:1.
Majors Accounting; automobile/automotive mechanics technology; baking and pastry arts; business administration and management; computer and information sciences; criminal justice/safety; culinary arts; diesel mechanics technology; early childhood education; education; environmental studies; general studies; health services/allied health/health sciences; human services; liberal arts and sciences/liberal studies; medical office assistant; office management; registered nursing/registered nurse; welding technology.
Academics *Calendar:* semesters. *Degree:* certificates, diplomas, and associate. *Special study options:* academic remediation for entering students, adult/continuing education programs, advanced placement credit, cooperative education, distance learning, double majors, external degree program, independent study, internships, part-time degree program, services for LD students, student-designed majors, summer session for credit.
Library Fortier Library with 17,550 titles, 859 audiovisual materials, an OPAC.
Student Life *Housing:* college housing not available. *Activities and Organizations:* Student Senate.
Standardized Tests *Required:* ACCUPLACER Placement Test; Test of Essential Academic Skills (TEAS) for Nursing AS Degree (for admission).
Costs (2015–16) *Tuition:* state resident $6000 full-time, $200 per credit part-time; nonresident $13,500 full-time, $450 per credit part-time. Full-time tuition and fees vary according to class time, location, and program. Part-time tuition and fees vary according to class time, location, and program. *Required fees:* $510 full-time, $17 per credit part-time. *Payment plans:* installment, deferred payment. *Waivers:* senior citizens and employees or children of employees.
Applying *Options:* electronic application, deferred entrance. *Application fee:* $20. *Required:* high school transcript, placement test. *Required for some:* essay or personal statement. *Application deadlines:* rolling (freshmen), rolling (transfers). *Notification:* continuous (freshmen), continuous (transfers).
Freshman Application Contact Ms. Kristen Miller, Admissions Counselor, White Mountains Community College, 2020 Riverside Drive, Berlin, NH 03570. *Phone:* 603-342-3002. *Toll-free phone:* 800-445-4525. *Fax:* 603-752-6335. *E-mail:* kmiller@ccsnh.edu.
Website: http://www.wmcc.edu/.

NEW JERSEY

Assumption College for Sisters
Mendham, New Jersey

Freshman Application Contact Sr. Gerardine Tantsits, Academic Dean/Registrar, Assumption College for Sisters, 350 Bernardsville Road, Mendham, NJ 07945-2923. *Phone:* 973-543-6528 Ext. 228. *Fax:* 973-543-1738. *E-mail:* deanregistrar@acs350.org.
Website: http://www.acs350.org/.

Atlantic Cape Community College
Mays Landing, New Jersey

Freshman Application Contact Mrs. Linda McLeod, Assistant Director, Admissions and College Recruitment, Atlantic Cape Community College, 5100 Black Horse Pike, Mays Landing, NJ 08330-2699. *Phone:* 609-343-5009. *Fax:* 609-343-4921. *E-mail:* accadmit@atlantic.edu.
Website: http://www.atlantic.edu/.

Bergen Community College
Paramus, New Jersey

Freshman Application Contact Admissions Office, Bergen Community College, 400 Paramus Road, Paramus, NJ 07652-1595. *Phone:* 201-447-7195. *E-mail:* admsoffice@bergen.edu.
Website: http://www.bergen.edu/.

Brookdale Community College
Lincroft, New Jersey

Director of Admissions Ms. Kim Toomey, Registrar, Brookdale Community College, 765 Newman Springs Road, Lincroft, NJ 07738-1597. *Phone:* 732-224-2268.
Website: http://www.brookdalecc.edu/.

Burlington County College
Pemberton, New Jersey

- **County-supported** 2-year, founded 1966
- **Suburban** 225-acre campus with easy access to Philadelphia
- **Coed,** 9,438 undergraduate students, 51% full-time, 58% women, 42% men

Undergraduates 4,827 full-time, 4,611 part-time. Students come from 20 states and territories; 0.7% are from out of state; 20% Black or African American, non-Hispanic/Latino; 5% Hispanic/Latino; 4% Asian, non-Hispanic/Latino; 0.2% Native Hawaiian or other Pacific Islander, non-Hispanic/Latino; 0.2% American Indian or Alaska Native, non-Hispanic/Latino; 8% Two or more races, non-Hispanic/Latino; 5% Race/ethnicity unknown; 2% international; 6% transferred in. *Retention:* 52% of full-time freshmen returned.
Freshmen *Admission:* 2,159 enrolled.
Faculty *Student/faculty ratio:* 26:1.
Majors Accounting; agribusiness; American Sign Language (ASL); animation, interactive technology, video graphics and special effects; art; automotive engineering technology; biological and physical sciences; biology/biological sciences; biotechnology; business administration and management; chemical engineering; chemistry; commercial and advertising art; communication disorders sciences and services related; computer graphics; computer science; construction engineering technology; criminal justice/police science; dental hygiene; drafting and design technology; dramatic/theater arts; education; electrical, electronic and communications engineering technology; engineering; engineering technologies and engineering related; English; environmental science; fashion/apparel design; fire science/firefighting; food service systems administration; geological and earth sciences/geosciences related; graphic and printing equipment operation/production; graphic design; health information/medical records technology; health services/allied health/health sciences; history; hospitality administration; human services; information technology; international/global studies; journalism; legal assistant/paralegal; liberal arts and sciences/liberal studies; management information systems; mathematics; music; philosophy; physics; psychology; registered nursing/registered nurse; respiratory care therapy; restaurant/food services management; retailing; sales, distribution, and marketing operations; sign language interpretation and translation; social sciences; sociology.
Academics *Calendar:* semesters plus 2 summer terms. *Degree:* certificates and associate. *Special study options:* academic remediation for entering students, accelerated degree program, adult/continuing education programs, advanced placement credit, cooperative education, distance learning, double majors, English as a second language, honors programs, independent study, internships, part-time degree program, services for LD students, study abroad, summer session for credit.
Library Burlington County College Library plus 1 other with 95,000 titles, an OPAC, a Web page.
Student Life *Housing:* college housing not available. *Activities and Organizations:* drama/theater group, student-run radio station, choral group, Student Government Association, Phi Theta Kappa, Creative Writing Guild. *Campus security:* 24-hour emergency response devices and patrols, late-night transport/escort service, electronic entrances to buildings and rooms, surveillance cameras. *Student services:* health clinic, personal/psychological counseling.
Athletics Member NJCAA. *Intercollegiate sports:* baseball M(s), basketball M(s)/W(s), golf M/W, soccer M/W, softball W. *Intramural sports:* archery M.
Costs (2014–15) *Tuition:* area resident $3000 full-time, $1500 per credit hour part-time; state resident $4350 full-time, $2175 per credit hour part-time; nonresident $6300 full-time, $3150 per credit hour part-time. *Required fees:* $885 full-time, $885 per credit hour part-time. *Payment plans:* installment, deferred payment. *Waivers:* senior citizens and employees or children of employees.

Financial Aid Of all full-time matriculated undergraduates who enrolled in 2013, 100 Federal Work-Study jobs (averaging $1200). 100 state and other part-time jobs (averaging $2000).
Applying *Options:* electronic application, early admission, deferred entrance. *Application fee:* $20. *Recommended:* high school transcript. *Application deadlines:* rolling (freshmen), rolling (out-of-state freshmen), rolling (transfers). *Notification:* continuous (freshmen), continuous (out-of-state freshmen), continuous (transfers).
Freshman Application Contact Burlington County College, 601 Pemberton Browns Mills Road, Pemberton, NJ 08068. *Phone:* 609-894-9311 Ext. 1200. *Website:* http://www.bcc.edu/.

Camden County College
Blackwood, New Jersey

- **State and locally supported** 2-year, founded 1967, part of New Jersey Commission on Higher Education
- **Suburban** 320-acre campus with easy access to Philadelphia
- **Coed,** 15,670 undergraduate students, 54% full-time, 61% women, 39% men

Undergraduates 8,529 full-time, 7,141 part-time. Students come from 9 states and territories. *Retention:* 67% of full-time freshmen returned.
Freshmen *Admission:* 7,889 applied, 2,203 enrolled.
Faculty *Total:* 729, 19% full-time.
Majors Accounting and business/management; administrative assistant and secretarial science; automotive engineering technology; banking and financial support services; biology/biotechnology laboratory technician; business administration and management; cinematography and film/video production; clinical/medical laboratory technology; criminal justice/law enforcement administration; data entry/microcomputer applications related; dental assisting; dental hygiene; desktop publishing and digital imaging design; dietetics; drafting and design technology; education; electrical, electronic and communications engineering technology; electromechanical technology; emergency medical technology (EMT paramedic); engineering science; fine/studio arts; fire prevention and safety technology; health information/medical records administration; health services/allied health/health sciences; industrial production technologies related; laser and optical technology; legal assistant/paralegal; liberal arts and sciences/liberal studies; management information systems; marketing/marketing management; massage therapy; mechanical engineering/mechanical technology; opticianry; real estate; registered nursing/registered nurse; sign language interpretation and translation; social work; sport and fitness administration/management; substance abuse/addiction counseling; veterinary/animal health technology.
Academics *Calendar:* semesters. *Degree:* certificates and associate. *Special study options:* academic remediation for entering students, adult/continuing education programs, cooperative education, distance learning, double majors, English as a second language, external degree program, freshman honors college, honors programs, independent study, internships, off-campus study, part-time degree program, services for LD students, study abroad, summer session for credit.
Library Learning Resource Center with 91,366 titles, 2,038 audiovisual materials, an OPAC.
Student Life *Housing:* college housing not available. *Activities and Organizations:* drama/theater group, student-run radio station, choral group. *Campus security:* 24-hour emergency response devices.
Athletics Member NJCAA. *Intercollegiate sports:* baseball M, basketball M/W, golf M, soccer M/W, softball W. *Intramural sports:* baseball M, basketball M/W, soccer M/W, softball W.
Costs (2014–15) *Tuition:* area resident $3210 full-time, $107 per credit part-time; state resident $3330 full-time, $111 per credit part-time; nonresident $3330 full-time, $111 per credit part-time. Full-time tuition and fees vary according to course load. Part-time tuition and fees vary according to course load. *Required fees:* $1110 full-time, $37 per credit part-time. *Payment plan:* deferred payment.
Financial Aid Of all full-time matriculated undergraduates who enrolled in 2013, 117 Federal Work-Study jobs (averaging $1126).
Applying *Options:* early admission. *Required for some:* high school transcript. *Application deadlines:* rolling (freshmen), rolling (transfers).
Freshman Application Contact Donald Delaney, Outreach Coordinator, School and Community Academic Programs, Camden County College, PO Box 200, Blackwood, NJ 08012-0200. *Phone:* 856-227-7200 Ext. 4371. *Fax:* 856-374-4916. *E-mail:* ddelaney@camdencc.edu.
Website: http://www.camdencc.edu/.

See display on next page and page 366 for the College Close-Up.

County College of Morris
Randolph, New Jersey

- **County-supported** 2-year, founded 1966
- **Suburban** 218-acre campus with easy access to New York City
- **Coed,** 8,096 undergraduate students, 51% full-time, 50% women, 50% men

Undergraduates 4,129 full-time, 3,967 part-time. Students come from 7 states and territories; 5% Black or African American, non-Hispanic/Latino; 18% Hispanic/Latino; 5% Asian, non-Hispanic/Latino; 0.2% Native Hawaiian or other Pacific Islander, non-Hispanic/Latino; 0.3% American Indian or Alaska Native, non-Hispanic/Latino; 2% Two or more races, non-Hispanic/Latino; 9% Race/ethnicity unknown; 2% international.

Freshmen *Admission:* 3,710 applied, 2,970 admitted.

Faculty *Total:* 552, 29% full-time. *Student/faculty ratio:* 19:1.

Majors Administrative assistant and secretarial science; agricultural business and management; airline pilot and flight crew; biology/biotechnology laboratory technician; business administration and management; business, management, and marketing related; chemical technology; criminal justice/police science; design and applied arts related; electrical, electronic and communications engineering technology; engineering science; fine/studio arts; fire prevention and safety technology; graphic design; hospitality and recreation marketing; kindergarten/preschool education; kinesiology and exercise science; liberal arts and sciences/liberal studies; management information systems; mechanical engineering/mechanical technology; multi/interdisciplinary studies related; music; photography; public administration; radiologic technology/science; registered nursing/registered nurse; respiratory care therapy; telecommunications technology; veterinary/animal health technology; web page, digital/multimedia and information resources design.

Academics *Calendar:* semesters. *Degree:* certificates and associate. *Special study options:* academic remediation for entering students, accelerated degree program, advanced placement credit, cooperative education, distance learning, double majors, English as a second language, independent study, internships, services for LD students, study abroad, summer session for credit.

Library Learning Resource Center plus 1 other.

Student Life *Housing:* college housing not available. *Activities and Organizations:* drama/theater group, student-run newspaper, choral group, Phi Theta Kappa Honor Society, EOF Student Alliance, Student Nurses Association, New Social Engine, Volunteer Club. *Campus security:* 24-hour emergency response devices and patrols, late-night transport/escort service. *Student services:* health clinic, personal/psychological counseling, women's center.

Athletics Member NJCAA. *Intercollegiate sports:* baseball M(s), basketball M(s)/W(s), golf M, ice hockey M(s), lacrosse M, soccer M/W(s), softball W(s), volleyball W. *Intramural sports:* badminton M, basketball M/W, bowling M/W, soccer M/W, table tennis M/W, tennis M/W, volleyball M/W.

Costs (2014–15) *Tuition:* area resident $3540 full-time, $118 per credit hour part-time; state resident $7080 full-time, $236 per credit hour part-time; nonresident $10,080 full-time, $336 per credit hour part-time. Full-time tuition and fees vary according to course load, location, and program. Part-time tuition and fees vary according to course load, location, and program. *Required fees:* $790 full-time, $20 per credit hour part-time, $19 per course part-time. *Waivers:* senior citizens and employees or children of employees.

Financial Aid Of all full-time matriculated undergraduates who enrolled in 2013, 588 Federal Work-Study jobs (averaging $1947).

Applying *Options:* electronic application. *Application fee:* $30. *Required:* high school transcript. *Application deadlines:* rolling (freshmen), rolling (out-of-state freshmen), rolling (transfers). *Notification:* continuous (freshmen), continuous (out-of-state freshmen), continuous (transfers).

Freshman Application Contact County College of Morris, 214 Center Grove Road, Randolph, NJ 07869-2086. *Phone:* 973-328-5100. *Website:* http://www.ccm.edu/.

Cumberland County College
Vineland, New Jersey

- **State and locally supported** 2-year, founded 1963, part of New Jersey Commission on Higher Education
- **Small-town** 100-acre campus with easy access to Philadelphia
- **Coed,** 3,844 undergraduate students, 60% full-time, 62% women, 38% men

Undergraduates 2,298 full-time, 1,546 part-time. 23% Black or African American, non-Hispanic/Latino; 28% Hispanic/Latino; 0.8% Asian, non-Hispanic/Latino; 0.9% Native Hawaiian or other Pacific Islander, non-Hispanic/Latino; 1% American Indian or Alaska Native, non-Hispanic/Latino; 0.5% Race/ethnicity unknown; 0.1% international. *Retention:* 66% of full-time freshmen returned.

Faculty *Total:* 272, 16% full-time. *Student/faculty ratio:* 23:1.

Majors Accounting; administrative assistant and secretarial science; aeronautical/aerospace engineering technology; building/construction finishing, management, and inspection related; business administration and management; computer and information sciences; computer systems networking and telecommunications; criminal justice/police science; education; fine/studio arts; health and medical administrative services related; horticultural science; industrial technology; legal assistant/paralegal; liberal arts and sciences/liberal studies; medical radiologic technology; ornamental horticulture; registered nursing/registered nurse; respiratory care therapy; social work.

Academics *Calendar:* semesters. *Degree:* certificates and associate. *Special study options:* academic remediation for entering students, advanced placement credit, cooperative education, distance learning, double majors, English as a second language, honors programs, independent study, part-time degree program, services for LD students, summer session for credit.

Library Cumberland County College Library with 51,000 titles, 480 audiovisual materials, an OPAC, a Web page.

Student Life *Housing:* college housing not available. *Activities and Organizations:* drama/theater group, student-run newspaper, television station, choral group. *Campus security:* 24-hour emergency response devices, late-night transport/escort service. *Student services:* personal/psychological counseling.

Athletics Member NJCAA. *Intercollegiate sports:* baseball M, basketball M/W, cross-country running M/W, softball W, track and field M. *Intramural sports:* fencing M/W, soccer M.

Costs (2014–15) *Tuition:* area resident $3390 full-time, $113 per credit hour part-time; state resident $3690 full-time, $123 per credit hour part-time; nonresident $13,560 full-time, $452 per credit hour part-time. *Required fees:* $900 full-time, $30 per credit hour part-time. *Payment plan:* installment. *Waivers:* employees or children of employees.

Financial Aid Of all full-time matriculated undergraduates who enrolled in 2013, 100 Federal Work-Study jobs (averaging $500). 100 state and other part-time jobs (averaging $600).

Applying *Options:* electronic application, early admission, deferred entrance. *Required:* high school transcript. *Application deadlines:* rolling (freshmen), rolling (transfers). *Notification:* continuous (freshmen), continuous (transfers).

Freshman Application Contact Ms. Anne Daly-Eimer, Director of Admissions and Registration, Cumberland County College, PO Box 1500, College Drive, Vineland, NJ 08362. *Phone:* 856-691-8600. *Website:* http://www.cccnj.edu/.

Eastern International College
Belleville, New Jersey

Admissions Office Contact Eastern International College, 251 Washington Avenue, Belleville, NJ 07109.
Website: http://www.eicollege.edu/.

Eastern International College
Jersey City, New Jersey

Admissions Office Contact Eastern International College, 684 Newark Avenue, Jersey City, NJ 07306.
Website: http://www.eicollege.edu/.

Eastwick College
Hackensack, New Jersey

Admissions Office Contact Eastwick College, 250 Moore Street, Hackensack, NJ 07601.
Website: http://www.eastwickcollege.edu/.

Eastwick College
Ramsey, New Jersey

Admissions Office Contact Eastwick College, 10 South Franklin Turnpike, Ramsey, NJ 07446.
Website: http://www.eastwickcollege.edu/.

Essex County College
Newark, New Jersey

Freshman Application Contact Ms. Marva Mack, Director of Admissions, Essex County College, 303 University Avenue, Newark, NJ 07102. *Phone:* 973-877-3119. *Fax:* 973-623-6449.
Website: http://www.essex.edu/.

Hudson County Community College
Jersey City, New Jersey

- **State and locally supported** 2-year, founded 1974
- **Urban** campus with easy access to New York City
- **Coed,** 9,203 undergraduate students, 65% full-time, 58% women, 42% men

Undergraduates 5,983 full-time, 3,220 part-time. Students come from 4 states and territories; 0.4% are from out of state; 14% Black or African American, non-Hispanic/Latino; 56% Hispanic/Latino; 7% Asian, non-Hispanic/Latino; 0.7% Native Hawaiian or other Pacific Islander, non-Hispanic/Latino; 0.2% American Indian or Alaska Native, non-Hispanic/Latino; 1% Two or more races, non-Hispanic/Latino; 9% Race/ethnicity unknown; 0.4% international; 4% transferred in. *Retention:* 56% of full-time freshmen returned.

Freshmen *Admission:* 2,419 enrolled.

Faculty *Total:* 661, 13% full-time.

Majors Biological and physical sciences; business administration and management; computer and information sciences; criminal justice/police science; culinary arts; electrical, electronic and communications engineering technology; emergency medical technology (EMT paramedic); engineering science; fine/studio arts; health information/medical records technology; health services/allied health/health sciences; legal assistant/paralegal; liberal arts and sciences/liberal studies; medical/clinical assistant; registered nursing/registered nurse; respiratory care therapy; social work.

Academics *Calendar:* semesters. *Degree:* certificates and associate. *Special study options:* academic remediation for entering students, advanced placement credit, distance learning, English as a second language, honors programs, independent study, internships, part-time degree program, services for LD students, summer session for credit.

Library Hudson County Community College Library.

Student Life *Housing:* college housing not available. *Activities and Organizations:* drama/theater group, student-run newspaper. *Campus security:* 24-hour emergency response devices. *Student services:* personal/psychological counseling.

Costs (2015–16) *Tuition:* area resident $3480 full-time, $116 per credit hour part-time; state resident $6960 full-time, $232 per credit hour part-time; nonresident $10,440 full-time, $348 per credit hour part-time. Full-time tuition and fees vary according to course load and program. Part-time tuition and fees vary according to course load and program. *Required fees:* $1203 full-time, $39 per credit hour part-time, $20 per term part-time. *Payment plan:* installment. *Waivers:* senior citizens and employees or children of employees.

Financial Aid Of all full-time matriculated undergraduates who enrolled in 2013, 102 Federal Work-Study jobs (averaging $3000).

Applying *Options:* electronic application. *Application fee:* $20. *Application deadlines:* 9/1 (freshmen), 9/1 (transfers). *Notification:* continuous until 9/1 (freshmen), continuous until 9/1 (transfers).

Freshman Application Contact Hudson County Community College, 70 Sip Avenue, Jersey City, NJ 07306. *Phone:* 201-360-4131.
Website: http://www.hccc.edu/.

ITT Technical Institute
Marlton, New Jersey

- **Proprietary** 2-year
- **Coed**

Academics *Degree:* associate.

Freshman Application Contact Director of Recruitment, ITT Technical Institute, 9000 Lincoln Drive East, Suite 100, Marlton, NJ 08053. *Phone:* 856-396-3500. *Toll-free phone:* 877-209-5410.
Website: http://www.itt-tech.edu/.

Jersey College
Teterboro, New Jersey

Admissions Office Contact Jersey College, 546 US Highway 46, Teterboro, NJ 07608.
Website: http://www.jerseycollege.edu/.

Mercer County Community College
Trenton, New Jersey

- **State and locally supported** 2-year, founded 1966
- **Suburban** 292-acre campus with easy access to New York City, Philadelphia
- **Coed**

Undergraduates 3,093 full-time, 5,408 part-time. Students come from 5 states and territories; 91 other countries; 7% are from out of state; 33% Black or African American, non-Hispanic/Latino; 13% Hispanic/Latino; 4% Asian,

non-Hispanic/Latino; 0.2% Native Hawaiian or other Pacific Islander, non-Hispanic/Latino; 0.5% American Indian or Alaska Native, non-Hispanic/Latino; 10% Race/ethnicity unknown; 4% international; 4% transferred in. *Retention:* 68% of full-time freshmen returned.
Faculty *Student/faculty ratio:* 15:1.
Academics *Calendar:* semesters. *Degree:* certificates and associate. *Special study options:* academic remediation for entering students, accelerated degree program, adult/continuing education programs, advanced placement credit, cooperative education, distance learning, double majors, English as a second language, external degree program, independent study, internships, part-time degree program, services for LD students, student-designed majors, summer session for credit. *ROTC:* Army (c), Air Force (c).
Student Life *Campus security:* 24-hour emergency response devices and patrols.
Athletics Member NJCAA.
Costs (2014–15) *Tuition:* area resident $2772 full-time, $116 per credit part-time; state resident $3888 full-time, $162 per credit part-time; nonresident $5976 full-time, $249 per credit part-time. Full-time tuition and fees vary according to program and reciprocity agreements. Part-time tuition and fees vary according to program and reciprocity agreements. *Required fees:* $756 full-time, $32 per credit part-time.
Financial Aid Of all full-time matriculated undergraduates who enrolled in 2013, 100 Federal Work-Study jobs (averaging $1500). 12 state and other part-time jobs (averaging $1500).
Applying *Options:* electronic application, deferred entrance. *Required:* high school transcript. *Recommended:* interview.
Freshman Application Contact Dr. L. Campbell, Dean for Student and Academic Services, Mercer County Community College, 1200 Old Trenton Road, PO Box B, Trenton, NJ 08690-1004. *Phone:* 609-586-4800 Ext. 3222. *Toll-free phone:* 800-392-MCCC. *Fax:* 609-586-6944. *E-mail:* admiss@mccc.edu.
Website: http://www.mccc.edu/.

Middlesex County College
Edison, New Jersey

- **County-supported** 2-year, founded 1964
- **Suburban** 200-acre campus with easy access to New York City
- **Coed,** 12,064 undergraduate students

Undergraduates 11% Black or African American, non-Hispanic/Latino; 29% Hispanic/Latino; 13% Asian, non-Hispanic/Latino; 0.8% Native Hawaiian or other Pacific Islander, non-Hispanic/Latino; 0.3% American Indian or Alaska Native, non-Hispanic/Latino; 3% Two or more races, non-Hispanic/Latino; 9% Race/ethnicity unknown; 2% international. *Retention:* 64% of full-time freshmen returned.
Faculty *Student/faculty ratio:* 20:1.
Majors Accounting; administrative assistant and secretarial science; automotive engineering technology; biology/biotechnology laboratory technician; biotechnology; business administration and management; civil engineering technology; clinical/medical laboratory technology; communications technologies and support services related; computer and information sciences; criminal justice/police science; dental hygiene; dietitian assistant; electrical, electronic and communications engineering technology; energy management and systems technology; engineering science; engineering technologies and engineering related; environmental control technologies related; fire prevention and safety technology; geology/earth science; graphic communications related; health professions related; health services/allied health/health sciences; hotel/motel administration; industrial production technologies related; legal assistant/paralegal; liberal arts and sciences/liberal studies; marketing/marketing management; mechanical engineering/mechanical technology; mechanical engineering technologies related; medical radiologic technology; merchandising, sales, and marketing operations related (specialized); physical sciences; registered nursing/registered nurse; rehabilitation and therapeutic professions related; respiratory care therapy; small business administration; surveying technology; teacher assistant/aide; visual and performing arts.
Academics *Calendar:* semesters. *Degree:* certificates and associate. *Special study options:* academic remediation for entering students, adult/continuing education programs, advanced placement credit, cooperative education, distance learning, English as a second language, independent study, internships, off-campus study, part-time degree program, services for LD students, study abroad, summer session for credit. *ROTC:* Army (c).
Library Middlesex County College Library plus 1 other with an OPAC, a Web page.
Student Life *Housing:* college housing not available. *Activities and Organizations:* drama/theater group, student-run newspaper, radio station, choral group. *Campus security:* 24-hour emergency response devices and patrols. *Student services:* health clinic, personal/psychological counseling.

Athletics Member NJCAA. *Intercollegiate sports:* baseball M, basketball M/W, cross-country running M/W, soccer M/W, softball W, track and field M/W, wrestling M.
Costs (2015–16) *Tuition:* $106 per credit part-time; state resident $212 per credit part-time; nonresident $212 per credit part-time. *Required fees:* $35 per credit part-time. *Waivers:* employees or children of employees.
Financial Aid Of all full-time matriculated undergraduates who enrolled in 2013, 69 Federal Work-Study jobs (averaging $3350).
Applying *Options:* early admission, deferred entrance. *Application fee:* $25. *Required:* high school transcript. *Application deadlines:* rolling (freshmen), rolling (transfers). *Notification:* continuous (freshmen), continuous (transfers).
Freshman Application Contact Middlesex County College, 2600 Woodbridge Avenue, PO Box 3050, Edison, NJ 08818-3050. *Phone:* 732-906-3130.
Website: http://www.middlesexcc.edu/.

Ocean County College
Toms River, New Jersey

- **County-supported** 2-year, founded 1964
- **Suburban** 275-acre campus with easy access to Philadelphia
- **Coed,** 9,296 undergraduate students, 53% full-time, 56% women, 44% men

Undergraduates 4,927 full-time, 4,369 part-time. Students come from 21 states and territories; 2% are from out of state; 6% Black or African American, non-Hispanic/Latino; 10% Hispanic/Latino; 2% Asian, non-Hispanic/Latino; 0.2% Native Hawaiian or other Pacific Islander, non-Hispanic/Latino; 0.3% American Indian or Alaska Native, non-Hispanic/Latino; 2% Two or more races, non-Hispanic/Latino; 5% Race/ethnicity unknown; 0.8% international; 2% transferred in. *Retention:* 71% of full-time freshmen returned.
Freshmen *Admission:* 2,049 applied, 2,049 admitted, 2,048 enrolled.
Faculty *Total:* 555, 17% full-time. *Student/faculty ratio:* 26:1.
Majors Broadcast journalism; business administration and management; business/commerce; communications technologies and support services related; computer and information sciences; criminal justice/police science; dental hygiene; engineering; engineering technologies and engineering related; environmental science; general studies; homeland security, law enforcement, firefighting and protective services related; human services; international/global studies; liberal arts and sciences/liberal studies; occupational therapist assistant; registered nursing/registered nurse; rehabilitation and therapeutic professions related; respiratory care therapy; sign language interpretation and translation; visual and performing arts.
Academics *Calendar:* semesters. *Degree:* certificates, diplomas, and associate. *Special study options:* academic remediation for entering students, accelerated degree program, adult/continuing education programs, advanced placement credit, cooperative education, distance learning, English as a second language, honors programs, independent study, internships, part-time degree program, services for LD students, study abroad, summer session for credit.
Library Ocean County College Library with 170,042 titles, 3,733 audiovisual materials, an OPAC, a Web page.
Student Life *Housing:* college housing not available. *Activities and Organizations:* drama/theater group, student-run newspaper, radio and television station, choral group, Student Activities Board, student government, OCC Vikings Cheerleaders, NJ STARS Club, Speech and Theater Club. *Campus security:* 24-hour emergency response devices and patrols, late-night transport/escort service, security cameras in hallways and parking lots. *Student services:* personal/psychological counseling.
Athletics Member NJCAA. *Intercollegiate sports:* baseball M, basketball M/W, cross-country running M/W, golf M/W, lacrosse M, soccer M/W, softball W, swimming and diving M/W, tennis M/W, volleyball W. *Intramural sports:* basketball M/W, cheerleading M(c)/W(c), ice hockey M(c), sailing M(c)/W(c), soccer M/W, softball W, tennis M/W, volleyball M/W.
Standardized Tests *Required for some:* ACCUPLACER is required for degree seeking students. Waiver may be obtained by meeting institution's minimum ACT or SAT scores, or English and math transfer credits.
Costs (2015–16) *Tuition:* area resident $3270 full-time, $109 per credit part-time; state resident $4050 full-time, $135 per credit part-time; nonresident $6750 full-time, $225 per credit part-time. Full-time tuition and fees vary according to program. Part-time tuition and fees vary according to program. *Required fees:* $846 full-time, $32 per credit part-time, $20 per term part-time. *Payment plan:* installment. *Waivers:* senior citizens and employees or children of employees.
Financial Aid Of all full-time matriculated undergraduates who enrolled in 2013, 76 Federal Work-Study jobs (averaging $1300). 45 state and other part-time jobs (averaging $850).
Applying *Options:* electronic application. *Required for some:* high school transcript, Accuplacer testing required for degree seeking students not meeting minimum ACT or SAT institutional requirements. Selective admissions for nursing students. *Application deadlines:* rolling (freshmen), rolling (out-of-

state freshmen), rolling (transfers). *Notification:* continuous (freshmen), continuous (out-of-state freshmen), continuous (transfers).
Freshman Application Contact Ms. Sheenah Hartigan, CRM Communications Administrator, Ocean County College, College Drive, PO Box 2001, Toms River, NJ 08754-2001. *Phone:* 732-255-0400 Ext. 2189. *E-mail:* shartigan@ocean.edu.
Website: http://www.ocean.edu/.

Passaic County Community College
Paterson, New Jersey

Freshman Application Contact Mr. Patrick Noonan, Director of Admissions, Passaic County Community College, One College Boulevard, Paterson, NJ 07505-1179. *Phone:* 973-684-6304.
Website: http://www.pccc.cc.nj.us/.

Raritan Valley Community College
Branchburg, New Jersey

- **State and locally supported** 2-year, founded 1965
- **Suburban** 225-acre campus with easy access to New York City, Philadelphia
- **Coed,** 8,214 undergraduate students, 42% full-time, 51% women, 49% men

Undergraduates 3,440 full-time, 4,774 part-time. Students come from 16 states and territories; 0.7% are from out of state; 9% Black or African American, non-Hispanic/Latino; 17% Hispanic/Latino; 6% Asian, non-Hispanic/Latino; 0.4% Native Hawaiian or other Pacific Islander, non-Hispanic/Latino; 0.2% American Indian or Alaska Native, non-Hispanic/Latino; 2% Two or more races, non-Hispanic/Latino; 8% Race/ethnicity unknown; 3% international; 61% transferred in. *Retention:* 66% of full-time freshmen returned.
Freshmen *Admission:* 1,526 enrolled. *Test scores:* SAT critical reading scores over 500: 73%; SAT math scores over 500: 79%; SAT writing scores over 500: 60%; SAT critical reading scores over 600: 21%; SAT math scores over 600: 26%; SAT writing scores over 600: 17%; SAT critical reading scores over 700: 3%; SAT math scores over 700: 2%; SAT writing scores over 700: 2%.
Faculty *Total:* 488, 25% full-time. *Student/faculty ratio:* 21:1.
Majors Accounting related; accounting technology and bookkeeping; administrative assistant and secretarial science; animation, interactive technology, video graphics and special effects; automotive engineering technology; biotechnology; business administration and management; business/commerce; chemical technology; child-care provision; cinematography and film/video production; communication and media related; computer and information sciences and support services related; computer programming (vendor/product certification); computer systems networking and telecommunications; construction engineering technology; corrections; criminal justice/law enforcement administration; criminal justice/police science; critical incident response/special police operations; dance; dental assisting; dental hygiene; design and applied arts related; diesel mechanics technology; digital communication and media/multimedia; engineering science; engineering technologies and engineering related; English; financial planning and services; fine/studio arts; health and physical education/fitness; health information/medical records technology; health services/allied health/health sciences; heating, ventilation, air conditioning and refrigeration engineering technology; information technology; interior design; international business/trade/commerce; kindergarten/preschool education; kinesiology and exercise science; legal assistant/paralegal; liberal arts and sciences/liberal studies; lineworker; management information systems; manufacturing engineering technology; marketing/marketing management; medical/clinical assistant; meeting and event planning; multi/interdisciplinary studies related; music; opticianry; optometric technician; registered nursing/registered nurse; respiratory care therapy; restaurant, culinary, and catering management; small business administration; web page, digital/multimedia and information resources design.
Academics *Calendar:* semesters. *Degree:* certificates and associate. *Special study options:* academic remediation for entering students, adult/continuing education programs, advanced placement credit, cooperative education, distance learning, double majors, English as a second language, honors programs, independent study, internships, off-campus study, part-time degree program, services for LD students, summer session for credit. *ROTC:* Army (c), Air Force (c).
Library Evelyn S. Field Library with 149,823 titles, 3,109 audiovisual materials, an OPAC, a Web page.
Student Life *Housing:* college housing not available. *Activities and Organizations:* drama/theater group, student-run radio station, choral group, Phi Theta Kappa, Orgullo Latino, Student Nurses Association, Business Club/SIFE, Environmental club. *Campus security:* 24-hour emergency response devices and patrols, late-night transport/escort service, 24-hour

outdoor and indoor surveillance cameras; 24-hr mobile patrols; 24-hr communication center. *Student services:* personal/psychological counseling.
Athletics Member NJCAA. *Intercollegiate sports:* baseball M(s), basketball M(s)/W(s), golf M/W, soccer M/W, softball W(s). *Intramural sports:* basketball M/W, volleyball M/W.
Costs (2014–15) *Tuition:* area resident $3096 full-time, $129 per credit hour part-time; state resident $3696 full-time, $154 per credit hour part-time; nonresident $3696 full-time, $154 per credit hour part-time. *Required fees:* $760 full-time, $22 per credit hour part-time, $96 per semester part-time. *Payment plan:* installment. *Waivers:* employees or children of employees.
Financial Aid Of all full-time matriculated undergraduates who enrolled in 2013, 12 Federal Work-Study jobs (averaging $2500).
Applying *Required:* high school transcript.
Freshman Application Contact Mr. Daniel Palubniak, Registrar, Enrollment Services, Raritan Valley Community College, 118 Lamington Road, Branchburg, NJ 08876-1265. *Phone:* 908-526-1200 Ext. 8206. *Fax:* 908-704-3442. *E-mail:* dpalubni@raritanval.edu.
Website: http://www.raritanval.edu/.

Rowan College at Gloucester County
Sewell, New Jersey

Freshman Application Contact Ms. Judy Atkinson, Registrar/Admissions, Rowan College at Gloucester County, 1400 Tanyard Road, Sewell, NJ 08080. *Phone:* 856-415-2209. *E-mail:* jatkinso@gccnj.edu.
Website: http://www.rcgc.edu/.

Salem Community College
Carneys Point, New Jersey

- **County-supported** 2-year, founded 1972
- **Small-town** campus with easy access to Philadelphia
- **Coed,** 1,107 undergraduate students, 54% full-time, 60% women, 40% men

Undergraduates 602 full-time, 505 part-time. 20% are from out of state; 18% Black or African American, non-Hispanic/Latino; 5% Hispanic/Latino; 2% Asian, non-Hispanic/Latino; 0.5% Native Hawaiian or other Pacific Islander, non-Hispanic/Latino; 0.6% American Indian or Alaska Native, non-Hispanic/Latino; 4% Two or more races, non-Hispanic/Latino; 18% Race/ethnicity unknown.
Freshmen *Admission:* 312 enrolled.
Faculty *Total:* 87, 20% full-time, 11% with terminal degrees. *Student/faculty ratio:* 19:1.
Majors Administrative assistant and secretarial science; adult health nursing; agricultural business and management; allied health diagnostic, intervention, and treatment professions related; biology/biological sciences; corrections; criminal justice/police science; culinary arts; education; engineering technologies and engineering related; fine arts related; fire science/firefighting; game and interactive media design; health and wellness; health information/medical records administration; homeland security; journalism; legal assistant/paralegal; liberal arts and sciences/liberal studies; licensed practical/vocational nurse training; medical insurance coding; nuclear/nuclear power technology; ornamental horticulture; pharmacy technician; political science and government; precision production related; psychology; registered nursing/registered nurse; respiratory care therapy; sculpture; social work; sociology; sport and fitness administration/management.
Academics *Calendar:* semesters. *Degree:* certificates and associate. *Special study options:* academic remediation for entering students, adult/continuing education programs, advanced placement credit, cooperative education, distance learning, double majors, English as a second language, independent study, off-campus study, part-time degree program, services for LD students, summer session for credit.
Library Michael S. Cettei Memorial Library with an OPAC.
Student Life *Housing:* college housing not available. *Activities and Organizations:* choral group. *Campus security:* 24-hour emergency response devices and patrols, late-night transport/escort service. *Student services:* personal/psychological counseling, women's center.
Costs (2014–15) *Tuition:* area resident $3060 full-time, $102 per credit hour part-time; state resident $3750 full-time, $125 per credit hour part-time; nonresident $3750 full-time, $125 per credit hour part-time. Full-time tuition and fees vary according to course load and program. Part-time tuition and fees vary according to course load and program. *Required fees:* $1044 full-time, $33 per credit hour part-time, $27 per term part-time. *Payment plan:* installment.
Financial Aid Of all full-time matriculated undergraduates who enrolled in 2010, 756 applied for aid, 624 were judged to have need, 35 had their need fully met. 34 Federal Work-Study jobs (averaging $1137). In 2010, 39 non-need-based awards were made. *Average percent of need met:* 47%. *Average*

financial aid package: $4663. *Average need-based loan:* $2304. *Average need-based gift aid:* $4284. *Average non-need-based aid:* $1652.
Applying *Options:* electronic application, early admission, deferred entrance. *Application fee:* $27. *Required:* high school transcript, Basic Skills test or minimum SAT scores. Students with a minimum score of 530 in math and 540 in English on the SAT are exempt from placement testing. HS GPA of 3.0 or higher needed for placement in Gateway courses. *Required for some:* essay or personal statement. *Application deadlines:* rolling (freshmen), rolling (out-of-state freshmen), rolling (transfers). *Notification:* continuous (freshmen), continuous (transfers).
Freshman Application Contact Kelly McShay, Director of Retention and Admissions, Salem Community College, 460 Hollywood Avenue, Carneys Point, NJ 08069. *Phone:* 856-351-2919. *E-mail:* kmcshay@salemcc.edu. *Website:* http://www.salemcc.edu/.

Sussex County Community College
Newton, New Jersey

- **State and locally supported** 2-year, founded 1981, part of New Jersey Commission on Higher Education
- **Small-town** 160-acre campus with easy access to New York City
- **Coed**

Undergraduates 2,059 full-time, 1,673 part-time. Students come from 3 states and territories; 12% are from out of state; 2% Black or African American, non-Hispanic/Latino; 9% Hispanic/Latino; 1% Asian, non-Hispanic/Latino; 0.2% American Indian or Alaska Native, non-Hispanic/Latino; 1% Two or more races, non-Hispanic/Latino; 0.7% Race/ethnicity unknown; 0.5% international; 5% transferred in. *Retention:* 66% of full-time freshmen returned.
Faculty *Student/faculty ratio:* 21:1.
Academics *Calendar:* 4-1-4. *Degree:* certificates and associate. *Special study options:* academic remediation for entering students, advanced placement credit, distance learning, double majors, English as a second language, internships, part-time degree program, services for LD students, summer session for credit.
Student Life *Campus security:* late-night transport/escort service, trained security personnel.
Athletics Member NJCAA.
Financial Aid Of all full-time matriculated undergraduates who enrolled in 2013, 29 Federal Work-Study jobs (averaging $1500).
Applying *Options:* electronic application. *Application fee:* $25.
Freshman Application Contact Mr. Todd Poltersdorf, Director of Admissions, Sussex County Community College, 1 College Hill Road, Newton, NJ 07860. *Phone:* 973-300-2253. *E-mail:* tpoltersdorf@sussex.edu. *Website:* http://www.sussex.edu/.

Union County College
Cranford, New Jersey

Freshman Application Contact Ms. Nina Hernandez, Director of Admissions, Records, and Registration, Union County College, Cranford, NJ 07016. *Phone:* 908-709-7127. *Fax:* 908-709-7125. *E-mail:* hernandez@ucc.edu. *Website:* http://www.ucc.edu/.

Warren County Community College
Washington, New Jersey

Freshman Application Contact Shannon Horwath, Associate Director of Admissions, Warren County Community College, 475 Route 57 West, Washington, NJ 07882-9605. *Phone:* 908-835-2300. *E-mail:* shorwath@warren.edu. *Website:* http://www.warren.edu/.

NEW MEXICO

Brown Mackie College–Albuquerque
Albuquerque, New Mexico

- **Proprietary** primarily 2-year, part of Education Management Corporation
- **Coed**

Academics *Degrees:* diplomas, associate, and bachelor's.
Freshman Application Contact Brown Mackie College–Albuquerque, 10500 Copper Avenue NE, Albuquerque, NM 87123. *Phone:* 505-559-5200. *Toll-free phone:* 877-271-3488.
Website: http://www.brownmackie.edu/albuquerque/.

Carrington College–Albuquerque
Albuquerque, New Mexico

- **Proprietary** 2-year, part of Carrington Colleges Group, Inc.
- **Coed**

Undergraduates 545 full-time, 102 part-time. 2% are from out of state; 3% Black or African American, non-Hispanic/Latino; 52% Hispanic/Latino; 2% Asian, non-Hispanic/Latino; 0.2% Native Hawaiian or other Pacific Islander, non-Hispanic/Latino; 16% American Indian or Alaska Native, non-Hispanic/Latino; 2% Two or more races, non-Hispanic/Latino; 2% Race/ethnicity unknown; 16% transferred in.
Faculty *Student/faculty ratio:* 24:1.
Academics *Degree:* certificates and associate.
Costs (2014–15) *Tuition:* $14,287 per degree program part-time. Full-time tuition and fees vary according to program. Part-time tuition and fees vary according to program. Total costs vary by program. Tuition provided is for largest program (Medical Assisting).
Applying *Required:* essay or personal statement, high school transcript, interview, Entrance test administered by Carrington College.
Freshman Application Contact Carrington College–Albuquerque, 1001 Menaul Boulevard NE, Albuquerque, NM 87107.
Website: http://carrington.edu/.

Central New Mexico Community College
Albuquerque, New Mexico

Freshman Application Contact Glenn Damiani, Sr. Director, Enrollment Services, Central New Mexico Community College, Albuquerque, NM 87106. *Phone:* 505-224-3223.
Website: http://www.cnm.edu/.

Clovis Community College
Clovis, New Mexico

Freshman Application Contact Ms. Rosie Corrie, Director of Admissions and Records/Registrar, Clovis Community College, Clovis, NM 88101-8381. *Phone:* 575-769-4962. *Toll-free phone:* 800-769-1409. *Fax:* 575-769-4190. *E-mail:* admissions@clovis.edu.
Website: http://www.clovis.edu/.

Doña Ana Community College
Las Cruces, New Mexico

Freshman Application Contact Mrs. Ricci Montes, Admissions Advisor, Doña Ana Community College, MSC-3DA, Box 30001, 3400 South Espina Street, Las Cruces, NM 88003-8001. *Phone:* 575-527-7683. *Toll-free phone:* 800-903-7503. *Fax:* 575-527-7515.
Website: http://dabcc-www.nmsu.edu/.

Eastern New Mexico University–Roswell
Roswell, New Mexico

Freshman Application Contact Eastern New Mexico University–Roswell, PO Box 6000, Roswell, NM 88202-6000. *Phone:* 505-624-7142. *Toll-free phone:* 800-243-6687 (in-state); 800-624-7000 (out-of-state).
Website: http://www.roswell.enmu.edu/.

ITT Technical Institute
Albuquerque, New Mexico

- **Proprietary** primarily 2-year, founded 1989, part of ITT Educational Services, Inc.
- **Coed**

Academics *Calendar:* quarters. *Degrees:* associate and bachelor's.
Freshman Application Contact Director of Recruitment, ITT Technical Institute, 5100 Masthead Street, NE, Albuquerque, NM 87109-4366. *Phone:* 505-828-1114. *Toll-free phone:* 800-636-1114.
Website: http://www.itt-tech.edu/.

Luna Community College
Las Vegas, New Mexico

Freshman Application Contact Ms. Henrietta Griego, Director of Admissions, Recruitment, and Retention, Luna Community College, PO Box 1510, Las Vegas, NM 87701. *Phone:* 505-454-2020. *Toll-free phone:* 800-588-7232 (in-state); 800-5888-7232 (out-of-state). *Fax:* 505-454-2588. *E-mail:* hgriego@luna.cc.nm.us.
Website: http://www.luna.edu/.

Mesalands Community College
Tucumcari, New Mexico

Director of Admissions Mr. Ken Brashear, Director of Enrollment Management, Mesalands Community College, 911 South Tenth Street, Tucumcari, NM 88401. *Phone:* 505-461-4413.
Website: http://www.mesalands.edu/.

National American University
Albuquerque, New Mexico

Freshman Application Contact Admissions Office, National American University, 10131 Coors Boulevard NW, Suite I-01, Albuquerque, NM 87114.
Website: http://www.national.edu/.

New Mexico Junior College
Hobbs, New Mexico

- **State and locally supported** 2-year, founded 1965, part of New Mexico Commission on Higher Education
- **Small-town** 185-acre campus
- **Coed**, 3,222 undergraduate students

Undergraduates Students come from 17 states and territories; 7 other countries; 10% are from out of state; 15% live on campus.
Freshmen *Average high school GPA:* 2.75.
Faculty *Total:* 120, 54% full-time. *Student/faculty ratio:* 19:1.
Majors Accounting; administrative assistant and secretarial science; agriculture; art; art teacher education; athletic training; automobile/automotive mechanics technology; biological and physical sciences; biology/biological sciences; business administration and management; business teacher education; carpentry; chemistry; clinical/medical laboratory technology; commercial and advertising art; computer graphics; computer programming; computer science; computer typography and composition equipment operation; construction engineering technology; cosmetology; criminal justice/police science; data processing and data processing technology; drafting and design technology; dramatic/theater arts; education; elementary education; emergency medical technology (EMT paramedic); engineering; English; environmental education; environmental studies; finance; fire science/firefighting; health professions related; history; legal administrative assistant/secretary; liberal arts and sciences/liberal studies; licensed practical/vocational nurse training; machine tool technology; marketing/marketing management; mathematics; medical administrative assistant and medical secretary; medical/clinical assistant; music; parks, recreation and leisure; petroleum technology; physical education teaching and coaching; real estate; registered nursing/registered nurse; trade and industrial teacher education; welding technology.
Academics *Calendar:* semesters. *Degree:* certificates and associate. *Special study options:* academic remediation for entering students, advanced placement credit, cooperative education, distance learning, internships, part-time degree program, services for LD students, summer session for credit.
Library Pannell Library with 118,500 titles, an OPAC, a Web page.
Student Life *Housing:* on-campus residence required for freshman year. *Options:* coed. Campus housing is university owned. *Activities and Organizations:* drama/theater group, choral group, Student Nurses Association, Phi Theta Kappa, Fellowship of Christian Athletes. *Campus security:* 24-hour emergency response devices and patrols, late-night transport/escort service, controlled dormitory access. *Student services:* health clinic, personal/psychological counseling.
Athletics Member NJCAA. *Intercollegiate sports:* baseball M(s), basketball M(s)/W(s), golf M(s). *Intramural sports:* badminton M/W, basketball M/W, cross-country running M/W, football M, racquetball M/W, table tennis M/W, volleyball M/W, weight lifting M/W.
Costs (2014–15) *Tuition:* area resident $1050 full-time, $35 per credit hour part-time; state resident $1620 full-time, $54 per credit hour part-time; nonresident $1860 full-time, $62 per credit hour part-time. Full-time tuition and fees vary according to course load. Part-time tuition and fees vary according to course load. *Required fees:* $100 full-time, $17 per credit hour part-time. *Room and board:* $4700; room only: $2400. Room and board charges vary according to board plan and housing facility. *Payment plan:* deferred payment. *Waivers:* senior citizens and employees or children of employees.
Applying *Options:* electronic application, early admission, deferred entrance. *Application deadlines:* rolling (freshmen), rolling (transfers).
Freshman Application Contact New Mexico Junior College, 5317 Lovington Highway, Hobbs, NM 88240-9123. *Phone:* 575-492-2587. *Toll-free phone:* 800-657-6260.
Website: http://www.nmjc.edu/.

New Mexico Military Institute
Roswell, New Mexico

Freshman Application Contact New Mexico Military Institute, Roswell, NM 88201-5173. *Phone:* 505-624-8050. *Toll-free phone:* 800-421-5376. *Fax:* 505-624-8058. *E-mail:* admissions@nmmi.edu.
Website: http://www.nmmi.edu/.

New Mexico State University–Alamogordo
Alamogordo, New Mexico

- **State-supported** 2-year, founded 1958, part of New Mexico State University System
- **Small-town** 540-acre campus
- **Endowment** $147,086
- **Coed**

Undergraduates 1,005 full-time, 2,366 part-time. Students come from 26 states and territories; 15% are from out of state; 4% Black or African American, non-Hispanic/Latino; 38% Hispanic/Latino; 2% Asian, non-Hispanic/Latino; 0.1% Native Hawaiian or other Pacific Islander, non-Hispanic/Latino; 3% American Indian or Alaska Native, non-Hispanic/Latino; 1% Two or more races, non-Hispanic/Latino; 6% Race/ethnicity unknown; 2% international; 6% transferred in. *Retention:* 50% of full-time freshmen returned.
Faculty *Student/faculty ratio:* 20:1.
Academics *Calendar:* semesters. *Degree:* certificates and associate. *Special study options:* academic remediation for entering students, adult/continuing education programs, advanced placement credit, distance learning, double majors, independent study, internships, off-campus study, part-time degree program, services for LD students, study abroad, summer session for credit.
Student Life *Campus security:* 24-hour emergency response devices.
Costs (2014–15) *Tuition:* area resident $1872 full-time, $78 per credit hour part-time; state resident $2232 full-time, $93 per credit hour part-time; nonresident $5184 full-time, $216 per credit hour part-time. Full-time tuition and fees vary according to course load. *Required fees:* $96 full-time, $4 per credit hour part-time. *Payment plans:* installment, deferred payment.
Financial Aid Of all full-time matriculated undergraduates who enrolled in 2013, 10 Federal Work-Study jobs (averaging $3300). 60 state and other part-time jobs (averaging $3300). *Financial aid deadline:* 5/1.
Applying *Options:* electronic application, early admission, deferred entrance. *Application fee:* $20. *Required:* high school transcript, minimum 2.0 GPA.
Freshman Application Contact Ms. Elma Hernandez, Coordinator of Admissions and Records, New Mexico State University–Alamogordo, 2400 North Scenic Drive, Alamogordo, NM 88311-0477. *Phone:* 575-439-3700. *E-mail:* advisor@nmsua.nmsu.edu.
Website: http://nmsua.edu/.

New Mexico State University–Carlsbad
Carlsbad, New Mexico

Freshman Application Contact Ms. Everal Shannon, Records Specialist, New Mexico State University–Carlsbad, 1500 University Drive, Carlsbad, NM 88220. *Phone:* 575-234-9222. *Fax:* 575-885-4951. *E-mail:* eshannon@nmsu.edu.
Website: http://www.cavern.nmsu.edu/.

New Mexico State University–Grants
Grants, New Mexico

Director of Admissions Ms. Irene Lutz, Campus Student Services Officer, New Mexico State University–Grants, 1500 3rd Street, Grants, NM 87020-2025. *Phone:* 505-287-7981.
Website: http://grants.nmsu.edu/.

Pima Medical Institute
Albuquerque, New Mexico

Freshman Application Contact Admissions Office, Pima Medical Institute, 4400 Cutler Avenue NE, Albuquerque, NM 87110. *Phone:* 505-881-1234. *Toll-free phone:* 800-477-PIMA (in-state); 888-477-PIMA (out-of-state). *Fax:* 505-881-5329.
Website: http://www.pmi.edu/.

Pima Medical Institute
Albuquerque, New Mexico

Freshman Application Contact Pima Medical Institute, RMTS 32, 8601 Golf Course Road, NW, Albuquerque, NM 87114. *Phone:* 505-816-0556.
Website: http://www.pmi.edu/.

San Juan College
Farmington, New Mexico

- **State-supported** 2-year, founded 1958, part of New Mexico Higher Education Department
- **Small-town** 698-acre campus
- **Endowment** $14.2 million
- **Coed,** 7,786 undergraduate students, 29% full-time, 63% women, 37% men

Undergraduates 2,229 full-time, 5,557 part-time. Students come from 51 states and territories; 33 other countries; 26% are from out of state; 0.9% Black or African American, non-Hispanic/Latino; 15% Hispanic/Latino; 0.8% Asian, non-Hispanic/Latino; 0.1% Native Hawaiian or other Pacific Islander, non-Hispanic/Latino; 30% American Indian or Alaska Native, non-Hispanic/Latino; 1% Two or more races, non-Hispanic/Latino; 4% Race/ethnicity unknown; 0.9% international; 5% transferred in.
Freshmen *Admission:* 937 applied, 937 admitted, 897 enrolled.
Faculty *Total:* 351, 48% full-time, 5% with terminal degrees. *Student/faculty ratio:* 20:1.
Majors Accounting technology and bookkeeping; American Indian/Native American studies; autobody/collision and repair technology; automobile/automotive mechanics technology; biology/biological sciences; business administration and management; carpentry; chemistry; child-care provision; clinical/medical laboratory technology; commercial and advertising art; cosmetology; criminal justice/police science; data processing and data processing technology; dental hygiene; diesel mechanics technology; drafting and design technology; electrical, electronic and communications engineering technology; elementary education; emergency medical technology (EMT paramedic); engineering; engineering technology; fire science/firefighting; general studies; geology/earth science; health and physical education/fitness; health information/medical records technology; industrial mechanics and maintenance technology; industrial technology; instrumentation technology; landscaping and groundskeeping; legal assistant/paralegal; liberal arts and sciences/liberal studies; machine shop technology; mathematics; occupational safety and health technology; occupational therapist assistant; parks, recreation and leisure; physical sciences; physical therapy technology; physics; premedical studies; psychology; registered nursing/registered nurse; respiratory care therapy; secondary education; social work; solar energy technology; special education; surgical technology; theater design and technology; veterinary/animal health technology; welding technology.
Academics *Calendar:* semesters. *Degree:* certificates, diplomas, and associate. *Special study options:* academic remediation for entering students, adult/continuing education programs, advanced placement credit, cooperative education, distance learning, double majors, English as a second language, freshman honors college, honors programs, independent study, internships, part-time degree program, services for LD students, summer session for credit.
Library San Juan College Library with 94,111 titles, 7,332 audiovisual materials, an OPAC, a Web page.
Student Life *Housing:* college housing not available. *Activities and Organizations:* drama/theater group, student-run newspaper, choral group, AGAVE, SJC National Society of Leadership and Success, Psychology/PSI Beta, National Honor Society of Leadership and Success (NSLS), American Indian Science and Leadership Society (AISES), national fraternities, national sororities. *Campus security:* 24-hour emergency response devices and patrols, late-night transport/escort service. *Student services:* personal/psychological counseling.
Athletics *Intramural sports:* badminton M/W, basketball M/W, cross-country running M/W, football M/W, rock climbing M/W, skiing (cross-country) M/W, skiing (downhill) M/W, soccer M/W, softball M/W, table tennis M/W, ultimate Frisbee M/W, volleyball M/W, weight lifting M/W.
Costs (2015–16) *Tuition:* state resident $984 full-time, $41 per credit hour part-time; nonresident $2520 full-time, $123 per credit hour part-time. Full-time tuition and fees vary according to reciprocity agreements. Part-time tuition and fees vary according to reciprocity agreements. *Required fees:* $336 full-time, $78 per term part-time. *Payment plans:* tuition prepayment, installment. *Waivers:* senior citizens and employees or children of employees.
Financial Aid Of all full-time matriculated undergraduates who enrolled in 2013, 150 Federal Work-Study jobs (averaging $2500). 175 state and other part-time jobs (averaging $2500).
Applying *Options:* electronic application, early admission, deferred entrance. *Application fee:* $10. *Required:* high school transcript. *Application deadlines:* rolling (freshmen), rolling (transfers). *Notification:* continuous (freshmen), continuous (transfers).
Freshman Application Contact Mrs. Abby Calcote, Enrollment Specialist, San Juan College, 4601 College Blvd, Farmington, NM 87402. *Phone:* 505-566-3572. *Fax:* 505-566-3500. *E-mail:* calcotea@sanjuancollege.edu.
Website: http://www.sanjuancollege.edu/.

Santa Fe Community College
Santa Fe, New Mexico

Freshman Application Contact Ms. Rebecca Estrada, Director of Recruitment, Santa Fe Community College, 6401 Richards Ave, Santa Fe, NM 87508. *Phone:* 505-428-1604. *Fax:* 505-428-1468. *E-mail:* rebecca.estrada@sfcc.edu.
Website: http://www.sfcc.edu/.

Southwestern Indian Polytechnic Institute
Albuquerque, New Mexico

- **Federally supported** 2-year, founded 1971
- **Suburban** 144-acre campus
- **Coed,** 481 undergraduate students, 88% full-time, 51% women, 49% men

Undergraduates 422 full-time, 59 part-time. Students come from 21 states and territories; 60% live on campus.
Freshmen *Admission:* 139 applied, 107 admitted, 177 enrolled. *Average high school GPA:* 2.11.
Faculty *Total:* 41, 56% full-time, 12% with terminal degrees. *Student/faculty ratio:* 16:1.
Majors Accounting technology and bookkeeping; business administration and management; business/commerce; early childhood education; engineering; geographic information science and cartography; institutional food workers; instrumentation technology; liberal arts and sciences/liberal studies; natural resources and conservation related; opticianry; system, networking, and LAN/WAN management.
Academics *Calendar:* trimesters. *Degree:* certificates and associate. *Special study options:* academic remediation for entering students, advanced placement credit, cooperative education, distance learning, double majors, internships, part-time degree program, services for LD students, summer session for credit.
Library Southwester Indian Polytechnic Institute Library with 27,000 titles.
Student Life *Housing Options:* men-only, women-only. Campus housing is university owned. *Activities and Organizations:* Dance club, Student Senate, Natural Resources, Pow-wow club. *Campus security:* 24-hour emergency response devices and patrols, late-night transport/escort service. *Student services:* personal/psychological counseling.
Athletics *Intramural sports:* basketball M/W, softball M/W, volleyball M/W.
Costs (2014–15) *Tuition:* state resident $0 full-time; nonresident $0 full-time. *Required fees:* $1095 full-time, $290 per term part-time. *Room and board:* $450. *Payment plan:* deferred payment.
Financial Aid Of all full-time matriculated undergraduates who enrolled in 2013, 350 applied for aid, 350 were judged to have need, 4 had their need fully met. 15 Federal Work-Study jobs (averaging $774). 16 state and other part-time jobs (averaging $813). *Average percent of need met:* 22%. *Average financial aid package:* $2590. *Average need-based gift aid:* $2590.

Applying *Required:* high school transcript, Certificate of Indian Blood, physical and immunization records. *Application deadlines:* 7/30 (freshmen), 7/30 (transfers). *Notification:* continuous (freshmen).
Freshman Application Contact Southwestern Indian Polytechnic Institute, 9169 Coors, NW, Box 10146, Albuquerque, NM 87184-0146. *Phone:* 505-346-2324. *Toll-free phone:* 800-586-7474.
Website: http://www.sipi.edu/.

University of New Mexico–Gallup
Gallup, New Mexico

Director of Admissions Ms. Pearl A. Morris, Admissions Representative, University of New Mexico–Gallup, 200 College Road, Gallup, NM 87301-5603. *Phone:* 505-863-7576.
Website: http://www.gallup.unm.edu/.

University of New Mexico–Los Alamos Branch
Los Alamos, New Mexico

- **State-supported** 2-year, founded 1980, part of New Mexico Commission on Higher Education
- **Small-town** 5-acre campus
- **Coed**

Undergraduates 191 full-time, 553 part-time. 1% are from out of state; 1% Black or African American, non-Hispanic/Latino; 43% Hispanic/Latino; 3% Asian, non-Hispanic/Latino; 0.4% Native Hawaiian or other Pacific Islander, non-Hispanic/Latino; 5% American Indian or Alaska Native, non-Hispanic/Latino; 2% Two or more races, non-Hispanic/Latino; 3% Race/ethnicity unknown; 3% transferred in. *Retention:* 57% of full-time freshmen returned.
Faculty *Student/faculty ratio:* 9:1.
Academics *Calendar:* semesters. *Degree:* certificates and associate. *Special study options:* academic remediation for entering students, adult/continuing education programs, advanced placement credit, cooperative education, distance learning, double majors, English as a second language, internships, off-campus study, part-time degree program, services for LD students, summer session for credit.
Standardized Tests *Recommended:* SAT or ACT (for admission).
Costs (2014–15) *Tuition:* state resident $1536 full-time, $64 per credit part-time; nonresident $4776 full-time, $199 per credit part-time. *Required fees:* $108 full-time, $5 per credit part-time.
Financial Aid Of all full-time matriculated undergraduates who enrolled in 2013, 15 Federal Work-Study jobs (averaging $5000). 10 state and other part-time jobs (averaging $7000).
Applying *Required:* high school transcript.
Freshman Application Contact Mrs. Irene K. Martinez, Enrollment Representative, University of New Mexico–Los Alamos Branch, 4000 University Drive, Los Alamos, NM 87544-2233. *Phone:* 505-662-0332. *E-mail:* L65130@unm.edu.
Website: http://losalamos.unm.edu/.

University of New Mexico–Taos
Taos, New Mexico

Director of Admissions Vickie Alvarez, Student Enrollment Associate, University of New Mexico–Taos, 115 Civic Plaza Drive, Taos, NM 87571. *Phone:* 575-737-6425. *E-mail:* valvarez@unm.edu.
Website: http://taos.unm.edu/.

University of New Mexico–Valencia Campus
Los Lunas, New Mexico

Director of Admissions Richard M. Hulett, Director of Admissions and Recruitment, University of New Mexico–Valencia Campus, 280 La Entrada, Los Lunas, NM 87031-7633. *Phone:* 505-277-2446. *E-mail:* mhulett@unm.edu.
Website: http://www.unm.edu/~unmvc/.

NEW YORK

Adirondack Community College
Queensbury, New York

Freshman Application Contact Office of Admissions, Adirondack Community College, 640 Bay Road, Queensbury, NY 12804. *Phone:* 518-743-2264. *Toll-free phone:* 888-SUNY-ADK. *Fax:* 518-743-2200.
Website: http://www.sunyacc.edu/.

American Academy McAllister Institute of Funeral Service
New York, New York

Freshman Application Contact Mr. Norman Provost, Registrar, American Academy McAllister Institute of Funeral Service, 450 West 56th Street, New York, NY 10019-3602. *Phone:* 212-757-1190. *Toll-free phone:* 866-932-2264.
Website: http://www.funeraleducation.org/.

American Academy of Dramatic Arts–New York
New York, New York

- **Independent** 2-year, founded 1884
- **Urban** campus
- **Endowment** $5.1 million
- **Coed,** 253 undergraduate students, 100% full-time, 68% women, 32% men

Undergraduates 253 full-time. Students come from 33 states and territories; 14 other countries; 50% are from out of state; 13% Black or African American, non-Hispanic/Latino; 7% Hispanic/Latino; 0.8% Asian, non-Hispanic/Latino; 4% Two or more races, non-Hispanic/Latino; 4% Race/ethnicity unknown; 30% international; 53% live on campus.
Freshmen *Admission:* 489 applied, 343 admitted. *Average high school GPA:* 2.74.
Faculty *Total:* 31, 32% full-time, 35% with terminal degrees. *Student/faculty ratio:* 13:1.
Majors Dramatic/theater arts.
Academics *Calendar:* semesters. *Degree:* certificates and associate. *Special study options:* academic remediation for entering students, honors programs.
Library Academy/CBS Library with 8,000 titles, 950 audiovisual materials, an OPAC.
Student Life *Housing Options:* coed. Campus housing is leased by the school. Freshman applicants given priority for college housing. *Activities and Organizations:* national fraternities. *Campus security:* 24-hour emergency response devices and patrols, controlled dormitory access, trained security guard during hours of operation and campus housing. *Student services:* personal/psychological counseling.
Costs (2014–15) *Tuition:* $29,900 full-time. *Required fees:* $750 full-time. *Room only:* $15,525. Room and board charges vary according to housing facility. *Payment plan:* installment. *Waivers:* employees or children of employees.
Financial Aid Of all full-time matriculated undergraduates who enrolled in 2012, 240 applied for aid, 231 were judged to have need. 50 Federal Work-Study jobs (averaging $900). 50 state and other part-time jobs (averaging $2000). In 2012, 59 non-need-based awards were made. *Average percent of need met:* 67%. *Average financial aid package:* $18,150. *Average need-based loan:* $4500. *Average need-based gift aid:* $7000. *Average non-need-based aid:* $7000. *Average indebtedness upon graduation:* $15,000. *Financial aid deadline:* 5/15.
Applying *Options:* electronic application, deferred entrance. *Application fee:* $50. *Required:* essay or personal statement, high school transcript, minimum 2.0 GPA, 2 letters of recommendation, interview, audition. *Application deadlines:* rolling (freshmen), rolling (transfers). *Notification:* continuous (freshmen), continuous (transfers).
Freshman Application Contact Kerin Reilly, Director of Admissions, American Academy of Dramatic Arts–New York, 120 Madison Avenue, New York, NY 10016. *Phone:* 212-686-9244 Ext. 333. *Toll-free phone:* 800-463-8990. *E-mail:* kreilly@aada.edu.
Website: http://www.aada.edu/.

ASA College
Brooklyn, New York

Freshman Application Contact Admissions Office, ASA College, 81 Willoughby Street, Brooklyn, NY 11201. *Phone:* 718-522-9073. *Toll-free phone:* 877-679-8772.
Website: http://www.asa.edu/.

The Belanger School of Nursing
Schenectady, New York

- **Independent** 2-year, founded 1906
- **Urban** campus
- **Coed, primarily women,** 124 undergraduate students, 30% full-time, 83% women, 17% men

Undergraduates 37 full-time, 87 part-time. Students come from 3 states and territories; 12% Black or African American, non-Hispanic/Latino; 6% Hispanic/Latino; 5% Asian, non-Hispanic/Latino; 2% American Indian or Alaska Native, non-Hispanic/Latino; 0.8% Two or more races, non-Hispanic/Latino.
Freshmen *Admission:* 2 enrolled. *Average high school GPA:* 3.2.
Faculty *Student/faculty ratio:* 6:1.
Majors Registered nursing/registered nurse.
Academics *Degree:* associate.
Student Life *Housing:* college housing not available.
Standardized Tests *Recommended:* SAT or ACT (for admission).
Costs (2014–15) *Tuition:* $8724 full-time, $6200 per year part-time. Full-time tuition and fees vary according to course level, course load, and student level. Part-time tuition and fees vary according to course level, course load, and student level. *Required fees:* $1004 full-time, $300 per credit hour part-time, $962 per year part-time. *Payment plan:* installment.
Applying *Required:* essay or personal statement, high school transcript, minimum 3.0 GPA, 2 letters of recommendation.
Freshman Application Contact Carolyn Lansing, Student Services Manager, The Belanger School of Nursing, 65 McClellan Street, Schenectady, NY 12304. *Phone:* 518-831-8810. *Fax:* 518-243-4470. *E-mail:* lansingc@ellismedicine.org.
Website: http://www.ellismedicine.org/school-of-nursing/.

Berkeley College–Westchester Campus
White Plains, New York

- **Proprietary** primarily 2-year, founded 1945
- **Suburban** campus with easy access to New York City
- **Coed,** 450 undergraduate students, 92% full-time, 63% women, 37% men

Undergraduates 412 full-time, 38 part-time. Students come from 22 states and territories; 24% are from out of state; 29% Black or African American, non-Hispanic/Latino; 26% Hispanic/Latino; 2% Asian, non-Hispanic/Latino; 0.4% Native Hawaiian or other Pacific Islander, non-Hispanic/Latino; 0.7% American Indian or Alaska Native, non-Hispanic/Latino; 22% Race/ethnicity unknown; 8% international; 11% transferred in. *Retention:* 61% of full-time freshmen returned.
Freshmen *Admission:* 104 enrolled.
Faculty *Student/faculty ratio:* 22:1.
Majors Business administration and management; criminal justice/law enforcement administration; criminal justice/police science; health/health-care administration; health information/medical records technology; marketing/marketing management.
Academics *Calendar:* quarters. *Degrees:* associate and bachelor's. *Special study options:* academic remediation for entering students, accelerated degree program, adult/continuing education programs, advanced placement credit, cooperative education, distance learning, honors programs, independent study, internships, off-campus study, part-time degree program, study abroad, summer session for credit.
Library an OPAC, a Web page.
Student Life *Housing Options:* coed. Campus housing is university owned. *Activities and Organizations:* student-run newspaper. *Campus security:* 24-hour emergency response devices, controlled dormitory access, monitored entrance with front desk security guard. *Student services:* personal/psychological counseling.
Athletics Member USCAA. *Intercollegiate sports:* basketball M/W, cross-country running M/W, soccer M/W.
Costs (2014–15) *Tuition:* $23,100 full-time, $525 per quarter hour part-time. Full-time tuition and fees vary according to course load. Part-time tuition and fees vary according to course load. No tuition increase for student's term of enrollment. *Required fees:* $1200 full-time, $275 per term part-time. *Room only:* $9000. *Payment plan:* installment. *Waivers:* employees or children of employees.

Applying *Options:* electronic application, deferred entrance. *Application fee:* $50. *Required:* high school transcript. *Recommended:* interview. *Application deadlines:* rolling (freshmen), rolling (out-of-state freshmen), rolling (transfers).
Freshman Application Contact Lynn Ovimeleh, Director of High School Admissions, Berkeley College–Westchester Campus, 99 Church Street, White Plains, NY 10601. *Phone:* 914-694-1122. *Toll-free phone:* 800-446-5400. *E-mail:* info@berkeleycollege.edu.
Website: http://www.berkeleycollege.edu/.

Bill and Sandra Pomeroy College of Nursing at Crouse Hospital
Syracuse, New York

Freshman Application Contact Ms. Amy Graham, Enrollment Management Supervisor, Bill and Sandra Pomeroy College of Nursing at Crouse Hospital, 765 Irving Avenue, Syracuse, NY 13210. *Phone:* 315-470-7481. *Fax:* 315-470-7925. *E-mail:* amygraham@crouse.org.
Website: http://www.crouse.org/nursing/.

Borough of Manhattan Community College of the City University of New York
New York, New York

- **State and locally supported** 2-year, founded 1963, part of City University of New York System
- **Urban** 5-acre campus
- **Coed,** 26,623 undergraduate students, 64% full-time, 57% women, 43% men

Undergraduates 17,131 full-time, 9,492 part-time. 2% are from out of state; 30% Black or African American, non-Hispanic/Latino; 40% Hispanic/Latino; 13% Asian, non-Hispanic/Latino; 0.3% American Indian or Alaska Native, non-Hispanic/Latino; 6% international; 7% transferred in.
Freshmen *Admission:* 25,547 applied, 25,294 admitted, 7,071 enrolled. *Test scores:* SAT critical reading scores over 500: 10%; SAT math scores over 500: 12%; SAT critical reading scores over 600: 1%; SAT math scores over 600: 2%.
Faculty *Total:* 1,453, 36% full-time.
Majors Accounting technology and bookkeeping; administrative assistant and secretarial science; biotechnology; business administration and management; community organization and advocacy; computer and information sciences; computer science; computer systems networking and telecommunications; criminal justice/law enforcement administration; criminal justice/safety; emergency medical technology (EMT paramedic); engineering; English; forensic science and technology; geographic information science and cartography; health information/medical records technology; liberal arts and sciences/liberal studies; mathematics; physical sciences; public health education and promotion; radio and television broadcasting technology; registered nursing/registered nurse; respiratory therapy technician; small business administration; teacher assistant/aide; visual and performing arts; web page, digital/multimedia and information resources design.
Academics *Calendar:* semesters. *Degree:* certificates and associate. *Special study options:* academic remediation for entering students, adult/continuing education programs, advanced placement credit, cooperative education, distance learning, English as a second language, honors programs, independent study, internships, off-campus study, part-time degree program, services for LD students, study abroad, summer session for credit.
Library A. Philip Randolph Library with 200,250 titles, an OPAC, a Web page.
Student Life *Housing:* college housing not available. *Activities and Organizations:* drama/theater group, student-run newspaper, choral group, Chinese Culture Association, Chinese Cultural Studies Society, Math Club, African Students Association, Student Nurses Association. *Campus security:* 24-hour patrols. *Student services:* health clinic, personal/psychological counseling, women's center.
Athletics Member NJCAA. *Intercollegiate sports:* basketball M/W, soccer M/W, volleyball W.
Standardized Tests *Recommended:* SAT or ACT (for admission).
Costs (2015–16) *Tuition:* state resident $4800 full-time; nonresident $7680 full-time. Full-time tuition and fees vary according to course load. Part-time tuition and fees vary according to course load. *Required fees:* $319 full-time. *Payment plans:* installment, deferred payment. *Waivers:* senior citizens and employees or children of employees.
Applying *Options:* electronic application, deferred entrance. *Application fee:* $65. *Required:* high school transcript. *Application deadlines:* rolling

(freshmen), rolling (transfers). *Notification:* continuous (freshmen), continuous (transfers).
Freshman Application Contact Dr. Eugenio Barrios, Director of Enrollment Management, Borough of Manhattan Community College of the City University of New York, 199 Chambers Street, Room S-310, New York, NY 10007. *Phone:* 212-220-1265. *Toll-free phone:* 866-583-5729. *Fax:* 212-220-2366. *E-mail:* admissions@bmcc.cuny.edu.
Website: http://www.bmcc.cuny.edu/.

Bramson ORT College
Forest Hills, New York

Freshman Application Contact Admissions Office, Bramson ORT College, 69-30 Austin Street, Forest Hills, NY 11375-4239. *Phone:* 718-261-5800. *Fax:* 718-575-5119. *E-mail:* admissions@bramsonort.edu.
Website: http://www.bramsonort.edu/.

Bronx Community College of the City University of New York
Bronx, New York

- **State and locally supported** 2-year, founded 1959, part of City University of New York System
- **Urban** 50-acre campus with easy access to New York City
- **Endowment** $469,572
- **Coed**

Undergraduates 6,598 full-time, 4,770 part-time. Students come from 119 other countries; 8% are from out of state; 9% transferred in. *Retention:* 65% of full-time freshmen returned.
Faculty *Student/faculty ratio:* 26:1.
Academics *Calendar:* semesters. *Degree:* certificates and associate. *Special study options:* academic remediation for entering students, accelerated degree program, adult/continuing education programs, advanced placement credit, cooperative education, distance learning, double majors, English as a second language, honors programs, independent study, internships, off-campus study, part-time degree program, services for LD students, study abroad, summer session for credit.
Student Life *Campus security:* 24-hour emergency response devices and patrols, late-night transport/escort service, A free shuttle bus service provides evening students with transportation from campus to several subway and bus lines between 5pm-11pm.
Athletics Member NJCAA.
Standardized Tests *Recommended:* SAT or ACT (for admission).
Applying *Options:* early admission. *Application fee:* $65. *Required:* high school transcript, copy of accredited high school diploma or GED scores.
Freshman Application Contact Ms. Patricia A. Ramos, Admissions Officer, Bronx Community College of the City University of New York, 2155 University Avenue, Bronx, NY 10453. *Phone:* 718-289-5888. *E-mail:* admission@bcc.cuny.edu.
Website: http://www.bcc.cuny.edu/.

Broome Community College
Binghamton, New York

Freshman Application Contact Ms. Jenae Norris, Director of Admissions, Broome Community College, PO Box 1017, Upper Front Street, Binghamton, NY 13902. *Phone:* 607-778-5001. *Fax:* 607-778-5394. *E-mail:* admissions@sunybroome.edu.
Website: http://www.sunybroome.edu/.

Bryant & Stratton College–Albany Campus
Albany, New York

Freshman Application Contact Mr. Robert Ferrell, Director of Admissions, Bryant & Stratton College–Albany Campus, 1259 Central Avenue, Albany, NY 12205. *Phone:* 518-437-1802 Ext. 205. *Fax:* 518-437-1048.
Website: http://www.bryantstratton.edu/.

Bryant & Stratton College–Amherst Campus
Clarence, New York

Freshman Application Contact Mr. Brian K. Dioguardi, Director of Admissions, Bryant & Stratton College–Amherst Campus, Audubon Business Center, 40 Hazelwood Drive, Amherst, NY 14228. *Phone:* 716-691-0012. *Fax:* 716-691-0012. *E-mail:* bkdioguardi@bryantstratton.edu.
Website: http://www.bryantstratton.edu/.

Bryant & Stratton College–Buffalo Campus
Buffalo, New York

Freshman Application Contact Mr. Philip J. Struebel, Director of Admissions, Bryant & Stratton College–Buffalo Campus, 465 Main Street, Suite 400, Buffalo, NY 14203. *Phone:* 716-884-9120. *Fax:* 716-884-0091. *E-mail:* pjstruebel@bryantstratton.edu.
Website: http://www.bryantstratton.edu/.

Bryant & Stratton College–Greece Campus
Rochester, New York

Freshman Application Contact Bryant & Stratton College–Greece Campus, 854 Long Pond Road, Rochester, NY 14612. *Phone:* 585-720-0660.
Website: http://www.bryantstratton.edu/.

Bryant & Stratton College–Henrietta Campus
Rochester, New York

Freshman Application Contact Bryant & Stratton College–Henrietta Campus, 1225 Jefferson Road, Rochester, NY 14623-3136. *Phone:* 585-292-5627 Ext. 101.
Website: http://www.bryantstratton.edu/.

Bryant & Stratton College–North Campus
Liverpool, New York

Freshman Application Contact Ms. Heather Macnik, Director of Admissions, Bryant & Stratton College–North Campus, 8687 Carling Road, Liverpool, NY 13090-1315. *Phone:* 315-652-6500.
Website: http://www.bryantstratton.edu/.

Bryant & Stratton College–Southtowns Campus
Orchard Park, New York

Freshman Application Contact Bryant & Stratton College–Southtowns Campus, 200 Redtail Road, Orchard Park, NY 14127. *Phone:* 716-677-9500.
Website: http://www.bryantstratton.edu/.

Bryant & Stratton College–Syracuse Campus
Syracuse, New York

Freshman Application Contact Ms. Dawn Rajkowski, Director of High School Enrollments, Bryant & Stratton College–Syracuse Campus, 953 James Street, Syracuse, NY 13203-2502. *Phone:* 315-472-6603 Ext. 248. *Fax:* 315-474-4383.
Website: http://www.bryantstratton.edu/.

Business Informatics Center, Inc.
Valley Stream, New York

Freshman Application Contact Admissions Office, Business Informatics Center, Inc., 134 South Central Avenue, Valley Stream, NY 11580-5431. *Phone:* 516-561-0050. *Fax:* 516-561-0074. *E-mail:* info@thecollegeforbusiness.com.
Website: http://www.thecollegeforbusiness.com/.

Cayuga County Community College
Auburn, New York

- **State and locally supported** 2-year, founded 1953, part of State University of New York System
- **Small-town** 50-acre campus with easy access to Rochester, Syracuse
- **Endowment** $6.4 million
- **Coed,** 3,269 undergraduate students, 61% full-time, 64% women, 36% men

Undergraduates 2,003 full-time, 1,266 part-time. 5% Black or African American, non-Hispanic/Latino; 4% Hispanic/Latino; 1% Asian, non-Hispanic/Latino; 0.4% American Indian or Alaska Native, non-Hispanic/Latino; 2% Two or more races, non-Hispanic/Latino; 10% Race/ethnicity unknown; 6% transferred in. *Retention:* 42% of full-time freshmen returned.
Freshmen *Admission:* 2,792 applied, 1,925 admitted, 655 enrolled.
Faculty *Total:* 234, 21% full-time. *Student/faculty ratio:* 22:1.
Majors Accounting technology and bookkeeping; art; business administration and management; child-care and support services management; communication and journalism related; communications systems installation and repair technology; computer and information sciences; computer and information sciences and support services related; corrections; criminal justice/police science; drafting and design technology; education (multiple levels); electrical, electronic and communications engineering technology; fine/studio arts; game and interactive media design; general studies; geography; graphic design; health services/allied health/health sciences; humanities; information science/studies; liberal arts and sciences/liberal studies; literature related; mathematics related; mechanical engineering; mechanical engineering/mechanical technology; music related; psychology related; radio, television, and digital communication related; registered nursing/registered nurse; science technologies related; sport and fitness administration/management; telecommunications technology; wine steward/sommelier; writing.
Academics *Calendar:* semesters. *Degree:* certificates and associate. *Special study options:* academic remediation for entering students, accelerated degree program, adult/continuing education programs, advanced placement credit, cooperative education, distance learning, double majors, honors programs, independent study, internships, off-campus study, part-time degree program, services for LD students, study abroad, summer session for credit. *ROTC:* Air Force (c).
Library Norman F. Bourke Memorial Library plus 2 others with 80,830 titles, 4,341 audiovisual materials, an OPAC, a Web page.
Student Life *Housing Options:* coed. Campus housing is provided by a third party. *Activities and Organizations:* drama/theater group, student-run newspaper, radio and television station, choral group, Student Activity Board, Student government, Criminal Justice Club, Tutor Club, Early Childhood Club. *Campus security:* security from 8 am to 9 pm. *Student services:* health clinic.
Athletics Member NJCAA. *Intercollegiate sports:* basketball M/W, bowling M/W, golf M/W, lacrosse M, soccer M/W, softball W, volleyball W. *Intramural sports:* basketball M/W, skiing (downhill) M/W, volleyball M/W.
Standardized Tests *Required for some:* SAT or ACT (for admission).
Costs (2014–15) *Tuition:* state resident $4200 full-time, $168 per credit hour part-time; nonresident $8400 full-time, $336 per credit hour part-time. Full-time tuition and fees vary according to course load. Part-time tuition and fees vary according to course load. *Required fees:* $441 full-time. *Payment plan:* installment. *Waivers:* senior citizens and employees or children of employees.
Financial Aid Of all full-time matriculated undergraduates who enrolled in 2013, 150 Federal Work-Study jobs (averaging $2000). 200 state and other part-time jobs (averaging $1000).
Applying *Options:* electronic application, deferred entrance. *Required:* high school transcript. *Required for some:* interview. *Application deadlines:* rolling (freshmen), rolling (transfers). *Notification:* continuous (freshmen), continuous (transfers).
Freshman Application Contact Cayuga County Community College, 197 Franklin Street, Auburn, NY 13021-3099. *Phone:* 315-255-1743 Ext. 2244. *Toll-free phone:* 866-598-8883.
Website: http://www.cayuga-cc.edu/.

Clinton Community College
Plattsburgh, New York

- **State and locally supported** 2-year, founded 1969, part of State University of New York System
- **Small-town** 100-acre campus
- **Coed,** 1,347 undergraduate students, 72% full-time, 55% women, 45% men

Undergraduates 967 full-time, 380 part-time. Students come from 10 states and territories; 20 other countries; 3% are from out of state, 8% Black or African American, non-Hispanic/Latino; 3% Hispanic/Latino; 3% Asian, non-Hispanic/Latino; 0.1% Native Hawaiian or other Pacific Islander, non-Hispanic/Latino; 0.5% American Indian or Alaska Native, non-Hispanic/Latino; 10% Race/ethnicity unknown; 7% transferred in; 10% live on campus. *Retention:* 56% of full-time freshmen returned.
Freshmen *Admission:* 1,292 applied, 427 admitted, 251 enrolled.
Faculty *Total:* 118, 43% full-time. *Student/faculty ratio:* 15:1.
Majors Accounting; biological and physical sciences; business administration and management; community organization and advocacy; computer/information technology services administration related; consumer merchandising/retailing management; criminal justice/law enforcement administration; criminal justice/police science; electrical, electronic and communications engineering technology; energy management and systems technology; engineering technologies and engineering related; humanities; industrial technology; liberal arts and sciences/liberal studies; physical education teaching and coaching; registered nursing/registered nurse; social sciences.
Academics *Calendar:* semesters. *Degree:* certificates and associate. *Special study options:* academic remediation for entering students, adult/continuing education programs, advanced placement credit, cooperative education, distance learning, English as a second language, external degree program, honors programs, independent study, internships, off-campus study, part-time degree program, services for LD students, student-designed majors, summer session for credit.
Library Clinton Community College Learning Resource Center plus 1 other with 40,665 titles, 1,687 audiovisual materials, an OPAC, a Web page.
Student Life *Housing Options:* coed, special housing for students with disabilities. Campus housing is provided by a third party. Freshman campus housing is guaranteed. *Activities and Organizations:* drama/theater group, student-run newspaper, choral group, Athletics, Future Human Services Professionals, PTK (Honor Society), Drama Club, Criminal Justice Club. *Campus security:* 24-hour emergency response devices and patrols, late-night transport/escort service, controlled dormitory access. *Student services:* health clinic, personal/psychological counseling.
Athletics Member NJCAA. *Intercollegiate sports:* baseball M, basketball M/W, soccer M/W. *Intramural sports:* volleyball M/W.
Costs (2014–15) *Tuition:* state resident $4060 full-time, $169 per hour part-time; nonresident $8800 full-time, $366 per hour part-time. Full-time tuition and fees vary according to course load and program. Part-time tuition and fees vary according to course load and program. *Required fees:* $430 full-time, $26 per hour part-time, $20 per year part-time. *Room and board:* $8490; room only: $4700. Room and board charges vary according to board plan.
Financial Aid Of all full-time matriculated undergraduates who enrolled in 2013, 45 Federal Work-Study jobs (averaging $1260).
Applying *Options:* electronic application, deferred entrance. *Required:* high school transcript. *Required for some:* essay or personal statement, 3 letters of recommendation, interview. *Application deadlines:* 8/26 (freshmen), 9/3 (transfers). *Notification:* continuous (freshmen), continuous (out-of-state freshmen), continuous (transfers).
Freshman Application Contact Clinton Community College, 136 Clinton Point Drive, Plattsburgh, NY 12901-9573. *Phone:* 518-562-4100. *Toll-free phone:* 800-552-1160.
Website: http://clintoncc.suny.edu/.

Cochran School of Nursing
Yonkers, New York

Freshman Application Contact Cochran School of Nursing, 967 North Broadway, Yonkers, NY 10701. *Phone:* 914-964-4606.
Website: http://www.cochranschoolofnursing.us/.

The College of Westchester
White Plains, New York

- **Proprietary** primarily 2-year, founded 1915
- **Suburban** campus with easy access to New York City
- **Coed,** 1,125 undergraduate students, 79% full-time, 64% women, 36% men

Undergraduates 892 full-time, 233 part-time. Students come from 4 states and territories; 4% are from out of state; 35% Black or African American, non-Hispanic/Latino; 43% Hispanic/Latino; 2% Asian, non-Hispanic/Latino; 0.4% American Indian or Alaska Native, non-Hispanic/Latino; 2% Two or more races, non-Hispanic/Latino; 3% Race/ethnicity unknown. *Retention:* 72% of full-time freshmen returned.
Freshmen *Admission:* 741 applied, 588 admitted, 186 enrolled.
Faculty *Total:* 83, 46% full-time. *Student/faculty ratio:* 18:1.
Majors Accounting; business administration and management; computer software and media applications related; health/health-care administration; health information/medical records administration; medical/clinical assistant;

network and system administration; web page, digital/multimedia and information resources design.

Academics *Calendar:* semesters. *Degrees:* certificates, associate, and bachelor's. *Special study options:* academic remediation for entering students, accelerated degree program, adult/continuing education programs, cooperative education, distance learning, double majors, honors programs, internships, part-time degree program, summer session for credit.

Library Dr. William R. Papallo Library plus 1 other.

Student Life *Housing:* college housing not available. *Activities and Organizations:* student-run newspaper. *Student services:* personal/psychological counseling.

Standardized Tests *Recommended:* SAT (for admission).

Applying *Options:* electronic application, deferred entrance. *Application fee:* $40. *Required:* high school transcript, interview. *Required for some:* essay or personal statement. *Application deadlines:* rolling (freshmen), rolling (out-of-state freshmen), rolling (transfers).

Freshman Application Contact Mr. Dale T. Smith, Vice President, The College of Westchester, 325 Central Avenue, PO Box 710, White Plains, NY 10602. *Phone:* 914-948-4442 Ext. 311. *Toll-free phone:* 800-660-7093. *Fax:* 914-948-5441. *E-mail:* admissions@cw.edu.
Website: http://www.cw.edu/.

Columbia-Greene Community College
Hudson, New York

- **State and locally supported** 2-year, founded 1969, part of State University of New York System
- **Rural** 143-acre campus
- **Coed,** 2,043 undergraduate students, 42% full-time, 61% women, 39% men

Undergraduates 851 full-time, 1,192 part-time. Students come from 3 states and territories; 0.1% are from out of state; 7% Black or African American, non-Hispanic/Latino; 7% Hispanic/Latino; 2% Asian, non-Hispanic/Latino; 0.1% Native Hawaiian or other Pacific Islander, non-Hispanic/Latino; 0.2% American Indian or Alaska Native, non-Hispanic/Latino; 3% Two or more races, non-Hispanic/Latino; 0.6% Race/ethnicity unknown; 6% transferred in. *Retention:* 64% of full-time freshmen returned.

Freshmen *Admission:* 345 enrolled.

Faculty *Total:* 172, 28% full-time. *Student/faculty ratio:* 19:1.

Majors Accounting technology and bookkeeping; administrative assistant and secretarial science; art; automobile/automotive mechanics technology; business administration and management; computer and information sciences; criminal justice/law enforcement administration; cyber/computer forensics and counterterrorism; environmental studies; general studies; health and physical education/fitness; humanities; human services; information technology; liberal arts and sciences/liberal studies; medical/clinical assistant; registered nursing/registered nurse.

Academics *Calendar:* semesters. *Degree:* certificates and associate. *Special study options:* academic remediation for entering students, adult/continuing education programs, advanced placement credit, distance learning, double majors, English as a second language, honors programs, independent study, internships, part-time degree program, services for LD students, summer session for credit.

Library CGCC Library with an OPAC, a Web page.

Student Life *Housing:* college housing not available. *Activities and Organizations:* student-run radio station, Criminal Justice Club, Human Services Club, Psychology Club, Student Senate, Animal Avocates. *Campus security:* 24-hour patrols, late-night transport/escort service.

Athletics Member NCAA, NJCAA. All NCAA Division III. *Intercollegiate sports:* baseball M, basketball M, bowling M/W, golf M/W, softball W.

Costs (2014–15) *Tuition:* state resident $4080 full-time, $170 per semester hour part-time; nonresident $8160 full-time, $340 per semester hour part-time. Full-time tuition and fees vary according to course load and program. Part-time tuition and fees vary according to course load and program. *Required fees:* $330 full-time, $14 per semester hour part-time, $5 per term part-time. *Payment plan:* installment. *Waivers:* senior citizens and employees or children of employees.

Applying *Required:* high school transcript. *Required for some:* interview.

Freshman Application Contact Mr. Josh Horn, Director of Admissions, Columbia-Greene Community College, 4400 Route 23, Hudson, NY 12534-0327. *Phone:* 518-828-4181 Ext. 3370. *E-mail:* josh.horn@sunycgcc.edu.
Website: http://www.sunycgcc.edu/.

Corning Community College
Corning, New York

- **State and locally supported** 2-year, founded 1956, part of State University of New York System
- **Rural** 500-acre campus
- **Endowment** $515,617
- **Coed,** 4,520 undergraduate students, 47% full-time, 58% women, 42% men

Undergraduates 2,114 full-time, 2,406 part-time. Students come from 12 states and territories; 14 other countries; 5% are from out of state; 3% Black or African American, non-Hispanic/Latino; 3% Hispanic/Latino; 0.9% Asian, non-Hispanic/Latino; 0.6% American Indian or Alaska Native, non-Hispanic/Latino; 2% Two or more races, non-Hispanic/Latino; 9% Race/ethnicity unknown; 0.1% international; 3% transferred in; 6% live on campus. *Retention:* 57% of full-time freshmen returned.

Freshmen *Admission:* 1,737 applied, 1,732 admitted, 781 enrolled. *Average high school GPA:* 3.25.

Faculty *Total:* 232, 38% full-time. *Student/faculty ratio:* 22:1.

Majors Accounting; art; autobody/collision and repair technology; automobile/automotive mechanics technology; business administration and management; CAD/CADD drafting/design technology; chemical technology; computer and information sciences; computer and information sciences and support services related; computer and information sciences related; computer/information technology services administration related; computer numerically controlled (CNC) machinist technology; computer science; computer support specialist; computer technology/computer systems technology; corrections and criminal justice related; criminal justice/police science; customer service management; digital arts; drafting/design engineering technologies related; early childhood education; education related; education (specific levels and methods) related; electrical and electronic engineering technologies related; electrical and electronics engineering; energy management and systems technology; engineering science; engineering technology; environmental science; fine arts related; fine/studio arts; graphic design; health and physical education/fitness; health and physical education related; health and wellness; health professions related; hospitality administration related; humanities; human services; information technology; liberal arts and sciences and humanities related; liberal arts and sciences/liberal studies; machine tool technology; manufacturing engineering technology; mathematics; mathematics related; mechanical drafting and CAD/CADD; mechanical engineering/mechanical technology; mechanical engineering technologies related; mechanic and repair technologies related; mechanics and repair; network and system administration; office management; office occupations and clerical services; outdoor education; parks, recreation and leisure; parks, recreation, leisure, and fitness studies related; pre-engineering; registered nursing/registered nurse; social sciences; substance abuse/addiction counseling; vehicle maintenance and repair technologies; vehicle maintenance and repair technologies related; web page, digital/multimedia and information resources design.

Academics *Calendar:* semesters. *Degree:* certificates and associate. *Special study options:* academic remediation for entering students, accelerated degree program, adult/continuing education programs, advanced placement credit, cooperative education, distance learning, double majors, English as a second language, honors programs, independent study, internships, off-campus study, part-time degree program, services for LD students, student-designed majors, study abroad, summer session for credit.

Library Arthur A. Houghton, Jr. Library with 46,427 titles, 1,107 audiovisual materials, an OPAC, a Web page.

Student Life *Housing Options:* coed. Campus housing is university owned. *Activities and Organizations:* drama/theater group, student-run newspaper, radio station, choral group, Student Association, EQUAL, Nursing Society, Muse of Fire theatre group, WCEB radio station. *Campus security:* 24-hour emergency response devices and patrols, late-night transport/escort service, controlled dormitory access. *Student services:* health clinic, personal/psychological counseling.

Athletics Member NJCAA. *Intercollegiate sports:* baseball M, basketball M/W, bowling M/W, golf M/W, soccer M/W, softball W, volleyball W. *Intramural sports:* badminton M/W, basketball M/W, soccer M/W, softball W, volleyball M/W.

Costs (2014–15) *Tuition:* state resident $4150 full-time, $173 per credit hour part-time; nonresident $8300 full-time, $346 per credit hour part-time. Part-time tuition and fees vary according to course load. *Required fees:* $538 full-time, $9 per credit hour part-time. *Room and board:* $8500; room only: $6200. Room and board charges vary according to housing facility. *Payment plan:* installment. *Waivers:* senior citizens and employees or children of employees.

Financial Aid Of all full-time matriculated undergraduates who enrolled in 2013, 264 Federal Work-Study jobs (averaging $1128).

Applying *Options:* electronic application, early admission. *Required:* high school transcript. *Required for some:* interview. *Application deadlines:*

rolling (freshmen), rolling (transfers). *Notification:* continuous (freshmen), continuous (transfers).

Freshman Application Contact Corning Community College, One Academic Drive, Corning, NY 14830-3297. *Phone:* 607-962-9427. *Toll-free phone:* 800-358-7171.

Website: http://www.corning-cc.edu/.

Dutchess Community College
Poughkeepsie, New York

- **State and locally supported** 2-year, founded 1957, part of State University of New York System
- **Suburban** 130-acre campus with easy access to New York City
- **Coed,** 9,905 undergraduate students, 47% full-time, 54% women, 46% men

Undergraduates 4,666 full-time, 5,239 part-time. 11% Black or African American, non-Hispanic/Latino; 17% Hispanic/Latino; 3% Asian, non-Hispanic/Latino; 0.1% Native Hawaiian or other Pacific Islander, non-Hispanic/Latino; 0.2% American Indian or Alaska Native, non-Hispanic/Latino; 3% Two or more races, non-Hispanic/Latino; 1% Race/ethnicity unknown; 1% international; 4% transferred in; 5% live on campus.

Freshmen *Admission:* 2,008 enrolled. *Average high school GPA:* 2.5.

Faculty *Total:* 551, 23% full-time, 6% with terminal degrees. *Student/faculty ratio:* 25:1.

Majors Accounting; accounting technology and bookkeeping; airline pilot and flight crew; architectural engineering technology; art; aviation/airway management; business administration and management; child-care and support services management; clinical/medical laboratory technology; commercial and advertising art; communications systems installation and repair technology; community health services counseling; computer/information technology services administration related; computer science; construction trades related; criminal justice/police science; electrical, electronic and communications engineering technology; emergency medical technology (EMT paramedic); engineering; fire services administration; general studies; humanities; human services; information science/studies; legal assistant/paralegal; liberal arts and sciences and humanities related; liberal arts and sciences/liberal studies; physical education teaching and coaching; registered nursing/registered nurse; speech communication and rhetoric; visual and performing arts.

Academics *Calendar:* semesters. *Degree:* certificates and associate. *Special study options:* academic remediation for entering students, adult/continuing education programs, advanced placement credit, distance learning, English as a second language, freshman honors college, honors programs, internships, off-campus study, part-time degree program, services for LD students, summer session for credit.

Library Dutchess Library plus 1 other with 197,933 titles, 2,588 audiovisual materials, an OPAC, a Web page.

Student Life *Housing Options:* coed. Campus housing is university owned. *Activities and Organizations:* drama/theater group, student-run newspaper, radio station, choral group, Rap, Poetry & Music, Outdoor Adventure, Gamers Guild, Masquers Guild, Christian Fellowship. *Campus security:* 24-hour emergency response devices and patrols, late-night transport/escort service. *Student services:* health clinic, personal/psychological counseling.

Athletics Member NJCAA. *Intercollegiate sports:* baseball M, basketball M/W, cross-country running M/W, soccer M, softball W, volleyball W.

Costs (2014–15) *Tuition:* state resident $3200 full-time, $133 per credit hour part-time; nonresident $6400 full-time, $266 per credit hour part-time. *Required fees:* $435 full-time, $10 per hour part-time, $19 per term part-time. *Room and board:* $9620. Room and board charges vary according to board plan. *Payment plan:* installment. *Waivers:* senior citizens and employees or children of employees.

Applying *Options:* electronic application, early admission, deferred entrance. *Required:* high school transcript. *Application deadlines:* rolling (freshmen), rolling (transfers). *Notification:* continuous (freshmen), continuous (transfers).

Freshman Application Contact Dutchess Community College, 53 Pendell Road, Poughkeepsie, NY 12601-1595. *Phone:* 845-431-8010.

Website: http://www.sunydutchess.edu/.

Elmira Business Institute
Elmira, New York

- **Private** 2-year, founded 1858
- **Urban** campus
- **Coed, primarily women**

Undergraduates 74 full-time, 24 part-time.

Faculty *Student/faculty ratio:* 9:1.

Academics *Calendar:* semesters. *Degree:* certificates and associate. *Special study options:* academic remediation for entering students, advanced placement credit, internships, part-time degree program.

Student Life *Campus security:* 24-hour emergency response devices.

Costs (2014–15) *Tuition:* $12,000 full-time, $400 per credit part-time. Full-time tuition and fees vary according to program. Part-time tuition and fees vary according to program. No tuition increase for student's term of enrollment. *Required fees:* $700 full-time.

Financial Aid Of all full-time matriculated undergraduates who enrolled in 2011, 316 applied for aid, 306 were judged to have need. *Average percent of need met:* 85. *Average financial aid package:* $30,450. *Average need-based loan:* $3500. *Average need-based gift aid:* $18,950. *Average indebtedness upon graduation:* $14,000.

Applying *Options:* electronic application. *Required:* high school transcript, interview. *Required for some:* essay or personal statement.

Freshman Application Contact Ms. Lindsay Dull, Director of Student services, Elmira Business Institute, Elmira, NY 14901. *Phone:* 607-733-7177. *Toll-free phone:* 800-843-1812. *E-mail:* info@ebi-college.com. *Website:* http://www.ebi-college.com/.

Erie Community College
Buffalo, New York

- **State and locally supported** 2-year, founded 1971, part of State University of New York System
- **Urban** 1-acre campus
- **Coed,** 2,880 undergraduate students, 76% full-time, 60% women, 40% men

Undergraduates 2,195 full-time, 685 part-time. Students come from 10 states and territories; 12 other countries; 0.6% are from out of state; 33% Black or African American, non-Hispanic/Latino; 10% Hispanic/Latino; 2% Asian, non-Hispanic/Latino; 0.2% Native Hawaiian or other Pacific Islander, non-Hispanic/Latino; 0.6% American Indian or Alaska Native, non-Hispanic/Latino; 5% Two or more races, non-Hispanic/Latino; 3% Race/ethnicity unknown; 7% international; 5% transferred in.

Freshmen *Admission:* 2,708 applied, 1,861 admitted, 668 enrolled.

Faculty *Student/faculty ratio:* 21:1.

Majors Building/property maintenance; business administration and management; child-care and support services management; criminal justice/law enforcement administration; crisis/emergency/disaster management; culinary arts; general studies; health and physical education/fitness; health and wellness; humanities; legal assistant/paralegal; liberal arts and sciences and humanities related; liberal arts and sciences/liberal studies; medical radiologic technology; registered nursing/registered nurse; substance abuse/addiction counseling.

Academics *Calendar:* semesters plus summer sessions, winter intersession. *Degree:* certificates, diplomas, and associate. *Special study options:* academic remediation for entering students, adult/continuing education programs, advanced placement credit, cooperative education, distance learning, double majors, English as a second language, honors programs, independent study, internships, part-time degree program, services for LD students, student-designed majors, study abroad, summer session for credit. *ROTC:* Army (c).

Library Leon E. Butler Library with 23,840 titles, 1,810 audiovisual materials, an OPAC, a Web page.

Student Life *Housing:* college housing not available. *Activities and Organizations:* HPER, Celestial, Campus Ministry. *Campus security:* 24-hour emergency response devices and patrols, late-night transport/escort service. *Student services:* health clinic, personal/psychological counseling, women's center.

Athletics Member NJCAA. *Intercollegiate sports:* baseball M, basketball M/W, bowling M/W, cheerleading W, football M, ice hockey M, lacrosse W, soccer M/W, softball W, volleyball W.

Costs (2014–15) *One-time required fee:* $75. *Tuition:* area resident $4295 full-time, $179 per credit hour part-time; state resident $8590 full-time, $358 per credit hour part-time; nonresident $8590 full-time, $358 per credit hour part-time. *Required fees:* $593 full-time, $15 per credit hour part-time, $70 per term part-time. *Payment plan:* installment. *Waivers:* senior citizens and employees or children of employees.

Applying *Options:* electronic application. *Application fee:* $25. *Required:* high school transcript. *Required for some:* interview. *Application deadlines:* rolling (freshmen), rolling (transfers). *Notification:* continuous (freshmen), continuous (transfers).

Freshman Application Contact Erie Community College, 121 Ellicott Street, Buffalo, NY 14203-2698. *Phone:* 716-851-1155. *Fax:* 716-270-2821. *E-mail:* admissions@ecc.edu. *Website:* http://www.ecc.edu/.

Erie Community College, North Campus
Williamsville, New York

- **State and locally supported** 2-year, founded 1946, part of State University of New York System
- **Suburban** 120-acre campus with easy access to Buffalo
- **Coed,** 5,855 undergraduate students, 66% full-time, 49% women, 51% men

Undergraduates 3,877 full-time, 1,978 part-time. Students come from 17 states and territories; 27 other countries; 0.5% are from out of state; 12% Black or African American, non-Hispanic/Latino; 5% Hispanic/Latino; 3% Asian, non-Hispanic/Latino; 0.1% Native Hawaiian or other Pacific Islander, non-Hispanic/Latino; 0.6% American Indian or Alaska Native, non-Hispanic/Latino; 3% Two or more races, non-Hispanic/Latino; 3% Race/ethnicity unknown; 5% international; 8% transferred in.
Freshmen *Admission:* 4,434 applied, 3,273 admitted, 1,221 enrolled. *Test scores:* SAT critical reading scores over 500: 82%; SAT math scores over 500: 87%; SAT critical reading scores over 600: 14%; SAT math scores over 600: 22%; SAT critical reading scores over 700: 2%; SAT math scores over 700: 1%.
Faculty *Student/faculty ratio:* 21:1.
Majors Biology/biotechnology laboratory technician; building/construction site management; business administration and management; civil engineering technology; clinical/medical laboratory technology; computer and information sciences; criminal justice/law enforcement administration; criminal justice/police science; culinary arts; dental hygiene; dietitian assistant; electrical, electronic and communications engineering technology; engineering; environmental engineering technology; environmental science; general studies; health and physical education/fitness; health and wellness; health information/medical records technology; humanities; industrial technology; information technology; liberal arts and sciences/liberal studies; mechanical engineering/mechanical technology; medical administrative assistant and medical secretary; nanotechnology; occupational therapist assistant; office management; opticianry; registered nursing/registered nurse; respiratory care therapy; restaurant/food services management.
Academics *Calendar:* semesters plus summer sessions, winter intersession. *Degree:* certificates, diplomas, and associate. *Special study options:* academic remediation for entering students, adult/continuing education programs, advanced placement credit, cooperative education, distance learning, double majors, English as a second language, honors programs, independent study, internships, part-time degree program, services for LD students, student-designed majors, study abroad, summer session for credit. *ROTC:* Army (c).
Library Richard R. Dry Memorial Library with 51,056 titles, 3,972 audiovisual materials, an OPAC, a Web page.
Student Life *Housing:* college housing not available. *Activities and Organizations:* Dental, American Public Works Association, Student Occupational Therapy Association. *Campus security:* 24-hour emergency response devices and patrols, late-night transport/escort service. *Student services:* health clinic, personal/psychological counseling, women's center.
Athletics Member NJCAA. *Intercollegiate sports:* baseball M, basketball M/W, bowling M/W, cheerleading W, football M, ice hockey M, lacrosse W, soccer M/W, softball W, volleyball W.
Costs (2014–15) *One-time required fee:* $75. *Tuition:* area resident $4295 full-time, $179 per credit hour part-time; state resident $8590 full-time, $358 per credit hour part-time; nonresident $8590 full-time, $358 per credit hour part-time. *Required fees:* $593 full-time, $15 per credit hour part-time, $70 per term part-time. *Payment plan:* installment. *Waivers:* senior citizens and employees or children of employees.
Applying *Options:* electronic application. *Application fee:* $25. *Required:* high school transcript. *Required for some:* interview. *Application deadlines:* rolling (freshmen), rolling (transfers). *Notification:* continuous (freshmen), continuous (transfers).
Freshman Application Contact Erie Community College, North Campus, 6205 Main Street, Williamsville, NY 14221-7095. *Phone:* 716-851-1455. *Fax:* 716-270-2961. *E-mail:* admissions@ecc.edu. *Website:* http://www.ecc.edu/.

Erie Community College, South Campus
Orchard Park, New York

- **State and locally supported** 2-year, founded 1974, part of State University of New York System
- **Suburban** 110-acre campus with easy access to Buffalo
- **Coed,** 3,935 undergraduate students, 59% full-time, 45% women, 55% men

Undergraduates 2,330 full-time, 1,605 part-time. Students come from 19 states and territories; 10 other countries; 1% are from out of state; 7% Black or African American, non-Hispanic/Latino; 5% Hispanic/Latino; 1% Asian, non-Hispanic/Latino; 1% American Indian or Alaska Native, non-Hispanic/Latino;

3% Two or more races, non-Hispanic/Latino; 4% Race/ethnicity unknown; 1% international; 5% transferred in.
Freshmen *Admission:* 2,372 applied, 1,966 admitted, 769 enrolled. *Test scores:* SAT critical reading scores over 500: 97%; SAT critical reading scores over 600: 13%; SAT critical reading scores over 700: 2%.
Faculty *Student/faculty ratio:* 21:1.
Majors Architectural engineering technology; autobody/collision and repair technology; automobile/automotive mechanics technology; business administration and management; CAD/CADD drafting/design technology; communications systems installation and repair technology; computer technology/computer systems technology; criminal justice/law enforcement administration; dental laboratory technology; emergency medical technology (EMT paramedic); fire services administration; general studies; graphic and printing equipment operation/production; health and physical education/fitness; health and wellness; humanities; information technology; liberal arts and sciences/liberal studies; office management; speech communication and rhetoric; telecommunications technology.
Academics *Calendar:* semesters plus summer sessions, winter intersession. *Degree:* certificates, diplomas, and associate. *Special study options:* academic remediation for entering students, adult/continuing education programs, advanced placement credit, cooperative education, distance learning, double majors, English as a second language, honors programs, independent study, internships, part-time degree program, services for LD students, student-designed majors, study abroad, summer session for credit. *ROTC:* Army (c).
Library 37,459 titles, 1,518 audiovisual materials, an OPAC, a Web page.
Student Life *Housing:* college housing not available. *Activities and Organizations:* HPER, Criminal Justice, Architecture. *Campus security:* 24-hour emergency response devices and patrols, late-night transport/escort service. *Student services:* health clinic, personal/psychological counseling, women's center.
Athletics Member NJCAA. *Intercollegiate sports:* baseball M, basketball M/W, bowling M/W, cheerleading W, football M, ice hockey M, lacrosse W, soccer M/W, softball W, volleyball W.
Costs (2014–15) *One-time required fee:* $75. *Tuition:* area resident $4295 full-time, $179 per credit hour part-time; state resident $8590 full-time, $358 per credit hour part-time; nonresident $8590 full-time, $358 per credit hour part-time. *Required fees:* $593 full-time, $15 per credit hour part-time, $70 per term part-time. *Payment plan:* installment. *Waivers:* senior citizens and employees or children of employees.
Applying *Options:* electronic application. *Application fee:* $25. *Required:* high school transcript. *Required for some:* interview. *Application deadlines:* rolling (freshmen), rolling (transfers). *Notification:* continuous (freshmen), continuous (transfers).
Freshman Application Contact Erie Community College, South Campus, 4041 Southwestern Boulevard, Orchard Park, NY 14127-2199. *Phone:* 716-851-1655. *Fax:* 716-851-1687. *E-mail:* admissions@ecc.edu. *Website:* http://www.ecc.edu/.

Eugenio María de Hostos Community College of the City University of New York
Bronx, New York

Freshman Application Contact Mr. Roland Velez, Director of Admissions, Eugenio María de Hostos Community College of the City University of New York, 120 149th Street, Bronx, NY 10451. *Phone:* 718-319-7968. *Fax:* 718-319-7919. *E-mail:* admissions@hostos.cuny.edu. *Website:* http://www.hostos.cuny.edu/.

Fashion Institute of Technology
New York, New York

- **State and locally supported** comprehensive, founded 1944, part of State University of New York System
- **Urban** 5-acre campus with easy access to New York City
- **Coed, primarily women,** 9,567 undergraduate students, 78% full-time, 85% women, 15% men

Undergraduates 7,454 full-time, 2,113 part-time. 32% are from out of state; 9% Black or African American, non-Hispanic/Latino; 17% Hispanic/Latino; 9% Asian, non-Hispanic/Latino; 0.3% Native Hawaiian or other Pacific Islander, non-Hispanic/Latino; 0.1% American Indian or Alaska Native, non-Hispanic/Latino; 4% Two or more races, non-Hispanic/Latino; 0.4% Race/ethnicity unknown; 14% international; 10% transferred in; 22% live on campus. *Retention:* 89% of full-time freshmen returned.
Freshmen *Admission:* 4,729 applied, 2,094 admitted, 1,322 enrolled. *Average high school GPA:* 3.6.
Faculty *Total:* 944, 25% full-time. *Student/faculty ratio:* 17:1.

Majors Advertising; animation, interactive technology, video graphics and special effects; apparel and textile manufacturing; cinematography and film/video production; commercial and advertising art; commercial photography; design and applied arts related; entrepreneurial and small business related; fashion/apparel design; fashion merchandising; fashion modeling; film/cinema/video studies; fine and studio arts management; fine/studio arts; graphic design; illustration; industrial and product design; interior design; international marketing; marketing research; merchandising, sales, and marketing operations related (specialized); metal and jewelry arts; special products marketing.

Academics *Calendar:* semesters. *Degrees:* certificates, associate, bachelor's, and master's. *Special study options:* academic remediation for entering students, adult/continuing education programs, advanced placement credit, distance learning, English as a second language, honors programs, independent study, internships, part-time degree program, services for LD students, study abroad, summer session for credit.

Library Gladys Marcus Library.

Student Life *Housing Options:* coed, women-only, special housing for students with disabilities. Campus housing is university owned. Freshman applicants given priority for college housing. *Activities and Organizations:* drama/theater group, student-run newspaper, radio and television station, choral group. *Campus security:* 24-hour emergency response devices and patrols, late-night transport/escort service, controlled dormitory access. *Student services:* health clinic, personal/psychological counseling.

Athletics Member NJCAA. *Intercollegiate sports:* cross-country running M/W, soccer W, swimming and diving M/W, table tennis M/W, tennis W, track and field M/W, volleyball W. *Intramural sports:* archery M(c)/W(c).

Standardized Tests *Recommended:* SAT or ACT (for admission).

Costs (2014–15) *Tuition:* state resident $4500 full-time, $257 per credit hour part-time; nonresident $13,500 full-time, $742 per credit hour part-time. Full-time tuition and fees vary according to degree level. Part-time tuition and fees vary according to degree level. *Required fees:* $700 full-time. *Room and board:* $13,162. Room and board charges vary according to board plan and housing facility. *Payment plan:* installment. *Waivers:* senior citizens and employees or children of employees.

Financial Aid Of all full-time matriculated undergraduates who enrolled in 2013, 4,713 applied for aid, 3,789 were judged to have need, 1,339 had their need fully met. In 2013, 99 non-need-based awards were made. *Average percent of need met:* 72%. *Average financial aid package:* $11,882. *Average need-based loan:* $3500. *Average need-based gift aid:* $5751. *Average non-need-based aid:* $955. *Average indebtedness upon graduation:* $27,303.

Applying *Options:* electronic application. *Application fee:* $50. *Required:* essay or personal statement, high school transcript. *Required for some:* portfolio for art and design programs. *Application deadlines:* 1/1 (freshmen), 1/1 (transfers). *Notification:* 4/1 (freshmen), 4/1 (transfers).

Freshman Application Contact Ms. Laura Arbogast, Director of Admissions and Strategic Recruitment, Fashion Institute of Technology, Seventh Avenue at 27th Street, New York, NY 10001-5992. *E-mail:* fitinfo@fitnyc.edu. *Website:* http://www.fitnyc.edu/.

See display below and page 368 for the College Close-Up.

Finger Lakes Community College
Canandaigua, New York

- **State and locally supported** 2-year, founded 1965, part of State University of New York System
- **Small-town** 300-acre campus with easy access to Rochester
- **Coed,** 6,800 undergraduate students, 49% full-time, 57% women, 43% men

Undergraduates 3,317 full-time, 3,483 part-time. Students come from 13 states and territories; 2 other countries; 0.4% are from out of state; 8% Black or African American, non-Hispanic/Latino; 5% Hispanic/Latino; 0.4% Asian, non-Hispanic/Latino; 0.1% Native Hawaiian or other Pacific Islander, non-Hispanic/Latino; 0.5% American Indian or Alaska Native, non-Hispanic/Latino; 3% Two or more races, non-Hispanic/Latino; 7% Race/ethnicity unknown; 0.2% international; 4% transferred in.

Freshmen *Admission:* 4,369 admitted, 1,354 enrolled.

Faculty *Total:* 378, 31% full-time. *Student/faculty ratio:* 22:1.

Majors Accounting; administrative assistant and secretarial science; animation, interactive technology, video graphics and special effects; architectural engineering technology; biological and physical sciences; biology/biological sciences; biology/biotechnology laboratory technician; business administration and management; chemistry; commercial and advertising art; computer and information sciences; computer science; criminal justice/law enforcement administration; criminal justice/police science; culinary arts; data processing and data processing technology; digital communication and media/multimedia; drafting and design technology; dramatic/theater arts; early childhood education; e-commerce; emergency medical technology (EMT paramedic); engineering science; environmental studies; fine/studio arts; fishing and fisheries sciences and management; hotel/motel administration; humanities; human services; instrumentation technology; kindergarten/preschool education; legal assistant/paralegal; liberal

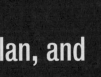

arts and sciences/liberal studies; marketing/marketing management; mass communication/media; mathematics; mechanical engineering/mechanical technology; music; natural resources/conservation; natural resources law enforcement and protective services; natural resources management and policy; natural resources management and policy related; ornamental horticulture; physical education teaching and coaching; physics; political science and government; pre-engineering; psychology; recording arts technology; registered nursing/registered nurse; resort management; social sciences; sociology; sports studies; substance abuse/addiction counseling; tourism and travel services management; viticulture and enology.

Academics *Calendar:* semesters. *Degree:* certificates and associate. *Special study options:* academic remediation for entering students, accelerated degree program, advanced placement credit, distance learning, honors programs, internships, off-campus study, part-time degree program, services for LD students, study abroad, summer session for credit. *ROTC:* Air Force (c).

Library Charles Meder Library with 75,610 titles, an OPAC.

Student Life *Housing Options:* Campus housing is provided by a third party. *Activities and Organizations:* drama/theater group, student-run radio station, choral group. *Campus security:* 24-hour emergency response devices and patrols, late-night transport/escort service. *Student services:* health clinic, personal/psychological counseling, legal services.

Athletics Member NJCAA. *Intercollegiate sports:* baseball M, basketball M/W, cross-country running M/W, lacrosse M, soccer M/W, softball W, track and field M/W, volleyball W. *Intramural sports:* basketball M/W, tennis M/W, volleyball M/W.

Costs (2014–15) *Tuition:* state resident $4022 full-time, $153 per credit hour part-time; nonresident $8044 full-time, $306 per credit hour part-time. Full-time tuition and fees vary according to course load. Part-time tuition and fees vary according to course load. *Required fees:* $360 full-time, $14 per credit hour part-time. *Payment plan:* installment. *Waivers:* senior citizens and employees or children of employees.

Financial Aid Of all full-time matriculated undergraduates who enrolled in 2011, 200 Federal Work-Study jobs (averaging $2200). 100 state and other part-time jobs (averaging $2200).

Applying *Options:* electronic application, early admission, deferred entrance. *Application fee:* $20. *Required:* high school transcript. *Application deadlines:* 8/22 (freshmen), 8/22 (transfers).

Freshman Application Contact Ms. Bonnie B. Ritts, Director of Admissions, Finger Lakes Community College, 3325 Marvin Sands Drive, Canandaigua, NY 14424-8395. *Phone:* 585-785-1279. *Fax:* 585-785-1734. *E-mail:* admissions@flcc.edu.
Website: http://www.flcc.edu/.

Fiorello H. LaGuardia Community College of the City University of New York

Long Island City, New York

- **State and locally supported** 2-year, founded 1970, part of City University of New York System
- **Urban** 10-acre campus with easy access to New York City
- **Coed,** 20,153 undergraduate students, 55% full-time, 57% women, 43% men

Undergraduates 11,054 full-time, 9,099 part-time. Students come from 14 states and territories; 157 other countries; 0.2% are from out of state; 19% Black or African American, non-Hispanic/Latino; 36% Hispanic/Latino; 16% Asian, non-Hispanic/Latino; 0.2% American Indian or Alaska Native, non-Hispanic/Latino; 0.7% Two or more races, non-Hispanic/Latino; 12% Race/ethnicity unknown; 4% international; 8% transferred in.

Freshmen *Admission:* 21,488 applied, 20,015 admitted, 3,106 enrolled.

Faculty *Total:* 1,246, 28% full-time, 26% with terminal degrees. *Student/faculty ratio:* 21:1.

Majors Accounting technology and bookkeeping; administrative assistant and secretarial science; adult development and aging; biology/biological sciences; business administration and management; civil engineering; commercial photography; computer and information sciences and support services related; computer installation and repair technology; computer programming; computer science; computer systems networking and telecommunications; criminal justice/safety; data entry/microcomputer applications; dietetic technology; digital arts; dramatic/theater arts; electrical and electronics engineering; emergency medical technology (EMT paramedic); English; environmental science; fine/studio arts; funeral service and mortuary science; industrial and product design; legal assistant/paralegal; liberal arts and sciences/liberal studies; licensed practical/vocational nurse training; mechanical engineering; medical radiologic technology; occupational therapist assistant; philosophy; physical therapy technology; psychiatric/mental health services technology; psychology; recording arts technology; registered nursing/registered nurse; restaurant/food services management; Spanish;

speech communication and rhetoric; teacher assistant/aide; tourism and travel services management; veterinary/animal health technology; visual and performing arts.

Academics *Calendar:* enhanced semester. *Degree:* certificates and associate. *Special study options:* academic remediation for entering students, accelerated degree program, adult/continuing education programs, advanced placement credit, cooperative education, distance learning, double majors, English as a second language, honors programs, independent study, internships, off-campus study, part-time degree program, services for LD students, student-designed majors, study abroad, summer session for credit.

Library Fiorello H. LaGuardia Community College Library Media Resources Center plus 1 other with 384,946 titles, 3,630 audiovisual materials, an OPAC, a Web page.

Student Life *Housing:* college housing not available. *Activities and Organizations:* drama/theater group, student-run newspaper, radio station, Bangladesh Student Association, Christian Club, Chinese Club, Web Radio, Black Student Union. *Campus security:* 24-hour emergency response devices and patrols, late-night transport/escort service. *Student services:* health clinic, personal/psychological counseling, women's center, legal services.

Athletics *Intercollegiate sports:* basketball M/W. *Intramural sports:* basketball M/W, bowling M/W, cheerleading M/W, soccer M/W, swimming and diving M/W, table tennis M/W, volleyball M/W.

Costs (2014–15) *Tuition:* state resident $4500 full-time, $195 per credit part-time; nonresident $9000 full-time, $300 per credit part-time. *Required fees:* $366 full-time, $92 per term part-time. *Payment plan:* installment. *Waivers:* senior citizens and employees or children of employees.

Financial Aid Of all full-time matriculated undergraduates who enrolled in 2012, 7,961 applied for aid, 7,741 were judged to have need, 286 had their need fully met. 352 Federal Work-Study jobs (averaging $1175). *Average percent of need met:* 45%. *Average financial aid package:* $5523. *Average need-based gift aid:* $5818.

Applying *Options:* electronic application, early admission, deferred entrance. *Application fee:* $65. *Required:* high school transcript. *Application deadlines:* rolling (freshmen), rolling (transfers). *Notification:* continuous (freshmen), continuous (transfers).

Freshman Application Contact Ms. LaVora Desvigne, Director of Admissions, Fiorello H. LaGuardia Community College of the City University of New York, RM-147, 31-10 Thomson Avenue, Long Island City, NY 11101. *Phone:* 718-482-5114. *Fax:* 718-482-5112. *E-mail:* admissions@lagcc.cuny.edu.
Website: http://www.lagcc.cuny.edu/.

Fulton-Montgomery Community College

Johnstown, New York

Freshman Application Contact Fulton-Montgomery Community College, 2805 State Highway 67, Johnstown, NY 12095-3790. *Phone:* 518-762-4651 Ext. 8301.
Website: http://www.fmcc.suny.edu/.

Genesee Community College

Batavia, New York

- **State and locally supported** 2-year, founded 1966, part of State University of New York System
- **Small-town** 256-acre campus with easy access to Buffalo, Rochester
- **Endowment** $3.9 million
- **Coed,** 6,883 undergraduate students, 46% full-time, 63% women, 37% men

Undergraduates 3,178 full-time, 3,705 part-time. Students come from 27 states and territories; 15 other countries; 2% are from out of state; 9% Black or African American, non-Hispanic/Latino; 5% Hispanic/Latino; 0.5% Asian, non-Hispanic/Latino; 1% American Indian or Alaska Native, non-Hispanic/Latino; 2% Two or more races, non-Hispanic/Latino; 4% Race/ethnicity unknown; 3% international; 6% transferred in; 5% live on campus.

Freshmen *Admission:* 3,462 applied, 2,674 admitted, 1,159 enrolled.

Faculty *Total:* 348, 23% full-time, 6% with terminal degrees. *Student/faculty ratio:* 18:1.

Majors Accounting; administrative assistant and secretarial science; biology/biological sciences; biology/biotechnology laboratory technician; biotechnology; business administration and management; business administration, management and operations related; business, management, and marketing related; business operations support and secretarial services related; chemistry; civil drafting and CAD/CADD; clinical/medical laboratory technology; computer and information sciences related; computer graphics; computer installation and repair technology; computer programming related; computer science; computer software and media applications related; computer support specialist; computer systems networking and

telecommunications; corrections and criminal justice related; criminal justice/law enforcement administration; criminal justice/police science; criminal justice/safety; criminology; digital arts; drafting and design technology; drafting/design engineering technologies related; dramatic/theater arts; dramatic/theater arts and stagecraft related; e-commerce; education; education (multiple levels); education related; elementary education; engineering; engineering science; entrepreneurship; fashion/apparel design; fashion merchandising; fine/studio arts; food technology and processing; foreign languages related; general studies; gerontology; graphic design; health and physical education/fitness; health and physical education related; health professions related; hospitality administration; hotel/motel administration; humanities; human services; information science/studies; kindergarten/preschool education; legal assistant/paralegal; liberal arts and sciences and humanities related; liberal arts and sciences/liberal studies; marketing/marketing management; mass communication/media; mathematics; mathematics related; medical administrative assistant and medical secretary; network and system administration; nursing practice; parks, recreation, leisure, and fitness studies related; physical education teaching and coaching; physical therapy; physical therapy technology; polysomnography; psychology; psychology related; radio and television; radio and television broadcasting technology; radio, television, and digital communication related; registered nursing, nursing administration, nursing research and clinical nursing related; registered nursing/registered nurse; respiratory care therapy; social sciences; social sciences related; social work; social work related; sports studies; substance abuse/addiction counseling; teacher assistant/aide; theater design and technology; theater/theater arts management; tourism and travel services management; tourism promotion; veterinary/animal health technology; web page, digital/multimedia and information resources design.
Academics *Calendar:* semesters. *Degree:* certificates and associate. *Special study options:* academic remediation for entering students, adult/continuing education programs, advanced placement credit, cooperative education, distance learning, double majors, English as a second language, honors programs, independent study, internships, part-time degree program, services for LD students, study abroad, summer session for credit. *ROTC:* Army (c).
Library Alfred C. OConnell Library with 133,065 titles, 6,912 audiovisual materials, an OPAC, a Web page.
Student Life *Housing Options:* special housing for students with disabilities. Campus housing is university owned. *Activities and Organizations:* drama/theater group, student-run newspaper, radio station, choral group, Cougarettes Dance Team, Honor Society, Multi Cultural Communications Club, Christian Students United, Theater Group. *Campus security:* 24-hour emergency response devices and patrols, student patrols, late-night transport/escort service, controlled dormitory access. *Student services:* health clinic, personal/psychological counseling.
Athletics Member NJCAA. *Intercollegiate sports:* baseball M(s), basketball M(s)/W(s), cheerleading M/W, golf M/W, lacrosse M(s)/W, soccer M/W, softball W, swimming and diving M/W, volleyball W(s). *Intramural sports:* badminton M/W, basketball M/W, soccer M/W, tennis M/W, track and field M/W, volleyball M/W, water polo M/W.
Standardized Tests *Recommended:* ACT (for admission).
Costs (2014–15) *Tuition:* state resident $3850 full-time, $155 per credit hour part-time; nonresident $4450 full-time, $175 per credit hour part-time. Full-time tuition and fees vary according to course load. Part-time tuition and fees vary according to course load. *Required fees:* $466 full-time, $2 per credit hour part-time, $42 per term part-time. *Room and board:* $8349; room only: $6100. Room and board charges vary according to board plan and housing facility. *Payment plan:* installment. *Waivers:* senior citizens and employees or children of employees.
Financial Aid Of all full-time matriculated undergraduates who enrolled in 2013, 2,875 applied for aid, 2,599 were judged to have need, 1,033 had their need fully met. 167 Federal Work-Study jobs (averaging $868). 93 state and other part-time jobs (averaging $1519). *Average percent of need met:* 82%. *Average financial aid package:* $4685. *Average need-based loan:* $3556. *Average need-based gift aid:* $3145. *Average indebtedness upon graduation:* $8995.
Applying *Options:* electronic application. *Required:* high school transcript. *Required for some:* 1 letter of recommendation. *Application deadlines:* rolling (freshmen), rolling (out-of-state freshmen), rolling (transfers). *Notification:* continuous (freshmen), continuous (out-of-state freshmen), continuous (transfers).
Freshman Application Contact Mrs. Tanya Lane-Martin, Director of Admissions, Genesee Community College, Batavia, NY 14020. *Phone:* 585-343-0055 Ext. 6413. *Toll-free phone:* 866-CALL GCC. *Fax:* 585-345-6892. *E-mail:* tmlanemartin@genesee.edu.
Website: http://www.genesee.edu/.

Helene Fuld College of Nursing of North General Hospital
New York, New York

Freshman Application Contact Helene Fuld College of Nursing of North General Hospital, 24 East 120th Street, New York, NY 10035. *Phone:* 212-616-7271.
Website: http://www.helenefuld.edu/.

Herkimer County Community College
Herkimer, New York

- **State and locally supported** 2-year, founded 1966, part of State University of New York System
- **Small-town** 500-acre campus with easy access to Syracuse
- **Endowment** $2.8 million
- **Coed**

Undergraduates 2,089 full-time, 1,134 part-time. Students come from 13 other countries; 3% are from out of state; 12% Black or African American, non-Hispanic/Latino; 5% Hispanic/Latino; 0.7% Asian, non-Hispanic/Latino; 0.7% American Indian or Alaska Native, non-Hispanic/Latino; 1% Two or more races, non-Hispanic/Latino; 11% Race/ethnicity unknown; 3% international; 6% transferred in; 19% live on campus.
Faculty *Student/faculty ratio:* 19:1.
Academics *Calendar:* semesters. *Degree:* certificates and associate. *Special study options:* academic remediation for entering students, adult/continuing education programs, advanced placement credit, distance learning, English as a second language, honors programs, independent study, internships, part-time degree program, services for LD students, summer session for credit. *ROTC:* Army (c).
Student Life *Campus security:* 24-hour emergency response devices and patrols.
Athletics Member NJCAA.
Costs (2014–15) *Tuition:* state resident $3840 full-time, $129 per credit part-time; nonresident $5900 full-time, $233 per credit part-time. *Required fees:* $620 full-time. *Room and board:* $8400. Room and board charges vary according to board plan and housing facility.
Financial Aid Of all full-time matriculated undergraduates who enrolled in 2013, 150 Federal Work-Study jobs (averaging $700).
Applying *Required:* high school transcript.
Freshman Application Contact Herkimer County Community College, 100 Reservoir Road, Herkimer, NY 13350. *Phone:* 315-866-0300 Ext. 8278. *Toll-free phone:* 888-464-4222 Ext. 8278.
Website: http://www.herkimer.edu/.

Hudson Valley Community College
Troy, New York

Freshman Application Contact Ms. Marie Claire Bauer, Director of Admissions, Hudson Valley Community College, 80 Vandenburgh Avenue, Troy, NY 12180-6096. *Phone:* 518-629-7309. *Toll-free phone:* 877-325-HVCC.
Website: http://www.hvcc.edu/.

Institute of Design and Construction
Brooklyn, New York

- **Independent** 2-year, founded 1947
- **Urban** campus
- **Coed**

Undergraduates 43 full-time, 60 part-time. Students come from 3 states and territories; 2 other countries; 42% Black or African American, non-Hispanic/Latino; 25% Hispanic/Latino; 9% Asian, non-Hispanic/Latino; 2% international; 10% transferred in. *Retention:* 47% of full-time freshmen returned.
Faculty *Student/faculty ratio:* 9:1.
Academics *Calendar:* semesters. *Degree:* associate. *Special study options:* academic remediation for entering students, adult/continuing education programs, advanced placement credit, cooperative education, part-time degree program, services for LD students, summer session for credit.
Student Life *Campus security:* 24-hour emergency response devices.
Costs (2014–15) *One-time required fee:* $30. *Tuition:* $8160 full-time, $340 per credit part-time. Full-time tuition and fees vary according to course load. Part-time tuition and fees vary according to course load. *Required fees:* $280 full-time, $140 per term part-time.

Applying *Options:* electronic application, deferred entrance. *Application fee:* $30. *Required:* high school transcript. *Recommended:* interview.

Freshman Application Contact Mr. Marquise Martin, Director of Admissions, Institute of Design and Construction, 141 Willoughby Street, Brooklyn, NY 11201. *Phone:* 718-855-3661. *Fax:* 718-852-5889. *E-mail:* mmartin@idc.edu.
Website: http://www.idc.edu/.

Island Drafting and Technical Institute
Amityville, New York

- **Proprietary** 2-year, founded 1957
- **Suburban** campus with easy access to New York City
- **Coed, primarily men,** 110 undergraduate students, 100% full-time, 10% women, 90% men

Undergraduates 110 full-time. Students come from 1 other state; 11% Black or African American, non-Hispanic/Latino; 22% Hispanic/Latino; 2% Asian, non-Hispanic/Latino; 0.9% Native Hawaiian or other Pacific Islander, non-Hispanic/Latino; 5% Two or more races, non-Hispanic/Latino; 18% Race/ethnicity unknown. *Retention:* 92% of full-time freshmen returned.

Freshmen *Admission:* 56 enrolled. *Average high school GPA:* 2.5.

Faculty *Total:* 11, 45% full-time. *Student/faculty ratio:* 15:1.

Majors Architectural drafting and CAD/CADD; computer and information sciences and support services related; computer and information systems security; computer systems networking and telecommunications; computer technology/computer systems technology; electrical, electronic and communications engineering technology; mechanical drafting and CAD/CADD; network and system administration.

Academics *Calendar:* semesters. *Degree:* certificates, diplomas, and associate. *Special study options:* accelerated degree program, adult/continuing education programs, summer session for credit.

Student Life *Housing:* college housing not available.

Costs (2015–16) *Tuition:* $15,750 full-time, $525 per credit part-time. No tuition increase for student's term of enrollment. *Required fees:* $450 full-time. *Payment plan:* installment.

Applying *Options:* early admission. *Application fee:* $40. *Required:* interview. *Recommended:* high school transcript. *Notification:* continuous (freshmen).

Freshman Application Contact Larry Basile, Island Drafting and Technical Institute, 128 Broadway, Amityville, NY 11701. *Phone:* 631-691-8733 Ext. 114. *Fax:* 631-691-8738. *E-mail:* info@idti.edu.
Website: http://www.idti.edu/.

ITT Technical Institute
Albany, New York

- **Proprietary** 2-year, founded 1998, part of ITT Educational Services, Inc.
- **Coed**

Academics *Calendar:* quarters. *Degree:* associate.

Freshman Application Contact Director of Recruitment, ITT Technical Institute, 13 Airline Drive, Albany, NY 12205. *Phone:* 518-452-9300. *Toll-free phone:* 800-489-1191.
Website: http://www.itt-tech.edu/.

ITT Technical Institute
Getzville, New York

- **Proprietary** 2-year, part of ITT Educational Services, Inc.
- **Coed**

Academics *Degree:* associate.

Freshman Application Contact Director of Recruitment, ITT Technical Institute, 2295 Millersport Highway, Getzville, NY 14068. *Phone:* 716-689-2200. *Toll-free phone:* 800-469-7593.
Website: http://www.itt-tech.edu/.

ITT Technical Institute
Liverpool, New York

- **Proprietary** 2-year, founded 1998, part of ITT Educational Services, Inc.
- **Coed**

Academics *Calendar:* semesters. *Degree:* associate.

Freshman Application Contact Director of Recruitment, ITT Technical Institute, 235 Greenfield Parkway, Liverpool, NY 13088. *Phone:* 315-461-8000. *Toll-free phone:* 877-488-0011.
Website: http://www.itt-tech.edu/.

Jamestown Business College
Jamestown, New York

- **Proprietary** primarily 2-year, founded 1886
- **Small-town** 1-acre campus
- **Coed,** 318 undergraduate students, 99% full-time, 71% women, 29% men

Undergraduates 314 full-time, 4 part-time. Students come from 2 states and territories; 7% are from out of state; 2% Black or African American, non-Hispanic/Latino; 16% Hispanic/Latino; 0.6% Native Hawaiian or other Pacific Islander, non-Hispanic/Latino; 6% American Indian or Alaska Native, non-Hispanic/Latino; 4% Two or more races, non-Hispanic/Latino; 0.9% Race/ethnicity unknown; 10% transferred in. *Retention:* 68% of full-time freshmen returned.

Freshmen *Admission:* 98 applied, 91 admitted, 114 enrolled.

Faculty *Total:* 25, 24% full-time, 8% with terminal degrees. *Student/faculty ratio:* 23:1.

Majors Administrative assistant and secretarial science; business administration and management; medical/clinical assistant; office management.

Academics *Calendar:* quarters. *Degrees:* certificates, associate, and bachelor's. *Special study options:* advanced placement credit, double majors, off-campus study, part-time degree program, summer session for credit.

Library James Prendergast Library with 279,270 titles, an OPAC, a Web page.

Student Life *Housing:* college housing not available. *Campus security:* 24-hour emergency response devices.

Athletics *Intramural sports:* basketball M(c)/W(c), racquetball M(c)/W(c), softball M(c)/W(c), swimming and diving M(c)/W(c), table tennis M(c)/W(c), tennis M(c)/W(c), volleyball M(c)/W(c), weight lifting M(c)/W(c).

Costs (2014–15) *One-time required fee:* $25. *Tuition:* $11,100 full-time, $308 per credit hour part-time. Full-time tuition and fees vary according to course load. Part-time tuition and fees vary according to course load. *Required fees:* $900 full-time, $150 per quarter part-time. *Waivers:* employees or children of employees.

Financial Aid Of all full-time matriculated undergraduates who enrolled in 2014, 316 applied for aid, 316 were judged to have need.

Applying *Application fee:* $25. *Required:* essay or personal statement, high school transcript, interview. *Application deadlines:* rolling (freshmen), rolling (transfers).

Freshman Application Contact Mrs. Brenda Salemme, Director of Admissions and Placement, Jamestown Business College, 7 Fairmount Avenue, Box 429, Jamestown, NY 14702-0429. *Phone:* 716-664-5100. *Fax:* 716-664-3144. *E-mail:* brendasalemme@jamestownbusinesscollege.edu.
Website: http://www.jamestownbusinesscollege.edu/.

Jamestown Community College
Jamestown, New York

- **State and locally supported** 2-year, founded 1950, part of State University of New York System
- **Small-town** 107-acre campus
- **Endowment** $12.5 million
- **Coed,** 3,368 undergraduate students, 74% full-time, 58% women, 42% men

Undergraduates 2,485 full-time, 883 part-time. Students come from 11 states and territories; 13 other countries; 8% are from out of state; 4% Black or African American, non-Hispanic/Latino; 7% Hispanic/Latino; 0.8% Asian, non-Hispanic/Latino; 0.1% Native Hawaiian or other Pacific Islander, non-Hispanic/Latino; 1% American Indian or Alaska Native, non-Hispanic/Latino; 3% Two or more races, non-Hispanic/Latino; 0.9% Race/ethnicity unknown; 0.8% international; 6% transferred in; 11% live on campus.

Freshmen *Admission:* 1,935 applied, 1,898 admitted, 1,033 enrolled. *Average high school GPA:* 3.25.

Faculty *Total:* 382, 23% full-time. *Student/faculty ratio:* 17:1.

Majors Accounting technology and bookkeeping; administrative assistant and secretarial science; airline pilot and flight crew; biology/biotechnology laboratory technician; business administration and management; computer and information sciences; criminal justice/law enforcement administration; criminal justice/police science; engineering; environmental science; fine/studio arts; general studies; health and physical education/fitness; health information/medical records technology; humanities; human services; information science/studies; information technology; international/global studies; liberal arts and sciences and humanities related; liberal arts and sciences/liberal studies; mechanical engineering/mechanical technology; music; occupational therapist assistant; registered nursing/registered nurse; speech communication and rhetoric; teacher assistant/aide; welding technology.

Academics *Calendar:* semesters. *Degree:* certificates and associate. *Special study options:* academic remediation for entering students, adult/continuing

education programs, advanced placement credit, distance learning, honors programs, independent study, internships, off-campus study, part-time degree program, services for LD students, study abroad, summer session for credit.

Library Hultquist Library plus 1 other with 89,159 titles, 7,773 audiovisual materials, an OPAC, a Web page.

Student Life *Housing Options:* coed. Campus housing is university owned. *Activities and Organizations:* drama/theater group, student-run radio station, choral group, Nursing Club, InterVarsity Christian Fellowship, Anime Club, Earth Awareness, Campus Activities Board. *Campus security:* 24-hour emergency response devices, controlled dormitory access. *Student services:* health clinic, personal/psychological counseling.

Athletics Member NJCAA. *Intercollegiate sports:* baseball M, basketball M/W, golf M/W, soccer M/W, softball W, swimming and diving M/W, volleyball W, wrestling M. *Intramural sports:* basketball M/W, bowling M/W, cross-country running M/W, softball M/W, volleyball M/W.

Costs (2014–15) *One-time required fee:* $85. *Tuition:* state resident $4410 full-time, $184 per credit hour part-time; nonresident $8820 full-time, $368 per credit hour part-time. Full-time tuition and fees vary according to course load and program. Part-time tuition and fees vary according to course load and program. *Required fees:* $602 full-time, $19 per credit hour part-time. *Room and board:* $10,380; room only: $7280. Room and board charges vary according to board plan. *Payment plan:* installment. *Waivers:* employees or children of employees.

Financial Aid Of all full-time matriculated undergraduates who enrolled in 2013, 85 Federal Work-Study jobs (averaging $1500). 85 state and other part-time jobs (averaging $1300).

Applying *Options:* electronic application, deferred entrance. *Required:* high school transcript. *Required for some:* standardized test scores used for placement, GEDs accepted. TOEFL (or equivalent) for international students. *Application deadlines:* rolling (freshmen), rolling (out-of-state freshmen), rolling (transfers). *Notification:* continuous (freshmen), continuous (out-of-state freshmen), continuous (transfers).

Freshman Application Contact Ms. Wendy Present, Director of Admissions, Jamestown Community College, 525 Falconer Street, PO Box 20, Jamestown, NY 14702-0020. *Phone:* 716-338-1001. *Toll-free phone:* 800-388-8557. *Fax:* 716-338-1450. *E-mail:* admissions@mail.sunyjcc.edu. *Website:* http://www.sunyjcc.edu/.

Jefferson Community College
Watertown, New York

- **State and locally supported** 2-year, founded 1961, part of State University of New York System
- **Small-town** 90-acre campus with easy access to Syracuse
- **Coed,** 3,931 undergraduate students, 57% full-time, 62% women, 38% men

Undergraduates 2,234 full-time, 1,697 part-time. 5% Black or African American, non-Hispanic/Latino; 11% Hispanic/Latino; 0.9% Asian, non-Hispanic/Latino; 0.2% Native Hawaiian or other Pacific Islander, non-Hispanic/Latino; 0.5% American Indian or Alaska Native, non-Hispanic/Latino; 4% Two or more races, non-Hispanic/Latino; 1% Race/ethnicity unknown; 0.4% international.

Freshmen *Admission:* 832 enrolled.

Faculty *Total:* 246, 33% full-time. *Student/faculty ratio:* 16:1.

Majors Accounting; accounting technology and bookkeeping; administrative assistant and secretarial science; animal/livestock husbandry and production; business administration and management; child-care and support services management; child development; community organization and advocacy; computer and information sciences; computer and information sciences and support services related; computer/information technology services administration related; computer science; computer technology/computer systems technology; criminal justice/law enforcement administration; early childhood education; emergency medical technology (EMT paramedic); engineering; engineering science; fire prevention and safety technology; fire services administration; forest technology; hospitality administration; humanities; human services; information science/studies; legal assistant/paralegal; liberal arts and sciences/liberal studies; mathematics; mechanical engineering technologies related; medical administrative assistant and medical secretary; office management; office occupations and clerical services; registered nursing/registered nurse; sport and fitness administration/management; teacher assistant/aide; tourism promotion.

Academics *Calendar:* semesters. *Degree:* certificates and associate. *Special study options:* academic remediation for entering students, advanced placement credit, cooperative education, distance learning, double majors, honors programs, independent study, internships, part-time degree program, services for LD students, student-designed majors, summer session for credit.

Library Melvil Dewey Library plus 1 other with 145,009 titles, 6,565 audiovisual materials, an OPAC, a Web page.

Student Life *Activities and Organizations:* student-run newspaper. *Campus security:* 24-hour emergency response devices and patrols. *Student services:* health clinic, personal/psychological counseling.

Athletics Member NJCAA. *Intercollegiate sports:* baseball M, basketball M/W, lacrosse M/W, soccer M/W, softball W, volleyball W.

Standardized Tests *Recommended:* SAT or ACT (for admission).

Costs (2014–15) *Tuition:* state resident $3984 full-time, $166 per credit hour part-time; nonresident $6072 full-time, $253 per credit hour part-time. Full-time tuition and fees vary according to course load, location, and program. Part-time tuition and fees vary according to course load, location, and program. *Required fees:* $563 full-time. *Room and board:* $10,700; room only: $7600. Room and board charges vary according to board plan. *Payment plan:* installment. *Waivers:* senior citizens and employees or children of employees.

Financial Aid Of all full-time matriculated undergraduates who enrolled in 2009, 1,748 applied for aid. 98 Federal Work-Study jobs (averaging $1093).

Applying *Options:* electronic application, early admission, deferred entrance. *Required:* high school transcript. *Required for some:* interview. *Application deadlines:* 9/6 (freshmen), rolling (transfers). *Notification:* continuous (freshmen), continuous (transfers).

Freshman Application Contact Ms. Rosanne N. Weir, Director of Admissions, Jefferson Community College, 1220 Coffeen Street, Watertown, NY 13601. *Phone:* 315-786-2277. *Toll-free phone:* 888-435-6522. *Fax:* 315-786-2459. *E-mail:* admissions@sunyjefferson.edu. *Website:* http://www.sunyjefferson.edu/.

Kingsborough Community College of the City University of New York
Brooklyn, New York

- **State and locally supported** 2-year, founded 1963, part of City University of New York System
- **Urban** 72-acre campus with easy access to New York City
- **Coed,** 17,495 undergraduate students, 58% full-time, 55% women, 45% men

Undergraduates 10,179 full-time, 7,316 part-time. Students come from 10 states and territories; 136 other countries; 1% are from out of state; 25% Black or African American, non-Hispanic/Latino; 18% Hispanic/Latino; 13% Asian, non-Hispanic/Latino; 0.5% Native Hawaiian or other Pacific Islander, non-Hispanic/Latino; 0.8% American Indian or Alaska Native, non-Hispanic/Latino; 17% Race/ethnicity unknown; 2% international; 8% transferred in. *Retention:* 66% of full-time freshmen returned.

Freshmen *Admission:* 2,557 enrolled. *Average high school GPA:* 2.7.

Majors Accounting; administrative assistant and secretarial science; art; biology/biological sciences; broadcast journalism; business administration and management; chemistry; commercial and advertising art; community health services counseling; computer and information sciences; computer science; cooking and related culinary arts; criminal justice/law enforcement administration; data processing and data processing technology; design and applied arts related; dramatic/theater arts; early childhood education; education; elementary education; engineering science; fashion merchandising; health and physical education related; human services; journalism; labor and industrial relations; liberal arts and sciences/liberal studies; marine maintenance and ship repair technology; marketing/marketing management; mathematics; mental health counseling; music; parks, recreation and leisure; physical therapy; physical therapy technology; physics; psychiatric/mental health services technology; registered nursing/registered nurse; sport and fitness administration/management; teacher assistant/aide; tourism and travel services management.

Academics *Calendar:* semesters. *Degree:* associate. *Special study options:* academic remediation for entering students, adult/continuing education programs, advanced placement credit, distance learning, English as a second language, honors programs, independent study, internships, off-campus study, part-time degree program, services for LD students, summer session for credit.

Library Robert J. Kibbee Library with 198,343 titles, 2,145 audiovisual materials, an OPAC.

Student Life *Housing:* college housing not available. *Activities and Organizations:* drama/theater group, student-run newspaper, radio station, choral group, Peer Advisors, Caribbean Club, DECA. *Campus security:* 24-hour emergency response devices and patrols. *Student services:* health clinic, personal/psychological counseling, women's center.

Athletics Member NJCAA. *Intercollegiate sports:* baseball M, basketball M/W, soccer M, softball W, tennis M/W, track and field M/W, volleyball W. *Intramural sports:* baseball M, basketball M/W, soccer M, softball W, tennis M/W, track and field M/W, volleyball W.

Costs (2014–15) *Tuition:* state resident $4500 full-time, $195 per credit part-time; nonresident $9000 full-time, $300 per credit part-time. *Required fees:* $350 full-time, $92 per term part-time. *Payment plan:* installment. *Waivers:* senior citizens.

Applying *Application fee:* $65. *Required:* high school transcript. *Application deadlines:* 8/15 (freshmen), rolling (transfers).
Freshman Application Contact Mr. Javier Morgades, Director of Admissions Information Center, Kingsborough Community College of the City University of New York, 2001 Oriental Boulevard, Brooklyn, NY 11235. *Phone:* 718-368-4600. *E-mail:* info@kbcc.cuny.edu.
Website: http://www.kbcc.cuny.edu/.

Long Island Business Institute
Flushing, New York

- **Proprietary** 2-year, founded 1968
- **Urban** campus with easy access to New York City
- **Coed, primarily women,** 391 undergraduate students, 73% full-time, 71% women, 29% men

Undergraduates 285 full-time, 106 part-time. Students come from 2 states and territories; 24 other countries; 12% Black or African American, non-Hispanic/Latino; 12% Hispanic/Latino; 42% Asian, non-Hispanic/Latino; 0.3% Two or more races, non-Hispanic/Latino; 0.8% Race/ethnicity unknown; 10% international; 7% transferred in.
Freshmen *Admission:* 166 applied, 105 admitted, 97 enrolled.
Faculty *Total:* 72, 19% full-time, 6% with terminal degrees. *Student/faculty ratio:* 10:1.
Majors Accounting; business administration and management; business, management, and marketing related; court reporting; homeland security; hospitality administration related; medical office management.
Academics *Calendar:* semesters. *Degrees:* certificates and associate (information provided for Commack and Flushing campuses). *Special study options:* academic remediation for entering students, adult/continuing education programs, advanced placement credit, cooperative education, English as a second language, honors programs, independent study, part-time degree program, summer session for credit.
Library Flushing Main Campus Library, Commack Campus Library with 7,314 titles, 1,209 audiovisual materials, an OPAC, a Web page.
Student Life *Housing:* college housing not available. *Activities and Organizations:* Small Business Club, Web Design Club, Investment Club, Court Reporting Alumni Association. *Campus security:* 24-hour emergency response devices.
Standardized Tests *Required:* ACT Compass, CELSA (for admission).
Costs (2015–16) *Tuition:* $13,299 full-time, $375 per credit part-time. *Required fees:* $1350 full-time, $450 per term part-time. *Payment plans:* installment, deferred payment.
Applying *Required:* high school transcript, interview. *Application deadlines:* rolling (freshmen), rolling (transfers).
Freshman Application Contact Ms. Jackie Chang, Director of Admissions, Long Island Business Institute, 136-18 39th Avenue, Flushing, NY 11354. *Phone:* 718-939-5100. *Fax:* 718-939-9235. *E-mail:* samw@libi.edu.
Website: http://www.libi.edu/.

Mandl School
New York, New York

Admissions Office Contact Mandl School, 254 West 54th Street, 9th Floor, New York, NY 10019.
Website: http://www.mandlschool.com/.

Memorial Hospital School of Nursing
Albany, New York

Freshman Application Contact Admissions Office, Memorial Hospital School of Nursing, 600 Northern Boulevard, Albany, NY 12204.
Website: http://www.nehealth.com/son/.

Mildred Elley–New York City
New York, New York

Admissions Office Contact Mildred Elley–New York City, 25 Broadway, 16th Floor, New York, NY 10004-1010.
Website: http://www.mildred-elley.edu/.

Mildred Elley School
Albany, New York

Director of Admissions Mr. Michael Cahalan, Enrollment Manager, Mildred Elley School, 855 Central Avenue, Albany, NY 12206. *Phone:* 518-786-3171 Ext. 227. *Toll-free phone:* 800-622-6327.
Website: http://www.mildred-elley.edu/.

Mohawk Valley Community College
Utica, New York

- **State and locally supported** 2-year, founded 1946, part of State University of New York System
- **Suburban** 80-acre campus
- **Coed,** 7,149 undergraduate students, 56% full-time, 53% women, 47% men

Undergraduates 4,024 full-time, 3,125 part-time. Students come from 20 states and territories; 17 other countries; 0.3% are from out of state; 8% Black or African American, non-Hispanic/Latino; 8% Hispanic/Latino; 5% Asian, non-Hispanic/Latino; 0.1% Native Hawaiian or other Pacific Islander, non-Hispanic/Latino; 0.5% American Indian or Alaska Native, non-Hispanic/Latino; 3% Two or more races, non-Hispanic/Latino; 0.4% Race/ethnicity unknown; 1% international; 4% transferred in; 7% live on campus.
Freshmen *Admission:* 3,348 applied, 3,328 admitted, 1,401 enrolled. *Average high school GPA:* 2.63.
Faculty *Total:* 533, 27% full-time, 11% with terminal degrees. *Student/faculty ratio:* 18:1.
Majors Accounting technology and bookkeeping; administrative assistant and secretarial science; advertising; airframe mechanics and aircraft maintenance technology; art; banking and financial support services; building/property maintenance; business administration and management; CAD/CADD drafting/design technology; chemical technology; civil engineering technology; commercial and advertising art; commercial photography; communications systems installation and repair technology; computer and information sciences; computer and information sciences and support services related; computer and information systems security; computer programming; criminal justice/law enforcement administration; dietetic technology; digital arts; electrical and electronic engineering technologies related; electrical, electronic and communications engineering technology; electrical/electronics maintenance and repair technology related; emergency care attendant (EMT ambulance); engineering; fire services administration; general studies; heating, air conditioning, ventilation and refrigeration maintenance technology; hotel/motel administration; humanities; human services; law enforcement investigation and interviewing; liberal arts and sciences and humanities related; liberal arts and sciences/liberal studies; manufacturing engineering technology; mechanical engineering/mechanical technology; mechanical engineering technologies related; medical/clinical assistant; medical radiologic technology; operations management; parks, recreation and leisure facilities management; registered nursing/registered nurse; respiratory care therapy; restaurant, culinary, and catering management; sign language interpretation and translation; substance abuse/addiction counseling; surveying technology; web page, digital/multimedia and information resources design; welding technology.
Academics *Calendar:* semesters. *Degree:* certificates and associate. *Special study options:* academic remediation for entering students, advanced placement credit, distance learning, double majors, English as a second language, honors programs, independent study, internships, off-campus study, part-time degree program, services for LD students, student-designed majors, summer session for credit. *ROTC:* Army (c), Air Force (c).
Library Mohawk Valley Community College Library plus 1 other with 127,754 titles, 7,036 audiovisual materials, an OPAC, a Web page.
Student Life *Housing Options:* coed, men-only, women-only, special housing for students with disabilities. Campus housing is provided by a third party. Freshman applicants given priority for college housing. *Activities and Organizations:* drama/theater group, Student Congress, Student Nurses Organization (SNO), Photography Club, Recreation Club, Phi Theta Kappa. *Campus security:* 24-hour emergency response devices and patrols, late-night transport/escort service, controlled dormitory access. *Student services:* health clinic, personal/psychological counseling.
Athletics Member NJCAA. *Intercollegiate sports:* baseball M, basketball M/W, bowling M/W, cross-country running M/W, golf M/W, ice hockey M, lacrosse M/W, soccer M/W, softball W, tennis M/W, track and field M/W, volleyball W. *Intramural sports:* badminton M/W, basketball M/W, volleyball M/W.
Costs (2014–15) *Tuition:* state resident $3810 full-time, $155 per credit hour part-time; nonresident $7620 full-time, $310 per credit hour part-time. *Required fees:* $605 full-time, $10 per credit hour part-time, $56 per term part-time. *Room and board:* $9800; room only: $5960. Room and board charges vary according to board plan. *Payment plans:* installment, deferred payment. *Waivers:* senior citizens and employees or children of employees.
Financial Aid Of all full-time matriculated undergraduates who enrolled in 2013, 229 Federal Work-Study jobs (averaging $1750).
Applying *Options:* electronic application, deferred entrance. *Required for some:* high school transcript. *Recommended:* interview. *Application deadlines:* rolling (freshmen), rolling (out-of-state freshmen), rolling

(transfers). *Notification:* continuous (freshmen), continuous (out-of-state freshmen), continuous (transfers).
Freshman Application Contact Ms. Michelle Collea, Data Processing Clerk, Admissions, Mohawk Valley Community College, Utica, NY 13501. *Phone:* 315-792-5640. *Toll-free phone:* 800-SEE-MVCC. *Fax:* 315-792-5527. *E-mail:* mcollea@mvcc.edu.
Website: http://www.mvcc.edu/.

Monroe Community College
Rochester, New York

- **State and locally supported** 2-year, founded 1961, part of State University of New York System
- **Suburban** 314-acre campus with easy access to Buffalo
- **Coed,** 15,335 undergraduate students, 61% full-time, 53% women, 47% men

Undergraduates 9,374 full-time, 5,961 part-time. 3% are from out of state; 21% Black or African American, non-Hispanic/Latino; 9% Hispanic/Latino; 4% Asian, non-Hispanic/Latino; 0.2% Native Hawaiian or other Pacific Islander, non-Hispanic/Latino; 0.4% American Indian or Alaska Native, non-Hispanic/Latino; 4% Two or more races, non-Hispanic/Latino; 0.2% Race/ethnicity unknown; 0.9% international.
Freshmen *Admission:* 3,409 enrolled. *Test scores:* SAT critical reading scores over 500: 33%; SAT math scores over 500: 40%; SAT writing scores over 500: 25%; ACT scores over 18: 74%; SAT critical reading scores over 600: 7%; SAT math scores over 600: 10%; SAT writing scores over 600: 4%; ACT scores over 24: 26%; SAT critical reading scores over 700: 1%; SAT math scores over 700: 1%; ACT scores over 30: 4%.
Faculty *Total:* 882, 36% full-time, 13% with terminal degrees. *Student/faculty ratio:* 23:1.
Majors Accounting; administrative assistant and secretarial science; art; automobile/automotive mechanics technology; behavioral sciences; biological and physical sciences; biology/biological sciences; biology/biotechnology laboratory technician; business administration and management; chemical engineering; chemistry; civil engineering technology; commercial and advertising art; computer and information sciences and support services related; computer and information sciences related; computer engineering related; computer engineering technology; computer science; construction engineering technology; consumer merchandising/retailing management; corrections; criminal justice/law enforcement administration; criminal justice/police science; data processing and data processing technology; dental hygiene; electrical, electronic and communications engineering technology; engineering science; environmental studies; family and consumer sciences/human sciences; fashion/apparel design; fashion merchandising; fire science/firefighting; food technology and processing; forestry; graphic and printing equipment operation/production; health information/medical records administration; heating, air conditioning, ventilation and refrigeration maintenance technology; history; hotel/motel administration; human services; industrial radiologic technology; industrial technology; information science/studies; information technology; instrumentation technology; interior design; international business/trade/commerce; landscape architecture; laser and optical technology; legal administrative assistant/secretary; liberal arts and sciences/liberal studies; marketing/marketing management; mass communication/media; mathematics; mechanical engineering/mechanical technology; music; parks, recreation and leisure; physical education teaching and coaching; physics; political science and government; pre-pharmacy studies; quality control technology; registered nursing/registered nurse; social sciences; special products marketing; telecommunications technology; tourism and travel services management.
Academics *Calendar:* semesters. *Degree:* certificates and associate. *Special study options:* academic remediation for entering students, accelerated degree program, adult/continuing education programs, advanced placement credit, cooperative education, English as a second language, honors programs, internships, off-campus study, part-time degree program, services for LD students, summer session for credit.
Library LeRoy V. Good Library with an OPAC.
Student Life *Housing Options:* coed, men-only, women-only. Campus housing is university owned. *Activities and Organizations:* drama/theater group, student-run newspaper, radio station, choral group, student newspaper, Phi Theta Kappa, student government. *Campus security:* 24-hour emergency response devices, late-night transport/escort service. *Student services:* health clinic, personal/psychological counseling.
Athletics Member NJCAA. *Intercollegiate sports:* baseball M(s), basketball M(s)/W(s), golf M, ice hockey M(s), lacrosse M(s), soccer M(s)/W(s), softball W, swimming and diving M(s)/W(s), tennis M/W, volleyball W. *Intramural sports:* archery M/W, basketball M/W, bowling M/W, cheerleading W, cross-country running M/W, football M, lacrosse W, racquetball M/W, rugby M, skiing (cross-country) M/W, soccer M/W, softball M/W, swimming and diving M/W, tennis M/W, volleyball M/W.

Costs (2015–16) *Tuition:* state resident $3416 full-time, $135 per credit hour part-time; nonresident $6832 full-time, $270 per credit hour part-time. Full-time tuition and fees vary according to program. Part-time tuition and fees vary according to course load and program. *Required fees:* $234 full-time. *Room and board:* room only: $6170. Room and board charges vary according to housing facility. *Payment plan:* installment. *Waivers:* senior citizens and employees or children of employees.
Applying *Options:* electronic application, early admission. *Required:* high school transcript. *Application deadlines:* rolling (freshmen), rolling (transfers). *Notification:* continuous (freshmen), continuous (transfers).
Freshman Application Contact Ms. Christine Casalinuovo-Adams, Director of Admissions, Monroe Community College, 1000 East Henrietta Road, Rochester, NY 14623. *Phone:* 585-292-2222. *Fax:* 585-292-3860. *E-mail:* admissions@monroecc.edu.
Website: http://www.monroecc.edu/.

Montefiore School of Nursing
Mount Vernon, New York

Director of Admissions Sandra Farrior, Coordinator of Student Services, Montefiore School of Nursing, 53 Valentine Street, Mount Vernon, NY 10550. *Phone:* 914-361-6472. *E-mail:* hopferadmissions@sshsw.org.
Website: http://www.montefiorehealthsystem.org/landing.cfm?id=19.

Nassau Community College
Garden City, New York

- **State and locally supported** 2-year, founded 1959, part of State University of New York System
- **Suburban** 225-acre campus with easy access to New York City
- **Coed,** 22,310 undergraduate students, 60% full-time, 50% women, 50% men

Undergraduates 13,282 full-time, 9,028 part-time. Students come from 19 states and territories; 69 other countries; 0.3% are from out of state; 22% Black or African American, non-Hispanic/Latino; 23% Hispanic/Latino; 6% Asian, non-Hispanic/Latino; 0.4% Native Hawaiian or other Pacific Islander, non-Hispanic/Latino; 0.3% American Indian or Alaska Native, non-Hispanic/Latino; 6% Race/ethnicity unknown; 0.9% international; 6% transferred in. *Retention:* 32% of full-time freshmen returned.
Freshmen *Admission:* 5,997 applied, 5,681 admitted, 4,623 enrolled. *Average high school GPA:* 2.51.
Faculty *Total:* 1,422, 35% full-time, 28% with terminal degrees. *Student/faculty ratio:* 21:1.
Majors Accounting; accounting technology and bookkeeping; administrative assistant and secretarial science; African American/Black studies; art; business administration and management; civil engineering technology; clinical/medical laboratory technology; commercial and advertising art; computer and information sciences; computer and information sciences related; computer graphics; computer science; computer systems networking and telecommunications; criminal justice/law enforcement administration; criminal justice/safety; dance; data processing and data processing technology; design and visual communications; dramatic/theater arts; engineering; entrepreneurship; fashion/apparel design; fashion merchandising; funeral service and mortuary science; general studies; hotel/motel administration; instrumentation technology; insurance; interior design; kindergarten/preschool education; legal administrative assistant/secretary; legal assistant/paralegal; liberal arts and sciences/liberal studies; management information systems; marketing/marketing management; mass communication/media; mathematics; medical administrative assistant and medical secretary; medical radiologic technology; music performance; photography; physical therapy technology; real estate; registered nursing/registered nurse; rehabilitation and therapeutic professions related; respiratory care therapy; retailing; speech communication and rhetoric; surgical technology; theater design and technology; transportation and materials moving related; visual and performing arts.
Academics *Calendar:* semesters. *Degree:* certificates and associate. *Special study options:* academic remediation for entering students, adult/continuing education programs, advanced placement credit, cooperative education, distance learning, English as a second language, honors programs, internships, off-campus study, part-time degree program, services for LD students, summer session for credit.
Library A. Holly Patterson Library with 186,782 titles, 18,903 audiovisual materials, an OPAC, a Web page.
Student Life *Housing:* college housing not available. *Activities and Organizations:* drama/theater group, student-run newspaper, radio station, choral group, Muslim Student Association, Make a Difference Club, Interact Club, Political Science Club, Investment Club. *Campus security:* 24-hour emergency response devices and patrols, late-night transport/escort service. *Student services:* personal/psychological counseling, women's center.

Athletics Member NJCAA. *Intercollegiate sports:* baseball M, basketball M/W, bowling M/W, cheerleading M/W, cross-country running M/W, football M, golf M/W, lacrosse M/W, soccer M/W, softball M, tennis M/W, track and field M/W, volleyball W, wrestling M. *Intramural sports:* badminton M/W, baseball M, basketball M/W, racquetball M/W, soccer M/W, softball M/W, swimming and diving M/W, table tennis M/W, tennis M/W, volleyball M/W.
Standardized Tests *Recommended:* SAT or ACT (for admission).
Costs (2014–15) *Tuition:* area resident $4234 full-time, $177 per credit hour part-time; state resident $8468 full-time, $354 per credit hour part-time; nonresident $8468 full-time, $354 per credit hour part-time. *Required fees:* $140 full-time. *Payment plan:* installment.
Financial Aid Of all full-time matriculated undergraduates who enrolled in 2013, 400 Federal Work-Study jobs (averaging $3000).
Applying *Options:* electronic application, deferred entrance. *Application fee:* $40. *Required:* high school transcript. *Required for some:* minimum 3.0 GPA, interview. *Recommended:* minimum 2.0 GPA. *Application deadlines:* 8/7 (freshmen), 8/7 (transfers). *Notification:* continuous (freshmen), continuous (transfers).
Freshman Application Contact Mr. Craig Wright, Vice President of Enrollment Management, Nassau Community College, Garden City, NY 11530. *Phone:* 516-572-7345. *E-mail:* admissions@sunynassau.edu.
Website: http://www.ncc.edu/.

New York Career Institute
New York, New York

- **Proprietary** 2-year, founded 1942
- **Urban** campus
- **Coed, primarily women**

Undergraduates 461 full-time, 241 part-time. 25% Black or African American, non-Hispanic/Latino; 17% Hispanic/Latino; 2% Asian, non-Hispanic/Latino; 0.7% American Indian or Alaska Native, non-Hispanic/Latino; 3% Two or more races, non-Hispanic/Latino; 19% Race/ethnicity unknown.
Academics *Calendar:* trimesters semesters for evening division. *Degree:* certificates and associate. *Special study options:* academic remediation for entering students, advanced placement credit, internships, part-time degree program, summer session for credit.
Costs (2014–15) *Tuition:* $13,350 full-time, $420 per credit hour part-time. Full-time tuition and fees vary according to class time. Part-time tuition and fees vary according to class time. *Required fees:* $150 full-time, $50 per term part-time.
Applying *Options:* electronic application. *Application fee:* $50. *Required:* high school transcript, interview.
Freshman Application Contact Mr. Larry Stieglitz, Director of Admissions, New York Career Institute, 11 Park Place, New York, NY 10007. *Phone:* 212-962-0002 Ext. 115. *Fax:* 212-385-7574. *E-mail:* lstieglitz@nyci.edu.
Website: http://www.nyci.com/.

Niagara County Community College
Sanborn, New York

- **State and locally supported** 2-year, founded 1962, part of State University of New York System
- **Rural** 287-acre campus with easy access to Buffalo
- **Endowment** $7.5 million
- **Coed,** 6,486 undergraduate students, 62% full-time, 58% women, 42% men

Undergraduates 3,991 full-time, 2,495 part-time. Students come from 15 states and territories; 1 other country; 1% are from out of state; 10% Black or African American, non-Hispanic/Latino; 3% Hispanic/Latino; 1% Asian, non-Hispanic/Latino; 0.1% Native Hawaiian or other Pacific Islander, non-Hispanic/Latino; 1% American Indian or Alaska Native, non-Hispanic/Latino; 2% Race/ethnicity unknown; 8% transferred in; 4% live on campus.
Freshmen *Admission:* 2,954 applied, 2,528 admitted, 1,418 enrolled. *Average high school GPA:* 2.48.
Faculty *Total:* 384, 29% full-time, 13% with terminal degrees. *Student/faculty ratio:* 17:1.
Majors Accounting; administrative assistant and secretarial science; animal sciences; baking and pastry arts; biological and physical sciences; business administration and management; business, management, and marketing related; chemical technology; computer science; consumer merchandising/retailing management; criminal justice/law enforcement administration; culinary arts; design and applied arts related; drafting and design technology; drafting/design engineering technologies related; dramatic/theater arts; elementary education; fine/studio arts; general studies; hospitality administration; humanities; human services; information science/studies; liberal arts and sciences/liberal studies; massage therapy; mass communication/media; mathematics; medical/clinical assistant; medical

radiologic technology; music; natural resources/conservation; occupational health and industrial hygiene; parks, recreation and leisure; physical education teaching and coaching; physical therapy technology; registered nursing/registered nurse; social sciences; sport and fitness administration/management; surgical technology; tourism and travel services management; web page, digital/multimedia and information resources design; wine steward/sommelier.
Academics *Calendar:* semesters. *Degree:* certificates and associate. *Special study options:* academic remediation for entering students, adult/continuing education programs, advanced placement credit, cooperative education, distance learning, double majors, honors programs, independent study, internships, off-campus study, part-time degree program, services for LD students, student-designed majors, study abroad, summer session for credit. *ROTC:* Army (c).
Library Henrietta G. Lewis Library with 83,146 titles, 4,837 audiovisual materials, an OPAC, a Web page.
Student Life *Housing Options:* coed. Campus housing is provided by a third party. *Activities and Organizations:* drama/theater group, student-run newspaper, radio station, choral group, student radio station, Student Nurses Association, Phi Theta Kappa, Alpha Beta Gamma, Physical Education Club. *Campus security:* 24-hour emergency response devices and patrols, student patrols, late-night transport/escort service. *Student services:* health clinic, personal/psychological counseling.
Athletics Member NJCAA. *Intercollegiate sports:* baseball M, basketball M(s)/W(s), golf M/W, lacrosse M/W, soccer M/W, softball W, volleyball W, wrestling M(s). *Intramural sports:* basketball M/W, racquetball M/W, soccer M/W, swimming and diving M/W, tennis M/W.
Costs (2014–15) *Tuition:* state resident $3888 full-time, $162 per credit hour part-time; nonresident $9720 full-time, $405 per credit hour part-time. Full-time tuition and fees vary according to course load and program. Part-time tuition and fees vary according to course load and program. *Required fees:* $386 full-time. *Room and board:* $11,028; room only: $8528. Room and board charges vary according to housing facility. *Payment plan:* installment. *Waivers:* senior citizens and employees or children of employees.
Financial Aid Of all full-time matriculated undergraduates who enrolled in 2013, 6,382 applied for aid, 6,382 were judged to have need. 99 Federal Work-Study jobs (averaging $921). 139 state and other part-time jobs (averaging $574). *Average percent of need met:* 79%. *Average financial aid package:* $5079. *Average need-based loan:* $2577. *Average need-based gift aid:* $633.
Applying *Options:* electronic application, early admission. *Required:* high school transcript. *Required for some:* minimum 2.0 GPA. *Notification:* continuous until 8/31 (freshmen), continuous until 8/31 (transfers).
Freshman Application Contact Ms. Kathy Saunders, Director of Enrollment Services, Niagara County Community College, 3111 Saunders Settlement Road, Sanborn, NY 14132. *Phone:* 716-614-6200. *Fax:* 716-614-6820. *E-mail:* admissions@niagaracc.suny.edu.
Website: http://www.niagaracc.suny.edu/.

North Country Community College
Saranac Lake, New York

Freshman Application Contact Enrollment Management Assistant, North Country Community College, 23 Santanoni Avenue, PO Box 89, Saranac Lake, NY 12983-0089. *Phone:* 518-891-2915 Ext. 686. *Toll-free phone:* 800-TRY-NCCC (in-state); 888-TRY-NCCC (out-of-state). *Fax:* 518-891-0898. *E-mail:* info@nccc.edu.
Website: http://www.nccc.edu/.

Onondaga Community College
Syracuse, New York

- **State and locally supported** 2-year, founded 1962, part of State University of New York System
- **Suburban** 280-acre campus
- **Endowment** $9.1 million
- **Coed**

Undergraduates 6,540 full-time, 6,301 part-time. Students come from 22 states and territories; 23 other countries; 6% are from out of state; 11% Black or African American, non-Hispanic/Latino; 4% Hispanic/Latino; 2% Asian, non-Hispanic/Latino; 0.1% Native Hawaiian or other Pacific Islander, non-Hispanic/Latino; 1% American Indian or Alaska Native, non-Hispanic/Latino; 2% Two or more races, non-Hispanic/Latino; 21% Race/ethnicity unknown; 0.5% international; 49% transferred in; 6% live on campus.
Faculty *Student/faculty ratio:* 25:1.
Academics *Calendar:* semesters. *Degree:* certificates, diplomas, and associate. *Special study options:* academic remediation for entering students, accelerated degree program, adult/continuing education programs, advanced placement credit, cooperative education, distance learning, double majors, English as a second language, external degree program, honors programs,

internships, part-time degree program, services for LD students, study abroad, summer session for credit. *ROTC:* Air Force (c).

Student Life *Campus security:* 24-hour emergency response devices and patrols, controlled dormitory access.

Athletics Member NJCAA.

Costs (2014–15) *Tuition:* state resident $4300 full-time, $164 per credit hour part-time; nonresident $8600 full-time, $328 per credit hour part-time. Full-time tuition and fees vary according to program. Part-time tuition and fees vary according to course load and program. *Required fees:* $584 full-time. *Room and board:* room only: $6270. Room and board charges vary according to board plan.

Financial Aid Of all full-time matriculated undergraduates who enrolled in 2013, 5,671 applied for aid, 5,090 were judged to have need, 263 had their need fully met. *Average percent of need met:* 58. *Average financial aid package:* $6716. *Average need-based loan:* $2997. *Average need-based gift aid:* $5422.

Applying *Options:* electronic application. *Required:* high school transcript, some programs require specific prerequisite courses and/or tests to be admitted directly to the program; an alternate program is offered. *Required for some:* minimum 2.0 GPA, interview.

Freshman Application Contact Mrs. Katherine Perry, Director of Admissions, Onondaga Community College, 4585 West Seneca Turnpike, Syracuse, NY 13215. *Phone:* 315-488-2602. *Fax:* 315-488-2107. *E-mail:* admissions@sunyocc.edu.

Website: http://www.sunyocc.edu/.

Orange County Community College
Middletown, New York

Freshman Application Contact Michael Roe, Director of Admissions and Recruitment, Orange County Community College, 115 South Street, Middletown, NY 10940. *Phone:* 845-341-4205. *Fax:* 845-343-1228. *E-mail:* apply@sunyorange.edu.

Website: http://www.sunyorange.edu/.

Phillips Beth Israel School of Nursing
New York, New York

Freshman Application Contact Mrs. Bernice Pass-Stern, Assistant Dean, Phillips Beth Israel School of Nursing, 776 Sixth Avenue, 4th Floor, New York, NY 10010-6354. *Phone:* 212-614-6176. *Fax:* 212-614-6109. *E-mail:* bstern@chpnet.org.

Website: http://www.pbisn.edu/.

Plaza College
Forest Hills, New York

- **Proprietary** primarily 2-year, founded 1916
- **Urban** campus with easy access to New York City
- **Coed,** 726 undergraduate students

Majors Accounting technology and bookkeeping; administrative assistant and secretarial science; allied health and medical assisting services related; business administration and management; business administration, management and operations related; health/health-care administration; health information/medical records technology.

Academics *Calendar:* semesters. *Degrees:* certificates, associate, and bachelor's. *Special study options:* academic remediation for entering students, English as a second language, internships, services for LD students, summer session for credit.

Student Life *Housing:* college housing not available. *Activities and Organizations:* drama/theater group, Ambassadors Club, VDAY, Performing Arts Society, Plaza College Psychology Society, Plaza College Social Media Society. *Campus security:* 24-hour emergency response devices.

Standardized Tests *Required:* ACT Compass (for admission).

Costs (2014–15) *Tuition:* $9900 full-time, $440 per credit hour part-time. Full-time tuition and fees vary according to program. Part-time tuition and fees vary according to program. *Required fees:* $1720 full-time, $860 per term part-time.

Applying *Application fee:* $100. *Required:* essay or personal statement, interview, placement test. *Required for some:* 2 letters of recommendation. *Application deadlines:* rolling (freshmen), rolling (transfers).

Freshman Application Contact Dean Vanessa Lopez, Dean of Admissions, Plaza College, 118-33 Queens Boulevard, Forest Hills, NY 11375. *Phone:* 718-779-1430. *E-mail:* info@plazacollege.edu.

Website: http://www.plazacollege.edu/.

Professional Business College
New York, New York

Admissions Office Contact Professional Business College, 408 Broadway, 2nd Floor, New York, NY 10013.

Website: http://www.pbcny.edu/.

Queensborough Community College of the City University of New York
Bayside, New York

- **State and locally supported** 2-year, founded 1958, part of City University of New York System
- **Urban** 34-acre campus with easy access to New York City
- **Coed,** 16,182 undergraduate students, 59% full-time, 54% women, 46% men

Undergraduates 9,551 full-time, 6,631 part-time. Students come from 8 states and territories; 138 other countries; 1% are from out of state; 23% Black or African American, non-Hispanic/Latino; 32% Hispanic/Latino; 21% Asian, non-Hispanic/Latino; 1% Native Hawaiian or other Pacific Islander, non-Hispanic/Latino; 0.8% American Indian or Alaska Native, non-Hispanic/Latino; 1% Two or more races, non-Hispanic/Latino; 6% international; 6% transferred in.

Freshmen *Admission:* 3,392 enrolled.

Faculty *Total:* 923, 42% full-time. *Student/faculty ratio:* 29:1.

Majors Accounting; business administration and management; business, management, and marketing related; clinical/medical laboratory technology; communication and journalism related; computer engineering technology; electrical, electronic and communications engineering technology; engineering science; environmental design/architecture; environmental health; fine/studio arts; health professions related; information science/studies; information technology; laser and optical technology; liberal arts and sciences/liberal studies; mechanical engineering/mechanical technology; musical instrument fabrication and repair; registered nursing/registered nurse; telecommunications technology; visual and performing arts.

Academics *Calendar:* semesters. *Degree:* certificates and associate. *Special study options:* academic remediation for entering students, accelerated degree program, advanced placement credit, cooperative education, double majors, English as a second language, honors programs, internships, off-campus study, part-time degree program, services for LD students, student-designed majors, study abroad, summer session for credit. *ROTC:* Army (c).

Library The Kurt R. Schmeller with an OPAC.

Student Life *Housing:* college housing not available. *Activities and Organizations:* drama/theater group, student-run newspaper, choral group, Phi Theta kappa, Student organization for disability Awareness (SODA), ASAP Club, CSTEP Club, NYPIRG. *Campus security:* 24-hour patrols, late-night transport/escort service. *Student services:* health clinic, personal/psychological counseling, legal services.

Athletics Member NJCAA. *Intercollegiate sports:* baseball M, basketball M/W, cross-country running M/W, soccer M, softball W, swimming and diving M/W, track and field M/W, volleyball W. *Intramural sports:* badminton M/W, basketball M/W, football M/W, swimming and diving M/W, table tennis M/W, volleyball M/W.

Costs (2015–16) *Tuition:* state resident $4500 full-time, $195 per credit part-time; nonresident $7200 full-time, $300 per credit part-time. *Required fees:* $341 full-time, $80 per term part-time.

Applying *Options:* electronic application, deferred entrance. *Application fee:* $65. *Required:* high school transcript. *Application deadlines:* rolling (freshmen), rolling (transfers). *Notification:* continuous (freshmen), continuous (transfers).

Freshman Application Contact Mr. Anthony Davis, Associate Director, Queensborough Community College of the City University of New York, 222-05 56th Avenue, Bayside, NY 11364. *Phone:* 718-281-5000. *Fax:* 718-281-5189.

Website: http://www.qcc.cuny.edu/.

Rockland Community College
Suffern, New York

- **State and locally supported** 2-year, founded 1959, part of State University of New York System
- **Suburban** 150-acre campus with easy access to New York City
- **Coed,** 7,434 undergraduate students, 56% full-time, 53% women, 47% men

Undergraduates 4,189 full-time, 3,245 part-time. Students come from 5 states and territories; 78 other countries; 1% are from out of state; 18% Black or African American, non-Hispanic/Latino; 19% Hispanic/Latino; 5% Asian, non-Hispanic/Latino; 0.3% Native Hawaiian or other Pacific Islander, non-

Hispanic/Latino; 0.2% American Indian or Alaska Native, non-Hispanic/Latino; 2% Two or more races, non-Hispanic/Latino; 17% Race/ethnicity unknown; 0.9% international; 6% transferred in. *Retention:* 70% of full-time freshmen returned.
Freshmen *Admission:* 1,471 applied, 1,471 admitted, 1,482 enrolled.
Faculty *Total:* 490, 23% full-time. *Student/faculty ratio:* 22:1.
Majors Accounting; administrative assistant and secretarial science; advertising; art; automobile/automotive mechanics technology; biological and physical sciences; business administration and management; commercial and advertising art; computer and information sciences related; computer graphics; computer/information technology services administration related; computer programming; computer programming related; computer programming (specific applications); computer systems networking and telecommunications; criminal justice/law enforcement administration; culinary arts; data processing and data processing technology; design and applied arts related; developmental and child psychology; dietetics; drafting and design technology; dramatic/theater arts; electrical, electronic and communications engineering technology; emergency medical technology (EMT paramedic); finance; fine/studio arts; fire science/firefighting; health information/medical records administration; hospitality administration; human services; liberal arts and sciences/liberal studies; marketing/marketing management; mass communication/media; mathematics; network and system administration; occupational therapy; photography; registered nursing/registered nurse; respiratory care therapy; tourism and travel services management.
Academics *Calendar:* semesters. *Degree:* certificates and associate. *Special study options:* academic remediation for entering students, accelerated degree program, adult/continuing education programs, advanced placement credit, cooperative education, distance learning, double majors, English as a second language, external degree program, freshman honors college, honors programs, independent study, internships, off-campus study, part-time degree program, services for LD students, study abroad, summer session for credit.
Library Rockland Community College Library with an OPAC, a Web page.
Student Life *Housing:* college housing not available. *Activities and Organizations:* drama/theater group, student-run newspaper, television station. *Campus security:* 24-hour emergency response devices and patrols, student patrols, late-night transport/escort service. *Student services:* personal/psychological counseling.
Athletics Member NJCAA. *Intercollegiate sports:* baseball M(s), basketball M/W, bowling M/W, golf M(s), soccer M/W, softball W, tennis M/W, volleyball W. *Intramural sports:* basketball M/W, bowling M/W, field hockey M/W, football M/W, golf M, racquetball M/W, soccer M/W, softball M/W, tennis M/W, volleyball M/W.
Costs (2014–15) *Tuition:* state resident $4299 full-time, $180 per credit part-time; nonresident $8598 full-time, $359 per credit part-time. Full-time tuition and fees vary according to course load and program. Part-time tuition and fees vary according to course load and program. *Required fees:* $355 full-time, $8 per credit part-time, $9 per term part-time. *Payment plans:* installment, deferred payment. *Waivers:* employees or children of employees.
Financial Aid Of all full-time matriculated undergraduates who enrolled in 2011, 68 Federal Work-Study jobs (averaging $2358). *Average need-based loan:* $4232. *Average need-based gift aid:* $3573.
Applying *Options:* early admission, deferred entrance. *Application fee:* $30. *Required:* high school transcript. *Application deadline:* rolling (freshmen).
Freshman Application Contact Rockland Community College, 145 College Road, Suffern, NY 10901-3699. *Phone:* 845-574-4484. *Toll-free phone:* 800-722-7666.
Website: http://www.sunyrockland.edu/.

St. Elizabeth College of Nursing
Utica, New York

- **Independent** 2-year, founded 1904
- **Small-town** 1-acre campus with easy access to Syracuse
- **Coed**
- 32% of applicants were admitted

Undergraduates 72 full-time, 87 part-time. Students come from 1 other state; 2% Black or African American, non-Hispanic/Latino; 2% Hispanic/Latino; 1% Asian, non-Hispanic/Latino; 3% Two or more races, non-Hispanic/Latino; 1% international; 51% transferred in. *Retention:* 75% of full-time freshmen returned.
Faculty *Student/faculty ratio:* 7:1.
Academics *Calendar:* semesters. *Degree:* associate. *Special study options:* academic remediation for entering students, advanced placement credit, off-campus study, part-time degree program, services for LD students.
Student Life *Campus security:* 24-hour emergency response devices and patrols.
Standardized Tests *Required:* SAT or ACT (for admission).

Applying *Options:* electronic application. *Application fee:* $65. *Required:* high school transcript, 2 letters of recommendation. *Recommended:* minimum 3.0 GPA.
Freshman Application Contact Donna Ernst, Director of Recruitment, St. Elizabeth College of Nursing, 2215 Genesee Street, Utica, NY 13501. *Phone:* 315-798-8189. *E-mail:* dernst@secon.edu.
Website: http://www.secon.edu/.

St. Joseph's College of Nursing
Syracuse, New York

Freshman Application Contact Ms. Felicia Corp, Recruiter, St. Joseph's College of Nursing, 206 Prospect Avenue, Syracuse, NY 13203. *Phone:* 315-448-5040. *Fax:* 315-448-5745. *E-mail:* collegeofnursing@sjhsyr.org.
Website: http://www.sjhsyr.org/nursing/.

St. Paul's School of Nursing
Rego Park, New York

Director of Admissions Nancy Wolinski, Chairperson of Admissions, St. Paul's School of Nursing, 97-77 Queens Boulevard, Rego Park, NY 11374. *Phone:* 718-357-0500 Ext. 131. *E-mail:* nwolinski@svcmcny.org.
Website: http://www.stpaulsschoolofnursing.com/.

St. Paul's School of Nursing
Staten Island, New York

Admissions Office Contact St. Paul's School of Nursing, Corporate Commons Two, 2 Teleport Drive, Suite 203, Staten Island, NY 10311.
Website: http://www.stpaulsschoolofnursing.com/.

Samaritan Hospital School of Nursing
Troy, New York

Director of Admissions Diane Dyer, Student Services Coordinator, Samaritan Hospital School of Nursing, 2215 Burdett Avenue, Troy, NY 12180. *Phone:* 518-271-3734. *Fax:* 518-271-3303. *E-mail:* marronej@nehealth.com.
Website: http://www.nehealth.com/.

Schenectady County Community College
Schenectady, New York

Freshman Application Contact Mr. David Sampson, Director of Admissions, Schenectady County Community College, 78 Washington Avenue, Schenectady, NY 12305-2294. *Phone:* 518-381-1370. *E-mail:* sampsodg@gw.sunysccc.edu.
Website: http://www.sunysccc.edu/.

State University of New York College of Technology at Alfred
Alfred, New York

- **State-supported** primarily 2-year, founded 1908, part of State University of New York System
- **Rural** 1084-acre campus with easy access to Rochester, Buffalo
- **Endowment** $4.5 million
- **Coed,** 3,661 undergraduate students, 91% full-time, 39% women, 61% men

Undergraduates 3,329 full-time, 332 part-time. Students come from 7 other countries; 6% are from out of state; 8% Black or African American, non-Hispanic/Latino; 6% Hispanic/Latino; 2% Asian, non-Hispanic/Latino; 0.1% Native Hawaiian or other Pacific Islander, non-Hispanic/Latino; 0.3% American Indian or Alaska Native, non-Hispanic/Latino; 2% Two or more races, non-Hispanic/Latino; 3% Race/ethnicity unknown; 9% transferred in; 66% live on campus. *Retention:* 86% of full-time freshmen returned.
Freshmen *Admission:* 6,034 applied, 3,273 admitted, 1,085 enrolled. *Average high school GPA:* 3.
Faculty *Total:* 233, 72% full-time, 17% with terminal degrees. *Student/faculty ratio:* 19:1.
Majors Accounting technology and bookkeeping; agribusiness; agriculture; animation, interactive technology, video graphics and special effects; architectural engineering technology; architecture; autobody/collision and repair technology; automobile/automotive mechanics technology; banking and financial support services; biology/biological sciences; business administration and management; business, management, and marketing related; computer and

information sciences; computer and information systems security; computer engineering technology; construction engineering technology; construction management; construction trades related; court reporting; culinary arts; diesel mechanics technology; drafting and design technology; drafting/design engineering technologies related; electrical and electronic engineering technologies related; electrical and power transmission installation; electrical, electronic and communications engineering technology; electromechanical technology; engineering; engineering technologies and engineering related; entrepreneurship; environmental engineering technology; environmental science; financial planning and services; forensic science and technology; general studies; health information/medical records technology; heating, air conditioning, ventilation and refrigeration maintenance technology; heavy/industrial equipment maintenance technologies related; humanities; human resources management; human services; interior design; liberal arts and sciences and humanities related; liberal arts and sciences/liberal studies; machine shop technology; manufacturing engineering technology; masonry; mechanical engineering/mechanical technology; registered nursing/registered nurse; sales, distribution, and marketing operations; sport and fitness administration/management; surveying technology; system, networking, and LAN/WAN management; vehicle maintenance and repair technologies related; veterinary/animal health technology; web/multimedia management and webmaster; welding technology.

Academics *Calendar:* semesters. *Degrees:* certificates, associate, and bachelor's. *Special study options:* academic remediation for entering students, adult/continuing education programs, advanced placement credit, cooperative education, distance learning, double majors, English as a second language, honors programs, independent study, internships, off-campus study, part-time degree program, services for LD students, student-designed majors, study abroad, summer session for credit. *ROTC:* Army (c).

Library Walter C. Hinkle Memorial Library plus 1 other with 55,429 titles, 3,487 audiovisual materials, an OPAC, a Web page.

Student Life *Housing Options:* coed, men-only, women-only, special housing for students with disabilities. Campus housing is university owned. Freshman campus housing is guaranteed. *Activities and Organizations:* drama/theater group, student-run newspaper, radio station, choral group, Outdoor Recreation Club, Caribbean Student Association, Alfred Programming Board, Pioneer Woodsmen, Disaster Relief Team. *Campus security:* 24-hour emergency response devices and patrols, late-night transport/escort service, controlled dormitory access, residence hall entrance guards. *Student services:* health clinic, personal/psychological counseling.

Athletics Member NCAA, USCAA. All Division III. *Intercollegiate sports:* baseball M, basketball M/W, cross-country running M/W, equestrian sports M/W, football M, lacrosse M, soccer M/W, softball W, swimming and diving M/W, track and field M/W, volleyball M, wrestling M. *Intramural sports:* basketball M/W, football M(c), golf M/W, ice hockey M(c)/W(c), lacrosse M(c)/W(c), rock climbing M/W, soccer M/W, softball M/W, swimming and diving M(c)/W(c), tennis M/W, ultimate Frisbee M/W, volleyball M/W.

Standardized Tests *Required for some:* SAT or ACT (for admission). *Recommended:* SAT or ACT (for admission).

Costs (2014–15) *One-time required fee:* $100. *Tuition:* state resident $6170 full-time, $257 per credit hour part-time; nonresident $9740 full-time, $406 per credit hour part-time. Full-time tuition and fees vary according to course load and degree level. Part-time tuition and fees vary according to course load and degree level. *Required fees:* $1476 full-time, $58 per credit hour part-time, $10 per credit hour part-time. *Room and board:* $11,910; room only: $7080. Room and board charges vary according to board plan and housing facility. *Payment plan:* installment. *Waivers:* employees or children of employees.

Financial Aid Of all full-time matriculated undergraduates who enrolled in 2014, 3,070 applied for aid, 2,751 were judged to have need, 227 had their need fully met. 208 Federal Work-Study jobs (averaging $1273). In 2014, 150 non-need-based awards were made. *Average percent of need met:* 56%. *Average financial aid package:* $10,970. *Average need-based loan:* $4089. *Average need-based gift aid:* $6638. *Average non-need-based aid:* $6130. *Average indebtedness upon graduation:* $31,247.

Applying *Options:* electronic application. *Application fee:* $50. *Required:* high school transcript, minimum 2.0 GPA. *Recommended:* essay or personal statement, interview. *Application deadlines:* rolling (freshmen), rolling (out-of-state freshmen), rolling (transfers). *Notification:* continuous (freshmen), continuous (out-of-state freshmen), continuous (transfers).

Freshman Application Contact Mrs. Goodrich Deborah, Associate Vice President for Enrollment Management, State University of New York College of Technology at Alfred, Huntington Administration Building, 10 Upper College Drive, Alfred, NY 14802. *Phone:* 607-587-3945. *Toll-free phone:* 800-4-ALFRED. *Fax:* 607-587-4299. *E-mail:* admissions@alfredstate.edu. *Website:* http://www.alfredstate.edu/.

Stella and Charles Guttman Community College
New York, New York

Admissions Office Contact Stella and Charles Guttman Community College, 50 West 40th Street, New York, NY 10018.
Website: http://guttman.cuny.edu/.

Suffolk County Community College
Selden, New York

Freshman Application Contact Suffolk County Community College, 533 College Road, Selden, NY 11784-2899. *Phone:* 631-451-4000.
Website: http://www.sunysuffolk.edu/.

Sullivan County Community College
Loch Sheldrake, New York

- **State and locally supported** 2-year, founded 1962, part of State University of New York System
- **Rural** 405-acre campus
- **Endowment** $1.1 million
- **Coed,** 1,647 undergraduate students, 57% full-time, 53% women, 47% men

Undergraduates 931 full-time, 716 part-time. Students come from 5 states and territories; 4 other countries; 2% are from out of state; 20% Black or African American, non-Hispanic/Latino; 18% Hispanic/Latino; 1% Asian, non-Hispanic/Latino; 0.1% Native Hawaiian or other Pacific Islander, non-Hispanic/Latino; 0.5% American Indian or Alaska Native, non-Hispanic/Latino; 2% Two or more races, non-Hispanic/Latino; 8% Race/ethnicity unknown; 0.4% international; 6% transferred in; 22% live on campus.

Freshmen *Admission:* 2,084 applied, 1,790 admitted, 344 enrolled. *Average high school GPA:* 2.8.

Faculty *Total:* 104, 46% full-time, 20% with terminal degrees. *Student/faculty ratio:* 17:1.

Majors Accounting; administrative assistant and secretarial science; baking and pastry arts; business administration and management; commercial and advertising art; computer graphics; computer programming (specific applications); construction engineering technology; consumer merchandising/retailing management; criminal justice/police science; crisis/emergency/disaster management; culinary arts; data entry/microcomputer applications; electrical, electronic and communications engineering technology; elementary education; environmental studies; fire prevention and safety technology; forensic science and technology; hospitality administration; human services; information science/studies; kindergarten/preschool education; legal assistant/paralegal; liberal arts and sciences/liberal studies; marketing/marketing management; mathematics; medical/clinical assistant; parks, recreation and leisure; photography; psychology; radio and television; radio, television, and digital communication related; registered nursing/registered nurse; respiratory care therapy; science technologies related; sport and fitness administration/management; tourism and travel services management.

Academics *Calendar:* semesters. *Degree:* certificates and associate. *Special study options:* academic remediation for entering students, adult/continuing education programs, advanced placement credit, distance learning, double majors, honors programs, independent study, internships, off-campus study, part-time degree program, services for LD students, summer session for credit.

Library Hermann Memorial Library plus 1 other with 131,870 titles, 8,857 audiovisual materials, an OPAC, a Web page.

Student Life *Housing Options:* coed. Campus housing is provided by a third party. Freshman applicants given priority for college housing. *Activities and Organizations:* student-run newspaper, radio station, Science Alliance, Black Student Union, Gay Straight Alliance, Dance Club, Honor Society. *Campus security:* 24-hour emergency response devices and patrols, student patrols, controlled dormitory access. *Student services:* health clinic, personal/psychological counseling, legal services.

Athletics Member NJCAA. *Intercollegiate sports:* basketball M/W, cross-country running M/W, softball W, volleyball W, wrestling M. *Intramural sports:* basketball M/W, bowling M/W, cross-country running M/W, football M, golf M/W, racquetball M/W, skiing (downhill) M/W, soccer M/W, softball M/W, table tennis M/W, tennis M/W, volleyball M/W, weight lifting M/W.

Costs (2015–16) *Tuition:* state resident $4474 full-time, $186 per credit hour part-time; nonresident $8948 full-time, $300 per credit hour part-time. Full-time tuition and fees vary according to program. Part-time tuition and fees vary according to program. *Required fees:* $826 full-time, $35 per credit hour part-time. *Room and board:* $9254; room only: $6050. Room and board charges vary according to board plan and housing facility. *Payment plans:* installment, deferred payment. *Waivers:* senior citizens and employees or children of employees.

Financial Aid Of all full-time matriculated undergraduates who enrolled in 2013, 1,068 applied for aid, 982 were judged to have need, 982 had their need fully met. 73 Federal Work-Study jobs (averaging $1129). 22 state and other part-time jobs (averaging $794). *Average percent of need met:* 100%. *Average financial aid package:* $5928. *Average need-based loan:* $2882. *Average need-based gift aid:* $5928.

Applying *Options:* electronic application, early admission, deferred entrance. *Required:* high school transcript. *Application deadlines:* rolling (freshmen), rolling (out-of-state freshmen), rolling (transfers). *Notification:* continuous (freshmen), continuous (out-of-state freshmen), continuous (transfers).

Freshman Application Contact Ms. Sari Rosenheck, Director of Admissions and Registration Services, Sullivan County Community College, 112 College Road, Loch Sheldrake, NY 12759. *Phone:* 845-434-5750 Ext. 4200. *Toll-free phone:* 800-577-5243. *Fax:* 845-434-4806. *E-mail:* sarir@sunysullivan.edu. *Website:* http://www.sullivan.suny.edu/.

TCI–The College of Technology
New York, New York

- **Proprietary** 2-year, founded 1909
- **Urban** campus
- **Coed**

Undergraduates 2,640 full-time, 380 part-time. 42% Black or African American, non-Hispanic/Latino; 34% Hispanic/Latino; 3% Asian, non-Hispanic/Latino; 0.1% Native Hawaiian or other Pacific Islander, non-Hispanic/Latino; 0.6% Two or more races, non-Hispanic/Latino; 14% Race/ethnicity unknown; 0.6% international.

Faculty *Student/faculty ratio:* 24:1.

Academics *Calendar:* semesters. *Degree:* certificates and associate. *Special study options:* academic remediation for entering students, adult/continuing education programs, advanced placement credit, distance learning, English as a second language, part-time degree program, summer session for credit.

Student Life *Campus security:* 24-hour patrols.

Applying *Options:* deferred entrance. *Required:* essay or personal statement, high school transcript, interview.

Freshman Application Contact TCI–The College of Technology, 320 West 31st Street, New York, NY 10001-2705. *Phone:* 212-594-4000. *Toll-free phone:* 800-878-8246.

Website: http://www.tcicollege.edu/.

Tompkins Cortland Community College
Dryden, New York

- **State and locally supported** 2-year, founded 1968, part of State University of New York System
- **Rural** 300-acre campus with easy access to Syracuse
- **Coed,** 5,560 undergraduate students, 42% full-time, 55% women, 45% men

Undergraduates 2,328 full-time, 3,232 part-time. Students come from 22 states and territories; 25 other countries; 3% are from out of state; 13% Black or African American, non-Hispanic/Latino; 11% Hispanic/Latino; 2% Asian, non-Hispanic/Latino; 0.3% American Indian or Alaska Native, non-Hispanic/Latino; 4% Two or more races, non-Hispanic/Latino; 3% Race/ethnicity unknown; 2% international; 5% transferred in.

Freshmen *Admission:* 825 enrolled.

Faculty *Total:* 349, 20% full-time, 14% with terminal degrees. *Student/faculty ratio:* 21:1.

Majors Accounting technology and bookkeeping; administrative assistant and secretarial science; agroecology and sustainable agriculture; biology/biotechnology laboratory technician; business administration and management; child-care and support services management; commercial and advertising art; computer and information sciences; computer support specialist; construction engineering technology; creative writing; criminal justice/law enforcement administration; criminal justice/police science; culinary arts; digital communication and media/multimedia; engineering; entrepreneurship; environmental studies; hotel, motel, and restaurant management; humanities; human services; information science/studies; international business/trade/commerce; international/global studies; legal assistant/paralegal; liberal arts and sciences and humanities related; liberal arts and sciences/liberal studies; parks, recreation and leisure; parks, recreation and leisure facilities management; photographic and film/video technology; radio and television broadcasting technology; registered nursing/registered nurse; special products marketing; speech communication and rhetoric; sport and fitness administration/management; substance abuse/addiction counseling.

Academics *Calendar:* semesters. *Degree:* certificates and associate. *Special study options:* academic remediation for entering students, adult/continuing education programs, advanced placement credit, cooperative education,

distance learning, double majors, English as a second language, freshman honors college, honors programs, independent study, internships, off-campus study, part-time degree program, services for LD students, study abroad, summer session for credit.

Library Gerald A. Barry Memorial Library plus 1 other with 65,386 titles, 3,445 audiovisual materials, an OPAC, a Web page.

Student Life *Housing Options:* coed. Campus housing is provided by a third party. *Activities and Organizations:* drama/theater group, College Entertainment Board, Sport Management Club, Nursing Club, Media Club, Writer's Guild. *Campus security:* 24-hour patrols, late-night transport/escort service, controlled dormitory access, armed peace officers. *Student services:* health clinic, personal/psychological counseling.

Athletics Member NJCAA. *Intercollegiate sports:* baseball M, basketball M/W, golf M/W, lacrosse M, soccer M/W, softball W, volleyball W. *Intramural sports:* archery M/W, badminton M/W, basketball M/W, bowling M/W, football M/W, golf M/W, lacrosse M/W, racquetball M/W, skiing (cross-country) M/W, skiing (downhill) M/W, soccer M/W, softball M/W, squash M/W, swimming and diving M/W, table tennis M/W, tennis M/W, ultimate Frisbee M/W, volleyball M/W, water polo M/W, weight lifting M/W, wrestling M/W.

Costs (2014–15) *Tuition:* state resident $4500 full-time, $157 per credit hour part-time; nonresident $9300 full-time, $324 per credit hour part-time. Part-time tuition and fees vary according to course load. *Required fees:* $991 full-time, $35 per credit hour part-time, $12 per term part-time. *Room and board:* $10,100. Room and board charges vary according to board plan and housing facility. *Payment plans:* installment, deferred payment. *Waivers:* employees or children of employees.

Financial Aid Of all full-time matriculated undergraduates who enrolled in 2013, 150 Federal Work-Study jobs (averaging $1000). 150 state and other part-time jobs (averaging $1000).

Applying *Options:* electronic application, early admission, deferred entrance. *Required:* high school transcript. *Required for some:* essay or personal statement, interview. *Application deadlines:* rolling (freshmen), rolling (out-of-state freshmen), rolling (transfers). *Notification:* continuous (freshmen), continuous (out-of-state freshmen), continuous (transfers).

Freshman Application Contact Mr. Sandy Drumluk, Director of Admissions, Tompkins Cortland Community College, 170 North Street, PO Box 139, Dryden, NY 13053-0139. *Phone:* 607-844-6580. *Toll-free phone:* 888-567-8211. *Fax:* 607-844-6538. *E-mail:* admissions@tc3.edu. *Website:* http://www.TC3.edu/.

Trocaire College
Buffalo, New York

- **Independent** primarily 2-year, founded 1958
- **Urban** 1-acre campus
- **Endowment** $10.8 million
- **Coed, primarily women,** 1,467 undergraduate students, 46% full-time, 87% women, 13% men

Undergraduates 671 full-time, 796 part-time. Students come from 4 states and territories; 1 other country; 0.2% are from out of state; 14% Black or African American, non-Hispanic/Latino; 3% Hispanic/Latino; 2% Asian, non-Hispanic/Latino; 0.1% Native Hawaiian or other Pacific Islander, non-Hispanic/Latino; 1% American Indian or Alaska Native, non-Hispanic/Latino; 0.7% Two or more races, non-Hispanic/Latino; 9% Race/ethnicity unknown; 0.1% international; 17% transferred in. *Retention:* 63% of full-time freshmen returned.

Freshmen *Admission:* 730 applied, 423 admitted, 137 enrolled.

Faculty *Total:* 169, 30% full-time. *Student/faculty ratio:* 11:1.

Majors Business administration and management; computer systems networking and telecommunications; diagnostic medical sonography and ultrasound technology; dietetic technology; general studies; health information/medical records technology; hospitality administration; human resources management; liberal arts and sciences/liberal studies; massage therapy; medical/clinical assistant; medical informatics; radiologic technology/science; surgical technology.

Academics *Calendar:* semesters. *Degrees:* certificates, associate, and bachelor's. *Special study options:* academic remediation for entering students, adult/continuing education programs, advanced placement credit, cooperative education, distance learning, double majors, external degree program, independent study, internships, off-campus study, part-time degree program, services for LD students, study abroad, summer session for credit.

Library The Rachel R. Savarino Library plus 1 other with 12,156 titles, 772 audiovisual materials, an OPAC, a Web page.

Student Life *Housing:* college housing not available. *Activities and Organizations:* student-run newspaper, Student Governance Association, TroGreen, Diversity Club. *Campus security:* 24-hour emergency response devices and patrols, late-night transport/escort service. *Student services:* personal/psychological counseling.

Costs (2015–16) *Tuition:* $15,970 full-time, $660 per hour part-time. Full-time tuition and fees vary according to course load. Part-time tuition and fees vary according to course load. *Required fees:* $320 full-time, $27 per credit hour part-time. *Payment plan:* installment. *Waivers:* employees or children of employees.
Applying *Options:* electronic application, deferred entrance. *Required:* high school transcript. *Required for some:* essay or personal statement, 1 letter of recommendation. *Recommended:* minimum 1.9 GPA, interview. *Application deadlines:* rolling (freshmen), rolling (transfers).
Freshman Application Contact Mrs. Sharon Kempton, Director of Admissions, Trocaire College, 360 Choate Avenue, Buffalo, NY 14220-2094. *Phone:* 716-827-2459. *Fax:* 716-828-6107. *E-mail:* info@trocaire.edu. *Website:* http://www.trocaire.edu/.

Ulster County Community College
Stone Ridge, New York

- **State and locally supported** 2-year, founded 1961, part of State University of New York System
- **Rural** 165-acre campus
- **Endowment** $4.9 million
- **Coed,** 3,540 undergraduate students, 50% full-time, 59% women, 41% men

Undergraduates 1,759 full-time, 1,781 part-time. Students come from 10 states and territories; 8 other countries; 6% transferred in.
Freshmen *Admission:* 618 applied, 618 admitted, 583 enrolled.
Faculty *Total:* 189, 35% full-time. *Student/faculty ratio:* 19:1.
Majors Accounting technology and bookkeeping; biology teacher education; business administration and management; chemistry teacher education; commercial and advertising art; community organization and advocacy; computer and information sciences; computer and information sciences and support services related; criminal justice/law enforcement administration; drafting/design engineering technologies related; dramatic/theater arts; engineering; kindergarten/preschool education; liberal arts and sciences/liberal studies; management information systems and services related; mathematics teacher education; natural resources/conservation; parks, recreation and leisure facilities management; public administration and social service professions related; registered nursing/registered nurse; science teacher education; social studies teacher education; Spanish language teacher education; speech communication and rhetoric; veterinary/animal health technology; visual and performing arts.
Academics *Calendar:* semesters. *Degree:* certificates, diplomas, and associate. *Special study options:* academic remediation for entering students, adult/continuing education programs, advanced placement credit, cooperative education, distance learning, double majors, English as a second language, honors programs, independent study, internships, off-campus study, part-time degree program, services for LD students, student-designed majors, study abroad, summer session for credit.
Library McDonald Dewitt Library with 86,597 titles, 4,828 audiovisual materials, an OPAC, a Web page.
Student Life *Housing:* college housing not available. *Activities and Organizations:* drama/theater group, choral group, Vet Tech, Biology Club, Nursing Club, Business Club, Visual Arts Club. *Campus security:* 24-hour emergency response devices and patrols. *Student services:* personal/psychological counseling.
Athletics Member NJCAA. *Intercollegiate sports:* baseball M, basketball M/W, golf M, soccer M, softball W, tennis M, volleyball W.
Costs (2014–15) *Tuition:* state resident $4230 full-time, $159 per credit hour part-time; nonresident $8460 full-time, $318 per credit hour part-time. *Required fees:* $797 full-time, $65 per credit hour part-time, $24 per term part-time. *Payment plans:* installment, deferred payment. *Waivers:* senior citizens and employees or children of employees.
Financial Aid Of all full-time matriculated undergraduates who enrolled in 2013, 45 Federal Work-Study jobs (averaging $1000).
Applying *Options:* electronic application, early admission, deferred entrance. *Required:* high school transcript. *Application deadlines:* rolling (freshmen), rolling (transfers). *Notification:* continuous (freshmen), continuous (transfers).
Freshman Application Contact Admissions Office, Ulster County Community College, 491 Cottekill Road, Stone Ridge, NY 12484. *Phone:* 845-687-5022. *Toll-free phone:* 800-724-0833. *E-mail:* admissionsoffice@sunyulster.edu. *Website:* http://www.sunyulster.edu/.

Utica School of Commerce
Utica, New York

Freshman Application Contact Senior Admissions Coordinator, Utica School of Commerce, 201 Bleecker Street, Utica, NY 13501-2280. *Phone:* 315-733-2300. *Toll-free phone:* 800-321-4USC. *Fax:* 315-733-9281. *Website:* http://www.uscny.edu/.

Westchester Community College
Valhalla, New York

- **State and locally supported** 2-year, founded 1946, part of State University of New York System
- **Suburban** 218-acre campus with easy access to New York City
- **Coed,** 13,916 undergraduate students, 54% full-time, 52% women, 48% men

Undergraduates 7,546 full-time, 6,370 part-time. 6% transferred in.
Freshmen *Admission:* 5,211 applied, 5,211 admitted, 2,495 enrolled.
Faculty *Total:* 1,090, 16% full-time.
Majors Accounting; administrative assistant and secretarial science; apparel and textile manufacturing; business administration and management; child development; civil engineering technology; clinical laboratory science/medical technology; clinical/medical laboratory technology; community organization and advocacy; computer and information sciences; computer and information sciences and support services related; computer and information sciences related; computer and information systems security; computer science; computer systems networking and telecommunications; consumer merchandising/retailing management; corrections; culinary arts; dance; data processing and data processing technology; design and applied arts related; dietetics; education (multiple levels); electrical, electronic and communications engineering technology; emergency medical technology (EMT paramedic); energy management and systems technology; engineering science; engineering technology; environmental control technologies related; environmental science; environmental studies; film/video and photographic arts related; finance; fine/studio arts; food technology and processing; humanities; information science/studies; international business/trade/commerce; journalism; legal assistant/paralegal; liberal arts and sciences/liberal studies; marketing/marketing management; mass communication/media; mechanical engineering/mechanical technology; public administration; registered nursing/registered nurse; respiratory care therapy; social sciences; substance abuse/addiction counseling; veterinary/animal health technology.
Academics *Calendar:* semesters. *Degree:* certificates and associate. *Special study options:* academic remediation for entering students, adult/continuing education programs, advanced placement credit, cooperative education, distance learning, double majors, English as a second language, honors programs, independent study, internships, off-campus study, part-time degree program, services for LD students, student-designed majors, study abroad, summer session for credit.
Library Harold L. Drimmer Library with an OPAC, a Web page.
Student Life *Housing:* college housing not available. *Activities and Organizations:* drama/theater group, student-run newspaper, radio station, choral group, Deca Fashion Retail, Future Educators, Respiratory Club, Black Student Union, Diversity Action. *Campus security:* 24-hour emergency response devices and patrols, late-night transport/escort service. *Student services:* health clinic, personal/psychological counseling, women's center.
Athletics Member NJCAA. *Intercollegiate sports:* baseball M, basketball M/W, bowling M/W, golf M, soccer M, softball W, volleyball W. *Intramural sports:* badminton M/W, basketball M/W, softball M/W, swimming and diving M/W, tennis M/W, volleyball M/W, weight lifting M/W.
Costs (2014–15) *Tuition:* state resident $4280 full-time, $179 per credit part-time; nonresident $11,770 full-time, $493 per credit part-time. Full-time tuition and fees vary according to location. Part-time tuition and fees vary according to location. *Required fees:* $443 full-time, $102 per term part-time. *Payment plan:* installment.
Financial Aid Of all full-time matriculated undergraduates who enrolled in 2013, 200 Federal Work-Study jobs (averaging $1000).
Applying *Options:* early admission. *Application fee:* $35. *Required:* high school transcript. *Recommended:* interview.
Freshman Application Contact Ms. Gloria Leon, Director of Admissions, Westchester Community College, 75 Grasslands Road, Administration Building, Valhalla, NY 10595-1698. *Phone:* 914-606-6735. *Fax:* 914-606-6540. *E-mail:* admissions@sunywcc.edu. *Website:* http://www.sunywcc.edu/.

Wood Tobe–Coburn School
New York, New York
- **Private** 2-year, founded 1879
- **Urban** campus
- **Coed,** 476 undergraduate students
- 72% of applicants were admitted

Freshmen *Admission:* 737 applied, 532 admitted.

Majors Accounting technology and bookkeeping; administrative assistant and secretarial science; computer programming; computer systems networking and telecommunications; fashion/apparel design; graphic design; hotel/motel administration; medical/clinical assistant; retailing.

Academics *Calendar:* semesters. *Degree:* diplomas and associate. *Special study options:* accelerated degree program, internships.

Student Life *Housing:* college housing not available.

Freshman Application Contact Admissions Office, Wood Tobe–Coburn School, 8 East 40th Street, New York, NY 10016. *Phone:* 212-686-9040. *Toll-free phone:* 800-394-9663.

Website: http://www.woodtobecoburn.edu/.

NORTH CAROLINA

Alamance Community College
Graham, North Carolina
- **State-supported** 2-year, founded 1959, part of North Carolina Community College System
- **Small-town** 48-acre campus
- **Endowment** $2.9 million
- **Coed,** 4,614 undergraduate students, 57% full-time, 58% women, 42% men

Undergraduates 2,651 full-time, 1,963 part-time. Students come from 7 states and territories; 3 other countries; 1% are from out of state; 20% Black or African American, non-Hispanic/Latino; 10% Hispanic/Latino; 2% Asian, non-Hispanic/Latino; 0.7% American Indian or Alaska Native, non-Hispanic/Latino; 4% Two or more races, non-Hispanic/Latino; 0.8% international; 28% transferred in.

Freshmen *Admission:* 710 applied, 710 admitted, 710 enrolled.

Faculty *Total:* 435, 26% full-time, 3% with terminal degrees. *Student/faculty ratio:* 12:1.

Majors Accounting technology and bookkeeping; animal sciences; applied horticulture/horticulture operations; automobile/automotive mechanics technology; banking and financial support services; biotechnology; business administration and management; carpentry; clinical/medical laboratory technology; commercial and advertising art; criminal justice/safety; culinary arts; electrical, electronic and communications engineering technology; executive assistant/executive secretary; heating, ventilation, air conditioning and refrigeration engineering technology; information science/studies; kindergarten/preschool education; legal administrative assistant/secretary; liberal arts and sciences/liberal studies; machine tool technology; mechanical engineering/mechanical technology; medical administrative assistant and medical secretary; medical/clinical assistant; office occupations and clerical services; registered nursing/registered nurse; retailing; teacher assistant/aide; welding technology.

Academics *Calendar:* semesters. *Degree:* certificates, diplomas, and associate. *Special study options:* academic remediation for entering students, adult/continuing education programs, cooperative education, distance learning, double majors, English as a second language, independent study, off-campus study, part-time degree program, services for LD students, summer session for credit.

Library Learning Resources Center with 22,114 titles, an OPAC, a Web page.

Student Life *Housing:* college housing not available. *Campus security:* 24-hour emergency response devices and patrols, student patrols, late-night transport/escort service. *Student services:* personal/psychological counseling.

Athletics *Intramural sports:* basketball M/W, bowling M/W, tennis M/W, volleyball M/W.

Costs (2014–15) *Tuition:* state resident $2160 full-time; nonresident $7920 full-time. Full-time tuition and fees vary according to course load. Part-time tuition and fees vary according to course load. *Required fees:* $30 full-time. *Waivers:* senior citizens.

Financial Aid Of all full-time matriculated undergraduates who enrolled in 2010, 4,000 applied for aid, 3,000 were judged to have need. 200 Federal Work-Study jobs. *Average percent of need met:* 30%. *Average financial aid package:* $4500. *Average need-based gift aid:* $4500. *Average indebtedness upon graduation:* $2500.

Applying *Options:* electronic application. *Required:* high school transcript. *Application deadlines:* rolling (freshmen), rolling (transfers). *Notification:* continuous (freshmen), continuous (transfers).

Freshman Application Contact Ms. Elizabeth Brehler, Director for Enrollment Management, Alamance Community College, Graham, NC 27253-8000. *Phone:* 336-506-4120. *Fax:* 336-506-4264. *E-mail:* brehlere@alamancecc.edu.

Website: http://www.alamancecc.edu/.

Asheville-Buncombe Technical Community College
Asheville, North Carolina

Freshman Application Contact Asheville-Buncombe Technical Community College, 340 Victoria Road, Asheville, NC 28801-4897. *Phone:* 828-254-1921 Ext. 7520.

Website: http://www.abtech.edu/.

Beaufort County Community College
Washington, North Carolina

Freshman Application Contact Mr. Gary Burbage, Director of Admissions, Beaufort County Community College, PO Box 1069, 5337 US Highway 264 East, Washington, NC 27889-1069. *Phone:* 252-940-6233. *Fax:* 252-940-6393. *E-mail:* garyb@beaufortccc.edu.

Website: http://www.beaufortccc.edu/.

Bladen Community College
Dublin, North Carolina

Freshman Application Contact Ms. Andrea Fisher, Enrollment Specialist, Bladen Community College, PO Box 266, Dublin, NC 28332. *Phone:* 910-879-5593. *Fax:* 910-879-5564. *E-mail:* acarterfisher@bladencc.edu.

Website: http://www.bladen.cc.nc.us/.

Blue Ridge Community College
Flat Rock, North Carolina

Freshman Application Contact Blue Ridge Community College, 180 West Campus Drive, Flat Rock, NC 28731. *Phone:* 828-694-1810.

Website: http://www.blueridge.edu/.

Brunswick Community College
Supply, North Carolina

Freshman Application Contact Admissions Counselor, Brunswick Community College, 50 College Road, PO Box 30, Supply, NC 28462-0030. *Phone:* 910-755-7300. *Toll-free phone:* 800-754-1050. *Fax:* 910-754-9609. *E-mail:* admissions@brunswickcc.edu.

Website: http://www.brunswickcc.edu/.

Caldwell Community College and Technical Institute
Hudson, North Carolina

Freshman Application Contact Carolyn Woodard, Director of Enrollment Management Services, Caldwell Community College and Technical Institute, 2855 Hickory Boulevard, Hudson, NC 28638. *Phone:* 828-726-2703. *Fax:* 828-726-2709. *E-mail:* cwoodard@cccti.edu.

Website: http://www.cccti.edu/.

Cape Fear Community College
Wilmington, North Carolina
- **State-supported** 2-year, founded 1959, part of North Carolina Community College System
- **Urban** 150-acre campus
- **Endowment** $7.4 million
- **Coed,** 9,300 undergraduate students, 45% full-time, 55% women, 45% men

Undergraduates 4,208 full-time, 5,092 part-time. Students come from 30 states and territories; 52 other countries; 4% are from out of state; 15% Black or African American, non-Hispanic/Latino; 6% Hispanic/Latino; 1% Asian, non-Hispanic/Latino; 0.2% Native Hawaiian or other Pacific Islander, non-Hispanic/Latino; 0.9% American Indian or Alaska Native, non-

Hispanic/Latino; 3% Two or more races, non-Hispanic/Latino; 2% Race/ethnicity unknown; 5% transferred in.

Freshmen *Admission:* 4,321 applied, 2,326 admitted, 1,920 enrolled.

Faculty *Total:* 781, 38% full-time. *Student/faculty ratio:* 14:1.

Majors Accounting technology and bookkeeping; architectural engineering technology; automobile/automotive mechanics technology; building/property maintenance; business administration and management; chemical technology; cinematography and film/video production; computer systems networking and telecommunications; computer technology/computer systems technology; criminal justice/police science; culinary arts; dental hygiene; diagnostic medical sonography and ultrasound technology; early childhood education; electrical, electronic and communications engineering technology; electrical/electronics equipment installation and repair; electromechanical and instrumentation and maintenance technologies related; executive assistant/executive secretary; fire prevention and safety technology; hotel/motel administration; instrumentation technology; interior design; landscaping and groundskeeping; language interpretation and translation; liberal arts and sciences/liberal studies; machine shop technology; marine maintenance and ship repair technology; mechanical engineering/mechanical technology; medical office management; medical radiologic technology; nuclear/nuclear power technology; occupational therapist assistant; oceanography (chemical and physical); registered nursing/registered nurse; surgical technology.

Academics *Calendar:* semesters. *Degree:* certificates, diplomas, and associate. *Special study options:* academic remediation for entering students, adult/continuing education programs, advanced placement credit, cooperative education, distance learning, double majors, English as a second language, independent study, off-campus study, part-time degree program, services for LD students, summer session for credit.

Library Cape Fear Community College Library with 83,653 titles, 16,156 audiovisual materials, an OPAC, a Web page.

Student Life *Housing:* college housing not available. *Activities and Organizations:* student-run newspaper, choral group, Nursing Club, Dental Hygiene Club, Pineapple Guild, Phi Theta Kappa, Occupational Therapy. *Campus security:* 24-hour emergency response devices and patrols, late-night transport/escort service, armed police officers. *Student services:* personal/psychological counseling.

Athletics Member NJCAA. *Intercollegiate sports:* basketball M/W, cheerleading M/W, golf M, soccer M/W, volleyball W. *Intramural sports:* basketball M/W, table tennis M/W.

Costs (2015–16) *Tuition:* state resident $2304 full-time; nonresident $8448 full-time. Full-time tuition and fees vary according to course load. Part-time tuition and fees vary according to course load. *Required fees:* $222 full-time. *Payment plan:* installment.

Financial Aid Of all full-time matriculated undergraduates who enrolled in 2012, 150 Federal Work-Study jobs (averaging $1687).

Applying *Options:* electronic application, early admission. *Required for some:* high school transcript, interview, placement testing. *Application deadlines:* 8/16 (freshmen), rolling (transfers). *Notification:* continuous (freshmen), continuous (transfers).

Freshman Application Contact Ms. Linda Kasyan, Director of Enrollment Management, Cape Fear Community College, 411 North Front Street, Wilmington, NC 28401-3993. *Phone:* 910-362-7054. *Toll-free phone:* 877-799-2322. *Fax:* 910-362-7080. *E-mail:* admissions@cfcc.edu. *Website:* http://www.cfcc.edu/.

Carolinas College of Health Sciences
Charlotte, North Carolina

- **Public** 2-year, founded 1990
- **Urban** 3-acre campus with easy access to Charlotte
- **Endowment** $1.8 million
- **Coed**

Undergraduates 58 full-time, 380 part-time. Students come from 4 states and territories; 6% are from out of state; 9% Black or African American, non-Hispanic/Latino; 4% Hispanic/Latino; 2% Asian, non-Hispanic/Latino; 0.7% Native Hawaiian or other Pacific Islander, non-Hispanic/Latino; 0.5% American Indian or Alaska Native, non-Hispanic/Latino; 3% Two or more races, non-Hispanic/Latino; 3% Race/ethnicity unknown.

Faculty *Student/faculty ratio:* 11:1.

Academics *Calendar:* semesters. *Degree:* certificates, diplomas, and associate. *Special study options:* advanced placement credit, distance learning, double majors, honors programs, independent study, services for LD students, summer session for credit.

Student Life *Campus security:* 24-hour emergency response devices and patrols, late-night transport/escort service.

Standardized Tests *Required for some:* SAT or ACT (for admission).

Costs (2014–15) *Tuition:* state resident $13,311 full-time, $317 per credit hour part-time; nonresident $13,311 full-time, $317 per credit hour part-time. Full-time tuition and fees vary according to course load and program. Part-time

tuition and fees vary according to course load and program. *Required fees:* $1240 full-time, $125 per term part-time.

Financial Aid Of all full-time matriculated undergraduates who enrolled in 2013, 8 Federal Work-Study jobs (averaging $2258).

Applying *Options:* electronic application. *Application fee:* $50. *Required:* minimum 2.5 GPA. *Required for some:* high school transcript, 1 letter of recommendation, interview, SAT or ACT scores.

Freshman Application Contact Ms. Laura Holland, Admissions Representative, Carolinas College of Health Sciences, 1200 Blythe Boulevard, Charlotte, NC 28203. *Phone:* 704-355-5583. *Fax:* 704-355-9336. *E-mail:* Laura.Holland@CarolinasCollege.edu. *Website:* http://www.carolinascollege.edu/.

Carteret Community College
Morehead City, North Carolina

- **State-supported** 2-year, founded 1963, part of North Carolina Community College System
- **Small-town** 25-acre campus
- **Coed**, 1,872 undergraduate students, 43% full-time, 69% women, 31% men

Undergraduates 804 full-time, 1,068 part-time. Students come from 27 states and territories; 2 other countries; 8% transferred in. *Retention:* 52% of full-time freshmen returned.

Freshmen *Admission:* 2,156 applied, 1,970 admitted, 304 enrolled.

Faculty *Total:* 253, 26% full-time, 7% with terminal degrees. *Student/faculty ratio:* 9:1.

Majors Administrative assistant and secretarial science; business administration and management; computer engineering technology; computer software and media applications related; computer systems networking and telecommunications; criminal justice/law enforcement administration; industrial radiologic technology; information technology; interior design; legal administrative assistant/secretary; legal assistant/paralegal; liberal arts and sciences/liberal studies; licensed practical/vocational nurse training; medical/clinical assistant; photography; respiratory care therapy; teacher assistant/aide.

Academics *Calendar:* semesters. *Degrees:* certificates, diplomas, associate, and postbachelor's certificates. *Special study options:* academic remediation for entering students, adult/continuing education programs, cooperative education, distance learning, double majors, internships, part-time degree program, services for LD students, summer session for credit.

Library Michael J. Smith Learning Resource Center with 22,000 titles, an OPAC, a Web page.

Student Life *Housing:* college housing not available. *Activities and Organizations:* drama/theater group, student-run newspaper, Student Government Association, Medical Assisting Club, Respiratory Therapy Club, Radiography Club, Chess Club. *Campus security:* late-night transport/escort service, security service from 7 am until 11:30 pm.

Standardized Tests *Recommended:* SAT or ACT (for admission).

Costs (2014–15) *Tuition:* state resident $1728 full-time, $72 per credit hour part-time; nonresident $6336 full-time, $264 per credit hour part-time. *Required fees:* $63 full-time, $19 per term part-time. *Payment plan:* installment.

Applying *Options:* electronic application. *Required for some:* high school transcript. *Application deadlines:* rolling (freshmen), rolling (out-of-state freshmen), rolling (transfers). *Notification:* continuous (freshmen), continuous (out-of-state freshmen), continuous (transfers).

Freshman Application Contact Ms. Margie Ward, Admissions Officer, Carteret Community College, 3505 Arendell Street, Morehead City, NC 28557-2989. *Phone:* 252-222-6155. *Fax:* 252-222-6265. *E-mail:* admissions@carteret.edu. *Website:* http://www.carteret.edu/.

Catawba Valley Community College
Hickory, North Carolina

- **State and locally supported** 2-year, founded 1960, part of North Carolina Community College System
- **Small-town** 50-acre campus with easy access to Charlotte
- **Endowment** $2.9 million
- **Coed**, 4,561 undergraduate students, 39% full-time, 59% women, 41% men

Undergraduates 1,779 full-time, 2,782 part-time. Students come from 4 states and territories; 9% Black or African American, non-Hispanic/Latino; 8% Hispanic/Latino; 7% Asian, non-Hispanic/Latino; 0.8% American Indian or Alaska Native, non-Hispanic/Latino; 0.9% Two or more races, non-Hispanic/Latino; 2% Race/ethnicity unknown; 23% transferred in.

Freshmen *Admission:* 1,939 applied, 1,303 admitted, 928 enrolled. *Average high school GPA:* 3.11.

Faculty *Total:* 422, 37% full-time. *Student/faculty ratio:* 10:1.

Majors Accounting technology and bookkeeping; applied horticulture/horticulture operations; architectural engineering technology; automobile/automotive mechanics technology; business administration and management; commercial and advertising art; computer engineering technology; computer programming; computer systems networking and telecommunications; criminal justice/safety; cyber/computer forensics and counterterrorism; dental hygiene; early childhood education; electrical, electronic and communications engineering technology; electromechanical and instrumentation and maintenance technologies related; electroneurodiagnostic/electroencephalographic technology; emergency medical technology (EMT paramedic); fire prevention and safety technology; forensic science and technology; general studies; health information/medical records technology; information science/studies; information technology; liberal arts and sciences/liberal studies; machine shop technology; mechanical engineering/mechanical technology; medical office management; medical radiologic technology; office management; photographic and film/video technology; polysomnography; registered nursing/registered nurse; respiratory care therapy; turf and turfgrass management.

Academics *Calendar:* semesters. *Degree:* certificates, diplomas, and associate. *Special study options:* academic remediation for entering students, adult/continuing education programs, advanced placement credit, cooperative education, distance learning, double majors, English as a second language, independent study, part-time degree program, services for LD students, student-designed majors, summer session for credit.

Library Learning Resource Center with 29,315 titles, 1,000 audiovisual materials, an OPAC, a Web page.

Student Life *Housing:* college housing not available. *Activities and Organizations:* drama/theater group, choral group, Skills USA, Campus Crusade for Christ, Emerging Entrepreneurs, Circle K, Phi Theta Kappa. *Campus security:* 24-hour patrols. *Student services:* personal/psychological counseling.

Athletics Member NJCAA. *Intercollegiate sports:* baseball M, basketball M/W, cheerleading M/W, volleyball W.

Standardized Tests *Required:* ACT Compass (for admission).

Costs (2014–15) *Tuition:* state resident $1728 full-time, $72 per credit part-time; nonresident $6336 full-time, $264 per credit hour part-time. Part-time tuition and fees vary according to course load. *Required fees:* $99 full-time, $5 per credit hour part-time, $17 per term part-time. *Payment plan:* installment.

Applying *Options:* electronic application. *Required:* high school transcript. *Required for some:* 1 letter of recommendation. *Application deadlines:* rolling (freshmen), rolling (out-of-state freshmen), rolling (transfers). *Notification:* continuous (freshmen), continuous (out-of-state freshmen), continuous (transfers).

Freshman Application Contact Catawba Valley Community College, 2550 Highway 70 SE, Hickory, NC 28602-9699. *Phone:* 828-327-7000 Ext. 4618. *Website:* http://www.cvcc.edu/.

Central Carolina Community College
Sanford, North Carolina

- **State and locally supported** 2-year, founded 1962, part of North Carolina Community College System
- **Small-town** 41-acre campus with easy access to Raleigh, Fayetteville, NC
- **Endowment** $3.0 million
- **Coed**

Undergraduates 2,138 full-time, 2,762 part-time. 6% are from out of state; 23% Black or African American, non-Hispanic/Latino; 9% Hispanic/Latino; 0.7% Asian, non-Hispanic/Latino; 0.1% Native Hawaiian or other Pacific Islander, non-Hispanic/Latino; 0.8% American Indian or Alaska Native, non-Hispanic/Latino; 1% Two or more races, non-Hispanic/Latino; 0.5% Race/ethnicity unknown; 0.4% international.

Academics *Calendar:* semesters. *Degree:* certificates, diplomas, and associate. *Special study options:* academic remediation for entering students, adult/continuing education programs, advanced placement credit, distance learning, double majors, English as a second language, independent study, internships, part-time degree program, services for LD students, summer session for credit.

Student Life *Campus security:* 24-hour emergency response devices and patrols, student patrols, patrols by trained security personnel during operating hours.

Athletics Member NJCAA.

Standardized Tests *Required for some:* accepts SAT, ACT, Compass, Asset, and ACCUPLACER test scores within the last five years. *Recommended:* SAT or ACT (for admission).

Costs (2014–15) *Tuition:* state resident $2288 full-time; nonresident $8432 full-time. Full-time tuition and fees vary according to course load. Part-time tuition and fees vary according to course load.

Financial Aid Of all full-time matriculated undergraduates who enrolled in 2013, 70 Federal Work-Study jobs (averaging $1361). *Financial aid deadline:* 5/4.

Applying *Options:* electronic application, early admission, deferred entrance. *Required:* high school transcript.

Freshman Application Contact Mrs. Jamie Tyson Childress, Dean of Enrollment/Registrar, Central Carolina Community College, 1105 Kelly Drive, Sanford, NC 27330-9000. *Phone:* 919-718-7239. *Toll-free phone:* 800-682-8353. *Fax:* 919-718-7380.

Website: http://www.cccc.edu/.

Central Piedmont Community College
Charlotte, North Carolina

Freshman Application Contact Ms. Linda McComb, Associate Dean, Central Piedmont Community College, PO Box 35009, Charlotte, NC 28235-5009. *Phone:* 704-330-6784. *Fax:* 704-330-6136.

Website: http://www.cpcc.edu/.

Cleveland Community College
Shelby, North Carolina

- **State-supported** 2-year, founded 1965, part of North Carolina Community College System
- **Small-town** 43-acre campus with easy access to Charlotte
- **Coed**, 2,990 undergraduate students, 34% full-time, 64% women, 36% men

Undergraduates 1,029 full-time, 1,961 part-time. 22% Black or African American, non-Hispanic/Latino; 4% Hispanic/Latino; 1% Asian, non-Hispanic/Latino; 0.1% Native Hawaiian or other Pacific Islander, non-Hispanic/Latino; 0.3% American Indian or Alaska Native, non-Hispanic/Latino; 2% Two or more races, non-Hispanic/Latino; 2% Race/ethnicity unknown.

Freshmen *Admission:* 512 enrolled.

Faculty *Total:* 308, 25% full-time. *Student/faculty ratio:* 10:1.

Majors Accounting; banking and financial support services; biotechnology; business administration and management; criminal justice/safety; early childhood education; electrical, electronic and communications engineering technology; electrician; elementary education; emergency medical technology (EMT paramedic); entrepreneurship; fire prevention and safety technology; general studies; information technology; language interpretation and translation; legal administrative assistant/secretary; liberal arts and sciences and humanities related; liberal arts and sciences/liberal studies; marketing/marketing management; mechanical drafting and CAD/CADD; medical/clinical assistant; medical office management; office management; operations management; radio and television broadcasting technology; radiologic technology/science; registered nursing/registered nurse.

Academics *Calendar:* semesters. *Degree:* certificates, diplomas, and associate. *Special study options:* academic remediation for entering students, adult/continuing education programs, advanced placement credit, cooperative education, distance learning, double majors, English as a second language, independent study, off-campus study, part-time degree program, summer session for credit.

Library Jim & Patsy Rose Library with an OPAC, a Web page.

Student Life *Housing:* college housing not available. *Activities and Organizations:* drama/theater group, student-run television station. *Campus security:* security personnel during open hours. *Student services:* personal/psychological counseling.

Costs (2014–15) *Tuition:* state resident $2304 full-time, $72 per credit hour part-time; nonresident $8448 full-time, $264 per credit hour part-time. Full-time tuition and fees vary according to course load. Part-time tuition and fees vary according to course load. *Required fees:* $94 full-time.

Financial Aid Of all full-time matriculated undergraduates who enrolled in 2013, 20 Federal Work-Study jobs.

Applying *Options:* electronic application, deferred entrance. *Required:* high school transcript. *Application deadlines:* rolling (freshmen), rolling (transfers). *Notification:* continuous (freshmen), continuous (transfers).

Freshman Application Contact Cleveland Community College, 137 South Post Road, Shelby, NC 28152. *Phone:* 704-669-4139.

Website: http://www.clevelandcc.edu/.

Coastal Carolina Community College
Jacksonville, North Carolina

Freshman Application Contact Ms. Heather Calihan, Counseling Coordinator, Coastal Carolina Community College, Jacksonville, NC 28546. *Phone:* 910-938-6241. *Fax:* 910-455-2767. *E-mail:* calihanh@coastal.cc.nc.us.

Website: http://www.coastalcarolina.edu/.

College of The Albemarle
Elizabeth City, North Carolina

Freshman Application Contact Angie Godfrey-Dawson, Director of Admissions and International Students, College of The Albemarle, PO Box 2327, Elizabeth City, NC 27906-2327. *Phone:* 252-335-0821. *Fax:* 252-335-2011.
Website: http://www.albemarle.edu/.

Craven Community College
New Bern, North Carolina

Freshman Application Contact Ms. Millicent Fulford, Recruiter, Craven Community College, 800 College Court, New Bern, NC 28562-4984. *Phone:* 252-638-7232.
Website: http://www.cravencc.edu/.

Davidson County Community College
Lexington, North Carolina

Freshman Application Contact Davidson County Community College, PO Box 1287, Lexington, NC 27293-1287. *Phone:* 336-249-8186 Ext. 6715. *Fax:* 336-224-0240. *E-mail:* admissions@davidsonccc.edu.
Website: http://www.davidsonccc.edu/.

Durham Technical Community College
Durham, North Carolina

Director of Admissions Ms. Penny Augustine, Director of Admissions and Testing, Durham Technical Community College, 1637 Lawson Street, Durham, NC 27703-5023. *Phone:* 919-686-3619.
Website: http://www.durhamtech.edu/.

ECPI University
Charlotte, North Carolina

Admissions Office Contact ECPI University, 4800 Airport Center Parkway, Charlotte, NC 28208. *Toll-free phone:* 866-708-6167.
Website: http://www.ecpi.edu/.

ECPI University
Greensboro, North Carolina

Admissions Office Contact ECPI University, 7802 Airport Center Drive, Greensboro, NC 27409. *Toll-free phone:* 866-708-6170.
Website: http://www.ecpi.edu/.

Edgecombe Community College
Tarboro, North Carolina

Freshman Application Contact Ms. Jackie Heath, Admissions Officer, Edgecombe Community College, 2009 West Wilson Street, Tarboro, NC 27886-9399. *Phone:* 252-823-5166 Ext. 254.
Website: http://www.edgecombe.edu/.

Fayetteville Technical Community College
Fayetteville, North Carolina

- **State-supported** 2-year, founded 1961, part of North Carolina Community College System
- **Suburban** 215-acre campus with easy access to Raleigh
- **Endowment** $39,050
- **Coed,** 12,103 undergraduate students, 40% full-time, 62% women, 38% men

Undergraduates 4,878 full-time, 7,225 part-time. Students come from 46 states and territories; 44 other countries; 20% are from out of state; 44% Black or African American, non-Hispanic/Latino; 9% Hispanic/Latino; 1% Asian, non-Hispanic/Latino; 0.5% Native Hawaiian or other Pacific Islander, non-Hispanic/Latino; 3% American Indian or Alaska Native, non-Hispanic/Latino; 4% Two or more races, non-Hispanic/Latino; 2% Race/ethnicity unknown; 0.7% international; 23% transferred in.
Freshmen *Admission:* 4,496 applied, 4,496 admitted, 2,167 enrolled. *Average high school GPA:* 2.56. *Test scores:* SAT critical reading scores over 500: 34%; SAT math scores over 500: 31%; SAT writing scores over 500: 16%; SAT critical reading scores over 600: 6%; SAT math scores over 600: 8%; SAT writing scores over 600: 7%; SAT math scores over 700: 4%.
Faculty *Total:* 535, 50% full-time, 6% with terminal degrees. *Student/faculty ratio:* 20:1.
Majors Accounting; applied horticulture/horticulture operations; architectural engineering technology; autobody/collision and repair technology; automobile/automotive mechanics technology; banking and financial support services; building/construction finishing, management, and inspection related; business administration and management; civil engineering technology; commercial and advertising art; computer and information systems security; computer programming; computer systems networking and telecommunications; cosmetology; criminal justice/safety; crisis/emergency/disaster management; culinary arts; dental hygiene; early childhood education; electrical, electronic and communications engineering technology; electrician; elementary education; emergency medical technology (EMT paramedic); fire prevention and safety technology; forensic science and technology; funeral service and mortuary science; game and interactive media design; general studies; health and physical education related; heating, air conditioning, ventilation and refrigeration maintenance technology; hotel, motel, and restaurant management; human resources management; information science/studies; information technology; legal assistant/paralegal; liberal arts and sciences and humanities related; liberal arts and sciences/liberal studies; machine shop technology; marketing/marketing management; medical office management; office management; operations management; pharmacy technician; physical therapy technology; public administration; radiologic technology/science; registered nursing/registered nurse; respiratory care therapy; speech-language pathology assistant; surgical technology; surveying technology.
Academics *Calendar:* semesters. *Degree:* certificates, diplomas, and associate. *Special study options:* academic remediation for entering students, accelerated degree program, adult/continuing education programs, advanced placement credit, cooperative education, distance learning, double majors, English as a second language, independent study, internships, off-campus study, part-time degree program, services for LD students, summer session for credit.
Library Paul H. Thompson Library plus 1 other with 61,181 titles, 561 audiovisual materials, an OPAC, a Web page.
Student Life *Housing:* college housing not available. *Activities and Organizations:* Parents for Higher Education, Phi Theta Kappa, Phi Beta Lambda, Association of Nursing Students, African-American Heritage Club. *Campus security:* 24-hour emergency response devices and patrols, late-night transport/escort service, campus-wide emergency notification system. *Student services:* personal/psychological counseling.
Athletics *Intramural sports:* basketball M/W, football M/W, soccer M/W, softball M/W, volleyball M/W.
Standardized Tests *Required:* ACCUPLACER is required or ACT and SAT scores in lieu of ACCUPLACER if the scores are no more than 5 years old or ASSET and ACT Compass scores are also accepted if they are no more than 3 years old. High school grade point average of 2.6 and successful completion of four units of English and Math (for admission).
Costs (2014–15) *One-time required fee:* $25. *Tuition:* state resident $2304 full-time, $72 per credit hour part-time; nonresident $8448 full-time, $264 per credit hour part-time. Full-time tuition and fees vary according to course load. Part-time tuition and fees vary according to course load. *Required fees:* $90 full-time, $45 per term part-time. *Payment plan:* installment. *Waivers:* employees or children of employees.
Financial Aid Of all full-time matriculated undergraduates who enrolled in 2013, 75 Federal Work-Study jobs (averaging $2000). *Financial aid deadline:* 6/1.
Applying *Options:* electronic application, deferred entrance. *Required for some:* essay or personal statement, high school transcript, interview. *Application deadlines:* rolling (freshmen), rolling (out-of-state freshmen), rolling (transfers). *Notification:* continuous (freshmen), continuous (out-of-state freshmen), continuous (transfers).
Freshman Application Contact Dr. Louanna Castleman, Director of Admissions, Fayetteville Technical Community College, 2201 Hull Road, PO Box 35236, Fayetteville, NC 28303. *Phone:* 910-678-0141. *Fax:* 910-678-0085. *E-mail:* castleml@faytechcc.edu.
Website: http://www.faytechcc.edu/.

Forsyth Technical Community College
Winston-Salem, North Carolina

- **State-supported** 2-year, founded 1964, part of North Carolina Community College System
- **Suburban** 38-acre campus
- **Coed,** 9,148 undergraduate students, 41% full-time, 60% women, 40% men

Undergraduates 3,726 full-time, 5,422 part-time. 1% are from out of state; 29% Black or African American, non-Hispanic/Latino; 8% Hispanic/Latino;

2% Asian, non-Hispanic/Latino; 0.1% Native Hawaiian or other Pacific Islander, non-Hispanic/Latino; 0.5% American Indian or Alaska Native, non-Hispanic/Latino; 2% Two or more races, non-Hispanic/Latino; 2% Race/ethnicity unknown; 0.7% international; 26% transferred in.
Freshmen *Admission:* 1,284 enrolled.
Faculty *Student/faculty ratio:* 13:1.
Majors Accounting; allied health diagnostic, intervention, and treatment professions related; animation, interactive technology, video graphics and special effects; applied horticulture/horticultural business services related; architectural engineering technology; automobile/automotive mechanics technology; biology/biotechnology laboratory technician; biophysics; business administration and management; cardiovascular science; cardiovascular technology; clinical/medical laboratory technology; communication sciences and disorders; computer and information sciences; computer engineering technology; computer hardware technology; computer programming; computer systems networking and telecommunications; criminal justice/safety; diagnostic medical sonography and ultrasound technology; early childhood education; e-commerce; electrical, electronic and communications engineering technology; emergency medical technology (EMT paramedic); fire prevention and safety technology; forensic science and technology; general studies; graphic design; health information/medical records administration; health professions related; human services; industrial technology; information science/studies; information technology; interior design; international business/trade/commerce; legal assistant/paralegal; liberal arts and sciences/liberal studies; logistics, materials, and supply chain management; machine shop technology; massage therapy; mechanical engineering/mechanical technology; medical/clinical assistant; medical office management; medical radiologic technology; nuclear medical technology; office management; radiologic technology/science; registered nursing/registered nurse.
Academics *Calendar:* semesters. *Degree:* certificates, diplomas, and associate. *Special study options:* academic remediation for entering students, adult/continuing education programs, advanced placement credit, cooperative education, distance learning, double majors, English as a second language, independent study, internships, off-campus study, part-time degree program, services for LD students, summer session for credit.
Library Forsyth Technical Community College Library plus 1 other with an OPAC, a Web page.
Student Life *Housing:* college housing not available. *Activities and Organizations:* student-run newspaper. *Campus security:* 24-hour emergency response devices and patrols, late-night transport/escort service. *Student services:* personal/psychological counseling, women's center.
Standardized Tests *Required:* ACT Compass (for admission).
Costs (2014–15) *Tuition:* state resident $1848 full-time; nonresident $6480 full-time. Full-time tuition and fees vary according to course load. Part-time tuition and fees vary according to course load. *Required fees:* $208 full-time, $195 per term part-time. *Payment plan:* installment. *Waivers:* senior citizens.
Financial Aid Of all full-time matriculated undergraduates who enrolled in 2013, 42 Federal Work-Study jobs (averaging $2083).
Applying *Required:* high school transcript.
Freshman Application Contact Admissions Office, Forsyth Technical Community College, 2100 Silas Creek Parkway, Winston-Salem, NC 27103-5197. *Phone:* 336-734-7556. *E-mail:* admissions@forsythtech.edu. *Website:* http://www.forsythtech.edu/.

Gaston College
Dallas, North Carolina

Freshman Application Contact Terry Basier, Director of Enrollment Management and Admissions, Gaston College, 201 Highway 321 South, Dallas, NC 28034. *Phone:* 704-922-6214. *Fax:* 704-922-6443. *Website:* http://www.gaston.edu/.

Guilford Technical Community College
Jamestown, North Carolina

- **State and locally supported** 2-year, founded 1958, part of North Carolina Community College System
- **Urban** 158-acre campus with easy access to Raleigh, Charlotte, Greensboro
- **Endowment** $3.4 million
- **Coed,** 12,430 undergraduate students, 47% full-time, 57% women, 43% men

Undergraduates 5,783 full-time, 6,647 part-time. Students come from 19 states and territories; 0.5% are from out of state; 42% Black or African American, non-Hispanic/Latino; 7% Hispanic/Latino; 4% Asian, non-Hispanic/Latino; 0.1% Native Hawaiian or other Pacific Islander, non-Hispanic/Latino; 0.8% American Indian or Alaska Native, non-Hispanic/Latino; 2% Two or more races, non-Hispanic/Latino; 2%

Race/ethnicity unknown; 1% international; 9% transferred in. *Retention:* 50% of full-time freshmen returned.
Freshmen *Admission:* 6,620 applied, 6,620 admitted, 2,347 enrolled. *Average high school GPA:* 2.55.
Faculty *Total:* 393, 80% full-time. *Student/faculty ratio:* 20:1.
Majors Accounting technology and bookkeeping; agricultural power machinery operation; airline pilot and flight crew; architectural engineering technology; automobile/automotive mechanics technology; avionics maintenance technology; biology/biotechnology laboratory technician; building/property maintenance; business administration and management; chemical technology; civil engineering technology; commercial and advertising art; computer programming; computer systems analysis; computer systems networking and telecommunications; cosmetology; criminal justice/safety; culinary arts; dental hygiene; early childhood education; education related; electrical, electronic and communications engineering technology; electrician; electromechanical technology; emergency medical technology (EMT paramedic); fire prevention and safety technology; general studies; heating, air conditioning, ventilation and refrigeration maintenance technology; hotel/motel administration; human resources management; industrial production technologies related; information science/studies; information technology; legal assistant/paralegal; liberal arts and sciences and humanities related; liberal arts and sciences/liberal studies; logistics, materials, and supply chain management; machine shop technology; mechanical engineering/mechanical technology; medical/clinical assistant; medical office management; office management; pharmacy technician; physical therapy technology; psychiatric/mental health services technology; recording arts technology; registered nursing/registered nurse; substance abuse/addiction counseling; surgical technology; surveying technology; system, networking, and LAN/WAN management; telecommunications technology; turf and turfgrass management; vehicle maintenance and repair technologies related.
Academics *Calendar:* semesters. *Degree:* certificates, diplomas, and associate. *Special study options:* academic remediation for entering students, adult/continuing education programs, advanced placement credit, cooperative education, distance learning, double majors, English as a second language, external degree program, independent study, internships, off-campus study, part-time degree program, services for LD students, student-designed majors, summer session for credit. *ROTC:* Army (c), Air Force (c).
Library M. W. Bell Library plus 2 others with 57,610 titles, 7,893 audiovisual materials, an OPAC, a Web page.
Student Life *Housing:* college housing not available. *Activities and Organizations:* drama/theater group, national sororities. *Campus security:* 24-hour emergency response devices and patrols, late-night transport/escort service. *Student services:* personal/psychological counseling.
Athletics Member NJCAA. *Intercollegiate sports:* baseball M(s), basketball M(s)/W(s), cheerleading M/W, volleyball W(s).
Costs (2014–15) *Tuition:* state resident $2304 full-time, $72 per credit hour part-time; nonresident $8488 full-time, $264 per credit hour part-time. Full-time tuition and fees vary according to course load and program. Part-time tuition and fees vary according to course load and program. *Required fees:* $185 full-time. *Payment plan:* deferred payment. *Waivers:* senior citizens and employees or children of employees.
Applying *Options:* electronic application, early admission, deferred entrance. *Required for some:* high school transcript, interview. *Application deadlines:* rolling (freshmen), rolling (transfers). *Notification:* continuous (freshmen), continuous (transfers).
Freshman Application Contact Guilford Technical Community College, PO Box 309, Jamestown, NC 27282-0309. *Phone:* 336-334-4822 Ext. 50125. *Website:* http://www.gtcc.edu/.

Halifax Community College
Weldon, North Carolina

- **State and locally supported** 2-year, founded 1967, part of North Carolina Community College System
- **Rural** 109-acre campus
- **Endowment** $1.0 million
- **Coed,** 1,293 undergraduate students, 53% full-time, 64% women, 36% men

Undergraduates 681 full-time, 612 part-time. 1% are from out of state; 53% Black or African American, non-Hispanic/Latino; 2% Hispanic/Latino; 0.3% Asian, non-Hispanic/Latino; 2% American Indian or Alaska Native, non-Hispanic/Latino; 1% Two or more races, non-Hispanic/Latino; 1% Race/ethnicity unknown; 0.3% international. *Retention:* 53% of full-time freshmen returned.
Freshmen *Admission:* 462 applied, 297 admitted, 281 enrolled. *Average high school GPA:* 2.5.
Faculty *Total:* 122, 47% full-time, 8% with terminal degrees. *Student/faculty ratio:* 11:1.
Majors Accounting; business administration and management; clinical/medical laboratory technology; clinical/medical social work;

commercial and advertising art; computer systems networking and telecommunications; criminal justice/police science; dental hygiene; early childhood education; health professions related; information technology; legal assistant/paralegal; medical administrative assistant and medical secretary; office management; registered nursing/registered nurse.

Academics *Calendar:* semesters. *Degree:* certificates, diplomas, and associate. *Special study options:* academic remediation for entering students, cooperative education, distance learning, double majors, English as a second language, independent study, internships, part-time degree program, services for LD students, summer session for credit.

Library Learning Resources Center plus 1 other with 32,611 titles, 1,944 audiovisual materials, an OPAC, a Web page.

Student Life *Housing:* college housing not available. *Activities and Organizations:* PTK, PRIDE, Women of Excellence. *Campus security:* 24-hour emergency response devices, 12-hour patrols by trained security personnel. *Student services:* health clinic.

Costs (2014–15) *Tuition:* state resident $2304 full-time, $72 per credit hour part-time; nonresident $8448 full-time, $264 per credit hour part-time. Full-time tuition and fees vary according to course load and program. Part-time tuition and fees vary according to course load and program. *Required fees:* $122 full-time, $122 per year part-time. *Payment plan:* installment.

Applying *Options:* electronic application, deferred entrance. *Required:* high school transcript. *Application deadlines:* rolling (freshmen), rolling (transfers). *Notification:* continuous (freshmen), continuous (transfers).

Freshman Application Contact Mr. James Washington, Director of Admissions, Halifax Community College, PO Drawer 809, Weldon, NC 27890-0809. *Phone:* 252-536-7220. *E-mail:* jwashington660@halifaxcc.edu. *Website:* http://www.halifaxcc.edu/.

Harrison College
Morrisville, North Carolina

- **Proprietary** 2-year, founded 2011, part of Harrison College
- **Suburban** campus with easy access to Raleigh
- **Coed**

Undergraduates 159 full-time, 41 part-time. 48% Black or African American, non-Hispanic/Latino; 7% Hispanic/Latino; 0.5% Asian, non-Hispanic/Latino; 3% Two or more races, non-Hispanic/Latino; 2% Race/ethnicity unknown.

Faculty *Student/faculty ratio:* 14:1.

Academics *Degree:* associate. *Special study options:* adult/continuing education programs, advanced placement credit, cooperative education, distance learning, double majors, internships, off-campus study, part-time degree program, summer session for credit.

Standardized Tests *Required:* Wonderlic Scholastic Level Exam (SLE) (for admission).

Applying *Options:* electronic application. *Required:* high school transcript, interview.

Freshman Application Contact Mr. Jason Howanec, Vice President of Enrollment, Harrison College, 500 N. Meridian St., Indianapolis, IN 46204. *Phone:* 800-919-2500. *E-mail:* Admissions@harrison.edu. *Website:* http://www.harrison.edu/.

Haywood Community College
Clyde, North Carolina

- **State and locally supported** 2-year, founded 1964, part of North Carolina Community College System
- **Rural** 85-acre campus
- **Coed,** 2,127 undergraduate students

Majors Accounting technology and bookkeeping; applied horticulture/horticulture operations; automobile/automotive mechanics technology; building/construction finishing, management, and inspection related; business administration and management; child-care and support services management; civil engineering related; computer systems analysis; computer systems networking and telecommunications; cosmetology; criminal justice/law enforcement administration; electrical, electronic and communications engineering technology; electrician; electromechanical technology; engineering technologies and engineering related; executive assistant/executive secretary; forest/forest resources management; forest technology; liberal arts and sciences and humanities related; liberal arts and sciences/liberal studies; machine shop technology; management information systems; manufacturing engineering; mechanical engineering/mechanical technology; medical/clinical assistant; precision production related; registered nursing/registered nurse; teacher assistant/aide; telecommunications technology; watchmaking and jewelrymaking; welding technology; wildlife, fish and wildlands science and management; wood science and wood products/pulp and paper technology; woodworking related.

Academics *Calendar:* semesters. *Degree:* certificates, diplomas, and associate. *Special study options:* academic remediation for entering students,

adult/continuing education programs, advanced placement credit, cooperative education, distance learning, double majors, English as a second language, honors programs, independent study, internships, part-time degree program, services for LD students, study abroad, summer session for credit.

Library Freedlander Learning Resource Center with 26,788 titles, an OPAC, a Web page.

Student Life *Housing:* college housing not available. *Campus security:* 24-hour emergency response devices and patrols.

Athletics *Intramural sports:* basketball M/W, bowling M/W, football M/W, golf M/W, softball M/W, volleyball M/W.

Financial Aid Of all full-time matriculated undergraduates who enrolled in 2013, 41 Federal Work-Study jobs (averaging $857).

Applying *Options:* electronic application. *Required:* high school transcript. *Required for some:* interview. *Application deadlines:* rolling (freshmen), rolling (transfers).

Freshman Application Contact Enrollment Technician, Haywood Community College, 185 Freedlander Drive, Clyde, NC 28721-9453. *Phone:* 828-627-4669. *Toll-free phone:* 866-GOTOHCC. *E-mail:* enrollment@haywood.edu. *Website:* http://www.haywood.edu/.

Isothermal Community College
Spindale, North Carolina

Freshman Application Contact Ms. Vickie Searcy, Enrollment Management Office, Isothermal Community College, PO Box 804, Spindale, NC 28160-0804. *Phone:* 828-286-3636 Ext. 251. *Fax:* 828-286-8109. *E-mail:* vsearcy@isothermal.edu. *Website:* http://www.isothermal.edu/.

ITT Technical Institute
Cary, North Carolina

- **Proprietary** primarily 2-year, part of ITT Educational Services, Inc.
- **Coed**

Academics *Degrees:* associate and bachelor's.

Freshman Application Contact Director of Recruitment, ITT Technical Institute, 5520 Dillard Drive, Suite 100, Cary, NC 27518. *Phone:* 919-233-2520. *Toll-free phone:* 877-203-5533. *Website:* http://www.itt-tech.edu/.

ITT Technical Institute
Charlotte, North Carolina

- **Proprietary** primarily 2-year
- **Coed**

Academics *Degrees:* associate and bachelor's.

Freshman Application Contact Director of Recruitment, ITT Technical Institute, 4135 Southstream Boulevard, Suite 200, Charlotte, NC 28217. *Phone:* 704-423-3100. *Toll-free phone:* 800-488-0173. *Website:* http://www.itt-tech.edu/.

ITT Technical Institute
High Point, North Carolina

- **Proprietary** primarily 2-year, founded 2007, part of ITT Educational Services, Inc.
- **Coed**

Academics *Calendar:* quarters. *Degrees:* associate and bachelor's.

Freshman Application Contact Director of Recruitment, ITT Technical Institute, 4050 Piedmont Parkway, Suite 110, High Point, NC 27265. *Phone:* 336-819-5900. *Toll-free phone:* 877-536-5231. *Website:* http://www.itt-tech.edu/.

James Sprunt Community College
Kenansville, North Carolina

- **State-supported** 2-year, founded 1964, part of North Carolina Community College System
- **Rural** 51-acre campus with easy access to Raleigh, Wilmington, NC
- **Endowment** $1.1 million
- **Coed,** 1,213 undergraduate students, 46% full-time, 68% women, 32% men

Undergraduates 560 full-time, 653 part-time. Students come from 5 states and territories; 1% are from out of state; 32% Black or African American, non-Hispanic/Latino; 15% Hispanic/Latino; 0.2% Asian, non-Hispanic/Latino; 0.1% Native Hawaiian or other Pacific Islander, non-Hispanic/Latino; 0.3%

American Indian or Alaska Native, non-Hispanic/Latino; 1% Two or more races, non-Hispanic/Latino; 0.2% international; 17% transferred in. *Retention:* 81% of full-time freshmen returned.

Freshmen *Admission:* 672 applied, 672 admitted, 137 enrolled.

Faculty *Total:* 74, 55% full-time, 7% with terminal degrees. *Student/faculty ratio:* 15:1.

Majors Accounting; agribusiness; animal sciences; business administration and management; child development; commercial and advertising art; criminal justice/safety; early childhood education; elementary education; general studies; information technology; institutional food workers; liberal arts and sciences and humanities related; liberal arts and sciences/liberal studies; medical/clinical assistant; registered nursing/registered nurse; viticulture and enology.

Academics *Calendar:* semesters. *Degree:* certificates, diplomas, and associate. *Special study options:* academic remediation for entering students, accelerated degree program, advanced placement credit, cooperative education, distance learning, double majors, English as a second language, independent study, internships, part-time degree program, services for LD students, summer session for credit.

Library James Sprunt Community College Library with 24,887 titles, 628 audiovisual materials, an OPAC, a Web page.

Student Life *Housing:* college housing not available. *Activities and Organizations:* student-run newspaper, Student Nurses Association, Art Club, Alumni Association, National Technical-Vocational Honor Society, Phi Theta Kappa, national sororities. *Campus security:* day, evening and Saturday trained security personnel. *Student services:* personal/psychological counseling.

Athletics *Intercollegiate sports:* softball M/W, volleyball M/W.

Costs (2014–15) *Tuition:* state resident $2304 full-time, $72 per credit part-time; nonresident $8448 full-time, $264 per credit part-time. Full-time tuition and fees vary according to course load. Part-time tuition and fees vary according to course load. *Required fees:* $70 full-time, $35 per term part-time.

Financial Aid Of all full-time matriculated undergraduates who enrolled in 2013, 35 Federal Work-Study jobs (averaging $1057).

Applying *Options:* electronic application. *Required:* high school transcript. *Application deadlines:* rolling (freshmen), rolling (out-of-state freshmen), rolling (transfers). *Notification:* continuous (freshmen), continuous (out-of-state freshmen), continuous (transfers).

Freshman Application Contact Ms. Lea Matthews, Admissions Specialist, James Sprunt Community College, Highway 11 South, 133 James Sprunt Drive, Kenansville, NC 28349. *Phone:* 910-296-6078. *Fax:* 910-296-1222. *E-mail:* lmatthews@jamessprunt.edu.

Website: http://www.jamessprunt.edu/.

Johnston Community College
Smithfield, North Carolina

- **State-supported** 2-year, founded 1969, part of North Carolina Community College System
- **Rural** 100-acre campus
- **Endowment** $4.6 million
- **Coed,** 4,021 undergraduate students, 45% full-time, 65% women, 35% men

Undergraduates 1,823 full-time, 2,198 part-time. 16% Black or African American, non-Hispanic/Latino; 11% Hispanic/Latino; 0.6% Asian, non-Hispanic/Latino; 0.2% Native Hawaiian or other Pacific Islander, non-Hispanic/Latino; 0.7% American Indian or Alaska Native, non-Hispanic/Latino; 1% Two or more races, non-Hispanic/Latino; 8% Race/ethnicity unknown.

Freshmen *Admission:* 568 enrolled.

Majors Accounting; administrative assistant and secretarial science; business administration and management; criminal justice/police science; diesel mechanics technology; early childhood education; heating, air conditioning, ventilation and refrigeration maintenance technology; legal assistant/paralegal; liberal arts and sciences/liberal studies; medical/clinical assistant; medical office management; office management; registered nursing/registered nurse.

Academics *Calendar:* semesters. *Degree:* certificates, diplomas, and associate. *Special study options:* academic remediation for entering students, adult/continuing education programs, advanced placement credit, cooperative education, distance learning, double majors, honors programs, independent study, part-time degree program, services for LD students, summer session for credit.

Library Johnston Community College Library plus 1 other with 35,722 titles, 9,409 audiovisual materials, an OPAC, a Web page.

Student Life *Housing:* college housing not available. *Activities and Organizations:* choral group. *Campus security:* 24-hour patrols. *Student services:* personal/psychological counseling.

Athletics Member NJCAA. *Intercollegiate sports:* golf M/W.

Standardized Tests *Required:* ACCUPLACER (for admission). *Recommended:* SAT or ACT (for admission).

Costs (2014–15) *Tuition:* state resident $2304 full-time, $72 per credit hour part-time; nonresident $8448 full-time, $264 per credit hour part-time. *Required fees:* $97 full-time. *Payment plan:* installment.

Financial Aid Of all full-time matriculated undergraduates who enrolled in 2013, 35 Federal Work-Study jobs (averaging $1853).

Applying *Options:* electronic application. *Required:* high school transcript, interview. *Application deadlines:* rolling (freshmen), rolling (transfers). *Notification:* continuous (freshmen), continuous (transfers).

Freshman Application Contact Dr. Pamela J. Harrell, Vice President of Student Services, Johnston Community College, Smithfield, NC 27577-2350. *Phone:* 919-209-2048. *Fax:* 919-989-7862. *E-mail:* pjharrell@ johnstoncc.edu.

Website: http://www.johnstoncc.edu/.

Kaplan College, Charlotte Campus
Charlotte, North Carolina

Freshman Application Contact Director of Admissions, Kaplan College, Charlotte Campus, 6070 East Independence Boulevard, Charlotte, NC 28212. *Phone:* 704-567-3700.

Website: http://www.kaplancollege.com/.

King's College
Charlotte, North Carolina

- **Private** 2-year, founded 1901
- **Suburban** campus
- **Coed,** 381 undergraduate students
- 78% of applicants were admitted

Freshmen *Admission:* 848 applied, 665 admitted.

Majors Accounting technology and bookkeeping; administrative assistant and secretarial science; computer programming; computer systems networking and telecommunications; graphic design; hotel/motel administration; legal administrative assistant/secretary; legal assistant/paralegal; medical/clinical assistant.

Academics *Calendar:* semesters. *Degree:* diplomas and associate.

Freshman Application Contact Admissions Office, King's College, 322 Lamar Avenue, Charlotte, NC 28204-2436. *Phone:* 704-372-0266. *Toll-free phone:* 800-768-2255.

Website: http://www.kingscollegecharlotte.edu/.

Lenoir Community College
Kinston, North Carolina

- **State-supported** 2-year, founded 1960, part of North Carolina Community College System
- **Small-town** 86-acre campus
- **Coed,** 3,251 undergraduate students, 40% full-time, 65% women, 35% men

Undergraduates 1,287 full-time, 1,964 part-time. Students come from 31 states and territories; 4 other countries; 3% are from out of state; 35% Black or African American, non-Hispanic/Latino; 8% Hispanic/Latino; 0.6% Asian, non-Hispanic/Latino; 0.1% Native Hawaiian or other Pacific Islander, non-Hispanic/Latino; 0.5% American Indian or Alaska Native, non-Hispanic/Latino; 1% Two or more races, non-Hispanic/Latino; 0.5% international; 9% transferred in.

Freshmen *Admission:* 1,830 applied, 1,325 admitted, 363 enrolled.

Faculty *Total:* 337, 33% full-time. *Student/faculty ratio:* 10:1.

Majors Airline pilot and flight crew; art; aviation/airway management; avionics maintenance technology; business administration and management; computer programming; consumer merchandising/retailing management; cosmetology; criminal justice/law enforcement administration; criminal justice/police science; elementary education; finance; food technology and processing; graphic and printing equipment operation/production; horticultural science; industrial technology; liberal arts and sciences/liberal studies; marketing/marketing management; medical administrative assistant and medical secretary; medical/clinical assistant; ornamental horticulture; pre-engineering; registered nursing/registered nurse; trade and industrial teacher education; welding technology.

Academics *Calendar:* semesters. *Degree:* certificates, diplomas, and associate. *Special study options:* academic remediation for entering students, adult/continuing education programs, advanced placement credit, cooperative education, distance learning, double majors, English as a second language, independent study, part-time degree program, summer session for credit.

Library Learning Resources Center plus 1 other with 55,636 titles.

Student Life *Housing:* college housing not available. *Activities and Organizations:* student-run newspaper, choral group, Student Government Association, Automotive Club, Electronics Club, Drafting Club, Cosmetology

Club. *Campus security:* 24-hour emergency response devices and patrols, student patrols. *Student services:* personal/psychological counseling.

Athletics Member NJCAA. *Intercollegiate sports:* baseball M, basketball M/W, volleyball W.

Standardized Tests *Required for some:* Assessment and Placement Services for Community Colleges. *Recommended:* SAT or ACT (for admission).

Costs (2014–15) *Tuition:* state resident $2160 full-time, $72 per credit part-time; nonresident $7920 full-time, $264 per credit part-time. Full-time tuition and fees vary according to course load. Part-time tuition and fees vary according to course load. *Required fees:* $60 full-time. *Waivers:* employees or children of employees.

Applying *Options:* electronic application, early admission. *Required:* high school transcript. *Application deadlines:* rolling (freshmen), rolling (transfers). *Notification:* continuous (freshmen), continuous (transfers).

Freshman Application Contact Mrs. Kim Hill, Enrollment Management Coordinator, Lenoir Community College, PO Box188, Kinston, NC 28502-0188. *Phone:* 252-527-6223 Ext. 301. *Fax:* 252-233-6895. *E-mail:* krhill01@lenoircc.edu.
Website: http://www.lenoircc.edu/.

Living Arts College
Raleigh, North Carolina

- **Proprietary** primarily 2-year, founded 1992
- **Suburban** campus with easy access to Raleigh
- **Coed**

Undergraduates 578 full-time. Students come from 8 states and territories; 1 other country; 1% are from out of state; 48% Black or African American, non-Hispanic/Latino; 5% Hispanic/Latino; 0.9% Asian, non-Hispanic/Latino; 0.7% American Indian or Alaska Native, non-Hispanic/Latino; 2% Two or more races, non-Hispanic/Latino; 3% Race/ethnicity unknown; 35% live on campus. *Retention:* 69% of full-time freshmen returned.

Faculty *Student/faculty ratio:* 10:1.

Academics *Calendar:* quarters. *Degree:* certificates, diplomas, and bachelor's. *Special study options:* cooperative education, summer session for credit.

Student Life *Campus security:* controlled dormitory access.

Standardized Tests *Required:* Wonderlic aptitude test (for admission).

Applying *Options:* electronic application, early admission, early decision, early action, deferred entrance. *Application fee:* $25. *Required:* essay or personal statement, high school transcript, interview, portfolio for selected program.

Freshman Application Contact Julie Wenta, Director of Admissions, Living Arts College, 3000 Wakefield Crossing Drive, Raleigh, NC 27614. *Phone:* 919-488-5902. *Toll-free phone:* 800-288-7442. *Fax:* 919-488-8490. *E-mail:* jwenta@living-arts-college.edu.
Website: http://www.living-arts-college.edu/.

Louisburg College
Louisburg, North Carolina

Freshman Application Contact Ms. Stephanie Tolbert, Vice President for Enrollment Management, Louisburg College, 501 North Main Street, Louisburg, NC 27549-2399. *Phone:* 919-497-3233. *Toll-free phone:* 800-775-0208. *Fax:* 919-496-1788. *E-mail:* admissions@louisburg.edu.
Website: http://www.louisburg.edu/.

Martin Community College
Williamston, North Carolina

Freshman Application Contact Martin Community College, 1161 Kehukee Park Road, Williamston, NC 27892. *Phone:* 252-792-1521 Ext. 243.
Website: http://www.martin.cc.nc.us/.

Mayland Community College
Spruce Pine, North Carolina

Director of Admissions Ms. Cathy Morrison, Director of Admissions, Mayland Community College, PO Box 547, Spruce Pine, NC 28777-0547. *Phone:* 828-765-7351 Ext. 224. *Toll-free phone:* 800-462-9526.
Website: http://www.mayland.edu/.

McDowell Technical Community College
Marion, North Carolina

Freshman Application Contact Mr. Rick L. Wilson, Director of Admissions, McDowell Technical Community College, 54 College Drive, Marion, NC 28752. *Phone:* 828-652-0632. *Fax:* 828-652-1014. *E-mail:* rickw@mcdowelltech.edu.
Website: http://www.mcdowelltech.edu/.

Miller-Motte College
Cary, North Carolina

Admissions Office Contact Miller-Motte College, 2205 Walnut Street, Cary, NC 27518.
Website: http://www.miller-motte.edu/.

Miller-Motte College
Fayetteville, North Carolina

Admissions Office Contact Miller-Motte College, 3725 Ramsey Street, Suite 103A, Fayetteville, NC 28311.
Website: http://www.miller-motte.edu/.

Miller-Motte College
Greenville, North Carolina

Admissions Office Contact Miller-Motte College, 1021 WH Smith Boulevard, Suite 102, Greenville, NC 27834.
Website: http://www.miller-motte.edu/.

Miller-Motte College
Jacksonville, North Carolina

Admissions Office Contact Miller-Motte College, 1291 Hargett Street, Jacksonville, NC 28540. *Toll-free phone:* 866-297-0267.
Website: http://www.miller-motte.edu/.

Miller-Motte College
Raleigh, North Carolina

Admissions Office Contact Miller-Motte College, 3901 Capital Boulevard, Suite 151, Raleigh, NC 27604-6072.
Website: http://www.miller-motte.edu/.

Miller-Motte College
Wilmington, North Carolina

Freshman Application Contact Admissions Office, Miller-Motte College, 5000 Market Street, Wilmington, NC 28405. *Toll-free phone:* 800-784-2110.
Website: http://www.miller-motte.edu/.

Mitchell Community College
Statesville, North Carolina

- **State-supported** 2-year, founded 1852, part of North Carolina Community College System
- **Small-town** 8-acre campus with easy access to Charlotte
- **Endowment** $2.5 million
- **Coed**

Undergraduates 1,532 full-time, 1,982 part-time. Students come from 27 states and territories; 15% Black or African American, non-Hispanic/Latino; 7% Hispanic/Latino; 2% Asian, non-Hispanic/Latino; 0.1% Native Hawaiian or other Pacific Islander, non-Hispanic/Latino; 0.7% American Indian or Alaska Native, non-Hispanic/Latino; 0.9% Two or more races, non-Hispanic/Latino; 2% Race/ethnicity unknown; 0.5% international; 3% transferred in. *Retention:* 46% of full-time freshmen returned.

Academics *Calendar:* semesters. *Degree:* certificates, diplomas, and associate. *Special study options:* academic remediation for entering students, adult/continuing education programs, advanced placement credit, distance learning, English as a second language, part-time degree program, services for LD students, summer session for credit. *ROTC:* Army (c).

Student Life *Campus security:* day and evening security guards.

Costs (2014–15) *Tuition:* state resident $2304 full-time, $72 per credit hour part-time; nonresident $8448 full-time, $264 per credit hour part-time. Full-time tuition and fees vary according to course load. Part-time tuition and fees vary according to course load. *Required fees:* $100 full-time, $1 per credit hour part-time, $18 per term part-time. *Payment plans:* tuition prepayment, installment.

Financial Aid Of all full-time matriculated undergraduates who enrolled in 2013, 30 Federal Work-Study jobs.

Applying *Required:* high school transcript.
Freshman Application Contact Mr. Doug Rhoney, Counselor, Mitchell Community College, 500 West Broad, Statesville, NC 28677-5293. *Phone:* 704-878-3280.
Website: http://www.mitchellcc.edu/.

Montgomery Community College
Troy, North Carolina

- **State-supported** 2-year, founded 1967, part of North Carolina Community College System
- **Rural** 159-acre campus
- **Coed,** 863 undergraduate students, 40% full-time, 61% women, 39% men

Undergraduates 342 full-time, 521 part-time. Students come from 10 states and territories; 1% are from out of state; 16% Black or African American, non-Hispanic/Latino; 13% Hispanic/Latino; 1% Asian, non-Hispanic/Latino; 0.7% American Indian or Alaska Native, non-Hispanic/Latino; 0.7% Two or more races, non-Hispanic/Latino; 0.1% international.
Freshmen *Admission:* 135 enrolled.
Faculty *Total:* 76, 47% full-time.
Majors Business administration and management; criminal justice/safety; early childhood education; electrician; electromechanical and instrumentation and maintenance technologies related; forest technology; gunsmithing; heating, air conditioning, ventilation and refrigeration maintenance technology; information technology; liberal arts and sciences/liberal studies; medical/clinical assistant; mental and social health services and allied professions related; office management.
Academics *Calendar:* semesters. *Degree:* certificates, diplomas, and associate. *Special study options:* academic remediation for entering students, advanced placement credit, distance learning, English as a second language, part-time degree program, services for LD students, summer session for credit.
Library Montgomery Community College Learning Resource Center with 47,380 titles, 1,430 audiovisual materials, an OPAC, a Web page.
Student Life *Housing:* college housing not available. *Activities and Organizations:* Student Government Association, Nursing Club, Gunsmithing Society, Medical Assisting Club, Forestry Club. *Campus security:* 24-hour emergency response devices. *Student services:* personal/psychological counseling.
Costs (2015–16) *Tuition:* state resident $2304 full-time; nonresident $8448 full-time. *Required fees:* $105 full-time. *Payment plan:* installment.
Financial Aid Of all full-time matriculated undergraduates who enrolled in 2013, 24 Federal Work-Study jobs (averaging $500).
Applying *Options:* electronic application, early admission, deferred entrance. *Required:* high school transcript. *Application deadlines:* rolling (freshmen), rolling (transfers). *Notification:* continuous (freshmen), continuous (transfers).
Freshman Application Contact Ms. Tavia Thompson, Enrollment Specialist, Montgomery Community College, 1011 Page Street, Troy, NC 27371. *Phone:* 910-576-6222 Ext. 220.
Website: http://www.montgomery.edu/.

Nash Community College
Rocky Mount, North Carolina

Freshman Application Contact Ms. Dorothy Gardner, Admissions Officer, Nash Community College, PO Box 7488, Rocky Mount, NC 27804. *Phone:* 252-451-8300. *E-mail:* dgardner@nashcc.edu.
Website: http://www.nashcc.edu/.

Pamlico Community College
Grantsboro, North Carolina

Director of Admissions Mr. Floyd H. Hardison, Admissions Counselor, Pamlico Community College, PO Box 185, Grantsboro, NC 28529-0185. *Phone:* 252-249-1851 Ext. 28.
Website: http://www.pamlicocc.edu/.

Piedmont Community College
Roxboro, North Carolina

- **State-supported** 2-year, founded 1970, part of North Carolina Community College System
- **Small-town** 178-acre campus
- **Coed,** 1,475 undergraduate students, 41% full-time, 63% women, 37% men

Undergraduates 602 full-time, 873 part-time.

Freshmen *Admission:* 710 applied, 710 admitted.
Faculty *Student/faculty ratio:* 11:1.
Majors Accounting; building/property maintenance; business administration and management; child-care and support services management; cinematography and film/video production; clinical/medical social work; computer programming (specific applications); computer systems networking and telecommunications; criminal justice/law enforcement administration; e-commerce; electrical and power transmission installation; electrician; electromechanical and instrumentation and maintenance technologies related; elementary education; general studies; graphic communications; health professions related; historic preservation and conservation; industrial technology; information technology; liberal arts and sciences and humanities related; liberal arts and sciences/liberal studies; medical administrative assistant and medical secretary; office management; registered nursing/registered nurse.
Academics *Calendar:* semesters. *Degree:* certificates, diplomas, and associate. *Special study options:* academic remediation for entering students, adult/continuing education programs, advanced placement credit, cooperative education, distance learning, double majors, English as a second language, off-campus study, part-time degree program, summer session for credit.
Library Learning Resource Center with 18,576 titles.
Student Life *Housing:* college housing not available. *Activities and Organizations:* drama/theater group, choral group. *Campus security:* routine patrols by the local sheriff's department.
Athletics *Intramural sports:* volleyball M/W.
Costs (2014–15) *Tuition:* state resident $1728 full-time, $72 per credit hour part-time; nonresident $6336 full-time, $264 per credit hour part-time. Full-time tuition and fees vary according to course load. Part-time tuition and fees vary according to course load. *Required fees:* $115 full-time, $57 per term part-time. *Payment plan:* installment.
Financial Aid Of all full-time matriculated undergraduates who enrolled in 2013, 30 Federal Work-Study jobs (averaging $1500).
Applying *Options:* electronic application, early admission, deferred entrance. *Required for some:* high school transcript. *Application deadlines:* rolling (freshmen), rolling (transfers). *Notification:* continuous until 9/29 (freshmen), continuous until 9/29 (transfers).
Freshman Application Contact Piedmont Community College, PO Box 1197, Roxboro, NC 27573-1197. *Phone:* 336-599-1181 Ext. 2163.
Website: http://www.piedmont.cc.nc.us/.

Pitt Community College
Greenville, North Carolina

- **State and locally supported** 2-year, founded 1961, part of North Carolina Community College System
- **Small-town** 294-acre campus
- **Coed**

Undergraduates 4,670 full-time, 4,232 part-time. 28% Black or African American, non-Hispanic/Latino; 2% Hispanic/Latino; 0.5% Asian, non-Hispanic/Latino; 0.1% Native Hawaiian or other Pacific Islander, non-Hispanic/Latino; 0.3% American Indian or Alaska Native, non-Hispanic/Latino; 0.2% Two or more races, non-Hispanic/Latino; 39% Race/ethnicity unknown; 0.7% international. *Retention:* 68% of full-time freshmen returned.
Academics *Calendar:* semesters. *Degree:* certificates, diplomas, and associate. *Special study options:* academic remediation for entering students, adult/continuing education programs, advanced placement credit, cooperative education, distance learning, double majors, English as a second language, external degree program, independent study, internships, part-time degree program, services for LD students, summer session for credit. *ROTC:* Army (b).
Student Life *Campus security:* 24-hour patrols, student patrols, late-night transport/escort service.
Athletics Member NJCAA.
Costs (2014–15) *Tuition:* state resident $2304 full-time, $72 per credit hour part-time; nonresident $8448 full-time, $264 per credit hour part-time. *Required fees:* $86 full-time, $86 per term part-time.
Financial Aid Of all full-time matriculated undergraduates who enrolled in 2013, 79 Federal Work-Study jobs (averaging $1772).
Applying *Options:* electronic application, deferred entrance. *Required:* high school transcript.
Freshman Application Contact Dr. Kimberly Williamson, Interim Coordinator of Counseling, Pitt Community College, PO Drawer 7007, Greenville, NC 27835-7007. *Phone:* 252-493-7217. *Fax:* 252-321-4612. *E-mail:* pittadm@pcc.pitt.cc.nc.us.
Website: http://www.pittcc.edu/.

Randolph Community College
Asheboro, North Carolina

- **State-supported** 2-year, founded 1962, part of North Carolina Community College System
- **Small-town** 40-acre campus with easy access to Greensboro, Winston-Salem, High Point
- **Endowment** $10.0 million
- **Coed,** 2,771 undergraduate students, 37% full-time, 62% women, 38% men

Undergraduates 1,036 full-time, 1,735 part-time. Students come from 2 states and territories; 13 other countries; 8% Black or African American, non-Hispanic/Latino; 13% Hispanic/Latino; 1% Asian, non-Hispanic/Latino; 1% American Indian or Alaska Native, non-Hispanic/Latino; 2% Two or more races, non-Hispanic/Latino; 0.2% Race/ethnicity unknown; 0.5% international; 28% transferred in. *Retention:* 72% of full-time freshmen returned.

Freshmen *Admission:* 2,633 applied, 2,633 admitted, 595 enrolled. *Average high school GPA:* 2.88.

Faculty *Total:* 254, 33% full-time. *Student/faculty ratio:* 9:1.

Majors Accounting; autobody/collision and repair technology; automobile/automotive mechanics technology; business administration and management; commercial and advertising art; commercial photography; computer systems networking and telecommunications; cosmetology; criminal justice/safety; early childhood education; electrician; electromechanical technology; funeral service and mortuary science; information technology; interior design; liberal arts and sciences and humanities related; liberal arts and sciences/liberal studies; logistics, materials, and supply chain management; machine shop technology; mechatronics, robotics, and automation engineering; medical/clinical assistant; medical office management; photographic and film/video technology; photojournalism; physical therapy technology; radiologic technology/science; registered nursing/registered nurse.

Academics *Calendar:* semesters. *Degree:* certificates, diplomas, and associate. *Special study options:* academic remediation for entering students, adult/continuing education programs, advanced placement credit, cooperative education, distance learning, double majors, English as a second language, independent study, internships, off-campus study, part-time degree program, services for LD students, summer session for credit. *ROTC:* Air Force (c).

Library R. Alton Cox Learning Resources Center with 22,000 titles, 2,000 audiovisual materials, an OPAC, a Web page.

Student Life *Housing:* college housing not available. *Activities and Organizations:* Student Government Association, Phi Theta Kappa, Student Nurse Association, Phi Beta Lambda, Campus Crusaders. *Campus security:* 24-hour emergency response devices, security officer during open hours. *Student services:* personal/psychological counseling.

Costs (2015–16) *Tuition:* state resident $2304 full-time, $72 per credit part-time; nonresident $8448 full-time, $264 per credit part-time. *Required fees:* $88 full-time, $3 per credit part-time. *Payment plan:* installment.

Applying *Options:* electronic application, deferred entrance. *Application deadlines:* rolling (freshmen), rolling (transfers). *Notification:* continuous (freshmen), continuous (transfers).

Freshman Application Contact Ms. Brandi F. Hagerman, Director of Enrollment Management/Registrar, Randolph Community College, 629 Industrial Park Avenue, Asheboro, NC 27205-7333. *Phone:* 336-633-0213. *Fax:* 336-629-9547. *E-mail:* bhagerman@randolph.edu. *Website:* http://www.randolph.edu/.

Richmond Community College
Hamlet, North Carolina

- **State-supported** 2-year, founded 1964, part of North Carolina Community College System
- **Rural** 163-acre campus
- **Coed,** 2,664 undergraduate students, 42% full-time, 67% women, 33% men

Undergraduates 1,112 full-time, 1,552 part-time. 0.5% are from out of state; 38% Black or African American, non-Hispanic/Latino; 2% Hispanic/Latino; 0.6% Asian, non-Hispanic/Latino; 9% American Indian or Alaska Native, non-Hispanic/Latino; 2% Two or more races, non-Hispanic/Latino; 6% Race/ethnicity unknown; 5% transferred in.

Freshmen *Admission:* 474 enrolled.

Faculty *Student/faculty ratio:* 17:1.

Majors Accounting; business administration and management; computer engineering technology; criminal justice/safety; early childhood education; electrical and power transmission installation; electrical, electronic and communications engineering technology; electromechanical and instrumentation and maintenance technologies related; electromechanical technology; elementary education; entrepreneurship; health information/medical records technology; health professions related; heating, air conditioning, ventilation and refrigeration maintenance technology; information technology; liberal arts and sciences/liberal studies; mechanical engineering/mechanical technology; medical/clinical assistant; medical office computer specialist; mental and social health services and allied professions related; office management; registered nursing/registered nurse; welding technology.

Academics *Calendar:* semesters. *Degree:* certificates, diplomas, and associate. *Special study options:* academic remediation for entering students, adult/continuing education programs, advanced placement credit, cooperative education, distance learning, double majors, English as a second language, independent study, internships, part-time degree program, student-designed majors, summer session for credit.

Library Richmond Community College Library with 30,088 titles, an OPAC.

Student Life *Housing:* college housing not available. *Campus security:* 24-hour emergency response devices, security guard during operating hours. *Student services:* personal/psychological counseling.

Costs (2014–15) *Tuition:* state resident $2304 full-time, $72 per credit hour part-time; nonresident $8448 full-time, $264 per credit hour part-time. Full-time tuition and fees vary according to course load. Part-time tuition and fees vary according to course load. *Required fees:* $78 full-time, $32 per term part-time. *Payment plan:* installment. *Waivers:* employees or children of employees.

Financial Aid Of all full-time matriculated undergraduates who enrolled in 2013, 35 Federal Work-Study jobs (averaging $2000).

Applying *Options:* electronic application, deferred entrance. *Required:* high school transcript. *Application deadlines:* rolling (freshmen), rolling (transfers). *Notification:* continuous until 8/1 (freshmen), continuous until 8/1 (transfers).

Freshman Application Contact Lori J. Graham, Registrar, Richmond Community College, PO Box 1189, 1042 W. Hamlet Ave., Hamlet, NC 28345. *Phone:* 910-410-1737. *Fax:* 910-582-7102. *E-mail:* ljgraham1273@richmondcc.edu. *Website:* http://www.richmondcc.edu/.

Roanoke-Chowan Community College
Ahoskie, North Carolina

Director of Admissions Miss Sandra Copeland, Director, Counseling Services, Roanoke-Chowan Community College, 109 Community College Road, Ahoskie, NC 27910. *Phone:* 252-862-1225. *Website:* http://www.roanokechowan.edu/.

Robeson Community College
Lumberton, North Carolina

Freshman Application Contact Ms. Patricia Locklear, College Recruiter, Robeson Community College, PO Box 1420, Lumberton, NC 28359. *Phone:* 910-272-3356 Ext. 251. *Fax:* 910-618-5686. *E-mail:* plocklear@robeson.edu. *Website:* http://www.robeson.edu/.

Rockingham Community College
Wentworth, North Carolina

Freshman Application Contact Mr. Derrick Satterfield, Director of Enrollment Services, Rockingham Community College, PO Box 38, Wentworth, NC 27375-0038. *Phone:* 336-342-4261 Ext. 2114. *Fax:* 336-342-1809. *E-mail:* admissions@rockinghamcc.edu. *Website:* http://www.rockinghamcc.edu/.

Rowan-Cabarrus Community College
Salisbury, North Carolina

Freshman Application Contact Mrs. Gail Cummins, Director of Admissions and Recruitment, Rowan-Cabarrus Community College, PO Box 1595, Salisbury, NC 28145-1595. *Phone:* 704-637-0760. *Fax:* 704-633-6804. *Website:* http://www.rccc.edu/.

Sampson Community College
Clinton, North Carolina

Director of Admissions Mr. William R. Jordan, Director of Admissions, Sampson Community College, PO Box 318, 1801 Sunset Avenue, Highway 24 West, Clinton, NC 28329-0318. *Phone:* 910-592-8084 Ext. 2022. *Website:* http://www.sampsoncc.edu/.

Sandhills Community College
Pinehurst, North Carolina

Freshman Application Contact Mr. Isai Robledo, Recruiter, Sandhills Community College, 3395 Airport Road, Pinehurst, NC 28374-8299. *Phone:* 910-246-5365. *Toll-free phone:* 800-338-3944. *Fax:* 910-695-3981. *E-mail:* robledoi@sandhills.edu.
Website: http://www.sandhills.edu/.

South College–Asheville
Asheville, North Carolina

Freshman Application Contact Director of Admissions, South College–Asheville, 1567 Patton Avenue, Asheville, NC 28806. *Phone:* 828-277-5521. *Fax:* 828-277-6151.
Website: http://www.southcollegenc.edu/.

Southeastern Community College
Whiteville, North Carolina

- **State-supported** 2-year, founded 1964, part of North Carolina Community College System
- **Rural** 106-acre campus
- **Coed**

Undergraduates 766 full-time, 636 part-time. 0.8% are from out of state; 24% Black or African American, non-Hispanic/Latino; 3% Hispanic/Latino; 0.4% Asian, non-Hispanic/Latino; 7% American Indian or Alaska Native, non-Hispanic/Latino; 2% Race/ethnicity unknown. *Retention:* 48% of full-time freshmen returned.
Faculty *Student/faculty ratio:* 20:1.
Academics *Calendar:* semesters. *Degree:* certificates, diplomas, and associate. *Special study options:* academic remediation for entering students, adult/continuing education programs, advanced placement credit, cooperative education, distance learning, double majors, English as a second language, honors programs, independent study, internships, part-time degree program, services for LD students, summer session for credit.
Student Life *Campus security:* 24-hour emergency response devices.
Athletics Member NJCAA.
Applying *Options:* electronic application, early admission, deferred entrance. *Required:* high school transcript.
Freshman Application Contact Ms. Sylvia McQueen, Registrar, Southeastern Community College, PO Box 151, Whiteville, NC 28472. *Phone:* 910-642-7141 Ext. 249. *Fax:* 910-642-5658.
Website: http://www.sccnc.edu/.

South Piedmont Community College
Polkton, North Carolina

- **State-supported** 2-year, founded 1962, part of North Carolina Community College System
- **Rural** 56-acre campus with easy access to Charlotte
- **Endowment** $27,818
- **Coed**, 2,658 undergraduate students, 28% full-time, 69% women, 31% men

Undergraduates 732 full-time, 1,926 part-time. Students come from 5 states and territories; 1% are from out of state; 19% Black or African American, non-Hispanic/Latino; 11% Hispanic/Latino; 2% Asian, non-Hispanic/Latino; 0.2% Native Hawaiian or other Pacific Islander, non-Hispanic/Latino; 0.3% American Indian or Alaska Native, non-Hispanic/Latino; 2% Two or more races, non-Hispanic/Latino; 4% Race/ethnicity unknown; 2% international; 5% transferred in. *Retention:* 58% of full-time freshmen returned.
Freshmen *Admission:* 740 applied, 618 admitted, 391 enrolled.
Faculty *Total:* 106. *Student/faculty ratio:* 17:1.
Majors Accounting; allied health diagnostic, intervention, and treatment professions related; automobile/automotive mechanics technology; biotechnology; business administration and management; commercial and advertising art; criminal justice/safety; cyber/computer forensics and counterterrorism; diagnostic medical sonography and ultrasound technology; early childhood education; electrician; electromechanical and instrumentation and maintenance technologies related; electromechanical technology; elementary education; entrepreneurship; fire prevention and safety technology; game and interactive media design; general studies; heating, air conditioning, ventilation and refrigeration maintenance technology; information science/studies; information technology; legal assistant/paralegal; liberal arts and sciences/liberal studies; massage therapy; mechanical engineering/mechanical technology; medical/clinical assistant; medical office management; mental and social health services and allied professions related; registered nursing/registered nurse.

Academics *Calendar:* semesters. *Degree:* certificates, diplomas, and associate. *Special study options:* academic remediation for entering students, accelerated degree program, adult/continuing education programs, cooperative education, distance learning, English as a second language, independent study, internships, off-campus study, part-time degree program, services for LD students, summer session for credit.
Library Martin Learning Resource Center with 18,917 titles, an OPAC.
Student Life *Housing:* college housing not available. *Activities and Organizations:* choral group, Student Association, Phi Beta Lambda, Phi Theta Kappa, Social Services Club, Criminal Justice Club. *Campus security:* 24-hour emergency response devices and patrols, evening security. *Student services:* personal/psychological counseling, women's center.
Costs (2014–15) *Tuition:* state resident $2304 full-time, $72 per semester hour part-time; nonresident $8448 full-time, $264 per semester hour part-time. *Required fees:* $169 full-time, $5 per semester hour part-time, $17 per term part-time. *Payment plan:* installment.
Applying *Options:* electronic application, early admission, deferred entrance. *Required:* high school transcript. *Application deadlines:* rolling (freshmen), rolling (transfers). *Notification:* continuous (freshmen), continuous (transfers).
Freshman Application Contact Ms. Amanda Secrest, Assistant Director Admissions and Testing, South Piedmont Community College, PO Box 126, Polkton, NC 28135. *Phone:* 704-290-5847. *Toll-free phone:* 800-766-0319. *E-mail:* asecrest@spcc.edu.
Website: http://www.spcc.edu/.

Southwestern Community College
Sylva, North Carolina

- **State-supported** 2-year, founded 1964, part of North Carolina Community College System
- **Small-town** 77-acre campus
- **Coed**

Faculty *Student/faculty ratio:* 16:1.
Academics *Calendar:* semesters. *Degree:* certificates, diplomas, and associate. *Special study options:* academic remediation for entering students, adult/continuing education programs, advanced placement credit, cooperative education, distance learning, double majors, English as a second language, honors programs, independent study, off-campus study, part-time degree program, services for LD students, summer session for credit.
Student Life *Campus security:* security during hours college is open.
Costs (2014–15) *Tuition:* state resident $4032 full-time, $72 per credit hour part-time; nonresident $14,784 full-time, $264 per credit hour part-time. *Required fees:* $85 full-time, $3 per credit hour part-time, $1 per year part-time.
Applying *Required:* high school transcript. *Required for some:* minimum 2.5 GPA, interview.
Freshman Application Contact Ms. Dominique Benson, Admissions Officer, Southwestern Community College, 447 College Dr, Sylva, NC 28779. *Phone:* 828-339-4217. *Toll-free phone:* 800-447-4091 (in-state); 800-447-7091 (out-of-state). *E-mail:* D_Benson@southwesterncc.edu.
Website: http://www.southwesterncc.edu/.

Stanly Community College
Albemarle, North Carolina

Freshman Application Contact Mrs. Denise B. Ross, Associate Dean, Admissions, Stanly Community College, 141 College Drive, Albemarle, NC 28001. *Phone:* 704-982-0121 Ext. 264. *Fax:* 704-982-0255. *E-mail:* dross7926@stanly.edu.
Website: http://www.stanly.edu/.

Surry Community College
Dobson, North Carolina

Freshman Application Contact Renita Hazelwood, Director of Admissions, Surry Community College, 630 South Main Street, Dobson, NC 27017. *Phone:* 336-386-3392. *Fax:* 336-386-3690. *E-mail:* hazelwoodr@surry.edu.
Website: http://www.surry.edu/.

Tri-County Community College
Murphy, North Carolina

Freshman Application Contact Dr. Jason Chambers, Director of Student Services and Admissions, Tri-County Community College, 21 Campus Circle, Murphy, NC 28906-7919. *Phone:* 828-837-6810. *Fax:* 828-837-3266. *E-mail:* jchambers@tricountycc.edu.
Website: http://www.tricountycc.edu/.

Vance-Granville Community College
Henderson, North Carolina

Freshman Application Contact Ms. Kathy Kutl, Admissions Officer, Vance-Granville Community College, PO Box 917, State Road 1126, Henderson, NC 27536. *Phone:* 252-492-2061 Ext. 3265. *Fax:* 252-430-0460. .
Website: http://www.vgcc.edu/.

Virginia College in Greensboro
Greensboro, North Carolina

Admissions Office Contact Virginia College in Greensboro, 3740 South Holden Road, Greensboro, NC 27406.
Website: http://www.vc.edu/.

Wake Technical Community College
Raleigh, North Carolina

Director of Admissions Ms. Susan Bloomfield, Director of Admissions, Wake Technical Community College, 9101 Fayetteville Road, Raleigh, NC 27603-5696. *Phone:* 919-866-5452. *E-mail:* srbloomfield@waketech.edu.
Website: http://www.waketech.edu/.

Wayne Community College
Goldsboro, North Carolina

- **State and locally supported** 2-year, founded 1957, part of North Carolina Community College System
- **Small-town** 175-acre campus with easy access to Raleigh
- **Endowment** $92,408
- **Coed**

Undergraduates 1,813 full-time, 2,024 part-time. 4% are from out of state; 27% Black or African American, non-Hispanic/Latino; 8% Hispanic/Latino; 2% Asian, non-Hispanic/Latino; 0.3% Native Hawaiian or other Pacific Islander, non-Hispanic/Latino; 0.6% American Indian or Alaska Native, non-Hispanic/Latino; 0.8% Two or more races, non-Hispanic/Latino; 2% Race/ethnicity unknown; 0.3% international; 26% transferred in.
Faculty *Student/faculty ratio:* 20:1.
Academics *Calendar:* semesters. *Degree:* certificates, diplomas, and associate. *Special study options:* academic remediation for entering students, adult/continuing education programs, advanced placement credit, cooperative education, distance learning, double majors, English as a second language, external degree program, honors programs, part-time degree program, services for LD students, summer session for credit.
Student Life *Campus security:* 24-hour emergency response devices and patrols.
Standardized Tests *Recommended:* SAT or ACT (for admission).
Costs (2014–15) *Tuition:* state resident $2288 full-time, $72 per credit part-time; nonresident $8432 full-time, $264 per credit part-time. Full-time tuition and fees vary according to course load. Part-time tuition and fees vary according to course load. *Required fees:* $92 full-time, $23 per term part-time.
Financial Aid Of all full-time matriculated undergraduates who enrolled in 2013, 100 Federal Work-Study jobs (averaging $2000).
Applying *Options:* electronic application. *Required:* high school transcript, interview.
Freshman Application Contact Mrs. Jennifer P Mayo, Associate Director of Admissions and Records, Wayne Community College, PO Box 8002, Goldsboro, NC 27533. *Phone:* 919-735-5151 Ext. 6721. *Fax:* 919-736-9425. *E-mail:* jbmayo@waynecc.edu.
Website: http://www.waynecc.edu/.

Western Piedmont Community College
Morganton, North Carolina

Freshman Application Contact Susan Williams, Director of Admissions, Western Piedmont Community College, 1001 Burkemont Avenue, Morganton, NC 28655-4511. *Phone:* 828-438-6051. *Fax:* 828-438-6065. *E-mail:* swilliams@wpcc.edu.
Website: http://www.wpcc.edu/.

Wilkes Community College
Wilkesboro, North Carolina

Freshman Application Contact Mr. Mac Warren, Director of Admissions, Wilkes Community College, PO Box 120, Wilkesboro, NC 28697. *Phone:* 336-838-6141. *Fax:* 336-838-6547. *E-mail:* mac.warren@wilkescc.edu.
Website: http://www.wilkescc.edu/.

Wilson Community College
Wilson, North Carolina

Freshman Application Contact Mrs. Maegan Williams, Admissions Technician, Wilson Community College, Wilson, NC 27893-0305. *Phone:* 252-246-1275. *Fax:* 252-243-7148. *E-mail:* mwilliams@wilsoncc.edu.
Website: http://www.wilsoncc.edu/.

NORTH DAKOTA

Bismarck State College
Bismarck, North Dakota

- **State-supported** primarily 2-year, founded 1939, part of North Dakota University System
- **Urban** 100-acre campus
- **Coed**

Undergraduates 2,365 full-time, 1,697 part-time. Students come from 6 other countries; 25% are from out of state; 3% Black or African American, non-Hispanic/Latino; 3% Hispanic/Latino; 0.4% Asian, non-Hispanic/Latino; 0.1% Native Hawaiian or other Pacific Islander, non-Hispanic/Latino; 2% American Indian or Alaska Native, non-Hispanic/Latino; 2% Two or more races, non-Hispanic/Latino; 2% Race/ethnicity unknown; 0.3% international; 7% transferred in; 9% live on campus.
Faculty *Student/faculty ratio:* 15:1.
Academics *Calendar:* semesters. *Degrees:* certificates, diplomas, associate, and bachelor's. *Special study options:* academic remediation for entering students, adult/continuing education programs, advanced placement credit, cooperative education, distance learning, independent study, internships, part-time degree program, services for LD students, study abroad, summer session for credit.
Student Life *Campus security:* late-night transport/escort service, controlled dormitory access.
Athletics Member NJCAA.
Standardized Tests *Required for some:* SAT or ACT (for admission).
Costs (2014–15) *Tuition:* state resident $2808 full-time, $117 per credit hour part-time; nonresident $7488 full-time, $312 per credit hour part-time. Full-time tuition and fees vary according to course level, course load, degree level, location, program, and reciprocity agreements. Part-time tuition and fees vary according to course level, course load, degree level, location, program, and reciprocity agreements. *Required fees:* $712 full-time, $30 per credit hour part-time. *Room and board:* $6801; room only: $2401. Room and board charges vary according to board plan and housing facility.
Financial Aid Of all full-time matriculated undergraduates who enrolled in 2013, 1,731 applied for aid, 1,133 were judged to have need, 429 had their need fully met. In 2013, 236. *Average percent of need met:* 49. *Average financial aid package:* $11,129. *Average need-based loan:* $4646. *Average need-based gift aid:* $4241. *Average non-need-based aid:* $709.
Applying *Options:* electronic application, early admission. *Application fee:* $35. *Required:* high school transcript. *Required for some:* interview.
Freshman Application Contact Karen Erickson, Director of Admissions and Enrollment Services, Bismarck State College, PO Box 5587, Bismarck, ND 58506. *Phone:* 701-224-5424. *Toll-free phone:* 800-445-5073. *Fax:* 701-224-5643. *E-mail:* karen.erickson@bismarckstate.edu.
Website: http://www.bismarckstate.edu/.

Cankdeska Cikana Community College
Fort Totten, North Dakota

Director of Admissions Mr. Ermen Brown Jr., Registrar, Cankdeska Cikana Community College, PO Box 269, Fort Totten, ND 58335-0269. *Phone:* 701-766-1342. *Toll-free phone:* 888-783-1463.
Website: http://www.littlehoop.edu/.

Dakota College at Bottineau
Bottineau, North Dakota

- **State-supported** 2-year, founded 1906, part of North Dakota University System
- **Rural** 35-acre campus
- **Coed**, 852 undergraduate students

Undergraduates Students come from 3 other countries; 23% are from out of state; 10% Black or African American, non-Hispanic/Latino; 3% Hispanic/Latino; 0.4% Asian, non-Hispanic/Latino; 0.3% Native Hawaiian or other Pacific Islander, non-Hispanic/Latino; 2% American Indian or Alaska

Native, non-Hispanic/Latino; 3% Two or more races, non-Hispanic/Latino; 17% Race/ethnicity unknown; 3% international.

Faculty *Total:* 88, 32% full-time, 6% with terminal degrees. *Student/faculty ratio:* 10:1.

Majors Accounting; accounting related; accounting technology and bookkeeping; administrative assistant and secretarial science; adult development and aging; advertising; agriculture; applied horticulture/horticultural business services related; applied horticulture/horticulture operations; biology/biological sciences; business administration and management; business automation/technology/data entry; chemistry; child-care and support services management; child-care provision; computer and information sciences; computer and information sciences and support services related; computer software and media applications related; computer technology/computer systems technology; crop production; education; entrepreneurial and small business related; environmental engineering technology; executive assistant/executive secretary; fishing and fisheries sciences and management; floriculture/floristry management; general studies; greenhouse management; health and physical education/fitness; health services/allied health/health sciences; history; horticultural science; hospitality and recreation marketing; humanities; information science/studies; information technology; landscaping and groundskeeping; land use planning and management; liberal arts and sciences and humanities related; liberal arts and sciences/liberal studies; licensed practical/vocational nurse training; marketing/marketing management; marketing related; mathematics; medical administrative assistant and medical secretary; medical/clinical assistant; medical insurance coding; medical office assistant; natural resources/conservation; network and system administration; office management; office occupations and clerical services; ornamental horticulture; parks, recreation and leisure; parks, recreation and leisure facilities management; parks, recreation, leisure, and fitness studies related; photography; physical sciences; physical sciences related; premedical studies; prenursing studies; pre-veterinary studies; psychology; receptionist; registered nursing/registered nurse; science technologies related; small business administration; social sciences; teacher assistant/aide; urban forestry; wildlife, fish and wildlands science and management; zoology/animal biology.

Academics *Calendar:* semesters. *Degree:* certificates, diplomas, and associate. *Special study options:* academic remediation for entering students, advanced placement credit, cooperative education, distance learning, double majors, off-campus study, part-time degree program, services for LD students, summer session for credit.

Library Dakota College at Bottineau Library plus 1 other with 41,411 titles, 1,339 audiovisual materials, an OPAC, a Web page.

Student Life *Housing:* on-campus residence required through sophomore year. *Options:* men-only, women-only. Campus housing is university owned. Freshman campus housing is guaranteed. *Activities and Organizations:* drama/theater group, Student Senate, Wildlife Club/Horticulture Club, Snowboarding Club, Phi Theta Kappa, Delta Epsilon Chi. *Campus security:* controlled dormitory access, security cameras. *Student services:* health clinic, personal/psychological counseling.

Athletics Member NJCAA. *Intercollegiate sports:* baseball M(s), basketball M(s)/W(s), football M, ice hockey M(s), softball W(s), volleyball W(s). *Intramural sports:* badminton M/W, basketball M/W, skiing (downhill) M/W, table tennis M/W, volleyball M/W.

Standardized Tests *Required:* SAT or ACT (for admission). *Recommended:* ACT (for admission).

Costs (2014–15) *Tuition:* state resident $4098 full-time, $174 per credit hour part-time; nonresident $5748 full-time, $240 per credit hour part-time. Full-time tuition and fees vary according to location, program, and reciprocity agreements. Part-time tuition and fees vary according to location, program, and reciprocity agreements. *Room and board:* $5669; room only: $2332. Room and board charges vary according to board plan and housing facility. *Payment plan:* installment.

Financial Aid Of all full-time matriculated undergraduates who enrolled in 2012, 290 applied for aid, 237 were judged to have need, 63 had their need fully met. 60 Federal Work-Study jobs (averaging $1500). In 2012, 33 non-need-based awards were made. *Average percent of need met:* 61%. *Average financial aid package:* $10,670. *Average need-based loan:* $4616. *Average need-based gift aid:* $4757. *Average non-need-based aid:* $664.

Applying *Options:* electronic application, early admission, deferred entrance. *Application fee:* $35. *Required:* high school transcript, immunization records, previous college official transcripts, ACT or SAT scores. *Application deadlines:* rolling (freshmen), rolling (out-of-state freshmen), rolling (transfers).

Freshman Application Contact Mrs. Luann Soland, Admissions Counselor, Dakota College at Bottineau, 105 Simrall Boulevard, Bottineau, ND 58318. *Phone:* 701-228-5487. *Toll-free phone:* 800-542-6866. *Fax:* 701-228-5499. *E-mail:* luann.soland@dakotacollege.edu. *Website:* http://www.dakotacollege.edu/.

Fort Berthold Community College
New Town, North Dakota

Freshman Application Contact Office of Admissions, Fort Berthold Community College, PO Box 490, 220 8th Avenue North, New Town, ND 58763-0490. *Phone:* 701-627-4738 Ext. 295. *Website:* http://www.fortbertholdcc.edu/.

Lake Region State College
Devils Lake, North Dakota

- **State-supported** 2-year, founded 1941, part of North Dakota University System
- **Small-town** 120-acre campus
- **Coed,** 1,988 undergraduate students, 27% full-time, 55% women, 45% men

Undergraduates 530 full-time, 1,458 part-time. Students come from 26 states and territories; 6 other countries; 12% are from out of state; 5% Black or African American, non-Hispanic/Latino; 4% Hispanic/Latino; 0.9% Asian, non-Hispanic/Latino; 0.3% Native Hawaiian or other Pacific Islander, non-Hispanic/Latino; 3% American Indian or Alaska Native, non-Hispanic/Latino; 3% Two or more races, non-Hispanic/Latino; 2% Race/ethnicity unknown; 6% international; 5% transferred in; 10% live on campus.

Freshmen *Admission:* 214 enrolled. *Test scores:* ACT scores over 18: 72%; ACT scores over 24: 17%.

Majors Administrative assistant and secretarial science; agricultural business and management; automobile/automotive mechanics technology; business administration and management; child-care provision; computer installation and repair technology; criminal justice/police science; electrical and electronic engineering technologies related; language interpretation and translation; liberal arts and sciences/liberal studies; management information systems; merchandising, sales, and marketing operations related (general); physical fitness technician; registered nursing/registered nurse; speech-language pathology.

Academics *Calendar:* semesters. *Degree:* certificates, diplomas, and associate. *Special study options:* academic remediation for entering students, cooperative education, distance learning, double majors, English as a second language, honors programs, internships, part-time degree program, services for LD students, summer session for credit.

Library Paul Hoghaug Library with 40,000 titles, 2,000 audiovisual materials, an OPAC.

Student Life *Housing Options:* coed, men-only, women-only. Campus housing is university owned and leased by the school. *Activities and Organizations:* drama/theater group, choral group, marching band, Student Senate, Phi Theta Kappa, Delta Epsilon Chi, Phi Theta Lambda, Student Nurse Organization. *Campus security:* 24-hour emergency response devices, controlled dormitory access. *Student services:* personal/psychological counseling.

Athletics Member NJCAA. *Intercollegiate sports:* baseball M(s), basketball M(s)/W(s), golf M(s)/W(s), softball W(s), volleyball W(s). *Intramural sports:* archery M/W, basketball M/W, golf M/W, riflery M/W, soccer M/W, volleyball M/W, weight lifting M/W.

Standardized Tests *Required for some:* SAT or ACT (for admission), ACT Compass.

Costs (2014–15) *Tuition:* state resident $3197 full-time, $133 per credit part-time; nonresident $3197 full-time, $133 per credit part-time. Full-time tuition and fees vary according to course load, location, and program. Part-time tuition and fees vary according to course load, location, and program. *Required fees:* $877 full-time, $29 per credit part-time. *Room and board:* $5950. Room and board charges vary according to board plan and housing facility. *Payment plan:* installment. *Waivers:* minority students, senior citizens, and employees or children of employees.

Financial Aid Of all full-time matriculated undergraduates who enrolled in 2014, 389 applied for aid, 305 were judged to have need, 128 had their need fully met. In 2014, 86 non-need-based awards were made. *Average percent of need met:* 80%. *Average financial aid package:* $9634. *Average need-based loan:* $5063. *Average need-based gift aid:* $5248. *Average non-need-based aid:* $821. *Average indebtedness upon graduation:* $9405.

Applying *Options:* electronic application. *Application fee:* $35. *Required:* Immunizations records and college transcripts required for some. *Required for some:* high school transcript, interview. *Application deadlines:* rolling (freshmen), rolling (out-of-state freshmen), rolling (transfers). *Notification:* continuous (freshmen), continuous (out-of-state freshmen), continuous (transfers).

Freshman Application Contact Samantha Cordrey, Administrative Assistant, Admissions Office, Lake Region State College, 1801 College Drive North, Devils Lake, ND 58301. *Phone:* 701-662-1514. *Toll-free phone:* 800-443-1313. *Fax:* 701-662-1581. *E-mail:* samantha.cordrey@lrsc.edu. *Website:* http://www.lrsc.edu/.

North Dakota State College of Science
Wahpeton, North Dakota

- **State-supported** 2-year, founded 1903, part of North Dakota University System
- **Rural** 128-acre campus
- **Endowment** $12.9 million
- **Coed**

Undergraduates 1,712 full-time, 1,456 part-time. Students come from 39 states and territories; 5 other countries; 40% are from out of state; 5% Black or African American, non-Hispanic/Latino; 1% Hispanic/Latino; 0.9% Asian, non-Hispanic/Latino; 1% American Indian or Alaska Native, non-Hispanic/Latino; 2% Two or more races, non-Hispanic/Latino; 1% Race/ethnicity unknown; 7% transferred in; 56% live on campus.
Faculty *Student/faculty ratio:* 13:1.
Academics *Calendar:* semesters. *Degree:* certificates, diplomas, and associate. *Special study options:* academic remediation for entering students, adult/continuing education programs, cooperative education, distance learning, double majors, English as a second language, independent study, internships, part-time degree program, services for LD students, student-designed majors, summer session for credit.
Student Life *Campus security:* 24-hour emergency response devices and patrols, student patrols, late-night transport/escort service, controlled dormitory access.
Athletics Member NJCAA.
Financial Aid Of all full-time matriculated undergraduates who enrolled in 2013, 1,433 applied for aid, 1,078 were judged to have need, 480 had their need fully met. 126 Federal Work-Study jobs (averaging $1597). In 2013, 332. *Average percent of need met:* 59. *Average financial aid package:* $12,193. *Average need-based loan:* $5182. *Average need-based gift aid:* $4179. *Average non-need-based aid:* $874. *Average indebtedness upon graduation:* $15,643. *Financial aid deadline:* 4/15.
Applying *Options:* electronic application, early admission. *Application fee:* $35. *Required:* high school transcript.
Freshman Application Contact Ms. Barb Mund, Director of Admissions and Records, North Dakota State College of Science, 800 North 6th Street, Wahpeton, ND 58076. *Phone:* 701-671-2204. *Toll-free phone:* 800-342-4325. *Fax:* 701-671-2201. *E-mail:* Barb.Mund@ndscs.edu.
Website: http://www.ndscs.edu/.

Turtle Mountain Community College
Belcourt, North Dakota

Director of Admissions Ms. Joni LaFontaine, Admissions/Records Officer, Turtle Mountain Community College, Box 340, Belcourt, ND 58316-0340. *Phone:* 701-477-5605 Ext. 217. *E-mail:* jlafontaine@tm.edu.
Website: http://my.tm.edu/.

United Tribes Technical College
Bismarck, North Dakota

Freshman Application Contact Ms. Vivian Gillette, Director of Admissions, United Tribes Technical College, Bismarck, ND 58504. *Phone:* 701-255-3285 Ext. 1334. *Fax:* 701-530-0640. *E-mail:* vgillette@uttc.edu.
Website: http://www.uttc.edu/.

Williston State College
Williston, North Dakota

- **State-supported** 2-year, founded 1957, part of North Dakota University System
- **Small-town** 80-acre campus
- **Endowment** $52,200
- **Coed,** 883 undergraduate students, 48% full-time, 62% women, 38% men

Undergraduates 421 full-time, 462 part-time. Students come from 33 states and territories; 6 other countries; 18% are from out of state; 5% Black or African American, non-Hispanic/Latino; 5% Hispanic/Latino; 1% Asian, non-Hispanic/Latino; 0.1% Native Hawaiian or other Pacific Islander, non-Hispanic/Latino; 2% American Indian or Alaska Native, non-Hispanic/Latino; 4% Two or more races, non-Hispanic/Latino; 4% Race/ethnicity unknown; 5% international; 26% transferred in. *Retention:* 47% of full-time freshmen returned.
Freshmen *Admission:* 294 applied, 236 admitted, 157 enrolled.
Faculty *Total:* 37, 100% full-time. *Student/faculty ratio:* 23:1.
Majors Accounting technology and bookkeeping; administrative assistant and secretarial science; agriculture; business administration, management and operations related; carpentry; diesel mechanics technology; health information/medical records technology; liberal arts and sciences/liberal studies; licensed practical/vocational nurse training; marketing/marketing management; massage therapy; multi/interdisciplinary studies related; petroleum technology; psychiatric/mental health services technology; registered nursing/registered nurse; speech-language pathology; system, networking, and LAN/WAN management; welding technology.
Academics *Calendar:* semesters. *Degree:* certificates, diplomas, and associate. *Special study options:* academic remediation for entering students, advanced placement credit, cooperative education, distance learning, double majors, independent study, part-time degree program, services for LD students, student-designed majors, study abroad, summer session for credit.
Library Williston State College Learning Commons with 17,439 titles, 478 audiovisual materials, an OPAC, a Web page.
Student Life *Housing Options:* coed, special housing for students with disabilities. Campus housing is university owned. *Activities and Organizations:* student-run newspaper, choral group, Phi Theta Kappa, Student Senate, Teton Activity Board, Biz-Tech, Student Nurses Organization. *Campus security:* 24-hour patrols, controlled dormitory access. *Student services:* personal/psychological counseling.
Athletics Member NJCAA. *Intercollegiate sports:* baseball M(s), basketball M(s)/W(s), ice hockey M(s), softball W(s), volleyball W(s). *Intramural sports:* basketball M/W, volleyball M/W.
Costs (2014–15) *One-time required fee:* $35. *Tuition:* state resident $3235 full-time, $108 per credit hour part-time; nonresident $3235 full-time, $108 per credit hour part-time. Full-time tuition and fees vary according to course load, location, program, and reciprocity agreements. Part-time tuition and fees vary according to course load, location, program, and reciprocity agreements. *Required fees:* $1103 full-time, $42 per credit hour part-time. *Room and board:* $7548; room only: $4300. Room and board charges vary according to board plan and housing facility. *Payment plan:* installment. *Waivers:* minority students, senior citizens, and employees or children of employees.
Applying *Options:* electronic application, deferred entrance. *Application fee:* $35. *Required:* high school transcript. *Application deadlines:* rolling (freshmen), rolling (out-of-state freshmen), rolling (transfers). *Notification:* continuous (freshmen), continuous (out-of-state freshmen), continuous (transfers).
Freshman Application Contact Ms. Brittney O'Neill, Enrollment Services Associate, Williston State College, 1410 University Avenue, Williston, ND 58801. *Phone:* 701-774-4202. *Toll-free phone:* 888-863-9455. *E-mail:* brittney.f.oneill@willistonstate.edu.
Website: http://www.willistonstate.edu/.

NORTHERN MARIANA ISLANDS

Northern Marianas College
Saipan, Northern Mariana Islands

Freshman Application Contact Ms. Leilani M. Basa-Alam, Admission Specialist, Northern Marianas College, PO Box 501250, Saipan, MP 96950-1250. *Phone:* 670-234-3690 Ext. 1539. *Fax:* 670-235-4967. *E-mail:* leilanib@nmcnet.edu.
Website: http://www.marianas.edu/.

OHIO

Akron Institute of Herzing University
Akron, Ohio

Admissions Office Contact Akron Institute of Herzing University, 1600 South Arlington Street, Suite 100, Akron, OH 44306. *Toll-free phone:* 800-311-0512.
Website: http://www.akroninstitute.com/.

American Institute of Alternative Medicine
Columbus, Ohio

Admissions Office Contact American Institute of Alternative Medicine, 6685 Doubletree Avenue, Columbus, OH 43229.
Website: http://www.aiam.edu/.

Antonelli College
Cincinnati, Ohio

Freshman Application Contact Antonelli Colleges, 124 East Seventh Street, Cincinnati, OH 45202. *Phone:* 513-241-4338. *Toll-free phone:* 877-500-4304.
Website: http://www.antonellicollege.edu/.

The Art Institute of Cincinnati
Cincinnati, Ohio

- **Independent** primarily 2-year, founded 1976
- **Urban** 3-acre campus with easy access to Cincinnati
- **Coed,** 34 undergraduate students, 88% full-time, 65% women, 35% men

Undergraduates 30 full-time, 4 part-time. Students come from 3 states and territories; 27% are from out of state; 18% Black or African American, non-Hispanic/Latino. *Retention:* 90% of full-time freshmen returned.
Freshmen *Admission:* 46 applied, 34 admitted, 6 enrolled. *Average high school GPA:* 3.3.
Faculty *Total:* 11, 36% full-time, 18% with terminal degrees. *Student/faculty ratio:* 5:1.
Majors Computer graphics.
Academics *Degrees:* associate and bachelor's. *Special study options:* academic remediation for entering students, accelerated degree program, advanced placement credit, cooperative education, part-time degree program, services for LD students.
Library The Art Institute of Cincinnati Library plus 1 other with 3,000 titles, 75 audiovisual materials, an OPAC, a Web page.
Student Life *Housing:* college housing not available. *Activities and Organizations:* AIGA Student Chapter. *Campus security:* 24-hour emergency response devices, SMS. *Student services:* personal/psychological counseling.
Standardized Tests *Recommended:* SAT or ACT (for admission).
Costs (2015–16) *Tuition:* $23,001 full-time, $511 per credit hour part-time. No tuition increase for student's term of enrollment. *Required fees:* $1017 full-time. *Payment plan:* installment. *Waivers:* employees or children of employees.
Applying *Options:* early admission, early decision, deferred entrance. *Application fee:* $100. *Required:* essay or personal statement, high school transcript, interview. *Recommended:* minimum 2.0 GPA, ACT or SAT score submission recommended. Placement testing is offered. *Application deadlines:* rolling (freshmen), rolling (out-of-state freshmen), rolling (transfers). *Early decision deadline:* rolling (for plan 1), rolling (for plan 2). *Notification:* continuous (freshmen), continuous (out-of-state freshmen), continuous (transfers), rolling (early decision plan 1), rolling (early decision plan 2).
Freshman Application Contact Megan Orsburn AIA, Admissions Assistant, The Art Institute of Cincinnati, 1171 E. Kemper Road, Cincinnati, OH 45246. *Phone:* 513-751-1206.
Website: http://www.aic-arts.edu/.

ATS Institute of Technology
Highland Heights, Ohio

Freshman Application Contact Admissions Office, ATS Institute of Technology, 325 Alpha Park, Highland Heights, OH 44143. *Phone:* 440-449-1700 Ext. 103. *E-mail:* info@atsinstitute.edu.
Website: http://www.atsinstitute.edu/cleveland/.

Beckfield College
Cincinnati, Ohio

Admissions Office Contact Beckfield College, 225 Pictoria Drive, Suite 200, Cincinnati, OH 45246.
Website: http://www.beckfield.edu/.

Belmont College
St. Clairsville, Ohio

Director of Admissions Michael Sterling, Director of Recruitment, Belmont College, 120 Fox Shannon Place, St. Clairsville, OH 43950-9735. *Phone:* 740-695-9500 Ext. 1563. *Toll-free phone:* 800-423-1188. *E-mail:* msterling@btc.edu.
Website: http://www.belmontcollege.edu/.

Bowling Green State University-Firelands College
Huron, Ohio

- **State-supported** primarily 2-year, founded 1968, part of Bowling Green State University System
- **Rural** 216-acre campus with easy access to Cleveland, Toledo
- **Coed,** 2,287 undergraduate students, 52% full-time, 63% women, 37% men

Undergraduates 1,191 full-time, 1,096 part-time. Students come from 8 states and territories; 6% Black or African American, non-Hispanic/Latino; 5% Hispanic/Latino; 0.5% Asian, non-Hispanic/Latino; 0.2% Native Hawaiian or other Pacific Islander, non-Hispanic/Latino; 0.4% American Indian or Alaska Native, non-Hispanic/Latino; 4% Two or more races, non-Hispanic/Latino; 4% Race/ethnicity unknown; 6% transferred in. *Retention:* 52% of full-time freshmen returned.
Freshmen *Admission:* 856 applied, 658 admitted, 385 enrolled. *Average high school GPA:* 2.8.
Faculty *Total:* 141, 37% full-time, 27% with terminal degrees. *Student/faculty ratio:* 19:1.
Majors Allied health and medical assisting services related; business administration and management; communications technologies and support services related; computer and information sciences and support services related; computer engineering technology; computer systems networking and telecommunications; criminal justice/safety; design and visual communications; diagnostic medical sonography and ultrasound technology; education; electrical, electronic and communications engineering technology; electromechanical technology; health information/medical records administration; health professions related; human services; industrial technology; interdisciplinary studies; liberal arts and sciences/liberal studies; management information systems and services related; manufacturing engineering technology; mechanical engineering/mechanical technology; medical radiologic technology; registered nursing/registered nurse; respiratory care therapy; social work.
Academics *Calendar:* semesters. *Degrees:* certificates, associate, and bachelor's (also offers some upper-level and graduate courses). *Special study options:* academic remediation for entering students, adult/continuing education programs, advanced placement credit, cooperative education, distance learning, double majors, honors programs, independent study, internships, part-time degree program, services for LD students, student-designed majors, study abroad, summer session for credit. *ROTC:* Army (c), Air Force (c).
Library BGSU Firelands College Library with 61,019 titles, 1,958 audiovisual materials, an OPAC, a Web page.
Student Life *Housing:* college housing not available. *Activities and Organizations:* drama/theater group, Society of Fandom and Gaming, Student Government, Student Theater Guild, Safe Space, Society of Leadership and Success. *Campus security:* 24-hour emergency response devices, late-night transport/escort service, patrols by trained security personnel.
Athletics *Intramural sports:* basketball M/W, bowling M/W, football M, table tennis M/W, volleyball M/W.
Costs (2015–16) *Tuition:* state resident $4706 full-time, $196 per credit hour part-time; nonresident $12,014 full-time, $501 per credit hour part-time. Full-time tuition and fees vary according to location. Part-time tuition and fees vary according to location. *Required fees:* $240 full-time, $9 per credit hour part-time, $120 per term part-time. *Payment plan:* installment. *Waivers:* employees or children of employees.
Applying *Options:* electronic application, early admission, deferred entrance. *Application fee:* $45. *Required:* high school transcript. *Application deadlines:* 8/6 (freshmen), 8/6 (transfers). *Notification:* continuous (freshmen), continuous (transfers).
Freshman Application Contact Debralee Divers, Director of Admissions and Financial Aid, Bowling Green State University-Firelands College, One University Drive, Huron, OH 44839-9791. *Phone:* 419-433-5560. *Toll-free phone:* 800-322-4787. *Fax:* 419-372-0604. *E-mail:* divers@bgsu.edu.
Website: http://www.firelands.bgsu.edu/.

Bradford School
Columbus, Ohio

- **Private** 2-year, founded 1911
- **Suburban** campus
- **Coed, primarily women,** 449 undergraduate students

Majors Cooking and related culinary arts; graphic design; medical/clinical assistant; physical therapy technology; veterinary/animal health technology.

Academics *Calendar:* semesters. *Degree:* diplomas and associate.
Freshman Application Contact Admissions Office, Bradford School, 2469 Stelzer Road, Columbus, OH 43219. *Phone:* 614-416-6200. *Toll-free phone:* 800-678-7981.
Website: http://www.bradfordschoolcolumbus.edu/.

Brown Mackie College–Akron
Akron, Ohio

- **Proprietary** primarily 2-year, founded 1968, part of Education Management Corporation
- **Suburban** campus
- **Coed**

Academics *Calendar:* quarters. *Degrees:* diplomas, associate, and bachelor's.
Freshman Application Contact Brown Mackie College–Akron, 755 White Pond Drive, Suite 101, Akron, OH 44320. *Phone:* 330-869-3600.
Website: http://www.brownmackie.edu/akron/.

Brown Mackie College–Cincinnati
Cincinnati, Ohio

- **Proprietary** primarily 2-year, founded 1927, part of Education Management Corporation
- **Suburban** campus
- **Coed**

Academics *Calendar:* quarters. *Degrees:* diplomas, associate, and bachelor's.
Freshman Application Contact Brown Mackie College–Cincinnati, 1011 Glendale-Milford Road, Cincinnati, OH 45215. *Phone:* 513-771-2424. *Toll-free phone:* 800-888-1445.
Website: http://www.brownmackie.edu/cincinnati/.

Brown Mackie College–Findlay
Findlay, Ohio

- **Proprietary** primarily 2-year, founded 1929, part of Education Management Corporation
- **Rural** campus
- **Coed**

Academics *Calendar:* continuous. *Degrees:* diplomas, associate, and bachelor's.
Freshman Application Contact Brown Mackie College–Findlay, 1700 Fostoria Avenue, Suite 100, Findlay, OH 45840. *Phone:* 419-423-2211. *Toll-free phone:* 800-842-3687.
Website: http://www.brownmackie.edu/findlay/.

Brown Mackie College–North Canton
Canton, Ohio

- **Proprietary** primarily 2-year, founded 1929, part of Education Management Corporation
- **Suburban** campus
- **Coed**

Academics *Calendar:* quarters. *Degrees:* diplomas, associate, and bachelor's.
Freshman Application Contact Brown Mackie College–North Canton, 4300 Munson Street NW, Canton, OH 44718-3674. *Phone:* 330-494-1214.
Website: http://www.brownmackie.edu/northcanton/.

Bryant & Stratton College–Eastlake Campus
Eastlake, Ohio

Freshman Application Contact Ms. Melanie Pettit, Director of Admissions, Bryant & Stratton College–Eastlake Campus, 35350 Curtis Boulevard, Eastlake, OH 44095. *Phone:* 440-510-1112.
Website: http://www.bryantstratton.edu/.

Bryant & Stratton College–Parma Campus
Parma, Ohio

Freshman Application Contact Bryant & Stratton College–Parma Campus, 12955 Snow Road, Parma, OH 44130-1013. *Phone:* 216-265-3151. *Toll-free phone:* 866-948-0571.
Website: http://www.bryantstratton.edu/.

Central Ohio Technical College
Newark, Ohio

- **State-supported** 2-year, founded 1971, part of Ohio Board of Regents
- **Small-town** 155-acre campus with easy access to Columbus
- **Endowment** $2.5 million
- **Coed**

Undergraduates 995 full-time, 2,653 part-time. 1% are from out of state; 11% Black or African American, non-Hispanic/Latino; 2% Hispanic/Latino; 0.5% Asian, non-Hispanic/Latino; 0.2% Native Hawaiian or other Pacific Islander, non-Hispanic/Latino; 0.4% American Indian or Alaska Native, non-Hispanic/Latino; 3% Two or more races, non-Hispanic/Latino; 4% Race/ethnicity unknown; 11% transferred in. *Retention:* 43% of full-time freshmen returned.
Faculty *Student/faculty ratio:* 15:1.
Academics *Calendar:* quarters. *Degree:* certificates and associate. *Special study options:* academic remediation for entering students, accelerated degree program, adult/continuing education programs, advanced placement credit, cooperative education, distance learning, double majors, internships, off-campus study, part-time degree program, services for LD students, summer session for credit.
Student Life *Campus security:* 24-hour emergency response devices and patrols, student patrols, late-night transport/escort service.
Costs (2014–15) *One-time required fee:* $40. *Tuition:* state resident $4296 full-time, $179 per semester hour part-time; nonresident $7056 full-time, $294 per semester hour part-time.
Financial Aid Of all full-time matriculated undergraduates who enrolled in 2013, 43 Federal Work-Study jobs (averaging $4000).
Applying *Options:* electronic application, early admission, deferred entrance. *Application fee:* $20. *Required:* high school transcript.
Freshman Application Contact Teri Holder, Interim Director of Gateway Operations, Central Ohio Technical College, 1179 University Drive, Newark, OH 43055-1767. *Phone:* 740-366-9222. *Toll-free phone:* 800-9NEWARK. *Fax:* 740-366-5047.
Website: http://www.cotc.edu/.

Chatfield College
St. Martin, Ohio

Freshman Application Contact Chatfield College, 20918 State Route 251, St. Martin, OH 45118-9705. *Phone:* 513-875-3344 Ext. 137.
Website: http://www.chatfield.edu/.

The Christ College of Nursing and Health Sciences
Cincinnati, Ohio

Freshman Application Contact Mr. Bradley Jackson, Admissions, The Christ College of Nursing and Health Sciences, 2139 Auburn Avenue, Cincinnati, OH 45219. *Phone:* 513-585-0016. *E-mail:* bradley.jackson@thechristcollege.edu.
Website: http://www.thechristcollege.edu/.

Cincinnati State Technical and Community College
Cincinnati, Ohio

- **State-supported** 2-year, founded 1966, part of Ohio Board of Regents
- **Urban** 46-acre campus
- **Coed,** 10,707 undergraduate students, 33% full-time, 55% women, 45% men

Undergraduates 3,581 full-time, 7,126 part-time. 9% are from out of state; 29% Black or African American, non-Hispanic/Latino; 2% Hispanic/Latino; 1% Asian, non-Hispanic/Latino; 0.1% Native Hawaiian or other Pacific Islander, non-Hispanic/Latino; 0.4% American Indian or Alaska Native, non-Hispanic/Latino; 3% Two or more races, non-Hispanic/Latino; 5% Race/ethnicity unknown; 2% international. *Retention:* 43% of full-time freshmen returned.
Freshmen *Admission:* 1,261 enrolled.
Faculty *Total:* 785, 27% full-time, 3% with terminal degrees. *Student/faculty ratio:* 15:1.
Majors Accounting; administrative assistant and secretarial science; aeronautical/aerospace engineering technology; allied health and medical assisting services related; applied horticulture/horticultural business services related; architectural engineering technology; audiovisual communications technologies related; automobile/automotive mechanics technology; automotive engineering technology; baking and pastry arts; biology/biological sciences; biomedical technology; business administration and management;

business administration, management and operations related; chemical technology; civil engineering technology; clinical/medical laboratory technology; commercial and advertising art; computer and information sciences; computer engineering technology; computer programming (specific applications); computer support specialist; computer systems analysis; crisis/emergency/disaster management; culinary arts; desktop publishing and digital imaging design; diagnostic medical sonography and ultrasound technology; dietetics; early childhood education; electrical, electronic and communications engineering technology; electromechanical technology; emergency medical technology (EMT paramedic); energy management and systems technology; engineering technologies and engineering related; entrepreneurship; environmental control technologies related; environmental engineering technology; executive assistant/executive secretary; financial planning and services; fire science/firefighting; general studies; health information/medical records technology; hospitality administration; industrial technology; information technology project management; landscaping and groundskeeping; liberal arts and sciences/liberal studies; marketing/marketing management; mechanical engineering/mechanical technology; medical office assistant; multi/interdisciplinary studies related; network and system administration; nuclear medical technology; occupational safety and health technology; occupational therapist assistant; parks, recreation, leisure, and fitness studies related; plastics and polymer engineering technology; real estate; registered nursing/registered nurse; restaurant, culinary, and catering management; sign language interpretation and translation; surgical technology; turf and turfgrass management.

Academics *Calendar:* 5 ten-week terms. *Degree:* certificates and associate. *Special study options:* academic remediation for entering students, advanced placement credit, cooperative education, distance learning, double majors, English as a second language, honors programs, independent study, internships, off-campus study, part-time degree program, services for LD students, student-designed majors, summer session for credit. *ROTC:* Army (c).

Library Johnnie Mae Berry Library with an OPAC, a Web page.

Student Life *Housing:* college housing not available. *Activities and Organizations:* Student government, Nursing Student Association, Phi Theta Kappa, American Society of Civil Engineers, Respiratory care club. *Campus security:* 24-hour emergency response devices and patrols, late-night transport/escort service. *Student services:* personal/psychological counseling.

Athletics Member NJCAA. *Intercollegiate sports:* basketball M(s)/W(s), golf M/W, soccer M(s)/W(s), volleyball W.

Costs (2014–15) *One-time required fee:* $15. *Tuition:* state resident $5351 full-time, $149 per credit hour part-time; nonresident $10,702 full-time, $297 per credit hour part-time. *Required fees:* $258 full-time, $9 per credit hour part-time, $47 per term part-time. *Payment plan:* installment. *Waivers:* senior citizens and employees or children of employees.

Financial Aid Of all full-time matriculated undergraduates who enrolled in 2013, 100 Federal Work-Study jobs (averaging $3500).

Applying *Options:* electronic application, deferred entrance. *Required:* high school transcript.

Freshman Application Contact Ms. Gabriele Boeckermann, Director of Admission, Cincinnati State Technical and Community College, Office of Admissions, 3520 Central Parkway, Cincinnati, OH 45223-2690. *Phone:* 513-569-1550. *Toll-free phone:* 877-569-0115. *Fax:* 513-569-1562. *E-mail:* adm@cincinnatistate.edu.

Website: http://www.cincinnatistate.edu/.

Clark State Community College
Springfield, Ohio

- **State-supported** 2-year, founded 1962, part of Ohio Board of Regents
- **Suburban** 60-acre campus with easy access to Columbus, Dayton
- **Endowment** $9.2 million
- **Coed**

Undergraduates 1,693 full-time, 3,960 part-time. Students come from 8 states and territories; 11 other countries; 0.5% are from out of state; 19% Black or African American, non-Hispanic/Latino; 1% Hispanic/Latino; 0.9% Asian, non-Hispanic/Latino; 0.2% Native Hawaiian or other Pacific Islander, non-Hispanic/Latino; 0.5% American Indian or Alaska Native, non-Hispanic/Latino; 5% Race/ethnicity unknown; 0.7% international; 15% transferred in. *Retention:* 39% of full-time freshmen returned.

Faculty *Student/faculty ratio:* 14:1.

Academics *Calendar:* quarters. *Degree:* certificates and associate. *Special study options:* academic remediation for entering students, adult/continuing education programs, advanced placement credit, cooperative education, distance learning, double majors, honors programs, independent study,

internships, off-campus study, part-time degree program, services for LD students, summer session for credit. *ROTC:* Army (c).

Student Life *Campus security:* late-night transport/escort service.

Athletics Member NJCAA.

Costs (2014–15) *Tuition:* state resident $2912 full-time, $139 per credit hour part-time; nonresident $5824 full-time, $261 per credit hour part-time. *Required fees:* $447 full-time, $8 per term part-time.

Applying *Options:* electronic application. *Application fee:* $15. *Required:* high school transcript.

Freshman Application Contact Admissions Office, Clark State Community College, PO Box 570, Springfield, OH 45501-0570. *Phone:* 937-328-3858. *Fax:* 937-328-6133. *E-mail:* admissions@clarkstate.edu.

Website: http://www.clarkstate.edu/.

Columbus Culinary Institute at Bradford School
Columbus, Ohio

- **Private** 2-year, founded 2006
- **Suburban** campus
- **Coed,** 148 undergraduate students
- **56%** of applicants were admitted

Freshmen *Admission:* 583 applied, 326 admitted.

Majors Cooking and related culinary arts.

Academics *Calendar:* semesters. *Degree:* associate.

Freshman Application Contact Admissions Office, Columbus Culinary Institute at Bradford School, 2435 Stelzer Road, Columbus, OH 43219. *Phone:* 614-944-4200. *Toll-free phone:* 877-506-5006.

Website: http://www.columbusculinary.com/.

Columbus State Community College
Columbus, Ohio

- **State-supported** 2-year, founded 1963, part of Ohio Board of Regents
- **Urban** 75-acre campus
- **Endowment** $3.9 million
- **Coed**

Undergraduates 8,817 full-time, 16,432 part-time. Students come from 50 other countries; 2% are from out of state; 20% Black or African American, non-Hispanic/Latino; 4% Hispanic/Latino; 3% Asian, non-Hispanic/Latino; 0.1% Native Hawaiian or other Pacific Islander, non-Hispanic/Latino; 0.3% American Indian or Alaska Native, non-Hispanic/Latino; 3% Two or more races, non-Hispanic/Latino; 5% Race/ethnicity unknown; 1% international; 24% transferred in. *Retention:* 50% of full-time freshmen returned.

Academics *Calendar:* quarters. *Degree:* certificates and associate. *Special study options:* academic remediation for entering students, adult/continuing education programs, advanced placement credit, cooperative education, distance learning, double majors, English as a second language, honors programs, independent study, internships, off-campus study, part-time degree program, services for LD students, student-designed majors, study abroad, summer session for credit. *ROTC:* Army (b), Air Force (c). *Unusual degree programs:* 3-2 business administration with Franklin University.

Student Life *Campus security:* 24-hour emergency response devices and patrols, late-night transport/escort service.

Athletics Member NJCAA.

Standardized Tests *Recommended:* ACT (for admission), Applicants can utilize ACT scores for course placement purposes and as part of determining their eligibility for Post Secondary Enrollment Options Program. TOEFL scores are utilized for admission of international applicants.

Costs (2014–15) *One-time required fee:* $50. *Tuition:* state resident $3808 full-time; nonresident $8430 full-time.

Financial Aid Of all full-time matriculated undergraduates who enrolled in 2013, 133 Federal Work-Study jobs (averaging $1500).

Applying *Options:* electronic application, early admission, deferred entrance. *Application fee:* $50. *Required for some:* essay or personal statement, high school transcript, minimum 3.0 GPA, 1 letter of recommendation, interview, Some special population applicants (e.g. Post Secondary Enrollment Options, International, Immigrant, Criminal Background) must submit additional documentation as part of their admission process. *Recommended:* high school transcript.

Freshman Application Contact Ms. Tari Blaney, Director of Admissions, Columbus State Community College, 550 East Spring Street, Columbus, OH 43215. *Phone:* 614-287-2669. *Toll-free phone:* 800-621-6407 Ext. 2669. *Fax:* 614-287-6019. *E-mail:* tblaney@cscc.edu.

Website: http://www.cscc.edu/.

Cuyahoga Community College
Cleveland, Ohio

Freshman Application Contact Mr. Kevin McDaniel, Director of Admissions and Records, Cuyahoga Community College, Cleveland, OH 44115. *Phone:* 216-987-4030. *Toll-free phone:* 800-954-8742. *Fax:* 216-696-2567. *Website:* http://www.tri-c.edu/.

Davis College
Toledo, Ohio

- **Proprietary** 2-year, founded 1858
- **Urban** 1-acre campus with easy access to Detroit
- **Coed,** 193 undergraduate students, 26% full-time, 81% women, 19% men

Undergraduates 50 full-time, 143 part-time. Students come from 2 states and territories; 2% are from out of state; 43% Black or African American, non-Hispanic/Latino; 3% Hispanic/Latino; 0.5% American Indian or Alaska Native, non-Hispanic/Latino; 2% Race/ethnicity unknown.
Freshmen *Admission:* 22 applied, 22 admitted, 19 enrolled.
Faculty *Total:* 25, 24% full-time. *Student/faculty ratio:* 8:1.
Majors Accounting related; administrative assistant and secretarial science; business administration and management; business operations support and secretarial services related; computer systems networking and telecommunications; early childhood education; graphic design; interior design; marketing/marketing management; medical administrative assistant and medical secretary; medical/clinical assistant; medical insurance coding.
Academics *Calendar:* quarters. *Degree:* certificates, diplomas, and associate. *Special study options:* academic remediation for entering students, adult/continuing education programs, advanced placement credit, distance learning, internships, part-time degree program, summer session for credit.
Library Davis College Resource Center with 3,387 titles, 117 audiovisual materials, an OPAC.
Student Life *Housing:* college housing not available. *Campus security:* security cameras for parking lot. *Student services:* personal/psychological counseling.
Standardized Tests *Required:* Admissions test (for admission).
Costs (2015–16) *Tuition:* $12,600 full-time, $350 per credit hour part-time. *Required fees:* $1050 full-time, $350 per credit hour part-time, $350 per term part-time. *Payment plan:* installment. *Waivers:* employees or children of employees.
Financial Aid Of all full-time matriculated undergraduates who enrolled in 2013, 10 Federal Work-Study jobs (averaging $3500).
Applying *Options:* electronic application, early admission, deferred entrance. *Application fee:* $30. *Required:* high school transcript, interview. *Application deadlines:* rolling (freshmen), rolling (transfers). *Notification:* continuous (freshmen), continuous (transfers).
Freshman Application Contact Ms. Dana Stern, Davis College, 4747 Monroe Street, Toledo, OH 43623-4307. *Phone:* 419-473-2700. *Toll-free phone:* 800-477-7021. *Fax:* 419-473-2472. *E-mail:* dstern@daviscollege.edu. *Website:* http://daviscollege.edu/.

Daymar College
Jackson, Ohio

Freshman Application Contact Admissions Office, Daymar College, 980 East Main Street, Jackson, OH 45640. *Phone:* 740-286-1554. *Toll-free phone:* 877-258-7796. *Fax:* 740-774-6317. *Website:* http://www.daymarcollege.edu/.

Daymar College
Lancaster, Ohio

Freshman Application Contact Holly Hankinson, Admissions Office, Daymar College, 1579 Victor Road, NW, Lancaster, OH 43130. *Phone:* 740-687-6126. *Toll-free phone:* 877-258-7796. *E-mail:* hhankinson@daymarcollege.edu. *Website:* http://www.daymarcollege.edu/.

Daymar College
New Boston, Ohio

Freshman Application Contact Mike Bell, Admissions Representative, Daymar College, 3879 Rhodes Avenue, New Boston, OH 45662. *Phone:* 740-456-4124. *Toll-free phone:* 877-258-7796. *Website:* http://www.daymarcollege.edu/.

Eastern Gateway Community College
Steubenville, Ohio

- **State and locally supported** 2-year, founded 1966, part of Ohio Board of Regents
- **Small-town** 83-acre campus with easy access to Pittsburgh
- **Endowment** $263,075
- **Coed,** 3,182 undergraduate students, 47% full-time, 64% women, 36% men

Undergraduates 1,504 full-time, 1,678 part-time. Students come from 5 states and territories; 1 other country; 27% Black or African American, non-Hispanic/Latino; 3% Hispanic/Latino; 0.7% Asian, non-Hispanic/Latino; 0.7% American Indian or Alaska Native, non-Hispanic/Latino; 4% Two or more races, non-Hispanic/Latino; 2% Race/ethnicity unknown; 0.2% international.
Freshmen *Admission:* 2,020 applied, 2,020 admitted, 766 enrolled.
Faculty *Total:* 269, 16% full-time. *Student/faculty ratio:* 17:1.
Majors Accounting; administrative assistant and secretarial science; business administration and management; child-care and support services management; computer engineering related; corrections; criminal justice/police science; data processing and data processing technology; dental assisting; drafting and design technology; electrical, electronic and communications engineering technology; emergency medical technology (EMT paramedic); industrial radiologic technology; industrial technology; legal administrative assistant/secretary; licensed practical/vocational nurse training; mechanical engineering/mechanical technology; medical administrative assistant and medical secretary; medical/clinical assistant; real estate; respiratory care therapy.
Academics *Calendar:* semesters. *Degree:* certificates and associate. *Special study options:* academic remediation for entering students, accelerated degree program, adult/continuing education programs, cooperative education, distance learning, double majors, off-campus study, part-time degree program, services for LD students, summer session for credit.
Library Eastern Gateway Community College Library with an OPAC.
Student Life *Housing:* college housing not available. *Activities and Organizations:* Student Senate, Phi Theta Kappa. *Campus security:* 24-hour emergency response devices, day and evening security.
Athletics *Intramural sports:* football M/W, softball M/W.
Standardized Tests *Required for some:* SAT or ACT (for admission).
Costs (2014–15) *Tuition:* area resident $3330 full-time, $111 per credit hour part-time; state resident $3510 full-time, $117 per credit hour part-time; nonresident $4350 full-time, $145 per credit hour part-time. Full-time tuition and fees vary according to program and reciprocity agreements. Part-time tuition and fees vary according to program and reciprocity agreements. *Payment plan:* deferred payment. *Waivers:* senior citizens and employees or children of employees.
Financial Aid Of all full-time matriculated undergraduates who enrolled in 2013, 30 Federal Work-Study jobs (averaging $1500).
Applying *Options:* electronic application, early admission, deferred entrance. *Application fee:* $20. *Required for some:* high school transcript. *Notification:* continuous (freshmen), continuous (out-of-state freshmen), continuous (transfers).
Freshman Application Contact Mrs. Marlana Featner, Director of Admissions-Jefferson Campus, Eastern Gateway Community College, 4000 Sunset Boulevard, Steubenville, OH 43952. *Phone:* 740-264-5591 Ext. 1642. *Toll-free phone:* 800-68-COLLEGE. *Fax:* 740-266-2944. *E-mail:* mfeatner@egcc.edu. *Website:* http://www.egcc.edu/.

Edison Community College
Piqua, Ohio

- **State-supported** 2-year, founded 1973, part of Ohio Board of Regents
- **Small-town** 131-acre campus with easy access to Dayton, Columbus, Cincinnati
- **Coed,** 3,042 undergraduate students, 26% full-time, 64% women, 36% men

Undergraduates 785 full-time, 2,257 part-time. Students come from 3 states and territories; 1 other country; 1% are from out of state; 4% Black or African American, non-Hispanic/Latino; 1% Hispanic/Latino; 1% Asian, non-Hispanic/Latino; 0.6% American Indian or Alaska Native, non-Hispanic/Latino; 2% Two or more races, non-Hispanic/Latino; 4% Race/ethnicity unknown; 3% transferred in. *Retention:* 52% of full-time freshmen returned.
Freshmen *Admission:* 688 applied, 593 admitted, 347 enrolled. *Average high school GPA:* 2.74. *Test scores:* ACT scores over 18: 79%; ACT scores over 24: 23%; ACT scores over 30: 2%.
Faculty *Total:* 202, 25% full-time, 10% with terminal degrees. *Student/faculty ratio:* 7:1.

Majors Accounting; art; biology/biological sciences; business administration and management; child development; clinical/medical laboratory technology; computer and information sciences; computer and information systems security; computer programming; computer systems networking and telecommunications; criminal justice/police science; dramatic/theater arts; economics; education; electrical, electronic and communications engineering technology; electromechanical technology; English; executive assistant/executive secretary; geology/earth science; health/medical preparatory programs related; history; human resources management; industrial technology; legal assistant/paralegal; liberal arts and sciences/liberal studies; logistics, materials, and supply chain management; manufacturing engineering technology; marketing/marketing management; mathematics; mechanical drafting and CAD/CADD; mechanical engineering/mechanical technology; medical administrative assistant and medical secretary; medical/clinical assistant; medium/heavy vehicle and truck technology; philosophy and religious studies related; physical therapy technology; prenursing studies; psychology; registered nursing/registered nurse; social work; speech communication and rhetoric.

Academics *Calendar:* semesters. *Degrees:* certificates, associate, and postbachelor's certificates. *Special study options:* academic remediation for entering students, accelerated degree program, adult/continuing education programs, advanced placement credit, distance learning, double majors, English as a second language, honors programs, independent study, internships, off-campus study, part-time degree program, services for LD students, student-designed majors, summer session for credit.

Library Edison Community College Library with 19,300 titles, 6,299 audiovisual materials, an OPAC, a Web page.

Student Life *Housing:* college housing not available. *Activities and Organizations:* drama/theater group, student-run newspaper. *Campus security:* late-night transport/escort service, 18-hour patrols by trained security personnel. *Student services:* health clinic.

Athletics Member NJCAA. *Intercollegiate sports:* basketball M(s)/W(s), volleyball W(s). *Intramural sports:* baseball M(c).

Standardized Tests *Required:* ACT Compass (for admission).

Costs (2014–15) *Tuition:* state resident $3609 full-time, $120 per credit hour part-time; nonresident $7219 full-time, $241 per credit hour part-time. Full-time tuition and fees vary according to class time, course level, course load, degree level, location, program, reciprocity agreements, and student level. Part-time tuition and fees vary according to class time, course level, course load, degree level, location, program, reciprocity agreements, and student level. *Required fees:* $609 full-time. *Payment plans:* installment, deferred payment. *Waivers:* senior citizens and employees or children of employees.

Financial Aid Of all full-time matriculated undergraduates who enrolled in 2013, 42 Federal Work-Study jobs (averaging $3000).

Applying *Options:* electronic application. *Application fee:* $20. *Required:* high school transcript. *Application deadlines:* rolling (freshmen), rolling (out-of-state freshmen), rolling (transfers).

Freshman Application Contact Ms. Teresa Roth, Director of Student Services, Edison Community College, 1973 Edison Drive, Piqua, OH 45356. *Phone:* 937-778-7850. *E-mail:* troth@edisonohio.edu. *Website:* http://www.edisonohio.edu/.

ETI Technical College of Niles
Niles, Ohio

Freshman Application Contact Ms. Diane Marsteller, Director of Admissions, ETI Technical College of Niles, 2076 Youngstown-Warren Road, Niles, OH 44446-4398. *Phone:* 330-652-9919 Ext. 16. *Fax:* 330-652-4399. *E-mail:* dianemarsteller@eticollege.edu. *Website:* http://eticollege.edu/.

Fortis College
Centerville, Ohio

Freshman Application Contact Fortis College, 555 East Alex Bell Road, Centerville, OH 45459. *Phone:* 937-433-3410. *Toll-free phone:* 855-4-FORTIS. *Website:* http://www.fortis.edu/.

Fortis College
Cincinnati, Ohio

Admissions Office Contact Fortis College, 11499 Chester Road, Suite 200, Cincinnati, OH 45246. *Website:* http://www.fortis.edu/.

Fortis College
Cuyahoga Falls, Ohio

Freshman Application Contact Admissions Office, Fortis College, 2545 Bailey Road, Cuyahoga Falls, OH 44221. *Phone:* 330-923-9959. *Fax:* 330-923-0886. *Website:* http://www.fortis.edu/.

Fortis College
Ravenna, Ohio

Freshman Application Contact Admissions Office, Fortis College, 653 Enterprise Parkway, Ravenna, OH 44266. *Toll-free phone:* 855-4-FORTIS. *Website:* http://www.fortis.edu/.

Fortis College
Westerville, Ohio

Admissions Office Contact Fortis College, 4151 Executive Parkway, Suite 120, Westerville, OH 43081. *Website:* http://www.fortis.edu/.

Gallipolis Career College
Gallipolis, Ohio

Freshman Application Contact Mr. Jack Henson, Director of Admissions, Gallipolis Career College, 1176 Jackson Pike, Suite 312, Gallipolis, OH 45631. *Phone:* 740-446-4367. *Toll-free phone:* 800-214-0452. *Fax:* 740-446-4124. *E-mail:* admissions@gallipoliscareercollege.com. *Website:* http://www.gallipoliscareercollege.com/.

Good Samaritan College of Nursing and Health Science
Cincinnati, Ohio

- **Proprietary** primarily 2-year
- **Urban** campus with easy access to Cincinnati
- **Coed,** 353 undergraduate students, 36% full-time, 91% women, 9% men

Undergraduates 128 full-time, 225 part-time. 14% are from out of state; 11% Black or African American, non-Hispanic/Latino; 3% Hispanic/Latino; 2% Asian, non-Hispanic/Latino; 0.8% Two or more races, non-Hispanic/Latino; 22% transferred in.

Freshmen *Admission:* 52 applied, 41 admitted, 40 enrolled. *Average high school GPA:* 2.8. *Test scores:* ACT scores over 18: 88%; ACT scores over 24: 18%; ACT scores over 30: 4%.

Faculty *Total:* 41, 73% full-time, 24% with terminal degrees. *Student/faculty ratio:* 7:1.

Majors Registered nursing/registered nurse.

Academics *Calendar:* semesters. *Degrees:* associate and bachelor's. *Special study options:* academic remediation for entering students, advanced placement credit, cooperative education, honors programs, part-time degree program, services for LD students, summer session for credit.

Student Life *Housing:* college housing not available. *Campus security:* 24-hour emergency response devices and patrols, late-night transport/escort service.

Standardized Tests *Required:* SAT or ACT (for admission).

Costs (2014–15) *Tuition:* $17,905 full-time, $499 per credit hour part-time. *Required fees:* $1515 full-time, $80 per credit hour part-time. *Payment plan:* installment. *Waivers:* employees or children of employees.

Financial Aid Of all full-time matriculated undergraduates who enrolled in 2010, 155 applied for aid, 149 were judged to have need. 8 state and other part-time jobs (averaging $750). In 2010, 8 non-need-based awards were made. *Average percent of need met:* 68%. *Average financial aid package:* $7488. *Average need-based loan:* $3477. *Average need-based gift aid:* $4260. *Average non-need-based aid:* $1100.

Applying *Options:* electronic application. *Application fee:* $40. *Required:* high school transcript, minimum 2.5 GPA, average GPA 2.25 in these high school courses: English, Math (Algebra required), Science (Chemistry required), and Social Studies.

Freshman Application Contact Admissions Office, Good Samaritan College of Nursing and Health Science, 375 Dixmyth Avenue, Cincinnati, OH 45220. *Phone:* 513-862-2743. *Fax:* 513-862-3572. *Website:* http://www.gscollege.edu/.

Herzing University
Toledo, Ohio

Admissions Office Contact Herzing University, 5212 Hill Avenue, Toledo, OH 43615. *Toll-free phone:* 800-596-0724.
Website: http://www.herzing.edu/toledo.

Hocking College
Nelsonville, Ohio

- **State-supported** 2-year, founded 1968, part of Ohio Board of Regents
- **Rural** 1600-acre campus with easy access to Columbus
- **Endowment** $4.8 million
- **Coed,** 4,094 undergraduate students, 74% full-time, 51% women, 49% men

Undergraduates 3,012 full-time, 1,082 part-time. Students come from 25 states and territories; 17 other countries; 3% are from out of state; 4% Black or African American, non-Hispanic/Latino; 2% Hispanic/Latino; 0.5% Asian, non-Hispanic/Latino; 0.5% American Indian or Alaska Native, non-Hispanic/Latino; 3% Two or more races, non-Hispanic/Latino; 2% Race/ethnicity unknown; 2% international; 18% live on campus. *Retention:* 44% of full-time freshmen returned.
Freshmen *Admission:* 2,270 applied, 2,270 admitted.
Faculty *Total:* 281, 62% full-time. *Student/faculty ratio:* 16:1.
Majors Accounting; business administration and management; ceramic sciences and engineering; child development; computer engineering technology; computer programming; computer science; corrections; criminal justice/law enforcement administration; criminal justice/police science; culinary arts; dietetics; drafting and design technology; ecology; electrical, electronic and communications engineering technology; emergency medical technology (EMT paramedic); equestrian studies; fire science/firefighting; fishing and fisheries sciences and management; food science; forestry; forest technology; health information/medical records administration; hospitality administration; hotel/motel administration; industrial technology; land use planning and management; licensed practical/vocational nurse training; marketing/marketing management; medical administrative assistant and medical secretary; medical/clinical assistant; natural resources/conservation; natural resources management and policy; natural resources management and policy related; ophthalmic laboratory technology; physical therapy technology; registered nursing/registered nurse; tourism and travel services management; wildlife, fish and wildlands science and management.
Academics *Calendar:* semesters. *Degree:* certificates, diplomas, and associate. *Special study options:* academic remediation for entering students, accelerated degree program, adult/continuing education programs, advanced placement credit, cooperative education, distance learning, double majors, English as a second language, internships, off-campus study, part-time degree program, services for LD students, student-designed majors, summer session for credit. *ROTC:* Army (c).
Library Hocking College Learning Resources Center with 13,259 titles, 2,781 audiovisual materials, an OPAC, a Web page.
Student Life *Housing Options:* coed. Campus housing is university owned and is provided by a third party. *Activities and Organizations:* drama/theater group, choral group, Phi Theta Kappa, Recycling Club, Kappa Beta Delta (Business Honor Society), Alpha Beta Gamma, Native American Club. *Campus security:* 24-hour emergency response devices and patrols, student patrols, late-night transport/escort service, controlled dormitory access. *Student services:* personal/psychological counseling.
Athletics *Intramural sports:* archery M/W, basketball M/W, cross-country running M/W, football M/W, golf M/W, soccer M/W, softball M/W, tennis M/W, volleyball M/W, weight lifting M/W.
Costs (2015–16) *Tuition:* state resident $4390 full-time, $183 per credit hour part-time; nonresident $8780 full-time, $366 per credit hour part-time. Full-time tuition and fees vary according to course load and program. Part-time tuition and fees vary according to program. *Room and board:* $6560. Room and board charges vary according to board plan and housing facility. *Payment plan:* installment. *Waivers:* senior citizens and employees or children of employees.
Financial Aid Of all full-time matriculated undergraduates who enrolled in 2013, 125 Federal Work-Study jobs (averaging $1700). 225 state and other part-time jobs (averaging $1700).
Applying *Options:* electronic application. *Application fee:* $15. *Required:* high school transcript. *Application deadlines:* rolling (freshmen), rolling (out-of-state freshmen), rolling (transfers). *Notification:* continuous (freshmen), continuous (out-of-state freshmen), continuous (transfers).
Freshman Application Contact Hocking College, 3301 Hocking Parkway, Nelsonville, OH 45764-9588. *Phone:* 740-753-3591 Ext. 7080.
Website: http://www.hocking.edu/.

Hondros College
Westerville, Ohio

Director of Admissions Ms. Carol Thomas, Operations Manager, Hondros College, 4140 Executive Parkway, Westerville, OH 43081-3855. *Phone:* 614-508-7244. *Toll-free phone:* 888-HONDROS.
Website: http://www.hondros.edu/.

International College of Broadcasting
Dayton, Ohio

- **Private** 2-year, founded 1968
- **Urban** 1-acre campus with easy access to Dayton
- **Coed,** 88 undergraduate students

Faculty *Total:* 16, 25% full-time, 6% with terminal degrees.
Majors Recording arts technology.
Academics *Calendar:* semesters. *Degree:* diplomas and associate. *Special study options:* academic remediation for entering students, internships, services for LD students.
Student Life *Housing:* college housing not available. *Activities and Organizations:* student-run radio station.
Standardized Tests *Required:* Wonderlic aptitude test (for admission).
Costs (2014–15) *Tuition:* $30,485 full-time. Full-time tuition and fees vary according to program. Part-time tuition and fees vary according to program. No tuition increase for student's term of enrollment. *Payment plans:* tuition prepayment, installment.
Applying *Options:* early admission. *Application fee:* $100. *Required:* high school transcript, interview, passing Wonderlic Test.
Freshman Application Contact International College of Broadcasting, 6 South Smithville Road, Dayton, OH 45431-1833. *Phone:* 937-258-8251. *Toll-free phone:* 800-517-7284.
Website: http://www.icb.edu/.

ITT Technical Institute
Akron, Ohio

- **Proprietary** primarily 2-year
- **Coed**

Academics *Degrees:* associate and bachelor's.
Freshman Application Contact Director of Recruitment, ITT Technical Institute, 3428 West Market Street, Akron, OH 44333. *Phone:* 330-865-8600. *Toll-free phone:* 877-818-0154.
Website: http://www.itt-tech.edu/.

ITT Technical Institute
Columbus, Ohio

- **Proprietary** primarily 2-year, part of ITT Educational Services, Inc.
- **Coed**

Academics *Calendar:* quarters. *Degrees:* associate and bachelor's.
Freshman Application Contact Director of Recruitment, ITT Technical Institute, 4717 Hilton Corporate Drive, Columbus, OH 43232. *Phone:* 614-868-2000. *Toll-free phone:* 877-233-8864.
Website: http://www.itt-tech.edu/.

ITT Technical Institute
Dayton, Ohio

- **Proprietary** primarily 2-year, founded 1935, part of ITT Educational Services, Inc.
- **Suburban** campus
- **Coed**

Academics *Calendar:* quarters. *Degrees:* associate and bachelor's.
Freshman Application Contact Director of Recruitment, ITT Technical Institute, 3325 Stop 8 Road, Dayton, OH 45414-3425. *Phone:* 937-264-7700. *Toll-free phone:* 800-568-3241.
Website: http://www.itt-tech.edu/.

ITT Technical Institute
Hilliard, Ohio

- **Proprietary** primarily 2-year, founded 2003, part of ITT Educational Services, Inc.
- **Coed**

Academics *Calendar:* quarters. *Degrees:* associate and bachelor's.
Freshman Application Contact Director of Recruitment, ITT Technical Institute, 3781 Park Mill Run Drive, Hilliard, OH 43026. *Phone:* 614-771-4888. *Toll-free phone:* 888-483-4888.
Website: http://www.itt-tech.edu/.

ITT Technical Institute
Maumee, Ohio

- **Proprietary** primarily 2-year
- **Coed**

Academics *Degrees:* associate and bachelor's.
Freshman Application Contact Director of Recruitment, ITT Technical Institute, 1656 Henthorne Drive, Suite B, Maumee, OH 43537. *Phone:* 419-861-6500. *Toll-free phone:* 877-205-4639.
Website: http://www.itt-tech.edu/.

ITT Technical Institute
Norwood, Ohio

- **Proprietary** primarily 2-year, founded 1995, part of ITT Educational Services, Inc.
- **Coed**

Academics *Calendar:* quarters. *Degrees:* associate and bachelor's.
Freshman Application Contact Director of Recruitment, ITT Technical Institute, 4750 Wesley Avenue, Norwood, OH 45212. *Phone:* 513-531-8300. *Toll-free phone:* 800-314-8324.
Website: http://www.itt-tech.edu/.

ITT Technical Institute
Strongsville, Ohio

- **Proprietary** primarily 2-year, founded 1994, part of ITT Educational Services, Inc.
- **Coed**

Academics *Calendar:* quarters. *Degrees:* associate and bachelor's.
Freshman Application Contact Director of Recruitment, ITT Technical Institute, 14955 Sprague Road, Strongsville, OH 44136. *Phone:* 440-234-9091. *Toll-free phone:* 800-331-1488.
Website: http://www.itt-tech.edu/.

ITT Technical Institute
Warrensville Heights, Ohio

- **Proprietary** primarily 2-year, founded 2005
- **Coed**

Academics *Calendar:* quarters. *Degrees:* associate and bachelor's.
Freshman Application Contact Director of Recruitment, ITT Technical Institute, 24865 Emery Road, Warrensville Heights, OH 44128. *Phone:* 216-896-6500. *Toll-free phone:* 800-741-3494.
Website: http://www.itt-tech.edu/.

ITT Technical Institute
Youngstown, Ohio

- **Proprietary** primarily 2-year, founded 1967, part of ITT Educational Services, Inc.
- **Suburban** campus
- **Coed**

Academics *Calendar:* quarters. *Degrees:* associate and bachelor's.
Financial Aid Of all full-time matriculated undergraduates who enrolled in 2013, 5 Federal Work-Study jobs (averaging $3979).
Freshman Application Contact Director of Recruitment, ITT Technical Institute, 1030 North Meridian Road, Youngstown, OH 44509-4098. *Phone:* 330-270-1600. *Toll-free phone:* 800-832-5001.
Website: http://www.itt-tech.edu/.

James A. Rhodes State College
Lima, Ohio

Freshman Application Contact Traci Cox, Director, Office of Admissions, James A. Rhodes State College, Lima, OH 45804-3597. *Phone:* 419-995-8040. *E-mail:* cox.t@rhodesstate.edu.
Website: http://www.rhodesstate.edu/.

Kaplan College, Dayton Campus
Dayton, Ohio

Freshman Application Contact Kaplan College, Dayton Campus, 2800 East River Road, Dayton, OH 45439. *Phone:* 937-294-6155. *Toll-free phone:* 800-935-1857.
Website: http://www.kaplancollege.com/.

Kent State University at Ashtabula
Ashtabula, Ohio

- **State-supported** primarily 2-year, founded 1958, part of Kent State University System
- **Small-town** 120-acre campus with easy access to Cleveland
- **Coed,** 2,278 undergraduate students, 51% full-time, 65% women, 35% men

Undergraduates 1,168 full-time, 1,110 part-time. Students come from 23 states and territories; 7 other countries; 4% are from out of state; 5% Black or African American, non-Hispanic/Latino; 3% Hispanic/Latino; 1% Asian, non-Hispanic/Latino; 0.1% Native Hawaiian or other Pacific Islander, non-Hispanic/Latino; 0.4% American Indian or Alaska Native, non-Hispanic/Latino; 2% Two or more races, non-Hispanic/Latino; 2% Race/ethnicity unknown; 0.4% international; 5% transferred in. *Retention:* 60% of full-time freshmen returned.
Freshmen *Admission:* 346 applied, 337 admitted, 221 enrolled. *Average high school GPA:* 2.86. *Test scores:* SAT critical reading scores over 500: 17%; SAT math scores over 500: 17%; SAT writing scores over 500: 17%; ACT scores over 18: 73%; SAT critical reading scores over 600: 8%; SAT math scores over 600: 17%; SAT writing scores over 600: 8%; ACT scores over 24: 10%.
Faculty *Total:* 107, 48% full-time. *Student/faculty ratio:* 22:1.
Majors Accounting technology and bookkeeping; administrative assistant and secretarial science; aerospace, aeronautical and astronautical/space engineering; business administration and management; business/commerce; computer programming (specific applications); criminal justice/safety; English; general studies; health and medical administrative services related; health/medical preparatory programs related; hospitality administration; liberal arts and sciences and humanities related; medical radiologic technology; occupational therapist assistant; physical therapy technology; psychology; registered nursing/registered nurse; respiratory care therapy; sociology; speech communication and rhetoric; viticulture and enology.
Academics *Calendar:* semesters. *Degrees:* certificates, associate, and bachelor's (also offers some upper-level and graduate courses). *Special study options:* academic remediation for entering students, advanced placement credit, distance learning, double majors, independent study, internships, part-time degree program, services for LD students, student-designed majors, study abroad, summer session for credit. *ROTC:* Army (c), Air Force (c).
Library Kent State at Ashtabula Library with 51,884 titles, 640 audiovisual materials, an OPAC, a Web page.
Student Life *Housing:* college housing not available. *Activities and Organizations:* student government, student veterans association, Student Nurses Association, Student Occupational Therapy Association, Media Club. *Campus security:* 24-hour emergency response devices.
Athletics *Intramural sports:* volleyball M/W.
Standardized Tests *Required for some:* SAT or ACT (for admission). *Recommended:* SAT or ACT (for admission).
Costs (2014–15) *One-time required fee:* $150. *Tuition:* state resident $5664 full-time, $258 per credit hour part-time; nonresident $13,624 full-time, $620 per credit hour part-time. Full-time tuition and fees vary according to course level and course load. Part-time tuition and fees vary according to course level and course load. *Payment plan:* installment. *Waivers:* senior citizens and employees or children of employees.
Financial Aid Of all full-time matriculated undergraduates who enrolled in 2014, 612 applied for aid, 568 were judged to have need, 17 had their need fully met. In 2014, 22 non-need-based awards were made. *Average percent of need met:* 40%. *Average financial aid package:* $7373. *Average need-based loan:* $3970. *Average need-based gift aid:* $4761. *Average non-need-based aid:* $1045.
Applying *Options:* electronic application, deferred entrance. *Application fee:* $40. *Required:* high school transcript. *Application deadlines:* rolling

(freshmen), rolling (transfers). *Notification:* continuous (freshmen), continuous (transfers).

Freshman Application Contact Kent State University at Ashtabula, 3300 Lake Road West, Ashtabula, OH 44004-2299. *Phone:* 440-964-4314. *Website:* http://www.ashtabula.kent.edu/.

Kent State University at East Liverpool
East Liverpool, Ohio

- **State-supported** primarily 2-year, founded 1967, part of Kent State University System
- **Small-town** 4-acre campus with easy access to Pittsburgh
- **Coed,** 1,481 undergraduate students, 55% full-time, 67% women, 33% men

Undergraduates 817 full-time, 664 part-time. Students come from 5 states and territories; 1 other country; 16% are from out of state; 6% Black or African American, non-Hispanic/Latino; 3% Hispanic/Latino; 0.9% Asian, non-Hispanic/Latino; 0.1% Native Hawaiian or other Pacific Islander, non-Hispanic/Latino; 0.2% American Indian or Alaska Native, non-Hispanic/Latino; 2% Two or more races, non-Hispanic/Latino; 3% Race/ethnicity unknown; 0.3% international; 5% transferred in. *Retention:* 58% of full-time freshmen returned.

Freshmen *Admission:* 121 applied, 116 admitted, 86 enrolled. *Average high school GPA:* 2.87. *Test scores:* ACT scores over 18: 83%; ACT scores over 24: 10%.

Faculty *Total:* 63, 43% full-time. *Student/faculty ratio:* 27:1.

Majors Accounting technology and bookkeeping; business/commerce; computer programming (specific applications); criminal justice/safety; English; general studies; legal assistant/paralegal; liberal arts and sciences and humanities related; occupational therapist assistant; physical therapy technology; psychology; registered nursing/registered nurse; speech communication and rhetoric.

Academics *Calendar:* semesters. *Degrees:* certificates, associate, bachelor's, and master's (also offers some upper-level and graduate courses). *Special study options:* academic remediation for entering students, accelerated degree program, advanced placement credit, distance learning, double majors, freshman honors college, honors programs, independent study, internships, part-time degree program, services for LD students, student-designed majors, summer session for credit. *ROTC:* Army (c), Air Force (c).

Library Blair Memorial Library with 31,320 titles, an OPAC, a Web page.

Student Life *Housing:* college housing not available. *Activities and Organizations:* student government, Student Nurses Association, Environmental Club, Student Occupational Therapist Assistants, Physical Therapist Assistant Club. *Campus security:* 24-hour emergency response devices, student patrols, late-night transport/escort service. *Student services:* personal/psychological counseling.

Standardized Tests *Required for some:* SAT or ACT (for admission). *Recommended:* SAT or ACT (for admission).

Costs (2014–15) *One-time required fee:* $150. *Tuition:* state resident $5664 full-time, $258 per credit hour part-time; nonresident $13,624 full-time, $620 per credit hour part-time. Full-time tuition and fees vary according to course level and course load. Part-time tuition and fees vary according to course level and course load. *Payment plan:* installment. *Waivers:* senior citizens and employees or children of employees.

Financial Aid Of all full-time matriculated undergraduates who enrolled in 2014, 283 applied for aid, 272 were judged to have need, 8 had their need fully met. In 2014, 1 non-need-based awards were made. *Average percent of need met:* 41%. *Average financial aid package:* $7450. *Average need-based loan:* $3983. *Average need-based gift aid:* $4866. *Average non-need-based aid:* $2116.

Applying *Options:* electronic application, deferred entrance. *Application fee:* $40. *Required:* high school transcript. *Application deadlines:* rolling (freshmen), rolling (transfers). *Notification:* continuous (freshmen), continuous (transfers).

Freshman Application Contact Kent State University at East Liverpool, OH. *Phone:* 330-385-3805. *Website:* http://www.eliv.kent.edu/.

Kent State University at Salem
Salem, Ohio

- **State-supported** primarily 2-year, founded 1966, part of Kent State University System
- **Rural** 98-acre campus
- **Coed,** 1,844 undergraduate students, 67% full-time, 71% women, 29% men

Undergraduates 1,220 full-time, 616 part-time. Students come from 11 states and territories; 4 other countries; 2% are from out of state; 3% Black or African American, non-Hispanic/Latino; 2% Hispanic/Latino; 0.7% Asian, non-Hispanic/Latino; 0.1% Native Hawaiian or other Pacific Islander, non-Hispanic/Latino; 0.5% American Indian or Alaska Native, non-Hispanic/Latino; 1% Two or more races, non-Hispanic/Latino; 3% Race/ethnicity unknown; 0.2% international; 7% transferred in. *Retention:* 56% of full-time freshmen returned.

Freshmen *Admission:* 342 applied, 331 admitted, 205 enrolled. *Average high school GPA:* 3.01. *Test scores:* SAT critical reading scores over 500: 50%; SAT math scores over 500: 17%; SAT writing scores over 500: 33%; ACT scores over 18: 76%; SAT critical reading scores over 600: 17%; SAT math scores over 600: 17%; SAT writing scores over 600: 17%; ACT scores over 24: 19%; ACT scores over 30: 2%.

Faculty *Total:* 130, 33% full-time. *Student/faculty ratio:* 20:1.

Majors Accounting technology and bookkeeping; administrative assistant and secretarial science; applied horticulture/horticulture operations; biological and biomedical sciences related; business administration and management; business/commerce; computer programming (specific applications); criminal justice/safety; early childhood education; education related; English; general studies; health and medical administrative services related; human development and family studies; insurance; liberal arts and sciences and humanities related; liberal arts and sciences/liberal studies; medical radiologic technology; psychology; registered nursing/registered nurse; speech communication and rhetoric.

Academics *Calendar:* semesters. *Degrees:* certificates, associate, and bachelor's (also offers some upper-level and graduate courses). *Special study options:* academic remediation for entering students, accelerated degree program, adult/continuing education programs, advanced placement credit, cooperative education, distance learning, double majors, freshman honors college, honors programs, independent study, internships, part-time degree program, services for LD students, student-designed majors, summer session for credit. *ROTC:* Army (c), Air Force (c).

Library Kent State Salem Library with 19,000 titles, 158 audiovisual materials, an OPAC, a Web page.

Student Life *Housing:* college housing not available. *Activities and Organizations:* Criminal Justice Club, Human Services Technology Club, Radiologic Technology Club, Student Government Association, Students for Professional Nursing. *Campus security:* 24-hour emergency response devices, late-night transport/escort service. *Student services:* personal/psychological counseling.

Athletics *Intramural sports:* basketball M/W, skiing (downhill) M/W, table tennis M/W, tennis M/W, volleyball M/W.

Standardized Tests *Required for some:* SAT or ACT (for admission). *Recommended:* SAT or ACT (for admission).

Costs (2014–15) *One-time required fee:* $150. *Tuition:* state resident $5664 full-time, $258 per credit hour part-time; nonresident $13,624 full-time, $620 per credit hour part-time. Full-time tuition and fees vary according to course level and course load. Part-time tuition and fees vary according to course level and course load. *Payment plan:* installment. *Waivers:* senior citizens and employees or children of employees.

Financial Aid Of all full-time matriculated undergraduates who enrolled in 2014, 732 applied for aid, 673 were judged to have need, 31 had their need fully met. In 2014, 19 non-need-based awards were made. *Average percent of need met:* 40%. *Average financial aid package:* $6673. *Average need-based loan:* $3857. *Average need-based gift aid:* $4620. *Average non-need-based aid:* $764.

Applying *Options:* electronic application, deferred entrance. *Application fee:* $40. *Required:* high school transcript. *Required for some:* essay or personal statement. *Application deadlines:* rolling (freshmen), rolling (out-of-state freshmen), rolling (transfers). *Notification:* continuous (freshmen), continuous (out-of-state freshmen), continuous (transfers).

Freshman Application Contact Kent State University at Salem, 2491 State Route 45 South, Salem, OH 44460-9412. *Phone:* 330-382-7415. *Website:* http://www.salem.kent.edu/.

Kent State University at Trumbull
Warren, Ohio

- **State-supported** primarily 2-year, founded 1954, part of Kent State University System
- **Suburban** 200-acre campus with easy access to Cleveland-Akron-Canton
- **Coed,** 2,796 undergraduate students, 65% full-time, 65% women, 35% men

Undergraduates 1,811 full-time, 985 part-time. Students come from 9 states and territories; 8 other countries; 2% are from out of state; 9% Black or African American, non-Hispanic/Latino; 2% Hispanic/Latino; 0.5% Asian, non-Hispanic/Latino; 2% Two or more races, non-Hispanic/Latino; 3% Race/ethnicity unknown; 0.6% international; 6% transferred in. *Retention:* 57% of full-time freshmen returned.

Freshmen *Admission:* 433 applied, 428 admitted, 326 enrolled. *Average high school GPA:* 2.81. *Test scores:* SAT critical reading scores over 500: 33%;

SAT math scores over 500: 33%; ACT scores over 18: 73%; ACT scores over 24: 16%.

Faculty *Total:* 110, 53% full-time. *Student/faculty ratio:* 28:1.

Majors Accounting technology and bookkeeping; administrative assistant and secretarial science; business administration and management; business/commerce; computer programming (specific applications); criminal justice/safety; electrical and electronic engineering technologies related; emergency medical technology (EMT paramedic); English; environmental engineering technology; general studies; health/health-care administration; industrial production technologies related; industrial technology; legal assistant/paralegal; liberal arts and sciences and humanities related; mechanical engineering/mechanical technology; psychology; public health; registered nursing/registered nurse; speech communication and rhetoric; urban forestry.

Academics *Calendar:* semesters. *Degrees:* associate and bachelor's (also offers some upper-level and graduate courses). *Special study options:* academic remediation for entering students, adult/continuing education programs, advanced placement credit, distance learning, double majors, freshman honors college, honors programs, independent study, internships, part-time degree program, services for LD students, student-designed majors, summer session for credit. *ROTC:* Army (c), Air Force (c).

Library Trumbull Campus Library with 65,951 titles, an OPAC, a Web page.

Student Life *Housing:* college housing not available. *Activities and Organizations:* Student Nurses Association, REACH, ENACTUS, Jurisprudence, If These Hands Could Talk - ASL. *Campus security:* 24-hour emergency response devices, late-night transport/escort service, patrols by trained security personnel during open hours. *Student services:* personal/psychological counseling.

Standardized Tests *Required for some:* SAT or ACT (for admission). *Recommended:* SAT or ACT (for admission).

Costs (2014–15) *One-time required fee:* $150. *Tuition:* state resident $5664 full-time, $258 per credit hour part-time; nonresident $13,624 full-time, $620 per credit hour part-time. Full-time tuition and fees vary according to course level and course load. Part-time tuition and fees vary according to course level and course load. *Payment plan:* installment. *Waivers:* senior citizens and employees or children of employees.

Financial Aid Of all full-time matriculated undergraduates who enrolled in 2014, 957 applied for aid, 890 were judged to have need, 21 had their need fully met. In 2014, 18 non-need-based awards were made. *Average percent of need met:* 41%. *Average financial aid package:* $7133. *Average need-based loan:* $3907. *Average need-based gift aid:* $4749. *Average non-need-based aid:* $1305.

Applying *Options:* electronic application, deferred entrance. *Application fee:* $40. *Required:* high school transcript. *Application deadlines:* rolling (freshmen), rolling (out-of-state freshmen), rolling (transfers). *Notification:* continuous (freshmen), continuous (out-of-state freshmen), continuous (transfers).

Freshman Application Contact Kent State University at Trumbull, Warren, OH 44483. *Phone:* 330-675-8935.

Website: http://www.trumbull.kent.edu/.

Kent State University at Tuscarawas
New Philadelphia, Ohio

- **State-supported** primarily 2-year, founded 1962, part of Kent State University System
- **Small-town** 172-acre campus with easy access to Cleveland-Akron-Canton
- **Coed,** 2,266 undergraduate students, 59% full-time, 57% women, 43% men

Undergraduates 1,347 full-time, 919 part-time. Students come from 4 states and territories; 3 other countries; 1% are from out of state; 3% Black or African American, non-Hispanic/Latino; 1% Hispanic/Latino; 0.6% Asian, non-Hispanic/Latino; 2% Two or more races, non-Hispanic/Latino; 3% Race/ethnicity unknown; 0.5% international; 4% transferred in. *Retention:* 59% of full-time freshmen returned.

Freshmen *Admission:* 354 applied, 331 admitted, 276 enrolled. *Average high school GPA:* 2.97. *Test scores:* SAT critical reading scores over 500: 33%; SAT math scores over 500: 33%; SAT writing scores over 500: 33%; ACT scores over 18: 80%; ACT scores over 24: 18%.

Faculty *Total:* 124, 44% full-time. *Student/faculty ratio:* 21:1.

Majors Accounting technology and bookkeeping; administrative assistant and secretarial science; agribusiness; business administration and management; business/commerce; CAD/CADD drafting/design technology; computer programming (specific applications); criminal justice/safety; early childhood education; education related; electrical and electronic engineering technologies related; engineering technology; English; general studies; industrial technology; liberal arts and sciences and humanities related; mechanical engineering/mechanical technology; psychology; registered nursing/registered

nurse; speech communication and rhetoric; veterinary/animal health technology.

Academics *Calendar:* semesters. *Degrees:* certificates, associate, and bachelor's (also offers some upper-level and graduate courses). *Special study options:* academic remediation for entering students, accelerated degree program, adult/continuing education programs, advanced placement credit, distance learning, double majors, freshman honors college, honors programs, independent study, internships, part-time degree program, services for LD students, student-designed majors, study abroad, summer session for credit. *ROTC:* Army (c), Air Force (c).

Library Tuscarawas Campus Library with 63,880 titles, 1,179 audiovisual materials, an OPAC, a Web page.

Student Life *Housing:* college housing not available. *Activities and Organizations:* Society of Manufacturing Engineers, IEEE, Animation Imagineers, Criminology & Justice Studies Club, Student Activities Council. *Campus security:* 24-hour emergency response devices.

Athletics *Intramural sports:* basketball M/W, volleyball M/W.

Standardized Tests *Required for some:* SAT or ACT (for admission). *Recommended:* SAT or ACT (for admission).

Costs (2014–15) *One-time required fee:* $150. *Tuition:* state resident $5664 full-time, $258 per credit hour part-time; nonresident $13,624 full-time, $620 per credit hour part-time. Full-time tuition and fees vary according to course level and course load. Part-time tuition and fees vary according to course level and course load. *Payment plan:* installment. *Waivers:* senior citizens and employees or children of employees.

Financial Aid Of all full-time matriculated undergraduates who enrolled in 2014, 797 applied for aid, 736 were judged to have need, 31 had their need fully met. In 2014, 31 non-need-based awards were made. *Average percent of need met:* 43%. *Average financial aid package:* $6761. *Average need-based loan:* $3940. *Average need-based gift aid:* $4339. *Average non-need-based aid:* $1344.

Applying *Options:* electronic application, deferred entrance. *Application fee:* $40. *Required:* high school transcript. *Application deadlines:* rolling (freshmen), rolling (out-of-state freshmen), rolling (transfers). *Notification:* continuous (freshmen), continuous (out-of-state freshmen), continuous (transfers).

Freshman Application Contact Kent State University at Tuscarawas, Kent State University at Tuscarawas, 330 University Drive Northeast, New Philadelphia, OH 44663-9403. *Phone:* 330-339-3391 Ext. 47425. *Fax:* 330-339-3321. *E-mail:* info@tusc.kent.edu.

Website: http://www.tusc.kent.edu/.

Lakeland Community College
Kirtland, Ohio

- **State and locally supported** 2-year, founded 1967, part of Ohio Board of Regents
- **Suburban** 380-acre campus with easy access to Cleveland
- **Endowment** $35,486
- **Coed,** 8,250 undergraduate students, 35% full-time, 60% women, 40% men

Undergraduates 2,905 full-time, 5,345 part-time. Students come from 5 states and territories; 16% Black or African American, non-Hispanic/Latino; 3% Hispanic/Latino; 1% Asian, non-Hispanic/Latino; 0.1% Native Hawaiian or other Pacific Islander, non-Hispanic/Latino; 0.5% American Indian or Alaska Native, non-Hispanic/Latino; 1% Two or more races, non-Hispanic/Latino; 4% Race/ethnicity unknown; 0.2% international; 5% transferred in. *Retention:* 45% of full-time freshmen returned.

Freshmen *Admission:* 1,268 enrolled.

Faculty *Total:* 653, 18% full-time. *Student/faculty ratio:* 16:1.

Majors Accounting; administrative assistant and secretarial science; biotechnology; business administration and management; child-care provision; civil engineering technology; clinical/medical laboratory technology; commercial and advertising art; computer engineering technology; computer programming (specific applications); computer systems analysis; computer systems networking and telecommunications; computer technology/computer systems technology; corrections; criminal justice/police science; dental hygiene; electrical, electronic and communications engineering technology; energy management and systems technology; fire prevention and safety technology; health professions related; homeland security, law enforcement, firefighting and protective services related; hospitality administration; instrumentation technology; legal assistant/paralegal; liberal arts and sciences/liberal studies; management information systems; marketing/marketing management; mechanical engineering/mechanical technology; medical radiologic technology; nuclear medical technology; ophthalmic technology; quality control technology; registered nursing/registered nurse; respiratory care therapy; restaurant, culinary, and catering management; sign language interpretation and translation; social work; surgical technology; tourism and travel services management.

Academics *Calendar:* semesters. *Degree:* certificates and associate. *Special study options:* academic remediation for entering students, adult/continuing education programs, advanced placement credit, cooperative education, distance learning, English as a second language, external degree program, independent study, internships, off-campus study, part-time degree program, services for LD students, study abroad, summer session for credit.

Library Lakeland Community College Library with 65,814 titles, 4,212 audiovisual materials, an OPAC, a Web page.

Student Life *Housing:* college housing not available. *Activities and Organizations:* drama/theater group, student-run newspaper, radio station, choral group, Campus Activities Board, Lakeland Student Government, Lakeland Signers, Gamer's Guild. *Campus security:* 24-hour emergency response devices and patrols, student patrols, late-night transport/escort service. *Student services:* health clinic, personal/psychological counseling, women's center.

Athletics Member NJCAA. *Intercollegiate sports:* baseball M(s), basketball M(s)/W(s), golf M(s), soccer M(s), softball W(s), volleyball W(s).

Standardized Tests *Required:* ACT Compass (for admission).

Costs (2014–15) *Tuition:* area resident $3287 full-time, $110 per credit hour part-time; state resident $4136 full-time, $138 per credit hour part-time; nonresident $9176 full-time, $306 per credit hour part-time. Full-time tuition and fees vary according to course load. Part-time tuition and fees vary according to course load. *Required fees:* $14 per term part-time. *Payment plan:* installment. *Waivers:* senior citizens and employees or children of employees.

Financial Aid Of all full-time matriculated undergraduates who enrolled in 2013, 3,429 applied for aid, 2,958 were judged to have need, 468 had their need fully met. 65 Federal Work-Study jobs (averaging $2253). *Average percent of need met:* 56%. *Average financial aid package:* $7026. *Average need-based loan:* $3232. *Average need-based gift aid:* $5251.

Applying *Options:* electronic application, early admission, deferred entrance. *Application fee:* $15. *Required:* high school transcript. *Application deadlines:* 9/1 (freshmen), 9/1 (transfers). *Notification:* continuous until 9/1 (freshmen), continuous until 9/1 (transfers).

Freshman Application Contact Lakeland Community College, 7700 Clocktower Drive, Kirtland, OH 44094-5198. *Phone:* 440-525-7230. *Toll-free phone:* 800-589-8520. *Website:* http://www.lakeland.cc.oh.us/.

Lorain County Community College
Elyria, Ohio

- **State and locally supported** 2-year, founded 1963, part of Ohio Board of Regents
- **Suburban** 280-acre campus with easy access to Cleveland
- **Endowment** $26.6 million
- **Coed,** 11,574 undergraduate students, 28% full-time, 62% women, 38% men

Undergraduates 3,287 full-time, 8,287 part-time. Students come from 15 states and territories; 25 other countries; 1% are from out of state; 10% Black or African American, non-Hispanic/Latino; 6% Hispanic/Latino; 1% Asian, non-Hispanic/Latino; 0.2% Native Hawaiian or other Pacific Islander, non-Hispanic/Latino; 0.4% American Indian or Alaska Native, non-Hispanic/Latino; 6% Two or more races, non-Hispanic/Latino; 1% Race/ethnicity unknown; 0.9% international. *Retention:* 59% of full-time freshmen returned.

Freshmen *Admission:* 2,153 applied, 2,153 admitted, 1,873 enrolled.

Faculty *Total:* 699, 18% full-time. *Student/faculty ratio:* 20:1.

Majors Accounting; administrative assistant and secretarial science; art; artificial intelligence; athletic training; biological and physical sciences; biology/biological sciences; business administration and management; chemistry; civil engineering technology; clinical/medical laboratory technology; computer and information sciences related; computer engineering technology; computer programming; computer programming related; computer programming (specific applications); computer programming (vendor/product certification); computer science; computer systems networking and telecommunications; computer technology/computer systems technology; consumer merchandising/retailing management; corrections; cosmetology; cosmetology and personal grooming arts related; criminal justice/police science; data entry/microcomputer applications; data entry/microcomputer applications related; diagnostic medical sonography and ultrasound technology; drafting and design technology; drafting/design engineering technologies related; dramatic/theater arts; education; electrical, electronic and communications engineering technology; elementary education; engineering; engineering technology; finance; fire science/firefighting; history; human services; industrial radiologic technology; industrial technology; information science/studies; information technology; journalism; kindergarten/preschool education; liberal arts and sciences/liberal studies; machine tool technology; marketing/marketing management; mass communication/media; mathematics; music; nuclear medical technology; pharmacy; physical education teaching and coaching; physical therapy technology; physics; plastics and polymer engineering technology; political science and government; pre-engineering; psychology; quality control technology; real estate; registered nursing/registered nurse; social sciences; social work; sociology; sport and fitness administration/management; surgical technology; tourism and travel services management; urban studies/affairs; word processing.

Academics *Calendar:* semesters. *Degree:* certificates and associate. *Special study options:* academic remediation for entering students, adult/continuing education programs, advanced placement credit, cooperative education, distance learning, double majors, English as a second language, external degree program, honors programs, independent study, internships, part-time degree program, services for LD students, student-designed majors, summer session for credit.

Library Learning Resource Center with 198,984 titles, 3,289 audiovisual materials, an OPAC.

Student Life *Housing:* college housing not available. *Activities and Organizations:* drama/theater group, student-run newspaper, radio station, choral group, Phi Beta Kappa, Black Progressives, Hispanic Club, national fraternities, national sororities. *Campus security:* 24-hour emergency response devices and patrols, late-night transport/escort service. *Student services:* health clinic, personal/psychological counseling, women's center, legal services.

Athletics *Intramural sports:* archery M/W, basketball M/W, softball M/W, volleyball M/W, weight lifting M/W, wrestling M.

Costs (2014–15) *Tuition:* area resident $3077 full-time, $118 per credit hour part-time; state resident $3679 full-time, $141 per credit hour part-time; nonresident $7302 full-time, $281 per credit hour part-time. *Payment plans:* installment, deferred payment. *Waivers:* senior citizens and employees or children of employees.

Applying *Options:* early admission, deferred entrance. *Required for some:* high school transcript. *Application deadlines:* rolling (freshmen), rolling (transfers). *Notification:* continuous (freshmen), continuous (transfers).

Freshman Application Contact Lorain County Community College, 1005 Abbe Road, North, Elyria, OH 44035. *Phone:* 440-366-7622. *Toll-free phone:* 800-995-5222 Ext. 4032. *Website:* http://www.lorainccc.edu/.

Marion Technical College
Marion, Ohio

Freshman Application Contact Mr. Joel Liles, Dean of Enrollment Services, Marion Technical College, 1467 Mount Vernon Avenue, Marion, OH 43302. *Phone:* 740-389-4636 Ext. 249. *Fax:* 740-389-6136. *E-mail:* enroll@mtc.edu. *Website:* http://www.mtc.edu/.

Miami-Jacobs Career College
Columbus, Ohio

Admissions Office Contact Miami-Jacobs Career College, 150 E. Gay Street, Columbus, OH 43215. *Website:* http://www.miamijacobs.edu/.

Miami-Jacobs Career College
Dayton, Ohio

Director of Admissions Mary Percell, Vice President of Information Services, Miami-Jacobs Career College, 110 N. Patterson Boulevard, Dayton, OH 45402. *Phone:* 937-461-5174 Ext. 118. *Website:* http://www.miamijacobs.edu/.

Miami-Jacobs Career College
Independence, Ohio

Freshman Application Contact Director of Admissions, Miami-Jacobs Career College, 6400 Rockside Road, Independence, OH 44131. *Phone:* 216-861-3222. *Toll-free phone:* 866-324-0142. *Fax:* 216-861-4517. *Website:* http://www.miamijacobs.edu/.

Miami-Jacobs Career College
Sharonville, Ohio

Admissions Office Contact Miami-Jacobs Career College, 2 Crowne Pointe Courte, Suite 100, Sharonville, OH 45241. *Website:* http://www.miamijacobs.edu/.

Miami-Jacobs Career College
Springboro, Ohio

Admissions Office Contact Miami-Jacobs Career College, 875 West Central Avenue, Springboro, OH 45066.
Website: http://www.miamijacobs.edu/.

Miami-Jacobs Career College
Troy, Ohio

Admissions Office Contact Miami-Jacobs Career College, 865 W. Market Street, Troy, OH 45373.
Website: http://www.miamijacobs.edu/.

Miami University Middletown
Middletown, Ohio

Freshman Application Contact Diane Cantonwine, Assistant Director of Admission and Financial Aid, Miami University Middletown, 4200 East University Boulevard, Middletown, OH 45042-3497. *Phone:* 513-727-3346. *Toll-free phone:* 866-426-4643. *Fax:* 513-727-3223. *E-mail:* cantondm@muohio.edu.
Website: http://regionals.miamioh.edu/.

National College
Canton, Ohio

Admissions Office Contact National College, 4736 Dressler Road NW, Canton, OH 44718.
Website: http://www.national-college.edu/.

National College
Cincinnati, Ohio

Director of Admissions Patrick M. Brown, Campus Director, National College, 6871 Steger Drive, Cincinnati, OH 45237. *Phone:* 513-761-1291.
Website: http://www.national-college.edu/.

National College
Cleveland, Ohio

Admissions Office Contact National College, 27557 Chardon Road, Cleveland, OH 44092.
Website: http://www.national-college.edu/.

National College
Columbus, Ohio

Admissions Office Contact National College, 5665 Forest Hills Boulevard, Columbus, OH 45420.
Website: http://www.national-college.edu/.

National College
Kettering, Ohio

Director of Admissions Gregory J. Shields, Director, National College, 1837 Woodman Center Drive, Kettering, OH 45420-1157. *Phone:* 937-299-9450.
Website: http://www.national-college.edu/.

National College
Stow, Ohio

Admissions Office Contact National College, 3855 Fishcreek Road, Stow, OH 44224.
Website: http://www.national-college.edu/.

National College
Youngstown, Ohio

Admissions Office Contact National College, 3487 Belmont Avenue, Youngstown, OH 44505.
Website: http://www.national-college.edu/.

North Central State College
Mansfield, Ohio

Freshman Application Contact Ms. Nikia L. Fletcher, Director of Admissions, North Central State College, 2441 Kenwood Circle, PO Box 698, Mansfield, OH 44901-0698. *Phone:* 419-755-4813. *Toll-free phone:* 888-755-4899. *E-mail:* nfletcher@ncstatecollege.edu.
Website: http://www.ncstatecollege.edu/.

Northwest State Community College
Archbold, Ohio

- **State-supported** 2-year, founded 1968, part of Ohio Board of Regents
- **Rural** 80-acre campus with easy access to Toledo
- **Coed,** 3,614 undergraduate students, 20% full-time, 46% women, 54% men

Undergraduates 713 full-time, 2,901 part-time. Students come from 6 states and territories; 2 other countries; 4% are from out of state; 3% Black or African American, non-Hispanic/Latino; 6% Hispanic/Latino; 0.7% Asian, non-Hispanic/Latino; 0.1% American Indian or Alaska Native, non-Hispanic/Latino; 1% Two or more races, non-Hispanic/Latino; 12% Race/ethnicity unknown; 3% transferred in.
Freshmen *Admission:* 1,360 applied, 1,360 admitted, 582 enrolled. *Average high school GPA:* 3.11. *Test scores:* ACT scores over 18: 82%; ACT scores over 24: 27%; ACT scores over 30: 2%.
Faculty *Total:* 142, 30% full-time, 75% with terminal degrees. *Student/faculty ratio:* 27:1.
Majors Accounting; accounting related; administrative assistant and secretarial science; banking and financial support services; business administration and management; business/commerce; CAD/CADD drafting/design technology; child-care and support services management; computer and information systems security; computer engineering; computer engineering technology; computer programming; construction engineering technology; corrections and criminal justice related; criminal justice/police science; criminal justice/safety; data entry/microcomputer applications; design and visual communications; electrical, electronic and communications engineering technology; energy management and systems technology; engineering/industrial management; engineering related; engineering technologies and engineering related; entrepreneurship; history; human development and family studies related; human resources management; industrial electronics technology; industrial mechanics and maintenance technology; industrial production technologies related; international business/trade/commerce; kindergarten/preschool education; legal administrative assistant/secretary; legal assistant/paralegal; liberal arts and sciences/liberal studies; logistics, materials, and supply chain management; machine tool technology; marketing/marketing management; mechanical engineering; mechanical engineering/mechanical technology; medical administrative assistant and medical secretary; medical/clinical assistant; network and system administration; nonprofit management; office management; plastics and polymer engineering technology; precision metal working related; registered nursing/registered nurse; social work; teacher assistant/aide; web page, digital/multimedia and information resources design.
Academics *Calendar:* semesters. *Degree:* certificates and associate. *Special study options:* academic remediation for entering students, adult/continuing education programs, advanced placement credit, cooperative education, distance learning, double majors, external degree program, independent study, internships, off-campus study, part-time degree program, services for LD students, student-designed majors, summer session for credit.
Library Northwest State Community College Library plus 1 other with 80,400 titles, 3,401 audiovisual materials, an OPAC, a Web page.
Student Life *Housing:* college housing not available. *Activities and Organizations:* Student Body Organziation (SBO), Students for Community Outreach and Awareness (SCOA), Phi Theta Kappa (PTK), Kappa Beta Delta (KBD), ev/Motorsports. *Campus security:* 24-hour emergency response devices, security patrols. *Student services:* personal/psychological counseling.
Athletics *Intramural sports:* basketball M/W, bowling M/W, soccer M/W, table tennis M/W, volleyball M/W.
Costs (2015–16) *Tuition:* state resident $3768 full-time, $157 per credit part-time; nonresident $7392 full-time, $308 per credit part-time. *Required fees:* $70 full-time, $35 per term part-time. *Payment plan:* installment. *Waivers:* employees or children of employees.
Financial Aid Of all full-time matriculated undergraduates who enrolled in 2013, 43 Federal Work-Study jobs (averaging $1077).
Applying *Options:* electronic application, early admission, deferred entrance. *Required:* high school transcript. *Required for some:* minimum 2.5 GPA, interview, Nursing requires the NLN PAX with a relative score greater than or equal to 50 in each of the 3 sections. *Application deadlines:* rolling (freshmen), rolling (out-of-state freshmen), rolling (transfers). *Notification:*

continuous (freshmen), continuous (out-of-state freshmen), continuous (transfers).

Freshman Application Contact Mrs. Amanda Potts, Director of Admissions, Northwest State Community College, 22600 State Route 34, Archbold, OH 43502. *Phone:* 419-267-1364. *Toll-free phone:* 855-267-5511. *Fax:* 419-267-3688. *E-mail:* apotts@northweststate.edu.
Website: http://www.northweststate.edu/.

Ohio Business College

Hilliard, Ohio

- **Proprietary** 2-year
- **Suburban** campus
- **Coed**

Academics *Degree:* diplomas and associate.
Freshman Application Contact Ohio Business College, 4525 Trueman Boulevard, Hilliard, OH 43026. *Toll-free phone:* 800-954-4274.
Website: http://www.ohiobusinesscollege.edu/.

Ohio Business College

Sandusky, Ohio

- **Proprietary** 2-year, founded 1982
- **Small-town** 1-acre campus with easy access to Cleveland or Toledo
- **Coed,** 265 undergraduate students, 64% full-time, 74% women, 26% men

Undergraduates 170 full-time, 95 part-time. Students come from 1 other state; 22% Black or African American, non-Hispanic/Latino; 5% Hispanic/Latino; 0.4% Asian, non-Hispanic/Latino; 0.4% American Indian or Alaska Native, non-Hispanic/Latino; 0.4% Two or more races, non-Hispanic/Latino; 2% Race/ethnicity unknown.
Freshmen *Admission:* 29 enrolled.
Faculty *Total:* 32, 19% full-time. *Student/faculty ratio:* 8:1.
Majors Accounting; administrative assistant and secretarial science; business administration and management; computer support specialist; hospitality and recreation marketing; human resources management; legal administrative assistant/secretary; medical administrative assistant and medical secretary.
Academics *Calendar:* quarters. *Degree:* diplomas and associate. *Special study options:* academic remediation for entering students, independent study, internships, part-time degree program, summer session for credit.
Library Main Library plus 1 other.
Student Life *Housing:* college housing not available.
Costs (2014–15) *Tuition:* $8140 full-time, $225 per credit hour part-time. Full-time tuition and fees vary according to course load. Part-time tuition and fees vary according to course load. No tuition increase for student's term of enrollment. *Payment plans:* tuition prepayment, installment. *Waivers:* employees or children of employees.
Applying *Required:* Valid HS diploma or GED.
Freshman Application Contact Ohio Business College, 5202 Timber Commons Drive, Sandusky, OH 44870. *Phone:* 419-627-8345. *Toll-free phone:* 888-627-8345.
Website: http://www.ohiobusinesscollege.edu/.

Ohio Business College

Sheffield Village, Ohio

Director of Admissions Mr. Jim Unger, Admissions Director, Ohio Business College, 5095 Waterford Drive, Sheffield Village, OH 44035. *Toll-free phone:* 888-514-3126.
Website: http://www.ohiobusinesscollege.edu/.

Ohio College of Massotherapy

Akron, Ohio

Director of Admissions Mr. John Atkins, Director of Admissions and Marketing, Ohio College of Massotherapy, 225 Heritage Woods Drive, Akron, OH 44321. *Phone:* 330-665-1084 Ext. 11. *Toll-free phone:* 888-888-4325. *E-mail:* johna@ocm.edu.
Website: http://www.ocm.edu/.

The Ohio State University Agricultural Technical Institute

Wooster, Ohio

- **State-supported** 2-year, founded 1971, part of The Ohio State University
- **Small-town** 1942-acre campus with easy access to Cleveland, Columbus, Akron, Canton
- **Coed,** 757 undergraduate students, 93% full-time, 45% women, 55% men

Undergraduates 702 full-time, 55 part-time. Students come from 8 states and territories; 2% are from out of state; 3% transferred in. *Retention:* 62% of full-time freshmen returned.
Freshmen *Admission:* 642 applied, 545 admitted, 372 enrolled. *Test scores:* ACT scores over 18: 57%; ACT scores over 24: 11%.
Faculty *Total:* 70, 47% full-time, 33% with terminal degrees. *Student/faculty ratio:* 17:1.
Majors Agribusiness; agricultural business and management; agricultural business technology; agricultural communication/journalism; agricultural economics; agricultural mechanization; agricultural power machinery operation; agricultural teacher education; agronomy and crop science; animal/livestock husbandry and production; animal sciences; biology/biotechnology laboratory technician; building/construction site management; construction engineering technology; construction management; crop production; dairy husbandry and production; dairy science; environmental science; equestrian studies; floriculture/floristry management; greenhouse management; heavy equipment maintenance technology; horse husbandry/equine science and management; horticultural science; hydraulics and fluid power technology; industrial technology; landscaping and groundskeeping; livestock management; natural resources management and policy; natural resources management and policy related; plant nursery management; soil science and agronomy; turf and turfgrass management.
Academics *Calendar:* semesters. *Degree:* certificates, diplomas, and associate. *Special study options:* academic remediation for entering students, accelerated degree program, adult/continuing education programs, advanced placement credit, cooperative education, distance learning, double majors, independent study, internships, off-campus study, part-time degree program, services for LD students, student-designed majors, study abroad. *ROTC:* Army (c), Navy (c), Air Force (c).
Library Agricultural Technical Institute Library plus 1 other with 9,000 titles, 100 audiovisual materials, an OPAC, a Web page.
Student Life *Housing:* on-campus residence required for freshman year. *Options:* coed, special housing for students with disabilities. Campus housing is university owned. *Activities and Organizations:* Hoof-n-Hide Club, Collegiate FFA, Campus Crusade for Christ, Phi Theta Kappa, Community Council. *Campus security:* 24-hour emergency response devices and patrols, controlled dormitory access. *Student services:* personal/psychological counseling.
Athletics *Intramural sports:* archery M/W, badminton M/W, basketball M/W, bowling M/W, football M/W, racquetball M/W, soccer M/W, softball M/W, volleyball M/W, weight lifting M/W.
Standardized Tests *Required for some:* SAT or ACT (for admission).
Costs (2014–15) *Tuition:* state resident $7104 full-time, $300 per credit hour part-time; nonresident $23,604 full-time, $988 per credit hour part-time. Full-time tuition and fees vary according to course load, location, and program. Part-time tuition and fees vary according to course load, location, and program. *Room and board:* $8130; room only: $6530. Room and board charges vary according to board plan and location. *Payment plan:* installment.
Financial Aid Of all full-time matriculated undergraduates who enrolled in 2010, 540 applied for aid, 474 were judged to have need, 25 had their need fully met. 64 Federal Work-Study jobs (averaging $2000). In 2010, 24 non-need-based awards were made. *Average percent of need met:* 44%. *Average financial aid package:* $6859. *Average need-based loan:* $3826. *Average need-based gift aid:* $4241. *Average non-need-based aid:* $2107.
Applying *Options:* electronic application. *Application fee:* $60. *Required:* high school transcript. *Application deadlines:* 6/1 (freshmen), 6/1 (out-of-state freshmen), 6/1 (transfers). *Notification:* continuous (freshmen).
Freshman Application Contact Ms. Julia Morris, Admissions Counselor, The Ohio State University Agricultural Technical Institute, 1328 Dover Road, Wooster, OH 44691. *Phone:* 330-287-1327. *Toll-free phone:* 800-647-8283 Ext. 1327. *Fax:* 330-287-1333. *E-mail:* morris.878@osu.edu.
Website: http://www.ati.osu.edu/.

Ohio Technical College

Cleveland, Ohio

Director of Admissions Mr. Marc Brenner, President, Ohio Technical College, 1374 East 51st Street, Cleveland, OH 44103. *Phone:* 216-881-1700.

Toll-free phone: 800-322-7000. *Fax:* 216-881-9145. *E-mail:* ohioauto@aol.com.
Website: http://www.ohiotechnicalcollege.com/.

Ohio Valley College of Technology
East Liverpool, Ohio

Freshman Application Contact Mr. Scott S. Rogers, Director, Ohio Valley College of Technology, 16808 St. Clair Avenue, PO Box 7000, East Liverpool, OH 43920. *Phone:* 330-385-1070.
Website: http://www.ovct.edu/.

Owens Community College
Toledo, Ohio

- **State-supported** 2-year, founded 1966
- **Suburban** 420-acre campus with easy access to Detroit
- **Endowment** $1.7 million
- **Coed,** 12,572 undergraduate students, 34% full-time, 51% women, 49% men

Undergraduates 4,257 full-time, 8,315 part-time. Students come from 25 states and territories; 6 other countries; 3% are from out of state; 15% Black or African American, non-Hispanic/Latino; 7% Hispanic/Latino; 1% Asian, non-Hispanic/Latino; 0.4% American Indian or Alaska Native, non-Hispanic/Latino; 3% Two or more races, non-Hispanic/Latino; 2% Race/ethnicity unknown; 1% international; 0.7% transferred in.
Freshmen *Admission:* 8,090 applied, 8,090 admitted, 1,735 enrolled. *Average high school GPA:* 2.71. *Test scores:* SAT critical reading scores over 500: 25%; SAT math scores over 500: 30%; SAT writing scores over 500: 25%; ACT scores over 18: 59%; SAT critical reading scores over 600: 4%; SAT writing scores over 600: 4%; ACT scores over 24: 9%.
Faculty *Total:* 1,259, 15% full-time, 9% with terminal degrees. *Student/faculty ratio:* 16:1.
Majors Accounting technology and bookkeeping; agricultural mechanization; architectural drafting and CAD/CADD; architectural engineering technology; automotive engineering technology; biomedical technology; business/commerce; commercial and advertising art; commercial photography; computer and information systems security; computer engineering technology; computer programming (specific applications); construction engineering technology; criminal justice/law enforcement administration; criminal justice/police science; dental hygiene; diagnostic medical sonography and ultrasound technology; dietetics; early childhood education; electrical, electronic and communications engineering technology; executive assistant/executive secretary; general studies; health information/medical records technology; homeland security, law enforcement, firefighting and protective services related; industrial technology; information technology; interdisciplinary studies; landscaping and groundskeeping; logistics, materials, and supply chain management; magnetic resonance imaging (MRI) technology; manufacturing engineering technology; massage therapy; medical administrative assistant and medical secretary; medical/health management and clinical assistant; medical radiologic technology; music technology; nuclear medical technology; occupational therapist assistant; office management; physical therapy technology; registered nursing/registered nurse; restaurant/food services management; sales, distribution, and marketing operations; surgical technology; welding technology.
Academics *Calendar:* semesters. *Degree:* certificates and associate. *Special study options:* academic remediation for entering students, accelerated degree program, adult/continuing education programs, advanced placement credit, cooperative education, distance learning, double majors, English as a second language, honors programs, independent study, internships, part-time degree program, services for LD students, study abroad, summer session for credit.
Library Owens Community College Library plus 1 other with 75,428 titles, 7,364 audiovisual materials, an OPAC, a Web page.
Student Life *Housing:* college housing not available. *Activities and Organizations:* drama/theater group, student-run newspaper, choral group. *Campus security:* 24-hour emergency response devices and patrols, student patrols, classroom doors that lock from the inside; campus alert system. *Student services:* personal/psychological counseling.
Athletics Member NJCAA. *Intercollegiate sports:* baseball M(s), basketball M(s)/W(s), golf M(s)/W, soccer M(s)/W(s), softball W(s), volleyball W(s). *Intramural sports:* basketball M/W, bowling M/W, football M, golf M/W, softball M/W, table tennis M/W, tennis M/W, volleyball M/W, weight lifting M.
Costs (2014–15) *Tuition:* state resident $4284 full-time, $153 per credit hour part-time; nonresident $8568 full-time, $306 per credit hour part-time. Full-time tuition and fees vary according to course load and reciprocity agreements. Part-time tuition and fees vary according to course load and reciprocity agreements. *Required fees:* $454 full-time, $16 per credit hour part-time, $10

per term part-time. *Payment plans:* installment, deferred payment. *Waivers:* senior citizens and employees or children of employees.
Financial Aid Of all full-time matriculated undergraduates who enrolled in 2014, 3,401 applied for aid, 2,884 were judged to have need, 456 had their need fully met. In 2014, 185 non-need-based awards were made. *Average percent of need met:* 70%. *Average financial aid package:* $6893. *Average need-based loan:* $7386. *Average need-based gift aid:* $4654. *Average non-need-based aid:* $1248.
Applying *Options:* electronic application, early admission, deferred entrance. *Application fee:* $20. *Required:* high school transcript. *Required for some:* minimum 2.0 GPA, interview, Health Technology, Peace Officer Academy, and Early Childhood Education programs require high school transcripts and standardized test scores for admission. *Application deadlines:* rolling (freshmen), rolling (out-of-state freshmen), rolling (transfers). *Notification:* continuous (freshmen), continuous (out-of-state freshmen), continuous (transfers).
Freshman Application Contact Ms. Meghan L Schmidbauer, Director, Admissions, Owens Community College, PO Box 10000, Toledo, OH 43699. *Phone:* 567-661-2155. *Toll-free phone:* 800-GO-OWENS. *Fax:* 567-661-7734. *E-mail:* meghan_schmidbauer@owens.edu.
Website: http://www.owens.edu/.

Professional Skills Institute
Toledo, Ohio

Director of Admissions Ms. Hope Finch, Director of Marketing, Professional Skills Institute, 1505 Holland Road, Maumee, Toledo, OH 43537. *Phone:* 419-531-9610.
Website: http://www.proskills.com/.

Remington College–Cleveland Campus
Cleveland, Ohio

Director of Admissions Director of Recruitment, Remington College–Cleveland Campus, 14445 Broadway Avenue, Cleveland, OH 44125. *Phone:* 216-475-7520. *Fax:* 216-475-6055.
Website: http://www.remingtoncollege.edu/.

Rosedale Bible College
Irwin, Ohio

Director of Admissions Mr. John Showalter, Director of Enrollment Services, Rosedale Bible College, 2270 Rosedale Road, Irwin, OH 43029-9501. *Phone:* 740-857-1311. *Fax:* 740-857-1577. *E-mail:* pweber@rosedale.edu.
Website: http://www.rosedale.edu/.

School of Advertising Art
Kettering, Ohio

- **Proprietary** 2-year, founded 1983
- **Suburban** 5-acre campus with easy access to Columbus
- **Coed,** 142 undergraduate students, 97% full-time, 68% women, 32% men

Undergraduates 138 full-time, 4 part-time. Students come from 3 states and territories; 2% are from out of state; 2% Black or African American, non-Hispanic/Latino; 1% Hispanic/Latino; 2% Asian, non-Hispanic/Latino; 0.7% Native Hawaiian or other Pacific Islander, non-Hispanic/Latino; 1% Race/ethnicity unknown; 6% transferred in. *Retention:* 68% of full-time freshmen returned.
Freshmen *Admission:* 412 applied, 203 admitted, 79 enrolled.
Faculty *Total:* 19, 53% full-time, 5% with terminal degrees. *Student/faculty ratio:* 11:1.
Majors Commercial and advertising art.
Academics *Calendar:* semesters. *Degree:* associate.
Library SAA Library with 820 titles, 12 audiovisual materials, an OPAC, a Web page.
Student Life *Housing:* college housing not available. *Activities and Organizations:* Fine Art Club. *Student services:* personal/psychological counseling.
Costs (2015–16) *Tuition:* $24,712 full-time. *Required fees:* $1349 full-time. *Payment plan:* installment. *Waivers:* employees or children of employees.
Applying *Options:* electronic application. *Required:* high school transcript, minimum 2.0 GPA, interview. *Required for some:* essay or personal statement, 2 letters of recommendation.
Freshman Application Contact Ms. Abigail Heaney, Admissions, School of Advertising Art, 1725 East David Road, Kettering, OH 45440. *Phone:* 937-

294-0592. *Toll-free phone:* 877-300-9866. *Fax:* 937-294-5869. *E-mail:* Abbie@saa.edu.
Website: http://www.saa.edu/.

Sinclair Community College
Dayton, Ohio

Freshman Application Contact Ms. Sara Smith, Director and Systems Manager, Outreach Services, Sinclair Community College, 444 West Third Street, Dayton, OH 45402-1460. *Phone:* 937-512-3060. *Toll-free phone:* 800-315-3000. *Fax:* 937-512-2393. *E-mail:* ssmith@sinclair.edu.
Website: http://www.sinclair.edu/.

Southern State Community College
Hillsboro, Ohio

- **State-supported** 2-year, founded 1975
- **Rural** 60-acre campus
- **Endowment** $1.9 million
- **Coed**

Undergraduates 1,175 full-time, 1,256 part-time. Students come from 2 states and territories; 2% Black or African American, non-Hispanic/Latino; 0.7% Hispanic/Latino; 0.5% Asian, non-Hispanic/Latino; 0.1% Native Hawaiian or other Pacific Islander, non-Hispanic/Latino; 0.3% American Indian or Alaska Native, non-Hispanic/Latino; 1% Two or more races, non-Hispanic/Latino; 2% Race/ethnicity unknown.
Faculty *Student/faculty ratio:* 16:1.
Academics *Calendar:* quarters. *Degree:* certificates and associate. *Special study options:* academic remediation for entering students, advanced placement credit, cooperative education, distance learning, double majors, independent study, internships, off-campus study, part-time degree program, services for LD students, student-designed majors, summer session for credit.
Athletics Member USCAA.
Costs (2014–15) *Tuition:* state resident $4232 full-time, $162 per semester hour part-time; nonresident $7938 full-time, $306 per semester hour part-time. Full-time tuition and fees vary according to course load and reciprocity agreements. Part-time tuition and fees vary according to course load and reciprocity agreements.
Financial Aid Of all full-time matriculated undergraduates who enrolled in 2011, 3,082 applied for aid, 3,082 were judged to have need, 2,537 had their need fully met. 61 Federal Work-Study jobs (averaging $2030). In 2011, 754. *Average percent of need met:* 92. *Average financial aid package:* $4570. *Average need-based loan:* $2247. *Average need-based gift aid:* $3560. *Average non-need-based aid:* $1675.
Applying *Options:* electronic application, early admission, deferred entrance. *Recommended:* high school transcript.
Freshman Application Contact Ms. Wendy Johnson, Director of Admissions, Southern State Community College, Hillsboro, OH 45133. *Phone:* 937-393-3431 Ext. 2720. *Toll-free phone:* 800-628-7722. *Fax:* 937-393-6682. *E-mail:* wjohnson@sscc.edu.
Website: http://www.sscc.edu/.

Stark State College
North Canton, Ohio

- **State-related** 2-year, founded 1970, part of University System of Ohio
- **Suburban** 34-acre campus with easy access to Cleveland
- **Endowment** $4.8 million
- **Coed,** 14,097 undergraduate students, 29% full-time, 59% women, 41% men

Undergraduates 4,111 full-time, 9,986 part-time. Students come from 38 states and territories; 6 other countries; 1% are from out of state; 17% Black or African American, non-Hispanic/Latino; 1% Hispanic/Latino; 1% Asian, non-Hispanic/Latino; 0.1% Native Hawaiian or other Pacific Islander, non-Hispanic/Latino; 0.4% American Indian or Alaska Native, non-Hispanic/Latino; 3% Two or more races, non-Hispanic/Latino; 8% Race/ethnicity unknown; 8% transferred in. *Retention:* 42% of full-time freshmen returned.
Freshmen *Admission:* 2,175 enrolled. *Test scores:* ACT scores over 18: 55%; ACT scores over 24: 10%; ACT scores over 30: 1%.
Faculty *Total:* 716, 28% full-time. *Student/faculty ratio:* 20:1.
Majors Accounting; administrative assistant and secretarial science; architectural engineering technology; automobile/automotive mechanics technology; biomedical technology; business administration and management; child development; civil engineering technology; clinical/medical laboratory technology; computer and information sciences and support services related; computer and information sciences related; computer engineering related; computer hardware engineering; computer/information technology services

administration related; computer programming; computer programming related; computer programming (specific applications); computer programming (vendor/product certification); computer software and media applications related; computer software engineering; computer systems networking and telecommunications; consumer merchandising/retailing management; court reporting; data entry/microcomputer applications; data entry/microcomputer applications related; dental hygiene; drafting and design technology; environmental studies; finance; fire science/firefighting; food technology and processing; health information/medical records administration; human services; industrial technology; information technology; international business/trade/commerce; legal administrative assistant/secretary; marketing/marketing management; mechanical engineering/mechanical technology; medical/clinical assistant; occupational therapy; operations management; physical therapy; registered nursing/registered nurse; respiratory care therapy; surveying technology; web/multimedia management and webmaster; web page, digital/multimedia and information resources design; word processing.
Academics *Calendar:* semesters. *Degree:* certificates and associate. *Special study options:* academic remediation for entering students, adult/continuing education programs, cooperative education, distance learning, double majors, external degree program, independent study, internships, off-campus study, part-time degree program, services for LD students, student-designed majors, summer session for credit.
Library Learning Resource Center plus 1 other with 82,728 titles, an OPAC, a Web page.
Student Life *Housing:* college housing not available. *Activities and Organizations:* student-run newspaper, Phi Theta Kappa, Business Student Club, Institute of Management Accountants, Stark State College Association of Medical Assistants, Student Health Information Management Association, national fraternities, national sororities. *Campus security:* 24-hour emergency response devices and patrols, student patrols, late-night transport/escort service, patrols by trained security personnel at anytime the campus is open. *Student services:* personal/psychological counseling.
Standardized Tests *Recommended:* SAT or ACT (for admission).
Costs (2014–15) *One-time required fee:* $85. *Tuition:* state resident $2796 full-time, $117 per credit hour part-time; nonresident $4980 full-time, $208 per credit hour part-time. Full-time tuition and fees vary according to course load and program. Part-time tuition and fees vary according to program. *Required fees:* $890 full-time, $37 per credit hour part-time, $30 per term part-time. *Payment plan:* installment. *Waivers:* senior citizens and employees or children of employees.
Financial Aid Of all full-time matriculated undergraduates who enrolled in 2013, 194 Federal Work-Study jobs (averaging $2383).
Applying *Required:* high school transcript.
Freshman Application Contact JP Cooney, Executive Director to Recruitment, Admissions and Marketing, Stark State College, 6200 Frank Road NE, Canton, OH 44720. *Phone:* 330-494-6170 Ext. 4401. *Toll-free phone:* 800-797-8275. *E-mail:* info@starkstate.edu.
Website: http://www.starkstate.edu/.

Stautzenberger College
Brecksville, Ohio

Admissions Office Contact Stautzenberger College, 8001 Katherine Boulevard, Brecksville, OH 44141. *Toll-free phone:* 800-437-2997.
Website: http://www.sctoday.edu/.

Stautzenberger College
Maumee, Ohio

Director of Admissions Ms. Karen Fitzgerald, Director of Admissions and Marketing, Stautzenberger College, 1796 Indian Wood Circle, Maumee, OH 43537. *Phone:* 419-866-0261. *Toll-free phone:* 800-552-5099. *Fax:* 419-867-9821. *E-mail:* klfitzgerald@stautzenberger.com.
Website: http://www.sctoday.edu/maumee/.

Terra State Community College
Fremont, Ohio

- **State-supported** 2-year, founded 1968, part of Ohio Board of Regents
- **Small-town** 100-acre campus with easy access to Toledo
- **Coed,** 2,603 undergraduate students, 32% full-time, 56% women, 44% men

Undergraduates 822 full-time, 1,781 part-time. 4% Black or African American, non-Hispanic/Latino; 9% Hispanic/Latino; 0.4% Asian, non-Hispanic/Latino; 0.5% American Indian or Alaska Native, non-Hispanic/Latino; 0.8% Two or more races, non-Hispanic/Latino; 2% Race/ethnicity unknown; 0.4% international.
Freshmen *Admission:* 371 applied, 371 admitted, 371 enrolled.

Faculty *Total:* 191, 21% full-time, 6% with terminal degrees. *Student/faculty ratio:* 15:1.

Majors Accounting; agricultural business and management; animation, interactive technology, video graphics and special effects; architectural engineering technology; art history, criticism and conservation; automotive engineering technology; banking and financial support services; biological and physical sciences; biology/biological sciences; business administration and management; business/commerce; chemistry; commercial and advertising art; computer and information sciences; computer programming; computer systems networking and telecommunications; criminal justice/police science; data processing and data processing technology; desktop publishing and digital imaging design; economics; education; electrical and electronic engineering technologies related; electrical, electronic and communications engineering technology; engineering; English; executive assistant/executive secretary; fine/studio arts; general studies; health/health-care administration; health information/medical records administration; health information/medical records technology; health professions related; heating, ventilation, air conditioning and refrigeration engineering technology; history; hospitality administration; humanities; kindergarten/preschool education; language interpretation and translation; liberal arts and sciences/liberal studies; manufacturing engineering technology; marketing/marketing management; mathematics; mechanical engineering/mechanical technology; mechanical engineering technologies related; medical administrative assistant and medical secretary; medical/clinical assistant; medical/health management and clinical assistant; medical insurance coding; medical office assistant; music; music management; music performance; music related; nuclear/nuclear power technology; operations management; physics; plastics and polymer engineering technology; psychology; real estate; registered nursing/registered nurse; robotics technology; sheet metal technology; social sciences; social work; teaching assistants/aides related; web page, digital/multimedia and information resources design; welding technology.

Academics *Calendar:* semesters. *Degree:* certificates, diplomas, and associate. *Special study options:* academic remediation for entering students, adult/continuing education programs, advanced placement credit, cooperative education, distance learning, double majors, independent study, internships, off-campus study, part-time degree program, services for LD students, student-designed majors, summer session for credit.

Library Learning Resource Center with 22,675 titles, an OPAC, a Web page.

Student Life *Housing:* college housing not available. *Activities and Organizations:* choral group, Phi Theta Kappa, Student Activities Club, Society of Plastic Engineers, Koinonia, Student Senate. *Campus security:* 24-hour emergency response devices. *Student services:* personal/psychological counseling, legal services.

Athletics *Intramural sports:* basketball M/W, bowling M/W, football M, golf M/W, table tennis M/W, volleyball M/W.

Costs (2015–16) *Tuition:* state resident $3396 full-time, $162 per semester hour part-time; nonresident $7149 full-time, $341 per semester hour part-time. *Required fees:* $357 full-time, $17 per semester hour part-time, $10 per term part-time. *Payment plan:* installment. *Waivers:* employees or children of employees.

Financial Aid Of all full-time matriculated undergraduates who enrolled in 2013, 57 Federal Work-Study jobs (averaging $1450).

Applying *Options:* electronic application, early admission, deferred entrance. *Required:* high school transcript. *Application deadlines:* rolling (freshmen), rolling (transfers).

Freshman Application Contact Mr. Heath Martin, Director of Admissions and Enrollment Services, Terra State Community College, 2830 Napoleon Road, Fremont, OH 43420. *Phone:* 419-559-2154. *Toll-free phone:* 866-AT-TERRA. *Fax:* 419-559-2352.
Website: http://www.terra.edu/.

Trumbull Business College
Warren, Ohio

Director of Admissions Admissions Office, Trumbull Business College, 3200 Ridge Road, Warren, OH 44484. *Phone:* 330-369-6792. *Toll-free phone:* 888-766-1598. *E-mail:* admissions@tbc-trumbullbusiness.com.
Website: http://www.tbc-trumbullbusiness.com/.

The University of Akron Wayne College
Orrville, Ohio

- **State-supported** primarily 2-year, founded 1972, part of The University of Akron
- **Rural** 157-acre campus
- **Coed**

Undergraduates 1,109 full-time, 1,244 part-time. Students come from 2 states and territories; 2 other countries; 3% Black or African American, non-Hispanic/Latino; 1% Hispanic/Latino; 0.6% Asian, non-Hispanic/Latino; 0.1%

Native Hawaiian or other Pacific Islander, non-Hispanic/Latino; 0.3% American Indian or Alaska Native, non-Hispanic/Latino; 2% Two or more races, non-Hispanic/Latino; 4% Race/ethnicity unknown; 2% transferred in. *Retention:* 55% of full-time freshmen returned.

Faculty *Student/faculty ratio:* 20:1.

Academics *Calendar:* semesters. *Degrees:* certificates, associate, and bachelor's. *Special study options:* academic remediation for entering students, adult/continuing education programs, advanced placement credit, cooperative education, distance learning, double majors, honors programs, independent study, internships, off-campus study, part-time degree program, services for LD students, summer session for credit. *ROTC:* Army (c), Air Force (c).

Student Life *Campus security:* 24-hour emergency response devices, late-night transport/escort service.

Standardized Tests *Required for some:* SAT or ACT (for admission), ACT Compass. *Recommended:* SAT or ACT (for admission), ACT Compass.

Costs (2014–15) *Tuition:* state resident $5940 full-time, $248 per credit hour part-time; nonresident $14,281 full-time, $526 per credit hour part-time. Full-time tuition and fees vary according to course level, course load, location, and reciprocity agreements. Part-time tuition and fees vary according to course level, location, and reciprocity agreements. *Required fees:* $176 full-time, $7 per credit hour part-time.

Financial Aid Of all full-time matriculated undergraduates who enrolled in 2013, 8 Federal Work-Study jobs (averaging $2200).

Applying *Options:* electronic application, early admission, deferred entrance. *Application fee:* $40. *Required for some:* high school transcript.

Freshman Application Contact Ms. Alicia Broadus, Student Services Counselor, The University of Akron Wayne College, Orrville, OH 44667. *Phone:* 800-221-8308 Ext. 8901. *Toll-free phone:* 800-221-8308. *Fax:* 330-684-8989. *E-mail:* wayneadmissions@uakron.edu.
Website: http://www.wayne.uakron.edu/.

University of Cincinnati Blue Ash
Cincinnati, Ohio

Freshman Application Contact Leigh Schlegal, Admission Counselor, University of Cincinnati Blue Ash, 9555 Plainfield Road, Cincinnati, OH 45236-1007. *Phone:* 513-745-5783. *Fax:* 513-745-5768.
Website: http://www.ucblueash.edu/.

University of Cincinnati Clermont College
Batavia, Ohio

- **State-supported** primarily 2-year, founded 1972, part of University of Cincinnati System
- **Rural** 91-acre campus with easy access to Cincinnati
- **Endowment** $338,141
- **Coed,** 3,246 undergraduate students, 58% full-time, 56% women, 44% men

Undergraduates 1,881 full-time, 1,365 part-time. 3% are from out of state; 2% Black or African American, non-Hispanic/Latino; 2% Hispanic/Latino; 0.8% Asian, non-Hispanic/Latino; 0.3% American Indian or Alaska Native, non-Hispanic/Latino; 1% Two or more races, non-Hispanic/Latino; 14% Race/ethnicity unknown; 0.3% international.

Freshmen *Admission:* 1,283 applied, 952 admitted, 693 enrolled.

Faculty *Student/faculty ratio:* 16:1.

Majors Accounting; aeronautics/aviation/aerospace science and technology; audiology and speech-language pathology; biology/biological sciences; business administration and management; business/commerce; chemistry; computer technology/computer systems technology; computer typography and composition equipment operation; criminal justice/safety; data processing and data processing technology; elementary education; emergency medical technology (EMT paramedic); environmental studies; general studies; health information/medical records technology; health professions related; information science/studies; kindergarten/preschool education; legal assistant/paralegal; liberal arts and sciences/liberal studies; manufacturing engineering technology; middle school education; multi/interdisciplinary studies related; organizational behavior; physical therapy technology; pre-law studies; pre-pharmacy studies; psychology; respiratory care therapy; science technologies related; secondary education; social sciences; social work; special education; sport and fitness administration/management; surgical technology.

Academics *Calendar:* semesters. *Degrees:* certificates, associate, bachelor's, and postbachelor's certificates. *Special study options:* academic remediation for entering students, adult/continuing education programs, advanced placement credit, cooperative education, distance learning, double majors, independent study, internships, off-campus study, part-time degree program, services for LD students, student-designed majors, study abroad, summer session for credit. *ROTC:* Air Force (c).

Library UC Clermont College Library with 1.4 million titles, an OPAC, a Web page.
Student Life *Housing:* college housing not available. *Activities and Organizations:* student-run newspaper, Active Minds, Art Collaborative, Education Club, Tribunal. *Campus security:* 24-hour emergency response devices, 24-hour patrols by trained security personnel. *Student services:* personal/psychological counseling.
Athletics *Intercollegiate sports:* baseball M, basketball M/W, cheerleading W, golf M, softball W, volleyball W.
Costs (2014–15) *Tuition:* state resident $2658 per term part-time; nonresident $6274 per term part-time. Full-time tuition and fees vary according to course load, degree level, program, and reciprocity agreements. Part-time tuition and fees vary according to course load, degree level, program, and reciprocity agreements. *Required fees:* $222 per semester hour part-time. *Payment plan:* installment. *Waivers:* senior citizens and employees or children of employees.
Applying *Options:* electronic application, deferred entrance. *Application fee:* $50. *Required:* high school transcript. *Application deadlines:* rolling (freshmen), rolling (transfers). *Notification:* continuous (freshmen), continuous (transfers).
Freshman Application Contact Mrs. Jamie Adkins, University Services Associate, University of Cincinnati Clermont College, 4200 Clermont College Drive, Batavia, OH 45103. *Phone:* 513-732-5294. *Toll-free phone:* 866-446-2822. *Fax:* 513-732-5303. *E-mail:* jamie.adkins@uc.edu.
Website: http://www.ucclermont.edu/.

Vatterott College
Broadview Heights, Ohio

Director of Admissions Mr. Jack Chalk, Director of Admissions, Vatterott College, 5025 East Royalton Road, Broadview Heights, OH 44147. *Phone:* 440-526-1660. *Toll-free phone:* 888-553-6627.
Website: http://www.vatterott.edu/.

Vet Tech Institute at Bradford School
Columbus, Ohio

- **Private** 2-year, founded 2005
- **Suburban** campus
- **Coed,** 156 undergraduate students
- 35% of applicants were admitted

Freshmen *Admission:* 556 applied, 193 admitted.
Majors Veterinary/animal health technology.
Academics *Calendar:* semesters. *Degree:* associate. *Special study options:* accelerated degree program, internships.
Freshman Application Contact Admissions Office, Vet Tech Institute at Bradford School, 2469 Stelzer Road, Columbus, OH 43219. *Phone:* 800-678-7981. *Toll-free phone:* 800-678-7981.
Website: http://columbus.vettechinstitute.edu/.

Virginia Marti College of Art and Design
Lakewood, Ohio

Freshman Application Contact Virginia Marti College of Art and Design, 11724 Detroit Avenue, PO Box 580, Lakewood, OH 44107-3002. *Phone:* 216-221-8584 Ext. 106.
Website: http://www.vmcad.edu/.

Washington State Community College
Marietta, Ohio

Freshman Application Contact Ms. Rebecca Peroni, Director of Admissions, Washington State Community College, 110 Colegate Drive, Marietta, OH 45750. *Phone:* 740-374-8716. *Fax:* 740-376-0257. *E-mail:* rperoni@wscc.edu.
Website: http://www.wscc.edu/.

Wright State University–Lake Campus
Celina, Ohio

- **State-supported** primarily 2-year, founded 1969, part of University System of Ohio
- **Rural** 173-acre campus
- **Endowment** $86.3 million
- **Coed,** 1,115 undergraduate students, 68% full-time, 53% women, 47% men

Undergraduates 761 full-time, 354 part-time. Students come from 10 states and territories; 4 other countries; 4% are from out of state; 3% Black or African American, non-Hispanic/Latino; 2% Hispanic/Latino; 0.8% Asian, non-Hispanic/Latino; 0.3% American Indian or Alaska Native, non-Hispanic/Latino; 2% Two or more races, non-Hispanic/Latino; 0.4% Race/ethnicity unknown; 2% international; 7% transferred in; 5% live on campus. *Retention:* 71% of full-time freshmen returned.
Freshmen *Admission:* 309 applied, 308 admitted, 235 enrolled. *Average high school GPA:* 3.05. *Test scores:* SAT critical reading scores over 500: 20%; SAT math scores over 500: 40%; SAT writing scores over 500: 20%; ACT scores over 18: 87%; SAT critical reading scores over 600: 20%; SAT math scores over 600: 40%; SAT writing scores over 600: 20%; ACT scores over 24: 27%; SAT math scores over 700: 20%; ACT scores over 30: 1%.
Faculty *Total:* 34. *Student/faculty ratio:* 27:1.
Majors Accounting; administrative assistant and secretarial science; agribusiness; biology/biological sciences; business administration and management; business/commerce; chemistry; criminology; early childhood education; elementary education; engineering; engineering technology; English; food service systems administration; geology/earth science; graphic communications related; graphic design; history; liberal arts and sciences/liberal studies; mass communication/media; mechanical engineering; mechanical engineering/mechanical technology; middle school education; psychology; social work; sociology; speech communication and rhetoric.
Academics *Calendar:* semesters. *Degrees:* certificates, associate, bachelor's, and master's. *Special study options:* academic remediation for entering students, accelerated degree program, advanced placement credit, cooperative education, distance learning, double majors, honors programs, independent study, internships, off-campus study, part-time degree program, services for LD students, student-designed majors, study abroad, summer session for credit. *ROTC:* Army (c), Air Force (c).
Library Wright State University, Lake Campus Learning Center plus 1 other with 1.3 million titles, 15,695 audiovisual materials, an OPAC, a Web page.
Student Life *Housing Options:* special housing for students with disabilities. Campus housing is leased by the school. *Activities and Organizations:* Circle K, Engineering Club, Business and Graphics Professionals. *Campus security:* 24-hour emergency response devices, WSU-Police Department presence, 40 hours per week. *Student services:* health clinic, personal/psychological counseling, legal services.
Athletics *Intercollegiate sports:* baseball M, basketball M/W.
Standardized Tests *Required:* SAT or ACT (for admission).
Costs (2014–15) *Tuition:* state resident $5842 full-time, $265 per credit hour part-time; nonresident $14,022 full-time, $641 per credit hour part-time. Full-time tuition and fees vary according to course load, location, and reciprocity agreements. Part-time tuition and fees vary according to course load, location, and reciprocity agreements. *Required fees:* $265 per credit hour part-time. *Room and board:* $7754; room only: $3160. Room and board charges vary according to board plan, housing facility, and location. *Payment plan:* installment. *Waivers:* senior citizens and employees or children of employees.
Applying *Options:* electronic application, early admission, deferred entrance. *Application fee:* $30. *Required:* high school transcript. *Recommended:* minimum 2.0 GPA. *Application deadlines:* rolling (freshmen), rolling (out-of-state freshmen), rolling (transfers). *Notification:* continuous (freshmen), continuous (out-of-state freshmen), continuous (transfers).
Freshman Application Contact Jill Puthoff, Admissions/Communications Coordinator, Wright State University–Lake Campus, 174 Dwyer Hall, Celina, OH 45822. *Phone:* 419-586-0363. *Toll-free phone:* 800-237-1477. *E-mail:* jill.puthoff@wright.edu.
Website: http://www.wright.edu/lake/.

Zane State College
Zanesville, Ohio

Director of Admissions Mr. Paul Young, Director of Admissions, Zane State College, 1555 Newark Road, Zanesville, OH 43701-2626. *Phone:* 740-454-2501 Ext. 1225. *Toll-free phone:* 800-686-8324. *E-mail:* pyoung@zanestate.edu.
Website: http://www.zanestate.edu/.

OKLAHOMA

Brown Mackie College–Oklahoma City
Oklahoma City, Oklahoma

- **Proprietary** primarily 2-year, part of Education Management Corporation
- **Coed**

Academics *Degrees:* associate and bachelor's.
Freshman Application Contact Brown Mackie College–Oklahoma City, 7101 Northwest Expressway, Suite 800, Oklahoma City, OK 73132. *Phone:* 405-621-8000. *Toll-free phone:* 888-229-3280.
Website: http://www.brownmackie.edu/oklahoma-city/.

Brown Mackie College–Tulsa
Tulsa, Oklahoma

- **Proprietary** primarily 2-year, part of Education Management Corporation
- **Coed**

Academics *Degrees:* diplomas, associate, and bachelor's.
Freshman Application Contact Brown Mackie College–Tulsa, 4608 South Garnett, Suite 110, Tulsa, OK 74146. *Phone:* 918-628-3700. *Toll-free phone:* 888-794-8411.
Website: http://www.brownmackie.edu/tulsa/.

Career Point College
Tulsa, Oklahoma

Admissions Office Contact Career Point College, 3138 South Garnett Road, Tulsa, OK 74145.
Website: http://www.careerpointcollege.edu/.

Carl Albert State College
Poteau, Oklahoma

- **State-supported** 2-year, founded 1934, part of Oklahoma State Regents for Higher Education
- **Small-town** 78-acre campus
- **Endowment** $5.7 million
- **Coed,** 2,460 undergraduate students, 56% full-time, 66% women, 34% men

Undergraduates 1,373 full-time, 1,087 part-time. Students come from 16 states and territories; 9 other countries; 12% live on campus.
Freshmen *Admission:* 733 applied, 733 admitted, 605 enrolled.
Faculty *Total:* 154, 33% full-time, 2% with terminal degrees. *Student/faculty ratio:* 16:1.
Majors Biology/biological sciences; business administration and management; business/commerce; child development; computer and information sciences; elementary education; engineering; engineering technologies and engineering related; English; film/cinema/video studies; fine arts related; foods, nutrition, and wellness; health professions related; health services/allied health/health sciences; hotel/motel administration; journalism; management information systems; mathematics; music related; physical education teaching and coaching; physical sciences; physical therapy technology; pre-law studies; radiologic technology/science; registered nursing/registered nurse; rhetoric and composition; secondary education; social sciences; telecommunications technology.
Academics *Calendar:* semesters. *Degree:* certificates and associate. *Special study options:* academic remediation for entering students, adult/continuing education programs, cooperative education, part-time degree program.
Library Joe E. White Library with 27,200 titles, an OPAC.
Student Life *Housing Options:* men-only, women-only. Campus housing is university owned. *Activities and Organizations:* drama/theater group, student-run newspaper, radio station, choral group, Student Government Association, Phi Theta Kappa, Baptist Student Union, BACCHUS, Student Physical Therapist Assistant Association. *Campus security:* security guards. *Student services:* health clinic, personal/psychological counseling.
Athletics Member NJCAA. *Intercollegiate sports:* baseball M, basketball M(s)/W(s), softball M. *Intramural sports:* tennis M/W, volleyball M/W, weight lifting M.
Costs (2014–15) *Tuition:* state resident $1401 full-time, $100 per credit hour part-time; nonresident $2803 full-time, $200 per credit hour part-time. Full-time tuition and fees vary according to course load. Part-time tuition and fees vary according to course load. *Required fees:* $930 full-time, $500 per term part-time. *Room and board:* $2110; room only: $1600. Room and board charges vary according to board plan. *Payment plan:* installment. *Waivers:* employees or children of employees.
Financial Aid Of all full-time matriculated undergraduates who enrolled in 2013, 112 Federal Work-Study jobs (averaging $2100).
Applying *Required:* high school transcript. *Application deadlines:* 8/13 (freshmen), 8/15 (transfers). *Notification:* continuous (freshmen), continuous (transfers).
Freshman Application Contact Admission Clerk, Carl Albert State College, 1507 South McKenna, Poteau, OK 74953-5208. *Phone:* 918-647-1300. *Fax:* 918-647-1306.
Website: http://www.carlalbert.edu/.

Clary Sage College
Tulsa, Oklahoma

- **Proprietary** 2-year, part of Dental Directions, Inc.
- **Urban** 6-acre campus with easy access to Tulsa
- **Coed, primarily women,** 312 undergraduate students, 100% full-time, 98% women, 2% men

Undergraduates 312 full-time. Students come from 3 states and territories; 1% are from out of state; 18% Black or African American, non-Hispanic/Latino; 8% Hispanic/Latino; 2% Asian, non-Hispanic/Latino; 12% American Indian or Alaska Native, non-Hispanic/Latino; 4% Two or more races, non-Hispanic/Latino; 4% Race/ethnicity unknown.
Freshmen *Admission:* 107 enrolled.
Faculty *Total:* 32, 100% full-time. *Student/faculty ratio:* 10:1.
Majors Cosmetology; fashion/apparel design; interior design.
Academics *Calendar:* continuous. *Degree:* diplomas and associate. *Special study options:* adult/continuing education programs, distance learning, internships, part-time degree program.
Student Life *Housing:* college housing not available. *Activities and Organizations:* Student Ambassadors. *Campus security:* security guard during hours of operation. *Student services:* personal/psychological counseling.
Applying *Options:* electronic application. *Application fee:* $100. *Required:* essay or personal statement, high school transcript, interview. *Application deadlines:* rolling (freshmen), rolling (out-of-state freshmen), rolling (transfers). *Notification:* continuous (freshmen), continuous (out-of-state freshmen), continuous (transfers).
Freshman Application Contact Ms. Teresa Knox, Chief Executive Officer, Clary Sage College, 3131 South Sheridan, Tulsa, OK 74145. *Phone:* 918-610-0027 Ext. 2005. *E-mail:* tknox@communitycarecollege.edu.
Website: http://www.clarysagecollege.com/.

College of the Muscogee Nation
Okmulgee, Oklahoma

Admissions Office Contact College of the Muscogee Nation, 2170 Raven Circle, Okmulgee, OK 74447-0917.
Website: http://www.mvsktc.org/.

Community Care College
Tulsa, Oklahoma

- **Proprietary** 2-year, founded 1995, part of Dental Directions, Inc.
- **Urban** 6-acre campus
- **Coed, primarily women,** 587 undergraduate students, 100% full-time, 90% women, 10% men

Undergraduates 587 full-time. Students come from 14 states and territories; 15% are from out of state; 18% Black or African American, non-Hispanic/Latino; 5% Hispanic/Latino; 2% Asian, non-Hispanic/Latino; 13% American Indian or Alaska Native, non-Hispanic/Latino; 1% Two or more races, non-Hispanic/Latino; 13% Race/ethnicity unknown.
Freshmen *Admission:* 175 enrolled.
Faculty *Total:* 37, 100% full-time. *Student/faculty ratio:* 29:1.
Majors Accounting technology and bookkeeping; business administration, management and operations related; dental assisting; early childhood education; health and physical education/fitness; health/health-care administration; legal assistant/paralegal; massage therapy; medical/clinical assistant; medical insurance coding; pharmacy technician; surgical technology; veterinary/animal health technology.
Academics *Calendar:* continuous. *Degree:* diplomas and associate. *Special study options:* adult/continuing education programs, distance learning, independent study, internships, services for LD students.
Student Life *Housing:* college housing not available. *Activities and Organizations:* Student Ambassadors. *Campus security:* campus security personnel are available during school hours.
Applying *Options:* electronic application. *Application fee:* $100. *Required:* essay or personal statement, high school transcript, interview. *Required for some:* 1 letter of recommendation. *Application deadlines:* rolling (freshmen),

rolling (out-of-state freshmen). *Notification:* continuous (freshmen), continuous (out-of-state freshmen).
Freshman Application Contact Ms. Teresa L. Knox, Chief Executive Officer, Community Care College, 4242 South Sheridan, Tulsa, OK 74145. *Phone:* 918-610-0027 Ext. 2005. *Fax:* 918-610-0029. *E-mail:* tknox@communitycarecollege.edu.
Website: http://www.communitycarecollege.edu/.

Connors State College
Warner, Oklahoma

Freshman Application Contact Ms. Sonya Baker, Registrar, Connors State College, Route 1 Box 1000, Warner, OK 74469-9700. *Phone:* 918-463-6233. *Website:* http://www.connorsstate.edu/.

Eastern Oklahoma State College
Wilburton, Oklahoma

Freshman Application Contact Ms. Leah McLaughlin, Director of Admissions, Eastern Oklahoma State College, 1301 West Main, Wilburton, OK 74578-4999. *Phone:* 918-465-1811. *Toll-free phone:* 855-534-3672. *Fax:* 918-465-2431. *E-mail:* lmiller@eosc.edu.
Website: http://www.eosc.edu/.

Heritage College
Oklahoma City, Oklahoma

Freshman Application Contact Admissions Office, Heritage College, 7202 I-35 Services Road, Suite 7118, Oklahoma City, OK 73149. *Phone:* 405-631-3399. *Toll-free phone:* 888-334-7339. *E-mail:* info@heritage-education.com. *Website:* http://www.heritage-education.com/.

ITT Technical Institute
Tulsa, Oklahoma

- **Proprietary** primarily 2-year, founded 2005
- **Coed**

Academics *Calendar:* quarters. *Degrees:* associate and bachelor's.
Freshman Application Contact Director of Recruitment, ITT Technical Institute, 4500 South 129th East Avenue, Suite 152, Tulsa, OK 74134. *Phone:* 918-615-3900. *Toll-free phone:* 800-514-6535.
Website: http://www.itt-tech.edu/.

Murray State College
Tishomingo, Oklahoma

Freshman Application Contact Murray State College, One Murray Campus, Tishomingo, OK 73460-3130. *Phone:* 580-371-2371 Ext. 171.
Website: http://www.mscok.edu/.

Northeastern Oklahoma Agricultural and Mechanical College
Miami, Oklahoma

Freshman Application Contact Amy Ishmael, Vice President for Enrollment Management, Northeastern Oklahoma Agricultural and Mechanical College, 200 I Street, NE, Miami, OK 74354-6434. *Phone:* 918-540-6212. *Toll-free phone:* 800-464-6636. *Fax:* 918-540-6946. *E-mail:* neoadmission@neo.edu. *Website:* http://www.neo.edu/.

Northern Oklahoma College
Tonkawa, Oklahoma

Freshman Application Contact Ms. Sheri Snyder, Director of College Relations, Northern Oklahoma College, 1220 East Grand Avenue, PO Box 310, Tonkawa, OK 74653-0310. *Phone:* 580-628-6290.
Website: http://www.noc.edu/.

Oklahoma City Community College
Oklahoma City, Oklahoma

- **State-supported** 2-year, founded 1969, part of Oklahoma State Regents for Higher Education
- **Urban** 143-acre campus with easy access to Oklahoma City
- **Endowment** $296,574
- **Coed,** 13,391 undergraduate students, 35% full-time, 58% women, 42% men

Undergraduates 4,666 full-time, 8,725 part-time. Students come from 22 states and territories; 58 other countries; 6% are from out of state; 10% Black or African American, non-Hispanic/Latino; 14% Hispanic/Latino; 5% Asian, non-Hispanic/Latino; 0.3% Native Hawaiian or other Pacific Islander, non-Hispanic/Latino; 4% American Indian or Alaska Native, non-Hispanic/Latino; 5% Two or more races, non-Hispanic/Latino; 7% Race/ethnicity unknown; 3% international.
Freshmen *Admission:* 4,574 applied, 4,574 admitted, 2,661 enrolled. *Test scores:* ACT scores over 18: 78%; ACT scores over 24: 25%; ACT scores over 30: 3%.
Faculty *Total:* 501, 28% full-time, 14% with terminal degrees. *Student/faculty ratio:* 27:1.
Majors Accounting; administrative assistant and secretarial science; airframe mechanics and aircraft maintenance technology; American government and politics; animation, interactive technology, video graphics and special effects; architectural drafting and CAD/CADD; art; automobile/automotive mechanics technology; automotive engineering technology; banking and financial support services; biology/biological sciences; biotechnology; broadcast journalism; business administration and management; business/commerce; chemistry; child development; cinematography and film/video production; commercial and advertising art; computer engineering technology; computer science; computer systems analysis; computer systems networking and telecommunications; cyber/electronic operations and warfare; design and applied arts related; design and visual communications; diagnostic medical sonography and ultrasound technology; diesel mechanics technology; digital communication and media/multimedia; drafting and design technology; dramatic/theater arts; electrical, electronic and communications engineering technology; elementary education; emergency medical technology (EMT paramedic); engineering technologies and engineering related; finance; fine/studio arts; foreign languages and literatures; game and interactive media design; general studies; geographic information science and cartography; graphic communications; health information/medical records administration; history; humanities; legal administrative assistant/secretary; liberal arts and sciences/liberal studies; literature; management information systems; manufacturing engineering technology; mass communication/media; mathematics; medical/clinical assistant; multi/interdisciplinary studies related; music; occupational therapy; orthotics/prosthetics; philosophy; photographic and film/video technology; physical therapy; physics; political science and government; pre-engineering; psychology; public relations, advertising, and applied communication; registered nursing/registered nurse; respiratory care therapy; sociology; speech-language pathology assistant; surgical technology; system, networking, and LAN/WAN management; web/multimedia management and webmaster.
Academics *Calendar:* semesters. *Degree:* certificates and associate. *Special study options:* academic remediation for entering students, accelerated degree program, advanced placement credit, cooperative education, distance learning, double majors, English as a second language, honors programs, independent study, internships, part-time degree program, services for LD students, student-designed majors, summer session for credit.
Library Keith Leftwich Memorial Library with 89,441 titles, 25,919 audiovisual materials, an OPAC, a Web page.
Student Life *Housing:* college housing not available. *Activities and Organizations:* drama/theater group, student-run newspaper, choral group, Health Professions Association, Black Student Association, Nursing Student Association, Hispanic Organization Promoting Education (H.O.P.E), The Gamers Guild. *Campus security:* 24-hour emergency response devices and patrols, late-night transport/escort service. *Student services:* personal/psychological counseling.
Athletics *Intramural sports:* badminton M/W, basketball M/W, football M/W, soccer M/W, table tennis M/W, ultimate Frisbee M/W, volleyball M/W, weight lifting M/W.
Standardized Tests *Required for some:* ACT (for admission). *Recommended:* ACT (for admission), SAT or ACT (for admission).
Costs (2015–16) *One-time required fee:* $25. *Tuition:* state resident $2477 full-time, $83 per credit hour part-time; nonresident $7511 full-time, $250 per credit hour part-time. Full-time tuition and fees vary according to class time and course level. Part-time tuition and fees vary according to class time and course level. *Required fees:* $764 full-time, $25 per credit hour part-time. *Payment plan:* installment. *Waivers:* senior citizens and employees or children of employees.

Financial Aid Of all full-time matriculated undergraduates who enrolled in 2012, 4,062 applied for aid, 3,608 were judged to have need, 1,576 had their need fully met. 315 Federal Work-Study jobs (averaging $4800). 240 state and other part-time jobs (averaging $2502). In 2012, 321 non-need-based awards were made. *Average percent of need met:* 70%. *Average financial aid package:* $7351. *Average need-based loan:* $2801. *Average need-based gift aid:* $4769. *Average non-need-based aid:* $589.

Applying *Options:* electronic application. *Application fee:* $25. *Required:* Proof of English Proficiency, All college and university transcripts. *Required for some:* high school transcript. *Application deadlines:* rolling (freshmen), rolling (out-of-state freshmen), rolling (transfers). *Notification:* continuous (freshmen), continuous (out-of-state freshmen), continuous (transfers).

Freshman Application Contact Mr. Jon Horinek, Director of Recruitment and Admissions, Oklahoma City Community College, 7777 South May Avenue, Oklahoma City, OK 73159. *Phone:* 405-682-7743. *Fax:* 405-682-7817. *E-mail:* jhorinek@occc.edu.
Website: http://www.occc.edu/.

Oklahoma State University Institute of Technology
Okmulgee, Oklahoma

- **State-supported** primarily 2-year, founded 1946, part of Oklahoma State University
- **Small-town** 160-acre campus with easy access to Tulsa
- **Endowment** $7.3 million
- **Coed,** 2,624 undergraduate students, 73% full-time, 37% women, 63% men

Undergraduates 1,910 full-time, 714 part-time. Students come from 30 states and territories; 13 other countries; 12% are from out of state; 5% Black or African American, non-Hispanic/Latino; 6% Hispanic/Latino; 1% Asian, non-Hispanic/Latino; 0.2% Native Hawaiian or other Pacific Islander, non-Hispanic/Latino; 18% American Indian or Alaska Native, non-Hispanic/Latino; 5% Two or more races, non-Hispanic/Latino; 4% Race/ethnicity unknown; 0.7% international; 8% transferred in; 28% live on campus. *Retention:* 56% of full-time freshmen returned.

Freshmen *Admission:* 1,805 applied, 843 admitted, 490 enrolled. *Average high school GPA:* 2.93. *Test scores:* ACT scores over 18: 57%; ACT scores over 24: 9%; ACT scores over 30: 1%.

Faculty *Total:* 182, 67% full-time, 5% with terminal degrees. *Student/faculty ratio:* 15:1.

Majors Autobody/collision and repair technology; automotive engineering technology; business/commerce; casino management; civil engineering technology; computer and information systems security; construction engineering technology; culinary arts related; diesel mechanics technology; education (multiple levels); engineering technology; graphic design; health services/allied health/health sciences; heating, air conditioning, ventilation and refrigeration maintenance technology; information technology; instrumentation technology; intermedia/multimedia; mechanical engineering/mechanical technology; mechanic and repair technologies related; multi/interdisciplinary studies related; office occupations and clerical services; orthotics/prosthetics; petroleum technology; photography; registered nursing/registered nurse.

Academics *Calendar:* trimesters. *Degrees:* associate and bachelor's. *Special study options:* academic remediation for entering students, adult/continuing education programs, advanced placement credit, distance learning, double majors, independent study, internships, part-time degree program, services for LD students, summer session for credit.

Library Oklahoma State University Institute of Technology Library with 8,074 titles, 1,401 audiovisual materials, an OPAC, a Web page.

Student Life *Housing:* on-campus residence required for freshman year. *Options:* coed, men-only. Campus housing is university owned. Freshman applicants given priority for college housing. *Activities and Organizations:* Phi Theta Kappa, Future Art Directors Club, Air Conditioning and Refrigeration Club, Future Chefs Association Club, Instrumentation, Society and Automation Club. *Campus security:* 24-hour emergency response devices and patrols, late-night transport/escort service, controlled dormitory access. *Student services:* health clinic, personal/psychological counseling.

Athletics *Intramural sports:* basketball M/W, football M/W, racquetball M/W, soccer M/W, softball M/W, table tennis M/W, volleyball M/W.

Standardized Tests *Required for some:* SAT or ACT (for admission). *Recommended:* ACT (for admission).

Costs (2015–16) *Tuition:* state resident $3465 full-time, $116 per credit hour part-time; nonresident $9075 full-time, $303 per credit hour part-time. Full-time tuition and fees vary according to course level, course load, location, program, and student level. Part-time tuition and fees vary according to course level, course load, location, program, and student level. *Required fees:* $1140 full-time, $38 per credit hour part-time. *Room and board:* $5902. Room and board charges vary according to board plan and housing facility. *Payment plan:* installment. *Waivers:* senior citizens and employees or children of employees.

Applying *Options:* deferred entrance. *Required:* high school transcript. *Application deadlines:* rolling (freshmen), rolling (out-of-state freshmen), rolling (transfers).

Freshman Application Contact Chenoa Worthington, Assistant Registrar, Oklahoma State University Institute of Technology, 1801 E 4th St, Okmulgee, OK 74447. *Phone:* 918-293-5274. *Toll-free phone:* 800-722-4471. *Fax:* 918-293-4643. *E-mail:* chenoa.worthington@okstate.edu.
Website: http://www.osuit.edu/.

Oklahoma State University, Oklahoma City
Oklahoma City, Oklahoma

- **State-supported** primarily 2-year, founded 1961, part of Oklahoma State University
- **Urban** 110-acre campus
- **Coed,** 6,712 undergraduate students, 32% full-time, 61% women, 39% men

Undergraduates 2,175 full-time, 4,537 part-time. Students come from 25 states and territories; 3% are from out of state; 15% Black or African American, non-Hispanic/Latino; 10% Hispanic/Latino; 3% Asian, non-Hispanic/Latino; 4% American Indian or Alaska Native, non-Hispanic/Latino; 9% Two or more races, non-Hispanic/Latino; 4% Race/ethnicity unknown; 12% transferred in.

Freshmen *Admission:* 952 admitted, 952 enrolled.

Faculty *Total:* 438, 20% full-time. *Student/faculty ratio:* 19:1.

Majors Accounting; American Sign Language (ASL); architectural engineering technology; art; building/home/construction inspection; business administration and management; civil engineering technology; construction engineering technology; construction management; construction trades; criminal justice/police science; drafting and design technology; early childhood education; economics; electrical and power transmission installation; electrical, electronic and communications engineering technology; electrocardiograph technology; emergency medical technology (EMT paramedic); engineering technology; fire prevention and safety technology; fire science/firefighting; general studies; health/health-care administration; history; horticultural science; humanities; human services; illustration; information science/studies; information technology; language interpretation and translation; occupational safety and health technology; physics; pre-engineering; prenursing studies; professional, technical, business, and scientific writing; psychology; public administration and social service professions related; radiologic technology/science; registered nursing/registered nurse; sign language interpretation and translation; substance abuse/addiction counseling; surveying technology; turf and turfgrass management; veterinary/animal health technology; web page, digital/multimedia and information resources design.

Academics *Calendar:* semesters. *Degrees:* certificates, associate, and bachelor's. *Special study options:* academic remediation for entering students, advanced placement credit, cooperative education, distance learning, double majors, honors programs, independent study, part-time degree program, services for LD students, study abroad, summer session for credit.

Library Oklahoma State University-Oklahoma City Campus Library with an OPAC, a Web page.

Student Life *Housing:* college housing not available. *Activities and Organizations:* Student Government Association, Go Green, Wind Energy Student Association, Hispanic Student Association, OSU-OKC Chapter of the OK Student Nurse Association. *Campus security:* 24-hour patrols, late-night transport/escort service.

Costs (2015–16) *Tuition:* state resident $2770 full-time, $115 per credit hour part-time; nonresident $7630 full-time, $318 per credit hour part-time. Full-time tuition and fees vary according to course level, degree level, program, and student level. Part-time tuition and fees vary according to course level, degree level, program, and student level. No tuition increase for student's term of enrollment. *Required fees:* $89 full-time, $12 per term part-time, $65 per year part-time. *Payment plans:* tuition prepayment, installment. *Waivers:* senior citizens and employees or children of employees.

Applying *Options:* electronic application, early admission. *Required:* high school transcript. *Application deadlines:* rolling (freshmen), rolling (transfers). *Notification:* continuous (freshmen), continuous (transfers).

Freshman Application Contact Mr. Kyle Williams, Director, Enrollment Management, Oklahoma State University, Oklahoma City, 900 North Portland Avenue, AD202, Oklahoma City, OK 73107. *Phone:* 405-945-9152. *Toll-free phone:* 800-560-4099. *E-mail:* wilkylw@osuokc.edu.
Website: http://www.osuokc.edu/.

Oklahoma Technical College
Tulsa, Oklahoma

- **Proprietary** 2-year, part of Dental Directions, Inc.
- **Urban** 9-acre campus with easy access to Tulsa
- **Coed,** 182 undergraduate students, 100% full-time, 13% women, 87% men

Undergraduates 182 full-time. Students come from 2 states and territories; 1% are from out of state; 26% Black or African American, non-Hispanic/Latino; 7% Hispanic/Latino; 11% American Indian or Alaska Native, non-Hispanic/Latino; 0.5% Two or more races, non-Hispanic/Latino; 5% Race/ethnicity unknown.
Freshmen *Admission:* 58 enrolled.
Faculty *Total:* 11, 100% full-time. *Student/faculty ratio:* 17:1.
Majors Automobile/automotive mechanics technology; diesel mechanics technology; heating, ventilation, air conditioning and refrigeration engineering technology; welding technology.
Academics *Degree:* diplomas and associate. *Special study options:* adult/continuing education programs, distance learning, internships, services for LD students.
Student Life *Housing:* college housing not available. *Activities and Organizations:* Student Ambassadors. *Campus security:* Campus security is available during school hours. *Student services:* personal/psychological counseling.
Applying *Options:* electronic application. *Application fee:* $100. *Required:* essay or personal statement, high school transcript, interview. *Application deadlines:* rolling (freshmen), rolling (out-of-state freshmen), rolling (transfers). *Notification:* continuous (freshmen), continuous (out-of-state freshmen), continuous (transfers).
Freshman Application Contact Ms. Teresa L. Knox, Chief Executive Officer, Oklahoma Technical College, 4242 South Sheridan, Tulsa, OK 74145. *Phone:* 918-610-0027 Ext. 2005. *Fax:* 918-610-0029. *E-mail:* tknox@communitycarecollege.edu.
Website: http://www.oklahomatechnicalcollege.com/.

Platt College
Moore, Oklahoma

Admissions Office Contact Platt College, 201 North Eastern Avenue, Moore, OK 73160.
Website: http://www.plattcolleges.edu/.

Platt College
Oklahoma City, Oklahoma

Freshman Application Contact Ms. Kim Lamb, Director of Admissions, Platt College, 309 South Ann Arbor, Oklahoma City, OK 73128. *Phone:* 405-946-7799. *Fax:* 405-943-2150. *E-mail:* klamb@plattcollege.org.
Website: http://www.plattcolleges.edu/.

Platt College
Tulsa, Oklahoma

Director of Admissions Mrs. Susan Rone, Director, Platt College, 3801 South Sheridan Road, Tulsa, OK 74145-111. *Phone:* 918-663-9000. *Fax:* 918-622-1240. *E-mail:* susanr@plattcollege.org.
Website: http://www.plattcolleges.edu/.

Redlands Community College
El Reno, Oklahoma

Freshman Application Contact Redlands Community College, 1300 South Country Club Road, El Reno, OK 73036-5304. *Phone:* 405-262-2552 Ext. 1263. *Toll-free phone:* 866-415-6367.
Website: http://www.redlandscc.edu/.

Rose State College
Midwest City, Oklahoma

Freshman Application Contact Ms. Mechelle Aitson-Roessler, Registrar and Director of Admissions, Rose State College, 6420 Southeast 15th Street, Midwest City, OK 73110-2799. *Phone:* 405-733-7308. *Toll-free phone:* 866-621-0987. *Fax:* 405-736-0203. *E-mail:* maitson@ms.rose.cc.ok.us.
Website: http://www.rose.edu/.

Seminole State College
Seminole, Oklahoma

- **State-supported** 2-year, founded 1931, part of Oklahoma State Regents for Higher Education
- **Small-town** 40-acre campus with easy access to Oklahoma City
- **Endowment** $3.1 million
- **Coed,** 1,895 undergraduate students, 56% full-time, 65% women, 35% men

Undergraduates 1,057 full-time, 838 part-time. Students come from 16 states and territories; 9 other countries; 4% are from out of state; 6% Black or African American, non-Hispanic/Latino; 3% Hispanic/Latino; 0.8% Asian, non-Hispanic/Latino; 0.2% Native Hawaiian or other Pacific Islander, non-Hispanic/Latino; 25% American Indian or Alaska Native, non-Hispanic/Latino; 0.5% Race/ethnicity unknown; 0.7% international; 5% transferred in; 8% live on campus.
Freshmen *Admission:* 601 applied, 601 admitted, 533 enrolled. *Test scores:* ACT scores over 18: 77%; ACT scores over 24: 18%; ACT scores over 30: 1%.
Faculty *Total:* 89, 43% full-time, 7% with terminal degrees. *Student/faculty ratio:* 25:1.
Majors Accounting; art; behavioral sciences; biological and biomedical sciences related; biology/biological sciences; business administration and management; business/commerce; child development; clinical/medical laboratory technology; computer science; criminal justice/law enforcement administration; criminal justice/police science; elementary education; engineering; English; fine arts related; general studies; humanities; liberal arts and sciences/liberal studies; management information systems and services related; mathematics; physical education teaching and coaching; physical sciences; pre-engineering; psychology related; registered nursing/registered nurse; social sciences.
Academics *Calendar:* semesters. *Degree:* diplomas and associate. *Special study options:* academic remediation for entering students, adult/continuing education programs, advanced placement credit, cooperative education, distance learning, double majors, English as a second language, independent study, off-campus study, part-time degree program, services for LD students, study abroad, summer session for credit.
Library Boren Library plus 1 other with 27,507 titles, 651 audiovisual materials, an OPAC, a Web page.
Student Life *Housing Options:* coed. Campus housing is university owned. *Activities and Organizations:* Student Government Association, Native American Student Association, Psi Beta Honor Society, Student Nurses Association, Phi Theta Kappa. *Campus security:* 24-hour emergency response devices and patrols, student patrols, late-night transport/escort service, controlled dormitory access.
Athletics Member NJCAA. *Intercollegiate sports:* baseball M(s), basketball M(s)/W(s), cheerleading W, golf M(s)/W(s), softball W(s), tennis M(s)/W(s), volleyball W(s).
Standardized Tests *Required for some:* ACT Compass if no ACT scores. *Recommended:* ACT (for admission).
Costs (2015–16) *One-time required fee:* $15. *Tuition:* state resident $2385 full-time, $80 per credit hour part-time; nonresident $7305 full-time, $244 per credit hour part-time. Full-time tuition and fees vary according to location and program. Part-time tuition and fees vary according to location and program. *Required fees:* $1245 full-time, $42 per credit hour part-time. *Room and board:* $6670; room only: $3900. *Payment plans:* installment, deferred payment. *Waivers:* senior citizens and employees or children of employees.
Financial Aid Of all full-time matriculated undergraduates who enrolled in 2012, 14 Federal Work-Study jobs (averaging $2750).
Applying *Options:* early admission, deferred entrance. *Application fee:* $15. *Required:* high school transcript. *Application deadlines:* rolling (freshmen), rolling (transfers). *Notification:* continuous (freshmen), continuous (transfers).
Freshman Application Contact Mrs. Corey Quiett, Registrar, Seminole State College, PO Box 351, 2701 Boren Boulevard, Seminole, OK 74818-0351. *Phone:* 405-382-9501. *Fax:* 405-382-9524. *E-mail:* c.quiett@sscok.edu.
Website: http://www.sscok.edu/.

Southwestern Oklahoma State University at Sayre
Sayre, Oklahoma

Freshman Application Contact Ms. Kim Seymour, Registrar, Southwestern Oklahoma State University at Sayre, 409 East Mississippi Avenue, Sayre, OK 73662. *Phone:* 580-928-5533 Ext. 101. *Fax:* 580-928-1140. *E-mail:* kim.seymour@swosu.edu.
Website: http://www.swosu.edu/sayre/.

Spartan College of Aeronautics and Technology
Tulsa, Oklahoma

Freshman Application Contact Mr. Mark Fowler, Vice President of Student Records and Finance, Spartan College of Aeronautics and Technology, 8820 East Pine Street, PO Box 582833, Tulsa, OK 74158-2833. *Phone:* 918-836-6886. *Toll-free phone:* 800-331-1204 (in-state); 800-331-124 (out-of-state). *Website:* http://www.spartan.edu/.

Tulsa Community College
Tulsa, Oklahoma

- **State-supported** 2-year, founded 1968, part of Oklahoma State Regents for Higher Education
- **Urban** 160-acre campus
- **Endowment** $4.8 million
- **Coed,** 17,253 undergraduate students, 35% full-time, 60% women, 40% men

Undergraduates 6,006 full-time, 11,247 part-time. 0.4% are from out of state; 9% Black or African American, non-Hispanic/Latino; 7% Hispanic/Latino; 4% Asian, non-Hispanic/Latino; 0.1% Native Hawaiian or other Pacific Islander, non-Hispanic/Latino; 8% American Indian or Alaska Native, non-Hispanic/Latino; 8% Two or more races, non-Hispanic/Latino; 3% Race/ethnicity unknown; 2% international; 3% transferred in.

Freshmen *Admission:* 3,538 enrolled. *Average high school GPA:* 2.95. *Test scores:* ACT scores over 18: 76%; ACT scores over 24: 21%; ACT scores over 30: 1%.

Faculty *Total:* 962, 32% full-time, 7% with terminal degrees. *Student/faculty ratio:* 19:1.

Majors Accounting technology and bookkeeping; aeronautical/aerospace engineering technology; air traffic control; applied horticulture/horticulture operations; biotechnology; business administration and management; business/commerce; business, management, and marketing related; child development; clinical/medical laboratory technology; communication; computer and information sciences and support services related; computer and information sciences related; computer installation and repair technology; computer science; criminal justice/police science; dental hygiene; diagnostic medical sonography and ultrasound technology; digital communication and media/multimedia; dramatic/theater arts; education; electrical, electronic and communications engineering technology; engineering-related technologies; environmental science; fine/studio arts; fire services administration; foreign languages related; general studies; graphic and printing equipment operation/production; health information/medical records technology; health/medical preparatory programs related; human resources management; interior design; international business/trade/commerce; legal assistant/paralegal; marketing/marketing management; mathematics; medical radiologic technology; multi/interdisciplinary studies related; music; nutrition sciences; occupational therapy; physical sciences; physical therapy technology; pre-engineering; prenursing studies; pre-pharmacy studies; registered nursing/registered nurse; respiratory care therapy; sign language interpretation and translation; social sciences; social work; sport and fitness administration/management; surgical technology; veterinary/animal health technology.

Academics *Calendar:* semesters. *Degree:* certificates and associate. *Special study options:* academic remediation for entering students, accelerated degree program, adult/continuing education programs, advanced placement credit, cooperative education, distance learning, English as a second language, freshman honors college, honors programs, independent study, internships, off-campus study, part-time degree program, services for LD students, student-designed majors, study abroad, summer session for credit.

Library 85,805 titles, 3,979 audiovisual materials, an OPAC, a Web page.

Student Life *Housing:* college housing not available. *Activities and Organizations:* drama/theater group, student-run newspaper, radio station, choral group. *Campus security:* 24-hour emergency response devices and patrols, student patrols, late-night transport/escort service. *Student services:* health clinic, personal/psychological counseling, women's center.

Athletics *Intramural sports:* basketball M/W, football M/W, soccer M/W, softball M/W, volleyball M/W.

Costs (2014–15) *Tuition:* state resident $3510 full-time, $87 per credit hour part-time; nonresident $9497 full-time, $287 per credit hour part-time. *Required fees:* $894 full-time, $29 per credit hour part-time, $5 per term part-time. *Payment plan:* installment. *Waivers:* senior citizens and employees or children of employees.

Financial Aid Of all full-time matriculated undergraduates who enrolled in 2014, 4,945 applied for aid, 3,806 were judged to have need, 437 had their need fully met. In 2014, 540 non-need-based awards were made. *Average percent of need met:* 74%. *Average financial aid package:* $4326. *Average need-based loan:* $1803. *Average need-based gift aid:* $2827. *Average non-need-based aid:* $1518.

Applying *Options:* electronic application, early admission. *Application fee:* $20. *Required:* high school transcript. *Application deadlines:* rolling (freshmen), rolling (transfers).

Freshman Application Contact Ms. Traci Heck, Dean of Enrollment Management, Tulsa Community College, 6111 East Skelly Drive, Tulsa, OK 74135. *Phone:* 918-595-3411. *E-mail:* traci.heck@tulsacc.edu. *Website:* http://www.tulsacc.edu/.

Tulsa Welding School
Tulsa, Oklahoma

Freshman Application Contact Mrs. Debbie Renee Burke, Vice President/Executive Director, Tulsa Welding School, 2545 East 11th Street, Tulsa, OK 74104. *Phone:* 918-587-6789 Ext. 2258. *Toll-free phone:* 888-765-5555. *Fax:* 918-295-6812. *E-mail:* dburke@twsweld.com. *Website:* http://www.weldingschool.com/.

Vatterott College
Tulsa, Oklahoma

Freshman Application Contact Mr. Terry Queeno, Campus Director, Vatterott College, 4343 South 118th East Avenue, Suite A, Tulsa, OK 74146. *Phone:* 918-836-6656. *Toll-free phone:* 888-553-6627. *Fax:* 918-836-9698. *E-mail:* tulsa@vatterott-college.edu. *Website:* http://www.vatterott.edu/.

Vatterott College
Warr Acres, Oklahoma

Freshman Application Contact Mr. Mark Hybers, Director of Admissions, Vatterott College, Oklahoma City, OK 73127. *Phone:* 405-945-0088 Ext. 4416. *Toll-free phone:* 888-553-6627. *Fax:* 405-945-0788. *E-mail:* mark.hybers@vatterott-college.edu. *Website:* http://www.vatterott.edu/.

Virginia College in Tulsa
Tulsa, Oklahoma

Admissions Office Contact Virginia College in Tulsa, 5124 South Peoria Avenue, Tulsa, OK 74105. *Website:* http://www.vc.edu/.

Western Oklahoma State College
Altus, Oklahoma

- **State-supported** 2-year, founded 1926, part of Oklahoma State Regents for Higher Education
- **Rural** 142-acre campus
- **Endowment** $5.4 million
- **Coed**

Undergraduates 675 full-time, 1,015 part-time. Students come from 6 other countries; 12% are from out of state; 10% Black or African American, non-Hispanic/Latino; 16% Hispanic/Latino; 0.9% Asian, non-Hispanic/Latino; 0.2% Native Hawaiian or other Pacific Islander, non-Hispanic/Latino; 2% American Indian or Alaska Native, non-Hispanic/Latino; 8% Two or more races, non-Hispanic/Latino; 9% Race/ethnicity unknown; 1% international; 48% transferred in; 6% live on campus. *Retention:* 49% of full-time freshmen returned.

Faculty *Student/faculty ratio:* 19:1.

Academics *Calendar:* semesters. *Degree:* certificates and associate. *Special study options:* academic remediation for entering students, adult/continuing education programs, advanced placement credit, distance learning, English as a second language, honors programs, independent study, off-campus study, part-time degree program, services for LD students, student-designed majors, summer session for credit.

Student Life *Campus security:* 24-hour emergency response devices, trained security personnel 8:00 AM - 10:00 PM M-F.

Athletics Member NJCAA.

Standardized Tests *Required for some:* ACT (for admission).

Costs (2014–15) *Tuition:* state resident $2118 full-time, $71 per credit part-time; nonresident $6473 full-time, $216 per credit part-time. *Required fees:* $1013 full-time, $34 per credit part-time. *Room and board:* $1900.

Financial Aid Of all full-time matriculated undergraduates who enrolled in 2013, 56 Federal Work-Study jobs (averaging $2700).

Applying *Options:* electronic application, early admission. *Application fee:* $15. *Required:* high school transcript.
Freshman Application Contact Dean Chad E. Wiginton, Dean of Student Support Services, Western Oklahoma State College, 2801 North Main, Altus, OK 73521. *Phone:* 580-477-7918. *Fax:* 580-477-7716. *E-mail:* chad.wiginton@wosc.edu.
Website: http://www.wosc.edu/.

Wright Career College
Oklahoma City, Oklahoma

- **Proprietary** primarily 2-year
- **Suburban** campus with easy access to Oklahoma City
- **Coed**

Undergraduates 180 full-time, 74 part-time. Students come from 2 states and territories; 44% Black or African American, non-Hispanic/Latino; 9% Hispanic/Latino; 0.8% Asian, non-Hispanic/Latino; 0.4% Native Hawaiian or other Pacific Islander, non-Hispanic/Latino; 4% American Indian or Alaska Native, non-Hispanic/Latino; 2% Two or more races, non-Hispanic/Latino; 1% Race/ethnicity unknown; 2% transferred in. *Retention:* 2% of full-time freshmen returned.
Academics *Degrees:* diplomas, associate, and bachelor's. *Special study options:* adult/continuing education programs, distance learning, internships, off-campus study.
Freshman Application Contact Wright Career College, 2219 W I-240 Service Road, Suite #124, Oklahoma City, OK 73159. *Phone:* 405-681-2300. *Toll-free phone:* 800-555-4003. *E-mail:* info@wrightcc.edu.
Website: http://www.wrightcc.edu/.

Wright Career College
Tulsa, Oklahoma

- **Proprietary** primarily 2-year
- **Suburban** campus with easy access to Tulsa
- **Coed**

Undergraduates 110 full-time, 199 part-time. Students come from 3 states and territories; 45% Black or African American, non-Hispanic/Latino; 2% Hispanic/Latino; 0.6% Native Hawaiian or other Pacific Islander, non-Hispanic/Latino; 6% American Indian or Alaska Native, non-Hispanic/Latino; 5% Two or more races, non-Hispanic/Latino; 0.3% Race/ethnicity unknown; 1% transferred in.
Academics *Degrees:* diplomas, associate, and bachelor's. *Special study options:* distance learning, internships, off-campus study.
Freshman Application Contact Wright Career College, 4908 S Sheridan, Tulsa, OK 74145. *Phone:* 918-628-7700. *Toll-free phone:* 800-555-4003. *E-mail:* info@wrightcc.edu.
Website: http://www.wrightcc.edu/.

OREGON

American College of Healthcare Sciences
Portland, Oregon

Freshman Application Contact Admissions Office, American College of Healthcare Sciences, 5940 SW Hood Avenue, Portland, OR 97239. *Phone:* 503-244-0726. *Toll-free phone:* 800-487-8839. *Fax:* 503-244-0727. *E-mail:* achs@achs.edu.
Website: http://www.achs.edu/.

Blue Mountain Community College
Pendleton, Oregon

Director of Admissions Ms. Theresa Bosworth, Director of Admissions, Blue Mountain Community College, 2411 Northwest Carden Avenue, PO Box 100, Pendleton, OR 97801-1000. *Phone:* 541-278-5774. *E-mail:* tbosworth@bluecc.edu.
Website: http://www.bluecc.edu/.

Carrington College–Portland
Portland, Oregon

Freshman Application Contact Admissions Office, Carrington College–Portland, 2004 Lloyd Center, 3rd Floor, Portland, OR 97232. *Phone:* 503-761-6100.
Website: http://carrington.edu/.

Central Oregon Community College
Bend, Oregon

- **District-supported** 2-year, founded 1949, part of Oregon Community College Association
- **Small-town** 193-acre campus
- **Endowment** $16.0 million
- **Coed,** 6,312 undergraduate students, 43% full-time, 54% women, 46% men

Undergraduates 2,736 full-time, 3,576 part-time. Students come from 28 states and territories; 5% are from out of state; 0.6% Black or African American, non-Hispanic/Latino; 9% Hispanic/Latino; 1% Asian, non-Hispanic/Latino; 0.4% Native Hawaiian or other Pacific Islander, non-Hispanic/Latino; 2% American Indian or Alaska Native, non-Hispanic/Latino; 3% Two or more races, non-Hispanic/Latino; 13% Race/ethnicity unknown; 8% transferred in; 1% live on campus. *Retention:* 51% of full-time freshmen returned.
Freshmen *Admission:* 1,508 applied, 1,508 admitted, 738 enrolled.
Faculty *Total:* 284, 42% full-time, 16% with terminal degrees. *Student/faculty ratio:* 20:1.
Majors Accounting; airline pilot and flight crew; art; automobile/automotive mechanics technology; biological and physical sciences; biology/biological sciences; business administration and management; CAD/CADD drafting/design technology; child-care and support services management; computer and information sciences related; computer science; computer systems networking and telecommunications; cooking and related culinary arts; customer service management; dental assisting; dietetics; drafting and design technology; early childhood education; education; electrical, electronic and communications engineering technology; emergency medical technology (EMT paramedic); engineering; entrepreneurship; fire science/firefighting; fishing and fisheries sciences and management; foreign languages and literatures; forestry; forest technology; health and physical education/fitness; health information/medical records technology; hotel/motel administration; humanities; industrial technology; kinesiology and exercise science; liberal arts and sciences/liberal studies; licensed practical/vocational nurse training; management information systems; manufacturing engineering technology; marketing/marketing management; massage therapy; mathematics; medical/clinical assistant; natural resources/conservation; physical sciences; physical therapy; polymer/plastics engineering; pre-law studies; premedical studies; pre-pharmacy studies; radiologic technology/science; registered nursing/registered nurse; retailing; social sciences; speech communication and rhetoric; sport and fitness administration/management; substance abuse/addiction counseling.
Academics *Calendar:* quarters. *Degree:* certificates and associate. *Special study options:* academic remediation for entering students, cooperative education, distance learning, double majors, English as a second language, independent study, internships, part-time degree program, services for LD students, student-designed majors, study abroad, summer session for credit. *ROTC:* Army (c).
Library COCC Library plus 1 other with 62,865 titles, 1,676 audiovisual materials, an OPAC, a Web page.
Student Life *Housing Options:* coed. Campus housing is university owned. *Activities and Organizations:* drama/theater group, student-run newspaper, choral group, club sports, student newspaper, Criminal Justice Club, Aviation Club. *Campus security:* 24-hour emergency response devices and patrols, late-night transport/escort service. *Student services:* personal/psychological counseling.
Athletics *Intercollegiate sports:* golf M/W. *Intramural sports:* baseball M, basketball M/W, cross-country running M/W, football M, rugby M, skiing (cross-country) M/W, skiing (downhill) M/W, soccer M/W, track and field M/W, volleyball M/W, weight lifting M/W.
Costs (2015–16) *Tuition:* area resident $3132 full-time, $87 per credit hour part-time; state resident $4140 full-time, $115 per credit hour part-time; nonresident $8532 full-time, $237 per credit hour part-time. *Required fees:* $261 full-time, $7 per credit hour part-time. *Room and board:* $9000. *Payment plan:* installment. *Waivers:* employees or children of employees.
Financial Aid Of all full-time matriculated undergraduates who enrolled in 2013, 725 Federal Work-Study jobs (averaging $2130).

Applying *Options:* electronic application. *Application fee:* $25. *Application deadlines:* rolling (freshmen), rolling (transfers). *Notification:* continuous (freshmen), continuous (transfers).
Freshman Application Contact Central Oregon Community College, 2600 Northwest College Way, Bend, OR 97701-5998. *Phone:* 541-383-7500. *Website:* http://www.cocc.edu/.

Chemeketa Community College
Salem, Oregon

Freshman Application Contact Admissions Office, Chemeketa Community College, PO Box 14009, Salem, OR 97309. *Phone:* 503-399-5001. *E-mail:* admissions@chemeketa.edu.
Website: http://www.chemeketa.edu/.

Clackamas Community College
Oregon City, Oregon

Freshman Application Contact Ms. Tara Sprehe, Registrar, Clackamas Community College, 19600 South Molalla Avenue, Oregon City, OR 97045. *Phone:* 503-657-6958 Ext. 2742. *Fax:* 503-650-6654. *E-mail:* pattyw@clackamas.edu.
Website: http://www.clackamas.edu/.

Clatsop Community College
Astoria, Oregon

- **County-supported** 2-year, founded 1958
- **Small-town** 20-acre campus
- **Coed**

Undergraduates 455 full-time, 616 part-time. Students come from 5 states and territories; 12% are from out of state; 0.6% Black or African American, non-Hispanic/Latino; 12% Hispanic/Latino; 1% Asian, non-Hispanic/Latino; 0.2% Native Hawaiian or other Pacific Islander, non-Hispanic/Latino; 2% American Indian or Alaska Native, non-Hispanic/Latino; 2% Two or more races, non-Hispanic/Latino; 8% Race/ethnicity unknown; 5% transferred in.
Faculty *Student/faculty ratio:* 13:1.
Academics *Calendar:* quarters. *Degree:* certificates and associate. *Special study options:* academic remediation for entering students, adult/continuing education programs, advanced placement credit, cooperative education, distance learning, English as a second language, freshman honors college, honors programs, independent study, internships, part-time degree program, services for LD students, summer session for credit.
Student Life *Campus security:* 24-hour emergency response devices, late-night transport/escort service.
Costs (2014–15) *One-time required fee:* $90. *Tuition:* state resident $3564 full-time, $99 per credit part-time; nonresident $7128 full-time, $198 per credit part-time. Full-time tuition and fees vary according to reciprocity agreements. Part-time tuition and fees vary according to reciprocity agreements. *Required fees:* $450 full-time, $10 per credit part-time, $30 per term part-time.
Financial Aid Of all full-time matriculated undergraduates who enrolled in 2013, 220 Federal Work-Study jobs (averaging $2175).
Applying *Options:* electronic application. *Application fee:* $15. *Recommended:* high school transcript.
Freshman Application Contact Ms. Monica Van Steenberg, Recruiting Coordinator, Clatsop Community College, 1651 Lexington Avenue, Astoria, OR 97103. *Phone:* 503-338-2417. *Toll-free phone:* 855-252-8767. *Fax:* 503-325-5738. *E-mail:* admissions@clatsopcc.edu.
Website: http://www.clatsopcc.edu/.

Columbia Gorge Community College
The Dalles, Oregon

- **State-supported** 2-year, founded 1977
- **Small-town** 78-acre campus
- **Coed**

Undergraduates 542 full-time, 703 part-time. Students come from 24 states and territories; 1% are from out of state; 0.6% Black or African American, non-Hispanic/Latino; 7% Hispanic/Latino; 0.8% Asian, non-Hispanic/Latino; 0.1% Native Hawaiian or other Pacific Islander, non-Hispanic/Latino; 5% American Indian or Alaska Native, non-Hispanic/Latino; 0.3% Two or more races, non-Hispanic/Latino; 17% Race/ethnicity unknown. *Retention:* 21% of full-time freshmen returned.
Academics *Calendar:* quarters. *Degree:* certificates, diplomas, and associate. *Special study options:* academic remediation for entering students, cooperative education, distance learning, English as a second language, honors programs,

independent study, part-time degree program, services for LD students, summer session for credit.
Student Life *Campus security:* 24-hour emergency response devices.
Costs (2014–15) *Tuition:* state resident $3204 full-time, $89 per credit hour part-time; nonresident $8100 full-time, $225 per credit hour part-time. Full-time tuition and fees vary according to course load. Part-time tuition and fees vary according to course load. *Required fees:* $432 full-time, $12 per credit hour part-time.
Applying *Options:* electronic application.
Freshman Application Contact Columbia Gorge Community College, 400 East Scenic Drive, The Dalles, OR 97058. *Phone:* 541-506-6025.
Website: http://www.cgcc.cc.or.us/.

Concorde Career College
Portland, Oregon

Admissions Office Contact Concorde Career College, 1425 NE Irving Street, Suite 300, Portland, OR 97232.
Website: http://www.concorde.edu/.

Everest College
Portland, Oregon

Freshman Application Contact Admissions Office, Everest College, 425 Southwest Washington Street, Portland, OR 97204. *Phone:* 503-222-3225. *Toll-free phone:* 888-741-4270. *Fax:* 503-228-6926.
Website: http://www.everest.edu/.

ITT Technical Institute
Portland, Oregon

- **Proprietary** primarily 2-year, founded 1971, part of ITT Educational Services, Inc.
- **Urban** campus
- **Coed**

Academics *Calendar:* quarters. *Degrees:* associate and bachelor's.
Financial Aid Of all full-time matriculated undergraduates who enrolled in 2013, 15 Federal Work-Study jobs (averaging $5000).
Freshman Application Contact Director of Recruitment, ITT Technical Institute, 9500 Northeast Cascades Parkway, Portland, OR 97220. *Phone:* 503-255-6500. *Toll-free phone:* 800-234-5488.
Website: http://www.itt-tech.edu/.

Klamath Community College
Klamath Falls, Oregon

Freshman Application Contact Tammi Garlock, Retention Coordinator, Klamath Community College, 7390 So. 6th St., Klamath Falls, OR 97603. *Phone:* 541-882-3521. *Fax:* 541-885-7758. *E-mail:* garlock@klamathcc.edu.
Website: http://www.klamathcc.edu/.

Lane Community College
Eugene, Oregon

- **State and locally supported** 2-year, founded 1964
- **Suburban** 240-acre campus
- **Coed**

Undergraduates 4,996 full-time, 6,006 part-time. 2% Black or African American, non-Hispanic/Latino; 9% Hispanic/Latino; 1% Asian, non-Hispanic/Latino; 0.6% Native Hawaiian or other Pacific Islander, non-Hispanic/Latino; 2% American Indian or Alaska Native, non-Hispanic/Latino; 5% Two or more races, non-Hispanic/Latino; 11% Race/ethnicity unknown; 0.7% international.
Academics *Calendar:* quarters. *Degree:* certificates and associate. *Special study options:* academic remediation for entering students, adult/continuing education programs, advanced placement credit, English as a second language, internships, part-time degree program, services for LD students, summer session for credit.
Student Life *Campus security:* 24-hour emergency response devices and patrols, student patrols, late-night transport/escort service.
Financial Aid Of all full-time matriculated undergraduates who enrolled in 2013, 400 Federal Work-Study jobs (averaging $3600).
Applying *Options:* early admission.
Freshman Application Contact Lane Community College, 4000 East 30th Avenue, Eugene, OR 97405-0640. *Phone:* 541-747-4501 Ext. 2686.
Website: http://www.lanecc.edu/.

Le Cordon Bleu College of Culinary Arts in Portland

Portland, Oregon

Admissions Office Contact Le Cordon Bleu College of Culinary Arts in Portland, 600 SW 10th Avenue, Suite 500, Portland, OR 97205. *Toll-free phone:* 888-891-6222.
Website: http://www.chefs.edu/Portland/.

Linn-Benton Community College

Albany, Oregon

- **State and locally supported** 2-year, founded 1966
- **Small-town** 104-acre campus
- **Coed**

Undergraduates 2,604 full-time, 3,013 part-time. 3% are from out of state; 1% Black or African American, non-Hispanic/Latino; 8% Hispanic/Latino; 2% Asian, non-Hispanic/Latino; 0.5% Native Hawaiian or other Pacific Islander, non-Hispanic/Latino; 2% American Indian or Alaska Native, non-Hispanic/Latino; 3% Two or more races, non-Hispanic/Latino; 4% Race/ethnicity unknown; 2% international; 10% transferred in. *Retention:* 55% of full-time freshmen returned.
Academics *Calendar:* quarters. *Degree:* certificates and associate. *Special study options:* academic remediation for entering students, advanced placement credit, cooperative education, distance learning, English as a second language, independent study, internships, part-time degree program, services for LD students, student-designed majors, study abroad, summer session for credit. *ROTC:* Army (c), Navy (c), Air Force (c).
Student Life *Campus security:* 24-hour emergency response devices and patrols, student patrols, late-night transport/escort service.
Costs (2014–15) *Tuition:* state resident $4221 full-time, $94 per credit part-time; nonresident $9171 full-time, $204 per credit part-time. Full-time tuition and fees vary according to program. Part-time tuition and fees vary according to program. *Required fees:* $232 full-time, $5 per credit hour part-time.
Financial Aid Of all full-time matriculated undergraduates who enrolled in 2013, 290 Federal Work-Study jobs (averaging $1800).
Applying *Options:* electronic application, deferred entrance. *Application fee:* $30.
Freshman Application Contact Ms. Kim Sullivan, Outreach Coordinator, Linn-Benton Community College, 6500 Pacific Boulevard, SW, Albany, OR 97321. *Phone:* 541-917-4847. *Fax:* 541-917-4838. *E-mail:* admissions@linnbenton.edu.
Website: http://www.linnbenton.edu/.

Mt. Hood Community College

Gresham, Oregon

Director of Admissions Dr. Craig Kolins, Associate Vice President of Enrollment Services, Mt. Hood Community College, 26000 Southeast Stark Street, Gresham, OR 97030-3300. *Phone:* 503-491-7265.
Website: http://www.mhcc.edu/.

Oregon Coast Community College

Newport, Oregon

- **Public** 2-year, founded 1987
- **Small-town** 24-acre campus
- **Coed,** 489 undergraduate students, 43% full-time, 61% women, 39% men

Undergraduates 208 full-time, 281 part-time. 1% are from out of state; 0.2% Black or African American, non-Hispanic/Latino; 11% Hispanic/Latino; 2% Asian, non-Hispanic/Latino; 0.2% Native Hawaiian or other Pacific Islander, non-Hispanic/Latino; 2% American Indian or Alaska Native, non-Hispanic/Latino; 6% Two or more races, non-Hispanic/Latino; 6% Race/ethnicity unknown; 8% transferred in. *Retention:* 45% of full-time freshmen returned.
Freshmen *Admission:* 64 applied, 64 admitted, 74 enrolled.
Faculty *Total:* 60, 13% full-time, 17% with terminal degrees. *Student/faculty ratio:* 14:1.
Majors Criminal justice/safety; general studies; liberal arts and sciences/liberal studies; marine biology and biological oceanography; registered nursing/registered nurse.
Academics *Calendar:* quarters. *Degree:* certificates and associate. *Special study options:* academic remediation for entering students, cooperative education, distance learning, English as a second language, honors programs, internships, part-time degree program, services for LD students, summer session for credit.

Library Oregon Coast Community College Library with 114,948 titles, 2,723 audiovisual materials, an OPAC, a Web page.
Student Life *Housing:* college housing not available. *Activities and Organizations:* Psych club, Triangle club, Writing club, ASG. *Campus security:* 24-hour emergency response devices.
Standardized Tests *Required for some:* nursing entrance exam.
Costs (2015–16) *Tuition:* state resident $3564 full-time, $99 per credit part-time; nonresident $7704 full-time, $214 per credit part-time. Full-time tuition and fees vary according to course load and program. Part-time tuition and fees vary according to course load and program. *Required fees:* $252 full-time, $7 per credit part-time. *Payment plan:* deferred payment. *Waivers:* employees or children of employees.
Applying *Required for some:* essay or personal statement, 2 letters of recommendation, interview.
Freshman Application Contact Student Services, Oregon Coast Community College, 400 SE College Way, Newport, OR 97366. *Phone:* 541-265-2283. *Fax:* 541-265-3820. *E-mail:* webinfo@occc.cc.or.us.
Website: http://www.oregoncoastcc.org.

Portland Community College

Portland, Oregon

Freshman Application Contact Admissions and Registration Office, Portland Community College, PO Box 19000, Portland, OR 97280. *Phone:* 503-977-8888. *Toll-free phone:* 866-922-1010.
Website: http://www.pcc.edu/.

Rogue Community College

Grants Pass, Oregon

- **State and locally supported** 2-year, founded 1970
- **Rural** 84-acre campus
- **Endowment** $8.8 million
- **Coed,** 5,099 undergraduate students, 38% full-time, 57% women, 43% men

Undergraduates 1,928 full-time, 3,171 part-time. Students come from 21 states and territories; 3 other countries; 3% are from out of state; 0.8% Black or African American, non-Hispanic/Latino; 13% Hispanic/Latino; 1% Asian, non-Hispanic/Latino; 0.6% Native Hawaiian or other Pacific Islander, non-Hispanic/Latino; 2% American Indian or Alaska Native, non-Hispanic/Latino; 3% Two or more races, non-Hispanic/Latino; 5% Race/ethnicity unknown; 68% transferred in.
Freshmen *Admission:* 730 enrolled. *Average high school GPA:* 3.68.
Faculty *Total:* 456, 17% full-time. *Student/faculty ratio:* 15:1.
Majors Accounting technology and bookkeeping; automobile/automotive mechanics technology; business administration and management; business/commerce; child-care and support services management; computer and information sciences; computer software technology; construction engineering technology; construction trades; criminal justice/police science; diesel mechanics technology; electrical and power transmission installation; electrical, electronic and communications engineering technology; emergency medical technology (EMT paramedic); fire prevention and safety technology; general studies; liberal arts and sciences/liberal studies; manufacturing engineering technology; marketing/marketing management; mechanics and repair; medical office computer specialist; registered nursing/registered nurse; social work; visual and performing arts; welding technology.
Academics *Calendar:* quarters. *Degree:* certificates and associate. *Special study options:* academic remediation for entering students, adult/continuing education programs, advanced placement credit, cooperative education, distance learning, double majors, English as a second language, independent study, internships, part-time degree program, services for LD students, study abroad, summer session for credit.
Library Rogue Community College Library with 33,000 titles, an OPAC.
Student Life *Activities and Organizations:* drama/theater group, student-run newspaper, choral group. *Campus security:* 24-hour emergency response devices and patrols, late-night transport/escort service. *Student services:* personal/psychological counseling.
Athletics *Intramural sports:* badminton M/W, basketball M/W, soccer M/W, softball M/W, volleyball M/W.
Costs (2014–15) *Tuition:* state resident $3276 full-time, $91 per credit hour part-time; nonresident $3996 full-time, $111 per credit hour part-time. *Required fees:* $549 full-time, $4 per credit hour part-time, $135 per term part-time. *Payment plan:* installment. *Waivers:* employees or children of employees.
Financial Aid Of all full-time matriculated undergraduates who enrolled in 2014, 1,585 applied for aid, 1,407 were judged to have need, 25 had their need fully met. 87 Federal Work-Study jobs (averaging $3072). In 2014, 24 non-need-based awards were made. *Average percent of need met:* 65%. *Average*

financial aid package: $8904. *Average need-based loan:* $3751. *Average need-based gift aid:* $6031. *Average non-need-based aid:* $1065.
Applying *Options:* electronic application, early admission. *Application deadlines:* rolling (freshmen), rolling (out-of-state freshmen), rolling (transfers).
Freshman Application Contact Ms. Claudia Sullivan, Director of Enrollment Services, Rogue Community College, 3345 Redwood Highway, Grants Pass, OR 97527-9291. *Phone:* 541-956-7176. *Fax:* 541-471-3585. *E-mail:* csullivan@roguecc.edu.
Website: http://www.roguecc.edu/.

Southwestern Oregon Community College
Coos Bay, Oregon

Freshman Application Contact Miss Lela Wells, Southwestern Oregon Community College, Student First Stop, 1988 Newmark Avenue, Coos Bay, OR 97420. *Phone:* 541-888-7611. *Toll-free phone:* 800-962-2838. *E-mail:* lwells@socc.edu.
Website: http://www.socc.edu/.

Sumner College
Portland, Oregon

Admissions Office Contact Sumner College, 8909 SW Barbur Boulevard, Suite 100, Portland, OR 97219.
Website: http://www.sumnercollege.edu/.

Tillamook Bay Community College
Tillamook, Oregon

Freshman Application Contact Lori Gates, Tillamook Bay Community College, 4301 Third Street, Tillamook, OR 97141. *Phone:* 503-842-8222. *Fax:* 503-842-2214. *E-mail:* gates@tillamookbay.cc.
Website: http://www.tbcc.cc.or.us/.

Treasure Valley Community College
Ontario, Oregon

- **State and locally supported** 2-year, founded 1962
- **Rural** 95-acre campus with easy access to Boise
- **Coed**

Undergraduates 1,212 full-time, 1,231 part-time. Students come from 14 states and territories; 2 other countries; 68% are from out of state; 2% Black or African American, non-Hispanic/Latino; 20% Hispanic/Latino; 1% Asian, non-Hispanic/Latino; 1% American Indian or Alaska Native, non-Hispanic/Latino; 18% Race/ethnicity unknown; 15% transferred in; 6% live on campus.
Faculty *Student/faculty ratio:* 21:1.
Academics *Calendar:* quarters. *Degree:* certificates and associate. *Special study options:* academic remediation for entering students, accelerated degree program, adult/continuing education programs, advanced placement credit, cooperative education, distance learning, English as a second language, honors programs, independent study, internships, part-time degree program, services for LD students, summer session for credit.
Student Life *Campus security:* 24-hour emergency response devices, late-night transport/escort service, controlled dormitory access, Emergency response phone and computer notifications.
Financial Aid Of all full-time matriculated undergraduates who enrolled in 2013, 90 Federal Work-Study jobs (averaging $1500).
Applying *Options:* electronic application, early admission, deferred entrance.
Freshman Application Contact Christina Coyne, Office of Admissions and Student Services, Treasure Valley Community College, 650 College Boulevard, Ontario, OR 97914. *Phone:* 541-881-5822. *E-mail:* ccoyne@tvcc.cc.
Website: http://www.tvcc.cc/.

Umpqua Community College
Roseburg, Oregon

- **State and locally supported** 2-year, founded 1964
- **Rural** 100-acre campus
- **Endowment** $7.3 million
- **Coed,** 2,046 undergraduate students, 47% full-time, 60% women, 40% men

Undergraduates 971 full-time, 1,075 part-time. Students come from 15 states and territories; 1% Black or African American, non-Hispanic/Latino; 12%

Hispanic/Latino; 1% Asian, non-Hispanic/Latino; 0.3% Native Hawaiian or other Pacific Islander, non-Hispanic/Latino; 2% American Indian or Alaska Native, non-Hispanic/Latino; 5% Two or more races, non-Hispanic/Latino; 3% Race/ethnicity unknown; 22% transferred in. *Retention:* 48% of full-time freshmen returned.
Freshmen *Admission:* 176 applied, 176 admitted, 176 enrolled.
Faculty *Total:* 149, 37% full-time. *Student/faculty ratio:* 14:1.
Majors Accounting; administrative assistant and secretarial science; agriculture; anthropology; art; art history, criticism and conservation; art teacher education; automobile/automotive mechanics technology; behavioral sciences; biological and physical sciences; biology/biological sciences; business administration and management; chemistry; child development; civil engineering technology; computer engineering technology; computer science; cosmetology; criminal justice/law enforcement administration; desktop publishing and digital imaging design; dramatic/theater arts; economics; education; electrical, electronic and communications engineering technology; elementary education; emergency medical technology (EMT paramedic); engineering; English; fire science/firefighting; forestry; health teacher education; history; humanities; human resources management; journalism; kindergarten/preschool education; legal administrative assistant/secretary; liberal arts and sciences/liberal studies; marketing/marketing management; mathematics; medical administrative assistant and medical secretary; music; music teacher education; natural sciences; physical education teaching and coaching; physical sciences; political science and government; pre-engineering; psychology; registered nursing/registered nurse; social sciences; social work; sociology.
Academics *Calendar:* quarters. *Degree:* certificates and associate. *Special study options:* academic remediation for entering students, accelerated degree program, adult/continuing education programs, advanced placement credit, cooperative education, distance learning, English as a second language, honors programs, independent study, internships, part-time degree program, services for LD students, study abroad, summer session for credit.
Library Umpqua Community College Library with 41,000 titles, an OPAC, a Web page.
Student Life *Housing:* college housing not available. *Activities and Organizations:* drama/theater group, student-run newspaper, choral group, Phi Theta Kappa, Computer Club, Phi Beta Lambda, Nursing Club, Umpqua Accounting Associates. *Campus security:* 24-hour emergency response devices and patrols. *Student services:* personal/psychological counseling.
Athletics *Intercollegiate sports:* basketball M(s)/W(s), volleyball W(s). *Intramural sports:* basketball M/W.
Costs (2014–15) *One-time required fee:* $25. *Tuition:* state resident $4343 full-time, $96 per credit hour part-time; nonresident $9428 full-time, $210 per credit hour part-time. *Required fees:* $302 full-time, $101 per term part-time. *Waivers:* employees or children of employees.
Financial Aid Of all full-time matriculated undergraduates who enrolled in 2013, 120 Federal Work-Study jobs (averaging $3000).
Applying *Options:* electronic application, early admission, deferred entrance. *Application fee:* $25. *Recommended:* high school transcript. *Application deadlines:* rolling (freshmen), rolling (transfers).
Freshman Application Contact Admissions Office, Umpqua Community College, PO Box 967, Roseburg, OR 97470-0226. *Phone:* 541-440-7743. *Fax:* 541-440-4612.
Website: http://www.umpqua.edu/.

PENNSYLVANIA

All-State Career School–Allied Health Campus
Essington, Pennsylvania

Admissions Office Contact All-State Career School–Allied Health Campus, 50 W Powhattan Ave, Essington, PA 19029.
Website: http://www.allstatecareer.edu/.

Antonelli Institute
Erdenheim, Pennsylvania

- **Proprietary** 2-year, founded 1938
- **Suburban** 15-acre campus with easy access to Philadelphia
- **Coed,** 189 undergraduate students
- **89%** of applicants were admitted

Freshmen *Admission:* 211 applied, 188 admitted.
Majors Graphic design; photography.
Academics *Calendar:* semesters. *Degree:* associate.

Financial Aid Of all full-time matriculated undergraduates who enrolled in 2013, 5 Federal Work-Study jobs (averaging $2000).
Freshman Application Contact Admissions Office, Antonelli Institute, 300 Montgomery Avenue, Erdenheim, PA 19038. *Phone:* 800-722-7871. *Toll-free phone:* 800-722-7871.
Website: http://www.antonelli.edu/.

Berks Technical Institute
Wyomissing, Pennsylvania

Freshman Application Contact Mr. Allan Brussolo, Academic Dean, Berks Technical Institute, 2205 Ridgewood Road, Wyomissing, PA 19610-1168. *Phone:* 610-372-1722. *Toll-free phone:* 866-591-8384. *Fax:* 610-376-4684. *E-mail:* abrussolo@berks.edu.
Website: http://www.berks.edu/.

Bidwell Training Center
Pittsburgh, Pennsylvania

Freshman Application Contact Admissions Office, Bidwell Training Center, 1815 Metropolitan Street, Pittsburgh, PA 15233. *Phone:* 412-322-1773. *Toll-free phone:* 800-516-1800. *E-mail:* admissions@mcg-btc.org.
Website: http://www.bidwell-training.org/.

Bradford School
Pittsburgh, Pennsylvania

- **Private** 2-year, founded 1968
- **Urban** campus
- **Coed,** 439 undergraduate students
- 84% of applicants were admitted

Freshmen *Admission:* 798 applied, 669 admitted.
Majors Accounting technology and bookkeeping; administrative assistant and secretarial science; computer programming; computer systems networking and telecommunications; dental assisting; graphic design; hotel/motel administration; legal administrative assistant/secretary; legal assistant/paralegal; medical/clinical assistant; retailing.
Academics *Calendar:* semesters. *Degree:* diplomas and associate.
Freshman Application Contact Admissions Office, Bradford School, 125 West Station Square Drive, Pittsburgh, PA 15219. *Phone:* 412-391-6710. *Toll-free phone:* 800-391-6810.
Website: http://www.bradfordpittsburgh.edu/.

Bucks County Community College
Newtown, Pennsylvania

- **County-supported** 2-year, founded 1964
- **Suburban** 200-acre campus with easy access to Philadelphia
- **Endowment** $6.2 million
- **Coed,** 8,979 undergraduate students, 34% full-time, 55% women, 45% men

Undergraduates 3,047 full-time, 5,932 part-time. Students come from 10 states and territories; 1% are from out of state; 5% Black or African American, non-Hispanic/Latino; 6% Hispanic/Latino; 3% Asian, non-Hispanic/Latino; 0.1% Native Hawaiian or other Pacific Islander, non-Hispanic/Latino; 0.9% American Indian or Alaska Native, non-Hispanic/Latino; 2% Two or more races, non-Hispanic/Latino; 22% Race/ethnicity unknown; 0.2% international; 73% transferred in. *Retention:* 67% of full-time freshmen returned.
Freshmen *Admission:* 4,625 applied, 4,489 admitted, 2,151 enrolled.
Faculty *Total:* 698, 23% full-time, 24% with terminal degrees. *Student/faculty ratio:* 17:1.
Majors Accounting technology and bookkeeping; American studies; baking and pastry arts; biology/biotechnology laboratory technician; biology teacher education; biotechnology; building/home/construction inspection; business administration and management; business/commerce; business, management, and marketing related; cabinetmaking and millwork; chemical technology; chemistry teacher education; child-care provision; cinematography and film/video production; commercial and advertising art; commercial photography; computer and information sciences; computer programming (specific applications); computer systems networking and telecommunications; criminal justice/safety; crisis/emergency/disaster management; culinary arts; dramatic/theater arts; early childhood education; education; engineering technology; environmental science; food service systems administration; health professions related; history; history teacher education; human development and family studies; humanities; industrial technology; information science/studies; journalism; legal professions and studies related; liberal arts and sciences and humanities related; liberal arts and sciences/liberal studies; mathematics; mathematics teacher education;

medical/clinical assistant; medical insurance coding; multi/interdisciplinary studies related; music; network and system administration; neuroscience; physical education teaching and coaching; psychology; registered nursing/registered nurse; retailing; small business administration; speech communication and rhetoric; sport and fitness administration/management; tourism and travel services management; visual and performing arts; web page, digital/multimedia and information resources design; women's studies.
Academics *Calendar:* semesters. *Degree:* certificates and associate. *Special study options:* academic remediation for entering students, adult/continuing education programs, advanced placement credit, cooperative education, distance learning, English as a second language, external degree program, independent study, internships, part-time degree program, services for LD students, student-designed majors, summer session for credit.
Library Bucks County Community College Library with 113,651 titles, 1,887 audiovisual materials, an OPAC, a Web page.
Student Life *Housing:* college housing not available. *Activities and Organizations:* drama/theater group, student-run newspaper, radio and television station, choral group, Phi Theta Kappa, Kappa Beta Delta, Students Student Success, Digital Gaming, Glass Arts. *Campus security:* 24-hour emergency response devices and patrols, late-night transport/escort service. *Student services:* personal/psychological counseling, women's center.
Athletics Member NJCAA. *Intercollegiate sports:* baseball M, basketball M, equestrian sports M/W, golf M, skiing (downhill) M/W, soccer M/W, tennis M/W, volleyball W. *Intramural sports:* baseball M, basketball M/W, equestrian sports M/W, football M, tennis M/W, ultimate Frisbee M/W, volleyball W.
Costs (2014–15) *Tuition:* area resident $3900 full-time, $130 per credit hour part-time; state resident $7800 full-time, $260 per credit hour part-time; nonresident $11,700 full-time, $390 per credit hour part-time. Full-time tuition and fees vary according to program. Part-time tuition and fees vary according to program. *Required fees:* $1130 full-time, $61 per credit hour part-time. *Payment plans:* installment, deferred payment. *Waivers:* senior citizens and employees or children of employees.
Applying *Options:* electronic application, early admission. *Required:* high school transcript. *Required for some:* essay or personal statement, interview.
Freshman Application Contact Ms. Marlene Barlow, Director of Admissions, Bucks County Community College, Newtown, PA 18940. *Phone:* 215-968-8137. *Fax:* 215-968-8110. *E-mail:* marlene.barlow@bucks.edu.
Website: http://www.bucks.edu/.

Butler County Community College
Butler, Pennsylvania

- **County-supported** 2-year, founded 1965
- **Rural** 300-acre campus with easy access to Pittsburgh
- **Coed,** 3,570 undergraduate students, 47% full-time, 59% women, 41% men

Undergraduates 1,684 full-time, 1,886 part-time. 1% are from out of state; 3% Black or African American, non-Hispanic/Latino; 2% Hispanic/Latino; 0.6% Asian, non-Hispanic/Latino; 0.1% Native Hawaiian or other Pacific Islander, non-Hispanic/Latino; 0.3% American Indian or Alaska Native, non-Hispanic/Latino; 1% Two or more races, non-Hispanic/Latino; 11% Race/ethnicity unknown; 0.2% international.
Faculty *Total:* 351, 18% full-time. *Student/faculty ratio:* 18:1.
Majors Administrative assistant and secretarial science; architectural drafting and CAD/CADD; biology/biological sciences; business administration and management; business/commerce; business, management, and marketing related; CAD/CADD drafting/design technology; civil engineering technology; computer and information sciences; computer and information systems security; computer programming (specific applications); computer technology/computer systems technology; cooking and related culinary arts; corrections; cosmetology; criminal justice/law enforcement administration; criminal justice/police science; digital communication and media/multimedia; education; electrical, electronic and communications engineering technology; elementary education; engineering; English; fine arts related; fire science/firefighting; food service systems administration; food technology and processing; general studies; health and medical administrative services related; health/health-care administration; heating, air conditioning, ventilation and refrigeration maintenance technology; homeland security; homeland security, law enforcement, firefighting and protective services related; hospitality administration related; human resources management; instrumentation technology; kindergarten/preschool education; legal administrative assistant/secretary; machine shop technology; machine tool technology; manufacturing engineering technology; massage therapy; mathematics; mechanical drafting and CAD/CADD; medical insurance coding; medical office assistant; network and system administration; office occupations and clerical services; organizational communication; parks, recreation and leisure facilities management; photography; physical sciences; physical therapy technology; precision production trades; psychology; radiologic

technology/science; registered nursing/registered nurse; robotics technology; selling skills and sales; social work related; sport and fitness administration/management; web page, digital/multimedia and information resources design.

Academics *Calendar:* semesters. *Degree:* certificates and associate. *Special study options:* academic remediation for entering students, adult/continuing education programs, advanced placement credit, cooperative education, distance learning, English as a second language, internships, part-time degree program, services for LD students, summer session for credit.

Library John A. Beck, Jr. Library with 70,000 titles.

Student Life *Housing:* college housing not available. *Activities and Organizations:* student-run newspaper. *Campus security:* 24-hour emergency response devices, late-night transport/escort service. *Student services:* personal/psychological counseling.

Athletics Member NJCAA. *Intercollegiate sports:* baseball M, basketball M, golf M/W, softball W, volleyball W. *Intramural sports:* basketball M/W, table tennis M/W, volleyball M/W.

Costs (2014–15) *Tuition:* area resident $2880 full-time, $96 per credit part-time; state resident $5760 full-time, $192 per credit part-time; nonresident $8640 full-time, $288 per credit part-time. *Required fees:* $930 full-time, $31 per credit part-time. *Payment plan:* installment. *Waivers:* employees or children of employees.

Financial Aid Of all full-time matriculated undergraduates who enrolled in 2013, 65 Federal Work-Study jobs (averaging $1545).

Applying *Options:* electronic application. *Application fee:* $25. *Required:* high school transcript. *Required for some:* interview. *Application deadlines:* 8/15 (freshmen), 8/15 (transfers). *Notification:* continuous until 8/15 (freshmen), continuous until 8/15 (transfers).

Freshman Application Contact Mr. Robert Morris, Director of Admissions, Butler County Community College, College Drive, PO Box 1205, Butler, PA 16003-1203. *Phone:* 724-287-8711 Ext. 344. *Toll-free phone:* 888-826-2829. *Fax:* 724-287-4961. *E-mail:* robert.morris@bc3.edu. *Website:* http://www.bc3.edu/.

Cambria-Rowe Business College
Indiana, Pennsylvania

- **Proprietary** 2-year, founded 1959
- **Small-town** 1-acre campus
- **Coed,** 93 undergraduate students, 99% full-time, 85% women, 15% men
- 60% of applicants were admitted

Undergraduates 92 full-time, 1 part-time. 1% Asian, non-Hispanic/Latino; 1% American Indian or Alaska Native, non-Hispanic/Latino; 2% Two or more races, non-Hispanic/Latino. *Retention:* 64% of full-time freshmen returned.

Freshmen *Admission:* 20 applied, 12 admitted, 17 enrolled.

Faculty *Total:* 7, 100% full-time, 86% with terminal degrees. *Student/faculty ratio:* 13:1.

Majors Accounting; administrative assistant and secretarial science; business administration and management; health services/allied health/health sciences; legal administrative assistant/secretary; medical office assistant.

Academics *Calendar:* quarters. *Degree:* diplomas and associate. *Special study options:* part-time degree program.

Library LIRN.

Student Life *Housing:* college housing not available. *Options:* Campus housing is provided by a third party.

Costs (2015–16) *Comprehensive fee:* $20,625 includes full-time tuition ($13,200) and room and board ($7425). Full-time tuition and fees vary according to course level and course load. Part-time tuition: $250 per credit. Part-time tuition and fees vary according to course level and course load. *Room and board:* Room and board charges vary according to housing facility and location. *Payment plan:* installment. *Waivers:* employees or children of employees.

Applying *Options:* electronic application. *Application fee:* $30. *Required:* high school transcript. *Recommended:* interview.

Freshman Application Contact Mrs. Stacey Bell-Leger, Representative at Indiana Campus, Cambria-Rowe Business College, 422 South 13th Street, Indiana, PA 15701. *Phone:* 724-463-0222. *Toll-free phone:* 800-NEW-CAREER. *Fax:* 724-463-7246. *E-mail:* sbell-leger@crbc.net. *Website:* http://www.crbc.net/.

Cambria-Rowe Business College
Johnstown, Pennsylvania

- **Proprietary** 2-year, founded 1891
- **Small-town** campus with easy access to Pittsburgh
- **Coed, primarily women**

Undergraduates 141 full-time, 1 part-time. 9% Black or African American, non-Hispanic/Latino; 0.7% American Indian or Alaska Native, non-

Hispanic/Latino; 2% Two or more races, non-Hispanic/Latino. *Retention:* 50% of full-time freshmen returned.

Faculty *Student/faculty ratio:* 13:1.

Academics *Calendar:* quarters. *Degree:* associate. *Special study options:* accelerated degree program, advanced placement credit, part-time degree program, summer session for credit.

Costs (2014–15) *Comprehensive fee:* $21,642 includes full-time tuition ($12,950), mandatory fees ($1330), and room and board ($7362). Full-time tuition and fees vary according to course load. Part-time tuition and fees vary according to course load. *Required fees:* $1330 per degree program part-time. *Room and board:* Room and board charges vary according to housing facility and location.

Financial Aid *Average need-based gift aid:* $8058. *Financial aid deadline:* 8/1.

Applying *Options:* electronic application, early admission. *Application fee:* $15. *Required:* high school transcript, entrance exam. *Recommended:* interview.

Freshman Application Contact Mrs. Riley McDonald, Admissions Representative, Cambria-Rowe Business College, 221 Central Avenue, Johnstown, PA 15902-2494. *Phone:* 814-536-5168. *Toll-free phone:* 800-NEWCAREER. *Fax:* 814-536-5160. *E-mail:* admissions@crbc.net. *Website:* http://www.crbc.net/.

Career Training Academy
Monroeville, Pennsylvania

Freshman Application Contact Career Training Academy, 4314 Old William Penn Highway, Suite 103, Monroeville, PA 15146. *Phone:* 412-372-3900. *Toll-free phone:* 866-673-7773. *Website:* http://www.careerta.edu/.

Career Training Academy
New Kensington, Pennsylvania

Freshman Application Contact Career Training Academy, 950 Fifth Avenue, New Kensington, PA 15068-6301. *Phone:* 724-337-1000. *Toll-free phone:* 866-673-7773. *Website:* http://www.careerta.edu/.

Career Training Academy
Pittsburgh, Pennsylvania

- **Proprietary** 2-year
- **Suburban** campus with easy access to Pittsburgh
- **Coed,** 70 undergraduate students, 100% full-time, 93% women, 7% men

Undergraduates 70 full-time. Students come from 1 other state; 33% Black or African American, non-Hispanic/Latino; 4% Hispanic/Latino; 1% Native Hawaiian or other Pacific Islander, non-Hispanic/Latino.

Freshmen *Admission:* 13 enrolled. *Average high school GPA:* 2.

Faculty *Total:* 9, 78% full-time. *Student/faculty ratio:* 9:1.

Majors Massage therapy; medical/clinical assistant; medical insurance coding.

Academics *Calendar:* continuous. *Degree:* diplomas and associate. *Special study options:* academic remediation for entering students, advanced placement credit, cooperative education, internships, services for LD students.

Library Career Training Academy.

Student Life *Housing:* college housing not available. *Campus security:* 24-hour emergency response devices and patrols, late-night transport/escort service.

Applying *Application fee:* $30. *Required:* essay or personal statement, high school transcript, minimum 1.5 GPA, interview. *Application deadlines:* rolling (freshmen), rolling (out-of-state freshmen).

Freshman Application Contact Jaimie Vignone, Career Training Academy, 1014 West View Park Drive, Pittsburgh, PA 15229. *Phone:* 412-367-4000. *Toll-free phone:* 866-673-7773. *Fax:* 412-369-7223. *E-mail:* admission3@careerta.edu. *Website:* http://www.careerta.edu/.

Commonwealth Technical Institute
Johnstown, Pennsylvania

- **State-supported** 2-year
- **Suburban** 59-acre campus
- **Coed,** 222 undergraduate students, 100% full-time, 35% women, 65% men

Undergraduates 222 full-time. Students come from 4 states and territories; 1% are from out of state; 7% Black or African American, non-Hispanic/Latino; 1% Asian, non-Hispanic/Latino; 0.5% Two or more races, non-

Hispanic/Latino; 25% Race/ethnicity unknown. *Retention:* 74% of full-time freshmen returned.
Freshmen *Admission:* 76 enrolled.
Faculty *Total:* 27, 100% full-time. *Student/faculty ratio:* 15:1.
Majors Architectural drafting and CAD/CADD; computer technology/computer systems technology; culinary arts; dental laboratory technology; mechanical drafting and CAD/CADD; medical office assistant.
Academics *Calendar:* trimesters. *Degree:* diplomas and associate. *Special study options:* academic remediation for entering students, advanced placement credit, services for LD students.
Library Commonwealth Technical Institute at the Hiram G.Andrews Center Library with 5,000 titles, 470 audiovisual materials.
Student Life *Housing Options:* men-only, women-only, special housing for students with disabilities. Campus housing is university owned. *Activities and Organizations:* drama/theater group, choral group. *Campus security:* 24-hour patrols, controlled dormitory access. *Student services:* health clinic, personal/psychological counseling.
Costs (2015–16) *Tuition:* state resident $11,224 full-time. *Room and board:* $5490. *Payment plan:* installment.
Financial Aid Of all full-time matriculated undergraduates who enrolled in 2011, 403 applied for aid, 259 were judged to have need. 35 Federal Work-Study jobs (averaging $1000). *Average percent of need met:* 30%. *Average financial aid package:* $2500. *Average need-based gift aid:* $2500.
Applying *Required for some:* high school transcript. *Recommended:* high school transcript. *Application deadline:* rolling (freshmen). *Notification:* continuous (freshmen).
Freshman Application Contact Mr. Jason Gies, Admissions Supervisor, Commonwealth Technical Institute, Commonwealth Technical Institute @ Hiram G. Andrews Center, 727 Goucher Street, Johnstown, PA 15905. *Phone:* 814-255-8200 Ext. 0564. *Toll-free phone:* 800-762-4211. *Fax:* 814-255-8283. *E-mail:* jgies@pa.gov.
Website: http://www.portal.state.pa.us/portal/server.pt/community/commonwealth_technical_institute/10361.

Community College of Allegheny County
Pittsburgh, Pennsylvania

- **County-supported** 2-year, founded 1966
- **Urban** 242-acre campus
- **Coed,** 17,148 undergraduate students, 35% full-time, 58% women, 42% men

Undergraduates 6,009 full-time, 11,139 part-time. 2% are from out of state.
Freshmen *Admission:* 3,012 enrolled.
Majors Accounting technology and bookkeeping; administrative assistant and secretarial science; airline pilot and flight crew; applied horticulture/horticulture operations; architectural drafting and CAD/CADD; art; athletic training; automotive engineering technology; aviation/airway management; banking and financial support services; biology/biological sciences; building/property maintenance; business administration and management; business automation/technology/data entry; business machine repair; carpentry; chemical technology; chemistry; child-care provision; child development; civil drafting and CAD/CADD; civil engineering technology; clinical/medical laboratory technology; commercial and advertising art; communications technologies and support services related; community health services counseling; computer engineering technology; computer systems networking and telecommunications; computer technology/computer systems technology; construction engineering technology; construction trades related; corrections; cosmetology and personal grooming arts related; court reporting; criminal justice/police science; culinary arts; diagnostic medical sonography and ultrasound technology; dietitian assistant; drafting and design technology; drafting/design engineering technologies related; dramatic/theater arts; education (specific levels and methods) related; education (specific subject areas) related; electrical, electronic and communications engineering technology; electroneurodiagnostic/electroencephalographic technology; energy management and systems technology; engineering technologies and engineering related; English; entrepreneurship; environmental engineering technology; fire prevention and safety technology; food service systems administration; foreign languages and literatures; general studies; greenhouse management; health and physical education/fitness; health information/medical records technology; health professions related; health unit coordinator/ward clerk; heating, air conditioning, ventilation and refrigeration maintenance technology; hotel/motel administration; housing and human environments related; human development and family studies related; humanities; human resources management; industrial technology; insurance; journalism; landscaping and groundskeeping; legal administrative assistant/secretary; legal assistant/paralegal; liberal arts and sciences/liberal studies; licensed practical/vocational nurse training; machine shop technology; management information systems; marketing/marketing management; mathematics; mechanical drafting and CAD/CADD; medical administrative

assistant and medical secretary; medical/clinical assistant; medical radiologic technology; music; nuclear medical technology; nursing assistant/aide and patient care assistant/aide; occupational therapist assistant; office management; ornamental horticulture; perioperative/operating room and surgical nursing; pharmacy technician; physical therapy technology; physics; plant nursery management; psychiatric/mental health services technology; psychology; quality control technology; real estate; registered nursing/registered nurse; respiratory care therapy; restaurant, culinary, and catering management; retailing; robotics technology; science technologies related; sheet metal technology; sign language interpretation and translation; social sciences; social work; sociology; solar energy technology; substance abuse/addiction counseling; surgical technology; therapeutic recreation; tourism promotion; turf and turfgrass management; visual and performing arts related; welding technology.
Academics *Calendar:* semesters. *Degree:* certificates, diplomas, and associate. *Special study options:* part-time degree program.
Library Community College of Allegheny County Library.
Student Life *Housing:* college housing not available. *Campus security:* 24-hour emergency response devices and patrols, late-night transport/escort service.
Athletics Member NJCAA. *Intercollegiate sports:* baseball M, basketball M/W, bowling M/W, golf M/W, ice hockey M, softball W, table tennis M/W, tennis M/W, volleyball W. *Intramural sports:* badminton M/W, basketball M/W, bowling M/W, cross-country running M/W, football M, golf M/W, lacrosse M, racquetball M/W, softball M/W, table tennis M/W, tennis M/W, volleyball M/W, weight lifting M/W.
Costs (2014–15) *Tuition:* area resident $3143 full-time, $105 per credit part-time; state resident $6285 full-time, $210 per credit part-time; nonresident $9428 full-time, $314 per credit part-time. Full-time tuition and fees vary according to program. Part-time tuition and fees vary according to program. *Payment plan:* installment. *Waivers:* senior citizens and employees or children of employees.
Applying *Options:* early decision, early action. *Recommended:* high school transcript.
Freshman Application Contact Admissions Office, Community College of Allegheny County, 808 Ridge Avenue, Pittsburgh, PA 15212. *Phone:* 412-237-2511.
Website: http://www.ccac.edu/.

Community College of Beaver County
Monaca, Pennsylvania

Freshman Application Contact Enrollment Management, Community College of Beaver County, One Campus Drive, Monaca, PA 15061-2588. *Phone:* 724-480-3500. *Toll-free phone:* 800-335-0222. *E-mail:* admissions@ccbc.edu.
Website: http://www.ccbc.edu/.

Community College of Philadelphia
Philadelphia, Pennsylvania

- **State and locally supported** 2-year, founded 1964
- **Urban** 14-acre campus
- **Coed,** 39,500 undergraduate students

Undergraduates Students come from 50 other countries.
Faculty *Total:* 1,109, 39% full-time.
Majors Accounting; architectural engineering technology; art; automobile/automotive mechanics technology; business administration and management; chemical technology; clinical/medical laboratory technology; computer science; construction engineering technology; criminal justice/law enforcement administration; culinary arts; dental hygiene; drafting and design technology; education; engineering; engineering technology; facilities planning and management; finance; fire science/firefighting; forensic science and technology; health information/medical records administration; health professions related; hotel/motel administration; human services; kindergarten/preschool education; liberal arts and sciences/liberal studies; medical administrative assistant and medical secretary; medical radiologic technology; mental health counseling; music; occupational therapist assistant; photography; pre-engineering; psychology; recording arts technology; registered nursing/registered nurse; respiratory care therapy; sign language interpretation and translation.
Academics *Calendar:* semesters. *Degree:* certificates, diplomas, and associate. *Special study options:* academic remediation for entering students, accelerated degree program, adult/continuing education programs, advanced placement credit, cooperative education, distance learning, English as a second language, external degree program, honors programs, independent study, internships, off-campus study, part-time degree program, services for LD students, student-designed majors, study abroad, summer session for credit. *ROTC:* Army (c).

Library Main Campus Library plus 2 others with 110,000 titles, an OPAC, a Web page.

Student Life *Housing:* college housing not available. *Activities and Organizations:* drama/theater group, student-run newspaper, choral group, Philadelphia L.E.A.D.S, Phi Theta Kappa, Student Government Association, Vanguard Student Newspaper, Fundraising Club. *Campus security:* 24-hour emergency response devices and patrols, phone/alert systems in classrooms/buildings. *Student services:* personal/psychological counseling, women's center.

Athletics Member NJCAA. *Intercollegiate sports:* baseball M, basketball M/W, cheerleading M/W, cross-country running M/W, soccer M, tennis M/W, track and field M/W, volleyball M/W. *Intramural sports:* basketball M/W, soccer M/W, tennis M/W, track and field M/W, volleyball M/W.

Costs (2014–15) *Tuition:* area resident $5100 full-time, $153 per credit hour part-time; state resident $9070 full-time, $306 per credit hour part-time; nonresident $13,040 full-time, $459 per credit hour part-time. Full-time tuition and fees vary according to program. Part-time tuition and fees vary according to program. *Payment plan:* installment. *Waivers:* senior citizens and employees or children of employees.

Applying *Options:* electronic application, early admission, deferred entrance. *Application fee:* $20. *Required for some:* high school transcript, allied health and nursing programs have specific entry requirements. *Application deadlines:* rolling (freshmen), rolling (transfers). *Notification:* continuous (freshmen), continuous (transfers).

Freshman Application Contact Community College of Philadelphia, 1700 Spring Garden Street, Philadelphia, PA 19130-3991. *Phone:* 215-751-8010. *Website:* http://www.ccp.edu/.

Consolidated School of Business
Lancaster, Pennsylvania

Freshman Application Contact Ms. Libby Paul, Admissions Representative, Consolidated School of Business, 2124 Ambassador Circle, Lancaster, PA 17603. *Phone:* 717-394-6211. *Toll-free phone:* 800-541-8298. *Fax:* 717-394-6213. *E-mail:* lpaul@csb.edu.
Website: http://www.csb.edu/.

Consolidated School of Business
York, Pennsylvania

Freshman Application Contact Ms. Sandra Swanger, Admissions Representative, Consolidated School of Business, 1605 Clugston Road, York, PA 17404. *Phone:* 717-764-9550. *Toll-free phone:* 800-520-0691. *Fax:* 717-764-9469. *E-mail:* sswanger@csb.edu.
Website: http://www.csb.edu/.

Dean Institute of Technology
Pittsburgh, Pennsylvania

Director of Admissions Mr. Richard D. Ali, Admissions Director, Dean Institute of Technology, 1501 West Liberty Avenue, Pittsburgh, PA 15226-1103. *Phone:* 412-531-4433.
Website: http://www.deantech.edu/.

Delaware County Community College
Media, Pennsylvania

Freshman Application Contact Ms. Hope Diehl, Director of Admissions and Enrollment Services, Delaware County Community College, 901 South Media Line Road, Media, PA 19063-1094. *Phone:* 610-359-5050. *Fax:* 610-723-1530. *E-mail:* admiss@dccc.edu.
Website: http://www.dccc.edu/.

Douglas Education Center
Monessen, Pennsylvania

Freshman Application Contact Ms. Sherry Lee Walters, Director of Enrollment Services, Douglas Education Center, 130 Seventh Street, Monessen, PA 15062. *Phone:* 724-684-3684 Ext. 2181. *Toll-free phone:* 800-413-6013.
Website: http://www.dec.edu/.

DuBois Business College
DuBois, Pennsylvania

Director of Admissions Terry Khoury, Director of Admissions, DuBois Business College, 1 Beaver Drive, DuBois, PA 15801-2401. *Phone:* 814-371-

6920. *Toll-free phone:* 800-692-6213. *Fax:* 814-371-3947. *E-mail:* dotylj@dbcollege.com.
Website: http://www.dbcollege.com/.

DuBois Business College
Huntingdon, Pennsylvania

Admissions Office Contact DuBois Business College, 1001 Moore Street, Huntingdon, PA 16652.
Website: http://www.dbcollege.com/.

DuBois Business College
Oil City, Pennsylvania

Admissions Office Contact DuBois Business College, 701 East Third Street, Oil City, PA 16301.
Website: http://www.dbcollege.com/.

Erie Institute of Technology
Erie, Pennsylvania

Freshman Application Contact Erie Institute of Technology, 940 Millcreek Mall, Erie, PA 16565. *Phone:* 814-868-9900. *Toll-free phone:* 866-868-3743.
Website: http://www.erieit.edu/.

Everest Institute
Pittsburgh, Pennsylvania

Director of Admissions Director of Admissions, Everest Institute, 100 Forbes Avenue, Suite 1200, Pittsburgh, PA 15222. *Phone:* 412-261-4520. *Toll-free phone:* 888-741-4270. *Fax:* 412-261-4546.
Website: http://www.everest.edu/.

Fortis Institute
Erie, Pennsylvania

Director of Admissions Guy M. Euliano, President, Fortis Institute, 5757 West 26th Street, Erie, PA 16506. *Phone:* 814-838-7673. *Fax:* 814-838-8642. *E-mail:* geuliano@tsbi.org.
Website: http://www.fortis.edu/.

Fortis Institute
Forty Fort, Pennsylvania

Freshman Application Contact Admissions Office, Fortis Institute, 166 Slocum Street, Forty Fort, PA 18704. *Phone:* 570-288-8400.
Website: http://www.fortis.edu/.

Fortis Institute
Scranton, Pennsylvania

Director of Admissions Ms. Heather Contardi, Director of Admissions, Fortis Institute, 517 Ash Street, Scranton, PA 18509-2903. *Phone:* 570-558-1818. *Fax:* 570-342-4537. *E-mail:* heatherp@markogroup.com.
Website: http://www.fortis.edu/.

Harcum College
Bryn Mawr, Pennsylvania

Freshman Application Contact Office of Enrollment Management, Harcum College, 750 Montgomery Avenue, Bryn Mawr, PA 19010-3476. *Phone:* 610-526-6050. *E-mail:* enroll@harcum.edu.
Website: http://www.harcum.edu/.

Harrisburg Area Community College
Harrisburg, Pennsylvania

- **State and locally supported** 2-year, founded 1964
- **Urban** 212-acre campus
- **Coed,** 20,230 undergraduate students, 30% full-time, 63% women, 37% men

Undergraduates 6,136 full-time, 14,094 part-time. 1% are from out of state; 12% Black or African American, non-Hispanic/Latino; 10% Hispanic/Latino; 3% Asian, non-Hispanic/Latino; 0.2% Native Hawaiian or other Pacific Islander, non-Hispanic/Latino; 0.3% American Indian or Alaska Native, non-

Hispanic/Latino; 2% Two or more races, non-Hispanic/Latino; 1% Race/ethnicity unknown; 2% international; 7% transferred in.
Freshmen *Admission:* 9,970 applied, 9,923 admitted, 769 enrolled.
Faculty *Total:* 1,064, 32% full-time, 58% with terminal degrees. *Student/faculty ratio:* 19:1.
Majors Accounting and business/management; accounting technology and bookkeeping; administrative assistant and secretarial science; agribusiness; architectural engineering technology; architecture; art; automobile/automotive mechanics technology; banking and financial support services; biology/biological sciences; building/home/construction inspection; business administration and management; business/commerce; cabinetmaking and millwork; cardiovascular technology; chemistry; civil engineering technology; clinical/medical laboratory technology; computer and information sciences; computer and information systems security; computer installation and repair technology; computer science; computer systems networking and telecommunications; construction engineering technology; construction trades; court reporting; crafts, folk art and artisanry; criminalistics and criminal science; criminal justice/law enforcement administration; criminal justice/police science; culinary arts; dental hygiene; design and visual communications; diagnostic medical sonography and ultrasound technology; dietetics; dramatic/theater arts; early childhood education; electrical, electronic and communications engineering technology; electrician; emergency medical technology (EMT paramedic); energy management and systems technology; engineering; engineering technologies and engineering related; environmental science; environmental studies; fire science/firefighting; food service systems administration; general studies; geographic information science and cartography; graphic design; health/health-care administration; health services administration; heating, air conditioning, ventilation and refrigeration maintenance technology; hospitality administration; hotel/motel administration; human services; international relations and affairs; landscaping and groundskeeping; legal assistant/paralegal; lineworker; management information systems and services related; mass communication/media; mathematics; mechanical engineering/mechanical technology; mechatronics, robotics, and automation engineering; medical/clinical assistant; music management; nuclear medical technology; philosophy; photography; physical sciences; psychology; radiologic technology/science; real estate; registered nursing/registered nurse; respiratory care therapy; sales, distribution, and marketing operations; secondary education; small business administration; social sciences; social work; surgical technology; tourism and travel services management; visual and performing arts; viticulture and enology; web page, digital/multimedia and information resources design.
Academics *Calendar:* semesters. *Degree:* certificates, diplomas, and associate. *Special study options:* academic remediation for entering students, adult/continuing education programs, advanced placement credit, distance learning, double majors, English as a second language, honors programs, independent study, internships, part-time degree program, services for LD students, student-designed majors, study abroad, summer session for credit. *ROTC:* Army (b).
Library McCormick Library with an OPAC, a Web page.
Student Life *Housing:* college housing not available. *Activities and Organizations:* drama/theater group, student-run newspaper, Student Government Association, Phi Theta Kappa, African American Student Association, Mosiaco Club, Fourth Estate. *Campus security:* 24-hour emergency response devices and patrols, late-night transport/escort service.
Athletics *Intercollegiate sports:* basketball M/W, soccer M, tennis M/W. *Intramural sports:* basketball M/W, soccer M/W, swimming and diving M/W, tennis M/W, volleyball M/W.
Costs (2014–15) *Tuition:* area resident $4575 full-time, $153 per credit hour part-time; state resident $6210 full-time, $207 per credit hour part-time; nonresident $9315 full-time, $311 per credit hour part-time. Full-time tuition and fees vary according to program. Part-time tuition and fees vary according to program. *Required fees:* $1230 full-time, $46 per credit hour part-time. *Payment plan:* installment. *Waivers:* employees or children of employees.
Financial Aid Of all full-time matriculated undergraduates who enrolled in 2013, 3,145 applied for aid.
Applying *Options:* electronic application, early admission, deferred entrance. *Application fee:* $35. *Required for some:* high school transcript, 1 letter of recommendation, interview.
Freshman Application Contact Mrs. Vanita L. Cowan, Administrative Clerk, Admissions, Harrisburg Area Community College, Harrisburg, PA 17110. *Phone:* 717-780-2694. *Toll-free phone:* 800-ABC-HACC. *Fax:* 717-231-7674. *E-mail:* admit@hacc.edu.
Website: http://www.hacc.edu/.

Hussian School of Art
Philadelphia, Pennsylvania

Freshman Application Contact Director of Admissions, Hussian School of Art, The Bourse, Suite 300, 111 South Independence Mall East, Philadelphia, PA 19106. *Phone:* 215-574-9600. *Fax:* 215-574-9800. *E-mail:* info@hussianart.edu.
Website: http://www.hussianart.edu/.

ITT Technical Institute
Dunmore, Pennsylvania

- **Proprietary** 2-year, part of ITT Educational Services, Inc.
- **Coed**

Academics *Calendar:* quarters. *Degree:* diplomas and associate.
Freshman Application Contact Director of Recruitment, ITT Technical Institute, 1000 Meade Street, Dunmore, PA 18512. *Phone:* 570-330-0600. *Toll-free phone:* 800-774-9791.
Website: http://www.itt-tech.edu/.

ITT Technical Institute
Harrisburg, Pennsylvania

- **Proprietary** 2-year, part of ITT Educational Services, Inc.
- **Coed**

Academics *Degree:* diplomas and associate.
Freshman Application Contact Director of Recruitment, ITT Technical Institute, 449 Eisenhower Boulevard, Suite 100, Harrisburg, PA 17111. *Phone:* 717-565-1700. *Toll-free phone:* 800-847-4756.
Website: http://www.itt-tech.edu/.

ITT Technical Institute
Levittown, Pennsylvania

- **Proprietary** 2-year, founded 2000, part of ITT Educational Services, Inc.
- **Coed**

Academics *Calendar:* quarters. *Degree:* diplomas and associate.
Freshman Application Contact Director of Recruitment, ITT Technical Institute, 311 Veterans Highway, Levittown, PA 19056. *Phone:* 215-702-6300. *Toll-free phone:* 866-488-8324.
Website: http://www.itt-tech.edu/.

ITT Technical Institute
Philadelphia, Pennsylvania

- **Proprietary** 2-year
- **Coed**

Freshman Application Contact Director of Recruiting, ITT Technical Institute, 105 South 7th Street, Philadelphia, PA 19106. *Phone:* 215-413-4300.
Website: http://www.itt-tech.edu/.

ITT Technical Institute
Pittsburgh, Pennsylvania

- **Proprietary** 2-year, part of ITT Educational Services, Inc.
- **Coed**

Academics *Calendar:* quarters. *Degree:* diplomas and associate.
Freshman Application Contact Director of Recruitment, ITT Technical Institute, 5460 Campbells Run Road, Pittsburgh, PA 15205. *Phone:* 412-446-2900. *Toll-free phone:* 800-353-8324.
Website: http://www.itt-tech.edu/.

ITT Technical Institute
Plymouth Meeting, Pennsylvania

- **Proprietary** 2-year, founded 2002, part of ITT Educational Services, Inc.
- **Coed**

Academics *Calendar:* quarters. *Degree:* diplomas and associate.
Freshman Application Contact Director of Recruitment, ITT Technical Institute, 220 West Germantown Pike, Suite 100, Plymouth Meeting, PA 19462. *Phone:* 610-832-3400. *Toll-free phone:* 866-902-8324.
Website: http://www.itt-tech.edu/.

ITT Technical Institute
Tarentum, Pennsylvania

- **Proprietary** 2-year, part of ITT Educational Services, Inc.
- **Coed**

Academics *Calendar:* quarters. *Degree:* diplomas and associate.

Freshman Application Contact Director of Recruitment, ITT Technical Institute, 100 Pittsburgh Mills Circle, Suite 100, Tarentum, PA 15084. *Phone:* 724-274-1400. *Toll-free phone:* 800-488-0121.

Website: http://www.itt-tech.edu/.

JNA Institute of Culinary Arts
Philadelphia, Pennsylvania

- **Proprietary** 2-year, founded 1988
- **Urban** campus with easy access to Philadelphia
- **Coed,** 59 undergraduate students, 100% full-time, 51% women, 49% men

Undergraduates 59 full-time. Students come from 7 states and territories; 10% are from out of state; 57% Black or African American, non-Hispanic/Latino; 11% Hispanic/Latino; 3% Asian, non-Hispanic/Latino. *Retention:* 60% of full-time freshmen returned.

Freshmen *Admission:* 28 enrolled.

Majors Restaurant, culinary, and catering management.

Academics *Calendar:* continuous. *Degree:* associate.

Freshman Application Contact Admissions Office, JNA Institute of Culinary Arts, 1212 South Broad Street, Philadelphia, PA 19146.

Website: http://www.culinaryarts.com/.

Johnson College
Scranton, Pennsylvania

Freshman Application Contact Ms. Melissa Ide, Director of Enrollment Management, Johnson College, 3427 North Main Avenue, Scranton, PA 18508. *Phone:* 570-702-8910. *Toll-free phone:* 800-2WE-WORK. *Fax:* 570-348-2181. *E-mail:* admit@johnson.edu.

Website: http://www.johnson.edu/.

Kaplan Career Institute, Broomall Campus
Broomall, Pennsylvania

Freshman Application Contact Kaplan Career Institute, Broomall Campus, 1991 Sproul Road, Suite 42, Broomall, PA 19008. *Phone:* 610-353-3300. *Toll-free phone:* 800-935-1857.

Website: http://www.kaplancareerinstitute.com/.

Kaplan Career Institute, Franklin Mills Campus
Philadelphia, Pennsylvania

Freshman Application Contact Kaplan Career Institute, Franklin Mills Campus, 177 Franklin Mills Boulevard, Philadelphia, PA 19154. *Phone:* 215-612-6600. *Toll-free phone:* 800-935-1857.

Website: http://www.kaplancareerinstitute.com/.

Kaplan Career Institute, Harrisburg Campus
Harrisburg, Pennsylvania

Freshman Application Contact Kaplan Career Institute, Harrisburg Campus, 5650 Derry Street, Harrisburg, PA 17111-3518. *Phone:* 717-558-1300. *Toll-free phone:* 800-935-1857.

Website: http://www.kaplancareerinstitute.com/.

Kaplan Career Institute, Philadelphia Campus
Philadelphia, Pennsylvania

Freshman Application Contact Admissions Director, Kaplan Career Institute, Philadelphia Campus, 3010 Market Street, Philadelphia, PA 19104. *Toll-free phone:* 800-935-1857.

Website: http://www.kaplancareerinstitute.com/.

Kaplan Career Institute, Pittsburgh Campus
Pittsburgh, Pennsylvania

Freshman Application Contact Kaplan Career Institute, Pittsburgh Campus, 933 Penn Avenue, Pittsburgh, PA 15222. *Phone:* 412-261-2647. *Toll-free phone:* 800-935-1857.

Website: http://www.kaplancareerinstitute.com/.

Keystone Technical Institute
Harrisburg, Pennsylvania

Freshman Application Contact Tom Bogush, Director of Admissions, Keystone Technical Institute, 2301 Academy Drive, Harrisburg, PA 17112. *Phone:* 717-545-4747. *Toll-free phone:* 800-400-3322. *Fax:* 717-901-9090. *E-mail:* info@acadcampus.com.

Website: http://www.kti.edu/.

Lackawanna College
Scranton, Pennsylvania

Freshman Application Contact Ms. Stacey Muchal, Associate Director of Admissions, Lackawanna College, 501 Vine Street, Scranton, PA 18509. *Phone:* 570-961-7868. *Toll-free phone:* 877-346-3552. *Fax:* 570-961-7843. *E-mail:* muchals@lackawanna.edu.

Website: http://www.lackawanna.edu/.

Lansdale School of Business
North Wales, Pennsylvania

Director of Admissions Ms. Marianne H. Johnson, Director of Admissions, Lansdale School of Business, 201 Church Road, North Wales, PA 19454-4148. *Phone:* 215-699-5700 Ext. 112. *Toll-free phone:* 800-219-0486. *Fax:* 215-699-8770. *E-mail:* mjohnson@lsb.edu.

Website: http://www.lsb.edu/.

Laurel Business Institute
Uniontown, Pennsylvania

Freshman Application Contact Mrs. Lisa Dolan, Laurel Business Institute, 11 East Penn Street, PO Box 877, Uniontown, PA 15401. *Phone:* 724-439-4900 Ext. 158. *Fax:* 724-439-3607. *E-mail:* ldolan@laurel.edu.

Website: http://www.laurel.edu/lbi/.

Laurel Technical Institute
Sharon, Pennsylvania

Freshman Application Contact Irene Lewis, Laurel Technical Institute, 200 Sterling Avenue, Sharon, PA 16146. *Phone:* 724-983-0700. *Fax:* 724-983-8355. *E-mail:* info@biop.edu.

Website: http://www.laurel.edu/lti/.

Lehigh Carbon Community College
Schnecksville, Pennsylvania

- **State and locally supported** 2-year, founded 1967
- **Suburban** 254-acre campus with easy access to Philadelphia
- **Endowment** $3.1 million
- **Coed,** 6,779 undergraduate students, 37% full-time, 60% women, 40% men

Undergraduates 2,525 full-time, 4,254 part-time. Students come from 10 states and territories; 0.3% are from out of state; 6% Black or African American, non-Hispanic/Latino; 13% Hispanic/Latino; 2% Asian, non-Hispanic/Latino; 0.2% American Indian or Alaska Native, non-Hispanic/Latino; 4% Two or more races, non-Hispanic/Latino; 11% Race/ethnicity unknown; 0.4% international; 56% transferred in.

Freshmen *Admission:* 4,515 applied, 4,515 admitted, 1,463 enrolled.

Faculty *Total:* 431, 20% full-time, 4% with terminal degrees. *Student/faculty ratio:* 17:1.

Majors Accounting technology and bookkeeping; aeronautics/aviation/aerospace science and technology; airline pilot and flight crew; animation, interactive technology, video graphics and special effects; art; biology/biological sciences; biotechnology; building/construction site management; business administration and management; business/commerce; chemical technology; chemistry; computer and information sciences; computer and information systems security; computer programming; computer programming (specific applications); computer systems networking and telecommunications; construction trades; criminal justice/law enforcement administration; criminal justice/safety; drafting and design technology; early childhood education; education; electrical, electronic and communications engineering technology; engineering; environmental science; fashion/apparel design; game and interactive media design; general studies; geographic information science and cartography; graphic design; health information/medical records technology; heating, air conditioning, ventilation and refrigeration maintenance technology; human resources management; human services; industrial electronics technology; interior design; kinesiology and exercise science; legal assistant/paralegal; liberal arts and sciences/liberal studies; manufacturing engineering technology; mathematics; mechanical engineering/mechanical technology; medical/clinical assistant; nanotechnology; occupational therapist assistant; physical sciences; physical therapy technology; psychology; public administration; radio and television broadcasting technology; recording arts technology; registered nursing/registered nurse; resort management; social work; special education; speech communication and rhetoric; sport and fitness administration/management; teacher assistant/aide; veterinary/animal health technology; web page, digital/multimedia and information resources design.

Academics *Calendar:* semesters. *Degree:* certificates, diplomas, and associate. *Special study options:* academic remediation for entering students, advanced placement credit, cooperative education, distance learning, English as a second language, external degree program, honors programs, independent study, internships, part-time degree program, services for LD students, summer session for credit. *ROTC:* Army (c).

Library Rothrock Library with 60,096 titles, 3,762 audiovisual materials, an OPAC, a Web page.

Student Life *Housing:* college housing not available. *Activities and Organizations:* drama/theater group, choral group, Phi Theta Kappa, Justice Society, PSI BETA (Psychology Club), Student Government Association, Teacher Education Student Association (TESA). *Campus security:* 24-hour emergency response devices. *Student services:* personal/psychological counseling.

Athletics Member NJCAA. *Intercollegiate sports:* baseball M, basketball M/W, golf M/W, soccer M, softball W, volleyball W. *Intramural sports:* basketball M/W, golf M/W, table tennis M/W, volleyball M/W.

Standardized Tests *Required for some:* TEAS (for those applying to Nursing Program).

Costs (2014–15) *Tuition:* area resident $3000 full-time, $100 per credit part-time; state resident $6270 full-time, $209 per credit part-time; nonresident $9540 full-time, $318 per credit part-time. *Required fees:* $510 full-time, $27 per credit part-time. *Payment plan:* installment. *Waivers:* senior citizens and employees or children of employees.

Applying *Options:* electronic application. *Required for some:* essay or personal statement, high school transcript, interview. *Application deadlines:* rolling (freshmen), rolling (out-of-state freshmen), rolling (transfers). *Notification:* continuous (freshmen), continuous (out-of-state freshmen), continuous (transfers).

Freshman Application Contact Mr. Louis Hegyes, Director of Recruitment/Admissions, Lehigh Carbon Community College, 4525 Education Park Drive, Schnecksville, PA 18078. *Phone:* 610-799-1575. *Fax:* 610-799-1527. *E-mail:* admissions@lccc.edu. *Website:* http://www.lccc.edu/.

Lincoln Technical Institute
Allentown, Pennsylvania

Freshman Application Contact Admissions Office, Lincoln Technical Institute, 5151 Tilghman Street, Allentown, PA 18104-3298. *Phone:* 610-398-5301. *Website:* http://www.lincolnedu.com/.

Lincoln Technical Institute
Philadelphia, Pennsylvania

Director of Admissions Mr. James Kuntz, Executive Director, Lincoln Technical Institute, 9191 Torresdale Avenue, Philadelphia, PA 19136-1595. *Phone:* 215-335-0800. *Fax:* 215-335-1443. *E-mail:* jkuntz@lincolntech.com. *Website:* http://www.lincolnedu.com/.

Luzerne County Community College
Nanticoke, Pennsylvania

- **County-supported** 2-year, founded 1966
- **Suburban** 122-acre campus with easy access to Philadelphia
- **Coed,** 6,049 undergraduate students, 46% full-time, 60% women, 40% men

Undergraduates 2,793 full-time, 3,256 part-time. 0.3% are from out of state; 5% Black or African American, non-Hispanic/Latino; 10% Hispanic/Latino;

1% Asian, non-Hispanic/Latino; 0.2% Native Hawaiian or other Pacific Islander, non-Hispanic/Latino; 0.2% American Indian or Alaska Native, non-Hispanic/Latino; 0.9% Two or more races, non-Hispanic/Latino; 8% Race/ethnicity unknown. *Retention:* 57% of full-time freshmen returned.

Freshmen *Admission:* 2,504 applied, 2,504 admitted, 1,417 enrolled.

Majors Accounting; administrative assistant and secretarial science; airline pilot and flight crew; architectural engineering; architectural engineering technology; automobile/automotive mechanics technology; aviation/airway management; baking and pastry arts; banking and financial support services; biological and physical sciences; building/property maintenance; business administration and management; child-care provision; commercial and advertising art; commercial photography; computer and information sciences; computer and information sciences related; computer graphics; computer programming related; computer science; computer systems networking and telecommunications; computer technology/computer systems technology; court reporting; criminal justice/law enforcement administration; culinary arts; data entry/microcomputer applications; data processing and data processing technology; dental assisting; dental hygiene; drafting and design technology; drafting/design engineering technologies related; drawing; early childhood education; education; electrical, electronic and communications engineering technology; electrician; emergency medical technology (EMT paramedic); engineering technology; executive assistant/executive secretary; fire science/firefighting; food technology and processing; funeral service and mortuary science; general studies; graphic and printing equipment operation/production; graphic design; health and physical education/fitness; health/health-care administration; heating, air conditioning, ventilation and refrigeration maintenance technology; horticultural science; hospitality and recreation marketing; hotel/motel administration; humanities; human services; industrial and product design; international business/trade/commerce; journalism; legal assistant/paralegal; liberal arts and sciences and humanities related; liberal arts and sciences/liberal studies; mathematics; medical administrative assistant and medical secretary; painting; photography; physical education teaching and coaching; plumbing technology; pre-pharmacy studies; radio and television broadcasting technology; real estate; registered nursing/registered nurse; respiratory care therapy; social sciences; surgical technology; tourism and travel services management; tourism and travel services marketing.

Academics *Calendar:* semesters. *Degree:* certificates, diplomas, and associate. *Special study options:* academic remediation for entering students, accelerated degree program, advanced placement credit, distance learning, external degree program, internships, part-time degree program, services for LD students, summer session for credit.

Library Learning Resources Center with an OPAC, a Web page.

Student Life *Housing:* college housing not available. *Activities and Organizations:* student-run newspaper, radio and television station, student government, Circle K, Nursing Forum, Science Club, SADAH. *Campus security:* 24-hour patrols.

Athletics Member NJCAA. *Intercollegiate sports:* baseball M, basketball M/W, cross-country running M/W, golf M/W, soccer M/W, softball W, volleyball W. *Intramural sports:* badminton M/W, basketball M/W, bowling M/W, softball M/W, tennis M/W, volleyball M/W.

Costs (2014–15) *Tuition:* area resident $3540 full-time, $118 per credit hour part-time; state resident $7080 full-time, $236 per credit hour part-time; nonresident $10,620 full-time, $354 per credit hour part-time. Full-time tuition and fees vary according to course load. Part-time tuition and fees vary according to course load. *Required fees:* $1050 full-time, $35 per credit hour part-time. *Payment plan:* installment. *Waivers:* senior citizens and employees or children of employees.

Applying *Options:* early admission, deferred entrance. *Recommended:* high school transcript.

Freshman Application Contact Mr. Francis Curry, Director of Admissions, Luzerne County Community College, 1333 South Prospect Street, Nanticoke, PA 18634-9804. *Phone:* 570-740-0337. *Toll-free phone:* 800-377-5222 Ext. 7337. *Fax:* 570-740-0238. *E-mail:* admissions@luzerne.edu. *Website:* http://www.luzerne.edu/.

Manor College
Jenkintown, Pennsylvania

- **Independent Byzantine Catholic** 2-year, founded 1947
- **Small-town** 35-acre campus with easy access to Philadelphia
- **Endowment** $2.2 million
- **Coed,** 780 undergraduate students, 60% full-time, 72% women, 28% men

Undergraduates 471 full-time, 309 part-time. Students come from 5 states and territories; 2% are from out of state; 38% Black or African American, non-Hispanic/Latino; 7% Hispanic/Latino; 3% Asian, non-Hispanic/Latino; 0.3% Native Hawaiian or other Pacific Islander, non-Hispanic/Latino; 0.5% American Indian or Alaska Native, non-Hispanic/Latino; 3% Two or more races, non-Hispanic/Latino; 2% Race/ethnicity unknown; 15% transferred in; 11% live on campus. *Retention:* 76% of full-time freshmen returned.

Freshmen *Admission:* 1,198 applied, 644 admitted, 200 enrolled. *Average high school GPA:* 2.71. *Test scores:* SAT critical reading scores over 500: 9%; SAT math scores over 500: 9%; SAT writing scores over 500: 6%; ACT scores over 18: 20%; SAT critical reading scores over 600: 4%; SAT math scores over 600: 1%; SAT writing scores over 600: 2%; ACT scores over 24: 10%; SAT critical reading scores over 700: 1%.

Faculty *Total:* 142, 18% full-time, 33% with terminal degrees. *Student/faculty ratio:* 9:1.

Majors Accounting; business administration and management; business, management, and marketing related; communication and media related; computer programming (specific applications); dental assisting; dental hygiene; education (specific subject areas) related; elementary education; health professions related; human resources management and services related; legal assistant/paralegal; liberal arts and sciences/liberal studies; marketing/marketing management; psychology; religious education; sport and fitness administration/management; veterinary/animal health technology.

Academics *Calendar:* semesters. *Degrees:* certificates, diplomas, associate, and postbachelor's certificates. *Special study options:* academic remediation for entering students, accelerated degree program, adult/continuing education programs, advanced placement credit, distance learning, double majors, honors programs, independent study, internships, part-time degree program, services for LD students, summer session for credit.

Library Basileiad Library with 42,000 titles, 30 audiovisual materials, an OPAC, a Web page.

Student Life *Housing Options:* coed. Campus housing is university owned. *Activities and Organizations:* Rotoract (Student service organization), Vet Tech Club, Campus Activities Board, Macrinian Yearbook, Phi Theta Kappa (Honor Society). *Campus security:* 24-hour emergency response devices and patrols, late-night transport/escort service. *Student services:* personal/psychological counseling.

Athletics Member NJCAA. *Intercollegiate sports:* basketball M/W, soccer M/W.

Standardized Tests *Required for some:* SAT or ACT (for admission). *Recommended:* SAT or ACT (for admission).

Costs (2015–16) *Comprehensive fee:* $23,324 includes full-time tuition ($15,470), mandatory fees ($600), and room and board ($7254). Full-time tuition and fees vary according to course load and program. Part-time tuition: $399 per credit. Part-time tuition and fees vary according to course load and program. *Required fees:* $100 per term part-time. *Payment plan:* installment. *Waivers:* adult students, senior citizens, and employees or children of employees.

Financial Aid Of all full-time matriculated undergraduates who enrolled in 2009, 35 Federal Work-Study jobs (averaging $3000). 10 state and other part-time jobs (averaging $3600).

Applying *Options:* electronic application, deferred entrance. *Required:* high school transcript. *Application deadlines:* rolling (freshmen), rolling (transfers). *Notification:* continuous (freshmen), continuous (transfers).

Freshman Application Contact Manor College, 700 Fox Chase Rd., Jenkintown, PA 19046. *Phone:* 215-885-2360 Ext. 205. *Website:* http://www.manor.edu/.

McCann School of Business & Technology
Hazelton, Pennsylvania

Admissions Office Contact McCann School of Business & Technology, 370 Maplewood Drive, Hazelton, PA 18202. *Website:* http://www.mccann.edu/.

McCann School of Business & Technology
Pottsville, Pennsylvania

Freshman Application Contact Mrs. Amelia Hopkins, Director, Pottsville Campus, McCann School of Business & Technology, 2650 Woodglen Rd., Pottsville, PA 17901. *Phone:* 570-622-7622. *Fax:* 570-622-7770. *Website:* http://www.mccann.edu/.

McCann School of Business & Technology
Sunbury, Pennsylvania

Admissions Office Contact McCann School of Business & Technology, 1147 North Fourth Street, Sunbury, PA 17801. *Website:* http://www.mccann.edu/.

Mercyhurst North East
North East, Pennsylvania

Director of Admissions Travis Lindahl, Director of Admissions, Mercyhurst North East, 16 West Division Street, North East, PA 16428. *Phone:* 814-725-6217. *Toll-free phone:* 866-846-6042. *Fax:* 814-725-6251. *E-mail:* neadmiss@mercyhurst.edu. *Website:* http://northeast.mercyhurst.edu/.

Metropolitan Career Center Computer Technology Institute
Philadelphia, Pennsylvania

Freshman Application Contact Admissions Office, Metropolitan Career Center Computer Technology Institute, 100 South Broad Street, Suite 830, Philadelphia, PA 19110. *Phone:* 215-568-7861. *Website:* http://www.careersinit.org/.

Montgomery County Community College
Blue Bell, Pennsylvania

- **County-supported** 2-year, founded 1964
- **Suburban** 186-acre campus with easy access to Philadelphia
- **Coed,** 12,805 undergraduate students, 34% full-time, 57% women, 43% men

Undergraduates 4,343 full-time, 8,462 part-time. Students come from 14 states and territories; 105 other countries; 0.3% are from out of state; 15% Black or African American, non-Hispanic/Latino; 6% Hispanic/Latino; 6% Asian, non-Hispanic/Latino; 0.3% Native Hawaiian or other Pacific Islander, non-Hispanic/Latino; 0.4% American Indian or Alaska Native, non-Hispanic/Latino; 3% Two or more races, non-Hispanic/Latino; 9% Race/ethnicity unknown; 2% international. *Retention:* 62% of full-time freshmen returned.

Freshmen *Admission:* 14,463 applied, 14,463 admitted, 3,071 enrolled.

Faculty *Total:* 755, 24% full-time. *Student/faculty ratio:* 19:1.

Majors Accounting; accounting technology and bookkeeping; administrative assistant and secretarial science; art; baking and pastry arts; biology/biological sciences; biotechnology; business administration and management; business/commerce; business/corporate communications; child-care and support services management; clinical/medical laboratory technology; commercial and advertising art; communications technologies and support services related; computer and information sciences; computer programming; computer systems networking and telecommunications; criminal justice/police science; culinary arts; dental hygiene; electrical, electronic and communications engineering technology; electromechanical technology; elementary education; engineering science; engineering technologies and engineering related; environmental science; fire prevention and safety technology; health and physical education/fitness; hospitality and recreation marketing; humanities; information science/studies; liberal arts and sciences/liberal studies; management information systems and services related; mathematics; mechanical engineering/mechanical technology; medical/clinical assistant; medical radiologic technology; network and system administration; physical education teaching and coaching; physical sciences; psychiatric/mental health services technology; psychology; radiologic technology/science; radio, television, and digital communication related; real estate; recording arts technology; registered nursing/registered nurse; sales, distribution, and marketing operations; secondary education; social sciences; speech communication and rhetoric; surgical technology; teacher assistant/aide; tourism and travel services marketing; web/multimedia management and webmaster.

Academics *Calendar:* semesters plus winter term. *Degree:* certificates and associate. *Special study options:* academic remediation for entering students, accelerated degree program, adult/continuing education programs, advanced placement credit, cooperative education, distance learning, English as a second language, honors programs, independent study, internships, part-time degree program, services for LD students, student-designed majors, study abroad, summer session for credit.

Library The Brendlinger Library/Branch Library Pottstown Campus with 86,001 titles, 13,533 audiovisual materials, an OPAC, a Web page.

Student Life *Housing:* college housing not available. *Activities and Organizations:* drama/theater group, student-run newspaper, radio and television station, choral group, student government, Thrive (Christian Fellowship), radio station, Drama Club, African - American Student League. *Campus security:* 24-hour emergency response devices and patrols, late-night transport/escort service, bicycle patrol. *Student services:* health clinic, personal/psychological counseling.

Athletics Member NJCAA. *Intercollegiate sports:* baseball M, basketball M/W, soccer M/W, softball W, volleyball W. *Intramural sports:* badminton M/W, basketball M/W, bowling M/W, cross-country running M/W, football M,

racquetball M/W, soccer M/W, table tennis M/W, tennis M/W, volleyball M/W, weight lifting M/W.
Costs (2014–15) *Tuition:* area resident $3870 full-time, $129 per credit part-time; state resident $8040 full-time, $258 per credit part-time; nonresident $12,210 full-time, $387 per credit part-time. Full-time tuition and fees vary according to program. Part-time tuition and fees vary according to program. *Required fees:* $870 full-time, $29 per credit part-time. *Payment plan:* deferred payment. *Waivers:* senior citizens and employees or children of employees.
Financial Aid Of all full-time matriculated undergraduates who enrolled in 2013, 60 Federal Work-Study jobs (averaging $2500).
Applying *Options:* electronic application, early admission, deferred entrance. *Application fee:* $25. *Required:* high school transcript. *Required for some:* interview. *Application deadline:* rolling (transfers). *Notification:* continuous (freshmen), continuous (transfers).
Freshman Application Contact Montgomery County Community College, Blue Bell, PA 19422. *Phone:* 215-641-6551. *Fax:* 215-619-7188. *E-mail:* admrec@admin.mc3.edu.
Website: http://www.mc3.edu/.

New Castle School of Trades
New Castle, Pennsylvania

- **Independent** 2-year, founded 1945, part of Educational Enterprises Incorporated
- **Rural** 20-acre campus with easy access to Pittsburgh
- **Coed, primarily men,** 601 undergraduate students, 100% full-time, 4% women, 96% men

Undergraduates 601 full-time. Students come from 3 states and territories; 40% are from out of state.
Freshmen *Admission:* 601 enrolled.
Faculty *Total:* 64, 72% full-time. *Student/faculty ratio:* 13:1.
Majors Automotive engineering technology; construction engineering technology; diesel mechanics technology; electrical, electronic and communications engineering technology; heating, ventilation, air conditioning and refrigeration engineering technology; industrial mechanics and maintenance technology; machine tool technology.
Academics *Calendar:* quarters. *Degree:* diplomas and associate. *Special study options:* part-time degree program.
Student Life *Housing:* college housing not available. *Campus security:* 24-hour emergency response devices. *Student services:* personal/psychological counseling.
Standardized Tests *Required:* Wonderlic aptitude test (for admission).
Applying *Required:* high school transcript, interview. *Required for some:* essay or personal statement.
Freshman Application Contact Mr. James Catheline, Admissions Director, New Castle School of Trades, 4117 Pulaski Road, New Castle, PA 16101. *Phone:* 724-964-8811. *Toll-free phone:* 800-837-8299.
Website: http://www.ncstrades.com/.

Northampton Community College
Bethlehem, Pennsylvania

- **State and locally supported** 2-year, founded 1967
- **Suburban** 165-acre campus with easy access to Philadelphia
- **Endowment** $40.6 million
- **Coed,** 10,531 undergraduate students, 43% full-time, 60% women, 40% men

Undergraduates 4,519 full-time, 6,012 part-time. Students come from 26 states and territories; 35 other countries; 1% are from out of state; 12% Black or African American, non-Hispanic/Latino; 20% Hispanic/Latino; 2% Asian, non-Hispanic/Latino; 0.2% Native Hawaiian or other Pacific Islander, non-Hispanic/Latino; 0.3% American Indian or Alaska Native, non-Hispanic/Latino; 2% Two or more races, non-Hispanic/Latino; 2% Race/ethnicity unknown; 0.8% international; 9% transferred in; 3% live on campus.
Freshmen *Admission:* 4,643 applied, 4,643 admitted, 2,125 enrolled.
Faculty *Total:* 722, 17% full-time, 14% with terminal degrees. *Student/faculty ratio:* 20:1.
Majors Accounting technology and bookkeeping; acting; administrative assistant and secretarial science; architectural engineering technology; athletic training; automobile/automotive mechanics technology; biology/biological sciences; biotechnology; business administration and management; business/commerce; CAD/CADD drafting/design technology; chemistry; computer and information systems security; computer installation and repair technology; computer programming; computer science; computer systems networking and telecommunications; construction management; criminal justice/safety; culinary arts; dental hygiene; diagnostic medical sonography and ultrasound technology; early childhood education; electrical, electronic

and communications engineering technology; electrician; electromechanical technology; engineering; environmental science; fine/studio arts; fire science/firefighting; fire services administration; funeral service and mortuary science; general studies; graphic design; heating, air conditioning, ventilation and refrigeration maintenance technology; hotel/motel administration; industrial electronics technology; interior design; journalism; legal administrative assistant/secretary; legal assistant/paralegal; liberal arts and sciences and humanities related; liberal arts and sciences/liberal studies; marketing/marketing management; mathematics; medical administrative assistant and medical secretary; meeting and event planning; middle school education; physics; public health education and promotion; quality control technology; radio and television broadcasting technology; radiologic technology/science; registered nursing/registered nurse; restaurant/food services management; secondary education; social work; speech communication and rhetoric; sport and fitness administration/management; teacher assistant/aide; veterinary/animal health technology; web page, digital/multimedia and information resources design.
Academics *Calendar:* semesters. *Degree:* certificates, diplomas, and associate. *Special study options:* academic remediation for entering students, adult/continuing education programs, advanced placement credit, distance learning, English as a second language, honors programs, independent study, internships, off-campus study, part-time degree program, services for LD students, student-designed majors, study abroad, summer session for credit.
Library Paul & Harriett Mack Library with 113,848 titles, 21,337 audiovisual materials, an OPAC, a Web page.
Student Life *Housing Options:* coed. Campus housing is university owned. *Activities and Organizations:* student-run newspaper, radio station, choral group, Phi Theta Kappa, Student Senate, College and Hospital Association of Radiologic Technologies Students (CHARTS), American Dental Hygiene Association (ADHA), International Student Organization. *Campus security:* 24-hour emergency response devices and patrols, controlled dormitory access. *Student services:* health clinic, personal/psychological counseling.
Athletics Member NJCAA. *Intercollegiate sports:* baseball M, basketball M/W, cross-country running M/W, golf M, lacrosse M, soccer M/W, softball W, tennis W, volleyball W. *Intramural sports:* basketball M/W, cheerleading M(c)/W(c), soccer M/W, volleyball M/W.
Costs (2014–15) *Tuition:* area resident $2730 full-time, $91 per credit hour part-time; state resident $5460 full-time, $182 per credit hour part-time; nonresident $8190 full-time, $273 per credit hour part-time. Full-time tuition and fees vary according to course load. Part-time tuition and fees vary according to course load. *Required fees:* $1110 full-time, $37 per credit hour part-time. *Room and board:* $8220; room only: $4726. Room and board charges vary according to board plan and housing facility. *Payment plan:* installment. *Waivers:* adult students, senior citizens, and employees or children of employees.
Financial Aid Of all full-time matriculated undergraduates who enrolled in 2014, 202 Federal Work-Study jobs (averaging $2400). 116 state and other part-time jobs (averaging $2000).
Applying *Options:* electronic application, deferred entrance. *Application fee:* $25. *Required for some:* high school transcript, minimum 2.5 GPA, interview, interview for rad and veterinary. *Recommended:* high school transcript. *Application deadlines:* rolling (freshmen), rolling (out-of-state freshmen), rolling (transfers). *Notification:* continuous (freshmen), continuous (out-of-state freshmen), continuous (transfers).
Freshman Application Contact Mr. James McCarthy, Director of Admissions, Northampton Community College, 3835 Green Pond Road, Bethlehem, PA 18020-7599. *Phone:* 610-861-5506. *Fax:* 610-861-5551. *E-mail:* jrmccarthy@northampton.edu.
Website: http://www.northampton.edu/.

Orleans Technical Institute
Philadelphia, Pennsylvania

Freshman Application Contact Mrs. Dorothy Stinson, Admissions Secretary, Orleans Technical Institute, 2770 Red Lion Road, Philadelphia, PA 19114. *Phone:* 215-728-4700. *Fax:* 215-745-1689. *E-mail:* stinsd@jevs.org. *Website:* http://www.orleanstech.edu/.

Penn Commercial Business and Technical School
Washington, Pennsylvania

Director of Admissions Mr. Michael John Joyce, Director of Admissions, Penn Commercial Business and Technical School, 242 Oak Spring Road, Washington, PA 15301. *Phone:* 724-222-5330 Ext. 1. *Toll-free phone:* 888-309-7484. *E-mail:* mjoyce@penn-commercial.com.
Website: http://www.penncommercial.net/.

Pennco Tech
Bristol, Pennsylvania

Freshman Application Contact Pennco Tech, 3815 Otter Street, Bristol, PA 19007-3696. *Phone:* 215-785-0111. *Toll-free phone:* 800-575-9399. *Website:* http://www.penncotech.com/.

Penn State DuBois
DuBois, Pennsylvania

- **State-related** primarily 2-year, founded 1935, part of Pennsylvania State University
- **Small-town** campus
- **Coed,** 615 undergraduate students, 76% full-time, 48% women, 52% men

Undergraduates 467 full-time, 148 part-time. 3% are from out of state; 1% Black or African American, non-Hispanic/Latino; 3% Hispanic/Latino; 0.8% Asian, non-Hispanic/Latino; 0.4% Two or more races, non-Hispanic/Latino; 1% Race/ethnicity unknown; 1% international; 3% transferred in. *Retention:* 77% of full-time freshmen returned.

Freshmen *Admission:* 378 applied, 335 admitted, 153 enrolled. *Average high school GPA:* 3.11. *Test scores:* SAT critical reading scores over 500: 29%; SAT math scores over 500: 36%; SAT writing scores over 500: 25%; ACT scores over 18: 50%; SAT critical reading scores over 600: 5%; SAT math scores over 600: 6%; SAT writing scores over 600: 3%; SAT math scores over 700: 1%; SAT writing scores over 700: 1%.

Faculty *Total:* 60, 65% full-time, 47% with terminal degrees. *Student/faculty ratio:* 11:1.

Majors Accounting; acting; actuarial science; adult and continuing education administration; advertising; aerospace, aeronautical and astronautical/space engineering; African American/Black studies; agribusiness; agricultural and extension education; agricultural business and management related; agricultural engineering; agricultural mechanization; agriculture; agronomy and crop science; animal sciences; animal sciences related; anthropology; applied economics; archeology; architectural engineering; art; art history, criticism and conservation; art teacher education; Asian studies (East); astronomy; atmospheric sciences and meteorology; biochemistry; bioengineering and biomedical engineering; biological and biomedical sciences related; biological and physical sciences; biology/biological sciences; biology/biotechnology laboratory technician; biomedical technology; business administration and management; business/commerce; business/managerial economics; chemical engineering; chemistry; civil engineering; classics and classical languages; clinical/medical laboratory technology; communication and journalism related; communication sciences and disorders; comparative literature; computer and information sciences; computer engineering; criminal justice/law enforcement administration; economics; electrical and electronics engineering; electrical, electronic and communications engineering technology; elementary education; engineering science; English; environmental/environmental health engineering; film/cinema/video studies; finance; food science; foreign language teacher education; forest sciences and biology; forest technology; French; geography; geological and earth sciences/geosciences related; geology/earth science; German; graphic design; health/health-care administration; history; horticultural science; hospitality administration related; human development and family studies; human nutrition; industrial engineering; information science/studies; international business/trade/commerce; international relations and affairs; Italian; Japanese; Jewish/Judaic studies; journalism; kinesiology and exercise science; labor and industrial relations; landscaping and groundskeeping; Latin American studies; liberal arts and sciences/liberal studies; management information systems; marketing/marketing management; materials science; mathematics; mechanical engineering; mechanical engineering/mechanical technology; medical microbiology and bacteriology; medieval and Renaissance studies; metallurgical technology; mining and mineral engineering; music; natural resources and conservation related; natural resources/conservation; nuclear engineering; occupational therapist assistant; organizational behavior; parks, recreation and leisure facilities management; petroleum engineering; philosophy; physical therapy technology; physics; political science and government; premedical studies; psychology; registered nursing/registered nurse; rehabilitation and therapeutic professions related; religious studies; Russian; secondary education; sociology; soil science and agronomy; Spanish; special education; speech communication and rhetoric; statistics; telecommunications technology; theater design and technology; toxicology; turf and turfgrass management; visual and performing arts; wildlife, fish and wildlands science and management; women's studies.

Academics *Calendar:* semesters. *Degrees:* certificates, associate, and bachelor's. *Special study options:* adult/continuing education programs, external degree program.

Student Life *Housing:* college housing not available.

Athletics Member NJCAA. *Intercollegiate sports:* basketball M, cross-country running M/W, golf M/W, volleyball W. *Intramural sports:* basketball M/W, football M, soccer M/W, table tennis M/W, volleyball M/W.

Standardized Tests *Required:* SAT or ACT (for admission).

Costs (2014–15) *Tuition:* state resident $12,718 full-time, $524 per credit hour part-time; nonresident $19,404 full-time, $809 per credit hour part-time. Full-time tuition and fees vary according to course level, degree level, location, program, and student level. Part-time tuition and fees vary according to course level, course load, degree level, location, program, and student level. *Required fees:* $810 full-time. *Payment plans:* installment, deferred payment. *Waivers:* senior citizens and employees or children of employees.

Financial Aid Of all full-time matriculated undergraduates who enrolled in 2013, 495 applied for aid, 444 were judged to have need, 25 had their need fully met. In 2013, 23 non-need-based awards were made. *Average percent of need met:* 62%. *Average financial aid package:* $11,013. *Average need-based loan:* $3810. *Average need-based gift aid:* $6293. *Average non-need-based aid:* $1954. *Average indebtedness upon graduation:* $36,935.

Applying *Options:* electronic application, early admission, deferred entrance. *Application fee:* $50. *Required:* high school transcript. *Required for some:* interview. *Recommended:* essay or personal statement. *Application deadlines:* rolling (freshmen), rolling (transfers). *Notification:* continuous (freshmen), continuous (transfers).

Freshman Application Contact Admissions Office, Penn State DuBois, 1 College Place, DuBois, PA 15801. *Phone:* 814-375-4720. *Toll-free phone:* 800-346-7627. *Fax:* 814-375-4784. *E-mail:* duboisinfo@psi.edu. *Website:* http://www.ds.psu.edu/.

Penn State Fayette, The Eberly Campus
Lemont Furnace, Pennsylvania

- **State-related** primarily 2-year, founded 1934, part of Pennsylvania State University
- **Small-town** campus
- **Coed,** 717 undergraduate students, 81% full-time, 58% women, 42% men

Undergraduates 578 full-time, 139 part-time. 4% are from out of state; 4% Black or African American, non-Hispanic/Latino; 2% Hispanic/Latino; 0.8% Asian, non-Hispanic/Latino; 0.2% American Indian or Alaska Native, non-Hispanic/Latino; 3% Two or more races, non-Hispanic/Latino; 0.8% Race/ethnicity unknown; 2% international; 7% transferred in. *Retention:* 77% of full-time freshmen returned.

Freshmen *Admission:* 579 applied, 484 admitted, 196 enrolled. *Average high school GPA:* 3.16. *Test scores:* SAT critical reading scores over 500: 34%; SAT math scores over 500: 36%; SAT writing scores over 500: 18%; ACT scores over 18: 85%; SAT critical reading scores over 600: 5%; SAT math scores over 600: 7%; SAT writing scores over 600: 3%; ACT scores over 24: 15%; SAT critical reading scores over 700: 1%; SAT math scores over 700: 1%; SAT writing scores over 700: 1%; ACT scores over 30: 8%.

Faculty *Total:* 76, 59% full-time, 32% with terminal degrees. *Student/faculty ratio:* 11:1.

Majors Accounting; acting; actuarial science; adult and continuing education administration; advertising; aerospace, aeronautical and astronautical/space engineering; African American/Black studies; agribusiness; agricultural and extension education; agricultural business and management related; agricultural engineering; agricultural mechanization; agriculture; agronomy and crop science; animal sciences; animal sciences related; anthropology; applied economics; archeology; architectural engineering; architectural engineering technology; art; art history, criticism and conservation; art teacher education; Asian studies (East); astronomy; atmospheric sciences and meteorology; biochemistry; bioengineering and biomedical engineering; biological and biomedical sciences related; biological and physical sciences; biology/biological sciences; biology/biotechnology laboratory technician; biomedical technology; business administration and management; business/commerce; business/managerial economics; chemical engineering; chemistry; civil engineering; classics and classical languages; communication and journalism related; communication sciences and disorders; comparative literature; computer and information sciences; computer engineering; criminal justice/law enforcement administration; criminal justice/safety; economics; electrical and electronics engineering; electrical, electronic and communications engineering technology; elementary education; engineering science; English; environmental/environmental health engineering; film/cinema/video studies; finance; food science; foreign language teacher education; forest sciences and biology; forest technology; French; geography; geological and earth sciences/geosciences related; geology/earth science; German; graphic design; health/health-care administration; history; horticultural science; hospitality administration related; human development and family studies; human nutrition; industrial engineering; information science/studies; international relations and affairs; Italian; Japanese; Jewish/Judaic studies; journalism; kinesiology and exercise science; labor and industrial relations; landscaping and groundskeeping; Latin American studies;

liberal arts and sciences/liberal studies; logistics, materials, and supply chain management; management information systems; manufacturing engineering; marketing/marketing management; materials science; mathematics; mechanical engineering; medical microbiology and bacteriology; medieval and Renaissance studies; metallurgical technology; mining and mineral engineering; natural resources and conservation related; natural resources/conservation; nuclear engineering; organizational behavior; parks, recreation and leisure facilities management; petroleum engineering; philosophy; physics; political science and government; premedical studies; psychology; registered nursing/registered nurse; rehabilitation and therapeutic professions related; religious studies; Russian; secondary education; sociology; soil science and agronomy; Spanish; special education; speech communication and rhetoric; statistics; telecommunications technology; theater design and technology; toxicology; turf and turfgrass management; visual and performing arts; women's studies.

Academics *Calendar:* semesters. *Degrees:* certificates, associate, and bachelor's. *Special study options:* adult/continuing education programs, external degree program. *ROTC:* Army (b).

Student Life *Housing:* college housing not available. *Campus security:* student patrols, 8-hour patrols by trained security personnel.

Athletics Member NJCAA. *Intercollegiate sports:* baseball M, basketball M, softball W, volleyball W. *Intramural sports:* badminton M/W, basketball M/W, cheerleading M(c)/W(c), equestrian sports M(c)/W(c), football M/W, golf M(c)/W(c), softball M/W, tennis M/W, volleyball M/W, weight lifting M/W.

Standardized Tests *Required:* SAT or ACT (for admission).

Costs (2014–15) *Tuition:* state resident $12,718 full-time, $524 per credit hour part-time; nonresident $19,404 full-time, $809 per credit hour part-time. Full-time tuition and fees vary according to course level, degree level, location, program, and student level. Part-time tuition and fees vary according to course level, course load, degree level, location, program, and student level. *Required fees:* $870 full-time. *Payment plans:* installment, deferred payment. *Waivers:* senior citizens and employees or children of employees.

Financial Aid Of all full-time matriculated undergraduates who enrolled in 2013, 578 applied for aid, 507 were judged to have need, 23 had their need fully met. In 2013, 57 non-need-based awards were made. *Average percent of need met:* 64%. *Average financial aid package:* $11,210. *Average need-based loan:* $4039. *Average need-based gift aid:* $6644. *Average non-need-based aid:* $2968. *Average indebtedness upon graduation:* $36,935.

Applying *Options:* electronic application, early admission, deferred entrance. *Application fee:* $50. *Required:* high school transcript. *Required for some:* interview. *Recommended:* essay or personal statement. *Application deadlines:* rolling (freshmen), rolling (transfers). *Notification:* continuous (freshmen), continuous (transfers).

Freshman Application Contact Admissions Office, Penn State Fayette, The Eberly Campus, 2201 University Drive, Lemont Furnace, PA 15456. *Phone:* 724-430-4130. *Toll-free phone:* 877-568-4130. *Fax:* 724-430-4175. *E-mail:* feadm@psu.edu.
Website: http://www.fe.psu.edu/.

Penn State Mont Alto
Mont Alto, Pennsylvania

- **State-related** primarily 2-year, founded 1929, part of Pennsylvania State University
- **Small-town** campus
- **Coed,** 940 undergraduate students, 72% full-time, 57% women, 43% men

Undergraduates 679 full-time, 261 part-time. 15% are from out of state; 8% Black or African American, non-Hispanic/Latino; 4% Hispanic/Latino; 1% Asian, non-Hispanic/Latino; 0.2% Native Hawaiian or other Pacific Islander, non-Hispanic/Latino; 3% Two or more races, non-Hispanic/Latino; 0.8% Race/ethnicity unknown; 0.1% international; 4% transferred in; 27% live on campus. *Retention:* 75% of full-time freshmen returned.

Freshmen *Admission:* 778 applied, 607 admitted, 276 enrolled. *Average high school GPA:* 3.08. *Test scores:* SAT critical reading scores over 500: 38%; SAT math scores over 500: 40%; SAT writing scores over 500: 27%; ACT scores over 18: 100%; SAT critical reading scores over 600: 8%; SAT math scores over 600: 10%; SAT writing scores over 600: 6%; ACT scores over 24: 25%; SAT critical reading scores over 700: 1%; SAT math scores over 700: 1%; ACT scores over 30: 13%.

Faculty *Total:* 95, 61% full-time, 36% with terminal degrees. *Student/faculty ratio:* 11:1.

Majors Accounting; acting; actuarial science; adult and continuing education administration; advertising; aerospace, aeronautical and astronautical/space engineering; African American/Black studies; agribusiness; agricultural and

extension education; agricultural business and management related; agricultural engineering; agricultural mechanization; agriculture; agronomy and crop science; animal sciences; animal sciences related; anthropology; applied economics; archeology; architectural engineering; art; art history, criticism and conservation; art teacher education; Asian studies (East); astronomy; atmospheric sciences and meteorology; biochemistry; bioengineering and biomedical engineering; biological and biomedical sciences related; biological and physical sciences; biology/biological sciences; biology/biotechnology laboratory technician; business administration and management; business/commerce; business/managerial economics; chemical engineering; chemistry; civil engineering; classics and classical languages; communication and journalism related; communication sciences and disorders; comparative literature; computer and information sciences; computer engineering; criminal justice/law enforcement administration; economics; electrical and electronics engineering; elementary education; engineering science; English; environmental/environmental health engineering; film/cinema/video studies; finance; food science; foreign language teacher education; forest sciences and biology; forest technology; French; geography; geological and earth sciences/geosciences related; geology/earth science; German; graphic design; health/health-care administration; history; horticultural science; hospitality administration related; human development and family studies; human nutrition; industrial engineering; information science/studies; international relations and affairs; Italian; Japanese; Jewish/Judaic studies; journalism; kinesiology and exercise science; labor and industrial relations; landscaping and groundskeeping; Latin American studies; liberal arts and sciences/liberal studies; management information systems; marketing/marketing management; materials science; mathematics; mechanical engineering; medical microbiology and bacteriology; medieval and Renaissance studies; mining and mineral engineering; music; natural resources and conservation related; natural resources/conservation; nuclear engineering; occupational therapist assistant; occupational therapy; organizational behavior; parks, recreation and leisure facilities management; petroleum engineering; philosophy; physical therapy technology; physics; political science and government; premedical studies; psychology; registered nursing/registered nurse; rehabilitation and therapeutic professions related; religious studies; Russian; secondary education; sociology; soil science and agronomy; Spanish; special education; speech communication and rhetoric; statistics; theater design and technology; toxicology; turf and turfgrass management; visual and performing arts; women's studies.

Academics *Calendar:* semesters. *Degrees:* certificates, associate, and bachelor's. *Special study options:* adult/continuing education programs, external degree program. *ROTC:* Army (c).

Student Life *Housing Options:* coed, special housing for students with disabilities. Campus housing is university owned. Freshman campus housing is guaranteed. *Campus security:* 24-hour patrols, controlled dormitory access.

Athletics Member NJCAA. *Intercollegiate sports:* basketball M/W, cheerleading M/W, cross-country running M/W, golf M/W, soccer M/W, softball W, tennis M/W, volleyball W. *Intramural sports:* badminton M/W, basketball M/W, cheerleading M(c)/W(c), racquetball M/W, soccer M/W, softball W, volleyball M/W.

Standardized Tests *Required:* SAT or ACT (for admission).

Costs (2014–15) *Tuition:* state resident $12,718 full-time, $524 per credit hour part-time; nonresident $19,404 full-time, $809 per credit hour part-time. Full-time tuition and fees vary according to course level, degree level, location, program, and student level. Part-time tuition and fees vary according to course level, course load, degree level, location, program, and student level. *Required fees:* $930 full-time. *Room and board:* $10,520; room only: $5460. Room and board charges vary according to board plan, housing facility, and location. *Payment plans:* installment, deferred payment. *Waivers:* senior citizens and employees or children of employees.

Financial Aid Of all full-time matriculated undergraduates who enrolled in 2013, 659 applied for aid, 581 were judged to have need, 38 had their need fully met. In 2013, 48 non-need-based awards were made. *Average percent of need met:* 60%. *Average financial aid package:* $11,314. *Average need-based loan:* $3979. *Average need-based gift aid:* $6314. *Average non-need-based aid:* $4557. *Average indebtedness upon graduation:* $36,935.

Applying *Options:* electronic application, early admission, deferred entrance. *Application fee:* $50. *Required:* high school transcript. *Required for some:* interview. *Recommended:* essay or personal statement. *Application deadlines:* rolling (freshmen), rolling (transfers). *Notification:* continuous (freshmen), continuous (transfers).

Freshman Application Contact Admissions Office, Penn State Mont Alto, 1 Campus Drive, Mont Alto, PA 17237-9703. *Phone:* 717-749-6130. *Toll-free phone:* 800-392-6173. *Fax:* 717-749-6132. *E-mail:* psuma@psu.edu.
Website: http://www.ma.psu.edu/.

Penn State Shenango
Sharon, Pennsylvania

- **State-related** primarily 2-year, founded 1965, part of Pennsylvania State University
- **Small-town** campus
- **Coed,** 539 undergraduate students, 57% full-time, 70% women, 30% men

Undergraduates 309 full-time, 230 part-time. 23% are from out of state; 9% Black or African American, non-Hispanic/Latino; 2% Hispanic/Latino; 1% Asian, non-Hispanic/Latino; 0.6% Native Hawaiian or other Pacific Islander, non-Hispanic/Latino; 3% Two or more races, non-Hispanic/Latino; 3% Race/ethnicity unknown; 9% transferred in. *Retention:* 59% of full-time freshmen returned.

Freshmen *Admission:* 201 applied, 135 admitted, 79 enrolled. *Average high school GPA:* 2.99. *Test scores:* SAT critical reading scores over 500: 24%; SAT math scores over 500: 24%; SAT writing scores over 500: 9%; ACT scores over 18: 60%; SAT critical reading scores over 600: 2%; SAT writing scores over 600: 2%; ACT scores over 24: 20%.

Faculty *Total:* 50, 52% full-time, 36% with terminal degrees. *Student/faculty ratio:* 11:1.

Majors Accounting; acting; actuarial science; adult and continuing education administration; advertising; aerospace, aeronautical and astronautical/space engineering; African American/Black studies; agribusiness; agricultural and extension education; agricultural business and management related; agricultural engineering; agricultural mechanization; agriculture; agronomy and crop science; animal sciences; animal sciences related; anthropology; applied economics; archeology; architectural engineering; art; art history, criticism and conservation; art teacher education; Asian studies (East); astronomy; atmospheric sciences and meteorology; biochemistry; bioengineering and biomedical engineering; biological and biomedical sciences related; biological and physical sciences; biology/biological sciences; biology/biotechnology laboratory technician; biomedical technology; business administration and management; business/commerce; business/managerial economics; chemical engineering; chemistry; civil engineering; classics and classical languages; communication and journalism related; communication sciences and disorders; comparative literature; computer and information sciences; computer engineering; criminal justice/law enforcement administration; economics; electrical and electronics engineering; electrical, electronic and communications engineering technology; elementary education; engineering science; English; environmental/environmental health engineering; film/cinema/video studies; finance; food science; foreign language teacher education; forest sciences and biology; forest technology; French; geography; geological and earth sciences/geosciences related; geology/earth science; German; graphic design; health/health-care administration; history; horticultural science; hospitality administration related; human development and family studies; human nutrition; industrial engineering; information science/studies; international relations and affairs; Italian; Japanese; Jewish/Judaic studies; journalism; kinesiology and exercise science; labor and industrial relations; landscaping and groundskeeping; Latin American studies; liberal arts and sciences/liberal studies; logistics, materials, and supply chain management; management information systems; marketing/marketing management; materials science; mathematics; mechanical engineering; mechanical engineering/mechanical technology; medical microbiology and bacteriology; medieval and Renaissance studies; metallurgical technology; mining and mineral engineering; music; natural resources and conservation related; natural resources/conservation; nuclear engineering; organizational behavior; parks, recreation and leisure facilities management; petroleum engineering; philosophy; physical therapy technology; physics; political science and government; premedical studies; psychology; registered nursing/registered nurse; rehabilitation and therapeutic professions related; religious studies; Russian; secondary education; sociology; soil science and agronomy; Spanish; special education; speech communication and rhetoric; statistics; telecommunications technology; theater design and technology; toxicology; turf and turfgrass management; visual and performing arts; women's studies.

Academics *Calendar:* semesters. *Degrees:* certificates, associate, and bachelor's. *Special study options:* adult/continuing education programs, external degree program.

Student Life *Housing:* college housing not available.

Athletics *Intramural sports:* basketball M(c)/W, bowling M/W, football M(c), golf M/W, softball M/W, tennis M/W, volleyball M/W.

Standardized Tests *Required:* SAT or ACT (for admission).

Costs (2014–15) *Tuition:* state resident $12,474 full-time, $504 per credit hour part-time; nonresident $19,030 full-time, $793 per credit hour part-time. Full-time tuition and fees vary according to course level, degree level, location, program, and student level. Part-time tuition and fees vary according to course level, course load, degree level, location, program, and student level. *Required fees:* $858 full-time. *Payment plans:* installment, deferred payment. *Waivers:* senior citizens and employees or children of employees.

Financial Aid Of all full-time matriculated undergraduates who enrolled in 2013, 292 applied for aid, 278 were judged to have need, 16 had their need fully met. In 2013, 16 non-need-based awards were made. *Average percent of need met:* 61%. *Average financial aid package:* $12,741. *Average need-based loan:* $4008. *Average need-based gift aid:* $6759. *Average non-need-based aid:* $4157. *Average indebtedness upon graduation:* $36,935.

Applying *Options:* electronic application, early admission, deferred entrance. *Application fee:* $50. *Required:* high school transcript. *Application deadlines:* rolling (freshmen), rolling (transfers). *Notification:* continuous (freshmen), continuous (transfers).

Freshman Application Contact Admissions Office, Penn State Shenango, 147 Shenango Avenue, Sharon, PA 16146-1537. *Phone:* 724-983-2803. *Fax:* 724-983-2820. *E-mail:* psushenango@psu.edu.

Website: http://www.shenango.psu.edu/.

Pennsylvania Highlands Community College
Johnstown, Pennsylvania

- **State and locally supported** 2-year, founded 1994
- **Small-town** campus
- **Coed,** 2,470 undergraduate students, 37% full-time, 60% women, 40% men

Undergraduates 903 full-time, 1,567 part-time. 3% Black or African American, non-Hispanic/Latino; 2% Hispanic/Latino; 1% Asian, non-Hispanic/Latino; 0.2% American Indian or Alaska Native, non-Hispanic/Latino; 2% Two or more races, non-Hispanic/Latino; 3% Race/ethnicity unknown.

Freshmen *Admission:* 342 enrolled.

Faculty *Total:* 130, 21% full-time. *Student/faculty ratio:* 24:1.

Majors Accounting; accounting technology and bookkeeping; airline pilot and flight crew; architectural drafting and CAD/CADD; business/commerce; child-care and support services management; communication and journalism related; computer and information sciences; computer science; corrections; criminal justice/law enforcement administration; early childhood education; education; emergency medical technology (EMT paramedic); engineering technologies and engineering related; environmental science; general studies; health information/medical records technology; health professions related; histologic technician; human services; medical/clinical assistant; operations management; psychology; radiologic technology/science; radio, television, and digital communication related; restaurant, culinary, and catering management; welding technology.

Academics *Calendar:* semesters. *Degree:* certificates, diplomas, and associate. *Special study options:* academic remediation for entering students, adult/continuing education programs, advanced placement credit, cooperative education, distance learning, honors programs, independent study, internships, part-time degree program, services for LD students, summer session for credit.

Library Mangarella Library at Pennsylvania Highlands Community College plus 1 other with an OPAC, a Web page.

Student Life *Housing:* college housing not available. *Activities and Organizations:* Student Senate Organization, Phi Theta Kappa Honor Society (PTK), National Society of Leadership and Success Organization (Sigma Alpha Pi), Black Bear Bowling Team, Anime Art Style Club.

Athletics Member NJCAA. *Intercollegiate sports:* basketball M, volleyball W. *Intramural sports:* basketball M/W, bowling M/W, cheerleading M/W, soccer M/W, table tennis M/W, volleyball M/W.

Costs (2015–16) *Tuition:* area resident $3810 full-time; state resident $5850 full-time; nonresident $8790 full-time. Full-time tuition and fees vary according to course load. Part-time tuition and fees vary according to course load. *Required fees:* $1770 full-time. *Payment plan:* installment. *Waivers:* employees or children of employees.

Financial Aid Of all full-time matriculated undergraduates who enrolled in 2013, 25 Federal Work-Study jobs (averaging $2500).

Applying *Options:* electronic application. *Application fee:* $20. *Required:* high school transcript.

Freshman Application Contact Mr. Jeff Maul, Admissions Officer, Pennsylvania Highlands Community College, 101 Community College Way, Johnstown, PA 15904. *Phone:* 814-262-6431. *Toll-free phone:* 888-385-7325. *Fax:* 814-269-9743. *E-mail:* jmaul@pennhighlands.edu.

Website: http://www.pennhighlands.edu/.

Pennsylvania Institute of Health and Technology
Mount Braddock, Pennsylvania

Admissions Office Contact Pennsylvania Institute of Health and Technology, 1015 Mount Braddock Road, Mount Braddock, PA 15465.

Website: http://www.piht.edu/.

Pennsylvania Institute of Technology
Media, Pennsylvania

- **Independent** 2-year, founded 1953
- **Small-town** 12-acre campus with easy access to Philadelphia
- **Coed,** 661 undergraduate students, 67% full-time, 76% women, 24% men

Undergraduates 444 full-time, 217 part-time. 59% Black or African American, non-Hispanic/Latino; 6% Hispanic/Latino; 3% Asian, non-Hispanic/Latino; 0.2% Native Hawaiian or other Pacific Islander, non-Hispanic/Latino; 0.2% American Indian or Alaska Native, non-Hispanic/Latino; 1% Two or more races, non-Hispanic/Latino; 16% Race/ethnicity unknown.
Freshmen *Admission:* 369 enrolled.
Faculty *Total:* 80, 30% full-time. *Student/faculty ratio:* 13:1.
Majors Allied health and medical assisting services related; business administration and management; communication; electrical, electronic and communications engineering technology; engineering technology; general studies; health information/medical records technology; health services/allied health/health sciences; medical office management; pharmacy technician; physical therapy technology.
Academics *Calendar:* semesters. *Degree:* certificates and associate. *Special study options:* academic remediation for entering students, adult/continuing education programs, advanced placement credit, cooperative education, part-time degree program, summer session for credit.
Library Pennsylvania Institute of Technology Library/Learning Resource Center with 16,500 titles, an OPAC, a Web page.
Student Life *Housing:* college housing not available. *Campus security:* 24-hour emergency response devices. *Student services:* personal/psychological counseling.
Athletics *Intramural sports:* basketball M/W.
Costs (2014–15) *Tuition:* $11,250 full-time, $375 per credit hour part-time. Full-time tuition and fees vary according to program. Part-time tuition and fees vary according to course load and program. *Required fees:* $1500 full-time, $50 per credit part-time. *Payment plan:* installment. *Waivers:* employees or children of employees.
Financial Aid Of all full-time matriculated undergraduates who enrolled in 2013, 15 Federal Work-Study jobs (averaging $1025). *Financial aid deadline:* 8/1.
Applying *Options:* electronic application, deferred entrance. *Application fee:* $25. *Required:* high school transcript, interview. *Required for some:* 2 letters of recommendation. *Recommended:* essay or personal statement. *Application deadlines:* 9/19 (freshmen), 9/19 (transfers). *Notification:* continuous until 9/19 (freshmen), continuous until 9/19 (transfers).
Freshman Application Contact Mr. John DeTurris, Director of Admissions, Pennsylvania Institute of Technology, 800 Manchester Avenue, Media, PA 19063-4036. *Phone:* 610-892-1543. *Toll-free phone:* 800-422-0025. *Fax:* 610-892-1510. *E-mail:* info@pit.edu.
Website: http://www.pit.edu/.

Pittsburgh Institute of Aeronautics
Pittsburgh, Pennsylvania

Freshman Application Contact Steven J. Sabold, Director of Admissions, Pittsburgh Institute of Aeronautics, PO Box 10897, Pittsburgh, PA 15236-0897. *Phone:* 412-346-2100. *Toll-free phone:* 800-444-1440. *Fax:* 412-466-5013. *E-mail:* admissions@pia.edu.
Website: http://www.pia.edu/.

Pittsburgh Institute of Mortuary Science, Incorporated
Pittsburgh, Pennsylvania

Freshman Application Contact Ms. Karen Rocco, Registrar, Pittsburgh Institute of Mortuary Science, Incorporated, 5808 Baum Boulevard, Pittsburgh, PA 15206-3706. *Phone:* 412-362-8500 Ext. 105. *Fax:* 412-362-1684. *E-mail:* pims5808@aol.com.
Website: http://www.pims.edu/.

Pittsburgh Technical Institute
Oakdale, Pennsylvania

- **Proprietary** 2-year, founded 1946
- **Suburban** 180-acre campus with easy access to Pittsburgh
- **Coed**
- 84% of applicants were admitted

Undergraduates 1,841 full-time. Students come from 22 states and territories; 19% are from out of state; 11% Black or African American, non-

Hispanic/Latino; 1% Hispanic/Latino; 0.9% Asian, non-Hispanic/Latino; 0.2% Native Hawaiian or other Pacific Islander, non-Hispanic/Latino; 0.1% American Indian or Alaska Native, non-Hispanic/Latino; 5% Two or more races, non-Hispanic/Latino; 12% Race/ethnicity unknown; 14% transferred in; 40% live on campus.
Faculty *Student/faculty ratio:* 25:1.
Academics *Calendar:* quarters. *Degree:* certificates and associate. *Special study options:* academic remediation for entering students, advanced placement credit, cooperative education, distance learning, double majors, internships, services for LD students.
Student Life *Campus security:* 24-hour emergency response devices and patrols, controlled dormitory access.
Costs (2014–15) *Comprehensive fee:* $24,252 includes full-time tuition ($15,657) and room and board ($8595). Full-time tuition and fees vary according to course load and program. No tuition increase for student's term of enrollment. *Room and board:* college room only: $6100. Room and board charges vary according to housing facility. *Payment plans:* installment, deferred payment.
Applying *Options:* electronic application, deferred entrance. *Required:* high school transcript. *Required for some:* essay or personal statement, certain programs require a criminal background check; some programs require applicants to be in top 50-80% of class; Practical Nursing certificate and Associate Degree in Nursing require entrance exam. *Recommended:* interview.
Freshman Application Contact Ms. Nancy Goodlin, Admissions Office Assistant, Pittsburgh Technical Institute, 1111 McKee Road, Oakdale, PA 15071. *Phone:* 412-809-5100. *Toll-free phone:* 800-784-9675. *Fax:* 412-809-5351. *E-mail:* goodlin.nancy@pti.edu.
Website: http://www.pti.edu/.

Reading Area Community College
Reading, Pennsylvania

- **County-supported** 2-year, founded 1971
- **Urban** 14-acre campus with easy access to Philadelphia
- **Coed,** 4,198 undergraduate students, 22% full-time, 63% women, 37% men

Undergraduates 913 full-time, 3,285 part-time. 0.4% are from out of state; 12% Black or African American, non-Hispanic/Latino; 31% Hispanic/Latino; 2% Asian, non-Hispanic/Latino; 0.1% Native Hawaiian or other Pacific Islander, non-Hispanic/Latino; 0.4% American Indian or Alaska Native, non-Hispanic/Latino; 2% Two or more races, non-Hispanic/Latino; 1% Race/ethnicity unknown.
Freshmen *Admission:* 803 enrolled.
Faculty *Total:* 228, 27% full-time. *Student/faculty ratio:* 17:1.
Majors Accounting; accounting and business/management; administrative assistant and secretarial science; art; business administration and management; child-care and support services management; child development; clinical/medical laboratory technology; communication and media related; computer and information sciences; computer technology/computer systems technology; creative writing; criminal justice/police science; elementary education; general studies; health information/medical records technology; health services/allied health/health sciences; human services; industrial mechanics and maintenance technology; interdisciplinary studies; liberal arts and sciences/liberal studies; machine tool technology; medical administrative assistant and medical secretary; occupational therapist assistant; physical sciences; physical therapy technology; psychology; registered nursing/registered nurse; respiratory care therapy; restaurant, culinary, and catering management; science technologies related; secondary education; social sciences; social work; substance abuse/addiction counseling; web page, digital/multimedia and information resources design.
Academics *Calendar:* semesters. *Degree:* certificates, diplomas, and associate. *Special study options:* academic remediation for entering students, adult/continuing education programs, advanced placement credit, cooperative education, distance learning, English as a second language, external degree program, honors programs, internships, part-time degree program, services for LD students, summer session for credit.
Library Yocum Library with 46,853 titles, 11,645 audiovisual materials, an OPAC, a Web page.
Student Life *Housing:* college housing not available. *Activities and Organizations:* student-run newspaper. *Campus security:* 24-hour emergency response devices, late-night transport/escort service. *Student services:* personal/psychological counseling.
Standardized Tests *Required for some:* TOEFL. *Recommended:* SAT (for admission), ACT (for admission).
Costs (2015–16) *Tuition:* area resident $3660 full-time, $122 per credit part-time; state resident $7320 full-time, $244 per credit part-time; nonresident $10,980 full-time, $366 per credit part-time. Full-time tuition and fees vary according to course load and program. Part-time tuition and fees vary according to course load and program. *Required fees:* $1470 full-time, $49 per

credit part-time. *Payment plan:* installment. *Waivers:* senior citizens and employees or children of employees.

Financial Aid Of all full-time matriculated undergraduates who enrolled in 2013, 80 Federal Work-Study jobs (averaging $5400). 20 state and other part-time jobs (averaging $3300).

Applying *Options:* electronic application, early admission. *Required for some:* essay or personal statement, high school transcript, 1 letter of recommendation, interview, background/criminal check, physical exam, proof of insurance: For selective admissions programs. *Recommended:* high school transcript. *Application deadlines:* rolling (freshmen), rolling (out-of-state freshmen), rolling (transfers). *Notification:* continuous (freshmen), continuous (out-of-state freshmen), continuous (transfers).

Freshman Application Contact Ms. Debbie Hettinger, Enrollment Services Processing Specialist, Reading Area Community College, PO Box 1706, Reading, PA 19603-1706. *Phone:* 610-372-4721 Ext. 5130. *E-mail:* Dhettinger@racc.edu.

Website: http://www.racc.edu/.

The Restaurant School at Walnut Hill College
Philadelphia, Pennsylvania

Freshman Application Contact Miss Toni Morelli, Director of Admissions, The Restaurant School at Walnut Hill College, 4207 Walnut Street, Philadelphia, PA 19104-3518. *Phone:* 267-295-2353. *Fax:* 215-222-4219. *E-mail:* tmorelli@walnuthillcollege.edu.

Website: http://www.walnuthillcollege.edu/.

Rosedale Technical Institute
Pittsburgh, Pennsylvania

Freshman Application Contact Ms. Debbie Bier, Director of Admissions, Rosedale Technical Institute, 215 Beecham Drive, Suite 2, Pittsburgh, PA 15205-9791. *Phone:* 412-521-6200. *Toll-free phone:* 800-521-6262. *Fax:* 412-521-2520. *E-mail:* admissions@rosedaletech.org.

Website: http://www.rosedaletech.org/.

South Hills School of Business & Technology
Altoona, Pennsylvania

Freshman Application Contact Ms. Holly J. Emerick, Director of Admissions, South Hills School of Business & Technology, 508 58th Street, Altoona, PA 16602. *Phone:* 814-944-6134. *Fax:* 814-944-4684. *E-mail:* hemerick@southhills.edu.

Website: http://www.southhills.edu/.

South Hills School of Business & Technology
State College, Pennsylvania

- **Proprietary** 2-year, founded 1970
- **Small-town** 6-acre campus
- **Coed,** 630 undergraduate students, 91% full-time, 66% women, 34% men

Undergraduates 574 full-time, 56 part-time. 2% Black or African American, non-Hispanic/Latino; 0.6% Hispanic/Latino; 0.5% Asian, non-Hispanic/Latino; 0.3% American Indian or Alaska Native, non-Hispanic/Latino; 1% Two or more races, non-Hispanic/Latino; 0.2% international; 15% transferred in. *Retention:* 70% of full-time freshmen returned.

Freshmen *Admission:* 439 applied, 402 admitted, 213 enrolled.

Faculty *Total:* 65, 63% full-time. *Student/faculty ratio:* 13:1.

Majors Accounting; administrative assistant and secretarial science; business administration and management; computer science; criminal justice/law enforcement administration; diagnostic medical sonography and ultrasound technology; graphic design; health information/medical records technology; industrial technology; medical administrative assistant and medical secretary; medical/clinical assistant.

Academics *Calendar:* quarters. *Degrees:* certificates, diplomas, and associate (also includes Altoona campus). *Special study options:* advanced placement credit, internships, part-time degree program.

Library Main Library plus 1 other with 123,422 titles, 50 audiovisual materials.

Student Life *Housing:* college housing not available. *Activities and Organizations:* Phi Beta Lambda, South Hills Ambassadors, Club IT, C.O.P.S., Student Forum. *Campus security:* 24-hour emergency response devices.

Standardized Tests *Required:* Wonderlic (for admission).

Costs (2015–16) *Tuition:* $16,521 full-time, $459 per credit part-time. Full-time tuition and fees vary according to program. Part-time tuition and fees vary according to course load.

Applying *Options:* electronic application. *Required:* high school transcript, interview. *Required for some:* essay or personal statement, 2 letters of recommendation. *Application deadline:* rolling (freshmen).

Freshman Application Contact Mr. Troy R. Otradovec, Regional Director of Admissions, South Hills School of Business & Technology, 480 Waupelani Drive, State College, PA 16801-4516. *Phone:* 814-234-7755 Ext. 2020. *Toll-free phone:* 888-282-7427. *Fax:* 814-234-0926. *E-mail:* admissions@southhills.edu.

Website: http://www.southhills.edu/.

Thaddeus Stevens College of Technology
Lancaster, Pennsylvania

Director of Admissions Ms. Erin Kate Nelsen, Director of Enrollment, Thaddeus Stevens College of Technology, 750 East King Street, Lancaster, PA 17602-3198. *Phone:* 717-299-7772. *Toll-free phone:* 800-842-3832.

Website: http://www.stevenscollege.edu/.

Triangle Tech, Bethlehem
Bethlehem, Pennsylvania

Freshman Application Contact Triangle Tech, Bethlehem, 3184 Airport Road, Bethlehem, PA 18017.

Website: http://www.triangle-tech.edu/.

Triangle Tech, DuBois
DuBois, Pennsylvania

Freshman Application Contact Terry Kucic, Director of Admissions, Triangle Tech, DuBois, PO Box 551, DuBois, PA 15801. *Phone:* 814-371-2090. *Toll-free phone:* 800-874-8324. *Fax:* 814-371-9227. *E-mail:* tkucic@triangle-tech.com.

Website: http://www.triangle-tech.edu/.

Triangle Tech, Erie
Erie, Pennsylvania

Freshman Application Contact Admissions Representative, Triangle Tech, Erie, 2000 Liberty Street, Erie, PA 16502-2594. *Phone:* 814-453-6016. *Toll-free phone:* 800-874-8324 (in-state); 800-TRI-TECH (out-of-state).

Website: http://www.triangle-tech.edu/.

Triangle Tech, Greensburg
Greensburg, Pennsylvania

Freshman Application Contact Mr. John Mazzarese, Vice President of Admissions, Triangle Tech, Greensburg, 222 East Pittsburgh Street, Greensburg, PA 15601. *Phone:* 412-359-1000. *Toll-free phone:* 800-874-8324.

Website: http://www.triangle-tech.edu/.

Triangle Tech, Pittsburgh
Pittsburgh, Pennsylvania

- **Proprietary** 2-year, founded 1944, part of Triangle Tech Group, Inc.
- **Urban** 5-acre campus
- **Coed, primarily men**

Undergraduates 103 full-time. Students come from 3 states and territories; 2% are from out of state; 29% Black or African American, non-Hispanic/Latino; 1% Hispanic/Latino; 0.2% Native Hawaiian or other Pacific Islander, non-Hispanic/Latino; 2% Two or more races, non-Hispanic/Latino; 1% transferred in. *Retention:* 78% of full-time freshmen returned.

Faculty *Student/faculty ratio:* 12:1.

Academics *Calendar:* semesters. *Degree:* associate. *Special study options:* academic remediation for entering students.

Student Life *Campus security:* 16-hour patrols by trained security personnel.

Financial Aid Of all full-time matriculated undergraduates who enrolled in 2013, 16 Federal Work-Study jobs (averaging $1500). *Financial aid deadline:* 7/1.

Applying *Required:* high school transcript, minimum 2.0 GPA, interview.
Freshman Application Contact Director of Admissions, Triangle Tech, Pittsburgh, 1940 Perrysville Avenue, Pittsburgh, PA 15214-3897. *Phone:* 412-359-1000. *Toll-free phone:* 800-874-8324. *Fax:* 412-359-1012. *E-mail:* info@triangle-tech.edu.
Website: http://www.triangle-tech.edu/.

Triangle Tech, Sunbury
Sunbury, Pennsylvania

Freshman Application Contact Triangle Tech, Sunbury, 191 Performance Road, Sunbury, PA 17801. *Phone:* 412-359-1000.
Website: http://www.triangle-tech.edu/.

University of Pittsburgh at Titusville
Titusville, Pennsylvania

Freshman Application Contact Mr. Robert J. Wyant, Director of Admissions, University of Pittsburgh at Titusville, 504 E Main St, Titusville, PA 16354. *Phone:* 814-827-4457. *Toll-free phone:* 888-878-0462. *Fax:* 814-827-4519. *E-mail:* wyant@pitt.edu.
Website: http://www.upt.pitt.edu/.

Valley Forge Military College
Wayne, Pennsylvania

Freshman Application Contact Maj. Greg Potts, Dean of Enrollment Management, Valley Forge Military College, 1001 Eagle Road, Wayne, PA 19087-3695. *Phone:* 610-989-1300. *Toll-free phone:* 800-234-8362. *Fax:* 610-688-1545. *E-mail:* admissions@vfmac.edu.
Website: http://www.vfmac.edu/.

Vet Tech Institute
Pittsburgh, Pennsylvania

- **Private** 2-year, founded 1958
- **Urban** campus
- **Coed,** 385 undergraduate students
- 61% of applicants were admitted

Freshmen *Admission:* 527 applied, 324 admitted.
Majors Veterinary/animal health technology.
Academics *Calendar:* semesters. *Degree:* associate. *Special study options:* accelerated degree program, internships, summer session for credit.
Freshman Application Contact Admissions Office, Vet Tech Institute, 125 7th Street, Pittsburgh, PA 15222-3400. *Phone:* 412-391-7021. *Toll-free phone:* 800-570-0693.
Website: http://pittsburgh.vettechinstitute.edu/.

Westmoreland County Community College
Youngwood, Pennsylvania

- **County-supported** 2-year, founded 1970
- **Rural** 85-acre campus with easy access to Pittsburgh
- **Endowment** $548,821
- **Coed,** 5,638 undergraduate students, 48% full-time, 63% women, 37% men

Undergraduates 2,679 full-time, 2,959 part-time. Students come from 5 states and territories; 0.2% are from out of state; 4% Black or African American, non-Hispanic/Latino; 2% Hispanic/Latino; 0.6% Asian, non-Hispanic/Latino; 0.2% American Indian or Alaska Native, non-Hispanic/Latino; 2% Two or more races, non-Hispanic/Latino; 22% transferred in. *Retention:* 62% of full-time freshmen returned.
Freshmen *Admission:* 2,357 applied, 2,357 admitted, 1,400 enrolled.
Faculty *Total:* 410, 20% full-time. *Student/faculty ratio:* 18:1.
Majors Accounting technology and bookkeeping; administrative assistant and secretarial science; applied horticulture/horticulture operations; architectural drafting and CAD/CADD; baking and pastry arts; banking and financial support services; biology/biotechnology laboratory technician; business administration and management; business/commerce; casino management; chemical technology; child-care provision; clinical laboratory science/medical technology; clinical/medical laboratory assistant; communications systems installation and repair technology; computer and information systems security; computer numerically controlled (CNC) machinist technology; computer programming; computer programming (specific applications); computer support specialist; computer systems networking and telecommunications; corrections; criminal justice/police science; criminal justice/safety; culinary arts; data entry/microcomputer applications; data processing and data processing technology; dental assisting; dental hygiene; diagnostic medical sonography and ultrasound technology; dietetic technology; early childhood education; electrical and power transmission installation; electrical, electronic and communications engineering technology; electromechanical technology; executive assistant/executive secretary; family and community services; fire prevention and safety technology; floriculture/floristry management; food service and dining room management; graphic communications related; graphic design; health and medical administrative services related; heating, air conditioning, ventilation and refrigeration maintenance technology; homeland security, law enforcement, firefighting and protective services related; hotel/motel administration; human resources management; industrial mechanics and maintenance technology; industrial technology; legal assistant/paralegal; liberal arts and sciences/liberal studies; library and information science; licensed practical/vocational nurse training; logistics, materials, and supply chain management; machine shop technology; machine tool technology; manufacturing engineering technology; mechanical drafting and CAD/CADD; mechanical engineering/mechanical technology; mechatronics, robotics, and automation engineering; medical/clinical assistant; medical office assistant; occupational safety and health technology; phlebotomy technology; physical science technologies related; pre-engineering; radio and television broadcasting technology; radiologic technology/science; real estate; registered nursing/registered nurse; restaurant, culinary, and catering management; sales, distribution, and marketing operations; special education–elementary school; tourism and travel services management; turf and turfgrass management; web page, digital/multimedia and information resources design; welding technology; well drilling.
Academics *Calendar:* semesters. *Degree:* certificates, diplomas, and associate. *Special study options:* academic remediation for entering students, accelerated degree program, adult/continuing education programs, advanced placement credit, cooperative education, distance learning, double majors, English as a second language, honors programs, independent study, internships, off-campus study, part-time degree program, services for LD students, summer session for credit.
Library Westmoreland County Community College Learning Resources Center with 46,499 titles, 4,346 audiovisual materials, an OPAC, a Web page.
Student Life *Housing:* college housing not available. *Activities and Organizations:* choral group, Phi Theta Kappa, Sigma Alpha Pi Leadership Society, Criminal Justice Fraternity, SNAP, SADAA/SADHA. *Campus security:* 24-hour emergency response devices and patrols, late-night transport/escort service, county police office on campus. *Student services:* personal/psychological counseling.
Athletics Member NJCAA. *Intercollegiate sports:* baseball M, basketball M/W, bowling M/W, cross-country running M/W, golf M/W, soccer M/W, softball W, volleyball W.
Costs (2014–15) *One-time required fee:* $25. *Tuition:* area resident $2940 full-time, $98 per credit part-time; state resident $5880 full-time, $196 per credit part-time; nonresident $8820 full-time, $294 per credit part-time. Full-time tuition and fees vary according to course load. Part-time tuition and fees vary according to course load. *Required fees:* $930 full-time, $31 per credit part-time. *Payment plans:* installment, deferred payment. *Waivers:* senior citizens and employees or children of employees.
Applying *Options:* electronic application, early admission. *Application fee:* $25. *Application deadlines:* rolling (freshmen), rolling (out-of-state freshmen), rolling (transfers). *Notification:* continuous (freshmen), continuous (out-of-state freshmen), continuous (transfers).
Freshman Application Contact Mr. James Pirlo, Admissions Coordinator, Westmoreland County Community College, 145 Pavillon Lane, Youngwood, PA 15697. *Phone:* 724-925-6953. *Toll-free phone:* 800-262-2103. *Fax:* 724-925-4292. *E-mail:* pirloj@wccc.edu.
Website: http://www.wccc.edu/.

The Williamson Free School of Mechanical Trades
Media, Pennsylvania

- **Independent** 2-year, founded 1888
- **Small-town** 222-acre campus with easy access to Philadelphia
- **Men only**

Undergraduates 270 full-time. Students come from 7 states and territories; 15% are from out of state; 100% live on campus.
Faculty *Student/faculty ratio:* 12:1.
Academics *Calendar:* semesters. *Degree:* diplomas and associate. *Special study options:* academic remediation for entering students, independent study, off-campus study.
Student Life *Campus security:* evening patrols, gate security.
Athletics Member NJCAA.
Standardized Tests *Required:* Armed Services Vocational Aptitude Battery (for admission).

Costs (2014–15) *Tuition:* $0 full-time. All Williamson students attend on full scholarships covering tuition, room, board, and textbooks. *Required fees:* $800 full-time.
Financial Aid *Financial aid deadline:* 2/23.
Applying *Required:* essay or personal statement, high school transcript, minimum 2.0 GPA, interview, Average performance or better on the Armed Services Vocational Aptitude Battery (ASVAB).
Freshman Application Contact Mr. Jay Merillat, Dean of Admissions, The Williamson Free School of Mechanical Trades, 106 South New Middletown Road, Media, PA 19063. *Phone:* 610-566-1776 Ext. 235. *E-mail:* jmerillat@williamson.edu.
Website: http://www.williamson.edu/.

WyoTech Blairsville
Blairsville, Pennsylvania

Freshman Application Contact Mr. Tim Smyers, WyoTech Blairsville, 500 Innovation Drive, Blairsville, PA 15717. *Phone:* 724-459-2311. *Toll-free phone:* 888-577-7559. *Fax:* 724-459-6499. *E-mail:* tsmyers@wyotech.edu.
Website: http://www.wyotech.edu/.

Yorktowne Business Institute
York, Pennsylvania

Director of Admissions Director of Admissions, Yorktowne Business Institute, West Seventh Avenue, York, PA 17404. *Phone:* 717-846-5000. *Toll-free phone:* 800-840-1004.
Website: http://www.ybi.edu/.

YTI Career Institute–Altoona
Altoona, Pennsylvania

Admissions Office Contact YTI Career Institute–Altoona, 2900 Fairway Drive, Altoona, PA 16602.
Website: http://www.yti.edu/.

YTI Career Institute–York
York, Pennsylvania

Freshman Application Contact YTI Career Institute–York, 1405 Williams Road, York, PA 17402-9017. *Phone:* 717-757-1100 Ext. 318. *Toll-free phone:* 800-557-6335.
Website: http://www.yti.edu/.

PUERTO RICO

The Center of Cinematography, Arts and Television
Bayamon, Puerto Rico

Admissions Office Contact The Center of Cinematography, Arts and Television, 51 Dr. Veve Street, Degetau Street Corner, Bayamon, PR 00960.
Website: http://ccatmiami.com/.

Centro de Estudios Multidisciplinarios
Rio Piedras, Puerto Rico

Director of Admissions Admissions Department, Centro de Estudios Multidisciplinarios, Calle 13 #1206, Ext. San Agustin, Rio Piedras, PR 00926. *Phone:* 787-765-4210 Ext. 115. *Toll-free phone:* 877-779-CDEM.
Website: http://www.cempr.edu/.

Dewey University–Bayamón
Bayamón, Puerto Rico

Admissions Office Contact Dewey University–Bayamón, Carr. #2, Km. 15.9, Parque Industrial Corujo, Hato Tejas, Bayamón, PR 00959.
Website: http://www.dewey.edu/.

Dewey University–Fajardo
Fajardo, Puerto Rico

Admissions Office Contact Dewey University–Fajardo, 267 Calle General Valero, Fajardo, PR 00910.
Website: http://www.dewey.edu/.

EDIC College
Caguas, Puerto Rico

Admissions Office Contact EDIC College, Ave. Rafael Cordero Calle Gnova Urb. Caguas Norte, Caguas, PR 00726.
Website: http://www.ediccollege.edu/.

Huertas Junior College
Caguas, Puerto Rico

Director of Admissions Mrs. Barbara Hassim López, Director of Admissions, Huertas Junior College, PO Box 8429, Caguas, PR 00726. *Phone:* 787-743-1242. *Fax:* 787-743-0203. *E-mail:* huertas@huertas.org.
Website: http://www.huertas.edu/.

Humacao Community College
Humacao, Puerto Rico

- **Independent** primarily 2-year
- **Urban** campus
- **Endowment** $799,498
- **Coed,** 639 undergraduate students, 74% full-time, 65% women, 35% men

Undergraduates 472 full-time, 167 part-time. Students come from 1 other state; 100% Hispanic/Latino; 3% transferred in. *Retention:* 40% of full-time freshmen returned.
Freshmen *Admission:* 220 applied, 174 admitted, 155 enrolled. *Average high school GPA:* 2.17.
Faculty *Total:* 27, 48% full-time, 100% with terminal degrees. *Student/faculty ratio:* 30:1.
Majors Biotechnology; business/commerce; computer programming (specific applications); dental assisting; electrical and electronics engineering; executive assistant/executive secretary; health information/medical records administration; heating, ventilation, air conditioning and refrigeration engineering technology; medical administrative assistant and medical secretary; pharmacy technician.
Academics *Calendar:* trimesters. *Degrees:* certificates, diplomas, associate, and bachelor's. *Special study options:* academic remediation for entering students, adult/continuing education programs, cooperative education, distance learning, English as a second language, internships, services for LD students.
Library SANTIAGO N. MAUNEZ EDUCATIONAL RESOURCES CENTER with 5,743 titles, 613 audiovisual materials, an OPAC.
Student Life *Housing:* college housing not available. *Campus security:* 24-hour emergency response devices and patrols. *Student services:* personal/psychological counseling.
Costs (2015–16) *Tuition:* $4680 full-time, $2340 per year part-time. Full-time tuition and fees vary according to degree level. Part-time tuition and fees vary according to degree level. *Required fees:* $450 full-time. *Payment plan:* installment. *Waivers:* employees or children of employees.
Financial Aid Of all full-time matriculated undergraduates who enrolled in 2013, 64 Federal Work-Study jobs (averaging $546).
Applying *Application fee:* $15. *Required:* high school transcript, interview, Certificate of Immunization for students under 21 years, be a US citizen, legal resident, or otherwise legally eligible to study in the US, complete and submit admission application, and pay the appropriate nonrefundable admission fee. *Notification:* continuous (freshmen).
Freshman Application Contact Mrs. Loalis Quinones, Director of Admissions, Humacao Community College, PO Box 9139, Humacao, PR 00792, Puerto Rico. *Phone:* 787-852-1430 Ext. 225. *Fax:* 787-850-1577. *E-mail:* lquinones@hccpr.edu.
Website: http://www.hccpr.edu/.

ICPR Junior College–Hato Rey Campus
Hato Rey, Puerto Rico

Freshman Application Contact Admissions Office, ICPR Junior College–Hato Rey Campus, 558 Munoz Rivera Avenue, PO Box 190304, Hato Rey, PR 00919-0304. *Phone:* 787-753-6335.
Website: http://www.icprjc.edu/.

RHODE ISLAND

Community College of Rhode Island
Warwick, Rhode Island

- **State-supported** 2-year, founded 1964
- **Urban** 205-acre campus with easy access to Boston
- **Coed,** 17,553 undergraduate students, 30% full-time, 59% women, 41% men

Undergraduates 5,272 full-time, 12,281 part-time. Students come from 20 states and territories; 4% are from out of state; 9% Black or African American, non-Hispanic/Latino; 19% Hispanic/Latino; 3% Asian, non-Hispanic/Latino; 0.6% American Indian or Alaska Native, non-Hispanic/Latino; 4% Two or more races, non-Hispanic/Latino; 4% Race/ethnicity unknown; 0.1% international.
Freshmen *Admission:* 7,458 applied, 7,413 admitted, 3,124 enrolled.
Faculty *Total:* 943, 35% full-time. *Student/faculty ratio:* 18:1.
Majors Accounting; administrative assistant and secretarial science; adult development and aging; art; banking and financial support services; biological and physical sciences; business administration and management; business/commerce; chemical technology; clinical/medical laboratory technology; computer and information sciences; computer engineering technology; computer programming (specific applications); computer support specialist; computer systems networking and telecommunications; criminal justice/police science; crisis/emergency/disaster management; customer service management; dental hygiene; diagnostic medical sonography and ultrasound technology; dramatic/theater arts; electromechanical technology; engineering; fire science/firefighting; general studies; histologic technician; jazz/jazz studies; kindergarten/preschool education; legal administrative assistant/secretary; legal assistant/paralegal; liberal arts and sciences/liberal studies; licensed practical/vocational nurse training; marketing/marketing management; massage therapy; medical administrative assistant and medical secretary; mental health counseling; music; occupational therapist assistant; opticianry; physical therapy technology; radiologic technology/science; registered nursing/registered nurse; respiratory care therapy; social work; special education; substance abuse/addiction counseling; surveying engineering; web/multimedia management and webmaster.
Academics *Calendar:* semesters. *Degree:* certificates, diplomas, and associate. *Special study options:* academic remediation for entering students, adult/continuing education programs, advanced placement credit, cooperative education, distance learning, double majors, English as a second language, external degree program, honors programs, independent study, internships, off-campus study, part-time degree program, services for LD students, study abroad, summer session for credit. *ROTC:* Army (c).
Library Community College of Rhode Island Learning Resources Center plus 3 others with an OPAC, a Web page.
Student Life *Housing:* college housing not available. *Activities and Organizations:* drama/theater group, student-run newspaper, choral group, Distributive Education Clubs of America, Theater group - Players, Skills USA, Phi Theta Kappa, student government. *Campus security:* 24-hour emergency response devices and patrols. *Student services:* health clinic, personal/psychological counseling.
Athletics Member NJCAA. *Intercollegiate sports:* baseball M(s), basketball M(s)/W(s), golf M/W, soccer M(s)/W(s), softball W(s), tennis M/W, track and field M/W, volleyball W(s). *Intramural sports:* basketball M/W, volleyball M/W.
Costs (2014–15) *Tuition:* state resident $3624 full-time, $165 per credit hour part-time; nonresident $10,256 full-time, $490 per credit hour part-time. Full-time tuition and fees vary according to program. Part-time tuition and fees vary according to course load and program. *Required fees:* $326 full-time, $12 per credit hour part-time. *Payment plans:* installment, deferred payment. *Waivers:* senior citizens and employees or children of employees.
Financial Aid Of all full-time matriculated undergraduates who enrolled in 2013, 500 Federal Work-Study jobs (averaging $2500).
Applying *Options:* deferred entrance. *Application fee:* $20. *Application deadlines:* rolling (freshmen), rolling (transfers). *Notification:* continuous (freshmen).
Freshman Application Contact Community College of Rhode Island, Flanagan Campus, 1762 Louisquisset Pike, Lincoln, RI 02865-4585. *Phone:* 401-333-7490. *Fax:* 401-333-7122. *E-mail:* webadmission@ccri.edu. *Website:* http://www.ccri.edu/.

SOUTH CAROLINA

Aiken Technical College
Aiken, South Carolina

Freshman Application Contact Ms. Lisa Sommers, Aiken Technical College, PO Drawer 696, Aiken, SC 29802. *Phone:* 803-593-9231 Ext. 1584. *Fax:* 803-593-6526. *E-mail:* sommersl@atc.edu. *Website:* http://www.atc.edu/.

Brown Mackie College–Greenville
Greenville, South Carolina

- **Proprietary** primarily 2-year, part of Education Management Corporation
- **Coed**

Academics *Degrees:* certificates, associate, and bachelor's.
Freshman Application Contact Brown Mackie College–Greenville, Two Liberty Square, 75 Beattie Place, Suite 100, Greenville, SC 29601. *Phone:* 864-239-5300. *Toll-free phone:* 877-479-8465. *Website:* http://www.brownmackie.edu/greenville/.

Central Carolina Technical College
Sumter, South Carolina

Freshman Application Contact Ms. Barbara Wright, Director of Admissions and Counseling, Central Carolina Technical College, 506 North Guignard Drive, Sumter, SC 29150. *Phone:* 803-778-6695. *Toll-free phone:* 800-221-8711. *Fax:* 803-778-6696. *E-mail:* wrightb@cctech.edu. *Website:* http://www.cctech.edu/.

Clinton College
Rock Hill, South Carolina

Director of Admissions Robert M. Copeland, Vice President for Student Affairs, Clinton College, 1029 Crawford Road, Rock Hill, SC 29730. *Phone:* 803-327-7402. *Toll-free phone:* 877-837-9645. *Fax:* 803-327-3261. *E-mail:* rcopeland@clintonjrcollege.org. *Website:* http://www.clintoncollege.edu/.

Denmark Technical College
Denmark, South Carolina

- **State-supported** 2-year, founded 1948, part of South Carolina State Board for Technical and Comprehensive Education
- **Rural** 53-acre campus
- **Coed,** 1,678 undergraduate students, 85% full-time, 61% women, 39% men

Undergraduates 1,422 full-time, 256 part-time. 3% are from out of state; 96% Black or African American, non-Hispanic/Latino; 0.3% Hispanic/Latino; 0.1% Asian, non-Hispanic/Latino; 0.3% American Indian or Alaska Native, non-Hispanic/Latino; 0.2% Race/ethnicity unknown; 1% transferred in. *Retention:* 45% of full-time freshmen returned.
Freshmen *Admission:* 351 enrolled.
Faculty *Total:* 47, 74% full-time. *Student/faculty ratio:* 21:1.
Majors Administrative assistant and secretarial science; automobile/automotive mechanics technology; business administration and management; computer and information sciences; criminal justice/law enforcement administration; engineering technology; human services; kindergarten/preschool education.
Academics *Calendar:* semesters. *Degree:* certificates, diplomas, and associate. *Special study options:* academic remediation for entering students, adult/continuing education programs, advanced placement credit, cooperative education, distance learning, independent study, internships, off-campus study, part-time degree program, summer session for credit.
Library Denmark Technical College Learning Resources Center with 9,644 titles, 762 audiovisual materials, an OPAC.
Student Life *Housing Options:* men-only, women-only. Campus housing is university owned. Freshman applicants given priority for college housing. *Activities and Organizations:* choral group, Student Government Association, DTC Choir, Athletics, Phi Theta Kappa Internal Honor Society, Esquire Club (men and women). *Campus security:* 24-hour patrols, late-night transport/escort service, 24-hour emergency contact line/alarm devices. *Student services:* health clinic, personal/psychological counseling.
Athletics Member NJCAA. *Intercollegiate sports:* basketball M/W, cheerleading W. *Intramural sports:* basketball M/W.

Standardized Tests *Required:* ACT, ASSET, ACT Compass, and TEAS (Nursing) (for admission). *Recommended:* SAT or ACT (for admission).
Costs (2014–15) *Tuition:* state resident $2734 full-time; nonresident $5158 full-time. *Room and board:* $3808.
Financial Aid Of all full-time matriculated undergraduates who enrolled in 2013, 250 Federal Work-Study jobs (averaging $2000).
Applying *Options:* electronic application, early admission, deferred entrance. *Application fee:* $10. *Required:* high school transcript. *Required for some:* essay or personal statement. *Recommended:* SLED Check, TEAS Testing, Drug Test, PPD Test (all requirement for LPN). *Application deadlines:* rolling (freshmen), rolling (out-of-state freshmen), rolling (transfers). *Notification:* continuous (freshmen), continuous (out-of-state freshmen), continuous (transfers).
Freshman Application Contact Ms. Kara Troy, Administrative Specialist II, Denmark Technical College, PO Box 327, 1126 Solomon Blatt Boulevard, Denmark, SC 29042. *Phone:* 803-793-5180. *Fax:* 803-793-5942. *E-mail:* troyk@denmarktech.edu.
Website: http://www.denmarktech.edu/.

ECPI University
Columbia, South Carolina

Admissions Office Contact ECPI University, 250 Berryhill Road, #300, Columbia, SC 29210. *Toll-free phone:* 866-708-6168.
Website: http://www.ecpi.edu/.

ECPI University
Greenville, South Carolina

Admissions Office Contact ECPI University, 1001 Keys Drive, #100, Greenville, SC 29615. *Toll-free phone:* 866-708-6171.
Website: http://www.ecpi.edu/.

ECPI University
North Charleston, South Carolina

Admissions Office Contact ECPI University, 7410 Northside Drive, Suite 100, North Charleston, SC 29420. *Toll-free phone:* 866-708-6166.
Website: http://www.ecpi.edu/.

Florence-Darlington Technical College
Florence, South Carolina

Director of Admissions Shelley Fortin, Vice President for Enrollment Management and Student Services, Florence-Darlington Technical College, 2715 West Lucas Street, PO Box 100548, Florence, SC 29501-0548. *Phone:* 843-661-8111 Ext. 117. *Toll-free phone:* 800-228-5745. *E-mail:* shelley.fortin@fdtc.edu.
Website: http://www.fdtc.edu/.

Forrest College
Anderson, South Carolina

- **Proprietary** 2-year, founded 1946
- **Small-town** 3-acre campus
- **Endowment** $60,000
- **Coed,** 120 undergraduate students, 72% full-time, 89% women, 11% men

Undergraduates 86 full-time, 34 part-time. Students come from 2 states and territories; 1% are from out of state.
Freshmen *Admission:* 13 enrolled.
Faculty *Total:* 20, 10% full-time, 20% with terminal degrees. *Student/faculty ratio:* 6:1.
Majors Accounting; business administration and management; child-care and support services management; computer installation and repair technology; computer technology/computer systems technology; legal administrative assistant/secretary; legal assistant/paralegal; medical/clinical assistant; medical office management; office management.
Academics *Calendar:* quarters. *Degree:* certificates, diplomas, and associate. *Special study options:* advanced placement credit, cooperative education, double majors, independent study, internships, part-time degree program, summer session for credit.
Library Forrest College Library plus 1 other with 40,000 titles, 2,200 audiovisual materials, an OPAC.
Student Life *Housing:* college housing not available. *Campus security:* 24-hour emergency response devices, late-night transport/escort service.
Standardized Tests *Required:* Gates-McGinnity (for admission).

Costs (2015–16) *One-time required fee:* $200. *Tuition:* $11,760 full-time, $245 per credit hour part-time. Full-time tuition and fees vary according to course load and program. Part-time tuition and fees vary according to course load and program. *Required fees:* $500 full-time, $500 per year part-time, $125 per term part-time. *Payment plan:* installment. *Waivers:* employees or children of employees.
Financial Aid Of all full-time matriculated undergraduates who enrolled in 2012, 135 applied for aid, 135 were judged to have need.
Applying *Required:* essay or personal statement, high school transcript, minimum 2.0 GPA, interview. *Recommended:* minimum 2.5 GPA.
Freshman Application Contact Ms. Veronica Wright, Admissions and Placement Coordinator/Representative, Forrest College, 601 East River Street, Anderson, SC 29624. *Phone:* 864-225-7653. *Fax:* 864-261-7471. *E-mail:* veronicawright@forrestcollege.edu.
Website: http://www.forrestcollege.edu/.

Fortis College
Columbia, South Carolina

Admissions Office Contact Fortis College, 246 Stoneridge Drive, Suite 101, Columbia, SC 29210.
Website: http://www.fortis.edu/.

Golf Academy of America
Myrtle Beach, South Carolina

Admissions Office Contact Golf Academy of America, 3268 Waccamaw Boulevard, Myrtle Beach, SC 29579.
Website: http://www.golfacademy.edu/.

Greenville Technical College
Greenville, South Carolina

- **State-supported** 2-year, founded 1962, part of South Carolina State Board for Technical and Comprehensive Education
- **Urban** 604-acre campus
- **Coed,** 12,592 undergraduate students, 39% full-time, 58% women, 42% men

Undergraduates 4,873 full-time, 7,719 part-time. Students come from 60 other countries; 4% are from out of state; 24% Black or African American, non-Hispanic/Latino; 8% Hispanic/Latino; 2% Asian, non-Hispanic/Latino; 0.1% Native Hawaiian or other Pacific Islander, non-Hispanic/Latino; 0.4% American Indian or Alaska Native, non-Hispanic/Latino; 2% Two or more races, non-Hispanic/Latino; 4% Race/ethnicity unknown; 0.2% international; 6% transferred in.
Freshmen *Admission:* 4,946 applied, 4,910 admitted, 2,145 enrolled.
Faculty *Total:* 792, 44% full-time. *Student/faculty ratio:* 15:1.
Majors Accounting; administrative assistant and secretarial science; architectural engineering technology; automobile/automotive mechanics technology; business administration and management; child-care and support services management; clinical/medical laboratory technology; construction engineering technology; criminal justice/safety; culinary arts; data processing and data processing technology; dental hygiene; diagnostic medical sonography and ultrasound technology; electrical, electronic and communications engineering technology; electromechanical and instrumentation and maintenance technologies related; emergency medical technology (EMT paramedic); fire science/firefighting; health information/medical records technology; institutional food workers; legal assistant/paralegal; liberal arts and sciences/liberal studies; machine tool technology; mechanical drafting and CAD/CADD; mechanical engineering/mechanical technology; mechanic and repair technologies related; medical radiologic technology; multi/interdisciplinary studies related; occupational therapist assistant; physical therapy technology; purchasing, procurement/acquisitions and contracts management; registered nursing/registered nurse; respiratory care therapy; sales, distribution, and marketing operations; social work.
Academics *Calendar:* semesters. *Degree:* certificates, diplomas, and associate. *Special study options:* academic remediation for entering students, advanced placement credit, cooperative education, distance learning, double majors, English as a second language, honors programs, independent study, internships, part-time degree program, services for LD students, summer session for credit.
Library J. Verne Smith Library plus 3 others with 38,784 titles, 2,482 audiovisual materials, an OPAC, a Web page.
Student Life *Housing:* college housing not available. *Activities and Organizations:* Phi Theta Kappa, AAMLI, Cosmetology Club, Engineering Club, SGA/SAT Club. *Campus security:* 24-hour emergency response devices and patrols, late-night transport/escort service.

Athletics *Intramural sports:* badminton M(c)/W(c), basketball M(c)/W(c), football M(c)/W(c), soccer M(c)/W(c), softball M(c)/W(c), tennis M(c)/W(c), volleyball M(c)/W(c).
Standardized Tests *Recommended:* SAT, ACT ASSET, or ACT Compass.
Costs (2015–16) *Tuition:* area resident $5060 full-time, $164 per credit hour part-time; state resident $5495 full-time, $179 per credit hour part-time; nonresident $10,490 full-time, $347 per credit hour part-time. Full-time tuition and fees vary according to course load and program. Part-time tuition and fees vary according to course load and program. *Required fees:* $5 per credit hour part-time, $55 per credit hour part-time. *Payment plans:* installment, deferred payment. *Waivers:* senior citizens.
Financial Aid Of all full-time matriculated undergraduates who enrolled in 2013, 105 Federal Work-Study jobs (averaging $3735).
Applying *Options:* electronic application, early admission, deferred entrance. *Application fee:* $35. *Required:* high school transcript. *Application deadlines:* rolling (freshmen), rolling (transfers). *Notification:* continuous until 8/18 (freshmen), continuous until 8/18 (transfers).
Freshman Application Contact Greenville Technical College, PO Box 5616, Greenville, SC 29606-5616. *Phone:* 864-250-8287. *Toll-free phone:* 800-992-1183 (in-state); 800-723-0673 (out-of-state).
Website: http://www.gvltec.edu/.

Horry-Georgetown Technical College
Conway, South Carolina

- **State and locally supported** 2-year, founded 1966, part of South Carolina State Board for Technical and Comprehensive Education
- **Small-town** campus
- **Coed,** 7,660 undergraduate students, 38% full-time, 64% women, 36% men

Undergraduates 2,911 full-time, 4,749 part-time. 22% Black or African American, non-Hispanic/Latino; 4% Hispanic/Latino; 1% Asian, non-Hispanic/Latino; 0.1% Native Hawaiian or other Pacific Islander, non-Hispanic/Latino; 0.5% American Indian or Alaska Native, non-Hispanic/Latino; 2% Two or more races, non-Hispanic/Latino; 0.6% Race/ethnicity unknown; 0.2% international. *Retention:* 57% of full-time freshmen returned.
Freshmen *Admission:* 1,105 enrolled. *Average high school GPA:* 2.5.
Faculty *Total:* 352, 42% full-time. *Student/faculty ratio:* 21:1.
Majors Administrative assistant and secretarial science; business administration and management; criminal justice/safety; culinary arts; electrical, electronic and communications engineering technology; forest technology; legal assistant/paralegal; machine tool technology; registered nursing/registered nurse.
Academics *Calendar:* semesters. *Degree:* certificates, diplomas, and associate. *Special study options:* academic remediation for entering students, adult/continuing education programs, advanced placement credit, cooperative education, distance learning, double majors, independent study, internships, part-time degree program, services for LD students, summer session for credit.
Library Conway Campus Library with a Web page.
Student Life *Housing:* college housing not available. *Campus security:* 24-hour emergency response devices and patrols. *Student services:* personal/psychological counseling.
Costs (2015–16) *Tuition:* area resident $1793 full-time, $150 per hour part-time; state resident $2250 full-time, $188 per hour part-time; nonresident $3229 full-time, $270 per hour part-time. *Required fees:* $402 full-time. *Waivers:* senior citizens and employees or children of employees.
Applying *Options:* early admission. *Application fee:* $25. *Required for some:* high school transcript. *Application deadlines:* rolling (freshmen), rolling (transfers). *Notification:* continuous (freshmen), continuous (transfers).
Freshman Application Contact Mr. George Swindoll, Associate Vice President for Enrollment, Development, and Registration, Horry-Georgetown Technical College, 2050 Highway 501 East, PO Box 261966, Conway, SC 29528-6066. *Phone:* 843-349-5277. *Fax:* 843-349-7501. *E-mail:* george.swindoll@hgtc.edu.
Website: http://www.hgtc.edu/.

ITT Technical Institute
Columbia, South Carolina

- **Proprietary** primarily 2-year, part of ITT Educational Services, Inc.
- **Coed**

Academics *Degrees:* associate and bachelor's.
Freshman Application Contact Director of Recruitment, ITT Technical Institute, 1628 Browning Road, Suite 180, Columbia, SC 29210. *Phone:* 803-216-6000. *Toll-free phone:* 800-242-5158.
Website: http://www.itt-tech.edu/.

ITT Technical Institute
Greenville, South Carolina

- **Proprietary** primarily 2-year, founded 1992, part of ITT Educational Services, Inc.
- **Coed**

Academics *Calendar:* quarters. *Degrees:* associate and bachelor's.
Financial Aid Of all full-time matriculated undergraduates who enrolled in 2013, 3 Federal Work-Study jobs.
Freshman Application Contact Director of Recruitment, ITT Technical Institute, 6 Independence Pointe, Greenville, SC 29615. *Phone:* 864-288-0777. *Toll-free phone:* 800-932-4488.
Website: http://www.itt-tech.edu/.

ITT Technical Institute
Myrtle Beach, South Carolina

- **Proprietary** primarily 2-year, part of ITT Educational Services, Inc.
- **Coed**

Academics *Calendar:* quarters. *Degrees:* associate and bachelor's.
Freshman Application Contact Director of Recruitment, ITT Technical Institute, 9654 N. Kings Highway, Suite 101, Myrtle Beach, SC 29572. *Phone:* 843-497-7820. *Toll-free phone:* 877-316-7054.
Website: http://www.itt-tech.edu/.

ITT Technical Institute
North Charleston, South Carolina

- **Proprietary** primarily 2-year, part of ITT Educational Services, Inc.
- **Coed**

Academics *Calendar:* quarters. *Degrees:* associate and bachelor's.
Freshman Application Contact Director of Recruitment, ITT Technical Institute, 2431 W. Aviation Avenue, North Charleston, SC 29406. *Phone:* 843-745-5700. *Toll-free phone:* 877-291-0900.
Website: http://www.itt-tech.edu/.

Midlands Technical College
Columbia, South Carolina

- **State and locally supported** 2-year, founded 1974, part of South Carolina State Board for Technical and Comprehensive Education
- **Suburban** 156-acre campus
- **Endowment** $4.2 million
- **Coed,** 11,424 undergraduate students, 46% full-time, 59% women, 41% men

Undergraduates 5,252 full-time, 6,172 part-time. Students come from 36 states and territories; 64 other countries; 2% are from out of state; 36% Black or African American, non-Hispanic/Latino; 4% Hispanic/Latino; 2% Asian, non-Hispanic/Latino; 0.2% Native Hawaiian or other Pacific Islander, non-Hispanic/Latino; 0.5% American Indian or Alaska Native, non-Hispanic/Latino; 3% Two or more races, non-Hispanic/Latino; 3% Race/ethnicity unknown; 10% transferred in.
Freshmen *Admission:* 5,753 applied, 3,763 admitted, 2,508 enrolled.
Faculty *Total:* 724, 30% full-time. *Student/faculty ratio:* 20:1.
Majors Accounting; administrative assistant and secretarial science; architectural engineering technology; automobile/automotive mechanics technology; building construction technology; business administration and management; business/commerce; child-care provision; civil engineering technology; clinical/medical laboratory technology; commercial and advertising art; computer and information sciences and support services related; computer installation and repair technology; computer systems networking and telecommunications; construction engineering technology; court reporting; criminal justice/safety; data processing and data processing technology; dental assisting; dental hygiene; electrical, electronic and communications engineering technology; engineering technology; gerontology; health information/medical records technology; health professions related; heating, air conditioning, ventilation and refrigeration maintenance technology; human services; industrial electronics technology; industrial mechanics and maintenance technology; legal assistant/paralegal; liberal arts and sciences/liberal studies; licensed practical/vocational nurse training; machine tool technology; mechanical drafting and CAD/CADD; mechanical engineering/mechanical technology; medical/clinical assistant; medical radiologic technology; multi/interdisciplinary studies related; nuclear medical technology; occupational therapist assistant; pharmacy technician; physical therapy technology; precision production related; precision production trades; registered nursing/registered nurse; respiratory care therapy; sales, distribution, and marketing operations; surgical technology; youth services.

Academics *Calendar:* semesters. *Degree:* certificates, diplomas, and associate. *Special study options:* academic remediation for entering students, adult/continuing education programs, advanced placement credit, cooperative education, distance learning, double majors, English as a second language, internships, part-time degree program, services for LD students, student-designed majors, summer session for credit. *ROTC:* Army (c), Navy (c), Air Force (c).

Library Midlands Technical College Library with 75,646 titles, 2,114 audiovisual materials, an OPAC, a Web page.

Student Life *Housing:* college housing not available. *Activities and Organizations:* drama/theater group, student-run newspaper. *Campus security:* 24-hour emergency response devices and patrols, late-night transport/escort service.

Athletics *Intramural sports:* basketball M, bowling M/W, equestrian sports M/W, football M, softball M/W, ultimate Frisbee M/W, volleyball M/W.

Standardized Tests *Required for some:* ACT ASSET. *Recommended:* SAT or ACT (for admission).

Financial Aid Of all full-time matriculated undergraduates who enrolled in 2011, 4,794 applied for aid, 4,160 were judged to have need, 118 had their need fully met. 154 Federal Work-Study jobs (averaging $2775). *Average percent of need met:* 13%. *Average financial aid package:* $6098. *Average need-based loan:* $3089. *Average need-based gift aid:* $4370.

Applying *Options:* electronic application, early admission, deferred entrance. *Application fee:* $35. *Recommended:* high school transcript. *Application deadline:* rolling (transfers). *Notification:* continuous (transfers).

Freshman Application Contact Ms. Sylvia Littlejohn, Director of Admissions, Midlands Technical College, PO Box 2408, Columbia, SC 29202. *Phone:* 803-738-8324. *Toll-free phone:* 800-922-8038. *Fax:* 803-790-7524. *E-mail:* admissions@midlandstech.edu. *Website:* http://www.midlandstech.edu/.

Miller-Motte Technical College
Conway, South Carolina

Admissions Office Contact Miller-Motte Technical College, 2451 Highway 501 East, Conway, SC 29526. *Toll-free phone:* 866-297-0267. *Website:* http://www.miller-motte.edu/.

Miller-Motte Technical College
North Charleston, South Carolina

Freshman Application Contact Ms. Elaine Cue, Campus President, Miller-Motte Technical College, 8085 Rivers Avenue, Suite E, North Charleston, SC 29406. *Phone:* 843-574-0101. *Toll-free phone:* 800-923-4162. *Fax:* 843-266-3424. *E-mail:* juliasc@miller-mott.net. *Website:* http://www.miller-motte.edu/.

Northeastern Technical College
Cheraw, South Carolina

- **State and locally supported** 2-year, founded 1967, part of South Carolina State Board for Technical and Comprehensive Education
- **Rural** 59-acre campus
- **Endowment** $31,355
- **Coed**

Undergraduates 446 full-time, 530 part-time. Students come from 3 states and territories; 1% are from out of state; 3% transferred in.

Faculty *Student/faculty ratio:* 25:1.

Academics *Calendar:* semesters. *Degree:* certificates, diplomas, and associate. *Special study options:* academic remediation for entering students, adult/continuing education programs, advanced placement credit, distance learning, independent study, part-time degree program, study abroad.

Student Life *Campus security:* 24-hour emergency response devices.

Standardized Tests *Required:* ACT Compass (for admission). *Required for some:* SAT (for admission).

Costs (2014–15) *Tuition:* area resident $2310 full-time; state resident $2445 full-time; nonresident $3945 full-time. Full-time tuition and fees vary according to class time, course level, course load, degree level, program, reciprocity agreements, and student level. Part-time tuition and fees vary according to class time, course level, course load, degree level, program, reciprocity agreements, and student level.

Financial Aid Of all full-time matriculated undergraduates who enrolled in 2013, 26 Federal Work-Study jobs (averaging $2800).

Applying *Options:* electronic application, early admission. *Application fee:* $25. *Required:* high school transcript, interview.

Freshman Application Contact Mrs. Mary K. Newton, Dean of Students, Northeastern Technical College, 1201 Chesterfield Highway, Cheraw, SC 29520-1007. *Phone:* 843-921-6935. *Toll-free phone:* 800-921-7399. *Fax:* 843-921-1476. *E-mail:* mpace@netc.edu. *Website:* http://www.netc.edu/.

Orangeburg-Calhoun Technical College
Orangeburg, South Carolina

Freshman Application Contact Mr. Dana Rickards, Director of Recruitment, Orangeburg-Calhoun Technical College, 3250 St Matthews Road, NE, Orangeburg, SC 29118-8299. *Phone:* 803-535-1219. *Toll-free phone:* 800-813-6519. *Website:* http://www.octech.edu/.

Piedmont Technical College
Greenwood, South Carolina

Director of Admissions Mr. Steve Coleman, Director of Admissions, Piedmont Technical College, 620 North Emerald Road, PO Box 1467, Greenwood, SC 29648-1467. *Phone:* 864-941-8603. *Toll-free phone:* 800-868-5528. *Website:* http://www.ptc.edu/.

Spartanburg Community College
Spartanburg, South Carolina

- **State-supported** 2-year, founded 1961, part of South Carolina State Board for Technical and Comprehensive Education
- **Suburban** 104-acre campus with easy access to Charlotte
- **Coed,** 5,495 undergraduate students, 47% full-time, 58% women, 42% men

Undergraduates 2,594 full-time, 2,901 part-time. Students come from 7 states and territories; 3 other countries; 1% are from out of state; 23% Black or African American, non-Hispanic/Latino; 6% Hispanic/Latino; 3% Asian, non-Hispanic/Latino; 0.1% Native Hawaiian or other Pacific Islander, non-Hispanic/Latino; 0.3% American Indian or Alaska Native, non-Hispanic/Latino; 2% Two or more races, non-Hispanic/Latino; 2% Race/ethnicity unknown; 8% transferred in. *Retention:* 33% of full-time freshmen returned.

Freshmen *Admission:* 1,169 enrolled.

Faculty *Total:* 345, 31% full-time. *Student/faculty ratio:* 16:1.

Majors Accounting; administrative assistant and secretarial science; applied horticulture/horticulture operations; automobile/automotive mechanics technology; business administration and management; clinical/medical laboratory technology; data processing and data processing technology; electrical, electronic and communications engineering technology; heating, air conditioning, ventilation and refrigeration maintenance technology; industrial electronics technology; liberal arts and sciences/liberal studies; machine tool technology; manufacturing engineering technology; mechanical engineering/mechanical technology; medical radiologic technology; multi/interdisciplinary studies related; radiation protection/health physics technology; registered nursing/registered nurse; respiratory care therapy.

Academics *Calendar:* semesters condensed semesters plus summer sessions. *Degree:* certificates, diplomas, and associate. *Special study options:* academic remediation for entering students, adult/continuing education programs, advanced placement credit, cooperative education, distance learning, English as a second language, part-time degree program, services for LD students, summer session for credit.

Library Spartanburg Community College Library with 40,078 titles, an OPAC, a Web page.

Student Life *Activities and Organizations:* drama/theater group, student-run newspaper. *Campus security:* 24-hour emergency response devices and patrols. *Student services:* personal/psychological counseling, women's center.

Standardized Tests *Required for some:* SAT or ACT (for admission).

Financial Aid Of all full-time matriculated undergraduates who enrolled in 2012, 47 Federal Work-Study jobs (averaging $3212).

Applying *Options:* electronic application, early admission. *Application fee:* $25. *Required:* high school transcript, high school diploma, GED or equivalent. *Recommended:* interview. *Application deadlines:* rolling (freshmen), rolling (transfers). *Notification:* continuous (freshmen), continuous (transfers).

Freshman Application Contact Sabrina Sims, Admissions Counselor, Spartanburg Community College, PO Box 4386, Spartanburg, SC 29305. *Phone:* 864-592-4816. *Toll-free phone:* 866-591-3700. *Fax:* 864-592-4564. *E-mail:* admissions@sccsc.edu. *Website:* http://www.sccsc.edu/.

Spartanburg Methodist College
Spartanburg, South Carolina

- **Independent Methodist** 2-year, founded 1911
- **Suburban** 110-acre campus with easy access to Charlotte
- **Endowment** $22.0 million
- **Coed,** 793 undergraduate students, 98% full-time, 44% women, 56% men

Undergraduates 776 full-time, 17 part-time. Students come from 12 states and territories; 5 other countries; 5% are from out of state; 31% Black or African American, non-Hispanic/Latino; 6% Hispanic/Latino; 0.5% Asian, non-Hispanic/Latino; 0.1% American Indian or Alaska Native, non-Hispanic/Latino; 2% Two or more races, non-Hispanic/Latino; 0.8% international; 5% transferred in; 65% live on campus.
Freshmen *Admission:* 1,289 applied, 846 admitted, 464 enrolled. *Average high school GPA:* 3.43. *Test scores:* SAT critical reading scores over 500: 20%; SAT math scores over 500: 23%; SAT writing scores over 500: 13%; ACT scores over 18: 55%; SAT math scores over 600: 3%; SAT writing scores over 600: 1%; ACT scores over 24: 8%.
Faculty *Total:* 70, 39% full-time, 31% with terminal degrees. *Student/faculty ratio:* 19:1.
Majors Business/commerce; criminal justice/law enforcement administration; liberal arts and sciences/liberal studies; religious studies related; visual and performing arts.
Academics *Calendar:* semesters. *Degree:* associate. *Special study options:* academic remediation for entering students, advanced placement credit, English as a second language, honors programs, independent study, part-time degree program, services for LD students, summer session for credit.
Library Marie Blair Burgess Learning Resource Center plus 1 other with 75,000 titles, 3,150 audiovisual materials, an OPAC, a Web page.
Student Life *Housing Options:* coed, men-only, women-only. Campus housing is university owned. Freshman campus housing is guaranteed. *Activities and Organizations:* drama/theater group, student-run newspaper, choral group, College Christian Movement, Alpha Phi Omega, Campus Union, Fellowship of Christian Athletes, Kappa Sigma Alpha. *Campus security:* 24-hour emergency response devices and patrols, student patrols, late-night transport/escort service, controlled dormitory access. *Student services:* health clinic, personal/psychological counseling.
Athletics Member NJCAA. *Intercollegiate sports:* baseball M(s), basketball M(s)/W(s), cross-country running M(s)/W(s), golf M(s)/W(s), soccer M(s)/W(s), softball W(s), tennis M(s)/W(s), volleyball W(s), wrestling M(s). *Intramural sports:* basketball M/W, cheerleading M/W, football M/W, softball M/W, table tennis M/W, volleyball M/W.
Standardized Tests *Required:* SAT or ACT (for admission).
Costs (2014–15) *One-time required fee:* $175. *Comprehensive fee:* $24,166 includes full-time tuition ($15,000), mandatory fees ($930), and room and board ($8236). Full-time tuition and fees vary according to course load. Part-time tuition: $405 per semester hour. Part-time tuition and fees vary according to course load. *Payment plan:* installment. *Waivers:* senior citizens and employees or children of employees.
Financial Aid Of all full-time matriculated undergraduates who enrolled in 2013, 80 Federal Work-Study jobs (averaging $1600). 90 state and other part-time jobs (averaging $1600). *Financial aid deadline:* 8/30.
Applying *Options:* electronic application, deferred entrance. *Application fee:* $25. *Required:* essay or personal statement, high school transcript, minimum 2.0 GPA, high school rank considered along with other criteria. *Required for some:* interview. *Recommended:* interview. *Application deadlines:* rolling (freshmen), rolling (transfers). *Notification:* continuous (freshmen), continuous (transfers).
Freshman Application Contact Mr. Daniel L. Philbeck, Vice President for Enrollment Management, Spartanburg Methodist College, 1000 Powell Mill Road, Spartanburg, SC 29301-5899. *Phone:* 864-587-4223. *Toll-free phone:* 800-772-7286. *Fax:* 864-587-4355. *E-mail:* admiss@smcsc.edu. *Website:* http://www.smcsc.edu/.

Technical College of the Lowcountry
Beaufort, South Carolina

- **State-supported** 2-year, founded 1972, part of South Carolina Technical and Comprehensive Education System
- **Small-town** 12-acre campus
- **Coed,** 2,529 undergraduate students, 29% full-time, 69% women, 31% men

Undergraduates 734 full-time, 1,795 part-time. 6% are from out of state; 35% Black or African American, non-Hispanic/Latino; 10% Hispanic/Latino; 0.8% Asian, non-Hispanic/Latino; 0.2% Native Hawaiian or other Pacific Islander, non-Hispanic/Latino; 0.3% American Indian or Alaska Native, non-Hispanic/Latino; 1% Two or more races, non-Hispanic/Latino; 4% Race/ethnicity unknown; 0.1% international; 11% transferred in.

Freshmen *Admission:* 475 enrolled.
Faculty *Student/faculty ratio:* 15:1.
Majors Administrative assistant and secretarial science; business/commerce; child-care provision; civil engineering technology; construction engineering technology; data processing and data processing technology; early childhood education; education; emergency medical technology (EMT paramedic); fire services administration; golf course operation and grounds management; hospitality administration; industrial electronics technology; legal assistant/paralegal; liberal arts and sciences and humanities related; liberal arts and sciences/liberal studies; medical radiologic technology; physical therapy technology; registered nursing/registered nurse.
Academics *Calendar:* semesters. *Degree:* certificates, diplomas, and associate. *Special study options:* academic remediation for entering students, adult/continuing education programs, advanced placement credit, distance learning, part-time degree program, summer session for credit.
Student Life *Housing:* college housing not available. *Campus security:* security during class hours.
Standardized Tests *Required:* ACT ASSET (for admission). *Recommended:* SAT and SAT Subject Tests or ACT (for admission).
Costs (2014–15) *Tuition:* area resident $3864 full-time, $161 per credit hour part-time; state resident $4464 full-time, $186 per credit hour part-time; nonresident $8616 full-time, $359 per credit hour part-time. *Required fees:* $196 full-time, $4 per credit hour part-time, $50 per term part-time. *Payment plan:* installment. *Waivers:* senior citizens.
Financial Aid Of all full-time matriculated undergraduates who enrolled in 2013, 56 Federal Work-Study jobs (averaging $1700).
Applying *Options:* early admission, deferred entrance. *Application fee:* $25. *Application deadlines:* rolling (freshmen), rolling (transfers).
Freshman Application Contact Rhonda Cole, Admissions Services Manager, Technical College of the Lowcountry, 921 Ribaut Road, PO Box 1288, Beaufort, SC 29901-1288. *Phone:* 843-525-8229. *Fax:* 843-525-8285. *E-mail:* rcole@tcl.edu. *Website:* http://www.tcl.edu/.

Tri-County Technical College
Pendleton, South Carolina

Director of Admissions Renae Frazier, Director, Recruitment and Admissions, Tri-County Technical College, PO Box 587, 7900 Highway 76, Pendleton, SC 29670-0587. *Phone:* 864-646-1550. *Fax:* 864-646-1890. *E-mail:* infocent@tctc.edu. *Website:* http://www.tctc.edu/.

Trident Technical College
Charleston, South Carolina

- **State and locally supported** 2-year, founded 1964, part of South Carolina State Board for Technical and Comprehensive Education
- **Urban** campus
- **Coed,** 16,139 undergraduate students, 45% full-time, 62% women, 38% men

Undergraduates 7,186 full-time, 8,953 part-time. Students come from 83 other countries; 2% are from out of state; 30% Black or African American, non-Hispanic/Latino; 5% Hispanic/Latino; 2% Asian, non-Hispanic/Latino; 0.3% Native Hawaiian or other Pacific Islander, non-Hispanic/Latino; 0.6% American Indian or Alaska Native, non-Hispanic/Latino; 2% Two or more races, non-Hispanic/Latino; 2% Race/ethnicity unknown; 0.9% transferred in.
Freshmen *Admission:* 2,403 admitted, 2,406 enrolled.
Faculty *Total:* 1,120, 30% full-time, 4% with terminal degrees. *Student/faculty ratio:* 17:1.
Majors Accounting; administrative assistant and secretarial science; airframe mechanics and aircraft maintenance technology; automobile/automotive mechanics technology; biological and physical sciences; business administration and management; child-care provision; civil engineering technology; clinical/medical laboratory technology; commercial and advertising art; computer engineering technology; computer graphics; computer/information technology services administration related; computer programming (specific applications); computer systems networking and telecommunications; criminal justice/law enforcement administration; culinary arts; dental hygiene; electrical, electronic and communications engineering technology; engineering technology; horticultural science; hotel/motel administration; human services; industrial technology; legal assistant/paralegal; legal studies; liberal arts and sciences/liberal studies; machine tool technology; marketing/marketing management; mechanical engineering/mechanical technology; medical administrative assistant and medical secretary; occupational therapy; physical therapy; registered nursing/registered nurse; respiratory care therapy; telecommunications technology; veterinary/animal health technology; web/multimedia

management and webmaster; web page, digital/multimedia and information resources design.

Academics *Calendar:* semesters. *Degree:* certificates, diplomas, and associate. *Special study options:* academic remediation for entering students, advanced placement credit, cooperative education, distance learning, double majors, English as a second language, internships, off-campus study, part-time degree program, services for LD students, study abroad, summer session for credit.

Library Learning Resource Center plus 2 others with 107,671 titles, 5,042 audiovisual materials, an OPAC, a Web page.

Student Life *Housing:* college housing not available. *Activities and Organizations:* drama/theater group, student-run newspaper, radio station, Phi Theta Kappa, Lex Artis Paralegal Society, Hospitality and Culinary Student Association, Partnership for Change in Communities and Families, Society of Student Leaders. *Campus security:* 24-hour emergency response devices and patrols, late-night transport/escort service. *Student services:* personal/psychological counseling.

Costs (2015–16) *Tuition:* area resident $3912 full-time; state resident $4340 full-time; nonresident $7404 full-time. Full-time tuition and fees vary according to course load and program. Part-time tuition and fees vary according to course load and program. *Payment plan:* installment. *Waivers:* senior citizens.

Applying *Options:* electronic application, early admission. *Application fee:* $30. *Required for some:* high school transcript. *Application deadlines:* 8/6 (freshmen), 8/6 (transfers). *Notification:* continuous (freshmen), continuous (transfers).

Freshman Application Contact Ms. Clara Martin, Admissions Director, Trident Technical College, Charleston, SC 29423-8067. *Phone:* 843-574-6326. *Fax:* 843-574-6109. *E-mail:* Clara.Martin@tridenttech.edu. *Website:* http://www.tridenttech.edu/.

University of South Carolina Lancaster
Lancaster, South Carolina

Freshman Application Contact Susan Vinson, Admissions Counselor, University of South Carolina Lancaster, PO Box 889, Lancaster, SC 29721. *Phone:* 803-313-7000. *Fax:* 803-313-7116. *E-mail:* vinsons@mailbox.sc.edu. *Website:* http://usclancaster.sc.edu/.

University of South Carolina Salkehatchie
Allendale, South Carolina

- **State-supported** 2-year, founded 1965, part of University of South Carolina System
- **Rural** 95-acre campus
- **Coed,** 1,076 undergraduate students

Undergraduates 5% are from out of state. *Retention:* 45% of full-time freshmen returned.

Freshmen *Admission:* 647 applied, 388 admitted.

Faculty *Student/faculty ratio:* 17:1.

Majors Liberal arts and sciences/liberal studies.

Academics *Calendar:* semesters. *Degree:* associate. *Special study options:* academic remediation for entering students, adult/continuing education programs, advanced placement credit, cooperative education, distance learning, independent study, internships, part-time degree program, services for LD students, study abroad, summer session for credit.

Library Salkehatchie Learning Resource Center with an OPAC, a Web page.

Student Life *Housing:* college housing not available. *Campus security:* 24-hour emergency response devices, late-night transport/escort service.

Athletics Member NJCAA. *Intercollegiate sports:* baseball M, basketball M, soccer M/W, softball W.

Standardized Tests *Required:* SAT or ACT (for admission).

Costs (2014–15) *Tuition:* state resident $6294 full-time; nonresident $15,738 full-time. Full-time tuition and fees vary according to course load, degree level, reciprocity agreements, and student level. Part-time tuition and fees vary according to course load, degree level, reciprocity agreements, and student level. *Required fees:* $246 full-time. *Payment plan:* installment. *Waivers:* senior citizens.

Applying *Options:* electronic application. *Application fee:* $40. *Required:* high school transcript, minimum 2.0 GPA. *Application deadlines:* rolling (freshmen), rolling (out-of-state freshmen), rolling (transfers).

Freshman Application Contact Ms. Carmen Brown, Admissions Coordinator, University of South Carolina Salkehatchie, PO Box 617,

Allendale, SC 29810. *Phone:* 803-584-3446. *Toll-free phone:* 800-922-5500. *Fax:* 803-584-3884. *E-mail:* cdbrown@mailbox.sc.edu. *Website:* http://uscsalkehatchie.sc.edu/.

University of South Carolina Sumter
Sumter, South Carolina

Freshman Application Contact Mr. Keith Britton, Director of Admissions, University of South Carolina Sumter, 200 Miller Road, Sumter, SC 29150-2498. *Phone:* 803-938-3882. *Fax:* 803-938-3901. *E-mail:* kbritton@usc.sumter.edu. *Website:* http://www.uscsumter.edu/.

University of South Carolina Union
Union, South Carolina

- **State-supported** primarily 2-year, founded 1965, part of University of South Carolina System
- **Small-town** campus with easy access to Charlotte
- **Coed,** 500 undergraduate students, 50% full-time, 60% women, 40% men

Undergraduates 250 full-time, 250 part-time.

Freshmen *Admission:* 400 enrolled. *Average high school GPA:* 3.

Faculty *Total:* 38, 26% full-time. *Student/faculty ratio:* 18:1.

Majors Biological and physical sciences; liberal arts and sciences/liberal studies.

Academics *Calendar:* semesters. *Degrees:* associate and bachelor's. *Special study options:* cooperative education, part-time degree program.

Library USC UNION CAMPUS LIBRARY plus 1 other.

Student Life *Housing:* college housing not available. *Activities and Organizations:* drama/theater group, student-run newspaper, choral group.

Athletics *Intramural sports:* baseball M(c).

Standardized Tests *Required:* SAT or ACT (for admission).

Costs (2015–16) *Tuition:* state resident $3147 full-time, $262 per credit hour part-time; nonresident $7869 full-time, $656 per credit hour part-time. Full-time tuition and fees vary according to course load, degree level, and student level. Part-time tuition and fees vary according to student level. *Required fees:* $361 full-time, $180 per term part-time. *Payment plan:* deferred payment. *Waivers:* senior citizens.

Financial Aid Of all full-time matriculated undergraduates who enrolled in 2013, 16 Federal Work-Study jobs (averaging $3400).

Applying *Options:* electronic application. *Application fee:* $40. *Required:* high school transcript. *Application deadline:* rolling (freshmen).

Freshman Application Contact Mr. Michael B. Greer, Director of Enrollment Services, University of South Carolina Union, PO Drawer 729, Union, SC 29379-0729. *Phone:* 864-429-8728. *E-mail:* tyoung@gwm.sc.edu. *Website:* http://uscunion.sc.edu/.

Virginia College in Charleston
North Charleston, South Carolina

Admissions Office Contact Virginia College in Charleston, 6185 Rivers Avenue, North Charleston, SC 29406. *Website:* http://www.vc.edu/.

Virginia College in Columbia
Columbia, South Carolina

Admissions Office Contact Virginia College in Columbia, 7201 Two Notch Road, Suite 1000, Columbia, SC 29223. *Website:* http://www.vc.edu/.

Virginia College in Florence
Florence, South Carolina

Admissions Office Contact Virginia College in Florence, 2400 David H. McLeod Boulevard, Florence, SC 29501. *Website:* http://www.vc.edu/.

Virginia College in Greenville
Greenville, South Carolina

Admissions Office Contact Virginia College in Greenville, 78 Global Drive, Suite 200, Greenville, SC 29607. *Website:* http://www.vc.edu/.

Virginia College in Spartanburg
Spartanburg, South Carolina

Admissions Office Contact Virginia College in Spartanburg, 8150 Warren H. Abernathy Highway, Spartanburg, SC 29301.
Website: http://www.vc.edu/.

Williamsburg Technical College
Kingstree, South Carolina

Freshman Application Contact Williamsburg Technical College, 601 Martin Luther King, Jr Avenue, Kingstree, SC 29556-4197. *Phone:* 843-355-4162. *Toll-free phone:* 800-768-2021.
Website: http://www.wiltech.edu/.

York Technical College
Rock Hill, South Carolina

Freshman Application Contact Mr. Kenny Aldridge, Admissions Department Manager, York Technical College, Rock Hill, SC 29730. *Phone:* 803-327-8008. *Toll-free phone:* 800-922-8324. *Fax:* 803-981-7237. *E-mail:* kaldridge@yorktech.com.
Website: http://www.yorktech.com/.

SOUTH DAKOTA

Kilian Community College
Sioux Falls, South Dakota

- **Independent** 2-year, founded 1977
- **Urban** 2-acre campus
- **Coed**

Undergraduates 34 full-time, 219 part-time. Students come from 3 states and territories; 2% are from out of state; 13% Black or African American, non-Hispanic/Latino; 1% Hispanic/Latino; 0.4% Asian, non-Hispanic/Latino; 7% American Indian or Alaska Native, non-Hispanic/Latino; 25% Race/ethnicity unknown; 15% transferred in. *Retention:* 33% of full-time freshmen returned.
Faculty *Student/faculty ratio:* 8:1.
Academics *Calendar:* trimesters. *Degree:* certificates and associate. *Special study options:* academic remediation for entering students, advanced placement credit, double majors, English as a second language, independent study, part-time degree program, services for LD students, summer session for credit.
Student Life *Campus security:* late-night transport/escort service.
Costs (2014–15) *Tuition:* $10,764 full-time, $319 per credit hour part-time. Part-time tuition and fees vary according to course load. *Required fees:* $1440 full-time, $50 per credit hour part-time.
Financial Aid Of all full-time matriculated undergraduates who enrolled in 2011, 31 applied for aid, 31 were judged to have need. 26 Federal Work-Study jobs (averaging $1500). *Average percent of need met:* 61. *Average financial aid package:* $9000. *Average need-based loan:* $4500. *Average need-based gift aid:* $4500.
Applying *Options:* electronic application, deferred entrance. *Application fee:* $25. *Required:* high school transcript.
Freshman Application Contact Ms. Mary Klockman, Director of Admissions, Kilian Community College, 300 East 6th Street, Sioux Falls, SD 57103. *Phone:* 605-221-3100. *Toll-free phone:* 800-888-1147. *Fax:* 605-336-2606. *E-mail:* info@killian.edu.
Website: http://www.kilian.edu/.

Lake Area Technical Institute
Watertown, South Dakota

- **State-supported** 2-year, founded 1964
- **Small-town** 40-acre campus
- **Endowment** $2.2 million
- **Coed,** 1,728 undergraduate students, 81% full-time, 48% women, 52% men

Undergraduates 1,402 full-time, 326 part-time. 1% Black or African American, non-Hispanic/Latino; 1% Hispanic/Latino; 2% American Indian or Alaska Native, non-Hispanic/Latino. *Retention:* 84% of full-time freshmen returned.
Freshmen *Admission:* 1,689 applied, 1,020 admitted, 685 enrolled.
Faculty *Total:* 157, 62% full-time. *Student/faculty ratio:* 16:1.

Majors Agricultural business and management; aircraft powerplant technology; autobody/collision and repair technology; automobile/automotive mechanics technology; banking and financial support services; building construction technology; clinical/medical laboratory technology; computer science; construction engineering technology; construction/heavy equipment/earthmoving equipment operation; criminal justice/police science; dental assisting; diesel mechanics technology; electrical, electronic and communications engineering technology; emergency medical technology (EMT paramedic); engine machinist; entrepreneurship; environmental science; human services; machine tool technology; manufacturing engineering technology; marketing/marketing management; medical/clinical assistant; occupational therapist assistant; physical therapy technology; robotics technology, welding technology.
Academics *Calendar:* semesters. *Degree:* certificates, diplomas, and associate. *Special study options:* academic remediation for entering students, distance learning, internships, services for LD students.
Library Leonard H. Timmerman Library plus 1 other with 5,000 titles.
Student Life *Housing:* college housing not available.
Athletics *Intramural sports:* basketball M/W, bowling M/W, softball M/W, volleyball M/W.
Standardized Tests *Required:* ACT (for admission).
Costs (2015–16) *Tuition:* state resident $104 per credit hour part-time; nonresident $104 per credit hour part-time. Full-time tuition and fees vary according to program. Part-time tuition and fees vary according to program. *Payment plan:* installment.
Financial Aid Of all full-time matriculated undergraduates who enrolled in 2014, 130 Federal Work-Study jobs (averaging $2100).
Applying *Options:* electronic application. *Application fee:* $25. *Required:* high school transcript. *Required for some:* essay or personal statement, 3 letters of recommendation, interview. *Application deadline:* rolling (freshmen).
Freshman Application Contact Ms. LuAnn Strait, Director of Student Services, Lake Area Technical Institute, 1201 Arrow Ave, Watertown, SD 57201. *Phone:* 605-882-5284 Ext. 241. *Toll-free phone:* 800-657-4344. *E-mail:* straitl@lakeareatech.edu.
Website: http://www.lakeareatech.edu/.

Mitchell Technical Institute
Mitchell, South Dakota

- **State-supported** 2-year, founded 1968, part of South Dakota Board of Education
- **Rural** 90-acre campus
- **Coed,** 1,245 undergraduate students, 72% full-time, 35% women, 65% men

Undergraduates 894 full-time, 351 part-time. Students come from 7 states and territories; 8% are from out of state; 0.2% Black or African American, non-Hispanic/Latino; 1% Hispanic/Latino; 0.2% Asian, non-Hispanic/Latino; 3% American Indian or Alaska Native, non-Hispanic/Latino; 1% Two or more races, non-Hispanic/Latino; 0.1% Race/ethnicity unknown; 11% transferred in. *Retention:* 78% of full-time freshmen returned.
Freshmen *Admission:* 660 applied, 495 admitted, 360 enrolled. *Average high school GPA:* 2.8. *Test scores:* ACT scores over 18: 72%; ACT scores over 24: 12%; ACT scores over 30: 1%.
Faculty *Total:* 89, 89% full-time, 1% with terminal degrees. *Student/faculty ratio:* 12:1.
Majors Accounting and business/management; agricultural mechanics and equipment technology; agricultural production; automation engineer technology; building construction technology; building/property maintenance; business automation/technology/data entry; clinical/medical laboratory technology; computer support specialist; construction trades related; culinary arts; electrician; energy management and systems technology; geographic information science and cartography; heating, air conditioning, ventilation and refrigeration maintenance technology; human services; lineworker; magnetic resonance imaging (MRI) technology; medical/clinical assistant; medical office assistant; medical radiologic technology; network and system administration; radiologic technology/science; radio, television, and digital communication related; small engine mechanics and repair technology; speech-language pathology assistant; telecommunications technology; welding engineering technology.
Academics *Calendar:* semesters. *Degree:* certificates, diplomas, and associate. *Special study options:* academic remediation for entering students, advanced placement credit, cooperative education, distance learning, internships, part-time degree program, services for LD students, summer session for credit.
Library Instructional Services Center with 1,657 titles, 148 audiovisual materials, an OPAC.
Student Life *Housing Options:* Campus housing is provided by a third party. *Activities and Organizations:* Student Representative Board, Skills USA, Post-

Secondary Agricultural Students, Rodeo Club. *Student services:* personal/psychological counseling.
Athletics *Intercollegiate sports:* equestrian sports M/W. *Intramural sports:* basketball M/W, bowling M/W, riflery M/W, softball M/W, volleyball M/W.
Standardized Tests *Required for some:* SAT or ACT (for admission). *Recommended:* SAT or ACT (for admission).
Costs (2014–15) *Tuition:* state resident $3328 full-time, $104 per credit hour part-time; nonresident $3328 full-time, $104 per credit hour part-time. Full-time tuition and fees vary according to course load and program. Part-time tuition and fees vary according to course load and program. *Required fees:* $2528 full-time, $79 per credit hour part-time. *Payment plan:* installment. *Waivers:* employees or children of employees.
Financial Aid Of all full-time matriculated undergraduates who enrolled in 2014, 720 applied for aid, 607 were judged to have need, 8 had their need fully met. *Average percent of need met:* 63%. *Average financial aid package:* $8443. *Average need-based loan:* $3473. *Average need-based gift aid:* $4392. *Average indebtedness upon graduation:* $6682.
Applying *Options:* electronic application. *Required:* high school transcript. *Required for some:* essay or personal statement, interview. *Recommended:* minimum 2.0 GPA. *Application deadlines:* rolling (freshmen), rolling (out-of-state freshmen), rolling (transfers). *Notification:* continuous (freshmen), continuous (out-of-state freshmen), continuous (transfers).
Freshman Application Contact Mr. Clayton Deuter, Director of Admissions, Mitchell Technical Institute, 1800 East Spruce Street, Mitchell, SD 57301. *Phone:* 605-995-3025. *Toll-free phone:* 800-684-1969. *Fax:* 605-995-3067. *E-mail:* clayton.deuter@mitchelltech.edu.
Website: http://www.mitchelltech.edu/.

National American University

Ellsworth AFB, South Dakota

Freshman Application Contact Admissions Office, National American University, 1000 Ellsworth Street, Suite 2400B, Ellsworth AFB, SD 57706. *Website:* http://www.national.edu/.

Sisseton-Wahpeton College

Sisseton, South Dakota

- **Federally supported** 2-year, founded 1979
- **Rural** 2-acre campus
- **Coed,** 165 undergraduate students, 61% full-time, 64% women, 36% men

Undergraduates 101 full-time, 64 part-time. 2% are from out of state; 0.6% Black or African American, non-Hispanic/Latino; 91% American Indian or Alaska Native, non-Hispanic/Latino; 0.6% Two or more races, non-Hispanic/Latino; 0.6% transferred in.
Freshmen *Admission:* 67 applied, 63 admitted, 31 enrolled.
Faculty *Total:* 30, 33% full-time, 33% with terminal degrees. *Student/faculty ratio:* 10:1.
Majors Accounting; American Indian/Native American studies; business administration and management; electrical, electronic and communications engineering technology; hospitality administration; information science/studies; kindergarten/preschool education; liberal arts and sciences/liberal studies; natural sciences; nutrition sciences; registered nursing/registered nurse; substance abuse/addiction counseling.
Academics *Calendar:* semesters. *Degree:* certificates and associate. *Special study options:* academic remediation for entering students, adult/continuing education programs, cooperative education, double majors, internships, off-campus study, part-time degree program, summer session for credit.
Library Sisseton-Wahpeton Community College Library with 15,481 titles, 885 audiovisual materials, an OPAC, a Web page.
Student Life *Activities and Organizations:* AIHEC, AISES, Student Senate, Student Nurses Association, AIBL. *Campus security:* 24-hour emergency response devices. *Student services:* personal/psychological counseling.
Standardized Tests *Required:* ACT Compass (for admission).
Financial Aid Of all full-time matriculated undergraduates who enrolled in 2013, 165 applied for aid, 165 were judged to have need. In 2013, 165 non-need-based awards were made. *Average need-based gift aid:* $800. *Average non-need-based aid:* $800.
Applying *Required:* high school transcript. *Required for some:* Certificate of Indian Blood for enrolled tribal members. *Recommended:* minimum 2.0 GPA, interview. *Application deadlines:* rolling (freshmen), 7/8 (out-of-state freshmen), rolling (transfers).
Freshman Application Contact Sisseton-Wahpeton College, Old Agency Box 689, Sisseton, SD 57262. *Phone:* 605-698-3966 Ext. 1180.
Website: http://www.swc.tc/.

Southeast Technical Institute

Sioux Falls, South Dakota

- **State-supported** 2-year, founded 1968
- **Urban** 138-acre campus
- **Endowment** $768,716
- **Coed**

Undergraduates 1,683 full-time, 784 part-time. Students come from 11 states and territories; 8% are from out of state; 3% Black or African American, non-Hispanic/Latino; 3% Hispanic/Latino; 0.8% Asian, non-Hispanic/Latino; 0.1% Native Hawaiian or other Pacific Islander, non-Hispanic/Latino; 2% American Indian or Alaska Native, non-Hispanic/Latino; 2% Two or more races, non-Hispanic/Latino; 5% Race/ethnicity unknown; 14% transferred in; 2% live on campus. *Retention:* 56% of full-time freshmen returned.
Faculty *Student/faculty ratio:* 18:1.
Academics *Calendar:* semesters. *Degree:* certificates, diplomas, and associate. *Special study options:* academic remediation for entering students, advanced placement credit, distance learning, double majors, independent study, internships, part-time degree program, services for LD students, summer session for credit.
Student Life *Campus security:* 24-hour patrols, late-night transport/escort service, controlled dormitory access.
Standardized Tests *Recommended:* ACT (for admission).
Costs (2014–15) *Tuition:* state resident $3120 full-time, $104 per credit part-time; nonresident $3120 full-time, $104 per credit part-time. Full-time tuition and fees vary according to program. Part-time tuition and fees vary according to program. *Required fees:* $2790 full-time, $91 per credit part-time. *Room and board:* room only: $4700.
Financial Aid Of all full-time matriculated undergraduates who enrolled in 2013, 35 Federal Work-Study jobs (averaging $2550).
Applying *Options:* electronic application. *Required:* high school transcript, minimum 2.2 GPA. *Required for some:* interview, background check and drug testing for certain programs.
Freshman Application Contact Mr. Scott Dorman, Recruiter, Southeast Technical Institute, Sioux Falls, SD 57107. *Phone:* 605-367-4458. *Toll-free phone:* 800-247-0789. *Fax:* 605-367-8305. *E-mail:* scott.dorman@southeasttech.edu.
Website: http://www.southeasttech.edu/.

Western Dakota Technical Institute

Rapid City, South Dakota

- **State-supported** 2-year, founded 1968
- **Small-town** 5-acre campus
- **Coed,** 876 undergraduate students, 78% full-time, 49% women, 51% men

Undergraduates 681 full-time, 195 part-time. Students come from 10 states and territories; 3% are from out of state; 3% Black or African American, non-Hispanic/Latino; 5% Hispanic/Latino; 1% Asian, non-Hispanic/Latino; 0.9% Native Hawaiian or other Pacific Islander, non-Hispanic/Latino; 15% American Indian or Alaska Native, non-Hispanic/Latino; 0.1% Two or more races, non-Hispanic/Latino; 1% Race/ethnicity unknown; 31% transferred in. *Retention:* 53% of full-time freshmen returned.
Freshmen *Admission:* 1,503 applied, 1,003 admitted, 199 enrolled. *Average high school GPA:* 2.75. *Test scores:* ACT scores over 18: 38%; ACT scores over 24: 11%.
Faculty *Total:* 71, 46% full-time. *Student/faculty ratio:* 16:1.
Majors Accounting; business administration and management; computer systems networking and telecommunications; criminal justice/police science; criminal justice/safety; drafting and design technology; electrician; emergency medical technology (EMT paramedic); environmental control technologies related; fire science/firefighting; heating, air conditioning, ventilation and refrigeration maintenance technology; legal assistant/paralegal; library and archives assisting; licensed practical/vocational nurse training; machine tool technology; medical/clinical assistant; medical transcription; pharmacy technician; precision metal working related; surgical technology; vehicle maintenance and repair technologies related.
Academics *Calendar:* semesters. *Degree:* certificates, diplomas, and associate. *Special study options:* academic remediation for entering students, advanced placement credit, distance learning, independent study, internships, part-time degree program, services for LD students, summer session for credit.
Library Western Dakota Technical Institute Library with 2,470 titles, 330 audiovisual materials, an OPAC, a Web page.
Student Life *Housing:* college housing not available. *Campus security:* 24-hour video surveillance.
Standardized Tests *Recommended:* SAT or ACT (for admission).
Costs (2015–16) *One-time required fee:* $250. *Tuition:* state resident $3744 full-time, $104 per credit hour part-time; nonresident $3744 full-time, $104 per credit hour part-time. Full-time tuition and fees vary according to course

load and program. Part-time tuition and fees vary according to course load. *Required fees:* $3103 full-time, $85 per credit hour part-time. *Payment plans:* installment, deferred payment. *Waivers:* employees or children of employees.
Financial Aid Of all full-time matriculated undergraduates who enrolled in 2013, 85 Federal Work-Study jobs (averaging $1400).
Applying *Options:* electronic application. *Application fee:* $20. *Required:* high school transcript, Placement test. *Required for some:* essay or personal statement, 3 letters of recommendation, interview. *Recommended:* minimum 2.0 GPA. *Application deadlines:* 8/1 (freshmen), 8/1 (transfers). *Notification:* continuous until 8/15 (freshmen), continuous until 8/15 (transfers).
Freshman Application Contact Jill Elder, Admissions Coordinator, Western Dakota Technical Institute, 800 Mickelson Drive, Rapid City, SD 57703. *Phone:* 605-718-2411. *Toll-free phone:* 800-544-8765. *Fax:* 605-394-2204. *E-mail:* jill.elder@wdt.edu.
Website: http://www.wdt.edu/.

TENNESSEE

Chattanooga College–Medical, Dental and Technical Careers
Chattanooga, Tennessee

- **Proprietary** 2-year
- **Urban** campus
- **Coed**

Academics *Degree:* associate.
Applying *Application fee:* $25.
Freshman Application Contact Chattanooga College–Medical, Dental and Technical Careers, 248 Northgate Mall Drive, Suite 130, Chattanooga, TN 37415. *Phone:* 423-305-7781. *Toll-free phone:* 877-313-2373.
Website: http://www.chattanoogacollege.edu/.

Chattanooga State Community College
Chattanooga, Tennessee

Freshman Application Contact Brad McCormick, Director of Admissions and Records, Chattanooga State Community College, 4501 Amnicola Highway, Chattanooga, TN 37406. *Phone:* 423-697-4401 Ext. 3264. *Toll-free phone:* 866-547-3733. *Fax:* 423-697-4709. *E-mail:* brad.mccormick@chattanoogastate.edu.
Website: http://www.chattanoogastate.edu/.

Cleveland State Community College
Cleveland, Tennessee

- **State-supported** 2-year, founded 1967, part of Tennessee Board of Regents
- **Suburban** 83-acre campus
- **Endowment** $7.9 million
- **Coed,** 3,522 undergraduate students, 51% full-time, 61% women, 39% men

Undergraduates 1,785 full-time, 1,737 part-time. Students come from 8 states and territories; 3 other countries; 1% are from out of state; 6% Black or African American, non-Hispanic/Latino; 4% Hispanic/Latino; 1% Asian, non-Hispanic/Latino; 0.1% Native Hawaiian or other Pacific Islander, non-Hispanic/Latino; 0.3% American Indian or Alaska Native, non-Hispanic/Latino; 1% Two or more races, non-Hispanic/Latino; 4% Race/ethnicity unknown; 0.1% international; 15% transferred in.
Freshmen *Admission:* 1,599 applied, 798 admitted, 798 enrolled. *Average high school GPA:* 3.08. *Test scores:* ACT scores over 18: 69%; ACT scores over 24: 10%.
Faculty *Total:* 174, 40% full-time, 15% with terminal degrees. *Student/faculty ratio:* 23:1.
Majors Administrative assistant and secretarial science; business administration and management; child development; community organization and advocacy; criminal justice/police science; general studies; industrial technology; kindergarten/preschool education; liberal arts and sciences and humanities related; liberal arts and sciences/liberal studies; public administration and social service professions related; registered nursing/registered nurse; science technologies related.
Academics *Calendar:* semesters. *Degree:* certificates and associate. *Special study options:* academic remediation for entering students, adult/continuing education programs, advanced placement credit, cooperative education, distance learning, double majors, external degree program, honors programs,

independent study, internships, off-campus study, part-time degree program, services for LD students, summer session for credit.
Library Cleveland State Community College Library with 158,562 titles, 8,151 audiovisual materials, an OPAC, a Web page.
Student Life *Housing:* college housing not available. *Activities and Organizations:* student-run newspaper, choral group, Human Services/Social Work, Computer Aided Design, Phi Theta Kappa, Student Nursing Association, Early Childhood Education. *Campus security:* 24-hour emergency response devices and patrols. *Student services:* personal/psychological counseling.
Athletics Member NJCAA. *Intercollegiate sports:* baseball M(s), basketball M(s)/W(s), softball W(s). *Intramural sports:* archery M/W, basketball M/W, bowling M/W, cheerleading M(c)/W(c), softball W, table tennis M/W, volleyball M/W.
Costs (2014–15) *Tuition:* state resident $3985 full-time, $147 per credit hour part-time; nonresident $15,601 full-time, $608 per credit hour part-time. Full-time tuition and fees vary according to course load. *Required fees:* $283 full-time, $14 per credit hour part-time, $29 per term part-time. *Payment plan:* deferred payment. *Waivers:* senior citizens and employees or children of employees.
Financial Aid Of all full-time matriculated undergraduates who enrolled in 2013, 52 Federal Work-Study jobs (averaging $1025).
Applying *Options:* electronic application, early admission, deferred entrance. *Application fee:* $20. *Required:* high school transcript. *Application deadlines:* rolling (freshmen), rolling (transfers). *Notification:* continuous (freshmen), continuous (transfers).
Freshman Application Contact Mrs. Suzanne Bayne, Assistant Director of Admissions and Recruitment, Cleveland State Community College, PO Box 3570, Cleveland, TN 37320-3570. *Phone:* 423-472-7141 Ext. 743. *Toll-free phone:* 800-604-2722. *Fax:* 423-614-8711. *E-mail:* SBayne@clevelandstatecc.edu.
Website: http://www.clevelandstatecc.edu/.

Columbia State Community College
Columbia, Tennessee

Freshman Application Contact Mr. Joey Scruggs, Coordinator of Recruitment, Columbia State Community College, PO Box 1315, Columbia, TN 38402-1315. *Phone:* 931-540-2540. *E-mail:* scruggs@coscc.cc.tn.us.
Website: http://www.columbiastate.edu/.

Concorde Career College
Memphis, Tennessee

Freshman Application Contact Dee Vickers, Director, Concorde Career College, 5100 Poplar Avenue, Suite 132, Memphis, TN 38137. *Phone:* 901-761-9494. *Fax:* 901-761-3293. *E-mail:* dvickers@concorde.edu.
Website: http://www.concorde.edu/.

Daymar Institute
Nashville, Tennessee

Director of Admissions Admissions Office, Daymar Institute, 340 Plus Park Boulevard, Nashville, TN 37217. *Phone:* 615-361-7555. *Fax:* 615-367-2736.
Website: http://www.daymarinstitute.edu/.

Dyersburg State Community College
Dyersburg, Tennessee

- **State-supported** 2-year, founded 1969, part of Tennessee Board of Regents
- **Small-town** 115-acre campus with easy access to Memphis
- **Endowment** $4.0 million
- **Coed,** 2,847 undergraduate students, 40% full-time, 65% women, 35% men

Undergraduates 1,141 full-time, 1,706 part-time. Students come from 5 states and territories; 2 other countries; 21% Black or African American, non-Hispanic/Latino; 2% Hispanic/Latino; 0.4% Asian, non-Hispanic/Latino; 0.3% American Indian or Alaska Native, non-Hispanic/Latino; 2% Two or more races, non-Hispanic/Latino; 0.8% Race/ethnicity unknown; 6% transferred in. *Retention:* 51% of full-time freshmen returned.
Freshmen *Admission:* 552 enrolled. *Average high school GPA:* 2.9. *Test scores:* ACT scores over 18: 64%; ACT scores over 24: 13%; ACT scores over 30: 1%.
Faculty *Total:* 182, 29% full-time, 12% with terminal degrees. *Student/faculty ratio:* 8:1.
Majors Agriculture; automation engineer technology; business administration and management; child development; computer and information systems

security; criminal justice/police science; criminal justice/safety; education; emergency medical technology (EMT paramedic); general studies; health information/medical records technology; health services/allied health/health sciences; industrial electronics technology; industrial mechanics and maintenance technology; information science/studies; liberal arts and sciences/liberal studies; medical informatics; music performance; registered nursing/registered nurse; web page, digital/multimedia and information resources design.

Academics *Calendar:* semesters. *Degree:* certificates and associate. *Special study options:* academic remediation for entering students, accelerated degree program, adult/continuing education programs, advanced placement credit, cooperative education, distance learning, double majors, honors programs, independent study, internships, off-campus study, part-time degree program, services for LD students, study abroad, summer session for credit.

Library Learning Resource Center with 20,384 titles, 362 audiovisual materials, an OPAC, a Web page.

Student Life *Activities and Organizations:* drama/theater group, choral group, Psychology Club, Phi Theta Kappa, student government, Student Nurses Association, Criminal Justice Association. *Campus security:* 24-hour emergency response devices and patrols. *Student services:* personal/psychological counseling.

Athletics Member NJCAA. *Intercollegiate sports:* baseball M(s), basketball M(s)/W(s), cheerleading M(s)/W(s), softball W(s). *Intramural sports:* basketball M/W, soccer M/W, table tennis M/W, ultimate Frisbee M/W, volleyball M/W.

Standardized Tests *Required:* SAT or ACT (for admission), an official copy of ACT scores is required for all first-time degree-seeking students under the age of 21. ACT scores may be used only if the ACT scores are no older than three years. Official SAT scores may be accepted in lieu of ACT scores. The ACT Compass is required by student who are over 21 (for admission).

Costs (2014–15) *Tuition:* state resident $3528 full-time, $147 per credit hour part-time; nonresident $14,592 full-time, $608 per credit hour part-time. Full-time tuition and fees vary according to course load. Part-time tuition and fees vary according to course load. *Required fees:* $299 full-time, $150 per term part-time. *Payment plan:* deferred payment. *Waivers:* senior citizens and employees or children of employees.

Financial Aid Of all full-time matriculated undergraduates who enrolled in 2013, 26 Federal Work-Study jobs (averaging $2900). 112 state and other part-time jobs (averaging $1258).

Applying *Required:* high school transcript.

Freshman Application Contact Mrs. Margaret Jones, Director of Admissions, Dyersburg State Community College, Dyersburg, TN 38024. *Phone:* 731-286-3327. *Fax:* 731-286-3325. *E-mail:* mjones@dscc.edu. *Website:* http://www.dscc.edu/.

Fortis Institute
Cookeville, Tennessee

Director of Admissions Ms. Sharon Mellott, Director of Admissions, Fortis Institute, 1025 Highway 111, Cookeville, TN 38501. *Phone:* 931-526-3660. *Toll-free phone:* 855-4-FORTIS.
Website: http://www.fortis.edu/.

Fortis Institute
Nashville, Tennessee

Admissions Office Contact Fortis Institute, 3354 Perimeter Hill Drive, Suite 105, Nashville, TN 37211.
Website: http://www.fortis.edu/.

Fountainhead College of Technology
Knoxville, Tennessee

- **Proprietary** primarily 2-year, founded 1947
- **Suburban** 2-acre campus
- **Coed,** 180 undergraduate students, 100% full-time, 17% women, 83% men

Undergraduates 180 full-time. Students come from 1 other state. *Retention:* 82% of full-time freshmen returned.

Faculty *Total:* 20, 65% full-time, 15% with terminal degrees. *Student/faculty ratio:* 8:1.

Majors Communications technology; computer and information systems security; computer engineering technology; computer programming; electrical, electronic and communications engineering technology; health

information/medical records technology; information technology; medical insurance coding.

Academics *Calendar:* semesters. *Degrees:* associate and bachelor's. *Special study options:* accelerated degree program, distance learning, double majors, part-time degree program, summer session for credit.

Library Library and Resource Center with an OPAC, a Web page.

Student Life *Housing:* college housing not available. *Campus security:* 24-hour emergency response devices.

Standardized Tests *Required for some:* SAT or ACT (for admission), Institutional Entrance Exam.

Applying *Required:* high school transcript, interview. *Application deadlines:* rolling (freshmen), rolling (transfers). *Notification:* continuous (freshmen), continuous (transfers).

Freshman Application Contact Mr. Joel B Southern, Director of Admissions, Fountainhead College of Technology, 10208 Technology Drive, Knoxville, TN 37932. *Phone:* 865-688-9422. *Toll-free phone:* 888-218-7335. *Fax:* 865-688-2419. *E-mail:* joel.southern@fountainheadcollege.edu.
Website: http://www.fountainheadcollege.edu/.

Hiwassee College
Madisonville, Tennessee

Director of Admissions Jamie Williamson, Director of Admission, Hiwassee College, 225 Hiwassee College Drive, Madisonville, TN 37354. *Phone:* 423-420-1891. *Toll-free phone:* 800-356-2187.
Website: http://www.hiwassee.edu/.

ITT Technical Institute
Chattanooga, Tennessee

- **Proprietary** primarily 2-year, part of ITT Educational Services, Inc.
- **Coed**

Academics *Degrees:* associate and bachelor's.

Freshman Application Contact Director of Recruitment, ITT Technical Institute, 5600 Brainerd Road, Suite G-1, Chattanooga, TN 37411. *Phone:* 423-510-6800. *Toll-free phone:* 877-474-8312.
Website: http://www.itt-tech.edu/.

ITT Technical Institute
Cordova, Tennessee

- **Proprietary** primarily 2-year, founded 1994, part of ITT Educational Services, Inc.
- **Suburban** campus
- **Coed**

Academics *Calendar:* quarters. *Degrees:* associate and bachelor's.

Freshman Application Contact Director of Recruitment, ITT Technical Institute, 7260 Goodlett Farms Parkway, Cordova, TN 38016. *Phone:* 901-381-0200. *Toll-free phone:* 866-444-5141.
Website: http://www.itt-tech.edu/.

ITT Technical Institute
Johnson City, Tennessee

- **Proprietary** primarily 2-year
- **Coed**

Academics *Degrees:* associate and bachelor's.

Freshman Application Contact Director of Recruitment, ITT Technical Institute, 4721 Lake Park Drive, Suite 100, Johnson City, TN 37615. *Phone:* 423-952-4400. *Toll-free phone:* 877-301-9691.
Website: http://www.itt-tech.edu/.

ITT Technical Institute
Knoxville, Tennessee

- **Proprietary** primarily 2-year, founded 1988, part of ITT Educational Services, Inc.
- **Suburban** campus
- **Coed**

Academics *Calendar:* quarters. *Degrees:* associate and bachelor's.

Freshman Application Contact Director of Recruitment, ITT Technical Institute, 9123 Executive Park Drive, Knoxville, TN 37923. *Phone:* 865-342-2300. *Toll-free phone:* 800-671-2801.
Website: http://www.itt-tech.edu/.

ITT Technical Institute

Nashville, Tennessee

- **Proprietary** primarily 2-year, founded 1984, part of ITT Educational Services, Inc.
- **Urban** campus
- **Coed**

Academics *Calendar:* quarters. *Degrees:* associate and bachelor's.
Freshman Application Contact Director of Recruitment, ITT Technical Institute, 2845 Elm Hill Pike, Nashville, TN 37214. *Phone:* 615-889-8700. *Toll-free phone:* 800-331-8386.
Website: http://www.itt-tech.edu/.

Jackson State Community College

Jackson, Tennessee

- **State-supported** 2-year, founded 1967, part of Tennessee Board of Regents
- **Suburban** 100-acre campus with easy access to Memphis
- **Coed,** 4,926 undergraduate students

Freshmen *Admission:* 1,219 applied, 927 admitted.
Faculty *Total:* 285, 31% full-time. *Student/faculty ratio:* 19:1.
Majors Agriculture; business administration and management; clinical/medical laboratory technology; computer science; education; general studies; industrial technology; liberal arts and sciences/liberal studies; management information systems; medical radiologic technology; physical therapy technology; registered nursing/registered nurse; science technologies related.
Academics *Calendar:* semesters. *Degree:* certificates, diplomas, and associate. *Special study options:* academic remediation for entering students, accelerated degree program, adult/continuing education programs, advanced placement credit, cooperative education, distance learning, external degree program, honors programs, independent study, internships, off-campus study, part-time degree program, services for LD students, study abroad, summer session for credit. *ROTC:* Army (c).
Library Jackson State Community College Library with 58,104 titles, 1,686 audiovisual materials, an OPAC, a Web page.
Student Life *Housing:* college housing not available. *Activities and Organizations:* choral group, Spanish Club, Gay/Straight Alliance, Art Club, H2O Wellness, Biology Club. *Campus security:* 24-hour patrols, late-night transport/escort service, field camera surveillance. *Student services:* personal/psychological counseling.
Athletics Member NJCAA. *Intercollegiate sports:* baseball M(s), basketball M(s)/W(s), softball W(s).
Standardized Tests *Required:* SAT or ACT (for admission), ACT Compass (for admission). *Recommended:* ACT (for admission).
Costs (2014–15) *Tuition:* state resident $3528 full-time, $147 per credit hour part-time; nonresident $9220 full-time, $461 per credit hour part-time. Full-time tuition and fees vary according to course load and program. Part-time tuition and fees vary according to course load and program. *Required fees:* $276 full-time, $9 per credit hour part-time, $30 per term part-time. *Payment plan:* installment. *Waivers:* senior citizens and employees or children of employees.
Financial Aid Of all full-time matriculated undergraduates who enrolled in 2013, 2,070 applied for aid, 1,907 were judged to have need, 46 had their need fully met. 38 Federal Work-Study jobs (averaging $1763). 14 state and other part-time jobs (averaging $1595). In 2013, 40 non-need-based awards were made. *Average percent of need met:* 45%. *Average financial aid package:* $4961. *Average need-based loan:* $643. *Average need-based gift aid:* $4717. *Average non-need-based aid:* $3204.
Applying *Options:* electronic application. *Required for some:* high school transcript. *Application deadlines:* 8/23 (freshmen), 8/23 (out-of-state freshmen), rolling (transfers). *Notification:* continuous (freshmen), continuous (out-of-state freshmen), continuous (transfers).
Freshman Application Contact Ms. Andrea Winchester, Director of High School Initiatives, Jackson State Community College, 2046 North Parkway, Jackson, TN 38301-3797. *Phone:* 731-424-3520 Ext. 50484. *Toll-free phone:* 800-355-5722. *Fax:* 731-425-9559. *E-mail:* awinchester@jscc.edu.
Website: http://www.jscc.edu/.

John A. Gupton College

Nashville, Tennessee

- **Independent** 2-year, founded 1946
- **Urban** 1-acre campus with easy access to Nashville
- **Endowment** $60,000
- **Coed,** 129 undergraduate students, 52% full-time, 57% women, 43% men

Undergraduates 67 full-time, 62 part-time. Students come from 11 states and territories; 10% are from out of state; 24% Black or African American, non-Hispanic/Latino; 0.8% Hispanic/Latino; 0.8% Asian, non-Hispanic/Latino; 0.8% Two or more races, non-Hispanic/Latino; 26% transferred in; 11% live on campus.
Freshmen *Admission:* 84 applied, 46 admitted, 17 enrolled.
Faculty *Total:* 13, 15% full-time. *Student/faculty ratio:* 8:1.
Majors Funeral service and mortuary science.
Academics *Calendar:* semesters. *Degree:* certificates, diplomas, and associate. *Special study options:* part-time degree program.
Library Memorial Library with 4,000 titles, a Web page.
Student Life *Housing Options:* coed. Campus housing is university owned. *Campus security:* controlled dormitory access, day patrols.
Standardized Tests *Required:* ACT (for admission).
Costs (2014–15) *Tuition:* $9600 full-time, $300 per semester hour part-time. Full-time tuition and fees vary according to course load. Part-time tuition and fees vary according to course load. *Required fees:* $70 full-time. *Room only:* $3600. *Payment plan:* installment.
Financial Aid *Financial aid deadline:* 6/1.
Applying *Options:* deferred entrance. *Application fee:* $50. *Required:* essay or personal statement, high school transcript, 2 letters of recommendation. *Application deadlines:* rolling (freshmen), rolling (transfers).
Freshman Application Contact John A. Gupton College, 1616 Church Street, Nashville, TN 37203-2920. *Phone:* 615-327-3927.
Website: http://www.guptoncollege.edu/.

Kaplan College, Nashville Campus

Nashville, Tennessee

Freshman Application Contact Kaplan College, Nashville Campus, 750 Envious Lane, Nashville, TN 37217. *Phone:* 615-269-9900. *Toll-free phone:* 800-935-1857.
Website: http://www.kaplancollege.com/.

L'Ecole Culinaire–Memphis

Cordova, Tennessee

Admissions Office Contact L'Ecole Culinaire–Memphis, 1245 N. Germantown Parkway, Cordova, TN 38016.
Website: http://www.lecole.edu/memphis/.

Lincoln College of Technology

Nashville, Tennessee

- **Proprietary** 2-year, founded 1919
- **Urban** 16-acre campus
- **Coed, primarily men**

Undergraduates 1,375 full-time. Students come from 50 states and territories; 83% are from out of state; 21% live on campus.
Faculty *Student/faculty ratio:* 30:1.
Academics *Calendar:* continuous. *Degree:* diplomas and associate. *Special study options:* advanced placement credit, cooperative education, honors programs.
Student Life *Campus security:* 24-hour emergency response devices and patrols.
Standardized Tests *Recommended:* SAT or ACT (for admission).
Applying *Options:* electronic application, deferred entrance. *Application fee:* $100. *Required:* high school transcript. *Required for some:* interview.
Freshman Application Contact Ms. Tanya Smith, Director of Admissions, Lincoln College of Technology, 1524 Gallatin Road, Nashville, TN 37206. *Phone:* 615-226-3990 Ext. 71703. *Toll-free phone:* 800-228-6232. *Fax:* 615-262-8466. *E-mail:* tlegg-smith@lincolntech.com.
Website: http://www.lincolnedu.com/campus/nashville-tn.

Miller-Motte Technical College

Chattanooga, Tennessee

Admissions Office Contact Miller-Motte Technical College, 6020 Shallowford Road, Suite 100, Chattanooga, TN 37421.
Website: http://www.miller-motte.edu/.

Miller-Motte Technical College
Clarksville, Tennessee

Director of Admissions Joseph Kuchno, Director of Admissions, Miller-Motte Technical College, 1820 Business Park Drive, Clarksville, TN 37040. *Phone:* 800-558-0071. *E-mail:* lisateague@hotmail.com. *Website:* http://www.miller-motte.edu/.

Miller-Motte Technical College
Madison, Tennessee

Admissions Office Contact Miller-Motte Technical College, 1515 Gallatin Pike North, Madison, TN 37115. *Website:* http://www.miller-motte.edu/.

Motlow State Community College
Tullahoma, Tennessee

- **State-supported** 2-year, founded 1969, part of Tennessee Board of Regents
- **Rural** 187-acre campus with easy access to Nashville
- **Endowment** $6.1 million
- **Coed,** 4,900 undergraduate students, 40% full-time, 49% women, 31% men

Undergraduates 1,951 full-time, 1,950 part-time. Students come from 13 states and territories; 1% are from out of state; 9% Black or African American, non-Hispanic/Latino; 4% Hispanic/Latino; 2% Asian, non-Hispanic/Latino; 0.1% Native Hawaiian or other Pacific Islander, non-Hispanic/Latino; 0.2% American Indian or Alaska Native, non-Hispanic/Latino; 1% Two or more races, non-Hispanic/Latino; 3% Race/ethnicity unknown; 0.4% international; 9% transferred in.
Faculty *Total:* 261, 36% full-time, 12% with terminal degrees.
Majors Business administration and management; education; electromechanical technology; general studies; liberal arts and sciences/liberal studies; registered nursing/registered nurse; special education–early childhood; web page, digital/multimedia and information resources design.
Academics *Calendar:* semesters. *Degree:* certificates and associate. *Special study options:* academic remediation for entering students, accelerated degree program, adult/continuing education programs, advanced placement credit, cooperative education, distance learning, double majors, honors programs, independent study, part-time degree program, services for LD students, study abroad, summer session for credit.
Library Clayton-Glass Library with 273,805 titles, 4,268 audiovisual materials, an OPAC, a Web page.
Student Life *Housing:* college housing not available. *Activities and Organizations:* drama/theater group, choral group, PTK Club, Communication Club, Student Government Association, Art Club, Baptist Student Union. *Campus security:* 24-hour patrols, late-night transport/escort service. *Student services:* personal/psychological counseling.
Athletics Member NJCAA. *Intercollegiate sports:* baseball M(s), basketball M(s)/W(s), softball W(s). *Intramural sports:* badminton M/W, basketball M/W, bowling M/W, golf M/W, tennis M/W, volleyball M/W.
Costs (2014–15) *Tuition:* state resident $3804 full-time; nonresident $14,868 full-time. *Payment plans:* installment, deferred payment. *Waivers:* senior citizens and employees or children of employees.
Financial Aid Of all full-time matriculated undergraduates who enrolled in 2013, 1,773 applied for aid, 1,422 were judged to have need, 72 had their need fully met. 2 Federal Work-Study jobs (averaging $1750). In 2013, 234 non-need-based awards were made. *Average percent of need met:* 55%. *Average financial aid package:* $5212. *Average need-based loan:* $2344. *Average need-based gift aid:* $4313. *Average non-need-based aid:* $2970.
Applying *Options:* electronic application, early admission, deferred entrance. *Application fee:* $10. *Required:* high school transcript. *Application deadlines:* 8/13 (freshmen), 8/13 (transfers). *Notification:* continuous (freshmen), continuous (transfers).
Freshman Application Contact Ms. Sheri Mason, Assistant Director of Student Services, Motlow State Community College, Lynchburg, TN 37352-8500. *Phone:* 931-393-1764. *Toll-free phone:* 800-654-4877. *Fax:* 931-393-1681. *E-mail:* smason@mscc.edu. *Website:* http://www.mscc.edu/.

Nashville State Community College
Nashville, Tennessee

Freshman Application Contact Mr. Beth Mahan, Coordinator of Recruitment, Nashville State Community College, 120 White Bridge Road, Nashville, TN 37209-4515. *Phone:* 615-353-3214. *Toll-free phone:* 800-272-7363. *E-mail:* beth.mahan@nscc.edu. *Website:* http://www.nscc.edu/.

National College
Bristol, Tennessee

Freshman Application Contact National College, 1328 Highway 11 West, Bristol, TN 37620. *Phone:* 423-878-4440. *Toll-free phone:* 888-9-JOBREADY. *Website:* http://www.national-college.edu/.

National College
Knoxville, Tennessee

Director of Admissions Frank Alvey, Campus Director, National College, 8415 Kingston Pike, Knoxville, TN 37919. *Phone:* 865-539-2011. *Toll-free phone:* 888-9-JOBREADY. *Fax:* 865-539-2049. *Website:* http://www.national-college.edu/.

National College
Nashville, Tennessee

Director of Admissions Jerry Lafferty, Campus Director, National College, 1638 Bell Road, Nashville, TN 37211. *Phone:* 615-333-3344. *Toll-free phone:* 888-9-JOBREADY. *Website:* http://www.national-college.edu/.

North Central Institute
Clarksville, Tennessee

Freshman Application Contact Dale Wood, Director of Admissions, North Central Institute, 168 Jack Miller Boulevard, Clarksville, TN 37042. *Phone:* 931-431-9700. *Toll-free phone:* 800-603-4116. *Fax:* 931-431-9771. *E-mail:* admissions@nci.edu. *Website:* http://www.nci.edu/.

Northeast State Community College
Blountville, Tennessee

Freshman Application Contact Dr. Jon P. Harr, Vice President for Student Affairs, Northeast State Community College, PO Box 246, Blountville, TN 37617. *Phone:* 423-323-0231. *Toll-free phone:* 800-836-7822. *Fax:* 423-323-0240. *E-mail:* jpharr@northeaststate.edu. *Website:* http://www.northeaststate.edu/.

Pellissippi State Community College
Knoxville, Tennessee

Freshman Application Contact Director of Admissions and Records, Pellissippi State Community College, PO Box 22990, Knoxville, TN 37933-0990. *Phone:* 865-694-6400. *Fax:* 865-539-7217. *Website:* http://www.pstcc.edu/.

Remington College–Memphis Campus
Memphis, Tennessee

Director of Admissions Randal Hayes, Director of Recruitment, Remington College–Memphis Campus, 2710 Nonconnah Boulevard, Memphis, TN 38132. *Phone:* 901-345-1000. *Fax:* 901-396-8310. *E-mail:* randal.hayes@remingtoncollege.edu. *Website:* http://www.remingtoncollege.edu/.

Remington College–Nashville Campus
Nashville, Tennessee

Director of Admissions Mr. Frank Vivelo, Campus President, Remington College–Nashville Campus, 441 Donelson Pike, Suite 150, Nashville, TN 37214. *Phone:* 615-889-5520. *Fax:* 615-889-5528. *E-mail:* frank.vivelo@remingtoncollege.edu. *Website:* http://www.remingtoncollege.edu/.

Roane State Community College
Harriman, Tennessee

- **State-supported** 2-year, founded 1971, part of Tennessee Board of Regents
- **Small-town** 104-acre campus with easy access to Knoxville
- **Endowment** $8.3 million
- **Coed,** 5,832 undergraduate students, 40% full-time, 66% women, 34% men

Undergraduates 2,358 full-time, 3,474 part-time. Students come from 11 states and territories; 5 other countries; 1% are from out of state; 3% Black or African American, non-Hispanic/Latino; 3% Hispanic/Latino; 0.7% Asian, non-Hispanic/Latino; 0.1% Native Hawaiian or other Pacific Islander, non-Hispanic/Latino; 0.3% American Indian or Alaska Native, non-Hispanic/Latino; 3% Two or more races, non-Hispanic/Latino; 2% Race/ethnicity unknown; 0.2% international; 4% transferred in. *Retention:* 62% of full-time freshmen returned.

Freshmen *Admission:* 1,817 applied, 1,754 admitted, 1,213 enrolled. *Average high school GPA:* 3.17. *Test scores:* ACT scores over 18: 59%; ACT scores over 24: 9%; ACT scores over 30: 2%.

Faculty *Total:* 385, 31% full-time. *Student/faculty ratio:* 17:1.

Majors Accounting; administrative assistant and secretarial science; art; art teacher education; biology/biological sciences; business administration and management; business teacher education; chemistry; clinical/medical laboratory technology; computer engineering technology; computer science; corrections; criminal justice/law enforcement administration; criminal justice/police science; dental hygiene; early childhood education; education; elementary education; emergency medical technology (EMT paramedic); engineering; environmental health; general studies; health information/medical records administration; industrial radiologic technology; information technology; kindergarten/preschool education; laser and optical technology; legal administrative assistant/secretary; liberal arts and sciences/liberal studies; mathematics; medical administrative assistant and medical secretary; music teacher education; occupational therapy; pharmacy technician; physical education teaching and coaching; physical sciences; physical therapy; pre-engineering; registered nursing/registered nurse; respiratory care therapy; social sciences; technology/industrial arts teacher education.

Academics *Calendar:* semesters. *Degree:* certificates and associate. *Special study options:* academic remediation for entering students, accelerated degree program, advanced placement credit, cooperative education, distance learning, double majors, honors programs, independent study, internships, off-campus study, services for LD students, study abroad, summer session for credit. *ROTC:* Army (c), Air Force (c).

Library Roane State Community College Library plus 3 others with 316,114 titles, 3,030 audiovisual materials, an OPAC, a Web page.

Student Life *Housing:* college housing not available. *Activities and Organizations:* drama/theater group, choral group, Baptist Student Union, American Chemical Society, Physical Therapy Student Association, Student Artists At Roane State (S.T.A.R.S.), Phi Theta Kappa. *Campus security:* 24-hour patrols. *Student services:* personal/psychological counseling.

Athletics Member NJCAA. *Intercollegiate sports:* baseball M(s), basketball M(s)/W(s), softball W(s). *Intramural sports:* basketball M/W, football M, golf M, soccer M, softball M/W, volleyball M/W, weight lifting M.

Costs (2015–16) *Tuition:* state resident $3528 full-time; nonresident $14,592 full-time. *Required fees:* $303 full-time.

Financial Aid Of all full-time matriculated undergraduates who enrolled in 2013, 2,890 applied for aid, 2,465 were judged to have need, 229 had their need fully met. 56 Federal Work-Study jobs (averaging $1791). In 2013, 55 non-need-based awards were made. *Average percent of need met:* 54%. *Average financial aid package:* $7044. *Average need-based loan:* $3195. *Average need-based gift aid:* $6144. *Average non-need-based aid:* $7309.

Applying *Options:* electronic application, early admission, deferred entrance. *Application fee:* $20. *Required:* high school transcript. *Application deadlines:* rolling (freshmen), rolling (transfers). *Notification:* continuous (freshmen), continuous (transfers).

Freshman Application Contact Admissions Office, Roane State Community College, 276 Patton Lane, Harriman, TN 37748. *Phone:* 865-882-4523. *Toll-free phone:* 866-462-7722 Ext. 4554. *E-mail:* admissionsrecords@roanestate.edu.
Website: http://www.roanestate.edu/.

SAE Institute of Technology
Nashville, Tennessee

Admissions Office Contact SAE Institute of Technology, 7 Music Circle N, Nashville, TN 37203.
Website: http://www.sae-nashville.com/.

Southwest Tennessee Community College
Memphis, Tennessee

Freshman Application Contact Ms. Cindy Meziere, Assistant Director of Recruiting, Southwest Tennessee Community College, PO Box 780, Memphis, TN 38103-0780. *Phone:* 901-333-4195. *Toll-free phone:* 877-717-STCC. *Fax:* 901-333-4473. *E-mail:* cmeziere@southwest.tn.edu.
Website: http://www.southwest.tn.edu/.

Vatterott College
Memphis, Tennessee

Admissions Office Contact Vatterott College, 2655 Dividend Drive, Memphis, TN 38132. *Toll-free phone:* 888-553-6627.
Website: http://www.vatterott.edu/.

Vatterott College
Memphis, Tennessee

Admissions Office Contact Vatterott College, 6991 Appling Farms Parkway, Memphis, TN 38133.
Website: http://www.vatterott.edu/.

Virginia College in Chattanooga
Chattanooga, Tennessee

Admissions Office Contact Virginia College in Chattanooga, 721 Eastgate Loop Road, Chattanooga, TN 37411.
Website: http://www.vc.edu/.

Virginia College in Knoxville
Knoxville, Tennessee

Admissions Office Contact Virginia College in Knoxville, 5003 North Broadway Street, Knoxville, TN 37918.
Website: http://www.vc.edu/.

Volunteer State Community College
Gallatin, Tennessee

- **State-supported** 2-year, founded 1970, part of Tennessee Board of Regents
- **Suburban** 110-acre campus with easy access to Nashville
- **Endowment** $4.1 million
- **Coed,** 7,664 undergraduate students, 44% full-time, 60% women, 40% men

Undergraduates 3,377 full-time, 4,287 part-time. Students come from 16 states and territories; 11 other countries; 1% are from out of state; 9% Black or African American, non-Hispanic/Latino; 4% Hispanic/Latino; 1% Asian, non-Hispanic/Latino; 0.1% Native Hawaiian or other Pacific Islander, non-Hispanic/Latino; 0.3% American Indian or Alaska Native, non-Hispanic/Latino; 2% Two or more races, non-Hispanic/Latino; 2% Race/ethnicity unknown; 0.7% international; 6% transferred in.

Freshmen *Admission:* 2,096 applied, 2,096 admitted, 1,507 enrolled. *Average high school GPA:* 2.97. *Test scores:* ACT scores over 18: 71%; ACT scores over 24: 13%.

Faculty *Total:* 376, 42% full-time, 17% with terminal degrees. *Student/faculty ratio:* 21:1.

Majors Business administration and management; child development; clinical/medical laboratory technology; computer and information sciences; criminal justice/police science; digital arts; education; fire science/firefighting; general studies; health information/medical records technology; health professions related; legal assistant/paralegal; liberal arts and sciences/liberal studies; medical informatics; medical radiologic technology; ophthalmic technology; physical therapy technology; respiratory care therapy; science technologies related; veterinary/animal health technology; web page, digital/multimedia and information resources design.

Academics *Calendar:* semesters. *Degree:* certificates and associate. *Special study options:* academic remediation for entering students, accelerated degree program, adult/continuing education programs, advanced placement credit, cooperative education, distance learning, double majors, English as a second language, honors programs, independent study, internships, part-time degree program, services for LD students, study abroad, summer session for credit.

Library Thigpen Library with 193,000 titles, 1,554 audiovisual materials, an OPAC, a Web page.

Student Life *Housing:* college housing not available. *Activities and Organizations:* drama/theater group, student-run newspaper, radio station, choral group, Gamma Beta Phi, Returning Woman's Organization, Phi Theta Kappa, Student Government Association, The Settler. *Campus security:* 24-hour emergency response devices and patrols, late-night transport/escort service. *Student services:* personal/psychological counseling.

Athletics Member NJCAA. *Intercollegiate sports:* baseball M(s), basketball M(s)/W(s), softball W(s).

Standardized Tests *Required for some:* SAT or ACT (for admission).

Costs (2015–16) *Tuition:* state resident $3528 full-time, $147 per credit hour part-time; nonresident $14,592 full-time, $608 per credit hour part-time. Full-time tuition and fees vary according to course load. Part-time tuition and fees vary according to course load. *Required fees:* $273 full-time, $33 per credit hour part-time. *Payment plan:* deferred payment. *Waivers:* senior citizens and employees or children of employees.

Financial Aid Of all full-time matriculated undergraduates who enrolled in 2014, 2,959 applied for aid, 2,275 were judged to have need, 112 had their need fully met. 40 Federal Work-Study jobs (averaging $1370). In 2014, 61 non-need-based awards were made. *Average percent of need met:* 45%. *Average financial aid package:* $5567. *Average need-based loan:* $2872. *Average need-based gift aid:* $4384. *Average non-need-based aid:* $2375.

Applying *Options:* electronic application, early admission, deferred entrance. *Application fee:* $20. *Required:* high school transcript. *Required for some:* minimum 2.0 GPA, interview. *Application deadlines:* 8/25 (freshmen), 8/25 (transfers). *Notification:* continuous (freshmen), continuous (transfers).

Freshman Application Contact Mr. Tim Amyx, Director of Admissions, Volunteer State Community College, 1480 Nashville Pike, Gallatin, TN 37066-3188. *Phone:* 615-452-8600 Ext. 3614. *Toll-free phone:* 888-335-8722. *Fax:* 615-230-4875. *E-mail:* admissions@volstate.edu. *Website:* http://www.volstate.edu/.

Walters State Community College
Morristown, Tennessee

- **State-supported** 2-year, founded 1970, part of Tennessee Board of Regents
- **Small-town** 100-acre campus
- **Coed,** 6,005 undergraduate students, 52% full-time, 60% women, 40% men

Undergraduates 3,106 full-time, 2,899 part-time. 3% Black or African American, non-Hispanic/Latino; 3% Hispanic/Latino; 0.6% Asian, non-Hispanic/Latino; 0.2% American Indian or Alaska Native, non-Hispanic/Latino; 2% Two or more races, non-Hispanic/Latino; 0.1% Race/ethnicity unknown; 1% international; 7% transferred in.

Freshmen *Admission:* 2,716 applied, 1,409 admitted, 1,409 enrolled. *Average high school GPA:* 3.13. *Test scores:* ACT scores over 18: 70%; ACT scores over 24: 14%.

Faculty *Total:* 372, 42% full-time, 23% with terminal degrees. *Student/faculty ratio:* 18:1.

Majors Business administration and management; child development; computer and information sciences; criminal justice/police science; criminal justice/safety; data processing and data processing technology; education; energy management and systems technology; general studies; health information/medical records technology; industrial technology; liberal arts and sciences/liberal studies; music performance; occupational therapist assistant; ornamental horticulture; physical therapy technology; registered nursing/registered nurse; respiratory care therapy; surgical technology; web page, digital/multimedia and information resources design.

Academics *Calendar:* semesters. *Degree:* certificates and associate. *Special study options:* academic remediation for entering students, accelerated degree program, advanced placement credit, cooperative education, distance learning, English as a second language, freshman honors college, honors programs, independent study, internships, off-campus study, part-time degree program, services for LD students, student-designed majors, study abroad, summer session for credit. *ROTC:* Army (c).

Library Walters State Library with an OPAC, a Web page.

Student Life *Housing:* college housing not available. *Activities and Organizations:* drama/theater group, choral group, Baptist Collegiate Ministry, Phi Theta Kappa, Debate Club, Student Government Association, Service Learners Club. *Campus security:* 24-hour emergency response devices and patrols, late-night transport/escort service, Security Cameras. *Student services:* health clinic, personal/psychological counseling.

Athletics Member NJCAA. *Intercollegiate sports:* baseball M(s), basketball M(s)/W(s), golf M(s), softball W(s), volleyball W(s). *Intramural sports:* baseball M, basketball M/W.

Standardized Tests *Required:* SAT or ACT (for admission).

Costs (2015–16) *Tuition:* state resident $3528 full-time, $147 per credit hour part-time; nonresident $14,592 full-time, $608 per credit hour part-time. Full-time tuition and fees vary according to course load and program. Part-time tuition and fees vary according to course load and program. *Required fees:*

$288 full-time. *Payment plan:* deferred payment. *Waivers:* senior citizens and employees or children of employees.

Financial Aid Of all full-time matriculated undergraduates who enrolled in 2013, 3,121 applied for aid, 2,730 were judged to have need, 184 had their need fully met. In 2013, 379 non-need-based awards were made. *Average percent of need met:* 53%. *Average financial aid package:* $5272. *Average need-based gift aid:* $4565. *Average non-need-based aid:* $3389.

Applying *Options:* electronic application, early admission. *Required:* high school transcript. *Application deadlines:* rolling (freshmen), rolling (transfers). *Notification:* continuous (freshmen), continuous (transfers).

Freshman Application Contact Mr. Michael Campbell, Assistant Vice President for Student Affairs, Walters State Community College, 500 South Davy Crockett Parkway, Morristown, TN 37813-6899. *Phone:* 423-585-2682. *Toll-free phone:* 800-225-4770. *Fax:* 423-585-6876. *E-mail:* mike.campbell@ws.edu. *Website:* http://www.ws.edu/.

West Tennessee Business College
Jackson, Tennessee

Admissions Office Contact West Tennessee Business College, 1186 Highway 45 Bypass, Jackson, TN 38343. *Website:* http://www.wtbc.edu/.

TEXAS

Alvin Community College
Alvin, Texas

- **State and locally supported** 2-year, founded 1949
- **Suburban** 114-acre campus with easy access to Houston
- **Coed,** 4,837 undergraduate students, 28% full-time, 56% women, 44% men

Undergraduates 1,369 full-time, 3,468 part-time. Students come from 17 states and territories; 0.7% are from out of state; 10% Black or African American, non-Hispanic/Latino; 31% Hispanic/Latino; 5% Asian, non-Hispanic/Latino; 0.4% Native Hawaiian or other Pacific Islander, non-Hispanic/Latino; 0.7% American Indian or Alaska Native, non-Hispanic/Latino; 2% Race/ethnicity unknown; 32% transferred in.

Freshmen *Admission:* 1,263 enrolled.

Faculty *Total:* 298, 37% full-time. *Student/faculty ratio:* 17:1.

Majors Accounting; administrative assistant and secretarial science; aeronautics/aviation/aerospace science and technology; art; biology/biological sciences; business administration and management; business/commerce; chemical technology; child development; computer engineering technology; computer programming; corrections; court reporting; criminal justice/police science; culinary arts; diagnostic medical sonography and ultrasound technology; drafting and design technology; dramatic/theater arts; early childhood education; electrical, electronic and communications engineering technology; electroneurodiagnostic/electroencephalographic technology; emergency medical technology (EMT paramedic); executive assistant/executive secretary; general studies; health services/allied health/health sciences; legal administrative assistant/secretary; legal assistant/paralegal; legal studies; liberal arts and sciences/liberal studies; marketing/marketing management; mathematics; medical administrative assistant and medical secretary; mental health counseling; middle school education; music; pharmacy technician; physical education teaching and coaching; physical sciences; psychiatric/mental health services technology; psychology; radio and television; registered nursing/registered nurse; respiratory care therapy; secondary education; sociology; substance abuse/addiction counseling; voice and opera.

Academics *Calendar:* semesters. *Degree:* certificates, diplomas, and associate. *Special study options:* academic remediation for entering students, accelerated degree program, adult/continuing education programs, advanced placement credit, cooperative education, distance learning, double majors, English as a second language, honors programs, independent study, internships, part-time degree program, services for LD students, student-designed majors, study abroad, summer session for credit.

Library Alvin Community College Library with an OPAC, a Web page.

Student Life *Housing:* college housing not available. *Activities and Organizations:* student-run radio station. *Campus security:* 24-hour patrols, late-night transport/escort service. *Student services:* personal/psychological counseling.

Athletics Member NJCAA. *Intercollegiate sports:* baseball M(s), softball W(s).

Costs (2015–16) *Tuition:* area resident $1080 full-time, $45 per credit hour part-time; state resident $2160 full-time, $90 per credit hour part-time;

nonresident $3360 full-time, $140 per credit hour part-time. Full-time tuition and fees vary according to course load and program. Part-time tuition and fees vary according to course load and program. *Required fees:* $197 per term part-time. *Payment plan:* installment.

Financial Aid Of all full-time matriculated undergraduates who enrolled in 2014, 17 Federal Work-Study jobs (averaging $3400). 3 state and other part-time jobs (averaging $10,000).

Applying *Options:* electronic application. *Required for some:* high school transcript. *Application deadlines:* rolling (freshmen), rolling (transfers).

Freshman Application Contact Alvin Community College, 3110 Mustang Road, Alvin, TX 77511-4898. *Phone:* 281-756-3531.

Website: http://www.alvincollege.edu/.

Amarillo College
Amarillo, Texas

- **State and locally supported** 2-year, founded 1929
- **Urban** 1542-acre campus
- **Endowment** $36.5 million
- **Coed**

Undergraduates *Retention:* 52% of full-time freshmen returned.

Faculty *Total:* 468, 47% full-time.

Majors Accounting; administrative assistant and secretarial science; airframe mechanics and aircraft maintenance technology; architectural engineering technology; art; automobile/automotive mechanics technology; behavioral sciences; biblical studies; biology/biological sciences; broadcast journalism; business administration and management; business teacher education; chemical technology; chemistry; child development; clinical laboratory science/medical technology; commercial and advertising art; computer engineering technology; computer programming; computer science; computer systems analysis; corrections; criminal justice/law enforcement administration; criminal justice/police science; dental hygiene; drafting and design technology; dramatic/theater arts; electrical, electronic and communications engineering technology; elementary education; emergency medical technology (EMT paramedic); engineering; English; environmental health; fine/studio arts; fire science/firefighting; funeral service and mortuary science; general studies; geology/earth science; health information/medical records administration; heating, air conditioning, ventilation and refrigeration maintenance technology; heavy equipment maintenance technology; history; industrial radiologic technology; information science/studies; instrumentation technology; interior design; journalism; laser and optical technology; legal administrative assistant/secretary; liberal arts and sciences/liberal studies; licensed practical/vocational nurse training; machine tool technology; mass communication/media; mathematics; medical administrative assistant and medical secretary; modern languages; music; music teacher education; natural sciences; nuclear medical technology; occupational therapy; photography; physical education teaching and coaching; physical sciences; physical therapy; physics; pre-engineering; pre-pharmacy studies; psychology; public relations/image management; radio and television; radiologic technology/science; real estate; registered nursing/registered nurse; religious studies; respiratory care therapy; rhetoric and composition; social sciences; social work; substance abuse/addiction counseling; telecommunications technology; tourism and travel services management; visual and performing arts.

Academics *Calendar:* semesters. *Degree:* certificates and associate. *Special study options:* academic remediation for entering students, adult/continuing education programs, advanced placement credit, cooperative education, distance learning, English as a second language, freshman honors college, honors programs, part-time degree program, services for LD students, summer session for credit.

Library Lynn Library Learning Center plus 2 others with 59,964 titles, an OPAC, a Web page.

Student Life *Housing:* college housing not available. *Activities and Organizations:* drama/theater group, student-run newspaper, radio station, choral group, Student Government Association, College Republicans. *Campus security:* 24-hour emergency response devices, late-night transport/escort service, campus police patrol Monday through Saturday 0700 to 2300.

Athletics *Intramural sports:* basketball M/W, soccer M/W, softball M/W, tennis M/W, volleyball M/W.

Costs (2014–15) *Tuition:* area resident $1914 full-time, $80 per semester hour part-time; state resident $2898 full-time, $121 per semester hour part-time; nonresident $4362 full-time, $182 per semester hour part-time. Full-time tuition and fees vary according to course load. Part-time tuition and fees vary according to course load. *Payment plan:* installment. *Waivers:* senior citizens and employees or children of employees.

Financial Aid Of all full-time matriculated undergraduates who enrolled in 2013, 100 Federal Work-Study jobs (averaging $3000).

Applying *Options:* early admission, deferred entrance. *Required:* high school transcript. *Notification:* continuous (freshmen), continuous (transfers).

Freshman Application Contact Amarillo College, PO Box 447, Amarillo, TX 79178-0001. *Phone:* 806-371-5000. *Toll-free phone:* 800-227-8784. *Fax:* 806-371-5497. *E-mail:* askac@actx.edu.

Website: http://www.actx.edu/.

Angelina College
Lufkin, Texas

Freshman Application Contact Angelina College, PO Box 1768, Lufkin, TX 75902-1768. *Phone:* 936-633-5213.

Website: http://www.angelina.cc.tx.us/.

Austin Community College District
Austin, Texas

- **State and locally supported** 2-year, founded 1972
- **Urban** campus with easy access to Austin
- **Endowment** $4.8 million
- **Coed,** 40,949 undergraduate students, 22% full-time, 56% women, 44% men

Undergraduates 9,040 full-time, 31,909 part-time. Students come from 111 other countries; 2% are from out of state; 7% Black or African American, non-Hispanic/Latino; 30% Hispanic/Latino; 5% Asian, non-Hispanic/Latino; 0.2% Native Hawaiian or other Pacific Islander, non-Hispanic/Latino; 0.8% American Indian or Alaska Native, non-Hispanic/Latino; 3% Two or more races, non-Hispanic/Latino; 5% Race/ethnicity unknown; 3% international.

Faculty *Total:* 1,852, 29% full-time, 23% with terminal degrees. *Student/faculty ratio:* 20:1.

Majors Accounting technology and bookkeeping; administrative assistant and secretarial science; animation, interactive technology, video graphics and special effects; anthropology; art; automobile/automotive mechanics technology; biology/biological sciences; biology/biotechnology laboratory technician; business administration and management; business/commerce; carpentry; chemistry; child development; clinical/medical laboratory technology; commercial and advertising art; commercial photography; computer and information sciences; computer programming; computer systems networking and telecommunications; corrections; creative writing; criminal justice/police science; culinary arts; dance; dental hygiene; diagnostic medical sonography and ultrasound technology; drafting and design technology; dramatic/theater arts; early childhood education; economics; electrical, electronic and communications engineering technology; emergency medical technology (EMT paramedic); engineering; environmental engineering technology; fire prevention and safety technology; foreign languages and literatures; French; general studies; geographic information science and cartography; geography; geology/earth science; German; health and physical education/fitness; health information/medical records technology; health teacher education; heating, ventilation, air conditioning and refrigeration engineering technology; history; hospitality administration; human services; international business/trade/commerce; Japanese; journalism; Latin; legal assistant/paralegal; marketing/marketing management; mathematics; middle school education; music; music management; occupational therapist assistant; philosophy; physical sciences; physical therapy technology; physics; political science and government; pre-dentistry studies; premedical studies; pre-pharmacy studies; pre-veterinary studies; professional, technical, business, and scientific writing; psychology; radio and television; radiologic technology/science; real estate; registered nursing/registered nurse; rhetoric and composition; Russian; secondary education; sign language interpretation and translation; social work; sociology; Spanish; substance abuse/addiction counseling; surgical technology; surveying technology; therapeutic recreation; tourism and travel services management; watchmaking and jewelrymaking; welding technology; writing.

Academics *Calendar:* semesters. *Degrees:* certificates, associate, and postbachelor's certificates. *Special study options:* academic remediation for entering students, accelerated degree program, adult/continuing education programs, advanced placement credit, cooperative education, distance learning, English as a second language, honors programs, independent study, internships, part-time degree program, services for LD students, summer session for credit. *ROTC:* Army (c), Air Force (c).

Library Main Library plus 10 others with 221,326 titles, 13,742 audiovisual materials, an OPAC, a Web page.

Student Life *Housing:* college housing not available. *Activities and Organizations:* student-run newspaper, choral group, Intramurals, Student Government Association (SGA), Phi Theta Kappa (PTK), Center for Student Political Studies (CSPS), Circle K International (CKI). *Campus security:* 24-hour emergency response devices and patrols, late-night transport/escort service, 24-hour patrols by police officers. *Student services:* personal/psychological counseling.

Athletics *Intramural sports:* basketball M/W, soccer M/W, volleyball W.

Costs (2014–15) *Tuition:* area resident $2010 full-time, $67 per credit hour part-time; state resident $8070 full-time, $269 per credit hour part-time; nonresident $10,290 full-time, $343 per credit hour part-time. Full-time tuition and fees vary according to course load. Part-time tuition and fees vary according to course load. *Required fees:* $540 full-time, $18 per credit hour part-time. *Payment plan:* installment. *Waivers:* senior citizens and employees or children of employees.

Financial Aid Of all full-time matriculated undergraduates who enrolled in 2014, 4,796 applied for aid, 3,890 were judged to have need. 57 Federal Work-Study jobs (averaging $1740). 10 state and other part-time jobs (averaging $1838). *Average need-based loan:* $1820. *Average need-based gift aid:* $2228.

Applying *Options:* electronic application. *Required:* high school transcript. *Application deadlines:* rolling (freshmen), rolling (transfers).

Freshman Application Contact Ms. Linda Kluck, Director, Admissions and Records, Austin Community College District, 5930 Middle Fiskville Road, Austin, TX 78752. *Phone:* 512-223-7503. *Fax:* 512-223-7665. *E-mail:* admission@austincc.edu.
Website: http://www.austincc.edu/.

Blinn College
Brenham, Texas

Freshman Application Contact Mrs. Stephanie Wehring, Coordinator, Recruitment and Admissions, Blinn College, 902 College Avenue, Brenham, TX 77833-4049. *Phone:* 979-830-4152. *Fax:* 979-830-4110. *E-mail:* recruit@blinn.edu.
Website: http://www.blinn.edu/.

Brazosport College
Lake Jackson, Texas

Freshman Application Contact Brazosport College, 500 College Drive, Lake Jackson, TX 77566-3199. *Phone:* 979-230-3020.
Website: http://www.brazosport.edu/.

Brookhaven College
Farmers Branch, Texas

- **County-supported** 2-year, founded 1978, part of Dallas County Community College District System
- **Suburban** 200-acre campus with easy access to Dallas-Fort Worth
- **Coed,** 12,403 undergraduate students, 17% full-time, 58% women, 42% men

Undergraduates 2,162 full-time, 10,241 part-time. Students come from 34 states and territories; 79 other countries; 0.2% are from out of state; 18% Black or African American, non-Hispanic/Latino; 36% Hispanic/Latino; 10% Asian, non-Hispanic/Latino; 0.4% American Indian or Alaska Native, non-Hispanic/Latino; 1% Two or more races, non-Hispanic/Latino; 4% Race/ethnicity unknown; 0.4% international; 8% transferred in.

Freshmen *Admission:* 1,294 enrolled.

Faculty *Total:* 567, 25% full-time. *Student/faculty ratio:* 17:1.

Majors Accounting; automobile/automotive mechanics technology; business administration and management; business/commerce; child development; computer engineering technology; computer programming; computer technology/computer systems technology; criminal justice/law enforcement administration; design and visual communications; e-commerce; education (multiple levels); emergency medical technology (EMT paramedic); executive assistant/executive secretary; general studies; geographic information science and cartography; graphic design; humanities; information science/studies; liberal arts and sciences/liberal studies; marketing/marketing management; music; office management; radiologic technology/science; registered nursing/registered nurse; secondary education; speech communication and rhetoric.

Academics *Calendar:* semesters. *Degree:* certificates and associate. *Special study options:* academic remediation for entering students, adult/continuing education programs, advanced placement credit, cooperative education, distance learning, English as a second language, honors programs, independent study, internships, off-campus study, part-time degree program, services for LD students, student-designed majors, study abroad, summer session for credit.

Library Brookhaven College Learning Resources Center plus 1 other with an OPAC, a Web page.

Student Life *Housing:* college housing not available. *Activities and Organizations:* drama/theater group, student-run newspaper, choral group. *Campus security:* 24-hour emergency response devices and patrols, late-night transport/escort service. *Student services:* health clinic, personal/psychological counseling.

Athletics Member NJCAA. *Intercollegiate sports:* baseball M, basketball M, soccer W, volleyball W. *Intramural sports:* weight lifting M/W.

Standardized Tests *Required:* State Developed test scores or an approved test for Reading, Writing and Math course placement. Test scores used for placement, not admission, purposes. Certain programs require specific tests (for admission).

Costs (2015–16) *Tuition:* area resident $1770 full-time, $59 per credit part-time; state resident $3330 full-time, $111 per credit part-time; nonresident $5220 full-time, $174 per credit part-time. *Payment plan:* installment. *Waivers:* senior citizens and employees or children of employees.

Applying *Options:* electronic application, early admission, deferred entrance. *Required:* high school transcript. *Required for some:* Admission to the nursing program is based on a point system consisting of three parts: (1) HESI score, (2)GPA of prerequisite courses, and (3) completion of support courses. *Application deadlines:* rolling (freshmen), rolling (transfers).

Freshman Application Contact Admissions Office, Brookhaven College, 3939 Valley View Lane, Farmers Branch, TX 75244-4997. *Phone:* 972-860-4883. *Fax:* 972-860-4886. *E-mail:* bhcAdmissions@dcccd.edu.
Website: http://www.brookhavencollege.edu/.

Cedar Valley College
Lancaster, Texas

- **State-supported** 2-year, founded 1977, part of Dallas County Community College District System
- **Suburban** 353-acre campus with easy access to Dallas-Fort Worth
- **Coed,** 6,953 undergraduate students, 22% full-time, 58% women, 42% men

Undergraduates 1,564 full-time, 5,389 part-time. Students come from 1 other state; 1% are from out of state; 54% Black or African American, non-Hispanic/Latino; 21% Hispanic/Latino; 2% Asian, non-Hispanic/Latino; 0.1% Native Hawaiian or other Pacific Islander, non-Hispanic/Latino; 0.3% American Indian or Alaska Native, non-Hispanic/Latino; 1% Two or more races, non-Hispanic/Latino; 2% Race/ethnicity unknown; 0.1% international; 20% transferred in. *Retention:* 44% of full-time freshmen returned.

Freshmen *Admission:* 815 enrolled.

Faculty *Total:* 296, 25% full-time, 100% with terminal degrees. *Student/faculty ratio:* 24:1.

Majors Accounting; automobile/automotive mechanics technology; business administration and management; business/commerce; computer programming; computer systems networking and telecommunications; criminal justice/safety; data processing and data processing technology; education; executive assistant/executive secretary; general studies; graphic design; heating, air conditioning, ventilation and refrigeration maintenance technology; marketing/marketing management; multi/interdisciplinary studies related; music management; music performance; music theory and composition; radio and television broadcasting technology; real estate; veterinary/animal health technology.

Academics *Calendar:* semesters. *Degree:* certificates and associate. *Special study options:* academic remediation for entering students, advanced placement credit, cooperative education, distance learning, double majors, English as a second language, internships, off-campus study, part-time degree program, services for LD students, summer session for credit.

Library Cedar Valley College Library with 2 audiovisual materials, an OPAC, a Web page.

Student Life *Housing:* college housing not available. *Activities and Organizations:* choral group, Phi Theta Kappa (PTK), Brother 2 Brother, Sustainability, Commercial Music Association, Family Music Club. *Campus security:* 24-hour emergency response devices and patrols, late-night transport/escort service. *Student services:* health clinic, personal/psychological counseling.

Athletics Member NCAA, NJCAA. *Intercollegiate sports:* baseball M, basketball M, soccer W, volleyball W.

Standardized Tests *Required:* SAT or ACT (for admission), TSI (for admission). *Required for some:* SAT and SAT Subject Tests or ACT (for admission).

Costs (2015–16) *Tuition:* area resident $1560 full-time, $59 per credit hour part-time; state resident $2910 full-time, $111 per credit hour part-time; nonresident $4590 full-time, $200 per credit hour part-time. Full-time tuition and fees vary according to class time, course level, course load, degree level, location, program, reciprocity agreements, and student level. Part-time tuition and fees vary according to class time, course level, course load, degree level, location, program, reciprocity agreements, and student level. No tuition increase for student's term of enrollment. *Required fees:* $59 per credit hour part-time. *Payment plans:* tuition prepayment, installment. *Waivers:* minority students, senior citizens, and employees or children of employees.

Applying *Required:* high school transcript, minimum 2.0 GPA.

Freshman Application Contact Admissions Office, Cedar Valley College, Lancaster, TX 75134-3799. *Phone:* 972-860-8206. *Fax:* 972-860-8207.
Website: http://www.cedarvalleycollege.edu/.

Center for Advanced Legal Studies
Houston, Texas

Freshman Application Contact Mr. James Scheffer, Center for Advanced Legal Studies, 3910 Kirby, Suite 200, Houston, TX 77098. *Phone:* 713-529-2778. *Toll-free phone:* 800-446-6931. *Fax:* 713-523-2715. *E-mail:* james.scheffer@paralegal.edu.
Website: http://www.paralegal.edu/.

Central Texas College
Killeen, Texas

- **State and locally supported** 2-year, founded 1967
- **Suburban** 500-acre campus with easy access to Austin
- **Endowment** $6.5 million
- **Coed,** 21,647 undergraduate students, 17% full-time, 47% women, 53% men

Undergraduates 3,754 full-time, 17,893 part-time. 24% Black or African American, non-Hispanic/Latino; 17% Hispanic/Latino; 3% Asian, non-Hispanic/Latino; 2% Native Hawaiian or other Pacific Islander, non-Hispanic/Latino; 1% American Indian or Alaska Native, non-Hispanic/Latino; 0.4% Two or more races, non-Hispanic/Latino; 13% Race/ethnicity unknown; 0.3% international; 1% live on campus.
Freshmen *Admission:* 3,515 enrolled.
Faculty *Total:* 1,237, 15% full-time, 21% with terminal degrees. *Student/faculty ratio:* 18:1.
Majors Administrative assistant and secretarial science; agriculture; aircraft powerplant technology; airline pilot and flight crew; autobody/collision and repair technology; automobile/automotive mechanics technology; biology/biological sciences; building/property maintenance; business administration and management; chemistry; child-care provision; clinical/medical laboratory technology; clinical/medical social work; commercial and advertising art; computer and information systems security; computer technology/computer systems technology; criminal justice/police science; diesel mechanics technology; drafting and design technology; dramatic/theater arts; early childhood education; emergency medical technology (EMT paramedic); engineering; environmental science; farm and ranch management; fine/studio arts; fire services administration; foreign languages and literatures; general studies; geology/earth science; graphic and printing equipment operation/production; health and physical education/fitness; heating, air conditioning, ventilation and refrigeration maintenance technology; hospitality administration; journalism; legal assistant/paralegal; liberal arts and sciences/liberal studies; licensed practical/vocational nurse training; marketing/marketing management; mathematics; music; public administration; radio and television; registered nursing/registered nurse; restaurant/food services management; social sciences; system, networking, and LAN/WAN management; telecommunications technology; welding technology.
Academics *Calendar:* semesters. *Degree:* certificates and associate. *Special study options:* academic remediation for entering students, accelerated degree program, adult/continuing education programs, advanced placement credit, distance learning, English as a second language, external degree program, internships, part-time degree program, services for LD students, student-designed majors, summer session for credit. *ROTC:* Army (b).
Library Oveta Culp Hobby Memorial Library with 65,205 titles, 1,796 audiovisual materials, an OPAC, a Web page.
Student Life *Housing Options:* coed. Campus housing is university owned. *Activities and Organizations:* drama/theater group, student-run newspaper, International Student Association, We Can Do It Club, Students in Free Enterprise (SIFE), Student Nurses Association, NAACP, national fraternities. *Campus security:* 24-hour emergency response devices and patrols.
Athletics *Intramural sports:* badminton M/W, basketball M/W, bowling M/W, football M/W, golf M/W, soccer M/W, softball M/W, table tennis M/W, tennis M/W, volleyball M/W.
Costs (2014–15) *Tuition:* area resident $2130 full-time, $71 per credit hour part-time; state resident $2790 full-time, $93 per credit hour part-time; nonresident $6270 full-time, $209 per credit hour part-time. Full-time tuition and fees vary according to location and program. Part-time tuition and fees vary according to location and program. *Room and board:* $5031. Room and board charges vary according to housing facility. *Payment plan:* installment. *Waivers:* senior citizens and employees or children of employees.
Financial Aid Of all full-time matriculated undergraduates who enrolled in 2013, 68 Federal Work-Study jobs (averaging $3658).
Applying *Options:* electronic application, early admission, deferred entrance. *Required:* high school transcript. *Application deadlines:* rolling (freshmen), rolling (out-of-state freshmen), rolling (transfers).
Freshman Application Contact Admissions Office, Central Texas College, PO Box 1800, Killeen, TX 76540-1800. *Phone:* 254-526-1696. *Toll-free*

phone: 800-223-4760 (in-state); 800-792-3348 (out-of-state). *E-mail:* admrec@ctcd.edu.
Website: http://www.ctcd.edu/.

Cisco College
Cisco, Texas

Freshman Application Contact Mr. Olin O. Odom III, Dean of Admission/Registrar, Cisco College, 101 College Heights, Cisco, TX 76437-9321. *Phone:* 254-442-2567 Ext. 5130. *E-mail:* oodom@cjc.edu.
Website: http://www.cisco.edu/.

Clarendon College
Clarendon, Texas

- **State and locally supported** 2-year, founded 1898
- **Rural** 109-acre campus
- **Endowment** $2.1 million
- **Coed**

Undergraduates 576 full-time, 638 part-time. Students come from 14 states and territories; 2 other countries; 4% are from out of state; 4% Black or African American, non-Hispanic/Latino; 21% Hispanic/Latino; 0.3% Asian, non-Hispanic/Latino; 1% American Indian or Alaska Native, non-Hispanic/Latino; 6% Race/ethnicity unknown; 0.8% international; 21% live on campus.
Faculty *Student/faculty ratio:* 19:1.
Academics *Calendar:* semesters. *Degree:* certificates and associate. *Special study options:* academic remediation for entering students, adult/continuing education programs, advanced placement credit, distance learning, double majors, English as a second language, independent study, part-time degree program, services for LD students, summer session for credit.
Student Life *Campus security:* 8-hour patrols by trained security personnel, Emergency notification system through text messaging.
Athletics Member NJCAA.
Financial Aid Of all full-time matriculated undergraduates who enrolled in 2010, 47 Federal Work-Study jobs (averaging $575). 12 state and other part-time jobs (averaging $485).
Applying *Options:* electronic application, early admission. *Required:* high school transcript. *Required for some:* interview.
Freshman Application Contact Ms. Martha Smith, Admissions Director, Clarendon College, PO Box 968, Clarendon, TX 79226. *Phone:* 806-874-3571 Ext. 106. *Toll-free phone:* 800-687-9737. *Fax:* 806-874-3201. *E-mail:* martha.smith@clarendoncollege.edu.
Website: http://www.clarendoncollege.edu/.

Coastal Bend College
Beeville, Texas

- **County-supported** 2-year, founded 1965
- **Rural** 100-acre campus
- **Endowment** $514,263
- **Coed,** 3,776 undergraduate students, 36% full-time, 62% women, 38% men

Undergraduates 1,353 full-time, 2,423 part-time. Students come from 2 states and territories; 1 other country; 1% are from out of state; 5% transferred in; 5% live on campus.
Freshmen *Admission:* 519 applied, 519 admitted, 519 enrolled.
Faculty *Total:* 157, 46% full-time, 4% with terminal degrees. *Student/faculty ratio:* 13:1.
Majors Accounting; administrative assistant and secretarial science; automobile/automotive mechanics technology; business administration and management; child development; computer and information sciences related; computer programming related; computer programming (specific applications); computer science; cosmetology; criminal justice/law enforcement administration; criminal justice/police science; dental hygiene; drafting and design technology; information technology; liberal arts and sciences/liberal studies; licensed practical/vocational nurse training; petroleum technology; registered nursing/registered nurse; welding technology.
Academics *Calendar:* semesters. *Degree:* certificates and associate. *Special study options:* academic remediation for entering students, adult/continuing education programs, advanced placement credit, cooperative education, distance learning, internships, part-time degree program, services for LD students, summer session for credit.
Library Grady C. Hogue Learning Resource Center with 43,004 titles, 2,179 audiovisual materials, an OPAC, a Web page.
Student Life *Housing Options:* coed, special housing for students with disabilities. Campus housing is university owned. *Activities and Organizations:* student government, Computer Science Club, Creative Writing

Club, Drama Club, Art Club. *Campus security:* 24-hour emergency response devices, night security. *Student services:* personal/psychological counseling.

Athletics Member NJCAA. *Intercollegiate sports:* basketball M, volleyball W. *Intramural sports:* archery M/W, badminton M/W, basketball M/W, bowling M/W, cross-country running M/W, golf M/W, soccer M/W, softball M/W, table tennis M/W, tennis M/W, track and field M/W, volleyball M/W, weight lifting M/W.

Financial Aid Of all full-time matriculated undergraduates who enrolled in 2013, 80 Federal Work-Study jobs (averaging $1484). 11 state and other part-time jobs (averaging $1159).

Applying *Options:* electronic application, deferred entrance. *Required:* high school transcript. *Application deadlines:* rolling (freshmen), rolling (out-of-state freshmen), rolling (transfers). *Notification:* continuous (freshmen), continuous (out-of-state freshmen), continuous (transfers).

Freshman Application Contact Mrs. Tammy Adams, Director of Admissions/Registrar, Coastal Bend College, Beeville, TX 78102-2197. *Phone:* 361-354-2245. *Toll-free phone:* 866-722-2838 (in-state); 866-262-2838 (out-of-state). *Fax:* 361-354-2254. *E-mail:* tadams@coastalbend.edu. *Website:* http://www.coastalbend.edu/.

The College of Health Care Professions
Austin, Texas

Admissions Office Contact The College of Health Care Professions, 6505 Airport Boulevard, Austin, TX 78752.
Website: http://www.chcp.edu/.

The College of Health Care Professions
Houston, Texas

Freshman Application Contact Admissions Office, The College of Health Care Professions, 240 Northwest Mall Boulevard, Houston, TX 77092. *Phone:* 713-425-3100. *Toll-free phone:* 800-487-6728. *Fax:* 713-425-3193. *Website:* http://www.chcp.edu/.

College of the Mainland
Texas City, Texas

- **State and locally supported** 2-year, founded 1967
- **Suburban** 128-acre campus with easy access to Houston
- **Coed**

Undergraduates 1,121 full-time, 3,067 part-time. Students come from 3 states and territories; 16% Black or African American, non-Hispanic/Latino; 27% Hispanic/Latino; 3% Asian, non-Hispanic/Latino; 0.2% Native Hawaiian or other Pacific Islander, non-Hispanic/Latino; 0.4% American Indian or Alaska Native, non-Hispanic/Latino; 0.5% Two or more races, non-Hispanic/Latino; 5% transferred in. *Retention:* 54% of full-time freshmen returned.

Faculty *Student/faculty ratio:* 15:1.

Academics *Calendar:* semesters. *Degree:* certificates, diplomas, and associate. *Special study options:* academic remediation for entering students, adult/continuing education programs, cooperative education, distance learning, English as a second language, honors programs, internships, part-time degree program, services for LD students, summer session for credit. *ROTC:* Air Force (c).

Student Life *Campus security:* 24-hour emergency response devices and patrols, student patrols, late-night transport/escort service, Vehicular assistance - lock outs, jump starts.

Standardized Tests *Recommended:* SAT or ACT (for admission).

Costs (2014–15) *Tuition:* area resident $1350 full-time, $540 per year part-time; state resident $2550 full-time, $1020 per year part-time; nonresident $3450 full-time, $1380 per year part-time. Full-time tuition and fees vary according to course load and program. Part-time tuition and fees vary according to course load and program. *Required fees:* $423 full-time, $390 per year part-time.

Financial Aid Of all full-time matriculated undergraduates who enrolled in 2013, 649 applied for aid, 585 were judged to have need, 40 had their need fully met. 54 Federal Work-Study jobs (averaging $1585). 42 state and other part-time jobs (averaging $1096). In 2013, 36. *Average percent of need met:* 58. *Average financial aid package:* $5368. *Average need-based loan:* $2190. *Average need-based gift aid:* $4655. *Average non-need-based aid:* $1116.

Applying *Options:* electronic application, early admission, deferred entrance. *Required for some:* high school transcript.

Freshman Application Contact Mr. Martin Perez, Director of Admissions/International Affairs, College of the Mainland, 1200 Amburn Road, Texas City, TX 77591. *Phone:* 409-933-8653. *Toll-free phone:* 888-258-8859 Ext. 8264. *E-mail:* mperez@com.edu. *Website:* http://www.com.edu/.

Collin County Community College District
McKinney, Texas

- **State and locally supported** 2-year, founded 1985
- **Suburban** 333-acre campus with easy access to Dallas-Fort Worth
- **Endowment** $9.6 million
- **Coed,** 27,991 undergraduate students, 35% full-time, 56% women, 44% men

Undergraduates 9,899 full-time, 18,092 part-time. Students come from 55 states and territories; 98 other countries; 12% Black or African American, non-Hispanic/Latino; 20% Hispanic/Latino; 8% Asian, non-Hispanic/Latino; 0.3% Native Hawaiian or other Pacific Islander, non-Hispanic/Latino; 0.4% American Indian or Alaska Native, non-Hispanic/Latino; 3% Two or more races, non-Hispanic/Latino; 0.5% Race/ethnicity unknown; 3% international; 7% transferred in. *Retention:* 54% of full-time freshmen returned.

Freshmen *Admission:* 4,525 applied, 4,525 admitted, 5,239 enrolled.

Faculty *Total:* 1,237, 30% full-time, 20% with terminal degrees. *Student/faculty ratio:* 24:1.

Majors Administrative assistant and secretarial science; baking and pastry arts; biology/biotechnology laboratory technician; business administration and management; business/commerce; child-care provision; child development; commercial and advertising art; computer and information sciences; computer and information systems security; computer science; criminal justice/police science; culinary arts; dental hygiene; drafting and design technology; early childhood education; electrical, electronic and communications engineering technology; electroneurodiagnostic/electroencephalographic technology; emergency medical technology (EMT paramedic); engineering; engineering technology; fire prevention and safety technology; fire science/firefighting; game and interactive media design; geographic information science and cartography; graphic design; health information/medical records technology; hospitality administration; illustration; integrated circuit design; interior design; legal assistant/paralegal; liberal arts and sciences/liberal studies; medical insurance coding; middle school education; music; music management; network and system administration; real estate; registered nursing/registered nurse; respiratory care therapy; retail management; secondary education; sign language interpretation and translation; speech communication and rhetoric; surgical technology; system, networking, and LAN/WAN management; telecommunications technology; web page, digital/multimedia and information resources design.

Academics *Calendar:* semesters. *Degree:* certificates and associate. *Special study options:* academic remediation for entering students, adult/continuing education programs, advanced placement credit, cooperative education, distance learning, English as a second language, honors programs, internships, part-time degree program, services for LD students, summer session for credit. *ROTC:* Air Force (c).

Library Collin College Library(Spring Creek, Preston Ridge, Central Park) with 344,207 titles, 41,008 audiovisual materials, an OPAC, a Web page.

Student Life *Housing:* college housing not available. *Activities and Organizations:* drama/theater group, choral group, student government, Phi Theta Kappa, Baptist Student Ministry, National Society of Leadership Success, Political Science Club. *Campus security:* 24-hour emergency response devices and patrols, late-night transport/escort service. *Student services:* personal/psychological counseling.

Athletics Member NJCAA. *Intercollegiate sports:* basketball M(s)/W(s), tennis M(s)/W(s).

Costs (2014–15) *Tuition:* area resident $960 full-time, $39 per credit hour part-time; state resident $2130 full-time, $78 per credit hour part-time; nonresident $3930 full-time, $138 per credit hour part-time. *Required fees:* $214 full-time, $7 per credit hour part-time, $2 per term part-time. *Payment plan:* installment. *Waivers:* senior citizens.

Applying *Options:* electronic application. *Required:* high school transcript. *Application deadlines:* rolling (freshmen), rolling (out-of-state freshmen), rolling (transfers). *Notification:* continuous (freshmen), continuous (out-of-state freshmen), continuous (transfers).

Freshman Application Contact Mr. Todd Fields, Registrar/Director of Admissions, Collin County Community College District, 2800 E. Spring Creek Pkwy., Plano, TX 75074. *Phone:* 972-881-5174. *Fax:* 972-881-5175. *E-mail:* tfields@collin.edu. *Website:* http://www.collin.edu/.

Commonwealth Institute of Funeral Service
Houston, Texas

Freshman Application Contact Ms. Patricia Moreno, Registrar, Commonwealth Institute of Funeral Service, 415 Barren Springs Drive,

Houston, TX 77090. *Phone:* 281-873-0262. *Toll-free phone:* 800-628-1580. *Fax:* 281-873-5232. *E-mail:* p.moreno@commonwealth.edu. *Website:* http://www.commonwealth.edu/.

Concorde Career College
Dallas, Texas

Admissions Office Contact Concorde Career College, 12606 Greenville Avenue, Suite 130, Dallas, TX 75243.
Website: http://www.concorde.edu/.

Concorde Career College
Grand Prairie, Texas

Admissions Office Contact Concorde Career College, 3015 West Interstate 20, Grand Prairie, TX 75052.
Website: http://www.concorde.edu/.

Concorde Career College
San Antonio, Texas

Admissions Office Contact Concorde Career College, 4803 NW Loop 410, San Antonio, TX 78229.
Website: http://www.concorde.edu/.

Court Reporting Institute of Dallas
Dallas, Texas

Director of Admissions Ms. Debra Smith-Armstrong, Director of Admissions, Court Reporting Institute of Dallas, 1341 West Mockingbird Lane, Suite 200E, Dallas, TX 75247. *Phone:* 214-350-9722 Ext. 227. *Toll-free phone:* 877-841-3557 (in-state); 888-841-3557 (out-of-state).
Website: http://www.crid.com/.

Culinary Institute LeNotre
Houston, Texas

- **Proprietary** 2-year
- **Urban** campus with easy access to Houston
- **Coed**

Undergraduates 248 full-time, 155 part-time. Students come from 6 states and territories; 3 other countries; 6% are from out of state; 22% Black or African American, non-Hispanic/Latino; 40% Hispanic/Latino; 2% Asian, non-Hispanic/Latino; 0.2% Native Hawaiian or other Pacific Islander, non-Hispanic/Latino; 0.5% Two or more races, non-Hispanic/Latino; 1% Race/ethnicity unknown.
Faculty *Student/faculty ratio:* 12:1.
Academics *Degree:* diplomas and associate. *Special study options:* academic remediation for entering students, adult/continuing education programs, cooperative education, internships, part-time degree program, study abroad.
Student Life *Campus security:* late-night transport/escort service.
Costs (2014–15) *Tuition:* $11,988 full-time, $333 per credit hour part-time. Full-time tuition and fees vary according to course load and program. Part-time tuition and fees vary according to course load and program.
Applying *Application fee:* $50. *Required:* essay or personal statement, high school transcript, minimum 2.0 GPA, interview.
Freshman Application Contact Admissions Office, Culinary Institute LeNotre, 7070 Allensby, Houston, TX 77022-4322. *Phone:* 713-358-5070. *Toll-free phone:* 888-LENOTRE.
Website: http://www.culinaryinstitute.edu/.

Dallas Institute of Funeral Service
Dallas, Texas

- **Independent** 2-year, founded 1945, part of Dallas Institute is one of the Pierce Mortuary Colleges, Inc.
- **Urban** 4-acre campus with easy access to Dallas-Fort Worth
- **Coed,** 141 undergraduate students, 100% full-time, 47% women, 53% men

Undergraduates 141 full-time. Students come from 7 states and territories; 11% are from out of state; 30% Black or African American, non-Hispanic/Latino; 15% Hispanic/Latino. *Retention:* 71% of full-time freshmen returned.
Freshmen *Admission:* 56 enrolled.
Faculty *Student/faculty ratio:* 17:1.
Majors Funeral service and mortuary science.

Academics *Calendar:* quarters. *Degree:* certificates and associate. *Special study options:* distance learning, services for LD students.
Student Life *Housing:* college housing not available. *Campus security:* 24-hour emergency response devices.
Applying *Options:* electronic application. *Application fee:* $50. *Required:* high school transcript. *Application deadline:* rolling (freshmen).
Freshman Application Contact Director of Admissions, Dallas Institute of Funeral Service, 3909 South Buckner Boulevard, Dallas, TX 75227. *Phone:* 214-388-5466. *Toll-free phone:* 800-235-5444. *Fax:* 214-388-0316. *E-mail:* difs@dallasinstitute.edu.
Website: http://www.dallasinstitute.edu/.

Dallas Nursing Institute
Dallas, Texas

Admissions Office Contact Dallas Nursing Institute, 12170 N. Abrams Road, Suite 200, Dallas, TX 75243.
Website: http://www.dni.edu/.

Del Mar College
Corpus Christi, Texas

Freshman Application Contact Ms. Frances P. Jordan, Director of Admissions and Registrar, Del Mar College, 101 Baldwin, Corpus Christi, TX 78404. *Phone:* 361-698-1255. *Toll-free phone:* 800-652-3357. *Fax:* 361-698-1595. *E-mail:* fjordan@delmar.edu.
Website: http://www.delmar.edu/.

Eastfield College
Mesquite, Texas

Freshman Application Contact Ms. Glynis Miller, Director of Admissions/Registrar, Eastfield College, 3737 Motley Drive, Mesquite, TX 75150-2099. *Phone:* 972-860-7010. *Fax:* 972-860-8306. *E-mail:* efc@dcccd.edu.
Website: http://www.efc.dcccd.edu/.

El Centro College
Dallas, Texas

- **County-supported** 2-year, founded 1966, part of Dallas County Community College District System
- **Urban** 2-acre campus
- **Coed,** 10,101 undergraduate students, 23% full-time, 66% women, 34% men

Undergraduates 2,314 full-time, 7,787 part-time. Students come from 49 other countries; 1% are from out of state; 19% Black or African American, non-Hispanic/Latino; 38% Hispanic/Latino; 3% Asian, non-Hispanic/Latino; 0.0% Native Hawaiian or other Pacific Islander, non-Hispanic/Latino; 0.3% American Indian or Alaska Native, non-Hispanic/Latino; 24% Two or more races, non-Hispanic/Latino; 2% Race/ethnicity unknown; 0.3% international; 74% transferred in. *Retention:* 39% of full-time freshmen returned.
Freshmen *Admission:* 1,935 enrolled.
Faculty *Total:* 493, 27% full-time, 8% with terminal degrees. *Student/faculty ratio:* 19:1.
Majors Accounting; apparel and accessories marketing; baking and pastry arts; biotechnology; business administration and management; business automation/technology/data entry; business/commerce; cardiovascular technology; clinical/medical laboratory technology; computer and information systems security; computer/information technology services administration related; computer programming; computer science; culinary arts; data processing and data processing technology; diagnostic medical sonography and ultrasound technology; emergency medical technology (EMT paramedic); executive assistant/executive secretary; fashion/apparel design; health information/medical records administration; information science/studies; interior design; legal administrative assistant/secretary; legal assistant/paralegal; licensed practical/vocational nurse training; medical/clinical assistant; medical radiologic technology; medical transcription; office occupations and clerical services; peace studies and conflict resolution; radiologic technology/science; registered nursing/registered nurse; respiratory care therapy; special products marketing; surgical technology; teacher assistant/aide; web page, digital/multimedia and information resources design.
Academics *Calendar:* semesters. *Degree:* certificates and associate. *Special study options:* academic remediation for entering students, adult/continuing education programs, advanced placement credit, cooperative education, distance learning, double majors, English as a second language, freshman

honors college, honors programs, internships, part-time degree program, services for LD students, summer session for credit. *ROTC:* Army (c).

Library El Centro College Library with 77,902 titles, 585 audiovisual materials, an OPAC, a Web page.

Student Life *Housing:* college housing not available. *Activities and Organizations:* choral group, Phi Theta Kappa, student government, Paralegal Student Association, El Centro Computer Society, Conflict Resolution Society. *Campus security:* 24-hour emergency response devices and patrols, late-night transport/escort service, e-mail and text message alerts. *Student services:* health clinic, personal/psychological counseling.

Applying *Required for some:* high school transcript, 1 letter of recommendation.

Freshman Application Contact Ms. Rebecca Garza, Director of Admissions and Registrar, El Centro College, Dallas, TX 75202. *Phone:* 214-860-2618. *Fax:* 214-860-2233. *E-mail:* rgarza@dcccd.edu.

Website: http://www.elcentrocollege.edu/.

El Paso Community College
El Paso, Texas

Freshman Application Contact Daryle Hendry, Director of Admissions, El Paso Community College, PO Box 20500, El Paso, TX 79998-0500. *Phone:* 915-831-2580. *E-mail:* daryleh@epcc.edu.

Website: http://www.epcc.edu/.

Everest College
Arlington, Texas

Freshman Application Contact Admissions Office, Everest College, 300 Six Flags Drive, Suite 200, Arlington, TX 76011. *Phone:* 817-652-7790. *Toll-free phone:* 888-741-4270. *Fax:* 817-649-6033.

Website: http://www.everest.edu/.

Everest College
Dallas, Texas

Freshman Application Contact Admissions Office, Everest College, 6080 North Central Expressway, Dallas, TX 75206. *Phone:* 214-234-4850. *Toll-free phone:* 888-741-4270. *Fax:* 214-696-6208.

Website: http://www.everest.edu/.

Everest College
Fort Worth, Texas

Admissions Office Contact Everest College, La Gran Plaza 4200, South Freeway, Suite 1940, Fort Worth, TX 76115.

Website: http://www.everest.edu/.

Frank Phillips College
Borger, Texas

- **State and locally supported** 2-year, founded 1948
- **Small-town** 60-acre campus
- **Endowment** $1.3 million
- **Coed**

Undergraduates 501 full-time, 647 part-time. Students come from 15 states and territories; 6 other countries; 10% are from out of state; 5% Black or African American, non-Hispanic/Latino; 17% Hispanic/Latino; 0.8% Asian, non-Hispanic/Latino; 0.2% Native Hawaiian or other Pacific Islander, non-Hispanic/Latino; 3% American Indian or Alaska Native, non-Hispanic/Latino; 5% Race/ethnicity unknown; 0.2% international; 7% transferred in; 20% live on campus. *Retention:* 41% of full-time freshmen returned.

Faculty *Student/faculty ratio:* 16:1.

Academics *Calendar:* semesters. *Degree:* certificates and associate. *Special study options:* academic remediation for entering students, accelerated degree program, adult/continuing education programs, advanced placement credit, cooperative education, distance learning, honors programs, internships, part-time degree program, services for LD students, summer session for credit.

Student Life *Campus security:* 24-hour emergency response devices and patrols, controlled dormitory access.

Athletics Member NJCAA.

Costs (2014–15) *Tuition:* area resident $1200 full-time, $40 per credit hour part-time; state resident $1890 full-time, $63 per credit hour part-time; nonresident $2100 full-time, $70 per credit hour part-time. Full-time tuition and fees vary according to course load. Part-time tuition and fees vary according to course load. *Required fees:* $1600 full-time, $48 per credit hour part-time. *Room and board:* $3111. Room and board charges vary according to housing facility.

Financial Aid Of all full-time matriculated undergraduates who enrolled in 2013, 24 Federal Work-Study jobs (averaging $5200). 6 state and other part-time jobs (averaging $4800). *Financial aid deadline:* 8/31.

Applying *Options:* electronic application, early admission, deferred entrance. *Required:* high school transcript.

Freshman Application Contact Ms. Michele Stevens, Director of Enrollment Management, Frank Phillips College, PO Box 5118, Borger, TX 79008-5118. *Phone:* 806-457-4200 Ext. 707. *Fax:* 806-457-4225. *E-mail:* mstevens@fpctx.edu.

Website: http://www.fpctx.edu/.

Galveston College
Galveston, Texas

- **State and locally supported** 2-year, founded 1967
- **Urban** 11-acre campus with easy access to Houston
- **Coed**

Undergraduates 577 full-time, 1,554 part-time. 17% Black or African American, non-Hispanic/Latino; 30% Hispanic/Latino; 3% Asian, non-Hispanic/Latino; 0.2% Native Hawaiian or other Pacific Islander, non-Hispanic/Latino; 0.3% American Indian or Alaska Native, non-Hispanic/Latino; 0.3% Two or more races, non-Hispanic/Latino; 4% Race/ethnicity unknown; 0.7% international; 13% transferred in. *Retention:* 52% of full-time freshmen returned.

Faculty *Student/faculty ratio:* 15:1.

Academics *Calendar:* semesters. *Degree:* certificates and associate. *Special study options:* adult/continuing education programs, advanced placement credit, cooperative education, distance learning, internships, off-campus study, part-time degree program, services for LD students, summer session for credit.

Student Life *Campus security:* 24-hour emergency response devices and patrols, late-night transport/escort service.

Athletics Member NJCAA.

Costs (2014–15) *Tuition:* area resident $1110 full-time; state resident $1470 full-time; nonresident $3360 full-time. *Required fees:* $790 full-time.

Financial Aid Of all full-time matriculated undergraduates who enrolled in 2013, 36 Federal Work-Study jobs (averaging $2000).

Applying *Required for some:* high school transcript.

Freshman Application Contact Galveston College, 4015 Avenue Q, Galveston, TX 77550-7496. *Phone:* 409-944-1216.

Website: http://www.gc.edu/.

Golf Academy of America
Farmers Branch, Texas

Admissions Office Contact Golf Academy of America, 1861 Valley View Lane, Suite 100, Farmers Branch, TX 75234. *Toll-free phone:* 800-342-7342.

Website: http://www.golfacademy.edu/.

Grayson College
Denison, Texas

- **State and locally supported** 2-year, founded 1964
- **Rural** 500-acre campus with easy access to Dallas-Fort Worth
- **Endowment** $8.7 million
- **Coed**

Undergraduates 2,101 full-time, 2,913 part-time. Students come from 14 states and territories; 18 other countries; 5% are from out of state; 7% Black or African American, non-Hispanic/Latino; 12% Hispanic/Latino; 1% Asian, non-Hispanic/Latino; 0.2% Native Hawaiian or other Pacific Islander, non-Hispanic/Latino; 2% American Indian or Alaska Native, non-Hispanic/Latino; 4% Two or more races, non-Hispanic/Latino; 0.4% Race/ethnicity unknown; 2% international; 12% transferred in; 17% live on campus. *Retention:* 53% of full-time freshmen returned.

Faculty *Student/faculty ratio:* 26:1.

Academics *Calendar:* semesters. *Degree:* certificates, diplomas, and associate. *Special study options:* academic remediation for entering students, adult/continuing education programs, advanced placement credit, distance learning, English as a second language, freshman honors college, honors programs, part-time degree program, summer session for credit.

Student Life *Campus security:* 24-hour emergency response devices and patrols, student patrols, late-night transport/escort service, controlled dormitory access.

Athletics Member NJCAA.

Costs (2014–15) *Tuition:* area resident $1176 full-time, $49 per credit hour part-time; state resident $2088 full-time, $87 per credit hour part-time; nonresident $3192 full-time, $133 per credit hour part-time. Full-time tuition and fees vary according to course load. Part-time tuition and fees vary according to course load. *Required fees:* $456 full-time, $19 per credit hour part-time, $12 per term part-time. *Room and board:* $5180.

Applying *Options:* electronic application, early admission, deferred entrance. **Freshman Application Contact** Charles Leslie, Enrollment Advisor, Grayson College, 6101Grayson Drive, Denison, TX 75020. *Phone:* 903-415-2532. *Fax:* 903-463-5284. *E-mail:* lesliec@grayson.edu. *Website:* http://www.grayson.edu/.

Hill College
Hillsboro, Texas

Freshman Application Contact Enrollment Management, Hill College, 112 Lamar Drive, Hillsboro, TX 76645. *Phone:* 254-659-7600. *Fax:* 254-582-7591. *E-mail:* enrollmentinfo@hillcollege.edu. *Website:* http://www.hillcollege.edu/.

Houston Community College
Houston, Texas

- **State and locally supported** 2-year, founded 1971
- **Urban** campus with easy access to Houston
- **Coed**, 58,276 undergraduate students, 30% full-time, 58% women, 42% men

Undergraduates 17,288 full-time, 40,988 part-time. Students come from 150 other countries; 32% Black or African American, non-Hispanic/Latino; 32% Hispanic/Latino; 9% Asian, non-Hispanic/Latino; 0.2% Native Hawaiian or other Pacific Islander, non-Hispanic/Latino; 0.2% American Indian or Alaska Native, non-Hispanic/Latino; 2% Two or more races, non-Hispanic/Latino; 2% Race/ethnicity unknown; 9% international; 8% transferred in.
Freshmen *Admission:* 3,544 applied, 3,544 admitted, 8,260 enrolled.
Faculty *Total:* 2,501, 30% full-time. *Student/faculty ratio:* 23:1.
Majors Accounting; animation, interactive technology, video graphics and special effects; applied horticulture/horticulture operations; automobile/automotive mechanics technology; banking and financial support services; biology/biotechnology laboratory technician; business administration and management; business automation/technology/data entry; business/corporate communications; cardiovascular technology; chemical technology; child development; cinematography and film/video production; clinical/medical laboratory science and allied professions related; clinical/medical laboratory technology; commercial photography; computer engineering technology; computer programming; computer programming (specific applications); computer systems networking and telecommunications; construction engineering technology; cosmetology; court reporting; criminal justice/police science; culinary arts; desktop publishing and digital imaging design; drafting and design technology; emergency medical technology (EMT paramedic); fashion/apparel design; fashion merchandising; fire prevention and safety technology; health and physical education/fitness; health information/medical records technology; histologic technician; hotel/motel administration; instrumentation technology; interior design; international business/trade/commerce; legal assistant/paralegal; logistics, materials, and supply chain management; manufacturing engineering technology; marketing/marketing management; music management; music performance; music theory and composition; network and system administration; nuclear medical technology; occupational therapist assistant; petroleum technology; physical therapy technology; psychiatric/mental health services technology; public administration; radio and television broadcasting technology; radiologic technology/science; real estate; registered nursing/registered nurse; respiratory care therapy; sign language interpretation and translation; tourism and travel services management; turf and turfgrass management.
Academics *Calendar:* semesters. *Degree:* certificates and associate. *Special study options:* academic remediation for entering students, advanced placement credit, cooperative education, distance learning, English as a second language, honors programs, internships, part-time degree program, services for LD students, study abroad, summer session for credit. *ROTC:* Army (c), Air Force (c).
Library 272,932 titles, 54,684 audiovisual materials, an OPAC, a Web page.
Student Life *Housing:* college housing not available. *Activities and Organizations:* drama/theater group, student-run newspaper. *Campus security:* 24-hour emergency response devices and patrols, late-night transport/escort service, Houston Community College Police Department provides law enforcement and crime prevention services. *Student services:* personal/psychological counseling.
Costs (2014–15) *Tuition:* area resident $1630 full-time, $410 per term part-time; state resident $3358 full-time, $842 per term part-time; nonresident $3754 full-time, $941 per term part-time. Full-time tuition and fees vary according to course load. Part-time tuition and fees vary according to course load. *Payment plan:* installment. *Waivers:* senior citizens and employees or children of employees.
Financial Aid Of all full-time matriculated undergraduates who enrolled in 2013, 46,382 applied for aid, 44,410 were judged to have need, 44,410 had

their need fully met. *Average percent of need met:* 77%. *Average financial aid package:* $6693. *Average need-based loan:* $3482. *Average indebtedness upon graduation:* $7800. *Financial aid deadline:* 6/30.
Applying *Options:* electronic application. *Required for some:* high school transcript, interview. *Application deadlines:* rolling (freshmen), rolling (out-of-state freshmen), rolling (transfers).
Freshman Application Contact Ms. Mary Lemburg, Registrar, Houston Community College, 3100 Main Street, PO Box 667517, Houston, TX 77266-7517. *Phone:* 713-718-2000. *Toll-free phone:* 877-422-6111. *Fax:* 713-718-2111. *E-mail:* student.info@hccs.edu. *Website:* http://www.hccs.edu/.

Howard College
Big Spring, Texas

Freshman Application Contact Ms. TaNeal Richardson, Assistant Registrar, Howard College, 1001 Birdwell Lane, Big Spring, TX 79720-3702. *Phone:* 432-264-5105. *Toll-free phone:* 866-HC-HAWKS. *Fax:* 432-264-5604. *E-mail:* trichardson@howardcollege.edu. *Website:* http://www.howardcollege.edu/.

Interactive College of Technology
Houston, Texas

Admissions Office Contact Interactive College of Technology, 4473 I-45 N. Freeway, Airline Plaza, Houston, TX 77022. *Website:* http://ict.edu/.

Interactive College of Technology
Pasadena, Texas

Admissions Office Contact Interactive College of Technology, 213 W. Southmore Street, Suite 101, Pasadena, TX 77502. *Website:* http://ict.edu/.

International Business College
El Paso, Texas

Admissions Office Contact International Business College, 1155 North Zaragosa Road, El Paso, TX 79907. *Website:* http://www.ibcelpaso.edu/.

International Business College
El Paso, Texas

Admissions Office Contact International Business College, 5700 Cromo Drive, El Paso, TX 79912. *Website:* http://www.ibcelpaso.edu/.

ITT Technical Institute
Arlington, Texas

- **Proprietary** primarily 2-year, founded 1982, part of ITT Educational Services, Inc.
- **Suburban** campus
- **Coed**

Academics *Calendar:* quarters. *Degrees:* associate and bachelor's.
Freshman Application Contact Director of Recruitment, ITT Technical Institute, 551 Ryan Plaza Drive, Arlington, TX 76011. *Phone:* 817-794-5100. *Toll-free phone:* 888-288-4950. *Website:* http://www.itt-tech.edu/.

ITT Technical Institute
Austin, Texas

- **Proprietary** primarily 2-year, founded 1985, part of ITT Educational Services, Inc.
- **Urban** campus
- **Coed**

Academics *Calendar:* quarters. *Degrees:* associate and bachelor's.
Financial Aid Of all full-time matriculated undergraduates who enrolled in 2013, 1 Federal Work-Study job.
Freshman Application Contact Director of Recruitment, ITT Technical Institute, 6330 East Highway 290, Suite 150, Austin, TX 78723-1061. *Phone:* 512-467-6800. *Toll-free phone:* 800-431-0677. *Website:* http://www.itt-tech.edu/.

ITT Technical Institute
DeSoto, Texas

- **Proprietary** primarily 2-year
- **Coed**

Academics *Degrees:* associate and bachelor's.
Freshman Application Contact Director of Recruitment, ITT Technical Institute, 921 West Belt Line Road, Suite 181, DeSoto, TX 75115. *Phone:* 972-274-8600. *Toll-free phone:* 877-854-5728. *Website:* http://www.itt-tech.edu/.

ITT Technical Institute
Houston, Texas

- **Proprietary** primarily 2-year, founded 1985, part of ITT Educational Services, Inc.
- **Suburban** campus
- **Coed**

Academics *Calendar:* quarters. *Degrees:* associate and bachelor's.
Freshman Application Contact Director of Recruitment, ITT Technical Institute, 15651 North Freeway, Houston, TX 77090. *Phone:* 281-873-0512. *Toll-free phone:* 800-879-6486. *Website:* http://www.itt-tech.edu/.

ITT Technical Institute
Houston, Texas

- **Proprietary** primarily 2-year, founded 1983, part of ITT Educational Services, Inc.
- **Urban** campus
- **Coed**

Academics *Calendar:* quarters. *Degrees:* associate and bachelor's.
Freshman Application Contact Director of Recruitment, ITT Technical Institute, 2950 South Gessner, Houston, TX 77063-3751. *Phone:* 713-952-2294. *Toll-free phone:* 800-235-4787. *Website:* http://www.itt-tech.edu/.

ITT Technical Institute
Richardson, Texas

- **Proprietary** primarily 2-year, founded 1989, part of ITT Educational Services, Inc.
- **Suburban** campus
- **Coed**

Academics *Calendar:* quarters. *Degrees:* associate and bachelor's.
Financial Aid Of all full-time matriculated undergraduates who enrolled in 2013, 5 Federal Work-Study jobs (averaging $5000).
Freshman Application Contact Director of Recruitment, ITT Technical Institute, 2101 Waterview Parkway, Richardson, TX 75080. *Phone:* 972-690-9100. *Toll-free phone:* 888-488-5761. *Website:* http://www.itt-tech.edu/.

ITT Technical Institute
San Antonio, Texas

- **Proprietary** primarily 2-year
- **Coed**

Academics *Degrees:* associate and bachelor's.
Freshman Application Contact Director of Recruiting, ITT Technical Institute, 2895 NE Loop 410, San Antonio, TX 78218. *Phone:* 210-651-8500. *Toll-free phone:* 877-400-8894. *Website:* http://www.itt-tech.edu/.

ITT Technical Institute
San Antonio, Texas

- **Proprietary** primarily 2-year, founded 1988, part of ITT Educational Services, Inc.
- **Urban** campus
- **Coed**

Academics *Calendar:* quarters. *Degrees:* associate and bachelor's.
Freshman Application Contact Director of Recruitment, ITT Technical Institute, 5700 Northwest Parkway, San Antonio, TX 78249-3303. *Phone:* 210-694-4612. *Toll-free phone:* 800-880-0570. *Website:* http://www.itt-tech.edu/.

ITT Technical Institute
Waco, Texas

- **Proprietary** primarily 2-year, part of ITT Educational Services, Inc.
- **Coed**

Academics *Calendar:* quarters. *Degrees:* associate and bachelor's.
Freshman Application Contact Director of Recruitment, ITT Technical Institute, 3700 S. Jack Kultgen Expressway, Suite 100, Waco, TX 76706. *Phone:* 254-523-3940. *Toll-free phone:* 877-201-7143. *Website:* http://www.itt-tech.edu/.

ITT Technical Institute
Webster, Texas

- **Proprietary** primarily 2-year, founded 1995, part of ITT Educational Services, Inc.
- **Coed**

Academics *Calendar:* quarters. *Degrees:* associate and bachelor's.
Freshman Application Contact Director of Recruitment, ITT Technical Institute, 1001 Magnolia Avenue, Webster, TX 77598. *Phone:* 281-316-4700. *Toll-free phone:* 888-488-9347. *Website:* http://www.itt-tech.edu/.

Jacksonville College
Jacksonville, Texas

Freshman Application Contact Danny Morris, Director of Admissions, Jacksonville College, 105 B.J. Albritton Drive, Jacksonville, TX 75766. *Phone:* 903-589-7110. *Toll-free phone:* 800-256-8522. *E-mail:* admissions@jacksonville-college.org. *Website:* http://www.jacksonville-college.edu/.

Kaplan College, Arlington Campus
Arlington, Texas

Freshman Application Contact Kaplan College, Arlington Campus, 2241 South Watson Road, Arlington, TX 76010. *Phone:* 866-249-2074. *Toll-free phone:* 800-935-1857. *Website:* http://www.kaplancollege.com/.

Kaplan College, Beaumont Campus
Beaumont, Texas

Freshman Application Contact Admissions Office, Kaplan College, Beaumont Campus, 6115 Eastex Freeway, Beaumont, TX 77706. *Phone:* 409-833-2722. *Toll-free phone:* 800-935-1857. *Website:* http://www.kaplancollege.com/.

Kaplan College, Brownsville Campus
Brownsville, Texas

Freshman Application Contact Director of Admissions, Kaplan College, Brownsville Campus, 1900 North Expressway, Suite O, Brownsville, TX 78521. *Phone:* 956-547-8200. *Website:* http://www.kaplancollege.com/.

Kaplan College, Corpus Christi Campus
Corpus Christi, Texas

Freshman Application Contact Admissions Director, Kaplan College, Corpus Christi Campus, 1620 South Padre Island Drive, Suite 600, Corpus Christi, TX 78416. *Phone:* 361-852-2900. *Website:* http://www.kaplancollege.com/.

Kaplan College, Dallas Campus
Dallas, Texas

Freshman Application Contact Kaplan College, Dallas Campus, 12005 Ford Road, Suite 100, Dallas, TX 75234. *Phone:* 972-385-1446. *Toll-free phone:* 800-935-1857. *Website:* http://www.kaplancollege.com/.

Kaplan College, El Paso Campus
El Paso, Texas

Freshman Application Contact Director of Admissions, Kaplan College, El Paso Campus, 8360 Burnham Road, Suite 100, El Paso, TX 79907. *Website:* http://www.kaplancollege.com/.

Kaplan College, Fort Worth Campus
Fort Worth, Texas

Freshman Application Contact Director of Admissions, Kaplan College, Fort Worth Campus, 2001 Beach Street, Suite 201, Fort Worth, TX 76103. *Phone:* 817-413-2000. *Website:* http://www.kaplancollege.com/.

Kaplan College, Laredo Campus
Laredo, Texas

Freshman Application Contact Admissions Office, Kaplan College, Laredo Campus, 6410 McPherson Road, Laredo, TX 78041. *Phone:* 956-717-5909. *Toll-free phone:* 800-935-1857. *Website:* http://www.kaplancollege.com/.

Kaplan College, Lubbock Campus
Lubbock, Texas

Freshman Application Contact Admissions Office, Kaplan College, Lubbock Campus, 1421 Ninth Street, Lubbock, TX 79401. *Phone:* 806-765-7051. *Toll-free phone:* 800-935-1857. *Website:* http://www.kaplancollege.com/.

Kaplan College, McAllen Campus
McAllen, Texas

Admissions Office Contact Kaplan College, McAllen Campus, 1500 South Jackson Road, McAllen, TX 78503. *Toll-free phone:* 800-935-1857. *Website:* http://www.kaplancollege.com/.

Kaplan College, San Antonio Campus
San Antonio, Texas

Freshman Application Contact Admissions Office, Kaplan College, San Antonio Campus, 6441 NW Loop 410, San Antonio, TX 78238. *Phone:* 210-308-8584. *Toll-free phone:* 800-935-1857. *Website:* http://www.kaplancollege.com/.

Kaplan College, San Antonio–San Pedro Area Campus
San Antonio, Texas

Freshman Application Contact Director of Admissions, Kaplan College, San Antonio–San Pedro Area Campus, 7142 San Pedro Avenue, Suite 100, San Antonio, TX 78216. *Toll-free phone:* 800-935-1857. *Website:* http://www.kaplancollege.com/.

KD College Conservatory of Film and Dramatic Arts
Dallas, Texas

- **Proprietary** 2-year, founded 1979
- **Urban** campus
- **Coed,** 236 undergraduate students, 100% full-time, 46% women, 54% men

Undergraduates 236 full-time. Students come from 11 states and territories; 1 other country; 5% are from out of state; 31% Black or African American, non-Hispanic/Latino; 19% Hispanic/Latino; 2% Asian, non-Hispanic/Latino; 0.4% American Indian or Alaska Native, non-Hispanic/Latino; 0.8% Two or more races, non-Hispanic/Latino; 12% Race/ethnicity unknown; 1% international. *Retention:* 69% of full-time freshmen returned.
Freshmen *Admission:* 70 applied, 24 admitted, 24 enrolled.
Faculty *Total:* 28, 100% full-time, 4% with terminal degrees. *Student/faculty ratio:* 12:1.
Majors Acting; film/cinema/video studies; musical theater.
Academics *Calendar:* semesters. *Degree:* associate.
Library KD Studio Library with 800 titles.

Student Life *Housing:* college housing not available. *Activities and Organizations:* drama/theater group, Student Council. *Campus security:* 24-hour emergency response devices and patrols.
Costs (2015–16) *Tuition:* $14,025 full-time. No tuition increase for student's term of enrollment. *Required fees:* $550 full-time. *Payment plans:* tuition prepayment, installment.
Applying *Options:* electronic application, deferred entrance. *Required:* essay or personal statement, high school transcript, interview, AUDITION AND/OR INTERVIEW WITH PROGRAM CHAIR AND DIRECTOR OF SCHOOL. *Application deadlines:* rolling (freshmen), rolling (transfers).
Freshman Application Contact Mr. T. A. Taylor, Director of Education, KD College Conservatory of Film and Dramatic Arts, 2600 Stemmons Freeway, Suite 117, Dallas, TX 75207. *Phone:* 214-638-0484. *Toll-free phone:* 877-278-2283. *Fax:* 214-630-5140. *E-mail:* tataylor@kdstudio.com. *Website:* http://www.kdstudio.com/.

Kilgore College
Kilgore, Texas

- **State and locally supported** 2-year, founded 1935
- **Small-town** 35-acre campus with easy access to Dallas-Fort Worth
- **Coed,** 5,768 undergraduate students, 45% full-time, 60% women, 40% men

Undergraduates 2,586 full-time, 3,182 part-time. Students come from 22 states and territories; 26 other countries; 0.4% are from out of state; 21% Black or African American, non-Hispanic/Latino; 15% Hispanic/Latino; 0.9% Asian, non-Hispanic/Latino; 0.1% Native Hawaiian or other Pacific Islander, non-Hispanic/Latino; 0.6% American Indian or Alaska Native, non-Hispanic/Latino; 3% Two or more races, non-Hispanic/Latino; 0.9% Race/ethnicity unknown; 0.7% international; 6% transferred in; 7% live on campus. *Retention:* 59% of full-time freshmen returned.
Freshmen *Admission:* 1,127 enrolled.
Faculty *Total:* 277, 62% full-time, 8% with terminal degrees. *Student/faculty ratio:* 18:1.
Majors Accounting technology and bookkeeping; aerospace, aeronautical and astronautical/space engineering; agriculture; architecture; art; autobody/collision and repair technology; automobile/automotive mechanics technology; biological and physical sciences; business administration and management; business/commerce; chemical engineering; chemistry; child-care and support services management; child-care provision; civil engineering; commercial and advertising art; commercial photography; computer and information sciences; computer programming; computer systems networking and telecommunications; criminal justice/law enforcement administration; dance; diesel mechanics technology; drafting and design technology; dramatic/theater arts; electrical, electronic and communications engineering technology; elementary education; emergency medical technology (EMT paramedic); English; executive assistant/executive secretary; forestry; general studies; geology/earth science; health teacher education; heating, air conditioning, ventilation and refrigeration maintenance technology; journalism; legal assistant/paralegal; management information systems; mathematics; mechanical engineering; medical radiologic technology; metallurgical technology; music; occupational safety and health technology; operations management; petroleum engineering; physical education teaching and coaching; physical therapy; physical therapy technology; physics; pre-dentistry studies; pre-law studies; premedical studies; pre-pharmacy studies; pre-veterinary studies; psychology; radiologic technology/science; registered nursing/registered nurse; religious studies; social sciences; surgical technology; welding technology.
Academics *Calendar:* semesters. *Degree:* certificates and associate. *Special study options:* academic remediation for entering students, adult/continuing education programs, advanced placement credit, cooperative education, distance learning, English as a second language, internships, part-time degree program, services for LD students, student-designed majors, summer session for credit.
Library Randolph C. Watson Library plus 1 other with 56,139 titles, 13,351 audiovisual materials, an OPAC, a Web page.
Student Life *Housing Options:* coed, men-only, women-only. Campus housing is university owned. *Activities and Organizations:* drama/theater group, student-run newspaper, choral group, marching band. *Campus security:* 24-hour emergency response devices and patrols. *Student services:* personal/psychological counseling.
Athletics Member NJCAA. *Intercollegiate sports:* basketball M(s)/W(s), cheerleading M(s)/W(s), football M(s), softball W. *Intramural sports:* basketball M/W, football M/W, racquetball M/W, tennis M/W, volleyball M/W.
Costs (2014–15) *Tuition:* area resident $720 full-time, $30 per semester hour part-time; state resident $2376 full-time, $99 per semester hour part-time; nonresident $3576 full-time, $149 per semester hour part-time. *Required fees:* $672 full-time. *Room and board:* $4370. Room and board charges vary according to board plan and housing facility. *Payment plan:* installment. *Waivers:* senior citizens and employees or children of employees.

Financial Aid Of all full-time matriculated undergraduates who enrolled in 2013, 80 Federal Work-Study jobs (averaging $2500). *Financial aid deadline:* 6/1.

Applying *Options:* electronic application, early admission. *Required:* high school transcript. *Required for some:* interview. *Application deadlines:* rolling (freshmen), rolling (out-of-state freshmen), rolling (transfers).

Freshman Application Contact Kilgore College, 1100 Broadway Boulevard, Kilgore, TX 75662-3299. *Phone:* 903-983-8200. *E-mail:* register@kilgore.cc.tx.us.

Website: http://www.kilgore.edu/.

Lamar Institute of Technology

Beaumont, Texas

Freshman Application Contact Admissions Office, Lamar Institute of Technology, 855 East Lavaca, Beaumont, TX 77705. *Phone:* 409-880-8354.

Toll-free phone: 800-950-6989.

Website: http://www.lit.edu/.

Lamar State College–Orange

Orange, Texas

- **State-supported** 2-year, founded 1969, part of Texas State University System
- **Small-town** 21-acre campus
- **Coed**

Undergraduates 992 full-time, 1,434 part-time. 16% Black or African American, non-Hispanic/Latino; 6% Hispanic/Latino; 2% Asian, non-Hispanic/Latino; 0.5% American Indian or Alaska Native, non-Hispanic/Latino. *Retention:* 47% of full-time freshmen returned.

Faculty *Student/faculty ratio:* 19:1.

Academics *Calendar:* semesters. *Degree:* certificates and associate. *Special study options:* academic remediation for entering students, distance learning, double majors, internships, part-time degree program, summer session for credit.

Student Life *Campus security:* 24-hour emergency response devices, late-night transport/escort service.

Financial Aid Of all full-time matriculated undergraduates who enrolled in 2013, 20 Federal Work-Study jobs (averaging $3000). 2 state and other part-time jobs (averaging $2000).

Applying *Required:* high school transcript.

Freshman Application Contact Kerry Olson, Director of Admissions and Financial Aid, Lamar State College–Orange, 410 Front Street, Orange, TX 77632. *Phone:* 409-882-3362. *Fax:* 409-882-3374.

Website: http://www.lsco.edu/.

Lamar State College–Port Arthur

Port Arthur, Texas

Freshman Application Contact Ms. Connie Nicholas, Registrar, Lamar State College–Port Arthur, PO Box 310, Port Arthur, TX 77641-0310. *Phone:* 409-984-6165. *Toll-free phone:* 800-477-5872. *Fax:* 409-984-6025. *E-mail:* nichoca@lamarpa.edu.

Website: http://www.lamarpa.edu/.

Laredo Community College

Laredo, Texas

Freshman Application Contact Ms. Josie Soliz, Admissions Records Supervisor, Laredo Community College, Laredo, TX 78040-4395. *Phone:* 956-721-5177. *Fax:* 956-721-5493.

Website: http://www.laredo.edu/.

Le Cordon Bleu College of Culinary Arts in Austin

Austin, Texas

Director of Admissions Paula Paulette, Vice President of Marketing and Admissions, Le Cordon Bleu College of Culinary Arts in Austin, 3110 Esperanza Crossing, Suite 100, Austin, TX 78758. *Phone:* 512-837-2665. *Toll-free phone:* 888-559-7222. *E-mail:* ppaulette@txca.com.

Website: http://www.chefs.edu/Austin/.

Le Cordon Bleu College of Culinary Arts in Dallas

Dallas, Texas

Admissions Office Contact Le Cordon Bleu College of Culinary Arts in Dallas, 11830 Webb Chapel Road, Dallas, TX 75234.

Website: http://www.chefs.edu/Dallas/.

Lee College

Baytown, Texas

Director of Admissions Ms. Becki Griffith, Registrar, Lee College, PO Box 818, Baytown, TX 77522-0818. *Phone:* 281-425-6399. *E-mail:* bgriffit@lee.edu.

Website: http://www.lee.edu/.

Lincoln College of Technology

Grand Prairie, Texas

Admissions Office Contact Lincoln College of Technology, 2915 Alouette Drive, Grand Prairie, TX 75052.

Website: http://www.lincolnedu.com/.

Lone Star College–CyFair

Cypress, Texas

- **State and locally supported** 2-year, founded 2002, part of Lone Star College
- **Suburban** campus with easy access to Houston
- **Coed,** 20,384 undergraduate students, 30% full-time, 57% women, 43% men

Undergraduates 6,170 full-time, 14,214 part-time. Students come from 67 other countries; 15% Black or African American, non-Hispanic/Latino; 41% Hispanic/Latino; 10% Asian, non-Hispanic/Latino; 0.2% American Indian or Alaska Native, non-Hispanic/Latino; 3% Two or more races, non-Hispanic/Latino; 3% Race/ethnicity unknown; 20% transferred in.

Freshmen *Admission:* 3,320 applied, 3,320 admitted, 3,320 enrolled.

Faculty *Total:* 1,045, 21% full-time, 17% with terminal degrees. *Student/faculty ratio:* 22:1.

Majors Accounting; accounting and computer science; animation, interactive technology, video graphics and special effects; business administration and management; computer and information sciences; computer science; criminal justice/law enforcement administration; dance; design and visual communications; diagnostic medical sonography and ultrasound technology; economics; education; electrical, electronic and communications engineering technology; emergency medical technology (EMT paramedic); fire science/firefighting; geographic information science and cartography; health information/medical records technology; industrial technology; information technology; liberal arts and sciences/liberal studies; logistics, materials, and supply chain management; marketing/marketing management; medical radiologic technology; music; office occupations and clerical services; radiation protection/health physics technology; registered nursing/registered nurse; sign language interpretation and translation; speech communication and rhetoric; welding technology.

Academics *Calendar:* semesters. *Degree:* certificates, diplomas, and associate. *Special study options:* academic remediation for entering students, accelerated degree program, adult/continuing education programs, advanced placement credit, cooperative education, distance learning, double majors, English as a second language, honors programs, independent study, internships, part-time degree program, services for LD students, study abroad, summer session for credit.

Library LSC-CyFair Library with an OPAC, a Web page.

Student Life *Housing:* college housing not available. *Activities and Organizations:* drama/theater group, choral group. *Campus security:* 24-hour emergency response devices and patrols, late-night transport/escort service. *Student services:* personal/psychological counseling.

Costs (2015–16) *Tuition:* area resident $1008 full-time, $42 per credit hour part-time; state resident $2688 full-time, $112 per credit hour part-time; nonresident $3048 full-time, $127 per credit hour part-time. Full-time tuition and fees vary according to program. Part-time tuition and fees vary according to program. *Required fees:* $496 full-time, $18 per credit hour part-time, $32 per credit hour part-time. *Payment plan:* installment.

Applying *Options:* electronic application, early admission.

Freshman Application Contact Admissions Office, Lone Star College–CyFair, 9191 Barker Cypress Road, Cypress, TX 77433-1383. *Phone:* 281-290-3200. *E-mail:* cfc.info@lonestar.edu.

Website: http://www.lonestar.edu/cyfair.

Lone Star College–Kingwood
Kingwood, Texas

- **State and locally supported** 2-year, founded 1984, part of Lone Star College
- **Suburban** 264-acre campus with easy access to Houston
- **Coed,** 12,837 undergraduate students, 32% full-time, 63% women, 37% men

Undergraduates 4,087 full-time, 8,750 part-time. Students come from 49 other countries; 17% Black or African American, non-Hispanic/Latino; 30% Hispanic/Latino; 4% Asian, non-Hispanic/Latino; 0.3% American Indian or Alaska Native, non-Hispanic/Latino; 3% Two or more races, non-Hispanic/Latino; 3% Race/ethnicity unknown; 21% transferred in.
Freshmen *Admission:* 1,687 applied, 1,687 admitted, 1,687 enrolled.
Faculty *Total:* 781, 18% full-time, 12% with terminal degrees. *Student/faculty ratio:* 20:1.
Majors Administrative assistant and secretarial science; business administration and management; computer and information sciences; computer science; cosmetology; criminal justice/law enforcement administration; dental hygiene; design and visual communications; education; electroneurodiagnostic/electroencephalographic technology; fire science/firefighting; interior design; marketing/marketing management; music; occupational therapy; registered nursing/registered nurse; respiratory care therapy.
Academics *Calendar:* semesters. *Degree:* certificates and associate. *Special study options:* academic remediation for entering students, accelerated degree program, adult/continuing education programs, advanced placement credit, cooperative education, distance learning, double majors, English as a second language, honors programs, independent study, internships, part-time degree program, services for LD students, study abroad, summer session for credit.
Library LSC-Kingwood Library with an OPAC, a Web page.
Student Life *Housing:* college housing not available. *Activities and Organizations:* drama/theater group, student-run television station, choral group. *Campus security:* 24-hour emergency response devices and patrols, late-night transport/escort service. *Student services:* personal/psychological counseling.
Athletics *Intramural sports:* baseball M.
Costs (2015–16) *Tuition:* area resident $1008 full-time, $42 per credit hour part-time; state resident $2688 full-time, $112 per credit hour part-time; nonresident $3048 full-time, $127 per credit hour part-time. Full-time tuition and fees vary according to program. Part-time tuition and fees vary according to program. *Required fees:* $496 full-time, $18 per credit hour part-time, $32 per term part-time. *Payment plan:* installment.
Financial Aid Of all full-time matriculated undergraduates who enrolled in 2009, 28 Federal Work-Study jobs, 6 state and other part-time jobs. *Financial aid deadline:* 4/1.
Applying *Options:* electronic application, early admission. *Application deadlines:* rolling (freshmen), rolling (transfers).
Freshman Application Contact Admissions Office, Lone Star College–Kingwood, 20000 Kingwood Drive, Kingwood, TX 77339. *Phone:* 281-312-1525. *Fax:* 281-312-1477. *E-mail:* kingwoodadvising@lonestar.edu.
Website: http://www.lonestar.edu/kingwood.htm.

Lone Star College–Montgomery
Conroe, Texas

- **State and locally supported** 2-year, founded 1995, part of Lone Star College
- **Suburban** campus with easy access to Houston
- **Coed,** 13,254 undergraduate students, 33% full-time, 61% women, 39% men

Undergraduates 4,334 full-time, 8,920 part-time. Students come from 54 other countries; 11% Black or African American, non-Hispanic/Latino; 27% Hispanic/Latino; 4% Asian, non-Hispanic/Latino; 0.4% American Indian or Alaska Native, non-Hispanic/Latino; 3% Two or more races, non-Hispanic/Latino; 2% Race/ethnicity unknown; 20% transferred in.
Freshmen *Admission:* 1,954 applied, 1,954 admitted, 1,954 enrolled.
Faculty *Total:* 682, 24% full-time, 15% with terminal degrees. *Student/faculty ratio:* 22:1.
Majors Accounting and business/management; automobile/automotive mechanics technology; biology/biotechnology laboratory technician; business administration and management; computer science; criminal justice/law enforcement administration; education; emergency medical technology (EMT paramedic); fire science/firefighting; human services; information technology; music; physical therapy technology; registered nursing/registered nurse.
Academics *Calendar:* semesters. *Degree:* certificates and associate. *Special study options:* academic remediation for entering students, adult/continuing education programs, advanced placement credit, cooperative education, distance learning, double majors, English as a second language, honors

programs, independent study, internships, part-time degree program, services for LD students, study abroad, summer session for credit.
Library LSC-Montgomery Library with an OPAC, a Web page.
Student Life *Housing:* college housing not available. *Activities and Organizations:* drama/theater group, student-run newspaper, choral group, Campus Crusade for Christ, Criminal Justice Club, Phi Theta Kappa, Latino-American Student Association, African-American Cultural Awareness. *Campus security:* 24-hour emergency response devices and patrols, late-night transport/escort service. *Student services:* personal/psychological counseling.
Costs (2015–16) *Tuition:* area resident $1008 full-time, $42 per credit hour part-time; state resident $2688 full-time, $112 per credit hour part-time; nonresident $3048 full-time, $127 per credit hour part-time. Full-time tuition and fees vary according to program. Part-time tuition and fees vary according to program. *Required fees:* $496 full-time, $18 per credit hour part-time, $32 per term part-time. *Payment plan:* installment.
Financial Aid Of all full-time matriculated undergraduates who enrolled in 2013, 25 Federal Work-Study jobs (averaging $2500). 4 state and other part-time jobs.
Applying *Options:* electronic application, early admission. *Application deadlines:* rolling (freshmen), rolling (transfers).
Freshman Application Contact Lone Star College–Montgomery, 3200 College Park Drive, Conroe, TX 77384. *Phone:* 281-290-2721.
Website: http://www.lonestar.edu/montgomery.

Lone Star College–North Harris
Houston, Texas

- **State and locally supported** 2-year, founded 1972, part of Lone Star College
- **Suburban** campus with easy access to Houston
- **Coed,** 17,721 undergraduate students, 30% full-time, 61% women, 39% men

Undergraduates 5,239 full-time, 12,482 part-time. Students come from 51 other countries; 33% Black or African American, non-Hispanic/Latino; 39% Hispanic/Latino; 5% Asian, non-Hispanic/Latino; 0.1% American Indian or Alaska Native, non-Hispanic/Latino; 3% Two or more races, non-Hispanic/Latino; 4% Race/ethnicity unknown; 20% transferred in.
Freshmen *Admission:* 2,965 applied, 2,965 admitted, 2,965 enrolled.
Faculty *Total:* 1,045, 21% full-time, 12% with terminal degrees. *Student/faculty ratio:* 19:1.
Majors Accounting; automobile/automotive mechanics technology; business administration and management; computer science; cosmetology; criminal justice/law enforcement administration; design and visual communications; drafting and design technology; education; educational/instructional technology; electrical, electronic and communications engineering technology; emergency medical technology (EMT paramedic); health information/medical records technology; heating, air conditioning, ventilation and refrigeration maintenance technology; industrial technology; legal assistant/paralegal; mechanical engineering; music; pharmacy technician; registered nursing/registered nurse; sign language interpretation and translation; welding technology.
Academics *Calendar:* semesters. *Degree:* certificates and associate. *Special study options:* academic remediation for entering students, adult/continuing education programs, advanced placement credit, cooperative education, distance learning, double majors, English as a second language, honors programs, independent study, internships, part-time degree program, services for LD students, study abroad, summer session for credit.
Library LSC-North Harris Library with an OPAC, a Web page.
Student Life *Activities and Organizations:* drama/theater group, student-run newspaper, choral group, Student Government Association, Phi Theta Kappa, Ambassadors, honors student organizations, Soccer Club. *Campus security:* 24-hour emergency response devices and patrols, late-night transport/escort service. *Student services:* personal/psychological counseling, women's center.
Athletics *Intramural sports:* badminton M/W, baseball M/W, basketball M/W, bowling M/W, football M/W, golf M/W, gymnastics M/W, racquetball M/W, soccer M/W, softball M/W, table tennis M/W, tennis M/W, track and field M/W, volleyball M/W, weight lifting M/W.
Costs (2015–16) *Tuition:* area resident $1008 full-time, $42 per credit hour part-time; state resident $2688 full-time, $112 per credit hour part-time; nonresident $3048 full-time, $127 per credit hour part-time. Full-time tuition and fees vary according to program. Part-time tuition and fees vary according to program. *Required fees:* $496 full-time, $18 per credit hour part-time, $32 per term part-time. *Payment plan:* installment.
Applying *Options:* electronic application, early admission. *Application deadlines:* rolling (freshmen), rolling (transfers).
Freshman Application Contact Admissions Office, Lone Star College–North Harris, 2700 W. W. Thorne Drive, Houston, TX 77073-3499. *Phone:* 281-618-5410. *E-mail:* nhcounselor@lonestar.edu.
Website: http://www.lonestar.edu/northharris.

Lone Star College–Tomball
Tomball, Texas

- **State and locally supported** 2-year, founded 1988, part of Lone Star College
- **Suburban** campus with easy access to Houston
- **Coed,** 9,361 undergraduate students, 31% full-time, 63% women, 37% men

Undergraduates 2,924 full-time, 6,437 part-time. Students come from 42 other countries; 15% Black or African American, non-Hispanic/Latino; 25% Hispanic/Latino; 5% Asian, non-Hispanic/Latino; 0.3% American Indian or Alaska Native, non-Hispanic/Latino; 3% Two or more races, non-Hispanic/Latino; 3% Race/ethnicity unknown; 21% transferred in.

Freshmen *Admission:* 1,306 applied, 1,306 admitted, 1,306 enrolled.

Faculty *Total:* 378, 29% full-time, 12% with terminal degrees. *Student/faculty ratio:* 26:1.

Majors Accounting; administrative assistant and secretarial science; animation, interactive technology, video graphics and special effects; business administration and management; computer programming; computer science; criminal justice/law enforcement administration; education; electrical, electronic and communications engineering technology; industrial technology; music; registered nursing/registered nurse; surgical technology; system, networking, and LAN/WAN management; veterinary/animal health technology.

Academics *Calendar:* semesters. *Degree:* certificates and associate. *Special study options:* academic remediation for entering students, adult/continuing education programs, advanced placement credit, cooperative education, distance learning, double majors, English as a second language, honors programs, independent study, internships, part-time degree program, services for LD students, study abroad, summer session for credit.

Library LSC-Tomball Community Library with an OPAC, a Web page.

Student Life *Housing:* college housing not available. *Activities and Organizations:* drama/theater group, student-run newspaper, choral group, Phi Theta Kappa, Occupational Therapy OTA, Veterinary Technicians Student Organization, STARS, Student Nurses Association. *Campus security:* 24-hour emergency response devices and patrols, late-night transport/escort service, trained security personnel during open hours. *Student services:* personal/psychological counseling.

Costs (2015–16) *Tuition:* area resident $1008 full-time, $42 per credit hour part-time; state resident $2688 full-time, $112 per credit hour part-time; nonresident $3048 full-time, $127 per credit hour part-time. Full-time tuition and fees vary according to program. Part-time tuition and fees vary according to program. *Required fees:* $496 full-time, $18 per credit hour part-time, $32 per term part-time. *Payment plan:* installment.

Financial Aid Of all full-time matriculated undergraduates who enrolled in 2013, 34 Federal Work-Study jobs (averaging $3000).

Applying *Options:* electronic application, early admission. *Application deadlines:* rolling (freshmen), rolling (transfers).

Freshman Application Contact Admissions Office, Lone Star College–Tomball, 30555 Tomball Parkway, Tomball, TX 77375-4036. *Phone:* 281-351-3310. *E-mail:* tcinfo@lonestar.edu.

Website: http://www.lonestar.edu/tomball.

Lone Star College–University Park
Houston, Texas

- **State and locally supported** 2-year, founded 2010, part of Lone Star College
- **Suburban** campus with easy access to Houston
- **Coed,** 9,261 undergraduate students, 30% full-time, 57% women, 43% men

Undergraduates 2,813 full-time, 6,448 part-time. Students come from 55 other countries; 16% Black or African American, non-Hispanic/Latino; 35% Hispanic/Latino; 11% Asian, non-Hispanic/Latino; 0.2% American Indian or Alaska Native, non-Hispanic/Latino; 3% Two or more races, non-Hispanic/Latino; 5% Race/ethnicity unknown; 18% transferred in.

Freshmen *Admission:* 1,521 enrolled.

Faculty *Total:* 385, 15% full-time, 10% with terminal degrees. *Student/faculty ratio:* 30:1.

Majors Accounting; business administration and management; criminal justice/law enforcement administration; speech communication and rhetoric.

Academics *Degree:* certificates and associate. *Special study options:* academic remediation for entering students, advanced placement credit, cooperative education, distance learning, English as a second language, honors programs, independent study, internships, off-campus study, part-time degree program, services for LD students, study abroad, summer session for credit.

Student Life *Housing:* college housing not available. *Campus security:* 24-hour emergency response devices and patrols, late-night transport/escort service.

Costs (2014–15) *Tuition:* area resident $1008 full-time, $42 per credit hour part-time; state resident $2688 full-time, $112 per credit hour part-time; nonresident $3048 full-time, $127 per credit hour part-time. Full-time tuition and fees vary according to program. Part-time tuition and fees vary according to program. *Required fees:* $496 full-time, $18 per credit hour part-time, $32 per term part-time. *Payment plan:* installment. *Waivers:* senior citizens.

Applying *Recommended:* high school transcript.

Freshman Application Contact Lone Star College–University Park, 20515 SH 249, Houston, TX 77070-2607. *Phone:* 281-290-2721.

Website: http://www.lonestar.edu/universitypark.

McLennan Community College
Waco, Texas

Freshman Application Contact Dr. Vivian G. Jefferson, Director, Admissions and Recruitment, McLennan Community College, 1400 College Drive, Waco, TX 76708. *Phone:* 254-299-8689. *Fax:* 254-299-8694. *E-mail:* vjefferson@mclennan.edu.

Website: http://www.mclennan.edu/.

Mountain View College
Dallas, Texas

- **State and locally supported** 2-year, founded 1970, part of Dallas County Community College District System
- **Urban** 200-acre campus
- **Coed**

Undergraduates 2,066 full-time, 7,002 part-time. Students come from 12 states and territories; 26% Black or African American, non-Hispanic/Latino; 53% Hispanic/Latino; 4% Asian, non-Hispanic/Latino; 0.3% American Indian or Alaska Native, non-Hispanic/Latino; 0.5% Two or more races, non-Hispanic/Latino; 3% Race/ethnicity unknown; 0.3% international; 18% transferred in. *Retention:* 57% of full-time freshmen returned.

Faculty *Student/faculty ratio:* 28:1.

Academics *Calendar:* semesters. *Degree:* certificates and associate. *Special study options:* academic remediation for entering students, adult/continuing education programs, advanced placement credit, cooperative education, distance learning, double majors, English as a second language, external degree program, freshman honors college, honors programs, independent study, internships, part-time degree program, services for LD students, summer session for credit.

Student Life *Campus security:* 24-hour patrols, late-night transport/escort service.

Athletics Member NJCAA.

Costs (2014–15) *Tuition:* area resident $1770 full-time, $59 per credit hour part-time; state resident $3330 full-time, $111 per credit hour part-time; nonresident $5220 full-time, $174 per credit hour part-time.

Financial Aid Of all full-time matriculated undergraduates who enrolled in 2013, 145 Federal Work-Study jobs (averaging $2700).

Applying *Options:* electronic application, early admission, deferred entrance. *Required:* high school transcript.

Freshman Application Contact Ms. Glenda Hall, Director of Admissions, Mountain View College, 4849 West Illinois Avenue, Dallas, TX 75211-6599. *Phone:* 214-860-8666. *Fax:* 214-860-8570. *E-mail:* ghall@dcccd.edu.

Website: http://www.mountainviewcollege.edu/.

Navarro College
Corsicana, Texas

- **State and locally supported** 2-year, founded 1946
- **Small-town** 275-acre campus with easy access to Dallas-Fort Worth
- **Coed,** 9,999 undergraduate students, 39% full-time, 59% women, 41% men

Undergraduates 3,944 full-time, 6,055 part-time. Students come from 34 other countries; 1% are from out of state; 21% Black or African American, non-Hispanic/Latino; 18% Hispanic/Latino; 0.7% Asian, non-Hispanic/Latino; 0.2% Native Hawaiian or other Pacific Islander, non-Hispanic/Latino; 0.6% American Indian or Alaska Native, non-Hispanic/Latino; 1% Two or more races, non-Hispanic/Latino; 1% international; 25% live on campus.

Freshmen *Admission:* 1,865 enrolled.

Faculty *Total:* 542, 23% full-time, 7% with terminal degrees.

Majors Accounting; administrative assistant and secretarial science; agricultural mechanization; airline pilot and flight crew; art; avionics maintenance technology; biological and physical sciences; biology/biological sciences; broadcast journalism; business administration and management; chemistry; clinical/medical laboratory technology; commercial and advertising art; computer graphics; computer programming; computer science; consumer merchandising/retailing management; corrections; criminal justice/law enforcement administration; criminal justice/police science; dance; data

processing and data processing technology; dental hygiene; developmental and child psychology; drafting and design technology; dramatic/theater arts; education; elementary education; engineering; English; fire science/firefighting; industrial and product design; industrial technology; journalism; legal administrative assistant/secretary; legal assistant/paralegal; legal studies; licensed practical/vocational nurse training; marketing/marketing management; mathematics; music; occupational therapy; pharmacy; physical education teaching and coaching; physical sciences; physics; pre-engineering; psychology; radio and television; real estate; registered nursing/registered nurse; rhetoric and composition; social sciences; sociology; voice and opera.
Academics *Calendar:* semesters. *Degree:* certificates, diplomas, and associate. *Special study options:* academic remediation for entering students, adult/continuing education programs, advanced placement credit, cooperative education, distance learning, freshman honors college, honors programs, part-time degree program, services for LD students, student-designed majors, summer session for credit.
Library Richard M. Sanchez Library with 40,000 titles.
Student Life *Housing Options:* Campus housing is university owned. *Activities and Organizations:* drama/theater group, student-run television station, choral group, marching band, Student Government Association, Phi Theta Kappa, Ebony Club, Que Pasa. *Campus security:* 24-hour patrols. *Student services:* personal/psychological counseling.
Athletics Member NJCAA. *Intercollegiate sports:* baseball M(s), basketball M(s), football M(s), soccer W, softball W, volleyball W(s). *Intramural sports:* basketball M/W, bowling M/W, football M, soccer M, softball M/W, volleyball M/W.
Costs (2015–16) *Tuition:* area resident $1110 full-time, $111 per credit hour part-time; state resident $1260 full-time, $126 per credit hour part-time; nonresident $2700 full-time, $270 per credit hour part-time. Full-time tuition and fees vary according to course load. Part-time tuition and fees vary according to course load. *Required fees:* $98 per credit hour part-time. *Room and board:* $64,790. Room and board charges vary according to board plan. *Payment plan:* installment. *Waivers:* employees or children of employees.
Applying *Options:* electronic application, early admission. *Required:* high school transcript.
Freshman Application Contact David Edwards, Registrar, Navarro College, 3200 West 7th Avenue, Corsicana, TX 75110-4899. *Phone:* 903-875-7348. *Toll-free phone:* 800-NAVARRO (in-state); 800-628-2776 (out-of-state). *Fax:* 903-875-7353. *E-mail:* david.edwards@navarrocollege.edu.
Website: http://www.navarrocollege.edu/.

North Central Texas College
Gainesville, Texas

- **State and locally supported** 2-year, founded 1924
- **Suburban** 132-acre campus with easy access to Dallas-Fort Worth
- **Endowment** $4.3 million
- **Coed,** 10,169 undergraduate students, 35% full-time, 58% women, 42% men

Undergraduates 3,520 full-time, 6,649 part-time. Students come from 32 states and territories; 34 other countries; 1% are from out of state; 9% Black or African American, non-Hispanic/Latino; 20% Hispanic/Latino; 2% Asian, non-Hispanic/Latino; 0.2% Native Hawaiian or other Pacific Islander, non-Hispanic/Latino; 0.6% American Indian or Alaska Native, non-Hispanic/Latino; 3% Two or more races, non-Hispanic/Latino; 0.4% Race/ethnicity unknown; 1% international; 13% transferred in; 1% live on campus. *Retention:* 42% of full-time freshmen returned.
Freshmen *Admission:* 2,686 applied, 2,686 admitted, 2,686 enrolled.
Faculty *Total:* 421, 33% full-time, 9% with terminal degrees. *Student/faculty ratio:* 24:1.
Majors Administrative assistant and secretarial science; agricultural mechanization; animal/livestock husbandry and production; automobile/automotive mechanics technology; biological and physical sciences; business administration and management; business and personal/financial services marketing; computer and information sciences and support services related; computer engineering technology; computer graphics; computer/information technology services administration related; computer programming; computer programming related; computer programming (specific applications); computer programming (vendor/product certification); computer science; criminal justice/law enforcement administration; criminal justice/police science; data processing and data processing technology; drafting and design technology; electrical, electronic and communications engineering technology; emergency medical technology (EMT paramedic); engineering technology; equestrian studies; farm and ranch management; health information/medical records administration; industrial mechanics and maintenance technology; information science/studies; legal administrative assistant/secretary; legal assistant/paralegal; liberal arts and sciences/liberal studies; machine shop technology; machine tool technology; merchandising; occupational therapy; pre-engineering; real estate; registered nursing/registered nurse; retailing; sales, distribution, and marketing operations; welding technology; word processing.
Academics *Calendar:* semesters. *Degree:* certificates, diplomas, and associate. *Special study options:* academic remediation for entering students, adult/continuing education programs, advanced placement credit, cooperative education, distance learning, internships, part-time degree program, services for LD students, summer session for credit. *ROTC:* Army (c).
Library North Central Texas College Library plus 1 other with 44,861 titles, an OPAC.
Student Life *Housing Options:* coed. Campus housing is university owned. *Activities and Organizations:* drama/theater group, choral group, Student Nursing Association, Residence Hall Association, Cosmetology Student Association, Student Government Association - Gainesville, Gainesville Program Council. *Campus security:* late-night transport/escort service, controlled dormitory access, cameras added to campus. *Student services:* personal/psychological counseling.
Athletics Member NJCAA. *Intercollegiate sports:* baseball M(s), equestrian sports M(s)/W(s), softball W(s), tennis W(s), volleyball W(s). *Intramural sports:* archery M/W, basketball M/W, bowling M/W, field hockey M/W, football M/W, golf M/W, soccer M/W, softball M/W, swimming and diving M/W, table tennis M/W, tennis M/W, ultimate Frisbee M/W, volleyball M/W.
Financial Aid Of all full-time matriculated undergraduates who enrolled in 2013, 108 Federal Work-Study jobs (averaging $1253). 29 state and other part-time jobs (averaging $392).
Applying *Options:* electronic application, early admission. *Required:* high school transcript. *Application deadlines:* rolling (freshmen), rolling (out-of-state freshmen), rolling (transfers).
Freshman Application Contact Melinda Carroll, Director of Admissions/Registrar, North Central Texas College, 1525 West California, Gainesville, TX 76240-4699. *Phone:* 940-668-7731. *Fax:* 940-668-7075. *E-mail:* mcarroll@nctc.edu.
Website: http://www.nctc.edu/.

Northeast Texas Community College
Mount Pleasant, Texas

- **State and locally supported** 2-year, founded 1985
- **Rural** 175-acre campus
- **Coed**

Undergraduates 1,104 full-time, 2,178 part-time. Students come from 19 states and territories; 4 other countries; 2% are from out of state; 13% Black or African American, non-Hispanic/Latino; 24% Hispanic/Latino; 0.4% Asian, non-Hispanic/Latino; 0.1% Native Hawaiian or other Pacific Islander, non-Hispanic/Latino; 0.2% American Indian or Alaska Native, non-Hispanic/Latino; 3% Two or more races, non-Hispanic/Latino; 2% Race/ethnicity unknown; 1% international. *Retention:* 50% of full-time freshmen returned.
Faculty *Student/faculty ratio:* 17:1.
Academics *Calendar:* semesters. *Degree:* certificates and associate. *Special study options:* academic remediation for entering students, adult/continuing education programs, advanced placement credit, cooperative education, distance learning, honors programs, independent study, part-time degree program, services for LD students, summer session for credit.
Student Life *Campus security:* 24-hour patrols.
Athletics Member NJCAA.
Financial Aid Of all full-time matriculated undergraduates who enrolled in 2009, 98 Federal Work-Study jobs (averaging $1600). 13 state and other part-time jobs (averaging $1600).
Applying *Options:* electronic application, early admission. *Required:* high school transcript.
Freshman Application Contact Linda Bond, Admissions Specialist, Northeast Texas Community College, PO Box 1307, Mount Pleasant, TX 75456-1307. *Phone:* 903-434-8140. *Toll-free phone:* 800-870-0142. *E-mail:* lbond@ntcc.edu.
Website: http://www.ntcc.edu/.

North Lake College
Irving, Texas

Freshman Application Contact Admissions/Registration Office, North Lake College, 5001 North MacArthur Boulevard, Irving, TX 75038. *Phone:* 972-273-3183.
Website: http://www.northlakecollege.edu/.

Northwest Vista College

San Antonio, Texas

Freshman Application Contact Dr. Elaine Lang, Interim Director of Enrollment Management, Northwest Vista College, 3535 North Ellison Drive, San Antonio, TX 78251. *Phone:* 210-348-2016. *E-mail:* elang@accd.edu. *Website:* http://www.alamo.edu/nvc/.

Odessa College

Odessa, Texas

Freshman Application Contact Ms. Tracy Hilliard, Associate Director, Admissions, Odessa College, 201 West University Avenue, Odessa, TX 79764. *Phone:* 432-335-6816. *Fax:* 432-335-6303. *E-mail:* thilliard@odessa.edu. *Website:* http://www.odessa.edu/.

Palo Alto College

San Antonio, Texas

Freshman Application Contact Ms. Rachel Montejano, Director of Enrollment Management, Palo Alto College, 1400 West Villaret Boulevard, San Antonio, TX 78224. *Phone:* 210-921-5279. *Fax:* 210-921-5310. *E-mail:* pacar@accd.edu. *Website:* http://www.alamo.edu/pac/.

Panola College

Carthage, Texas

- **State and locally supported** 2-year, founded 1947
- **Small-town** 35-acre campus
- **Endowment** $2.8 million
- **Coed,** 2,564 undergraduate students, 51% full-time, 66% women, 34% men

Undergraduates 1,316 full-time, 1,248 part-time. Students come from 18 states and territories; 12 other countries; 8% are from out of state; 21% Black or African American, non-Hispanic/Latino; 10% Hispanic/Latino; 0.4% Asian, non-Hispanic/Latino; 0.5% American Indian or Alaska Native, non-Hispanic/Latino; 1% Two or more races, non-Hispanic/Latino; 2% international; 12% transferred in; 9% live on campus. *Retention:* 42% of full-time freshmen returned.
Freshmen *Admission:* 431 enrolled.
Faculty *Total:* 147, 47% full-time, 5% with terminal degrees. *Student/faculty ratio:* 18:1.
Majors Administrative assistant and secretarial science; business automation/technology/data entry; clinical/medical laboratory technology; early childhood education; education; general studies; health information/medical records technology; industrial technology; information science/studies; information technology; medical/clinical assistant; middle school education; music; occupational therapist assistant; petroleum technology; registered nursing/registered nurse.
Academics *Calendar:* semesters. *Degree:* certificates and associate. *Special study options:* academic remediation for entering students, advanced placement credit, cooperative education, distance learning, English as a second language, part-time degree program, services for LD students, summer session for credit.
Library M. P. Baker Library with 247,592 titles, 4,397 audiovisual materials, an OPAC, a Web page.
Student Life *Housing Options:* coed. Campus housing is university owned. *Activities and Organizations:* drama/theater group, student-run newspaper, choral group, Student Government Organization, Student Occupational Therapy Assistant Club, Baptist Student Ministries, Texas Nursing Student Association, Phi Theta Kappa. *Campus security:* controlled dormitory access, 24 hour campus police department.
Athletics Member NCAA, NJCAA. *Intercollegiate sports:* baseball M(s), basketball M(s)/W(s), volleyball W(s). *Intramural sports:* basketball M/W, football M/W, racquetball M/W, table tennis M/W, weight lifting M/W.
Costs (2015–16) *Tuition:* area resident $750 full-time, $73 per semester hour part-time; state resident $2190 full-time, $121 per semester hour part-time; nonresident $3120 full-time, $152 per semester hour part-time. Full-time tuition and fees vary according to reciprocity agreements. Part-time tuition and fees vary according to reciprocity agreements. *Required fees:* $1440 full-time. *Room and board:* $4700. Room and board charges vary according to housing facility. *Payment plan:* deferred payment. *Waivers:* employees or children of employees.

Applying *Required for some:* high school transcript. *Recommended:* high school transcript.
Freshman Application Contact Mr. Jeremy Dorman, Registrar/Director of Admissions, Panola College, 1109 West Panola Street, Carthage, TX 75633-2397. *Phone:* 903-693-2009. *Fax:* 903-693-2031. *E-mail:* bsimpson@panola.edu. *Website:* http://www.panola.edu/.

Paris Junior College

Paris, Texas

- **State and locally supported** 2-year, founded 1924
- **Rural** 54-acre campus with easy access to Dallas-Fort Worth
- **Endowment** $21.7 million
- **Coed,** 5,086 undergraduate students, 44% full-time, 60% women, 40% men

Undergraduates 2,229 full-time, 2,857 part-time. Students come from 26 states and territories; 4 other countries; 3% are from out of state; 11% Black or African American, non-Hispanic/Latino; 12% Hispanic/Latino; 0.9% Asian, non-Hispanic/Latino; 0.1% Native Hawaiian or other Pacific Islander, non-Hispanic/Latino; 2% American Indian or Alaska Native, non-Hispanic/Latino; 0.9% Two or more races, non-Hispanic/Latino; 0.2% international; 6% transferred in; 4% live on campus.
Freshmen *Admission:* 806 applied, 806 admitted, 1,027 enrolled.
Faculty *Total:* 248, 37% full-time, 6% with terminal degrees. *Student/faculty ratio:* 22:1.
Majors Accounting; agricultural mechanization; agriculture; art; biological and physical sciences; biology/biological sciences; business administration and management; business automation/technology/data entry; business/commerce; business teacher education; chemistry; computer and information sciences; computer engineering technology; computer typography and composition equipment operation; cosmetology; criminal justice/safety; criminology; drafting and design technology; dramatic/theater arts; early childhood education; education; education (multiple levels); electrical; electronic and communications engineering technology; electromechanical technology; elementary education; emergency medical technology (EMT paramedic); engineering; English; foreign languages and literatures; general studies; health and physical education/fitness; health information/medical records technology; health services/allied health/health sciences; heating, air conditioning, ventilation and refrigeration maintenance technology; history; information science/studies; journalism; liberal arts and sciences/liberal studies; mathematics; medical insurance coding; metal and jewelry arts; music; nursing administration; physical sciences; physics; political science and government; pre-law studies; premedical studies; prenursing studies; pre-pharmacy studies; psychology; radiologic technology/science; registered nursing/registered nurse; rhetoric and composition; secondary education; social sciences; social work; sociology; surgical technology; system, networking, and LAN/WAN management; watchmaking and jewelrymaking; welding technology.
Academics *Calendar:* semesters. *Degree:* certificates, diplomas, and associate. *Special study options:* academic remediation for entering students, adult/continuing education programs, advanced placement credit, cooperative education, distance learning, English as a second language, part-time degree program, services for LD students, summer session for credit.
Library Mike Rheudasil Learning Center with 52,272 titles, an OPAC.
Student Life *Housing Options:* men-only, women-only. Campus housing is university owned. *Activities and Organizations:* drama/theater group, student-run newspaper, choral group, Student Government Organization, Blends Club for all ethic groups. *Campus security:* 24-hour emergency response devices and patrols, late-night transport/escort service, controlled dormitory access. *Student services:* personal/psychological counseling.
Athletics Member NJCAA. *Intercollegiate sports:* baseball M(s), basketball M(s)/W(s), golf M(s), soccer M(s)/W(s), softball W(s), volleyball W(s). *Intramural sports:* basketball M, football M, table tennis M/W, tennis M/W, volleyball M/W.
Costs (2014–15) *Tuition:* area resident $1890 full-time, $50 per credit hour part-time; state resident $2820 full-time, $81 per credit hour part-time; nonresident $4230 full-time, $128 per credit hour part-time. Full-time tuition and fees vary according to class time, course level, course load, degree level, location, program, and student level. Part-time tuition and fees vary according to class time, course level, course load, degree level, location, program, and student level. *Required fees:* $390 full-time. *Room and board:* $4740. Room and board charges vary according to board plan and housing facility. *Payment plan:* installment. *Waivers:* employees or children of employees.
Financial Aid Of all full-time matriculated undergraduates who enrolled in 2013, 54 Federal Work-Study jobs (averaging $3600). 8 state and other part-time jobs (averaging $3600).
Applying *Options:* electronic application, early admission. *Required:* high school transcript. *Application deadlines:* rolling (freshmen), rolling (out-of-

state freshmen), rolling (transfers). *Notification:* continuous (freshmen), continuous (out-of-state freshmen), continuous (transfers). **Freshman Application Contact** Paris Junior College, 2400 Clarksville Street, Paris, TX 75460-6298. *Phone:* 903-782-0211. *Toll-free phone:* 800-232-5804.
Website: http://www.parisjc.edu/.

Pima Medical Institute
Houston, Texas
Freshman Application Contact Christopher Luebke, Corporate Director of Admissions, Pima Medical Institute, 2160 South Power Road, Mesa, AZ 85209. *Phone:* 480-610-6063. *E-mail:* cluebke@pmi.edu.
Website: http://www.pmi.edu/.

Quest College
San Antonio, Texas
Admissions Office Contact Quest College, 5430 Fredericksburg Road, Suite 310, San Antonio, TX 78229.
Website: http://www.questcollege.edu/.

Ranger College
Ranger, Texas
Freshman Application Contact Dr. Jim Davis, Dean of Students, Ranger College, 1100 College Circle, Ranger, TX 76470. *Phone:* 254-647-3234 Ext. 110.
Website: http://www.rangercollege.edu/.

Remington College–Dallas Campus
Garland, Texas
Director of Admissions Ms. Shonda Wisenhunt, Remington College–Dallas Campus, 1800 Eastgate Drive, Garland, TX 75041. *Phone:* 972-686-7878. *Fax:* 972-686-5116. *E-mail:* shonda.wisenhunt@remingtoncollege.edu.
Website: http://www.remingtoncollege.edu/.

Remington College–Fort Worth Campus
Fort Worth, Texas
Director of Admissions Marcia Kline, Director of Recruitment, Remington College–Fort Worth Campus, 300 East Loop 820, Fort Worth, TX 76112. *Phone:* 817-451-0017. *Toll-free phone:* 800-560-6192. *Fax:* 817-496-1257. *E-mail:* marcia.kline@remingtoncollege.edu.
Website: http://www.remingtoncollege.edu/.

Remington College–Houston Campus
Houston, Texas
Director of Admissions Kevin Wilkinson, Director of Recruitment, Remington College–Houston Campus, 3110 Hayes Road, Suite 380, Houston, TX 77082. *Phone:* 281-899-1240. *Fax:* 281-597-8466. *E-mail:* kevin.wilkinson@remingtoncollege.edu.
Website: http://www.remingtoncollege.edu/.

Remington College–Houston Southeast
Webster, Texas
Director of Admissions Lori Minor, Director of Recruitment, Remington College–Houston Southeast, 20985 Interstate 45 South, Webster, TX 77598. *Phone:* 281-554-1700. *Fax:* 281-554-1765. *E-mail:* lori.minor@ remingtoncollege.edu.
Website: http://www.remingtoncollege.edu/.

Remington College–North Houston Campus
Houston, Texas
Director of Admissions Edmund Flores, Director of Recruitment, Remington College–North Houston Campus, 11310 Greens Crossing Boulevard, Suite 300, Houston, TX 77067. *Phone:* 281-885-4450. *Fax:* 281-875-9964. *E-mail:* edmund.flores@remingtoncollege.edu.
Website: http://www.remingtoncollege.edu/.

Richland College
Dallas, Texas
Freshman Application Contact Ms. Carol McKinney, Department Assistant, Richland College, 12800 Abrams Road, Dallas, TX 75243-2199. *Phone:* 972-238-6100.
Website: http://www.rlc.dcccd.edu/.

St. Philip's College
San Antonio, Texas
- **District-supported** 2-year, founded 1898, part of Alamo Community College District System
- **Urban** 68-acre campus with easy access to San Antonio
- **Coed,** 10,238 undergraduate students, 17% full-time, 56% women, 44% men

Undergraduates 1,769 full-time, 8,469 part-time. Students come from 11 other countries; 1% are from out of state; 10% Black or African American, non-Hispanic/Latino; 52% Hispanic/Latino; 3% Asian, non-Hispanic/Latino; 0.1% Native Hawaiian or other Pacific Islander, non-Hispanic/Latino; 0.2% American Indian or Alaska Native, non-Hispanic/Latino; 3% Two or more races, non-Hispanic/Latino; 1% Race/ethnicity unknown; 0.4% international; 6% transferred in.
Freshmen *Admission:* 1,130 enrolled.
Faculty *Total:* 389, 41% full-time, 9% with terminal degrees. *Student/faculty ratio:* 19:1.
Majors Accounting; administrative assistant and secretarial science; aircraft powerplant technology; airframe mechanics and aircraft maintenance technology; art; autobody/collision and repair technology; automobile/automotive mechanics technology; biology/biological sciences; biomedical technology; building/construction finishing, management, and inspection related; business administration and management; CAD/CADD drafting/design technology; chemistry; clinical/medical laboratory technology; computer and information systems security; computer systems networking and telecommunications; computer technology/computer systems technology; construction engineering technology; criminal justice/law enforcement administration; culinary arts; data entry/microcomputer applications; diesel mechanics technology; dramatic/theater arts; dramatic/theater arts and stagecraft related; early childhood education; e-commerce; economics; education; electrical/electronics equipment installation and repair; electromechanical technology; energy management and systems technology; English; environmental science; geology/earth science; health information/medical records technology; heating, air conditioning, ventilation and refrigeration maintenance technology; history; hotel/motel administration; kinesiology and exercise science; legal administrative assistant/secretary; liberal arts and sciences/liberal studies; mathematics; medical administrative assistant and medical secretary; medical radiologic technology; music; natural resources/conservation; occupational safety and health technology; occupational therapist assistant; philosophy; physical therapy technology; political science and government; pre-dentistry studies; pre-engineering; pre-law studies; premedical studies; prenursing studies; pre-pharmacy studies; psychology; respiratory care therapy; restaurant/food services management; rhetoric and composition; social work; sociology; Spanish; system, networking, and LAN/WAN management; teacher assistant/aide; telecommunications technology; welding technology.
Academics *Calendar:* semesters. *Degree:* certificates, diplomas, and associate. *Special study options:* academic remediation for entering students, adult/continuing education programs, advanced placement credit, cooperative education, distance learning, double majors, English as a second language, honors programs, independent study, internships, off-campus study, part-time degree program, services for LD students, study abroad, summer session for credit. *ROTC:* Army (c).
Library Library plus 1 other with 112,745 titles, 11,520 audiovisual materials, an OPAC, a Web page.
Student Life *Housing:* college housing not available. *Activities and Organizations:* drama/theater group, choral group, student government, Future United Latino Leaders of Change, African American Men on the Move. *Campus security:* 24-hour emergency response devices and patrols, late-night transport/escort service. *Student services:* health clinic.
Athletics *Intramural sports:* basketball M/W, cheerleading M/W, table tennis M/W, volleyball M/W, weight lifting M/W.
Costs (2014–15) *Tuition:* area resident $2008 full-time, $69 per semester hour part-time; state resident $5470 full-time, $185 per semester hour part-time; nonresident $10,660 full-time, $358 per semester hour part-time. Full-time tuition and fees vary according to program. Part-time tuition and fees vary according to program. *Required fees:* $80 full-time, $1 per semester hour part-time, $25 per term part-time.

Applying *Options:* electronic application, early admission. *Required:* high school transcript. *Application deadlines:* rolling (freshmen), rolling (transfers). *Notification:* continuous (freshmen), continuous (transfers).
Freshman Application Contact Ms. Angela Molina, Records and Reports Tech II, St. Philip's College, 1801 Martin Luther King Drive, San Antonio, TX 78203-2098. *Phone:* 210-486-2403. *Fax:* 210-486-2103. *E-mail:* amolina@alamo.edu.
Website: http://www.alamo.edu/spc/.

San Antonio College
San Antonio, Texas

Director of Admissions Mr. J. Martin Ortega, Director of Admissions and Records, San Antonio College, 1300 San Pedro Avenue, San Antonio, TX 78212-4299. *Phone:* 210-733-2582.
Website: http://www.alamo.edu/sac/.

San Jacinto College District
Pasadena, Texas

- **State and locally supported** 2-year, founded 1961
- **Suburban** 445-acre campus with easy access to Houston
- **Endowment** $4.2 million
- **Coed,** 27,911 undergraduate students, 25% full-time, 56% women, 44% men

Undergraduates 7,087 full-time, 20,824 part-time. Students come from 48 states and territories; 70 other countries; 1% are from out of state; 10% Black or African American, non-Hispanic/Latino; 49% Hispanic/Latino; 5% Asian, non-Hispanic/Latino; 0.1% Native Hawaiian or other Pacific Islander, non-Hispanic/Latino; 0.2% American Indian or Alaska Native, non-Hispanic/Latino; 2% Two or more races, non-Hispanic/Latino; 3% Race/ethnicity unknown; 2% international; 4% transferred in. *Retention:* 53% of full-time freshmen returned.
Freshmen *Admission:* 13,185 applied, 13,185 admitted, 5,449 enrolled. *Test scores:* SAT critical reading scores over 500: 100%; ACT scores over 18: 100%; SAT critical reading scores over 600: 38%; ACT scores over 24: 64%; SAT critical reading scores over 700: 2%; ACT scores over 30: 7%.
Faculty *Total:* 1,491, 35% full-time, 7% with terminal degrees. *Student/faculty ratio:* 17:1.
Majors Accounting; administrative assistant and secretarial science; agribusiness; agriculture; airline pilot and flight crew; art; autobody/collision and repair technology; automobile/automotive mechanics technology; aviation/airway management; baking and pastry arts; behavioral sciences; biology/biological sciences; business administration and management; business/commerce; chemical process technology; chemical technology; chemistry; child development; clinical/medical laboratory technology; commercial and advertising art; computer and information sciences; construction engineering technology; cosmetology; cosmetology, barber/styling, and nail instruction; criminal justice/police science; culinary arts; dance; diagnostic medical sonography and ultrasound technology; diesel mechanics technology; digital communication and media/multimedia; drafting and design technology; dramatic/theater arts; electrical and power transmission installation; electrical, electronic and communications engineering technology; emergency medical technology (EMT paramedic); engineering; English; environmental science; fire science/firefighting; food service systems administration; foreign languages and literatures; general studies; geology/earth science; health and physical education/fitness; health information/medical records technology; heating, air conditioning, ventilation and refrigeration maintenance technology; Hispanic-American, Puerto Rican, and Mexican-American/Chicano studies; history; instrumentation technology; interior design; international business/trade/commerce; journalism; legal assistant/paralegal; management information systems; marine science/merchant marine officer; mathematics; music; occupational safety and health technology; optometric technician; philosophy; physical sciences; physical therapy technology; physics; political science and government; psychology; radio and television broadcasting technology; radiologic technology/science; real estate; registered nursing/registered nurse; respiratory care therapy; restaurant, culinary, and catering management; rhetoric and composition; science teacher education; secondary education; social sciences; sociology; surgical technology; welding technology.
Academics *Calendar:* semesters. *Degree:* certificates and associate. *Special study options:* academic remediation for entering students, accelerated degree program, adult/continuing education programs, advanced placement credit, cooperative education, distance learning, double majors, English as a second language, honors programs, off-campus study, part-time degree program, services for LD students, student-designed majors, study abroad, summer session for credit. *ROTC:* Army (c), Air Force (c).

Library Lee Davis Library (C), Edwin E. Lehr (N), and Parker Williams (S) with 193,411 titles, 1,117 audiovisual materials, an OPAC, a Web page.
Student Life *Housing:* college housing not available. *Activities and Organizations:* drama/theater group, student-run newspaper, choral group, Phi Theta Kappa honor society, Nurses Association, Student Government Association, ABG Radiography, Texas Student Education Association. *Campus security:* 24-hour emergency response devices and patrols, late-night transport/escort service.
Athletics Member NJCAA. *Intercollegiate sports:* baseball M(s), basketball M(s)/W(s), soccer M(s), softball W(s), volleyball W(s). *Intramural sports:* basketball M/W, football M/W, golf M/W, soccer M/W, softball M/W, table tennis M/W, tennis M/W, volleyball M/W, weight lifting M/W.
Costs (2014–15) *Tuition:* area resident $1408 full-time, $47 per credit part-time; state resident $2416 full-time, $89 per credit part-time; nonresident $3688 full-time, $142 per credit part-time. Full-time tuition and fees vary according to course load. Part-time tuition and fees vary according to course load. *Required fees:* $280 full-time. *Payment plan:* installment. *Waivers:* senior citizens.
Applying *Options:* electronic application, early admission. *Required:* high school transcript. *Required for some:* interview. *Application deadlines:* rolling (freshmen), rolling (out-of-state freshmen), rolling (transfers). *Notification:* continuous (freshmen), continuous (out-of-state freshmen), continuous (transfers).
Freshman Application Contact San Jacinto College District, 4624 Fairmont Parkway, Pasadena, TX 77504-3323. *Phone:* 281-998-6150.
Website: http://www.sanjac.edu/.

School of Automotive Machinists
Houston, Texas

Admissions Office Contact School of Automotive Machinists, 1911 Antoine Drive, Houston, TX 77055-1803.
Website: http://www.samracing.com/.

South Plains College
Levelland, Texas

- **State and locally supported** 2-year, founded 1958
- **Small-town** 177-acre campus
- **Endowment** $3.0 million
- **Coed**

Undergraduates 4,382 full-time, 5,062 part-time. Students come from 21 states and territories; 8 other countries; 4% are from out of state; 6% Black or African American, non-Hispanic/Latino; 38% Hispanic/Latino; 2% Asian, non-Hispanic/Latino; 0.3% Native Hawaiian or other Pacific Islander, non-Hispanic/Latino; 3% American Indian or Alaska Native, non-Hispanic/Latino; 0.7% international; 10% transferred in; 10% live on campus. *Retention:* 45% of full-time freshmen returned.
Faculty *Student/faculty ratio:* 20:1.
Academics *Calendar:* semesters. *Degree:* certificates and associate. *Special study options:* academic remediation for entering students, accelerated degree program, adult/continuing education programs, advanced placement credit, distance learning, double majors, internships, off-campus study, part-time degree program, services for LD students, study abroad, summer session for credit. *ROTC:* Army (c), Air Force (c).
Student Life *Campus security:* 24-hour emergency response devices and patrols, controlled dormitory access.
Athletics Member NJCAA.
Standardized Tests *Recommended:* ACT (for admission), SAT Subject Tests (for admission).
Costs (2014–15) *Tuition:* area resident $696 full-time, $29 per credit hour part-time; state resident $1440 full-time, $60 per credit hour part-time; nonresident $1824 full-time, $76 per credit hour part-time. Full-time tuition and fees vary according to course load and location. Part-time tuition and fees vary according to course load and location. *Required fees:* $1544 full-time, $70 per credit hour part-time. *Room and board:* $3400. Room and board charges vary according to housing facility.
Financial Aid Of all full-time matriculated undergraduates who enrolled in 2013, 80 Federal Work-Study jobs (averaging $2000). 22 state and other part-time jobs (averaging $2000).
Applying *Options:* electronic application, early admission. *Required:* high school transcript.
Freshman Application Contact Mrs. Andrea Rangel, Dean of Admissions and Records, South Plains College, 1401 College Avenue, Levelland, TX 78336. *Phone:* 806-894-9611 Ext. 2370. *Fax:* 806-897-3167. *E-mail:* arangel@southplainscollege.edu.
Website: http://www.southplainscollege.edu/.

South Texas College

McAllen, Texas

Freshman Application Contact Mr. Matthew Hebbard, Director of Enrollment Services and Registrar, South Texas College, 3201 West Pecan, McAllen, TX 78501. *Phone:* 956-872-2147. *Toll-free phone:* 800-742-7822. *E-mail:* mshebbar@southtexascollege.edu.
Website: http://www.southtexascollege.edu/.

Southwest Texas Junior College

Uvalde, Texas

Director of Admissions Carol LaRue, Dean of Admissions and Student Services, Southwest Texas Junior College, 2401 Garner Field Road, Uvalde, TX 78801-6297. *Phone:* 830-278-4401 Ext. 7284.
Website: http://www.swtjc.edu/.

Tarrant County College District

Fort Worth, Texas

- **County-supported** 2-year, founded 1967
- **Urban** 667-acre campus with easy access to Dallas-Fort Worth
- **Endowment** $5.8 million
- **Coed**

Undergraduates 17,466 full-time, 32,973 part-time. 19% Black or African American, non-Hispanic/Latino; 26% Hispanic/Latino; 6% Asian, non-Hispanic/Latino; 0.2% Native Hawaiian or other Pacific Islander, non-Hispanic/Latino; 0.5% American Indian or Alaska Native, non-Hispanic/Latino; 1% Two or more races, non-Hispanic/Latino; 0.9% Race/ethnicity unknown; 0.8% international.
Faculty *Student/faculty ratio:* 29:1.
Academics *Calendar:* semesters. *Degree:* certificates and associate. *Special study options:* academic remediation for entering students, adult/continuing education programs, advanced placement credit, distance learning, English as a second language, honors programs, part-time degree program, services for LD students, summer session for credit. *ROTC:* Army (c), Air Force (c).
Student Life *Campus security:* 24-hour emergency response devices and patrols, late-night transport/escort service.
Costs (2014–15) *Tuition:* area resident $1320 full-time, $55 per credit hour part-time; state resident $2064 full-time, $86 per credit hour part-time; nonresident $4920 full-time, $205 per credit hour part-time. Full-time tuition and fees vary according to course load and program. Part-time tuition and fees vary according to course load and program. *Payment plans:* installment, deferred payment.
Financial Aid Of all full-time matriculated undergraduates who enrolled in 2013, 12,236 applied for aid, 11,070 were judged to have need. 263 Federal Work-Study jobs (averaging $2021). 50 state and other part-time jobs (averaging $4416). In 2013, 167. *Average need-based loan:* $3234. *Average need-based gift aid:* $4387. *Average non-need-based aid:* $1235.
Applying *Options:* electronic application.
Freshman Application Contact Mr. Vikas Rajpurohit, Assistant Director of Admissions Services, Tarrant County College District, 300 Trinity Campus Circle, Fort Worth, TX 76102-6599. *Phone:* 817-515-1581. *E-mail:* vikas.rajpurohit@tccd.edu.
Website: http://www.tccd.edu/.

Temple College

Temple, Texas

- **District-supported** 2-year, founded 1926
- **Suburban** 106-acre campus with easy access to Austin
- **Endowment** $638,964
- **Coed**

Undergraduates 1,821 full-time, 3,685 part-time. Students come from 24 states and territories; 6 other countries; 2% are from out of state; 20% Black or African American, non-Hispanic/Latino; 21% Hispanic/Latino; 2% Asian, non-Hispanic/Latino; 0.2% Native Hawaiian or other Pacific Islander, non-Hispanic/Latino; 0.7% American Indian or Alaska Native, non-Hispanic/Latino; 3% Race/ethnicity unknown; 0.1% international; 6% transferred in.
Faculty *Student/faculty ratio:* 25:1.
Academics *Calendar:* semesters. *Degree:* certificates and associate. *Special study options:* academic remediation for entering students, adult/continuing education programs, advanced placement credit, cooperative education, distance learning, English as a second language, internships, off-campus study,

part-time degree program, services for LD students, study abroad, summer session for credit.
Student Life *Campus security:* 24-hour emergency response devices and patrols.
Athletics Member NJCAA.
Costs (2014–15) *Tuition:* area resident $2640 full-time, $88 per semester hour part-time; state resident $4620 full-time, $154 per semester hour part-time; nonresident $7020 full-time, $330 per semester hour part-time. Full-time tuition and fees vary according to course load and location. Part-time tuition and fees vary according to course load and location. *Required fees:* $150 full-time, $24 per year part-time, $48 per term part-time.
Applying *Options:* electronic application, early admission. *Required:* high school transcript.
Freshman Application Contact Ms. Carey Rose, Director of Admissions and Records, Temple College, 2600 South First Street, Temple, TX 76504. *Phone:* 254-298-8303. *Toll-free phone:* 800-460-4636. *E-mail:* carey.rose@templejc.edu.
Website: http://www.templejc.edu/.

Texarkana College

Texarkana, Texas

- **State and locally supported** 2-year, founded 1927
- **Urban** 90-acre campus
- **Coed**

Undergraduates 1,587 full-time, 2,524 part-time. Students come from 7 states and territories; 27% are from out of state; 23% Black or African American, non-Hispanic/Latino; 5% Hispanic/Latino; 1% Asian, non-Hispanic/Latino; 0.8% American Indian or Alaska Native, non-Hispanic/Latino; 3% Two or more races, non-Hispanic/Latino; 3% Race/ethnicity unknown; 1% live on campus.
Faculty *Student/faculty ratio:* 21:1.
Academics *Calendar:* semesters. *Degree:* certificates and associate. *Special study options:* academic remediation for entering students, adult/continuing education programs, advanced placement credit, cooperative education, honors programs, part-time degree program, services for LD students, summer session for credit.
Student Life *Campus security:* 24-hour patrols.
Athletics Member NJCAA.
Financial Aid Of all full-time matriculated undergraduates who enrolled in 2013, 30 Federal Work-Study jobs (averaging $3090).
Applying *Options:* electronic application, early admission, deferred entrance. *Required:* high school transcript. *Recommended:* Interview recommended for nursing program. Must have meningitis vaccine before student can start.
Freshman Application Contact Mr. Lee Williams, Director of Admissions, Texarkana College, 2500 North Robison Road, Texarkana, TX 75599-0001. *Phone:* 903-823-3016. *Fax:* 903-823-3451. *E-mail:* lee.williams@texarkanacollege.edu.
Website: http://www.texarkanacollege.edu/.

Texas School of Business, Friendswood Campus

Friendswood, Texas

Freshman Application Contact Admissions Office, Texas School of Business, Friendswood Campus, 3208 Farm to Market Road 528, Friendswood, TX 77546.
Website: http://www.friendswood.tsb.edu/.

Texas School of Business, Houston North Campus

Houston, Texas

Freshman Application Contact Admissions Office, Texas School of Business, Houston North Campus, 711 East Airtex Drive, Houston, TX 77073. *Phone:* 281-443-8900.
Website: http://www.north.tsb.edu/.

Texas Southmost College

Brownsville, Texas

Freshman Application Contact New Student Relations, Texas Southmost College, 80 Fort Brown, Brownsville, TX 78520-4991. *Phone:* 956-882-8860. *Toll-free phone:* 877-882-8721. *Fax:* 956-882-8959.
Website: http://www.utb.edu/.

Texas State Technical College Harlingen
Harlingen, Texas

- **State-supported** 2-year, founded 1967, part of Texas State Technical College System
- **Small-town** 125-acre campus
- **Coed,** 5,225 undergraduate students, 41% full-time, 52% women, 48% men

Undergraduates 2,128 full-time, 3,097 part-time. Students come from 14 states and territories; 1 other country; 0.6% are from out of state; 0.4% Black or African American, non-Hispanic/Latino; 90% Hispanic/Latino; 0.6% Asian, non-Hispanic/Latino; 0.1% Native Hawaiian or other Pacific Islander, non-Hispanic/Latino; 0.1% American Indian or Alaska Native, non-Hispanic/Latino; 2% Race/ethnicity unknown; 5% live on campus.

Freshmen *Admission:* 702 enrolled.

Faculty *Total:* 206, 75% full-time, 2% with terminal degrees. *Student/faculty ratio:* 19:1.

Majors Agricultural business technology; airframe mechanics and aircraft maintenance technology; autobody/collision and repair technology; automobile/automotive mechanics technology; biology/biological sciences; biomedical technology; chemical technology; commercial and advertising art; computer programming; computer systems networking and telecommunications; computer technology/computer systems technology; construction engineering technology; dental hygiene; dental laboratory technology; drafting and design technology; electromechanical technology; engineering; health information/medical records technology; heating, air conditioning, ventilation and refrigeration maintenance technology; information technology; institutional food workers; mathematics; medical/clinical assistant; registered nursing/registered nurse; surgical technology; teacher assistant/aide; telecommunications technology; tool and die technology; welding technology.

Academics *Calendar:* semesters. *Degree:* certificates and associate. *Special study options:* academic remediation for entering students, adult/continuing education programs, cooperative education, distance learning, double majors, internships, part-time degree program, services for LD students, summer session for credit.

Library Dr. J. Gilbert Leal Learning Resource Center with 23,500 titles, 649 audiovisual materials, an OPAC, a Web page.

Student Life *Housing Options:* men-only, women-only, special housing for students with disabilities. Campus housing is university owned. *Activities and Organizations:* student-run newspaper, Student Government Association, VICA (Vocational Industrial Clubs of America), Business Professionals of America. *Campus security:* 24-hour emergency response devices and patrols, late-night transport/escort service, night watchman for housing area. *Student services:* health clinic, personal/psychological counseling, women's center.

Athletics *Intramural sports:* badminton M/W, basketball M/W, football M/W, racquetball M/W, soccer M/W, softball M/W, table tennis M/W, tennis M/W, track and field M/W, volleyball M/W, weight lifting M/W.

Costs (2014–15) *Tuition:* state resident $2160 full-time, $90 per credit hour part-time; nonresident $6096 full-time, $254 per credit hour part-time. Full-time tuition and fees vary according to class time, course level, course load, program, and student level. Part-time tuition and fees vary according to class time, course level, course load, program, and student level. *Required fees:* $1104 full-time, $46 per credit hour part-time, $552 per term part-time. *Room and board:* $4950; room only: $2175. Room and board charges vary according to board plan and housing facility. *Payment plan:* installment. *Waivers:* senior citizens and employees or children of employees.

Financial Aid Of all full-time matriculated undergraduates who enrolled in 2012, 850 applied for aid, 827 were judged to have need, 568 had their need fully met. 144 Federal Work-Study jobs (averaging $2159). 31 state and other part-time jobs (averaging $3689). In 2012, 1 non-need-based awards were made. *Average percent of need met:* 85%. *Average financial aid package:* $6056. *Average need-based gift aid:* $5497. *Average non-need-based aid:* $2500.

Applying *Options:* electronic application, early admission, deferred entrance. *Required:* high school transcript. *Application deadlines:* rolling (freshmen), rolling (transfers). *Notification:* continuous (freshmen), continuous (transfers).

Freshman Application Contact Texas State Technical College Harlingen, 1902 North Loop 499, Harlingen, TX 78550-3697. *Phone:* 956-364-4329. *Toll-free phone:* 800-852-8784.

Website: http://www.harlingen.tstc.edu/.

Texas State Technical College–Marshall
Marshall, Texas

Director of Admissions Pat Robbins, Registrar, Texas State Technical College–Marshall, 2650 East End Boulevard South, Marshall, TX 75671. *Phone:* 903-935-1010. *Toll-free phone:* 888-382-8782. *Fax:* 903-923-3282. *E-mail:* Pat.Robbins@marshall.tstc.edu.

Website: http://www.marshall.tstc.edu/.

Texas State Technical College Waco
Waco, Texas

- **State-supported** 2-year, founded 1965, part of Texas State Technical College System
- **Suburban** 200-acre campus
- **Coed**

Undergraduates 5,357 full-time, 1,912 part-time. 1% are from out of state; 14% Black or African American, non-Hispanic/Latino; 20% Hispanic/Latino; 0.9% Asian, non-Hispanic/Latino; 0.2% Native Hawaiian or other Pacific Islander, non-Hispanic/Latino; 0.5% American Indian or Alaska Native, non-Hispanic/Latino; 0.2% Two or more races, non-Hispanic/Latino; 4% Race/ethnicity unknown; 0.1% international; 16% transferred in. *Retention:* 48% of full-time freshmen returned.

Faculty *Student/faculty ratio:* 17:1.

Academics *Calendar:* trimesters. *Degree:* certificates and associate. *Special study options:* academic remediation for entering students, adult/continuing education programs, cooperative education, distance learning, internships, part-time degree program, services for LD students, summer session for credit.

Student Life *Campus security:* 24-hour emergency response devices and patrols, late-night transport/escort service, controlled dormitory access.

Standardized Tests *Required:* Texas Success Initiative assessment (for admission).

Costs (2014–15) *Tuition:* state resident $2238 full-time, $97 per credit hour part-time; nonresident $6096 full-time, $254 per credit hour part-time. Full-time tuition and fees vary according to course load. Part-time tuition and fees vary according to course load. *Required fees:* $1104 full-time, $1104 per year part-time. *Room and board:* $6027. Room and board charges vary according to board plan, housing facility, and location.

Applying *Options:* electronic application, early admission. *Required:* high school transcript. *Required for some:* interview.

Freshman Application Contact Ms. Mary Daniel, Registrar/Director of Admission and Records, Texas State Technical College Waco, 3801 Campus Drive, Waco, TX 76705. *Phone:* 254-867-3363. *Toll-free phone:* 800-792-8784 Ext. 2362. *E-mail:* mary.daniel@tstc.edu.

Website: http://waco.tstc.edu/.

Texas State Technical College West Texas
Sweetwater, Texas

Freshman Application Contact Ms. Maria Aguirre-Acuna, Texas State Technical College West Texas, 300 Homer K Taylor Drive, Sweetwater, TX 79556-4108. *Phone:* 325-235-7349. *Toll-free phone:* 800-592-8784. *Fax:* 325-235-7443. *E-mail:* maria.aquirre@sweetwater.tstc.edu.

Website: http://www.westtexas.tstc.edu/.

Trinity Valley Community College
Athens, Texas

- **State and locally supported** 2-year, founded 1946
- **Rural** 65-acre campus with easy access to Dallas-Fort Worth
- **Coed,** 5,172 undergraduate students, 52% full-time, 62% women, 38% men

Undergraduates 2,685 full-time, 2,487 part-time. Students come from 28 states and territories; 15 other countries; 1% are from out of state; 17% Black or African American, non-Hispanic/Latino; 7% Hispanic/Latino; 0.4% Asian, non-Hispanic/Latino; 0.4% American Indian or Alaska Native, non-Hispanic/Latino; 11% Two or more races, non-Hispanic/Latino; 2% Race/ethnicity unknown; 0.3% international; 14% live on campus.

Freshmen *Admission:* 1,320 enrolled.

Faculty *Total:* 277, 52% full-time, 3% with terminal degrees. *Student/faculty ratio:* 16:1.

Majors Accounting; agricultural teacher education; animal sciences; art; automobile/automotive mechanics technology; biology/biological sciences; business administration and management; business teacher education; chemistry; child development; commercial photography; computer science; corrections; cosmetology; criminal justice/law enforcement administration; criminal justice/police science; dance; data processing and data processing technology; developmental and child psychology; drafting and design technology; dramatic/theater arts; education; elementary education; emergency medical technology (EMT paramedic); English; farm and ranch management; fashion merchandising; finance; geology/earth science; heating, air conditioning, ventilation and refrigeration maintenance technology; history; horticultural science; insurance; journalism; kindergarten/preschool education; legal administrative assistant/secretary; liberal arts and sciences/liberal studies; licensed practical/vocational nurse training; marketing/marketing management; mathematics; music; physical education teaching and coaching;

physical sciences; political science and government; pre-engineering; psychology; range science and management; real estate; registered nursing/registered nurse; religious studies; rhetoric and composition; sociology; Spanish; surgical technology; welding technology.

Academics *Calendar:* semesters. *Degree:* certificates, diplomas, and associate. *Special study options:* academic remediation for entering students, adult/continuing education programs, advanced placement credit, cooperative education, distance learning, double majors, English as a second language, honors programs, independent study, internships, part-time degree program, services for LD students, summer session for credit.

Library Ginger Murchison Learning Resource Center plus 3 others with 177,016 titles, 20,908 audiovisual materials, an OPAC, a Web page.

Student Life *Housing Options:* coed, men-only, women-only. Campus housing is university owned. *Activities and Organizations:* drama/theater group, student-run newspaper, choral group, marching band, Student Senate, Phi Theta Kappa, Delta Epsilon Chi. *Campus security:* 24-hour emergency response devices and patrols, controlled dormitory access. *Student services:* personal/psychological counseling.

Athletics Member NJCAA. *Intercollegiate sports:* basketball M(s)/W(s), cheerleading M(s)/W(s), football M(s), softball W(s), volleyball W(s). *Intramural sports:* baseball M/W, basketball M/W, football M, table tennis M/W, volleyball M/W.

Costs (2014–15) *Tuition:* area resident $2220 full-time, $32 per semester hour part-time; state resident $3660 full-time, $80 per semester hour part-time; nonresident $4500 full-time, $108 per semester hour part-time. Full-time tuition and fees vary according to course load. Part-time tuition and fees vary according to course load. *Required fees:* $42 per semester hour part-time. *Room and board:* $5370. Room and board charges vary according to board plan. *Payment plan:* installment. *Waivers:* employees or children of employees.

Financial Aid Of all full-time matriculated undergraduates who enrolled in 2013, 80 Federal Work-Study jobs (averaging $1544). 40 state and other part-time jobs (averaging $1544).

Applying *Options:* electronic application, early admission. *Required:* high school transcript. *Application deadlines:* rolling (freshmen), rolling (transfers). *Notification:* continuous (freshmen), continuous (transfers).

Freshman Application Contact Dr. Colette Hilliard, Dean of Enrollment Management and Registrar, Trinity Valley Community College, 100 Cardinal Drive, Athens, TX 75751. *Phone:* 903-675-6209 Ext. 209. *Website:* http://www.tvcc.edu/.

Tyler Junior College
Tyler, Texas
- **State and locally supported** 2-year, founded 1926
- **Suburban** 85-acre campus
- **Endowment** $39.7 million
- **Coed,** 11,168 undergraduate students, 56% full-time, 59% women, 41% men

Undergraduates 6,243 full-time, 4,925 part-time. Students come from 35 other countries; 2% are from out of state; 23% Black or African American, non-Hispanic/Latino; 16% Hispanic/Latino; 1% Asian, non-Hispanic/Latino; 0.1% Native Hawaiian or other Pacific Islander, non-Hispanic/Latino; 0.6% American Indian or Alaska Native, non-Hispanic/Latino; 2% Two or more races, non-Hispanic/Latino; 0.6% Race/ethnicity unknown; 0.8% international; 6% transferred in; 9% live on campus. *Retention:* 53% of full-time freshmen returned.

Freshmen *Admission:* 10,727 applied, 10,264 admitted, 2,845 enrolled.
Faculty *Total:* 538, 54% full-time, 21% with terminal degrees. *Student/faculty ratio:* 21:1.

Majors Accounting; administrative assistant and secretarial science; art; athletic training; automobile/automotive mechanics technology; behavioral sciences; biology/biological sciences; business administration and management; CAD/CADD drafting/design technology; chemistry; child development; clinical/medical laboratory technology; commercial and advertising art; commercial photography; computer and information sciences; computer and information sciences related; computer engineering technology; computer graphics; computer programming; computer programming related; computer science; computer systems networking and telecommunications; computer technology/computer systems technology; criminalistics and criminal science; criminal justice/law enforcement administration; criminal justice/police science; criminal justice/safety; dance; data entry/microcomputer applications; dental hygiene; diagnostic medical sonography and ultrasound technology; drafting and design technology; dramatic/theater arts; economics; education (multiple levels); electromechanical technology; emergency medical technology (EMT paramedic); engineering; English literature (British and Commonwealth); environmental science; family and consumer sciences/human sciences; fire science/firefighting; foreign languages and literatures; general studies; geology/earth science; health and physical education/fitness; health/health-

care administration; health information/medical records technology; heating, air conditioning, ventilation and refrigeration maintenance technology; history; industrial electronics technology; industrial radiologic technology; information technology; legal administrative assistant/secretary; legal assistant/paralegal; liberal arts and sciences/liberal studies; licensed practical/vocational nurse training; mathematics; medical administrative assistant and medical secretary; middle school education; modern languages; music; natural sciences; occupational therapist assistant; photography; physical education teaching and coaching; physical therapy technology; physics; political science and government; prenursing studies; psychology; public administration; radiologic technology/science; registered nursing/registered nurse; respiratory care therapy; secondary education; sign language interpretation and translation; social sciences; social work; sociology; speech communication and rhetoric; substance abuse/addiction counseling; surgical technology; surveying technology; system, networking, and LAN/WAN management; welding technology.

Academics *Calendar:* semesters. *Degree:* certificates, diplomas, and associate. *Special study options:* academic remediation for entering students, accelerated degree program, adult/continuing education programs, advanced placement credit, distance learning, freshman honors college, honors programs, part-time degree program, services for LD students, study abroad, summer session for credit.

Library Vaughn Library and Learning Resource Center with 107,395 titles, an OPAC.

Student Life *Housing Options:* coed, men-only, women-only. Campus housing is university owned. *Activities and Organizations:* drama/theater group, student-run newspaper, choral group, marching band, student government, religious affiliation clubs, Phi Theta Kappa, national sororities. *Campus security:* 24-hour emergency response devices and patrols, controlled dormitory access. *Student services:* health clinic, personal/psychological counseling.

Athletics Member NJCAA. *Intercollegiate sports:* baseball M, basketball M(s)/W(s), cheerleading W(s), football M(s), golf M/W, soccer M(s)/W(s), softball W(s), tennis M(s)/W(s), volleyball W(s). *Intramural sports:* basketball M/W, cheerleading W, racquetball M/W, volleyball M/W, weight lifting M/W.

Standardized Tests *Required:* TXSI (for admission).

Costs (2014–15) *Tuition:* area resident $900 full-time, $30 per credit hour part-time; state resident $2310 full-time, $77 per credit hour part-time; nonresident $2910 full-time, $97 per credit hour part-time. *Required fees:* $1452 full-time. *Room and board:* $7200. Room and board charges vary according to housing facility. *Payment plan:* installment. *Waivers:* senior citizens and employees or children of employees.

Financial Aid Of all full-time matriculated undergraduates who enrolled in 2013, 4,721 applied for aid, 4,168 were judged to have need, 73 had their need fully met. 41 Federal Work-Study jobs (averaging $1296). 36 state and other part-time jobs (averaging $1814). In 2013, 710 non-need-based awards were made. *Average percent of need met:* 62%. *Average financial aid package:* $3780. *Average need-based loan:* $1316. *Average need-based gift aid:* $2503. *Average non-need-based aid:* $361. *Average indebtedness upon graduation:* $2255.

Applying *Options:* electronic application, early admission. *Required:* high school transcript. *Application deadlines:* rolling (freshmen), rolling (out-of-state freshmen), rolling (transfers). *Notification:* continuous (freshmen), continuous (out-of-state freshmen), continuous (transfers).

Freshman Application Contact Ms. Janna Chancey, Director of Enrollment Management, Tyler Junior College, PO Box 9020, Tyler, TX 75711-9020. *Phone:* 903-510-3325. *Toll-free phone:* 800-687-5680. *E-mail:* jcha@tjc.edu. *Website:* http://www.tjc.edu/.

Vernon College
Vernon, Texas
Director of Admissions Mr. Joe Hite, Dean of Admissions/Registrar, Vernon College, 4400 College Drive, Vernon, TX 76384-4092. *Phone:* 940-552-6291 Ext. 2204.
Website: http://www.vernoncollege.edu/.

Vet Tech Institute of Houston
Houston, Texas
- **Private** 2-year, founded 1958
- **Suburban** campus
- **Coed,** 196 undergraduate students
- 65% of applicants were admitted

Freshmen *Admission:* 502 applied, 325 admitted.
Majors Veterinary/animal health technology.
Academics *Calendar:* semesters. *Degree:* associate. *Special study options:* accelerated degree program, internships.

Student Life *Housing:* college housing not available.
Freshman Application Contact Admissions Office, Vet Tech Institute of Houston, 4669 Southwest Freeway, Suite 100, Houston, TX 77027. *Phone:* 800-275-2736. *Toll-free phone:* 800-275-2736.
Website: http://houston.vettechinstitute.edu/.

Victoria College
Victoria, Texas

- **County-supported** 2-year, founded 1925
- **Urban** 80-acre campus
- **Coed,** 4,169 undergraduate students, 28% full-time, 65% women, 35% men

Undergraduates 1,154 full-time, 3,015 part-time. Students come from 10 states and territories; 4 other countries; 0.3% are from out of state; 6% Black or African American, non-Hispanic/Latino; 46% Hispanic/Latino; 1% Asian, non-Hispanic/Latino; 0.1% Native Hawaiian or other Pacific Islander, non-Hispanic/Latino; 0.3% American Indian or Alaska Native, non-Hispanic/Latino; 1% Two or more races, non-Hispanic/Latino; 0.5% Race/ethnicity unknown; 7% transferred in.
Freshmen *Admission:* 680 applied, 680 admitted, 691 enrolled.
Faculty *Total:* 225, 40% full-time. *Student/faculty ratio:* 16:1.
Majors Administrative assistant and secretarial science; business administration and management; chemical technology; clinical/medical laboratory technology; computer systems networking and telecommunications; criminal justice/police science; early childhood education; electrical, electronic and communications engineering technology; emergency medical technology (EMT paramedic); fire science/firefighting; general studies; physical therapy technology; registered nursing/registered nurse; respiratory care therapy.
Academics *Calendar:* semesters. *Degree:* certificates and associate. *Special study options:* academic remediation for entering students, advanced placement credit, distance learning, off-campus study, part-time degree program, services for LD students, summer session for credit.
Library Victoria College/University of Houston-Victoria Library (VC/UHV Librar with 222,510 titles, 23,309 audiovisual materials, an OPAC, a Web page.
Student Life *Housing:* college housing not available. *Activities and Organizations:* drama/theater group, choral group, Student Senate. *Campus security:* 24-hour emergency response devices. *Student services:* personal/psychological counseling.
Athletics *Intramural sports:* basketball M/W, bowling M/W, soccer M/W, softball M/W, tennis M/W, volleyball W.
Costs (2014–15) *Tuition:* area resident $1380 full-time, $46 per credit hour part-time; state resident $1410 full-time, $93 per credit hour part-time; nonresident $3390 full-time, $113 per credit hour part-time. Full-time tuition and fees vary according to program. Part-time tuition and fees vary according to program. *Required fees:* $1260 full-time, $42 per credit hour part-time. *Payment plan:* installment. *Waivers:* employees or children of employees.
Applying *Options:* electronic application, early admission. *Required:* high school transcript. *Application deadlines:* rolling (freshmen), rolling (transfers).
Freshman Application Contact Missy Klimitchek, Registrar, Victoria College, 2200 E Red River, Victoria, TX 77901. *Phone:* 361-573-3291 Ext. 6407. *Toll-free phone:* 877-843-4369. *Fax:* 361-582-2525. *E-mail:* registrar@victoriacollege.edu.
Website: http://www.victoriacollege.edu/.

Virginia College in Austin
Austin, Texas

Admissions Office Contact Virginia College in Austin, 6301 East Highway 290, Austin, TX 78723.
Website: http://www.vc.edu/.

Vista College
El Paso, Texas

Director of Admissions Ms. Sarah Hernandez, Registrar, Vista College, 6101 Montana Avenue, El Paso, TX 79925. *Phone:* 915-779-8031. *Toll-free phone:* 866-442-4197.
Website: http://www.vistacollege.edu/.

Wade College
Dallas, Texas

Freshman Application Contact Wade College, INFOMart, 1950 Stemmons Freeway, Suite 4080, LB 562, Dallas, TX 75207. *Phone:* 214-637-3530. *Toll-free phone:* 800-624-4850.
Website: http://www.wadecollege.edu/.

Weatherford College
Weatherford, Texas

Freshman Application Contact Mr. Ralph Willingham, Director of Admissions, Weatherford College, 225 College Park Drive, Weatherford, TX 76086-5699. *Phone:* 817-598-6248. *Toll-free phone:* 800-287-5471. *Fax:* 817-598-6205. *E-mail:* willingham@wc.edu.
Website: http://www.wc.edu/.

Western Technical College
El Paso, Texas

Freshman Application Contact Laura Pena, Director of Admissions, Western Technical College, 9451 Diana Drive, El Paso, TX 79930-2610. *Phone:* 915-566-9621. *Toll-free phone:* 800-201-9232. *E-mail:* lpena@westerntech.edu.
Website: http://www.westerntech.edu/.

Western Technical College
El Paso, Texas

Freshman Application Contact Mr. Bill Terrell, Chief Admissions Officer, Western Technical College, 9624 Plaza Circle, El Paso, TX 79927. *Phone:* 915-532-3737 Ext. 117. *Fax:* 915-532-6946. *E-mail:* bterrell@wtc-ep.edu.
Website: http://www.westerntech.edu/.

Western Texas College
Snyder, Texas

- **State and locally supported** 2-year, founded 1969
- **Small-town** 165-acre campus
- **Coed**

Undergraduates 702 full-time, 1,771 part-time. Students come from 22 other countries; 5% are from out of state; 8% Black or African American, non-Hispanic/Latino; 29% Hispanic/Latino; 0.9% Asian, non-Hispanic/Latino; 0.1% Native Hawaiian or other Pacific Islander, non-Hispanic/Latino; 0.3% American Indian or Alaska Native, non-Hispanic/Latino; 2% Two or more races, non-Hispanic/Latino; 2% international. *Retention:* 50% of full-time freshmen returned.
Faculty *Student/faculty ratio:* 21:1.
Academics *Calendar:* semesters. *Degree:* certificates and associate. *Special study options:* academic remediation for entering students, adult/continuing education programs, advanced placement credit, internships, part-time degree program, services for LD students, student-designed majors, summer session for credit.
Student Life *Campus security:* 24-hour emergency response devices and patrols.
Athletics Member NJCAA.
Costs (2014–15) *Tuition:* area resident $2370 full-time; state resident $3240 full-time; nonresident $4350 full-time. *Required fees:* $400 full-time. *Room and board:* $2550.
Financial Aid Of all full-time matriculated undergraduates who enrolled in 2013, 19 Federal Work-Study jobs (averaging $1600).
Applying *Options:* early admission, deferred entrance. *Required:* high school transcript.
Freshman Application Contact Western Texas College, 6200 College Avenue, Snyder, TX 79549. *Phone:* 325-573-8511 Ext. 204. *Toll-free phone:* 888-GO-TO-WTC.
Website: http://www.wtc.edu/.

Wharton County Junior College
Wharton, Texas

Freshman Application Contact Mr. Albert Barnes, Dean of Admissions and Registration, Wharton County Junior College, 911 Boling Highway, Wharton, TX 77488-3298. *Phone:* 979-532-6381. *E-mail:* albertb@wcjc.edu.
Website: http://www.wcjc.edu/.

UTAH

AmeriTech College
Draper, Utah

Admissions Office Contact AmeriTech College, 12257 South Business Park Drive, Suite 108, Draper, UT 84020-6545.
Website: http://www.ameritech.edu/.

Eagle Gate College
Salt Lake City, Utah

Admissions Office Contact Eagle Gate College, 405 South Main Street, 7th Floor, Salt Lake City, UT 84111.
Website: http://eaglegatecollege.edu/.

ITT Technical Institute
Murray, Utah

- **Proprietary** primarily 2-year, founded 1984, part of ITT Educational Services, Inc.
- **Suburban** campus
- **Coed**

Academics *Calendar:* quarters. *Degrees:* associate and bachelor's.
Freshman Application Contact Director of Recruitment, ITT Technical Institute, 920 West Levoy Drive, Murray, UT 84123-2500. *Phone:* 801-263-3313. *Toll-free phone:* 800-365-2136.
Website: http://www.itt-tech.edu/.

LDS Business College
Salt Lake City, Utah

- **Independent** 2-year, founded 1886, affiliated with The Church of Jesus Christ of Latter-day Saints, part of Latter-day Saints Church Educational System
- **Urban** 2-acre campus with easy access to Salt Lake City
- **Coed**

Undergraduates 1,589 full-time, 602 part-time. Students come from 60 other countries; 45% are from out of state; 0.2% Black or African American, non-Hispanic/Latino; 11% Hispanic/Latino; 1% Asian, non-Hispanic/Latino; 2% Native Hawaiian or other Pacific Islander, non-Hispanic/Latino; 0.5% American Indian or Alaska Native, non-Hispanic/Latino; 4% Two or more races, non-Hispanic/Latino; 3% Race/ethnicity unknown; 13% international; 34% transferred in. *Retention:* 48% of full-time freshmen returned.
Faculty *Student/faculty ratio:* 25:1.
Academics *Calendar:* semesters. *Degree:* certificates and associate. *Special study options:* academic remediation for entering students, adult/continuing education programs, advanced placement credit, internships, part-time degree program, services for LD students, summer session for credit. *ROTC:* Army (c), Air Force (c).
Student Life *Campus security:* 24-hour emergency response devices and patrols.
Standardized Tests *Recommended:* SAT or ACT (for admission).
Costs (2014–15) *Tuition:* $3060 full-time, $128 per credit part-time. Full-time tuition and fees vary according to course load. Part-time tuition and fees vary according to course load.
Applying *Options:* electronic application, deferred entrance. *Application fee:* $35. *Required:* essay or personal statement, high school transcript, interview.
Freshman Application Contact Miss Dawn Fellows, Assistant Director of Admissions, LDS Business College, 95 North 300 West, Salt Lake City, UT 84101-3500. *Phone:* 801-524-8146. *Toll-free phone:* 800-999-5767. *Fax:* 801-524-1900. *E-mail:* DFellows@ldsbc.edu.
Website: http://www.ldsbc.edu/.

Nightingale College
Ogden, Utah

- **Proprietary** primarily 2-year
- **Suburban** campus with easy access to Salt Lake City
- **Coed**

Undergraduates *Retention:* 95% of full-time freshmen returned.
Academics *Calendar:* semesters. *Degree:* diplomas and bachelor's.
Standardized Tests *Required:* Nightingale Entrance Exam (for admission).
Applying *Options:* early admission. *Required:* essay or personal statement, high school transcript, interview.
Freshman Application Contact Nightingale College, 4155 Harrison Boulevard #100, Ogden, UT 84403.
Website: http://www.nightingale.edu/.

Provo College
Provo, Utah

Director of Admissions Mr. Gordon Peters, College Director, Provo College, 1450 West 820 North, Provo, UT 84601. *Phone:* 801-375-1861. *Toll-free phone:* 877-777-5886. *Fax:* 801-375-9728. *E-mail:* gordonp@provocollege.org.
Website: http://www.provocollege.edu/.

Salt Lake Community College
Salt Lake City, Utah

- **State-supported** 2-year, founded 1948, part of Utah System of Higher Education
- **Urban** 114-acre campus with easy access to Salt Lake City
- **Endowment** $828,523
- **Coed,** 29,537 undergraduate students, 27% full-time, 51% women, 49% men

Undergraduates 7,865 full-time, 21,672 part-time. 2% Black or African American, non-Hispanic/Latino; 15% Hispanic/Latino; 4% Asian, non-Hispanic/Latino; 1% Native Hawaiian or other Pacific Islander, non-Hispanic/Latino; 0.9% American Indian or Alaska Native, non-Hispanic/Latino; 2% Two or more races, non-Hispanic/Latino; 4% Race/ethnicity unknown; 1% international; 5% transferred in.
Freshmen *Admission:* 2,715 applied, 2,715 admitted, 2,715 enrolled.
Faculty *Total:* 1,498, 23% full-time. *Student/faculty ratio:* 20:1.
Majors Accounting technology and bookkeeping; airline pilot and flight crew; architectural engineering technology; autobody/collision and repair technology; avionics maintenance technology; biology/biological sciences; biology/biotechnology laboratory technician; building/construction finishing, management, and inspection related; business administration and management; chemistry; clinical/medical laboratory technology; computer and information sciences; computer science; cosmetology; criminal justice/law enforcement administration; culinary arts; dental hygiene; design and visual communications; diesel mechanics technology; drafting and design technology; economics; electrical, electronic and communications engineering technology; engineering; engineering technology; English; entrepreneurship; environmental engineering technology; finance; general studies; geology/earth science; graphic design; health professions related; heating, air conditioning, ventilation and refrigeration maintenance technology; history; human development and family studies; humanities; industrial radiologic technology; information science/studies; information technology; instrumentation technology; international/global studies; international relations and affairs; kinesiology and exercise science; legal assistant/paralegal; marketing/marketing management; mass communication/media; medical/clinical assistant; medical radiologic technology; music; occupational therapist assistant; photographic and film/video technology; physical sciences; physical therapy technology; physics; political science and government; psychology; public health related; quality control technology; radio and television broadcasting technology; registered nursing/registered nurse; sign language interpretation and translation; social work; sociology; speech communication and rhetoric; sport and fitness administration/management; surveying technology; teacher assistant/aide; telecommunications technology; welding technology.
Academics *Calendar:* semesters. *Degree:* certificates, diplomas, and associate. *Special study options:* academic remediation for entering students, advanced placement credit, cooperative education, distance learning, double majors, English as a second language, internships, part-time degree program, services for LD students, student-designed majors, study abroad, summer session for credit. *ROTC:* Army (c), Air Force (c).
Library Markosian Library plus 2 others with 152,537 titles, 20,645 audiovisual materials, an OPAC, a Web page.
Student Life *Housing:* college housing not available. *Activities and Organizations:* drama/theater group, student-run newspaper, radio and television station, choral group, marching band. *Campus security:* 24-hour emergency response devices and patrols, late-night transport/escort service. *Student services:* health clinic, personal/psychological counseling.
Athletics Member NJCAA. *Intercollegiate sports:* baseball M(s), basketball M(s)/W(s), cheerleading M(s)/W(s), soccer M(c)/W(c), softball W(s), volleyball W(s).
Costs (2014–15) *Tuition:* state resident $3040 full-time, $126 per credit hour part-time; nonresident $10,582 full-time, $440 per credit hour part-time.

Required fees: $429 full-time. *Payment plan:* installment. *Waivers:* senior citizens and employees or children of employees.
Financial Aid Of all full-time matriculated undergraduates who enrolled in 2013, 132 Federal Work-Study jobs (averaging $2567).
Applying *Options:* electronic application, early admission. *Application fee:* $40. *Application deadlines:* rolling (freshmen), rolling (transfers).
Freshman Application Contact Ms. Kathy Thompson, Salt Lake Community College, Salt Lake City, UT 84130. *Phone:* 801-957-4485. *E-mail:* kathy.thompson@slcc.edu.
Website: http://www.slcc.edu/.

Snow College
Ephraim, Utah

- **State-supported** 2-year, founded 1888, part of Utah System of Higher Education
- **Rural** 50-acre campus
- **Endowment** $6.2 million
- **Coed**

Undergraduates 2,813 full-time, 1,792 part-time. Students come from 24 other countries; 6% are from out of state; 1% Black or African American, non-Hispanic/Latino; 4% Hispanic/Latino; 0.7% Asian, non-Hispanic/Latino; 2% Native Hawaiian or other Pacific Islander, non-Hispanic/Latino; 2% American Indian or Alaska Native, non-Hispanic/Latino; 1% Two or more races, non-Hispanic/Latino; 1% Race/ethnicity unknown; 3% international; 2% transferred in; 20% live on campus. *Retention:* 34% of full-time freshmen returned.
Faculty *Student/faculty ratio:* 21:1.
Academics *Calendar:* semesters. *Degree:* certificates, diplomas, and associate. *Special study options:* academic remediation for entering students, adult/continuing education programs, advanced placement credit, cooperative education, distance learning, English as a second language, external degree program, honors programs, independent study, part-time degree program, services for LD students, summer session for credit.
Student Life *Campus security:* 24-hour emergency response devices and patrols, student patrols, late-night transport/escort service, controlled dormitory access.
Athletics Member NJCAA.
Standardized Tests *Recommended:* SAT or ACT (for admission).
Costs (2014–15) *Tuition:* state resident $2830 full-time, $153 per credit part-time; nonresident $10,332 full-time, $561 per credit part-time. Full-time tuition and fees vary according to degree level. *Required fees:* $390 full-time. *Room and board:* room only: $3500. Room and board charges vary according to board plan, housing facility, and location.
Financial Aid *Average financial aid package:* $2351. *Average need-based loan:* $2903. *Average need-based gift aid:* $2395.
Applying *Options:* electronic application, early admission. *Application fee:* $30. *Required:* high school transcript.
Freshman Application Contact Ms. Lorie Parry, Admissions Advisor, Snow College, 150 East College Avenue, Ephraim, UT 84627. *Phone:* 435-283-7144. *Fax:* 435-283-7157. *E-mail:* snowcollege@snow.edu.
Website: http://www.snow.edu/.

Vista College
Clearfield, Utah

Admissions Office Contact Vista College, 775 South 2000 East, Clearfield, UT 84015.
Website: http://www.vistacollege.edu/.

VERMONT

Community College of Vermont
Montpelier, Vermont

- **State-supported** 2-year, founded 1970, part of Vermont State Colleges System
- **Rural** campus
- **Coed**

Undergraduates 995 full-time, 5,624 part-time. Students come from 22 states and territories; 4% are from out of state; 2% Black or African American, non-Hispanic/Latino; 3% Hispanic/Latino; 2% Asian, non-Hispanic/Latino; 0.2% Native Hawaiian or other Pacific Islander, non-Hispanic/Latino; 1% American Indian or Alaska Native, non-Hispanic/Latino; 4% Two or more races, non-Hispanic/Latino; 4% Race/ethnicity unknown. *Retention:* 57% of full-time freshmen returned.

Faculty *Student/faculty ratio:* 13:1.
Academics *Calendar:* semesters. *Degree:* certificates and associate. *Special study options:* academic remediation for entering students, accelerated degree program, adult/continuing education programs, advanced placement credit, cooperative education, distance learning, double majors, English as a second language, external degree program, independent study, internships, part-time degree program, services for LD students, student-designed majors, study abroad, summer session for credit.
Standardized Tests *Required for some:* ACCUPLACER assessments are required for degree seeking applicants and some continuing education applicants. SAT/ACT scores as well as college transcripts may be used to waive the ACCUPLACER. *Recommended:* SAT or ACT (for admission).
Costs (2014–15) *Tuition:* state resident $7170 full-time, $239 per credit hour part-time; nonresident $14,340 full-time, $478 per credit hour part-time. *Required fees:* $150 full-time, $75 per term part-time.
Financial Aid Of all full-time matriculated undergraduates who enrolled in 2014, 52 Federal Work-Study jobs (averaging $2756).
Applying *Options:* electronic application.
Freshman Application Contact Community College of Vermont, 660 Elm Street, Montpelier, VT 05602. *Phone:* 802-654-0505. *Toll-free phone:* 800-CCV-6686.
Website: http://www.ccv.edu/.

Landmark College
Putney, Vermont

- **Independent** primarily 2-year, founded 1983
- **Small-town** 125-acre campus
- **Endowment** $19.1 million
- **Coed,** 514 undergraduate students, 96% full-time, 27% women, 73% men

Undergraduates 494 full-time, 20 part-time. Students come from 39 states and territories; 7 other countries; 93% are from out of state; 4% Black or African American, non-Hispanic/Latino; 4% Hispanic/Latino; 2% Asian, non-Hispanic/Latino; 0.2% Native Hawaiian or other Pacific Islander, non-Hispanic/Latino; 0.2% American Indian or Alaska Native, non-Hispanic/Latino; 2% Two or more races, non-Hispanic/Latino; 14% Race/ethnicity unknown; 2% international; 15% transferred in; 95% live on campus. *Retention:* 66% of full-time freshmen returned.
Freshmen *Admission:* 266 applied, 230 admitted, 119 enrolled.
Faculty *Total:* 78, 100% full-time, 13% with terminal degrees. *Student/faculty ratio:* 6:1.
Majors Biology/biological sciences; business administration and management; business/commerce; computer science; fine/studio arts; general studies; liberal arts and sciences/liberal studies.
Academics *Calendar:* semesters. *Degrees:* certificates, associate, and bachelor's. *Special study options:* academic remediation for entering students, advanced placement credit, distance learning, internships, services for LD students, study abroad, summer session for credit.
Library Landmark College Library with 140 titles, 1,500 audiovisual materials, an OPAC, a Web page.
Student Life *Housing:* on-campus residence required for freshman year. *Options:* coed, special housing for students with disabilities. Campus housing is university owned. Freshman campus housing is guaranteed. *Activities and Organizations:* drama/theater group, student-run newspaper, radio station, choral group, Student Government Association, Campus Activities Board, Phi Theta Kappa Honor Society, Equestrian Club, PBL Business Club. *Campus security:* 24-hour emergency response devices and patrols, late-night transport/escort service, controlled dormitory access. *Student services:* health clinic, personal/psychological counseling, women's center.
Athletics *Intercollegiate sports:* baseball M(c), basketball M(c)/W(c), cross-country running M(c)/W(c), equestrian sports M/W, rock climbing M(c)/W(c), soccer M/W, softball W(c). *Intramural sports:* badminton M(c)/W(c), basketball M(c)/W(c), fencing M(c)/W(c), skiing (cross-country) M(c)/W(c), tennis M(c)/W(c), volleyball M(c)/W(c), weight lifting M(c)/W(c).
Standardized Tests *Required:* Cognitive and achievement tests such as the Wechsler Adult Intelligence Scale III and the Nelson Denny Reading Test are required (for admission).
Costs (2014–15) *Comprehensive fee:* $60,530 includes full-time tuition ($49,950), mandatory fees ($130), and room and board ($10,450). *Room and board:* college room only: $5390. Room and board charges vary according to board plan and housing facility. *Payment plan:* installment. *Waivers:* employees or children of employees.
Financial Aid Of all full-time matriculated undergraduates who enrolled in 2010, 341 applied for aid, 243 were judged to have need, 3 had their need fully met. 85 Federal Work-Study jobs (averaging $1000). 3 state and other part-time jobs (averaging $1000). In 2010, 18 non-need-based awards were made. *Average percent of need met:* 45%. *Average financial aid package:* $26,000. *Average need-based loan:* $4500. *Average need-based gift aid:* $21,000.

Average non-need-based aid: $7800. *Average indebtedness upon graduation:* $6100.

Applying *Options:* electronic application, early action, deferred entrance. *Application fee:* $75. *Required:* essay or personal statement, high school transcript, diagnosis of LD and/or ADHD and cognitive testing. *Recommended:* 2 letters of recommendation, interview. *Application deadlines:* rolling (freshmen), rolling (transfers), 12/1 (early action). *Notification:* continuous (freshmen), continuous (transfers), 1/5 (early action). **Freshman Application Contact** Admissions Main Desk, Landmark College, Admissions Office, River Road South, Putney, VT 05346. *Phone:* 802-387-6718. *Fax:* 802-387-6868. *E-mail:* admissions@landmark.edu. *Website:* http://www.landmark.edu/.

New England Culinary Institute
Montpelier, Vermont

- **Proprietary** primarily 2-year, founded 1980
- **Small-town** campus
- **Coed,** 422 undergraduate students, 80% full-time, 45% women, 55% men

Undergraduates 338 full-time, 84 part-time. Students come from 39 states and territories; 6 other countries; 80% are from out of state; 4% Black or African American, non-Hispanic/Latino; 6% Hispanic/Latino; 2% Asian, non-Hispanic/Latino; 0.5% Native Hawaiian or other Pacific Islander, non-Hispanic/Latino; 1% Two or more races, non-Hispanic/Latino; 11% Race/ethnicity unknown; 1% international; 80% live on campus. *Retention:* 93% of full-time freshmen returned.

Freshmen *Admission:* 249 applied, 92 admitted.

Faculty *Total:* 39, 62% full-time. *Student/faculty ratio:* 13:1.

Majors Baking and pastry arts; culinary arts; restaurant, culinary, and catering management.

Academics *Calendar:* quarters. *Degrees:* certificates, associate, and bachelor's. *Special study options:* academic remediation for entering students, accelerated degree program, advanced placement credit, cooperative education, distance learning, honors programs, internships, services for LD students.

Library New England Culinary Institute Library with 4,075 titles, 325 audiovisual materials, an OPAC, a Web page.

Student Life *Housing:* on-campus residence required for freshman year. *Options:* coed, men-only, women-only. Campus housing is leased by the school. Freshman applicants given priority for college housing. *Activities and Organizations:* American Culinary Federation, Slow Food, Student Council, Special Guest Lecture Series, Student Ambassadors (Leadership Program). *Campus security:* 24-hour emergency response devices, student patrols.

Standardized Tests *Recommended:* SAT or ACT (for admission).

Costs (2014–15) *Comprehensive fee:* $28,625 includes full-time tuition ($20,625) and room and board ($8000). Full-time tuition and fees vary according to course load, degree level, program, reciprocity agreements, and student level. Part-time tuition and fees vary according to course load, degree level, program, reciprocity agreements, and student level. *Room and board:* Room and board charges vary according to housing facility. *Payment plan:* installment. *Waivers:* employees or children of employees.

Financial Aid Of all full-time matriculated undergraduates who enrolled in 2013, 320 Federal Work-Study jobs (averaging $1000).

Applying *Options:* electronic application, early admission, deferred entrance. *Required:* high school transcript. *Required for some:* interview. *Recommended:* essay or personal statement, 2 letters of recommendation, culinary experience. *Application deadline:* rolling (freshmen). **Freshman Application Contact** Adonica Williams, New England Culinary Institute, 56 College Street, Montpelier, VT 05602-3115. *Phone:* 802-225-3210. *Toll-free phone:* 877-223-6324. *Fax:* 802-225-3280. *E-mail:* admissions@neci.edu. *Website:* http://www.neci.edu/.

VIRGINIA

Advanced Technology Institute
Virginia Beach, Virginia

Freshman Application Contact Admissions Office, Advanced Technology Institute, 5700 Southern Boulevard, Suite 100, Virginia Beach, VA 23462. *Phone:* 757-490-1241. *Toll-free phone:* 888-468-1093. *Website:* http://www.auto.edu/.

American National University
Charlottesville, Virginia

Director of Admissions Kimberly Moore, Campus Director, American National University, 3926 Seminole Trail, Charlottesville, VA 22911. *Phone:* 434-295-0136. *Toll-free phone:* 888-9-JOBREADY. *Fax:* 434-979-8061. *Website:* http://www.national-college.edu/.

American National University
Danville, Virginia

Freshman Application Contact Admissions Office, American National University, 336 Old Riverside Drive, Danville, VA 24541. *Phone:* 434-793-6822. *Toll-free phone:* 888-9-JOBREADY. *Website:* http://www.national-college.edu/.

American National University
Harrisonburg, Virginia

Director of Admissions Jack Evey, Campus Director, American National University, 1515 Country Club Road, Harrisonburg, VA 22802. *Phone:* 540-432-0943. *Toll-free phone:* 888-9-JOBREADY. *Website:* http://www.national-college.edu/.

American National University
Lynchburg, Virginia

Freshman Application Contact Admissions Representative, American National University, 104 Candlewood Court, Lynchburg, VA 24502-2653. *Phone:* 804-239-3500. *Toll-free phone:* 888-9-JOBREADY. *Website:* http://www.national-college.edu/.

American National University
Martinsville, Virginia

Director of Admissions Mr. John Scott, Campus Director, American National University, 905 Memorial Boulevard North, Martinsville, VA 24112. *Phone:* 276-632-5621. *Toll-free phone:* 888-9-JOBREADY. *Website:* http://www.national-college.edu/.

Blue Ridge Community College
Weyers Cave, Virginia

Freshman Application Contact Blue Ridge Community College, PO Box 80, Weyers Cave, VA 24486-0080. *Phone:* 540-453-2217. *Toll-free phone:* 888-750-2722. *Website:* http://www.brcc.edu/.

Bryant & Stratton College–Richmond Campus
Richmond, Virginia

Freshman Application Contact Mr. David K. Mayle, Director of Admissions, Bryant & Stratton College–Richmond Campus, 8141 Hull Street Road, Richmond, VA 23235-6411. *Phone:* 804-745-2444. *Fax:* 804-745-6884. *E-mail:* tlawson@bryanstratton.edu. *Website:* http://www.bryantstratton.edu/.

Bryant & Stratton College–Virginia Beach Campus
Virginia Beach, Virginia

Freshman Application Contact Bryant & Stratton College–Virginia Beach Campus, 301 Centre Pointe Drive, Virginia Beach, VA 23462-4417. *Phone:* 757-499-7900 Ext. 173. *Website:* http://www.bryantstratton.edu/.

Career Training Solutions
Fredericksburg, Virginia

Admissions Office Contact Career Training Solutions, 10304 Spotsylvania Avenue, Suite 400, Fredericksburg, VA 22408. *Website:* http://www.careertrainingsolutions.com/.

Central Virginia Community College
Lynchburg, Virginia

- **State-supported** 2-year, founded 1966, part of Virginia Community College System
- **Suburban** 104-acre campus
- **Coed,** 4,519 undergraduate students, 33% full-time, 51% women, 49% men

Undergraduates 1,513 full-time, 3,006 part-time. Students come from 14 states and territories; 1% are from out of state; 16% Black or African American, non-Hispanic/Latino; 3% Hispanic/Latino; 2% Asian, non-Hispanic/Latino; 0.1% Native Hawaiian or other Pacific Islander, non-Hispanic/Latino; 0.3% American Indian or Alaska Native, non-Hispanic/Latino; 3% Two or more races, non-Hispanic/Latino; 0.6% Race/ethnicity unknown; 0.2% international. *Retention:* 40% of full-time freshmen returned.

Freshmen *Admission:* 2,006 applied, 2,005 admitted.

Faculty *Total:* 302, 21% full-time. *Student/faculty ratio:* 18:1.

Majors Accounting related; business administration and management; business/commerce; business operations support and secretarial services related; computer and information sciences; criminal justice/law enforcement administration; culinary arts; design and visual communications; education; emergency medical technology (EMT paramedic); engineering; engineering technology; industrial technology; liberal arts and sciences/liberal studies; management science; medical/clinical assistant; radiologic technology/science; respiratory care therapy; science technologies.

Academics *Calendar:* semesters. *Degree:* certificates, diplomas, and associate. *Special study options:* academic remediation for entering students, advanced placement credit, cooperative education, distance learning, independent study, internships, part-time degree program, services for LD students, summer session for credit.

Library Bedford Learning Resources Center with an OPAC, a Web page.

Student Life *Activities and Organizations:* drama/theater group. *Campus security:* 24-hour emergency response devices.

Athletics Member NJCAA. *Intercollegiate sports:* baseball M.

Costs (2014–15) *Tuition:* state resident $4260 full-time, $142 per credit hour part-time; nonresident $10,068 full-time, $336 per credit hour part-time. *Payment plan:* installment.

Financial Aid Of all full-time matriculated undergraduates who enrolled in 2013, 65 Federal Work-Study jobs (averaging $2700).

Applying *Options:* electronic application, early admission, deferred entrance. *Application deadlines:* rolling (freshmen), rolling (out-of-state freshmen), rolling (transfers). *Notification:* continuous (freshmen), continuous (out-of-state freshmen), continuous (transfers).

Freshman Application Contact Admissions Office, Central Virginia Community College, 3506 Wards Road, Lynchburg, VA 24502. *Phone:* 434-832-7633. *Toll-free phone:* 800-562-3060. *Fax:* 434-832-7793. *Website:* http://www.cvcc.vccs.edu/.

Centura College
Chesapeake, Virginia

Director of Admissions Director of Admissions, Centura College, 932 Ventures Way, Chesapeake, VA 23320. *Phone:* 757-549-2121. *Toll-free phone:* 877-575-5627. *Fax:* 575-549-1196. *Website:* http://www.centuracollege.edu/.

Centura College
Newport News, Virginia

Director of Admissions Victoria Whitehead, Director of Admissions, Centura College, 616 Denbigh Boulevard, Newport News, VA 23608. *Phone:* 757-874-2121. *Toll-free phone:* 877-575-5627. *Fax:* 757-874-3857. *E-mail:* admdircpen@centura.edu. *Website:* http://www.centuracollege.edu/.

Centura College
Norfolk, Virginia

Director of Admissions Director of Admissions, Centura College, 7020 North Military Highway, Norfolk, VA 23518. *Phone:* 757-853-2121. *Toll-free phone:* 877-575-5627. *Fax:* 757-852-9017. *Website:* http://www.centuracollege.edu/.

Centura College
North Chesterfield, Virginia

Freshman Application Contact Admissions Office, Centura College, 7914 Midlothian Turnpike, North Chesterfield, VA 23235-5230. *Phone:* 804-330-0111. *Toll-free phone:* 877-575-5627. *Fax:* 804-330-3809. *Website:* http://www.centuracollege.edu/.

Centura College
Virginia Beach, Virginia

Freshman Application Contact Admissions Office, Centura College, 2697 Dean Drive, Suite 100, Virginia Beach, VA 23452. *Phone:* 757-340-2121. *Toll-free phone:* 877-575-5627. *Fax:* 757-340-9704. *Website:* http://www.centuracollege.edu/.

Columbia College
Fairfax, Virginia

Admissions Office Contact Columbia College, 8300 Merrifield Avenue, Fairfax, VA 22031. *Website:* http://www.ccdc.edu/.

Dabney S. Lancaster Community College
Clifton Forge, Virginia

- **State-supported** 2-year, founded 1964, part of Virginia Community College System
- **Rural** 117-acre campus
- **Endowment** $3.3 million
- **Coed,** 1,284 undergraduate students, 24% full-time, 55% women, 45% men

Undergraduates 314 full-time, 970 part-time. Students come from 4 states and territories; 2% are from out of state; 5% Black or African American, non-Hispanic/Latino; 2% Hispanic/Latino; 0.1% Asian, non-Hispanic/Latino; 0.8% American Indian or Alaska Native, non-Hispanic/Latino; 2% Two or more races, non-Hispanic/Latino; 32% transferred in.

Freshmen *Admission:* 174 enrolled.

Faculty *Total:* 97, 24% full-time. *Student/faculty ratio:* 16:1.

Majors Administrative assistant and secretarial science; biological and physical sciences; business administration and management; computer programming; criminal justice/law enforcement administration; data processing and data processing technology; drafting and design technology; drafting/design engineering technologies related; education; electrical, electronic and communications engineering technology; forest technology; information science/studies; legal administrative assistant/secretary; liberal arts and sciences/liberal studies; medical administrative assistant and medical secretary; registered nursing/registered nurse; wood science and wood products/pulp and paper technology.

Academics *Calendar:* semesters. *Degree:* certificates and associate. *Special study options:* academic remediation for entering students, adult/continuing education programs, advanced placement credit, cooperative education, distance learning, honors programs, independent study, internships, part-time degree program, services for LD students, study abroad, summer session for credit.

Library DSLCC Library plus 1 other with 34,397 titles, 1,260 audiovisual materials, an OPAC.

Student Life *Housing:* college housing not available. *Activities and Organizations:* choral group. *Campus security:* 24-hour emergency response devices. *Student services:* personal/psychological counseling.

Athletics *Intramural sports:* basketball M/W, volleyball M/W.

Standardized Tests *Required for some:* SAT (for admission), ACT (for admission), SAT or ACT (for admission), SAT and SAT Subject Tests or ACT (for admission), SAT Subject Tests (for admission), Virginia Placement Test.

Costs (2014–15) *Tuition:* state resident $3324 full-time, $139 per credit part-time; nonresident $7994 full-time, $333 per credit part-time. Full-time tuition and fees vary according to reciprocity agreements. Part-time tuition and fees vary according to reciprocity agreements. *Required fees:* $264 full-time, $11 per credit hour part-time. *Payment plan:* installment. *Waivers:* senior citizens.

Applying *Recommended:* high school transcript.

Freshman Application Contact Mrs. Lorrie Wilhelm Ferguson, Registrar, Dabney S. Lancaster Community College, Backels Hall, Clifton Forge, VA 24422. *Phone:* 540-863-2823. *Toll-free phone:* 877-73-DSLCC. *Fax:* 540-863-2915. *E-mail:* lwferguson@dslcc.edu. *Website:* http://www.dslcc.edu/.

Danville Community College
Danville, Virginia

Freshman Application Contact Cathy Pulliam, Coordinator of Student Recruitment and Enrollment, Danville Community College, 1008 South Main Street, Danville, VA 24541-4088. *Phone:* 434-797-8538. *Toll-free phone:* 800-560-4291. *E-mail:* cpulliam@dcc.vccs.edu. *Website:* http://www.dcc.vccs.edu/.

Eastern Shore Community College
Melfa, Virginia

- **State-supported** 2 year, founded 1971, part of Virginia Community College System
- **Rural** 117-acre campus with easy access to Hampton Roads/Virginia Beach, Norfolk
- **Coed**

Undergraduates 264 full-time, 593 part-time. 39% Black or African American, non-Hispanic/Latino; 6% Hispanic/Latino; 1% Asian, non-Hispanic/Latino; 0.2% American Indian or Alaska Native, non-Hispanic/Latino; 0.8% Race/ethnicity unknown.
Faculty *Student/faculty ratio:* 13:1.
Academics *Calendar:* semesters. *Degree:* certificates and associate. *Special study options:* academic remediation for entering students, adult/continuing education programs, distance learning, internships, off-campus study, part-time degree program, services for LD students, summer session for credit.
Student Life *Campus security:* security guards, day and night during classes when the college is in session.
Standardized Tests *Required:* The Virginia Community College System (VCCS) has a placement test designed for and utilized by all schools in its system (for admission).
Costs (2014–15) *Tuition:* area resident $3892 full-time; state resident $3800 full-time, $128 per credit hour part-time; nonresident $9340 full-time, $304 per credit hour part-time. Full-time tuition and fees vary according to course load. Part-time tuition and fees vary according to course load. *Required fees:* $128 full-time, $12 per credit hour part-time, $18 per term part-time.
Financial Aid Of all full-time matriculated undergraduates who enrolled in 2013, 11 Federal Work-Study jobs.
Applying *Options:* electronic application. *Required:* high school transcript, high school diploma or GED.
Freshman Application Contact P. Bryan Smith, Dean of Student Services, Eastern Shore Community College, 29300 Lankford Highway, Melfa, VA 23410. *Phone:* 757-789-1732. *Toll-free phone:* 877-871-8455. *Fax:* 757-789-1737. *E-mail:* bsmith@es.vccs.edu. *Website:* http://www.es.vccs.edu/.

ECPI University
Richmond, Virginia

Freshman Application Contact Director, ECPI University, 800 Moorefield Park Drive, Richmond, VA 23236. *Phone:* 804-330-5533. *Toll-free phone:* 800-986-1200. *Fax:* 804-330-5577. *E-mail:* agerard@ecpi.edu. *Website:* http://www.ecpi.edu/.

Everest College
Chesapeake, Virginia

Admissions Office Contact Everest College, 825 Greenbrier Circle, Chesapeake, VA 23320-2637. *Website:* http://www.everest.edu/.

Everest College
Newport News, Virginia

Admissions Office Contact Everest College, 803 Diligence Drive, Newport News, VA 23606. *Website:* http://www.everest.edu/.

Fortis College
Norfolk, Virginia

Admissions Office Contact Fortis College, 6300 Center Drive, Suite 100, Norfolk, VA 23502. *Website:* http://www.fortis.edu/.

Fortis College
Richmond, Virginia

Admissions Office Contact Fortis College, 2000 Westmoreland Street, Suite A, Richmond, VA 23230. *Website:* http://www.fortis.edu/.

Germanna Community College
Locust Grove, Virginia

Freshman Application Contact Ms. Rita Dunston, Registrar, Germanna Community College, 10000 Germanna Point Drive, Fredericksburg, VA 22408. *Phone:* 540-891-3020. *Fax:* 540-891-3092. *Website:* http://www.germanna.edu/.

Global Health College
Alexandria, Virginia

Admissions Office Contact Global Health College, 25 South Quaker Lane, 1st Floor, Alexandria, VA 22314. *Website:* http://www.global.edu/.

ITT Technical Institute
Chantilly, Virginia

- **Proprietary** primarily 2-year, founded 2002, part of ITT Educational Services, Inc.
- **Coed**

Academics *Calendar:* quarters. *Degrees:* associate and bachelor's.
Freshman Application Contact Director of Recruitment, ITT Technical Institute, 14420 Albemarle Point Place, Suite 100, Chantilly, VA 20151. *Phone:* 703-263-2541. *Toll-free phone:* 888-895-8324. *Website:* http://www.itt-tech.edu/.

ITT Technical Institute
Norfolk, Virginia

- **Proprietary** primarily 2-year, founded 1988, part of ITT Educational Services, Inc.
- **Suburban** campus
- **Coed**

Academics *Calendar:* quarters. *Degrees:* associate and bachelor's.
Financial Aid Of all full-time matriculated undergraduates who enrolled in 2013, 3 Federal Work-Study jobs (averaging $5000).
Freshman Application Contact Director of Recruitment, ITT Technical Institute, 5425 Robin Hood Road, Norfolk, VA 23513. *Phone:* 757-466-1260. *Toll-free phone:* 888-253-8324. *Website:* http://www.itt-tech.edu/.

ITT Technical Institute
Richmond, Virginia

- **Proprietary** primarily 2-year, founded 1999, part of ITT Educational Services, Inc.
- **Coed**

Academics *Calendar:* quarters. *Degrees:* associate and bachelor's.
Freshman Application Contact Director of Recruitment, ITT Technical Institute, 300 Gateway Centre Parkway, Richmond, VA 23235. *Phone:* 804-330-4992. *Toll-free phone:* 888-330-4888. *Website:* http://www.itt-tech.edu/.

ITT Technical Institute
Salem, Virginia

- **Proprietary** primarily 2-year
- **Coed**

Academics *Degrees:* associate and bachelor's.
Freshman Application Contact Director of Recruitment, ITT Technical Institute, 2159 Apperson Drive, Salem, VA 24153. *Phone:* 540-989-2500. *Toll-free phone:* 877-208-6132. *Website:* http://www.itt-tech.edu/.

ITT Technical Institute

Springfield, Virginia

- **Proprietary** primarily 2-year, founded 2002, part of ITT Educational Services, Inc.
- **Coed**

Academics *Calendar:* quarters. *Degrees:* associate and bachelor's.
Freshman Application Contact Director of Recruitment, ITT Technical Institute, 7300 Boston Boulevard, Springfield, VA 22153. *Phone:* 703-440-9535. *Toll-free phone:* 866-817-8324.
Website: http://www.itt-tech.edu/.

John Tyler Community College

Chester, Virginia

- **State-supported** 2-year, founded 1967, part of Virginia Community College System
- **Suburban** 160-acre campus with easy access to Richmond
- **Coed,** 9,875 undergraduate students, 27% full-time, 57% women, 43% men

Undergraduates 2,697 full-time, 7,178 part-time. Students come from 43 states and territories; 24 other countries; 1% are from out of state; 24% Black or African American, non-Hispanic/Latino; 7% Hispanic/Latino; 3% Asian, non-Hispanic/Latino; 0.2% Native Hawaiian or other Pacific Islander, non-Hispanic/Latino; 0.5% American Indian or Alaska Native, non-Hispanic/Latino; 1% Race/ethnicity unknown; 6% transferred in.
Freshmen *Admission:* 1,633 enrolled.
Faculty *Total:* 568, 21% full-time. *Student/faculty ratio:* 19:1.
Majors Accounting related; architectural technology; business administration and management; business administration, management and operations related; business/commerce; child-care provision; computer and information sciences; criminal justice/law enforcement administration; engineering; funeral service and mortuary science; general studies; humanities; human services; industrial electronics technology; industrial technology; information technology; liberal arts and sciences/liberal studies; management information systems; mechanical engineering technologies related; mental and social health services and allied professions related; registered nursing/registered nurse; visual and performing arts related.
Academics *Calendar:* semesters. *Degree:* certificates and associate. *Special study options:* academic remediation for entering students, adult/continuing education programs, advanced placement credit, distance learning, external degree program, honors programs, off-campus study, part-time degree program, services for LD students, study abroad, summer session for credit. *ROTC:* Army (c).
Library John Tyler Community College Learning Resource and Technology Center with 52,000 titles, 1,335 audiovisual materials, an OPAC, a Web page.
Student Life *Housing:* college housing not available. *Activities and Organizations:* drama/theater group, choral group, Phi Theta Kappa, Human Services Club, Future Teachers Club, Student Nurses' Association, Student Veteran's Organization. *Campus security:* 24-hour emergency response devices and patrols.
Athletics *Intramural sports:* basketball M(c)/W(c), golf M(c)/W(c), ultimate Frisbee M(c)/W(c).
Costs (2014–15) *Tuition:* state resident $3264 full-time, $136 per credit hour part-time; nonresident $7934 full-time, $331 per credit hour part-time. Full-time tuition and fees vary according to course load. Part-time tuition and fees vary according to course load. *Required fees:* $70 full-time, $35 per semester part-time. *Payment plan:* installment. *Waivers:* senior citizens.
Financial Aid Of all full-time matriculated undergraduates who enrolled in 2013, 60 Federal Work-Study jobs (averaging $2437).
Applying *Options:* early admission, deferred entrance. *Recommended:* high school transcript. *Application deadline:* rolling (freshmen). *Notification:* continuous (freshmen).
Freshman Application Contact Ms. Joy James, Director of Admissions and Records/Veterans Affairs and Registrar, John Tyler Community College, 13101 Jefferson Davis Highway, Chester, VA 23831. *Phone:* 804-706-5214. *Toll-free phone:* 800-552-3490. *Fax:* 804-796-4362. *E-mail:* jjames@jtcc.edu.
Website: http://www.jtcc.edu/.

J. Sargeant Reynolds Community College

Richmond, Virginia

- **State-supported** 2-year, founded 1972, part of Virginia Community College System
- **Suburban** 207-acre campus with easy access to Richmond
- **Coed,** 11,949 undergraduate students, 28% full-time, 62% women, 38% men

Undergraduates 3,344 full-time, 8,605 part-time. Students come from 31 states and territories; 19 other countries; 1% are from out of state; 36% Black or African American, non-Hispanic/Latino; 2% Hispanic/Latino; 5% Asian, non-Hispanic/Latino; 0.2% Native Hawaiian or other Pacific Islander, non-Hispanic/Latino; 0.5% American Indian or Alaska Native, non-Hispanic/Latino; 6% Two or more races, non-Hispanic/Latino; 1% Race/ethnicity unknown; 5% transferred in. *Retention:* 50% of full-time freshmen returned.
Freshmen *Admission:* 1,821 enrolled.
Faculty *Total:* 666, 21% full-time. *Student/faculty ratio:* 20:1.
Majors Accounting related; allied health and medical assisting services related; applied horticulture/horticulture operations; architectural and building sciences; automobile/automotive mechanics technology; baking and pastry arts; biological and physical sciences; building/construction site management; business administration and management; business administration, management and operations related; business operations support and secretarial services related; CAD/CADD drafting/design technology; child-care provision; civil engineering; civil engineering technology; clinical/medical laboratory technology; computer and information sciences; computer/information technology services administration related; computer programming; computer science; computer systems networking and telecommunications; consumer merchandising/retailing management; cooking and related culinary arts; criminal justice/law enforcement administration; dental assisting; dental laboratory technology; diesel mechanics technology; emergency care attendant (EMT ambulance); emergency medical technology (EMT paramedic); engineering; fire science/firefighting; floriculture/floristry management; food preparation; health information/medical records technology; hospitality administration; hospitality administration related; hotel/motel administration; industrial electronics technology; legal assistant/paralegal; liberal arts and sciences and humanities related; licensed practical/vocational nurse training; mathematics; mental and social health services and allied professions related; opticianry; pharmacy technician; real estate; registered nursing/registered nurse; respiratory care therapy; restaurant/food services management; sign language interpretation and translation; small business administration; social sciences; substance abuse/addiction counseling; web page, digital/multimedia and information resources design; welding technology.
Academics *Calendar:* semesters. *Degree:* certificates and associate. *Special study options:* academic remediation for entering students, adult/continuing education programs, advanced placement credit, distance learning, double majors, English as a second language, independent study, internships, off-campus study, part-time degree program, services for LD students, summer session for credit.
Library J. Sargeant Reynolds Community College Library plus 2 others with 130,000 titles, 3,000 audiovisual materials, an OPAC, a Web page.
Student Life *Housing:* college housing not available. *Campus security:* 24-hour emergency response devices and patrols, late-night transport/escort service, security during open hours. *Student services:* personal/psychological counseling.
Costs (2015–16) *Tuition:* state resident $3702 full-time, $148 per credit part-time; nonresident $8219 full-time, $331 per credit part-time. Full-time tuition and fees vary according to course load and program. Part-time tuition and fees vary according to course load and program. *Required fees:* $510 full-time. *Payment plan:* installment. *Waivers:* senior citizens.
Financial Aid Of all full-time matriculated undergraduates who enrolled in 2009, 14,628 applied for aid, 11,184 were judged to have need. 64 Federal Work-Study jobs (averaging $2600). In 2009, 121 non-need-based awards were made. *Average percent of need met:* 49%. *Average financial aid package:* $6950. *Average need-based loan:* $2792. *Average need-based gift aid:* $3400. *Average non-need-based aid:* $891. *Average indebtedness upon graduation:* $3891.
Applying *Options:* electronic application. *Required:* high school transcript. *Required for some:* interview, Interviews with some departments; A few require criminal background checks and/or drug screening; At least one has minimal physical standards. *Application deadlines:* rolling (freshmen), rolling (transfers). *Notification:* continuous (freshmen), continuous (transfers).
Freshman Application Contact Ms. Karen Pettis-Walden, Director of Admissions and Records, J. Sargeant Reynolds Community College, PO Box

85622, Richmond, VA 23285-5622. *Phone:* 804-523-5029. *Fax:* 804-371-3650. *E-mail:* kpettis-walden@reynolds.edu. *Website:* http://www.reynolds.edu/.

Lord Fairfax Community College
Middletown, Virginia

Freshman Application Contact Karen Bucher, Director of Enrollment Management, Lord Fairfax Community College, 173 Skirmisher Lane, Middletown, VA 22645. *Phone:* 540-868-7132. *Toll-free phone:* 800-906-LFCC. *Fax:* 540-868-7005. *E-mail:* kbucher@lfcc.edu. *Website:* http://www.lfcc.edu/.

Miller-Motte Technical College
Lynchburg, Virginia

Director of Admissions Ms. Betty J. Dierstein, Director, Miller-Motte Technical College, 1011 Creekside Lane, Lynchburg, VA 24502. *Phone:* 434-239-5222. *Fax:* 434-239-1069. *E-mail:* bjdierstein@miller-mott.com. *Website:* http://www.miller-motte.edu/.

Miller-Motte Technical College
Roanoke, Virginia

Admissions Office Contact Miller-Motte Technical College, 4444 Electric Road, Roanoke, VA 24018. *Website:* http://www.miller-motte.edu/.

Mountain Empire Community College
Big Stone Gap, Virginia

- **State-supported** 2-year, founded 1972, part of Virginia Community College System
- **Rural** campus
- **Coed**

Undergraduates 1,310 full-time, 1,614 part-time. Students come from 9 states and territories; 4% are from out of state; 2% Black or African American, non-Hispanic/Latino; 0.4% Hispanic/Latino; 0.2% Asian, non-Hispanic/Latino; 0.3% American Indian or Alaska Native, non-Hispanic/Latino; 0.3% Race/ethnicity unknown. *Retention:* 61% of full-time freshmen returned.
Academics *Calendar:* semesters. *Degree:* certificates and associate. *Special study options:* academic remediation for entering students, adult/continuing education programs, advanced placement credit, cooperative education, distance learning, double majors, external degree program, independent study, internships, part-time degree program, student-designed majors, summer session for credit.
Student Life *Campus security:* 24-hour emergency response devices and patrols.
Costs (2014–15) *Tuition:* state resident $3336 full-time, $139 per credit hour part-time; nonresident $8006 full-time, $334 per credit hour part-time. Full-time tuition and fees vary according to course load. Part-time tuition and fees vary according to course load.
Financial Aid Of all full-time matriculated undergraduates who enrolled in 2013, 150 Federal Work-Study jobs (averaging $1200). 30 state and other part-time jobs (averaging $650).
Applying *Options:* electronic application, early admission, deferred entrance. *Required:* high school transcript. *Required for some:* minimum 2.0 GPA.
Freshman Application Contact Mountain Empire Community College, 3441 Mountain Empire Road, Big Stone Gap, VA 24219. *Phone:* 276-523-2400 Ext. 219. *Website:* http://www.mecc.edu/.

New River Community College
Dublin, Virginia

Freshman Application Contact Ms. Margaret G. Taylor, Director of Student Services, New River Community College, PO Box 1127, Dublin, VA 24084-1127. *Phone:* 540-674-3600. *Toll-free phone:* 866-462-6722. *Fax:* 540-674-3644. *E-mail:* nrtaylm@nr.edu. *Website:* http://www.nr.edu/.

Northern Virginia Community College
Annandale, Virginia

- **State-supported** 2-year, founded 1965, part of Virginia Community College System
- **Suburban** 435-acre campus with easy access to Washington, DC
- **Coed,** 51,803 undergraduate students, 38% full-time, 51% women, 49% men

Undergraduates 19,700 full-time, 32,103 part-time. 3% are from out of state; 18% Black or African American, non-Hispanic/Latino; 19% Hispanic/Latino; 14% Asian, non-Hispanic/Latino; 10% Native Hawaiian or other Pacific Islander, non-Hispanic/Latino; 3% Two or more races, non-Hispanic/Latino; 3% Race/ethnicity unknown; 3% international.
Freshmen *Admission:* 9,128 enrolled.
Faculty *Total:* 2,657, 27% full-time.
Majors Administrative assistant and secretarial science; agricultural business and management; agricultural business and management related; architectural engineering technology; biological and physical sciences; business administration and management; business/commerce; clinical/medical laboratory technology; computer and information sciences; dental hygiene; electrical, electronic and communications engineering technology; emergency medical technology (EMT paramedic); engineering; engineering technologies and engineering related; environmental control technologies related; general studies; graphic and printing equipment operation/production; health information/medical records administration; homeland security, law enforcement, firefighting and protective services related; industrial technology; information technology; interior design; liberal arts and sciences/liberal studies; management information systems; medical radiologic technology; mental and social health services and allied professions related; parks, recreation and leisure; physical therapy; respiratory care therapy; social sciences; special education; transportation and materials moving related; vehicle maintenance and repair technologies related; visual and performing arts; visual and performing arts related.
Academics *Calendar:* semesters. *Degree:* certificates and associate. *Special study options:* academic remediation for entering students, adult/continuing education programs, advanced placement credit, cooperative education, distance learning, double majors, English as a second language, external degree program, honors programs, part-time degree program, services for LD students, study abroad, summer session for credit.
Library 228,009 titles, 12,227 audiovisual materials, an OPAC, a Web page.
Student Life *Housing:* college housing not available. *Activities and Organizations:* student-run newspaper, television station. *Campus security:* 24-hour emergency response devices, campus police.
Athletics *Intramural sports:* basketball M/W, football M/W, soccer M/W, volleyball M/W.
Costs (2014–15) *Tuition:* state resident $3677 full-time; nonresident $8411 full-time.
Applying *Options:* early admission, deferred entrance. *Required for some:* high school transcript. *Application deadlines:* rolling (freshmen), rolling (transfers). *Notification:* continuous (freshmen), continuous (transfers).
Freshman Application Contact Northern Virginia Community College, 4001 Wakefield Chapel Road, Annandale, VA 22003-3796. *Phone:* 703-323-3195. *Website:* http://www.nvcc.edu/.

Patrick Henry Community College
Martinsville, Virginia

- **State-supported** 2-year, founded 1962, part of Virginia Community College System
- **Rural** 137-acre campus with easy access to Greensboro
- **Endowment** $10.6 million
- **Coed**

Undergraduates 1,486 full-time, 1,677 part-time. Students come from 6 states and territories; 1% are from out of state; 24% Black or African American, non-Hispanic/Latino; 4% Hispanic/Latino; 0.5% Asian, non-Hispanic/Latino; 0.3% American Indian or Alaska Native, non-Hispanic/Latino; 2% Two or more races, non-Hispanic/Latino; 0.1% Race/ethnicity unknown; 0.3% international. *Retention:* 59% of full-time freshmen returned.
Faculty *Student/faculty ratio:* 18:1.
Academics *Calendar:* semesters. *Degree:* certificates and associate. *Special study options:* academic remediation for entering students, adult/continuing education programs, advanced placement credit, cooperative education, distance learning, independent study, internships, part-time degree program, services for LD students, summer session for credit.
Student Life *Campus security:* 24-hour emergency response devices and patrols, late-night transport/escort service.
Athletics Member NJCAA.
Financial Aid Of all full-time matriculated undergraduates who enrolled in 2013, 41 Federal Work-Study jobs (averaging $2000).

Applying *Options:* electronic application, early admission. *Required:* high school transcript.
Freshman Application Contact Mr. Travis Tisdale, Coordinator, Admissions and Records, Patrick Henry Community College, 645 Patriot Avenue, Martinsville, VA 24112. *Phone:* 276-656-0311. *Toll-free phone:* 800-232-7997. *Fax:* 276-656-0352.
Website: http://www.ph.vccs.edu/.

Paul D. Camp Community College
Franklin, Virginia

Freshman Application Contact Mrs. Trina Jones, Dean Student Services, Paul D. Camp Community College, PO Box 737, 100 N College Drive, Franklin, VA 23851. *Phone:* 757-569-6720. *E-mail:* tjones@pdc.edu.
Website: http://www.pdc.edu/.

Piedmont Virginia Community College
Charlottesville, Virginia

- **State-supported** 2-year, founded 1972, part of Virginia Community College System
- **Suburban** 114-acre campus with easy access to Richmond
- **Endowment** $6.8 million
- **Coed,** 5,554 undergraduate students, 22% full-time, 58% women, 42% men

Undergraduates 1,234 full-time, 4,320 part-time. Students come from 22 states and territories; 13% Black or African American, non-Hispanic/Latino; 5% Hispanic/Latino; 4% Asian, non-Hispanic/Latino; 0.2% Native Hawaiian or other Pacific Islander, non-Hispanic/Latino; 0.3% American Indian or Alaska Native, non-Hispanic/Latino; 4% Two or more races, non-Hispanic/Latino; 1% Race/ethnicity unknown; 0.6% international; 6% transferred in.
Freshmen *Admission:* 710 enrolled.
Faculty *Total:* 75. *Student/faculty ratio:* 19:1.
Academics *Calendar:* semesters. *Degree:* certificates and associate. *Special study options:* academic remediation for entering students, adult/continuing education programs, advanced placement credit, cooperative education, distance learning, English as a second language, honors programs, independent study, internships, part-time degree program, services for LD students, summer session for credit. *ROTC:* Army (c).
Library Jessup Library with 38,816 titles, 1,239 audiovisual materials, an OPAC, a Web page.
Student Life *Housing:* college housing not available. *Activities and Organizations:* drama/theater group, student-run newspaper, choral group. *Campus security:* 24-hour emergency response devices and patrols, late-night transport/escort service, establishment of Campus Police.
Athletics *Intramural sports:* basketball M/W, golf M/W, soccer M/W, table tennis M/W, tennis M/W, ultimate Frisbee M/W, volleyball M/W, weight lifting M/W.
Costs (2015–16) *Tuition:* state resident $3855 full-time, $129 per credit part-time; nonresident $9153 full-time, $305 per hour part-time. Full-time tuition and fees vary according to course load. Part-time tuition and fees vary according to course load. *Required fees:* $380 full-time, $13 part-time. *Payment plan:* installment. *Waivers:* senior citizens and employees or children of employees.
Financial Aid Of all full-time matriculated undergraduates who enrolled in 2014, 35 Federal Work-Study jobs.
Applying *Options:* electronic application, early admission, deferred entrance. *Required for some:* high school transcript, Admission to programs in Nursing, Practical Nursing, Radiography, Sonography, Surgical Technology, Emergency Medical Services, Health Information Management, and Patient Admissions Coordination is competitive and/or requires completion of specific prerequisites. *Application deadlines:* rolling (freshmen), rolling (transfers). *Notification:* continuous (freshmen), continuous (transfers).
Freshman Application Contact Ms. Mary Lee Walsh, Dean of Student Services, Piedmont Virginia Community College, 501 College Drive, Charlottesville, VA 22902-7589. *Phone:* 434-961-6540. *Fax:* 434-961-5425.
E-mail: mwalsh@pvcc.edu.
Website: http://www.pvcc.edu/.

Rappahannock Community College
Glenns, Virginia

- **State and locally supported** 2-year, founded 1970, part of Virginia Community College System
- **Rural** campus
- **Coed,** 3,555 undergraduate students, 23% full-time, 62% women, 38% men

Undergraduates 832 full-time, 2,723 part-time.
Majors Accounting; administrative assistant and secretarial science; biological and physical sciences; business administration and management; business administration, management and operations related; criminal justice/law enforcement administration; criminal justice/police science; engineering technology; information science/studies; liberal arts and sciences/liberal studies; registered nursing/registered nurse.
Academics *Calendar:* semesters. *Degree:* certificates and associate. *Special study options:* academic remediation for entering students, adult/continuing education programs, distance learning, honors programs, internships, off-campus study, part-time degree program, services for LD students, summer session for credit.
Library an OPAC, a Web page.
Student Life *Student services:* personal/psychological counseling.
Athletics *Intercollegiate sports:* softball W.
Costs (2014–15) *Tuition:* state resident $3825 full-time, $128 per credit hour part-time; nonresident $9123 full-time, $304 per credit hour part-time. Full-time tuition and fees vary according to course load. Part-time tuition and fees vary according to course load. *Required fees:* $426 full-time, $14 per credit hour part-time. *Payment plan:* deferred payment. *Waivers:* senior citizens.
Financial Aid Of all full-time matriculated undergraduates who enrolled in 2013, 40 Federal Work-Study jobs (averaging $1015).
Applying *Options:* electronic application, early admission. *Application deadlines:* rolling (freshmen), rolling (out-of-state freshmen), rolling (transfers). *Notification:* continuous (freshmen), continuous (out-of-state freshmen), continuous (transfers).
Freshman Application Contact Ms. Felicia Packett, Admissions and Records Officer, Rappahannock Community College, 12745 College Drive, Glenns, VA 23149-0287. *Phone:* 804-758-6740. *Toll-free phone:* 800-836-9381.
Website: http://www.rappahannock.edu/.

Richard Bland College of The College of William and Mary
Petersburg, Virginia

Freshman Application Contact Office of Admissions, Richard Bland College of The College of William and Mary, 8311 Halifax Road, Petersburg, VA 23805. *Phone:* 804-862-6100 Ext. 6249. *E-mail:* apply@rbc.edu.
Website: http://www.rbc.edu/.

Riverside School of Health Careers
Newport News, Virginia

Admissions Office Contact Riverside School of Health Careers, 316 Main Street, Newport News, VA 23601.
Website: http://www.riversideonline.com/rshc/.

Southside Regional Medical Center Professional Schools
Colonial Heights, Virginia

Admissions Office Contact Southside Regional Medical Center Professional Schools, 430 Clairmont Court, Suite 200, Colonial Heights, VA 23834.
Website: http://www.srmconline.com/Southside-Regional-Medical-Center/nursingeducation.aspx.

Southside Virginia Community College
Alberta, Virginia

Freshman Application Contact Mr. Brent Richey, Dean of Enrollment Management, Southside Virginia Community College, 109 Campus Drive, Alberta, VA 23821. *Phone:* 434-949-1012. *Fax:* 434-949-7863. *E-mail:* rhina.jones@sv.vccs.edu.
Website: http://www.southside.edu/.

Southwest Virginia Community College
Richlands, Virginia

- **State-supported** 2-year, founded 1968, part of Virginia Community College System
- **Rural** 100-acre campus
- **Endowment** $18.0 million
- **Coed,** 2,546 undergraduate students, 48% full-time, 61% women, 39% men

Undergraduates 1,212 full-time, 1,337 part-time. Students come from 7 states and territories; 1% are from out of state; 2% Black or African American, non-Hispanic/Latino; 0.5% Hispanic/Latino; 0.6% Asian, non-Hispanic/Latino; 0.4% American Indian or Alaska Native, non-Hispanic/Latino; 1% Two or more races, non-Hispanic/Latino; 0.2% Race/ethnicity unknown; 29% transferred in. *Retention:* 60% of full-time freshmen returned.
Freshmen *Admission:* 367 enrolled.
Faculty *Total:* 129, 31% full-time. *Student/faculty ratio:* 23:1.
Majors Accounting related; business administration, management and operations related; business operations support and secretarial services related; child-care provision; computer and information sciences; criminal justice/law enforcement administration; electrical, electronic and communications engineering technology; emergency medical technology (EMT paramedic); liberal arts and sciences/liberal studies; mental and social health services and allied professions related; radiologic technology/science; registered nursing/registered nurse.
Academics *Calendar:* semesters. *Degree:* certificates, diplomas, and associate. *Special study options:* academic remediation for entering students, accelerated degree program, adult/continuing education programs, advanced placement credit, distance learning, double majors, honors programs, internships, off-campus study, part-time degree program, summer session for credit.
Library Southwest Virginia Community College Library with 53,795 titles, 1,000 audiovisual materials, an OPAC, a Web page.
Student Life *Housing:* college housing not available. *Activities and Organizations:* choral group, Phi Theta Kappa, Phi Beta Lambda, Intervoice, Helping Minds Club, Project ACHEIVE. *Campus security:* 24-hour emergency response devices and patrols, student patrols, heavily saturated camera system. *Student services:* personal/psychological counseling.
Standardized Tests *Required:* VCCS Math and English Assessments (for admission).
Costs (2014–15) *Tuition:* area resident $3060 full-time; state resident $3030 full-time, $128 per credit hour part-time; nonresident $7298 full-time, $304 per credit hour part-time. Full-time tuition and fees vary according to reciprocity agreements. Part-time tuition and fees vary according to reciprocity agreements. *Required fees:* $252 full-time, $11 per credit hour part-time, $29 per credit hour part-time.
Financial Aid Of all full-time matriculated undergraduates who enrolled in 2013, 150 Federal Work-Study jobs (averaging $1140).
Applying *Options:* electronic application, early admission, deferred entrance. *Required:* high school transcript, interview. *Application deadlines:* rolling (freshmen), rolling (transfers).
Freshman Application Contact Ms. Dionne Cook, Admissions Counselor, Southwest Virginia Community College, Box SVCC, Richlands, VA 24641. *Phone:* 276-964-7301. *Toll-free phone:* 800-822-7822. *Fax:* 276-964-7716. *E-mail:* dionne.cook@sw.edu.
Website: http://www.sw.edu/.

Thomas Nelson Community College
Hampton, Virginia

Freshman Application Contact Ms. Geraldine Newson, Sr. Admission Specialist, Thomas Nelson Community College, PO Box 9407, Hampton, VA 23670-0407. *Phone:* 757-825-2800. *Fax:* 757-825-2763. *E-mail:* admissions@tncc.edu.
Website: http://www.tncc.edu/.

Tidewater Community College
Norfolk, Virginia

Freshman Application Contact Kellie Sorey PhD, Registrar, Tidewater Community College, Norfolk, VA 23510. *Phone:* 757-822-1900. *E-mail:* CentralRecords@tcc.edu.
Website: http://www.tcc.edu/.

Virginia College in Richmond
Richmond, Virginia

Admissions Office Contact Virginia College in Richmond, 7200 Midlothian Turnpike, Richmond, VA 23225.
Website: http://www.vc.edu/.

Virginia Highlands Community College
Abingdon, Virginia

Freshman Application Contact Karen Cheers, Acting Director of Admissions, Records, and Financial Aid, Virginia Highlands Community College, PO Box 828, 100 VHCC Drive Abingdon, Abingdon, VA 24212. *Phone:* 276-739-2490. *Toll-free phone:* 877-207-6115. *E-mail:* kcheers@vhcc.edu.
Website: http://www.vhcc.edu/.

Virginia Western Community College
Roanoke, Virginia

- **State-supported** 2-year, founded 1966, part of Virginia Community College System
- **Suburban** 70-acre campus
- **Endowment** $3.0 million
- **Coed,** 8,652 undergraduate students, 17% full-time, 55% women, 45% men

Undergraduates 1,477 full-time, 7,175 part-time. Students come from 9 states and territories; 54 other countries; 2% are from out of state; 12% Black or African American, non-Hispanic/Latino; 3% Hispanic/Latino; 0.4% Asian, non-Hispanic/Latino; 0.3% American Indian or Alaska Native, non-Hispanic/Latino; 3% Two or more races, non-Hispanic/Latino; 0.7% Race/ethnicity unknown; 0.6% international; 4% transferred in. *Retention:* 55% of full-time freshmen returned.
Freshmen *Admission:* 2,464 enrolled.
Faculty *Total:* 432, 22% full-time. *Student/faculty ratio:* 19:1.
Majors Accounting; administrative assistant and secretarial science; art; automobile/automotive mechanics technology; biological and physical sciences; business administration and management; child development; civil engineering technology; commercial and advertising art; computer science; criminal justice/law enforcement administration; data processing and data processing technology; dental hygiene; education; electrical, electronic and communications engineering technology; engineering; industrial radiologic technology; kindergarten/preschool education; liberal arts and sciences/liberal studies; mechanical engineering/mechanical technology; mental health counseling; pre-engineering; radio and television; radiologic technology/science; registered nursing/registered nurse.
Academics *Calendar:* semesters. *Degree:* certificates and associate. *Special study options:* academic remediation for entering students, advanced placement credit, cooperative education, distance learning, double majors, English as a second language, honors programs, independent study, internships, part-time degree program, services for LD students, summer session for credit.
Library Brown Library with an OPAC, a Web page.
Student Life *Housing:* college housing not available. *Activities and Organizations:* drama/theater group, student-run newspaper. *Campus security:* 24-hour emergency response devices and patrols, late-night transport/escort service. *Student services:* personal/psychological counseling.
Athletics *Intramural sports:* basketball M/W, soccer M, volleyball W.
Costs (2015–16) *Tuition:* state resident $4473 full-time, $149 per credit part-time; nonresident $10,311 full-time, $344 per credit part-time. *Payment plan:* installment. *Waivers:* senior citizens and employees or children of employees.
Applying *Options:* electronic application, early admission, deferred entrance. *Required for some:* high school transcript. *Recommended:* high school transcript. *Application deadlines:* rolling (freshmen), rolling (transfers). *Notification:* continuous (freshmen), continuous (transfers).
Freshman Application Contact Admissions Office, Virginia Western Community College, PO Box 14007, Roanoke, VA 24038. *Phone:* 540-857-7231.
Website: http://www.virginiawestern.edu/.

Wytheville Community College

Wytheville, Virginia

- **State-supported** 2-year, founded 1967, part of Virginia Community College System
- **Rural** 141-acre campus
- **Coed,** 3,468 undergraduate students, 35% full-time, 64% women, 36% men

Undergraduates 1,209 full-time, 2,259 part-time. 8% Black or African American, non-Hispanic/Latino; 1% Hispanic/Latino; 1% Asian, non-Hispanic/Latino; 0.3% American Indian or Alaska Native, non-Hispanic/Latino; 3% Two or more races, non-Hispanic/Latino; 0.1% Race/ethnicity unknown. *Retention:* 55% of full-time freshmen returned.

Faculty *Total:* 163, 28% full-time. *Student/faculty ratio:* 17:1.

Majors Accounting; administrative assistant and secretarial science; biological and physical sciences; business administration and management; civil engineering technology; clinical/medical laboratory technology; corrections; criminal justice/law enforcement administration; criminal justice/police science; dental hygiene; drafting and design technology; education; electrical, electronic and communications engineering technology; information science/studies; liberal arts and sciences/liberal studies; machine tool technology; mass communication/media; mechanical engineering/mechanical technology; medical administrative assistant and medical secretary; physical therapy; registered nursing/registered nurse.

Academics *Calendar:* semesters. *Degree:* certificates, diplomas, and associate. *Special study options:* academic remediation for entering students, adult/continuing education programs, advanced placement credit, distance learning, external degree program, independent study, part-time degree program, services for LD students, summer session for credit.

Library Wytheville Community College Library.

Student Life *Housing:* college housing not available. *Activities and Organizations:* drama/theater group, student-run newspaper. *Campus security:* 24-hour emergency response devices and patrols.

Athletics Member NJCAA. *Intercollegiate sports:* basketball M, volleyball W.

Costs (2014–15) *Tuition:* state resident $3825 full-time, $128 per credit part-time; nonresident $9123 full-time, $304 per credit part-time. *Required fees:* $345 full-time, $21 per credit part-time.

Financial Aid Of all full-time matriculated undergraduates who enrolled in 2013, 125 Federal Work-Study jobs (averaging $2592).

Applying *Options:* early admission. *Required:* high school transcript. *Required for some:* interview. *Application deadlines:* rolling (freshmen), rolling (transfers). *Notification:* continuous (freshmen), continuous (transfers).

Freshman Application Contact Wytheville Community College, 1000 East Main Street, Wytheville, VA 24382-3308. *Phone:* 276-223-4701. *Toll-free phone:* 800-468-1195.

Website: http://www.wcc.vccs.edu/.

WASHINGTON

Bates Technical College

Tacoma, Washington

Director of Admissions Director of Admissions, Bates Technical College, 1101 South Yakima Avenue, Tacoma, WA 98405-4895. *Phone:* 253-680-7000. *E-mail:* registration@bates.ctc.edu.

Website: http://www.bates.ctc.edu/.

Bellevue College

Bellevue, Washington

Freshman Application Contact Morenika Jacobs, Associate Dean of Enrollment Services, Bellevue College, 3000 Landerholm Circle, SE, Bellevue, WA 98007-6484. *Phone:* 425-564-2205. *Fax:* 425-564-4065.

Website: http://www.bcc.ctc.edu/.

Bellingham Technical College

Bellingham, Washington

- **State-supported** 2-year, founded 1957, part of Washington State Board for Community and Technical Colleges
- **Suburban** 21-acre campus with easy access to Vancouver
- **Coed,** 2,864 undergraduate students

Freshmen *Admission:* 2,527 applied, 2,527 admitted.

Faculty *Total:* 189, 67% full-time. *Student/faculty ratio:* 24:1.

Majors Accounting technology and bookkeeping; autobody/collision and repair technology; automobile/automotive mechanics technology; building/property maintenance; civil engineering technology; communications systems installation and repair technology; computer systems networking and telecommunications; culinary arts; data entry/microcomputer applications; diesel mechanics technology; electrician; executive assistant/executive secretary; fishing and fisheries sciences and management; heating, air conditioning, ventilation and refrigeration maintenance technology; heavy/industrial equipment maintenance technologies related; industrial mechanics and maintenance technology; instrumentation technology; legal assistant/paralegal; machine tool technology; marketing/marketing management; medical radiologic technology; registered nursing/registered nurse; surgical technology; surveying technology; welding technology.

Academics *Calendar:* quarters. *Degree:* certificates and associate. *Special study options:* academic remediation for entering students, distance learning, English as a second language, internships, part-time degree program, services for LD students, summer session for credit.

Library Information Technology Resource Center with an OPAC, a Web page.

Student Life *Housing:* college housing not available. *Student services:* personal/psychological counseling.

Standardized Tests *Required:* ACCUPLACER entrance exam or waiver (for admission).

Costs (2014–15) *Tuition:* state resident $3518 full-time, $106 per credit hour part-time; nonresident $8708 full-time, $278 per credit hour part-time. Full-time tuition and fees vary according to course load. Part-time tuition and fees vary according to course load. *Waivers:* employees or children of employees.

Financial Aid Of all full-time matriculated undergraduates who enrolled in 2013, 13 Federal Work-Study jobs (averaging $4050). 32 state and other part-time jobs (averaging $2027).

Applying *Options:* electronic application, early admission, deferred entrance. *Required for some:* high school transcript, some programs have prerequisites. *Application deadlines:* rolling (freshmen), rolling (out-of-state freshmen), rolling (transfers).

Freshman Application Contact Bellingham Technical College, 3028 Lindbergh Avenue, Bellingham, WA 98225. *Phone:* 360-752-8324.

Website: http://www.btc.ctc.edu/.

Big Bend Community College

Moses Lake, Washington

- **State-supported** 2-year, founded 1962
- **Small-town** 159-acre campus
- **Coed,** 1,991 undergraduate students, 72% full-time, 57% women, 43% men

Undergraduates 1,440 full-time, 551 part-time. 1% Black or African American, non-Hispanic/Latino; 33% Hispanic/Latino; 2% Asian, non-Hispanic/Latino; 0.9% American Indian or Alaska Native, non-Hispanic/Latino; 2% Two or more races, non-Hispanic/Latino; 2% Race/ethnicity unknown; 0.2% international; 5% live on campus.

Freshmen *Admission:* 310 enrolled.

Faculty *Student/faculty ratio:* 21:1.

Majors Accounting technology and bookkeeping; agricultural production; airline pilot and flight crew; automobile/automotive mechanics technology; avionics maintenance technology; computer support specialist; computer systems networking and telecommunications; early childhood education; industrial electronics technology; industrial mechanics and maintenance technology; liberal arts and sciences/liberal studies; licensed practical/vocational nurse training; medical/clinical assistant; medical office management; network and system administration; office management; registered nursing/registered nurse; welding technology.

Academics *Calendar:* quarters. *Degree:* certificates and associate. *Special study options:* academic remediation for entering students, advanced placement credit, cooperative education, distance learning, English as a second language, part-time degree program, services for LD students, summer session for credit.

Library Big Bend Community College Library with 42,603 titles, 4,131 audiovisual materials, an OPAC, a Web page.

Student Life *Housing Options:* coed. Campus housing is university owned. *Activities and Organizations:* choral group. *Campus security:* 24-hour emergency response devices, student patrols, late-night transport/escort service, controlled dormitory access, daytime security on campus during the week, student security in dorms four evenings a week, Enhanced Campus Notification System. *Student services:* personal/psychological counseling.

Athletics *Intercollegiate sports:* baseball M, basketball M/W, softball W, volleyball W.

Costs (2014–15) *Tuition:* state resident $4150 full-time, $112 per credit hour part-time; nonresident $4550 full-time, $125 per credit hour part-time. Full-time tuition and fees vary according to course load and program. Part-time tuition and fees vary according to course load and program. *Required fees:*

$150 full-time, $5 per credit hour part-time. *Room and board:* $7140. *Payment plan:* installment. *Waivers:* senior citizens.
Applying *Options:* electronic application, early admission, deferred entrance. *Application fee:* $30. *Required for some:* high school transcript. *Application deadlines:* rolling (freshmen), rolling (transfers). *Notification:* continuous (freshmen), continuous (transfers).
Freshman Application Contact Candis Lacher, Associate Vice President of Student Services, Big Bend Community College, 7662 Chanute Street, Moses Lake, WA 98837. *Phone:* 509-793-2061. *Toll-free phone:* 877-745-1212. *Fax:* 509-793-6243. *E-mail:* admissions@bigbend.edu.
Website: http://www.bigbend.edu/.

Carrington College–Spokane
Spokane, Washington

- **Proprietary** 2-year, founded 1976, part of Carrington Colleges Group, Inc.
- **Coed**

Undergraduates 538 full-time. 18% are from out of state; 4% Black or African American, non-Hispanic/Latino; 8% Hispanic/Latino; 1% Asian, non-Hispanic/Latino; 0.4% Native Hawaiian or other Pacific Islander, non-Hispanic/Latino; 3% American Indian or Alaska Native, non-Hispanic/Latino; 3% Two or more races, non-Hispanic/Latino; 1% Race/ethnicity unknown; 15% transferred in.
Faculty *Student/faculty ratio:* 33:1.
Academics *Degree:* certificates and associate.
Applying *Required:* essay or personal statement, high school transcript, interview, Entrance test administered by Carrington College.
Freshman Application Contact Carrington College–Spokane, 10102 East Knox Avenue, Suite 200, Spokane, WA 99206.
Website: http://carrington.edu/.

Cascadia Community College
Bothell, Washington

- **State-supported** 2-year, founded 1999
- **Suburban** 128-acre campus
- **Coed**

Undergraduates 1,060 full-time, 1,610 part-time. 3% Black or African American, non-Hispanic/Latino; 9% Hispanic/Latino; 11% Asian, non-Hispanic/Latino; 1% American Indian or Alaska Native, non-Hispanic/Latino; 3% Two or more races, non-Hispanic/Latino; 11% Race/ethnicity unknown; 4% international.
Faculty *Student/faculty ratio:* 23:1.
Academics *Calendar:* quarters. *Degree:* certificates and associate. *Special study options:* academic remediation for entering students, accelerated degree program, adult/continuing education programs, advanced placement credit, cooperative education, distance learning, double majors, English as a second language, independent study, internships, off-campus study, part-time degree program, services for LD students, study abroad, summer session for credit.
Student Life *Campus security:* 24-hour emergency response devices, late-night transport/escort service.
Costs (2014–15) *One-time required fee:* $30. *Tuition:* state resident $4020 full-time, $107 per credit part-time; nonresident $4818 full-time, $279 per credit part-time. Full-time tuition and fees vary according to course load and program. Part-time tuition and fees vary according to course load and program. *Required fees:* $270 full-time.
Applying *Options:* electronic application.
Freshman Application Contact Ms. Erin Blakeney, Dean for Student Success, Cascadia Community College, 18345 Campus Way, NE, Bothell, WA 98011. *Phone:* 425-352-8000. *Fax:* 425-352-8137. *E-mail:* admissions@cascadia.edu.
Website: http://www.cascadia.edu/.

Centralia College
Centralia, Washington

Freshman Application Contact Admissions Office, Centralia College, Centralia, WA 98531. *Phone:* 360-736-9391 Ext. 221. *Fax:* 360-330-7503. *E-mail:* admissions@centralia.edu.
Website: http://www.centralia.edu/.

Clark College
Vancouver, Washington

- **State-supported** 2-year, founded 1933, part of Washington State Board for Community and Technical Colleges
- **Urban** 101-acre campus with easy access to Portland
- **Coed,** 10,911 undergraduate students, 48% full-time, 57% women, 43% men

Undergraduates 5,254 full-time, 5,657 part-time. 4% are from out of state; 2% Black or African American, non-Hispanic/Latino; 9% Hispanic/Latino; 4% Asian, non-Hispanic/Latino; 0.1% Native Hawaiian or other Pacific Islander, non-Hispanic/Latino; 0.8% American Indian or Alaska Native, non-Hispanic/Latino; 8% Two or more races, non-Hispanic/Latino; 5% Race/ethnicity unknown; 1% international; 3% transferred in.
Freshmen *Admission:* 1,145 applied, 1,145 admitted, 1,436 enrolled.
Faculty *Total:* 626, 32% full-time, 15% with terminal degrees. *Student/faculty ratio:* 21:1.
Majors Accounting technology and bookkeeping; applied horticulture/horticulture operations; automobile/automotive mechanics technology; baking and pastry arts; business administration and management; business automation/technology/data entry; computer programming; computer systems networking and telecommunications; construction engineering technology; culinary arts; data entry/microcomputer applications; dental hygiene; diesel mechanics technology; early childhood education; electrical, electronic and communications engineering technology; emergency medical technology (EMT paramedic); executive assistant/executive secretary; graphic communications; human resources management; landscaping and groundskeeping; legal administrative assistant/secretary; legal assistant/paralegal; liberal arts and sciences/liberal studies; machine tool technology; manufacturing engineering technology; medical administrative assistant and medical secretary; medical/clinical assistant; radiologic technology/science; registered nursing/registered nurse; retailing; selling skills and sales; sport and fitness administration/management; substance abuse/addiction counseling; surveying technology; telecommunications technology; web/multimedia management and webmaster; welding technology.
Academics *Calendar:* quarters. *Degree:* certificates, diplomas, and associate. *Special study options:* adult/continuing education programs, part-time degree program. *ROTC:* Army (c), Air Force (c).
Library Lewis D. Cannell Library.
Student Life *Housing:* college housing not available. *Campus security:* 24-hour patrols, late-night transport/escort service, security staff during hours of operation.
Athletics *Intercollegiate sports:* baseball M, basketball M(s)/W(s), cross-country running M(s)/W(s), fencing M(c)/W(c), soccer M(s)/W(s), softball W, track and field M(s)/W(s), volleyball W(s). *Intramural sports:* basketball M/W, fencing M/W, soccer M/W, softball M/W, volleyball M/W.
Costs (2014–15) *Tuition:* state resident $4154 full-time, $110 per credit hour part-time; nonresident $9389 full-time, $282 per credit hour part-time. Full-time tuition and fees vary according to course load and program. Part-time tuition and fees vary according to course load and program. *Payment plan:* installment. *Waivers:* senior citizens and employees or children of employees.
Applying *Options:* electronic application, early admission, deferred entrance. *Application fee:* $25.
Freshman Application Contact Ms. Sheryl Anderson, Director of Admissions, Clark College, Vancouver, WA 98663. *Phone:* 360-992-2308. *Fax:* 360-992-2867. *E-mail:* admissions@clark.edu.
Website: http://www.clark.edu/.

Clover Park Technical College
Lakewood, Washington

Director of Admissions Ms. Judy Richardson, Registrar, Clover Park Technical College, 4500 Steilacoom Boulevard, SW, Lakewood, WA 98499. *Phone:* 253-589-5570.
Website: http://www.cptc.edu/.

Columbia Basin College
Pasco, Washington

Freshman Application Contact Admissions Department, Columbia Basin College, 2600 North 20th Avenue, Pasco, WA 99301-3397. *Phone:* 509-542-4524. *Fax:* 509-544-2023. *E-mail:* admissions@columbiabasin.edu.
Website: http://www.columbiabasin.edu/.

Edmonds Community College
Lynnwood, Washington

Freshman Application Contact Ms. Nancy Froemming, Enrollment Services Office Manager, Edmonds Community College, 20000 68th Avenue West, Lynwood, WA 98036-5999. *Phone:* 425-640-1853. *Fax:* 425-640-1159. *E-mail:* nanci.froemming@edcc.edu.
Website: http://www.edcc.edu/.

Everest College
Bremerton, Washington

Admissions Office Contact Everest College, 155 Washington Avenue, Suite 200, Bremerton, WA 98337.
Website: http://www.everest.edu/.

Everest College
Tacoma, Washington

Admissions Office Contact Everest College, 2156 Pacific Avenue, Tacoma, WA 98402.
Website: http://www.everest.edu/.

Everest College
Vancouver, Washington

Director of Admissions Ms. Renee Schiffhauer, Director of Admissions, Everest College, 120 Northeast 136th Avenue, Suite 130, Vancouver, WA 98684. *Phone:* 360-254-3282. *Toll-free phone:* 888-741-4270. *Fax:* 360-254-3035. *E-mail:* rschiffhauer@cci.edu.
Website: http://www.everest.edu/.

Everett Community College
Everett, Washington

Freshman Application Contact Ms. Linda Baca, Entry Services Manager, Everett Community College, 2000 Tower Street, Everett, WA 98201-1327. *Phone:* 425-388-9219. *Fax:* 425-388-9173. *E-mail:* admissions@everettcc.edu.
Website: http://www.everettcc.edu/.

Grays Harbor College
Aberdeen, Washington

- **State-supported** 2-year, founded 1930, part of Washington State Board for Community and Technical Colleges
- **Small-town** 125-acre campus
- **Endowment** $8.6 million
- **Coed**

Undergraduates 1,312 full-time, 654 part-time. Students come from 1 other state; 4% Black or African American, non-Hispanic/Latino; 8% Hispanic/Latino; 2% Asian, non-Hispanic/Latino; 0.5% Native Hawaiian or other Pacific Islander, non-Hispanic/Latino; 3% American Indian or Alaska Native, non-Hispanic/Latino; 6% Two or more races, non-Hispanic/Latino; 2% Race/ethnicity unknown; 0.2% international; 23% transferred in. *Retention:* 57% of full-time freshmen returned.
Faculty *Student/faculty ratio:* 19:1.
Academics *Calendar:* quarters. *Degree:* certificates, diplomas, and associate. *Special study options:* academic remediation for entering students, accelerated degree program, adult/continuing education programs, advanced placement credit, cooperative education, distance learning, double majors, English as a second language, external degree program, honors programs, independent study, internships, part-time degree program, services for LD students, study abroad, summer session for credit.
Student Life *Campus security:* 24-hour emergency response devices, late-night transport/escort service.
Financial Aid Of all full-time matriculated undergraduates who enrolled in 2012, 1,458 applied for aid, 1,415 were judged to have need. 58 Federal Work-Study jobs (averaging $1315). 132 state and other part-time jobs (averaging $2089). *Average financial aid package:* $5932. *Average need-based gift aid:* $6094.
Applying *Options:* electronic application, early admission. *Recommended:* high school transcript.
Freshman Application Contact Ms. Brenda Dell, Admissions Officer, Grays Harbor College, 1620 Edward P. Smith Drive, Aberdeen, WA 98520. *Phone:* 360-532-4216. *Toll-free phone:* 800-562-4830.
Website: http://www.ghc.edu/.

Green River College
Auburn, Washington

Freshman Application Contact Ms. Peggy Morgan, Program Support Supervisor, Green River College, 12401 Southeast 320th Street, Auburn, WA 98092-3699. *Phone:* 253-833-9111. *Fax:* 253-288-3454.
Website: http://www.greenriver.edu/.

Highline College
Des Moines, Washington

Freshman Application Contact Ms. Michelle Kuwasaki, Director of Admissions, Highline College, 2400 South 240th Street, Des Moines, WA 98198-9800. *Phone:* 206-878-3710 Ext. 9800.
Website: http://www.highline.edu/.

ITT Technical Institute
Everett, Washington

- **Proprietary** primarily 2-year, part of ITT Educational Services, Inc.
- **Coed**

Academics *Degrees:* associate and bachelor's.
Freshman Application Contact Director of Recruitment, ITT Technical Institute, 1615 75th Street SW, Everett, WA 98203. *Phone:* 425-583-0200. *Toll-free phone:* 800-272-3791.
Website: http://www.itt-tech.edu/.

ITT Technical Institute
Seattle, Washington

- **Proprietary** primarily 2-year, founded 1932, part of ITT Educational Services, Inc.
- **Urban** campus
- **Coed**

Academics *Calendar:* quarters. *Degrees:* associate and bachelor's.
Freshman Application Contact Director of Recruitment, ITT Technical Institute, 12720 Gateway Drive, Suite 100, Seattle, WA 98168-3333. *Phone:* 206-244-3300. *Toll-free phone:* 800-422-2029.
Website: http://www.itt-tech.edu/.

ITT Technical Institute
Spokane Valley, Washington

- **Proprietary** primarily 2-year, founded 1985, part of ITT Educational Services, Inc.
- **Suburban** campus
- **Coed**

Academics *Calendar:* quarters. *Degrees:* associate and bachelor's.
Freshman Application Contact Director of Recruitment, ITT Technical Institute, 13518 East Indiana Avenue, Spokane Valley, WA 99216. *Phone:* 509-926-2900. *Toll-free phone:* 800-777-8324.
Website: http://www.itt-tech.edu/.

Lake Washington Institute of Technology
Kirkland, Washington

Freshman Application Contact Shawn Miller, Registrar, Enrollment Services, Lake Washington Institute of Technology, 11605 132nd Avenue NE, Kirkland, WA 98034-8506. *Phone:* 425-739-8104. *E-mail:* info@lwtc.edu.
Website: http://www.lwtech.edu/.

Lower Columbia College
Longview, Washington

- **State-supported** 2-year, founded 1934, part of Washington State Board for Community and Technical Colleges
- **Rural** 39-acre campus with easy access to Portland
- **Endowment** $14.9 million
- **Coed,** 3,152 undergraduate students, 52% full-time, 64% women, 36% men

Undergraduates 1,633 full-time, 1,519 part-time.
Freshmen *Admission:* 304 enrolled.
Faculty *Total:* 196, 34% full-time. *Student/faculty ratio:* 15:1.
Majors Accounting; accounting technology and bookkeeping; administrative assistant and secretarial science; automobile/automotive mechanics technology; business administration and management; criminal justice/law enforcement administration; data entry/microcomputer applications; diesel

mechanics technology; early childhood education; fire science/firefighting; industrial mechanics and maintenance technology; instrumentation technology; legal administrative assistant/secretary; liberal arts and sciences/liberal studies; machine tool technology; medical administrative assistant and medical secretary; medical/clinical assistant; registered nursing/registered nurse; substance abuse/addiction counseling; welding technology.

Academics *Calendar:* quarters. *Degree:* certificates, diplomas, and associate. *Special study options:* academic remediation for entering students, adult/continuing education programs, advanced placement credit, cooperative education, distance learning, English as a second language, external degree program, independent study, internships, part-time degree program, services for LD students, student-designed majors, summer session for credit.

Library Alan Thompson Library plus 1 other with 27,936 titles, 2,618 audiovisual materials, an OPAC, a Web page.

Student Life *Housing:* college housing not available. *Activities and Organizations:* drama/theater group, choral group, Phi Theta Kappa, Electric Vehicle Club, Multicultural Club, Global Medical Brigade, Sustainability Club. *Campus security:* 24-hour emergency response devices and patrols. *Student services:* personal/psychological counseling.

Athletics *Intercollegiate sports:* baseball M(s), basketball M(s)/W(s), soccer W(s), softball W(s), volleyball W(s).

Costs (2014–15) *One-time required fee:* $30. *Tuition:* state resident $4281 full-time, $115 per credit part-time; nonresident $4820 full-time, $129 per credit part-time. Full-time tuition and fees vary according to course load and reciprocity agreements. Part-time tuition and fees vary according to course load and reciprocity agreements. *Required fees:* $293 full-time, $20 per credit part-time. *Payment plan:* deferred payment. *Waivers:* senior citizens and employees or children of employees.

Financial Aid Of all full-time matriculated undergraduates who enrolled in 2013, 440 Federal Work-Study jobs (averaging $708). 447 state and other part-time jobs (averaging $2415).

Applying *Options:* electronic application. *Application fee:* $30. *Recommended:* high school transcript. *Application deadlines:* rolling (freshmen), rolling (transfers). *Notification:* continuous (freshmen).

Freshman Application Contact Ms. Nichole Seroshek, Director of Registration, Lower Columbia College, 1600 Maple Street, Longview, WA 98632. *Phone:* 360-442-2372. *Toll-free phone:* 866-900-2311. *Fax:* 360-442-2379. *E-mail:* registration@lowercolumbia.edu. *Website:* http://www.lowercolumbia.edu/.

North Seattle College
Seattle, Washington

Freshman Application Contact Ms. Betsy Abts, Registrar, North Seattle College, Seattle, WA 98103-3599. *Phone:* 206-934-3663. *Fax:* 206-934-3671. *E-mail:* arrc@seattlecolleges.edu. *Website:* http://www.northseattle.edu/.

Northwest Indian College
Bellingham, Washington

Freshman Application Contact Office of Admissions, Northwest Indian College, 2522 Kwina Road, Bellingham, WA 98226. *Phone:* 360-676-2772. *Toll-free phone:* 866-676-2772. *Fax:* 360-392-4333. *E-mail:* admissions@nwic.edu. *Website:* http://www.nwic.edu/.

Northwest School of Wooden Boatbuilding
Port Hadlock, Washington

- **Independent** 2-year, founded 1980
- **Small-town** campus
- **Coed**

Faculty *Total:* 98, 98% full-time. *Student/faculty ratio:* 12:1.

Majors Marine maintenance and ship repair technology.

Academics *Calendar:* quarters. *Degree:* diplomas and associate.

Library School Library with 1,200 titles.

Student Life *Housing:* college housing not available.

Costs (2015–16) *Tuition:* $19,400 full-time. No tuition increase for student's term of enrollment. *Required fees:* $100 full-time.

Applying *Options:* electronic application.

Freshman Application Contact Northwest School of Wooden Boatbuilding, 42 North Water Street, Port Hadlock, WA 98339. *Phone:* 360-385-4948. *Website:* http://www.nwboatschool.org/.

Olympic College
Bremerton, Washington

- **State-supported** primarily 2-year, founded 1946, part of Washington State Board for Community and Technical Colleges
- **Suburban** 33-acre campus with easy access to Seattle by ferry 30 miles, Tacoma by hwy 35 miles
- **Coed,** 8,058 undergraduate students

Undergraduates 5% Black or African American, non-Hispanic/Latino; 7% Hispanic/Latino; 9% Asian, non-Hispanic/Latino; 2% American Indian or Alaska Native, non-Hispanic/Latino; 1% international; 1% live on campus.

Freshmen *Admission:* 3,803 applied, 3,803 admitted.

Faculty *Total:* 475, 25% full-time.

Majors Accounting technology and bookkeeping; administrative assistant and secretarial science; business administration and management; chemical engineering; computer systems networking and telecommunications; cosmetology; culinary arts; drafting and design technology; early childhood education; electrical, electronic and communications engineering technology; engineering technology; industrial technology; information technology; legal administrative assistant/secretary; liberal arts and sciences/liberal studies; marine maintenance and ship repair technology; medical/clinical assistant; organizational leadership; physical therapy technology; registered nursing/registered nurse; substance abuse/addiction counseling; welding technology.

Academics *Calendar:* quarters. *Degrees:* certificates, diplomas, associate, and bachelor's. *Special study options:* academic remediation for entering students, adult/continuing education programs, advanced placement credit, cooperative education, distance learning, English as a second language, honors programs, independent study, internships, off-campus study, part-time degree program, services for LD students, summer session for credit.

Library Haselwood Library with an OPAC, a Web page.

Student Life *Housing Options:* coed. Campus housing is university owned. *Activities and Organizations:* drama/theater group, student-run newspaper, choral group, Phi Theta Kappa, International Club, Gaming Club, Engineering Club, Public Communications Club. *Campus security:* 24-hour emergency response devices and patrols, student patrols, late-night transport/escort service. *Student services:* personal/psychological counseling.

Athletics *Intercollegiate sports:* baseball M(s), basketball M(s)/W(s), cross-country running M/W, golf M(s)/W(s), softball W(s), track and field M/W, volleyball W(s). *Intramural sports:* basketball M/W, table tennis M/W, volleyball M/W.

Costs (2014–15) *Tuition:* state resident $107 per credit part-time; nonresident $120 per credit part-time. Full-time tuition and fees vary according to course load and degree level. Part-time tuition and fees vary according to course load and degree level. *Payment plan:* installment. *Waivers:* senior citizens and employees or children of employees.

Financial Aid Of all full-time matriculated undergraduates who enrolled in 2013, 105 Federal Work-Study jobs (averaging $2380). 31 state and other part-time jobs (averaging $2880).

Applying *Options:* electronic application. *Required for some:* high school transcript. *Application deadlines:* rolling (freshmen), rolling (out-of-state freshmen), rolling (transfers).

Freshman Application Contact Ms. Nora Downard, Program Support Supervisor, Olympic College, 1600 Chester Avenue, Bremerton, WA 98337-1699. *Phone:* 360-475-7445. *Toll-free phone:* 800-259-6718. *Fax:* 360-475-7202. *E-mail:* ndownard@olympic.edu. *Website:* http://www.olympic.edu/.

Peninsula College
Port Angeles, Washington

Freshman Application Contact Ms. Pauline Marvin, Peninsula College, 1502 East Lauridsen Boulevard, Port Angeles, WA 98362. *Phone:* 360-417-6596. *Toll-free phone:* 877-452-9277. *Fax:* 360-457-8100. *E-mail:* admissions@pencol.edu. *Website:* http://www.pc.ctc.edu/.

Pierce College at Puyallup
Puyallup, Washington

Freshman Application Contact Pierce College at Puyallup, 1601 39th Avenue Southeast, Puyallup, WA 98374. *Phone:* 253-840-8400. *Website:* http://www.pierce.ctc.edu/.

Pima Medical Institute
Renton, Washington

Freshman Application Contact Pima Medical Institute, 555 South Renton Village Place, Renton, WA 98057. *Phone:* 425-228-9600. *Website:* http://www.pmi.edu/.

Pima Medical Institute
Seattle, Washington

Freshman Application Contact Admissions Office, Pima Medical Institute, 9709 Third Avenue NE, Suite 400, Seattle, WA 98115. *Phone:* 206-322-6100. *Toll-free phone:* 800-477-PIMA (in-state); 888-477-PIMA (out-of-state). *Website:* http://www.pmi.edu/.

Renton Technical College
Renton, Washington

- **State-supported** primarily 2-year, founded 1942, part of Washington State Board for Community and Technical Colleges
- **Suburban** 30-acre campus with easy access to Seattle
- **Coed,** 9,301 undergraduate students, 43% full-time, 43% women, 57% men

Undergraduates 4,019 full-time, 5,282 part-time. Students come from 9 states and territories; 13 other countries.
Faculty *Total:* 282, 30% full-time. *Student/faculty ratio:* 15:1.
Majors Accounting; administrative assistant and secretarial science; automobile/automotive mechanics technology; business administration and management; civil engineering technology; clinical laboratory science/medical technology; communications technology; computer science; culinary arts; electrical, electronic and communications engineering technology; heating, air conditioning, ventilation and refrigeration maintenance technology; legal administrative assistant/secretary; machine tool technology; medical administrative assistant and medical secretary; medical/clinical assistant; musical instrument fabrication and repair; surgical technology; surveying technology; teacher assistant/aide.
Academics *Calendar:* quarters. *Degrees:* certificates, diplomas, associate, and bachelor's. *Special study options:* academic remediation for entering students, adult/continuing education programs, advanced placement credit, cooperative education, distance learning, English as a second language, internships, off-campus study, part-time degree program, services for LD students, summer session for credit.
Library Renton Technical College Library with 12,876 titles, 321 audiovisual materials, an OPAC.
Student Life *Housing:* college housing not available. *Campus security:* patrols by security, security system. *Student services:* personal/psychological counseling.
Standardized Tests *Required for some:* ACT ASSET, CLEP, ACT Compass.
Costs (2014–15) *Tuition:* state resident $4735 full-time, $113 per credit hour part-time; nonresident $5028 full-time, $126 per credit hour part-time. Full-time tuition and fees vary according to course load and program. Part-time tuition and fees vary according to course load and program. *Payment plan:* installment.
Applying *Options:* electronic application, early admission. *Application fee:* $30. *Required for some:* essay or personal statement, high school transcript, interview. *Application deadlines:* rolling (freshmen), rolling (out-of-state freshmen), rolling (transfers). *Notification:* continuous (freshmen), continuous (out-of-state freshmen), continuous (transfers).
Freshman Application Contact Linh Bracking, Student Success Advisor, Renton Technical College, 3000 NE 4th St, Reton, WA 98056. *Phone:* 425-235-2352 Ext. 5543. *E-mail:* lbracking@rtc.edu. *Website:* http://www.rtc.edu/.

Seattle Central College
Seattle, Washington

Freshman Application Contact Admissions Office, Seattle Central College, 1701 Broadway, Seattle, WA 98122-2400. *Phone:* 206-587-5450. *Website:* http://www.seattlecentral.edu/.

Shoreline Community College
Shoreline, Washington

- **State-supported** 2-year, founded 1964, part of Washington State Board for Community and Technical Colleges
- **Suburban** 80-acre campus
- **Coed**

Faculty *Student/faculty ratio:* 21:1.

Academics *Calendar:* quarters. *Degree:* certificates, diplomas, and associate. *Special study options:* academic remediation for entering students, adult/continuing education programs, advanced placement credit, cooperative education, distance learning, English as a second language, independent study, internships, part-time degree program, services for LD students, study abroad, summer session for credit.
Student Life *Campus security:* 24-hour emergency response devices and patrols.
Standardized Tests *Recommended:* ACT ASSET or ACT Compass.
Applying *Options:* electronic application. *Required:* high school transcript.
Freshman Application Contact Shoreline Community College, 16101 Greenwood Avenue North, Shoreline, WA 98133-5696. *Phone:* 206-546-4613. *Website:* http://www.shoreline.edu/.

Skagit Valley College
Mount Vernon, Washington

Freshman Application Contact Ms. Karen Marie Bade, Admissions and Recruitment Coordinator, Skagit Valley College, 2405 College Way, Mount Vernon, WA 98273-5899. *Phone:* 360-416-7620. *E-mail:* karenmarie.bade@skagit.edu. *Website:* http://www.skagit.edu/.

South Puget Sound Community College
Olympia, Washington

Freshman Application Contact Ms. Heidi Dearborn, South Puget Sound Community College, 2011 Mottman Road, SW, Olympia, WA 98512-6292. *Phone:* 360-754-7711 Ext. 5358. *E-mail:* hdearborn@spcc.edu. *Website:* http://www.spscc.ctc.edu/.

South Seattle College
Seattle, Washington

Director of Admissions Ms. Kim Manderbach, Dean of Student Services/Registration, South Seattle College, 6000 16th Avenue, SW, Seattle, WA 98106-1499. *Phone:* 206-764-5378. *Fax:* 206-764-7947. *E-mail:* kimmanderb@sccd.ctc.edu. *Website:* http://southseattle.edu/.

Spokane Community College
Spokane, Washington

Freshman Application Contact Ann Hightower-Chavez, Researcher, District Institutional Research, Spokane Community College, Spokane, WA 99217-5399. *Phone:* 509-434-5242. *Toll-free phone:* 800-248-5644. *Fax:* 509-434-5249. *E-mail:* mlee@ccs.spokane.edu. *Website:* http://www.scc.spokane.edu/.

Spokane Falls Community College
Spokane, Washington

Freshman Application Contact Admissions Office, Spokane Falls Community College, Admissions MS 3011, 3410 West Fort George Wright Drive, Spokane, WA 99224. *Phone:* 509-533-3401. *Toll-free phone:* 888-509-7944. *Fax:* 509-533-3852. *Website:* http://www.spokanefalls.edu/.

Tacoma Community College
Tacoma, Washington

Freshman Application Contact Enrollment Services, Tacoma Community College, 6501 South 19th Street, Tacoma, WA 98466. *Phone:* 253-566-5325. *Fax:* 253-566-6034. *Website:* http://www.tacomacc.edu/.

Walla Walla Community College
Walla Walla, Washington

- **State-supported** 2-year, founded 1967, part of Washington State Board for Community and Technical Colleges
- **Small-town** 125-acre campus
- **Coed**

Undergraduates 2,969 full-time, 2,140 part-time. Students come from 11 states and territories; 24% are from out of state; 4% Black or African American, non-Hispanic/Latino; 17% Hispanic/Latino; 1% Asian, non-

Hispanic/Latino; 0.4% Native Hawaiian or other Pacific Islander, non-Hispanic/Latino; 1% American Indian or Alaska Native, non-Hispanic/Latino; 5% Two or more races, non-Hispanic/Latino; 5% Race/ethnicity unknown; 0.1% international; 15% transferred in. *Retention:* 67% of full-time freshmen returned.

Faculty *Student/faculty ratio:* 20:1.

Academics *Calendar:* quarters. *Degree:* certificates, diplomas, and associate. *Special study options:* academic remediation for entering students, adult/continuing education programs, advanced placement credit, cooperative education, distance learning, external degree program, off-campus study, part-time degree program, summer session for credit.

Student Life *Campus security:* student patrols, late-night transport/escort service.

Costs (2014–15) *Tuition:* state resident $4376 full-time, $119 per credit part-time; nonresident $5675 full-time, $132 per credit part-time.

Financial Aid Of all full-time matriculated undergraduates who enrolled in 2013, 95 Federal Work-Study jobs (averaging $1600). 20 state and other part-time jobs (averaging $2000).

Applying *Options:* electronic application. *Required for some:* interview. *Recommended:* high school transcript.

Freshman Application Contact Walla Walla Community College, 500 Tausick Way, Walla Walla, WA 99362-9267. *Phone:* 509-522-2500. *Toll-free phone:* 877-992-9922.

Website: http://www.wwcc.edu/.

Wenatchee Valley College
Wenatchee, Washington

- **State and locally supported** 2-year, founded 1939, part of Washington State Board for Community and Technical Colleges
- **Small-town** 56-acre campus
- **Coed,** 3,510 undergraduate students, 73% full-time, 57% women, 43% men

Undergraduates 2,578 full-time, 932 part-time. 0.7% Black or African American, non-Hispanic/Latino; 35% Hispanic/Latino; 1% Asian, non-Hispanic/Latino; 2% American Indian or Alaska Native, non-Hispanic/Latino; 3% Two or more races, non-Hispanic/Latino; 4% Race/ethnicity unknown; 0.1% international.

Freshmen *Admission:* 527 enrolled.

Majors Accounting; accounting technology and bookkeeping; administrative assistant and secretarial science; agricultural production; athletic training; automobile/automotive mechanics technology; biology/biological sciences; business administration and management; casino management; chemistry; clinical/medical laboratory assistant; clinical/medical laboratory technology; computer systems networking and telecommunications; criminal justice/police science; design and applied arts related; early childhood education; economics; education; electrical/electronics equipment installation and repair; heating, air conditioning, ventilation and refrigeration maintenance technology; history; industrial electronics technology; kindergarten/preschool education; legal administrative assistant/secretary; liberal arts and sciences/liberal studies; licensed practical/vocational nurse training; mathematics; medical administrative assistant and medical secretary; medical/clinical assistant; music; music teacher education; natural resource recreation and tourism; office management; physical sciences; pre-engineering; radiologic technology/science; registered nursing/registered nurse; sociology; substance abuse/addiction counseling.

Academics *Calendar:* quarters. *Degree:* certificates, diplomas, and associate. *Special study options:* academic remediation for entering students, adult/continuing education programs, advanced placement credit, cooperative education, distance learning, English as a second language, external degree program, independent study, internships, part-time degree program, services for LD students, study abroad, summer session for credit.

Library John Brown Library plus 1 other with an OPAC, a Web page.

Student Life *Housing Options:* coed. Campus housing is university owned. *Activities and Organizations:* drama/theater group, choral group. *Campus security:* 24-hour patrols, controlled dormitory access.

Athletics *Intercollegiate sports:* baseball M, basketball M(s)/W(s), soccer M/W, softball W(s), volleyball W(s). *Intramural sports:* basketball M/W, racquetball M/W, skiing (cross-country) M/W, skiing (downhill) M/W, tennis M/W, volleyball M/W, weight lifting M/W.

Costs (2014–15) *Tuition:* state resident $3523 full-time; nonresident $3917 full-time. Full-time tuition and fees vary according to course load. *Required*

fees: $188 full-time. *Room and board:* $5755. *Payment plan:* installment. *Waivers:* senior citizens and employees or children of employees.

Applying *Options:* electronic application, early admission, deferred entrance. *Required for some:* high school transcript. *Application deadline:* rolling (freshmen).

Freshman Application Contact Wenatchee Valley College, 1300 Fifth Street, Wenatchee, WA 98801-1799. *Phone:* 509-682-6835 Ext. 2145. *Toll-free phone:* 877-982-4968.

Website: http://www.wvc.edu/.

Whatcom Community College
Bellingham, Washington

- **State-supported** 2-year, founded 1970, part of Washington State Board for Community and Technical Colleges
- **Small-town** 52-acre campus with easy access to Vancouver
- **Endowment** $2.0 million
- **Coed,** 6,233 undergraduate students

Undergraduates Students come from 30 other countries; 5% are from out of state.

Faculty *Total:* 225, 33% full-time.

Majors Accounting; administrative assistant and secretarial science; business administration and management; commercial and advertising art; computer engineering technology; computer science; criminal justice/police science; kindergarten/preschool education; legal assistant/paralegal; liberal arts and sciences/liberal studies; medical administrative assistant and medical secretary; medical/clinical assistant; physical therapy technology; registered nursing/registered nurse.

Academics *Calendar:* quarters. *Degree:* certificates, diplomas, and associate. *Special study options:* academic remediation for entering students, accelerated degree program, adult/continuing education programs, advanced placement credit, cooperative education, distance learning, English as a second language, external degree program, honors programs, independent study, internships, part-time degree program, services for LD students, student-designed majors, study abroad, summer session for credit.

Library Whatcom Community College Library with 14,680 titles, 3,653 audiovisual materials, an OPAC, a Web page.

Student Life *Housing:* college housing not available. *Activities and Organizations:* drama/theater group, student-run newspaper, choral group, Japanime, Ethnic Student Association, Queer/Straight Alliance, Phi Theta Kappa, International Friendship Club. *Campus security:* 24-hour emergency response devices. *Student services:* personal/psychological counseling.

Athletics *Intercollegiate sports:* basketball M(s)/W(s), cross-country running M(s)/W(s), soccer M(s)/W(s), volleyball W(s). *Intramural sports:* basketball M/W, cross-country running M/W, soccer M/W, tennis M/W, ultimate Frisbee M/W, volleyball W.

Costs (2014–15) *Tuition:* state resident $4180 full-time, $113 per credit part-time; nonresident $9415 full-time, $285 per credit part-time. Full-time tuition and fees vary according to course load and program. Part-time tuition and fees vary according to course load and program. *Required fees:* $284 full-time, $6 per credit part-time. *Payment plans:* installment, deferred payment. *Waivers:* senior citizens and employees or children of employees.

Financial Aid Of all full-time matriculated undergraduates who enrolled in 2013, 30 Federal Work-Study jobs (averaging $3780). 80 state and other part-time jobs (averaging $3620).

Applying *Options:* electronic application. *Application deadline:* rolling (freshmen). *Notification:* continuous (freshmen).

Freshman Application Contact Entry and Advising Center, Whatcom Community College, 237 West Kellogg Road, Bellingham, WA 98226-8003. *Phone:* 360-676-2170. *Fax:* 360-676-2171. *E-mail:* admit@whatcom.ctc.edu. *Website:* http://www.whatcom.ctc.edu/.

Yakima Valley Community College
Yakima, Washington

Freshman Application Contact Denise Anderson, Registrar and Director for Enrollment Services, Yakima Valley Community College, PO Box 1647, Yakima, WA 98907-1647. *Phone:* 509-574-4702. *Fax:* 509-574-6879. *E-mail:* admis@yvcc.edu.

Website: http://www.yvcc.edu/.

WEST VIRGINIA

Blue Ridge Community and Technical College
Martinsburg, West Virginia

- **State-supported** 2-year, founded 1974, part of Community and Technical College System of West Virginia
- **Small-town** 46-acre campus
- **Coed,** 5,553 undergraduate students, 20% full-time, 66% women, 34% men

Undergraduates 1,123 full-time, 4,430 part-time. 5% are from out of state; 10% Black or African American, non-Hispanic/Latino; 4% Hispanic/Latino; 0.7% Asian, non-Hispanic/Latino; 0.3% Native Hawaiian or other Pacific Islander, non-Hispanic/Latino; 0.4% American Indian or Alaska Native, non-Hispanic/Latino; 2% Two or more races, non-Hispanic/Latino; 0.8% Race/ethnicity unknown; 4% transferred in. *Retention:* 51% of full-time freshmen returned.
Freshmen *Admission:* 612 applied, 574 admitted, 410 enrolled. *Test scores:* SAT critical reading scores over 500: 45%; SAT critical reading scores over 600: 10%.
Faculty *Total:* 177, 36% full-time, 10% with terminal degrees. *Student/faculty ratio:* 25:1.
Majors Accounting; allied health and medical assisting services related; automation engineer technology; baking and pastry arts; business administration and management; business administration, management and operations related; clinical/medical laboratory technology; computer and information systems security; criminal justice/safety; culinary arts; data entry/microcomputer applications related; electrical and electronic engineering technologies related; emergency medical technology (EMT paramedic); general studies; information technology; legal assistant/paralegal; liberal arts and sciences/liberal studies; medical/clinical assistant; multi/interdisciplinary studies related; operations management; physical therapy technology; registered nursing/registered nurse; restaurant, culinary, and catering management; science technologies related; system, networking, and LAN/WAN management.
Academics *Calendar:* semesters. *Degree:* certificates and associate. *Special study options:* academic remediation for entering students, accelerated degree program, adult/continuing education programs, advanced placement credit, double majors, English as a second language, independent study, internships, part-time degree program, services for LD students.
Library Martinsburg Public Library with 188,774 titles, 17,081 audiovisual materials, an OPAC, a Web page.
Student Life *Housing:* college housing not available. *Activities and Organizations:* drama/theater group, Student Leadership Academy, Drama Club, Phi Theta Kappa, Skills USA, Student Nurses Association, national fraternities. *Campus security:* late-night transport/escort service. *Student services:* personal/psychological counseling.
Standardized Tests *Recommended:* SAT and SAT Subject Tests or ACT (for admission).
Costs (2014–15) *Tuition:* state resident $3432 full-time, $143 per credit hour part-time; nonresident $6192 full-time, $258 per credit hour part-time. Full-time tuition and fees vary according to class time and course load. Part-time tuition and fees vary according to class time and course load. *Payment plan:* installment. *Waivers:* employees or children of employees.
Applying *Options:* deferred entrance. *Application fee:* $25. *Required:* high school transcript. *Required for some:* interview.
Freshman Application Contact Brenda K. Neal, Director of Access, Blue Ridge Community and Technical College, 13650 Apple Harvest Drive, Martinsburg, WV 25403. *Phone:* 304-260-4380 Ext. 2109. *Fax:* 304-260-4376. *E-mail:* bneal@blueridgectc.edu.
Website: http://www.blueridgectc.edu/.

BridgeValley Community and Technical College
Montgomery, West Virginia

Director of Admissions Ms. Lisa Graham, Director of Admissions, BridgeValley Community and Technical College, 619 2nd Avenue, Montgomery, WV 25136. *Phone:* 304-442-3167.
Website: http://www.bridgevalley.edu/.

BridgeValley Community and Technical College
South Charleston, West Virginia

Freshman Application Contact Mr. Bryce Casto, Vice President, Student Affairs, BridgeValley Community and Technical College, 2001 Union Carbide Drive, South Charleston, WV 25303. *Phone:* 304-766-3140. *Fax:* 304-766-4158. *E-mail:* castosb@wvstateu.edu.
Website: http://www.bridgevalley.edu/.

Eastern West Virginia Community and Technical College
Moorefield, West Virginia

Freshman Application Contact Learner Support Services, Eastern West Virginia Community and Technical College, HC 65 Box 402, Moorefield, WV 26836. *Phone:* 304-434-8000. *Toll-free phone:* 877-982-2322. *Fax:* 304-434-7000. *E-mail:* askeast@eastern.wvnet.edu.
Website: http://www.eastern.wvnet.edu/.

Huntington Junior College
Huntington, West Virginia

Director of Admissions Mr. James Garrett, Educational Services Director, Huntington Junior College, 900 Fifth Avenue, Huntington, WV 25701-2004. *Phone:* 304-697-7550. *Toll-free phone:* 800-344-4522.
Website: http://www.huntingtonjuniorcollege.com/.

ITT Technical Institute
Huntington, West Virginia

- **Proprietary** 2-year, part of ITT Educational Services, Inc.
- **Coed**

Academics *Calendar:* quarters. *Degree:* associate.
Freshman Application Contact Director of Recruitment, ITT Technical Institute, 5183 US Route 60, Building 1, Suite 40, Huntington, WV 25705. *Phone:* 304-733-8700. *Toll-free phone:* 800-224-4695.
Website: http://www.itt-tech.edu/.

Mountain State College
Parkersburg, West Virginia

- **Proprietary** 2-year, founded 1888
- **Small-town** campus
- **Coed,** 176 undergraduate students, 99% full-time, 92% women, 8% men

Undergraduates 174 full-time, 2 part-time. Students come from 2 states and territories; 3% transferred in. *Retention:* 70% of full-time freshmen returned.
Freshmen *Admission:* 28 enrolled.
Faculty *Total:* 11, 64% full-time, 36% with terminal degrees. *Student/faculty ratio:* 17:1.
Majors Accounting and business/management; administrative assistant and secretarial science; computer and information sciences; legal assistant/paralegal; medical/clinical assistant; medical transcription; substance abuse/addiction counseling.
Academics *Calendar:* quarters. *Degree:* diplomas and associate. *Special study options:* distance learning, double majors, honors programs, independent study, internships, part-time degree program.
Library Mountain State College Library with an OPAC.
Student Life *Housing:* college housing not available. *Student services:* personal/psychological counseling.
Standardized Tests *Required:* CPAt (for admission).
Costs (2014–15) *Tuition:* $8100 full-time, $2700 per term part-time. Full-time tuition and fees vary according to program. Part-time tuition and fees vary according to program. No tuition increase for student's term of enrollment. *Payment plan:* installment.
Applying *Required:* interview.
Freshman Application Contact Ms. Judith Sutton, President, Mountain State College, 1508 Spring Street, Parkersburg, WV 26101-3993. *Phone:* 304-485-5487. *Toll-free phone:* 800-841-0201. *Fax:* 304-485-3524. *E-mail:* jsutton@msc.edu.
Website: http://www.msc.edu/.

Mountwest Community & Technical College
Huntington, West Virginia

Freshman Application Contact Dr. Tammy Johnson, Admissions Director, Mountwest Community & Technical College, 1 John Marshall Drive, Huntington, WV 25755. *Phone:* 304-696-3160. *Toll-free phone:* 866-676-5533. *Fax:* 304-696-3135. *E-mail:* admissions@marshall.edu. *Website:* http://www.mctc.edu/.

New River Community and Technical College
Beckley, West Virginia

Director of Admissions Dr. Allen B. Withers, Vice President, Student Services, New River Community and Technical College, 167 Dye Drive, Beckley, WV 25801. *Phone:* 304-929-5011. *E-mail:* awithers@newriver.edu. *Website:* http://www.newriver.edu/.

Pierpont Community & Technical College
Fairmont, West Virginia

Freshman Application Contact Mr. Steve Leadman, Director of Admissions and Recruiting, Pierpont Community & Technical College, 1201 Locust Avenue, Fairmont, WV 26554. *Phone:* 304-367-4892. *Toll-free phone:* 800-641-5678. *Fax:* 304-367-4789. *Website:* http://www.pierpont.edu/.

Potomac State College of West Virginia University
Keyser, West Virginia

- **State-supported** primarily 2-year, founded 1901, part of West Virginia Higher Education Policy Commission
- **Small-town** 18-acre campus
- **Coed,** 1,540 undergraduate students, 80% full-time, 55% women, 45% men

Undergraduates 1,235 full-time, 305 part-time. Students come from 22 states and territories; 2 other countries; 35% are from out of state; 17% Black or African American, non-Hispanic/Latino; 3% Hispanic/Latino; 2% Asian, non-Hispanic/Latino; 0.2% Native Hawaiian or other Pacific Islander, non-Hispanic/Latino; 1% American Indian or Alaska Native, non-Hispanic/Latino; 0.5% Two or more races, non-Hispanic/Latino; 2% Race/ethnicity unknown; 0.4% international; 3% transferred in; 35% live on campus. *Retention:* 42% of full-time freshmen returned.

Freshmen *Admission:* 2,846 applied, 1,154 admitted, 639 enrolled. *Average high school GPA:* 2.83. *Test scores:* SAT critical reading scores over 500: 20%; SAT math scores over 500: 17%; ACT scores over 18: 63%; SAT critical reading scores over 600: 4%; SAT math scores over 600: 3%; ACT scores over 24: 17%; SAT critical reading scores over 700: 1%; SAT math scores over 700: 1%; ACT scores over 30: 1%.

Faculty *Total:* 86, 52% full-time, 14% with terminal degrees. *Student/faculty ratio:* 22:1.

Majors Administrative assistant and secretarial science; agricultural and extension education; agricultural business and management; agriculture; agriculture and agriculture operations related; agronomy and crop science; animal sciences; biology/biological sciences; business administration and management; business automation/technology/data entry; chemistry; civil engineering; communication; computer and information sciences; criminal justice/safety; criminology; data entry/microcomputer applications related; early childhood education; economics; electrical and electronics engineering; elementary education; English; forensic science and technology; forest resources production and management; geological and earth sciences/geosciences related; geology/earth science; history; horse husbandry/equine science and management; horticultural science; hospitality administration; journalism; liberal arts and sciences/liberal studies; mathematics; mechanical engineering; medical/clinical assistant; modern languages; parks, recreation and leisure facilities management; physical education teaching and coaching; physics; political science and government; pre-dentistry studies; pre-law studies; premedical studies; prenursing studies; pre-occupational therapy; pre-pharmacy studies; pre-physical therapy; pre-veterinary studies; psychology; secondary education; social work; sociology; wildlife, fish and wildlands science and management; wood science and wood products/pulp and paper technology.

Academics *Calendar:* semesters. *Degrees:* associate and bachelor's. *Special study options:* academic remediation for entering students, adult/continuing education programs, advanced placement credit, distance learning, double majors, honors programs, independent study, internships, part-time degree program, services for LD students, study abroad, summer session for credit.

Library Mary F. Shipper Library with 34,549 titles, 410 audiovisual materials, an OPAC, a Web page.

Student Life *Housing:* on-campus residence required through sophomore year. *Options:* coed. Campus housing is university owned. Freshman applicants given priority for college housing. *Activities and Organizations:* drama/theater group, student-run newspaper, choral group, Agriculture & Forestry Club, Black Student Alliance, Gamers & Geeks Club, Campus & Community Ministries. *Campus security:* 24-hour patrols, late-night transport/escort service, controlled dormitory access. *Student services:* health clinic, personal/psychological counseling.

Athletics Member NJCAA. *Intercollegiate sports:* baseball M(s), basketball M(s)/W(s), cross-country running M(s)/W(s), lacrosse M(s)/W(s), soccer M/W, softball W(s), volleyball W(s). *Intramural sports:* basketball M/W, football M/W, soccer M/W, softball M/W, table tennis M/W, ultimate Frisbee M/W, volleyball M/W.

Standardized Tests *Recommended:* SAT or ACT (for admission).

Costs (2014–15) *Tuition:* state resident $3480 full-time, $145 per credit hour part-time; nonresident $9456 full-time, $394 per credit hour part-time. Full-time tuition and fees vary according to course load and degree level. Part-time tuition and fees vary according to course load and degree level. *Room and board:* $8230; room only: $4334. Room and board charges vary according to board plan and housing facility. *Payment plan:* installment. *Waivers:* senior citizens and employees or children of employees.

Financial Aid Of all full-time matriculated undergraduates who enrolled in 2013, 70 Federal Work-Study jobs (averaging $1300).

Applying *Options:* electronic application. *Required:* high school transcript. *Application deadlines:* rolling (freshmen), rolling (transfers).

Freshman Application Contact Ms. Beth Little, Director of Enrollment Services, Potomac State College of West Virginia University, 75 Arnold Street, Keyser, WV 26726. *Phone:* 304-788-6820. *Toll-free phone:* 800-262-7332 Ext. 6820. *Fax:* 304-788-6939. *E-mail:* go2psc@mail.wvu.edu. *Website:* http://www.potomacstatecollege.edu/.

Southern West Virginia Community and Technical College
Mount Gay, West Virginia

Freshman Application Contact Mr. Roy Simmons, Registrar, Southern West Virginia Community and Technical College, PO Box 2900, Mt. Gay, WV 25637. *Phone:* 304-792-7160 Ext. 120. *Fax:* 304-792-7096. *E-mail:* admissions@southern.wvnet.edu. *Website:* http://southernwv.edu/.

West Virginia Business College
Nutter Fort, West Virginia

Director of Admissions Robert Wright, Campus Director, West Virginia Business College, 116 Pennsylvania Avenue, Nutter Fort, WV 26301. *Phone:* 304-624-7695. *E-mail:* info@wvbc.edu. *Website:* http://www.wvbc.edu/.

West Virginia Business College
Wheeling, West Virginia

Freshman Application Contact Ms. Karen D. Shaw, Director, West Virginia Business College, 1052 Main Street, Wheeling, WV 26003. *Phone:* 304-232-0361. *Fax:* 304-232-0363. *E-mail:* wvbcwheeling@stratuswave.net. *Website:* http://www.wvbc.edu/.

West Virginia Junior College–Bridgeport
Bridgeport, West Virginia

- **Proprietary** 2-year, founded 1922, part of West Virginia Junior College-Charleston, WV; West Virginia Junior College-Morgantown, WV; Pennsylvania Institute of Health & Technology-Uniontown, PA; Ohio Institute of Health & Technology, E. Liverpool, OH
- **Small-town** 3-acre campus with easy access to Pittsburgh
- **Coed,** 389 undergraduate students, 100% full-time, 85% women, 15% men

Undergraduates 389 full-time. Students come from 4 states and territories; 0.5% Black or African American, non-Hispanic/Latino; 10% transferred in. *Retention:* 80% of full-time freshmen returned.

Freshmen *Admission:* 389 enrolled. *Average high school GPA:* 2.5.
Faculty *Total:* 19, 42% full-time, 79% with terminal degrees. *Student/faculty ratio:* 15:1.
Majors Dental assisting; information technology; medical/clinical assistant; medical office management; pharmacy technician.
Academics *Calendar:* quarters. *Degree:* diplomas and associate. *Special study options:* cooperative education, distance learning, independent study, internships, services for LD students, summer session for credit.
Library WVJC Resource Center plus 1 other with an OPAC.
Student Life *Housing:* college housing not available. *Activities and Organizations:* Medical Club, Business Club, Computer Club, Dental Assisting Club, Pharmacy Tech Club. *Campus security:* 24-hour emergency response devices.
Standardized Tests *Recommended:* SAT or ACT (for admission).
Financial Aid Of all full-time matriculated undergraduates who enrolled in 2013, 10 Federal Work-Study jobs.
Applying *Options:* electronic application. *Application fee:* $25. *Required:* essay or personal statement, minimum 2.5 GPA, interview, Applicants are required to meet with an Admissions Representative. *Required for some:* 1 letter of recommendation. *Recommended:* high school transcript. *Application deadline:* rolling (freshmen). *Notification:* continuous (freshmen).
Freshman Application Contact Mr. Adam Pratt, High School Admissions Coordinator, West Virginia Junior College–Bridgeport, 176 Thompson Drive, Bridgeport, WV 26330. *Phone:* 304-842-4007 Ext. 112. *Toll-free phone:* 800-470-5627. *Fax:* 304-842-8191. *E-mail:* apratt@wvjcinfo.net.
Website: http://www.wvjc.edu/.

West Virginia Junior College–Charleston
Charleston, West Virginia

Freshman Application Contact West Virginia Junior College–Charleston, 1000 Virginia Street East, Charleston, WV 25301-2817. *Phone:* 304-345-2820. *Toll-free phone:* 800-924-5208.
Website: http://www.wvjc.edu/.

West Virginia Junior College– Morgantown
Morgantown, West Virginia

Freshman Application Contact Admissions Office, West Virginia Junior College–Morgantown, 148 Willey Street, Morgantown, WV 26505-5521. *Phone:* 304-296-8282.
Website: http://www.wvjcmorgantown.edu/.

West Virginia Northern Community College
Wheeling, West Virginia

Freshman Application Contact Mrs. Janet Fike, Vice President of Student Services, West Virginia Northern Community College, 1704 Market Street, Wheeling, WV 26003. *Phone:* 304-214-8837. *E-mail:* jfike@northern.wvnet.edu.
Website: http://www.wvncc.edu/.

West Virginia University at Parkersburg
Parkersburg, West Virginia

Freshman Application Contact Christine Post, Associate Dean of Enrollment Management, West Virginia University at Parkersburg, 300 Campus Drive, Parkersburg, WV 26104. *Phone:* 304-424-8223 Ext. 223. *Toll-free phone:* 800-WVA-WVUP. *Fax:* 304-424-8332. *E-mail:* christine.post@mail.wvu.edu.
Website: http://www.wvup.edu/.

WISCONSIN

Blackhawk Technical College
Janesville, Wisconsin

- **District-supported** 2-year, founded 1968, part of Wisconsin Technical College System
- **Small-town** 84-acre campus
- **Coed**

Undergraduates 997 full-time, 1,525 part-time. Students come from 3 states and territories; 1% are from out of state; 9% Black or African American, non-Hispanic/Latino; 8% Hispanic/Latino; 0.8% Asian, non-Hispanic/Latino; 0.1% Native Hawaiian or other Pacific Islander, non-Hispanic/Latino; 0.4% American Indian or Alaska Native, non-Hispanic/Latino; 3% Two or more races, non-Hispanic/Latino; 2% Race/ethnicity unknown. *Retention:* 83% of full-time freshmen returned.
Faculty *Student/faculty ratio:* 10:1.
Academics *Calendar:* semesters. *Degree:* associate. *Special study options:* academic remediation for entering students, accelerated degree program, adult/continuing education programs, advanced placement credit, cooperative education, distance learning, English as a second language, independent study, internships, part-time degree program, services for LD students, student-designed majors, summer session for credit.
Student Life *Campus security:* student patrols.
Costs (2014–15) *Tuition:* state resident $3778 full-time, $126 per credit hour part-time; nonresident $5664 full-time, $189 per credit hour part-time. Full-time tuition and fees vary according to course load. Part-time tuition and fees vary according to course load. *Required fees:* $502 full-time, $6 per credit hour part-time.
Financial Aid Of all full-time matriculated undergraduates who enrolled in 2013, 33 Federal Work-Study jobs (averaging $1150).
Applying *Options:* electronic application. *Application fee:* $30. *Required:* high school transcript.
Freshman Application Contact Blackhawk Technical College, PO Box 5009, Janesville, WI 53547-5009. *Phone:* 608-757-7713.
Website: http://www.blackhawk.edu/.

Bryant & Stratton College–Bayshore Campus
Glendale, Wisconsin

Admissions Office Contact Bryant & Stratton College–Bayshore Campus, 500 West Silver Spring Road, Suite K340, Glendale, WI 53217.
Website: http://www.bryantstratton.edu/.

Bryant & Stratton College–Milwaukee Campus
Milwaukee, Wisconsin

Freshman Application Contact Mr. Dan Basile, Director of Admissions, Bryant & Stratton College–Milwaukee Campus, 310 West Wisconsin Avenue, Suite 500 East, Milwaukee, WI 53203-2214. *Phone:* 414-276-5200.
Website: http://www.bryantstratton.edu/.

Chippewa Valley Technical College
Eau Claire, Wisconsin

- **District-supported** 2-year, founded 1912, part of Wisconsin Technical College System
- **Suburban** 255-acre campus
- **Coed**

Undergraduates 2,445 full-time, 3,172 part-time. 2% are from out of state; 1% Black or African American, non-Hispanic/Latino; 2% Hispanic/Latino; 4% Asian, non-Hispanic/Latino; 0.1% Native Hawaiian or other Pacific Islander, non-Hispanic/Latino; 0.5% American Indian or Alaska Native, non-Hispanic/Latino; 2% Two or more races, non-Hispanic/Latino; 7% Race/ethnicity unknown. *Retention:* 59% of full-time freshmen returned.
Faculty *Student/faculty ratio:* 14:1.
Academics *Calendar:* semesters. *Degree:* certificates, diplomas, and associate. *Special study options:* academic remediation for entering students, accelerated degree program, adult/continuing education programs, advanced placement credit, cooperative education, distance learning, double majors, English as a second language, honors programs, independent study, internships, part-time degree program, services for LD students, student-designed majors, summer session for credit.

Student Life *Campus security:* 24-hour emergency response devices, late-night transport/escort service, security cameras.
Standardized Tests *Required:* ACT Compass, ACCUPLACER (for admission). *Recommended:* ACT (for admission).
Financial Aid Of all full-time matriculated undergraduates who enrolled in 2013, 218 Federal Work-Study jobs (averaging $875).
Applying *Options:* electronic application, early admission, deferred entrance. *Application fee:* $30. *Required for some:* high school transcript.
Freshman Application Contact Admissions Office, Chippewa Valley Technical College, 620 W. Clairemont Avenue, Eau Claire, WI 54701. *Phone:* 715-833-6200. *Toll-free phone:* 800-547-2882. *Fax:* 715-833-6470. *E-mail:* infocenter@cvtc.edu.
Website: http://www.cvtc.edu/.

College of Menominee Nation
Keshena, Wisconsin

Director of Admissions Tessa James, Admissions Coordinator, College of Menominee Nation, PO Box 1179, Keshena, WI 54135. *Phone:* 715-799-5600 Ext. 3053. *Toll-free phone:* 800-567-2344. *E-mail:* tjames@menominee.edu. *Website:* http://www.menominee.edu/.

Fox Valley Technical College
Appleton, Wisconsin

- **State and locally supported** 2-year, founded 1967, part of Wisconsin Technical College System
- **Suburban** 100-acre campus
- **Endowment** $3.0 million
- **Coed,** 10,488 undergraduate students, 25% full-time, 48% women, 52% men

Undergraduates 2,673 full-time, 7,815 part-time. Students come from 14 states and territories; 17 other countries; 2% are from out of state; 2% Black or African American, non-Hispanic/Latino; 4% Hispanic/Latino; 5% Asian, non-Hispanic/Latino; 0.1% Native Hawaiian or other Pacific Islander, non-Hispanic/Latino; 1% American Indian or Alaska Native, non-Hispanic/Latino; 0.4% Two or more races, non-Hispanic/Latino; 8% Race/ethnicity unknown; 0.1% international.
Freshmen *Admission:* 2,470 applied, 1,977 admitted, 963 enrolled.
Faculty *Total:* 881, 35% full-time. *Student/faculty ratio:* 11:1.
Majors Accounting; administrative assistant and secretarial science; agricultural/farm supplies retailing and wholesaling; agricultural mechanization; airline pilot and flight crew; autobody/collision and repair technology; automation engineer technology; automobile/automotive mechanics technology; avionics maintenance technology; banking and financial support services; biology/biotechnology laboratory technician; building/construction site management; business administration and management; computer programming; computer support specialist; computer systems networking and telecommunications; court reporting; criminal justice/police science; culinary arts; dental hygiene; diesel mechanics technology; early childhood education; electrical and electronic engineering technologies related; electrical, electronic and communications engineering technology; electromechanical technology; emergency medical technology (EMT paramedic); energy management and systems technology; fire protection related; fire science/firefighting; forensic science and technology; graphic and printing equipment operation/production; graphic communications; health information/medical records technology; homeland security related; hospitality administration; human resources management; industrial safety technology; interdisciplinary studies; interior design; legal assistant/paralegal; logistics, materials, and supply chain management; manufacturing engineering technology; marketing/marketing management; mechanical drafting and CAD/CADD; medical office management; meeting and event planning; multi/interdisciplinary studies related; natural resources/conservation; occupational therapist assistant; office management; professional, technical, business, and scientific writing; radio, television, and digital communication related; registered nursing/registered nurse; substance abuse/addiction counseling; web/multimedia management and webmaster; welding technology; wildland/forest firefighting and investigation.
Academics *Calendar:* semesters. *Degree:* certificates, diplomas, and associate. *Special study options:* academic remediation for entering students, accelerated degree program, advanced placement credit, cooperative education, distance learning, double majors, English as a second language, independent study, internships, off-campus study, part-time degree program, services for LD students, student-designed majors, study abroad, summer session for credit.
Library Student Success Center Library with 155,000 titles, 1,000 audiovisual materials, an OPAC, a Web page.
Student Life *Housing:* college housing not available. *Activities and Organizations:* student-run newspaper, Student Government Association, Phi

Theta Kappa, Culinary Arts, Machine Tool, Post Secondary Agribusiness. *Campus security:* 24-hour emergency response devices, late-night transport/escort service, trained security personnel patrol during the colleges hours of operation. *Student services:* health clinic, personal/psychological counseling.
Athletics *Intercollegiate sports:* basketball M/W, volleyball W. *Intramural sports:* table tennis M/W.
Costs (2014–15) *Tuition:* state resident $3776 full-time, $143 per credit part-time; nonresident $5664 full-time, $206 per credit part-time. *Required fees:* $513 full-time, $17 per credit part-time. *Payment plan:* installment.
Applying *Options:* electronic application, early admission, deferred entrance. *Application fee:* $30. *Required:* high school transcript. *Application deadlines:* rolling (freshmen), rolling (transfers).
Freshman Application Contact Admissions Center, Fox Valley Technical College, 1825 North Bluemound Drive, PO Box 2277, Appleton, WI 54912-2277. *Phone:* 920-735-5643. *Toll-free phone:* 800-735-3882. *Fax:* 920-735-2582.
Website: http://www.fvtc.edu/.

Gateway Technical College
Kenosha, Wisconsin

- **State and locally supported** 2-year, founded 1911, part of Wisconsin Technical College System
- **Urban** 10-acre campus with easy access to Chicago, Milwaukee
- **Endowment** $156.8 million
- **Coed,** 7,410 undergraduate students, 19% full-time, 59% women, 41% men

Undergraduates 1,421 full-time, 5,989 part-time. Students come from 8 states and territories; 2% are from out of state; 14% Black or African American, non-Hispanic/Latino; 15% Hispanic/Latino; 1% Asian, non-Hispanic/Latino; 0.5% American Indian or Alaska Native, non-Hispanic/Latino; 3% Two or more races, non-Hispanic/Latino; 1% Race/ethnicity unknown; 9% transferred in. *Retention:* 56% of full-time freshmen returned.
Freshmen *Admission:* 1,366 enrolled.
Faculty *Total:* 741, 32% full-time. *Student/faculty ratio:* 9:1.
Majors Accounting; airline pilot and flight crew; applied horticulture/horticultural business services related; applied horticulture/horticulture operations; architectural engineering technology; automobile/automotive mechanics technology; biology/biotechnology laboratory technician; business administration and management; business operations support and secretarial services related; civil engineering technology; computer and information systems security; computer programming; computer software and media applications related; computer support specialist; computer systems analysis; computer systems networking and telecommunications; criminal justice/police science; diesel mechanics technology; early childhood education; electrical, electronic and communications engineering technology; electromechanical technology; emergency medical technology (EMT paramedic); fire science/firefighting; graphic design; health information/medical records technology; heating, air conditioning, ventilation and refrigeration maintenance technology; heating, ventilation, air conditioning and refrigeration engineering technology; hotel, motel, and restaurant management; industrial mechanics and maintenance technology; interior design; marketing/marketing management; marketing related; mechanical drafting and CAD/CADD; mental and social health services and allied professions related; multi/interdisciplinary studies related; operations management; physical therapy technology; professional, technical, business, and scientific writing; quality control technology; registered nursing/registered nurse; restaurant, culinary, and catering management; surgical technology; surveying technology; teacher assistant/aide; transportation and highway engineering; veterinary/animal health technology; water quality and wastewater treatment management and recycling technology; web/multimedia management and webmaster.
Academics *Calendar:* semesters. *Degree:* certificates, diplomas, and associate. *Special study options:* academic remediation for entering students, advanced placement credit, cooperative education, distance learning, double majors, English as a second language, independent study, internships, off-campus study, part-time degree program, services for LD students, student-designed majors, summer session for credit.
Library Library/Learning Resources Center plus 3 others with 36,916 titles, 2,980 audiovisual materials, an OPAC, a Web page.
Student Life *Housing:* college housing not available. *Activities and Organizations:* student-run newspaper, International Club. *Campus security:* 24-hour emergency response devices and patrols, late-night transport/escort service. *Student services:* personal/psychological counseling.
Costs (2014–15) *Tuition:* state resident $3092 full-time, $129 per credit hour part-time; nonresident $4531 full-time, $189 per credit hour part-time. *Required fees:* $108 full-time, $5 per credit part-time. *Payment plan:* installment. *Waivers:* senior citizens and employees or children of employees.

Applying *Options:* electronic application, early admission, deferred entrance. *Application fee:* $30. *Required:* high school transcript. *Application deadlines:* rolling (freshmen), rolling (out-of-state freshmen), rolling (transfers). *Notification:* continuous (freshmen), continuous (out-of-state freshmen), continuous (transfers).
Freshman Application Contact Admissions, Gateway Technical College, 3520 30th Avenue, Kenosha, WI 53144-1690. *Phone:* 262-564-2300. *Fax:* 262-564-2301. *E-mail:* admissions@gtc.edu.
Website: http://www.gtc.edu/.

ITT Technical Institute
Green Bay, Wisconsin

- **Proprietary** primarily 2-year, founded 2000, part of ITT Educational Services, Inc.
- **Coed**

Academics *Calendar:* quarters. *Degrees:* associate and bachelor's.
Freshman Application Contact Director of Recruitment, ITT Technical Institute, 470 Security Boulevard, Green Bay, WI 54313. *Phone:* 920-662-9000. *Toll-free phone:* 888-884-3626.
Website: http://www.itt-tech.edu/.

ITT Technical Institute
Greenfield, Wisconsin

- **Proprietary** primarily 2-year, founded 1968, part of ITT Educational Services, Inc.
- **Suburban** campus
- **Coed**

Academics *Calendar:* quarters. *Degrees:* associate and bachelor's.
Freshman Application Contact Director of Recruitment, ITT Technical Institute, 6300 West Layton Avenue, Greenfield, WI 53220-4612. *Phone:* 414-282-9494.
Website: http://www.itt-tech.edu/.

ITT Technical Institute
Madison, Wisconsin

- **Proprietary** primarily 2-year, part of ITT Educational Services, Inc.
- **Coed**

Academics *Degrees:* associate and bachelor's.
Freshman Application Contact Director of Recruitment, ITT Technical Institute, 2450 Rimrock Road, Suite 100, Madison, WI 53713. *Phone:* 608-288-6301. *Toll-free phone:* 877-628-5960.
Website: http://www.itt-tech.edu/.

Lac Courte Oreilles Ojibwa Community College
Hayward, Wisconsin

Freshman Application Contact Ms. Annette Wiggins, Registrar, Lac Courte Oreilles Ojibwa Community College, 13466 West Trepania Road, Hayward, WI 54843-2181. *Phone:* 715-634-4790 Ext. 104. *Toll-free phone:* 888-526-6221.
Website: http://www.lco.edu/.

Lakeshore Technical College
Cleveland, Wisconsin

Freshman Application Contact Lakeshore Technical College, 1290 North Avenue, Cleveland, WI 53015. *Phone:* 920-693-1339. *Toll-free phone:* 888-GO TO LTC. *Fax:* 920-693-3561.
Website: http://www.gotoltc.com/.

Madison Area Technical College
Madison, Wisconsin

Director of Admissions Ms. Maureen Menendez, Interim Admissions Administrator, Madison Area Technical College, 1701 Wright Street, Madison, WI 53704. *Phone:* 608-246-6212. *Toll-free phone:* 800-322-6282.
Website: http://madisoncollege.edu/.

Madison Media Institute
Madison, Wisconsin

Freshman Application Contact Mr. Chris K. Hutchings, President/Director, Madison Media Institute, 2702 Agriculture Drive, Madison, WI 53718. *Phone:* 608-237-8301. *Toll-free phone:* 800-236-4997.
Website: http://www.mediainstitute.edu/.

Mid-State Technical College
Wisconsin Rapids, Wisconsin

Freshman Application Contact Ms. Carole Prochnow, Admissions Assistant, Mid-State Technical College, 500 32nd Street North, Wisconsin Rapids, WI 54494-5599. *Phone:* 715-422-5444.
Website: http://www.mstc.edu/.

Milwaukee Area Technical College
Milwaukee, Wisconsin

Freshman Application Contact Sarah Adams, Director, Enrollment Services, Milwaukee Area Technical College, 700 West State Street, Milwaukee, WI 53233-1443. *Phone:* 414-297-6595. *Fax:* 414-297-7800. *E-mail:* adamss4@matc.edu.
Website: http://www.matc.edu/.

Milwaukee Career College
Milwaukee, Wisconsin

Admissions Office Contact Milwaukee Career College, 3077 N. Mayfair Road, Suite 300, Milwaukee, WI 53222.
Website: http://www.mkecc.edu/.

Moraine Park Technical College
Fond du Lac, Wisconsin

- **District-supported** 2-year, founded 1967, part of Wisconsin Technical College System
- **Small-town** 40-acre campus with easy access to Milwaukee
- **Coed,** 6,613 undergraduate students

Faculty *Total:* 270, 54% full-time.
Majors Accounting; administrative assistant and secretarial science; automobile/automotive mechanics technology; business administration and management; chiropractic assistant; clinical/medical laboratory technology; computer programming related; computer support specialist; computer systems networking and telecommunications; corrections; court reporting; culinary arts; early childhood education; electrical and electronic engineering technologies related; electromechanical technology; emergency medical technology (EMT paramedic); graphic design; health information/medical records technology; heating, ventilation, air conditioning and refrigeration engineering technology; hotel/motel administration; human resources management; legal administrative assistant/secretary; legal assistant/paralegal; machine tool technology; marketing/marketing management; mechanical drafting and CAD/CADD; mechanical engineering technologies related; medical radiologic technology; multi/interdisciplinary studies related; office management; registered nursing/registered nurse; respiratory care therapy; structural engineering; substance abuse/addiction counseling; surgical technology; teacher assistant/aide; water quality and wastewater treatment management and recycling technology.
Academics *Calendar:* semesters. *Degree:* certificates, diplomas, and associate. *Special study options:* academic remediation for entering students, accelerated degree program, adult/continuing education programs, advanced placement credit, distance learning, double majors, English as a second language, external degree program, independent study, internships, part-time degree program, services for LD students, student-designed majors, study abroad, summer session for credit.
Library Moraine Park Technical College Library/Learning Resource Center with 19,906 titles, 25,948 audiovisual materials, an OPAC, a Web page.
Student Life *Housing:* college housing not available. *Activities and Organizations:* Student Government, Student Nurses Association Club, Electrical Power Distribution Club, Electricity Club, Auto Technician Club. *Campus security:* late-night transport/escort service, Campus Security Services between 5-10 pm M-Th during the academic year. Services include night patrols. *Student services:* personal/psychological counseling.
Standardized Tests *Required:* ACT, ACCUPLACER OR ACT Compass (for admission). *Required for some:* ACT (for admission).
Costs (2015–16) *One-time required fee:* $30. *Tuition:* state resident $3947 full-time, $132 per credit hour part-time; nonresident $5920 full-time, $197 per credit hour part-time. Full-time tuition and fees vary according to program.

Part-time tuition and fees vary according to program. *Required fees:* $316 full-time, $10 per credit hour part-time. *Payment plans:* installment, deferred payment. *Waivers:* senior citizens.

Applying *Required:* high school transcript, interview, Placement test required for all; Criminal background ground check required for some. *Required for some:* interview.

Freshman Application Contact Karen Jarvis, Student Services, Moraine Park Technical College, 235 North National Avenue, Fond du Lac, WI 54935. *Phone:* 920-924-3200. *Toll-free phone:* 800-472-4554. *Fax:* 920-924-3421. *E-mail:* kjarvis@morainepark.edu. *Website:* http://www.morainepark.edu/.

Nicolet Area Technical College
Rhinelander, Wisconsin

Freshman Application Contact Ms. Susan Kordula, Director of Admissions, Nicolet Area Technical College, PO Box 518, Rhinelander, WI 54501. *Phone:* 715-365-4451. *Toll-free phone:* 800-544-3039. *E-mail:* inquire@nicoletcollege.edu. *Website:* http://www.nicoletcollege.edu/.

Northcentral Technical College
Wausau, Wisconsin

- **District-supported** 2-year, founded 1912, part of Wisconsin Technical College System
- **Rural** 96-acre campus
- **Coed,** 4,401 undergraduate students, 38% full-time, 61% women, 39% men

Undergraduates 1,659 full-time, 2,742 part-time. 1% Black or African American, non-Hispanic/Latino; 0.3% Hispanic/Latino; 5% Asian, non-Hispanic/Latino; 0.2% Native Hawaiian or other Pacific Islander, non-Hispanic/Latino; 1% American Indian or Alaska Native, non-Hispanic/Latino; 23% Race/ethnicity unknown.

Freshmen *Admission:* 810 enrolled.

Faculty *Student/faculty ratio:* 23:1.

Majors Accounting; administrative assistant and secretarial science; architectural engineering technology; automobile/automotive mechanics technology; business administration and management; clinical/medical laboratory technology; computer and information sciences and support services related; computer systems analysis; computer systems networking and telecommunications; criminal justice/police science; dental hygiene; early childhood education; electromechanical technology; emergency medical technology (EMT paramedic); furniture design and manufacturing; general studies; graphic communications; manufacturing engineering technology; marketing/marketing management; mechanical drafting and CAD/CADD; medical insurance/medical billing; medical radiologic technology; mental and social health services and allied professions related; merchandising, sales, and marketing operations related (general); multi/interdisciplinary studies related; operations management; registered nursing/registered nurse; sign language interpretation and translation; teacher assistant/aide.

Academics *Calendar:* semesters. *Degree:* certificates, diplomas, and associate. *Special study options:* academic remediation for entering students, accelerated degree program, adult/continuing education programs, advanced placement credit, cooperative education, distance learning, double majors, English as a second language, independent study, internships, off-campus study, part-time degree program, services for LD students, student-designed majors, summer session for credit.

Library Northcentral Technical College, Wausau Campus Library plus 1 other with 30,000 titles, an OPAC, a Web page.

Student Life *Housing Options:* Campus housing is provided by a third party. *Campus security:* 24-hour emergency response devices, student patrols, late-night transport/escort service. *Student services:* personal/psychological counseling, women's center.

Athletics *Intramural sports:* basketball M/W, field hockey M/W, football M/W, soccer M/W, softball M/W, volleyball M/W.

Costs (2014–15) *Tuition:* state resident $4140 full-time; nonresident $6029 full-time. Full-time tuition and fees vary according to course level, course load, and program. Part-time tuition and fees vary according to course level, course load, and program. *Payment plans:* installment, deferred payment. *Waivers:* senior citizens.

Financial Aid Of all full-time matriculated undergraduates who enrolled in 2013, 366 Federal Work-Study jobs (averaging $2000).

Applying *Options:* electronic application, early admission, deferred entrance. *Application fee:* $30. *Required:* high school transcript. *Required for some:*

interview. *Application deadlines:* rolling (freshmen), rolling (transfers). *Notification:* continuous (freshmen), continuous (transfers).

Freshman Application Contact Northcentral Technical College, 1000 West Campus Drive, Wausau, WI 54401-1899. *Phone:* 715-675-3331. *Website:* http://www.ntc.edu/.

Northeast Wisconsin Technical College
Green Bay, Wisconsin

Freshman Application Contact Christine Lemerande, Program Enrollment Supervisor, Northeast Wisconsin Technical College, 2740 W Mason Street, PO Box 19042, Green Bay, WI 54307-9042. *Phone:* 920-498-5444. *Toll-free phone:* 888-385-6982. *Fax:* 920-498-6882. *Website:* http://www.nwtc.edu/.

Southwest Wisconsin Technical College
Fennimore, Wisconsin

Freshman Application Contact Student Services, Southwest Wisconsin Technical College, 1800 Bronson Boulevard, Fennimore, WI 53809-9778. *Phone:* 608-822-2354. *Toll-free phone:* 800-362-3322. *Fax:* 608-822-6019. *E-mail:* student-services@swtc.edu. *Website:* http://www.swtc.edu/.

University of Wisconsin–Baraboo/Sauk County
Baraboo, Wisconsin

Freshman Application Contact Ms. Jan Gerlach, Assistant Director of Student Services, University of Wisconsin–Baraboo/Sauk County, Baraboo, WI 53913-1015. *Phone:* 608-355-5270. *E-mail:* booinfo@uwc.edu. *Website:* http://www.baraboo.uwc.edu/.

University of Wisconsin–Barron County
Rice Lake, Wisconsin

Freshman Application Contact Assistant Dean for Student Services, University of Wisconsin–Barron County, 1800 College Drive, Rice Lake, WI 54868-2497. *Phone:* 715-234-8024. *Fax:* 715-234-8024. *Website:* http://www.barron.uwc.edu/.

University of Wisconsin–Fond du Lac
Fond du Lac, Wisconsin

- **State-supported** 2-year, founded 1968, part of University of Wisconsin System
- **Small-town** 182-acre campus with easy access to Milwaukee
- **Coed,** 626 undergraduate students

Undergraduates Students come from 3 states and territories; 1% are from out of state. *Retention:* 58% of full-time freshmen returned.

Freshmen *Admission:* 381 applied, 325 admitted. *Average high school GPA:* 2.5. *Test scores:* ACT scores over 18: 93%; ACT scores over 24: 20%; ACT scores over 30: 1%.

Faculty *Total:* 27, 59% full-time, 70% with terminal degrees. *Student/faculty ratio:* 18:1.

Majors Liberal arts and sciences/liberal studies.

Academics *Calendar:* semesters. *Degree:* associate. *Special study options:* academic remediation for entering students, accelerated degree program, adult/continuing education programs, advanced placement credit, cooperative education, distance learning, independent study, off-campus study, part-time degree program, services for LD students, study abroad, summer session for credit.

Library 41,891 titles.

Student Life *Housing:* college housing not available. *Activities and Organizations:* drama/theater group, student-run newspaper, choral group, student government, Campus Ambassadors, Multicultural Club, chorus, band. *Campus security:* 24-hour emergency response devices. *Student services:* personal/psychological counseling.

Athletics Member NJCAA. *Intercollegiate sports:* basketball M/W, golf M/W, soccer M/W, tennis M/W, volleyball W. *Intramural sports:* basketball M/W, bowling M/W, golf M/W, volleyball M/W.

Standardized Tests *Required:* SAT or ACT (for admission).

Costs (2015–16) *One-time required fee:* $135. *Tuition:* state resident $5200 full-time; nonresident $11,734 full-time. Full-time tuition and fees vary according to course load and reciprocity agreements. Part-time tuition and fees vary according to course load and reciprocity agreements. *Required fees:* $221 full-time. *Payment plan:* installment.

Applying *Options:* electronic application. *Required:* high school transcript. *Application deadlines:* rolling (freshmen), rolling (out-of-state freshmen), rolling (transfers).
Freshman Application Contact University of Wisconsin–Fond du Lac, 400 University Drive, Fond du Lac, WI 54935. *Phone:* 920-929-1122.
Website: http://www.fdl.uwc.edu/.

University of Wisconsin–Fox Valley
Menasha, Wisconsin

- **State-supported** 2-year, founded 1933, part of University of Wisconsin System
- **Urban** 33-acre campus
- **Coed,** 1,797 undergraduate students, 58% full-time, 52% women, 48% men

Undergraduates 1,037 full-time, 760 part-time. Students come from 3 states and territories; 4 other countries; 1% are from out of state. *Retention:* 60% of full-time freshmen returned.
Freshmen *Admission:* 1,166 enrolled. *Average high school GPA:* 2.5.
Faculty *Total:* 91, 34% full-time. *Student/faculty ratio:* 20:1.
Majors Liberal arts and sciences/liberal studies.
Academics *Calendar:* semesters. *Degree:* certificates and associate. *Special study options:* academic remediation for entering students, accelerated degree program, adult/continuing education programs, advanced placement credit, cooperative education, distance learning, honors programs, independent study, internships, off-campus study, part-time degree program, services for LD students, study abroad, summer session for credit.
Library UW Fox Library with 30,000 titles, an OPAC, a Web page.
Student Life *Housing:* college housing not available. *Options:* Campus housing is provided by a third party. *Activities and Organizations:* drama/theater group, student-run newspaper, radio and television station, choral group, Business Club, Education Club, Ballroom Dance Club, Campus Crusade for Christ, Computer Science Club. *Campus security:* 24-hour emergency response devices, late-night transport/escort service. *Student services:* personal/psychological counseling.
Athletics Member NJCAA. *Intercollegiate sports:* basketball M/W, golf M/W, soccer M/W, tennis M/W, volleyball M/W. *Intramural sports:* baseball M(c), basketball M/W, volleyball M/W, wrestling M(c).
Standardized Tests *Required:* ACT (for admission).
Costs (2014–15) *Tuition:* state resident $5019 full-time, $209 per credit part-time; nonresident $12,003 full-time, $500 per credit part-time. Full-time tuition and fees vary according to course load. Part-time tuition and fees vary according to course load. *Required fees:* $275 full-time. *Payment plan:* installment. *Waivers:* senior citizens.
Applying *Required:* high school transcript. *Required for some:* interview. *Recommended:* essay or personal statement.
Freshman Application Contact University of Wisconsin–Fox Valley, 1478 Midway Road, Menasha, WI 54952. *Phone:* 920-832-2620.
Website: http://www.uwfox.uwc.edu/.

University of Wisconsin–Manitowoc
Manitowoc, Wisconsin

Freshman Application Contact Dr. Christopher Lewis, Assistant Campus Dean for Student Services, University of Wisconsin–Manitowoc, 705 Viebahn Street, Manitowoc, WI 54220-6699. *Phone:* 920-683-4707. *Fax:* 920-683-4776. *E-mail:* christopher.lewis@uwc.edu.
Website: http://www.manitowoc.uwc.edu/.

University of Wisconsin–Marathon County
Wausau, Wisconsin

Freshman Application Contact Dr. Nolan Beck, Director of Student Services, University of Wisconsin–Marathon County, 518 South Seventh Avenue, Wausau, WI 54401-5396. *Phone:* 715-261-6238. *Toll-free phone:* 888-367-8962. *Fax:* 715-848-3568.
Website: http://www.uwmc.uwc.edu/.

University of Wisconsin–Marinette
Marinette, Wisconsin

Freshman Application Contact Ms. Cynthia M. Bailey, Assistant Campus Dean for Student Services, University of Wisconsin–Marinette, 750 West Bay

Shore, Marinette, WI 54143-4299. *Phone:* 715-735-4301. *E-mail:* cynthia.bailey@uwc.edu.
Website: http://www.marinette.uwc.edu/.

University of Wisconsin–Marshfield/Wood County
Marshfield, Wisconsin

Freshman Application Contact Brittany Lueth, Director of Student Services, University of Wisconsin–Marshfield/Wood County, 2000 West 5th Street, Marshfield, WI 54449. *Phone:* 715-389-6500. *Fax:* 715-384-1718.
Website: http://marshfield.uwc.edu/.

University of Wisconsin–Richland
Richland Center, Wisconsin

Freshman Application Contact Mr. John D. Poole, Assistant Campus Dean, University of Wisconsin–Richland, 1200 Highway 14 West, Richland Center, WI 53581. *Phone:* 608-647-8422. *Fax:* 608-647-2275. *E-mail:* john.poole@uwc.edu.
Website: http://richland.uwc.edu/.

University of Wisconsin–Rock County
Janesville, Wisconsin

Freshman Application Contact University of Wisconsin–Rock County, 2909 Kellogg Avenue, Janesville, WI 53546-5699. *Phone:* 608-758-6523. *Toll-free phone:* 888-INFO-UWC.
Website: http://rock.uwc.edu/.

University of Wisconsin–Sheboygan
Sheboygan, Wisconsin

- **State-supported** 2-year, founded 1933, part of University of Wisconsin System
- **Small-town** 75-acre campus with easy access to Milwaukee
- **Coed,** 769 undergraduate students, 40% full-time, 51% women, 49% men

Undergraduates 305 full-time, 464 part-time. 2% Black or African American, non-Hispanic/Latino; 2% Hispanic/Latino; 11% Asian, non-Hispanic/Latino; 0.4% American Indian or Alaska Native, non-Hispanic/Latino; 0.4% Race/ethnicity unknown.
Freshmen *Admission:* 355 applied, 355 admitted, 470 enrolled.
Faculty *Total:* 17, 100% full-time. *Student/faculty ratio:* 16:1.
Majors Liberal arts and sciences/liberal studies.
Academics *Calendar:* semesters. *Degree:* associate. *Special study options:* academic remediation for entering students, adult/continuing education programs, advanced placement credit, cooperative education, distance learning, English as a second language, independent study, off-campus study, part-time degree program, services for LD students, summer session for credit.
Library University Library - Open for use by all Sheboygan County residents with an OPAC.
Student Life *Housing:* college housing not available. *Activities and Organizations:* drama/theater group, student-run newspaper, choral group, Student Government Association (SGA), English Club, University Theatre, Intramural Athletics, Southeast Asian Club. *Campus security:* 24-hour patrols by city police. *Student services:* personal/psychological counseling.
Athletics *Intercollegiate sports:* basketball M, golf M/W, soccer M/W, tennis M/W, volleyball W. *Intramural sports:* basketball M/W, football M/W, ultimate Frisbee M/W, volleyball M/W.
Standardized Tests *Required:* SAT or ACT (for admission).
Costs (2015–16) *Tuition:* state resident $4750 full-time, $198 per credit part-time; nonresident $11,737 full-time. Full-time tuition and fees vary according to course load. Part-time tuition and fees vary according to course load. *Required fees:* $354 full-time, $15 part-time. *Payment plan:* installment.
Applying *Options:* electronic application. *Application fee:* $44. *Required:* essay or personal statement, high school transcript. *Required for some:* ACT Scores required for students under age 21. *Application deadlines:* rolling (freshmen), rolling (out-of-state freshmen), rolling (transfers). *Notification:* continuous (freshmen), continuous (out-of-state freshmen), continuous (transfers).
Freshman Application Contact Mrs. Elisa Carr, High School Relations and Recruitment Coordinator, University of Wisconsin–Sheboygan, One University Drive, Sheboygan, WI 53081. *Phone:* 920-459-5956. *Fax:* 920-459-6602. *E-mail:* elisa.carr@uwc.edu.
Website: http://www.sheboygan.uwc.edu/.

University of Wisconsin–Washington County
West Bend, Wisconsin

Freshman Application Contact Mr. Dan Cebrario, Associate Director of Student Services, University of Wisconsin–Washington County, Student Services Office, 400 University Drive, West Bend, WI 53095. *Phone:* 262-335-5201. *Fax:* 262-335-5220. *E-mail:* dan.cibrario@uwc.edu. *Website:* http://www.washington.uwc.edu/.

University of Wisconsin–Waukesha
Waukesha, Wisconsin

- **State-supported** primarily 2-year, founded 1966, part of University of Wisconsin System
- **Suburban** 86-acre campus with easy access to Milwaukee
- **Coed,** 2,239 undergraduate students, 48% full-time, 47% women, 53% men

Undergraduates 1,069 full-time, 1,170 part-time. Students come from 16 states and territories; 1 other country; 7% are from out of state; 4% Black or African American, non-Hispanic/Latino; 4% Hispanic/Latino; 3% Asian, non-Hispanic/Latino; 0.9% Native Hawaiian or other Pacific Islander, non-Hispanic/Latino; 0.1% American Indian or Alaska Native, non-Hispanic/Latino; 0.1% Race/ethnicity unknown; 0.1% international; 7% transferred in.
Freshmen *Admission:* 1,418 enrolled.
Faculty *Total:* 92, 67% full-time, 93% with terminal degrees. *Student/faculty ratio:* 24:1.
Majors Liberal arts and sciences/liberal studies.
Academics *Calendar:* semesters. *Degrees:* associate and bachelor's. *Special study options:* academic remediation for entering students, accelerated degree program, advanced placement credit, distance learning, honors programs, internships, off-campus study, part-time degree program, services for LD students, study abroad, summer session for credit.
Library University of Wisconsin-Waukesha Library plus 1 other with 68,600 titles, 5,121 audiovisual materials, a Web page.
Student Life *Housing:* college housing not available. *Activities and Organizations:* drama/theater group, student-run newspaper, choral group, Student Government, Student Activities Committee, Campus Crusade, Phi Theta Kappa, Circle K. *Campus security:* late-night transport/escort service, part-time patrols by trained security personnel. *Student services:* personal/psychological counseling.
Athletics Member NJCAA. *Intercollegiate sports:* basketball M/W, golf M/W, soccer M/W, tennis M/W, volleyball W. *Intramural sports:* basketball M, bowling M/W, cheerleading W, cross-country running W, football M/W, skiing (downhill) M/W, table tennis M/W, volleyball M(c).
Standardized Tests *Required:* SAT or ACT (for admission).
Costs (2014–15) *Tuition:* state resident $5091 full-time, $215 per credit part-time; nonresident $12,072 full-time, $506 per credit part-time. Full-time tuition and fees vary according to course load. Part-time tuition and fees vary according to course load. *Required fees:* $230 full-time. *Payment plan:* installment.
Applying *Options:* electronic application, early admission, deferred entrance. *Application fee:* $44. *Required:* high school transcript. *Required for some:* interview. *Recommended:* essay or personal statement, Admission interview may be recommended. *Application deadline:* rolling (freshmen). *Notification:* continuous (freshmen).
Freshman Application Contact Ms. Deb Kusick, Sr. Admission Specialist, University of Wisconsin–Waukesha, 1500 North University Drive, Waukesha, WI 53188-2799. *Phone:* 262-521-5040. *Fax:* 262-521-5530. *E-mail:* deborah.kusick@uwc.edu. *Website:* http://www.waukesha.uwc.edu/.

Waukesha County Technical College
Pewaukee, Wisconsin

- **State and locally supported** 2-year, founded 1923, part of Wisconsin Technical College System
- **Suburban** 137-acre campus with easy access to Milwaukee
- **Coed,** 8,692 undergraduate students, 20% full-time, 47% women, 53% men

Undergraduates 1,729 full-time, 6,963 part-time. 9% Black or African American, non-Hispanic/Latino; 7% Hispanic/Latino; 2% Asian, non-Hispanic/Latino; 0.1% Native Hawaiian or other Pacific Islander, non-Hispanic/Latino; 0.6% American Indian or Alaska Native, non-Hispanic/Latino; 3% Race/ethnicity unknown.
Freshmen *Admission:* 486 enrolled.
Faculty *Total:* 858, 22% full-time. *Student/faculty ratio:* 18:1.

Majors Accounting; administrative assistant and secretarial science; architectural drafting and CAD/CADD; autobody/collision and repair technology; automobile/automotive mechanics technology; baking and pastry arts; business administration and management; business administration, management and operations related; computer and information sciences and support services related; computer programming; computer support specialist; computer systems networking and telecommunications; criminal justice/police science; dental hygiene; digital arts; early childhood education; electrical, electronic and communications engineering technology; electromechanical and instrumentation and maintenance technologies related; emergency medical technology (EMT paramedic); fire prevention and safety technology; graphic communications; graphic design; health information/medical records technology; hotel, motel, and restaurant management; human resources management; interior design; international marketing; marketing/marketing management; mechanical drafting and CAD/CADD; medical radiologic technology; mental and social health services and allied professions related; metal fabricator; multi/interdisciplinary studies related; operations management; physical therapy technology; real estate; registered nursing/registered nurse; restaurant, culinary, and catering management; surgical technology; teacher assistant/aide.
Academics *Calendar:* semesters. *Degree:* certificates, diplomas, and associate. *Special study options:* academic remediation for entering students, accelerated degree program, advanced placement credit, cooperative education, distance learning, English as a second language, part-time degree program, services for LD students, student-designed majors, summer session for credit.
Student Life *Housing:* college housing not available. *Campus security:* patrols by police officers 8 am to 10 pm.
Costs (2014–15) *Tuition:* state resident $3776 full-time, $126 per credit hour part-time; nonresident $5664 full-time, $189 per credit hour part-time. Full-time tuition and fees vary according to program. Part-time tuition and fees vary according to program. *Required fees:* $227 full-time, $8 per credit hour part-time. *Payment plans:* installment, deferred payment. *Waivers:* senior citizens.
Financial Aid Of all full-time matriculated undergraduates who enrolled in 2013, 285 Federal Work-Study jobs (averaging $3245). 197 state and other part-time jobs (averaging $1425).
Applying *Options:* electronic application. *Application fee:* $30. *Required:* high school transcript. *Required for some:* interview. *Application deadlines:* rolling (freshmen), rolling (transfers).
Freshman Application Contact Waukesha County Technical College, 800 Main Street, Pewaukee, WI 53072-4601. *Phone:* 262-691-5464. *Website:* http://www.wctc.edu/.

Western Technical College
La Crosse, Wisconsin

Freshman Application Contact Ms. Jane Wells, Manager of Admissions, Registration, and Records, Western Technical College, PO Box 908, La Crosse, WI 54602-0908. *Phone:* 608-785-9158. *Toll-free phone:* 800-322-9982. *Fax:* 608-785-9094. *E-mail:* mildes@wwtc.edu. *Website:* http://www.westerntc.edu/.

Wisconsin Indianhead Technical College
Shell Lake, Wisconsin

- **District-supported** 2-year, founded 1912, part of Wisconsin Technical College System
- **Urban** 118-acre campus
- **Endowment** $3.5 million
- **Coed,** 3,045 undergraduate students, 40% full-time, 60% women, 40% men

Undergraduates 1,221 full-time, 1,824 part-time. Students come from 8 states and territories; 8% are from out of state; 0.9% Black or African American, non-Hispanic/Latino; 0.6% Hispanic/Latino; 0.5% Asian, non-Hispanic/Latino; 2% American Indian or Alaska Native, non-Hispanic/Latino; 2% Two or more races, non-Hispanic/Latino; 1% Race/ethnicity unknown.
Freshmen *Admission:* 465 enrolled.
Faculty *Total:* 348, 44% full-time. *Student/faculty ratio:* 17:1.
Majors Accounting; administrative assistant and secretarial science; architectural engineering technology; business administration and management; computer/information technology services administration related; computer installation and repair technology; computer systems networking and telecommunications; corrections; criminal justice/police science; early childhood education; emergency medical technology (EMT paramedic); engineering design; finance; health information/medical records technology; human resources management; industrial production technologies related; marketing/marketing management; medical administrative assistant and medical secretary; multi/interdisciplinary studies related; occupational therapist assistant; office management; operations management; registered

nursing/registered nurse; web page, digital/multimedia and information resources design.

Academics *Calendar:* semesters. *Degree:* certificates, diplomas, and associate.

Student Life *Housing:* college housing not available. *Student services:* health clinic.

Costs (2014–15) *Tuition:* state resident $3776 full-time, $126 per credit part-time; nonresident $5664 full-time, $189 per credit part-time. Full-time tuition and fees vary according to course load, program, and reciprocity agreements. Part-time tuition and fees vary according to course load, program, and reciprocity agreements. *Required fees:* $395 full-time, $126 per credit part-time. *Payment plans:* installment, deferred payment.

Applying *Options:* electronic application. *Application fee:* $30. *Application deadline:* rolling (freshmen).

Freshman Application Contact Mr. Steve Bitzer, Vice President, Student Affairs and Campus Administrator, Wisconsin Indianhead Technical College, 2100 Beaser Avenue, Ashland, WI 54806. *Phone:* 715-468-2815 Ext. 3149. *Toll-free phone:* 800-243-9482. *Fax:* 715-468-2819. *E-mail:* Steve.Bitzer@ witc.edu.

Website: http://www.witc.edu/.

WYOMING

Casper College
Casper, Wyoming

- **State and locally supported** 2-year, founded 1945
- **Small-town** 200-acre campus
- **Coed,** 3,993 undergraduate students, 43% full-time, 59% women, 41% men

Undergraduates 1,717 full-time, 2,276 part-time. Students come from 35 states and territories; 15 other countries; 11% are from out of state; 1% Black or African American, non-Hispanic/Latino; 5% Hispanic/Latino; 0.7% Asian, non-Hispanic/Latino; 0.2% Native Hawaiian or other Pacific Islander, non-Hispanic/Latino; 0.4% American Indian or Alaska Native, non-Hispanic/Latino; 2% Two or more races, non-Hispanic/Latino; 3% Race/ethnicity unknown; 0.7% international; 5% transferred in; 10% live on campus.

Freshmen *Admission:* 1,063 applied, 1,063 admitted, 581 enrolled. *Average high school GPA:* 3.1. *Test scores:* ACT scores over 18: 76%; ACT scores over 24: 18%; ACT scores over 30: 1%.

Faculty *Total:* 258, 57% full-time, 23% with terminal degrees. *Student/faculty ratio:* 13:1.

Majors Accounting; accounting technology and bookkeeping; acting; administrative assistant and secretarial science; agricultural business and management; agriculture; airline pilot and flight crew; animal sciences; anthropology; art; art teacher education; athletic training; autobody/collision and repair technology; automobile/automotive mechanics technology; biology/biological sciences; business administration and management; business automation/technology/data entry; chemistry; clinical laboratory science/medical technology; computer and information systems security; computer programming; construction management; construction trades; criminal justice/law enforcement administration; crisis/emergency/disaster management; dance; diesel mechanics technology; drafting and design technology; economics; electrical, electronic and communications engineering technology; elementary education; emergency medical technology (EMT paramedic); energy management and systems technology; engineering; English; entrepreneurship; environmental science; fine/studio arts; fire science/firefighting; foreign languages and literatures; forensic science and technology; general studies; geographic information science and cartography; geology/earth science; graphic design; health services/allied health/health sciences; history; hospitality administration; industrial mechanics and maintenance technology; international relations and affairs; journalism; kindergarten/preschool education; legal assistant/paralegal; liberal arts and sciences/liberal studies; machine tool technology; manufacturing engineering technology; marketing/marketing management; mass communication/media; mathematics; mining technology; museum studies; music; musical theater; music performance; music teacher education; nutrition sciences; occupational therapist assistant; pharmacy technician; photography; physical education teaching and coaching; physics; political science and government; pre-dentistry studies; pre-law studies; premedical studies; pre-occupational therapy; pre-optometry; pre-pharmacy studies; pre-physical therapy; pre-veterinary studies; psychology; radiologic technology/science; range science and management; registered nursing/registered nurse; respiratory care therapy; retailing; robotics technology; social studies teacher education; social work; sociology; speech communication and rhetoric; statistics related; substance abuse/addiction counseling; technology/industrial arts teacher education;

theater design and technology; water quality and wastewater treatment management and recycling technology; web/multimedia management and webmaster; web page, digital/multimedia and information resources design; welding technology; wildlife, fish and wildlands science and management; women's studies.

Academics *Calendar:* semesters. *Degree:* certificates and associate. *Special study options:* academic remediation for entering students, accelerated degree program, advanced placement credit, cooperative education, distance learning, English as a second language, honors programs, independent study, internships, off-campus study, part-time degree program, services for LD students, summer session for credit.

Library Goodstein Foundation Library with 128,000 titles, an OPAC, a Web page.

Student Life *Housing Options:* coed. Campus housing is university owned. *Activities and Organizations:* drama/theater group, student-run newspaper, choral group, Student Senate, Student Activities Board, Agriculture Club, Theater Club, Phi Theta Kappa. *Campus security:* 24-hour patrols, late-night transport/escort service. *Student services:* health clinic, personal/psychological counseling.

Athletics Member NJCAA. *Intercollegiate sports:* basketball M(s)/W(s), equestrian sports M/W, volleyball W(s). *Intramural sports:* basketball M/W, bowling M/W, football M/W, golf M/W, racquetball M/W, soccer M/W, softball M/W, tennis M/W.

Costs (2015–16) *Tuition:* state resident $1992 full-time, $83 per credit part-time; nonresident $5976 full-time, $249 per credit part-time. Part-time tuition and fees vary according to course load. *Required fees:* $600 full-time, $25 per credit part-time. *Room and board:* $6050. Room and board charges vary according to board plan and housing facility. *Payment plan:* installment. *Waivers:* senior citizens and employees or children of employees.

Financial Aid Of all full-time matriculated undergraduates who enrolled in 2013, 80 Federal Work-Study jobs (averaging $2000).

Applying *Options:* electronic application, early admission. *Required:* high school transcript. *Application deadlines:* 8/15 (freshmen), 8/15 (transfers). *Notification:* continuous until 8/15 (freshmen), continuous until 8/15 (transfers).

Freshman Application Contact Mrs. Kyla Foltz, Director of Admissions Services, Casper College, 125 College Drive, Casper, WY 82601. *Phone:* 307-268-2111. *Toll-free phone:* 800-442-2963. *Fax:* 307-268-2611. *E-mail:* kfoltz@caspercollege.edu.

Website: http://www.caspercollege.edu/.

Central Wyoming College
Riverton, Wyoming

- **State and locally supported** 2-year, founded 1966, part of Wyoming Community College Commission
- **Small-town** 200-acre campus
- **Endowment** $17.4 million
- **Coed,** 2,036 undergraduate students, 36% full-time, 56% women, 44% men

Undergraduates 738 full-time, 1,298 part-time. Students come from 45 states and territories; 6 other countries; 13% are from out of state; 1% Black or African American, non-Hispanic/Latino; 10% Hispanic/Latino; 0.7% Asian, non-Hispanic/Latino; 0.2% Native Hawaiian or other Pacific Islander, non-Hispanic/Latino; 10% American Indian or Alaska Native, non-Hispanic/Latino; 2% Two or more races, non-Hispanic/Latino; 2% Race/ethnicity unknown; 0.4% international; 5% transferred in; 10% live on campus. *Retention:* 48% of full-time freshmen returned.

Freshmen *Admission:* 527 applied, 527 admitted, 271 enrolled. *Average high school GPA:* 3.01. *Test scores:* SAT critical reading scores over 500: 33%; SAT math scores over 500: 67%; ACT scores over 18: 68%; SAT math scores over 600: 17%; ACT scores over 24: 18%; ACT scores over 30: 1%.

Faculty *Total:* 209, 39% full-time, 31% with terminal degrees. *Student/faculty ratio:* 9:1.

Majors Accounting; accounting technology and bookkeeping; acting; administrative assistant and secretarial science; agricultural business and management; American Indian/Native American studies; art; athletic training; automobile/automotive mechanics technology; biology/biological sciences; building/property maintenance; business administration and management; business/commerce; carpentry; commercial photography; computer science; computer technology/computer systems technology; criminal justice/law enforcement administration; culinary arts; customer service support/call center/teleservice operation; dramatic/theater arts; early childhood education; elementary education; engineering; English; entrepreneurship; environmental/environmental health engineering; environmental science; equestrian studies; fire science/firefighting; general studies; geology/earth science; graphic design; homeland security, law enforcement, firefighting and protective services related; hotel/motel administration; international/global studies; mathematics; medical office assistant; music; occupational safety and health technology; parks, recreation and leisure; parks, recreation and leisure facilities management; physical sciences; pre-law studies; psychology; radio and television; range science and management; registered nursing/registered nurse; rehabilitation and therapeutic professions related; secondary education; social sciences; teacher assistant/aide; theater design and technology; welding technology.

Academics *Calendar:* semesters. *Degree:* certificates, diplomas, and associate. *Special study options:* academic remediation for entering students, adult/continuing education programs, advanced placement credit, cooperative education, distance learning, double majors, English as a second language, honors programs, independent study, off-campus study, part-time degree program, services for LD students, summer session for credit.

Library Central Wyoming College Library with 54,974 titles, 1,450 audiovisual materials, an OPAC, a Web page.

Student Life *Housing Options:* coed. Campus housing is university owned. *Activities and Organizations:* drama/theater group, student-run radio and television station, choral group, Multi-Cultural Club, La Vida Nueva Club, Fellowship of College Christians, Quality Leaders, Science Club. *Campus security:* 24-hour emergency response devices, late-night transport/escort service, controlled dormitory access. *Student services:* personal/psychological counseling.

Athletics Member NJCAA. *Intercollegiate sports:* basketball M(s)/W(s), cross-country running M/W, equestrian sports M(s)/W(s), golf M/W, volleyball W(s). *Intramural sports:* badminton M/W, basketball M/W, football M/W, rock climbing M/W, skiing (cross-country) M/W, skiing (downhill) M/W, soccer M/W, softball M/W, swimming and diving M/W, table tennis M/W, tennis M/W, ultimate Frisbee M/W, volleyball M/W, weight lifting M/W.

Costs (2015–16) *Tuition:* state resident $1992 full-time, $83 per credit part-time; nonresident $5976 full-time, $249 per credit part-time. Full-time tuition and fees vary according to course load, program, and reciprocity agreements. Part-time tuition and fees vary according to course load, program, and reciprocity agreements. *Required fees:* $720 full-time, $30 part-time. *Room and board:* $5130; room only: $2530. Room and board charges vary according to board plan and housing facility. *Payment plans:* installment, deferred payment. *Waivers:* senior citizens and employees or children of employees.

Financial Aid Of all full-time matriculated undergraduates who enrolled in 2013, 407 applied for aid, 327 were judged to have need. 39 Federal Work-Study jobs (averaging $2291). *Financial aid deadline:* 6/30.

Applying *Options:* electronic application, early admission, deferred entrance. *Recommended:* high school transcript. *Application deadlines:* rolling (freshmen), rolling (out-of-state freshmen), rolling (transfers).

Freshman Application Contact Mrs. Deborah Graham, Admissions Assistant, Central Wyoming College, 2660 Peck Avenue, Riverton, WY 82501-2273. *Phone:* 307-855-2061. *Toll-free phone:* 800-735-8418. *Fax:* 307-855-2065. *E-mail:* admit@cwc.edu.
Website: http://www.cwc.edu/.

Eastern Wyoming College
Torrington, Wyoming

- **State and locally supported** 2-year, founded 1948, part of Wyoming Community College Commission
- **Rural** 40-acre campus
- **Coed,** 1,750 undergraduate students, 38% full-time, 57% women, 43% men

Undergraduates 662 full-time, 1,088 part-time. 1% Black or African American, non-Hispanic/Latino; 7% Hispanic/Latino; 0.6% Asian, non-Hispanic/Latino; 0.4% Native Hawaiian or other Pacific Islander, non-Hispanic/Latino; 1% American Indian or Alaska Native, non-Hispanic/Latino; 0.9% Two or more races, non-Hispanic/Latino; 0.1% Race/ethnicity unknown; 0.1% international.

Freshmen *Admission:* 185 enrolled.

Faculty *Total:* 76, 58% full-time. *Student/faculty ratio:* 24:1.

Majors Accounting; administrative assistant and secretarial science; agribusiness; agricultural teacher education; art; biology/biological sciences; business administration and management; business teacher education; computer systems networking and telecommunications; corrections administration; cosmetology; criminal justice/law enforcement administration; criminal justice/police science; criminal justice/safety; early childhood education; economics; elementary education; English; environmental biology; farm and ranch management; foreign languages and literatures; general studies; health/medical preparatory programs related; liberal arts and sciences/liberal studies; mathematics; mathematics teacher education; music; music teacher education; office management; physical education teaching and coaching; pre-dentistry studies; premedical studies; pre-pharmacy studies; pre-veterinary studies; range science and management; secondary education; social sciences; speech communication and rhetoric; statistics; veterinary/animal health technology; welding technology; wildlife, fish and wildlands science and management.

Academics *Calendar:* semesters. *Degree:* certificates, diplomas, and associate. *Special study options:* academic remediation for entering students,

accelerated degree program, advanced placement credit, distance learning, English as a second language, independent study, internships, part-time degree program, services for LD students, student-designed majors, summer session for credit.

Library Eastern Wyoming College Library plus 1 other with an OPAC, a Web page.

Student Life *Housing Options:* coed, men-only, women-only. Campus housing is university owned. *Activities and Organizations:* drama/theater group, student-run newspaper, choral group, Criminal Justice Club, Veterinary Technology Club, Student Senate, Music Club, Rodeo Club. *Campus security:* 24-hour emergency response devices, controlled dormitory access. *Student services:* personal/psychological counseling.

Athletics Member NJCAA. *Intercollegiate sports:* basketball M/W, equestrian sports M/W, golf M, volleyball W.

Costs (2015–16) *Tuition:* state resident $1992 full-time, $83 per credit part-time; nonresident $5976 full-time, $249 per credit part-time. Full-time tuition and fees vary according to location. Part-time tuition and fees vary according to location. *Required fees:* $576 full-time, $24 per credit part-time. *Room and board:* $6136; room only: $3292. Room and board charges vary according to housing facility. *Payment plan:* installment. *Waivers:* senior citizens and employees or children of employees.

Applying *Recommended:* high school transcript.

Freshman Application Contact Dr. Rex Cogdill, Vice President for Students Services, Eastern Wyoming College, 3200 West C Street, Torrington, WY 82240. *Phone:* 307-532-8257. *Toll-free phone:* 866-327-8996. *Fax:* 307-532-8222. *E-mail:* rex.cogdill@ewc.wy.edu.
Website: http://www.ewc.wy.edu/.

Laramie County Community College
Cheyenne, Wyoming

- **District-supported** 2-year, founded 1968, part of Wyoming Community College Commission
- **Small-town** 271-acre campus
- **Coed,** 4,271 undergraduate students, 43% full-time, 59% women, 41% men

Undergraduates 1,844 full-time, 2,427 part-time. 14% are from out of state; 3% Black or African American, non-Hispanic/Latino; 12% Hispanic/Latino; 1% Asian, non-Hispanic/Latino; 0.4% Native Hawaiian or other Pacific Islander, non-Hispanic/Latino; 1% American Indian or Alaska Native, non-Hispanic/Latino; 0.5% Two or more races, non-Hispanic/Latino; 2% Race/ethnicity unknown; 0.6% international; 19% transferred in; 7% live on campus.

Freshmen *Admission:* 1,718 applied, 1,718 admitted, 412 enrolled. *Average high school GPA:* 2.92. *Test scores:* ACT scores over 18: 72%; ACT scores over 24: 15%; ACT scores over 30: 2%.

Faculty *Total:* 387, 28% full-time, 5% with terminal degrees. *Student/faculty ratio:* 13:1.

Majors Accounting; agribusiness; agricultural business technology; agricultural production; agriculture; anthropology; art; autobody/collision and repair technology; automobile/automotive mechanics technology; biological and physical sciences; biology/biological sciences; business administration and management; business/commerce; chemistry; computer programming; computer science; corrections; criminal justice/law enforcement administration; dental hygiene; diagnostic medical sonography and ultrasound technology; diesel mechanics technology; digital communication and media/multimedia; drafting and design technology; early childhood education; economics; education; emergency medical technology (EMT paramedic); energy management and systems technology; engineering; English; entrepreneurship; equestrian studies; fire science/firefighting; general studies; heating, air conditioning, ventilation and refrigeration maintenance technology; history; homeland security, law enforcement, firefighting and protective services related; humanities; human services; kinesiology and exercise science; legal assistant/paralegal; mass communication/media; mathematics; mechanic and repair technologies related; medical insurance coding; music; physical education teaching and coaching; physical therapy technology; political science and government; pre-law studies; pre-pharmacy studies; psychology; public administration; radiologic technology/science; registered nursing/registered nurse; religious studies; social sciences; sociology; Spanish; speech communication and rhetoric; surgical technology; wildlife, fish and wildlands science and management.

Academics *Calendar:* semesters. *Degree:* certificates and associate. *Special study options:* academic remediation for entering students, adult/continuing education programs, advanced placement credit, cooperative education, distance learning, double majors, English as a second language, honors programs, independent study, internships, off-campus study, part-time degree program, services for LD students, summer session for credit. *ROTC:* Army (c), Air Force (c).

Library Ludden Library with an OPAC, a Web page.

Student Life *Housing Options:* coed. Campus housing is university owned. *Activities and Organizations:* drama/theater group, student-run newspaper, choral group, Student Government Association, Phi Theta Kappa, Block and Bridle, Student Nursing Club, Skills USA. *Campus security:* 24-hour emergency response devices and patrols, late-night transport/escort service, controlled dormitory access. *Student services:* health clinic, personal/psychological counseling.

Athletics Member NJCAA. *Intercollegiate sports:* basketball M(s), cheerleading M(s)/W(s), equestrian sports M(s)/W(s), soccer M(s)/W(s), volleyball W(s). *Intramural sports:* basketball M/W, equestrian sports M/W, racquetball M/W, rock climbing M/W, skiing (cross-country) M/W, soccer M/W, softball M/W, table tennis M/W, ultimate Frisbee M/W, volleyball M/W.

Costs (2014–15) *Tuition:* state resident $1992 full-time, $83 per credit part-time; nonresident $5976 full-time, $249 per credit part-time. Part-time tuition and fees vary according to course load. *Required fees:* $840 full-time, $35 per credit part-time. *Room and board:* $7922; room only: $4208. Room and board charges vary according to housing facility. *Payment plan:* installment. *Waivers:* senior citizens and employees or children of employees.

Financial Aid Of all full-time matriculated undergraduates who enrolled in 2013, 1,385 applied for aid, 1,087 were judged to have need, 241 had their need fully met. In 2013, 90 non-need-based awards were made. *Average percent of need met:* 62%. *Average financial aid package:* $6423. *Average need-based loan:* $3029. *Average need-based gift aid:* $1738. *Average non-need-based aid:* $1501.

Applying *Options:* electronic application, deferred entrance. *Required for some:* high school transcript, interview.

Freshman Application Contact Ms. Holly Bruegman, Director of Admissions, Laramie County Community College, 1400 East College Drive, Cheyenne, WY 82007. *Phone:* 307-778-1117. *Toll-free phone:* 800-522-2993 Ext. 1357. *Fax:* 307-778-1360. *E-mail:* learnmore@lccc.wy.edu. *Website:* http://www.lccc.wy.edu/.

Northwest College
Powell, Wyoming

- **State and locally supported** 2-year, founded 1946, part of Wyoming Community College System
- **Rural** 132-acre campus
- **Coed,** 1,652 undergraduate students, 62% full-time, 60% women, 40% men

Undergraduates 1,023 full-time, 629 part-time. Students come from 42 states and territories; 32 other countries; 25% are from out of state; 0.7% Black or African American, non-Hispanic/Latino; 7% Hispanic/Latino; 0.5% Asian, non-Hispanic/Latino; 0.1% Native Hawaiian or other Pacific Islander, non-Hispanic/Latino; 1% American Indian or Alaska Native, non-Hispanic/Latino; 2% Two or more races, non-Hispanic/Latino; 4% international. *Retention:* 61% of full-time freshmen returned.

Freshmen *Admission:* 388 enrolled.

Faculty *Total:* 151, 52% full-time. *Student/faculty ratio:* 12:1.

Majors Accounting; administrative assistant and secretarial science; aeronautics/aviation/aerospace science and technology; agribusiness; agricultural communication/journalism; agricultural production; agricultural teacher education; animal sciences; anthropology; archeology; art; athletic training; biology/biological sciences; business administration and management; business/commerce; CAD/CADD drafting/design technology; chemistry; cinematography and film/video production; commercial and advertising art; commercial photography; criminal justice/law enforcement administration; crop production; desktop publishing and digital imaging design; elementary education; engineering; English; equestrian studies; farm and ranch management; French; general studies; graphic and printing equipment operation/production; health and physical education/fitness; health/medical preparatory programs related; health services/allied health/health sciences; history; international relations and affairs; journalism; kindergarten/preschool education; liberal arts and sciences/liberal studies; mathematics; music; natural resources management and policy; parks, recreation and leisure; physics; playwriting and screenwriting; political science and government; pre-pharmacy studies; psychology; radio and television; radio, television, and digital communication related; range science and management; registered nursing/registered nurse; secondary education; social sciences; sociology; Spanish; speech communication and rhetoric; veterinary/animal health technology; visual and performing arts related; welding technology.

Academics *Calendar:* semesters. *Degree:* certificates and associate. *Special study options:* academic remediation for entering students, adult/continuing education programs, advanced placement credit, cooperative education, distance learning, double majors, English as a second language, external degree program, independent study, internships, off-campus study, part-time degree program, services for LD students, study abroad, summer session for credit.

Library John Taggart Hinckley Library with an OPAC, a Web page.

Student Life *Housing:* on-campus residence required for freshman year. *Options:* coed, women-only, special housing for students with disabilities. Campus housing is university owned. Freshman campus housing is guaranteed. *Activities and Organizations:* drama/theater group, student-run newspaper, radio and television station, choral group. *Campus security:* 24-hour emergency response devices and patrols, late-night transport/escort service, controlled dormitory access. *Student services:* health clinic, personal/psychological counseling.

Athletics Member NJCAA. *Intercollegiate sports:* basketball M(s)/W(s), equestrian sports M(s)/W(s), soccer M(s)/W(s), volleyball W(s), wrestling M(s). *Intramural sports:* basketball M/W, football M/W, golf M/W, softball M/W, tennis M/W, ultimate Frisbee M/W, volleyball M/W.

Standardized Tests *Recommended:* SAT or ACT (for admission), ACT Compass.

Costs (2014–15) *Tuition:* state resident $1992 full-time, $83 per credit hour part-time; nonresident $5976 full-time, $249 per credit hour part-time. Full-time tuition and fees vary according to course load, location, and program. Part-time tuition and fees vary according to course load, location, and program. *Required fees:* $797 full-time, $26 per credit hour part-time. *Room and board:* $5100; room only: $2280. Room and board charges vary according to board plan and housing facility. *Payment plan:* installment. *Waivers:* children of alumni, senior citizens, and employees or children of employees.

Financial Aid Of all full-time matriculated undergraduates who enrolled in 2013, 115 Federal Work-Study jobs (averaging $2700). 215 state and other part-time jobs (averaging $2700).

Applying *Options:* electronic application. *Required:* high school transcript. *Required for some:* minimum 2.0 GPA. *Recommended:* minimum 2.0 GPA. *Application deadlines:* rolling (freshmen), rolling (out-of-state freshmen), rolling (transfers). *Notification:* continuous (freshmen), continuous (out-of-state freshmen), continuous (transfers).

Freshman Application Contact Mr. West Hernandez, Admissions Manager, Northwest College, 231 West 6th Street, Orendorff Building 1, Powell, WY 82435-1898. *Phone:* 307-754-6103. *Toll-free phone:* 800-560-4692. *Fax:* 307-754-6249. *E-mail:* west.hernandez@nwc.edu. *Website:* http://www.nwc.edu/.

Sheridan College
Sheridan, Wyoming

- **State and locally supported** 2-year, founded 1948, part of Wyoming Community College Commission
- **Small-town** 124-acre campus
- **Endowment** $29.0 million
- **Coed,** 4,374 undergraduate students, 32% full-time, 46% women, 54% men

Undergraduates 1,399 full-time, 2,975 part-time. Students come from 41 states and territories; 12 other countries; 18% are from out of state; 1% Black or African American, non-Hispanic/Latino; 6% Hispanic/Latino; 0.6% Asian, non-Hispanic/Latino; 2% American Indian or Alaska Native, non-Hispanic/Latino; 2% Two or more races, non-Hispanic/Latino; 0.5% international; 2% transferred in; 10% live on campus. *Retention:* 60% of full-time freshmen returned.

Freshmen *Admission:* 490 enrolled.

Faculty *Total:* 237, 42% full-time, 12% with terminal degrees. *Student/faculty ratio:* 16:1.

Majors Agricultural business and management; agriculture; agriculture and agriculture operations related; animal sciences; art; biological and physical sciences; biology/biological sciences; building construction technology; business/commerce; CAD/CADD drafting/design technology; community organization and advocacy; computer and information sciences; computer and information systems security; criminal justice/safety; culinary arts; dental hygiene; diesel mechanics technology; dramatic/theater arts; early childhood education; electrical and electronic engineering technologies related; elementary education; engineering; English; environmental engineering technology; general studies; health and physical education/fitness; health services/allied health/health sciences; history; horticultural science; hospitality administration; information science/studies; kinesiology and exercise science; machine tool technology; massage therapy; mathematics; mining technology; multi/interdisciplinary studies related; music; physical fitness technician; precision production related; psychology; range science and management; registered nursing/registered nurse; secondary education; surveying technology; web/multimedia management and webmaster; welding technology.

Academics *Calendar:* semesters. *Degree:* certificates and associate. *Special study options:* academic remediation for entering students, accelerated degree program, advanced placement credit, cooperative education, distance learning, double majors, English as a second language, independent study, internships, off-campus study, part-time degree program, services for LD students, summer session for credit.

Library Mary Brown Kooi Library plus 1 other with 47,864 titles, 5,571 audiovisual materials, an OPAC, a Web page.

Student Life *Housing Options:* coed. Campus housing is university owned and leased by the school. *Activities and Organizations:* drama/theater group, choral group, National Society of Leadership and Success, Student Senate, Baptist Collegiate Ministries, Nursing Club, Dental Hygiene Club. *Campus security:* 24-hour emergency response devices, student patrols, controlled dormitory access, night patrols by certified officers. *Student services:* personal/psychological counseling.

Athletics Member NJCAA. *Intercollegiate sports:* basketball M(s)/W(s), cross-country running M(s)/W(s), equestrian sports M(s)/W(s), soccer M(s)/W(s), volleyball W(s). *Intramural sports:* basketball M/W, bowling M/W, football M/W, golf M/W, lacrosse M/W, soccer M/W, softball M/W, table tennis M/W, ultimate Frisbee M/W, volleyball M/W, wrestling M/W.

Costs (2015–16) *Tuition:* state resident $1992 full-time, $83 per credit part-time; nonresident $5976 full-time, $249 per credit part-time. Full-time tuition and fees vary according to course load, location, and reciprocity agreements. Part-time tuition and fees vary according to location and reciprocity agreements. *Required fees:* $960 full-time, $32 per hour part-time. *Room and board:* Room and board charges vary according to board plan, housing facility, and location. *Payment plan:* installment. *Waivers:* senior citizens and employees or children of employees.

Applying *Options:* electronic application, early admission, deferred entrance. *Required for some:* high school transcript. *Recommended:* high school transcript. *Application deadlines:* rolling (freshmen), rolling (out-of-state freshmen), rolling (transfers). *Notification:* continuous (freshmen), continuous (out-of-state freshmen), continuous (transfers).

Freshman Application Contact Mr. Matt Adams, Admissions Coordinator, Sheridan College, PO Box 1500, Sheridan, WY 82801-1500. *Phone:* 307-674-6446 Ext. 2005. *Toll-free phone:* 800-913-9139 Ext. 2002. *Fax:* 307-674-3373. *E-mail:* madams@sheridan.edu.
Website: http://www.sheridan.edu/.

Western Wyoming Community College
Rock Springs, Wyoming

- **State and locally supported** 2-year, founded 1959
- **Small-town** 342-acre campus
- **Endowment** $20.0 million
- **Coed,** 3,621 undergraduate students, 34% full-time, 53% women, 47% men

Undergraduates 1,222 full-time, 2,399 part-time. Students come from 27 states and territories; 18 other countries; 13% are from out of state; 2% Black or African American, non-Hispanic/Latino; 11% Hispanic/Latino; 0.8% Asian, non-Hispanic/Latino; 0.1% Native Hawaiian or other Pacific Islander, non-Hispanic/Latino; 0.6% American Indian or Alaska Native, non-Hispanic/Latino; 2% Two or more races, non-Hispanic/Latino; 0.1% Race/ethnicity unknown; 0.7% international; 2% transferred in; 41% live on campus. *Retention:* 73% of full-time freshmen returned.

Freshmen *Admission:* 428 enrolled. *Average high school GPA:* 3.41. *Test scores:* ACT scores over 18: 51%; ACT scores over 24: 14%.

Faculty *Total:* 314, 25% full-time. *Student/faculty ratio:* 16:1.

Majors Accounting; administrative assistant and secretarial science; anthropology; archeology; art; automobile/automotive mechanics technology; biological and physical sciences; biology/biological sciences; business administration and management; chemistry; computer and information sciences; computer programming (specific applications); computer science; criminal justice/law enforcement administration; criminology; dance; data entry/microcomputer applications; data processing and data processing technology; diesel mechanics technology; dramatic/theater arts; early childhood education; economics; education; education (multiple levels); electrical, electronic and communications engineering technology; electrical/electronics equipment installation and repair; electrician; elementary education; engineering technology; English; environmental science; forestry; general studies; geology/earth science; health/medical preparatory programs related; health services/allied health/health sciences; heavy equipment maintenance technology; history; humanities; human services; industrial electronics technology; industrial mechanics and maintenance technology; information science/studies; information technology; instrumentation technology; international relations and affairs; journalism; kinesiology and exercise science; legal administrative assistant/secretary; liberal arts and sciences/liberal studies; licensed practical/vocational nurse training; marketing/marketing management; mathematics; mechanics and repair; medical administrative assistant and medical secretary; medical/clinical assistant; medical office assistant; medical office computer specialist; mining technology; music; nursing assistant/aide and patient care assistant/aide; photography; political science and government; pre-dentistry studies; pre-engineering; pre-law studies; premedical studies; prenursing studies; pre-pharmacy studies; pre-veterinary studies; psychology; secondary education; social sciences; social work; sociology; Spanish; speech communication and rhetoric; theater design and technology; visual and performing arts; web/multimedia management and webmaster; web page, digital/multimedia and information resources design; welding technology; wildlife, fish and wildlands science and management; word processing.

Academics *Calendar:* semesters. *Degree:* certificates, diplomas, and associate. *Special study options:* academic remediation for entering students, advanced placement credit, cooperative education, distance learning, English as a second language, honors programs, independent study, internships, part-time degree program, services for LD students, summer session for credit.

Library Hay Library with 115,615 titles, 2,763 audiovisual materials, an OPAC, a Web page.

Student Life *Housing Options:* coed, special housing for students with disabilities. Campus housing is university owned. *Activities and Organizations:* drama/theater group, student-run newspaper, radio station, choral group, Association of Non-Traditional Students (ANTS), Spanish Club, Residence Hall Association, International Club, Latter Day Saints Student Association. *Campus security:* 24-hour emergency response devices and patrols, late-night transport/escort service, controlled dormitory access, patrols by trained security personnel from 4 pm to 8 am, 24-hour patrols on weekends and holidays. *Student services:* personal/psychological counseling.

Athletics Member NJCAA. *Intercollegiate sports:* basketball M(s)/W(s), cheerleading M(s)/W(s), soccer M(s)/W(s), volleyball W(s), wrestling M(s).

Standardized Tests *Recommended:* SAT or ACT (for admission).

Costs (2015–16) *Tuition:* state resident $996 full-time, $83 per credit hour part-time; nonresident $2988 full-time, $249 per credit hour part-time. *Required fees:* $204 full-time, $18 per credit hour part-time, $18 per credit hour part-time. *Room and board:* $4090; room only: $2054. Room and board charges vary according to board plan and housing facility. *Waivers:* employees or children of employees.

Financial Aid Of all full-time matriculated undergraduates who enrolled in 2013, 20 Federal Work-Study jobs (averaging $1500).

Applying *Options:* electronic application, early admission, deferred entrance. *Recommended:* high school transcript. *Application deadlines:* rolling (freshmen), rolling (transfers).

Freshman Application Contact Ms. Erin M. Grey, Director of Admissions, Western Wyoming Community College, 2500 College Drive, PO Box 428, Rock Springs, WY 82901. *Phone:* 307-382-1647. *Toll-free phone:* 800-226-1181. *Fax:* 307-382-1636. *E-mail:* admissions@wwcc.wy.edu.
Website: http://www.wwcc.wy.edu/.

WyoTech Laramie
Laramie, Wyoming

Director of Admissions Director of Admissions, WyoTech Laramie, 4373 North Third Street, Laramie, WY 82072-9519. *Phone:* 307-742-3776. *Toll-free phone:* 888-577-7559. *Fax:* 307-721-4854.
Website: http://www.wyotech.edu/.

CANADA

Southern Alberta Institute of Technology
Calgary, Alberta, Canada

Freshman Application Contact Southern Alberta Institute of Technology, 1301 16th Avenue NW, Calgary, AB T2M 0L4, Canada. *Phone:* 403-284-8857. *Toll-free phone:* 877-284-SAIT.
Website: http://www.sait.ca/.

INTERNATIONAL

MEXICO

Westhill University
Sante Fe, Mexico

- **Independent** primarily 2-year, founded 1996
- **Urban** campus with easy access to Mexico City
- **Coed,** 1,206 undergraduate students, 100% full-time, 57% women, 43% men

Undergraduates 1,206 full-time. *Retention:* 86% of full-time freshmen returned.

Majors Architecture related; business administration, management and operations related; liberal arts and sciences and humanities related.

Academics *Calendar:* trimesters. *Degrees:* associate, bachelor's, and master's. *Special study options:* accelerated degree program, adult/continuing education programs, distance learning, part-time degree program, study abroad.

Library an OPAC.

Student Life *Housing:* college housing not available. *Activities and Organizations:* drama/theater group. *Campus security:* 24-hour patrols. *Student services:* health clinic, personal/psychological counseling.

Athletics *Intramural sports:* gymnastics W, soccer M/W, swimming and diving M/W, water polo M/W, weight lifting M/W.

Costs (2015–16) *Tuition:* 178,200 Mexican pesos full-time. Full-time tuition and fees vary according to degree level, program, reciprocity agreements, and student level. *Payment plans:* tuition prepayment, installment, deferred payment. *Waivers:* employees or children of employees.

Applying *Required:* high school transcript, interview, Local Test and Psychological Profile. *Application deadlines:* rolling (freshmen), rolling (out-of-state freshmen), rolling (transfers).

Freshman Application Contact Admissions, Westhill University, 56 Domingo Garcia Ramos, Zona Escolar, Prados de la Montana I, 05610 Sante Fe, Cuajimalpa, Mexico. *Phone:* 52-55 88517010. *Toll-free phone:* 800-838-7711. *E-mail:* admissions@westhill.edu.mx. *Website:* http://www.westhill.edu.mx/.

PALAU

Palau Community College
Koror, Palau

Freshman Application Contact Ms. Dahlia Katosang, Director of Admissions and Financial Aid, Palau Community College, PO Box 9, Koror, PW 96940-0009. *Phone:* 680-488-2471 Ext. 233. *Fax:* 680-488-4468. *E-mail:* dahliapcc@palaunet.com. *Website:* http://www.palau.edu/.

Featured Two-Year Colleges

BAY STATE COLLEGE
BOSTON, MASSACHUSETTS

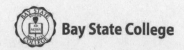

The College and Its Mission

Founded in 1946, Bay State College is a private, independent, coeducational institution located in Boston's historic Back Bay. Since its founding, Bay State College has been preparing graduates for outstanding careers and continued education.

Bay State College is a small, private college focused on passionate students who want to turn their interests into a rewarding career. The College offers associate and bachelor's degrees in a number of rewarding fields. Everyone at Bay State—from admissions counselors and professors to the career services team—helps to assist, guide, and advise students, from the moment they apply and throughout their careers. Located in Boston's Back Bay, the College offers the city of Boston as a campus, small classes, and one-on-one attention. For students seeking a career in one of the professions offered by Bay State, a degree program at the College could be a strong first step on their career path.

The College offers associate degrees and bachelor's degrees. The educational experience offered through the variety of programs prepares students to excel in the careers of their choice. Personalized attention is the cornerstone of a Bay State College education. Through the transformative power of its core values of quality, respect, and support, Bay State College has been able to assist students with setting and achieving goals that prepare them for careers and continued education.

Recognizing that one of the most important aspects of college is life outside the classroom, the Office of Student Affairs seeks to provide services from orientation through graduation and beyond. Special events throughout the year include a fashion show and a host of events produced by the Entertainment Management Association. Students also enjoy professional sports teams such as the Boston Celtics and Boston Red Sox.

Bay State College's campus experience can be whatever the student chooses it to be. It's not the typical college campus—its residence halls are actually brownstones along Boston's trendy Commonwealth Avenue and Bay State's quad could be Boston Common, the banks of the Charles River by the Esplanade, or Copley Square. That's the advantage of being located in Boston's Back Bay, which is also the safest neighborhood in the city. Students can relax at a favorite coffee shop, bike along the Charles River, ice skate on the Frog Pond, check out the city's nightlife, or take in a ball game at Fenway Park.

Bay State College is accredited by the New England Association of Schools and Colleges and is authorized to award the Associate in Science, Associate in Applied Science, and three Bachelor of Science degrees by the Commonwealth of Massachusetts. Bay State is a member of several professional educational associations. Its medical assisting program is accredited by the Accrediting Bureau of Health Education Schools (ABHES). The physical therapist assistant program is accredited by the Commission on Accreditation in Physical Therapy Education (CAPTE) of the American Physical Therapy Association (APTA).

Academic Programs

Bay State College operates on a semester calendar. The fall semester runs from early September to late December. The spring semester runs from late January until mid-May. A satellite campus is located in Taunton, Massachusetts.

Bachelor's degrees are offered in criminal justice, entertainment management, fashion merchandising, information technology, management, and RN to B.S.N.

Associate degrees are offered in business administration, criminal justice, entertainment management (with a concentration in audio production), fashion design, fashion merchandising, health studies, information technology, marketing, medical assisting, nursing, physical therapist assistant studies, retail business management, and hospitality management.

Bay State College also offers courses on-ground and online to working adults in its Evening and Online Division. The courses are offered in eight-week sessions and allow more flexibility for students who must balance work and family commitments while pursuing their education.

Bay State College reviews, enhances, and adds new programs to help graduates remain industry-current in their respective fields.

Off-Campus Programs

Many students cite Bay State's internship program as a turning point for them. Bay State internships allow students to gain hands-on experience and spend time working in their chosen fields. These valuable opportunities can give students an advantage when they apply for positions after they have completed school.

Bay State's Boston location allows the College to offer internships at many well-known companies and organizations. Students are able to apply what they've learned in the classroom and do meaningful work in their field of study. In addition, they build working relationships with people in their chosen profession. For more information on internships, prospective students may contact Tom Corrigan, Director of Career Services, at 617-217-9000.

Costs

Tuition charges are assessed on a per-credit-hour basis and vary depending upon program of study. This provides students with maximum flexibility based on individual financial and academic needs, making a Bay State College education more accommodating and affordable. Rates quoted below by program are for the 2015–16 academic year. Charges are not prorated unless noted. Program flow sheets may require more or less than 30 credits per academic year.

Medical assisting, and health studies: $786 per credit, $23,580 (30 credits). Business, criminal justice, fashion merchandising, fashion design, entertainment management, and hospitality management: $876 per credit, $26,280 (30 credits). Nursing and physical therapy assistant: $876 per credit, $30,660 (35 credits).

Room and board are $11,800 per year, the student services fee is $400 (for day students only), and the student activity fee is $50. The cost of books and additional fees vary by major. A residence hall security deposit of $300 and a technology fee of $300 are required of all resident students.

The fall tuition payment due date is July 1; the spring tuition payment is due December 1.

Financial Aid

Each student works with a personal advocate to thoroughly explain financial options and guide them through the financial aid application process. Many options are available: aid, grants and scholarships, federal programs, and private loans. Bay State College's Financial Aid Department and tuition planners can help students determine what aid may apply. Approximately 85 percent of students receive some form of financial assistance. Bay State College requires a completed Free Application for Federal Student Aid (FAFSA) form and signed federal tax forms. The College's institutional financial aid priority deadline is March 31. Financial aid is granted on a rolling basis.

Faculty

There are 72 faculty members, many holding advanced degrees and several holding doctoral degrees. The student-faculty ratio is 20:1.

Student Body Profile

There are approximately 1,200 students in degree programs in both the day and evening divisions.

Student Activities

Bay State College students participate in a multitude of activities offered by the College through existing student organizations. Students also have the opportunity to create clubs and organizations that meet their interests. Existing organizations include the Student Government Association, Entertainment Management Association, Justice Society, and the Criminal Justice Society. Students produce an annual talent show as well as an annual fashion show that showcases student work from the College's fashion design program. An annual literary magazine also features the work of students throughout the College.

Facilities and Resources

Advisement/Counseling: Trained staff members assist students in selecting courses and programs of study. A counseling center is available to provide mental and physical health referrals to all students in need of such services. Referral networks are extensive, within a wide range of geographic areas, and provide access to a variety of public and private health agencies.

Specialized Services: The Office of Academic Development at Bay State College is designed to meet and support the various academic needs of the student body and serve as a resource for supplemental instruction, academic plans, learning accommodations, and other types of support. The Office of Academic Development operates on the belief that all students can achieve success in their courses by accessing support services and creating individual academic plans.

The Center for Learning and Academic Success (CLAS) at Bay State College is a key component available to help students achieve academic success. Students come to CLAS to get support in specific subject areas as well as study skills such as note-taking, reading comprehension, writing research papers, time management, and coping with exam anxiety. They utilize CLAS to develop study plans and strategies that positively impact their grades in all subjects. Students can also take advantage of the tutoring and seminars CLAS offers. CLAS's goal is to ensure that students are provided with exceptional academic support in all areas of study.

Career Planning/Placement: For many college students, the transition from student life to professional life is filled with questions and uncharted realities. Bay State College's Career Services Department offers students their own personal career advancement team. The department can help students learn to write a resume and cover letter, use social networks, practice interviewing skills, find the right job opportunity, and learn other career-related functions. Students even receive a Professionalism Grade, which lets future employers know they have what it takes to start contributing on day one. The Career Services Department at is determined to see each student succeed and offers valuable instruction that will serve students throughout their professional careers.

Library and Audiovisual Services: The library is staffed with trained librarians who are available to guide students in their research process. The library's resources include 7,500 books, eighty-five periodical subscriptions, and a dramatically increased reach through its online library resource databases that include ProQuest, InfoTrac, and LexisNexis. In addition, the library provides computer access and study space for students. The library catalog and databases are accessible from any Internet-ready terminal.

First-Year Experience: The First-Year Experience (FYE) is a 1-credit course that is required of all first-year students and takes place during the first three days that students are on campus. FYE combines social activities with an academic syllabus that is designed to ease the transition into the college experience. Through FYE, students have the opportunity to connect with their academic advisers as well as with other students in their academic programs. At the conclusion of FYE, students are on the road to mapping out their personal action plan for success. The plan, designed by students, guided by academic advisers, and revisited each semester, helps students set, monitor, and achieve academic and life goals. It also builds the preparation for lifelong accomplishment.

Location

Located in the historic city of Boston, Massachusetts, and surrounded by dozens of colleges and universities, Bay State College is an ideal setting in which to pursue a college degree. Tree-lined streets around the school are mirrored in the skyscrapers of the Back Bay. The College is located within walking distance of several major league sport franchises, concert halls, museums, the Freedom Trail, Boston Symphony Hall, the Boston Public Library, and the Boston Public Garden. World-class shopping and major cultural and sporting events help make college life a memorable experience.

The College is accessible by the MBTA and commuter rail and bus, and it is near Boston Logan International Airport.

Admission Requirements

Applicants must be a high school graduate, a current high school student working toward graduation, or a recipient of a GED certificate. The Office of Admissions requires that applicants to the associate degree programs have a minimum of a 2.0 GPA (on a 4.0 scale); if available, applicants may submit SAT and/or ACT scores. Applicants to bachelor's degree programs must have a minimum 2.3 GPA (on a 4.0 scale) and must also submit SAT or ACT scores. International applicants must also submit high school transcripts translated to English with an explanation of the grading system, financial documentation, and a minimum TOEFL score of 500 on the paper-based exam or 173 on the computer-based exam if English is not their native language.

The physical therapist assistant studies and nursing programs require a minimum 2.7 GPA (on a 4.0 scale) and the Evening Division has different or additional admission requirements. For more information about these programs, interested students should visit the website at http://www.baystate.edu.

A personal interview is required for all prospective students—parents are encouraged to attend. Applicants must receive the recommendation of a Bay State College Admissions Officer.

Application and Information

Applications are accepted on a rolling basis. Students are responsible for arranging for their official high school transcripts, test scores, and letters of recommendation to be submitted to Bay State College.

The Bay State College Admissions Office notifies applicants of a decision within one week of receipt of the transcript and other required documents. There is a $100 nonrefundable tuition deposit required upon acceptance to ensure a place in the class; the deposit is credited toward the tuition fee. Deposits are due within thirty days of acceptance. Once a student is accepted, a Bay State College representative creates a personalized financial plan that provides payment options for a Bay State College education.

Applications should be submitted to:

Admissions Office
Bay State College
122 Commonwealth Avenue
Boston, Massachusetts 02116
Phone: 800-81-LEARN (53276)
Fax: 617-249-0400 (eFax)
E-mail: admissions@baystate.edu
Website: http://www.baystate.edu
　　　　http://www.facebook.com/baystatecollege
　　　　http://twitter.com/baystatecollege

Giving students access is an essential part of a Bay State College education. Students have access to a community of support, experiential learning, faculty with real-world experience, and a dynamic location in the heart of the city.

CAMDEN COUNTY COLLEGE
BLACKWOOD, NEW JERSEY

The College and Its Mission

Camden County College (CCC) is a fully accredited comprehensive public community college located in New Jersey, near Philadelphia. CCC provides accessible and affordable education through 100-plus associate degree and occupational certificate programs along with noncredit development courses and job training. CCC is one of the largest community colleges in New Jersey and one of the most sophisticated in the nation. Recognized as a leader in technology programs, the College is also regionally acknowledged for nursing and healthcare education and as a vital resource for transfer education, customized training, and cultural events.

Although housing is not available on campus, students may reside at local apartment complexes within walking distance of the main campus in Blackwood and near the College's other locations in Camden and Cherry Hill.

More than 20 student clubs and service organizations, honor societies, and other activities are available. The College also has a student newspaper, *The Campus Press,* and a radio station.

Varsity sports teams compete against other two-year colleges in the Garden State Athletic Conference and Region XIX of the National Junior College Athletic Association. Men compete in baseball, basketball, cross-country, golf, soccer, and wrestling. Women compete in basketball, cross-country, golf, soccer, softball, and tennis. Intramural sports are also offered, and students may use College athletic facilities, including an all-weather quarter-mile track; a fitness center; basketball/volleyball courts; and outdoor fields.

Academic Programs

http://camdencc.edu/academics/cataloginfo.cfm

Camden County College offers the following associate degrees: A.A., A.S., A.F.A., and A.A.S. The College also offers C.T., C.A., and C.P.S. certificates. Baccalaureate-completion programs also are offered on CCC's campuses, many of which allow students to earn Rutgers University degrees.

The College's fall and spring semesters include a 15-week session along with 13-week, 10-week, 7-week, 5-week, and weekend sessions. Summer sessions and a winter intersession are offered as well. On-campus, online, and hybrid courses are available. Classes are offered in arts, humanities, social sciences, business, computers, mathematics, healthcare, and the hard sciences. The College's academic calendar is available at **www.camdencc.edu**.

In general, approximately 60 credits are required to earn an associate degree and approximately 30 credits are required for a certificate. The total number of credits required varies by program.

Career Programs (A.A.S.) include accounting; addictions counseling; automotive technology (apprentice); automotive technology: GM/ASEP; biotechnology; biotechnology: cell and tissue culture option; biotechnology: forensic science option; CADD: computer-aided drafting and design; computer graphics; computer graphics: game design and development; computer information systems; computer integrated manufacturing/engineering technology; computer systems technology; dental assisting; dental hygiene; dietetic technology; engineering technology: electrical electronic engineering; engineering technology: electromechanical engineering; engineering technology: mechanical engineering; film and television production; finance; fire science technology; fire science technology: health information technology; health science; health science: certified medical assistant option; health science: surgical technology option; hospitality technology; management; management: business paraprofessional management option; management: small business management

option; marketing; massage therapy; medical laboratory technology; office systems technology administrative assistant; office systems technology administrative assistant: information processing option; ophthalmic science technology; paralegal studies; paramedic sciences; paramedic sciences: paramedic educational management option; photonics: laser/electro-optic technology; photonics: laser/electro-optic technology fiber-optic option; preschool teacher education; respiratory therapy; sign language interpreter education; technical studies; veterinary technology; video imaging; and Web design and development.

Transfer Programs (A.A./ A.S. /A.F.A.) include business administration (A.S); computer science (A.A.) and (A.S.); criminal justice (A.S.); elementary/secondary education (A.S.); engineering science (A.S.); human services (A.S.); human services: developmental disabilities option (AS); human services: early childhood education option (A.S.); liberal arts and science (LAS) (A.A.); LAS: applied and fine arts option (A.A.); LAS: communications option (A.A.); LAS: public relations/advertising track (A.A.); LAS: computer graphics option (A.A.); LAS: electronic publishing track (A.A.); LAS: deaf studies option (A.A.); LAS English option (A.A.); LAS history option (A.A.); LAS: languages and international studies option (A.A.); LAS: law, government, and politics option (A.A.); LAS: music option (A.A.); LAS: photography option (A.A.); LAS: psychology option (A.A.); LAS: theatre option (A.A.); liberal arts and science (LAS) (A.S.); LAS: biology option (A.S.); LAS: chemistry option (A.S.); LAS: environmental science option (A.S.); LAS: food science option (A.S.); LAS: health and exercise science option (A.S.); LAS: mathematics option (A.S.); LAS: nursing, pre-nursing option; LAS: physics option (A.S.); LAS: pre-pharmacy option (A.S.); LAS: secondary education in biology option; LAS: secondary education in mathematics option (A.S.); management of information systems; nursing: Our Lady of Lourdes School of Nursing (A.S.); occupational therapy assistant (A.S.); psychosocial rehabilitation and treatment (A.S.); sport management (A.S.); and studio art (A.F.A).

Academic Certificate Programs (C.T.) offered are computer applications programming; computer graphics; computer integrated manufacturing technology; computer programming; computer systems technology; dental assisting; homeland security; medical coding; nutrition care manager; office assistant; photonics: fiber-optic technical specialist; practical nursing; and social services.

Certificate of Achievement Programs (C.A.) include ASL; ASL and English interpreting; addictions counseling; automotive general technician; CADD: computer-aided drafting and design; computer-aided manufacturing technician; culinary; educational interpreter training; emergency and disaster management; fundamentals of policing; industrial controls: precision machining technology; programmable logic controller; international healthcare; Linux/UNIX administration; massage therapy; meeting and event planning; multi-skilled technician; music recording; ophthalmic medical technician; ophthalmic science apprentice; paramedic sciences; personal trainer; relational database management system using ORACLE; SQL analyst; and surgical technology.

A Certificate of Postsecondary Study (C.P.S.) is offered in vocational skills.

Off-Campus Programs

Camden County College offers a cooperative program with Our Lady of Lourdes School of Nursing, through which associate degree students complete their nursing studies at Lourdes in Camden. Much of the training available through CCC's Camden County Career Institute is offered on the Sicklerville Campus of Camden County Technical Schools.

Credit for Nontraditional Learning Experiences

CCC offers a number of credit-earning opportunities including evaluating educational experiences approved by the American Council on Education and the Program on Non-Collegiate Sponsored Instruction and validating armed services training. Details are in the *Camden County College Catalog* at **www.camdencc.edu/academics/cataloginfo.cfm**.

Costs

For students who enter in September 2015, tuition costs are $107 per credit for in-county residents, $111 per credit for out-of-county residents, and $199 per credit for international students. The general service fee per credit is $30, and the facility fee per credit is $7. Other fees vary depending on courses taken.

The cost of books and supplies is estimated at $1,600 for one year for a full-time student. Actual costs depend on specific courses taken. Students who choose e-textbooks instead of new print books can reduce costs by up to 50 percent, and those who rent books or participate in buy-back programs can also save.

Financial Aid

Financial aid comes in the form of scholarships, grants, loans, and work-study employment. Students are required to file a Free Application for Federal Student Aid (FAFSA) as soon as possible after January 1 of each year using the College's school code of 006865, along with the College's authorization and certification form. Financial aid applications filed by May 1 and completed by June 1 of each year are given priority. Students must be admitted before an offer of financial aid can be made.

Faculty

The student-faculty ratio is 25:1. Faculty members are dedicated to teaching and supporting students throughout the academic year. In addition to the College's advisement staff, some faculty members may assist in providing academic advisement for their field of specialization. Most full-time and adjunct faculty members hold advanced degrees.

Student Body Profile

Of the College's 19,959 credit students served in fiscal year 2014, 73 percent were Camden County residents and 96 percent were New Jersey residents. Approximately 52.4 percent of the students were Caucasian, 21.5 percent African American, 5.7 percent Asian, 8.4 percent Hispanic, 1.3 percent American Indian/Alaskan native, 0.3 percent Native Hawaiian/Pacific Islander, 5.1 percent two or more, and 5.8 unknown/not reported. The mean student age is 28.

Academic Facilities

On the Blackwood Campus, the Kevin G. Halpern Hall for Science and Health Education houses state-of-the-art biology, chemistry, and physics labs; a dental hygiene clinic; a café and classroom kitchen; and a healthcare education suite with a laboratory, a surgical suite, and patient care areas for nursing, medical laboratory technology, veterinary technology, and surgical technology students. The library is located on the Blackwood Campus, and an e-library is available at the Cherry Hill location. Students on the Camden City Campus have access to the Rutgers University library and gym. CCC offers open-access computer labs, laser labs, an automotive facility, a vision care facility, and numerous other laboratories. The Otto R. Mauke Community Center houses a Barnes & Noble bookstore, a cyber café, student activities offices, a cafeteria, and student lounge areas. The Papiano Gymnasium hosts a fitness center and a variety of indoor and outdoor sports.

Location

The College has four primary locations: a 320-acre main campus in Blackwood, a branch campus in Camden in the University District, the William G. Rohrer Center in Cherry Hill, and the Regional Emergency Training Center (RETC) in Blackwood. The Blackwood Campus is accessible from many directions, particularly Route 42 via Exit 7B, which leads directly into the main entrance, and is easily reached from the interstate highway system, is located a short distance from the PATCO high-speed train line to and from Philadelphia, and is on NJ Transit bus routes.

A capital initiative has transformed many of the facilities and structural amenities of the Blackwood Campus: an all-in-one, fully networked Student Services Center was added during the renovation of Taft Hall; the Kevin G. Halpern Hall for Science and Health Education was constructed; and a traffic-flow-improving ring road, new athletic fields, and improved parking lots were completed. The Marlin Art Gallery, Dennis Flyer Memorial Theatre, Little Theatre, and Civic Hall, home to the Center for Civic Leadership and Responsibility, are venues for College, county, and community performances, presentations, and events. The Camden Conference Center on the Camden City Campus is used by College, business, community, and government groups. The RETC is home to the Camden County College Police Academy and the Camden County College Fire Academy.

Admission Requirements

The College has open enrollment. A few select programs have additional admission criteria. Students must be 18 years of age. Prospective students should apply online at **www.camdencc.edu**. There is no cost to apply to CCC.

Application and Information

Processing of admissions applications begins no later than February 15 for the fall semester and no later than October 1 for the spring semester. Rolling admission runs through the last day of a semester.

For more information, contact:

Office of Admissions, Records and Registration Services
Camden County College
200 College Drive
Blackwood, New Jersey 08012
Phone: 856-227-7200
Website: www.camdencc.edu

Camden County College provides accessible and affordable education through its more than 100 associate degree and occupational certificate programs along with noncredit development courses and job training.

FASHION INSTITUTE OF TECHNOLOGY
State University of New York
NEW YORK, NEW YORK

The College and Its Mission

The Fashion Institute of Technology (FIT) is New York's celebrated urban college for creative and business talent. A State University of New York (SUNY) college of art, design, business, and technology, FIT is a dynamic mix of innovative achievers, original thinkers, and industry pioneers. FIT balances a real-world-based curriculum and hands-on instruction with a rigorous liberal arts foundation. The college marries design and business and supports individual creativity in a collaborative environment. It offers a complete college experience with a vibrant student and residential life.

With an extraordinary location at the center of New York City—world capital of the arts, business, and media—FIT maintains close ties with the design, fashion, advertising, communications, and international commerce industries. Academic departments consult with advisory boards of noted experts to ensure that the curricula and classroom technology reflect current industry practices. The college's faculty of successful professionals brings experience to the classroom, while field trips, guest lectures, and sponsored competitions introduce students to the opportunities and challenges of their disciplines.

FIT's mission is to produce well-rounded graduates—doers and thinkers who raise the professional bar to become the next generation of business pacesetters and creative icons.

FIT's four residence halls house 2,300 students in fully furnished traditional or apartment-style accommodations. Various dining options and meal plans are available. Residential counselors and student staff members live in the residence halls, helping students adjust to college life and New York City.

FIT is accredited by the Middle States Commission on Higher Education, the National Association of Schools of Art and Design, and the Council for Interior Design Accreditation.

Academic Programs

FIT serves approximately 10,000 full-time, part-time, and evening/weekend students from the metropolitan area, New York State, across the country, and around the world, offering nearly fifty programs leading to the A.A.S., B.F.A., B.S., M.A., M.F.A., and M.P.S. degrees. Each undergraduate program includes a core of traditional liberal arts courses, providing students with a global perspective, critical-thinking skills, and the ability to communicate effectively. All degree programs are designed to prepare students for creative and business careers and to provide them with the prerequisite studies to go on to baccalaureate, master's, or doctoral degrees, if they wish.

All students complete a two-year A.A.S. program in their major area and the liberal arts. They may then choose to go on to a related, two-year B.F.A. or B.S. program or begin their careers with their A.A.S. degree, which qualifies them for entry-level positions.

Associate Degree Programs: For the A.A.S. degree, FIT offers ten majors through the School of Art and Design, four through the Jay and Patty Baker School of Business and Technology, and one through the School of Liberal Arts. The A.A.S. programs are accessories design*, advertising and marketing communications*, communication design foundation*, fashion design*, fashion merchandising management* (with an online option), film and media, fine arts, illustration, interior design, jewelry design, menswear, photography, production management: fashion and related industries, textile development and marketing*, and textile/surface design*. Programs with an asterisk (*) are also available in a one-year format for students with sufficient transferable credits.

Bachelor's Degree Programs: Many A.A.S. graduates choose to pursue a related, two-year baccalaureate program at the college. FIT offers twenty-six baccalaureate programs—fourteen B.F.A. programs through the School of Art and Design, ten B.S. programs through the Baker School of Business and Technology, and two B.S. programs through the School of Liberal Arts. The B.F.A. programs are accessories design, advertising design, computer animation and interactive media, fabric styling, fashion design (with specializations in children's wear, intimate apparel, knitwear, special occasion, and sportswear), fine

arts, graphic design, illustration, interior design, packaging design, photography and the digital image, textile/surface design, toy design, and visual presentation and exhibition design. The B.S. programs are advertising and marketing communications, art history and museum professions, cosmetics and fragrance marketing, direct and interactive marketing, entrepreneurship for the fashion and design industries, fashion merchandising management, film and media, home products development, international trade and marketing for the fashion industries, production management: fashion and related industries, technical design, and textile development and marketing.

Liberal Arts Minors: The School of Liberal Arts offers FIT students the opportunity to minor in a variety of liberal arts areas in two forms: traditional subject-based minors and interdisciplinary minors unique to the FIT liberal arts curriculum. Selected minors include economics, English literature, ethics and sustainability, international politics, Asian studies, and psychology.

Evening/Weekend Programs: FIT provides evening and weekend credit and noncredit classes to students and working professionals interested in pursuing a degree or furthering their knowledge of a particular industry, while balancing the demands of career or family. There are nine degree programs available through evening/weekend study: advertising and marketing communications (A.A.S.* and B.S.), communication design foundation (A.A.S.), fashion design (A.A.S.), fashion merchandising management (A.A.S.* and B.S.), graphic design (B.F.A.), illustration (B.F.A.), and international trade and marketing for the fashion industries (B.S.). Programs with an asterisk (*) are also available in a one-year format for students with sufficient transferable credits.

Certificate Programs: FIT's Center for Continuing and Professional Studies offers credit and noncredit certificates through its two divisions: Enterprise Studies and Digital Design and Professional Studies. Certificates available include leather apparel, millinery, retail management, fashion styling, pet product design and marketing, and sustainable design entrepreneurship. The center also provides career and personal development courses designed for adults with busy schedules.

Honors Program: The Presidential Scholars honors program, available to academically exceptional students in all majors, offers special courses, projects, colloquia, and off-campus activities that broaden horizons and stimulate discourse. Presidential Scholars receive priority course registration and an annual merit stipend.

Internships: Internships are a required element of most programs and are available to all matriculated students. Nearly one third of FIT student interns are offered employment on completion of their internships; past sponsors include American Eagle Outfitters, Bloomingdale's, Calvin Klein, Estée Lauder, Hearst Magazines, MTV, and Saatchi & Saatchi.

Precollege Programs: Precollege programs (Saturday Live, Sunday Live, and Summer Live) are available to middle and high school students during the fall, spring, and summer. More than 100 courses provide the chance to learn in an innovative environment, develop art and design portfolios, explore the business and technological sides of many creative careers, and discover natural talents and abilities.

Off-Campus Programs

The study-abroad experience lets students immerse themselves in diverse cultures and prepares them to live and work in a global community. FIT has two campuses in Italy—one in Milan, one in Florence—where students study fashion design or fashion merchandising management and gain firsthand experience in the dynamics of European fashion. FIT also offers study-abroad options in countries like Australia, China, England, France, and Mexico. Students can study abroad during the winter or summer sessions, for a semester, or for a full academic year.

Costs

As a SUNY college, FIT offers affordable tuition for both New York State residents and nonresidents. The 2014–15 associate-level tuition per semester for in-state residents was $2,250; for nonresidents, $6,750. Baccalaureate-level tuition per semester was $3,084 for in-state residents and $8,905 for nonresidents. Per-semester housing costs were $6,485–$6,680 for traditional residence hall accommodations with mandatory meal plan and $6,060–$10,095 for apartment-style accommodations. Meal plans ranged from $1,745 to $2,233 per semester. Textbook costs and other nominal fees, such as locker rental or laboratory use, vary per program. All costs are subject to change.

Financial Aid

FIT offers scholarships, grants, loans, and work-study employment for students with financial need. Overall, two-thirds of full-time, matriculated undergraduate students who complete the federal financial aid application process receive some type of assistance through loans and/or grants. The college directly administers its own institutional grants and scholarships, which are provided by the FIT Foundation.

College-administered funding includes Federal Pell Grants, Federal Perkins Loans, Federal Supplemental Educational Opportunity Grants, Federal Work-Study, and the Federal Family Educational Loan Program, which includes student and parent loans. New York State residents who meet eligibility guidelines may also receive Tuition Assistance Program (TAP) and/or Educational Opportunity Program (EOP) grants. Financial aid applicants must file the Free Application for Federal Student Aid (FAFSA) and should also apply to all available outside sources of aid. Additional documentation may be requested by the Financial Aid Office. Applications for financial aid should be completed prior to February 15 for fall admission or November 1 for spring admission.

Faculty

FIT's faculty is drawn from top professionals in academia, art, design, communications, and business, providing a curriculum rich in real-world experience and traditional educational values. Student-instructor interaction is encouraged, with a maximum class size of 25, and courses are structured to foster participation, independent thinking, and self-expression.

Student Body Profile

Fall 2014 enrollment was 9,764 with 8,455 students enrolled in degree programs. Thirty-six percent of degree-seeking students are enrolled in the School of Art and Design; 48 percent were in the Baker School of Business and Technology. The average age of full-time degree seekers was 23. Thirty-seven percent of FIT's students were New York City residents, 25 percent were New York State (non–New York City) residents, and 37 percent were out-of-state residents or international students. The ethnic/racial makeup of the student body was approximately 10 percent Asian; 10 percent black; 16 percent Hispanic; 3 percent multiracial; and 46 percent white. There were 1,211 international students.

Student Activities

Participation in campus life is encouraged, and the college is home to more than sixty student organizations, societies, athletic teams, major-related groups, and special-interest clubs. Each organization is open to all students who have paid their activity fee.

Student Government: The Student Council, the governing body of the Student Association, grants all students the privileges and responsibilities of citizens in a self-governing college community. Faculty committees often include student representatives, and the president of the student government sits on FIT's Board of Trustees.

Athletics: FIT has intercollegiate teams in cross-country, half marathon, track and field, table tennis, tennis, women's soccer, swimming and diving, and women's volleyball. Athletics and Recreation offers a full array of group fitness classes, including aerobics, dance, spin, and yoga at no extra cost. Students can also work out on their own in a 5,000-square-foot fitness center. Open gym activities allow students to participate in both team and individual sports.

Events: Concerts, dances, field trips, films, flea markets, and other events are planned by the FIT Student Association and Programming Board and various clubs. Student-run publications include a campus newspaper and a literary and art magazine.

Facilities and Resources

FIT's campus provides its students with classrooms, laboratories, and studios that reflect the most advanced educational and industry practices. The Fred P. Pomerantz Art and Design Center houses drawing, painting, photography, printmaking, and sculpture studios; display and exhibition design rooms; a model-making workshop; and a graphics printing service bureau. The Peter G. Scotese Computer-Aided Design and Communications Center provides the latest technology in computer graphics, design, photography, and animation.

Other cutting-edge facilities include a professionally equipped fragrance-development laboratory—the only one of its kind on a U.S. college campus—cutting and sewing labs, a design/research lighting laboratory, knitting lab, broadcasting studio, multimedia foreign languages laboratory, and forty-six computer labs containing Mac and PC workstations.

The Museum at FIT, New York City's only museum dedicated to fashion, contains one of the most important collections of fashion and textiles in the world. The museum, which is accredited by the American Alliance of Museums, operates year-round, and its exhibitions are free and open to the public. The Gladys Marcus Library provides more than 300,000 volumes of print, nonprint, and electronic materials. The periodicals collection includes over 500 current subscriptions, with a specialization in international design and trade publications; online resources include more than 90 searchable databases.

The David Dubinsky Student Center offers student lounges, a game room, a student radio station, the Style Shop (a student-run boutique), a full-service dining hall and Starbucks, student government and club offices, disability services, comprehensive health services and a counseling center, two gyms, a state-of-the-art fitness center, and a dance studio.

Location

Occupying an entire block in Manhattan's Chelsea neighborhood, FIT makes extensive use of the city's creative, commercial, and cultural resources, providing students with unrivaled internship opportunities and professional connections. A wide range of cultural and entertainment options are available within a short walk of the campus, as is convenient access to several subway and bus lines and the city's major rail and bus transportation hubs.

Admission Requirements

Applicants for admission must be either candidates for or recipients of a high school diploma or a General Educational Development (GED) certificate. Admission is based on strength and performance in college-preparatory coursework and the student essay. A portfolio evaluation is required for art and design majors. Specific portfolio requirements are explained on FIT's website. SAT and ACT scores are required for placement in math and English classes and they are required for students applying to the Presidential Scholars honors program. International applicants whose native language is not English must submit scores from TOEFL, PTE, or IELTS examinations.

Transfer students must submit official transcripts for admission and credit evaluation. Students may qualify for the one-year A.A.S. option if they hold a bachelor's degree or if they have a minimum of 30 transferable college credits, including 24 credits equivalent to FIT's liberal arts requirements.

Students seeking admission to a B.F.A. or B.S. program must hold an A.A.S. degree from FIT or an equivalent college degree and must meet the prerequisites for the specific major. Further requirements may include an interview with a departmental committee, review of academic standing, and portfolio review for applicants to B.F.A. programs. Any student who applies for baccalaureate-level transfer to FIT from a four-year program must have completed a minimum of 60 credits, including the requisite art or technical courses and the liberal arts requirements.

Application and Information

Students wishing to visit FIT are encouraged to attend an admissions information session and take a tour of FIT's campus. The visit schedule is available online at fitnyc.edu/visitfit. A virtual tour of the campus can be found at fitnyc.edu/virtualtour. Candidates may apply online at fitnyc.edu/admissions. More information is available by contacting:

Office of Admissions

Fashion Institute of Technology
227 West 27 Street, Room C139
New York, New York 10001-5992
Phone: 212-217-3760
       800-GO-TO-FIT (toll-free)
E-mail: fitinfo@fitnyc.edu
Website: http://www.fitnyc.edu
      http://www.facebook.com/FashionInstituteofTechnology

FIDM/FASHION INSTITUTE OF DESIGN & MERCHANDISING
LOS ANGELES, CALIFORNIA

The Institute and Its Mission

For more than 45 years, FIDM/Fashion Institute of Design & Merchandising has been educating students for professional careers in fashion, entertainment, and digital media, offering bachelor's and associate degrees in 26 creative majors. The talented and supportive faculty, dedicated staff, and renowned industry partners work together to create an academically rigorous, career-focused curriculum that results in skilled, marketable, and in-demand graduates. FIDM students complete more specialized and industry-driven classes in their major in two years than most four-year college students do throughout their education. FIDM's four vibrant campuses are strategically located in California's entertainment, fashion, action sports industry, and business hubs. FIDM's Career Center team has exceptional connections and offers one-on-one targeted career planning and placement services. Last year, 10,000 companies posted over 21,000 jobs on FIDM's online job board, open only to current students and alumni.

Established in 1969, FIDM is a private college of about 7,000 students with over 65,000 alumni. Graduates receive membership in the Alumni Association, which keeps them well connected while providing up-to-the-minute alumni news and information. FIDM alumni chapters can be found in 44 locations around the United States, Europe, and Asia.

FIDM offers two-year and four-year degree programs—Associate of Arts (A.A.), A.A. Professional Designation, A.A. Advanced Study, Bachelor of Science (B.S.), and Bachelor of Arts (B.A.).

Career Services: Career planning and job placement are among the most important services offered by the college. Career assistance includes job search techniques, preparation for employment interviews, resume preparation, virtual portfolios, and job transition assistance. FIDM's full-time Career Center department and advisors partner one-on-one with current students and graduates to help them move forward on their career path. Employers post over 21,000 jobs a year on FIDM's alumni job search site, which is available 24/7 exclusively to FIDM students and graduates. FIDM Career Advisors connect students to internships and directly to professionals in the industry. FIDM also offers job fairs, open portfolio days, and networking days to allow students to personally meet alumni and industry leaders. Because of the college's long-standing industry relationships, many firms come to FIDM first to recruit for internships and staff positions. FIDM grads are highly marketable, and have a strong employment rate across all majors. Everything about FIDM's curriculum and resources is geared toward ensuring that its grads are highly sought-after in the marketplace. Some of FIDM's successful graduates include celebrity designers Nick Verreos, Monique Lhuillier, and Pam Skaist-Levy, co-founder of Juicy Couture, as well as Hollywood costume designer Marlene Stewart.

Student Life: FIDM's ethnically and culturally diverse student body attracts students from around the world. The current population includes students from more than 30 different countries. The Student Activities Office plans and coordinates social activities, cultural events, and community projects. Student organizations include the ASID student chapter, Cross-Cultural Student Alliance, American Association of Textile Chemists and Colorists, Phi Theta Kappa honor society, Student Veterans of America (SVA), and the Alumni Association. Students from all majors and campuses collaborate to produce *FIDM MODE*™, a glossy lifestyle magazine that promotes awareness about the design industry, current events, alumni news, and FIDM student life. The current issue is available to view online at FIDMMODE.com.

FIDM's unique industry partnerships offer exciting opportunities for students through internships, job fair events, and informative guest speakers from companies such as Forever 21, JCPenney, Mattel, NBC Universal, Oakley, Smashbox, and Stila.

Accreditation: FIDM is accredited by the Senior College and University Commission of the Western Association of Schools and Colleges (WASC) and the National Association of Schools of Art and Design (NASAD).

Academic Programs

FIDM offers Associate of Arts (A.A.), A.A. Advanced Study, A.A. Professional Designation, and bachelor's (B.A. and B.S.) degree programs. There are 26 specialized creative business and design majors to choose from.

FIDM's Admissions Advisors help students explore the career paths available and choose the right program.

Associate degree programs include:

Associate of Arts: A foundation of liberal arts combined with two years of specialized education in one of the following majors: Apparel Industry Management, Beauty Industry Merchandising & Marketing, Digital Media, Fashion Design, Fashion Knitwear Design, Graphic Design, Interior Design, Jewelry Design, Merchandise Marketing, Merchandise Product Development, Social Media, Textile Design, and Visual Communications.

Associate of Arts Professional Designation: One-year programs designed for transfer students and college grads. Specialties include Apparel Industry Management, Beauty Industry Merchandising & Marketing, Digital Media, Fashion Design, Fashion Knitwear Design, Graphic Design, Interior Design, Jewelry Design, Merchandise Marketing, Merchandise Product Development, Social Media, Textile Design, and Visual Communications.

Associate of Arts Advanced Study: For students holding an A.A. degree from FIDM in a related discipline, programs include: Advanced Fashion Design, Beauty Industry Management, Entertainment Set Design & Decoration, Film & TV Costume Design, Footwear Design, International Manufacturing & Product Development, Menswear, Textile Production & Development, and Theatre Costume Design.

Students who complete an A.A. degree at FIDM are qualified to apply for FIDM's specialized bachelor's degree programs including:

B.A. degrees in Design, Digital Media, Graphic Design, Interior Design, Professional Studies (both A.A. and A.A. Advanced Study required), and Social Media.

B.S. degrees in Apparel Technical Design and Business Management.

For specific information and requirements concerning the above programs, prospective students should contact an Admissions Advisor at any FIDM campus.

FIDM operates on a four-quarter academic calendar. New students may begin their studies at the start of any quarter throughout the year. Detailed information about FIDM majors and curriculum is also available online at http://fidm.edu/en/Majors/.

FIDM's eLearning program ensures that a student's educational experience can take place anywhere. The online courses are designed to replicate the experience of classes on campus. Students in the eLearning program are granted the same high-quality education as students on campus and have immediate access to valuable campus resources, including the FIDM Library, Career Advisors, and instructors.

Off-Campus Programs

Internships are available within each major. Paid and volunteer positions provide work experience for students to gain practical application of classroom skills. Some of the companies that recruit FIDM interns include Smashbox, Stila, Saks Fifth Avenue, BCBG, GUESS, Rachel Zoe, Old Navy, Alexander McQueen, NBC Universal, Mattel, and Charlotte Russe.

FIDM provides the opportunity for students to participate in academic study tours in Europe, Asia, and New York. These tours are specifically designed to broaden and enhance the specialized education offered at FIDM. Participants may earn academic credit under faculty-supervised directed studies. Exchange programs are also available with L'Accademia Internazionale d'Alta Moda E

D'Arte del Costume Koefia, Rome; Instituto Europeo di Design, Milan, Turin, Rome, and Barcelona; Créapole, École de Création Management, Paris; Janette Klein Instituto de la Moda, Mexico City; Pearl Academy of Fashion, New Delhi; and RMIT University, Melbourne, Australia.

Costs

For the 2015–16 academic year, tuition, fees, books, and most supplies start at $30,085, depending on the selected major. First-year application fees range from $225 for California residents to $525 for international students.

Financial Aid

There are several sources of financial funding available, including federal financial aid and education loan programs, California state aid programs, institutional loan programs, and FIDM awards and scholarships. The FIDM Financial Services Office and FIDM Admissions Advisors work one-on-one with students and parents to help them find funding for their FIDM education. More information on FIDM scholarships and financial aid can be found at http://fidm.edu/go/fidmscholarships.

Faculty

FIDM faculty members are selected as specialists in their fields, working professionals with impressive resumes and invaluable industry connections. They bring daily exposure from their industry into the classroom for the benefit of the students. In pursuit of the best faculty members, consideration is given to both academic excellence and practical experience.

Facilities and Resources

FIDM's award-winning campuses feature design studios with computer labs and innovative study spaces, spacious classrooms, imaginative common areas, and state-of-the-industry technology. Computer labs support and enhance the educational programs of the Institute. Specialized labs offer computerized cutting and marking; graphic, interior, and textile design; word processing; and database management.

The FIDM Library goes beyond traditional sources of information. It houses a print and electronic collection of over 2.5 million titles that encompass all subject areas, with an emphasis on fashion, interior design, retailing, and costume. The library subscribes to over 160 international and national periodicals, offering the latest information on art, design, graphics, fashion, beauty, business, and current trends. The FIDM Library also features an international video library, subscriptions to major predictive services, interior design workrooms, textile samples, a trimmings/findings collection, and access to the Internet.

The FIDM Museum & Galleries' permanent and study collections contain more than 12,000 garments from the 18th century to present day, including film and theater costumes. One of the largest collections in the United States, it features top designer holdings including Chanel, Yves Saint Laurent, Dior, and Lacroix. The collection also includes items from the California Historical Society (First Families), the Hollywood Collection, and the Rudi Gernreich Collection.

Location

FIDM's main campus is in the heart of the gentrified South Park neighborhood downtown Los Angeles near the famed California Market Center and Fashion District. There are additional California campuses in San Francisco, San Diego, and Orange County. A virtual tour of the campuses and their locations is available at http://fidm.edu/en/Visit+FIDM/Launch+Virtual+Tour.

FIDM Los Angeles is nestled at the center of an incredibly vibrant apparel and entertainment hub, surrounded by the fashion, entertainment, jewelry, and financial districts. It is situated next to beautiful Grand Hope Park, a tree-filled oasis amid the hustle and bustle of downtown Los Angeles. Newly renovated by acclaimed architect Clive Wilkinson, FIDM San Francisco stands in the heart of historic Union Square. The country's third-largest shopping area and stimulating atmosphere combined with the industry-based staff and faculty make this campus as incredible as the city in which it is located.

The FIDM Orange County campus is a dynamic visual experience with ultramodern lofts, an indoor/outdoor student lounge, eye-popping colors, and a one-of-a-kind audiovisual igloo. Also designed by world-renowned architect Clive Wilkinson, this campus has received several prestigious architectural awards and has been featured in numerous national magazines.

FIDM San Diego's gorgeous campus overlooks PETCO Park and is near the historic Gaslamp district and the San Diego harbor. FIDM's newest campus is sophisticated, stylish, and tech savvy, reflecting the importance of California's fastest-growing city and its appeal to the global industry.

Admission Requirements

Students are accepted into one of FIDM's specialized Associate of Arts degree programs which offer 16–25 challenging courses per major. Associate of Arts programs are designed for high school graduates or applicants with strong GED scores. These programs offer the highly specialized curriculum of a specific major, as well as a traditional liberal arts/ general studies foundation.

Official transcripts from high school/secondary schools and all colleges/universities attended are needed to apply. International students must send transcripts accompanied by official English translations. Three recommendations from teachers, counselors, or employers are also required for admission. FIDM provides a reference request form on its website in the Admissions section under "How To Apply." All references must be sealed and mailed to the school when applying. An admissions essay portion and portfolio/entrance project requirement, which is specific to the student's selected major, are also available on the website's Admissions section under "How To Apply."

For more information on the application process, prospective students can go to www.fidm.edu.

Application and Information

FIDM/Fashion Institute of Design & Merchandising
919 South Grand Avenue
Los Angeles, California 90015
United States
Phone: 800-624-1200 (toll-free)
Fax: 213-624-4799
Website: http://www.fidm.edu
http://www.facebook.com/home.php/#!/FIDMCollege
http://twitter.com/#!/FIDM

FIDM Los Angeles (exterior campus)

MIRACOSTA COLLEGE
OCEANSIDE, CALIFORNIA

The College and Its Mission

MiraCosta College offers a friendly and safe suburban environment within easy driving distance of world famous attractions in Southern California. The sunny climate and ocean views make the campus a great place to study. Facilities include library and technology center, student computer labs, free academic tutoring and writing center, cafeteria and patio, an outdoor amphitheater, tennis courts, track, gymnasium, and fitness center.

The MiraCosta Community College District is located in North San Diego County, along the Southern California coast between Orange County to the north and the metropolitan area of San Diego to the south. Classes and resources are available in four separate locations within the district.

The MiraCosta Community College District's mission is to provide superior educational opportunities and student support services to a diverse population of learners with a focus on their success. MiraCosta offers associate degrees, university transfer courses, career and technical education, certificate programs, basic skills education, and lifelong learning opportunities that strengthen the economic, cultural, social, and educational well-being of the communities it serves.

Academic Programs

MiraCosta Community College offers students a wide range of subjects to pursue. Most classes are also available online. Academic programs include:

Accounting
Administration of justice
American college English
Anthropology
Art
Astronomy
Athletics
Automotive technology
Biology
Biotechnology
Business administration
Business office technology
Career and life planning
Chemistry
Child development
Chinese
Communication
Computer studies and
  information technology
Computer science
Counseling
Dance
Design
Dramatic arts
Earth science
Economics
Education
English
English as a second
  language

Film
French
Geography
Geology
German
Gerontology
Health education
History
Horticulture
Hospitality management
Humanities
Internship studies and
  cooperative education
Italian
Japanese
Kinesiology
Learning skills
Library science
Linguistics
Literature
Mathematics
Media arts and technologies
Medical administrative
  professional
Massage therapy
Music
Nursing
Nutrition
Oceanography
Pharmacology

Philosophy
Physical science
Physics
Political science
Psychology
Reading

Real estate
Religious studies
Sociology
Spanish
Surgical technology

Costs

For the 2015–16 academic year, tuition at MiraCosta College is $46 per credit unit for California residents and $246 per credit unit for nonresident and international students.

Financial Aid

In fiscal year 2014, a total of $11,321,677 in financial aid was distributed to 11,330 students.

Faculty

The College has 178 full-time faculty members and 540 part-time faculty members.

Student Body Profile

There are approximately 18,500 students enrolled at MiraCosta College. The diverse student body includes people from a variety of ages, ethnicities, and cultural backgrounds. Fifty-six percent of the students are women and 44 percent are men; 64 percent are age 24 or younger, while 36 percent are 25 and older. Ethnicity of the student body is 46 percent white, 34 percent Hispanic, 8 percent Asian/Pacific Islander, 4 percent African American, and 8 percent multiethnic or other.

Student Activities

The Offices of Student Activities supports a wide range of activities and events, provides information and resources centers, and serves as a focal point for service and leadership development programs. MiraCosta has more than forty active student clubs including the Accounting and Business Club, the International Club, the Black Student Union, the Dance Club, the Martial Arts Club, the Performance Writers Club, and many others.

Facilities and Resources

Advisement/Counseling: The Counseling Center offers individualized academic, career, and personal counseling to assist both prospective and current students develop their educational programs; coordinate their career and academic goals; and understand graduation, major, certificate, and transfer requirements.

Specialized Services: With an average class size of about 30 to 45, MiraCosta students rave about their professors and the personal attention they receive. Both students and staff enjoy a friendly atmosphere and a shared belief in helping one another.

Career Planning/Placement: The mission of the Center for Career Studies and Services is to empower students to make informed, intentional career decisions. Career Center resources include a computer lab, resource library, workshops, and career counseling by appointment.

Library and Audiovisual Services: Maintaining thousands of academic research databases, periodicals, reference materials, and professional research guides, the Library and Information Hub is the center for learning and academic support for MiraCosta students. The Library is also home to the Academic Tutoring Center, the Math Learning Center, the Writing Center, and a large computer lab. All services are free to MiraCosta students.

Location

MiraCosta College's district is coastal North San Diego County, approximately 35 miles north of San Diego and 90 miles south of Los Angeles. The Oceanside Campus is a 121-acre hilltop location with coastal and mountain views; the San Elijo Campus is on 42 acres in Cardiff facing the San Elijo Lagoon and Nature Preserve; the Community Learning Center is a 7.6-acre urban facility in downtown Oceanside; and a Technical Career Institute is located in Carlsbad.

Admission Requirements

Adults and high school students (sophomore level and higher) are able to enroll. International students who are at least 18 years old with a high school diploma can apply with a written application to the International Office.

Application and Information

For more information, prospective students should contact:

Admissions Office
MiraCosta College
1 Barnard Drive
Oceanside, California 92056
Phone: 760-757-2121
Website: www.miracosta.edu
        www.facebook.com/MiraCostaCC
        www.twitter.com/MiraCosta

Indexes

Institutional Changes Since *Peterson's® Two-Year Colleges 2015*

The following is an alphabetical listing of institutions that have closed, merged with other institutions, or changed their names or status since the release of *Peterson's® Two-Year Colleges 2015.*

Acacia University (Tempe, AZ): *no longer offers undergraduate degrees.*

Altamaha Technical College (Jesup, GA): *merged into new Coastal Pines Technical College (Waycross, GA).*

American Business & Technology University (Saint Joseph, MO): *now classified as 4-year college.*

American National University (Salem, VA): *now classified as 4-year college.*

Anamarc College (El Paso, TX): *closed.*

Anthem Career College (Memphis, TN): *closed.*

Anthem Career College–Nashville (Nashville, TN): *closed.*

Anthem College–Atlanta (Atlanta, GA): *closed.*

Anthem College–Aurora (Aurora, CO): *closed.*

Anthem College–Brookfield (Brookfield, WI): *closed.*

Anthem College–Fenton (Fenton, MO): *closed.*

Anthem College–Kansas City (Kansas City, MO): *closed.*

Anthem College–Las Vegas (Las Vegas, NV): *closed.*

Anthem College–Maryland Heights (Maryland Heights, MO): *closed.*

Anthem College–Phoenix (Phoenix, AZ): *closed.*

Anthem College–Sacramento (Sacramento, CA): *closed.*

Anthem College–St. Louis Park (St. Louis Park, MN): *closed.*

The Art Institute of New York City (New York, NY): *closed.*

Austin Community College (Austin, TX): *name changed to Austin Community College District.*

Blue Cliff College–Lafayette (Lafayette, LA): *no longer degree granting.*

Bryan University (Springfield, MO): *now classified as 4-year college.*

The Bryman School of Arizona (Phoenix, AZ): *closed.*

Carrington College California–Citrus Heights (Citrus Heights, CA): *name changed to Carrington College–Citrus Heights.*

Carrington College California–Pleasant Hill (Pleasant Hill, CA): *name changed to Carrington College–Pleasant Hill.*

Carrington College California–Pomona (Pomona, CA): *name changed to Carrington College–Pomona.*

Carrington College California–Sacramento (Sacramento, CA): *name changed to Carrington College–Sacramento.*

Carrington College California–San Jose (San Jose, CA): *name changed to Carrington College–San Jose.*

Carrington College California–San Leandro (San Leandro, CA): *name changed to Carrington College–San Leandro.*

Carrington College California–Stockton (Stockton, CA): *name changed to Carrington College–Stockton.*

Central Florida Institute (Palm Harbor, FL): *closed.*

Central Maine Medical Center College of Nursing and Health Professions (Lewiston, ME): *name changed to Maine College of Health Professions.*

Cleveland Institute of Electronics (Cleveland, OH): *no longer degree granting.*

Clinton Junior College (Rock Hill, SC): *name changed to Clinton College.*

Coleman University (San Marcos, CA): *closed.*

Computer Career Center (El Paso, TX): *name changed to Vista College.*

Concorde Career Institute (Arlington, TX): *name changed to Concorde Career College.*

Crouse Hospital School of Nursing (Syracuse, NY): *name changed to Bill and Sandra Pomeroy College of Nursing at Crouse Hospital.*

Daymar College (Bellevue, KY): *closed.*

Daymar College (Louisville, KY): *closed.*

Daymar College (Paducah, KY): *closed.*

Daymar College (Chillicothe, OH): *closed.*

Dorothea Hopfer School of Nursing at The Mount Vernon Hospital (Mount Vernon, NY): *name changed to Montefiore School of Nursing.*

Edison State College (Fort Myers, FL): *name changed to Florida SouthWestern State College.*

Erie Business Center, Main (Erie, PA): *closed.*

Erie Business Center, South (New Castle, PA): *closed.*

Everest College (Phoenix, AZ): *closed.*

Everest College (City of Industry, CA): *closed.*

Everest College (Los Angeles, CA): *closed.*

Everest College (Ontario, CA): *closed.*

Everest College (West Valley City, UT): *closed.*

Everest Institute (Miami, FL): *closed.*

Everest Institute (Rochester, NY): *closed.*

Everest Institute (Cross Lanes, WV): *closed.*

Florida College of Natural Health (Bradenton, FL): *closed.*

Gloucester County College (Sewell, NJ): *name changed to Rowan College at Gloucester County.*

Green River Community College (Auburn, WA): *name changed to Green River College.*

Hallmark College of Technology (San Antonio, TX) *name changed to Hallmark University and now classified as 4-year college.*

Hallmark Institute of Aeronautics (San Antonio, TX: *merged as a unit into Hallmark University (San Antonio, TX).*

Heald College–Concord (Concord, CA): *closed.*

Heald College–Fresno (Fresno, CA): *closed.*

Heald College–Hayward (Hayward, CA): *closed.*

Heald College–Honolulu (Honolulu, HI): *closed.*

Heald College–Modesto (Salida, CA): *closed.*

Heald College–Portland (Portland, OR): *closed.*

Heald College–Rancho Cordova (Rancho Cordova, CA): *closed.*

Heald College–Roseville (Roseville, CA): *closed.*

Heald College–Salinas (Salinas, CA): *closed.*

Heald College–San Francisco (San Francisco, CA): *closed.*

Heald College–San Jose (Milpitas, CA): *closed.*

Heald College–Stockton (Stockton, CA): *closed.*

Highline Community College (Des Moines, WA): *name changed to Highline College.*

Houston Community College System (Houston, TX): *name changed to Houston Community College.*

Hutchinson Community College and Area Vocational School (Hutchinson, KS): *name changed to Hutchinson Community College.*

Institute of Business & Medical Careers (Fort Collins, CO): *name changed to IBMC College.*

ITT Technical Institute (West Covina, CA): *closed.*

J. F. Drake State Technical College (Huntsville, AL): *name changed to J. F. Drake State Community and Technical College.*

Kaplan Career Institute, Cleveland Campus (Brooklyn, OH): *closed.*

Kaplan Career Institute, Nashville Campus (Nashville, TN): *name changed to Kaplan College, Nashville Campus.*

Kaplan College (North Hollywood, CA): *name changed to Kaplan College, North Hollywood Campus.*

Kaplan College, Jacksonville Campus (Jacksonville, FL): *closed.*

Kaplan University (Lewiston, ME): *name changed to Kaplan University, Lewiston.*

Kaplan University (South Portland, ME): *name changed to Kaplan University, South Portland.*

KD Studio (Dallas, TX): *name changed to KD College Conservatory of Film and Dramatic Arts.*

L'Ecole Culinaire (Cordova, TN): *name changed to L'Ecole Culinaire–Memphis.*

Linn State Technical College (Linn, MO): *name changed to State Technical College of Missouri.*

Los Angeles Film School (Hollywood, CA): *now classified as 4-year college.*

Mesabi Range Community and Technical College (Virginia, MN): *name changed to Mesabi Range College.*

Miami University–Middletown Campus (Middletown, OH): *name changed to Miami University Middletown.*

Mount Washington College (Nashua, NH): *closed.*

Mount Washington College (Salem, NH): *closed.*

National College of Business and Technology (Stow, OH): *name changed to National College.*

National College of Business and Technology (Nashville, TN): *name changed to National College.*

Navajo Technical University (Crownpoint, NM): *now classified as 4-year college.*

Northern New Mexico College (Española, NM): *now classified as 4-year college.*

Northland Community and Technical College–Thief River Falls & East Grand Forks (Thief River Falls, MN): *name changed to Northland Community College.*

North Seattle Community College (Seattle, WA): *name changed to North Seattle College.*

Nossi College of Art (Nashville, TN): *now classified as 4-year college.*

Okefenokee Technical College (Waycross, GA): *merged into new Coastal Pines Technical College (Waycross, GA).*

Penn State Beaver (Monaca, PA): *now classified as 4-year college.*

Penn State Brandywine (Media, PA): *now classified as 4-year college.*

Penn State Greater Allegheny (McKeesport, PA): *now classified as 4-year college.*

Penn State Hazleton (Hazleton, PA): *now classified as 4-year college.*

Penn State Lehigh Valley (Fogelsville, PA): *now classified as 4-year college.*

Penn State New Kensington (New Kensington, PA): *now classified as 4-year college.*

Penn State Schuylkill (Schuylkill Haven, PA): *now classified as 4-year college.*

Penn State Wilkes-Barre (Lehman, PA): *now classified as 4-year college.*

Penn State Worthington Scranton (Dunmore, PA): *now classified as 4-year college.*

Penn State York (York, PA): *now classified as 4-year college.*

Pennsylvania College of Health Sciences (Lancaster, PA): *now classified as 4-year college.*

Pennsylvania School of Business (Allentown, PA): *closed.*

Pine Technical College (Pine City, MN): *name changed to Pine Technical and Community College.*

Prince Institute of Professional Studies (Montgomery, AL): *closed.*

Prince Institute–Rocky Mountains Campus (Westminster, CO): *closed.*

Prism Career Institute (Upper Darby, PA): *closed.*

Saint Charles Community College (Cottleville, MO): *name changed to St. Charles Community College.*

Sanford-Brown College (Tampa, FL): *closed.*

Sanford-Brown College (Mendota Heights, MN): *closed.*

Sanford-Brown Institute (Fort Lauderdale, FL): *closed.*

Sanford-Brown Institute (Jacksonville, FL): *closed.*

SBI Campus–an affiliate of Sanford-Brown (Melville, NY): *closed.*

Seattle Central Community College (Seattle, WA): *name changed to Seattle Central College.*

Sitting Bull College (Fort Yates, ND): *now classified as 4-year college.*

South Seattle Community College (Seattle, WA): *name changed to South Seattle College.*

Southwest Florida College (Tampa, FL): *name changed to Southern Technical College.*

Triangle Tech–Greensburg School (Greensburg, PA): *name changed to Triangle Tech, Greensburg.*

Triangle Tech Inc–Bethlehem (Bethlehem, PA): *name changed to Triangle Tech, Bethlehem.*

Triangle Tech, Inc.–DuBois School (DuBois, PA): *name changed to Triangle Tech, DuBois.*

Triangle Tech, Inc.–Erie School (Erie, PA): *name changed to Triangle Tech, Erie.*

Triangle Tech, Inc.–Pittsburgh School (Pittsburgh, PA): *name changed to Triangle Tech, Pittsburgh.*

Triangle Tech, Inc.–Sunbury School (Sunbury, PA): *name changed to Triangle Tech, Sunbury.*

Universal Technical Institute (Houston, TX): *no longer degree granting.*

Valley College (Martinsburg, WV): *no longer degree granting.*

Vatterott College (Omaha, NE): *closed.*

Virginia College (Columbus, GA): *name changed to Virginia College in Columbus.*

Virginia College (Savannah, GA): *name changed to Virginia College in Savannah.*

Virginia College (Bossier City, LA): *name changed to Virginia College in Shreveport/Bossier City.*

Virginia College (Tulsa, OK): *name changed to Virginia College in Tulsa.*

Virginia College (Florence, SC): *name changed to Virginia College in Florence.*

Virginia College (Knoxville, TN): *name changed to Virginia College in Knoxville.*

Virginia College School of Business and Health at Chattanooga (Chattanooga, TN): *name changed to Virginia College in Chattanooga.*

Wright State University, Lake Campus (Celina, OH): *name changed to Wright State University–Lake Campus.*

WyoTech Fremont (Fremont, CA): *closed.*

WyoTech Long Beach (Long Beach, CA): *closed.*

YTI Career Institute–Capital Region (Mechanicsburg, PA): *closed.*

Associate Degree Programs at Two-Year Colleges

ACCOUNTING
Alexandria Tech and Comm Coll (MN)
Allen Comm Coll (KS)
Alvin Comm Coll (TX)
Amarillo Coll (TX)
American Samoa Comm Coll (AS)
Anoka-Ramsey Comm Coll (MN)
Anoka-Ramsey Comm Coll, Cambridge Campus (MN)
Anoka Tech Coll (MN)
Arizona Western Coll (AZ)
Bainbridge State Coll (GA)
Blue Ridge Comm and Tech Coll (WV)
Brookhaven Coll (TX)
Bunker Hill Comm Coll (MA)
Burlington County Coll (NJ)
Cambria-Rowe Business Coll, Indiana (PA)
Casper Coll (WY)
Cedar Valley Coll (TX)
Central Maine Comm Coll (ME)
Central Oregon Comm Coll (OR)
Central Wyoming Coll (WY)
Century Coll (MN)
Chandler-Gilbert Comm Coll (AZ)
Chipola Coll (FL)
Cincinnati State Tech and Comm Coll (OH)
City Colls of Chicago, Olive-Harvey College (IL)
Cleveland Comm Coll (NC)
Clinton Comm Coll (NY)
Coastal Bend Coll (TX)
Coll of Southern Idaho (ID)
The Coll of Westchester (NY)
Colorado Northwestern Comm Coll (CO)
Comm Coll of Denver (CO)
Comm Coll of Philadelphia (PA)
Comm Coll of Rhode Island (RI)
Copiah-Lincoln Comm Coll (MS)
Corning Comm Coll (NY)
Cumberland County Coll (NJ)
Dakota Coll at Bottineau (ND)
Darton State Coll (GA)
Daytona State Coll (FL)
Delaware Tech & Comm Coll, Terry Campus (DE)
Delgado Comm Coll (LA)
Des Moines Area Comm Coll (IA)
Dutchess Comm Coll (NY)
Eastern Gateway Comm Coll (OH)
Eastern Idaho Tech Coll (ID)
Eastern Wyoming Coll (WY)
Edison Comm Coll (OH)
El Centro Coll (TX)
Elgin Comm Coll (IL)
Fayetteville Tech Comm Coll (NC)
Finger Lakes Comm Coll (NY)
Forrest Coll (SC)
Forsyth Tech Comm Coll (NC)
Fox Valley Tech Coll (WI)
Frederick Comm Coll (MD)
Gateway Comm Coll (CT)
Gateway Tech Coll (WI)
Genesee Comm Coll (NY)
George C. Wallace Comm Coll (AL)
Golden West Coll (CA)
Greenville Tech Coll (SC)
Guam Comm Coll (GU)
Gwinnett Tech Coll (GA)
Halifax Comm Coll (NC)
Harford Comm Coll (MD)
Harper Coll (IL)
Hawkeye Comm Coll (IA)
Hennepin Tech Coll (MN)
Highland Comm Coll (IL)

Hinds Comm Coll (MS)
Hocking Coll (OH)
Housatonic Comm Coll (CT)
Houston Comm Coll (TX)
Howard Comm Coll (MD)
Illinois Eastern Comm Colls, Olney Central College (IL)
Iowa Central Comm Coll (IA)
Iowa Lakes Comm Coll (IA)
James Sprunt Comm Coll (NC)
Jefferson Comm Coll (NY)
J. F. Drake State Comm and Tech Coll (AL)
Johnston Comm Coll (NC)
Kaskaskia Coll (IL)
Kellogg Comm Coll (MI)
Kingsborough Comm Coll of the City U of New York (NY)
Lakeland Comm Coll (OH)
Lakes Region Comm Coll (NH)
Lamar Comm Coll (CO)
Laramie County Comm Coll (WY)
Lone Star Coll–CyFair (TX)
Lone Star Coll–North Harris (TX)
Lone Star Coll–Tomball (TX)
Lone Star Coll–U Park (TX)
Long Island Business Inst (NY)
Lorain County Comm Coll (OH)
Los Angeles Trade-Tech Coll (CA)
Lower Columbia Coll (WA)
Luzerne County Comm Coll (PA)
Macomb Comm Coll (MI)
Manchester Comm Coll (CT)
Manor Coll (PA)
Massachusetts Bay Comm Coll (MA)
McHenry County Coll (IL)
Mesa Comm Coll (AZ)
Middlesex County Coll (NJ)
Midlands Tech Coll (SC)
Minneapolis Comm and Tech Coll (MN)
Minnesota State Coll–Southeast Tech (MN)
Minnesota West Comm and Tech Coll (MN)
Mohave Comm Coll (AZ)
Monroe Comm Coll (NY)
Monroe County Comm Coll (MI)
Montcalm Comm Coll (MI)
Montgomery County Comm Coll (PA)
Moraine Park Tech Coll (WI)
Morgan Comm Coll (CO)
Mt. San Antonio Coll (CA)
Nassau Comm Coll (NY)
Navarro Coll (TX)
New Mexico Jr Coll (NM)
Niagara County Comm Coll (NY)
Northcentral Tech Coll (WI)
Northeastern Jr Coll (CO)
Northeast Iowa Comm Coll (IA)
Northern Essex Comm Coll (MA)
North Hennepin Comm Coll (MN)
North Iowa Area Comm Coll (IA)
Northland Comm Coll (MN)
North Shore Comm Coll (MA)
Northwest Coll (WY)
Northwest State Comm Coll (OH)
Northwest Tech Coll (MN)
Norwalk Comm Coll (CT)
Ohio Business Coll, Sandusky (OH)
Ohlone Coll (CA)
Oklahoma City Comm Coll (OK)
Oklahoma State U, Oklahoma City (OK)
Orange Coast Coll (CA)
Ozarks Tech Comm Coll (MO)
Paris Jr Coll (TX)
Pasadena City Coll (CA)
Penn Foster Coll (AZ)

Pennsylvania Highlands Comm Coll (PA)
Pensacola State Coll (FL)
Phoenix Coll (AZ)
Piedmont Comm Coll (NC)
Queensborough Comm Coll of the City U of New York (NY)
Randolph Comm Coll (NC)
Rappahannock Comm Coll (VA)
Reading Area Comm Coll (PA)
Renton Tech Coll (WA)
Richland Comm Coll (IL)
Richmond Comm Coll (NC)
Ridgewater Coll (MN)
Roane State Comm Coll (TN)
Rockland Comm Coll (NY)
Rock Valley Coll (IL)
St. Philip's Coll (TX)
San Diego Miramar Coll (CA)
San Jacinto Coll District (TX)
San Joaquin Delta Coll (CA)
Scottsdale Comm Coll (AZ)
Seminole State Coll (OK)
Seminole State Coll of Florida (FL)
Shawnee Comm Coll (IL)
Sierra Coll (CA)
Sisseton-Wahpeton Coll (SD)
Southeastern Comm Coll (IA)
Southern U at Shreveport (LA)
South Florida State Coll (FL)
South Hills School of Business & Technology, State College (PA)
South Piedmont Comm Coll (NC)
South Suburban Coll (IL)
Southwestern Illinois Coll (IL)
Spartanburg Comm Coll (SC)
Springfield Tech Comm Coll (MA)
Stark State Coll (OH)
State Fair Comm Coll (MO)
Sullivan County Comm Coll (NY)
Terra State Comm Coll (OH)
Three Rivers Comm Coll (CT)
Trident Tech Coll (SC)
Trinity Valley Comm Coll (TX)
Tunxis Comm Coll (CT)
Tyler Jr Coll (TX)
Umpqua Comm Coll (OR)
U of Cincinnati Clermont Coll (OH)
Virginia Western Comm Coll (VA)
Waukesha County Tech Coll (WI)
Wenatchee Valley Coll (WA)
Westchester Comm Coll (NY)
Western Dakota Tech Inst (SD)
Western Iowa Tech Comm Coll (IA)
Western Nevada Coll (NV)
Western Wyoming Comm Coll (WY)
Whatcom Comm Coll (WA)
White Mountains Comm Coll (NH)
Wisconsin Indianhead Tech Coll (WI)
Wright State U–Lake Campus (OH)
Wytheville Comm Coll (VA)
York County Comm Coll (ME)

ACCOUNTING AND BUSINESS/ MANAGEMENT
Camden County Coll (NJ)
Des Moines Area Comm Coll (IA)
Harrisburg Area Comm Coll (PA)
IntelliTec Coll, Grand Junction (CO)
Lone Star Coll–Montgomery (TX)
Mitchell Tech Inst (SD)
Mountain State Coll (WV)
Reading Area Comm Coll (PA)

ACCOUNTING AND COMPUTER SCIENCE
Lone Star Coll–CyFair (TX)
State Fair Comm Coll (MO)

ACCOUNTING RELATED
Central Virginia Comm Coll (VA)
Dakota Coll at Bottineau (ND)
Davis Coll (OH)
John Tyler Comm Coll (VA)
J. Sargeant Reynolds Comm Coll (VA)
Northwest State Comm Coll (OH)
Raritan Valley Comm Coll (NJ)
Southwest Virginia Comm Coll (VA)

ACCOUNTING TECHNOLOGY AND BOOKKEEPING
Alamance Comm Coll (NC)
Anne Arundel Comm Coll (MD)
Anoka-Ramsey Comm Coll (MN)
Anoka-Ramsey Comm Coll, Cambridge Campus (MN)
Arapahoe Comm Coll (CO)
Austin Comm Coll District (TX)
Bellingham Tech Coll (WA)
Big Bend Comm Coll (WA)
Borough of Manhattan Comm Coll of the City U of New York (NY)
Bradford School (PA)
Bucks County Comm Coll (PA)
Ca&nnada Coll (CA)
Cape Fear Comm Coll (NC)
Carroll Comm Coll (MD)
Casper Coll (WY)
Catawba Valley Comm Coll (NC)
Cayuga County Comm Coll (NY)
Central Maine Comm Coll (ME)
Central Wyoming Coll (WY)
Chandler-Gilbert Comm Coll (AZ)
Chesapeake Coll (MD)
Clark Coll (WA)
Coll of Central Florida (FL)
Coll of Marin (CA)
Coll of Southern Maryland (MD)
Coll of the Canyons (CA)
Columbia-Greene Comm Coll (NY)
Comm Care Coll (OK)
Comm Coll of Allegheny County (PA)
Comm Coll of Aurora (CO)
The Comm Coll of Baltimore County (MD)
Comm Coll of Denver (CO)
Dakota Coll at Bottineau (ND)
Danville Area Comm Coll (IL)
Delta Coll (MI)
Des Moines Area Comm Coll (IA)
Duluth Business U (MN)
Dutchess Comm Coll (NY)
Fiorello H. LaGuardia Comm Coll of the City U of New York (NY)
Florida SouthWestern State Coll (FL)
Fox Coll (IL)
Front Range Comm Coll (CO)
Gadsden State Comm Coll (AL)
Great Falls Coll Montana State U (MT)
Greenfield Comm Coll (MA)
Guilford Tech Comm Coll (NC)
Gulf Coast State Coll (FL)
Hagerstown Comm Coll (MD)
Harrisburg Area Comm Coll (PA)
Haywood Comm Coll (NC)
H. Councill Trenholm State Tech Coll (AL)
Hillsborough Comm Coll (FL)
Hinds Comm Coll (MS)
Holyoke Comm Coll (MA)
IBMC Coll (CO)
International Business Coll, Indianapolis (IN)
Iowa Lakes Comm Coll (IA)
Jamestown Comm Coll (NY)
Jefferson Comm Coll (NY)

Jefferson State Comm Coll (AL)
J. F. Drake State Comm and Tech Coll (AL)
Kalamazoo Valley Comm Coll (MI)
Kennebec Valley Comm Coll (ME)
Kent State U at Ashtabula (OH)
Kent State U at East Liverpool (OH)
Kent State U at Salem (OH)
Kent State U at Trumbull (OH)
Kent State U at Tuscarawas (OH)
Kilgore Coll (TX)
King's Coll (NC)
Lake Land Coll (IL)
Lehigh Carbon Comm Coll (PA)
Lower Columbia Coll (WA)
Miami Dade Coll (FL)
Minneapolis Business Coll (MN)
Minneapolis Comm and Tech Coll (MN)
Minnesota State Coll–Southeast Tech (MN)
MiraCosta Coll (CA)
Mohawk Valley Comm Coll (NY)
Montgomery Coll (MD)
Montgomery County Comm Coll (PA)
Mott Comm Coll (MI)
Nassau Comm Coll (NY)
Northampton Comm Coll (PA)
North Hennepin Comm Coll (MN)
North Iowa Area Comm Coll (IA)
Northwestern Coll (IL)
Northwestern Michigan Coll (MI)
Oakton Comm Coll (IL)
Olympic Coll (WA)
Owens Comm Coll, Toledo (OH)
Palomar Coll (CA)
Pasadena City Coll (CA)
Pennsylvania Highlands Comm Coll (PA)
Pensacola State Coll (FL)
Plaza Coll (NY)
Pueblo Comm Coll (CO)
Raritan Valley Comm Coll (NJ)
Rogue Comm Coll (OR)
St. Charles Comm Coll (MO)
St. Clair County Comm Coll (MI)
Salt Lake Comm Coll (UT)
San Juan Coll (NM)
Schoolcraft Coll (MI)
Southern U at Shreveport (LA)
South Florida State Coll (FL)
South Suburban Coll (IL)
Southwestern Indian Polytechnic Inst (NM)
Southwestern Michigan Coll (MI)
Sowela Tech Comm Coll (LA)
State U of New York Coll of Technology at Alfred (NY)
Tallahassee Comm Coll (FL)
Three Rivers Comm Coll (CT)
Tompkins Cortland Comm Coll (NY)
Tulsa Comm Coll (OK)
Ulster County Comm Coll (NY)
Vincennes U (IN)
Wayne County Comm Coll District (MI)
Wenatchee Valley Coll (WA)
Western Iowa Tech Comm Coll (IA)
Westmoreland County Comm Coll (PA)
Williston State Coll (ND)
Wood Tobe–Coburn School (NY)
Wor-Wic Comm Coll (MD)

ACTING
Casper Coll (WY)
Central Wyoming Coll (WY)
Greenfield Comm Coll (MA)

KD Coll Conservatory of Film and Dramatic Arts (TX)
Northampton Comm Coll (PA)

ACTUARIAL SCIENCE
South Florida State Coll (FL)

ADMINISTRATIVE ASSISTANT AND SECRETARIAL SCIENCE
Allen Comm Coll (KS)
Alvin Comm Coll (TX)
Amarillo Coll (TX)
Anoka Tech Coll (MN)
Antelope Valley Coll (CA)
Austin Comm Coll District (TX)
Bainbridge State Coll (GA)
Bevill State Comm Coll (AL)
Borough of Manhattan Comm Coll of the City U of New York (NY)
Bossier Parish Comm Coll (LA)
Bradford School (PA)
Butler County Comm Coll (PA)
Cambria-Rowe Business Coll, Indiana (PA)
Camden County Coll (NJ)
Ca&nnada Coll (CA)
Career Tech Coll, Monroe (LA)
Carroll Comm Coll (MD)
Carteret Comm Coll (NC)
Casper Coll (WY)
Cecil Coll (MD)
Central Maine Comm Coll (ME)
Central Texas Coll (TX)
Central Wyoming Coll (WY)
Century Coll (MN)
Cincinnati State Tech and Comm Coll (OH)
Citrus Coll (CA)
Cleveland State Comm Coll (TN)
Cloud County Comm Coll (KS)
Coastal Bend Coll (TX)
Cochise Coll, Douglas (AZ)
Coll of Southern Idaho (ID)
Coll of the Canyons (CA)
Collin County Comm Coll District (TX)
Columbia-Greene Comm Coll (NY)
Comm Coll of Allegheny County (PA)
The Comm Coll of Baltimore County (MD)
Comm Coll of Denver (CO)
Comm Coll of Rhode Island (RI)
County Coll of Morris (NJ)
Crowder Coll (MO)
Cumberland County Coll (NJ)
Dabney S. Lancaster Comm Coll (VA)
Dakota Coll at Bottineau (ND)
Davis Coll (OH)
Daytona State Coll (FL)
Delta Coll (MI)
Denmark Tech Coll (SC)
Eastern Gateway Comm Coll (OH)
Eastern Idaho Tech Coll (ID)
Eastern Wyoming Coll (WY)
Elgin Comm Coll (IL)
Finger Lakes Comm Coll (NY)
Fiorello H. LaGuardia Comm Coll of the City U of New York (NY)
Fox Coll (IL)
Fox Valley Tech Coll (WI)
Gadsden State Comm Coll (AL)
Genesee Comm Coll (NY)
George-C. Wallace Comm Coll (AL)
Golden West Coll (CA)
Greenfield Comm Coll (MA)
Greenville Tech Coll (SC)
Gwinnett Tech Coll (GA)
Harford Comm Coll (MD)
Harper Coll (IL)
Harrisburg Area Comm Coll (PA)
H. Councill Trenholm State Tech Coll (AL)
Hennepin Tech Coll (MN)
Hinds Comm Coll (MS)
Holyoke Comm Coll (MA)
Hopkinsville Comm Coll (KY)
Horry-Georgetown Tech Coll (SC)
Housatonic Comm Coll (CT)
Hutchinson Comm Coll (KS)
International Business Coll, Indianapolis (IN)
Iowa Central Comm Coll (IA)
Iowa Lakes Comm Coll (IA)
James H. Faulkner State Comm Coll (AL)
Jamestown Business Coll (NY)
Jamestown Comm Coll (NY)
Jefferson Coll (MO)

Jefferson Comm Coll (NY)
Jefferson State Comm Coll (AL)
J. F. Drake State Comm and Tech Coll (AL)
Johnston Comm Coll (NC)
Kankakee Comm Coll (IL)
Kellogg Comm Coll (MI)
Kent State U at Ashtabula (OH)
Kent State U at Salem (OH)
Kent State U at Trumbull (OH)
Kent State U at Tuscarawas (OH)
Kingsborough Comm Coll of the City U of New York (NY)
King's Coll (NC)
Kirtland Comm Coll (MI)
Kishwaukee Coll (IL)
Lake Land Coll (IL)
Lakeland Comm Coll (OH)
Lake Region State Coll (ND)
Lone Star Coll–Kingwood (TX)
Lone Star Coll–Tomball (TX)
Lorain County Comm Coll (OH)
Louisiana Delta Comm Coll, Monroe (LA)
Lower Columbia Coll (WA)
Lurleen B. Wallace Comm Coll (AL)
Luzerne County Comm Coll (PA)
Macomb Comm Coll (MI)
Manchester Comm Coll (CT)
McHenry County Coll (IL)
Mesabi Range Coll (MN)
Mesa Comm Coll (AZ)
Miami Dade Coll (FL)
Middlesex County Coll (NJ)
Midlands Tech Coll (SC)
Mid-Plains Comm Coll, North Platte (NE)
Minneapolis Business Coll (MN)
Minneapolis Comm and Tech Coll (MN)
Minnesota State Coll–Southeast Tech (MN)
Minnesota West Comm and Tech Coll (MN)
MiraCosta Coll (CA)
Mohawk Valley Comm Coll (NY)
Monroe Comm Coll (NY)
Monroe County Comm Coll (MI)
Montcalm Comm Coll (MI)
Montgomery County Comm Coll (PA)
Moraine Park Tech Coll (WI)
Moraine Valley Comm Coll (IL)
Morgan Comm Coll (CO)
Mountain State Coll (WV)
Mt. San Antonio Coll (CA)
Nassau Comm Coll (NY)
Navarro Coll (TX)
New Mexico Jr Coll (NM)
Niagara County Comm Coll (NY)
Northampton Comm Coll (PA)
Northcentral Tech Coll (WI)
North Central Texas Coll (TX)
Northeast Iowa Comm Coll (IA)
Northern Essex Comm Coll (MA)
Northern Virginia Comm Coll (VA)
North Iowa Area Comm Coll (IA)
Northland Comm Coll (MN)
North Shore Comm Coll (MA)
Northwest Coll (WY)
Northwest-Shoals Comm Coll (AL)
Northwest State Comm Coll (OH)
Northwest Tech Coll (MN)
Norwalk Comm Coll (CT)
Oakton Comm Coll (IL)
Ohio Business Coll, Sandusky (OH)
Ohlone Coll (CA)
Oklahoma City Comm Coll (OK)
Olympic Coll (WA)
Orange Coast Coll (CA)
Otero Jr Coll (CO)
Ozarks Tech Comm Coll (MO)
Palomar Coll (CA)
Panola Coll (TX)
Pasadena City Coll (CA)
Pensacola State Coll (FL)
Phoenix Coll (AZ)
Plaza Coll (NY)
Potomac State Coll of West Virginia U (WV)
Rainy River Comm Coll (MN)
Rappahannock Comm Coll (VA)
Raritan Valley Comm Coll (NJ)
Reading Area Comm Coll (PA)
Reid State Tech Coll (AL)
Renton Tech Coll (WA)
Richland Comm Coll (IL)
Ridgewater Coll (MN)
Riverland Comm Coll (MN)
Roane State Comm Coll (TN)

Rockland Comm Coll (NY)
Rock Valley Coll (IL)
St. Philip's Coll (TX)
Salem Comm Coll (NJ)
San Diego Miramar Coll (CA)
San Jacinto Coll District (TX)
Scottsdale Comm Coll (AZ)
Seminole State Coll of Florida (FL)
Shawnee Comm Coll (IL)
Sierra Coll (CA)
Southeastern Comm Coll (IA)
South Hills School of Business & Technology, State College (PA)
South Louisiana Comm Coll (LA)
Southwestern Illinois Coll (IL)
Sowela Tech Comm Coll (LA)
Spartanburg Comm Coll (SC)
Springfield Tech Comm Coll (MA)
Stark State Coll (OH)
Sullivan County Comm Coll (NY)
Tech Coll of the Lowcountry (SC)
Tompkins Cortland Comm Coll (NY)
Trident Tech Coll (SC)
Truckee Meadows Comm Coll (NV)
Tunxis Comm Coll (CT)
Tyler Jr Coll (TX)
Umpqua Comm Coll (OR)
Victoria Coll (TX)
Victor Valley Coll (CA)
Vincennes U (IN)
Virginia Western Comm Coll (VA)
Waukesha County Tech Coll (WI)
Wenatchee Valley Coll (WA)
Westchester Comm Coll (NY)
Western Iowa Tech Comm Coll (IA)
Western Wyoming Comm Coll (WY)
Westmoreland County Comm Coll (PA)
Whatcom Comm Coll (WA)
Williston State Coll (ND)
Wisconsin Indianhead Tech Coll (WI)
Wood Tobe–Coburn School (NY)
Wor-Wic Comm Coll (MD)
Wright State U–Lake Campus (OH)
Wytheville Comm Coll (VA)

ADULT AND CONTINUING EDUCATION
Cochise Coll, Douglas (AZ)

ADULT DEVELOPMENT AND AGING
Comm Coll of Rhode Island (RI)
Dakota Coll at Bottineau (ND)
Fiorello H. LaGuardia Comm Coll of the City U of New York (NY)
MiraCosta Coll (CA)

ADULT HEALTH NURSING
Salem Comm Coll (NJ)

ADVERTISING
Coll of Central Florida (FL)
Dakota Coll at Bottineau (ND)
Fashion Inst of Technology (NY)
Harford Comm Coll (MD)
Mohawk Valley Comm Coll (NY)
Mt. San Antonio Coll (CA)
Palomar Coll (CA)
Rockland Comm Coll (NY)
South Florida State Coll (FL)

AERONAUTICAL/AEROSPACE ENGINEERING TECHNOLOGY
Cincinnati State Tech and Comm Coll (OH)
Cumberland County Coll (NJ)
Tulsa Comm Coll (OK)

AERONAUTICS/AVIATION/ AEROSPACE SCIENCE AND TECHNOLOGY
Alvin Comm Coll (TX)
Cecil Coll (MD)
The Comm Coll of Baltimore County (MD)
Comm Coll of the Air Force (AL)
Hinds Comm Coll (MS)
Lehigh Carbon Comm Coll (PA)
Miami Dade Coll (FL)
Northland Comm Coll (MN)
Northwest Coll (WY)
Orange Coast Coll (CA)
U of Cincinnati Clermont Coll (OH)

AEROSPACE, AERONAUTICAL AND ASTRONAUTICAL/SPACE ENGINEERING
Kent State U at Ashtabula (OH)
Kilgore Coll (TX)

South Florida State Coll (FL)

AESTHETICIAN/ESTHETICIAN AND SKIN CARE
IBMC Coll (CO)
Southeastern Coll–Greenacres (FL)

AFRICAN AMERICAN/BLACK STUDIES
Nassau Comm Coll (NY)

AGRIBUSINESS
Burlington County Coll (NJ)
Coll of Central Florida (FL)
Coll of the Desert (CA)
Copiah-Lincoln Comm Coll (MS)
Crowder Coll (MO)
Eastern Wyoming Coll (WY)
Harford Comm Coll (MD)
Harrisburg Area Comm Coll (PA)
Hinds Comm Coll (MS)
Iowa Lakes Comm Coll (IA)
James Sprunt Comm Coll (NC)
Laramie County Comm Coll (WY)
Minnesota West Comm and Tech Coll (MN)
Northeast Iowa Comm Coll (IA)
Northwest Coll (WY)
The Ohio State U Ag Tech Inst (OH)
Ridgewater Coll (MN)
San Jacinto Coll District (TX)
South Florida State Coll (FL)
State Fair Comm Coll (MO)
State U of New York Coll of Technology at Alfred (NY)
Wright State U–Lake Campus (OH)

AGRICULTURAL AND EXTENSION EDUCATION
Potomac State Coll of West Virginia U (WV)

AGRICULTURAL AND FOOD PRODUCTS PROCESSING
Minnesota West Comm and Tech Coll (MN)
Northeast Iowa Comm Coll (IA)

AGRICULTURAL BUSINESS AND MANAGEMENT
American Samoa Comm Coll (AS)
Arizona Western Coll (AZ)
Casper Coll (WY)
Central Wyoming Coll (WY)
Cloud County Comm Coll (KS)
Cochise Coll, Douglas (AZ)
Coll of Southern Idaho (ID)
Copiah-Lincoln Comm Coll (MS)
County Coll of Morris (NJ)
Danville Area Comm Coll (IL)
Delaware Tech & Comm Coll, Terry Campus (DE)
Highland Comm Coll (IL)
Illinois Eastern Comm Colls, Wabash Valley College (IL)
Iowa Lakes Comm Coll (IA)
Lake Area Tech Inst (SD)
Lake Land Coll (IL)
Lake Region State Coll (ND)
Lamar Comm Coll (CO)
Mesa Comm Coll (AZ)
Mt. San Antonio Coll (CA)
Northeastern Jr Coll (CO)
Northern Virginia Comm Coll (VA)
The Ohio State U Ag Tech Inst (OH)
Otero Jr Coll (CO)
Pensacola State Coll (FL)
Potomac State Coll of West Virginia U (WV)
Richland Comm Coll (IL)
Salem Comm Coll (NJ)
San Joaquin Delta Coll (CA)
Shawnee Comm Coll (IL)
Sheridan Coll (WY)
Southeastern Comm Coll (IA)
Terra State Comm Coll (OH)
Trinidad State Jr Coll (CO)
Vincennes U (IN)

AGRICULTURAL BUSINESS AND MANAGEMENT RELATED
Coll of Southern Idaho (ID)
Copiah-Lincoln Comm Coll (MS)
Iowa Lakes Comm Coll (IA)
Northern Virginia Comm Coll (VA)
Penn State DuBois (PA)
Penn State Fayette, The Eberly Campus (PA)
Penn State Mont Alto (PA)
Penn State Shenango (PA)

AGRICULTURAL BUSINESS TECHNOLOGY
Iowa Lakes Comm Coll (IA)
Laramie County Comm Coll (WY)
The Ohio State U Ag Tech Inst (OH)
Texas State Tech Coll Harlingen (TX)

AGRICULTURAL COMMUNICATION/ JOURNALISM
Northwest Coll (WY)
The Ohio State U Ag Tech Inst (OH)

AGRICULTURAL ECONOMICS
Copiah-Lincoln Comm Coll (MS)
Iowa Lakes Comm Coll (IA)
James H. Faulkner State Comm Coll (AL)
Northeastern Jr Coll (CO)
North Iowa Area Comm Coll (IA)
The Ohio State U Ag Tech Inst (OH)
South Florida State Coll (FL)

AGRICULTURAL ENGINEERING
South Florida State Coll (FL)
Vincennes U (IN)

AGRICULTURAL/FARM SUPPLIES RETAILING AND WHOLESALING
Cloud County Comm Coll (KS)
Copiah-Lincoln Comm Coll (MS)
Des Moines Area Comm Coll (IA)
Fox Valley Tech Coll (WI)
Hawkeye Comm Coll (IA)
Iowa Lakes Comm Coll (IA)
Minnesota West Comm and Tech Coll (MN)
North Iowa Area Comm Coll (IA)
Western Iowa Tech Comm Coll (IA)

AGRICULTURAL MECHANICS AND EQUIPMENT TECHNOLOGY
Hutchinson Comm Coll (KS)
Iowa Lakes Comm Coll (IA)
Mitchell Tech Inst (SD)

AGRICULTURAL MECHANIZATION
Crowder Coll (MO)
Fox Valley Tech Coll (WI)
Iowa Lakes Comm Coll (IA)
Kishwaukee Coll (IL)
Lake Land Coll (IL)
Mesa Comm Coll (AZ)
Navarro Coll (TX)
North Central Texas Coll (TX)
Northeastern Jr Coll (CO)
The Ohio State U Ag Tech Inst (OH)
Owens Comm Coll, Toledo (OH)
Paris Jr Coll (TX)
San Joaquin Delta Coll (CA)

AGRICULTURAL MECHANIZATION RELATED
Hinds Comm Coll (MS)

AGRICULTURAL POWER MACHINERY OPERATION
Guilford Tech Comm Coll (NC)
Hawkeye Comm Coll (IA)
Iowa Lakes Comm Coll (IA)
Northeast Iowa Comm Coll (IA)
The Ohio State U Ag Tech Inst (OH)

AGRICULTURAL PRODUCTION
Allen Comm Coll (KS)
Big Bend Comm Coll (WA)
Hopkinsville Comm Coll (KY)
Illinois Eastern Comm Colls, Wabash Valley College (IL)
Iowa Lakes Comm Coll (IA)
Lake Land Coll (IL)
Laramie County Comm Coll (WY)
Minnesota West Comm and Tech Coll (MN)
Mitchell Tech Inst (SD)
Northeast Iowa Comm Coll (IA)
North Iowa Area Comm Coll (IA)
Northwest Coll (WY)
Owensboro Comm and Tech Coll (KY)
Ridgewater Coll (MN)
Wenatchee Valley Coll (WA)

AGRICULTURAL PRODUCTION RELATED
Iowa Lakes Comm Coll (IA)
Northwestern Michigan Coll (MI)

AGRICULTURAL TEACHER EDUCATION

Eastern Wyoming Coll (WY)
Iowa Lakes Comm Coll (IA)
Northeastern Jr Coll (CO)
Northwest Coll (WY)
The Ohio State U Ag Tech Inst (OH)
South Florida State Coll (FL)
Trinity Valley Comm Coll (TX)
Victor Valley Coll (CA)

AGRICULTURE

American Samoa Comm Coll (AS)
Arizona Western Coll (AZ)
Bainbridge State Coll (GA)
Casper Coll (WY)
Central Texas Coll (TX)
Chipola Coll (FL)
Coll of Central Florida (FL)
Coll of Southern Idaho (ID)
Coll of the Desert (CA)
Copiah-Lincoln Comm Coll (MS)
Crowder (MO)
Dakota Coll at Bottineau (ND)
Darton State Coll (GA)
Dyersburg State Comm Coll (TN)
Georgia Highlands Coll (GA)
Harford Comm Coll (MD)
Hinds Comm Coll (MS)
Hutchinson Comm Coll (KS)
Iowa Lakes Comm Coll (IA)
Jackson State Comm Coll (TN)
Kankakee Comm Coll (IL)
Kaskaskia Coll (IL)
Kilgore Coll (TX)
Lamar Comm Coll (CO)
Laramie County Comm Coll (WY)
Macomb Comm Coll (MI)
Miami Dade Coll (FL)
Minnesota West Comm and Tech Coll (MN)
Mt. San Antonio Coll (CA)
New Mexico Jr Coll (NM)
Northeastern Jr Coll (CO)
Paris Jr Coll (TX)
Pensacola State Coll (FL)
Potomac State Coll of West Virginia U (WV)
Ridgewater Coll (MN)
San Jacinto Coll District (TX)
San Joaquin Delta Coll (CA)
Shawnee Comm Coll (IL)
Sheridan Coll (WY)
Sierra Coll (CA)
South Florida State Coll (FL)
State U of New York Coll of Technology at Alfred (NY)
Umpqua Comm Coll (OR)
Vincennes U (IN)
Williston State Coll (ND)

AGRICULTURE AND AGRICULTURE OPERATIONS RELATED

Potomac State Coll of West Virginia U (WV)
Sheridan Coll (WY)

AGROECOLOGY AND SUSTAINABLE AGRICULTURE

Kennebec Valley Comm Coll (ME)
Tompkins Cortland Comm Coll (NY)

AGRONOMY AND CROP SCIENCE

Chipola Coll (FL)
Iowa Lakes Comm Coll (IA)
Lamar Comm Coll (CO)
Mesa Comm Coll (AZ)
Minnesota West Comm and Tech Coll (MN)
Northeastern Jr Coll (CO)
The Ohio State U Ag Tech Inst (OH)
Potomac State Coll of West Virginia U (WV)
Ridgewater Coll (MN)
Shawnee Comm Coll (IL)
Southeastern Comm Coll (IA)

AIR AND SPACE OPERATIONS TECHNOLOGY

Cochise Coll, Douglas (AZ)

AIRCRAFT POWERPLANT TECHNOLOGY

Antelope Valley Coll (CA)
Central Texas Coll (TX)
Colorado Northwestern Comm Coll (CO)
Lake Area Tech Inst (SD)
Middlesex Comm Coll (MA)
St. Philip's Coll (TX)

Somerset Comm Coll (KY)
South Louisiana Comm Coll (LA)
Sowela Tech Comm Coll (LA)
U of Arkansas Comm Coll at Batesville (AR)
Vincennes U (IN)
Wayne County Comm Coll District (MI)

AIRFRAME MECHANICS AND AIRCRAFT MAINTENANCE TECHNOLOGY

Amarillo Coll (TX)
Antelope Valley Coll (CA)
Comm Coll of the Air Force (AL)
Florida State Coll at Jacksonville (FL)
Hinds Comm Coll (MS)
Mohawk Valley Comm Coll (NY)
Mt. San Antonio Coll (CA)
Oklahoma City Comm Coll (OK)
St. Philip's Coll (TX)
San Diego Miramar Coll (CA)
San Joaquin Valley Coll—Fresno Aviation Campus (CA)
Southwestern Illinois Coll (IL)
Texas State Tech Coll Harlingen (TX)
Three Rivers Comm Coll (CT)
Trident Tech Coll (SC)
Wayne County Comm Coll District (MI)

AIRLINE PILOT AND FLIGHT CREW

Big Bend Comm Coll (WA)
Casper Coll (WY)
Central Oregon Comm Coll (OR)
Central Texas Coll (TX)
Chandler-Gilbert Comm Coll (AZ)
Cochise Coll, Douglas (AZ)
Colorado Northwestern Comm Coll (CO)
Comm Coll of Allegheny County (PA)
County Coll of Morris (NJ)
Dutchess Comm Coll (NY)
Florida State Coll at Jacksonville (FL)
Fox Valley Tech Coll (WI)
Gateway Tech Coll (WI)
Guilford Tech Comm Coll (NC)
Iowa Central Comm Coll (IA)
Iowa Lakes Comm Coll (IA)
Jamestown Comm Coll (NY)
Kishwaukee Coll (IL)
Lehigh Carbon Comm Coll (PA)
Lenoir Comm Coll (NC)
Luzerne County Comm Coll (PA)
Miami Dade Coll (FL)
Mt. San Antonio Coll (CA)
Navarro Coll (TX)
North Shore Comm Coll (MA)
Northwestern Michigan Coll (MI)
Orange Coast Coll (CA)
Palomar Coll (CA)
Pennsylvania Highlands Comm Coll (PA)
Salt Lake Comm Coll (UT)
San Jacinto Coll District (TX)
Southwestern Illinois Coll (IL)
Vincennes U (IN)

AIR TRAFFIC CONTROL

Cecil Coll (MD)
Comm Coll of the Air Force (AL)
Miami Dade Coll (FL)
Mt. San Antonio Coll (CA)
Tulsa Comm Coll (OK)

AIR TRANSPORTATION RELATED

Cochise Coll, Douglas (AZ)

ALLIED HEALTH AND MEDICAL ASSISTING SERVICES RELATED

Blue Ridge Comm and Tech Coll (WV)
Bowling Green State U-Firelands Coll (OH)
Cincinnati State Tech and Comm Coll (OH)
J. Sargeant Reynolds Comm Coll (VA)
Mount Wachusett Comm Coll (MA)
Pennsylvania Inst of Technology (PA)
Plaza Coll (NY)

ALLIED HEALTH DIAGNOSTIC, INTERVENTION, AND TREATMENT PROFESSIONS RELATED

Forsyth Tech Comm Coll (NC)
Minneapolis Comm and Tech Coll (MN)
Salem Comm Coll (NJ)

South Piedmont Comm Coll (NC)

ALTERNATIVE AND COMPLEMENTARY MEDICAL SUPPORT SERVICES RELATED

Mount Wachusett Comm Coll (MA)

ALTERNATIVE AND COMPLEMENTARY MEDICINE RELATED

Quinsigamond Comm Coll (MA)

AMERICAN GOVERNMENT AND POLITICS

Oklahoma City Comm Coll (OK)

AMERICAN INDIAN/NATIVE AMERICAN STUDIES

Arizona Western Coll (AZ)
Central Wyoming Coll (WY)
Nebraska Indian Comm Coll (NE)
Saginaw Chippewa Tribal Coll (MI)
San Juan Coll (NM)
Sisseton-Wahpeton Coll (SD)

AMERICAN SIGN LANGUAGE (ASL)

Burlington County Coll (NJ)
Coll of Southern Idaho (ID)
Montgomery Coll (MD)
Ohlone Coll (CA)
Oklahoma State U, Oklahoma City (OK)
Quinsigamond Comm Coll (MA)
Sierra Coll (CA)
Vincennes U (IN)

AMERICAN STUDIES

Bucks County Comm Coll (PA)
Greenfield Comm Coll (MA)
Miami Dade Coll (FL)
South Florida State Coll (FL)

ANATOMY

Northeastern Jr Coll (CO)

ANIMAL/LIVESTOCK HUSBANDRY AND PRODUCTION

Hawkeye Comm Coll (IA)
Hopkinsville Comm Coll (KY)
Iowa Lakes Comm Coll (IA)
Jefferson Comm Coll (NY)
North Central Texas Coll (TX)
The Ohio State U Ag Tech Inst (OH)
Ridgewater Coll (MN)
Sierra Coll (CA)

ANIMAL SCIENCES

Alamance Comm Coll (NC)
Casper Coll (WY)
Coll of Central Florida (FL)
Coll of Southern Idaho (ID)
Iowa Lakes Comm Coll (IA)
James Sprunt Comm Coll (NC)
Kaskaskia Coll (IL)
Lamar Comm Coll (CO)
Mt. San Antonio Coll (CA)
Niagara County Comm Coll (NY)
Northeastern Jr Coll (CO)
Northwest Coll (WY)
The Ohio State U Ag Tech Inst (OH)
Potomac State Coll of West Virginia U (WV)
San Joaquin Delta Coll (CA)
Shawnee Comm Coll (IL)
Sheridan Coll (WY)
South Florida State Coll (FL)
Trinity Valley Comm Coll (TX)

ANIMAL TRAINING

Lamar Comm Coll (CO)

ANIMATION, INTERACTIVE TECHNOLOGY, VIDEO GRAPHICS AND SPECIAL EFFECTS

Austin Comm Coll District (TX)
Burlington County Coll (NJ)
Ca&nnada Coll (CA)
Cecil Coll (MD)
Coll of Marin (CA)
Coll of the Canyons (CA)
Elgin Comm Coll (IL)
Finger Lakes Comm Coll (NY)
Forsyth Tech Comm Coll (NC)
Front Range Comm Coll (CO)
Hagerstown Comm Coll (MD)
Houston Comm Coll (TX)
Kalamazoo Valley Comm Coll (MI)
Kirtland Comm Coll (MI)
Lakes Region Comm Coll (NH)
Lehigh Carbon Comm Coll (PA)

Lone Star Coll–CyFair (TX)
Lone Star Coll–Tomball (TX)
McHenry County Coll (IL)
Minneapolis Comm and Tech Coll (MN)
Montgomery Coll (MD)
Oklahoma City Comm Coll (OK)
Palomar Coll (CA)
Pasadena City Coll (CA)
Pueblo Comm Coll (CO)
Raritan Valley Comm Coll (NJ)
Springfield Tech Comm Coll (MA)
State U of New York Coll of Technology at Alfred (NY)
Sullivan Coll of Technology and Design (KY)
Terra State Comm Coll (OH)
Western Iowa Tech Comm Coll (IA)
York County Comm Coll (ME)

ANTHROPOLOGY

Austin Comm Coll District (TX)
Ca&nnada Coll (CA)
Casper Coll (WY)
Coll of Southern Idaho (ID)
Coll of the Desert (CA)
Darton State Coll (GA)
Eastern Arizona Coll (AZ)
Great Basin Coll (NV)
Harford Comm Coll (MD)
Laramie County Comm Coll (WY)
Miami Dade Coll (FL)
Northwest Coll (WY)
Ohlone Coll (CA)
Orange Coast Coll (CA)
Pasadena City Coll (CA)
San Diego Miramar Coll (CA)
San Joaquin Delta Coll (CA)
South Florida State Coll (FL)
Truckee Meadows Comm Coll (NV)
Umpqua Comm Coll (OR)
Vincennes U (IN)
Western Wyoming Comm Coll (WY)

APPAREL AND ACCESSORIES MARKETING

Des Moines Area Comm Coll (IA)
El Centro Coll (TX)
FIDM/Fashion Inst of Design & Merchandising, Los Angeles Campus (CA)
FIDM/Fashion Inst of Design & Merchandising, San Francisco Campus (CA)
FIDM/The Fashion Inst of Design & Merchandising, San Diego Campus (CA)

APPAREL AND TEXTILE MANUFACTURING

Ca&nnada Coll (CA)
Fashion Inst of Technology (NY)
Sierra Coll (CA)
Westchester Comm Coll (NY)

APPAREL AND TEXTILE MARKETING MANAGEMENT

Comm Coll of the Air Force (AL)
FIDM/Fashion Inst of Design & Merchandising, Los Angeles Campus (CA)
FIDM/Fashion Inst of Design & Merchandising, Orange County Campus (CA)
Palomar Coll (CA)
Sierra Coll (CA)

APPAREL AND TEXTILES

Antelope Valley Coll (CA)
FIDM/Fashion Inst of Design & Merchandising, Los Angeles Campus (CA)
FIDM/Fashion Inst of Design & Merchandising, Orange County Campus (CA)
FIDM/Fashion Inst of Design & Merchandising, San Francisco Campus (CA)
Mt. San Antonio Coll (CA)

APPLIED HORTICULTURE/ HORTICULTURAL BUSINESS SERVICES RELATED

Cincinnati State Tech and Comm Coll (OH)
Dakota Coll at Bottineau (ND)
Des Moines Area Comm Coll (IA)
Forsyth Tech Comm Coll (NC)
Gateway Tech Coll (WI)
Hinds Comm Coll (MS)

APPLIED HORTICULTURE/ HORTICULTURE OPERATIONS

Alamance Comm Coll (NC)
Catawba Valley Comm Coll (NC)
Cecil Coll (MD)
Clark Coll (WA)
Coll of Southern Idaho (ID)
Coll of the Desert (CA)
Comm Coll of Allegheny County (PA)
The Comm Coll of Baltimore County (MD)
Dakota Coll at Bottineau (ND)
Fayetteville Tech Comm Coll (NC)
Front Range Comm Coll (CO)
Gateway Tech Coll (WI)
Hawkeye Comm Coll (IA)
Haywood Comm Coll (NC)
Houston Comm Coll (TX)
J. Sargeant Reynolds Comm Coll (VA)
Kankakee Comm Coll (IL)
Kaskaskia Coll (IL)
Kent State U at Salem (OH)
Kishwaukee Coll (IL)
McHenry County Coll (IL)
Montgomery Coll (MD)
Owensboro Comm and Tech Coll (KY)
Sierra Coll (CA)
Southwestern Illinois Coll (IL)
Spartanburg Comm Coll (SC)
State Fair Comm Coll (MO)
Tulsa Comm Coll (OK)
Vincennes U (IN)
Westmoreland County Comm Coll (PA)

APPLIED MATHEMATICS

Northeastern Jr Coll (CO)
San Diego Miramar Coll (CA)
South Florida State Coll (FL)

AQUACULTURE

Coll of Southern Idaho (ID)
Hillsborough Comm Coll (FL)
Trinidad State Jr Coll (CO)

ARCHEOLOGY

Ca&nnada Coll (CA)
Northwest Coll (WY)
Palomar Coll (CA)
Western Wyoming Comm Coll (WY)

ARCHITECTURAL AND BUILDING SCIENCES

J. Sargeant Reynolds Comm Coll (VA)

ARCHITECTURAL DRAFTING AND CAD/CADD

American Samoa Comm Coll (AS)
Anne Arundel Comm Coll (MD)
Anoka Tech Coll (MN)
Benjamin Franklin Inst of Technology (MA)
Butler County Comm Coll (PA)
Carroll Comm Coll (MD)
Coll of the Canyons (CA)
Commonwealth Tech Inst (PA)
Comm Coll of Allegheny County (PA)
The Comm Coll of Baltimore County (MD)
Des Moines Area Comm Coll (IA)
Dunwoody Coll of Technology (MN)
Guam Comm Coll (GU)
Harper Coll (IL)
Hennepin Tech Coll (MN)
Hutchinson Comm Coll (KS)
Island Drafting and Tech Inst (NY)
Kaskaskia Coll (IL)
Macomb Comm Coll (MI)
Miami Dade Coll (FL)
Montgomery Coll (MD)
Oakton Comm Coll (IL)
Oklahoma City Comm Coll (OK)
Owens Comm Coll, Toledo (OH)
Palomar Coll (CA)
Pennsylvania Highlands Comm Coll (PA)
Phoenix Coll (AZ)
Sierra Coll (CA)
South Suburban Coll (IL)
Sullivan Coll of Technology and Design (KY)
Three Rivers Comm Coll (CT)
Vincennes U (IN)
Waukesha County Tech Coll (WI)
Westmoreland County Comm Coll (PA)
York County Comm Coll (ME)

ARCHITECTURAL ENGINEERING
Luzerne County Comm Coll (PA)
Springfield Tech Comm Coll (MA)

ARCHITECTURAL ENGINEERING TECHNOLOGY
Amarillo Coll (TX)
Arapahoe Comm Coll (CO)
Benjamin Franklin Inst of Technology (MA)
Cape Fear Comm Coll (NC)
Catawba Valley Comm Coll (NC)
Central Maine Comm Coll (ME)
Cincinnati State Tech and Comm Coll (OH)
Comm Coll of Philadelphia (PA)
Daytona State Coll (FL)
Delaware Tech & Comm Coll, Terry Campus (DE)
Delgado Comm Coll (LA)
Delta Coll (MI)
Dutchess Comm Coll (NY)
Erie Comm Coll, South Campus (NY)
Fayetteville Tech Comm Coll (NC)
Finger Lakes Comm Coll (NY)
Forsyth Tech Comm Coll (NC)
Front Range Comm Coll (CO)
Gateway Tech Coll (WI)
Golden West Coll (CA)
Greenville Tech Coll (SC)
Guilford Tech Comm Coll (NC)
Harper Coll (IL)
Harrisburg Area Comm Coll (PA)
Hillsborough Comm Coll (FL)
Hinds Comm Coll (MS)
Lake Land Coll (IL)
Los Angeles Trade-Tech Coll (CA)
Luzerne County Comm Coll (PA)
Miami Dade Coll (FL)
Midlands Tech Coll (SC)
Monroe County Comm Coll (MI)
Mott Comm Coll (MI)
Mt. San Antonio Coll (CA)
Northampton Comm Coll (PA)
Northcentral Tech Coll (WI)
Northern Virginia Comm Coll (VA)
Northland Comm Coll (MN)
Norwalk Comm Coll (CT)
Oklahoma State U, Oklahoma City (OK)
Orange Coast Coll (CA)
Owens Comm Coll, Toledo (OH)
Penn State Fayette, The Eberly Campus (PA)
Salt Lake Comm Coll (UT)
Seminole State Coll of Florida (FL)
Stark State Coll (OH)
State U of New York Coll of Technology at Alfred (NY)
Sullivan Coll of Technology and Design (KY)
Terra State Comm Coll (OH)
Three Rivers Comm Coll (CT)
Western Iowa Tech Comm Coll (IA)
Wisconsin Indianhead Tech Coll (WI)

ARCHITECTURAL TECHNOLOGY
Arizona Western Coll (AZ)
Coll of Marin (CA)
Coll of the Desert (CA)
Dunwoody Coll of Technology (MN)
Florida SouthWestern State Coll (FL)
Florida State Coll at Jacksonville (FL)
Grand Rapids Comm Coll (MI)
John Tyler Comm Coll (VA)
Miami Dade Coll (FL)
MiraCosta Coll (CA)
Palomar Coll (CA)

ARCHITECTURE
Allen Comm Coll (KS)
Coll of Central Florida (FL)
Copiah-Lincoln Comm Coll (MS)
Grand Rapids Comm Coll (MI)
Harrisburg Area Comm Coll (PA)
Hinds Comm Coll (MS)
Kilgore Coll (TX)
Pasadena City Coll (CA)
South Florida State Coll (FL)
Truckee Meadows Comm Coll (NV)

ARCHITECTURE RELATED
Sullivan Coll of Technology and Design (KY)
Westhill U (Mexico)

AREA STUDIES RELATED
Ca&nnada Coll (CA)

ART
Allen Comm Coll (KS)
Alvin Comm Coll (TX)
Amarillo Coll (TX)
American Samoa Comm Coll (AS)
Austin Comm Coll District (TX)
Bainbridge State Coll (GA)
Bunker Hill Comm Coll (MA)
Burlington County Coll (NJ)
Ca&nnada Coll (CA)
Carroll Comm Coll (MD)
Casper Coll (WY)
Cayuga County Comm Coll (NY)
Central Oregon Comm Coll (OR)
Central Wyoming Coll (WY)
Chipola Coll (FL)
Citrus Coll (CA)
Cochise Coll, Douglas (AZ)
Coll of Central Florida (FL)
Coll of Marin (CA)
Coll of Southern Idaho (ID)
Coll of the Canyons (CA)
Coll of the Desert (CA)
Columbia-Greene Comm Coll (NY)
Comm Coll of Allegheny County (PA)
Comm Coll of Philadelphia (PA)
Comm Coll of Rhode Island (RI)
Corning Comm Coll (NY)
Crowder Coll (MO)
Darton State Coll (GA)
Dutchess Comm Coll (NY)
Eastern Arizona Coll (AZ)
Eastern Wyoming Coll (WY)
Edison Comm Coll (OH)
Frederick Comm Coll (MD)
Georgia Highlands Coll (GA)
Golden West Coll (CA)
Grand Rapids Comm Coll (MI)
Great Basin Coll (NV)
Greenfield Comm Coll (MA)
Harper Coll (IL)
Harrisburg Area Comm Coll (PA)
Hinds Comm Coll (MS)
Holyoke Comm Coll (MA)
Housatonic Comm Coll (CT)
Howard Comm Coll (MD)
Kankakee Comm Coll (IL)
Kilgore Coll (TX)
Kingsborough Comm Coll of the City U of New York (NY)
Kirtland Comm Coll (MI)
Kishwaukee Coll (IL)
Laramie County Comm Coll (WY)
Lehigh Carbon Comm Coll (PA)
Lenoir Comm Coll (NC)
Lorain County Comm Coll (OH)
Mesa Comm Coll (AZ)
Miami Dade Coll (FL)
Middlesex Comm Coll (MA)
MiraCosta Coll (CA)
Mohave Comm Coll (AZ)
Mohawk Valley Comm Coll (NY)
Monroe Comm Coll (NY)
Monroe County Comm Coll (MI)
Montgomery Coll (MD)
Montgomery County Comm Coll (PA)
Mount Wachusett Comm Coll (MA)
Nassau Comm Coll (NY)
Navarro Coll (TX)
New Mexico Jr Coll (NM)
Northeastern Jr Coll (CO)
Northwest Coll (WY)
Northwestern Michigan Coll (MI)
Norwalk Comm Coll (CT)
Ohlone Coll (CA)
Oklahoma City Comm Coll (OK)
Oklahoma State U, Oklahoma City (OK)
Orange Coast Coll (CA)
Palomar Coll (CA)
Paris Jr Coll (TX)
Pasadena City Coll (CA)
Pensacola State Coll (FL)
Phoenix Coll (AZ)
Reading Area Comm Coll (PA)
Roane State Comm Coll (TN)
Rockland Comm Coll (NY)
St. Philip's Coll (TX)
San Diego Miramar Coll (CA)
San Jacinto Coll District (TX)
San Joaquin Delta Coll (CA)
Seminole State Coll (OK)
Sheridan Coll (WY)
Sierra Coll (CA)
South Florida State Coll (FL)
Trinity Valley Comm Coll (TX)
Tunxis Comm Coll (CT)

Tyler Jr Coll (TX)
Umpqua Comm Coll (OR)
Victor Valley Coll (CA)
Vincennes U (IN)
Virginia Western Comm Coll (VA)
Wayne County Comm Coll District (MI)
Western Wyoming Comm Coll (WY)

ART HISTORY, CRITICISM AND CONSERVATION
South Florida State Coll (FL)
Terra State Comm Coll (OH)
Umpqua Comm Coll (OR)

ARTIFICIAL INTELLIGENCE
Lorain County Comm Coll (OH)
Southeastern Comm Coll (IA)
Sullivan Coll of Technology and Design (KY)

ART TEACHER EDUCATION
Casper Coll (WY)
Cochise Coll, Douglas (AZ)
Copiah-Lincoln Comm Coll (MS)
Darton State Coll (GA)
Eastern Arizona Coll (AZ)
Iowa Lakes Comm Coll (IA)
New Mexico Jr Coll (NM)
Northeastern Jr Coll (CO)
Pensacola State Coll (FL)
Roane State Comm Coll (TN)
South Florida State Coll (FL)
Umpqua Comm Coll (OR)
Vincennes U (IN)

ART THERAPY
Vincennes U (IN)

ASIAN STUDIES
Miami Dade Coll (FL)

ASTRONOMY
Iowa Lakes Comm Coll (IA)
Palomar Coll (CA)
South Florida State Coll (FL)

ATHLETIC TRAINING
Allen Comm Coll (KS)
Casper Coll (WY)
Central Wyoming Coll (WY)
Coll of the Canyons (CA)
Comm Coll of Allegheny County (PA)
Dean Coll (MA)
Iowa Lakes Comm Coll (IA)
Lorain County Comm Coll (OH)
New Mexico Jr Coll (NM)
Northampton Comm Coll (PA)
Northwest Coll (WY)
Orange Coast Coll (CA)
Tyler Jr Coll (TX)
Wenatchee Valley Coll (WA)

ATMOSPHERIC SCIENCES AND METEOROLOGY
Comm Coll of the Air Force (AL)
South Florida State Coll (FL)

AUDIOLOGY AND SPEECH-LANGUAGE PATHOLOGY
Miami Dade Coll (FL)
Pasadena City Coll (CA)
South Florida State Coll (FL)
U of Cincinnati Clermont Coll (OH)

AUDIOVISUAL COMMUNICATIONS TECHNOLOGIES RELATED
Bossier Parish Comm Coll (LA)
Cincinnati State Tech and Comm Coll (OH)

AUTOBODY/COLLISION AND REPAIR TECHNOLOGY
American Samoa Comm Coll (AS)
Antelope Valley Coll (CA)
Bellingham Tech Coll (WA)
Casper Coll (WY)
Central Texas Coll (TX)
Coll of Marin (CA)
Coll of Southern Idaho (ID)
Corning Comm Coll (NY)
Crowder Coll (MO)
Danville Area Comm Coll (IL)
Des Moines Area Comm Coll (IA)
Dunwoody Coll of Technology (MN)
Erie Comm Coll, South Campus (NY)
Fayetteville Tech Comm Coll (NC)
Florida State Coll at Jacksonville (FL)

Fox Valley Tech Coll (WI)
George C. Wallace Comm Coll (AL)
Hawkeye Comm Coll (IA)
Hennepin Tech Coll (MN)
Highland Comm Coll (IL)
Hutchinson Comm Coll (KS)
Illinois Eastern Comm Colls, Olney Central College (IL)
Iowa Lakes Comm Coll (IA)
Kaskaskia Coll (IL)
Kilgore Coll (TX)
Kishwaukee Coll (IL)
Lake Area Tech Inst (SD)
Laramie County Comm Coll (WY)
Mid-Plains Comm Coll, North Platte (NE)
Minnesota State Coll–Southeast Tech (MN)
Northland Comm Coll (MN)
Oklahoma State U Inst of Technology (OK)
Ozarks Tech Comm Coll (MO)
Palomar Coll (CA)
Pueblo Comm Coll (CO)
Randolph Comm Coll (NC)
Ridgewater Coll (MN)
Riverland Comm Coll (MN)
St. Philip's Coll (TX)
Salt Lake Comm Coll (UT)
San Jacinto Coll District (TX)
San Juan Coll (NM)
Southwestern Illinois Coll (IL)
State U of New York Coll of Technology at Alfred (NY)
Texas State Tech Coll Harlingen (TX)
U of Arkansas Comm Coll at Morrilton (AR)
Vincennes U (IN)
Waukesha County Tech Coll (WI)
Wayne County Comm Coll District (MI)
Western Iowa Tech Comm Coll (IA)

AUTOMATION ENGINEER TECHNOLOGY
Alexandria Tech and Comm Coll (MN)
Blue Ridge Comm and Tech Coll (WV)
Dyersburg State Comm Coll (TN)
Fox Valley Tech Coll (WI)
Gulf Coast State Coll (FL)
Hennepin Tech Coll (MN)
Miami Dade Coll (FL)
Mitchell Tech Inst (SD)
St. Clair County Comm Coll (MI)
Southwestern Michigan Coll (MI)

AUTOMOBILE/AUTOMOTIVE MECHANICS TECHNOLOGY
Alamance Comm Coll (NC)
Amarillo Coll (TX)
American Samoa Comm Coll (AS)
Anoka Tech Coll (MN)
Antelope Valley Coll (CA)
Arapahoe Comm Coll (CO)
Austin Comm Coll District (TX)
Bellingham Tech Coll (WA)
Benjamin Franklin Inst of Technology (MA)
Big Bend Comm Coll (WA)
Brookhaven Coll (TX)
Cape Fear Comm Coll (NC)
Casper Coll (WY)
Catawba Valley Comm Coll (NC)
Cedar Valley Coll (TX)
Central Maine Comm Coll (ME)
Central Oregon Comm Coll (OR)
Central Texas Coll (TX)
Central Wyoming Coll (WY)
Cincinnati State Tech and Comm Coll (OH)
Citrus Coll (CA)
Clark Coll (WA)
Coastal Bend Coll (TX)
Cochise Coll, Douglas (AZ)
Coll of Marin (CA)
Coll of Southern Idaho (ID)
Coll of the Canyons (CA)
Coll of the Desert (CA)
Columbia-Greene Comm Coll (NY)
The Comm Coll of Baltimore County (MD)
Comm Coll of Philadelphia (PA)
Comm Coll of the Air Force (AL)
Corning Comm Coll (NY)
Crowder Coll (MO)
Danville Area Comm Coll (IL)
Daytona State Coll (FL)
Delgado Comm Coll (LA)

Delta Coll (MI)
Denmark Tech Coll (SC)
Des Moines Area Comm Coll (IA)
Dunwoody Coll of Technology (MN)
Eastern Arizona Coll (AZ)
Eastern Idaho Tech Coll (ID)
Elgin Comm Coll (IL)
Elizabethtown Comm and Tech Coll, Elizabethtown (KY)
Erie Comm Coll, South Campus (NY)
Fayetteville Tech Comm Coll (NC)
Florida State Coll at Jacksonville (FL)
Forsyth Tech Comm Coll (NC)
Fox Valley Tech Coll (WI)
Front Range Comm Coll (CO)
Gateway Comm Coll (CT)
Gateway Tech Coll (WI)
George C. Wallace Comm Coll (AL)
Golden West Coll (CA)
Grand Rapids Comm Coll (MI)
Greenville Tech Coll (SC)
Guam Comm Coll (GU)
Guilford Tech Comm Coll (NC)
Gwinnett Tech Coll (GA)
Harrisburg Area Comm Coll (PA)
Hawkeye Comm Coll (IA)
Haywood Comm Coll (NC)
Hennepin Tech Coll (MN)
Highland Comm Coll (IL)
Houston Comm Coll (TX)
Hutchinson Comm Coll (KS)
Illinois Eastern Comm Colls, Frontier Community College (IL)
Illinois Eastern Comm Colls, Olney Central College (IL)
Iowa Central Comm Coll (IA)
Iowa Lakes Comm Coll (IA)
Jefferson Coll (MO)
J. F. Drake State Comm and Tech Coll (AL)
J. Sargeant Reynolds Comm Coll (VA)
Kalamazoo Valley Comm Coll (MI)
Kankakee Comm Coll (IL)
Kaskaskia Coll (IL)
Kilgore Coll (TX)
Kirtland Comm Coll (MI)
Kishwaukee Coll (IL)
Lake Area Tech Inst (SD)
Lake Land Coll (IL)
Lake Region State Coll (ND)
Lakes Region Comm Coll (NH)
Laramie County Comm Coll (WY)
Lone Star Coll–Montgomery (TX)
Lone Star Coll–North Harris (TX)
Los Angeles Trade-Tech Coll (CA)
Lower Columbia Coll (WA)
Luzerne County Comm Coll (PA)
Macomb Comm Coll (MI)
Mesa Comm Coll (AZ)
Midlands Tech Coll (SC)
Mid-Plains Comm Coll, North Platte (NE)
Minnesota West Comm and Tech Coll (MN)
Mohave Comm Coll (AZ)
Monroe Comm Coll (NY)
Montcalm Comm Coll (MI)
Montgomery Coll (MD)
Moraine Park Tech Coll (WI)
Moraine Valley Comm Coll (IL)
Morgan Comm Coll (CO)
Mott Comm Coll (MI)
Mount Wachusett Comm Coll (MA)
New Mexico Jr Coll (NM)
Northampton Comm Coll (PA)
Northcentral Tech Coll (WI)
North Central Texas Coll (TX)
Northeastern Jr Coll (CO)
Northeast Iowa Comm Coll (IA)
North Iowa Area Comm Coll (IA)
Northland Comm Coll (MN)
Northwestern Michigan Coll (MI)
Northwest Tech Coll (MN)
Oakton Comm Coll (IL)
Oklahoma City Comm Coll (OK)
Oklahoma Tech Coll (OK)
Otero Jr Coll (CO)
Ozarks Tech Comm Coll (MO)
Palomar Coll (CA)
Pasadena City Coll (CA)
Pueblo Comm Coll (CO)
Quinsigamond Comm Coll (MA)
Randolph Comm Coll (NC)
Renton Tech Coll (WA)
Richland Comm Coll (IL)
Ridgewater Coll (MN)
Rockland Comm Coll (NY)

Rock Valley Coll (IL)
Rogue Comm Coll (OR)
St. Philip's Coll (TX)
San Diego Miramar Coll (CA)
San Jacinto Coll District (TX)
San Joaquin Delta Coll (CA)
San Juan Coll (NM)
Seminole State Coll of Florida (FL)
Shawnee Comm Coll (IL)
Sierra Coll (CA)
Southeastern Comm Coll (IA)
South Louisiana Comm Coll (LA)
South Piedmont Comm Coll (NC)
Southwestern Michigan Coll (MI)
Spartanburg Comm Coll (SC)
Stark State Coll (OH)
State Fair Comm Coll (MO)
State U of New York Coll of Technology at Alfred (NY)
Texas State Tech Coll Harlingen (TX)
Trident Tech Coll (SC)
Trinidad State Jr Coll (CO)
Trinity Valley Comm Coll (TX)
Truckee Meadows Comm Coll (NV)
Tyler Jr Coll (TX)
Umpqua Comm Coll (OR)
U of Arkansas Comm Coll at Morrilton (AR)
Victor Valley Coll (CA)
Vincennes U (IN)
Virginia Western Comm Coll (VA)
Waukesha County Tech Coll (WI)
Wayne County Comm Coll District (MI)
Wenatchee Valley Coll (WA)
Western Iowa Tech Comm Coll (IA)
Western Nevada Coll (NV)
Western Wyoming Comm Coll (WY)
White Mountains Comm Coll (NH)

AUTOMOTIVE ENGINEERING TECHNOLOGY
Benjamin Franklin Inst of Technology (MA)
Burlington County Coll (NJ)
Camden County Coll (NJ)
Cincinnati State Tech and Comm Coll (OH)
Comm Coll of Allegheny County (PA)
Florida State Coll at Jacksonville (FL)
H. Councill Trenholm State Tech Coll (AL)
IntelliTec Coll, Grand Junction (CO)
J. F. Drake State Comm and Tech Coll (AL)
Macomb Comm Coll (MI)
Massachusetts Bay Comm Coll (MA)
Middlesex County Coll (NJ)
New Castle School of Trades (PA)
Oklahoma City Comm Coll (OK)
Oklahoma State U Inst of Technology (OK)
Owens Comm Coll, Toledo (OH)
Raritan Valley Comm Coll (NJ)
Springfield Tech Comm Coll (MA)
Terra State Comm Coll (OH)

AVIATION/AIRWAY MANAGEMENT
Anoka Tech Coll (MN)
Comm Coll of Allegheny County (PA)
Dutchess Comm Coll (NY)
Florida State Coll at Jacksonville (FL)
Hinds Comm Coll (MS)
Iowa Central Comm Coll (IA)
Iowa Lakes Comm Coll (IA)
Lenoir Comm Coll (NC)
Luzerne County Comm Coll (PA)
Miami Dade Coll (FL)
Northland Comm Coll (MN)
Palomar Coll (CA)
San Jacinto Coll District (TX)
Southwestern Illinois Coll (IL)

AVIONICS MAINTENANCE TECHNOLOGY
Antelope Valley Coll (CA)
Big Bend Comm Coll (WA)
Cochise Coll, Douglas (AZ)
Comm Coll of the Air Force (AL)
Fox Valley Tech Coll (WI)
Gateway Comm Coll (CT)
Guilford Tech Comm Coll (NC)
Housatonic Comm Coll (CT)
Lenoir Comm Coll (NC)
Mt. San Antonio Coll (CA)
Navarro Coll (TX)
Orange Coast Coll (CA)
Rock Valley Coll (IL)
Salt Lake Comm Coll (UT)
San Diego Miramar Coll (CA)
Southern U at Shreveport (LA)

BAKING AND PASTRY ARTS
Blue Ridge Comm and Tech Coll (WV)
Bucks County Comm Coll (PA)
Cincinnati State Tech and Comm Coll (OH)
Clark Coll (WA)
Collin County Comm Coll District (TX)
El Centro Coll (TX)
Elgin Comm Coll (IL)
J. Sargeant Reynolds Comm Coll (VA)
Luzerne County Comm Coll (PA)
Montgomery County Comm Coll (PA)
Moraine Valley Comm Coll (IL)
Mott Comm Coll (MI)
New England Culinary Inst (VT)
Niagara County Comm Coll (NY)
San Jacinto Coll District (TX)
Sullivan County Comm Coll (NY)
Waukesha County Tech Coll (WI)
Westmoreland County Comm Coll (PA)
White Mountains Comm Coll (NH)

BANKING AND FINANCIAL SUPPORT SERVICES
Alamance Comm Coll (NC)
Allen Comm Coll (KS)
Arapahoe Comm Coll (CO)
Camden County Coll (NJ)
Cleveland Comm Coll (NC)
Colorado Northwestern Comm Coll (CO)
Comm Coll of Allegheny County (PA)
Comm Coll of Rhode Island (RI)
Fayetteville Tech Comm Coll (NC)
Fox Valley Tech Coll (WI)
Harper Coll (IL)
Harrisburg Area Comm Coll (PA)
Hinds Comm Coll (MS)
Houston Comm Coll (TX)
Lake Area Tech Inst (SD)
Luzerne County Comm Coll (PA)
Miami Dade Coll (FL)
Mohawk Valley Comm Coll (NY)
Northwest State Comm Coll (OH)
Oakton Comm Coll (IL)
Oklahoma City Comm Coll (OK)
Phoenix Coll (AZ)
Seminole State Coll of Florida (FL)
Southern U at Shreveport (LA)
South Florida State Coll (FL)
State U of New York Coll of Technology at Alfred (NY)
Terra State Comm Coll (OH)
Three Rivers Comm Coll (CT)
Westmoreland County Comm Coll (PA)

BEHAVIORAL ASPECTS OF HEALTH
Darton State Coll (GA)

BEHAVIORAL SCIENCES
Amarillo Coll (TX)
Ancilla Coll (IN)
Citrus Coll (CA)
Iowa Lakes Comm Coll (IA)
Miami Dade Coll (FL)
Monroe Comm Coll (NY)
Orange Coast Coll (CA)
San Jacinto Coll District (TX)
Seminole State Coll (OK)
Tyler Jr Coll (TX)
Umpqua Comm Coll (OR)
Vincennes U (IN)

BIBLICAL STUDIES
Amarillo Coll (TX)

BILINGUAL AND MULTILINGUAL EDUCATION
Coll of Southern Idaho (ID)
Delaware Tech & Comm Coll, Terry Campus (DE)

BIOCHEMISTRY
Pasadena City Coll (CA)
Pensacola State Coll (FL)
South Florida State Coll (FL)
Vincennes U (IN)

BIOENGINEERING AND BIOMEDICAL ENGINEERING
Anoka-Ramsey Comm Coll (MN)
Anoka-Ramsey Comm Coll, Cambridge Campus (MN)
Benjamin Franklin Inst of Technology (MA)
Bunker Hill Comm Coll (MA)
Quinsigamond Comm Coll (MA)

BIOLOGICAL AND BIOMEDICAL SCIENCES RELATED
Darton State Coll (GA)
Seminole State Coll (OK)
Vincennes U (IN)

BIOLOGICAL AND PHYSICAL SCIENCES
Ancilla Coll (IN)
Burlington County Coll (NJ)
Ca&nnada Coll (CA)
Central Oregon Comm Coll (OR)
Chipola Coll (FL)
Citrus Coll (CA)
City Colls of Chicago, Olive-Harvey College (IL)
Clinton Comm Coll (NY)
Coll of Marin (CA)
Coll of the Canyons (CA)
Coll of the Desert (CA)
The Comm Coll of Baltimore County (MD)
Comm Coll of Rhode Island (RI)
Copiah-Lincoln Comm Coll (MS)
Dabney S. Lancaster Comm Coll (VA)
Delgado Comm Coll (LA)
Elgin Comm Coll (IL)
Finger Lakes Comm Coll (NY)
Georgia Highlands Coll (GA)
Golden West Coll (CA)
Highland Comm Coll (IL)
Howard Comm Coll (MD)
Hudson County Comm Coll (NJ)
Illinois Eastern Comm Colls, Frontier Community College (IL)
Illinois Eastern Comm Colls, Lincoln Trail College (IL)
Illinois Eastern Comm Colls, Olney Central College (IL)
Illinois Eastern Comm Colls, Wabash Valley College (IL)
Iowa Central Comm Coll (IA)
Iowa Lakes Comm Coll (IA)
J. Sargeant Reynolds Comm Coll (VA)
Kaskaskia Coll (IL)
Kilgore Coll (TX)
Kishwaukee Coll (IL)
Lake Land Coll (IL)
Lamar Comm Coll (CO)
Laramie County Comm Coll (WY)
Lorain County Comm Coll (OH)
Luzerne County Comm Coll (PA)
Massachusetts Bay Comm Coll (MA)
McHenry County Coll (IL)
MiraCosta Coll (CA)
Monroe Comm Coll (NY)
Moraine Valley Comm Coll (IL)
Morgan Comm Coll (CO)
Mt. San Antonio Coll (CA)
Navarro Coll (TX)
New Mexico Jr Coll (NM)
Niagara County Comm Coll (NY)
North Central Texas Coll (TX)
Northeastern Jr Coll (CO)
Northern Essex Comm Coll (MA)
Northern Virginia Comm Coll (VA)
Oakton Comm Coll (IL)
Otero Jr Coll (CO)
Palomar Coll (CA)
Paris Jr Coll (TX)
Pasadena City Coll (CA)
Penn State DuBois (PA)
Penn State Fayette, The Eberly Campus (PA)
Penn State Shenango (PA)
Rainy River Comm Coll (MN)
Rappahannock Comm Coll (VA)
Richland Comm Coll (IL)
Rockland Comm Coll (NY)
Shawnee Comm Coll (IL)
Sheridan Coll (WY)
Sierra Coll (CA)
South Florida State Coll (FL)
South Suburban Coll (IL)
Southwestern Illinois Coll (IL)
Terra State Comm Coll (OH)
Trident Tech Coll (SC)
Trinidad State Jr Coll (CO)
Umpqua Comm Coll (OR)
U of South Carolina Union (SC)
Victor Valley Coll (CA)
Vincennes U (IN)
Virginia Western Comm Coll (VA)
Western Wyoming Comm Coll (WY)
Wor-Wic Comm Coll (MD)
Wytheville Comm Coll (VA)

BIOLOGY/BIOLOGICAL SCIENCES
Allen Comm Coll (KS)
Alvin Comm Coll (TX)
Amarillo Coll (TX)
Anoka-Ramsey Comm Coll (MN)
Anoka-Ramsey Comm Coll, Cambridge Campus (MN)
Antelope Valley Coll (CA)
Arizona Western Coll (AZ)
Austin Comm Coll District (TX)
Bainbridge State Coll (GA)
Bunker Hill Comm Coll (MA)
Burlington County Coll (NJ)
Butler County Comm Coll (PA)
Ca&nnada Coll (CA)
Carl Albert State Coll (OK)
Casper Coll (WY)
Cecil Coll (MD)
Central Oregon Comm Coll (OR)
Central Texas Coll (TX)
Central Wyoming Coll (WY)
Cincinnati State Tech and Comm Coll (OH)
Citrus Coll (CA)
Cochise Coll, Douglas (AZ)
Coll of Central Florida (FL)
Coll of Marin (CA)
Coll of Southern Idaho (ID)
Coll of the Desert (CA)
Comm Coll of Allegheny County (PA)
Copiah-Lincoln Comm Coll (MS)
Crowder Coll (MO)
Dakota Coll at Bottineau (ND)
Darton State Coll (GA)
Dean Coll (MA)
Eastern Arizona Coll (AZ)
Eastern Wyoming Coll (WY)
Edison Comm Coll (OH)
Finger Lakes Comm Coll (NY)
Fiorello H. LaGuardia Comm Coll of the City U of New York (NY)
Frederick Comm Coll (MD)
Genesee Comm Coll (NY)
Golden West Coll (CA)
Harford Comm Coll (MD)
Harper Coll (IL)
Harrisburg Area Comm Coll (PA)
Hinds Comm Coll (MS)
Hutchinson Comm Coll (KS)
Iowa Lakes Comm Coll (IA)
Kankakee Comm Coll (IL)
Kingsborough Comm Coll of the City U of New York (NY)
Lamar Comm Coll (CO)
Landmark Coll (VT)
Laramie County Comm Coll (WY)
Lehigh Carbon Comm Coll (PA)
Lorain County Comm Coll (OH)
Macomb Comm Coll (MI)
Mesa Comm Coll (AZ)
Miami Dade Coll (FL)
Middlesex Comm Coll (MA)
Minneapolis Comm and Tech Coll (MN)
Monroe Comm Coll (NY)
Monroe County Comm Coll (MI)
Montgomery County Comm Coll (PA)
Mott Comm Coll (MI)
Navarro Coll (TX)
New Mexico Jr Coll (NM)
Northampton Comm Coll (PA)
Northeastern Jr Coll (CO)
North Hennepin Comm Coll (MN)
Northwest Coll (WY)
Northwestern Michigan Coll (MI)
Ohlone Coll (CA)
Oklahoma City Comm Coll (OK)
Orange Coast Coll (CA)
Otero Jr Coll (CO)
Palomar Coll (CA)
Paris Jr Coll (TX)
Pasadena City Coll (CA)
Pensacola State Coll (FL)
Potomac State Coll of West Virginia U (WV)
Ridgewater Coll (MN)
Roane State Comm Coll (TN)
St. Charles Comm Coll (MO)
St. Philip's Coll (TX)
Salem Comm Coll (NJ)
Salt Lake Comm Coll (UT)
San Diego Miramar Coll (CA)
San Jacinto Coll District (TX)
San Joaquin Delta Coll (CA)
San Juan Coll (NM)
Seminole State Coll (OK)
Sheridan Coll (WY)
Sierra Coll (CA)
Southern U at Shreveport (LA)
South Florida State Coll (FL)
Springfield Tech Comm Coll (MA)
State U of New York Coll of Technology at Alfred (NY)
Terra State Comm Coll (OH)
Texas State Tech Coll Harlingen (TX)
Trinidad State Jr Coll (CO)
Trinity Valley Comm Coll (TX)
Truckee Meadows Comm Coll (NV)
Tyler Jr Coll (TX)
Umpqua Comm Coll (OR)
U of Cincinnati Clermont Coll (OH)
Victor Valley Coll (CA)
Vincennes U (IN)
Wenatchee Valley Coll (WA)
Western Nevada Coll (NV)
Western Wyoming Comm Coll (WY)
Wright State U–Lake Campus (OH)

BIOLOGY/BIOTECHNOLOGY LABORATORY TECHNICIAN
Austin Comm Coll District (TX)
Bucks County Comm Coll (PA)
Camden County Coll (NJ)
Collin County Comm Coll District (TX)
County Coll of Morris (NJ)
Elgin Comm Coll (IL)
Erie Comm Coll, North Campus (NY)
Finger Lakes Comm Coll (NY)
Florida SouthWestern State Coll (FL)
Florida State Coll at Jacksonville (FL)
Forsyth Tech Comm Coll (NC)
Fox Valley Tech Coll (WI)
Gateway Tech Coll (WI)
Genesee Comm Coll (NY)
Guilford Tech Comm Coll (NC)
Hagerstown Comm Coll (MD)
Hillsborough Comm Coll (FL)
Houston Comm Coll (TX)
Hutchinson Comm Coll (KS)
Jamestown Comm Coll (NY)
Kennebec Valley Comm Coll (ME)
Lone Star Coll–Montgomery (TX)
Massachusetts Bay Comm Coll (MA)
Middlesex Comm Coll (MA)
Middlesex County Coll (NJ)
Minnesota West Comm and Tech Coll (MN)
Monroe Comm Coll (NY)
Montgomery Coll (MD)
North Shore Comm Coll (MA)
The Ohio State U Ag Tech Inst (OH)
Salt Lake Comm Coll (UT)
Tompkins Cortland Comm Coll (NY)
Westmoreland County Comm Coll (PA)

BIOLOGY TEACHER EDUCATION
Bucks County Comm Coll (PA)
Ulster County Comm Coll (NY)

BIOMEDICAL TECHNOLOGY
Anoka-Ramsey Comm Coll (MN)
Anoka-Ramsey Comm Coll, Cambridge Campus (MN)
Anoka Tech Coll (MN)
Benjamin Franklin Inst of Technology (MA)
Cincinnati State Tech and Comm Coll (OH)
Comm Coll of the Air Force (AL)
Delaware Tech & Comm Coll, Terry Campus (DE)
Delgado Comm Coll (LA)
Des Moines Area Comm Coll (IA)
Florida State Coll at Jacksonville (FL)
Gateway Comm Coll (CT)
Howard Comm Coll (MD)
Miami Dade Coll (FL)
Minnesota State Coll–Southeast Tech (MN)
MiraCosta Coll (CA)
Owens Comm Coll, Toledo (OH)
Penn State DuBois (PA)
Penn State Fayette, The Eberly Campus (PA)
Penn State Shenango (PA)
St. Philip's Coll (TX)
Schoolcraft Coll (MI)
Southeastern Comm Coll (IA)
South Florida State Coll (FL)
Spencerian Coll–Lexington (KY)
Stark State Coll (OH)
Texas State Tech Coll Harlingen (TX)
Wayne County Comm Coll District (MI)
Western Iowa Tech Comm Coll (IA)

BIOPHYSICS
Forsyth Tech Comm Coll (NC)

BIOTECHNOLOGY
Alamance Comm Coll (NC)
Borough of Manhattan Comm Coll of the City U of New York (NY)
Bucks County Comm Coll (PA)
Bunker Hill Comm Coll (MA)
Burlington County Coll (NJ)
Cecil Coll (MD)
Cleveland Comm Coll (NC)
El Centro Coll (TX)
Genesee Comm Coll (NY)
Howard Comm Coll (MD)
Humacao Comm Coll (PR)
Lakeland Comm Coll (OH)
Lehigh Carbon Comm Coll (PA)
Miami Dade Coll (FL)
Middlesex County Coll (NJ)
Montgomery County Comm Coll (PA)
Mount Wachusett Comm Coll (MA)
Northampton Comm Coll (PA)
Ohlone Coll (CA)
Oklahoma City Comm Coll (OK)
Quinsigamond Comm Coll (MA)
Raritan Valley Comm Coll (NJ)
South Piedmont Comm Coll (NC)
Springfield Tech Comm Coll (MA)
Tulsa Comm Coll (OK)
Vincennes U (IN)

BOTANY/PLANT BIOLOGY
Iowa Lakes Comm Coll (IA)
Pensacola State Coll (FL)
South Florida State Coll (FL)

BROADCAST JOURNALISM
Amarillo Coll (TX)
Iowa Central Comm Coll (IA)
Kingsborough Comm Coll of the City U of New York (NY)
Navarro Coll (TX)
Ocean County Coll (NJ)
Ohlone Coll (CA)
Oklahoma City Comm Coll (OK)
Palomar Coll (CA)
Pasadena City Coll (CA)
San Joaquin Delta Coll (CA)

BUILDING/CONSTRUCTION FINISHING, MANAGEMENT, AND INSPECTION RELATED
Coll of Southern Idaho (ID)
Coll of Southern Maryland (MD)
The Comm Coll of Baltimore County (MD)
Cumberland County Coll (NJ)
Delgado Comm Coll (LA)
Delta Coll (MI)
Fayetteville Tech Comm Coll (NC)
Frederick Comm Coll (MD)
Gwinnett Tech Coll (GA)
Haywood Comm Coll (NC)
Mid-Plains Comm Coll, North Platte (NE)
Mohave Comm Coll (AZ)
Montgomery Coll (MD)
Mt. San Antonio Coll (CA)
Nebraska Indian Comm Coll (NE)
Oakton Comm Coll (IL)
St. Philip's Coll (TX)
Salt Lake Comm Coll (UT)
Seminole State Coll of Florida (FL)
Springfield Tech Comm Coll (MA)
Victor Valley Coll (CA)

BUILDING/CONSTRUCTION SITE MANAGEMENT
Coll of the Canyons (CA)
Coll of the Desert (CA)
The Comm Coll of Baltimore County (MD)
Dunwoody Coll of Technology (MN)
Erie Comm Coll, North Campus (NY)
Fox Valley Tech Coll (WI)
J. Sargeant Reynolds Comm Coll (VA)
Lehigh Carbon Comm Coll (PA)
The Ohio State U Ag Tech Inst (OH)
State Fair Comm Coll (MO)

BUILDING CONSTRUCTION TECHNOLOGY
Central Maine Comm Coll (ME)
Cochise Coll, Douglas (AZ)
Kennebec Valley Comm Coll (ME)
Lake Area Tech Inst (SD)
Midlands Tech Coll (SC)
Mitchell Tech Inst (SD)
Penn Foster Coll (AZ)
Sheridan Coll (WY)
Truckee Meadows Comm Coll (NV)

BUILDING/HOME/CONSTRUCTION INSPECTION
Bucks County Comm Coll (PA)
Harrisburg Area Comm Coll (PA)
Oklahoma State U, Oklahoma City (OK)
Orange Coast Coll (CA)
Palomar Coll (CA)
Pasadena City Coll (CA)
Phoenix Coll (AZ)
South Suburban Coll (IL)
Vincennes U (IN)

BUILDING/PROPERTY MAINTENANCE
Bellingham Tech Coll (WA)
Cape Fear Comm Coll (NC)
Central Texas Coll (TX)
Central Wyoming Coll (WY)
Century Coll (MN)
Comm Coll of Allegheny County (PA)
Delgado Comm Coll (LA)
Delta Coll (MI)
Erie Comm Coll (NY)
Guilford Tech Comm Coll (NC)
Luzerne County Comm Coll (PA)
Mitchell Tech Inst (SD)
Mohawk Valley Comm Coll (NY)
Pensacola State Coll (FL)
Piedmont Comm Coll (NC)
Wayne County Comm Coll District (MI)

BUSINESS ADMINISTRATION AND MANAGEMENT
Alamance Comm Coll (NC)
Alexandria Tech and Comm Coll (MN)
Allen Comm Coll (KS)
Alvin Comm Coll (TX)
Amarillo Coll (TX)
American Samoa Comm Coll (AS)
Ancilla Coll (IN)
Anne Arundel Comm Coll (MD)
Anoka-Ramsey Comm Coll (MN)
Anoka-Ramsey Comm Coll, Cambridge Campus (MN)
Antelope Valley Coll (CA)
Arapahoe Comm Coll (CO)
Arizona Western Coll (AZ)
Austin Comm Coll District (TX)
Bainbridge State Coll (GA)
Berkeley Coll–Westchester Campus (NY)
Blue Ridge Comm and Tech Coll (WV)
Borough of Manhattan Comm Coll of the City U of New York (NY)
Bowling Green State U-Firelands Coll (OH)
Brookhaven Coll (TX)
Bucks County Comm Coll (PA)
Bunker Hill Comm Coll (MA)
Burlington County Coll (NJ)
Butler County Comm Coll (PA)
Cambria-Rowe Business Coll, Indiana (PA)
Camden County Coll (NJ)
Ca&nnada Coll (CA)
Cape Fear Comm Coll (NC)
Career Tech Coll, Monroe (LA)
Carl Albert State Coll (OK)
Carroll Comm Coll (MD)
Carteret Comm Coll (NC)
Casper Coll (WY)
Catawba Valley Comm Coll (NC)
Cayuga County Comm Coll (NY)
Cecil Coll (MD)
Cedar Valley Coll (TX)
Central Maine Comm Coll (ME)
Central Oregon Comm Coll (OR)
Central Texas Coll (TX)
Central Virginia Comm Coll (VA)
Central Wyoming Coll (WY)
Century Coll (MN)
Chandler-Gilbert Comm Coll (AZ)
Chesapeake Coll (MD)
Chipola Coll (FL)
Cincinnati State Tech and Comm Coll (OH)
Citrus Coll (CA)
City Colls of Chicago, Olive-Harvey College (IL)
Clark Coll (WA)
Cleveland Comm Coll (NC)
Cleveland State Comm Coll (TN)
Clinton Comm Coll (NY)
Cloud County Comm Coll (KS)
Coastal Bend Coll (TX)
Cochise Coll, Douglas (AZ)

CollAmerica–Flagstaff (AZ)
Coll of Central Florida (FL)
Coll of Marin (CA)
Coll of Southern Idaho (ID)
Coll of Southern Maryland (MD)
Coll of the Canyons (CA)
Coll of the Desert (CA)
The Coll of Westchester (NY)
Collin County Comm Coll District (TX)
Columbia-Greene Comm Coll (NY)
Comm Coll of Allegheny County (PA)
The Comm Coll of Baltimore County (MD)
Comm Coll of Denver (CO)
Comm Coll of Philadelphia (PA)
Comm Coll of Rhode Island (RI)
Copiah-Lincoln Comm Coll (MS)
Corning Comm Coll (NY)
County Coll of Morris (NJ)
Crowder Coll (MO)
Cumberland County Coll (NJ)
Dabney S. Lancaster Comm Coll (VA)
Dakota Coll at Bottineau (ND)
Darton State Coll (GA)
Davis Coll (OH)
Daytona State Coll (FL)
Dean Coll (MA)
Delaware Tech & Comm Coll, Terry Campus (DE)
Delgado Comm Coll (LA)
Delta Coll (MI)
Denmark Tech Coll (SC)
Des Moines Area Comm Coll (IA)
Duluth Business U (MN)
Dutchess Comm Coll (NY)
Dyersburg State Comm Coll (TN)
Eastern Arizona Coll (AZ)
Eastern Gateway Comm Coll (OH)
Eastern Wyoming Coll (WY)
Edison Comm Coll (OH)
El Centro Coll (TX)
Elgin Comm Coll (IL)
Elizabethtown Comm and Tech Coll, Elizabethtown (KY)
Erie Comm Coll (NY)
Erie Comm Coll, North Campus (NY)
Erie Comm Coll, South Campus (NY)
Fayetteville Tech Comm Coll (NC)
Finger Lakes Comm Coll (NY)
Fiorello H. LaGuardia Comm Coll of the City U of New York (NY)
Florida SouthWestern State Coll (FL)
Florida State Coll at Jacksonville (FL)
Forrest Coll (SC)
Forsyth Tech Comm Coll (NC)
Fox Valley Tech Coll (WI)
Frederick Comm Coll (MD)
Front Range Comm Coll (CO)
Garrett Coll (MD)
Gateway Comm and Tech Coll (KY)
Gateway Comm Coll (CT)
Gateway Tech Coll (WI)
Genesee Comm Coll (NY)
George C. Wallace Comm Coll (AL)
Georgia Highlands Coll (GA)
Golden West Coll (CA)
Goodwin Coll (CT)
Grand Rapids Comm Coll (MI)
Great Basin Coll (NV)
Great Falls Coll Montana State U (MT)
Greenfield Comm Coll (MA)
Greenville Tech Coll (SC)
Guilford Tech Comm Coll (NC)
Gulf Coast State Coll (FL)
Gwinnett Tech Coll (GA)
Hagerstown Comm Coll (MD)
Halifax Comm Coll (NC)
Harford Comm Coll (MD)
Harper Coll (IL)
Harrisburg Area Comm Coll (PA)
Haywood Comm Coll (NC)
Hennepin Tech Coll (MN)
Hillsborough Comm Coll (FL)
Hocking Coll (OH)
Holyoke Comm Coll (MA)
Hopkinsville Comm Coll (KY)
Horry-Georgetown Tech Coll (SC)
Housatonic Comm Coll (CT)
Houston Comm Coll (TX)
Howard Comm Coll (MD)
Hudson County Comm Coll (NJ)
IBMC Coll (CO)
Illinois Eastern Comm Colls, Olney Central College (IL)

Illinois Eastern Comm Colls, Wabash Valley College (IL)
Iowa Central Comm Coll (IA)
Iowa Lakes Comm Coll (IA)
Jackson State Comm Coll (TN)
James H. Faulkner State Comm Coll (AL)
James Sprunt Comm Coll (NC)
Jamestown Business Coll (NY)
Jamestown Comm Coll (NY)
Jefferson Coll (MO)
Jefferson Comm Coll (NY)
Johnston Comm Coll (NC)
John Tyler Comm Coll (VA)
J. Sargeant Reynolds Comm Coll (VA)
Kalamazoo Valley Comm Coll (MI)
Kankakee Comm Coll (IL)
Kellogg Comm Coll (MI)
Kilgore Coll (TX)
Kingsborough Comm Coll of the City U of New York (NY)
Kirtland Comm Coll (MI)
Kishwaukee Coll (IL)
Lake Land Coll (IL)
Lakeland Comm Coll (OH)
Lake Region State Coll (ND)
Lamar Comm Coll (CO)
Landmark Coll (VT)
Laramie County Comm Coll (WY)
Lehigh Carbon Comm Coll (PA)
Lenoir Comm Coll (NC)
Lone Star Coll–CyFair (TX)
Lone Star Coll–Kingwood (TX)
Lone Star Coll–Montgomery (TX)
Lone Star Coll–North Harris (TX)
Lone Star Coll–Tomball (TX)
Lone Star Coll–U Park (TX)
Long Island Business Inst (NY)
Lorain County Comm Coll (OH)
Los Angeles Trade-Tech Coll (CA)
Lower Columbia Coll (WA)
Luzerne County Comm Coll (PA)
Macomb Comm Coll (MI)
Manchester Comm Coll (CT)
Manor Coll (PA)
Massachusetts Bay Comm Coll (MA)
Maysville Comm and Tech Coll, Maysville (KY)
McHenry County Coll (IL)
Mesa Comm Coll (AZ)
Miami Dade Coll (FL)
Middlesex Comm Coll (MA)
Middlesex County Coll (NJ)
Midlands Tech Coll (SC)
Mid-Plains Comm Coll, North Platte (NE)
Minneapolis Comm and Tech Coll (MN)
Minnesota State Coll–Southeast Tech (MN)
Minnesota West Comm and Tech Coll (MN)
MiraCosta Coll (CA)
Mohave Comm Coll (AZ)
Mohawk Valley Comm Coll (NY)
Monroe Comm Coll (NY)
Monroe County Comm Coll (MI)
Montcalm Comm Coll (MI)
Montgomery Comm Coll (NC)
Montgomery County Comm Coll (PA)
Moraine Park Tech Coll (WI)
Moraine Valley Comm Coll (IL)
Morgan Comm Coll (CO)
Motlow State Comm Coll (TN)
Mott Comm Coll (MI)
Mt. San Antonio Coll (CA)
Mount Wachusett Comm Coll (MA)
Nassau Comm Coll (NY)
Navarro Coll (TX)
Nebraska Indian Comm Coll (NE)
New Mexico Jr Coll (NM)
Niagara County Comm Coll (NY)
Northampton Comm Coll (PA)
Northcentral Tech Coll (WI)
North Central Texas Coll (TX)
Northeastern Jr Coll (CO)
Northeast Iowa Comm Coll (IA)
Northern Essex Comm Coll (MA)
Northern Virginia Comm Coll (VA)
North Hennepin Comm Coll (MN)
North Iowa Area Comm Coll (IA)
Northland Comm Coll (MN)
North Shore Comm Coll (MA)
Northwest Coll (WY)
Northwestern Coll (IL)
Northwestern Michigan Coll (MI)
Northwest State Comm Coll (OH)
Northwest Tech Coll (MN)
Norwalk Comm Coll (CT)

Ocean County Coll (NJ)
Ohio Business Coll, Sandusky (OH)
Ohlone Coll (CA)
Oklahoma City Comm Coll (OK)
Oklahoma State U, Oklahoma City (OK)
Olympic Coll (WA)
Orange Coast Coll (CA)
Otero Jr Coll (CO)
Owensboro Comm and Tech Coll (KY)
Ozarks Tech Comm Coll (MO)
Palomar Coll (CA)
Paris Jr Coll (TX)
Pasadena City Coll (CA)
Pasco-Hernando State Coll (FL)
Penn Foster Coll (AZ)
Pennsylvania Inst of Technology (PA)
Pensacola State Coll (FL)
Phoenix Coll (AZ)
Piedmont Comm Coll (NC)
Plaza Coll (NY)
Potomac State Coll of West Virginia U (WV)
Pueblo Comm Coll (CO)
Queensborough Comm Coll of the City U of New York (NY)
Quinsigamond Comm Coll (MA)
Rainy River Comm Coll (MN)
Randolph Comm Coll (NC)
Rappahannock Comm Coll (VA)
Raritan Valley Comm Coll (NJ)
Reading Area Comm Coll (PA)
Renton Tech Coll (WA)
Richland Comm Coll (IL)
Richmond Comm Coll (NC)
Ridgewater Coll (MN)
Riverland Comm Coll (MN)
Roane State Comm Coll (TN)
Rockland Comm Coll (NY)
Rock Valley Coll (IL)
Rogue Comm Coll (OR)
St. Philip's Coll (TX)
Salt Lake Comm Coll (UT)
San Diego Miramar Coll (CA)
San Jacinto Coll District (TX)
San Joaquin Delta Coll (CA)
San Joaquin Valley Coll, Bakersfield (CA)
San Joaquin Valley Coll–Online (CA)
San Juan Coll (NM)
Schoolcraft Coll (MI)
Scottsdale Comm Coll (AZ)
Seminole State Coll (OK)
Seminole State Coll of Florida (FL)
Shawnee Comm Coll (IL)
Sierra Coll (CA)
Sisseton-Wahpeton Coll (SD)
Somerset Comm Coll (KY)
Southeastern Comm Coll (IA)
South Florida State Coll (FL)
South Hills School of Business & Technology, State College (PA)
South Piedmont Comm Coll (NC)
Southwestern Indian Polytechnic Inst (NM)
Southwestern Michigan Coll (MI)
Spartanburg Comm Coll (SC)
Springfield Tech Comm Coll (MA)
Stark State Coll (OH)
State Fair Comm Coll (MO)
State U of New York Coll of Technology at Alfred (NY)
Sullivan County Comm Coll (NY)
Terra State Comm Coll (OH)
Tohono O'odham Comm Coll (AZ)
Tompkins Cortland Comm Coll (NY)
Trident Tech Coll (SC)
Trinidad State Jr Coll (CO)
Trinity Valley Comm Coll (TX)
Trocaire Coll (NY)
Truckee Meadows Comm Coll (NV)
Tulsa Comm Coll (OK)
Tunxis Comm Coll (CT)
Tyler Jr Coll (TX)
Ulster County Comm Coll (NY)
Umpqua Comm Coll (OR)
U of Alaska Southeast, Sitka Campus (AK)
U of Cincinnati Clermont Coll (OH)
Victoria Coll (TX)
Victor Valley Coll (CA)
Vincennes U (IN)
Virginia Western Comm Coll (VA)
Volunteer State Comm Coll (TN)
Walters State Comm Coll (TN)
Waukesha County Tech Coll (WI)
Wayne County Comm Coll District (MI)
Wenatchee Valley Coll (WA)

Westchester Comm Coll (NY)
Western Dakota Tech Inst (SD)
Western Iowa Tech Comm Coll (IA)
Western Wyoming Comm Coll (WY)
Westmoreland County Comm Coll (PA)
Whatcom Comm Coll (WA)
White Mountains Comm Coll (NH)
Wisconsin Indianhead Tech Coll (WI)
Wor-Wic Comm Coll (MD)
Wright State U–Lake Campus (OH)
Wytheville Comm Coll (VA)
York County Comm Coll (ME)

BUSINESS ADMINISTRATION, MANAGEMENT AND OPERATIONS RELATED
Anne Arundel Comm Coll (MD)
Blue Ridge Comm and Tech Coll (WV)
Bunker Hill Comm Coll (MA)
Chandler-Gilbert Comm Coll (AZ)
Cincinnati State Tech and Comm Coll (OH)
Coll of Central Florida (FL)
Comm Care Coll (OK)
Genesee Comm Coll (NY)
John Tyler Comm Coll (VA)
J. Sargeant Reynolds Comm Coll (VA)
Pensacola State Coll (FL)
Rappahannock Comm Coll (VA)
Southwest Virginia Comm Coll (VA)
Waukesha County Tech Coll (WI)
Westhill U (Mexico)
Williston State Coll (ND)

BUSINESS AND PERSONAL/ FINANCIAL SERVICES MARKETING
Hutchinson Comm Coll (KS)
North Central Texas Coll (TX)
Northwestern Michigan Coll (MI)

BUSINESS AUTOMATION/ TECHNOLOGY/DATA ENTRY
Casper Coll (WY)
Clark Coll (WA)
Comm Coll of Allegheny County (PA)
Crowder Coll (MO)
Dakota Coll at Bottineau (ND)
Danville Area Comm Coll (IL)
Delaware Tech & Comm Coll, Terry Campus (DE)
El Centro Coll (TX)
Garrett Coll (MD)
Guam Comm Coll (GU)
Houston Comm Coll (TX)
Illinois Eastern Comm Colls, Frontier Community College (IL)
Illinois Eastern Comm Colls, Lincoln Trail College (IL)
Illinois Eastern Comm Colls, Olney Central College (IL)
Illinois Eastern Comm Colls, Wabash Valley College (IL)
Iowa Lakes Comm Coll (IA)
Kaskaskia Coll (IL)
Lakes Region Comm Coll (NH)
Macomb Comm Coll (MI)
Miami Dade Coll (FL)
Minneapolis Comm and Tech Coll (MN)
Mitchell Tech Inst (SD)
Northeast Iowa Comm Coll (IA)
Northwestern Michigan Coll (MI)
Panola Coll (TX)
Paris Jr Coll (TX)
Pasadena City Coll (CA)
Potomac State Coll of West Virginia U (WV)
Pueblo Comm Coll (CO)
Schoolcraft Coll (MI)
Shawnee Comm Coll (IL)
Trinidad State Jr Coll (CO)
Western Iowa Tech Comm Coll (IA)

BUSINESS/COMMERCE
Allen Comm Coll (KS)
Alvin Comm Coll (TX)
Anne Arundel Comm Coll (MD)
Anoka-Ramsey Comm Coll (MN)
Anoka-Ramsey Comm Coll, Cambridge Campus (MN)
Antelope Valley Coll (CA)
Arizona Western Coll (AZ)
Arkansas Northeastern Coll (AR)
Austin Comm Coll District (TX)
Bossier Parish Comm Coll (LA)
Brookhaven Coll (TX)
Bucks County Comm Coll (PA)
Butler County Comm Coll (PA)

Carl Albert State Coll (OK)
Cecil Coll (MD)
Cedar Valley Coll (TX)
Central Virginia Comm Coll (VA)
Central Wyoming Coll (WY)
Chandler-Gilbert Comm Coll (AZ)
Chesapeake Coll (MD)
Citrus Coll (CA)
Coll of Central Florida (FL)
Coll of Marin (CA)
Coll of Southern Maryland (MD)
Coll of the Desert (CA)
Collin County Comm Coll District (TX)
The Comm Coll of Baltimore County (MD)
Comm Coll of Rhode Island (RI)
Delaware Tech & Comm Coll, Terry Campus (DE)
El Centro Coll (TX)
Garrett Coll (MD)
Goodwin Coll (CT)
Great Basin Coll (NV)
Greenfield Comm Coll (MA)
Hagerstown Comm Coll (MD)
Harrisburg Area Comm Coll (PA)
Hinds Comm Coll (MS)
Humacao Comm Coll (PR)
Hutchinson Comm Coll (KS)
Jefferson Coll (MO)
John Tyler Comm Coll (VA)
Kaskaskia Coll (IL)
Kent State U at Ashtabula (OH)
Kent State U at East Liverpool (OH)
Kent State U at Salem (OH)
Kent State U at Trumbull (OH)
Kent State U at Tuscarawas (OH)
Kilgore Coll (TX)
Lakes Region Comm Coll (NH)
Landmark Coll (VT)
Laramie County Comm Coll (WY)
Lehigh Carbon Comm Coll (PA)
Louisiana Delta Comm Coll, Monroe (LA)
Macomb Comm Coll (MI)
Massachusetts Bay Comm Coll (MA)
Mesabi Range Coll (MN)
Midlands Tech Coll (SC)
Minnesota West Comm and Tech Coll (MN)
Montgomery Coll (MD)
Montgomery County Comm Coll (PA)
Moraine Valley Comm Coll (IL)
Mott Comm Coll (MI)
Mount Wachusett Comm Coll (MA)
Northampton Comm Coll (PA)
Northern Virginia Comm Coll (VA)
Northwest Coll (WY)
Northwest State Comm Coll (OH)
Nunez Comm Coll (LA)
Ocean County Coll (NJ)
Oklahoma City Comm Coll (OK)
Oklahoma State U Inst of Technology (OK)
Owens Comm Coll, Toledo (OH)
Palomar Coll (CA)
Paris Jr Coll (TX)
Penn State DuBois (PA)
Penn State Fayette, The Eberly Campus (PA)
Penn State Mont Alto (PA)
Penn State Shenango (PA)
Pennsylvania Highlands Comm Coll (PA)
Pensacola State Coll (FL)
Phoenix Coll (AZ)
Quinsigamond Comm Coll (MA)
Raritan Valley Comm Coll (NJ)
Rogue Comm Coll (OR)
Saginaw Chippewa Tribal Coll (MI)
St. Clair County Comm Coll (MI)
San Jacinto Coll District (TX)
San Joaquin Valley Coll, Visalia (CA)
Schoolcraft Coll (MI)
Seminole State Coll (OK)
Sheridan Coll (WY)
Sierra Coll (CA)
Southern U at Shreveport (LA)
South Florida State Coll (FL)
South Louisiana Comm Coll (LA)
Southwestern Indian Polytechnic Inst (NM)
Spartanburg Methodist Coll (SC)
Springfield Tech Comm Coll (MA)
Tech Coll of the Lowcountry (SC)
Terra State Comm Coll (OH)
Three Rivers Comm Coll (CT)
Tulsa Comm Coll (OK)
U of Arkansas Comm Coll at Batesville (AR)

U of Arkansas Comm Coll at Hope (AR)
U of Arkansas Comm Coll at Morrilton (AR)
U of Cincinnati Clermont Coll (OH)
Victor Valley Coll (CA)
Vincennes U (IN)
Western Nevada Coll (NV)
Westmoreland County Comm Coll (PA)
Wor-Wic Comm Coll (MD)
Wright State U–Lake Campus (OH)

BUSINESS/CORPORATE COMMUNICATIONS
Cecil Coll (MD)
Houston Comm Coll (TX)
Montgomery County Comm Coll (PA)

BUSINESS MACHINE REPAIR
Comm Coll of Allegheny County (PA)
Iowa Lakes Comm Coll (IA)
Ozarks Tech Comm Coll (MO)

BUSINESS, MANAGEMENT, AND MARKETING RELATED
Bucks County Comm Coll (PA)
Butler County Comm Coll (PA)
Chandler-Gilbert Comm Coll (AZ)
Cloud County Comm Coll (KS)
County Coll of Morris (NJ)
Eastern Arizona Coll (AZ)
Genesee Comm Coll (NY)
Long Island Business Inst (NY)
Manor Coll (PA)
Niagara County Comm Coll (NY)
Northwestern Michigan Coll (MI)
Queensborough Comm Coll of the City U of New York (NY)
Southeastern Coll–Greenacres (FL)
Tulsa Comm Coll (OK)

BUSINESS/MANAGERIAL ECONOMICS
Morgan Comm Coll (CO)
South Florida State Coll (FL)

BUSINESS OPERATIONS SUPPORT AND SECRETARIAL SERVICES RELATED
Bunker Hill Comm Coll (MA)
Central Virginia Comm Coll (VA)
Davis Coll (OH)
Eastern Arizona Coll (AZ)
Gateway Tech Coll (WI)
Genesee Comm Coll (NY)
J. Sargeant Reynolds Comm Coll (VA)
Southwest Virginia Comm Coll (VA)

BUSINESS TEACHER EDUCATION
Allen Comm Coll (KS)
Amarillo Coll (TX)
Bainbridge State Coll (GA)
Darton State Coll (GA)
Eastern Arizona Coll (AZ)
Eastern Wyoming Coll (WY)
Hinds Comm Coll (MS)
Iowa Central Comm Coll (IA)
Iowa Lakes Comm Coll (IA)
Morgan Comm Coll (CO)
Mt. San Antonio Coll (CA)
New Mexico Jr Coll (NM)
Northeastern Jr Coll (CO)
Northern Essex Comm Coll (MA)
Paris Jr Coll (TX)
Rio Hondo Coll (CA)
Roane State Comm Coll (TN)
South Florida State Coll (FL)
Trinity Valley Comm Coll (TX)

CABINETMAKING AND MILLWORK
Bucks County Comm Coll (PA)
Coll of Southern Idaho (ID)
George C. Wallace Comm Coll (AL)
Harrisburg Area Comm Coll (PA)
Macomb Comm Coll (MI)
Palomar Coll (CA)
Sierra Coll (CA)

CAD/CADD DRAFTING/DESIGN TECHNOLOGY
Arizona Western Coll (AZ)
Butler County Comm Coll (PA)
Central Oregon Comm Coll (OR)
Century Coll (MN)
Corning Comm Coll (NY)
Danville Area Comm Coll (IL)
Dunwoody Coll of Technology (MN)
Elgin Comm Coll (IL)

Erie Comm Coll, South Campus (NY)
Front Range Comm Coll (CO)
Gateway Comm and Tech Coll (KY)
Gulf Coast State Coll (FL)
Hennepin Tech Coll (MN)
J. Sargeant Reynolds Comm Coll (VA)
Kalamazoo Valley Comm Coll (MI)
Kent State U at Tuscarawas (OH)
Kishwaukee Coll (IL)
Miami Dade Coll (FL)
Minnesota State Coll–Southeast Tech (MN)
Mohawk Valley Comm Coll (NY)
Northampton Comm Coll (PA)
Northwest Coll (WY)
Northwest State Comm Coll (OH)
St. Philip's Coll (TX)
Sheridan Coll (WY)
South Suburban Coll (IL)
State Fair Comm Coll (MO)
Sullivan Coll of Technology and Design (KY)
Tallahassee Comm Coll (FL)
Tyler Jr Coll (TX)
Wayne County Comm Coll District (MI)

CARDIOVASCULAR SCIENCE
Forsyth Tech Comm Coll (NC)

CARDIOVASCULAR TECHNOLOGY
Bunker Hill Comm Coll (MA)
Comm Coll of the Air Force (AL)
Darton State Coll (GA)
El Centro Coll (TX)
Florida SouthWestern State Coll (FL)
Florida State Coll at Jacksonville (FL)
Forsyth Tech Comm Coll (NC)
Harper Coll (IL)
Harrisburg Area Comm Coll (PA)
Houston Comm Coll (TX)
Howard Comm Coll (MD)
Kirtland Comm Coll (MI)
Northland Comm Coll (MN)
Orange Coast Coll (CA)
St. Vincent's Coll (CT)
Southern U at Shreveport (LA)

CARPENTRY
Alamance Comm Coll (NC)
Arizona Western Coll (AZ)
Austin Comm Coll District (TX)
Central Wyoming Coll (WY)
Comm Coll of Allegheny County (PA)
Delta Coll (MI)
George C. Wallace Comm Coll (AL)
Hawkeye Comm Coll (IA)
Hennepin Tech Coll (MN)
Hutchinson Comm Coll (KS)
Iowa Central Comm Coll (IA)
Iowa Lakes Comm Coll (IA)
Kaskaskia Coll (IL)
Los Angeles Trade-Tech Coll (CA)
Minnesota State Coll–Southeast Tech (MN)
Nebraska Indian Comm Coll (NE)
New Mexico Jr Coll (NM)
North Iowa Area Comm Coll (IA)
Northland Comm Coll (MN)
Palomar Coll (CA)
Ridgewater Coll (MN)
San Juan Coll (NM)
South Louisiana Comm Coll (LA)
Southwestern Illinois Coll (IL)
Southwestern Michigan Coll (MI)
Western Iowa Tech Comm Coll (IA)
Williston State Coll (ND)

CASINO MANAGEMENT
Oklahoma State U Inst of Technology (OK)
Wenatchee Valley Coll (WA)
Westmoreland County Comm Coll (PA)

CERAMIC ARTS AND CERAMICS
Palomar Coll (CA)

CERAMIC SCIENCES AND ENGINEERING
Hocking Coll (OH)

CHEMICAL ENGINEERING
Burlington County Coll (NJ)
Kilgore Coll (TX)
Los Angeles Trade-Tech Coll (CA)
Monroe Comm Coll (NY)
Olympic Coll (WA)
South Florida State Coll (FL)

CHEMICAL PROCESS TECHNOLOGY
San Jacinto Coll District (TX)

CHEMICAL TECHNOLOGY
Alvin Comm Coll (TX)
Amarillo Coll (TX)
Bucks County Comm Coll (PA)
Cape Fear Comm Coll (NC)
Cincinnati State Tech and Comm Coll (OH)
Comm Coll of Allegheny County (PA)
Comm Coll of Philadelphia (PA)
Comm Coll of Rhode Island (RI)
Corning Comm Coll (NY)
County Coll of Morris (NJ)
Delta Coll (MI)
Guilford Tech Comm Coll (NC)
Houston Comm Coll (TX)
Kalamazoo Valley Comm Coll (MI)
Kellogg Comm Coll (MI)
Lehigh Carbon Comm Coll (PA)
Massachusetts Bay Comm Coll (MA)
Mohawk Valley Comm Coll (NY)
Niagara County Comm Coll (NY)
Pensacola State Coll (FL)
Raritan Valley Comm Coll (NJ)
San Jacinto Coll District (TX)
Texas State Tech Coll Harlingen (TX)
Victoria Coll (TX)
Westmoreland County Comm Coll (PA)

CHEMISTRY
Allen Comm Coll (KS)
Amarillo Coll (TX)
Arizona Western Coll (AZ)
Austin Comm Coll District (TX)
Bainbridge State Coll (GA)
Bunker Hill Comm Coll (MA)
Burlington County Coll (NJ)
Ca&nnada Coll (CA)
Casper Coll (WY)
Cecil Coll (MD)
Central Texas Coll (TX)
Cochise Coll, Douglas (AZ)
Coll of Central Florida (FL)
Coll of Marin (CA)
Coll of Southern Idaho (ID)
Coll of the Desert (CA)
Comm Coll of Allegheny County (PA)
Copiah-Lincoln Comm Coll (MS)
Dakota Coll at Bottineau (ND)
Darton State Coll (GA)
Eastern Arizona Coll (AZ)
Finger Lakes Comm Coll (NY)
Frederick Comm Coll (MD)
Genesee Comm Coll (NY)
Georgia Highlands Coll (GA)
Grand Rapids Comm Coll (MI)
Great Basin Coll (NV)
Harford Comm Coll (MD)
Harper Coll (IL)
Harrisburg Area Comm Coll (PA)
Hinds Comm Coll (MS)
Iowa Lakes Comm Coll (IA)
Kankakee Comm Coll (IL)
Kilgore Coll (TX)
Kingsborough Comm Coll of the City U of New York (NY)
Laramie County Comm Coll (WY)
Lehigh Carbon Comm Coll (PA)
Lorain County Comm Coll (OH)
Macomb Comm Coll (MI)
Miami Dade Coll (FL)
Minneapolis Comm and Tech Coll (MN)
Monroe Comm Coll (NY)
Navarro Coll (TX)
New Mexico Jr Coll (NM)
Northampton Comm Coll (PA)
North Hennepin Comm Coll (MN)
Northwest Coll (WY)
Oklahoma City Comm Coll (OK)
Orange Coast Coll (CA)
Palomar Coll (CA)
Paris Jr Coll (TX)
Pasadena City Coll (CA)
Pensacola State Coll (FL)
Potomac State Coll of West Virginia U (WV)
Ridgewater Coll (MN)
Roane State Comm Coll (TN)
St. Charles Comm Coll (MO)
St. Philip's Coll (TX)
Salt Lake Comm Coll (UT)
San Diego Miramar Coll (CA)
San Jacinto Coll District (TX)
San Joaquin Delta Coll (CA)
San Juan Coll (NM)
Sierra Coll (CA)
Southern U at Shreveport (LA)

South Florida State Coll (FL)
Springfield Tech Comm Coll (MA)
Terra State Comm Coll (OH)
Trinidad State Jr Coll (CO)
Trinity Valley Comm Coll (TX)
Truckee Meadows Comm Coll (NV)
Tyler Jr Coll (TX)
Umpqua Comm Coll (OR)
U of Cincinnati Clermont Coll (OH)
Vincennes U (IN)
Wenatchee Valley Coll (WA)
Western Wyoming Comm Coll (WY)
Wright State U–Lake Campus (OH)

CHEMISTRY RELATED
South Florida State Coll (FL)
Vincennes U (IN)

CHEMISTRY TEACHER EDUCATION
Anne Arundel Comm Coll (MD)
Bucks County Comm Coll (PA)
Carroll Comm Coll (MD)
The Comm Coll of Baltimore County (MD)
Harford Comm Coll (MD)
Montgomery Coll (MD)
Ulster County Comm Coll (NY)
Vincennes U (IN)

CHILD-CARE AND SUPPORT SERVICES MANAGEMENT
Anne Arundel Comm Coll (MD)
Antelope Valley Coll (CA)
Bevill State Comm Coll (AL)
Carroll Comm Coll (MD)
Cayuga County Comm Coll (NY)
Cecil Coll (MD)
Central Oregon Comm Coll (OR)
Chesapeake Coll (MD)
Cloud County Comm Coll (KS)
Coll of Southern Idaho (ID)
Coll of Southern Maryland (MD)
Coll of the Desert (CA)
The Comm Coll of Baltimore County (MD)
Dakota Coll at Bottineau (ND)
Dutchess Comm Coll (NY)
Eastern Gateway Comm Coll (OH)
Erie Comm Coll (NY)
Florida State Coll at Jacksonville (FL)
Forrest Coll (SC)
Gadsden State Comm Coll (AL)
Goodwin Coll (CT)
Grand Rapids Comm Coll (MI)
Greenville Tech Coll (SC)
Hagerstown Comm Coll (MD)
Haywood Comm Coll (NC)
H. Councill Trenholm State Tech Coll (AL)
Hillsborough Comm Coll (FL)
Holyoke Comm Coll (MA)
Hopkinsville Comm Coll (KY)
Hutchinson Comm Coll (KS)
Jefferson Coll (MO)
Jefferson Comm Coll (NY)
Jefferson State Comm Coll (AL)
Kilgore Coll (TX)
Kishwaukee Coll (IL)
Lake Land Coll (IL)
Lurleen B. Wallace Comm Coll (AL)
Macomb Comm Coll (MI)
Massachusetts Bay Comm Coll (MA)
Minneapolis Comm and Tech Coll (MN)
Minnesota West Comm and Tech Coll (MN)
MiraCosta Coll (CA)
Montcalm Comm Coll (MI)
Montgomery County Comm Coll (PA)
Mount Wachusett Comm Coll (MA)
Nebraska Indian Comm Coll (NE)
Northwestern Michigan Coll (MI)
Northwest-Shoals Comm Coll (AL)
Northwest State Comm Coll (OH)
Northwest Tech Coll (MN)
Orange Coast Coll (CA)
Palomar Coll (CA)
Pennsylvania Highlands Comm Coll (PA)
Pensacola State Coll (FL)
Phoenix Coll (AZ)
Piedmont Comm Coll (NC)
Reading Area Comm Coll (PA)
Reid State Tech Coll (AL)
Rogue Comm Coll (OR)
St. Clair County Comm Coll (MI)
State Fair Comm Coll (MO)
Three Rivers Comm Coll (CT)

Tompkins Cortland Comm Coll (NY)
U of Arkansas Comm Coll at Hope (AR)
Victor Valley Coll (CA)
Vincennes U (IN)
Wayne County Comm Coll District (MI)
Western Nevada Coll (NV)
Wor-Wic Comm Coll (MD)

CHILD-CARE PROVISION
Bossier Parish Comm Coll (LA)
Bucks County Comm Coll (PA)
Ca&nnada Coll (CA)
Central Texas Coll (TX)
City Colls of Chicago, Olive-Harvey College (IL)
Coll of Marin (CA)
Coll of the Canyons (CA)
Collin County Comm Coll District (TX)
Comm Coll of Allegheny County (PA)
Dakota Coll at Bottineau (ND)
Danville Area Comm Coll (IL)
Delta Coll (MI)
Des Moines Area Comm Coll (IA)
Elizabethtown Comm and Tech Coll, Elizabethtown (KY)
Florida SouthWestern State Coll (FL)
Florida State Coll at Jacksonville (FL)
Gulf Coast State Coll (FL)
Harper Coll (IL)
Hawkeye Comm Coll (IA)
Highland Comm Coll (IL)
Hinds Comm Coll (MS)
Hopkinsville Comm Coll (KY)
Iowa Lakes Comm Coll (IA)
John Tyler Comm Coll (VA)
J. Sargeant Reynolds Comm Coll (VA)
Kaskaskia Coll (IL)
Kilgore Coll (TX)
Kishwaukee Coll (IL)
Lakeland Comm Coll (OH)
Lake Region State Coll (ND)
Louisiana Delta Comm Coll, Monroe (LA)
Luzerne County Comm Coll (PA)
McHenry County Coll (IL)
Miami Dade Coll (FL)
Midlands Tech Coll (SC)
MiraCosta Coll (CA)
Montcalm Comm Coll (MI)
Montgomery Coll (MD)
Moraine Valley Comm Coll (IL)
Mott Comm Coll (MI)
Northland Comm Coll (MN)
Nunez Comm Coll (LA)
Oakton Comm Coll (IL)
Orange Coast Coll (CA)
Owensboro Comm and Tech Coll (KY)
Palomar Coll (CA)
Pensacola State Coll (FL)
Raritan Valley Comm Coll (NJ)
St. Charles Comm Coll (MO)
San Juan Coll (NM)
Somerset Comm Coll (KY)
South Suburban Coll (IL)
Southwestern Illinois Coll (IL)
Southwest Virginia Comm Coll (VA)
Tech Coll of the Lowcountry (SC)
Trident Tech Coll (SC)
Vincennes U (IN)
Western Iowa Tech Comm Coll (IA)
Westmoreland County Comm Coll (PA)

CHILD DEVELOPMENT
Alexandria Tech and Comm Coll (MN)
Allen Comm Coll (KS)
Alvin Comm Coll (TX)
Amarillo Coll (TX)
Antelope Valley Coll (CA)
Austin Comm Coll District (TX)
Brookhaven Coll (TX)
Carl Albert State Coll (OK)
Central Maine Comm Coll (ME)
Citrus Coll (CA)
Cleveland State Comm Coll (TN)
Cloud County Comm Coll (KS)
Coastal Bend Coll (TX)
Collin County Comm Coll District (TX)
Comm Coll of Allegheny County (PA)
Comm Coll of Aurora (CO)
Comm Coll of Denver (CO)
Copiah-Lincoln Comm Coll (MS)

Daytona State Coll (FL)
Dyersburg State Comm Coll (TN)
Edison Comm Coll (OH)
Frederick Comm Coll (MD)
Goodwin Coll (CT)
Hennepin Tech Coll (MN)
Hocking Coll (OH)
Housatonic Comm Coll (CT)
Houston Comm Coll (TX)
Howard Comm Coll (MD)
Illinois Eastern Comm Colls, Wabash Valley College (IL)
Iowa Lakes Comm Coll (IA)
James Sprunt Comm Coll (NC)
Jefferson Comm Coll (NY)
Kennebec Valley Comm Coll (ME)
Mesa Comm Coll (AZ)
Miami Dade Coll (FL)
Minneapolis Comm and Tech Coll (MN)
Monroe County Comm Coll (MI)
Mt. San Antonio Coll (CA)
Mount Wachusett Comm Coll (MA)
Northeastern Jr Coll (CO)
Northland Comm Coll (MN)
North Shore Comm Coll (MA)
Northwest-Shoals Comm Coll (AL)
Ohlone Coll (CA)
Oklahoma City Comm Coll (OK)
Otero Jr Coll (CO)
Pasadena City Coll (CA)
Reading Area Comm Coll (PA)
Richland Comm Coll (IL)
Rock Valley Coll (IL)
San Jacinto Coll District (TX)
Schoolcraft Coll (MI)
Seminole State Coll (OK)
Seminole State Coll of Florida (FL)
Shawnee Comm Coll (IL)
Sierra Coll (CA)
Southeastern Comm Coll (IA)
Stark State Coll (OH)
Tohono O'odham Comm Coll (AZ)
Trinity Valley Comm Coll (TX)
Tulsa Comm Coll (OK)
Tyler Jr Coll (TX)
Umpqua Comm Coll (OR)
U of Arkansas Comm Coll at Morrilton (AR)
Victor Valley Coll (CA)
Virginia Western Comm Coll (VA)
Volunteer State Comm Coll (TN)
Walters State Comm Coll (TN)
Westchester Comm Coll (NY)

CHIROPRACTIC ASSISTANT
Moraine Park Tech Coll (WI)

CINEMATOGRAPHY AND FILM/VIDEO PRODUCTION
Antelope Valley Coll (CA)
Bucks County Comm Coll (PA)
Camden County Coll (NJ)
Cape Fear Comm Coll (NC)
Coll of Marin (CA)
Coll of the Canyons (CA)
Comm Coll of Aurora (CO)
FIDM/Fashion Inst of Design & Merchandising, Los Angeles Campus (CA)
Hillsborough Comm Coll (FL)
Houston Comm Coll (TX)
Miami Dade Coll (FL)
Minneapolis Comm and Tech Coll (MN)
Mott Comm Coll (MI)
Northwest Coll (WY)
Oklahoma City Comm Coll (OK)
Orange Coast Coll (CA)
Pasadena City Coll (CA)
Piedmont Comm Coll (NC)
Raritan Valley Comm Coll (NJ)
Western Iowa Tech Comm Coll (IA)

CITY/URBAN, COMMUNITY AND REGIONAL PLANNING
South Florida State Coll (FL)

CIVIL DRAFTING AND CAD/CADD
Comm Coll of Allegheny County (PA)
Genesee Comm Coll (NY)
Harford Comm Coll (MD)
Sullivan Coll of Technology and Design (KY)

CIVIL ENGINEERING
American Samoa Comm Coll (AS)
Fiorello H. LaGuardia Comm Coll of the City U of New York (NY)

J. Sargeant Reynolds Comm Coll (VA)
Kilgore Coll (TX)
Potomac State Coll of West Virginia U (WV)
St. Charles Comm Coll (MO)
South Florida State Coll (FL)
Truckee Meadows Comm Coll (NV)
Vincennes U (IN)

CIVIL ENGINEERING RELATED
Haywood Comm Coll (NC)

CIVIL ENGINEERING TECHNOLOGY
Arapahoe Comm Coll (CO)
Arizona Western Coll (AZ)
Bellingham Tech Coll (WA)
Butler County Comm Coll (PA)
Central Maine Comm Coll (ME)
Cincinnati State Tech and Comm Coll (OH)
Comm Coll of Allegheny County (PA)
Copiah-Lincoln Comm Coll (MS)
Delaware Tech & Comm Coll, Terry Campus (DE)
Delgado Comm Coll (LA)
Des Moines Area Comm Coll (IA)
Eastern Arizona Coll (AZ)
Erie Comm Coll, North Campus (NY)
Fayetteville Tech Comm Coll (NC)
Florida SouthWestern State Coll (FL)
Gadsden State Comm Coll (AL)
Gateway Tech Coll (WI)
Guilford Tech Comm Coll (NC)
Gulf Coast State Coll (FL)
Harrisburg Area Comm Coll (PA)
Hawkeye Comm Coll (IA)
J. Sargeant Reynolds Comm Coll (VA)
Lake Land Coll (IL)
Lakeland Comm Coll (OH)
Lorain County Comm Coll (OH)
Macomb Comm Coll (MI)
Miami Dade Coll (FL)
Middlesex County Coll (NJ)
Midlands Tech Coll (SC)
Mohawk Valley Comm Coll (NY)
Monroe Comm Coll (NY)
Mt. San Antonio Coll (CA)
Nassau Comm Coll (NY)
Northern Essex Comm Coll (MA)
Oklahoma State U, Oklahoma City (OK)
Pensacola State Coll (FL)
Phoenix Coll (AZ)
Renton Tech Coll (WA)
San Joaquin Delta Coll (CA)
Seminole State Coll of Florida (FL)
South Florida State Coll (FL)
Springfield Tech Comm Coll (MA)
Stark State Coll (OH)
Tech Coll of the Lowcountry (SC)
Three Rivers Comm Coll (CT)
Trident Tech Coll (SC)
Umpqua Comm Coll (OR)
Virginia Western Comm Coll (VA)
Westchester Comm Coll (NY)
Wytheville Comm Coll (VA)

CLASSICS AND CLASSICAL LANGUAGES
Pasadena City Coll (CA)

CLINICAL LABORATORY SCIENCE/MEDICAL TECHNOLOGY
Amarillo Coll (TX)
Casper Coll (WY)
Chipola Coll (FL)
Coll of Central Florida (FL)
Coll of Southern Idaho (ID)
Darton State Coll (GA)
Georgia Highlands Coll (GA)
Hinds Comm Coll (MS)
Howard Comm Coll (MD)
Monroe County Comm Coll (MI)
Northeastern Jr Coll (CO)
Orange Coast Coll (CA)
Renton Tech Coll (WA)
South Florida State Coll (FL)
Westchester Comm Coll (NY)
Westmoreland County Comm Coll (PA)

CLINICAL/MEDICAL LABORATORY ASSISTANT
IntelliTec Coll, Grand Junction (CO)
Somerset Comm Coll (KY)
Wenatchee Valley Coll (WA)

Westmoreland County Comm Coll (PA)

CLINICAL/MEDICAL LABORATORY SCIENCE AND ALLIED PROFESSIONS RELATED
Houston Comm Coll (TX)

CLINICAL/MEDICAL LABORATORY TECHNOLOGY
Alamance Comm Coll (NC)
Alexandria Tech and Comm Coll (MN)
Anne Arundel Comm Coll (MD)
Arapahoe Comm Coll (CO)
Austin Comm Coll District (TX)
Blue Ridge Comm and Tech Coll (WV)
Bunker Hill Comm Coll (MA)
Camden County Coll (NJ)
Central Texas Coll (TX)
Cincinnati State Tech and Comm Coll (OH)
Coll of Southern Maryland (MD)
Coll of the Canyons (CA)
Comm Coll of Allegheny County (PA)
The Comm Coll of Baltimore County (MD)
Comm Coll of Philadelphia (PA)
Comm Coll of Rhode Island (RI)
Comm Coll of the Air Force (AL)
Copiah-Lincoln Comm Coll (MS)
Delgado Comm Coll (LA)
Des Moines Area Comm Coll (IA)
Dutchess Comm Coll (NY)
Edison Comm Coll (OH)
El Centro Coll (TX)
Elgin Comm Coll (IL)
Erie Comm Coll, North Campus (NY)
Florida State Coll at Jacksonville (FL)
Forsyth Tech Comm Coll (NC)
Gadsden State Comm Coll (AL)
Genesee Comm Coll (NY)
George C. Wallace Comm Coll (AL)
Greenville Tech Coll (SC)
Halifax Comm Coll (NC)
Harrisburg Area Comm Coll (PA)
Hawkeye Comm Coll (IA)
Hinds Comm Coll (MS)
Housatonic Comm Coll (CT)
Houston Comm Coll (TX)
Hutchinson Comm Coll (KS)
Iowa Central Comm Coll (IA)
Jackson State Comm Coll (TN)
Jefferson State Comm Coll (AL)
J. Sargeant Reynolds Comm Coll (VA)
Kankakee Comm Coll (IL)
Kaskaskia Coll (IL)
Lake Area Tech Inst (SD)
Lakeland Comm Coll (OH)
Lorain County Comm Coll (OH)
Manchester Comm Coll (CT)
Miami Dade Coll (FL)
Middlesex County Coll (NJ)
Midlands Tech Coll (SC)
Mid-Plains Comm Coll, North Platte (NE)
Minnesota West Comm and Tech Coll (MN)
Mitchell Tech Inst (SD)
Montgomery County Comm Coll (PA)
Moraine Park Tech Coll (WI)
Mount Wachusett Comm Coll (MA)
Nassau Comm Coll (NY)
Navarro Coll (TX)
New Mexico Jr Coll (NM)
Northcentral Tech Coll (WI)
Northeast Iowa Comm Coll (IA)
Northern Virginia Comm Coll (VA)
North Hennepin Comm Coll (MN)
North Iowa Area Comm Coll (IA)
Oakton Comm Coll (IL)
Panola Coll (TX)
Phoenix Coll (AZ)
Queensborough Comm Coll of the City U of New York (NY)
Reading Area Comm Coll (PA)
Roane State Comm Coll (TN)
St. Philip's Coll (TX)
Salt Lake Comm Coll (UT)
San Jacinto Coll District (TX)
San Juan Coll (NM)
Seminole State Coll (OK)
Shawnee Comm Coll (IL)
Southern U at Shreveport (LA)
South Louisiana Comm Coll (LA)
Southwestern Illinois Coll (IL)

Spartanburg Comm Coll (SC)
Spencerian Coll (KY)
Spencerian Coll–Lexington (KY)
Springfield Tech Comm Coll (MA)
Stark State Coll (OH)
Trident Tech Coll (SC)
Tulsa Comm Coll (OK)
Tyler Jr Coll (TX)
Victoria Coll (TX)
Volunteer State Comm Coll (TN)
Wenatchee Valley Coll (WA)
Westchester Comm Coll (NY)
Western Nevada Coll (NV)
Wytheville Comm Coll (VA)

CLINICAL/MEDICAL SOCIAL WORK
Central Texas Coll (TX)
Halifax Comm Coll (NC)
Piedmont Comm Coll (NC)

COMMERCIAL AND ADVERTISING ART
Alamance Comm Coll (NC)
Alexandria Tech and Comm Coll (MN)
Amarillo Coll (TX)
Austin Comm Coll District (TX)
Bucks County Comm Coll (PA)
Burlington County Coll (NJ)
Catawba Valley Comm Coll (NC)
Central Texas Coll (TX)
Cincinnati State Tech and Comm Coll (OH)
Coll of Southern Idaho (ID)
Collin County Comm Coll District (TX)
Comm Coll of Allegheny County (PA)
The Comm Coll of Baltimore County (MD)
Comm Coll of the Air Force (AL)
Delaware Tech & Comm Coll, Terry Campus (DE)
Delgado Comm Coll (LA)
Des Moines Area Comm Coll (IA)
Duluth Business U (MN)
Dutchess Comm Coll (NY)
Eastern Arizona Coll (AZ)
Fashion Inst of Technology (NY)
Fayetteville Tech Comm Coll (NC)
FIDM/Fashion Inst of Design & Merchandising, Los Angeles Campus (CA)
FIDM/Fashion Inst of Design & Merchandising, Orange County Campus (CA)
FIDM/Fashion Inst of Design & Merchandising, San Francisco Campus (CA)
FIDM/The Fashion Inst of Design & Merchandising, San Diego Campus (CA)
Finger Lakes Comm Coll (NY)
Golden West Coll (CA)
Guilford Tech Comm Coll (NC)
Hagerstown Comm Coll (MD)
Halifax Comm Coll (NC)
Housatonic Comm Coll (CT)
Iowa Lakes Comm Coll (IA)
James H. Faulkner State Comm Coll (AL)
James Sprunt Comm Coll (NC)
J. F. Drake State Comm and Tech Coll (AL)
Kilgore Coll (TX)
Kingsborough Comm Coll of the City U of New York (NY)
Lakeland Comm Coll (OH)
Los Angeles Trade-Tech Coll (CA)
Luzerne County Comm Coll (PA)
Macomb Comm Coll (MI)
Manchester Comm Coll (CT)
Miami Dade Coll (FL)
Middlesex Comm Coll (MA)
Midlands Tech Coll (SC)
Mid-Plains Comm Coll, North Platte (NE)
Mohawk Valley Comm Coll (NY)
Monroe Comm Coll (NY)
Montgomery Coll (MD)
Montgomery County Comm Coll (PA)
Mt. San Antonio Coll (CA)
Nassau Comm Coll (NY)
Navarro Coll (TX)
New Mexico Jr Coll (NM)
Northern Essex Comm Coll (MA)
Northwest Coll (WY)
Northwestern Michigan Coll (MI)
Norwalk Comm Coll (CT)
Ohlone Coll (CA)
Oklahoma City Comm Coll (OK)
Orange Coast Coll (CA)

Owens Comm Coll, Toledo (OH)
Palomar Coll (CA)
Pensacola State Coll (FL)
Phoenix Coll (AZ)
Randolph Comm Coll (NC)
Rockland Comm Coll (NY)
St. Charles Comm Coll (MO)
St. Clair County Comm Coll (MI)
San Jacinto Coll District (TX)
San Joaquin Delta Coll (CA)
San Juan Coll (NM)
School of Advertising Art (OH)
South Piedmont Comm Coll (NC)
Sowela Tech Comm Coll (LA)
Springfield Tech Comm Coll (MA)
Sullivan County Comm Coll (NY)
Tallahassee Comm Coll (FL)
Terra State Comm Coll (OH)
Texas State Tech Coll Harlingen (TX)
Tompkins Cortland Comm Coll (NY)
Trident Tech Coll (SC)
Tunxis Comm Coll (CT)
Tyler Jr Coll (TX)
Ulster County Comm Coll (NY)
U of Arkansas Comm Coll at Morrilton (AR)
Vincennes U (IN)
Virginia Western Comm Coll (VA)
Whatcom Comm Coll (WA)

COMMERCIAL PHOTOGRAPHY
Austin Comm Coll District (TX)
Bucks County Comm Coll (PA)
Cecil Coll (MD)
Central Wyoming Coll (WY)
Fashion Inst of Technology (NY)
Fiorello H. LaGuardia Comm Coll of the City U of New York (NY)
Hawkeye Comm Coll (IA)
Houston Comm Coll (TX)
Kilgore Coll (TX)
Kirtland Comm Coll (MI)
Luzerne County Comm Coll (PA)
McHenry County Coll (IL)
Minneapolis Comm and Tech Coll (MN)
Mohawk Valley Comm Coll (NY)
Montgomery Coll (MD)
Northwest Coll (WY)
Owens Comm Coll, Toledo (OH)
Phoenix Coll (AZ)
Randolph Comm Coll (NC)
Ridgewater Coll (MN)
Sierra Coll (CA)
Springfield Tech Comm Coll (MA)
Trinity Valley Comm Coll (TX)
Tyler Jr Coll (TX)
Western Iowa Tech Comm Coll (IA)

COMMUNICATION
Ohlone Coll (CA)
Pennsylvania Inst of Technology (PA)
Potomac State Coll of West Virginia U (WV)
Tulsa Comm Coll (OK)

COMMUNICATION AND JOURNALISM RELATED
Cayuga County Comm Coll (NY)
Delgado Comm Coll (LA)
Gadsden State Comm Coll (AL)
Georgia Highlands Coll (GA)
Iowa Lakes Comm Coll (IA)
Pennsylvania Highlands Comm Coll (PA)
Queensborough Comm Coll of the City U of New York (NY)

COMMUNICATION AND MEDIA RELATED
Coll of Southern Maryland (MD)
Manor Coll (PA)
Raritan Valley Comm Coll (NJ)
Reading Area Comm Coll (PA)

COMMUNICATION DISORDERS SCIENCES AND SERVICES RELATED
Burlington County Coll (NJ)

COMMUNICATION SCIENCES AND DISORDERS
Forsyth Tech Comm Coll (NC)

COMMUNICATIONS SYSTEMS INSTALLATION AND REPAIR TECHNOLOGY
Bellingham Tech Coll (WA)
Cayuga County Comm Coll (NY)
Des Moines Area Comm Coll (IA)
Dutchess Comm Coll (NY)
Erie Comm Coll, South Campus (NY)

Mohawk Valley Comm Coll (NY)
Westmoreland County Comm Coll (PA)

COMMUNICATIONS TECHNOLOGIES AND SUPPORT SERVICES RELATED
Anne Arundel Comm Coll (MD)
Bowling Green State U-Firelands Coll (OH)
Comm Coll of Allegheny County (PA)
Middlesex County Coll (NJ)
Montgomery Coll (MD)
Montgomery County Comm Coll (PA)
Ocean County Coll (NJ)

COMMUNICATIONS TECHNOLOGY
Comm Coll of the Air Force (AL)
Daytona State Coll (FL)
Fountainhead Coll of Technology (TN)
Gulf Coast State Coll (FL)
Hutchinson Comm Coll (KS)
Mott Comm Coll (MI)
Orange Coast Coll (CA)
Pensacola State Coll (FL)
Pueblo Comm Coll (CO)
Renton Tech Coll (WA)
Vincennes U (IN)

COMMUNITY HEALTH AND PREVENTIVE MEDICINE
Anoka-Ramsey Comm Coll (MN)
Anoka-Ramsey Comm Coll, Cambridge Campus (MN)

COMMUNITY HEALTH SERVICES COUNSELING
Comm Coll of Allegheny County (PA)
Dutchess Comm Coll (NY)
Greenfield Comm Coll (MA)
Kingsborough Comm Coll of the City U of New York (NY)
Miami Dade Coll (FL)
Mott Comm Coll (MI)

COMMUNITY ORGANIZATION AND ADVOCACY
Borough of Manhattan Comm Coll of the City U of New York (NY)
Cleveland State Comm Coll (TN)
Clinton Comm Coll (NY)
Iowa Central Comm Coll (IA)
Jefferson Comm Coll (NY)
Minneapolis Comm and Tech Coll (MN)
Sheridan Coll (WY)
Ulster County Comm Coll (NY)
Westchester Comm Coll (NY)

COMPARATIVE LITERATURE
Iowa Lakes Comm Coll (IA)
Miami Dade Coll (FL)
Otero Jr Coll (CO)
San Joaquin Delta Coll (CA)

COMPUTER AND INFORMATION SCIENCES
Ancilla Coll (IN)
Anne Arundel Comm Coll (MD)
Antelope Valley Coll (CA)
Arapahoe Comm Coll (CO)
Arizona Western Coll (AZ)
Austin Comm Coll District (TX)
Bevill State Comm Coll (AL)
Borough of Manhattan Comm Coll of the City U of New York (NY)
Bucks County Comm Coll (PA)
Butler County Comm Coll (PA)
Carl Albert State Coll (OK)
Cayuga County Comm Coll (NY)
Central Virginia Comm Coll (VA)
Chandler-Gilbert Comm Coll (AZ)
Cincinnati State Tech and Comm Coll (OH)
Coll of Central Florida (FL)
Coll of Southern Maryland (MD)
Collin County Comm Coll District (TX)
Columbia-Greene Comm Coll (NY)
The Comm Coll of Baltimore County (MD)
Comm Coll of Denver (CO)
Comm Coll of Rhode Island (RI)
Corning Comm Coll (NY)
Cumberland County Coll (NJ)
Dakota Coll at Bottineau (ND)
Darton State Coll (GA)
Delaware Tech & Comm Coll, Terry Campus (DE)
Denmark Tech Coll (SC)

Edison Comm Coll (OH)
Elizabethtown Comm and Tech Coll, Elizabethtown (KY)
Erie Comm Coll, North Campus (NY)
Finger Lakes Comm Coll (NY)
Florida Gateway Coll (FL)
Forsyth Tech Comm Coll (NC)
Front Range Comm Coll (CO)
Gadsden State Comm Coll (AL)
Gateway Comm and Tech Coll (KY)
George C. Wallace Comm Coll (AL)
Georgia Highlands Coll (GA)
Grand Rapids Comm Coll (MI)
Greenfield Comm Coll (MA)
Hagerstown Comm Coll (MD)
Harford Comm Coll (MD)
Harper Coll (IL)
Harrisburg Area Comm Coll (PA)
H. Councill Trenholm State Tech Coll (AL)
Hinds Comm Coll (MS)
Hopkinsville Comm Coll (KY)
Hudson County Comm Coll (NJ)
Hutchinson Comm Coll (KS)
James H. Faulkner State Comm Coll (AL)
Jamestown Comm Coll (NY)
Jefferson Comm Coll (NY)
Jefferson State Comm Coll (AL)
J. F. Drake State Comm and Tech Coll (AL)
John Tyler Comm Coll (VA)
J. Sargeant Reynolds Comm Coll (VA)
Kilgore Coll (TX)
Kingsborough Comm Coll of the City U of New York (NY)
Lakes Region Comm Coll (NH)
Lehigh Carbon Comm Coll (PA)
Lone Star Coll–CyFair (TX)
Lone Star Coll–Kingwood (TX)
Lurleen B. Wallace Comm Coll (AL)
Luzerne County Comm Coll (PA)
Massachusetts Bay Comm Coll (MA)
Maysville Comm and Tech Coll, Maysville (KY)
Middlesex Comm Coll (MA)
Middlesex County Coll (NJ)
Mid-Plains Comm Coll, North Platte (NE)
Mohawk Valley Comm Coll (NY)
Montgomery Coll (MD)
Montgomery County Comm Coll (PA)
Mountain State Coll (WV)
Mt. San Antonio Coll (CA)
Mount Wachusett Comm Coll (MA)
Nassau Comm Coll (NY)
Northern Essex Comm Coll (MA)
Northern Virginia Comm Coll (VA)
Northwest-Shoals Comm Coll (AL)
Ocean County Coll (NJ)
Ohlone Coll (CA)
Owensboro Comm and Tech Coll (KY)
Paris Jr Coll (TX)
Penn Foster Coll (AZ)
Pennsylvania Highlands Comm Coll (PA)
Pensacola State Coll (FL)
Phoenix Coll (AZ)
Potomac State Coll of West Virginia U (WV)
Pueblo Comm Coll (CO)
Reading Area Comm Coll (PA)
Reid State Tech Coll (AL)
Rogue Comm Coll (OR)
Salt Lake Comm Coll (UT)
San Jacinto Coll District (TX)
Sheridan Coll (WY)
Somerset Comm Coll (KY)
South Florida State Coll (FL)
Southwestern Illinois Coll (IL)
Southwest Virginia Comm Coll (VA)
State U of New York Coll of Technology at Alfred (NY)
Sullivan Coll of Technology and Design (KY)
Terra State Comm Coll (OH)
Tompkins Cortland Comm Coll (NY)
Tyler Jr Coll (TX)
Ulster County Comm Coll (NY)
U of Arkansas Comm Coll at Hope (AR)
U of Arkansas Comm Coll at Morrilton (AR)
Victor Valley Coll (CA)
Vincennes U (IN)
Volunteer State Comm Coll (TN)
Walters State Comm Coll (TN)
Westchester Comm Coll (NY)
Western Nevada Coll (NV)

Western Wyoming Comm Coll (WY)
White Mountains Comm Coll (NH)
Wor-Wic Comm Coll (MD)

COMPUTER AND INFORMATION SCIENCES AND SUPPORT SERVICES RELATED
Arapahoe Comm Coll (CO)
Bowling Green State U-Firelands Coll (OH)
Bunker Hill Comm Coll (MA)
Career Tech Coll, Monroe (LA)
Cayuga County Comm Coll (NY)
Chandler-Gilbert Comm Coll (AZ)
Chesapeake Coll (MD)
Corning Comm Coll (NY)
Dakota Coll at Bottineau (ND)
Darton State Coll (GA)
Des Moines Area Comm Coll (IA)
Fiorello H. LaGuardia Comm Coll of the City U of New York (NY)
Greenfield Comm Coll (MA)
Island Drafting and Tech Inst (NY)
Jefferson Comm Coll (NY)
Middlesex Comm Coll (MA)
Midlands Tech Coll (SC)
Mohawk Valley Comm Coll (NY)
Monroe Comm Coll (NY)
Northcentral Tech Coll (WI)
North Central Texas Coll (TX)
Northland Comm Coll (MN)
Raritan Valley Comm Coll (NJ)
Riverland Comm Coll (MN)
San Joaquin Valley Coll, Visalia (CA)
Seminole State Coll of Florida (FL)
Sierra Coll (CA)
Southeastern Coll–Greenacres (FL)
Stark State Coll (OH)
Sullivan Coll of Technology and Design (KY)
Tulsa Comm Coll (OK)
Ulster County Comm Coll (NY)
Waukesha County Tech Coll (WI)
Westchester Comm Coll (NY)

COMPUTER AND INFORMATION SCIENCES RELATED
Central Oregon Comm Coll (OR)
Chipola Coll (FL)
Citrus Coll (CA)
Coastal Bend Coll (TX)
Corning Comm Coll (NY)
Daytona State Coll (FL)
Delta Coll (MI)
Gateway Comm Coll (CT)
Genesee Comm Coll (NY)
Howard Comm Coll (MD)
Iowa Lakes Comm Coll (IA)
Lorain County Comm Coll (OH)
Luzerne County Comm Coll (PA)
Mohave Comm Coll (AZ)
Monroe Comm Coll (NY)
Monroe County Comm Coll (MI)
Nassau Comm Coll (NY)
Northland Comm Coll (MN)
North Shore Comm Coll (MA)
Pensacola State Coll (FL)
Richland Comm Coll (IL)
Rockland Comm Coll (NY)
Seminole State Coll of Florida (FL)
Stark State Coll (OH)
Tulsa Comm Coll (OK)
Tyler Jr Coll (TX)
Westchester Comm Coll (NY)

COMPUTER AND INFORMATION SYSTEMS SECURITY
Anne Arundel Comm Coll (MD)
Blue Ridge Comm and Tech Coll (WV)
Bunker Hill Comm Coll (MA)
Butler County Comm Coll (PA)
Casper Coll (WY)
Central Texas Coll (TX)
Century Coll (MN)
Chesapeake Coll (MD)
Cochise Coll, Douglas (AZ)
Coll of Southern Maryland (MD)
Collin County Comm Coll District (TX)
The Comm Coll of Baltimore County (MD)
Delta Coll (MI)
Dyersburg State Comm Coll (TN)
Edison Comm Coll (OH)
El Centro Coll (TX)
Elgin Comm Coll (IL)
Fayetteville Tech Comm Coll (NC)
Gateway Tech Coll (WI)
Grand Rapids Comm Coll (MI)

Hagerstown Comm Coll (MD)
Harrisburg Area Comm Coll (PA)
Hinds Comm Coll (MS)
Island Drafting and Tech Inst (NY)
Lehigh Carbon Comm Coll (PA)
Minneapolis Comm and Tech Coll (MN)
Minnesota West Comm and Tech Coll (MN)
Mohawk Valley Comm Coll (NY)
Montgomery Coll (MD)
Northampton Comm Coll (PA)
Northwest State Comm Coll (OH)
Norwalk Comm Coll (CT)
Ohlone Coll (CA)
Owens Comm Coll, Toledo (OH)
Pensacola State Coll (FL)
Quinsigamond Comm Coll (MA)
Riverland Comm Coll (MN)
St. Philip's Coll (TX)
Seminole State Coll of Florida (FL)
Sheridan Coll (WY)
Spencerian Coll–Lexington (KY)
Springfield Tech Comm Coll (MA)
Sullivan Coll of Technology and Design (KY)
Westchester Comm Coll (NY)
Westmoreland County Comm Coll (PA)

COMPUTER ENGINEERING
Carroll Comm Coll (MD)
Coll of Southern Maryland (MD)
The Comm Coll of Baltimore County (MD)
Daytona State Coll (FL)
Northwest State Comm Coll (OH)
Ohlone Coll (CA)
Pensacola State Coll (FL)
South Florida State Coll (FL)

COMPUTER ENGINEERING RELATED
Daytona State Coll (FL)
Eastern Gateway Comm Coll (OH)
Gateway Comm Coll (CT)
Monroe Comm Coll (NY)
Seminole State Coll of Florida (FL)
Stark State Coll (OH)

COMPUTER ENGINEERING TECHNOLOGY
Alvin Comm Coll (TX)
Amarillo Coll (TX)
Benjamin Franklin Inst of Technology (MA)
Bowling Green State U-Firelands Coll (OH)
Brookhaven Coll (TX)
Carteret Comm Coll (NC)
Catawba Valley Comm Coll (NC)
Cincinnati State Tech and Comm Coll (OH)
Comm Coll of Allegheny County (PA)
Comm Coll of Rhode Island (RI)
Delaware Tech & Comm Coll, Terry Campus (DE)
Delgado Comm Coll (LA)
Des Moines Area Comm Coll (IA)
Forsyth Tech Comm Coll (NC)
Fountainhead Coll of Technology (TN)
Gateway Comm Coll (CT)
Hocking Coll (OH)
Houston Comm Coll (TX)
Iowa Central Comm Coll (IA)
Kellogg Comm Coll (MI)
Lakeland Comm Coll (OH)
Lorain County Comm Coll (OH)
Los Angeles Trade-Tech Coll (CA)
Massachusetts Bay Comm Coll (MA)
Miami Dade Coll (FL)
Middlesex Comm Coll (MA)
Minnesota West Comm and Tech Coll (MN)
Monroe Comm Coll (NY)
Monroe County Comm Coll (MI)
Mt. San Antonio Coll (CA)
North Central Texas Coll (TX)
Northeastern Jr Coll (CO)
Northern Essex Comm Coll (MA)
North Shore Comm Coll (MA)
Northwest State Comm Coll (OH)
Oklahoma City Comm Coll (OK)
Orange Coast Coll (CA)
Owens Comm Coll, Toledo (OH)
Paris Jr Coll (TX)
Queensborough Comm Coll of the City U of New York (NY)
Quinsigamond Comm Coll (MA)

Richmond Comm Coll (NC)
Roane State Comm Coll (TN)
Rock Valley Coll (IL)
Seminole State Coll of Florida (FL)
South Florida State Coll (FL)
Spencerian Coll–Lexington (KY)
Springfield Tech Comm Coll (MA)
State U of New York Coll of Technology at Alfred (NY)
Sullivan Coll of Technology and Design (KY)
Three Rivers Comm Coll (CT)
Trident Tech Coll (SC)
Tyler Jr Coll (TX)
Umpqua Comm Coll (OR)
Whatcom Comm Coll (WA)

COMPUTER GRAPHICS
Antelope Valley Coll (CA)
Arizona Western Coll (AZ)
The Art Inst of Cincinnati (OH)
Burlington County Coll (NJ)
Carroll Comm Coll (MD)
Citrus Coll (CA)
Coll of the Desert (CA)
Daytona State Coll (FL)
Florida State Coll at Jacksonville (FL)
Gateway Comm Coll (CT)
Genesee Comm Coll (NY)
Howard Comm Coll (MD)
Iowa Lakes Comm Coll (IA)
Kellogg Comm Coll (MI)
Luzerne County Comm Coll (PA)
Mesabi Range Coll (MN)
Miami Dade Coll (FL)
Monroe County Comm Coll (MI)
Moraine Valley Comm Coll (IL)
Mt. San Antonio Coll (CA)
Mount Wachusett Comm Coll (MA)
Nassau Comm Coll (NY)
Navarro Coll (TX)
New Mexico Jr Coll (NM)
North Central Texas Coll (TX)
Northern Essex Comm Coll (MA)
Northland Comm Coll (MN)
North Shore Comm Coll (MA)
Orange Coast Coll (CA)
Palomar Coll (CA)
Phoenix Coll (AZ)
Quinsigamond Comm Coll (MA)
Richland Comm Coll (IL)
Rockland Comm Coll (NY)
Schoolcraft Coll (MI)
Seminole State Coll of Florida (FL)
Shawnee Comm Coll (IL)
Spencerian Coll–Lexington (KY)
Sullivan Coll of Technology and Design (KY)
Sullivan County Comm Coll (NY)
Tallahassee Comm Coll (FL)
Trident Tech Coll (SC)
Tyler Jr Coll (TX)

COMPUTER HARDWARE ENGINEERING
Seminole State Coll of Florida (FL)
Stark State Coll (OH)
Sullivan Coll of Technology and Design (KY)

COMPUTER HARDWARE TECHNOLOGY
Forsyth Tech Comm Coll (NC)
Sullivan Coll of Technology and Design (KY)

COMPUTER/INFORMATION TECHNOLOGY SERVICES ADMINISTRATION RELATED
Bossier Parish Comm Coll (LA)
Bunker Hill Comm Coll (MA)
Clinton Comm Coll (NY)
Corning Comm Coll (NY)
Daytona State Coll (FL)
Dutchess Comm Coll (NY)
El Centro Coll (TX)
Hawkeye Comm Coll (IA)
Hillsborough Comm Coll (FL)
Howard Comm Coll (MD)
Iowa Lakes Comm Coll (IA)
Jefferson Comm Coll (NY)
J. Sargeant Reynolds Comm Coll (VA)
Mesabi Range Coll (MN)
North Central Texas Coll (TX)
Pasadena City Coll (CA)
Rockland Comm Coll (NY)
Seminole State Coll of Florida (FL)
Southwestern Illinois Coll (IL)

Stark State Coll (OH)
Trident Tech Coll (SC)
Vincennes U (IN)
Western Iowa Tech Comm Coll (IA)
Wisconsin Indianhead Tech Coll (WI)

COMPUTER INSTALLATION AND REPAIR TECHNOLOGY
Central Maine Comm Coll (ME)
Delgado Comm Coll (LA)
Delta Coll (MI)
Fiorello H. LaGuardia Comm Coll of the City U of New York (NY)
Forrest Coll (SC)
Genesee Comm Coll (NY)
Harrisburg Area Comm Coll (PA)
Hinds Comm Coll (MS)
Lake Region State Coll (ND)
Miami Dade Coll (FL)
Midlands Tech Coll (SC)
Montcalm Comm Coll (MI)
Northampton Comm Coll (PA)
Penn Foster Coll (AZ)
Riverland Comm Coll (MN)
Sierra Coll (CA)
Sullivan Coll of Technology and Design (KY)
Tulsa Comm Coll (OK)
Wisconsin Indianhead Tech Coll (WI)

COMPUTER NUMERICALLY CONTROLLED (CNC) MACHINIST TECHNOLOGY
Anoka Tech Coll (MN)
Corning Comm Coll (NY)
Hennepin Tech Coll (MN)
Wayne County Comm Coll District (MI)
Westmoreland County Comm Coll (PA)

COMPUTER PROGRAMMING
Alvin Comm Coll (TX)
Amarillo Coll (TX)
Antelope Valley Coll (CA)
Austin Comm Coll District (TX)
Bradford School (PA)
Brookhaven Coll (TX)
Bunker Hill Comm Coll (MA)
Casper Coll (WY)
Catawba Valley Comm Coll (NC)
Cedar Valley Coll (TX)
Chandler-Gilbert Comm Coll (AZ)
Clark Coll (WA)
Cochise Coll, Douglas (AZ)
Coll of Southern Maryland (MD)
Copiah-Lincoln Comm Coll (MS)
Dabney S. Lancaster Comm Coll (VA)
Daytona State Coll (FL)
Delta Coll (MI)
Edison Comm Coll (OH)
El Centro Coll (TX)
Fayetteville Tech Comm Coll (NC)
Fiorello H. LaGuardia Comm Coll of the City U of New York (NY)
Florida Gateway Coll (FL)
Florida SouthWestern State Coll (FL)
Forsyth Tech Comm Coll (NC)
Fountainhead Coll of Technology (TN)
Fox Valley Tech Coll (WI)
Gateway Tech Coll (WI)
Grand Rapids Comm Coll (MI)
Guilford Tech Comm Coll (NC)
Gulf Coast State Coll (FL)
Gwinnett Tech Coll (GA)
Harper Coll (IL)
Hennepin Tech Coll (MN)
Hinds Comm Coll (MS)
Hocking Coll (OH)
Houston Comm Coll (TX)
International Business Coll, Indianapolis (IN)
Iowa Lakes Comm Coll (IA)
J. Sargeant Reynolds Comm Coll (VA)
Kalamazoo Valley Comm Coll (MI)
Kellogg Comm Coll (MI)
Kilgore Coll (TX)
King's Coll (NC)
Lamar Comm Coll (CO)
Laramie County Comm Coll (WY)
Lehigh Carbon Comm Coll (PA)
Lenoir Comm Coll (NC)
Lone Star Coll–Tomball (TX)
Lorain County Comm Coll (OH)
Los Angeles Trade-Tech Coll (CA)
Macomb Comm Coll (MI)
Miami Dade Coll (FL)

Middlesex Comm Coll (MA)
Minneapolis Business Coll (MN)
Minneapolis Comm and Tech Coll (MN)
Minnesota State Coll–Southeast Tech (MN)
MiraCosta Coll (CA)
Mohawk Valley Comm Coll (NY)
Montgomery County Comm Coll (PA)
Mott Comm Coll (MI)
Navarro Coll (TX)
New Mexico Jr Coll (NM)
Northampton Comm Coll (PA)
North Central Texas Coll (TX)
Northern Essex Comm Coll (MA)
North Shore Comm Coll (MA)
Northwest State Comm Coll (OH)
Oakton Comm Coll (IL)
Ohlone Coll (CA)
Orange Coast Coll (CA)
Palomar Coll (CA)
Pensacola State Coll (FL)
Ridgewater Coll (MN)
Rockland Comm Coll (NY)
St. Clair County Comm Coll (MI)
Schoolcraft Coll (MI)
Seminole State Coll of Florida (FL)
Sierra Coll (CA)
Southeastern Comm Coll (IA)
South Florida State Coll (FL)
Southwestern Illinois Coll (IL)
Southwestern Michigan Coll (MI)
Sowela Tech Comm Coll (LA)
Stark State Coll (OH)
Tallahassee Comm Coll (FL)
Terra State Comm Coll (OH)
Texas State Tech Coll Harlingen (TX)
Truckee Meadows Comm Coll (NV)
Tyler Jr Coll (TX)
Vincennes U (IN)
Waukesha County Tech Coll (WI)
Wayne County Comm Coll District (MI)
Western Nevada Coll (NV)
Westmoreland County Comm Coll (PA)
Wood Tobe–Coburn School (NY)

COMPUTER PROGRAMMING RELATED
Coastal Bend Coll (TX)
Genesee Comm Coll (NY)
Lorain County Comm Coll (OH)
Luzerne County Comm Coll (PA)
Mesabi Range Coll (MN)
Moraine Park Tech Coll (WI)
North Central Texas Coll (TX)
Northern Essex Comm Coll (MA)
Pasco-Hernando State Coll (FL)
Rockland Comm Coll (NY)
Seminole State Coll of Florida (FL)
Stark State Coll (OH)
Tyler Jr Coll (TX)

COMPUTER PROGRAMMING (SPECIFIC APPLICATIONS)
Bucks County Comm Coll (PA)
Bunker Hill Comm Coll (MA)
Butler County Comm Coll (PA)
Cincinnati State Tech and Comm Coll (OH)
Coastal Bend Coll (TX)
Comm Coll of Rhode Island (RI)
Danville Area Comm Coll (IL)
Daytona State Coll (FL)
Des Moines Area Comm Coll (IA)
Grand Rapids Comm Coll (MI)
Harper Coll (IL)
Hillsborough Comm Coll (FL)
Holyoke Comm Coll (MA)
Houston Comm Coll (TX)
Humacao Comm Coll (PR)
Kellogg Comm Coll (MI)
Kent State U at Ashtabula (OH)
Kent State U at East Liverpool (OH)
Kent State U at Salem (OH)
Kent State U at Trumbull (OH)
Kent State U at Tuscarawas (OH)
Lake Land Coll (IL)
Lakeland Comm Coll (OH)
Lehigh Carbon Comm Coll (PA)
Lorain County Comm Coll (OH)
Macomb Comm Coll (MI)
Manor Coll (PA)
Mesabi Range Coll (MN)
Miami Dade Coll (FL)
Mohave Comm Coll (AZ)
Monroe County Comm Coll (MI)
Mott Comm Coll (MI)
North Central Texas Coll (TX)

Northeast Iowa Comm Coll (IA)
Northern Essex Comm Coll (MA)
North Shore Comm Coll (MA)
Orange Coast Coll (CA)
Owens Comm Coll, Toledo (OH)
Pasco-Hernando State Coll (FL)
Pensacola State Coll (FL)
Piedmont Comm Coll (NC)
Quinsigamond Comm Coll (MA)
Richland Comm Coll (IL)
Riverland Comm Coll (MN)
Rockland Comm Coll (NY)
Schoolcraft Coll (MI)
Seminole State Coll of Florida (FL)
Springfield Tech Comm Coll (MA)
Stark State Coll (OH)
State Fair Comm Coll (MO)
Sullivan County Comm Coll (NY)
Tallahassee Comm Coll (FL)
Trident Tech Coll (SC)
Victor Valley Coll (CA)
Western Iowa Tech Comm Coll (IA)
Western Wyoming Comm Coll (WY)
Westmoreland County Comm Coll (PA)

COMPUTER PROGRAMMING (VENDOR/PRODUCT CERTIFICATION)
Chandler-Gilbert Comm Coll (AZ)
Gulf Coast State Coll (FL)
Lorain County Comm Coll (OH)
Miami Dade Coll (FL)
North Central Texas Coll (TX)
Pensacola State Coll (FL)
Raritan Valley Comm Coll (NJ)
Riverland Comm Coll (MN)
Seminole State Coll of Florida (FL)
Stark State Coll (OH)
Sullivan Coll of Technology and Design (KY)

COMPUTER SCIENCE
Allen County Comm Coll (KS)
Amarillo Coll (TX)
Anoka-Ramsey Comm Coll (MN)
Anoka-Ramsey Comm Coll, Cambridge Campus (MN)
Benjamin Franklin Inst of Technology (MA)
Borough of Manhattan Comm Coll of the City U of New York (NY)
Bunker Hill Comm Coll (MA)
Burlington County Coll (NJ)
Ca&nnada Coll (CA)
Central Oregon Comm Coll (OR)
Central Wyoming Coll (WY)
Century Coll (MN)
Chesapeake Coll (MD)
Chipola Coll (FL)
Citrus Coll (CA)
Coastal Bend Coll (TX)
Cochise Coll, Douglas (AZ)
Coll of Marin (CA)
Coll of Southern Idaho (ID)
Coll of the Canyons (CA)
Coll of the Desert (CA)
Collin County Comm Coll District (TX)
Comm Coll of Philadelphia (PA)
Corning Comm Coll (NY)
Darton State Coll (GA)
Daytona State Coll (FL)
Dutchess Comm Coll (NY)
El Centro Coll (TX)
Finger Lakes Comm Coll (NY)
Fiorello H. LaGuardia Comm Coll of the City U of New York (NY)
Frederick Comm Coll (MD)
Genesee Comm Coll (NY)
George C. Wallace Comm Coll (AL)
Guam Comm Coll (GU)
Gwinnett Tech Coll (GA)
Harford Comm Coll (MD)
Harper Coll (IL)
Harrisburg Area Comm Coll (PA)
Hocking Coll (OH)
Howard Comm Coll (MD)
Iowa Lakes Comm Coll (IA)
Jackson State Comm Coll (TN)
Jefferson Comm Coll (NY)
J. Sargeant Reynolds Comm Coll (VA)
Kingsborough Comm Coll of the City U of New York (NY)
Lake Area Tech Inst (SD)
Lamar Comm Coll (CO)
Landmark Coll (VT)
Laramie County Comm Coll (WY)
Lone Star Coll–CyFair (TX)

Lone Star Coll–Kingwood (TX)
Lone Star Coll–Montgomery (TX)
Lone Star Coll–North Harris (TX)
Lone Star Coll–Tomball (TX)
Lorain County Comm Coll (OH)
Luzerne County Comm Coll (PA)
Massachusetts Bay Comm Coll (MA)
Miami Dade Coll (FL)
Minnesota West Comm and Tech Coll (MN)
MiraCosta Coll (CA)
Mohave Comm Coll (AZ)
Monroe Comm Coll (NY)
Mt. San Antonio Coll (CA)
Nassau Comm Coll (NY)
Navarro Coll (TX)
New Mexico Jr Coll (NM)
Niagara County Comm Coll (NY)
Normandale Comm Coll (MN)
Northampton Comm Coll (PA)
North Central Texas Coll (TX)
Northeastern Jr Coll (CO)
Northern Essex Comm Coll (MA)
North Hennepin Comm Coll (MN)
Northland Comm Coll (MN)
North Shore Comm Coll (MA)
Ohlone Coll (CA)
Oklahoma City Comm Coll (OK)
Pasadena City Coll (CA)
Pennsylvania Highlands Comm Coll (PA)
Pensacola State Coll (FL)
Quinsigamond Comm Coll (MA)
Renton Tech Coll (WA)
Ridgewater Coll (MN)
Roane State Comm Coll (TN)
Rock Valley Coll (IL)
Salt Lake Comm Coll (UT)
San Joaquin Delta Coll (CA)
Seminole State Coll (OK)
Southern U at Shreveport (LA)
South Hills School of Business & Technology, State College (PA)
Springfield Tech Comm Coll (MA)
Trinity Valley Comm Coll (TX)
Tulsa Comm Coll (OK)
Tyler Jr Coll (TX)
Umpqua Comm Coll (OR)
Victor Valley Coll (CA)
Vincennes U (IN)
Virginia Western Comm Coll (VA)
Westchester Comm Coll (NY)
Western Wyoming Comm Coll (WY)
Whatcom Comm Coll (WA)
York County Comm Coll (ME)

COMPUTER SOFTWARE AND MEDIA APPLICATIONS RELATED

Carteret Comm Coll (NC)
The Coll of Westchester (NY)
Dakota Coll at Bottineau (ND)
Delta Coll (MI)
Gateway Tech Coll (WI)
Genesee Comm Coll (NY)
Kellogg Comm Coll (MI)
Mesabi Range Coll (MN)
Northland Comm Coll (MN)
Riverland Comm Coll (MN)
Seminole State Coll of Florida (FL)
Stark State Coll (OH)

COMPUTER SOFTWARE ENGINEERING

Seminole State Coll of Florida (FL)
Stark State Coll (OH)

COMPUTER SOFTWARE TECHNOLOGY

Iowa Lakes Comm Coll (IA)
Miami Dade Coll (FL)
Rogue Comm Coll (OR)

COMPUTER SUPPORT SPECIALIST

Big Bend Comm Coll (WA)
Cincinnati State Tech and Comm Coll (OH)
Comm Coll of Rhode Island (RI)
Corning Comm Coll (NY)
Fox Valley Tech Coll (WI)
Gateway Tech Coll (WI)
Genesee Comm Coll (NY)
Grand Rapids Comm Coll (MI)
IBMC Coll (CO)
Miami Dade Coll (FL)
Mitchell Tech Inst (SD)
Moraine Park Tech Coll (WI)
Ohio Business Coll, Sandusky (OH)
Southwestern Michigan Coll (MI)
Tompkins Cortland Comm Coll (NY)
Waukesha County Tech Coll (WI)

Westmoreland County Comm Coll (PA)

COMPUTER SYSTEMS ANALYSIS

Amarillo Coll (TX)
Chandler-Gilbert Comm Coll (AZ)
Cincinnati State Tech and Comm Coll (OH)
Crowder Coll (MO)
Gateway Tech Coll (WI)
Guilford Tech Comm Coll (NC)
Haywood Comm Coll (NC)
Hillsborough Comm Coll (FL)
Hutchinson Comm Coll (KS)
Kalamazoo Valley Comm Coll (MI)
Kirtland Comm Coll (MI)
Lakeland Comm Coll (OH)
Northcentral Tech Coll (WI)
Oklahoma City Comm Coll (OK)
Pensacola State Coll (FL)
Phoenix Coll (AZ)
Quinsigamond Comm Coll (MA)
Tohono O'odham Comm Coll (AZ)
Wor-Wic Comm Coll (MD)

COMPUTER SYSTEMS NETWORKING AND TELECOMMUNICATIONS

Alexandria Tech and Comm Coll (MN)
Allen Comm Coll (KS)
Anne Arundel Comm Coll (MD)
Anoka-Ramsey Comm Coll (MN)
Anoka-Ramsey Comm Coll, Cambridge Campus (MN)
Austin Comm Coll District (TX)
Bellingham Tech Coll (WA)
Big Bend Comm Coll (WA)
Borough of Manhattan Comm Coll of the City U of New York (NY)
Bowling Green State U-Firelands Coll (OH)
Bradford School (PA)
Bucks County Comm Coll (PA)
Bunker Hill Comm Coll (MA)
Ca&nnada Coll (CA)
Cape Fear Comm Coll (NC)
Carteret Comm Coll (NC)
Catawba Valley Comm Coll (NC)
Cedar Valley Coll (TX)
Central Oregon Comm Coll (OR)
Century Coll (MN)
Chandler-Gilbert Comm Coll (AZ)
Clark Coll (WA)
Cochise Coll, Douglas (AZ)
CollAmerica–Flagstaff (AZ)
Coll of Marin (CA)
Coll of Southern Idaho (ID)
Coll of the Canyons (CA)
Comm Coll of Allegheny County (PA)
The Comm Coll of Baltimore County (MD)
Comm Coll of Rhode Island (RI)
Crowder Coll (MO)
Cumberland County Coll (NJ)
Danville Area Comm Coll (IL)
Davis Coll (OH)
Daytona State Coll (FL)
Delaware Tech & Comm Coll, Terry Campus (DE)
Delta Coll (MI)
Dunwoody Coll of Technology (MN)
Eastern Idaho Tech Coll (ID)
Eastern Wyoming Coll (WY)
Edison Comm Coll (OH)
Fayetteville Tech Comm Coll (NC)
Fiorello H. LaGuardia Comm Coll of the City U of New York (NY)
Florida SouthWestern State Coll (FL)
Forsyth Tech Comm Coll (NC)
Fox Valley Tech Coll (WI)
Front Range Comm Coll (CO)
Gateway Tech Coll (WI)
Genesee Comm Coll (NY)
Grand Rapids Comm Coll (MI)
Great Falls Coll Montana State U (MT)
Guam Comm Coll (GU)
Guilford Tech Comm Coll (NC)
Gulf Coast State Coll (FL)
Gwinnett Tech Coll (GA)
Halifax Comm Coll (NC)
Harrisburg Area Comm Coll (PA)
Hawkeye Comm Coll (IA)
Haywood Comm Coll (NC)
Hennepin Tech Coll (MN)
Hinds Comm Coll (MS)
Houston Comm Coll (TX)
Howard Comm Coll (MD)
Hutchinson Comm Coll (KS)

Illinois Eastern Comm Colls, Lincoln Trail College (IL)
International Business Coll, Indianapolis (IN)
Iowa Lakes Comm Coll (IA)
Island Drafting and Tech Inst (NY)
Jefferson Coll (MO)
J. Sargeant Reynolds Comm Coll (VA)
Kilgore Coll (TX)
King's Coll (NC)
Lake Land Coll (IL)
Lakeland Comm Coll (OH)
Lehigh Carbon Comm Coll (PA)
Lorain County Comm Coll (OH)
Luzerne County Comm Coll (PA)
McHenry County Coll (IL)
Mesabi Range Coll (MN)
Miami Dade Coll (FL)
Midlands Tech Coll (SC)
Minneapolis Business Coll (MN)
Minneapolis Comm and Tech Coll (MN)
Minnesota State Coll–Southeast Tech (MN)
Minnesota West Comm and Tech Coll (MN)
MiraCosta Coll (CA)
Montgomery County Comm Coll (PA)
Moraine Park Tech Coll (WI)
Mott Comm Coll (MI)
Nassau Comm Coll (NY)
Northampton Comm Coll (PA)
Northcentral Tech Coll (WI)
Northern Essex Comm Coll (MA)
North Iowa Area Comm Coll (IA)
Northwest Tech Coll (MN)
Norwalk Comm Coll (CT)
Ohlone Coll (CA)
Oklahoma City Comm Coll (OK)
Olympic Coll (WA)
Ozarks Tech Comm Coll (MO)
Palomar Coll (CA)
Pasco-Hernando State Coll (FL)
Piedmont Comm Coll (NC)
Randolph Comm Coll (NC)
Raritan Valley Comm Coll (NJ)
Ridgewater Coll (MN)
Riverland Comm Coll (MN)
Rockland Comm Coll (NY)
Rock Valley Coll (IL)
St. Clair County Comm Coll (MI)
St. Philip's Coll (TX)
Seminole State Coll of Florida (FL)
Shawnee Comm Coll (IL)
Sierra Coll (CA)
Southeastern Coll–Greenacres (FL)
South Louisiana Comm Coll (LA)
Southwestern Michigan Coll (MI)
Sowela Tech Comm Coll (LA)
Stark State Coll (OH)
State Fair Comm Coll (MO)
Sullivan Coll of Technology and Design (KY)
Tallahassee Comm Coll (FL)
Terra State Comm Coll (OH)
Texas State Tech Coll Harlingen (TX)
Trident Tech Coll (SC)
Trocaire Coll (NY)
Tyler Jr Coll (TX)
Victoria Coll (TX)
Vincennes U (IN)
Waukesha County Tech Coll (WI)
Wenatchee Valley Coll (WA)
Westchester Comm Coll (NY)
Western Dakota Tech Inst (SD)
Westmoreland County Comm Coll (PA)
Wisconsin Indianhead Tech Coll (WI)
Wood Tobe–Coburn School (NY)

COMPUTER TECHNOLOGY/ COMPUTER SYSTEMS TECHNOLOGY

Anoka Tech Coll (MN)
Benjamin Franklin Inst of Technology (MA)
Brookhaven Coll (TX)
Butler County Comm Coll (PA)
Cape Fear Comm Coll (NC)
Central Texas Coll (TX)
Central Wyoming Coll (WY)
Century Coll (MN)
Commonwealth Tech Inst (PA)
Comm Coll of Allegheny County (PA)
Corning Comm Coll (NY)
Dakota Coll at Bottineau (ND)
Daytona State Coll (FL)
Delaware Tech & Comm Coll, Terry Campus (DE)
Erie Comm Coll, South Campus (NY)

Forrest Coll (SC)
Hillsborough Comm Coll (FL)
Island Drafting and Tech Inst (NY)
ITI Tech Coll (LA)
Jefferson Comm Coll (NY)
Lakeland Comm Coll (OH)
Lorain County Comm Coll (OH)
Luzerne County Comm Coll (PA)
Miami Dade Coll (FL)
Minnesota State Coll–Southeast Tech (MN)
Minnesota West Comm and Tech Coll (MN)
Montgomery Coll (MD)
Normandale Comm Coll (MN)
Pasadena City Coll (CA)
Pasco-Hernando State Coll (FL)
Reading Area Comm Coll (PA)
Ridgewater Coll (MN)
St. Philip's Coll (TX)
Sullivan Coll of Technology and Design (KY)
Texas State Tech Coll Harlingen (TX)
Tyler Jr Coll (TX)
U of Arkansas Comm Coll at Morrilton (AR)
U of Cincinnati Clermont Coll (OH)

COMPUTER TYPOGRAPHY AND COMPOSITION EQUIPMENT OPERATION

Gateway Comm Coll (CT)
Housatonic Comm Coll (CT)
Lamar Comm Coll (CO)
New Mexico Jr Coll (NM)
Northern Essex Comm Coll (MA)
Ohlone Coll (CA)
Orange Coast Coll (CA)
Paris Jr Coll (TX)
U of Cincinnati Clermont Coll (OH)

CONCRETE FINISHING

Southwestern Illinois Coll (IL)

CONSTRUCTION ENGINEERING

Bossier Parish Comm Coll (LA)

CONSTRUCTION ENGINEERING TECHNOLOGY

Antelope Valley Coll (CA)
Bossier Parish Comm Coll (LA)
Burlington County Coll (NJ)
Clark Coll (WA)
Coll of Central Florida (FL)
Comm Coll of Allegheny County (PA)
Comm Coll of Philadelphia (PA)
Comm Coll of the Air Force (AL)
Crowder Coll (MO)
Delta Coll (MI)
Greenville Tech Coll (SC)
Gulf Coast State Coll (FL)
Harrisburg Area Comm Coll (PA)
Hinds Comm Coll (MS)
Houston Comm Coll (TX)
Iowa Lakes Comm Coll (IA)
Jefferson State Comm Coll (AL)
Lake Area Tech Inst (SD)
Los Angeles Trade-Tech Coll (CA)
Macomb Comm Coll (MI)
Miami Dade Coll (FL)
Midlands Tech Coll (SC)
Mid-Plains Comm Coll, North Platte (NE)
Monroe Comm Coll (NY)
New Castle School of Trades (PA)
New Mexico Jr Coll (NM)
Northwest State Comm Coll (OH)
Norwalk Comm Coll (CT)
The Ohio State U Ag Tech Inst (OH)
Oklahoma State U Inst of Technology (OK)
Oklahoma State U, Oklahoma City (OK)
Orange Coast Coll (CA)
Owens Comm Coll, Toledo (OH)
Ozarks Tech Comm Coll (MO)
Pensacola State Coll (FL)
Raritan Valley Comm Coll (NJ)
Richland Comm Coll (IL)
Rock Valley Coll (IL)
Rogue Comm Coll (OR)
St. Philip's Coll (TX)
San Jacinto Coll District (TX)
San Joaquin Delta Coll (CA)
Seminole State Coll of Florida (FL)
Southeastern Comm Coll (IA)
South Florida State Coll (FL)
South Suburban Coll (IL)
State U of New York Coll of Technology at Alfred (NY)
Sullivan County Comm Coll (NY)
Tallahassee Comm Coll (FL)

Tech Coll of the Lowcountry (SC)
Texas State Tech Coll Harlingen (TX)
Tompkins Cortland Comm Coll (NY)
Victor Valley Coll (CA)

CONSTRUCTION/HEAVY EQUIPMENT/EARTHMOVING EQUIPMENT OPERATION

Lake Area Tech Inst (SD)
Trinidad State Jr Coll (CO)

CONSTRUCTION MANAGEMENT

Arizona Western Coll (AZ)
Casper Coll (WY)
Delaware Tech & Comm Coll, Terry Campus (DE)
Dunwoody Coll of Technology (MN)
Iowa Lakes Comm Coll (IA)
Kankakee Comm Coll (IL)
Kaskaskia Coll (IL)
McHenry County Coll (IL)
Northampton Comm Coll (PA)
North Hennepin Comm Coll (MN)
The Ohio State U Ag Tech Inst (OH)
Oklahoma State U, Oklahoma City (OK)
Phoenix Coll (AZ)
San Joaquin Valley Coll, Ontario (CA)
San Joaquin Valley Coll–Online (CA)
State U of New York Coll of Technology at Alfred (NY)
Three Rivers Comm Coll (CT)
Truckee Meadows Comm Coll (NV)

CONSTRUCTION TRADES

American Samoa Comm Coll (AS)
Casper Coll (WY)
Crowder Coll (MO)
Harrisburg Area Comm Coll (PA)
Illinois Eastern Comm Colls, Frontier Community College (IL)
Illinois Eastern Comm Colls, Lincoln Trail College (IL)
Iowa Lakes Comm Coll (IA)
Lamar Comm Coll (CO)
Lehigh Carbon Comm Coll (PA)
Northeast Iowa Comm Coll (IA)
Oklahoma State U, Oklahoma City (OK)
Owensboro Comm and Tech Coll (KY)
Pasadena City Coll (CA)
Rogue Comm Coll (OR)
Sierra Coll (CA)
Southwestern Illinois Coll (IL)
Trinidad State Jr Coll (CO)
Vincennes U (IN)

CONSTRUCTION TRADES RELATED

Arizona Western Coll (AZ)
Central Maine Comm Coll (ME)
Citrus Coll (CA)
Comm Coll of Allegheny County (PA)
Dutchess Comm Coll (NY)
Mitchell Tech Inst (SD)
Palomar Coll (CA)
State U of New York Coll of Technology at Alfred (NY)
York County Comm Coll (ME)

CONSUMER MERCHANDISING/ RETAILING MANAGEMENT

Clinton Comm Coll (NY)
FIDM/Fashion Inst of Design & Merchandising, Los Angeles Campus (CA)
FIDM/Fashion Inst of Design & Merchandising, Orange County Campus (CA)
FIDM/Fashion Inst of Design & Merchandising, San Francisco Campus (CA)
FIDM/The Fashion Inst of Design & Merchandising, San Diego Campus (CA)
Gateway Comm Coll (CT)
Golden West Coll (CA)
Iowa Lakes Comm Coll (IA)
J. Sargeant Reynolds Comm Coll (VA)
Lenoir Comm Coll (NC)
Lorain County Comm Coll (OH)
Monroe Comm Coll (NY)
Navarro Coll (TX)
Niagara County Comm Coll (NY)
Northland Comm Coll (MN)
Stark State Coll (OH)
Sullivan County Comm Coll (NY)
Westchester Comm Coll (NY)

CONSUMER SERVICES AND ADVOCACY
Ohlone Coll (CA)
Pensacola State Coll (FL)

COOKING AND RELATED CULINARY ARTS
Bradford School (OH)
Butler County Comm Coll (PA)
Central Oregon Comm Coll (OR)
Columbus Culinary Inst at Bradford School (OH)
Culinary Inst of St. Louis at Hickey Coll (MO)
Hinds Comm Coll (MS)
J. Sargeant Reynolds Comm Coll (VA)
Kennebec Valley Comm Coll (ME)
Kingsborough Comm Coll of the City U of New York (NY)
Miami Dade Coll (FL)
Pensacola State Coll (FL)
Pueblo Comm Coll (CO)

CORRECTIONS
Alvin Comm Coll (TX)
Amarillo Coll (TX)
Antelope Valley Coll (CA)
Austin Comm Coll District (TX)
Butler County Comm Coll (PA)
Cayuga County Comm Coll (NY)
Comm Coll of Allegheny County (PA)
Danville Area Comm Coll (IL)
Delta Coll (MI)
Eastern Gateway Comm Coll (OH)
Florida Gateway Coll (FL)
Garrett Coll (MD)
Grand Rapids Comm Coll (MI)
Hocking Coll (OH)
Illinois Eastern Comm Colls, Frontier Community College (IL)
Illinois Eastern Comm Colls, Lincoln Trail College (IL)
Iowa Lakes Comm Coll (IA)
Kellogg Comm Coll (MI)
Lake Land Coll (IL)
Lakeland Comm Coll (OH)
Laramie County Comm Coll (WY)
Lorain County Comm Coll (OH)
Miami Dade Coll (FL)
Monroe Comm Coll (NY)
Montcalm Comm Coll (MI)
Moraine Park Tech Coll (WI)
Mt. San Antonio Coll (CA)
Mount Wachusett Comm Coll (MA)
Navarro Coll (TX)
Northeastern Jr Coll (CO)
Pennsylvania Highlands Comm Coll (PA)
Raritan Valley Comm Coll (NJ)
Riverland Comm Coll (MN)
Roane State Comm Coll (TN)
St. Clair County Comm Coll (MI)
Salem Comm Coll (NJ)
San Diego Miramar Coll (CA)
San Joaquin Delta Coll (CA)
San Joaquin Valley Coll, Bakersfield (CA)
San Joaquin Valley Coll, Fresno (CA)
San Joaquin Valley Coll, Lancaster (CA)
San Joaquin Valley Coll, Ontario (CA)
San Joaquin Valley Coll, Visalia (CA)
Sierra Coll (CA)
Tallahassee Comm Coll (FL)
Trinity Valley Comm Coll (TX)
Tunxis Comm Coll (CT)
Vincennes U (IN)
Wayne County Comm Coll District (MI)
Westchester Comm Coll (NY)
Western Nevada Coll (NV)
Westmoreland County Comm Coll (PA)
Wisconsin Indianhead Tech Coll (WI)
Wytheville Comm Coll (VA)

CORRECTIONS ADMINISTRATION
Eastern Wyoming Coll (WY)
Kirtland Comm Coll (MI)

CORRECTIONS AND CRIMINAL JUSTICE RELATED
Career Tech Coll, Monroe (LA)
Chesapeake Coll (MD)
Corning Comm Coll (NY)
Genesee Comm Coll (NY)
Hinds Comm Coll (MS)

Miami Dade Coll (FL)
Nebraska Indian Comm Coll (NE)
Northwestern Michigan Coll (MI)
Northwest State Comm Coll (OH)

COSMETOLOGY
Butler County Comm Coll (PA)
Century Coll (MN)
Citrus Coll (CA)
Clary Sage Coll (OK)
Coastal Bend Coll (TX)
Colorado Northwestern Comm Coll (CO)
Copiah-Lincoln Comm Coll (MS)
Eastern Arizona Coll (AZ)
Eastern Wyoming Coll (WY)
Fayetteville Tech Comm Coll (NC)
Golden West Coll (CA)
Guilford Tech Comm Coll (NC)
Haywood Comm Coll (NC)
Houston Comm Coll (TX)
J. F. Drake State Comm and Tech Coll (AL)
Kaskaskia Coll (IL)
Kirtland Comm Coll (MI)
Lamar Comm Coll (CO)
Lenoir Comm Coll (NC)
Lone Star Coll–Kingwood (TX)
Lone Star Coll–North Harris (TX)
Lorain County Comm Coll (OH)
Los Angeles Trade-Tech Coll (CA)
Minnesota State Coll–Southeast Tech (MN)
Montcalm Comm Coll (MI)
New Mexico Jr Coll (NM)
Northeastern Jr Coll (CO)
Northeast Iowa Comm Coll (IA)
Olympic Coll (WA)
Paris Jr Coll (TX)
Pasadena City Coll (CA)
Pueblo Comm Coll (CO)
Randolph Comm Coll (NC)
Ridgewater Coll (MN)
Salt Lake Comm Coll (UT)
San Jacinto Coll District (TX)
San Juan Coll (NM)
Shawnee Comm Coll (IL)
Southeastern Comm Coll (IA)
Trinity Valley Comm Coll (TX)
Umpqua Comm Coll (OR)
Vincennes U (IN)

COSMETOLOGY AND PERSONAL GROOMING ARTS RELATED
Comm Coll of Allegheny County (PA)
Lorain County Comm Coll (OH)

COSMETOLOGY, BARBER/STYLING, AND NAIL INSTRUCTION
IBMC Coll (CO)
Pasadena City Coll (CA)
San Jacinto Coll District (TX)

COSTUME DESIGN
FIDM/Fashion Inst of Design & Merchandising, Los Angeles Campus (CA)
Ohlone Coll (CA)

COUNSELING PSYCHOLOGY
Trinidad State Jr Coll (CO)

COURT REPORTING
Alvin Comm Coll (TX)
Anoka Tech Coll (MN)
Coll of Marin (CA)
Comm Coll of Allegheny County (PA)
Fox Valley Tech Coll (WI)
Gadsden State Comm Coll (AL)
Harrisburg Area Comm Coll (PA)
Hinds Comm Coll (MS)
Houston Comm Coll (TX)
Long Island Business Inst (NY)
Luzerne County Comm Coll (PA)
Miami Dade Coll (FL)
Midlands Tech Coll (SC)
Moraine Park Tech Coll (WI)
South Suburban Coll (IL)
Stark State Coll (OH)
State U of New York Coll of Technology at Alfred (NY)

CRAFTS, FOLK ART AND ARTISANRY
Harrisburg Area Comm Coll (PA)

CREATIVE WRITING
Anoka-Ramsey Comm Coll (MN)

Anoka-Ramsey Comm Coll, Cambridge Campus (MN)
Austin Comm Coll District (TX)
Coll of the Desert (CA)
Normandale Comm Coll (MN)
North Hennepin Comm Coll (MN)
Reading Area Comm Coll (PA)
Tompkins Cortland Comm Coll (NY)

CRIMINALISTICS AND CRIMINAL SCIENCE
Harrisburg Area Comm Coll (PA)
Tyler Jr Coll (TX)

CRIMINAL JUSTICE/LAW ENFORCEMENT ADMINISTRATION
Allen Comm Coll (KS)
Amarillo Coll (TX)
Anne Arundel Comm Coll (MD)
Antelope Valley Coll (CA)
Arapahoe Comm Coll (CO)
Arizona Western Coll (AZ)
Bainbridge State Coll (GA)
Borough of Manhattan Comm Coll of the City U of New York (NY)
Brookhaven Coll (TX)
Bunker Hill Comm Coll (MA)
Butler County Comm Coll (PA)
Camden County Coll (NJ)
Carteret Comm Coll (NC)
Casper Coll (WY)
Central Maine Comm Coll (ME)
Central Virginia Comm Coll (VA)
Central Wyoming Coll (WY)
Citrus Coll (CA)
Clinton Comm Coll (NY)
Coastal Bend Coll (TX)
Coll of Central Florida (FL)
Coll of Southern Idaho (ID)
Coll of Southern Maryland (MD)
Columbia-Greene Comm Coll (NY)
Comm Coll of Aurora (CO)
Comm Coll of Philadelphia (PA)
Comm Coll of the Air Force (AL)
Dabney S. Lancaster Comm Coll (VA)
Darton State Coll (GA)
Daytona State Coll (FL)
Delaware Tech & Comm Coll, Terry Campus (DE)
Denmark Tech Coll (SC)
Des Moines Area Comm Coll (IA)
Eastern Arizona Coll (AZ)
Eastern Wyoming Coll (WY)
Elizabethtown Comm and Tech Coll, Elizabethtown (KY)
Erie Comm Coll (NY)
Erie Comm Coll, North Campus (NY)
Erie Comm Coll, South Campus (NY)
Finger Lakes Comm Coll (NY)
Florida Gateway Coll (FL)
Florida SouthWestern State Coll (FL)
Florida State Coll at Jacksonville (FL)
Frederick Comm Coll (MD)
Gateway Comm and Tech Coll (KY)
Genesee Comm Coll (NY)
Golden West Coll (CA)
Goodwin Coll (CT)
Grand Rapids Comm Coll (MI)
Guam Comm Coll (GU)
Gulf Coast State Coll (FL)
Harper Coll (IL)
Harrisburg Area Comm Coll (PA)
Haywood Comm Coll (NC)
Hillsborough Comm Coll (FL)
Hocking Coll (OH)
Hopkinsville Comm Coll (KY)
Housatonic Comm Coll (CT)
Howard Comm Coll (MD)
Iowa Lakes Comm Coll (IA)
James H. Faulkner State Comm Coll (AL)
Jamestown Comm Coll (NY)
Jefferson Coll (MO)
Jefferson Comm Coll (NY)
John Tyler Comm Coll (VA)
J. Sargeant Reynolds Comm Coll (VA)
Kankakee Comm Coll (IL)
Kaskaskia Coll (IL)
Kilgore Coll (TX)
Kingsborough Comm Coll of the City U of New York (NY)
Kirtland Comm Coll (MI)
Laramie County Comm Coll (WY)
Lehigh Carbon Comm Coll (PA)
Lenoir Comm Coll (NC)

Lone Star Coll–CyFair (TX)
Lone Star Coll–Kingwood (TX)
Lone Star Coll–Montgomery (TX)
Lone Star Coll–North Harris (TX)
Lone Star Coll–Tomball (TX)
Lone Star Coll–U Park (TX)
Lower Columbia Coll (WA)
Luzerne County Comm Coll (PA)
Macomb Comm Coll (MI)
Manchester Comm Coll (CT)
Massachusetts Bay Comm Coll (MA)
Mesa Comm Coll (AZ)
Miami Dade Coll (FL)
Middlesex Comm Coll (MA)
Mohawk Valley Comm Coll (NY)
Monroe Comm Coll (NY)
Montcalm Comm Coll (MI)
Mount Wachusett Comm Coll (MA)
Nassau Comm Coll (NY)
Navarro Coll (TX)
Niagara County Comm Coll (NY)
North Central Texas Coll (TX)
Northern Essex Comm Coll (MA)
Northland Comm Coll (MN)
North Shore Comm Coll (MA)
Northwest Coll (WY)
Northwestern Coll (IL)
Norwalk Comm Coll (CT)
Ohlone Coll (CA)
Owens Comm Coll, Toledo (OH)
Pasadena City Coll (CA)
Pasco-Hernando State Coll (FL)
Penn Foster Coll (AZ)
Pennsylvania Highlands Comm Coll (PA)
Pensacola State Coll (FL)
Piedmont Comm Coll (NC)
Pueblo Comm Coll (CO)
Rappahannock Comm Coll (VA)
Raritan Valley Comm Coll (NJ)
Rio Hondo Coll (CA)
Roane State Comm Coll (TN)
Rockland Comm Coll (NY)
Rock Valley Coll (IL)
St. Clair County Comm Coll (MI)
St. Philip's Coll (TX)
Salt Lake Comm Coll (UT)
San Diego Miramar Coll (CA)
San Joaquin Valley Coll, Hanford (CA)
San Joaquin Valley Coll, Hesperia (CA)
Scottsdale Comm Coll (AZ)
Seminole State Coll (OK)
Seminole State Coll of Florida (FL)
Somerset Comm Coll (KY)
Southeastern Comm Coll (IA)
Southern U at Shreveport (LA)
South Florida State Coll (FL)
South Hills School of Business & Technology, State College (PA)
Southwestern Illinois Coll (IL)
Southwest Virginia Comm Coll (VA)
Spartanburg Methodist Coll (SC)
Tallahassee Comm Coll (FL)
Tompkins Cortland Comm Coll (NY)
Trident Tech Coll (SC)
Trinidad State Jr Coll (CO)
Trinity Valley Comm Coll (TX)
Truckee Meadows Comm Coll (NV)
Tunxis Comm Coll (CT)
Tyler Jr Coll (TX)
Ulster County Comm Coll (NY)
Umpqua Comm Coll (OR)
U of Alaska Southeast, Sitka Campus (AK)
U of Arkansas Comm Coll at Morrilton (AR)
Virginia Western Comm Coll (VA)
Western Nevada Coll (NV)
Western Wyoming Comm Coll (WY)
Wytheville Comm Coll (VA)

CRIMINAL JUSTICE/POLICE SCIENCE
Alexandria Tech and Comm Coll (MN)
Alvin Comm Coll (TX)
Amarillo Coll (TX)
Anne Arundel Comm Coll (MD)
Antelope Valley Coll (CA)
Arkansas Northeastern Coll (AR)
Austin Comm Coll District (TX)
Berkeley Coll–Westchester Campus (NY)
Bunker Hill Comm Coll (MA)
Burlington County Coll (NJ)
Butler County Comm Coll (PA)
Cape Fear Comm Coll (NC)
Carroll Comm Coll (MD)

Cayuga County Comm Coll (NY)
Cecil Coll (MD)
Central Texas Coll (TX)
Century Coll (MN)
Citrus Coll (CA)
Cleveland State Comm Coll (TN)
Clinton Comm Coll (NY)
Cloud County Comm Coll (KS)
Coastal Bend Coll (TX)
Cochise Coll, Douglas (AZ)
Coll of Marin (CA)
Coll of the Canyons (CA)
Coll of the Desert (CA)
Collin County Comm Coll District (TX)
Comm Coll of Allegheny County (PA)
The Comm Coll of Baltimore County (MD)
Comm Coll of Rhode Island (RI)
Copiah-Lincoln Comm Coll (MS)
Corning Comm Coll (NY)
County Coll of Morris (NJ)
Cumberland County Coll (NJ)
Danville Area Comm Coll (IL)
Daytona State Coll (FL)
Delaware Tech & Comm Coll, Terry Campus (DE)
Delgado Comm Coll (LA)
Delta Coll (MI)
Dutchess Comm Coll (NY)
Dyersburg State Comm Coll (TN)
Eastern Arizona Coll (AZ)
Eastern Gateway Comm Coll (OH)
Eastern Wyoming Coll (WY)
Edison Comm Coll (OH)
Elgin Comm Coll (IL)
Erie Comm Coll, North Campus (NY)
Finger Lakes Comm Coll (NY)
Florida State Coll at Jacksonville (FL)
Fox Valley Tech Coll (WI)
Gadsden State Comm Coll (AL)
Gateway Tech Coll (WI)
Genesee Comm Coll (NY)
George C. Wallace Comm Coll (AL)
Georgia Highlands Coll (GA)
Golden West Coll (CA)
Grand Rapids Comm Coll (MI)
Greenfield Comm Coll (MA)
Hagerstown Comm Coll (MD)
Halifax Comm Coll (NC)
Harford Comm Coll (MD)
Harrisburg Area Comm Coll (PA)
Hawkeye Comm Coll (IA)
Hocking Coll (OH)
Hopkinsville Comm Coll (KY)
Houston Comm Coll (TX)
Hudson County Comm Coll (NJ)
Hutchinson Comm Coll (KS)
Iowa Central Comm Coll (IA)
Iowa Lakes Comm Coll (IA)
Jamestown Comm Coll (NY)
Jefferson Coll (MO)
Jefferson State Comm Coll (AL)
Johnston Comm Coll (NC)
Kalamazoo Valley Comm Coll (MI)
Kankakee Comm Coll (IL)
Kellogg Comm Coll (MI)
Kirtland Comm Coll (MI)
Kishwaukee Coll (IL)
Lake Area Tech Inst (SD)
Lake Land Coll (IL)
Lakeland Comm Coll (OH)
Lake Region State Coll (ND)
Lenoir Comm Coll (NC)
Lorain County Comm Coll (OH)
Macomb Comm Coll (MI)
McHenry County Coll (IL)
Miami Dade Coll (FL)
Middlesex County Coll (NJ)
Minneapolis Comm and Tech Coll (MN)
Minnesota West Comm and Tech Coll (MN)
MiraCosta Coll (CA)
Mohave Comm Coll (AZ)
Monroe Comm Coll (NY)
Monroe County Comm Coll (MI)
Montgomery Coll (MD)
Montgomery County Comm Coll (PA)
Moraine Valley Comm Coll (IL)
Mott Comm Coll (MI)
Mt. San Antonio Coll (CA)
Navarro Coll (TX)
New Mexico Jr Coll (NM)
Normandale Comm Coll (MN)
Northcentral Tech Coll (WI)
North Central Texas Coll (TX)
Northeastern Jr Coll (CO)
North Hennepin Comm Coll (MN)

North Iowa Area Comm Coll (IA)
Northland Comm Coll (MN)
Northwest-Shoals Comm Coll (AL)
Northwest State Comm Coll (OH)
Oakton Comm Coll (IL)
Ocean County Coll (NJ)
Ohlone Coll (CA)
Oklahoma State U, Oklahoma City (OK)
Owens Comm Coll, Toledo (OH)
Quinsigamond Comm Coll (MA)
Rappahannock Comm Coll (VA)
Raritan Valley Comm Coll (NJ)
Reading Area Comm Coll (PA)
Richland Comm Coll (IL)
Ridgewater Coll (MN)
Riverland Comm Coll (MN)
Roane State Comm Coll (TN)
Rogue Comm Coll (OR)
St. Charles Comm Coll (MO)
Salem Comm Coll (NJ)
San Diego Miramar Coll (CA)
San Jacinto Coll District (TX)
San Joaquin Delta Coll (CA)
San Juan Coll (NM)
Schoolcraft Coll (MI)
Seminole State Coll (OK)
Shawnee Comm Coll (IL)
Sierra Coll (CA)
Springfield Tech Comm Coll (MA)
State Fair Comm Coll (MO)
Sullivan County Comm Coll (NY)
Tallahassee Comm Coll (FL)
Terra State Comm Coll (OH)
Three Rivers Comm Coll (CT)
Tompkins Cortland Comm Coll (NY)
Trinity Valley Comm Coll (TX)
Tulsa Comm Coll (OK)
Tyler Jr Coll (TX)
Victoria Coll (TX)
Victor Valley Coll (CA)
Vincennes U (IN)
Volunteer State Comm Coll (TN)
Walters State Comm Coll (TN)
Waukesha County Tech Coll (WI)
Wayne County Comm Coll District (MI)
Wenatchee Valley Coll (WA)
Western Iowa Tech Comm Coll (IA)
Western Nevada Coll (NV)
Westmoreland County Comm Coll (PA)
Whatcom Comm Coll (WA)
Wisconsin Indianhead Tech Coll (WI)
Wor-Wic Comm Coll (MD)
Wytheville Comm Coll (VA)

CRIMINAL JUSTICE/SAFETY
Alamance Comm Coll (NC)
American Samoa Comm Coll (AS)
Ancilla Coll (IN)
Blue Ridge Comm and Tech Coll (WV)
Borough of Manhattan Comm Coll of the City U of New York (NY)
Bossier Parish Comm Coll (LA)
Bowling Green State U-Firelands Coll (OH)
Bucks County Comm Coll (PA)
Catawba Valley Comm Coll (NC)
Cedar Valley Coll (TX)
Central Maine Comm Coll (ME)
Century Coll (MN)
Chandler-Gilbert Comm Coll (AZ)
Cleveland Comm Coll (NC)
Dean Coll (MA)
Dyersburg State Comm Coll (TN)
Eastern Wyoming Coll (WY)
Fayetteville Tech Comm Coll (NC)
Fiorello H. LaGuardia Comm Coll of the City U of New York (NY)
Forsyth Tech Comm Coll (NC)
Genesee Comm Coll (NY)
Georgia Highlands Coll (GA)
Great Basin Coll (NV)
Greenville Tech Coll (SC)
Guilford Tech Comm Coll (NC)
Hinds Comm Coll (MS)
Holyoke Comm Coll (MA)
Horry-Georgetown Tech Coll (SC)
James Sprunt Comm Coll (NC)
Kellogg Comm Coll (MI)
Kent State U at Ashtabula (OH)
Kent State U at East Liverpool (OH)
Kent State U at Salem (OH)
Kent State U at Trumbull (OH)
Kent State U at Tuscarawas (OH)
Kishwaukee Coll (IL)
Lamar Comm Coll (CO)
Lehigh Carbon Comm Coll (PA)

Midlands Tech Coll (SC)
Minneapolis Comm and Tech Coll (MN)
Minnesota State Coll–Southeast Tech (MN)
Monroe County Comm Coll (MI)
Montgomery Comm Coll (NC)
Nassau Comm Coll (NY)
Normandale Comm Coll (MN)
Northampton Comm Coll (PA)
North Hennepin Comm Coll (MN)
Northwest State Comm Coll (OH)
Oregon Coast Comm Coll (OR)
Paris Jr Coll (TX)
Phoenix Coll (AZ)
Potomac State Coll of West Virginia U (WV)
Randolph Comm Ooll (NC)
Richmond Comm Coll (NC)
Sheridan Coll (WY)
South Florida State Coll (FL)
South Louisiana Comm Coll (LA)
South Piedmont Comm Coll (NC)
South Suburban Coll (IL)
Southwestern Michigan Coll (MI)
Sowela Tech Comm Coll (LA)
Tyler Jr Coll (TX)
U of Arkansas Comm Coll at Batesville (AR)
U of Cincinnati Clermont Coll (OH)
Walters State Comm Coll (TN)
Western Dakota Tech Inst (SD)
Westmoreland County Comm Coll (PA)
White Mountains Comm Coll (NH)
York County Comm Coll (ME)

CRIMINOLOGY
Coll of Central Florida (FL)
Genesee Comm Coll (NY)
Northland Comm Coll (MN)
Paris Jr Coll (TX)
Potomac State Coll of West Virginia U (WV)
Western Wyoming Comm Coll (WY)

CRISIS/EMERGENCY/DISASTER MANAGEMENT
Bucks County Comm Coll (PA)
Casper Coll (WY)
Cincinnati State Tech and Comm Coll (OH)
City Colls of Chicago, Olive-Harvey College (IL)
Comm Coll of Rhode Island (RI)
Erie Comm Coll (NY)
Fayetteville Tech Comm Coll (NC)
Florida State Coll at Jacksonville (FL)
Guam Comm Coll (GU)
Montgomery Coll (MD)
Sullivan County Comm Coll (NY)
Western Iowa Tech Comm Coll (IA)

CRITICAL INCIDENT RESPONSE/SPECIAL POLICE OPERATIONS
Raritan Valley Comm Coll (NJ)

CROP PRODUCTION
Arizona Western Coll (AZ)
Coll of the Desert (CA)
Dakota Coll at Bottineau (ND)
Greenfield Comm Coll (MA)
Iowa Lakes Comm Coll (IA)
Northeast Iowa Comm Coll (IA)
Northwest Coll (WY)
Northwestern Michigan Coll (MI)
The Ohio State U Ag Tech Inst (OH)
Ridgewater Coll (MN)
San Joaquin Delta Coll (CA)

CULINARY ARTS
Alamance Comm Coll (NC)
Alvin Comm Coll (TX)
Arizona Western Coll (AZ)
Austin Comm Coll District (TX)
Bellingham Tech Coll (WA)
Blue Ridge Comm and Tech Coll (WV)
Bossier Parish Comm Coll (LA)
Bucks County Comm Coll (PA)
Bunker Hill Comm Coll (MA)
Cape Fear Comm Coll (NC)
Central Virginia Comm Coll (VA)
Central Wyoming Coll (WY)
Cincinnati State Tech and Comm Coll (OH)
Clark Coll (WA)
Cochise Coll, Douglas (AZ)
Coll of Southern Idaho (ID)
Coll of the Desert (CA)

Collin County Comm Coll District (TX)
Commonwealth Tech Inst (PA)
Comm Coll of Allegheny County (PA)
Comm Coll of Philadelphia (PA)
Daytona State Coll (FL)
Delaware Tech & Comm Coll, Terry Campus (DE)
Des Moines Area Comm Coll (IA)
El Centro Coll (TX)
Elgin Comm Coll (IL)
Erie Comm Coll (NY)
Erie Comm Coll, North Campus (NY)
Fayetteville Tech Comm Coll (NC)
Finger Lakes Comm Coll (NY)
Florida State Coll at Jacksonville (FL)
Fox Valley Tech Coll (WI)
Grand Rapids Comm Coll (MI)
Greenville Tech Coll (SC)
Guilford Tech Comm Coll (NC)
Harrisburg Area Comm Coll (PA)
H. Councill Trenholm State Tech Coll (AL)
Hocking Coll (OH)
Horry-Georgetown Tech Coll (SC)
Houston Comm Coll (TX)
Hudson County Comm Coll (NJ)
Jefferson Coll (MO)
J. F. Drake State Comm and Tech Coll (AL)
Kaskaskia Coll (IL)
Lakes Region Comm Coll (NH)
Los Angeles Trade-Tech Coll (CA)
Luzerne County Comm Coll (PA)
Macomb Comm Coll (MI)
Miami Dade Coll (FL)
Mitchell Tech Inst (SD)
Mohave Comm Coll (AZ)
Monroe County Comm Coll (MI)
Montgomery County Comm Coll (PA)
Moraine Park Tech Coll (WI)
Mott Comm Coll (MI)
New England Culinary Inst (VT)
Niagara County Comm Coll (NY)
Northampton Comm Coll (PA)
North Shore Comm Coll (MA)
Northwestern Michigan Coll (MI)
Olympic Coll (WA)
Orange Coast Coll (CA)
Ozarks Tech Comm Coll (MO)
Phoenix Coll (AZ)
Renton Tech Coll (WA)
Rockland Comm Coll (NY)
St. Philip's Coll (TX)
Salem Comm Coll (NJ)
Salt Lake Comm Coll (UT)
San Jacinto Coll District (TX)
San Joaquin Delta Coll (CA)
Schoolcraft Coll (MI)
Scottsdale Comm Coll (AZ)
Sheridan Coll (WY)
South Louisiana Comm Coll (LA)
Sowela Tech Comm Coll (LA)
State U of New York Coll of Technology at Alfred (NY)
Sullivan County Comm Coll (NY)
Tompkins Cortland Comm Coll (NY)
Trident Tech Coll (SC)
Truckee Meadows Comm Coll (NV)
Vincennes U (IN)
Westchester Comm Coll (NY)
Westmoreland County Comm Coll (PA)
White Mountains Comm Coll (NH)
York County Comm Coll (ME)

CULINARY ARTS RELATED
Guam Comm Coll (GU)
Iowa Lakes Comm Coll (IA)
Oklahoma State U Inst of Technology (OK)

CUSTOMER SERVICE MANAGEMENT
Central Oregon Comm Coll (OR)
Comm Coll of Rhode Island (RI)
Corning Comm Coll (NY)

CUSTOMER SERVICE SUPPORT/ CALL CENTER/TELESERVICE OPERATION
Central Wyoming Coll (WY)
Miami Dade Coll (FL)

CYBER/COMPUTER FORENSICS AND COUNTERTERRORISM
Catawba Valley Comm Coll (NC)
Century Coll (MN)
Columbia-Greene Comm Coll (NY)
Harper Coll (IL)
Pensacola State Coll (FL)
South Piedmont Comm Coll (NC)

CYBER/ELECTRONIC OPERATIONS AND WARFARE
Oklahoma City Comm Coll (OK)

DAIRY HUSBANDRY AND PRODUCTION
Northeast Iowa Comm Coll (IA)
The Ohio State U Ag Tech Inst (OH)
Ridgewater Coll (MN)

DAIRY SCIENCE
Mt. San Antonio Coll (CA)
The Ohio State U Ag Tech Inst (OH)

DANCE
Austin Comm Coll District (TX)
Casper Coll (WY)
Citrus Coll (CA)
Coll of Marin (CA)
Darton State Coll (GA)
Dean Coll (MA)
Greenfield Comm Coll (MA)
Hinds Comm Coll (MS)
Kilgore Coll (TX)
Lone Star Coll–CyFair (TX)
Miami Dade Coll (FL)
MiraCosta Coll (CA)
Nassau Comm Coll (NY)
Navarro Coll (TX)
Northern Essex Comm Coll (MA)
Orange Coast Coll (CA)
Palomar Coll (CA)
Pasadena City Coll (CA)
Raritan Valley Comm Coll (NJ)
San Jacinto Coll District (TX)
San Joaquin Delta Coll (CA)
Trinity Valley Comm Coll (TX)
Truckee Meadows Comm Coll (NV)
Tyler Jr Coll (TX)
Westchester Comm Coll (NY)
Western Wyoming Comm Coll (WY)

DANCE RELATED
Citrus Coll (CA)

DATA ENTRY/ MICROCOMPUTER APPLICATIONS
Arizona Western Coll (AZ)
Bellingham Tech Coll (WA)
Bunker Hill Comm Coll (MA)
Chandler-Gilbert Comm Coll (AZ)
Clark Coll (WA)
Elgin Comm Coll (IL)
Fiorello H. LaGuardia Comm Coll of the City U of New York (NY)
Gateway Comm Coll (CT)
Iowa Lakes Comm Coll (IA)
Lorain County Comm Coll (OH)
Lower Columbia Coll (WA)
Luzerne County Comm Coll (PA)
MiraCosta Coll (CA)
Montgomery Coll (MD)
Nebraska Indian Comm Coll (NE)
Northland Comm Coll (MN)
North Shore Comm Coll (MA)
Northwest State Comm Coll (OH)
Richland Comm Coll (IL)
Riverland Comm Coll (MN)
St. Philip's Coll (TX)
Seminole State Coll of Florida (FL)
Sierra Coll (CA)
Stark State Coll (OH)
Sullivan County Comm Coll (NY)
Tyler Jr Coll (TX)
Western Wyoming Comm Coll (WY)
Westmoreland County Comm Coll (PA)

DATA ENTRY/ MICROCOMPUTER APPLICATIONS RELATED
Blue Ridge Comm and Tech Coll (WV)
Camden County Coll (NJ)
Kellogg Comm Coll (MI)
Lorain County Comm Coll (OH)
Northland Comm Coll (MN)
Orange Coast Coll (CA)
Pasadena City Coll (CA)
Potomac State Coll of West Virginia U (WV)
Richland Comm Coll (IL)
Riverland Comm Coll (MN)
Seminole State Coll of Florida (FL)
Stark State Coll (OH)

DATA MODELING/ WAREHOUSING AND DATABASE ADMINISTRATION
Chandler-Gilbert Comm Coll (AZ)
Coll of Marin (CA)

Northland Comm Coll (MN)
Quinsigamond Comm Coll (MA)
Seminole State Coll of Florida (FL)
Southwestern Illinois Coll (IL)

DATA PROCESSING AND DATA PROCESSING TECHNOLOGY
Allen Comm Coll (KS)
Ancilla Coll (IN)
Antelope Valley Coll (CA)
Bainbridge State Coll (GA)
Cedar Valley Coll (TX)
Citrus Coll (CA)
Copiah-Lincoln Comm Coll (MS)
Dabney S. Lancaster Comm Coll (VA)
Delgado Comm Coll (LA)
Eastern Gateway Comm Coll (OH)
El Centro Coll (TX)
Elizabethtown Comm and Tech Coll, Elizabethtown (KY)
Finger Lakes Comm Coll (NY)
Gateway Comm Coll (CT)
Great Basin Coll (NV)
Greenville Tech Coll (SC)
Housatonic Comm Coll (CT)
Iowa Central Comm Coll (IA)
Iowa Lakes Comm Coll (IA)
Kingsborough Comm Coll of the City U of New York (NY)
Lamar Comm Coll (CO)
Los Angeles Trade-Tech Coll (CA)
Luzerne County Comm Coll (PA)
Mesa Comm Coll (AZ)
Midlands Tech Coll (SC)
Monroe Comm Coll (NY)
Monroe County Comm Coll (MI)
Montcalm Comm Coll (MI)
Mt. San Antonio Coll (CA)
Nassau Comm Coll (NY)
Navarro Coll (TX)
New Mexico Jr Coll (NM)
North Central Texas Coll (TX)
Northern Essex Comm Coll (MA)
Orange Coast Coll (CA)
Otero Jr Coll (CO)
Rockland Comm Coll (NY)
St. Clair County Comm Coll (MI)
San Juan Coll (NM)
Seminole State Coll of Florida (FL)
Spartanburg Comm Coll (SC)
Tech Coll of the Lowcountry (SC)
Terra State Comm Coll (OH)
Trinity Valley Comm Coll (TX)
Tunxis Comm Coll (CT)
U of Cincinnati Clermont Coll (OH)
Virginia Western Comm Coll (VA)
Walters State Comm Coll (TN)
Westchester Comm Coll (NY)
Western Wyoming Comm Coll (WY)
Westmoreland County Comm Coll (PA)

DEAF STUDIES
Ohlone Coll (CA)

DENTAL ASSISTING
Bradford School (PA)
Camden County Coll (NJ)
Central Oregon Comm Coll (OR)
Century Coll (MN)
Citrus Coll (CA)
Coll of Central Florida (FL)
Coll of Marin (CA)
Coll of Southern Idaho (ID)
Comm Care Coll (OK)
Comm Coll of the Air Force (AL)
Delta Coll (MI)
Eastern Gateway Comm Coll (OH)
H. Councill Trenholm State Tech Coll (AL)
Hennepin Tech Coll (MN)
Hinds Comm Coll (MS)
Humacao Comm Coll (PR)
IBMC Coll (CO)
International Business Coll, Indianapolis (IN)
James H. Faulkner State Comm Coll (AL)
J. Sargeant Reynolds Comm Coll (VA)
Kaskaskia Coll (IL)
Lake Area Tech Inst (SD)
Luzerne County Comm Coll (PA)
Manor Coll (PA)
Middlesex Comm Coll (MA)
Midlands Tech Coll (SC)
Mid-Plains Comm Coll, North Platte (NE)
Minneapolis Comm and Tech Coll (MN)

Minnesota West Comm and Tech Coll (MN)
Mohave Comm Coll (AZ)
Mott Comm Coll (MI)
Northern Essex Comm Coll (MA)
Northwestern Michigan Coll (MI)
Northwest Tech Coll (MN)
Palomar Coll (CA)
Pasadena City Coll (CA)
Phoenix Coll (AZ)
Pueblo Comm Coll (CO)
Raritan Valley Comm Coll (NJ)
Tallahassee Comm Coll (FL)
Western Iowa Tech Comm Coll (IA)
Westmoreland County Comm Coll (PA)
West Virginia Jr Coll–Bridgeport (WV)

DENTAL HYGIENE
Amarillo Coll (TX)
Austin Comm Coll District (TX)
Burlington County Coll (NJ)
Camden County Coll (NJ)
Cape Fear Comm Coll (NC)
Catawba Valley Comm Coll (NC)
Century Coll (MN)
Clark Coll (WA)
Coastal Bend Coll (TX)
Collin County Comm Coll District (TX)
Colorado Northwestern Comm Coll (CO)
The Comm Coll of Baltimore County (MD)
Comm Coll of Denver (CO)
Comm Coll of Philadelphia (PA)
Comm Coll of Rhode Island (RI)
Darton State Coll (GA)
Daytona State Coll (FL)
Delgado Comm Coll (LA)
Delta Coll (MI)
Des Moines Area Comm Coll (IA)
Elizabethtown Comm and Tech Coll, Elizabethtown (KY)
Erie Comm Coll, North Campus (NY)
Fayetteville Tech Comm Coll (NC)
Florida SouthWestern State Coll (FL)
Florida State Coll at Jacksonville (FL)
Fox Valley Tech Coll (WI)
Georgia Highlands Coll (GA)
Goodwin Coll (CT)
Grand Rapids Comm Coll (MI)
Great Falls Coll Montana State U (MT)
Greenville Tech Coll (SC)
Guilford Tech Comm Coll (NC)
Gulf Coast State Coll (FL)
Hagerstown Comm Coll (MD)
Halifax Comm Coll (NC)
Harper Coll (IL)
Harrisburg Area Comm Coll (PA)
Hawkeye Comm Coll (IA)
Hillsborough Comm Coll (FL)
Hinds Comm Coll (MS)
Kalamazoo Valley Comm Coll (MI)
Kellogg Comm Coll (MI)
Lake Land Coll (IL)
Lakeland Comm Coll (OH)
Laramie County Comm Coll (WY)
Lone Star Coll–Kingwood (TX)
Luzerne County Comm Coll (PA)
Manor Coll (PA)
Miami Dade Coll (FL)
Middlesex Comm Coll (MA)
Middlesex County Coll (NJ)
Midlands Tech Coll (SC)
Mohave Comm Coll (AZ)
Monroe Comm Coll (NY)
Montgomery County Comm Coll (PA)
Mott Comm Coll (MI)
Mount Wachusett Comm Coll (MA)
Navarro Coll (TX)
Normandale Comm Coll (MN)
Northampton Comm Coll (PA)
Northcentral Tech Coll (WI)
Northern Virginia Comm Coll (VA)
Ocean County Coll (NJ)
Orange Coast Coll (CA)
Owens Comm Coll, Toledo (OH)
Pasadena City Coll (CA)
Pasco-Hernando State Coll (FL)
Pensacola State Coll (FL)
Phoenix Coll (AZ)
Pueblo Comm Coll (CO)
Quinsigamond Comm Coll (MA)
Raritan Valley Comm Coll (NJ)
Roane State Comm Coll (TN)
Rock Valley Coll (IL)

Salt Lake Comm Coll (UT)
San Joaquin Valley Coll, Chula Vista (CA)
San Joaquin Valley Coll, Ontario (CA)
San Joaquin Valley Coll, Visalia (CA)
San Juan Coll (NM)
Sheridan Coll (WY)
Southern U at Shreveport (LA)
South Florida State Coll (FL)
Springfield Tech Comm Coll (MA)
Stark State Coll (OH)
State Fair Comm Coll (MO)
Tallahassee Comm Coll (FL)
Texas State Tech Coll Harlingen (TX)
Trident Tech Coll (SC)
Truckee Meadows Comm Coll (NV)
Tulsa Comm Coll (OK)
Tunxis Comm Coll (CT)
Tyler Jr Coll (TX)
Virginia Western Comm Coll (VA)
Waukesha County Tech Coll (WI)
Wayne County Comm Coll District (MI)
Westmoreland County Comm Coll (PA)
Wytheville Comm Coll (VA)

DENTAL LABORATORY TECHNOLOGY
Commonwealth Tech Inst (PA)
Comm Coll of the Air Force (AL)
Delgado Comm Coll (LA)
Erie Comm Coll, South Campus (NY)
J. Sargeant Reynolds Comm Coll (VA)
Middlesex Comm Coll (MA)
Pasadena City Coll (CA)
Texas State Tech Coll Harlingen (TX)

DENTAL SERVICES AND ALLIED PROFESSIONS RELATED
Quinsigamond Comm Coll (MA)

DESIGN AND APPLIED ARTS RELATED
County Coll of Morris (NJ)
Howard Comm Coll (MD)
Iowa Lakes Comm Coll (IA)
Kingsborough Comm Coll of the City U of New York (NY)
Niagara County Comm Coll (NY)
Oklahoma City Comm Coll (OK)
Raritan Valley Comm Coll (NJ)
Rockland Comm Coll (NY)
Tunxis Comm Coll (CT)
Vincennes U (IN)
Wenatchee Valley Comm Coll (WA)
Westchester Comm Coll (NY)

DESIGN AND VISUAL COMMUNICATIONS
Brookhaven Coll (TX)
Bunker Hill Comm Coll (MA)
Cecil Coll (MD)
Central Virginia Comm Coll (VA)
Coll of Marin (CA)
Elgin Comm Coll (IL)
FIDM/Fashion Inst of Design & Merchandising, Los Angeles Campus (CA)
FIDM/Fashion Inst of Design & Merchandising, Orange County Campus (CA)
FIDM/Fashion Inst of Design & Merchandising, San Francisco Campus (CA)
FIDM/The Fashion Inst of Design & Merchandising, San Diego Campus (CA)
Guam Comm Coll (GU)
Harrisburg Area Comm Coll (PA)
Hutchinson Comm Coll (KS)
Lone Star Coll–CyFair (TX)
Lone Star Coll–Kingwood (TX)
Lone Star Coll–North Harris (TX)
Minneapolis Comm and Tech Coll (MN)
Moraine Valley Comm Coll (IL)
Nassau Comm Coll (NY)
Northwest State Comm Coll (OH)
Oklahoma City Comm Coll (OK)
Palomar Coll (CA)
Salt Lake Comm Coll (UT)

DESKTOP PUBLISHING AND DIGITAL IMAGING DESIGN
Camden County Coll (NJ)

Cincinnati State Tech and Comm Coll (OH)
Des Moines Area Comm Coll (IA)
Dunwoody Coll of Technology (MN)
Hennepin Tech Coll (MN)
Houston Comm Coll (TX)
Iowa Lakes Comm Coll (IA)
Kankakee Comm Coll (IL)
Lake Land Coll (IL)
Northeast Iowa Comm Coll (IA)
North Iowa Area Comm Coll (IA)
Northwest Coll (WY)
Palomar Coll (CA)
Pasadena City Coll (CA)
Ridgewater Coll (MN)
South Louisiana Comm Coll (LA)
Southwestern Illinois Coll (IL)
Sullivan Coll of Technology and Design (KY)
Terra State Comm Coll (OH)
Umpqua Comm Coll (OR)
Western Iowa Tech Comm Coll (IA)

DEVELOPMENTAL AND CHILD PSYCHOLOGY
Iowa Lakes Comm Coll (IA)
Navarro Coll (TX)
Rockland Comm Coll (NY)
San Diego Miramar Coll (CA)
Trinity Valley Comm Coll (TX)

DEVELOPMENTAL SERVICES WORKER
Anoka Tech Coll (MN)

DIAGNOSTIC MEDICAL SONOGRAPHY AND ULTRASOUND TECHNOLOGY
Alvin Comm Coll (TX)
Austin Comm Coll District (TX)
Bowling Green State U-Firelands Coll (OH)
Bunker Hill Comm Coll (MA)
Cape Fear Comm Coll (NC)
Cincinnati State Tech and Comm Coll (OH)
Comm Coll of Allegheny County (PA)
Comm Coll of Rhode Island (RI)
Darton State Coll (GA)
Delta Coll (MI)
El Centro Coll (TX)
Forsyth Tech Comm Coll (NC)
Greenville Tech Coll (SC)
Gulf Coast State Coll (FL)
Harper Coll (IL)
Harrisburg Area Comm Coll (PA)
H. Councill Trenholm State Tech Coll (AL)
Hillsborough Comm Coll (FL)
Hinds Comm Coll (MS)
Howard Comm Coll (MD)
Kennebec Valley Comm Coll (ME)
Laramie County Comm Coll (WY)
Lone Star Coll–CyFair (TX)
Lorain County Comm Coll (OH)
Lurleen B. Wallace Comm Coll (AL)
Miami Dade Coll (FL)
Middlesex Comm Coll (MA)
Montgomery Coll (MD)
Northampton Comm Coll (PA)
Northwestern Coll (IL)
Oklahoma City Comm Coll (OK)
Owens Comm Coll, Toledo (OH)
Pensacola State Coll (FL)
San Jacinto Coll District (TX)
South Hills School of Business & Technology, State College (PA)
South Piedmont Comm Coll (NC)
Springfield Tech Comm Coll (MA)
Tallahassee Comm Coll (FL)
Tulsa Comm Coll (OK)
Tyler Jr Coll (TX)
Westmoreland County Comm Coll (PA)

DIESEL MECHANICS TECHNOLOGY
Alexandria Tech and Comm Coll (MN)
Bellingham Tech Coll (WA)
Casper Coll (WY)
Central Texas Coll (TX)
Citrus Coll (CA)
City Colls of Chicago, Olive-Harvey College (IL)
Clark Coll (WA)
Coll of Southern Idaho (ID)
Des Moines Area Comm Coll (IA)
Eastern Arizona Coll (AZ)
Eastern Idaho Tech Coll (ID)

Elizabethtown Comm and Tech Coll, Elizabethtown (KY)
Fox Valley Tech Coll (WI)
Gateway Tech Coll (WI)
Great Basin Coll (NV)
Hawkeye Comm Coll (IA)
Hinds Comm Coll (MS)
Illinois Eastern Comm Colls, Wabash Valley College (IL)
Johnston Comm Coll (NC)
J. Sargeant Reynolds Comm Coll (VA)
Kilgore Coll (TX)
Kishwaukee Coll (IL)
Lake Area Tech Inst (SD)
Laramie County Comm Coll (WY)
Lower Columbia Coll (WA)
Mid-Plains Comm Coll, North Platte (NE)
Minnesota West Comm and Tech Coll (MN)
New Castle School of Trades (PA)
Oklahoma City Comm Coll (OK)
Oklahoma State U Inst of Technology (OK)
Oklahoma Tech Coll (OK)
Ozarks Tech Comm Coll (MO)
Palomar Coll (CA)
Raritan Valley Comm Coll (NJ)
Riverland Comm Coll (MN)
Rogue Comm Coll (OR)
St. Philip's Coll (TX)
Salt Lake Comm Coll (UT)
San Jacinto Coll District (TX)
San Juan Coll (NM)
Sheridan Coll (WY)
South Louisiana Comm Coll (LA)
State U of New York Coll of Technology at Alfred (NY)
Trinidad State Jr Coll (CO)
Truckee Meadows Comm Coll (NV)
Vincennes U (IN)
Western Wyoming Comm Coll (WY)
White Mountains Comm Coll (NH)
Williston State Coll (ND)

DIETETICS
Camden County Coll (NJ)
Central Oregon Comm Coll (OR)
Cincinnati State Tech and Comm Coll (OH)
Comm Coll of the Air Force (AL)
Delgado Comm Coll (LA)
Gateway Comm Coll (CT)
Harper Coll (IL)
Harrisburg Area Comm Coll (PA)
Hocking Coll (OH)
Miami Dade Coll (FL)
Orange Coast Coll (CA)
Owens Comm Coll, Toledo (OH)
Pensacola State Coll (FL)
Rockland Comm Coll (NY)
South Florida State Coll (FL)
Truckee Meadows Comm Coll (NV)
Vincennes U (IN)
Westchester Comm Coll (NY)

DIETETIC TECHNOLOGY
Chandler-Gilbert Comm Coll (AZ)
Coll of the Desert (CA)
Fiorello H. LaGuardia Comm Coll of the City U of New York (NY)
Harper Coll (IL)
Miami Dade Coll (FL)
Mohawk Valley Comm Coll (NY)
Normandale Comm Coll (MN)
Trocaire Coll (NY)
Truckee Meadows Comm Coll (NV)
Westmoreland County Comm Coll (PA)

DIETITIAN ASSISTANT
Chandler-Gilbert Comm Coll (AZ)
Comm Coll of Allegheny County (PA)
Erie Comm Coll, North Campus (NY)
Hillsborough Comm Coll (FL)
Middlesex County Coll (NJ)

DIGITAL ARTS
Corning Comm Coll (NY)
Fiorello H. LaGuardia Comm Coll of the City U of New York (NY)
Genesee Comm Coll (NY)
Gulf Coast State Coll (FL)
Harford Comm Coll (MD)
Mohawk Valley Comm Coll (NY)
Volunteer State Comm Coll (TN)
Waukesha County Tech Coll (WI)

DIGITAL COMMUNICATION AND MEDIA/MULTIMEDIA
Butler County Comm Coll (PA)
Century Coll (MN)
Cochise Coll, Douglas (AZ)
Coll of Southern Maryland (MD)
Delaware Tech & Comm Coll, Terry Campus (DE)
Finger Lakes Comm Coll (NY)
Gulf Coast State Coll (FL)
Hawkeye Comm Coll (IA)
Hinds Comm Coll (MS)
Laramie County Comm Coll (WY)
Minneapolis Comm and Tech Coll (MN)
Oklahoma City Comm Coll (OK)
Pasadena City Coll (CA)
Raritan Valley Comm Coll (NJ)
Ridgewater Coll (MN)
San Jacinto Coll District (TX)
Sierra Coll (CA)
Sullivan Coll of Technology and Design (KY)
Tompkins Cortland Comm Coll (NY)
Tulsa Comm Coll (OK)
Wayne County Comm Coll District (MI)

DRAFTING AND DESIGN TECHNOLOGY
Allen Comm Coll (KS)
Alvin Comm Coll (TX)
Amarillo Coll (TX)
Antelope Valley Coll (CA)
Austin Comm Coll District (TX)
Bainbridge State Coll (GA)
Benjamin Franklin Inst of Technology (MA)
Bevill State Comm Coll (AL)
Bossier Parish Comm Coll (LA)
Burlington County Coll (NJ)
Camden County Coll (NJ)
Casper Coll (WY)
Cayuga County Comm Coll (NY)
Central Oregon Comm Coll (OR)
Central Texas Coll (TX)
Citrus Coll (CA)
Coastal Bend Coll (TX)
Coll of Central Florida (FL)
Coll of Southern Idaho (ID)
Coll of the Desert (CA)
Collin County Comm Coll District (TX)
Comm Coll of Allegheny County (PA)
Comm Coll of Denver (CO)
Comm Coll of Philadelphia (PA)
Copiah-Lincoln Comm Coll (MS)
Crowder Coll (MO)
Dabney S. Lancaster Comm Coll (VA)
Daytona State Coll (FL)
Delaware Tech & Comm Coll, Terry Campus (DE)
Delgado Comm Coll (LA)
Eastern Arizona Coll (AZ)
Eastern Gateway Comm Coll (OH)
Finger Lakes Comm Coll (NY)
Florida State Coll at Jacksonville (FL)
Frederick Comm Coll (MD)
Gadsden State Comm Coll (AL)
Genesee Comm Coll (NY)
George C. Wallace Comm Coll (AL)
Golden West Coll (CA)
Gwinnett Tech Coll (GA)
H. Councill Trenholm State Tech Coll (AL)
Hinds Comm Coll (MS)
Hocking Coll (OH)
Houston Comm Coll (TX)
Hutchinson Comm Coll (KS)
Iowa Central Comm Coll (IA)
ITI Tech Coll (LA)
J. F. Drake State Comm and Tech Coll (AL)
Kankakee Comm Coll (IL)
Kellogg Comm Coll (MI)
Kilgore Coll (TX)
Lake Land Coll (IL)
Laramie County Comm Coll (WY)
Lehigh Carbon Comm Coll (PA)
Lone Star Coll–North Harris (TX)
Lorain County Comm Coll (OH)
Los Angeles Trade-Tech Coll (CA)
Louisiana Delta Comm Coll, Monroe (LA)
Luzerne County Comm Coll (PA)
Macomb Comm Coll (MI)
Massachusetts Bay Comm Coll (MA)
Mesa Comm Coll (AZ)

Miami Dade Coll (FL)
MiraCosta Coll (CA)
Mohave Comm Coll (AZ)
Monroe County Comm Coll (MI)
Montcalm Comm Coll (MI)
Mott Comm Coll (MI)
Mt. San Antonio Coll (CA)
Navarro Coll (TX)
New Mexico Jr Coll (NM)
Niagara County Comm Coll (NY)
North Central Texas Coll (TX)
Northland Comm Coll (MN)
Northwestern Michigan Coll (MI)
Northwest-Shoals Comm Coll (AL)
Ohlone Coll (CA)
Oklahoma City Comm Coll (OK)
Oklahoma State U, Oklahoma City (OK)
Olympic Coll (WA)
Orange Coast Coll (CA)
Palomar Coll (CA)
Paris Jr Coll (TX)
Pasadena City Coll (CA)
Pasco-Hernando State Coll (FL)
Pensacola State Coll (FL)
Richland Comm Coll (IL)
Rockland Comm Coll (NY)
St. Charles Comm Coll (MO)
St. Clair County Comm Coll (MI)
Salt Lake Comm Coll (UT)
San Jacinto Coll District (TX)
San Juan Coll (NM)
Schoolcraft Coll (MI)
Seminole State Coll of Florida (FL)
Southeastern Comm Coll (IA)
South Louisiana Comm Coll (LA)
Sowela Tech Comm Coll (LA)
Stark State Coll (OH)
State U of New York Coll of Technology at Alfred (NY)
Sullivan Coll of Technology and Design (KY)
Tallahassee Comm Coll (FL)
Texas State Tech Coll Harlingen (TX)
Trinity Valley Comm Coll (TX)
Truckee Meadows Comm Coll (NV)
Tyler Jr Coll (TX)
U of Arkansas Comm Coll at Morrilton (AR)
Western Dakota Tech Inst (SD)
Western Nevada Coll (NV)
Wytheville Comm Coll (VA)

DRAFTING/DESIGN ENGINEERING TECHNOLOGIES RELATED
Comm Coll of Allegheny County (PA)
Corning Comm Coll (NY)
Dabney S. Lancaster Comm Coll (VA)
Genesee Comm Coll (NY)
Hennepin Tech Coll (MN)
Kennebec Valley Comm Coll (ME)
Lorain County Comm Coll (OH)
Luzerne County Comm Coll (PA)
Macomb Comm Coll (MI)
Mt. San Antonio Coll (CA)
Niagara County Comm Coll (NY)
Rock Valley Coll (IL)
State U of New York Coll of Technology at Alfred (NY)
Sullivan Coll of Technology and Design (KY)
Ulster County Comm Coll (NY)

DRAMA AND DANCE TEACHER EDUCATION
Darton State Coll (GA)
Hutchinson Comm Coll (KS)

DRAMATIC/THEATER ARTS
Allen Comm Coll (KS)
Alvin Comm Coll (TX)
Amarillo Coll (TX)
American Academy of Dramatic Arts (CA)
American Academy of Dramatic Arts–New York (NY)
Anoka-Ramsey Comm Coll (MN)
Anoka-Ramsey Comm Coll, Cambridge Campus (MN)
Arizona Western Coll (AZ)
Austin Comm Coll District (TX)
Bainbridge State Coll (GA)
Bossier Parish Comm Coll (LA)
Bucks County Comm Coll (PA)
Bunker Hill Comm Coll (MA)
Burlington County Coll (NJ)
Ca&nnada Coll (CA)
Central Texas Coll (TX)
Central Wyoming Coll (WY)
Chandler-Gilbert Comm Coll (AZ)

Citrus Coll (CA)
Cochise Coll, Douglas (AZ)
Coll of Central Florida (FL)
Coll of Marin (CA)
Coll of Southern Idaho (ID)
Coll of the Canyons (CA)
Coll of the Desert (CA)
Comm Coll of Allegheny County (PA)
Comm Coll of Rhode Island (RI)
Crowder Coll (MO)
Darton State Coll (GA)
Dean Coll (MA)
Eastern Arizona Coll (AZ)
Edison Comm Coll (OH)
Finger Lakes Comm Coll (NY)
Fiorello H. LaGuardia Comm Coll of the City U of New York (NY)
Genesee Comm Coll (NY)
Harrisburg Area Comm Coll (PA)
Hinds Comm Coll (MS)
Howard Comm Coll (MD)
Kilgore Coll (TX)
Kingsborough Comm Coll of the City U of New York (NY)
Lorain County Comm Coll (OH)
Manchester Comm Coll (CT)
Miami Dade Coll (FL)
Minneapolis Comm and Tech Coll (MN)
Nassau Comm Coll (NY)
Navarro Coll (TX)
New Mexico Jr Coll (NM)
Niagara County Comm Coll (NY)
Normandale Comm Coll (MN)
Northeastern Jr Coll (CO)
Northern Essex Comm Coll (MA)
North Hennepin Comm Coll (MN)
Northwestern Michigan Coll (MI)
Oklahoma City Comm Coll (OK)
Orange Coast Coll (CA)
Otero Jr Coll (CO)
Owensboro Comm and Tech Coll (KY)
Palomar Coll (CA)
Paris Jr Coll (TX)
Pasadena City Coll (CA)
Pensacola State Coll (FL)
Phoenix Coll (AZ)
Rockland Comm Coll (NY)
St. Charles Comm Coll (MO)
St. Philip's Coll (TX)
San Jacinto Coll District (TX)
San Joaquin Delta Coll (CA)
Scottsdale Comm Coll (AZ)
Sheridan Coll (WY)
South Florida State Coll (FL)
Trinidad State Jr Coll (CO)
Trinity Valley Comm Coll (TX)
Truckee Meadows Comm Coll (NV)
Tulsa Comm Coll (OK)
Tyler Jr Coll (TX)
Ulster County Comm Coll (NY)
Umpqua Comm Coll (OR)
Victor Valley Coll (CA)
Vincennes U (IN)
Western Wyoming Comm Coll (WY)

DRAMATIC/THEATER ARTS AND STAGECRAFT RELATED
Genesee Comm Coll (NY)
St. Philip's Coll (TX)

DRAWING
Cecil Coll (MD)
Luzerne County Comm Coll (PA)
Northeastern Jr Coll (CO)
Palomar Coll (CA)

DRYWALL INSTALLATION
Palomar Coll (CA)

EARLY CHILDHOOD EDUCATION
Alvin Comm Coll (TX)
Ancilla Coll (IN)
Anne Arundel Comm Coll (MD)
Arizona Western Coll (AZ)
Austin Comm Coll District (TX)
Big Bend Comm Coll (WA)
Bucks County Comm Coll (PA)
Bunker Hill Comm Coll (MA)
Cape Fear Comm Coll (NC)
Carroll Comm Coll (MD)
Catawba Valley Comm Coll (NC)
Central Maine Comm Coll (ME)
Central Oregon Comm Coll (OR)
Central Texas Coll (TX)
Central Wyoming Coll (WY)
Chesapeake Coll (MD)
Cincinnati State Tech and Comm Coll (OH)
Clark Coll (WA)

Cleveland Comm Coll (NC)
Cochise Coll, Douglas (AZ)
Coll of Central Florida (FL)
Coll of Southern Maryland (MD)
Collin County Comm Coll District (TX)
Colorado Northwestern Comm Coll (CO)
Comm Care Coll (OK)
The Comm Coll of Baltimore County (MD)
Corning Comm Coll (NY)
Davis Coll (OH)
Dean Coll (MA)
Delaware Tech & Comm Coll, Terry Campus (DE)
Eastern Arizona Coll (AZ)
Eastern Wyoming Coll (WY)
Fayetteville Tech Comm Coll (NC)
Finger Lakes Comm Coll (NY)
Florida Gateway Coll (FL)
Florida SouthWestern State Coll (FL)
Forsyth Tech Comm Coll (NC)
Fox Valley Tech Coll (WI)
Frederick Comm Coll (MD)
Front Range Comm Coll (CO)
Garrett Coll (MD)
Gateway Comm and Tech Coll (KY)
Gateway Tech Coll (WI)
Greenfield Comm Coll (MA)
Guam Comm Coll (GU)
Guilford Tech Comm Coll (NC)
Gulf Coast State Coll (FL)
Hagerstown Comm Coll (MD)
Halifax Comm Coll (NC)
Harford Comm Coll (MD)
Harper Coll (IL)
Harrisburg Area Comm Coll (PA)
Highland Comm Coll (IL)
Hopkinsville Comm Coll (KY)
Iowa Lakes Comm Coll (IA)
James Sprunt Comm Coll (NC)
Jefferson Comm Coll (NY)
Johnston Comm Coll (NC)
Kankakee Comm Coll (IL)
Kingsborough Comm Coll of the City U of New York (NY)
Lakes Region Comm Coll (NH)
Laramie County Comm Coll (WY)
Lehigh Carbon Comm Coll (PA)
Lower Columbia Coll (WA)
Luzerne County Comm Coll (PA)
Miami Dade Coll (FL)
Minnesota State Coll–Southeast Tech (MN)
Montgomery Coll (MD)
Montgomery Comm Coll (NC)
Moraine Park Tech Coll (WI)
Mott Comm Coll (MI)
Nebraska Indian Comm Coll (NE)
Northampton Comm Coll (PA)
Northcentral Tech Coll (WI)
North Iowa Area Comm Coll (IA)
Norwalk Comm Coll (CT)
Ohlone Coll (CA)
Oklahoma State U, Oklahoma City (OK)
Olympic Coll (WA)
Owens Comm Coll, Toledo (OH)
Panola Coll (TX)
Paris Jr Coll (TX)
Penn Foster Coll (AZ)
Pennsylvania Highlands Comm Coll (PA)
Pensacola State Coll (FL)
Potomac State Coll of West Virginia U (WV)
Pueblo Comm Coll (CO)
Randolph Comm Coll (NC)
Richmond Comm Coll (NC)
Ridgewater Coll (MN)
Roane State Comm Coll (TN)
St. Philip's Coll (TX)
Sheridan Coll (WY)
South Florida State Coll (FL)
South Piedmont Comm Coll (NC)
Southwestern Indian Polytechnic Inst (NM)
Southwestern Michigan Coll (MI)
Springfield Tech Comm Coll (MA)
Tallahassee Comm Coll (FL)
Tech Coll of the Lowcountry (SC)
Tohono O'odham Comm Coll (AZ)
Trinidad State Jr Coll (CO)
Truckee Meadows Comm Coll (NV)
U of Arkansas Comm Coll at Batesville (AR)
Victoria Coll (TX)
Vincennes U (IN)
Waukesha County Tech Coll (WI)
Wenatchee Valley Coll (WA)

Western Wyoming Comm Coll (WY)
Westmoreland County Comm Coll (PA)
White Mountains Comm Coll (NH)
Wisconsin Indianhead Tech Coll (WI)
Wor-Wic Comm Coll (MD)
York County Comm Coll (ME)

ECOLOGY
Hocking Coll (OH)
Iowa Lakes Comm Coll (IA)

E-COMMERCE
Brookhaven Coll (TX)
Century Coll (MN)
Delaware Tech & Comm Coll, Terry Campus (DE)
Finger Lakes Comm Coll (NY)
Forsyth Tech Comm Coll (NC)
Genesee Comm Coll (NY)
Kalamazoo Valley Comm Coll (MI)
Pasco-Hernando State Coll (FL)
Piedmont Comm Coll (NC)
St. Philip's Coll (TX)
Three Rivers Comm Coll (CT)
Wayne County Comm Coll District (MI)

ECONOMICS
Allen Comm Coll (KS)
Austin Comm Coll District (TX)
Ca&nnada Coll (CA)
Casper Coll (WY)
Cochise Coll, Douglas (AZ)
Coll of Central Florida (FL)
Coll of the Desert (CA)
Copiah-Lincoln Comm Coll (MS)
Darton State Coll (GA)
Eastern Wyoming Coll (WY)
Edison Comm Coll (OH)
Georgia Highlands Coll (GA)
Greenfield Comm Coll (MA)
Iowa Lakes Comm Coll (IA)
Laramie County Comm Coll (WY)
Lone Star Coll–CyFair (TX)
Miami Dade Coll (FL)
Northeastern Jr Coll (CO)
Ohlone Coll (CA)
Oklahoma State U, Oklahoma City (OK)
Orange Coast Coll (CA)
Palomar Coll (CA)
Potomac State Coll of West Virginia U (WV)
St. Charles Comm Coll (MO)
St. Philip's Coll (TX)
Salt Lake Comm Coll (UT)
San Joaquin Delta Coll (CA)
South Florida State Coll (FL)
Terra State Comm Coll (OH)
Tyler Jr Coll (TX)
Umpqua Comm Coll (OR)
Vincennes U (IN)
Wenatchee Valley Coll (WA)
Western Wyoming Comm Coll (WY)

EDUCATION
American Samoa Comm Coll (AS)
Bainbridge State Coll (GA)
Bossier Parish Comm Coll (LA)
Bowling Green State U-Firelands Coll (OH)
Bucks County Comm Coll (PA)
Bunker Hill Comm Coll (MA)
Burlington County Coll (NJ)
Butler County Comm Coll (PA)
Camden County Coll (NJ)
Carroll Comm Coll (MD)
Cecil Coll (MD)
Cedar Valley Coll (TX)
Central Oregon Comm Coll (OR)
Central Virginia Comm Coll (VA)
Century Coll (MN)
Chesapeake Coll (MD)
Chipola Coll (FL)
Coll of Southern Idaho (ID)
Coll of Southern Maryland (MD)
The Comm Coll of Baltimore County (MD)
Comm Coll of Philadelphia (PA)
Copiah-Lincoln Comm Coll (MS)
Crowder Coll (MO)
Cumberland County Coll (NJ)
Dabney S. Lancaster Comm Coll (VA)
Dakota Coll at Bottineau (ND)
Dyersburg State Comm Coll (TN)
Edison Comm Coll (OH)
Frederick Comm Coll (MD)
Garrett Coll (MD)
Genesee Comm Coll (NY)
Greenfield Comm Coll (MA)

Guam Comm Coll (GU)
Hagerstown Comm Coll (MD)
Harford Comm Coll (MD)
Hutchinson Comm Coll (KS)
Iowa Central Comm Coll (IA)
Iowa Lakes Comm Coll (IA)
Jackson State Comm Coll (TN)
Kankakee Comm Coll (IL)
Kingsborough Comm Coll of the City U of New York (NY)
Lakes Region Comm Coll (NH)
Laramie County Comm Coll (WY)
Lehigh Carbon Comm Coll (PA)
Lone Star Coll–CyFair (TX)
Lone Star Coll–Kingwood (TX)
Lone Star Coll–Montgomery (TX)
Lone Star Coll–North Harris (TX)
Lone Star Coll–Tomball (TX)
Lorain County Comm Coll (OH)
Louisiana Delta Comm Coll, Monroe (LA)
Luzerne County Comm Coll (PA)
Miami Dade Coll (FL)
Minneapolis Comm and Tech Coll (MN)
Mohave Comm Coll (AZ)
Motlow State Comm Coll (TN)
Navarro Coll (TX)
New Mexico Jr Coll (NM)
Northeastern Jr Coll (CO)
Northern Essex Comm Coll (MA)
North Hennepin Comm Coll (MN)
Northwestern Michigan Coll (MI)
Nunez Comm Coll (LA)
Palomar Coll (CA)
Panola Coll (TX)
Paris Jr Coll (TX)
Pennsylvania Highlands Comm Coll (PA)
Pensacola State Coll (FL)
Roane State Comm Coll (TN)
St. Charles Comm Coll (MO)
St. Philip's Coll (TX)
Salem Comm Coll (NJ)
Schoolcraft Coll (MI)
South Louisiana Comm Coll (LA)
Tech Coll of the Lowcountry (SC)
Terra State Comm Coll (OH)
Three Rivers Comm Coll (CT)
Trinidad State Jr Coll (CO)
Trinity Valley Comm Coll (TX)
Tulsa Comm Coll (OK)
Umpqua Comm Coll (OR)
Vincennes U (IN)
Virginia Western Comm Coll (VA)
Volunteer State Comm Coll (TN)
Walters State Comm Coll (TN)
Wenatchee Valley Coll (WA)
Western Wyoming Comm Coll (WY)
White Mountains Comm Coll (NH)
Wor-Wic Comm Coll (MD)
Wytheville Comm Coll (VA)
York County Comm Coll (ME)

EDUCATIONAL/ INSTRUCTIONAL TECHNOLOGY
Bossier Parish Comm Coll (LA)
Comm Coll of the Air Force (AL)
Gateway Comm and Tech Coll (KY)
Lone Star Coll–North Harris (TX)

EDUCATIONAL LEADERSHIP AND ADMINISTRATION
Comm Coll of the Air Force (AL)

EDUCATION (MULTIPLE LEVELS)
Brookhaven Coll (TX)
Cayuga County Comm Coll (NY)
Delaware Tech & Comm Coll, Terry Campus (DE)
Genesee Comm Coll (NY)
Kishwaukee Coll (IL)
Minneapolis Comm and Tech Coll (MN)
Oklahoma State U Inst of Technology (OK)
Paris Jr Coll (TX)
Tyler Jr Coll (TX)
U of Arkansas Comm Coll at Hope (AR)
U of Arkansas Comm Coll at Morrilton (AR)
Westchester Comm Coll (NY)
Western Wyoming Comm Coll (WY)

EDUCATION RELATED
Corning Comm Coll (NY)
Genesee Comm Coll (NY)
Georgia Highlands Coll (GA)
Guilford Tech Comm Coll (NC)

Kent State U at Salem (OH)
Kent State U at Tuscarawas (OH)
Miami Dade Coll (FL)

EDUCATION (SPECIFIC LEVELS AND METHODS) RELATED
Comm Coll of Allegheny County (PA)
Corning Comm Coll (NY)
Harford Comm Coll (MD)
Jefferson Coll (MO)
Miami Dade Coll (FL)

EDUCATION (SPECIFIC SUBJECT AREAS) RELATED
Comm Coll of Allegheny County (PA)
Harford Comm Coll (MD)
Manor Coll (PA)
St. Charles Comm Coll (MO)
State Fair Comm Coll (MO)

ELECTRICAL AND ELECTRONIC ENGINEERING TECHNOLOGIES RELATED
Benjamin Franklin Inst of Technology (MA)
Blue Ridge Comm and Tech Coll (WV)
Corning Comm Coll (NY)
Fox Valley Tech Coll (WI)
Kent State U at Trumbull (OH)
Kent State U at Tuscarawas (OH)
Lake Region State Coll (ND)
Miami Dade Coll (FL)
Mohawk Valley Comm Coll (NY)
Moraine Park Tech Coll (WI)
Pasadena City Coll (CA)
Sheridan Coll (WY)
Spencerian Coll–Lexington (KY)
State U of New York Coll of Technology at Alfred (NY)
Sullivan Coll of Technology and Design (KY)
Terra State Comm Coll (OH)
Wayne County Comm Coll District (MI)

ELECTRICAL AND ELECTRONICS ENGINEERING
Allen Comm Coll (KS)
Anne Arundel Comm Coll (MD)
Carroll Comm Coll (MD)
Coll of Southern Maryland (MD)
The Comm Coll of Baltimore County (MD)
Corning Comm Coll (NY)
Fiorello H. LaGuardia Comm Coll of the City U of New York (NY)
Garrett Coll (MD)
Humacao Comm Coll (PR)
Pasadena City Coll (CA)
Potomac State Coll of West Virginia U (WV)
Southern Tech Coll, Orlando (FL)
South Florida State Coll (FL)

ELECTRICAL AND POWER TRANSMISSION INSTALLATION
Benjamin Franklin Inst of Technology (MA)
Delta Coll (MI)
Minnesota West Comm and Tech Coll (MN)
Oklahoma State U, Oklahoma City (OK)
Orange Coast Coll (CA)
Piedmont Comm Coll (NC)
Richmond Comm Coll (NC)
Rogue Comm Coll (OR)
San Jacinto Coll District (TX)
Southwestern Illinois Coll (IL)
State U of New York Coll of Technology at Alfred (NY)
Western Nevada Coll (NV)
Westmoreland County Comm Coll (PA)

ELECTRICAL AND POWER TRANSMISSION INSTALLATION RELATED
Minnesota West Comm and Tech Coll (MN)

ELECTRICAL, ELECTRONIC AND COMMUNICATIONS ENGINEERING TECHNOLOGY
Alamance Comm Coll (NC)
Allen Comm Coll (KS)
Alvin Comm Coll (TX)
Amarillo Coll (TX)
American Samoa Comm Coll (AS)
Anne Arundel Comm Coll (MD)

Anoka Tech Coll (MN)
Antelope Valley Coll (CA)
Arapahoe Comm Coll (CO)
Arizona Western Coll (AZ)
Austin Comm Coll District (TX)
Bainbridge State Coll (GA)
Benjamin Franklin Inst of Technology (MA)
Bowling Green State U–Firelands Coll (OH)
Burlington County Coll (NJ)
Butler County Comm Coll (PA)
Camden County Coll (NJ)
Cape Fear Comm Coll (NC)
Casper Coll (WY)
Catawba Valley Comm Coll (NC)
Cayuga County Comm Coll (NY)
Cecil Coll (MD)
Central Oregon Comm Coll (OR)
Cincinnati State Tech and Comm Coll (OH)
Citrus Coll (CA)
Clark Coll (WA)
Cleveland Comm Coll (NC)
Clinton Comm Coll (NY)
Cochise Coll, Douglas (AZ)
Collin County Comm Coll District (TX)
Comm Coll of Allegheny County (PA)
Comm Coll of the Air Force (AL)
Copiah-Lincoln Comm Coll (MS)
County Coll of Morris (NJ)
Crowder Coll (MO)
Dabney S. Lancaster Comm Coll (VA)
Daytona State Coll (FL)
Delaware Tech & Comm Coll, Terry Campus (DE)
Delgado Comm Coll (LA)
Des Moines Area Comm Coll (IA)
Dunwoody Coll of Technology (MN)
Dutchess Comm Coll (NY)
Eastern Gateway Comm Coll (OH)
Edison Comm Coll (OH)
Erie Comm Coll, North Campus (NY)
Fayetteville Tech Comm Coll (NC)
Forsyth Tech Comm Coll (NC)
Fountainhead Coll of Technology (TN)
Fox Valley Tech Coll (WI)
Gadsden State Comm Coll (AL)
Gateway Comm Coll (CT)
Gateway Tech Coll (WI)
George C. Wallace Comm Coll (AL)
Golden West Coll (CA)
Grand Rapids Comm Coll (MI)
Great Basin Coll (NV)
Greenville Tech Coll (SC)
Guilford Tech Comm Coll (NC)
Gulf Coast State Coll (FL)
Gwinnett Tech Coll (GA)
Harper Coll (IL)
Harrisburg Area Comm Coll (PA)
Hawkeye Comm Coll (IA)
Haywood Comm Coll (NC)
Hennepin Tech Coll (MN)
Hillsborough Comm Coll (FL)
Hinds Comm Coll (MS)
Hocking Coll (OH)
Hopkinsville Comm Coll (KY)
Horry-Georgetown Tech Coll (SC)
Howard Comm Coll (MD)
Hudson County Comm Coll (NJ)
Hutchinson Comm Coll (KS)
Iowa Central Comm Coll (IA)
Iowa Lakes Comm Coll (IA)
Island Drafting and Tech Inst (NY)
ITI Tech Coll (LA)
Jefferson Coll (MO)
J. F. Drake State Comm and Tech Coll (AL)
Kalamazoo Valley Comm Coll (MI)
Kaskaskia Coll (IL)
Kennebec Valley Comm Coll (ME)
Kilgore Coll (TX)
Kirtland Comm Coll (MI)
Kishwaukee Coll (IL)
Lake Area Tech Inst (SD)
Lake Land Coll (IL)
Lakeland Comm Coll (OH)
Lehigh Carbon Comm Coll (PA)
Lone Star Coll–CyFair (TX)
Lone Star Coll–North Harris (TX)
Lone Star Coll–Tomball (TX)
Lorain County Comm Coll (OH)
Los Angeles Trade-Tech Coll (CA)
Luzerne County Comm Coll (PA)
Macomb Comm Coll (MI)
Mesa Comm Coll (AZ)
Miami Dade Coll (FL)

Middlesex Comm Coll (MA)
Middlesex County Coll (NJ)
Midlands Tech Coll (SC)
Minnesota State Coll–Southeast Tech (MN)
Mohawk Valley Comm Coll (NY)
Monroe Comm Coll (NY)
Monroe County Comm Coll (MI)
Montcalm Comm Coll (MI)
Montgomery County Comm Coll (PA)
Mott Comm Coll (MI)
Mt. San Antonio Coll (CA)
New Castle School of Trades (PA)
Northampton Comm Coll (PA)
North Central Texas Coll (TX)
Northeast Iowa Comm Coll (IA)
Northern Essex Comm Coll (MA)
Northern Virginia Comm Coll (VA)
North Iowa Area Comm Coll (IA)
Northland Comm Coll (MN)
Northwestern Michigan Coll (MI)
Northwest State Comm Coll (OH)
Oakton Comm Coll (IL)
Ohlone Coll (CA)
Oklahoma City Comm Coll (OK)
Oklahoma State U, Oklahoma City (OK)
Olympic Coll (WA)
Orange Coast Coll (CA)
Owens Comm Coll, Toledo (OH)
Ozarks Tech Comm Coll (MO)
Paris Jr Coll (TX)
Penn State DuBois (PA)
Penn State Fayette, The Eberly Campus (PA)
Penn State Shenango (PA)
Pennsylvania Inst of Technology (PA)
Pensacola State Coll (FL)
Pueblo Comm Coll (CO)
Queensborough Comm Coll of the City U of New York (NY)
Quinsigamond Comm Coll (MA)
Reid State Tech Coll (AL)
Renton Tech Coll (WA)
Richland Comm Coll (IL)
Richmond Comm Coll (NC)
Ridgewater Coll (MN)
Rockland Comm Coll (NY)
Rock Valley Coll (IL)
Rogue Comm Coll (OR)
St. Clair County Comm Coll (MI)
Salt Lake Comm Coll (UT)
San Jacinto Coll District (TX)
San Joaquin Delta Coll (CA)
San Juan Coll (NM)
Schoolcraft Coll (MI)
Scottsdale Comm Coll (AZ)
Seminole State Coll of Florida (FL)
Shawnee Comm Coll (IL)
Sisseton-Wahpeton Coll (SD)
Southeastern Comm Coll (IA)
Southern U at Shreveport (LA)
South Florida State Coll (FL)
South Suburban Coll (IL)
Southwestern Illinois Coll (IL)
Southwest Virginia Comm Coll (VA)
Spartanburg Comm Coll (SC)
Spencerian Coll–Lexington (KY)
Springfield Tech Comm Coll (MA)
State U of New York Coll of Technology at Alfred (NY)
Sullivan Coll of Technology and Design (KY)
Sullivan County Comm Coll (NY)
Terra State Comm Coll (OH)
Three Rivers Comm Coll (CT)
Trident Tech Coll (SC)
Tulsa Comm Coll (OK)
Umpqua Comm Coll (OR)
U of Arkansas Comm Coll at Hope (AR)
Victoria Coll (TX)
Victor Valley Coll (CA)
Vincennes U (IN)
Virginia Western Comm Coll (VA)
Waukesha County Tech Coll (WI)
Wayne County Comm Coll District (MI)
Westchester Comm Coll (NY)
Western Nevada Coll (NV)
Western Wyoming Comm Coll (WY)
Westmoreland County Comm Coll (PA)
Wor-Wic Comm Coll (MD)
Wytheville Comm Coll (VA)

ELECTRICAL/ELECTRONICS DRAFTING AND CAD/CADD
Dunwoody Coll of Technology (MN)
Middlesex Comm Coll (MA)

Palomar Coll (CA)

ELECTRICAL/ELECTRONICS EQUIPMENT INSTALLATION AND REPAIR
Cape Fear Comm Coll (NC)
Delgado Comm Coll (LA)
Hinds Comm Coll (MS)
Hutchinson Comm Coll (KS)
Iowa Lakes Comm Coll (IA)
Lakes Region Comm Coll (NH)
Macomb Comm Coll (MI)
Mesabi Range Coll (MN)
Orange Coast Coll (CA)
Riverland Comm Coll (MN)
St. Philip's Coll (TX)
Sierra Coll (CA)
Sullivan Coll of Technology and Design (KY)
U of Arkansas Comm Coll at Batesville (AR)
Wenatchee Valley Coll (WA)
Western Wyoming Comm Coll (WY)

ELECTRICAL/ELECTRONICS MAINTENANCE AND REPAIR TECHNOLOGY RELATED
Bunker Hill Comm Coll (MA)
Kennebec Valley Comm Coll (ME)
Mohawk Valley Comm Coll (NY)
Southern Tech Coll, Orlando (FL)
Sullivan Coll of Technology and Design (KY)

ELECTRICIAN
Bellingham Tech Coll (WA)
Bevill State Comm Coll (AL)
Cleveland Comm Coll (NC)
Danville Area Comm Coll (IL)
Delta Coll (MI)
Dunwoody Coll of Technology (MN)
Elizabethtown Comm and Tech Coll, Elizabethtown (KY)
Fayetteville Tech Comm Coll (NC)
George C. Wallace Comm Coll (AL)
Guilford Tech Comm Coll (NC)
Harrisburg Area Comm Coll (PA)
Haywood Comm Coll (NC)
H. Councill Trenholm State Tech Coll (AL)
Hinds Comm Coll (MS)
J. F. Drake State Comm and Tech Coll (AL)
Kaskaskia Coll (IL)
Kennebec Valley Comm Coll (ME)
Luzerne County Comm Coll (PA)
Miami Dade Coll (FL)
Minnesota West Comm and Tech Coll (MN)
Mitchell Tech Inst (SD)
Montgomery Comm Coll (NC)
Northampton Comm Coll (PA)
Northeast Iowa Comm Coll (IA)
Palomar Coll (CA)
Piedmont Comm Coll (NC)
Randolph Comm Coll (NC)
Ridgewater Coll (MN)
Rock Valley Coll (IL)
South Louisiana Comm Coll (LA)
South Piedmont Comm Coll (NC)
Southwestern Illinois Coll (IL)
Western Dakota Tech Inst (SD)
Western Iowa Tech Comm Coll (IA)
Western Wyoming Comm Coll (WY)

ELECTROCARDIOGRAPH TECHNOLOGY
Oklahoma State U, Oklahoma City (OK)

ELECTROMECHANICAL AND INSTRUMENTATION AND MAINTENANCE TECHNOLOGIES RELATED
Cape Fear Comm Coll (NC)
Catawba Valley Comm Coll (NC)
Greenville Tech Coll (SC)
Montgomery Comm Coll (NC)
Northwestern Michigan Coll (MI)
Piedmont Comm Coll (NC)
Pueblo Comm Coll (CO)
Richmond Comm Coll (NC)
South Piedmont Comm Coll (NC)
Sullivan Coll of Technology and Design (KY)
Waukesha County Tech Coll (WI)

ELECTROMECHANICAL TECHNOLOGY
Bowling Green State U-Firelands Coll (OH)
Camden County Coll (NJ)
Central Maine Comm Coll (ME)
Chandler-Gilbert Comm Coll (AZ)
Cincinnati State Tech and Comm Coll (OH)
Comm Coll of Rhode Island (RI)
Delaware Tech & Comm Coll, Terry Campus (DE)
Edison Comm Coll (OH)
Fox Valley Tech Coll (WI)
Gateway Tech Coll (WI)
Guilford Tech Comm Coll (NC)
Haywood Comm Coll (NC)
Kirtland Comm Coll (MI)
Lake Land Coll (IL)
Macomb Comm Coll (MI)
Maysville Comm and Tech Coll, Maysville (KY)
Montgomery County Comm Coll (PA)
Moraine Park Tech Coll (WI)
Motlow State Comm Coll (TN)
Northampton Comm Coll (PA)
Northcentral Tech Coll (WI)
Paris Jr Coll (TX)
Quinsigamond Comm Coll (MA)
Randolph Comm Coll (NC)
Richmond Comm Coll (NC)
Ridgewater Coll (MN)
St. Philip's Coll (TX)
South Piedmont Comm Coll (NC)
Springfield Tech Comm Coll (MA)
State U of New York Coll of Technology at Alfred (NY)
Texas State Tech Coll Harlingen (TX)
Tyler Jr Coll (TX)
Westmoreland County Comm Coll (PA)

ELECTRONEURODIAGNOSTIC/ELECTROENCEPHALOGRAPHIC TECHNOLOGY
Alvin Comm Coll (TX)
Catawba Valley Comm Coll (NC)
Collin County Comm Coll District (TX)
Comm Coll of Allegheny County (PA)
Comm Coll of Denver (CO)
Harford Comm Coll (MD)
Lone Star Coll–Kingwood (TX)

ELEMENTARY EDUCATION
Allen Comm Coll (KS)
Amarillo Coll (TX)
Ancilla Coll (IN)
Arizona Western Coll (AZ)
Bainbridge State Coll (GA)
Butler County Comm Coll (PA)
Carl Albert State Coll (OK)
Carroll Comm Coll (MD)
Casper Coll (WY)
Cecil Coll (MD)
Central Wyoming Coll (WY)
Chandler-Gilbert Comm Coll (AZ)
Chesapeake Coll (MD)
Cleveland Comm Coll (NC)
Cochise Coll, Douglas (AZ)
Coll of Central Florida (FL)
Coll of Southern Idaho (ID)
Coll of Southern Maryland (MD)
The Comm Coll of Baltimore County (MD)
Copiah-Lincoln Comm Coll (MS)
Crowder Coll (MO)
Delaware Tech & Comm Coll, Terry Campus (DE)
Eastern Arizona Coll (AZ)
Eastern Wyoming Coll (WY)
Fayetteville Tech Comm Coll (NC)
Frederick Comm Coll (MD)
Garrett Coll (MD)
Genesee Comm Coll (NY)
Grand Rapids Comm Coll (MI)
Great Basin Coll (NV)
Hagerstown Comm Coll (MD)
Harford Comm Coll (MD)
Harper Coll (IL)
Hinds Comm Coll (MS)
Howard Comm Coll (MD)
Iowa Lakes Comm Coll (IA)
James Sprunt Comm Coll (NC)
Kalamazoo Valley Comm Coll (MI)
Kankakee Comm Coll (IL)
Kellogg Comm Coll (MI)
Kilgore Coll (TX)
Kingsborough Comm Coll of the City U of New York (NY)

Lenoir Comm Coll (NC)
Lorain County Comm Coll (OH)
Manor Coll (PA)
Miami Dade Coll (FL)
Middlesex Comm Coll (MA)
Monroe County Comm Coll (MI)
Montgomery Coll (MD)
Montgomery County Comm Coll (PA)
Navarro Coll (TX)
New Mexico Jr Coll (NM)
Niagara County Comm Coll (NY)
Normandale Comm Coll (MN)
Northeastern Jr Coll (CO)
Northern Essex Comm Coll (MA)
Northwest Coll (WY)
Oklahoma City Comm Coll (OK)
Otero Jr Coll (CO)
Paris Jr Coll (TX)
Pensacola State Coll (FL)
Phoenix Coll (AZ)
Piedmont Comm Coll (NC)
Potomac State Coll of West Virginia U (WV)
Quinsigamond Comm Coll (MA)
Reading Area Comm Coll (PA)
Richmond Comm Coll (NC)
Roane State Comm Coll (TN)
San Juan Coll (NM)
Seminole State Coll (OK)
Sheridan Coll (WY)
South Florida State Coll (FL)
South Piedmont Comm Coll (NC)
Springfield Tech Comm Coll (MA)
Sullivan County Comm Coll (NY)
Trinity Valley Comm Coll (TX)
Truckee Meadows Comm Coll (NV)
Umpqua Comm Coll (OR)
U of Cincinnati Clermont Coll (OH)
Vincennes U (IN)
Wayne County Comm Coll District (MI)
Western Wyoming Comm Coll (WY)
Wor-Wic Comm Coll (MD)

EMERGENCY CARE ATTENDANT (EMT AMBULANCE)
Illinois Eastern Comm Colls, Frontier Community College (IL)
Iowa Lakes Comm Coll (IA)
J. Sargeant Reynolds Comm Coll (VA)
Mohawk Valley Comm Coll (NY)

EMERGENCY MEDICAL TECHNOLOGY (EMT PARAMEDIC)
Allen Comm Coll (KS)
Alvin Comm Coll (TX)
Amarillo Coll (TX)
Arapahoe Comm Coll (CO)
Arizona Western Coll (AZ)
Austin Comm Coll District (TX)
Bevill State Comm Coll (AL)
Blue Ridge Comm and Tech Coll (WV)
Borough of Manhattan Comm Coll of the City U of New York (NY)
Bossier Parish Comm Coll (LA)
Brookhaven Coll (TX)
Camden County Coll (NJ)
Carroll Comm Coll (MD)
Casper Coll (WY)
Catawba Valley Comm Coll (NC)
Cecil Coll (MD)
Central Oregon Comm Coll (OR)
Central Texas Coll (TX)
Central Virginia Comm Coll (VA)
Century Coll (MN)
Chesapeake Coll (MD)
Cincinnati State Tech and Comm Coll (OH)
Clark Coll (WA)
Cleveland Comm Coll (NC)
Cochise Coll, Douglas (AZ)
Coll of Central Florida (FL)
Coll of Southern Idaho (ID)
Coll of Southern Maryland (MD)
Collin County Comm Coll District (TX)
Colorado Northwestern Comm Coll (CO)
Comm Coll of Aurora (CO)
The Comm Coll of Baltimore County (MD)
Crowder Coll (MO)
Darton State Coll (GA)
Daytona State Coll (FL)
Delaware Tech & Comm Coll, Terry Campus (DE)
Delgado Comm Coll (LA)
Dutchess Comm Coll (NY)

Dyersburg State Comm Coll (TN)
Eastern Arizona Coll (AZ)
Eastern Gateway Comm Coll (OH)
El Centro Coll (TX)
Erie Comm Coll, South Campus (NY)
Fayetteville Tech Comm Coll (NC)
Finger Lakes Comm Coll (NY)
Fiorello H. LaGuardia Comm Coll of the City U of New York (NY)
Florida Gateway Coll (FL)
Florida SouthWestern State Coll (FL)
Florida State Coll at Jacksonville (FL)
Forsyth Tech Comm Coll (NC)
Fox Valley Tech Coll (WI)
Frederick Comm Coll (MD)
Gadsden State Comm Coll (AL)
Gateway Tech Coll (WI)
George C. Wallace Comm Coll (AL)
Great Falls Coll Montana State U (MT)
Greenville Tech Coll (SC)
Guilford Tech Comm Coll (NC)
Gulf Coast State Coll (FL)
Gwinnett Tech Coll (GA)
Hagerstown Comm Coll (MD)
Harper Coll (IL)
Harrisburg Area Comm Coll (PA)
Hawkeye Comm Coll (IA)
H. Councill Trenholm State Tech Coll (AL)
Highland Comm Coll (IL)
Hillsborough Comm Coll (FL)
Hinds Comm Coll (MS)
Hocking Coll (OH)
Houston Comm Coll (TX)
Howard Comm Coll (MD)
Hudson County Comm Coll (NJ)
Hutchinson Comm Coll (KS)
Jefferson Coll (MO)
Jefferson Comm Coll (NY)
Jefferson State Comm Coll (AL)
J. Sargeant Reynolds Comm Coll (VA)
Kalamazoo Valley Comm Coll (MI)
Kankakee Comm Coll (IL)
Kaskaskia Coll (IL)
Kellogg Comm Coll (MI)
Kennebec Valley Comm Coll (ME)
Kent State U at Trumbull (OH)
Kilgore Coll (TX)
Kirtland Comm Coll (MI)
Kishwaukee Coll (IL)
Lake Area Tech Inst (SD)
Lamar Comm Coll (CO)
Laramie County Comm Coll (WY)
Lone Star Coll–CyFair (TX)
Lone Star Coll–Montgomery (TX)
Lone Star Coll–North Harris (TX)
Lurleen B. Wallace Comm Coll (AL)
Luzerne County Comm Coll (PA)
Macomb Comm Coll (MI)
McHenry County Coll (IL)
Miami Dade Coll (FL)
Mohave Comm Coll (AZ)
Montcalm Comm Coll (MI)
Moraine Park Tech Coll (WI)
Moraine Valley Comm Coll (IL)
Mott Comm Coll (MI)
Mt. San Antonio Coll (CA)
New Mexico Jr Coll (NM)
Northcentral Tech Coll (WI)
North Central Texas Coll (TX)
Northeastern Jr Coll (CO)
Northeast Iowa Comm Coll (IA)
Northern Virginia Comm Coll (VA)
North Iowa Area Comm Coll (IA)
Northland Comm Coll (MN)
Northwest-Shoals Comm Coll (AL)
Oklahoma City Comm Coll (OK)
Oklahoma State U, Oklahoma City (OK)
Orange Coast Coll (CA)
Owensboro Comm and Tech Coll (KY)
Ozarks Tech Comm Coll (MO)
Palomar Coll (CA)
Paris Jr Coll (TX)
Pasco-Hernando State Coll (FL)
Pennsylvania Highlands Comm Coll (PA)
Pensacola State Coll (FL)
Phoenix Coll (AZ)
Pueblo Comm Coll (CO)
Quinsigamond Comm Coll (MA)
Roane State Comm Coll (TN)
Rockland Comm Coll (NY)
Rogue Comm Coll (OR)
St. Charles Comm Coll (MO)
San Diego Miramar Coll (CA)
San Jacinto Coll District (TX)
San Juan Coll (NM)

Schoolcraft Coll (MI)
Seminole State Coll of Florida (FL)
Southeastern Coll–Greenacres (FL)
Southeastern Comm Coll (IA)
South Florida State Coll (FL)
South Louisiana Comm Coll (LA)
Southwestern Illinois Coll (IL)
Southwestern Michigan Coll (MI)
Southwest Virginia Comm Coll (VA)
Tallahassee Comm Coll (FL)
Tech Coll of the Lowcountry (SC)
Trinidad State Jr Coll (CO)
Trinity Valley Comm Coll (TX)
Tyler Jr Coll (TX)
Umpqua Comm Coll (OR)
U of Arkansas Comm Coll at Batesville (AR)
U of Arkansas Comm Coll at Hope (AR)
U of Cincinnati Clermont Coll (OH)
Victoria Coll (TX)
Vincennes U (IN)
Waukesha County Tech Coll (WI)
Wayne County Comm Coll District (MI)
Westchester Comm Coll (NY)
Western Dakota Tech Inst (SD)
Western Iowa Tech Comm Coll (IA)
Wisconsin Indianhead Tech Coll (WI)
Wor-Wic Comm Coll (MD)

ENERGY MANAGEMENT AND SYSTEMS TECHNOLOGY
Casper Coll (WY)
Century Coll (MN)
Cincinnati State Tech and Comm Coll (OH)
Clinton Comm Coll (NY)
Comm Coll of Allegheny County (PA)
Corning Comm Coll (NY)
Crowder Coll (MO)
Danville Area Comm Coll (IL)
Delaware Tech & Comm Coll, Terry Campus (DE)
Delta Coll (MI)
Fox Valley Tech Coll (WI)
Front Range Comm Coll (CO)
Harrisburg Area Comm Coll (PA)
Hawkeye Comm Coll (IA)
Illinois Eastern Comm Colls, Wabash Valley College (IL)
Iowa Lakes Comm Coll (IA)
Lakeland Comm Coll (OH)
Lakes Region Comm Coll (NH)
Laramie County Comm Coll (WY)
Macomb Comm Coll (MI)
Middlesex County Coll (NJ)
Minnesota West Comm and Tech Coll (MN)
Mitchell Tech Inst (SD)
Mount Wachusett Comm Coll (MA)
Northeast Iowa Comm Coll (IA)
Northwest State Comm Coll (OH)
Northwest Tech Coll (MN)
Quinsigamond Comm Coll (MA)
Rock Valley Coll (IL)
St. Clair County Comm Coll (MI)
St. Philip's Coll (TX)
South Louisiana Comm Coll (LA)
Walters State Comm Coll (TN)
Westchester Comm Coll (NY)
Western Iowa Tech Comm Coll (IA)

ENGINEERING
Allen Comm Coll (KS)
Amarillo Coll (TX)
Anne Arundel Comm Coll (MD)
Antelope Valley Coll (CA)
Arizona Western Coll (AZ)
Austin Comm Coll District (TX)
Borough of Manhattan Comm Coll of the City U of New York (NY)
Bossier Parish Comm Coll (LA)
Bunker Hill Comm Coll (MA)
Burlington County Coll (NJ)
Butler County Comm Coll (PA)
Ca&nnada Coll (CA)
Carl Albert State Coll (OK)
Casper Coll (WY)
Central Oregon Comm Coll (OR)
Central Texas Coll (TX)
Central Virginia Comm Coll (VA)
Central Wyoming Coll (WY)
Citrus Coll (CA)
Cochise Coll, Douglas (AZ)
Coll of Central Florida (FL)
Coll of Marin (CA)
Coll of Southern Idaho (ID)
Coll of Southern Maryland (MD)
Collin County Comm Coll District (TX)

The Comm Coll of Baltimore County (MD)
Comm Coll of Philadelphia (PA)
Comm Coll of Rhode Island (RI)
Copiah-Lincoln Comm Coll (MS)
Danville Area Comm Coll (IL)
Daytona State Coll (FL)
Dutchess Comm Coll (NY)
Elgin Comm Coll (IL)
Erie Comm Coll, North Campus (NY)
Frederick Comm Coll (MD)
Genesee Comm Coll (NY)
Grand Rapids Comm Coll (MI)
Hagerstown Comm Coll (MD)
Harford Comm Coll (MD)
Harper Coll (IL)
Harrisburg Area Comm Coll (PA)
Highland Comm Coll (IL)
Hinds Comm Coll (MS)
Holyoke Comm Coll (MA)
Howard Comm Coll (MD)
Hutchinson Comm Coll (KS)
Illinois Eastern Comm Colls, Frontier Community College (IL)
Illinois Eastern Comm Colls, Olney Central College (IL)
Illinois Eastern Comm Colls, Wabash Valley College (IL)
Jamestown Comm Coll (NY)
Jefferson Coll (MO)
Jefferson Comm Coll (NY)
John Tyler Comm Coll (VA)
J. Sargeant Reynolds Comm Coll (VA)
Kalamazoo Valley Comm Coll (MI)
Kankakee Comm Coll (IL)
Kaskaskia Coll (IL)
Kellogg Comm Coll (MI)
Kishwaukee Coll (IL)
Laramie County Comm Coll (WY)
Lehigh Carbon Comm Coll (PA)
Lorain County Comm Coll (OH)
Los Angeles Trade-Tech Coll (CA)
McHenry County Coll (IL)
Miami Dade Coll (FL)
Mohawk Valley Comm Coll (NY)
Montgomery Coll (MD)
Nassau Comm Coll (NY)
Navarro Coll (TX)
New Mexico Jr Coll (NM)
Northampton Comm Coll (PA)
Northern Virginia Comm Coll (VA)
Northwest Coll (WY)
Northwestern Michigan Coll (MI)
Oakton Comm Coll (IL)
Ocean County Coll (NJ)
Ohlone Coll (CA)
Orange Coast Coll (CA)
Paris Jr Coll (TX)
Pensacola State Coll (FL)
Roane State Comm Coll (TN)
St. Charles Comm Coll (MO)
St. Clair County Comm Coll (MI)
Salt Lake Comm Coll (UT)
San Jacinto Coll District (TX)
San Joaquin Delta Coll (CA)
San Juan Coll (NM)
Schoolcraft Coll (MI)
Seminole State Coll (OK)
Sheridan Coll (WY)
Sierra Coll (CA)
South Florida State Coll (FL)
Southwestern Indian Polytechnic Inst (NM)
Springfield Tech Comm Coll (MA)
State U of New York Coll of Technology at Alfred (NY)
Terra State Comm Coll (OH)
Texas State Tech Coll Harlingen (TX)
Tompkins Cortland Comm Coll (NY)
Truckee Meadows Comm Coll (NV)
Tunxis Comm Coll (CT)
Tyler Jr Coll (TX)
Ulster County Comm Coll (NY)
Umpqua Comm Coll (OR)
Virginia Western Comm Coll (VA)
Western Nevada Coll (NV)

ENGINEERING DESIGN
Wisconsin Indianhead Tech Coll (WI)

ENGINEERING/INDUSTRIAL MANAGEMENT
Northwest State Comm Coll (OH)

ENGINEERING RELATED
Macomb Comm Coll (MI)
Miami Dade Coll (FL)
Northwest State Comm Coll (OH)
San Joaquin Delta Coll (CA)
Southeastern Comm Coll (IA)

ENGINEERING-RELATED TECHNOLOGIES
Chesapeake Coll (MD)
Gateway Comm Coll (CT)
Tulsa Comm Coll (OK)

ENGINEERING SCIENCE
Camden County Coll (NJ)
City Colls of Chicago, Olive-Harvey College (IL)
Corning Comm Coll (NY)
County Coll of Morris (NJ)
Finger Lakes Comm Coll (NY)
Genesee Comm Coll (NY)
Greenfield Comm Coll (MA)
Hudson County Comm Coll (NJ)
Jefferson Comm Coll (NY)
Kingsborough Comm Coll of the City U of New York (NY)
Manchester Comm Coll (CT)
Middlesex County Coll (NJ)
Monroe Comm Coll (NY)
Montgomery County Comm Coll (PA)
Northern Essex Comm Coll (MA)
North Shore Comm Coll (MA)
Norwalk Comm Coll (CT)
Queensborough Comm Coll of the City U of New York (NY)
Raritan Valley Comm Coll (NJ)
South Florida State Coll (FL)
Three Rivers Comm Coll (CT)
Westchester Comm Coll (NY)

ENGINEERING TECHNOLOGIES AND ENGINEERING RELATED
Burlington County Coll (NJ)
Carl Albert State Coll (OK)
Cincinnati State Tech and Comm Coll (OH)
Clinton Comm Coll (NY)
Coll of Southern Maryland (MD)
Comm Coll of Allegheny County (PA)
The Comm Coll of Baltimore County (MD)
Hagerstown Comm Coll (MD)
Harrisburg Area Comm Coll (PA)
Haywood Comm Coll (NC)
Middlesex Comm Coll (MA)
Middlesex County Coll (NJ)
Montgomery County Comm Coll (PA)
Mott Comm Coll (MI)
Northern Virginia Comm Coll (VA)
Northwest State Comm Coll (OH)
Ocean County Coll (NJ)
Oklahoma City Comm Coll (OK)
Pennsylvania Highlands Comm Coll (PA)
Quinsigamond Comm Coll (MA)
Raritan Valley Comm Coll (NJ)
Salem Comm Coll (NJ)
Sullivan Coll of Technology and Design (KY)
Wor-Wic Comm Coll (MD)

ENGINEERING TECHNOLOGY
Allen Comm Coll (KS)
Antelope Valley Coll (CA)
Arapahoe Comm Coll (CO)
Benjamin Franklin Inst of Technology (MA)
Bucks County Comm Coll (PA)
Central Virginia Comm Coll (VA)
Citrus Coll (CA)
Coll of Central Florida (FL)
Coll of Marin (CA)
Collin County Comm Coll District (TX)
Comm Coll of Philadelphia (PA)
Corning Comm Coll (NY)
Darton State Coll (GA)
Denmark Tech Coll (SC)
Elizabethtown Comm and Tech Coll, Elizabethtown (KY)
Florida Gateway Coll (FL)
Florida State Coll at Jacksonville (FL)
Gateway Comm and Tech Coll (KY)
Gateway Comm Coll (CT)
Golden West Coll (CA)
Gulf Coast State Coll (FL)
Harford Comm Coll (MD)
Hillsborough Comm Coll (FL)
Hopkinsville Comm Coll (KY)
Iowa Lakes Comm Coll (IA)
Jefferson State Comm Coll (AL)
Kalamazoo Valley Comm Coll (MI)
Lorain County Comm Coll (OH)
Luzerne County Comm Coll (PA)
Massachusetts Bay Comm Coll (MA)
Maysville Comm and Tech Coll, Maysville (KY)
Mesa Comm Coll (AZ)
Miami Dade Coll (FL)

Midlands Tech Coll (SC)
Mt. San Antonio Coll (CA)
North Central Texas Coll (TX)
Oklahoma State U Inst of Technology (OK)
Oklahoma State U, Oklahoma City (OK)
Olympic Coll (WA)
Owensboro Comm and Tech Coll (KY)
Pasadena City Coll (CA)
Penn Foster Coll (AZ)
Pennsylvania Inst of Technology (PA)
Pensacola State Coll (FL)
Pueblo Comm Coll (CO)
Rappahannock Comm Coll (VA)
Salt Lake Comm Coll (UT)
San Joaquin Delta Coll (CA)
San Juan Coll (NM)
Somerset Comm Coll (KY)
South Florida State Coll (FL)
Southwestern Michigan Coll (MI)
Sullivan Coll of Technology and Design (KY)
Three Rivers Comm Coll (CT)
Trident Tech Coll (SC)
Tunxis Comm Coll (CT)
Vincennes U (IN)
Westchester Comm Coll (NY)
Western Wyoming Comm Coll (WY)
Wright State U–Lake Campus (OH)

ENGINE MACHINIST
Lake Area Tech Inst (SD)
Northwest Tech Coll (MN)

ENGLISH
Amarillo Coll (TX)
Arizona Western Coll (AZ)
Bainbridge State Coll (GA)
Borough of Manhattan Comm Coll of the City U of New York (NY)
Bunker Hill Comm Coll (MA)
Burlington County Coll (NJ)
Butler County Comm Coll (PA)
Ca&nnada Coll (CA)
Carl Albert State Coll (OK)
Casper Coll (WY)
Central Wyoming Coll (WY)
Citrus Coll (CA)
Cochise Coll, Douglas (AZ)
Coll of Central Florida (FL)
Coll of Marin (CA)
Coll of Southern Idaho (ID)
Coll of the Canyons (CA)
Coll of the Desert (CA)
Comm Coll of Allegheny County (PA)
Copiah-Lincoln Comm Coll (MS)
Darton State Coll (GA)
Dean Coll (MA)
Eastern Arizona Coll (AZ)
Eastern Wyoming Coll (WY)
Edison Comm Coll (OH)
Fiorello H. LaGuardia Comm Coll of the City U of New York (NY)
Georgia Highlands Coll (GA)
Grand Rapids Comm Coll (MI)
Great Basin Coll (NV)
Greenfield Comm Coll (MA)
Harford Comm Coll (MD)
Harper Coll (IL)
Hinds Comm Coll (MS)
Hutchinson Comm Coll (KS)
Kankakee Comm Coll (IL)
Kilgore Coll (TX)
Laramie County Comm Coll (WY)
Miami Dade Coll (FL)
Mohave Comm Coll (AZ)
Monroe County Comm Coll (MI)
Navarro Coll (TX)
New Mexico Jr Coll (NM)
Northeastern Jr Coll (CO)
Northwest Coll (WY)
Northwestern Michigan Coll (MI)
Ohlone Coll (CA)
Orange Coast Coll (CA)
Palomar Coll (CA)
Paris Jr Coll (TX)
Pensacola State Coll (FL)
Potomac State Coll of West Virginia U (WV)
Raritan Valley Comm Coll (NJ)
St. Charles Comm Coll (MO)
St. Philip's Coll (TX)
Salt Lake Comm Coll (UT)
San Diego Miramar Coll (CA)
San Jacinto Coll District (TX)
San Joaquin Delta Coll (CA)
Seminole State Coll (OK)
Sheridan Coll (WY)

Sierra Coll (CA)
South Florida State Coll (FL)
Terra State Comm Coll (OH)
Trinidad State Jr Coll (CO)
Trinity Valley Comm Coll (TX)
Truckee Meadows Comm Coll (NV)
Umpqua Comm Coll (OR)
Vincennes U (IN)
Western Wyoming Comm Coll (WY)

ENGLISH LANGUAGE AND LITERATURE RELATED
Citrus Coll (CA)
Mt. San Antonio Coll (CA)

ENGLISH/LANGUAGE ARTS TEACHER EDUCATION
Anne Arundel Comm Coll (MD)
Carroll Comm Coll (MD)
Cecil Coll (MD)
Darton State Coll (GA)
Hagerstown Comm Coll (MD)
Harford Comm Coll (MD)
Montgomery Coll (MD)
South Florida State Coll (FL)
Vincennes U (IN)

ENGLISH LITERATURE (BRITISH AND COMMONWEALTH)
Tyler Jr Coll (TX)

ENTOMOLOGY
South Florida State Coll (FL)

ENTREPRENEURIAL AND SMALL BUSINESS RELATED
Dakota Coll at Bottineau (ND)

ENTREPRENEURSHIP
Anne Arundel Comm Coll (MD)
Bunker Hill Comm Coll (MA)
Casper Coll (WY)
Central Oregon Comm Coll (OR)
Central Wyoming Coll (WY)
Cincinnati State Tech and Comm Coll (OH)
Cleveland Comm Coll (NC)
Coll of Southern Idaho (ID)
Comm Coll of Allegheny County (PA)
Delaware Tech & Comm Coll, Terry Campus (DE)
Eastern Arizona Coll (AZ)
Elgin Comm Coll (IL)
Genesee Comm Coll (NY)
Great Falls Coll Montana State U (MT)
Harford Comm Coll (MD)
Lake Area Tech Inst (SD)
Lamar Comm Coll (CO)
Laramie County Comm Coll (WY)
Miami Dade Coll (FL)
Montcalm Comm Coll (MI)
Mott Comm Coll (MI)
Nassau Comm Coll (NY)
North Hennepin Comm Coll (MN)
North Iowa Area Comm Coll (IA)
Northland Comm Coll (MN)
Northwest State Comm Coll (OH)
Richmond Comm Coll (NC)
Salt Lake Comm Coll (UT)
South Piedmont Comm Coll (NC)
State U of New York Coll of Technology at Alfred (NY)
Tallahassee Comm Coll (FL)
Three Rivers Comm Coll (CT)
Tompkins Cortland Comm Coll (NY)
Truckee Meadows Comm Coll (NV)

ENVIRONMENTAL BIOLOGY
Eastern Arizona Coll (AZ)
Eastern Wyoming Coll (WY)

ENVIRONMENTAL CONTROL TECHNOLOGIES RELATED
Cincinnati State Tech and Comm Coll (OH)
Hillsborough Comm Coll (FL)
Holyoke Comm Coll (MA)
Middlesex County Coll (NJ)
Northern Virginia Comm Coll (VA)
Westchester Comm Coll (NY)
Western Dakota Tech Inst (SD)

ENVIRONMENTAL DESIGN/ARCHITECTURE
Iowa Lakes Comm Coll (IA)
Queensborough Comm Coll of the City U of New York (NY)
Scottsdale Comm Coll (AZ)

ENVIRONMENTAL EDUCATION
Iowa Lakes Comm Coll (IA)
New Mexico Jr Coll (NM)

ENVIRONMENTAL ENGINEERING TECHNOLOGY
Austin Comm Coll District (TX)
Cincinnati State Tech and Comm Coll (OH)
Comm Coll of Allegheny County (PA)
Crowder Coll (MO)
Dakota Coll at Bottineau (ND)
Delta Coll (MI)
Erie Comm Coll, North Campus (NY)
Harford Comm Coll (MD)
IntelliTec Coll, Grand Junction (CO)
Iowa Lakes Comm Coll (IA)
James H. Faulkner State Comm Coll (AL)
Kent State U at Trumbull (OH)
Massachusetts Bay Comm Coll (MA)
Miami Dade Coll (FL)
Northwest-Shoals Comm Coll (AL)
Salt Lake Comm Coll (UT)
Schoolcraft Coll (MI)
Sheridan Coll (WY)
State U of New York Coll of Technology at Alfred (NY)
Three Rivers Comm Coll (CT)
Trinidad State Jr Coll (CO)
Wor-Wic Comm Coll (MD)

ENVIRONMENTAL/ENVIRONMENTAL HEALTH ENGINEERING
Central Wyoming Coll (WY)
South Florida State Coll (FL)

ENVIRONMENTAL HEALTH
Amarillo Coll (TX)
Comm Coll of the Air Force (AL)
Queensborough Comm Coll of the City U of New York (NY)
Roane State Comm Coll (TN)

ENVIRONMENTAL SCIENCE
Anoka-Ramsey Comm Coll (MN)
Anoka-Ramsey Comm Coll, Cambridge Campus (MN)
Arizona Western Coll (AZ)
Bucks County Comm Coll (PA)
Burlington County Coll (NJ)
Casper Coll (WY)
Central Texas Coll (TX)
Central Wyoming Coll (WY)
Coll of the Desert (CA)
Corning Comm Coll (NY)
Erie Comm Coll, North Campus (NY)
Fiorello H. LaGuardia Comm Coll of the City U of New York (NY)
Florida State Coll at Jacksonville (FL)
Greenfield Comm Coll (MA)
Harford Comm Coll (MD)
Harrisburg Area Comm Coll (PA)
Jamestown Comm Coll (NY)
Lake Area Tech Inst (SD)
Lehigh Carbon Comm Coll (PA)
Miami Dade Coll (FL)
Montgomery County Comm Coll (PA)
Northampton Comm Coll (PA)
Ocean County Coll (NJ)
The Ohio State U Ag Tech Inst (OH)
Ohlone Coll (CA)
Pennsylvania Highlands Comm Coll (PA)
St. Philip's Coll (TX)
San Jacinto Coll District (TX)
South Florida State Coll (FL)
State U of New York Coll of Technology at Alfred (NY)
Tallahassee Comm Coll (FL)
Truckee Meadows Comm Coll (NV)
Tulsa Comm Coll (OK)
Tyler Jr Coll (TX)
Westchester Comm Coll (NY)
Western Wyoming Comm Coll (WY)

ENVIRONMENTAL STUDIES
Ancilla Coll (IN)
Coll of Central Florida (FL)
Coll of the Desert (CA)
Columbia-Greene Comm Coll (NY)
Comm Coll of the Air Force (AL)
Darton State Coll (GA)
Dean Coll (MA)
Finger Lakes Comm Coll (NY)
Goodwin Coll (CT)
Harper Coll (IL)
Harrisburg Area Comm Coll (PA)

Housatonic Comm Coll (CT)
Howard Comm Coll (MD)
Iowa Lakes Comm Coll (IA)
Monroe Comm Coll (NY)
Mount Wachusett Comm Coll (MA)
New Mexico Jr Coll (NM)
Ohlone Coll (CA)
Stark State Coll (OH)
Sullivan County Comm Coll (NY)
Tompkins Cortland Comm Coll (NY)
U of Cincinnati Clermont Coll (OH)
Westchester Comm Coll (NY)
Western Nevada Coll (NV)
White Mountains Comm Coll (NH)

EQUESTRIAN STUDIES
Allen Comm Coll (KS)
Central Wyoming Coll (WY)
Cochise Coll, Douglas (AZ)
Coll of Central Florida (FL)
Coll of Southern Idaho (ID)
Colorado Northwestern Comm Coll (CO)
Hocking Coll (OH)
Lamar Comm Coll (CO)
Laramie County Comm Coll (WY)
North Central Texas Coll (TX)
Northeastern Jr Coll (CO)
Northwest Coll (WY)
The Ohio State U Ag Tech Inst (OH)
Scottsdale Comm Coll (AZ)
Sierra Coll (CA)

ETHNIC, CULTURAL MINORITY, GENDER, AND GROUP STUDIES RELATED
Coll of Marin (CA)

EXECUTIVE ASSISTANT/EXECUTIVE SECRETARY
Alamance Comm Coll (NC)
Alvin Comm Coll (TX)
Bellingham Tech Coll (WA)
Brookhaven Coll (TX)
Cape Fear Comm Coll (NC)
Cedar Valley Coll (TX)
Cincinnati State Tech and Comm Coll (OH)
Clark Coll (WA)
Crowder Coll (MO)
Dakota Coll at Bottineau (ND)
Danville Area Comm Coll (IL)
Edison Comm Coll (OH)
El Centro Coll (TX)
Elgin Comm Coll (IL)
Elizabethtown Comm and Tech Coll, Elizabethtown (KY)
Hawkeye Comm Coll (IA)
Haywood Comm Coll (NC)
Hillsborough Comm Coll (FL)
Hopkinsville Comm Coll (KY)
Humacao Comm Coll (PR)
Illinois Eastern Comm Colls, Frontier Community College (IL)
Illinois Eastern Comm Colls, Wabash Valley College (IL)
Kalamazoo Valley Comm Coll (MI)
Kaskaskia Coll (IL)
Kellogg Comm Coll (MI)
Kilgore Coll (TX)
Lake Land Coll (IL)
Luzerne County Comm Coll (PA)
Maysville Comm and Tech Coll, Maysville (KY)
Northwestern Michigan Coll (MI)
Owensboro Comm and Tech Coll (KY)
Owens Comm Coll, Toledo (OH)
Pensacola State Coll (FL)
Quinsigamond Comm Coll (MA)
St. Clair County Comm Coll (MI)
Schoolcraft Coll (MI)
Somerset Comm Coll (KY)
South Suburban Coll (IL)
Southwestern Michigan Coll (MI)
Terra State Comm Coll (OH)
Westmoreland County Comm Coll (PA)

FACILITIES PLANNING AND MANAGEMENT
Comm Coll of Philadelphia (PA)

FAMILY AND COMMUNITY SERVICES
Palomar Coll (CA)
Phoenix Coll (AZ)
Westmoreland County Comm Coll (PA)

FAMILY AND CONSUMER ECONOMICS RELATED
American Samoa Comm Coll (AS)
Orange Coast Coll (CA)

FAMILY AND CONSUMER SCIENCES/HOME ECONOMICS TEACHER EDUCATION
Antelope Valley Coll (CA)
Copiah-Lincoln Comm Coll (MS)
South Florida State Coll (FL)
Vincennes U (IN)

FAMILY AND CONSUMER SCIENCES/HUMAN SCIENCES
Allen Comm Coll (KS)
Arizona Western Coll (AZ)
Bainbridge State Coll (GA)
Coll of Central Florida (FL)
Hinds Comm Coll (MS)
Hutchinson Comm Coll (KS)
Iowa Lakes Comm Coll (IA)
Mesa Comm Coll (AZ)
Monroe Comm Coll (NY)
Mt. San Antonio Coll (CA)
Northeastern Jr Coll (CO)
Ohlone Coll (CA)
Orange Coast Coll (CA)
Palomar Coll (CA)
Phoenix Coll (AZ)
San Joaquin Delta Coll (CA)
Tyler Jr Coll (TX)
Vincennes U (IN)

FAMILY SYSTEMS
Goodwin Coll (CT)
Maysville Comm and Tech Coll, Maysville (KY)

FARM AND RANCH MANAGEMENT
Allen Comm Coll (KS)
Central Texas Coll (TX)
Copiah-Lincoln Comm Coll (MS)
Crowder Coll (MO)
Eastern Wyoming Coll (WY)
Hutchinson Comm Coll (KS)
Iowa Lakes Comm Coll (IA)
Lamar Comm Coll (CO)
North Central Texas Coll (TX)
Northeastern Jr Coll (CO)
Northland Comm Coll (MN)
Northwest Coll (WY)
Trinity Valley Comm Coll (TX)

FASHION AND FABRIC CONSULTING
Harper Coll (IL)

FASHION/APPAREL DESIGN
Burlington County Coll (NJ)
Ca&nnada Coll (CA)
Clary Sage Coll (OK)
El Centro Coll (TX)
Fashion Inst of Technology (NY)
FIDM/Fashion Inst of Design & Merchandising, Los Angeles Campus (CA)
FIDM/Fashion Inst of Design & Merchandising, Orange County Campus (CA)
FIDM/Fashion Inst of Design & Merchandising, San Francisco Campus (CA)
FIDM/The Fashion Inst of Design & Merchandising, San Diego Campus (CA)
Genesee Comm Coll (NY)
Harper Coll (IL)
Houston Comm Coll (TX)
Lehigh Carbon Comm Coll (PA)
Los Angeles Trade-Tech Coll (CA)
Monroe Comm Coll (NY)
Nassau Comm Coll (NY)
Palomar Coll (CA)
Pasadena City Coll (CA)
Phoenix Coll (AZ)
Wood Tobe–Coburn School (NY)

FASHION MERCHANDISING
Alexandria Tech and Comm Coll (MN)
Fashion Inst of Technology (NY)
FIDM/Fashion Inst of Design & Merchandising, Los Angeles Campus (CA)
FIDM/Fashion Inst of Design & Merchandising, Orange County Campus (CA)

FIDM/Fashion Inst of Design & Merchandising, San Francisco Campus (CA)
FIDM/The Fashion Inst of Design & Merchandising, San Diego Campus (CA)
Gateway Comm Coll (CT)
Genesee Comm Coll (NY)
Grand Rapids Comm Coll (MI)
Harper Coll (IL)
Hinds Comm Coll (MS)
Houston Comm Coll (TX)
Iowa Lakes Comm Coll (IA)
Kingsborough Comm Coll of the City U of New York (NY)
Los Angeles Trade-Tech Coll (CA)
Mesa Comm Coll (AZ)
Middlesex Comm Coll (MA)
Monroe Comm Coll (NY)
Mt. San Antonio Coll (CA)
Nassau Comm Coll (NY)
Ohlone Coll (CA)
Orange Coast Coll (CA)
Pasadena City Coll (CA)
Penn Foster Coll (AZ)
Phoenix Coll (AZ)
San Joaquin Delta Coll (CA)
Scottsdale Comm Coll (AZ)
Trinity Valley Comm Coll (TX)
Vincennes U (IN)

FASHION MODELING
Fashion Inst of Technology (NY)

FIBER, TEXTILE AND WEAVING ARTS
Antelope Valley Coll (CA)
FIDM/Fashion Inst of Design & Merchandising, Orange County Campus (CA)

FILM/CINEMA/VIDEO STUDIES
Carl Albert State Coll (OK)
Coll of Marin (CA)
Fashion Inst of Technology (NY)
KD Coll Conservatory of Film and Dramatic Arts (TX)
Orange Coast Coll (CA)
Palomar Coll (CA)

FILM/VIDEO AND PHOTOGRAPHIC ARTS RELATED
Greenfield Comm Coll (MA)
Westchester Comm Coll (NY)

FINANCE
Bunker Hill Comm Coll (MA)
Chipola Coll (FL)
Comm Coll of Philadelphia (PA)
Comm Coll of the Air Force (AL)
Harper Coll (IL)
Iowa Lakes Comm Coll (IA)
Lenoir Comm Coll (NC)
Lorain County Comm Coll (OH)
Macomb Comm Coll (MI)
Mesa Comm Coll (AZ)
Miami Dade Coll (FL)
Monroe County Comm Coll (MI)
Mt. San Antonio Coll (CA)
New Mexico Jr Coll (NM)
Northern Essex Comm Coll (MA)
North Hennepin Comm Coll (MN)
Norwalk Comm Coll (CT)
Oklahoma City Comm Coll (OK)
Penn Foster Coll (AZ)
Rockland Comm Coll (NY)
Salt Lake Comm Coll (UT)
Scottsdale Comm Coll (AZ)
Seminole State Coll of Florida (FL)
South Florida State Coll (FL)
Springfield Tech Comm Coll (MA)
Stark State Coll (OH)
Trinity Valley Comm Coll (TX)
Vincennes U (IN)
Westchester Comm Coll (NY)
Western Iowa Tech Comm Coll (IA)
Wisconsin Indianhead Tech Coll (WI)

FINANCIAL PLANNING AND SERVICES
Cecil Coll (MD)
Cincinnati State Tech and Comm Coll (OH)
Howard Comm Coll (MD)
Raritan Valley Comm Coll (NJ)

FINE ARTS RELATED
Butler County Comm Coll (PA)
Carl Albert State Coll (OK)
Corning Comm Coll (NY)
Ohlone Coll (CA)

Salem Comm Coll (NJ)
Schoolcraft Coll (MI)
Seminole State Coll (OK)

FINE/STUDIO ARTS
Amarillo Coll (TX)
Anoka-Ramsey Comm Coll (MN)
Anoka-Ramsey Comm Coll, Cambridge Campus (MN)
Arizona Western Comm Coll (AZ)
Camden County Coll (NJ)
Casper Coll (WY)
Cayuga County Comm Coll (NY)
Cecil Coll (MD)
Central Texas Coll (TX)
Century Coll (MN)
Chandler-Gilbert Comm Coll (AZ)
City Colls of Chicago, Olive-Harvey College (IL)
Corning Comm Coll (NY)
County Coll of Morris (NJ)
Cumberland County Coll (NJ)
Delta Coll (MI)
Elgin Comm Coll (IL)
Fashion Inst of Technology (NY)
Finger Lakes Comm Coll (NY)
Fiorello H. LaGuardia Comm Coll of the City U of New York (NY)
Genesee Comm Coll (NY)
Greenfield Comm Coll (MA)
Harford Comm Coll (MD)
Harper Coll (IL)
Hudson County Comm Coll (NJ)
Iowa Lakes Comm Coll (IA)
Jamestown Comm Coll (NY)
Kishwaukee Coll (IL)
Lakes Region Comm Coll (NH)
Manchester Comm Coll (CT)
McHenry County Coll (IL)
Minneapolis Comm and Tech Coll (MN)
Niagara County Comm Coll (NY)
Normandale Comm Coll (MN)
Northampton Comm Coll (PA)
Northeastern Jr Coll (CO)
North Hennepin Comm Coll (MN)
Norwalk Comm Coll (CT)
Oklahoma City Comm Coll (OK)
Owensboro Comm and Tech Coll (KY)
Phoenix Coll (AZ)
Queensborough Comm Coll of the City U of New York (NY)
Raritan Valley Comm Coll (NJ)
Rockland Comm Coll (NY)
San Diego Miramar Coll (CA)
South Florida State Coll (FL)
South Suburban Coll (IL)
Southwestern Illinois Coll (IL)
Springfield Tech Comm Coll (MA)
Terra State Comm Coll (OH)
Three Rivers Comm Coll (CT)
Truckee Meadows Comm Coll (NV)
Tulsa Comm Coll (OK)
Westchester Comm Coll (NY)

FIRE PREVENTION AND SAFETY TECHNOLOGY
Anne Arundel Comm Coll (MD)
Antelope Valley Coll (CA)
Austin Comm Coll District (TX)
Bunker Hill Comm Coll (MA)
Camden County Coll (NJ)
Cape Fear Comm Coll (NC)
Catawba Valley Comm Coll (NC)
Cleveland Comm Coll (NC)
Coll of the Canyons (CA)
Collin County Comm Coll District (TX)
Comm Coll of Allegheny County (PA)
County Coll of Morris (NJ)
Delgado Comm Coll (LA)
Delta Coll (MI)
Des Moines Area Comm Coll (IA)
Fayetteville Tech Comm Coll (NC)
Florida SouthWestern State Coll (FL)
Florida State Coll at Jacksonville (FL)
Forsyth Tech Comm Coll (NC)
Greenfield Comm Coll (MA)
Guilford Tech Comm Coll (NC)
Gulf Coast State Coll (FL)
Hillsborough Comm Coll (FL)
Houston Comm Coll (TX)
Jefferson Coll (MO)
Jefferson Comm Coll (NY)
Lakeland Comm Coll (OH)
Lakes Region Comm Coll (NH)
Macomb Comm Coll (MI)
Miami Dade Coll (FL)
Middlesex County Coll (NJ)
Montgomery Coll (MD)

Montgomery County Comm Coll (PA)
Moraine Valley Comm Coll (IL)
Mott Comm Coll (MI)
Mount Wachusett Comm Coll (MA)
North Iowa Area Comm Coll (IA)
Northland Comm Coll (MN)
Oklahoma State U, Oklahoma City (OK)
Palomar Coll (CA)
Pasadena City Coll (CA)
Pensacola State Coll (FL)
Rogue Comm Coll (OR)
South Florida State Coll (FL)
South Piedmont Comm Coll (NC)
Springfield Tech Comm Coll (MA)
Sullivan County Comm Coll (NY)
Victor Valley Coll (CA)
Waukesha County Tech Coll (WI)
Wayne County Comm Coll District (MI)
Western Nevada Coll (NV)
Westmoreland County Comm Coll (PA)

FIRE PROTECTION RELATED
Fox Valley Tech Coll (WI)

FIRE SCIENCE/FIREFIGHTING
Amarillo Coll (TX)
Arizona Western Coll (AZ)
Burlington County Coll (NJ)
Butler County Comm Coll (PA)
Casper Coll (WY)
Cecil Coll (MD)
Central Oregon Comm Coll (OR)
Central Wyoming Coll (WY)
Cincinnati State Tech and Comm Coll (OH)
Cochise Coll, Douglas (AZ)
Coll of Central Florida (FL)
Coll of Southern Maryland (MD)
Coll of the Desert (CA)
Collin County Comm Coll District (TX)
Comm Coll of Aurora (CO)
Comm Coll of Philadelphia (PA)
Comm Coll of Rhode Island (RI)
Comm Coll of the Air Force (AL)
Crowder Coll (MO)
Danville Area Comm Coll (IL)
Daytona State Coll (FL)
Delta Coll (MI)
Eastern Arizona Coll (AZ)
Eastern Idaho Tech Coll (ID)
Elgin Comm Coll (IL)
Elizabethtown Comm and Tech Coll, Elizabethtown (KY)
Florida State Coll at Jacksonville (FL)
Fox Valley Tech Coll (WI)
Frederick Comm Coll (MD)
Gateway Comm and Tech Coll (KY)
Gateway Comm Coll (CT)
Gateway Tech Coll (WI)
Greenville Tech Coll (SC)
Harper Coll (IL)
Harrisburg Area Comm Coll (PA)
Hawkeye Comm Coll (IA)
Hennepin Tech Coll (MN)
Hocking Coll (OH)
Hutchinson Comm Coll (KS)
Illinois Eastern Comm Colls, Frontier Community College (IL)
J. Sargeant Reynolds Comm Coll (VA)
Kalamazoo Valley Comm Coll (MI)
Lakes Region Comm Coll (NH)
Laramie County Comm Coll (WY)
Lone Star Coll–CyFair (TX)
Lone Star Coll–Kingwood (TX)
Lone Star Coll–Montgomery (TX)
Lorain County Comm Coll (OH)
Lower Columbia Coll (WA)
Luzerne County Comm Coll (PA)
McHenry County Coll (IL)
Mesa Comm Coll (AZ)
Miami Dade Coll (FL)
Middlesex Comm Coll (MA)
Mid-Plains Comm Coll, North Platte (NE)
Mohave Comm Coll (AZ)
Monroe Comm Coll (NY)
Moraine Valley Comm Coll (IL)
Mt. San Antonio Coll (CA)
Navarro Coll (TX)
New Mexico Jr Coll (NM)
Northampton Comm Coll (PA)
Northeast Iowa Comm Coll (IA)
North Shore Comm Coll (MA)
Norwalk Comm Coll (CT)
Oakton Comm Coll (IL)

Oklahoma State U, Oklahoma City (OK)
Owensboro Comm and Tech Coll (KY)
Ozarks Tech Comm Coll (MO)
Pensacola State Coll (FL)
Phoenix Coll (AZ)
Pueblo Comm Coll (CO)
Richland Comm Coll (IL)
Rockland Comm Coll (NY)
Rock Valley Coll (IL)
St. Charles Comm Coll (MO)
St. Clair County Comm Coll (MI)
Salem Comm Coll (NJ)
San Diego Miramar Coll (CA)
San Jacinto Coll District (TX)
San Joaquin Delta Coll (CA)
San Juan Coll (NM)
Schoolcraft Coll (MI)
Seminole State Coll of Florida (FL)
Sierra Coll (CA)
Southwestern Illinois Coll (IL)
Southwestern Michigan Coll (MI)
Stark State Coll (OH)
Tallahassee Comm Coll (FL)
Trinidad State Jr Coll (CO)
Truckee Meadows Comm Coll (NV)
Tyler Jr Coll (TX)
Umpqua Comm Coll (OR)
Victoria Coll (TX)
Victor Valley Coll (CA)
Vincennes U (IN)
Volunteer State Comm Coll (TN)
Western Dakota Tech Inst (SD)
Western Iowa Tech Comm Coll (IA)

FIRE SERVICES ADMINISTRATION
Central Texas Coll (TX)
Delta Coll (MI)
Dutchess Comm Coll (NY)
Erie Comm Coll, South Campus (NY)
Florida State Coll at Jacksonville (FL)
Jefferson Comm Coll (NY)
Jefferson State Comm Coll (AL)
Mohawk Valley Comm Coll (NY)
Northampton Comm Coll (PA)
Quinsigamond Comm Coll (MA)
Tech Coll of the Lowcountry (SC)
Three Rivers Comm Coll (CT)
Tulsa Comm Coll (OK)

FISHING AND FISHERIES SCIENCES AND MANAGEMENT
Bellingham Tech Coll (WA)
Central Oregon Comm Coll (OR)
Dakota Coll at Bottineau (ND)
Finger Lakes Comm Coll (NY)
Hocking Coll (OH)
Iowa Lakes Comm Coll (IA)
U of Alaska Southeast, Sitka Campus (AK)

FLIGHT INSTRUCTION
Iowa Lakes Comm Coll (IA)

FLORICULTURE/FLORISTRY MANAGEMENT
Dakota Coll at Bottineau (ND)
Danville Area Comm Coll (IL)
J. Sargeant Reynolds Comm Coll (VA)
The Ohio State U Ag Tech Inst (OH)
Westmoreland County Comm Coll (PA)

FOOD PREPARATION
Iowa Lakes Comm Coll (IA)
J. Sargeant Reynolds Comm Coll (VA)

FOODS AND NUTRITION RELATED
Iowa Lakes Comm Coll (IA)

FOOD SCIENCE
Greenfield Comm Coll (MA)
Hocking Coll (OH)
Miami Dade Coll (FL)
Normandale Comm Coll (MN)
Ohlone Coll (CA)
Orange Coast Coll (CA)
South Florida State Coll (FL)
Vincennes U (IN)

FOOD SERVICE AND DINING ROOM MANAGEMENT
Iowa Lakes Comm Coll (IA)
Pasadena City Coll (CA)
Westmoreland County Comm Coll (PA)

FOOD SERVICE SYSTEMS ADMINISTRATION
Bucks County Comm Coll (PA)
Burlington County Coll (NJ)
Butler County Comm Coll (PA)
Comm Coll of Allegheny County (PA)
Harper Coll (IL)
Harrisburg Area Comm Coll (PA)
Mott Comm Coll (MI)
Pensacola State Coll (FL)
Phoenix Coll (AZ)
San Jacinto Coll District (TX)
Wayne County Comm Coll District (MI)
Wright State U–Lake Campus (OH)

FOODS, NUTRITION, AND WELLNESS
Antelope Valley Coll (CA)
Bossier Parish Comm Coll (LA)
Carl Albert State Coll (OK)
North Shore Comm Coll (MA)
Ohlone Coll (CA)
Orange Coast Coll (CA)
Pensacola State Coll (FL)

FOOD TECHNOLOGY AND PROCESSING
Butler County Comm Coll (PA)
Copiah-Lincoln Comm Coll (MS)
Genesee Comm Coll (NY)
Lenoir Comm Coll (NC)
Luzerne County Comm Coll (PA)
Monroe Comm Coll (NY)
Orange Coast Coll (CA)
Richland Comm Coll (IL)
Stark State Coll (OH)
Victor Valley Coll (CA)
Westchester Comm Coll (NY)

FOREIGN LANGUAGES AND LITERATURES
Austin Comm Coll District (TX)
Bunker Hill Comm Coll (MA)
Casper Coll (WY)
Central Oregon Comm Coll (OR)
Central Texas Coll (TX)
Coll of Central Florida (FL)
Coll of Marin (CA)
Coll of Southern Idaho (ID)
Comm Coll of Allegheny County (PA)
Darton State Coll (GA)
Eastern Arizona Coll (AZ)
Eastern Wyoming Coll (WY)
Georgia Highlands Coll (GA)
Grand Rapids Comm Coll (MI)
Hutchinson Comm Coll (KS)
Iowa Lakes Comm Coll (IA)
Oklahoma City Comm Coll (OK)
Palomar Coll (CA)
Paris Jr Coll (TX)
St. Charles Comm Coll (MO)
San Jacinto Coll District (TX)
South Florida State Coll (FL)
Tyler Jr Coll (TX)
Vincennes U (IN)

FOREIGN LANGUAGES RELATED
Genesee Comm Coll (NY)
Tulsa Comm Coll (OK)
Vincennes U (IN)

FOREIGN LANGUAGE TEACHER EDUCATION
South Florida State Coll (FL)

FORENSIC SCIENCE AND TECHNOLOGY
American Samoa Comm Coll (AS)
Borough of Manhattan Comm Coll of the City U of New York (NY)
Carroll Comm Coll (MD)
Casper Coll (WY)
Catawba Valley Comm Coll (NC)
Comm Coll of Philadelphia (PA)
Darton State Coll (GA)
Fayetteville Tech Comm Coll (NC)
Florida SouthWestern State Coll (FL)
Forsyth Tech Comm Coll (NC)
Fox Valley Tech Coll (WI)
Gulf Coast State Coll (FL)
Kishwaukee Coll (IL)
Louisiana Delta Comm Coll, Monroe (LA)
Macomb Comm Coll (MI)
Massachusetts Bay Comm Coll (MA)
Miami Dade Coll (FL)
Palomar Coll (CA)
Pensacola State Coll (FL)
Phoenix Coll (AZ)

Potomac State Coll of West Virginia U (WV)
South Florida State Coll (FL)
Sullivan County Comm Coll (NY)
Tunxis Comm Coll (CT)
U of Arkansas Comm Coll at Morrilton (AR)

FOREST/FOREST RESOURCES MANAGEMENT
Haywood Comm Coll (NC)
Northwestern Michigan Coll (MI)

FOREST RESOURCES PRODUCTION AND MANAGEMENT
Potomac State Coll of West Virginia U (WV)

FORESTRY
Allen Comm Coll (KS)
Bainbridge State Coll (GA)
Central Oregon Comm Coll (OR)
Coll of Central Florida (FL)
Coll of Southern Idaho (ID)
Copiah-Lincoln Comm Coll (MS)
Darton State Coll (GA)
Eastern Arizona Coll (AZ)
Grand Rapids Comm Coll (MI)
Hinds Comm Coll (MS)
Hocking Coll (OH)
Iowa Lakes Comm Coll (IA)
Kilgore Coll (TX)
Miami Dade Coll (FL)
Monroe Comm Coll (NY)
Sierra Coll (CA)
South Florida State Coll (FL)
Umpqua Comm Coll (OR)
Western Wyoming Comm Coll (WY)

FOREST TECHNOLOGY
Central Oregon Comm Coll (OR)
Dabney S. Lancaster Comm Coll (VA)
Haywood Comm Coll (NC)
Hocking Coll (OH)
Horry-Georgetown Tech Coll (SC)
Jefferson Comm Coll (NY)
Lurleen B. Wallace Comm Coll (AL)
Montgomery Comm Coll (NC)
Mt. San Antonio Coll (CA)
Penn State Mont Alto (PA)

FRENCH
Austin Comm Coll District (TX)
Citrus Coll (CA)
Coll of Marin (CA)
Coll of the Canyons (CA)
Coll of the Desert (CA)
Miami Dade Coll (FL)
Northwest Coll (WY)
Orange Coast Coll (CA)
Palomar Coll (CA)
St. Charles Comm Coll (MO)
South Florida State Coll (FL)

FUNERAL SERVICE AND MORTUARY SCIENCE
Allen Comm Coll (KS)
Amarillo Coll (TX)
Arapahoe Comm Coll (CO)
The Comm Coll of Baltimore County (MD)
Dallas Inst of Funeral Service (TX)
Delgado Comm Coll (LA)
Des Moines Area Comm Coll (IA)
Fayetteville Tech Comm Coll (NC)
Fiorello H. LaGuardia Comm Coll of the City U of New York (NY)
Florida State Coll at Jacksonville (FL)
Jefferson State Comm Coll (AL)
John A. Gupton Coll (TN)
John Tyler Comm Coll (VA)
Luzerne County Comm Coll (PA)
Miami Dade Coll (FL)
Monroe County Comm Coll (MI)
Nassau Comm Coll (NY)
Northampton Comm Coll (PA)
Randolph Comm Coll (NC)
U of Arkansas Comm Coll at Hope (AR)
Vincennes U (IN)

FURNITURE DESIGN AND MANUFACTURING
Northcentral Tech Coll (WI)

GAME AND INTERACTIVE MEDIA DESIGN
Cayuga County Comm Coll (NY)

Collin County Comm Coll District (TX)
Fayetteville Tech Comm Coll (NC)
Hinds Comm Coll (MS)
Lehigh Carbon Comm Coll (PA)
Oklahoma City Comm Coll (OK)
Salem Comm Coll (NJ)
South Piedmont Comm Coll (NC)
Western Iowa Tech Comm Coll (IA)

GENERAL STUDIES
Allen Comm Coll (KS)
Alvin Comm Coll (TX)
Amarillo Coll (TX)
Ancilla Coll (IN)
Arizona Western Coll (AZ)
Arkansas Northeastern Coll (AR)
Austin Comm Coll District (TX)
Bevill State Comm Coll (AL)
Blue Ridge Comm and Tech Coll (WV)
Bossier Parish Comm Coll (LA)
Brookhaven Coll (TX)
Bunker Hill Comm Coll (MA)
Butler County Comm Coll (PA)
Carroll Comm Coll (MD)
Casper Coll (WY)
Catawba Valley Comm Coll (NC)
Cayuga County Comm Coll (NY)
Cecil Coll (MD)
Cedar Valley Coll (TX)
Central Texas Coll (TX)
Central Wyoming Coll (WY)
Chandler-Gilbert Comm Coll (AZ)
Chesapeake Coll (MD)
Cincinnati State Tech and Comm Coll (OH)
City Colls of Chicago, Olive-Harvey College (IL)
Cleveland Comm Coll (NC)
Cleveland State Comm Coll (TN)
Cochise Coll, Douglas (AZ)
Colorado Northwestern Comm Coll (CO)
Columbia-Greene Comm Coll (NY)
Comm Coll of Allegheny County (PA)
Comm Coll of Aurora (CO)
Comm Coll of Denver (CO)
Comm Coll of Rhode Island (RI)
Crowder Coll (MO)
Dakota Coll at Bottineau (ND)
Danville Area Comm Coll (IL)
Darton State Coll (GA)
Dean Coll (MA)
Delgado Comm Coll (LA)
Delta Coll (MI)
Dutchess Comm Coll (NY)
Dyersburg State Comm Coll (TN)
Eastern Wyoming Coll (WY)
Erie Comm Coll (NY)
Erie Comm Coll, North Campus (NY)
Erie Comm Coll, South Campus (NY)
Fayetteville Tech Comm Coll (NC)
Forsyth Tech Comm Coll (NC)
Frederick Comm Coll (MD)
Front Range Comm Coll (CO)
Gadsden State Comm Coll (AL)
Gateway Comm and Tech Coll (KY)
Genesee Comm Coll (NY)
Georgia Highlands Coll (GA)
Guilford Tech Comm Coll (NC)
Harford Comm Coll (MD)
Harrisburg Area Comm Coll (PA)
Highland Comm Coll (IL)
Hinds Comm Coll (MS)
Howard Comm Coll (MD)
Illinois Eastern Comm Colls, Frontier Community College (IL)
Illinois Eastern Comm Colls, Lincoln Trail College (IL)
Illinois Eastern Comm Colls, Olney Central College (IL)
Illinois Eastern Comm Colls, Wabash Valley College (IL)
Iowa Lakes Comm Coll (IA)
Jackson State Comm Coll (TN)
James H. Faulkner State Comm Coll (AL)
James Sprunt Comm Coll (NC)
Jamestown Comm Coll (NY)
Jefferson State Comm Coll (AL)
John Tyler Comm Coll (VA)
Kalamazoo Valley Comm Coll (MI)
Kankakee Comm Coll (IL)
Kaskaskia Coll (IL)
Kellogg Comm Coll (MI)
Kilgore Coll (TX)
Kirtland Comm Coll (MI)
Lake Land Coll (IL)

Lakes Region Comm Coll (NH)
Landmark Coll (VT)
Laramie County Comm Coll (WY)
Lehigh Carbon Comm Coll (PA)
Louisiana Delta Comm Coll, Monroe (LA)
Lurleen B. Wallace Comm Coll (AL)
Luzerne County Comm Coll (PA)
Macomb Comm Coll (MI)
Manchester Comm Coll (CT)
Massachusetts Bay Comm Coll (MA)
McHenry County Coll (IL)
Miami Dade Coll (FL)
Middlesex Comm Coll (MA)
Mohawk Valley Comm Coll (NY)
Montcalm Comm Coll (MI)
Motlow State Comm Coll (TN)
Mott Comm Coll (MI)
Mount Wachusett Comm Coll (MA)
Nassau Comm Coll (NY)
Niagara County Comm Coll (NY)
Northampton Comm Coll (PA)
Northcentral Tech Coll (WI)
Northern Essex Comm Coll (MA)
Northern Virginia Comm Coll (VA)
Northwest Coll (WY)
Northwest-Shoals Comm Coll (AL)
Norwalk Comm Coll (CT)
Nunez Comm Coll (LA)
Ocean County Coll (NJ)
Oklahoma City Comm Coll (OK)
Oklahoma State U, Oklahoma City (OK)
Oregon Coast Comm Coll (OR)
Owens Comm Coll, Toledo (OH)
Panola Coll (TX)
Paris Jr Coll (TX)
Pennsylvania Highlands Comm Coll (PA)
Pennsylvania Inst of Technology (PA)
Phoenix Coll (AZ)
Piedmont Comm Coll (NC)
Pueblo Comm Coll (CO)
Quinsigamond Comm Coll (MA)
Reading Area Comm Coll (PA)
Roane State Comm Coll (TN)
Rogue Comm Coll (OR)
St. Charles Comm Coll (MO)
St. Vincent's Coll (CT)
Salt Lake Comm Coll (UT)
San Jacinto Coll District (TX)
San Juan Coll (NM)
Schoolcraft Coll (MI)
Seminole State Coll (OK)
Sheridan Coll (WY)
Sierra Coll (CA)
Southern U at Shreveport (LA)
South Florida State Coll (FL)
South Louisiana Comm Coll (LA)
South Piedmont Comm Coll (NC)
Southwestern Illinois Coll (IL)
Southwestern Michigan Coll (MI)
Sowela Tech Comm Coll (LA)
Springfield Tech Comm Coll (MA)
State U of New York Coll of Technology at Alfred (NY)
Terra State Comm Coll (OH)
Three Rivers Comm Coll (CT)
Trinidad State Jr Coll (CO)
Trocaire Coll (NY)
Truckee Meadows Comm Coll (NV)
Tulsa Comm Coll (OK)
Tyler Jr Coll (TX)
U of Alaska Southeast, Sitka Campus (AK)
U of Arkansas Comm Coll at Hope (AR)
U of Arkansas Comm Coll at Morrilton (AR)
U of Cincinnati Clermont Coll (OH)
Victoria Coll (TX)
Volunteer State Comm Coll (TN)
Walters State Comm Coll (TN)
Wayne County Comm Coll District (MI)
Western Nevada Coll (NV)
Western Wyoming Comm Coll (WY)
White Mountains Comm Coll (NH)

GEOGRAPHIC INFORMATION SCIENCE AND CARTOGRAPHY
Austin Comm Coll District (TX)
Borough of Manhattan Comm Coll of the City U of New York (NY)
Brookhaven Coll (TX)
Casper Coll (WY)
Collin County Comm Coll District (TX)
Harrisburg Area Comm Coll (PA)
Hinds Comm Coll (MS)

Lehigh Carbon Comm Coll (PA)
Lone Star Coll—CyFair (TX)
Mitchell Tech Inst (SD)
Oklahoma City Comm Coll (OK)
Southwestern Indian Polytechnic Inst (NM)

GEOGRAPHY
Allen Comm Coll (KS)
Austin Comm Coll District (TX)
Ca&nnada Coll (CA)
Cayuga County Comm Coll (NY)
Coll of Marin (CA)
Coll of Southern Idaho (ID)
Coll of the Canyons (CA)
Coll of the Desert (CA)
The Comm Coll of Baltimore County (MD)
Darton State Coll (GA)
Montgomery Coll (MD)
Ohlone Coll (CA)
Orange Coast Coll (CA)
Palomar Coll (CA)
San Diego Miramar Coll (CA)
South Florida State Coll (FL)

GEOGRAPHY RELATED
Palomar Coll (CA)

GEOLOGICAL AND EARTH SCIENCES/GEOSCIENCES RELATED
Burlington County Coll (NJ)
Potomac State Coll of West Virginia U (WV)
Truckee Meadows Comm Coll (NV)

GEOLOGY/EARTH SCIENCE
Amarillo Coll (TX)
Arizona Western Coll (AZ)
Austin Comm Coll District (TX)
Casper Coll (WY)
Central Texas Coll (TX)
Central Wyoming Coll (WY)
Coll of Marin (CA)
Coll of Southern Idaho (ID)
Coll of the Canyons (CA)
Coll of the Desert (CA)
Eastern Arizona Coll (AZ)
Edison Comm Coll (OH)
Georgia Highlands Coll (GA)
Grand Rapids Comm Coll (MI)
Great Basin Coll (NV)
Hinds Comm Coll (MS)
Iowa Lakes Comm Coll (IA)
Kilgore Coll (TX)
Miami Dade Coll (FL)
Middlesex County Coll (NJ)
Ohlone Coll (CA)
Orange Coast Coll (CA)
Palomar Coll (CA)
Pensacola State Coll (FL)
Potomac State Coll of West Virginia U (WV)
St. Philip's Coll (TX)
Salt Lake Comm Coll (UT)
San Jacinto Coll District (TX)
San Joaquin Delta Coll (CA)
San Juan Coll (NM)
Sierra Coll (CA)
South Florida State Coll (FL)
Trinity Valley Comm Coll (TX)
Tyler Jr Coll (TX)
Vincennes U (IN)
Western Wyoming Comm Coll (WY)
Wright State U–Lake Campus (OH)

GERMAN
Austin Comm Coll District (TX)
Citrus Coll (CA)
Miami Dade Coll (FL)
Orange Coast Coll (CA)

GERONTOLOGY
Anne Arundel Comm Coll (MD)
Gateway Comm Coll (CT)
Genesee Comm Coll (NY)
Lakes Region Comm Coll (NH)
Midlands Tech Coll (SC)
North Shore Comm Coll (MA)
South Florida State Coll (FL)

GOLF COURSE OPERATION AND GROUNDS MANAGEMENT
Anoka Tech Coll (MN)
Tech Coll of the Lowcountry (SC)

GRAPHIC AND PRINTING EQUIPMENT OPERATION/PRODUCTION
Burlington County Coll (NJ)

Central Maine Comm Coll (ME)
Central Texas Coll (TX)
Erie Comm Coll, South Campus (NY)
Fox Valley Tech Coll (WI)
Golden West Coll (CA)
Iowa Lakes Comm Coll (IA)
Lake Land Coll (IL)
Lakes Region Comm Coll (NH)
Lenoir Comm Coll (NC)
Los Angeles Trade-Tech Coll (CA)
Luzerne County Comm Coll (PA)
Macomb Comm Coll (MI)
Monroe Comm Coll (NY)
Northern Virginia Comm Coll (VA)
Northwest Coll (WY)
Ozarks Tech Comm Coll (MO)
Palomar Coll (CA)
Pasadena City Coll (CA)
Rock Valley Coll (IL)
Sullivan Coll of Technology and Design (KY)
Tulsa Comm Coll (OK)
Vincennes U (IN)

GRAPHIC COMMUNICATIONS
Central Maine Comm Coll (ME)
Clark Coll (WA)
Fox Valley Tech Coll (WI)
Hawkeye Comm Coll (IA)
Iowa Lakes Comm Coll (IA)
Northcentral Tech Coll (WI)
Oklahoma City Comm Coll (OK)
Piedmont Comm Coll (NC)
Sullivan Coll of Technology and Design (KY)
Waukesha County Tech Coll (WI)

GRAPHIC COMMUNICATIONS RELATED
H. Councill Trenholm State Tech Coll (AL)
Middlesex County Coll (NJ)
Sullivan Coll of Technology and Design (KY)
Westmoreland County Comm Coll (PA)
Wright State U–Lake Campus (OH)

GRAPHIC DESIGN
Anne Arundel Comm Coll (MD)
Antonelli Inst (PA)
Arapahoe Comm Coll (CO)
Bradford School (OH)
Bradford School (PA)
Brookhaven Coll (TX)
Burlington County Coll (NJ)
Casper Coll (WY)
Cayuga County Comm Coll (NY)
Cedar Valley Coll (TX)
Central Wyoming Coll (WY)
Cloud County Comm Coll (KS)
Coll of the Canyons (CA)
Collin County Comm Coll District (TX)
Comm Coll of Denver (CO)
Corning Comm Coll (NY)
County Coll of Morris (NJ)
Davis Coll (OH)
Dunwoody Coll of Technology (MN)
Elgin Comm Coll (IL)
FIDM/Fashion Inst of Design & Merchandising, Los Angeles Campus (CA)
FIDM/Fashion Inst of Design & Merchandising, Orange County Campus (CA)
FIDM/Fashion Inst of Design & Merchandising, San Francisco Campus (CA)
Florida Gateway Coll (FL)
Forsyth Tech Comm Coll (NC)
Fox Coll (IL)
Gateway Tech Coll (WI)
Genesee Comm Coll (NY)
Great Falls Coll Montana State U (MT)
Harford Comm Coll (MD)
Harrisburg Area Comm Coll (PA)
Hennepin Tech Coll (MN)
Highland Comm Coll (IL)
Hinds Comm Coll (MS)
International Business Coll, Indianapolis (IN)
Iowa Lakes Comm Coll (IA)
Kalamazoo Valley Comm Coll (MI)
King's Coll (NC)
Kirtland Comm Coll (MI)
Lehigh Carbon Comm Coll (PA)
Luzerne County Comm Coll (PA)

Minneapolis Business Coll (MN)
Moraine Park Tech Coll (WI)
Mott Comm Coll (MI)
Northampton Comm Coll (PA)
North Hennepin Comm Coll (MN)
Norwalk Comm Coll (CT)
Oakton Comm Coll (IL)
Oklahoma State U Inst of Technology (OK)
Palomar Coll (CA)
Pasadena City Coll (CA)
Penn Foster Coll (AZ)
Pensacola State Coll (FL)
Phoenix Coll (AZ)
Salt Lake Comm Coll (UT)
Sierra Coll (CA)
South Florida State Coll (FL)
South Hills School of Business & Technology, State College (PA)
Southwestern Michigan Coll (MI)
Sullivan Coll of Technology and Design (KY)
Three Rivers Comm Coll (CT)
Waukesha County Tech Coll (WI)
Westmoreland County Comm Coll (PA)
Wood Tobe–Coburn School (NY)
Wright State U–Lake Campus (OH)

GREENHOUSE MANAGEMENT
Century Coll (MN)
Comm Coll of Allegheny County (PA)
Dakota Coll at Bottineau (ND)
Hennepin Tech Coll (MN)
The Ohio State U Ag Tech Inst (OH)

GUNSMITHING
Montgomery Comm Coll (NC)
Trinidad State Jr Coll (CO)

HAIR STYLING AND HAIR DESIGN
IBMC Coll (CO)

HAZARDOUS MATERIALS MANAGEMENT AND WASTE TECHNOLOGY
Pensacola State Coll (FL)
Sierra Coll (CA)

HEALTH AIDE
Allen Comm Coll (KS)

HEALTH AND MEDICAL ADMINISTRATIVE SERVICES RELATED
Butler County Comm Coll (PA)
Cumberland County Coll (NJ)
Hinds Comm Coll (MS)
Kent State U at Ashtabula (OH)
Kent State U at Salem (OH)
North Iowa Area Comm Coll (IA)
Owensboro Comm and Tech Coll (KY)
San Joaquin Valley Coll, Visalia (CA)
Westmoreland County Comm Coll (PA)

HEALTH AND PHYSICAL EDUCATION/FITNESS
Allen Comm Coll (KS)
Anne Arundel Comm Coll (MD)
Antelope Valley Coll (CA)
Arapahoe Comm Coll (CO)
Arizona Western Coll (AZ)
Austin Comm Coll District (TX)
Ca&nnada Coll (CA)
Central Oregon Comm Coll (OR)
Central Texas Coll (TX)
Citrus Coll (CA)
Cochise Coll, Douglas (AZ)
Coll of Marin (CA)
Coll of the Canyons (CA)
Coll of the Desert (CA)
Columbia-Greene Comm Coll (NY)
Comm Care Coll (OK)
Comm Coll of Allegheny County (PA)
Corning Comm Coll (NY)
Dakota Coll at Bottineau (ND)
Darton State Coll (GA)
Eastern Arizona Coll (AZ)
Elgin Comm Coll (IL)
Erie Comm Coll (NY)
Erie Comm Coll, North Campus (NY)
Erie Comm Coll, South Campus (NY)
Genesee Comm Coll (NY)
Holyoke Comm Coll (MA)
Houston Comm Coll (TX)
Iowa Lakes Comm Coll (IA)
Jamestown Comm Coll (NY)
Luzerne County Comm Coll (PA)
McHenry County Coll (IL)
Montgomery County Comm Coll (PA)
Mt. San Antonio Coll (CA)
North Hennepin Comm Coll (MN)
Northwest Coll (WY)
Paris Jr Coll (TX)
Raritan Valley Comm Coll (NJ)
San Jacinto Coll District (TX)
San Juan Coll (NM)
Sheridan Coll (WY)
Sierra Coll (CA)
Tyler Jr Coll (TX)
Vincennes U (IN)

HEALTH AND PHYSICAL EDUCATION RELATED
Coll of Southern Maryland (MD)
Corning Comm Coll (NY)
Fayetteville Tech Comm Coll (NC)
Genesee Comm Coll (NY)
Kingsborough Comm Coll of the City U of New York (NY)

HEALTH AND WELLNESS
Corning Comm Coll (NY)
Dean Coll (MA)
Erie Comm Coll (NY)
Erie Comm Coll, North Campus (NY)
Erie Comm Coll, South Campus (NY)
Salem Comm Coll (NJ)

HEALTH/HEALTH-CARE ADMINISTRATION
Berkeley Coll–Westchester Campus (NY)
Butler County Comm Coll (PA)
Comm Care Coll (OK)
Comm Coll of the Air Force (AL)
Des Moines Area Comm Coll (IA)
Harrisburg Area Comm Coll (PA)
Iowa Lakes Comm Coll (IA)
Kent State U at Trumbull (OH)
Luzerne County Comm Coll (PA)
Oklahoma State U, Oklahoma City (OK)
Penn Foster Coll (AZ)
Pensacola State Coll (FL)
South Florida State Coll (FL)
Terra State Comm Coll (OH)
Tyler Jr Coll (TX)
Ultimate Medical Academy Online (FL)

HEALTH INFORMATION/ MEDICAL RECORDS ADMINISTRATION
Amarillo Coll (TX)
Bowling Green State U-Firelands Coll (OH)
Bunker Hill Comm Coll (MA)
Camden County Coll (NJ)
The Coll of Westchester (NY)
Comm Coll of Philadelphia (PA)
Darton State Coll (GA)
Daytona State Coll (FL)
El Centro Coll (TX)
Florida Gateway Coll (FL)
Forsyth Tech Comm Coll (NC)
Georgia Highlands Coll (GA)
Hinds Comm Coll (MS)
Hocking Coll (OH)
Humacao Comm Coll (PR)
Illinois Eastern Comm Colls, Lincoln Trail College (IL)
Miami Dade Coll (FL)
Monroe Comm Coll (NY)
Mount Wachusett Comm Coll (MA)
North Central Texas Coll (TX)
Northern Essex Comm Coll (MA)
Northern Virginia Comm Coll (VA)
Oakton Comm Coll (IL)
Oklahoma City Comm Coll (OK)
Pensacola State Coll (FL)
Roane State Comm Coll (TN)
Rockland Comm Coll (NY)
Salem Comm Coll (NJ)
Southern U at Shreveport (LA)
South Florida State Coll (FL)
Stark State Coll (OH)
Terra State Comm Coll (OH)
U of Alaska Southeast, Sitka Campus (AK)

HEALTH INFORMATION/ MEDICAL RECORDS TECHNOLOGY
Anne Arundel Comm Coll (MD)
Anoka Tech Coll (MN)
Arapahoe Comm Coll (CO)
Austin Comm Coll District (TX)
Berkeley Coll–Westchester Campus (NY)
Borough of Manhattan Comm Coll of the City U of New York (NY)
Burlington County Coll (NJ)
Carroll Comm Coll (MD)
Catawba Valley Comm Coll (NC)
Central Oregon Comm Coll (OR)
Cincinnati State Tech and Comm Coll (OH)
Coll of Central Florida (FL)
Coll of Southern Maryland (MD)
Collin County Comm Coll District (TX)
Comm Coll of Allegheny County (PA)
Crowder Coll (MO)
Danville Area Comm Coll (IL)
Darton State Coll (GA)
Delgado Comm Coll (LA)
Duluth Business U (MN)
Dyersburg State Comm Coll (TN)
Erie Comm Coll, North Campus (NY)
Florida SouthWestern State Coll (FL)
Florida State Coll at Jacksonville (FL)
Fountainhead Coll of Technology (TN)
Fox Valley Tech Coll (WI)
Front Range Comm Coll (CO)
Gateway Tech Coll (WI)
Great Falls Coll Montana State U (MT)
Greenville Tech Coll (SC)
Highland Comm Coll (IL)
Hinds Comm Coll (MS)
Houston Comm Coll (TX)
Hudson County Comm Coll (NJ)
Hutchinson Comm Coll (KS)
Illinois Eastern Comm Colls, Frontier Community College (IL)
Jamestown Comm Coll (NY)
J. Sargeant Reynolds Comm Coll (VA)
Kaskaskia Coll (IL)
Kennebec Valley Comm Coll (ME)
Kirtland Comm Coll (MI)
Lehigh Carbon Comm Coll (PA)
Lone Star Coll–CyFair (TX)
Lone Star Coll–North Harris (TX)
Miami Dade Coll (FL)
Midlands Tech Coll (SC)
Montgomery Coll (MD)
Moraine Park Tech Coll (WI)
Moraine Valley Comm Coll (IL)
Northeast Iowa Comm Coll (IA)
Northwestern Coll (IL)
Owens Comm Coll, Toledo (OH)
Ozarks Tech Comm Coll (MO)
Panola Coll (TX)
Paris Jr Coll (TX)
Penn Foster Coll (AZ)
Pennsylvania Highlands Comm Coll (PA)
Pennsylvania Inst of Technology (PA)
Pensacola State Coll (FL)
Phoenix Coll (AZ)
Plaza Coll (NY)
Raritan Valley Comm Coll (NJ)
Reading Area Comm Coll (PA)
Richmond Comm Coll (NC)
Ridgewater Coll (MN)
St. Charles Comm Coll (MO)
St. Clair County Comm Coll (MI)
St. Philip's Coll (TX)
San Jacinto Coll District (TX)
San Juan Coll (NM)
Schoolcraft Coll (MI)
Shawnee Comm Coll (IL)
Southern U at Shreveport (LA)
South Hills School of Business & Technology, State College (PA)
Southwestern Illinois Coll (IL)
Southwestern Michigan Coll (MI)
State Fair Comm Coll (MO)
State U of New York Coll of Technology at Alfred (NY)
Tallahassee Comm Coll (FL)
Terra State Comm Coll (OH)
Texas State Tech Coll Harlingen (TX)
Trocaire Coll (NY)
Tulsa Comm Coll (OK)
Tyler Jr Coll (TX)
Ultimate Medical Academy Online (FL)
U of Alaska Southeast, Sitka Campus (AK)
U of Cincinnati Clermont Coll (OH)
Vincennes U (IN)
Volunteer State Comm Coll (TN)
Walters State Comm Coll (TN)
Waukesha County Tech Coll (WI)
Williston State Coll (ND)
Wisconsin Indianhead Tech Coll (WI)
York County Comm Coll (ME)

HEALTH/MEDICAL PREPARATORY PROGRAMS RELATED
Coll of Central Florida (FL)
Darton State Coll (GA)
Eastern Arizona Coll (AZ)
Eastern Wyoming Coll (WY)
Edison Comm Coll (OH)
Miami Dade Coll (FL)
Northwest Coll (WY)
Tulsa Comm Coll (OK)
Western Wyoming Comm Coll (WY)

HEALTH PROFESSIONS RELATED
Bowling Green State U-Firelands Coll (OH)
Bucks County Comm Coll (PA)
Carl Albert State Coll (OK)
Carroll Comm Coll (MD)
Comm Coll of Allegheny County (PA)
Comm Coll of Philadelphia (PA)
Corning Comm Coll (NY)
Forsyth Tech Comm Coll (NC)
Gateway Comm and Tech Coll (KY)
Genesee Comm Coll (NY)
Greenfield Comm Coll (MA)
Halifax Comm Coll (NC)
Hinds Comm Coll (MS)
Lakeland Comm Coll (OH)
Manor Coll (PA)
Miami Dade Coll (FL)
Middlesex County Coll (NJ)
Midlands Tech Coll (SC)
Moraine Valley Comm Coll (IL)
New Mexico Jr Coll (NM)
Northeastern Jr Coll (CO)
North Shore Comm Coll (MA)
Northwestern Michigan Coll (MI)
Ohlone Coll (CA)
Orange Coast Coll (CA)
Pennsylvania Highlands Comm Coll (PA)
Piedmont Comm Coll (NC)
Queensborough Comm Coll of the City U of New York (NY)
Richmond Comm Coll (NC)
Salt Lake Comm Coll (UT)
Southeastern Coll–Greenacres (FL)
Terra State Comm Coll (OH)
U of Cincinnati Clermont Coll (OH)
Volunteer State Comm Coll (TN)

HEALTH SERVICES ADMINISTRATION
Florida Gateway Coll (FL)
Harrisburg Area Comm Coll (PA)

HEALTH SERVICES/ALLIED HEALTH/HEALTH SCIENCES
Alvin Comm Coll (TX)
American Samoa Comm Coll (AS)
Ancilla Coll (IN)
Anoka-Ramsey Comm Coll (MN)
Anoka-Ramsey Comm Coll, Cambridge Campus (MN)
Arizona Western Coll (AZ)
Burlington County Coll (NJ)
Cambria-Rowe Business Coll, Indiana (PA)
Camden County Coll (NJ)
Carl Albert State Coll (OK)
Casper Coll (WY)
Cayuga County Comm Coll (NY)
Cecil Coll (MD)
Century Coll (MN)
Coll of Central Florida (FL)
Dakota Coll at Bottineau (ND)
Dyersburg State Comm Coll (TN)
Goodwin Coll (CT)
Gulf Coast State Coll (FL)
Hudson County Comm Coll (NJ)
Miami Dade Coll (FL)
Middlesex County Coll (NJ)
Northwest Coll (WY)
Oklahoma State U Inst of Technology (OK)
Paris Jr Coll (TX)
Pennsylvania Inst of Technology (PA)
Quinsigamond Comm Coll (MA)
Raritan Valley Comm Coll (NJ)
Reading Area Comm Coll (PA)
Schoolcraft Coll (MI)
Sheridan Coll (WY)
South Florida State Coll (FL)
Ultimate Medical Academy Clearwater (FL)
Ultimate Medical Academy Online (FL)
Ultimate Medical Academy Tampa (FL)
U of Alaska Southeast, Sitka Campus (AK)
Western Wyoming Comm Coll (WY)
White Mountains Comm Coll (NH)
York County Comm Coll (ME)

HEALTH TEACHER EDUCATION
Austin Comm Coll District (TX)
Bainbridge State Coll (GA)
Copiah-Lincoln Comm Coll (MS)
Harper Coll (IL)
Howard Comm Coll (MD)
Kilgore Coll (TX)
South Florida State Coll (FL)
Umpqua Comm Coll (OR)

HEALTH UNIT COORDINATOR/ WARD CLERK
Comm Coll of Allegheny County (PA)
Riverland Comm Coll (MN)

HEATING, AIR CONDITIONING, VENTILATION AND REFRIGERATION MAINTENANCE TECHNOLOGY
Amarillo Coll (TX)
Antelope Valley Coll (CA)
Arizona Western Coll (AZ)
Bellingham Tech Coll (WA)
Butler County Comm Coll (PA)
Cedar Valley Coll (TX)
Central Texas Coll (TX)
Century Coll (MN)
Coll of the Desert (CA)
Comm Coll of Allegheny County (PA)
Delta Coll (MI)
Des Moines Area Comm Coll (IA)
Dunwoody Coll of Technology (MN)
Elgin Comm Coll (IL)
Fayetteville Tech Comm Coll (NC)
Gateway Tech Coll (WI)
George C. Wallace Comm Coll (AL)
Grand Rapids Comm Coll (MI)
Guilford Tech Comm Coll (NC)
Harper Coll (IL)
Harrisburg Area Comm Coll (PA)
Hennepin Tech Coll (MN)
Hinds Comm Coll (MS)
Iowa Lakes Comm Coll (IA)
Jefferson Coll (MO)
Johnston Comm Coll (NC)
Kankakee Comm Coll (IL)
Kaskaskia Coll (IL)
Kellogg Comm Coll (MI)
Kilgore Coll (TX)
Kirtland Comm Coll (MI)
Laramie County Comm Coll (WY)
Lehigh Carbon Comm Coll (PA)
Lone Star Coll–North Harris (TX)
Los Angeles Trade-Tech Coll (CA)
Louisiana Delta Comm Coll, Monroe (LA)
Luzerne County Comm Coll (PA)
Macomb Comm Coll (MI)
Miami Dade Coll (FL)
Midlands Tech Coll (SC)
Mid-Plains Comm Coll, North Platte (NE)
Minneapolis Comm and Tech Coll (MN)
Minnesota State Coll–Southeast Tech (MN)
Mitchell Tech Inst (SD)
Mohave Comm Coll (AZ)
Mohawk Valley Comm Coll (NY)
Monroe Comm Coll (NY)
Montgomery Comm Coll (NC)
Moraine Valley Comm Coll (IL)
Mt. San Antonio Coll (CA)
Northampton Comm Coll (PA)
North Iowa Area Comm Coll (IA)
Northland Comm Coll (MN)
Oklahoma State U Inst of Technology (OK)
Orange Coast Coll (CA)
Ozarks Tech Comm Coll (MO)
Paris Jr Coll (TX)
Renton Tech Coll (WA)
Richmond Comm Coll (NC)
St. Philip's Coll (TX)
Salt Lake Comm Coll (UT)
San Jacinto Coll District (TX)
San Joaquin Delta Coll (CA)
San Joaquin Valley Coll, Hesperia (CA)
San Joaquin Valley Coll, Lancaster (CA)
San Joaquin Valley Coll, Ontario (CA)
San Joaquin Valley Coll, Temecula (CA)
South Louisiana Comm Coll (LA)
South Piedmont Comm Coll (NC)

Southwestern Illinois Coll (IL)
Spartanburg Comm Coll (SC)
State U of New York Coll of Technology at Alfred (NY)
Texas State Tech Coll Harlingen (TX)
Trinity Valley Comm Coll (TX)
Tyler Jr Coll (TX)
U of Arkansas Comm Coll at Morrilton (AR)
Wayne County Comm Coll District (MI)
Wenatchee Valley Coll (WA)
Western Dakota Tech Inst (SD)
Western Iowa Tech Comm Coll (IA)
Westmoreland County Comm Coll (PA)

HEATING, VENTILATION, AIR CONDITIONING AND REFRIGERATION ENGINEERING TECHNOLOGY
Alamance Comm Coll (NC)
Austin Comm Coll District (TX)
Bevill State Comm Coll (AL)
The Comm Coll of Baltimore County (MD)
Dunwoody Coll of Technology (MN)
Front Range Comm Coll (CO)
Gadsden State Comm Coll (AL)
Gateway Tech Coll (WI)
George C. Wallace Comm Coll (AL)
H. Councill Trenholm State Tech Coll (AL)
Humacao Comm Coll (PR)
Iowa Lakes Comm Coll (IA)
J. F. Drake State Comm and Tech Coll (AL)
Kalamazoo Valley Comm Coll (MI)
Kennebec Valley Comm Coll (ME)
Macomb Comm Coll (MI)
Miami Dade Coll (FL)
Moraine Park Tech Coll (WI)
Mott Comm Coll (MI)
New Castle School of Trades (PA)
Oakton Comm Coll (IL)
Oklahoma Tech Coll (OK)
Raritan Valley Comm Coll (NJ)
San Joaquin Valley Coll, Bakersfield (CA)
San Joaquin Valley Coll, Fresno (CA)
San Joaquin Valley Coll, Visalia (CA)
Springfield Tech Comm Coll (MA)
Sullivan Coll of Technology and Design (KY)
Terra State Comm Coll (OH)
Truckee Meadows Comm Coll (NV)

HEAVY EQUIPMENT MAINTENANCE TECHNOLOGY
Amarillo Coll (TX)
Comm Coll of Aurora (CO)
Highland Comm Coll (IL)
Los Angeles Trade-Tech Coll (CA)
Mesa Comm Coll (AZ)
The Ohio State U Ag Tech Inst (OH)
Ozarks Tech Comm Coll (MO)
Trinidad State Jr Coll (CO)
Western Wyoming Comm Coll (WY)

HEAVY/INDUSTRIAL EQUIPMENT MAINTENANCE TECHNOLOGIES RELATED
Bellingham Tech Coll (WA)
State U of New York Coll of Technology at Alfred (NY)

HEMATOLOGY TECHNOLOGY
Comm Coll of the Air Force (AL)

HISPANIC-AMERICAN, PUERTO RICAN, AND MEXICAN-AMERICAN/CHICANO STUDIES
San Jacinto Coll District (TX)

HISTOLOGIC TECHNICIAN
Comm Coll of Rhode Island (RI)
Darton State Coll (GA)
Florida State Coll at Jacksonville (FL)
Goodwin Coll (CT)
Houston Comm Coll (TX)
Miami Dade Coll (FL)
Mott Comm Coll (MI)
Pennsylvania Highlands Comm Coll (PA)

HISTOLOGIC TECHNOLOGY/ HISTOTECHNOLOGIST
Miami Dade Coll (FL)
North Hennepin Comm Coll (MN)
Phoenix Coll (AZ)

HISTORIC PRESERVATION AND CONSERVATION
Piedmont Comm Coll (NC)

HISTORY
Allen Comm Coll (KS)
Amarillo Coll (TX)
Ancilla Coll (IN)
Arizona Western Coll (AZ)
Austin Comm Coll District (TX)
Bainbridge State Coll (GA)
Bucks County Comm Coll (PA)
Bunker Hill Comm Coll (MA)
Burlington County Coll (NJ)
Ca&nnada Coll (CA)
Casper Coll (WY)
Citrus Coll (CA)
Coll of Central Florida (FL)
Coll of Marin (CA)
Coll of Southern Idaho (ID)
Coll of the Canyons (CA)
Coll of the Desert (CA)
Copiah-Lincoln Comm Coll (MS)
Dakota Coll at Bottineau (ND)
Darton State Coll (GA)
Dean Coll (MA)
Eastern Arizona Coll (AZ)
Edison Comm Coll (OH)
Georgia Highlands Coll (GA)
Great Basin Coll (NV)
Harford Comm Coll (MD)
Harper Coll (IL)
Hinds Comm Coll (MS)
Iowa Lakes Comm Coll (IA)
Kankakee Comm Coll (IL)
Lamar Comm Coll (CO)
Laramie County Comm Coll (WY)
Lorain County Comm Coll (OH)
Miami Dade Coll (FL)
MiraCosta Coll (CA)
Mohave Comm Coll (AZ)
Monroe Comm Coll (NY)
New Mexico Jr Coll (NM)
Northeastern Jr Coll (CO)
Northern Essex Comm Coll (MA)
Northwest Coll (WY)
Northwest State Comm Coll (OH)
Ohlone Coll (CA)
Oklahoma City Comm Coll (OK)
Oklahoma State U, Oklahoma City (OK)
Orange Coast Coll (CA)
Otero Jr Coll (CO)
Paris Jr Coll (TX)
Pasadena City Coll (CA)
Pensacola State Coll (FL)
Potomac State Coll of West Virginia U (WV)
St. Charles Comm Coll (MO)
St. Philip's Coll (TX)
Salt Lake Comm Coll (UT)
San Jacinto Coll District (TX)
San Joaquin Delta Coll (CA)
Sheridan Coll (WY)
South Florida State Coll (FL)
Terra State Comm Coll (OH)
Trinity Valley Comm Coll (TX)
Truckee Meadows Comm Coll (NV)
Tyler Jr Coll (TX)
Umpqua Comm Coll (OR)
Vincennes U (IN)
Wenatchee Valley Coll (WA)
Western Wyoming Comm Coll (WY)
Wright State U–Lake Campus (OH)

HISTORY TEACHER EDUCATION
Bucks County Comm Coll (PA)
Cochise Coll, Douglas (AZ)
Darton State Coll (GA)

HOLISTIC HEALTH
Anoka-Ramsey Comm Coll (MN)
Anoka-Ramsey Comm Coll, Cambridge Campus (MN)
Front Range Comm Coll (CO)

HOME HEALTH AIDE/HOME ATTENDANT
Allen Comm Coll (KS)

HOMELAND SECURITY
Butler County Comm Coll (PA)
City Colls of Chicago, Olive-Harvey College (IL)
Coll of Southern Maryland (MD)
Goodwin Coll (CT)
Harper Coll (IL)
Long Island Business Inst (NY)
Palomar Coll (CA)

Salem Comm Coll (NJ)

HOMELAND SECURITY, LAW ENFORCEMENT, FIREFIGHTING AND PROTECTIVE SERVICES RELATED
Butler County Comm Coll (PA)
Central Wyoming Comm Coll (WY)
Century Coll (MN)
Goodwin Coll (CT)
Lakeland Comm Coll (OH)
Laramie County Comm Coll (WY)
Northern Virginia Comm Coll (VA)
Ocean County Coll (NJ)
Owens Comm Coll, Toledo (OH)
San Joaquin Valley Coll, Bakersfield (CA)
Schoolcraft Coll (MI)
Westmoreland County Comm Coll (PA)

HOMELAND SECURITY RELATED
Fox Valley Tech Coll (WI)
Pensacola State Coll (FL)
Tallahassee Comm Coll (FL)

HORSE HUSBANDRY/EQUINE SCIENCE AND MANAGEMENT
Cecil Coll (MD)
Highland Comm Coll (IL)
The Ohio State U Ag Tech Inst (OH)
Potomac State Coll of West Virginia U (WV)

HORTICULTURAL SCIENCE
Century Coll (MN)
Cumberland County Coll (NJ)
Dakota Coll at Bottineau (ND)
Gwinnett Tech Coll (GA)
Lenoir Comm Coll (NC)
Luzerne County Comm Coll (PA)
Mesa Comm Coll (AZ)
Miami Dade Coll (FL)
Mt. San Antonio Coll (CA)
The Ohio State U Ag Tech Inst (OH)
Oklahoma State U, Oklahoma City (OK)
Orange Coast Coll (CA)
Potomac State Coll of West Virginia U (WV)
Sheridan Coll (WY)
South Florida State Coll (FL)
Trident Tech Coll (SC)
Trinity Valley Comm Coll (TX)
Victor Valley Coll (CA)

HOSPITAL AND HEALTH-CARE FACILITIES ADMINISTRATION
Allen Comm Coll (KS)
Bossier Parish Comm Coll (LA)
Minnesota West Comm and Tech Coll (MN)

HOSPITALITY ADMINISTRATION
Arizona Western Coll (AZ)
Austin Comm Coll District (TX)
Bunker Hill Comm Coll (MA)
Burlington County Coll (NJ)
Casper Coll (WY)
Central Texas Coll (TX)
Chesapeake Coll (MD)
Cincinnati State Tech and Comm Coll (OH)
Coll of Southern Maryland (MD)
Coll of the Canyons (CA)
Coll of the Desert (CA)
Collin County Comm Coll District (TX)
Daytona State Coll (FL)
Delgado Comm Coll (LA)
Des Moines Area Comm Coll (IA)
Fox Valley Tech Coll (WI)
Front Range Comm Coll (CO)
Genesee Comm Coll (NY)
Greenfield Comm Coll (MA)
Gulf Coast State Coll (FL)
Harper Coll (IL)
Harrisburg Area Comm Coll (PA)
Hillsborough Comm Coll (FL)
Hinds Comm Coll (MS)
Hocking Coll (OH)
Iowa Lakes Comm Coll (IA)
James H. Faulkner State Comm Coll (AL)
Jefferson Comm Coll (NY)
Jefferson State Comm Coll (AL)
J. Sargeant Reynolds Comm Coll (VA)

Lakeland Comm Coll (OH)
Lakes Region Comm Coll (NH)
Massachusetts Bay Comm Coll (MA)
Miami Dade Coll (FL)
MiraCosta Coll (CA)
Moraine Valley Comm Coll (IL)
Niagara County Comm Coll (NY)
Normandale Comm Coll (MN)
North Iowa Area Comm Coll (IA)
North Shore Comm Coll (MA)
Pasadena City Coll (CA)
Penn Foster Coll (AZ)
Pensacola State Coll (FL)
Potomac State Coll of West Virginia U (WV)
Quinsigamond Comm Coll (MA)
Rockland Comm Coll (NY)
Scottsdale Comm Coll (AZ)
Sheridan Coll (WY)
Sisseton-Wahpeton Coll (SD)
Southern U at Shreveport (LA)
South Florida State Coll (FL)
Sullivan County Comm Coll (NY)
Tech Coll of the Lowcountry (SC)
Terra State Comm Coll (OH)
Three Rivers Comm Coll (CT)
Trocaire Coll (NY)
Vincennes U (IN)
Wor-Wic Comm Coll (MD)

HOSPITALITY ADMINISTRATION RELATED
Bunker Hill Comm Coll (MA)
Butler County Comm Coll (PA)
Corning Comm Coll (NY)
Holyoke Comm Coll (MA)
J. Sargeant Reynolds Comm Coll (VA)
Long Island Business Inst (NY)

HOSPITALITY AND RECREATION MARKETING
County Coll of Morris (NJ)
Dakota Coll at Bottineau (ND)
Iowa Central Comm Coll (IA)
Luzerne County Comm Coll (PA)
Montgomery County Comm Coll (PA)
Ohio Business Coll, Sandusky (OH)

HOTEL/MOTEL ADMINISTRATION
Anne Arundel Comm Coll (MD)
Bradford School (PA)
Cape Fear Comm Coll (NC)
Carl Albert State Coll (OK)
Central Oregon Comm Coll (OR)
Central Wyoming Coll (WY)
Coll of Southern Idaho (ID)
Coll of the Canyons (CA)
Comm Coll of Allegheny County (PA)
The Comm Coll of Baltimore County (MD)
Comm Coll of Philadelphia (PA)
Comm Coll of the Air Force (AL)
Daytona State Coll (FL)
Delaware Tech & Comm Coll, Terry Campus (DE)
Finger Lakes Comm Coll (NY)
Florida State Coll at Jacksonville (FL)
Gateway Comm Coll (CT)
Genesee Comm Coll (NY)
Guam Comm Coll (GU)
Guilford Tech Comm Coll (NC)
Gwinnett Tech Coll (GA)
Harrisburg Area Comm Coll (PA)
Hocking Coll (OH)
Houston Comm Coll (TX)
International Business Coll, Indianapolis (IN)
Iowa Lakes Comm Coll (IA)
J. Sargeant Reynolds Comm Coll (VA)
King's Coll (NC)
Luzerne County Comm Coll (PA)
Manchester Comm Coll (CT)
Miami Dade Coll (FL)
Middlesex Comm Coll (MA)
Middlesex County Coll (NJ)
Minneapolis Business Coll (MN)
Mohawk Valley Comm Coll (NY)
Monroe Comm Coll (NY)
Montgomery Coll (MD)
Moraine Park Tech Coll (WI)
Mt. San Antonio Coll (CA)
Nassau Comm Coll (NY)
Northampton Comm Coll (PA)
Northern Essex Comm Coll (MA)
Norwalk Comm Coll (CT)
Orange Coast Coll (CA)

Ozarks Tech Comm Coll (MO)
Pensacola State Coll (FL)
St. Philip's Coll (TX)
Scottsdale Comm Coll (AZ)
Southern U at Shreveport (LA)
Trident Tech Coll (SC)
Vincennes U (IN)
Westmoreland County Comm Coll (PA)
Wood Tobe–Coburn School (NY)

HOTEL, MOTEL, AND RESTAURANT MANAGEMENT
Fayetteville Tech Comm Coll (NC)
Gateway Tech Coll (WI)
Pensacola State Coll (FL)
Tompkins Cortland Comm Coll (NY)
Waukesha County Tech Coll (WI)

HOUSING AND HUMAN ENVIRONMENTS
Orange Coast Coll (CA)
Sullivan Coll of Technology and Design (KY)

HOUSING AND HUMAN ENVIRONMENTS RELATED
Comm Coll of Allegheny County (PA)
Hinds Comm Coll (MS)

HUMAN DEVELOPMENT AND FAMILY STUDIES
Bucks County Comm Coll (PA)
City Colls of Chicago, Olive-Harvey College (IL)
Ohlone Coll (CA)
Orange Coast Coll (CA)
Penn State DuBois (PA)
Penn State Fayette, The Eberly Campus (PA)
Penn State Mont Alto (PA)
Penn State Shenango (PA)
Salt Lake Comm Coll (UT)

HUMAN DEVELOPMENT AND FAMILY STUDIES RELATED
Comm Coll of Allegheny County (PA)
Northwest State Comm Coll (OH)

HUMANITIES
Allen Comm Coll (KS)
Brookhaven Coll (TX)
Bucks County Comm Coll (PA)
Ca&nnada Coll (CA)
Cayuga County Comm Coll (NY)
Central Oregon Comm Coll (OR)
Clinton Comm Coll (NY)
Cochise Coll, Douglas (AZ)
Coll of Central Florida (FL)
Coll of Marin (CA)
Coll of the Canyons (CA)
Coll of the Desert (CA)
Columbia-Greene Comm Coll (NY)
Comm Coll of Allegheny County (PA)
Corning Comm Coll (NY)
Dakota Coll at Bottineau (ND)
Dutchess Comm Coll (NY)
Erie Comm Coll (NY)
Erie Comm Coll, North Campus (NY)
Erie Comm Coll, South Campus (NY)
Finger Lakes Comm Coll (NY)
Genesee Comm Coll (NY)
Golden West Coll (CA)
Harper Coll (IL)
Housatonic Comm Coll (CT)
Iowa Lakes Comm Coll (IA)
Jamestown Comm Coll (NY)
Jefferson Comm Coll (NY)
John Tyler Comm Coll (VA)
Laramie County Comm Coll (WY)
Luzerne County Comm Coll (PA)
Miami Dade Coll (FL)
Mohawk Valley Comm Coll (NY)
Montgomery County Comm Coll (PA)
Mt. San Antonio Coll (CA)
Niagara County Comm Coll (NY)
Northeastern Jr Coll (CO)
Oklahoma City Comm Coll (OK)
Oklahoma State U, Oklahoma City (OK)
Orange Coast Coll (CA)
Otero Jr Coll (CO)
Palomar Coll (CA)
Pasadena City Coll (CA)
Salt Lake Comm Coll (UT)
San Diego Miramar Coll (CA)
San Joaquin Delta Coll (CA)
Seminole State Coll (OK)
South Florida State Coll (FL)

State U of New York Coll of
 Technology at Alfred (NY)
Terra State Comm Coll (OH)
Tompkins Cortland Comm Coll (NY)
Umpqua Comm Coll (OR)
Victor Valley Coll (CA)
Westchester Comm Coll (NY)
Western Wyoming Comm Coll (WY)

HUMAN RESOURCES MANAGEMENT
Anoka-Ramsey Comm Coll (MN)
Anoka-Ramsey Comm Coll,
 Cambridge Campus (MN)
Butler County Comm Coll (PA)
Cecil Coll (MD)
Clark Coll (WA)
Comm Coll of Allegheny County (PA)
Comm Coll of the Air Force (AL)
Delaware Tech & Comm Coll, Terry
 Campus (DE)
Edison Comm Coll (OH)
Fayetteville Tech Comm Coll (NC)
Fox Valley Tech Coll (WI)
Guilford Tech Comm Coll (NC)
Harford Comm Coll (MD)
Hawkeye Comm Coll (IA)
Illinois Eastern Comm Colls, Olney
 Central College (IL)
Lehigh Carbon Comm Coll (PA)
Moraine Park Tech Coll (WI)
Moraine Valley Comm Coll (IL)
Northwest State Comm Coll (OH)
Ohio Business Coll, Sandusky (OH)
Penn Foster Coll (AZ)
San Joaquin Valley Coll, Visalia (CA)
South Florida State Coll (FL)
Trocaire Coll (NY)
Tulsa Comm Coll (OK)
Umpqua Comm Coll (OR)
Waukesha County Tech Coll (WI)
Western Iowa Tech Comm Coll (IA)
Westmoreland County Comm Coll
 (PA)
Wisconsin Indianhead Tech Coll (WI)

HUMAN RESOURCES MANAGEMENT AND SERVICES RELATED
Iowa Lakes Comm Coll (IA)
Manor Coll (PA)
San Joaquin Valley Coll–Online (CA)

HUMAN SERVICES
Alexandria Tech and Comm Coll
 (MN)
American Samoa Comm Coll (AS)
Austin Comm Coll District (TX)
Bowling Green State U-Firelands Coll
 (OH)
Bunker Hill Comm Coll (MA)
Burlington County Coll (NJ)
Ca&nnada Coll (CA)
Central Maine Comm Coll (ME)
Century Coll (MN)
Coll of Central Florida (FL)
Coll of Southern Idaho (ID)
Columbia-Greene Comm Coll (NY)
Comm Coll of Denver (CO)
Comm Coll of Philadelphia (PA)
Corning Comm Coll (NY)
Daytona State Coll (FL)
Delaware Tech & Comm Coll, Terry
 Campus (DE)
Denmark Tech Coll (SC)
Dutchess Comm Coll (NY)
Finger Lakes Comm Coll (NY)
Forsyth Tech Comm Coll (NC)
Frederick Comm Coll (MD)
Gateway Comm Coll (CT)
Genesee Comm Coll (NY)
Georgia Highlands Coll (GA)
Goodwin Coll (CT)
Guam Comm Coll (GU)
Harper Coll (IL)
Harrisburg Area Comm Coll (PA)
Hopkinsville Comm Coll (KY)
Housatonic Comm Coll (CT)
Jamestown Comm Coll (NY)
Jefferson Comm Coll (NY)
John Tyler Comm Coll (VA)
Kellogg Comm Coll (MI)
Kingsborough Comm Coll of the City
 U of New York (NY)
Lake Area Tech Inst (SD)
Lake Land Coll (IL)
Lakes Region Comm Coll (NH)
Laramie County Comm Coll (WY)
Lehigh Carbon Comm Coll (PA)
Lone Star Coll–Montgomery (TX)
Lorain County Comm Coll (OH)
Luzerne County Comm Coll (PA)

Manchester Comm Coll (CT)
Massachusetts Bay Comm Coll (MA)
Mesabi Range Coll (MN)
Miami Dade Coll (FL)
Midlands Tech Coll (SC)
Minneapolis Comm and Tech Coll
 (MN)
Minnesota West Comm and Tech
 Coll (MN)
Mitchell Tech Inst (SD)
Mohawk Valley Comm Coll (NY)
Monroe Comm Coll (NY)
Mount Wachusett Comm Coll (MA)
Nebraska Indian Comm Coll (NE)
Niagara County Comm Coll (NY)
Northern Essex Comm Coll (MA)
Norwalk Comm Coll (CT)
Ocean County Coll (NJ)
Oklahoma State U, Oklahoma City
 (OK)
Owensboro Comm and Tech Coll
 (KY)
Pasco-Hernando State Coll (FL)
Pennsylvania Highlands Comm Coll
 (PA)
Phoenix Coll (AZ)
Quinsigamond Comm Coll (MA)
Reading Area Comm Coll (PA)
Riverland Comm Coll (MN)
Rockland Comm Coll (NY)
Rock Valley Coll (IL)
St. Charles Comm Coll (MO)
Shawnee Comm Coll (IL)
Southern U at Shreveport (LA)
Stark State Coll (OH)
State U of New York Coll of
 Technology at Alfred (NY)
Sullivan County Comm Coll (NY)
Tohono O'odham Comm Coll (AZ)
Tompkins Cortland Comm Coll (NY)
Trident Tech Coll (SC)
Tunxis Comm Coll (CT)
Ultimate Medical Academy Online
 (FL)
U of Arkansas Comm Coll at Hope
 (AR)
Western Wyoming Comm Coll (WY)
White Mountains Comm Coll (NH)
York County Comm Coll (ME)

HYDRAULICS AND FLUID POWER TECHNOLOGY
The Comm Coll of Baltimore County
 (MD)
Hennepin Tech Coll (MN)
Minnesota West Comm and Tech
 Coll (MN)
The Ohio State U Ag Tech Inst (OH)

HYDROLOGY AND WATER RESOURCES SCIENCE
Citrus Coll (CA)
Coll of Southern Idaho (ID)
Iowa Lakes Comm Coll (IA)
Los Angeles Trade-Tech Coll (CA)

ILLUSTRATION
Collin County Comm Coll District
 (TX)
Fashion Inst of Technology (NY)
Kalamazoo Valley Comm Coll (MI)
Oklahoma State U, Oklahoma City
 (OK)

INDUSTRIAL AND PRODUCT DESIGN
Fiorello H. LaGuardia Comm Coll of
 the City U of New York (NY)
Luzerne County Comm Coll (PA)
Mt. San Antonio Coll (CA)
Navarro Coll (TX)
Orange Coast Coll (CA)
Rock Valley Coll (IL)

INDUSTRIAL ELECTRONICS TECHNOLOGY
Bevill State Comm Coll (AL)
Big Bend Comm Coll (WA)
Danville Area Comm Coll (IL)
Des Moines Area Comm Coll (IA)
Dyersburg State Comm Coll (TN)
Eastern Arizona Coll (AZ)
Elizabethtown Comm and Tech Coll,
 Elizabethtown (KY)
J. F. Drake State Comm and Tech
 Coll (AL)
John Tyler Comm Coll (VA)
J. Sargeant Reynolds Comm Coll
 (VA)
Kankakee Comm Coll (IL)
Lehigh Carbon Comm Coll (PA)

Louisiana Delta Comm Coll, Monroe
 (LA)
Lurleen B. Wallace Comm Coll (AL)
Midlands Tech Coll (SC)
Moraine Valley Comm Coll (IL)
Northampton Comm Coll (PA)
Northland Comm Coll (MN)
Northwest-Shoals Comm Coll (AL)
Northwest State Comm Coll (OH)
Pasadena City Coll (CA)
Penn Foster Coll (AZ)
Sierra Coll (CA)
South Louisiana Comm Coll (LA)
Spartanburg Comm Coll (SC)
Sullivan Coll of Technology and
 Design (KY)
Tech Coll of the Lowcountry (SC)
Tyler Jr Coll (TX)
Wenatchee Valley Coll (WA)
Western Wyoming Comm Coll (WY)

INDUSTRIAL ENGINEERING
Manchester Comm Coll (CT)
Montcalm Comm Coll (MI)
South Florida State Coll (FL)

INDUSTRIAL MECHANICS AND MAINTENANCE TECHNOLOGY
Alexandria Tech and Comm Coll
 (MN)
Arkansas Northeastern Coll (AR)
Bellingham Tech Coll (WA)
Big Bend Comm Coll (WA)
Bossier Parish Comm Coll (LA)
Casper Coll (WY)
Danville Area Comm Coll (IL)
Delta Coll (MI)
Des Moines Area Comm Coll (IA)
Dyersburg State Comm Coll (TN)
Eastern Arizona Coll (AZ)
Elgin Comm Coll (IL)
Elizabethtown Comm and Tech Coll,
 Elizabethtown (KY)
Gadsden State Comm Coll (AL)
Gateway Tech Coll (WI)
George C. Wallace Comm Coll (AL)
H. Councill Trenholm State Tech Coll
 (AL)
Illinois Eastern Comm Colls, Olney
 Central College (IL)
J. F. Drake State Comm and Tech
 Coll (AL)
Kaskaskia Coll (IL)
Kennebec Valley Comm Coll (ME)
Lower Columbia Coll (WA)
Macomb Comm Coll (MI)
Midlands Tech Coll (SC)
Minnesota State Coll–Southeast
 Tech (MN)
New Castle School of Trades (PA)
North Central Texas Coll (TX)
Northwest-Shoals Comm Coll (AL)
Northwest State Comm Coll (OH)
Reading Area Comm Coll (PA)
Riverland Comm Coll (MN)
San Joaquin Valley Coll, Lancaster
 (CA)
San Joaquin Valley Coll, Ontario (CA)
San Juan Coll (NM)
Somerset Comm Coll (KY)
South Louisiana Comm Coll (LA)
Southwestern Illinois Coll (IL)
Southwestern Michigan Coll (MI)
Sullivan Coll of Technology and
 Design (KY)
Western Iowa Tech Comm Coll (IA)
Western Wyoming Comm Coll (WY)
Westmoreland County Comm Coll
 (PA)

INDUSTRIAL PRODUCTION TECHNOLOGIES RELATED
Arkansas Northeastern Coll (AR)
Camden County Coll (NJ)
Guilford Tech Comm Coll (NC)
Kent State U at Trumbull (OH)
Louisiana Delta Comm Coll, Monroe
 (LA)
Middlesex County Coll (NJ)
Northwest State Comm Coll (OH)
Southwestern Michigan Coll (MI)
Wisconsin Indianhead Tech Coll (WI)

INDUSTRIAL RADIOLOGIC TECHNOLOGY
Amarillo Coll (TX)
Carteret Comm Coll (NC)
Copiah-Lincoln Comm Coll (MS)
Daytona State Coll (FL)
Eastern Gateway Comm Coll (OH)
Gateway Comm Coll (CT)
Iowa Central Comm Coll (IA)

Lorain County Comm Coll (OH)
Monroe Comm Coll (NY)
Mt. San Antonio Coll (CA)
Northern Essex Comm Coll (MA)
Orange Coast Coll (CA)
Roane State Comm Coll (TN)
Salt Lake Comm Coll (UT)
Southeastern Comm Coll (IA)
South Louisiana Comm Coll (LA)
Tyler Jr Coll (TX)
Virginia Western Comm Coll (VA)

INDUSTRIAL SAFETY TECHNOLOGY
Fox Valley Tech Coll (WI)
Northwest Tech Coll (MN)

INDUSTRIAL TECHNOLOGY
Allen Comm Coll (KS)
Arizona Western Coll (AZ)
Arkansas Northeastern Coll (AR)
Bossier Parish Comm Coll (LA)
Bowling Green State U-Firelands Coll
 (OH)
Bucks County Comm Coll (PA)
Central Oregon Comm Coll (OR)
Central Virginia Comm Coll (VA)
Cincinnati State Tech and Comm Coll
 (OH)
Cleveland State Comm Coll (TN)
Clinton Comm Coll (NY)
Comm Coll of Allegheny County (PA)
Comm Coll of the Air Force (AL)
Crowder Coll (MO)
Cumberland County Coll (NJ)
Daytona State Coll (FL)
Eastern Gateway Comm Coll (OH)
Edison Comm Coll (OH)
Erie Comm Coll, North Campus (NY)
FIDM/Fashion Inst of Design &
 Merchandising, Orange County
 Campus (CA)
Forsyth Tech Comm Coll (NC)
Gateway Comm and Tech Coll (KY)
Gateway Comm Coll (CT)
Grand Rapids Comm Coll (MI)
Great Basin Coll (NV)
Hagerstown Comm Coll (MD)
Highland Comm Coll (IL)
Hocking Coll (OH)
Hopkinsville Comm Coll (KY)
Illinois Eastern Comm Colls, Wabash
 Valley College (IL)
Jackson State Comm Coll (TN)
John Tyler Comm Coll (VA)
Kellogg Comm Coll (MI)
Kent State U at Trumbull (OH)
Kent State U at Tuscarawas (OH)
Lake Land Coll (IL)
Lenoir Comm Coll (NC)
Lone Star Coll–CyFair (TX)
Lone Star Coll–North Harris (TX)
Lone Star Coll–Tomball (TX)
Lorain County Comm Coll (OH)
Los Angeles Trade-Tech Coll (CA)
Macomb Comm Coll (MI)
Manchester Comm Coll (CT)
Mesa Comm Coll (AZ)
Miami Dade Coll (FL)
Monroe Comm Coll (NY)
Monroe County Comm Coll (MI)
Montcalm Comm Coll (MI)
Navarro Coll (TX)
Northern Virginia Comm Coll (VA)
Northwestern Michigan Coll (MI)
Northwest Tech Coll (MN)
Nunez Comm Coll (LA)
The Ohio State U Ag Tech Inst (OH)
Olympic Coll (WA)
Owens Comm Coll, Toledo (OH)
Ozarks Tech Comm Coll (MO)
Panola Coll (TX)
Piedmont Comm Coll (NC)
Richland Comm Coll (IL)
Rock Valley Coll (IL)
St. Charles Comm Coll (MO)
San Joaquin Valley Coll, Hesperia
 (CA)
San Joaquin Valley Coll, Salida (CA)
San Joaquin Valley Coll, Visalia (CA)
San Juan Coll (NM)
Seminole State Coll of Florida (FL)
South Hills School of Business &
 Technology, State College (PA)
South Louisiana Comm Coll (LA)
Stark State Coll (OH)
Trident Tech Coll (SC)
Walters State Comm Coll (TN)
Western Nevada Coll (NV)
Westmoreland County Comm Coll
 (PA)

INFORMATION SCIENCE/ STUDIES
Alamance Comm Coll (NC)
Alexandria Tech and Comm Coll
 (MN)
Allen Comm Coll (KS)
Amarillo Coll (TX)
Bainbridge State Coll (GA)
Bossier Parish Comm Coll (LA)
Brookhaven Coll (TX)
Bucks County Comm Coll (PA)
Catawba Valley Comm Coll (NC)
Cayuga County Comm Coll (NY)
Century Coll (MN)
Cochise Coll, Douglas (AZ)
Dabney S. Lancaster Comm Coll
 (VA)
Dakota Coll at Bottineau (ND)
Dutchess Comm Coll (NY)
Dyersburg State Comm Coll (TN)
Eastern Arizona Coll (AZ)
El Centro Coll (TX)
Fayetteville Tech Comm Coll (NC)
Forsyth Tech Comm Coll (NC)
Genesee Comm Coll (NY)
Guilford Tech Comm Coll (NC)
Gwinnett Tech Coll (GA)
Harford Comm Coll (MD)
Howard Comm Coll (MD)
ITI Tech Coll (LA)
Jamestown Comm Coll (NY)
Jefferson Comm Coll (NY)
J. F. Drake State Comm and Tech
 Coll (AL)
Kaskaskia Coll (IL)
Kirtland Comm Coll (MI)
Lamar Comm Coll (CO)
Lorain County Comm Coll (OH)
Los Angeles Trade-Tech Coll (CA)
Manchester Comm Coll (CT)
Massachusetts Bay Comm Coll (MA)
Miami Dade Coll (FL)
Monroe Comm Coll (NY)
Montgomery County Comm Coll (PA)
Niagara County Comm Coll (NY)
North Central Texas Coll (TX)
North Shore Comm Coll (MA)
Norwalk Comm Coll (CT)
Oklahoma State U, Oklahoma City
 (OK)
Orange Coast Coll (CA)
Ozarks Tech Comm Coll (MO)
Panola Coll (TX)
Paris Jr Coll (TX)
Penn State DuBois (PA)
Pensacola State Coll (FL)
Queensborough Comm Coll of the
 City U of New York (NY)
Rappahannock Comm Coll (VA)
Richland Comm Coll (IL)
Salt Lake Comm Coll (UT)
San Diego Miramar Coll (CA)
Scottsdale Comm Coll (AZ)
Seminole State Coll of Florida (FL)
Shawnee Comm Coll (IL)
Sheridan Coll (WY)
Sisseton-Wahpeton Coll (SD)
Southeastern Comm Coll (IA)
South Florida State Coll (FL)
South Piedmont Comm Coll (NC)
Sullivan County Comm Coll (NY)
Tompkins Cortland Comm Coll (NY)
Tunxis Comm Coll (CT)
U of Cincinnati Clermont Coll (OH)
Victor Valley Coll (CA)
Westchester Comm Coll (NY)
Western Wyoming Comm Coll (WY)
Wytheville Comm Coll (VA)

INFORMATION TECHNOLOGY
Blue Ridge Comm and Tech Coll
 (WV)
Burlington County Coll (NJ)
Carteret Comm Coll (NC)
Catawba Valley Comm Coll (NC)
Chandler-Gilbert Comm Coll (AZ)
City Colls of Chicago, Olive-Harvey
 College (IL)
Cleveland Comm Coll (NC)
Coastal Bend Coll (TX)
Coll of Central Florida (FL)
Coll of Southern Maryland (MD)
Coll of the Desert (CA)
Columbia-Greene Comm Coll (NY)
Corning Comm Coll (NY)
Dakota Coll at Bottineau (ND)
Daytona State Coll (FL)
Des Moines Area Comm Coll (IA)
Erie Comm Coll, North Campus (NY)
Erie Comm Coll, South Campus (NY)
Fayetteville Tech Comm Coll (NC)

Florida Gateway Coll (FL)
Florida State Coll at Jacksonville (FL)
Forsyth Tech Comm Coll (NC)
Fountainhead Coll of Technology (TN)
Frederick Comm Coll (MD)
Great Falls Coll Montana State U (MT)
Guilford Tech Comm Coll (NC)
Halifax Comm Coll (NC)
Highland Comm Coll (IL)
Howard Comm Coll (MD)
Illinois Eastern Comm Colls, Olney Central College (IL)
Iowa Lakes Comm Coll (IA)
ITI Tech Coll (LA)
James Sprunt Comm Coll (NC)
Jamestown Comm Coll (NY)
Jefferson Coll (MO)
John Tyler Comm Coll (VA)
Kishwaukee Coll (IL)
Lake Land Coll (IL)
Lone Star Coll–CyFair (TX)
Lone Star Coll–Montgomery (TX)
Lorain County Comm Coll (OH)
McHenry County Coll (IL)
Mesabi Range Coll (MN)
Miami Dade Coll (FL)
Minnesota West Comm and Tech Coll (MN)
Mohave Comm Coll (AZ)
Monroe Comm Coll (NY)
Monroe County Comm Coll (MI)
Montgomery Comm Coll (NC)
Nebraska Indian Comm Coll (NE)
Northern Virginia Comm Coll (VA)
Northland Comm Coll (MN)
Norwalk Comm Coll (CT)
Oakton Comm Coll (IL)
Oklahoma State U Inst of Technology (OK)
Oklahoma State U, Oklahoma City (OK)
Owens Comm Coll, Toledo (OH)
Palomar Coll (CA)
Panola Coll (TX)
Pasco-Hernando State Coll (FL)
Piedmont Comm Coll (NC)
Queensborough Comm Coll of the City U of New York (NY)
Randolph Comm Coll (NC)
Raritan Valley Comm Coll (NJ)
Richmond Comm Coll (NC)
Roane State Comm Coll (TN)
Salt Lake Comm Coll (UT)
Seminole State Coll of Florida (FL)
Sierra Coll (CA)
South Piedmont Comm Coll (NC)
South Suburban Coll (IL)
Southwestern Illinois Coll (IL)
Stark State Coll (OH)
Sullivan Coll of Technology and Design (KY)
Tallahassee Comm Coll (FL)
Texas State Tech Coll Harlingen (TX)
Tyler Jr Coll (TX)
Western Wyoming Comm Coll (WY)
West Virginia Jr Coll–Bridgeport (WV)

INFORMATION TECHNOLOGY PROJECT MANAGEMENT
Cincinnati State Tech and Comm Coll (OH)

INSTITUTIONAL FOOD WORKERS
Greenville Tech Coll (SC)
Hinds Comm Coll (MS)
Iowa Lakes Comm Coll (IA)
James Sprunt Comm Coll (NC)
Southwestern Indian Polytechnic Inst (NM)
Texas State Tech Coll Harlingen (TX)

INSTRUMENTATION TECHNOLOGY
Amarillo Coll (TX)
Bellingham Tech Coll (WA)
Butler County Comm Coll (PA)
Cape Fear Comm Coll (NC)
Finger Lakes Comm Coll (NY)
Hagerstown Comm Coll (MD)
Houston Comm Coll (TX)
ITI Tech Coll (LA)
Lakeland Comm Coll (OH)
Louisiana Delta Comm Coll, Monroe (LA)
Lower Columbia Coll (WA)

Mesabi Range Coll (MN)
Monroe Comm Coll (NY)
Nassau Comm Coll (NY)
Ozarks Tech Comm Coll (MO)
Ridgewater Coll (MN)
Salt Lake Comm Coll (UT)
San Jacinto Coll District (TX)
San Juan Coll (NM)
Southwestern Indian Polytechnic Inst (NM)
Sowela Tech Comm Coll (LA)
Western Wyoming Comm Coll (WY)

INSURANCE
Comm Coll of Allegheny County (PA)
Mesa Comm Coll (AZ)
Nassau Comm Coll (NY)
North Iowa Area Comm Coll (IA)
Palomar Coll (CA)
Richland Comm Coll (IL)
South Florida State Coll (FL)
Trinity Valley Comm Coll (TX)

INTEGRATED CIRCUIT DESIGN
Collin County Comm Coll District (TX)

INTELLIGENCE
Cochise Coll, Douglas (AZ)

INTERDISCIPLINARY STUDIES
Anoka-Ramsey Comm Coll (MN)
Anoka-Ramsey Comm Coll, Cambridge Campus (MN)
Bowling Green State U-Firelands Coll (OH)
Elizabethtown Comm and Tech Coll, Elizabethtown (KY)
Fox Valley Tech Coll (WI)
Great Basin Coll (NV)
Maysville Comm and Tech Coll, Maysville (KY)
North Shore Comm Coll (MA)
Owens Comm Coll, Toledo (OH)
Reading Area Comm Coll (PA)

INTERIOR ARCHITECTURE
Coll of Central Florida (FL)
Delgado Comm Coll (LA)

INTERIOR DESIGN
Alexandria Tech and Comm Coll (MN)
Amarillo Coll (TX)
Antelope Valley Coll (CA)
Arapahoe Comm Coll (CO)
Ca&nnada Coll (CA)
Cape Fear Comm Coll (NC)
Carteret Comm Coll (NC)
Century Coll (MN)
Clary Sage Coll (OK)
Coll of Marin (CA)
Coll of the Canyons (CA)
Collin County Comm Coll District (TX)
Davis Coll (OH)
Daytona State Coll (FL)
Delaware Tech & Comm Coll, Terry Campus (DE)
El Centro Coll (TX)
Fashion Inst of Technology (NY)
FIDM/Fashion Inst of Design & Merchandising, Los Angeles Campus (CA)
FIDM/Fashion Inst of Design & Merchandising, Orange County Campus (CA)
FIDM/Fashion Inst of Design & Merchandising, San Francisco Campus (CA)
FIDM/The Fashion Inst of Design & Merchandising, San Diego Campus (CA)
Florida State Coll at Jacksonville (FL)
Forsyth Tech Comm Coll (NC)
Fox Valley Tech Coll (WI)
Front Range Comm Coll (CO)
Gateway Tech Coll (WI)
Gwinnett Tech Coll (GA)
Harford Comm Coll (MD)
Harper Coll (IL)
Hawkeye Comm Coll (IA)
Houston Comm Coll (TX)
Lehigh Carbon Comm Coll (PA)
Lone Star Coll–Kingwood (TX)
Mesa Comm Coll (AZ)
Miami Dade Coll (FL)
Monroe Comm Coll (NY)
Montgomery Coll (MD)

Mt. San Antonio Coll (CA)
Nassau Comm Coll (NY)
Northampton Comm Coll (PA)
Northern Virginia Comm Coll (VA)
Norwalk Comm Coll (CT)
Ohlone Coll (CA)
Orange Coast Coll (CA)
Palomar Coll (CA)
Phoenix Coll (AZ)
Randolph Comm Coll (NC)
Raritan Valley Comm Coll (NJ)
San Jacinto Coll District (TX)
Scottsdale Comm Coll (AZ)
Seminole State Coll of Florida (FL)
State U of New York Coll of Technology at Alfred (NY)
Sullivan Coll of Technology and Design (KY)
Tulsa Comm Coll (OK)
Waukesha County Tech Coll (WI)
Western Iowa Tech Comm Coll (IA)

INTERMEDIA/MULTIMEDIA
Oklahoma State U Inst of Technology (OK)

INTERNATIONAL BUSINESS/ TRADE/COMMERCE
Austin Comm Coll District (TX)
Bunker Hill Comm Coll (MA)
Forsyth Tech Comm Coll (NC)
Harper Coll (IL)
Houston Comm Coll (TX)
Luzerne County Comm Coll (PA)
Monroe Comm Coll (NY)
Northwest State Comm Coll (OH)
Palomar Coll (CA)
Pasadena City Coll (CA)
Raritan Valley Comm Coll (NJ)
San Jacinto Coll District (TX)
South Florida State Coll (FL)
Stark State Coll (OH)
Tompkins Cortland Comm Coll (NY)
Tulsa Comm Coll (OK)
Westchester Comm Coll (NY)

INTERNATIONAL/GLOBAL STUDIES
Burlington County Coll (NJ)
Central Wyoming Coll (WY)
Jamestown Comm Coll (NY)
Kalamazoo Valley Comm Coll (MI)
Macomb Comm Coll (MI)
Ocean County Coll (NJ)
Pasadena City Coll (CA)
Salt Lake Comm Coll (UT)
Tompkins Cortland Comm Coll (NY)

INTERNATIONAL MARKETING
Waukesha County Tech Coll (WI)

INTERNATIONAL RELATIONS AND AFFAIRS
Ca&nnada Coll (CA)
Casper Coll (WY)
Coll of Marin (CA)
Greenfield Comm Coll (MA)
Harford Comm Coll (MD)
Harrisburg Area Comm Coll (PA)
Massachusetts Bay Comm Coll (MA)
Miami Dade Coll (FL)
Northern Essex Comm Coll (MA)
Northwest Coll (WY)
Salt Lake Comm Coll (UT)
South Florida State Coll (FL)
Western Wyoming Comm Coll (WY)

IRONWORKING
Southwestern Illinois Coll (IL)

ITALIAN
Coll of the Desert (CA)
Miami Dade Coll (FL)

JAPANESE
Austin Comm Coll District (TX)
Citrus Coll (CA)

JAZZ/JAZZ STUDIES
Comm Coll of Rhode Island (RI)
Iowa Lakes Comm Coll (IA)
South Florida State Coll (FL)

JOURNALISM
Allen Comm Coll (KS)
Amarillo Coll (TX)
Austin Comm Coll District (TX)
Bainbridge State Coll (GA)
Bucks County Comm Coll (PA)
Burlington County Coll (NJ)
Carl Albert State Coll (OK)

Casper Coll (WY)
Central Texas Coll (TX)
Citrus Coll (CA)
Cloud County Comm Coll (KS)
Cochise Coll, Douglas (AZ)
Coll of Central Florida (FL)
Coll of the Canyons (CA)
Coll of the Desert (CA)
Comm Coll of Allegheny County (PA)
Copiah-Lincoln Comm Coll (MS)
Darton State Coll (GA)
Delta Coll (MI)
Georgia Highlands Coll (GA)
Golden West Coll (CA)
Grand Rapids Comm Coll (MI)
Hinds Comm Coll (MS)
Housatonic Comm Coll (CT)
Iowa Central Comm Coll (IA)
Iowa Lakes Comm Coll (IA)
Kilgore Coll (TX)
Kingsborough Comm Coll of the City U of New York (NY)
Lorain County Comm Coll (OH)
Los Angeles Trade-Tech Coll (CA)
Luzerne County Comm Coll (PA)
Manchester Comm Coll (CT)
Miami Dade Coll (FL)
Monroe County Comm Coll (MI)
Mt. San Antonio Coll (CA)
Navarro Coll (TX)
Northampton Comm Coll (PA)
Northeastern Jr Coll (CO)
Northern Essex Comm Coll (MA)
Northwest Coll (WY)
Ohlone Coll (CA)
Orange Coast Coll (CA)
Palomar Coll (CA)
Paris Jr Coll (TX)
Pensacola State Coll (FL)
Potomac State Coll of West Virginia U (WV)
Salem Comm Coll (NJ)
San Jacinto Coll District (TX)
San Joaquin Delta Coll (CA)
South Florida State Coll (FL)
Trinity Valley Comm Coll (TX)
Umpqua Comm Coll (OR)
Vincennes U (IN)
Westchester Comm Coll (NY)
Western Wyoming Comm Coll (WY)

JUVENILE CORRECTIONS
Danville Area Comm Coll (IL)
Kaskaskia Coll (IL)

KEYBOARD INSTRUMENTS
Iowa Lakes Comm Coll (IA)

KINDERGARTEN/PRESCHOOL EDUCATION
Alamance Comm Coll (NC)
Bainbridge State Coll (GA)
Butler County Comm Coll (PA)
Casper Coll (WY)
Cleveland State Comm Coll (TN)
Comm Coll of Philadelphia (PA)
Comm Coll of Rhode Island (RI)
County Coll of Morris (NJ)
Daytona State Coll (FL)
Delaware Tech & Comm Coll, Terry Campus (DE)
Delgado Comm Coll (LA)
Denmark Tech Coll (SC)
Finger Lakes Comm Colf (NY)
Gateway Comm Coll (CT)
Genesee Comm Coll (NY)
Great Basin Coll (NV)
Howard Comm Coll (MD)
Iowa Lakes Comm Coll (IA)
Lorain County Comm Coll (OH)
Manchester Comm Coll (CT)
Miami Dade Coll (FL)
Middlesex Comm Coll (MA)
Mt. San Antonio Coll (CA)
Nassau Comm Coll (NY)
Northeastern Jr Coll (CO)
Northern Essex Comm Coll (MA)
North Shore Comm Coll (MA)
Northwest Coll (WY)
Northwest State Comm Coll (OH)
Nunez Comm Coll (LA)
Ohlone Coll (CA)
Orange Coast Coll (CA)
Otero Jr Coll (CO)
Ozarks Tech Comm Coll (MO)
Quinsigamond Comm Coll (MA)
Raritan Valley Comm Coll (NJ)
Roane State Comm Coll (TN)
Sisseton-Wahpeton Coll (SD)
Southern U at Shreveport (LA)

Sullivan County Comm Coll (NY)
Terra State Comm Coll (OH)
Trinity Valley Comm Coll (TX)
Tunxis Comm Coll (CT)
Ulster County Comm Coll (NY)
Umpqua Comm Coll (OR)
U of Cincinnati Clermont Coll (OH)
Victor Valley Coll (CA)
Virginia Western Comm Coll (VA)
Wenatchee Valley Coll (WA)
Whatcom Comm Coll (WA)

KINESIOLOGY AND EXERCISE SCIENCE
Ancilla Coll (IN)
Carroll Comm Coll (MD)
Central Oregon Comm Coll (OR)
Chandler-Gilbert Comm Coll (AZ)
County Coll of Morris (NJ)
Laramie County Comm Coll (WY)
Lehigh Carbon Comm Coll (PA)
Norwalk Comm Coll (CT)
Ohlone Coll (CA)
Orange Coast Coll (CA)
Palomar Coll (CA)
Raritan Valley Comm Coll (NJ)
St. Philip's Coll (TX)
Salt Lake Comm Coll (UT)
Sheridan Coll (WY)
South Florida State Coll (FL)
South Suburban Coll (IL)
Three Rivers Comm Coll (CT)
Western Wyoming Comm Coll (WY)

LABOR AND INDUSTRIAL RELATIONS
Kingsborough Comm Coll of the City U of New York (NY)
Los Angeles Trade-Tech Coll (CA)

LANDSCAPE ARCHITECTURE
Hinds Comm Coll (MS)
Monroe Comm Coll (NY)
Mt. San Antonio Coll (CA)
Truckee Meadows Comm Coll (NV)

LANDSCAPING AND GROUNDSKEEPING
Anoka Tech Coll (MN)
Cape Fear Comm Coll (NC)
Century Coll (MN)
Cincinnati State Tech and Comm Coll (OH)
Clark Coll (WA)
Coll of Central Florida (FL)
Coll of Marin (CA)
Comm Coll of Allegheny County (PA)
Dakota Coll at Bottineau (ND)
Danville Area Comm Coll (IL)
Grand Rapids Comm Coll (MI)
Harrisburg Area Comm Coll (PA)
Hennepin Tech Coll (MN)
Hinds Comm Coll (MS)
Iowa Lakes Comm Coll (IA)
James H. Faulkner State Comm Coll (AL)
Kishwaukee Coll (IL)
Miami Dade Coll (FL)
Northwestern Michigan Coll (MI)
The Ohio State U Ag Tech Inst (OH)
Owens Comm Coll, Toledo (OH)
Pensacola State Coll (FL)
San Juan Coll (NM)
South Florida State Coll (FL)
Springfield Tech Comm Coll (MA)

LAND USE PLANNING AND MANAGEMENT
Dakota Coll at Bottineau (ND)
Hocking Coll (OH)

LANGUAGE INTERPRETATION AND TRANSLATION
Allen Comm Coll (KS)
Cape Fear Comm Coll (NC)
Century Coll (MN)
Cleveland Comm Coll (NC)
Des Moines Area Comm Coll (IA)
Lake Region State Coll (ND)
Oklahoma State U, Oklahoma City (OK)
Terra State Comm Coll (OH)

LASER AND OPTICAL TECHNOLOGY
Amarillo Coll (TX)
Camden County Coll (NJ)
Monroe Comm Coll (NY)
Queensborough Comm Coll of the City U of New York (NY)
Roane State Comm Coll (TN)

Springfield Tech Comm Coll (MA)
Three Rivers Comm Coll (CT)

LATIN
Austin Comm Coll District (TX)

LATIN AMERICAN STUDIES
Miami Dade Coll (FL)

LAW ENFORCEMENT INVESTIGATION AND INTERVIEWING
Mohawk Valley Comm Coll (NY)

LEGAL ADMINISTRATIVE ASSISTANT/SECRETARY
Alamance Comm Coll (NC)
Alexandria Tech and Comm Coll (MN)
Alvin Comm Coll (TX)
Amarillo Coll (TX)
Anoka Tech Coll (MN)
Arizona Western Coll (AZ)
Bradford School (PA)
Butler County Comm Coll (PA)
Cambria-Rowe Business Coll, Indiana (PA)
Career Tech Coll, Monroe (LA)
Carteret Comm Coll (NC)
Clark Coll (WA)
Cleveland Comm Coll (NC)
Comm Coll of Allegheny County (PA)
Comm Coll of Rhode Island (RI)
Crowder Coll (MO)
Dabney S. Lancaster Comm Coll (VA)
Delaware Tech & Comm Coll, Terry Campus (DE)
Eastern Gateway Comm Coll (OH)
El Centro Coll (TX)
Forrest Coll (SC)
Gateway Comm Coll (CT)
Golden West Coll (CA)
Harper Coll (IL)
Howard Comm Coll (MD)
IBMC Coll (CO)
International Business Coll, Indianapolis (IN)
Iowa Lakes Comm Coll (IA)
Jefferson Coll (MO)
Kellogg Comm Coll (MI)
King's Coll (NC)
Kirtland Comm Coll (MI)
Lake Land Coll (IL)
Lower Columbia Coll (WA)
Manchester Comm Coll (CT)
Miami Dade Coll (FL)
Minneapolis Business Coll (MN)
Minnesota State Coll–Southeast Tech (MN)
Monroe Comm Coll (NY)
Monroe County Comm Coll (MI)
Moraine Park Tech Coll (WI)
Mt. San Antonio Coll (CA)
Nassau Comm Coll (NY)
Navarro Coll (TX)
New Mexico Jr Coll (NM)
Northampton Comm Coll (PA)
North Central Texas Coll (TX)
Northeastern Jr Coll (CO)
North Iowa Area Comm Coll (IA)
North Shore Comm Coll (MA)
Northwestern Michigan Coll (MI)
Northwest State Comm Coll (OH)
Ohio Business Coll, Sandusky (OH)
Oklahoma City Comm Coll (OK)
Olympic Coll (WA)
Otero Jr Coll (CO)
Pensacola State Coll (FL)
Renton Tech Coll (WA)
Richland Comm Coll (IL)
Ridgewater Coll (MN)
Riverland Comm Coll (MN)
Roane State Comm Coll (TN)
St. Philip's Coll (TX)
Shawnee Comm Coll (IL)
Southwestern Illinois Coll (IL)
Stark State Coll (OH)
Trinity Valley Comm Coll (TX)
Tyler Jr Coll (TX)
Umpqua Comm Coll (OR)
Wenatchee Valley Coll (WA)
Western Wyoming Comm Coll (WY)

LEGAL ASSISTANT/PARALEGAL
Alexandria Tech and Comm Coll (MN)
Alvin Comm Coll (TX)
Anne Arundel Comm Coll (MD)
Arapahoe Comm Coll (CO)
Austin Comm Coll District (TX)
Bellingham Tech Coll (WA)

Bevill State Comm Coll (AL)
Blue Ridge Comm and Tech Coll (WV)
Bradford School (PA)
Bunker Hill Comm Coll (MA)
Burlington County Coll (NJ)
Camden County Coll (NJ)
Ca&nnada Coll (CA)
Carteret Comm Coll (NC)
Casper Coll (WY)
Central Texas Coll (TX)
Chesapeake Coll (MD)
Clark Coll (WA)
Cloud County Comm Coll (KS)
Coll of Central Florida (FL)
Coll of the Canyons (CA)
Collin County Comm Coll District (TX)
Comm Care Coll (OK)
Comm Coll of Allegheny County (PA)
The Comm Coll of Baltimore County (MD)
Comm Coll of Denver (CO)
Comm Coll of Rhode Island (RI)
Comm Coll of the Air Force (AL)
Cumberland County Coll (NJ)
Daytona State Coll (FL)
Delta Coll (MI)
Des Moines Area Comm Coll (IA)
Dutchess Comm Coll (NY)
Eastern Idaho Tech Coll (ID)
Edison Comm Coll (OH)
El Centro Coll (TX)
Elgin Comm Coll (IL)
Erie Comm Coll (NY)
Fayetteville Tech Comm Coll (NC)
Finger Lakes Comm Coll (NY)
Fiorello H. LaGuardia Comm Coll of the City U of New York (NY)
Florida SouthWestern State Coll (FL)
Florida State Coll at Jacksonville (FL)
Forrest Coll (SC)
Forsyth Tech Comm Coll (NC)
Fox Valley Tech Coll (WI)
Frederick Comm Coll (MD)
Front Range Comm Coll (CO)
Gadsden State Comm Coll (AL)
Genesee Comm Coll (NY)
Greenville Tech Coll (SC)
Guilford Tech Comm Coll (NC)
Halifax Comm Coll (NC)
Harford Comm Coll (MD)
Harper Coll (IL)
Harrisburg Area Comm Coll (PA)
Hillsborough Comm Coll (FL)
Hinds Comm Coll (MS)
Horry-Georgetown Tech Coll (SC)
Houston Comm Coll (TX)
Hudson County Comm Coll (NJ)
Hutchinson Comm Coll (KS)
IBMC Coll (CO)
Illinois Eastern Comm Colls, Wabash Valley College (IL)
International Business Coll, Indianapolis (IN)
Iowa Lakes Comm Coll (IA)
James H. Faulkner State Comm Coll (AL)
Jefferson Comm Coll (NY)
Johnston Comm Coll (NC)
J. Sargeant Reynolds Comm Coll (VA)
Kankakee Comm Coll (IL)
Kellogg Comm Coll (MI)
Kent State U at East Liverpool (OH)
Kent State U at Trumbull (OH)
Kilgore Coll (TX)
King's Coll (NC)
Lakeland Comm Coll (OH)
Laramie County Comm Coll (WY)
Lehigh Carbon Comm Coll (PA)
Lone Star Coll–North Harris (TX)
Luzerne County Comm Coll (PA)
Macomb Comm Coll (MI)
Manchester Comm Coll (CT)
Manor Coll (PA)
Massachusetts Bay Comm Coll (MA)
Miami Dade Coll (FL)
Middlesex Comm Coll (MA)
Middlesex County Coll (NJ)
Midlands Tech Coll (SC)
Minneapolis Business Coll (MN)
Mohave Comm Coll (AZ)
Montgomery Coll (MD)
Moraine Park Tech Coll (WI)
Mountain State Coll (WV)
Mt. San Antonio Coll (CA)
Mount Wachusett Comm Coll (MA)
Nassau Comm Coll (NY)
Navarro Coll (TX)
Northampton Comm Coll (PA)

North Central Texas Coll (TX)
Northern Essex Comm Coll (MA)
North Hennepin Comm Coll (MN)
North Shore Comm Coll (MA)
Northwestern Coll (IL)
Northwest State Comm Coll (OH)
Norwalk Comm Coll (CT)
Nunez Comm Coll (LA)
Pasadena City Coll (CA)
Pasco-Hernando State Coll (FL)
Penn Foster Coll (AZ)
Pensacola State Coll (FL)
Phoenix Coll (AZ)
Raritan Valley Comm Coll (NJ)
Salem Comm Coll (NJ)
Salt Lake Comm Coll (UT)
San Diego Miramar Coll (CA)
San Jacinto Coll District (TX)
San Juan Coll (NM)
Seminole State Coll of Florida (FL)
Southern U at Shreveport (LA)
South Florida State Coll (FL)
South Piedmont Comm Coll (NC)
South Suburban Coll (IL)
Southwestern Illinois Coll (IL)
Sullivan County Comm Coll (NY)
Tallahassee Comm Coll (FL)
Tech Coll of the Lowcountry (SC)
Tompkins Cortland Comm Coll (NY)
Trident Tech Coll (SC)
Truckee Meadows Comm Coll (NV)
Tulsa Comm Coll (OK)
Tyler Jr Coll (TX)
U of Cincinnati Clermont Coll (OH)
Vincennes U (IN)
Volunteer State Comm Coll (TN)
Wayne County Comm Coll District (MI)
Westchester Comm Coll (NY)
Western Dakota Tech Inst (SD)
Western Iowa Tech Comm Coll (IA)
Westmoreland County Comm Coll (PA)
Whatcom Comm Coll (WA)

LEGAL PROFESSIONS AND STUDIES RELATED
Bucks County Comm Coll (PA)

LEGAL STUDIES
Alvin Comm Coll (TX)
Carroll Comm Coll (MD)
Coll of Southern Maryland (MD)
Iowa Lakes Comm Coll (IA)
Macomb Comm Coll (MI)
Navarro Coll (TX)
Palomar Coll (CA)
Trident Tech Coll (SC)

LIBERAL ARTS AND SCIENCES AND HUMANITIES RELATED
Anne Arundel Comm Coll (MD)
Bossier Parish Comm Coll (LA)
Bucks County Comm Coll (PA)
Chandler-Gilbert Comm Coll (AZ)
Chesapeake Coll (MD)
Cleveland Comm Coll (NC)
Cleveland State Comm Coll (TN)
Coll of Central Florida (FL)
Coll of Southern Maryland (MD)
Comm Coll of Aurora (CO)
The Comm Coll of Baltimore County (MD)
Corning Comm Coll (NY)
Dakota Coll at Bottineau (ND)
Dutchess Comm Coll (NY)
Erie Comm Coll (NY)
Fayetteville Tech Comm Coll (NC)
Front Range Comm Coll (CO)
Garrett Coll (MD)
Genesee Comm Coll (NY)
Great Falls Coll Montana State U (MT)
Guilford Tech Comm Coll (NC)
Hagerstown Comm Coll (MD)
Haywood Comm Coll (NC)
Holyoke Comm Coll (MA)
Iowa Lakes Comm Coll (IA)
James Sprunt Comm Coll (NC)
Jamestown Comm Coll (NY)
J. Sargeant Reynolds Comm Coll (VA)
Kent State U at Ashtabula (OH)
Kent State U at East Liverpool (OH)
Kent State U at Salem (OH)
Kent State U at Trumbull (OH)
Kent State U at Tuscarawas (OH)
Louisiana Delta Comm Coll, Monroe (LA)
Luzerne County Comm Coll (PA)
Minnesota West Comm and Tech Coll (MN)

Mohawk Valley Comm Coll (NY)
Montgomery Coll (MD)
Northampton Comm Coll (PA)
Nunez Comm Coll (LA)
Piedmont Comm Coll (NC)
Pueblo Comm Coll (CO)
Randolph Comm Coll (NC)
Ridgewater Coll (MN)
Southern U at Shreveport (LA)
South Florida State Coll (FL)
Sowela Tech Comm Coll (LA)
State U of New York Coll of Technology at Alfred (NY)
Tech Coll of the Lowcountry (SC)
Tompkins Cortland Comm Coll (NY)
Wor-Wic Comm Coll (MD)

LIBERAL ARTS AND SCIENCES/ LIBERAL STUDIES
Alamance Comm Coll (NC)
Alexandria Tech and Comm Coll (MN)
Alvin Comm Coll (TX)
Amarillo Coll (TX)
American Samoa Comm Coll (AS)
Anne Arundel Comm Coll (MD)
Anoka-Ramsey Comm Coll (MN)
Anoka-Ramsey Comm Coll, Cambridge Campus (MN)
Antelope Valley Coll (CA)
Arapahoe Comm Coll (CO)
Bainbridge State Coll (GA)
Bevill State Comm Coll (AL)
Big Bend Comm Coll (WA)
Blue Ridge Comm and Tech Coll (WV)
Borough of Manhattan Comm Coll of the City U of New York (NY)
Bossier Parish Comm Coll (LA)
Bowling Green State U-Firelands Coll (OH)
Brookhaven Coll (TX)
Bucks County Comm Coll (PA)
Burlington County Coll (NJ)
Camden County Coll (NJ)
Ca&nnada Coll (CA)
Cape Fear Comm Coll (NC)
Carroll Comm Coll (MD)
Carteret Comm Coll (NC)
Casper Coll (WY)
Catawba Valley Comm Coll (NC)
Cayuga County Comm Coll (NY)
Cecil Coll (MD)
Central Maine Comm Coll (ME)
Central Oregon Comm Coll (OR)
Central Texas Coll (TX)
Central Virginia Comm Coll (VA)
Century Coll (MN)
Chandler-Gilbert Comm Coll (AZ)
Chesapeake Coll (MD)
Chipola Coll (FL)
Cincinnati State Tech and Comm Coll (OH)
Citrus Coll (CA)
City Colls of Chicago, Olive-Harvey College (IL)
Clark Coll (WA)
Cleveland Comm Coll (NC)
Cleveland State Comm Coll (TN)
Clinton Comm Coll (NY)
Cloud County Comm Coll (KS)
Coastal Bend Coll (TX)
Coastline Comm Coll (CA)
Coll of Central Florida (FL)
Coll of Marin (CA)
Coll of Southern Idaho (ID)
Coll of Southern Maryland (MD)
Coll of the Canyons (CA)
Coll of the Desert (CA)
Collin County Comm Coll District (TX)
Colorado Northwestern Comm Coll (CO)
Columbia-Greene Comm Coll (NY)
Comm Coll of Allegheny County (PA)
Comm Coll of Aurora (CO)
The Comm Coll of Baltimore County (MD)
Comm Coll of Denver (CO)
Comm Coll of Philadelphia (PA)
Comm Coll of Rhode Island (RI)
Copiah-Lincoln Comm Coll (MS)
Corning Comm Coll (NY)
County Coll of Morris (NJ)
Crowder Coll (MO)
Cumberland County Coll (NJ)
Dabney S. Lancaster Comm Coll (VA)
Dakota Coll at Bottineau (ND)
Danville Area Comm Coll (IL)
Deep Springs Coll (CA)

Delta Coll (MI)
Des Moines Area Comm Coll (IA)
Donnelly Coll (KS)
Dutchess Comm Coll (NY)
Dyersburg State Comm Coll (TN)
Eastern Arizona Coll (AZ)
Eastern Wyoming Coll (WY)
Edison Comm Coll (OH)
Elgin Comm Coll (IL)
Elizabethtown Comm and Tech Coll, Elizabethtown (KY)
Erie Comm Coll (NY)
Erie Comm Coll, North Campus (NY)
Erie Comm Coll, South Campus (NY)
Fayetteville Tech Comm Coll (NC)
Finger Lakes Comm Coll (NY)
Fiorello H. LaGuardia Comm Coll of the City U of New York (NY)
Florida Gateway Coll (FL)
Florida SouthWestern State Coll (FL)
Florida State Coll at Jacksonville (FL)
Forsyth Tech Comm Coll (NC)
Frederick Comm Coll (MD)
Front Range Comm Coll (CO)
Gadsden State Comm Coll (AL)
Garrett Coll (MD)
Gateway Comm Coll (CT)
Genesee Comm Coll (NY)
Georgia Highlands Coll (GA)
Golden West Coll (CA)
Goodwin Coll (CT)
Grand Rapids Comm Coll (MI)
Greenfield Comm Coll (MA)
Greenville Tech Coll (SC)
Guam Comm Coll (GU)
Guilford Tech Comm Coll (NC)
Gulf Coast State Coll (FL)
Hagerstown Comm Coll (MD)
Harper Coll (IL)
Hawaii Tokai International Coll (HI)
Hawkeye Comm Coll (IA)
Haywood Comm Coll (NC)
Highland Comm Coll (IL)
Hillsborough Comm Coll (FL)
Holyoke Comm Coll (MA)
Hopkinsville Comm Coll (KY)
Housatonic Comm Coll (CT)
Howard Comm Coll (MD)
Hudson County Comm Coll (NJ)
Hutchinson Comm Coll (KS)
Illinois Eastern Comm Colls, Frontier Community College (IL)
Illinois Eastern Comm Colls, Lincoln Trail College (IL)
Illinois Eastern Comm Colls, Olney Central College (IL)
Illinois Eastern Comm Colls, Wabash Valley College (IL)
Iowa Central Comm Coll (IA)
Iowa Lakes Comm Coll (IA)
Jackson State Comm Coll (TN)
James H. Faulkner State Comm Coll (AL)
James Sprunt Comm Coll (NC)
Jamestown Comm Coll (NY)
Jefferson Coll (MO)
Jefferson Comm Coll (NY)
Jefferson State Comm Coll (AL)
Johnston Comm Coll (NC)
John Tyler Comm Coll (VA)
Kalamazoo Valley Comm Coll (MI)
Kaskaskia Coll (IL)
Kellogg Comm Coll (MI)
Kennebec Valley Comm Coll (ME)
Kent State U at Salem (OH)
Kingsborough Comm Coll of the City U of New York (NY)
Kirtland Comm Coll (MI)
Kishwaukee Coll (IL)
Lake Land Coll (IL)
Lakeland Comm Coll (OH)
Lake Region State Coll (ND)
Lakes Region Comm Coll (NH)
Lamar Comm Coll (CO)
Landmark Coll (VT)
Lehigh Carbon Comm Coll (PA)
Lenoir Comm Coll (NC)
Lone Star Coll–CyFair (TX)
Lorain County Comm Coll (OH)
Los Angeles Trade-Tech Coll (CA)
Louisiana Delta Comm Coll, Monroe (LA)
Lower Columbia Coll (WA)
Lurleen B. Wallace Comm Coll (AL)
Luzerne County Comm Coll (PA)
Macomb Comm Coll (MI)
Manchester Comm Coll (CT)
Manor Coll (PA)
Massachusetts Bay Comm Coll (MA)
Maysville Comm and Tech Coll, Maysville (KY)

McHenry County Coll (IL)
Mesabi Range Coll (MN)
Mesa Comm Coll (AZ)
Miami Dade Coll (FL)
Middlesex Comm Coll (MA)
Middlesex County Coll (NJ)
Midlands Tech Coll (SC)
Mid-Plains Comm Coll, North Platte (NE)
Minneapolis Comm and Tech Coll (MN)
Minnesota West Comm and Tech Coll (MN)
MiraCosta Coll (CA)
Mohave Comm Coll (AZ)
Mohawk Valley Comm Coll (NY)
Monroe Comm Coll (NY)
Monroe County Comm Coll (MI)
Montcalm Comm Coll (MI)
Montgomery Coll (MD)
Montgomery Comm Coll (NC)
Montgomery County Comm Coll (PA)
Moraine Valley Comm Coll (IL)
Morgan Comm Coll (CO)
Motlow State Comm Coll (TN)
Mott Comm Coll (MI)
Mount Wachusett Comm Coll (MA)
Nassau Comm Coll (NY)
Nebraska Indian Comm Coll (NE)
New Mexico Jr Coll (NM)
Niagara County Comm Coll (NY)
Normandale Comm Coll (MN)
Northampton Comm Coll (PA)
North Central Texas Coll (TX)
Northeastern Jr Coll (CO)
Northeast Iowa Comm Coll (IA)
Northern Essex Comm Coll (MA)
Northern Virginia Comm Coll (VA)
North Hennepin Comm Coll (MN)
North Iowa Area Comm Coll (IA)
Northland Comm Coll (MN)
North Shore Comm Coll (MA)
Northwest Coll (WY)
Northwestern Michigan Coll (MI)
Northwest-Shoals Comm Coll (AL)
Northwest State Comm Coll (OH)
Norwalk Comm Coll (CT)
Oakton Comm Coll (IL)
Ocean County Coll (NJ)
Ohlone Coll (CA)
Oklahoma City Comm Coll (OK)
Olympic Coll (WA)
Orange Coast Coll (CA)
Oregon Coast Comm Coll (OR)
Otero Jr Coll (CO)
Owensboro Comm and Tech Coll (KY)
Ozarks Tech Comm Coll (MO)
Palomar Coll (CA)
Paris Jr Coll (TX)
Pasadena City Coll (CA)
Pasco-Hernando State Coll (FL)
Penn State DuBois (PA)
Penn State Fayette, The Eberly Campus (PA)
Penn State Mont Alto (PA)
Penn State Shenango (PA)
Pensacola State Coll (FL)
Phoenix Coll (AZ)
Piedmont Comm Coll (NC)
Potomac State Coll of West Virginia U (WV)
Pueblo Comm Coll (CO)
Queensborough Comm Coll of the City U of New York (NY)
Quinsigamond Comm Coll (MA)
Rainy River Comm Coll (MN)
Randolph Comm Coll (NC)
Rappahannock Comm Coll (VA)
Raritan Valley Comm Coll (NJ)
Reading Area Comm Coll (PA)
Richland Comm Coll (IL)
Richmond Comm Coll (NC)
Ridgewater Coll (MN)
Rio Hondo Coll (CA)
Riverland Comm Coll (MN)
Roane State Comm Coll (TN)
Rockland Comm Coll (NY)
Rock Valley Coll (IL)
Rogue Comm Coll (OR)
Saginaw Chippewa Tribal Coll (MI)
St. Charles Comm Coll (MO)
St. Clair County Comm Coll (MI)
St. Philip's Coll (TX)
Salem Comm Coll (NJ)
San Diego Miramar Coll (CA)
San Joaquin Delta Coll (CA)
San Juan Coll (NM)
Seminole State Coll (OK)
Seminole State Coll of Florida (FL)

Shawnee Comm Coll (IL)
Sierra Coll (CA)
Sisseton-Wahpeton Coll (SD)
Somerset Comm Coll (KY)
Southeastern Comm Coll (IA)
South Florida State Coll (FL)
South Piedmont Comm Coll (NC)
South Suburban Coll (IL)
Southwestern Illinois Coll (IL)
Southwestern Indian Polytechnic Inst (NM)
Southwestern Michigan Coll (MI)
Southwest Virginia Comm Coll (VA)
Spartanburg Comm Coll (SC)
Spartanburg Methodist Coll (SC)
Springfield Tech Comm Coll (MA)
State Fair Comm Coll (MO)
State U of New York Coll of Technology at Alfred (NY)
Sullivan County Comm Coll (NY)
Tallahassee Comm Coll (FL)
Tech Coll of the Lowcountry (SC)
Terra State Comm Coll (OH)
Three Rivers Comm Coll (CT)
Tohono O'odham Comm Coll (AZ)
Tompkins Cortland Comm Coll (NY)
Trident Tech Coll (SC)
Trinidad State Jr Coll (CO)
Trinity Valley Comm Coll (TX)
Trocaire Coll (NY)
Tunxis Comm Coll (CT)
Tyler Jr Coll (TX)
Ulster County Comm Coll (NY)
Umpqua Comm Coll (OR)
U of Alaska Southeast, Sitka Campus (AK)
U of Arkansas Comm Coll at Batesville (AR)
U of Arkansas Comm Coll at Hope (AR)
U of Arkansas Comm Coll at Morrilton (AR)
U of Cincinnati Clermont Coll (OH)
U of South Carolina Salkehatchie (SC)
U of South Carolina Union (SC)
U of Wisconsin–Fond du Lac (WI)
U of Wisconsin–Fox Valley (WI)
U of Wisconsin–Sheboygan (WI)
U of Wisconsin–Waukesha (WI)
Victor Valley Coll (CA)
Vincennes U (IN)
Virginia Western Comm Coll (VA)
Volunteer State Comm Coll (TN)
Walters State Comm Coll (TN)
Wenatchee Valley Coll (WA)
Westchester Comm Coll (NY)
Western Iowa Tech Comm Coll (IA)
Western Nevada Coll (NV)
Western Wyoming Comm Coll (WY)
Westmoreland County Comm Coll (PA)
Whatcom Comm Coll (WA)
White Mountains Comm Coll (NH)
Williston State Coll (ND)
Wor-Wic Comm Coll (MD)
Wright State U–Lake Campus (OH)
Wytheville Comm Coll (VA)

LIBRARY AND ARCHIVES ASSISTING
Citrus Coll (CA)
Minneapolis Comm and Tech Coll (MN)
Palomar Coll (CA)
Pueblo Comm Coll (CO)
Western Dakota Tech Inst (SD)

LIBRARY AND INFORMATION SCIENCE
Allen Comm Coll (KS)
Citrus Coll (CA)
Coll of Central Florida (FL)
Coll of Southern Idaho (ID)
Copiah-Lincoln Comm Coll (MS)
Grand Rapids Comm Coll (MI)
Mesa Comm Coll (AZ)
Westmoreland County Comm Coll (PA)

LIBRARY SCIENCE RELATED
Pasadena City Coll (CA)

LICENSED PRACTICAL/ VOCATIONAL NURSE TRAINING
Amarillo Coll (TX)
Anoka Tech Coll (MN)
Bainbridge State Coll (GA)
Big Bend Comm Coll (WA)

Carroll Comm Coll (MD)
Carteret Comm Coll (NC)
Central Maine Comm Coll (ME)
Central Oregon Comm Coll (OR)
Central Texas Coll (TX)
Citrus Coll (CA)
Coastal Bend Coll (TX)
Coll of Southern Idaho (ID)
Coll of the Desert (CA)
Comm Coll of Allegheny County (PA)
Comm Coll of Denver (CO)
Comm Coll of Rhode Island (RI)
Dakota Coll at Bottineau (ND)
Des Moines Area Comm Coll (IA)
Eastern Gateway Comm Coll (OH)
El Centro Coll (TX)
Fiorello H. LaGuardia Comm Coll of the City U of New York (NY)
George C. Wallace Comm Coll (AL)
Grand Rapids Comm Coll (MI)
Great Falls Coll Montana State U (MT)
Hennepin Tech Coll (MN)
Hocking Coll (OH)
Howard Comm Coll (MD)
Iowa Central Comm Coll (IA)
James H. Faulkner State Comm Coll (AL)
Jefferson Coll (MO)
J. F. Drake State Comm and Tech Coll (AL)
J. Sargeant Reynolds Comm Coll (VA)
Kellogg Comm Coll (MI)
Kirtland Comm Coll (MI)
Lamar Comm Coll (CO)
Midlands Tech Coll (SC)
Mid-Plains Comm Coll, North Platte (NE)
MiraCosta Coll (CA)
Navarro Coll (TX)
New Mexico Jr Coll (NM)
Northeastern Jr Coll (CO)
North Iowa Area Comm Coll (IA)
Northland Comm Coll (MN)
Northwest Tech Coll (MN)
Pasadena City Coll (CA)
St. Charles Comm Coll (MO)
Salem Comm Coll (NJ)
San Joaquin Delta Coll (CA)
San Joaquin Valley Coll, Visalia (CA)
Sierra Coll (CA)
Southeastern Coll–Greenacres (FL)
Southeastern Comm Coll (IA)
South Louisiana Comm Coll (LA)
Trinity Valley Comm Coll (TX)
Tyler Jr Coll (TX)
Wenatchee Valley Coll (WA)
Western Dakota Tech Inst (SD)
Western Iowa Tech Comm Coll (IA)
Western Wyoming Comm Coll (WY)
Westmoreland County Comm Coll (PA)
Williston State Coll (ND)

LINEWORKER
Chandler-Gilbert Comm Coll (AZ)
Coll of Southern Maryland (MD)
Harrisburg Area Comm Coll (PA)
Kennebec Valley Comm Coll (ME)
Minnesota West Comm and Tech Coll (MN)
Mitchell Tech Inst (SD)
Raritan Valley Comm Coll (NJ)
Trinidad State Jr Coll (CO)

LINGUISTICS
Ca&nnada Coll (CA)
South Florida State Coll (FL)

LITERATURE
Oklahoma City Comm Coll (OK)

LITERATURE RELATED
Cayuga County Comm Coll (NY)

LIVESTOCK MANAGEMENT
The Ohio State U Ag Tech Inst (OH)

LOGISTICS, MATERIALS, AND SUPPLY CHAIN MANAGEMENT
Ancilla Coll (IN)
Arizona Western Coll (AZ)
Cecil Coll (MD)
City Colls of Chicago, Olive-Harvey College (IL)
Cochise Coll, Douglas (AZ)
Comm Coll of the Air Force (AL)
Edison Comm Coll (OH)

FIDM/Fashion Inst of Design & Merchandising, Los Angeles Campus (CA)
Florida Gateway Coll (FL)
Forsyth Tech Comm Coll (NC)
Fox Valley Tech Coll (WI)
Goodwin Coll (CT)
Guilford Tech Comm Coll (NC)
Houston Comm Coll (TX)
Lone Star Coll–CyFair (TX)
Miami Dade Coll (FL)
Northwest State Comm Coll (OH)
Owens Comm Coll, Toledo (OH)
Randolph Comm Coll (NC)
Truckee Meadows Comm Coll (NV)
Westmoreland County Comm Coll (PA)

MACHINE SHOP TECHNOLOGY
Butler County Comm Coll (PA)
Cape Fear Comm Coll (NC)
Catawba Valley Comm Coll (NC)
Comm Coll of Allegheny County (PA)
Comm Coll of Denver (CO)
Daytona State Coll (FL)
Delta Coll (MI)
Eastern Arizona Coll (AZ)
Fayetteville Tech Comm Coll (NC)
Forsyth Tech Comm Coll (NC)
Guilford Tech Comm Coll (NC)
Haywood Comm Coll (NC)
Maysville Comm and Tech Coll, Maysville (KY)
North Central Texas Coll (TX)
Northwestern Michigan Coll (MI)
Orange Coast Coll (CA)
Pasadena City Coll (CA)
Pueblo Comm Coll (CO)
Randolph Comm Coll (NC)
Riverland Comm Coll (MN)
San Juan Coll (NM)
State U of New York Coll of Technology at Alfred (NY)
Westmoreland County Comm Coll (PA)

MACHINE TOOL TECHNOLOGY
Alamance Comm Coll (NC)
Amarillo Coll (TX)
Bellingham Tech Coll (WA)
Butler County Comm Coll (PA)
Casper Coll (WY)
Central Maine Comm Coll (ME)
Clark Coll (WA)
Coll of Marin (CA)
Corning Comm Coll (NY)
Des Moines Area Comm Coll (IA)
Elgin Comm Coll (IL)
George C. Wallace Comm Coll (AL)
Greenville Tech Coll (SC)
Gwinnett Tech Coll (GA)
Hawkeye Comm Coll (IA)
H. Councill Trenholm State Tech Coll (AL)
Hennepin Tech Coll (MN)
Horry-Georgetown Tech Coll (SC)
Hutchinson Comm Coll (KS)
Illinois Eastern Comm Colls, Wabash Valley College (IL)
Iowa Central Comm Coll (IA)
Jefferson Coll (MO)
J. F. Drake State Comm and Tech Coll (AL)
Kalamazoo Valley Comm Coll (MI)
Kellogg Comm Coll (MI)
Kennebec Valley Comm Coll (ME)
Lake Area Tech Inst (SD)
Lorain County Comm Coll (OH)
Lower Columbia Coll (WA)
Macomb Comm Coll (MI)
Midlands Tech Coll (SC)
Moraine Park Tech Coll (WI)
Mt. San Antonio Coll (CA)
New Castle School of Trades (PA)
New Mexico Jr Coll (NM)
North Central Texas Coll (TX)
Northern Essex Comm Coll (MA)
Northwest State Comm Coll (OH)
Orange Coast Coll (CA)
Ozarks Tech Comm Coll (MO)
Reading Area Comm Coll (PA)
Renton Tech Coll (WA)
Ridgewater Coll (MN)
San Joaquin Delta Coll (CA)
Sheridan Coll (WY)
Southeastern Comm Coll (IA)
South Louisiana Comm Coll (LA)
Southwestern Illinois Coll (IL)
Southwestern Michigan Coll (MI)
Spartanburg Comm Coll (SC)

State Fair Comm Coll (MO)
Trident Tech Coll (SC)
Western Dakota Tech Inst (SD)
Western Nevada Coll (NV)
Westmoreland County Comm Coll (PA)
Wytheville Comm Coll (VA)
York County Comm Coll (ME)

MAGNETIC RESONANCE IMAGING (MRI) TECHNOLOGY
Mitchell Tech Inst (SD)
Owens Comm Coll, Toledo (OH)

MANAGEMENT INFORMATION SYSTEMS
Anne Arundel Comm Coll (MD)
Burlington County Coll (NJ)
Camden County Coll (NJ)
Carl Albert State Coll (OK)
Carroll Comm Coll (MD)
Cecil Coll (MD)
Central Oregon Comm Coll (OR)
Comm Coll of Allegheny County (PA)
Comm Coll of Aurora (CO)
The Comm Coll of Baltimore County (MD)
Comm Coll of Denver (CO)
Comm Coll of the Air Force (AL)
County Coll of Morris (NJ)
Delaware Tech & Comm Coll, Terry Campus (DE)
Florida SouthWestern State Coll (FL)
Garrett Coll (MD)
Gulf Coast State Coll (FL)
Gwinnett Tech Coll (GA)
Hagerstown Comm Coll (MD)
Haywood Comm Coll (NC)
Hennepin Tech Coll (MN)
Jackson State Comm Coll (TN)
John Tyler Comm Coll (VA)
Kennebec Valley Comm Coll (ME)
Kilgore Coll (TX)
Kirtland Comm Coll (MI)
Lakeland Comm Coll (OH)
Lake Region State Coll (ND)
Lamar Comm Coll (CO)
Manchester Comm Coll (CT)
Miami Dade Coll (FL)
Moraine Valley Comm Coll (IL)
Nassau Comm Coll (NY)
Normandale Comm Coll (MN)
Northern Virginia Comm Coll (VA)
North Hennepin Comm Coll (MN)
Northwestern Michigan Coll (MI)
Oklahoma City Comm Coll (OK)
Ozarks Tech Comm Coll (MO)
Pensacola State Coll (FL)
Raritan Valley Comm Coll (NJ)
San Jacinto Coll District (TX)
South Florida State Coll (FL)
Three Rivers Comm Coll (CT)
Victor Valley Coll (CA)
Western Nevada Coll (NV)

MANAGEMENT INFORMATION SYSTEMS AND SERVICES RELATED
Anne Arundel Comm Coll (MD)
Bowling Green State U-Firelands Coll (OH)
Harrisburg Area Comm Coll (PA)
Hillsborough Comm Coll (FL)
Montgomery County Comm Coll (PA)
Pensacola State Coll (FL)
Seminole State Coll (OK)
Ulster County Comm Coll (NY)

MANAGEMENT SCIENCE
Career Tech Coll, Monroe (LA)
Central Virginia Comm Coll (VA)
Pensacola State Coll (FL)
South Florida State Coll (FL)

MANUFACTURING ENGINEERING
Haywood Comm Coll (NC)
Penn State Fayette, The Eberly Campus (PA)

MANUFACTURING ENGINEERING TECHNOLOGY
Arizona Western Coll (AZ)
Bowling Green State U-Firelands Coll (OH)
Butler County Comm Coll (PA)
Casper Coll (WY)
Central Oregon Comm Coll (OR)
City Colls of Chicago, Olive-Harvey College (IL)

Clark Coll (WA)
Coll of Southern Idaho (ID)
Corning Comm Coll (NY)
Crowder Coll (MO)
Danville Area Comm Coll (IL)
Delta Coll (MI)
Edison Comm Coll (OH)
Fox Valley Tech Coll (WI)
Gadsden State Comm Coll (AL)
Gateway Comm and Tech Coll (KY)
Gulf Coast State Coll (FL)
Hawkeye Comm Coll (IA)
H. Councill Trenholm State Tech Coll (AL)
Hennepin Tech Coll (MN)
Houston Comm Coll (TX)
Hutchinson Comm Coll (KS)
Illinois Eastern Comm Colls, Wabash Valley College (IL)
ITI Tech Coll (LA)
Jefferson Coll (MO)
Lake Area Tech Inst (SD)
Lehigh Carbon Comm Coll (PA)
Macomb Comm Coll (MI)
Miami Dade Coll (FL)
Minnesota West Comm and Tech Coll (MN)
Mohawk Valley Comm Coll (NY)
Normandale Comm Coll (MN)
Northcentral Tech Coll (WI)
North Iowa Area Comm Coll (IA)
Northwest Tech Coll (MN)
Oakton Comm Coll (IL)
Oklahoma City Comm Coll (OK)
Owens Comm Coll, Toledo (OH)
Pueblo Comm Coll (CO)
Quinsigamond Comm Coll (MA)
Raritan Valley Comm Coll (NJ)
Rogue Comm Coll (OR)
St. Clair County Comm Coll (MI)
Schoolcraft Coll (MI)
Sierra Coll (CA)
Southwestern Illinois Coll (IL)
Spartanburg Comm Coll (SC)
State Fair Comm Coll (MO)
Sullivan Coll of Technology and Design (KY)
Tallahassee Comm Coll (FL)
Terra State Comm Coll (OH)
Three Rivers Comm Coll (CT)
Trinidad State Jr Coll (CO)
Truckee Meadows Comm Coll (NV)
U of Cincinnati Clermont Coll (OH)
Vincennes U (IN)
Wayne County Comm Coll District (MI)
Westmoreland County Comm Coll (PA)

MARINE BIOLOGY AND BIOLOGICAL OCEANOGRAPHY
Oregon Coast Comm Coll (OR)
South Florida State Coll (FL)

MARINE MAINTENANCE AND SHIP REPAIR TECHNOLOGY
Cape Fear Comm Coll (NC)
Iowa Lakes Comm Coll (IA)
Kingsborough Comm Coll of the City U of New York (NY)
Lakes Region Comm Coll (NH)
The Landing School (ME)
Northwest School of Wooden Boatbuilding (WA)
Olympic Coll (WA)
Orange Coast Coll (CA)
State Fair Comm Coll (MO)

MARINE SCIENCE/MERCHANT MARINE OFFICER
American Samoa Comm Coll (AS)
San Jacinto Coll District (TX)

MARITIME STUDIES
Northwestern Michigan Coll (MI)

MARKETING/MARKETING MANAGEMENT
Alexandria Tech and Comm Coll (MN)
Alvin Comm Coll (TX)
Antelope Valley Coll (CA)
Arizona Western Coll (AZ)
Arkansas Northeastern Coll (AR)
Austin Comm Coll District (TX)
Bainbridge State Coll (GA)
Bellingham Tech Coll (WA)
Berkeley Coll–Westchester Campus (NY)
Brookhaven Coll (TX)
Camden County Coll (NJ)
Casper Coll (WY)

Cecil Coll (MD)
Cedar Valley Coll (TX)
Central Oregon Comm Coll (OR)
Central Texas Coll (TX)
Century Coll (MN)
Cincinnati State Tech and Comm Coll (OH)
Cleveland Comm Coll (NC)
Coll of Central Florida (FL)
Comm Coll of Allegheny County (PA)
Comm Coll of Rhode Island (RI)
Dakota Coll at Bottineau (ND)
Davis Coll (OH)
Delaware Tech & Comm Coll, Terry Campus (DE)
Delta Coll (MI)
Des Moines Area Comm Coll (IA)
Eastern Idaho Tech Coll (ID)
Edison Comm Coll (OH)
Elgin Comm Coll (IL)
Fayetteville Tech Comm Coll (NC)
FIDM/Fashion Inst of Design & Merchandising, Los Angeles Campus (CA)
FIDM/Fashion Inst of Design & Merchandising, Orange County Campus (CA)
Finger Lakes Comm Coll (NY)
Florida State Coll at Jacksonville (FL)
Fox Valley Tech Coll (WI)
Gateway Tech Coll (WI)
Genesee Comm Coll (NY)
Golden West Coll (CA)
Guam Comm Coll (GU)
Gwinnett Tech Coll (GA)
Harford Comm Coll (MD)
Harper Coll (IL)
Hinds Comm Coll (MS)
Hocking Coll (OH)
Houston Comm Coll (TX)
Iowa Lakes Comm Coll (IA)
Kalamazoo Valley Comm Coll (MI)
Kennebec Valley Comm Coll (ME)
Kingsborough Comm Coll of the City U of New York (NY)
Lake Area Tech Inst (SD)
Lake Land Coll (IL)
Lakeland Comm Coll (OH)
Lamar Comm Coll (CO)
Lenoir Comm Coll (NC)
Lone Star Coll–CyFair (TX)
Lone Star Coll–Kingwood (TX)
Lorain County Comm Coll (OH)
Macomb Comm Coll (MI)
Manchester Comm Coll (CT)
Manor Coll (PA)
Mesa Comm Coll (AZ)
Miami Dade Coll (FL)
Middlesex County Coll (NJ)
Monroe Comm Coll (NY)
Monroe County Comm Coll (MI)
Moraine Park Tech Coll (WI)
Mott Comm Coll (MI)
Mt. San Antonio Coll (CA)
Nassau Comm Coll (NY)
Navarro Coll (TX)
New Mexico Jr Coll (NM)
Normandale Comm Coll (MN)
Northampton Comm Coll (PA)
Northcentral Tech Coll (WI)
Northeastern Jr Coll (CO)
Northern Essex Comm Coll (MA)
North Hennepin Comm Coll (MN)
Northland Comm Coll (MN)
North Shore Comm Coll (MA)
Northwestern Michigan Coll (MI)
Northwest State Comm Coll (OH)
Norwalk Comm Coll (CT)
Oakton Comm Coll (IL)
Ohlone Coll (CA)
Orange Coast Coll (CA)
Pasadena City Coll (CA)
Pasco-Hernando State Coll (FL)
Penn Foster Coll (AZ)
Phoenix Coll (AZ)
Raritan Valley Comm Coll (NJ)
Ridgewater Coll (MN)
Rockland Comm Coll (NY)
Rock Valley Coll (IL)
Rogue Comm Coll (OR)
St. Charles Comm Coll (MO)
St. Clair County Comm Coll (MI)
Salt Lake Comm Coll (UT)
Schoolcraft Coll (MI)
Seminole State Coll of Florida (FL)
South Florida State Coll (FL)
Springfield Tech Comm Coll (MA)
Stark State Coll (OH)
Sullivan County Comm Coll (NY)
Terra State Comm Coll (OH)
Three Rivers Comm Coll (CT)

Trident Tech Coll (SC)
Trinity Valley Comm Coll (TX)
Tulsa Comm Coll (OK)
Tunxis Comm Coll (CT)
Umpqua Comm Coll (OR)
Vincennes U (IN)
Waukesha County Tech Coll (WI)
Westchester Comm Coll (NY)
Western Wyoming Comm Coll (WY)
Williston State Coll (ND)
Wisconsin Indianhead Tech Coll (WI)

MARKETING RELATED
Dakota Coll at Bottineau (ND)
Gateway Tech Coll (WI)

MARKETING RESEARCH
Penn Foster Coll (AZ)

MASONRY
Palomar Coll (CA)
Southwestern Illinois Coll (IL)
State U of New York Coll of Technology at Alfred (NY)
Tallahassee Comm Coll (FL)

MASSAGE THERAPY
Arizona Western Coll (AZ)
Butler County Comm Coll (PA)
Camden County Coll (NJ)
Career Tech Coll, Monroe (LA)
Career Training Academy, Pittsburgh (PA)
Central Oregon Comm Coll (OR)
Chandler-Gilbert Comm Coll (AZ)
Coll of Southern Maryland (MD)
Comm Care Coll (OK)
The Comm Coll of Baltimore County (MD)
Comm Coll of Rhode Island (RI)
Duluth Business U (MN)
Forsyth Tech Comm Coll (NC)
IBMC Coll (CO)
Iowa Lakes Comm Coll (IA)
Miami Dade Coll (FL)
Minnesota State Coll–Southeast Tech (MN)
Niagara County Comm Coll (NY)
Northwestern Coll (IL)
Owens Comm Coll, Toledo (OH)
Phoenix Coll (AZ)
St. Charles Comm Coll (MO)
St. Clair County Comm Coll (MI)
San Joaquin Valley Coll, Salida (CA)
Schoolcraft Coll (MI)
Sheridan Coll (WY)
Southeastern Coll–Greenacres (FL)
South Piedmont Comm Coll (NC)
Southwestern Illinois Coll (IL)
Spencerian Coll (KY)
Spencerian Coll–Lexington (KY)
Springfield Tech Comm Coll (MA)
Trinidad State Jr Coll (CO)
Trocaire Coll (NY)
Vincennes U (IN)
Williston State Coll (ND)

MASS COMMUNICATION/ MEDIA
Amarillo Coll (TX)
Ancilla Coll (IN)
Arizona Western Coll (AZ)
Bunker Hill Comm Coll (MA)
Casper Coll (WY)
Chipola Coll (FL)
Coll of Marin (CA)
Coll of the Desert (CA)
Crowder Coll (MO)
Dean Coll (MA)
Finger Lakes Comm Coll (NY)
Genesee Comm Coll (NY)
Harford Comm Coll (MD)
Harrisburg Area Comm Coll (PA)
Iowa Central Comm Coll (IA)
Iowa Lakes Comm Coll (IA)
James H. Faulkner State Comm Coll (AL)
Laramie County Comm Coll (WY)
Lorain County Comm Coll (OH)
Miami Dade Coll (FL)
Monroe Comm Coll (NY)
Monroe County Comm Coll (MI)
Nassau Comm Coll (NY)
Niagara County Comm Coll (NY)
Northland Comm Coll (MN)
Ohlone Coll (CA)
Oklahoma City Comm Coll (OK)
Orange Coast Coll (CA)
Rockland Comm Coll (NY)
Salt Lake Comm Coll (UT)
Westchester Comm Coll (NY)
Wright State U–Lake Campus (OH)

Wytheville Comm Coll (VA)

MATERIALS ENGINEERING
South Florida State Coll (FL)

MATERIALS SCIENCE
Mt. San Antonio Coll (CA)
Northern Essex Comm Coll (MA)

MATHEMATICS
Allen Comm Coll (KS)
Alvin Comm Coll (TX)
Amarillo Coll (TX)
Anne Arundel Comm Coll (MD)
Antelope Valley Coll (CA)
Arizona Western Coll (AZ)
Austin Comm Coll District (TX)
Bainbridge State Coll (GA)
Borough of Manhattan Comm Coll of the City U of New York (NY)
Bucks County Comm Coll (PA)
Bunker Hill Comm Coll (MA)
Burlington County Coll (NJ)
Butler County Comm Coll (PA)
Carl Albert State Coll (OK)
Casper Coll (WY)
Cecil Coll (MD)
Central Oregon Comm Coll (OR)
Central Texas Coll (TX)
Central Wyoming Coll (WY)
Citrus Coll (CA)
Cochise Coll, Douglas (AZ)
Coll of Central Florida (FL)
Coll of Marin (CA)
Coll of Southern Idaho (ID)
Coll of the Canyons (CA)
Coll of the Desert (CA)
Comm Coll of Allegheny County (PA)
Corning Comm Coll (NY)
Crowder Coll (MO)
Dakota Coll at Bottineau (ND)
Darton State Coll (GA)
Dean Coll (MA)
Eastern Arizona Coll (AZ)
Eastern Wyoming Coll (WY)
Edison Comm Coll (OH)
Finger Lakes Comm Coll (NY)
Frederick Comm Coll (MD)
Genesee Comm Coll (NY)
Golden West Coll (CA)
Great Basin Coll (NV)
Harford Comm Coll (MD)
Harper Coll (IL)
Harrisburg Area Comm Coll (PA)
Hinds Comm Coll (MS)
Housatonic Comm Coll (CT)
Hutchinson Comm Coll (KS)
Iowa Lakes Comm Coll (IA)
Jefferson Comm Coll (NY)
J. Sargeant Reynolds Comm Coll (VA)
Kankakee Comm Coll (IL)
Kilgore Coll (TX)
Kingsborough Comm Coll of the City U of New York (NY)
Laramie County Comm Coll (WY)
Lehigh Carbon Comm Coll (PA)
Lorain County Comm Coll (OH)
Luzerne County Comm Coll (PA)
Macomb Comm Coll (MI)
Mesa Comm Coll (AZ)
Miami Dade Coll (FL)
Minneapolis Comm and Tech Coll (MN)
MiraCosta Coll (CA)
Mohave Comm Coll (AZ)
Monroe Comm Coll (NY)
Monroe County Comm Coll (MI)
Montgomery County Comm Coll (PA)
Mt. San Antonio Coll (CA)
Nassau Comm Coll (NY)
Navarro Coll (TX)
New Mexico Jr Coll (NM)
Niagara County Comm Coll (NY)
Northampton Comm Coll (PA)
Northeastern Jr Coll (CO)
North Hennepin Comm Coll (MN)
Northwest Coll (WY)
Northwestern Michigan Coll (MI)
Ohlone Coll (CA)
Oklahoma City Comm Coll (OK)
Orange Coast Coll (CA)
Otero Jr Coll (CO)
Palomar Coll (CA)
Paris Jr Coll (TX)
Pasadena City Coll (CA)
Pensacola State Coll (FL)
Potomac State Coll of West Virginia U (WV)
Roane State Comm Coll (TN)
Rockland Comm Coll (NY)
St. Charles Comm Coll (MO)

St. Philip's Coll (TX)
San Diego Miramar Coll (CA)
San Jacinto Coll District (TX)
San Joaquin Delta Coll (CA)
San Juan Coll (NM)
Scottsdale Comm Coll (AZ)
Seminole State Coll (OK)
Sheridan Coll (WY)
Sierra Coll (CA)
Southern U at Shreveport (LA)
South Florida State Coll (FL)
Springfield Tech Comm Coll (MA)
Sullivan County Comm Coll (NY)
Terra State Comm Coll (OH)
Texas State Tech Coll Harlingen (TX)
Trinity Valley Comm Coll (TX)
Truckee Meadows Comm Coll (NV)
Tulsa Comm Coll (OK)
Tyler Jr Coll (TX)
Umpqua Comm Coll (OR)
Victor Valley Coll (CA)
Vincennes U (IN)
Wenatchee Valley Coll (WA)
Western Nevada Coll (NV)
Western Wyoming Comm Coll (WY)

MATHEMATICS AND COMPUTER SCIENCE
Crowder Coll (MO)

MATHEMATICS AND STATISTICS RELATED
Georgia Highlands Coll (GA)

MATHEMATICS RELATED
Cayuga County Comm Coll (NY)
Corning Comm Coll (NY)
Genesee Comm Coll (NY)

MATHEMATICS TEACHER EDUCATION
Anne Arundel Comm Coll (MD)
Bucks County Comm Coll (PA)
Carroll Comm Coll (MD)
Chesapeake Coll (MD)
The Comm Coll of Baltimore County (MD)
Darton State Coll (GA)
Delaware Tech & Comm Coll, Terry Campus (DE)
Eastern Wyoming Coll (WY)
Frederick Comm Coll (MD)
Harford Comm Coll (MD)
Highland Comm Coll (IL)
Kankakee Comm Coll (IL)
Kaskaskia Coll (IL)
Montgomery Coll (MD)
Moraine Valley Comm Coll (IL)
South Florida State Coll (FL)
Southwestern Illinois Coll (IL)
Ulster County Comm Coll (NY)
Vincennes U (IN)

MECHANICAL DRAFTING AND CAD/CADD
Alexandria Tech and Comm Coll (MN)
Anoka Tech Coll (MN)
Butler County Comm Coll (PA)
Cleveland Comm Coll (NC)
Commonwealth Tech Inst (PA)
Comm Coll of Allegheny County (PA)
Corning Comm Coll (NY)
Des Moines Area Comm Coll (IA)
Edison Comm Coll (OH)
Fox Valley Tech Coll (WI)
Gateway Tech Coll (WI)
Greenville Tech Coll (SC)
Hutchinson Comm Coll (KS)
Island Drafting and Tech Inst (NY)
Macomb Comm Coll (MI)
Midlands Tech Coll (SC)
Moraine Park Tech Coll (WI)
Northcentral Tech Coll (WI)
North Iowa Area Comm Coll (IA)
Ozarks Tech Comm Coll (MO)
Ridgewater Coll (MN)
Sierra Coll (CA)
Southwestern Illinois Coll (IL)
Sullivan Coll of Technology and Design (KY)
Vincennes U (IN)
Waukesha County Tech Coll (WI)
Western Iowa Tech Comm Coll (IA)
Westmoreland County Comm Coll (PA)

MECHANICAL ENGINEERING
Cayuga County Comm Coll (NY)
Fiorello H. LaGuardia Comm Coll of the City U of New York (NY)
Kilgore Coll (TX)

Lone Star Coll–North Harris (TX)
Northwest State Comm Coll (OH)
Pasadena City Coll (CA)
Potomac State Coll of West Virginia U (WV)
St. Charles Comm Coll (MO)
South Florida State Coll (FL)

MECHANICAL ENGINEERING/ MECHANICAL TECHNOLOGY
Alamance Comm Coll (NC)
Benjamin Franklin Inst of Technology (MA)
Bowling Green State U-Firelands Coll (OH)
Camden County Coll (NJ)
Cape Fear Comm Coll (NC)
Catawba Valley Comm Coll (NC)
Cayuga County Comm Coll (NY)
Cincinnati State Tech and Comm Coll (OH)
Citrus Coll (CA)
Corning Comm Coll (NY)
County Coll of Morris (NJ)
Delta Coll (MI)
Eastern Gateway Comm Coll (OH)
Edison Comm Coll (OH)
Erie Comm Coll, North Campus (NY)
Finger Lakes Comm Coll (NY)
Forsyth Tech Comm Coll (NC)
Gateway Comm Coll (CT)
Greenville Tech Coll (SC)
Guilford Tech Comm Coll (NC)
Hagerstown Comm Coll (MD)
Harrisburg Area Comm Coll (PA)
Haywood Comm Coll (NC)
Illinois Eastern Comm Colls, Lincoln Trail College (IL)
Jamestown Comm Coll (NY)
Kalamazoo Valley Comm Coll (MI)
Kent State U at Trumbull (OH)
Kent State U at Tuscarawas (OH)
Lakeland Comm Coll (OH)
Lehigh Carbon Comm Coll (PA)
Los Angeles Trade-Tech Coll (CA)
Macomb Comm Coll (MI)
Massachusetts Bay Comm Coll (MA)
Middlesex County Coll (NJ)
Midlands Tech Coll (SC)
Mohawk Valley Comm Coll (NY)
Monroe Comm Coll (NY)
Montgomery County Comm Coll (PA)
Moraine Valley Comm Coll (IL)
Mott Comm Coll (MI)
Northwest State Comm Coll (OH)
Oakton Comm Coll (IL)
Oklahoma State U Inst of Technology (OK)
Penn State DuBois (PA)
Penn State Shenango (PA)
Queensborough Comm Coll of the City U of New York (NY)
Richmond Comm Coll (NC)
San Joaquin Delta Coll (CA)
Southeastern Comm Coll (IA)
Southern U at Shreveport (LA)
South Piedmont Comm Coll (NC)
Spartanburg Comm Coll (SC)
Springfield Tech Comm Coll (MA)
Stark State Coll (OH)
State U of New York Coll of Technology at Alfred (NY)
Sullivan Coll of Technology and Design (KY)
Terra State Comm Coll (OH)
Three Rivers Comm Coll (CT)
Trident Tech Coll (SC)
Vincennes U (IN)
Virginia Western Comm Coll (VA)
Westchester Comm Coll (NY)
Westmoreland County Comm Coll (PA)
Wytheville Comm Coll (VA)

MECHANICAL ENGINEERING TECHNOLOGIES RELATED
Corning Comm Coll (NY)
Jefferson Comm Coll (NY)
John Tyler Comm Coll (VA)
Middlesex County Coll (NJ)
Mohawk Valley Comm Coll (NY)
Moraine Park Tech Coll (WI)
Terra State Comm Coll (OH)

MECHANIC AND REPAIR TECHNOLOGIES RELATED
Chandler-Gilbert Comm Coll (AZ)
Cloud County Comm Coll (KS)
Corning Comm Coll (NY)
Greenville Tech Coll (SC)

Laramie County Comm Coll (WY)
Macomb Comm Coll (MI)
Oklahoma State U Inst of Technology (OK)
State Fair Comm Coll (MO)

MECHANICS AND REPAIR
Corning Comm Coll (NY)
Kalamazoo Valley Comm Coll (MI)
Owensboro Comm and Tech Coll (KY)
Rogue Comm Coll (OR)
Western Wyoming Comm Coll (WY)

MECHATRONICS, ROBOTICS, AND AUTOMATION ENGINEERING
Anne Arundel Comm Coll (MD)
Cochise Coll, Douglas (AZ)
Harrisburg Area Comm Coll (PA)
Randolph Comm Coll (NC)
Westmoreland County Comm Coll (PA)

MEDICAL ADMINISTRATIVE ASSISTANT AND MEDICAL SECRETARY
Alamance Comm Coll (NC)
Alexandria Tech and Comm Coll (MN)
Alvin Comm Coll (TX)
Amarillo Coll (TX)
Anne Arundel Comm Coll (MD)
Anoka Tech Coll (MN)
Antelope Valley Coll (CA)
Bunker Hill Comm Coll (MA)
Century Coll (MN)
Clark Coll (WA)
Coll of Marin (CA)
Comm Coll of Allegheny County (PA)
The Comm Coll of Baltimore County (MD)
Comm Coll of Philadelphia (PA)
Comm Coll of Rhode Island (RI)
Crowder Coll (MO)
Dabney S. Lancaster Comm Coll (VA)
Dakota Coll at Bottineau (ND)
Danville Area Comm Coll (IL)
Davis Coll (OH)
Daytona State Coll (FL)
Delta Coll (MI)
Des Moines Area Comm Coll (IA)
Eastern Gateway Comm Coll (OH)
Edison Comm Coll (OH)
Elizabethtown Comm and Tech Coll, Elizabethtown (KY)
Erie Comm Coll, North Campus (NY)
Frederick Comm Coll (MD)
Gateway Comm Coll (CT)
Genesee Comm Coll (NY)
Grand Rapids Comm Coll (MI)
Gulf Coast State Coll (FL)
Halifax Comm Coll (NC)
Harper Coll (IL)
Hawkeye Comm Coll (IA)
Hennepin Tech Coll (MN)
Hocking Coll (OH)
Howard Comm Coll (MD)
Humacao Comm Coll (PR)
IBMC Coll (CO)
Illinois Eastern Comm Colls, Olney Central College (IL)
Iowa Lakes Comm Coll (IA)
Jefferson Coll (MO)
Jefferson Comm Coll (NY)
Kellogg Comm Coll (MI)
Kennebec Valley Comm Coll (ME)
Kirtland Comm Coll (MI)
Lake Land Coll (IL)
Lenoir Comm Coll (NC)
Lower Columbia Coll (WA)
Luzerne County Comm Coll (PA)
Manchester Comm Coll (CT)
Mesa Comm Coll (AZ)
Minnesota State Coll–Southeast Tech (MN)
Minnesota West Comm and Tech Coll (MN)
Monroe County Comm Coll (MI)
Montcalm Comm Coll (MI)
Mt. San Antonio Coll (CA)
Nassau Comm Coll (NY)
New Mexico Jr Coll (NM)
Northampton Comm Coll (PA)
Northeastern Jr Coll (CO)
Northern Essex Comm Coll (MA)
North Iowa Area Comm Coll (IA)
Northland Comm Coll (MN)
North Shore Comm Coll (MA)

Northwest State Comm Coll (OH)
Northwest Tech Coll (MN)
Ohio Business Coll, Sandusky (OH)
Ohlone Coll (CA)
Orange Coast Coll (CA)
Otero Jr Coll (CO)
Owensboro Comm and Tech Coll (KY)
Owens Comm Coll, Toledo (OH)
Palomar Coll (CA)
Piedmont Comm Coll (NC)
Quinsigamond Comm Coll (MA)
Reading Area Comm Coll (PA)
Renton Tech Coll (WA)
Richland Comm Coll (IL)
Ridgewater Coll (MN)
Riverland Comm Coll (MN)
Roane State Comm Coll (TN)
St. Charles Comm Coll (MO)
St. Clair County Comm Coll (MI)
St. Philip's Coll (TX)
San Joaquin Valley Coll, Visalia (CA)
Scottsdale Comm Coll (AZ)
Shawnee Comm Coll (IL)
Somerset Comm Coll (KY)
South Hills School of Business & Technology, State College (PA)
Springfield Tech Comm Coll (MA)
State Fair Comm Coll (MO)
Terra State Comm Coll (OH)
Trident Tech Coll (SC)
Tunxis Comm Coll (CT)
Tyler Jr Coll (TX)
Ultimate Medical Academy Online (FL)
Umpqua Comm Coll (OR)
Wenatchee Valley Coll (WA)
Western Iowa Tech Comm Coll (IA)
Western Wyoming Comm Coll (WY)
Whatcom Comm Coll (WA)
Wisconsin Indianhead Tech Coll (WI)
Wytheville Comm Coll (VA)

MEDICAL/CLINICAL ASSISTANT
Alamance Comm Coll (NC)
Anoka Tech Coll (MN)
Big Bend Comm Coll (WA)
Blue Ridge Comm and Tech Coll (WV)
Bossier Parish Comm Coll (LA)
Bradford School (OH)
Bradford School (PA)
Bucks County Comm Coll (PA)
Ca&nnada Coll (CA)
Career Tech Coll, Monroe (LA)
Career Training Academy, Pittsburgh (PA)
Carteret Comm Coll (NC)
Central Maine Comm Coll (ME)
Central Oregon Comm Coll (OR)
Central Virginia Comm Coll (VA)
Clark Coll (WA)
Cleveland Comm Coll (NC)
Coll of Marin (CA)
The Coll of Westchester (NY)
Columbia-Greene Comm Coll (NY)
Comm Care Coll (OK)
Comm Coll of Allegheny County (PA)
Dakota Coll at Bottineau (ND)
Davis Coll (OH)
Delaware Tech & Comm Coll, Terry Campus (DE)
Des Moines Area Comm Coll (IA)
Duluth Business U (MN)
Eastern Gateway Comm Coll (OH)
Eastern Idaho Tech Coll (ID)
Edison Comm Coll (OH)
El Centro Coll (TX)
Forrest Coll (SC)
Forsyth Tech Comm Coll (NC)
Fox Coll (IL)
Frederick Comm Coll (MD)
George C. Wallace Comm Coll (AL)
Goodwin Coll (CT)
Great Falls Coll Montana State U (MT)
Guam Comm Coll (GU)
Guilford Tech Comm Coll (NC)
Gwinnett Tech Coll (GA)
Harper Coll (IL)
Harrisburg Area Comm Coll (PA)
Haywood Comm Coll (NC)
H. Councill Trenholm State Tech Coll (AL)
Highland Comm Coll (IL)
Hinds Comm Coll (MS)
Hocking Coll (OH)
Hudson County Comm Coll (NJ)
IBMC Coll (CO)

Illinois Eastern Comm Colls, Lincoln Trail College (IL)
International Business Coll, Indianapolis (IN)
Iowa Central Comm Coll (IA)
Iowa Lakes Comm Coll (IA)
James Sprunt Comm Coll (NC)
Jamestown Business Coll (NY)
J. F. Drake State Comm and Tech Coll (AL)
Johnston Comm Coll (NC)
Kankakee Comm Coll (IL)
Kennebec Valley Comm Coll (ME)
King's Coll (NC)
Kirtland Comm Coll (MI)
Lake Area Tech Inst (SD)
Lehigh Carbon Comm Coll (PA)
Lenoir Comm Coll (NC)
Lower Columbia Coll (WA)
Macomb Comm Coll (MI)
Miami Dade Coll (FL)
Middlesex Comm Coll (MA)
Midlands Tech Coll (SC)
Minneapolis Business Coll (MN)
Minnesota West Comm and Tech Coll (MN)
MiraCosta Coll (CA)
Mitchell Tech Inst (SD)
Mohave Comm Coll (AZ)
Mohawk Valley Comm Coll (NY)
Montgomery Comm Coll (NC)
Montgomery County Comm Coll (PA)
Mountain State Coll (WV)
Mount Wachusett Comm Coll (MA)
New Mexico Jr Coll (NM)
Niagara County Comm Coll (NY)
North Iowa Area Comm Coll (IA)
Northwestern Coll (IL)
Northwestern Michigan Coll (MI)
Northwest-Shoals Comm Coll (AL)
Northwest State Comm Coll (OH)
Ohlone Coll (CA)
Oklahoma City Comm Coll (OK)
Olympic Coll (WA)
Orange Coast Coll (CA)
Panola Coll (TX)
Pasadena City Coll (CA)
Penn Foster Coll (AZ)
Pennsylvania Highlands Comm Coll (PA)
Phoenix Coll (AZ)
Potomac State Coll of West Virginia U (WV)
Randolph Comm Coll (NC)
Raritan Valley Comm Coll (NJ)
Renton Tech Coll (WA)
Richmond Comm Coll (NC)
Ridgewater Coll (MN)
St. Clair County Comm Coll (MI)
St. Vincent's Coll (CT)
Salt Lake Comm Coll (UT)
San Joaquin Valley Coll, Bakersfield (CA)
San Joaquin Valley Coll, Fresno (CA)
San Joaquin Valley Coll, Hanford (CA)
San Joaquin Valley Coll, Hesperia (CA)
San Joaquin Valley Coll, Lancaster (CA)
San Joaquin Valley Coll, Ontario (CA)
San Joaquin Valley Coll, Salida (CA)
San Joaquin Valley Coll, Temecula (CA)
San Joaquin Valley Coll, Visalia (CA)
San Joaquin Valley Coll–Online (CA)
Southeastern Coll–Greenacres (FL)
Southeastern Comm Coll (IA)
Southern Tech Coll, Orlando (FL)
South Hills School of Business & Technology, State College (PA)
South Piedmont Comm Coll (NC)
Southwestern Illinois Coll (IL)
Southwestern Michigan Coll (MI)
Springfield Tech Comm Coll (MA)
Stark State Coll (OH)
Sullivan County Comm Coll (NY)
Terra State Comm Coll (OH)
Texas State Tech Coll Harlingen (TX)
Trocaire Coll (NY)
Wenatchee Valley Coll (WA)
Western Dakota Tech Inst (SD)
Western Iowa Tech Comm Coll (IA)
Western Wyoming Comm Coll (WY)
Westmoreland County Comm Coll (PA)
West Virginia Jr Coll–Bridgeport (WV)
Whatcom Comm Coll (WA)

Wood Tobe–Coburn School (NY)
York County Comm Coll (ME)

MEDICAL/HEALTH MANAGEMENT AND CLINICAL ASSISTANT
CollAmerica–Flagstaff (AZ)
Owens Comm Coll, Toledo (OH)
Terra State Comm Coll (OH)

MEDICAL INFORMATICS
The Comm Coll of Baltimore County (MD)
Dyersburg State Comm Coll (TN)
Volunteer State Comm Coll (TN)

MEDICAL INSURANCE CODING
Bucks County Comm Coll (PA)
Butler County Comm Coll (PA)
Career Training Academy, Pittsburgh (PA)
Collin County Comm Coll District (TX)
Comm Care Coll (OK)
Dakota Coll at Bottineau (ND)
Davis Coll (OH)
Fountainhead Coll of Technology (TN)
Goodwin Coll (CT)
Hawkeye Comm Coll (IA)
Laramie County Comm Coll (WY)
Minnesota West Comm and Tech Coll (MN)
Paris Jr Coll (TX)
Salem Comm Coll (NJ)
Southeastern Coll–Greenacres (FL)
Spencerian Coll (KY)
Springfield Tech Comm Coll (MA)
Terra State Comm Coll (OH)

MEDICAL INSURANCE/ MEDICAL BILLING
Goodwin Coll (CT)
Great Falls Coll Montana State U (MT)
Northcentral Tech Coll (WI)
Pasadena City Coll (CA)
San Joaquin Valley Coll, Bakersfield (CA)
San Joaquin Valley Coll, Hanford (CA)
San Joaquin Valley Coll, Hesperia (CA)
Southeastern Coll–Greenacres (FL)
Southern Tech Coll, Orlando (FL)
Ultimate Medical Academy Online (FL)

MEDICAL MICROBIOLOGY AND BACTERIOLOGY
South Florida State Coll (FL)

MEDICAL OFFICE ASSISTANT
Butler County Comm Coll (PA)
Cambria-Rowe Business Coll, Indiana (PA)
Central Wyoming Coll (WY)
Cincinnati State Tech and Comm Coll (OH)
Commonwealth Tech Inst (PA)
Dakota Coll at Bottineau (ND)
Front Range Comm Coll (CO)
Harford Comm Coll (MD)
Iowa Lakes Comm Coll (IA)
Kankakee Comm Coll (IL)
Mitchell Tech Inst (SD)
Pasadena City Coll (CA)
Phoenix Coll (AZ)
San Joaquin Valley Coll, Fresno (CA)
San Joaquin Valley Coll, Lancaster (CA)
San Joaquin Valley Coll, Ontario (CA)
San Joaquin Valley Coll, Salida (CA)
San Joaquin Valley Coll, Temecula (CA)
San Joaquin Valley Coll, Visalia (CA)
Southwestern Illinois Coll (IL)
Terra State Comm Coll (OH)
Trinidad State Jr Coll (CO)
Western Wyoming Comm Coll (WY)
Westmoreland County Comm Coll (PA)
White Mountains Comm Coll (NH)

MEDICAL OFFICE COMPUTER SPECIALIST
Iowa Lakes Comm Coll (IA)
Lamar Comm Coll (CO)
Normandale Comm Coll (MN)
Richmond Comm Coll (NC)

Rogue Comm Coll (OR)
Western Wyoming Comm Coll (WY)

MEDICAL OFFICE MANAGEMENT
Arapahoe Comm Coll (CO)
Big Bend Comm Coll (WA)
Cape Fear Comm Coll (NC)
Career Tech Coll, Monroe (LA)
Catawba Valley Comm Coll (NC)
Cleveland Comm Coll (NC)
Fayetteville Tech Comm Coll (NC)
Forrest Coll (SC)
Forsyth Tech Comm Coll (NC)
Fox Valley Tech Coll (WI)
Guilford Tech Comm Coll (NC)
Johnston Comm Coll (NC)
Long Island Business Inst (NY)
Norwalk Comm Coll (CT)
Pennsylvania Inst of Technology (PA)
Pueblo Comm Coll (CO)
Randolph Comm Coll (NC)
San Joaquin Valley Coll–Online (CA)
South Piedmont Comm Coll (NC)
Spencerian Coll–Lexington (KY)
U of Arkansas Comm Coll at Batesville (AR)
U of Arkansas Comm Coll at Hope (AR)
Western Iowa Tech Comm Coll (IA)
West Virginia Jr Coll–Bridgeport (WV)

MEDICAL RADIOLOGIC TECHNOLOGY
Anne Arundel Comm Coll (MD)
Bellingham Tech Coll (WA)
Bowling Green State U–Firelands Coll (OH)
Bunker Hill Comm Coll (MA)
Cape Fear Comm Coll (NC)
Catawba Valley Comm Coll (NC)
Chesapeake Coll (MD)
Coll of Central Florida (FL)
Coll of Southern Idaho (ID)
Comm Coll of Allegheny County (PA)
The Comm Coll of Baltimore County (MD)
Comm Coll of Philadelphia (PA)
Comm Coll of the Air Force (AL)
Cumberland County Coll (NJ)
Delgado Comm Coll (LA)
Delta Coll (MI)
Dunwoody Coll of Technology (MN)
El Centro Coll (TX)
Elizabethtown Comm and Tech Coll, Elizabethtown (KY)
Erie Comm Coll (NY)
Fiorello H. LaGuardia Comm Coll of the City U of New York (NY)
Florida SouthWestern State Coll (FL)
Florida State Coll at Jacksonville (FL)
Forsyth Tech Comm Coll (NC)
George C. Wallace Comm Coll (AL)
Greenville Tech Coll (SC)
Gulf Coast State Coll (FL)
Gwinnett Tech Coll (GA)
Hagerstown Comm Coll (MD)
Hillsborough Comm Coll (FL)
Holyoke Comm Coll (MA)
Hutchinson Comm Coll (KS)
Illinois Eastern Comm Colls, Olney Central College (IL)
Jackson State Comm Coll (TN)
Kellogg Comm Coll (MI)
Kent State U at Ashtabula (OH)
Kent State U at Salem (OH)
Kilgore Coll (TX)
Lakeland Comm Coll (OH)
Lone Star Coll–CyFair (TX)
Massachusetts Bay Comm Coll (MA)
Miami Dade Coll (FL)
Middlesex Comm Coll (MA)
Middlesex County Coll (NJ)
Midlands Tech Coll (SC)
Mitchell Tech Inst (SD)
Mohawk Valley Comm Coll (NY)
Montgomery Coll (MD)
Montgomery County Comm Coll (PA)
Moraine Park Tech Coll (WI)
Mott Comm Coll (MI)
Nassau Comm Coll (NY)
Niagara County Comm Coll (NY)
Northcentral Tech Coll (WI)
Northern Virginia Comm Coll (VA)
North Shore Comm Coll (MA)
Owensboro Comm and Tech Coll (KY)
Owens Comm Coll, Toledo (OH)
Pensacola State Coll (FL)
Riverland Comm Coll (MN)
St. Clair County Comm Coll (MI)

St. Philip's Coll (TX)
St. Vincent's Coll (CT)
Salt Lake Comm Coll (UT)
Somerset Comm Coll (KY)
Southern U at Shreveport (LA)
South Florida State Coll (FL)
Spartanburg Comm Coll (SC)
Tallahassee Comm Coll (FL)
Tech Coll of the Lowcountry (SC)
Tulsa Comm Coll (OK)
Vincennes U (IN)
Volunteer State Comm Coll (TN)
Waukesha County Tech Coll (WI)
Wor-Wic Comm Coll (MD)

MEDICAL RECEPTION
Iowa Lakes Comm Coll (IA)

MEDICAL TRANSCRIPTION
El Centro Coll (TX)
Great Falls Coll Montana State U (MT)
Iowa Lakes Comm Coll (IA)
Mountain State Coll (WV)
Northern Essex Comm Coll (MA)
Western Dakota Tech Inst (SD)

MEDIUM/HEAVY VEHICLE AND TRUCK TECHNOLOGY
Edison Comm Coll (OH)
Hennepin Tech Coll (MN)

MEETING AND EVENT PLANNING
Fox Valley Tech Coll (WI)
Northampton Comm Coll (PA)
Raritan Valley Comm Coll (NJ)

MENTAL AND SOCIAL HEALTH SERVICES AND ALLIED PROFESSIONS RELATED
Chesapeake Coll (MD)
Coll of Southern Maryland (MD)
Gateway Tech Coll (WI)
John Tyler Comm Coll (VA)
J. Sargeant Reynolds Comm Coll (VA)
Kennebec Valley Comm Coll (ME)
Montgomery Comm Coll (NC)
Northcentral Tech Coll (WI)
Northern Virginia Comm Coll (VA)
Richmond Comm Coll (NC)
South Piedmont Comm Coll (NC)
Southwest Virginia Comm Coll (VA)
Waukesha County Tech Coll (WI)

MENTAL HEALTH COUNSELING
Alvin Comm Coll (TX)
Comm Coll of Denver (CO)
Comm Coll of Philadelphia (PA)
Comm Coll of Rhode Island (RI)
Comm Coll of the Air Force (AL)
Gateway Comm Coll (CT)
Housatonic Comm Coll (CT)
Kingsborough Comm Coll of the City U of New York (NY)
Macomb Comm Coll (MI)
Mt. San Antonio Coll (CA)
Northern Essex Comm Coll (MA)
North Shore Comm Coll (MA)
Southern U at Shreveport (LA)
Truckee Meadows Comm Coll (NV)
Virginia Western Comm Coll (VA)

MERCHANDISING
Delta Coll (MI)
North Central Texas Coll (TX)

MERCHANDISING, SALES, AND MARKETING OPERATIONS RELATED (GENERAL)
Iowa Lakes Comm Coll (IA)
Lake Region State Coll (ND)
Northcentral Tech Coll (WI)

MERCHANDISING, SALES, AND MARKETING OPERATIONS RELATED (SPECIALIZED)
Middlesex County Coll (NJ)

METAL AND JEWELRY ARTS
Fashion Inst of Technology (NY)
FIDM/Fashion Inst of Design & Merchandising, Los Angeles Campus (CA)
Palomar Coll (CA)
Paris Jr Coll (TX)

METAL FABRICATOR
Waukesha County Tech Coll (WI)

METALLURGICAL TECHNOLOGY
Arkansas Northeastern Coll (AR)
Comm Coll of the Air Force (AL)
Kilgore Coll (TX)
Macomb Comm Coll (MI)
Penn State DuBois (PA)
Penn State Fayette, The Eberly Campus (PA)
Penn State Shenango (PA)
Schoolcraft Coll (MI)

MIDDLE SCHOOL EDUCATION
Alvin Comm Coll (TX)
Arkansas Northeastern Coll (AR)
Austin Comm Coll District (TX)
Collin County Comm Coll District (TX)
Darton State Coll (GA)
Delaware Tech & Comm Coll, Terry Campus (DE)
Miami Dade Coll (FL)
Northampton Comm Coll (PA)
Panola Coll (TX)
South Florida State Coll (FL)
Tyler Jr Coll (TX)
U of Cincinnati Clermont Coll (OH)

MINING TECHNOLOGY
Casper Coll (WY)
Eastern Arizona Coll (AZ)
Illinois Eastern Comm Colls, Wabash Valley College (IL)
Sheridan Coll (WY)
Western Wyoming Comm Coll (WY)

MODERN LANGUAGES
Amarillo Coll (TX)
Citrus Coll (CA)
Otero Jr Coll (CO)
Potomac State Coll of West Virginia U (WV)
Tyler Jr Coll (TX)

MORTUARY SCIENCE AND EMBALMING
Gupton-Jones Coll of Funeral Service (GA)
Wayne County Comm Coll District (MI)

MOTORCYCLE MAINTENANCE AND REPAIR TECHNOLOGY
Iowa Lakes Comm Coll (IA)
Western Iowa Tech Comm Coll (IA)

MOVEMENT AND MIND-BODY THERAPIES AND EDUCATION RELATED
Moraine Valley Comm Coll (IL)

MULTI/INTERDISCIPLINARY STUDIES RELATED
Alexandria Tech and Comm Coll (MN)
Anne Arundel Comm Coll (MD)
Anoka-Ramsey Comm Coll (MN)
Anoka-Ramsey Comm Coll, Cambridge Campus (MN)
Arkansas Northeastern Coll (AR)
Blue Ridge Comm and Tech Coll (WV)
Bucks County Comm Coll (PA)
Carroll Comm Coll (MD)
Cedar Valley Coll (TX)
Central Maine Comm Coll (ME)
Century Coll (MN)
Cincinnati State Tech and Comm Coll (OH)
Coll of Southern Maryland (MD)
Coll of the Desert (CA)
County Coll of Morris (NJ)
Eastern Arizona Coll (AZ)
Fox Valley Tech Coll (WI)
Gateway Tech Coll (WI)
Greenville Tech Coll (SC)
Hawkeye Comm Coll (IA)
Hopkinsville Comm Coll (KY)
J. F. Drake State Comm and Tech Coll (AL)
Kennebec Valley Comm Coll (ME)
Midlands Tech Coll (SC)
Minnesota State Coll–Southeast Tech (MN)
Moraine Park Tech Coll (WI)
Normandale Comm Coll (MN)
Northcentral Tech Coll (WI)
North Hennepin Comm Coll (MN)
North Iowa Area Comm Coll (IA)
Northwest-Shoals Comm Coll (AL)
Oklahoma City Comm Coll (OK)

Oklahoma State U Inst of Technology (OK)
Raritan Valley Comm Coll (NJ)
Sheridan Coll (WY)
Somerset Comm Coll (KY)
South Florida State Coll (FL)
Spartanburg Comm Coll (SC)
Tulsa Comm Coll (OK)
U of Arkansas Comm Coll at Batesville (AR)
U of Arkansas Comm Coll at Hope (AR)
U of Cincinnati Clermont Coll (OH)
Waukesha County Tech Comm Coll (WI)
Western Iowa Tech Comm Coll (IA)
Williston State Coll (ND)
Wisconsin Indianhead Tech Coll (WI)
York County Comm Coll (ME)

MUSEUM STUDIES
Casper Coll (WY)

MUSIC
Allen Comm Coll (KS)
Alvin Comm Coll (TX)
Amarillo Coll (TX)
American Samoa Comm Coll (AS)
Anoka-Ramsey Comm Coll (MN)
Anoka-Ramsey Comm Coll, Cambridge Campus (MN)
Antelope Valley Coll (CA)
Arizona Western Coll (AZ)
Austin Comm Coll District (TX)
Bossier Parish Comm Coll (LA)
Brookhaven Coll (TX)
Bucks County Comm Coll (PA)
Bunker Hill Comm Coll (MA)
Burlington County Coll (NJ)
Ca&nnada Coll (CA)
Carroll Comm Coll (MD)
Casper Coll (WY)
Central Texas Coll (TX)
Central Wyoming Coll (WY)
Century Coll (MN)
Citrus Coll (CA)
Cochise Coll, Douglas (AZ)
Coll of Central Florida (FL)
Coll of Marin (CA)
Coll of Southern Idaho (ID)
Coll of the Canyons (CA)
Coll of the Desert (CA)
Collin County Comm Coll District (TX)
Comm Coll of Allegheny County (PA)
Comm Coll of Philadelphia (PA)
Comm Coll of Rhode Island (RI)
County Coll of Morris (NJ)
Crowder Coll (MO)
Darton State Coll (GA)
Eastern Arizona Coll (AZ)
Eastern Wyoming Coll (WY)
Elgin Comm Coll (IL)
Finger Lakes Comm Coll (NY)
Georgia Highlands Coll (GA)
Golden West Coll (CA)
Grand Rapids Comm Coll (MI)
Harford Comm Coll (MD)
Harper Coll (IL)
Hinds Comm Coll (MS)
Holyoke Comm Coll (MA)
Howard Comm Coll (MD)
Iowa Lakes Comm Coll (IA)
Jamestown Comm Coll (NY)
Kaskaskia Coll (IL)
Kilgore Coll (TX)
Kingsborough Comm Coll of the City U of New York (NY)
Laramie County Comm Coll (WY)
Lone Star Coll–CyFair (TX)
Lone Star Coll–Kingwood (TX)
Lone Star Coll–Montgomery (TX)
Lone Star Coll–North Harris (TX)
Lone Star Coll–Tomball (TX)
Lorain County Comm Coll (OH)
Manchester Comm Coll (CT)
McHenry County Coll (IL)
Mesa Comm Coll (AZ)
Miami Dade Coll (FL)
MiraCosta Coll (CA)
Monroe Comm Coll (NY)
Moraine Valley Comm Coll (IL)
Mt. San Antonio Coll (CA)
Navarro Coll (TX)
New Mexico Jr Coll (NM)
Niagara County Comm Coll (NY)
Normandale Comm Coll (MN)
Northeastern Jr Coll (CO)
Northern Essex Comm Coll (MA)
North Hennepin Comm Coll (MN)
Northwest Coll (WY)
Northwestern Michigan Coll (MI)
Oakton Comm Coll (IL)

Ohlone Coll (CA)
Oklahoma City Comm Coll (OK)
Orange Coast Coll (CA)
Palomar Coll (CA)
Panola Coll (TX)
Paris Jr Coll (TX)
Pensacola State Coll (FL)
Raritan Valley Comm Coll (NJ)
St. Philip's Coll (TX)
Salt Lake Comm Coll (UT)
San Jacinto Coll District (TX)
San Joaquin Delta Coll (CA)
Sheridan Coll (WY)
Sierra Coll (CA)
South Florida State Coll (FL)
Southwestern Illinois Coll (IL)
Terra State Comm Coll (OH)
Trinity Valley Comm Coll (TX)
Truckee Meadows Comm Coll (NV)
Tulsa Comm Coll (OK)
Tyler Jr Coll (TX)
Umpqua Comm Coll (OR)
Victor Valley Coll (CA)
Vincennes U (IN)
Wenatchee Valley Coll (WA)
Western Wyoming Comm Coll (WY)

MUSICAL INSTRUMENT FABRICATION AND REPAIR
Queensborough Comm Coll of the City U of New York (NY)
Renton Tech Coll (WA)
Western Iowa Tech Comm Coll (IA)

MUSICAL THEATER
Casper Coll (WY)
KD Coll Conservatory of Film and Dramatic Arts (TX)

MUSIC HISTORY, LITERATURE, AND THEORY
Ohlone Coll (CA)
St. Charles Comm Coll (MO)
South Florida State Coll (FL)

MUSIC MANAGEMENT
Austin Comm Coll District (TX)
Cedar Valley Coll (TX)
Chandler-Gilbert Comm Coll (AZ)
Collin County Comm Coll District (TX)
Georgia Highlands Coll (GA)
Harrisburg Area Comm Coll (PA)
Houston Comm Coll (TX)
Orange Coast Coll (CA)
Phoenix Coll (AZ)
Terra State Comm Coll (OH)

MUSIC PERFORMANCE
Casper Coll (WY)
Cedar Valley Coll (TX)
Comm Coll of the Air Force (AL)
Dyersburg State Comm Coll (TN)
Greenfield Comm Coll (MA)
Houston Comm Coll (TX)
Macomb Comm Coll (MI)
Miami Dade Coll (FL)
Nassau Comm Coll (NY)
Ohlone Coll (CA)
South Florida State Coll (FL)
Terra State Comm Coll (OH)
Walters State Comm Coll (TN)

MUSIC RELATED
Carl Albert State Coll (OK)
Cayuga County Comm Coll (NY)
Terra State Comm Coll (OH)

MUSIC TEACHER EDUCATION
Amarillo Coll (TX)
Casper Coll (WY)
Coll of Central Florida (FL)
Copiah-Lincoln Comm Coll (MS)
Darton State Coll (GA)
Eastern Wyoming Coll (WY)
Grand Rapids Comm Coll (MI)
Iowa Lakes Comm Coll (IA)
Miami Dade Coll (FL)
Northeastern Jr Coll (CO)
Pensacola State Coll (FL)
Roane State Comm Coll (TN)
South Florida State Coll (FL)
Southwestern Illinois Coll (IL)
Umpqua Comm Coll (OR)
Vincennes U (IN)
Wenatchee Valley Coll (WA)

MUSIC TECHNOLOGY
Gulf Coast State Coll (FL)
Miami Dade Coll (FL)
Mott Comm Coll (MI)
Ohlone Coll (CA)

Owens Comm Coll, Toledo (OH)

MUSIC THEORY AND COMPOSITION
Cedar Valley Coll (TX)
Houston Comm Coll (TX)
Ohlone Coll (CA)
South Florida State Coll (FL)

MUSIC THERAPY
South Florida State Coll (FL)

NAIL TECHNICIAN AND MANICURIST
IBMC Coll (CO)

NANOTECHNOLOGY
Erie Comm Coll, North Campus (NY)
Harper Coll (IL)
Lehigh Carbon Comm Coll (PA)

NATURAL RESOURCE RECREATION AND TOURISM
Wenatchee Valley Coll (WA)

NATURAL RESOURCES AND CONSERVATION RELATED
Southwestern Indian Polytechnic Inst (NM)

NATURAL RESOURCES/ CONSERVATION
American Samoa Comm Coll (AS)
Central Oregon Comm Coll (OR)
Coll of the Desert (CA)
Colorado Northwestern Comm Coll (CO)
Dakota Coll at Bottineau (ND)
Finger Lakes Comm Coll (NY)
Florida Gateway Coll (FL)
Fox Valley Tech Coll (WI)
Hocking Coll (OH)
Iowa Lakes Comm Coll (IA)
Nebraska Indian Comm Coll (NE)
Niagara County Comm Coll (NY)
St. Philip's Coll (TX)
Ulster County Comm Coll (NY)
Vincennes U (IN)

NATURAL RESOURCES/ CONSERVATION RELATED
Greenfield Comm Coll (MA)

NATURAL RESOURCES LAW ENFORCEMENT AND PROTECTIVE SERVICES
Finger Lakes Comm Coll (NY)

NATURAL RESOURCES MANAGEMENT AND POLICY
Finger Lakes Comm Coll (NY)
Hawkeye Comm Coll (IA)
Hocking Coll (OH)
Hutchinson Comm Coll (KS)
Northwest Coll (WY)
The Ohio State U Ag Tech Inst (OH)
Pensacola State Coll (FL)
San Joaquin Delta Coll (CA)
Trinidad State Jr Coll (CO)

NATURAL RESOURCES MANAGEMENT AND POLICY RELATED
Finger Lakes Comm Coll (NY)
Hocking Coll (OH)
The Ohio State U Ag Tech Inst (OH)

NATURAL SCIENCES
Amarillo Coll (TX)
Bossier Parish Comm Coll (LA)
Citrus Coll (CA)
Golden West Coll (CA)
Iowa Lakes Comm Coll (IA)
Miami Dade Coll (FL)
Northeastern Jr Coll (CO)
Ohlone Coll (CA)
Orange Coast Coll (CA)
Phoenix Coll (AZ)
San Joaquin Delta Coll (CA)
Sisseton-Wahpeton Coll (SD)
Tyler Jr Coll (TX)
Umpqua Comm Coll (OR)
Victor Valley Coll (CA)

NETWORK AND SYSTEM ADMINISTRATION
Big Bend Comm Coll (WA)
Bucks County Comm Coll (PA)
Butler County Comm Coll (PA)
Ca&nnada Coll (CA)
Central Maine Comm Coll (ME)

Cincinnati State Tech and Comm Coll (OH)
The Coll of Westchester (NY)
Collin County Comm Coll District (TX)
Corning Comm Coll (NY)
Dakota Coll at Bottineau (ND)
Florida State Coll at Jacksonville (FL)
Genesee Comm Coll (NY)
Gulf Coast State Coll (FL)
Houston Comm Coll (TX)
Island Drafting and Tech Inst (NY)
Kaskaskia Coll (IL)
Kishwaukee Coll (IL)
Louisiana Delta Comm Coll, Monroe (LA)
Miami Dade Coll (FL)
Minneapolis Comm and Tech Coll (MN)
Mitchell Tech Inst (SD)
Montgomery County Comm Coll (PA)
North Iowa Area Comm Coll (IA)
Northland Comm Coll (MN)
Northwest State Comm Coll (OH)
Ohlone Coll (CA)
Ridgewater Coll (MN)
Rockland Comm Coll (NY)
Seminole State Coll of Florida (FL)
Sierra Coll (CA)
Southwestern Illinois Coll (IL)
Sullivan Coll of Technology and Design (KY)
Truckee Meadows Comm Coll (NV)

NEUROSCIENCE
Bucks County Comm Coll (PA)

NONPROFIT MANAGEMENT
Goodwin Coll (CT)
Miami Dade Coll (FL)
Northwest State Comm Coll (OH)

NUCLEAR ENGINEERING
South Florida State Coll (FL)

NUCLEAR ENGINEERING TECHNOLOGY
Coll of Southern Maryland (MD)

NUCLEAR MEDICAL TECHNOLOGY
Amarillo Coll (TX)
Cincinnati State Tech and Comm Coll (OH)
Comm Coll of Allegheny County (PA)
Comm Coll of the Air Force (AL)
Darton State Coll (GA)
Forsyth Tech Comm Coll (NC)
Frederick Comm Coll (MD)
Gateway Comm Coll (CT)
Gulf Coast State Coll (FL)
Harrisburg Area Comm Coll (PA)
Hillsborough Comm Coll (FL)
Houston Comm Coll (TX)
Howard Comm Coll (MD)
Lakeland Comm Coll (OH)
Lorain County Comm Coll (OH)
Maine Coll of Health Professions (ME)
Miami Dade Coll (FL)
Midlands Tech Coll (SC)
Orange Coast Coll (CA)
Owens Comm Coll, Toledo (OH)
Vincennes U (IN)

NUCLEAR/NUCLEAR POWER TECHNOLOGY
Allen Comm Coll (KS)
Cape Fear Comm Coll (NC)
Salem Comm Coll (NJ)
Terra State Comm Coll (OH)
Three Rivers Comm Coll (CT)

NURSING ADMINISTRATION
Paris Jr Coll (TX)
South Suburban Coll (IL)

NURSING ASSISTANT/AIDE AND PATIENT CARE ASSISTANT/AIDE
Allen Comm Coll (KS)
Comm Coll of Allegheny County (PA)
North Iowa Area Comm Coll (IA)
Pensacola State Coll (FL)
Riverland Comm Coll (MN)
Tallahassee Comm Coll (FL)
Trinidad State Jr Coll (CO)
U of Alaska Southeast, Sitka Campus (AK)
Western Iowa Tech Comm Coll (IA)

Western Wyoming Comm Coll (WY)

NURSING PRACTICE
Genesee Comm Coll (NY)

NURSING SCIENCE
Ultimate Medical Academy Tampa (FL)

NUTRITION SCIENCES
Casper Coll (WY)
Sisseton-Wahpeton Coll (SD)
Tulsa Comm Coll (OK)

OCCUPATIONAL HEALTH AND INDUSTRIAL HYGIENE
Niagara County Comm Coll (NY)

OCCUPATIONAL SAFETY AND HEALTH TECHNOLOGY
Anne Arundel Comm Coll (MD)
Central Wyoming Coll (WY)
Cincinnati State Tech and Comm Coll (OH)
The Comm Coll of Baltimore County (MD)
Comm Coll of the Air Force (AL)
Delgado Comm Coll (LA)
Kilgore Coll (TX)
Mt. San Antonio Coll (CA)
Oklahoma State U, Oklahoma City (OK)
St. Philip's Coll (TX)
San Diego Miramar Coll (CA)
San Jacinto Coll District (TX)
San Juan Coll (NM)
Trinidad State Jr Coll (CO)
Westmoreland County Comm Coll (PA)

OCCUPATIONAL THERAPIST ASSISTANT
Anoka Tech Coll (MN)
Austin Comm Coll District (TX)
Bossier Parish Comm Coll (LA)
Cape Fear Comm Coll (NC)
Casper Coll (WY)
Cincinnati State Tech and Comm Coll (OH)
Comm Coll of Allegheny County (PA)
Comm Coll of Philadelphia (PA)
Comm Coll of Rhode Island (RI)
Crowder Coll (MO)
Darton State Coll (GA)
Daytona State Coll (FL)
Delgado Comm Coll (LA)
Erie Comm Coll, North Campus (NY)
Fiorello H. LaGuardia Comm Coll of the City U of New York (NY)
Florida State Coll at Jacksonville (FL)
Fox Valley Tech Coll (WI)
Goodwin Coll (CT)
Greenville Tech Coll (SC)
Hawkeye Comm Coll (IA)
Houston Comm Coll (TX)
Jamestown Comm Coll (NY)
Jefferson Coll (MO)
Kaskaskia Coll (IL)
Kennebec Valley Comm Coll (ME)
Kent State U at Ashtabula (OH)
Kent State U at East Liverpool (OH)
Lake Area Tech Inst (SD)
Lehigh Carbon Comm Coll (PA)
Macomb Comm Coll (MI)
Manchester Comm Coll (CT)
McHenry County Coll (IL)
Midlands Tech Coll (SC)
Mott Comm Coll (MI)
Northland Comm Coll (MN)
Ocean County Coll (NJ)
Owens Comm Coll, Toledo (OH)
Ozarks Tech Comm Coll (MO)
Panola Coll (TX)
Penn State DuBois (PA)
Penn State Mont Alto (PA)
Pueblo Comm Coll (CO)
Reading Area Comm Coll (PA)
St. Charles Comm Coll (MO)
St. Philip's Coll (TX)
Salt Lake Comm Coll (UT)
San Juan Coll (NM)
Shawnee Comm Coll (IL)
South Suburban Coll (IL)
Springfield Tech Comm Coll (MA)
State Fair Comm Coll (MO)
Tyler Jr Coll (TX)
Walters State Comm Coll (TN)
Wisconsin Indianhead Tech Coll (WI)
Wor-Wic Comm Coll (MD)

OCCUPATIONAL THERAPY
Amarillo Coll (TX)
Coll of Central Florida (FL)
The Comm Coll of Baltimore County (MD)
Hinds Comm Coll (MS)
Iowa Central Comm Coll (IA)
Lone Star Coll–Kingwood (TX)
Morgan Comm Coll (CO)
Navarro Coll (TX)
North Central Texas Coll (TX)
North Shore Comm Coll (MA)
Oklahoma City Comm Coll (OK)
Ozarks Tech Comm Coll (MO)
Quinsigamond Comm Coll (MA)
Roane State Comm Coll (TN)
Rockland Comm Coll (NY)
South Florida State Coll (FL)
Stark State Coll (OH)
Trident Tech Coll (SC)
Tulsa Comm Coll (OK)

OCEAN ENGINEERING
South Florida State Coll (FL)

OCEANOGRAPHY (CHEMICAL AND PHYSICAL)
Cape Fear Comm Coll (NC)

OFFICE MANAGEMENT
Alexandria Tech and Comm Coll (MN)
Anoka Tech Coll (MN)
Arizona Western Coll (AZ)
Big Bend Comm Coll (WA)
Brookhaven Coll (TX)
Catawba Valley Comm Coll (NC)
Cecil Coll (MD)
Cleveland Comm Coll (NC)
Coll of Central Florida (FL)
Coll of Marin (CA)
Coll of the Desert (CA)
Comm Coll of Allegheny County (PA)
Comm Coll of Aurora (CO)
Comm Coll of Denver (CO)
Comm Coll of the Air Force (AL)
Corning Comm Coll (NY)
Dakota Coll at Bottineau (ND)
Delaware Tech & Comm Coll, Terry Campus (DE)
Des Moines Area Comm Coll (IA)
Eastern Wyoming Coll (WY)
Erie Comm Coll, North Campus (NY)
Erie Comm Coll, South Campus (NY)
Fayetteville Tech Comm Coll (NC)
Florida Gateway Coll (FL)
Florida State Coll at Jacksonville (FL)
Forrest Coll (SC)
Forsyth Tech Comm Coll (NC)
Fox Valley Tech Coll (WI)
Goodwin Coll (CT)
Great Basin Coll (NV)
Guam Comm Coll (GU)
Guilford Tech Comm Coll (NC)
Gulf Coast State Coll (FL)
Halifax Comm Coll (NC)
Howard Comm Coll (MD)
Iowa Lakes Comm Coll (IA)
Jamestown Business Coll (NY)
Jefferson Comm Coll (NY)
Jefferson State Comm Coll (AL)
Johnston Comm Coll (NC)
Lake Land Coll (IL)
Miami Dade Coll (FL)
MiraCosta Coll (CA)
Montgomery Comm Coll (NC)
Moraine Park Tech Coll (WI)
Northwest State Comm Coll (OH)
Owens Comm Coll, Toledo (OH)
Piedmont Comm Coll (NC)
Richmond Comm Coll (NC)
St. Clair County Comm Coll (MI)
South Florida State Coll (FL)
South Suburban Coll (IL)
Tallahassee Comm Coll (FL)
Wayne County Comm Coll District (MI)
Wenatchee Valley Coll (WA)
White Mountains Comm Coll (NH)
Wisconsin Indianhead Tech Coll (WI)

OFFICE OCCUPATIONS AND CLERICAL SERVICES
Alamance Comm Coll (NC)
American Samoa Comm Coll (AS)
Butler County Comm Coll (PA)
Cloud County Comm Coll (KS)
Corning Comm Coll (NY)

Dakota Coll at Bottineau (ND)
El Centro Coll (TX)
Gateway Comm and Tech Coll (KY)
IBMC Coll (CO)
Iowa Lakes Comm Coll (IA)
ITI Tech Coll (LA)
Jefferson Comm Coll (NY)
Lone Star Coll–CyFair (TX)
Middlesex Comm Coll (MA)
Oklahoma State U Inst of Technology (OK)
San Joaquin Valley Coll, Fresno (CA)
San Joaquin Valley Coll, Hanford (CA)
San Joaquin Valley Coll, Hesperia (CA)
San Joaquin Valley Coll, Lancaster (CA)
San Joaquin Valley Coll, Ontario (CA)
San Joaquin Valley Coll, Salida (CA)
San Joaquin Valley Coll, Temecula (CA)

OPERATIONS MANAGEMENT
Blue Ridge Comm and Tech Coll (WV)
Bunker Hill Comm Coll (MA)
Cleveland Comm Coll (NC)
Fayetteville Tech Comm Coll (NC)
Florida State Coll at Jacksonville (FL)
Gateway Tech Coll (WI)
Great Basin Coll (NV)
Hillsborough Comm Coll (FL)
Kilgore Coll (TX)
Macomb Comm Coll (MI)
McHenry County Coll (IL)
Miami Dade Coll (FL)
Mohawk Valley Comm Coll (NY)
Northcentral Tech Coll (WI)
Oakton Comm Coll (IL)
Pennsylvania Highlands Comm Coll (PA)
Stark State Coll (OH)
Terra State Comm Coll (OH)
Waukesha County Tech Coll (WI)
Wisconsin Indianhead Tech Coll (WI)

OPHTHALMIC AND OPTOMETRIC SUPPORT SERVICES AND ALLIED PROFESSIONS RELATED
Vincennes U (IN)

OPHTHALMIC LABORATORY TECHNOLOGY
Comm Coll of the Air Force (AL)
Hocking Coll (OH)

OPHTHALMIC TECHNOLOGY
Florida State Coll at Jacksonville (FL)
Lakeland Comm Coll (OH)
Miami Dade Coll (FL)
Volunteer State Comm Coll (TN)

OPTICIANRY
Benjamin Franklin Inst of Technology (MA)
Camden County Coll (NJ)
Comm Coll of Rhode Island (RI)
Erie Comm Coll, North Campus (NY)
Goodwin Coll (CT)
Hillsborough Comm Coll (FL)
Holyoke Comm Coll (MA)
J. Sargeant Reynolds Comm Coll (VA)
Miami Dade Coll (FL)
Raritan Valley Comm Coll (NJ)
Southwestern Indian Polytechnic Inst (NM)

OPTOMETRIC TECHNICIAN
Hillsborough Comm Coll (FL)
Raritan Valley Comm Coll (NJ)
San Jacinto Coll District (TX)

ORGANIZATIONAL BEHAVIOR
Chandler-Gilbert Comm Coll (AZ)
Phoenix Coll (AZ)
U of Cincinnati Clermont Coll (OH)

ORGANIZATIONAL COMMUNICATION
Butler County Comm Coll (PA)

ORGANIZATIONAL LEADERSHIP
Olympic Coll (WA)

ORNAMENTAL HORTICULTURE
Antelope Valley Coll (CA)
Comm Coll of Allegheny County (PA)
Cumberland County Coll (NJ)
Dakota Coll at Bottineau (ND)
Finger Lakes Comm Coll (NY)
Golden West Coll (CA)
Gwinnett Tech Coll (GA)
Kishwaukee Coll (IL)
Lenoir Comm Coll (NC)
Mesa Comm Coll (AZ)
Miami Dade Coll (FL)
Mt. San Antonio Coll (CA)
Orange Coast Coll (CA)
Pensacola State Coll (FL)
Salem Comm Coll (NJ)
San Joaquin Delta Coll (CA)
Victor Valley Coll (CA)
Walters State Comm Coll (TN)

ORTHOTICS/PROSTHETICS
Century Coll (MN)
Oklahoma City Comm Coll (OK)
Oklahoma State U Inst of Technology (OK)

OUTDOOR EDUCATION
Corning Comm Coll (NY)

PAINTING
Luzerne County Comm Coll (PA)

PAINTING AND WALL COVERING
Southwestern Illinois Coll (IL)

PARKS, RECREATION AND LEISURE
Central Wyoming Coll (WY)
Coll of Central Florida (FL)
Coll of the Canyons (CA)
The Comm Coll of Baltimore County (MD)
Comm Coll of the Air Force (AL)
Corning Comm Coll (NY)
Dakota Coll at Bottineau (ND)
Iowa Lakes Comm Coll (IA)
Kingsborough Comm Coll of the City U of New York (NY)
Miami Dade Coll (FL)
Monroe Comm Coll (NY)
Mt. San Antonio Coll (CA)
New Mexico Jr Coll (NM)
Niagara County Comm Coll (NY)
Northern Essex Comm Coll (MA)
Northern Virginia Comm Coll (VA)
Northwest Coll (WY)
Norwalk Comm Coll (CT)
Palomar Coll (CA)
Phoenix Coll (AZ)
San Juan Coll (NM)
Sierra Coll (CA)
Sullivan County Comm Coll (NY)
Tompkins Cortland Comm Coll (NY)
Vincennes U (IN)

PARKS, RECREATION AND LEISURE FACILITIES MANAGEMENT
Allen Comm Coll (KS)
Arizona Western Coll (AZ)
Butler County Comm Coll (PA)
Central Wyoming Coll (WY)
Coll of the Desert (CA)
Dakota Coll at Bottineau (ND)
James H. Faulkner State Comm Coll (AL)
Mohawk Valley Comm Coll (NY)
Moraine Valley Comm Coll (IL)
Mt. San Antonio Coll (CA)
Potomac State Coll of West Virginia U (WV)
Southeastern Coll–Greenacres (FL)
South Florida State Coll (FL)
Tompkins Cortland Comm Coll (NY)
Ulster County Comm Coll (NY)

PARKS, RECREATION, LEISURE, AND FITNESS STUDIES RELATED
Cincinnati State Tech and Comm Coll (OH)
The Comm Coll of Baltimore County (MD)
Corning Comm Coll (NY)
Dakota Coll at Bottineau (ND)
Genesee Comm Coll (NY)

PEACE STUDIES AND CONFLICT RESOLUTION
Delta Coll (MI)
El Centro Coll (TX)

PERCUSSION INSTRUMENTS
Iowa Lakes Comm Coll (IA)

PERIOPERATIVE/OPERATING ROOM AND SURGICAL NURSING
Comm Coll of Allegheny County (PA)

PERSONAL AND CULINARY SERVICES RELATED
Mohave Comm Coll (AZ)

PETROLEUM ENGINEERING
Kilgore Coll (TX)

PETROLEUM TECHNOLOGY
Bossier Parish Comm Coll (LA)
Coastal Bend Coll (TX)
Houston Comm Coll (TX)
New Mexico Jr Coll (NM)
Oklahoma State U Inst of Technology (OK)
Panola Coll (TX)
U of Arkansas Comm Coll at Morrilton (AR)
Williston State Coll (ND)

PHARMACY
Iowa Lakes Comm Coll (IA)
Lorain County Comm Coll (OH)
Navarro Coll (TX)
South Florida State Coll (FL)

PHARMACY TECHNICIAN
Alvin Comm Coll (TX)
Anoka-Ramsey Comm Coll, Cambridge Campus (MN)
Bossier Parish Comm Coll (LA)
Casper Coll (WY)
Comm Care Coll (OK)
Comm Coll of Allegheny County (PA)
Comm Coll of the Air Force (AL)
Eastern Arizona Coll (AZ)
Fayetteville Tech Comm Coll (NC)
Guilford Tech Comm Coll (NC)
Humacao Comm Coll (PR)
Hutchinson Comm Coll (KS)
IBMC Coll (CO)
J. Sargeant Reynolds Comm Coll (VA)
Kirtland Comm Coll (MI)
Lone Star Coll–North Harris (TX)
Miami Dade Coll (FL)
Midlands Tech Coll (SC)
Mohave Comm Coll (AZ)
Northland Comm Coll (MN)
Pennsylvania Inst of Technology (PA)
Pensacola State Coll (FL)
Riverland Comm Coll (MN)
Roane State Comm Coll (TN)
Salem Comm Coll (NJ)
San Joaquin Valley Coll, Bakersfield (CA)
San Joaquin Valley Coll, Fresno (CA)
San Joaquin Valley Coll, Hesperia (CA)
San Joaquin Valley Coll, Lancaster (CA)
San Joaquin Valley Coll, Ontario (CA)
San Joaquin Valley Coll, Salida (CA)
San Joaquin Valley Coll, Temecula (CA)
San Joaquin Valley Coll, Visalia (CA)
Southeastern Coll–Greenacres (FL)
Tallahassee Comm Coll (FL)
Ultimate Medical Academy Online (FL)
Vincennes U (IN)
Wayne County Comm Coll District (MI)
Western Dakota Tech Inst (SD)
Western Iowa Tech Comm Coll (IA)
West Virginia Jr Coll–Bridgeport (WV)

PHILOSOPHY
Allen Comm Coll (KS)
Arizona Western Coll (AZ)
Austin Comm Coll District (TX)
Burlington County Coll (NJ)
Ca&nnada Coll (CA)
Cochise Coll, Douglas (AZ)
Coll of Central Florida (FL)
Coll of the Canyons (CA)
Coll of the Desert (CA)
Darton State Coll (GA)
Fiorello H. LaGuardia Comm Coll of the City U of New York (NY)
Georgia Highlands Coll (GA)
Harford Comm Coll (MD)
Harper Coll (IL)
Harrisburg Area Comm Coll (PA)

(column 3)
Iowa Lakes Comm Coll (IA)
Miami Dade Coll (FL)
Minneapolis Comm and Tech Coll (MN)
Ohlone Coll (CA)
Oklahoma City Comm Coll (OK)
Orange Coast Coll (CA)
Pensacola State Coll (FL)
St. Charles Comm Coll (MO)
St. Philip's Coll (TX)
San Diego Miramar Coll (CA)
San Jacinto Coll District (TX)
San Joaquin Delta Coll (CA)
Sierra Coll (CA)
South Florida State Coll (FL)
Truckee Meadows Comm Coll (NV)
Vincennes U (IN)

PHILOSOPHY AND RELIGIOUS STUDIES RELATED
Edison Comm Coll (OH)
South Florida State Coll (FL)

PHLEBOTOMY TECHNOLOGY
Duluth Business U (MN)
Miami Dade Coll (FL)
Westmoreland County Comm Coll (PA)

PHOTOGRAPHIC AND FILM/VIDEO TECHNOLOGY
Catawba Valley Comm Coll (NC)
Daytona State Coll (FL)
Hinds Comm Coll (MS)
Miami Dade Coll (FL)
Minneapolis Comm and Tech Coll (MN)
MiraCosta Coll (CA)
Oklahoma City Comm Coll (OK)
Palomar Coll (CA)
Randolph Comm Coll (NC)
Salt Lake Comm Coll (UT)
Tompkins Cortland Comm Coll (NY)

PHOTOGRAPHY
Amarillo Coll (TX)
Antelope Valley Coll (CA)
Antonelli Inst (PA)
Butler County Comm Coll (PA)
Carteret Comm Coll (NC)
Casper Coll (WY)
Cecil Coll (MD)
Citrus Coll (CA)
Coll of Southern Idaho (ID)
Coll of the Canyons (CA)
Comm Coll of Philadelphia (PA)
County Coll of Morris (NJ)
Dakota Coll at Bottineau (ND)
Delaware Tech & Comm Coll, Terry Campus (DE)
Gwinnett Tech Coll (GA)
Harford Comm Coll (MD)
Harrisburg Area Comm Coll (PA)
Hennepin Tech Coll (MN)
Howard Comm Coll (MD)
Iowa Lakes Comm Coll (IA)
Los Angeles Trade-Tech Coll (CA)
Luzerne County Comm Coll (PA)
Miami Dade Coll (FL)
Mott Comm Coll (MI)
Mt. San Antonio Coll (CA)
Nassau Comm Coll (NY)
Oklahoma State U Inst of Technology (OK)
Orange Coast Coll (CA)
Pasadena City Coll (CA)
Pensacola State Coll (FL)
Rockland Comm Coll (NY)
San Joaquin Delta Coll (CA)
Scottsdale Comm Coll (AZ)
Sullivan County Comm Coll (NY)
Tyler Jr Coll (TX)
Western Wyoming Comm Coll (WY)

PHOTOJOURNALISM
Pasadena City Coll (CA)
Randolph Comm Coll (NC)
Vincennes U (IN)

PHYSICAL EDUCATION TEACHING AND COACHING
Alvin Comm Coll (TX)
Amarillo Coll (TX)
Bucks County Comm Coll (PA)
Carl Albert State Coll (OK)
Casper Coll (WY)
Citrus Coll (CA)
Clinton Comm Coll (NY)
Coll of Central Florida (FL)
Coll of Southern Idaho (ID)
Copiah-Lincoln Comm Coll (MS)
Crowder Coll (MO)

(column 4)
Dutchess Comm Coll (NY)
Eastern Wyoming Coll (WY)
Finger Lakes Comm Coll (NY)
Genesee Comm Coll (NY)
Grand Rapids Comm Coll (MI)
Harper Coll (IL)
Hinds Comm Coll (MS)
Iowa Lakes Comm Coll (IA)
Kilgore Coll (TX)
Laramie County Comm Coll (WY)
Lorain County Comm Coll (OH)
Luzerne County Comm Coll (PA)
Miami Dade Coll (FL)
Monroe Comm Coll (NY)
Montgomery County Comm Coll (PA)
Navarro Coll (TX)
New Mexico Jr Coll (NM)
Niagara County Comm Coll (NY)
Northeastern Jr Coll (CO)
Northern Essex Comm Coll (MA)
North Hennepin Comm Coll (MN)
North Iowa Area Comm Coll (IA)
Orange Coast Coll (CA)
Potomac State Coll of West Virginia U (WV)
Roane State Comm Coll (TN)
San Diego Miramar Coll (CA)
San Joaquin Delta Coll (CA)
Seminole State Coll (OK)
Trinidad State Jr Coll (CO)
Trinity Valley Comm Coll (TX)
Tyler Jr Coll (TX)
Umpqua Comm Coll (OR)
Vincennes U (IN)

PHYSICAL FITNESS TECHNICIAN
Alexandria Tech and Comm Coll (MN)
Lake Region State Coll (ND)
Sheridan Coll (WY)
Tallahassee Comm Coll (FL)
Western Iowa Tech Comm Coll (IA)

PHYSICAL SCIENCES
Alvin Comm Coll (TX)
Amarillo Coll (TX)
Antelope Valley Coll (CA)
Austin Comm Coll District (TX)
Borough of Manhattan Comm Coll of the City U of New York (NY)
Butler County Comm Coll (PA)
Carl Albert State Coll (OK)
Central Oregon Comm Coll (OR)
Central Wyoming Coll (WY)
Chandler-Gilbert Comm Coll (AZ)
Citrus Coll (CA)
Coll of Marin (CA)
Crowder Coll (MO)
Dakota Coll at Bottineau (ND)
Golden West Coll (CA)
Harper Coll (IL)
Harrisburg Area Comm Coll (PA)
Hinds Comm Coll (MS)
Howard Comm Coll (MD)
Hutchinson Comm Coll (KS)
Iowa Lakes Comm Coll (IA)
Lehigh Carbon Comm Coll (PA)
Miami Dade Coll (FL)
Middlesex Comm Coll (MA)
Middlesex County Coll (NJ)
Montgomery County Comm Coll (PA)
Navarro Coll (TX)
Northeastern Jr Coll (CO)
Northwestern Michigan Coll (MI)
Ohlone Coll (CA)
Ozarks Tech Comm Coll (MO)
Paris Jr Coll (TX)
Phoenix Coll (AZ)
Reading Area Comm Coll (PA)
Roane State Comm Coll (TN)
Salt Lake Comm Coll (UT)
San Diego Miramar Coll (CA)
San Jacinto Coll District (TX)
San Joaquin Delta Coll (CA)
San Juan Coll (NM)
Seminole State Coll (OK)
Trinity Valley Comm Coll (TX)
Tulsa Comm Coll (OK)
Umpqua Comm Coll (OR)
Victor Valley Coll (CA)
Vincennes U (IN)
Wenatchee Valley Coll (WA)
Western Nevada Coll (NV)

PHYSICAL SCIENCES RELATED
Dakota Coll at Bottineau (ND)
Mt. San Antonio Coll (CA)

(column 5)

PHYSICAL SCIENCE TECHNOLOGIES RELATED
Westmoreland County Comm Coll (PA)

PHYSICAL THERAPY
Allen Comm Coll (KS)
Amarillo Coll (TX)
Bossier Parish Comm Coll (LA)
Central Oregon Comm Coll (OR)
Chesapeake Coll (MD)
Coll of Central Florida (FL)
Daytona State Coll (FL)
Genesee Comm Coll (NY)
Gwinnett Tech Coll (GA)
Hinds Comm Coll (MS)
Housatonic Comm Coll (CT)
Iowa Central Comm Coll (IA)
Kilgore Coll (TX)
Kingsborough Comm Coll of the City U of New York (NY)
Monroe County Comm Coll (MI)
Morgan Comm Coll (CO)
Northern Virginia Comm Coll (VA)
Ohlone Coll (CA)
Oklahoma City Comm Coll (OK)
Roane State Comm Coll (TN)
Seminole State Coll of Florida (FL)
Stark State Coll (OH)
Trident Tech Coll (SC)
Wytheville Comm Coll (VA)

PHYSICAL THERAPY TECHNOLOGY
Anne Arundel Comm Coll (MD)
Anoka-Ramsey Comm Coll (MN)
Arapahoe Comm Coll (CO)
Austin Comm Coll District (TX)
Blue Ridge Comm and Tech Coll (WV)
Bossier Parish Comm Coll (LA)
Bradford School (OH)
Butler County Comm Coll (PA)
Carl Albert State Coll (OK)
Carroll Comm Coll (MD)
Coll of Central Florida (FL)
Coll of Southern Maryland (MD)
Comm Coll of Allegheny County (PA)
Comm Coll of Rhode Island (RI)
Comm Coll of the Air Force (AL)
Darton State Coll (GA)
Delgado Comm Coll (LA)
Delta Coll (MI)
Edison Comm Coll (OH)
Elgin Comm Coll (IL)
Fayetteville Tech Comm Coll (NC)
Fiorello H. LaGuardia Comm Coll of the City U of New York (NY)
Florida Gateway Coll (FL)
Florida State Coll at Jacksonville (FL)
Fox Coll (IL)
Gateway Tech Coll (WI)
Genesee Comm Coll (NY)
George C. Wallace Comm Coll (AL)
Great Falls Coll Montana State U (MT)
Greenville Tech Coll (SC)
Guilford Tech Comm Coll (NC)
Gulf Coast State Coll (FL)
Gwinnett Tech Coll (GA)
Hawkeye Comm Coll (IA)
Hinds Comm Coll (MS)
Hocking Coll (OH)
Houston Comm Coll (TX)
Howard Comm Coll (MD)
Hutchinson Comm Coll (KS)
Jackson State Comm Coll (TN)
Jefferson Coll (MO)
Jefferson State Comm Coll (AL)
Kankakee Comm Coll (IL)
Kaskaskia Coll (IL)
Kellogg Comm Coll (MI)
Kennebec Valley Comm Coll (ME)
Kent State U at Ashtabula (OH)
Kent State U at East Liverpool (OH)
Kilgore Coll (TX)
Kingsborough Comm Coll of the City U of New York (NY)
Lake Area Tech Inst (SD)
Lake Land Coll (IL)
Laramie County Comm Coll (WY)
Lehigh Carbon Comm Coll (PA)
Lone Star Coll–Montgomery (TX)
Lorain County Comm Coll (OH)
Macomb Comm Coll (MI)
Manchester Comm Coll (CT)
Massachusetts Bay Comm Coll (MA)
Miami Dade Coll (FL)
Midlands Tech Coll (SC)
Mohave Comm Coll (AZ)
Montgomery Coll (MD)
Mott Comm Coll (MI)

Mount Wachusett Comm Coll (MA)
Nassau Comm Coll (NY)
Niagara County Comm Coll (NY)
North Iowa Area Comm Coll (IA)
Northland Comm Coll (MN)
North Shore Comm Coll (MA)
Oakton Comm Coll (IL)
Ohlone Coll (CA)
Olympic Coll (WA)
Owens Comm Coll, Toledo (OH)
Ozarks Tech Comm Coll (MO)
Penn State DuBois (PA)
Penn State Mont Alto (PA)
Penn State Shenango (PA)
Pennsylvania Inst of Technology (PA)
Pensacola State Coll (FL)
Pueblo Comm Coll (CO)
Randolph Comm Coll (NC)
Reading Area Comm Coll (PA)
St. Philip's Coll (TX)
Salt Lake Comm Coll (UT)
San Jacinto Coll District (TX)
San Juan Coll (NM)
Somerset Comm Coll (KY)
Southern U at Shreveport (LA)
Southwestern Illinois Coll (IL)
Springfield Tech Comm Coll (MA)
State Fair Comm Coll (MO)
Tech Coll of the Lowcountry (SC)
Tulsa Comm Coll (OK)
Tyler Jr Coll (TX)
U of Cincinnati Clermont Coll (OH)
Victoria Coll (TX)
Vincennes U (IN)
Volunteer State Comm Coll (TN)
Walters State Comm Coll (TN)
Waukesha County Tech Coll (WI)
Western Iowa Tech Comm Coll (IA)
Whatcom Comm Coll (WA)

PHYSICIAN ASSISTANT
Georgia Highlands Coll (GA)
Miami Dade Coll (FL)
San Joaquin Valley Coll, Visalia (CA)
Wayne County Comm Coll District (MI)

PHYSICS
Allen Comm Coll (KS)
Amarillo Coll (TX)
Arizona Western Coll (AZ)
Austin Comm Coll District (TX)
Bunker Hill Comm Coll (MA)
Burlington County Coll (NJ)
Ca&nnada Coll (CA)
Casper Coll (WY)
Cecil Coll (MD)
Cochise Coll, Douglas (AZ)
Coll of Central Florida (FL)
Coll of Marin (CA)
Coll of Southern Idaho (ID)
Coll of the Canyons (CA)
Coll of the Desert (CA)
Comm Coll of Allegheny County (PA)
Darton State Coll (GA)
Eastern Arizona Coll (AZ)
Finger Lakes Comm Coll (NY)
Georgia Highlands Coll (GA)
Great Basin Coll (NV)
Harford Comm Coll (MD)
Kankakee Comm Coll (IL)
Kilgore Coll (TX)
Kingsborough Comm Coll of the City U of New York (NY)
Lorain County Comm Coll (OH)
Miami Dade Coll (FL)
Monroe Comm Coll (NY)
Navarro Coll (TX)
Northampton Comm Coll (PA)
Northwest Coll (WY)
Ohlone Coll (CA)
Oklahoma City Comm Coll (OK)
Oklahoma State U, Oklahoma City (OK)
Orange Coast Coll (CA)
Paris Jr Coll (TX)
Pensacola State Coll (FL)
Potomac State Coll of West Virginia U (WV)
Salt Lake Comm Coll (UT)
San Diego Miramar Coll (CA)
San Jacinto Coll District (TX)
San Juan Coll (NM)
Sierra Coll (CA)
South Florida State Coll (FL)
Springfield Tech Comm Coll (MA)
Terra State Comm Coll (OH)
Truckee Meadows Comm Coll (NV)
Tyler Jr Coll (TX)

PHYSICS RELATED
South Florida State Coll (FL)

PHYSICS TEACHER EDUCATION
Anne Arundel Comm Coll (MD)
Chesapeake Coll (MD)
The Comm Coll of Baltimore County (MD)
Harford Comm Coll (MD)
Montgomery Coll (MD)

PHYSIOLOGY
Comm Coll of the Air Force (AL)

PIPEFITTING AND SPRINKLER FITTING
Delta Coll (MI)
Kellogg Comm Coll (MI)
Los Angeles Trade-Tech Coll (CA)
Miami Dade Coll (FL)
Southwestern Illinois Coll (IL)

PLANT NURSERY MANAGEMENT
Coll of Marin (CA)
Comm Coll of Allegheny County (PA)
Miami Dade Coll (FL)
MiraCosta Coll (CA)
The Ohio State U Ag Tech Inst (OH)

PLANT SCIENCES
South Florida State Coll (FL)

PLASTICS AND POLYMER ENGINEERING TECHNOLOGY
Cincinnati State Tech and Comm Coll (OH)
Daytona State Coll (FL)
Grand Rapids Comm Coll (MI)
Hennepin Tech Coll (MN)
Lorain County Comm Coll (OH)
Macomb Comm Coll (MI)
Mount Wachusett Comm Coll (MA)
Northwest State Comm Coll (OH)
Terra State Comm Coll (OH)

PLAYWRITING AND SCREENWRITING
Minneapolis Comm and Tech Coll (MN)
Northwest Coll (WY)

PLUMBING TECHNOLOGY
Arizona Western Coll (AZ)
Delta Coll (MI)
Hinds Comm Coll (MS)
Luzerne County Comm Coll (PA)
Macomb Comm Coll (MI)
Miami Dade Coll (FL)
Minnesota West Comm and Tech Coll (MN)
Northeast Iowa Comm Coll (IA)
Northland Comm Coll (MN)

POLITICAL SCIENCE AND GOVERNMENT
Allen Comm Coll (KS)
American Samoa Comm Coll (AS)
Arizona Western Coll (AZ)
Austin Comm Coll District (TX)
Bainbridge State Coll (GA)
Ca&nnada Coll (CA)
Casper Coll (WY)
Coll of Marin (CA)
Coll of Southern Idaho (ID)
Coll of the Canyons (CA)
Coll of the Desert (CA)
Darton State Coll (GA)
Eastern Arizona Coll (AZ)
Finger Lakes Comm Coll (NY)
Frederick Comm Coll (MD)
Georgia Highlands Coll (GA)
Harford Comm Coll (MD)
Hinds Comm Coll (MS)
Iowa Lakes Comm Coll (IA)
Kankakee Comm Coll (IL)
Laramie County Comm Coll (WY)
Lorain County Comm Coll (OH)
Miami Dade Coll (FL)
Monroe Comm Coll (NY)
Northern Essex Comm Coll (MA)
Northwest Coll (WY)
Oklahoma City Comm Coll (OK)
Orange Coast Coll (CA)
Otero Jr Coll (CO)
Paris Jr Coll (TX)
Potomac State Coll of West Virginia U (WV)
St. Charles Comm Coll (MO)
St. Philip's Coll (TX)

Salem Comm Coll (NJ)
Salt Lake Comm Coll (UT)
San Jacinto Coll District (TX)
San Joaquin Delta Coll (CA)
South Florida State Coll (FL)
Trinity Valley Comm Coll (TX)
Tyler Jr Coll (TX)
Umpqua Comm Coll (OR)
Vincennes U (IN)
Western Wyoming Comm Coll (WY)

POLYMER/PLASTICS ENGINEERING
Central Oregon Comm Coll (OR)

POLYSOMNOGRAPHY
Catawba Valley Comm Coll (NC)
Genesee Comm Coll (NY)
Minneapolis Comm and Tech Coll (MN)
Moraine Valley Comm Coll (IL)

PORTUGUESE
Miami Dade Coll (FL)

PRECISION METAL WORKING RELATED
Delta Coll (MI)
Northwest State Comm Coll (OH)
Western Dakota Tech Inst (SD)

PRECISION PRODUCTION RELATED
Delta Coll (MI)
Haywood Comm Coll (NC)
Jefferson Coll (MO)
Midlands Tech Coll (SC)
Mott Comm Coll (MI)
St. Charles Comm Coll (MO)
Salem Comm Coll (NJ)
Sheridan Coll (WY)

PRECISION PRODUCTION TRADES
Butler County Comm Coll (PA)
Midlands Tech Coll (SC)
Owensboro Comm and Tech Coll (KY)

PRE-DENTISTRY STUDIES
Allen Comm Coll (KS)
Austin Comm Coll District (TX)
Casper Coll (WY)
Darton State Coll (GA)
Eastern Wyoming Coll (WY)
Hinds Comm Coll (MS)
Iowa Lakes Comm Coll (IA)
Kilgore Coll (TX)
Pensacola State Coll (FL)
Potomac State Coll of West Virginia U (WV)
St. Philip's Coll (TX)
Vincennes U (IN)
Western Wyoming Comm Coll (WY)

PRE-ENGINEERING
Alexandria Tech and Comm Coll
Amarillo Coll (TX)
Anoka-Ramsey Comm Coll (MN)
Anoka-Ramsey Comm Coll, Cambridge Campus (MN)
Century Coll (MN)
Chipola Coll (FL)
Coll of the Canyons (CA)
Comm Coll of Philadelphia (PA)
Corning Comm Coll (NY)
Crowder Coll (MO)
Darton State Coll (GA)
Finger Lakes Comm Coll (NY)
Housatonic Comm Coll (CT)
Iowa Lakes Comm Coll (IA)
Lamar Comm Coll (CO)
Lenoir Comm Coll (NC)
Lorain County Comm Coll (OH)
Macomb Comm Coll (MI)
Mesabi Range Coll (MN)
Mesa Comm Coll (AZ)
Miami Dade Coll (FL)
Monroe County Comm Coll (MI)
Mt. San Antonio Coll (CA)
Navarro Coll (TX)
Normandale Comm Coll (MN)
North Central Texas Coll (TX)
Northeastern Jr Coll (CO)
North Hennepin Comm Coll (MN)
North Shore Comm Coll (MA)
Ohlone Coll (CA)
Oklahoma City Comm Coll (OK)
Oklahoma State U, Oklahoma City (OK)

Otero Jr Coll (CO)
Palomar Coll (CA)
Rainy River Comm Coll (MN)
Richland Comm Coll (IL)
Roane State Comm Coll (TN)
Rock Valley Coll (IL)
St. Philip's Coll (TX)
Seminole State Coll (OK)
Trinidad State Jr Coll (CO)
Trinity Valley Comm Coll (TX)
Tulsa Comm Coll (OK)
Umpqua Comm Coll (OR)
Virginia Western Comm Coll (VA)
Wayne County Comm Coll District (MI)
Wenatchee Valley Coll (WA)
Western Wyoming Comm Coll (WY)
Westmoreland County Comm Coll (PA)

PRE-LAW STUDIES
Allen Comm Coll (KS)
American Samoa Comm Coll (AS)
Anne Arundel Comm Coll (MD)
Carl Albert State Coll (OK)
Casper Coll (WY)
Central Oregon Comm Coll (OR)
Central Wyoming Coll (WY)
Coll of Central Florida (FL)
Coll of Southern Idaho (ID)
Darton State Coll (GA)
Hinds Comm Coll (MS)
Iowa Lakes Comm Coll (IA)
Kilgore Coll (TX)
Laramie County Comm Coll (WY)
Paris Jr Coll (TX)
Pensacola State Coll (FL)
Potomac State Coll of West Virginia U (WV)
St. Philip's Coll (TX)
U of Cincinnati Clermont Coll (OH)
Western Wyoming Comm Coll (WY)

PREMEDICAL STUDIES
Allen Comm Coll (KS)
Austin Comm Coll District (TX)
Casper Coll (WY)
Central Oregon Comm Coll (OR)
Coll of Central Florida (FL)
Dakota Coll at Bottineau (ND)
Darton State Coll (GA)
Eastern Arizona Coll (AZ)
Eastern Wyoming Coll (WY)
Hinds Comm Coll (MS)
Howard Comm Coll (MD)
Iowa Lakes Comm Coll (IA)
Kilgore Coll (TX)
Paris Jr Coll (TX)
Pensacola State Coll (FL)
Potomac State Coll of West Virginia U (WV)
St. Philip's Coll (TX)
San Juan Coll (NM)
Springfield Tech Comm Coll (MA)
Vincennes U (IN)
Western Wyoming Comm Coll (WY)

PRENURSING STUDIES
Arizona Western Coll (AZ)
Dakota Coll at Bottineau (ND)
Edison Comm Coll (OH)
Hinds Comm Coll (MS)
Iowa Lakes Comm Coll (IA)
Oklahoma State U, Oklahoma City (OK)
Paris Jr Coll (TX)
Pensacola State Coll (FL)
Potomac State Coll of West Virginia U (WV)
St. Philip's Coll (TX)
Southwestern Michigan Coll (MI)
Tulsa Comm Coll (OK)
Tyler Jr Coll (TX)
Western Wyoming Comm Coll (WY)

PRE-OCCUPATIONAL THERAPY
Casper Coll (WY)
Potomac State Coll of West Virginia U (WV)

PRE-OPTOMETRY
Casper Coll (WY)

PRE-PHARMACY STUDIES
Allen Comm Coll (KS)
Amarillo Coll (TX)
Austin Comm Coll District (TX)
Casper Coll (WY)
Central Oregon Comm Coll (OR)
Coll of Central Florida (FL)

Coll of Southern Idaho (ID)
Darton State Coll (GA)
Eastern Arizona Coll (AZ)
Eastern Wyoming Coll (WY)
Georgia Highlands Coll (GA)
Hinds Comm Coll (MS)
Howard Comm Coll (MD)
Iowa Lakes Comm Coll (IA)
Kilgore Coll (TX)
Laramie County Comm Coll (WY)
Luzerne County Comm Coll (PA)
Monroe County Comm Coll (NY)
Northwest Coll (WY)
Paris Jr Coll (TX)
Pensacola State Coll (FL)
Potomac State Coll of West Virginia U (WV)
Quinsigamond Comm Coll (MA)
St. Philip's Coll (TX)
Schoolcraft Coll (MI)
Tulsa Comm Coll (OK)
U of Cincinnati Clermont Coll (OH)
Vincennes U (IN)
Western Wyoming Comm Coll (WY)

PRE-PHYSICAL THERAPY
Casper Coll (WY)
Georgia Highlands Coll (GA)
Potomac State Coll of West Virginia U (WV)

PRE-VETERINARY STUDIES
Allen Comm Coll (KS)
Austin Comm Coll District (TX)
Casper Coll (WY)
Coll of Central Florida (FL)
Dakota Coll at Bottineau (ND)
Darton State Coll (GA)
Eastern Wyoming Coll (WY)
Hinds Comm Coll (MS)
Iowa Lakes Comm Coll (IA)
Kilgore Coll (TX)
Pensacola State Coll (FL)
Potomac State Coll of West Virginia U (WV)
Vincennes U (IN)
Western Wyoming Comm Coll (WY)

PRINTING PRESS OPERATION
Dunwoody Coll of Technology (MN)
Lake Land Coll (IL)

PROFESSIONAL, TECHNICAL, BUSINESS, AND SCIENTIFIC WRITING
Austin Comm Coll District (TX)
Fox Valley Tech Coll (WI)
Gateway Tech Coll (WI)
Oklahoma State U, Oklahoma City (OK)
Southwestern Michigan Coll (MI)

PSYCHIATRIC/MENTAL HEALTH SERVICES TECHNOLOGY
Alvin Comm Coll (TX)
Anne Arundel Comm Coll (MD)
Coll of Southern Idaho (ID)
Comm Coll of Allegheny County (PA)
The Comm Coll of Baltimore County (MD)
Fiorello H. LaGuardia Comm Coll of the City U of New York (NY)
Guilford Tech Comm Coll (NC)
Hagerstown Comm Coll (MD)
Hillsborough Comm Coll (FL)
Houston Comm Coll (TX)
Kingsborough Comm Coll of the City U of New York (NY)
Middlesex Comm Coll (MA)
Montgomery Coll (MD)
Montgomery County Comm Coll (PA)
Pueblo Comm Coll (CO)
Three Rivers Comm Coll (CT)
Williston State Coll (ND)

PSYCHOLOGY
Allen Comm Coll (KS)
Alvin Comm Coll (TX)
Amarillo Coll (TX)
Arizona Western Coll (AZ)
Austin Comm Coll District (TX)
Bainbridge State Coll (GA)
Bucks County Comm Coll (PA)
Bunker Hill Comm Coll (MA)
Burlington County Coll (NJ)
Butler County Comm Coll (PA)
Ca&nnada Coll (CA)
Carroll Comm Coll (MD)
Casper Coll (WY)

Central Wyoming Coll (WY)
Chandler-Gilbert Comm Coll (AZ)
Citrus Coll (CA)
Cochise Coll, Douglas (AZ)
Coll of Central Florida (FL)
Coll of Marin (CA)
Coll of Southern Idaho (ID)
Coll of the Canyons (CA)
Coll of the Desert (CA)
Comm Coll of Allegheny County (PA)
Comm Coll of Philadelphia (PA)
Crowder Coll (MO)
Dakota Coll at Bottineau (ND)
Darton State Coll (GA)
Dean Coll (MA)
Eastern Arizona Coll (AZ)
Edison Comm Coll (OH)
Finger Lakes Comm Coll (NY)
Fiorello H. LaGuardia Comm Coll of
the City U of New York (NY)
Frederick Comm Coll (MD)
Genesee Comm Coll (NY)
Georgia Highlands Coll (GA)
Great Basin Coll (NV)
Harford Comm Coll (MD)
Harper Coll (IL)
Harrisburg Area Comm Coll (PA)
Hinds Comm Coll (MS)
Hutchinson Comm Coll (KS)
Iowa Lakes Comm Coll (IA)
Kankakee Comm Coll (IL)
Kilgore Coll (TX)
Laramie County Comm Coll (WY)
Lehigh Carbon Comm Coll (PA)
Lorain County Comm Coll (OH)
Manor Coll (PA)
Miami Dade Coll (FL)
MiraCosta Coll (CA)
Mohave Comm Coll (AZ)
Monroe County Comm Coll (MI)
Montgomery County Comm Coll (PA)
Navarro Coll (TX)
Northeastern Jr Coll (CO)
Northwest Coll (WY)
Norwalk Comm Coll (CT)
Ohlone Coll (CA)
Oklahoma City Comm Coll (OK)
Oklahoma State U, Oklahoma City
(OK)
Otero Jr Coll (CO)
Palomar Coll (CA)
Paris Jr Coll (TX)
Pasadena City Coll (CA)
Pennsylvania Highlands Comm Coll
(PA)
Pensacola State Coll (FL)
Potomac State Coll of West Virginia
U (WV)
Reading Area Comm Coll (PA)
St. Charles Comm Coll (MO)
St. Philip's Coll (TX)
Salem Comm Coll (NJ)
Salt Lake Comm Coll (UT)
San Diego Miramar Coll (CA)
San Jacinto Coll District (TX)
San Joaquin Delta Coll (CA)
San Juan Coll (NM)
Sheridan Coll (WY)
Sierra Coll (CA)
South Florida State Coll (FL)
Sullivan County Comm Coll (NY)
Terra State Comm Coll (OH)
Trinidad State Jr Coll (CO)
Trinity Valley Comm Coll (TX)
Truckee Meadows Comm Coll (NV)
Tyler Jr Coll (TX)
Umpqua Comm Coll (OR)
U of Cincinnati Clermont Coll (OH)
Vincennes U (IN)
Western Wyoming Comm Coll (WY)
Wright State U–Lake Campus (OH)

PSYCHOLOGY RELATED
Cayuga County Comm Coll (NY)
Genesee Comm Coll (NY)
MiraCosta Coll (CA)
Seminole State Coll (OK)

PUBLIC ADMINISTRATION
Central Texas Coll (TX)
Citrus Coll (CA)
County Coll of Morris (NJ)
Fayetteville Tech Comm Coll (NC)
Housatonic Comm Coll (CT)
Houston Comm Coll (TX)
Laramie County Comm Coll (WY)
Lehigh Carbon Comm Coll (PA)
Miami Dade Coll (FL)
Minneapolis Comm and Tech Coll
(MN)
Palomar Coll (CA)
Scottsdale Comm Coll (AZ)

Southern U at Shreveport (LA)
South Florida State Coll (FL)
Tyler Jr Coll (TX)
Westchester Comm Coll (NY)

PUBLIC ADMINISTRATION AND SOCIAL SERVICE PROFESSIONS RELATED
Cleveland State Comm Coll (TN)
Oklahoma State U, Oklahoma City
(OK)
Ulster County Comm Coll (NY)

PUBLIC HEALTH
Anne Arundel Comm Coll (MD)

PUBLIC HEALTH EDUCATION AND PROMOTION
Borough of Manhattan Comm Coll of
the City U of New York (NY)
Coll of Southern Idaho (ID)
Northampton Comm Coll (PA)

PUBLIC HEALTH RELATED
Salt Lake Comm Coll (UT)

PUBLIC RELATIONS, ADVERTISING, AND APPLIED COMMUNICATION
Oklahoma City Comm Coll (OK)

PUBLIC RELATIONS, ADVERTISING, AND APPLIED COMMUNICATION RELATED
Harper Coll (IL)

PUBLIC RELATIONS/IMAGE MANAGEMENT
Amarillo Coll (TX)
Comm Coll of the Air Force (AL)
Crowder Coll (MO)
South Florida State Coll (FL)
Vincennes U (IN)

PURCHASING, PROCUREMENT/ ACQUISITIONS AND CONTRACTS MANAGEMENT
Cecil Coll (MD)
Comm Coll of the Air Force (AL)
Greenville Tech Coll (SC)

QUALITY CONTROL AND SAFETY TECHNOLOGIES RELATED
Comm Coll of Denver (CO)
Elizabethtown Comm and Tech Coll,
Elizabethtown (KY)
Macomb Comm Coll (MI)

QUALITY CONTROL TECHNOLOGY
Comm Coll of Allegheny County (PA)
Gateway Tech Coll (WI)
Goodwin Coll (CT)
Grand Rapids Comm Coll (MI)
Illinois Eastern Comm Colls, Frontier
Community College (IL)
Illinois Eastern Comm Colls, Lincoln
Trail College (IL)
Lakeland Comm Coll (OH)
Lorain County Comm Coll (OH)
Macomb Comm Coll (MI)
Mesa Comm Coll (AZ)
Monroe Comm Coll (NY)
Mt. San Antonio Coll (CA)
Northampton Comm Coll (PA)
Rock Valley Coll (IL)
Salt Lake Comm Coll (UT)

RADIATION PROTECTION/ HEALTH PHYSICS TECHNOLOGY
Lone Star Coll–CyFair (TX)
Spartanburg Comm Coll (SC)

RADIO AND TELEVISION
Alvin Comm Coll (TX)
Amarillo Coll (TX)
Austin Comm Coll District (TX)
Central Texas Coll (TX)
Central Wyoming Coll (WY)
Coll of the Canyons (CA)
Daytona State Coll (FL)
Delta Coll (MI)
Genesee Comm Coll (NY)
Golden West Coll (CA)
Hinds Comm Coll (MS)
Illinois Eastern Comm Colls, Wabash
Valley College (IL)
Iowa Central Comm Coll (IA)
Iowa Lakes Comm Coll (IA)
Lake Land Coll (IL)
Miami Dade Coll (FL)

Mt. San Antonio Coll (CA)
Navarro Coll (TX)
Northwest Coll (WY)
Ohlone Coll (CA)
Palomar Coll (CA)
Pasadena City Coll (CA)
South Florida State Coll (FL)
Sullivan County Comm Coll (NY)
Virginia Western Comm Coll (VA)

RADIO AND TELEVISION BROADCASTING TECHNOLOGY
Arizona Western Coll (AZ)
Borough of Manhattan Comm Coll of
the City U of New York (NY)
Cedar Valley Coll (TX)
Cleveland Comm Coll (NC)
Cloud County Comm Coll (KS)
Genesee Comm Coll (NY)
Hinds Comm Coll (MS)
Houston Comm Coll (TX)
Hutchinson Comm Coll (KS)
Iowa Lakes Comm Coll (IA)
Lehigh Carbon Comm Coll (PA)
Luzerne County Comm Coll (PA)
Miami Dade Coll (FL)
Mount Wachusett Comm Coll (MA)
Northampton Comm Coll (PA)
Ohlone Coll (CA)
Ozarks Tech Comm Coll (MO)
Pasadena City Coll (CA)
Salt Lake Comm Coll (UT)
San Jacinto Coll District (TX)
Schoolcraft Coll (MI)
Springfield Tech Comm Coll (MA)
Tompkins Cortland Comm Coll (NY)
Vincennes U (IN)
Westmoreland County Comm Coll
(PA)

RADIOLOGIC TECHNOLOGY/ SCIENCE
Amarillo Coll (TX)
Arizona Western Coll (AZ)
Austin Comm Coll District (TX)
Brookhaven Coll (TX)
Butler County Comm Coll (PA)
Ca&nnada Coll (CA)
Career Tech Coll, Monroe (LA)
Carl Albert State Coll (OK)
Casper Coll (WY)
Central Oregon Comm Coll (OR)
Central Virginia Comm Coll (VA)
Century Coll (MN)
Clark Coll (WA)
Cleveland Comm Coll (NC)
Comm Coll of Denver (CO)
Comm Coll of Rhode Island (RI)
County Coll of Morris (NJ)
Danville Area Comm Coll (IL)
El Centro Coll (TX)
Elgin Comm Coll (IL)
Fayetteville Tech Comm Coll (NC)
Forsyth Tech Comm Coll (NC)
Gadsden State Comm Coll (AL)
George C. Wallace Comm Coll (AL)
Great Falls Coll Montana State U
(MT)
Harper Coll (IL)
Harrisburg Area Comm Coll (PA)
H. Councill Trenholm State Tech Coll
(AL)
Hinds Comm Coll (MS)
Houston Comm Coll (TX)
Jefferson State Comm Coll (AL)
Kankakee Comm Coll (IL)
Kaskaskia Coll (IL)
Kennebec Valley Comm Coll (ME)
Kilgore Coll (TX)
Kishwaukee Coll (IL)
Laramie County Comm Coll (WY)
Maine Coll of Health Professions
(ME)
Miami Dade Coll (FL)
Minnesota State Coll–Southeast
Tech (MN)
Minnesota West Comm and Tech
Coll (MN)
Mitchell Tech Inst (SD)
Montgomery County Comm Coll (PA)
Moraine Valley Comm Coll (IL)
Northampton Comm Coll (PA)
Northeast Iowa Comm Coll (IA)
Northern Essex Comm Coll (MA)
Northland Comm Coll (MN)
Northwestern Coll (IL)
Oklahoma State U, Oklahoma City
(OK)
Paris Jr Coll (TX)
Pasadena City Coll (CA)
Pasco-Hernando State Coll (FL)

Pennsylvania Highlands Comm Coll
(PA)
Pueblo Comm Coll (CO)
Quinsigamond Comm Coll (MA)
Randolph Comm Coll (NC)
Ridgewater Coll (MN)
St. Luke's Coll (IA)
San Jacinto Coll District (TX)
Southern U at Shreveport (LA)
South Suburban Coll (IL)
Southwestern Illinois Coll (IL)
Southwest Virginia Comm Coll (VA)
Spencerian Coll (KY)
Spencerian Coll–Lexington (KY)
Springfield Tech Comm Coll (MA)
State Fair Comm Coll (MO)
Truckee Meadows Comm Coll (NV)
Tyler Jr Coll (TX)
Virginia Western Comm Coll (VA)
Wenatchee Valley Coll (WA)
Westmoreland County Comm Coll
(PA)

RADIO, TELEVISION, AND DIGITAL COMMUNICATION RELATED
Cayuga County Comm Coll (NY)
Fox Valley Tech Coll (WI)
Genesee Comm Coll (NY)
Mitchell Tech Inst (SD)
Montgomery County Comm Coll (PA)
Northwest Coll (WY)
Pennsylvania Highlands Comm Coll
(PA)
Sullivan County Comm Coll (NY)

RANGE SCIENCE AND MANAGEMENT
Casper Coll (WY)
Central Wyoming Coll (WY)
Eastern Wyoming Coll (WY)
Northwest Coll (WY)
Sheridan Coll (WY)
Trinity Valley Comm Coll (TX)

REAL ESTATE
Amarillo Coll (TX)
Antelope Valley Coll (CA)
Austin Comm Coll District (TX)
Camden County Coll (NJ)
Cedar Valley Coll (TX)
Cincinnati State Tech and Comm Coll
(OH)
Citrus Coll (CA)
Coll of Marin (CA)
Coll of Southern Idaho (ID)
Coll of the Canyons (CA)
Collin County Comm Coll District
(TX)
Comm Coll of Allegheny County (PA)
Eastern Gateway Comm Coll (OH)
Florida State Coll at Jacksonville (FL)
Golden West Coll (CA)
Harrisburg Area Comm Coll (PA)
Hinds Comm Coll (MS)
Houston Comm Coll (TX)
Iowa Lakes Comm Coll (IA)
J. Sargeant Reynolds Comm Coll
(VA)
Lorain County Comm Coll (OH)
Los Angeles Trade-Tech Coll (CA)
Luzerne County Comm Coll (PA)
Mesa Comm Coll (AZ)
Miami Dade Coll (FL)
MiraCosta Coll (CA)
Montgomery County Comm Coll (PA)
Mt. San Antonio Coll (CA)
Nassau Comm Coll (NY)
Navarro Coll (TX)
New Mexico Jr Coll (NM)
North Central Texas Coll (TX)
Northern Essex Comm Coll (MA)
Oakton Comm Coll (IL)
Ohlone Coll (CA)
Palomar Coll (CA)
San Jacinto Coll District (TX)
Scottsdale Comm Coll (AZ)
Sierra Coll (CA)
South Florida State Coll (FL)
Terra State Comm Coll (OH)
Trinity Valley Comm Coll (TX)
Victor Valley Coll (CA)
Waukesha County Tech Coll (WI)
Westmoreland County Comm Coll
(PA)

RECEPTIONIST
Dakota Coll at Bottineau (ND)
Iowa Lakes Comm Coll (IA)

RECORDING ARTS TECHNOLOGY
Bossier Parish Comm Coll (LA)
Citrus Coll (CA)
Comm Coll of Philadelphia (PA)
Finger Lakes Comm Coll (NY)
Fiorello H. LaGuardia Comm Coll of
the City U of New York (NY)
Grand Rapids Comm Coll (MI)
Guilford Tech Comm Coll (NC)
Hennepin Tech Coll (MN)
International Coll of Broadcasting
(OH)
Lehigh Carbon Comm Coll (PA)
Miami Dade Coll (FL)
Minneapolis Comm and Tech Coll
(MN)
MiraCosta Coll (CA)
Montgomery County Comm Coll (PA)
Phoenix Coll (AZ)
Ridgewater Coll (MN)
Schoolcraft Coll (MI)
Springfield Tech Comm Coll (MA)
Vincennes U (IN)
Western Iowa Tech Comm Coll (IA)

REGISTERED NURSING, NURSING ADMINISTRATION, NURSING RESEARCH AND CLINICAL NURSING RELATED
Genesee Comm Coll (NY)
Harford Comm Coll (MD)

REGISTERED NURSING/ REGISTERED NURSE
Alamance Comm Coll (NC)
Alexandria Tech and Comm Coll
(MN)
Alvin Comm Coll (TX)
Amarillo Coll (TX)
Ancilla Coll (IN)
Anne Arundel Comm Coll (MD)
Anoka-Ramsey Comm Coll (MN)
Anoka-Ramsey Comm Coll,
Cambridge Campus (MN)
Antelope Valley Coll (CA)
Arapahoe Comm Coll (CO)
Arkansas Northeastern Coll (AR)
Austin Comm Coll District (TX)
Bainbridge State Coll (GA)
The Belanger School of Nursing (NY)
Bellingham Tech Coll (WA)
Bevill State Comm Coll (AL)
Big Bend Comm Coll (WA)
Blue Ridge Comm and Tech Coll
(WV)
Borough of Manhattan Comm Coll of
the City U of New York (NY)
Bossier Parish Comm Coll (LA)
Bowling Green State U-Firelands Coll
(OH)
Brookhaven Coll (TX)
Bucks County Comm Coll (PA)
Bunker Hill Comm Coll (MA)
Burlington County Coll (NJ)
Butler County Comm Coll (PA)
Camden County Coll (NJ)
Cape Fear Comm Coll (NC)
Carl Albert State Coll (OK)
Carroll Comm Coll (MD)
Casper Coll (WY)
Catawba Valley Comm Coll (NC)
Cayuga County Comm Coll (NY)
Cecil Coll (MD)
Central Maine Comm Coll (ME)
Central Oregon Comm Coll (OR)
Central Texas Coll (TX)
Central Wyoming Coll (WY)
Century Coll (MN)
Chandler-Gilbert Comm Coll (AZ)
Chesapeake Coll (MD)
Chipola Coll (FL)
Cincinnati State Tech and Comm Coll
(OH)
Citrus Coll (CA)
City Colls of Chicago, Olive-Harvey
College (IL)
Clark Coll (WA)
Cleveland Comm Coll (NC)
Cleveland State Comm Coll (TN)
Clinton Comm Coll (NY)
Cloud County Comm Coll (KS)
Coastal Bend Coll (TX)
Cochise Coll, Douglas (AZ)
Coll of Central Florida (FL)
Coll of Marin (CA)
Coll of Southern Idaho (ID)
Coll of Southern Maryland (MD)
Coll of the Canyons (CA)
Coll of the Desert (CA)
Collin County Comm Coll District
(TX)

Colorado Northwestern Comm Coll (CO)
Columbia-Greene Comm Coll (NY)
Comm Coll of Allegheny County (PA)
The Comm Coll of Baltimore County (MD)
Comm Coll of Denver (CO)
Comm Coll of Philadelphia (PA)
Comm Coll of Rhode Island (RI)
Copiah-Lincoln Comm Coll (MS)
Corning Comm Coll (NY)
County Coll of Morris (NJ)
Crowder Coll (MO)
Cumberland County Coll (NJ)
Dabney S. Lancaster Comm Coll (VA)
Dakota Coll at Bottineau (ND)
Danville Area Comm Coll (IL)
Darton State Coll (GA)
Daytona State Coll (FL)
Delaware Tech & Comm Coll, Terry Campus (DE)
Delgado Comm Coll (LA)
Delta Coll (MI)
Des Moines Area Comm Coll (IA)
Dutchess Comm Coll (NY)
Dyersburg State Comm Coll (TN)
Eastern Arizona Coll (AZ)
Eastern Idaho Tech Coll (ID)
Edison Comm Coll (OH)
El Centro Coll (TX)
Elgin Comm Coll (IL)
Elizabethtown Comm and Tech Coll, Elizabethtown (KY)
Erie Comm Coll (NY)
Erie Comm Coll, North Campus (NY)
Fayetteville Tech Comm Coll (NC)
Finger Lakes Comm Coll (NY)
Fiorello H. LaGuardia Comm Coll of the City U of New York (NY)
Florida Gateway Coll (FL)
Florida SouthWestern State Coll (FL)
Florida State Coll at Jacksonville (FL)
Forsyth Tech Comm Coll (NC)
Fox Valley Tech Coll (WI)
Frederick Comm Coll (MD)
Front Range Comm Coll (CO)
Gadsden State Comm Coll (AL)
Gateway Comm and Tech Coll (KY)
Gateway Comm Coll (CT)
Gateway Tech Coll (WI)
Genesee Comm Coll (NY)
George C. Wallace Comm Coll (AL)
Georgia Highlands Coll (GA)
Golden West Coll (CA)
Good Samaritan Coll of Nursing and Health Science (OH)
Goodwin Coll (CT)
Grand Rapids Comm Coll (MI)
Great Basin Coll (NV)
Greenfield Comm Coll (MA)
Greenville Tech Coll (SC)
Guilford Tech Comm Coll (NC)
Gulf Coast State Coll (FL)
Hagerstown Comm Coll (MD)
Halifax Comm Coll (NC)
Harper Coll (IL)
Harrisburg Area Comm Coll (PA)
Hawkeye Comm Coll (IA)
Haywood Comm Coll (NC)
Highland Comm Coll (IL)
Hillsborough Comm Coll (FL)
Hinds Comm Coll (MS)
Hocking Coll (OH)
Holyoke Comm Coll (MA)
Hopkinsville Comm Coll (KY)
Horry-Georgetown Tech Coll (SC)
Housatonic Comm Coll (CT)
Houston Comm Coll (TX)
Howard Comm Coll (MD)
Hudson County Comm Coll (NJ)
Hutchinson Comm Coll (KS)
Illinois Eastern Comm Colls, Frontier Community College (IL)
Illinois Eastern Comm Colls, Olney Central College (IL)
Iowa Central Comm Coll (IA)
Iowa Lakes Comm Coll (IA)
Jackson State Comm Coll (TN)
James H. Faulkner State Comm Coll (AL)
James Sprunt Comm Coll (NC)
Jamestown Comm Coll (NY)
Jefferson Coll (MO)
Jefferson Comm Coll (NY)
Jefferson State Comm Coll (AL)
Johnston Comm Coll (NC)
John Tyler Comm Coll (VA)
J. Sargeant Reynolds Comm Coll (VA)
Kalamazoo Valley Comm Coll (MI)
Kankakee Comm Coll (IL)
Kaskaskia Coll (IL)
Kellogg Comm Coll (MI)
Kennebec Valley Comm Coll (ME)
Kent State U at Ashtabula (OH)
Kent State U at East Liverpool (OH)
Kent State U at Tuscarawas (OH)
Kilgore Coll (TX)
Kingsborough Comm Coll of the City U of New York (NY)
Kirtland Comm Coll (MI)
Kishwaukee Coll (IL)
Lake Land Coll (IL)
Lakeland Comm Coll (OH)
Lake Region State Coll (ND)
Lakes Region Comm Coll (NH)
Lamar Comm Coll (CO)
Laramie County Comm Coll (WY)
Lehigh Carbon Comm Coll (PA)
Lenoir Comm Coll (NC)
Lone Star Coll–CyFair (TX)
Lone Star Coll–Kingwood (TX)
Lone Star Coll–Montgomery (TX)
Lone Star Coll–North Harris (TX)
Lone Star Coll–Tomball (TX)
Lorain County Comm Coll (OH)
Los Angeles Trade-Tech Coll (CA)
Louisiana Delta Comm Coll, Monroe (LA)
Lower Columbia Coll (WA)
Lurleen B. Wallace Comm Coll (AL)
Luzerne County Comm Coll (PA)
Macomb Comm Coll (MI)
Maine Coll of Health Professions (ME)
Massachusetts Bay Comm Coll (MA)
Maysville Comm and Tech Coll, Maysville (KY)
McHenry County Coll (IL)
Mesa Comm Coll (AZ)
Miami Dade Coll (FL)
Middlesex Comm Coll (MA)
Middlesex County Coll (NJ)
Midlands Tech Coll (SC)
Mid-Plains Comm Coll, North Platte (NE)
Minneapolis Comm and Tech Coll (MN)
Minnesota State Coll–Southeast Tech (MN)
Minnesota West Comm and Tech Coll (MN)
MiraCosta Coll (CA)
Mohave Comm Coll (AZ)
Mohawk Valley Comm Coll (NY)
Monroe Comm Coll (NY)
Monroe County Comm Coll (MI)
Montcalm Comm Coll (MI)
Montgomery Coll (MD)
Montgomery County Comm Coll (PA)
Moraine Park Tech Coll (WI)
Moraine Valley Comm Coll (IL)
Motlow State Comm Coll (TN)
Mott Comm Coll (MI)
Mt. San Antonio Coll (CA)
Mount Wachusett Comm Coll (MA)
Nassau Comm Coll (NY)
Navarro Coll (TX)
New Mexico Jr Coll (NM)
Niagara County Comm Coll (NY)
Normandale Comm Coll (MN)
Northampton Comm Coll (PA)
Northcentral Tech Coll (WI)
North Central Texas Coll (TX)
Northeastern Jr Coll (CO)
Northeast Iowa Comm Coll (IA)
Northern Essex Comm Coll (MA)
North Hennepin Comm Coll (MN)
North Iowa Area Comm Coll (IA)
Northland Comm Coll (MN)
North Shore Comm Coll (MA)
Northwest Coll (WY)
Northwestern Coll (IL)
Northwestern Michigan Coll (MI)
Northwest-Shoals Comm Coll (AL)
Northwest State Comm Coll (OH)
Northwest Tech Coll (MN)
Norwalk Comm Coll (CT)
Oakton Comm Coll (IL)
Ocean County Coll (NJ)
Ohlone Coll (CA)
Oklahoma City Comm Coll (OK)
Oklahoma State U Inst of Technology (OK)
Oklahoma State U, Oklahoma City (OK)
Olympic Coll (WA)
Oregon Coast Comm Coll (OR)
Otero Jr Coll (CO)
Owensboro Comm and Tech Coll (KY)
Owens Comm Coll, Toledo (OH)
Palomar Coll (CA)
Panola Coll (TX)
Paris Jr Coll (TX)
Pasadena City Coll (CA)
Pasco-Hernando State Coll (FL)
Penn State Fayette, The Eberly Campus (PA)
Penn State Mont Alto (PA)
Pensacola State Coll (FL)
Phoenix Coll (AZ)
Piedmont Comm Coll (NC)
Pueblo Comm Coll (CO)
Queensborough Comm Coll of the City U of New York (NY)
Quinsigamond Comm Coll (MA)
Randolph Comm Coll (NC)
Rappahannock Comm Coll (VA)
Raritan Valley Comm Coll (NJ)
Reading Area Comm Coll (PA)
Richland Comm Coll (IL)
Richmond Comm Coll (NC)
Ridgewater Coll (MN)
Rio Hondo Coll (CA)
Riverland Comm Coll (MN)
Roane State Comm Coll (TN)
Rockland Comm Coll (NY)
Rock Valley Coll (IL)
Rogue Comm Coll (OR)
St. Charles Comm Coll (MO)
St. Luke's Coll (IA)
St. Vincent's Coll (CT)
Salem Comm Coll (NJ)
Salt Lake Comm Coll (UT)
San Jacinto Coll District (TX)
San Joaquin Delta Coll (CA)
San Joaquin Valley Coll, Visalia (CA)
San Juan Coll (NM)
Schoolcraft Coll (MI)
Scottsdale Comm Coll (AZ)
Seminole State Coll (OK)
Seminole State Coll of Florida (FL)
Shawnee Comm Coll (IL)
Sheridan Coll (WY)
Sierra Coll (CA)
Sisseton-Wahpeton Coll (SD)
Somerset Comm Coll (KY)
Southeastern Comm Coll (IA)
Southern U at Shreveport (LA)
South Florida State Coll (FL)
South Louisiana Comm Coll (LA)
South Piedmont Comm Coll (NC)
Southwestern Illinois Coll (IL)
Southwestern Michigan Coll (MI)
Southwest Virginia Comm Coll (VA)
Spartanburg Comm Coll (SC)
Spencerian Coll (KY)
Springfield Tech Comm Coll (MA)
Stark State Coll (OH)
State Fair Comm Coll (MO)
State U of New York Coll of Technology at Alfred (NY)
Sullivan County Comm Coll (NY)
Tallahassee Comm Coll (FL)
Tech Coll of the Lowcountry (SC)
Terra State Comm Coll (OH)
Texas State Tech Coll Harlingen (TX)
Three Rivers Comm Coll (CT)
Tompkins Cortland Comm Coll (NY)
Trident Tech Coll (SC)
Trinidad State Jr Coll (CO)
Trinity Valley Comm Coll (TX)
Truckee Meadows Comm Coll (NV)
Tulsa Comm Coll (OK)
Tyler Jr Coll (TX)
Ulster County Comm Coll (NY)
Umpqua Comm Coll (OR)
U of Arkansas Comm Coll at Batesville (AR)
U of Arkansas Comm Coll at Hope (AR)
U of Arkansas Comm Coll at Morrilton (AR)
Victoria Coll (TX)
Victor Valley Coll (CA)
Vincennes U (IN)
Virginia Western Comm Coll (VA)
Walters State Comm Coll (TN)
Waukesha County Tech Coll (WI)
Wayne County Comm Coll District (MI)
Wenatchee Valley Coll (WA)
Westchester Comm Coll (NY)
Western Iowa Tech Comm Coll (IA)
Western Nevada Coll (NV)
Westmoreland County Comm Coll (PA)
Whatcom Comm Coll (WA)
White Mountains Comm Coll (NH)
Williston State Coll (ND)
Wisconsin Indianhead Tech Coll (WI)
Wor-Wic Comm Coll (MD)
Wytheville Comm Coll (VA)

REHABILITATION AND THERAPEUTIC PROFESSIONS RELATED

Central Wyoming Coll (WY)
Iowa Lakes Comm Coll (IA)
Middlesex County Coll (NJ)
Nassau Comm Coll (NY)
Ocean County Coll (NJ)

RELIGIOUS EDUCATION

Manor Coll (PA)

RELIGIOUS STUDIES

Allen Comm Coll (KS)
Amarillo Coll (TX)
Coll of Central Florida (FL)
Kilgore Coll (TX)
Laramie County Comm Coll (WY)
Orange Coast Coll (CA)
Pensacola State Coll (FL)
San Joaquin Delta Coll (CA)
South Florida State Coll (FL)
Trinity Valley Comm Coll (TX)

RELIGIOUS STUDIES RELATED

Spartanburg Methodist Coll (SC)

RESORT MANAGEMENT

Coll of the Desert (CA)
Finger Lakes Comm Coll (NY)
Lehigh Carbon Comm Coll (PA)

RESPIRATORY CARE THERAPY

Alvin Comm Coll (TX)
Amarillo Coll (TX)
Bossier Parish Comm Coll (LA)
Bowling Green State U-Firelands Coll (OH)
Burlington County Coll (NJ)
Carteret Comm Coll (NC)
Casper Coll (WY)
Catawba Valley Comm Coll (NC)
Central Virginia Comm Coll (VA)
City Colls of Chicago, Olive-Harvey College (IL)
Cochise Coll, Douglas (AZ)
Collin County Comm Coll District (TX)
Comm Coll of Allegheny County (PA)
The Comm Coll of Baltimore County (MD)
Comm Coll of Philadelphia (PA)
Comm Coll of Rhode Island (RI)
County Coll of Morris (NJ)
Cumberland County Coll (NJ)
Darton State Coll (GA)
Daytona State Coll (FL)
Delgado Comm Coll (LA)
Delta Coll (MI)
Des Moines Area Comm Coll (IA)
Eastern Gateway Comm Coll (OH)
El Centro Coll (TX)
Elizabethtown Comm and Tech Coll, Elizabethtown (KY)
Erie Comm Coll, North Campus (NY)
Fayetteville Tech Comm Coll (NC)
Florida SouthWestern State Coll (FL)
Florida State Coll at Jacksonville (FL)
Frederick Comm Coll (MD)
Genesee Comm Coll (NY)
George C. Wallace Comm Coll (AL)
Goodwin Coll (CT)
Great Falls Coll Montana State U (MT)
Greenville Tech Coll (SC)
Gulf Coast State Coll (FL)
Gwinnett Tech Coll (GA)
Harrisburg Area Comm Coll (PA)
Hawkeye Comm Coll (IA)
Hillsborough Comm Coll (FL)
Hinds Comm Coll (MS)
Houston Comm Coll (TX)
Hudson County Comm Coll (NJ)
J. Sargeant Reynolds Comm Coll (VA)
Kalamazoo Valley Comm Coll (MI)
Kankakee Comm Coll (IL)
Kaskaskia Coll (IL)
Kennebec Valley Comm Coll (ME)
Kent State U at Ashtabula (OH)
Lakeland Comm Coll (OH)
Lone Star Coll–Kingwood (TX)
Luzerne County Comm Coll (PA)
Macomb Comm Coll (MI)
Manchester Comm Coll (CT)
Massachusetts Bay Comm Coll (MA)
Maysville Comm and Tech Coll, Maysville (KY)
Miami Dade Coll (FL)
Middlesex County Coll (NJ)
Midlands Tech Coll (SC)
Mohawk Valley Comm Coll (NY)
Monroe County Comm Coll (MI)
Moraine Park Tech Coll (WI)
Moraine Valley Comm Coll (IL)
Mott Comm Coll (MI)
Mt. San Antonio Coll (CA)
Nassau Comm Coll (NY)
Northeast Iowa Comm Coll (IA)
Northern Essex Comm Coll (MA)
Northern Virginia Comm Coll (VA)
Northland Comm Coll (MN)
North Shore Comm Coll (MA)
Norwalk Comm Coll (CT)
Ocean County Coll (NJ)
Ohlone Coll (CA)
Oklahoma City Comm Coll (OK)
Orange Coast Coll (CA)
Ozarks Tech Comm Coll (MO)
Pueblo Comm Coll (CO)
Quinsigamond Comm Coll (MA)
Raritan Valley Comm Coll (NJ)
Reading Area Comm Coll (PA)
Roane State Comm Coll (TN)
Rockland Comm Coll (NY)
Rock Valley Coll (IL)
St. Luke's Coll (IA)
St. Philip's Coll (TX)
Salem Comm Coll (NJ)
San Jacinto Coll District (TX)
San Joaquin Valley Coll, Bakersfield (CA)
San Joaquin Valley Coll, Ontario (CA)
San Joaquin Valley Coll, Temecula (CA)
San Joaquin Valley Coll, Visalia (CA)
San Juan Coll (NM)
Seminole State Coll of Florida (FL)
Somerset Comm Coll (KY)
Southeastern Comm Coll (IA)
Southern U at Shreveport (LA)
South Florida State Coll (FL)
Southwestern Illinois Coll (IL)
Spartanburg Comm Coll (SC)
Spencerian Coll (KY)
Springfield Tech Comm Coll (MA)
Stark State Coll (OH)
Sullivan County Comm Coll (NY)
Tallahassee Comm Coll (FL)
Trident Tech Coll (SC)
Tulsa Comm Coll (OK)
Tyler Jr Coll (TX)
U of Cincinnati Clermont Coll (OH)
Victoria Coll (TX)
Victor Valley Coll (CA)
Volunteer State Comm Coll (TN)
Walters State Comm Coll (TN)
Westchester Comm Coll (NY)

RESPIRATORY THERAPY TECHNICIAN

Borough of Manhattan Comm Coll of the City U of New York (NY)
Bunker Hill Comm Coll (MA)
Career Tech Coll, Monroe (LA)
Georgia Highlands Coll (GA)
Hutchinson Comm Coll (KS)
Miami Dade Coll (FL)
Northern Essex Comm Coll (MA)
San Joaquin Valley Coll, Rancho Cordova (CA)

RESTAURANT, CULINARY, AND CATERING MANAGEMENT

Blue Ridge Comm and Tech Coll (WV)
Cincinnati State Tech and Comm Coll (OH)
Coll of Central Florida (FL)
Coll of the Canyons (CA)
Comm Coll of Allegheny County (PA)
Elgin Comm Coll (IL)
Florida State Coll at Jacksonville (FL)
Gateway Tech Coll (WI)
Grand Rapids Comm Coll (MI)
Guam Comm Coll (GU)
Gulf Coast State Coll (FL)
Hillsborough Comm Coll (FL)

Iowa Lakes Comm Coll (IA)
JNA Inst of Culinary Arts (PA)
Lakeland Comm Coll (OH)
McHenry County Coll (IL)
Miami Dade Coll (FL)
MiraCosta Coll (CA)
Mohawk Valley Comm Coll (NY)
New England Culinary Inst (VT)
Orange Coast Coll (CA)
Pennsylvania Highlands Comm Coll (PA)
Pensacola State Coll (FL)
Raritan Valley Comm Coll (NJ)
Reading Area Comm Coll (PA)
San Jacinto Coll District (TX)
Southwestern Illinois Coll (IL)
Vincennes U (IN)
Waukesha County Tech Coll (WI)
Westmoreland County Comm Coll (PA)

RESTAURANT/FOOD SERVICES MANAGEMENT
Burlington County Coll (NJ)
Central Texas Coll (TX)
Erie Comm Coll, North Campus (NY)
Fiorello H. LaGuardia Comm Coll of the City U of New York (NY)
Hillsborough Comm Coll (FL)
Iowa Lakes Comm Coll (IA)
J. Sargeant Reynolds Comm Coll (VA)
Lakes Region Comm Coll (NH)
Miami Dade Coll (FL)
Minneapolis Comm and Tech Coll (MN)
Northampton Comm Coll (PA)
Norwalk Comm Coll (CT)
Owens Comm Coll, Toledo (OH)
Quinsigamond Comm Coll (MA)
St. Philip's Coll (TX)

RETAILING
Alamance Comm Coll (NC)
Bradford School (PA)
Bucks County Comm Coll (PA)
Burlington County Coll (NJ)
Ca&nnada Coll (CA)
Casper Coll (WY)
Central Oregon Comm Coll (OR)
Clark Coll (WA)
Comm Coll of Allegheny County (PA)
Delta Coll (MI)
Elgin Comm Coll (IL)
Holyoke Comm Coll (MA)
Hutchinson Comm Coll (KS)
Iowa Lakes Comm Coll (IA)
Minnesota State Coll–Southeast Tech (MN)
Nassau Comm Coll (NY)
North Central Texas Coll (TX)
Orange Coast Coll (CA)
Western Iowa Tech Comm Coll (IA)
Wood Tobe–Coburn School (NY)

RETAIL MANAGEMENT
Collin County Comm Coll District (TX)
Penn Foster Coll (AZ)

RHETORIC AND COMPOSITION
Allen Comm Coll (KS)
Amarillo Coll (TX)
Austin Comm Coll District (TX)
Bainbridge State Coll (GA)
Carl Albert State Coll (OK)
Iowa Lakes Comm Coll (IA)
Monroe County Comm Coll (MI)
Navarro Coll (TX)
Paris Jr Coll (TX)
St. Philip's Coll (TX)
San Jacinto Coll District (TX)
San Joaquin Delta Coll (CA)
Sierra Coll (CA)
South Florida State Coll (FL)
Trinity Valley Comm Coll (TX)

ROBOTICS TECHNOLOGY
Butler County Comm Coll (PA)
Casper Coll (WY)
Comm Coll of Allegheny County (PA)
Daytona State Coll (FL)
Dunwoody Coll of Technology (MN)
Kaskaskia Coll (IL)
Kirtland Comm Coll (MI)
Lake Area Tech Inst (SD)
Macomb Comm Coll (MI)
McHenry County Coll (IL)
Minnesota West Comm and Tech Coll (MN)
Southern U at Shreveport (LA)

Sullivan Coll of Technology and Design (KY)
Terra State Comm Coll (OH)
Vincennes U (IN)

ROOFING
Penn Foster Coll (AZ)

RUSSIAN
Austin Comm Coll District (TX)

SALES, DISTRIBUTION, AND MARKETING OPERATIONS
Alexandria Tech and Comm Coll (MN)
Anoka-Ramsey Comm Coll (MN)
Anoka-Ramsey Comm Coll, Cambridge Campus (MN)
Burlington County Coll (NJ)
Coll of the Canyons (CA)
Des Moines Area Comm Coll (IA)
Gadsden State Comm Coll (AL)
Greenfield Comm Coll (MA)
Greenville Tech Coll (SC)
Guam Comm Coll (GU)
Harper Coll (IL)
Harrisburg Area Comm Coll (PA)
Hawkeye Comm Coll (IA)
Iowa Lakes Comm Coll (IA)
Midlands Tech Coll (SC)
Minnesota State Coll–Southeast Tech (MN)
MiraCosta Coll (CA)
Montgomery County Comm Coll (PA)
North Central Texas Coll (TX)
Northeast Iowa Comm Coll (IA)
North Iowa Area Comm Coll (IA)
Northwest Tech Coll (MN)
Oakton Comm Coll (IL)
Owens Comm Coll, Toledo (OH)
Ridgewater Coll (MN)
Sierra Coll (CA)
State U of New York Coll of Technology at Alfred (NY)
Western Iowa Tech Comm Coll (IA)
Westmoreland County Comm Coll (PA)

SALON/BEAUTY SALON MANAGEMENT
Delta Coll (MI)
Mott Comm Coll (MI)
Northwest-Shoals Comm Coll (AL)
Schoolcraft Coll (MI)
Southeastern Coll–Greenacres (FL)

SCIENCE TEACHER EDUCATION
Darton State Coll (GA)
Iowa Central Comm Coll (IA)
Iowa Lakes Comm Coll (IA)
Moraine Valley Comm Coll (IL)
San Jacinto Coll District (TX)
South Florida State Coll (FL)
Ulster County Comm Coll (NY)
Vincennes U (IN)

SCIENCE TECHNOLOGIES
Central Virginia Comm Coll (VA)

SCIENCE TECHNOLOGIES RELATED
Blue Ridge Comm and Tech Coll (WV)
Cayuga County Comm Coll (NY)
Cleveland State Comm Coll (TN)
Comm Coll of Allegheny County (PA)
Comm Coll of Aurora (CO)
Comm Coll of Denver (CO)
Dakota Coll at Bottineau (ND)
Front Range Comm Coll (CO)
Jackson State Comm Coll (TN)
Pueblo Comm Coll (CO)
Reading Area Comm Coll (PA)
Sullivan County Comm Coll (NY)
Trinidad State Jr Coll (CO)
U of Cincinnati Clermont Coll (OH)
Victor Valley Coll (CA)
Volunteer State Comm Coll (TN)

SCULPTURE
Palomar Coll (CA)
Salem Comm Coll (NJ)

SECONDARY EDUCATION
Allen Comm Coll (KS)
Alvin Comm Coll (TX)
Ancilla Coll (IN)
Arizona Western Coll (AZ)
Austin Comm Coll District (TX)
Brookhaven Coll (TX)
Carl Albert State Coll (OK)

Cecil Coll (MD)
Central Wyoming Coll (WY)
Coll of Central Florida (FL)
Collin County Comm Coll District (TX)
Eastern Arizona Coll (AZ)
Eastern Wyoming Coll (WY)
Georgia Highlands Coll (GA)
Grand Rapids Comm Coll (MI)
Harrisburg Area Comm Coll (PA)
Hinds Comm Coll (MS)
Howard Comm Coll (MD)
Kankakee Comm Coll (IL)
Montgomery County Comm Coll (PA)
Northampton Comm Coll (PA)
Northwest Coll (WY)
Paris Jr Coll (TX)
Potomac State Coll of West Virginia U (WV)
Reading Area Comm Coll (PA)
San Jacinto Coll District (TX)
San Juan Coll (NM)
Sheridan Coll (WY)
South Florida State Coll (FL)
Springfield Tech Comm Coll (MA)
Tyler Jr Coll (TX)
U of Cincinnati Clermont Coll (OH)
Vincennes U (IN)
Western Wyoming Comm Coll (WY)

SECURITIES SERVICES ADMINISTRATION
Vincennes U (IN)
Western Iowa Tech Comm Coll (IA)

SECURITY AND LOSS PREVENTION
Citrus Coll (CA)
Comm Coll of the Air Force (AL)
Delta Coll (MI)
Miami Dade Coll (FL)
Tallahassee Comm Coll (FL)
Vincennes U (IN)

SELLING SKILLS AND SALES
Butler County Comm Coll (PA)
Clark Coll (WA)
Danville Area Comm Coll (IL)
Iowa Lakes Comm Coll (IA)
McHenry County Coll (IL)
Minnesota State Coll–Southeast Tech (MN)
Orange Coast Coll (CA)
Ridgewater Coll (MN)
Southwestern Illinois Coll (IL)

SHEET METAL TECHNOLOGY
Comm Coll of Allegheny County (PA)
Delta Coll (MI)
Macomb Comm Coll (MI)
Miami Dade Coll (FL)
Palomar Coll (CA)
Rock Valley Coll (IL)
Shawnee Comm Coll (IL)
Southwestern Illinois Coll (IL)
Terra State Comm Coll (OH)
Vincennes U (IN)

SIGNAL/GEOSPATIAL INTELLIGENCE
Northland Comm Coll (MN)

SIGN LANGUAGE INTERPRETATION AND TRANSLATION
Austin Comm Coll District (TX)
Burlington County Coll (NJ)
Camden County Coll (NJ)
Cincinnati State Tech and Comm Coll (OH)
Coll of the Canyons (CA)
Collin County Comm Coll District (TX)
Comm Coll of Allegheny County (PA)
The Comm Coll of Baltimore County (MD)
Comm Coll of Philadelphia (PA)
Delgado Comm Coll (LA)
Front Range Comm Coll (CO)
Golden West Coll (CA)
Hinds Comm Coll (MS)
Houston Comm Coll (TX)
J. Sargeant Reynolds Comm Coll (VA)
Lakeland Comm Coll (OH)
Lone Star Coll–CyFair (TX)
Lone Star Coll–North Harris (TX)
Miami Dade Coll (FL)
Mohawk Valley Comm Coll (NY)
Mott Comm Coll (MI)
Mt. San Antonio Coll (CA)
Northcentral Tech Coll (WI)

Northern Essex Comm Coll (MA)
Ocean County Coll (NJ)
Ohlone Coll (CA)
Oklahoma State U, Oklahoma City (OK)
Palomar Coll (CA)
Phoenix Coll (AZ)
Salt Lake Comm Coll (UT)
Southwestern Illinois Coll (IL)
Tulsa Comm Coll (OK)
Tyler Jr Coll (TX)

SMALL BUSINESS ADMINISTRATION
Borough of Manhattan Comm Coll of the City U of New York (NY)
Bucks County Comm Coll (PA)
Ca&nnada Coll (CA)
Coll of the Canyons (CA)
Colorado Northwestern Comm Coll (CO)
Dakota Coll at Bottineau (ND)
Delta Coll (MI)
Harper Coll (IL)
Harrisburg Area Comm Coll (PA)
Iowa Lakes Comm Coll (IA)
J. Sargeant Reynolds Comm Coll (VA)
Middlesex County Coll (NJ)
MiraCosta Coll (CA)
Moraine Valley Comm Coll (IL)
Pensacola State Coll (FL)
Raritan Valley Comm Coll (NJ)
Schoolcraft Coll (MI)
Sierra Coll (CA)
South Suburban Coll (IL)
Southwestern Illinois Coll (IL)
Springfield Tech Comm Coll (MA)

SMALL ENGINE MECHANICS AND REPAIR TECHNOLOGY
Iowa Lakes Comm Coll (IA)
Mitchell Tech Inst (SD)

SOCIAL PSYCHOLOGY
Macomb Comm Coll (MI)
South Florida State Coll (FL)

SOCIAL SCIENCES
Amarillo Coll (TX)
Arizona Western Coll (AZ)
Burlington County Coll (NJ)
Carl Albert State Coll (OK)
Central Oregon Comm Coll (OR)
Central Texas Coll (TX)
Central Wyoming Coll (WY)
Citrus Coll (CA)
Clinton Comm Coll (NY)
Cochise Coll, Douglas (AZ)
Coll of Central Florida (FL)
Coll of Marin (CA)
Coll of Southern Idaho (ID)
Coll of the Canyons (CA)
Coll of the Desert (CA)
Comm Coll of Allegheny County (PA)
Corning Comm Coll (NY)
Dakota Coll at Bottineau (ND)
Eastern Wyoming Coll (WY)
Finger Lakes Comm Coll (NY)
Genesee Comm Coll (NY)
Greenfield Comm Coll (MA)
Harrisburg Area Comm Coll (PA)
Hinds Comm Coll (MS)
Housatonic Comm Coll (CT)
Howard Comm Coll (MD)
Hutchinson Comm Coll (KS)
Iowa Lakes Comm Coll (IA)
J. Sargeant Reynolds Comm Coll (VA)
Kilgore Coll (TX)
Laramie County Comm Coll (WY)
Lorain County Comm Coll (OH)
Luzerne County Comm Coll (PA)
Massachusetts Bay Comm Coll (MA)
Miami Dade Coll (FL)
Monroe Comm Coll (NY)
Montgomery County Comm Coll (PA)
Mt. San Antonio Coll (CA)
Navarro Coll (TX)
Niagara County Comm Coll (NY)
Northeastern Jr Coll (CO)
Northern Virginia Comm Coll (VA)
Northwest Coll (WY)
Northwestern Michigan Coll (MI)
Ohlone Coll (CA)
Orange Coast Coll (CA)
Otero Jr Coll (CO)
Palomar Coll (CA)
Paris Jr Coll (TX)
Reading Area Comm Coll (PA)
Roane State Comm Coll (TN)
San Diego Miramar Coll (CA)

San Jacinto Coll District (TX)
San Joaquin Delta Coll (CA)
Seminole State Coll (OK)
Sierra Coll (CA)
South Florida State Coll (FL)
Terra State Comm Coll (OH)
Tulsa Comm Coll (OK)
Tyler Jr Coll (TX)
Umpqua Comm Coll (OR)
U of Cincinnati Clermont Coll (OH)
Victor Valley Coll (CA)
Wayne County Comm Coll District (MI)
Westchester Comm Coll (NY)
Western Wyoming Comm Coll (WY)

SOCIAL SCIENCES RELATED
Genesee Comm Coll (NY)
Greenfield Comm Coll (MA)

SOCIAL SCIENCE TEACHER EDUCATION
South Florida State Coll (FL)

SOCIAL STUDIES TEACHER EDUCATION
Casper Coll (WY)
Ulster County Comm Coll (NY)

SOCIAL WORK
Allen Comm Coll (KS)
Amarillo Coll (TX)
Austin Comm Coll District (TX)
Bowling Green State U-Firelands Coll (OH)
Camden County Coll (NJ)
Casper Coll (WY)
Chandler-Gilbert Comm Coll (AZ)
Chipola Coll (FL)
Cochise Coll, Douglas (AZ)
Coll of Central Florida (FL)
Comm Coll of Allegheny County (PA)
Comm Coll of Rhode Island (RI)
Comm Coll of the Air Force (AL)
Cumberland County Coll (NJ)
Darton State Coll (GA)
Edison Comm Coll (OH)
Elgin Comm Coll (IL)
Elizabethtown Comm and Tech Coll, Elizabethtown (KY)
Genesee Comm Coll (NY)
Greenville Tech Coll (SC)
Harford Comm Coll (MD)
Harrisburg Area Comm Coll (PA)
Holyoke Comm Coll (MA)
Hopkinsville Comm Coll (KY)
Hudson County Comm Coll (NJ)
Illinois Eastern Comm Colls, Wabash Valley College (IL)
Iowa Central Comm Coll (IA)
Iowa Lakes Comm Coll (IA)
Lake Land Coll (IL)
Lakeland Comm Coll (OH)
Lehigh Carbon Comm Coll (PA)
Lorain County Comm Coll (OH)
Manchester Comm Coll (CT)
Miami Dade Coll (FL)
Monroe County Comm Coll (MI)
Nebraska Indian Comm Coll (NE)
Northampton Comm Coll (PA)
Northeastern Jr Coll (CO)
Northeast Iowa Comm Coll (IA)
Northwest State Comm Coll (OH)
Oakton Comm Coll (IL)
Paris Jr Coll (TX)
Potomac State Coll of West Virginia U (WV)
Reading Area Comm Coll (PA)
Rogue Comm Coll (OR)
St. Charles Comm Coll (MO)
St. Philip's Coll (TX)
Salem Comm Coll (NJ)
Salt Lake Comm Coll (UT)
San Juan Coll (NM)
Shawnee Comm Coll (IL)
South Florida State Coll (FL)
South Suburban Coll (IL)
Southwestern Illinois Coll (IL)
Southwestern Michigan Coll (MI)
Terra State Comm Coll (OH)
Tulsa Comm Coll (OK)
Tyler Jr Coll (TX)
Umpqua Comm Coll (OR)
U of Cincinnati Clermont Coll (OH)
Vincennes U (IN)
Wayne County Comm Coll District (MI)
Western Wyoming Comm Coll (WY)
Wright State U–Lake Campus (OH)

SOCIAL WORK RELATED
Butler County Comm Coll (PA)

Genesee Comm Coll (NY)

SOCIOLOGY
Allen Comm Coll (KS)
Alvin Comm Coll (TX)
Austin Comm Coll District (TX)
Bainbridge State Coll (GA)
Bunker Hill Comm Coll (MA)
Burlington County Coll (NJ)
Ca&nnada Coll (CA)
Casper Coll (WY)
Citrus Coll (CA)
Coll of Central Florida (FL)
Coll of Southern Idaho (ID)
Coll of the Canyons (CA)
Coll of the Desert (CA)
Comm Coll of Allegheny County (PA)
Darton State Coll (GA)
Dean Coll (MA)
Eastern Arizona Coll (AZ)
Finger Lakes Comm Coll (NY)
Georgia Highlands Coll (GA)
Great Basin Coll (NV)
Harford Comm Coll (MD)
Hinds Comm Coll (MS)
Iowa Central Comm Coll (IA)
Iowa Lakes Comm Coll (IA)
Kankakee Comm Coll (IL)
Laramie County Comm Coll (WY)
Lorain County Comm Coll (OH)
Miami Dade Coll (FL)
MiraCosta Coll (CA)
Mohave Comm Coll (AZ)
Navarro Coll (TX)
Northwest Coll (WY)
Ohlone Coll (CA)
Oklahoma City Comm Coll (OK)
Orange Coast Coll (CA)
Palomar Coll (CA)
Paris Jr Coll (TX)
Pasadena City Coll (CA)
Pensacola State Coll (FL)
Potomac State Coll of West Virginia U (WV)
St. Charles Comm Coll (MO)
St. Philip's Coll (TX)
Salem Comm Coll (NJ)
Salt Lake Comm Coll (UT)
San Diego Miramar Coll (CA)
San Jacinto Coll District (TX)
San Joaquin Delta Coll (CA)
Southern U at Shreveport (LA)
South Florida State Coll (FL)
Trinity Valley Comm Coll (TX)
Tyler Jr Coll (TX)
Umpqua Comm Coll (OR)
Vincennes U (IN)
Wenatchee Valley Coll (WA)
Western Wyoming Comm Coll (WY)
Wright State U–Lake Campus (OH)

SOCIOLOGY AND ANTHROPOLOGY
Harper Coll (IL)

SOIL SCIENCE AND AGRONOMY
Iowa Lakes Comm Coll (IA)
The Ohio State U Ag Tech Inst (OH)
South Florida State Coll (FL)

SOLAR ENERGY TECHNOLOGY
Arizona Western Coll (AZ)
Comm Coll of Allegheny County (PA)
Crowder Coll (MO)
San Juan Coll (NM)

SPANISH
Arizona Western Coll (AZ)
Austin Comm Coll District (TX)
Ca&nnada Coll (CA)
Citrus Coll (CA)
Coll of Marin (CA)
Coll of the Canyons (CA)
Coll of the Desert (CA)
Fiorello H. LaGuardia Comm Coll of the City U of New York (NY)
Iowa Lakes Comm Coll (IA)
Laramie County Comm Coll (WY)
Miami Dade Coll (FL)
Northwest Coll (WY)
Ohlone Coll (CA)
Orange Coast Coll (CA)
Pasadena City Coll (CA)
St. Charles Comm Coll (MO)
St. Philip's Coll (TX)
San Diego Miramar Coll (CA)
South Florida State Coll (FL)
Trinity Valley Comm Coll (TX)
Western Wyoming Comm Coll (WY)

SPANISH LANGUAGE TEACHER EDUCATION
Anne Arundel Comm Coll (MD)
Carroll Comm Coll (MD)
The Comm Coll of Baltimore County (MD)
Frederick Comm Coll (MD)
Harford Comm Coll (MD)
Montgomery Coll (MD)
Ulster County Comm Coll (NY)

SPECIAL EDUCATION
Coll of Central Florida (FL)
Comm Coll of Rhode Island (RI)
Darton State Coll (GA)
Harford Comm Coll (MD)
Highland Comm Coll (IL)
Kankakee Comm Coll (IL)
Lehigh Carbon Comm Coll (PA)
McHenry County Coll (IL)
Miami Dade Coll (FL)
Moraine Valley Comm Coll (IL)
Normandale Comm Coll (MN)
Northern Virginia Comm Coll (VA)
Pensacola State Coll (FL)
San Juan Coll (NM)
South Florida State Coll (FL)
Truckee Meadows Comm Coll (NV)
U of Cincinnati Clermont Coll (OH)
Vincennes U (IN)

SPECIAL EDUCATION–EARLY CHILDHOOD
Harford Comm Coll (MD)
Motlow State Comm Coll (TN)
Palomar Coll (CA)

SPECIAL EDUCATION–ELEMENTARY SCHOOL
Harford Comm Coll (MD)
Truckee Meadows Comm Coll (NV)
Westmoreland County Comm Coll (PA)

SPECIAL EDUCATION–INDIVIDUALS WITH EMOTIONAL DISTURBANCES
South Florida State Coll (FL)

SPECIAL EDUCATION–INDIVIDUALS WITH HEARING IMPAIRMENTS
Florida State Coll at Jacksonville (FL)
Hillsborough Comm Coll (FL)
Miami Dade Coll (FL)

SPECIAL EDUCATION–INDIVIDUALS WITH INTELLECTUAL DISABILITIES
South Florida State Coll (FL)

SPECIAL EDUCATION–INDIVIDUALS WITH SPECIFIC LEARNING DISABILITIES
South Florida State Coll (FL)

SPECIAL EDUCATION–INDIVIDUALS WITH VISION IMPAIRMENTS
South Florida State Coll (FL)

SPECIAL PRODUCTS MARKETING
Copiah-Lincoln Comm Coll (MS)
El Centro Coll (TX)
Gateway Comm Coll (CT)
Monroe Comm Coll (NY)
Orange Coast Coll (CA)
Scottsdale Comm Coll (AZ)
State Fair Comm Coll (MO)
Tompkins Cortland Comm Coll (NY)

SPEECH COMMUNICATION AND RHETORIC
Ancilla Coll (IN)
Brookhaven Coll (TX)
Bucks County Comm Coll (PA)
Bunker Hill Comm Coll (MA)
Ca&nnada Coll (CA)
Casper Coll (WY)
Central Oregon Comm Coll (OR)
Citrus Coll (CA)
Cochise Coll, Douglas (AZ)
Coll of Marin (CA)
Coll of Southern Idaho (ID)
Coll of the Canyons (CA)
Coll of the Desert (CA)
Collin County Comm Coll District (TX)

Dutchess Comm Coll (NY)
Eastern Wyoming Coll (WY)
Edison Comm Coll (OH)
Erie Comm Coll, South Campus (NY)
Fiorello H. LaGuardia Comm Coll of the City U of New York (NY)
Harper Coll (IL)
Hinds Comm Coll (MS)
Hutchinson Comm Coll (KS)
Jamestown Comm Coll (NY)
Laramie County Comm Coll (WY)
Lehigh Carbon Comm Coll (PA)
Lone Star Coll–CyFair (TX)
Lone Star Coll–U Park (TX)
Macomb Comm Coll (MI)
Manchester Comm Coll (CT)
Massachusetts Bay Comm Coll (MA)
Montgomery Coll (MD)
Montgomery County Comm Coll (PA)
Nassau Comm Coll (NY)
Northampton Comm Coll (PA)
Northwest Coll (WY)
Northwestern Michigan Coll (MI)
Norwalk Comm Coll (CT)
Palomar Coll (CA)
Pasadena City Coll (CA)
Salt Lake Comm Coll (UT)
South Florida State Coll (FL)
Tompkins Cortland Comm Coll (NY)
Tyler Jr Coll (TX)
Ulster County Comm Coll (NY)
Western Wyoming Comm Coll (WY)
Wright State U–Lake Campus (OH)

SPEECH-LANGUAGE PATHOLOGY
Lake Region State Coll (ND)
Williston State Coll (ND)

SPEECH-LANGUAGE PATHOLOGY ASSISTANT
Alexandria Tech and Comm Coll (MN)
Fayetteville Tech Comm Coll (NC)
Mitchell Tech Inst (SD)
Oklahoma City Comm Coll (OK)

SPEECH TEACHER EDUCATION
Darton State Coll (GA)

SPORT AND FITNESS ADMINISTRATION/ MANAGEMENT
Bucks County Comm Coll (PA)
Butler County Comm Coll (PA)
Camden County Coll (NJ)
Ca&nnada Coll (CA)
Cayuga County Comm Coll (NY)
Central Oregon Comm Coll (OR)
Clark Coll (WA)
Dean Coll (MA)
Delta Coll (MI)
Des Moines Area Comm Coll (IA)
Garrett Coll (MD)
Holyoke Comm Coll (MA)
Howard Comm Coll (MD)
Hutchinson Comm Coll (KS)
Illinois Eastern Comm Colls, Frontier Community College (IL)
Illinois Eastern Comm Colls, Lincoln Trail College (IL)
Illinois Eastern Comm Colls, Wabash Valley College (IL)
Iowa Lakes Comm Coll (IA)
Jefferson Comm Coll (NY)
Kingsborough Comm Coll of the City U of New York (NY)
Lehigh Carbon Comm Coll (PA)
Lorain County Comm Coll (OH)
Manor Coll (PA)
Niagara County Comm Coll (NY)
Northampton Comm Coll (PA)
North Iowa Area Comm Coll (IA)
Rock Valley Coll (IL)
Salem Comm Coll (NJ)
Springfield Tech Comm Coll (MA)
State U of New York Coll of Technology at Alfred (NY)
Sullivan County Comm Coll (NY)
Three Rivers Comm Coll (CT)
Tompkins Cortland Comm Coll (NY)
Tulsa Comm Coll (OK)
U of Cincinnati Clermont Coll (OH)
Vincennes U (IN)

SPORTS STUDIES
Finger Lakes Comm Coll (NY)
Genesee Comm Coll (NY)

STATISTICS
Coll of Central Florida (FL)
Eastern Wyoming Coll (WY)
South Florida State Coll (FL)

STATISTICS RELATED
Casper Coll (WY)

STRUCTURAL ENGINEERING
Moraine Park Tech Coll (WI)

SUBSTANCE ABUSE/ ADDICTION COUNSELING
Alvin Comm Coll (TX)
Amarillo Coll (TX)
Anne Arundel Comm Coll (MD)
Austin Comm Coll District (TX)
Camden County Coll (NJ)
Casper Coll (WY)
Central Oregon Comm Coll (OR)
Century Coll (MN)
Clark Coll (WA)
Coll of the Desert (CA)
Comm Coll of Allegheny County (PA)
The Comm Coll of Baltimore County (MD)
Comm Coll of Rhode Island (RI)
Corning Comm Coll (NY)
Delaware Tech & Comm Coll, Terry Campus (DE)
Erie Comm Coll (NY)
Finger Lakes Comm Coll (NY)
Fox Valley Tech Coll (WI)
Gadsden State Comm Coll (AL)
Gateway Comm Coll (CT)
Genesee Comm Coll (NY)
Guilford Tech Comm Coll (NC)
Housatonic Comm Coll (CT)
Howard Comm Coll (MD)
J. Sargeant Reynolds Comm Coll (VA)
Lower Columbia Coll (WA)
Mesabi Range Coll (MN)
Miami Dade Coll (FL)
Minneapolis Comm and Tech Coll (MN)
Mohave Comm Coll (AZ)
Mohawk Valley Comm Coll (NY)
Moraine Park Tech Coll (WI)
Moraine Valley Comm Coll (IL)
Mountain State Coll (WV)
North Shore Comm Coll (MA)
Oakton Comm Coll (IL)
Oklahoma State U, Oklahoma City (OK)
Olympic Coll (WA)
Palomar Coll (CA)
Reading Area Comm Coll (PA)
Sisseton-Wahpeton Coll (SD)
Southeastern Comm Coll (IA)
Tompkins Cortland Comm Coll (NY)
Truckee Meadows Comm Coll (NV)
Tyler Jr Coll (TX)
Wenatchee Valley Coll (WA)
Westchester Comm Coll (NY)
Wor-Wic Comm Coll (MD)

SURGICAL TECHNOLOGY
Anne Arundel Comm Coll (MD)
Anoka Tech Coll (MN)
Austin Comm Coll District (TX)
Bellingham Tech Coll (WA)
Cape Fear Comm Coll (NC)
Career Tech Coll, Monroe (LA)
Cincinnati State Tech and Comm Coll (OH)
Coll of Southern Idaho (ID)
Collin County Comm Coll District (TX)
Comm Care Coll (OK)
Comm Coll of Allegheny County (PA)
Comm Coll of the Air Force (AL)
Delta Coll (MI)
Eastern Idaho Tech Coll (ID)
El Centro Coll (TX)
Fayetteville Tech Comm Coll (NC)
Frederick Comm Coll (MD)
Gateway Tech Coll (WI)
Great Falls Coll Montana State U (MT)
Guilford Tech Comm Coll (NC)
Gulf Coast State Coll (FL)
Harrisburg Area Comm Coll (PA)
Hinds Comm Coll (MS)
Hutchinson Comm Coll (KS)
Iowa Lakes Comm Coll (IA)
James H. Faulkner State Comm Coll (AL)
Kalamazoo Valley Comm Coll (MI)
Kilgore Coll (TX)

Kirtland Comm Coll (MI)
Lakeland Comm Coll (OH)
Laramie County Comm Coll (WY)
Lone Star Coll–Tomball (TX)
Lorain County Comm Coll (OH)
Luzerne County Comm Coll (PA)
Macomb Comm Coll (MI)
Manchester Comm Coll (CT)
Midlands Tech Coll (SC)
Minnesota West Comm and Tech Coll (MN)
MiraCosta Coll (CA)
Mohave Comm Coll (AZ)
Montgomery Coll (MD)
Montgomery County Comm Coll (PA)
Moraine Park Tech Coll (WI)
Nassau Comm Coll (NY)
Niagara County Comm Coll (NY)
Northland Comm Coll (MN)
Oklahoma City Comm Coll (OK)
Owensboro Comm and Tech Coll (KY)
Owens Comm Coll, Toledo (OH)
Paris Jr Coll (TX)
Pueblo Comm Coll (CO)
Renton Tech Coll (WA)
Richland Comm Coll (IL)
Rock Valley Coll (IL)
San Jacinto Coll District (TX)
San Joaquin Valley Coll, Bakersfield (CA)
San Joaquin Valley Coll, Fresno (CA)
San Juan Coll (NM)
Somerset Comm Coll (KY)
Southeastern Coll–Greenacres (FL)
Southern U at Shreveport (LA)
South Louisiana Comm Coll (LA)
Spencerian Coll (KY)
Springfield Tech Comm Coll (MA)
Tallahassee Comm Coll (FL)
Texas State Tech Coll Harlingen (TX)
Trinity Valley Comm Coll (TX)
Trocaire Coll (NY)
Tulsa Comm Coll (OK)
Tyler Jr Coll (TX)
U of Cincinnati Clermont Coll (OH)
Vincennes U (IN)
Walters State Comm Coll (TN)
Waukesha County Tech Coll (WI)
Wayne County Comm Coll District (MI)
Western Dakota Tech Inst (SD)
Western Iowa Tech Comm Coll (IA)

SURVEYING ENGINEERING
Comm Coll of Rhode Island (RI)
Des Moines Area Comm Coll (IA)

SURVEYING TECHNOLOGY
Austin Comm Coll District (TX)
Bellingham Tech Coll (WA)
Clark Coll (WA)
Coll of the Canyons (CA)
The Comm Coll of Baltimore County (MD)
Fayetteville Tech Comm Coll (NC)
Gateway Tech Coll (WI)
Guam Comm Coll (GU)
Guilford Tech Comm Coll (NC)
Macomb Comm Coll (MI)
Middlesex County Coll (NJ)
Mohawk Valley Comm Coll (NY)
Mt. San Antonio Coll (CA)
Oklahoma State U, Oklahoma City (OK)
Phoenix Coll (AZ)
Renton Tech Coll (WA)
Salt Lake Comm Coll (UT)
Sheridan Coll (WY)
South Florida State Coll (FL)
South Louisiana Comm Coll (LA)
Stark State Coll (OH)
State U of New York Coll of Technology at Alfred (NY)
Tyler Jr Coll (TX)
U of Arkansas Comm Coll at Morrilton (AR)
Vincennes U (IN)

SYSTEM, NETWORKING, AND LAN/WAN MANAGEMENT
Arapahoe Comm Coll (CO)
Blue Ridge Comm and Tech Coll (WV)
Central Texas Coll (TX)
Cloud County Comm Coll (KS)
Collin County Comm Coll District (TX)
Guilford Tech Comm Coll (NC)
Iowa Lakes Comm Coll (IA)

Lone Star Coll–Tomball (TX)
Moraine Valley Comm Coll (IL)
Oklahoma City Comm Coll (OK)
Paris Jr Coll (TX)
St. Philip's Coll (TX)
Southwestern Indian Polytechnic Inst (NM)
Tyler Jr Coll (TX)
Williston State Coll (ND)

SYSTEMS ENGINEERING
South Florida State Coll (FL)

TEACHER ASSISTANT/AIDE
Alamance Comm Coll (NC)
Antelope Valley Coll (CA)
Borough of Manhattan Comm Coll of the City U of New York (NY)
Carteret Comm Coll (NC)
Central Wyoming Comm Coll (WY)
Century Coll (MN)
Cloud County Comm Coll (KS)
Coll of Southern Idaho (ID)
Comm Coll of Denver (CO)
Dakota Coll at Bottineau (ND)
Danville Area Comm Coll (IL)
El Centro Coll (TX)
Elizabethtown Comm and Tech Coll, Elizabethtown (KY)
Fiorello H. LaGuardia Comm Coll of the City U of New York (NY)
Gateway Comm and Tech Coll (KY)
Gateway Tech Coll (WI)
Genesee Comm Coll (NY)
Harford Comm Coll (MD)
Haywood Comm Coll (NC)
Highland Comm Coll (IL)
Hopkinsville Comm Coll (KY)
Illinois Eastern Comm Colls, Lincoln Trail College (IL)
Jamestown Comm Coll (NY)
Jefferson Comm Coll (NY)
Kankakee Comm Coll (IL)
Kaskaskia Coll (IL)
Kingsborough Comm Coll of the City U of New York (NY)
Kishwaukee Coll (IL)
Lehigh Carbon Comm Coll (PA)
Manchester Comm Coll (CT)
Mesa Comm Coll (AZ)
Miami Dade Coll (FL)
Middlesex County Comm Coll (NJ)
Montcalm Comm Coll (MI)
Montgomery County Comm Coll (PA)
Moraine Park Tech Coll (WI)
Moraine Valley Comm Coll (IL)
Northampton Comm Coll (PA)
Northcentral Tech Coll (WI)
Northwest State Comm Coll (OH)
Owensboro Comm and Tech Coll (KY)
Phoenix Coll (AZ)
Renton Tech Coll (WA)
Ridgewater Coll (MN)
St. Charles Comm Coll (MO)
St. Philip's Coll (TX)
Salt Lake Comm Coll (UT)
Somerset Comm Coll (KY)
Southern U at Shreveport (LA)
Southwestern Illinois Coll (IL)
State Fair Comm Coll (MO)
Texas State Tech Coll Harlingen (TX)
Victor Valley Coll (CA)
Vincennes U (IN)
Waukesha County Tech Coll (WI)
Western Iowa Tech Comm Coll (IA)

TEACHING ASSISTANTS/AIDES RELATED
Comm Coll of Denver (CO)
Terra State Comm Coll (OH)

TECHNICAL TEACHER EDUCATION
State Fair Comm Coll (MO)

TECHNOLOGY/INDUSTRIAL ARTS TEACHER EDUCATION
Allen Comm Coll (KS)
Casper Coll (WY)
Delta Coll (MI)
Eastern Arizona Coll (AZ)
Hinds Comm Coll (MS)
Iowa Lakes Comm Coll (IA)
Roane State Comm Coll (TN)

TELECOMMUNICATIONS TECHNOLOGY
Amarillo Coll (TX)
Carl Albert State Coll (OK)
Cayuga County Comm Coll (NY)
Central Texas Coll (TX)

Clark Coll (WA)
Collin County Comm Coll District (TX)
County Coll of Morris (NJ)
Erie Comm Coll, South Campus (NY)
Guilford Tech Comm Coll (NC)
Haywood Comm Coll (NC)
Hinds Comm Coll (MS)
Howard Comm Coll (MD)
Illinois Eastern Comm Colls, Lincoln Trail College (IL)
Iowa Central Comm Coll (IA)
Lake Land Coll (IL)
Miami Dade Coll (FL)
Mitchell Tech Inst (SD)
Monroe Comm Coll (NY)
Northern Essex Comm Coll (MA)
Penn State DuBois (PA)
Penn State Fayette, The Eberly Campus (PA)
Penn State Shenango (PA)
Pensacola State Coll (FL)
Queensborough Comm Coll of the City U of New York (NY)
Quinsigamond Comm Coll (MA)
Ridgewater Coll (MN)
St. Philip's Coll (TX)
Salt Lake Comm Coll (UT)
Seminole State Coll of Florida (FL)
Springfield Tech Comm Coll (MA)
Texas State Tech Coll Harlingen (TX)
Trident Tech Coll (SC)
Western Iowa Tech Comm Coll (IA)

THEATER DESIGN AND TECHNOLOGY
Carroll Comm Coll (MD)
Casper Coll (WY)
Central Wyoming Coll (WY)
Florida State Coll at Jacksonville (FL)
Genesee Comm Coll (NY)
Harford Comm Coll (MD)
Howard Comm Coll (MD)
Miami Dade Coll (FL)
MiraCosta Coll (CA)
Nassau Comm Coll (NY)
Normandale Comm Coll (MN)
Ohlone Coll (CA)
Pasadena City Coll (CA)
San Juan Coll (NM)
Vincennes U (IN)
Western Wyoming Comm Coll (WY)

THEATER/THEATER ARTS MANAGEMENT
Genesee Comm Coll (NY)
Harper Coll (IL)
Ohlone Coll (CA)

THERAPEUTIC RECREATION
Austin Comm Coll District (TX)
Comm Coll of Allegheny County (PA)
Ridgewater Coll (MN)

TOOL AND DIE TECHNOLOGY
Bevill State Comm Coll (AL)
Delta Coll (MI)
Des Moines Area Comm Coll (IA)
Dunwoody Coll of Technology (MN)
Gadsden State Comm Coll (AL)
George C. Wallace Comm Coll (AL)
Hennepin Tech Coll (MN)
J. F. Drake State Comm and Tech Coll (AL)
Macomb Comm Coll (MI)
North Iowa Area Comm Coll (IA)
Ridgewater Coll (MN)
Rock Valley Coll (IL)
Texas State Tech Coll Harlingen (TX)
Vincennes U (IN)

TOURISM AND TRAVEL SERVICES MANAGEMENT
Amarillo Coll (TX)
Austin Comm Coll District (TX)
Bucks County Comm Coll (PA)
Bunker Hill Comm Coll (MA)
Daytona State Coll (FL)
Finger Lakes Comm Coll (NY)
Fiorello H. LaGuardia Comm Coll of the City U of New York (NY)
Genesee Comm Coll (NY)
Guam Comm Coll (GU)
Gwinnett Tech Coll (GA)
Harrisburg Area Comm Coll (PA)
Hinds Comm Coll (MS)
Hocking Coll (OH)
Houston Comm Coll (TX)
Kingsborough Comm Coll of the City U of New York (NY)
Lakeland Comm Coll (OH)
Lorain County Comm Coll (OH)

Luzerne County Comm Coll (PA)
Miami Dade Coll (FL)
Monroe Comm Coll (NY)
Moraine Valley Comm Coll (IL)
Niagara County Comm Coll (NY)
Northern Essex Comm Coll (MA)
North Shore Comm Coll (MA)
Rockland Comm Coll (NY)
Southern U at Shreveport (LA)
Sullivan County Comm Coll (NY)
Westmoreland County Comm Coll (PA)

TOURISM AND TRAVEL SERVICES MARKETING
Luzerne County Comm Coll (PA)
Montgomery County Comm Coll (PA)

TOURISM PROMOTION
Comm Coll of Allegheny County (PA)
Genesee Comm Coll (NY)
Jefferson Comm Coll (NY)

TRADE AND INDUSTRIAL TEACHER EDUCATION
Copiah-Lincoln Comm Coll (MS)
Darton State Coll (GA)
Iowa Lakes Comm Coll (IA)
Lenoir Comm Coll (NC)
New Mexico Jr Coll (NM)
Northeastern Jr Coll (CO)
Quinsigamond Comm Coll (MA)
Southeastern Comm Coll (IA)
South Florida State Coll (FL)
Victor Valley Coll (CA)

TRANSPORTATION AND HIGHWAY ENGINEERING
Gateway Tech Coll (WI)

TRANSPORTATION AND MATERIALS MOVING RELATED
Cecil Coll (MD)
Los Angeles Trade-Tech Coll (CA)
Mid-Plains Comm Coll, North Platte (NE)
Mt. San Antonio Coll (CA)
Nassau Comm Coll (NY)
Northern Virginia Comm Coll (VA)
San Diego Miramar Coll (CA)

TRANSPORTATION/MOBILITY MANAGEMENT
Cecil Coll (MD)
Florida State Coll at Jacksonville (FL)
Gulf Coast State Coll (FL)
Hagerstown Comm Coll (MD)
South Florida State Coll (FL)

TRUCK AND BUS DRIVER/COMMERCIAL VEHICLE OPERATION/INSTRUCTION
Mohave Comm Coll (AZ)

TURF AND TURFGRASS MANAGEMENT
Catawba Valley Comm Coll (NC)
Cincinnati State Tech and Comm Coll (OH)
Coll of the Desert (CA)
Comm Coll of Allegheny County (PA)
Danville Area Comm Coll (IL)
Guilford Tech Comm Coll (NC)
Houston Comm Coll (TX)
Iowa Lakes Comm Coll (IA)
Northwestern Michigan Coll (MI)
The Ohio State U Ag Tech Inst (OH)
Oklahoma State U, Oklahoma City (OK)
Ozarks Tech Comm Coll (MO)
Westmoreland County Comm Coll (PA)

URBAN FORESTRY
Dakota Coll at Bottineau (ND)
Hennepin Tech Coll (MN)
Kent State U at Trumbull (OH)

URBAN STUDIES/AFFAIRS
Lorain County Comm Coll (OH)

VEHICLE MAINTENANCE AND REPAIR TECHNOLOGIES
Coll of the Desert (CA)
Corning Comm Coll (NY)

VEHICLE MAINTENANCE AND REPAIR TECHNOLOGIES RELATED
Corning Comm Coll (NY)
Guilford Tech Comm Coll (NC)
Northern Virginia Comm Coll (VA)

State U of New York Coll of Technology at Alfred (NY)
Victor Valley Coll (CA)
Western Dakota Tech Inst (SD)

VETERINARY/ANIMAL HEALTH TECHNOLOGY
Bradford School (OH)
Camden County Coll (NJ)
Cedar Valley Coll (TX)
Coll of Central Florida (FL)
Coll of Southern Idaho (ID)
Comm Care Coll (OK)
The Comm Coll of Baltimore County (MD)
Comm Coll of Denver (CO)
County Coll of Morris (NJ)
Crowder Coll (MO)
Des Moines Area Comm Coll (IA)
Duluth Business U (MN)
Eastern Wyoming Coll (WY)
Fiorello H. LaGuardia Comm Coll of the City U of New York (NY)
Florida Gateway Coll (FL)
Fox Coll (IL)
Front Range Comm Coll (CO)
Gateway Tech Coll (WI)
Genesee Comm Coll (NY)
Gwinnett Tech Coll (GA)
Hillsborough Comm Coll (FL)
Hinds Comm Coll (MS)
Holyoke Comm Coll (MA)
International Business Coll, Indianapolis (IN)
Jefferson Coll (MO)
Jefferson State Comm Coll (AL)
Kaskaskia Coll (IL)
Kent State U at Tuscarawas (OH)
Lehigh Carbon Comm Coll (PA)
Lone Star Coll–Tomball (TX)
Macomb Comm Coll (MI)
Manor Coll (PA)
Miami Dade Coll (FL)
Northampton Comm Coll (PA)
North Shore Comm Coll (MA)
Northwest Coll (WY)
Oklahoma State U, Oklahoma City (OK)
Owensboro Comm and Tech Coll (KY)
Penn Foster Coll (AZ)
Pensacola State Coll (FL)
Ridgewater Coll (MN)
San Joaquin Valley Coll, Fresno (CA)
San Juan Coll (NM)
Shawnee Comm Coll (IL)
State U of New York Coll of Technology at Alfred (NY)
Trident Tech Coll (SC)
Truckee Meadows Comm Coll (NV)
Tulsa Comm Coll (OK)
Ulster County Comm Coll (NY)
Vet Tech Inst (PA)
Vet Tech Inst at Bradford School (OH)
Vet Tech Inst at Fox Coll (IL)
Vet Tech Inst at Hickey Coll (MO)
Vet Tech Inst at International Business Coll, Fort Wayne (IN)
Vet Tech Inst at International Business Coll, Indianapolis (IN)
Vet Tech Inst of Houston (TX)
Volunteer State Comm Coll (TN)
Wayne County Comm Coll District (MI)
Westchester Comm Coll (NY)
Western Iowa Tech Comm Coll (IA)
York County Comm Coll (ME)

VISUAL AND PERFORMING ARTS
Amarillo Coll (TX)
Borough of Manhattan Comm Coll of the City U of New York (NY)
Bucks County Comm Coll (PA)
Chandler-Gilbert Comm Coll (AZ)
Citrus Coll (CA)
The Comm Coll of Baltimore County (MD)
Dutchess Comm Coll (NY)
Fiorello H. LaGuardia Comm Coll of the City U of New York (NY)
Harrisburg Area Comm Coll (PA)
Hutchinson Comm Coll (KS)
Kankakee Comm Coll (IL)
Middlesex County Coll (NJ)
Moraine Valley Comm Coll (IL)
Mott Comm Coll (MI)
Mt. San Antonio Coll (CA)
Nassau Comm Coll (NY)
Northern Virginia Comm Coll (VA)
Ocean County Coll (NJ)
Phoenix Coll (AZ)

Queensborough Comm Coll of the City U of New York (NY)
Rogue Comm Coll (OR)
Sierra Coll (CA)
Spartanburg Methodist Coll (SC)
Ulster County Comm Coll (NY)
Western Wyoming Comm Coll (WY)

VISUAL AND PERFORMING ARTS RELATED
Bossier Parish Comm Coll (LA)
Comm Coll of Allegheny County (PA)
John Tyler Comm Coll (VA)
Northern Virginia Comm Coll (VA)
Northwest Coll (WY)

VITICULTURE AND ENOLOGY
Finger Lakes Comm Coll (NY)
Harrisburg Area Comm Coll (PA)
James Sprunt Comm Coll (NC)
Kent State U at Ashtabula (OH)

VOCATIONAL REHABILITATION COUNSELING
South Florida State Coll (FL)

VOICE AND OPERA
Alvin Comm Coll (TX)
Iowa Lakes Comm Coll (IA)
Navarro Coll (TX)

WATCHMAKING AND JEWELRYMAKING
Austin Comm Coll District (TX)
Haywood Comm Coll (NC)
Paris Jr Coll (TX)

WATER QUALITY AND WASTEWATER TREATMENT MANAGEMENT AND RECYCLING TECHNOLOGY
Arizona Western Coll (AZ)
Casper Coll (WY)
Citrus Coll (CA)
Coll of Southern Idaho (ID)
Coll of the Canyons (CA)
Delta Coll (MI)
Gateway Tech Coll (WI)
Moraine Park Tech Coll (WI)
Palomar Coll (CA)

WATER, WETLANDS, AND MARINE RESOURCES MANAGEMENT
Iowa Lakes Comm Coll (IA)
South Florida State Coll (FL)

WEB/MULTIMEDIA MANAGEMENT AND WEBMASTER
Casper Coll (WY)
Clark Coll (WA)
Comm Coll of Rhode Island (RI)
Delta Coll (MI)
Fox Valley Tech Coll (WI)
Gateway Tech Coll (WI)
Kalamazoo Valley Comm Coll (MI)
Kaskaskia Coll (IL)
Kirtland Comm Coll (MI)
MiraCosta Coll (CA)
Monroe County Comm Coll (MI)
Montgomery County Comm Coll (PA)
Moraine Valley Comm Coll (IL)
Northern Essex Comm Coll (MA)
Northland Comm Coll (MN)
Oklahoma City Comm Coll (OK)
Riverland Comm Coll (MN)
St. Clair County Comm Coll (MI)
Seminole State Coll of Florida (FL)
Sheridan Coll (WY)
Southwestern Illinois Coll (IL)
Stark State Coll (OH)
Trident Tech Coll (SC)
Truckee Meadows Comm Coll (NV)
Vincennes U (IN)
Western Wyoming Comm Coll (WY)

WEB PAGE, DIGITAL/MULTIMEDIA AND INFORMATION RESOURCES DESIGN
Borough of Manhattan Comm Coll of the City U of New York (NY)
Bucks County Comm Coll (PA)
Bunker Hill Comm Coll (MA)
Butler County Comm Coll (PA)
Casper Coll (WY)
Cecil Coll (MD)
City Colls of Chicago, Olive-Harvey College (IL)
Cloud County Comm Coll (KS)

Coll of Southern Idaho (ID)
The Coll of Westchester (NY)
Collin County Comm Coll District (TX)
Corning Comm Coll (NY)
County Coll of Morris (NJ)
Dunwoody Coll of Technology (MN)
Dyersburg State Comm Coll (TN)
El Centro Coll (TX)
Florida State Coll at Jacksonville (FL)
Genesee Comm Coll (NY)
Great Falls Coll Montana State U (MT)
Gulf Coast State Coll (FL)
Hagerstown Comm Coll (MD)
Harper Coll (IL)
Harrisburg Area Comm Coll (PA)
Hawkeye Comm Coll (IA)
Hennepin Tech Coll (MN)
Hutchinson Comm Coll (KS)
J. Sargeant Reynolds Comm Coll (VA)
Kalamazoo Valley Comm Coll (MI)
Lehigh Carbon Comm Coll (PA)
Mesabi Range Coll (MN)
Miami Dade Coll (FL)
Middlesex Comm Coll (MA)
Minneapolis Comm and Tech Coll (MN)
Minnesota State Coll–Southeast Tech (MN)
Mohawk Valley Comm Coll (NY)
Monroe County Comm Coll (MI)
Montgomery Coll (MD)
Motlow State Comm Coll (TN)
Mott Comm Coll (MI)
Mount Wachusett Comm Coll (MA)
Niagara County Comm Coll (NY)
Northampton Comm Coll (PA)
Northern Essex Comm Coll (MA)
North Iowa Area Comm Coll (IA)
Northland Comm Coll (MN)
North Shore Comm Coll (MA)
Northwest State Comm Coll (OH)
Norwalk Comm Coll (CT)
Oklahoma State U, Oklahoma City (OK)
Palomar Coll (CA)
Pasco-Hernando State Coll (FL)
Phoenix Coll (AZ)
Pueblo Comm Coll (CO)
Quinsigamond Comm Coll (MA)
Raritan Valley Comm Coll (NJ)
Reading Area Comm Coll (PA)
Ridgewater Coll (MN)
Riverland Comm Coll (MN)
Schoolcraft Coll (MI)
Seminole State Coll of Florida (FL)

Sierra Coll (CA)
South Louisiana Comm Coll (LA)
Stark State Coll (OH)
State Fair Comm Coll (MO)
Sullivan Coll of Technology and Design (KY)
Tallahassee Comm Coll (FL)
Terra State Comm Coll (OH)
Trident Tech Coll (SC)
Volunteer State Comm Coll (TN)
Walters State Comm Coll (TN)
Western Iowa Tech Comm Coll (IA)
Western Wyoming Comm Coll (WY)
Westmoreland County Comm Coll (PA)
Wisconsin Indianhead Tech Coll (WI)

WELDING ENGINEERING TECHNOLOGY

Mitchell Tech Inst (SD)
St. Clair County Comm Coll (MI)

WELDING TECHNOLOGY

Alamance Comm Coll (NC)
American Samoa Comm Coll (AS)
Anoka Tech Coll (MN)
Antelope Valley Coll (CA)
Arizona Western Coll (AZ)
Austin Comm Coll District (TX)
Bainbridge State Coll (GA)
Bellingham Tech Coll (WA)
Big Bend Comm Coll (WA)
Casper Coll (WY)
Central Texas Coll (TX)
Central Wyoming Coll (WY)
Clark Coll (WA)
Coastal Bend Coll (TX)
Cochise Coll, Douglas (AZ)
Coll of Southern Idaho (ID)
Coll of the Canyons (CA)
Comm Coll of Allegheny County (PA)
Comm Coll of Denver (CO)
Crowder Coll (MO)
Delta Coll (MI)
Dunwoody Coll of Technology (MN)
Eastern Arizona Coll (AZ)
Eastern Idaho Tech Coll (ID)
Eastern Wyoming Coll (WY)
Elizabethtown Comm and Tech Coll, Elizabethtown (KY)
Fox Valley Tech Coll (WI)
Front Range Comm Coll (CO)
George C. Wallace Comm Coll (AL)
Grand Rapids Comm Coll (MI)
Great Basin Coll (NV)
Great Falls Coll Montana State U (MT)
Haywood Comm Coll (NC)
Hinds Comm Coll (MS)

Hutchinson Comm Coll (KS)
Iowa Central Comm Coll (IA)
Iowa Lakes Comm Coll (IA)
Jamestown Comm Coll (NY)
Jefferson Coll (MO)
J. Sargeant Reynolds Comm Coll (VA)
Kalamazoo Valley Comm Coll (MI)
Kankakee Comm Coll (IL)
Kaskaskia Coll (IL)
Kellogg Comm Coll (MI)
Kennebec Valley Comm Coll (ME)
Kilgore Coll (TX)
Kirtland Comm Coll (MI)
Lake Area Tech Inst (SD)
Lenoir Comm Coll (NC)
Lone Star Coll–CyFair (TX)
Lone Star Coll–North Harris (TX)
Los Angeles Trade-Tech Coll (CA)
Lower Columbia Coll (WA)
Macomb Comm Coll (MI)
Maysville Comm and Tech Coll, Maysville (KY)
Mid-Plains Comm Coll, North Platte (NE)
Mohave Comm Coll (AZ)
Mohawk Valley Comm Coll (NY)
Monroe County Comm Coll (MI)
Montcalm Comm Coll (MI)
Mt. San Antonio Coll (CA)
New Mexico Jr Coll (NM)
North Central Texas Coll (TX)
North Iowa Area Comm Coll (IA)
Northland Comm Coll (MN)
Northwest Coll (WY)
Oklahoma Tech Coll (OK)
Olympic Coll (WA)
Orange Coast Coll (CA)
Owens Comm Coll, Toledo (OH)
Ozarks Tech Comm Coll (MO)
Palomar Coll (CA)
Paris Jr Coll (TX)
Pasadena City Coll (CA)
Pennsylvania Highlands Comm Coll (PA)
Pueblo Comm Coll (CO)
Richmond Comm Coll (NC)
Ridgewater Coll (MN)
Rock Valley Coll (IL)
Rogue Comm Coll (OR)
St. Philip's Coll (TX)
Salt Lake Comm Coll (UT)
San Jacinto Coll District (TX)
San Juan Coll (NM)
Schoolcraft Coll (MI)
Shawnee Comm Coll (IL)
Sheridan Coll (WY)
Southeastern Comm Coll (IA)
South Louisiana Comm Coll (LA)

Southwestern Illinois Coll (IL)
State U of New York Coll of Technology at Alfred (NY)
Tallahassee Comm Coll (FL)
Terra State Comm Coll (OH)
Texas State Tech Coll Harlingen (TX)
Trinidad State Jr Coll (CO)
Trinity Valley Comm Coll (TX)
Truckee Meadows Comm Coll (NV)
Tyler Jr Coll (TX)
Victor Valley Coll (CA)
Wayne County Comm Coll District (MI)
Western Iowa Tech Comm Coll (IA)
Western Nevada Coll (NV)
Western Wyoming Comm Coll (WY)
Westmoreland County Comm Coll (PA)
White Mountains Comm Coll (NH)
Williston State Coll (ND)

WELL DRILLING

Westmoreland County Comm Coll (PA)

WILDLAND/FOREST FIREFIGHTING AND INVESTIGATION

Fox Valley Tech Coll (WI)
Trinidad State Jr Coll (CO)

WILDLIFE BIOLOGY

Eastern Arizona Coll (AZ)
Iowa Lakes Comm Coll (IA)

WILDLIFE, FISH AND WILDLANDS SCIENCE AND MANAGEMENT

Casper Coll (WY)
Dakota Coll at Bottineau (ND)
Eastern Wyoming Coll (WY)
Front Range Comm Coll (CO)
Garrett Coll (MD)
Haywood Comm Coll (NC)
Hocking Coll (OH)
Iowa Lakes Comm Coll (IA)
Laramie County Comm Coll (WY)
Mt. San Antonio Coll (CA)
Penn State DuBois (PA)
Potomac State Coll of West Virginia U (WV)
Shawnee Comm Coll (IL)
Western Wyoming Comm Coll (WY)

WINE STEWARD/SOMMELIER

Cayuga County Comm Coll (NY)
Niagara County Comm Coll (NY)

WOMEN'S STUDIES

Bucks County Comm Coll (PA)

Casper Coll (WY)
Greenfield Comm Coll (MA)
Northern Essex Comm Coll (MA)
Palomar Coll (CA)
Sierra Coll (CA)

WOOD SCIENCE AND WOOD PRODUCTS/PULP AND PAPER TECHNOLOGY

Dabney S. Lancaster Comm Coll (VA)
Haywood Comm Coll (NC)
Kennebec Valley Comm Coll (ME)
Potomac State Coll of West Virginia U (WV)

WOODWIND INSTRUMENTS

Iowa Lakes Comm Coll (IA)

WOODWORKING

Vincennes U (IN)

WOODWORKING RELATED

Haywood Comm Coll (NC)

WORD PROCESSING

Gateway Comm Coll (CT)
Iowa Lakes Comm Coll (IA)
Kellogg Comm Coll (MI)
Lorain County Comm Coll (OH)
Monroe County Comm Coll (MI)
North Central Texas Coll (TX)
Northland Comm Coll (MN)
Orange Coast Coll (CA)
Richland Comm Coll (IL)
Riverland Comm Coll (MN)
Seminole State Coll of Florida (FL)
Stark State Coll (OH)
Western Wyoming Comm Coll (WY)

WORK AND FAMILY STUDIES

Antelope Valley Coll (CA)
Arizona Western Coll (AZ)

WRITING

Allen Comm Coll (KS)
Austin Comm Coll District (TX)
Cayuga County Comm Coll (NY)

YOUTH SERVICES

Midlands Tech Coll (SC)

ZOOLOGY/ANIMAL BIOLOGY

Dakota Coll at Bottineau (ND)
Northeastern Jr Coll (CO)
Pensacola State Coll (FL)
South Florida State Coll (FL)

Associate Degree Programs at Four-Year Colleges

ACCOUNTING
Baker Coll (MI)
Berkeley Coll–New York City Campus (NY)
California U of Pennsylvania (PA)
Calumet Coll of Saint Joseph (IN)
Caribbean U (PR)
Central Penn Coll (PA)
Champlain Coll (VT)
Clarke U (IA)
Davenport U, Grand Rapids (MI)
Elizabethtown Coll School of Continuing and Professional Studies (PA)
Ellis U (IL)
Fisher Coll (MA)
Franciscan U of Steubenville (OH)
Franklin U (OH)
Gwynedd Mercy U (PA)
Hawai'i Pacific U (HI)
Hobe Sound Bible Coll (FL)
Husson U (ME)
Immaculata U (PA)
Indian River State Coll (FL)
Inter American U of Puerto Rico, Aguadilla Campus (PR)
Inter American U of Puerto Rico, Bayamón Campus (PR)
Inter American U of Puerto Rico, Fajardo Campus (PR)
Inter American U of Puerto Rico, Guayama Campus (PR)
Inter American U of Puerto Rico, Ponce Campus (PR)
Inter American U of Puerto Rico, San Germán Campus (PR)
Johnson State Coll (VT)
Keiser U, Fort Lauderdale (FL)
Keystone Coll (PA)
Lincoln Coll of New England, Southington (CT)
Maria Coll (NY)
Missouri Southern State U (MO)
Morrisville State Coll (NY)
Mount Aloysius Coll (PA)
Mount Marty Coll (SD)
Mount St. Joseph U (OH)
Muhlenberg Coll (PA)
National U Coll, Bayam&on (PR)
Palm Beach State Coll (FL)
Post U (CT)
Rasmussen Coll Appleton (WI)
Rasmussen Coll Aurora (IL)
Rasmussen Coll Bismarck (ND)
Rasmussen Coll Blaine (MN)
Rasmussen Coll Bloomington (MN)
Rasmussen Coll Brooklyn Park (MN)
Rasmussen Coll Eagan (MN)
Rasmussen Coll Fort Myers (FL)
Rasmussen Coll Green Bay (WI)
Rasmussen Coll Kansas City/Overland Park (KS)
Rasmussen Coll Lake Elmo/Woodbury (MN)
Rasmussen Coll Land O' Lakes (FL)
Rasmussen Coll Mankato (MN)
Rasmussen Coll Mokena/Tinley Park (IL)
Rasmussen Coll Moorhead (MN)
Rasmussen Coll New Port Richey (FL)
Rasmussen Coll Ocala (FL)
Rasmussen Coll Romeoville/Joliet (IL)
Rasmussen Coll St. Cloud (MN)
Rasmussen Coll Tampa/Brandon (FL)
Rasmussen Coll Topeka (KS)
Rasmussen Coll Wausau (WI)

Saint Francis U (PA)
Saint Mary-of-the-Woods Coll (IN)
Shawnee State U (OH)
Siena Heights U (MI)
Southern Adventist U (TN)
Southern New Hampshire U (NH)
Southern Tech Coll, Fort Myers (FL)
Southwest Minnesota State U (MN)
State Coll of Florida Manatee-Sarasota (FL)
Stratford U, Glen Allen (VA)
Stratford U, Newport News (VA)
Stratford U, Woodbridge (VA)
Thiel Coll (PA)
Thomas More Coll (KY)
Tiffin U (OH)
Trine U (IN)
Union Coll (NE)
Universidad del Turabo (PR)
U of Alaska Anchorage (AK)
U of Cincinnati (OH)
The U of Findlay (OH)
U of Northwestern–St. Paul (MN)
U of Rio Grande (OH)
U of the Virgin Islands (VI)
Urbana U (OH)
Utah Valley U (UT)
Walsh U (OH)
Webber International U (FL)
Youngstown State U (OH)

ACCOUNTING AND BUSINESS/MANAGEMENT
Kansas State U (KS)

ACCOUNTING RELATED
Florida National U (FL)
Franklin U (OH)
Montana State U Billings (MT)

ACCOUNTING TECHNOLOGY AND BOOKKEEPING
American Public U System (WV)
DeVry U, Pomona (CA)
DeVry U, Westminster (CO)
DeVry U, Miramar (FL)
DeVry U, Orlando (FL)
DeVry U, Decatur (GA)
DeVry U Online (IL)
Ferris State U (MI)
Florida National U (FL)
Gannon U (PA)
Hickey Coll (MO)
Hilbert Coll (NY)
International Business Coll, Fort Wayne (IN)
Kent State U at Geauga (OH)
Lewis-Clark State Coll (ID)
Mercy Coll (NY)
Miami U (OH)
Montana State U Billings (MT)
Montana Tech of The U of Montana (MT)
Morrisville State Coll (NY)
New York City Coll of Technology of the City U of New York (NY)
New York Inst of Technology (NY)
Pennsylvania Coll of Technology (PA)
Polk State Coll (FL)
Post U (CT)
State U of New York Coll of Agriculture and Technology at Cobleskill (NY)
State U of New York Coll of Technology at Canton (NY)
State U of New York Coll of Technology at Delhi (NY)
Sullivan U (KY)
The U of Akron (OH)

U of Alaska Fairbanks (AK)
U of Cincinnati (OH)
The U of Montana (MT)
U of Rio Grande (OH)
U of the District of Columbia (DC)
The U of Toledo (OH)
Valencia Coll (FL)

ACTING
Academy of Art U (CA)

ADMINISTRATIVE ASSISTANT AND SECRETARIAL SCIENCE
Arkansas Tech U (AR)
Baker Coll (MI)
Ball State U (IN)
Black Hills State U (SD)
Campbellsville U (KY)
Clarion U of Pennsylvania (PA)
Clayton State U (GA)
Columbia Centro Universitario, Caguas (PR)
Columbia Centro Universitario, Yauco (PR)
Concordia Coll–New York (NY)
Dickinson State U (ND)
Eastern Kentucky U (KY)
EDP U of Puerto Rico (PR)
EDP U of Puerto Rico–San Sebastian (PR)
Faith Baptist Bible Coll and Theological Seminary (IA)
Florida National U (FL)
Fort Hays State U (KS)
Fort Valley State U (GA)
Hickey Coll (MO)
Hobe Sound Bible Coll (FL)
Idaho State U (ID)
Indian River State Coll (FL)
Inter American U of Puerto Rico, San Germán Campus (PR)
International Business Coll, Fort Wayne (IN)
Kuyper Coll (MI)
Lewis-Clark State Coll (ID)
Miami U (OH)
Montana State U Billings (MT)
Montana Tech of The U of Montana (MT)
Morrisville State Coll (NY)
Northern Michigan U (MI)
Oakland City U (IN)
Palm Beach State Coll (FL)
Rider U (NJ)
State Coll of Florida Manatee-Sarasota (FL)
Summit U (PA)
Tennessee State U (TN)
The U of Akron (OH)
U of Puerto Rico in Ponce (PR)
U of Rio Grande (OH)
U of the District of Columbia (DC)
Washburn U (KS)
Weber State U (UT)
Welch Coll (TN)
Williams Baptist Coll (AR)

ADULT AND CONTINUING EDUCATION
Fisher Coll (MA)

ADULT AND CONTINUING EDUCATION ADMINISTRATION
Concordia Coll–New York (NY)

ADULT DEVELOPMENT AND AGING
Madonna U (MI)

ADVERTISING
Academy of Art U (CA)
Fashion Inst of Technology (NY)
State Coll of Florida Manatee-Sarasota (FL)

AERONAUTICAL/AEROSPACE ENGINEERING TECHNOLOGY
Purdue U (IN)
U of the District of Columbia (DC)
Vaughn Coll of Aeronautics and Technology (NY)

AERONAUTICS/AVIATION/AEROSPACE SCIENCE AND TECHNOLOGY
Embry-Riddle Aeronautical U–Worldwide (FL)
Liberty U (VA)
Montana State U (MT)
Ohio U (OH)
Purdue U (IN)
U of Alaska Anchorage (AK)
U of Cincinnati (OH)
U of the District of Columbia (DC)
Vaughn Coll of Aeronautics and Technology (NY)
Walla Walla U (WA)

AFRICAN AMERICAN/BLACK STUDIES
State Coll of Florida Manatee-Sarasota (FL)

AGRIBUSINESS
Southern Arkansas U–Magnolia (AR)
Southwest Minnesota State U (MN)
State U of New York Coll of Agriculture and Technology at Cobleskill (NY)
Vermont Tech Coll (VT)

AGRICULTURAL BUSINESS AND MANAGEMENT
Coll of Coastal Georgia (GA)
Colorado Mesa U (CO)
Dickinson State U (ND)
Indian River State Coll (FL)
Michigan State U (MI)
Morrisville State Coll (NY)
North Carolina State U (NC)
State U of New York Coll of Agriculture and Technology at Cobleskill (NY)

AGRICULTURAL BUSINESS AND MANAGEMENT RELATED
Penn State Abington (PA)
Penn State Altoona (PA)
Penn State Beaver (PA)
Penn State Berks (PA)
Penn State Brandywine (PA)
Penn State Erie, The Behrend Coll (PA)
Penn State Greater Allegheny (PA)
Penn State Hazleton (PA)
Penn State Lehigh Valley (PA)
Penn State New Kensington (PA)
Penn State Schuylkill (PA)
Penn State U Park (PA)
Penn State Wilkes-Barre (PA)
Penn State Worthington Scranton (PA)
Penn State York (PA)
U of Guelph (ON, Canada)

AGRICULTURAL BUSINESS TECHNOLOGY
Wright State U (OH)

AGRICULTURAL ENGINEERING
Morrisville State Coll (NY)

AGRICULTURAL MECHANICS AND EQUIPMENT TECHNOLOGY
Morrisville State Coll (NY)

AGRICULTURAL PRODUCTION
Eastern New Mexico U (NM)
U of the Fraser Valley (BC, Canada)
Western Kentucky U (KY)

AGRICULTURE
Lubbock Christian U (TX)
Morrisville State Coll (NY)
North Carolina State U (NC)
South Dakota State U (SD)
State U of New York Coll of Agriculture and Technology at Cobleskill (NY)
U of Delaware (DE)
U of Guelph (ON, Canada)

AGRICULTURE AND AGRICULTURE OPERATIONS RELATED
Murray State U (KY)

AGRONOMY AND CROP SCIENCE
State U of New York Coll of Agriculture and Technology at Cobleskill (NY)

AIRCRAFT POWERPLANT TECHNOLOGY
Embry-Riddle Aeronautical U–Daytona (FL)
Embry-Riddle Aeronautical U–Worldwide (FL)
Hallmark U (TX)
Idaho State U (ID)
Pennsylvania Coll of Technology (PA)
U of Alaska Fairbanks (AK)

AIRFRAME MECHANICS AND AIRCRAFT MAINTENANCE TECHNOLOGY
Hallmark U (TX)
Lewis U (IL)
Northern Michigan U (MI)
U of Alaska Anchorage (AK)

AIRLINE FLIGHT ATTENDANT
Liberty U (VA)

AIRLINE PILOT AND FLIGHT CREW
Indian River State Coll (FL)
Lewis U (IL)
Palm Beach State Coll (FL)
Polk State Coll (FL)
Santa Fe Coll (FL)
Southern Illinois U Carbondale (IL)
Southern Utah U (UT)
U of Alaska Anchorage (AK)
U of Alaska Fairbanks (AK)
Utah Valley U (UT)

AIR TRAFFIC CONTROL
LeTourneau U (TX)
Lewis U (IL)
U of Alaska Anchorage (AK)

ALLIED HEALTH AND MEDICAL ASSISTING SERVICES RELATED
Clarion U of Pennsylvania (PA)
Eastern U (PA)
Florida National U (FL)

National U (CA)
Nebraska Methodist Coll (NE)
Stratford U, Falls Church (VA)
Widener U (PA)

ALLIED HEALTH DIAGNOSTIC, INTERVENTION, AND TREATMENT PROFESSIONS RELATED
Ball State U (IN)
Cameron U (OK)
Gwynedd Mercy U (PA)
Pennsylvania Coll of Technology (PA)

AMERICAN GOVERNMENT AND POLITICS
State Coll of Florida Manatee-Sarasota (FL)

AMERICAN INDIAN/NATIVE AMERICAN STUDIES
Inst of American Indian Arts (NM)

AMERICAN NATIVE/NATIVE AMERICAN LANGUAGES
Idaho State U (ID)
U of Alaska Fairbanks (AK)

AMERICAN SIGN LANGUAGE (ASL)
Bethel Coll (IN)
Idaho State U (ID)
Madonna U (MI)

AMERICAN STUDIES
State Coll of Florida Manatee-Sarasota (FL)

ANIMAL/LIVESTOCK HUSBANDRY AND PRODUCTION
Michigan State U (MI)
North Carolina State U (NC)
Southern Utah U (UT)
U of Connecticut (CT)
U of the Fraser Valley (BC, Canada)

ANIMAL SCIENCES
Becker Coll (MA)
State U of New York Coll of Agriculture and Technology at Cobleskill (NY)
U of Connecticut (CT)
U of New Hampshire (NH)

ANIMAL SCIENCES RELATED
Santa Fe Coll (FL)

ANIMAL TRAINING
Becker Coll (MA)

ANIMATION, INTERACTIVE TECHNOLOGY, VIDEO GRAPHICS AND SPECIAL EFFECTS
Academy of Art U (CA)
Colorado Mesa U (CO)
Ferris State U (MI)
New England Inst of Technology (RI)

ANTHROPOLOGY
Indian River State Coll (FL)

APPAREL AND ACCESSORIES MARKETING
The U of Montana (MT)

APPAREL AND TEXTILE MANUFACTURING
Fashion Inst of Technology (NY)

APPAREL AND TEXTILE MARKETING MANAGEMENT
U of the Incarnate Word (TX)

APPAREL AND TEXTILES
Indian River State Coll (FL)
Palm Beach State Coll (FL)

APPLIED HORTICULTURE/HORTICULTURAL BUSINESS SERVICES RELATED
Morrisville State Coll (NY)
U of Massachusetts Amherst (MA)

APPLIED HORTICULTURE/HORTICULTURE OPERATIONS
Oakland City U (IN)
Pennsylvania Coll of Technology (PA)

State U of New York Coll of Technology at Delhi (NY)
U of Connecticut (CT)
U of Massachusetts Amherst (MA)
U of New Hampshire (NH)
U of the Fraser Valley (BC, Canada)

APPLIED MATHEMATICS
Central Methodist U (MO)
Clarion U of Pennsylvania (PA)

APPLIED PSYCHOLOGY
Christian Brothers U (TN)

AQUACULTURE
Morrisville State Coll (NY)

ARCHEOLOGY
Weber State U (UT)

ARCHITECTURAL DRAFTING AND CAD/CADD
Indiana U–Purdue U Indianapolis (IN)
Indian River State Coll (FL)
Morrisville State Coll (NY)
New York City Coll of Technology of the City U of New York (NY)
Universidad del Turabo (PR)

ARCHITECTURAL ENGINEERING TECHNOLOGY
Baker Coll (MI)
Bluefield State Coll (WV)
Ferris State U (MI)
Indiana U–Purdue U Fort Wayne (IN)
Morrisville State Coll (NY)
New England Inst of Technology (RI)
Norfolk State U (VA)
Northern Kentucky U (KY)
Penn State Worthington Scranton (PA)
State U of New York Coll of Technology at Delhi (NY)
U of Alaska Anchorage (AK)
U of the District of Columbia (DC)
Valencia Coll (FL)
Vermont Tech Coll (VT)
Wentworth Inst of Technology (MA)

ARCHITECTURAL TECHNOLOGY
New York Inst of Technology (NY)
Pennsylvania Coll of Technology (PA)

ARCHITECTURE
Morrisville State Coll (NY)
South Dakota State U (SD)

ARCHITECTURE RELATED
Abilene Christian U (TX)

ART
Coll of Coastal Georgia (GA)
Eastern New Mexico U (NM)
Hannibal-LaGrange U (MO)
Lourdes U (OH)
Mount St. Joseph U (OH)
Northern Michigan U (MI)
Palm Beach State Coll (FL)
State Coll of Florida Manatee-Sarasota (FL)
State U of New York Empire State Coll (NY)
U of Rio Grande (OH)

ART HISTORY, CRITICISM AND CONSERVATION
Clarke U (IA)
John Cabot U (Italy)
Palm Beach State Coll (FL)
State Coll of Florida Manatee-Sarasota (FL)
Thomas More Coll (KY)
U of Saint Francis (IN)

ARTS, ENTERTAINMENT, AND MEDIA MANAGEMENT RELATED
EDP U of Puerto Rico–San Sebastian (PR)

ART TEACHER EDUCATION
Indian River State Coll (FL)

ASIAN STUDIES
State Coll of Florida Manatee-Sarasota (FL)

ASTRONOMY
State Coll of Florida Manatee-Sarasota (FL)

ATHLETIC TRAINING
The U of Akron (OH)

AUDIOLOGY AND SPEECH-LANGUAGE PATHOLOGY
U of Cincinnati (OH)

AUTOBODY/COLLISION AND REPAIR TECHNOLOGY
Idaho State U (ID)
Lewis-Clark State Coll (ID)
Montana State U Billings (MT)
Morrisville State Coll (NY)
New England Inst of Technology (RI)
Pennsylvania Coll of Technology (PA)
Utah Valley U (UT)

AUTOMOBILE/AUTOMOTIVE MECHANICS TECHNOLOGY
Baker Coll (MI)
Colorado Mesa U (CO)
Dixie State U (UT)
Ferris State U (MI)
Idaho State U (ID)
Indian River State Coll (FL)
Lewis-Clark State Coll (ID)
Midland Coll (TX)
Montana State U Billings (MT)
Montana Tech of The U of Montana (MT)
Morrisville State Coll (NY)
New England Inst of Technology (RI)
Northern Michigan U (MI)
Pennsylvania Coll of Technology (PA)
Pittsburg State U (KS)
Southern Adventist U (TN)
State U of New York Coll of Technology at Canton (NY)
State U of New York Coll of Technology at Delhi (NY)
U of Alaska Anchorage (AK)
U of the District of Columbia (DC)
Utah Valley U (UT)
Walla Walla U (WA)
Weber State U (UT)

AUTOMOTIVE ENGINEERING TECHNOLOGY
Farmingdale State Coll (NY)
Northern Kentucky U (KY)
Santa Fe Coll (FL)
Vermont Tech Coll (VT)

AVIATION/AIRWAY MANAGEMENT
Northern Kentucky U (KY)
Polk State Coll (FL)
Santa Fe Coll (FL)
U of Alaska Anchorage (AK)
U of the District of Columbia (DC)
Vaughn Coll of Aeronautics and Technology (NY)

AVIONICS MAINTENANCE TECHNOLOGY
Excelsior Coll (NY)
Hallmark U (TX)
U of Alaska Anchorage (AK)
Vaughn Coll of Aeronautics and Technology (NY)

BAKING AND PASTRY ARTS
Colorado Mesa U (CO)
The Culinary Inst of America (NY)
Johnson & Wales U (FL)
Johnson & Wales U (NC)
Johnson & Wales U (RI)
Keiser U, Fort Lauderdale (FL)
Newbury Coll (MA)
Pennsylvania Coll of Technology (PA)
Southern New Hampshire U (NH)
Stratford U (MD)
Stratford U, Falls Church (VA)
Stratford U, Glen Allen (VA)
Stratford U, Newport News (VA)
Stratford U, Woodbridge (VA)
Sullivan U (KY)
Valencia Coll (FL)

BANKING AND FINANCIAL SUPPORT SERVICES
Hilbert Coll (NY)
Indian River State Coll (FL)
Universidad Metropolitana (PR)

BEHAVIORAL SCIENCES
Granite State Coll (NH)
Lewis-Clark State Coll (ID)

BIBLICAL STUDIES
Barclay Coll (KS)
Bethel Coll (IN)
Beulah Heights U (GA)
Calvary Bible Coll and Theological Seminary (MO)
Campbellsville U (KY)
Cincinnati Christian U (OH)
Coll of Biblical Studies–Houston (TX)
Corban U (OR)
Covenant Coll (GA)
Dallas Baptist U (TX)
Davis Coll (NY)
Faith Baptist Bible Coll and Theological Seminary (IA)
Grace Coll (IN)
Houghton Coll (NY)
Howard Payne U (TX)
Kentucky Mountain Bible Coll (KY)
Kuyper Coll (MI)
Laurel U (NC)
Lincoln Christian U (IL)
Manhattan Christian Coll (KS)
Mid-Atlantic Christian U (NC)
Nyack Coll (NY)
Point U (GA)
Selma U (AL)
Shasta Bible Coll (CA)
Simpson U (CA)
Southeastern Bible Coll (AL)
Southern Adventist U (TN)
Southern California Seminary (CA)
Southwestern Assemblies of God U (TX)
Trinity Coll of Florida (FL)
U of Valley Forge (PA)
Welch Coll (TN)

BIOCHEMISTRY
Saint Joseph's Coll (IN)

BIOLOGICAL AND BIOMEDICAL SCIENCES RELATED
Gwynedd Mercy U (PA)
Roberts Wesleyan Coll (NY)

BIOLOGICAL AND PHYSICAL SCIENCES
Ferris State U (MI)
Jefferson Coll of Health Sciences (VA)
Oklahoma Wesleyan U (OK)
Penn State Altoona (PA)
Penn State Beaver (PA)
Penn State Greater Allegheny (PA)
Penn State New Kensington (PA)
Penn State Schuylkill (PA)
Trine U (IN)
Valparaiso U (IN)
Welch Coll (TN)

BIOLOGY/BIOLOGICAL SCIENCES
Coll of Coastal Georgia (GA)
Cumberland U (TN)
Dallas Baptist U (TX)
Immaculata U (PA)
Indian River State Coll (FL)
Lourdes U (OH)
Oklahoma Wesleyan U (OK)
Palm Beach State Coll (FL)
Pine Manor Coll (MA)
Shawnee State U (OH)
Siena Heights U (MI)
State Coll of Florida Manatee-Sarasota (FL)
State U of New York Coll of Agriculture and Technology at Cobleskill (NY)
Thomas More Coll (KY)
U of Cincinnati (OH)
U of New Hampshire at Manchester (NH)
U of Puerto Rico in Ponce (PR)
U of Rio Grande (OH)
The U of Tampa (FL)
Utah Valley U (UT)
Welch Coll (TN)
Wright State U (OH)
York Coll of Pennsylvania (PA)

BIOLOGY/BIOTECHNOLOGY LABORATORY TECHNICIAN
Santa Fe Coll (FL)

State U of New York Coll of Agriculture and Technology at Cobleskill (NY)
Weber State U (UT)

BIOLOGY TEACHER EDUCATION
State Coll of Florida Manatee-Sarasota (FL)

BIOMEDICAL TECHNOLOGY
Penn State Altoona (PA)
Penn State Berks (PA)
Penn State Erie, The Behrend Coll (PA)
Penn State Hazleton (PA)
Penn State New Kensington (PA)
Penn State Schuylkill (PA)
Penn State York (PA)
Santa Fe Coll (FL)

BIOTECHNOLOGY
Inter American U of Puerto Rico, Guayama Campus (PR)
Keiser U, Fort Lauderdale (FL)
Universidad del Turabo (PR)

BLOOD BANK TECHNOLOGY
Rasmussen Coll St. Cloud (MN)

BOTANY/PLANT BIOLOGY
Palm Beach State Coll (FL)

BROADCAST JOURNALISM
Evangel U (MO)

BUILDING/CONSTRUCTION FINISHING, MANAGEMENT, AND INSPECTION RELATED
Baker Coll (MI)
John Brown U (AR)
Palm Beach State Coll (FL)
Pratt Inst (NY)
Weber State U (UT)

BUILDING/CONSTRUCTION SITE MANAGEMENT
State U of New York Coll of Technology at Canton (NY)
Wentworth Inst of Technology (MA)

BUILDING CONSTRUCTION TECHNOLOGY
Wentworth Inst of Technology (MA)

BUILDING/HOME/ CONSTRUCTION INSPECTION
Utah Valley U (UT)

BUILDING/PROPERTY MAINTENANCE
Southern Adventist U (TN)
Utah Valley U (UT)

BUSINESS ADMINISTRATION AND MANAGEMENT
Alaska Pacific U (AK)
Albertus Magnus Coll (CT)
The American U of Rome (Italy)
Anderson U (IN)
Austin Peay State U (TN)
Baker Coll (MI)
Ball State U (IN)
Bay Path U (MA)
Beacon Coll (FL)
Benedictine U (IL)
Berkeley Coll, Woodland Park (NJ)
Berkeley Coll–New York City Campus (NY)
Bethel Coll (IN)
Beulah Heights U (GA)
Bryan Coll (TN)
California U of Pennsylvania (PA)
Calumet Coll of Saint Joseph (IN)
Cameron U (OK)
Campbellsville U (KY)
Cardinal Stritch U (WI)
Caribbean U (PR)
Carroll Coll (MT)
Castleton State Coll (VT)
Cazenovia Coll (NY)
Central Penn Coll (PA)
Clarion U of Pennsylvania (PA)
Coll of Coastal Georgia (GA)
Coll of Saint Mary (NE)
Columbia Centro Universitario, Yauco (PR)
Columbia Southern U (AL)
Concordia Coll–New York (NY)
Concord U (WV)
Corban U (OR)

Cornerstone U (MI)
Dakota State U (SD)
Dallas Baptist U (TX)
Davenport U, Grand Rapids (MI)
Defiance Coll (OH)
Dixie State U (UT)
Edinboro U of Pennsylvania (PA)
EDP U of Puerto Rico (PR)
EDP U of Puerto Rico–San Sebastian (PR)
Elizabethtown Coll School of Continuing and Professional Studies (PA)
Ellis U (IL)
Elmira Coll (NY)
Excelsior Coll (NY)
Farmingdale State Coll (NY)
Faulkner U (AL)
Fisher Coll (MA)
Five Towns Coll (NY)
Florida National U (FL)
Franciscan U of Steubenville (OH)
Franklin U (OH)
Geneva Coll (PA)
Gwynedd Mercy U (PA)
Hallmark U (TX)
Hawai'i Pacific U (HI)
Heritage U (WA)
Hilbert Coll (NY)
Husson U (ME)
Immaculata U (PA)
Indian River State Coll (FL)
Inter American U of Puerto Rico, Aguadilla Campus (PR)
Inter American U of Puerto Rico, Bayamón Campus (PR)
Inter American U of Puerto Rico, Fajardo Campus (PR)
Inter American U of Puerto Rico, Guayama Campus (PR)
Inter American U of Puerto Rico, Ponce Campus (PR)
Inter American U of Puerto Rico, San Germán Campus (PR)
John Cabot U (Italy)
Johnson State Coll (VT)
Kansas Wesleyan U (KS)
Keiser U, Fort Lauderdale (FL)
Kent State U (OH)
Keystone Coll (PA)
King's Coll (PA)
Lincoln Coll of New England, Southington (CT)
Lock Haven U of Pennsylvania (PA)
Long Island U–LIU Brooklyn (NY)
Madonna U (MI)
Maria Coll (NY)
Marian U (IN)
Marietta Coll (OH)
McKendree U (IL)
Medaille Coll (NY)
Medgar Evers Coll of the City U of New York (NY)
Mercy Coll (NY)
Missouri Baptist U (MO)
Missouri Western State U (MO)
Montana State U Billings (MT)
Montreat Coll, Montreat (NC)
Morrisville State Coll (NY)
Mount Aloysius Coll (PA)
Mount Marty Coll (SD)
Mount St. Joseph U (OH)
Mount Saint Mary's U (CA)
Muhlenberg Coll (PA)
National U (CA)
Newbury Coll (MA)
New England Coll (NH)
New England Inst of Technology (RI)
Newman U (KS)
New Mexico Inst of Mining and Technology (NM)
New York Inst of Technology (NY)
Niagara U (NY)
Nichols Coll (MA)
Northwood U, Michigan Campus (MI)
Nyack Coll (NY)
Oakland City U (IN)
Ohio Dominican U (OH)
Oklahoma Wesleyan U (OK)
Peirce Coll (PA)
Pennsylvania Coll of Technology (PA)
Pine Manor Coll (MA)
Point U (GA)
Post U (CT)
Providence Coll (RI)
Rasmussen Coll Appleton (WI)
Rasmussen Coll Aurora (IL)
Rasmussen Coll Blaine (MN)
Rasmussen Coll Bloomington (MN)
Rasmussen Coll Brooklyn Park (MN)
Rasmussen Coll Eagan (MN)

Rasmussen Coll Fort Myers (FL)
Rasmussen Coll Green Bay (WI)
Rasmussen Coll Kansas City/ Overland Park (KS)
Rasmussen Coll Lake Elmo/ Woodbury (MN)
Rasmussen Coll Land O' Lakes (FL)
Rasmussen Coll Mankato (MN)
Rasmussen Coll Mokena/Tinley Park (IL)
Rasmussen Coll Moorhead (MN)
Rasmussen Coll New Port Richey (FL)
Rasmussen Coll Ocala (FL)
Rasmussen Coll Romeoville/Joliet (IL)
Rasmussen Coll St. Cloud (MN)
Rasmussen Coll Tampa/Brandon (FL)
Rasmussen Coll Topeka (KS)
Rasmussen Coll Wausau (WI)
Regent U (VA)
Rider U (NJ)
Robert Morris U Illinois (IL)
Roger Williams U (RI)
Rust Coll (MS)
St. Catharine Coll (KY)
St. Francis Coll (NY)
Saint Francis U (PA)
St. Gregory's U, Shawnee (OK)
St. John's U (NY)
Saint Joseph's U (PA)
Saint Leo U (FL)
Saint Peter's U (NJ)
St. Thomas Aquinas Coll (NY)
Santa Fe Coll (FL)
Shawnee State U (OH)
Siena Heights U (MI)
Southern Adventist U (TN)
Southern California Inst of Technology (CA)
Southern New Hampshire U (NH)
Southwestern Assemblies of God U (TX)
Southwest Minnesota State U (MN)
State Coll of Florida Manatee-Sarasota (FL)
State U of New York Coll of Agriculture and Technology at Cobleskill (NY)
State U of New York Coll of Technology at Canton (NY)
State U of New York Coll of Technology at Delhi (NY)
Stevens–The Inst of Business & Arts (MO)
Stratford U, Falls Church (VA)
Stratford U, Glen Allen (VA)
Stratford U, Newport News (VA)
Stratford U, Woodbridge (VA)
Sullivan U (KY)
Taylor U (IN)
Thomas More Coll (KY)
Tiffin U (OH)
Toccoa Falls Coll (GA)
Trine U (IN)
Tulane U (LA)
Union Coll (NE)
Universidad del Turabo (PR)
The U of Akron (OH)
U of Alaska Anchorage (AK)
U of Alaska Fairbanks (AK)
U of Arkansas–Fort Smith (AR)
U of Cincinnati (OH)
The U of Findlay (OH)
U of Maine at Augusta (ME)
U of Maine at Fort Kent (ME)
The U of Montana Western (MT)
U of New Hampshire (NH)
U of New Hampshire at Manchester (NH)
U of New Haven (CT)
U of Pennsylvania (PA)
U of Pikeville (KY)
U of Rio Grande (OH)
U of Saint Francis (IN)
The U of Scranton (PA)
U of the Cumberlands (KY)
U of the Fraser Valley (BC, Canada)
U of the Incarnate Word (TX)
U of the Virgin Islands (VI)
The U of Toledo (OH)
Upper Iowa U (IA)
Urbana U (OH)
Utah Valley U (UT)
Valencia Coll (FL)
Vermont Tech Coll (VT)
Villa Maria Coll (NY)
Walla Walla U (WA)
Walsh U (OH)
Wayland Baptist U (TX)

Webber International U (FL)
Welch Coll (TN)
Western Kentucky U (KY)
Williams Baptist Coll (AR)
Wright State U (OH)
Xavier U (OH)
York Coll of Pennsylvania (PA)
Youngstown State U (OH)

BUSINESS ADMINISTRATION, MANAGEMENT AND OPERATIONS RELATED
Bay Path U (MA)
Columbia Centro Universitario, Caguas (PR)
Dixie State U (UT)
Embry-Riddle Aeronautical U–Worldwide (FL)

BUSINESS AND PERSONAL/ FINANCIAL SERVICES MARKETING
Dixie State U (UT)

BUSINESS AUTOMATION/ TECHNOLOGY/DATA ENTRY
Colorado Mesa U (CO)
Hallmark U (TX)
Montana State U Billings (MT)
Northern Michigan U (MI)
The U of Akron (OH)
U of Alaska Anchorage (AK)
U of Rio Grande (OH)
U of the District of Columbia (DC)
The U of Toledo (OH)
Utah Valley U (UT)

BUSINESS/COMMERCE
Adams State U (CO)
Alvernia U (PA)
American Public U System (WV)
Cardinal Stritch U (WI)
Castleton State Coll (VT)
Champlain Coll (VT)
Christian Brothers U (TN)
Coll of Staten Island of the City U of New York (NY)
Columbia Coll (MO)
Cumberland U (TN)
Ferris State U (MI)
Gannon U (PA)
Granite State Coll (NH)
Hillsdale Free Will Baptist Coll (OK)
Idaho State U (ID)
Indiana U Northwest (IN)
Kent State U at Geauga (OH)
Limestone Coll (SC)
Lourdes U (OH)
Mayville State U (ND)
Metropolitan Coll of New York (NY)
Miami U (OH)
Midland Coll (TX)
Montana State U Billings (MT)
Mount Vernon Nazarene U (OH)
Murray State U (KY)
New Mexico State U (NM)
New York U (NY)
Northern Kentucky U (KY)
Northern Michigan U (MI)
Olivet Nazarene U (IL)
Penn State Abington (PA)
Penn State Altoona (PA)
Penn State Beaver (PA)
Penn State Berks (PA)
Penn State Brandywine (PA)
Penn State Erie, The Behrend Coll (PA)
Penn State Greater Allegheny (PA)
Penn State Harrisburg (PA)
Penn State Hazleton (PA)
Penn State Lehigh Valley (PA)
Penn State New Kensington (PA)
Penn State Schuylkill (PA)
Penn State U Park (PA)
Penn State Wilkes-Barre (PA)
Penn State Worthington Scranton (PA)
Penn State York (PA)
Saint Mary-of-the-Woods Coll (IN)
Southern Arkansas U–Magnolia (AR)
Southwest Baptist U (MO)
Southwestern Assemblies of God U (TX)
Spalding U (KY)
State Coll of Florida Manatee-Sarasota (FL)
State U of New York Empire State Coll (NY)
Thomas More Coll (KY)
Troy U (AL)
Tulane U (LA)
U of Alaska Anchorage (AK)

U of Bridgeport (CT)
U of Cincinnati (OH)
U of Maine at Fort Kent (ME)
U of Massachusetts Lowell (MA)
U of New Hampshire (NH)
U of Puerto Rico in Ponce (PR)
U of Southern Indiana (IN)
Wright State U (OH)
Youngstown State U (OH)

BUSINESS, MANAGEMENT, AND MARKETING RELATED
Ball State U (IN)
Five Towns Coll (NY)
Florida National U (FL)
Oklahoma Wesleyan U (OK)
Purdue U North Central (IN)
Sacred Heart U (CT)

BUSINESS/MANAGERIAL ECONOMICS
Campbellsville U (KY)
Saint Peter's U (NJ)
State Coll of Florida Manatee-Sarasota (FL)
Urbana U (OH)

BUSINESS TEACHER EDUCATION
Wright State U (OH)

CABINETMAKING AND MILLWORK
Utah Valley U (UT)

CAD/CADD DRAFTING/DESIGN TECHNOLOGY
Ferris State U (MI)
Idaho State U (ID)
Keiser U, Fort Lauderdale (FL)
Missouri Southern State U (MO)
Montana Tech of The U of Montana (MT)
Morrisville State Coll (NY)
Northern Michigan U (MI)
Shawnee State U (OH)
State U of New York Coll of Technology at Delhi (NY)
U of Arkansas–Fort Smith (AR)

CARDIOVASCULAR TECHNOLOGY
Arkansas Tech U (AR)
Gwynedd Mercy U (PA)
Molloy Coll (NY)
Nebraska Methodist Coll (NE)
Pennsylvania Coll of Health Sciences (PA)
Polk State Coll (FL)
Santa Fe Coll (FL)
Sentara Coll of Health Sciences (VA)
Valencia Coll (FL)

CARPENTRY
Indian River State Coll (FL)
Liberty U (VA)
Montana State U Billings (MT)
Montana Tech of The U of Montana (MT)
New England Inst of Technology (RI)
Southern Utah U (UT)
U of Alaska Fairbanks (AK)

CELL BIOLOGY AND ANATOMICAL SCIENCES RELATED
National U (CA)

CERAMIC ARTS AND CERAMICS
Palm Beach State Coll (FL)

CHEMICAL TECHNOLOGY
Ball State U (IN)
Indiana U–Purdue U Fort Wayne (IN)
Inter American U of Puerto Rico, Guayama Campus (PR)
Lawrence Technological U (MI)
New York City Coll of Technology of the City U of New York (NY)
State U of New York Coll of Agriculture and Technology at Cobleskill (NY)
Weber State U (UT)

CHEMISTRY
Central Methodist U (MO)
Clarke U (IA)
Coll of Coastal Georgia (GA)
Immaculata U (PA)
Indian River State Coll (FL)
Lindsey Wilson Coll (KY)
Oklahoma Wesleyan U (OK)
Palm Beach State Coll (FL)

Siena Heights U (MI)
Southern Arkansas U–Magnolia (AR)
State Coll of Florida Manatee-Sarasota (FL)
Thomas More Coll (KY)
U of Cincinnati (OH)
U of Rio Grande (OH)
The U of Tampa (FL)
U of the Incarnate Word (TX)
Utah Valley U (UT)
Wright State U (OH)
York Coll of Pennsylvania (PA)

CHEMISTRY TEACHER EDUCATION
State Coll of Florida Manatee-Sarasota (FL)

CHILD-CARE AND SUPPORT SERVICES MANAGEMENT
Eastern New Mexico U (NM)
Ferris State U (MI)
Morrisville State Coll (NY)
Mount Vernon Nazarene U (OH)
Nicholls State U (LA)
Polk State Coll (FL)
Siena Heights U (MI)
Southeast Missouri State U (MO)
State U of New York Coll of Agriculture and Technology at Cobleskill (NY)
State U of New York Coll of Technology at Canton (NY)
U of the Fraser Valley (BC, Canada)
Youngstown State U (OH)

CHILD-CARE PROVISION
American Public U System (WV)
Eastern Kentucky U (KY)
Mayville State U (ND)
Pennsylvania Coll of Technology (PA)
St. Catharine Coll (KY)
Santa Fe Coll (FL)
U of Alaska Anchorage (AK)

CHILD DEVELOPMENT
Arkansas Tech U (AR)
Ellis U (IL)
Evangel U (MO)
Franciscan U of Steubenville (OH)
Indian River State Coll (FL)
Kuyper Coll (MI)
Lewis-Clark State Coll (ID)
Lincoln Coll of New England, Southington (CT)
Madonna U (MI)
Midland Coll (TX)
Northern Michigan U (MI)
Ohio U (OH)
Polk State Coll (FL)
Southern Utah U (UT)
State Coll of Florida Manatee-Sarasota (FL)
Tougaloo Coll (MS)
Weber State U (UT)
Youngstown State U (OH)

CHRISTIAN STUDIES
Oklahoma Baptist U (OK)
Oklahoma Wesleyan U (OK)
Regent U (VA)
Wayland Baptist U (TX)

CINEMATOGRAPHY AND FILM/ VIDEO PRODUCTION
Academy of Art U (CA)
Inst of American Indian Arts (NM)
New England Inst of Technology (RI)
Valencia Coll (FL)

CIVIL ENGINEERING TECHNOLOGY
Bluefield State Coll (WV)
Fairmont State U (WV)
Ferris State U (MI)
Idaho State U (ID)
Indiana U–Purdue U Fort Wayne (IN)
Indian River State Coll (FL)
Montana Tech of The U of Montana (MT)
Murray State U (KY)
New York City Coll of Technology of the City U of New York (NY)
Pennsylvania Coll of Technology (PA)
State Coll of Florida Manatee-Sarasota (FL)
State U of New York Coll of Technology at Canton (NY)
U of Massachusetts Lowell (MA)
U of New Hampshire (NH)
U of Puerto Rico in Ponce (PR)
The U of Toledo (OH)

Valencia Coll (FL)
Vermont Tech Coll (VT)
Youngstown State U (OH)

CLINICAL LABORATORY SCIENCE/MEDICAL TECHNOLOGY
Arkansas State U (AR)
Dixie State U (UT)
New England Inst of Technology (RI)
Shawnee State U (OH)
U of Cincinnati (OH)

CLINICAL/MEDICAL LABORATORY ASSISTANT
New England Inst of Technology (RI)
U of Alaska Fairbanks (AK)
U of Maine at Augusta (ME)

CLINICAL/MEDICAL LABORATORY SCIENCE AND ALLIED PROFESSIONS RELATED
State U of New York Coll of Agriculture and Technology at Cobleskill (NY)
Youngstown State U (OH)

CLINICAL/MEDICAL LABORATORY TECHNOLOGY
Baker Coll (MI)
Coll of Coastal Georgia (GA)
Colorado Mesa U (CO)
Eastern Kentucky U (KY)
Farmingdale State Coll (NY)
Ferris State U (MI)
The George Washington U (DC)
Indian River State Coll (FL)
Keiser U, Fort Lauderdale (FL)
Marshall U (WV)
Mount Aloysius Coll (PA)
Penn State Hazleton (PA)
Penn State Schuylkill (PA)
Rasmussen Coll Bismarck (ND)
Rasmussen Coll Green Bay (WI)
Rasmussen Coll Lake Elmo/Woodbury (MN)
Rasmussen Coll Mankato (MN)
Rasmussen Coll Moorhead (MN)
Rasmussen Coll St. Cloud (MN)
Tarleton State U (TX)
U of Alaska Anchorage (AK)
U of Maine at Presque Isle (ME)
U of Rio Grande (OH)
Weber State U (UT)
Youngstown State U (OH)

COMMERCIAL AND ADVERTISING ART
Academy of Art U (CA)
Baker Coll (MI)
California U of Pennsylvania (PA)
Fashion Inst of Technology (NY)
Mitchell Coll (CT)
Mount Saint Mary's U (CA)
New York City Coll of Technology of the City U of New York (NY)
Northern State U (SD)
Nossi Coll of Art (TN)
Palm Beach State Coll (FL)
Pennsylvania Coll of Technology (PA)
Pratt Inst (NY)
Robert Morris U Illinois (IL)
Santa Fe Coll (FL)
Southern Adventist U (TN)
State Coll of Florida Manatee-Sarasota (FL)
State U of New York Coll of Agriculture and Technology at Cobleskill (NY)
U of Cincinnati (OH)
Valencia Coll (FL)
Villa Maria Coll (NY)

COMMERCIAL PHOTOGRAPHY
Fashion Inst of Technology (NY)
Nossi Coll of Art (TN)

COMMUNICATION
Elizabethtown Coll School of Continuing and Professional Studies (PA)
Inter American U of Puerto Rico, Ponce Campus (PR)
Keystone Coll (PA)
National U (CA)
Thomas More Coll (KY)

COMMUNICATION AND JOURNALISM RELATED
Clarke U (IA)
Immaculata U (PA)
Madonna U (MI)
Tulane U (LA)
Valparaiso U (IN)

COMMUNICATION AND MEDIA RELATED
Keystone Coll (PA)

COMMUNICATION DISORDERS SCIENCES AND SERVICES RELATED
Granite State Coll (NH)

COMMUNICATIONS TECHNOLOGIES AND SUPPORT SERVICES RELATED
Southern Adventist U (TN)

COMMUNICATIONS TECHNOLOGY
Colorado Mesa U (CO)
East Stroudsburg U of Pennsylvania (PA)

COMMUNITY HEALTH AND PREVENTIVE MEDICINE
National U (CA)
Utah Valley U (UT)

COMMUNITY HEALTH SERVICES COUNSELING
State Coll of Florida Manatee-Sarasota (FL)

COMMUNITY ORGANIZATION AND ADVOCACY
Metropolitan Coll of New York (NY)
Morrisville State Coll (NY)
State U of New York Empire State Coll (NY)
The U of Akron (OH)
U of Alaska Fairbanks (AK)
The U of Findlay (OH)
U of New Hampshire (NH)

COMPARATIVE LITERATURE
John Cabot U (Italy)
Palm Beach State Coll (FL)

COMPUTER AND INFORMATION SCIENCES
Ball State U (IN)
Beacon Coll (FL)
Black Hills State U (SD)
California U of Pennsylvania (PA)
Calumet Coll of Saint Joseph (IN)
Clarke U (IA)
Columbia Coll (MO)
Edinboro U of Pennsylvania (PA)
Excelsior Coll (NY)
Fisher Coll (MA)
Husson U (ME)
Inter American U of Puerto Rico, Fajardo Campus (PR)
Inter American U of Puerto Rico, Ponce Campus (PR)
King's Coll (PA)
Lewis-Clark State Coll (ID)
Lincoln U (MO)
Manchester U (IN)
Montana State U Billings (MT)
Morrisville State Coll (NY)
National U (CA)
New England Inst of Technology (RI)
New York City Coll of Technology of the City U of New York (NY)
Penn State Schuylkill (PA)
St. John's U (NY)
Southern New Hampshire U (NH)
State Coll of Florida Manatee-Sarasota (FL)
State U of New York Coll of Agriculture and Technology at Cobleskill (NY)
Troy U (AL)
Tulane U (LA)
Union Coll (NE)
Universidad del Turabo (PR)
U of Alaska Anchorage (AK)
U of Maine at Augusta (ME)
The U of Tampa (FL)
The U of Toledo (OH)
Utah Valley U (UT)
Washburn U (KS)
Webber International U (FL)
Youngstown State U (OH)

COMPUTER AND INFORMATION SCIENCES AND SUPPORT SERVICES RELATED
Indiana U–Purdue U Indianapolis (IN)
Inter American U of Puerto Rico, Guayama Campus (PR)
Montana State U Billings (MT)
New York U (NY)
Pace U (NY)
Palm Beach State Coll (FL)

COMPUTER AND INFORMATION SCIENCES RELATED
Limestone Coll (SC)
Lindsey Wilson Coll (KY)
Madonna U (MI)
State Coll of Florida Manatee-Sarasota (FL)

COMPUTER AND INFORMATION SYSTEMS SECURITY
Davenport U, Grand Rapids (MI)
St. John's U (NY)
Stratford U, Woodbridge (VA)
U of Maine at Fort Kent (ME)

COMPUTER ENGINEERING
Johnson & Wales U (RI)
New England Inst of Technology (RI)
The U of Scranton (PA)

COMPUTER ENGINEERING TECHNOLOGIES RELATED
Universidad del Turabo (PR)

COMPUTER ENGINEERING TECHNOLOGY
California U of Pennsylvania (PA)
Eastern Kentucky U (KY)
Indian River State Coll (FL)
Morrisville State Coll (NY)
Northern Michigan U (MI)
Oakland City U (IN)
Penn State New Kensington (PA)
Polk State Coll (FL)
State Coll of Florida Manatee-Sarasota (FL)
U of Alaska Anchorage (AK)
U of Hartford (CT)
U of the District of Columbia (DC)
Valencia Coll (FL)
Vermont Tech Coll (VT)
Weber State U (UT)

COMPUTER GRAPHICS
EDP U of Puerto Rico (PR)
Purdue U (IN)
State Coll of Florida Manatee-Sarasota (FL)

COMPUTER/INFORMATION TECHNOLOGY SERVICES ADMINISTRATION RELATED
Berkeley Coll, Woodland Park (NJ)
Berkeley Coll–New York City Campus (NY)
Limestone Coll (SC)
Maria Coll (NY)
Mercy Coll (NY)
Pennsylvania Coll of Technology (PA)
Valencia Coll (FL)

COMPUTER INSTALLATION AND REPAIR TECHNOLOGY
Inter American U of Puerto Rico, Aguadilla Campus (PR)
Inter American U of Puerto Rico, Bayamón Campus (PR)
Inter American U of Puerto Rico, Fajardo Campus (PR)
Universidad Metropolitana (PR)
U of Alaska Fairbanks (AK)

COMPUTER PROGRAMMING
Baker Coll (MI)
Black Hills State U (SD)
Caribbean U (PR)
Champlain Coll (VT)
Coll of Staten Island of the City U of New York (NY)
Columbia Centro Universitario, Caguas (PR)
EDP U of Puerto Rico (PR)
EDP U of Puerto Rico–San Sebastian (PR)
Gwynedd Mercy U (PA)
Indian River State Coll (FL)

International Business Coll, Fort Wayne (IN)
Johnson & Wales U (RI)
Limestone Coll (SC)
Medgar Evers Coll of the City U of New York (NY)
Missouri Southern State U (MO)
Morrisville State Coll (NY)
New England Inst of Technology (RI)
Oakland City U (IN)
Palm Beach State Coll (FL)
Polk State Coll (FL)
Rasmussen Coll Fargo (ND)
Saint Francis U (PA)
State Coll of Florida Manatee-Sarasota (FL)
Stratford U, Falls Church (VA)
U of Arkansas at Little Rock (AR)
The U of Toledo (OH)
Walla Walla U (WA)
Youngstown State U (OH)

COMPUTER PROGRAMMING RELATED
Florida National U (FL)
State Coll of Florida Manatee-Sarasota (FL)
Stratford U, Falls Church (VA)

COMPUTER PROGRAMMING (SPECIFIC APPLICATIONS)
Academy of Art U (CA)
Florida National U (FL)
Indiana U South Bend (IN)
Kent State U at Geauga (OH)
Palm Beach State Coll (FL)
U of Alaska Anchorage (AK)
Valencia Coll (FL)

COMPUTER SCIENCE
Baker Coll (MI)
Black Hills State U (SD)
Carroll Coll (MT)
Central Methodist U (MO)
Central Penn Coll (PA)
Coll of Coastal Georgia (GA)
Creighton U (NE)
Florida National U (FL)
Franklin U (OH)
Hawai'i Pacific U (HI)
Heritage U (WA)
Indian River State Coll (FL)
Inter American U of Puerto Rico, Aguadilla Campus (PR)
Inter American U of Puerto Rico, Bayamón Campus (PR)
Inter American U of Puerto Rico, Ponce Campus (PR)
Inter American U of Puerto Rico, San Germán Campus (PR)
Madonna U (MI)
Morrisville State Coll (NY)
New England Inst of Technology (RI)
New York City Coll of Technology of the City U of New York (NY)
Oakland City U (IN)
Palm Beach State Coll (FL)
Sacred Heart U (CT)
Southern California Inst of Technology (CA)
Southwest Baptist U (MO)
Universidad Metropolitana (PR)
The U of Findlay (OH)
U of Maine at Fort Kent (ME)
U of New Haven (CT)
U of Rio Grande (OH)
U of the Virgin Islands (VI)
Utah Valley U (UT)
Walsh U (OH)
Weber State U (UT)

COMPUTER SOFTWARE AND MEDIA APPLICATIONS RELATED
American Public U System (WV)
Champlain Coll (VT)
Hobe Sound Bible Coll (FL)
Polytechnic U of Puerto Rico (PR)
Southern Tech Coll, Fort Myers (FL)

COMPUTER SOFTWARE ENGINEERING
Ohio Dominican U (OH)
Rasmussen Coll Appleton (WI)
Rasmussen Coll Bismarck (ND)
Rasmussen Coll Blaine (MN)
Rasmussen Coll Bloomington (MN)
Rasmussen Coll Brooklyn Park (MN)
Rasmussen Coll Eagan (MN)
Rasmussen Coll Fargo (ND)

Rasmussen Coll Fort Myers (FL)
Rasmussen Coll Green Bay (WI)
Rasmussen Coll Kansas City/Overland Park (KS)
Rasmussen Coll Lake Elmo/Woodbury (MN)
Rasmussen Coll Land O' Lakes (FL)
Rasmussen Coll Mankato (MN)
Rasmussen Coll Moorhead (MN)
Rasmussen Coll New Port Richey (FL)
Rasmussen Coll Ocala (FL)
Rasmussen Coll St. Cloud (MN)
Rasmussen Coll Tampa/Brandon (FL)
Rasmussen Coll Topeka (KS)
Rasmussen Coll Wausau (WI)
Vermont Tech Coll (VT)

COMPUTER SUPPORT SPECIALIST
Sullivan U (KY)

COMPUTER SYSTEMS ANALYSIS
Davenport U, Grand Rapids (MI)
Johnson & Wales U (RI)
Santa Fe Coll (FL)
The U of Akron (OH)
Valencia Coll (FL)

COMPUTER SYSTEMS NETWORKING AND TELECOMMUNICATIONS
Baker Coll (MI)
Clayton State U (GA)
Colorado Mesa U (CO)
DeVry Coll of New York (NY)
DeVry U, Phoenix (AZ)
DeVry U, Pomona (CA)
DeVry U, Westminster (CO)
DeVry U, Miramar (FL)
DeVry U, Orlando (FL)
DeVry U, Decatur (GA)
DeVry U, Chicago (IL)
DeVry U, Kansas City (MO)
DeVry U, North Brunswick (NJ)
DeVry U, Columbus (OH)
DeVry U, Fort Washington (PA)
DeVry U, Irving (TX)
DeVry U, Arlington (VA)
DeVry U Online (IL)
Florida National U (FL)
Hickey Coll (MO)
Idaho State U (ID)
International Business Coll, Fort Wayne (IN)
Montana Tech of The U of Montana (MT)
Pace U (NY)
Robert Morris U Illinois (IL)
Southern Tech Coll, Fort Myers (FL)
Stratford U, Falls Church (VA)
The U of Akron (OH)
U of Alaska Anchorage (AK)
The U of Toledo (OH)
Weber State U (UT)

COMPUTER TECHNOLOGY/COMPUTER SYSTEMS TECHNOLOGY
Capitol Technology U (MD)
Morrisville State Coll (NY)
New England Inst of Technology (RI)
Southeast Missouri State U (MO)
U of Alaska Anchorage (AK)
U of Cincinnati (OH)
Valencia Coll (FL)

COMPUTER TYPOGRAPHY AND COMPOSITION EQUIPMENT OPERATION
Indian River State Coll (FL)
U of Cincinnati (OH)

CONSTRUCTION ENGINEERING TECHNOLOGY
Baker Coll (MI)
Ferris State U (MI)
Lawrence Technological U (MI)
New York City Coll of Technology of the City U of New York (NY)
Pennsylvania Coll of Technology (PA)
Santa Fe Coll (FL)
State Coll of Florida Manatee-Sarasota (FL)
State U of New York Coll of Technology at Delhi (NY)
The U of Akron (OH)

The U of Toledo (OH)
Valencia Coll (FL)
Vermont Tech Coll (VT)

CONSTRUCTION/HEAVY EQUIPMENT/EARTHMOVING EQUIPMENT OPERATION
U of Alaska Anchorage (AK)

CONSTRUCTION MANAGEMENT
U of Alaska Anchorage (AK)
U of Alaska Fairbanks (AK)
U of the District of Columbia (DC)
Utah Valley U (UT)
Vermont Tech Coll (VT)
Wentworth Inst of Technology (MA)

CONSTRUCTION TRADES
Colorado Mesa U (CO)
Liberty U (VA)
Morrisville State Coll (NY)
Northern Michigan U (MI)

CONSTRUCTION TRADES RELATED
John Brown U (AR)
Morrisville State Coll (NY)

CONSUMER MERCHANDISING/ RETAILING MANAGEMENT
Indian River State Coll (FL)

COOKING AND RELATED CULINARY ARTS
Colorado Mesa U (CO)
Hickey Coll (MO)

CORRECTIONS
Baker Coll (MI)
California U of Pennsylvania (PA)
Indian River State Coll (FL)
Mount Aloysius Coll (PA)
U of the District of Columbia (DC)
Xavier U (OH)
Youngstown State U (OH)

CORRECTIONS AND CRIMINAL JUSTICE RELATED
Cameron U (OK)
Inter American U of Puerto Rico, Aguadilla Campus (PR)
Inter American U of Puerto Rico, Fajardo Campus (PR)
Morrisville State Coll (NY)
Rasmussen Coll Appleton (WI)
Rasmussen Coll Aurora (IL)
Rasmussen Coll Bismarck (ND)
Rasmussen Coll Blaine (MN)
Rasmussen Coll Bloomington (MN)
Rasmussen Coll Brooklyn Park (MN)
Rasmussen Coll Eagan (MN)
Rasmussen Coll Fort Myers (FL)
Rasmussen Coll Green Bay (WI)
Rasmussen Coll Kansas City/ Overland Park (KS)
Rasmussen Coll Lake Elmo/ Woodbury (MN)
Rasmussen Coll Land O' Lakes (FL)
Rasmussen Coll Mankato (MN)
Rasmussen Coll Mokena/Tinley Park (IL)
Rasmussen Coll Moorhead (MN)
Rasmussen Coll New Port Richey (FL)
Rasmussen Coll Ocala (FL)
Rasmussen Coll Rockford (IL)
Rasmussen Coll Romeoville/Joliet (IL)
Rasmussen Coll St. Cloud (MN)
Rasmussen Coll Tampa/Brandon (FL)
Rasmussen Coll Topeka (KS)
Rasmussen Coll Wausau (WI)
U of Saint Francis (IN)

COSMETOLOGY
Indian River State Coll (FL)
Midland Coll (TX)

COUNSELING PSYCHOLOGY
Hobe Sound Bible Coll (FL)

CREATIVE WRITING
Inst of American Indian Arts (NM)
National U (CA)
U of Maine at Presque Isle (ME)

CRIMINALISTICS AND CRIMINAL SCIENCE
Keiser U, Fort Lauderdale (FL)

CRIMINAL JUSTICE/LAW ENFORCEMENT ADMINISTRATION
American Public U System (WV)
Anderson U (IN)
Arkansas State U (AR)
Bemidji State U (MN)
Calumet Coll of Saint Joseph (IN)
Campbellsville U (KY)
Castleton State Coll (VT)
Clarion U of Pennsylvania (PA)
Coll of Coastal Georgia (GA)
Colorado Mesa U (CO)
Columbia Coll (MO)
Fisher Coll (MA)
Fort Valley State U (GA)
Hannibal-LaGrange U (MO)
Hawai`i Pacific U (HI)
Husson U (ME)
Indian River State Coll (FL)
Keiser U, Fort Lauderdale (FL)
Keystone Coll (PA)
Lincoln Coll of New England, Southington (CT)
Lincoln U (MO)
Lock Haven U of Pennsylvania (PA)
Mansfield U of Pennsylvania (PA)
Miami U (OH)
Morrisville State Coll (NY)
National U (CA)
New England Inst of Technology (RI)
Northern Michigan U (MI)
Palm Beach State Coll (FL)
Peirce Coll (PA)
Polk State Coll (FL)
Regent U (VA)
Reinhardt U (GA)
Roger Williams U (RI)
St. John's U (NY)
Salve Regina U (RI)
Santa Fe Coll (FL)
Southern Tech Coll, Fort Myers (FL)
Tiffin U (OH)
Trine U (IN)
U of Arkansas at Pine Bluff (AR)
U of Arkansas–Fort Smith (AR)
The U of Findlay (OH)
U of Maine at Fort Kent (ME)
U of Maine at Presque Isle (ME)
Urbana U (OH)
Utah Valley U (UT)
Valencia Coll (FL)
Washburn U (KS)
Wayland Baptist U (TX)
Webber International U (FL)
Wright State U (OH)
York Coll of Pennsylvania (PA)
Youngstown State U (OH)

CRIMINAL JUSTICE/POLICE SCIENCE
Arkansas State U (AR)
Armstrong State U (GA)
Berkeley Coll, Woodland Park (NJ)
Berkeley Coll–New York City Campus (NY)
Caribbean U (PR)
Columbia Southern U (AL)
Eastern Kentucky U (KY)
Elizabethtown Coll School of Continuing and Professional Studies (PA)
Ferris State U (MI)
Hilbert Coll (NY)
Idaho State U (ID)
Indian River State Coll (FL)
Inter American U of Puerto Rico, Ponce Campus (PR)
Midland Coll (TX)
Missouri Southern State U (MO)
Missouri Western State U (MO)
Northern Kentucky U (KY)
Palm Beach State Coll (FL)
Rasmussen Coll Blaine (MN)
Rasmussen Coll Bloomington (MN)
Rasmussen Coll Brooklyn Park (MN)
Rasmussen Coll Eagan (MN)
Rasmussen Coll Lake Elmo/ Woodbury (MN)
Rasmussen Coll Mankato (MN)
Rasmussen Coll St. Cloud (MN)
Southern Utah U (UT)
State U of New York Coll of Technology at Canton (NY)
Sullivan U (KY)
Universidad del Turabo (PR)
Universidad Metropolitana (PR)
The U of Akron (OH)
U of Arkansas at Little Rock (AR)
U of Arkansas at Pine Bluff (AR)
U of New Haven (CT)

U of the Virgin Islands (VI)
Youngstown State U (OH)

CRIMINAL JUSTICE/SAFETY
American Public U System (WV)
Arkansas Tech U (AR)
Ball State U (IN)
Bethel Coll (IN)
Calumet Coll of Saint Joseph (IN)
Cazenovia Coll (NY)
Central Penn Coll (PA)
Chaminade U of Honolulu (HI)
Columbus State U (GA)
Defiance Coll (OH)
Dixie State U (UT)
Edinboro U of Pennsylvania (PA)
Fisher Coll (MA)
Florida National U (FL)
Gannon U (PA)
Georgia Regents U (GA)
Husson U (ME)
Idaho State U (ID)
Indiana U Northwest (IN)
Inter American U of Puerto Rico, Aguadilla Campus (PR)
Kent State U at Stark (OH)
King's Coll (PA)
Liberty U (VA)
Lourdes U (OH)
Madonna U (MI)
Manchester U (IN)
Morrisville State Coll (NY)
Northern Michigan U (MI)
Penn State Altoona (PA)
St. Francis Coll (NY)
State Coll of Florida Manatee-Sarasota (FL)
Thomas More Coll (KY)
Universidad Metropolitana (PR)
U of Cincinnati (OH)
U of Maine at Augusta (ME)
U of Pikeville (KY)
The U of Scranton (PA)
U of the Cumberlands (KY)
U of the Fraser Valley (BC, Canada)
Weber State U (UT)
Xavier U (OH)
Youngstown State U (OH)

CRIMINOLOGY
Elizabethtown Coll School of Continuing and Professional Studies (PA)

CRISIS/EMERGENCY/DISASTER MANAGEMENT
Arkansas State U (AR)
Eastern New Mexico U (NM)
Universidad del Turabo (PR)

CROP PRODUCTION
North Carolina State U (NC)
U of Massachusetts Amherst (MA)

CULINARY ARTS
Baker Coll (MI)
Bob Jones U (SC)
The Culinary Inst of America (NY)
Eastern New Mexico U (NM)
Indian River State Coll (FL)
Johnson & Wales U (CO)
Johnson & Wales U (FL)
Johnson & Wales U (NC)
Johnson & Wales U (RI)
Keiser U, Fort Lauderdale (FL)
Keystone Coll (PA)
Newbury Coll (MA)
Nicholls State U (LA)
Pennsylvania Coll of Technology (PA)
Robert Morris U Illinois (IL)
Southern Adventist U (TN)
Southern New Hampshire U (NH)
State U of New York Coll of Agriculture and Technology at Cobleskill (NY)
State U of New York Coll of Technology at Delhi (NY)
Stratford U (MD)
Stratford U, Falls Church (VA)
Stratford U, Glen Allen (VA)
Stratford U, Newport News (VA)
Stratford U, Woodbridge (VA)
Sullivan U (KY)
The U of Akron (OH)
U of Alaska Anchorage (AK)
U of Alaska Fairbanks (AK)
The U of Montana (MT)
Utah Valley U (UT)
Valencia Coll (FL)

CULINARY ARTS RELATED
Johnson & Wales U (CO)

Johnson & Wales U (FL)
Johnson & Wales U (RI)
Morrisville State Coll (NY)

CRIMINAL JUSTICE/SAFETY

CULINARY SCIENCE
Wright State U (OH)

CURRICULUM AND INSTRUCTION
Ohio Dominican U (OH)
State U of New York Coll of Technology at Delhi (NY)

DAIRY HUSBANDRY AND PRODUCTION
Morrisville State Coll (NY)

DAIRY SCIENCE
Michigan State U (MI)
Vermont Tech Coll (VT)

DANCE
Dixie State U (UT)
Southern Utah U (UT)
U of Saint Francis (IN)
Utah Valley U (UT)

DATA MODELING/ WAREHOUSING AND DATABASE ADMINISTRATION
American Public U System (WV)
Limestone Coll (SC)

DATA PROCESSING AND DATA PROCESSING TECHNOLOGY
American Public U System (WV)
Baker Coll (MI)
Campbellsville U (KY)
Hallmark U (TX)
Miami U (OH)
Montana State U Billings (MT)
Mount Vernon Nazarene U (OH)
Northern Kentucky U (KY)
Northern State U (SD)
Palm Beach State Coll (FL)
U of Puerto Rico in Ponce (PR)
Youngstown State U (OH)

DENTAL ASSISTING
Lincoln Coll of New England, Southington (CT)
National U Coll, Bayam&,on (PR)
U of Alaska Anchorage (AK)
U of Alaska Fairbanks (AK)
U of Southern Indiana (IN)

DENTAL HYGIENE
Baker Coll (MI)
Coll of Coastal Georgia (GA)
Dixie State U (UT)
Farmingdale State Coll (NY)
Ferris State U (MI)
Florida National U (FL)
Indiana U Northwest (IN)
Indiana U–Purdue U Fort Wayne (IN)
Indiana U–Purdue U Indianapolis (IN)
Indiana U South Bend (IN)
Indian River State Coll (FL)
Missouri Southern State U (MO)
New York City Coll of Technology of the City U of New York (NY)
New York U (NY)
Palm Beach State Coll (FL)
Pennsylvania Coll of Technology (PA)
Rutgers, The State U of New Jersey, New Brunswick (NJ)
Santa Fe Coll (FL)
Shawnee State U (OH)
Southern Adventist U (TN)
State U of New York Coll of Technology at Canton (NY)
Tennessee State U (TN)
U of Alaska Anchorage (AK)
U of Alaska Fairbanks (AK)
U of Bridgeport (CT)
U of Cincinnati (OH)
U of Maine at Augusta (ME)
U of New Haven (CT)
Utah Valley U (UT)
Valencia Coll (FL)
Vermont Tech Coll (VT)
Weber State U (UT)
Western Kentucky U (KY)
West Liberty U (WV)

DENTAL LABORATORY TECHNOLOGY
Florida National U (FL)
Indiana U–Purdue U Fort Wayne (IN)
Louisiana State U Health Sciences Center (LA)

New York City Coll of Technology of the City U of New York (NY)

DENTAL SERVICES AND ALLIED PROFESSIONS RELATED
Valdosta State U (GA)

DESIGN AND APPLIED ARTS RELATED
U of Maine at Presque Isle (ME)
U of Saint Francis (IN)
Washburn U (KS)

DESIGN AND VISUAL COMMUNICATIONS
Keiser U, Fort Lauderdale (FL)
U of Saint Francis (IN)
Utah Valley U (UT)

DESKTOP PUBLISHING AND DIGITAL IMAGING DESIGN
New England Inst of Technology (RI)

DIAGNOSTIC MEDICAL SONOGRAPHY AND ULTRASOUND TECHNOLOGY
Adventist U of Health Sciences (FL)
Baker Coll (MI)
Ferris State U (MI)
Florida National U (FL)
Keiser U, Fort Lauderdale (FL)
Keystone Coll (PA)
Lincoln U (CA)
Mercy Coll of Health Sciences (IA)
Midland Coll (TX)
Nebraska Methodist Coll (NE)
Pennsylvania Coll of Health Sciences (PA)
Polk State Coll (FL)
St. Catharine Coll (KY)
St. Catherine U (MN)
Santa Fe Coll (FL)
Southern Tech Coll, Fort Myers (FL)
U of Charleston (WV)
Valencia Coll (FL)

DIESEL MECHANICS TECHNOLOGY
Idaho State U (ID)
Lewis-Clark State Coll (ID)
Midland Coll (TX)
Montana State U Billings (MT)
Morrisville State Coll (NY)
Pennsylvania Coll of Technology (PA)
State U of New York Coll of Agriculture and Technology at Cobleskill (NY)
Utah Valley U (UT)
Vermont Tech Coll (VT)
Weber State U (UT)

DIETETICS
Ferris State U (MI)
Lincoln Coll of New England, Southington (CT)
State Coll of Florida Manatee-Sarasota (FL)

DIETETIC TECHNOLOGY
Morrisville State Coll (NY)
Youngstown State U (OH)

DIETITIAN ASSISTANT
Lincoln Coll of New England, Southington (CT)
Youngstown State U (OH)

DIGITAL ARTS
Academy of Art U (CA)

DIGITAL COMMUNICATION AND MEDIA/MULTIMEDIA
Florida National U (FL)
Indiana U–Purdue U Indianapolis (IN)
National U (CA)
Vaughn Coll of Aeronautics and Technology (NY)

DISABILITY STUDIES
U of Alaska Anchorage (AK)

DIVINITY/MINISTRY
Carson-Newman U (TN)
Christian Life Coll (IL)
Cincinnati Christian U (OH)
Great Lakes Christian Coll (MI)
Nebraska Christian Coll (NE)
Providence Coll (RI)
Southeastern Baptist Theological Seminary (NC)
U of Valley Forge (PA)

DOG/PET/ANIMAL GROOMING
Becker Coll (MA)

DRAFTING AND DESIGN TECHNOLOGY
Baker Coll (MI)
Black Hills State U (SD)
California U of Pennsylvania (PA)
Caribbean U (PR)
Indian River State Coll (FL)
Johnson & Wales U (RI)
Kentucky State U (KY)
Langston U (OK)
LeTourneau U (TX)
Lewis-Clark State Coll (ID)
Lincoln U (MO)
Montana State U (MT)
Montana State U Billings (MT)
Morrisville State Coll (NY)
Palm Beach State Coll (FL)
State Coll of Florida Manatee-
  Sarasota (FL)
Universidad Metropolitana (PR)
The U of Akron (OH)
U of Alaska Anchorage (AK)
U of Alaska Fairbanks (AK)
U of Puerto Rico in Ponce (PR)
U of Rio Grande (OH)
Utah Valley U (UT)
Valencia Coll (FL)
Weber State U (UT)
Wright State U (OH)
Youngstown State U (OH)

DRAFTING/DESIGN ENGINEERING TECHNOLOGIES RELATED
Morrisville State Coll (NY)
Pennsylvania Coll of Technology
  (PA)

DRAMATIC/THEATER ARTS
Adams State U (CO)
Clarke U (IA)
Indian River State Coll (FL)
Palm Beach State Coll (FL)
Pine Manor Coll (MA)
State Coll of Florida Manatee-
  Sarasota (FL)
Thomas More Coll (KY)
U of the Fraser Valley (BC, Canada)
Utah Valley U (UT)

DRAWING
Pratt Inst (NY)

EARLY CHILDHOOD EDUCATION
Adams State U (CO)
Bethel Coll (IN)
Chaminade U of Honolulu (HI)
Clarion U of Pennsylvania (PA)
Coll of Saint Mary (NE)
Cornerstone U (MI)
Davis Coll (NY)
Dixie State U (UT)
Gannon U (PA)
Granite State Coll (NH)
Great Lakes Christian Coll (MI)
Keystone Coll (PA)
Lincoln Christian U (IL)
Lincoln U (MO)
Lindsey Wilson Coll (KY)
Manchester U (IN)
Maranatha Baptist U (WI)
Morrisville State Coll (NY)
Mount Aloysius Coll (PA)
Mount Saint Mary's U (CA)
National U (CA)
Nazarene Bible Coll (CO)
Nova Southeastern U (FL)
Oakland City U (IN)
Oklahoma Wesleyan U (OK)
Pine Manor Coll (MA)
Rasmussen Coll Appleton (WI)
Rasmussen Coll Aurora (IL)
Rasmussen Coll Bismarck (ND)
Rasmussen Coll Blaine (MN)
Rasmussen Coll Bloomington (MN)
Rasmussen Coll Brooklyn Park (MN)
Rasmussen Coll Eagan (MN)
Rasmussen Coll Fargo (ND)
Rasmussen Coll Fort Myers (FL)
Rasmussen Coll Green Bay (WI)
Rasmussen Coll Kansas City/
  Overland Park (KS)
Rasmussen Coll Lake Elmo/
  Woodbury (MN)
Rasmussen Coll Land O' Lakes (FL)
Rasmussen Coll Mankato (MN)

Rasmussen Coll Mokena/Tinley Park
  (IL)
Rasmussen Coll Moorhead (MN)
Rasmussen Coll New Port Richey
  (FL)
Rasmussen Coll Ocala (FL)
Rasmussen Coll Rockford (IL)
Rasmussen Coll Romeoville/Joliet
  (IL)
Rasmussen Coll St. Cloud (MN)
Rasmussen Coll Tampa/Brandon
  (FL)
Rasmussen Coll Topeka (KS)
Rasmussen Coll Wausau (WI)
Rust Coll (MS)
St. Gregory's U, Shawnee (OK)
Shasta Bible Coll (CA)
Southern Tech Coll, Fort Myers (FL)
Southwestern Assemblies of God U
  (TX)
Sullivan U (KY)
Summit U (PA)
Taylor U (IN)
Tougaloo Coll (MS)
U of Alaska Fairbanks (AK)
U of Arkansas–Fort Smith (AR)
U of Cincinnati (OH)
U of Great Falls (MT)
The U of Montana Western (MT)
U of Southern Indiana (IN)
U of the Virgin Islands (VI)
U of Valley Forge (PA)
Utah Valley U (UT)
Washburn U (KS)
Wayland Baptist U (TX)
Western Kentucky U (KY)
Wilmington U (DE)
Xavier U (OH)

E-COMMERCE
Limestone Coll (SC)

ECONOMICS
Hawai`i Pacific U (HI)
Immaculata U (PA)
Indian River State Coll (FL)
John Cabot U (Italy)
Palm Beach State Coll (FL)
State Coll of Florida Manatee-
  Sarasota (FL)
Thomas More Coll (KY)
The U of Tampa (FL)

EDUCATION
Baker Coll (MI)
Cincinnati Christian U (OH)
Corban U (OR)
Cumberland U (TN)
Florida National U (FL)
Indian River State Coll (FL)
Kent State U (OH)
Montana State U Billings (MT)
Montreat Coll, Montreat (NC)
Morrisville State Coll (NY)
National U (CA)
Palm Beach State Coll (FL)
Saint Francis U (PA)
Southwestern Assemblies of God U
  (TX)
State U of New York Empire State
  Coll (NY)
U of the District of Columbia (DC)

EDUCATIONAL/ INSTRUCTIONAL TECHNOLOGY
Cameron U (OK)

EDUCATIONAL LEADERSHIP AND ADMINISTRATION
Ohio Dominican U (OH)

EDUCATION (MULTIPLE LEVELS)
Coll of Coastal Georgia (GA)
Midland Coll (TX)

EDUCATION RELATED
The U of Akron (OH)

EDUCATION (SPECIFIC SUBJECT AREAS) RELATED
National U (CA)

ELECTRICAL AND ELECTRONIC ENGINEERING TECHNOLOGIES RELATED
Capitol Technology U (MD)
Lawrence Technological U (MI)
Northern Michigan U (MI)
Rochester Inst of Technology (NY)

Vaughn Coll of Aeronautics and
  Technology (NY)
Youngstown State U (OH)

ELECTRICAL AND ELECTRONICS ENGINEERING
New England Inst of Technology (RI)
Southern California Inst of
  Technology (CA)
The U of Scranton (PA)

ELECTRICAL AND POWER TRANSMISSION INSTALLATION
Polk State Coll (FL)
State U of New York Coll of
  Technology at Delhi (NY)

ELECTRICAL, ELECTRONIC AND COMMUNICATIONS ENGINEERING TECHNOLOGY
Baker Coll (MI)
Bluefield State Coll (WV)
California U of Pennsylvania (PA)
Capitol Technology U (MD)
Coll of Staten Island of the City U of
  New York (NY)
DeVry Coll of New York (NY)
DeVry U, Phoenix (AZ)
DeVry U, Pomona (CA)
DeVry U, Westminster (CO)
DeVry U, Miramar (FL)
DeVry U, Orlando (FL)
DeVry U, Decatur (GA)
DeVry U, Chicago (IL)
DeVry U, Kansas City (MO)
DeVry U, North Brunswick (NJ)
DeVry U, Columbus (OH)
DeVry U, Fort Washington (PA)
DeVry U, Irving (TX)
DeVry U Online (IL)
Fairmont State U (WV)
Fort Valley State U (GA)
Hallmark U (TX)
Idaho State U (ID)
Indiana U–Purdue U Fort Wayne (IN)
Indian River State Coll (FL)
Inter American U of Puerto Rico,
  Aguadilla Campus (PR)
Inter American U of Puerto Rico, San
  Germán Campus (PR)
Kentucky State U (KY)
Langston U (OK)
Lawrence Technological U (MI)
Morrisville State Coll (NY)
New York City Coll of Technology of
  the City U of New York (NY)
New York Inst of Technology (NY)
Northern Michigan U (MI)
Palm Beach State Coll (FL)
Penn State Altoona (PA)
Penn State Berks (PA)
Penn State Brandywine (PA)
Penn State Erie, The Behrend Coll
  (PA)
Penn State Hazleton (PA)
Penn State New Kensington (PA)
Penn State Schuylkill (PA)
Penn State Wilkes-Barre (PA)
Penn State Worthington Scranton
  (PA)
Penn State York (PA)
Pennsylvania Coll of Technology
  (PA)
Purdue U (IN)
Purdue U North Central (IN)
State Coll of Florida Manatee-
  Sarasota (FL)
State U of New York Coll of
  Technology at Canton (NY)
State U of New York Coll of
  Technology at Delhi (NY)
Universidad del Turabo (PR)
The U of Akron (OH)
U of Alaska Anchorage (AK)
U of Arkansas at Little Rock (AR)
U of Hartford (CT)
U of Massachusetts Lowell (MA)
The U of Montana (MT)
U of the District of Columbia (DC)
The U of Toledo (OH)
Valencia Coll (FL)
Vermont Tech Coll (VT)
Weber State U (UT)
Youngstown State U (OH)

ELECTRICAL/ELECTRONICS EQUIPMENT INSTALLATION AND REPAIR
Lewis-Clark State Coll (ID)
New England Inst of Technology (RI)

Pittsburg State U (KS)
U of Arkansas–Fort Smith (AR)

ELECTRICIAN
Liberty U (VA)
Michigan State U (MI)
Pennsylvania Coll of Technology
  (PA)
Universidad del Turabo (PR)
Weber State U (UT)

ELECTROCARDIOGRAPH TECHNOLOGY
Pennsylvania Coll of Health
  Sciences (PA)

ELECTROMECHANICAL AND INSTRUMENTATION AND MAINTENANCE TECHNOLOGIES RELATED
Excelsior Coll (NY)

ELECTROMECHANICAL TECHNOLOGY
Excelsior Coll (NY)
John Brown U (AR)
Midland Coll (TX)
New York City Coll of Technology of
  the City U of New York (NY)
Northern Michigan U (MI)
Pennsylvania Coll of Technology
  (PA)
Shawnee State U (OH)
State U of New York Coll of
  Technology at Delhi (NY)
The U of Toledo (OH)

ELECTRONEURODIAGNOSTIC/ ELECTROENCEPHALOGRAPHIC TECHNOLOGY
DeVry U, North Brunswick (NJ)

ELEMENTARY EDUCATION
Adams State U (CO)
Edinboro U of Pennsylvania (PA)
Ferris State U (MI)
Hillsdale Free Will Baptist Coll (OK)
Morrisville State Coll (NY)
New Mexico Highlands U (NM)
Palm Beach State Coll (FL)
Saint Mary-of-the-Woods Coll (IN)
U of Cincinnati (OH)
Weber State U (UT)

EMERGENCY MEDICAL TECHNOLOGY (EMT PARAMEDIC)
Arkansas Tech U (AR)
Baker Coll (MI)
Colorado Mesa U (CO)
Creighton U (NE)
Dixie State U (UT)
Eastern Kentucky U (KY)
EDP U of Puerto Rico (PR)
EDP U of Puerto Rico–San
  Sebastian (PR)
Idaho State U (ID)
Indiana U–Purdue U Indianapolis
  (IN)
Indian River State Coll (FL)
Mercy Coll of Health Sciences (IA)
Midland Coll (TX)
Montana State U Billings (MT)
Pennsylvania Coll of Technology
  (PA)
Polk State Coll (FL)
Purdue U Calumet (IN)
Saint Joseph's Coll (IN)
Santa Fe Coll (FL)
Shawnee State U (OH)
Southwest Baptist U (MO)
Spalding U (KY)
State U of New York Coll of
  Agriculture and Technology at
  Cobleskill (NY)
The U of Akron (OH)
U of Alaska Anchorage (AK)
U of Cincinnati (OH)
U of New Haven (CT)
U of Saint Francis (IN)
The U of West Alabama (AL)
Valencia Coll (FL)
Weber State U (UT)
Western Kentucky U (KY)
Youngstown State U (OH)

ENERGY MANAGEMENT AND SYSTEMS TECHNOLOGY
Idaho State U (ID)
Montana State U Billings (MT)
U of Rio Grande (OH)

ENGINEERING
Cameron U (OK)
Coll of Staten Island of the City U of
  New York (NY)
Dixie State U (UT)
Ferris State U (MI)
Geneva Coll (PA)
Indian River State Coll (FL)
Lindsey Wilson Coll (KY)
Morrisville State Coll (NY)
Palm Beach Atlantic U (FL)
Purdue U North Central (IN)
Southern Adventist U (TN)
State Coll of Florida Manatee-
  Sarasota (FL)
State U of New York Coll of
  Technology at Canton (NY)
Union Coll (NE)
Weber State U (UT)

ENGINEERING RELATED
Eastern Kentucky U (KY)

ENGINEERING SCIENCE
National U (CA)
Rochester Inst of Technology (NY)
U of Pittsburgh at Bradford (PA)

ENGINEERING TECHNOLOGIES AND ENGINEERING RELATED
Arkansas State U (AR)
Excelsior Coll (NY)
Missouri Southern State U (MO)
Morrisville State Coll (NY)
State U of New York Coll of
  Agriculture and Technology at
  Cobleskill (NY)
State U of New York Coll of
  Technology at Canton (NY)
State U of New York Maritime Coll
  (NY)

ENGINEERING TECHNOLOGY
Austin Peay State U (TN)
Edinboro U of Pennsylvania (PA)
Fairmont State U (WV)
Indian River State Coll (FL)
Kansas State U (KS)
Lincoln U (MO)
Miami U (OH)
Michigan Technological U (MI)
Morehead State U (KY)
National U (CA)
Northern Kentucky U (KY)
Polk State Coll (FL)
Southern Utah U (UT)
U of Alaska Anchorage (AK)
The U of Toledo (OH)
Wentworth Inst of Technology (MA)
Wright State U (OH)
Youngstown State U (OH)

ENGLISH
Calumet Coll of Saint Joseph (IN)
Carroll Coll (MT)
Central Methodist U (MO)
Coll of Coastal Georgia (GA)
Hannibal-LaGrange U (MO)
Hillsdale Free Will Baptist Coll (OK)
Immaculata U (PA)
Indian River State Coll (FL)
John Cabot U (Italy)
Liberty U (VA)
Lourdes U (OH)
Madonna U (MI)
Ohio Dominican U (OH)
Palm Beach State Coll (FL)
Pine Manor Coll (MA)
Southwestern Assemblies of God U
  (TX)
State Coll of Florida Manatee-
  Sarasota (FL)
Thomas More Coll (KY)
U of Cincinnati (OH)
The U of Tampa (FL)
Utah Valley U (UT)
Xavier U (OH)

ENGLISH AS A SECOND/ FOREIGN LANGUAGE (TEACHING)
Cornerstone U (MI)
Lincoln Christian U (IL)
Ohio Dominican U (OH)
Union Coll (NE)

ENGLISH LANGUAGE AND LITERATURE RELATED
State U of New York Empire State
  Coll (NY)

ENGLISH/LANGUAGE ARTS TEACHER EDUCATION
State Coll of Florida Manatee-Sarasota (FL)

ENTREPRENEURIAL AND SMALL BUSINESS RELATED
National U Coll, Bayam&,on (PR)

ENTREPRENEURSHIP
Baker Coll (MI)
Central Penn Coll (PA)
Universidad Metropolitana (PR)
U of Alaska Anchorage (AK)

ENVIRONMENTAL CONTROL TECHNOLOGIES RELATED
Montana Tech of The U of Montana (MT)

ENVIRONMENTAL ENGINEERING TECHNOLOGY
Baker Coll (MI)
New York City Coll of Technology of the City U of New York (NY)

ENVIRONMENTAL SCIENCE
Madonna U (MI)
U of Saint Francis (IN)

ENVIRONMENTAL STUDIES
Columbia Coll (MO)
Dickinson State U (ND)
State U of New York Coll of Agriculture and Technology at Cobleskill (NY)

EQUESTRIAN STUDIES
Morrisville State Coll (NY)
Saint Mary-of-the-Woods Coll (IN)
The U of Findlay (OH)
U of Massachusetts Amherst (MA)
The U of Montana Western (MT)

EXECUTIVE ASSISTANT/EXECUTIVE SECRETARY
Northern Kentucky U (KY)
Santa Fe Coll (FL)
Sullivan U (KY)
U of Arkansas–Fort Smith (AR)
The U of Montana (MT)

FAMILY AND COMMUNITY SERVICES
Baker Coll (MI)

FAMILY AND CONSUMER SCIENCES/HOME ECONOMICS TEACHER EDUCATION
State Coll of Florida Manatee-Sarasota (FL)

FAMILY AND CONSUMER SCIENCES/HUMAN SCIENCES
Eastern New Mexico U (NM)
Indian River State Coll (FL)
Mount Vernon Nazarene U (OH)
Palm Beach State Coll (FL)
U of Alaska Anchorage (AK)

FASHION AND FABRIC CONSULTING
Academy of Art U (CA)

FASHION/APPAREL DESIGN
Academy of Art U (CA)
EDP U of Puerto Rico (PR)
EDP U of Puerto Rico–San Sebastian (PR)
Fashion Inst of Technology (NY)
Fisher Coll (MA)
Palm Beach State Coll (FL)
Universidad del Turabo (PR)

FASHION MERCHANDISING
Berkeley Coll, Woodland Park (NJ)
Berkeley Coll–New York City Campus (NY)
Fashion Inst of Technology (NY)
Fisher Coll (MA)
Immaculata U (PA)
Indian River State Coll (FL)
LIM Coll (NY)
Lincoln Coll of New England, Southington (CT)
New York City Coll of Technology of the City U of New York (NY)
Palm Beach State Coll (FL)
Southern New Hampshire U (NH)
Stevens–The Inst of Business & Arts (MO)
The U of Akron (OH)
U of Bridgeport (CT)

U of the District of Columbia (DC)

FASHION MODELING
Fashion Inst of Technology (NY)

FILM/CINEMA/VIDEO STUDIES
Fashion Inst of Technology (NY)
Los Angeles Film School (CA)

FINANCE
Davenport U, Grand Rapids (MI)
Ellis U (IL)
Franklin U (OH)
Hawai`i Pacific U (HI)
Indian River State Coll (FL)
John Cabot U (Italy)
Palm Beach State Coll (FL)
Saint Peter's U (NJ)
State Coll of Florida Manatee-Sarasota (FL)
The U of Findlay (OH)
Youngstown State U (OH)

FINANCIAL PLANNING AND SERVICES
Berkeley Coll, Woodland Park (NJ)
Berkeley Coll–New York City Campus (NY)

FINE ARTS RELATED
Heritage U (WA)
Madonna U (MI)
Pennsylvania Coll of Technology (PA)
Saint Francis U (PA)

FINE/STUDIO ARTS
Academy of Art U (CA)
Adams State U (CO)
Beacon Coll (FL)
Fashion Inst of Technology (NY)
Inst of American Indian Arts (NM)
Keystone Coll (PA)
Lindsey Wilson Coll (KY)
Pratt Inst (NY)
State Coll of Florida Manatee-Sarasota (FL)
Thomas More Coll (KY)
U of Maine at Augusta (ME)
U of Saint Francis (IN)
Villa Maria Coll (NY)
York Coll of Pennsylvania (PA)

FIRE PREVENTION AND SAFETY TECHNOLOGY
Montana State U Billings (MT)
Northern Kentucky U (KY)
Polk State Coll (FL)
Santa Fe Coll (FL)
The U of Akron (OH)
U of New Haven (CT)

FIRE SCIENCE/FIREFIGHTING
American Public U System (WV)
Columbia Southern U (AL)
Idaho State U (ID)
Indian River State Coll (FL)
Keiser U, Fort Lauderdale (FL)
Lewis-Clark State Coll (ID)
Madonna U (MI)
Midland Coll (TX)
Palm Beach State Coll (FL)
Polk State Coll (FL)
Southwestern Adventist U (TX)
State Coll of Florida Manatee-Sarasota (FL)
U of Alaska Anchorage (AK)
U of Alaska Fairbanks (AK)
U of Cincinnati (OH)
U of New Haven (CT)
U of the District of Columbia (DC)
Utah Valley U (UT)
Valencia Coll (FL)
Vermont Tech Coll (VT)

FIRE SERVICES ADMINISTRATION
American Public U System (WV)
Columbia Coll (MO)

FISHING AND FISHERIES SCIENCES AND MANAGEMENT
State U of New York Coll of Agriculture and Technology at Cobleskill (NY)

FOOD PREPARATION
Washburn U (KS)

FOODS AND NUTRITION RELATED
U of Guelph (ON, Canada)

FOOD SERVICE SYSTEMS ADMINISTRATION
Inter American U of Puerto Rico, Aguadilla Campus (PR)
Lincoln Coll of New England, Southington (CT)
Morrisville State Coll (NY)
Northern Michigan U (MI)
U of New Hampshire (NH)

FOODS, NUTRITION, AND WELLNESS
Indian River State Coll (FL)
Madonna U (MI)
Morrisville State Coll (NY)
Palm Beach State Coll (FL)
Southern Adventist U (TN)
Youngstown State U (OH)

FOREIGN LANGUAGES AND LITERATURES
Coll of Coastal Georgia (GA)
Southwestern Assemblies of God U (TX)

FOREIGN LANGUAGES RELATED
U of Alaska Fairbanks (AK)

FOREIGN LANGUAGE TEACHER EDUCATION
State Coll of Florida Manatee-Sarasota (FL)

FORENSIC SCIENCE AND TECHNOLOGY
Arkansas State U (AR)
U of Arkansas–Fort Smith (AR)
U of Saint Francis (IN)

FORESTRY
Coll of Coastal Georgia (GA)
Indian River State Coll (FL)

FOREST TECHNOLOGY
Pennsylvania Coll of Technology (PA)
State U of New York Coll of Environmental Science and Forestry (NY)
U of Maine at Fort Kent (ME)
U of New Hampshire (NH)

FRENCH
Indian River State Coll (FL)
State Coll of Florida Manatee-Sarasota (FL)
Thomas More Coll (KY)
The U of Tampa (FL)
Xavier U (OH)

FUNERAL SERVICE AND MORTUARY SCIENCE
Cincinnati Coll of Mortuary Science (OH)
Ferris State U (MI)
Lincoln Coll of New England, Southington (CT)
U of the District of Columbia (DC)

GAME AND INTERACTIVE MEDIA DESIGN
Academy of Art U (CA)
Keiser U, Fort Lauderdale (FL)
National U (CA)

GENERAL STUDIES
Adventist U of Health Sciences (FL)
Alverno Coll (WI)
American Baptist Coll of American Baptist Theological Seminary (TN)
American Public U System (WV)
Arkansas State U (AR)
Arkansas Tech U (AR)
Asbury U (KY)
Austin Peay State U (TN)
Barclay Coll (KS)
Belhaven U (MS)
Bethel Coll (IN)
Black Hills State U (SD)
Butler U (IN)
Cabarrus Coll of Health Sciences (NC)
Calumet Coll of Saint Joseph (IN)
Cameron U (OK)
Cardinal Stritch U (WI)
Castleton State Coll (VT)
Chaminade U of Honolulu (HI)
Christian Brothers U (TN)
Columbia Coll (MO)
Columbia Southern U (AL)
Concordia U, St. Paul (MN)
Concordia U Texas (TX)

Dakota State U (SD)
Dixie State U (UT)
Eastern Connecticut State U (CT)
Eastern Kentucky U (KY)
Ferris State U (MI)
Fisher Coll (MA)
Fort Hays State U (KS)
Franciscan U of Steubenville (OH)
Friends U (KS)
Granite State Coll (NH)
Great Lakes Christian Coll (MI)
Hillsdale Free Will Baptist Coll (OK)
Hope International U (CA)
Idaho State U (ID)
Indiana U Northwest (IN)
Indiana U South Bend (IN)
John Brown U (AR)
Johnson State Coll (VT)
La Salle U (PA)
Lawrence Technological U (MI)
Liberty U (VA)
Lincoln Christian U (IL)
Lipscomb U (TN)
Louisiana Tech U (LA)
McNeese State U (LA)
Medaille Coll (NY)
Miami U (OH)
Midland Coll (TX)
Monmouth U (NJ)
Montana State U Billings (MT)
Morehead State U (KY)
Morrisville State Coll (NY)
Mount Aloysius Coll (PA)
Mount Marty Coll (SD)
Mount St. Joseph U (OH)
Mount Vernon Nazarene U (OH)
Newbury Coll (MA)
New Mexico Inst of Mining and Technology (NM)
Nicholls State U (LA)
Northern Kentucky U (KY)
Northern Michigan U (MI)
Northwest Christian U (OR)
Northwest U (WA)
Ohio Dominican U (OH)
The Ohio State U at Lima (OH)
The Ohio State U at Marion (OH)
The Ohio State U–Mansfield Campus (OH)
The Ohio State U–Newark Campus (OH)
Oklahoma Wesleyan U (OK)
Peirce Coll (PA)
Point U (GA)
Regent U (VA)
Rider U (NJ)
Sacred Heart U (CT)
Shawnee State U (OH)
Siena Heights U (MI)
Simpson U (CA)
South Dakota School of Mines and Technology (SD)
South Dakota State U (SD)
Southern Arkansas U–Magnolia (AR)
Southern Utah U (UT)
Southwest Baptist U (MO)
Southwestern Adventist U (TX)
Southwestern Assemblies of God U (TX)
State U of New York Coll of Technology at Canton (NY)
State U of New York Coll of Technology at Delhi (NY)
Summit U (PA)
Temple U (PA)
Tiffin U (OH)
Toccoa Falls Coll (GA)
Trevecca Nazarene U (TN)
Trinity Coll of Florida (FL)
U of Arkansas at Little Rock (AR)
U of Arkansas–Fort Smith (AR)
U of Bridgeport (CT)
U of Central Arkansas (AR)
U of Cincinnati (OH)
U of Hartford (CT)
U of Maine at Fort Kent (ME)
U of Mobile (AL)
U of Rio Grande (OH)
U of the Fraser Valley (BC, Canada)
U of Wisconsin–Superior (WI)
Utah State U (UT)
Utah Valley U (UT)
Viterbo U (WI)
Wayland Baptist U (TX)
Weber State U (UT)
Western Kentucky U (KY)
Wichita State U (KS)
Widener U (PA)
Wilmington U (DE)
York Coll of Pennsylvania (PA)

GEOGRAPHIC INFORMATION SCIENCE AND CARTOGRAPHY
The U of Akron (OH)

GEOGRAPHY
The U of Tampa (FL)
Wright State U (OH)

GEOGRAPHY RELATED
Adams State U (CO)

GEOLOGY/EARTH SCIENCE
Coll of Coastal Georgia (GA)
Wright State U (OH)

GERMAN
State Coll of Florida Manatee-Sarasota (FL)
Xavier U (OH)

GERONTOLOGY
Holy Cross Coll (IN)
Madonna U (MI)
Manchester U (IN)
Ohio Dominican U (OH)
Siena Heights U (MI)
Thomas More Coll (KY)

GOLF COURSE OPERATION AND GROUNDS MANAGEMENT
Keiser U, Fort Lauderdale (FL)

GRAPHIC AND PRINTING EQUIPMENT OPERATION/PRODUCTION
Chowan U (NC)
Dixie State U (UT)
Lewis-Clark State Coll (ID)

GRAPHIC COMMUNICATIONS
New England Inst of Technology (RI)
Walla Walla U (WA)

GRAPHIC COMMUNICATIONS RELATED
Rasmussen Coll Moorhead (MN)
U of the District of Columbia (DC)

GRAPHIC DESIGN
Academy of Art U (CA)
California U of Pennsylvania (PA)
Columbia Centro Universitario, Caguas (PR)
Creative Center (NE)
Defiance Coll (OH)
Ferris State U (MI)
Hickey Coll (MO)
Inter American U of Puerto Rico, San Germán Campus (PR)
International Business Coll, Fort Wayne (IN)
Madonna U (MI)
Mount St. Joseph U (OH)
Pratt Inst (NY)
State U of New York Coll of Agriculture and Technology at Cobleskill (NY)
Union Coll (NE)
U of the District of Columbia (DC)
U of the Fraser Valley (BC, Canada)
Villa Maria Coll (NY)
Wright State U (OH)

HEALTH AIDE
National U (CA)

HEALTH AND MEDICAL ADMINISTRATIVE SERVICES RELATED
National U (CA)

HEALTH AND PHYSICAL EDUCATION/FITNESS
Coll of Coastal Georgia (GA)
Robert Morris U Illinois (IL)
State U of New York Coll of Technology at Delhi (NY)
Universidad del Turabo (PR)
Universidad Metropolitana (PR)
Utah Valley U (UT)

HEALTH AND PHYSICAL EDUCATION RELATED
Pennsylvania Coll of Technology (PA)

HEALTH/HEALTH-CARE ADMINISTRATION
Baker Coll (MI)
Berkeley Coll, Woodland Park (NJ)
Berkeley Coll–New York City Campus (NY)

Elizabethtown Coll School of
Continuing and Professional
Studies (PA)
Mount Saint Mary's U (CA)
National U (CA)
Park U (MO)
Southern Tech Coll, Fort Myers (FL)
State Coll of Florida Manatee-
Sarasota (FL)
The U of Scranton (PA)
Washburn U (KS)

**HEALTH INFORMATION/
MEDICAL RECORDS
ADMINISTRATION**
Indian River State Coll (FL)
Keiser U, Fort Lauderdale (FL)
Lincoln Coll of New England,
Southington (CT)
Montana State U Billings (MT)
Santa Fe Coll (FL)

**HEALTH INFORMATION/
MEDICAL RECORDS
TECHNOLOGY**
Baker Coll (MI)
Berkeley Coll, Woodland Park (NJ)
Berkeley Coll–New York City
Campus (NY)
Dakota State U (SD)
Davenport U, Grand Rapids (MI)
DeVry U, Pomona (CA)
DeVry U, Westminster (CO)
DeVry U, Decatur (GA)
DeVry U, Chicago (IL)
DeVry U, North Brunswick (NJ)
DeVry U, Columbus (OH)
DeVry U, Fort Washington (PA)
DeVry U, Irving (TX)
DeVry U Online (IL)
Ferris State U (MI)
Fisher Coll (MA)
Gwynedd Mercy U (PA)
Hodges U (FL)
Idaho State U (ID)
Indiana U Northwest (IN)
Keiser U, Fort Lauderdale (FL)
Lincoln Coll of New England,
Southington (CT)
Louisiana Tech U (LA)
Midland Coll (TX)
Missouri Western State U (MO)
National U (CA)
New England Inst of Technology (RI)
Northern Michigan U (MI)
Peirce Coll (PA)
Pennsylvania Coll of Technology
(PA)
Rasmussen Coll Appleton (WI)
Rasmussen Coll Aurora (IL)
Rasmussen Coll Bismarck (ND)
Rasmussen Coll Blaine (MN)
Rasmussen Coll Bloomington (MN)
Rasmussen Coll Brooklyn Park (MN)
Rasmussen Coll Eagan (MN)
Rasmussen Coll Fort Myers (FL)
Rasmussen Coll Green Bay (WI)
Rasmussen Coll Kansas City/
Overland Park (KS)
Rasmussen Coll Lake Elmo/
Woodbury (MN)
Rasmussen Coll Land O' Lakes (FL)
Rasmussen Coll Mankato (MN)
Rasmussen Coll Mokena/Tinley Park
(IL)
Rasmussen Coll Moorhead (MN)
Rasmussen Coll New Port Richey
(FL)
Rasmussen Coll Ocala (FL)
Rasmussen Coll Rockford (IL)
Rasmussen Coll Romeoville/Joliet
(IL)
Rasmussen Coll St. Cloud (MN)
Rasmussen Coll Tampa/Brandon
(FL)
Rasmussen Coll Topeka (KS)
Rasmussen Coll Wausau (WI)
St. Catherine U (MN)
Santa Fe Coll (FL)
Sullivan U (KY)
U of Cincinnati (OH)
Washburn U (KS)
Weber State U (UT)
Western Kentucky U (KY)

**HEALTH/MEDICAL
PREPARATORY PROGRAMS
RELATED**
Immaculata U (PA)
Mount Saint Mary's U (CA)

Northwest Christian U (OR)
Ohio Valley U (WV)

**HEALTH PROFESSIONS
RELATED**
American Public U System (WV)
Caribbean U (PR)
Ferris State U (MI)
Fisher Coll (MA)
Lock Haven U of Pennsylvania (PA)
Morrisville State Coll (NY)
Newman U (KS)
New York U (NY)
Northwest U (WA)
Saint Peter's U (NJ)
U of Cincinnati (OH)
U of Hartford (CT)
U of Saint Francis (IN)
Villa Maria Coll (NY)

**HEALTH SERVICES
ADMINISTRATION**
Florida National U (FL)
Keiser U, Fort Lauderdale (FL)

**HEALTH SERVICES/ALLIED
HEALTH/HEALTH SCIENCES**
Berkeley Coll, Woodland Park (NJ)
Cameron U (OK)
Fisher Coll (MA)
Howard Payne U (TX)
Keystone Coll (PA)
Lindsey Wilson Coll (KY)
Pennsylvania Coll of Technology
(PA)
Pine Manor Coll (MA)
St. Catharine Coll (KY)
State U of New York Coll of
Agriculture and Technology at
Cobleskill (NY)
U of Hartford (CT)
U of Maine at Fort Kent (ME)
U of the Incarnate Word (TX)
Weber State U (UT)

**HEALTH TEACHER
EDUCATION**
Palm Beach State Coll (FL)
State Coll of Florida Manatee-
Sarasota (FL)

**HEATING, AIR CONDITIONING,
VENTILATION AND
REFRIGERATION
MAINTENANCE TECHNOLOGY**
Indian River State Coll (FL)
Lewis-Clark State Coll (ID)
Montana State U Billings (MT)
New England Inst of Technology (RI)
Santa Fe Coll (FL)
State U of New York Coll of
Technology at Delhi (NY)
U of Alaska Anchorage (AK)

**HEATING, VENTILATION, AIR
CONDITIONING AND
REFRIGERATION ENGINEERING
TECHNOLOGY**
Ferris State U (MI)
Midland Coll (TX)
Northern Michigan U (MI)
Pennsylvania Coll of Technology
(PA)
State U of New York Coll of
Technology at Canton (NY)

**HEAVY EQUIPMENT
MAINTENANCE TECHNOLOGY**
Ferris State U (MI)
Pennsylvania Coll of Technology
(PA)
U of Alaska Anchorage (AK)
The U of Montana (MT)

HEBREW
Yeshiva U (NY)

HISTOLOGIC TECHNICIAN
Indiana U–Purdue U Indianapolis
(IN)
Northern Michigan U (MI)
Tarleton State U (TX)

**HISTOLOGIC TECHNOLOGY/
HISTOTECHNOLOGIST**
Keiser U, Fort Lauderdale (FL)
Tarleton State U (TX)

**HISTORIC PRESERVATION AND
CONSERVATION**
Montana Tech of The U of Montana
(MT)

HISTORY
American Public U System (WV)
Clarke U (IA)
Coll of Coastal Georgia (GA)
Indian River State Coll (FL)
John Cabot U (Italy)
Lindsey Wilson Coll (KY)
Lourdes U (OH)
Oklahoma Wesleyan U (OK)
Palm Beach State Coll (FL)
Regent U (VA)
State Coll of Florida Manatee-
Sarasota (FL)
State U of New York Empire State
Coll (NY)
Thomas More Coll (KY)
U of Rio Grande (OH)
The U of Tampa (FL)
Utah Valley U (UT)
Wright State U (OH)
Xavier U (OH)

HOMELAND SECURITY
Keiser U, Fort Lauderdale (FL)

**HOMELAND SECURITY, LAW
ENFORCEMENT, FIREFIGHTING
AND PROTECTIVE SERVICES
RELATED**
Idaho State U (ID)

**HORSE HUSBANDRY/EQUINE
SCIENCE AND MANAGEMENT**
Michigan State U (MI)
Southern Utah U (UT)
U of Guelph (ON, Canada)

HORTICULTURAL SCIENCE
Andrews U (MI)
Morrisville State Coll (NY)
Temple U (PA)
U of Connecticut (CT)
U of Guelph (ON, Canada)

**HOSPITAL AND HEALTH-CARE
FACILITIES ADMINISTRATION**
State Coll of Florida Manatee-
Sarasota (FL)

**HOSPITALITY
ADMINISTRATION**
Colorado Mesa U (CO)
Florida National U (FL)
Keiser U, Fort Lauderdale (FL)
Lewis-Clark State Coll (ID)
Morrisville State Coll (NY)
National U (CA)
New York City Coll of Technology of
the City U of New York (NY)
Stratford U (MD)
Tougaloo Coll (MS)
The U of Akron (OH)
U of Cincinnati (OH)
Utah Valley U (UT)
Valencia Coll (FL)
Webber International U (FL)
Youngstown State U (OH)

**HOSPITALITY
ADMINISTRATION RELATED**
Morrisville State Coll (NY)
Penn State Beaver (PA)
Penn State Berks (PA)
U of the District of Columbia (DC)

**HOSPITALITY AND
RECREATION MARKETING**
Ferris State U (MI)

**HOTEL/MOTEL
ADMINISTRATION**
Baker Coll (MI)
Ferris State U (MI)
Indian River State Coll (FL)
Inter American U of Puerto Rico,
Fajardo Campus (PR)
International Business Coll, Fort
Wayne (IN)
Lincoln Coll of New England,
Southington (CT)
Palm Beach State Coll (FL)
State U of New York Coll of
Agriculture and Technology at
Cobleskill (NY)
Stratford U, Falls Church (VA)
Stratford U, Woodbridge (VA)

The U of Akron (OH)
Valencia Coll (FL)

**HOTEL, MOTEL, AND
RESTAURANT MANAGEMENT**
Stratford U, Glen Allen (VA)
Stratford U, Newport News (VA)
Sullivan U (KY)

**HUMAN DEVELOPMENT AND
FAMILY STUDIES**
Penn State Abington (PA)
Penn State Altoona (PA)
Penn State Berks (PA)
Penn State Brandywine (PA)
Penn State Erie, The Behrend Coll
(PA)
Penn State New Kensington (PA)
Penn State Schuylkill (PA)
Penn State Worthington Scranton
(PA)
Penn State York (PA)

**HUMAN DEVELOPMENT AND
FAMILY STUDIES RELATED**
Utah State U (UT)

HUMANITIES
Aquinas Coll (TN)
Calumet Coll of Saint Joseph (IN)
Fisher Coll (MA)
Harrison Middleton U (AZ)
Indian River State Coll (FL)
John Cabot U (Italy)
Michigan Technological U (MI)
Ohio U (OH)
Saint Mary-of-the-Woods Coll (IN)
Saint Peter's U (NJ)
State Coll of Florida Manatee-
Sarasota (FL)
State U of New York Coll of
Agriculture and Technology at
Cobleskill (NY)
State U of New York Coll of
Technology at Delhi (NY)
Thomas More Coll (KY)
Utah Valley U (UT)
Valparaiso U (IN)
Washburn U (KS)

**HUMAN RESOURCES
DEVELOPMENT**
Hawai'i Pacific U (HI)
Park U (MO)

**HUMAN RESOURCES
MANAGEMENT**
Baker Coll (MI)
King's Coll (PA)
Montana State U Billings (MT)
Rasmussen Coll Appleton (WI)
Rasmussen Coll Blaine (MN)
Rasmussen Coll Bloomington (MN)
Rasmussen Coll Brooklyn Park (MN)
Rasmussen Coll Eagan (MN)
Rasmussen Coll Fargo (ND)
Rasmussen Coll Fort Myers (FL)
Rasmussen Coll Green Bay (WI)
Rasmussen Coll Kansas City/
Overland Park (KS)
Rasmussen Coll Lake Elmo/
Woodbury (MN)
Rasmussen Coll Land O' Lakes (FL)
Rasmussen Coll Mankato (MN)
Rasmussen Coll Moorhead (MN)
Rasmussen Coll New Port Richey
(FL)
Rasmussen Coll Ocala (FL)
Rasmussen Coll Tampa/Brandon
(FL)
Rasmussen Coll Topeka (KS)
Rasmussen Coll Wausau (WI)
The U of Findlay (OH)
U of Saint Francis (IN)
The U of Scranton (PA)
Urbana (OH)

**HUMAN RESOURCES
MANAGEMENT AND SERVICES
RELATED**
American Public U System (WV)

HUMAN SERVICES
Arkansas Tech U (AR)
Baker Coll (MI)
Beacon Coll (FL)
Bethel Coll (IN)
Caribbean U (PR)
Cazenovia Coll (NY)
Columbia Coll (MO)
Cornerstone U (MI)

Elizabethtown Coll School of
Continuing and Professional
Studies (PA)
Hilbert Coll (NY)
Indian River State Coll (FL)
Lincoln Coll of New England,
Southington (CT)
Mercy Coll (NY)
Morrisville State Coll (NY)
Mount Saint Mary's U (CA)
Mount Vernon Nazarene U (OH)
New York City Coll of Technology of
the City U of New York (NY)
Rasmussen Coll Appleton (WI)
Rasmussen Coll Bismarck (ND)
Rasmussen Coll Blaine (MN)
Rasmussen Coll Bloomington (MN)
Rasmussen Coll Brooklyn Park (MN)
Rasmussen Coll Eagan (MN)
Rasmussen Coll Fargo (ND)
Rasmussen Coll Fort Myers (FL)
Rasmussen Coll Green Bay (WI)
Rasmussen Coll Kansas City/
Overland Park (KS)
Rasmussen Coll Lake Elmo/
Woodbury (MN)
Rasmussen Coll Land O' Lakes (FL)
Rasmussen Coll Mankato (MN)
Rasmussen Coll Moorhead (MN)
Rasmussen Coll New Port Richey
(FL)
Rasmussen Coll Ocala (FL)
Rasmussen Coll St. Cloud (MN)
Rasmussen Coll Tampa/Brandon
(FL)
Rasmussen Coll Topeka (KS)
Rasmussen Coll Wausau (WI)
U of Alaska Anchorage (AK)
U of Great Falls (MT)
U of Maine at Fort Kent (ME)
The U of Scranton (PA)
U of the Cumberlands (KY)
U of Valley Forge (PA)
Walsh U (OH)
Wayland Baptist U (TX)

**HYDROLOGY AND WATER
RESOURCES SCIENCE**
Indian River State Coll (FL)

ILLUSTRATION
Academy of Art U (CA)
Fashion Inst of Technology (NY)
Pratt Inst (NY)

**INDUSTRIAL AND PRODUCT
DESIGN**
Academy of Art U (CA)

**INDUSTRIAL ELECTRONICS
TECHNOLOGY**
Ferris State U (MI)
Lewis-Clark State Coll (ID)
National U Coll, Bayam&,on (PR)
Pennsylvania Coll of Technology
(PA)

**INDUSTRIAL MECHANICS AND
MAINTENANCE TECHNOLOGY**
Northern Michigan U (MI)
Pennsylvania Coll of Technology
(PA)
U of Alaska Anchorage (AK)
The U of West Alabama (AL)

**INDUSTRIAL PRODUCTION
TECHNOLOGIES RELATED**
Austin Peay State U (TN)
California U of Pennsylvania (PA)
Clarion U of Pennsylvania (PA)
Ferris State U (MI)
U of Alaska Fairbanks (AK)

**INDUSTRIAL RADIOLOGIC
TECHNOLOGY**
The George Washington U (DC)
Indian River State Coll (FL)
Palm Beach State Coll (FL)
Widener U (PA)

INDUSTRIAL TECHNOLOGY
Arkansas Tech U (AR)
Eastern Kentucky U (KY)
Indiana U–Purdue U Fort Wayne (IN)
Millersville U of Pennsylvania (PA)
Murray State U (KY)
Penn State York (PA)
Pittsburg State U (KS)
Southeastern Louisiana U (LA)
Southern Arkansas U–Magnolia
(AR)

U of Alaska Anchorage (AK)
U of Arkansas at Pine Bluff (AR)
U of Puerto Rico in Ponce (PR)
U of Rio Grande (OH)
Washburn U (KS)

INFORMATION RESOURCES MANAGEMENT
Rasmussen Coll Fort Myers (FL)
Rasmussen Coll Land O' Lakes (FL)
Rasmussen Coll New Port Richey (FL)
Rasmussen Coll Ocala (FL)
Rasmussen Coll Tampa/Brandon (FL)

INFORMATION SCIENCE/ STUDIES
Campbellsville U (KY)
Elizabethtown Coll School of Continuing and Professional Studies (PA)
Immaculata U (PA)
Indiana U–Purdue U Fort Wayne (IN)
Indian River State Coll (FL)
Johnson State Coll (VT)
Mansfield U of Pennsylvania (PA)
Morrisville State Coll (NY)
Newman U (KS)
Oakland City U (IN)
Penn State Abington (PA)
Penn State Altoona (PA)
Penn State Berks (PA)
Penn State Erie, The Behrend Coll (PA)
Penn State Hazleton (PA)
Penn State Lehigh Valley (PA)
Penn State New Kensington (PA)
Penn State Schuylkill (PA)
Penn State York (PA)
Saint Peter's U (NJ)
State Coll of Florida Manatee-Sarasota (FL)
State U of New York Coll of Agriculture and Technology at Cobleskill (NY)
State U of New York Coll of Technology at Canton (NY)
State U of New York Coll of Technology at Delhi (NY)
Tulane U (LA)
U of Alaska Anchorage (AK)
U of Cincinnati (OH)
U of Massachusetts Lowell (MA)
U of Pittsburgh at Bradford (PA)
The U of Scranton (PA)
Wright State U (OH)

INFORMATION TECHNOLOGY
Arkansas Tech U (AR)
Cameron U (OK)
Ferris State U (MI)
Florida National U (FL)
Franklin U (OH)
Hallmark U (TX)
Indiana U–Purdue U Fort Wayne (IN)
Keiser U, Fort Lauderdale (FL)
Keystone Coll (PA)
Life U (GA)
Limestone Coll (SC)
Mercy Coll (NY)
National U Coll, Bayam&,on (PR)
New England Inst of Technology (RI)
Peirce Coll (PA)
Purdue U (IN)
Regent U (VA)
Southern Utah U (UT)
Thomas More Coll (KY)
Tiffin U (OH)
Trevecca Nazarene U (TN)
Vermont Tech Coll (VT)
Youngstown State U (OH)

INSTITUTIONAL FOOD WORKERS
Immaculata U (PA)

INSTRUMENTATION TECHNOLOGY
Idaho State U (ID)
U of Alaska Anchorage (AK)

INTERCULTURAL/ MULTICULTURAL AND DIVERSITY STUDIES
Baptist U of the Americas (TX)
Nyack Coll (NY)

INTERDISCIPLINARY STUDIES
Central Methodist U (MO)
John Brown U (AR)
Keiser U, Fort Lauderdale (FL)

Lesley U (MA)
U of North Florida (FL)

INTERIOR ARCHITECTURE
Villa Maria Coll (NY)

INTERIOR DESIGN
Academy of Art U (CA)
Baker Coll (MI)
Bay Path U (MA)
Berkeley Coll, Woodland Park (NJ)
Chaminade U of Honolulu (HI)
EDP U of Puerto Rico (PR)
Fashion Inst of Technology (NY)
Indiana U–Purdue U Fort Wayne (IN)
Indiana U–Purdue U Indianapolis (IN)
Indian River State Coll (FL)
Montana State U (MT)
New England Inst of Technology (RI)
New York School of Interior Design (NY)
Palm Beach State Coll (FL)
Robert Morris U Illinois (IL)
Southern Tech Coll, Fort Myers (FL)
Stevens–The Inst of Business & Arts (MO)
Villa Maria Coll (NY)
Weber State U (UT)

INTERNATIONAL BUSINESS/ TRADE/COMMERCE
The American U of Rome (Italy)
Berkeley Coll, Woodland Park (NJ)
Berkeley Coll–New York City Campus (NY)
John Cabot U (Italy)
Saint Peter's U (NJ)

INTERNATIONAL/GLOBAL STUDIES
Holy Cross Coll (IN)
Thomas More Coll (KY)

INTERNATIONAL RELATIONS AND AFFAIRS
John Cabot U (Italy)

ITALIAN STUDIES
John Cabot U (Italy)

JAZZ/JAZZ STUDIES
Five Towns Coll (NY)
State Coll of Florida Manatee-Sarasota (FL)
Villa Maria Coll (NY)

JEWISH/JUDAIC STUDIES
State Coll of Florida Manatee-Sarasota (FL)

JOURNALISM
Academy of Art U (CA)
Indian River State Coll (FL)
John Brown U (AR)
Madonna U (MI)
Manchester U (IN)
Morrisville State Coll (NY)
Palm Beach State Coll (FL)
State Coll of Florida Manatee-Sarasota (FL)

JOURNALISM RELATED
Adams State U (CO)
National U (CA)

KINDERGARTEN/PRESCHOOL EDUCATION
Baker Coll (MI)
California U of Pennsylvania (PA)
Fisher Coll (MA)
Indian River State Coll (FL)
Maria Coll (NY)
Miami U (OH)
Mitchell Coll (CT)
Mount Saint Mary's U (CA)
Palm Beach State Coll (FL)
Shawnee State U (OH)
State Coll of Florida Manatee-Sarasota (FL)
Tennessee State U (TN)
U of Cincinnati (OH)
U of Great Falls (MT)
U of Rio Grande (OH)

KINESIOLOGY AND EXERCISE SCIENCE
Ohio Dominican U (OH)
Southwestern Adventist U (TX)

LABOR AND INDUSTRIAL RELATIONS
Indiana U–Purdue U Fort Wayne (IN)
Rider U (NJ)

State U of New York Empire State Coll (NY)
Youngstown State U (OH)

LABOR STUDIES
Indiana U Bloomington (IN)
Indiana U Northwest (IN)
Indiana U–Purdue U Indianapolis (IN)

LANDSCAPE ARCHITECTURE
Academy of Art U (CA)
Keystone Coll (PA)
Morrisville State Coll (NY)

LANDSCAPING AND GROUNDSKEEPING
Michigan State U (MI)
North Carolina State U (NC)
Pennsylvania Coll of Technology (PA)
State U of New York Coll of Technology at Delhi (NY)
U of Massachusetts Amherst (MA)
Valencia Coll (FL)
Vermont Tech Coll (VT)

LANGUAGE INTERPRETATION AND TRANSLATION
Indian River State Coll (FL)

LATIN AMERICAN STUDIES
State Coll of Florida Manatee-Sarasota (FL)

LAW ENFORCEMENT INVESTIGATION AND INTERVIEWING
U of the District of Columbia (DC)

LAY MINISTRY
Howard Payne U (TX)
Maranatha Baptist U (WI)
Southeastern Bible Coll (AL)
U of Saint Francis (IN)

LEGAL ADMINISTRATIVE ASSISTANT/SECRETARY
Baker Coll (MI)
Clarion U of Pennsylvania (PA)
Hickey Coll (MO)
International Business Coll, Fort Wayne (IN)
Lewis-Clark State Coll (ID)
National U Coll, Bayam&,on (PR)
Palm Beach State Coll (FL)
Shawnee State U (OH)
Sullivan U (KY)
The U of Montana (MT)
U of Rio Grande (OH)
U of the District of Columbia (DC)
The U of Toledo (OH)
Washburn U (KS)
Youngstown State U (OH)

LEGAL ASSISTANT/PARALEGAL
American Public U System (WV)
Bay Path U (MA)
Calumet Coll of Saint Joseph (IN)
Central Penn Coll (PA)
Champlain Coll (VT)
Clayton State U (GA)
Coll of Saint Mary (NE)
Davenport U, Grand Rapids (MI)
Eastern Kentucky U (KY)
Ellis U (IL)
Elms Coll (MA)
Ferris State U (MI)
Florida National U (FL)
Gannon U (PA)
Hickey Coll (MO)
Hilbert Coll (NY)
Hodges U (FL)
Husson U (ME)
Idaho State U (ID)
Indian River State Coll (FL)
International Business Coll, Fort Wayne (IN)
Keiser U, Fort Lauderdale (FL)
Lewis-Clark State Coll (ID)
Lincoln Coll of New England, Southington (CT)
Madonna U (MI)
Maria Coll (NY)
McNeese State U (LA)
Midland Coll (TX)
Missouri Western State U (MO)
Mount Aloysius Coll (PA)
Mount St. Joseph U (OH)
National Paralegal Coll (AZ)
National U (CA)
Newman U (KS)
New York City Coll of Technology of the City U of New York (NY)

Peirce Coll (PA)
Pennsylvania Coll of Technology (PA)
Post U (CT)
Rasmussen Coll Appleton (WI)
Rasmussen Coll Aurora (IL)
Rasmussen Coll Bismarck (ND)
Rasmussen Coll Blaine (MN)
Rasmussen Coll Bloomington (MN)
Rasmussen Coll Brooklyn Park (MN)
Rasmussen Coll Eagan (MN)
Rasmussen Coll Fargo (ND)
Rasmussen Coll Fort Myers (FL)
Rasmussen Coll Green Bay (WI)
Rasmussen Coll Kansas City/ Overland Park (KS)
Rasmussen Coll Lake Elmo/ Woodbury (MN)
Rasmussen Coll Land O' Lakes (FL)
Rasmussen Coll Mankato (MN)
Rasmussen Coll Mokena/Tinley Park (IL)
Rasmussen Coll Moorhead (MN)
Rasmussen Coll New Port Richey (FL)
Rasmussen Coll Ocala (FL)
Rasmussen Coll Rockford (IL)
Rasmussen Coll Romeoville/Joliet (IL)
Rasmussen Coll St. Cloud (MN)
Rasmussen Coll Tampa/Brandon (FL)
Rasmussen Coll Topeka (KS)
Rasmussen Coll Wausau (WI)
Robert Morris U Illinois (IL)
Saint Mary-of-the-Woods Coll (IN)
Santa Fe Coll (FL)
Shawnee State U (OH)
Southern Utah U (UT)
State Coll of Florida Manatee-Sarasota (FL)
Stevens–The Inst of Business & Arts (MO)
Suffolk U (MA)
Sullivan U (KY)
Tulane U (LA)
The U of Akron (OH)
U of Alaska Fairbanks (AK)
U of Arkansas–Fort Smith (AR)
U of Great Falls (MT)
U of Hartford (CT)
U of Louisville (KY)
The U of Montana (MT)
Utah Valley U (UT)
Valencia Coll (FL)
Washburn U (KS)
Western Kentucky U (KY)
Widener U (PA)

LEGAL PROFESSIONS AND STUDIES RELATED
Berkeley Coll, Woodland Park (NJ)
Berkeley Coll–New York City Campus (NY)
U of the District of Columbia (DC)

LEGAL STUDIES
Maria Coll (NY)
St. John's U (NY)
U of Hartford (CT)
The U of Montana (MT)
U of New Haven (CT)

LIBERAL ARTS AND SCIENCES AND HUMANITIES RELATED
Adams State U (CO)
Anderson U (IN)
Ball State U (IN)
Colorado Mesa U (CO)
Ferris State U (MI)
Heritage U (WA)
Kent State U at Geauga (OH)
Kent State U at Stark (OH)
Long Island U–LIU Post (NY)
Marymount California U (CA)
Morrisville State Coll (NY)
Mount Aloysius Coll (PA)
New York U (NY)
Pennsylvania Coll of Technology (PA)
Sacred Heart U (CT)
State U of New York Coll of Technology at Delhi (NY)
Taylor U (IN)
U of Maryland U Coll (MD)
U of Wisconsin–Green Bay (WI)
U of Wisconsin–La Crosse (WI)
Walsh U (OH)
Wayland Baptist U (TX)
William Penn U (IA)
Williamson Christian Coll (TN)

LIBERAL ARTS AND SCIENCES/ LIBERAL STUDIES
Adams State U (CO)
Adelphi U (NY)
Alverno Coll (WI)
American International Coll (MA)
American U (DC)
The American U of Rome (Italy)
Amridge U (AL)
Aquinas Coll (MI)
Arizona Christian U (AZ)
Arkansas State U (AR)
Armstrong State U (GA)
Averett U (VA)
Ball State U (IN)
Bard Coll (NY)
Bard Coll at Simon's Rock (MA)
Bay Path U (MA)
Beacon Coll (FL)
Bemidji State U (MN)
Bethel Coll (IN)
Bethel U (MN)
Brenau U (GA)
Bryan Coll (TN)
California U of Pennsylvania (PA)
Calumet Coll of Saint Joseph (IN)
Cazenovia Coll (NY)
Charter Oak State Coll (CT)
Chestnut Hill Coll (PA)
Christendom Coll (VA)
Clarion U of Pennsylvania (PA)
Clarke U (IA)
Clayton State U (GA)
Colby-Sawyer Coll (NH)
Coll of Coastal Georgia (GA)
Coll of Staten Island of the City U of New York (NY)
Colorado Mesa U (CO)
Columbia Coll (MO)
Columbus State U (GA)
Concordia Coll–New York (NY)
Concordia U (CA)
Concordia U Texas (TX)
Crossroads Coll (MN)
Cumberland U (TN)
Dallas Baptist U (TX)
Dickinson State U (ND)
Dominican Coll (NY)
Eastern New Mexico U (NM)
Eastern U (PA)
Elmira Coll (NY)
Emmanuel Coll (GA)
Endicott Coll (MA)
Excelsior Coll (NY)
Fairleigh Dickinson U, Metropolitan Campus (NJ)
Farmingdale State Coll (NY)
Faulkner U (AL)
Ferris State U (MI)
Fisher Coll (MA)
Five Towns Coll (NY)
Florida A&M U (FL)
Florida Atlantic U (FL)
Florida Coll (FL)
Gannon U (PA)
Georgia Regents U (GA)
Gwynedd Mercy U (PA)
Hilbert Coll (NY)
Hobe Sound Bible Coll (FL)
Holy Cross Coll (IN)
Houghton Coll (NY)
Indiana U of Pennsylvania (PA)
Indian River State Coll (FL)
Johnson State Coll (VT)
Kent State U at Stark (OH)
Kentucky State U (KY)
Keystone Coll (PA)
Kuyper Coll (MI)
Lewis-Clark State Coll (ID)
Limestone Coll (SC)
Long Island U–LIU Brooklyn (NY)
Loras Coll (IA)
Lourdes U (OH)
Mansfield U of Pennsylvania (PA)
Maria Coll (NY)
Marian U (IN)
Marymount California U (CA)
Medaille Coll (NY)
Medgar Evers Coll of the City U of New York (NY)
Mercy Coll (NY)
Mercy Coll of Health Sciences (IA)
MidAmerica Nazarene U (KS)
Midwestern State U (TX)
Minnesota State U Mankato (MN)
Minnesota State U Moorhead (MN)
Mitchell Coll (CT)
Molloy Coll (NY)
Montana State U (MT)
Montana State U Billings (MT)
Montreat Coll, Montreat (NC)

Morrisville State Coll (NY)
Mount Aloysius Coll (PA)
Mount Marty Coll (SD)
Mount Saint Mary's U (CA)
Murray State U (KY)
Neumann U (PA)
New England Coll (NH)
Newman U (KS)
New Saint Andrews Coll (ID)
New York City Coll of Technology of the City U of New York (NY)
New York U (NY)
Niagara U (NY)
Northern Kentucky U (KY)
Northern State U (SD)
Nyack Coll (NY)
Oakland City U (IN)
Ohio Dominican U (OH)
The Ohio State U at Marion (OH)
The Ohio State U–Mansfield Campus (OH)
The Ohio State U–Newark Campus (OH)
Ohio U (OH)
Ohio Valley U (WV)
Palm Beach State Coll (FL)
Penn State Abington (PA)
Penn State Altoona (PA)
Penn State Beaver (PA)
Penn State Berks (PA)
Penn State Brandywine (PA)
Penn State Erie, The Behrend Coll (PA)
Penn State Greater Allegheny (PA)
Penn State Harrisburg (PA)
Penn State Hazleton (PA)
Penn State Lehigh Valley (PA)
Penn State New Kensington (PA)
Penn State Schuylkill (PA)
Penn State U Park (PA)
Penn State Wilkes-Barre (PA)
Penn State Worthington Scranton (PA)
Penn State York (PA)
Pine Manor Coll (MA)
Polk State Coll (FL)
Providence Coll (RI)
Quincy U (IL)
Reinhardt U (GA)
Rivier U (NH)
Rocky Mountain Coll (MT)
Roger Williams U (RI)
St. Catharine Coll (KY)
St. Catherine U (MN)
St. Francis Coll (NY)
St. Gregory's U, Shawnee (OK)
St. John's U (NY)
Saint Joseph's U (PA)
Saint Leo U (FL)
Saint Louis Christian Coll (MO)
St. Thomas Aquinas Coll (NY)
Salve Regina U (RI)
San Diego Christian Coll (CA)
Santa Fe Coll (FL)
Savannah State U (GA)
Shiloh U (IA)
Southeastern Baptist Theological Seminary (NC)
Southern Adventist U (TN)
Southern Vermont Coll (VT)
State Coll of Florida Manatee-Sarasota (FL)
State U of New York Coll of Agriculture and Technology at Cobleskill (NY)
State U of New York Coll of Technology at Delhi (NY)
Stephens Coll (MO)
Suffolk U (MA)
Syracuse U (NY)
Thiel Coll (PA)
Thomas More Coll (KY)
Trine U (IN)
Troy U (AL)
Unity Coll (ME)
The U of Akron (OH)
U of Alaska Fairbanks (AK)
U of Arkansas–Fort Smith (AR)
U of Cincinnati (OH)
U of Delaware (DE)
U of Hartford (CT)
U of Maine at Augusta (ME)
U of Maine at Fort Kent (ME)
U of Maine at Presque Isle (ME)
The U of Montana Western (MT)
U of New Hampshire at Manchester (NH)
U of North Georgia (GA)
U of Northwestern–St. Paul (MN)
U of Pittsburgh at Bradford (PA)

U of Saint Francis (IN)
U of South Carolina Beaufort (SC)
The U of South Dakota (SD)
U of South Florida, St. Petersburg (FL)
U of the District of Columbia (DC)
U of the Fraser Valley (BC, Canada)
U of the Incarnate Word (TX)
U of West Florida (FL)
U of Wisconsin–Eau Claire (WI)
U of Wisconsin–Oshkosh (WI)
U of Wisconsin–Stevens Point (WI)
U of Wisconsin–Superior (WI)
U of Wisconsin–Whitewater (WI)
Upper Iowa U (IA)
Urbana U (OH)
Valdosta State U (GA)
Valencia Coll (FL)
Villa Maria Coll (NY)
Waldorf Coll (IA)
Washburn U (KS)
Western New England U (MA)
Wichita State U (KS)
Williams Baptist Coll (AR)
William Woods U (MO)
Winona State U (MN)
Xavier U (OH)
Youngstown State U (OH)

LIBRARY AND ARCHIVES ASSISTING
U of Maine at Augusta (ME)
U of the Fraser Valley (BC, Canada)

LIBRARY AND INFORMATION SCIENCE
Indian River State Coll (FL)

LICENSED PRACTICAL/VOCATIONAL NURSE TRAINING
Arkansas Tech U (AR)
Campbellsville U (KY)
Dickinson State U (ND)
Indian River State Coll (FL)
Inter American U of Puerto Rico, Aguadilla Campus (PR)
Inter American U of Puerto Rico, Bayamón Campus (PR)
Inter American U of Puerto Rico, Ponce Campus (PR)
Inter American U of Puerto Rico, San Germán Campus (PR)
Lewis-Clark State Coll (ID)
Maria Coll (NY)
Medgar Evers Coll of the City U of New York (NY)
Montana State U Billings (MT)
National U (CA)
Selma U (AL)
The U of Montana (MT)
U of the Fraser Valley (BC, Canada)
Virginia State U (VA)

LOGISTICS, MATERIALS, AND SUPPLY CHAIN MANAGEMENT
Park U (MO)
Polytechnic U of Puerto Rico (PR)
Sullivan U (KY)
U of Alaska Anchorage (AK)

MACHINE SHOP TECHNOLOGY
Missouri Southern State U (MO)

MACHINE TOOL TECHNOLOGY
Colorado Mesa U (CO)
Idaho State U (ID)
Pennsylvania Coll of Technology (PA)

MANAGEMENT INFORMATION SYSTEMS
Arkansas State U (AR)
Columbia Centro Universitario, Yauco (PR)
Inter American U of Puerto Rico, Ponce Campus (PR)
Johnson State Coll (VT)
Lindsey Wilson Coll (KY)
Lock Haven U of Pennsylvania (PA)
Morehead State U (KY)
Shawnee State U (OH)
Thiel Coll (PA)
U of the Virgin Islands (VI)
Weber State U (UT)
Wright State U (OH)

MANAGEMENT INFORMATION SYSTEMS AND SERVICES RELATED
Mount Aloysius Coll (PA)

Purdue U North Central (IN)
Rasmussen Coll Appleton (WI)
Rasmussen Coll Aurora (IL)
Rasmussen Coll Bismarck (ND)
Rasmussen Coll Blaine (MN)
Rasmussen Coll Bloomington (MN)
Rasmussen Coll Brooklyn Park (MN)
Rasmussen Coll Eagan (MN)
Rasmussen Coll Fargo (ND)
Rasmussen Coll Fort Myers (FL)
Rasmussen Coll Green Bay (WI)
Rasmussen Coll Kansas City/Overland Park (KS)
Rasmussen Coll Lake Elmo/Woodbury (MN)
Rasmussen Coll Land O' Lakes (FL)
Rasmussen Coll Mankato (MN)
Rasmussen Coll Mokena/Tinley Park (IL)
Rasmussen Coll Moorhead (MN)
Rasmussen Coll New Port Richey (FL)
Rasmussen Coll Ocala (FL)
Rasmussen Coll Rockford (IL)
Rasmussen Coll Romeoville/Joliet (IL)
Rasmussen Coll St. Cloud (MN)
Rasmussen Coll Tampa/Brandon (FL)
Rasmussen Coll Wausau (WI)
Santa Fe Coll (FL)

MANAGEMENT SCIENCE
Ellis U (IL)
U of Alaska Anchorage (AK)

MANUFACTURING ENGINEERING
Penn State Greater Allegheny (PA)
Penn State Hazleton (PA)
Penn State Wilkes-Barre (PA)
Penn State York (PA)

MANUFACTURING ENGINEERING TECHNOLOGY
Colorado Mesa U (CO)
Edinboro U of Pennsylvania (PA)
Excelsior Coll (NY)
Lawrence Technological U (MI)
Lewis-Clark State Coll (ID)
Missouri Southern State U (MO)
Missouri Western State U (MO)
Morehead State U (KY)
New England Inst of Technology (RI)
Pennsylvania Coll of Technology (PA)
Purdue U (IN)
The U of Akron (OH)
U of Cincinnati (OH)
Weber State U (UT)
Wright State U (OH)

MARINE BIOLOGY AND BIOLOGICAL OCEANOGRAPHY
Savannah State U (GA)

MARINE MAINTENANCE AND SHIP REPAIR TECHNOLOGY
New England Inst of Technology (RI)

MARINE SCIENCE/MERCHANT MARINE OFFICER
Indian River State Coll (FL)

MARKETING/MARKETING MANAGEMENT
Baker Coll (MI)
Berkeley Coll–New York City Campus (NY)
Central Penn Coll (PA)
Chaminade U of Honolulu (HI)
Ellis U (IL)
Ferris State U (MI)
Hawai`i Pacific U (HI)
Idaho State U (ID)
Indian River State Coll (FL)
John Cabot U (Italy)
Madonna U (MI)
Miami U (OH)
New York City Coll of Technology of the City U of New York (NY)
Palm Beach State Coll (FL)
Post U (CT)
Rasmussen Coll Appleton (WI)
Rasmussen Coll Bismarck (ND)
Rasmussen Coll Blaine (MN)
Rasmussen Coll Bloomington (MN)
Rasmussen Coll Brooklyn Park (MN)
Rasmussen Coll Eagan (MN)
Rasmussen Coll Fargo (ND)
Rasmussen Coll Fort Myers (FL)

Rasmussen Coll Green Bay (WI)
Rasmussen Coll Kansas City/Overland Park (KS)
Rasmussen Coll Lake Elmo/Woodbury (MN)
Rasmussen Coll Land O' Lakes (FL)
Rasmussen Coll Mankato (MN)
Rasmussen Coll Moorhead (MN)
Rasmussen Coll New Port Richey (FL)
Rasmussen Coll Ocala (FL)
Rasmussen Coll St. Cloud (MN)
Rasmussen Coll Tampa/Brandon (FL)
Rasmussen Coll Topeka (KS)
Rasmussen Coll Wausau (WI)
Saint Peter's U (NJ)
Southern New Hampshire U (NH)
Southwest Minnesota State U (MN)
Tulane U (LA)
The U of Akron (OH)
Urbana U (OH)
Walsh U (OH)
Webber International U (FL)
Wright State U (OH)
Youngstown State U (OH)

MASONRY
Pennsylvania Coll of Technology (PA)

MASSAGE THERAPY
Columbia Centro Universitario, Caguas (PR)
Idaho State U (ID)
Keiser U, Fort Lauderdale (FL)
Morrisville State Coll (NY)

MASS COMMUNICATION/MEDIA
Adams State U (CO)
Black Hills State U (SD)
Elizabethtown Coll School of Continuing and Professional Studies (PA)
John Cabot U (Italy)
Palm Beach State Coll (FL)
Southern Adventist U (TN)
Southwestern Assemblies of God U (TX)
State Coll of Florida Manatee-Sarasota (FL)
U of Rio Grande (OH)
U of the Incarnate Word (TX)
York Coll of Pennsylvania (PA)

MATERNAL AND CHILD HEALTH
Universidad del Turabo (PR)

MATHEMATICS
Clarke U (IA)
Coll of Coastal Georgia (GA)
Creighton U (NE)
Hawai`i Pacific U (HI)
Idaho State U (ID)
Indian River State Coll (FL)
Oklahoma Wesleyan U (OK)
Palm Beach State Coll (FL)
Shawnee State U (OH)
State U of New York Coll of Agriculture and Technology at Cobleskill (NY)
Thomas More Coll (KY)
Trine U (IN)
U of Great Falls (MT)
U of Rio Grande (OH)
The U of Tampa (FL)
Utah Valley U (UT)

MATHEMATICS AND COMPUTER SCIENCE
Immaculata U (PA)

MATHEMATICS TEACHER EDUCATION
State Coll of Florida Manatee-Sarasota (FL)

MECHANICAL DRAFTING AND CAD/CADD
Baker Coll (MI)
Midland Coll (TX)
New York City Coll of Technology of the City U of New York (NY)

MECHANICAL ENGINEERING
New England Inst of Technology (RI)

MECHANICAL ENGINEERING/MECHANICAL TECHNOLOGY
Baker Coll (MI)
Bluefield State Coll (WV)
Fairmont State U (WV)
Farmingdale State Coll (NY)
Ferris State U (MI)
Idaho State U (ID)
Indiana U–Purdue U Fort Wayne (IN)
Lawrence Technological U (MI)
Miami U (OH)
Morrisville State Coll (NY)
New York City Coll of Technology of the City U of New York (NY)
Penn State Altoona (PA)
Penn State Berks (PA)
Penn State Erie, The Behrend Coll (PA)
Penn State Hazleton (PA)
Penn State New Kensington (PA)
Penn State York (PA)
Purdue U (IN)
State U of New York Coll of Agriculture and Technology at Cobleskill (NY)
State U of New York Coll of Technology at Canton (NY)
Universidad del Turabo (PR)
The U of Akron (OH)
U of Arkansas at Little Rock (AR)
U of Rio Grande (OH)
Vermont Tech Coll (VT)
Weber State U (UT)
Youngstown State U (OH)

MECHANICAL ENGINEERING TECHNOLOGIES RELATED
Polytechnic U of Puerto Rico (PR)
Purdue U North Central (IN)
U of Massachusetts Lowell (MA)

MECHANIC AND REPAIR TECHNOLOGIES RELATED
Inter American U of Puerto Rico, Guayama Campus (PR)
Pennsylvania Coll of Technology (PA)
Washburn U (KS)

MECHANICS AND REPAIR
Idaho State U (ID)
Lewis-Clark State Coll (ID)
Utah Valley U (UT)

MECHATRONICS, ROBOTICS, AND AUTOMATION ENGINEERING
Johnson & Wales U (RI)
U of the Fraser Valley (BC, Canada)
Utah Valley U (UT)

MEDICAL ADMINISTRATIVE ASSISTANT AND MEDICAL SECRETARY
Arkansas Tech U (AR)
Baker Coll (MI)
Dickinson State U (ND)
Florida National U (FL)
Hallmark U (TX)
Indian River State Coll (FL)
Lincoln Coll of New England, Southington (CT)
Montana State U Billings (MT)
Morrisville State Coll (NY)
National U Coll, Bayam&,on (PR)
Rasmussen Coll Appleton (WI)
Rasmussen Coll Aurora (IL)
Rasmussen Coll Bismarck (ND)
Rasmussen Coll Blaine (MN)
Rasmussen Coll Bloomington (MN)
Rasmussen Coll Brooklyn Park (MN)
Rasmussen Coll Eagan (MN)
Rasmussen Coll Fargo (ND)
Rasmussen Coll Fort Myers (FL)
Rasmussen Coll Green Bay (WI)
Rasmussen Coll Kansas City/Overland Park (KS)
Rasmussen Coll Lake Elmo/Woodbury (MN)
Rasmussen Coll Land O' Lakes (FL)
Rasmussen Coll Mankato (MN)
Rasmussen Coll Mokena/Tinley Park (IL)
Rasmussen Coll Moorhead (MN)
Rasmussen Coll New Port Richey (FL)
Rasmussen Coll Ocala (FL)
Rasmussen Coll Rockford (IL)
Rasmussen Coll Romeoville/Joliet (IL)

Rasmussen Coll St. Cloud (MN)
Rasmussen Coll Tampa/Brandon (FL)
Rasmussen Coll Wausau (WI)
U of Cincinnati (OH)
The U of Montana (MT)
U of Rio Grande (OH)

MEDICAL/CLINICAL ASSISTANT
Arkansas Tech U (AR)
Baker Coll (MI)
Berkeley Coll, Woodland Park (NJ)
Cabarrus Coll of Health Sciences (NC)
Central Penn Coll (PA)
Colorado Mesa U (CO)
Davenport U, Grand Rapids (MI)
Florida National U (FL)
Hallmark U (TX)
Hodges U (FL)
Idaho State U (ID)
International Business Coll, Fort Wayne (IN)
Keiser U, Fort Lauderdale (FL)
Lincoln Coll of New England, Southington (CT)
Mercy Coll of Health Sciences (IA)
Montana State U Billings (MT)
Montana Tech of The U of Montana (MT)
Mount Aloysius Coll (PA)
New England Inst of Technology (RI)
Rasmussen Coll Appleton (WI)
Rasmussen Coll Aurora (IL)
Rasmussen Coll Bismarck (ND)
Rasmussen Coll Blaine (MN)
Rasmussen Coll Bloomington (MN)
Rasmussen Coll Brooklyn Park (MN)
Rasmussen Coll Eagan (MN)
Rasmussen Coll Fort Myers (FL)
Rasmussen Coll Green Bay (WI)
Rasmussen Coll Kansas City/Overland Park (KS)
Rasmussen Coll Lake Elmo/Woodbury (MN)
Rasmussen Coll Land O' Lakes (FL)
Rasmussen Coll Mankato (MN)
Rasmussen Coll Mokena/Tinley Park (IL)
Rasmussen Coll Moorhead (MN)
Rasmussen Coll New Port Richey (FL)
Rasmussen Coll Ocala (FL)
Rasmussen Coll Rockford (IL)
Rasmussen Coll Romeoville/Joliet (IL)
Rasmussen Coll St. Cloud (MN)
Rasmussen Coll Tampa/Brandon (FL)
Rasmussen Coll Topeka (KS)
Rasmussen Coll Wausau (WI)
Robert Morris U Illinois (IL)
Southern Tech Coll, Fort Myers (FL)
Stratford U, Glen Allen (VA)
Stratford U, Newport News (VA)
Sullivan U (KY)
The U of Akron (OH)
U of Alaska Anchorage (AK)
U of Alaska Fairbanks (AK)
U of Cincinnati (OH)
Youngstown State U (OH)

MEDICAL/HEALTH MANAGEMENT AND CLINICAL ASSISTANT
Florida National U (FL)
Lewis-Clark State Coll (ID)
Stratford U, Woodbridge (VA)

MEDICAL INFORMATICS
Champlain Coll (VT)
Montana Tech of The U of Montana (MT)
National U (CA)
Southern New Hampshire U (NH)

MEDICAL INSURANCE CODING
Columbia Southern U (AL)
National U (CA)
Stratford U, Woodbridge (VA)

MEDICAL INSURANCE/MEDICAL BILLING
Stratford U, Glen Allen (VA)
Stratford U, Newport News (VA)

MEDICAL MICROBIOLOGY AND BACTERIOLOGY
Florida National U (FL)

MEDICAL OFFICE ASSISTANT
Hickey Coll (MO)

Lewis-Clark State Coll (ID)
Sullivan U (KY)

MEDICAL OFFICE MANAGEMENT
Ohio Dominican U (OH)
The U of Akron (OH)

MEDICAL RADIOLOGIC TECHNOLOGY
Arkansas State U (AR)
Ball State U (IN)
Bluefield State Coll (WV)
Coll of Coastal Georgia (GA)
Drexel U (PA)
Ferris State U (MI)
Idaho State U (ID)
Indiana U–Purdue U Fort Wayne (IN)
Inter American U of Puerto Rico, Aguadilla Campus (PR)
Inter American U of Puerto Rico, Ponce Campus (PR)
Inter American U of Puerto Rico, San Germán Campus (PR)
Keiser U, Fort Lauderdale (FL)
Keystone Coll (PA)
La Roche Coll (PA)
Missouri Southern State U (MO)
Morehead State U (KY)
Mount Aloysius Coll (PA)
Newman U (KS)
New York City Coll of Technology of the City U of New York (NY)
Northern Kentucky U (KY)
Penn State New Kensington (PA)
Penn State Schuylkill (PA)
Pennsylvania Coll of Health Sciences (PA)
Pennsylvania Coll of Technology (PA)
Polk State Coll (FL)
St. Catherine U (MN)
Santa Fe Coll (FL)
Shawnee State U (OH)
State Coll of Florida Manatee-Sarasota (FL)
The U of Akron (OH)
U of Charleston (WV)
U of Cincinnati (OH)
U of New Mexico (NM)
U of Saint Francis (IN)
Valencia Coll (FL)
Weber State U (UT)

MEDICAL STAFF SERVICES TECHNOLOGY
Southern Tech Coll, Fort Myers (FL)

MEETING AND EVENT PLANNING
Sullivan U (KY)

MENTAL AND SOCIAL HEALTH SERVICES AND ALLIED PROFESSIONS RELATED
Clarion U of Pennsylvania (PA)
U of Alaska Fairbanks (AK)
U of Maine at Augusta (ME)
Washburn U (KS)

MERCHANDISING
The U of Akron (OH)

MERCHANDISING, SALES, AND MARKETING OPERATIONS RELATED (GENERAL)
Inter American U of Puerto Rico, Aguadilla Campus (PR)
Inter American U of Puerto Rico, Ponce Campus (PR)
Post U (CT)
State U of New York Coll of Technology at Delhi (NY)

METAL AND JEWELRY ARTS
Academy of Art U (CA)
Fashion Inst of Technology (NY)

METALLURGICAL TECHNOLOGY
Penn State Altoona (PA)
Penn State Berks (PA)
Penn State Erie, The Behrend Coll (PA)
Penn State Hazleton (PA)
Penn State New Kensington (PA)
Penn State Schuylkill (PA)
Penn State Wilkes-Barre (PA)
Penn State York (PA)

MIDDLE SCHOOL EDUCATION
U of Cincinnati (OH)
Wright State U (OH)

MILITARY HISTORY
American Public U System (WV)

MILITARY STUDIES
Hawai`i Pacific U (HI)

MINING AND PETROLEUM TECHNOLOGIES RELATED
U of the Virgin Islands (VI)

MISSIONARY STUDIES AND MISSIOLOGY
Faith Baptist Bible Coll and Theological Seminary (IA)
Hillsdale Free Will Baptist Coll (OK)
Hobe Sound Bible Coll (FL)
Manhattan Christian Coll (KS)
U of the Cumberlands (KY)

MORTUARY SCIENCE AND EMBALMING
U of the District of Columbia (DC)

MULTI/INTERDISCIPLINARY STUDIES RELATED
Arkansas Tech U (AR)
Heritage U (WA)
Liberty U (VA)
Miami U (OH)
Montana Tech of The U of Montana (MT)
Northwest Missouri State U (MO)
Pennsylvania Coll of Technology (PA)
State U of New York Empire State Coll (NY)
The U of Akron (OH)
U of Alaska Fairbanks (AK)
U of Arkansas–Fort Smith (AR)
U of Cincinnati (OH)
The U of Montana Western (MT)
Utah Valley U (UT)
Washburn U (KS)

MUSEUM STUDIES
Inst of American Indian Arts (NM)

MUSIC
Clayton State U (GA)
Five Towns Coll (NY)
Hannibal-LaGrange U (MO)
Hillsdale Free Will Baptist Coll (OK)
Indian River State Coll (FL)
Marian U (IN)
Mount Vernon Nazarene U (OH)
Nyack Coll (NY)
Palm Beach State Coll (FL)
Southwestern Assemblies of God U (TX)
State Coll of Florida Manatee-Sarasota (FL)
Thomas More Coll (KY)
U of Maine at Augusta (ME)
U of Rio Grande (OH)
U of the District of Columbia (DC)
Utah Valley U (UT)
Villa Maria Coll (NY)
Williams Baptist Coll (AR)
York Coll of Pennsylvania (PA)

MUSICAL INSTRUMENT FABRICATION AND REPAIR
Indiana U Bloomington (IN)

MUSIC MANAGEMENT
Five Towns Coll (NY)
U of Central Oklahoma (OK)
Villa Maria Coll (NY)

MUSIC PERFORMANCE
Five Towns Coll (NY)
State Coll of Florida Manatee-Sarasota (FL)
Villa Maria Coll (NY)

MUSIC RELATED
Academy of Art U (CA)
Alverno Coll (WI)
Five Towns Coll (NY)
Hobe Sound Bible Coll (FL)
Mercy Coll (NY)
Valencia Coll (FL)

MUSIC TEACHER EDUCATION
State Coll of Florida Manatee-Sarasota (FL)
Wright State U (OH)

MUSIC TECHNOLOGY
Mercy Coll (NY)
U of Saint Francis (IN)

MUSIC THEORY AND COMPOSITION
State Coll of Florida Manatee-Sarasota (FL)

NATURAL RESOURCES/CONSERVATION
Heritage U (WA)
Morrisville State Coll (NY)
State U of New York Coll of Environmental Science and Forestry (NY)

NATURAL RESOURCES MANAGEMENT AND POLICY
Morrisville State Coll (NY)
U of Alaska Fairbanks (AK)

NATURAL RESOURCES MANAGEMENT AND POLICY RELATED
State U of New York Coll of Technology at Delhi (NY)
U of Guelph (ON, Canada)

NATURAL SCIENCES
Lourdes U (OH)
Madonna U (MI)
Roberts Wesleyan Coll (NY)
Universidad Metropolitana (PR)
U of Alaska Fairbanks (AK)
Washburn U (KS)

NETWORK AND SYSTEM ADMINISTRATION
Florida National U (FL)
Palm Beach State Coll (FL)
Polk State Coll (FL)

NUCLEAR ENGINEERING TECHNOLOGY
Arkansas Tech U (AR)
Idaho State U (ID)

NUCLEAR MEDICAL TECHNOLOGY
Ball State U (IN)
The George Washington U (DC)
Keiser U, Fort Lauderdale (FL)
Molloy Coll (NY)
Pennsylvania Coll of Health Sciences (PA)
Santa Fe Coll (FL)
U of Cincinnati (OH)

NUCLEAR/NUCLEAR POWER TECHNOLOGY
Excelsior Coll (NY)

NURSING ASSISTANT/AIDE AND PATIENT CARE ASSISTANT/AIDE
Cabarrus Coll of Health Sciences (NC)

NURSING EDUCATION
U of the District of Columbia (DC)

NURSING SCIENCE
Dixie State U (UT)
EDP U of Puerto Rico (PR)
EDP U of Puerto Rico–San Sebastian (PR)
U of Alaska Anchorage (AK)

OCCUPATIONAL SAFETY AND HEALTH TECHNOLOGY
Columbia Southern U (AL)
Fairmont State U (WV)
U of Alaska Anchorage (AK)

OCCUPATIONAL THERAPIST ASSISTANT
Adventist U of Health Sciences (FL)
Arkansas State U (AR)
Arkansas Tech U (AR)
Baker Coll (MI)
Cabarrus Coll of Health Sciences (NC)
California U of Pennsylvania (PA)
Central Penn Coll (PA)
Inter American U of Puerto Rico, Ponce Campus (PR)
Jefferson Coll of Health Sciences (VA)
Keiser U, Fort Lauderdale (FL)
Lincoln Coll of New England, Southington (CT)
Maria Coll (NY)
Mercy Coll (NY)
New England Inst of Technology (RI)
Newman U (KS)
Penn State Berks (PA)

MUSIC THEORY AND COMPOSITION
Pennsylvania Coll of Technology (PA)
Polk State Coll (FL)
Rutgers, The State U of New Jersey, New Brunswick (NJ)
St. Catherine U (MN)
State Coll of Florida Manatee-Sarasota (FL)
U of Charleston (WV)
U of Southern Indiana (IN)
Washburn U (KS)

OCCUPATIONAL THERAPY
Coll of Coastal Georgia (GA)
Keystone Coll (PA)
Palm Beach State Coll (FL)
Shawnee State U (OH)
Southern Adventist U (TN)
State Coll of Florida Manatee-Sarasota (FL)

OFFICE MANAGEMENT
Emmanuel Coll (GA)
Inter American U of Puerto Rico, Aguadilla Campus (PR)
Inter American U of Puerto Rico, Bayamón Campus (PR)
Inter American U of Puerto Rico, Fajardo Campus (PR)
Inter American U of Puerto Rico, Guayama Campus (PR)
Inter American U of Puerto Rico, Ponce Campus (PR)
Inter American U of Puerto Rico, San Germán Campus (PR)
Maranatha Baptist U (WI)
Miami U (OH)
Morrisville State Coll (NY)
Shawnee State U (OH)
Universidad del Turabo (PR)
Universidad Metropolitana (PR)
The U of Akron (OH)
Washburn U (KS)

OFFICE OCCUPATIONS AND CLERICAL SERVICES
Bob Jones U (SC)
Midland Coll (TX)
Morrisville State Coll (NY)

OPERATIONS MANAGEMENT
Indiana U–Purdue U Fort Wayne (IN)
Northern Kentucky U (KY)
Polk State Coll (FL)

OPTICAL SCIENCES
Indiana U of Pennsylvania (PA)

OPTICIANRY
New York City Coll of Technology of the City U of New York (NY)

OPTOMETRIC TECHNICIAN
Indiana U Bloomington (IN)
Inter American U of Puerto Rico, Ponce Campus (PR)

ORGANIZATIONAL BEHAVIOR
Hawai`i Pacific U (HI)
U of Cincinnati (OH)

ORGANIZATIONAL COMMUNICATION
Creighton U (NE)
Franklin U (OH)

ORGANIZATIONAL LEADERSHIP
Beulah Heights U (GA)
Grace Coll (IN)
Point U (GA)
Purdue U (IN)

ORNAMENTAL HORTICULTURE
Farmingdale State Coll (NY)
State U of New York Coll of Agriculture and Technology at Cobleskill (NY)
U of the Fraser Valley (BC, Canada)
Vermont Tech Coll (VT)

ORTHOTICS/PROSTHETICS
Baker Coll (MI)

PAINTING
Pratt Inst (NY)

PALLIATIVE CARE NURSING
Madonna U (MI)

PARKS, RECREATION AND LEISURE
Eastern New Mexico U (NM)

PARKS, RECREATION AND LEISURE FACILITIES MANAGEMENT
Coll of Coastal Georgia (GA)
Webber International U (FL)

PASTORAL STUDIES/ COUNSELING
Marian U (IN)
Nebraska Christian Coll (NE)
William Jessup U (CA)

PERSONAL AND CULINARY SERVICES RELATED
U of Cincinnati (OH)

PETROLEUM TECHNOLOGY
Mansfield U of Pennsylvania (PA)
Montana State U Billings (MT)
Nicholls State U (LA)
U of Alaska Anchorage (AK)
U of Pittsburgh at Bradford (PA)

PHARMACEUTICAL SCIENCES
Universidad del Turabo (PR)

PHARMACOLOGY
Universidad del Turabo (PR)

PHARMACY
Indian River State Coll (FL)

PHARMACY, PHARMACEUTICAL SCIENCES, AND ADMINISTRATION RELATED
EDP U of Puerto Rico–San Sebastian (PR)
Universidad del Turabo (PR)

PHARMACY TECHNICIAN
Baker Coll (MI)
Cabarrus Coll of Health Sciences (NC)
Inter American U of Puerto Rico, Aguadilla Campus (PR)
National U Coll, Bayam&on (PR)
Rasmussen Coll Appleton (WI)
Rasmussen Coll Aurora (IL)
Rasmussen Coll Blaine (MN)
Rasmussen Coll Bloomington (MN)
Rasmussen Coll Brooklyn Park (MN)
Rasmussen Coll Eagan (MN)
Rasmussen Coll Fort Myers (FL)
Rasmussen Coll Green Bay (WI)
Rasmussen Coll Kansas City/ Overland Park (KS)
Rasmussen Coll Lake Elmo/ Woodbury (MN)
Rasmussen Coll Land O' Lakes (FL)
Rasmussen Coll Mankato (MN)
Rasmussen Coll Mokena/Tinley Park (IL)
Rasmussen Coll Moorhead (MN)
Rasmussen Coll New Port Richey (FL)
Rasmussen Coll Ocala (FL)
Rasmussen Coll Rockford (IL)
Rasmussen Coll Romeoville/Joliet (IL)
Rasmussen Coll St. Cloud (MN)
Rasmussen Coll Tampa/Brandon (FL)
Rasmussen Coll Topeka (KS)
Rasmussen Coll Wausau (WI)
Robert Morris U Illinois (IL)
Stratford U, Glen Allen (VA)
Stratford U, Newport News (VA)
Stratford U, Woodbridge (VA)
Sullivan U (KY)

PHILOSOPHY
Carroll Coll (MT)
Coll of Coastal Georgia (GA)
Indian River State Coll (FL)
Palm Beach State Coll (FL)
State Coll of Florida Manatee-Sarasota (FL)
Thomas More Coll (KY)
The U of Tampa (FL)
Utah Valley U (UT)

PHLEBOTOMY TECHNOLOGY
Stratford U, Glen Allen (VA)
Stratford U, Newport News (VA)
Stratford U, Woodbridge (VA)

PHOTOGRAPHIC AND FILM/ VIDEO TECHNOLOGY
St. John's U (NY)
U of Cincinnati (OH)

Villa Maria Coll (NY)

PHOTOGRAPHY
Paier Coll of Art, Inc. (CT)
Palm Beach State Coll (FL)
Villa Maria Coll (NY)

PHYSICAL EDUCATION TEACHING AND COACHING
Hillsdale Free Will Baptist Coll (OK)
Indian River State Coll (FL)
Palm Beach State Coll (FL)
State Coll of Florida Manatee-Sarasota (FL)
U of Rio Grande (OH)

PHYSICAL SCIENCES
Hillsdale Free Will Baptist Coll (OK)
New York City Coll of Technology of the City U of New York (NY)
Oklahoma Wesleyan U (OK)
Palm Beach State Coll (FL)
Roberts Wesleyan Coll (NY)
U of the Fraser Valley (BC, Canada)
Utah Valley U (UT)

PHYSICAL SCIENCES RELATED
State U of New York Empire State Coll (NY)

PHYSICAL THERAPY
Coll of Coastal Georgia (GA)
EDP U of Puerto Rico–San Sebastian (PR)
Indian River State Coll (FL)
Palm Beach State Coll (FL)
Southern Adventist U (TN)
State Coll of Florida Manatee-Sarasota (FL)

PHYSICAL THERAPY TECHNOLOGY
Arkansas State U (AR)
Arkansas Tech U (AR)
Baker Coll (MI)
California U of Pennsylvania (PA)
Central Penn Coll (PA)
Dixie State U (UT)
EDP U of Puerto Rico (PR)
EDP U of Puerto Rico–San Sebastian (PR)
Idaho State U (ID)
Indian River State Coll (FL)
Inter American U of Puerto Rico, Ponce Campus (PR)
Jefferson Coll of Health Sciences (VA)
Keiser U, Fort Lauderdale (FL)
Louisiana Coll (LA)
Mercy Coll of Health Sciences (IA)
Missouri Western State U (MO)
Mount Aloysius Coll (PA)
Nebraska Methodist Coll (NE)
New England Inst of Technology (RI)
Penn State Hazleton (PA)
Polk State Coll (FL)
St. Catherine U (MN)
Shawnee State U (OH)
Southern Illinois U Carbondale (IL)
State Coll of Florida Manatee-Sarasota (FL)
State U of New York Coll of Technology at Canton (NY)
U of Cincinnati (OH)
U of Evansville (IN)
U of Indianapolis (IN)
U of Maine at Presque Isle (ME)
U of Puerto Rico in Ponce (PR)
U of Saint Francis (IN)
Villa Maria Coll (NY)
Washburn U (KS)

PHYSICIAN ASSISTANT
Coll of Coastal Georgia (GA)
Ohio Dominican U (OH)
State Coll of Florida Manatee-Sarasota (FL)

PHYSICS
Coll of Coastal Georgia (GA)
Idaho State U (ID)
Indian River State Coll (FL)
State Coll of Florida Manatee-Sarasota (FL)
Thomas More Coll (KY)
U of the Virgin Islands (VI)
Utah Valley U (UT)
York Coll of Pennsylvania (PA)

PHYSICS TEACHER EDUCATION
State Coll of Florida Manatee-Sarasota (FL)

PIPEFITTING AND SPRINKLER FITTING
New England Inst of Technology (RI)
State U of New York Coll of Technology at Delhi (NY)

PLANT NURSERY MANAGEMENT
Dalhousie U (NS, Canada)

PLANT PROTECTION AND INTEGRATED PEST MANAGEMENT
Dalhousie U (NS, Canada)
North Carolina State U (NC)

PLANT SCIENCES
Michigan State U (MI)
State U of New York Coll of Agriculture and Technology at Cobleskill (NY)

PLASTICS AND POLYMER ENGINEERING TECHNOLOGY
Ferris State U (MI)
Penn State Erie, The Behrend Coll (PA)
Pennsylvania Coll of Technology (PA)
Shawnee State U (OH)

POLITICAL SCIENCE AND GOVERNMENT
Adams State U (CO)
Coll of Coastal Georgia (GA)
Holy Cross Coll (IN)
Immaculata U (PA)
Indian River State Coll (FL)
John Cabot U (Italy)
Liberty U (VA)
Palm Beach State Coll (FL)
Thomas More Coll (KY)
The U of Tampa (FL)
Xavier U (OH)

POLITICAL SCIENCE AND GOVERNMENT RELATED
Inter American U of Puerto Rico, Fajardo Campus (PR)

POULTRY SCIENCE
State U of New York Coll of Agriculture and Technology at Cobleskill (NY)

PRACTICAL NURSING, VOCATIONAL NURSING AND NURSING ASSISTANTS RELATED
Caribbean U (PR)
Rasmussen Coll Ocala School of Nursing (FL)

PRECISION METAL WORKING RELATED
Montana Tech of The U of Montana (MT)

PRE-DENTISTRY STUDIES
Coll of Coastal Georgia (GA)
Concordia U Wisconsin (WI)
U of Cincinnati (OH)

PRE-ENGINEERING
Coll of Coastal Georgia (GA)
Columbia Coll (MO)
Dixie State U (UT)
Fort Valley State U (GA)
Indian River State Coll (FL)
Newman U (KS)
Northern State U (SD)
Palm Beach State Coll (FL)
Siena Heights U (MI)
Southern Utah U (UT)
Utah Valley U (UT)
Weber State U (UT)

PRE-LAW STUDIES
Calumet Coll of Saint Joseph (IN)
Ferris State U (MI)
Florida National U (FL)
Immaculata U (PA)
Thomas More Coll (KY)
U of Cincinnati (OH)
Wayland Baptist U (TX)

PREMEDICAL STUDIES
Coll of Coastal Georgia (GA)
Concordia U Wisconsin (WI)
U of Cincinnati (OH)

PRENURSING STUDIES
Concordia U Wisconsin (WI)
Eastern New Mexico U (NM)
Keystone Coll (PA)
Lincoln Christian U (IL)
National U (CA)
Reinhardt U (GA)

PRE-PHARMACY STUDIES
Coll of Coastal Georgia (GA)
Edinboro U of Pennsylvania (PA)
Ferris State U (MI)
Keystone Coll (PA)
Madonna U (MI)
State Coll of Florida Manatee-Sarasota (FL)
U of Cincinnati (OH)

PRE-PHYSICAL THERAPY
Keystone Coll (PA)

PRE-THEOLOGY/PRE-MINISTERIAL STUDIES
Nazarene Bible Coll (CO)

PRE-VETERINARY STUDIES
Coll of Coastal Georgia (GA)
U of Cincinnati (OH)

PROFESSIONAL, TECHNICAL, BUSINESS, AND SCIENTIFIC WRITING
Ferris State U (MI)
Florida National U (FL)

PSYCHIATRIC/MENTAL HEALTH SERVICES TECHNOLOGY
Pennsylvania Coll of Technology (PA)
U of Alaska Anchorage (AK)

PSYCHOLOGY
Beacon Coll (FL)
Calumet Coll of Saint Joseph (IN)
Central Methodist U (MO)
Cincinnati Christian U (OH)
Coll of Coastal Georgia (GA)
Eastern New Mexico U (NM)
Ferris State U (MI)
Fisher Coll (MA)
Hillsdale Free Will Baptist Coll (OK)
Indian River State Coll (FL)
Liberty U (VA)
Life U (GA)
Montana State U Billings (MT)
Muhlenberg Coll (PA)
New England Coll (NH)
Palm Beach State Coll (FL)
Regent U (VA)
Siena Heights U (MI)
Southwestern Assemblies of God U (TX)
State Coll of Florida Manatee-Sarasota (FL)
State U of New York Empire State Coll (NY)
Thomas More Coll (KY)
U of Cincinnati (OH)
U of Rio Grande (OH)
The U of Tampa (FL)
U of the Cumberlands (KY)
U of Valley Forge (PA)
Utah Valley U (UT)
Wright State U (OH)
Xavier U (OH)

PSYCHOLOGY RELATED
Morrisville State Coll (NY)

PUBLIC ADMINISTRATION
Central Methodist U (MO)
Ferris State U (MI)
Florida National U (FL)
Hawai'i Pacific U (HI)
Indiana U Bloomington (IN)
Indiana U Northwest (IN)
State Coll of Florida Manatee-Sarasota (FL)
Universidad del Turabo (PR)
U of Maine at Augusta (ME)

PUBLIC ADMINISTRATION AND SOCIAL SERVICE PROFESSIONS RELATED
The U of Akron (OH)

PUBLIC HEALTH
American Public U System (WV)
U of Alaska Fairbanks (AK)

PUBLIC HEALTH EDUCATION AND PROMOTION
U of Cincinnati (OH)

PUBLIC POLICY ANALYSIS
Saint Peter's U (NJ)

PUBLIC RELATIONS, ADVERTISING, AND APPLIED COMMUNICATION RELATED
John Brown U (AR)
U of Maine at Presque Isle (ME)

PUBLIC RELATIONS/IMAGE MANAGEMENT
Franklin U (OH)
John Brown U (AR)
Xavier U (OH)

QUALITY CONTROL AND SAFETY TECHNOLOGIES RELATED
Madonna U (MI)

QUALITY CONTROL TECHNOLOGY
Universidad del Turabo (PR)
Weber State U (UT)

RADIATION PROTECTION/ HEALTH PHYSICS TECHNOLOGY
Keiser U, Fort Lauderdale (FL)

RADIO AND TELEVISION
Lawrence Technological U (MI)
State Coll of Florida Manatee-Sarasota (FL)
U of Northwestern–St. Paul (MN)
Xavier U (OH)

RADIO AND TELEVISION BROADCASTING TECHNOLOGY
Lincoln Coll of New England, Southington (CT)
New England Inst of Technology (RI)
State Coll of Florida Manatee-Sarasota (FL)

RADIOLOGIC TECHNOLOGY/ SCIENCE
Adventist U of Health Sciences (FL)
Allen Coll (IA)
Alvernia U (PA)
Baker Coll (MI)
Champlain Coll (VT)
Colorado Mesa U (CO)
Dixie State U (UT)
Fairleigh Dickinson U, Metropolitan Campus (NJ)
Florida National U (FL)
Fort Hays State U (KS)
Gannon U (PA)
Holy Family U (PA)
Indiana U Kokomo (IN)
Indiana U Northwest (IN)
Indiana U–Purdue U Indianapolis (IN)
Indiana U South Bend (IN)
Keystone Coll (PA)
Lewis-Clark State Coll (ID)
Mansfield U of Pennsylvania (PA)
Mercy Coll of Health Sciences (IA)
Montana Tech of The U of Montana (MT)
Nebraska Methodist Coll (NE)
Newman U (KS)
Northern Michigan U (MI)
Pennsylvania Coll of Health Sciences (PA)
Regis Coll (MA)
St. Catharine Coll (KY)
State Coll of Florida Manatee-Sarasota (FL)
U of Alaska Anchorage (AK)
U of Arkansas–Fort Smith (AR)
The U of Montana (MT)
U of Rio Grande (OH)
U of Saint Francis (IN)
Washburn U (KS)
Widener U (PA)
Xavier U (OH)

RADIO, TELEVISION, AND DIGITAL COMMUNICATION RELATED
Keystone Coll (PA)
Lawrence Technological U (MI)
Madonna U (MI)

REAL ESTATE
American Public U System (WV)
National U (CA)
Northern Kentucky U (KY)
Saint Francis U (PA)

RECEPTIONIST
The U of Montana (MT)

RECORDING ARTS TECHNOLOGY
Columbia Centro Universitario, Caguas (PR)
Indiana U Bloomington (IN)
Los Angeles Film School (CA)

REGIONAL STUDIES
Arkansas Tech U (AR)

REGISTERED NURSING, NURSING ADMINISTRATION, NURSING RESEARCH AND CLINICAL NURSING RELATED
Rasmussen Coll Ocala School of Nursing (FL)

REGISTERED NURSING/ REGISTERED NURSE
Alcorn State U (MS)
Aquinas Coll (TN)
Arkansas State U (AR)
Arkansas Tech U (AR)
Becker Coll (MA)
Bethel Coll (IN)
Bluefield State Coll (WV)
Cabarrus Coll of Health Sciences (NC)
California U of Pennsylvania (PA)
Campbellsville U (KY)
Cardinal Stritch U (WI)
Castleton State Coll (VT)
Chamberlain Coll of Nursing, Columbus (OH)
Clarion U of Pennsylvania (PA)
Coll of Coastal Georgia (GA)
Coll of Saint Mary (NE)
Coll of Staten Island of the City U of New York (NY)
Colorado Mesa U (CO)
Columbia Centro Universitario, Caguas (PR)
Columbia Centro Universitario, Yauco (PR)
Columbia Coll (MO)
Dixie State U (UT)
Eastern Kentucky U (KY)
Excelsior Coll (NY)
Fairmont State U (WV)
Florida National U (FL)
Gwynedd Mercy U (PA)
Hallmark U (TX)
Hannibal-LaGrange U (MO)
Heritage U (WA)
Idaho State U (ID)
Indian River State Coll (FL)
Inter American U of Puerto Rico, Guayama Campus (PR)
Judson Coll (AL)
Keiser U, Fort Lauderdale (FL)
Kent State U (OH)
Kent State U at Geauga (OH)
Kentucky State U (KY)
Lamar U (TX)
La Roche Coll (PA)
Lincoln Memorial U (TN)
Lincoln U (MO)
Lock Haven U of Pennsylvania (PA)
Louisiana Tech U (LA)
Maria Coll (NY)
Marshall U (WV)
Mercy Coll of Health Sciences (IA)
Miami U (OH)
Midland Coll (TX)
Mississippi U for Women (MS)
Montana State U Billings (MT)
Montana Tech of The U of Montana (MT)
Morehead State U (KY)
Morrisville State Coll (NY)
Mount Aloysius Coll (PA)
Mount Saint Mary's U (CA)
National U (CA)
National U Coll, Bayam&,on (PR)
New England Inst of Technology (RI)

New York City Coll of Technology of the City U of New York (NY)
Norfolk State U (VA)
Palm Beach State Coll (FL)
Park U (MO)
Penn State Altoona (PA)
Penn State Berks (PA)
Penn State Erie, The Behrend Coll (PA)
Penn State U Park (PA)
Penn State Worthington Scranton (PA)
Pennsylvania Coll of Health Sciences (PA)
Pennsylvania Coll of Technology (PA)
Polk State Coll (FL)
Regis Coll (MA)
Reinhardt U (GA)
Rivier U (NH)
Robert Morris U Illinois (IL)
St. Catharine Coll (KY)
Shawnee State U (OH)
Southern Adventist U (TN)
Southern Arkansas U–Magnolia (AR)
Southern Tech Coll, Fort Myers (FL)
Southwest Baptist U (MO)
State Coll of Florida Manatee-Sarasota (FL)
State U of New York Coll of Technology at Canton (NY)
State U of New York Coll of Technology at Delhi (NY)
Sul Ross State U (TX)
Tennessee State U (TN)
Troy U (AL)
Universidad Metropolitana (PR)
U of Alaska Anchorage (AK)
U of Arkansas at Little Rock (AR)
U of Charleston (WV)
U of Cincinnati (OH)
U of Guam (GU)
U of Maine at Augusta (ME)
U of North Georgia (GA)
U of Pikeville (KY)
U of Pittsburgh at Bradford (PA)
U of Rio Grande (OH)
U of Saint Francis (IN)
U of the Virgin Islands (VI)
The U of South Dakota (SD)
The U of West Alabama (AL)
Utah Valley U (UT)
Valencia Coll (FL)
Vermont Tech Coll (VT)
Weber State U (UT)
Western Kentucky U (KY)

REHABILITATION AND THERAPEUTIC PROFESSIONS RELATED
National U (CA)
Rutgers, The State U of New Jersey, Newark (NJ)
Rutgers, The State U of New Jersey, New Brunswick (NJ)

RELIGIOUS EDUCATION
Cincinnati Christian U (OH)
Dallas Baptist U (TX)
Hillsdale Free Will Baptist Coll (OK)
Kuyper Coll (MI)
Manhattan Christian Coll (KS)
Marian U (IN)
Nazarene Bible Coll (CO)
Nebraska Christian Coll (NE)
Oakland City U (IN)

RELIGIOUS/SACRED MUSIC
Calvary Bible Coll and Theological Seminary (MO)
Cincinnati Christian U (OH)
Dallas Baptist U (TX)
Hillsdale Free Will Baptist Coll (OK)
Immaculata U (PA)
Manhattan Christian Coll (KS)
Mount Vernon Nazarene U (OH)
Nazarene Bible Coll (CO)
Nebraska Christian Coll (NE)

RELIGIOUS STUDIES
Beulah Heights U (GA)
Calumet Coll of Saint Joseph (IN)
Concordia Coll–New York (NY)
Corban U (OR)
Liberty U (VA)
Lourdes U (OH)
Madonna U (MI)
Mount Marty Coll (SD)
Mount Vernon Nazarene U (OH)
Northwest U (WA)
Palm Beach State Coll (FL)
Southern Adventist U (TN)

State Coll of Florida Manatee-Sarasota (FL)
Thomas More Coll (KY)
Tougaloo Coll (MS)
Xavier U (OH)

RESORT MANAGEMENT
State U of New York Coll of Technology at Delhi (NY)

RESPIRATORY CARE THERAPY
Clarion U of Pennsylvania (PA)
Coll of Coastal Georgia (GA)
Dakota State U (SD)
Dixie State U (UT)
Ferris State U (MI)
Gannon U (PA)
Gwynedd Mercy U (PA)
Idaho State U (ID)
Indian River State Coll (FL)
Jefferson Coll of Health Sciences (VA)
Keiser U, Fort Lauderdale (FL)
Mansfield U of Pennsylvania (PA)
Midland Coll (TX)
Missouri Southern State U (MO)
Molloy Coll (NY)
Morehead State U (KY)
Nebraska Methodist Coll (NE)
Newman U (KS)
Pennsylvania Coll of Health Sciences (PA)
Polk State Coll (FL)
Rutgers, The State U of New Jersey, New Brunswick (NJ)
Santa Fe Coll (FL)
Shawnee State U (OH)
Southern Adventist U (TN)
State Coll of Florida Manatee-Sarasota (FL)
Universidad del Turabo (PR)
Universidad Metropolitana (PR)
U of Cincinnati (OH)
The U of Montana (MT)
U of Southern Indiana (IN)
U of the District of Columbia (DC)
Valencia Coll (FL)
Vermont Tech Coll (VT)
Washburn U (KS)
Weber State U (UT)
York Coll of Pennsylvania (PA)

RESPIRATORY THERAPY TECHNICIAN
Florida National U (FL)
Keiser U, Fort Lauderdale (FL)
Northern Michigan U (MI)
U of the District of Columbia (DC)

RESTAURANT, CULINARY, AND CATERING MANAGEMENT
Arkansas Tech U (AR)
Ferris State U (MI)
Morrisville State Coll (NY)
State U of New York Coll of Agriculture and Technology at Cobleskill (NY)
State U of New York Coll of Technology at Delhi (NY)
Stratford U (MD)

RESTAURANT/FOOD SERVICES MANAGEMENT
Morrisville State Coll (NY)
Pennsylvania Coll of Technology (PA)
The U of Akron (OH)
Valencia Coll (FL)

RETAILING
American Public U System (WV)
International Business Coll, Fort Wayne (IN)
Stevens–The Inst of Business & Arts (MO)
Weber State U (UT)

RHETORIC AND COMPOSITION
Ferris State U (MI)
Indian River State Coll (FL)
State Coll of Florida Manatee-Sarasota (FL)

ROBOTICS TECHNOLOGY
California U of Pennsylvania (PA)
Idaho State U (ID)
Indiana U–Purdue U Indianapolis (IN)
Pennsylvania Coll of Technology (PA)
U of Rio Grande (OH)
Utah Valley U (UT)

RUSSIAN
Idaho State U (ID)

RUSSIAN, CENTRAL EUROPEAN, EAST EUROPEAN AND EURASIAN STUDIES
State Coll of Florida Manatee-Sarasota (FL)

RUSSIAN STUDIES
State Coll of Florida Manatee-Sarasota (FL)

SALES AND MARKETING/ MARKETING AND DISTRIBUTION TEACHER EDUCATION
Wright State U (OH)

SALES, DISTRIBUTION, AND MARKETING OPERATIONS
Baker Coll (MI)
Inter American U of Puerto Rico, Aguadilla Campus (PR)
Southern Adventist U (TN)
Sullivan U (KY)
The U of Findlay (OH)

SCIENCE TEACHER EDUCATION
State Coll of Florida Manatee-Sarasota (FL)
Wright State U (OH)

SCIENCE TECHNOLOGIES
Washburn U (KS)

SCIENCE TECHNOLOGIES RELATED
Madonna U (MI)
Maria Coll (NY)
Ohio Valley U (WV)
State U of New York Coll of Agriculture and Technology at Cobleskill (NY)
U of Alaska Fairbanks (AK)
U of Cincinnati (OH)

SECONDARY EDUCATION
Ferris State U (MI)
U of Cincinnati (OH)

SELLING SKILLS AND SALES
Inter American U of Puerto Rico, San Germán Campus (PR)
The U of Akron (OH)
The U of Toledo (OH)

SHEET METAL TECHNOLOGY
Montana State U Billings (MT)

SIGN LANGUAGE INTERPRETATION AND TRANSLATION
Cincinnati Christian U (OH)
Mount Aloysius Coll (PA)
Nebraska Christian Coll (NE)
St. Catherine U (MN)
U of Arkansas at Little Rock (AR)

SMALL BUSINESS ADMINISTRATION
Lewis-Clark State Coll (ID)
The U of Akron (OH)
U of Alaska Anchorage (AK)

SMALL ENGINE MECHANICS AND REPAIR TECHNOLOGY
The U of Montana (MT)

SOCIAL PSYCHOLOGY
State Coll of Florida Manatee-Sarasota (FL)

SOCIAL SCIENCES
Campbellsville U (KY)
Fisher Coll (MA)
Heritage U (WA)
Hillsdale Free Will Baptist Coll (OK)
Indian River State Coll (FL)
Long Island U–LIU Brooklyn (NY)
Marymount Manhattan Coll (NY)
Palm Beach State Coll (FL)
St. Gregory's U, Shawnee (OK)
Saint Peter's U (NJ)
Shawnee State U (OH)
Southwestern Assemblies of God U (TX)
State Coll of Florida Manatee-Sarasota (FL)
State U of New York Empire State Coll (NY)
Trine U (IN)
Universidad del Turabo (PR)
U of Cincinnati (OH)
U of Puerto Rico in Ponce (PR)

U of Southern Indiana (IN)
Valparaiso U (IN)
Wayland Baptist U (TX)

SOCIAL SCIENCES RELATED
Concordia U Texas (TX)

SOCIAL SCIENCE TEACHER EDUCATION
Montana State U (MT)

SOCIAL STUDIES TEACHER EDUCATION
State Coll of Florida Manatee-Sarasota (FL)

SOCIAL WORK
Edinboro U of Pennsylvania (PA)
Elizabethtown Coll School of Continuing and Professional Studies (PA)
Ferris State U (MI)
Indian River State Coll (FL)
Northern State U (SD)
Palm Beach State Coll (FL)
State Coll of Florida Manatee-Sarasota (FL)
State U of New York Coll of Agriculture and Technology at Cobleskill (NY)
U of Cincinnati (OH)
U of Rio Grande (OH)
U of Saint Francis (IN)
U of the Fraser Valley (BC, Canada)
Wright State U (OH)
Youngstown State U (OH)

SOCIAL WORK RELATED
The U of Akron (OH)

SOCIOLOGY
Coll of Coastal Georgia (GA)
Holy Cross Coll (IN)
Indian River State Coll (FL)
Lourdes U (OH)
Montana State U Billings (MT)
New England Coll (NH)
Thomas More Coll (KY)
U of Rio Grande (OH)
The U of Scranton (PA)
The U of Tampa (FL)
Wright State U (OH)
Xavier U (OH)

SOIL SCIENCES RELATED
Michigan State U (MI)

SOLAR ENERGY TECHNOLOGY
Pennsylvania Coll of Technology (PA)

SPANISH
Holy Cross Coll (IN)
Immaculata U (PA)
Indian River State Coll (FL)
State Coll of Florida Manatee-Sarasota (FL)
Thomas More Coll (KY)
The U of Tampa (FL)
Xavier U (OH)

SPECIAL EDUCATION
Edinboro U of Pennsylvania (PA)
Montana State U Billings (MT)
U of Cincinnati (OH)

SPECIAL EDUCATION– INDIVIDUALS WHO ARE DEVELOPMENTALLY DELAYED
Saint Mary-of-the-Woods Coll (IN)

SPECIAL EDUCATION RELATED
Minot State U (ND)

SPECIAL PRODUCTS MARKETING
Indian River State Coll (FL)
Palm Beach State Coll (FL)

SPEECH COMMUNICATION AND RHETORIC
American Public U System (WV)
Central Penn Coll (PA)
Chaminade U of Honolulu (HI)
Lincoln Coll of New England, Southington (CT)
Mount St. Joseph U (OH)
State U of New York Coll of Agriculture and Technology at Cobleskill (NY)
Trine U (IN)
Tulane U (LA)
U of Cincinnati (OH)
U of Rio Grande (OH)

Utah Valley U (UT)
Wright State U (OH)

SPEECH-LANGUAGE PATHOLOGY
Elms Coll (MA)
Southern Adventist U (TN)

SPORT AND FITNESS ADMINISTRATION/ MANAGEMENT
Keiser U, Fort Lauderdale (FL)
Morrisville State Coll (NY)
Mount Vernon Nazarene U (OH)
National U (CA)
Ohio Dominican U (OH)
Southwestern Adventist U (TX)
State U of New York Coll of Technology at Delhi (NY)
U of Cincinnati (OH)
Webber International U (FL)

STATISTICS
State Coll of Florida Manatee-Sarasota (FL)

SUBSTANCE ABUSE/ ADDICTION COUNSELING
Midland Coll (TX)
National U (CA)
U of Great Falls (MT)
Washburn U (KS)

SURGICAL TECHNOLOGY
Baker Coll (MI)
Berkeley Coll, Woodland Park (NJ)
Cabarrus Coll of Health Sciences (NC)
Keiser U, Fort Lauderdale (FL)
Lincoln U (MO)
Mercy Coll of Health Sciences (IA)
Montana State U Billings (MT)
Mount Aloysius Coll (PA)
Nebraska Methodist Coll (NE)
New England Inst of Technology (RI)
Northern Michigan U (MI)
Pennsylvania Coll of Health Sciences (PA)
Pennsylvania Coll of Technology (PA)
Rasmussen Coll Brooklyn Park (MN)
Rasmussen Coll St. Cloud (MN)
Robert Morris U Illinois (IL)
St. Catharine Coll (KY)
Sentara Coll of Health Sciences (VA)
Southern Tech Coll, Fort Myers (FL)
The U of Akron (OH)
U of Arkansas–Fort Smith (AR)
U of Cincinnati (OH)
The U of Montana (MT)
U of Saint Francis (IN)
Washburn U (KS)

SURVEYING TECHNOLOGY
Ferris State U (MI)
Indian River State Coll (FL)
Palm Beach State Coll (FL)
Penn State Wilkes-Barre (PA)
Pennsylvania Coll of Technology (PA)
Polytechnic U of Puerto Rico (PR)
State U of New York Coll of Environmental Science and Forestry (NY)
The U of Akron (OH)
U of Alaska Anchorage (AK)
Utah Valley U (UT)

SYSTEM, NETWORKING, AND LAN/WAN MANAGEMENT
Baker Coll (MI)
Dakota State U (SD)
Midland Coll (TX)
Stratford U, Falls Church (VA)

TEACHER ASSISTANT/AIDE
Alverno Coll (WI)
Indian River State Coll (FL)
National U (CA)
Saint Mary-of-the-Woods Coll (IN)
State U of New York Coll of Agriculture and Technology at Cobleskill (NY)
The U of Montana Western (MT)
Valparaiso U (IN)

TECHNICAL TEACHER EDUCATION
Northern Kentucky U (KY)
Western Kentucky U (KY)

TECHNOLOGY/INDUSTRIAL ARTS TEACHER EDUCATION
State Coll of Florida Manatee-Sarasota (FL)

TELECOMMUNICATIONS TECHNOLOGY
New York City Coll of Technology of the City U of New York (NY)
Pace U (NY)
Penn State Hazleton (PA)
Penn State New Kensington (PA)
Penn State Schuylkill (PA)
Penn State Wilkes-Barre (PA)
Penn State York (PA)
St. John's U (NY)

TERRORISM AND COUNTERTERRORISM OPERATIONS
American Public U System (WV)

THEATER DESIGN AND TECHNOLOGY
Johnson State Coll (VT)
U of Rio Grande (OH)
Utah Valley U (UT)

THEOLOGICAL AND MINISTERIAL STUDIES RELATED
Bob Jones U (SC)
California Christian Coll (CA)
Lincoln Christian U (IL)
Manhattan Christian Coll (KS)
Providence Coll (RI)

THEOLOGY
Calvary Bible Coll and Theological Seminary (MO)
Creighton U (NE)
Franciscan U of Steubenville (OH)
Immaculata U (PA)
King's U (TX)
Marian U (IN)
Missouri Baptist U (MO)
Ohio Dominican U (OH)
William Jessup U (CA)
Williams Baptist Coll (AR)

THEOLOGY AND RELIGIOUS VOCATIONS RELATED
Anderson U (IN)
Southeastern U (FL)

TOOL AND DIE TECHNOLOGY
Ferris State U (MI)

TOURISM AND TRAVEL SERVICES MANAGEMENT
Black Hills State U (SD)
Fisher Coll (MA)
Morrisville State Coll (NY)
Stevens–The Inst of Business & Arts (MO)

TOURISM AND TRAVEL SERVICES MARKETING
Morrisville State Coll (NY)
State U of New York Coll of Agriculture and Technology at Cobleskill (NY)
State U of New York Coll of Technology at Delhi (NY)

TRADE AND INDUSTRIAL TEACHER EDUCATION
Eastern Kentucky U (KY)
Murray State U (KY)
State Coll of Florida Manatee-Sarasota (FL)

TRANSPORTATION AND MATERIALS MOVING RELATED
Baker Coll (MI)

TRANSPORTATION/MOBILITY MANAGEMENT
Polk State Coll (FL)
The U of Toledo (OH)

TURF AND TURFGRASS MANAGEMENT
Michigan State U (MI)
North Carolina State U (NC)
U of Guelph (ON, Canada)
U of Massachusetts Amherst (MA)

URBAN MINISTRY
Tabor Coll (KS)

URBAN STUDIES/AFFAIRS
Saint Peter's U (NJ)

VEHICLE AND VEHICLE PARTS AND ACCESSORIES MARKETING
Pennsylvania Coll of Technology (PA)

VETERINARY/ANIMAL HEALTH TECHNOLOGY
Baker Coll (MI)
Becker Coll (MA)
Dalhousie U (NS, Canada)
Fort Valley State U (GA)
Hickey Coll (MO)
International Business Coll, Fort Wayne (IN)
Lincoln Memorial U (TN)
Medaille Coll (NY)
Michigan State U (MI)
Morehead State U (KY)
New England Inst of Technology (RI)
Purdue U (IN)
State U of New York Coll of Technology at Canton (NY)
State U of New York Coll of Technology at Delhi (NY)
Universidad del Turabo (PR)
U of Cincinnati (OH)
U of Guelph (ON, Canada)

U of Maine at Augusta (ME)
U of New Hampshire (NH)
Vermont Tech Coll (VT)

VISUAL AND PERFORMING ARTS
Pine Manor Coll (MA)

VISUAL AND PERFORMING ARTS RELATED
Valencia Coll (FL)

VITICULTURE AND ENOLOGY
Michigan State U (MI)

VOCATIONAL REHABILITATION COUNSELING
State Coll of Florida Manatee-Sarasota (FL)

WATER QUALITY AND WASTEWATER TREATMENT MANAGEMENT AND RECYCLING TECHNOLOGY
Colorado Mesa U (CO)
Western Kentucky U (KY)

WEAPONS OF MASS DESTRUCTION
American Public U System (WV)

WEB/MULTIMEDIA MANAGEMENT AND WEBMASTER
American Public U System (WV)
Lewis-Clark State Coll (ID)
Montana Tech of The U of Montana (MT)

WEB PAGE, DIGITAL/ MULTIMEDIA AND INFORMATION RESOURCES DESIGN
Academy of Art U (CA)
Baker Coll (MI)
Champlain Coll (VT)
DeVry U, Phoenix (AZ)
DeVry U, Pomona (CA)
DeVry U, Westminster (CO)
DeVry U, Miramar (FL)
DeVry U, Orlando (FL)
DeVry U, Decatur (GA)
DeVry U, Chicago (IL)
DeVry U, Kansas City (MO)
DeVry U, North Brunswick (NJ)
DeVry U, Columbus (OH)
DeVry U, Fort Washington (PA)
DeVry U, Irving (TX)
DeVry U, Arlington (VA)
DeVry U Online (IL)
Florida National U (FL)
Limestone Coll (SC)
New England Inst of Technology (RI)
Palm Beach State Coll (FL)
Polk State Coll (FL)
Rasmussen Coll Appleton (WI)
Rasmussen Coll Aurora (IL)
Rasmussen Coll Bismarck (ND)
Rasmussen Coll Blaine (MN)
Rasmussen Coll Bloomington (MN)
Rasmussen Coll Brooklyn Park (MN)
Rasmussen Coll Eagan (MN)
Rasmussen Coll Fargo (ND)
Rasmussen Coll Fort Myers (FL)
Rasmussen Coll Green Bay (WI)

Rasmussen Coll Kansas City/ Overland Park (KS)
Rasmussen Coll Lake Elmo/ Woodbury (MN)
Rasmussen Coll Land O' Lakes (FL)
Rasmussen Coll Mankato (MN)
Rasmussen Coll Mokena/Tinley Park (IL)
Rasmussen Coll Moorhead (MN)
Rasmussen Coll New Port Richey (FL)
Rasmussen Coll Ocala (FL)
Rasmussen Coll Romeoville/Joliet (IL)
Rasmussen Coll St. Cloud (MN)
Rasmussen Coll Tampa/Brandon (FL)
Rasmussen Coll Topeka (KS)
Rasmussen Coll Wausau (WI)
Stratford U, Woodbridge (VA)
Thomas More Coll (KY)
Universidad del Turabo (PR)
Utah Valley U (UT)
Wilmington U (DE)

WELDING TECHNOLOGY
Ferris State U (MI)
Idaho State U (ID)
Lewis-Clark State Coll (ID)
Liberty U (VA)
Midland Coll (TX)
Pennsylvania Coll of Technology (PA)
State U of New York Coll of Technology at Delhi (NY)
U of Alaska Anchorage (AK)
The U of Montana (MT)
Weber State U (UT)

WILDLAND/FOREST FIREFIGHTING AND INVESTIGATION
Colorado Mesa U (CO)

WILDLIFE, FISH AND WILDLANDS SCIENCE AND MANAGEMENT
State U of New York Coll of Agriculture and Technology at Cobleskill (NY)

WOMEN'S STUDIES
Indiana U–Purdue U Fort Wayne (IN)
State Coll of Florida Manatee-Sarasota (FL)

WOOD SCIENCE AND WOOD PRODUCTS/PULP AND PAPER TECHNOLOGY
Morrisville State Coll (NY)

WORD PROCESSING
Palm Beach State Coll (FL)

WRITING
Carroll Coll (MT)
The U of Tampa (FL)

YOUTH MINISTRY
Calvary Bible Coll and Theological Seminary (MO)
U of Valley Forge (PA)

ZOOLOGY/ANIMAL BIOLOGY
Palm Beach State Coll (FL)

Alphabetical Listing of Two-Year Colleges

In this index, the page numbers of the profiles are printed in regular type, the displays are in *italic*, and the Close-Ups are in **bold**.